Not a week goes by that I don't receive a letter from a grateful parent stating that his or her child learned to read thanks to the Garfield comic strip. Some children are very young and simply learned to read for the first time. Other children (and even adults) have a learning disability. Something about putting a visual with the words cuts through the muck allowing the cognitive process to kick in!

After twenty years of receiving such letters, it's clear to me that there's a trend here. Seeing a word along with a specific gesture or expression brings more senses to bear when it comes to comprehending that word.

It's common knowledge that we retain 20 percent of what we hear and up to 80 percent of what we see. Words accompanied by pictures are much easier to recall for one simple reason ... association ... one of the fundamental ways our mind remembers.

Another advantage of using the comic strip to build the vocabulary is that the words are utilized squarely within the American vernacular, and not in a dry way. One educator once told me that, first, you have to get a student's attention. With that accomplished, teaching is easy.

The use of humor is not only a pleasurable way to learn but also a most effective way.

A classic novel or a comic strip ... what difference does it make what a person reads as long as he or she is reading? As reading skills develop, reading becomes easier and more rewarding. Readers can then naturally move on to weightier material.

My deepest gratitude goes to the folks at Merriam-Webster and their publisher, John Morse, who have shown faith in Garfield by boldly publishing this landmark edition of *The Merriam-Webster Dictionary*.

Enjoy!

JIM DAVIS
Garfield Creator

The
Merriam-Webster
and

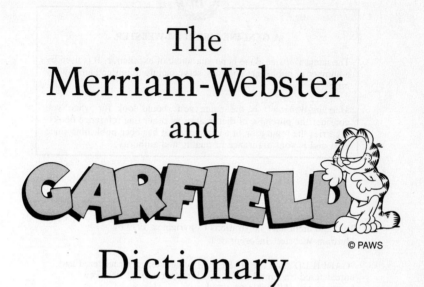

© PAWS

Dictionary

Merriam-Webster, Incorporated
Springfield, Massachusetts, U.S.A.

A GENUINE MERRIAM-WEBSTER

The name *Webster* alone is no guarantee of excellence. It is used by a number of publishers and may serve mainly to mislead an unwary buyer.

Merriam-Webster™ is the name you should look for when you consider the purchase of dictionaries or other fine reference books. It carries the reputation of a company that has been publishing since 1831 and is your assurance of quality and authority.

Text and dictionary illustrations Copyright © 1999 by
Merriam-Webster, Incorporated

"GARFIELD" and the GARFIELD characters are registered and unregistered trademarks of Paws, Incorporated. © 1999 Paws, Incorporated. All rights reserved.

Library of Congress Cataloging in Publication Data
Main entry under title:

The Merriam-Webster and Garfield dictionary.
        p.   cm.
   ". . . combines the text of a Merriam-Webster dictionary with a collection of Jim Davis's Garfield cartoon strips carefully selected for the ways they illustrate the use of language"—Pref.
   ISBN 0-87779-626-2 (alk. paper)
   1. English language — Dictionaries. 2. English language — Caricatures and cartoons. 3. Garfield (Fictitious character)
I. Davis, Jim. II. Merriam-Webster, Inc.
PE1628.M33   1999
423—dc21   99-25351
                                                     CIP

Made in the United States of America

5RRD01

Contents

Preface

THE MERRIAM-WEBSTER AND GARFIELD DIC-
TIONARY introduces a new approach to
dictionary-making. It combines the text of
a Merriam-Webster dictionary with a collection of Jim Davis's Garfield cartoon
strips carefully selected for the ways they
illustrate the use of language. Like all
Merriam-Webster dictionaries, this one is
designed to meet the day-to-day language-
information needs of users in the home,
school, or office. In addition, the special
goal of this dictionary is to use the humor
and fun of the Garfield comic strips to help
illustrate the meanings and usage of
words, to make the information more
memorable, and to make browsing the dictionary more enjoyable than ever.

The heart of this dictionary is the A-Z
vocabulary section. Within this section,
one finds the core of the English vocabulary; obsolete, rare, and highly technical
words and obsolete meanings of common
words have been omitted. The vocabulary
is thus a compilation of the words most
likely to be looked up by a person searching for a meaning, pronunciation, or end-
of-line division point. Every definition in
this section is based on examples of actual
usage found among the more than 15 million citations in the Merriam-Webster citation file. In addition, hundreds of entries
in this section are illustrated with examples of the word in use in a Garfield cartoon strip specially chosen by Merriam-
Webster editors.

The A-Z section is followed by several
sections that dictionary users have long
found helpful: a list of Common English
Given Names; a list of Foreign Words and
Phrases that often occur in English texts
but that have not yet become part of the
English vocabulary; a section including Biographical, Biblical, and Mythological
Names; a Geographical Names section; a
section devoted to widely used Signs and
Symbols; a Handbook of Style section;
and a section on Documentation of Sources. In addition, following these sections
there is a special section of Daffy Definitions, illustrating Garfield's distinctive and
unconventional approach to defining
words.

The A-Z section is preceded by a section
of Explanatory Notes that should be read
carefully by every user of this dictionary.
An understanding of the information contained in these notes will add to the satisfaction and pleasure that comes from
looking into the pages of this dictionary.
Following these notes is a list of Abbreviations Used in This Work and a page that
lists and explains the pronunciation symbols used in this dictionary.

The idea for *The Merriam-Webster and
Garfield Dictionary* was conceived by Jim
Davis. The creation of the book is the result of a collaboration between Jim Davis
and Merriam-Webster, a company that has
been publishing dictionaries for more than
150 years. Jim Davis and the editors of
Merriam-Webster together offer this book
in the firm belief that it will serve well
those who want an easy-to-read and fun-
to-use record of today's English words.

Explanatory Notes

Entries

A boldface letter or a combination of such letters, including punctuation marks and diacritics where needed, that is set flush with the left-hand margin of each column of type is a main entry. The main entry may consist of letters set solid, of letters joined by a hyphen or a diagonal, or of letters separated by one or more spaces:

> **alone** . . . *adj*
> **avant–garde** . . . *n*
> **and/or** . . . *conj*
> **assembly language** *n*

The material in lightface type that follows each main entry on the same line and on succeeding indented lines presents information about the main entry.

The main entries follow one another in alphabetical order letter by letter: *bill of health* follows *billion; Day of Atonement* follows *daylight saving time*. Those containing an Arabic numeral are alphabetized as if the numeral were spelled out: *4-H* comes between *fourfold* and *Four Hundred; 3-D* comes between *three* and *three-dimensional*. Those that often begin with the abbreviation *St.* in common usage have the abbreviation spelled out: *Saint Valentine's Day*.

A pair of guide words is printed at the top of each page. These indicate that the entries falling alphabetically between the words at the top of the outer column of each page are found on that page.

The guide words are usually the alphabetically first and the alphabetically last entries on the page:

> **behindhand • belongings**

Occasionally the last printed entry is not the alphabetically last entry. On page 87, for example, *canteen* is the last main entry, but *canteloupe*, a variant entry at *cantaloupe*, is the alphabetically last entry and is therefore the second guide word. The alphabetically last entry is not used, however, if it follows alphabetically the first guide word on the succeeding page. Thus on page 183 *doughy* is not a guide word because it follows alphabetically the entry *doughnut* which is the first guide word on page 184.

Any boldface word—a main entry with definition, a variant, an inflected form, a defined or undefined run-on, or a run-in entry—may be used as a guide word.

When one main entry has exactly the same written form as another, the two are distinguished by superscript numerals preceding each word:

> [1]**melt** . . . *vb*   [1]**pine** . . . *n*
> [2]**melt** *n*   [2]**pine** *vb*

Full words come before parts of words made up of the same letters; solid compounds come before hyphenated compounds; hyphenated compounds come before open compounds; and lowercase entries come before those with an initial capital:

> [2]**super** *adj*
> **super-** . . . *prefix*
> **run•down** . . . *n*
> **run–down** . . . *adj*
> **run down** *vb*
> **dutch** . . . *adv*
> **Dutch** . . . *n*

The centered dots within entry words indicate division points at which a hyphen may be put at the end of a line of print or writing. Thus the noun *cap•puc•ci•no* may be ended on one line and continued on the next in this manner:

> cap-
> puccino
>
> cappuc-
> cino
>
> cappucci-
> no

Centered dots are not shown after a single initial letter or before a single terminal letter because typesetters seldom cut off a single letter:

> **abyss** . . . *n*
> **flighty** . . . *adj*
> **idea** . . . *n*

Nor are they usually shown at the second and succeeding homographs unless they differ among themselves:

> [1]**sig•nal** . . . *n*
> [2]**signal** *vb*
> [3]**signal** *adj*
> [1]**min•ute** . . . *n*
> [2]**mi•nute** . . . *adj*

There are acceptable alternative end-of-line divisions just as there are acceptable variant spellings and pronunciations, but no more than one division is shown for any entry in this dictionary.

A double hyphen at the end of a line in this dictionary (as in the definition at **ant lion**) stands for a hyphen that is retained when the word is written as a unit on one line. This kind of fixed hyphen is always represented in boldface words in this dictionary with an en dash.

When a main entry is followed by the word *or* and another spelling, the two spellings are equal variants. Both are standard, and either one may be used according to personal inclination:

ocher *or* **ochre**

If two variants joined by *or* are out of alphabetical order, they remain equal variants. The one printed first is, however, slightly more common than the second:

¹plow *or* **plough**

When another spelling is joined to the main entry by the word *also*, the spelling after *also* is a secondary variant and occurs less frequently than the first:

absinthe *also* **absinth**

Secondary variants belong to standard usage and may be used according to personal inclination. Once the word *also* is used to signal a secondary variant, all following variants are joined by *or:*

²wool•ly *also* **wool•ie** *or* **wooly**

Variants whose spelling puts them alphabetically more than a column away from the main entry are entered at their own alphabetical places and usually not at the main entry:

li•chee *var of* LITCHI

Variants having a usage label appear only at their own alphabetical places:

me•tre . . . *chiefly Brit var of* METER

To show all the stylings that are found for English compounds would require space that can be better used for other information. So this dictionary limits itself to a single styling for a compound:

peace•mak•er

pell–mell

boom box

When a compound is widely used and one styling predominates, that styling is shown. When a compound is uncommon or when the evidence indicates that two or three stylings are approximately equal in frequency, the styling shown is based on the comparison of other similar compounds.

A main entry may be followed by one or more derivatives or by a homograph with a different functional label. These are run-on entries. Each is introduced by a boldface dash and each has a functional label. They are not defined, however, since their meanings are readily understood from the meaning of the root word:

fear•less . . . *adj* . . . — **fear•less•ly** *adv*

— **fear•less•ness** *n*

hic•cup . . . *n* . . . — **hiccup** *vb*

A main entry may be followed by one or more phrases containing the entry word or an inflected form of it. These are also run-on entries. Each is introduced by a boldface dash but there is no functional label. They are, however, defined since their meanings are more than the sum of the meanings of their elements:

¹set . . . *vb* . . . — **set sail** : . . .

¹hand . . . *n* . . . — **at hand** : . . .

Defined phrases of this sort are run on at the entry defining the first major word in the phrase. When there are variants, however, the run-on appears at the entry defining the first major word which is invariable in the phrase:

¹seed . . . *n* . . . — **go to seed** *or* **run to seed 1** : . . .

Boldface words that appear within parentheses (as **co•ca** at **co•caine** and **jet engine** and **jet propulsion** at **jet–propelled**) are run-in entries.

Attention is called to the definition of *vocabulary entry* on page 678. The term *dictionary entry* includes all vocabulary entries as well as all boldface entries in the section headed "Foreign Words and Phrases."

Pronunciation

The matter between a pair of reversed virgules \ \ following the entry word indicates the pronunciation. The symbols used are explained in the chart on page 16a.

A hyphen is used in the pronunciation to show syllabic division. These hyphens sometimes coincide with the centered dots in the entry word that indicate end-of-line division:

ab•sen•tee \ˌab-sən-ˈtē\

Sometimes they do not:

met•ric \ˈme-trik\

A high-set mark ˈ indicates major (primary) stress or accent; a low-set mark ˌ indicates minor (secondary) stress or accent:

heart·beat \ˈhärt-ˌbēt\

The stress mark stands at the beginning of the syllable that receives the stress.

A syllable with neither a high-set mark nor a low-set mark is unstressed:

¹struc·ture \ˈstrək-chər\

The presence of variant pronunciations indicates that not all educated speakers pronounce words the same way. A second-place variant is not to be regarded as less acceptable than the pronunciation that is given first. It may, in fact, be used by as many educated speakers as the first variant, but the requirements of the printed page are such that one must precede the other:

apri·cot \ˈa-prə-ˌkät, ˈā-\

pro·vost \ˈprō-ˌvōst, ˈprä-vəst\

Symbols enclosed by parentheses represent elements that are present in the pronunciation of some speakers but are absent from the pronunciation of other speakers, or elements that are present in some but absent from other utterances of the same speaker:

¹om·ni·bus \ˈäm-ni-(ˌ)bəs\

ad·di·tion·al \ə-ˈdi-sh(ə-)nəl\

Thus, the above parentheses indicate that some people say \ˈäm-ni-ˌbəs\ and others say \ˈäm-ni-bəs\; some \ə-ˈdi-shə-nəl\, others \ə-ˈdi-shnəl\.

When a main entry has less than a full pronunciation, the missing part is to be supplied from a pronunciation in a preceding entry or within the same pair of reversed virgules:

cham·pi·on·ship \-ˌship\

pa·la·ver \pə-ˈla-vər, -ˈlä-\

The pronunciation of the first three syllables of *championship* is found at the main entry *champion*. The hyphens before and after \ˈlä\ in the pronunciation of *palaver* indicate that both the first and the last parts of the pronunciation are to be taken from the immediately preceding pronunciation.

In general, no pronunciation is indicated for open compounds consisting of two or more English words that have own-place entry:

witch doctor *n*

Only the first entry in a sequence of numbered homographs is given a pronunciation if their pronunciations are the same:

¹re·ward \ri-ˈwȯrd\ *vb*

²reward *n*

The absent but implied pronunciation of derivatives and compounds run on after a main entry is a combination of the pronunciation at the main entry and the pronunciation of the other element as given at its alphabetical place in the vocabulary:

— **quick·ness** *n*

— **hold forth**

Thus, the pronunciation of *quickness* is the sum of the pronunciations given at *quick* and *-ness;* that of *hold forth*, the sum of the pronunciations of the two elements that make up the phrase.

Functional Labels

An italic label indicating a part of speech or another functional classification follows the pronunciation or, if no pronunciation is given, the main entry. The eight traditional parts of speech are indicated as follows:

bold . . . *adj*

forth·with . . . *adv*

¹but . . . *conj*

ge·sund·heit . . . *interj*

bo·le·ro . . . *n*

²un·der . . . *prep*

¹it . . . *pron*

slap . . . *vb*

Other italicized labels used to indicate functional classifications that are not traditional parts of speech include:

ATM *abbr*

self- *comb form*

un- . . . *prefix*

-ial *adj suffix*

²-ly *adv suffix*

²-er . . . *n suffix*

-ize . . . *vb suffix*

Fe *symbol*

may . . . *verbal auxiliary*

Functional labels are sometimes combined:

afloat . . . *adj or adv*

Inflected Forms

Nouns

The plurals of nouns are shown in this dictionary when suffixation brings about a change of final -y to -i-, when the noun ends in a consonant plus -o or in -ey, when the noun ends in -oo, when the noun has an irregular plural or a zero plural or a foreign plural, when the noun is a compound that pluralizes any element but the last, when a final consonant is doubled, when the noun has variant plurals, and when it is believed that the dictionary user might have reasonable doubts about the spelling of the plural or when the plural is spelled in a way contrary to what is expected:

> ²spy *n, pl* spies
> si·lo . . . *n, pl* silos
> val·ley . . . *n, pl* valleys
> ²shampoo *n, pl* shampoos
> ¹quiz . . . *n, pl* quiz·zes
> ¹fish . . . *n, pl* fish *or* fish·es
> mouse . . . *n, pl* mice
> moose . . . *n, pl* moose
> cri·te·ri·on . . . *n, pl* -ria
> son–in–law . . . *n, pl* sons–in–law
> pi . . . *n, pl* pis
> ³dry *n, pl* drys

Cutback inflected forms are used when the noun has three or more syllables:

> ame·ni·ty . . . *n, pl* -ties

The plurals of nouns are usually not shown when the base word is unchanged by suffixation, when the noun is a compound whose second element is readily recognizable as a regular free form entered at its own place, or when the noun is unlikely to occur in the plural:

> night . . . *n*
> fore·foot . . . *n*
> mo·nog·a·my . . . *n*

Nouns that are plural in form and that regularly occur in plural construction are labeled *n pl*:

> munch·ies . . . *n pl*

Nouns that are plural in form but that are not always construed as plurals are appropriately labeled:

> lo·gis·tics . . . *n sing or pl*

Verbs

The principal parts of verbs are shown in this dictionary when suffixation brings about a doubling of a final consonant or an elision of a final -e or a change of final -y to -i-, when final -c changes to -ck in suffixation, when the verb ends in -ey, when the inflection is irregular,

when there are variant inflected forms, and when it is believed that the dictionary user might have reasonable doubts about the spelling of an inflected form or when the inflected form is spelled in a way contrary to what is expected:

> ²snag *vb* snagged; snag·ging
> ¹move . . . *vb* moved; mov·ing
> ¹cry . . . *vb* cried; cry·ing
> ¹frol·ic . . . *vb* frol·icked; frol·ick·ing
> ¹sur·vey . . . *vb* sur·veyed; sur·vey·ing
> ¹drive . . . *vb* drove . . .; driv·en . . .; driv·ing
> ²bus *vb* bused *or* bussed; bus·ing *or* bus·sing
> ²visa *vb* vi·saed . . .; vi·sa·ing
> ²chagrin *vb* cha·grined . . .; cha·grin·ing

The principal parts of a regularly inflected verb are shown when it is desirable to indicate the pronunciation of one of the inflected forms:

> learn . . . *vb* learned \'lərnd, 'lərnt\; learn·ing
> ¹al·ter \'ȯl-tər\ *vb* al·tered; al·ter·ing \-t(ə-)riŋ\

Cutback inflected forms are usually used when the verb has three or more syllables, when it is a two-syllable word that ends in -l and has variant spellings, and when it is a compound whose second element is readily recognized as an irregular verb:

> elim·i·nate . . . *vb* -nat·ed; -nat·ing
> ²quarrel *vb* -reled *or* -relled; -rel·ing *or* -rel·ling
> ¹re·take . . . *vb* -took . . .; -tak·en . . .; -tak·ing

The principal parts of verbs are usually not shown when the base word is unchanged by suffixation or when the verb is a compound whose second element is readily recognizable as a regular free form entered at its own place:

> ¹jump . . . *vb*
> pre·judge . . . *vb*

Another inflected form of English verbs is the third person singular of the present tense, which is regularly formed by the addition of -s or -es to the base form of the verb. This inflected form is not shown except at a handful of entries (as *have* and *do*) for which it is in some way anomalous.

Adjectives & Adverbs

The comparative and superlative forms of adjectives and adverbs are shown in this dictionary when suffixation brings about a doubling of a final consonant or an elision of a final -e or a change of final -y to -i-, when the word ends in -ey, when the inflection is irregular, and when there are variant inflected forms:

> ¹red . . . *adj* red·der; red·dest

¹tame . . . *adj* tam•er; tam•est

¹kind•ly . . . *adj* kind•li•er; -est

hors•ey *or* horsy . . . *adj* hors•i•er; -est

¹good . . . *adj* bet•ter . . .; best

¹far . . . *adv* far•ther . . . *or* fur•ther . . .;
  far•thest *or* fur•thest

The superlative forms of adjectives and adverbs of two or more syllables are usually cut back:

³fancy *adj* fan•ci•er; -est

¹ear•ly . . . *adv* ear•li•er; -est

The comparative and superlative forms of regularly inflected adjectives and adverbs are shown when it is desirable to indicate the pronunciation of the inflected forms:

¹young \ˈyəŋ\ *adj* youn•ger \ˈyəŋ-gər\; youn•gest \ˈyəŋ-gəst\

The inclusion of inflected forms in -*er* and -*est* at adjective and adverb entries means nothing more about the use of *more* and *most* with these adjectives and adverbs than that their comparative and superlative degrees may be expressed in either way: *lazier* or *more lazy; laziest* or *most lazy.*

At a few adjective entries only the superlative form is shown:

²mere *adj, superlative* mer•est

The absence of the comparative form indicates that there is no evidence of its use.

The comparative and superlative forms of adjectives and adverbs are usually not shown when the base word is unchanged by suffixation, when the inflected forms of the word are identical with those of a preceding homograph, or when the word is a compound whose second element is readily recognizable as a regular free form entered at its own place:

¹near . . . *adv*

³good *adv*

un•wor•thy . . . *adj*

Inflected forms are not shown at undefined run-ons.

Capitalization

Most entries in this dictionary begin with a lowercase letter. A few of these have an italicized label *often cap*, which indicates that the word is as likely to be capitalized as not and that it is as acceptable with an uppercase initial as it is with one in lowercase. Some entries begin with an uppercase letter, which indicates that the word is usually capitalized. The absence of an initial capital or of an *often cap* label indicates that the word is not ordinarily capitalized:

salm•on . . . *n*

gar•gan•tuan . . . *adj, often cap*

Mo•hawk . . . *n*

The capitalization of entries that are open or hyphenated compounds is similarly indicated by the form of the entry or by an italicized label:

dry goods . . . *n pl*

french fry *vb, often cap 1st F*

un–Amer•i•can . . . *adj*

Par•kin•son's disease . . . *n*

lazy Su•san . . . *n*

Jack Frost *n*

A word that is capitalized in some senses and lowercase in others shows variations from the form of the main entry by the use of italicized labels at the appropriate senses:

Trin•i•ty . . . *n* . . . 2 *not cap*

To•ry . . . *n* . . . 3 *often not cap*

ti•tan . . . *n* 1 *cap*

re•nais•sance . . . *n* . . . 1 *cap* . . . 2 *often cap*

Etymology

This dictionary gives the etymologies for a number of the vocabulary entries. These etymologies are in boldface square brackets preceding the definition. Meanings given in roman type within these brackets are not definitions of the entry, but are meanings of the Middle English, Old English, or non-English words within the brackets.

The etymology gives the language from which words borrowed into English have come. It also gives the form of the word in that language or a representation of the word in our alphabet if the form in that language differs from that in English:

philo•den•dron . . . [NL, fr. Gk, neut. of *philodendros* loving trees . . .]

¹sav•age . . . [ME *sauvage*, fr. MF, fr. ML *salvaticus*, alter. of L *silvaticus* of the woods, wild . . .]

An etymology beginning with the name of a language (including ME or OE) and not giving the foreign (or Middle English or Old English) form indicates that this form is the same as the form of the entry word:

le•gume . . . [F]

¹jour•ney . . . [ME, fr. OF . . .]

An etymology beginning with the name of a language (including ME or OE) and not giving the foreign (or Middle English or Old English) meaning indicates that this meaning is the same as the meaning expressed in the first definition in the entry:

ug·ly . . . *adj* . . . [ME, fr. ON *uggligr* . . .] **1**
: FRIGHTFUL, DIRE

Usage

Three types of status labels are used in this dictionary—temporal, regional, and stylistic—to signal that a word or a sense of a word is not part of the standard vocabulary of English.

The temporal label *obs* for "obsolete" means that there is no evidence of use since 1755:

³**post** *n* **1** *obs*

The label *obs* is a comment on the word being defined. When a thing, as distinguished from the word used to designate it, is obsolete, appropriate orientation is usually given in the definition:

cat·a·pult . . . *n* **1** : an ancient military machine for hurling missiles

The temporal label *archaic* means that a word or sense once in common use is found today only sporadically or in special contexts:

¹**mete** . . . *vb* . . . **1** *archaic*
¹**thou** . . . *pron, archaic*

A word or sense limited in use to a specific region of the U.S. has an appropriate label. The adverb *chiefly* precedes a label when the word has some currency outside the specified region, and a double label is used to indicate considerable currency in each of two specific regions:

²**wash** *n* . . . **5** *West*
do·gie . . . *n, chiefly West*
crul·ler . . . *n* . . . **2** *Northern & Midland*

Words current in all regions of the U.S. have no label.

A word or sense limited in use to one of the other countries of the English-speaking world has an appropriate regional label:

chem·ist . . . *n* . . . **2** *Brit*
loch . . . *n, Scot*
²**wireless** *n* . . . **2** *chiefly Brit*

The label *dial* for "dialect" indicates that the pattern of use of a word or sense is too complex for summary labeling: it usually includes several regional varieties of American English or of American and British English:

²**mind** *vb* **1** *chiefly dial*

The stylistic label *slang* is used with words or senses that are especially appropriate in contexts of extreme informality:

³**can** . . . *vb* . . . **2** *slang*
²**grand** *n, slang*

There is no satisfactory objective test for slang, especially with reference to a word out of context. No word, in fact, is invariably slang, and many standard words can be given slang applications.

Definitions are sometimes followed by verbal illustrations that show a typical use of the word in context. These illustrations are enclosed in angle brackets, and the word being illustrated is usually replaced by a lightface swung dash. The swung dash stands for the boldface entry word, and it may be followed by an italicized suffix:

¹**jump** . . . *vb* . . . **5** . . . ⟨∼ the gun⟩
all–around . . . *adj* **1** . . . ⟨best ∼ performance⟩
¹**can·on** . . . *n* . . . **3** . . . ⟨the ∼*s* of good taste⟩
en·joy . . . *vb* . . . **2** . . . ⟨∼*ed* the concert⟩

The swung dash is not used when the form of the boldface entry word is changed in suffixation, and it is not used for open compounds:

²**deal** *vb* . . . **2** . . . ⟨*dealt* him a blow⟩
drum up *vb* **1** . . . ⟨*drum up* business⟩

Definitions are sometimes followed by usage notes that give supplementary information about such matters as idiom, syntax, and semantic relationship. A usage note is introduced by a lightface dash:

²**cry** *n* . . . **5** . . . — usu. used in the phrase *a far cry*
²**drum** *vb* . . . **4** . . . — usu. used with *out*
¹**jaw** . . . *n* . . . **2** . . . — usu. used in pl.
¹**ada·gio** . . . *adv or adj* . . . — used as a direction in music
hajji . . . *n* . . . — often used as a title

Sometimes a usage note is used in place of a definition. Some function words (as conjunctions and prepositions) have chiefly grammatical meaning and little or no lexical meaning; most interjections express feelings but are otherwise untranslatable into lexical meaning; and some other words (as honorific titles) are more amenable to comment than to definition:

or . . . *conj* — used as a function word to indicate an alternative

¹at . . . *prep* 1 — used to indicate a point in time or space

auf Wie•der•seh•en . . . *interj* . . . — used to express farewell

sir . . . *n* . . . 2 — used as a usu. respectful form of address

Sense Division

A boldface colon is used in this dictionary to introduce a definition:

equine . . . *adj* . . . : of or relating to the horse

It is also used to separate two or more definitions of a single sense:

no•ti•fy . . . *vb* . . . 1 : to give notice of : report the occurrence of

Boldface Arabic numerals separate the senses of a word that has more than one sense:

add . . . *vb* 1 : to join to something else so as to increase in number or amount 2 : to say further . . . 3 : to combine (numbers) into one sum

A particular semantic relationship between senses is sometimes suggested by the use of one of the two italic sense dividers *esp* or *also*. The sense divider *esp* (for *especially*) is used to introduce the most common meaning included in the more general preceding definition:

crys•tal . . . *n* . . . 2 : something resembling crystal (as in transparency); *esp* : a clear glass used for table articles

The sense divider *also* is used to introduce a meaning related to the preceding sense by an easily understood extension of that sense:

chi•na . . . *n* : porcelain ware; *also* : domestic pottery in general

The order of senses is historical: the sense known to have been first used in English is entered first. This is not to be taken to mean, however, that each sense of a multisense word developed from the immediately preceding sense. It is altogether possible that sense 1 of a word has given rise to sense 2 and sense 2 to sense 3, but frequently sense 2 and sense 3 may have developed independently of one another from sense 1.

When an italicized label follows a boldface numeral, the label applies only to that specific numbered sense. It does not apply to any other boldface numbered senses:

craft . . . *n* . . . 3 *pl usu* **craft**

¹fa•ther . . . *n* . . . 2 *cap* . . . 5 *often cap*

dul•ci•mer . . . *n* . . . 2 *or* dul•ci•more \-₁mōr\

²lift *n* . . . 5 *chiefly Brit*

At *craft* the *pl* label applies to sense 3 but to none of the other numbered senses. At *father* the *cap* label applies only to sense 2 and the *often cap* label only to sense 5. At *dulcimer* the variant spelling and pronunciation apply only to sense 2, and the *chiefly Brit* label at *lift* applies only to sense 5.

Cross-Reference

Four different kinds of cross-references are used in this dictionary: directional, synonymous, cognate, and inflectional. In each instance the cross-reference is readily recognized by the lightface small capitals in which it is printed.

A cross-reference following a lightface dash and beginning with *see* is a directional cross-reference. It directs the dictionary user to look elsewhere for further information:

ri•al . . . *n* — see MONEY table

A cross-reference following a boldface colon is a synonymous cross-reference. It may stand alone as the only definition for an entry or for a sense of an entry; it may follow an analytical definition; it may be one of two or more synonymous cross-references separated by commas:

pa•pa . . . *n* : FATHER

¹par•tic•u•lar . . . *adj* . . . 4 : attentive to details : PRECISE

²main *adj* 1 : CHIEF, PRINCIPAL

¹fig•ure . . . *n* . . . 6 : SHAPE, FORM, OUTLINE

A synonymous cross-reference indicates that an entry, a definition at the entry, or a specific sense at the entry cross-referred to can be substituted as a definition for the entry or the sense in which the cross-reference appears.

A cross-reference following an italic *var of* ("variant of") is a cognate cross-reference:

pick•a•back . . . *var of* PIGGYBACK

Occasionally a cognate cross-reference has a limiting label preceding *var of* as an indication that the variant is not standard English:

aero•plane . . . *chiefly Brit var of* AIRPLANE

A cross-reference following an italic label that identifies an entry as an inflected form (as of a noun or verb) is an inflectional cross-reference:

calves *pl of* CALF

woven *past part of* WEAVE

Inflectional cross-references appear only when the inflected form falls at least a column away from the entry cross-referred to.

Synonyms

A boldface **syn** near the end of an entry introduces words that are synonymous with the word being defined:

alone . . . *adj* . . . **syn** lonely, lonesome, lone, solitary

Synonyms are not definitions although they may often be substituted for each other in context.

Combining Forms, Prefixes, & Suffixes

An entry that begins or ends with a hyphen is a word element that forms part of an English compound:

-wise . . . *adv comb form* . . . ⟨slant*wise*⟩

ex- . . . *prefix* . . . ⟨*ex*-president⟩

-let . . . *n suffix* **1** . . . ⟨book*let*⟩

Combining forms, prefixes, and suffixes are entered in this dictionary for two reasons: to make understandable the meaning of many undefined run-ons and to make recognizable the meaningful elements of words that are not entered in the dictionary.

Lists of Undefined Words

Lists of undefined words occur after the entries *anti-*, *in-*, *non-*, *over-*, *re-*, *self-*, *semi-*, *sub-*, *super-*, and *un-*. These words are undefined because they are self-explanatory: their meanings are simply the sum of a meaning of the prefix or combining form and a meaning of the root word.

Abbreviations & Symbols

Abbreviations and symbols for chemical elements are included as main entries in the vocabulary:

RSVP *abbr* . . . please reply

Ca *symbol* calcium

Abbreviations have been normalized to one form. In practice, however, there is considerable variation in the use of periods and in capitalization (as *vhf*, *v.h.f.*, *VHF*, and *V.H.F.*), and stylings other than those given in this dictionary are often acceptable.

Symbols that are not capable of being alphabetized are included in a separate section of the back matter headed "Signs and Symbols."

Comic Strips

Each Garfield comic strip that appears in this work contains a word that is entered and defined on the same page as the strip or on the page facing the strip. The entry that is being illustrated by each strip is indicated by a picture of Garfield and appears within a box.

Abbreviations Used in This Work

ab	about	*AmerF*	American French
abbr	abbreviation	*AmerInd*	American Indian
abl	ablative	*AmerSp*	American Spanish
acc	accusative	*Ar*	Arabic
A.D.	anno Domini	*Aram*	Aramaic
adj	adjective	*B.C.*	before Christ
adv	adverb	*Brit*	British
alter	alteration	*C*	Celsius
Am	American	*Calif*	California

CanF	Canadian French		*NGk*	New Greek
cap	capital, capitalized		*NHeb*	New Hebrew
Celt	Celtic		*NL*	New Latin
cent	century		*No*	North
Chin	Chinese		*Norw*	Norwegian
comb	combining		*n pl*	noun plural
compar	comparative		*obs*	obsolete
conj	conjunction		*OE*	Old English
D	Dutch		*OF*	Old French
Dan	Danish		*OIt*	Old Italian
dat	dative		*ON*	Old Norse
deriv	derivative		*OPer*	Old Persian
dial	dialect		*OProv*	Old Provençal
dim	diminutive		*orig*	originally
E	English		*part*	participle
Egypt	Egyptian		*Per*	Persian
Eng	English		*perh*	perhaps
esp	especially		*Pg*	Portuguese
F	Fahrenheit, French		*pl*	plural
fem	feminine		*Pol*	Polish
fr	from		*pp*	past participle
G	German		*prep*	preposition
Gk	Greek		*pres*	present
Gmc	Germanic		*prob*	probably
Heb	Hebrew		*pron*	pronoun, pronunci-
Hung	Hungarian			ation
Icel	Icelandic		*Prov*	Provençal
imit	imitative		*prp*	present participle
imper	imperative		*Russ*	Russian
interj	interjection		*Sc*	Scotch, Scots
Ir	Irish		*Scand*	Scandinavian
irreg	irregular		*ScGael*	Scottish Gaelic
It, Ital	Italian		*Scot*	Scottish
Jp	Japanese		*sing*	singular
K	Kelvin		*Skt*	Sanskrit
L	Latin		*Slav*	Slavic
LaF	Louisiana French		*So*	South
LG	Low German		*Sp*	Spanish
LGk	Late Greek		*St*	Saint
LHeb	Late Hebrew		*superl*	superlative
lit	literally		*Sw*	Swedish
LL	Late Latin		*syn*	synonym, synonymy
masc	masculine		*trans*	translation
MD	Middle Dutch		*Turk*	Turkish
ME	Middle English		*US*	United States
MexSp	Mexican Spanish		*USSR*	Union of Soviet
MF	Middle French			Socialist Republics
MGk	Middle Greek		*usu*	usually
ML	Medieval Latin		*var*	variant
modif	modification		*vb*	verb
MS	manuscript		*vi*	verb intransitive
n	noun		*VL*	Vulgar Latin
neut	neuter		*vt*	verb transitive
NewEng	New England		*W*	Welsh

Pronunciation Symbols

ə . . . . . abut, collect, suppose

ˈə, ˌə . . humdrum

ᵊ . . . . . (in ᵊl, ᵊn) battle, cotton; (in lᵊ, mᵊ, rᵊ) French table, prisme, titre

ər . . . . operation, further

a . . . . . map, patch

ā . . . . . day, fate

ä . . . . . bother, cot, father

à . . . . . a sound between \a\ and \ä\, as in an Eastern New England pronunciation of aunt, ask

au̇ . . . . now, out

b . . . . . baby, rib

ch . . . . chin, catch

d . . . . . did, adder

e . . . . . set, red

ē . . . . . beat, easy

f . . . . . fifty, cuff

g . . . . . go, big

h . . . . . hat, ahead

hw . . . . whale

i . . . . . tip, banish

ī . . . . . site, buy

j . . . . job, edge

k . . . . . kin, cook

ḵ . . . . . German Bach, Scots loch

l . . . . . lily, cool

m . . . . murmur, dim

n . . . . . nine, own

ⁿ . . . . . indicates that a preceding vowel is pronounced through both nose and mouth, as in French bon \bōⁿ\

ŋ . . . . . sing, singer, finger, ink

ō . . . . . bone, hollow

ȯ . . . . . saw

œ . . . . French bœuf, German Hölle

œ̄ . . . . French feu, German Höhle

ȯi . . . . toy

p . . . . . pepper, lip

r . . . . . rarity

s . . . . . source, less

sh . . . . shy, mission

t . . . . . tie, attack

th . . . . thin, ether

th . . . . then, either

ü . . . . . boot, few \ˈfyü\

u̇ . . . . . put, pure \ˈpyu̇r\

ᵫ . . . . German füllen

ᵫ̄ . . . . French rue, German fühlen

v . . . . . vivid, give

w . . . . we, away

y . . . . . yard, cue \ˈkyü\

ʸ . . . . . indicates that a preceding \l\, \n\, or \w\ is modified by having the tongue approximate the position for \y\, as in French digne \dēnʸ\

z . . . . . zone, raise

zh . . . . vision, pleasure

\ . . . . . slant line used in pairs to mark the beginning and end of a transcription: \ˈpen\

ˈ . . . . . mark at the beginning of a syllable that has primary (strongest) stress: \ˈshə-fəl-ˌbȯrd\

ˌ . . . . . mark at the beginning of a syllable that has secondary (next-strongest) stress: \ˈshə-fəl-ˌbȯrd\

- . . . . . mark of a syllable division in pronunciations (the mark of end-of-line division in boldface entries is a centered dot •)

( ) . . . . indicate that what is symbolized between sometimes occurs and sometimes does not occur in the pronunciation of the word: bakery \ˈbā-k(ə-)rē\ = \ˈbā-kə-rē, ˈbā-krē\

A

¹a \¹ā\ *n, pl* a's *or* as \¹āz\ *often cap* 1 : the 1st letter of the English alphabet 2 : a grade rating a student's work as superior

²a \ə, (¹)ā\ *indefinite article* : ONE, SOME — used to indicate an unspecified or unidentified individual ⟨there's ∼ man outside⟩

³a *abbr, often cap* 1 absent 2 acre 3 alto 4 answer 5 are 6 area

AA *abbr* 1 Alcoholics Anonymous 2 antiaircraft 3 associate in arts

AAA *abbr* American Automobile Association

A and M *abbr* agricultural and mechanical

A and R *abbr* artists and repertory

aard·vark \¹ärd-ˌvärk\ *n* [obs. Afrikaans, fr. Afrikaans *aard* earth + *vark* pig] : a large burrowing African ungulate mammal that feeds on ants and termites with its sticky tongue

¹ab \¹ab\ *n* : an abdominal muscle

²ab *abbr* about

AB *abbr* 1 able-bodied seaman 2 airman basic 3 [NL *artium baccalaureus*] bachelor of arts

ABA *abbr* American Bar Association

aback \ə-¹bak\ *adv* : by surprise ⟨taken ∼⟩

aba·cus \¹a-bə-kəs\ *n, pl* aba·ci \-ˌsī, -ˌkē\ *or* aba·cus·es : an instrument for making calculations by sliding counters along rods or grooves

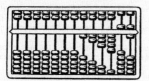

abacus

¹abaft \ə-¹baft\ *prep* : to the rear of

²abaft *adv* : toward or at the stern : AFT

ab·a·lo·ne \ˌa-bə-¹lō-nē, ¹a-bə-ˌ\ *n* : a large edible sea mollusk with a flattened slightly spiral shell with holes along the edge

¹aban·don \ə-¹ban-dən\ *vb* [ME *abandounen*, fr. MF *abandoner*, fr. *abandon*, n., surrender, fr. *a bandon* in one's power] : to give up completely : FORSAKE, DESERT — aban·don·ment *n*

²abandon *n* : a thorough yielding to natural impulses; *esp* : EXUBERANCE

aban·doned \ə-¹ban-dənd\ *adj* : morally unrestrained

syn profligate, dissolute, reprobate

abase \ə-¹bās\ *vb* abased; abas·ing : HUMBLE, DEGRADE — abase·ment *n*

abash \ə-¹bash\ *vb* : to destroy the composure of : EMBARRASS — abash·ment *n*

abate \ə-¹bāt\ *vb* abat·ed; abat·ing 1 : to put an end to ⟨∼ a nuisance⟩ 2 : to decrease in amount, number, or degree

abate·ment \ə-¹bāt-mənt\ *n* 1 : DECREASE 2 : an amount abated; *esp* : a deduction from a tax

ab·at·toir \¹a-bə-ˌtwär\ *n* [F] : SLAUGHTERHOUSE

ab·ba·cy \¹a-bə-sē\ *n, pl* -cies : the office or term of office of an abbot or abbess

ab·bé \a-¹bā, ¹a-ˌ\ *n* : a member of the French secular clergy — used as a title

ab·bess \¹a-bəs\ *n* : the superior of a convent for nuns

ab·bey \¹a-bē\ *n, pl* abbeys 1 : MONASTERY 2 : CONVENT 3 : an abbey church

ab·bot \¹a-bət\ *n* [ME *abbod*, fr. OE, fr. LL *abbat-, abbas*, fr. LGk *abbas*, fr. Aramaic *abbā* father] : the superior of a monastery for men

abbr *abbr* abbreviation

ab·bre·vi·ate \ə-¹brē-vē-ˌāt\ *vb* -at·ed; -at·ing : SHORTEN, CURTAIL; *esp* : to reduce to an abbreviation

ab·bre·vi·a·tion \ə-ˌbrē-vē-¹ā-shən\ *n* 1 : the act or result of abbreviating 2 : a shortened form of a word or phrase used for brevity esp. in writing

¹ABC \ˌā-(ˌ)bē-¹sē\ *n, pl* ABC's *or* ABCs \-¹sēz\ 1 : ALPHABET — usu. used in pl. 2 : RUDIMENTS

²ABC *abbr* American Broadcasting Company

Ab·di·as \ab-¹dī-əs\ *n* : OBADIAH

ab·di·cate \¹ab-di-ˌkāt\ *vb* -cat·ed; -cat·ing : to give up (as a throne) formally — ab·di·ca·tion \ˌab-di-¹kā-shən\ *n*

ab·do·men \¹ab-də-mən, ab-¹dō-\ *n* 1 : the cavity in or area of the body between the chest and the pelvis 2 : the part of the body posterior to the thorax in an arthropod — ab·dom·i·nal \ab-¹dä-mən- əl\ *adj* — ab·dom·i·nal·ly *adv*

ab·duct \ab-¹dəkt\ *vb* : to take away (a person) by force : KIDNAP — ab·duc·tion \-¹dək-shən\ *n* — ab·duc·tor \-tər\ *n*

abeam \ə-¹bēm\ *adv or adj* : on a line at right angles to a ship's keel

abed \ə-¹bed\ *adv or adj* : in bed

Abe·na·ki \ˌa-bə-¹nä-kē\ *n, pl* Abenaki *or* Abenakis : a member of a group of American Indian peoples of northern New England and southern Quebec

ab·er·ra·tion \ˌa-bə-¹rā-shən\ *n* 1 : deviation esp. from a moral standard or normal state 2 : failure of a mirror or lens to produce exact point-to-point correspondence between an object and its image 3 : unsoundness of mind : DERANGEMENT — ab·er·rant \a-¹ber-ənt\ *adj*

abet \ə-¹bet\ *vb* abet·ted; abet·ting [ME *abetten*, fr. MF *abeter*, fr. OF *beter* to bait] 1 : INCITE, ENCOURAGE 2 : to assist or support in the achievement of a purpose — abet·tor *or* abet·ter \-¹be-tər\ *n*

abey·ance \ə-¹bā-əns\ *n* : a condition of suspended activity

ab·hor \əb-¹hòr, ab-\ *vb* ab·horred; ab·hor·ring [ME *abhorren*, fr. L *abhorrēre*, fr. *ab-* + *horrēre* to shudder] : LOATHE, DETEST — ab·hor·rence \-əns\ *n*

ab·hor·rent \-ənt\ *adj* : LOATHSOME, DETESTABLE

abide \ə-¹bīd\ *vb* abode \-¹bōd\ *or* abid·ed; abid·ing 1 : BEAR, ENDURE 2 : DWELL, REMAIN, LAST

abil·i·ty \ə-¹bi-lə-tē\ *n, pl* -ties : the quality of being able : POWER, SKILL

-ability *also* -ibility *n suffix* : capacity, fitness, or tendency to act or be acted on in a (specified) way ⟨flammability⟩

ab·ject \¹ab-jekt, ab-¹jekt\ *adj* : low in spirit or hope : CRINGING — ab·jec·tion \ab-¹jek-shən\ *n* — ab·ject·ly *adv* — ab·ject·ness *n*

ab·jure \ab-¹jùr\ *vb* ab·jured; ab·jur·ing 1 : to renounce solemnly : RECANT 2 : to abstain from — ab·ju·ra·tion \ˌab-jə-¹rā-shən\ *n*

abl *abbr* ablative

ab·late \a-¹blāt\ *vb* ab·lat·ed; ab·lat·ing : to remove or become removed esp. by cutting, abrading, or vaporizing

ab·la·tion \a-¹blā-shən\ *n* 1 : surgical cutting and removal 2 : loss of a part (as the outside of a nose cone) by melting or vaporization

ab·la·tive \¹ab-lə-tiv\ *adj* : of, relating to, or constituting a grammatical case (as in Latin) expressing typically the relation of separation and source — ablative *n*

ablaze \ə-¹blāz\ *adj or adv* : being on fire : BLAZING

able \¹ā-bəl\ *adj* abler \-b(ə-)lər\; ablest \-b(ə-)ləst\ 1 : having sufficient power, skill, or resources to accomplish an object 2 : marked by skill or efficiency — ably \-blē\ *adv*

-able *also* -ible *adj suffix* 1 : capable of, fit for, or worthy of (being so acted upon or toward) ⟨break*able*⟩ ⟨collect*ible*⟩ **2** : tending, given, or liable to ⟨knowl-edge*able*⟩ ⟨perish*able*⟩

able-bod·ied \'ā-bəl-'bä-dēd\ *adj* : having a sound strong body

abloom \ə-'blüm\ *adj* : BLOOMING

ab·lu·tion \ə-'blü-shən, a-\ *n* : the washing of one's body or part of it

ABM \ᵊā-(ᵢ)bē-'em\ *n, pl* **ABM's** *or* **ABMs** : ANTIBAL-LISTIC MISSILE

Ab·na·ki \ab-'nä-kē\ *var of* ABENAKI

ab·ne·gate \'ab-ni-ᵢgāt\ *vb* **-gat·ed; -gat·ing 1** : DENY, RENOUNCE **2** : SURRENDER, RELINQUISH — **ab·ne·ga·tion** \ᵢab-ni-'gā-shən\ *n*

ab·nor·mal \ab-'nòr-məl\ *adj* : deviating from the nor-mal or average — **ab·nor·mal·i·ty** \ᵢab-nòr-'ma-lə-tē\ *n* — **ab·nor·mal·ly** *adv*

¹**aboard** \ə-'bōrd\ *adv* **1** : ALONGSIDE **2** : on, onto, or within a car, ship, or aircraft **3** : in or into a group or association ⟨welcome new workers ∼⟩

²**aboard** *prep* : ON, ONTO, ABOARD

abode \ə-'bōd\ *n* **1** : STAY, SOJOURN **2** : HOME, RESI-DENCE

abol·ish \ə-'bä-lish\ *vb* : to do away with : ANNUL — **ab·o·li·tion** \ᵢa-bə-'li-shən\ *n*

ab·o·li·tion·ism \ᵢa-bə-'li-shə-ᵢni-zəm\ *n* : advocacy of the abolition of slavery — **ab·o·li·tion·ist** \-'li-sh(ə-)nist\ *n or adj*

A–bomb \'ā-ᵢbäm\ *n* : ATOMIC BOMB — **A–bomb** *vb*

abom·i·na·ble \ə-'bä-mə-nə-bəl\ *adj* : ODIOUS, LOATH-SOME, DETESTABLE

abominable snow·man \-'snō-mən, -ᵢman\ *n, often cap A&S* : a mysterious creature with human or ape-like characteristics reported to exist in the high Hi-malayas

abom·i·nate \ə-'bä-mə-ᵢnāt\ *vb* **-nat·ed; -nat·ing** [L *abominari*, lit., to deprecate as an ill omen, fr. *ab-* away + *omen* omen] : LOATHE, DETEST

abom·i·na·tion \ᵢa-bä-mə-'nä-shən\ *n* **1** : something abominable **2** : DISGUST, LOATHING

ab·orig·i·nal \ᵢa-bə-'ri-jə-nəl\ *adj* : ORIGINAL, INDIGE-NOUS, PRIMITIVE

ab·orig·i·ne \ᵢa-bə-'ri-jə-nē\ *n* : a member of the orig-inal race of inhabitants of a region : NATIVE

aborn·ing \ə-'bòr-niŋ\ *adv* : while being born or pro-duced

¹**abort** \ə-'bòrt\ *vb* **1** : to cause or undergo abortion **2** : to terminate prematurely ⟨∼ a spaceflight⟩ — **abor·tive** \-'bòr-tiv\ *adj*

²**abort** *n* : the premature termination of a mission or of a procedure relating to an aircraft or spacecraft

abor·tion \ə-'bòr-shən\ *n* : the spontaneous or induced termination of a pregnancy after, accompanied by, resulting in, or closely followed by the death of the embryo or fetus

abor·tion·ist \-sh(ə-)nist\ *n* : one who induces abor-tions

abound \ə-'baund\ *vb* **1** : to be plentiful : TEEM **2** : to be fully supplied

¹**about** \ə-'baut\ *adv* **1** : reasonably close to; *also* : on the verge of ⟨∼ to join the army⟩ **2** : on all sides **3** : NEARBY

²**about** *prep* **1** : on every side of **2** : near to **3** : CON-CERNING

about–face \-'fās\ *n* : a reversal of direction or attitude — **about–face** *vb*

¹**above** \ə-'bəv\ *adv* **1** : in the sky; *also* : in or to heaven **2** : in or to a higher place; *also* : higher on the same page or on a preceding page

²**above** *prep* **1** : in or to a higher place than : OVER ⟨storm clouds ∼ the bay⟩ **2** : superior to ⟨he thought her far ∼ him⟩ **3** : more than : EXCEEDING **4** : as dis-tinct from ⟨∼ the noise⟩

above·board \-ᵢbōrd\ *adv or adj* : without conceal-ment or deception : OPENLY

abp *abbr* archbishop

abr *abbr* abridged; abridgment

ab·ra·ca·dab·ra \ᵢa-brə-kə-'da-brə\ *n* **1** : a magical charm or incantation against calamity **2** : GIBBERISH

abrade \ə-'brād\ *vb* **abrad·ed; abrad·ing 1** : to wear away by friction **2** : to wear down in spirit : IRRITATE — **abra·sion** \-'brā-zhən\ *n*

¹**abra·sive** \ə-'brā-siv\ *n* : a substance (as pumice) for abrading, smoothing, or polishing

²**abrasive** *adj* : tending to abrade : causing irritation ⟨∼ relationships⟩ — **abra·sive·ly** *adv* — **abra·sive·ness** *n*

abreast \ə-'brest\ *adv or adj* **1** : side by side **2** : up to a standard or level esp. of knowledge

abridge \ə-'brij\ *vb* **abridged; abridg·ing** [ME *abre-gen*, fr. MF *abregier*, fr. LL *abbreviare*, fr. L *ad* to + *brevis* short] : to lessen in length or extent : SHORT-EN — **abridg·ment** *or* **abridge·ment** *n*

abroad \ə-'bròd\ *adv or adj* **1** : over a wide area **2** : away from one's home **3** : outside one's country

ab·ro·gate \'a-brə-ᵢgāt\ *vb* **-gat·ed; -gat·ing** : ANNUL, REVOKE — **ab·ro·ga·tion** \ᵢa-brə-'gā-shən\ *n*

abrupt \ə-'brəpt\ *adj* **1** : broken or as if broken off **2** : SUDDEN, HASTY **3** : so quick as to seem rude **4** : DIS-CONNECTED **5** : STEEP — **abrupt·ly** *adv*

abs *abbr* absolute

ab·scess \'ab-ᵢses\ *n, pl* **ab·scess·es** [L *abscessus*, lit., act of going away, fr. *abscedere* to go away, fr. *abs-*, *ab-* away + *cedere* to go] : a localized collection of pus surrounded by inflamed tissue — **ab·scessed** \-ᵢsest\ *adj*

ab·scis·sa \ab-'si-sə\ *n, pl* **abscissas** *also* **ab·scis·sae** \-'si-(ᵢ)sē\ : the horizontal coordinate of a point in a plane coordinate system obtained by measuring par-allel to the x-axis

ab·scis·sion \ab-'si-zhən\ *n* **1** : the act or process of cutting off **2** : the natural separation of flowers, fruits, or leaves from plants — **ab·scise** \ab-'sīz\ *vb*

ab·scond \ab-'skänd\ *vb* : to depart secretly and hide oneself

ab·sence \'ab-səns\ *n* **1** : the state or time of being ab-sent **2** : WANT, LACK **3** : INATTENTION

¹**ab·sent** \'ab-sənt\ *adj* **1** : not present **2** : LACKING **3** : INATTENTIVE

²**ab·sent** \ab-'sent\ *vb* : to keep (oneself) away

³**ab·sent** \'ab-sənt\ *prep* : in the absence of : WITHOUT

ab·sen·tee \ᵢab-sən-'tē\ *n* : one that is absent or keeps away

absentee ballot *n* : a ballot submitted (as by mail) in advance of an election by a voter who is unable to be present at the polls

ab·sen·tee·ism \ᵢab-sən-'tē-ᵢi-zəm\ *n* : chronic absence (as from work or school)

ab·sent–mind·ed \ᵢab-sənt-'mīn-dəd\ *adj* : unaware of one's surroundings or actions : INATTENTIVE — **ab·sent–mind·ed·ly** *adv* — **ab·sent–mind·ed·ness** *n*

ab·sinthe *also* **ab·sinth** \'ab-ᵢsinth\ *n* [F] : a liqueur fla-vored esp. with wormwood and anise

---

ab·so·lute \'ab-sə-ᵢlüt, ᵢab-sə-'lüt\ *adj* **1** : free from imperfection or mixture **2** : free from control, restriction, or qual-ification **3** : lacking grammatical con-nection with any other word in a sentence ⟨∼ con-struction⟩ **4** : POSITIVE ⟨∼ proof⟩ **5** : relating to the fundamental units of length, mass, and time **6** : FUN-DAMENTAL, ULTIMATE — **ab·so·lute·ly** *adv*

---

absolute pitch *n* **1** : the position of a tone in a standard scale independently determined by its rate of vibra-tion **2** : the ability to sing a note asked for or to name a note heard

absolute value *n* : the numerical value of a real number that for a positive number or zero is equal to the num-ber itself and for a negative number is equal to the

positive number which when added to it is equal to zero

ab·so·lute zero *n* : a theoretical temperature marked by a complete absence of heat and equivalent to exactly −273.15°C or −459.67°F

ab·so·lu·tion \ab-sə-ˈlü-shən\ *n* : the act of absolving; *esp* : a remission of sins pronounced by a priest in the sacrament of reconciliation

ab·so·lut·ism \ˈab-sə-lü-ti-zəm\ *n* **1** : the theory that a ruler or government should have unlimited power **2** : government by an absolute ruler or authority

ab·solve \əb-ˈzälv, -ˈsälv\ *vb* **ab·solved; ab·solv·ing** : to set free from an obligation or the consequences of guilt

ab·sorb \əb-ˈsòrb, -ˈzòrb\ *vb* **1** : to take in and make part of an existent whole **2** : to suck up or take in in the manner of a sponge **3** : to engage (one's attention) : ENGROSS **4** : to receive without recoil or echo ⟨a ceiling that ∼s sound⟩ **5** : ASSUME, BEAR ⟨∼ all costs⟩ **6** : to transform (radiant energy) into a different form usu. with a resulting rise in temperature — **ab·sorb·ing** *adj* — **ab·sorb·ing·ly** *adv*

ab·sor·bent *also* **ab·sor·bant** \əb-ˈsòr-bənt, -ˈzòr-\ *adj* : able to absorb ⟨∼ cotton⟩ — **ab·sor·ben·cy** \-bən-sē\ *n* — **absorbent** *also* **absorbant** *n*

ab·sorp·tion \əb-ˈsòrp-shən, -ˈzòrp-\ *n* **1** : a process of absorbing or being absorbed **2** : concentration of attention — **ab·sorp·tive** \-tiv\ *adj*

ab·stain \əb-ˈstān\ *vb* : to refrain from an action or practice — **ab·stain·er** *n* — **ab·sten·tion** \-ˈsten-chən\ *n*

ab·ste·mi·ous \ab-ˈstē-mē-əs\ *adj* : sparing in use of food or drink : TEMPERATE — **ab·ste·mi·ous·ly** *adv* — **ab·ste·mi·ous·ness** *n*

ab·sti·nence \ˈab-stə-nəns\ *n* : voluntary refraining esp. from eating certain foods or drinking liquor — **ab·sti·nent** \-nənt\ *adj*

abstr *abbr* abstract

¹ab·stract \ab-ˈstrakt, ˈab-strakt\ *adj* **1** : considered apart from a particular instance **2** : expressing a quality apart from an object ⟨*whiteness* is an ∼ word⟩ **3** : having only intrinsic form with little or no pictorial representation ⟨∼ painting⟩ — **ab·stract·ly** *adv* — **ab·stract·ness** *n*

²ab·stract \ˈab-strakt; 2 *also* ab-ˈstrakt\ *n* **1** : SUMMARY, EPITOME **2** : an abstract thing or state

³ab·stract \ab-ˈstrakt, ˈab-strakt; 2 *usu* ˈab-strakt\ *vb* **1** : REMOVE, SEPARATE **2** : to make an abstract of : SUMMARIZE **3** : to draw away the attention of **4** : STEAL — **ab·stract·ed·ly** \ab-ˈstrak-təd-lē, ˈab-strak-\ *adv*

abstract expressionism *n* : art that expresses the artist's attitudes and emotions through abstract forms — **abstract expressionist** *n*

ab·strac·tion \ab-ˈstrak-shən\ *n* **1** : the act of abstracting : the state of being abstracted **2** : an abstract idea **3** : an abstract work of art

ab·struse \ab-ˈstrüs\ *adj* : hard to understand : RECONDITE — **ab·struse·ly** *adv* — **ab·struse·ness** *n*

ab·surd \əb-ˈsərd, -ˈzərd\ *adj* [MF *absurde*, fr. L *absurdus*, fr. *ab-* from + *surdus* deaf, stupid] : RIDICULOUS, UNREASONABLE — **ab·sur·di·ty** \-ˈsər-də-tē, -ˈzər-\ *n* — **ab·surd·ly** *adv*

abun·dant \ə-ˈbən-dənt\ *adj* [ME, fr. MF, fr. L *abundant-, abundans*, prp. of *abundare* to abound, fr. *ab-* from + *unda* wave] : more than enough : amply sufficient **syn** copious, plentiful, ample, bountiful — **abun·dance** \-dəns\ *n* — **abun·dant·ly** *adv*

¹abuse \ə-ˈbyüs\ *n* **1** : a corrupt practice **2** : MISUSE ⟨drug ∼⟩ **3** : coarse and insulting speech **4** : MISTREATMENT ⟨child ∼⟩

²abuse \ə-ˈbyüz\ *vb* **abused; abus·ing 1** : to put to a wrong use : MISUSE **2** : MISTREAT **3** : to attack in words : REVILE — **abus·er** *n* — **abu·sive** \-ˈbyü-siv\ *adj* — **abu·sive·ly** *adv* — **abu·sive·ness** *n*

abut \ə-ˈbət\ *vb* **abut·ted; abut·ting** : to touch along a border : border on

abut·ment \ə-ˈbət-mənt\ *n* : the part of a structure (as a bridge) that supports weight or withstands lateral pressure

abut·ter \ə-ˈbə-tər\ *n* : one that abuts; *esp* : the owner of a contiguous property

abys·mal \ə-ˈbiz-məl\ *adj* **1** : immeasurably deep : BOTTOMLESS **2** : absolutely wretched ⟨∼ living conditions of the poor⟩ — **abys·mal·ly** *adv*

abyss \ə-'bis\ *n* **1** : the bottomless pit in old accounts of the universe **2** : an immeasurable depth

abys·sal \ə-'bi-səl\ *adj* : of or relating to the bottom waters of the ocean depths

ac *abbr* account

-ac *n suffix* : one affected with ⟨hypochondri*ac*⟩

Ac *symbol* actinium

AC *abbr* **1** air-conditioning **2** alternating current **3** [L *ante Christum*] before Christ **4** [L *ante cibum*] before meals **5** area code

aca·cia \ə-'kā-shə\ *n* : any of numerous leguminous trees or shrubs with round white or yellow flower clusters and often fernlike leaves

acad *abbr* academic; academy

ac·a·deme \'a-kə-ˌdēm, ˌa-kə-'\ *n* : SCHOOL; *also* : academic environment

¹**ac·a·dem·ic** \ˌa-kə-'de-mik\ *n* : a person who is academic in background, outlook, or methods

²**academic** *adj* **1** : of, relating to, or associated with schools or colleges **2** : literary or general rather than technical **3** : theoretical rather than practical — **ac·a·dem·i·cal·ly** \-mi-k(ə-)lē\ *adv*

ac·a·de·mi·cian \ˌa-kə-də-'mi-shən, ə-ˌka-də-\ *n* **1** : a member of a society of scholars or artists **2** : ACADEMIC

ac·a·dem·i·cism \ˌa-kə-'de-mə-ˌsi-zəm\ *also* **acad·e·mism** \ə-'ka-də-ˌmi-zəm\ *n* **1** : a formal academic quality **2** : purely speculative thinking

acad·e·my \ə-'ka-də-mē\ *n, pl* **-mies** [Gk *Akadēmeia*, school of philosophy founded by Plato, fr. *Akadēmeia*, gymnasium where Plato taught, fr. *Akadēmos* Greek mythological hero] **1** : a school above the elementary level; *esp* : a private high school **2** : a society of scholars or artists

acan·thus \ə-'kan-thəs\ *n, pl* **acanthus 1** : any of a genus of prickly herbs of the Mediterranean region **2** : an ornamentation (as on a column) representing the leaves of the acanthus

a cap·pel·la *also* **a ca·pel·la** \ˌä-kə-'pe-lə\ *adv or adj* [It *a cappella* in chapel style] : without instrumental accompaniment

acc *abbr* accusative

ac·cede \ak-'sēd\ *vb* **ac·ced·ed; ac·ced·ing 1** : to become a party to an agreement **2** : to express approval **3** : to enter upon an office **syn** agree, acquiesce, assent, consent, subscribe

ac·cel·er·ate \ik-'se-lə-ˌrāt, ak-\ *vb* **-at·ed; -at·ing 1** : to bring about earlier **2** : to speed up : QUICKEN — **ac·cel·er·a·tion** \-ˌse-lə-'rā-shən\ *n*

ac·cel·er·a·tor \ik-'se-lə-ˌrā-tər, ak-\ *n* **1** : one that accelerates **2** : a pedal for controlling the speed of a motor-vehicle engine **3** : an apparatus for imparting high velocities to charged particles

ac·cel·er·om·e·ter \ik-ˌse-lə-'rä-mə-tər, ak-\ *n* : an instrument for measuring acceleration or vibrations

¹**ac·cent** \'ak-ˌsent, ak-'sent\ *vb* : STRESS, EMPHASIZE

²**ac·cent** \'ak-ˌsent\ *n* **1** : a distinctive manner of pronunciation ⟨a foreign ∼⟩ **2** : prominence given to one syllable of a word esp. by stress **3** : a mark (as ´, `, ˆ) over a vowel used usu. to indicate a difference in pronunciation from a vowel not so marked — **ac·cen·tu·al** \ak-'sen-chə-wəl\ *adj*

ac·cen·tu·ate \ak-'sen-chə-ˌwāt\ *vb* **-at·ed; -at·ing** : ACCENT — **ac·cen·tu·a·tion** \-ˌsen-chə-'wā-shən\ *n*

ac·cept \ik-'sept, ak-\ *vb* **1** : to receive willingly **2** : to agree to **3** : to assume an obligation to pay

ac·cept·able \ik-'sep-tə-bəl, ak-\ *adj* : capable of or worthy of being accepted — **ac·cept·abil·i·ty** \ik-ˌsep-tə-'bi-lə-tē, ak-\ *n*

ac·cep·tance \ik-'sep-təns, ak-\ *n* **1** : the act of accepting **2** : the state of being accepted or acceptable **3** : an accepted bill of exchange

ac·cep·ta·tion \ˌak-ˌsep-'tā-shən\ *n* : the generally understood meaning of a word

¹**ac·cess** \'ak-ˌses\ *n* **1** : capacity to enter or approach **2** : a way of approach : ENTRANCE

²**access** *vb* : to get at : gain access to

ac·ces·si·ble \ik-'se-sə-bəl, ak-, ek-\ *adj* **1** : capable of being reached ⟨∼ by train⟩ **2** : capable of being used, seen, or known : OBTAINABLE ⟨∼ information⟩ — **ac·ces·si·bil·i·ty** \-ˌse-sə-'bi-lə-tē-\ *n*

ac·ces·sion \ik-'se-shən, ak-\ *n* **1** : increase by something added **2** : something added **3** : the act of coming to a high office or position

ac·ces·so·ry *also* **ac·ces·sa·ry** \ik-'se-sə-rē, ak-\ *n, pl* **-ries 1** : a person who though not present abets or assists in the commission of an offense **2** : something helpful but not essential **syn** appurtenance, adjunct, appendage, appendix — **accessory** *adj*

ac·ci·dent \'ak-sə-dənt\ *n* **1** : an event occurring by chance or unintentionally **2** : CHANCE ⟨met by ∼⟩ **3** : a nonessential property

¹**ac·ci·den·tal** \ˌak-sə-'dent-ᵊl\ *adj* **1** : happening unexpectedly or by chance **2** : happening without intent or through carelessness **syn** casual, fortuitous, incidental, chance — **ac·ci·den·tal·ly** \-'den-tə-lē\ *also* **ac·ci·dent·ly** \-'dent-lē\ *adv*

²**accidental** *n* : a musical note foreign to a key indicated by a signature

ac·claim \ə-'klām\ *vb* **1** : APPLAUD, PRAISE **2** : to declare by acclamation **syn** extol, laud, commend, hail — **acclaim** *n*

ac·cla·ma·tion \ˌa-klə-'mā-shən\ *n* **1** : loud eager applause **2** : an overwhelming affirmative vote by shouting or applause rather than by ballot

ac·cli·mate \'a-klə-ˌmāt, ə-'klī-mət\ *vb* **-mat·ed; -mat·ing** : ACCLIMATIZE — **ac·cli·ma·tion** \ˌa-klə-'mā-shən, -ˌklī-\ *n*

ac·cli·ma·tise *Brit var of* ACCLIMATIZE

ac·cli·ma·tize \ə-'klī-mə-ˌtīz\ *vb* **-tized; -tiz·ing** : to accustom or become accustomed to a new climate or situation — **ac·cli·ma·ti·za·tion** \-ˌklī-mə-tə-'zā-shən\ *n*

ac·cliv·i·ty \ə-'kli-və-tē\ *n, pl* **-ties** : an ascending slope

ac·co·lade \'a-kə-ˌlād\ *n* [F, fr. *accoler* to embrace, fr. L *ad-* to + *collum* neck] : an expression of praise : AWARD

ac·com·mo·date \ə-'kä-mə-ˌdāt\ *vb* **-dat·ed; -dat·ing 1** : to make fit or suitable : ADAPT, ADJUST **2** : HARMONIZE, RECONCILE **3** : to provide with something needed **4** : to hold without crowding **5** : to undergo visual accommodation

ac·com·mo·dat·ing *adj* : OBLIGING

ac·com·mo·da·tion \ə-ˌkä-mə-'dā-shən\ *n* **1** : something supplied to satisfy a need; *esp* : LODGINGS — usu. used in pl. **2** : the act of accommodating : ADJUSTMENT **3** : the automatic adjustment of the eye for seeing at different distances

ac·com·pa·ni·ment \ə-'kəm-pə-nē-mənt, -'kəmp-nē-\ *n* : something that accompanies another; *esp* : subordinate music to support a principal voice or instrument

ac·com·pa·ny \-nē\ *vb* **-nied; -ny·ing 1** : to go or occur with : ATTEND **2** : to play an accompaniment for — **ac·com·pa·nist** \-nist\ *n*

ac·com·plice \ə-'käm-pləs, -'kəm-\ *n* : an associate in crime

ac·com·plish \ə-'käm-plish, -'kəm-\ *vb* : to bring to completion **syn** achieve, effect, execute, perform — **ac·com·plish·er** *n*

ac·com·plished *adj* **1** : EXPERT, SKILLED **2** : established beyond doubt

ac·com·plish·ment \ə-'käm-plish-mənt, -'kəm-\ *n* **1** : COMPLETION **2** : something completed or effected **3** : an acquired excellence or skill

¹**ac·cord** \ə-'kord\ *vb* [ME, fr. OF *acorder*, fr. L *ad-* to + *cord-, cor* heart] **1** : GRANT, CONCEDE **2** : AGREE, HARMONIZE — **ac·cor·dant** \-'kord-ᵊnt\ *adj*

²**accord** *n* **1** : AGREEMENT, HARMONY **2** : willingness to act ⟨gave of their own ∼⟩

ac·cor·dance \ə-'kord-ᵊns\ *n* **1** : ACCORD **2** : the act of granting

ac·cord·ing·ly \ə-ˈkòr-diŋ-lē\ adv 1 : in accordance 2 : CONSEQUENTLY, SO

according to prep 1 : in conformity with ⟨paid according to ability⟩ 2 : as stated or attested by ⟨according to you⟩

¹**ac·cor·di·on** \ə-ˈkòr-dē-ən\ n [G Akkordion, fr. Akkord chord] : a portable keyboard instrument with a bellows and reeds — **ac·cor·di·on·ist** \-ə-nist\ n

accordion

²**accordion** adj : folding like the bellows of an accordion ⟨∼ pleats⟩

ac·cost \ə-ˈkòst\ vb [MF accoster, ultim. fr. L ad- to + costa rib, side] : to approach and speak to esp. aggressively

¹**ac·count** \ə-ˈkaùnt\ n 1 : a statement of business transactions 2 : an arrangement with a vendor to supply credit 3 : a statement of reasons, causes, or motives 4 : VALUE, IMPORTANCE 5 : a sum of money deposited in a bank and subject to withdrawal by the depositor — **on account of** : BECAUSE OF — **on no account** : under no circumstances — **on one's own account** : on one's own behalf

²**account** vb 1 : CONSIDER ⟨I ∼ him lucky⟩ 2 : to give an explanation — used with for

ac·count·able \ə-ˈkaùn-tə-bəl\ adj 1 : ANSWERABLE, RESPONSIBLE 2 : EXPLICABLE — **ac·count·abil·i·ty** \-ˌkaùn-tə-ˈbi-lə-tē\ n

ac·coun·tant \ə-ˈkaùnt-ᵊnt\ n : a person skilled in accounting — **ac·coun·tan·cy** \-ᵊn-sē\ n

account executive n : a business executive in charge of a client's account

ac·count·ing \ə-ˈkaùn-tiŋ\ n : the art or system of keeping and analyzing financial records

ac·cou·tre or **ac·cou·ter** \ə-ˈkü-tər\ vb -**cou·tred** or -**cou·tered**; -**cou·tring** or -**cou·ter·ing** \-ˈkü-t(ə-)riŋ\ : EQUIP, OUTFIT

ac·cou·tre·ment or **ac·cou·ter·ment** \ə-ˈkü-trə-mənt, -ˈkü-tər-\ n [F] 1 : an accessory item — usu. used in pl. 2 : an identifying characteristic

ac·cred·it \ə-ˈkre-dət\ vb 1 : to endorse or approve officially 2 : CREDIT — **ac·cred·i·ta·tion** \-ˌkre-də-ˈtā-shən\ n

ac·cre·tion \ə-ˈkrē-shən\ n 1 : growth or enlargement esp. by addition from without 2 : a product of accretion

ac·crue \ə-ˈkrü\ vb **ac·crued**; **ac·cru·ing** 1 : to come by way of increase 2 : to be added by periodic growth — **ac·cru·al** \-əl\ n

acct abbr account; accountant

ac·cul·tur·a·tion \ə-ˌkəl-chə-ˈrā-shən\ n : cultural modification of an individual or group by borrowing and adapting traits from another culture

ac·cu·mu·late \ə-ˈkyü-myə-ˌlāt\ vb -**lat·ed**; -**lat·ing** [L accumulare, fr. ad- to + cumulare to heap up] : to heap or pile up syn amass, gather, collect, stockpile — **ac·cu·mu·la·tion** \-ˌkyü-myə-ˈlā-shən\ n — **ac·cu·mu·la·tive** \-ˈkyü-myə-lə-tiv\ adj — **ac·cu·mu·la·tor** \-ˈkyü-myə-ˌlā-tər\ n

---

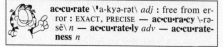

ac·cu·rate \ˈa-kyə-rət\ adj : free from error : EXACT, PRECISE — **ac·cu·ra·cy** \-rə-sē\ n — **ac·cu·rate·ly** adv — **ac·cu·rate·ness** n

---

ac·cursed \ə-ˈkərst, -ˈkər-səd\ or **ac·curst** \ə-ˈkərst\ adj 1 : being under a curse 2 : DAMNABLE, EXECRABLE

ac·cus·al \ə-ˈkyü-zəl\ n : ACCUSATION

ac·cu·sa·tive \ə-ˈkyü-zə-tiv\ adj : of, relating to, or being a grammatical case marking the direct object of a verb or the object of a preposition — **accusative** n

ac·cuse \ə-ˈkyüz\ vb **ac·cused**; **ac·cus·ing** : to charge with an offense : BLAME — **ac·cu·sa·tion** \ˌa-kyə-ˈzā-shən\ n — **ac·cus·er** n

ac·cused \ə-ˈkyüzd\ n, pl **accused** : the defendant in a criminal case

ac·cus·tom \ə-ˈkəs-təm\ vb : to make familiar through use or experience

ac·cus·tomed \ə-ˈkəs-təmd\ adj : USUAL, CUSTOMARY

¹**ace** \ˈās\ n [ME as a die face marked with one spot, fr. OF, fr. L, unit, a copper coin] 1 : a playing card bearing a single large pip in its center 2 : a point (as in tennis) won on a serve that goes untouched 3 : a golf score of one stroke on a hole 4 : a combat pilot who has downed five or more enemy planes 5 : one that excels

²**ace** vb **aced**; **ac·ing** 1 : to score an ace against (an opponent) or on (a golf hole) 2 : to defeat decisively

³**ace** adj : of first rank or quality

acer·bic \ə-ˈsər-bik, a-\ adj : acid in temper, mood, or tone

acer·bi·ty \ə-ˈsər-bə-tē\ n, pl -**ties** : SOURNESS, BITTERNESS

acet·amin·o·phen \ə-ˌsē-tə-ˈmi-nə-fən\ n : a crystalline compound used in chemical synthesis and in medicine to relieve pain and fever

ac·e·tate \ˈa-sə-ˌtāt\ n 1 : a salt or ester of acetic acid 2 : a textile fiber made from cellulose and acetic acid; also : a fabric or plastic made of this fiber

ace·tic acid \ə-ˈsē-tik-\ n : a colorless pungent liquid acid that is the chief acid of vinegar and is used esp. in making chemical compounds

ac·e·tone \ˈa-sə-ˌtōn\ n : a volatile flammable fragrant

liquid compound used in making other chemical compounds and as a solvent

ace·tyl·cho·line \ə-ˌsēt-ᵊl-ˈkō-ˌlēn\ *n* : a compound that is released at nerve endings of the autonomic nervous system and is active in the transmission of nerve impulses

acet·y·lene \ə-ˈset-ᵊl-ən, -ᵊl-ˌēn\ *n* : a colorless flammable gas used as a fuel (as in welding and soldering)

ace·tyl·sal·i·cyl·ic acid \ə-ˌsēt-ᵊl-ˌsa-lə-ˌsi-lik-\ *n* : ASPIRIN 1

ache \ˈāk\ *vb* **ached; ach·ing 1** : to suffer a usu. dull persistent pain **2** : LONG, YEARN — **ache** *n*

achieve \ə-ˈchēv\ *vb* **achieved; achiev·ing** [ME *acheven,* fr. MF *achever* to finish, fr. *a-* to (fr. L *ad-*) + *chief* end, head, fr. L *caput*] : to gain by work or effort **syn** accomplish, attain, realize — **achiev·able** \-ˈchē-və-bəl\ *adj* — **achieve·ment** *n* — **achiev·er** *n*

Achil·les' heel \ə-ˌki-lēz-\ *n* [fr. the story that the Greek warrior Achilles was vulnerable only in the heel] : a vulnerable point

Achil·les tendon \ə-ˌki-lēz-\ *n* : the tendon joining the muscles in the calf of the leg to the bone of the heel

ach·ro·mat·ic \ˌa-krə-ˈma-tik\ *adj* : giving an image almost free from extraneous colors ⟨~ lens⟩

achy \ˈā-kē\ *adj* **ach·i·er; ach·i·est** : afflicted with aches — **ach·i·ness** *n*

¹ac·id \ˈa-səd\ *adj* **1** : sour or biting to the taste; *also* : sharp or sour in manner **2** : of or relating to an acid — **acid·i·ty** \ə-ˈsi-də-tē\ *n* — **acid·ly** *adv*

²acid *n* **1** : a sour substance **2** : a usu. water-soluble chemical compound that has a sour taste, reacts with a base to form a salt, and reddens litmus **3** : LSD — **acid·ic** \ə-ˈsi-dik\ *adj*

acid·i·fy \ə-ˈsi-də-ˌfī\ *vb* **-fied; -fy·ing 1** : to make or become acid **2** : to change into an acid — **acid·i·fi·ca·tion** \-ˌsi-də-fə-ˈkā-shən\ *n*

ac·i·do·sis \ˌa-sə-ˈdō-səs\ *n, pl* **-do·ses** \-ˌsēz\ : an abnormal state of reduced alkalinity of the blood and body tissues

acid precipitation *n* : precipitation with above normal acidity that is caused esp. by atmospheric pollutants

acid rain *n* : acid precipitation in the form of rain

acid test *n* : a severe or crucial test

acid·u·lous \ə-ˈsi-jə-ləs\ *adj* : somewhat acid or harsh in taste or manner

ack *abbr* acknowledge; acknowledgment

ac·knowl·edge \ik-ˈnä-lij, ak-\ *vb* **-edged; -edg·ing 1** : to recognize the rights or authority of **2** : to admit as true **3** : to express thanks for; *also* : to report receipt of **4** : to recognize as valid — **ac·knowl·edg·ment** *or* **ac·knowl·edge·ment** *n*

ACLU *abbr* American Civil Liberties Union

ac·me \ˈak-mē\ *n* [Gk *akmē*] : the highest point

ac·ne \ˈak-nē\ *n* [Gk *aknē,* MS var. of *akmē,* lit., point] : a skin disorder marked by inflammation of skin glands and hair follicles and by pimple formation esp. on the face

ac·o·lyte \ˈa-kə-ˌlīt\ *n* **1** : one who assists a member of the clergy in a liturgical service **2** : FOLLOWER

ac·o·nite \ˈa-kə-ˌnīt\ *n* **1** : MONKSHOOD **2** : a drug obtained from a common Old World monkshood

acorn \ˈā-ˌkȯrn, -kərn\ *n* : the nut of the oak

acorn squash *n* : an acorn-shaped dark green winter squash with a ridged surface

acous·tic \ə-ˈkü-stik\ *or* **acous·ti·cal** \-sti-kəl\ *adj* **1** : of or relating to the sense or organs of hearing, to sound, or to the science of sounds **2** : deadening sound ⟨~ tile⟩ **3** : operated by or utilizing sound waves — **acous·ti·cal·ly** \-k(ə-)lē\ *adv*

acous·tics \ə-ˈkü-stiks\ *n sing or pl* **1** : the science of sound **2** : the qualities in a room that make it easy or hard for a person in it to hear distinctly

ac·quaint \ə-ˈkwānt\ *vb* [ME, ultim. fr. L *ad-* + *cognoscere* to know] **1** : to cause to know personally **2** : INFORM

ac·quain·tance \ə-ˈkwānt-ᵊns\ *n* **1** : personal knowledge **2** : a person with whom one is acquainted — **ac·quain·tance·ship** *n*

ac·qui·esce \ˌa-kwē-ˈes\ *vb* **-esced; -esc·ing** : to accept, comply, or submit without open opposition **syn** consent, agree, assent, accede — **ac·qui·es·cence** \-ˈes-ᵊns\ *n* — **ac·qui·es·cent** \-ᵊnt\ *adj* — **ac·qui·es·cent·ly** *adv*

ac·quire \ə-ˈkwīr\ *vb* **ac·quired; ac·quir·ing** : to gain possession of : GET — **ac·quir·able** \-ˈkwī-rə-bəl\ *adj*

ac·quired \ə-ˈkwīrd\ *adj* **1** : gained by or as a result of effort or experience **2** : caused by environmental forces and not passed from parent to offspring in the genes ⟨~ characteristics⟩

---

acquired immune deficiency syndrome *n* : AIDS

acquired immunodeficiency syndrome *n* : AIDS

ac·quire·ment *n* **1** : ATTAINMENT, ACCOMPLISHMENT **2** : the act of acquiring

ac·qui·si·tion \ˌa-kwə-ˈzi-shən\ *n* **1** : ACQUIREMENT **2** : something acquired

ac·quis·i·tive \ə-ˈkwi-zə-tiv\ *adj* : eager to acquire : GREEDY — **ac·quis·i·tive·ly** *adv* — **ac·quis·i·tive·ness** *n*

ac·quit \ə-ˈkwit\ *vb* **ac·quit·ted; ac·quit·ting 1** : to pronounce not guilty **2** : to conduct (oneself) usu. satisfactorily — **ac·quit·tal** \-ᵊl\ *n*

acre \ˈā-kər\ *n* **1** *pl* : LANDS, ESTATE **2** — see WEIGHT table

acre·age \ˈā-k(ə-)rij\ *n* : area in acres

ac·rid \ˈa-krəd\ *adj* **1** : sharp and biting in taste or odor **2** : deeply bitter : CAUSTIC — **acrid·i·ty** \a-ˈkri-də-tē\ *n* — **ac·rid·ly** *adv* — **ac·rid·ness** *n*

ac·ri·mo·ny \ˈa-krə-ˌmō-nē\ *n, pl* **-nies** : harsh or biting sharpness of language or feeling — **ac·ri·mo·ni·ous** \ˌa-krə-ˈmō-nē-əs\ *adj* — **ac·ri·mo·ni·ous·ly** *adv* — **ac·ri·mo·ni·ous·ness** *n*

ac·ro·bat \ˈa-krə-ˌbat\ *n* [F *acrobate,* fr. Gk *akrobatēs,* fr. *akros* topmost + *bainein* to go] : a performer of gymnastic feats — **ac·ro·bat·ic** \ˌa-krə-ˈba-tik\ *adj* — **ac·ro·bat·i·cal·ly** \-ti-k(ə-)lē\ *adv*

ac·ro·bat·ics \ˌa-krə-ˈba-tiks\ *n sing or pl* : the performance of an acrobat

ac·ro·nym \ˈa-krə-ˌnim\ *n* : a word (as *radar*) formed from the initial letter or letters of each of the successive parts or major parts of a compound term

ac·ro·pho·bia \ˌa-krə-ˈfō-bē-ə\ *n* : abnormal dread of being at a great height

ac·rop·o·lis \ə-ˈkrä-pə-ləs\ *n* [Gk *akropolis,* fr. *akros* topmost + *polis* city] : the upper fortified part of an ancient Greek city

¹**across** \ə-ˈkrȯs\ *adv* **1** : to or on the opposite side **2** : so as to be understandable ⟨get the point ∼⟩

²**across** *prep* **1** : to or on the opposite side of ⟨ran ∼ the street⟩ **2** : on so as to cross or pass at an angle ⟨a log ∼ the road⟩

across–the–board *adj* **1** : placed to win if a competitor wins, places, or shows ⟨an ∼ bet⟩ **2** : including all classes or categories ⟨an ∼ wage increase⟩

acros·tic \ə-ˈkrȯs-tik\ *n* : a composition usu. in verse in which the initial or final letters of the lines taken in order form a word or phrase — **acrostic** *adj*

acryl·ic \ə-ˈkri-lik\ *n* **1** : ACRYLIC RESIN **2** : a paint in which the vehicle is acrylic resin **3** : a quick-drying synthetic textile fiber

acrylic resin *n* : a glassy thermoplastic used for cast and molded parts or as coatings and adhesives

¹**act** \ˈakt\ *n* **1** : a thing done : DEED **2** : STATUTE, DECREE **3** : a main division of a play; *also* : an item on a variety program **4** : an instance of insincere behavior : PRETENSE

²**act** *vb* **1** : to perform by action esp. on the stage; *also* : FEIGN, SIMULATE, PRETEND **2** : to take action **3** : to conduct oneself : BEHAVE **4** : to perform a specified function **5** : to produce an effect

³**act** *abbr* **1** active **2** actual

ACT *abbr* Australian Capital Territory

actg *abbr* acting

ACTH \ˌā-(ˌ)sē-(ˌ)tē-ˈāch\ *n* : a protein hormone of the pituitary gland that stimulates the adrenal cortex

act·ing \ˈak-tiŋ\ *adj* : doing duty temporarily or for another ⟨∼ president⟩

ac·tin·i·um \ak-ˈti-nē-əm\ *n* : a radioactive metallic chemical element — see ELEMENT table

ac·tion \ˈak-shən\ *n* **1** : a legal proceeding **2** : the manner or method of performing **3** : ACTIVITY **4** : ACT, DEED **5** : the accomplishment of a thing usu. over a period of time, in stages, or with the possibility of repetition **6** *pl* : CONDUCT **7** : COMBAT, BATTLE **8** : the events of a literary plot **9** : an operating mechanism ⟨the ∼ of a gun⟩; *also* : the way it operates ⟨stiff ∼⟩

ac·tion·able \ˈak-sh(ə-)nə-bəl\ *adj* : affording ground for an action or suit at law — **action·ably** \-blē\ *adv*

ac·ti·vate \ˈak-tə-ˌvāt\ *vb* **-vat·ed; -vat·ing 1** : to spur into action; *also* : to make active, reactive, or radioactive **2** : to treat (as carbon) so as to improve adsorptive properties **3** : to set up (a military unit)

formally; *also* : to call to active duty — **ac·ti·va·tion** \ˌak-tə-ˈvā-shən\ *n* — **ac·ti·va·tor** \ˈak-tə-ˌvā-tər\ *n*

ac·tive \ˈak-tiv\ *adj* **1** : causing or involving action or change **2** : asserting that the grammatical subject performs the action represented by the verb ⟨∼ voice⟩ **3** : BRISK, LIVELY **4** : erupting or likely to erupt ⟨∼ volcano⟩ **5** : presently in operation or use **6** : tending to progress or to cause degeneration ⟨∼ tuberculosis⟩ — **active** *n* — **ac·tive·ly** *adv* — **ac·tive·ness** *n*

ac·tiv·ism \ˈak-ti-ˌvi-zəm\ *n* : a doctrine or practice that emphasizes vigorous action for political ends — **ac·tiv·ist** \-vist\ *n or adj*

ac·tiv·i·ty \ak-ˈti-və-tē\ *n, pl* **-ties 1** : the quality or state of being active **2** : forceful or energetic action **3** : an occupation in which one is engaged

ac·tor \ˈak-tər\ *n* : a person who acts in a play or motion picture

ac·tress \ˈak-trəs\ *n* : a woman who is an actor

Acts \ˈakts\ *or* **Acts of the Apostles** *n* — see BIBLE table

ac·tu·al \ˈak-chə-wəl, -shə-\ *adj* : really existing : REAL — **ac·tu·al·i·ty** \ˌak-chə-ˈwa-lə-tē, -shə-\ *n* — **ac·tu·al·iza·tion** \ˌak-chə-wə-lə-ˈzā-shən, -shə-\ *n* — **ac·tu·al·ize** \ˈak-chə-wə-ˌlīz, -shə-\ *vb*

ac·tu·al·ly \ˈak-chə-wə-lē, -shə-\ *adv* : in fact or in truth : REALLY

ac·tu·ary \ˈak-chə-ˌwer-ē, -shə-\ *n, pl* **-ar·ies** : a person who calculates insurance risks and premiums — **ac·tu·ar·i·al** \ˌak-chə-ˈwer-ē-əl, -shə-\ *adj*

ac·tu·ate \ˈak-chə-ˌwāt\ *vb* **-at·ed; -at·ing 1** : to put into action **2** : to move to action — **ac·tu·a·tion** \ˌak-chə-ˈwā-shən, -shə-\ *n* — **ac·tu·a·tor** \ˈak-chə-ˌwā-tər, -shə-\ *n*

act up *vb* **1** : MISBEHAVE **2** : to function improperly

acu·ity \ə-ˈkyü-ə-tē\ *n, pl* **-ities** : keenness of perception

acu·men \ə-ˈkyü-mən\ *n* : mental keenness and penetration **syn** discernment, insight, percipience, perspicacity

acu·pres·sure \ˈa-kyu-ˌpre-shər\ *n* : SHIATSU

acu·punc·ture \-ˌpəŋk-chər\ *n* : an orig. Chinese practice of puncturing the body (as with needles) at specific points to cure disease or relieve pain — **acu·punc·tur·ist** \ˌa-kyu-ˈpəŋk-chə-rist\ *n*

acute \ə-ˈkyüt\ *adj* **acut·er; acut·est** [L *acutus,* pp. of *acuere* to sharpen, fr. *acus* needle] **1** : SHARP, POINTED **2** : containing less than 90 degrees ⟨an ∼ angle⟩ **3** : sharply perceptive; *esp* : mentally keen **4** : SEVERE ⟨∼ distress⟩; *also* : having a sudden onset, sharp rise, and short duration ⟨∼ inflammation⟩ **5** : of, marked by, or being an accent mark having the form ´ — **acute·ly** *adv* — **acute·ness** *n*

acy·clo·vir \(ˌ)ā-ˈsī-klō-ˌvir\ *n* : a drug used esp. to treat the genital form of herpes simplex

ad \ˈad\ *n* : ADVERTISEMENT

AD *abbr* **1** after date **2** [L *anno Domini*] in the year of our Lord — often printed in small capitals and often punctuated **3** assistant director **4** athletic director

ad·age \ˈa-dij\ *n* : an old familiar saying : PROVERB, MAXIM

¹ada·gio \ə-'dä-j(ē-₁)ō, -zh(ē-₁)ō\ *adv or adj* [It] : at a slow tempo — used as a direction in music

²adagio *n, pl* **-gios 1** : an adagio movement **2** : a ballet duet or trio displaying feats of lifting and balancing

¹ad·a·mant \'a-də-mənt, -₁mant\ *n* [ME, fr. OF, fr. L *adamant-, adamas* hardest metal, diamond, fr. Gk] : a stone believed to be impenetrably hard — **ad·a·man·tine** \₁a-də-'man-₁tēn, -₁tīn\ *adj*

²adamant *adj* : INFLEXIBLE, UNYIELDING — **ad·a·mant·ly** *adv*

Ad·am's apple \'a-dəmz-\ *n* : the projection in front of the neck formed by the largest cartilage of the larynx

adapt \ə-'dapt\ *vb* : to make suitable or fit (as for a new use or for different conditions) **syn** adjust, accommodate, conform — **adapt·abil·i·ty** \ə-₁dap-tə-'bi-lə-tē\ *n* — **adapt·able** *adj* — **ad·ap·ta·tion** \₁a-₁dap-'tā-shən\ *n* — **ad·ap·ta·tion·al** \-sh(ə-)nəl\ *adj* — **adap·tive** \ə-'dap-tiv\ *adj* — **ad·ap·tiv·i·ty** \₁a-₁dap-'ti-və-tē\ *n*

adapt·er *also* **adap·tor** \ə-'dap-tər\ *n* **1** : one that adapts **2** : a device for connecting two dissimilar parts of an apparatus **3** : an attachment for adapting apparatus for uses not orig. intended

ADC *abbr* **1** aide-de-camp **2** Aid to Dependent Children

add \'ad\ *vb* **1** : to join to something else so as to increase in number or amount **2** : to say further ⟨let me ∼ this⟩ **3** : to combine (numbers) into one sum

ad·dend \'a-₁dend\ *n* : a number to be added to another

ad·den·dum \a-'den-dəm\ *n, pl* **-da** \-də\ [L] : something added; *esp* : a supplement to a book

¹ad·der \'a-dər\ *n* **1** : a poisonous European viper or a related snake **2** : any of various harmless No. American snakes (as the hognose snake)

²add·er \'a-dər\ *n* : one that adds; *esp* : a device that performs addition

¹ad·dict \ə-'dikt\ *vb* **1** : to devote or surrender (oneself) to something habitually or excessively **2** : to cause addiction to a substance in (as a person) — **ad·dic·tive** \-'dik-tiv\ *adj*

²ad·dict \'a-(₁)dikt\ *n* : one who is addicted to a substance

ad·dic·tion \ə-'dik-shən\ *n* **1** : the quality or state of being addicted **2** : compulsive need for and use of a habit-forming substance (as heroin, nicotine, or alcohol) characterized by well-defined physiological symptoms upon withdrawal; *also* : persistent compulsive use of a substance known by the user to be harmful

ad·di·tion \ə-'di-shən\ *n* **1** : the act or process of adding; *also* : something added **2** : the operation of combining numbers to obtain their sum **syn** accretion, increment, accession, augmentation

ad·di·tion·al \ə-'di-sh(ə-)nəl\ *adj* : coming by way of addition : ADDED, EXTRA

ad·di·tion·al·ly \ə-'di-sh(ə-)nə-lē\ *adv* : in or by way of addition : FURTHERMORE

¹ad·di·tive \'a-də-tiv\ *adj* **1** : of, relating to, or characterized by addition **2** : produced by addition — **ad·di·tiv·i·ty** \₁a-də-'ti-və-tē\ *n*

²additive *n* : a substance added to another in small quantities to effect a desired change in properties ⟨food ∼s⟩

ad·dle \'ad-²l\ *vb* **ad·dled; ad·dling 1** : to throw into confusion : MUDDLE **2** : to become rotten ⟨addled eggs⟩

addn *abbr* addition

addnl *abbr* additional

add-on \'ad-₁ȯn, -₁än\ *n* : something (as a feature or accessory) added esp. as an enhancement

¹ad·dress \ə-'dres\ *vb* **1** : to direct the attention of (oneself) **2** : to direct one's remarks to : deliver an address to **3** : to mark directions for delivery on **4** : to identify (as a memory location) by an address

²ad·dress \ə-'dres, 'a-₁dres\ *n* **1** : skillful management

2 : a formal speech : LECTURE **3** : the place where a person or organization may be communicated with **4** : the directions for delivery placed on mail **5** : a location (as in a computer's memory) where particular data is stored

ad·dress·ee \₁a-₁dre-'sē, ə-₁dre-'sē\ *n* : one to whom something is addressed

ad·duce \ə-'düs, -'dyüs\ *vb* **ad·duced; ad·duc·ing** : to offer as argument, reason, or proof **syn** advance, allege, cite, submit — **ad·duc·er** *n*

-ade *n suffix* **1** : act : action ⟨block*ade*⟩ **2** : product; *esp* : sweet drink ⟨lime*ade*⟩

ad·e·nine \'ad-²n-₁ēn\ *n* : one of the purine bases that make up the genetic code of DNA and RNA

ad·e·noid \'ad-₁nȯid, -²n-₁ȯid\ *n* : an enlarged mass of tissue near the opening of the nose into the throat — usu. used in pl. — **adenoid** *or* **ad·e·noi·dal** \₁ad-'nȯi-dəl, -²n-'ȯi-\ *adj*

aden·o·sine tri·phos·phate \ə-'de-nə-₁sēn-trī-'fäs-₁fāt\ *n* : ATP

¹ad·ept \'a-₁dept\ *n* : EXPERT

²adept \ə-'dept\ *adj* : highly skilled : EXPERT — **adept·ly** *adv* — **adept·ness** *n*

ad·e·quate \'a-di-kwət\ *adj* : equal to or sufficient for a specific requirement — **ad·e·qua·cy** \-kwə-sē\ *n* — **ad·e·quate·ly** *adv* — **ad·e·quate·ness** *n*

ad·here \ad-'hir\ *vb* **ad·hered; ad·her·ing 1** : to give support : maintain loyalty **2** : to stick fast : CLING — **ad·her·ence** \-'hir-əns\ *n* — **ad·her·ent** \-ənt\ *adj or n*

ad·he·sion \ad-'hē-zhən\ *n* **1** : the act or state of adhering **2** : the union of bodily tissues abnormally grown together after inflammation; *also* : the newly formed uniting tissue **3** : the molecular attraction between the surfaces of bodies in contact

¹ad·he·sive \-'hē-siv, -ziv\ *adj* **1** : tending to adhere : STICKY **2** : prepared for adhering

²adhesive *n* : an adhesive substance

adhesive tape *n* : tape coated on one side with an adhesive mixture; *esp* : one used for covering wounds

¹ad hoc \'ad-'häk, -'hōk\ *adv* [L, for this] : for the case at hand apart from other applications

²ad hoc *adj* : concerned with or formed for a particular purpose ⟨an ad hoc committee⟩ ⟨ad hoc solutions⟩

adi·a·bat·ic \₁a-dē-ə-'ba-tik\ *adj* : occurring without loss or gain of heat — **adi·a·bat·i·cal·ly** \-ti-k(ə-)lē\ *adv*

adieu \ə-'dü, -'dyü\ *n, pl* **adieus** *or* **adieux** \ə-'düz, -'dyüz\ : FAREWELL — often used interjectionally

ad in·fi·ni·tum \₁ad-₁in-fə-'nī-təm\ *adv or adj* : without end or limit

ad in·ter·im \ad-'in-tə-rəm, -₁rim\ *adv* : for the intervening time — **ad interim** *adj*

adi·os \₁a-dē-'ōs, ₁ä-\ *interj* [Sp *adiós*, lit., to God] — used to express farewell

ad·i·pose \'a-də-₁pōs\ *adj* : of or relating to animal fat : FATTY

adj *abbr* **1** adjective **2** adjutant

ad·ja·cent \ə-'jās-²nt\ *adj* : situated near or next **syn** adjoining, contiguous, abutting, juxtaposed, conterminous — **ad·ja·cent·ly** *adv*

ad·jec·tive \'a-jik-tiv\ *n* : a word that typically serves as a modifier of a noun — **ad·jec·ti·val** \₁a-jik-'tī-vəl\ *adj* — **ad·jec·ti·val·ly** *adv*

ad·join \ə-'jȯin\ *vb* : to be situated next to

ad·join·ing *adj* : touching or bounding at a point or line

ad·journ \ə-'jərn\ *vb* **1** : to suspend indefinitely or until a stated time **2** : to transfer to another place — **ad·journ·ment** *n*

ad·judge \ə-'jəj\ *vb* **ad·judged; ad·judg·ing 1** : JUDGE, ADJUDICATE **2** : to hold or pronounce to be : DEEM **3** : to award by judicial decision

ad·ju·di·cate \ə-'jü-di-₁kāt\ *vb* **-cat·ed; -cat·ing** : to settle judicially — **ad·ju·di·ca·tion** \ə-₁jü-di-'kā-shən\ *n*

ad·junct \'a-₁jəŋkt\ *n* : something joined or added to another but not essentially a part of it **syn** appendage, appurtenance, accessory, appendix

ad·jure \ə-ˈju̇r\ *vb* **ad·jured; ad·jur·ing** : to command solemnly : urge earnestly **syn** beg, beseech, implore — **ad·ju·ra·tion** \ˌa-jə-ˈrā-shən\ *n*

ad·just \ə-ˈjəst\ *vb* **1** : to bring to agreement : SETTLE **2** : to cause to conform : ADAPT, FIT **3** : REGULATE ⟨∼ a watch⟩ — **ad·just·able** *adj* — **ad·just·er** *also* **ad·jus·tor** \ə-ˈjəs-tər\ *n* — **ad·just·ment** \ə-ˈjəst-mənt\ *n*

ad·ju·tant \ˈa-jə-tənt\ *n* : one who assists; *esp* : an officer who assists a commanding officer by handling correspondence and keeping records

ad·ju·vant \ˈa-jə-vənt\ *n* : one that helps or facilitates; *esp* : something that enhances the effectiveness of medical treatment — **adjuvant** *adj*

¹ad–lib \ˈad-ˈlib\ *vb* **ad–libbed; ad–lib·bing** : IMPROVISE — **ad–lib** *n*

²ad–lib *adj* : spoken, composed, or performed without preparation

ad lib \ˈad-ˈlib\ *adv* [NL *ad libitum*] **1** : at one's pleasure **2** : without limit

adm *abbr* administration; administrative

ADM *abbr* admiral

ad·man \ˈad-ˌman\ *n* : one who writes, solicits, or places advertisements

admin *abbr* administration; administrative

ad·min·is·ter \əd-ˈmi-nə-stər\ *vb* **1** : MANAGE, SUPERINTEND **2** : to mete out : DISPENSE **3** : to give ritually or remedially ⟨∼ quinine for malaria⟩ **4** : to perform the office of administrator — **ad·min·is·tra·ble** \-strə-bəl\ *adj* — **ad·min·is·trant** \-strənt\ *n*

ad·min·is·tra·tion \əd-ˌmi-nə-ˈstrā- shən\ *n* **1** : the act or process of administering **2** : MANAGEMENT **3** : the officials directing the government of a country **4** : the term of office of an administrative officer or body — **ad·min·is·tra·tive** \əd-ˈmi-nə-ˌstrā-tiv\ *adj* — **ad·min·is·tra·tive·ly** *adv*

ad·min·is·tra·tor \əd-ˈmi-nə-ˌstrā-tər\ *n* : one that administers; *esp* : one who settles an intestate estate

ad·mi·ra·ble \ˈad-m(ə-)rə-bəl\ *adj* : worthy of admiration : EXCELLENT — **ad·mi·ra·bil·i·ty** \ˌad-m(ə-)rə-ˈbi-lə-tē\ *n* — **ad·mi·ra·ble·ness** *n* — **ad·mi·ra·bly** \-blē\ *adv*

ad·mi·ral \ˈad-m(ə-)rəl\ *n* [ME, ultim. fr. Ar *amīr-al-* commander of the (as in *amīr-al-baḥr* commander of the sea)] : a commissioned officer in the navy ranking next below a fleet admiral

ad·mi·ral·ty \ˈad-m(ə-)rəl-tē\ *n* **1** *cap* : a British government department formerly having authority over naval affairs **2** : the court having jurisdiction over questions of maritime law

ad·mire \əd-ˈmīr\ *vb* **ad·mired; ad·mir·ing** [MF *admirer*, fr. L *admirari*, fr. *ad-* to + *mirari* to wonder] : to regard with high esteem — **ad·mi·ra·tion** \ˌad-mə-ˈrā-shən\ *n* — **ad·mir·er** *n* — **ad·mir·ing·ly** \-ˈmī-riŋ-lē\ *adv*

ad·mis·si·ble \əd-ˈmi-sə-bəl\ *adj* : that can be or is worthy to be admitted or allowed : ALLOWABLE ⟨∼ evidence⟩ — **ad·mis·si·bil·i·ty** \-ˌmi-sə-ˈbi-lə-tē\ *n*

ad·mis·sion \əd-ˈmi-shən\ *n* **1** : the act of admitting **2** : the privilege of being admitted **3** : a fee paid for admission **4** : the granting of an argument **5** : the acknowledgment of a fact

ad·mit \əd-ˈmit\ *vb* **ad·mit·ted; ad·mit·ting 1** : PERMIT, ALLOW **2** : to recognize as genuine or valid **3** : to allow to enter

ad·mit·tance \əd-ˈmit-ᵊns\ *n* : permission to enter

ad·mit·ted·ly \əd-ˈmi-təd-lē\ *adv* **1** : as has been or must be admitted **2** : it must be admitted

ad·mix \ad-ˈmiks\ *vb* : to mix in

ad·mix·ture \ad-ˈmiks-chər\ *n* **1** : something added in mixing **2** : MIXTURE

ad·mon·ish \ad-ˈmä-nish\ *vb* : to warn gently : reprove with a warning **syn** chide, reproach, rebuke, reprimand, reprove — **ad·mon·ish·er** *n* — **ad·mon·ish·ing·ly** *adv* — **ad·mon·ish·ment** *n* — **ad·mo·ni·tion** \ˌad-mə-ˈni-shən\ *n* — **ad·mon·i·to·ry** \ad-ˈmä-nə-ˌtōr-ē\ *adj*

ad nau·se·am \ad-ˈnȯ-zē-əm\ *adv* [L] : to a sickening or excessive degree

ado \ə-ˈdü\ *n* **1** : bustling excitement : FUSS **2** : TROUBLE

ado·be \ə-ˈdō-bē\ *n* **1** : sun-dried brick; *also* : clay for making such bricks **2** : a structure made of adobe bricks

ad·o·les·cence \ˌad-ᵊl-ˈes-ᵊns\ *n* : the process or period of growth between childhood and maturity — **ad·o·les·cent** \-ᵊnt\ *adj or n*

adopt \ə-ˈdäpt\ *vb* **1** : to take (a child of other parents) as one's own child **2** : to take up and practice as one's own **3** : to accept formally and put into effect — **adopt·able** \-ˈdäp-tə-bəl\ *adj* — **adopt·er** *n* — **adop·tion** \-ˈdäp-shən\ *n*

adop·tive \ə-ˈdäp-tiv\ *adj* : made or acquired by adoption ⟨∼ father⟩ — **adop·tive·ly** *adv*

ador·able \ə-ˈdȯr-ə-bəl\ *adj* **1** : worthy of adoration **2** : extremely charming — **ador·able·ness** *n* — **ador·ably** \-blē\ *adv*

adore \ə-ˈdȯr\ *vb* **adored; ador·ing** [ME *adouren*, fr. MF *adorer*, fr. L *adorare*, fr. *ad-* + *orare* to speak, pray] **1** : WORSHIP **2** : to regard with loving admiration **3** : to be extremely fond of — **ad·o·ra·tion** \ˌa-də-ˈrā-shən\ *n*

adorn \ə-ˈdȯrn\ *vb* : to enhance the appearance of esp. with ornaments — **adorn·ment** *n*

ad·re·nal \ə-ˈdrēn-ᵊl\ *adj* : of, relating to, or being a pair of endocrine organs (**adrenal glands**) that are located near the kidneys and produce several hormones and esp. epinephrine

adren·a·line \ə-ˈdren-ᵊl-ən\ *n* : EPINEPHRINE

adrift \ə-ˈdrift\ *adv or adj* **1** : afloat without motive power or moorings **2** : without guidance or purpose

adroit \ə-ˈdrȯit\ *adj* [F, fr. OF, fr. *a-* to + *droit* right] **1** : dexterous with one's hands **2** : SHREWD, RESOURCEFUL **syn** canny, clever, cunning, ingenious — **adroit·ly** *adv* — **adroit·ness** *n*

ad·sorb \ad-ˈsȯrb, -ˈzȯrb\ *vb* : to take up (as molecules

of gases) and hold on the surface of a solid or liquid — **ad·sorp·tion** \-'sȯrp-shən, -'zȯrp-\ n

ad·u·late \'a-jə-ˌlāt\ vb **-lat·ed; -lat·ing** : to flatter or admire excessively — **ad·u·la·tion** \ˌa-jə-'lā-shən\ n — **ad·u·la·tor** \'a-jə-ˌlā-tər\ n — **ad·u·la·to·ry** \-lə-ˌtȯr-ē\ adj

¹**adult** \ə-'dəlt, 'a-ˌ\ adj [L adultus, pp. of adolescere to grow up, fr. ad- to + alescere to grow] : fully developed and mature — **adult·hood** n

²**adult** n : one that is adult; esp : a human being after an age (as 18) specified by law

adul·ter·ant \ə-'dəl-tə-rənt\ n : something used to adulterate another

adul·ter·ate \ə-'dəl-tə-ˌrāt\ vb **-at·ed; -at·ing** [L adulterare, fr. ad- to + alter other] : to make impure by mixing in a foreign or inferior substance — **adul·ter·a·tion** \-ˌdəl-tə-'rā-shən\ n

adul·tery \ə-'dəl-t(ə-)rē\ n, pl **-ter·ies** : sexual unfaithfulness of a married person — **adul·ter·er** \-tər-ər\ n — **adul·ter·ess** \-t(ə-)rəs\ n — **adul·ter·ous** \-t(ə-)rəs\ adj

ad·um·brate \'a-dəm-ˌbrāt\ vb **-brat·ed; -brat·ing 1** : to foreshadow vaguely : INTIMATE **2** : to suggest or disclose partially **3** : SHADE, OBSCURE — **ad·um·bra·tion** \ˌa-dəm-'brā-shən\ n

adv abbr **1** adverb **2** advertisement

ad va·lor·em \ˌad-və-'lȯr-əm\ adj [L, according to the value] : imposed at a percentage of the value (an ad valorem tax)

¹**ad·vance** \əd-'vans\ vb **ad·vanced; ad·vanc·ing 1** : to assist the progress of **2** : to bring or move forward **3** : to promote in rank **4** : to make earlier in time **5** : PROPOSE **6** : LEND **7** : to raise in rate : INCREASE — **ad·vance·ment** n

²**advance** n **1** : a forward movement **2** : IMPROVEMENT **3** : a rise esp. in price or value **4** : OFFER — **in advance** : BEFOREHAND

³**advance** adj : made, sent, or furnished ahead of time

ad·van·tage \əd-'van-tij\ n **1** : superiority of position **2** : BENEFIT, GAIN **3** : the 1st point won in tennis after deuce — **ad·van·ta·geous** \ˌad-van-'tā-jəs\ adj — **ad·van·ta·geous·ly** adv

ad·vent \'ad-ˌvent\ n **1** cap : a penitential period beginning four Sundays before Christmas **2** cap : the coming of Christ **3** : a coming into being or use

ad·ven·ti·tious \ˌad-vən-'ti-shəs\ adj **1** : ACCIDENTAL, INCIDENTAL **2** : arising or occurring sporadically or in other than the usual location ⟨∼ buds⟩ — **ad·ven·ti·tious·ly** adv

¹**ad·ven·ture** \əd-'ven-chər\ n **1** : a risky undertaking **2** : a remarkable and exciting experience — **ad·ven·tur·ous** \-ch(ə-)rəs\ adj

²**adventure** vb **-ven·tured; -ven·tur·ing** \-'ven-ch(ə-)riŋ\ : RISK, HAZARD

ad·ven·tur·er \əd-'ven-ch(ə-)rər\ n **1** : a person who engages in new and risky undertakings **2** : a person who follows a military career for adventure or profit **3** : a person who tries to gain wealth by questionable means

ad·ven·ture·some \əd-'ven-chər-səm\ adj : inclined to take risks

ad·ven·tur·ess \əd-'ven-ch(ə-)rəs\ n : a female adventurer

ad·verb \'ad-ˌvərb\ n : a word that typically serves as a modifier of a verb, an adjective, or another adverb — **ad·ver·bi·al** \ad-'vər-bē-əl\ adj — **ad·ver·bi·al·ly** adv

¹**ad·ver·sary** \'ad-vər-ˌser-ē\ n, pl **-sar·ies** : FOE

²**adversary** adj : involving antagonistic parties or interests

ad·verse \ad-'vərs, 'ad-ˌvərs\ adj **1** : acting against or in a contrary direction **2** : UNFAVORABLE — **ad·verse·ly** adv

ad·ver·si·ty \ad-'vər-sə-tē\ n, pl **-ties** : hard times : MISFORTUNE

ad·vert \ad-'vərt\ vb : REFER

ad·ver·tise \'ad-vər-ˌtīz\ vb **-tised; -tis·ing 1** : INFORM, NOTIFY **2** : to call public attention to esp. in order to sell — **ad·ver·tis·er** n

ad·ver·tise·ment \ˌad-vər-'tīz-mənt; əd-'vər-təs-mənt\ n **1** : the act of advertising **2** : a public notice intended to advertise something

ad·ver·tis·ing \'ad-vər-ˌtī-ziŋ\ n : the business of preparing advertisements

ad·vice \əd-'vīs\ n **1** : recommendation with regard to a course of action : COUNSEL **2** : INFORMATION, REPORT

ad·vis·able \əd-'vī-zə-bəl\ adj : proper to be done : EXPEDIENT — **ad·vis·abil·i·ty** \-ˌvī-zə-'bi-lə-tē\ n

ad·vise \əd-'vīz\ vb **ad·vised; ad·vis·ing 1** : to give advice to : COUNSEL **2** : INFORM, NOTIFY **3** : CONSULT, CONFER — **ad·vis·er** or **ad·vi·sor** \-'vī-zər\ n

ad·vised \əd-'vīzd\ adj : thought out : CONSIDERED ⟨well-advised⟩ — **ad·vis·ed·ly** \-'vī-zəd-lē\ adv

ad·vise·ment \əd-'vīz-mənt\ n **1** : careful consideration **2** : the act of advising

ad·vi·so·ry \əd-'vī-zə-rē\ adj **1** : having or exercising power to advise **2** : containing advice

¹**ad·vo·cate** \'ad-və-kət, -ˌkāt\ n [ultim. fr. L advocare to summon, fr. ad- to + vocare to call] **1** : one who pleads another's cause **2** : one who argues or pleads for a cause or proposal — **ad·vo·ca·cy** \-və-kə-sē\ n

²**ad·vo·cate** \-ˌkāt\ vb **-cat·ed; -cat·ing** : to plead in favor of — **ad·vo·ca·tion** \ˌad-və-'kā-shən\ n

advt abbr advertisement

adze also **adz** \'adz\ n : a tool with a curved blade set at right angles to the handle that is used in shaping wood

adze

AEC abbr Atomic Energy Commission

ae·gis \'ē-jəs\ n **1** : SHIELD, PROTECTION **2** : PATRONAGE, SPONSORSHIP

ae·o·li·an harp \ē-'ō-lē-ən-\ n : a box with strings that produce musical sounds when the wind blows on them

ae·on \'ē-ən, -ˌän\ n : an indefinitely long time : AGE

aer·ate \'a(-ə)r-ˌāt\ vb **aer·at·ed; aer·at·ing 1** : to supply (blood) with oxygen by respiration **2** : to supply, impregnate, or combine with a gas and esp. air — **aer·a·tion** \ˌa(-ə)r-'ā-shən\ n — **aer·a·tor** \'a(-ə)r-ˌā-tər\ n

¹**ae·ri·al** \'ar-ē-əl\ adj **1** : inhabiting, occurring in, or done in the air **2** : AIRY **3** : of or relating to aircraft

²**aer·i·al** \'ar-ē-əl\ n : ANTENNA 2

ae·ri·al·ist \'ar-ē-ə-list\ n : a performer of feats above the ground esp. on a trapeze

ae·rie \'ar-ē, 'ir-ē\ n : a highly placed nest (as of an eagle)

aer·o·bat·ics \ˌar-ə-'ba-tiks\ n sing or pl : spectacular flying feats and maneuvers

aer·o·bic \a(-ə)r-'rō-bik\ adj **1** : living or active only in the presence of oxygen ⟨∼ bacteria⟩ **2** : of or relating to aerobics — **aer·o·bi·cal·ly** \-bi-k(ə-)lē\ adv

aer·o·bics \-biks\ n sing or pl : strenuous exercises that produce a marked temporary increase in respiration and heart rate; also : a system of physical conditioning involving these

aero·drome \'ar-ə-ˌdrōm\ n, chiefly Brit : AIRPORT

aero·dy·nam·ics \ˌar-ō-dī-'na-miks\ n : the science dealing with the forces acting on bodies in motion in a gas (as air) — **aero·dy·nam·ic** \-mik\ also **aero·dy·nam·i·cal** \-mi-kəl\ adj — **aero·dy·nam·i·cal·ly** \-mi-k(ə-)lē\ adv

aero·naut \\'ar-ə-‚nòt\ *n* : one who operates or travels in an airship or balloon

aero·nau·tics \‚ar-ə-'nò-tiks\ *n* : the science of aircraft operation — **aero·nau·ti·cal** \-ti-kəl\ *also* **aero·nau·tic** \-tik\ *adj*

aero·plane \\'ar-ə-‚plān\ *chiefly Brit var of* AIRPLANE

aero·sol \\'ar-ə-‚säl, -‚sòl\ *n* 1 : a suspension of fine solid or liquid particles in a gas 2 : a substance (as an insecticide) dispensed from a pressurized container as an aerosol

aero·space \\'ar-ō-‚spās\ *n* : the earth's atmosphere and the space beyond — **aerospace** *adj*

aery \\'ar-ē\ *adj* **aer·i·er; -est** : having an aerial quality : ETHEREAL

aes·thete \\'es-‚thēt\ *n* : a person having or affecting sensitivity to beauty esp. in art

aes·thet·ic \es-'the-tik\ *adj* 1 : of or relating to aesthetics : ARTISTIC 2 : appreciative of the beautiful — **aes·thet·i·cal·ly** \-ti-k(ə-)lē\ *adv*

aes·thet·ics \-tiks\ *n* : a branch of philosophy dealing with the nature, creation, and appreciation of beauty

ae·ti·ol·o·gy *chiefly Brit var of* ETIOLOGY

AF *abbr* 1 air force 2 audio frequency

[1]afar \ə-'fär\ *adv* : from, at, or to a great distance

[2]afar *n* : a great distance

AFB *abbr* air force base

AFC *abbr* 1 American Football Conference 2 automatic frequency control

AFDC *abbr* Aid to Families with Dependent Children

af·fa·ble \\'a-fə-bəl\ *adj* : courteous and agreeable in conversation — **af·fa·bil·i·ty** \‚a-fə-'bi-lə-tē\ *n* — **af·fa·bly** \\'a-fə-blē\ *adv*

af·fair \ə-'far\ *n* [ME *affaire,* fr. MF, fr. *a faire* to do] 1 : something that relates to or involves one : CONCERN 2 : a romantic or sexual attachment of limited duration

[1]af·fect \ə-'fekt, a-\ *vb* 1 : to be fond of using or wearing 2 : SIMULATE, ASSUME, PRETEND

[2]affect *vb* : to produce an effect on : INFLUENCE

af·fec·ta·tion \‚a-fek-'tā-shən\ *n* : an attitude or behavior that is assumed by a person but not genuinely felt

af·fect·ed \a-'fek-təd\ *adj* 1 : given to affectation 2 : artificially assumed to impress others — **af·fect·ed·ly** *adv*

af·fect·ing \a-'fek-tiŋ\ *adj* : arousing pity, sympathy, or sorrow 〈an ∼ story〉 — **af·fect·ing·ly** *adv*

af·fec·tion \ə-'fek-shən\ *n* : tender attachment — **af·fec·tion·ate** \-sh(ə-)nət\ *adj* — **af·fec·tion·ate·ly** *adv*

af·fer·ent \\'a-fə-rənt, -‚fer-ənt\ *adj* : bearing or conducting inward toward a more central part and esp. a nerve center (as the brain or spinal cord)

af·fi·ance \ə-'fī-əns\ *vb* **-anced; -anc·ing** : BETROTH, ENGAGE

af·fi·da·vit \‚a-fə-'dā-vət\ *n* [ML, he has made an oath] : a sworn statement in writing

[1]af·fil·i·ate \ə-'fi-lē-‚āt\ *vb* **-at·ed; -at·ing** : to associate as a member or branch — **af·fil·i·a·tion** \-‚fi-lē-'ā-shən\ *n*

[2]af·fil·i·ate \ə-'fi-lē-ət\ *n* : an affiliated person or organization

af·fin·i·ty \ə-'fi-nə-tē\ *n, pl* **-ties** 1 : KINSHIP, RELATIONSHIP 2 : attractive force : ATTRACTION, SYMPATHY

af·firm \ə-'fərm\ *vb* 1 : CONFIRM 2 : to assert positively 3 : to make a solemn and formal declaration or assertion in place of an oath **syn** aver, avow, avouch, declare, assert — **af·fir·ma·tion** \‚a-fər-'mā-shən\ *n*

[1]af·fir·ma·tive \ə-'fər-mə-tiv\ *adj* : asserting that the fact is so : POSITIVE

[2]affirmative *n* 1 : an expression of affirmation or assent 2 : the side that upholds the proposition stated in a debate

affirmative action *n* : an active effort to improve the employment or educational opportunities of members of minority groups and women

[1]af·fix \ə-'fiks\ *vb* : ATTACH, ADD

[2]af·fix \\'a-‚fiks\ *n* : one or more sounds or letters attached to the beginning or end of a word that produce a derivative word or an inflectional form

af·fla·tus \ə-'flā-təs\ *n* : divine inspiration

af·flict \ə-'flikt\ *vb* : to cause pain and distress to **syn** rack, try, torment, torture — **af·flic·tion** \-'flik-shən\ *n*

af·flic·tive \ə-'flik-tiv\ *adj* : causing affliction : DISTRESSING — **af·flic·tive·ly** *adv*

af·flu·ence \\'a-‚flü-ən(t)s, a-'flü-\ *n* : abundant supply; *also* : WEALTH, RICHES — **af·flu·ent** \-ənt\ *adj*

af·ford \ə-'fòrd\ *vb* 1 : to manage to bear or bear the cost of without serious harm or loss 2 : PROVIDE, FURNISH

af·for·es·ta·tion \a-‚fòr-ə-'stā-shən\ *n* : the act or process of establishing a forest — **af·for·est** \a-'fòr-əst, -'fär-\ *vb*

af·fray \ə-'frā\ *n* : FIGHT, FRAY

af·fright \ə-'frīt\ *vb* : FRIGHTEN, ALARM — **affright** *n*

af·front \ə-'frənt\ *vb* 1 : INSULT 2 : CONFRONT — **affront** *n*

af·ghan \\'af-‚gan\ *n* 1 *cap* : a native or inhabitant of Afghanistan 2 : a blanket or shawl of colored wool knitted or crocheted in sections — **Afghan** *adj*

Afghan hound *n* : any of a breed of tall slim swift hunting dogs with a coat of silky thick hair and a long silky top knot

af·gha·ni \af-'ga-nē\ *n* — see MONEY table

afi·cio·na·do \ə-‚fi-sh(ē-)ə-'nä-dō, -sē-ə-\ *n, pl* **-dos** [Sp, fr. pp. of *aficionar* to inspire affection] : DEVOTEE, FAN

afield \ə-'fēld\ *adv or adj* 1 : to, in, or on the field 2 : away from home 3 : out of the way : ASTRAY

afire \ə-'fīr\ *adj or adv* : being on fire : BURNING

AFL *abbr* American Football League

aflame \ə-'flām\ *adj or adv* : FLAMING

AFL–CIO *abbr* American Federation of Labor and Congress of Industrial Organizations

afloat \ə-'flōt\ *adj or adv* 1 : borne on or as if on the water 2 : CIRCULATING 〈rumors were ∼〉 3 : ADRIFT

I KNOW WHAT YOU NEED, GARFIELD

YOU NEED TO BE REASSURED OF MY AFFECTION

YOU NEED A PAT ON THE HEAD

I NEED TO KNOW IF I'M IN YOUR WILL

JIM DAVIS 10-21

aflut·ter \ə-'flə-tər\ adj 1 : FLUTTERING 2 : nervously excited

afoot \ə-'füt\ adv or adj 1 : on foot 2 : in action : in progress

afore·men·tioned \ə-'fōr-'men-chənd\ adj : mentioned previously

afore·said \-ˌsed\ : said or named before

afore·thought \-ˌthȯt\ adj : PREMEDITATED ⟨with malice ∼⟩

a for·ti·o·ri \ˌä-ˌfȯr-tē-'ōr-ē\ adv [NL, lit., from the stronger (argument)] : with even greater reason

afoul of \ə-'faúl-əv\ prep 1 : in or into conflict with 2 : in or into collision or entanglement with

Afr abbr Africa; African

afraid \ə-'frād\ adj 1 : FRIGHTENED, FEARFUL 2 : filled with concern or regret

A–frame \'ā-ˌfrām\ n : a building having triangular front and rear walls with the roof reaching to the ground

afresh \ə-'fresh\ adv : ANEW, AGAIN

Af·ri·can \'a-fri-kən\ n 1 : a native or inhabitant of Africa 2 : a person of African ancestry — **African** adj

Af·ri·can–Amer·i·can \-ə-'mer-ə-kən\ n : AFRO–AMERICAN — **African–American** adj

Af·ri·can·ized bee \'a-fri-kə-ˌnīzd-\ n : a highly aggressive hybrid honeybee accidentally produced from Brazilian and African stocks that has spread from So. America into Mexico and the southern U.S.

Africanized honeybee n : AFRICANIZED BEE

African violet n : a tropical African plant widely grown indoors for its velvety fleshy leaves and showy purple, pink, or white flowers

Af·ri·kaans \ˌa-fri-'käns\ n : a language developed from 17th century Dutch that is one of the official languages of the Republic of So. Africa

¹Af·ro \'a-frō\ adj : having the hair shaped into a round bushy mass

²Afro n, pl **Afros** : an Afro hairstyle

Afro–Amer·i·can \ˌa-frō-ə-'mer-ə-kən\ n : an American of African and esp. of black African descent — **Afro–American** adj

aft \'aft\ adv : near, toward, or in the stern of a ship or the tail of an aircraft

AFT abbr American Federation of Teachers

¹af·ter \'af-tər\ adv : AFTERWARD, SUBSEQUENTLY

²after prep 1 : behind in place 2 : later than 3 : in pursuit or search of ⟨he's ∼ your job⟩

³after conj : following the time when

⁴after adj 1 : LATER 2 : located toward the rear

af·ter·birth \'af-tər-ˌbərth\ n : the placenta and membranes of the fetus that are expelled after childbirth

af·ter·burn·er \-ˌbər-nər\ n : a device incorporated in the tail pipe of a turbojet engine for injecting fuel into the hot exhaust gases and burning it to provide extra thrust

af·ter·care \-ˌker\ n : the care, nursing, or treatment of a convalescent patient

af·ter·deck \-ˌdek\ n : the rear half of the deck of a ship

af·ter·ef·fect \-ə-ˌfekt\ n : an effect that follows its cause after an interval

af·ter·glow \-ˌglō\ n : a glow remaining where a light has disappeared

af·ter·im·age \-ˌim-ij\ n : a usu. visual sensation continuing after the stimulus causing it has ended

af·ter·life \-ˌlīf\ n : an existence after death

af·ter·math \-ˌmath\ n 1 : a second-growth crop esp. of hay : CONSEQUENCES, EFFECTS syn aftereffect, upshot, result, outcome

af·ter·noon \ˌaf-tər-'nün\ n : the time between noon and evening

af·ter·shave \'af-tər-ˌshāv\ n : a usu. scented lotion for the face after shaving

af·ter·taste \-ˌtāst\ n : a sensation (as of flavor) continuing after the stimulus causing it has ended

af·ter–tax \'af-tər-'taks\ adj : remaining after payment of taxes and esp. of income tax ⟨an ∼ profit⟩

af·ter·thought \-ˌthȯt\ n : a later thought; also : something thought of later

af·ter·ward \-wərd\ or **af·ter·wards** \-wərdz\ adv : at a later time

Ag symbol [L argentum] silver

AG abbr 1 adjutant general 2 attorney general

again \ə-'gen, -'gin\ adv 1 : once more : ANEW 2 : on the other hand 3 : in addition : BESIDES

against \ə-'genst\ prep 1 : in opposition to 2 : directly opposite to : FACING 3 : as defense from 4 : so as to touch or strike ⟨threw him ∼ the wall⟩; also : TOUCHING

¹aga·pe \ä-'gä-pā, 'ä-gə-ˌpā\ n [Gk, lit., love] : unselfish unconditional love for another

²agape \ə-'gāp\ adj or adv : having the mouth open in wonder or surprise : GAPING

agar \'ä-ˌgär\ n 1 : a jellylike substance extracted from a red alga and used esp. as a gelling and stabilizing agent in foods 2 : a culture medium containing agar

agar–agar \ˌä-gär-'ä-ˌgär\ n : AGAR

ag·ate \'a-gət\ n 1 : a striped or clouded quartz 2 : a playing marble of agate or of glass

aga·ve \ə-'gä-vē\ n : any of a genus of spiny–leaved plants (as a century plant) related to the amaryllis

agcy abbr agency

¹age \'āj\ n 1 : the length of time during which a being or thing has lived or existed 2 : the time of life at which some particular qualification is achieved; esp : MAJORITY 3 : the latter part of life 4 : a long time 5 : a period in history

²age vb **aged; ag·ing** or **age·ing** 1 : to grow old or cause to grow old 2 : to become or cause to become mature or mellow

-age n suffix 1 : aggregate : collection ⟨trackage⟩ 2 : action : process ⟨haulage⟩ 3 : cumulative result of ⟨breakage⟩ 4 : rate of ⟨dosage⟩ 5 : house or place of ⟨orphanage⟩ 6 : state : rank ⟨vassalage⟩ 7 : fee : charge ⟨postage⟩

aged \'ā-jəd for 1; 'ājd for 2\ adj 1 : of advanced age

2 : having attained a specified age ⟨a man ∼ 40 years⟩

age·less \ˈāj-ləs\ *adj* **1** : not growing old or showing the effects of age **2** : TIMELESS, ETERNAL ⟨∼ truths⟩

agen·cy \ˈā-jən-sē\ *n, pl* **-cies 1** : one through which something is accomplished : INSTRUMENTALITY **2** : the office or function of an agent **3** : an establishment doing business for another **4** : an administrative division (as of a government) **syn** means, medium, vehicle

agen·da \ə-ˈjen-də\ *n* : a list of things to be done : PROGRAM

agent \ˈā-jənt\ *n* **1** : one that acts **2** : MEANS, INSTRUMENT **3** : a person acting or doing business for another **syn** attorney, deputy, proxy, delegate

Agent Orange *n* : an herbicide widely used in the Vietnam War that is composed of 2,4-D and 2,4,5-T and contains a toxic contaminant

agent pro·vo·ca·teur \ˈä-ˌzhäⁿ-prō-ˌvä-kə-ˈtər, ˈä-jənt-\ *n, pl* **agents provocateurs** \ˈä-ˌzhäⁿ-prō-ˌväk-ə-ˈtər, ˈā-jənts-prō-\ [F] : a person hired to infiltrate a group and incite its members to illegal action

age of consent : the age at which one is legally competent to give consent esp. to marriage or to sexual intercourse

age–old \ˈāj-ˈōld\ *adj* : having existed for ages : ANCIENT

ag·er·a·tum \ˌa-jə-ˈrā-təm\ *n, pl* **-tum** *also* **-tums** : any of a large genus of tropical American plants that are related to the daisies and have small showy heads of blue or white flowers

Ag·ge·us \a-ˈgē-əs\ *n* : HAGGAI

¹**ag·glom·er·ate** \ə-ˈglä-mə-ˌrāt\ *vb* **-at·ed; -at·ing** [L *agglomerare* to heap up, join, fr. *ad-* to + *glomer-, glomus* ball] : to gather into a mass : CLUSTER — **ag·glom·er·a·tion** \-ˌglä-mə-ˈrā-shən\ *n*

²**ag·glom·er·ate** \-rət\ *n* : rock composed of volcanic fragments

ag·glu·ti·nate \ə-ˈglüt-ᵊn-ˌāt\ *vb* **-nat·ed; -nat·ing 1** : to cause to adhere : gather into a group or mass **2** : to cause (as red blood cells or bacteria) to collect into clumps — **ag·glu·ti·na·tion** \-ˌglüt-ᵊn-ˈā-shən\ *n*

ag·gran·dise *Brit var of* AGGRANDIZE

ag·gran·dize \ə-ˈgran-ˌdīz, ˈa-grən-\ *vb* **-dized; -diz·ing** : to make great or greater — **ag·gran·dize·ment** \ə-ˈgran-dəz-mənt, -ˌdīz-; ˌa-grən-ˈdīz-\ *n*

ag·gra·vate \ˈa-grə-ˌvāt\ *vb* **-vat·ed; -vat·ing 1** : to make more severe : INTENSIFY **2** : IRRITATE — **ag·gra·va·tion** \ˌa-grə-ˈvā-shən\ *n*

¹**ag·gre·gate** \ˈa-gri-gət\ *adj* : formed by the gathering of units into one mass

²**ag·gre·gate** \-ˌgāt\ *vb* **-gat·ed; -gat·ing** : to collect into one mass

³**ag·gre·gate** \-gət\ *n* : a mass or body of units or parts somewhat loosely associated with one another; *also* : the whole amount

ag·gre·ga·tion \ˌa-gri-ˈgā-shən\ *n* **1** : a group, body, or mass composed of many distinct parts **2** : the collecting of units or parts into a mass or whole

ag·gres·sion \ə-ˈgre-shən\ *n* **1** : an unprovoked attack **2** : the practice of making attacks **3** : hostile, injurious, or destructive behavior or outlook esp. when caused by frustration — **ag·gres·sor** \-ˈgre-sər\ *n*

ag·gres·sive \ə-ˈgre-siv\ *adj* **1** : tending toward or exhibiting aggression; *esp* : marked by combative readiness **2** : marked by driving energy or initiative : ENTERPRISING **3** : more intensive or comprehensive esp. in dosage or extent — **ag·gres·sive·ly** *adv* — **ag·gres·sive·ness** *n*

ag·grieve \ə-ˈgrēv\ *vb* **ag·grieved; ag·griev·ing 1** : to cause grief to **2** : to inflict injury on : WRONG

aghast \ə-ˈgast\ *adj* : struck with amazement or horror

ag·ile \ˈa-jəl\ *adj* : able to move quickly and easily — **agil·i·ty** \ə-ˈji-lə-tē\ *n*

ag·i·tate \ˈa-jə-ˌtāt\ *vb* **-tat·ed; -tat·ing 1** : to move with an irregular rapid motion **2** : to stir up : EXCITE **3** : to discuss earnestly **4** : to attempt to arouse public

feeling — **ag·i·ta·tion** \ˌa-jə-ˈtā-shən\ *n* — **ag·i·ta·tor** \ˈa-jə-ˌtā-tər\ *n*

ag·it·prop \ˈa-jət-ˌpräp\ *n* [Russ] : political propaganda promulgated esp. through the arts

agleam \ə-ˈglēm\ *adj* : GLEAMING

aglit·ter \ə-ˈgli-tər\ *adj* : GLITTERING

aglow \ə-ˈglō\ *adj* : GLOWING

ag·nos·tic \ag-ˈnäs-tik\ *adj* [Gk *agnōstos* unknown, unknowable, fr. *a-* un- + *gnōstos* known] : of or relating to the belief that the existence of any ultimate reality (as God) is unknown and prob. unknowable — **agnostic** *n* — **ag·nos·ti·cism** \-ˈnäs-tə-ˌsi-zəm\ *n*

ago \ə-ˈgō\ *adj or adv* : earlier than the present time

agog \ə-ˈgäg\ *adj* [MF *en gogues* in mirth] : full of excitement : EAGER

a-go-go \ä-ˈgō-ˌgō\ *adj* [*Whisky à Gogo*, café and disco in Paris, France, fr. F *à gogo* galore] : GO-GO

ag·o·nise *Brit var of* AGONIZE

ag·o·nize \ˈa-gə-ˌnīz\ *vb* **-nized; -niz·ing** : to suffer or cause to suffer agony — **ag·o·niz·ing·ly** *adv*

ag·o·ny \ˈa-gə-nē\ *n, pl* **-nies** [ME *agonie*, fr. L *agonia*, fr. Gk *agōnia* struggle, anguish, fr. *agōn* gathering, contest for a prize] : extreme pain of mind or body **syn** suffering, distress, misery

ago·ra \ˈä-gə-ˈrä\ *n, pl* **ago·rot** \-ˈrōt\ — see *shekel* at MONEY table

ag·o·ra·pho·bia \ˌa-gə-rə-ˈfō-bē-ə\ *n* : abnormal fear of being in a helpless, embarrassing, or inescapable situation characterized esp. by avoidance of open or public places — **ag·o·ra·pho·bic** \-ˈfō-bik, -ˈfä-\ *adj or n*

agr *abbr* agricultural; agriculture

agrar·i·an \ə-ˈgrer-ē-ən\ *adj* **1** : of or relating to land or its ownership ⟨∼ reforms⟩ **2** : of or relating to farmers or farming interests — **agrarian** *n* — **agrar·i·an·ism** *n*

agree \ə-ˈgrē\ *vb* **agreed; agree·ing 1** : ADMIT, CONCEDE **2** : to be similar : CORRESPOND **3** : to express agreement or approval **4** : to be in harmony **5** : to settle by common consent **6** : to be fitting or healthful : SUIT

agree·able \ə-ˈgrē-ə-bəl\ *adj* **1** : PLEASING, PLEASANT **2** : ready to consent **3** : being in harmony : CONSONANT — **agree·able·ness** *n* — **agree·ably** \-blē\ *adv*

agree·ment \ə-ˈgrē-mənt\ *n* **1** : harmony of opinion or action **2** : mutual understanding or arrangement; *also* : a document containing such an arrangement

ag·ri·busi·ness \ˈa-grə-ˌbiz-nəs, -nəz\ *n* : an industry engaged in the manufacture and sale of farm equipment and supplies and in the production, processing, storage, and sale of farm commodities

agric *abbr* agricultural; agriculture

ag·ri·cul·ture \ˈa-gri-ˌkəl-chər\ *n* : FARMING, HUSBANDRY — **ag·ri·cul·tur·al** \ˌa-gri-ˈkəl-ch(ə-)rəl\ *adj* — **ag·ri·cul·tur·ist** \-ch(ə-)rist\ *or* **ag·ri·cul·tur·al·ist** \-ch(ə-)rə-list\ *n*

agron·o·my \ə-ˈgrä-nə-mē\ *n* : a branch of agriculture that deals with the raising of crops and the care of the soil — **ag·ro·nom·ic** \ˌa-grə-ˈnä-mik\ *adj* — **agron·o·mist** \ə-ˈgrä-nə-mist\ *n*

aground \ə-ˈgraünd\ *adv or adj* : on or onto the bottom or shore ⟨ran ∼⟩

agt *abbr* agent

ague \ˈā-gyü\ *n* : a fever (as malaria) with recurrent chills and sweating

ahead \ə-ˈhed\ *adv or adj* **1** : in or toward the front **2** : into or for the future ⟨plan ∼⟩ **3** : in or toward a more advantageous position

ahead of *prep* **1** : in front or advance of **2** : in excess of : ABOVE

AHL *abbr* American Hockey League

ahoy \ə-ˈhȯi\ *interj* — used in hailing ⟨ship ∼⟩

AI *abbr* artificial intelligence

¹**aid** \ˈād\ *vb* : to provide with what is useful in achieving an end : ASSIST

²**aid** *n* **1** : ASSISTANCE **2** : ASSISTANT

AID *abbr* Agency for International Development
aide \ˈād\ *n* : a person who acts as an assistant; *esp* : a military officer assisting a superior
aide–de–camp \ˈād-di-ˈkamp, -ˈkäm\ *n, pl* **aides–de–camp** \ˌādz-di-\ [F] : AIDE
AIDS \ˈādz\ *n* [*acquired immunodeficiency syndrome*] : a serious disease of the human immune system that is caused by infection with HIV, that is characterized by severe reduction in the numbers of helper T cells, that in modern industrialized nations occurs esp. in intravenous users of illicit drugs and in homosexual and bisexual men, and that is transmitted esp. in blood and bodily secretions (as semen)
AIDS–related complex *n* : a group of symptoms (as fever, weight loss, and lymphadenopathy) that is associated with the presence of antibodies to HIV and is followed by the development of AIDS in a certain proportion of cases
AIDS virus *n* : HIV
ai·grette \ā-ˈgret, ˈā-ˌ\ *n* [F, plume, egret] : a plume or decorative tuft for the head
ail \ˈāl\ *vb* **1** : to be the matter with : TROUBLE **2** : to be unwell
ai·lan·thus \ā-ˈlan-thəs\ *n* : any of a genus of Asian trees or shrubs with pinnate leaves and ill-scented greenish flowers
ai·le·ron \ˈā-lə-ˌrän\ *n* : a movable part of an airplane wing used in banking
ail·ment \ˈāl-mənt\ *n* : a bodily disorder
¹aim \ˈām\ *vb* [ME, fr. MF *aesmer* & *esmer*; MF *aesmer*, fr. OF, fr. *a-* to (fr. L *ad-*) + *esmer* to estimate, fr. L *aestimare*] **1** : to point a weapon at an object **2** : to direct one's efforts : ASPIRE **3** : to direct to or toward a specified object or goal

²aim *n* **1** : the pointing of a weapon at an object **2** : the ability to hit a target **3** : OBJECT, PURPOSE — **aim·less** \-ləs\ *adj* — **aim·less·ly** *adv* — **aim·less·ness** *n*

AIM *abbr* American Indian Movement
ain't \ˈānt\ **1** : are not **2** : is not **3** : am not — though disapproved by many and more common in less educated speech, used orally in most parts of the U.S. by many educated speakers esp. in the phrase *ain't I*
Ai·nu \ˈī-nü\ *n, pl* **Ainu** *or* **Ainus 1** : a member of an indigenous people of northern Japan **2** : the language of the Ainu people
¹air \ˈar\ *n* **1** : the gaseous mixture surrounding the earth **2** : a light breeze **3** : MELODY, TUNE **4** : the outward appearance of a person or thing : MANNER **5** : an artificial manner **6** : COMPRESSED AIR ⟨~ sprayer⟩ **7** : AIRCRAFT ⟨~ patrol⟩ **8** : AVIATION ⟨~ safety⟩ **9** : the medium of transmission of radio waves; *also* : RADIO, TELEVISION
²air *vb* **1** : to expose to the air **2** : to expose to public view
air bag *n* : a bag designed to inflate automatically to protect automobile occupants in case of collision

air·boat \ˈar-ˌbōt\ *n* : a shallow-draft boat driven by an airplane propeller
air·borne \-ˌbōrn\ *adj* : done or being in the air
air brake *n* **1** : a brake operated by a piston driven by compressed air **2** : a surface projected into the airflow to lower an airplane's speed
air·brush \ˈar-ˌbrəsh\ *n* : a device for applying a fine spray (as of paint) by compressed air — **airbrush** *vb*
air–con·di·tion \ˌar-kən-ˈdi-shən\ *vb* : to equip with an apparatus for filtering air and controlling its humidity and temperature — **air con·di·tion·er** \-ˈdi-sh(ə-)nər\ *n*
air·craft \ˈar-ˌkraft\ *n, pl* **aircraft** : a vehicle for traveling through the air
aircraft carrier *n* : a warship with a deck on which airplanes can be launched and landed
air·drop \ˈar-ˌdräp\ *n* : delivery of cargo or personnel by parachute from an airplane in flight — **air–drop** *vb*
Aire·dale terrier \ˈar-ˌdāl-\ *n* : any of a breed of large terriers with a hard wiry coat
air·fare \ˈar-ˌfar\ *n* : fare for travel by airplane
air·field \-ˌfēld\ *n* : AIRPORT
air·flow \-ˌflō\ *n* : the motion of air relative to a body in it
air·foil \-ˌfòil\ *n* : an airplane surface designed to produce reaction forces from the air through which it moves
air force *n* : the military organization of a nation for air warfare
air·frame \ˈar-ˌfrām\ *n* : the structure of an aircraft, rocket, or missile without the power plant
air·freight \-ˈfrāt\ *n* : freight transport by aircraft in volume; *also* : the charge for this service
air gun *n* **1** : a gun operated by compressed air **2** : a hand tool that works by compressed air; *esp* : AIRBRUSH
air·head \ˈar-ˌhed\ *n* : a mindless or stupid person
air lane *n* : AIRWAY 1
air·lift \ˈar-ˌlift\ *n* : transportation (as of supplies or passengers) by aircraft — **airlift** *vb*
air·line \-ˌlīn\ *n* : a transportation system using airplanes
air·lin·er \-ˌlī-nər\ *n* : a large passenger airplane operated by an airline
air lock *n* : an airtight chamber separating areas of different pressure
air·mail \ˈar-ˌmāl\ *n* : the system of transporting mail by aircraft; *also* : mail so transported — **airmail** *vb*
air·man \-mən\ *n* **1** : AVIATOR, PILOT **2** : an enlisted man in the air force in one of the three ranks below sergeant
airman basic *n* : an enlisted man of the lowest rank in the air force
airman first class *n* : an enlisted man in the air force with a rank just below that of sergeant
air mass *n* : a large horizontally homogeneous body of air
air·mo·bile \ˈar-mō-bəl, -ˌbēl\ *adj* : of, relating to, or

being a military unit whose members are transported to combat areas usu. by helicopter

air·plane \-ˌplān\ *n* : a powered heavier-than-air aircraft that has fixed wings from which it derives lift

air·play \-ˌplā\ *n* : the playing of a musical recording on the air by a radio station

air pocket *n* : a condition of the atmosphere that causes an airplane to drop suddenly

air police *n* : the military police of an air force

air·port \ˈar-ˌpōrt\ *n* : a place from which aircraft operate that usu. has paved runways and a terminal

air raid *n* : an attack by armed airplanes on a surface target

air·ship \ˈar-ˌship\ *n* : a lighter-than-air aircraft having propulsion and steering systems

air·sick \-ˌsik\ *adj* : affected with motion sickness associated with flying — **air·sick·ness** *n*

air·space \-ˌspās\ *n* : the space above a nation and under its jurisdiction

air·speed \-ˌspēd\ *n* : the speed of an object (as an airplane) with relation to the surrounding air

air·strip \-ˌstrip\ *n* : a runway without normal airport facilities

air·tight \ˈar-ˈtīt\ *adj* **1** : so tightly sealed that no air can enter or escape **2** : leaving no opening for attack

air–to–air *adj* : launched from one airplane in flight at another; *also* : involving aircraft in flight

air·waves \ˈar-ˌwāvz\ *n pl* : AIR 9

air·way \-ˌwā\ *n* **1** : a regular route for airplanes **2** : AIRLINE

air·wor·thy \-ˌwər-thē\ *adj* : fit for operation in the air ⟨an ~ plane⟩ — **air·wor·thi·ness** *n*

airy \ˈar-ē\ *adj* **air·i·er; -est** **1** : LOFTY **2** : lacking in reality : EMPTY **3** : DELICATE **4** : BREEZY

aisle \ˈīl\ *n* [ME *ile*, fr. MF *ele* wing, fr. L *ala*] **1** : the side of a church nave separated by piers from the nave proper **2** : a passage between sections of seats

ajar \ə-ˈjär\ *adj or adv* : partly open

AK *abbr* Alaska

aka *abbr* also known as

AKC *abbr* American Kennel Club

akim·bo \ə-ˈkim-bō\ *adj or adv* : having the hand on the hip and the elbow turned outward

akin \ə-ˈkin\ *adj* **1** : related by blood **2** : similar in kind

Al *symbol* aluminum

AL *abbr* **1** Alabama **2** American League **3** American Legion

[1]-al *adj suffix* : of, relating to, or characterized by ⟨directional⟩

[2]-al *n suffix* : action : process ⟨rehearsal⟩

Ala *abbr* Alabama

al·a·bas·ter \ˈa-lə-ˌbas-tər\ *n* **1** : a compact fine-textured usu. white and translucent gypsum often carved into objects (as vases) **2** : a hard translucent calcite

à la carte \ˌä-lə-ˈkärt, ˌä-\ *adv or adj* [F] : with a separate price for each item on the menu

alac·ri·ty \ə-ˈla-krə-tē\ *n* : cheerful readiness : BRISKNESS

à la mode \ˌä-lə-ˈmōd, ˌä-\ *adj* [F, according to the fashion] **1** : FASHIONABLE, STYLISH **2** : topped with ice cream

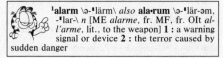

[1]alarm \ə-ˈlärm\ *also* **ala·rum** \ə-ˈlär-əm, -ˈlar-\ *n* [ME *alarme*, fr. MF, fr. OIt *all'arme*, lit., to the weapon] **1** : a warning signal or device **2** : the terror caused by sudden danger

[2]alarm *also* **alarum** *vb* **1** : to warn of danger **2** : FRIGHTEN

alarm·ist \ə-ˈlär-mist\ *n* : a person who alarms others esp. needlessly

alas \ə-ˈlas\ *interj* — used to express unhappiness, pity, or concern

al·ba·core \ˈal-bə-ˌkōr\ *n, pl* **-core** *or* **-cores** : a large tuna that is a source of canned tuna

Al·ba·nian \al-ˈbā-nē-ən\ *n* : a native or inhabitant of Albania

al·ba·tross \ˈal-bə-ˌtrós, -ˌträs\ *n, pl* **-tross** *or* **-tross·es** : any of a family of large web-footed seabirds

al·be·do \al-ˈbē-(ˌ)dō\ *n, pl* **-dos** : the fraction of incident radiation that is reflected by a body or surface

al·be·it \ól-ˈbē-ət, al-\ *conj* : even though : ALTHOUGH

al·bi·no \al-ˈbī-nō\ *n, pl* **-nos** : a person or nonhuman mammal lacking coloring matter in the skin, hair, and eyes — **al·bi·nism** \ˈal-bə-ˌni-zəm\ *n*

al·bum \ˈal-bəm\ *n* **1** : a book with blank pages used for making a collection (as of stamps) **2** : one or more recordings (as on tape or disk) produced as a single unit

al·bu·men \al-ˈbyü-mən\ *n* **1** : the white of an egg **2** : ALBUMIN

al·bu·min \al-ˈbyü-mən\ *n* : any of numerous water-soluble proteins of blood, milk, egg white, and plant and animal tissues

al·bu·min·ous \al-ˈbyü-mə-nəs\ *adj* : containing or resembling albumen or albumin

alc *abbr* alcohol

al·cal·de \al-ˈkäl-dē\ *n* : the chief administrative and judicial officer of a Spanish or Spanish-American town

al·ca·zar \al-ˈkä-zər, -ˈka-\ *n* [Sp *alcázar*, fr. Ar *al-qaṣr* the castle] : a Spanish fortress or palace

al·che·my \ˈal-kə-mē\ *n* : medieval chemistry chiefly concerned with efforts to turn base metals into gold — **al·che·mist** \ˈal-kə-mist\ *n*

al·co·hol \ˈal-kə-ˌhòl\ *n* [NL, fr. ML, powdered antimony, fr. Sp, fr. Ar *al-kuḥul* the powdered antimony] **1** : a colorless flammable liquid that is the intoxicating agent in fermented and distilled liquors **2** : any of various carbon compounds similar to alcohol **3** : beverages containing alcohol

[1]al·co·hol·ic \ˌal-kə-ˈhò-lik, -ˈhä-\ *adj* **1** : of, relating to, caused by, or containing alcohol **2** : affected with alcoholism — **al·co·hol·i·cal·ly** \-li-k(ə-)lē\ *adv*

[2]alcoholic *n* : a person affected with alcoholism

al·co·hol·ism \ˈal-kə-ˌhò-ˌli-zəm\ *n* : continued excessive and usu. uncontrollable use of alcoholic drinks;

also : a complex chronic psychological and nutritional disorder associated with such use

al·cove \'al-ˌkōv\ *n* **1** : a nook or small recess opening off a larger room **2** : a niche or arched opening (as in a wall)

ald *abbr* alderman

al·der \'ȯl-dər\ *n* : a tree or shrub related to the birches and growing in wet areas

al·der·man \'ȯl-dər-mən\ *n* : a member of a city legislative body

ale \'āl\ *n* : an alcoholic beverage brewed from malt and hops that is usu. more bitter than beer

ale·a·tor·ic \ˌā-lē-ə-'tȯr-ik\ *adj* : characterized by chance or random elements ⟨∼ music⟩

ale·a·to·ry \'ā-lē-ə-ˌtōr-ē\ *adj* : ALEATORIC

alee \ə-'lē\ *adv* : on or toward the lee

ale·house \'āl-ˌhau̇s\ *n* : a place where ale is sold to be drunk on the premises

¹alert \ə-'lərt\ *adj* [It *all' erta,* lit., on the ascent] **1** : watchful against danger **2** : quick to perceive and act — **alert·ly** *adv* — **alert·ness** *n*

²alert *n* **1** : ALARM 1 **2** : the period during which an alert is in effect

³alert *vb* **1** : WARN **2** : to make aware of

Aleut \ˌa-lē-'üt, ə-'lüt\ *n* **1** : a member of a people of the Aleutian and Shumagin islands and the western part of Alaska Peninsula **2** : the language of the Aleuts

ale·wife \'āl-ˌwīf\ *n* : a food fish of the herring family abundant esp. on the Atlantic coast

Al·ex·an·dri·an \ˌa-lig-'zan-drē-ən\ *adj* **1** : of or relating to Alexander the Great **2** : HELLENISTIC

al·ex·an·drine \-'zan-drən\ *n, often cap* : a line of six iambic feet

al·fal·fa \al-'fal-fə\ *n* : a leguminous plant widely grown for hay and forage

al·fres·co \al-'fres-kō\ *adj or adv* [It] : taking place in the open air

alg *abbr* algebra

al·ga \'al-gə\ *n, pl* **al·gae** \'al-(ˌ)jē\ : any of a group of lower plants having chlorophyll but no vascular system and including seaweeds and related freshwater plants — **al·gal** \-gəl\ *adj*

al·ge·bra \'al-jə-brə\ *n* [ML, fr. Ar *al-jabr*] : a branch of mathematics using symbols (as letters) to explore the relationships between numbers and the operations used to work with them — **al·ge·bra·ic** \ˌal-jə-'brā-ik\ *adj* — **al·ge·bra·i·cal·ly** \-'brā-ə-k(ə-)lē\ *adv*

Al·ge·ri·an \al-'jir-ē-ən\ *n* : a native or inhabitant of Algeria — **Algerian** *adj*

Al·gon·quin \al-'gän-kwən, -'gäŋ-\ *n* : a member of an American Indian people of the Ottawa River valley

al·go·rithm \'al-gə-ˌri-thəm\ *n* : a procedure for solving a problem esp. in mathematics or computing — **al·go·rith·mic** \ˌal-gə-'rith-mik\ *adj* — **al·go·rith·mi·cal·ly** \-mi-k(ə-)lē\ *adv*

¹alias \'ā-lē-əs, 'āl-yəs\ *adv* [L, otherwise, fr. *alius* other] : otherwise called

²alias *n* : an assumed name

¹al·i·bi \'a-lə-ˌbī\ *n* [L, elsewhere, fr. *alius* other] **1** : a plea offered by an accused person of not having been at the scene of an offense **2** : an excuse (as for failure)

²alibi *vb* **-bied; -bi·ing 1** : to furnish an excuse for **2** : to offer an excuse

¹alien \'ā-lē-ən, 'āl-yən\ *adj* : belonging to another : FOREIGN

²alien *n* **1** : a foreign-born resident who has not been naturalized **2** : EXTRATERRESTRIAL

alien·able \'āl-yə-nə-bəl, 'ā-lē-ə-nə-\ *adj* : transferable to the ownership of another ⟨∼ property⟩

alien·ate \'ā-lē-ə-ˌnāt, 'āl-yə-\ *vb* **-at·ed; -at·ing 1** : to make hostile : ESTRANGE **2** : to transfer (property) to another — **alien·ation** \ˌā-lē-ə-'nā-shən, ˌāl-yə-\ *n*

alien·ist \'ā-lē-ə-nist, 'āl-yə-\ *n* : PSYCHIATRIST

¹alight \ə-'līt\ *vb* **alight·ed** *also* **alit** \ə-'lit\ **alight·ing 1** : to get down (as from a vehicle) **2** : to come to rest from the air **syn** settle, land, perch

²alight *adj* : lighted up

align *also* **aline** \ə-'līn\ *vb* **1** : to bring into line **2** : to array on the side of or against a cause — **align·er** *n* — **align·ment** *also* **aline·ment** *n*

¹alike \ə-'līk\ *adv* : EQUALLY

²alike *adj* : LIKE **syn** akin, analogous, similar, comparable

al·i·ment \'a-lə-mənt\ *n* : NOURISHMENT 1 — **aliment** *vb*

al·i·men·ta·ry \ˌa-lə-'men-t(ə-)rē\ *adj* : of, relating to, or functioning in nourishment or nutrition

alimentary canal *n* : the tube that extends from the mouth to the anus and functions in the digestion and absorption of food and the elimination of residues

al·i·mo·ny \'a-lə-ˌmō-nē\ *n, pl* **-nies** [L *alimonia* sustenance, fr. *alere* to nourish] : an allowance made to one spouse by the other for support pending or after legal separation or divorce

A–line \'ā-ˌlīn\ *adj* : having a flared bottom and a close⸗ fitting top ⟨an ∼ skirt⟩

alive \ə-'līv\ *adj* **1** : having life **2** : being in force or operation **3** : SENSITIVE ⟨∼ to the danger⟩ **4** : ALERT, BRISK **5** : ANIMATED ⟨streets ∼ with traffic⟩ — **alive·ness** *n*

alk *abbr* alkaline

al·ka·li \'al-kə-ˌlī\ *n, pl* **-lies** *or* **-lis 1** : a substance (as a hydroxide) that has a bitter taste and neutralizes acids **2** : a mixture of salts in the soil of some dry regions in such amount as to make ordinary farming impossible — **al·ka·line** \-kə-lən, -ˌlīn\ *adj* — **al·ka·lin·i·ty** \ˌal-kə-'li-nə-tē\ *n*

al·ka·loid \'al-kə-ˌlȯid\ *n* : any of various usu. basic and bitter organic compounds found esp. in seed plants

al·kane \'al-ˌkān\ *n* : a hydrocarbon in which each carbon atom is bonded to 4 other atoms

al·kyd \'al-kəd\ *n* : any of numerous synthetic resins used esp. for protective coatings and in paint

¹all \'ȯl\ *adj* **1** : the whole of **2** : every member of **3** : EVERY ⟨∼ manner of problems⟩ **4** : any whatever ⟨beyond ∼ doubt⟩ **5** : nothing but ⟨∼ ears⟩ **6** : being more than one person or thing ⟨who ∼ is coming⟩

²all *adv* **1** : WHOLLY **2** : selected as the best — used in combination ⟨*all*-state champs⟩ **3** : so much ⟨∼ the better for it⟩ **4** : for each side ⟨the score is two ∼⟩

³all *pron* **1** : the whole number, quantity, or amount ⟨∼ of it is gone⟩ **2** : EVERYBODY, EVERYTHING ⟨that is ∼⟩

⁴all *n* : the whole of one's resources ⟨gave his ∼⟩

Al·lah \'ä-lä, 'a-; ä-'lä\ *n* [Ar] : GOD 1 — used in Islam

all along *adv* : all the time ⟨knew it *all along*⟩

all–Amer·i·can \ˌȯl-ə-'mer-ə-kən\ *adj* **1** : selected as the best in the U.S. **2** : composed wholly of American elements **3** : typical of the U.S. — **all–American** *n*

all–around \ˌȯl-ə-'rau̇nd\ *adj* **1** : considered in all aspects ⟨best ∼ performance⟩ **2** : competent in many fields : VERSATILE ⟨an ∼ athlete⟩

al·lay \ə-'lā\ *vb* **1** : ALLEVIATE **2** : CALM **syn** lighten, relieve, ease, assuage

all clear *n* : a signal that a danger has passed

al·lege \ə-'lej\ *vb* **al·leged; al·leg·ing 1** : to assert without proof **2** : to offer as a reason — **al·le·ga·tion** \ˌa-li-'gā-shən\ *n* — **al·leg·ed·ly** \ə-'le-jəd-lē\ *adv*

al·le·giance \ə-'lē-jəns\ *n* **1** : loyalty owed by a citizen to a government **2** : loyalty to a person or cause

al·le·go·ry \'a-lə-ˌgȯr-ē\ *n, pl* **-ries** : the expression through symbolism of truths or generalizations about human experience — **al·le·gor·i·cal** \ˌa-lə-'gȯr-i-kəl\ *adj* — **al·le·gor·i·cal·ly** \-k(ə-)lē\ *adv*

¹al·le·gro \ə-'le-grō, -'lā-\ *n, pl* **-gros** : an allegro movement

²allegro *adv or adj* [It, merry] : at a brisk lively tempo — used as a direction in music

al·le·lu·ia \ˌa-lə-'lü-yə\ *interj* : HALLELUJAH

Al·len wrench \'a-lən-\ *n* [*Allen* Manufacturing Company, Hartford, Conn.] : an L-shaped hexagonal metal bar of which either end fits the socket of a screw or bolt

al·ler·gen \'a-lər-jən\ *n* : something that causes allergy — **al·ler·gen·ic** \₁a-lər-'je-nik\ *adj*

al·ler·gist \'a-lər-jist\ *n* : a specialist in allergies

al·ler·gy \'a-lər-jē\ *n, pl* **-gies** [G *Allergie*, fr. Gk *allos* other + *ergon* work] : exaggerated or abnormal reaction (as by sneezing) to substances or situations harmless to most people — **al·ler·gic** \ə-'lər-jik\ *adj*

al·le·vi·ate \ə-'lē-vē-₁āt\ *vb* **-at·ed; -at·ing** : RELIEVE, LESSEN **syn** lighten, mitigate, allay — **al·le·vi·a·tion** \ə-₁lē-vē-'ā-shən\ *n*

al·ley \'a-lē\ *n, pl* **alleys 1** : a garden or park walk **2** : a place for bowling **3** : a narrow passageway esp. between buildings

al·ley–oop \₁a-lē-'yüp\ *n* : a basketball play in which a player catches a pass above the basket and immediately dunks the ball

al·ley·way \'a-lē-₁wā\ *n* : ALLEY 3

All·hal·lows \òl-'ha-lōz\ *n, pl* **Allhallows** : ALL SAINTS' DAY

al·li·ance \ə-'lī-əns\ *n* : a union to promote common interests **syn** league, coalition, confederacy, federation

al·li·ga·tor \'a-lə-₁gā-tər\ *n* [Sp *el lagarto* the lizard] : either of two large short-legged reptiles resembling crocodiles but having a shorter and broader snout

alligator

alligator pear *n* : AVOCADO

al·lit·er·ate \ə-'li-tə-₁rāt\ *vb* **-at·ed; -at·ing 1** : to form an alliteration **2** : to arrange so as to make alliteration

al·lit·er·a·tion \ə-₁li-tə-'rā-shən\ *n* : the repetition of initial sounds in adjacent words or syllables — **al·lit·er·a·tive** \-'li-tə-₁rā-tiv\ *adj*

al·lo·cate \'a-lə-₁kāt\ *vb* **-cat·ed; -cat·ing** : ALLOT, ASSIGN — **al·lo·ca·tion** \₁a-lə-'kā-shən\ *n*

al·lot \ə-'lät\ *vb* **al·lot·ted; al·lot·ting** : to distribute as a share **syn** assign, apportion, allocate — **al·lot·ment** *n*

all–out \'òl-'aut\ *adj* : made with maximum effort

all over *adv* : EVERYWHERE

al·low \ə-'lau\ *vb* **1** : to assign as a share ⟨~ time for rest⟩ **2** : to count as a deduction **3** : to make allowance ⟨~ for expansion⟩ **4** : ADMIT, CONCEDE **5** : PERMIT ⟨~s the dog to roam⟩ — **al·low·able** *adj*

al·low·ance \-əns\ *n* **1** : an allotted share **2** : money given regularly for expenses **3** : a taking into account of extenuating circumstances

al·loy \'a-₁lói, ə-'lói\ *n* **1** : a substance composed of metals melted together **2** : an admixture that lessens value — **al·loy** \ə-'lói, 'a-₁lói\ *vb*

all right *adv* **1** : very well ⟨*all right*, let's go⟩ **2** : beyond doubt **3** : SATISFACTORILY — **all right** *adj*

All Saints' Day *n* : a Christian feast on November 1 in honor of all the saints

All Souls' Day *n* : a day of prayer observed by some Christian churches on November 2 for the souls of the faithful departed

all·spice \'òl-₁spīs\ *n* : the berry of a West Indian tree related to the European myrtle; *also* : the mildly pungent and aromatic spice made from it

all–star \'òl-₁stär\ *n* : a member of a team of star performers — **all–star** *adj*

all told *adv* : with everything counted

al·lude \ə-'lüd\ *vb* **al·lud·ed; al·lud·ing** [L *alludere*, lit., to play with] : to refer indirectly — **al·lu·sion**

\-'lü-zhən\ *n* — **al·lu·sive** \-'lü-siv\ *adj* — **al·lu·sive·ly** *adv* — **al·lu·sive·ness** *n*

al·lure \ə-'lúr\ *vb* **al·lured; al·lur·ing** : CHARM, ENTICE — **allure** *n* — **al·lur·ing·ly** *adv*

al·lu·vi·um \ə-'lü-vē-əm\ *n, pl* **-vi·ums** *or* **-via** \-vē-ə\ : soil material (as clay) deposited by running water — **al·lu·vi·al** \-vē-əl\ *adj or n*

al·ly \ə-'lī, 'a-₁lī\ *vb* **al·lied; al·ly·ing** : to enter into an alliance — **al·ly** \'a-₁lī, ə-'lī\ *n*

-ally *adv suffix* : ²-LY ⟨specifically⟩

al·ma ma·ter \₁al-mə-'mä-tər\ *n* [L, fostering mother] **1** : an educational institute that one has attended **2** : the song or hymn of an alma mater

al·ma·nac \'òl-mə-₁nak, 'al-\ *n* **1** : a publication esp. of astronomical and meteorological data **2** : a usu. annual publication of miscellaneous information

al·man·dite \'al-mən-₁dīt\ *n* : a deep red garnet

al·mighty \òl-'mī-tē\ *adj* **1** *often cap* : having absolute power over all ⟨*Almighty* God⟩ **2** : relatively unlimited in power — **al·might·i·ness** *n*

Almighty *n* : GOD 1

al·mond \'ä-mənd, 'a-; 'al-\ *n* : a small tree related to the peach; *also* : the edible nutlike kernel of its fruit

al·mon·er \'al-mə-nər, 'ä-mə-\ *n* : a person who distributes alms

al·most \'òl-₁mōst, òl-'mōst\ *adv* : very nearly but not exactly

alms \'ämz, 'älmz\ *n, pl* **alms** [ME *almesse, almes*, fr. OE *ælmesse, ælms*, fr. L *eleemosyna* alms, fr. Gk *eleēmosynē* pity, alms, fr. *eleēmōn* merciful] : something given freely to relieve the poor

alms·house \-₁haus\ *n* : POORHOUSE

al·oe \'a-lō\ *n* **1** : any of a large genus of succulent chiefly southern African plants related to the lilies **2** *pl* : the dried juice of the leaves of an aloe used esp. formerly as a laxative

aloft \ə-'lòft\ *adv* **1** : high in the air **2** : in flight

alo·ha \ə-'lō-ə, ä-'lō-hä\ *interj* [Hawaiian] — used to greet or bid farewell

alone \ə-'lōn\ *adj* **1** : separated from others **2** : not including anyone or anything else : ONLY **syn** lonely, lonesome, lone, solitary — **alone** *adv*

¹**along** \ə-'lòn\ *prep* **1** : in line with the direction of ⟨sail ~ the coast⟩ **2** : at a point on or during ⟨stopped ~ the way⟩

²**along** *adv* **1** : FORWARD, ON **2** : as a companion ⟨bring her ~⟩ **3** : at an advanced point ⟨plans are far ~⟩

along·shore \ə-'lòn-'shòr\ *adv or adj* : along the shore or coast

¹**along·side** \-'sīd\ *adv* : along or by the side

²**alongside** *prep* **1** : along or by the side of **2** : in association with

alongside of *prep* : ALONGSIDE

aloof \ə-'lüf\ *adj* : removed or distant physically or emotionally — **aloof·ness** *n*

al·o·pe·cia \₁a-lə-'pē-sh(ē-)ə\ *n* : BALDNESS

aloud \ə-'laud\ *adv* : with a loud voice

alp \'alp\ *n* : a high rugged mountain

al·paca \al-'pa-kə\ *n* : a domesticated mammal esp. of Peru that is related to the llama; *also* : its woolly hair or cloth made from this

al·pha \'al-fə\ *n* **1** : the 1st letter of the Greek alphabet — A or α **2** : something first : BEGINNING

al·pha·bet \'al-fə-₁bet\ *n* : the set of letters or characters used in writing a language

al·pha·bet·i·cal \₁al-fə-'be-ti-kəl\ *or* **al·pha·bet·ic** \-'be-tik\ *adj* **1** : arranged in the order of the letters of the alphabet **2** : of or employing an alphabet — **al·pha·bet·i·cal·ly** \-ti-k(ə-)lē\ *adv*

al·pha·bet·ize \'al-fə-bə-₁tīz\ *vb* **-ized; -iz·ing** : to arrange in alphabetical order — **al·pha·bet·iz·er** *n*

al·pha·nu·mer·ic \₁al-fə-nu-'mer-ik, -nyu-\ *adj* : consisting of letters and numbers and often other symbols ⟨an ~ code⟩; *also* : being a character in an alphanumeric system

alpha particle *n* : a positively charged particle identical with the nucleus of a helium atom that is ejected at high speed in certain radioactive transformations

alpha rhythm *n* : ALPHA WAVE

alpha wave *n* : an electrical rhythm of the brain often associated with a state of wakeful relaxation

Al·pine \'al-₁pīn\ *adj* **1** : relating to, located in, or resembling the Alps mountains **2** *often not cap* : of, relating to, or growing on upland slopes above timberline **3** : of or relating to competitive ski events consisting of slalom and downhill racing

al·ready \ȯl-'re-dē\ *adv* : by this time : PREVIOUSLY

al·right \ȯl-'rīt\ *adv* : ALL RIGHT

al·so \'ȯl-sō\ *adv* : in addition : TOO

al·so–ran \-₁ran\ *n* **1** : a horse or dog that finishes out of the money in a race **2** : a contestant that does not win

alt *abbr* **1** alternate **2** altitude

Alta *abbr* Alberta

al·tar \'ȯl-tər\ *n* **1** : a structure on which sacrifices are offered or incense is burned **2** : a table used as a center of ritual or worship

altar boy *n* : a boy who assists the celebrant at a church service

¹**al·ter** \'ȯl-tər\ *vb* **al·tered; al·ter·ing** \-t(ə-)riŋ\ **1** : to make or become different **2** : CASTRATE, SPAY — **al·ter·a·tion** \₁ȯl-tə-'rā-shən\ *n*

²**alter** *abbr* alteration

al·ter·ca·tion \₁ȯl-tər-'kā-shən\ *n* : a noisy or angry dispute

al·ter ego \₁ȯl-tər-'ē-gō\ *n* [L, lit., second I] : a second self; *esp* : a trusted friend

¹**al·ter·nate** \'ȯl-tər-nət, 'al-\ *adj* **1** : arranged or succeeding by turns **2** : every other **3** : being an alternative (an ~ route) — **al·ter·nate·ly** *adv*

²**al·ter·nate** \-₁nāt\ *vb* **-nat·ed; -nat·ing** : to occur or cause to occur by turns — **al·ter·na·tion** \₁ȯl-tər-'nā-shən, ₁al-\ *n*

³**alternate** *n* : SUBSTITUTE

alternating current *n* : an electric current that reverses its direction at regular intervals

al·ter·na·tive \ȯl-'tər-nə-tiv, al-\ *adj* : offering a choice — **alternative** *n*

al·ter·na·tor \'ȯl-tər-₁nā-tər, 'al-\ *n* : an electric generator for producing alternating current

al·though *also* **al·tho** \ȯl-'thō\ *conj* : in spite of the fact that : even though

al·tim·e·ter \al-'ti-mə-tər, 'al-tə-₁mē-tər\ *n* : an instrument for measuring altitude

al·ti·tude \'al-tə-₁tüd, -₁tyüd\ *n* **1** : angular distance above the horizon **2** : vertical distance : HEIGHT **3** : the perpendicular distance in a geometric figure from the vertex to the base, from the vertex of an angle to the side opposite, or from the base to a parallel side or face

al·to \'al-tō\ *n, pl* **altos** [It, lit., high, fr. L *altus*] : the lower female voice part in a 4-part chorus; *also* : a singer having this voice or part

¹**al·to·geth·er** \₁ȯl-tə-'ge-thər\ *adv* **1** : WHOLLY **2** : in all **3** : on the whole

²**altogether** *n* : NUDE (posed in the ~)

al·tru·ism \'al-trü-₁i-zəm\ *n* : unselfish interest in the welfare of others — **al·tru·ist** \-ist\ *n* — **al·tru·is·tic** \₁al-trü-'is-tik\ *adj* — **al·tru·is·ti·cal·ly** \-ti-k(ə-)lē\ *adv*

al·um \'a-ləm\ *n* : either of two colorless crystalline aluminum-containing compounds used esp. as an emetic or as an astringent and styptic

alu·mi·na \ə-'lü-mə-nə\ *n* : the oxide of aluminum occurring in nature as corundum and in bauxite

al·u·min·i·um \₁al-yə-'mi-nē-əm\ *n, chiefly Brit* : ALUMINUM

alu·mi·nize \ə-'lü-mə-₁nīz\ *vb* **-nized; -niz·ing** : to treat with aluminum

alu·mi·num \ə-'lü-mə-nəm\ *n* : a silver-white malleable ductile light metallic element that is the most abundant metal in the earth's crust — see ELEMENT table

alum·na \ə-'ləm-nə\ *n, pl* **-nae** \-(₁)nē\ : a woman graduate or former student of a college or school

alum·nus \ə-'ləm-nəs\ *n, pl* **-ni** \-₁nī\ [L, foster son, pupil, fr. *alere* to nourish] : a graduate or former student of a college or school

al·ways \'ȯl-wēz, -wəz, -(₁)wāz\ *adv* **1** : at all times : INVARIABLY **2** : FOREVER

Alz·hei·mer's disease \'älts-₁hī-mərz-, 'alts-\ *n* : a degenerative disease of the central nervous system characterized esp. by premature senile mental deterioration

am *pres 1st sing of* BE

¹**Am** *abbr* America; American

²**Am** *symbol* americium

¹**AM** \'ā-₁em\ *n* : a broadcasting system using amplitude modulation; *also* : a radio receiver for broadcasts made by such a system

²**AM** *abbr* **1** ante meridiem — often not cap. and often punctuated **2** [NL *artium magister*] master of arts

AMA *abbr* American Medical Association

amah \'ä-(₁)mä\ *n* : an Oriental female servant; *esp* : a Chinese nurse

amain \ə-'mān\ *adv, archaic* : with full force or speed

amal·gam \ə-'mal-gəm\ *n* **1** : an alloy of mercury with another metal used in making dental cements **2** : a mixture of different elements

amal·gam·ate \ə-'mal-gə-₁māt\ *vb* **-at·ed; -at·ing** : to unite or merge into one body — **amal·ga·ma·tion** \-₁mal-gə-'mā-shən\ *n*

aman·u·en·sis \ə-₁man-yə-'wen-səs\ *n, pl* **-en·ses** \-₁sēz\ : one employed to write from dictation or to copy what another has written : SECRETARY

am·a·ranth \'a-mə-₁ranth\ *n* **1** : any of a large genus of coarse herbs sometimes grown for their showy flowers **2** : a flower that never fades

am·a·ran·thine \₁a-mə-'ran-thən, -₁thīn\ *adj* **1** : relating to or resembling an amaranth **2** : UNDYING

am·a·ryl·lis \₁a-mə-'ri-ləs\ *n* : any of various plants related to the lilies; *esp* : any of several African herbs having bulbs and grown for their clusters of large showy flowers

amass \ə-'mas\ *vb* : ACCUMULATE

am·a·teur \'a-mə-(ˌ)tər, -ˌtür, -ˌtyür, -ˌchür, -chər\ *n* [F, fr. L *amator* lover, fr. *amare* to love] **1** : a person who engages in a pursuit for pleasure and not as a profession **2** : a person who is not expert — **am·a·teur·ish** \ˌa-mə-'tər-ish, -'tür-, -'tyür-, -'chür-, -'chər-\ *adj* — **am·a·teur·ism** \'a-mə-(ˌ)tər-i-zəm, -ˌtür-, -ˌtyür-, -ˌchür-, -ˌchər-\ *n*

am·a·tive \'a-mə-tiv\ *adj* : indicative of love : AMOROUS — **am·a·tive·ly** *adv* — **am·a·tive·ness** *n*

am·a·to·ry \'a-mə-ˌtōr-ē\ *adj* : of or expressing sexual love

amaze \ə-'māz\ *vb* **amazed; amaz·ing** : to fill with wonder : ASTOUND **syn** astonish, surprise, dumbfound — **amaze·ment** *n* — **amaz·ing·ly** *adv*

am·a·zon \'a-mə-ˌzän, -zən\ *n* **1** *cap* : a member of a race of female warriors of Greek mythology **2** : a tall strong often masculine woman — **am·a·zo·ni·an** \ˌa-mə-'zō-nē-ən\ *adj, often cap*

amb *abbr* ambassador

am·bas·sa·dor \am-'ba-sə-dər\ *n* : a representative esp. of a government — **am·bas·sa·do·ri·al** \-ˌba-sə-'dōr-ē-əl\ *adj* — **am·bas·sa·dor·ship** *n*

am·ber \'am-bər\ *n* : a yellowish or brownish fossil resin used esp. for ornamental objects; *also* : the color of this resin

am·ber·gris \'am-bər-ˌgris, -ˌgrēs\ *n* : a waxy substance from the sperm whale used in making perfumes

am·bi·dex·trous \ˌam-bi-'dek-strəs\ *adj* : using both hands with equal ease — **am·bi·dex·trous·ly** *adv*

am·bi·ence *or* **am·bi·ance** \'am-bē-əns, äⁿ-'byäⁿs\ *n* : a pervading atmosphere

am·bi·ent \'am-bē-ənt\ *adj* : existing on all sides

am·big·u·ous \am-'bi-gyə-wəs\ *adj* : capable of being understood in more than one way — **am·bi·gu·i·ty** \ˌam-bə-'gyü-ə-tē\ *n* — **am·big·u·ous·ly** *adv*

am·bi·tion \am-'bi-shən\ *n* [ME, fr. MF or L; MF, fr. L *ambition-, ambitio*, lit., act of soliciting for votes, fr. *ambire* to go around] : eager desire for success or power

am·bi·tious \-shəs\ *adj* : characterized by ambition — **am·bi·tious·ly** *adv*

am·biv·a·lence \am-'bi-və-ləns\ *n* : simultaneous attraction toward and repulsion from a person, object, or action — **am·biv·a·lent** \-lənt\ *adj*

¹am·ble \'am-bəl\ *vb* **am·bled; am·bling** \-b(ə-)liŋ\ : to go at an amble

²amble *n* : an easy gait esp. of a horse

am·bro·sia \am-'brō-zh(ē-)ə\ *n* : the food of the Greek and Roman gods — **am·bro·sial** \-zh(ē-)əl\ *adj*

am·bu·lance \'am-byə-ləns\ *n* : a vehicle equipped for carrying the injured or sick

am·bu·lant \'am-byə-lənt\ *adj* : AMBULATORY

¹am·bu·la·to·ry \'am-byə-lə-ˌtōr-ē\ *adj* **1** : of, relating to, or adapted to walking **2** : able to walk or move about

²ambulatory *n, pl* **-ries** : a sheltered place (as in a cloister) for walking

am·bus·cade \'am-bə-ˌskād\ *n* : AMBUSH

am·bush \'am-ˌbùsh\ *n* : a trap in which concealed persons wait to attack by surprise — **ambush** *vb*

amdt *abbr* amendment

ame·ba, ame·boid *var of* AMOEBA, AMOEBOID

ame·lio·rate \ə-'mēl-yə-ˌrāt\ *vb* **-rat·ed; -rat·ing** : to make or grow better : IMPROVE — **ame·lio·ra·tion** \-ˌmēl-yə-'rā-shən\ *n*

amen \(ˌ)ā-'men, (ˌ)ä-\ *interj* — used esp. at the end of prayers to affirm or express approval

ame·na·ble \ə-'mē-nə-bəl, -'me-\ *adj* **1** : ANSWERABLE **2** : COMPLIANT

amend \ə-'mend\ *vb* **1** : to change for the better : IMPROVE **2** : to alter formally in phraseology — **amend·able** \-'men-də-bəl\ *adj*

amend·ment \ə-'mend-mənt\ *n* **1** : correction of faults **2** : the process of amending a parliamentary motion

or a constitution; *also* : the alteration so proposed or made

amends \ə-'mendz\ *n sing or pl* : compensation for injury or loss

ame·ni·ty \ə-'me-nə-tē, -'mē-\ *n, pl* **-ties 1** : AGREEABLENESS **2** : a gesture observed in social relationships **3** : something that serves as a comfort or convenience

Amer *abbr* America; American

amerce \ə-'mərs\ *vb* **amerced; amerc·ing 1** : to penalize by a fine determined by the court **2** : PUNISH — **amerce·ment** *n*

Amer·i·can \ə-'mer-ə-kən\ *n* **1** : a native or inhabitant of No. or So. America **2** : a citizen of the U.S. — **American** *adj* — **Amer·i·can·ism** \-ə-kə-ˌni-zəm\ *n* — **Amer·i·can·iza·tion** \ə-ˌmer-ə-kə-nə-'zā-shən\ *n* — **Amer·i·can·ize** \ə-'mer-ə-kə-ˌnīz\ *vb* — **Amer·i·can·ness** *n*

Amer·i·ca·na \ə-ˌmer-ə-'ka-nə, -'kä-\ *n pl* : materials concerning or characteristic of America, its civilization, or its culture

American Indian *n* : a member of any of the aboriginal peoples of No. and So. America except the Eskimos

American plan *n* : a hotel plan whereby the daily rates cover the cost of room and three meals

American Sign Language *n* : a sign language for the deaf in which meaning is conveyed by a system of hand gestures and placement

amer·i·ci·um \ˌa-mə-'rish-ē-əm, -'ris-\ *n* : a radioactive metallic chemical element produced artificially from plutonium — see ELEMENT table

AmerInd *abbr* American Indian

Am·er·in·di·an \ˌa-mə-'rin-dē-ən\ *n* : AMERICAN INDIAN — **Amerindian** *adj*

am·e·thyst \'a-mə-thəst\ *n* [ME *amatiste*, fr. OF & L; OF, fr. L *amethystus*, fr. Gk *amethystos*, lit., remedy against drunkenness, fr. *a-* not + *methyein* to be drunk, fr. *methy* wine] : a gemstone consisting of clear purple or bluish violet quartz

ami·a·ble \'ā-mē-ə-bəl\ *adj* **1** : AGREEABLE **2** : having a friendly and sociable disposition — **ami·a·bil·i·ty** \ˌā-mē-ə-'bi-lə-tē\ *n* — **ami·a·ble·ness** *n* — **ami·a·bly** \'ā-mē-ə-blē\ *adv*

am·i·ca·ble \'a-mi-kə-bəl\ *adj* : FRIENDLY, PEACEABLE — **am·i·ca·bil·i·ty** \ˌa-mi-kə-'bi-lə-tē\ *n* — **am·i·ca·bly** \'a-mi-kə-blē\ *adv*

amid \ə-'mid\ *or* **amidst** \-'midst\ *prep* : in or into the middle of : AMONG

amid·ships \ə-'mid-ˌships\ *adv* : in or near the middle of a ship

ami·no acid \ə-ˌmē-nō-\ *n* : any of numerous nitrogen-containing acids that include some which are used by cells to build proteins

¹amiss \ə-'mis\ *adv* **1** : WRONGLY **2** : ASTRAY **3** : IMPERFECTLY

²amiss *adj* **1** : WRONG **2** : out of place

am·i·ty \'a-mə-tē\ *n, pl* **-ties** : FRIENDSHIP; *esp* : friendly relations between nations

am·me·ter \'a-ˌmē-tər\ *n* : an instrument for measuring electric current in amperes

am·mo \'a-mō\ *n* : AMMUNITION

am·mo·nia \ə-'mōn-yə\ *n* [NL, fr. L *sal ammoniacus* sal ammoniac (ammonium chloride), lit., salt of Ammon, fr. Gk *ammōniakos* of Ammon, fr. *Ammōn* Ammon, Amen, an Egyptian god near one of whose temples it was prepared] **1** : a colorless gaseous compound of nitrogen and hydrogen used in refrigeration and in the making of fertilizers and explosives **2** : a solution (**ammonia water**) of ammonia in water

am·mo·ni·um \ə-'mō-nē-əm\ *n* : an ion or chemical group derived from ammonia by combination with hydrogen

ammonium chloride *n* : a white crystalline volatile salt used in batteries and as an expectorant

am·mu·ni·tion \ˌam-yə-'ni-shən\ *n* **1** : projectiles fired

from guns **2** : explosive items used in war **3** : material for use in attack or defense

Amn *abbr* airman

am·ne·sia \am-'nē-zhə\ *n* **1** : abnormal loss of memory **2** : the selective overlooking of events or acts not favorable to one's purpose — **am·ne·si·ac** \-zhē-ˌak, -zē-\ *or* **am·ne·sic** \-zik, -sik\ *adj or n*

am·nes·ty \'am-nə-stē\ *n, pl* **-ties** : an act granting a pardon to a group of individuals — **amnesty** *vb*

am·nio·cen·te·sis \ˌam-nē-ō-ˌsen-'tē-səs\ *n, pl* **-te·ses** \-ˌsēz\ : the surgical insertion of a hollow needle through the abdominal wall and uterus of a pregnant female esp. to obtain fluid used to check the fetus for chromosomal abnormality and to determine sex

amoe·ba \ə-'mē-bə\ *n, pl* **-bas** *or* **-bae** \-(ˌ)bē\ : any of various tiny one-celled protozoans that lack permanent cell organs and occur esp. in water and soil — **amoe·bic** \-bik\ *adj*

amoe·boid \-ˌbȯid\ *adj* : resembling an amoeba esp. in moving or readily changing shape

amok \ə-'mək, -'mäk\ *or* **amuck** \-'mək\ *adv* : in a violent, frenzied, or uncontrolled manner ⟨run ∼⟩

among \ə-'məŋ\ *also* **amongst** \-'məŋst\ *prep* **1** : in or through the midst of **2** : in the number, class, or company of **3** : in shares to each of **4** : by common action of

amon·til·la·do \ə-ˌmän-tə-'lä-dō\ *n, pl* **-dos** [Sp] : a medium dry sherry

amor·al \ā-'mȯr-əl\ *adj* **1** : neither moral nor immoral; *esp* : being outside the sphere to which moral judgments apply **2** : lacking moral sensibility — **amor·al·ly** *adv*

am·o·rous \'a-mə-rəs\ *adj* **1** : inclined to love **2** : being in love **3** : of or indicative of love — **am·o·rous·ly** *adv* — **am·o·rous·ness** *n*

amor·phous \ə-'mȯr-fəs\ *adj* **1** : SHAPELESS, FORMLESS **2** : not crystallized

am·or·tize \'a-mər-ˌtīz, ə-'mȯr-\ *vb* **-tized; -tiz·ing** : to extinguish (as a mortgage) usu. by payment on the principal at the time of each periodic interest payment — **amor·ti·za·tion** \ˌa-mər-tə-'zā-shən, ə-ˌmȯr-\ *n*

Amos \'ā-məs\ — see BIBLE table

¹**amount** \ə-'maȯnt\ *vb* **1** : to be equivalent **2** : to reach a total : add up

²**amount** *n* **1** : the total number or quantity **2** : a principal sum plus the interest on it

amour \ə-'mu̇r, ä-, a-\ *n* **1** : a love affair esp. when illicit **2** : LOVER

amour pro·pre \ˌa-ˌmu̇r-'prōprª, ˌä-, -'prȯprª\ *n* [F] : SELF-ESTEEM

¹**amp** \'amp\ *n* : AMPLIFIER; *also* : a unit consisting of an electronic amplifier and a loudspeaker

²**amp** *abbr* ampere

am·per·age \'am-p(ə-)rij\ *n* : the strength of a current of electricity expressed in amperes

am·pere \'am-ˌpir\ *n* : a unit of electric current equiv-

alent to a steady current produced by one volt applied across a resistance of one ohm

am·per·sand \'am-pər-ˌsand\ *n* [alter. of *and per se and*, spoken form of the phrase & *per se and*, lit., (the character) & by itself (stands for the word) *and*] : a character & used for the word *and*

am·phet·amine \am-'fe-tə-ˌmēn, -mən\ *n* : a compound or one of its derivatives that stimulates the central nervous system and is used esp. to treat hyperactive children and to suppress appetite

am·phib·i·an \am-'fi-bē-ən\ *n* **1** : an amphibious organism; *esp* : any of a class of vertebrate animals (as frogs and salamanders) intermediate between fishes and reptiles **2** : an airplane that can land on and take off from either land or water

am·phib·i·ous \am-'fi-bē-əs\ *adj* [Gk *amphibios*, lit., living a double life, fr. *amphi-* on both sides + *bios* mode of life] **1** : able to live both on land and in water **2** : adapted for both land and water **3** : made by joint action of land, sea, and air forces invading from the sea; *also* : trained for such action

am·phi·bole \'am-fə-ˌbōl\ *n* : any of a group of rock-forming minerals of similar crystal structure

am·phi·the·ater \'am-fə-ˌthē-ə-tər\ *n* **1** : an oval or circular structure with rising tiers of seats around an arena **2** : a very large auditorium

am·pho·ra \'am-fə-rə\ *n, pl* **-rae** \-ˌrē\ *or* **-ras** : an ancient Greek jar or vase with two handles that rise almost to the level of the mouth

am·ple \'am-pəl\ *adj* **am·pler** \-plər\ **am·plest** \-pləst\ **1** : LARGE, CAPACIOUS **2** : enough to satisfy : ABUNDANT — **am·ply** \-plē\ *adv*

am·pli·fy \'am-plə-ˌfī\ *vb* **-fied; -fy·ing 1** : to expand by extended treatment **2** : to increase in magnitude or strength; *esp* : to make louder — **am·pli·fi·ca·tion** \ˌam-plə-fə-'kā-shən\ *n* — **am·pli·fi·er** \'am-plə-ˌfī(-ə)r\ *n*

am·pli·tude \-ˌtüd, -ˌtyüd\ *n* **1** : ample extent : FULLNESS **2** : the extent of a vibratory movement (as of a pendulum) or of an oscillation (as of an alternating current or a radio wave)

amplitude modulation *n* : modulation of the amplitude of a radio carrier wave in accordance with the strength of the signal; *also* : a broadcasting system using such modulation

am·poule *or* **am·pule** *also* **am·pul** \'am-ˌpyül, -ˌpül\ *n* : a small sealed bulbous glass vessel used to hold a solution for hypodermic injection

---

am·pu·tate \'am-pyə-ˌtāt\ *vb* **-tat·ed; -tat·ing** : to cut off ⟨∼ a leg⟩ — **am·pu·ta·tion** \ˌam-pyə-'tā-shən\ *n*

---

am·pu·tee \ˌam-pyə-'tē\ *n* : one who has had a limb amputated

AMSLAN *abbr* American Sign Language

amt *abbr* amount

amuck \ə-'mək\ *var of* AMOK

am·u·let \'am-yə-lət\ *n* : an ornament worn as a charm against evil

amuse \ə-'myüz\ *vb* **amused; amus·ing** : to entertain in a light or playful manner : DIVERT — **amuse·ment** *n*

AM·VETS \'am-₁vets\ *abbr* American Veterans (of World War II)

am·y·lase \'a-mə-₁lās, -₁lāz\ *n* : any of several enzymes that accelerate the breakdown of starch and glycogen

an \ən, (')an\ *indefinite article* : A — used before words beginning with a vowel sound

¹**-an** *or* **-ian** *also* **-ean** *n suffix* 1 : one that belongs to ⟨American⟩ ⟨crustacean⟩ 2 : one skilled in or specializing in ⟨phonetician⟩

²**-an** *or* **-ian** *also* **-ean** *adj suffix* 1 : of or belonging to ⟨American⟩ 2 : characteristic of : resembling ⟨Mozartean⟩

AN *abbr* airman (Navy)

an·a·bol·ic steroid \₁a-nə-'bä-lik-\ *n* : any of a group of synthetic steroid hormones sometimes abused by athletes in training to increase temporarily the size of their muscles

anach·ro·nism \ə-'na-krə-₁ni-zəm\ *n* 1 : the error of placing a person or thing in the wrong period 2 : one that is chronologically out of place — **anach·ro·nis·tic** \ə-₁na-krə-'nis-tik\ *adj* — **anach·ro·nous** \-'na-krə-nəs\ *adj*

an·a·con·da \₁a-nə-'kän-də\ *n* : a large So. American snake that suffocates and kills its prey by constriction

anae·mia, anae·mic *chiefly Brit var of* ANEMIA, ANEMIC

an·aer·obe \'a-nə-₁rōb\ *n* : an anaerobic organism

an·aer·o·bic \₁a-nə-'rō-bik\ *adj* : living, active, occurring, or existing in the absence of free oxygen

an·aes·the·sia, an·aes·thet·ic *chiefly Brit var of* ANESTHESIA, ANESTHETIC

ana·gram \'a-nə-₁gram\ *n* : a word or phrase made by transposing the letters of another word or phrase

¹**anal** \'ān-ᵊl\ *adj* 1 : of, relating to, or situated near the anus 2 : of, relating to, or characterized by the stage of psychosexual development in psychoanalytic theory during which one is concerned esp. with feces 3 : of, relating to, or characterized by personality traits (as parsimony and ill humor) considered typical of fixation at the anal stage of development — **anal·ly** *adv*

²**anal** *abbr* 1 analogy 2 analysis; analytic

an·al·ge·sia \₁an-ᵊl-'jē-zhə\ *n* : insensibility to pain — **an·al·ge·sic** \-'jē-zik, -sik\ *adj*

an·al·ge·sic \-'jē-zik, -sik\ *n* : an agent for producing analgesia

analog computer \'an-ᵊl-₁òg-, -₁äg-\ *n* : a computer that operates with numbers represented by directly measurable quantities (as voltages)

anal·o·gous \ə-'na-lə-gəs\ *adj* : similar in one or more respects

an·a·logue *or* **an·a·log** \'an-ᵊl-₁òg, -₁ag\ *n* 1 : something that is analogous to something else 2 : an organ

similar in function to one of another animal or plant but different in structure or origin

anal·o·gy \ə-'na-lə-jē\ *n, pl* **-gies** 1 : inference that if two or more things agree in some respects they will probably agree in others 2 : a likeness in one or more ways between things otherwise unlike — **an·a·log·i·cal** \₁an-ᵊl-'ä-ji-kəl\ *adj* — **an·a·log·i·cal·ly** \-k(ə-)lē\ *adv*

an·a·lyse *chiefly Brit var of* ANALYZE

anal·y·sis \ə-'na-lə-səs\ *n, pl* **-yses** \-₁sēz\ [NL, fr. Gk, fr. *analyein* to break up, fr. *ana-* up + *lyein* to loosen] 1 : separation of a thing into the parts or elements of which it is composed 2 : an examination of a thing to determine its parts or elements; *also* : a statement showing the results of such an examination 3 : PSYCHOANALYSIS — **an·a·lyst** \'an-ᵊl-ist\ *n* — **an·a·lyt·ic** \₁an-ᵊl-'i-tik\ *or* **an·a·lyt·i·cal** \-ti-kəl\ *adj* — **an·a·lyt·i·cal·ly** *adv*

an·a·lyze \'an-ᵊl-₁īz\ *vb* **-lyzed; -lyz·ing** : to make an analysis of

an·a·pest \'a-nə-₁pest\ *n* : a metrical foot of two unaccented syllables followed by one accented syllable — **an·a·pes·tic** \₁a-nə-'pes-tik\ *adj or n*

an·ar·chism \'a-nər-₁ki-zəm\ *n* : the theory that all government is undesirable — **an·ar·chist** \-kist\ *n or adj* — **an·ar·chis·tic** \₁a-nər-'kis-tik\ *adj*

an·ar·chy \'an-ər-kē\ *n* 1 : a social structure without government or law and order 2 : utter confusion — **an·ar·chic** \a-'när-kik\ *adj* — **an·ar·chi·cal·ly** \-ki-k(ə-)lē\ *adv*

anas·to·mo·sis \ə-₁nas-tə-'mō-səs\ *n, pl* **-mo·ses** \-₁sēz\ 1 : the union of parts or branches (as of blood vessels) 2 : NETWORK

anat *abbr* anatomical; anatomy

anath·e·ma \ə-'na-thə-mə\ *n* 1 : a solemn curse 2 : a person or thing accursed; *also* : one intensely disliked

anath·e·ma·tize \-₁tīz\ *vb* **-tized; -tiz·ing** : to pronounce an anathema against : CURSE

anat·o·mise *Brit var of* ANATOMIZE

anat·o·mize \ə-'na-tə-₁mīz\ *vb* **-mized; -miz·ing** : to dissect so as to examine the structure and parts; *also* : ANALYZE

anat·o·my \ə-'na-tə-mē\ *n, pl* **-mies** [LL *anatomia* dissection, fr. Gk *anatomē*, fr. *anatemnein* to dissect, fr. *ana-* up + *temnein* to cut] 1 : a branch of science dealing with the structure of organisms 2 : structural makeup esp. of an organism or any of its parts 3 : a separating into parts for detailed study : ANALYSIS — **an·a·tom·ic** \₁a-nə-'tä-mik\ *or* **an·a·tom·i·cal** \-mi-kəl\ *adj* — **an·a·tom·i·cal·ly** \-mi-k(ə-)lē\ *adv* — **anat·o·mist** \ə-'na-tə-mist\ *n*

anc *abbr* ancient

-ance *n suffix* 1 : action or process ⟨furtherance⟩ : instance of an action or process ⟨performance⟩ 2 : quality or state : instance of a quality or state ⟨protuberance⟩ 3 : amount or degree ⟨conductance⟩

an·ces·tor \'an-₁ses-tər\ *n* [ME *ancestre*, fr. OF, fr. L *antecessor* predecessor, fr. *antecedere* to go before, fr. *ante-* before + *cedere* to go] : one from whom an individual is descended

an·ces·tress \'an-₁ses-trəs\ n : a female ancestor

an·ces·try \'an-₁ses-trē\ n 1 : line of descent : LINEAGE 2 : ANCESTORS — an·ces·tral \an-'ses-trəl\ adj

¹an·chor \'aŋ-kər\ n 1 : a heavy metal device attached to a ship that catches hold of the bottom and holds the ship in place 2 : ANCHORPERSON

²anchor vb : to hold or become held in place by or as if by an anchor

an·chor·age \'aŋ-k(ə-)rij\ n : a place suitable for ships to anchor

an·cho·rite \'aŋ-kə-₁rīt\ n : HERMIT

an·chor·man \'aŋ-kər-₁man\ n 1 : the member of a team who competes last 2 : an anchorperson who is a man

an·chor·per·son \-₁pər-sən\ n : a broadcaster who reads the news and introduces the reports of other broadcasters

an·chor·wom·an \-₁wù-mən\ n 1 : a woman who competes last 2 : an anchorperson who is a woman

an·cho·vy \'an-₁chō-vē, an-'chō-\ n, pl -vies or -vy : a small herringlike fish used esp. for sauces and relishes

an·cien ré·gime \äⁿs-yaⁿ-rā-'zhēm\ n 1 : the political and social system of France before the Revolution of 1789 2 : a system no longer prevailing

¹an·cient \'ān-shənt\ adj 1 : having existed for many years 2 : belonging to times long past; esp : belonging to the period before the Middle Ages

²ancient n 1 : an aged person 2 pl : the peoples of ancient Greece and Rome; esp : the classical authors of Greece and Rome

an·cil·lary \'an-sə-₁ler-ē\ adj 1 : SUBORDINATE, SUBSIDIARY 2 : AUXILIARY, SUPPLEMENTARY — ancillary n

-ancy n suffix : quality or state ⟨flamboyancy⟩

and \ənd, (')and\ conj 1 — used to indicate connection or addition esp. of items within the same class or type or to join words or phrases of the same grammatical rank or function 2 — used to join one finite verb to another so that together they are equivalent to an infinitive of purpose ⟨come ~ see me⟩

¹an·dan·te \än-'dän-₁tā, -₁tē\ adv or adj [It., lit., going, prp. of andare to go] : moderately slow — used as a direction in music

²andante n : an andante movement

and·iron \'an-₁dī(-ə)rn\ n : one of a pair of metal supports for firewood in a fireplace

and/or \'and-'ȯr\ conj — used to indicate that either and or or may apply ⟨men ~ women means men and women or men or women⟩

An·dor·ran \an-'dȯr-ən\ n : a native or inhabitant of Andorra

an·dro·gen \'an-drə-jən\ n : a male sex hormone

an·drog·y·nous \an-'drä-jə-nəs\ adj 1 : having the characteristics of both male and female 2 : suitable for either sex ⟨~ clothing⟩

an·droid \'an-₁drȯid\ n : a mobile robot usu. with a human form

an·ec·dot·al \₁a-nik-'dōt-ᵊl\ adj 1 : relating to or consisting of anecdotes 2 : based on reports of an unscientific nature — an·ec·dot·al·ly adv

an·ec·dote \an-ik-₁dōt\ n, pl -dotes also -dota \₁a-nik-'dō-tə\ [F, fr. Gk anekdota unpublished items, fr. a- not + ekdidonai to publish] : a brief story of an interesting, amusing, or biographical incident

ane·mia \ə-'nē-mē-ə\ n 1 : a condition in which blood is deficient in quantity, in red blood cells, or in hemoglobin and which is marked by pallor, weakness, and irregular heart action 2 : lack of vitality — ane·mic \ə-'nē-mik\ adj

an·e·mom·e·ter \₁a-nə-'mä-mə-tər\ n : an instrument for measuring the force or speed of the wind

anem·o·ne \ə-'ne-mə-nē\ n : any of a large genus of herbs related to the buttercups that have showy flowers without petals but with conspicuous often colored sepals

anent \ə-'nent\ prep : CONCERNING

an·es·the·sia \₁a-nəs-'thē-zhə\ n : loss of bodily sensation

an·es·the·si·ol·o·gy \₁-₁thē-zē-'ä-lə-jē\ n : a branch of medical science dealing with anesthesia and anesthetics — an·es·the·si·ol·o·gist \-jist\ n

¹an·es·thet·ic \₁a-nəs-'the-tik\ adj : of, relating to, or capable of producing anesthesia

²anesthetic n : an agent that produces anesthesia — anes·the·tist \ə-'nes-thə-tist\ n — anes·the·tize \-thə-₁tīz\ vb

anew \ə-'nü, -'nyü\ adv 1 : over again 2 : in a new form

an·gel \'ān-jəl\ n [ME, fr. OF angele, fr. L angelus, fr. Gk angelos, lit., messenger] 1 : a spiritual being superior to man 2 : an attendant spirit 3 : a winged figure of human form in art 4 : MESSENGER, HARBINGER 5 : a person held to resemble an angel 6 : a financial backer — an·gel·ic \an-'je-lik\ or an·gel·i·cal \-li-kəl\ adj — an·gel·i·cal·ly \-k(ə-)lē\ adv

an·gel·fish \'ān-jəl-₁fish\ n : any of several bright-colored tropical fishes that are flattened from side to side

an·gel·i·ca \an-'je-li-kə\ n : a biennial herb related to the carrot whose roots and fruit furnish a flavoring oil

¹an·ger \'aŋ-gər\ vb : to make angry

²anger n [ME, affliction, anger, fr. ON angr grief] : a strong feeling of displeasure syn wrath, ire, rage, fury, indignation

an·gi·na \an-'jī-nə\ n : a disorder (as of the heart) marked by attacks of intense pain; esp : ANGINA PECTORIS — an·gi·nal \an-'jīn-ᵊl\ adj

angina pec·to·ris \-'pek-t(ə-)rəs\ n : a heart disease marked by brief attacks of sharp chest pain caused by deficient oxygenation of heart muscles

an·gio·gram \'an-jē-ə-₁gram\ n : an X-ray photograph made by angiography

an·gi·og·ra·phy \₁an-jē-'ä-grə-fē\ n : the use of X rays to make blood vessels visible (as by photography) after injection of a substance opaque to radiation

an·gio·plas·ty \'an-jē-ə-₁plas-tē\ n : surgical repair of a blood vessel esp. by using an inflatable catheter to unblock arteries clogged by atherosclerotic deposits

an·gio·sperm \-₁spərm\ n : FLOWERING PLANT

¹an·gle \'aŋ-gəl\ n 1 : a sharp projecting corner 2 : the figure formed by the meeting of two lines in a point 3 : a point of view 4 : a special technique or plan : GIMMICK — an·gled adj

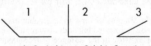

angle 2: 1 obtuse, 2 right, 3 acute

²angle vb an·gled; an·gling \-g(ə-)liŋ\ : to turn, move, or direct at an angle

³angle vb an·gled; an·gling \-g(ə-)liŋ\ : to fish with a hook and line — an·gler \-glər\ n — an·gling \-gliŋ\ n

an·gle·worm \'aŋ-gəl-₁wərm\ n : EARTHWORM

An·gli·can \'aŋ-gli-kən\ adj 1 : of or relating to the established episcopal Church of England 2 : of or relating to England or the English nation — Anglican n — An·gli·can·ism \-kə-₁ni-zəm\ n

an·gli·cize \'aŋ-glə-₁sīz\ vb -cized; -ciz·ing often cap 1 : to make English (as in habits, speech, character, or outlook) 2 : to borrow (a foreign word or phrase) into English without changing form or spelling and sometimes without changing pronunciation — an·gli·ci·za·tion \₁aŋ-glə-sə-'zā-shən\ n, often cap

An·glo \'aŋ-glō\ n, pl Anglos : a non-Hispanic white inhabitant of the U.S.; esp : one of English origin and descent

An·glo–French \₁aŋ-glō-'french\ n : the French language used in medieval England

An·glo·phile \'aŋ-glə-₁fīl\ also An·glo·phil \-₁fil\ n

: one who greatly admires England and things English

An·glo·phobe \'aŋ-glə-ˌfōb\ *n* : one who is averse to England and things English

An·glo–Sax·on \ˌaŋ-glō-'sak-sən\ *n* **1** : a member of any of the Germanic peoples who invaded England in the 5th century A.D. **2** : a member of the English people **3** : Old English — **Anglo–Saxon** *adj*

an·go·ra \aŋ-'gōr-ə, an-\ *n* **1** : yarn or cloth made from the hair of an Angora goat or rabbit **2** *cap* : any of a breed of cats, goats, or rabbits with a long silky coat

an·gry \'aŋ-grē\ *adj* **an·gri·er; -est** : feeling or showing anger **syn** enraged, wrathful, irate, indignant, mad — **an·gri·ly** \-grə-lē\ *adv*

angst \'äŋst\ *n* [G] : a feeling of anxiety

ang·strom \'aŋ-strəm\ *n* : a unit of length equal to one ten-billionth of a meter

an·guish \'aŋ-gwish\ *n* : extreme pain or distress esp. of mind — **an·guished** \-gwisht\ *adj*

an·gu·lar \'aŋ-gyə-lər\ *adj* **1** : sharp-cornered **2** : having one or more angles **3** : being thin and bony — **an·gu·lar·i·ty** \ˌaŋ-gyə-'lar-ə-tē\ *n*

An·gus \'aŋ-gəs\ *n* : any of a breed of usu. black hornless beef cattle originating in Scotland

an·hy·drous \an-'hī-drəs\ *adj* : free from water

an·i·line \'an-ᵊl-ən\ *n* : an oily poisonous liquid used in making dyes, medicines, and explosives

an·i·mad·vert \ˌa-nə-ˌmad-'vərt\ *vb* : to remark critically : express censure — **an·i·mad·ver·sion** \-'vər-zhən\ *n*

¹an·i·mal \'a-nə-məl\ *n* **1** : any of a kingdom of living things typically differing from plants in capacity for active movement, in rapid response to stimulation, and in lack of cellulose cell walls **2** : a lower animal as distinguished from human beings; *also* : MAMMAL

²animal *adj* **1** : of, relating to, or derived from animals **2** : of or relating to the physical as distinguished from the mental or spiritual **syn** carnal, fleshly, sensual

an·i·mal·cule \ˌa-nə-'mal-kyül\ *n* : a tiny animal usu. invisible to the naked eye

¹an·i·mate \'a-nə-mət\ *adj* : having life

²an·i·mate \-ˌmāt\ *vb* **-mat·ed; -mat·ing 1** : to impart life to **2** : to give spirit and vigor to **3** : to make appear to move ⟨~ a cartoon for motion pictures⟩ — **an·i·mat·ed** *adj*

an·i·ma·tion \ˌa-nə-'mā-shən\ *n* **1** : VIVACITY, LIVELINESS **2** : a motion picture made from a series of drawings simulating motions by means of slight progressive changes

an·i·mism \'a-nə-ˌmi-zəm\ *n* : attribution of conscious life to objects and in phenomena of nature or to inanimate objects — **an·i·mist** \-mist\ *n* — **an·i·mis·tic** \ˌa-nə-'mis-tik\ *adj*

an·i·mos·i·ty \ˌa-nə-'mä-sə-tē\ *n*, *pl* **-ties** : ILL WILL, RESENTMENT

an·i·mus \'a-nə-məs\ *n* : deep-seated resentment and hostility

an·ion \'a-ˌnī-ən, -ˌnī-ˌän\ *n* : a negatively charged ion

an·ise \'a-nəs\ *n* : an herb related to the carrot with aromatic seeds (**aniseed** \-sēd\) used in flavoring

an·is·ette \ˌa-nə-'set, -'zet\ *n* [F] : a usu. colorless sweet liqueur flavored with aniseed

ankh \'äŋk\ *n* : a cross having a loop for its upper vertical arm and serving esp. in ancient Egypt as an emblem of life

an·kle \'aŋ-kəl\ *n* : the joint or region between the foot and the leg

an·kle·bone \'aŋ-kəl-ˌbōn\ *n* : the bone that in human beings bears the weight of the body and with the tibia and fibula forms the ankle joint

an·klet \'aŋ-klət\ *n* **1** : something (as an ornament) worn around the ankle **2** : a short sock reaching slightly above the ankle

ann *abbr* **1** annals **2** annual

an·nals \'an-ᵊlz\ *n pl* **1** : a record of events in chronological order **2** : historical records — **an·nal·ist** \-ᵊl-ist\ *n*

an·neal \ə-'nēl\ *vb* **1** : to make (as glass or steel) less brittle by heating and then cooling **2** : STRENGTHEN, TOUGHEN

¹an·nex \ə-'neks, 'a-ˌneks\ *vb* **1** : to attach as an addition **2** : to incorporate (as a territory) within a political domain — **an·nex·a·tion** \ˌa-ˌnek-'sā-shən\ *n*

²an·nex \'a-ˌneks, -niks\ *n* : a subsidiary or supplementary structure

an·nexe *chiefly Brit var of* ANNEX

an·ni·hi·late \ə-'nī-ə-ˌlāt\ *vb* **-lat·ed; -lat·ing** : to destroy completely — **an·ni·hi·la·tion** \-ˌnī-ə-'lā-shən\ *n*

an·ni·ver·sa·ry \ˌa-nə-'vər-sə-rē\ *n*, *pl* **-ries** : the annual return of the date of a notable event and esp. a wedding

an·no Do·mi·ni \ˌa-nō-'dä-mə-nē, -'dō-, -ˌnī\ *adv, often cap A* [ML, in the year of the Lord] — used to indicate that a time division falls within the Christian era

an·no·tate \'a-nə-ˌtāt\ *vb* **-tat·ed; -tat·ing** : to furnish with notes — **an·no·ta·tion** \ˌa-nə-'tā-shən\ *n* — **an·no·ta·tor** \'a-nə-ˌtā-tər\ *n*

an·nounce \ə-'naůns\ *vb* **an·nounced; an·nounc·ing 1** : to make known publicly **2** : to give notice of the arrival or presence of — **an·nounce·ment** *n*

an·nounc·er \ə-'naůn-sər\ *n* : a person who introduces radio or television programs, makes commercial announcements, or gives station identification

an·noy \ə-'nȯi\ *vb* : to disturb or irritate esp. by repeated acts : VEX **syn** irk, bother, pester, tease, harass — **an·noy·ing·ly** *adv*

an·noy·ance \ə-'nȯi-əns\ *n* **1** : the act of annoying **2** : the state of being annoyed **3** : NUISANCE

¹an·nu·al \'an-yə-wəl\ *adj* **1** : covering the period of a year **2** : occurring once a year : YEARLY **3** : completing the life cycle in one growing season ⟨~ plants⟩ — **an·nu·al·ly** *adv*

²annual *n* **1** : a publication appearing once a year **2** : an annual plant

annual ring *n* : the layer of wood produced by a single year's growth of a woody plant

an·nu·i·tant \ə-'nü-ə-tənt, -'nyü-\ *n* : a beneficiary of an annuity

an·nu·i·ty \ə-'nü-ə-tē, -'nyü-\ *n*, *pl* **-i·ties** : an amount payable annually; *also* : the right to receive such a payment

an·nul \ə-'nəl\ *vb* **an·nulled; an·nul·ling** : to make legally void — **an·nul·ment** *n*

an·nu·lar \'an-yə-lər\ *adj* : ring-shaped

an·nun·ci·ate \ə-'nən-sē-ˌāt\ *vb* **-at·ed; -at·ing** : ANNOUNCE

an·nun·ci·a·tion \ə-ˌnən-sē-'ā-shən\ *n* **1** : ANNOUNCEMENT **2** *cap* : March 25 observed as a church festival commemorating the announcement of the Incarnation

an·nun·ci·a·tor \ə-'nən-sē-ˌā-tər\ *n* : one that annunciates; *specif* : a usu. electrically controlled signal board or indicator

an·ode \'a-ˌnōd\ *n* **1** : the positive electrode of an electrolytic cell **2** : the negative terminal of a battery **3** : the electron-collecting electrode of an electron tube — **an·od·ic** \a-'nä-dik\ *also* **an·od·al** \-'nōd-ᵊl\ *adj*

an·od·ize \'a-nə-ˌdīz\ *vb* **-ized; -iz·ing** : to subject (a metal) to electrolytic action as the anode of a cell in order to coat with a protective or decorative film

an·o·dyne \'a-nə-ˌdīn\ *n* : something that relieves pain : a soothing agent

anoint \ə-'nȯint\ *vb* **1** : to apply oil to esp. as a sacred rite **2** : CONSECRATE — **anoint·ment** *n*

anom·a·lous \ə-'nä-mə-ləs\ *adj* : deviating from a general rule : ABNORMAL

anom·a·ly \ə-'nä-mə-lē\ *n*, *pl* **-lies** : something anomalous : IRREGULARITY

¹anon \ə-'nän\ *adv, archaic* : SOON

²anon *abbr* anonymous; anonymously

anon·y·mous \ə-'nä-nə-məs\ *adj* : of unknown or un-

declared origin or authorship — **an·o·nym·i·ty** \ˌa-nə-ˈni-mə-tē\ n — **anon·y·mous·ly** adv

anoph·e·les \ə-ˈnä-fə-ˌlēz\ n [NL, genus name, fr. Gk anōphelēs useless, fr. a- not + ophelos advantage, help] : any of a genus of mosquitoes that includes all mosquitoes which transmit malaria to human beings

an·o·rec·tic \ˌa-nə-ˈrek-tik\ adj : ANOREXIC — **anorectic** n

an·orex·ia \ˌa-nə-ˈrek-sē-ə\ n **1** : loss of appetite esp. when prolonged **2** : ANOREXIA NERVOSA

anorexia ner·vo·sa \-nər-ˈvō-sə\ n : a serious disorder in eating behavior marked esp. by a pathological fear of weight gain leading to faulty eating patterns, malnutrition, and usu. excessive weight loss

an·orex·ic \ˌa-nə-ˈrek-sik\ adj **1** : lacking or causing loss of appetite **2** : affected with or as if with anorexia nervosa — **anorexic** n

¹an·oth·er \ə-ˈnə-thər\ adj **1** : some other **2** : being one in addition : one more

²another pron **1** : an additional one : one more **2** : one that is different from the first or present one

ans abbr answer

¹an·swer \ˈan-sər\ n **1** : something spoken or written in reply to a question **2** : a solution of a problem

²answer vb **1** : to speak or write in reply to **2** : to be responsible **3** : to be adequate — **an·swer·er** n

an·swer·able \ˈan-sə-rə-bəl\ adj **1** : subject to taking blame or responsibility **2** : capable of being refuted

answering machine n : a machine that receives telephone calls by playing a recorded message and usu. by recording messages from callers

answering service n : a commercial service that answers telephone calls for its clients

¹ant \ˈant\ n : any of a family of small social insects related to the bees and living in communities usu. in earth or wood

²ant abbr antonym

Ant abbr Antarctica

ant- — see ANTI-

¹-ant n suffix **1** : one that performs or promotes (a specified action) ⟨coolant⟩ **2** : thing that is acted upon (in a specified manner) ⟨inhalant⟩

²-ant adj suffix **1** : performing (a specified action) or being (in a specified condition) ⟨propellant⟩ **2** : promoting (a specified action or process) ⟨expectorant⟩

ant·ac·id \ant-ˈa-səd\ n : an agent that counteracts acidity — **antacid** adj

an·tag·o·nism \an-ˈta-gə-ˌni-zəm\ n **1** : active opposition or hostility **2** : opposition in physiological action — **an·tag·o·nis·tic** \-ˌta-gə-ˈnis-tik\ adj

an·tag·o·nist \-nist\ n : ADVERSARY, OPPONENT

an·tag·o·nize \an-ˈta-gə-ˌnīz\ vb **-nized; -niz·ing** : to provoke the hostility of

ant·arc·tic \ant-ˈärk-tik, -ˈär-tik\ adj, often cap : of or relating to the south pole or the region near it

antarctic circle n, often cap A&C : the parallel of latitude that is approximately 66½ degrees south of the equator

¹an·te \ˈan-tē\ n : a poker stake put up before the deal to build the pot; also : an amount paid : PRICE

²ante vb **an·ted; an·te·ing 1** : to put up (an ante) **2** : PAY

ant·eat·er \ˈant-ˌē-tər\ n : any of several mammals (as an aardvark) that feed mostly on ants or termites

an·te·bel·lum \ˌan-ti-ˈbe-ləm\ adj : existing before a war; esp : existing before the U.S. Civil War of 1861-65

an·te·ced·ent \ˌan-tə-ˈsēd-ᵊnt\ n **1** : a noun, pronoun, phrase, or clause referred to by a personal or relative pronoun **2** : a preceding event or cause **3** pl : the significant conditions of one's earlier life **4** pl : ANCESTORS — **antecedent** adj

an·te·cham·ber \ˈan-ti-ˌchām-bər\ n : ANTEROOM

an·te·date \ˈan-ti-ˌdāt\ vb **1** : to date (a paper) as of an earlier day than that on which the actual writing or signing is done **2** : to precede in time

an·te·di·lu·vi·an \ˌan-ti-də-ˈlü-vē-ən, -dī-\ adj **1** : of the period before the biblical flood **2** : ANTIQUATED

an·te·lope \ˈant-ᵊl-ˌōp\ n, pl **-lope** or **-lopes** [ME, fabulous heraldic beast, prob. fr. MF antelop savage animal with sawlike horns, fr. ML anthalopus, fr. LGk antholops] **1** : any of various Old World cud-chewing mammals related to the oxen but with smaller lighter bodies and horns that extend upward and backward **2** : PRONGHORN

an·te me·ri·di·em \ˈan-ti-mə-ˈri-dē-əm\ adj [L] : being before noon

an·ten·na \an-ˈte-nə\ n, pl **-nae** \-(ˌ)nē\ or **-nas** [ML, fr. L, sail yard] **1** : one of the long slender paired segmented sensory organs on the head of an arthropod (as an insect or crab) **2** pl usu **-nas** : a metallic device (as a rod or wire) for sending out or receiving radio waves

an·te·pe·nult \ˌan-ti-ˈpē-ˌnəlt\ also **an·te·pen·ul·ti·ma** \-pi-ˈnəl-tə-mə\ n : the 3d syllable of a word counting from the end — **an·te·pen·ul·ti·mate** \-pi-ˈnəl-tə-mət\ adj or n

an·te·ri·or \an-ˈtir-ē-ər\ adj **1** : situated before or toward the front **2** : situated near or nearer to the head **3** : coming before in time syn preceding, previous, prior, antecedent

an·te·room \ˈan-ti-ˌrüm, -ˌrùm\ n : a room forming the entrance to another and often used as a waiting room

an·them \ˈan-thəm\ n **1** : a sacred vocal composition **2** : a song or hymn of praise or gladness

an·ther \ˈan-thər\ n : the part of a stamen of a seed plant that produces and contains pollen

ant·hill \ˈant-ˌhil\ n : a mound thrown up by ants or termites in digging their nest

an·thol·o·gy \an-ˈthä-lə-jē\ n, pl **-gies** [NL anthologia collection of epigrams, fr. MGk, fr. Gk, flower gathering, fr. anthos flower + logia collecting, fr. legein to gather] : a collection of literary selections — **an·thol·o·gist** \-jist\ n — **an·thol·o·gize** \-ˌjīz\ vb

an·thra·cite \ˈan-thrə-ˌsīt\ n : a hard glossy coal that burns without much smoke

an·thrax \ˈan-ˌthraks\ n : an infectious and usu. fatal

bacterial disease of warm-blooded animals (as cattle and sheep) that is transmissible to humans; *also* : a bacterium causing anthrax

an·thro·po·cen·tric \ˌan-thrə-pə-ˈsen- trik\ *adj* : interpreting or regarding the world in terms of human values and experiences

an·thro·poid \ˈan-thrə-ˌpòid\ *n* **1** : any of several large tailless apes (as a gorilla) **2** : a person resembling an ape — **anthropoid** *adj*

an·thro·pol·o·gy \ˌan-thrə-ˈpä-lə-jē\ *n* : the science of human beings and esp. of their physical characteristics, their origin and the distribution of races, their environment and social relations, and their culture — **an·thro·po·log·i·cal** \-pə-ˈlä-ji-kəl\ *adj* — **an·thro·pol·o·gist** \-ˈpä-lə-jist\ *n*

an·thro·po·mor·phism \ˌan-thrə-pə-ˈmòr-ˌfi-zəm\ *n* : an interpretation of what is not human or personal in terms of human or personal characteristics : HUMANIZATION — **an·thro·po·mor·phic** \-fik\ *adj*

an·ti \ˈan-ˌtī, -tē\ *n, pl* **antis** : one who is opposed

anti- \an-ti, -tē, -ˌtī\ *or* **ant-** *or* **anth-** *prefix* **1** : opposite in kind, position, or action **2** : opposing : hostile toward **3** : counteractive **4** : preventive of : curative of

antiaging	antigovernment
anti-AIDS	anti-imperialism
antiaircraft	anti-imperialist
antialcohol	antiknock
anti-American	antilabor
antiapartheid	antimalarial
antibacterial	antimicrobial
anticapitalist	antinausea
anti-Catholic	antipoverty
anticholesterol	antislavery
anticlerical	antispasmodic
anticolonial	antistatic
anticommunism	antisubmarine
anticommunist	antitank
antidemocratic	antitumor
antiestablishment	antiviral
antifascist	

an·ti·abor·tion \ˌan-tē-ə-ˈbòr-shən, ˌan-ˌtī-\ *adj* : opposed to abortion

an·ti·bal·lis·tic missile \ˌan-ti-bə-ˈlis-tik-, ˌan-ˌtī-\ *n* : a missile for intercepting and destroying ballistic missiles

an·ti·bi·ot·ic \-bī-ˈä-tik, -bē-\ *n* : a substance produced by or derived by chemical alteration of a substance produced by a microorganism (as a fungus or bacterium) that in dilute solution inhibits or kills another microorganism — **antibiotic** *adj*

an·ti·body \ˈan-ti-ˌbä-dē\ *n* : any of a large number of proteins of high molecular weight produced normally by specialized B cells after stimulation by an antigen and acting specifically against the antigen in an immune response

¹an·tic \ˈan-tik\ *n* : an often wildly playful or funny act or action

²antic *adj* [It *antico* ancient, fr. L *antiquus*] **1** *archaic* : GROTESQUE **2** : PLAYFUL

an·ti·can·cer \ˌan-ti-ˈkan-sər, ˌan-ˌtī-\ *adj* : used against or tending to arrest cancer ⟨~ drugs⟩

An·ti·christ \ˈan-ti-ˌkrīst\ *n* **1** : one who denies or opposes Christ **2** : a false Christ

an·tic·i·pate \an-ˈti-sə-ˌpāt\ *vb* **-pat·ed; -pat·ing** **1** : to foresee and provide for beforehand **2** : to look forward to — **an·tic·i·pa·tion** \-ˌti-sə-ˈpā-shən\ *n* — **an·tic·i·pa·to·ry** \-ˈti-sə-pə-ˌtòr-ē\ *adj*

an·ti·cli·max \ˌan-ti-ˈklī-ˌmaks\ *n* : something closing a series that is strikingly less important than what has preceded it — **an·ti·cli·mac·tic** \-klī-ˈmak-tik\ *adj*

an·ti·cline \ˈan-ti-ˌklīn\ *n* : an arch of layers of rock in the earth's crust

an·ti·co·ag·u·lant \ˌan-ti-kō-ˈa-gyə-lənt\ *n* : a substance that hinders the clotting of blood — **anticoagulant** *adj*

an·ti·cy·clone \ˌan-ti-ˈsī-ˌklōn\ *n* : a system of winds that rotates about a center of high atmospheric pressure — **an·ti·cy·clon·ic** \-sī-ˈklä-nik\ *adj*

¹an·ti·de·pres·sant \ˌan-ti-di-ˈpres-ᵊnt, ˌan-ˌtī-\ *adj* : used or tending to relieve psychic depression ⟨~ drugs⟩

²antidepressant *n* : an antidepressant drug

an·ti·dote \ˈan-ti-ˌdōt\ *n* : a remedy to counteract the effects of poison

an·ti·drug \ˈan-ˌtī-ˌdrəg\ *adj* : acting against or opposing illicit drugs

an·ti·fer·til·i·ty \ˌan-ti-fər-ˈti-lə-tē\ *adj* : tending to control excess or unwanted fertility : CONTRACEPTIVE ⟨~ agents⟩

an·ti·freeze \ˈan-ti-ˌfrēz\ *n* : a substance added to a liquid to lower its freezing temperature

an·ti·gen \ˈan-ti-jən\ *n* : a usu. protein or carbohydrate substance (as a toxin or an enzyme) capable of stimulating an immune response — **an·ti·gen·ic** \ˌan-ti-ˈje-nik\ *adj* — **an·ti·ge·nic·i·ty** \-jə-ˈni-sə-tē\ *n*

an·ti·grav·i·ty \ˌan-ti-ˈgra-və-tē, ˌan-ˌtī-\ *adj* : reducing or canceling the effect of gravity

an·ti·hero \ˈan-ti-ˌhē-rō, ˈan-ˌtī-\ *n* : a protagonist who is notably lacking in heroic qualities (as courage)

an·ti·his·ta·mine \ˌan-ti-ˈhis-tə-ˌmēn, ˌan-ˌtī-, -mən\ *n* : any of various drugs used in treating allergies and colds

an·ti·hy·per·ten·sive \-ˌhī-pər-ˈten-siv\ *n* : a substance that is effective against high blood pressure — **antihypertensive** *adj*

an·ti-in·flam·ma·to·ry \-in-ˈfla-mə-ˌtōr-ē\ *adj* : counteracting inflammation — **anti–inflammatory** *n*

an·ti–in·tel·lec·tu·al \-ˌint-ᵊl-ˈek-chə- wəl\ *adj* : opposing or hostile to intellectuals or to an intellectual view or approach

an·ti·lock \ˈan-ti-ˌläk, ˈan-ˌtī-\ *adj* : being a braking system designed to prevent the wheels from locking

an·ti·log·a·rithm \ˌan-ti-ˈlò-gə-ˌri-thəm, ˌan-ˌtī-, -ˈlä-\ *n* : the number corresponding to a given logarithm

an·ti·ma·cas·sar \ˌan-ti-mə-ˈka-sər\ *n* : a cover to protect the back or arms of furniture

an·ti·mat·ter \ˈan-ti-ˌma-tər, ˈan-ˌtī-\ *n* : matter composed of antiparticles

an·ti·mo·ny \ˈan-tə-ˌmō-nē\ *n* : a brittle silvery white metallic chemical element used esp. in alloys — see ELEMENT table

an·ti·neu·tron \ˌan-ti-ˈnü-ˌträn, ˌan-ˌtī-, -ˈnyü-\ *n* : the antiparticle of the neutron

an·ti·no·mi·an \ˌan-ti-ˈnō-mē-ən\ *n* : one who denies the validity of moral laws

an·tin·o·my \an-ˈti-nə-mē\ *n, pl* **-mies** : a contradiction between two seemingly true statements

an·ti·nov·el \ˈan-ti-ˌnä-vəl, ˈan-ˌtī-\ *n* : a work of fiction that lacks all or most of the traditional features of the novel

an·ti·nu·cle·ar \ˌan-ti-ˈnü-klē-ər, -ˈnyü-\ *adj* : opposing the use or production of nuclear power plants

an·ti·ox·i·dant \ˌan-tē-ˈäk-sə-dənt, ˌan-ˌtī-\ *n* : a substance that inhibits oxidation — **antioxidant** *adj*

an·ti·par·ti·cle \ˈan-ti-ˌpär-ti-kəl, ˈan-ˌtī-\ *n* : a subatomic particle identical to another subatomic particle in mass but opposite to it in electric and magnetic properties

an·ti·pas·to \ˌan-ti-ˈpas-tō, ˌän-ti-ˈpäs-\ *n, pl* **-ti** \-(ˌ)tē\ : any of various typically Italian hors d'oeuvres

an·tip·a·thy \an-ˈti-pə-thē\ *n, pl* **-thies** **1** : settled aversion or dislike **2** : an object of aversion — **an·ti·pa·thet·ic** \ˌan-ti-pə-ˈthe-tik\ *adj*

an·ti·per·son·nel \ˌan-ti-ˌpərs-ᵊn-ˈel, ˌan-ˌtī-\ *adj* : designed for use against military personnel ⟨~ mine⟩

an·ti·per·spi·rant \-ˈpər-spə-rənt\ *n* : a preparation used to check perspiration

an·tiph·o·nal \an-ˈti-fən-ᵊl\ *adj* : performed by two alternating groups — **an·tiph·o·nal·ly** *adv*

an·ti·pode \ˈan-tə-ˌpōd\ *n, pl* **an·tip·o·des** \an-ˈti-pə-

ˌdēz\ [ME *antipodes*, pl., persons dwelling at opposite points on the globe, fr. L. fr. Gk. fr. pl. of *antipod-, antipous* with feet opposite, fr. *anti-* against + *pod-, pous* foot] : the parts of the earth diametrically opposite — usu. used in pl. — **an·tip·o·dal** \-ˈti-pəd-ᵊl\ *adj* — **an·tip·o·de·an** \(ˌ)an-ˌti-pə-ˈdē-ən\ *adj*

an·ti·pol·lu·tion \ˌan-ti-pə-ˈlü-shən\ *adj* : designed to prevent, reduce, or eliminate pollution ⟨~ laws⟩

an·ti·pope \ˈan-ti-ˌpōp\ *n* : one elected or claiming to be pope in opposition to the pope canonically chosen

an·ti·pro·ton \ˌan-ti-ˈprō-ˌtän\ *n* : the antiparticle of the proton

an·ti·quar·i·an \ˌan-tə-ˈkwer-ē-ən\ *adj* 1 : of or relating to antiquities 2 : dealing in old books — **antiquarian** *n* — **an·ti·quar·i·an·ism** *n*

an·ti·quary \ˈan-tə-ˌkwer-ē\ *n, pl* **-quar·ies** : a person who collects or studies antiquities

an·ti·quat·ed \ˈan-tə-ˌkwā-təd\ *adj* : OUT-OF-DATE, OLD-FASHIONED

¹**an·tique** \an-ˈtēk\ *n* : an object made in a bygone period

²**antique** *adj* 1 : belonging to antiquity 2 : OLD-FASHIONED 3 : of a bygone style or period

³**antique** *vb* **-tiqued; -tiqu·ing** 1 : to finish or refinish in antique style : give an appearance of age to 2 : to shop around for antiques — **an·tiqu·er** *n*

an·tiq·ui·ty \an-ˈti-kwə-tē\ *n, pl* **-ties** 1 : ancient times 2 : great age 3 *pl* : relics of ancient times 4 *pl* : matters relating to ancient culture

an·tis *pl of* ANTI

an·ti–Sem·i·tism \ˌan-ti-ˈse-mə-ˌti-zəm, ˌan-ˌtī-\ *n* : hostility toward Jews as a religious or social minority — **an·ti–Se·mit·ic** \-sə-ˈmi-tik\ *adj*

an·ti·sep·tic \ˌan-tə-ˈsep-tik\ *adj* 1 : killing or checking the growth of germs that cause decay or infection 2 : scrupulously clean : ASEPTIC — **antiseptic** *n* — **an·ti·sep·ti·cal·ly** *adv*

an·ti·se·rum \ˈan-ti-ˌsir-əm, ˈan-ˌtī-\ *n* : a serum containing antibodies

an·ti·so·cial \ˌan-ti-ˈsō-shəl\ *adj* 1 : disliking the society of others 2 : contrary or hostile to the well-being of society ⟨crime is ~⟩ — **an·ti·so·cial·ly** *adv*

an·tith·e·sis \an-ˈti-thə-səs\ *n, pl* **-e·ses** \-ˌsēz\ 1 : the opposition or contrast of ideas 2 : the direct opposite — **an·ti·thet·i·cal** \ˌan-tə-ˈthe-ti-kəl\ *also* **an·ti·thet·ic** \-tik\ *adj* : constituting or marked by antithesis — **an·ti·thet·i·cal·ly** \-ti-k(ə-)lē\ *adv*

an·ti·tox·in \ˌan-ti-ˈtäk-sən\ *n* : an antibody that is able to neutralize a particular toxin or disease-causing agent; *also* : an antiserum containing an antitoxin

an·ti·trust \ˌan-ti-ˈtrəst\ *adj* : of or relating to legislation against trusts; *also* : consisting of laws to protect trade and commerce from unlawful restraints and monopolies or unfair business practices

an·ti·ven·in \-ˈve-nən\ *n* : an antitoxin to a venom; *also* : a serum containing such antitoxin

ant·ler \ˈant-lər\ *n* [ME *aunteler*, fr. MF *antoillier*, fr. (assumed) VL *anteocularis* located before the eye, fr. L *ante-* before + *oculus* eye] : one of the paired de-

ciduous solid bone processes on the head of a deer; *also* : a branch of this — **ant·lered** \-lərd\ *adj*

ant lion *n* : any of various insects having a long-jawed larva that digs a conical pit in which it lies in wait for insects (as ants) on which it feeds

an·to·nym \ˈan-tə-ˌnim\ *n* : a word of opposite meaning

anus \ˈā-nəs\ *n* [L] : the lower or posterior opening of the alimentary canal

an·vil \ˈan-vəl\ *n* 1 : a heavy iron block on which metal is shaped 2 : INCUS

anx·i·ety \aŋ-ˈzī-ə-tē\ *n, pl* **-et·ies** 1 : painful uneasiness of mind usu. over an anticipated ill 2 : abnormal apprehension and fear often accompanied by physiological signs (as sweating and increased pulse), by doubt about the nature and reality of the threat itself, and by self-doubt

anx·ious \ˈaŋk-shəs\ *adj* 1 : uneasy in mind : WORRIED 2 : earnestly wishing : EAGER — **anx·ious·ly** *adv*

¹**any** \ˈe-nē\ *adj* 1 : one chosen at random 2 : of whatever number or quantity

²**any** *pron* 1 : any one or ones ⟨take ~ of the books you like⟩ 2 : any amount ⟨~ of the money not used is to be returned⟩

³**any** *adv* : to any extent or degree : AT ALL ⟨could not walk ~ farther⟩

any·body \-ˌbä-dē, -bə-\ *pron* : ANYONE

any·how \-ˌhaù\ *adv* 1 : in any way 2 : NEVERTHELESS; *also* : in any case

any·more \ˌe-nē-ˈmōr\ *adv* 1 : any longer 2 : at the present time

any·one \ˈe-nē-(ˌ)wən\ *pron* : any person

any·place \-ˌplās\ *adv* : ANYWHERE

any·thing \-ˌthiŋ\ *pron* : any thing whatever

any·time \ˈe-nē-ˌtīm\ *adv* : at any time whatever

any·way \-ˌwā\ *adv* : ANYHOW

any·where \-ˌhwer\ *adv* : in or to any place

any·wise \-ˌwīz\ *adv* : in any way whatever

A–OK \ˌā-ō-ˈkā\ *adv or adj* : very definitely OK

A1 \ˈā-ˈwən\ *adj* : of the finest quality

aor·ta \ā-ˈor-tə\ *n, pl* **-tas** *or* **-tae** \-ˌtē\ : the main artery that carries blood from the heart — **aor·tic** \-tik\ *adj*

ap *abbr* 1 apostle 2 apothecaries'

AP *abbr* 1 American plan 2 Associated Press

apace \ə-ˈpās\ *adv* : SWIFTLY

Apache \ə-ˈpa-chē\ *n, pl* **Apache** *or* **Apach·es** \-ˈpa-chēz, -ˈpa-shəz\ : a member of an American Indian people of the southwestern U.S.; *also* : any of the languages of the Apache people — **Apach·e·an** \ə-ˈpa-chē-ən\ *adj or n*

ap·a·nage *var of* APPANAGE

apart \ə-ˈpärt\ *adv* 1 : separately in place or time 2 : ASIDE 3 : in two or more parts : to pieces

apart·heid \ə-ˈpär-ˌtāt, -ˌtīt\ *n* [Afrikaans] : a policy of racial segregation practiced in the Republic of So. Africa

© 1986 United Feature Syndicate,Inc.

apart·ment \ə-'pärt-mənt\ *n* : a room or set of rooms occupied as a dwelling; *also* : a building divided into individual dwelling units

 **ap·a·thy** \'a-pə-thē\ *n* **1** : lack of emotion **2** : lack of interest : INDIFFERENCE — **ap·a·thet·ic** \ₐa-pə-'the-tik\ *adj* — **ap·a·thet·i·cal·ly** \-ti-k(ə-)lē\ *adv*

ap·a·tite \'a-pə-ₐtīt\ *n* : any of a group of minerals that are phosphates of calcium and occur esp. in phosphate rock and in bones and teeth

APB *abbr* all points bulletin

¹ape \'āp\ *n* **1** : any of the larger tailless primates (as a baboon or gorilla); *also* : MONKEY **2** : MIMIC, IMITATOR; *also* : a large uncouth person

²ape *vb* **aped; ap·ing** : IMITATE, MIMIC

ape–man \'āp-ₐman\ *n* : a primate intermediate in character between Homo sapiens and the higher apes

aper·çu \ₐä-per-sǖ, ₐa-pər-'sü\ *n, pl* **aperçus** \-sǖ(z), -'süz\ : an immediate impression; *esp* : INSIGHT

aper·i·tif \ä-ₐper-ə-'tēf\ *n* : an alcoholic drink taken as an appetizer

ap·er·ture \'a-pər-ₐchůr, -chər\ *n* : OPENING, HOLE

apex \'ā-ₐpeks\ *n, pl* **apex·es** *or* **api·ces** \'ā-pə-ₐsēz, 'a-\ : the highest point : PEAK

apha·sia \ə-'fā-zh(ē-)ə\ *n* : loss or impairment of the power to use or comprehend words — **apha·sic** \-zik\ *adj or n*

aph·elion \a-'fēl-yən\ *n, pl* **-elia** \-yə\ [NL, fr. *apo-* away from + Gk *hēlios* sun] : the point in an object's orbit most distant from the sun

aphid \'ā-fəd\ *n* : any of numerous small insects that suck the juices of plants

aphis \'ā-fəs, 'a-\ *n, pl* **aphi·des** \-fə-ₐdēz\ : APHID

aph·o·rism \'a-fə-ₐri-zəm\ *n* : a short saying stating a general truth : MAXIM — **aph·o·ris·tic** \ₐa-fə-'ris-tik\ *adj*

aph·ro·di·si·ac \ₐa-frə-'di-zē-ₐak, -'dē-zē-\ *n* : an agent that excites sexual desire — **aphrodisiac** *adj*

api·ary \'ā-pē-ₐer-ē\ *n, pl* **-ar·ies** : a place where bees are kept — **api·a·rist** \-pē-ə-rist\ *n*

api·cal \'ā-pi-kəl, 'a-\ *adj* : of, relating to, or situated at an apex — **api·cal·ly** \-k(ə-)lē\ *adv*

apiece \ə-'pēs\ *adv* : for each one

aplen·ty \ə-'plen-tē\ *adj* : being in plenty or abundance

aplomb \ə-'pläm, -'pləm\ *n* [F, lit., perpendicularity, fr. MF, fr. *a plomb*, lit., according to the plummet] : complete composure or self-assurance

APO *abbr* army post office

Apoc *abbr* **1** Apocalypse **2** Apocrypha

apoc·a·lypse \ə-'pä-kə-ₐlips\ *n* **1** : a writing prophesying a cataclysm in which evil forces are destroyed **2** *cap* — see BIBLE table — **apoc·a·lyp·tic** \-ₐpä-kə-'lip-tik\ *also* **apoc·a·lyp·ti·cal** \-ti-kəl\ *adj*

Apoc·ry·pha \ə-'pä-krə-fə\ *n* **1** *not cap* : writings of dubious authenticity **2** : books included in the Septuagint and Vulgate but excluded from the Jewish and Protestant canons of the Old Testament — see BIBLE

table **3** : early Christian writings not included in the New Testament

apoc·ry·phal \-fəl\ *adj* **1** : not canonical : SPURIOUS **2** *often cap* : of or resembling the Apocrypha — **apoc·ry·phal·ly** *adv* — **apoc·ry·phal·ness** *n*

apo·gee \'a-pə-(ₐ)jē\ *n* [F *apogée*, fr. NL *apogaeum*, fr. Gk *apogaion*, fr. *apo* away from + *gē* earth] : the point at which an orbiting object is farthest from the body being orbited

apo·lit·i·cal \ₐā-pə-'li-ti-kəl\ *adj* **1** : having an aversion for or no interest in political affairs **2** : having no political significance — **apo·lit·i·cal·ly** \-k(ə-)lē\ *adv*

apol·o·get·ic \ə-ₐpä-lə-'je-tik\ *adj* : expressing apology — **apol·o·get·i·cal·ly** \-ti-k(ə-)lē\ *adv*

ap·o·lo·gia \ₐa-pə-'lō-j(ē-)ə\ *n* : APOLOGY; *esp* : an argument in support or justification

apol·o·gise *Brit var of* APOLOGIZE

apol·o·gize \ə-'pä-lə-ₐjīz\ *vb* **-gized; -giz·ing** : to make an apology : express regret — **apol·o·gist** \-jist\ *n*

apol·o·gy \ə-'pä-lə-jē\ *n, pl* **-gies** **1** : a formal justification : DEFENSE **2** : an expression of regret for a wrong

apo·plexy \'a-pə-ₐplek-sē\ *n* : STROKE **3** — **ap·o·plec·tic** \ₐa-pə-'plek-tik\ *adj*

aport \ə-'pōrt\ *adv* : on or toward the left side of a ship

apos·ta·sy \ə-'päs-tə-sē\ *n, pl* **-sies** : a renunciation or abandonment of a former loyalty (as to a religion) — **apos·tate** \ə-'päs-ₐtāt, -tət\ *adj or n*

a pos·te·ri·o·ri \ₐä-pō-ₐstir-ē-'ōr-ē\ *adj* [L, lit., from the latter] : relating to or derived by reasoning from observed facts — **a posteriori** *adv*

apos·tle \ə-'pä-səl\ *n* **1** : one of the group composed of Jesus' 12 original disciples and Paul **2** : the first prominent missionary to a region or group **3** : a person who initiates or first advocates a great reform — **apos·tle·ship** *n*

ap·os·tol·ic \ₐa-pə-'stä-lik\ *adj* **1** : of or relating to an apostle or to the New Testament apostles **2** : of or relating to a succession of spiritual authority from the apostles **3** : PAPAL

¹apos·tro·phe \ə-'päs-trə-(ₐ)fē\ *n* : the rhetorical addressing of a usu. absent person or a usu. personified thing (as in "O grave, where is thy victory?")

²apostrophe *n* : a punctuation mark ' used esp. to indicate the possessive case or the omission of a letter or figure

apos·tro·phise *Brit var of* APOSTROPHIZE

apos·tro·phize \ə-'päs-trə-ₐfīz\ *vb* **-phized; -phiz·ing** : to address as if present or capable of understanding

apothecaries' weight *n* : a system of weights based on the troy pound and ounce and used chiefly by pharmacists — see WEIGHT table

apoth·e·cary \ə-'pä-thə-ₐker-ē\ *n, pl* **-car·ies** [ME *apothecarie*, fr. ML *apothecarius*, fr. LL, shopkeeper, fr. L *apotheca* storehouse, fr. Gk *apothēkē*, fr. *apotithenai* to put away] : DRUGGIST

ap·o·thegm \'a-pə-ₐthem\ *n* : APHORISM

apo·the·o·sis \ə-ₐpä-thē-'ō-səs, ₐa-pə-'thē-ə-səs\ *n, pl* **-o·ses** \-ₐsēz\ **1** : DEIFICATION **2** : the perfect example

app *abbr* **1** apparatus **2** appendix

ap•pall also **ap•pal** \ə-'pȯl\ vb **ap•palled; ap•pall•ing** : to overcome with horror : DISMAY

Ap•pa•loo•sa \ˌa-pə-'lü-sə\ n : any of a breed of saddle horses developed in western No. America and usu. having a white or solid-colored coat with small spots

Appaloosa

ap•pa•nage \'a-pə-nij\ n **1** : provision (as a grant of land) made by a sovereign or legislative body for dependent members of the royal family **2** : a rightful adjunct

ap•pa•ra•tus \ˌa-pə-'ra-təs, -'rā-\ n, pl **-tus•es** or **-tus** [L] **1** : a set of materials or equipment for a particular use **2** : a complex machine or device : MECHANISM **3** : the organization of a political party or underground movement

¹**ap•par•el** \ə-'par-əl\ vb **-eled** or **-elled; -el•ing** or **-el•ling 1** : CLOTHE **2** : ADORN

²**apparel** n : CLOTHING, DRESS

ap•par•ent \ə-'par-ənt\ adj **1** : open to view : VISIBLE **2** : EVIDENT, OBVIOUS **3** : appearing as real or true : SEEMING

ap•par•ent•ly \-lē\ adv : it seems apparent

ap•pa•ri•tion \ˌa-pə-'ri-shən\ n : a supernatural appearance : GHOST

ap•peal \ə-'pēl\ vb **1** : to take steps to have (a case) reheard in a higher court **2** : to plead for help, corroboration, or decision **3** : to arouse a sympathetic response — **appeal** n

ap•pear \ə-'pir\ vb **1** : to become visible **2** : to come formally before an authority **3** : SEEM **4** : to become evident **5** : to come before the public

ap•pear•ance \ə-'pir-əns\ n **1** : outward aspect : LOOK **2** : the act of appearing **3** : PHENOMENON

ap•pease \ə-'pēz\ vb **ap•peased; ap•peas•ing 1** : to cause to subside : ALLAY **2** : PACIFY, CONCILIATE; esp : to buy off by concessions — **ap•pease•ment** n — **ap•peas•able** \-'pē-zə-bəl\ adj

ap•pel•lant \ə-'pe-lənt\ n : one who appeals esp. from a judicial decision

ap•pel•late \ə-'pe-lət\ adj : having power to review decisions of a lower court

ap•pel•la•tion \ˌa-pə-'lā-shən\ n : NAME, DESIGNATION

ap•pel•lee \ˌa-pə-'lē\ n : one against whom an appeal is taken

ap•pend \ə-'pend\ vb : to attach esp. as something additional : AFFIX

ap•pend•age \ə-'pen-dij\ n **1** : something appended to a principal or greater thing **2** : a projecting part of the body (as an antenna) esp. when paired with one on each side **syn** accessory, adjunct, appendix, appurtenance

ap•pen•dec•to•my \ˌa-pən-'dek-tə-mē\ n, pl **-mies** : surgical removal of the intestinal appendix

ap•pen•di•ci•tis \ə-ˌpen-də-'sī-təs\ n : inflammation of the intestinal appendix

ap•pen•dix \ə-'pen-diks\ n, pl **-dix•es** or **-di•ces** \-də-ˌsēz\ [L] **1** : supplementary matter added at the end of a book **2** : a narrow blind tube usu. about three or four inches long that extends from the cecum in the lower right-hand part of the abdomen

ap•per•tain \ˌa-pər-'tān\ vb : to belong as a rightful part or privilege

ap•pe•tis•er, ap•pe•tis•ing Brit var of APPETIZER, APPETIZING

ap•pe•tite \'a-pə-ˌtīt\ n [ME apetit, fr. MF, fr. L appetitus, fr. appetere to strive after, fr. ad- to + petere to go to] **1** : natural desire for satisfying some want or need esp. for food **2** : TASTE, PREFERENCE

ap•pe•tiz•er \'a-pə-ˌtī-zər\ n : a food or drink taken just before a meal to stimulate the appetite

ap•pe•tiz•ing \-ziŋ\ adj : tempting to the appetite — **ap•pe•tiz•ing•ly** adv

appl abbr applied

ap•plaud \ə-'plȯd\ vb : to show approval esp. by clapping

ap•plause \ə-'plȯz\ n : approval publicly expressed (as by clapping)

ap•ple \'a-pəl\ n : a rounded fruit with firm white flesh and a seedy core; also : a tree that bears this fruit

ap•ple•jack \-ˌjak\ n : a liquor distilled from fermented cider

ap•pli•ance \ə-'plī-əns\ n **1** : INSTRUMENT, DEVICE **2** : a piece of household equipment (as a stove or toaster) operated by gas or electricity

ap•pli•ca•ble \'a-pli-kə-bəl, ə-'pli-kə-\ adj : capable of being applied : RELEVANT — **ap•pli•ca•bil•i•ty** \ˌa-pli-kə-'bi-lə-tē, ə-ˌpli-kə-\ n

ap•pli•cant \'a-pli-kənt\ n : one who applies

ap•pli•ca•tion \ˌa-plə-'kā-shən\ n **1** : the act of applying **2** : assiduous attention **3** : REQUEST; also : a form used in making a request **4** : something placed or spread on a surface **5** : capacity for use

ap•pli•ca•tor \'a-plə-ˌkā-tər\ n : a device for applying a substance (as medicine or polish)

ap•plied \ə-'plīd\ adj : put to practical use ⟨~ art⟩

ap•pli•qué \ˌa-plə-'kā\ n [F] : a fabric decoration cut out and fastened to a larger piece of material — **ap•pliqué** vb

ap•ply \ə-'plī\ vb **ap•plied; ap•ply•ing 1** : to put to practical use **2** : to place in contact : put or spread on a surface **3** : to employ with close attention **4** : to have reference or connection **5** : to submit a request

ap•point \ə-'pȯint\ vb **1** : to fix or set officially ⟨~ a day for trial) **2** : to name officially **3** : to fit out : EQUIP

ap·poin·tee \ə-ˌpȯin-ˈtē, ˌa-\ *n* : a person appointed

ap·point·ive \ə-ˈpȯin-tiv\ *adj* : subject to appointment

ap·point·ment \ə-ˈpȯint-mənt\ *n* **1** : the act of appointing **2** : an arrangement for a meeting **3** *pl* : FURNISHINGS, EQUIPMENT **4** : a nonelective office or position

ap·por·tion \ə-ˈpȯr-shən\ *vb* : to distribute proportionately : ALLOT — **ap·por·tion·ment** *n*

ap·po·site \ˈa-pə-zət\ *adj* : APPROPRIATE, RELEVANT — **ap·po·site·ly** *adv* — **ap·po·site·ness** *n*

ap·po·si·tion \ˌa-pə-ˈzi-shən\ *n* : a grammatical construction in which a noun or pronoun is followed by another that has the same referent (as *the poet* and *Burns* in "a biography of the poet Burns")

ap·pos·i·tive \ə-ˈpä-zə-tiv, a-\ *adj* : of, relating to, or standing in grammatical apposition — **appositive** *n*

ap·praise \ə-ˈprāz\ *vb* **ap·praised; ap·prais·ing** : to set a value on — **ap·prais·al** \-ˈprā-zəl\ *n* — **ap·prais·er** *n*

ap·pre·cia·ble \ə-ˈprē-shə-bəl\ *adj* : large enough to be recognized and measured — **ap·pre·cia·bly** *adv*

ap·pre·ci·ate \ə-ˈprē-shē-ˌāt\ *vb* **-at·ed; -at·ing** **1** : to value justly **2** : to be aware of **3** : to be grateful for **4** : to increase in value — **ap·pre·ci·a·tion** \-ˌprē-shē-ˈā-shən\ *n*

ap·pre·cia·tive \ə-ˈprē-shə-tiv, -shē-ˌāt-\ *adj* : having or showing appreciation — **ap·pre·cia·tive·ly** *adv* — **ap·pre·hen·sive·ness** *n*

ap·pre·hend \ˌa-pri-ˈhend\ *vb* **1** : ARREST **2** : to become aware of **3** : to look forward to with dread **4** : UNDERSTAND — **ap·pre·hen·sion** \-ˈhen-chən\ *n*

ap·pre·hen·sive \-ˈhen-siv\ *adj* : viewing the future with anxiety — **ap·pre·hen·sive·ly** *adv* — **ap·pre·hen·sive·ness** *n*

¹ap·pren·tice \ə-ˈpren-təs\ *n* **1** : a person learning a craft under a skilled worker **2** : BEGINNER — **ap·pren·tice·ship** *n*

²apprentice *vb* **-ticed; -tic·ing** : to bind or set at work as an apprentice

ap·prise \ə-ˈprīz\ *vb* **ap·prised; ap·pris·ing** : INFORM

ap·proach \ə-ˈprōch\ *vb* **1** : to move nearer to **2** : to be almost the same as **3** : to make advances to esp. for the purpose of creating a desired result **4** : to take preliminary steps toward — **approach** *n* — **ap·proach·able** *adj*

ap·pro·ba·tion \ˌa-prə-ˈbā-shən\ *n* : APPROVAL

¹ap·pro·pri·ate \ə-ˈprō-prē-ˌāt\ *vb* **-at·ed; -at·ing** **1** : to take possession of **2** : to set apart for a particular use

²ap·pro·pri·ate \ə-ˈprō-prē-ət\ *adj* : fitted to a purpose or use : SUITABLE **syn** proper, fit, apt, befitting — **ap·pro·pri·ate·ly** *adv* — **ap·pro·pri·ate·ness** *n*

ap·pro·pri·a·tion \ə-ˌprō-prē-ˈā-shən\ *n* : something (as money) set aside by formal action for a specific use

ap·prov·al \ə-ˈprü-vəl\ *n* : an act of approving — **on approval** : subject to a prospective buyer's acceptance or refusal

ap·prove \ə-ˈprüv\ *vb* **ap·proved; ap·prov·ing** **1** : to have or express a favorable opinion of **2** : to accept as satisfactory : RATIFY

approx *abbr* approximate; approximately

¹ap·prox·i·mate \ə-ˈpräk-sə-mət\ *adj* : nearly correct or exact — **ap·prox·i·mate·ly** *adv*

²ap·prox·i·mate \-ˌmāt\ *vb* **-mat·ed; -mat·ing** : to come near : APPROACH — **ap·prox·i·ma·tion** \ə-ˌpräk-sə-ˈmā-shən\ *n*

appt *abbr* appoint; appointed; appointment

ap·pur·te·nance \ə-ˈpərt-nəns, -ᵊn-əns\ *n* : something that belongs to or goes with another thing **syn** accessory, adjunct, appendage, appendix — **ap·pur·te·nant** \ə-ˈpərt-nənt, -ᵊn-ənt\ *adj*

Apr *abbr* April

APR *abbr* annual percentage rate

apri·cot \ˈa-prə-ˌkät, ˈā-\ *n* [deriv. of Ar *al-birqûq*] : an oval orange-colored fruit resembling the related peach and plum in flavor; *also* : a tree bearing apricots

April \ˈā-prəl\ *n* [ME, fr. OF & L; OF *avrill*, fr. L *Aprilis*] : the 4th month of the year

a pri·o·ri \ˌä-prē-ˈȯr-ē\ *adj* [L, from the former] **1** : characterized by or derived by reasoning from self-evident propositions **2** : independent of experience — **a priori** *adv*

apron \ˈā-prən\ *n* [ME, alter. (resulting fr. misdivision of *a napron*) of *napron*, fr. MF *naperon*, dim. of *nape* cloth, modif. of L *mappa* napkin] **1** : a garment tied over the front of the body to protect the clothes **2** : a paved area for parking or handling airplanes — **aproned** *adj*

¹ap·ro·pos \ˌa-prə-ˈpō, ˈa-prə-ˌpō\ *adv* [F *à propos*, lit., to the purpose] **1** : OPPORTUNELY **2** : in passing : INCIDENTALLY

²apropos *adj* : being to the point

apropos of *prep* : with regard to

apse \ˈaps\ *n* : a projecting usu. semicircular and vaulted part of a building (as a church)

¹apt \ˈapt\ *adj* **1** : well adapted : SUITABLE **2** : having an habitual tendency : LIKELY **3** : quick to learn — **apt·ly** *adv* — **apt·ness** \ˈapt-nəs\ *n*

²apt *abbr* **1** apartment **2** aptitude

ap·ti·tude \ˈap-tə-ˌtüd, -ˌtyüd\ *n* **1** : natural ability : TALENT **2** : capacity for learning **3** : APPROPRIATENESS

aqua \ˈa-kwə, ˈä-\ *n* : a light greenish blue color

aqua·cul·ture *also* **aqui·cul·ture** \ˈa-kwə-ˌkəl-chər, ˈä-\ *n* : the cultivation of aquatic plants or animals (as fish or shellfish) for human use

aqua·ma·rine \ˌa-kwə-mə-ˈrēn, ˌä-\ *n* **1** : a bluish green gem **2** : a pale blue to light greenish blue

aqua·naut \ˈa-kwə-ˌnȯt, ˈä-\ *n* : a person who lives in an underwater shelter for an extended period

aqua·plane \-ˌplān\ *n* : a board towed behind a motorboat and ridden by a person standing on it — **aqua·plane** *vb*

aqua re·gia \ˌa-kwə-ˈrē-j(ē-)ə\ *n* [NL, lit., royal water] : a mixture of nitric and hydrochloric acids that dissolves gold or platinum

aquar·i·um \ə-ˈkwar-ē-əm\ *n, pl* **-i·ums** *or* **-ia** \-ē-ə\ **1**

: a container (as a glass tank) in which living aquatic animals or plants are kept **2** : a place where aquatic animals and plants are kept and shown

Aquar·i·us \ə-ˈkwar-ē-əs\ *n* [L, lit., water carrier] **1** : a zodiacal constellation between Capricorn and Pisces usu. pictured as a man pouring water **2** : the 11th sign of the zodiac in astrology; *also* : one born under this sign

¹aquat·ic \ə-ˈkwä-tik, -ˈkwa-\ *adj* **1** : growing or living in or frequenting water **2** : performed in or on water

²aquatic *n* : an aquatic animal or plant

aqua·vit \ˈä-kwə-ˌvēt\ *n* : a clear liquor flavored with caraway seeds

aqua vi·tae \ˌa-kwə-ˈvī-tē, ˌä-\ *n* [ME, fr. ML, lit., water of life] : a strong alcoholic liquor (as brandy)

aq·ue·duct \ˈa-kwə-ˌdəkt\ *n* **1** : a conduit for carrying running water **2** : a structure carrying a canal over a river or hollow **3** : a passage in a bodily part

aqueduct 1

aque·ous \ˈä-kwē-əs, ˈa-\ *adj* **1** : WATERY **2** : made of, by, or with water

aqueous humor *n* : a clear fluid occupying the space between the lens and the cornea of the eye

aqui·fer \ˈa-kwə-fər, ˈä-\ *n* : a water-bearing stratum of permeable rock, sand, or gravel

aq·ui·line \ˈa-kwə-ˌlīn, -lən\ *adj* **1** : of or resembling an eagle **2** : hooked like an eagle's beak ⟨an ∼ nose⟩

ar *abbr* arrival; arrive

Ar *symbol* argon

AR *abbr* Arkansas

-ar *adj suffix* : of or relating to ⟨molecul*ar*⟩ : being ⟨spectacul*ar*⟩ : resembling ⟨oracul*ar*⟩

Ar·ab \ˈar-əb\ *n* **1** : a member of a Semitic people of the Arabian peninsula in southwestern Asia **2** : a member of an Arabic-speaking people — **Arab** *adj* — **Ara·bi·an** \ə-ˈrā-bē-ən\ *adj or n*

ar·a·besque \ˌar-ə-ˈbesk\ *n* : a design of interlacing lines forming figures of flowers, foliage, and sometimes animals — **arabesque** *adj*

¹Ar·a·bic \ˈar-ə-bik\ *n* : a Semitic language of southwestern Asia and northern Africa

²Arabic *adj* **1** : of or relating to the Arabs, Arabic, or the Arabian peninsula in southwestern Asia **2** : expressed in or making use of Arabic numerals

Arabic numeral *n* : any of the number symbols 0, 1, 2, 3, 4, 5, 6, 7, 8, 9

ar·a·ble \ˈar-ə-bəl\ *adj* : fit for or used for the growing of crops

arach·nid \ə-ˈrak-nəd\ *n* : any of a class of usu. 8-legged arthropods comprising the spiders, scorpions, mites, and ticks — **arachnid** *adj*

Ar·a·ma·ic \ˌar-ə-ˈmā-ik\ *n* : an ancient Semitic language

ar·a·mid \ˈar-ə-məd, -ˌmid\ *n* : any of several light but very strong heat-resistant synthetic materials used esp. in textiles and plastics

Arap·a·ho *or* **Arap·a·hoe** \ə-ˈra-pə-ˌhō\ *n, pl* **-ho** *or* **-hos** *or* **-hoe** *or* **-hoes** : a member of an American Indian people of the western U.S.

ar·bi·ter \ˈär-bə-tər\ *n* : one having power to decide : JUDGE

ar·bi·trage \ˈär-bə-ˌträzh\ *n* [F, fr. MF, arbitration] : the purchase and sale of the same or equivalent securities in different markets in order to profit from price discrepancies

ar·bi·tra·geur \ˌär-bə-(ˌ)trä-ˈzhər\ *or* **ar·bi·trag·er** \ˈär-bə-ˌträ-zhər\ *n* : one who practices arbitrage

ar·bit·ra·ment \är-ˈbi-trə-mənt\ *n* **1** : the act of deciding a dispute **2** : the judgment given by an arbitrator

ar·bi·trary \ˈär-bə-ˌtrer-ē\ *adj* **1** : AUTOCRATIC, DESPOTIC **2** : determined by will or caprice : selected at random — **ar·bi·trari·ly** \ˌär-bə-ˈtrer-ə-lē\ *adv* — **ar·bi·trari·ness** \ˈär-bə-ˌtrer-ē-nəs\ *n*

ar·bi·trate \ˈär-bə-ˌtrāt\ *vb* **-trat·ed; -trat·ing** **1** : to act as arbitrator **2** : to act on as arbitrator **3** : to submit for decision to an arbitrator — **ar·bi·tra·tion** \ˌär-bə-ˈträ-shən\ *n*

ar·bi·tra·tor \ˈär-bə-ˌträ-tər\ *n* : one chosen to settle differences between two parties in a controversy

ar·bor \ˈär-bər\ *n* [ME *erber* plot of grass, arbor, fr. OF *herbier* plot of grass, fr. *herbe* herb, grass] : a shelter formed of or covered with vines or branches

ar·bo·re·al \är-ˈbōr-ē-əl\ *adj* **1** : of, relating to, or resembling a tree **2** : living in trees ⟨∼ monkeys⟩

ar·bo·re·tum \ˌär-bə-ˈrē-təm\ *n, pl* **-retums** *or* **-re·ta** \-tə\ [L, plantation of trees, fr. *arbor* tree] : a place where trees and plants are grown for scientific and educational purposes

ar·bor·vi·tae \ˌär-bər-ˈvī-tē\ *n* : any of various evergreen trees and shrubs with scalelike leaves that are related to the cypresses

ar·bour *chiefly Brit var of* ARBOR

ar·bu·tus \är-ˈbyü-təs\ *n* : TRAILING ARBUTUS

¹arc \ˈärk\ *n* **1** : a sustained luminous discharge of electricity (as between two electrodes) **2** : a continuous portion of a curved line (as part of the circumference of a circle)

²arc *vb* **arced** \ˈärkt\; **arc·ing** \ˈär-kiŋ\ : to form an electric arc

ARC *abbr* **1** AIDS-related complex **2** American Red Cross

ar·cade \är-ˈkād\ *n* **1** : an arched or covered passageway; *esp* : one lined with shops **2** : a row of arches with their supporting columns

ar·cane \är-ˈkān\ *adj* : SECRET, MYSTERIOUS

¹arch \ˈärch\ *n* **1** : a curved structure spanning an opening (as a door) **2** : something resembling an arch **3** : ARCHWAY

²arch *vb* **1** : to cover with an arch **2** : to form or bend into an arch

³arch *adj* **1** : CHIEF, EMINENT **2** : ROGUISH, MISCHIEVOUS — **arch·ly** *adv* — **arch·ness** *n*

⁴arch *abbr* architect; architectural; architecture

ar·chae·ol·o·gy *or* **ar·che·ol·o·gy** \ˌär-kē-ˈä-lə-jē\ *n* : the study of past human life as revealed by relics left by ancient peoples — **ar·chae·o·log·i·cal** \-ə-ˈlä-ji-kəl\ *adj* — **ar·chae·ol·o·gist** \-ˈä-lə-jist\ *n*

ar·cha·ic \är-ˈkā-ik\ *adj* **1** : having the characteristics of the language of the past and surviving chiefly in specialized uses ⟨∼ words⟩ **2** : belonging to an earlier time : ANTIQUATED — **ar·cha·i·cal·ly** \-i-k(ə-)lē\ *adv*

arch·an·gel \ˈärk-ˌān-jəl\ *n* : a chief angel

arch·bish·op \ärch-ˈbi-shəp\ *n* : a bishop of high rank

arch·bish·op·ric \-shə-(ˌ)prik\ *n* : the jurisdiction or office of an archbishop

arch·con·ser·va·tive \(ˌ)ärch-kən-ˈsər-və-tiv\ *n* : an extreme conservative — **archconservative** *adj*

arch·dea·con \-ˈdē-kən\ *n* : a church official who assists a diocesan bishop in ceremonial or administrative functions

arch·di·o·cese \-ˈdī-ə-səs, -ˌsēz\ *n* : the diocese of an archbishop

arch·duke \-ˈdük, -ˈdyük\ *n* **1** : a sovereign prince **2** : a prince of the imperial family of Austria

Ar·che·an \är-ˈkē-ən\ *adj* : of, relating to, or being the earliest eon of geologic history — **Archean** *n*

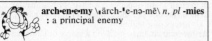

arch·en·e·my \ˌärch-ʹe-nə-mē\ *n, pl* **-mies** : a principal enemy

Ar·cheo·zo·ic \ˌär-kē-ə-ʹzō-ik\ *adj* : ARCHEAN — **Ar-cheozoic** *n*

ar·chery \ʹär-chə-rē\ *n* : the art or practice of shooting with bow and arrows — **ar·cher** \ʹär-chər\ *n*

ar·che·type \ʹär-ki-ˌtīp\ *n* : the original pattern or model of all things of the same type

arch·fiend \ˈärch-ʹfēnd\ *n* : a chief fiend; *esp* : SATAN

ar·chi·epis·co·pal \ˌär-kē-ə-ʹpis-kə-pəl\ *adj* : of or relating to an archbishop

ar·chi·man·drite \ˌär-kə-ʹman-ˌdrīt\ *n* : a dignitary in an Eastern church ranking below a bishop

ar·chi·pel·a·go \ˌär-kə-ʹpe-lə-ˌgō, ˌär-chə-\ *n, pl* **-goes** *or* **-gos** : a group of islands

ar·chi·tect \ʹär-kə-ˌtekt\ *n* **1** : a person who plans buildings and oversees their construction **2** : a person who designs and guides a plan or undertaking

ar·chi·tec·ture \ʹär-kə-ˌtek-chər\ *n* **1** : the art or science of planning and building structures **2** : a method or style of building **3** : the manner in which the elements (as of a design) are arranged or organized — **ar·chi·tec·tur·al** \ˌär-kə-ʹtek-chə-rəl, -ʹtek-shrəl\ *adj* — **ar·chi·tec·tur·al·ly** *adv*

ar·chi·trave \ʹär-kə-ˌtrāv\ *n* : the supporting horizontal member just above the columns in a building in the classical style of architecture

ar·chive \ʹär-ˌkīv\ *n* : a place for keeping public records; *also* : public records — often used in pl.

ar·chi·vist \ʹär-kə-vist, -ˌkī-\ *n* : a person in charge of archives

ar·chon \ʹär-ˌkän, -kən\ *n* : a chief magistrate of ancient Athens

arch·way \ʹärch-ˌwā\ *n* : a passageway under an arch; *also* : an arch over a passage

arc lamp *n* : a gas-filled electric lamp that produces light when a current arcs between incandescent electrodes

¹**arc·tic** \ʹärk-tik, ʹär-tik\ *adj* [ME *artik,* fr. L *arcticus,* fr. Gk *arktikos,* fr. *arktos* bear, Ursa Major, north] **1** *often cap* : of or relating to the north pole or the region near it **2** : FRIGID

²**arc·tic** \ʹär-tik, ʹärk-tik\ *n* : a rubber overshoe that reaches to the ankle or above

arctic circle *n, often cap A&C* : the parallel of latitude that is approximately 66½ degrees north of the equator

-ard *also* **-art** *n suffix* : one that is characterized by performing some action, possessing some quality, or being associated with some thing esp. conspicuously or excessively ⟨bragg*art*⟩ ⟨dull*ard*⟩

ar·dent \ʹär-dᵊnt\ *adj* **1** : characterized by warmth of feeling : PASSIONATE **2** : FIERY, HOT **3** : GLOWING — **ar·dent·ly** *adv*

ar·dor \ʹär-dər\ *n* **1** : warmth of feeling : ZEAL **2** : sexual excitement

ar·dour *chiefly Brit var of* ARDOR

ar·du·ous \ʹär-jə-wəs, -dyu̇-wəs\ *adj* : DIFFICULT, LABORIOUS — **ar·du·ous·ly** *adv* — **ar·du·ous·ness** *n*

¹**are** *pres 2d sing or pres pl of* BE

²**are** \ʹär\ *n* — see METRIC SYSTEM table

ar·ea \ʹar-ē-ə\ *n* **1** : a flat surface or space **2** : the amount of surface included (as within the lines of a geometric figure) **3** : range or extent of some thing or concept : FIELD **4** : REGION

area code *n* : a 3-digit number that identifies each telephone service area in a country (as the U.S. or Canada)

are·na \ə-ʹrē-nə\ *n* [L *harena, arena* sand, sandy place] **1** : an enclosed area used for public entertainment **2** : a sphere of activity or competition

Ar·gen·tine \ʹär-jən-ˌtēn, -ˌtīn\ *or* **Ar·gen·tin·ean** *or* **Ar·gen·tin·i·an** \ˌär-jən-ʹti-nē-ən\ *n* : a native or inhabitant of Argentina — **Argentine** *or* **Argentinean** *or* **Argentinian** *adj*

ar·gen·tite \ʹär-jən-ˌtīt\ *n* : a dark gray mineral that is an important ore of silver

ar·gon \ʹär-ˌgän\ *n* [Gk, neut. of *argos* idle, lazy, fr. *a-* not + *ergon* work; fr. its relative inertness] : a colorless odorless gaseous chemical element found in the air and used for filling electric lamps — see ELEMENT table

ar·go·sy \ʹär-gə-sē\ *n, pl* **-sies 1** : a large merchant ship **2** : FLEET

ar·got \ʹär-gət, -ˌgō\ *n* : the language of a particular group or class

ar·gu·able \ʹär-gyü-ə-bəl\ *adj* : open to argument, dispute, or question

ar·gu·ably \ʹär-gyü-(ə-)blē\ *adv* : it can be argued

ar·gue \ʹär-gyü\ *vb* **ar·gued; ar·gu·ing 1** : to give reasons for or against something **2** : to contend in words : DISPUTE **3** : DEBATE **4** : to persuade by giving reasons

ar·gu·ment \ʹär-gyə-mənt\ *n* **1** : a reason offered in proof **2** : discourse intended to persuade **3** : QUARREL

ar·gu·men·ta·tion \ˌär-gyə-mən-ʹtā-shən\ *n* : the art of formal discussion

ar·gu·men·ta·tive \ˌär-gyə-ʹmen-tə-tiv\ *adj* : inclined to argue

ar·gyle *also* **ar·gyll** \ʹär-ˌgīl\ *n, often cap* : a geometric knitting pattern of varicolored diamonds on a single background color; *also* : a sock knit in this pattern

aria \ʹär-ē-ə\ *n* : an accompanied elaborate vocal solo forming part of a larger work

ar·id \ʹar-əd\ *adj* : very dry; *esp* : having insufficient rainfall to support agriculture — **arid·i·ty** \ə-ʹri-də-tē\ *n*

Ar·ies \ʹar-ˌēz, -ē-ˌēz\ *n* [L, lit., ram] **1** : a zodiacal constellation between Pisces and Taurus pictured as a ram **2** : the 1st sign of the zodiac in astrology; *also* : one born under this sign

aright \ə-ʹrīt\ *adv* : RIGHT, CORRECTLY

arise \ə-ʹrīz\ *vb* **arose** \-ʹrōz\; **aris·en** \-ʹriz-ᵊn\; **aris·ing** \-ʹrī-ziŋ\ **1** : to get up **2** : ORIGINATE **3** : ASCEND **syn** rise, derive, spring, issue

aris·toc·ra·cy \ˌar-ə-ˈstä-krə-sē\ *n, pl* **-cies** **1** : government by a noble or privileged class; *also* : a state so governed **2** : the governing class of an aristocracy **3** : UPPER CLASS — **aris·to·crat** \ə-ˈris-tə-ˌkrat\ *n* — **aris·to·crat·ic** \ə-ˌris-tə-ˈkra-tik\ *adj*

arith *abbr* arithmetic; arithmetical

arith·me·tic \ə-ˈrith-mə-ˌtik\ *n* **1** : a branch of mathematics that deals with computations usu. with nonnegative real numbers **2** : COMPUTATION, CALCULATION — **ar·ith·met·ic** \ˌar-ith-ˈme-tik\ *or* **ar·ith·met·i·cal** \-ti-kəl\ *adj* — **ar·ith·met·i·cal·ly** \-ti-k(ə-)lē\ *adv* — **arith·me·ti·cian** \ə-ˌrith-mə-ˈti-shən\ *n*

arithmetic mean *n* : the sum of a set of numbers divided by the number of numbers in the set

Ariz *abbr* Arizona

ark \ˈärk\ *n* **1** : a boat held to resemble that of Noah's at the time of the Flood **2** : the sacred chest in a synagogue representing to Hebrews the presence of God; *also* : the repository for the scrolls of the Torah

Ark *abbr* Arkansas

¹arm \ˈärm\ *n* **1** : a human upper limb; *also* : a corresponding limb of a lower animal with a backbone **2** : something resembling an arm in shape or position ⟨an ∼ of a chair⟩ **3** : POWER, MIGHT ⟨the ∼ of the law⟩ — **armed** \ˈärmd\ *adj* — **arm·less** *adj*

²arm *vb* : to furnish with weapons

³arm *n* **1** : WEAPON **2** : a branch of the military forces **3** *pl* : the hereditary heraldic devices of a family

ar·ma·da \är-ˈmä-də, -ˈmä-\ *n* : a fleet of warships

ar·ma·dil·lo \ˌär-mə-ˈdi-lō\ *n, pl* **-los** : any of several small burrowing mammals with the head and body protected by an armor of bony plates

armadillo

Ar·ma·ged·don \ˌär-mə-ˈged-ᵊn\ *n* : a final conclusive battle between the forces of good and evil; *also* : the site or time of this

ar·ma·ment \ˈär-mə-mənt\ *n* **1** : military strength **2** : arms and equipment (as of a tank or combat unit) **3** : the process of preparing for war

ar·ma·ture \ˈär-mə-ˌchür, -chər\ *n* **1** : a protective covering or structure (as the spines of a cactus) **2** : the rotating part of an electric generator or motor; *also* : the movable part in an electromagnetic device (as a loudspeaker)

arm·chair \ˈärm-ˌcher\ *n* : a chair with armrests

armed forces *n pl* : the combined military, naval, and air forces of a nation

Ar·me·nian \är-ˈmē-nē-ən\ *n* : a native or inhabitant of Armenia

arm·ful \ˈärm-ˌfül\ *n, pl* **armfuls** *or* **arms·ful** \ˈärmzˌfül\ : as much as the arm or arms can hold

arm·hole \ˈärm-ˌhōl\ *n* : an opening for the arm in a garment

ar·mi·stice \ˈär-mə-stəs\ *n* : temporary suspension of hostilities by mutual agreement : TRUCE

arm·let \ˈärm-lət\ *n* : a band worn around the upper arm

ar·mor \ˈär-mər\ *n* **1** : protective covering **2** : armored forces and vehicles — **ar·mored** \-mərd\ *adj*

ar·mor·er \ˈär-mər-ər\ *n* **1** : a person who makes arms and armor **2** : a person who services firearms

ar·mo·ri·al \är-ˈmōr-ē-əl\ *adj* : of or bearing heraldic arms

ar·mory \ˈär-mə-rē\ *n, pl* **ar·mor·ies** **1** : a place where arms are stored **2** : a factory where arms are made

ar·mour, ar·moury *chiefly Brit var of* ARMOR, ARMORY

arm·pit \ˈärm-ˌpit\ *n* : the hollow under the junction of the arm and shoulder

arm·rest \-ˌrest\ *n* : a support for the arm

ar·my \ˈär-mē\ *n, pl* **armies** **1** : a body of men organized for war **2** *often cap* : the complete military organization of a country for land warfare **3** : a great number **4** : a body of persons organized to advance a cause

army ant *n* : any of various nomadic social ants

ar·my·worm \ˈär-mē-ˌwərm\ *n* : any of numerous moths whose larvae move about destroying crops

aro·ma \ə-ˈrō-mə\ *n* : a usu. pleasing odor : FRAGRANCE — **ar·o·mat·ic** \ˌar-ə-ˈmatik\ *adj*

aro·ma·ther·a·py \ə-ˌrō-mə-ˈther-ə-pē\ *n* : massage with a preparation of fragrant oils extracted from herbs, flowers, and fruits

arose *past of* ARISE

¹around \ə-ˈraùnd\ *adv* **1** : in a circle or in circumference ⟨a tree five feet ∼⟩ **2** : in or along a circuit ⟨the road goes ∼ by the lake⟩ **3** : on all sides ⟨nothing for miles ∼⟩ **4** : NEARBY ⟨wait ∼ awhile⟩ **5** : from one place to another ⟨travels ∼ on business⟩ **6** : in an opposite direction ⟨turn ∼⟩

²around *prep* **1** : SURROUNDING ⟨trees ∼ the house⟩ **2** : to or on another side of ⟨∼ the corner⟩ **3** : NEAR ⟨stayed right ∼ home⟩ **4** : along the circuit of ⟨go ∼ the world⟩

arouse \ə-ˈraùz\ *vb* **aroused; arous·ing** **1** : to awaken from sleep **2** : to stir up — **arous·al** \-ˈraù-zəl\ *n*

ar·peg·gio \är-ˈpe-jē-ˌō, -ˈpe-jō\ *n, pl* **-gios** [It fr. *peggiare* to play on the harp, fr. *arpa* harp] : a chord whose notes are performed in succession and not simultaneously

arr *abbr* **1** arranged **2** arrival; arrive

ar·raign \ə-'rān\ vb 1 : to call before a court to answer to an indictment 2 : to accuse of wrong or imperfection — **ar·raign·ment** n

ar·range \ə-'rānj\ vb **ar·ranged; ar·rang·ing** 1 : to put in order 2 : to adapt (a musical composition) to voices or instruments other than those for which it was orig. written 3 : to come to an agreement about : SETTLE — **ar·range·ment** n — **ar·rang·er** n

ar·rant \'ar-ənt\ adj : being notoriously without moderation : EXTREME

ar·ras \'ar-əs\ n, pl **arras** 1 : TAPESTRY 2 : a wall hanging or screen of tapestry

¹**ar·ray** \ə-'rā\ vb 1 : to dress esp. splendidly 2 : to arrange in order

²**array** n 1 : a regular arrangement 2 : rich apparel 3 : an imposing group

ar·rears \ə-'rirz\ n pl 1 : a state of being behind in the discharge of obligations ⟨in ∼ with the rent⟩ 2 : overdue debts

¹**ar·rest** \ə-'rest\ vb 1 : STOP, CHECK 2 : to take into legal custody

²**arrest** n 1 : the act of stopping; also : the state of being stopped 2 : the taking into custody by legal authority

ar·riv·al \ə-'rī-vəl\ n 1 : the act of arriving 2 : one that arrives

ar·rive \ə-'rīv\ vb **ar·rived; ar·riv·ing** 1 : to reach a destination 2 : to make an appearance ⟨the guests have arrived⟩ 3 : to attain success

ar·ro·gant \'ar-ə-gənt\ adj : offensively exaggerating one's own importance — **ar·ro·gance** \-gəns\ n — **ar·ro·gant·ly** adv

ar·ro·gate \-ˌgāt\ vb **-gat·ed; -gat·ing** : to claim or seize without justification as one's right — **ar·ro·ga·tion** \ˌar-ə-'gā-shən\ n

ar·row \'ar-ō\ n 1 : a missile shot from a bow and usu. having a slender shaft, a pointed head, and feathers at the butt 2 : a pointed mark used to indicate direction

ar·row·head \'ar-ō-ˌhed\ n : the pointed end of an arrow

ar·row·root \-ˌrüt, -ˌrút\ n : an edible starch from the roots of any of several tropical American plants; also : a plant yielding arrowroot

ar·roy·o \ə-'rói-ə, -ō\ n, pl **-roy·os** [Sp] 1 : a watercourse in a dry region 2 : a water-carved gully or channel

ar·se·nal \'ärs-nəl, 'ärs-ᵊn-əl\ n [ultim. fr. Ar dārṣiṇā'ah house of manufacture] 1 : a place for making and storing arms and military equipment 2 : STORE, REPERTORY

ar·se·nic \'ärs-nik, 'ärs-ᵊn-ik\ n 1 : a solid brittle poisonous chemical element of grayish metallic luster — see ELEMENT table 2 : a very poisonous oxygen compound of arsenic used in making insecticides

ar·son \'ärs-ᵊn\ n : the willful or malicious burning of property — **ar·son·ist** \-ist\ n

¹**art** \'ärt\ n 1 : skill acquired by experience or study 2 : a branch of learning; esp : one of the humanities 3 : an occupation requiring knowledge or skill 4 : the use of skill and imagination in the production of

things of beauty; also : works so produced 5 : ARTFULNESS

²**art** abbr 1 article 2 artificial 3 artillery

-art — see -ARD

ar·te·fact chiefly Brit var of ARTIFACT

ar·te·ri·al \är-'tir-ē-əl\ adj 1 : of or relating to an artery; also : relating to or being the oxygenated blood found in most arteries 2 : of, relating to, or being a route for through traffic

ar·te·ri·ole \är-'tir-ē-ˌōl\ n : one of the small terminal branches of an artery that ends in capillaries — **ar·te·ri·o·lar** \-ˌtir-ē-'ō-lər\ adj

ar·te·rio·scle·ro·sis \är-ˌtir-ē-ō-sklə-'rō-səs\ n : a chronic disease in which arterial walls are abnormally thickened and hardened — **ar·te·rio·scle·rot·ic** \-'rä-tik\ adj or n

ar·tery \'är-tə-rē\ n, pl **-ter·ies** 1 : one of the tubular vessels that carry blood from the heart 2 : a main channel of transportation or communication

ar·te·sian well \är-'tē-zhən-\ n : a well from which the water flows to the surface by natural pressure; also : a deep well

art·ful \'ärt-fəl\ adj 1 : INGENIOUS 2 : CRAFTY — **art·ful·ly** adv — **art·ful·ness** n

ar·thri·tis \är-'thrī-təs\ n, pl **-thri·ti·des** \-'thri-tə-ˌdēz\ : inflammation of the joints — **ar·thrit·ic** \-'thri-tik\ adj or n

ar·thro·pod \'är-thrə-ˌpäd\ n : any of a phylum of invertebrate animals comprising those (as insects, spiders, or crabs) with segmented bodies and jointed limbs — **arthropod** adj

ar·thros·co·py \är-'thräs-kə-pē\ n, pl **-pies** : visual examination of the interior of a joint (as the knee) with a special surgical instrument; also : joint surgery using arthroscopy — **ar·thro·scope** \'är-thrə-ˌskōp\ n — **ar·thro·scop·ic** \ˌär-thrə-'skä-pik\ adj

ar·ti·choke \'är-tə-ˌchōk\ n [It dial. articiocco, ultim. fr. Ar al-khurshūf] : a tall herb related to the daisies; also : its edible flower head

artichoke

ar·ti·cle \'är-ti-kəl\ n [ME, fr. OF, fr. L articulus joint, division, dim. of *artus* joint, limb] **1** : a distinct part of a written document **2** : a nonfictional prose composition forming an independent part of a publication **3** : a word (as *an, the*) used with a noun to limit or give definiteness to its application **4** : a member of a class of things; *esp* : COMMODITY

ar·tic·u·lar \är-ˈti-kyə-lər\ *adj* : of or relating to a joint

¹ar·tic·u·late \är-ˈti-kyə-lət\ *adj* **1** : divided into meaningful parts : INTELLIGIBLE **2** : able to speak; *also* : expressing oneself readily and effectively **3** : JOINTED — **ar·tic·u·late·ly** *adv* — **ar·tic·u·late·ness** *n*

²ar·tic·u·late \-ˌlāt\ *vb* **-lat·ed; -lat·ing 1** : to utter distinctly **2** : to unite by or as if by joints — **ar·tic·u·la·tion** \-ˌti-kyə-ˈlā-shən\ *n*

ar·ti·fact \ˈär-tə-ˌfakt\ *n* : something made or modified by humans usu. for a purpose; *esp* : an object remaining from another time or culture ⟨prehistoric ∼s⟩

ar·ti·fice \ˈär-tə-fəs\ *n* **1** : TRICK; *also* : TRICKERY **2** : an ingenious device; *also* : INGENUITY

ar·ti·fi·cer \är-ˈti-fə-sər, ˈär-tə-fə-sər\ *n* : a skilled worker

ar·ti·fi·cial \ˌär-tə-ˈfi-shəl\ *adj* **1** : produced by art rather than nature; *also* : made by humans to imitate nature **2** : not genuine : FEIGNED — **ar·ti·fi·ci·al·i·ty** \-ˌfi-shē-ˈa-lə-tē\ *n* — **ar·ti·fi·cial·ly** *adv* — **ar·ti·fi·cial·ness** *n*

artificial insemination *n* : introduction of semen into the uterus or oviduct by other than natural means

artificial intelligence *n* : the capability of a machine to imitate intelligent human behavior

artificial respiration *n* : the rhythmic forcing of air into and out of the lungs of a person whose breathing has stopped

ar·til·lery \är-ˈti-lə-rē\ *n, pl* **-ler·ies 1** : crew-served mounted firearms (as guns) **2** : a branch of the army armed with artillery — **ar·til·ler·ist** \-rist\ *n*

ar·ti·san \ˈär-tə-zən, -sən\ *n* : a skilled manual worker

art·ist \ˈär-tist\ *n* **1** : one who practices an art; *esp* : one who creates objects of beauty **2** : ARTISTE

ar·tiste \är-ˈtēst\ *n* : a skilled public performer

ar·tis·tic \är-ˈtis-tik\ *adj* : showing taste and skill — **ar·tis·ti·cal·ly** \-ti-k(ə-)lē\ *adv*

art·ist·ry \ˈär-tə-strē\ *n* : artistic quality or ability

art·less \ˈärt-ləs\ *adj* **1** : lacking art or skill **2** : free from artificiality : NATURAL **3** : free from guile : SINCERE — **art·less·ly** *adv* — **art·less·ness** *n*

art nou·veau \ˌär-nü-ˈvō, ˌärt-\ *n, often cap A&N* [F, lit., new art] : a late 19th century design style characterized by sinuous lines and leaf-shaped forms

arty \ˈär-tē\ *adj* **art·i·er; -est** : showily or pretentiously artistic — **art·i·ly** \ˈärt-ᵊl-ē\ *adv* — **art·i·ness** *n*

ar·um \ˈar-əm\ *n* : any of a family of plants (as the jack-in-the-pulpit or a skunk cabbage) with flowers in a fleshy enclosed spike

ARV *abbr* American Revised Version

¹-ary *n suffix* : thing or person belonging to or connected with ⟨function*ary*⟩

²-ary *adj suffix* : of, relating to, or connected with ⟨budget*ary*⟩

Ary·an \ˈar-ē-ən, ˈer-; ˈär-yən\ *adj* **1** : INDO-EUROPEAN **2** : NORDIC — **Aryan** *n*

¹as \əz, (ˌ)az\ *adv* **1** : to the same degree or amount : EQUALLY ⟨∼ green as grass⟩ **2** : for instance ⟨various trees, ∼ oak or pine⟩ **3** : when considered in a specified relation ⟨my opinion ∼ distinguished from his⟩

²as *conj* **1** : in the same amount or degree in which ⟨green ∼ grass⟩ **2** : in the same way that ⟨farmed ∼ his father before him had farmed⟩ **3** : WHILE, WHEN ⟨spoke to me ∼ I was leaving⟩ **4** : THOUGH ⟨improbable ∼ it seems⟩ **5** : SINCE, BECAUSE ⟨∼ I'm not wanted, I'll go⟩ **6** : that the result is ⟨so guilty ∼ to leave no doubt⟩

³as *pron* **1** : THAT — used after *same* or *such* ⟨it's the same price ∼ before⟩ **2** : a fact that ⟨he's rich, ∼ you know⟩

⁴as *prep* : in the capacity or character of ⟨this will serve ∼ a substitute⟩

As *symbol* arsenic

AS *abbr* **1** American Samoa **2** Anglo-Saxon **3** associate in science

asa·fet·i·da *or* **asa·foe·ti·da** \ˌa-sə-ˈfi-tə-dē, -ˈfe-tə-də\ *n* : an ill-smelling plant gum formerly used in medicine

ASAP *abbr* as soon as possible

as·bes·tos \as-ˈbes-təs, az-\ *n* : a noncombustible grayish mineral that occurs in fibrous form and has been used as a fireproof material

as·cend \ə-ˈsend\ *vb* **1** : to move upward : MOUNT, CLIMB **2** : to succeed to : OCCUPY ⟨he ∼ed the throne⟩

as·cen·dan·cy *also* **as·cen·den·cy** \ə-ˈsen-dən-sē\ *n* : controlling influence : DOMINATION

¹as·cen·dant *also* **as·cen·dent** \ə-ˈsen-dənt\ *n* : a dominant position

²ascendant *also* **ascendent** *adj* **1** : moving upward **2** : DOMINANT

as·cen·sion \ə-ˈsen-chən\ *n* : the act or process of ascending

Ascension Day *n* : the Thursday 40 days after Easter observed in commemoration of Christ's ascension into heaven

as·cent \ə-ˈsent\ *n* **1** : the act of mounting upward : CLIMB **2** : degree of upward slope

as·cer·tain \ˌas-ər-ˈtān\ *vb* : to learn with certainty — **as·cer·tain·able** *adj*

as·cet·ic \ə-ˈse-tik\ *adj* : practicing self-denial esp. for spiritual reasons : AUSTERE — **ascetic** *n* — **as·cet·i·cism** \-ˈse-tə-ˌsi-zəm\ *n*

ASCII \ˈas-kē\ *n* [American Standard Code for Information Interchange] : a computer code for representing alphanumeric information

ascor·bic acid \ə-ˈskȯr-bik-\ *n* : VITAMIN C

as·cot \ˈas-kət, -ˌkät\ *n* [*Ascot* Heath, racetrack near Ascot, England] : a broad neck scarf that is looped under the chin

as·cribe \ə-ˈskrīb\ *vb* **as·cribed; as·crib·ing** : to refer to a supposed cause, source, or author : ATTRIBUTE — **as·crib·able** *adj* — **as·crip·tion** \-ˈskrip-shən\ *n*

asep·tic \ā-ˈsep-tik\ *adj* : free or freed from disease-causing germs

asex·u·al \ā-ˈsek-shə-wəl\ *adj* **1** : lacking sex or functional sex organs **2** : occurring or formed without the production and union of two kinds of germ cells ⟨∼ reproduction⟩ — **asex·u·al·ly** *adv*

as for *prep* : with regard to : CONCERNING ⟨*as for* the others, they were late⟩

¹ash \ˈash\ *n* **1** : any of a genus of trees related to the olive and having winged seeds and bark with grooves and ridges **2** : the tough elastic wood of an ash

²ash *n* **1** : the solid matter left when material is burned **2** : fine mineral particles from a volcano **3** *pl* : the remains of the dead human body after cremation or disintegration

ashamed \ə-ˈshāmd\ *adj* **1** : feeling shame **2** : restrained by anticipation of shame ⟨∼ to say anything⟩ — **asham·ed·ly** \-ˈshā-məd-lē\ *adv*

ash·en \ˈa-shən\ *adj* : resembling ashes (as in color); *esp* : deadly pale

ash·lar \ˈash-lər\ *n* : hewn or squared stone; *also* : masonry of such stone

ashore \ə-ˈshȯr\ *adv* : on or to the shore

as how *conj* : THAT ⟨allowed *as how* she was glad to be here⟩

ash·ram \ˈäsh-rəm\ *n* : a religious retreat esp. of a Hindu sage

ash·tray \ˈash-ˌtrā\ *n* : a receptacle for tobacco ashes

Ash Wednesday *n* : the 1st day of Lent

ashy \ˈa-shē\ *adj* **ash·i·er; -est** : ASHEN

Asian \ˈā-zhən\ *adj* : of, relating to, or characteristic of the continent of Asia or its people — **Asian** *n*

Asi·at·ic \ˌā-zhē-ˈa-tik\ *adj* : ASIAN — sometimes taken to be offensive — **Asiatic** *n*

¹aside \ə-ˈsīd\ *adv* **1** : to or toward the side **2** : out of the way : AWAY

²aside *n* : an actor's words heard by the audience but supposedly not by other characters on stage

aside from *prep* **1** : BESIDES ⟨*aside from* being pretty, she's intelligent⟩ **2** : with the exception of ⟨*aside from* one D his grades are excellent⟩

as if *conj* **1** : as it would be if ⟨it's *as if* nothing had changed⟩ **2** : as one would if ⟨he acts *as if* he'd never been away⟩ **3** : THAT ⟨it seems *as if* nothing ever happens around here⟩

as·i·nine \ˈas-ᵊn-ˌīn\ *adj* [L *asininus*, fr. *asinus* ass] : STUPID, FOOLISH — **as·i·nin·i·ty** \ˌa-sə-ˈni-nə-tē\ *n*

ask \ˈask\ *vb* **asked** \ˈaskt\; **ask·ing 1** : to call on for an answer **2** : UTTER ⟨∼ a question⟩ **3** : to make a request of ⟨∼ him for help⟩ **4** : to make a request for ⟨∼ help of her⟩ **5** : to set as a price ⟨∼ed $800 for the car⟩ **6** : INVITE

askance \ə-ˈskans\ *adv* **1** : with a side glance **2** : with distrust

askew \ə-ˈskyü\ *adv or adj* : out of line : AWRY

ASL *abbr* American Sign Language

¹aslant \ə-ˈslant\ *adv or adj* : in a slanting direction

²aslant *prep* : over or across in a slanting direction

asleep \ə-ˈslēp\ *adv or adj* **1** : in or into a state of sleep **2** : DEAD **3** : NUMB **4** : INACTIVE

as long as *conj* **1** : provided that ⟨do as you like *as long as* you get home on time⟩ **2** : INASMUCH AS, SINCE ⟨*as long as* you're up, turn on the light⟩

aso·cial \(ˌ)ā-ˈsō-shəl\ *adj* : ANTISOCIAL

as of *prep* : AT, DURING, FROM, ON ⟨takes effect *as of* July 1⟩

asp \ˈasp\ *n* : a small poisonous African snake

as·par·a·gus \ə-ˈspar-ə-gəs\ *n* : a tall branching perennial herb related to the lilies; *also* : its edible young stalks

as·par·tame \as-ˈpär-ˌtām\ *n* : a crystalline low-calorie sweetener

ASPCA *abbr* American Society for the Prevention of Cruelty to Animals

as·pect \ˈas-ˌpekt\ *n* **1** : a position facing a particular direction **2** : APPEARANCE, LOOK **3** : PHASE

as·pen \ˈas-pən\ *n* : any of several poplars with leaves that flutter in the slightest breeze

as per \ˈaz-ˌpər\ *prep* : in accordance with ⟨*as per* instructions⟩

as·per·i·ty \a-ˈsper-ə-tē\ *n, pl* **-ties 1** : ROUGHNESS **2** : harshness of temper

as·per·sion \ə-ˈspər-zhən\ *n* : a slanderous or defamatory remark

as·phalt \ˈas-ˌfȯlt\ *also* **as·phal·tum** \as-ˈfȯl-təm\ *n* : a dark substance found in natural beds or obtained as a residue in petroleum refining and used esp. in paving streets

asphalt jungle *n* : a big city or a specified part of a big city

as·pho·del \ˈas-fə-ˌdel\ *n* : any of several Old World herbs related to the lilies and bearing flowers in long erect spikes

as·phyx·ia \as-ˈfik-sē-ə\ *n* : a lack of oxygen or excess of carbon dioxide in the body usu. caused by interruption of breathing and causing unconsciousness

as·phyx·i·ate \-sē-ˌāt\ *vb* **-at·ed; -at·ing** : SUFFOCATE — **as·phyx·i·a·tion** \-ˌfik-sē-ˈā-shən\ *n*

as·pic \ˈas-pik\ *n* [F, lit., asp] : a savory meat jelly

as·pi·rant \ˈas-pə-rənt, ə-ˈspī-rənt\ *n* : one who aspires **syn** candidate, applicant, seeker

¹as·pi·rate \ˈas-pə-rət\ *n* **1** : an independent sound \h\ or a character (as the letter *h*) representing it **2** : a consonant having aspiration as its final component

²as·pi·rate \ˈas-pə-ˌrāt\ *vb* **-rat·ed; -rat·ing** : to draw, remove, or take up or into by suction

as·pi·ra·tion \ˌas-pə-ˈrā-shən\ *n* **1** : the pronunciation or addition of an aspirate; *also* : the aspirate or its symbol **2** : a drawing of something in, out, up, or through by or as if by suction **3** : a strong desire to

achieve something noble; *also* : an object of this desire

as·pire \ə-ˈspīr\ *vb* **as·pired; as·pir·ing 1** : to seek to attain or accomplish a particular goal **2** : to rise aloft

as·pi·rin \ˈas-pə-rən\ *n, pl* **aspirin** *or* **aspirins 1** : a white crystalline drug used to relieve pain and fever **2** : a tablet of aspirin

as regards *also* **as respects** *prep* : in regard to : with respect to

ass \ˈas\ *n* **1** : any of several long-eared mammals smaller than the related horses; *esp* : one of Africa ancestral to the donkey **2** : a stupid person

as·sail \ə-ˈsāl\ *vb* : to attack violently — **as·sail·able** *adj* — **as·sail·ant** *n*

as·sas·sin \ə-ˈsas-ᵊn\ *n* [ML *assassinus*, fr. Ar *ḥash-shāshīn*, pl. of *ḥashshāsh* hashish-user, fr. *hashīsh* hashish] : a murderer esp. for hire or fanatical reasons

as·sas·si·nate \ə-ˈsas-ᵊn-ˌāt\ *vb* **-nat·ed; -nat·ing** : to murder by sudden or secret attack — **as·sas·si·na·tion** \-ˌsas-ᵊn-ˈā-shən\ *n*

as·sault \ə-ˈsȯlt\ *n* **1** : a violent attack **2** : an unlawful attempt or threat to do harm to another — **assault** *vb*

assault rifle *n* : a military automatic rifle with a large-capacity magazine

¹as·say \ˈa-ˌsā, a-ˈsā\ *n* : analysis to determine the quantity of one or more components present in a sample (as of an ore or drug)

²as·say \a-ˈsā, ˈa-ˌsā\ *vb* **1** : TRY, ATTEMPT **2** : to subject (as an ore or drug) to an assay **3** : JUDGE 3

as·sem·blage \ə-ˈsem-blij, *3 & 4 also* ˌas-äm-ˈbläzh\ *n* **1** : a collection of persons or things : GATHERING **2** : the act of assembling **3** : an artistic composition made from scraps, junk, and odds and ends **4** : the art of making assemblages

as·sem·ble \ə-ˈsem-bəl\ *vb* **-bled; -bling 1** : to collect into one place : CONGREGATE **2** : to fit together the parts of **3** : to meet together : CONVENE

as·sem·bly \ə-ˈsem-blē\ *n, pl* **-blies 1** : a gathering of persons : MEETING **2** *cap* : a legislative body; *esp* : the lower house of a legislature **3** : a signal for troops to assemble **4** : the fitting together of parts (as of a machine)

assembly language *n* : a computer language consisting of mnemonic codes corresponding to machine-language instructions

assembly line *n* : an arrangement of machines, equipment, and workers in which work passes from operation to operation in a direct line

as·sem·bly·man \ə-ˈsem-blē-mən\ *n* : a member of a legislative assembly

as·sem·bly·wom·an \-ˌwu̇-mən\ *n* : a woman who is a member of an assembly

as·sent \ə-ˈsent\ *vb* : AGREE, CONCUR — **assent** *n*

as·sert \ə-ˈsərt\ *vb* **1** : to state positively **2** : to demonstrate the existence of **syn** declare, affirm, protest, avow, claim — **as·ser·tive** \-ˈsər-tiv\ *adj* — **as·ser·tive·ness** *n*

as·ser·tion \ə-ˈsər-shən\ *n* : a positive statement

as·sess \ə-ˈses\ *vb* **1** : to fix the rate or amount of **2** : to impose (as a tax) at a specified rate **3** : to evaluate for taxation — **as·sess·ment** *n* — **as·ses·sor** \-ˈse-sər\ *n*

as·set \ˈa-ˌset\ *n* **1** *pl* : the entire property of a person or company that may be used to pay debts **2** : ADVANTAGE, RESOURCE

as·sev·er·ate \ə-ˈse-və-ˌrāt\ *vb* **-at·ed; -at·ing** : to assert earnestly — **as·sev·er·a·tion** \-ˌse-və-ˈrā-shən\ *n*

as·sid·u·ous \ə-ˈsi-jə-wəs\ *adj* : steadily attentive : DILIGENT — **as·si·du·i·ty** \ˌa-sə-ˈdü-ə-tē, -ˈdyü-\ *n* — **as·sid·u·ous·ly** *adv* — **as·sid·u·ous·ness** *n*

as·sign \ə-ˈsīn\ *vb* **1** : to transfer (property) to another **2** : to appoint to or as a duty ⟨∼ a lesson⟩ **3** : FIX, SPECIFY ⟨∼ a limit⟩ **4** : ASCRIBE ⟨∼ a reason⟩ — **as·sign·able** *adj*

as·sig·na·tion \ˌa-sig-ˈnā-shən\ *n* : an appointment for a meeting; *esp* : TRYST

assigned risk *n* : a poor risk (as an accident‑prone motorist) that an insurance company is forced to insure by state law

as·sign·ment \ə-'sīn-mənt\ *n* **1** : the act of assigning **2** : something assigned

as·sim·i·late \ə-'si-mə-ˌlāt\ *vb* **-lat·ed; -lat·ing 1** : to take up and absorb as nourishment; *also* : to absorb into a cultural tradition **2** : COMPREHEND **3** : to make or become similar — **as·sim·i·la·tion** \-ˌsi-mə-'lā-shən\ *n*

¹as·sist \ə-'sist\ *vb* : HELP, AID — **as·sis·tance** \-'sis-təns\ *n*

²assist *n* **1** : an act of assistance **2** : the action of a player who enables a teammate to make a putout (as in baseball) or score a goal (as in hockey)

as·sis·tant \ə-'sis-tənt\ *n* : a person who assists : HELPER

as·size \ə-'sīz\ *n* **1** : a judicial inquest **2** *pl* : the former regular sessions of superior courts in English counties

assn *abbr* association

assoc *abbr* associate; associated; association

¹as·so·ci·ate \ə-'sō-shē-ˌāt, -sē-\ *vb* **-at·ed; -at·ing 1** : to join in companionship or partnership **2** : to connect in thought

²as·so·ci·ate \-shē-ət, -sē-; -shət\ *n* **1** : a fellow worker : PARTNER **2** : COMPANION **3** *often cap* : a degree conferred esp. by a junior college 〈～ in arts〉 — **associate** *adj*

as·so·ci·a·tion \ə-ˌsō-shē-'ā-shən, -sē-\ *n* **1** : the act of associating **2** : an organization of persons : SOCIETY

as·so·cia·tive \ə-'sō-shē-ˌā-tiv, -sē-; -shə-tiv\ *adj* : of, relating to, or involved in association esp. of ideas or images

as·so·nance \'a-sə-nəns\ *n* : repetition of vowels esp. as an alternative to rhyme in verse — **as·so·nant** \-nənt\ *adj or n*

as soon as *conj* : immediately at or shortly after the time that (we'll start *as soon as* they arrive)

as·sort \ə-'sȯrt\ *vb* **1** : to distribute into like groups : CLASSIFY **2** : HARMONIZE

as·sort·ed \-'sȯr-təd\ *adj* : consisting of various kinds

as·sort·ment \-'sȯrt-mənt\ *n* : a collection of assorted things or persons

asst *abbr* assistant

as·suage \ə-'swāj\ *vb* **as·suaged; as·suag·ing 1** : to make (as pain or grief) less : EASE **2** : SATISFY **syn** alleviate, relieve, lighten, mitigate

as·sume \ə-'süm\ *vb* **as·sumed; as·sum·ing 1** : to take upon oneself **2** : to pretend to have or be **3** : to take as granted or true though not proved

as·sump·tion \ə-'səmp-shən\ *n* **1** : the taking up of a person into heaven **2** *cap* : August 15 observed in commemoration of the Assumption of the Virgin Mary **3** : a taking upon oneself **4** : PRETENSION **5** : SUPPOSITION

as·sur·ance \ə-'shùr-əns\ *n* **1** : PLEDGE **2** *chiefly Brit* : INSURANCE **3** : SECURITY **4** : SELF-CONFIDENCE; *also* : AUDACITY

as·sure \ə-'shùr\ *vb* **as·sured; as·sur·ing 1** : INSURE **2** : to give confidence to **3** : to state confidently to **4** : to make certain the coming or attainment of

as·sured \ə-'shùrd\ *n, pl* **assured** *or* **assureds** : INSURED

as·ta·tine \'as-tə-ˌtēn\ *n* : an unstable radioactive chemical element — see ELEMENT table

as·ter \'as-tər\ *n* : any of various mostly fall-blooming leafy-stemmed composite herbs with daisy-like purple, white, pink, or yellow flower heads

as·ter·isk \'as-tə-ˌrisk\ *n* [L *asteriscus*, fr. Gk *asteriskos*, lit., little star, dim. of *astēr*] : a character * used as a reference mark or as an indication of the omission of letters or words

astern \ə-'stərn\ *adv or adj* **1** : in, at, or toward the stern **2** : BACKWARD

as·ter·oid \'as-tə-ˌrȯid\ *n* : any of the numerous small celestial bodies found esp. between Mars and Jupiter

asth·ma \'az-mə\ *n* : an often allergic disorder marked by difficulty in breathing and a cough — **asth·mat·ic** \az-'ma-tik\ *adj or n*

as though *conj* : AS IF

astig·ma·tism \ə-'stig-mə-ˌti-zəm\ *n* : a defect in a lens or an eye causing improper focusing — **as·tig·mat·ic** \ˌas-tig-'ma-tik\ *adj*

astir \ə-'stər\ *adj* **1** : being in action : MOVING **2** : being out of bed

as to *prep* **1** : ABOUT, CONCERNING 〈uncertain *as to* what went on〉 **2** : ACCORDING TO 〈graded *as to* size〉

as·ton·ish \ə-'stä-nish\ *vb* : to strike with sudden and usu. great wonder : AMAZE — **as·ton·ish·ing·ly** *adv* — **as·ton·ish·ment** *n*

as·tound \ə-'staùnd\ *vb* : to fill with bewilderment or wonder — **as·tound·ing·ly** *adv*

¹astrad·dle \ə-'strad-ᵊl\ *adv* : on or above and extending onto both sides

²astraddle *prep* : ASTRIDE

as·tra·khan \'as-trə-kən, -ˌkan\ *n, often cap* **1** : karakul of Russian origin **2** : a cloth with a usu. wool, curled, and looped pile resembling karakul

as·tral \'as-trəl\ *adj* : of, relating to, or coming from the stars

astray \ə-'strā\ *adv or adj* **1** : off the right path or route **2** : into error

¹astride \ə-'strīd\ *adv* **1** : with one leg on each side **2** : with legs apart

²astride *prep* : with one leg on each side of

¹as·trin·gent \ə-'strin-jənt\ *adj* : able or tending to shrink body tissues — **as·trin·gen·cy** \-jən-sē\ *n*

²astringent *n* : an astringent agent or substance

astrol *abbr* astrologer; astrology

as·tro·labe \'as-trə-ˌlāb\ *n* : an instrument formerly used for observing the positions of celestial bodies

as·trol·o·gy \ə-'strä-lə-jē\ *n* : divination based on the supposed influence of the stars upon human events — **as·trol·o·ger** \-jər\ *n* — **as·tro·log·i·cal** \ˌas-trə-'lä-ji-kəl\ *adj*

astron *abbr* astronomer; astronomy

as·tro·naut \'as-trə-ˌnȯt\ *n* : a traveler in a spacecraft

as·tro·nau·tics \ˌas-trə-'nȯ-tiks\ *n* : the science of the construction and operation of spacecraft — **as·tro·nau·tic** \-tik\ *or* **as·tro·nau·ti·cal** \-ti-kəl\ *adj*

as·tro·nom·i·cal \ˌas-trə-'nä-mi-kəl\ *also* **as·tro·nom·ic** \-mik\ *adj* **1** : of or relating to astronomy **2** : extremely large 〈an ～ amount of money〉

astronomical unit *n* : a unit of length used in astronomy equal to the mean distance of the earth from the sun or about 93 million miles (150 million kilometers)

as·tron·o·my \ə-'strä-nə-mē\ *n, pl* **-mies** : the science of objects and matter beyond the earth's atmosphere — **as·tron·o·mer** \-mər\ *n*

as·tro·phys·ics \ˌas-trə-'fi-ziks\ *n* : astronomy dealing esp. with the physical properties and dynamic processes of celestial objects — **as·tro·phys·i·cal** \-zi-kəl\ *adj* — **as·tro·phys·i·cist** \-'fi-zə-sist\ *n*

as·tute \ə-'stüt, -'styüt, a-\ *adj* [L *astutus*, fr. *astus* craft] : shrewdly discerning; *also* : WILY — **as·tute·ly** *adv* — **as·tute·ness** *n*

asun·der \ə-'sən-dər\ *adv or adj* **1** : into separate pieces 〈torn ～〉 **2** : separated in position from each other

ASV *abbr* American Standard Version

¹as well as *conj* : and in addition : and moreover 〈brave *as well as* loyal〉

²as well as *prep* : in addition to : BESIDES 〈the coach, *as well as* the team, is ready〉

asy·lum \ə-'sī-ləm\ *n* [ME, fr. L, fr. Gk *asylon*, neut. of *asylos* inviolable, fr. a- not + *sylon* right of seizure] **1** : a place of refuge **2** : protection given to esp. political fugitives **3** : an institution for the care of the needy or sick and esp. of the insane

asym·met·ri·cal \ˌā-sə-'me-tri-kəl\ *or* **asym·met·ric** \-trik\ *adj* : not symmetrical — **asym·me·try** \(ˌ)ā-'si-mə-trē\ *n*

as·ymp·tote \'a-səmp-ˌtōt\ *n* : a straight line that is associated with a curve and tends to approximate it along an infinite branch — **as·ymp·tot·ic** \ˌa-səmp-'tä-tik\ *adj* — **as·ymp·tot·i·cal·ly** \-ti-k(ə-)lē\ *adv*

¹at \ət, (')at\ *prep* **1** — used to indicate a point in time or space ⟨be here ∼ 3 o'clock⟩ **2** — used to indicate a goal ⟨swung ∼ the ball⟩ **3** — used to indicate position or condition ⟨∼ rest⟩ **4** — used to indicate means, cause, or manner ⟨sold ∼ auction⟩

²at \'ät\ *n, pl* **at** — see *kip* at MONEY table

At *symbol* astatine

AT *abbr* automatic transmission

at all *adv* : in any way : in any circumstances ⟨not *at all* likely⟩

at·a·vism \'a-tə-ˌvi-zəm\ *n* : appearance in an individual of a character typical of an ancestral form; *also* : such an individual or character — **at·a·vis·tic** \ˌa-tə-'vis-tik\ *adj*

ate *past of* EAT

¹-ate *n suffix* **1** : one acted upon (in a specified way) ⟨distill*ate*⟩ **2** : chemical compound or complex derived from a (specified) compound or element ⟨ace*tate*⟩

²-ate *n suffix* **1** : office : function : rank : group of persons holding a (specified) office or rank ⟨episcop*ate*⟩ **2** : state : dominion : jurisdiction ⟨emir*ate*⟩

³-ate *adj suffix* **1** : acted on (in a specified way) : being in a (specified) state ⟨temper*ate*⟩ ⟨degener*ate*⟩ **2** : marked by having ⟨vertebr*ate*⟩

⁴-ate *vb suffix* : cause to be modified or affected by ⟨pollin*ate*⟩ : cause to become ⟨activ*ate*⟩ : furnish with ⟨aer*ate*⟩

ate·lier \ˌat-ᵊl-'yā\ *n* **1** : an artist's or designer's studio **2** : WORKSHOP

athe·ist \'ā-thē-ist\ *n* : one who denies the existence of God — **athe·ism** \-ˌi-zəm\ *n* — **athe·is·tic** \ˌā-thē-'is-tik\ *adj*

ath·e·nae·um *or* **ath·e·ne·um** \ˌa-thə-'nē-əm\ *n* : LIBRARY 1

ath·ero·scle·ro·sis \ˌa-thə-rō-sklə-'rō-səs\ *n* : arteriosclerosis characterized by the deposition of fatty substances in and the hardening of the inner layer of the arteries — **ath·ero·scle·rot·ic** \-'rä-tik\ *adj*

athirst \ə-'thərst\ *adj* **1** *archaic* : THIRSTY **2** : EAGER, LONGING

ath·lete \'ath-ˌlēt\ *n* [ME, fr. L *athleta*, fr. Gk *athlētēs*, fr. *athlein* to contend for a prize, fr. *athlon* prize, contest] : a person who is trained to compete in athletics

athlete's foot *n* : ringworm of the feet

ath·let·ic \ath-'le-tik\ *adj* **1** : of or relating to athletes or athletics **2** : VIGOROUS, ACTIVE **3** : STURDY, MUSCULAR

ath·let·ics \ath-'le-tiks\ *n sing or pl* : exercises and games requiring physical skill, strength, and endurance

athletic supporter *n* : an elastic pouch used to support the male genitals and worn esp. during athletic activity

¹athwart \ə-'thwȯrt\ *prep* **1** : ACROSS **2** : in opposition to

²athwart *adv* : obliquely across

atilt \ə-'tilt\ *adv or adj* **1** : in a tilted position **2** : with lance in hand

-ation *n suffix* : action or process ⟨flirt*ation*⟩ : something connected with an action or process ⟨discolor*ation*⟩

Atl *abbr* Atlantic

at·las \'at-ləs\ *n* : a book of maps

atm *abbr* atmosphere; atmospheric

ATM *abbr* automated teller machine

at·mo·sphere \'at-mə-ˌsfir\ *n* **1** : the gaseous envelope of a celestial body; *esp* : the mass of air surrounding the earth **2** : a surrounding influence **3** : a unit of pressure equal to the pressure of air at sea level or about 14.7 pounds per square inch (10 newtons per square centimeter) **4** : a dominant effect — **at·mo·spher-**

ic \ˌat-mə-'sfir-ik, -'sfer-\ *adj* — **at·mo·spher·i·cal·ly** \-i-k(ə-)lē\ *adv*

at·mo·sphe·rics \ˌat-mə-'sfir-iks, -'sfer-\ *n pl* : radio noise from atmospheric electrical phenomena

atoll \'a-ˌtȯl, -ˌtäl, 'ā-\ *n* : a coral island consisting of a reef surrounding a lagoon

atoll

at·om \'a-təm\ *n* [ME, fr. L *atomus*, fr. Gk *atomos*, fr. *atomos* indivisible, fr. *a-* not + *temnein* to cut] **1** : a tiny particle : BIT **2** : the smallest particle of a chemical element that can exist alone or in combination

atom·ic \ə-'tä-mik\ *adj* **1** : of or relating to atoms; *also* : NUCLEAR **2** ⟨∼ energy⟩ **2** : extremely small

atomic bomb *n* : a very destructive bomb utilizing the energy released by splitting the atom

atomic clock *n* : a very precise clock regulated by the natural vibration of atoms or molecules (as of cesium)

atomic number *n* : the number of protons in the nucleus of an element

atomic weight *n* : the mass of one atom of an element

at·om·ise, at·om·is·er *Brit var of* ATOMIZE, ATOMIZER

at·om·ize \'a-tə-ˌmīz\ *vb* **-ized; -iz·ing** : to reduce to minute particles

at·om·iz·er \'a-tə-ˌmī-zər\ *n* : a device for dispensing a liquid (as perfume) as a mist

atom smasher *n* : ACCELERATOR 3

aton·al \ā-'tōn-ᵊl\ *adj* : marked by avoidance of traditional musical tonality — **ato·nal·i·ty** \ˌā-tō-'na-lə-tē\ *n* — **aton·al·ly** \ā-'tōn-ᵊl-ē\ *adv*

atone \ə-'tōn\ *vb* **atoned; aton·ing** **1** : to make amends **2** : EXPIATE

atone·ment \ə-'tōn-mənt\ *n* **1** : the reconciliation of God and man through the death of Jesus Christ **2** : reparation for an offense : SATISFACTION

¹atop \ə-'täp\ *prep* : on top of

²atop *adv or adj* : on, to, or at the top

ATP \ˌā-ˌtē-'pē\ *n* [adenosine *tri*phosphate] : a compound that occurs widely in living tissue and supplies energy for many cellular processes by undergoing enzymatic hydrolysis

atri·um \'ā-trē-əm\ *n, pl* **atria** \-trē-ə\ *also* **atri·ums** **1** : the central room of a Roman house; *also* : an open patio or court in the center of a building (as a hotel) **2** : an anatomical cavity or passage; *esp* : one of the chambers of the heart that receives blood from the veins — **atri·al** \-əl\ *adj*

atro·cious \ə-'trō-shəs\ *adj* **1** : savagely brutal, cruel, or wicked **2** : very bad : ABOMINABLE — **atro·cious·ly** *adv* — **atro·cious·ness** *n*

atroc·i·ty \ə-'trä-sə-tē\ *n, pl* **-ties** **1** : ATROCIOUSNESS **2** : an atrocious act or object ⟨the *atrocities* of war⟩

at·ro·phy \'a-trə-fē\ *n, pl* **-phies** : decrease in size or wasting away of a bodily part or tissue — **atrophy** *vb*

at·ro·pine \'a-trə-ˌpēn\ *n* : a drug from belladonna and related plants used esp. to relieve spasms and to dilate the pupil of the eye

att *abbr* **1** attached **2** attention **3** attorney

at·tach \ə-'tach\ *vb* **1** : to seize legally in order to force payment of a debt **2** : to bind by personal ties **3** : FASTEN, CONNECT **4** : to be fastened or connected

at·ta·ché \ˌa-tə-'shā, ˌa-ˌta-, ə-ˌta-\ *n* [F] : a technical expert on the diplomatic staff of an ambassador

at·ta·ché case \ə-'ta-shā-, ˌa-tə-'shā-\ *n* : a small thin suitcase used esp. for carrying business papers; *also* : BRIEFCASE

at·tach·ment \ə-'tach-mənt\ *n* **1** : legal seizure of prop-

erty **2** : connection by ties of affection and regard **3** : a device attached to a machine or implement **4** : a connection by which one thing is attached to another

¹**at·tack** \ə-'tak\ *vb* **1** : to set upon with force or words : ASSAIL, ASSAULT **2** : to set to work on

²**attack** *n* **1** : an offensive action **2** : a fit of sickness

at·tain \ə-'tān\ *vb* **1** : ACHIEVE, ACCOMPLISH **2** : to arrive at : REACH — **at·tain·abil·i·ty** \-'tā-nə-'bi-lə-tē\ *n* — **at·tain·able** *adj*

at·tain·der \ə-'tān-dər\ *n* : extinction of the civil rights of a person upon sentence of death or outlawry

at·tain·ment \ə-'tān-mənt\ *n* **1** : the act of attaining **2** : ACCOMPLISHMENT

at·taint \ə-'tānt\ *vb* : to condemn to loss of civil rights

at·tar \'a-tər\ *n* [Per *'aṭir* perfumed, fr. Ar., fr. *'iṭr* perfume] : a fragrant floral oil

at·tempt \ə-'tempt\ *vb* : to make an effort toward : TRY — **attempt** *n*

at·tend \ə-'tend\ *vb* **1** : to look after : TEND **2** : to be present with **3** : to be present at **4** : to apply oneself **5** : to pay attention **6** : to direct one's attention

at·ten·dance \ə-'ten-dəns\ *n* **1** : the act or fact of attending **2** : the number of persons present; *also* : the number of times a person attends

¹**at·ten·dant** \ə-'ten-dənt\ *n* : one that attends another to render a service

²**attendant** *adj* : ACCOMPANYING ⟨∼ circumstances⟩

at·ten·tion \ə-'ten-chən\ *n* **1** : the act or state of applying the mind to an object **2** : CONSIDERATION **3** : an act of courtesy **4** : a position of readiness assumed on command by a soldier — **at·ten·tive** \-'ten-tiv\ *adj* — **at·ten·tive·ly** *adv* — **at·ten·tive·ness** *n*

at·ten·u·ate \ə-'ten-yə-₁wāt\ *vb* **-at·ed; -at·ing 1** : to make or become thin **2** : WEAKEN — **attenuate** \-wət\ *adj* — **at·ten·u·a·tion** \-₁ten-yə-'wā-shən\ *n*

at·test \ə-'test\ *vb* **1** : to certify as genuine by signing as a witness **2** : MANIFEST **3** : TESTIFY — **at·tes·ta·tion** \₁a-₁tes-'tā-shən\ *n*

at·tic \'a-tik\ *n* : the space or room in a building immediately below the roof

¹**at·tire** \ə-'tīr\ *vb* **at·tired; at·tir·ing** : to put garments on : DRESS, ARRAY

²**attire** *n* : DRESS, CLOTHES

at·ti·tude \'a-tə-₁tüd, -₁tyüd\ *n* **1** : POSTURE **2** : a mental position or feeling with regard to a fact or state **3** : the position of something in relation to something else **4** : a negative or hostile state of mind **5** : a cocky or arrogant manner

at·ti·tu·di·nise *Brit var of* ATTITUDINIZE

at·ti·tu·di·nize \₁a-tə-'tüd-ᵊn-₁iz, -'tyüd-\ *vb* **-nized; -niz·ing** : to assume an affected mental attitude : POSE

attn *abbr* attention

at·tor·ney \ə-'tər-nē\ *n, pl* **-neys** : a legal agent qualified to act for persons in legal proceedings

attorney general *n, pl* **attorneys general** *or* **attorney**

generals : the chief legal representative and adviser of a nation or state

at·tract \ə-'trakt\ *vb* **1** : to draw to or toward oneself : cause to approach **2** : to draw by emotional or aesthetic appeal **syn** charm, fascinate, allure, captivate, enchant — **at·trac·tive** \-'trak-tiv\ *adj* — **at·trac·tive·ly** *adv* — **at·trac·tive·ness** *n*

at·trac·tant \ə-'trak-tənt\ *n* : a substance (as a pheromone) used to attract insects or other animals

at·trac·tion \ə-'trak-shən\ *n* **1** : the act or power of attracting; *esp* : personal charm **2** : an attractive quality, object, or feature **3** : a force tending to draw particles together

attrib *abbr* attributive

¹**at·tri·bute** \'a-trə-₁byüt\ *n* **1** : an inherent characteristic **2** : a word ascribing a quality; *esp* : ADJECTIVE

²**at·trib·ute** \ə-'tri-₁byüt, -byət\ *vb* **-ut·ed; -ut·ing 1** : to explain as to cause or origin ⟨∼ the illness to fatigue⟩ **2** : to regard as a characteristic **syn** ascribe, credit, charge, impute — **at·trib·ut·able** *adj* — **at·tri·bu·tion** \₁a-trə-'byü-shən\ *n*

at·trib·u·tive \ə-'trib-yə-tiv\ *adj* : joined directly to a modified noun without a linking verb ⟨red in *red hair* is an ∼ adjective⟩ — **attributive** *n*

at·tri·tion \ə-'tri-shən\ *n* **1** : the act of wearing away by or as if by rubbing **2** : a reduction in numbers as a result of resignation, retirement, or death

at·tune \ə-'tün, -'tyün\ *vb* : to bring into harmony : TUNE — **at·tune·ment** *n*

atty *abbr* attorney

ATV *abbr* all-terrain vehicle

atyp·i·cal \ā-'ti-pi-kəl\ *adj* : not typical : IRREGULAR — **atyp·i·cal·ly** \-k(ə-)lē\ *adv*

Au *symbol* [L *aurum*] gold

au·burn \'ȯ-bərn\ *adj* : reddish brown — **auburn** *n*

au cou·rant \₁ō-kü-'rä^n\ *adj* [F, lit., in the current] : UP-TO-DATE, STYLISH

¹**auc·tion** \'ȯk-shən\ *n* [L *auction-, auctio*, fr. *augēre* to increase] : public sale of property to the highest bidder

²**auction** *vb* **auc·tioned; auc·tion·ing** \-shə-niŋ\ : to sell at auction

auc·tion·eer \₁ȯk-shə-'nir\ *n* : an agent who conducts an auction

aud *abbr* audit; auditor

au·da·cious \ȯ-'dā-shəs\ *adj* **1** : DARING, BOLD **2** : INSOLENT — **au·da·cious·ly** *adv* — **au·da·cious·ness** *n* — **au·dac·i·ty** \-'da-sə-tē\ *n*

¹**au·di·ble** \'ȯ-də-bəl\ *adj* : capable of being heard — **au·di·bil·i·ty** \₁ȯ-də-'bi-lə-tē\ *n* — **au·di·bly** \'ȯ-də-blē\ *adv*

²**audible** *n* : a play called at the line of scrimmage

au·di·ence \'ȯ-dē-əns\ *n* **1** : a formal interview **2** : an opportunity of being heard **3** : an assembly of listeners or spectators

¹**au·dio** \'ȯ-dē-₁ō\ *adj* **1** : of or relating to frequencies (as of radio waves) corresponding to those of audible sound waves **2** : of or relating to sound or its reproduction and esp. high-fidelity reproduction **3** : relat-

ing to or used in the transmission or reception of sound

²au·dio *n* **1** : the transmission, reception, or reproduction of sound **2** : the section of television or motion‑picture equipment that deals with sound

au·di·ol·o·gy \ȯ-dē-'ä-lə-jē\ *n* : a branch of science dealing with hearing and esp. with the treatment of individuals having trouble with hearing — **au·di·o·log·i·cal** \-ə-'lä-ji-kəl\ *adj* — **au·di·ol·o·gist** \-'ä-lə-jist\ *n*

au·dio·phile \'ȯ-dē-ō-ˌfīl\ *n* : one who is enthusiastic about high-fidelity sound reproduction

au·dio·tape \'ȯ-dē-ō-ˌtāp\ *n* : a tape recording of sound

au·dio·vi·su·al \ˌȯ-dē-ō-'vi-zhə-wəl\ *adj* : of, relating to, or making use of both hearing and sight

au·dio·vi·su·als \-wəlz\ *n pl* : audiovisual teaching materials (as videotapes)

¹au·dit \'ȯ-dət\ *n* : a formal examination and verification of financial accounts

²audit *vb* **1** : to perform an audit on or for **2** : to attend (a course) without expecting formal credit

¹au·di·tion \ȯ-'di-shən\ *n* : HEARING; *esp* : a trial performance to appraise an entertainer's merits

²audition *vb* **-tioned; -tion·ing** \-'di-shə-niŋ\ : to give an audition to; *also* : to give a trial performance

au·di·tor \'ȯ-də-tər\ *n* **1** : LISTENER **2** : a person who audits

au·di·to·ri·um \ˌȯ-də-'tȯr-ē-əm\ *n, pl* **-riums** *or* **-ria** \-rē-ə\ **1** : the part of a public building where an audience sits **2** : a hall or building used for public gatherings

au·di·to·ry \'ȯ-də-ˌtȯr-ē\ *adj* : of or relating to hearing or to the sense or organs of hearing

auditory tube *n* : EUSTACHIAN TUBE

auf Wie·der·seh·en \auf-'vē-dər-ˌzän\ *interj* [G] — used to express farewell

Aug *abbr* August

au·ger \'ȯ-gər\ *n* : a tool for boring

aught \'ȯt, 'ät\ *n* : ZERO, CIPHER

aug·ment \ȯg-'ment\ *vb* : ENLARGE, INCREASE — **aug·men·ta·tion** \ˌȯg-mən-'tā-shən\ *n*

au gra·tin \ō-'grat-ᵊn, ȯ-, -'grät-\ *adj* [F, lit., with the burnt scrapings from the pan] : covered with bread crumbs or grated cheese and browned

¹au·gur \'ȯ-gər\ *n* : DIVINER, SOOTHSAYER

²augur *vb* **1** : to foretell esp. from omens **2** : to give promise of : PRESAGE

au·gu·ry \'ȯ-gyə-rē, -gə-\ *n, pl* **-ries** **1** : divination from omens **2** : OMEN, PORTENT

au·gust \ȯ-'gəst\ *adj* : marked by majestic dignity or grandeur — **au·gust·ly** *adv* — **au·gust·ness** *n*

Au·gust \'ȯ-gəst\ *n* [ME, fr. OE, fr. L *Augustus*, fr. *Augustus* Caesar] : the 8th month of the year

au jus \ō-'zhü, -'zhüs, -'jüs; ō-zhǖ\ *adj* [F] : served in the juice obtained from roasting

auk \'ȯk\ *n* : any of several stocky black-and‑white diving seabirds that breed in colder parts of the northern hemisphere

auld \'ȯl, 'ȯld, 'äl, 'äld\ *adj, chiefly Scot* : OLD

aunt \'ant, 'änt\ *n* **1** : the sister of one's father or mother **2** : the wife of one's uncle

au pair \'ō-'par\ *n* [F, on even terms] : a usu. young foreign person who does domestic work for a family in return for room and board and to learn the family's language

au·ra \'ȯr-ə\ *n* **1** : a distinctive atmosphere surrounding a given source **2** : a luminous radiation

au·ral \'ȯr-əl\ *adj* : of or relating to the ear or to the sense of hearing

aurar *pl of* EYRIR

au·re·ole \'ȯr-ē-ˌōl\ *or* **au·re·o·la** \ȯ-'rē-ə-lə\ *n* : HALO, NIMBUS

au re·voir \ˌō-rə-'vwär\ *n* [F, lit., till seeing again] : GOOD-BYE

au·ri·cle \'ȯr-i-kəl\ *n* : an atrium of the heart

au·ric·u·lar \ȯ-'ri-kyə-lər\ *adj* **1** : told privately ⟨∼ confession⟩ **2** : known or recognized by the sense of hearing

au·ro·ra \ə-'rȯr-ə\ *n, pl* **auroras** *or* **au·ro·rae** \-(ˌ)ē\ : a luminous phenomenon of streamers or arches of light appearing in the upper atmosphere esp. of a planet's polar regions — **au·ro·ral** \-əl\ *adj*

aurora aus·tra·lis \-ȯ-'strā-ləs\ *n* : an aurora that occurs in earth's southern hemisphere

aurora bo·re·al·is \-ˌbȯr-ē-'a-ləs\ *n* : an aurora that occurs in earth's northern hemisphere

AUS *abbr* Army of the United States

aus·pice \'ȯ-spəs\ *n, pl* **aus·pic·es** \-spə-səz, -ˌsēz\ [L *auspicium,* fr. *auspic-, auspex* diviner by birds, fr. *avis* bird + *specere* to look, look at] **1** : observation of birds by an augur **2** *pl* : kindly patronage and protection **3** : a prophetic sign or omen

aus·pi·cious \ȯ-'spi-shəs\ *adj* **1** : promising success : PROPITIOUS **2** : FORTUNATE, PROSPEROUS — **aus·pi·cious·ly** *adv* — **aus·pi·cious·ness** *n*

aus·tere \ȯ-'stir\ *adj* **1** : STERN, SEVERE, STRICT **2** : AB‑STEMIOUS **3** : UNADORNED ⟨∼ style⟩ — **aus·tere·ly** *adv* — **aus·ter·i·ty** \-'ster-ə-tē\ *n*

aus·tral \'ȯs-trəl\ *adj* : SOUTHERN

Aus·tra·lian \ȯ-'strāl-yən\ *n* : a native or inhabitant of Australia — **Australian** *adj*

Aus·tri·an \'ȯ-strē-ən\ *n* : a native or inhabitant of Austria — **Austrian** *adj*

Aus·tro·ne·sian \ˌȯs-trə-'nē-zhən\ *adj* : of, relating to, or constituting a family of languages spoken in the area extending from Madagascar eastward through the Malay Peninsula to Hawaii and Easter Island

auth *abbr* **1** authentic **2** author **3** authorized

au·then·tic \ə-'then-tik, ȯ-\ *adj* : GENUINE, REAL — **au·then·ti·cal·ly** \-ti-k(ə-)lē\ *adv* — **au·then·tic·i·ty** \ˌȯ-ˌthen-'ti-sə-tē\ *n*

au·then·ti·cate \ə-'then-ti-ˌkāt, ȯ-\ *vb* **-cat·ed; -cat·ing** : to prove genuine — **au·then·ti·ca·tion** \-ˌthen-ti-'kā-shən\ *n*

au·thor \'ȯ-thər\ *n* [ME *autour,* ultim. fr. L *auctor* originator, author, fr. *augēre* to increase] **1** : one that originates or creates **2** : one that writes or composes a literary work

au·thor·ess \'ȯ-thə-rəs\ *n* : a woman author

au·tho·rise *Brit var of* AUTHORIZE

au·thor·i·tar·i·an \ȯ-ˌthär-ə-'ter-ē-ən, ə-, -ˌthȯr-\ *adj* **1** : characterized by or favoring the principle of blind obedience to authority **2** : characterized by or favoring concentration of political power in an authority not responsible to the people — **authoritarian** *n*

au·thor·i·ta·tive \ə-'thär-ə-ˌtā-tiv, ȯ-, -'thȯr-\ *adj* : supported by, proceeding from, or being an authority — **au·thor·i·ta·tive·ly** *adv* — **au·thor·i·ta·tive·ness** *n*

au·thor·i·ty \ə-'thär-ə-tē, ȯ-, -'thȯr-\ *n, pl* **-ties** **1** : a citation used in support of a statement or in defense of an action; *also* : the source of such a citation **2** : one appealed to as an expert **3** : power to influence thought or behavior **4** : freedom granted : RIGHT **5** : persons in command; *esp* : GOVERNMENT **6** : convincing force

au·tho·rize \'ȯ-thə-ˌrīz\ *vb* **-rized; -riz·ing** **1** : SANCTION **2** : to give legal power to — **au·tho·ri·za·tion** \ˌȯ-thə-rə-'zā-shən\ *n*

au·thor·ship \'ȯ-thər-ˌship\ *n* **1** : the state of being an author **2** : the source of a piece of writing, music, or art

au·tism \'ȯ-ˌti-zəm\ *n* **1** : absorption in self-centered mental activity (as delusions and hallucinations) esp. when accompanied by withdrawal from reality **2** : a mental disorder orginating in infancy that is characterized esp. by inability to interact socially, repetitive behavior, and language disorder — **au·tis·tic** \ȯ-'tis-tik\ *adj*

¹au·to \'ȯ-tō\ *n, pl* **autos** : AUTOMOBILE

²**auto** *abbr* automatic

au·to·bahn \'ò-tō-ˌbän, 'aù-\ *n* : a German, Swiss, or Austrian expressway

au·to·bi·og·ra·phy \ˌò-tə-bī-'ä-grə-fē\ *n* : the biography of a person narrated by that person — **au·to·bi·og·ra·pher** \-fər\ *n* — **au·to·bi·o·graph·i·cal** \-ˌbī-ə-'gra-fi-kəl\ *adj* — **au·to·bi·o·graph·i·cal·ly** \-k(ə-)lē\ *adv*

au·toch·tho·nous \ò-'täk-thə-nəs\ *adj* : INDIGENOUS, NATIVE

au·to·clave \'ò-tō-ˌklāv\ *n* : an apparatus (as for sterilizing) using superheated high-pressure steam

au·toc·ra·cy \ò-'tä-krə-sē\ *n, pl* **-cies** : government by one person having unlimited power — **au·to·crat** \'ò-tə-ˌkrat\ *n* — **au·to·crat·ic** \ˌò-tə-'kra-tik\ *adj* — **au·to·crat·i·cal·ly** \-ti-k(ə-)lē\ *adv*

¹**au·to·graph** \'ò-tə-ˌgraf\ *n* **1** : an original manuscript **2** : a person's signature written by hand

²**autograph** *vb* : to write one's signature on

au·to·im·mune \ˌò-tō-i-'myün\ *adj* : of, relating to, or caused by antibodies or lymphocytes that attack molecules, cells, or tissues of the organism producing them ⟨~ diseases⟩ — **au·to·im·mu·ni·ty** \-i-'myü-nə-tē\ *n*

au·to·mate \'ò-tə-ˌmāt\ *vb* **-mat·ed; -mat·ing 1** : to operate automatically using mechanical or electronic devices **2** : to convert to automatic operation — **au·to·ma·tion** \ˌò-tə-'mā-shən\ *n*

automated teller machine *n* : a computer terminal allowing access to one's own bank accounts

¹**au·to·mat·ic** \ˌò-tə-'ma-tik\ *adj* **1** : INVOLUNTARY **2** : made so that certain parts act in a desired manner at the proper time : SELF-ACTING — **au·to·mat·i·cal·ly** \-ti-k(ə-)lē\ *adv*

²**automatic** *n* : an automatic device; *esp* : an automatic firearm

au·tom·a·ton \ò-'tä-mə-tən, -ˌtän\ *n, pl* **-atons** *or* **-a·ta** \-ə-tə, -ə-ˌtä\ **1** : an automatic machine; *esp* : ROBOT **2** : an individual who acts mechanically

au·to·mo·bile \'ò-tə-mō-ˌbēl, ˌò-tə-mə-'bēl\ *n* : a usu. 4-wheeled automotive vehicle for passenger transportation

au·to·mo·tive \ˌò-tə-'mō-tiv\ *adj* **1** : of or relating to automobiles, trucks, or buses **2** : SELF-PROPELLED

au·to·nom·ic nervous system \ˌò-tə-'nä-mik-\ *n* : a part of the vertebrate nervous system that governs involuntary actions and that consists of the sympathetic nervous system and the parasympathetic nervous system

au·ton·o·mous \ò-'tä-nə-məs\ *adj* : having the right or power of self-government — **au·ton·o·mous·ly** *adv* — **au·ton·o·my** \-mē\ *n*

au·top·sy \'ò-ˌtäp-sē, 'ò-təp-\ *n, pl* **-sies** [Gk *autopsia* act of seeing with one's own eyes, fr. *autos* self + *opsis* sight] : examination of a dead body usu. with dissection sufficient to determine the cause of death or extent of change produced by disease — **autopsy** *vb*

au·tumn \'ò-təm\ *n* : the season between summer and winter — **au·tum·nal** \ò-'təm-nəl\ *adj*

aux *abbr* auxiliary

¹**aux·il·ia·ry** \òg-'zil-yə-rē, -'zi-lə-rē\ *adj* **1** : providing help **2** : functioning in a subsidiary capacity **3** : accompanying a verb form to express person, number, mood, or tense ⟨~ verbs⟩

²**auxiliary** *n, pl* **-ries 1** : an auxiliary person, group, or device **2** : an auxiliary verb

aux·in \'òk-sən\ *n* : a plant hormone that stimulates growth in length

av *abbr* **1** avenue **2** average **3** avoirdupois

AV *abbr* **1** ad valorem **2** audiovisual **3** Authorized Version

¹**avail** \ə-'vāl\ *vb* : to be of use or advantage : HELP, BENEFIT

²**avail** *n* : USE (effort was of no ~)

avail·able \ə-'vā-lə-bəl\ *adj* **1** : USABLE **2** : ACCESSIBLE — **avail·abil·i·ty** \-ˌvā-lə-'bi-lə-tē\ *n*

av·a·lanche \'a-və-ˌlanch\ *n* : a mass of snow, ice, earth, or rock sliding down a mountainside

avant–garde \ä-ˌvän-'gärd, -ˌvänt-\ *n* [F, vanguard] : those esp. in the arts who create or apply new or experimental ideas and techniques — **avant–garde** *adj*

av·a·rice \'a-və-rəs\ *n* : excessive desire for wealth : GREED — **av·a·ri·cious** \ˌa-və-'ri-shəs\ *adj*

avast \ə-'vast\ *vb imper* — a nautical command to stop or cease

av·a·tar \'a-və-ˌtär\ *n* [Skt *avatāra* descent] : INCARNATION

avaunt \ə-'vònt\ *adv* : AWAY, HENCE

avdp *abbr* avoirdupois

ave *abbr* avenue

Ave Ma·ria \ˌä-ˌvä-mə-'rē-ə\ *n* : HAIL MARY

avenge \ə-'venj\ *vb* **avenged; aveng·ing** : to take vengeance for — **aveng·er** *n*

av·e·nue \'a-və-ˌnü, -ˌnyü\ *n* **1** : a way or route to a place or goal : PATH **2** : a broad street

aver \ə-'vər\ *vb* **averred; aver·ring** : ALLEGE, ASSERT; *also* : DECLARE

¹**av·er·age** \'a-və-rij, 'a-vrij\ *n* [modif. of MF *avarie* damage to ship or cargo, fr. OIt *avaria*, fr. Ar *'awārīyah* damaged merchandise] **1** : ARITHMETIC MEAN **2** : a ratio of successful tries to total tries esp. in athletics (batting ~ of .303)

²**average** *adj* **1** : equaling or approximating an arithmetic mean **2** : being about midway between extremes **3** : not out of the ordinary : COMMON

³**average** *vb* **av·er·aged; av·er·ag·ing 1** : to be at or come to an average **2** : to be, do, or get usually **3** : to find the average of

averse \ə-'vərs\ *adj* : having an active feeling of dislike or reluctance ⟨~ to exercise⟩

© 1995 PAWS, INC./Distributed by Universal Press Syndicate

aver·sion \ə-'vər-zhən\ *n* **1** : a feeling of repugnance for something with a desire to avoid it **2** : something decidedly disliked

avert \ə-'vərt\ *vb* **1** : to turn aside or away ⟨∼ the eyes⟩ **2** : to ward off

avg *abbr* average

avi·an \'ā-vē-ən\ *adj* [L *avis* bird] : of, relating to, or derived from birds

avi·ary \'ā-vē-ˌer-ē\ *n, pl* **-ar·ies** : a place for keeping birds confined

avi·a·tion \ˌā-vē-'ā-shən, ˌa-\ *n* **1** : the operation of heavier-than-air aircraft **2** : aircraft manufacture, development, and design

avi·a·tor \'ā-vē-ˌā-tər, 'a-\ *n* : an airplane pilot

avi·a·trix \ˌā-vē-'ā-triks, ˌa-\ *n, pl* **-trix·es** \-trik-səz\ *or* **-tri·ces** \-trə-ˌsēz\ : a woman airplane pilot

avid \'a-vəd\ *adj* **1** : craving eagerly : GREEDY **2** : enthusiastic in pursuit of an interest — **avid·i·ty** \ə-'vi-də-tē, a-\ *n* — **avid·ly** *adv* — **avid·ness** *n*

avi·on·ics \ˌā-vē-'ä-niks, ˌa-\ *n pl* : electronics designed for use in aerospace vehicles — **avi·on·ic** \-nik\ *adj*

avo \'a-(ˌ)vü\ *n, pl* **avos** — see *pataca* at MONEY table

avo·ca·do \ˌa-və-'kä-dō, ˌä-\ *n, pl* **-dos** *also* **-does** [modif. of Sp *aguacate*, fr. Nahuatl *āhuacatl*, avocado, testicle] : a pulpy green to purple nutty-flavored edible fruit of a tropical American tree; *also* : this tree

avo·ca·tion \ˌa-və-'kā-shən\ *n* : HOBBY

avo·cet \'a-və-ˌset\ *n* : any of several long-legged shorebirds with webbed feet and slender upward-curving bills

avoid \ə-'vȯid\ *vb* **1** : to keep away from : SHUN **2** : to prevent the occurrence of **3** : to refrain from — **avoid·able** *adj* — **avoid·ably** *adv* — **avoid·ance** \-ᵊns\ *n*

avoir·du·pois \ˌa-vər-də-'pȯiz\ *n* [ME *avoir de pois* goods sold by weight, fr. OF, lit., goods of weight] **1** : AVOIRDUPOIS WEIGHT **2** : WEIGHT, HEAVINESS; *esp* : personal weight

avoirdupois weight *n* : a system of weights based on a pound of 16 ounces and an ounce of 16 drams (28 grams) — see WEIGHT table

avouch \ə-'vau̇ch\ *vb* **1** : to declare positively : AVER **2** : to vouch for

avow \ə-'vau̇\ *vb* : to declare openly — **avow·al** \-'vau̇-(ə)l\ *n*

avun·cu·lar \ə-'vəŋ-kyə-lər\ *adj* : of, relating to, or resembling an uncle

await \ə-'wāt\ *vb* : to wait for : EXPECT

¹**awake** \ə-'wāk\ *vb* **awoke** \-'wōk\ *also* **awaked** \-'wākt\; **awo·ken** \-'wō-kən\ *or* **awaked** *also* **awoke**; **awak·ing** : to bring back to consciousness : wake up

²**awake** *adj* : not asleep; *also* : ALERT

awak·en \ə-'wā-kən\ *vb* **awak·ened**; **awak·en·ing** \-'wā-kə-niŋ\ : AWAKE

¹**award** \ə-'wȯrd\ *vb* **1** : to give by judicial decision ⟨∼ damages⟩ **2** : to give in recognition of merit or achievement

²**award** *n* **1** : a final decision : JUDGMENT **2** : something awarded : PRIZE

aware \ə-'war\ *adj* : having perception or knowledge : CONSCIOUS, INFORMED — **aware·ness** *n*

awash \ə-'wȯsh, -'wäsh\ *adj* **1** : washed by waves or tide **2** : AFLOAT **3** : FLOODED

¹**away** \ə-'wā\ *adv* **1** : from this or that place ⟨go ∼⟩ **2** : out of the way **3** : in another direction ⟨turn ∼⟩ **4** : out of existence ⟨fade ∼⟩ **5** : from one's possession ⟨give ∼⟩ **6** : without interruption ⟨chatter ∼⟩ **7** : at a distance in space or time ⟨far ∼⟩ ⟨∼ back in 1910⟩

²**away** *adj* **1** : ABSENT **2** : distant in space or time ⟨a lake 10 miles ∼⟩

¹**awe** \'ȯ\ *n* **1** : profound and reverent dread of the supernatural **2** : respectful fear inspired by authority

²**awe** *vb* **awed; aw·ing** : to inspire with awe

aweigh \ə-'wā\ *adj* : just clear of the bottom ⟨anchors ∼⟩

awe·some \'ȯ-səm\ *adj* **1** : expressive of awe **2** : inspiring awe

awe·struck \-ˌstrək\ *also* **awe·strick·en** \-ˌstri-kən\ *adj* : filled with awe

aw·ful \'ȯ-fəl\ *adj* **1** : inspiring awe **2** : extremely disagreeable **3** : very great ⟨an ∼ lot of money⟩ — **aw·ful·ly** *adv*

awhile \ə-'hwīl\ *adv* : for a while

awhirl \ə-'hwərl\ *adj* : being in a whirl

awk·ward \'ȯ-kwərd\ *adj* **1** : CLUMSY **2** : UNGRACEFUL **3** : difficult to explain : EMBARRASSING **4** : difficult to deal with — **awk·ward·ly** *adv* — **awk·ward·ness** *n*

awl \'ȯl\ *n* : a pointed instrument for making small holes

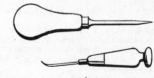

awls

aw·ning \'ȯ-niŋ\ *n* : a rooflike cover (as of canvas) extended over or in front of a place as a shelter

AWOL \'ā-ˌwȯl, ˌā-ˌdə-bəl-yü-ˌō-'el\ *n* : a person who is absent without leave — **AWOL** *adj or adv*

awry \ə-'rī\ *adv or adj* **1** : ASKEW **2** : AMISS

ax *or* **axe** \'aks\ *n* : a chopping or cutting tool with an edged head fitted parallel to a handle

axi·al \'ak-sē-əl\ *adj* **1** : of, relating to, or functioning as an axis **2** : situated around, in the direction of, on, or along an axis — **axi·al·ly** *adv*

axi·om \'ak-sē-əm\ *n* [L *axioma*, fr. Gk *axiōma*, lit., something worthy, fr. *axioun* to think worthy, fr. *axios* worth, worthy] **1** : a statement generally accepted as true : MAXIM **2** : a proposition regarded as a self-evident truth — **axi·om·at·ic** \ˌak-sē-ə-'ma-tik\ *adj* — **axi·om·at·i·cal·ly** \-ti-k(ə-)lē\ *adv*

ax·is \\'ak-səs\ *n, pl* **ax·es** \\-ˌsēz\ **1** : a straight line around which a body rotates **2** : a straight line or structure with respect to which a body or figure is symmetrical **3** : one of the reference lines of a system of coordinates **4** : an alliance between major powers

ax·le \\'ak-səl\ *n* : a shaft on which a wheel revolves

ayah \\'ī-ə\ *n* [Hindi *āyā*, fr. Pg *aia*, fr. L *avia* grandmother] : a nurse or maid native to India

aya·tol·lah \ˌī-ə-'tō-lə\ *n* [Per, lit., sign of God, fr. Ar *aya* sign, miracle + *allāh* God] : an Islamic religious leader — used as a title of respect

¹**aye** *also* **ay** \\'ā\ *adv* : ALWAYS, EVER

²**aye** *also* **ay** \\'ī\ *adv* : YES

³**aye** *also* **ay** \\'ī\ *n, pl* **ayes** : an affirmative vote

AZ *abbr* Arizona

aza·lea \ə-'zāl-yə\ *n* : any of numerous rhododendrons with funnel-shaped blossoms and usu. deciduous leaves

az·i·do·thy·mi·dine \ə-ˌzi-dō-'thī-mə-ˌdēn\ *n* : AZT

az·i·muth \\'a-zə-məth\ *n* : horizontal direction expressed as an angular distance from a fixed point

AZT \ˌā-(ˌ)zē-'tē\ *n* : an antiviral drug used to treat AIDS

Az·tec \\'az-ˌtek\ *n* : a member of a Nahuatl-speaking people that founded the Mexican empire and were conquered by Hernan Cortes in 1519 — **Az·tec·an** *adj*

azure \\'a-zhər\ *n* : the blue of the clear sky — **azure** *adj*

B

¹**b** \\'bē\ *n, pl* **b's** *or* **bs** \\'bēz\ *often cap* **1** : the 2d letter of the English alphabet **2** : a grade rating a student's work as good

²**b** *abbr, often cap* **1** bachelor **2** bass **3** bishop **4** book **5** born

B *symbol* boron

Ba *symbol* barium

BA *abbr* **1** bachelor of arts **2** batting average

bab·bitt \\'ba-bət\ *n* : an alloy used for lining bearings; *esp* : one containing tin, copper, and antimony

bab·ble \\'ba-bəl\ *vb* **bab·bled; bab·bling 1** : to talk enthusiastically or excessively **2** : to utter meaningless sounds — **babble** *n* — **bab·bler** \-b(ə-)lər\ *n*

babe \\'bāb\ *n* **1** : BABY **2** *slang* : GIRL, WOMAN

ba·bel \\'bā-bəl, 'ba-\ *n, often cap* [fr. the Tower of *Babel*, Gen 11:4–9] : a place or scene of noise and confusion; *also* : a confused sound **syn** hubbub, racket, din, uproar, clamor

ba·boon \ba-'bün\ *n* [ME *babewin*, fr. MF *babouin*, fr. *baboue* grimace] : any of several large apes of Asia and Africa with doglike muzzles

ba·bush·ka \bə-'büsh-kə, -'bùsh-\ *n* [Russ, grandmother, dim. of *baba* old woman] : a kerchief for the head

¹**ba·by** \\'bā-bē\ *n, pl* **babies 1** : a very young child : INFANT **2** : the youngest or smallest of a group **3** : a childish person — **baby** *adj* — **ba·by·hood** *n* — **ba·by·ish** *adj*

²**baby** *vb* **ba·bied; ba·by·ing** : to tend or treat often with excessive care

baby boom *n* : a marked rise in birthrate — **baby boom·er** \-'bü-mər\ *n*

baby's breath *n* : any of a genus of herbs that are related to the pinks and have small delicate flowers

ba·by-sit \\'bā-bē-ˌsit\ *vb* **-sat** \-ˌsat\; **-sit·ting** : to care for children usu. during a short absence of the parents — **ba·by-sit·ter** *n*

bac·ca·lau·re·ate \ˌba-kə-'lòr-ē-ət\ *n* **1** : the degree of bachelor conferred by colleges and universities **2** : a sermon delivered to a graduating class

bac·ca·rat \ˌbä-kə-'rä, ˌba-\ *n* : a card game played esp. in European casinos

bac·cha·nal \\'ba-kən-ᵊl, ˌba-kə-'nal, ˌbä-kə-'näl\ *n* **1** : ORGY **2** : REVELER

bac·cha·na·lia \ˌba-kə-'näl-yə\ *n, pl* **bacchanalia** : a drunken orgy — **bac·cha·na·lian** \-'näl-yən\ *adj or n*

bach·e·lor \\'ba-chə-lər\ *n* **1** : a person who has received the usu. lowest degree conferred by a 4-year college **2** : an unmarried man — **bach·e·lor·hood** *n*

bach·e·lor·ette \ˌba-chə-lə-'ret\ *n* : a young unmarried woman

bachelor's button *n* : a European plant related to the daisies and having blue, pink, or white flower heads

ba·cil·lus \bə-'si-ləs\ *n, pl* **-li** \-ˌlī\ [NL, fr. ML, small staff, dim. of L *baculus* staff] : any of numerous rod-shaped bacteria; *also* : a disease-producing bacterium — **bac·il·lary** \\'ba-sə-ˌler-ē\ *adj*

¹**back** \\'bak\ *n* **1** : the rear or dorsal part of the human body; *also* : the corresponding part of a lower animal **2** : the part or surface opposite the front **3** : a player in the backfield in football — **back·less** \-ləs\ *adj*

²**back** *adv* **1** : to, toward, or at the rear **2** : AGO **3** : so as to be restrained or retarded **4** : to, toward, or in a former place or state **5** : in return or reply

³**back** *adj* **1** : located at or in the back; *also* : REMOTE **2** : OVERDUE **3** : moving or operating backward **4** : not current

⁴**back** *vb* **1** : SUPPORT, UPHOLD **2** : to go or cause to go backward or in reverse **3** : to furnish with a back : form the back of

back·ache \\'ba-ˌkāk\ *n* : a pain in the lower back

back–bench·er \-'ben-chər\ *n* : a rank-and-file member of a British legislature

back·bite \\'bak-ˌbīt\ *vb* **-bit** \-ˌbit\; **-bit·ten** \-ˌbit-ᵊn\; **-bit·ing** \-ˌbī-tiŋ\ : to say mean or spiteful things about someone who is absent — **back·bit·er** *n*

back·board \-ˌbòrd\ *n* : a board placed at or serving as the back of something

back·bone \-ˌbōn\ *n* **1** : the bony column in the back of a vertebrate that is the chief support of the trunk and consists of a jointed series of vertebrae enclosing and protecting the spinal cord **2** : firm resolute character

back·drop \\'bak-ˌdräp\ *n* : a painted cloth hung across the rear of a stage

back·er \\'ba-kər\ *n* : one that supports

back·field \-ˌfēld\ *n* : the football players whose positions are behind the line

¹**back·fire** \-ˌfīr\ *n* : a loud noise caused by the improperly timed explosion of fuel in the cylinder of an internal combustion engine

²**backfire** *vb* **1** : to make or undergo a backfire **2** : to have a result opposite to what was intended

back·gam·mon \\'bak-ˌga-mən\ *n* : a game played with pieces on a double board in which the moves are determined by throwing dice

back·ground \\'bak-ˌgraund\ *n* **1** : the scenery behind something **2** : the setting within which something takes place; *also* : the sum of a person's experience, training, and understanding

back·hand \\'bak-ˌhand\ *n* : a stroke (as in tennis) made with the back of the hand turned in the direction of movement; *also* : the side on which such a stroke is made — **back·hand** *vb*

back·hand·ed \\'bak-'han-dəd\ *adj* **1** : INDIRECT, DEVIOUS; *esp* : SARCASTIC **2** : using or made with a backhand

back·hoe \\'bak-ˌhō\ *n* : an excavating machine having a bucket that is drawn toward the machine

back·ing \\'ba-kiŋ\ *n* **1** : something forming a back **2** : SUPPORT, AID; *also* : a body of supporters

back·lash \\'bak-ˌlash\ *n* **1** : a sudden violent backward

backhand

movement or reaction **2** : a strong adverse reaction

¹**back·log** \-ₗlȯg, -ₗläg\ *n* **1** : a large log at the back of a hearth fire **2** : an accumulation of tasks unperformed or materials not processed

²**backlog** *vb* : to accumulate in reserve

back of *prep* : BEHIND

back out *vb* : to withdraw esp. from a commitment or contest

¹**back·pack** \ˈbak-ₗpak\ *n* : a camping pack supported by an aluminum frame and carried on the back

²**backpack** *vb* : to hike with a backpack — **back·pack·er** *n*

back·ped·al \ˈbak-ₗped-ᵊl\ *vb* : RETREAT

back·rest \-ₗrest\ *n* : a rest for the back

back·side \-ₗsīd\ *n* : BUTTOCKS

back·slap \-ₗslap\ *vb* : to display excessive cordiality — **back·slap·per** *n*

back·slide \-ₗslīd\ *vb* **-slid** \-ₗslid\; **-slid** *or* **-slid·den** \-ₗslid-ᵊn\; **-slid·ing** \-ₗslī-diŋ\ : to lapse morally or in religious practice — **back·slid·er** *n*

back·spin \-ₗspin\ *n* : a backward rotary motion of a ball

¹**back·stage** \ˈbak-ₗstāj\ *adj* **1** : relating to or occurring in the area behind a stage **2** : of or relating to the private lives of theater people **3** : of or relating to the inner working or operation

²**back·stage** \ˈbak-ˈstāj\ *adv* **1** : in or to a backstage area **2** : SECRETLY

back·stairs \-ₗstarz\ *adj* : SECRET, FURTIVE; *also* : SORDID, SCANDALOUS

¹**back·stop** \-ₗstäp\ *n* : something serving as a stop behind something else; *esp* : a screen or fence to keep a ball from leaving the field of play

²**backstop** *vb* **1** : SUPPORT **2** : to serve as a backstop to

back·stretch \ˈbak-ˈstrech\ *n* : the side opposite the homestretch on a racecourse

back·stroke \-ₗstrōk\ *n* : a swimming stroke executed on the back

back talk *n* : impudent, insolent, or argumentative replies

back·track \ˈbak-ₗtrak\ *vb* **1** : to retrace one's course **2** : to reverse a position or stand

back·up \-ₗəp\ *n* : one that serves as a substitute or alternative

¹**back·ward** \ˈbak-wərd\ *or* **back·wards** \-wərdz\ *adv* **1** : toward the back **2** : with the back foremost **3** : in a reverse or contrary direction or way **4** : toward the past; *also* : toward a worse state

²**backward** *adj* **1** : directed, turned, or done backward **2** : DIFFIDENT, SHY **3** : retarded in development — **back·ward·ly** *adv* — **back·ward·ness** *n*

back·wash \ˈbak-ₗwȯsh, -ₗwäsh\ *n* : a backward flow or movement (as of water or air) produced by a propelling force (as the motion of oars)

back·wa·ter \-ₗwȯ-tər, -ₗwä-\ *n* **1** : water held or turned back in its course **2** : an isolated or backward place or condition

back·woods \-ˈwu̇dz\ *n pl* **1** : wooded or partly cleared areas far from cities **2** : a remote or isolated place

ba·con \ˈbā-kən\ *n* : salted and smoked meat from the sides or back of a pig

bacteria *pl of* BACTERIUM

bac·te·ri·cid·al \bak-ₗtir-ə-ˈsīd-ᵊl\ *adj* : destroying bacteria — **bac·te·ri·cide** \-ˈtir-ə-ₗsīd\ *n*

bac·te·ri·ol·o·gy \bak-ₗtir-ē-ˈä-lə-jē\ *n* **1** : a science dealing with bacteria **2** : bacterial life and phenomena — **bac·te·ri·o·log·ic** \-ᵊ-ˈlä-jik\ *or* **bac·te·ri·o·log·i·cal** \-ᵊ-ˈlä-ji-kəl\ *adj* — **bac·te·ri·ol·o·gist** \-ˈä-lə-jist\ *n*

bac·te·rio·phage \bak-ˈtir-ē-ə-ₗfāj\ *n* : any of various viruses that attack specific bacteria

bac·te·ri·um \bak-ˈtir-ē-əm\ *n, pl* **-ria** \-ē-ə\ [NL, fr. Gk *baktērion* staff] : any of a group of single-celled microorganisms including some that are disease producers and others that are valued esp. for their chemical effects (as fermentation) — **bac·te·ri·al** \-ē-əl\ *adj*

bad \ˈbad\ *adj* **worse** \ˈwərs\; **worst** \ˈwərst\ **1** : below standard : POOR; *also* : UNFAVORABLE ⟨a ∼ report⟩ **2** : SPOILED, DECAYED **3** : WICKED; *also* : not well-behaved : NAUGHTY **4** : DISAGREEABLE ⟨a ∼ taste⟩; *also* : HARMFUL **5** : DEFECTIVE, FAULTY ⟨∼ wiring⟩; *also* : not valid ⟨a ∼ check⟩ **6** : UNWELL, ILL **7** : SORRY, REGRETFUL **syn** evil, wrong, immoral, iniquitous — **bad·ly** *adv* — **bad·ness** *n*

bade *past and past part of* BID

badge \ˈbaj\ *n* : a device or token usu. worn as a sign of status

¹**bad·ger** \ˈba-jər\ *n* : any of several sturdy burrowing mammals with long claws on their forefeet

badger

²**badger** *vb* : to harass or annoy persistently

ba·di·nage \ₗbad-ᵊn-ˈäzh\ *n* [F] : playful talk back and forth : BANTER

bad·land \ˈbad-ₗland\ *n* : a region marked by intricate erosional sculpturing and scanty vegetation — usu. used in pl.

bad·min·ton \ˈbad-ₗmint-ᵊn\ *n* : a court game played with light rackets and a shuttlecock volleyed over a net

bad–mouth \ˈbad-ₗmau̇th\ *vb* : to criticize severely

Bae·de·ker \ˈbā-di-kər, ˈbe-\ *n* : GUIDEBOOK

¹**baf·fle** \ˈba-fəl\ *vb* **baf·fled; baf·fling** \-fə-liŋ\ : FRUSTRATE, THWART, FOIL; *also* : PERPLEX — **baf·fle·ment** *n*

²**baffle** *n* : a device (as a wall or screen) to deflect, check, or regulate flow (as of liquid or sound) — **baffled** \ˈba-fəld\ *adj*

¹**bag** \ˈbag\ *n* : a flexible usu. closable container (as for storing or carrying)

²**bag** *vb* **bagged; bag·ging 1** : DISTEND, BULGE **2** : to put in a bag **3** : to get possession of; *esp* : to take in hunting **syn** trap, snare, catch, capture, collar

ba·gasse \bə-ˈgas\ *n* [F] : plant residue (as of sugarcane) left after a product (as juice) has been extracted

bag·a·telle \ₗba-gə-ˈtel\ *n* [F] : TRIFLE

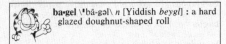

ba·gel \'bā-gəl\ *n* [Yiddish *beygl*] : a hard glazed doughnut-shaped roll

bag·gage \'ba-gij\ *n* **1** : the traveling bags and personal belongings of a traveler : LUGGAGE **2** : things that get in the way

bag·gy \'ba-gē\ *adj* **bag·gi·er; -est** : puffed out or hanging like a bag — **bag·gi·ly** \-gə-lē\ *adv* — **bag·gi·ness** \-gē-nəs\ *n*

bag·man \'bag-mən\ *n* : a person who collects or distributes illicitly gained money on behalf of another

ba·gnio \'ban-yō\ *n, pl* **bagnios** [It *bagno*, lit., public bath] : BROTHEL

bag of waters : a double-walled fluid-filled sac that encloses and protects the fetus in the womb and that breaks releasing its fluid during the process of birth

bag·pipe \'bag-ˌpīp\ *n* : a musical wind instrument consisting of a bag, a tube with valves, and sounding pipes — often used in pl.

ba·guette \ba-'get\ *n* [F, lit., rod] **1** : a gem having the shape of a narrow rectangle; *also* : the shape itself **2** : a long thin loaf of French bread

Ba·ha·mi·an \bə-'hä-mē-ən, -'hä-\ *n* : a native or inhabitant of the Bahama Islands

baht \'bät\ *n, pl* **baht** *also* **bahts** — see MONEY table

¹bail \'bāl\ *n* : a container for ladling water out of a boat

²bail *vb* : to dip and throw out water from a boat — **bail·er** *n*

³bail *n* : security given to guarantee a prisoner's appearance when legally required; *also* : one giving such security or the release secured

⁴bail *vb* : to release under bail; *also* : to procure the release of by giving bail — **bail·able** \'bā-lə-bəl\ *adj*

⁵bail *n* : the arched handle (as of a pail or kettle)

bai·liff \'bā-ləf\ *n* **1** : an aide of a British sheriff who serves writs and makes arrests; *also* : a minor officer of a U.S. court **2** : an estate or farm manager esp. in Britain : STEWARD

bai·li·wick \'bā-li-ˌwik\ *n* : one's special province or domain syn territory, field, sphere

bail·out \'bā-ˌlaůt\ *n* : a rescue from financial distress

bairn \'barn\ *n, chiefly Scot* : CHILD

¹bait \'bāt\ *vb* **1** : to persecute by continued attacks **2** : to harass with dogs usu. for sport ⟨~ a bear⟩ **3** : to furnish (as a hook) with bait **4** : ALLURE, ENTICE **5** : to give food and drink to (as an animal) syn badger, heckle, hound

²bait *n* **1** : a lure for catching animals (as fish) **2** : LURE, TEMPTATION syn snare, trap, decoy, come-on, enticement

bai·za \'bī-(ˌ)zä\ *n, pl* **baiza** *or* **baizas** — see *rial* at MONEY table

baize \'bāz\ *n* : a coarse feltlike fabric

¹bake \'bāk\ *vb* **baked; bak·ing 1** : to cook or become cooked in dry heat esp. in an oven **2** : to dry and harden by heat ⟨~ bricks⟩ — **bak·er** *n*

²bake *n* : a social gathering featuring baked food

baker's dozen *n* : THIRTEEN

bak·ery \'bā-k(ə-)rē\ *n, pl* **-er·ies** : a place for baking or selling baked goods

bake·shop \'bāk-ˌshäp\ *n* : BAKERY

baking powder *n* : a powder that consists of a carbonate, an acid, and a starch and that makes the dough rise in baking cakes and biscuits

baking soda *n* : SODIUM BICARBONATE

bak·sheesh \'bak-ˌshēsh\ *n* : payment (as a tip or bribe) to expedite service

bal *abbr* balance

bal·a·lai·ka \ˌba-lə-'lī-kə\ *n* : a triangular 3-stringed instrument of Russian origin played by plucking or strumming

¹bal·ance \'ba-ləns\ *n* [ME, fr. OF, fr. LL *bilanc-, bilanx* having two scalepans, fr. L *bi* two + *lanc-, lanx* plate] **1** : a weighing device : SCALE **2** : a weight, force, or influence counteracting the effect of another **3** : an oscillating wheel used to regulate a timepiece **4** : a state of equilibrium **5** : REMAINDER, REST; *esp* : an amount in excess esp. on the credit side of an account — **bal·anced** \-lənst\ *adj*

²balance *vb* **bal·anced; bal·anc·ing 1** : to compute the balance of an account **2** : to arrange so that one set of elements equals another; *also* : to equal or equalize in weight, number, or proportions **3** : WEIGH **4** : to bring or come to a state or position of balance; *also* : to bring into harmony or proportion

bal·boa \bal-'bō-ə\ *n* — see MONEY table

bal·brig·gan \bal-'bri-gən\ *n* : a knitted cotton fabric used esp. for underwear

bal·co·ny \'bal-kə-nē\ *n, pl* **-nies 1** : a platform projecting from the side of a building and enclosed by a railing **2** : a gallery inside a building

bald \'bȯld\ *adj* **1** : lacking a natural or usual covering (as of hair) **2** : UNADORNED, PLAIN syn bare, barren, naked, nude — **bald·ly** *adv* — **bald·ness** *n*

bal·da·chin \'bȯl-də-kən, 'bal-\ *or* **bal·da·chi·no** \ˌbal-də-'kē-nō\ *n, pl* **-chins** *or* **-chinos** : a canopylike structure over an altar

bald cypress *n* : either of two large swamp trees of the southern U.S. with hard red wood

bald eagle *n* : an eagle of No. America that when mature has white head and neck feathers and a white tail

bal·der·dash \'bȯl-dər-ˌdash\ *n* : NONSENSE

bald·ing \'bȯl-diŋ\ *adj* : getting bald

bal·dric \'bȯl-drik\ *n* : a belt worn over the shoulder to carry a sword or bugle

¹bale \'bāl\ *n* : a large or closely packed bundle

²bale *vb* **baled; bal·ing** : to pack in a bale — **bal·er** *n*

ba·leen \bə-'lēn\ *n* : a horny substance attached in plates to the upper jaw of some large whales (**baleen whales**)

bale·ful \'bāl-fəl\ *adj* : DEADLY, HARMFUL; *also* : OMINOUS syn sinister, malefic, maleficent, malign

¹balk \'bȯk\ *n* **1** : HINDRANCE, CHECK, SETBACK **2** : an illegal motion of the pitcher in baseball while in position

²balk *vb* **1** : BLOCK, THWART **2** : to stop short and refuse

to go on **3** : to commit a balk in sports **syn** frustrate, baffle, foil, thwart — **balky** \'bȯ-kē\ *adj*

¹ball \'bȯl\ *n* **1** : a rounded body or mass (as at the base of the thumb or for use as a missile or in a game) **2** : a game played with a ball **3** : a pitched baseball that misses the strike zone and is not swung at by the batter **4** : a hit or thrown ball in various games ⟨foul ∼⟩ — **on the ball** : COMPETENT, KNOWLEDGEABLE, ALERT

²ball *vb* : to form into a ball

³ball *n* : a large formal dance

bal·lad \'ba-ləd\ *n* **1** : a narrative poem of strongly marked rhythm suitable for singing **2** : a simple song : AIR **3** : a slow romantic song

bal·lad·eer \ba-lə-'dir\ *n* : a singer of ballads

¹bal·last \'ba-ləst\ *n* **1** : heavy material used to stabilize a ship or control a balloon's ascent **2** : crushed stone laid in a railroad bed or used in making concrete

²ballast *vb* : to provide with ballast **syn** balance, stabilize, steady

ball bearing *n* : a bearing in which the revolving part turns upon steel balls that roll easily in a groove; *also* : one of the balls in such a bearing

ball·car·ri·er \'bȯl-ˌkar-ē-ər\ *n* : the football player carrying the ball in an offensive play

bal·le·ri·na \ˌba-lə-'rē-nə\ *n* : a female ballet dancer

bal·let \'ba-ˌlā, ba-'lā\ *n* **1** : dancing in which fixed poses and steps are combined with light flowing movements often to convey a story; *also* : a theatrical art form using ballet dancing **2** : a company of ballet dancers

bal·let·o·mane \ba-'le-tə-ˌmān\ *n* : a devotee of ballet

bal·lis·tic missile \bə-'lis-tik-\ *n* : a missile that is guided during ascent and that falls freely during descent

bal·lis·tics \-tiks\ *n sing or pl* **1** : the science of the motion of projectiles (as bullets) in flight **2** : the flight characteristics of a projectile — **ballistic** *adj*

ball of fire : an unusually energetic person

¹bal·loon \bə-'lün\ *n* **1** : a bag filled with gas or heated air so as to rise and float in the atmosphere **2** : a toy consisting of an inflatable bag — **bal·loon·ist** *n*

²balloon *vb* **1** : to swell or puff out **2** : to travel in a balloon **3** : to increase rapidly

¹bal·lot \'ba-lət\ *n* [It *ballotta* small ball used in secret voting, fr. It dial., dim. of *balla* ball] **1** : a piece of paper used to cast a vote **2** : the action or a system of voting; *also* : the right to vote

²ballot *vb* : to decide by ballot : VOTE

¹ball·park \'bȯl-ˌpark\ *n* : a park in which ball games are played

²ballpark *adj* : approximately correct ⟨∼ estimate⟩

ball·point \'bȯl-ˌpȯint\ *n* : a pen whose writing point is a small rotating metal ball that inks itself from an inner container

ball·room \'bȯl-ˌrüm, -ˌrùm\ *n* : a large room for dances

bal·ly·hoo \'ba-lē-ˌhü\ *n, pl* **-hoos** : extravagant statements and claims made for publicity — **ballyhoo** *vb*

balm \'bäm, 'bälm\ *n* **1** : a fragrant healing or soothing lotion or ointment **2** : any of several spicy fragrant herbs of the mint family **3** : something that comforts or soothes

balmy \'bä-mē, 'bäl-\ *adj* **balm·i·er; -est** **1** : gently soothing : MILD **2** : FOOLISH, ABSURD **syn** soft, bland, mild, gentle — **balm·i·ness** *n*

ba·lo·ney \bə-'lō-nē\ *n* : NONSENSE

bal·sa \'bȯl-sə\ *n* : the extremely light strong wood of a tropical American tree; *also* : the tree

bal·sam \'bȯl-səm\ *n* **1** : a fragrant aromatic and usu. resinous substance oozing from various plants; *also* : a preparation containing or smelling like balsam **2** : a balsam-yielding tree (as balsam fir) **3** : a common garden ornamental plant — **bal·sam·ic** \bȯl-'sa-mik\ *adj*

balsam fir *n* : a resinous American evergreen tree that is widely used for pulpwood and as a Christmas tree

Bal·ti·more oriole \'bȯl-tə-ˌmȯr-\ *n* : a common American oriole in which the male is brightly colored with orange, black, and white

bal·us·ter \'ba-lə-stər\ *n* [F *balustre*, fr. It *balaustro*, fr. *balaustra* wild pomegranate flower, fr. L *balaustium;* fr. its shape] : an upright support for a rail (as of a staircase)

bal·us·trade \'ba-lə-ˌstrād\ *n* : a row of balusters topped by a rail

bam·boo \bam-'bü\ *n, pl* **bamboos** : any of various woody mostly tall tropical grasses including some with strong hollow stems used for building, furniture, or utensils

bamboo curtain *n, often cap B&C* : a political, military, and ideological barrier in the Orient

bam·boo·zle \bam-'bü-zəl\ *vb* **-boo·zled; -boo·zling** : TRICK, HOODWINK

¹ban \'ban\ *vb* **banned; ban·ning** : PROHIBIT, FORBID

²ban *n* **1** : CURSE **2** : a legal or formal prohibiting

³ban \'bän\ *n, pl* **ba·ni** \'bä-nē\ — see *leu* at MONEY table

ba·nal \bə-'näl, -'nal; 'bān-ᵊl\ *adj* [F] : COMMONPLACE, TRITE — **ba·nal·i·ty** \bā-'na-lə-tē\ *n*

ba·nana \bə-'na-nə\ *n* : a treelike tropical plant bearing thick clusters of yellow or reddish finger-shaped fruit; *also* : this fruit

¹band \'band\ *n* **1** : something that binds, ties, or goes around **2** : a strip or stripe that can be distinguished (as by color or texture) from nearby matter **3** : a range of wavelengths (as in radio)

²band *vb* **1** : to tie up, finish, or enclose with a band **2** : to gather together or unite esp. for some common end — **band·er** *n*

³band *n* : a group of persons, animals, or things; *esp* : a group of musicians organized for playing together

¹ban·dage \'ban-dij\ *n* : a strip of material used esp. in dressing wounds

²bandage *vb* **ban·daged; ban·dag·ing** : to dress or cover with a bandage

ban·dan·na *or* **ban·dana** \ban-'da-nə\ *n* : a large colored figured handkerchief

B and B *abbr* bed-and-breakfast

band·box \'band-ˌbäks\ *n* : a usu. cylindrical box for carrying clothing

band·ed \'ban-dəd\ *adj* : having or marked with bands

ban·de·role *or* **ban·de·rol** \'ban-də-ˌrōl\ *n* : a long narrow forked flag or streamer

ban·dit \'ban-dət\ *n* [It *bandito*, fr. *bandire* to banish] 1 *pl also* **ban·dit·ti** \ban-'di-tē\ : an outlaw who lives by plunder; *esp* : a member of a band of marauders 2 : ROBBER — **ban·dit·ry** \'ban-də-trē\ *n*

ban·do·lier *or* **ban·do·leer** \ˌban-də-'lir\ *n* : a belt slung over the shoulder esp. to carry ammunition

band saw *n* : a saw in the form of an endless steel belt running over pulleys

band·stand \'band-ˌstand\ *n* : a usu. roofed platform on which a band or orchestra performs outdoors

b and w *abbr* black and white

band·wag·on \'band-ˌwa-gən\ *n* 1 : a wagon carrying musicians in a parade 2 : a movement that attracts growing support

¹**ban·dy** \'ban-dē\ *vb* **ban·died; ban·dy·ing** 1 : to exchange (as blows or quips) esp. in rapid succession 2 : to use in a glib or offhand way

²**bandy** *adj* : curved outward 〈~ legs〉

bane \'bān\ *n* 1 : POISON 2 : WOE, HARM; *also* : a source of this — **bane·ful** *adj*

¹**bang** \'baŋ\ *vb* 1 : BUMP (fell and ~ed his knee) 2 : to strike, thrust, or move usu. with a loud noise

²**bang** *n* 1 : a resounding blow 2 : a sudden loud noise

³**bang** *adv* : DIRECTLY, RIGHT

⁴**bang** *n* : a fringe of hair cut short (as across the forehead) — usu. used in pl.

⁵**bang** *vb* : to cut a bang in

Ban·gla·deshi \ˌbäŋ-glə-'de-shē\ *n* : a native or inhabitant of Bangladesh — **Bangladeshi** *adj*

ban·gle \'baŋ-gəl\ *n* : BRACELET; *also* : a loose‑hanging ornament

bang–up \'baŋ-ˌəp\ *adj* : FIRST-RATE, EXCELLENT (a ~ job)

bani *pl of* ³BAN

ban·ish \'ba-nish\ *vb* 1 : to require by authority to leave a country 2 : to drive out : EXPEL **syn** exile, ostracize, deport, relegate — **ban·ish·ment** *n*

ban·is·ter \'ba-nə-stər\ *n* 1 : BALUSTER 2 : a handrail with its supporting posts 3 : HANDRAIL

ban·jo \'ban-ˌjō\ *n, pl* **banjos** *also* **banjoes** : a musical instrument with a long neck, a drumlike body, and usu. five strings — **ban·jo·ist** \-ist\ *n*

¹**bank** \'baŋk\ *n* 1 : a piled-up mass (as of cloud or earth) 2 : an undersea elevation 3 : rising ground bordering a lake, river, or sea 4 : the sideways slope of a surface along a curve or of a vehicle as it rounds a curve

²**bank** *vb* 1 : to form a bank about 2 : to cover (as a fire) with fuel to keep inactive 3 : to build (a curve) with the roadbed or track inclined laterally upward from the inside edge 4 : to pile or heap in a bank; *also* : to arrange in a tier 5 : to incline (an airplane) laterally

³**bank** *n* [ME, fr. MF or It; MF *banque*, fr. It *banca*, lit., bench] 1 : an establishment concerned esp. with the custody, loan, exchange, or issue of money, the extension of credit, and the transmission of funds 2 : a stock of or a place for holding something in reserve 〈a blood ~〉

⁴**bank** *vb* 1 : to conduct the business of a bank 2 : to deposit money or have an account in a bank — **bank·er** *n* — **bank·ing** *n*

⁵**bank** *n* : a group of objects arranged close together (as in a row or tier) 〈a ~ of file drawers〉

bank·book \'baŋk-ˌbùk\ *n* : the depositor's book in which a bank records deposits and withdrawals

bank·card \-ˌkärd\ *n* : a credit card issued by a bank

bank·note \-ˌnōt\ *n* : a promissory note issued by a bank and circulating as money

bank·roll \-ˌrōl\ *n* : supply of money : FUNDS

¹**bank·rupt** \'baŋ-(ˌ)krəpt\ *n* : an insolvent person; *esp* : one whose property is turned over by court action to a trustee to be handled for the benefit of his creditors — **bankrupt** *vb*

²**bankrupt** *adj* 1 : reduced to financial ruin; *esp* : legally declared a bankrupt 2 : wholly lacking in or deprived of some essential (morally ~) — **bank·rupt·cy** \'baŋ-(ˌ)krəpt-sē\ *n*

¹**ban·ner** \'ba-nər\ *n* 1 : a piece of cloth attached to a staff and used by a leader as his standard 2 : FLAG

²**banner** *adj* : distinguished from all others esp. in excellence 〈a ~ year〉

ban·nock \'ba-nək\ *n* : a flat oatmeal or barley cake usu. cooked on a griddle

banns \'banz\ *n pl* : public announcement esp. in church of a proposed marriage

ban·quet \'baŋ-kwət\ *n* [MF, fr. It *banchetto*, fr. dim. of *banca* bench, bank] : a ceremonial dinner — **banquet** *vb*

ban·quette \baŋ-'ket\ *n* : a long upholstered bench esp. along a wall

ban·shee \'ban-shē\ *n* [Ir *bean sídhe* & ScGael *bean sith*, lit., woman of fairyland] : a female spirit in Gaelic folklore whose wailing warns a family that one of them will soon die

ban·tam \'ban-təm\ *n* 1 : any of numerous small domestic fowls that are often miniatures of standard breeds 2 : a small but pugnacious person

¹**ban·ter** \'ban-tər\ *vb* : to speak to in a witty and teasing manner

²**banter** *n* : good-natured witty joking

Ban·tu \'ban-ˌtü\ *n, pl* **Bantu** *or* **Bantus** 1 : a member of a group of African peoples of central and southern Africa 2 : a group of African languages spoken by the Bantu

Ban·tu·stan \ˌban-tù-'stan, ˌbän-tù-'stän\ *n* : an all‑black enclave in the Republic of So. Africa with a limited degree of self-government

ban·yan \'ban-yən\ *n* [earlier *banyan* Hindu merchant, fr. Hindi *baniyā;* fr. a merchant's pagoda erected under a tree of the species in Iran] : a large East Indian tree whose aerial roots grow downward to the ground and form new trunks

banyan

ban·zai \bän-'zī\ *n* : a Japanese cheer or cry of triumph

bao·bab \'baù-ə-ˌbab, 'bā-ə-\ *n* : an Old World tropical tree with short swollen trunk and sour edible gourd-like fruits

bap·tism \'bap-ˌti-zəm\ *n* 1 : a Christian sacrament signifying spiritual rebirth and symbolized by the ritual use of water 2 : an act of baptizing — **bap·tis·mal** \bap-'tiz-məl\ *adj*

baptismal name *n* : GIVEN NAME

Bap·tist \'bap-tist\ *n* : a member of any of several Protestant denominations emphasizing baptism by immersion of believers only

bap·tis·tery *or* **bap·tis·try** \'bap-tə-strē\ *n, pl* **-ter·ies** *or* **-tries** : a place esp. in a church used for baptism

bap·tize \bap-'tīz, 'bap-ˌtīz\ *vb* **bap·tized; bap·tiz·ing** [ME, fr. OF *baptiser*, fr. L *baptizare*, fr. Gk *baptizein* to dip, baptize, fr. *baptein* to dip] 1 : to administer baptism to; *also* : CHRISTEN 2 : to purify esp. by an ordeal

© 1997 PAWS, INC./Distributed by Universal Press Syndicate

¹**bar** \'bär\ *n* **1** : a long narrow piece of material (as wood or metal) used esp. for a lever, fastening, or support **2** : BARRIER, OBSTACLE **3** : the railing in a law court at which prisoners are stationed; *also* : the legal profession or the whole body of lawyers **4** : a stripe, band, or line much longer than wide **5** : a counter at which food or esp. drink is served; *also* : BARROOM **6** : a vertical line across the musical staff

²**bar** *vb* **barred; bar•ring 1** : to fasten, confine, or obstruct with or as if with a bar or bars **2** : to mark with bars : STRIPE **3** : to shut or keep out : EXCLUDE **4** : FORBID, PREVENT

³**bar** *prep* : EXCEPT

⁴**bar** *abbr* barometer; barometric

Bar *abbr* Baruch

barb \'bärb\ *n* **1** : a sharp projection extending backward (as from the point of an arrow) **2** : a biting critical remark — **barbed** \'bärbd\ *adj*

bar•bar•ian \bär-'ber-ē-ən\ *adj* **1** : of, relating to, or being a land, culture, or people alien to and usu. believed to be inferior to another's **2** : lacking refinement, learning, or artistic or literary culture — **barbarian** *n*

> **bar•bar•ic** \bär-'bar-ik\ *adj* **1** : BARBARIAN **2** : marked by a lack of restraint : WILD **3** : PRIMITIVE, UNSOPHISTICATED

bar•ba•rism \'bär-bə-ɹri-zəm\ *n* **1** : the social condition of barbarians; *also* : the use or display of barbarian or barbarous acts, attitudes, or ideas **2** : a word or expression that offends standards of correctness or purity

bar•ba•rous \'bär-bə-rəs\ *adj* **1** : lacking culture or refinement **2** : using linguistic barbarisms **3** : mercilessly harsh or cruel — **bar•bar•i•ty** \bär-'bar-ə-tē\ *n* — **bar•ba•rous•ly** *adv*

¹**bar•be•cue** \'bär-bi-ɹkyü\ *n* : a social gathering at which barbecued food is served

²**barbecue** *vb* **-cued; -cu•ing 1** : to cook over hot coals or on a revolving spit **2** : to cook in a highly seasoned vinegar sauce

bar•bell \'bär-ɹbel\ *n* : a bar with adjustable weights attached to each end used for exercise and in weight-lifting competition

bar•ber \'bär-bər\ *n* [ME, fr. MF *barbeor*, fr. *barbe* beard, fr. L *barba*] : one whose business is cutting and dressing hair and shaving and trimming beards

bar•ber•ry \'bär-ɹber-ē\ *n* : any of a genus of spiny shrubs bearing yellow flowers and oblong red berries

bar•bi•tu•rate \bär-'bi-chə-rət\ *n* : any of various compounds (as a salt or ester) formed from an organic acid (**bar•bi•tu•ric acid** \ˌbär-bə-'tür-ik-, -'tyür-\); *esp* : one used as a sedative or hypnotic

bar•ca•role *or* **bar•ca•rolle** \'bär-kə-ɹrōl\ *n* : a Venetian boat song characterized by a beat suggesting a rowing rhythm; *also* : a piece of music imitating this

bar chart *n* : BAR GRAPH

bar code *n* : a set of printed and variously spaced bars

and sometimes numerals that is designed to be scanned to identify the object it labels

bard \'bärd\ *n* : POET

¹**bare** \'bar\ *adj* **bar•er; bar•est 1** : NAKED **2** : UNCONCEALED, EXPOSED **3** : EMPTY **4** : leaving nothing to spare : MERE **5** : PLAIN, UNADORNED **syn** nude, bald — **bare•ness** *n*

²**bare** *vb* **bared; bar•ing** : to make or lay bare : UNCOVER

bare•back \-ɹbak\ *or* **bare•backed** \-'bakt\ *adv or adj* : without a saddle

bare•faced \-'fāst\ *adj* **1** : having the face uncovered; *esp* : BEARDLESS **2** : not concealed : OPEN — **bare•faced•ly** \-'fā-səd-lē, -'fāst-lē\ *adv*

bare•foot \-ɹfüt\ *or* **bare•foot•ed** \-'fü-təd\ *adv or adj* : with bare feet

bare–hand•ed \-'han-dəd\ *adv or adj* **1** : without gloves **2** : without tools or weapons

bare•head•ed \-'he-dəd\ *adv or adj* : without a hat

bare•ly \'bar-lē\ *adv* **1** : PLAINLY, MEAGERLY **2** : by a narrow margin : only just ⟨~ enough money⟩

bar•fly \'bär-ɹflī\ *n* : a drinker who frequents bars

¹**bar•gain** \'bär-gən\ *n* **1** : AGREEMENT **2** : an advantageous purchase **3** : a transaction, situation, or event regarded in the light of its results

²**bargain** *vb* **1** : to negotiate over the terms of an agreement; *also* : to come to terms **2** : BARTER

bar•gain–base•ment \'bär-gən-'bās-mənt\ *adj* : markedly inexpensive

¹**barge** \'bärj\ *n* **1** : a broad flat-bottomed boat usu. moved by towing **2** : a motorboat supplied to a flagship (as for an admiral) **3** : a ceremonial boat elegantly furnished — **barge•man** \-mən\ *n*

²**barge** *vb* **barged; barg•ing 1** : to carry by barge **2** : to move or thrust oneself clumsily or rudely

bar graph *n* : a graphic technique for comparing amounts by rectangles whose lengths are proportional to the amounts they represent

bari•tone \'bar-ə-ɹtōn\ *n* [F *baryton* or It *baritono*, fr. Gk *barytonos* deep sounding, fr. *barys* heavy + *tonos* tone] : a male voice between bass and tenor; *also* : a man with such a voice

bar•i•um \'bar-ē-əm\ *n* : a silver-white metallic chemical element that occurs only in combination — see ELEMENT table

¹**bark** \'bärk\ *vb* **1** : to make the short loud cry of a dog **2** : to speak or utter in a curt loud tone : SNAP

²**bark** *n* : the sound made by a barking dog

³**bark** *n* : the tough corky outer covering of a woody stem or root

⁴**bark** *vb* **1** : to strip the bark from **2** : to rub the skin from : ABRADE

⁵**bark** *n* : a ship of three or more masts with the aft mast fore-and-aft rigged and the others square-rigged

bar•keep \'bär-ɹkēp\ *also* **bar•keep•er** \-ɹkē-pər\ *n* : BARTENDER

bark•er \'bär-kər\ *n* : a person who stands at the entrance esp. to a show and tries to attract customers to it

bar·ley \'bär-lē\ *n* : a cereal grass with seeds used as food and in making malt liquors; *also* : its seed

bar mitz·vah \bär-'mits-və\ *n, often cap B&M* [Heb *bar miṣwāh*, lit., son of the (divine) law] **1** : a Jewish boy who at about 13 years of age assumes religious responsibilities **2** : the ceremony recognizing a boy as a bar mitzvah

barn \'bärn\ *n* [ME *bern*, fr. OE *bereærn*, fr. *bere* barley + *ærn* house, store] : a building used esp. for storing hay and grain and for housing livestock or farm equipment

bar·na·cle \'bär-ni-kəl\ *n* : any of numerous small marine crustaceans free-swimming when young but permanently fixed (as to rocks, whales, or ships) when adult

barn·storm \'bärn-ıstòrm\ *vb* : to travel through the country making brief stops to entertain (as with shows or flying stunts) or to campaign for political office

barn·yard \-ıyärd\ *n* : a usu. fenced area adjoining a barn

baro·graph \'bar-ə-ıgraf\ *n* : a recording barometer

ba·rom·e·ter \bə-'räm-ə-tər\ *n* : an instrument for measuring atmospheric pressure — **baro·met·ric** \ıbar-ə-'me-trik\ *adj*

bar·on \'bar-ən\ *n* : a member of the lowest grade of the British peerage — **ba·ro·ni·al** \bə-'rō-nē-əl\ *adj* — **bar·ony** \'bar-ə-nē\ *n*

bar·on·age \'bar-ə-nij\ *n* : PEERAGE

bar·on·ess \'bar-ə-nəs\ *n* **1** : the wife or widow of a baron **2** : a woman holding a baronial title in her own right

bar·on·et \'bar-ə-nət\ *n* : a man holding a rank of honor below a baron but above a knight — **bar·on·et·cy** \-sē\ *n*

ba·roque \bə-'rōk, -'räk\ *adj* : marked by the use of complex forms, bold ornamentation, and the juxtapositioning of contrasting elements

ba·rouche \bə-'rüsh\ *n* [G *Barutsche*, fr. It *biroccio*, ultim. fr. LL *birotus* two-wheeled, fr. L *bi* two + *rota* wheel] : a 4-wheeled carriage with a high driver's seat in front and a folding top

bar·racks \'bar-əks\ *n sing or pl* : a building or group of buildings for lodging soldiers

bar·ra·cu·da \ıbar-ə-'kü-də\ *n, pl* **-da** *or* **-das** : any of several large predaceous sea fishes including some used for food

bar·rage \bə-'räzh, -'räj\ *n* : a heavy concentration of fire (as of artillery)

barred \'bärd\ *adj* : STRIPED

¹**bar·rel** \'bar-əl\ *n* **1** : a round bulging cask with flat ends of equal diameter **2** : the amount contained in a barrel **3** : a cylindrical or tubular part ⟨gun ∼⟩ — **bar·reled** \-əld\ *adj*

²**barrel** *vb* **-reled** *or* **-relled; -rel·ing** *or* **-rel·ling 1** : to pack in a barrel **2** : to travel at high speed

bar·rel·head \-ıhed\ *n* : the flat end of a barrel — **on the barrelhead** : asking for or granting no credit ⟨paid cash *on the barrelhead*⟩

barrel roll *n* : an airplane maneuver in which a complete revolution about the longitudinal axis is made

¹**bar·ren** \'bar-ən\ *adj* **1** : STERILE, UNFRUITFUL **2** : unproductive of results ⟨a ∼ scheme⟩ **3** : lacking interest or charm **4** : DULL, STUPID — **bar·ren·ness** \-nəs\ *n*

²**barren** *n* : a tract of barren land

bar·rette \bä-'ret, bə-\ *n* : a clasp or bar for holding the hair in place

¹**bar·ri·cade** \'bar-ə-ıkād, ıbar-ə-'kād\ *vb* **-cad·ed; -cad·ing** : to block, obstruct, or fortify with a barricade

²**barricade** *n* [F, fr. MF, fr. *barriquer* to barricade, fr. *barrique* barrel] **1** : a hastily thrown-up obstruction or fortification **2** : BARRIER, OBSTACLE

bar·ri·er \'bar-ē-ər\ *n* : something that separates, demarcates, or serves as a barricade ⟨racial ∼s⟩

barrier island *n* : a long broad sandy island lying parallel to a shore

barrier reef *n* : a coral reef roughly parallel to a shore and separated from it by a lagoon

bar·ring \'bar-iŋ\ *prep* : excluding by exception : EXCEPTING

bar·rio \'bär-ē-ıō, 'bar-\ *n, pl* **-ri·os 1** : a district of a city or town in a Spanish-speaking country **2** : a Spanish-speaking quarter in a U.S. city

bar·ris·ter \'bar-ə-stər\ *n* : a British counselor admitted to plead in the higher courts

bar·room \'bär-ırüm, -ırùm\ *n* : a room or establishment whose main feature is a bar for the sale of liquor

¹**bar·row** \'bar-ō\ *n* : a large burial mound of earth and stones

²**barrow** *n* **1** : WHEELBARROW **2** : a cart with a boxlike body and two shafts for pushing it

Bart *abbr* baronet

bar·tend·er \'bär-ıten-dər\ *n* : one that serves liquor at a bar

bar·ter \'bär-tər\ *vb* : to trade by exchange of goods — **barter** *n* — **bar·ter·er** *n*

Ba·ruch \'bär-ıük, bə-'rük\ *n* — see BIBLE table

bas·al \'bā-səl\ *adj* **1** : situated at or forming the base **2** : BASIC

basal metabolism *n* : the turnover of energy in a fasting and resting organism using energy solely to maintain vital cellular activity, respiration, and circulation as measured by the rate at which heat is given off

ba·salt \bə-'sòlt, 'bā-ısòlt\ *n* : a dark fine-grained igneous rock — **ba·sal·tic** \bə-'sòl-tik\ *adj*

¹**base** \'bās\ *n, pl* **bas·es 1** : BOTTOM, FOUNDATION **2** : a side or face on which a geometrical figure stands; *also* : the length of a base **3** : a main ingredient or fundamental part **4** : the point of beginning an act or operation **5** : a place on which a force depends for supplies **6** : a number (as 5 in 5⁷) that is raised to a power; *esp* : a number that when raised to a power equal to the logarithm of a number yields the number itself (the logarithm of 100 to ∼ 10 is 2 since $10^2 =$ 100) **7** : the number of units in a given digit's place of a number system that is required to give the numeral 1 in the next higher place (the decimal system uses a ∼ of 10); *also* : such a system using an indicated base ⟨convert from ∼ 10 to ∼ 2⟩ **8** : any of the four stations at the corners of a baseball diamond **9** : a chemical compound (as lime or ammonia) that reacts with an acid to form a salt, has a bitter taste, and turns litmus blue **syn** basis, ground, groundwork, footing, foundation — **base·man** \'bās-mən\ *n*

²**base** *vb* **based; bas·ing 1** : to form or serve as a base for **2** : ESTABLISH

³**base** *adj* **1** : of inferior quality : DEBASED, ALLOYED **2** : CONTEMPTIBLE, IGNOBLE **3** : MENIAL, DEGRADING **4** : of little value **syn** low, vile, despicable, wretched — **base·ly** *adv* — **base·ness** *n*

base·ball \'bās-ıbòl\ *n* : a game played with a bat and ball by two teams on a field with four bases arranged in a diamond; *also* : the ball used in this game

base·board \-ıbòrd\ *n* : a line of boards or molding covering the joint of a wall and the adjoining floor

base·born \-'bòrn\ *adj* **1** : MEAN, IGNOBLE **2** : of humble birth **3** : of illegitimate birth

base exchange *n* : a post exchange at a naval or air force base

base hit *n* : a hit in baseball that enables the batter to reach base safely with no error made and no base runner forced out

base·less \-ləs\ *adj* : having no base or basis : GROUNDLESS

base·line \'bās-ılīn\ *n* **1** : a line serving as a basis esp. to calculate or locate something **2** : the area within which a baseball player must keep when running between bases

base·ment \-mənt\ *n* **1** : the part of a building that is

wholly or partly below ground level **2** : the lowest or fundamental part of something

base on balls : an advance to first base given to a baseball player who receives four balls

base runner *n* : a baseball player who is on base or is attempting to reach a base

¹**bash** \\'bash\ *vb* **1** : to strike violently : HIT **2** : to smash by a blow **3** : to attack physically or verbally

²**bash** *n* **1** : a heavy blow **2** : a festive social gathering : PARTY

bash·ful \\'bash-fəl\ *adj* : inclined to shrink from public attention — **bash·ful·ness** *n*

ba·sic \\'bā-sik\ *adj* **1** : of, relating to, or forming the base or essence : FUNDAMENTAL **2** : of, relating to, or having the character of a chemical base **syn** underlying, basal, primary — **ba·sic·i·ty** \bā-'si-sə-tē\ *n*

BA·SIC \\'bā-sik\ *n* [*B*eginner's *A*ll-purpose *S*ymbolic *I*nstruction *C*ode] : a simplified language for programming a computer

ba·si·cal·ly \\'bā-si-k(ə-)lē\ *adv* **1** : at a basic level **2** : for the most part **3** : in a basic manner

ba·sil \\'bā-zəl, 'ba-, -səl\ *n* : any of several mints with fragrant leaves used in cooking

ba·sil·i·ca \bə-'si-li-kə, -'zi-\ *n* [L, fr. Gk *basilikē*, fr. fem. of *basilikos* royal, fr. *basileus* king] **1** : an early Christian church building consisting of nave and aisles with clerestory and apse **2** : a Roman Catholic church given ceremonial privileges

ba·si·lisk \\'ba-sə-ˌlisk, 'ba-zə-\ *n* [ME, fr. L *basiliscus*, fr. Gk *basiliskos*, fr. dim. of *basileus* king] : a legendary reptile with fatal breath and glance

ba·sin \\'bās-ᵊn\ *n* **1** : an open usu. circular vessel with sloping sides for holding liquid (as water) **2** : a hollow or enclosed place containing water; *also* : the region drained by a river

ba·sis \\'bā-səs\ *n, pl* **ba·ses** \-ˌsēz\ **1** : FOUNDATION, BASE **2** : a fundamental principle

bask \\'bask\ *vb* **1** : to expose oneself to comfortable heat **2** : to enjoy something warmly comforting ⟨~*ing* in his friends' admiration⟩

bas·ket \\'bas-kət\ *n* : a container made of woven material (as twigs or grasses); *also* : any of various lightweight usu. wood containers — **bas·ket·ful** *n*

bas·ket·ball \-ˌbȯl\ *n* : a game played on a court by two teams who try to throw an inflated ball through a raised goal; *also* : the ball used in this game

basket case *n* **1** : a person who has all four limbs amputated **2** : one that is totally incapacitated or inoperative

basket weave *n* : a textile weave resembling the checkered pattern of a plaited basket

bas mitz·vah \bäs-'mits-və\ *n, often cap B&M* [Heb *bath miswāh*, lit., daughter of the (divine) law] **1** : a Jewish girl who at about 13 years of age assumes religious responsibilities **2** : the ceremony recognizing a girl as a bas mitzvah

Basque \\'bask\ *n* **1** : a member of a people inhabiting a region bordering on the Bay of Biscay in northern

Spain and southwestern France **2** : the language of the Basque people — **Basque** *adj*

bas–re·lief \ˌbä-ri-'lēf\ *n* [F] : a sculpture in relief with the design raised very slightly from the background

¹**bass** \\'bas\ *n, pl* **bass** *or* **bass·es** : any of numerous sport and food bony fishes (as a striped bass)

²**bass** \\'bās\ *adj* : of low pitch

³**bass** \\'bās\ *n* **1** : a deep sound or tone **2** : the lower half of the musical pitch range **3** : the lowest part in a 4-part chorus; *also* : a singer having this voice or part

bas·set hound \\'ba-sət-\ *n* : any of an old breed of short-legged hunting dogs of French origin having long ears and crooked front legs

bas·si·net \ˌba-sə-'net\ *n* : a baby's bed that resembles a basket and often has a hood over one end

bas·so \\'ba-sō, 'bä-\ *n, pl* **bassos** *or* **bas·si** \\'bä-ˌsē\ [It] : a bass singer

bas·soon \bə-'sün\ *n* : a musical wind instrument lower in pitch than the oboe

bass·wood \\'bas-ˌwu̇d\ *n* : any of several New World lindens or their wood

bast \\'bast\ *n* : BAST FIBER

¹**bas·tard** \\'bas-tərd\ *n* **1** : an illegitimate child **2** : an offensive or disagreeable person

²**bastard** *adj* **1** : ILLEGITIMATE **2** : of an inferior or nontypical kind, size, or form; *also* : SPURIOUS — **bastardy** *n*

bas·tard·ise *Brit var of* BASTARDIZE

bas·tard·ize \\'bas-tər-ˌdīz\ *vb* **-ized; -iz·ing** : to reduce from a higher to a lower state : DEBASE

¹**baste** \\'bāst\ *vb* **bast·ed; bast·ing** : to sew with long stitches so as to keep temporarily in place

²**baste** *vb* **bast·ed; bast·ing** : to moisten (as meat) at intervals with liquid while cooking

bast fiber *n* : a strong woody plant fiber obtained chiefly from phloem and used esp. in making ropes

bas·ti·na·do \ˌbas-tə-'nä-dō, -'nä-\ *or* **bas·ti·nade** \ˌbas-tə-'nād, -'nād\ *n, pl* **-na·does** *or* **-nades 1** : a blow or beating esp. with a stick **2** : a punishment consisting of beating the soles of the feet

bas·tion \\'bas-chən\ *n* : a projecting part of a fortification; *also* : a fortified position

¹**bat** \\'bat\ *n* **1** : a stout stick : CLUB **2** : a sharp blow **3** : an implement (as of wood) used to hit a ball (as in baseball) **4** : a turn at batting — usu. used with *at*

²**bat** *vb* **bat·ted; bat·ting** : to hit with or as if with a bat

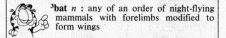

³**bat** *n* : any of an order of night-flying mammals with forelimbs modified to form wings

⁴**bat** *vb* **bat·ted; bat·ting** : WINK, BLINK

batch \\'bach\ *n* **1** : a quantity (as of bread) baked at one time **2** : a quantity of material for use at one time or produced at one operation

bate \\'bāt\ *vb* **bat·ed; bat·ing** : MODERATE, REDUCE

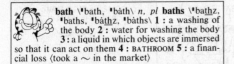

bath \'bath, 'bȧth\ *n, pl* **baths** \'baᵗhz, 'baths, 'bȧᵗhz, 'bȧths\ **1** : a washing of the body **2** : water for washing the body **3** : a liquid in which objects are immersed so that it can act on them **4** : BATHROOM **5** : a financial loss ⟨took a ∼ in the market⟩

bathe \'bāᵗh\ *vb* **bathed; bath•ing 1** : to wash in liquid and esp. water; *also* : to apply water or a medicated liquid to ⟨*bathed* her eyes⟩ **2** : to take a bath; *also* : to take a swim **3** : to wash along, over, or against so as to wet **4** : to suffuse with or as if with light — **bath•er** *n*

bath•house \'bath-,hau̇s, 'bȧth-\ *n* **1** : a building equipped for bathing **2** : a building containing dressing rooms for bathers

bathing suit *n* : SWIMSUIT

ba•thos \'bā-,thäs\ *n* [Gk, lit., depth] **1** : the sudden appearance of the commonplace in otherwise elevated matter or style **2** : insincere or overdone pathos — **ba•thet•ic** \bǝ-'the-tik\ *adj*

bath•robe \'bath-,rōb, 'bȧth-\ *n* : a loose often absorbent robe worn before and after bathing or as a dressing gown

bath•room \-,rüm, -,ru̇m\ *n* : a room containing a bathtub or shower and usu. a sink and toilet

bath•tub \-,tǝb\ *n* : a usu. fixed tub for bathing

ba•tik \bǝ-'tēk, 'ba-tik\ *n* [Javanese *baṭik*] **1** : an Indonesian method of hand-printing textiles by coating with wax the parts not to be dyed; *also* : a design so executed **2** : a fabric printed by batik

ba•tiste \bǝ-'tēst\ *n* : a fine sheer fabric of plain weave

bat•man \'bat-mǝn\ *n* : an orderly of a British military officer

ba•ton \bǝ-'tän\ *n* : STAFF, ROD; *esp* : a stick with which the leader directs an orchestra or band

bats•man \'bats-mǝn\ *n* : a batter esp. in cricket

bat•tal•ion \bǝ-'tal-yǝn\ *n* **1** : a large body of troops organized to act together : ARMY **2** : a military unit composed of a headquarters and two or more units (as companies)

¹bat•ten \'bat-ᵊn\ *vb* **1** : to grow or make fat **2** : THRIVE

²batten *n* : a strip of wood used esp. to seal or strengthen a joint

³batten *vb* : to fasten with battens

¹bat•ter \'ba-tǝr\ *vb* : to beat or damage with repeated blows

²batter *n* : a soft mixture (as for cake) basically of flour and liquid

³batter *n* : one that bats; *esp* : the player whose turn it is to bat

battering ram *n* **1** : an ancient military machine for battering down walls **2** : a heavy metal bar with handles used to batter down doors

bat•tery \'ba-tǝ-rē\ *n, pl* **-ter•ies 1** : BEATING; *esp* : unlawful beating or use of force on a person **2** : a grouping of artillery pieces for tactical purposes; *also* : the guns of a warship **3** : a group of electric cells for furnishing electric current; *also* : a single electric cell (a

flashlight ∼) **4** : a number of similar items grouped or used as a unit ⟨a ∼ of tests⟩ **5** : the pitcher and catcher of a baseball team

bat•ting \'ba-tiŋ\ *n* : layers or sheets of cotton or wool (as for lining quilts)

¹bat•tle \'bat-ᵊl\ *n* [ME *batel*, fr. OF *bataille* battle, fortifying tower, battalion, fr. LL *battalia* combat, alter. of *battualia* fencing exercises, fr. L *battuere* to beat] : a general military engagement; *also* : an extended contest or controversy

²battle *vb* **bat•tled; bat•tling** : to engage in battle : CONTEND, FIGHT

bat•tle–ax \'bat-ᵊl-,aks\ *n* **1** : a long-handled ax formerly used as a weapon **2** : a quarrelsome domineering woman

battle fatigue *n* : COMBAT FATIGUE

bat•tle•field \'bat-ᵊl-,fēld\ *n* : a place where a battle is fought

bat•tle•ment \-mǝnt\ *n* : a decorative or defensive parapet on top of a wall

bat•tle•ship \-,ship\ *n* : a warship of the most heavily armed and armored class

bat•tle•wag•on \-,wa-gǝn\ *n* : BATTLESHIP

bat•ty \'ba-tē\ *adj* **bat•ti•er; -est** : CRAZY, FOOLISH

bau•ble \'bȯ-bǝl\ *n* : TRINKET

baud \'bȯd, Brit 'bōd\ *n, pl* **baud** *also* **bauds** : a unit of data transmission speed

baulk *chiefly Brit var of* BALK

baux•ite \'bȯk-,sīt\ *n* : a clayey mixture that is the chief ore of aluminum

bawd \'bȯd\ *n* **1** : MADAM **2 2** : PROSTITUTE

bawdy \'bȯ-dē\ *adj* **bawd•i•er; -est** : OBSCENE, LEWD — **bawd•i•ly** \'bȯd-ᵊl-ē\ *adv* — **bawd•i•ness** \-dē-nǝs\ *n*

¹bawl \'bȯl\ *vb* : to cry or cry out loudly; *also* : to scold harshly

²bawl *n* : a long loud cry : BELLOW

¹bay \'bā\ *adj* : reddish brown

²bay *n* **1** : a bay-colored animal **2** : a reddish brown color

³bay *n* **1** : a section or compartment of a building or vehicle **2** : a compartment projecting outward from the wall of a building and containing a window (**bay window**)

⁴bay *vb* : to bark with deep long tones

⁵bay *n* **1** : the position of one unable to escape and forced to face danger **2** : a baying of dogs

⁶bay *n* : an inlet of a body of water (as the sea) usu. smaller than a gulf

⁷bay *n* : the European laurel; *also* : a shrub or tree resembling this

bay•ber•ry \'bā-,ber-ē\ *n* : a hardy deciduous shrub of coastal eastern No. America bearing small hard berries coated with a white wax used for candles; *also* : its fruit

bay leaf *n* : the dried leaf of the European laurel used in cooking

¹bay•o•net \'bā-ǝ-nǝt, ,bā-ǝ-'net\ *n* : a daggerlike weapon made to fit on the muzzle end of a rifle

GAVE YOUR BEAR A BATH?

HOW'D YOU GUESS?

JPM DAVIS

2-23

²bayonet *vb* **-net•ed** *also* **-net•ted; -net•ing** *also* **-net-ting** : to use or stab with a bayonet

bay•ou \'bī-yü, -ō\ *n* [Louisiana French, fr. Choctaw *bayuk*] : a marshy or sluggish body of water

bay rum *n* : a fragrant liquid used esp. as a cologne or after-shave lotion

ba•zaar \bə-'zär\ *n* **1** : a group of shops : MARKET-PLACE **2** : a fair for the sale of articles usu. for charity

ba•zoo•ka \bə-'zü-kə\ *n* [*bazooka* (a crude musical instrument made of pipes and a funnel)] : a weapon consisting of a tube and launching an explosive rocket able to pierce armor

¹BB \'bē-(ˌ)bē\ *n* : a small round shot pellet

²BB *abbr* base on balls

BBB *abbr* Better Business Bureau

BBC *abbr* British Broadcasting Corporation

bbl *abbr* barrel; barrels

BC *abbr* **1** before Christ — often printed in small capitals and often punctuated **2** British Columbia

B cell *n* [bone-marrow-derived *cell*] : any of the lymphocytes that secrete antibodies when mature

B complex *n* : VITAMIN B COMPLEX

bd *abbr* **1** board **2** bound

bdl *or* **bdle** *abbr* bundle

bdrm *abbr* bedroom

be \'bē\ *vb, past 1st & 3d sing* **was** \'wəz, 'wäz\; *2d sing* **were** \'wər\; *pl* **were;** *past subjunctive* **were;** *past part* **been** \'bin\; *pres part* **be•ing** \'bē-iŋ\; *pres 1st sing* **am** \əm, 'am\; *2d sing* **are** \ər, 'är\; *3d sing* **is** \'iz, əz\; *pl* **are;** *pres subjunctive* **be 1** : to equal in meaning or symbolically ⟨God *is* love⟩; *also* : to have a specified qualification or relationship ⟨leaves *are* green⟩ ⟨this fish *is* a trout⟩ **2** : to have objective existence ⟨I think, therefore I *am*⟩; *also* : to have or occupy a particular place ⟨here *is* your pen⟩ **3** : to take place : OCCUR ⟨the meeting *is* tonight⟩ **4** — used with the past participle of transitive verbs as a passive voice auxiliary ⟨the door *was* opened⟩ **5** — used as the auxiliary of the present participle in expressing continuous action ⟨he *is* sleeping⟩ **6** — used as an auxiliary with the past participle of some intransitive verbs to form archaic perfect tenses **7** — used as an auxiliary with *to* and the infinitive to express futurity, prearrangement, or obligation ⟨you *are* to come when called⟩

Be *symbol* beryllium

---

¹beach \'bēch\ *n* : a sandy or gravelly part of the shore of an ocean or lake

---

²beach *vb* : to run or drive ashore

beach buggy *n* : DUNE BUGGY

beach•comb•er \'bēch-ˌkō-mər\ *n* : a person who searches along a shore for something of use or value

beach•head \'bēch-ˌhed\ *n* : a small area on an enemy-held shore occupied in the initial stages of an invasion

bea•con \'bē-kən\ *n* **1** : a signal fire **2** : a guiding or warning signal (as a lighthouse) **3** : a radio transmitter emitting signals for guidance of aircraft

¹bead \'bēd\ *n* [ME *bede* prayer, prayer bead, fr. OE *bed, gebed* prayer] **1** *pl* : a series of prayers and meditations made with a rosary **2** : a small piece of material pierced for threading on a line (as in a rosary) **3** : a small globular body **4** : a narrow projecting rim or band — **bead•ing** *n* — **beady** *adj*

²bead *vb* : to form into a bead

bea•dle \'bēd-ᵊl\ *n* : a usu. English parish officer whose duties include keeping order in church

bea•gle \'bē-gəl\ *n* : a small short-legged smooth-coated hound

beagle

beak \'bēk\ *n* : the bill of a bird and esp. of a bird of prey; *also* : a pointed projecting part — **beaked** \'bēkt\ *adj*

bea•ker \'bē-kər\ *n* **1** : a large widemouthed drinking cup **2** : a widemouthed thin-walled laboratory vessel

¹beam \'bēm\ *n* **1** : a large long piece of timber or metal **2** : the bar of a balance from which the scales hang **3** : the breadth of a ship at its widest part **4** : a ray or shaft of light **5** : a collection of nearly parallel rays (as X rays) or particles (as electrons) **6** : a constant radio signal transmitted for the guidance of pilots; *also* : the course indicated by this signal

²beam *vb* **1** : to send out light **2** : to aim (a broadcast) by directional antennas **3** : to smile with joy

¹bean \'bēn\ *n* : the edible seed borne in pods by some leguminous plants; *also* : a plant or a pod bearing these

²bean *vb* : to strike on the head with an object

bean•bag \'bēn-ˌbag\ *n* : a cloth bag partially filled typically with dried beans and used as a toy

bean•ball \'bēn-ˌbȯl\ *n* : a pitch thrown at a batter's head

bean curd *n* : TOFU

bean•ie \'bē-nē\ *n* : a small round tight-fitting skullcap

beano \'bē-nō\ *n, pl* **beanos** : BINGO

¹bear \'bar\ *n, pl* **bears 1** *or pl* **bear** : any of a family of large heavy mammals with shaggy hair and small tails **2** : a gruff or sullen person **3** : one who sells (as securities) in expectation of a price decline — **bear•ish** *adj*

²bear *vb* **bore** \'bōr\; **borne** \'bōrn\ *also* **born** \'bȯrn\;

bear·ing 1 : CARRY **2** : to be equipped with **3** : to give as testimony ⟨∼ witness to the facts of the case⟩ **4** : to give birth to; *also* : PRODUCE, YIELD ⟨a tree that ∼s regularly⟩ **5** : ENDURE, SUSTAIN ⟨∼ pain⟩ ⟨*bore* the weight on piles⟩; *also* : to exert pressure or influence **6** : to go in an indicated direction ⟨∼ to the right⟩ — **bear·able** *adj* — **bear·er** *n*

¹**beard** \'bird\ *n* **1** : the hair that grows on the face of a man **2** : a growth of bristly hairs (as on a goat's chin) — **beard·ed** \'bir-dəd\ *adj* — **beard·less** *adj*

²**beard** *vb* : to confront boldly

bear·ing \'bar-iŋ\ *n* **1** : manner of carrying oneself : COMPORTMENT **2** : a supporting object, purpose, or point **3** : a machine part in which another part (as an axle or pin) turns **4** : an emblem in a coat of arms **5** : the position or direction of one point with respect to another or to the compass; *also* : a determination of position **6** *pl* : comprehension of one's situation **7** : connection with or influence on something; *also* : SIGNIFICANCE

bear·skin \'bar-ˌskin\ *n* : an article made of the skin of a bear

beast \'bēst\ *n* **1** : ANIMAL 1; *esp* : a 4-footed mammal **2** : a contemptible person

¹**beast·ly** \'bēst-lē\ *adj* **beast·li·er; -est 1** : BESTIAL **2** : ABOMINABLE, DISAGREEABLE — **beast·li·ness** \-nəs\ *n*

²**beastly** *adv* : VERY

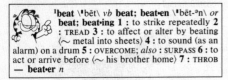

¹**beat** \'bēt\ *vb* **beat; beat·en** \'bēt-ᵊn\ *or* **beat; beat·ing 1** : to strike repeatedly **2** : TREAD **3** : to affect or alter by beating ⟨∼ metal into sheets⟩ **4** : to sound (as an alarm) on a drum **5** : OVERCOME; *also* : SURPASS **6** : to act or arrive before ⟨∼ his brother home⟩ **7** : THROB — **beat·er** *n*

²**beat** *n* **1** : a single stroke or blow esp. of a series; *also* : PULSATION **2** : a rhythmic stress in poetry or music or the rhythmic effect of these **3** : a regularly traversed course

³**beat** *adj* **1** : EXHAUSTED **2** : of or relating to beatniks

⁴**beat** *n* : BEATNIK

be·atif·ic \ˌbē-ə-'ti-fik\ *adj* : giving or indicative of great joy or bliss

be·at·i·fy \bē-'a-tə-ˌfī\ *vb* **-fied; -fy·ing 1** : to make supremely happy **2** : to declare to have attained the blessedness of heaven and authorize the title "Blessed" for — **be·at·i·fi·ca·tion** \-ˌa-tə-fə-'kā-shən\ *n*

be·at·i·tude \bē-'a-tə-ˌtüd, -ˌtyüd\ *n* **1** : a state of utmost bliss **2** : any of the declarations made in the Sermon on the Mount (Mt 5:3–12) beginning "Blessed are"

beat·nik \'bēt-nik\ *n* : a person who rejects the mores of established society and indulges in exotic philosophizing and self-expression

beau \'bō\ *n*, *pl* **beaux** \'bōz\ *or* **beaus** [F, fr. *beau* beautiful, fr. L *bellus* pretty] **1** : a man of fashion : DANDY **2** : SUITOR, LOVER

beau geste \bō-'zhest\ *n*, *pl* **beaux gestes** *or* **beau**

gestes \bō-'zhest\ : a graceful or magnanimous gesture

beau ide·al \ˌbō-ī-'dē(-ə)l\ *n*, *pl* **beau ideals** : the perfect type or model

Beau·jo·lais \ˌbō-zhō-'lā\ *n* : a French red table wine

beau monde \bō-'mänd, -'mōⁿd\ *n*, *pl* **beau mondes** \-'mänz, -'mändz\ *or* **beaux mondes** \bō-'mōⁿd\ : the world of high society and fashion

beau·te·ous \'byü-tē-əs\ *adj* : BEAUTIFUL — **beau·te·ous·ly** *adv*

beau·ti·cian \byü-'ti-shən\ *n* : COSMETOLOGIST

beau·ti·ful \'byü-ti-fəl\ *adj* : characterized by beauty : LOVELY **syn** pretty, fair, comely — **beau·ti·ful·ly** \-f(ə-)lē\ *adv*

beautiful people *n pl*, *often cap B&P* : wealthy or famous people whose lifestyle is usu. expensive and well-publicized

beau·ti·fy \'byü-tə-ˌfī\ *vb* **-fied; -fy·ing** : to make more beautiful — **beau·ti·fi·ca·tion** \ˌbyü-tə-fə-'kā-shən\ *n* — **beau·ti·fi·er** *n*

beau·ty \'byü-tē\ *n*, *pl* **beauties** : qualities that give pleasure to the senses or exalt the mind : LOVELINESS; *also* : something having such qualities

beauty shop *n* : an establishment where hairdressing, facials, and manicures are done

beaux arts \bō-'zär\ *n pl* [F] : FINE ARTS

bea·ver \'bē-vər\ *n*, *pl* **beavers** : a large fur-bearing herbivorous rodent that builds dams and underwater houses of mud and sticks; *also* : its fur

be·calm \bi-'käm, -'kälm\ *vb* : to keep (as a ship) motionless by lack of wind

be·cause \bi-'kòz, -'kəz\ *conj* : for the reason that

because of *prep* : by reason of

beck \'bek\ *n* : a beckoning gesture; *also* : SUMMONS

beck·on \'be-kən\ *vb* : to summon or signal esp. by a nod or gesture; *also* : ATTRACT

be·cloud \bi-'klaùd\ *vb* : OBSCURE

be·come \bi-'kəm\ *vb* **-came** \-'kām\; **-come; -com·ing 1** : to come to be ⟨∼ tired⟩ **2** : to suit or be suitable to ⟨her dress ∼s her⟩

be·com·ing *adj* : SUITABLE, FIT; *also* : ATTRACTIVE — **be·com·ing·ly** *adv*

¹**bed** \'bed\ *n* **1** : an article of furniture to sleep on **2** : a plot of ground prepared for plants **3** : FOUNDATION, BOTTOM **4** : LAYER, STRATUM

²**bed** *vb* **bed·ded; bed·ding 1** : to put or go to bed **2** : to fix in a foundation : EMBED **3** : to plant in beds **4** : to lay or lie flat or in layers

bed–and–breakfast *n* : an establishment offering lodging and breakfast

be·daub \bi-'dòb\ *vb* : SMEAR

be·daz·zle \bi-'da-zəl\ *vb* : to confuse by or as if by a strong light; *also* : FASCINATE — **be·daz·zle·ment** *n*

bed·bug \'bed-ˌbəg\ *n* : a wingless bloodsucking bug infesting houses and esp. beds

bed·clothes \'bed-ˌklōthz\ *n pl* : BEDDING 1

bed·ding \'be-diŋ\ *n* **1** : materials for making up a bed **2** : FOUNDATION

be·deck \bi-'dek\ *vb* : ADORN

be·dev·il \bi-'de-vəl\ *vb* **1** : HARASS, TORMENT **2** : CON-
FUSE, MUDDLE
be·dew \bi-'dü, -'dyü\ *vb* : to wet with or as if with
dew
bed·fast \'bed-ˌfast\ *adj* : BEDRIDDEN
bed·fel·low \-ˌfe-lō\ *n* **1** : one sharing the bed of another **2** : a close associate : ALLY
be·di·zen \bi-'dīz-ᵊn, -'diz-\ *vb* : to dress or adorn with
showy or vulgar finery
bed·lam \'bed-ləm\ *n* [*Bedlam*, popular name for the
Hospital of St. Mary of Bethlehem, London, an insane asylum, fr. ME *Bedlem* Bethlehem] **1** : an insane
asylum **2** : a scene of uproar and confusion
bed·ou·in *or* **bed·u·in** \'be-də-wən\ *n, pl* **bedouin** *or*
bedouins *or* **beduin** *or* **beduins** *often cap* [ME *Be-
doyne*, fr. MF *bedoïn*, fr. Ar *badawī* desert dweller]
: a nomadic Arab of the Arabian, Syrian, or No. African deserts
bed·pan \'bed-ˌpan\ *n* : a shallow vessel used by a
bedridden person for urination or defecation
bed·post \-ˌpōst\ *n* : the post of a bed
be·drag·gled \bi-'dra-gəld\ *adj* : soiled and disordered
as if by being drenched
bed·rid·den \'bed-ˌrid-ᵊn\ *adj* : kept in bed by illness
or weakness
¹**bed·rock** \-'räk\ *n* : the solid rock underlying surface
materials (as soil)
²**bedrock** *adj* : solidly fundamental, basic, or reliable
⟨traditional ∼ values⟩
bed·roll \'bed-ˌrōl\ *n* : bedding rolled up for carrying
bed·room \-ˌrüm, -ˌrům\ *n* : a room containing a bed
and used esp. for sleeping
bed·side \-ˌsīd\ *n* : the place beside a bed esp. of a sick
or dying person
bed·sore \-ˌsōr\ *n* : an ulceration of tissue deprived of
adequate blood supply by prolonged pressure
bed·spread \-ˌspred\ *n* : a usu. ornamental cloth cover
for a bed
bed·stead \-ˌsted\ *n* : the framework of a bed
bed·time \-ˌtīm\ *n* : time for going to bed
bed–wet·ting \-ˌwe-tiŋ\ *n* : involuntary discharge of
urine esp. in bed during sleep — **bed–wet·ter** *n*
¹**bee** \'bē\ *n* : HONEYBEE; *also* : any of various related
insects
²**bee** *n* : a gathering of people for a specific purpose
⟨quilting ∼⟩
beech \'bēch\ *n, pl* **beech·es** *or* **beech** : any of a genus
of deciduous hardwood trees with smooth gray bark
and small sweet triangular nuts; *also* : the wood of a
beech — **beech·en** \'bē-chən\ *adj*
beech·nut \'bēch-ˌnət\ *n* : the nut of a beech
¹**beef** \'bēf\ *n, pl* **beefs** \'bēfs\ *or* **beeves** \'bēvz\ **1** : the
flesh of a steer, cow, or bull; *also* : the dressed car-
cass of a beef animal **2** : a steer, cow, or bull esp.
when fattened for food **3** : MUSCLE, BRAWN **4** *pl* **beefs**
: COMPLAINT
²**beef** *vb* **1** : STRENGTHEN — usu. used with *up* **2** : COM-
PLAIN
beef·eat·er \'bē-ˌfē-tər\ *n* : a yeoman of the guard of an
English monarch
beef·steak \-ˌstāk\ *n* : a slice of beef suitable for broiling or frying
beefy \'bē-fē\ *adj* **beef·i·er; -est** : THICKSET, BRAWNY
bee·hive \'bē-ˌhīv\ *n* : HIVE 1, 3
bee·keep·er \-ˌkē-pər\ *n* : a person who raises bees —
bee·keep·ing *n*
bee·line \-ˌlīn\ *n* : a straight direct course
been *past part of* BE
beep·er \'bē-pər\ *n* : a small radio receiver that beeps
when signaled to alert the person carrying it
beer \'bir\ *n* : an alcoholic beverage brewed from malt
and hops — **beery** *adj*
bees·wax \'bēz-ˌwaks\ *n* : WAX 1
beet \'bēt\ *n* : a garden plant with edible leaves and a
thick sweet root used as a vegetable, as a source of
sugar, or as forage; *also* : its root

¹**bee·tle** \'bēt-ᵊl\ *n* : any of an order of insects having
four wings of which the stiff outer pair covers the
membranous inner pair when not in flight
²**beetle** *vb* **bee·tled; bee·tling** : to jut out : PROJECT
be·fall \bi-'fȯl\ *vb* **-fell** \-'fel\; **-fall·en** \-'fȯ-lən\ : to
happen to : OCCUR
be·fit \bi-'fit\ *vb* : to be suitable to
be·fog \bi-'fȯg, -'fäg\ *vb* : OBSCURE; *also* : CONFUSE
¹**be·fore** \bi-'fōr\ *adv or adj* **1** : in front **2** : EARLIER
²**before** *prep* **1** : in front of ⟨stood ∼ him⟩ **2** : earlier than
⟨got there ∼ me⟩ **3** : in a more important category
than ⟨put quality ∼ quantity⟩
³**before** *conj* **1** : earlier than the time that ⟨he got here
∼ I did⟩ **2** : more willingly than ⟨she'd starve ∼ she'd
steal⟩
be·fore·hand \bi-'fōr-ˌhand\ *adv or adj* : in advance
be·foul \bi-'faůl\ *vb* : SOIL
be·friend \bi-'frend\ *vb* : to act as friend to
be·fud·dle \bi-'fəd-ᵊl\ *vb* : MUDDLE, CONFUSE
beg \'beg\ *vb* **begged; beg·ging 1** : to ask as a charity;
also : ENTREAT **2** : EVADE; *also* : assume as established, settled, or proved ⟨∼ the question⟩
be·get \bi-'get\ *vb* **-got** \-'gät\; **-got·ten** \-'gät-ᵊn\ *or*
-got; -get·ting : to become the father of : SIRE
¹**beg·gar** \'be-gər\ *n* : one that begs; *esp* : a person who
begs as a way of life
²**beggar** *vb* : IMPOVERISH
beg·gar·ly \'be-gər-lē\ *adj* **1** : contemptibly mean or inadequate **2** : marked by unrelieved poverty ⟨a ∼ life⟩
beg·gary \'be-gə-rē\ *n* : extreme poverty
be·gin \bi-'gin\ *vb* **be·gan** \-'gan\; **be·gun** \-'gən\; **be·
gin·ning 1** : to do the first part of an action : COM-
MENCE **2** : to come into being : ARISE; *also* : FOUND **3**
: ORIGINATE, INVENT — **be·gin·ner** *n*
beg off *vb* : to ask to be excused from something
be·gone \bi-'gȯn\ *vb* : to go away : DEPART — used
esp. in the imperative
be·go·nia \bi-'gōn-yə\ *n* : any of a genus of tropical
herbs widely grown for their showy leaves and waxy
flowers
be·grime \bi-'grīm\ *vb* **be·grimed; be·grim·ing** : to
make dirty
be·grudge \bi-'grəj\ *vb* **1** : to give or concede reluc-
tantly **2** : to be reluctant to grant or allow
be·guile \-'gil\ *vb* **be·guiled; be·guil·ing 1** : DECEIVE **2**
: to while away **3** : to engage the interest of by guile
be·guine \bi-'gēn\ *n* [AmerF *béguine*, fr. F *béguin* flir-
tation] : a vigorous popular dance of the islands of
Saint Lucia and Martinique
be·gum \'bā-gəm, 'bē-\ *n* : a Muslim woman of high
rank
be·half \bi-'haf, -'håf\ *n* : BENEFIT, SUPPORT, DEFENSE
be·have \bi-'hāv\ *vb* **be·haved; be·hav·ing 1** : to bear,
comport, or conduct oneself in a particular and esp.
a proper way **2** : to act, function, or react in a particular way
be·hav·ior \bi-'hā-vyər\ *n* : way of behaving; *esp* : personal conduct — **be·hav·ior·al** \-vyə-rəl\ *adj*
be·hav·ior·ism \bi-'hā-vyə-ˌri-zəm\ *n* : a school of psychology concerned with the objective evidence of behavior without reference to conscious experience
be·hav·iour, be·hav·iour·ism *chiefly Brit var of* BE-
HAVIOR, BEHAVIORISM
be·head \bi-'hed\ *vb* : to cut off the head of
be·he·moth \bi-'hē-məth, 'bē-ə-ˌmäth\ *n* : a huge powerful animal described in Job 40:15–24; *also* : something of monstrous size or power
be·hest \bi-'hest\ *n* **1** : COMMAND **2** : an urgent prompt-
ing
¹**be·hind** \bi-'hīnd\ *adv or adj* **1** : BACK, BACKWARD
⟨look ∼ ⟩ **2** : LATE, SLOW
²**behind** *prep* **1** : in or to a place or situation in back of
or to the rear of ⟨look ∼ you⟩ ⟨the staff stayed ∼ the
troops⟩ **2** : inferior to ⟨as in rank⟩ : BELOW ⟨three
games ∼ the first-place team⟩ **3** : in support of : SUP-
PORTING ⟨we're ∼ you all the way⟩

be·hind·hand \bi-'hīnd-ˌhand\ *adj* : being in arrears **syn** tardy, late, overdue, belated

be·hold \bi-'hōld\ *vb* -**held** \-'held\; -**hold·ing 1** : to have in sight : SEE **2** — used imperatively to direct the attention **syn** view, observe, notice, espy — **be·hold·er** *n*

be·hold·en \bi-'hōl-dən\ *adj* : OBLIGATED, INDEBTED

be·hoof \bi-'hüf\ *n* : ADVANTAGE, PROFIT

be·hoove \bi-'hüv\ *vb* **be·hooved; be·hoov·ing** : to be necessary, proper, or advantageous for

be·hove *chiefly Brit var of* BEHOOVE

beige \'bāzh\ *n* : a pale dull yellowish brown — **beige** *adj*

be·ing \'bē-iŋ\ *n* **1** : EXISTENCE; *also* : LIFE **2** : the qualities or constitution of an existent thing **3** : a living thing; *esp* : PERSON

be·la·bor \bi-'lā-bər\ *vb* : to assail (as with words) tiresomely or at length

be·la·bour *chiefly Brit var of* BELABOR

be·lat·ed \bi-'lā-təd\ *adj* : DELAYED, LATE

be·lay \bi-'lā\ *vb* **1** : to wind (a rope) around a pin or cleat in order to hold secure **2** : QUIT, STOP — used in the imperative

belch \'belch\ *vb* **1** : to expel (gas) from the stomach through the mouth **2** : to gush forth ⟨a volcano ∼*ing* lava⟩ — **belch** *n*

bel·dam *or* **bel·dame** \'bel-dəm\ *n* [ME *beldam* grandmother, fr. MF *bel* beautiful + ME *dam* lady, mother] : an old woman

be·lea·guer \bi-'lē-gər\ *vb* **1** : BESIEGE **2** : HARASS ⟨∼*ed* parents⟩

bel·fry \'bel-frē\ *n, pl* **belfries** : a tower for a bell (as on a church); *also* : the part of the tower in which the bell hangs

Belg *abbr* Belgian; Belgium

Bel·gian \'bel-jən\ *n* : a native or inhabitant of Belgium — **Belgian** *adj*

be·lie \bi-'lī\ *vb* -**lied; -ly·ing 1** : MISREPRESENT **2** : to show (something) to be false **3** : to run counter to

be·lief \bə-'lēf\ *n* **1** : CONFIDENCE, TRUST **2** : something (as a tenet or creed) believed **syn** conviction, opinion, persuasion, sentiment

be·lieve \bə-'lēv\ *vb* **be·lieved; be·liev·ing 1** : to have religious convictions **2** : to have a firm conviction about something : accept as true **3** : to hold as an opinion : SUPPOSE — **be·liev·able** *adj* — **be·liev·er** *n*

be·like \bi-'līk\ *adv, archaic* : PROBABLY

be·lit·tle \bi-'lit-ᵊl\ *vb* -**lit·tled; -lit·tling** : to make seem little or less; *also* : DISPARAGE

¹bell \'bel\ *n* **1** : a hollow metallic device that makes a ringing sound when struck **2** : the sounding or stroke of a bell (as on shipboard to tell the time); *also* : time so indicated **3** : something with the flared form of a typical bell

²bell *vb* : to provide with a bell

bel·la·don·na \ˌbe-lə-'dä-nə\ *n* [It, lit., beautiful lady; fr. its cosmetic use] : a medicinal extract (as atropine) from a poisonous European herb related to the potato; *also* : this herb

bell–bot·toms \'bel-'bä-təmz\ *n pl* : pants with wide flaring bottoms — **bell–bottom** *adj*

bell·boy \'bel-ˌbȯi\ *n* : BELLHOP

belle \'bel\ *n* : an attractive and popular girl or woman

belles let·tres \bel-'letrᵊ\ *n pl* [F] : literature that is an end in itself and not practical or purely informative — **bel·le·tris·tic** \ˌbe-lə-'tris-tik\ *adj*

bell·hop \'bel-ˌhäp\ *n* : a hotel or club employee who takes guests to rooms, carries luggage, and runs errands

bel·li·cose \'be-li-ˌkōs\ *adj* : WARLIKE, PUGNACIOUS **syn** belligerent, quarrelsome, combative, contentious — **bel·li·cos·i·ty** \ˌbe-li-'kä-sə-tē\ *n*

bel·lig·er·en·cy \bə-'li-jə-rən-sē\ *n* **1** : the status of a nation engaged in war **2** : BELLIGERENCE, TRUCULENCE

bel·lig·er·ent \-rənt\ *adj* **1** : waging war **2** : TRUCULENT **syn** bellicose, pugnacious, combative, contentious, warlike — **bel·lig·er·ence** \-rəns\ *n* — **belligerent** *n*

bel·low \'be-lō\ *vb* **1** : to make the deep hollow sound characteristic of a bull **2** : to shout in a deep voice — **bellow** *n*

bel·lows \-lōz, -ləz\ *n sing or pl* : a closed device with sides that can be spread apart and then pressed together to draw in air and expel it through a tube

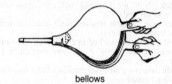

bellows

bell·weth·er \'bel-'we-thər, -ˌwe-\ *n* : one that takes the lead or initiative

¹bel·ly \'be-lē\ *n, pl* **bellies** [ME *bely* bellows, belly, fr. OE *belg* bag, skin] **1** : ABDOMEN; *also* : POTBELLY **2** : the underpart of an animal's body

²belly *vb* **bel·lied; bel·ly·ing** : BULGE

¹bel·ly·ache \'be-lē-ˌāk\ *n* : pain in the abdomen

²bellyache *vb* : COMPLAIN

belly button *n* : the human navel

belly dance *n* : a usu. solo dance emphasizing movement of the belly — **belly dance** *vb* — **belly dancer** *n*

belly laugh *n* : a deep hearty laugh

be·long \bi-'lȯŋ\ *vb* **1** : to be suitable or appropriate; *also* : to be properly situated ⟨shoes ∼ in the closet⟩ **2** : to be the property ⟨this ∼*s* to me⟩; *also* : to be attached (as through birth or membership) ⟨∼ to a club⟩ **3** : to form an attribute or part ⟨this wheel ∼*s* to the cart⟩ **4** : to be classified ⟨whales ∼ among the mammals⟩

be·long·ings \-'lȯŋ-iŋz\ *n pl* : GOODS, EFFECTS, POSSESSIONS

be·loved \bi-'ləvd, -'lə-vəd\ *adj* : dearly loved — **beloved** *n*

¹be·low \bi-'lō\ *adv* **1** : in or to a lower place or rank **2** : on earth **3** : in hell

²below *prep* **1** : lower than **2** : inferior to (as in rank)

be·low·decks \bi-ılō-ıdeks, -'lō-ıdeks\ *adv* : inside the superstructure of a boat or down to a lower deck

¹belt \'belt\ *n* **1** : a strip (as of leather) worn about the waist **2** : a flexible continuous band to communicate motion or convey material **3** : a region marked by some distinctive feature; *esp* : one suited to a particular crop

²belt *vb* **1** : to encircle or secure with a belt **2** : to beat with or as if with a belt **3** : to mark with an encircling band **4** : to sing loudly

³belt *n* **1** : a jarring blow : WHACK **2** : DRINK ⟨a ∼ of whiskey⟩

belt–tightening *n* : a reduction in spending

belt·way \'belt-ıwā\ *n* : a highway around a city

be·lu·ga \bə-'lü-gə\ *n* [Russ] : a white sturgeon of the Black Sea, Caspian Sea, and their tributaries that is a source of caviar; *also* : caviar from beluga roe

bel·ve·dere \'bel-və-ıdir\ *n* [It, lit., beautiful view] : a structure (as a summerhouse) designed to command a view

be·mire \bi-'mīr\ *vb* : to cover or soil with or sink in mire

be·moan \bi-'mōn\ *vb* : LAMENT, DEPLORE **syn** bewail, grieve, moan, weep

be·muse \bi-'myüz\ *vb* : BEWILDER, CONFUSE

¹bench \'bench\ *n* **1** : a long seat for two or more persons **2** : the seat of a judge in court; *also* : the office or dignity of a judge **3** : COURT; *also* : JUDGES **4** : a table for holding work and tools ⟨a carpenter's ∼⟩

²bench \'bench\ *vb* **1** : to furnish with benches **2** : to seat on a bench **3** : to remove from or keep out of a game

bench mark *n* **1** : a mark on a permanent object serving as an elevation reference in topographical surveys **2** *usu* **bench·mark** : a point of reference for measurement; *also* : STANDARD

bench press *n* : a press in weight lifting performed by a lifter lying on a bench — **bench–press** *vb*

bench warrant *n* : a warrant issued by a presiding judge or by a court against a person guilty of contempt or indicted for a crime

¹bend \'bend\ *vb* **bent** \'bent\; **bend·ing 1** : to draw (as a bow) taut **2** : to curve or cause a change of shape in ⟨∼ a bar⟩ **3** : to make fast : SECURE **4** : DEFLECT **5** : to turn in a certain direction ⟨*bent* his steps toward town⟩ **6** : APPLY ⟨*bent* themselves to the task⟩ **7** : SUBDUE **8** : to curve downward **9** : YIELD, SUBMIT

²bend *n* **1** : an act or process of bending **2** : something bent; *esp* : CURVE **3** *pl* : a painful and sometimes fatal disorder caused by release of gas bubbles in the tissues upon too rapid decrease in air pressure after a stay in a compressed atmosphere

³bend *n* : a knot by which a rope is fastened (as to another rope)

bend·er \'ben-dər\ *n* : SPREE

¹be·neath \bi-'nēth\ *adv* : BELOW **syn** under, underneath

²beneath *prep* **1** : BELOW, UNDER ⟨stood ∼ a tree⟩ **2** : unworthy of ⟨considered such behavior ∼ her⟩ **3** : concealed by

bene·dic·tion \ıbe-nə-'dik-shən\ *n* : the invocation of a blessing *esp.* at the close of a public worship service

ben·e·fac·tion \-'fak-shən\ *n* : a charitable donation **syn** contribution, alms, beneficence, offering

ben·e·fac·tor \'ben-ə-ıfak-tər\ *n* : one that confers a benefit and esp. a benefaction

ben·e·fac·tress \-ıfak-trəs\ *n* : a woman who is a benefactor

ben·e·fice \'be-nə-fəs\ *n* : an ecclesiastical office to which the revenue from an endowment is attached

be·nef·i·cence \bə-'ne-fə-səns\ *n* **1** : beneficent quality **2** : BENEFACTION

be·nef·i·cent \-sənt\ *adj* : doing or producing good (as by acts of kindness or charity); *also* : BENEFICIAL

ben·e·fi·cial \ıbe-nə-'fi-shəl\ *adj* : being of benefit or help : HELPFUL **syn** advantageous, profitable, favorable, propitious — **ben·e·fi·cial·ly** *adv*

ben·e·fi·cia·ry \ıbe-nə-'fi-shē-ıer-ē, -'fi-shə-rē\ *n, pl* **-ries** : one that receives a benefit (as the income of a trust or the proceeds of an insurance)

¹ben·e·fit \'be-nə-ıfit\ *n* **1** : ADVANTAGE ⟨the ∼s of exercise⟩ **2** : useful aid : HELP; *also* : material aid provided or due (as in sickness or unemployment) as a right **3** : a performance or event to raise funds

²benefit *vb* **-fit·ed** \-ıfi-təd\ *also* **-fit·ted; -fit·ing** *also* **-fit·ting 1** : to be useful or profitable to **2** : to receive benefit

be·nev·o·lence \bə-'ne-və-ləns\ *n* **1** : charitable nature **2** : an act of kindness : CHARITY — **be·nev·o·lent** \-lənt\ *adj* — **be·nev·o·lent·ly** *adv*

be·night·ed \bi-'nī-təd\ *adj* **1** : overtaken by darkness or night **2** : living in ignorance

be·nign \bi-'nīn\ *adj* [ME benigne, fr. MF, fr. L benignus] **1** : of a gentle disposition; *also* : showing kindness **2** : of a mild kind; *esp* : not malignant ⟨∼ tumors⟩ **syn** benignant, kind, kindly, good-hearted — **be·nig·ni·ty** \-'nig-nə-tē\ *n*

be·nig·nant \-'nig-nənt\ *adj* : BENIGN 1 **syn** kind, kindly, good-hearted

ben·i·son \'be-nə-sən, -zən\ *n* : BLESSING, BENEDICTION

bent \'bent\ *n* **1** : strong inclination or interest; *also* : TALENT **2** : power of endurance **syn** talent, aptitude, gift, flair, knack, genius

ben·thic \'ben-thik\ *adj* : of, relating to, or occurring at the bottom of a body of water

ben·ton·ite \'bent-ᵊn-ıīt\ *n* : an absorptive clay used esp. as a filler (as in paper)

bent·wood \'bent-ıwùd\ *adj* : made of wood bent into shape ⟨a ∼ rocker⟩

be·numb \bi-'nəm\ *vb* **1** : DULL, DEADEN **2** : to make numb esp. by cold

ben·zene \'ben-ızēn\ *n* : a colorless volatile flammable liquid hydrocarbon used in organic synthesis and as a solvent

ben·zine \'ben-ızēn\ *n* : any of various flammable petroleum distillates used as solvents or as motor fuels

ben·zo·ate \'ben-zə-ıwāt\ *n* : a salt or ester of benzoic acid

ben·zo·ic acid \ben-ızō-ik-\ *n* : a white crystalline acid used as a preservative and antiseptic and in synthesizing chemicals

ben·zo·in \'ben-zə-wən, -ızóin\ *n* : a balsamlike resin from trees of southern Asia used esp. in medicine and perfumes

be·queath \bi-'kwēth, -'kwēth\ *vb* [ME bequethen, fr. OE becwethan, fr. be- + cwethan to say] **1** : to leave by will **2** : to hand down

be·quest \bi-'kwest\ *n* **1** : the action of bequeathing **2** : something bequeathed : LEGACY

be·rate \-'rāt\ *vb* : to scold harshly

Ber·ber \'bər-bər\ *n* : a member of any of various peoples living in northern Africa west of Tripoli

ber·ceuse \ber-'sœz, -'süz\ *n, pl* **berceuses** *same or* -'sü-zəz\ [F, fr. bercer to rock] **1** : LULLABY **2** : a musical composition that resembles a lullaby

¹be·reaved \bi-'rēvd\ *adj* : suffering the death of a loved one — **be·reave·ment** *n*

²bereaved *n, pl* **bereaved** : one who is bereaved

be·reft \-'reft\ *adj* **1** : deprived of or lacking something — usu. used with *of* **2** : BEREAVED

be·ret \bə-'rā\ *n* : a round soft cap with no visor

berg \'bərg\ *n* : ICEBERG

beri·beri \ıber-ē-'ber-ē\ *n* : a deficiency disease marked by weakness, wasting, and nerve damage and caused by lack of thiamine

berke·li·um \'bər-klē-əm\ *n* : an artificially prepared radioactive chemical element — see ELEMENT table

berm \'bərm\ n : a narrow shelf or path at the top or bottom of a slope; *also* : a mound or bank of earth

Ber·mu·das \bər-'myü-dəz\ n pl : BERMUDA SHORTS

Bermuda shorts n pl : knee-length walking shorts

ber·ry \'ber-ē\ n, pl **berries 1** : a small pulpy fruit (as a strawberry) **2** : a simple fruit (as a grape, tomato, or banana) with the wall of the ripened ovary thick and pulpy **3** : the dry seed of some plants (as coffee)

ber·serk \bər-'sərk, -'zərk\ adj [ON *berserkr* warrior frenzied in battle, fr. *bjǫrn* bear + *serkr* shirt] : FRENZIED, CRAZED — **berserk** adv

¹berth \'bərth\ n **1** : adequate distance esp. for a ship to maneuver **2** : the place where a ship is anchored or a vehicle rests **3** : ACCOMMODATIONS **4** : JOB, POSITION **syn** post, situation, office, appointment

²berth vb **1** : to bring or come into a berth **2** : to allot a berth to

ber·yl \'ber-əl\ n : a hard silicate mineral occurring as green, yellow, pink, or white crystals

be·ryl·li·um \bə-'ri-lē-əm\ n : a light strong metallic chemical element used as a hardener in alloys — see ELEMENT table

be·seech \bi-'sēch\ vb **-sought** \-'sòt\ or **-seeched; -seech·ing** : to beg urgently : ENTREAT **syn** implore, plead, supplicate, importune

be·seem \bi-'sēm\ vb, archaic : BEFIT

be·set \-'set\ vb **1** : TROUBLE, HARASS **2** : ASSAIL; also : SURROUND

be·set·ting adj : persistently present

¹be·side \bi-'sīd\ prep **1** : by the side of ⟨sit ∼ me⟩ **2** : BESIDES **3** : not relevant to

²beside adv, archaic : BESIDES

¹be·sides \bi-'sīdz\ prep **1** : other than **2** : together with

²besides adv **1** : as well : ALSO **2** : MOREOVER

be·siege \bi-'sēj\ vb : to lay siege to; also : to press with requests — **be·sieg·er** n

be·smear \-'smir\ vb : SMEAR

be·smirch \-'smərch\ vb : SMIRCH, SOIL

be·som \'bē-zəm\ n : BROOM

be·sot \bi-'sät\ vb **be·sot·ted; be·sot·ting 1** : INFATUATE **2** : to make dull esp. by drinking

be·spat·ter \-'spa-tər\ vb : SPATTER

be·speak \bi-'spēk\ vb **-spoke** \-'spōk\; **-spo·ken** \-'spō-kən\; **-speak·ing 1** : PREARRANGE **2** : ADDRESS **3** : REQUEST **4** : INDICATE, SIGNIFY **5** : FORETELL

be·sprin·kle \-'spriŋ-kəl\ vb : SPRINKLE

¹best \'best\ adj, superlative of GOOD **1** : excelling all others **2** : most productive (as of good or satisfaction) **3** : LARGEST, MOST

²best adv, superlative of WELL **1** : in the best way **2** : MOST

³best n : something that is best

⁴best vb : to get the better of : OUTDO

bes·tial \'bes-chəl\ adj **1** : of or relating to beasts **2** : resembling a beast esp. in brutality or lack of intelligence

bes·ti·al·i·ty \,bes-chē-'a-lə-tē, ,bēs-\ n, pl **-ties 1** : the condition or status of a lower animal **2** : display or gratification of bestial traits or impulses

bes·ti·ary \'bes-chē-,er-ē\ n, pl **-ar·ies** : a medieval allegorical or moralizing work on the appearance and habits of animals

be·stir \bi-'stər\ vb : to rouse to action

best man n : the principal groomsman at a wedding

be·stow \bi-'stō\ vb **1** : PUT, PLACE, STOW **2** : to present as a gift — **be·stow·al** n

be·stride \bi-'strīd\ vb **-strode** \-'strōd\; **-strid·den** \-'strid-ᵊn\; **-strid·ing** : to ride, sit, or stand astride

¹bet \'bet\ n **1** : something that is wagered, risked, or pledged usu. between two parties on the outcome of a contest; also : the making of such a bet **2** : OPTION ⟨the back road is your best ∼⟩

²bet vb **bet** also **bet·ted; bet·ting 1** : to stake on the outcome of an issue or a contest ⟨*bet* $2 on the race⟩ **2** : to make a bet with **3** : to lay a bet

³bet abbr between

be·ta \'bā-tə\ n : the 2d letter of the Greek alphabet — B or β

beta block·er \-,blä-kər\ n : any of a group of drugs that tend to decrease heart action and increase coronary blood flow

be·ta–car·o·tene \-'kar-ə-,tēn\ n : an isomer of carotene found in dark green and dark yellow vegetables and fruits

be·take \bi-'tāk\ vb **-took** \-'tùk\; **-tak·en** \-'tā-kən\; **-tak·ing** : to cause (oneself) to go

beta particle n : a high-speed electron; esp : one emitted by a radioactive nucleus

beta ray n **1** : BETA PARTICLE **2** : a stream of beta particles

be·tel \'bēt-ᵊl\ n : a climbing pepper whose leaves are chewed together with lime and betel nut as a stimulant esp. by southern Asians

betel nut n : the astringent seed of an Asian palm that is chewed with betel leaves

bête noire \,bet-'nwär, ,bāt-\ n, pl **bêtes noires** \same or -'nwärz\ [F, lit., black beast] : a person or thing strongly disliked or avoided

beth·el \'be-thəl\ n [Heb *bēth'ēl* house of God] : a place of worship esp. for seamen

be·think \bi-'think\ vb **-thought** \-'thòt\; **-think·ing 1** : REMEMBER; also : PONDER

be·tide \bi-'tīd\ vb : to happen to

be·times \bi-'tīmz\ adv : in good time : EARLY **syn** soon, seasonably, timely

be·to·ken \bi-'tō-kən\ vb **1** : PRESAGE **2** : to give evidence of **syn** indicate, attest, bespeak, testify

be·tray \bi-'trā\ vb **1** : to lead astray; esp : SEDUCE **2** : to deliver to an enemy **3** : ABANDON **4** : to prove unfaithful to **5** : to reveal unintentionally; also : SHOW, INDICATE **syn** mislead, delude, deceive, beguile — **be·tray·al** n — **be·tray·er** n

be·troth \bi-'trōth, -'tròth\ vb : to promise to marry — **be·troth·al** n

be·trothed n : the person to whom one is betrothed

---

¹bet·ter \'be-tər\ adj, comparative of GOOD **1** : greater than half **2** : improved in health **3** : more attractive, favorable, or commendable **4** : more advantageous or effective **5** : improved in accuracy or performance

²better vb **1** : to make or become better **2** : SURPASS, EXCEL

³better adv, comparative of WELL **1** : in a superior manner **2** : to a higher or greater degree; also : MORE

⁴better n **1** : something better; also : a superior esp. in merit or rank **2** : ADVANTAGE

⁵better verbal auxiliary : had better ⟨you ∼ hurry⟩

bet·ter·ment \'be-tər-mənt\ n : IMPROVEMENT

bet·tor or **bet·ter** \'be-tər\ n : one that bets

¹be·tween \bi-'twēn\ prep **1** : by the common action of ⟨earned $10,000 ∼ the two of them⟩ **2** : in the interval separating ⟨an alley ∼ two buildings⟩; also : in intermediate relation to **3** : in point of comparison of ⟨choose ∼ two cars⟩

²between adv : in an intervening space or interval

be·twixt \bi-'twikst\ adv or prep : BETWEEN

¹bev·el \'be-vəl\ n **1** : a device for adjusting the slant of the surfaces of a piece of work **2** : the angle or slant that one surface or line makes with another when not at right angles

²bevel vb **-eled** or **-elled; -el·ing** or **-el·ling 1** : to cut or shape to a bevel **2** : INCLINE, SLANT

bev·er·age \'bev-rij\ n : a drinkable liquid

bevy \'be-vē\ n, pl **bev·ies 1** : a large group or collection **2** : a group of animals and esp. quail together

be·wail \bi-'wāl\ vb : LAMENT **syn** deplore, bemoan, grieve, moan, weep

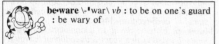

be·ware \-ˈwar\ *vb* : to be on one's guard : be wary of

be·wil·der \bi-ˈwil-dər\ *vb* : PERPLEX, CONFUSE **syn** mystify, distract, puzzle — **be·wil·der·ment** *n*
be·witch \-ˈwich\ *vb* **1** : to affect by witchcraft **2** : CHARM, FASCINATE **syn** enchant, attract, captivate — **be·witch·ment** *n*
bey \ˈbā\ *n* **1** : a former Turkish provincial governor **2** : the former native ruler of Tunis or Tunisia
¹be·yond \bē-ˈänd\ *adv* **1** : FARTHER **2** : BESIDES
²beyond *prep* **1** : on or to the farther side of **2** : out of the reach or sphere of **3** : BESIDES
be·zel \ˈbē-zəl, ˈbe-\ *n* **1** : a rim that holds a transparent covering (as on a watch) **2** : the faceted part of a cut gem that rises above the setting
bf *abbr* boldface
BG *or* **B Gen** *abbr* brigadier general
bhang \ˈbaŋ\ *n* [Hindi *bhāng*] : a mildly intoxicating preparation of the leaves and flowering tops of uncultivated hemp
Bi *symbol* bismuth
BIA *abbr* Bureau of Indian Affairs
bi·an·nu·al \(ˌ)bī-ˈan-yə-wəl\ *adj* : occurring twice a year — **bi·an·nu·al·ly** *adv*
¹bi·as \ˈbī-əs\ *n* **1** : a line diagonal to the grain of a fabric **2** : PREJUDICE, BENT
²bias *adv* : on the bias : DIAGONALLY
³bias *vb* **bi·ased** *or* **bi·assed**; **bi·as·ing** *or* **bi·as·sing** : PREJUDICE
bi·ath·lon \bī-ˈath-lən, -ˌlän\ *n* : a composite athletic contest consisting of cross-country skiing and target shooting with a rifle
¹bib \ˈbib\ *n* : a cloth or plastic shield tied under the chin to protect the clothes while eating
²bib *abbr* Bible; biblical
bi·be·lot \ˈbē-bə-ˌlō\ *n, pl* **bibelots** *same or* -ˌlōz\ : a small household ornament or decorative object
bi·ble \ˈbī-bəl\ *n* [ME, fr. OF, fr. ML *biblia*, fr. Gk, pl. of *biblion* book, fr. *byblos* papyrus, book, fr. Byblos, ancient Phoenician city from which papyrus was ex-

ported] **1** *cap* : the sacred scriptures of Christians comprising the Old and New Testaments **2** *cap* : the sacred scriptures of Judaism; *also* : those of some other religion **3** : a publication that is considered authoritative for its subject — **bib·li·cal** \ˈbi-bli-kəl\ *adj* ☞ For table, see next page.
bib·li·og·ra·phy \ˌbi-blē-ˈä-grə-fē\ *n, pl* **-phies 1** : the history or description of writings or publications **2** : a list of writings (as on a subject or of an author) — **bib·li·og·ra·pher** \-fər\ *n* — **bib·li·o·graph·ic** \-ə-ˈgra-fik\ *also* **bib·li·o·graph·i·cal** \-fi-kəl\ *adj*
bib·lio·phile \ˈbi-blē-ə-ˌfīl\ *n* : a lover of books
bib·u·lous \ˈbi-byə-ləs\ *adj* **1** : highly absorbent **2** : fond of alcoholic beverages
bi·cam·er·al \ˈbī-ˈka-mə-rəl\ *adj* : having or consisting of two legislative branches
bicarb \(ˌ)bī-ˈkärb, ˈbī-ˌ\ *n* : SODIUM BICARBONATE
bi·car·bon·ate \(ˌ)bī-ˈkär-bə-ˌnāt, -nət\ *n* : an acid carbonate
bicarbonate of soda : SODIUM BICARBONATE
bi·cen·te·na·ry \ˌbī-sen-ˈte-nə-rē, bī-ˈsent-ᵊn-ˌer-ē\ *n* : BICENTENNIAL — **bicentenary** *adj*
bi·cen·ten·ni·al \ˌbī-sen-ˈte-nē-əl\ *n* : a 200th anniversary or its celebration — **bicentennial** *adj*
bi·ceps \ˈbī-ˌseps\ *n, pl* **biceps** *also* **bicepses** [NL, fr. L, two-headed, fr. *bi-* two + *caput* head] : a muscle (as in the front of the upper arm) having two points of origin
¹bick·er \ˈbi-kər\ *n* : ALTERCATION
²bicker *vb* : to engage in a petty quarrel
bi·coast·al \bī-ˈkōst-ᵊl\ *adj* : living or working on both the East and West coasts of the U.S.
bi·con·cave \ˌbī-(ˌ)kän-ˈkāv, (ˌ)bī-ˈkän-ˌkāv\ *adj* : concave on both sides
bi·con·vex \ˌbī-(ˌ)kän-ˈveks, (ˌ)bī-ˈkän-ˌveks\ *adj* : convex on both sides
bi·cus·pid \bī-ˈkəs-pəd\ *n* : PREMOLAR
¹bi·cy·cle \ˈbī-ˌsi-kəl\ *n* : a light 2-wheeled vehicle with a steering handle, saddle, and pedals
²bicycle *vb* **-cy·cled**; **-cy·cling** \-ˌsi-k(ə-)liŋ, -ˌsī-\ : to ride a bicycle — **bi·cy·cler** \-k(ə-)lər\ *n* — **bi·cy·clist** \-k(ə-)list\ *n*
¹bid \ˈbid\ *vb* **bade** \ˈbad, ˈbād\ *or* **bid**; **bid·den** \ˈbid-ᵊn\ *or* **bid** *also* **bade**; **bid·ding 1** : COMMAND, ORDER

BOOKS OF THE OLD TESTAMENT

ROMAN CATHOLIC CANON	PROTESTANT CANON
Genesis	Genesis
Exodus	Exodus
Leviticus	Leviticus
Numbers	Numbers
Deuteronomy	Deuteronomy
Joshua	Joshua
Judges	Judges
Ruth	Ruth
1 & 2 Samuel	1 & 2 Samuel
1 & 2 Kings	1 & 2 Kings
1 & 2 Chronicles	1 & 2 Chronicles
Ezra	Ezra
Nehemiah	Nehemiah
Tobit	
Judith	
Esther	Esther
Job	Job
Psalms	Psalms
Proverbs	Proverbs
Ecclesiastes	Ecclesiastes
Song of Songs	Song of Solomon
Wisdom	
Sirach	
Isaiah	Isaiah
Jeremiah	Jeremiah
Lamentations	Lamentations
Baruch	
Ezekiel	Ezekiel
Daniel	Daniel
Hosea	Hosea
Joel	Joel
Amos	Amos
Obadiah	Obadiah
Jonah	Jonah
Micah	Micah
Nahum	Nahum
Habakkuk	Habakkuk
Zephaniah	Zephaniah
Haggai	Haggai
Zechariah	Zechariah
Malachi	Malachi
1 & 2 Macabees	

JEWISH SCRIPTURE

Law
Genesis
Exodus
Leviticus
Numbers
Deuteronomy
Prophets
Joshua
Judges
1 & 2 Samuel
1 & 2 Kings
Isaiah
Jeremiah
Ezekiel
Hosea
Joel
Amos
Obadiah
Jonah
Micah
Nahum
Habakkuk
Zephaniah
Haggai
Zechariah
Malachi
Hagiographa
Psalms
Proverbs
Job
Song of Songs
Ruth
Lamentations
Ecclesiastes
Esther
Daniel
Ezra
Nehemiah
1 & 2 Chronicles

PROTESTANT APOCRYPHA

1 & 2 Esdras
Tobit
Judith
Additions to Esther
Wisdom of Solomon
Ecclesiasticus *or* the Wisdom of Jesus Son of Sirach
Baruch
Prayer of Azariah and the Song of the Three Holy Children
Susanna
Bel and the Dragon
The Prayer of Manasses
1 & 2 Maccabees

BOOKS OF THE NEW TESTAMENT

Matthew
Mark
Luke
John
Acts of the Apostles
Romans
1 & 2 Corinthians
Galatians
Ephesians
Philippians
Colossians
1 & 2 Thessalonians
1 & 2 Timothy
Titus
Philemon
Hebrews
James
1 & 2 Peter
1, 2, 3 John
Jude
Revelation *or* Apocalypse

---

2 : INVITE 3 : to give expression to 4 : to make a bid : OFFER — **bid·der** *n*
²bid *n* 1 : the act of one who bids; *also* : an offer for something 2 : INVITATION 3 : an announcement in a card game of what a player proposes to accomplish 4 : an attempt to win or gain ⟨a ∼ for mayor⟩
bid·da·ble \'bi-də-bəl\ *adj* 1 : OBEDIENT, DOCILE 2 : capable of being bid
bid·dy \'bi-dē\ *n, pl* **biddies** : HEN; *also* : a young chicken
bide \'bīd\ *vb* **bode** \'bōd\ *or* **bid·ed; bided; bid·ing** 1 : to wait for 2 : WAIT, TARRY 3 : DWELL
bi·det \bi-'dā\ *n* : a bathroom fixture used esp. for bathing the external genitals and the posterior parts of the body
bi·di·rec·tion·al \ˌbī-də-'rek-sh(ə-)nəl\ *adj* : involving, moving, or taking place in two usu. opposite directions — **bi·di·rec·tion·al·ly** *adv*
bi·en·ni·al \bī-'e-nē-əl\ *adj* 1 : taking place once in two years 2 : lasting two years 3 : producing leaves the first year and fruiting and dying the second year — **biennial** *n* — **bi·en·ni·al·ly** *adv*
bi·en·ni·um \bī-'e-nē-əm\ *n, pl* **-niums** *or* **-nia** \-ə\ [L, fr. *bi-* two + *annus* year] : a period of two years
bier \'bir\ *n* : a stand bearing a coffin or corpse
bi·fo·cal \'bī-ˌfō-kəl\ *adj* : having two focal lengths
bifocals \-kəlz\ *n pl* : eyeglasses with lenses that have one part that corrects for near vision and one for distant vision
bi·fur·cate \'bī-fər-ˌkāt, bī-'fər-\ *vb* **-cated; -cat·ing** : to divide into two branches or parts — **bi·fur·ca·tion** \ˌbī-fər-'kā-shən\ *n*
big \'big\ *adj* **big·ger; big·gest** 1 : large in size, amount, or scope 2 : PREGNANT; *also* : SWELLING 3 : IMPORTANT, IMPOSING 4 : NOBLE, GENEROUS 5 : POPULAR — **big·ness** *n* — **big on** : strongly favoring or liking
big·a·my \'bi-gə-mē\ *n* : the act of marrying one person while still legally married to another — **big·a·mist** \-mist\ *n* — **big·a·mous** \-məs\ *adj*
big bang theory *n* : a theory in astronomy: the universe originated in an explosion (**big bang**) from a single point of nearly infinite energy density
big brother *n* 1 : an older brother 2 : a man who befriends a delinquent or friendless boy 3 *cap both Bs* : the leader of an authoritarian state or movement
Big Dipper *n* : the seven principal stars of Ursa Major in a form resembling a dipper
big·foot \'big-ˌfut\ *n* : SASQUATCH
big·horn \'big-ˌhorn\ *n, pl* **bighorn** *or* **bighorns** : a wild sheep of mountainous western No. America

bighorn

bight \'bīt\ *n* 1 : a curve in a coast; *also* : the bay formed by such a curve 2 : a slack part in a rope
big–name \'big-'nām\ *adj* : widely popular ⟨a ∼ performer⟩ — **big name** *n*
big·ot \'bi-gət\ *n* : one intolerantly devoted to his or

her own prejudices or opinions **syn** fanatic, enthusiast, zealot — **big·ot·ed** \-gə-təd\ *adj* — **big·ot·ry** \-trē\ *n*

big shot \'big-ˌshät\ *n* : an important person

big time \-ˌtīm\ *n* **1** : a high-paying vaudeville circuit requiring only two performances a day **2** : the top rank of an activity or enterprise — **big–tim·er** *n*
big top *n* **1** : the main tent of a circus **2** : CIRCUS
big·wig \'big-ˌwig\ *n* : BIG SHOT
bike \'bīk\ *n* **1** : BICYCLE **2** : MOTORCYCLE
bik·er *n* : MOTORCYCLIST; *esp* : one who is a member of an organized gang
bike·way \'bīk-ˌwā\ *n* : a thoroughfare for bicycles
bi·ki·ni \bə-'kē-nē\ *n* : a woman's brief 2-piece bathing suit
bi·lat·er·al \bī-'la-tə-rəl\ *adj* **1** : having or involving two sides **2** : affecting reciprocally two sides or parties — **bi·lat·er·al·ly** *adv*
bile \'bīl\ *n* **1** : a bitter greenish fluid secreted by the liver that aids in the digestion of fats **2** : an ill-humored mood
bilge \'bilj\ *n* **1** : the part of a ship that lies between the bottom and the point where the sides go straight up **2** : stale or worthless remarks or ideas
bi·lin·gual \bī-'liŋ-gwəl\ *adj* : expressed in, knowing, or using two languages
bil·ious \'bil-yəs\ *adj* **1** : marked by or suffering from disordered liver function **2** : IRRITABLE, ILL-TEMPERED — **bil·ious·ness** *n*
bilk \'bilk\ *vb* : CHEAT, SWINDLE
¹bill \'bil\ *n* : the jaws of a bird together with their horny covering; *also* : a mouth structure (as of a turtle) resembling these — **billed** \'bild\ *adj*
²bill *vb* : to caress fondly
³bill *n* **1** : an itemized statement of particulars; *also* : INVOICE **2** : a written document or note **3** : a printed advertisement (as a poster) announcing an event **4** : a draft of a law presented to a legislature for enactment **5** : a written statement of a legal wrong suffered or of some breach of law **6** : a piece of paper money
⁴bill *vb* **1** : to enter in or prepare a bill; *also* : to submit a bill or account to **2** : to advertise by bills or posters
bill·board \-ˌbȯrd\ *n* : a flat surface on which advertising bills are posted
¹bil·let \'bi-lət\ *n* **1** : an order requiring a person to provide lodging for a soldier; *also* : quarters assigned by or as if by such an order **2** : POSITION, APPOINTMENT
²billet *vb* : to assign lodging to by billet
bil·let–doux \ˌbi-lā-'dü\ *n, pl* **billets–doux** *same or* -'düz\ [F *billet doux*, lit., sweet letter] : a love letter
bill·fold \'bil-ˌfōld\ *n* : WALLET
bil·liards \'bil-yərdz\ *n* : any of several games played on an oblong table by driving balls against each other or into pockets with a cue
bil·lings·gate \'bi-liŋz-ˌgāt, *Brit usu* -git\ *n* [*Billings-*

gate, old gate and fish market, London, England] : coarsely abusive language
bil·lion \'bil-yən\ *n* **1** : a thousand millions **2** *Brit* : a million millions — **billion** *adj* — **bil·lionth** \-yənth\ *adj or n*
bill of health : a usu. favorable report following an examination
bill of sale : a legal document transferring ownership of goods
¹bil·low \'bi-lō\ *n* **1** : WAVE; *esp* : a great wave **2** : a rolling mass (as of fog or flame) like a great wave — **bil·lowy** \'bi-lə-wē\ *adj*
²billow *vb* : to rise and roll in waves; *also* : to swell out ⟨~*ing* sails⟩
bil·ly \'bi-lē\ *n, pl* **billies** : BILLY CLUB
billy club *n* : a heavy usu. wooden club; *esp* : a police officer's club
bil·ly goat \'bi-lē-\ *n* : a male goat
bi·met·al \'bī-ˌmet-ᵊl\ *adj* : BIMETALLIC — **bimetal** *n*
bi·me·tal·lic \ˌbī-mə-'ta-lik\ *adj* : made of two different metals — often used of devices having a bonded expansive part — **bimetallic** *n*
bi·met·al·lism \bī-'met-ᵊl-ˌi-zəm\ *n* : the use of two metals at fixed ratios to form a standard of value for a monetary system
¹bi·month·ly \bī-'mənth-lē\ *adj* **1** : occurring every two months **2** : occurring twice a month : SEMIMONTHLY — **bimonthly** *adv*
²bimonthly *n* : a bimonthly publication
bin \'bin\ *n* : a box, crib, or enclosure used for storage
bi·na·ry \'bī-nə-rē, -ˌner-ē\ *adj* **1** : consisting of two things or parts **2** : relating to, being, or belonging to a system of numbers having 2 as its base ⟨the ~ digits 0 and 1⟩ **3** : involving a choice between or condition of two alternatives only (as on-off, yes-no) — **binary** *n*
binary star *n* : a system of two stars revolving around each other
bin·au·ral \bī-'nȯr-əl\ *adj* : of or relating to sound reproduction involving the use of two separated microphones and two transmission channels to achieve a stereophonic effect
bind \'bīnd\ *vb* **bound** \'baȯnd\; **bind·ing** **1** : TIE; *also* : to restrain as if by tying **2** : to put under an obligation; *also* : to constrain with legal authority **3** : BANDAGE **4** : to unite into a mass **5** : to compel as if by a pledge ⟨a handshake ~*s* the deal⟩ **6** : to strengthen or decorate with a band **7** : to fasten together and enclose in a cover ⟨~ books⟩ **8** : to exert a tying, restraining, or compelling effect — **bind·er** *n*
bind·ing \'bīn-diŋ\ *n* : something (as a ski fastening, a cover, or an edging fabric) used to bind
¹binge \'binj\ *n* : SPREE
²binge *vb* **binged; binge·ing** *or* **bing·ing** : to go on a binge and esp. an eating binge — **bing·er** *n*
bin·go \'biŋ-gō\ *n, pl* **bingos** : a game of chance played with cards having numbered squares corresponding to numbered balls drawn at random and won by covering five squares in a row
bin·na·cle \'bi-ni-kəl\ *n* [alter. of ME *bitakle*, fr. Pg or

Sp; Pg *bitácola* & Sp *bitácula*, fr. L *habitaculum* dwelling place, fr. *habitare* to inhabit] : a container holding a ship's compass

¹bin·oc·u·lar \bī-ˈnä-kyə-lər, bə-\ *adj* : of, relating to, or adapted to the use of both eyes — **bin·oc·u·lar·ly** *adv*

²bin·oc·u·lar \bə-ˈnä-kyə-lər, bī-\ *n* **1** : a binocular optical instrument (as a microscope) **2** : a hand-held optical instrument composed of two telescopes and a focusing device — usu. used in pl.

bi·no·mi·al \bī-ˈnō-mē-əl\ *n* **1** : a mathematical expression consisting of two terms connected by the sign plus (+) or minus (−) **2** : a biological species name consisting of two terms — **binomial** *adj*

bio·chem·is·try \ˌbī-ō-ˈke-mə-strē\ *n* : chemistry that deals with the chemical compounds and processes occurring in living things — **bio·chem·i·cal** \-mi-kəl\ *adj or n* — **bio·chem·ist** \-mist\ *n*

bio·de·grad·able \-di-ˈgrā-də-bəl\ *adj* : capable of being broken down esp. into innocuous products by the actions of living things (as microorganisms) ⟨a ~ detergent⟩ — **bio·de·grad·abil·i·ty** \-ˌgrā-də-ˈbi-lə-tē\ *n* — **bio·deg·ra·da·tion** \-ˌde-grə-ˈdā-shən\ *n* — **bio·de·grade** \-di-ˈgrād\ *vb*

bio·di·ver·si·ty \-də-ˈvər-sə-tē, -dī-\ *n* : biological diversity in an environment as indicated by numbers of different species of plants and animals

bio·eth·ics \-ˈe-thiks\ *n* : the ethics of biological research and its applications esp. in medicine — **bio·eth·i·cal** \-ˈe-thi-kəl\ *adj* — **bio·eth·i·cist** \-ˈe-thə-sist\ *n*

bio·feed·back \-ˈfēd-ˌbak\ *n* : the technique of making unconscious or involuntary bodily processes (as heartbeats or brain waves) objectively perceptible to the senses (as by use of an oscilloscope) in order to manipulate them by conscious mental control

biog *abbr* biographer; biographical; biography

bio·ge·og·ra·phy \ˌbī-ō-jē-ˈä-grə-fē\ *n* : a branch of biology that deals with the distribution of plants and animals — **bio·ge·og·ra·pher** *n*

bi·og·ra·phy \bī-ˈä-grə-fē, bē-\ *n, pl* **-phies** : a written history of a person's life; *also* : such writings in general — **bi·og·ra·pher** *n* — **bio·graph·i·cal** \ˌbī-ə-ˈgra-fi-kəl\ *also* **bio·graph·ic** \-fik\ *adj*

biol *abbr* biologic; biological; biologist; biology

bi·o·log·i·cal \ˌbī-ə-ˈlä-ji-kəl\ *also* **bi·o·log·ic** \-jik\ *adj* **1** : of, relating to, or produced by biology or life and living processes **2** : related by direct genetic relationship rather than by adoption or marriage ⟨~ parents⟩ — **bi·o·log·i·cal·ly** \-ji-k(ə-)lē\ *adv*

biological clock *n* : an inherent timing mechanism inferred to exist in some living systems (as a cell) in order to explain various cyclic physiological and behavioral responses

biological warfare *n* : warfare in which living organisms (as bacteria) are used as weapons

bi·ol·o·gy \bī-ˈä-lə-jē\ *n* [G *Biologie*, fr. Gk *bios* mode of life + *logos* word] **1** : a science that deals with living beings and life processes **2** : the life processes of an organism or group — **bi·ol·o·gist** \bī-ˈä-lə-jist\ *n*

bio·med·i·cal \ˌbī-ō-ˈme-di-kəl\ *adj* : of, relating to, or involving biological, medical, and physical science

bi·on·ic \bī-ˈä-nik\ *adj* : having normal biological capability or performance enhanced by or as if by electronic or mechanical devices

bio·phys·ics \ˌbī-ō-ˈfi-ziks\ *n* : a branch of science concerned with the application of physical principles and methods to biological problems — **bio·phys·i·cal** \-zi-kəl\ *adj* — **bio·phys·i·cist** \-ˈfi-zə-sist\ *n*

bi·op·sy \ˈbī-ˌäp-sē\ *n, pl* **-sies** : the removal of tissue, cells, or fluids from the living body for examination

bio·rhythm \ˈbī-ō-ˌri-thəm\ *n* : an inherent rhythm that appears to control or initiate various biological processes

bio·sphere \ˈbī-ə-ˌsfir\ *n* **1** : the part of the world in which life can exist **2** : living beings together with their environment

bio·tech \ˈbī-ō-ˌtek\ *n* : BIOTECHNOLOGY

bio·tech·nol·o·gy \ˌbī-ō-tek-ˈnä-lə-jē\ *n* : biological science when applied esp. in genetic engineering and recombinant DNA technology

bi·ot·ic \bī-ˈä-tik\ *adj* : of or relating to life; *esp* : caused by living beings

bi·o·tin \ˈbī-ə-tən\ *n* : a vitamin of the vitamin B complex found esp. in yeast, liver, and egg yolk and active in growth promotion

bi·o·tite \ˈbī-ə-ˌtīt\ *n* : a dark mica containing iron, magnesium, potassium, and aluminum

bi·par·ti·san \bī-ˈpär-tə-zən\ *adj* : representing or composed of members of two parties

bi·par·tite \-ˈpär-ˌtīt\ *adj* **1** : being in two parts **2** : shared by two ⟨~ treaty⟩

bi·ped \ˈbī-ˌped\ *n* : a 2-footed animal — **bi·ped·al** \(ˌ)bī-ˈped-ᵊl\ *adj*

bi·plane \ˈbī-ˌplān\ *n* : an aircraft with two wings placed one above the other

bi·po·lar \ˈbī-ˈpō-lər\ *adj* : having or involving the use of two poles — **bi·po·lar·i·ty** \ˌbī-pō-ˈlar-ə-tē\ *n*

bi·ra·cial \bī-ˈrā-shəl\ *adj* : of, relating to, or involving members of two races

¹birch \ˈbərch\ *n* **1** : any of a genus of mostly short-lived deciduous shrubs and trees with membranous outer bark and pale close-grained wood; *also* : this wood **2** : a birch rod or bundle of twigs for flogging — **birch** *or* **birch·en** \ˈbər-chən\ *adj*

²birch *vb* : WHIP, FLOG

¹bird \ˈbərd\ *n* : any of a class of warm-blooded egg-laying vertebrates having the body feathered and the forelimbs modified to form wings

²bird *vb* : to observe or identify wild birds in their native habitat — **bird·er** *n*

bird·bath \ˈbərd-ˌbath, -ˌbàth\ *n* : a usu. ornamental basin set up for birds to bathe in

bird·house \-ˌhau̇s\ *n* : an artificial nesting place for birds; *also* : AVIARY

bird·ie \ˈbər-dē\ *n* : a score of one under par on a hole in golf

bird·lime \-ˌlīm\ *n* : a sticky substance smeared on twigs to snare small birds

bird of paradise : any of numerous brilliantly colored plumed birds of the New Guinea area

bird of prey : a carnivorous bird that feeds wholly or chiefly on carrion or on meat taken by hunting

bird·seed \ˈbərd-ˌsēd\ *n* : a mixture of small seeds (as of hemp or millet) used for feeding birds

bird's-eye \ˈbərdz-ˌī\ *adj* **1** : marked with spots resembling birds' eyes ⟨~ maple⟩ **2** : seen from above as if by a flying bird ⟨~ view⟩; *also* : CURSORY

bi·ret·ta \bə-ˈre-tə\ *n* : a square cap with three ridges on top worn esp. by Roman Catholic clergymen

birr \ˈbir, ˈbər\ *n, pl* **birr** — see MONEY table

birth \ˈbərth\ *n* **1** : the act or fact of being born or of bringing forth young **2** : LINEAGE, DESCENT **3** : ORIGIN, BEGINNING

birth canal *n* : the channel formed by the cervix, vagina, and vulva through which the fetus passes during birth

birth control *n* : control of the number of children born esp. by preventing or lessening the frequency of conception

birth·day \ˈbərth-ˌdā\ *n* : the day or anniversary of one's birth

birth defect *n* : a physical or biochemical defect present at birth and inherited or environmentally induced

birth·mark \ˈbərth-ˌmärk\ *n* : an unusual mark or blemish on the skin at birth

birth·place \-ˌplās\ *n* : place of birth or origin

birth·rate \-₁rāt\ *n* : the number of births per number of individuals in a given area or group during a given time

birth·right \-₁rīt\ *n* : a right, privilege, or possession to which one is entitled by birth *syn* legacy, patrimony, heritage, inheritance

birth·stone \-₁stōn\ *n* : a gemstone associated symbolically with the month of one's birth

bis·cuit \'bis-kət\ *n* [ME *bisquite*, fr. MF *bescuit*, fr. (*pain*) *bescuit* twice-cooked bread] **1** : a crisp flat cake; *esp, Brit* : CRACKER 2 **2** : a small quick bread made from dough that has been rolled and cut or dropped from a spoon

bi·sect \'bī-₁sekt\ *vb* : to divide into two usu. equal parts; *also* : CROSS, INTERSECT — **bi·sec·tion** \'bī-₁sek-shən\ *n* — **bi·sec·tor** \-tər\ *n*

bi·sex·u·al \bī-'sek-shə-wəl\ *adj* **1** : possessing characters of or having sexual desire for both sexes **2** : of, relating to, or involving both sexes — **bisexual** *n* — **bi·sex·u·al·i·ty** \₁bī-₁sek-shə-'wal-ə-tē\ *n*

bish·op \'bi-shəp\ *n* [ME *bisshop*, fr. OE *bisceop*, fr. LL *episcopus*, fr. Gk *episkopos*, lit., overseer, fr. *epi-* on, over + *skeptesthai* to look] **1** : a member of the clergy ranking above a priest and typically governing a diocese **2** : any of various Protestant church officials who superintend other clergy **3** : a chess piece that can move diagonally across any number of adjoining unoccupied squares

bish·op·ric \'bi-shə-prik\ *n* **1** : DIOCESE **2** : the office of bishop

bis·muth \'biz-məth\ *n* : a heavy brittle grayish white metallic chemical element used in alloys and medicine — see ELEMENT table

bi·son \'bīs-ᵊn, 'bīz-\ *n, pl* **bison** : BUFFALO 2

bisque \'bisk\ *n* : a thick cream soup

bis·tro \'bēs-trō, 'bis-\ *n, pl* **bistros** [F] **1** : a small or unpretentious restaurant **2** : BAR; *also* : NIGHTCLUB

¹bit \'bit\ *n* **1** : the biting or cutting edge or part of a tool **2** : the part of a bridle that is placed in a horse's mouth

²bit *n* **1** : a morsel of food; *also* : a small piece or quantity of something **2** : a small coin; *also* : a unit of value equal to 12½ cents **3** : something small or trivial **4** : an indefinite usu. small degree or extent ⟨a ~ tired⟩

³bit *n* [*binary digit*] : a unit of computer information equivalent to the result of a choice between two alternatives; *also* : its physical representation

¹bitch \'bich\ *n* **1** : a female canine; *esp* : a female dog **2** : a malicious, spiteful, and domineering woman

²bitch *vb* : COMPLAIN

¹bite \'bīt\ *vb* **bit** \'bit\; **bit·ten** \'bit-ᵊn\ *also* **bit**; **bit·ing** \'bī-tiŋ\ **1** : to grip with teeth or jaws; *also* : to wound or sting with or as if with fangs **2** : to cut or pierce with or as if with an edged instrument **3** : to cause to smart or sting **4** : CORRODE **5** : to take bait

²bite *n* **1** : the act or manner of biting **2** : FOOD **3** : a wound made by biting; *also* : a penetrating effect

bit·ing \'bī-tiŋ\ *adj* : SHARP, CUTTING

bit·ter \'bi-tər\ *adj* **1** : being or inducing the one of the basic taste sensations that is acrid, astringent, or dis-

agreeable and is suggestive of hops **2** : marked by intensity or severity (as of distress or hatred) **3** : extremely harsh or cruel — **bit·ter·ly** *adv* — **bit·ter·ness** *n*

bit·tern \'bi-tərn\ *n* : any of various small or medium-sized herons

bit·ters \'bi-tərz\ *n sing or pl* : a usu. alcoholic solution of bitter and often aromatic plant products used in mixing drinks and as a mild tonic

¹bit·ter·sweet \'bi-tər-₁swēt\ *n* **1** : a poisonous nightshade with purple flowers and orange-red berries **2** : a woody vine with yellow capsules that open when ripe and disclose scarlet seed coverings

²bittersweet *adj* : being at once both bitter and sweet

bi·tu·mi·nous coal \bə-'tü-mə-nəs-, bi-, -'tyü-\ *n* : a coal that when heated yields considerable volatile waste matter

bi·valve \'bī-₁valv\ *n* : an animal (as a clam) with a shell composed of two separate parts that open and shut — **bivalve** *adj*

¹biv·ouac \'bi-və-₁wak\ *n* [F, fr. LG *biwacht*, fr. *bi* at + *wacht* guard] : a temporary encampment or shelter : CAMP

²bivouac *vb* **-ouacked; -ouack·ing** : to form a bivouac

¹bi·week·ly \₁bī-'wē-klē\ *adj* **1** : occurring twice a week **2** : occurring every two weeks : FORTNIGHTLY — **biweekly** *adv*

²biweekly *n* : a biweekly publication

bi·year·ly \-'yir-lē\ *adj* **1** : BIANNUAL **2** : BIENNIAL

bi·zarre \bə-'zär\ *adj* : ODD, ECCENTRIC, FANTASTIC — **bi·zarre·ly** *adv*

bk *abbr* **1** bank **2** book

Bk *symbol* berkelium

bkg *abbr* banking

bkgd *abbr* background

bks *abbr* barracks

bkt *abbr* **1** basket **2** bracket

bl *abbr* **1** bale **2** barrel **3** blue

blab \'blab\ *vb* **blabbed; blab·bing** : TATTLE, GOSSIP

¹black \'blak\ *adj* **1** : of the color black; *also* : very dark **2** : SWARTHY **3** : of or relating to various groups of dark-skinned people **4** : of or relating to the Afro-American people or their culture **5** : SOILED, DIRTY **6** : lacking light ⟨a ~ night⟩ **7** : WICKED, EVIL ⟨~ magic⟩ **8** : DISMAL, GLOOMY ⟨a ~ outlook⟩ **9** : SULLEN ⟨a ~ mood⟩ — **black·ish** *adj* — **black·ly** *adv* — **black·ness** *n*

²black *n* **1** : a black pigment or dye; *also* : something (as clothing) that is black **2** : the characteristic color of soot or coal **3** : a person of a dark-skinned race **4** : AFRO-AMERICAN

³black *vb* : BLACKEN

black·a·moor \'bla-kə-₁múr\ *n* : a dark-skinned person

black-and-blue \₁bla-kən-'blü\ *adj* : darkly discolored from blood effused by bruising

black·ball \'blak-₁bȯl\ *vb* **1** : to vote against; *esp* : to exclude from membership by casting a negative vote **2** : OSTRACIZE — **black·ball** *n*

black bass *n* : any of several freshwater sunfishes native to eastern and central No. America

¹black belt \'blak-ˌbelt\ *n, often cap both Bs* : an area densely populated by blacks

²black belt \-'belt\ *n* : one who holds the rating of expert (as in judo or karate); *also* : the rating itself

black·ber·ry \-ˌber-ē\ *n* : the usu. black or purple juicy but seedy edible fruit of various brambles; *also* : a plant bearing this fruit

black·bird \-ˌbərd\ *n* : any of various birds (as the red= winged blackbird) of which the male is largely or wholly black

black·board \-ˌbōrd\ *n* : a smooth usu. dark surface used for writing or drawing on with chalk

black·body \-'bä-dē\ *n* : a body or surface that completely absorbs incident radiation with no reflection

black box *n* 1 : a usu. complicated electronic device whose components and workings are unknown or mysterious to the user 2 : a device used in aircraft to record cockpit conversations and flight data

black death *n* : an epidemic of bacterial plague and esp. bubonic plague that spread rapidly in Europe and Asia in the 14th century

black·en \'bla-kən\ *vb* **black·ened; black·en·ing** 1 : to make or become black 2 : DEFAME, SULLY

black·ened *adj* : coated with spices and quickly seared in a very hot skillet ⟨∼ swordfish⟩

black eye *n* : a discoloration of the skin around the eye from bruising

black–eyed Su·san \ˌblak-ˌīd-'süz-ᵊn\ *n* : either of two No. American plants that are related to the daisies and have deep yellow to orange flower heads with dark conical centers

Black·foot \'blak-ˌfut\ *n, pl* **Black·feet** *or* **Blackfoot** : a member of an American Indian people of Montana, Alberta, and Saskatchewan

black·guard \'bla-gərd, -ˌgärd\ *n* : SCOUNDREL, RASCAL

black·head \'blak-ˌhed\ *n* : a small usu. dark oily mass plugging the outlet of a skin gland

black hole *n* : a hypothetical celestial object with a gravitational field so strong that light cannot escape from it

black·ing \'bla-kiŋ\ *n* : a substance applied to something to make it black

¹black·jack \'blak-ˌjak\ *n* 1 : a leather-covered club with a flexible handle 2 : a card game in which the object is to be dealt cards having a higher count than the dealer but not exceeding 21

²blackjack *vb* : to hit with or as if with a blackjack

black light *n* : invisible ultraviolet light

black·list \'blak-ˌlist\ *n* : a list of persons who are disapproved of and are to be punished or boycotted — **blacklist** *vb*

black·mail \'blak-ˌmāl\ *n* : extortion by threats esp. of public exposure; *also* : something so extorted — **blackmail** *vb* — **black·mail·er** *n*

black market *n* : illicit trade in goods; *also* : a place where such trade is carried on

Black Mass *n* : a travesty of the Christian mass ascribed to worshipers of Satan

Black Muslim *n* : a member of a chiefly black group that professes Islamic religious belief

black nationalist *n, often cap B&N* : a member of a group of militant blacks who advocate separatism from whites and the formation of self-governing black communities — **black nationalism** *n, often cap B&N*

black·out \'bla-ˌkaut\ *n* 1 : a period of darkness due to electrical power failure 2 : a transitory loss or dulling of vision or consciousness 3 : the prohibition or restriction of the telecasting of a sports event — **black out** *vb*

black power *n* : the mobilization of the political and economic power of black Americans esp. to compel respect for their rights and improve their condition

black sheep *n* : a discreditable member of an otherwise respectable group

black·smith \'blak-ˌsmith\ *n* : a smith who forges iron — **black·smith·ing** *n*

black·thorn \-ˌthȯrn\ *n* : a European thorny plum

black·top \'blak-ˌtäp\ *n* : a dark tarry material (as asphalt) used esp. for surfacing roads — **blacktop** *vb*

black widow *n* : a venomous New World spider having the female black with an hourglass-shaped red mark on the underside of the abdomen

blad·der \'bla-dər\ *n* : a sac in which liquid or gas is stored; *esp* : one in a vertebrate into which urine passes from the kidneys

blade \'blād\ *n* 1 : a leaf of a plant and esp. of a grass; *also* : the flat part of a leaf as distinguished from its stalk 2 : something (as the flat part of an oar or an arm of a propeller) resembling the blade of a leaf 3 : the cutting part of an instrument or tool 4 : SWORD; *also* : SWORDSMAN 5 : a dashing fellow ⟨a gay ∼⟩ 6 : the runner of an ice skate — **blad·ed** \'blā-dəd\ *adj*

blain \'blān\ *n* : an inflammatory swelling or sore

¹blame \'blām\ *vb* **blamed; blam·ing** [ME, fr. OF blamer, fr. L blasphemare to blaspheme, fr. Gk blasphēmein] 1 : to find fault with 2 : to hold responsible or responsible for **syn** censure, denounce, condemn, criticize — **blam·able** *adj*

²blame *n* 1 : CENSURE, REPROOF 2 : responsibility for fault or error **syn** guilt, fault, culpability, onus — **blame·less** *adj* — **blame·less·ly** *adv* — **blame·less·ness** *n*

blame·wor·thy \-ˌwər-thē\ *adj* : deserving blame — **blame·wor·thi·ness** *n*

blanch \'blanch\ *vb* : to make or become white or pale : BLEACH

blanc·mange \blə-'mänj, -'mänzh\ *n* [ME blancmanger, fr. MF blanc manger, lit., white food] : a dessert made from gelatin or a starchy substance and milk usu. sweetened and flavored

bland \'bland\ *adj* 1 : smooth in manner : SUAVE 2 : gently soothing ⟨a ∼ diet⟩; *also* : INSIPID **syn** gentle, mild, soft, balmy — **bland·ly** *adv* — **bland·ness** *n*

blan·dish·ment \'blan-dish-mənt\ *n* : flattering or coaxing speech or action : CAJOLERY

¹blank \'blaŋk\ *adj* 1 : showing or causing an appearance of dazed dismay; *also* : EXPRESSIONLESS 2 : free from writing or marks; *also* : having spaces to be filled in 3 : DULL, EMPTY ⟨∼ moments⟩ 4 : ABSOLUTE, DOWNRIGHT ⟨a ∼ refusal⟩ 5 : not shaped in final form — **blank·ly** *adv* — **blank·ness** *n*

²blank *n* 1 : an empty space 2 : a form with spaces for the entry of data 3 : an unfinished form (as of a key) 4 : a cartridge with propellant and a seal but no projectile

³blank *vb* 1 : to cover or close up : OBSCURE 2 : to keep from scoring

blank check *n* 1 : a signed check with the amount unspecified 2 : complete freedom of action

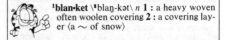

¹blan·ket \'blaŋ-kət\ *n* 1 : a heavy woven often woolen covering 2 : a covering layer ⟨a ∼ of snow⟩

²blanket *vb* : to cover with a blanket

³blanket *adj* : covering a group or class ⟨∼ insurance⟩; *also* : applicable in all instances ⟨∼ rules⟩

blank verse *n* : unrhymed iambic pentameter

blare \'blar\ *vb* **blared; blar·ing** : to sound loud and harsh; *also* : to proclaim loudly — **blare** *n*

blar·ney \'blär-nē\ *n* [Blarney stone, a stone in Blarney Castle, near Cork, Ireland, held to bestow skill in flattery on those who kiss it] : skillful flattery : BLANDISHMENT

bla·sé \blä-'zā\ *adj* [F] : apathetic to pleasure or excitement as a result of excessive indulgence; *also* : SOPHISTICATED

blas·pheme \blas-'fēm, 'blas-ˌ\ *vb* **blas·phemed; blas-**

phem·ing 1 : to speak of or address with irreverence **2** : to utter blasphemy — **blas·phem·er** *n*
blas·phe·my \'blas-fə-mē\ *n, pl* **-mies 1** : the act of expressing lack of reverence for God **2** : irreverence toward something considered sacred — **blas·phe·mous** \-məs\ *adj*
¹**blast** \'blast\ *n* **1** : a violent gust of wind; *also* : its effect **2** : sound made by a wind instrument **3** : a current of air forced at high pressure through a hole in a furnace (**blast furnace**) **4** : a sudden withering esp. of plants : BLIGHT **5** : EXPLOSION; *also* : the often destructive shock wave of an explosion
²**blast** *vb* : to shatter by or as if by an explosive
blast off *vb* : TAKE OFF **4** — used esp. of rocket-propelled vehicles — **blast·off** \'blast-‚òf\ *n*
bla·tant \'blāt-ᵊnt\ *adj* : offensively obtrusive : vulgarly showy **syn** vociferous, boisterous, clamorous, obstreperous — **bla·tan·cy** \-ᵊn-sē\ *n* — **bla·tant·ly** *adv*
blath·er \'bla-thər\ *vb* : to talk foolishly at length — **blather** *n*
blath·er·skite \'bla-thər-‚skīt\ *n* : a person who blathers
¹**blaze** \'blāz\ *n* **1** : FIRE **2** : intense direct light accompanied by heat **3** : something (as a dazzling display or sudden outburst) suggesting fire ⟨a ~ of autumn leaves⟩ **syn** glare, glow, flame
²**blaze** *vb* **blazed; blaz·ing 1** : to burn brightly; *also* : to flare up **2** : to be conspicuously bright : GLITTER
³**blaze** *vb* **blazed; blaz·ing** : to make public or conspicuous
⁴**blaze** *n* **1** : a usu. white stripe on the face of an animal **2** : a trail marker; *esp* : one made on a tree
⁵**blaze** *vb* **blazed; blaz·ing** : to mark (as a tree or trail) with blazes

blaz·er \'blā-zər\ *n* : a sports jacket often with notched collar and pockets that are stitched on

¹**bla·zon** \'blāz-ᵊn\ *n* **1** : COAT OF ARMS **2** : ostentatious display
²**blazon** *vb* **1** : to publish widely : PROCLAIM **2** : DECK, ADORN

bldg *abbr* building
bldr *abbr* builder
¹**bleach** \'blēch\ *vb* : WHITEN, BLANCH
²**bleach** *n* : a preparation used in bleaching
bleach·ers \'blē-chərz\ *n sing or pl* : a usu. uncovered stand of tiered seats for spectators
bleak \'blēk\ *adj* **1** : desolately barren and often wind-swept **2** : lacking warm or cheering qualities — **bleak·ish** *adj* — **bleak·ly** *adv* — **bleak·ness** *n*
blear \'blir\ *adj* : dim with water or tears ⟨~ eyes⟩
bleary \'blir-ē\ *adj* **1** : dull or dimmed esp. from fatigue or sleep **2** : poorly outlined or defined
bleat \'blēt\ *n* : the cry of a sheep or goat or a sound like it — **bleat** *vb*
bleed \'blēd\ *vb* **bled** \'bled\; **bleed·ing 1** : to lose or shed blood **2** : to be wounded; *also* : to feel pain or distress **3** : to flow or ooze from a wounded surface; *also* : to draw fluid from ⟨~ a tire⟩ **4** : to extort money from
bleed·er \'blē-dər\ *n* : one that bleeds; *esp* : HEMOPHILIAC
bleeding heart *n* **1** : a garden plant related to the poppies that has usu. deep pink drooping heart-shaped flowers **2** : a person who shows extreme sympathy esp. for an object of alleged persecution
¹**blem·ish** \'ble-mish\ *vb* : to spoil by a flaw : MAR
²**blemish** *n* : a noticeable flaw
¹**blench** \'blench\ *vb* [ME, to deceive, blench, fr. OE *blencan* to deceive] : FLINCH, QUAIL **syn** shrink, recoil, wince, start
²**blench** *vb* : to grow or make pale
¹**blend** \'blend\ *vb* **blend·ed; blend·ing 1** : to mix thoroughly **2** : to prepare (as coffee) by mixing different varieties **3** : to combine into an integrated whole **4** : HARMONIZE **syn** fuse, merge, mingle, coalesce — **blend·er** *n*
²**blend** *n* : a product of blending **syn** compound, composite, alloy, mixture
bless \'bles\ *vb* **blessed** \'blest\ *also* **blest** \'blest\; **bless·ing** [ME, fr. OE *blētsian*, fr. *blōd* blood; fr. the use of blood in consecration] **1** : to consecrate by religious rite or word **2** : to sanctify with the sign of the cross **3** : to invoke divine care for **4** : PRAISE, GLORIFY **5** : to confer happiness upon

bless·ed \'ble-səd\ *also* blest \'blest\ *adj* 1 : HOLY 2 : BEATIFIED 3 : DELIGHTFUL — bless·ed·ly *adv* — bless·ed·ness *n*

bless·ing \'ble-siŋ\ *n* 1 : the act or words of one who blesses; *also* : APPROVAL 2 : a thing conducive to happiness 3 : grace said at a meal

blew *past of* BLOW

¹blight \'blīt\ *n* 1 : a plant disease or injury marked by withering; *also* : an organism causing a blight 2 : an impairing or frustrating influence; *also* : a deteriorated condition ⟨urban ∼⟩

²blight *vb* : to affect with or suffer from blight

blimp \'blimp\ *n* : a nonrigid airship

¹blind \'blīnd\ *adj* 1 : lacking or grossly deficient in ability to see; *also* : intended for blind persons 2 : not based on reason, evidence, or knowledge ⟨∼ faith⟩ 3 : not intelligently controlled or directed ⟨∼ chance⟩ 4 : performed solely by using aircraft instruments ⟨a ∼ landing⟩ 5 : hard to discern or make out : HIDDEN ⟨a ∼ seam⟩ 6 : lacking an opening or outlet ⟨a ∼ alley⟩ — blind·ly *adv* — blind·ness \'blīnd-nəs\ *n*

²blind *vb* 1 : to make blind 2 : DAZZLE 3 : DARKEN; *also* : HIDE

³blind *n* 1 : something (as a shutter) to hinder vision or keep out light 2 : a place of concealment 3 : SUBTERFUGE

blind date *n* : a date between persons who have not previously met; *also* : either of these persons

blind·er \'blīn-dər\ *n* : either of two flaps on a horse's bridle to prevent it from seeing to the side

blind·fold \'blīnd-ˌfōld\ *vb* : to cover the eyes of with or as if with a bandage — blindfold *n*

¹blink \'bliŋk\ *vb* 1 : WINK 2 : TWINKLE 3 : EVADE, IGNORE

²blink *n* 1 : GLIMMER, SPARKLE 2 : a usu. involuntary shutting and opening of the eye

blink·er \'bliŋ-kər\ *n* : a blinking light used as a signal

blin·tze \'blint-sə\ *or* blintz \'blints\ *n* [Yiddish *blintse*] : a thin rolled pancake with a filling usu. of cream cheese

blip \'blip\ *n* 1 : a spot on a radar screen 2 : ABERRATION 1

bliss \'blis\ *n* : complete happiness : JOY syn beatitude, blessedness — bliss·ful \-fəl\ *adj* — bliss·ful·ly *adv*

¹blis·ter \'blis-tər\ *n* 1 : a raised area of skin containing watery fluid; *also* : an agent that causes blisters 2 : something (as a raised spot in paint) suggesting a blister 3 : a disease of plants marked by large swollen patches on the leaves

²blister *vb* : to develop a blister; *also* : to cause blisters

blithe \'blīth, 'blīth\ *adj* blith·er; blith·est : happily lighthearted syn merry, jovial, jolly, jocund — blithe·ly *adv* — blithe·some \-səm\ *adj*

blitz \'blits\ *n* 1 : an intensive series of air raids 2 : a fast intensive campaign 3 : a rush of the passer by the defensive linebackers in football — blitz *vb*

blitz·krieg \-ˌkrēg\ *n* [G. lit., lightning war, fr. *Blitz*

lightning + *Krieg* war] : a sudden violent enemy attack

bliz·zard \'bli-zərd\ *n* : a long severe snowstorm

blk *abbr* 1 black 2 block

bloat \'blōt\ *vb* : to swell by or as if by filling with water or air

blob \'bläb\ *n* : a small lump or drop of a thick consistency

bloc \'bläk\ *n* [F, lit., block] : a combination of individuals or groups (as nations) working for a common purpose

¹block \'bläk\ *n* 1 : a solid piece of substantial material (as wood or stone) 2 : HINDRANCE, OBSTRUCTION; *also* : interruption of normal function of body or mind ⟨heart ∼⟩ 3 : a frame enclosing one or more pulleys and having a hook or strap by which it may be attached 4 : a piece of material with a hand-cut design on its surface from which copies are to be made 5 : a large building divided into separate units (as apartments or offices) 6 : a row of houses or shops 7 : a city square; *also* : the distance along one of the sides of such a square 8 : a quantity of things considered as a unit ⟨a ∼ of seats⟩

²block *vb* 1 : OBSTRUCT, CHECK 2 : to outline roughly ⟨∼ out a design⟩ 3 : to provide or support with a block ⟨∼ up a wheel⟩ syn bar, impede, hinder, obstruct

block·ade \blä-'kād\ *n* : the isolation of a place usu. by troops or ships — blockade *vb* — block·ad·er *n*

block·age \'blä-kij\ *n* : an act or instance of obstructing : the state of being blocked

block·bust·er \'bläk-ˌbəs-tər\ *n* : one that is very large, successful, or violent ⟨a ∼ of a movie⟩

block·head \'bläk-ˌhed\ *n* : DOLT, DUNCE

block·house \-ˌhaüs\ *n* : a small strong building used as a shelter (as from enemy fire) or observation post

¹blond *or* blonde \'bländ\ *adj* : fair in complexion; *also* : of a light or bleached color ⟨∼ mahogany⟩ — blond·ish \'blän-dish\ *adj*

²blond *or* blonde *n* : a person having blond hair

blood \'bləd\ *n* 1 : a usu. red liquid that circulates in the heart, arteries, and veins of animals 2 : LIFEBLOOD; *also* : LIFE 3 : LINEAGE, STOCK 4 : KINSHIP; *also* : KINDRED 5 : the taking of life 6 : TEMPER, PASSION 7 : DANDY 1 — blood·less *adj* — bloody *adj*

blood bank *n* : a place where blood or plasma is stored

blood·bath \'bləd-ˌbath, -ˌbäth\ *n* : MASSACRE

blood count *n* : the determination of the number of blood cells in a specific volume of blood; *also* : the number of cells so determined

blood·cur·dling \'bləd-kərd-liŋ, -ˌkər-dᵊl-iŋ\ *adj* : arousing fright or horror

blood·ed \'blə-dəd\ *adj* 1 : having blood of a specified kind ⟨warm-*blooded* animals⟩ 2 : entirely or largely purebred ⟨∼ horses⟩

blood group *n* : one of the classes into which human beings can be separated by the presence or absence in their blood of specific antigens

blood·hound \'bləd-ˌhaünd\ *n* : any of a breed of large powerful hounds with long drooping ears, a wrinkled face, and keen sense of smell

blood·let·ting \-ˌle-tiŋ\ n 1 : PHLEBOTOMY 2 : BLOOD-SHED

blood·line \-ˌlīn\ n : a sequence of direct ancestors esp. in a pedigree

blood·mo·bile \-mō-ˌbēl\ n : a motor vehicle equipped for collecting blood from donors

blood poisoning n : invasion of the bloodstream by virulent microorganisms from a focus of infection accompanied esp. by chills, fever, and prostration

blood pressure n : pressure of the blood on the walls of blood vessels and esp. arteries

blood·root \'bləd-ˌrüt, -ˌrůt\ n : a plant related to the poppy that has a red root and sap, a solitary leaf, and a white flower in early spring

blood·shed \-ˌshed\ n : wounding or taking of life : CARNAGE, SLAUGHTER

blood·shot \-ˌshät\ adj : inflamed to redness ⟨~ eyes⟩

blood·stain \-ˌstān\ n : a discoloration caused by blood — **blood·stained** \-ˌstānd\ adj

blood·stone \-ˌstōn\ n : a green quartz sprinkled with red spots

blood·stream \-ˌstrēm\ n : the flowing blood in a circulatory system

blood·suck·er \-ˌsə-kər\ n : an animal that sucks blood; esp : LEECH — **blood·suck·ing** adj

blood test n : a test of the blood; esp : one for syphilis

blood·thirsty \'bləd-ˌthər-stē\ adj : eager to shed blood — **blood·thirst·i·ly** \-ˌthər-stə-lē\ adv — **blood·thirst·i·ness** \-stē-nəs\ n

blood type n : BLOOD GROUP — **blood–typ·ing** n

blood vessel n : a vessel (as a vein or artery) in which blood circulates in the body

Bloody Mary \-ˈmer-ē\ n, pl **Bloody Marys** : a drink made essentially of vodka and tomato juice

¹bloom \'blüm\ n 1 : FLOWER 1; also : flowers or amount of flowers (as of a plant) 2 : the period or state of flowering 3 : a state or time of beauty and vigor 4 : a powdery coating esp. on fruits and leaves 5 : rosy color; also : an appearance of freshness or health — **bloomy** adj

²bloom vb 1 : to produce or yield flowers 2 : MATURE 3 : to glow esp. with healthy color **syn** flower, blossom

bloo·mers \'blü-mərz\ n pl [Amelia Bloomer †1894 Am. reformer] : a woman's garment of short loose trousers gathered at the knee

bloop·er \'blü-pər\ n 1 : a fly ball hit barely beyond a baseball infield 2 : an embarrassing public blunder

¹blos·som \'blä-səm\ n 1 : the flower of a plant 2 : the period or state of flowering

²blossom vb 1 : FLOWER, BLOOM

¹blot \'blät\ n 1 : SPOT, STAIN ⟨ink ~s⟩ 2 : BLEMISH **syn** stigma, brand, slur

²blot vb **blot·ted; blot·ting** 1 : SPOT, STAIN 2 : OBSCURE, ECLIPSE ⟨~ out the sun⟩ 3 obs : MAR; esp : DISGRACE 4 : to dry or remove with or as if with an absorbing material 5 : to make a blot

blotch \'bläch\ n : a usu. large and irregular spot or mark (as of ink or color) — **blotch** vb — **blotchy** adj

blot·ter \'blä-tər\ n 1 : a piece of blotting paper 2 : a book for preliminary records (as of sales or arrests)

blot·ting paper n : a spongy paper used to absorb ink

blouse \'blaůs, 'blaůz\ n 1 : a loose outer garment like a smock 2 : a usu. loose garment reaching from the neck to about the waist

¹blow \'blō\ vb **blew** \'blü\; **blown** \'blōn\; **blow·ing** 1 : to move forcibly ⟨the wind blew⟩ 2 : to send forth a current of gas (as air) 3 : to act on with a current of gas or vapor; esp : to drive with such a current 4 : to sound or cause to sound ⟨~ a horn⟩ 5 : PANT, GASP; also : to expel moist air in breathing ⟨the whale blew⟩ 6 : BOAST; also : BLUSTER 7 : MELT — used of an electrical fuse 8 : to shape or form by blown or injected air ⟨~ glass⟩ 9 : to shatter or destroy by or as if by explosion 10 : to make breathless by exertion 11 : to spend recklessly 12 : to foul up hopelessly ⟨blew her lines⟩ — **blow·er** n

²blow n 1 : a usu. strong blowing of air : GALE 2 : BOASTING, BRAG 3 : an act or instance of blowing

³blow vb **blew** \'blü\; **blown** \'blōn\; **blow·ing** : FLOWER, BLOOM

⁴blow n 1 : a forcible stroke 2 : COMBAT ⟨come to ~s⟩ 3 : a severe and usu. unexpected calamity

blow–by–blow adj : minutely detailed ⟨~ account⟩

blow–dry \-ˌdrī\ vb : to dry and usu. style hair with a blow-dryer

blow–dryer \-ˌdrī-(ə)r\ n : a hand-held hair dryer

blow·fly \'blō-ˌflī\ n : any of a family of dipteran flies (as a bluebottle) that deposit their eggs or maggots on meat or in wounds

blow·gun \-ˌgən\ n : a tube from which an arrow or a dart may be shot by the force of the breath

blow·out \'blō-ˌaůt\ n : a bursting of something (as a tire) because of pressure of the contents (as air)

blow·sy also **blow·zy** \'blaů-zē\ adj : DISHEVELED, SLOVENLY

blow·torch \'blō-ˌtȯrch\ n : a small portable burner whose flame is made hotter by a blast of air or oxygen

blow·up \'blō-ˌəp\ n 1 : EXPLOSION 2 : an outburst of temper 3 : a photographic enlargement

blowy \'blō-ē\ adj : WINDY

BLT \ˌbē-ˌel-ˈtē\ n : a bacon, lettuce, and tomato sandwich

¹blub·ber \'blə-bər\ vb : to cry noisily

²blubber n 1 : the fat of large sea mammals (as whales) 2 : a noisy crying

¹blud·geon \'blə-jən\ n : a short often loaded club

²bludgeon vb : to strike with or as if with a bludgeon

¹blue \'blü\ adj **blu·er; blu·est** 1 : of the color blue; also : BLUISH 2 : MELANCHOLY; also : DEPRESSING 3 : PURITANICAL 4 : INDECENT — **blue·ness** n

²blue n 1 : a color between green and violet in the spectrum : the color of the clear daytime sky 2 : something (as clothing or the sky) that is blue

blue baby n : a baby with bluish skin due to faulty circulation caused by a heart defect

blue·bell \-₁bel\ *n* : any of various plants with blue bellshaped flowers

blue·ber·ry \'blü-₁ber-ē, -bə-rē\ *n* : the edible blue or blackish berry of various shrubs of the heath family; *also* : one of these shrubs

blue·bird \-₁bərd\ *n* : any of several small No. American thrushes that are blue above and reddishbrown or pale blue below

blue·bon·net \'blü-₁bä-nət\ *n* : either of two lowgrowing annual lupines of Texas with silky foliage and blue flowers

blue·bot·tle \'blü-₁bät-ᵊl\ *n* : any of several blowflies with iridescent blue bodies or abdomens

blue cheese *n* : cheese having veins of greenish blue mold

blue–col·lar \'blü-₁kä-lər\ *adj* : of, relating to, or being the class of workers whose duties call for work clothes

blue·fish \-₁fish\ *n* : a marine sport and food fish bluish above and silvery below

blue·grass \-₁gras\ *n* **1** : KENTUCKY BLUEGRASS **2** : country music played on stringed instruments having free improvisation and close harmonies

blue jay \-₁jā\ *n* : a crested bright blue No. American jay

blue jeans *n pl* : pants usu. made of blue denim

blue·nose \'blü-₁nōz\ *n* : a person who advocates a rigorous moral code

blue·point \-₁póint\ *n* : a small oyster typically from the south shore of Long Island, New York

blue·print \-₁print\ *n* **1** : a photographic print in white on a blue ground used esp. for copying mechanical drawings and architects' plans **2** : a detailed plan of action — **blueprint** *vb*

blues \'blüz\ *n pl* **1** : MELANCHOLY **2** : music in a style marked by recurrent minor intervals and melancholy lyrics

blue·stock·ing \'blü-₁stä-kiŋ\ *n* : a woman having intellectual interests

blu·et \'blü-ət\ *n* : a low No. American herb with dainty bluish flowers

blue whale *n* : a very large baleen whale that may reach a weight of 150 tons (135 metric tons) and a length of 100 feet (30 meters)

¹bluff \'bləf\ *adj* **1** : having a broad flattened front **2** : rising steeply with a broad flat front **3** : OUTSPOKEN, FRANK **syn** abrupt, blunt, brusque, curt, gruff

²bluff *n* : a high steep bank : CLIFF

³bluff *vb* : to frighten or deceive by pretense or a mere show of strength

⁴bluff *n* : an act or instance of bluffing; *also* : one who bluffs

blu·ing *or* **blue·ing** \'blü-iŋ\ *n* : a preparation used in laundering to counteract yellowing of white fabrics

blu·ish \'blü-ish\ *adj* : somewhat blue

¹blun·der \'blən-dər\ *vb* **1** : to move clumsily or unsteadily **2** : to make a stupid or needless mistake

²blunder *n* : an avoidable and usu. serious mistake

blun·der·buss \'blən-dər-₁bəs\ *n* [obs. D *donderbus*, fr. D *donder* thunder + obs. D *bus* gun] : an obsolete short-barreled firearm with a flaring muzzle

blunderbuss

¹blunt \'blənt\ *adj* **1** : not sharp : DULL **2** : lacking in tact : BLUFF **syn** brusque, curt, gruff, abrupt, crusty — **blunt·ly** *adv* — **blunt·ness** *n*

²blunt *vb* : to make or become dull

¹blur \'blər\ *n* **1** : a smear or stain that obscures **2**

: something vaguely perceived; *esp* : something moving too quickly to be clearly perceived — **blur·ry** \-ē\ *adj*

²blur *vb* **blurred; blur·ring** : DIM, CLOUD, OBSCURE

blurb \'blərb\ *n* : a short publicity notice (as on a book jacket)

blurt \'blərt\ *vb* : to utter suddenly and impulsively

blush \'bləsh\ *n* : a reddening of the face (as from modesty or confusion) : FLUSH — **blush** *vb* — **blushful** *adj*

blus·ter \'bləs-tər\ *vb* **1** : to blow in stormy noisy gusts **2** : to talk or act with noisy swaggering threats — **bluster** *n* — **blus·tery** \-tə-rē\ *adj*

blvd *abbr* boulevard

B lymphocyte *n* : B CELL

BM *abbr* bowel movement

B movie *n* : a cheaply produced motion picture

BO *abbr* **1** best offer **2** body odor **3** box office **4** branch office

boa \'bō-ə\ *n* **1** : a large snake (as the **boa con·stric·tor** \-kən-'strik-tər\ or the related anaconda) that suffocates and kills its prey by constriction **2** : a fluffy scarf usu. of fur or feathers

boar \'bōr\ *n* : a male swine; *also* : WILD BOAR

¹board \'bōrd\ *n* **1** : the side of a ship **2** : a thin flat length of sawed lumber; *also* : material (as cardboard) or a piece of material formed as a thin flat firm sheet **3** *pl* : STAGE 1 **4** : a table spread with a meal; *also* : daily meals esp. when furnished for pay **5** : a table at which a council or magistrates sit **6** : a group or association of persons organized for a special responsibility (as the management of a business or institution); *also* : an organized commercial exchange **7** : a sheet of insulating material carrying circuit elements and inserted in an electronic device

²board *vb* **1** : to go or put aboard ⟨∼ a boat⟩ **2** : to cover with boards **3** : to provide or be provided with meals and often lodging — **board·er** *n*

board·ing·house \'bōr-diŋ-₁haús\ *n* : a house at which persons are boarded

board·walk \'bōrd-₁wók\ *n* : a promenade (as of planking) along a beach

boast \'bōst\ *vb* **1** : to praise oneself **2** : to mention or assert with excessive pride **3** : to prize as a possession; *also* : HAVE ⟨the house ∼s a fireplace⟩ — **boast** *n* — **boast·ful** \-fəl\ *adj* — **boast·ful·ly** *adv*

boat \'bōt\ *n* : a small vessel for travel on water; *also* : SHIP

boat·er \'bō-tər\ *n* **1** : one that travels in a boat **2** : a stiff straw hat

boat·man \'bōt-mən\ *n* : a man who operates, works on, or deals in boats

boat people *n pl* : refugees fleeing by boat

boat·swain \'bōs-ᵊn\ *n* : a subordinate officer of a ship in charge of the hull and related equipment

¹bob \'bäb\ *vb* **bobbed; bob·bing** **1** : to move up and down jerkily or repeatedly **2** : to emerge, arise, or appear suddenly or unexpectedly

²bob *n* : a bobbing movement

³bob *n* **1** : a knob, knot, twist, or curl esp. of ribbons, yarn, or hair **2** : a short haircut of a woman or child **3** : FLOAT 2 **4** : a weight hanging from a line

⁴bob *vb* **bobbed; bob·bing** : to cut hair in a bob

⁵bob *n, pl* **bob** *slang Brit* : SHILLING

bob·bin \'bä-bən\ *n* : a cylinder or spindle for holding or dispensing thread (as in a sewing machine)

bob·ble \'bä-bəl\ *vb* **bob·bled; bob·bling** : FUMBLE — **bobble** *n*

bob·by \'bä-bē\ *n, pl* **bobbies** [*Bobby*, nickname for Sir *Robert* Peel, who organized the London police force] *Brit* : a police officer

bobby pin *n* : a flat wire hairpin with prongs that press close together

bob·cat \'bäb-ˌkat\ *n* : a small usu. rusty-colored No. American lynx

bob·o·link \'bä-bə-ˌliŋk\ *n* : an American migratory songbird related to the meadowlarks

bob·sled \'bäb-ˌsled\ *n* **1** : a short sled usu. used as one of a joined pair **2** : a racing sled with two pairs of runners, a steering wheel, and a hand brake — **bobsled** *vb*

bob·white \(ˌ)bäb-'hwīt\ *n* : any of a genus of quail; *esp* : a popular game bird of the eastern and central U.S.

boc·cie *or* **boc·ci** *or* **boc·ce** \'bä-chē\ *n* : Italian lawn bowling played on a long narrow court

bock \'bäk\ *n* : a dark heavy beer usu. sold in early spring

bod \'bäd\ *n* : BODY

¹bode \'bōd\ *vb* **bod·ed; bod·ing** : to indicate by signs : PRESAGE

²bode *past of* BIDE

bo·de·ga \bō-'dä-gə\ *n* [Sp, fr. L *apotheca* storehouse] : a store specializing in Hispanic groceries

bod·ice \'bä-dəs\ *n* [alter. of *bodies*, pl. of *body*] : the usu. close-fitting part of a dress above the waist

bod·i·less \'bä-di-ləs\ *adj* : lacking a body or material form

¹bod·i·ly \'bäd-ᵊl-ē\ *adj* : of or relating to the body ⟨∼ contact⟩

²bodily *adv* **1** : in the flesh **2** : as a whole ⟨lifted the crate up ∼⟩

bod·kin \'bäd-kən\ *n* **1** : DAGGER **2** : a pointed implement for punching holes in cloth **3** : a blunt needle for drawing tape or ribbon through a loop or hem

body \'bä-dē\ *n, pl* **bod·ies 1** : the physical whole of a living or dead organism; *also* : the trunk or main mass of an organism as distinguished from its appendages **2** : a human being : PERSON **3** : the main part of something **4** : a mass of matter distinct from other masses **5** : GROUP **6** : VISCOSITY, FIRMNESS **7** : richness of flavor — used esp. of wines — **bod·ied** \'bä-dēd\ *adj*

body English *n* : bodily motions made in a usu. unconscious effort to influence the movement of a propelled object (as a ball)

body·guard \'bä-dē-ˌgärd\ *n* : a personal guard; *also* : RETINUE

body stocking *n* : a sheer close-fitting one-piece garment for the torso that often has sleeves and legs

body·work \'bä-dē-ˌwərk\ *n* : the making or repairing of vehicle bodies

Boer \'bōr, 'bu̇r\ *n* [D, lit., farmer] : a South African of Dutch or Huguenot descent

¹bog \'bäg, 'bȯg\ *n* : wet, spongy, poorly drained, and usu. acid ground — **bog·gy** *adj*

²bog *vb* **bogged; bog·ging** : to sink into or as if into a bog

bo·gey *also* **bo·gie** *or* **bo·gy** \'bu̇-gē, 'bō- *for 1;* 'bō- *for 2*\ *n, pl* **bogeys** *also* **bogies 1** : SPECTER, HOBGOBLIN; *also* : a source of fear or annoyance **2** : a score of one over par on a hole in golf

bo·gey·man \'bu̇-gē-ˌman, 'bō-, 'bü-\ *n* : an imaginary monster used in threatening children

bog·gle \'bä-gəl\ *vb* **bog·gled; bog·gling** : to overwhelm or be overwhelmed with fright or amazement

bo·gus \'bō-gəs\ *adj* : SPURIOUS, SHAM

Bo·he·mi·an \bō-'hē-mē-ən\ *n* **1** : a native or inhabitant of Bohemia **2** *often not cap* : VAGABOND, WANDERER **3** *often not cap* : a person (as a writer or artist) living an unconventional life — **bohemian** *adj, often cap*

¹boil \'bȯil\ *n* : an inflamed swelling on the skin containing pus

²boil *vb* **1** : to heat or become heated to a temperature ⟨**boil·ing point**⟩ at which vapor is formed and rises in bubbles ⟨water ∼s and changes to steam⟩; *also* : to act on or be acted on by a boiling liquid ⟨∼ eggs⟩ **2** : to be in a state of seething agitation

³boil *n* : the act or state of boiling

boil·er \'bȯi-lər\ *n* **1** : a container in which something is boiled **2** : a strong vessel used in making steam **3** : a tank holding hot water

boil·er·mak·er \'bȯi-lər-ˌmā-kər\ *n* : whiskey with a beer chaser

bois·ter·ous \'bȯi-st(ə-)rəs\ *adj* : noisily turbulent or exuberant — **bois·ter·ous·ly** *adv*

bok choy \'bäk-'chȯi\ *n* : a Chinese vegetable related to the mustards that forms a loose head of green leaves with long thick white stalks

bo·la \'bō-lə\ *or* **bo·las** \-ləs\ *n, pl* **bolas** \-ləz\ *also* **bo·las·es** [AmerSp *bolas*, fr. Sp *bola* ball] : a cord with weights attached to the ends for hurling at and entangling an animal

bola

bold \'bōld\ *adj* **1** : COURAGEOUS, INTREPID **2** : IMPUDENT **3** : STEEP **4** : ADVENTUROUS, FREE ⟨a ∼ thinker⟩ **syn** dauntless, brave, valiant — **bold·ly** *adv* — **bold·ness** \'bōld-nəs\ *n*

bold·face \'bōld-ˌfās\ *n* : a heavy-faced type; *also* : printing in boldface — **bold–faced** \-'fāst\ *adj*

bole \'bōl\ *n* : the trunk of a tree

bo·le·ro \bə-'ler-ō\ *n, pl* **-ros 1** : a Spanish dance or its music **2** : a short loose jacket open at the front

bo·li·var \bə-'lē-ˌvär, 'bä-lə-vər\ *n, pl* **-va·res** \ˌbä-lə-'vär-ˌās, ˌbō-\ *or* **-vars** : see MONEY table

Bo·liv·i·an \bə-'li-vē-ən\ *n* : a native or inhabitant of Bolivia — **Bolivian** *adj*

bo·li·vi·a·no \bə-ˌli-vē-'ä-(ˌ)nō\ *n, pl* **-nos** — see MONEY table

boll \'bōl\ *n* : a seed pod (as of cotton)

boll weevil *n* : a small grayish weevil that infests the cotton plant both as a larva and as an adult

boll·worm \'bōl-ˌwərm\ *n* : any of several moths and esp. the corn earworm whose larvae feed on cotton bolls

bo·lo·gna \bə-'lō-nē\ *n* [short for *Bologna sausage*, fr. *Bologna*, Italy] : a large smoked sausage of beef, veal, and pork

Bol·she·vik \'bōl-shə-ˌvik\ *n, pl* **Bolsheviks** *also* **Bol·she·vi·ki** \ˌbōl-shə-'vi-kē\ [Russ *bol'shevik*, fr. *bol'shiĭ* larger] **1** : a member of the party that seized power in Russia in the revolution of November 1917 **2** : COMMUNIST — **Bolshevik** *adj*

bol·she·vism \'bōl-shə-ˌvi-zəm\ *n, often cap* : the doctrine or program of the Bolsheviks advocating violent overthrow of capitalism

¹bol·ster \'bōl-stər\ *n* : a long pillow or cushion

²bolster *vb* : to support with or as if with a bolster; *also* : REINFORCE

¹bolt \'bōlt\ *n* **1** : a missile (as an arrow) for a crossbow or catapult **2** : a flash of lightning : THUNDERBOLT **3** : a sliding bar used to fasten a door **4** : a roll of cloth or wallpaper of specified length **5** : a rod with a head at one end and a screw thread at the other used with a nut to fasten objects together **6** : a metal cylinder

that drives the cartridge into the chamber of a firearm
²**bolt** vb **1** : to move suddenly (as in fright or hurry) : START, DASH **2** : to break away (as from association) ⟨∼ from a political platform⟩ **3** : to produce seed prematurely **4** : to secure or fasten with a bolt **5** : to swallow hastily or without chewing

³**bolt** n : an act of bolting

bo·lus \'bō-ləs\ n **1** : a large pill **2** : a soft mass of chewed food

¹**bomb** \'bäm\ n **1** : a fused explosive device designed to detonate under specified conditions (as impact) **2** : an aerosol or foam dispenser (as of insecticide or hair spray) : SPRAY CAN **3** : a long pass in football

²**bomb** vb : to attack with bombs

bom·bard \bäm-'bärd\ vb **1** : to attack esp. with artillery or bombers **2** : to assail persistently **3** : to subject to the impact of rapidly moving particles (as electrons) — **bom·bard·ment** n

bom·bar·dier \ˌbäm-bər-'dir\ n : a bomber-crew member who releases the bombs

bom·bast \'bäm-ˌbast\ n [ME, cotton padding, fr. MF *bombace*, fr. ML *bombax* cotton, alter. of L *bombyx* silkworm, silk, fr. Gk] : pretentious wordy speech or writing — **bom·bas·tic** \bäm-'bas-tik\ adj — **bom·bas·ti·cal·ly** \-ti-k(ə-)lē\ adv

bom·ba·zine \ˌbäm-bə-'zēn\ n **1** : a twilled fabric with silk warp and worsted filling **2** : a silk fabric in twill weave dyed black

bomb·er \'bä-mər\ n : one that bombs; esp : an airplane for dropping bombs

bomb·proof \'bäm-ˌprüf\ adj : safe against the explosive force of bombs

bomb·shell \'bäm-ˌshel\ n **1** : BOMB 1 **2** : one that stuns, amazes, or completely upsets

bona fide \'bō-nə-ˌfīd, 'bä-; ˌbō-nə-'fī-dē, -də\ adj [L, in good faith] **1** : made in good faith ⟨a *bona fide* agreement⟩ **2** : GENUINE, REAL ⟨a *bona fide* bargain⟩

bo·nan·za \bə-'nan-zə\ n [Sp, lit., calm sea, fr. ML *bonacia*, alter. of L *malacia*, fr. Gk *malakia*, lit., softness, fr. *malakos* soft] : something yielding a rich return

bon·bon \'bän-ˌbän\ n : a candy with a creamy center and a soft covering (as of chocolate)

¹**bond** \'bänd\ n **1** : FETTER **2** : a binding or uniting force or tie ⟨∼s of friendship⟩ **3** : an agreement or obligation often made binding by a pledge of money or goods **4** : a person who acts as surety for another **5** : an interest-bearing certificate of public or private indebtedness **6** : the state of goods subject to supervision pending payment of taxes or duties due

²**bond** vb **1** : to assure payment of duties or taxes on (goods) by giving a bond **2** : to insure against losses caused by the acts of ⟨∼ a bank teller⟩ **3** : to make or become firmly united as if by bonds ⟨∼ iron to copper⟩

bond·age \'bän-dij\ n : SLAVERY, SERVITUDE

bond·hold·er \'bänd-ˌhōl-dər\ n : one that owns a government or corporation bond

bond·ing n **1** : the formation of a close personal relationship esp. through frequent or constant associa-

tion **2** : the attaching of a material (as porcelain) to a tooth surface esp. for cosmetic purposes

bond·man \'bänd-mən\ n : SLAVE, SERF

¹**bonds·man** \'bändz-mən\ n : SURETY 3

²**bondsman** n : BONDMAN

bond·wom·an \'bänd-ˌwu̇-mən\ n : a female slave or serf

¹**bone** \'bōn\ n **1** : a hard largely calcareous tissue forming most of the skeleton of a vertebrate animal; also : one of the pieces of bone making up a vertebrate skeleton **2** : a hard animal substance (as ivory or baleen) similar to true bone **3** : something made of bone — **bone·less** adj — **bony** also **bon·ey** \'bō-nē\ adj

²**bone** vb **boned; bon·ing** : to free from bones ⟨∼ a chicken⟩

bone black n : the black carbon residue from calcined bones used esp. as a pigment

bone meal n : crushed or ground bone used esp. as fertilizer or feed

bon·er \'bō-nər\ n : a stupid and ridiculous blunder

bone up vb **1** : CRAM 3 **2** : to refresh one's memory ⟨*boned up* on the speech before giving it⟩

bon·fire \'bän-ˌfir\ n [ME *bonefire* a fire of bones, fr. *bon* bone + *fire*] : a large fire built in the open air

bon·go \'bäŋ-gō\ n, pl **bongos** also **bongoes** [AmerSp *bongó*] : one of a pair of small tuned drums played with the hands

bon·ho·mie \ˌbä-nə-'mē\ n [F *bonhomie*, fr. *bonhomme* good-natured man, fr. *bon* good + *homme* man] : good-natured easy friendliness

bo·ni·to \bə-'nē-tō\ n, pl **-tos** or **-to** : any of several medium-sized tunas

bon mot \bōⁿ-'mō\ n, pl **bons mots** \same\ or **bon mots** \same or -'mō\ [F, lit., good word] : a clever remark

bon·net \'bä-nət\ n : a covering (as a cap) for the head; esp : a hat for a woman or infant tied under the chin

bon·ny \'bä-nē\ adj **bon·ni·er; -est** chiefly Brit : ATTRACTIVE, FAIR; also : FINE, EXCELLENT

bon·sai \bōn-'sī\ n, pl **bonsai** [Jp] : a potted plant (as a tree) dwarfed by special methods of culture; also : the art of growing such a plant

bo·nus \'bō-nəs\ n : something in addition to what is expected

bon vi·vant \ˌbän-vē-'vänt, ˌbōⁿ-vē-'väⁿ\ n, pl **bons vivants** \ˌbän-vē-'vänts, ˌbōⁿ-vē-'väⁿ\ or **bon vivants** \same\ [F, lit., good liver] : a person having cultivated, refined, and sociable tastes esp. in food and drink

bon voy·age \ˌbōⁿ-ˌvȯi-'äzh, ˌbän-; ˌbōⁿ-ˌvwä-'yäzh\ n : FAREWELL — often used as an interjection

bony fish n : any of a very large group of fishes (as a salmon or marlin) with a bony rather than a cartilaginous skeleton

bonze \'bänz\ n : a Buddhist monk

boo \'bü\ n, pl **boos** : a shout of disapproval or contempt — **boo** vb

boo·by \'bü-bē\ *n, pl* **boobies** : an awkward foolish person : DOPE
booby hatch *n* : an insane asylum
booby prize *n* : an award for the poorest performance in a contest
booby trap *n* : a trap for the unwary; *esp* : a concealed explosive device set to go off when some harmless-looking object is touched — **booby-trap** *vb*
boo·dle \'büd-ᵊl\ *n* **1** : bribe money **2** : a large amount of money

¹book \'búk\ *n* **1** : a set of sheets bound into a volume **2** : a long written or printed narrative or record **3** : a major division of a long literary work **4** *cap* : BIBLE

²book *vb* **1** : to engage, reserve, or schedule by or as if by writing in a book ⟨∼ seats on a plane⟩ **2** : to enter charges against in a police register
book·case \-ˌkās\ *n* : a piece of furniture consisting of shelves to hold books
book·end \-ˌend\ *n* : a support to hold up a row of books
book·ie \'bú-kē\ *n* : BOOKMAKER
book·ish \'bú-kish\ *adj* **1** : fond of books and reading **2** : inclined to rely unduly on book knowledge
book·keep·er \'búk-ˌkē-pər\ *n* : one who records the accounts or transactions of a business — **book·keep·ing** *n*
book·let \'búk-lət\ *n* : PAMPHLET
book·mak·er \'búk-ˌmā-kər\ *n* : one who determines odds and receives and pays off bets — **book·mak·ing** *n*
book·mark \-ˌmärk\ *or* **book·mark·er** \-ˌmär-kər\ *n* : a marker for finding a place in a book
book·mo·bile \'búk-mō-ˌbēl\ *n* : a truck that serves as a traveling library
book·plate \'búk-ˌplāt\ *n* : a label pasted in a book to show who owns it
book·sell·er \'búk-ˌse-lər\ *n* : one who sells books; *esp* : the proprietor of a bookstore
book·shelf \-ˌshelf\ *n* : a shelf for books
book·worm \'búk-ˌwərm\ *n* : a person unusually devoted to reading and study
¹boom \'büm\ *vb* **1** : to make a deep hollow sound : RESOUND **2** : to grow or cause to grow rapidly esp. in value, esteem, or importance
²boom *n* **1** : a booming sound or cry **2** : a rapid expansion or increase esp. of economic activity
³boom *n* **1** : a long spar used to extend the bottom of a sail **2** : a line of floating timbers used to obstruct passage or catch floating objects **3** : a beam projecting from the upright pole of a derrick to support or guide the object lifted
boom box *n* : a large portable radio and often tape player
boo·mer·ang \'bü-mə-ˌraŋ\ *n* [Dharuk (an Australian aboriginal language *bumariny*)] : a bent or angular club that can be so thrown as to return near the starting point

¹boon \'bün\ *n* [ME, fr. ON *bōn* petition] : BENEFIT, BLESSING **syn** favor, gift, largess, present
²boon *adj* [ME *bon*, fr. MF, good] : CONVIVIAL ⟨a ∼ companion⟩
boon·docks \'bün-ˌdäks\ *n pl* [Tagalog (language of the Philippines) *bundok* mountain] **1** : rough country filled with dense brush **2** : a rural area
boon·dog·gle \'bün-ˌdä-gəl, -ˌdò-\ *n* : a useless or wasteful project or activity
boor \'búr\ *n* **1** : YOKEL : a rude or insensitive person **syn** churl, lout, clown, clodhopper — **boor·ish** *adj*
boost \'büst\ *vb* **1** : to push up from below **2** : INCREASE, RAISE ⟨∼ prices⟩ **3** : AID, PROMOTE ⟨voted a bonus to ∼ morale⟩ — **boost** *n* — **boost·er** *n*
¹boot \'büt\ *n, chiefly dial* : something to equalize a trade — **to boot** : BESIDES
²boot *vb, archaic* : AVAIL, PROFIT
³boot *n* **1** : a covering for the foot and leg **2** : a protective sheath (as of a flower) **3** *Brit* : an automobile trunk **4** : KICK; *also* : a discharge from employment **5** : a navy or marine corps trainee
⁴boot *vb* **1** : KICK **2** : to eject or discharge summarily
boot·black \'büt-ˌblak\ *n* : a person who shines shoes
boo·tee *or* **boo·tie** \'bü-tē\ *n* : an infant's knitted or crocheted sock
booth \'büth\ *n, pl* **booths** \'büthz, 'büths\ **1** : a small enclosed stall (as at a fair) **2** : a small enclosure giving privacy for a person ⟨voting ∼⟩ ⟨telephone ∼⟩ **3** : a restaurant accommodation having a table between backed benches
boot·leg \'büt-ˌleg\ *vb* : to make, transport, or sell (as liquor) illegally — **boot·leg** *adj or n* — **boot·leg·ger** *n*
boot·less \'büt-ləs\ *adj* : USELESS **syn** futile, vain, abortive, fruitless — **boot·less·ly** *adv* — **boot·less·ness** *n*
boo·ty \'bü-tē\ *n, pl* **booties** : PLUNDER, SPOIL
¹booze \'büz\ *vb* **boozed; booz·ing** : to drink liquor to excess — **booz·er** *n*
²booze *n* : intoxicating liquor — **boozy** *adj*
bop \'bäp\ *vb* **bopped; bop·ping** : HIT, SOCK — **bop** *n*
BOQ *abbr* bachelor officers' quarters
bor *abbr* borough
bo·rate \'bōr-ˌāt\ *n* : a salt or ester of boric acid
bo·rax \'bōr-ˌaks\ *n* : a crystalline borate of sodium that occurs as a mineral and is used as a flux and cleanser
bor·del·lo \bòr-'de-lō\ *n, pl* **-los** [It] : BROTHEL
¹bor·der \'bòr-dər\ *n* **1** : EDGE, MARGIN **2** : BOUNDARY, FRONTIER **syn** rim, brim, brink, fringe, perimeter
²border *vb* **bor·dered; bor·der·ing 1** : to put a border on **2** : ADJOIN **3** : VERGE
bor·der·land \'bòr-dər-ˌland\ *n* **1** : territory at or near a border **2** : an outlying or intermediate region often not clearly defined
bor·der·line \-ˌlīn\ *adj* : being in an intermediate position or state; *esp* : not quite up to what is standard or expected ⟨∼ intelligence⟩
¹bore \'bōr\ *vb* **bored; bor·ing 1** : to make a hole in with or as if with a drill **2** : to make (as a well) by bor-

ing or digging away material **syn** perforate, drill, prick, puncture — **bor·er** *n*

²bore *n* **1** : a hole made by or as if by boring **2** : a cylindrical cavity **3** : the diameter of a hole or tube; *esp* : the interior diameter of a gun barrel or engine cylinder

³bore *past of* BEAR

⁴bore *n* : a tidal flood with a high abrupt front

⁵bore *n* : one that causes boredom

⁶bore *vb* **bored; bor·ing** : to weary with tedious dullness

bo·re·al \'bōr-ē-əl\ *adj* : of, relating to, or located in northern regions

bore·dom \'bōr-dəm\ *n* : the condition of being bored

bo·ric acid \'bōr-ik-\ *n* : a white crystalline weak acid that contains boron and is used esp. as an antiseptic

born \'bȯrn\ *adj* **1** : brought into life by birth **2** : NATIVE ⟨American-*born*⟩ **3** : having special natural abilities or character from birth ⟨a ∼ leader⟩

born–again *adj* : having experienced a revival of a personal faith or conviction ⟨∼ believer⟩ ⟨∼ liberal⟩

borne *past part of* BEAR

bo·ron \'bōr-ˌän\ *n* : a chemical element that occurs in nature only in combination (as in borax) — see ELEMENT table

bor·ough \'bər-ō\ *n* **1** : a British town that sends one or more members to Parliament; *also* : an incorporated British urban area **2** : an incorporated town or village in some U.S. states; *also* : any of the five political divisions of New York City **3** : a civil division of the state of Alaska corresponding to a county in most other states

bor·row \'bär-ō\ *vb* **1** : to take or receive (something) temporarily and with intent to return **2** : to take into possession or use from another source : DERIVE, APPROPRIATE ⟨∼ a metaphor⟩

borscht \'bȯrsht\ *or* **borsch** \'bȯrsh\ *n* [Yiddish *borsht* & Ukrainian & Russ *borshch*] : a soup made mainly from beets

bosh \'bäsh\ *n* [Turk *boş* empty] : foolish talk or action : NONSENSE

bosky \'bäs-kē\ *adj* : covered with trees or shrubs

¹bos·om \'bu̇-zəm, 'bü-\ *n* **1** : the front of the human chest; *esp* : the female breasts **2** : the seat of secret thoughts and feelings **3** : the part of a garment covering the breast — **bos·omed** \-zəmd\ *adj*

²bosom *adj* : CLOSE, INTIMATE

¹boss \'bäs, 'bȯs\ *n* : a knoblike ornament : STUD

²boss *vb* : to ornament with bosses

³boss \'bȯs\ *n* **1** : one (as a foreman or manager) exercising control or supervision **2** : a politician who controls votes or dictates policies — **bossy** *adj*

⁴boss \'bȯs\ *vb* : to act as a boss : SUPERVISE

bo·sun \'bōs-ᵊn\ *var of* BOATSWAIN

bot *abbr* botanical; botanist; botany

bot·a·ny \'bät-ᵊn-ē, 'bät-nē\ *n, pl* **-nies** **1** : a branch of biology dealing with plants and plant life **2** : plant life (as of a given region); *also* : the biology of a plant or plant group — **bo·tan·i·cal** \bə-'ta-ni-kəl\ *adj* — **bot·a·nist** \'bät-ᵊn-ist, 'bät-nist\ *n* — **bot·a·nize** \-ᵊn-ˌīz\ *vb*

botch \'bäch\ *vb* : to foul up hopelessly : BUNGLE — **botch** *n*

¹both \'bōth\ *pron* : both ones : the one as well as the other

²both *conj* — used as a function word to indicate and stress the inclusion of each of two or more things specified by coordinated words, phrases, or clauses ⟨∼ New York and London⟩

³both *adj* : being the two : affecting the one and the other

both·er \'bä-thər\ *vb* : WORRY, PESTER, TROUBLE **syn** vex, annoy, irk, provoke — **bother** *n* — **both·er·some** \-səm\ *adj*

¹bot·tle \'bät-ᵊl\ *n* **1** : a container (as of glass) with a narrow neck and usu. no handles **2** : the quantity held by a bottle **3** : intoxicating liquor

²bottle *vb* **bot·tled; bot·tling** **1** : to confine as if in a bottle : RESTRAIN **2** : to put into a bottle

bot·tle·neck \'bät-ᵊl-ˌnek\ *n* **1** : a narrow passage or point of congestion **2** : something that obstructs or impedes

¹bot·tom \'bä-təm\ *n* **1** : an under or supporting surface; *also* : BUTTOCKS **2** : the surface on which a body of water lies **3** : the lowest part or place; *also* : an inferior position ⟨start at the ∼⟩ **4** : BOTTOMLAND — **bottom** *adj* — **bot·tom·less** *adj*

²bottom *vb* **1** : to furnish with a bottom **2** : to reach the bottom **3** : to reach a low point before rebounding — usu. used with *out*

bot·tom·land \'bä-təm-ˌland\ *n* : low land along a river

bottom line *n* **1** : the essential point : CRUX **2** : the final result : OUTCOME

bot·u·lism \'bä-chə-ˌli-zəm\ *n* : an acute paralytic disease caused by a bacterial toxin esp. in food

bou·doir \'bü-ˌdwär, 'bu̇-, ˌbü-', ˌbu̇-'\ *n* [F, fr. *bouder* to pout] : a woman's dressing room or bedroom

bouf·fant \bü-'fänt, 'bü-ˌfänt\ *adj* [F] : puffed out ⟨∼ hairdos⟩

bough \'bau̇\ *n* : a usu. large or main branch of a tree

bought *past and past part of* BUY

bouil·la·baisse \ˌbü-yə-'bäs\ *n* [F] : a highly seasoned fish stew made with at least two kinds of fish

bouil·lon \'bü-ˌyän; 'bu̇l-ˌyän, -yən\ *n* : a clear soup made usu. from beef

boul·der \'bōl-dər\ *n* : a large detached rounded or worn mass of rock — **boul·dered** \-dərd\ *adj*

bou·le·vard \'bu̇-lə-ˌvärd, 'bü-\ *n* [F, modif. of MD *bolwerc* bulwark] : a broad often landscaped thoroughfare

bounce \'bau̇ns\ *vb* **bounced; bounc·ing** **1** : to cause to rebound ⟨∼ a ball⟩ **2** : to rebound after striking — **bounce** *n* — **bouncy** \'bau̇n-sē\ *adj*

bounc·er \'bau̇n-sər\ *n* : a person employed in a public place to remove disorderly persons

¹bound \'bau̇nd\ *adj* : intending to go

²bound *n* : LIMIT, BOUNDARY — **bound·less** *adj* — **bound·less·ness** *n*

³bound *vb* **1** : to set limits to **2** : to form the boundary of **3** : to name the boundaries of

⁴bound *past and past part of* BIND

⁵bound *adj* **1** : constrained by or as if by bonds : CONFINED, OBLIGED **2** : enclosed in a binding or cover **3** : RESOLVED, DETERMINED; *also* : SURE

⁶bound *n* **1** : LEAP, JUMP **2** : REBOUND, BOUNCE

⁷bound *vb* : SPRING, BOUNCE

bound·ary \'bau̇n-drē\ *n, pl* **-aries** : something that marks or fixes a limit (as of territory) **syn** border, frontier, march

bound·en \'bau̇n-dən\ *adj* : BINDING

boun·te·ous \'bau̇n-tē-əs\ *adj* **1** : GENEROUS **2** : ABUNDANT — **boun·te·ous·ly** *adv* — **boun·te·ous·ness** *n*

boun·ti·ful \'bau̇n-ti-fəl\ *adj* **1** : giving freely **2** : PLENTIFUL — **boun·ti·ful·ly** *adv* — **boun·ti·ful·ness** *n*

boun·ty \'bau̇n-tē\ *n, pl* **bounties** [ME *bounte* goodness, fr. OF *bonté*, fr. L *bonitas*, fr. *bonus* good] **1** : GENEROSITY **2** : something given liberally **3** : a reward, premium, or subsidy given usu. for doing something

bou·quet \bō-'kā, bü-\ *n* [F, fr. MF, thicket, fr. OF *bosc* forest] **1** : flowers picked and fastened together in a bunch **2** : a distinctive aroma (as of wine) **syn** scent, fragrance, perfume, redolence

bour·bon \'bər-bən\ *n* : a whiskey distilled from a corn mash

bour·geois \'bu̇rzh-ˌwä, bu̇rzh-'wä\ *n, pl* **bourgeois** *same or* -ˌwäz, -'wäz\ [MF, lit., citizen of a town, fr. *borc* town, borough, fr. L *burgus* fortified place, of Gmc origin] : a middle-class person — **bourgeois** *adj*

bour·geoi·sie \ˌbu̇rzh-ˌwä-'zē\ *n* : a social order dominated by bourgeois

bourne *also* **bourn** \'bōrn, 'bu̇rn\ *n* : BOUNDARY; *also* : DESTINATION

bourse \'bu̇rs\ *n* : a European stock exchange

bout \'bau̇t\ *n* **1** : CONTEST, MATCH **2** : OUTBREAK, ATTACK ⟨a ∼ of measles⟩ **3** : SESSION

bou·tique \bü-'tēk\ *n* : a small fashionable specialty shop

bou·ton·niere \,büt-ᵊn-'iᵊr\ *n* : a flower or bouquet worn in a buttonhole

¹bo·vine \'bō-,vīn, -,vēn\ *adj* **1** : of or relating to bovines **2** : having qualities (as placidity or dullness) characteristic of oxen or cows

²bovine *n* : any of a group of mammals including oxen, buffalo, and their close relatives

¹bow \'bau̇\ *vb* **1** : SUBMIT, YIELD **2** : to bend the head or body (as in submission, courtesy, or assent)

²bow *n* : an act or posture of bowing

³bow \'bō\ *n* **1** : BEND, ARCH; *esp* : RAINBOW **2** : a weapon for shooting arrows; *also* : ARCHER **3** : a knot formed by doubling a line into two or more loops **4** : a wooden rod strung with horsehairs for playing an instrument of the violin family

⁴bow \'bō\ *vb* **1** : BEND, CURVE **2** : to play (an instrument) with a bow

⁵bow \'bau̇\ *n* : the forward part of a ship — **bow** *adj*

bowd·ler·ise *Brit var of* BOWDLERIZE

bowd·ler·ize \'bōd-lə-,rīz, 'bau̇d-\ *vb* **-ized; -iz·ing** : to expurgate by omitting parts considered vulgar

bow·el \'bau̇(-ə)l\ *n* **1** : INTESTINE; *also* : one of the divisions of the intestine — usu. used in pl. **2** *pl* : the inmost parts ⟨the ∼s of the earth⟩

bow·er \'bau̇(-ə)r\ *n* : a shelter of boughs or vines : ARBOR

¹bowl \'bōl\ *n* **1** : a concave vessel used to hold liquids **2** : a drinking vessel **3** : a bowl-shaped part or structure — **bowl·ful** \-,fu̇l\ *n*

²bowl *n* **1** : a ball for rolling on a level surface in bowling **2** : a cast of the ball in bowling

³bowl *vb* **1** : to play a game of bowling; *also* : to roll a ball in bowling **2** : to travel (as in a vehicle) rapidly and smoothly **3** : to strike or knock down with a moving object; *also* : to overwhelm with surprise

bowlder *var of* BOULDER

bow·legged \'bō-,le-gəd\ *adj* : having legs that bow outward at or below the knee — **bow·leg** \'bō-,leg\ *n*

¹bowl·er \'bō-lər\ *n* : a person who bowls

²bowl·er \'bō-lər\ *n* : DERBY 3

bow·line \'bō-lən, -,līn\ *n* : a knot used to form a loop that neither slips nor jams

bowl·ing \'bō-liŋ\ *n* : any of various games in which balls are rolled on a green or alley at an object or a group of objects; *esp* : TENPINS

bow·man \'bō-mən\ *n* : ARCHER

bow·sprit \'bau̇-,sprit\ *n* : a spar projecting forward from the prow of a ship

bow·string \'bō-,striŋ\ *n* : the cord connecting the two ends of a shooting bow

¹box \'bäks\ *n, pl* **box** *or* **box·es** : an evergreen shrub or small tree used esp. for hedges

²box *n* **1** : a rigid typically rectangular receptacle often with a cover; *also* : the quantity held by a box **2** : a small compartment (as for a group of theater patrons); *also* : a boxlike receptacle or division **3** : any of six spaces on a baseball diamond where the batter, pitcher, coaches, and catcher stand **4** : PREDICAMENT

³box *vb* : to enclose in or as if in a box

⁴box *n* : a punch or slap esp. on the ear

⁵box *vb* **1** : to strike with the hand **2** : to engage in boxing with

box·car \'bäks-,kär\ *n* : a roofed freight car usu. with sliding doors in the sides

¹box·er \'bäk-sər\ *n* : a person who engages in boxing

²boxer *n* : a compact short-haired usu. fawn or brindled dog of a breed of German origin

box·ing \'bäk-siŋ\ *n* : the sport of fighting with the fists

box office *n* : an office (as in a theater) where admission tickets are sold

box·wood \'bäks-,wu̇d\ *n* : the tough hard wood of the box; *also* : a box tree or shrub

boy \'bȯi\ *n* **1** : a male child : YOUTH **2** : SON — **boy·hood** \-,hu̇d\ *n* — **boy·ish** *adj* — **boy·ish·ly** *adv* — **boy·ish·ness** *n*

boy·cott \'bȯi-,kät\ *vb* [Charles C. *Boycott* †1897 Eng. land agent in Ireland who was ostracized for refusing to reduce rents] : to refrain from having any dealings with — **boycott** *n*

boy·friend \'bȯi-,frend\ *n* **1** : a male friend **2** : a frequent or regular male companion of a girl or woman

Boy Scout *n* : a member of any of various national scouting programs (as the Boy Scouts of America)

boy·sen·ber·ry \'bȯiz-ᵊn-,ber-ē, 'bȯis-\ *n* : a large bramble fruit with a raspberry flavor; *also* : the hybrid plant bearing it developed by crossing blackberries and raspberries

bo·zo \'bō-,zō\ *n, pl* **bozos** : a foolish or incompetent person

bp *abbr* **1** bishop **2** birthplace

BP *abbr* **1** batting practice **2** blood pressure **3** boiling point

bpl *abbr* birthplace

BPOE *abbr* Benevolent and Protective Order of Elks

br *abbr* **1** branch **2** brass **3** brown

¹Br *abbr* Britain; British

²Br *symbol* bromine

BR *abbr* bedroom

bra \'brä\ *n* : BRASSIERE

¹brace \'brās\ *vb* **braced; brac·ing** **1** *archaic* : to make fast ; BIND **2** : to tighten preparatory to use; *also* : to get ready for : prepare oneself **3** : INVIGORATE **4** : to furnish or support with a brace; *also* : STRENGTHEN **5** : to set firmly **6** : to gain courage or confidence

²brace *n, pl* **brac·es 1** *or pl* **brace** : two of a kind ⟨a ∼ of dogs⟩ **2** : a crank-shaped device for turning a bit **3** : something (as a tie, prop, or clamp) that distributes, directs, or resists pressure or weight **4** *pl* : SUSPENDERS **5** : an appliance for supporting a body part (as the shoulders) **6** *pl* : dental appliances used to exert pressure to straighten misaligned teeth **7** : one of two marks { } used to connect words or items to be considered together

brace·let \'brā-slət\ *n* [ME, fr. MF, dim. of *bras* arm, fr. L *bracchium*, fr. Gk *brachiōn*] : an ornamental band or chain worn around the wrist

bra·ce·ro \brä-'ser-ō\ *n, pl* **-ros** : a Mexican laborer admitted to the U.S. esp. for seasonal farm work

brack·en \'bra-kən\ *n* : a large coarse fern; *also* : a growth of such ferns

¹brack·et \'bra-kət\ *n* **1** : a projecting framework or arm designed to support weight; *also* : a shelf on such framework **2** : one of a pair of punctuation marks [ ] used esp. to enclose interpolated matter **3** : a continuous section of a series; *esp* : one of a graded series of income groups

²bracket *vb* **1** : to furnish or fasten with brackets **2** : to place within brackets; *also* : to separate or group with or as if with brackets

brack·ish \'bra-kish\ *adj* : somewhat salty — **brack·ish·ness** *n*

bract \'brakt\ *n* : an often modified leaf on or at the base of a flower stalk

brad \'brad\ *n* : a slender nail with a small head

brae \'brā\ *n, chiefly Scot* : a hillside esp. along a river

brag \'brag\ *vb* **bragged; brag·ging** : to talk or assert boastfully — **brag** *n* — **brag·ger** *n*

brag·ga·do·cio \,bra-gə-'dō-shē-,ō, -sē-, -chē-\ *n, pl* **-cios 1** : BRAGGART, BOASTER **2** : empty boasting **3** : arrogant pretension : COCKINESS

brag·gart \'bra-gərt\ *n* : one who brags

Brah·man *or* **Brah·min** \'brä-mən *for 1*; 'brā-, 'brä-, 'bra- *for 2*\ *n* **1** : a Hindu of the highest caste traditionally assigned to the priesthood **2** : any of a breed of large vigorous humped cattle developed in the southern U.S. from Indian stock **3** *usu* **Brahmin** : a person of high social standing and cultivated intellect and taste

Brah·man·ism \'brä-mə-ˌni-zəm\ *n* : orthodox Hinduism

¹**braid** \'brād\ *vb* **1** : to form (strands) into a braid : PLAIT; *also* : to make from braids **2** : to ornament with braid

²**braid** *n* **1** : a length of braided hair **2** : a cord or ribbon of three or more interwoven strands

braille \'brāl\ *n, often cap* : a system of writing for the blind that uses characters made up of raised dots

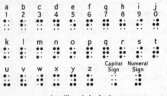

braille alphabet

¹**brain** \'brān\ *n* **1** : the part of the vertebrate nervous system that is the organ of thought and nervous co-ordination, is made up of nerve cells and their fibers, and is enclosed in the skull; *also* : a centralized mass of nerve tissue in an invertebrate **2** : INTELLECT, INTELLIGENCE — often used in pl. — **brained** \'brānd\ *adj* — **brain·less** *adj* — **brainy** *adj*

²**brain** *vb* **1** : to kill by smashing the skull **2** : to hit on the head

brain·child \'brān-ˌchīld\ *n* : a product of one's creative imagination

brain death *n* : final cessation of activity in the central nervous system esp. as indicated by a flat electroencephalogram — **brain–dead** \-ˌded\ *adj*

brain drain *n* : the departure of educated or professional people from one country, sector, or field to another esp. for better pay or living conditions

brain·storm \-ˌstȯrm\ *n* : a sudden inspiration or idea — **brainstorm** *vb*

brain·teas·er \-ˌtē-zər\ *n* : a challenging puzzle

brain·wash·ing \'brān-ˌwȯ-shiŋ, -ˌwä-\ *n* **1** : a forcible indoctrination to induce someone to give up basic political, social, or religious beliefs and attitudes and to accept contrasting regimented ideas **2** : persuasion by propaganda or salesmanship — **brain·wash** *vb*

brain wave *n* **1** : BRAINSTORM **2** : rhythmic fluctuations of voltage between parts of the brain; *also* : a current produced by brain waves

braise \'brāz\ *vb* **braised; brais·ing** : to cook (meat) slowly in fat and little moisture in a closed pot

¹**brake** \'brāk\ *n* : a common bracken fern

²**brake** *n* : rough or wet land heavily overgrown (as with thickets or reeds)

³**brake** *n* : a device for slowing or stopping motion esp. by friction — **brake·less** *adj*

⁴**brake** *vb* **braked; brak·ing** **1** : to slow or stop by or as if by a brake **2** : to apply a brake

brake·man \'brāk-mən\ *n* : a train crew member who inspects the train and assists the conductor

bram·ble \'bram-bəl\ *n* : any of a large genus of prickly shrubs (as a blackberry) related to the roses; *also* : any rough prickly shrub or vine — **bram·bly** \-b(ə-)lē\ *adj*

bran \'bran\ *n* : the edible broken husks of cereal grain sifted from flour or meal

¹**branch** \'branch\ *n* [ME, fr. OF *branche*, fr. LL *branca* paw] **1** : a natural subdivision (as a bough or twig) of a plant stem **2** : a division (as of an antler or a river) related to a whole like a plant branch to its stem **3** : a

discrete element of a complex system ⟨the executive ∼⟩; *esp* : a division of a family descended from one ancestor — **branched** \'brancht\ *adj*

²**branch** *vb* **1** : to develop branches **2** : DIVERGE **3** : to extend activities ⟨the business is ∼*ing* out⟩

¹**brand** \'brand\ *n* **1** : a piece of charred or burning wood **2** : a mark made (as by burning) usu. to identify; *also* : a mark of disgrace : STIGMA **3** : a class of goods identified as the product of a particular firm or producer **4** : a distinctive kind ⟨my own ∼ of humor⟩

²**brand** *vb* **1** : to mark with a brand **2** : STIGMATIZE

bran·dish \'bran-dish\ *vb* : to shake or wave menacingly **syn** flourish, flash, flaunt

brand–new \'bran-ˈnü, -ˈnyü\ *adj* : conspicuously new and unused

bran·dy \'bran-dē\ *n, pl* **brandies** [short for *brandywine*, fr. D *brandewijn*, fr. MD *brantwijn*, fr. *brant* distilled + *wijn* wine] : a liquor distilled from wine or fermented fruit juice — **brandy** *vb*

brash \'brash\ *adj* **1** : IMPETUOUS, AUDACIOUS **2** : aggressively self-assertive

brass \'bras\ *n* **1** : an alloy of copper and zinc; *also* : an object of brass **2** : brazen self-assurance **3** : persons of high rank (as in the military) — **brassy** *adj*

bras·siere \brə-ˈzir\ *n* : a woman's close-fitting undergarment designed to support the breasts

brat \'brat\ *n* : an ill-behaved child — **brat·ti·ness** *n* — **brat·ty** *adj*

bra·va·do \brə-ˈvä-dō\ *n, pl* **-does** *or* **-dos** **1** : blustering swaggering conduct **2** : a show of bravery

¹**brave** \'brāv\ *adj* **brav·er; brav·est** [MF, fr. It & Sp *bravo* courageous, wild, prob. fr. L *barbarus* barbarous] **1** : showing courage **2** : EXCELLENT, SPLENDID **syn** bold, intrepid, courageous, valiant — **brave·ly** *adv*

²**brave** *vb* **braved; brav·ing** : to face or endure bravely

³**brave** *n* : an American Indian warrior

brav·ery \'brā-və-rē\ *n, pl* **-er·ies** : COURAGE

bra·vo \'brä-vō\ *n, pl* **bravos** : a shout of approval — often used as an interjection in applauding

bra·vu·ra \brə-ˈvyuṙ-ə, -ˈvuṙ-\ *n* **1** : a florid brilliant musical style **2** : self-assured brilliant performance — **bravura** *adj*

brawl \'brȯl\ *n* : a noisy quarrel **syn** fracas, row, rumpus, scrap, fray, melee — **brawl** *vb* — **brawl·er** *n*

brawn \'brȯn\ *n* : strong muscles; *also* : muscular strength — **brawn·i·ness** *n* — **brawny** *adj*

bray \'brā\ *n* : the characteristic harsh cry of a donkey — **bray** *vb*

braze \'brāz\ *vb* **brazed; braz·ing** : to solder with an alloy (as brass) that melts at a lower temperature than the metals being joined — **braz·er** *n*

¹**bra·zen** \'brāz-ᵊn\ *adj* **1** : made of brass **2** : sounding harsh and loud **3** : of the color of brass **4** : marked by contemptuous boldness — **bra·zen·ly** *adv* — **bra·zen·ness** *n*

²**brazen** *vb* : to face boldly or defiantly

¹**bra·zier** \'brā-zhər\ *n* : a worker in brass

²**brazier** *n* **1** : a vessel holding burning coals (as for heating) **2** : a device on which food is grilled

Bra·zil·ian \brə-ˈzil-yən\ *n* : a native or inhabitant of Brazil — **Brazilian** *adj*

Bra·zil nut \brə-ˈzil-\ *n* : a triangular oily edible nut borne in large capsules by a tall So. American tree; *also* : the tree

¹**breach** \'brēch\ *n* **1** : a breaking of a law, obligation, tie (as of friendship), or standard (as of conduct) **2** : an interruption or opening made by or as if by breaking through **syn** violation, transgression, infringement, trespass

²**breach** *vb* **1** : to make a breach in **2** : to leap out of water ⟨whales ∼*ing*⟩

¹**bread** \'bred\ *n* **1** : baked food made basically of flour or meal **2** : FOOD

²**bread** *vb* : to cover with bread crumbs before cooking

bread·bas·ket \'bred-ᵢbas-kət\ *n* : a major cereal≈ producing region

bread·fruit \-ᵢfrüt\ *n* : a round usu. seedless fruit resembling bread in color and texture when baked; *also* : a tall tropical tree related to the mulberry and bearing breadfruit

bread·stuff \-ᵢstəf\ *n* : GRAIN, FLOUR

breadth \'bredth, 'bretth\ *n* **1** : WIDTH **2** : comprehensive quality : SCOPE ⟨∼ of knowledge⟩

bread·win·ner \'bred-ᵢwi-nər\ *n* : a member of a family whose wages supply its livelihood

¹**break** \'brāk\ *vb* **broke** \'brōk\; **bro·ken** \'brō-kən\; **break·ing 1** : to separate into parts usu. suddenly or violently : come or force apart **2** : TRANSGRESS ⟨∼ a law⟩ **3** : to force a way into, out of, or through **4** : to disrupt the order or unity of ⟨∼ ranks⟩ ⟨∼ up a gang⟩; *also* : to bring to submission or helplessness **5** : EXCEED, SURPASS ⟨∼ a record⟩ **6** : RUIN **7** : to make known **8** : HALT, INTERRUPT; *also* : to act or change abruptly (as a course or activity) **9** : to come esp. suddenly into being or notice ⟨as day ∼s⟩ **10** : to fail under stress **11** : HAPPEN, DEVELOP — **break·able** *adj or n*

²**break** *n* **1** : an act of breaking **2** : a result of breaking; *esp* : an interruption of continuity ⟨coffee ∼⟩ ⟨a ∼ for the commercial⟩ **3** : a stroke of good luck

break·age \'brā-kij\ *n* **1** : the action of breaking **2** : articles or amount broken **3** : loss due to things broken

break·down \'brāk-ᵢdaün\ *n* **1** : functional failure; *esp* : a physical, mental, or nervous collapse **2** : DISINTEGRATION **3** : DECOMPOSITION **4** : ANALYSIS, CLASSIFICATION — **break down** *vb*

break·er \'brā-kər\ *n* **1** : one that breaks **2** : a wave that breaks into foam (as against the shore)

break·fast \'brek-fəst\ *n* : the first meal of the day — **breakfast** *vb*

break in *vb* **1** : to enter a building by force **2** : INTERRUPT; *also* : INTRUDE **3** : TRAIN — **break–in** \'brāk-ᵢin\ *n*

break·neck \'brāk-'nek\ *adj* : very fast or dangerous ⟨∼ speed⟩

break out *vb* **1** : to develop or erupt suddenly or with force **2** : to develop a skin rash

break·through \'brāk-ᵢthrü\ *n* **1** : an act or instance of breaking through an obstruction or defensive line **2** : a sudden advance in knowledge or technique

break·up \-ᵢəp\ *n* **1** : DISSOLUTION **2** : a division into smaller units — **break up** *vb*

break·wa·ter \'brāk-ᵢwȯ-tər, -ᵢwä-\ *n* : a structure protecting a harbor or beach from the force of waves

bream \'brim, 'brēm\ *n, pl* **bream** *or* **breams** : any of various small freshwater sunfishes

breast \'brest\ *n* **1** : either of the pair of mammary glands extending from the front of the chest esp. in pubescent and adult human females **2** : the front part of the body between the neck and the abdomen **3** : the seat of emotion and thought

breast·bone \'brest-ᵢbōn\ *n* : STERNUM

breast–feed \-ᵢfēd\ *vb* : to feed (a baby) from a mother's breast rather than from a bottle

breast·plate \-ᵢplāt\ *n* : a metal plate of armor for the breast

breast·stroke \-ᵢstrōk\ *n* : a swimming stroke executed by extending both arms forward and then sweeping them back with palms out while kicking backward and outward with both legs

breast·work \-ᵢwərk\ *n* : a temporary fortification

breath \'breth\ *n* **1** : the act or power of breathing **2** : a slight breeze **3** : air inhaled or exhaled in breathing **4** : spoken sound **5** : SPIRIT — **breath·less** *adj* — **breath·less·ly** *adv* — **breath·less·ness** *n* — **breathy** \'bre-thē\ *adj*

breathe \'brēth\ *vb* **breathed; breath·ing 1** : to inhale and exhale **2** : LIVE **3** : to halt for rest **4** : to utter softly or secretly — **breath·able** *adj*

breath·er \'brē-thər\ *n* **1** : one that breathes **2** : a short rest

breath·tak·ing \'breth-ᵢtā-kiŋ\ *adj* **1** : making one out of breath **2** : EXCITING, THRILLING ⟨∼ beauty⟩ — **breath·tak·ing·ly** *adv*

brec·cia \'bre-chē-ə, -chə\ *n* : a rock consisting of sharp fragments held in fine-grained material

breech \'brēch\ *n* **1** *pl* \usu 'bri-chəz\ : trousers ending near the knee; *also* : PANTS **2** : BUTTOCKS, RUMP **3** : the part of a firearm at the rear of the barrel

¹**breed** \'brēd\ *vb* **bred** \'bred\; **breed·ing 1** : BEGET; *also* : ORIGINATE **2** : to propagate sexually; *also* : MATE **3** : BRING UP, NURTURE **4** : to produce (fissionable material) from material that is not fissionable **syn** generate, reproduce, procreate, propagate — **breed·er** *n*

²**breed** *n* **1** : a strain of similar and presumably related plants or animals usu. developed in domestication **2** : KIND, SORT, CLASS

breed·ing *n* **1** : ANCESTRY **2** : training in polite social interaction **3** : sexual propagation of plants or animals

¹**breeze** \'brēz\ *n* **1** : a light wind **2** : CINCH, SNAP — **breeze·less** *adj*

²**breeze** *vb* **breezed; breez·ing** : to progress quickly and easily

breeze·way \'brēz-ᵢwā\ *n* : a roofed open passage connecting two buildings (as a house and garage)

breezy \'brē-zē\ *adj* **1** : swept by breezes **2** : briskly informal — **breez·i·ly** \'brē-zə-lē\ *adv* — **breez·i·ness** \-zē-nəs\ *n*

breth·ren \'breth-rən, 'bre-thə-; 'bre-thərn\ *pl of* BROTHER — used esp. in formal or solemn address

Brethren *n pl* : members of one of several Protestant denominations originating chiefly in a German religious movement and stressing personal religious experience

bre·via·ry \'brē-vyə-rē, -vē-ᵢer-ē\ *n, pl* **-ries** *often cap* : a book of prayers, hymns, psalms, and readings used by Roman Catholic priests

brev·i·ty \'bre-və-tē\ *n, pl* **-ties 1** : shortness or conciseness of expression **2** : shortness of duration

brew \'brü\ *vb* **1** : to prepare (as beer) by steeping, boiling, and fermenting **2** : to prepare (as tea) by steeping in hot water — **brew** *n* — **brew·er** *n* — **brew·ery** \'brü-ə-rē, 'brü-(ə)r-ē\ *n*

¹bri·ar \'brī-ər\ *var of* BRIER

²briar *n* : a tobacco pipe made from the root or stem of a brier

bribe \'brīb\ *n* [ME, something stolen, fr. MF, bread given to a beggar] : something (as money or a favor) given or promised to a person to influence conduct

²bribe *vb* **bribed; brib·ing** : to influence by offering a bribe — **brib·able** *adj* — **brib·er** *n* — **brib·ery** \'brī-bə-rē\ *n*

bric-a-brac \'brik-ə-ˌbrak\ *n pl* [F] : small ornamental articles

¹brick \'brik\ *n* : a block molded from moist clay and hardened by heat used esp. for building

²brick *vb* : to close, cover, or pave with bricks

brick·bat \'brik-ˌbat\ *n* **1** : a piece of a hard material (as a brick) esp. when thrown as a missile **2** : an uncomplimentary remark

brick·lay·er \'brik-ˌlā-ər\ *n* : a person who builds or paves with bricks — **brick·lay·ing** *n*

¹brid·al \'brīd-ᵊl\ *n* [ME *bridale*, fr. OE *brȳdealu*, fr. *brȳd* bride + *ealu* ale] : MARRIAGE, WEDDING

²bridal *adj* : of or relating to a bride or a wedding

bride \'brīd\ *n* : a woman just married or about to be married

bride·groom \'brīd-ˌgrüm, -ˌgrum\ *n* : a man just married or about to be married

brides·maid \'brīdz-ˌmād\ *n* : a woman who attends a bride at her wedding

¹bridge \'brij\ *n* **1** : a structure built over a depression or obstacle for use as a passageway **2** : something (as the upper part of the nose) resembling a bridge in form or function **3** : a curved piece raising the strings of a musical instrument **4** : the forward part of a ship's superstructure from which it is navigated **5** : an artificial replacement for missing teeth

²bridge *vb* **bridged; bridg·ing** : to build a bridge over — **bridge·able** *adj*

³bridge *n* : a card game for four players developed from whist

bridge·head \-ˌhed\ *n* : an advanced position seized in enemy territory

bridge·work \-ˌwərk\ *n* : dental bridges

¹bri·dle \'brīd-ᵊl\ *n* **1** : headgear with which a horse is controlled **2** : CURB, RESTRAINT

²bridle *vb* **bri·dled; bri·dling 1** : to put a bridle on; *also* : to restrain with or as if with a bridle **2** : to show hostility or scorn usu. by tossing the head

Brie \'brē\ *n* : a soft cheese with a whitish rind and a pale yellow interior

¹brief \'brēf\ *adj* **1** : short in duration or extent **2** : CONCISE; *also* : CURT — **brief·ly** *adv* — **brief·ness** *n*

²brief *n* **1** : a concise statement or document; *esp* : one

summarizing a law client's case or a legal argument **2** *pl* : short snug underpants

³brief *vb* : to give final instructions or essential information to

brief·case \'brēf-ˌkās\ *n* : a flat flexible case for carrying papers

¹bri·er \'brī(-ə)r\ *n* : a plant (as a bramble or rose) with a thorny or prickly woody stem; *also* : a mass or twig of these — **bri·ery** \'brī(-ə)r-ē\ *adj*

²brier *or* **briar** *n* : a heath of southern Europe whose roots and knotted stems are used for making tobacco pipes

¹brig \'brig\ *n* : a 2-masted square-rigged sailing ship

²brig *n* : the place of confinement for offenders on a naval ship

³brig *abbr* brigade

bri·gade \bri-'gād\ *n* **1** : a military unit composed of a headquarters, one or more units of infantry or armored forces, and supporting units **2** : a group organized for a particular purpose (as fire fighting)

brig·a·dier general \ˌbri-gə-ˌdir-\ *n* : a commissioned officer (as in the army) ranking next below a major general

brig·and \'bri-gənd\ *n* : BANDIT — **brig·and·age** \-gən-dij\ *n*

brig·an·tine \'bri-gən-ˌtēn\ *n* : a 2-masted square-rigged ship with a fore-and-aft mainsail

Brig Gen *abbr* brigadier general

bright \'brīt\ *adj* **1** : SHINING, RADIANT **2** : ILLUSTRIOUS, GLORIOUS **3** : INTELLIGENT, CLEVER; *also* : LIVELY, CHEERFUL **syn** brilliant, lustrous, beaming — **bright** *adv* — **bright·ly** *adv* — **bright·ness** *n*

bright·en \'brīt-ᵊn\ *vb* : to make or become bright or brighter — **bright·en·er** *n*

¹bril·liant \'bril-yənt\ *adj* [F *brillant*, prp. of *briller* to shine, fr. It *brillare*] **1** : very bright **2** : STRIKING, DISTINCTIVE **3** : very intelligent **syn** radiant, lustrous, beaming, lucid, bright, lambent — **bril·liance** \-yəns\ *n* — **bril·lian·cy** \-yən-sē\ *n* — **bril·liant·ly** *adv*

²brilliant *n* : a gem cut in a particular form with many facets

¹brim \'brim\ *n* : EDGE, RIM **syn** brink, border, verge, fringe — **brim·less** *adj*

²brim *vb* **brimmed; brim·ming** : to be or become full often to overflowing

brim·ful \-'ful\ *adj* : full to the brim

brim·stone \'brim-ˌstōn\ *n* : SULFUR

brin·dled \'brin-dᵊld\ *adj* : having dark streaks or flecks on a gray or tawny ground ⟨a ∼ Great Dane⟩

brine \'brīn\ *n* **1** : water saturated with salt **2** : OCEAN — **brin·i·ness** \'brī-nē-nəs\ *n* — **briny** \'brī-nē\ *adj*

bring \'briŋ\ *vb* **brought** \'brȯt\; **bring·ing** \'briŋ-iŋ\ **1** : to cause to come with one **2** : INDUCE, PERSUADE, LEAD **3** : PRODUCE, EFFECT **4** : to sell for ⟨∼ a good price⟩ — **bring·er** *n*

bring about *vb* : to cause to take place

bring up *vb* **1** : to give a parent's fostering care to **2** : to come or bring to a sudden halt **3** : to call to notice

brink \'briŋk\ *n* **1** : an edge at the top of a steep place **2** : the point of onset

brio \'brē-ō\ *n* : VIVACITY, SPIRIT

bri·quet *or* **bri·quet** \bri-'ket\ *n* : a compacted often brick-shaped mass of fine material ⟨a charcoal ∼⟩

brisk \'brisk\ *adj* 1 : ALERT, LIVELY 2 : INVIGORATING **syn** agile, spry, nimble — **brisk·ly** *adv* — **brisk·ness** *n*

bris·ket \'bris-kət\ *n* : the breast or lower chest of a quadruped; *also* : a cut of beef from the brisket

bris·ling \'briz-liŋ, 'bris-\ *n* : SPRAT 1

¹**bris·tle** \'bri-səl\ *n* : a short stiff coarse hair — **bris·tle·like** \'bri-səl-ˌlik\ *adj* — **bris·tly** *adj*

²**bristle** *vb* **bris·tled; bris·tling** 1 : to stand stiffly erect 2 : to show angry defiance 3 : to appear as if covered with bristles

Brit *abbr* Britain; British

Bri·tan·nic \bri-'ta-nik\ *adj* : BRITISH

britch·es \'bri-chəz\ *n pl* : BREECHES, TROUSERS

Brit·ish \'bri-tish\ *n pl* : the people of Great Britain or the Commonwealth — **British** *adj* — **Brit·ish·ness** *n*

British thermal unit *n* : the quantity of heat needed to raise the temperature of one pound of water one degree Fahrenheit

Brit·on \'brit-ᵊn\ *n* 1 : a member of a people inhabiting Britain before the Anglo-Saxon invasion 2 : a native or inhabitant of Great Britain

brit·tle \'brit-ᵊl\ *adj* **brit·tler; brit·tlest** : easily broken : FRAGILE **syn** crisp, crumbly, friable — **brit·tle·ness** *n*

bro *abbr* brother

¹**broach** \'brōch\ *n* : a pointed tool

²**broach** *vb* 1 : to pierce (as a cask) in order to draw the contents 2 : to introduce as a topic of conversation

¹**broad** \'brôd\ *adj* 1 : WIDE 2 : SPACIOUS 3 : CLEAR, OPEN 4 : OBVIOUS ⟨a ∼ hint⟩ 5 : COARSE, CRUDE ⟨∼ stories⟩ 6 : tolerant in outlook 7 : GENERAL 8 : dealing with essential points — **broad·ly** *adv* — **broad·ness** *n*

²**broad** *n, slang* : WOMAN

¹**broad·cast** \'brôd-ˌkast\ *vb* **broadcast** *also* **broadcast·ed; broad·cast·ing** 1 : to scatter or sow broadcast 2 : to make widely known 3 : to transmit a broadcast — **broad·cast·er** *n*

²**broadcast** *adv* : to or over a wide area

³**broadcast** *n* 1 : the transmission of sound or images by radio or television 2 : a single radio or television program

broad·cloth \-ˌklôth\ *n* 1 : a smooth dense woolen cloth 2 : a fine soft cloth of cotton, silk, or synthetic fiber

broad·en \'brôd-ᵊn\ *vb* : WIDEN

broad·loom \-ˌlüm\ *adj* : woven on a wide loom esp. in a solid color

broad–mind·ed \-'mīn-dəd\ *adj* : tolerant of varied opinions — **broad–mind·ed·ly** *adv* — **broad–mind·ed·ness** *n*

¹**broad·side** \-ˌsīd\ *n* 1 : a sheet of paper printed usu. on one side (as an advertisement) 2 : all of the guns on one side of a ship; *also* : their simultaneous firing 3 : a volley of abuse or denunciation

²**broadside** *adv* 1 : with one side forward : SIDEWAYS 2 : from the side (the car was hit ∼)

broad–spectrum *adj* : effective against a wide range of organisms ⟨∼ antibiotics⟩

broad·sword \'brôd-ˌsôrd\ *n* : a broad-bladed sword

broad·tail \-ˌtāl\ *n* : a karakul esp. with flat and wavy fur

bro·cade \brō-'kād\ *n* : a usu. silk fabric with a raised design

broc·co·li \'brä-kə-lē\ *n* [It, pl. of *broccolo* flowering top of a cabbage, dim. of *brocco* small nail, sprout, fr. L *broccus* projecting] : the stems and immature usu. green or purple flower heads of either of two garden vegetable plants closely related to the cabbage; *also* : either of the plants

bro·chette \brō-'shet\ *n* : SKEWER

bro·chure \brō-'shủr\ *n* [F, fr. *brocher* to sew, fr. MF,

to prick, fr. OF *brochier*, fr. *broche* pointed tool] : PAMPHLET, BOOKLET

bro·gan \'brō-gən, brō-'gan\ *n* : a heavy shoe

brogue \'brōg\ *n* : a dialect or regional pronunciation; *esp* : an Irish accent

broil \'brôil\ *vb* : to cook by exposure to radiant heat : GRILL — **broil** *n*

broil·er \'brôi-lər\ *n* 1 : a utensil for broiling 2 : a young chicken fit for broiling

¹**broke** \'brōk\ *past of* BREAK

²**broke** *adj* : PENNILESS

¹**bro·ken** \'brō-kən\ *past part of* BREAK

²**broken** *adj* 1 : SHATTERED 2 : having gaps or breaks : INTERRUPTED, DISRUPTED 3 : SUBDUED, CRUSHED 4 : BANKRUPT 5 : imperfectly spoken ⟨∼ English⟩ — **bro·ken·ly** *adv*

bro·ken·heart·ed \ˌbrō-kən-'här-təd\ *adj* : overcome by grief or despair

bro·ker \'brō-kər\ *n* : an agent who negotiates contracts of purchase and sale — **broker** *vb*

bro·ker·age \'brō-kə-rij\ *n* 1 : the business of a broker 2 : the fee or commission charged by a broker

bro·mide \'brō-ˌmīd\ *n* : a compound of bromine and another element or chemical group including some (as potassium bromide) used as sedatives

bro·mid·ic \brō-'mi-dik\ *adj* : TRITE, UNORIGINAL

bro·mine \'brō-ˌmēn\ *n* [F *brome* bromine, fr. Gk *brōmos* stink] : a deep red liquid corrosive chemical element that gives off an irritating vapor — see ELEMENT table

bronc \'bräŋk\ *n* : an unbroken or partly broken range horse of western No. America; *also* : MUSTANG

bron·chi·al \'bräŋ-kē-əl\ *adj* : of, relating to, or affecting the bronchi or their branches

bron·chi·tis \brän-'kī-təs, bräŋ-\ *n* : inflammation of the bronchi and their branches — **bron·chit·ic** \-'ki-tik\ *adj*

bron·chus \'bräŋ-kəs\ *n, pl* **bron·chi** \'bräŋ-ˌkī, -ˌkē\ : either of the main divisions of the windpipe each leading to a lung

bron·co \'bräŋ-kō\ *n, pl* **broncos** [MexSp, fr. Sp, rough, wild] : BRONC

bron·to·sau·rus \ˌbrän-tə-'sòr-əs\ *also* **bron·to·saur** \'brän-tə-ˌsòr\ *n* [NL, fr. Gk *brontē* thunder + *sauros* lizard] : any of a genus of large 4-footed and probably herbivorous sauropod dinosaurs of the Jurassic

Bronx cheer \'bräŋks-\ *n* : RASPBERRY 2

¹**bronze** \'bränz\ *vb* **bronzed; bronz·ing** : to give the appearance of bronze to

²**bronze** *n* 1 : an alloy of copper and tin and sometimes other elements; *also* : something made of bronze 2 : a yellowish brown color — **bronzy** \'brän-zē\ *adj*

brooch \'brōch, 'brüch\ *n* : an ornamental clasp or pin

¹**brood** \'brüd\ *n* : a family of young animals or children and esp. of birds

²**brood** *adj* : kept for breeding ⟨a ∼ mare⟩

³**brood** *vb* 1 : to sit on eggs to hatch them; *also* : to shelter (hatched young) with the wings 2 : to think anxiously or gloomily about something — **brood·ing·ly** *adv*

brood·er \'brü-dər\ *n* 1 : one that broods 2 : a heated structure for raising young birds

¹**brook** \'brủk\ *n* : a small natural stream

²**brook** *vb* : TOLERATE, BEAR

brook·let \'brủk-lət\ *n* : a small brook

brook trout *n* : a common speckled cold-water char of No. America

broom \'brüm, 'brủm\ *n* 1 : any of several shrubs of the legume family with long slender branches and usu. yellow flowers 2 : an implement with a long handle (**broom·stick** \-ˌstik\) used for sweeping

bros *abbr* brothers

broth \'brôth\ *n, pl* **broths** \'brôths, 'brôthz\ 1 : liquid in which meat or sometimes vegetable food has been cooked 2 : a fluid culture medium

broth·el \'brä-thəl, 'brö-\ *n* : a house of prostitution

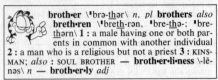

broth·er \'brə-thər\ *n, pl* **brothers** *also* **breth·ren** \'breth-rən, 'bre-thə-; 'bre-thərn\ **1** : a male having one or both parents in common with another individual **2** : a man who is a religious but not a priest **3** : KINSMAN; *also* : SOUL BROTHER — **broth·er·li·ness** \-lē-nəs\ *n* — **broth·er·ly** *adj*

broth·er·hood \'brə-thər-,hùd\ *n* **1** : the state of being brothers or a brother **2** : ASSOCIATION, FRATERNITY **3** : the whole body of persons in a business or profession

broth·er–in–law \'brə-thə-rən-,lò, 'brə-thərn-,lò\ *n, pl* **brothers–in–law** \'brə-thər-zən-\ : the brother of one's spouse; *also* : the husband of one's sister or of one's spouse's sister

brougham \'brü(-ə)m, 'brō(-ə)m\ *n* : a light closed horse-drawn carriage with the driver outside in front

brought *past and past part of* BRING

brou·ha·ha \'brü-,hä-,hä\ *n* : HUBBUB, UPROAR

brow \'braù\ *n* **1** : the eyebrow or the ridge on which it grows; *also* : FOREHEAD **2** : the projecting upper part of a steep place

brow·beat \'braù-,bēt\ *vb* **-beat; -beat·en** \-'bēt-ᵊn\ *or* **-beat; -beat·ing** : to intimidate by sternness or arrogance

¹brown \'braùn\ *adj* : of the color brown; *also* : of dark or tanned complexion

²brown *n* : a color like that of coffee or chocolate that is a blend of red and yellow darkened by black — **brown·ish** *adj*

³brown *vb* : to make or become brown

brown bag·ging \-'ba-giŋ\ *n* : the practice of carrying one's lunch usu. in a brown bag — **brown bag·ger** *n*

brown·ie \'braù-nē\ *n* **1** : a legendary cheerful elf who performs good deeds at night **2** *cap* : a member of a program of the Girl Scouts for girls in the first through third grades

brown·out \'braù-,naùt\ *n* : a period of reduced voltage of electricity caused esp. by high demand and resulting in reduced illumination

brown rice *n* : hulled but unpolished rice that retains most of the bran layers

brown·stone \'braùn-,stōn\ *n* : a dwelling faced with reddish brown sandstone

¹browse \'braùz\ *vb* **browsed; brows·ing 1** : to feed on browse; *also* : GRAZE **2** : to read or look over something in a casual way

²browse *n* : tender shoots, twigs, and leaves fit for food for cattle

bru·in \'brü-ən\ *n* : BEAR

¹bruise \'brüz\ *vb* **bruised; bruis·ing 1** : to inflict a bruise on; *also* : to become bruised **2** : to break down (as leaves or berries) by pounding

²bruise *n* : a surface injury to flesh : CONTUSION

bruis·er \'brü-zər\ *n* : a big husky man

bruit \'brüt\ *vb* : to make widely known by common report

brunch \'brənch\ *n* : a meal that combines a late breakfast and an early lunch

bru·net *or* **bru·nette** \brü-'net\ *adj* [F *brunet,* masc., *brunette,* fem., brownish, fr. OF, fr. *brun* brown] : having brown or black hair and usu. a relatively dark complexion — **brunet** *or* **brunette** *n*

brunt \'brənt\ *n* : the main shock, force, or stress esp. of an attack; *also* : the greater burden

¹brush \'brəsh\ *n* **1** : BRUSHWOOD **2** : scrub vegetation or land covered with it

²brush *n* **1** : a device composed of bristles set in a handle and used esp. for cleaning or painting **2** : a bushy tail (as of a fox) **3** : an electrical conductor that makes contact between a stationary and a moving part (as of a motor) **4** : a quick light touch in passing

³brush *vb* **1** : to treat (as in cleaning or painting) with a brush **2** : to remove with or as if with a brush; *also* : to dismiss in an offhand manner **3** : to touch gently in passing

⁴brush *n* : SKIRMISH **syn** encounter, run-in

brush–off \'brəsh-,òf\ *n* : a curt offhand dismissal

brush up *vb* : to renew one's skill

brush·wood \'brəsh-,wùd\ *n* **1** : small branches of wood esp. when cut **2** : a thicket of shrubs and small trees

brusque \'brəsk\ *adj* [F *brusque,* fr. It *brusco,* fr. ML *bruscus* a plant with stiff twigs used for brooms] : CURT, BLUNT, ABRUPT **syn** gruff, bluff, crusty, short — **brusque·ly** *adv*

brus·sels sprout \'brəs-əlz-\ *n, often cap B* : one of the edible small heads borne on the stalk of a plant closely related to the cabbage; *also, pl* : this plant

bru·tal \'brüt-ᵊl\ *adj* **1** : befitting a brute : UNFEELING, CRUEL **2** : HARSH, SEVERE ⟨~ weather⟩ **3** : unpleasantly accurate — **bru·tal·i·ty** \brü-'ta-lə-tē\ *n* — **bru·tal·ly** *adv*

bru·tal·ise *Brit var of* BRUTALIZE

bru·tal·ize \'brüt-ᵊl-,īz\ *vb* **-ized; -iz·ing 1** : to make brutal **2** : to treat brutally

¹brute \'brüt\ *adj* [ME, fr. MF *brut* rough, fr. L *brutus* brutish, lit., heavy] **1** : of or relating to beasts **2** : BRUTAL **3** : UNREASONING; *also* : purely physical ⟨~ strength⟩

²brute *n* **1** : BEAST 1 **2** : a brutal person

brut·ish \'brü-tish\ *adj* **1** : BRUTE 1 **2** : strongly sensual; *also* : showing little intelligence

BS *abbr* bachelor of science

BSA *abbr* Boy Scouts of America

bskt *abbr* basket

Bt *abbr* baronet

btry *abbr* battery

Btu *abbr* British thermal unit

bu *abbr* bushel

¹bub·ble \'bə-bəl\ *n* **1** : a globule of gas in a liquid **2** : a thin film of liquid filled with gas **3** : something lacking firmness or solidity — **bub·bly** *adj*

²bubble *vb* **bub·bled; bub·bling** : to form, rise in, or give off bubbles

bu·bo \'bü-bō, 'byü-\ *n, pl* **buboes** : an inflammatory swelling of a lymph gland

bu·bon·ic plague \bü-'bä-nik-, byü-\ n : plague caused by a bacterium transmitted to human beings by flea bites and marked esp. by chills and fever and by buboes usu. in the groin
buc·ca·neer \ˌbə-kə-'nir\ n : PIRATE
¹buck \'bək\ n, pl **bucks 1** or pl **buck** : a male animal (as a deer or antelope) **2** : DANDY **3** : DOLLAR
²buck vb **1** : to spring with an arching leap ⟨a ~ing horse⟩ **2** : to charge against something; also : to strive for advancement sometimes without regard to ethical behavior
buck·board \-ˌbōrd\ n : a 4-wheeled horse-drawn wagon with a floor of long springy boards

buckboard

buck·et \'bə-kət\ n **1** : PAIL **2** : an object resembling a bucket in collecting, scooping, or carrying something — **buck·et·ful** n
bucket seat n : a low separate seat for one person (as in an automobile)
buck·eye \'bə-ˌkī\ n : a tree related to the horse chestnut that occurs chiefly in the central U.S.; also : its large nutlike seed
buck fever n : nervous excitement of an inexperienced hunter at the sight of game
¹buck·le \'bə-kəl\ n : a clasp (as on a belt) for two loose ends
²buckle vb **buck·led; buck·ling 1** : to fasten with a buckle **2** : to apply oneself with vigor **3** : to crumple up : BEND, COLLAPSE
³buckle n : BEND, FOLD, KINK
buck·ler \'bə-klər\ n : SHIELD
buck·ram \'bə-krəm\ n : a coarse stiff cloth used esp. for binding books
buck·saw \'bək-ˌsò\ n : a saw set in a usu. H-shaped frame for sawing wood
buck·shot \'bək-ˌshät\ n : lead shot that is from .24 to .33 inch (about 6.1 to 8.4 millimeters) in diameter
buck·skin \-ˌskin\ n **1** : the skin of a buck **2** : a soft usu. suede-finished leather — **buckskin** adj
buck·tooth \-'tüth\ n : a large projecting front tooth — **buck–toothed** \-'tütht\ adj
buck·wheat \-ˌhwēt\ n : either of two plants grown for their triangular seeds which are used as a cereal grain; also : these seeds
bu·col·ic \byü-'kä-lik\ adj [L bucolicus, fr. Gk boukolikos, fr. boukolos one who tends cattle, fr. bous head of cattle + -kolos (akin to L colere to cultivate)] : PASTORAL, RURAL
¹bud \'bəd\ n **1** : an undeveloped plant shoot (as of a leaf or a flower); also : a partly opened flower **2** : an asexual reproductive structure that detaches from the parent and forms a new individual **3** : something not yet fully developed ⟨nipped in the ~⟩
²bud vb **bud·ded; bud·ding 1** : to form or put forth buds; also : to reproduce by asexual buds **2** : to be or develop like a bud **3** : to reproduce a desired variety (as of peach) by inserting a bud in a plant of a different variety
Bud·dhism \'bü-ˌdi-zəm, 'bù-\ n : a religion of eastern and central Asia growing out of the teachings of Gautama Buddha — **Bud·dhist** \'bü-dist, 'bù-\ n or adj
bud·dy \'bə-dē\ n, pl **buddies 1** : COMPANION; also : FRIEND **2** : FELLOW

budge \'bəj\ vb **budged; budg·ing** : MOVE, SHIFT; also : YIELD
bud·ger·i·gar \'bə-jə-rē-ˌgar\ n : a small brightly colored Australian parrot often kept as a pet
¹bud·get \'bə-jət\ n [ME bowgette, fr. MF bougette, dim. of bouge leather bag, fr. L bulga] **1** : STOCK, SUPPLY **2** : a financial report containing estimates of income and expenses; also : a plan for coordinating income and expenses **3** : the amount of money available for a particular use — **bud·get·ary** \'bə-jə-ˌter-ē\ adj
²budget vb **1** : to allow for in a budget **2** : to draw up a budget
³budget adj : INEXPENSIVE
bud·gie \'bə-jē\ n : BUDGERIGAR
¹buff \'bəf\ n **1** : a yellow to orange yellow color **2** : FAN, ENTHUSIAST
²buff adj : of the color buff
³buff vb : POLISH, SHINE
buf·fa·lo \'bə-fə-ˌlō\ n, pl **-lo** or **-loes** also **-los 1** : WATER BUFFALO **2** : a large shaggy-maned No. American wild bovine mammal that has short horns and heavy forequarters with a large muscular hump
¹buf·fer \'bə-fər\ n : something or someone that protects or shields (as from physical damage or a financial blow)
²buffer n : one that buffs
¹buf·fet \'bə-fət\ n : BLOW, SLAP
²buffet vb **1** : to strike with the hand; also : to pound repeatedly **2** : to struggle against or on syn beat, batter, drub, pummel, thrash
³buf·fet \(ˌ)bə-'fā, bü-\ n **1** : SIDEBOARD **2** : a counter for refreshments; also : a meal at which people serve themselves informally
buff leather n : a strong supple oil-tanned leather
buf·foon \(ˌ)bə-'fün\ n [MF bouffon, fr. It buffone] : CLOWN **2** — **buf·foon·ery** \-'fü-nə-rē\ n
¹bug \'bəg\ n **1** : an insect or other creeping or crawling invertebrate animal; esp : an insect pest (as a bedbug) **2** : any of an order of insects with sucking mouthparts and incomplete metamorphosis that includes many plant pests **3** : an unexpected flaw or imperfection ⟨a ~ in a computer program⟩ **4** : a disease-producing germ; also : a disease caused by it **5** : a concealed listening device
²bug vb **bugged; bug·ging 1** : BOTHER, ANNOY **2** : to plant a concealed microphone in
³bug vb **bugged; bug·ging** of the eyes : PROTRUDE, BULGE
bug·a·boo \'bə-gə-ˌbü\ n, pl **-boos** : BOGEY 1
bug·bear \'bəg-ˌbar\ n : BOGEY 1; also : a source of dread
bug·gy \'bə-gē\ n, pl **buggies** : a light horse-drawn carriage; also : a carriage for a baby
bu·gle \'byü-gəl\ n [ME, buffalo, instrument made of buffalo horn, bugle, fr. OF, fr. L buculus, dim. of bos head of cattle] : a valveless brass instrument resembling a trumpet and used esp. for military calls — **bu·gler** n
¹build \'bild\ vb **built** \'bilt\; **build·ing 1** : to form or have formed by ordering and uniting materials ⟨~ a house⟩; also : to bring into being or develop **2** : to produce or create gradually ⟨~ an argument on facts⟩ **3** : INCREASE, ENLARGE; also : ENHANCE **4** : to engage in building — **build·er** n
²build n : form or mode of structure; esp : PHYSIQUE
build·ing \'bil-diŋ\ n **1** : a usu. roofed and walled structure (as a house) for permanent use **2** : the art or business of constructing buildings
build·up \'bil-ˌdəp\ n : the act or process of building up; also : something produced by this
built–in \'bil-'tin\ adj **1** : forming an integral part of a structure **2** : INHERENT
bulb \'bəlb\ n **1** : an underground resting stage of a plant (as a lily or an onion) consisting of a short stem base bearing one or more buds enclosed in overlap-

ping leaves; *also* : a fleshy plant structure (as a tuber) resembling a bulb **2** : a plant having or growing from a bulb **3** : a rounded more or less bulb-shaped object or part (as for an electric lamp) — **bul·bous** \ˈbəl-bəs\ *adj*

Bul·gar·i·an \ˌbəl-ˈgar-ē-ən, bùl-\ *n* : a native or inhabitant of Bulgaria — **Bulgarian** *adj*

¹**bulge** \ˈbəlj\ *vb* **bulged; bulg·ing** : to become or cause to become protuberant

²**bulge** *n* : a swelling projecting part

bu·li·mia \bü-ˈlē-mē-ə, byü-, -ˈli-\ *n* **1** : an abnormal and constant craving for food **2** : a serious eating disorder chiefly of females that is characterized by compulsive overeating usu. followed by self-induced vomiting or laxative or diuretic abuse — **bu·lim·ic** \-ˈlē-mik, -ˈli-\ *adj or n*

¹**bulk** \ˈbəlk\ *n* **1** : MAGNITUDE, VOLUME **2** : material that forms a mass in the intestine; *esp* : FIBER 2 **3** : a large mass **4** : the major portion

²**bulk** *vb* **1** : to cause to swell or bulge **2** : to appear as a factor : LOOM

bulk·head \ˈbəlk-ˌhed\ *n* **1** : a partition separating compartments **2** : a structure built to cover a shaft or a cellar stairway

bulky \ˈbəl-kē\ *adj* **bulk·i·er; -est** : having bulk; *esp* : being large and unwieldy

¹**bull** \ˈbùl\ *n* **1** : a male bovine animal; *also* : a usu. adult male of various large animals (as the moose, elephant, or whale) **2** : one who buys securities or commodities in expectation of a price increase — **bull·ish** *adj*

²**bull** *adj* **1** : of, relating to, or suggestive of a bull : MALE **2** : large of its kind

³**bull** *n* [ME *bulle,* fr. ML *bulla,* fr. L, bubble, amulet] **1** : a papal letter **2** : DECREE

⁴**bull** *n, slang* : NONSENSE

⁵**bull** *abbr* bulletin

¹**bull·dog** \ˈbùl-ˌdòg\ *n* : any of a breed of compact muscular short-haired dogs of English origin

bulldog

²**bulldog** *vb* : to throw (a steer) by seizing the horns and twisting the neck

bull·doze \-ˌdōz\ *vb* **1** : to move, clear, or level with a tractor-driven machine (**bull·doz·er**) having a broad

blade for pushing **2** : to force as if by using a bulldozer

bul·let \ˈbù-lət\ *n* [MF *boulette* small ball & *boulet* missile, dims. of *boule* ball] : a missile to be shot from a firearm — **bul·let·proof** \-ˌprüf\ *adj*

bul·le·tin \ˈbù-lət-ᵊn\ *n* **1** : a brief public report intended for immediate release on a matter of public interest **2** : a periodical publication (as of a college) — **bulletin** *vb*

bull·fight \ˈbùl-ˌfīt\ *n* : a spectacle in which people ceremonially fight with and usu. kill bulls in an arena — **bull·fight·er** *n*

bull·frog \-ˌfròg, -ˌfräg\ *n* : a large deep-voiced frog

bull·head \-ˌhed\ *n* : any of several common freshwater catfishes of the U.S.

bull·head·ed \-ˈhe-dəd\ *adj* : stupidly stubborn : HEADSTRONG

bul·lion \ˈbùl-yən\ *n* : gold or silver esp. in bars or ingots

bull·ock \ˈbù-lək\ *n* : a young bull; *also* : STEER

bull pen *n* : a place on a baseball field where pitchers warm up; *also* : the relief pitchers of a baseball team

bull session *n* : an informal discussion

bull's-eye \ˈbùl-ˌzī\ *n, pl* **bull's-eyes** : the center of a target; *also* : a shot that hits the bull's-eye

¹**bul·ly** \ˈbù-lē\ *n, pl* **bullies** : a person habitually cruel to others who are weaker

²**bully** *adj* : EXCELLENT, FIRST-RATE — often used interjectionally

³**bully** *vb* **bul·lied; bul·ly·ing** : to behave as a bully toward : DOMINEER **syn** browbeat, intimidate, hector

bul·rush \ˈbùl-ˌrəsh\ *n* : any of several large rushes or sedges of wetlands

bul·wark \ˈbùl-(ˌ)wərk, -ˌwòrk; ˈbəl-(ˌ)wərk\ *n* **1** : a wall-like defensive structure **2** : a strong support or protection

¹**bum** \ˈbəm\ *adj* **1** : of poor quality ⟨~ advice⟩ **2** : DISABLED ⟨a ~ knee⟩

²**bum** *vb* **bummed; bum·ming 1** : to spend time unemployed and wandering; *also* : LOAF **2** : to obtain by begging

³**bum** *n* **1** : LOAFER **2** : a devotee of a recreational activity ⟨a ski ~⟩ **3** : TRAMP

bum·ble·bee \ˈbəm-bəl-ˌbē\ *n* : any of numerous large hairy social bees

bum·mer \ˈbə-mər\ *n* **1** : an unpleasant experience **2** : FAILURE

¹**bump** \ˈbəmp\ *n* **1** : a local bulge; *esp* : a swelling of tissue **2** : a sudden forceful blow or impact — **bumpy** *adj*

²**bump** *vb* **1** : to strike or knock forcibly; *also* : to move by or as if by bumping **2** : to collide with

¹**bum·per** \ˈbəm-pər\ *n* **1** : a cup or glass filled to the brim **2** : something unusually large — **bumper** *adj*

²**bump·er** \ˈbəm-pər\ *n* : a device for absorbing shock or preventing damage; *esp* : a usu. metal bar at either end of an automobile

bump·kin \\'bəmp-kən\\ *n* : an awkward and unsophisticated country person

bump·tious \\'bəmp-shəs\\ *adj* : obtusely and often noisily self-assertive

bun \\'bən\\ *n* : a sweet biscuit or roll

¹**bunch** \\'bənch\\ *n* **1** : SWELLING **2** : CLUSTER, GROUP — **bunchy** *adj*

²**bunch** *vb* : to form into a group or bunch

bun·co *or* **bun·ko** \\'bəŋ-kō\\ *n, pl* **buncos** *or* **bunkos** : a swindling scheme — **bunco** *vb*

¹**bun·dle** \\'bən-dᵊl\\ *n* **1** : several items bunched and fastened together; *also* : something wrapped for carrying **2** : a considerable amount : LOT **3** : a small band of mostly parallel nerve or muscle fibers

²**bundle** *vb* **bun·dled; bun·dling** : to gather or tie in a bundle

bun·dling \\'bənd-(ᵊ-)liŋ\\ *n* : a former custom of a courting couple's occupying the same bed without undressing

bung \\'bəŋ\\ *n* : the stopper in the bunghole of a cask

bun·ga·low \\'bəŋ-gə-ˌlō\\ *n* : a one-storied house with a low-pitched roof

bun·gee cord \\'bən-jē-\\ *n* : a long elastic cord used esp. in a sport (**bungee jump·ing**) in which it is fastened to a person to arrest a free fall from a high place (as a bridge)

bung·hole \\'bəŋ-ˌhōl\\ *n* : a hole for emptying or filling a cask

bun·gle \\'bəŋ-gəl\\ *vb* **bun·gled; bun·gling** : to do badly : BOTCH — **bungle** *n* — **bun·gler** *n*

bun·ion \\'bən-yən\\ *n* : an inflamed swelling of the first joint of the big toe

¹**bunk** \\'bəŋk\\ *n* : BED; *esp* : a built-in bed that is often one of a tier

²**bunk** *n* : BUNKUM, NONSENSE

bunk bed *n* : one of two single beds usu. placed one above the other

bun·ker \\'bəŋ-kər\\ *n* **1** : a bin or compartment for storage (as for coal on a ship) **2** : a protective embankment or dugout **3** : a sand trap or embankment constituting a hazard on a golf course

bun·kum *or* **bun·combe** \\'bəŋ-kəm\\ *n* [*Buncombe* County, N.C.; fr. a remark made by its congressman, who defended an irrelevant speech by claiming that he was speaking to Buncombe] : insincere or foolish talk

bun·ny \\'bə-nē\\ *n, pl* **-nies** : RABBIT

Bun·sen burner \\'bən-sən-\\ *n* : a gas burner usu. consisting of a straight tube with air holes at the bottom

¹**bunt** \\'bənt\\ *vb* **1** : ¹BUTT **2** : to push or tap a baseball lightly without swinging the bat

²**bunt** *n* : an act or instance of bunting; *also* : a bunted ball

¹**bun·ting** \\'bən-tiŋ\\ *n* : any of numerous small stout-billed finches

²**bunting** *n* : a thin fabric used esp. for flags; *also* : FLAGS

¹**buoy** \\'bü-ē, 'bȯi\\ *n* **1** : a floating object anchored in water to mark something (as a channel) **2** : a float consisting of a ring of buoyant material to support a person who has fallen into the water

²**buoy** *vb* **1** : to mark by a buoy **2** : to keep afloat **3** : to raise the spirits of

buoy·an·cy \\'bȯi-ən-sē, 'bü-yən-\\ *n* **1** : the tendency of a body to float or rise when submerged in a fluid **2** : the power of a fluid to exert an upward force on a body placed in it **3** : resilience of spirit — **buoy·ant** \\-ənt, -yənt\\ *adj*

¹**bur** \\'bər\\ *var of* BURR

²**bur** *abbr* bureau

¹**bur·den** \\'bərd-ᵊn\\ *n* **1** : LOAD; *also* : CARE, RESPONSIBILITY **2** : something oppressive : ENCUMBRANCE **3** : CARGO; *also* : capacity for cargo

²**burden** *vb* : LOAD, OPPRESS — **bur·den·some** \\-səm\\ *adj*

³**burden** *n* **1** : REFRAIN, CHORUS **2** : a main theme or idea : GIST

bur·dock \\'bər-ˌdäk\\ *n* : any of a genus of coarse composite herbs with globe-shaped flower heads surrounded by prickly bracts

bu·reau \\'byu̇r-ō\\ *n, pl* **bureaus** *also* **bu·reaux** \\-ōz\\ [F, desk, cloth covering for desks, fr. OF *burel* woolen cloth, ultim. fr. L *burra* shaggy cloth] **1** : a chest of drawers **2** : an administrative unit (as of a government department) **3** : a branch of a publication or wire service in an important news center

bu·reau·cra·cy \\byu̇-'rä-krə-sē\\ *n, pl* **-cies 1** : a body of appointive government officials **2** : government marked by specialization of functions under fixed rules and a hierarchy of authority; *also* : an unwieldy administrative system burdened with excessive complexity and lack of flexibility — **bu·reau·crat** \\'byu̇r-ə-ˌkrat\\ *n* — **bu·reau·crat·ic** \\ˌbyu̇r-ə-'kra-tik\\ *adj*

bur·geon \\'bər-jən\\ *vb* : to put forth fresh growth (as from buds) : grow vigorously : FLOURISH

burgh \\'bər-ō\\ *n* : a Scottish town

bur·gher \\'bər-gər\\ *n* **1** : TOWNSMAN **2** : a prosperous solid citizen

bur·glary \\'bər-glə-rē\\ *n, pl* **-glar·ies** : forcible entry into a building esp. at night with the intent to commit a crime (as theft) — **bur·glar** \\-glər\\ *n* — **bur·glar·ize** \\'bər-glə-ˌrīz\\ *vb*

bur·gle \\'bər-gəl\\ *vb* **bur·gled; bur·gling** : to commit burglary on

bur·go·mas·ter \\'bər-gə-ˌmas-tər\\ *n* : the chief magistrate of a town in some European countries

bur·gun·dy \\'bər-gən-dē\\ *n, pl* **-dies** *often cap* **1** : a red or white table wine from the Burgundy region of France **2** : an American red table wine

buri·al \\'ber-ē-əl\\ *n* : the act or process of burying

burl \\'bərl\\ *n* : a hard woody often flattened hemispherical outgrowth on a tree

bur·lap \\'bər-ˌlap\\ *n* : a coarse fabric usu. of jute or hemp used esp. for bags

¹**bur·lesque** \\(ˌ)bər-'lesk\\ *n* [*burlesque*, adj., comic, droll, fr. F, fr. It *burlesco*, fr. *burla* joke, fr. Sp] **1** : a witty or derisive literary or dramatic imitative work **2** : broadly humorous theatrical entertainment consisting of several items (as songs, skits, or dances)

²**burlesque** *vb* **bur·lesqued; bur·lesqu·ing** : to make ludicrous by burlesque syn caricature, parody, travesty

bur·ly \\'bər-lē\\ *adj* **bur·li·er, -est** : strongly and heavily built : HUSKY syn muscular, brawny, beefy, hefty

Bur·mese \\ˌbər-'mēz, -'mēs\\ *n, pl* **Burmese** : a native or inhabitant of Burma (Myanmar) — **Burmese** *adj*

¹**burn** \\'bərn\\ *vb* **burned** \\'bərnd, 'bərnt\\ *or* **burnt** \\'bərnt\\; **burn·ing 1** : to be on fire **2** : to feel or look as if on fire **3** : to alter or become altered by or as if by the action of fire or heat **4** : to use as fuel ⟨~ coal⟩; *also* : to destroy by fire ⟨~ trash⟩ **5** : to cause or make by fire ⟨~ a hole⟩; *also* : to affect as if by heat

²**burn** *n* : an injury or effect produced by or as if by burning

burn·er \\'bər-nər\\ *n* : the part of a fuel-burning or heat-producing device where the flame or heat is produced

bur·nish \\'bər-nish\\ *vb* : to make shiny esp. by rubbing : POLISH — **bur·nish·er** *n* — **bur·nish·ing** *adj or n*

bur·noose *or* **bur·nous** \\(ˌ)bər-'nüs\\ *n* : a hooded cloak worn esp. by Arabs

burn·out \\'bər-ˌnau̇t\\ *n* **1** : the cessation of operation of a jet or rocket engine **2** : exhaustion of one's physical or emotional strength; *also* : a person suffering from burnout

burp \\'bərp\\ *n* : an act of belching — **burp** *vb*

burp gun *n* : a small submachine gun

burr \\'bər\\ *n* **1** *usu* **bur** : a rough or prickly envelope of a fruit; *also* : a plant that bears burs **2** : roughness left in cutting or shaping metal **3** : WHIR — **bur·ry** *adj*

bur·ri·to \\bə-'rē-tō\\ *n* [AmerSp, fr. Sp, little donkey, dim. of *burro*] : a flour tortilla rolled around a filling and baked

bur·ro \'bər-ō, 'bu̇r-\ *n, pl* **burros** [Sp] : a usu. small donkey

¹bur·row \'bər-ō\ *n* : a hole in the ground made by an animal (as a rabbit)

²burrow *vb* **1** : to form by tunneling; *also* : to make a burrow **2** : to progress by or as if by digging — **bur·row·er** *n*

bur·sar \'bər-sər\ *n* : a treasurer esp. of a college

bur·si·tis \(̣)bər-'sī-təs\ *n* : inflammation of the serous sac (**bur·sa** \'bər-sə\) of a joint (as the elbow or shoulder)

¹burst \'bərst\ *vb* **burst** *or* **burst·ed; burst·ing 1** : to fly apart or into pieces **2** : to show one's feelings suddenly; *also* : PLUNGE ⟨~ into song⟩ **3** : to enter or emerge suddenly : SPRING **4** : to be filled to the breaking point

²burst *n* **1** : a sudden outbreak : SPURT **2** : EXPLOSION **3** : result of bursting

Bu·run·di·an \bu̇-'run-dē-ən\ *n* : a native or inhabitant of Burundi

---

bury \'ber-ē\ *vb* **bur·ied; bury·ing 1** : to deposit in the earth; *also* : to inter with funeral ceremonies **2** : CONCEAL, HIDE **3** : SUBMERGE, ENGROSS — usu. used with *in*

---

¹bus \'bəs\ *n, pl* **bus·es** *or* **bus·ses** [short for *omnibus*, fr. F, fr. L, for all, dat. pl. of *omnis* all] : a large motor vehicle for carrying passengers

²bus *vb* **bused** *or* **bussed; bus·ing** *or* **bus·sing 1** : to travel or transport by bus **2** : to work as a busboy

³bus *abbr* business

bus·boy \'bəs-ˌbȯi\ *n* : a waiter's helper

bus·by \'bəz-bē\ *n, pl* **busbies** : a military full-dress fur hat

bush \'bu̇sh\ *n* **1** : SHRUB **2** : rough uncleared country **3** : a thick tuft ⟨a ~ of hair⟩ — **bushy** *adj*

bushed \'bu̇sht\ *adj* : TIRED, EXHAUSTED

bush·el \'bu̇-shəl\ *n* — see WEIGHT table

bush·ing \'bu̇-shiŋ\ *n* : a usu. removable cylindrical lining for an opening of a mechanical part to limit the size of the opening, resist wear, or serve as a guide

bush·mas·ter \'bu̇sh-ˌmas-tər\ *n* : a large venomous tropical American pit viper

bush·whack \-ˌhwak\ *vb* **1** : AMBUSH **2** : to clear a path through esp. by chopping down bushes and branches — **bush·whack·er** *n*

busi·ly \'bi-zə-lē\ *adv* : in a busy manner

busi·ness \'biz-nəs, -nəz\ *n* **1** : OCCUPATION; *also* : TASK, MISSION **2** : a commercial or industrial enterprise; *also* : TRADE ⟨~ is good⟩ **3** : AFFAIR, MATTER **4** : personal concern

busi·ness·man \-ˌman\ *n* : a man engaged in business esp. as an executive

busi·ness·per·son \-ˌpərs-ᵊn\ *n* : a businessman or businesswoman

busi·ness·wom·an \-ˌwu̇-mən\ *n* : a woman engaged in business esp. as an executive

bus·kin \'bəs-kən\ *n* **1** : a laced boot reaching halfway to the knee **2** : tragic drama

buss \'bəs\ *n* : KISS — **buss** *vb*

¹bust \'bəst\ *n* [F *buste*, fr. It *busto*, fr. L *bustum* tomb] **1** : sculpture representing the upper part of the human figure **2** : the part of the human torso between the neck and the waist; *esp* : the breasts of a woman

²bust *vb* **bust·ed** *also* **bust; bust·ing 1** : BREAK, SMASH; *also* : BURST **2** : to ruin financially **3** : TAME **4** : DEMOTE **5** *slang* : ARREST; *also* : RAID

³bust *n* **1** : a drinking session **2** : a complete failure : FLOP **3** : a business depression **4** : PUNCH, SOCK **5** *slang* : a police raid; *also* : ARREST

¹bus·tle \'bə-səl\ *vb* **bus·tled; bus·tling** : to move or work in a brisk busy manner

²bustle *n* : briskly energetic activity

³bustle *n* : a pad or frame worn to support the fullness at the back of a woman's skirt

¹busy \'bi-zē\ *adj* **busi·er; -est 1** : engaged in action : not idle **2** : being in use ⟨~ telephones⟩ **3** : full of activity ⟨~ streets⟩ **4** : MEDDLING

²busy *vb* **bus·ied; busy·ing** : to make or keep busy : OCCUPY

busy·body \'bi-zē-ˌbä-dē\ *n* : MEDDLER

busy·work \-ˌwərk\ *n* : work that appears productive but only keeps one occupied

¹but \'bət\ *conj* **1** : except for the fact ⟨would have protested ~ that he was afraid⟩ **2** : THAT ⟨there's no doubt ~ he won⟩ **3** : without the certainty that ⟨never rains ~ it pours⟩ **4** : on the contrary ⟨not one, ~ two job offers⟩ **5** : YET ⟨poor ~ proud⟩ **6** : with the exception of ⟨none ~ the strongest attempt it⟩

²but *prep* : other than : EXCEPT ⟨this letter is nothing ~ an insult⟩; *also* : with the exception of ⟨no one here ~ me⟩

bu·tane \'byü-ˌtān\ *n* : either of two gaseous hydrocarbons used as a fuel

¹butch·er \'bu̇-chər\ *n* [ME *bocher*, fr. OF *bouchier*, fr. *bouc* he-goat] **1** : one who slaughters animals or dresses their flesh; *also* : a dealer in meat **2** : one that kills brutally or needlessly **3** : one that botches — **butch·ery** \-chə-rē\ *n*

²butcher *vb* **1** : to slaughter and dress for meat ⟨~ hogs⟩ **2** : to kill barbarously **3** : BOTCH

but·ler \'bət-lər\ *n* [ME *buteler*, fr. OF *bouteillier* bottle bearer, fr. *bouteille* bottle] : the chief male servant of a household

¹butt \'bət\ *vb* : to strike with the head or horns

²butt *n* : a blow or thrust with the head or horns

³butt *n* : a large cask

⁴butt *n* **1** : TARGET **2** : an object of abuse or ridicule

⁵butt *n* : a large, thicker, or bottom end of something

⁶butt *vb* **1** : ABUT **2** : to place or join edge to edge without overlapping

butte \'byüt\ *n* : an isolated steep hill

¹but·ter \'bə-tər\ *n* [ME, fr. OE *butere*, fr. L *butyrum* butter, fr. Gk *boutyron*, fr. *bous* cow + *tyros* cheese] **1** : a solid edible emulsion of fat obtained from cream by churning **2** : a substance resembling butter — **but·tery** *adj*

²butter *vb* : to spread with or as if with butter

but·ter–and–eggs \ˌbə-tə-rə-'negz\ *n sing or pl* : a

common perennial herb related to the snapdragon that has showy yellow and orange flowers

but·ter·cup \'bə-tər-ˌkəp\ n : any of a genus of herbs having usu. yellow flowers with five petals and sepals

but·ter·fat \-ˌfat\ n : the natural fat of milk and chief constituent of butter

but·ter·fin·gered \-ˌfiŋ-gərd\ adj : likely to let things fall or slip through the fingers — **but·ter·fin·gers** \-gərz\ n sing or pl

but·ter·fly \-ˌflī\ n : any of a group of slender day= flying insects with four broad wings covered with bright-colored scales

but·ter·milk \-ˌmilk\ n : the liquid remaining after butter is churned

but·ter·nut \-ˌnət\ n : the sweet egg-shaped nut of an American tree related to the walnut; also : this tree

but·ter·scotch \-ˌskäch\ n : a candy made from brown sugar, corn syrup, and water; also : the flavor of such candy

but·tock \'bə-tək\ n 1 : the back of a hip that forms one of the fleshy parts on which a person sits 2 pl : the seat of the body : RUMP

¹but·ton \'bət-ᵊn\ n 1 : a small knob secured to an article (as of clothing) and used as a fastener by passing it through a buttonhole or loop 2 : something that resembles a button 3 : PUSH BUTTON

²button vb : to close or fasten with or as if with buttons

¹but·ton·hole \'bət-ᵊn-ˌhōl\ n : a slit or loop for a button to pass through

²buttonhole vb : to detain in conversation by or as if by holding on to the outer garments of

¹but·tress \'bə-trəs\ n 1 : a projecting structure to support a wall 2 : PROP, SUPPORT

buttress 1

²buttress vb : PROP, SUPPORT

bu·tut \bù-'tüt\ n, pl bututs or butut — see dalasi at MONEY table

bux·om \'bək-səm\ adj : healthily plump; esp : full= bosomed

¹buy \'bī\ vb bought \'bòt\; buy·ing 1 : to obtain for a price : PURCHASE; also : BRIBE 2 : to accept as true — buy·er n

²buy n 1 : PURCHASE 1, 2 2 : an exceptional value : BARGAIN

¹buzz \'bəz\ vb 1 : to make a buzz 2 : to fly fast and close to

²buzz n 1 : a low humming sound 2 : RUMOR, GOSSIP

buz·zard \'bə-zərd\ n : any of various usu. large birds of prey and esp. the turkey vulture

buzz·er \'bə-zər\ n : a device that signals with a buzzing sound

buzz saw n : CIRCULAR SAW

buzz·word \'bəz-ˌwərd\ n : a voguish word or phrase often from technical jargon

BV abbr Blessed Virgin

BWI abbr British West Indies

bx abbr box

BX abbr base exchange

¹by \'bī, bə\ prep 1 : NEAR ⟨stood ∼ the window⟩ 2 : through or through the medium of : VIA ⟨left ∼ the door⟩ 3 : PAST ⟨drove ∼ the house⟩ 4 : DURING, AT ⟨studied ∼ night⟩ 5 : no later than ⟨get here ∼ 3 p.m.⟩ 6 : through the means or direct agency of ⟨∼ force⟩ 7 : in conformity with; also : ACCORDING TO ⟨did it ∼ the book⟩ 8 : with respect to ⟨a vet ∼ profession⟩ 9 : to the amount or extent of ⟨won ∼ a nose⟩ 10 — used to express relationship in multiplication, in division, and in measurements ⟨divide a ∼ b⟩ ⟨multiply ∼ 6⟩ ⟨15 feet ∼ 20 feet⟩

²by \'bī\ adv 1 : near at hand; also : IN ⟨stop ∼⟩ 2 : PAST 3 : ASIDE, APART

bye \'bī\ n : a position of a participant in a tournament who advances to the next round without playing

by–elec·tion also **bye–election** \'bī-ə-ˌlek-shən\ n : a special election held between regular elections in order to fill a vacancy

by·gone \'bī-ˌgòn\ adj : gone by : PAST — **bygone** n

by·law or **bye·law** \'bī-ˌlò\ n : a rule adopted by an organization for managing its internal affairs

by–line \'bī-ˌlīn\ n : a line at the beginning of a news story or magazine article giving the writer's name

BYO abbr bring your own

BYOB abbr bring your own beer; bring your own booze; bring your own bottle

¹by·pass \'bī-ˌpas\ n : a passage to one side or around a blocked or congested area; also : a surgical procedure establishing this ⟨a coronary ∼⟩

²bypass vb : to avoid by means of a bypass

by·path \-ˌpath, -ˌpàth\ n : BYWAY

by·play \'bī-ˌplā\ n : action engaged in on the side (as of a stage) while the main action proceeds

by–prod·uct \-ˌprä-(ˌ)dəkt\ n : a sometimes unexpected product or result produced in addition to the main product or result

by·stand·er \-ˌstan-dər\ n : one present but not participating syn onlooker, witness, spectator, eyewitness

byte \'bīt\ n : a group of 8 bits that a computer processes as a unit

by·way \'bī-ˌwā\ n 1 : a little-traveled side road 2 : a secondary aspect

by·word \-ˌwərd\ n 1 : PROVERB 2 : one that is noteworthy or notorious

Byz·an·tine \'biz-ᵊn-ˌtēn, 'bī-, -ˌtīn; bə-'zan-, bī-\ adj 1 : of, relating to, or characteristic of the ancient city of Byzantium or the Byzantine Empire 2 often not cap : intricately involved and often devious

C

¹c \'sē\ n, pl c's or cs \'sēz\ often cap 1 : the 3d letter of the English alphabet 2 slang : a sum of $100 3 : a grade rating a student's work as fair or mediocre in quality

²c abbr, often cap 1 calorie 2 carat 3 Celsius 4 cent 5 centigrade 6 centimeter 7 century 8 chapter 9 circa 10 cocaine 11 copyright

C symbol carbon

ca abbr circa

Ca symbol calcium

CA abbr 1 California 2 chartered accountant 3 chief accountant 4 chronological age

cab \'kab\ n 1 : a light closed horse-drawn carriage 2 : TAXICAB 3 : the covered compartment for the engineer and controls of a locomotive; also : a similar compartment (as on a truck)

CAB abbr Civil Aeronautics Board

ca·bal \kə-'bäl, -'bal\ n [F cabale, fr. ML cabbala ca-

bala, fr. Heb *qabbālāh*, lit., received (lore)] : a secret group of plotters or political conspirators

ca·ba·la \'ka-bə-lə, kə-'bä-\ *n, often cap* **1** : a medieval Jewish mysticism marked by belief in creation through emanation and a cipher method of interpreting Scripture **2** : esoteric or mysterious doctrine

ca·bana \kə-'ban-yə, -'ba-nə\ *n* : a shelter at a beach or swimming pool

cab·a·ret \ˌka-bə-'rā\ *n* : NIGHTCLUB

cab·bage \'ka-bij\ *n* [ME *caboche*, fr. OF, head] : a vegetable related to the mustard with a dense head of leaves

cab·bie *or* **cab·by** \'ka-bē\ *n, pl* **cabbies** : a driver of a cab

cab·er·net sau·vi·gnon \ˌka-bər-'nā-sō-vē-'nyōⁿ\ *n* : a dry red wine made from a single variety of black grape

cab·in \'ka-bən\ *n* **1** : a private room on a ship; *also* : a compartment below deck on a boat for passengers or crew **2** : an aircraft or spacecraft compartment for passengers, crew, or cargo **3** : a small simple one-story house

cabin boy *n* : a boy working as servant on a ship

cabin class *n* : a class of accommodations on a passenger ship superior to tourist class and inferior to first class

cabin cruiser *n* : CRUISER 3

cab·i·net \'kab-nit\ *n* **1** : a case or cupboard for holding or displaying articles **2** : the advisory council of a head of state (as a president or sovereign)

cab·i·net·mak·er \-ˌmā-kər\ *n* : a woodworker who makes fine furniture — **cab·i·net·mak·ing** *n*

cab·i·net·work \-ˌwərk\ *n* : the finished work of a cabinetmaker

¹ca·ble \'kā-bəl\ *n* **1** : a very strong rope, wire, or chain **2** : a bundle of insulated wires usu. twisted around a central core **3** : CABLEGRAM **4** : CABLE TELEVISION

²cable *vb* **ca·bled; ca·bling** : to telegraph by cable

cable car *n* : a vehicle moved by an endless cable

ca·ble·gram \'kā-bəl-ˌgram\ *n* : a message sent by a submarine telegraph cable

cable television *n* : a system of television reception in which signals from distant stations are sent by cable to the receivers of paying subscribers

cab·o·chon \'ka-bə-ˌshän\ *n* : a gem or bead cut in convex form and highly polished but not given facets; *also* : this style of cutting — **cabochon** *adv*

ca·boose \kə-'büs\ *n* : a car usu. at the rear of a freight train for the use of the train crew and railroad workers

cab·ri·o·let \ˌka-brē-ə-'lā\ *n* [F] **1** : a light 2-wheeled one-horse carriage **2** : a convertible coupe

cab·stand \'kab-ˌstand\ *n* : a place where cabs wait for passengers

ca·cao \kə-'kaù, -'kä-ō\ *n, pl* **cacaos** [Sp] : a So. American tree whose seeds (**cacao beans**) are the source of cocoa and chocolate; *also* : its dried fatty seeds

cac·cia·to·re \ˌkä-chə-'tōr-ē\ *adj* [It] : cooked with tomatoes and herbs (chicken ∼)

cache \'kash\ *n* [F] : a hiding place esp. for preserving

provisions; *also* : something hidden or stored in a cache — **cache** *vb*

ca·chet \ka-'shā\ *n* [F] **1** : a seal used esp. as a mark of official approval **2** : a feature or quality conferring prestige; *also* : PRESTIGE **3** : a design, inscription, or advertisement printed or stamped on mail

cack·le \'ka-kəl\ *vb* **cack·led; cack·ling** **1** : to make the sharp broken cry characteristic of a hen **2** : to laugh or chatter noisily — **cackle** *n* — **cack·ler** *n*

ca·coph·o·ny \ka-'kä-fə-nē\ *n, pl* **-nies** : harsh or discordant sound — **ca·coph·o·nous** \-nəs\ *adj*

cac·tus \'kak-təs\ *n, pl* **cac·ti** \-ˌtī\ *or* **cac·tus·es** *also* **cactus** : any of a large family of drought-resistant flowering plants with succulent stems and with leaves replaced by scales or prickles

cad \'kad\ *n* : a man who deliberately disregards another's feelings — **cad·dish** \'ka-dish\ *adj* — **cad·dish·ly** *adv* — **cad·dish·ness** *n*

ca·dav·er \kə-'da-vər\ *n* : a dead body

ca·dav·er·ous \kə-'da-və-rəs\ *adj* : suggesting a corpse esp. in gauntness or pallor **syn** wasted, emaciated, gaunt — **ca·dav·er·ous·ly** *adv*

---

cad·die *or* **cad·dy** \'ka-dē\ *n, pl* **caddies** [F *cadet* military cadet] : a person who assists a golfer esp. by carrying the clubs — **caddie** *or* **caddy** *vb*

---

cad·dy \'ka-dē\ *n, pl* **caddies** [Malay *kati* a unit of weight] : a small box, can, or chest; *esp* : one to keep tea in

ca·dence \'kād-ᵊns\ *n* : the measure or beat of a rhythmical flow : RHYTHM — **ca·denced** \-ᵊnst\ *adj*

ca·den·za \kə-'den-zə\ *n* [It] : a brilliant sometimes improvised passage usu. toward the close of a musical composition

ca·det \kə-'det\ *n* [F, fr. Prov (Gascony) *capdet* chief, fr. L *capitellum*, fr. L *caput* head] **1** : a younger son or brother **2** : a student in a service academy

Ca·dette \kə-'det\ *n* : a member of a Girl Scout program for girls in sixth through ninth grades

cadge \'kaj\ *vb* **cadged; cadg·ing** : SPONGE, BEG — **cadg·er** *n*

cad·mi·um \'kad-mē-əm\ *n* : a bluish white metallic chemical element used esp. in protective platings — see ELEMENT table

cad·re \'ka-ˌdrā, 'kä-, -drē\ *n* [F] **1** : FRAMEWORK **2** : a central unit esp. of trained personnel able to assume control and train others **3** : a group of indoctrinated leaders active in promoting the interests of a revolutionary party

ca·du·ceus \kə-'dü-sē-əs, -'dyü-, -shəs\ *n, pl* **-cei** \-sē-ˌī\ [L] **1** : the staff of a herald; *esp* : a representation of a staff with two entwined snakes and two wings at the top **2** : an insignia bearing a caduceus and symbolizing a physician

cae·cum *var of* CECUM

Cae·sar \'sē-zər\ *n* **1** : any of the Roman emperors succeeding Augustus Caesar — used as a title **2** *often* *not cap* : a powerful ruler : AUTOCRAT, DICTATOR; *also* : the civil or temporal power

caesarean *also* **caesarian** *var of* CESAREAN

cae·si·um *chiefly Brit var of* CESIUM

cae·su·ra \si-'zhùr-ə\ *n, pl* **-suras** *or* **-su·rae** \-'zhùr-(ˌ)ē\ : a break in the flow of sound usu. in the middle of a line of verse

ca·fé \ka-'fā\ *n* [F, lit., coffee] **1** : RESTAURANT **2** : BAR-ROOM **3** : NIGHTCLUB

ca·fé au lait \(ˌ)ka-ˌfā-ō-'lā\ *n* : coffee with hot milk in about equal parts

caf·e·te·ria \ˌka-fə-'tir-ē-ə\ *n* [AmerSp *cafetería* coffeehouse] : a restaurant in which the customers serve themselves or are served at a counter

caf·feine \ka-'fēn, 'ka-ˌfēn\ *n* : a stimulating alkaloid found esp. in coffee and tea

caf·fe lat·te \ˌkä-fā-'lä-tā\ *n* [It] : espresso mixed with hot or steamed milk

caf·tan \kaf-'tan, 'kaf-ˌtan\ *n* [Russ *kaftan*, fr. Turk, fr. Per *qaftān*] : an ankle-length garment with long sleeves worn in countries of the eastern Mediterranean

¹cage \'kāj\ *n* **1** : an openwork enclosure for confining an animal **2** : something resembling a cage

²cage *vb* **caged; cag·ing** : to put or keep in or as if in a cage

ca·gey *also* **ca·gy** \'kā-jē\ *adj* **ca·gi·er; -est** : wary of being trapped or deceived : SHREWD — **ca·gi·ly** \-jə-lē\ *adv* — **ca·gi·ness** \-jē-nəs\ *n*

CAGS *abbr* Certificate of Advanced Graduate Study

ca·hoot \kə-'hüt\ *n* : PARTNERSHIP, LEAGUE — usu. used in pl. ⟨officials in ∼s with the underworld⟩

cai·man \'kā-mən; kā-'man, kī-\ *n* : any of several Central and So. American reptiles closely related to alligators and crocodiles

cairn \'karn\ *n* : a heap of stones serving as a memorial or a landmark

cais·son \'kā-ˌsän, 'kās-ᵊn\ *n* **1** : a usu. 2-wheeled vehicle for artillery ammunition **2** : a watertight chamber used in underwater construction work or as a foundation

caisson disease *n* : ²BEND 3

cai·tiff \'kā-təf\ *adj* [ME *caitif*, fr. OF, captive, vile, fr. L *captivus* captive] : being base, cowardly, or despicable — **caitiff** *n*

ca·jole \kə-'jōl\ *vb* **ca·joled; ca·jol·ing** [F *cajoler*] : to persuade or coax esp. with flattery or false promises — **ca·jole·ment** *n* — **ca·jol·ery** \-'jō-lə-rē\ *n*

Ca·jun \'kā-jən\ *n* : a Louisianian descended from French-speaking immigrants from Acadia (Nova Scotia) — **Cajun** *adj*

¹cake \'kāk\ *n* **1** : a baked or fried breadlike food usu. in a small flat shape **2** : a sweet baked food made from batter or dough usu. containing flour, sugar, or shortening, and a leaven (as baking powder) **3** : a hardened or compacted substance ⟨a ∼ of soap⟩

²cake *vb* **caked; cak·ing 1** : ENCRUST **2** : to form or harden into a cake

cake·walk \'kāk-ˌwòk\ *n* **1** : a stage dance typically involving a high prance with backward tilt **2** : a one-sided contest or an easy task

cal *abbr* **1** calendar **2** caliber

Cal *abbr* **1** California **2** calorie

cal·a·bash \'ka-lə-ˌbash\ *n* : the fruit of a gourd; *also* : a utensil made from its hard shell

cal·a·boose \'ka-lə-ˌbüs\ *n* [Sp *calabozo* dungeon] : JAIL

ca·la·di·um \kə-'lā-dē-əm\ *n* : any of a genus of tropical American ornamental plants related to the arums

cal·a·mari \ˌkä-lə-'mär-ē\ *n* [It] : squid used as food

cal·a·mine \'ka-lə-ˌmīn\ *n* : a lotion of oxides of zinc and iron

ca·lam·i·ty \kə-'la-mə-tē\ *n, pl* **-ties 1** : great distress or misfortune **2** : an event causing great harm or loss and affliction : DISASTER — **ca·lam·i·tous** \-təs\ *adj* — **ca·lam·i·tous·ly** *adv* — **ca·lam·i·tous·ness** *n*

calc *abbr* calculate; calculated

cal·car·e·ous \kal-'kar-ē-əs\ *adj* : resembling calcium carbonate in hardness; *also* : containing calcium or calcium carbonate

cal·cif·er·ous \kal-'si-fə-rəs\ *adj* : producing or containing calcium carbonate

cal·ci·fy \'kal-sə-ˌfī\ *vb* **-fied; -fy·ing** : to make or become calcareous — **cal·ci·fi·ca·tion** \ˌkal-sə-fə-'kā-shən\ *n*

cal·ci·mine \'kal-sə-ˌmīn\ *n* : a thin water paint used esp. on plastered surfaces — **calcimine** *vb*

cal·cine \kal-'sīn\ *vb* **cal·cined; cal·cin·ing** : to heat to a high temperature but without fusing to drive off volatile matter and often to reduce to powder — **cal·ci·na·tion** \ˌkal-sə-'nā-shən\ *n*

cal·cite \'kal-ˌsīt\ *n* : a crystalline mineral consisting of calcium carbonate — **cal·cit·ic** \kal-'si-tik\ *adj*

cal·ci·um \'kal-sē-əm\ *n* : a silver-white soft metallic chemical element occurring only in combination — see ELEMENT table

calcium carbonate *n* : a substance found in nature as limestone and marble and in plant ashes, bones, and shells

cal·cu·late \'kal-kyə-ˌlāt\ *vb* **-lat·ed; -lat·ing** [L *calculare*, fr. *calculus* small stone, pebble used in reckoning] **1** : to determine by mathematical processes : COMPUTE **2** : to reckon by exercise of practical judgment : ESTIMATE **3** : to design or adapt for a purpose **4** : COUNT, RELY — **cal·cu·la·ble** \-lə-bəl\ *adj* — **cal·cu·la·tor** \-ˌlā-tər\ *n*

cal·cu·lat·ed \-ˌlā-təd\ *adj* **1** : undertaken after estimating the probability of success or failure ⟨a ∼ risk⟩ **2** : planned purposefully : DELIBERATE

cal·cu·lat·ing \-ˌlā-tiŋ\ *adj* : marked by shrewd consideration esp. of self-interest — **cal·cu·lat·ing·ly** *adv*

cal·cu·la·tion \ˌkal-kyə-'lā-shən\ *n* **1** : the process or an act of calculating **2** : the result of an act of calculating **3** : studied care; *also* : cold heartless planning to promote self-interest

cal·cu·lus \'kal-kyə-ləs\ *n, pl* **-li** \-ˌlī\ *also* **-lus·es** [L,

ONE MORE SIP OF COFFEE WOULD PROBABLY BE A MISTAKE

I KNOW MY CAFFEINE

JRM DAVES 1-26

pebble (used in reckoning)] **1** : a method of computation or calculation in a special notation (as of logic) **2** : a branch of higher mathematics comprising differential and integral calculus **3** : a concretion usu. of mineral salts esp. in hollow organs or ducts

cal·de·ra \kal-'der-ə, kòl-, -'dir-\ *n* [Sp, lit., caldron] : a large crater usu. formed by the collapse of a volcanic cone

cal·dron *var of* CAULDRON

¹cal·en·dar \'ka-lən-dər\ *n* **1** : an arrangement of time into days, weeks, months, and years; *also* : a sheet or folder containing such an arrangement for a period **2** : an orderly list

²calendar *vb* : to enter in a calendar

¹cal·en·der \'ka-lən-dər\ *vb* : to press (as cloth or paper) between rollers or plates so as to make smooth or glossy or to thin into sheets

²calender *n* : a machine for calendering

ca·lends \'ka-ləndz, 'ka-\ *n sing or pl* : the first day of the ancient Roman month

ca·len·du·la \kə-'len-jə-lə\ *n* : any of a genus of yellow‑flowered herbs related to the daisies

¹calf \'kaf, 'kàf\ *n, pl* **calves** \'kavz, 'kàvz\ **1** : the young of the domestic cow; *also* : the young of various large mammals (as the elephant or whale) **2** : CALFSKIN

²calf *n, pl* **calves** \'kavz, 'kàvz\ : the fleshy back of the leg below the knee

calf·skin \'kaf-ˌskin, 'kàf-\ *n* : leather made of the skin of a calf

cal·i·ber *or* **cal·i·bre** \'ka-lə-bər\ *n* [MF calibre, fr. It calibro, fr. Ar qālib shoemaker's last] **1** : degree of mental capacity, excellence, or importance **2** : the diameter of a projectile **3** : the diameter of the bore of a gun

cal·i·brate \'ka-lə-ˌbrāt\ *vb* **-brat·ed; -brat·ing** : to adjust precisely

cal·i·bra·tion \ˌka-lə-'brā-shən\ *n* : a set of graduated marks indicating values or positions — usu. used in pl.

¹cal·i·co \'ka-li-ˌkō\ *n, pl* **-coes** *or* **-cos** : printed cotton fabric

²calico *adj* **1** : made of calico **2** : having blotched or spotted markings ⟨a ~ cat⟩

Calif *abbr* California

Cal·i·for·nia poppy \ˌka-lə-'fòr-nyə-\ *n* : a widely cultivated herb with usu. yellow or orange flowers that is related to the poppies

cal·i·for·ni·um \ˌka-lə-'fòr-nē-əm\ *n* : an artificially prepared radioactive chemical element — see ELEMENT table

cal·i·per \'ka-lə-pər\ *n* **1** : any of various instruments having two arms, legs, or jaws used esp. to measure diameter or thickness — usu. used in pl. **2** : a device consisting of two plates lined with a frictional material that press against the sides of a rotating wheel or disk in certain brake systems

ca·liph \'kā-ləf, 'ka-\ *n* : a successor of Muhammad as head of Islam — used as a title — **ca·liph·ate** \-lə-ˌfāt, -fət\ *n*

cal·is·then·ics \ˌka-ləs-'the-niks\ *n sing or pl* [Gk kalos beautiful + sthenos strength] : bodily exercises usu. done without apparatus — **cal·is·then·ic** *adj*

calk \'kòk\ *var of* CAULK

¹call \'kòl\ *vb* **1** : SHOUT, CRY; *also* : to utter a characteristic note or cry **2** : to utter in a loud clear voice **3** : to announce authoritatively **4** : SUMMON **5** : to make a request or demand ⟨~ for an investigation⟩ **6** : to halt (as a baseball game) because of unsuitable conditions **7** : to demand payment of (a loan); *also* : to demand surrender of (as a bond) for redemption **8** : to get or try to get in communication by telephone **9** : to make a brief visit **10** : to speak of or address by name : give a name to **11** : to estimate or consider for practical purposes ⟨~ it ten miles⟩ **12** : to temporarily transfer control of computer processing to (as a subroutine or procedure) — **call·er** *n*

²call *n* **1** : SHOUT **2** : the cry of an animal (as a bird) **3** : a request or a command to come or assemble : INVITATION, SUMMONS **4** : DEMAND, CLAIM; *also* : REQUEST **5** : a brief usu. formal visit **6** : an act of calling on the telephone **7** : DECISION ⟨a tough ~⟩ **8** : a temporary transfer of control of computer processing to a particular set of instructions

cal·la lily \'ka-lə-\ *n* : a plant whose flowers form a fleshy yellow spike surrounded by a lilylike usu. white leaf

call·back \'kòl-ˌbak\ *n* a calling back; *esp* : RECALL 5

call–board \-ˌbòrd\ *n* : a board for posting notices (as of rehearsal calls)

call down *vb* : REPRIMAND

call girl *n* : a prostitute with whom appointments are made by phone

cal·lig·ra·phy \kə-'li-grə-fē\ *n* : artistic or elegant handwriting; *also* : the art of producing such writing — **cal·lig·ra·pher** \-fər\ *n*

call–in \'kòl-ˌin\ *adj* : allowing listeners to engage in broadcast telephone conversations ⟨a ~ show⟩

call in *vb* **1** : to order to return or be returned **2** : to summon to one's aid **3** : to report by telephone

call·ing \'kò-liŋ\ *n* **1** : a strong inner impulse toward a particular course of action **2** : the activity in which one customarily engages as an occupation

cal·li·ope \kə-'lī-ə-(ˌ)pē, 'ka-lē-ˌōp\ *n* [fr. Calliope, chief of the Muses, fr. L, fr. Gk Kalliopē] : a keyboard musical instrument similar to an organ and made up of a series of whistles

cal·li·per *chiefly Brit var of* CALIPER

call number *n* : a combination of characters assigned to a library book to indicate its place on a shelf

call off *vb* : CANCEL

cal·los·i·ty \ka-'lä-sə-tē\ *n, pl* **-ties** **1** : the quality or state of being callous **2** : CALLUS 1

¹cal·lous \'ka-ləs\ *adj* **1** : being thickened and hardened ⟨~ skin⟩ **2** : feeling no emotion or sympathy — **cal·lous·ly** *adv* — **cal·lous·ness** *n*

²callous *vb* : to make callous

cal·low \\'ka-lō\ *adj* [ME *calu* bald, fr. OE] : lacking adult sophistication ⟨a ~ youth⟩ — **cal·low·ness** *n*

call–up \\'kȯ-ˌləp\ *n* : an order to report for active military service

call up *vb* : to summon for active military duty

cal·lus \\'ka-ləs\ *n* **1** : a callous area on skin or bark **2** : tissue that is converted into bone in the healing of a bone fracture — **callus** *vb*

call–waiting *n* : a telephone service by which during a call in progress an incoming call is signaled (as by a click)

¹**calm** \\'käm, 'kälm\ *n* **1** : a period or a condition free from storms, high winds, or rough water **2** : complete or almost complete absence of wind **3** : a state of tranquillity

²**calm** *vb* : to make or become calm

³**calm** *adj* : marked by calm : STILL, UNRUFFLED — **calm·ly** *adv* — **calm·ness** *n*

cal·o·mel \\'ka-lə-məl, -ˌmel\ *n* : a chloride of mercury used esp. as a fungicide

ca·lor·ic \kə-'lȯ-rik\ *adj* **1** : of or relating to heat **2** : of or relating to calories

cal·o·rie *also* **cal·o·ry** \\'ka-lə-rē\ *n, pl* **-ries** : a unit for measuring heat; *esp* : one for measuring the value of foods for producing heat and energy in the human body equivalent to the amount of heat required to raise the temperature of one kilogram of water one degree Celsius

cal·o·rim·e·ter \ˌka-lə-'ri-mə-tər\ *n* : an apparatus for measuring quantities of heat — **cal·o·rim·e·try** \-trē\ *n*

cal·u·met \\'kal-yə-ˌmet, -mət\ *n* : an American Indian ceremonial pipe

ca·lum·ni·ate \kə-'ləm-nē-ˌāt\ *vb* **-at·ed; -at·ing** : to make false and malicious statements about **syn** defame, malign, libel, slander, traduce — **ca·lum·ni·a·tion** \-ˌləm-nē-'ā-shən\ *n* — **ca·lum·ni·a·tor** \-'ləm-nē-ˌā-tər\ *n*

ca·lum·ny \\'ka-ləm-nē\ *n, pl* **-nies** : false and malicious accusation — **ca·lum·ni·ous** \kə-'ləm-nē-əs\ *adj*

calve \\'kav, 'kȧv\ *vb* **calved; calv·ing** : to give birth to a calf

calves *pl of* CALF

Cal·vin·ism \\'kal-və-ˌni-zəm\ *n* : the theological system of John Calvin and his followers — **Cal·vin·ist** \-nist\ *n or adj* — **Cal·vin·is·tic** \ˌkal-və-'nis-tik\ *adj*

ca·lyp·so \kə-'lip-sō\ *n, pl* **-sos** : a style of music originating in the British West Indies and having lyrics that usu. satirize local personalities and events

ca·lyx \\'kā-liks, 'ka-\ *n, pl* **ca·lyx·es** *or* **ca·ly·ces** \\'kā-lə-ˌsēz, 'ka-\ : the usu. green or leaflike outer part of a flower consisting of sepals

cam \\'kam\ *n* : a rotating or sliding piece in a mechanical linkage by which rotary motion is transformed into linear motion or vice versa

ca·ma·ra·de·rie \ˌkäm-'rä-də-rē, ˌkam-, -'ra-\ *n* [F] : friendly feeling and goodwill among comrades

cam·bi·um \\'kam-bē-əm\ *n, pl* **-bi·ums** *or* **-bia** \-bē-ə\ : a thin cellular layer between xylem and phloem of most higher plants from which new tissues develop — **cam·bi·al** \-əl\ *adj*

Cam·bo·di·an \kam-'bō-dē-ən\ *n* : a native or inhabitant of Cambodia — **Cambodian** *adj*

Cam·bri·an \\'kam-brē-ən, 'käm-\ *adj* : of, relating to, or being the earliest period of the Paleozoic era — **Cambrian** *n*

cam·bric \\'kām-brik\ *n* : a fine thin white linen or cotton fabric

cam·cord·er \\'kam-ˌkȯr-dər\ *n* : a small portable video camera and recorder

came *past of* COME

cam·el \\'ka-məl\ *n* : either of two large hoofed cud‑chewing mammals used esp. in desert regions of Asia and Africa for carrying and riding

camel hair *also* **camel's hair** *n* **1** : the hair of a camel or a substitute for it **2** : cloth made of camel hair or of camel hair and wool

ca·mel·lia \kə-'mēl-yə\ *n* : any of a genus of shrubs and trees related to the tea plant and grown in warm regions and greenhouses for their showy roselike flowers

Cam·em·bert \\'ka-məm-ˌber\ *n* : a soft cheese with a grayish rind and yellow interior

cam·eo \\'ka-mē-ˌō\ *n, pl* **-eos 1** : a gem carved in relief; *also* : a small medallion with a profiled head in relief **2** : a brief appearance esp. by a well-known actor in a play or movie

---

cam·era \\'kam-rə, 'ka-mər-ə\ *n* : a device with a lightproof chamber fitted with a lens through which the image of an object is projected onto a surface for recording (as on film) or for conversion into electrical signals (as for television broadcast) — **cam·era·man** \-ˌman, -mən\ *n* — **cam·era·wom·an** *n*

Cam·er·oo·ni·an \ˌka-mə-'rü-nē-ən\ *n* : a native or inhabitant of the Republic of Cameroon or the Cameroons region — **Cameroonian** *adj*

cam·i·sole \\'ka-mə-ˌsōl\ *n* : a short sleeveless garment for women

camomile *var of* CHAMOMILE

cam·ou·flage \\'ka-mə-ˌfläzh, -ˌfläj\ *n* [F] **1** : the disguising of military equipment with paint, nets, or foliage; *also* : the disguise itself **2** : deceptive behavior — **camouflage** *vb*

¹**camp** \\'kamp\ *n* **1** : a place where tents or buildings are erected for usu. temporary shelter **2** : a collection of tents or other shelters **3** : a body of persons encamped — **camp·ground** \-ˌgraünd\ *n* — **camp·site** \-ˌsīt\ *n*

²**camp** *vb* **1** : to make or occupy a camp **2** : to live in a camp or outdoors

³**camp** *n* **1** : exaggerated effeminate mannerisms **2** : something so outrageous, inappropriate, or theatrical as to be considered amusing — **camp** *adj* — **camp·i·ly** \\'kam-pə-lē\ *adv* — **camp·i·ness** \-pē-nəs\ *n* — **campy** \-pē\ *adj*

⁴**camp** vb : to engage in camp : exhibit the qualities of camp

cam·paign \kam-'pān\ n 1 : a series of military operations forming one distinct stage in a war 2 : a series of activities designed to bring about a particular result ⟨advertising ∼⟩ — **campaign** vb — **cam·paign·er** n

cam·pa·ni·le \₁kam-pə-'nē-lē\ n, pl **-ni·les** or **-ni·li** \-'nē-lē\ : a usu. freestanding bell tower

cam·pa·nol·o·gy \₁kam-pə-'näl-ə-jē\ n : the art of bell ringing — **cam·pa·nol·o·gist** \-jist\ n

camp·er \'kam-pər\ n 1 : one that camps 2 : a portable dwelling (as a specially equipped vehicle) for use during casual travel and camping

Camp Fire Girl n : a member of a national organization of girls from ages 5 to 18

camp follower n 1 : a civilian (as a prostitute) who follows a military unit to attend or exploit its personnel 2 : a follower of a group who is not an adherent; esp : a politician who joins a movement solely for personal gain

cam·phor \'kam-fər\ n : a gummy volatile aromatic compound obtained from an evergreen Asian tree (**camphor tree**) and used esp. in medicine

camp meeting n : a series of evangelistic meetings usu. held outdoors

camp·o·ree \₁kam-pə-'rē\ n : a gathering of Boy Scouts or Girl Scouts from a given geographic area

cam·pus \'kam-pəs\ n [L, plain] : the grounds and buildings of a college or school; also : grounds resembling a campus ⟨hospital ∼⟩

cam·shaft \'kam-₁shaft\ n : a shaft to which a cam is fastened

¹**can** \kən, 'kan\ vb, past **could** \kəd, 'kud\; pres sing & pl **can** 1 : be able to 2 : may perhaps ⟨∼ he still be alive⟩ 3 : be permitted by conscience or feeling to ⟨you ∼ hardly blame her⟩ 4 : have permission to ⟨you ∼ go now⟩

²**can** \'kan\ n 1 : a usu. cylindrical container or receptacle ⟨garbage ∼⟩ ⟨coffee ∼⟩ 2 : JAIL 3 : TOILET

³**can** \'kan\ vb **canned; can·ning** 1 : to put in a can : preserve by sealing in airtight cans or jars 2 slang : to discharge from employment 3 slang : to put a stop or an end to — **can·ner** n

Can or **Canad** abbr Canada; Canadian

Can·a·da goose \'ka-nə-də-\ n : a common wild goose of No. America

Ca·na·di·an \kə-'nā-dē-ən\ n : a native or inhabitant of Canada — **Canadian** adj

ca·naille \kə-'nī, -'näl\ n [F, fr. It canaglia, fr. cane dog] : RABBLE, RIFFRAFF

ca·nal \kə-'nal\ n 1 : a tubular passage in the body : DUCT 2 : an artificial waterway (as for boats or irrigation)

can·a·lize \'kan-ᵊl-₁īz\ vb **-lized; -liz·ing** 1 : to provide with a canal or make into or like a channel 2 : to provide with an outlet; esp : to direct into preferred channels — **ca·nal·i·za·tion** \₁kan-ᵊl-ə-'zā-shən\ n

can·a·pé \'ka-nə-pē, -₁pā\ n [F, lit., sofa, fr. ML canopeum, canapeum mosquito net] : a piece of bread or toast or a cracker topped with a savory food

ca·nard \kə-'närd\ n : a false or unfounded report or story

ca·nary \kə-'ner-ē\ n, pl **ca·nar·ies** [fr. the Canary islands] 1 : a usu. sweet wine similar to Madeira 2 : a usu. yellow or greenish finch often kept in a cage as a pet

ca·nas·ta \kə-'nas-tə\ n [Sp, lit., basket] : rummy played with two full decks of cards plus four jokers

canc abbr canceled

¹**can·cel** \'kan-səl\ vb **-celed** or **-celled; -cel·ing** or **-celling** [ME cancellen, fr. MF canceller, fr. LL cancellare, fr. L, to make like a lattice, fr. cancelli lattice] 1 : to destroy the force or validity of : ANNUL 2 : to

match in force or effect : OFFSET 3 : to cross out : DELETE 4 : to remove (a common divisor) from a numerator and denominator; also : to remove (equivalents) on opposite sides of an equation or account 5 : to mark (a postage stamp or check) so that it cannot be reused 6 : to neutralize each other's strength or effect — **can·cel·la·tion** \₁kan-sə-'lā-shən\ n — **can·cel·er** or **can·cel·ler** n

²**cancel** n 1 : CANCELLATION 2 : a deleted part

can·cer \'kan-sər\ n [L, lit., crab] 1 cap : a zodiacal constellation between Gemini and Leo usu. pictured as a crab 2 cap : the 4th sign of the zodiac in astrology; also : one born under this sign 3 : a malignant tumor that tends to spread in the body 4 : a malignant evil that spreads destructively — **can·cer·ous** \-sə-rəs\ adj — **can·cer·ous·ly** adv

can·de·la·bra \₁kan-də-'lä-brə, -'la-\ n : an ornamental branched candlestick or lamp with several lights

candelabra

can·de·la·brum \-brəm\ n, pl **-bra** also **-brums** : CANDELABRA

can·did \'kan-dəd\ adj 1 : FRANK, STRAIGHTFORWARD 2 : relating to photography of subjects acting naturally or spontaneously without being posed — **can·did·ly** adv — **can·did·ness** n

can·di·da·cy \'kan-də-də-sē\ n, pl **-cies** : the state of being a candidate

can·di·date \'kan-də-₁dāt, 'ka-nə-, -dət\ n [L candidatus, fr. candidatus clothed in white, fr. candidus white; fr. the white toga worn by office seekers in ancient Rome] : one who seeks or is proposed for an office, honor, or membership

can·di·da·ture \'kan-də-də-₁chur, 'ka-nə-\ n, chiefly Brit : CANDIDACY

can·died \'kan-dēd\ adj : preserved in or encrusted with sugar

¹**can·dle** \'kan-dᵊl\ n : a usu. slender mass of tallow or wax molded around a wick that is burned to give light

²**candle** vb **can·dled; can·dling** : to examine (as eggs) by holding between the eye and a light — **can·dler** n

can·dle·light \'kan-dᵊl-₁līt\ n 1 : the light of a candle; also : any soft artificial light 2 : the time when candles are lit : TWILIGHT

can·dle·lit \-₁lit\ adj : illuminated by candlelight ⟨a ∼ dinner⟩

Can·dle·mas \'kan-dᵊl-məs\ n : February 2 observed as a church festival in commemoration of the presentation of Christ in the temple

can·dle·stick \-₁stik\ n : a holder with a socket for a candle

can·dle·wick \-₁wik\ n : a soft cotton yarn; also : embroidery made with this yarn usu. in tufts

can·dor \'kan-dər\ n : FRANKNESS, OUTSPOKENNESS

can·dour chiefly Brit var of CANDOR

C and W abbr country and western

¹**can·dy** \'kan-dē\ n, pl **candies** : a confection made from sugar often with flavoring and filling

²**candy** vb **can·died; can·dy·ing** : to encrust in sugar often by cooking in a syrup

candy strip•er \-'strī-pər\ n : a teenage volunteer worker at a hospital

¹cane \'kān\ n 1 : a slender hollow or pithy stem (as of a reed or bramble) 2 : a tall woody grass or reed (as sugarcane) 3 : a walking stick; also : a rod for flogging

²cane vb caned; can•ing 1 : to beat with a cane 2 : to weave or make with cane — can•er n

cane•brake \'kān-ˌbrāk\ n : a thicket of cane

¹ca•nine \'kā-ˌnīn\ n 1 : a pointed tooth between the outer incisor and the first premolar 2 : a canine mammal (as a domestic dog)

²canine adj [L caninus, fr. canis dog] : of or relating to dogs or to the family to which they belong

can•is•ter \'ka-nə-stər\ n 1 : an often cylindrical container

can•ker \'kaŋ-kər\ n : a spreading sore that eats into tissue — can•ker•ous \-kə-rəs\ adj

can•ker•worm \-ˌwərm\ n : either of two moths and esp. their larvae that are pests of fruit and shade trees

can•na \'ka-nə\ n : any of a genus of tropical herbs with large leaves and racemes of bright-colored flowers

can•na•bis \'ka-nə-bəs\ n : any of the psychoactive preparations (as marijuana) or chemicals (as THC) derived from hemp; also : HEMP

canned \'kand\ adj : prepared in standardized form for general use or wide distribution

can•nery \'ka-nə-rē\ n, pl -ner•ies : a factory for the canning of foods

can•ni•bal \'ka-nə-bəl\ n [NL Canibalis a member of a Caribbean Indian people, fr. Sp Caníbal] : one that eats the flesh of its own kind — can•ni•bal•ism \-bə-ˌli-zəm\ n — can•ni•bal•is•tic \-bə-'lis-tik\ adj

can•ni•bal•ise Brit var of CANNIBALIZE

can•ni•bal•ize \'ka-nə-bə-ˌlīz\ vb -ized; -iz•ing 1 : to take usable parts from (as an inoperative machine) to construct or repair another machine 2 : to practice cannibalism

can•non \'ka-nən\ n, pl cannons or cannon [MF canon, fr. It cannone, lit., large tube, fr. canna reed, tube, fr. L, cane, reed] : a large heavy gun; esp : one mounted on a carriage

can•non•ade \ˌka-nə-'nād\ n : a heavy fire of artillery — cannonade vb

can•non•ball \'ka-nən-ˌbȯl\ n : a usu. round solid missile for a cannon

can•non•eer \ˌka-nə-'nir\ n : an artillery gunner

can•not \'ka-ˌnät; kə-'nät\: can not — cannot but : to be unable to do otherwise than

can•nu•la \'kan-yə-lə\ n, pl -las or -lae \-ˌlē\ : a small tube for insertion into a body cavity or into a duct or vessel

can•ny \'ka-nē\ adj can•ni•er; -est : PRUDENT, SHREWD — can•ni•ly \'kan-ᵊl-ē\ adv — can•ni•ness \'ka-nē-nəs\ n

ca•noe \kə-'nü\ n : a light narrow boat with sharp ends and curved sides that is usu. propelled by paddles — canoe vb — ca•noe•ist n

ca•no•la \kə-'nō-lə\ n : a rape plant producing seeds that are low in a toxic acid and yield an edible oil (ca-

canoe

nola oil) high in monounsaturated fatty acids; also : this oil

¹can•on \'ka-nən\ n 1 : a regulation decreed by a church council; also : a provision of canon law 2 : an official or authoritative list (as of the saints or the books of the Bible) 3 : an accepted principle ⟨the ∼s of good taste⟩

²canon n : a clergyman on the staff of a cathedral

ca•non•i•cal \kə-'nä-ni-kəl\ adj 1 : of, relating to, or forming a canon 2 : conforming to a general rule or acceptable procedure : ORTHODOX 3 : of or relating to a clergyman who is a canon — ca•non•i•cal•ly \-k(ə-)lē\ adv

can•on•ize \'ka-nə-ˌnīz\ vb can•on•ized \-ˌnīzd\; can•on•iz•ing 1 : to declare (a deceased person) an officially recognized saint 2 : GLORIFY, EXALT — can•on•i•za•tion \ˌka-nə-nə-'zā-shən\ n

canon law n : the law governing a church

can•o•py \'ka-nə-pē\ n, pl -pies [ME canope, fr. ML canopeum mosquito net, fr. L conopeum, fr. Gk kōnōpion, fr. kōnōps mosquito] 1 : an overhanging cover, shelter, or shade 2 : a transparent cover for an airplane cockpit 3 : the fabric part of a parachute — canopy vb

¹cant \'kant\ vb : to give a slant to

²cant n 1 : an oblique or slanting surface 2 : TILT, SLANT

³cant vb 1 : to beg in a whining manner 2 : to talk hypocritically

⁴cant n 1 : the special idiom of a profession or trade : JARGON 2 : insincere speech; esp : insincerely pious words or statements

Cant abbr Canticle of Canticles

can•ta•bi•le \kän-'tä-bə-ˌlā\ adv or adj [It] : in a singing manner — used as a direction in music

can•ta•loupe also can•te•loupe \'kant-ᵊl-ˌōp\ n : MUSKMELON; esp : one with orange flesh and rough skin

can•tan•ker•ous \kan-'taŋ-kə-rəs\ adj : ILL-NATURED, QUARRELSOME — can•tan•ker•ous•ly adv — can•tan•ker•ous•ness n

can•ta•ta \kən-'tä-tə\ n [It] : a choral composition usu. sung to instrumental accompaniment

can•teen \kan-'tēn\ n [F cantine bottle case, canteen (store), fr. It cantina wine cellar] 1 : a flask for carrying liquids 2 : a place of recreation and entertain-

ment for military personnel **3** : a small cafeteria or counter at which snacks are served

can·ter \'kan-tər\ *n* : a horse's 3-beat gait resembling but smoother and slower than a gallop — **canter** *vb*

Can·ter·bury bell \'kant-ər-ˌber-ē-\ *n* : any of several plants related to the bluebell that are cultivated for their showy flowers

can·ti·cle \'kan-ti-kəl\ *n* : SONG; *esp* : any of several liturgical songs taken from the Bible

Canticle of Canticles *n* : SONG OF SONGS

¹**can·ti·le·ver** \'kant-ᵊl-ˌē-vər\ *n* : a projecting beam or structure supported only at one end; *also* : either of a pair of such structures projecting toward each other so that when joined they form a bridge

²**cantilever** *vb* **1** : to support by a cantilever ⟨a ∼ed shelf⟩ **2** : to build as a cantilever **3** : to project as a cantilever

can·tle \'kant-ᵊl\ *n* : the upwardly projecting rear part of a saddle

can·to \'kan-ˌtō\ *n*, *pl* **cantos** [It., fr. L *cantus* song] : one of the major divisions of a long poem

can·ton \'kant-ᵊn, 'kan-ˌtän\ *n* : a small territorial division of a country; *esp* : one of the political divisions of Switzerland — **can·ton·al** \'kant-ᵊn-əl, kan-'tän-ᵊl\ *adj*

can·ton·ment \kan-'tōn-mənt, -'tän-\ *n* : usu. temporary quarters for troops

can·tor \'kan-tər\ *n* **1** : a choir leader **2** : a synagogue official who sings liturgical music and leads the congregation in prayer

can·vas *also* **can·vass** \'kan-vəs\ *n* **1** : a strong cloth formerly much used for making tents and sails **2** : a set of sails **3** : a group of tents **4** : a piece of cloth prepared as a surface to receive oil paint; *also* : an oil painting **5** : the canvas-covered floor of a boxing or wrestling ring

can·vas·back \'kan-vəs-ˌbak\ *n* : a No. American wild duck with red head and gray back

¹**can·vass** *also* **can·vas** \'kan-vəs\ *vb* : to go through (a district) or to (persons) to solicit votes or orders for goods or to determine public opinion or sentiment — **can·vass·er** *n*

²**canvass** *n* : an act or instance of canvassing

can·yon \'kan-yən\ *n* : a deep narrow valley with high steep sides

¹**cap** \'kap\ *n* **1** : a covering for the head esp. with a visor and no brim; *also* : something resembling such a covering **2** : a container holding an explosive charge **3** : an upper limit (as on expenditures)

²**cap** *vb* **capped; cap·ping 1** : to provide or protect with a cap **2** : to form a cap over : CROWN **3** : OUTDO, SURPASS **4** : CLIMAX

³**cap** *abbr* **1** capacity **2** capital **3** capitalize; capitalized

CAP *abbr* Civil Air Patrol

ca·pa·ble \'kā-pə-bəl\ *adj* : having ability, capacity, or power to do something : ABLE, COMPETENT — **ca·pa·bil·i·ty** \ˌkā-pə-'bi-lə-tē\ *n* — **ca·pa·bly** *adv*

ca·pa·cious \kə-'pā-shəs\ *adj* : able to contain much — **ca·pa·cious·ly** *adv* — **ca·pa·cious·ness** *n*

ca·pac·i·tance \kə-'pa-sə-təns\ *n* : the property of an electric nonconductor that permits the storage of energy

ca·pac·i·tor \kə-'pa-sə-tər\ *n* : an electronic circuit device for temporary storage of electrical energy

¹**ca·pac·i·ty** \kə-'pa-sə-tē\ *n*, *pl* **-ties 1** : legal qualification or fitness **2** : the ability to contain, receive, or accommodate **3** : the maximum amount or number that can be contained — see METRIC SYSTEM table, WEIGHT table **4** : ABILITY **5** : position or character assigned or assumed

²**capacity** *adj* : equaling maximum capacity ⟨a ∼ crowd⟩

cap–a–pie *or* **cap–à–pie** \ˌka-pə-'pē\ *adv* [MF] : from head to foot : at all points

ca·par·i·son \kə-'par-ə-sən\ *n* **1** : an ornamental cov-

ering for a horse **2** : TRAPPINGS, ADORNMENT — **caparison** *vb*

¹**cape** \'kāp\ *n* **1** : a point of land jutting out into water **2** *often cap* : CAPE COD COTTAGE

²**cape** *n* : a sleeveless garment hanging from the neck over the shoulders — **caped** *adj*

Cape Cod cottage \'kāp-'käd-\ *n* : a compact rectangular dwelling of one or one-and-a-half stories usu. with a steep gable roof

¹**ca·per** \'kā-pər\ *n* : the flower bud or young berry of a Mediterranean shrub pickled for use as a relish; *also* : this shrub

²**caper** *vb* **ca·pered; ca·per·ing** : to leap about in a playful manner

³**caper** *n* **1** : a frolicsome leap **2** : a capricious escapade **3** : an illegal or questionable act

cape·skin \'kāp-ˌskin\ *n* : a light flexible leather made from sheepskins

Cape Verd·ean \-'vər-dē-ən\ *n* : a native or inhabitant of the Republic of Cape Verde

cap·ful \'kap-ˌfůl\ *n*, *pl* **cap·fuls** *also* **caps·ful** \'kaps-\ : as much as a cap will hold

cap·il·lar·i·ty \ˌka-pə-'lar-ə-tē\ *n*, *pl* **-ties** : the action by which the surface of a liquid where it is in contact with a solid (as in a slender tube) is raised or lowered depending on the relative attraction of the molecules of the liquid for each other and for those of the solid

¹**cap·il·lary** \'ka-pə-ˌler-ē\ *adj* **1** : resembling a hair **2** : having a very small bore ⟨∼ tube⟩ **3** : of or relating to capillaries or to capillarity

²**capillary** *n*, *pl* **-lar·ies** : any of the tiny thin-walled blood vessels that carry blood between the smallest arteries and their corresponding veins

¹**cap·i·tal** \'ka-pət-ᵊl\ *n* : the top part or piece of an architectural column

²**capital** *adj* **1** : conforming to the series A, B, C rather than a, b, c ⟨∼ letters⟩ ⟨∼ G⟩ **2** : punishable by death ⟨a ∼ crime⟩ **3** : most serious ⟨a ∼ error⟩ **4** : first in importance or position : CHIEF; *also* : being the seat of government ⟨the ∼ city⟩ **5** : of or relating to capital ⟨∼ expenditures⟩; *esp* : relating to or being assets that add to the long-term net worth of a corporation **6** : FIRST-RATE, EXCELLENT

³**capital** *n* **1** : accumulated wealth esp. as used to produce more wealth **2** : the total face value of shares of stock issued by a company **3** : persons holding capital **4** : ADVANTAGE, GAIN **5** : a letter larger than the ordinary small letter and often different in form **6** : the capital city of a state or country; *also* : a city preeminent in some activity ⟨the fashion ∼⟩

capital gain *n* : the increase in value of an asset (as stock or real estate) between the time it is bought and the time it is sold

capital goods *n pl* : machinery, tools, factories, and commodities used in the production of goods

cap·i·tal·ise *Brit var of* CAPITALIZE

cap·i·tal·ism \'ka-pət-ᵊl-ˌi-zəm\ *n* : an economic system characterized by private or corporate ownership of capital goods and by prices, production, and distribution of goods that are determined mainly by competition in a free market

¹**cap·i·tal·ist** \-ist\ *n* **1** : a person who has capital esp. invested in business **2** : a person of great wealth : PLUTOCRAT **3** : a believer in capitalism

²**capitalist** *or* **cap·i·tal·is·tic** \ˌka-pət-ᵊl-'is-tik\ *adj* **1** : owning capital **2** : practicing or advocating capitalism **3** : marked by capitalism — **cap·i·tal·is·ti·cal·ly** \-ti-k(ə-)lē\ *adv*

cap·i·tal·iza·tion \ˌka-pət-ᵊl-ə-'zā-shən\ *n* **1** : the act or process of capitalizing **2** : the total amount of money used as capital in a business

cap·i·tal·ize \'ka-pət-ᵊl-ˌīz\ *vb* **-ized; -iz·ing 1** : to write or print with an initial capital or in capitals **2** : to convert into or use as capital **3** : to supply capital for **4** : to gain by turning something to advantage : PROFIT

cap·i·tal·ly \'ka-pət-ʾl-ē\ *adv* : ADMIRABLY, EXCELLENTLY

cap·i·ta·tion \ˌka-pə-'tā-shən\ *n* : a direct uniform tax levied on each person

cap·i·tol \'ka-pət-ʾl\ *n* : the building in which a legislature holds its sessions

ca·pit·u·late \kə-'pi-chə-ˌlāt\ *vb* **-lat·ed; -lat·ing 1** : to surrender esp. on conditions agreed upon **2** : to cease resisting : ACQUIESCE **syn** submit, yield, succumb, cave, defer — **ca·pit·u·la·tion** \-ˌpi-chə-'lā-shən\ *n*

ca·pon \'kā-ˌpän, -pən\ *n* : a castrated male chicken

cap·puc·ci·no \ˌka-pə-'chē-nō, ˌkä-\ *n* [It, lit., Capuchin; fr. the likeness of its color to that of a Capuchin's habit] : espresso mixed with foamy hot milk or cream and often flavored with cinnamon

ca·pric·cio \kə-'prē-chē-ˌō, -chō\ *n, pl* **-cios** : an instrumental piece in free form usu. lively in tempo and brilliant in style

ca·price \kə-'prēs\ *n* [F, fr. It *capriccio*] **1** : a sudden whim or fancy **2** : an inclination to do things impulsively **3** : CAPRICCIO — **ca·pri·cious** \-'pri-shəs\ *adj* — **ca·pri·cious·ly** *adv* — **ca·pri·cious·ness** *n*

Cap·ri·corn \'ka-pri-ˌkȯrn\ *n* **1** : a zodiacal constellation between Sagittarius and Aquarius usu. pictured as a goat **2** : the 10th sign of the zodiac in astrology; *also* : one born under this sign

cap·ri·ole \'ka-prē-ˌōl\ *n* : ³CAPER 1; *also* : an upward leap of a horse with a backward kick at the height of the leap — **capriole** *vb*

caps *abbr* **1** capitals **2** capsule

cap·si·cum \'kap-si-kəm\ *n* : PEPPER 2

cap·size \'kap-ˌsīz, kap-'sīz\ *vb* **cap·sized; cap·siz·ing** : UPSET, OVERTURN

cap·stan \'kap-stən, -ˌstan\ *n* **1** : a machine for moving or raising heavy weights that consists of a vertical drum which can be rotated and around which cable is turned **2** : a rotating shaft that drives recorder tape

cap·su·lar \'kap-sə-lər\ *adj* : of, relating to, or resembling a capsule

cap·su·lat·ed \-ˌlā-təd\ *adj* : enclosed in a capsule

¹cap·sule \'kap-səl, -sül\ *n* **1** : a membrane or sac enclosing a body part (as of a joint) **2** : a case bearing spores or seeds **3** : a shell usu. of gelatin that is used for packaging something (as a drug); *also* : such a shell together with its contents **4** : a small pressurized compartment or vehicle (as for space flight)

²capsule *adj* **1** : very brief **2** : very compact

Capt *abbr* captain

¹cap·tain \'kap-tən\ *n* **1** : a commander of a body of troops **2** : a commissioned officer in the army, air force, or marine corps ranking next below a major **3** : an officer in charge of a ship **4** : a commissioned officer in the navy ranking next below a rear admiral or a commodore **5** : a leader of a side or team **6** : a dominant figure — **cap·tain·cy** *n*

²captain *vb* : to be captain of : LEAD

cap·tion \'kap-shən\ *n* **1** : a heading esp. of an article or document : TITLE **2** : the explanatory matter accompanying an illustration **3** : a motion-picture subtitle — **caption** *vb*

cap·tious \'kap-shəs\ *adj* : marked by an inclination to find fault — **cap·tious·ly** *adv* — **cap·tious·ness** *n*

cap·ti·vate \'kap-tə-ˌvāt\ *vb* **-vat·ed; -vat·ing** : to attract and hold irresistibly by some special charm or art — **cap·ti·va·tion** \ˌkap-tə-'vā-shən\ *n* — **cap·ti·va·tor** \'kap-tə-ˌvā-tər\ *n*

cap·tive \'kap-tiv\ *adj* **1** : made prisoner esp. in war **2** : kept within bounds : CONFINED **3** : held under control — **captive** *n* — **cap·tiv·i·ty** \kap-'ti-və-tē\ *n*

cap·tor \'kap-tər\ *n* : one that captures

¹cap·ture \'kap-chər\ *n* **1** : the act of capturing **2** : one that has been captured

²capture *vb* **cap·tured; cap·tur·ing 1** : to take captive : WIN, GAIN **2** : to preserve in a relatively permanent form

Ca·pu·chin \'ka-pyə-shən\ *n* : a member of an austere branch of the order of St. Francis of Assisi engaged in missionary work and preaching

car \'kär\ *n* **1** : a vehicle moving on wheels **2** : the compartment of an elevator **3** : the part of a balloon or airship that carries passengers or equipment

car·a·cole \'kar-ə-ˌkōl\ *n* : a half turn to right or left executed by a mounted horse — **caracole** *vb*

car·a·cul \'kar-ə-ˌkəl\ *n* : the pelt of a karakul lamb after the curl begins to loosen

ca·rafe \kə-'raf, -'räf\ *n* : a bottle with a flaring lip used esp. to hold wine

car·am·bo·la \ˌkar-əm-'bō-lə\ *n* **1** : a five-angled green to yellow edible tropical fruit of star-shaped cross section **2** : a tropical tree widely cultivated for carambolas

car·a·mel \'kar-ə-məl, 'kär-məl\ *n* **1** : an amorphous substance obtained by heating sugar and used for flavoring and coloring **2** : a firm chewy candy

car·a·pace \'kar-ə-ˌpās\ *n* : a protective case or shell on the back of some animals (as turtles or crabs)

¹carat *var of* KARAT

²car·at \'kar-ət\ *n* : a unit of weight for precious stones equal to 200 milligrams

car·a·van \'kar-ə-ˌvan\ *n* **1** : a group of travelers journeying together through desert or hostile regions **2** : a group of vehicles traveling in a file

car·a·van·sa·ry \ˌkar-ə-'van-sə-rē\ *or* **car·a·van·se·rai** \-sə-ˌrī\ *n, pl* **-ries** *or* **-rais** *or* **-rai** [Per *kārwānsarāī*, fr. *kārwān* caravan + *sarāī* palace, inn] **1** : an inn in eastern countries where caravans rest at night **2** : HOTEL, INN

car·a·vel \'kar-ə-ˌvel\ *n* : a small 15th and 16th century ship with a broad bow, high narrow poop, and usu. three masts

caravel

car·a·way \'kar-ə-ˌwā\ *n* : an aromatic herb related to the carrot with fruits (**caraway seed**) used in seasoning and medicine; *also* : its fruit

car·bide \'kär-ˌbīd\ *n* : a compound of carbon with another element

car·bine \'kär-ˌbēn, -ˌbīn\ *n* : a short-barreled lightweight rifle

car·bo·hy·drate \ˌkär-bō-'hī-ˌdrāt, -drət\ *n* : any of various compounds composed of carbon, hydrogen, and oxygen (as sugars and starches)

car·bol·ic acid \ˌkär-ˈbä-lik-\ *n* : PHENOL

car·bon \'kär-bən\ *n* **1** : a nonmetallic chemical element occurring in nature esp. as diamond and graphite and as a constituent of coal, petroleum, and limestone — see ELEMENT table **2** : a sheet of carbon paper; *also* : CARBON COPY 1 — **car·bon·less** \-ləs\ *adj*

car·bo·na·ceous \ˌkär-bə-'nā-shəs\ *adj* : relating to, containing, or composed of carbon

¹car·bon·ate \'kär-bə-ˌnāt, -nət\ *n* : a salt or ester of carbonic acid

²car·bon·ate \-ˌnāt\ *vb* **-at·ed; -at·ing** : to combine or impregnate with carbon dioxide (carbonated beverages) — **car·bon·ation** \ˌkär-bə-'nā-shən\ *n*

carbon black *n* : any of various black substances consisting chiefly of carbon and used esp. as pigments

carbon copy *n* **1** : a copy made by carbon paper **2** : DUPLICATE

carbon dating *n* : the determination of the age of old material (as an archaeological specimen) by its content of carbon 14

carbon dioxide *n* : a heavy colorless gas that does not support combustion and is formed in animal respiration and in the combustion and decomposition of organic substances

carbon 14 *n* : a heavy radioactive form of carbon used esp. in dating archaeological materials

car•bon•ic acid \kär-'bä-nik-\ *n* : a weak acid that decomposes readily into water and carbon dioxide

car•bon•if•er•ous \,kär-bə-'ni-fə-rəs\ *adj* **1** : producing or containing carbon or coal **2** *cap* : of, relating to, or being the period of the Paleozoic era between the Devonian and the Permian — **Carboniferous** *n*

carbon monoxide *n* : a colorless odorless very poisonous gas formed by the incomplete burning of carbon

carbon paper *n* : a thin paper coated with a pigment and used for making copies

carbon tet•ra•chlo•ride \-,te-trə-'klōr-,īd\ *n* : a colorless nonflammable toxic liquid used esp. as a solvent

carbon 12 *n* : the most abundant isotope of carbon having a nucleus of 6 protons and 6 neutrons and used as a standard for measurements of atomic weight

car•boy \'kär-,bòi\ *n* [Per *qarāba*, fr. Ar *qarrābah* demijohn] : a large container for liquids

car•bun•cle \'kär-,bəŋ-kəl\ *n* : a painful inflammation of the skin and underlying tissue that discharges pus from several openings

car•bu•re•tor \'kär-bə-,rā-tər, -byə-\ *n* : an apparatus for supplying an internal combustion engine with an explosive mixture of vaporized fuel and air

car•bu•ret•tor *also* car•bu•ret•ter \,kär-byə-'re-tər, 'kär-byə-,\ *chiefly Brit var of* CARBURETOR

car•case *Brit var of* CARCASS

car•cass \'kär-kəs\ *n* : a dead body; *esp* : one of an animal dressed for food

car•cin•o•gen \kär-'si-nə-jən\ *n* : an agent causing or inciting cancer — car•ci•no•gen•ic \,kärs-ᵊn-ō-'je-nik\ *adj* — car•ci•no•ge•nic•i•ty \-jə-'ni-sə-tē\ *n*

car•ci•no•ma \,kärs-ᵊn-'ō-mə\ *n, pl* -mas *or* -ma•ta \-tə\ : a malignant tumor of epithelial origin — car•ci•no•ma•tous \-təs\ *adj*

¹card \'kärd\ *vb* : to comb with a card : cleanse and untangle before spinning — card•er *n*

²card *n* : an instrument for combing fibers (as wool or cotton)

³card *n* **1** : PLAYING CARD **2** *pl* : a game played with playing cards; *also* : card playing **3** : a usu. clownishly amusing person : WAG **4** : a flat stiff usu. small piece of paper, cardboard, or plastic **5** : PROGRAM; *esp* : a sports program

⁴card *vb* **1** : to list or schedule on a card **2** : SCORE

⁵card *abbr* cardinal

car•da•mom \'kär-də-məm\ *n* : the aromatic capsular fruit of an East Indian herb related to the ginger whose seeds are used as a spice or condiment and in medicine; *also* : this plant

card•board \'kärd-,bòrd\ *n* : PAPERBOARD

card–car•ry•ing \'kärd-,kar-ē-iŋ\ *adj* : being a regularly enrolled member of an organized group and esp. of the Communist party

card catalog *n* : a catalog (as of books) in which the entries are arranged systematically on cards

car•di•ac \'kär-dē-,ak\ *adj* **1** : of, relating to, or located near the heart **2** : of, relating to, or affected with heart disease

car•di•gan \'kär-di-gən\ *n* : a sweater or jacket usu. without a collar and with a full-length opening in the front

¹car•di•nal \'kärd-nəl, 'kär-dᵊn-əl\ *n* **1** : an ecclesiastical official of the Roman Catholic Church ranking next below the pope **2** : a crested No. American finch that is nearly completely red in the male

²cardinal *adj* [ME, fr. LL *cardinalis*, fr. L serving as a hinge, fr. *cardo* hinge] : of basic importance : CHIEF, MAIN, PRIMARY — car•di•nal•ly *adv*

car•di•nal•ate \'kärd-nə-lət, -'kär-dᵊn-ə-let, -,lāt\ *n* : the office, rank, or dignity of a cardinal

cardinal flower *n* : a No. American plant that bears a spike of brilliant red flowers

cardinal number *n* : a number (as 1, 5, 82, 357) that is used in simple counting and answers the question "how many?"

cardinal point *n* : one of the four principal compass points north, south, east, and west

car•di•ol•o•gy \,kär-dē-'ä-lə-jē\ *n* : the study of the heart and its action and diseases — car•di•ol•o•gist \-jist\ *n*

car•dio•pul•mo•nary resuscitation \,kär-dē-ō-'pùl-mə-,ner-ē-\ *n* : a procedure to restore normal breathing after cardiac arrest that includes the clearance of air passages to the lungs, mouth-to-mouth method of artificial respiration, and heart massage by the exertion of pressure on the chest

car•dio•vas•cu•lar \-'vas-kyə-lər\ *adj* : of or relating to the heart and blood vessels

card•sharp•er \'kärd-,shär-pər\ *or* card•sharp \-,shärp\ *n* : a cheater at cards

¹care \'ker\ *n* **1** : a disquieted state of uncertainty and responsibility : ANXIETY **2** : watchful attention : HEED **3** : CHARGE, SUPERVISION **4** : a person or thing that is an object of anxiety or solicitude

²care *vb* cared; car•ing **1** : to feel anxiety **2** : to feel interest **3** : to give care **4** : to have a liking, fondness, taste, or inclination **5** : to be concerned about ⟨what happens⟩

CARE *abbr* Cooperative for American Relief to Everywhere

ca•reen \kə-'rēn\ *vb* **1** : to put (a ship or boat) on a beach esp. in order to clean or repair its hull **2** : to sway from side to side **3** : CAREER

¹ca•reer \kə-'rir\ n [MF *carrière,* fr. OProv *carriera* street, fr. ML *carraria* road for vehicles, fr. L *carrus* car] **1** : COURSE, PASSAGE; *also* : speed in a course ⟨ran at full ∿⟩ **2** : an occupation or profession followed as a life's work

²career vb : to go at top speed esp. in a headling manner

care•free \'ker-₁frē\ adj : free from care or worry

care•ful \-fəl\ adj care•ful•ler; care•ful•lest **1** : using or taking care : VIGILANT **2** : marked by solicitude, caution, or prudence — care•ful•ly adv — care•ful•ness n

care•giv•er \-₁gi-vər\ n : a person who provides direct care (as for children, the disabled, or the chronically ill)

care•less \-ləs\ adj **1** : free from care : UNTROUBLED **2** : UNCONCERNED, INDIFFERENT **3** : not taking care **4** : not showing or receiving care — care•less•ly adv — care•less•ness n

¹ca•ress \kə-'res\ n : a tender or loving touch or embrace

²caress vb : to touch or stroke tenderly or lovingly — ca•ress•er n

car•et \'kar-ət\ n [L, there is lacking, fr. *carēre* to lack, be without] : a mark ʌ used to indicate the place where something is to be inserted

care•tak•er \'ker-₁tā-kər\ n **1** : one in charge usu. as occupant in place of an absent owner **2** : one temporarily fulfilling the functions of an office

care•worn \-₁wörn\ adj : showing the effects of grief or anxiety

car•fare \'kär-₁far\ n : passenger fare (as on a streetcar or bus)

car•go \'kär-gō\ n, pl cargoes or cargos : the goods carried in a ship, airplane, or vehicle : FREIGHT

Ca•rib•be•an \₁kar-ə-'bē-ən, kə-'ri-bē-ən\ adj : of or relating to the eastern and southern West Indies or the Caribbean Sea

car•i•bou \'kar-ə-₁bü\ n, pl caribou or caribous : a large circumpolar gregarious deer of northern taiga and tundra that usu. has palmate antlers in both sexes — used esp. for one of the New World

car•i•ca•ture \'kar-i-kə-₁chür\ n **1** : distorted representation to produce a ridiculous effect **2** : a representation esp. in literature or art having the qualities of caricature — caricature vb — car•i•ca•tur•ist \-ist\ n

car•ies \'kar-ēz\ n, pl caries : tooth decay

car•il•lon \'kar-ə-₁län\ n : a set of tuned bells sounded by hammers controlled from a keyboard

car•i•ous \'kar-ē-əs\ adj : affected with caries

car•jack•ing \'kär-₁ja-kiŋ\ n : the theft of an automobile by force or intimidation — car•jack•er n

car•load \'kär-₁lōd\ n : a load that fills a car

car•mi•na•tive \kär-'mi-nə-tiv\ adj : expelling gas from the alimentary canal — carminative n

car•mine \'kär-mən, -₁mīn\ n : a vivid red

car•nage \'kär-nij\ n : great destruction of life : SLAUGHTER

car•nal \'kärn-ᵊl\ adj [ME, fr. LL *carnalis,* fr. L *carn-, caro* flesh] **1** : of or relating to the body **2** : relating to or given to sensual pleasures and appetites — car•nal•i•ty \kär-'na-lə-tē\ n — car•nal•ly adv

car•na•tion \kär-'nā-shən\ n : a cultivated pink of any of numerous usu. double-flowered varieties derived from an Old World species

car•nau•ba wax \kär-'nȯ-bə-, -'naů-; ₁kär-nə-'ü-bə-\ n : a brittle yellowish wax from a Brazilian palm that is used esp. in polishes

car•ne•lian \kär-'nēl-yən\ n : a hard tough reddish quartz used as a gem

car•ni•val \'kär-nə-vəl\ n [It *carnevale,* alter. of *carnelevare,* lit., removal of meat] **1** : a season of merrymaking just before Lent **2** : a boisterous merrymaking **3** : a traveling enterprise offering amusements **4** : an organized program of entertainment

car•niv•o•ra \kär-'ni-və-rə\ n pl : carnivorous mammals

car•ni•vore \'kär-nə-₁vōr\ n : a flesh-eating animal; *esp* : any of an order of mammals (as dogs, cats, bears, minks, and seals) feeding mostly on animal flesh

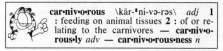

car•niv•o•rous \kär-'ni-və-rəs\ adj **1** : feeding on animal tissues **2** : of or relating to the carnivores — car•niv•o•rous•ly adv — car•niv•o•rous•ness n

car•ny or car•ney or car•nie \'kär-nē\ n, pl carnies or carneys **1** : CARNIVAL **3 2** : one who works with a carnival

car•ol \'kar-əl\ n : a song of joy or devotion — carol vb — car•ol•er or car•ol•ler n

car•om \'kar-əm\ n **1** : a shot in billiards in which the cue ball strikes two other balls **2** : a rebounding esp. at an angle — carom vb

car•o•tene \'kar-ə-₁tēn\ n : any of several orange to red pigments (as beta-carotene) formed esp. in plants and used as a source of vitamin A

ca•rot•id \kə-'rä-təd\ adj : of, relating to, or being the chief artery or pair of arteries that pass up the neck and supply the head — carotid n

ca•rous•al \kə-'raů-zəl\ n : CAROUSE

ca•rouse \kə-'raůz\ n [MF *carrousse,* fr. *carous,* adv., all out (in *boire carous* to empty the cup), fr. G *garaus*] : a drunken revel — carouse vb — ca•rous•er n

car•ou•sel \₁kar-ə-'sel, 'kar-ə-₁sel\ n **1** : MERRY-GO-ROUND **2** : a circular conveyor

¹carp \'kärp\ vb : to find fault : CAVIL, COMPLAIN — carp n — car•per n

²carp n, pl carp or carps : a large variable Asian freshwater fish of sluggish waters often raised for food

¹car•pal \'kär-pəl\ adj : relating to the wrist or the bones of the wrist

²carpal n : a carpal element or bone

carpal tunnel syndrome n : a condition characterized esp. by weakness, pain, and disturbances of sensation (as numbness) in the hand and caused by compression of a nerve in the wrist

car•pe di•em \'kär-pe-'dē-₁em, -'dī-\ n [L, lit., pluck

the day] : enjoyment of the present without concern for the future

car·pel \'kär-pəl\ *n* : one of the highly modified leaves that together form the ovary of a flower of a seed plant

car·pen·ter \'kär-pən-tər\ *n* : one who builds or repairs wooden structures — **carpenter** *vb* — **car·pen·try** \-trē\ *n*

car·pet \'kär-pət\ *n* : a heavy fabric used as a floor covering — **carpet** *vb*

car·pet·bag \-ˌbag\ *n* : a traveling bag common in the 19th century

car·pet·bag·ger \-ˌba-gər\ *n* : a Northerner in the South after the American Civil War usu. seeking private gain under the reconstruction governments

car·pet·ing \'kär-pə-tiŋ\ *n* : material for carpets; *also* : CARPETS

car pool *n* : an arrangement in which a group of people commute together by car; *also* : a group having this arrangement — **car·pool** \-ˌpül\ *vb*

car·port \'kär-ˌpȯrt\ *n* : an open-sided automobile shelter

car·pus \'kär-pəs\ *n* : the wrist or its bones

car·ra·geen·an *or* **car·ra·geen·in** \ˌkar-ə-ˈgē-nən\ *n* : a colloid extracted esp. from a dark purple branching seaweed and used in foods esp. to stabilize and thicken them

car·rel \'kar-əl\ *n* : a table often partitioned or enclosed for individual study in a library

car·riage \'kar-ij\ *n* 1 : the act of carrying 2 : manner of holding the body 3 : a wheeled vehicle 4 *Brit* : a railway passenger coach 5 : a movable part of a machine for supporting some other moving part ⟨a typewriter ~⟩

carriage trade *n* : trade from well-to-do or upper‑class people

car·ri·er \'kar-ē-ər\ *n* 1 : one that carries 2 : a person or organization in the transportation business 3 : AIRCRAFT CARRIER 4 : one whose system carries germs of a disease but who is immune to the disease 5 : an individual having a gene for a trait or condition that is not expressed bodily 6 : an electromagnetic wave whose amplitude or frequency is varied in order to convey a radio or television signal

carrier pigeon *n* : a pigeon used esp. to carry messages

car·ri·on \'kar-ē-ən\ *n* : dead and decaying flesh

car·rot \'kar-ət\ *n* : the elongated usu. orange root of a common garden plant that is eaten as a vegetable; *also* : this plant

car·rou·sel *var of* CAROUSEL

¹car·ry \'kar-ē\ *vb* **car·ried; car·ry·ing** 1 : to move while supporting : TRANSPORT, CONVEY, TAKE 2 : to influence by mental or emotional appeal 3 : to get possession or control of : CAPTURE, WIN 4 : to transfer from one place to another ⟨~ a number in adding⟩ 5 : to have or wear on one's person; *also* : to bear within one 6 : INVOLVE, IMPLY 7 : to hold or bear (oneself) in a specified way 8 : to keep in stock for sale 9 : to sustain the weight or bur-

den of : SUPPORT 10 : to prolong in space, time, or degree 11 : to keep on one's books as a debtor 12 : to succeed in (an election) 13 : to win adoption (as in a legislature) 14 : PUBLISH, PRINT 15 : to reach or penetrate to a distance

²carry *n* 1 : the range of a gun or projectile or of a struck or thrown ball 2 : PORTAGE 3 : an act or method of carrying ⟨fireman's ~⟩

car·ry·all \'kar-ē-ˌȯl\ *n* : a capacious bag or case

carry away *vb* : to arouse to a high and often excessive degree of emotion

carrying charge *n* : a charge added to the price of merchandise sold on the installment plan

car·ry-on *n* : a piece of luggage suitable for being carried aboard an airplane by a passenger — **carry-on** *adj*

carry on *vb* 1 : CONDUCT, MANAGE 2 : to behave in a foolish, excited, or improper manner 3 : to continue in spite of hindrance or discouragement

carry out *vb* 1 : to put into execution 2 : to bring to a successful conclusion

---

car·sick \'kär-ˌsik\ *adj* : affected with motion sickness esp. in an automobile — **car sickness** *n*

---

¹cart \'kärt\ *n* 1 : a heavy 2-wheeled wagon 2 : a small wheeled vehicle

²cart *vb* : to convey in or as if in a cart — **cart·er** *n*

cart·age \'kär-tij\ *n* : the act of or rate charged for carting

carte blanche \'kärt-ˈblänsh\ *n*, *pl* **cartes blanches** *same or* -ˈblän-shəz\ [F, lit., blank document] : full discretionary power

car·tel \kär-ˈtel\ *n* : a combination of independent business enterprises designed to limit competition **syn** pool, syndicate, monopoly, trust

car·ti·lage \'kärt-ᵊl-ij\ *n* : a usu. translucent somewhat elastic tissue that composes most of the skeleton of young vertebrate embryos and later is mostly converted to bone in higher vertebrates — **car·ti·lag·i·nous** \ˌkärt-ᵊl-ˈa-jə-nəs\ *adj*

cartilaginous fish *n* : any of a class of fishes (as a shark or ray having the skeleton wholly or largely composed of cartilage

car·tog·ra·phy \kär-ˈtä-grə-fē\ *n* : the making of maps — **car·tog·ra·pher** *n*

car·ton \'kärt-ᵊn\ *n* : a paperboard box or container

car·toon \kär-ˈtün\ *n* 1 : a preparatory sketch (as for a painting) 2 : a drawing intended as humor, caricature, or satire 3 : COMIC STRIP — **cartoon** *vb* — **car·toon·ist** *n*

car·tridge \'kär-trij\ *n* 1 : a tube containing a complete charge for a firearm 2 : a container of material for insertion into an apparatus 3 : a small case containing a phonograph needle and transducer that is attached to a tonearm 4 : a case containing a magnetic tape or disk **5** : a case for holding integrated circuits containing a computer program

cart·wheel \'kärt-ˌhwēl\ n **1** : a large coin (as a silver dollar) **2** : a lateral handspring with arms and legs extended

carve \kärv\ vb **carved; carv·ing 1** : to cut with care or precision : shape by cutting **2** : to cut into pieces or slices **3** : to slice and serve meat at table — **carv·er** n

cary·at·id \ˌkar-ē-'a-təd\ n, pl **-ids** or **-i·des** \-'a-təˌdēz\ : a sculptured draped female figure used as an architectural column

CAS abbr certificate of advanced study

ca·sa·ba \kə-'sä-bə\ n : any of several muskmelons with a yellow rind and sweet flesh

¹cas·cade \kas-'kād\ n **1** : a steep usu. small waterfall **2** : something arranged in a series or succession of stages so that each stage derives from or acts upon the product of the preceding

²cascade vb **cas·cad·ed; cas·cad·ing** : to fall, pass, or connect in or as if in a cascade

cas·cara \kas-'kar-ə\ n : the dried bark of a small Pacific coastal tree of the U.S. and southern Canada used as a laxative; also : this tree

¹case \'kās\ n [ME cas, fr. OF, fr. L casus fall, chance, fr. cadere to fall] **1** : a particular instance or situation **2** : an inflectional form of a noun, pronoun, or adjective indicating its grammatical relation to other words; also : such a relation whether indicated by inflection or not **3** : what actually exists or happens : FACT **4** : a suit or action in law : CAUSE **5** : a convincing argument **6** : an instance of disease or injury; also : PATIENT **7** : INSTANCE, EXAMPLE — **in case** : as a precaution — **in case of** : in the event of

²case n [ME cas, fr. OF casse, fr. L capsa] **1** : a box or container for holding something; also : a box with its contents **2** : an outer covering **3** : a divided tray for holding printing type **4** : CASING 2

³case vb **cased; cas·ing 1** : to enclose in or cover with a case **2** : to inspect esp. with intent to rob

ca·sein \'kā-ˌsēn, kā-'\ n : any of several phosphorus-containing proteins occurring in or produced from milk

case·ment \'kās-mənt\ n : a window that opens like a door

case·work \-ˌwərk\ n : social work that involves the individual person or family — **case·work·er** n

¹cash \'kash\ n [MF or It; MF casse money box, fr. It cassa, fr. L capsa chest, case] **1** : ready money **2** : money or its equivalent paid at the time of purchase or delivery

²cash vb : to pay or obtain cash for

ca·shew \'ka-shü, kə-'shü\ n : an edible kidney-shaped nut of a tropical American tree related to the sumacs; also : the tree

¹ca·shier \ka-'shir\ vb : to dismiss from service; esp : to dismiss in disgrace

²cash·ier \ka-'shir\ n **1** : a bank official responsible for moneys received and paid out **2** : a person who receives and records payments

cashier's check n : a check drawn by a bank upon its own funds and signed by its cashier

cash in vb **1** : to convert into cash ⟨cash in bonds⟩ **2** : to settle accounts and withdraw from a gambling game or business deal **3** : to obtain financial profit or advantage

cash·mere \'kazh-ˌmir, 'kash-\ n : fine wool from the undercoat of an Indian goat (**cashmere goat**) or a yarn spun of this; also : a soft twilled fabric orig. woven from this yarn

cash register n : a business machine that usu. has a money drawer, indicates each sale, and records the money received

cas·ing \'kā-siŋ\ n **1** : something that encases **2** : the frame of a door or window

ca·si·no \kə-'sē-nō\ n, pl **-nos** [It, fr. casa house] **1** : a

building or room for social amusements; esp : one used for gambling **2** also **cas·si·no** : a card game in which players win cards by matching those on the table

cask \'kask\ n : a barrel-shaped container usu. for liquids; also : the quantity held by such a container

cas·ket \'kas-kət\ n **1** : a small box (as for jewels) **2** : COFFIN

casque \'kask\ n : HELMET

cas·sa·va \kə-'sä-və\ n : any of several tropical spurges with rootstocks yielding a nutritious starch from which tapioca is prepared; also : the rootstock or its starch

cas·se·role \'ka-sə-ˌrōl\ n **1** : a dish in which food may be baked and served **2** : food cooked and served in a casserole

cas·sette also **ca·sette** \kə-'set\ n **1** : a lightproof container for photographic plates or film **2** : a plastic case containing magnetic tape

cas·sia \'ka-shə\ n **1** : a coarse cinnamon bark **2** : any of a genus of leguminous herbs, shrubs, and trees of warm regions including several which yield senna

cas·sit·er·ite \kə-'si-tə-ˌrīt\ n : a dark mineral that is the chief tin ore

cas·sock \'ka-sək\ n : an ankle-length garment worn esp. by Roman Catholic and Anglican clergy

cas·so·wary \'ka-sə-ˌwer-ē\ n, pl **-war·ies** : any of a genus of large birds closely related to the emu

¹cast \'kast\ vb **cast; cast·ing 1** : THROW, FLING **2** : DIRECT ⟨∼ a glance⟩ **3** : to deposit (a ballot) formally **4** : to throw off, out, or away : DISCARD, SHED **5** : COMPUTE; esp : to add up **6** : to assign the parts of (a play) to actors; also : to assign to a role or part **7** : to shape (a substance) by pouring in liquid or plastic form into a mold and letting harden without pressure **8** : to make (as a knot or stitch) by looping or catching up

²cast n **1** : THROW, FLING **2** : a throw of dice **3** : the set of actors in a dramatic production **4** : something formed in or as if in a mold; also : a rigid surgical dressing (as for protecting and supporting a fractured bone) **5** : TINGE, HUE **6** : APPEARANCE, LOOK **7** : something thrown out or off, shed, or expelled ⟨worm ∼s⟩

cas·ta·net \ˌkas-tə-'net\ n [Sp castañeta, fr. castaña chestnut, fr. L castanea] : a rhythm instrument consisting of two small wooden, ivory, or plastic shells held in the hand and clicked together

cast·away \'kas-tə-ˌwā\ adj **1** : thrown away : REJECTED **2** : cast adrift or ashore as a survivor of a shipwreck — **castaway** n

caste \'kast\ n [Port casta, lit., race, lineage, fr. fem. of casto pure, chaste, fr. L castus] **1** : one of the hereditary social classes in Hinduism **2** : a division of a society based on wealth, inherited rank, or occupation **3** : social position : PRESTIGE **4** : a system of rigid social stratification

cas·tel·lat·ed \'kas-tə-ˌlā-təd\ adj : having battlements like a castle

cast·er \'kas-tər\ n **1** or **cas·tor** : a small container to hold salt or pepper at the table **2** : a small wheel that turns freely and is used to support and move furniture, trucks, and equipment

cas·ti·gate \'kas-tə-ˌgāt\ vb **-gat·ed; -gat·ing** : to punish or criticize severely — **cas·ti·ga·tion** \ˌkas-tə-'gā-shən\ n — **cas·ti·ga·tor** \'kas-tə-ˌgā-tər\ n

cast·ing \'kas-tiŋ\ n **1** : CAST 7 **2** : something cast in a mold

casting vote n : a deciding vote cast by a presiding officer to break a tie

cast iron n : a hard brittle alloy of iron, carbon, and silicon cast in a mold

cas·tle \'ka-səl\ n **1** : a large fortified building or set of buildings **2** : a large or imposing house **3** : ³ROOK

castle in the air : an impracticable project

cast-off \'kas-ˌtȯf\ adj : thrown away or aside — **cast·off** n

cas·tor oil \'kas-tər-\ n : a thick yellowish oil extracted

from the poisonous seeds of an herb (**castor–oil plant**) and used as a lubricant and purgative

cas·trate \'kas-ˌtrāt\ vb **cas·trat·ed; cas·trat·ing** : to deprive of sex glands and esp. testes — **cas·tra·tion** \kas-'trā-shən\ n — **cas·tra·tor** \-ər\ n

ca·su·al \'ka-zhə-wəl\ adj 1 : resulting from or occurring by chance 2 : OCCASIONAL, INCIDENTAL 3 : OFFHAND, NONCHALANT 4 : designed for informal use ⟨∼ clothing⟩ — **ca·su·al·ly** adv — **ca·su·al·ness** n

ca·su·al·ty \'ka-zhəl-tē, 'ka-zhə-wəl-\ n, pl **-ties** 1 : serious or fatal accident 2 : a military person lost through death, injury, sickness, or capture or through being missing in action 3 : a person or thing injured, lost, or destroyed

ca·su·ist·ry \'ka-zhə-wə-strē\ n, pl **-ries** : specious argument : RATIONALIZATION — **ca·su·ist** \-wist\ n — **ca·su·is·tic** \ˌka-zhə-'wis-tik\ or **ca·su·is·ti·cal** \-ti-kəl\ adj

ca·sus bel·li \ˌkä-səs-'be-ˌlē, ˌkä-səs-'be-ˌlī\ n, pl **ca·sus belli** \ˌkä-ˌsüs-, ˌkä-\ [NL, occasion of war] : a cause or pretext for a declaration of war

¹**cat** \'kat\ n 1 : a carnivorous mammal long domesticated as a pet and for catching rats and mice 2 : any of a family of animals (as the lion, lynx, or leopard) including the domestic cat 3 : a spiteful woman 4 : GUY

²**cat** abbr catalog

ca·tab·o·lism \kə-'ta-bə-ˌli-zəm\ n : destructive metabolism involving the release of energy and resulting in the breakdown of complex materials — **cat·a·bol·ic** \ˌka-tə-'bä-lik\ adj

cat·a·clysm \'ka-tə-ˌkli-zəm\ n : a violent change or upheaval — **cat·a·clys·mal** \ˌka-tə-'kliz-məl\ or **cat·a·clys·mic** \-'kliz-mik\ adj

cat·a·comb \'ka-tə-ˌkōm\ n : an underground burial place with galleries and recesses for tombs

cat·a·falque \'ka-tə-ˌfalk, -ˌfȯlk, -ˌfȯk\ n : an ornamental structure sometimes used in solemn funerals to hold the body

cat·a·lep·sy \'ka-tə-ˌlep-sē\ n, pl **-sies** : a trancelike nervous condition characterized esp. by loss of voluntary motion — **cat·a·lep·tic** \ˌka-tə-'lep-tik\ adj or n

¹**cat·a·log** or **cat·a·logue** \'kat-əl-ˌȯg\ n 1 : LIST, REGISTER 2 : a systematic list of items with descriptive details; also : a book containing such a list

²**catalog** or **catalogue** vb **-loged** or **-logued; -log·ing** or **-logu·ing** 1 : to make a catalog of 2 : to enter in a catalog — **cat·a·log·er** or **cat·a·logu·er** n

ca·tal·pa \kə-'tal-pə\ n : a broad-leaved tree with showy flowers and long slim pods

ca·tal·y·sis \kə-'ta-lə-səs\ n, pl **-y·ses** \-ˌsēz\ : a change and esp. increase in the rate of a chemical reaction brought about by a substance (**cat·a·lyst** \'kat-əl-ist\) that is itself unchanged at the end of the reaction — **cat·a·lyt·ic** \ˌkat-əl-'i-tik\ adj — **cat·a·lyt·i·cal·ly** \-ti-k(ə-)lē\ adv

catalytic converter n : an automobile exhaust system component in which a catalyst changes harmful gases into mostly harmless products

cat·a·lyze \'kat-əl-ˌīz\ vb **-lyzed; -lyz·ing** : to bring about the catalysis of (a chemical reaction)

cat·a·ma·ran \ˌka-tə-mə-'ran\ n [Tamil (a language of southern India) kaṭṭumaram, fr. kaṭṭu to tie + maram tree] : a boat with twin hulls

cat·a·mount \'ka-tə-ˌmaunt\ n : COUGAR; also : LYNX

cat·a·pult \'ka-tə-ˌpəlt, -ˌpult\ n 1 : an ancient military machine for hurling missiles 2 : a device for launching an airplane (as from an aircraft carrier) — **catapult** vb

cat·a·ract \'ka-tə-ˌrakt\ n 1 : a cloudiness of the lens of the eye obstructing vision 2 : a large waterfall; also : steep rapids in a river

ca·tarrh \kə-'tär\ n : inflammation of a mucous membrane esp. of the nose and throat — **ca·tarrh·al** \-əl\ adj

ca·tas·tro·phe \kə-'tas-trə-(ˌ)fē\ n [Gk katastrophē, fr. katastrephein to overturn, fr. kata- down + strephein to turn] 1 : a great disaster or misfortune 2 : utter failure — **cat·a·stroph·ic** \ˌka-tə-'strä-fik\ adj — **cat·a·stroph·i·cal·ly** \-fi-k(ə-)lē\ adv

cat·a·ton·ic \ˌka-tə-'tä-nik\ adj : of, relating to, or marked by schizophrenia characterized esp. by stupor, negativism, rigidity, purposeless excitement, and abnormal posturing — **catatonic** n

cat·bird \'kat-ˌbərd\ n : an American songbird with a catlike mewing call

cat·boat \'kat-ˌbōt\ n : a single-masted sailboat with a single large sail extended by a long boom

cat·call \-ˌkȯl\ n : a loud cry made esp. to express disapproval — **catcall** vb

¹**catch** \'kach, 'kech\ vb **caught** \'kȯt\; **catch·ing** 1 : to capture esp. after pursuit 2 : TRAP 3 : to discover unexpectedly ⟨caught in the act⟩ 4 : to become suddenly aware of 5 : to take hold of : SNATCH ⟨∼ at a straw⟩ 6 : INTERCEPT 7 : to get entangled 8 : to become affected with or by ⟨∼ fire⟩ ⟨∼ cold⟩ 9 : to seize and hold firmly; also : FASTEN 10 : OVERTAKE 11 : to be in time for ⟨∼ a train⟩ 12 : to take in and retain 13 : to look at or listen to

²**catch** n 1 : something caught 2 : the act of catching; also : a game consisting of throwing and catching a ball 3 : something that catches or checks or holds immovable ⟨a door ∼⟩ 4 : one worth catching esp. as a mate 5 : FRAGMENT, SNATCH 6 : a concealed difficulty or complication

catch·all \'ka-ˌchȯl, 'ke-\ n : something to hold a variety of odds and ends

catch–as–catch–can adj : using any means available

catch·er \'ka-chər, 'ke-\ n : one that catches; esp : a player positioned behind home plate in baseball

catch·ing adj 1 : INFECTIOUS, CONTAGIOUS 2 : ALLURING, CATCHY

catch·ment \'kach-mənt, 'kech-\ n 1 : something that catches water 2 : the action of catching water

catch on vb 1 : UNDERSTAND 2 : to become popular

catch·pen·ny \\'kach-ıpe-nē, 'kech-\\ *adj* : using sensationalism or cheapness for appeal ⟨a ∼ newspaper⟩
catch–22 \\-ıtwen-tē-'tü\\ *n*, *pl* **catch–22's** *or* **catch–22s**
often cap C [fr. *Catch-22*, a paradoxical rule found in
the novel *Catch-22* (1961) by Joseph Heller] : a prob-
lematic situation for which the only solution is denied
by a circumstance inherent in the problem or by a
rule; *also* : the circumstance or rule that denies a solution
catch·up \\'ke-chəp, 'ka-\\ *var of* KETCHUP
catch up *vb* : to travel or work fast enough to overtake
or complete
catch·word \\'kach-ıwərd, 'kech-\\ *n* **1** : GUIDE WORD **2**
: a word or expression representative of a party,
school, or point of view
catchy \\'ka-chē, 'ke-\\ *adj* **catch·i·er; -est 1** : likely to
catch the interest or attention **2** : TRICKY
cat·e·chism \\'ka-tə-ıki-zəm\\ *n* : a summary or test (as
of religious doctrine) usu. in the form of questions
and answers — **cat·e·chist** \\-ıkist\\ *n* — **cat·e·chize**
\\-ıkīz\\ *vb*
cat·e·chu·men \\ıka-tə-'kyü-mən\\ *n* : a religious convert receiving training before baptism
cat·e·gor·i·cal \\ıka-tə-'gör-i-kəl\\ *adj* **1** : ABSOLUTE, UN-
QUALIFIED **2** : of, relating to, or constituting a category — **cat·e·gor·i·cal·ly** \\-i-k(ə-)lē\\ *adv*
cat·e·go·rise *Brit var of* CATEGORIZE
cat·e·go·rize \\'ka-ti-gə-ırīz\\ *vb* **-rized; -riz·ing** : to put
into a category : CLASSIFY — **cat·e·go·ri·za·tion** \\ıka-
ti-gə-rə-'zā-shən\\ *n*
cat·e·go·ry \\'ka-tə-ıgör-ē\\ *n*, *pl* **-ries** : a division used
in classification; *also* : CLASS, GROUP, KIND
ca·ter \\'kā-tər\\ *vb* **1** : to provide a supply of food **2** : to
supply what is wanted — **ca·ter·er** *n*
cat·er-cor·ner \\ıka-tē-'kör-nər, ıka-tə-, ıki-tē-\\ *or* **cater–cor·nered** *adv or adj* [obs. *cater* four + *corner*]
: in a diagonal or oblique position
cat·er·pil·lar \\'ka-tər-ıpi-lər\\ *n* [ME *catyrpel*, fr. OF
catepelose, lit., hairy cat] : a wormlike often hairy insect larva esp. of a butterfly or moth
cat·er·waul \\'ka-tər-ıwòl\\ *vb* : to make a harsh cry —
caterwaul *n*
cat·fish \\'kat-ıfish\\ *n* : any of an order of chiefly freshwater stout-bodied fishes with slender tactile processes around the mouth

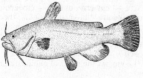

catfish

cat·gut \\-ıgət\\ *n* : a tough cord made usu. from sheep
intestines
ca·thar·sis \\kə-'thär-səs\\ *n*, *pl* **ca·thar·ses** \\-ısēz\\ **1** : an

act of purging or purification **2** : elimination of a complex by bringing it to consciousness and affording it
expression
¹ca·thar·tic \\kə-'thär-tik\\ *adj* : of, relating to, or producing catharsis
²cathartic *n* : PURGATIVE
ca·the·dral \\kə-'thē-drəl\\ *n* : the principal church of a
diocese
cath·e·ter \\'ka-thə-tər\\ *n* : a tube for insertion into a
bodily passage or cavity usu. for injecting or drawing
off material or for keeping a passage open
cath·ode \\'ka-ıthōd\\ *n* **1** : the negative electrode of an
electrolytic cell **2** : the positive terminal of a battery
3 : the electron-emitting electrode of an electron tube
— **cath·od·al** \\'ka-ıthō-dəl\\ *adj* — **ca·thod·ic** \\ka-
'thä-dik\\ *adj*
cathode–ray tube *n* : a vacuum tube in which a beam
of electrons is projected on a fluorescent screen to
produce a luminous spot
cath·o·lic \\'kath-lik, 'ka-thə-\\ *adj* **1** *cap* : of or relating
to Catholics and esp. Roman Catholics **2** : GENERAL,
UNIVERSAL
Cath·o·lic \\'kath-lik, 'ka-thə-\\ *n* : a member of a
church claiming historical continuity from the ancient
undivided Christian church; *esp* : a member of the
Roman Catholic Church — **Ca·thol·i·cism** \\kə-'thä-
lə-ısi-zəm\\ *n*
cath·o·lic·i·ty \\ıka-thə-'li-sə-tē\\ *n*, *pl* **-ties 1** *cap* : the
character of being in conformity with a Catholic
church **2** : liberality of sentiments or views **3** : comprehensive range
cat·ion \\'kat-ıī-ən\\ *n* : the ion in an electrolyte that migrates to the cathode; *also* : a positively charged ion
cat·kin \\'kat-kən\\ *n* : a long flower cluster (as of a
willow) bearing crowded flowers and prominent
bracts
cat·like \\-ılīk\\ *adj* : resembling a cat or its behavior;
esp : STEALTHY
cat·nap \\-ınap\\ *n* : a very short light nap — **catnap** *vb*

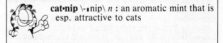

cat·nip \\-ınip\\ *n* : an aromatic mint that is
esp. attractive to cats

cat–o'–nine–tails \\ıka-tə-'nīn-ıtālz\\ *n*, *pl* **cat–o'–
nine–tails** : a whip made of usu. nine knotted cords
fastened to a handle
CAT scan \\'kat-\\ *n* [computerized *a*xial *t*omography]
: an image made by computed tomography
CAT scanner *n* : a medical instrument consisting of integrated X-ray and computing equipment that is used
to make CAT scans
cat's cradle *n* : a game played with a string looped on
the fingers in such a way as to resemble a small cradle
cat's–eye \\'kats-ıī\\ *n*, *pl* **cat's–eyes** : any of various iridescent gems
cat's–paw \\-ıpò\\ *n*, *pl* **cat's–paws** : a person used by
another as a tool

cat·sup \'ke-chəp, 'ka-; 'kat-səp\ *var of* KETCHUP

cat·tail \'kat-₁tāl\ *n* : a tall reedlike marsh plant with furry brown spikes of tiny flowers

cat·tle \'kat-ᵊl\ *n pl* : LIVESTOCK; *esp* : domestic bovines (as cows, bulls, or calves) — **cat·tle·man** \-mən, -₁man\ *n*

cat·ty \'ka-tē\ *adj* **cat·ti·er, -est** : slyly spiteful — **cat·ti·ly** \'ka-tᵊl-ē\ *adv* — **cat·ti·ness** *n*

cat·ty–cor·ner *or* **cat·ty–cor·nered** *var of* CATER-CORNER

CATV *abbr* community antenna television

cat·walk \'kat-₁wȯk\ *n* : a narrow walk (as along a bridge)

Cau·ca·sian \kȯ-'kā-zhən\ *adj* : of or relating to the white race of mankind — **Caucasian** *n* — **Cau·ca·soid** \'kȯ-kə-₁sȯid\ *adj or n*

cau·cus \'kȯ-kəs\ *n* : a meeting of a group of persons belonging to the same political party or faction usu. to decide upon policies and candidates — **caucus** *vb*

cau·dal \'kȯ-dᵊl\ *adj* : of, relating to, or located near the tail or the hind end of the body — **cau·dal·ly** *adv*

cau·di·llo \kau̇-'thē-(₁)yō, -'thēl-\ *n, pl* **-llos** : a Spanish or Latin-American military dictator

caught \'kȯt\ *past and past part of* CATCH

caul \'kȯl\ *n* : the inner fetal membrane of higher vertebrates esp. when covering the head at birth

caul·dron \'kȯl-drən\ *n* : a large kettle

cau·li·flow·er \'kȯ-li-₁flau̇(-ə)r\ *n* [It *cavolfiore*, fr. *cavolo* cabbage + *fiore* flower] : a garden plant closely related to cabbage and grown for its compact edible head of undeveloped flowers; *also* : this head used as a vegetable

cauliflower ear *n* : an ear deformed from injury and excessive growth of scar tissue

¹**caulk** \'kȯk\ *vb* [ME, fr. OF *cauquer* to trample, fr. L *calcare*, fr. *calx* heel] : to stop up and make tight against leakage (as a boat or its seams) — **caulk·er** *n*

²**caulk** *also* **caulk·ing** *n* : material used to caulk

caus·al \'kȯ-zəl\ *adj* **1** : expressing or indicating cause **2** : relating to or acting as a cause — **cau·sal·i·ty** \kȯ-'za-lə-tē\ *n* — **caus·al·ly** *adv*

cau·sa·tion \kȯ-'zā-shən\ *n* **1** : the act or process of causing **2** : the means by which an effect is produced

¹**cause** \'kȯz\ *n* **1** : REASON, MOTIVE **2** : something that brings about a result: *esp* : a person or thing that is the agent of bringing something about **3** : a suit or action in court : CASE **4** : a question or matter to be decided **5** : a principle or movement earnestly supported — **cause·less** *adj*

²**cause** *vb* **caused; caus·ing** : to be the cause or occasion of — **caus·a·tive** \'kȯ-zə-tiv\ *adj* — **caus·er** *n*

cause cé·lè·bre \₁kȯz-sā-'lebrᵊ, ₁kȯz-\ *n, pl* **causes célèbres** *same* \ [F, lit., celebrated case] **1** : a legal case that excites widespread interest **2** : a notorious person, thing, incident, or episode

cau·se·rie \₁kōz-'rē, ₁kō-zə-\ *n* [F] **1** : an informal conversation : CHAT **2** : a short informal essay

cause·way \'kȯz-₁wā\ *n* : a raised way or road across wet ground or water

¹**caus·tic** \'kȯ-stik\ *adj* **1** : CORROSIVE **2** : SHARP, INCISIVE ⟨~ wit⟩

²**caustic** *n* **1** : a substance that burns or destroys organic tissue by chemical action **2** : SODIUM HYDROXIDE

cau·ter·ize \'kȯ-tə-₁rīz\ *vb* **-ized; -iz·ing** : to burn or sear usu. to prevent infection or bleeding — **cau·ter·i·za·tion** \₁kȯ-tə-rə-'zā-shən\ *n*

¹**cau·tion** \'kȯ-shən\ *n* **1** : ADMONITION, WARNING **2** : prudent forethought to minimize risk **3** : one that astonishes — **cau·tion·ary** \-shə-₁ner-ē\ *adj*

²**caution** *vb* : to advise caution to

cau·tious \'kȯ-shəs\ *adj* : marked by or given to caution : CAREFUL — **cau·tious·ly** *adv* — **cau·tious·ness** *n*

cav *abbr* **1** cavalry **2** cavity

cav·al·cade \₁ka-vəl-'kād\ *n* **1** : a procession of riders or carriages; *also* : a procession of vehicles **2** : a dramatic sequence or procession

¹**cav·a·lier** \₁ka-və-'lir\ *n* [MF, fr. It *cavaliere*, fr. OProv *cavalier*, fr. LL *caballarius* horseman, fr. L *caballus* horse] **1** : a mounted soldier : KNIGHT **2** *cap* : an adherent of Charles I of England **3** : GALLANT

²**cavalier** *adj* **1** : DEBONAIR **2** : DISDAINFUL, HAUGHTY — **cav·a·lier·ly** *adv*

cav·al·ry \'ka-vəl-rē\ *n, pl* **-ries** : troops mounted on horseback or moving in motor vehicles — **cav·al·ry·man** \-mən, -₁man\ *n*

¹**cave** \'kāv\ *n* : a natural underground chamber open to the surface

²**cave** *vb* **caved; cav·ing 1** : to collapse or cause to collapse **2** : to cease to resist : SUBMIT — usu. used with *in*

ca·ve·at \'ka-vē-₁ät, -₁at; 'kä-vē-₁ät\ *n* [L, let him beware] : WARNING

caveat emp·tor \-'emp-tər, -₁tȯr\ *n* [NL, let the buyer beware] : a principle in commerce: without a warranty the buyer takes a risk

cave–in \'kā-₁vin\ *n* **1** : the action of caving in **2** : a place where earth has caved in

cave·man \'kāv-₁man\ *n* **1** : a cave dweller esp. of the Stone Age **2** : a man who acts in a rough or crude manner

cav·ern \'ka-vərn\ *n* : CAVE; *esp* : one of large or unknown size — **cav·ern·ous** *adj* — **cav·ern·ous·ly** *adv*

cav·i·ar *or* **cav·i·are** \'ka-vē-₁är, 'kä-\ *n* : the salted roe of a large fish (as sturgeon) used as an appetizer

cav·il \'ka-vəl\ *vb* **-iled** *or* **-illed; -il·ing** *or* **-il·ling** : to make frivolous objections or raise trivial objections to — **cavil** *n* — **cav·il·er** *or* **cav·il·ler** *n*

cav·ing \'kā-viŋ\ *n* : the sport of exploring caves : SPELUNKING

cav·i·ta·tion \₁ka-və-'tā-shən\ *n* : the formation of partial vacuums in a liquid by a swiftly moving solid body (as a propeller) or by high-intensity sound waves

cav·i·ty \'ka-və-tē\ *n, pl* **-ties 1** : an unfilled space with-

in a mass : a hollow place **2** : an area of decay in a tooth

ca·vort \kə-'vòrt\ *vb* : PRANCE, CAPER

ca·vy \'kā-vē\ *n, pl* **cavies** : GUINEA PIG 1

caw \'kò\ *vb* : to utter the harsh call of the crow or a similar cry — **caw** *n*

cay \'kē, 'kā\ *n* : ⁴KEY

cay·enne pepper \ˌkī-'en-, ˌkā-\ *n* : a condiment consisting of ground dried fruits or seeds of a hot pepper

cay·man *var of* CAIMAN

Ca·yu·ga \kā-'ü-gə, kī-\ *n, pl* **Cayuga** *or* **Cayugas** : a member of an American Indian people of New York

Cay·use \'kī-ˌyüs, kī-'\ *n* **1** *pl* **Cayuse** *or* **Cayuses** : a member of an American Indian people of Oregon and Washington **2** *pl* **cayuses,** *not cap, West* : a native range horse

Cb *symbol* columbium

CB \'sē-'bē\ *n* **1** : CITIZENS BAND; *also* : the radio set used for citizens-band communications

CBC *abbr* Canadian Broadcasting Corporation

CBD *abbr* cash before delivery

CBS *abbr* Columbia Broadcasting System

CBW *abbr* chemical and biological warfare

cc *abbr* cubic centimeter

CC *abbr* **1** carbon copy **2** community college **3** country club

CCD \ˌsē-ˌsē-'dē\ *n* : CHARGE-COUPLED DEVICE

CCTV *abbr* closed-circuit television

CCU *abbr* **1** cardiac care unit **2** coronary care unit **3** critical care unit

ccw *abbr* counterclockwise

cd *abbr* cord

Cd *symbol* cadmium

¹CD \ˌsē-'dē\ *n* : COMPACT DISC

²CD *abbr* **1** certificate of deposit **2** Civil Defense

CDR *abbr* commander

CD–ROM \ˌsē-ˌdē-'räm\ *n* : a compact disc containing data that can be read by a computer

CDT *abbr* central daylight (saving) time

Ce *symbol* cerium

CE *abbr* **1** chemical engineer **2** civil engineer **3** Corps of Engineers

cease \'sēs\ *vb* **ceased; ceas·ing** : to come or bring to an end : STOP

cease–fire \'sēs-'fīr\ *n* : a suspension of active hostilities

cease·less \'sēs-ləs\ *adj* : being without pause or stop : CONTINUOUS — **cease·less·ly** *adv* — **cease·less·ness** *n*

ce·cum \'sē-kəm\ *n, pl* **ce·ca** \-kə\ : the blind pouch at the beginning of the large intestine into which the small intestine opens — **ce·cal** \-kəl\ *adj*

ce·dar \'sē-dər\ *n* : any of numerous coniferous trees (as a juniper) noted for their fragrant durable wood; *also* : this wood

cede \'sēd\ *vb* **ced·ed; ced·ing 1** : to yield or give up esp. by treaty **2** : ASSIGN, TRANSFER — **ced·er** *n*

ce·di \'sā-dē\ *n* — see MONEY table

ce·dil·la \si-'di-lə\ *n* : a mark placed under the letter *c* (as ç) to show that the *c* is to be pronounced like *s*

ceil·ing \'sē-liŋ\ *n* **1** : the overhead inside lining of a room **2** : the height above the ground of the base of the lowest layer of clouds when over half of the sky is obscured **3** : the greatest height at which an airplane can operate efficiently **4** : a prescribed upper limit ⟨price ∼⟩

cel·an·dine \'se-lən-ˌdīn, -ˌdēn\ *n* : a yellow-flowered herb related to the poppies

cel·e·brate \'se-lə-ˌbrāt\ *vb* **-brat·ed; -brat·ing 1** : to perform (as a sacrament) with appropriate rites **2** : to honor (as a holiday) by solemn ceremonies or by refraining from ordinary business **3** : to observe a notable occasion with festivities **4** : EXTOL — **cel·e·brant** \-brənt\ *n* — **cel·e·bra·tion** \ˌse-lə-'brā-shən\ *n* — **cel·e·bra·tor** \'se-lə-brā-tər\ *n* — **cel·e·bra·to·ry** \-brə-ˌtōr-ē, -ˌtòr-; ˌse-lə-'brā-tə-rē\ *adj*

cel·e·brat·ed *adj* : widely known and often referred to **syn** distinguished, renowned, noted, famous, illustrious, notorious

ce·leb·ri·ty \sə-'le-brə-tē\ *n, pl* **-ties 1** : the state of being celebrated : RENOWN **2** : a celebrated person

ce·ler·i·ty \sə-'ler-ə-tē\ *n* : SPEED, RAPIDITY

---

cel·ery \'se-lə-rē\ *n, pl* **-er·ies** : a European herb related to the carrot and widely grown for the crisp edible stems of its leaves

---

celery cabbage *n* : CHINESE CABBAGE 2

ce·les·ta \sə-'les-tə\ *or* **ce·leste** \sə-'lest\ *n* : a keyboard instrument with hammers that strike steel plates

ce·les·tial \sə-'les-chəl\ *adj* **1** : HEAVENLY, DIVINE **2** : of or relating to the sky — **ce·les·tial·ly** *adv*

celestial navigation *n* : navigation by observation of the positions of stars

celestial sphere *n* : an imaginary sphere of infinite radius against which the celestial bodies appear to be projected

cel·i·ba·cy \'se-lə-bə-sē\ *n* **1** : the state of being unmarried; *esp* : abstention by vow from marriage **2** : abstention from sexual intercourse

cel·i·bate \'se-lə-bət\ *n* : one who lives in celibacy — **celibate** *adj*

cell \'sel\ *n* **1** : a small room (as in a convent or prison) usu. for one person; *also* : a small compartment, cavity, or bounded space **2** : a tiny mass of protoplasm that usu. contains a nucleus, is enclosed by a membrane, and forms the smallest structural unit of living matter capable of functioning independently **3** : a container holding an electrolyte either for generating electricity or for use in electrolysis **4** : a single unit in a device for converting radiant energy into electrical energy — **celled** \'seld\ *adj*

cel·lar \'se-lər\ *n* **1** : BASEMENT 1 **2** : the lowest position (as in an athletic league) **3** : a stock of wines

cel·lar·ette *or* **cel·lar·et** \ˌse-lə-'ret\ *n* : a case or cabinet for a few bottles of wine or liquor

cel·lo \'che-lō\ *n, pl* **cellos** : a bass member of the violin family tuned an octave below the viola — **cel·list** \-list\ *n*

cel·lo·phane \'se-lə-ˌfān\ *n* : a thin transparent material made from cellulose and used as a wrapping

cel·lu·lar \'sel-yə-lər\ *adj* **1** : of, relating to, or consisting of cells **2** : of, relating to, or being a radiotelephone system in which a geographical area is divided into small sections each served by a transmitter of limited range

cel·lu·lite \'sel-yə-ˌlīt\ *n* : lumpy fat in the thighs, hips, and buttocks of some women

cel·lu·lose \'sel-yə-ˌlōs\ *n* : a complex carbohydrate of the cell walls of plants used esp. in making paper or rayon — **cel·lu·los·ic** \ˌsel-yə-'lō-sik\ *adj or n*

Cel·si·us \'sel-sē-əs\ *adj* : relating to or having a scale for measuring temperature on which the interval between the triple point and the boiling point of water is divided into 99.99 degrees with 0.01° being the triple point and 100.00° the boiling point

Celt \'kelt, 'selt\ *n* : a member of any of a group of peoples (as the Irish or Welsh) of western Europe — **Celt·ic** *adj*

cem·ba·lo \'chem-bə-ˌlō\ *n, pl* **-ba·li** \-ˌlē\ *or* **-balos** [It] : HARPSICHORD

¹**ce·ment** \si-'ment\ *n* **1** : a powder that is produced from a burned mixture chiefly of clay and limestone and that is used in mortar and concrete; *also* : CONCRETE **2** : a binding element or agency **3** : CEMENTUM; *also* : a substance for filling cavities in teeth

²**cement** *vb* **1** : to unite by or as if by cement **2** : to cover with concrete — **ce·ment·er** *n*

ce·men·tum \si-'men-təm\ *n* : a specialized external bony layer covering the dentin of the part of a tooth normally within the gum

cem·e·tery \'se-mə-ˌter-ē\ *n, pl* **-ter·ies** [ME *cimitery*, fr. MF *cimitere*, fr. LL *coemeterium*, fr. Gk *koimētērion* sleeping chamber, burial place, fr. *koiman* to put to sleep] : a burial ground : GRAVEYARD

cen·o·bite \'se-nə-ˌbīt\ *n* : a member of a religious group living together in a monastic community — **cen·o·bit·ic** \ˌse-nə-'bi-tik\ *adj*

cen·o·taph \'se-nə-ˌtaf\ *n* [F *cénotaphe*, fr. L *cenotaphium*, fr. Gk *kenotaphion*, fr. *kenos* empty + *taphos* tomb] : a tomb or a monument erected in honor of a person whose body is elsewhere

Ce·no·zo·ic \ˌsē-nə-'zō-ik, ˌse-\ *adj* : of, relating to, or being the era of geologic history that extends from about 65 million years ago to the present — **Cenozoic** *n*

cen·ser \'sen-sər\ *n* : a vessel for burning incense (as in a religious ritual)

¹**cen·sor** \'sen-sər\ *n* **1** : one of two early Roman magistrates whose duties included taking the census **2** : an official who inspects printed matter or sometimes motion pictures with power to suppress anything objectionable — **cen·so·ri·al** \sen-'sōr-ē-əl\ *adj*

²**censor** *vb* : to subject to censorship

cen·so·ri·ous \sen-'sōr-ē-əs\ *adj* : marked by or given to censure : CRITICAL — **cen·so·ri·ous·ly** *adv* — **cen·so·ri·ous·ness** *n*

cen·sor·ship \'sen-sər-ˌship\ *n* **1** : the action of a censor esp. in stopping the transmission or publication of matter considered objectionable **2** : the office of a Roman censor

¹**cen·sure** \'sen-chər\ *n* **1** : the act of blaming or condemning sternly **2** : an official reprimand

²**censure** *vb* **cen·sured; cen·sur·ing** : to find fault with and criticize as blameworthy — **cen·sur·able** *adj* — **cen·sur·er** *n*

cen·sus \'sen-səs\ *n* **1** : a periodic governmental count of population **2** : COUNT, TALLY — **cen·sus** *vb*

¹**cent** \'sent\ *n* [MF, hundred, fr. L *centum*] **1** : a monetary unit equal to ¹⁄₁₀₀ of a basic unit of value — see *birr, dollar, gulden, leone, lilangeni, lira, pound, rand, rupee, shilling* at MONEY table **2** : a coin, token, or note representing one cent

²**cent** *abbr* **1** centigrade **2** central **3** century

cen·taur \'sen-ˌtör\ *n* : any of a race of creatures in Greek mythology half man and half horse

¹**cen·ta·vo** \sen-'tä-(ˌ)vō\ *n, pl* **-vos** — see *boliviano, colón, cordoba, lempira, peso, quetzal, sol, sucre* at MONEY table

²**cen·ta·vo** \-'tä-(ˌ)vü, -(ˌ)vō\ *n, pl* **-vos** — see *escudo, metical, real* at MONEY table

cen·te·nar·i·an \ˌsent-ᵊn-'er-ē-ən\ *n* : a person who is 100 or more years old

cen·te·na·ry \sen-'te-nə-rē, 'sent-ᵊn-ˌer-ē\ *n, pl* **-ries** : CENTENNIAL — **centenary** *adj*

cen·ten·ni·al \sen-'te-nē-əl\ *n* : a 100th anniversary or its celebration — **centennial** *adj*

¹**cen·ter** \'sen-tər\ *n* **1** : the point that is equally distant from all points on the circumference of a circle or surface of a sphere; *also* : MIDDLE 1 **2** : the point about which an activity concentrates or from which something originates **3** : a region of concentrated population **4** : a middle part **5** *often cap* : political figures holding moderate views esp. between those of conservatives and liberals **6** : a player occupying a middle position (as in football or basketball)

²**center** *vb* **1** : to place or fix at or around a center or central area **2** : to give a central focus or basis : CONCENTRATE **3** : to have a center : FOCUS

cen·ter·board \'sen-tər-ˌbōrd\ *n* : a retractable keel used esp. in sailboats

cen·ter·piece \-ˌpēs\ *n* **1** : an object in a central position; *esp* : an adornment in the center of a table **2** : one that is of central importance or interest in a larger whole

cen·tes·i·mal \sen-'te-sə-məl\ *adj* : marked by or relating to division into hundredths

¹**cen·tes·i·mo** \chen-'te-zə-ˌmō\ *n, pl* **-mi** \-(ˌ)mē\ — see *lira* at MONEY table

²**cen·tes·i·mo** \sen-'te-sə-ˌmō\ *n, pl* **-mos** — see *balboa, peso* at MONEY table

cen·ti·grade \'sen-tə-ˌgrād, 'sän-\ *adj* : relating to, conforming to, or having a thermometer scale on which the interval between the freezing and boiling points of water is divided into 100 degrees with 0°

representing the freezing point and 100° the boiling point ⟨10° ∼⟩

cen•ti•gram \-ˌgram\ *n* — see METRIC SYSTEM table

cen•ti•li•ter \'sen-ti-ˌlē-tər\ *n* — see METRIC SYSTEM table

cen•time \'sän-ˌtēm\ *n* — see *dinar, dirham, franc, gourde* at MONEY table

cen•ti•me•ter \'sen-tə-ˌmē-tər, 'sän-\ *n* — see METRIC SYSTEM table

centimeter–gram–second *adj* : of, relating to, or being a system of units based on the centimeter as the unit of length, the gram as the unit of mass, and the second as the unit of time

cen•ti•mo \'sen-tə-ˌmō\ *n, pl* **-mos** — see *bolivar, colón, dobra, guarani, peseta* at MONEY table

cen•ti•pede \'sen-tə-ˌpēd\ *n* [L *centipeda,* fr. *centum* hundred + *pes* foot] : any of a class of long flattened segmented arthropods with one pair of legs on each segment except the first which has a pair of poison fangs

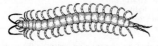

centipede

¹**cen•tral** \'sen-trəl\ *adj* **1** : constituting a center **2** : ESSENTIAL, PRINCIPAL **3** : situated at, in, or near the center **4** : centrally placed and superseding separate units ⟨∼ heating⟩ — **cen•tral•ly** *adv*

²**central** *n* : a central controlling office

cen•tral•ise *Brit var of* CENTRALIZE

cen•tral•ize \'sen-trə-ˌlīz\ *vb* **-ized; -iz•ing** : to bring to a central point or under central control — **cen•tral•i•za•tion** \ˌsen-trə-lə-ˈzā-shən\ *n* — **cen•tral•iz•er** \'sen-trə-ˌlī-zər\ *n*

central nervous system *n* : the part of the nervous system which integrates nervous function and activity and which in vertebrates consists of the brain and spinal cord

cen•tre *chiefly Brit var of* CENTER

cen•trif•u•gal \sen-ˈtri-fyə-gəl, -fi-\ *adj* [NL *centrifugus,* fr. *centr-* center + L *fugere* to flee] **1** : proceeding or acting in a direction away from a center or axis **2** : using or acting by centrifugal force

centrifugal force *n* : the force that tends to impel a thing or parts of a thing outward from a center of rotation

cen•tri•fuge \'sen-trə-ˌfyüj\ *n* : a machine using centrifugal force (as for separating substances of different densities or for removing moisture)

cen•trip•e•tal \sen-ˈtri-pət-ᵊl\ *adj* [NL *centripetus,* fr. *centr-* center + L *petere* seek] : proceeding or acting in a direction toward a center or axis

centripetal force *n* : the force needed to keep an object revolving about a point moving in a circular path

cen•trist \'sen-trist\ *n* **1** *often cap* : a member of a center party **2** : one who holds moderate views

cen•tu•ri•on \sen-ˈtür-ē-ən, -ˈtyür-\ *n* : an officer commanding a Roman century

cen•tu•ry \'sen-chə-rē\ *n, pl* **-ries** **1** : a subdivision of a Roman legion **2** : a group or sequence of 100 like things **3** : a period of 100 years

century plant *n* : a Mexican agave maturing and flowering only once in many years and then dying

CEO \ˌsē-(ˌ)ē-ˈō\ *n* : the executive with the chief decision-making authority in an organization or business

ce•phal•ic \sə-ˈfa-lik\ *adj* **1** : of or relating to the head **2** : directed toward or situated on or in or near the head

ce•ram•ic \sə-ˈra-mik\ *n* **1** *pl* : the art or process of making articles from a nonmetallic mineral (as clay)

by firing **2** : a product produced by ceramics — **ceramic** *adj*

ce•ra•mist \sə-ˈra-mist\ *or* **ce•ram•i•cist** \sə-ˈra-mə-sist\ *n* : one who engages in ceramics

¹**ce•re•al** \'sir-ē-əl\ *adj* [L *cerealis,* fr. *Ceres,* the Roman goddess of agriculture] : relating to grain or to the plants that produce it; *also* : made of grain

²**cereal** *n* **1** : a grass (as wheat) yielding grain suitable for food; *also* : its grain **2** : a food and esp. a breakfast food prepared from the grain of a cereal

cer•e•bel•lum \ˌser-ə-ˈbe-ləm\ *n, pl* **-bellums** *or* **-bel•la** \-lə\ [ML, fr. L, dim. of *cerebrum*] : a part of the brain that projects over the medulla and is concerned esp. with coordination of muscular action and with bodily balance — **cer•e•bel•lar** \-lər\ *adj*

ce•re•bral \sə-ˈrē-brəl, 'ser-ə-\ *adj* **1** : of or relating to the brain, intellect, or cerebrum **2** : appealing to or involving the intellect — **ce•re•bral•ly** *adv*

cerebral cortex *n* : the surface layer of gray matter of the cerebrum that functions chiefly in coordination of sensory and motor information

cerebral palsy *n* : a disorder caused by brain damage usu. before, during, or shortly after birth and marked esp. by defective muscle control

cer•e•brate \'ser-ə-ˌbrāt\ *vb* **-brat•ed; -brat•ing** : THINK — **cer•e•bra•tion** \ˌser-ə-ˈbrā-shən\ *n*

ce•re•brum \sə-ˈrē-brəm, 'ser-ə-\ *n, pl* **-brums** *or* **-bra** \-brə\ [L] : the enlarged front and upper part of the brain that contains the higher nervous centers

cere•ment \'ser-ə-mənt, 'sir-mənt\ *n* : a shroud for the dead

¹**cer•e•mo•ni•al** \ˌser-ə-ˈmō-nē-əl\ *adj* : of, relating to, or forming a ceremony; *also* : stressing careful attention to form and detail — **cer•e•mo•ni•al•ly** *adv*

²**ceremonial** *n* : a ceremonial act or system : RITUAL, FORM

cer•e•mo•ni•ous \ˌser-ə-ˈmō-nē-əs\ *adj* **1** : devoted to forms and ceremony **2** : CEREMONIAL **3** : according to formal usage or procedure **4** : marked by ceremony — **cer•e•mo•ni•ous•ly** *adv* — **cer•e•mo•ni•ous•ness** *n*

cer•e•mo•ny \'ser-ə-ˌmō-nē\ *n, pl* **-nies** **1** : a formal act or series of acts prescribed by law, ritual, or convention **2** : a conventional act of politeness **3** : a mere outward form with no deeper significance **4** : FORMALITY

ce•re•us \'sir-ē-əs\ *n* : any of various cacti of the western U.S. and tropical America

ce•rise \sə-ˈrēs\ *n* [F, lit., cherry] : a moderate red color

ce•ri•um \'sir-ē-əm\ *n* : a malleable metallic chemical element used esp. in alloys — see ELEMENT table

cer•met \'sər-ˌmet\ *n* : a strong alloy of a heat-resistant compound and a metal used esp. for turbine blades

cert *abbr* certificate; certification; certified; certify

¹**cer•tain** \'sərt-ᵊn\ *adj* **1** : FIXED, SETTLED **2** : of a specific but unspecified character ⟨∼ people in authority⟩ **3** : DEPENDABLE, RELIABLE **4** : INDISPUTABLE, UNDENIABLE **5** : assured in mind or action — **cer•tain•ly** *adv*

²**certain** *pron* : certain ones

cer•tain•ty \-tē\ *n, pl* **-ties** **1** : something that is certain **2** : the quality or state of being certain

cer•tif•i•cate \sər-ˈti-fi-kət\ *n* **1** : a document testifying to the truth of a fact **2** : a document testifying that one has fulfilled certain requirements (as of a course or school) **3** : a document giving evidence of ownership or debt ⟨∼ of deposit⟩

cer•ti•fi•ca•tion \ˌsər-tə-fə-ˈkā-shən\ *n* **1** : the act of certifying : the state of being certified **2** : a certified statement

certified mail *n* : first class mail for which proof of delivery may be secured but no indemnity value is claimed

certified milk *n* : milk produced in dairies that operate

© 1985 PAWS, INC.

under the rules and regulations of an authorized medical milk commission

certified public accountant *n* : an accountant who has met the requirements of a state law and has been granted a certificate

cer·ti·fy \'sər-tə-ˌfī\ *vb* **-fied; -fy·ing 1** : VERIFY, CONFIRM **2** : to endorse officially **3** : to guarantee (a bank check) as good by a statement to that effect stamped on its face **4** : to provide with a usu. professional certificate or license *syn* accredit, approve, sanction, endorse — **cer·ti·fi·able** \-ə-bəl\ *adj* — **cer·ti·fi·ably** \-blē\ *adv* — **cer·ti·fi·er** *n*

cer·ti·tude \'sər-tə-ˌtüd, -ˌtyüd\ *n* : the state of being or feeling certain

ce·ru·le·an \sə-'rü-lē-ən\ *adj* : AZURE

ce·ru·men \sə-'rü-mən\ *n* : EARWAX

cer·vi·cal \'sər-vi-kəl\ *adj* : of or relating to a neck or cervix

cervical cap *n* : a contraceptive device in the form of a thimble-shaped molded cap that fits over the uterine cervix and blocks sperm from entering the uterus

cer·vix \'sər-viks\ *n, pl* **cer·vi·ces** \-və-ˌsēz\ *or* **cer·vix·es 1** : NECK; *esp* : the back part of the neck **2** : a constricted portion of an organ or part; *esp* : the narrow outer end of the uterus

ce·sar·e·an *also* **ce·sar·i·an** \si-'zar-ē-ən, -'zer-\ *n* : CESAREAN SECTION — **cesarean** *also* **cesarian** *adj*

cesarean section *also* **cesarian section** *n* [fr. the belief that Julius Caesar was born this way] : surgical incision of the walls of the abdomen and uterus for delivery of offspring

ce·si·um \'sē-zē-əm\ *n* : a silver-white soft ductile chemical element — see ELEMENT table

ces·sa·tion \se-'sā-shən\ *n* : a temporary or final ceasing (as of action)

ces·sion \'se-shən\ *n* : a yielding (as of rights) to another

cess·pool \'ses-ˌpül\ *n* : an underground pit or tank for receiving household sewage

ce·ta·cean \si-'tā-shən\ *n* : any of an order of aquatic mostly marine mammals that includes whales, porpoises, dolphins, and related forms — **cetacean** *adj*

cf *abbr* [L *confer*] compare

Cf *symbol* californium

CF *abbr* cystic fibrosis

CFC *abbr* chlorofluorocarbon

cg *abbr* centigram

CG *abbr* **1** coast guard **2** commanding general

cgs *abbr* centimeter-gram-second

ch *abbr* **1** chain **2** champion **3** chapter **4** church

CH *abbr* **1** clearinghouse **2** courthouse **3** customhouse

Cha·blis \sha-'blē, shə-, shä-; 'sha-ˌblē\ *n, pl* **Chablis** \-'blēz, -(ˌ)blēz\ **1** : a dry sharp white Burgundy wine **2** : a white California wine

cha–cha \'chä-ˌchä\ *n* : a fast rhythmic ballroom dance of Latin American origin

Chad·ian \'cha-dē-ən\ *n* : a native or inhabitant of Chad — **Chadian** *adj*

chafe \'chāf\ *vb* **chafed; chaf·ing 1** : IRRITATE, VEX **2**

: FRET **3** : to warm by rubbing **4** : to rub so as to wear away; *also* : to make sore by rubbing

cha·fer \'chā-fər\ *n* : any of various scarab beetles

¹chaff \'chaf\ *n* **1** : debris (as husks) separated from grain in threshing **2** : something comparatively worthless — **chaffy** *adj*

²chaff *n* : light jesting talk : BANTER

³chaff *vb* : to tease good-naturedly

chaf·fer \'cha-fər\ *vb* : BARGAIN, HAGGLE — **chaf·fer·er** *n*

chaf·finch \'cha-ˌfinch\ *n* : a common European finch with a cheerful song

chaf·ing dish \'chā-fiŋ-\ *n* : a utensil for cooking food at the table

¹cha·grin \shə-'grin\ *n* : mental uneasiness or annoyance caused by failure, disappointment, or humiliation

²chagrin *vb* **cha·grined** \-'grind\; **cha·grin·ing** : to cause to feel chagrin

¹chain \'chān\ *n* [ME *cheyne*, fr. MF *chaeine*, fr. L *catena*] **1** : a flexible series of connected links **2** : a chainlike surveying instrument; *also* : a unit of length equal to 66 feet (about 20 meters) **3** *pl* : BONDS, FETTERS **4** : a series of things linked together *syn* train, string, sequence, succession, series

²chain *vb* : to fasten, bind, or connect with a chain; *also* : FETTER

chain gang *n* : a gang of convicts chained together

chain letter *n* : a letter sent to several persons with a request that each send copies to an equal number of persons

chain mail *n* : flexible armor of interlocking metal rings

chain reaction *n* **1** : a series of events in which each event initiates the succeeding one **2** : a chemical or nuclear reaction yielding products that cause further reactions of the same kind

chain saw *n* : a portable power saw that has teeth linked together to form an endless chain — **chain·saw** \'chān-ˌsó\ *vb*

chain–smoke \'chān-'smōk\ *vb* : to smoke esp. cigarettes continuously

chain store *n* : any of numerous stores under the same ownership that sell the same lines of goods

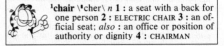

¹chair \'cher\ *n* **1** : a seat with a back for one person **2** : ELECTRIC CHAIR **3** : an official seat; *also* : an office or position of authority or dignity **4** : CHAIRMAN

²chair *vb* : to act as chairman of

chair·lift \'cher-ˌlift\ *n* : a motor-driven conveyor for skiers consisting of seats hung from a moving cable

chair·man \-mən\ *n* : the presiding officer of a meeting or of a committee — **chair·man·ship** *n*

chair·per·son \-ˌpər-sən\ *n* : CHAIRMAN

chair·wom·an \-ˌwü-mən\ *n* : a woman who acts as chairman

chaise \'shāz\ *n* : a 2-wheeled horse-drawn carriage with a folding top

chaise longue \'shāz-'lòŋ\ *n, pl* **chaise longues** *same or* -'lòŋz\ [F *chaise longue,* lit., long chair] : a long reclining chair
chaise lounge \-'laùnj\ *n* : CHAISE LONGUE
chal·ced·o·ny \kal-'sed-ᵊn-ē\ *n, pl* **-nies** : a translucent pale blue or gray quartz
chal·co·py·rite \,kal-kə-'pī-,rīt\ *n* : a yellow mineral constituting an important ore of copper
cha·let \sha-'lā\ *n* 1 : a herdsman's cabin in the Swiss mountains 2 : a building in the style of a Swiss cottage with a wide roof overhang

chalet 2

chal·ice \'cha-ləs\ *n* : a drinking cup; *esp* : the eucharistic cup
¹**chalk** \'chòk\ *n* 1 : a soft limestone 2 : chalk or chalky material esp. when used as a crayon — **chalky** *adj*
²**chalk** *vb* 1 : to rub or mark with chalk 2 : to record with or as if with chalk — usu. used with *up*
chalk·board \'chòk-,bòrd\ *n* : BLACKBOARD
chalk up *vb* 1 : ASCRIBE, CREDIT 2 : ATTAIN, ACHIEVE
¹**chal·lenge** \'cha-lənj\ *vb* **chal·lenged; chal·leng·ing** [ME *chalengen* to accuse, fr. OF *chalengier,* fr. L *calumniari* to accuse falsely, fr. *calumnia* calumny] 1 : to order to halt and prove identity 2 : to take exception to : DISPUTE 3 : to issue an invitation to compete against one esp. in single combat : DARE, DEFY — **chal·leng·er** *n*
²**challenge** *n* 1 : a summons to a duel 2 : an invitation to compete in a sport 3 : a calling into question 4 : an exception taken to a juror 5 : a sentry's command to halt and prove identity 6 : a stimulating or interesting task or problem
chal·lis \'sha-lē\ *n, pl* **chal·lises** \-lēz\ : a lightweight clothing fabric of wool, cotton, or synthetic yarns
cham·ber \'chām-bər\ *n* 1 : ROOM; *esp* : BEDROOM 2 : an enclosed space or cavity 3 : a hall for meetings of a legislative body 4 : a judge's consultation room — usu. used in pl. 5 : a legislative or judicial body; *also* : a council for a business purpose 6 : the part of a firearm that holds the cartridge or powder charge during firing — **cham·bered** \-bərd\ *adj*
cham·ber·lain \'chām-bər-lən\ *n* 1 : a chief officer in the household of a king or nobleman 2 : TREASURER
cham·ber·maid \-,mād\ *n* : a maid who takes care of bedrooms
chamber music *n* : music intended for performance by a few musicians before a small audience
chamber of commerce : an association of businesspeople for promoting commercial and industrial interests in the community
cham·bray \'sham-,brā\ *n* : a lightweight clothing fabric of white and colored threads
cha·me·leon \kə-'mēl-yən\ *n* [ME *camelion,* fr. MF, fr. L *chamaeleon,* fr. Gk *chamaileōn,* fr. *chamai* on the ground + *leōn* lion] : a small lizard whose skin changes color esp. according to its surroundings
¹**cham·fer** \'cham-fər\ *vb* 1 : to cut a furrow in (as a column) : GROOVE 2 : to make a chamfer on : BEVEL
²**chamfer** *n* : a beveled edge
cham·ois \'sha-mē\ *n, pl* **cham·ois** *same or* -mēz\ 1 : a small goatlike antelope of Europe and the Caucasus region of Russia 2 *also* **cham·my** \'sha-mē\ : a soft

leather made esp. from the skin of the sheep or goat 3 : a cotton fabric made in imitation of chamois leather
cham·o·mile \'ka-mə-,mīl, -,mēl\ *n* : any of a genus of strong-scented herbs related to the daisies and having flower heads that yield a bitter substance used esp. in tonics and teas
¹**champ** \'champ, 'chämp\ *vb* 1 : to chew noisily 2 : to show impatience of delay or restraint
²**champ** \'champ\ *n* : CHAMPION
cham·pagne \sham-'pān\ *n* : a white effervescent wine
¹**cham·pi·on** \'cham-pē-ən\ *n* 1 : a militant advocate or defender 2 : one that wins first prize or place in a contest 3 : one that is acknowledged to be better than all others
²**champion** *vb* : to protect or fight for as a champion **syn** back, advocate, uphold, support
cham·pi·on·ship \-,ship\ *n* 1 : the position or title of a champion 2 : the act of championing : DEFENSE 3 : a contest held to determine a champion
¹**chance** \'chans\ *n* 1 : something that happens without apparent cause 2 : the unpredictable element in existence : LUCK, FORTUNE 3 : OPPORTUNITY 4 : the likelihood of a particular outcome in an uncertain situation : PROBABILITY 5 : RISK 6 : a raffle ticket — **chance** *adj* — **by chance** : in the haphazard course of events
²**chance** *vb* **chanced; chanc·ing** 1 : to take place by chance : HAPPEN 2 : to come casually and unexpectedly — used with *upon* 3 : to leave to chance 4 : to accept the risk of
chan·cel \'chan-səl\ *n* : the part of a church including the altar and choir
chan·cel·lery *or* **chan·cel·lory** \'chan-sə-lə-rē\ *n, pl* **-ler·ies** *or* **-lor·ies** 1 : the position or office of a chancellor 2 : the building or room where a chancellor works 3 : the office or staff of an embassy or consulate
chan·cel·lor \'chan-sə-lər\ *n* 1 : a high state official in various countries 2 : the head of a university 3 : a judge in the equity court in various states of the U.S. 4 : the chief minister of state in some European countries — **chan·cel·lor·ship** *n*
chan·cery \'chan-sə-rē\ *n, pl* **-cer·ies** 1 : any of various courts of equity in the U.S. and Britain 2 : a record office for public or diplomatic archives 3 : a chancellor's court or office 4 : the office of an embassy
chan·cre \'shaŋ-kər\ *n* [F, fr. L *cancer*] : a primary sore or ulcer at the site of entry of an infective agent (as of syphilis)
chan·croid \'shaŋ-,kròid\ *n* : a sexually transmitted disease caused by a bacterium and characterized by chancres that differ from those of syphilis in lacking hardened margins
chancy \'chan-sē\ *adj* **chanc·i·er; -est** 1 *Scot* : AUSPICIOUS 2 : RISKY
chan·de·lier \,shan-də-'lir\ *n* : a branched lighting fixture suspended from a ceiling
chan·dler \'chand-lər\ *n* [ME *chandeler* a maker or seller of candles, fr. MF *chandelier,* fr. OF, fr. *chandelle* candle, fr. L *candela*] : a dealer in provisions and supplies of a specified kind ⟨ship's ∼⟩ — **chan·dlery** *n*
¹**change** \'chānj\ *vb* **changed; chang·ing** 1 : to make or become different : ALTER 2 : to replace with another 3 : to give or receive an equivalent sum in notes or coins of usu. smaller denominations or of another currency 4 : to put fresh clothes or covering on ⟨∼ a bed⟩ 5 : to put on different clothes 6 : EXCHANGE — **change·able** *adj* — **chang·er** *n*
²**change** *n* 1 : the act, process, or result of changing 2 : a fresh set of clothes 3 : money given in exchange for other money of higher denomination 4 : money returned when a payment exceeds the sum due 5 : coins esp. of small denominations — **change·ful** *adj*

change•ling \'chānj-liŋ\ *n* : a child secretly exchanged for another in infancy

change of life : MENOPAUSE

change•over \'chānj-ı̄ō-vər\ *n* : CONVERSION, TRANSITION

change ringing *n* : the art or practice of ringing a set of tuned bells in continually varying order

¹**chan•nel** \'chan-əl\ *n* **1** : the bed of a stream **2** : the deeper part of a waterway **3** : STRAIT **4** : a means of passage or transmission **5** : a range of frequencies of sufficient width for a single radio or television transmission **6** : a usu. tubular enclosed passage : CONDUIT **7** : a long gutter, groove, or furrow

²**channel** *vb* **-neled** *or* **-nelled; -neling** *or* **-nel•ling 1** : to make a channel in **2** : to direct into or through a channel

chan•nel•ize \'chan-əl-ı̄z\ *vb* **-ized; -iz•ing** : CHANNEL — **chan•nel•iza•tion** \ıchan-əl-ə-'zā-shən\ *n*

chan•son \shäⁿ-'sōⁿ\ *n, pl* **chan•sons** *same or* -'sōⁿz\ : SONG; *esp* : a cabaret song

¹**chant** \'chant\ *vb* **1** : SING; *esp* : to sing a chant **2** : to utter or recite in the manner of a chant **3** : to celebrate or praise in song — **chant•er** *n*

²**chant** *n* **1** : a repetitive melody in which several words are sung to one tone : SONG; *esp* : a liturgical melody **2** : a manner of singing or speaking in musical monotones

chan•teuse \shäⁿ-'tərz, shan-'tüz\ *n, pl* **chan•teuses** *same or* -'tər-zəz, -'tü-zəz\ [F] : a woman who is a concert or nightclub singer

chan•tey *or* **chan•ty** \'shan-tē, 'chan-\ *n, pl* **chanteys** *or* **chanties** : a song sung by sailors in rhythm with their work

chan•ti•cleer \ıchan-tə-'klir, ıshan-\ *n* : ROOSTER

Cha•nu•kah \'kä-nə-kə, 'hä-\ *var of* HANUKKAH

cha•os \'kā-ıäs\ *n* **1** *often cap* : the confused unorganized state existing before the creation of distinct forms **2** : the inherent unpredictability in the behavior of a natural system (as the atmosphere or the beating heart) **3** : complete disorder **syn** confusion, jumble, snarl, muddle, disarray — **cha•ot•ic** \kā-'ä-tik\ *adj* — **cha•ot•i•cal•ly** \-ti-k(ə)lē\ *adv*

¹**chap** \'chap\ *vb* **chapped; chap•ping** : to dry and crack open usu. from wind and cold (*chapped* lips)

²**chap** *n* : a jaw with its fleshy covering — usu. used in pl.

³**chap** *n* : FELLOW

⁴**chap** *abbr* chapter

chap•ar•ral \ısha-pə-'ral\ *n* **1** : a dense impenetrable thicket of shrubs or dwarf trees **2** : an ecological community esp. of southern California composed of shrubby plants

chap•book \'chap-ıbùk\ *n* : a small book of ballads, tales, or tracts

cha•peau \sha-'pō\ *n, pl* **cha•peaus** \-'pōz\ *or* **cha•peaux** \-'pō, -'pōz\ [MF] : HAT

cha•pel \'cha-pəl\ *n* [ME, fr. OF *chapele*, fr. ML *cappella*, fr. LL *cappa* cloak; fr. the cloak of St. Martin of Tours preserved as a sacred relic in a chapel built for that purpose] **1** : a private or subordinate place of worship **2** : an assembly at an educational institution usu. including devotional exercises **3** : a place of worship used by a Christian group other than an established church

¹**chap•er•on** *or* **chap•er•one** \'sha-pə-ırōn\ *n* [F *chaperon*, lit., hood, fr. MF, head covering, fr. *chape* cape, fr. LL *cappa*] **1** : a person (as a matron) who accompanies young unmarried women in public for propriety **2** : an older person who accompanies young people at a social gathering to ensure proper behavior

²**chaperon** *or* **chaperone** *vb* **-oned; -on•ing 1** : ESCORT, GUIDE **2** : to act as a chaperon to or for — **chap•er•on•age** \-ırō-nij\ *n*

chap•fall•en \'chap-ıfȯ-lən, 'chäp-\ *adj* **1** : having the lower jaw hanging loosely **2** : DEJECTED, DEPRESSED

chap•lain \'cha-plən\ *n* **1** : a member of the clergy officially attached to a special group (as the army) **2** : a person chosen to conduct religious exercises (as for a club) — **chap•lain•cy** \-sē\ *n*

chap•let \'cha-plət\ *n* **1** : a wreath for the head **2** : a string of beads : NECKLACE

chap•man \'chap-mən\ *n, Brit* : an itinerant dealer : PEDDLER

chaps \'shaps, 'chaps\ *n pl* [MexSp *chaparreras*] : leather leggings resembling trousers without a seat that are worn esp. by western ranch hands

chap•ter \'chap-tər\ *n* **1** : a main division of a book **2** : a body of canons (as of a cathedral) **3** : a local branch of a society or fraternity

¹**char** \'chär\ *n, pl* **char** *or* **chars** : any of a genus of trouts (as the common brook trout) with small scales

²**char** *vb* **charred; char•ring 1** : to burn or become burned to charcoal **2** : SCORCH

³**char** *vb* **charred; char•ring** : to work as a cleaning woman

char•ac•ter \'kar-ik-tər\ *n* [ME *caracter*, fr. MF *caractère*, fr. L *character* mark, distinctive quality, fr. Gk *charaktēr*, fr. *charassein* to scratch, engrave] **1** : a graphic symbol (as a letter) used in writing or printing **2** : a symbol that represents information; *also* : a representation of such a character that may be accepted by a computer **3** : a distinguishing feature : ATTRIBUTE **4** : the complex of mental and ethical traits marking a person or a group **5** : a person marked by conspicuous often peculiar traits **6** : one of the persons in a novel or play **7** : REPUTATION **8** : moral excellence

¹**char•ac•ter•is•tic** \ıkar-ik-tə-'ris-tik\ *n* : a distinguishing trait, quality, or property

²**characteristic** *adj* : serving to mark individual character **syn** individual, peculiar, distinctive — **char•ac•ter•is•ti•cal•ly** \-ti-k(ə)lē\ *adv*

char•ac•ter•ize \'kar-ik-tə-ırı̄z\ *vb* **-ized; -iz•ing 1** : to describe the character of **2** : to be a characteristic of — **char•ac•ter•iza•tion** \ıkar-ik-tə-rə-'zā-shən\ *n*

cha•rades \shə-'rādz\ *n sing or pl* : a game in which some of the players try to guess a word or phrase from the actions of another player who may not speak

char•coal \'chär-ıkōl\ *n* **1** : a porous carbon prepared from vegetable or animal substances **2** : a piece of fine charcoal used in drawing; *also* : a drawing made with charcoal

chard \'chärd\ *n* : SWISS CHARD

char•don•nay \ıshard-ən-'ā\ *n, often cap* [F] : a dry white wine made from a single variety of white grape

¹**charge** \'chärj\ *n* **1** : a quantity (as of fuel or ammunition) required to fill something to capacity **2** : a store or accumulation of force **3** : an excess or deficiency of electrons in a body **4** : THRILL, KICK **5** : a task or duty imposed **6** : CARE, RESPONSIBILITY **7** : one given into another's care **8** : instructions from a judge to a jury **9** : COST, EXPENSE, PRICE; *also* : a debit to an account **10** : ACCUSATION, INDICTMENT **11** : ATTACK, ASSAULT

²**charge** *vb* **charged; charg•ing 1** : to load or fill to capacity **2** : to give an electric charge to; *also* : to restore the activity of (a storage battery) by means of an electric current **3** : to impose a task or responsibility on **4** : COMMAND, ORDER **5** : ACCUSE **6** : to rush against : rush forward in assault **7** : to make liable for payment; *also* : to record a debt or liability against **8** : to fix as a price — **charge•able** *adj*

charge–coupled device *n* : a semiconductor device used esp. as an optical sensor

char•gé d'af•faires \shär-ızhä-də-'far\ *n, pl* **chargés d'affaires** \-ızhä-, -ızhäz-\ [F] : a diplomat who substitutes for an ambassador or minister

¹**charg•er** \'chär-jər\ *n* : a large platter

²**charg•er** *n* **1** : a device or a workman that charges something **2** : WARHORSE

char•i•ot \'char-ē-ət\ *n* : a 2-wheeled horse-drawn vehicle of ancient times used esp. in war and in races — **char·i·o·teer** \ˌchar-ē-ə-ˈtir\ *n*

cha·ris·ma \kə-ˈriz-mə\ *n* : a personal quality of leadership arousing popular loyalty or enthusiasm — **char·is·mat·ic** \ˌkar-əz-ˈma-tik\ *adj*

char·i·ta·ble \ˈchar-ə-tə-bəl\ *adj* **1** : liberal in giving to needy people **2** : merciful or lenient in judging others **syn** benevolent, philanthropic, altruistic, humanitarian — **char·i·ta·ble·ness** *n* — **char·i·ta·bly** \-blē\ *adv*

char·i·ty \ˈchar-ə-tē\ *n, pl* **-ties 1** : goodwill toward or love of humanity **2** : an act or feeling of generosity **3** : the giving of aid to the poor; *also* : an institution engaged in relief of the poor **5** : leniency in judging others **syn** mercy, clemency, lenity

char·la·tan \ˈshär-lə-tən\ *n* : a person making usu. showy pretenses to knowledge or ability : FRAUD, FAKER

Charles·ton \ˈchärl-stən\ *n* : a lively dance in which the knees are swung in and out and the heels are turned sharply outward on each step

char·ley horse \ˈchär-lē-ˌhȯrs\ *n* : a muscular pain, cramping, or stiffness from a strain or bruise

¹charm \ˈchärm\ *n* [ME *charme*, fr. MF, fr. L *carmen* song, fr. *canere* to sing] **1** : a practice or expression believed to have magic power **2** : something worn about the person to ward off evil or bring good fortune : AMULET **3** : a trait that fascinates or allures **4** : physical grace or attraction **5** : a small ornament worn on a bracelet or chain

²charm *vb* **1** : to affect by or as if by a magic spell **2** : to protect by or as if by charms **3** : FASCINATE, ENCHANT **syn** allure, captivate, bewitch, attract — **charm·er** *n*

charm·ing \ˈchär-miŋ\ *adj* : PLEASING, DELIGHTFUL — **charm·ing·ly** *adv*

char·nel house \ˈchärn-ᵊl-\ *n* : a building or chamber in which bodies or bones are deposited

¹chart \ˈchärt\ *n* **1** : MAP **2** : a sheet giving information in the form of a table, list, or diagram; *also* : GRAPH

²chart *vb* **1** : to make a chart of **2** : PLAN

¹char·ter \ˈchär-tər\ *n* **1** : an official document granting rights or privileges (as to a colony, town, or college) from a sovereign or a governing body **2** : CONSTITUTION **3** : a written instrument from a society creating a branch **4** : a mercantile lease of a ship

²charter *vb* **1** : to grant a charter to **2** *Brit* : CERTIFY ⟨~ed engineer⟩ **3** : to hire, rent, or lease for temporaly use — **char·ter·er** *n*

charter member *n* : an original member of an organization

char·treuse \shär-ˈtrüz, -ˈtrüs\ *n* : a brilliant yellow green

char·wom·an \ˈchär-ˌwu̇-mən\ *n* : a cleaning woman esp. in large buildings

chary \ˈchar-ē\ *adj* **chari·er; -est** [ME, sorrowful, dear, fr. OE *cearig* sorrowful, fr. *caru* sorrow] **1**

: CAUTIOUS, CIRCUMSPECT **2** : SPARING — **char·i·ly** \-ə-lē\ *adv*

¹chase \ˈchās\ *n* **1** : PURSUIT; *also* : HUNTING **2** : QUARRY **3** : a tract of unenclosed land used as a game preserve

²chase *vb* **chased; chas·ing 1** : to follow rapidly : PURSUE **2** : HUNT **3** : to seek out ⟨*chasing* down clues⟩ **4** : to cause to depart or flee : drive away **5** : RUSH, HASTEN

³chase *vb* **chased; chas·ing** : to decorate (a metal surface) by embossing or engraving

⁴chase *n* : FURROW, GROOVE

chas·er \ˈchā-sər\ *n* **1** : one that chases **2** : a mild drink (as beer) taken after hard liquor

chasm \ˈka-zəm\ *n* : GORGE **2**

chas·sis \ˈcha-sē, ˈsha-sē\ *n, pl* **chas·sis** \-sēz\ : the supporting frame of a structure (as an automobile or television set)

chaste \ˈchāst\ *adj* **chast·er; chast·est 1** : innocent of unlawful sexual intercourse : VIRTUOUS, PURE **2** : CELIBATE **3** : pure in thought : MODEST **4** : severe or simple in design — **chaste·ly** *adv* — **chaste·ness** *n*

chas·ten \ˈchās-ᵊn\ *vb* : to correct through punishment or suffering : DISCIPLINE; *also* : PURIFY — **chas·ten·er** *n*

chas·tise \chas-ˈtīz\ *vb* **chas·tised; chas·tis·ing** [ME *chastisen*, alter. of *chasten*] **1** : to punish esp. bodily **2** : to censure severely : CASTIGATE — **chas·tise·ment** \-mənt, ˈchas-təz-\ *n*

chas·ti·ty \ˈchas-tə-tē\ *n* : the quality or state of being chaste; *esp* : sexual purity

cha·su·ble \ˈcha-zə-bəl, -sə-\ *n* : the outer vestment of the priest at mass

chat \ˈchat\ *n* : light familiar informal talk — **chat** *vb*

châ·teau \sha-ˈtō\ *n, pl* **châ·teaus** \-ˈtōz\ *or* **châ·teaux** \-ˈtō, -ˈtōz\ [F, fr. L *castellum* castle, dim. of *castra* camp] **1** : a feudal castle in France **2** : a large country house **3** : a French vineyard estate

chat·e·laine \ˈshat-ᵊl-ˌān\ *n* **1** : the mistress of a chateau **2** : a clasp or hook for a watch, purse, or keys

chat·tel \ˈchat-ᵊl\ *n* **1** : an item of tangible property other than real estate **2** : SLAVE, BONDMAN

chat·ter \ˈcha-tər\ *vb* **1** : to utter speechlike but meaningless sounds **2** : to talk idly, incessantly, or fast **3** : to click repeatedly or uncontrollably — **chatter** *n* — **chat·ter·er** *n*

chat·ter·box \ˈcha-tər-ˌbäks\ *n* : one who talks incessantly

chat·ty \ˈcha-tē\ *adj* **chat·ti·er; -est** : TALKATIVE — **chat·ti·ly** \-tə-lē\ *adv* — **chat·ti·ness** \-tē-nəs\ *n*

¹chauf·feur \ˈshō-fər, shō-ˈfər\ *n* [F, lit., stoker, fr. *chauffer* to heat] : a person employed to drive an automobile

²chauffeur *vb* **chauf·feured; chauf·feur·ing 1** : to do the work of a chauffeur **2** : to transport in the manner of a chauffeur

chaunt \ˈchȯnt, ˈchänt\ *var of* CHANT

chau·vin·ism \ˈshō-və-ˌni-zəm\ *n* [F *chauvinisme*, fr. Nicolas *Chauvin*, fictional soldier of excessive patriotism and devotion to Napoleon] **1** : excessive or blind patriotism **2** : an attitude of superiority toward

members of the opposite sex — **chau·vin·ist** \-nist\ *n or adj* — **chau·vin·is·tic** \₁shō-və-ˈnis-tik\ *adj* — **chau·vin·is·ti·cal·ly** \-ti-k(ə-)lē\ *adv*

cheap \ˈchēp\ *adj* **1** : INEXPENSIVE **2** : costing little effort to obtain **3** : worth little : SHODDY, TAWDRY **4** : worthy of scorn **5** : STINGY — **cheap** *adv* — **cheap·ly** *adv* — **cheap·ness** *n*

cheap·en \ˈchē-pən\ *vb* **1** : to make or become cheap or cheaper in price or value **2** : to make tawdry

cheap·skate \ˈchēp-₁skāt\ *n* : a miserly or stingy person; *esp* : one who tries to avoid paying a fair share of costs

¹cheat \ˈchēt\ *vb* **1** : to deprive of something through fraud or deceit **2** : to practice fraud or trickery **3** : to violate rules (as of a game) dishonestly — **cheat·er** *n*

²cheat *n* **1** : the act of deceiving : FRAUD, DECEPTION **2** : one that cheats : a dishonest person

¹check \ˈchek\ *n* **1** : a sudden stoppage of progress **2** : a sudden pause or break **3** : something that stops or restrains **4** : a standard for testing or evaluation **5** : EXAMINATION, INVESTIGATION **6** : the act of testing or verifying **7** : a written order to a bank to pay money **8** : a ticket or token showing ownership or identity **9** : a slip indicating an amount due **10** : a pattern in squares; *also* : a fabric in such a pattern **11** : a mark typically ✔ placed beside an item to show that it has been noted **12** : CRACK, SPLIT

²check *vb* **1** : to slow down or stop : BRAKE **2** : to restrain the action or force of : CURB **3** : to compare with a source, original, or authority : VERIFY **4** : to inspect or test for satisfactory condition **5** : to mark with a check as examined **6** : to consign for shipment for one holding a passenger ticket **7** : to mark into squares **8** : to leave or accept for safekeeping in a checkroom **9** : to prove to be consistent or truthful **10** : CRACK, SPLIT

check·book \ˈchek-₁buk\ *n* : a book containing blank checks

¹check·er \ˈche-kər\ *n* : a piece in the game of checkers

²checker *vb* **1** : to variegate with different colors or shades **2** : to vary with contrasting elements (a ~ed career) **3** : to mark into squares

³checker *n* : one that checks; *esp* : one who checks out purchases in a supermarket

check·er·ber·ry \ˈche-kər-₁ber-ē\ *n* : WINTERGREEN 1; *also* : the spicy red fruit of this plant

check·er·board \-₁bȯrd\ *n* : a board of 64 squares of alternate colors used in various games

check·ers \ˈche-kərz\ *n* : a game for two played on a checkerboard with each player having 12 pieces

check in *vb* : to report one's presence or arrival (as at a hotel)

check·list \ˈchek-₁list\ *n* : a list of things to be checked or done; *also* : a comprehensive list

check·mate \ˈchek-₁māt\ *vb* [ME *chekmaten*, fr. *chekmate*, interj. used to announce checkmate, fr. MF *eschec mat*, fr. Ar *shāh māt*, fr. Per, lit., the king is left unable to escape] **1** : to thwart completely : DEFEAT,

FRUSTRATE **2** : to attack (an opponent's king) in chess so that escape is impossible — **checkmate** *n*

check-off \ˈche-₁kȯf\ *n* : the deduction of union dues from a worker's paycheck by the employer

check·out \ˈche-₁kaut\ *n* **1** : the action or an instance of checking out **2** : a counter at which checking out is done **3** : the process of examining and testing something as to readiness for intended use

check out *vb* **1** : to settle one's account (as at a hotel) and leave **2** : to total or have totaled the cost of purchases in a store and to make or receive payment for them

check·point \ˈchek-₁pȯint\ *n* : a point at which a check is performed

check·room \-₁rüm, -₁rum\ *n* : a room at which baggage, parcels, or clothing is checked

check·up \ˈche-₁kəp\ *n* : EXAMINATION; *esp* : a general physical examination

ched·dar \ˈche-dər\ *n, often cap* : a hard mild to sharp white or yellow cheese of smooth texture

cheek \ˈchēk\ *n* **1** : the fleshy side part of the face **2** : IMPUDENCE, BOLDNESS, AUDACITY **3** : BUTTOCK 1 — **cheeked** \ˈchēkt\ *adj*

cheek·bone \ˈchēk-₁bōn\ *n* : the bone or bony ridge below the eye

cheeky \ˈchē-kē\ *adj* **cheek·i·er; -est** : IMPUDENT, SAUCY — **cheek·i·ly** \-kə-lē\ *adv* — **cheek·i·ness** \-kē-nəs\ *n*

cheep \ˈchēp\ *vb* : to utter faint shrill sounds : PEEP — **cheep** *n*

¹cheer \ˈchir\ *n* [ME *chere* face, cheer, fr. OF, face, fr. ML *cara*, prob. fr. GK *kara* head, face] **1** : state of mind or heart : SPIRIT **2** : ANIMATION, GAIETY **3** : hospitable entertainment : WELCOME **4** : food and drink for a feast **5** : something that gladdens **6** : a shout of applause or encouragement

²cheer *vb* **1** : to give hope or courage to : COMFORT **2** : to make glad **3** : to urge on esp. by shouts **4** : to applaud with shouts **5** : to grow or be cheerful — usu. used with *up* — **cheer·er** *n*

cheer·ful \ˈchir-fəl\ *adj* : having or showing good spirits **2** : conducive to good spirits : pleasant and bright — **cheer·ful·ly** *adv* — **cheer·ful·ness** *n*

cheer·lead·er \ˈchir-₁lē-dər\ *n* : a person who directs organized cheering esp. at a sports event

cheer·less \ˈchir-ləs\ *adj* : BLEAK, DISPIRITING — **cheer·less·ly** *adv* — **cheer·less·ness** *n*

cheery \ˈchir-ē\ *adj* **cheer·i·er; -est** : CHEERFUL — **cheer·i·ly** \-ə-lē\ *adv* — **cheer·i·ness** \-ē-nəs\ *n*

cheese \ˈchēz\ *n* : the curd of milk usu. pressed into cakes and cured for use as food

cheese·burg·er \-₁bər-gər\ *n* : a hamburger topped with cheese

cheese·cake \-₁kāk\ *n* **1** : a dessert consisting of a creamy filling usu. containing cheese baked in a shell **2** : photographs of shapely scantily clad women

cheese·cloth \-ˌklȯth\ *n* : a lightweight coarse cotton gauze

cheese·par·ing \-ˌpar-iŋ\ *n* : miserly economizing — **cheeseparing** *adj*

cheesy \'chē-zē\ *adj* **chees·i·er; -est 1** : resembling, suggesting, or containing cheese **2** *slang* : CHEAP **3**

chee·tah \'chē-tə\ *n* [Hindu *cītā* leopard, fr. Skt *citra-ka*, fr. *citra* bright, variegated] : a large long-legged spotted swift-moving African and formerly Asian cat

cheetah

chef \'shef\ *n* **1** : a cook who manages the kitchen (as of a restaurant) **2** : COOK

chef d'oeu·vre \shā-'dœvrᵊ\ *n, pl* **chefs d'oeuvre** *same* \ : MASTERPIECE

chem *abbr* chemical; chemist; chemistry

¹**chem·i·cal** \'ke-mi-kəl\ *adj* **1** : of, relating to, used in, or produced by chemistry **2** : acting or operated or produced by chemicals — **chem·i·cal·ly** \-k(ə-)lē\ *adv*

²**chemical** *n* : a substance obtained by a chemical process or used for producing a chemical effect

chemical engineering *n* : engineering dealing with the industrial application of chemistry

chemical warfare *n* : warfare using incendiary mixtures, smokes, or irritant, burning, or asphyxiating gases

chemical weapon *n* : a weapon used in chemical warfare

che·mise \shə-'mēz\ *n* **1** : a woman's one-piece undergarment **2** : a loose straight-hanging dress

chem·ist \'ke-mist\ *n* **1** : one trained in chemistry **2** *Brit* : PHARMACIST

chem·is·try \'ke-mə-strē\ *n, pl* **-tries 1** : the science that deals with the composition, structure, and properties of substances and of the changes they undergo **2** : chemical composition or properties ⟨the ∼ of gasoline⟩ **3** : a strong mutual attraction

che·mo·ther·a·py \ˌkē-mō-'ther-ə-pē\ *n* : the use of chemicals in the treatment or control of disease — **che·mo·ther·a·peu·tic** \-ˌther-ə-'pyü-tik\ *adj*

che·nille \shə-'nēl\ *n* [F, lit., caterpillar, fr. L *canicula*, dim. of *canis* dog] : a fabric with a deep fuzzy pile often used for bedspreads and rugs

cheque \'chek\ *chiefly Brit var of* ¹CHECK 7

che·quer *chiefly Brit var of* CHECKER

cher·ish \'cher-ish\ *vb* **1** : to hold dear : treat with care and affection **2** : to keep deeply in mind — **cher·ish·able** *adj* — **cher·ish·er** *n*

Cher·o·kee \'cher-ə-(ˌ)kē\ *n, pl* **Cherokee** *or* **Cherokees** : a member of an American Indian people orig. of Tennessee and No. Carolina; *also* : their language

che·root \shə-'rüt\ *n* : a cigar cut square at both ends

cher·ry \'cher-ē\ *n, pl* **cherries** [ME *chery*, fr. OF *cherise* (taken as a plural), fr. LL *ceresia*, fr. L *cerasus* cherry tree, fr. Gk *kerasos*] **1** : the small fleshy pale yellow to deep blackish red fruit of a tree related to the roses; *also* : the tree or its wood **2** : a moderate red

chert \'chərt, 'chat\ *n* : a rock resembling flint and consisting essentially of fine crystalline quartz and fibrous chalcedony — **cherty** *adj*

cher·ub \'cher-əb\ *n* **1** *pl* **cher·u·bim** \'cher-ə-ˌbim\ : an angel of the 2d highest rank **2** *pl* **cherubs** : a chubby rosy person — **che·ru·bic** \chə-'rü-bik\ *adj*

chess \'ches\ *n* : a game for two played on a chessboard with each player having 16 pieces — **chess·man** \-ˌman, -mən\ *n*

chess·board \'ches-ˌbȯrd\ *n* : a checkerboard used in the game of chess

chest \'chest\ *n* **1** : a box, case, or boxlike receptacle for storage or shipping **2** : the part of the body enclosed by the ribs and sternum — **chest·ed** \'ches-təd\ *adj* — **chest·ful** \'chest-ˌfùl\ *n*

ches·ter·field \'ches-tər-ˌfēld\ *n* : an overcoat with a velvet collar

chest·nut \'ches-(ˌ)nət\ *n* **1** : the edible nut of any of a genus of trees related to the beech and oaks; *also* : this tree **2** : a grayish to reddish brown **3** : an old joke or story

chet·rum \'che-trəm\ *n, pl* **chetrums** *or* **chetrum** — see *ngultrum* at MONEY table

che·val glass \shə-'val-\ *n* : a full-length mirror that may be tilted in a frame

che·va·lier \ˌshe-və-'lir, shə-'val-ˌyā\ *n* : a member of one of various orders of knighthood or of merit

chev·iot \'she-vē-ət\ *n, often cap* **1** : a twilled fabric with a rough nap **2** : a sturdy soft-finished cotton fabric

chev·ron \'she-vrən\ *n* : a sleeve badge of one or more V-shaped or inverted V-shaped stripes worn to indicate rank or service (as in the armed forces)

¹**chew** \'chü\ *vb* : to crush or grind with the teeth — **chew·able** *adj* — **chew·er** *n*

²**chew** *n* **1** : an act of chewing **2** : something for chewing

chewy \'chü-ē\ *adj* : requiring much chewing ⟨∼ candy⟩

Chey·enne \shī-'an, -'en\ *n, pl* **Cheyenne** *or* **Cheyennes** [CanF, fr. Dakota *šahíyena*] : a member of an American Indian people of the western plains of the U.S.; *also* : their language

chg *abbr* **1** change **2** charge

chi \'kī\ *n* : the 22d letter of the Greek alphabet — Χ or χ

Chi·an·ti \kē-'än-tē, -'an-\ *n* : a dry usu. red wine

chiar·oscu·ro \kē-ˌär-ə-'skùr-ō, -'skyùr-\ *n, pl* **-ros** [It, fr. *chiaro* clear, light + *oscuro* obscure, dark] **1** : pictorial representation in terms of light and shade without regard to color **2** : the arrangement or treatment of light and dark parts in a pictorial work of art

¹**chic** \'shēk\ *n* : STYLISHNESS

²**chic** *adj* : cleverly stylish : SMART; *also* : currently fashionable

Chi·ca·na \chi-'kä-nə *also* shi-\ *n* : an American woman or girl of Mexican descent — **Chicana** *adj*

chi·cane \shi-'kān\ *n* : CHICANERY

chi·ca·nery \-'kā-nə-rē\ *n, pl* **-ner·ies** : TRICKERY, DECEPTION

Chi·ca·no \chi-'kä-nō\ *n, pl* **-nos** : an American of Mexican descent — **Chicano** *adj*

chi·chi \'shē-(ˌ)shē, 'chē-(ˌ)chē\ *adj* [F] **1** : SHOWY, FRILLY **2** : ARTY, PRECIOUS **3** : CHIC — **chichi** *n*

chick \'chik\ *n* **1** : a young chicken; *also* : a young bird **2** *slang* : a young woman

chick·a·dee \'chi-kə-(ˌ)dē\ *n* : any of several small grayish American birds with black or brown caps

Chick·a·saw \'chi-kə-ˌsȯ\ *n, pl* **Chickasaw** *or* **Chickasaws** : a member of an American Indian people of Mississippi and Alabama

¹**chick·en** \'chi-kən\ *n* **1** : a common domestic fowl esp. when young; *also* : its flesh used as food **2** : COWARD

²**chicken** *adj* **1** : COWARDLY **2** *slang* : insistent on petty esp. military discipline

chicken feed *n, slang* : an insignificant sum of money

chick·en·heart·ed \ˌchi-kən-'här-təd\ *adj* : TIMID, COWARDLY

chicken out *vb* : to lose one's courage

chicken pox *n* : an acute contagious virus disease esp. of children characterized by a low fever and vesicles

chicken wire *n* : a light wire netting of hexagonal mesh

chick–pea \'chik-ˌpē\ *n* : an Asian leguminous herb cultivated for its short pods with one or two edible seeds; *also* : its seed

chick·weed \'chik-ˌwēd\ *n* : any of several low-

growing small-leaved weeds related to the pinks

chi•cle \\'chi-kəl\\ *n* : a gum from the latex of a tropical tree used as the chief ingredient of chewing gum

chic•o•ry \\'chi-kə-rē\\ *n, pl* **-ries** : a usu. blue‑flowered herb related to the daisies and grown for its root and for use in salads; *also* : its dried ground root used to flavor or adulterate coffee

chide \\'chīd\\ *vb* **chid** \\'chid\\ *or* **chid•ed** \\'chī-dəd\\; **chid** *or* **chid•den** \\'chid-ᵊn\\ *or* **chided; chid•ing** : to speak disapprovingly to **syn** reproach, reprove, reprimand, admonish, scold, rebuke

¹chief \\'chēf\\ *adj* **1** : highest in rank **2** : most important **syn** principal, main, leading, major — **chief•ly** *adv*

²chief *n* **1** : the leader of a body or organization : HEAD **2** : the principal or most valuable part — **chief•dom** *n*

chief master sergeant *n* : a noncommissioned officer of the highest rank in the air force

chief of staff 1 : the ranking officer of a staff in the armed forces **2** : the ranking office of the army or air force

chief of state : the formal head of a national state as distinguished from the head of the government

chief petty officer *n* : an enlisted man in the navy ranking next below a senior chief petty officer

chief•tain \\'chēf-tən\\ *n* : a chief esp. of a band, tribe, or clan — **chief•tain•cy** \\-sē\\ *n* — **chief•tain•ship** *n*

chief warrant officer *n* : a warrant officer of senior rank

chif•fon \\shi-'fän, 'shi-ₐ\\ *n* [F, lit., rag, fr. *chiffe* old rag] : a sheer fabric esp. of silk

chif•fo•nier \\ₐshi-fə-'nir\\ *n* : a high narrow chest of drawers

chig•ger \\'chi-gər\\ *n* : a bloodsucking larval mite that causes intense itching

chi•gnon \\'shēn-ₐyän\\ *n* [F, fr. MF *chignon* chain, collar, nape] : a knot of hair worn at the back of the head

Chi•hua•hua \\chə-'wä-ₐwä\\ *n* : any of a breed of very small large-eared dogs that originated in Mexico

chil•blain \\'chil-ₐblān\\ *n* : a sore or inflamed swelling (as on the feet or hands) caused by exposure to cold

child \\'chīld\\ *n, pl* **chil•dren** \\'chil-drən\\ **1** : an unborn or recently born person **2** : a young person between the periods of infancy and youth **3** : a male or female offspring : SON, DAUGHTER **4** : one strongly influenced by another or by a place or state of affairs — **child•ish** *adj* — **child•ish•ly** *adv* — **child•ish•ness** *n* — **child•less** *adj* — **child•less•ness** *n* — **child•like** *adj*

child•bear•ing \\'chīld-ₐbar-iŋ\\ *n* : CHILDBIRTH — **childbearing** *adj*

child•birth \\-ₐbərth\\ *n* : the act or process of giving birth to offspring

child•hood \\-ₐhůd\\ *n* : the state or time of being a child

child•proof \\-ₐprüf\\ *adj* : made to prevent tampering or opening by children

child's play *n* : a simple task or act

Chil•ean \\'chi-lē-ən, chə-'lā-ən\\ *n* : a native or inhabitant of Chile — **Chilean** *adj*

chili *or* **chile** *or* **chil•li** \\'chi-lē\\ *n, pl* **chil•ies** *or* **chil‑**

es *or* **chil•ies 1** : a pungent pepper related to the tomato **2** : a thick sauce of meat and chilies **3** : CHILI CON CARNE

chili con car•ne \\ₐchi-lē-kän-'kär-nē\\ *n* [Sp *chile con carne* chili with meat] : a spiced stew of ground beef and chilies or chili powder usu. with beans

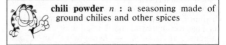

chili powder *n* : a seasoning made of ground chilies and other spices

chili sauce *n* : a spiced tomato sauce usu. made with red and green peppers

¹chill \\'chil\\ *n* **1** : a feeling of coldness accompanied by shivering **2** : moderate coldness **3** : a check to enthusiasm or warmth of feeling

²chill *adj* **1** : moderately cold **2** : COLD, RAW **3** : DISTANT, FORMAL ⟨a ∼ reception⟩ **4** : DEPRESSING, DISPIRITING

³chill *vb* **1** : to make or become cold or chilly **2** : to make cool esp. without freezing — **chill•er** *n*

chilly \\'chi-lē\\ *adj* **chill•i•er; -est 1** : noticeably cold **2** : unpleasantly affected by cold **3** : lacking warmth of feeling — **chill•i•ness** *n*

¹chime \\'chīm\\ *n* **1** : a set of bells musically tuned **2** : the sound of a set of bells — usu. used in pl. **3** : a musical sound suggesting bells

²chime *vb* **chimed; chim•ing 1** : to make bell‑like sounds **2** : to indicate (as the time of day) by chiming **3** : to be or act in accord : be in harmony

chime in *vb* : to break into or join in a conversation

chi•me•ra *or* **chi•mae•ra** \\kī-'mir-ə, kə-\\ *n* [L *chimaera*, fr. Gk *chimaira* she-goat, chimera] **1** : an imaginary monster made up of incongruous parts **2** : an illusion or fabrication of the mind; *esp* : an impossible dream

chi•me•ri•cal \\ki-'mer-i-kəl\\ *also* **chi•me•ric** \\-ik\\ *adj* **1** : FANTASTIC, IMAGINARY **2** : inclined to fantastic schemes

chim•ney \\'chim-nē\\ *n, pl* **chimneys 1** : a vertical structure extending above the roof of a building for carrying off smoke **2** : a glass tube around a lamp flame

chimp \\'chimp\\ *n* : CHIMPANZEE

chim•pan•zee \\ₐchim-ₐpan-'zē, chim-'pan-zē\\ *n* : an African ape related to the much larger gorilla

¹chin \\'chin\\ *n* : the part of the face below the lower lip including the prominence of the lower jaw — **chin•less** *adj*

²chin *vb* **chinned; chin•ning** : to raise (oneself) while hanging by the hands until the chin is level with the support

chi•na \\'chī-nə\\ *n* : porcelain ware; *also* : domestic pottery in general

Chi•na•town \\-ₐtaůn\\ *n* : the Chinese quarter of a city

chinch bug \\'chinch-\\ *n* : a small black and white bug destructive to cereal grasses

chin·chil·la \chin-'chi-lə\ *n* **1** : either of two small So. American rodents with soft pearl-gray fur; *also* : this fur **2** : a heavy long-napped woolen cloth

chinchilla 1

chine \'chīn\ *n* : BACKBONE, SPINE; *also* : a cut of meat including all or part of the backbone
Chi·nese \chī-'nēz, -'nēs\ *n, pl* **Chinese 1** : a native or inhabitant of China **2** : any of a group of related languages of China — **Chinese** *adj*
Chinese cabbage *n* **1** : BOK CHOY **2** : an Asian garden plant related to the cabbage and widely grown in the U.S. for its tight elongate cylindrical heads of pale green to cream-colored leaves
Chinese checkers *n* : a game in which each player in turn transfers a set of marbles from a home point to the opposite point of a pitted 6-pointed star
Chinese gooseberry *n* : a subtropical vine that bears kiwifruit; *also* : KIWIFRUIT
Chinese lantern *n* : a collapsible translucent cover for a light
¹chink \'chiŋk\ *n* : a small crack or fissure
²chink *vb* : to fill the chinks of : stop up
³chink *n* : a slight sharp metallic sound
⁴chink *vb* : to make a slight sharp metallic sound
chi·no \'chē-nō\ *n, pl* **chinos 1** : a usu. khaki cotton twill **2** *pl* : an article of clothing made of chino
Chi·nook \shə-'núk, chə-, -'nük\ *n, pl* **Chinook** *or* **Chinooks** : a member of an American Indian people of Oregon
chintz \'chints\ *n* : a usu. glazed printed cotton cloth
chintzy \'chint-sē\ *adj* **chintz·i·er; -est 1** : decorated with or as if with chintz **2** : GAUDY, CHEAP **3** : STINGY
chin–up \'chi-nəp\ *n* : the act of chinning oneself
¹chip \'chip\ *n* **1** : a small usu. thin and flat piece (as of wood) cut or broken off **2** : a thin crisp morsel of food **3** : a counter used in games (as poker) **4** *pl, slang* : MONEY **5** : a flaw left after a chip is removed **6** : INTEGRATED CIRCUIT **7** : a very small slice of silicon containing electronic circuits
²chip *vb* **chipped; chip·ping 1** : to cut or break chips from **2** : to break off in small pieces at the edges **3** : to play a chip shot
chip in *vb* : CONTRIBUTE
chip·munk \'chip-məŋk\ *n* : any of a genus of small striped No. American and Asian rodents closely related to the squirrels and marmots
chipped beef \'chipt-\ *n* : smoked dried beef sliced thin
¹chip·per \'chi-pər\ *n* : one that chips

²chipper *adj* : LIVELY, CHEERFUL
Chip·pe·wa \'chi-pə-ˌwȯ, -ˌwä, -ˌwā, -wə\ *n, pl* **Chippewa** *or* **Chippewas** : OJIBWA
chip shot *n* : a short usu. low shot to the green in golf
chi·rog·ra·phy \kī-'rä-grə-fē\ *n* : HANDWRITING, PENMANSHIP — **chi·ro·graph·ic** \ˌkī-rə-'gra-fik\ *adj*
chi·rop·o·dy \kə-'rä-pə-dē, shə-\ *n* : PODIATRY — **chi·rop·o·dist** \-dist\ *n*
chi·ro·prac·tic \'kī-rə-ˌprak-tik\ *n* : a system of therapy based esp. on manipulation of body structures — **chi·ro·prac·tor** \-tər\ *n*
chirp \'chərp\ *n* : a short sharp sound characteristic of a small bird or cricket — **chirp** *vb*

¹chis·el \'chi-zəl\ *n* : a metal tool with a sharpened edge at one end used to chip, carve, or cut into a solid material (as wood or stone)

²chisel *vb* **-eled** *or* **-elled; -el·ing** *or* **-el·ling 1** : to work with or as if with a chisel **2** : to obtain by shrewd often unfair methods; *also* : CHEAT — **chis·el·er** *n*
¹chit \'chit\ *n* [ME *chitte* kitten, cub] **1** : CHILD **2** : a pert young woman
²chit *n* [Hindi *ciṭṭhī* letter, note] : a signed voucher for a small debt
chit·chat \'chit-ˌchat\ *n* : casual or trifling conversation — **chitchat** *vb*
chi·tin \'kīt-ᵊn\ *n* : a sugar polymer that forms part of the hard outer integument esp. of insects — **chi·tin·ous** *adj*
chit·ter·lings *or* **chit·lins** \'chit-lənz\ *n pl* : the intestines of hogs esp. when prepared as food
chi·val·ric \shə-'val-rik\ *adj* : relating to chivalry : CHIVALROUS
chiv·al·rous \'shi-vəl-rəs\ *adj* **1** : of or relating to chivalry **2** : marked by honor, courtesy, and generosity **3** : marked by especial courtesy to women — **chiv·al·rous·ly** *adv* — **chiv·al·rous·ness** *n*
chiv·al·ry \'shi-vəl-rē\ *n, pl* **-ries 1** : mounted men-at-arms **2** : the system or practices of knighthood **3** : the spirit or character of the ideal knight
chive \'chīv\ *n* : an herb related to the onion that has leaves used for flavoring
chla·myd·ia \klə-'mi-dē-ə\ *n, pl* **-i·ae** \-dē-ˌē\ **1** : any of a genus of bacteria that cause various diseases of the eye and urogenital tract **2** : a disease or infection caused by chlamydiae
chlo·ral hydrate \'klōr-əl-\ *n* : a white crystalline compound used as a hypnotic and sedative
chlor·dane \'klōr-ˌdān\ *n* : a highly chlorinated persistent insecticide
chlo·ride \'klōr-ˌīd\ *n* : a compound of chlorine with another element or group
chlo·ri·nate \'klōr-ə-ˌnāt\ *vb* **-nat·ed; -nat·ing** : to treat or combine with chlorine or a chlorine compound — **chlo·ri·na·tion** \ˌklōr-ə-'nā-shən\ *n* — **chlo·ri·na·tor** \'klōr-ə-ˌnā-tər\ *n*
chlo·rine \'klōr-ˌēn\ *n* : a nonmetallic chemical element that is found alone as a strong-smelling greenish

yellow irritating gas and is used as a bleach, oxidizing agent, and disinfectant — see ELEMENT table

chlo·rite \\'klōr-ˌīt\ n : a usu. green mineral found with and resembling mica

chlo·ro·flu·o·ro·car·bon \ˌklōr-ə-ˈflōr-ə-ˌkär-bən, -ˈflur-\ n : any of several gaseous compounds that contain carbon, chlorine, fluorine, and sometimes hydrogen and are used esp. as solvents, refrigerants, and aerosol propellants

¹chlo·ro·form \\'klōr-ə-ˌfōrm\ n : a colorless heavy fluid with etherlike odor used as a solvent and anesthetic

²chloroform vb : to treat with chloroform to produce anesthesia or death

chlo·ro·phyll \-ˌfil\ n : the green coloring matter of plants that functions in photosynthesis

chm abbr chairman

chock \\'chäk\ n : a wedge for steadying something or for blocking the movement of a wheel — **chock** vb

chock·a·block \\'chä-kə-ˌbläk\ adj : very full : CROWDED

chock–full \\'chək-ˈful, 'chäk-\ adj : full to the limit : CRAMMED

choc·o·late \\'chä-k(ə-)lət, 'chò-\ n [Sp, fr. Nahuatl chocolātl] 1 : a food prepared from ground roasted cacao beans; also : a drink prepared from this 2 : a candy made of or with a coating of chocolate 3 : a dark brown color

Choc·taw \\'chäk-ˌtò\ n, pl **Choctaw** or **Choctaws** : a member of an American Indian people of Mississippi, Alabama, and Louisiana; also : their language

¹choice \\'chòis\ n 1 : the act of choosing : SELECTION 2 : the power or opportunity of choosing : OPTION 3 : the best part 4 : a person or thing selected 5 : a variety offered for selection

²choice adj **choic·er; choic·est** 1 : worthy of being chosen 2 : selected with care 3 : of high quality

choir \\'kwī(-ə)r\ n 1 : an organized company of singers (as in a church service) 2 : the part of a church occupied by the singers or by the clergy

choir·boy \\'kwī(-ə)r-ˌbòi\ n : a boy member of a church choir

choir·mas·ter \-ˌmas-tər\ n : the director of a choir (as in a church)

¹choke \\'chōk\ vb **choked; chok·ing** 1 : to hinder breathing (as by obstructing the windpipe) : STRANGLE 2 : to check the growth or action of 3 : CLOG, OBSTRUCT 4 : to enrich the fuel mixture of (a motor) by restricting the carburetor air intake 5 : to perform badly in a critical situation

²choke n 1 : the act of choking 2 : a narrowing in size toward the muzzle in the bore of a gun 3 : a valve for choking a gasoline engine

chok·er \\'chō-kər\ n : something (as a necklace) worn tightly around the neck

cho·ler \\'kä-lər, 'kō-\ n : a tendency toward anger : IRASCIBILITY

chol·era \\'kä-lə-rə\ n : a disease marked by severe vomiting and dysentery; esp : an often fatal epidemic disease (**Asiatic cholera**) chiefly of southeastern Asia caused by a bacillus

cho·ler·ic \\'kä-lə-rik, kə-ˈler-ik\ adj 1 : IRASCIBLE 2 : ANGRY, IRATE

cho·les·ter·ol \kə-ˈles-tə-ˌròl\ n : a physiologically important waxy steroid alcohol found in animal tissues and in high concentrations implicated as a cause of arteriosclerosis

chomp \\'chämp, 'chòmp\ vb : to chew or bite on something heavily

chon \\'chän\ n, pl **chon** — see won at MONEY table

choose \\'chüz\ vb **chose** \\'chōz\; **cho·sen** \\'chōz-ᵊn\; **choos·ing** \\'chü-ziŋ\ 1 : to select esp. after consideration 2 : DECIDE 3 : to have a preference for — **choos·er** n

choosy or **choos·ey** \\'chü-zē\ adj **choos·i·er; -est** : very particular in making choices

¹chop \\'chäp\ vb **chopped; chop·ping** 1 : to cut by repeated blows 2 : to cut into small pieces : MINCE 3 : to strike (a ball) with a short quick downward stroke

²chop n 1 : a sharp downward blow or stroke 2 : a small cut of meat often including part of a rib 3 : a short abrupt motion (as of a wave)

³chop n 1 : an official seal or stamp 2 : a mark on goods to indicate quality or kind; also : QUALITY, GRADE

chop·house \\'chäp-ˌhaus\ n : RESTAURANT

chop·per \\'chä-pər\ n 1 : one that chops 2 pl, slang : TEETH 3 : HELICOPTER

chop·pi·ness \\'chä-pē-nəs\ n : the quality or state of being choppy

¹chop·py \\'chä-pē\ adj **chop·pi·er; -est** 1 : rough with small waves 2 : JERKY, DISCONNECTED — **chop·pi·ly** \-pə-lē\ adv

²choppy adj **chop·pi·er; -est** : CHANGEABLE, VARIABLE ⟨a ∼ wind⟩

chops \\'chäps\ n pl : the fleshy covering of the jaws

chop·stick \\'chäp-ˌstik\ n : one of a pair of sticks used chiefly in oriental countries for lifting food to the mouth

chop su·ey \chäp-ˈsü-ē\ n, pl **chop sueys** : a dish made of vegetables (as bean sprouts, bamboo shoots, water chestnuts, onions, mushrooms) and meat or fish and served with rice

cho·ral \\'kōr-əl\ adj : of, relating to, or sung by a choir or chorus or in chorus — **cho·ral·ly** adv

cho·rale \kə-ˈral, -ˈräl\ n 1 : a hymn or psalm sung in church; also : a harmonization of a traditional melody 2 : CHORUS, CHOIR

¹chord \\'kòrd\ n [alter. of ME cord, short for accord] : three or more musical tones sounded simultaneously

²chord n 1 : CORD 2 2 : a straight line joining two points on a curve

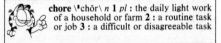

chore \\'chōr\ n 1 pl : the daily light work of a household or farm 2 : a routine task or job 3 : a difficult or disagreeable task

cho·rea \kə-ˈrē-ə\ n : a nervous disorder marked by spasmodic uncontrolled movements

GARFIELD, I HAVE SOME CHORES FOR YOU

HAPPY TO HELP

ONE OF THESE DAYS

JiM DAViS 9-20

cho·re·og·ra·phy \ˌkōr-ē-ˈä-grə-fē\ *n, pl* **-phies** : the art of composing and arranging dances and esp. ballets — **cho·reo·graph** \ˈkōr-ē-ə-ˌgraf\ *vb* — **cho·re·og·ra·pher** \ˌkōr-ē-ˈä-grə-fər\ *n* — **cho·reo·graph·ic** \ˌkōr-ē-ə-ˈgra-fik\ *adj* — **cho·reo·graph·i·cal·ly** \-fi-k(ə-)lē\ *adv*

cho·ris·ter \ˈkor-ə-stər\ *n* : a singer in a choir

chor·tle \ˈchort-ᵊl\ *vb* **chor·tled; chor·tling** : to laugh or chuckle esp. in satisfaction or exultation — **chor·tle** *n*

¹**cho·rus** \ˈkor-əs\ *n* **1** : an organized company of singers : CHOIR **2** : a group of dancers and singers (as in a musical comedy) **3** : a part of a song repeated at intervals **4** : a composition to be sung by a chorus; *also* : group singing **5** : sounds uttered by a number of persons or animals together ⟨a ∼ of boos⟩

²**chorus** *vb* : to sing or utter in chorus

chose *past of* CHOOSE

cho·sen \ˈchōz-ᵊn\ *adj* : selected or marked for special favor or privilege

¹**chow** \ˈchau̇\ *n* : FOOD

²**chow** *vb* : EAT — often used with *down*

³**chow** *n* : CHOW CHOW

chow·chow \ˈchau̇-ˌchau̇\ *n* : chopped mixed pickles in mustard sauce

chow chow \ˈchau̇-ˌchau̇\ *n* : any of a breed of thick-coated straight-legged muscular dogs of Chinese origin with a blue-black tongue and a short tail curled close to the back

chow·der \ˈchau̇-dər\ *n* : a soup or stew made from seafood or vegetables and containing milk or tomatoes

chow mein \ˈchau̇-ˈmān\ *n* : a seasoned stew of shredded or diced meat, mushrooms, and vegetables that is usu. served with fried noodles

chrism \ˈkri-zəm\ *n* : consecrated oil used esp. in baptism, confirmation, and ordination

Christ \ˈkrīst\ *n* [L *Christus*, fr. Gk *Christos*, lit., anointed] : Jesus esp. as the Messiah — **Christ·like** *adj* — **Christ·ly** *adj*

chris·ten \ˈkris-ᵊn\ *vb* **1** : BAPTIZE **2** : to name at baptism **3** : to name or dedicate (as a ship) by a ceremony suggestive of baptism — **chris·ten·ing** *n*

Chris·ten·dom \ˈkris-ᵊn-dəm\ *n* **1** : CHRISTIANITY **2** : the part of the world in which Christianity prevails

¹**Chris·tian** \ˈkris-chən\ *n* : an adherent of Christianity

²**Christian** *adj* **1** : of or relating to Christianity **2** : based on or conforming with Christianity **3** : of or relating to a Christian **4** : professing Christianity

chris·ti·a·nia \ˌkris-chē-ˈa-nē-ə, ˌkris-tē-\ *n* : CHRISTIE

Chris·ti·an·i·ty \ˌkris-chē-ˈa-nə-tē\ *n* : the religion derived from Jesus Christ, based on the Bible as sacred scripture, and professed by Christians

Chris·tian·ize \ˈkris-chə-ˌnīz\ *vb* **-ized; -iz·ing** : to make Christian

Christian name *n* : GIVEN NAME

Christian Science *n* : a religion and system of healing founded by Mary Baker Eddy and taught by the Church of Christ, Scientist — **Christian Scientist** *n*

chris·tie *or* **chris·ty** \ˈkris-tē\ *n, pl* **christies** : a skiing turn made by shifting body weight forward and skidding into a turn with parallel skis

Christ·mas \ˈkris-məs\ *n* : December 25 celebrated as a church festival in commemoration of the birth of Christ and observed as a legal holiday

Christmas club *n* : a savings account in which regular deposits are made to provide money for Christmas shopping

Christ·mas·tide \ˈkris-məs-ˌtīd\ *n* : the season of Christmas

chro·mat·ic \krō-ˈma-tik\ *adj* **1** : of or relating to color **2** : proceeding by half steps of the musical scale — **chro·mat·i·cism** \-tə-ˌsi-zəm\ *n*

chro·mato·graph \krō-ˈma-tə-ˌgraf\ *n* : an instrument used in chromatography

chro·ma·tog·ra·phy \ˌkrō-mə-ˈtä-grə-fē\ *n* : the separation of a complex mixture into its component compounds as a result of the different rates at which the compounds travel through or over a stationary substance due to differing affinities for the substance — **chro·mato·graph·ic** \ˌkrō-ˌma-tə-ˈgra-fik\ *adj* — **chro·mato·graph·i·cal·ly** \-fi-k(ə-)lē\ *adv*

chrome \ˈkrōm\ *n* **1** : CHROMIUM **2** : a chromium pigment **3** : something plated with an alloy of chromium

chro·mi·um \ˈkrō-mē-əm\ *n* : a bluish white metallic element used esp. in alloys and chrome plating — see ELEMENT table

chro·mo·some \ˈkrō-mə-ˌsōm, -ˌzōm\ *n* : any of the linear or sometimes circular DNA-containing bodies of viruses, bacteria, and the nucleus of higher organisms that contain most or all of the individual's genes — **chro·mo·som·al** \ˌkrō-mə-ˈsō-məl, -ˈzō-\ *adj*

chro·mo·sphere \ˈkrō-mə-ˌsfir\ *n* : the lower part of a star's atmosphere

chron *abbr* **1** chronicle **2** chronological; chronology

Chron *abbr* Chronicles

chron·ic \ˈkrä-nik\ *adj* : marked by long duration or frequent recurrence ⟨a ∼ disease⟩; *also* : HABITUAL ⟨a ∼ grumbler⟩ — **chron·i·cal·ly** \-ni-k(ə-)lē\ *adv*

¹**chron·i·cle** \ˈkrä-ni-kəl\ *n* : HISTORY, NARRATIVE

²**chronicle** *vb* **-cled; -cling** : to record in or as if in a chronicle — **chron·i·cler** *n*

Chronicles *n* — see BIBLE table

chro·no·graph \ˈkrä-nə-ˌgraf\ *n* : an instrument for measuring and recording time intervals with accuracy — **chro·no·graph·ic** \ˌkrä-nə-ˈgra-fik\ *adj* — **chro·nog·ra·phy** \krə-ˈnä-grə-fē\ *n*

chro·nol·o·gy \krə-ˈnä-lə-jē\ *n, pl* **-gies 1** : the science that deals with measuring time and dating events **2** : a chronological list or table **3** : arrangement of events in the order of their occurrence — **chron·o·log·i·cal** \ˌkrän-ᵊl-ˈä-ji-kəl\ *adj* — **chron·o·log·i·cal·ly** \-k(ə-)lē\ *adv* — **chro·nol·o·gist** \krə-ˈnä-lə-jist\ *n*

chro·nom·e·ter \krə-ˈnä-mə-tər\ *n* : a very accurate timepiece

chrys·a·lid \ˈkri-sə-ləd\ *n* : CHRYSALIS

chrys·a·lis \ˈkri-sə-ləs\ *n, pl* **chrys·al·i·des** \kri-ˈsa-lə-ˌdēz\ *or* **chrys·a·lis·es** : an insect pupa in a firm case without a cocoon

chry·san·the·mum \kri-ˈsan-thə-məm\ *n* [L, fr. Gk *chrysanthemon*, fr. *chrysos* gold + *anthemon* flower] : any of various plants related to the daisies including some grown for their showy flowers or for medicinal products or insecticides; *also* : a flower of a chrysanthemum

chub \ˈchəb\ *n, pl* **chub** *or* **chubs** : any of various small freshwater fishes related to the carp

chub·by \ˈchə-bē\ *adj* **chub·bi·er; -est** : PLUMP — **chub·bi·ness** *n*

¹**chuck** \ˈchək\ *vb* **1** : to give a pat or tap **2** : TOSS **3** : DISCARD; *also* : EJECT **4** : to have done with

²**chuck** *n* **1** : a light pat under the chin **2** : TOSS

³**chuck** *n* **1** : a cut of beef including most of the neck and the parts around the shoulder blade and the first three ribs **2** : a device for holding work or a tool in a machine (as a lathe)

chuck·hole \ˈchək-ˌhōl\ *n* : POTHOLE

chuck·le \ˈchə-kəl\ *vb* **chuck·led; chuck·ling** : to laugh in a quiet hardly audible manner — **chuckle** *n*

chuck wagon *n* : a wagon equipped with a stove and food supplies

¹**chug** \ˈchəg\ *n* : a dull explosive sound made by or as if by a laboring engine

²**chug** *vb* **chugged; chug·ging** : to move or go with chugs

chuk·ka \ˈchə-kə\ *n* : a usu. ankle-length leather boot

chuk·ker \\'chə-kər\ *also* **chuk·ka** \\'chə-kə\ *n* : a playing period of a polo game

¹chum \\'chəm\ *n* : a close friend

²chum *vb* **chummed; chum·ming 1** : to room together **2** : to be a close friend

chum·my \\'chə-mē\ *adj* **chum·mi·er; -est** : INTIMATE, SOCIABLE — **chum·mi·ly** \-mə-lē\ *adv* — **chum·mi·ness** \-mē-nəs\ *n*

chump \\'chəmp\ *n* : FOOL, BLOCKHEAD

chunk \\'chəŋk\ *n* **1** : a short thick piece **2** : a sizable amount

chunky \\'chəŋ-kē\ *adj* **chunk·i·er; -est 1** : STOCKY **2** : containing chunks

church \\'chərch\ *n* [OE *cirice*, ultim. fr. LGk *kyriakon*, fr. Gk. neut. of *kyriakos* of the lord, fr. *kyrios* lord, master] **1** : a building esp. for Christian public worship **2** : the whole body of Christians **3** : DENOMINATION **4** : CONGREGATION **5** : public divine worship

church·go·er \\'chərch-ˌgō(-ə)r\ *n* : one who habitually attends church — **church·go·ing** *adj or n*

church·less \\'chərch-ləs\ *adj* : not affiliated with a church

church·man \\'chərch-mən\ *n* **1** : CLERGYMAN **2** : a member of a church

church·war·den \\'chərch-ˌwȯrd-ᵊn\ *n* : WARDEN 5

church·yard \-ˌyärd\ *n* : a yard that belongs to a church and is often used as a burial ground

churl \\'chərl\ *n* **1** : a medieval peasant **2** : RUSTIC **3** : a rude ill-bred person — **churl·ish** *adj* — **churl·ish·ly** *adv* — **churl·ish·ness** *n*

¹churn \\'chərn\ *n* : a container in which milk or cream is violently stirred in making butter

²churn *vb* **1** : to stir in a churn; *also* : to make (butter) by such stirring **2** : to shake around violently

churn out *vb* : to produce mechanically or in large quantity

chute \\'shüt\ *n* **1** : an inclined surface, trough, or passage down or through which something may pass ⟨coal ∼⟩ ⟨a mail ∼⟩ **2** : PARACHUTE

chut·ney \\'chət-nē\ *n, pl* **chutneys** : a thick sauce containing fruits, vinegar, sugar, and spices

chutz·pah \\'hut-spə, -ˈkut-, -(ˌ)spä\ *n* : supreme self-confidence

CIA *abbr* Central Intelligence Agency

cía *abbr* [Sp *compañía*] company

ciao \\'chau̇\ *interj* — used to express greeting or farewell

ci·ca·da \sə-ˈkā-də\ *n* : any of a family of stout-bodied insects related to the aphids and having wide blunt heads and large transparent wings

cicada

ci·ca·trix \\'si-kə-ˌtriks\ *n, pl* **ci·ca·tri·ces** \ˌsi-kə-ˈtrī-ˌsēz\ [L] : a scar resulting from formation and contraction of fibrous tissue in a wound

ci·ce·ro·ne \ˌsi-sə-ˈrō-nē, ˌchē-chə-\ *n, pl* **-ni** \-(ˌ)nē\ : a guide who conducts sightseers

CID *abbr* Criminal Investigation Department

ci·der \\'sī-dər\ *n* : juice pressed from fruit (as apples) and used as a beverage, vinegar, or flavoring

cie *abbr* [F *compagnie*] company

ci·gar \si-ˈgär\ *n* : a roll of tobacco for smoking

cig·a·rette \ˌsi-gə-ˈret, ˈsi-gə-ˌret\ *n* [F, dim. of *cigare*

cigar] : a slender roll of cut tobacco enclosed in paper for smoking

cig·a·ril·lo \ˌsi-gə-ˈri-lō, -ˈrē-ō\ *n, pl* **-los** [Sp] **1** : a very small cigar **2** : a cigarette wrapped in tobacco rather than paper

ci·lan·tro \si-ˈlän-trō, -ˈlan-\ *n* : leaves of coriander used as a flavoring or garnish; *also* : the coriander plant

cil·i·ate \\'si-lē-ˌāt\ *n* : any of a group of protozoans characterized by cilia

cil·i·um \\'si-lē-əm\ *n, pl* **-ia** \-lē-ə\ **1** : a minute short hairlike process; *esp* : one of a cell **2** : EYELASH

C in C *abbr* commander in chief

cinch \\'sinch\ *n* **1** : a girth for a pack or saddle **2** : a sure or an easy thing — **cinch** *vb*

cin·cho·na \siŋ-ˈkō-nə\ *n* : any of a genus of So. American trees related to the madder; *also* : the bitter quinine-containing bark of a cinchona

cinc·ture \\'siŋk-chər\ *n* : BELT, SASH

cin·der \\'sin-dər\ *n* **1** : SLAG **2** *pl* : ASHES **3** : a hot piece of partly burned wood or coal **4** : a fragment of lava from an erupting volcano — **cinder** *vb* — **cin·dery** *adj*

cinder block *n* : a building block made of cement and coal cinders

cin·e·ma \\'si-nə-mə\ *n* **1** : a motion-picture theater **2** : MOVIES — **cin·e·mat·ic** \ˌsi-nə-ˈma-tik\ *adj*

cin·e·ma·theque \ˌsi-nə-mə-ˈtek\ *n* : a small movie house specializing in avant-garde films

cin·e·ma·tog·ra·phy \ˌsi-nə-mə-ˈtä-grə-fē\ *n* : motion-picture photography — **cin·e·ma·tog·ra·pher** *n* — **cin·e·mat·o·graph·ic** \-ˌma-tə-ˈgra-fik\ *adj*

cin·e·plex \\'si-nə-ˌpleks\ *n* : a complex that houses several movie theaters

cin·er·ar·i·um \ˌsi-nə-ˈrer-ē-əm\ *n, pl* **-ia** \-ē-ə\ : a place to receive the ashes of the cremated dead — **cin·er·ary** \\'si-nə-ˌrer-ē\ *adj*

cin·na·bar \\'si-nə-ˌbär\ *n* : a red mineral that is the only important ore of mercury

cin·na·mon \\'si-nə-mən\ *n* : a spice prepared from the highly aromatic bark of any of several trees related to the true laurel; *also* : a tree that yields cinnamon

cinque·foil \\'siŋk-ˌfȯil, ˈsaŋk-\ *n* : any of a genus of plants related to the roses with leaves having five lobes

¹ci·pher \\'sī-fər\ *n* [ME, fr. MF *cifre*, fr. ML *cifra*, fr. Ar *ṣifr* empty, zero] **1** : ZERO, NAUGHT **2** : a method of secret writing

²cipher *vb* : to compute arithmetically

cir *or* **circ** *abbr* circular

cir·ca \\'sər-kə\ *prep* : ABOUT ⟨∼ 1600⟩

cir·ca·di·an \ˌsər-ˈka-dē-ən, ˌsər-kə-ˈdī-ən\ *adj* : being, having, characterized by, or occurring in approximately 24-hour intervals (as of biological activity)

¹cir·cle \\'sər-kəl\ *n* **1** : a closed curve every point of which is equally distant from a fixed point within it **2** : something circular **3** : an area of action or influence **4** : CYCLE **5** : a group bound by a common tie

²circle *vb* **cir·cled; cir·cling 1** : to enclose in a circle **2** : to move or revolve around; *also* : to move in a circle

cir·clet \\'sər-klət\ *n* : a small circle; *esp* : a circular ornament

cir·cuit \\'sər-kət\ *n* **1** : a boundary around an enclosed space **2** : a course around a periphery **3** : a regular tour (as by a judge) around an assigned territory **4** : the complete path of an electric current; *also* : an assemblage of electronic components **5** : LEAGUE; *also* : a chain of theaters — **cir·cuital** \-ᵊl\ *adj*

circuit breaker *n* : a switch that automatically interrupts an electric circuit under an abnormal condition

circuit court *n* : a court that sits at two or more places within one judicial district

cir·cu·i·tous \ˌsər-ˈkyü-ə-təs\ *adj* **1** : having a circular or winding course **2** : not being forthright or direct in language or action

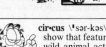

cir·cuit·ry \'sər-kə-trē\ n, pl **-ries** : the plan or the components of an electric circuit

cir·cu·ity \sər-'kyü-ə-tē\ n, pl **-ities** : INDIRECTION

¹**cir·cu·lar** \'sər-kyə-lər\ adj 1 : having the form of a circle : ROUND 2 : moving in or around a circle 3 : CIRCUITOUS 4 : intended for circulation ⟨a ∼ letter⟩ — **cir·cu·lar·i·ty** \sər-kyə-'lar-ə-tē\ n

²**circular** n : a paper (as a leaflet) intended for wide distribution

cir·cu·lar·ise Brit var of CIRCULARIZE

cir·cu·lar·ize \'sər-kyə-lə-ərīz\ vb **-ized; -iz·ing** 1 : to send circulars to 2 : to poll by questionnaire

circular saw n : a power saw with a round cutting blade

cir·cu·late \'sər-kyə-ərlāt\ vb **-lat·ed; -lat·ing** 1 : to move or cause to move in a circle, circuit, or orbit 2 : to pass from place to place or from person to person — **cir·cu·la·tion** \sər-kyə-'lā-shən\ n

cir·cu·la·to·ry \'sər-kyə-lə-ətōr-ē\ adj : of or relating to circulation or the circulatory system

circulatory system n : the system of blood, blood vessels, lymphatic vessels, and heart concerned with the circulation of the blood and lymph

cir·cum·am·bu·late \sər-kəm-'am-byə-ərlāt\ vb **-lat·ed; -lat·ing** : to circle on foot esp. as part of a ritual

cir·cum·cise \'sər-kəm-əsīz\ vb **-cised; -cis·ing** : to cut off the foreskin of — **cir·cum·ci·sion** \sər-kəm-'si-zhən\ n

cir·cum·fer·ence \sər-'kəm-f(ə-)rəns\ n 1 : the perimeter of a circle 2 : the external boundary or surface of a figure or object

cir·cum·flex \'sər-kəm-əfleks\ n : the mark ^ over a vowel

cir·cum·lo·cu·tion \sər-kəm-lō-'kyü-shən\ n : the use of unnecessary words in expressing an idea

cir·cum·lu·nar \-'lü-nər\ adj : revolving about or surrounding the moon

cir·cum·nav·i·gate \-'na-və-əgāt\ vb : to go completely around (as the earth) esp. by water — **cir·cum·nav·i·ga·tion** \-əna-və-'gā-shən\ n

cir·cum·po·lar \-'pō-lər\ adj 1 : continually visible above the horizon ⟨a ∼ star⟩ 2 : surrounding or found near a pole of the earth

cir·cum·scribe \'sər-kəm-əskrīb\ vb 1 : to constrict the range or activity of 2 : to draw a line around — **cir·cum·scrip·tion** \sər-kəm-'skrip-shən\ n

cir·cum·spect \'sər-kəm-əspekt\ adj : careful to consider all circumstances and consequences : PRUDENT — **cir·cum·spec·tion** \sər-kəm-'spek-shən\ n

cir·cum·stance \'sər-kəm-əstans\ n 1 : a fact or event that must be considered along with another fact or event 2 : surrounding conditions 3 : CHANCE, FATE 4 pl : situation with regard to wealth 5 : CEREMONY

cir·cum·stan·tial \sər-kəm-'stan-chəl\ adj 1 : consisting of or depending on circumstances 2 : INCIDENTAL 3 : containing full details — **cir·cum·stan·tial·ly** adv

cir·cum·vent \sər-kəm-'vent\ vb : to check or defeat esp. by stratagem — **cir·cum·ven·tion** \'vent-shən\ n

cir·cus \'sər-kəs\ n 1 : a usu. traveling show that features feats of physical skill, wild animal acts, and performances by clowns 2 : a circus performance; also : the equipment, livestock, and personnel of a circus

cirque \'sərk\ n : a deep steep-walled mountain basin usu. forming the blunt end of a valley

cir·rho·sis \sə-'rō-səs\ n, pl **-rho·ses** \-əsēz\ [NL, fr. Gk kirrhos orange-colored] : fibrosis of the liver — **cir·rhot·ic** \-'rä-tik\ adj or n

cir·rus \'sir-əs\ n, pl **cir·ri** \'sir-əī\ : a wispy white cloud usu. of minute ice crystals at high altitudes

cis·lu·nar \(ə)sis-'lü-nər\ adj : lying between the earth and the moon or the moon's orbit

cis·sy Brit var of SISSY

cis·tern \'sis-tərn\ n : an often underground tank for storing water

cit abbr 1 citation; cited 2 citizen

cit·a·del \'si-tə-dəl, -ədel\ n 1 : a fortress commanding a city 2 : STRONGHOLD

ci·ta·tion \sī-'tā-shən\ n 1 : an official summons to appear (as before a court) 2 : QUOTATION 3 : a formal statement of the achievements of a person; also : a specific reference in a military dispatch to meritorious performance of duty

cite \'sīt\ vb **cit·ed; cit·ing** 1 : to summon to appear before a court 2 : QUOTE 3 : to refer to esp. in commendation or praise

cit·i·fied \'si-ti-əfīd\ adj : of, relating to, or characterized by an urban style of living

cit·i·zen \'si-tə-zən\ n 1 : an inhabitant of a city or town 2 : a person who owes allegiance to a government and is entitled to its protection — **cit·i·zen·ship** n

cit·i·zen·ry \-rē\ n, pl **-ries** : a whole body of citizens

citizens band n : a range of radio frequencies set aside for private radio communications

cit·ric acid \'si-trik-\ n : a sour organic acid obtained from lemon and lime juices or by fermentation of sugars and used as a flavoring

cit·ron \'si-trən\ n 1 : the oval lemonlike fruit of an Asian citrus tree; also : the tree 2 : a small hard-fleshed watermelon used esp. in pickles and preserves

cit·ro·nel·la \si-trə-'ne-lə\ n : an oil obtained from a fragrant grass of southern Asia and used in perfumes and as an insect repellent

cit·rus \'si-trəs\ n, pl **citrus** or **cit·rus·es** : any of a genus of often thorny evergreen trees or shrubs grown in warm regions for their fruits (as the orange, lemon, lime, and grapefruit); also : the fruit

city \'si-tē\ n, pl **cit·ies** [ME citie large or small town, fr. OF cité, fr. ML civitas, fr. L citizenship, state, city of Rome, fr. civis citizen] 1 : an inhabited place larger or more important than a town 2 : a municipality in the U.S. governed under a charter granted by the state; also : an incorporated municipal unit of the highest class in Canada

city manager n : an official employed by an elected

council to direct the administration of a city government

city–state \'si-tē-ˌstāt\ *n* : an autonomous state consisting of a city and surrounding territory

civ *abbr* **1** civil; civilian **2** civilization

civ·et \'si-vət\ *n* : a yellowish strong-smelling substance obtained from a catlike mammal (**civet cat**) of Africa or Asia and used in making perfumes

civ·ic \'si-vik\ *adj* : of or relating to a city, citizenship, or civil affairs

civ·ics \-viks\ *n* : a social science dealing with the rights and duties of citizens

civ·il \'si-vəl\ *adj* **1** : of or relating to citizens or to the state as a political body **2** : COURTEOUS, POLITE **3** : of or relating to legal proceedings in connection with private rights and obligations ⟨the ~ code⟩ **4** : of or relating to the general population : not military or ecclesiastical

civil defense *n* : protective measures and emergency relief activities conducted by civilians in case of enemy attack or natural disaster

civil disobedience *n* : refusal to obey governmental commands esp. as a nonviolent means of protest

civil engineer *n* : an engineer whose training or occupation is in the design and construction esp. of public works (as roads or harbors) — **civil engineering** *n*

ci·vil·ian \sə-'vil-yən\ *n* : a person not on active duty in a military, police, or fire-fighting force

civ·i·li·sa·tion, civ·i·lise *chiefly Brit var of* CIVILIZATION, CIVILIZE

ci·vil·i·ty \sə-'vi-lə-tē\ *n, pl* **-ties 1** : POLITENESS, COURTESY **2** : a polite act or expression

civ·i·li·za·tion \ˌsi-və-lə-'zā-shən\ *n* **1** : a relatively high level of cultural and technological development **2** : the culture characteristic of a time or place

civ·i·lize \'si-və-ˌlīz\ *vb* **-lized; -liz·ing 1** : to raise from a primitive state to an advanced and ordered stage of cultural development **2** : REFINE — **civ·i·lized** *adj*

civil liberty *n* : freedom from arbitrary governmental interference specifically by denial of governmental power — usu. used in pl.

civ·il·ly \'si-vəl-lē\ *adv* **1** : in terms of civil rights, matters, or law ⟨~ dead⟩ **2** : in a civil manner : POLITELY

civil rights *n pl* : the nonpolitical rights of a citizen; *esp* : those guaranteed by the 13th and 14th amendments to the Constitution and by acts of Congress

civil servant *n* : a member of a civil service

civil service *n* : the administrative service of a government

civil war *n* : a war between opposing groups of citizens of the same country

civ·vies \'si-vēz\ *n pl* : civilian clothes as distinguished from a military uniform

CJ *abbr* chief justice

ck *abbr* **1** cask **2** check

cl *abbr* **1** centiliter **2** class

Cl *symbol* chlorine

¹clack \'klak\ *vb* **1** : CHATTER, PRATTLE **2** : to make or cause to make a clatter

²clack *n* **1** : rapid continuous talk : CHATTER **2** : a sound of clacking ⟨the ~ of a typewriter⟩

clad \'klad\ *adj* **1** : CLOTHED, COVERED **2** : being or consisting of coins made of outer layers of one metal bonded to a core of a different metal

¹claim \'klām\ *vb* [ME, fr. MF *clamer*, fr. L *clamare* to cry out, shout] **1** : to ask for as one's own; *also* : to take as the rightful owner **2** : to call for : REQUIRE **3** : to state as a fact : MAINTAIN

²claim *n* **1** : a demand for something due **2** : a right to something usu. in another's possession **3** : an assertion open to challenge **4** : something claimed (as a tract of land)

claim·ant \'klā-mənt\ *n* : a person making a claim

clair·voy·ant \klar-'vȯi-ənt\ *adj* [F, fr. *clair* clear + *voyant* seeing] **1** : unusually perceptive **2** : having the

power of discerning objects not present to the senses — **clair·voy·ance** \-əns\ *n* — **clairvoyant** *n*

clam \'klam\ *n* **1** : any of numerous bivalve mollusks including many that are edible **2** : DOLLAR

clam·bake \-ˌbāk\ *n* : a party or gathering (as at the seashore) at which food is cooked usu. on heated rocks covered by seaweed

clam·ber \'klam-bər\ *vb* : to climb awkwardly — **clam·ber·er** *n*

clam·my \'kla-mē\ *adj* **clam·mi·er; -est** : being damp, soft, sticky, and usu. cool — **clam·mi·ness** *n*

clam·or \'kla-mər\ *n* **1** : a noisy shouting **2** : a loud continuous noise **3** : insistent public expression (as of support or protest) — **clamor** *vb* — **clam·or·ous** *adj*

clam·our *chiefly Brit var of* CLAMOR

¹clamp \'klamp\ *n* : a device that holds or presses parts together firmly

²clamp *vb* : to fasten with or as if with a clamp

clamp down *vb* : to impose restrictions : become repressive — **clamp·down** \'klamp-ˌdaủn\ *n*

clam·shell \'klam-ˌshel\ *n* : a bucket or grapnel (as on a dredge) having two hinged jaws

clam up *vb* : to become silent

clan \'klan\ *n* [ME, fr. ScGael *clann* offspring, clan, fr. Old Irish *cland* plant, offspring, fr. L *planta* plant] : a group (as in the Scottish Highlands) made up of households whose heads claim descent from a common ancestor — **clan·nish** *adj* — **clan·nish·ness** *n*

clan·des·tine \klan-'des-tən\ *adj* : held in or conducted with secrecy

clang \'klaŋ\ *n* : a loud metallic ringing sound — **clang** *vb*

clan·gor \'klaŋ-ər, -gər\ *n* : a resounding clang or medley of clangs

clan·gour *chiefly Brit var of* CLANGOR

clank \'klaŋk\ *n* : a sharp brief metallic ringing sound — **clank** *vb*

¹clap \'klap\ *vb* **clapped; clap·ping 1** : to strike noisily **2** : APPLAUD

²clap *n* **1** : a loud noisy crash **2** : the noise made by clapping the hands

³clap *n* : GONORRHEA

clap·board \'kla-bərd, -ˌbȯrd; 'klap-ˌbȯrd\ *n* : a narrow board thicker at one edge than the other used for siding — **clapboard** *vb*

clap·per \'kla-pər\ *n* : one that claps; *esp* : the tongue of a bell

clap·trap \'klap-ˌtrap\ *n* : pretentious nonsense

claque \'klak\ *n* [F, fr. *claquer* to clap] **1** : a group hired to applaud at a performance **2** : a group of sycophants

clar·et \'klar-ət\ *n* [ME, fr. MF ⟨*vin*⟩ *claret* clear wine] : a dry red wine

clar·i·fy \'klar-ə-ˌfī\ *vb* **-fied; -fy·ing** : to make or become clear — **clar·i·fi·ca·tion** \ˌklar-ə-fə-'kā-shən\ *n*

clar·i·net \ˌklar-ə-'net\ *n* : a single-reed woodwind instrument in the form of a cylindrical tube with a moderately flaring end — **clar·i·net·ist** *or* **clar·i·net·tist** \-'ne-tist\ *n*

clarinet

clar·i·on \'klar-ē-ən\ *adj* : brilliantly clear ⟨a ~ call⟩

clar·i·ty \'klar-ə-tē\ *n* : CLEARNESS

¹clash \'klash\ *vb* **1** : to make or cause to make a clash **2** : CONFLICT, COLLIDE

²clash *n* **1** : a noisy usu. metallic sound of collision **2** : a hostile encounter; *also* : a conflict of opinion

clasp \'klasp\ *n* **1** : a device (as a hook) for holding objects or parts together **2** : EMBRACE, GRASP — **clasp** *vb*

¹class \'klas\ *n* **1** : a group of students meeting regularly in a course; *also* : a group graduating together **2** : a

course of instruction; *also* : the period when such a course is taught **3** : social rank; *also* : high quality **4** : a group of the same general status or nature; *esp* : a major category in biological classification that is above the order and below the phylum **5** : a division or rating based on grade or quality — **class·less** *adj*

²**class** *vb* : CLASSIFY

class action *n* : a legal action undertaken in behalf of the plaintiffs and all others having an identical interest in the alleged wrong

¹**clas·sic** \'kla-sik\ *adj* **1** : serving as a standard of excellence; *also* : TRADITIONAL **2** : CLASSICAL 2 **3** : notable esp. as the best example **4** : AUTHENTIC

²**classic** *n* **1** : a work of enduring excellence and esp. of ancient Greece or Rome; *also* : its author **2** : a traditional event

clas·si·cal \'kla-si-kəl\ *adj* **1** : CLASSIC **2** : of or relating to the ancient Greek and Roman classics **3** : of or relating to a form or system of primary significance before modern times ⟨∼ economics⟩ **4** : concerned with a general study of the arts and sciences — **clas·si·cal·ly** \-k(ə-)lē\ *adv*

clas·si·cism \'kla-sə-ˌsi-zəm\ *n* **1** : the principles or style of the literature or art of ancient Greece and Rome **2** : adherence to traditional standards believed to be universally valid — **clas·si·cist** \-sist\ *n*

clas·si·fied \'kla-sə-ˌfīd\ *adj* : withheld from general circulation for reasons of national security

clas·si·fy \'kla-sə-ˌfī\ *vb* **-fied; -fy·ing** : to arrange in or assign to classes — **clas·si·fi·able** *adj* — **clas·si·fi·ca·tion** \ˌkla-sə-fə-'kā-shən\ *n* — **clas·si·fi·er** *n*

class·mate \'klas-ˌmāt\ *n* : a member of the same class (as in a college)

class·room \-ˌrüm-, -ˌrùm\ *n* : a place where classes meet

classy \'kla-sē\ *adj* **class·i·er; -est** : ELEGANT, STYLISH — **class·i·ness** *n*

clat·ter \'kla-tər\ *n* : a rattling sound ⟨the ∼ of dishes⟩ — **clatter** *vb*

clause \'klòz\ *n* **1** : a group of words having its own subject and predicate but forming only part of a compound or complex sentence **2** : a separate part of an article or document

claus·tro·pho·bia \ˌklò-strə-'fō-bē-ə\ *n* : abnormal dread of being in closed or narrow spaces — **claus·tro·pho·bic** \-bik\ *adj*

clav·i·chord \'kla-və-ˌkòrd\ *n* : an early keyboard instrument in use before the piano

clav·i·cle \'kla-vi-kəl\ *n* [F *clavicule*, fr. NL *clavicula*, fr. L, dim. of L *clavis* key] : COLLARBONE

cla·vier \klə-'vir; 'klā-vē-ər\ *n* **1** : the keyboard of a musical instrument **2** : an early keyboard instrument

¹**claw** \'klò\ *n* **1** : a sharp usu. curved nail on the toe of an animal **2** : a sharp curved process (as on the foot of an insect); *also* : a pincerlike organ at the end of a limb of some arthropods (as a lobster) — **clawed** \'klòd\ *adj*

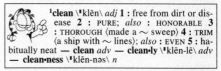

²**claw** *vb* : to rake, seize, or dig with or as if with claws

clay \'klā\ *n* **1** : an earthy material that is plastic when moist but hard when fired and is used in making pottery; *also* : finely divided soil consisting largely of such clay **2** : EARTH, MUD **3** : a plastic substance used for modeling **4** : the mortal human body — **clay·ey** \'klā-ē\ *adj*

clay·more \'klā-ˌmōr\ *n* : a large 2-edged sword formerly used by Scottish Highlanders

clay pigeon *n* : a saucer-shaped target thrown from a trap in trapshooting

¹**clean** \'klēn\ *adj* **1** : free from dirt or disease **2** : PURE; *also* : HONORABLE **3** : THOROUGH ⟨made a ∼ sweep⟩ **4** : TRIM ⟨a ship with ∼ lines⟩; *also* : EVEN **5** : habitually neat — **clean** *adv* — **clean·ly** \'klēn-lē\ *adv* — **clean·ness** \'klēn-nəs\ *n*

²**clean** *vb* : to make or become clean — **clean·er** *n*

clean-cut \'klēn-'kət\ *adj* **1** : cut so that the surface or edge is smooth and even **2** : sharply defined or outlined **3** : giving an effect of wholesomeness

clean·ly \'klen-lē\ *adj* **clean·li·er; -est** **1** : careful to

keep clean **2** : habitually kept clean — **clean·li·ness** n

clean room \'klēn-ₗrüm, -ₗrům\ n : an uncontaminated room maintained for the manufacture or assembly of objects (as precision parts)

cleanse \'klenz\ vb **cleansed; cleans·ing** : to make clean — **cleans·er** n

¹**clean·up** \'klē-ₗnəp\ n **1** : an act or instance of cleaning **2** : a very large profit

²**cleanup** adj : being 4th in the batting order of a baseball team

clean up vb : to make a spectacular business profit

¹**clear** \'klir\ adj **1** : BRIGHT, LUMINOUS; also : UNTROUBLED, SERENE **2** : CLOUDLESS **3** : CLEAN, PURE; also : TRANSPARENT **4** : easily heard, seen, or understood **5** : capable of sharp discernment; also : free from doubt **6** : INNOCENT **7** : free from restriction, obstruction, or entanglement — **clear** adv — **clear·ness** n

²**clear** vb **1** : to make or become clear **2** : to go away : DISPERSE **3** : to free from accusation or blame; also : to certify as trustworthy **4** : EXPLAIN **5** : to get free from obstruction **6** : SETTLE **7** : NET **8** : to get rid of : REMOVE **9** : to jump or go by without touching; also : PASS

³**clear** n : a clear space or part

clear·ance \'klir-əns\ n **1** : an act or process of clearing **2** : the distance by which one object clears another **3** : AUTHORIZATION

clear–cut \'klir-'kət\ adj **1** : sharply outlined **2** : DEFINITE, UNEQUIVOCAL

clear–head·ed \-'he-dəd\ adj : having a clear understanding : PERCEPTIVE

clear·ing \'klir-iŋ\ n **1** : a tract of land cleared of wood and brush **2** : the passage of checks and claims through a clearinghouse

clear·ing·house \-ₗhaůs\ n : an institution maintained by banks for making an exchange of checks and claims held by each bank against other banks; also : an informal channel for information or assistance

clear·ly \'klir-lē\ adv **1** : in a clear manner **2** : it is clear

cleat \'klēt\ n : a piece of wood or metal fastened on or projecting from something to give strength, provide a grip, or prevent slipping

cleav·age \'klē-vij\ n **1** : a splitting apart : SPLIT **2** : the depression between a woman's breasts esp. when exposed by a low-cut dress

¹**cleave** \'klēv\ vb **cleaved** \'klēvd\ or **clove** \'klōv\; **cleaved; cleav·ing** : ADHERE, CLING

²**cleave** vb **cleaved** \'klēvd\ also **cleft** \'kleft\ or **clove** \'klōv\; **cleaved** also **cleft** or **clo·ven** \'klō-vən\; **cleav·ing 1** : to divide by force : split asunder **2** : DIVIDE

cleav·er \'klē-vər\ n : a heavy chopping knife for cutting meat

clef \'klef\ n : a sign placed on the staff in music to show what pitch is represented by each line and space

cleft \'kleft\ n : FISSURE, CRACK

cleft palate n : a split in the roof of the mouth that appears as a birth defect

clem·a·tis \'kle-mə-təs; kli-'ma-təs\ n : any of a genus of vines or herbs related to the buttercups that have showy usu. white or purple flowers

clem·en·cy \'kle-mən-sē\ n, pl **-cies 1** : disposition to be merciful **2** : mildness of weather

clem·ent \'kle-mənt\ adj **1** : MERCIFUL, LENIENT **2** : TEMPERATE, MILD

clench \'klench\ vb **1** : CLINCH 1 **2** : to hold fast **3** : to set or close tightly

clere·sto·ry \'klir-ₗstōr-ē\ n : an outside wall of a room or building that rises above an adjoining roof and contains windows

cler·gy \'klər-jē\ n : a body of religious officials authorized to conduct services

cler·gy·man \-mən\ n : a member of the clergy

cler·ic \'kler-ik\ n : a member of the clergy

cler·i·cal \'kler-i-kəl\ adj **1** : of or relating to the clergy **2** : of or relating to a clerk

cler·i·cal·ism \'kler-i-kə-ₗli-zəm\ n : a policy of maintaining or increasing the power of a religious hierarchy

clerk \'klərk, Brit 'klärk\ n **1** : CLERIC **2** : an official responsible for correspondence, records, and accounts; also : a person employed to perform general office work **3** : a store salesperson — **clerk** vb — **clerk·ship** n

clev·er \'kle-vər\ adj **1** : showing skill or resourcefulness **2** : marked by wit or ingenuity — **clev·er·ly** adv — **clev·er·ness** n

clev·is \'kle-vəs\ n : a U-shaped shackle used for fastening

¹**clew** \'klü\ n **1** : CLUE **2** : a metal loop on a lower corner of a sail

²**clew** vb : to haul (a sail) up or down by ropes through the clews

cli·ché \kli-'shā\ n [F] : a trite phrase or expression — **cli·chéd** \-'shād\ adj

¹**click** \'klik\ vb **1** : to make or cause to make a click **2** : to fit or work together smoothly

²**click** n : a slight sharp noise

cli·ent \'klī-ənt\ n **1** : DEPENDENT **2** : a person who engages the professional services of another; also : PATRON, CUSTOMER

cli·en·tele \ₗklī-ən-'tel, ₗklē-\ n : a body of clients and esp. customers

cliff \'klif\ n : a high steep face of rock, earth, or ice

cliff–hang·er \-ₗhaŋ-ər\ n **1** : an adventure serial or melodrama usu. presented in installments each of which ends in suspense **2** : a contest whose outcome is in doubt up to the very end

cli·mac·ter·ic \klī-'mak-tə-rik\ n **1** : a major turning point or critical stage **2** : MENOPAUSE; also : a corresponding period in the male

cli·mate \'klī-mət\ n [ME climat, fr. MF, fr. LL clima, fr. Gk klima inclination, latitude, climate, fr. klinein to lean] **1** : a region having specific climatic conditions **2** : the average weather conditions at a place over a period of years **3** : the prevailing set of conditions (as temperature and humidity) indoors **4** : a prevailing atmosphere or environment (the ~ of opinion) — **cli·mat·ic** \klī-'ma-tik\ adj — **cli·mat·i·cal·ly** \-ti-k(ə-)lē\ adv

cli·ma·tol·o·gy \ₗklī-mə-'tä-lə-jē\ n : the science that deals with climates — **cli·ma·to·log·i·cal** \-mət-ºl-'ä-ji-kəl\ adj — **cli·ma·to·log·i·cal·ly** \-k(ə-)lē\ adv — **cli·ma·tol·o·gist** \-mə-'tä-lə-jist\ n

¹**cli·max** \'klī-ₗmaks\ n [L, fr. Gk klimax ladder, fr. klinein to lean] **1** : a series of ideas or statements so arranged that they increase in force and power from the first to the last; also : the last member of such a series **2** : the highest point **3** : ORGASM — **cli·mac·tic** \klī-'mak-tik\ adj

²**climax** vb : to come or bring to a climax

¹**climb** \'klīm\ vb **1** : to rise to a higher point **2** : to go up or down esp. by use of hands and feet; also : to ascend in growing — **climb·er** n

²**climb** n **1** : a place where climbing is necessary **2** : the act of climbing : ascent by climbing

clime \'klīm\ n : CLIMATE

¹**clinch** \'klinch\ vb **1** : to turn over or flatten the end of something sticking out (~ a nail); also : to fasten by clinching **2** : to make final : SETTLE **3** : to hold fast or firmly

²**clinch** n **1** : a fastening by means of a clinched nail, rivet, or bolt **2** : an act or instance of clinching in boxing

clinch·er \'klin-chər\ n : one that clinches; esp : a decisive fact, argument, act, or remark

cling \'kliŋ\ vb **clung** \'kləŋ\; **cling·ing 1** : to adhere as if glued; also : to hold or hold on tightly **2** : to have a strong emotional attachment

cling·stone \'kliŋ-ₗstōn\ n : any of various fruits (as some peaches) whose flesh adheres strongly to the pit

clin·ic \'kli-nik\ n 1 : a medical class in which patients are examined and discussed 2 : a group meeting for teaching a certain skill and working on individual problems (a reading ∼) 3 : a facility (as of a hospital) for diagnosis and treatment of outpatients

clin·i·cal \'kli-ni-kəl\ adj 1 : of, relating to, or typical of a clinic; esp : involving direct observation of the patient 2 : scientifically dispassionate — clin·i·cal·ly \-k(ə-)lē\ adv

cli·ni·cian \kli-'ni-shən\ n : a person qualified in the clinical practice of medicine, psychiatry, or psychology as distinguished from one specializing in laboratory or research techniques or in theory

¹clink \'kliŋk\ vb : to make or cause to make a sharp short metallic sound

²clink n : a clinking sound

clin·ker \'kliŋ-kər\ n : stony matter fused together : SLAG

¹clip \'klip\ vb clipped; clip·ping : to fasten with a clip

²clip n 1 : a device that grips, clasps, or hooks 2 : a cartridge holder for a rifle

³clip vb clipped; clip·ping 1 : to cut or cut off with shears 2 : CURTAIL, DIMINISH 3 : HIT, PUNCH 4 : to illegally block (an opponent) in football

⁴clip n 1 : a 2-bladed instrument for cutting esp. the nails 2 : a sharp blow 3 : a rapid pace

clip·board \'klip-ˌbōrd\ n : a small writing board with a spring clip at the top for holding papers

clip joint n, slang : an establishment (as a nightclub) that makes a practice of defrauding its customers

clip·per \'kli-pər\ n 1 : an implement for clipping esp. the hair or nails — usu. used in pl. 2 : a fast sailing ship

clip·ping \'kli-piŋ\ n : a piece clipped from something (as a newspaper)

clique \'klēk, 'klik\ n [F] : a small exclusive group of people : COTERIE — cliqu·ey \'klē-kē, 'kli-\ adj — cliqu·ish \-kish\ adj

cli·to·ris \'kli-tə-rəs\ n, pl cli·to·ri·des \kli-'tòr-ə-ˌdēz\ : a small erectile organ at the anterior or ventral part of the vulva homologous to the penis — cli·to·ral \-rəl\ adj

clk abbr clerk

clo abbr clothing

¹cloak \'klōk\ n 1 : a loose outer garment 2 : something that conceals

²cloak vb : to cover or hide with a cloak

cloak–and–dagger adj : involving or suggestive of espionage

clob·ber \'klä-bər\ vb 1 : to pound mercilessly; also : to hit with force : SMASH 2 : to defeat overwhelmingly

cloche \'klōsh\ n [F, lit., bell] : a woman's small close-fitting hat

¹clock \'kläk\ n : a timepiece not intended to be carried on the person

²clock vb 1 : to time (a person or a performance) by a timing device 2 : to register (as speed) on a mechanical recording device — clock·er n

³clock n : an ornamental figure on a stocking or sock

clock·wise \'kläk-ˌwīz\ adv : in the direction in which the hands of a clock move — clockwise adj

clock·work \-ˌwərk\ n 1 : the machinery that runs a mechanical device (as a clock or toy) 2 : the precision or regularity associated with a clock

clod \'kläd\ n 1 : a lump esp. of earth or clay 2 : a dull or insensitive person

clod·hop·per \-ˌhä-pər\ n 1 : an uncouth rustic 2 : a large heavy shoe

¹clog \'kläg\ n 1 : a weight so attached as to impede motion 2 : a thick-soled shoe

²clog vb clogged; clog·ging 1 : to impede with a clog : HINDER 2 : to obstruct passage through 3 : to become filled with extraneous matter

cloi·son·né \ˌklòiz-ᵊn-'ā\ adj : a colored decoration made of enamels poured into the divided areas in a design outlined with wire or metal strips

¹clois·ter \'klòi-stər\ n [ME cloistre, fr. OF, fr. ML claustrum, fr. L, bar, bolt, fr. claudere to close] 1 : a monastic establishment 2 : a covered usu. colonnaded passage on the side of a court — clois·tral \-strəl\ adj

²cloister vb : to shut away from the world

clone \'klōn\ n [Gk klōn twig, slip] 1 : the offspring produced asexually from an individual (as a plant increased by grafting); also : a group of replicas of all or part of a large biological molecule (as DNA) 2 : an individual grown from a single body cell of its parent and genetically identical to the parent 3 : one that appears to be a copy of an original form — clon·al \'klōn-ᵊl\ adj — clone vb

clop \'kläp\ n : a sound made by or as if by a hoof or wooden shoe against pavement — clop vb

¹close \'klōz\ vb closed; clos·ing 1 : to bar passage through : SHUT 2 : to suspend the operations (as of a school) 3 : END, TERMINATE 4 : to bring together the parts or edges of; also : to fill up 5 : GRAPPLE (∼ with the enemy) 6 : to enter into an agreement — clos·able or close·able adj

²close \'klōz\ n : CONCLUSION, END

³close \'klōs\ adj clos·er; clos·est 1 : having no openings 2 : narrowly restricting or restricted 3 : limited to a privileged class 4 : SECLUDED; also : SECRETIVE 5 : RIGOROUS 6 : SULTRY, STUFFY 7 : STINGY 8 : having little space between items or units 9 : fitting tightly; also : SHORT (∼ haircut) 10 : NEAR 11 : INTIMATE (∼ friends) 12 : ACCURATE 13 : decided by a narrow margin (a ∼ game) — close adv — close·ly adv — close·ness n

closed–circuit \'klōzd-'sər-kət\ adj : used in, shown on, or being a television installation in which the signal is transmitted by wire to a limited number of receivers

closed shop n : an establishment having only members of a labor union on the payroll

close·fist·ed \'klōz-'fis-təd, 'klōs-\ adj : STINGY

close–knit \'klōs-'nit\ *adj* : closely bound together by social, cultural, economic, or political ties

close•mouthed \'klōz-'maūthd, 'klōs-'maūtht\ *adj* : cautious or reticent in speaking

close•out \'klō-,zaūt\ *n* : a sale of a business's entire stock at low prices

close out *vb* 1 : to dispose of by a closeout 2 : to dispose of a business : SELL OUT

¹**clos•et** \'klä-zət, 'klò-\ *n* 1 : a small room for privacy 2 : a small compartment for household utensils or clothing 3 : a state or condition of secrecy ⟨came out of the ∼⟩

²**closet** *vb* : to take into a private room for an interview

close–up \'klō-,ṣəp\ *n* 1 : a photograph or movie shot taken at close range 2 : an intimate view or examination

clo•sure \'klō-zhər\ *n* 1 : an act of closing : the condition of being closed 2 : something that closes 3 : CLOTURE

clot \'klät\ *n* : a mass formed by a portion of liquid (as blood) thickening and sticking together — **clot** *vb*

cloth \'klòth\ *n, pl* **cloths** \'klòthz, 'klòths\ 1 : a pliable fabric made usu. by weaving or knitting natural or synthetic fibers and filaments 2 : TABLECLOTH 3 : distinctive dress of the clergy; *also* : CLERGY

clothe \'klōth\ *vb* **clothed** *or* **clad** \'klad\; **cloth•ing** 1 : DRESS 2 : to express by suitably significant language

clothes \'klōthz, 'klòz\ *n pl* 1 : CLOTHING 2 : BEDDING 1

clothes•horse \-,hòrs\ *n* 1 : a frame on which to hang clothes 2 : a conspicuously dressy person

clothes moth *n* : any of several small pale moths whose larvae eat wool, fur, and feathers

clothes•pin \'klōthz-,pin, 'klòz-\ *n* : a device for fastening clothes on a line

clothes•press \-,pres\ *n* : a receptacle for clothes

cloth•ier \'klōth-yər, 'klò-thē-ər\ *n* : a maker or seller of clothing

cloth•ing \'klō-thiŋ\ *n* : garments in general

clo•ture \'klō-chər\ *n* : the closing or limitation (as by calling for a vote) of debate in a legislative body

¹**cloud** \'klaūd\ *n* [ME, rock, cloud, fr. OE *clūd*] 1 : a visible mass of particles of condensed vapor (as water or ice) suspended in the atmosphere 2 : a usu. visible mass of minute airborne particles; *also* : a mass of obscuring matter in interstellar space 3 : CROWD, SWARM ⟨a ∼ of mosquitoes⟩ 4 : something having a dark or threatening aspect — **cloud•i•ness** \'klaū-dē-nəs\ *n* — **cloud•less** *adj* — **cloudy** *adj*

²**cloud** *vb* 1 : to darken or hide with or as if with a cloud 2 : OBSCURE 3 : TAINT, SULLY

cloud•burst \-,bərst\ *n* : a sudden heavy rainfall

cloud•let \-lət\ *n* : a small cloud

cloud nine *n* : a feeling of extreme well-being or elation — usu. used with *on*

¹**clout** \'klaūt\ *n* 1 : a blow esp. with the hand 2 : PULL, INFLUENCE

²**clout** *vb* : to hit forcefully

¹**clove** \'klōv\ *n* : one of the small bulbs that grows at the base of the scales of a large bulb ⟨a ∼ of garlic⟩

²**clove** *past of* CLEAVE

³**clove** *n* [ME *clowe*, fr. OF *clou (de girofle)*, lit., nail of clove, fr. L *clavus* nail] : the dried flower bud of an East Indian tree used esp. as a spice

clo•ven \'klō-vən\ *past part of* CLEAVE

cloven foot *n* : CLOVEN HOOF — **cloven–foot•ed** \-'fü-təd\ *adj*

cloven hoof *n* : a foot (as of a sheep) with the front part divided into two parts — **cloven–hoofed** \-'hüft, -'hüvd\ *adj*

clo•ver \'klō-vər\ *n* : any of a genus of leguminous herbs with usu. 3-parted leaves and dense flower heads

clo•ver•leaf \-,lēf\ *n, pl* **cloverleafs** \-,lēfs\ *or* **clo•ver•leaves** \-,lēvz\ : an interchange between two major highways that from above resembles a four-leaf clover

¹**clown** \'klaūn\ *n* 1 : BOOR 2 : a fool or comedian in an entertainment (as a circus) — **clown•ish** *adj* — **clown•ish•ly** *adv* — **clown•ish•ness** *n*

²**clown** *vb* : to act like a clown

cloy \'klòi\ *vb* : to disgust or nauseate with excess of something orig. pleasing — **cloy•ing•ly** *adv*

clr *abbr* clear

¹**club** \'kləb\ *n* 1 : a heavy wooden stick or staff used as a weapon; *also* : BAT 2 : any of a suit of playing cards marked with a black figure resembling a clover leaf 3 : a group of persons associated for a common purpose; *also* : the meeting place of such a group

²**club** *vb* **clubbed; club•bing** 1 : to strike with a club 2 : to unite or combine for a common cause

club•foot \'kləb-'füt\ *n* : a misshapen foot twisted out of position from birth; *also* : this deformed condition — **club•foot•ed** \-'fü-təd\ *adj*

club•house \'kləb-,haūs\ *n* 1 : a house occupied by a club 2 : locker rooms used by an athletic team

club sandwich *n* : a sandwich of three slices of bread with two layers of meat (as turkey) and lettuce, tomato, and mayonnaise

club soda *n* : SODA WATER

cluck \'klək\ *n* : the call of a hen esp. to her chicks — **cluck** *vb*

¹**clue** \'klü\ *n* : something that guides through an intricate procedure or maze; *esp* : a piece of evidence leading to the solution of a problem

²**clue** *vb* **clued; clue•ing** *or* **clu•ing** : to provide with a clue; *also* : to give information to ⟨∼ me in⟩

¹**clump** \'kləmp\ *n* 1 : a group of things clustered together 2 : a heavy tramping sound

²**clump** *vb* : to tread clumsily and noisily

clum•sy \'kləm-zē\ *adj* **clum•si•er; -est** 1 : lacking dexterity, nimbleness, or grace 2 : not tactful or subtle — **clum•si•ly** \-zə-lē\ *adv* — **clum•si•ness** \-zē-nəs\ *n*

clung *past and past part of* CLING

clunk•er \'kləŋ-kər\ *n* 1 : a dilapidated automobile 2 : a notable failure

¹**clus•ter** \'kləs-tər\ *n* : GROUP, BUNCH

²**cluster** *vb* : to grow or gather in a cluster

¹**clutch** \'kləch\ *vb* : to grasp with or as if with the hand

²**clutch** *n* 1 : the claws or a hand in the act of grasping; *also* : CONTROL, POWER 2 : a device for gripping an object 3 : a coupling used to connect and disconnect a driving and a driven part of a mechanism; *also* : a lever or pedal operating such a coupling 4 : a crucial situation

³**clutch** *adj* : made, done, or successful in a crucial situation

⁴**clutch** *n* 1 : a nest or batch of eggs; *also* : a brood of chicks 2 : GROUP, BUNCH

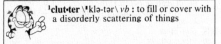
¹**clut•ter** \'klə-tər\ *vb* : to fill or cover with a disorderly scattering of things

²**clutter** *n* : a crowded mass

cm *abbr* centimeter

Cm *symbol* curium

CM *abbr* [Commonwealth of the Northern Mariana Islands] Northern Mariana Islands

cmdr *abbr* commander

cml *abbr* commercial

CMSgt *abbr* chief master sergeant

CNO *abbr* chief of naval operations

CNS *abbr* central nervous system

co *abbr* 1 company 2 county

Co *symbol* cobalt

CO *abbr* 1 Colorado 2 commanding officer 3 conscientious objector

c/o *abbr* care of

¹coach \'kōch\ *n* **1** : a large closed 4-wheeled carriage with an elevated outside front seat for the driver **2** : a railroad passenger car esp. for day travel **3** : BUS **4** : a private tutor; *also* : one who instructs or trains a team of performers

coach 1

²coach *vb* : to instruct, direct, or prompt as a coach
coach·man \-mən\ *n* : a man who drives a coach or carriage
co·ad·ju·tor \ˌkō-ə-'jü-tər, kō-'a-jə-tər\ *n* : ASSISTANT; *esp* : an assistant bishop having the right of succession
co·ag·u·lant \kō-'a-gyə-lənt\ *n* : something that produces coagulation
co·ag·u·late \-ˌlāt\ *vb* **-lat·ed; -lat·ing** : CLOT — **co·ag·u·la·tion** \kō-ˌa-gyə-'lā-shən\ *n*
¹coal \'kōl\ *n* **1** : EMBER **2** : a black solid combustible mineral used as fuel
²coal *vb* **1** : to supply with coal **2** : to take in coal
co·a·lesce \ˌkō-ə-'les\ *vb* **co·a·lesced; co·a·lesc·ing** : to grow together; *also* : FUSE **syn** merge, blend, mingle, mix — **co·a·les·cence** \-ᵊns\ *n*
coal·field \'kōl-ˌfēld\ *n* : a region rich in coal deposits
coal gas *n* : gas from coal; *esp* : gas distilled from bituminous coal and used for heating
co·a·li·tion \ˌkō-ə-'li-shən\ *n* : UNION; *esp* : a temporary union for a common purpose — **co·a·li·tion·ist** *n*
coal oil *n* : KEROSENE
coal tar *n* : tar distilled from bituminous coal and used in dyes and drugs
co·an·chor \'kō-ˌaŋ-kər\ *n* : a newscaster who shares the duties of head broadcaster

coarse \'kōrs\ *adj* **coars·er; coars·est 1** : of ordinary or inferior quality **2** : composed of large parts or particles ⟨∼ sand⟩ **3** : CRUDE ⟨∼ manners⟩ **4** : ROUGH, HARSH — **coarse·ly** *adv* — **coarse·ness** *n*
coars·en \'kōrs-ᵊn\ *vb* : to make or become coarse
¹coast \'kōst\ *n* [ME *cost*, fr. MF *coste*, fr. L *costa* rib, side] **1** : SEASHORE **2** : a slide down a slope **3** : the immediate area of view — used in the phrase *the coast is clear* — **coast·al** *adj*
²coast *vb* **1** : to sail along the shore **2** : to move (as downhill on a sled) without effort

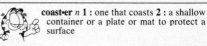
coast·er *n* **1** : one that coasts **2** : a shallow container or a plate or mat to protect a surface

coaster brake *n* : a brake in the hub of the rear wheel of a bicycle
coast guard *n* : a military force employed in guarding or patrolling a coast — **coast·guards·man** \'kōst-ˌgärdz-mən\ *n*
coast·line \'kōst-ˌlīn\ *n* : the outline or shape of a coast
¹coat \'kōt\ *n* **1** : an outer garment for the upper part of the body **2** : an external growth (as of fur or feathers) on an animal **3** : a covering layer — **coat·ed** \'kō-təd\ *adj*
²coat *vb* : to cover usu. with a finishing or protective coat
coat·ing \'kō-tiŋ\ *n* : COAT, COVERING
coat of arms : the heraldic bearings (as of a person) usu. depicted on an escutcheon
coat of mail : a garment of metal scales or rings worn as armor
co·au·thor \'kō-'ȯ-thər\ *n* : a joint or associate author — **coauthor** *vb*
coax \'kōks\ *vb* : WHEEDLE; *also* : to gain by gentle urging or flattery
co·ax·i·al \'kō-'ak-sē-əl\ *adj* : having coincident axes — **co·ax·i·al·ly** *adv*
coaxial cable *n* : a cable that consists of a tube of electrically conducting material surrounding a central conductor

cob \'käb\ n 1 : a male swan 2 : CORN-COB 3 : a short-legged stocky horse

co·balt \'kō-ˌbȯlt\ n [G Kobalt, alter. of Kobold, lit., goblin; fr. its occurrence in silver ore, believed to be due to goblins] : a tough shiny silver-white magnetic metallic chemical element found with iron and nickel — see ELEMENT table

cob·ble \'kä-bəl\ vb cob·bled; cob·bling : to make or put together roughly or hastily

cob·bler \'kä-blər\ n 1 : a mender or maker of shoes 2 : a deep-dish fruit pie with a thick crust

cob·ble·stone \'kä-bəl-ˌstōn\ n : a naturally rounded stone larger than a pebble and smaller than a boulder

co·bra \'kō-brə\ n [Pg cobra (de capello), lit., hooded snake] : any of several venomous snakes of Asia and Africa that when excited expand the skin of the neck into a broad hood

cob·web \'käb-ˌweb\ n [ME coppeweb, fr. coppe spider, fr. OE ātorcoppe] 1 : SPIDERWEB; also : a thread spun by a spider or insect larva 2 : something flimsy or entangling

co·caine \kō-'kān, 'kō-ˌkān\ n : a drug obtained from the leaves of a So. American shrub (co·ca \'kō-kə\) that can result in severe psychological dependence and is sometimes used in medicine as a local anesthetic and illegally to stimulate the central nervous system

coc·cus \'kä-kəs\ n, pl coc·ci \'käk-ˌsī\ : a spherical bacterium

coc·cyx \'käk-siks\ n, pl coc·cy·ges \'käk-sə-ˌjēz\ also coc·cyx·es \'käk-sik-səz\ : the end of the spinal column beyond the sacrum esp. in humans

co·chi·neal \'kä-chə-ˌnēl\ n : a red dye made from the dried bodies of females of a tropical American insect (cochineal insect)

co·chlea \'kō-klē-ə, 'kä-\ n, pl co·chle·as or co·chle·ae \-klē-ˌē, -ˌī\ : the usu. spiral part of the inner ear containing nerve endings which carry information about sound to the brain — co·chle·ar \-klē-ər\ adj

¹cock \'käk\ n 1 : the adult male of a bird and esp. of the common domestic chicken 2 : VALVE, FAUCET 3 : LEADER 4 : the hammer of a firearm; also : the position of the hammer when ready for firing

²cock vb 1 : to draw back the hammer of a firearm 2 : to set or draw back in readiness for some action (~ your arm to throw) 3 : to turn or tilt usu. to one side

³cock n : a small pile (as of hay)

cock·ade \kä-'kād\ n : an ornament worn on the hat as a badge

cock·a·tiel \ˌkä-kə-'tēl\ n : a small crested parrot often kept as a cage bird

cock·a·too \'kä-kə-ˌtü\ n, pl -toos [D kaketoe, fr. Malay kakatua] : any of various large noisy Australian crested parrots

cock·a·trice \'kä-kə-trəs, -ˌtrīs\ n : a legendary serpent with a deadly glance

cock·crow \'käk-ˌkrō\ n : DAWN

cocked hat \'käkt-\ n : a hat with the brim turned up on two or three sides

cock·er·el \'kä-kə-rəl\ n : a young male domestic chicken

cock·er spaniel \'kä-kər-\ n [cocking woodcock hunting] : any of a breed of small spaniels with long ears, square muzzle, and silky coat

cock·eyed \'kä-'kīd\ adj 1 : turned or tilted to one side 2 : slightly crazy : FOOLISH

cock·fight \'käk-ˌfīt\ n : a contest of gamecocks usu. fitted with metal spurs

¹cock·le \'kä-kəl\ n : any of several weedy plants related to the pinks

²cockle n : a bivalve mollusk with a heart-shaped shell

cock·le·shell \-ˌshel\ n 1 : the shell of a cockle 2 : a light flimsy boat

cockleshell 1

cock·ney \'käk-nē\ n, pl cockneys : a native of London and esp. of the East End of London; also : the dialect of a cockney

cock·pit \'käk-ˌpit\ n 1 : a pit for cockfights 2 : a space or compartment in a vehicle from which it is steered, piloted, or driven

cock·roach \'käk-ˌrōch\ n [Sp cucaracha] : any of an order or suborder of active nocturnal insects including some which infest houses and ships

cock·sure \'käk-'shùr\ adj 1 : perfectly sure : CERTAIN 2 : COCKY

cock·tail \'käk-ˌtāl\ n 1 : an iced drink made of liquor and flavoring ingredients 2 : an appetizer (as tomato juice) served as a first course of a meal

cocky \'kä-kē\ adj cock·i·er; -est : marked by overconfidence : PERT, CONCEITED — cock·i·ly \-kə-lē\ adv — cock·i·ness \-kē-nəs\ n

co·coa \'kō-kō\ n 1 : CACAO 2 : chocolate deprived of some of its fat and powdered; also : a drink made of this heated with water or milk

co·co·nut \'kō-kə-(ˌ)nət\ n : a large edible nut produced by a tall tropical palm (co·conut palm)

co·coon \kə-'kün\ n : a case usu. of silk formed by some insect larvae for protection during the pupal stage

cod \'käd\ n, pl cod also cods : a bottom-dwelling

bony fish of the No. Atlantic that is an important food fish; *also* : a related fish of the Pacific Ocean

COD *abbr* **1** cash on delivery **2** collect on delivery

co•da \'kō-də\ *n* : a closing section in a musical composition that is formally distinct from the main structure

cod•dle \'käd-əl\ *vb* **cod•dled; cod•dling 1** : to cook slowly in water below the boiling point **2** : PAMPER

¹code \'kōd\ *n* **1** : a systematic statement of a body of law **2** : a system of principles or rules ⟨moral ∼⟩ **3** : a system of signals **4** : a system of symbols (as in secret communication) with special meanings **5** : GENETIC CODE

²code *vb* **cod•ed; cod•ing** : to put into the form or symbols of a code

co•deine \'kō-ₐdēn\ *n* : a narcotic drug obtained from opium and used esp. in cough remedies

co•dex \'kō-ₐdeks\ *n*, *pl* **co•di•ces** \'kō-də-ₐsēz, 'kä-\ : a manuscript book (as of the Scriptures or classics)

cod•fish \'käd-ₐfish\ *n* : COD

cod•ger \'kä-jər\ *n* : an odd or cranky and usu. elderly fellow

cod•i•cil \'kä-də-səl, -ₐsil\ *n* : a legal instrument modifying an earlier will

cod•i•fy \'kä-də-ₐfī, 'kō-\ *vb* **-fied; -fy•ing** : to arrange in a systematic form — **cod•i•fi•ca•tion** \ₐkä-də-fə-'kä-shən, ₐkō-\ *n*

co•ed \'kō-ₐed\ *n* : a female student in a coeducational institution — **coed** *adj*

co•ed•u•ca•tion \ₐkō-ₐe-jə-'kä-shən\ *n* : the education of male and female students at the same institution — **co•ed•u•ca•tion•al** \-shə-nəl\ *adj* — **co•ed•u•ca•tion•al•ly** *adv*

co•ef•fi•cient \ₐkō-ə-'fi-shənt\ *n* **1** : a constant factor as distinguished from a variable in a mathematical term **2** : a number that serves as a measure of some property (as of a substance, device, or process)

coe•len•ter•ate \si-'len-tə-ₐrāt, -rət\ *n* : any of a phylum of radially symmetrical invertebrate animals including the corals, sea anemones, and jellyfishes

co•equal \kō-'ē-kwəl\ *adj* : equal with another — **co•equal** *n* — **co•equal•i•ty** \ₐkō-ē-'kwä-lə-tē\ *n* — **co•equal•ly** *adv*

co•erce \kō-'ərs\ *vb* **co•erced; co•erc•ing 1** : RESTRAIN, REPRESS **2** : COMPEL **3** : ENFORCE — **co•er•cion** \-'ər-zhən, -shən\ *n* — **co•er•cive** \-'ər-siv\ *adj*

co•e•val \kō-'ē-vəl\ *adj* : of the same age — **coeval** *n*

co•ex•ist \ₐkō-ig-'zist\ *vb* **1** : to exist together or at the same time **2** : to live in peace with each other — **co•ex•is•tence** \-'zis-təns\ *n*

co•ex•ten•sive \ₐkō-ik-'sten-siv\ *adj* : having the same scope or extent in space or time

C of C *abbr* Chamber of Commerce

cof•fee \'kȯ-fē\ *n* [It & Turk; It *caffè*, fr. Turk *kahve*, fr. Ar *qahwa*] : a drink made from the roasted and ground seeds of a fruit of a tropical shrub or tree; *also* : these seeds (**coffee beans**) or a plant producing them

cof•fee•house \-ₐhau̇s\ *n* : a place where refreshments (as coffee) are sold

coffee klatch \-ₐklach\ *n* : KAFFEE-KLATSCH

cof•fee•pot \-ₐpät\ *n* : a pot for brewing or serving coffee

coffee shop *n* : a small restaurant

coffee table *n* : a low table customarily placed in front of a sofa

cof•fer \'kȯ-fər\ *n* : a chest or box used esp. for valuables

cof•fer•dam \-ₐdam\ *n* : a watertight enclosure from which water is pumped to expose the bottom of a body of water and permit construction

cof•fin \'kȯ-fən\ *n* : a box or chest for a corpse to be buried in

C of S *abbr* chief of staff

¹cog \'käg\ *n* : a tooth on the rim of a wheel or gear — **cogged** \'kägd\ *adj*

²cog *abbr* cognate

co•gen•e•ra•tion \ₐkō-ₐje-nə-'rā-shən\ *n* : the simultaneous generation of electricity and heat from the same fuel

co•gent \'kō-jənt\ *adj* : having power to compel or constrain : CONVINCING — **co•gen•cy** \-jən-sē\ *n*

cog•i•tate \'kä-jə-ₐtāt\ *vb* **-tat•ed; -tat•ing** : THINK, PONDER — **cog•i•ta•tion** \ₐkä-jə-'tā-shən\ *n* — **cog•i•ta•tive** \'kä-jə-ₐtā-tiv\ *adj*

co•gnac \'kōn-ₐyak\ *n* : a French brandy

cog•nate \'käg-ₐnāt\ *adj* **1** : of the same or similar nature **2** : RELATED; *esp* : related by descent from the same ancestral language — **cognate** *n*

cog•ni•tive \'käg-nə-tiv\ *adj* : of, relating to, or being conscious mental activity (as thinking, remembering, learning, or using language) — **cog•ni•tion** \käg-'ni-shən\ *n*

cog•ni•zance \'käg-nə-zəns\ *n* **1** : apprehension by the mind : AWARENESS **2** : NOTICE, HEED — **cog•ni•zant** \'käg-nə-zənt\ *adj*

cog•no•men \käg-'nō-mən, 'käg-nə-\ *n*, *pl* **cognomens** *or* **cog•no•mi•na** \käg-'nä-mə-nə, -'nō-\ : NAME; *esp* : NICKNAME

co•gno•scen•te \ₐkän-yə-'shen-tē\ *n*, *pl* **-scen•ti** \-tē\ [obs. It] : CONNOISSEUR

cog•wheel \'käg-ₐhwēl\ *n* : a wheel with cogs or teeth

co•hab•it \kō-'ha-bət\ *vb* : to live together as husband and wife — **co•hab•i•ta•tion** \-ₐha-bə-'tā-shən\ *n*

co•here \kō-'hir\ *vb* **co•hered; co•her•ing** : to stick together

co•her•ent \kō-'hir-ənt\ *adj* **1** : having the quality of cohering **2** : logically consistent — **co•her•ence** \-əns\ *n* — **co•her•ent•ly** *adv*

co•he•sion \kō-'hē-zhən\ *n* **1** : a sticking together **2** : molecular attraction by which the particles of a body are united — **co•he•sive** \-siv\ *adj* — **co•he•sive•ly** *adv* — **co•he•sive•ness** *n*

co•ho \'kō-ₐhō\ *n*, *pl* **cohos** *or* **coho** : a rather small Pacific salmon with light-colored flesh

co•hort \'kō-ₐhȯrt\ *n* **1** : a group of warriors or followers **2** : COMPANION, ACCOMPLICE

coif \'kȯif; *2 usu* 'kwäf\ *n* **1** : a close-fitting hat **2** : COIFFURE

coif•feur \kwä-'fər\ *n* [F] : HAIRDRESSER

coif•feuse \kwä-'fərz, -'fəz, -'füz, -'fyüz\ *n* : a female hairdresser

coif•fure \kwä-'fyu̇r\ *n* : a manner of arranging the hair

¹coil \'kȯil\ *vb* : to wind in a spiral shape

²coil *n* : a series of rings or loops (as of coiled rope, wire, or pipe) : RING, LOOP

¹coin \'kȯin\ *n* [ME, fr. MF, wedge, corner, fr. L *cuneus* wedge] **1** : a piece of metal issued by government authority as money **2** : metal money

²coin *vb* **1** : to make (a coin) esp. by stamping : MINT **2** : CREATE, INVENT ⟨∼ a phrase⟩ — **coin•er** *n*

coin•age \'kȯi-nij\ *n* **1** : the act or process of coining **2** : COINS

co•in•cide \ₐkō-ən-'sīd, 'kō-ən-ₐsīd\ *vb* **-cid•ed; -cid•ing 1** : to occupy the same place in space or time **2** : to correspond or agree exactly

co•in•ci•dence \kō-'in-sə-dəns\ *n* **1** : exact agreement **2** : occurrence together apparently without reason; *also* : an event that so occurs

co•in•ci•dent \-sə-dənt\ *adj* **1** : of similar nature **2** : occupying the same space or time — **co•in•ci•den•tal** \kō-ₐin-sə-'dent-əl\ *adj*

co•i•tus \'kō-ə-təs\ *n* [L, fr. *coire* to come together] : SEXUAL INTERCOURSE — **co•i•tal** \-əl\ *adj*

¹coke \'kōk\ *n* : a hard gray porous fuel made by heating soft coal to drive off most of its volatile material

²coke *n* : COCAINE

¹col *abbr* **1** colonial; colony **2** column

²col *or* **coll** *abbr* **1** collect, collected, collection **2** college, collegiate

Col *abbr* **1** colonel **2** Colorado **3** Colossians

COL *abbr* **1** colonel **2** cost of living

co•la \'kō-lə\ *n* : a carbonated soft drink usu. containing sugar. caffeine, caramel, and special flavoring

col•an•der \\'kə-lən-dər, 'kä-\\ *n* : a perforated utensil for draining food

¹cold \\'kōld\\ *adj* **1** : having a low or decidedly subnormal temperature **2** : lacking warmth of feeling **3** : suffering or uncomfortable from lack of warmth — **cold•ly** *adv* — **cold•ness** *n* — **in cold blood** : with premeditation : DELIBERATELY

²cold *n* **1** : a condition marked by low temperature; *also* : cold weather **2** : a chilly feeling **3** : a bodily disorder popularly associated with chilling; *esp* : COMMON COLD

³cold *adv* : TOTALLY, FINALLY

cold–blood•ed \\'kōld-'blə-dəd\\ *adj* **1** : lacking normal human feelings **2** : having a body temperature not internally regulated but close to that of the environment **3** : sensitive to cold

cold feet *n pl* : doubt or fear that prevents action

cold front *n* : an advancing edge of a cold air mass

cold shoulder *n* : cold or unsympathetic behavior — **cold–shoul•der** *vb*

cold sore *n* : a group of blisters appearing in or about the mouth in the oral form of herpes simplex

cold sweat *n* : concurrent perspiration and chill usu. associated with fear, pain, or shock

¹cold turkey *n* : abrupt complete cessation of the use of an addictive drug

²cold turkey *adv* : without a period of adjustment : all at once

cold war *n* : a conflict characterized by the use of means short of sustained overt military action

cole•slaw \\'kōl-ˌslȯ\\ *n* [D *koolsla*, fr. *kool* cabbage + *sla* salad] : a salad made of raw cabbage

col•ic \\'kä-lik\\ *n* : sharp sudden abdominal pain — **col•icky** \\'kä-li-kē\\ *adj*

col•i•se•um \\ˌkä-lə-'sē-əm\\ *n* : a large structure esp. for athletic contests

col•lab•o•rate \\kə-'la-bə-ˌrāt\\ *vb* **-rat•ed; -rat•ing 1** : to work jointly with others (as in writing a book) **2** : to cooperate with an enemy force occupying one's country — **col•lab•o•ra•tion** \\-ˌla-bə-'rā-shən\\ *n* — **col•lab•o•ra•tor** \\-'la-bə-ˌrā-tər\\ *n*

col•lage \\kə-'läzh\\ *n* [F, lit., gluing] : an artistic composition of fragments (as of printed matter) pasted on a surface

¹col•lapse \\kə-'laps\\ *vb* **col•lapsed; col•laps•ing 1** : to shrink together abruptly **2** : DISINTEGRATE; *also* : to fall in : give way **3** : to break down physically or mentally; *esp* : to fall helpless or unconscious **4** : to fold down compactly — **col•laps•ible** *adj*

²collapse *n* : BREAKDOWN

¹col•lar \\'kä-lər\\ *n* **1** : a band, strip, or chain worn around the neck or the neckline of a garment **2** : something resembling a collar — **col•lar•less** *adj*

²collar *vb* : to seize by the collar; *also* : ARREST, GRAB

col•lar•bone \\-ˌbōn\\ *n* : the bone of the shoulder that joins the breastbone and the shoulder blade

col•lard \\'kä-lərd\\ *n* : a stalked smooth-leaved kale — usu. used in pl.

col•late \\kə-'lāt; 'kä-ˌlāt, 'kō-\\ *vb* **col•lat•ed; col•lat•ing 1** : to compare (as two texts) carefully and critically **2** : to assemble in proper order

¹col•lat•er•al \\kə-'la-tə-rəl\\ *adj* **1** : associated but of secondary importance **2** : descended from the same ancestors but not in the same line **3** : PARALLEL **4** : of, relating to, or being collateral used as security; *also* : secured by collateral

²collateral *n* : property (as stocks) used as security for the repayment of a loan

col•la•tion \\kä-'lā-shən, kō-\\ *n* **1** : a light meal **2** : the act, process, or result of collating

col•league \\'kä-ˌlēg\\ *n* : an associate esp. in a profession

¹col•lect \\'kä-likt, -ˌlekt\\ *n* : a short prayer comprising an invocation, petition, and conclusion

²col•lect \\kə-'lekt\\ *vb* **1** : to bring or come together into

one body or place : GATHER **2** : to gain control of (⁓ his thoughts) **3** : to receive payment of — **col•lect•ible** *or* **col•lect•able** *adj or n* — **col•lec•tor** \\-'lek-tər\\ *n*

³col•lect \\kə-'lekt\\ *adv or adj* : to be paid for by the receiver

col•lect•ed \\kə-'lek-təd\\ *adj* : SELF-POSSESSED, CALM

col•lec•tion \\kə-'lek-shən\\ *n* **1** : the act or process of collecting ⟨garbage ⁓⟩ **2** : something collected ⟨a stamp ⁓⟩ **3** : GROUP, AGGREGATE

¹col•lec•tive \\kə-'lek-tiv\\ *adj* **1** : of, relating to, or denoting a group of individuals considered as a whole **2** : involving all members of a group as distinct from its individuals **3** : shared or assumed by all members of the group — **col•lec•tive•ly** *adv*

²collective *n* **1** : GROUP **2** : a cooperative unit or organization

collective bargaining *n* : negotiation between an employer and a labor union

col•lec•tiv•ise *chiefly Brit var of* COLLECTIVIZE

col•lec•tiv•ism \\kə-'lek-ti-ˌvi-zəm\\ *n* : a political or economic theory advocating collective control esp. over production and distribution

col•lec•tiv•ize \\-ˌvīz\\ *vb* **-ized; -iz•ing** : to organize under collective control — **col•lec•tiv•i•za•tion** \\-ˌlek-ti-və-'zā-shən\\ *n*

col•leen \\kä-'lēn, 'kä-ˌlēn\\ *n* : an Irish girl

col•lege \\'kä-lij\\ *n* [ME, fr. MF, fr. L *collegium* society, fr. *collega* colleague, fr. *com-* with + *legare* to appoint] **1** : a building used for an educational or religious purpose **2** : an institution of higher learning granting a bachelor's degree; *also* : an institution offering instruction esp. in a vocational or technical field ⟨barber ⁓⟩ **3** : an organized body of persons having common interests or duties ⟨⁓ of cardinals⟩ — **col•le•giate** \\kə-'lē-jət\\ *adj*

col•le•gi•al•i•ty \\kə-ˌlē-jē-'a-lə-tē\\ *n* : the relationship of colleagues

col•le•gian \\kə-'lē-jən\\ *n* : a college student or recent college graduate

col•le•gi•um \\kə-'le-gē-əm, -'lā-\\ *n, pl* **-gia** \\-gē-ə\\ *or* **-giums** : a group in which each member has approximately equal power

col•lide \\kə-'līd\\ *vb* **col•lid•ed; col•lid•ing 1** : to come together with solid impact **2** : to come into conflict : CLASH

col•lid•er \\kə-'lī-dər\\ *n* : a particle accelerator in which two beams of particles are made to collide

col•lie \\'kä-lē\\ *n* : a large dog of a breed with rough⸗coated and smooth-coated varieties developed in Scotland for herding sheep

collie

col•lier \\'käl-yər\\ *n* **1** : a coal miner **2** : a ship for carrying coal

col•liery \\'käl-yə-rē\\ *n, pl* **-lier•ies** : a coal mine and its associated buildings

col•li•mate \\'kä-lə-ˌmāt\\ *vb* **-mat•ed; -mat•ing** : to make (as light rays) parallel

col·li·sion \kə-'li-zhən\ *n* : an act or instance of colliding

col·lo·ca·tion \ˌkä-lə-'kā-shən\ *n* : the act or result of placing or arranging together; *esp* : a noticeable arrangement or conjoining of linguistic elements (as words)

col·loid \'kä-ˌlȯid\ *n* : a substance in the form of submicroscopic particles that when in solution or suspension do not settle out; *also* : such a substance together with the medium in which it is dispersed — **col·loi·dal** \kə-'lȯid-ᵊl\ *adj*

colloq *abbr* colloquial

col·lo·qui·al \kə-'lō-kwē-əl\ *adj* : of, relating to, or characteristic of conversation and esp. of familiar and informal conversation

col·lo·qui·al·ism \-'lō-kwē-ə-ˌli-zəm\ *n* : a colloquial expression

col·lo·qui·um \kə-'lō-kwē-əm\ *n*, *pl* **-qui·ums** *or* **-quia** \-ə\ : CONFERENCE, SEMINAR

col·lo·quy \'kä-lə-kwē\ *n*, *pl* **-quies** : a usu. formal conversation or conference

col·lu·sion \kə-'lü-zhən\ *n* : secret agreement or cooperation for an illegal or deceitful purpose — **col·lu·sive** \-siv\ *adj*

Colo *abbr* Colorado

co·logne \kə-'lōn\ *n* [*Cologne*, Germany] : a perfumed liquid — **co·logned** \-'lōnd\ *adj*

Co·lom·bi·an \kə-'ləm-bē-ən\ *n* : a native or inhabitant of Colombia — **Colombian** *adj*

¹co·lon \'kō-lən\ *n*, *pl* **colons** *or* **co·la** \-lə\ : the part of the large intestine extending from the cecum to the rectum — **co·lon·ic** \kō-'lä-nik\ *adj*

²colon *n*, *pl* **colons** : a punctuation mark : used esp. to direct attention to following matter (as a list)

co·lón *also* **co·lone** \kə-'lōn\ *n*, *pl* **co·lo·nes** \-'lō-ˌnäs\ — see MONEY table

col·o·nel \'kərn-ᵊl\ *n* [alter. of *coronel*, fr. MF, fr. It *colonnello* column of soldiers, colonel, ultim. fr. L *columna*] : a commissioned officer (as in the army) ranking next below a brigadier general

¹co·lo·nial \kə-'lō-nē-əl\ *adj* **1** : of, relating to, or characteristic of a colony; *also* : possessing or composed of colonies **2** *often cap* : of or relating to the original 13 colonies forming the U.S.

²colonial *n* : a member or inhabitant of a colony

co·lo·nial·ism \-ə-ˌli-zəm\ *n* : control by one power over a dependent area or people; *also* : a policy advocating or based on such control — **co·lo·nial·ist** \-list\ *n or adj*

col·o·nise *Brit var of* COLONIZE

col·o·nist \'kä-lə-nist\ *n* **1** : COLONIAL **2** : one that colonizes or settles in a new country

col·o·nize \'kä-lə-ˌnīz\ *vb* **-nized; -niz·ing 1** : to establish a colony in or on **2** : SETTLE — **col·o·ni·za·tion** \ˌkä-lə-nə-'zā-shən\ *n* — **col·o·niz·er** *n*

col·on·nade \ˌkä-lə-'nād\ *n* : an evenly spaced row of columns usu. supporting the base of a roof structure

col·o·ny \'kä-lə-nē\ *n*, *pl* **-nies 1** : a body of people living in a new territory; *also* : the territory inhabited by these people **2** : a localized population of organisms ⟨a ∼ of bees⟩ **3** : a group with common interests situated in close association ⟨a writers' ∼⟩; *also* : the area occupied by such a group

col·o·phon \'kä-lə-fən, -ˌfän\ *n* **1** : an inscription placed at the end of a book with facts relative to its production **2** : a distinctive symbol used by a printer or publisher

¹col·or \'kə-lər\ *n* **1** : a phenomenon of light (as red or blue) or visual perception that enables one to differentiate otherwise identical objects; *also* : a hue as contrasted with black, white, or gray **2** : APPEARANCE **3** : complexion tint **4** *pl* : FLAG; *also* : military service ⟨a call to the ∼s⟩ **5** : VIVIDNESS, INTEREST — **col·or·ful** *adj* — **col·or·less** *adj*

²color *vb* **1** : to give color to; *also* : to change the color of **2** : BLUSH

Col·o·ra·do potato beetle \ˌkä-lə-'ra-dō-, -'rä-\ *n* : a black-and-yellow striped beetle that feeds on the leaves of the potato

col·or·ation \ˌkə-lə-'rā-shən\ *n* : use or arrangement of colors

col·or·a·tu·ra \ˌkə-lə-rə-'tùr-ə, -'tyùr-\ *n* **1** : elaborate ornamentation in vocal music **2** : a soprano specializing in coloratura

col·or–blind \'kə-lər-ˌblīnd\ *adj* **1** : partially or totally unable to distinguish one or more chromatic colors **2** : not recognizing differences of race — **color blindness** *n*

col·ored \'kə-lərd\ *adj* **1** : having color **2** : SLANTED, BIASED **3** : of a race other than the white; *esp* : BLACK **4** — sometimes taken to be offensive

col·or·fast \'kə-lər-ˌfast\ *adj* : having color that does not fade or run — **col·or·fast·ness** *n*

col·or·ize \'kə-lə-ˌrīz\ *vb* **-ized; -iz·ing** : to add color to by means of a computer — **col·or·i·za·tion** \ˌkə-lə-rə-'zā-shən\ *n*

co·los·sal \kə-'lä-səl\ *adj* : of very great size or degree

Co·los·sians \kə-'lä-shənz\ *n* — see BIBLE table

co·los·sus \kə-'lä-səs\ *n*, *pl* **co·los·si** \-ˌsī\ [L] : a gigantic statue; *also* : something of great size or scope

col·our *chiefly Brit var of* COLOR

col·por·teur \'käl-ˌpȯr-tər\ *n* [F] : a peddler of religious books

colt \'kōlt\ *n* : FOAL; *also* : a young male horse, ass, or zebra — **colt·ish** *adj*

col·um·bine \'kä-ləm-ˌbīn\ *n* [ME, fr. ML *columbina*, fr. L, fem. of *columbinus* dovelike, fr. *columba* dove] : any of a genus of plants with showy spurred flowers that are related to the buttercups

co·lum·bi·um \kə-'ləm-bē-əm\ *n* : NIOBIUM

Columbus Day \kə-'ləm-bəs-\ *n* : the 2d Monday in October or formerly October 12 observed as a legal holiday in many states in commemoration of the landing of Columbus

col·umn \'kä-ləm\ *n* **1** : one of two or more vertical

sections of a printed page; *also* : one in a usu. regular series of articles (as in a newspaper) **2** : a supporting pillar; *esp* : one consisting of a usu. round shaft, a capital, and a base **3** : something resembling a column ⟨a ∼ of water⟩ **4** : a long row (as of soldiers) — **co·lum·nar** \kə-'ləm-nər\ *adj*

col·um·nist \'kä-ləm-nist\ *n* : a person who writes a newspaper or magazine column

com *abbr* **1** comedy; comic **2** comma

co·ma \'kō-mə\ *n* : a state of deep unconsciousness caused by disease, injury, or poison — **co·ma·tose** \'kō-mə-₁tōs, 'kä-\ *adj*

Co·man·che \kə-'man-chē\ *n, pl* **Comanche** *or* **Co·manches** : a member of an American Indian people ranging from Wyoming and Nebraska south into New Mexico and Texas

¹comb \'kōm\ *n* **1** : a toothed instrument for arranging the hair or for separating and cleaning textile fibers **2** : a fleshy crest on the head of a fowl **3** : HONEYCOMB — **comb** *vb* — **combed** \'kōmd\ *adj*

²comb *abbr* combination; combining

com·bat \kəm-'bat, 'käm-₁bat\ *vb* **-bat·ed** *or* **-bat·ted; -bat·ing** *or* **-bat·ting 1** : FIGHT, CONTEND **2** : to struggle against : OPPOSE — **com·bat** \'käm-₁bat\ *n* — **com·bat·ant** \kəm-'bat-ᵊnt, 'käm-bə-tənt\ *n* — **com·bat·ive** \kəm-'ba-tiv\ *adj*

combat fatigue *n* : a traumatic neurotic or psychotic reaction occurring under conditions (as wartime combat) that cause intense stress

comb·er \'kō-mər\ *n* **1** : one that combs **2** : a long curling wave of the sea

com·bi·na·tion \₁käm-bə-'nā-shən\ *n* **1** : a result or product of combining **2** : a sequence of letters or numbers chosen in setting a lock **3** : the act or process of combining; *also* : the quality or state of being combined

¹com·bine \kəm-'bīn\ *vb* **com·bined; com·bin·ing** : to become one : UNITE

²com·bine \'käm-₁bīn\ *n* **1** : a combination esp. of business or political interests **2** : a machine that harvests and threshes grain while moving over a field

comb·ings \'kō-miɲz\ *n pl* : loose hairs or fibers removed by a comb

combining form *n* : a linguistic form that occurs only in compounds or derivatives

com·bo \'käm-bō\ *n, pl* **combos** : a small jazz or dance band

com·bus·ti·ble \kəm-'bəs-tə-bəl\ *adj* : capable of being burned — **com·bus·ti·bil·i·ty** \-₁bəs-tə-'bi-lə-tē\ *n* — **combustible** *n*

com·bus·tion \kəm-'bəs-chən\ *n* **1** : an act or instance of burning **2** : slow oxidation (as in the animal body)

comdg *abbr* commanding

comdr *abbr* commander

comdt *abbr* commandant

come \'kəm\ *vb* **came** \'kām\; **come; com·ing** \'kə-miɲ\ **1** : APPROACH **2** : ARRIVE **3** : to reach the point of being or becoming ⟨∼ to a boil⟩ **4** : AMOUNT ⟨the bill *came* to $10⟩ **5** : to take place **6** : ORIGINATE, ARISE **7** : to be available **8** : REACH, EXTEND — **come clean**

: CONFESS — **come into** : ACQUIRE, ACHIEVE — **come to pass** : HAPPEN — **come to terms** : to reach an agreement

come·back \'kəm-₁bak\ *n* **1** : RETORT **2** : a return to a former position or condition — **come back** *vb*

co·me·di·an \kə-'mē-dē-ən\ *n* **1** : an actor in comedy **2** : a comic person; *esp* : an entertainer specializing in comedy

co·me·di·enne \-₁mē-dē-'en\ *n* : a woman who is a comedian

come·down \'kəm-₁daùn\ *n* : a descent in rank or dignity

com·e·dy \'kä-mə-dē\ *n, pl* **-dies** [ME, fr. MF *comedie*, fr. L *comoedia*, fr. Gk *kōmōidia*, fr. *kōmos* revel + *aeidein* to sing] **1** : a light amusing play with a happy ending **2** : a literary work treating a comic theme or written in a comic style **3** : humorous entertainment

come·ly \'kəm-lē\ *adj* **come·li·er; -est** : ATTRACTIVE, HANDSOME — **come·li·ness** *n*

come off *vb* : SUCCEED

come-on \'kə-₁mȯn, -₁män\ *n* : INDUCEMENT, LURE

come out *vb* **1** : to come into public view **2** : to declare oneself **3** : TURN OUT **5** ⟨everything *came out* all right⟩ — **come out with** : SAY **1**

com·er \'kə-mər\ *n* **1** : one that comes ⟨all ∼s⟩ **2** : a promising beginner

¹co·mes·ti·ble \kə-'mes-tə-bəl\ *adj* : EDIBLE

²comestible *n* : FOOD — usu. used in pl.

com·et \'kä-mət\ *n* [ME *comete*, fr. OE *cometa*, fr. L, fr. Gk *komētēs*, lit., long-haired, fr. *komē* hair] : a small bright celestial body that develops a long tail when near the sun

come to *vb* : to regain consciousness

come·up·pance \kə-'mə-pəns\ *n* : a deserved rebuke or penalty

com·fit \'kəm-fət\ *n* : a candied fruit or nut

¹com·fort \'kəm-fərt\ *vb* **1** : to give strength and hope to **2** : CONSOLE

²comfort *n* **1** : CONSOLATION **2** : freedom from pain, trouble, or anxiety; *also* : something that gives such freedom

---

com·fort·able \'kəm-fər-tə-bəl, 'kəmf-tər-\ *adj* **1** : providing comfort or security **2** : feeling at ease — **com·fort·ably** \-blē\ *adv*

---

com·fort·er \'kəm-fər-tər\ *n* **1** : one that comforts **2** : QUILT

com·fy \'kəm-fē\ *adj* : COMFORTABLE

¹com·ic \'kä-mik\ *adj* **1** : relating to comedy or comic strips **2** : provoking laughter or amusement **syn** laughable, funny, farcical — **com·i·cal** *adj*

²comic *n* **1** : COMEDIAN **2** *pl* : the part of a newspaper devoted to comic strips

comic book *n* : a magazine containing sequences of comic strips

comic strip *n* : a group of cartoons in narrative sequence

com·ing \'kə-miŋ\ *adj* **1** : APPROACHING, NEXT **2** : gaining importance
co·mi·ty \'kä-mə-tē, 'kō-\ *n, pl* **-ties** : friendly civility : COURTESY
coml *abbr* commercial
comm *abbr* **1** command; commander **2** commerce; commercial **3** commission; commissioner **4** committee **5** common **6** commonwealth
com·ma \'kä-mə\ *n* : a punctuation mark , used esp. as a mark of separation within the sentence
¹com·mand \kə-'mand\ *vb* **1** : to direct authoritatively : ORDER **2** : DOMINATE, CONTROL, GOVERN **3** : to overlook from a strategic position
²command *n* **1** : an order given **2** : ability to control : MASTERY **3** : the act of commanding **4** : a signal that actuates a device (as a computer); *also* : the activation of a device by means of a signal **5** : a body of troops under a commander; *also* : an area or position that one commands **6** : a position of highest authority
com·man·dant \'kä-mən-ˌdant, -ˌdänt\ *n* : an officer in command
com·man·deer \ˌkä-mən-'dir\ *vb* : to take possession of by force
com·mand·er \kə-'man-dər\ *n* **1** : LEADER, CHIEF; *esp* : an officer commanding an army or subdivision of an army **2** : a commissioned officer in the navy ranking next below a captain
commander in chief : the supreme commander of the armed forces
com·mand·ment \kə-'mand-mənt\ *n* : COMMAND, ORDER; *esp* : any of the Ten Commandments
command module *n* : a space vehicle module designed to carry the crew and reentry equipment
com·man·do \kə-'man-dō\ *n, pl* **-dos** *or* **-does** [Afrikaans *kommando*, fr. Dutch *commando* command] : a member of a military unit trained for surprise raids
command sergeant major *n* : a noncommissioned officer in the army ranking above a first sergeant
com·mem·o·rate \kə-'me-mə-ˌrāt\ *vb* **-rat·ed; -rat·ing** **1** : to call or recall to mind **2** : to serve as a memorial of — **com·mem·o·ra·tion** \-ˌme-mə-ˌrā-shən\ *n*
com·mem·o·ra·tive \kə-'mem-rə-tiv, -'me-mə-ˌrā-tiv\ *adj* : intended to commemorate an event
com·mence \kə-'mens\ *vb* **com·menced; com·menc·ing** : BEGIN, START
com·mence·ment \-mənt\ *n* **1** : the act or time of a beginning **2** : the graduation exercises of a school or college
com·mend \kə-'mend\ *vb* **1** : to commit to one's care **2** : RECOMMEND **3** : PRAISE — **com·mend·able** \-'men-də-bəl\ *adj* — **com·mend·ably** \-blē\ *adv* — **com·men·da·tion** \ˌkä-mən-'dā-shən, -ˌmen-\ *n* — **com·mend·er** *n*
com·men·su·ra·ble \kə-'men-sə-rə-bəl\ *adj* : having a common measure or a common divisor
com·men·su·rate \kə-'men-sə-rət, -'men-chə-\ *adj* : equal in measure or extent; *also* : PROPORTIONAL, CORRESPONDING ⟨a job ∼ with her abilities⟩

com·ment \'kä-ˌment\ *n* **1** : an expression of opinion **2** : an explanatory, illustrative, or critical note or observation : REMARK — **comment** *vb*
com·men·tary \'kä-mən-ˌter-ē\ *n, pl* **-tar·ies** : a systematic series of comments
com·men·ta·tor \-ˌtā-tər\ *n* : one who comments; *esp* : a person who discusses news events on radio or television
com·merce \'kä-(ˌ)mərs\ *n* : the buying and selling of commodities : TRADE
¹com·mer·cial \kə-'mər-shəl\ *adj* : having to do with commerce; *also* : designed for profit or for mass appeal — **com·mer·cial·ly** *adv*

> **²commercial** *n* : an advertisement broadcast on radio or television

com·mer·cial·ise *Brit var of* COMMERCIALIZE
com·mer·cial·ism \kə-'mər-shə-ˌli-zəm\ *n* **1** : a spirit, method, or practice characteristic of business **2** : excessive emphasis on profit
com·mer·cial·ize \-ˌlīz\ *vb* **-ized; -iz·ing** **1** : to manage on a business basis for profit **2** : to exploit for profit
com·mi·na·tion \ˌkä-mə-'nā-shən\ *n* : DENUNCIATION — **com·mi·na·to·ry** \'kä-mə-nə-ˌtōr-ē\ *adj*
com·min·gle \kə-'miŋ-gəl\ *vb* : MINGLE, BLEND
com·mis·er·ate \kə-'mi-zə-ˌrāt\ *vb* **-at·ed; -at·ing** : to feel or express pity : SYMPATHIZE — **com·mis·er·a·tion** \-ˌmi-zə-'rā-shən\ *n*
com·mis·sar \'kä-mə-ˌsär\ *n* [Russ *komissar*] : a Communist party official
com·mis·sar·i·at \ˌkä-mə-'ser-ē-ət\ *n* **1** : a system for supplying troops with food **2** : a department headed by a commissar
com·mis·sary \'kä-mə-ˌser-ē\ *n, pl* **-sar·ies** : a store for equipment and provisions esp. for military personnel
¹com·mis·sion \kə-'mi-shən\ *n* **1** : a warrant granting certain powers and imposing certain duties **2** : a certificate conferring military rank and authority **3** : authority to act as agent for another; *also* : something to be done by an agent **4** : a body of persons charged with performing a duty **5** : the doing of some act; *also* : the thing done **6** : the allowance made to an agent for transacting business for another
²commission *vb* **1** : to give a commission to **2** : to order to be made **3** : to put (a ship) into a state of readiness for service
commissioned officer *n* : an officer of the armed forces holding rank by a commission from the president
com·mis·sion·er \kə-'mi-shə-nər\ *n* **1** : a member of a commission **2** : an official in charge of a department of public service **3** : the administrative head of a professional sport — **com·mis·sion·er·ship** *n*
com·mit \kə-'mit\ *vb* **com·mit·ted; com·mit·ting** **1** : to put into charge or trust : ENTRUST **2** : to put in a prison or mental institution **3** : TRANSFER, CONSIGN **4** : to carry into action : PERPETRATE ⟨∼ a crime⟩ **5** : to

pledge or assign to some particular course or use — **com·mit·ment** *n* — **com·mit·tal** *n*

com·mit·tee \kə-'mi-tē\ *n* : a body of persons selected to consider and act or report on some matter — **com·mit·tee·man** \-mən\ *n* — **com·mit·tee·wom·an** \-ˌwu̇-mən\ *n*

commo *abbr* commodore

com·mode \kə-'mōd\ *n* [F, fr. *commode*, adj., suitable, convenient, fr. L *commodus*, fr. *com*- with + *modus* measure] **1** : a movable washstand with cupboard below **2** : TOILET 3

com·mo·di·ous \kə-'mō-dē-əs\ *adj* : comfortably spacious : ROOMY

com·mod·i·ty \kə-'mä-də-tē\ *n, pl* **-ties 1** : a product of agriculture or mining **2** : an article of commerce **3** : something useful or valued ⟨that valuable ∼ patience⟩

com·mo·dore \'kä-mə-ˌdōr\ *n* **1** : a commissioned officer in the navy ranking next below a rear admiral **2** : an officer commanding a group of merchant ships **3** : the chief officer of a yacht club

¹com·mon \'kä-mən\ *adj* **1** : belonging to or serving the community : PUBLIC **2** : shared by a number in a group **3** : widely or generally known, found, or observed : FAMILIAR ⟨∼ knowledge⟩ **4** : VERNACULAR 3 ⟨∼ names of plants⟩ **5** : not above the average esp. in social status **syn** universal, general, generic — **com·mon·ly** *adv*

²common *n* **1** *pl* : the common people **2** *pl* : a dining hall **3** *pl, cap* : the lower house of the British and Canadian parliaments **4** : a piece of land subject to common use — **in common** : shared together

com·mon·al·ty \'kä-mən-əl-tē\ *n, pl* **-ties** : the common people

common cold *n* : a contagious respiratory disease caused by a virus and characterized by a sore, swollen, and inflamed nose and throat, usu. by much mucus, and by coughing and sneezing

common denominator *n* **1** : a common multiple of the denominators of a number of fractions **2** : a common trait or theme

common divisor *n* : a number or expression that divides two or more numbers or expressions without remainder

com·mon·er \'kä-mə-nər\ *n* : one of the common people : a person having no rank of nobility

common fraction *n* : a fraction in which the numerator and denominator are both integers and are separated by a horizontal or slanted line

common law *n* : a group of legal practices and traditions based on judges' decisions and social customs and usu. having the same force as laws passed by legislative bodies

common logarithm *n* : a logarithm whose base is 10

common market *n* : an economic association formed to remove trade barriers among members

common multiple *n* : a multiple of each of two or more numbers or expressions

¹com·mon·place \'kä-mən-ˌplās\ *n* : something that is ordinary or trite

²commonplace *adj* : ORDINARY

common sense *n* : ordinary good sense and judgment

com·mon·weal \'kä-mən-ˌwēl\ *n* **1** *archaic* : COMMONWEALTH **2** : the general welfare

com·mon·wealth \-ˌwelth\ *n* **1** : the body of people politically organized into a state **2** : STATE; *also* : an association or federation of autonomous states

com·mo·tion \kə-'mō-shən\ *n* **1** : DISTURBANCE, UPRISING **2** : AGITATION

com·mu·nal \kə-'myün-əl, 'käm-yən-əl\ *adj* **1** : of or relating to a commune or community **2** : marked by collective ownership and use of property **3** : shared or used in common

¹com·mune \kə-'myün\ *vb* **com·muned**; **com·mun·ing** : to communicate intimately

²com·mune \'käm-ˌyün; kə-'myün\ *n* **1** : the smallest administrative district in some European countries **2** : a community organized on a communal basis

com·mu·ni·ca·ble \kə-'myü-ni-kə-bəl\ *adj* : capable of being communicated ⟨∼ diseases⟩ — **com·mu·ni·ca·bil·i·ty** \-ˌmyü-ni-kə-'bi-lə-tē\ *n*

com·mu·ni·cant \-'myü-ni-kənt\ *n* **1** : a church member entitled to receive Communion **2** : one that communicates; *esp* : INFORMANT

com·mu·ni·cate \kə-'myü-nə-ˌkāt\ *vb* **-cat·ed**; **-cat·ing 1** : to make known **2** : to pass from one to another : TRANSMIT **3** : to receive Communion **4** : to be in communication **5** : JOIN, CONNECT

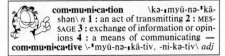

com·mu·ni·ca·tion \kə-ˌmyü-nə-'kā-shən\ *n* **1** : an act of transmitting **2** : MESSAGE **3** : exchange of information or opinions **4** : a means of communicating — **com·mu·ni·ca·tive** \-'myü-nə-ˌkā-tiv, -ni-kə-tiv\ *adj*

com·mu·nion \kə-'myü-nyən\ *n* **1** : a sharing of something with others **2** *cap* : a Christian sacrament in which bread and wine are consumed as the substance or symbols of Christ's body and blood in commemoration of the death of Christ **3** : intimate fellowship or rapport **4** : a body of Christians having a common faith and discipline

com·mu·ni·qué \kə-'myü-nə-ˌkā, -ˌmyü-nə-'kā\ *n* : BULLETIN 1

com·mu·nism \'käm-yə-ˌni-zəm\ *n* **1** : social organization in which goods are held in common **2** : a theory of social organization advocating common ownership of means of production and a distribution of products of industry based on need **3** *cap* : a political doctrine based on revolutionary Marxist socialism that was the official ideology of the U.S.S.R. and some other countries; *also* : a system of government in which one party controls state-owned means of production — **com·mu·nist** \-nist\ *n or adj, often cap* — **com·mu·nis·tic** \ˌkäm-yə-'nis-tik\ *adj, often cap*

com·mu·ni·ty \kə-'myü-nə-tē\ *n, pl* **-ties 1** : a body of people living in the same place under the same laws; *also* : a natural population of plants and animals that interact ecologically and live in one place (as a pond)

2 : society at large **3** : joint ownership **4** : SIMILARITY, LIKENESS

community college *n* : a 2-year government-supported college that offers an associate degree

community property *n* : property held jointly by husband and wife

com·mu·ta·tion \ˌkäm-yə-ˈtā-shən\ *n* : substitution of one form of payment or penalty for another

com·mu·ta·tive \ˈkäm-yə-ˌtā-tiv, kə-ˈmyü-tə-\ *adj* : of, relating to, having, or being the property that a given mathematical operation and set have when the result obtained using any two elements of the set with the operation does not differ with the order in which the numbers are used — **com·mu·ta·tiv·i·ty** \kə-ˌmyü-tə-ˈti-və-tē, ˌkäm-yə-tə-\ *n*

com·mu·ta·tor \ˈkäm-yə-ˌtā-tər\ *n* : a device (as on a generator or motor) for changing the direction of electric current

¹**com·mute** \kə-ˈmyüt\ *vb* **com·mut·ed; com·mut·ing 1** : EXCHANGE **2** : to revoke (a sentence) and impose a milder penalty **3** : to travel back and forth regularly — **com·mut·er** *n*

²**commute** *n* : a trip made in commuting

comp *abbr* **1** comparative; compare **2** compensation **3** compiled; compiler **4** composition; compositor **5** compound **6** comprehensive **7** comptroller

¹**com·pact** \kəm-ˈpakt, ˈkäm-ˌpakt\ *adj* **1** : SOLID, DENSE **2** : BRIEF, SUCCINCT **3** : occupying a small volume by efficient use of space ⟨∼ camera⟩ — **com·pact·ly** *adv* — **com·pact·ness** *n*

²**compact** *vb* : to pack together : COMPRESS — **com·pac·tor** \kəm-ˈpak-tər, ˈkäm-ˌpak-\ *n*

³**com·pact** \ˈkäm-ˌpakt\ *n* **1** : a small case for cosmetics **2** : a small automobile

⁴**com·pact** \ˈkäm-ˌpakt\ *n* : AGREEMENT, COVENANT

compact disc \ˈkäm-ˌpakt-\ *n* : a small plastic optical disc usu. containing recorded music

¹**com·pan·ion** \kəm-ˈpan-yən\ *n* [OF *compagnon*, fr. LL *companion-, companio*, fr. L *com-* together + *panis* bread] **1** : an intimate friend or associate : COMRADE **2** : one that is closely connected with something similar — **com·pan·ion·able** *adj* — **com·pan·ion·ship** *n*

²**companion** *n* : COMPANIONWAY

com·pan·ion·way \-ˌwā\ *n* : a ship's stairway from one deck to another

com·pa·ny \ˈkəm-pə-nē\ *n, pl* **-nies 1** : association with others : FELLOWSHIP; *also* : COMPANIONS **2** : GUESTS **3** : a group of persons or things **4** : an infantry unit consisting of two or more platoons and normally commanded by a captain **5** : a group of musical or dramatic performers **6** : the officers and crew of a ship **7** : an association of persons for carrying on a business **syn** party, band, troop, troupe, corps, outfit

com·pa·ra·ble \ˈkäm-pə-rə-bəl, -prə-\ *adj* : capable of being compared **syn** parallel, similar, like, alike, corresponding — **com·pa·ra·bil·i·ty** \ˌkäm-pə-rə-ˈbi-lə-tē\ *n*

¹**com·par·a·tive** \kəm-ˈpar-ə-tiv\ *adj* **1** : of, relating to, or constituting the degree of grammatical comparison that denotes increase in quality, quantity, or relation **2** : RELATIVE ⟨a ∼ stranger⟩ — **com·par·a·tive·ly** *adv*

²**comparative** *n* : the comparative degree or form in a language

¹**com·pare** \kəm-ˈpar\ *vb* **com·pared; com·par·ing 1** : to represent as similar : LIKEN **2** : to examine for likenesses and differences **3** : to inflect or modify (an adjective or adverb) according to the degrees of comparison

²**compare** *n* : the possibility of comparing ⟨beauty beyond ∼⟩

com·par·i·son \kəm-ˈpar-ə-sən\ *n* **1** : the act of comparing **2** : change in the form of an adjective or adverb to show different levels of quality, quantity, or relation

com·part·ment \kəm-ˈpärt-mənt\ *n* **1** : a separate division **2** : a section of an enclosed space : ROOM

com·part·men·tal·ise *Brit var of* COMPARTMENTALIZE

com·part·men·tal·ize \kəm-ˌpärt-ˈment-əl-ˌīz\ *vb* **-ized; -iz·ing** : to separate into compartments

¹**com·pass** \ˈkəm-pəs, ˈkäm-\ *vb* [ME, fr. OF *compasser* to measure, fr. (assumed) VL *compassare* to pace off, fr. L *com-* + *passus* pace] **1** : CONTRIVE, PLOT **2** : ENCIRCLE, ENCOMPASS **3** : BRING ABOUT, ACHIEVE

²**compass** *n* **1** : BOUNDARY, CIRCUMFERENCE **2** : an enclosed space **3** : RANGE, SCOPE **4** : a device for determining direction by means of a magnetic needle swinging freely and pointing to the magnetic north; *also* : a nonmagnetic device that indicates direction **5** : an instrument for drawing circles or transferring measurements consisting of two legs joined by a pivot

com·pas·sion \kəm-ˈpa-shən\ *n* : sympathetic feeling : PITY, MERCY — **com·pas·sion·ate** \-shə-nət\ *adj* — **com·pas·sion·ate·ly** *adv*

com·pat·i·ble \kəm-ˈpa-tə-bəl\ *adj* : able to exist or act together harmoniously ⟨∼ colors⟩ ⟨∼ drugs⟩ **syn** consonant, congenial, sympathetic — **com·pat·i·bil·i·ty** \-ˌpa-tə-ˈbi-lə-tē\ *n*

com·pa·tri·ot \kəm-ˈpā-trē-ət, -ˌät\ *n* : a fellow countryman

com·peer \ˈkäm-ˌpir\ *n* : EQUAL, PEER

com·pel \kəm-ˈpel\ *vb* **com·pelled; com·pel·ling** : to drive or urge with force

com·pen·di·ous \kəm-ˈpen-dē-əs\ *adj* : concise and comprehensive; *also* : COMPREHENSIVE

com·pen·di·um \kəm-ˈpen-dē-əm\ *n, pl* **-diums** *or* **-dia** \-ə\ **1** : a brief summary of a larger work or of a field of knowledge **2** : COLLECTION

com·pen·sate \ˈkäm-pən-ˌsāt\ *vb* **-sat·ed; -sat·ing 1** : to be equivalent to : make up for **2** : PAY, REMUNERATE **syn** balance, offset, counterbalance, counterpoise — **com·pen·sa·tion** \ˌkäm-pən-ˈsā-shən\ *n* — **com·pen·sa·to·ry** \kəm-ˈpen-sə-ˌtōr-ē\ *adj*

com·pete \kəm-ˈpēt\ *vb* **com·pet·ed; com·pet·ing** : CONTEND, VIE

com·pe·tence \ˈkäm-pə-təns\ *n* **1** : adequate means for subsistence **2** : FITNESS, ABILITY

com·pe·ten·cy \-tən-sē\ *n, pl* **-cies** : COMPETENCE

com·pe·tent \-tənt\ *adj* : CAPABLE, FIT, QUALIFIED

com·pe·ti·tion \ˌkäm-pə-ˈti-shən\ *n* **1** : the act of competing : RIVALRY **2** : CONTEST, MATCH; *also* : one's competitors — **com·pet·i·tive** \kəm-ˈpe-tə-tiv\ *adj* — **com·pet·i·tive·ly** *adv* — **com·pet·i·tive·ness** *n*

com·pet·i·tor \kəm-ˈpe-tə-tər\ *n* : one that competes : RIVAL

com·pile \kəm-ˈpīl\ *vb* **com·piled; com·pil·ing** [ME, MF *compiler*, fr. L *compilare* to plunder] **1** : to compose out of materials from other documents **2** : to collect and edit into a volume **3** : to translate (a computer program) with a compiler **4** : to build up gradually ⟨∼ a record of four wins and two losses⟩ — **com·pi·la·tion** \ˌkäm-pə-ˈlā-shən\ *n*

com·pil·er \kəm-ˈpī-lər\ *n* **1** : one that compiles **2** : a computer program that translates any program correctly written in a specific programming language into machine language

com·pla·cence \kəm-ˈplās-ᵊns\ *n* : COMPLACENCY — **com·pla·cent** \-ᵊnt\ *adj* — **com·pla·cent·ly** *adv*

com·pla·cen·cy \-ᵊn-sē\ *n, pl* **-cies** : SATISFACTION; *esp* : SELF-SATISFACTION

com·plain \kəm-ˈplān\ *vb* **1** : to express grief, pain, or discontent **2** : to make a formal accusation — **com·plain·ant** *n* — **com·plain·er** *n*

com·plaint \kəm-ˈplānt\ *n* **1** : expression of grief, pain, or dissatisfaction **2** : a bodily ailment or disease **3** : a formal accusation against a person

com·plai·sance \kəm-ˈplās-ᵊns, ˌkäm-plā-ˈzans\ *n* [F] : disposition to please — **com·plai·sant** \-ᵊnt, -ˈzant\ *adj*

com·pleat \kəm-ˈplēt\ *adj* : PROFICIENT

com·plect·ed \kəm-ˈplek-təd\ adj : having a specified facial complexion ⟨dark-*complected*⟩

¹**com·ple·ment** \ˈkäm-plə-mənt\ n 1 : something that fills up or completes; also : the full quantity, number, or amount that makes a thing complete 2 : an added word by which a predicate is made complete 3 : a group of proteins in blood that combines with antibodies to destroy antigens — **com·ple·men·ta·ry** \ˌkäm-plə-ˈmen-t(ə-)rē\ adj

²**com·ple·ment** \-ˌment\ vb : to be complementary to : fill out

¹**com·plete** \kəm-ˈplēt\ adj **com·plet·er**; **-est** 1 : having all parts or elements 2 : brought to an end 3 : fully carried out; also : ABSOLUTE 2 ⟨∼ silence⟩ — **com·plete·ly** adv — **com·plete·ness** n — **com·ple·tion** \-ˈplē-shən\ n

²**complete** vb **com·plet·ed**; **com·plet·ing** 1 : FINISH, CONCLUDE 2 : to make whole or perfect ⟨the hat ∼s the outfit⟩

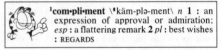

¹**com·plex** \ˈkäm-ˌpleks\ n 1 : a whole made up of or involving intricately interrelated elements 2 : a group of repressed desires and memories that exert a dominating influence on one's personality and behavior ⟨a guilt ∼⟩

²**com·plex** \käm-ˈpleks, ˈkäm-ˌpleks\ adj 1 : composed of two or more parts 2 : consisting of a main clause and one or more subordinate clauses ⟨∼ sentence⟩ 3 : hard to separate, analyze, or solve — **com·plex·i·ty** \käm-ˈplek-sə-tē\ n — **com·plex·ly** adv

complex fraction n : a fraction with a fraction or mixed number in the numerator or denominator or both

com·plex·ion \kəm-ˈplek-shən\ n 1 : the hue or appearance of the skin esp. of the face 2 : overall appearance — **com·plex·ioned** \-shənd\ adj

complex number n : a number (as $3 + 4\sqrt{-1}$) formed by adding a real number to the product of a real number and the square root of minus one

com·pli·ance \kəm-ˈplī-əns\ n 1 : the act of complying to a demand or proposal 2 : a disposition to yield — **com·pli·ant** \-ənt\ adj

com·pli·cate \ˈkäm-plə-ˌkāt\ vb **-cat·ed**; **-cat·ing** : to make or become complex or intricate

com·pli·cat·ed \ˈkäm-plə-ˌkā-təd\ adj 1 : consisting of parts intricately combined 2 : difficult to analyze, understand, or explain — **com·pli·cat·ed·ly** adv

com·pli·ca·tion \ˌkäm-plə-ˈkā-shən\ n 1 : the quality or state of being complicated; also : a complex feature 2 : a disease or condition that develops during and affects the course of a primary disease or condition

com·plic·i·ty \kəm-ˈpli-sə-tē\ n, pl **-ties** : the state of being an accomplice

¹**com·pli·ment** \ˈkäm-plə-ment\ n 1 : an expression of approval or admiration; esp : a flattering remark 2 pl : best wishes : REGARDS

²**com·pli·ment** \-ˌment\ vb : to pay a compliment to

com·pli·men·ta·ry \ˌkäm-plə-ˈmen-t(ə-)rē\ adj 1 : containing or expressing a compliment 2 : given free as a courtesy ⟨∼ ticket⟩

com·ply \kəm-ˈplī\ vb **com·plied**; **com·ply·ing** : CONFORM, YIELD

¹**com·po·nent** \kəm-ˈpō-nənt, ˈkäm-ˌpō-\ n : a component part syn ingredient, element, factor, constituent

²**component** adj : serving to form a part of : CONSTITUENT

com·port \kəm-ˈpōrt\ vb 1 : AGREE, ACCORD 2 : CONDUCT syn behave, acquit, deport — **com·port·ment** n

com·pose \kəm-ˈpōz\ vb **com·posed**; **com·pos·ing** 1 : to form by putting together : FASHION 2 : to produce (as pages of type) by composition 3 : ADJUST, ARRANGE 4 : CALM, QUIET 5 : to practice composition ⟨∼ music⟩ — **com·pos·er** n

¹**com·pos·ite** \käm-ˈpä-zət\ adj 1 : made up of distinct parts or elements 2 : of, relating to, or being a large family of flowering plants (as a daisy or aster) that bear many small flowers united into compact heads resembling single flowers

²**composite** n 1 : something composite 2 : a plant of the composite family syn blend, compound, mixture, amalgamation

com·po·si·tion \ˌkäm-pə-ˈzi-shən\ n 1 : the act or process of composing; *esp* : arrangement esp. in artistic form **2** : the arrangement or production of type for printing **3** : general makeup **4** : a product of mixing various elements or ingredients **5** : a literary, musical, or artistic product; *esp* : ESSAY

com·pos·i·tor \kəm-'pä-zə-tər\ *n* : one who sets type

com·post \'käm-₁pōst\ *n* : a fertilizing material consisting largely of decayed organic matter

com·po·sure \kəm-'pō-zhər\ *n* : CALMNESS, SELF═POSSESSION

com·pote \'käm-₁pōt\ *n* **1** : fruits cooked in syrup **2** : a bowl (as of glass) usu. with a base and stem for serving esp. fruit or compote

¹com·pound \käm-'paund, 'käm-₁\ *vb* [ME *compounen*, fr. MF *compondre*, fr. L *componere*, fr. *com-* together + *ponere* to put] **1** : COMBINE **2** : to form by combining parts ⟨∼ a medicine⟩ **3** : SETTLE ⟨∼ a dispute⟩; *also* : to refrain from prosecuting (an offense) in return for a consideration **4** : to increase (as interest) by an amount that can itself vary; *also* : to add to

²com·pound \'käm-₁paund\ *adj* **1** : made up of individual parts **2** : composed of united similar parts esp. of a kind usu. independent ⟨a ∼ plant ovary⟩ **3** : formed by the combination of two or more otherwise independent elements ⟨∼ sentence⟩

³com·pound \'käm-₁paund\ *n* **1** : a word consisting of parts that are words **2** : something formed from a union of elements or parts; *esp* : a distinct substance formed by the union of two or more chemical elements **syn** mixture, composite, blend, admixture, alloy

⁴com·pound \'käm-₁paund\ *n* [by folk etymology fr. Malay *kampung* group of buildings, village] : an enclosure containing buildings

compound interest *n* : interest computed on the sum of an original principal and accrued interest

com·pre·hend \₁käm-pri-'hend\ *vb* **1** : UNDERSTAND **2** : INCLUDE — **com·pre·hen·si·ble** \-'hen-sə-bəl\ *adj* — **com·pre·hen·sion** \-'hen-chən\ *n* — **com·pre·hen·sive** \-siv\ *adj*

¹com·press \kəm-'pres\ *vb* : to squeeze together **syn** constrict, contract, shrink — **com·pres·sion** \-'pre-shən\ *n* — **com·pres·sor** \-'pre-sər\ *n*

²com·press \'käm-₁pres\ *n* : a folded pad or cloth used to press upon a body part

compressed air *n* : air under pressure greater than that of the atmosphere

com·prise \kəm-'prīz\ *vb* **com·prised; com·pris·ing 1** : INCLUDE, CONTAIN **2** : to be made up of **3** : COMPOSE, CONSTITUTE

¹com·pro·mise \'käm-prə-₁mīz\ *n* : a settlement of differences reached by mutual concessions

²compromise *vb* **-mised; -mis·ing 1** : to settle by compromise **2** : to expose to suspicion or loss of reputation

comp·trol·ler \kən-'trō-lər, 'kämp-₁trō-\ *n* : an official who audits and supervises expenditures and accounts

com·pul·sion \kəm-'pəl-shən\ *n* **1** : an act of compelling **2** : a force that compels **3** : an irresistible impulse **syn** constraint, force, violence, duress — **com·pul·sive** \-siv\ *adj* — **com·pul·so·ry** \-sə-rē\ *adj*

com·punc·tion \kəm-'pəŋk-shən\ *n* : anxiety arising from guilt : REMORSE

com·pute \kəm-'pyüt\ *vb* **com·put·ed; com·put·ing** : CALCULATE, RECKON — **com·pu·ta·tion** \₁käm-pyü-'tā-shən\ *n* — **com·pu·ta·tion·al** *adj*

computed tomography *n* : radiography in which a three-dimensional image of a body structure is constructed by computer from a series of plane cross-sectional images made along an axis

com·put·er \kəm-'pyü-tər\ *n* : a programmable electronic device that can store, retrieve, and process data

com·put·er·ise *chiefly Brit var of* COMPUTERIZE

com·put·er·ize \kəm-'pyü-tə-₁rīz\ *vb* **-ized; -iz·ing 1**

: to carry out, control, or produce by means of a computer **2** : to provide with computers **3** : to store in a computer; *also* : put into a form that a computer can use — **com·put·er·iza·tion** \-₁pyü-tə-rə-'zā-shən\ *n*

computerized axial tomography *n* : COMPUTED TOMOGRAPHY

com·rade \'käm-₁rad\ *n* [MF *comarade* group sleeping in one room, roommate, companion, fr. Sp *comarada*, fr. *cámara* room, fr. LL *camera*] : COMPANION, ASSOCIATE — **com·rade·ly** *adj* — **com·rade·ship** *n*

¹con \'kän\ *vb* **conned; con·ning 1** : MEMORIZE **2** : STUDY

²con *adv* : in opposition : AGAINST

³con *n* : an opposing argument, person, or position ⟨pros and ∼s⟩

⁴con *vb* **conned; con·ning 1** : SWINDLE **2** : PERSUADE, CAJOLE

⁵con *n* : CONVICT

conc *abbr* concentrated

con·cat·e·nate \kän-'ka-tə-₁nāt\ *vb* **-nat·ed; -nat·ing** : to link together in a series or chain — **con·cat·e·na·tion** \(₁)kän-₁ka-tə-'nā-shən\ *n*

con·cave \kän-'kāv, 'kän-₁\ *adj* : curved or rounded inward like the inside of a bowl — **con·cav·i·ty** \kän-'ka-və-tē\ *n*

con·ceal \kən-'sēl\ *vb* : to place out of sight : HIDE — **con·ceal·ment** *n*

con·cede \kən-'sēd\ *vb* **con·ced·ed; con·ced·ing 1** : to admit to be true **2** : GRANT, YIELD **syn** allow, acknowledge, avow, confess

con·ceit \kən-'sēt\ *n* **1** : excessively high opinion of one's self or ability : VANITY **2** : an elaborate or strained metaphor — **con·ceit·ed** *adj*

con·ceive \kən-'sēv\ *vb* **con·ceived; con·ceiv·ing 1** : to become pregnant or pregnant with ⟨∼ a child⟩ **2** : to form an idea of : THINK, IMAGINE — **con·ceiv·able** \-'sē-və-bəl\ *adj* — **con·ceiv·ably** \-blē\ *adv*

con·cel·e·brant \kən-'se-lə-brənt\ *n* : one that jointly participates in celebrating the Eucharist

¹con·cen·trate \'kän-sən-₁trāt\ *vb* **-trat·ed; -trat·ing 1** : to gather into one body, mass, or force **2** : to make less dilute **3** : to fix one's powers, efforts, or attentions

²concentrate *n* : something concentrated

con·cen·tra·tion \₁kän-sən-'trā-shən\ *n* **1** : the act or process of concentrating : the state of being concentrated; *esp* : direction of attention on a single object **2** : the amount of a component in a given area or volume

concentration camp *n* : a camp where persons (as prisoners of war or political prisoners) are confined

con·cen·tric \kən-'sen-trik\ *adj* **1** : having a common center ⟨∼ circles⟩ **2** : COAXIAL

con·cept \'kän-₁sept\ *n* : THOUGHT, NOTION, IDEA — **con·cep·tu·al** \kən-'sep-chə-wəl\ *adj*

con·cep·tion \kən-'sep-shən\ *n* **1** : the process of conceiving or being conceived **2** : the power to form or understand ideas or concepts **3** : IDEA, CONCEPT **4** : the originating of something

con·cep·tu·al·ise *Brit var of* CONCEPTUALIZE

con·cep·tu·al·ize \-'sep-chə-wə-₁līz\ *vb* **-ized; -iz·ing** : to form a conception of

¹con·cern \kən-'sərn\ *vb* **1** : to relate to **2** : to be the business of : INVOLVE **3** : ENGAGE, OCCUPY

²concern *n* **1** : INTEREST, ANXIETY **2** : AFFAIR, MATTER **3** : a business organization **syn** care, worry, disquiet, unease

con·cerned *adj* **1** : ANXIOUS, UNEASY **2** : INVOLVED

con·cern·ing *prep* : relating to : REGARDING

con·cern·ment \kən-'sərn-mənt\ *n* **1** : something in which one is concerned **2** : IMPORTANCE, CONSEQUENCE

¹con·cert \'kän-(₁)sərt\ *n* **1** : agreement in a plan or design **2** : a concerted action **3** : a public performance (as of music)

²con·cert \kən-'sərt\ *vb* : to plan together

con·cert·ed \kən-'sər-təd\ adj : mutually agreed on; also : performed in unison

con·cer·ti·na \ˌkän-sər-'tē-nə\ n : an instrument of the accordion family

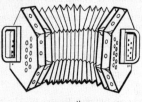

concertina

con·cert·mas·ter \'kän-sərt-ˌmas-tər\ or **con·cert·meis·ter** \-ˌmī-stər\ n : the leader of the first violins of an orchestra and assistant to the conductor

con·cer·to \kən-'cher-tō\ n, pl **-ti** \-(ˌ)tē\ or **-tos** [It] : a piece for one or more solo instruments and orchestra in three movements

con·ces·sion \kən-'se-shən\ n 1 : an act of conceding or yielding 2 : something yielded 3 : a grant by a government of land or of a right to use it 4 : a grant of a portion of premises for some specific purpose; also : the activities or enterprise carried on — **con·ces·sion·ary** \-'se-shə-ˌner-ē\ adj

con·ces·sion·aire \kən-ˌse-shə-'nar, -'ner\ n : one that owns or operates a concession

conch \'käŋk, 'känch\ n, pl **conchs** \'käŋks\ or **conch·es** \'kän-chəz\ : a large spiral-shelled marine gastropod mollusk; also : its shell

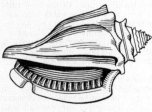

conch

con·cierge \kōⁿ-'syerzh\ n, pl **con·cierges** \same or -'syer-zhəz\ [F] 1 : a resident in an apartment building who performs services for the tenants 2 : a usu. multilingual hotel staff member

con·cil·i·ate \kən-'si-lē-ˌāt\ vb **-at·ed; -at·ing** 1 : to bring into agreement : RECONCILE 2 : to gain the goodwill of — **con·cil·i·a·tion** \-ˌsi-lē-'ā-shən\ n — **con·cil·ia·to·ry** \-'si-lē-ə-ˌtȯr-ē\ adj

con·cise \kən-'sīs\ adj : expressing much in few words : BRIEF — **con·cise·ly** adv — **con·cise·ness** n

con·clave \'kän-ˌklāv\ n [ML, fr. L, room that can be locked, fr. com- together + clavis key] : a private gathering; also : CONVENTION

con·clude \kən-'klüd\ vb **con·clud·ed; con·clud·ing** 1 : to bring to a close : END 2 : DECIDE, JUDGE 3 : to bring about as a result syn close, finish, terminate, complete, halt

con·clu·sion \kən-'klü-zhən\ n 1 : the logical consequence of a reasoning process 2 : TERMINATION, END 3 : OUTCOME, RESULT — **con·clu·sive** \-siv\ adj — **con·clu·sive·ly** adv

con·coct \kən-'käkt, kän-\ vb 1 : to prepare by combining raw materials 2 : DEVISE — **con·coc·tion** \-'käk-shən\ n

con·com·i·tant \-'kä-mə-tənt\ adj : ACCOMPANYING, ATTENDING — **concomitant** n

con·cord \'kän-ˌkȯrd, 'käŋ-\ n : AGREEMENT, HARMONY

con·cor·dance \kən-'kȯr-dᵊns\ n 1 : an alphabetical index of words in a book or in an author's works with the passages in which they occur 2 : AGREEMENT, COVENANT

con·cor·dant \-dᵊnt\ adj : HARMONIOUS, AGREEING

con·cor·dat \kən-'kȯr-ˌdat\ n : CONCORDANCE 2

con·course \'kän-ˌkȯrs\ n 1 : a spontaneous coming together : GATHERING 2 : an open space or hall (as in a bus terminal) where crowds gather

¹**con·crete** \'kän-ˌkrēt, kän-'krēt\ adj 1 : naming a real thing or class of things : not abstract 2 : not theoretical : ACTUAL 3 : made of or relating to concrete

²**con·crete** \'kän-ˌkrēt, kän-'krēt\ vb **con·cret·ed; con·cret·ing** 1 : SOLIDIFY 2 : to cover with concrete

³**con·crete** \'kän-ˌkrēt, kän-'krēt\ n : a hard building material made by mixing cement, sand, and gravel with water

con·cre·tion \kän-'krē-shən\ n : a hard mass esp. when formed abnormally in the body

con·cu·bine \'käŋ-kyü-ˌbīn\ n [ME, fr. MF, fr. L concubina, fr. com- with + cubare to lie] : a woman who is not legally a wife but lives with a man and sometimes has a recognized position in his household; also : MISTRESS — **con·cu·bi·nage** \kän-'kyü-bə-nij\ n

con·cu·pis·cence \kän-'kyü-pə-səns\ n : ardent sexual desire : LUST

con·cur \kən-'kər\ vb **con·curred; con·cur·ring** 1 : to act together 2 : AGREE 3 : COINCIDE syn unite, combine, cooperate, band, join

con·cur·rence \-'kər-əns\ n 1 : agreement in action or opinion 2 : occurrence together : CONJUNCTION

con·cur·rent \-'kər-ənt\ adj 1 : happening or operating at the same time 2 : joint and equal in authority

con·cus·sion \kən-'kə-shən\ n 1 : a hard blow or collision; also : bodily injury (as to the brain) resulting from a sudden jar 2 : AGITATION, SHAKING

con·demn \kən-'dem\ vb 1 : to declare to be wrong 2 : to convict of guilt 3 : to sentence judicially 4 : to pronounce unfit for use ⟨~ a building⟩ 5 : to declare forfeited or taken for public use syn denounce, cen-

sure, blame, criticize, reprehend — con·dem·na·tion \ˌkän-ˌdem-ˈnä-shən\ n — con·dem·na·to·ry \kən-ˈdem-nə-ˌtōr-ē\ adj
con·den·sate \ˈkän-dən-ˌsāt, kən-ˈden-\ n : a product of condensation
con·dense \kən-ˈdens\ vb con·densed; con·dens·ing 1 : to make or become more compact or dense : CONCENTRATE 2 : to change from vapor to liquid syn contract, shrink, compress, constrict — con·den·sa·tion \ˌkän-den-ˈsä-shən\ n
con·dens·er \kən-ˈden-sər\ n 1 : one that condenses 2 : CAPACITOR
con·de·scend \ˌkän-di-ˈsend\ vb : to assume an air of superiority — con·de·scend·ing·ly \-ˈsen-diŋ-lē\ adv — con·de·scen·sion \-ˈsen-chən\ n
con·dign \kən-ˈdīn, ˈkän-ˌdīn\ adj : DESERVED, APPROPRIATE (∼ punishment)
con·di·ment \ˈkän-də-mənt\ n : something used to make food savory; esp : a pungent seasoning (as pepper)
¹con·di·tion \kən-ˈdi-shən\ n 1 : something essential to the occurrence of some other thing 2 : state of being 3 : social status 4 pl : state of affairs : CIRCUMSTANCES 5 : a bodily state in which something is wrong (a heart ∼) 6 : a state of health, fitness, or working order (in good ∼)
²condition vb 1 : to put into proper condition for action or use 2 : to adapt, modify, or mold to respond in a particular way 3 : to modify so that an act or response previously associated with one stimulus becomes associated with another
con·di·tion·al \kən-ˈdi-shə-nəl\ adj : containing, implying, or depending on a condition — con·di·tion·al·ly adv
con·di·tioned adj : determined or established by conditioning
con·do \ˈkän-(ˌ)dō\ n : CONDOMINIUM 3
con·dole \kən-ˈdōl\ vb con·doled; con·dol·ing : to express sympathetic sorrow — con·do·lence \kən-ˈdō-ləns\ n
con·dom \ˈkän-dəm, ˈkən-\ n : a usu. rubber sheath worn over the penis (as to prevent pregnancy or venereal infection during sexual intercourse)
con·do·min·i·um \ˌkän-də-ˈmi-nē-əm\ n, pl -ums 1 : joint sovereignty (as by two or more nations) 2 : a politically dependent territory under condominium 3 : individual ownership of a unit (as an apartment) in a multiunit structure; also : a unit so owned
con·done \kən-ˈdōn\ vb con·doned; con·don·ing : to overlook or forgive esp. by treating (an offense) as harmless or trivial syn excuse, pardon, forgive, remit — con·do·na·tion \ˌkän-də-ˈnä-shən\ n
con·dor \ˈkän-dər, -ˌdōr\ n [Sp cóndor, fr. Quechua (a So. American Indian language) kuntur] : a very large American vulture of the high Andes; also : a related nearly extinct vulture of southern California now resident only in captivity
con·duce \kən-ˈdüs, -ˈdyüs\ vb con·duced; con·duc·ing : to lead or contribute to a particular result — con·du·cive adj
¹con·duct \ˈkän-(ˌ)dəkt\ n 1 : MANAGEMENT, DIRECTION 2 : BEHAVIOR
²con·duct \kən-ˈdəkt\ vb 1 : GUIDE, ESCORT 2 : MANAGE, DIRECT 3 : to act as a medium for conveying or transmitting 4 : BEHAVE — con·duc·tion \-ˈdək-shən\ n
con·duc·tance \kən-ˈdək-təns\ n : the readiness with which a conductor transmits an electric current
con·duc·tive \kən-ˈdək-tiv\ adj : having the power to conduct (as heat or electricity) — con·duc·tiv·i·ty \ˌkän-ˌdək-ˈti-və-tē\ n
con·duc·tor \kən-ˈdək-tər\ n 1 : one that conducts; esp : a material that permits an electric current to flow easily 2 : a collector of fares in a public conveyance 3 : the leader of a musical ensemble
con·duit \ˈkän-ˌdü-ət, ˌdyü-, -dwət\ n 1 : a channel for conveying fluid 2 : a tube or trough for protecting

electric wires or cables 3 : a means of transmitting or distributing
con·dyle \ˈkän-ˌdīl, -dᵊl\ n : an articular prominence of a bone — con·dy·lar \-də-lər\ adj
cone \ˈkōn\ n 1 : the scaly fruit of trees of the pine family 2 : a solid figure formed by rotating a right triangle about one of its legs 3 : a solid figure that slopes evenly to a point from a usu. circular base 4 : any of the conical light-sensitive receptor cells of the retina that function in color vision 5 : something shaped like a cone
Con·es·to·ga wagon \ˌkä-nə-ˈstō-gə-\ n : a broad⸗ wheeled covered wagon used esp. for transporting freight across the prairies
co·ney \ˈkō-nē\ n, pl coneys 1 : RABBIT; also : its fur 2 : PIKA
conf abbr 1 conference 2 confidential
con·fab \ˈkän-ˌfab, kən-ˈfab\ n : CONFABULATION 1
con·fab·u·la·tion \kən-ˌfab-yə-ˈlā-shən\ n 1 : CHAT; also : CONFERENCE 2 : a filling in of gaps in memory by fabrication
con·fec·tion \kən-ˈfek-shən\ n : a fancy dish or sweet; also : CANDY
con·fec·tion·er \-sh(ə-)nər\ n : a maker of or dealer in confections
con·fec·tion·ery \-shə-ˌner-ē\ n, pl -er·ies 1 : sweet foods 2 : a confectioner's place of business
Confed abbr Confederate
con·fed·er·a·cy \kən-ˈfe-də-rə-sē\ n, pl -cies 1 : LEAGUE, ALLIANCE 2 cap : the 11 southern states that seceded from the U.S. in 1860 and 1861
¹con·fed·er·ate \kən-ˈfe-də-rət\ adj 1 : united in a league : ALLIED 2 cap : of or relating to the Confederacy
²confederate n 1 : ALLY, ACCOMPLICE 2 cap : an adherent of the Confederacy
³con·fed·er·ate \-ˈfe-də-ˌrāt\ vb -at·ed; -at·ing : to unite in a confederacy
con·fed·er·a·tion \kən-ˌfe-də-ˈrā-shən\ n 1 : an act of confederating : ALLIANCE 2 : LEAGUE
con·fer \kən-ˈfər\ vb con·ferred; con·fer·ring 1 : GRANT, BESTOW 2 : to exchange views : CONSULT — con·fer·ee \ˌkän-fə-ˈrē\ n
con·fer·ence \ˈkän-f(ə-)rəns\ n 1 : an interchange of views; also : a meeting for this purpose 2 : an association of athletic teams
con·fess \kən-ˈfes\ vb 1 : to acknowledge or disclose one's misdeed, fault, or sin 2 : to acknowledge one's sins to God or to a priest 3 : to receive the confession of (a penitent) syn admit, own, avow, concede, grant
con·fess·ed·ly \-ˈfe-səd-lē\ adv : by confession : ADMITTEDLY
con·fes·sion \-ˈfe-shən\ n 1 : an act of confessing (as in the sacrament of penance) 2 : an acknowledgment of guilt 3 : a formal statement of religious beliefs 4 : a religious body having a common creed — con·fes·sion·al adj
con·fes·sion·al \-ˈfe-shə-nəl\ n : a place where a priest hears confessions
con·fes·sor \kən-ˈfe-sər\ n 1 : one that confesses 2 : a priest who hears confessions
con·fet·ti \kən-ˈfe-tē\ n [It, pl. of confetto sweetmeat, fr. ML confectum, fr. L, neut. of confectus, pp. of conficere to prepare] : bits of colored paper or ribbon for throwing (as at weddings)
con·fi·dant \ˈkän-fə-ˌdänt, -ˌdant\ n : one to whom secrets are confided
con·fi·dante \-ˌdänt, -ˌdant\ n : CONFIDANT; esp : one who is a woman
con·fide \kən-ˈfīd\ vb con·fid·ed; con·fid·ing 1 : to have or show faith : TRUST (∼ in a friend) 2 : to tell confidentially (∼ a secret) 3 : ENTRUST
¹con·fi·dence \ˈkän-fə-dəns\ n 1 : TRUST, RELIANCE 2 : SELF-ASSURANCE, BOLDNESS 3 : a state of trust or intimacy 4 : SECRET 2 — con·fi·dent \-dənt\ adj — con·fi·dent·ly adv

²**confidence** *adj* : of or relating to swindling by false promises ⟨a ~ game⟩

con·fi·den·tial \ˌkän-fə-ˈden-chəl\ *adj* **1** : SECRET, PRIVATE **2** : entrusted with confidences ⟨~ clerk⟩ — **con·fi·den·tial·ly** *adv*

con·fig·u·ra·tion \kən-ˌfi-gyə-ˈrā-shən\ *n* : structural arrangement of parts : SHAPE

con·fig·ure \kən-ˈfi-gyər\ *vb* **-ured; -ur·ing** : to set up for operation esp. in a particular way

con·fine \kən-ˈfīn\ *vb* **con·fined; con·fin·ing 1** : to hold within a location; *also* : IMPRISON **2** : to keep within limits ⟨will ~ my remarks to one subject⟩ — **con·fine·ment** *n* — **con·fin·er** *n*

con·fines \ˈkän-ˌfīnz\ *n pl* : BOUNDS, BORDERS

con·firm \kən-ˈfərm\ *vb* **1** : to give approval to : RATIFY **2** : to make firm or firmer **3** : to administer the rite of confirmation to **4** : VERIFY, CORROBORATE — **con·fir·ma·to·ry** \-ˈfər-mə-ˌtōr-ē\ *adj*

con·fir·ma·tion \ˌkän-fər-ˈmä-shən\ *n* **1** : a religious ceremony admitting a person to full membership in a church or synagogue **2** : an act of ratifying or corroborating; *also* : PROOF

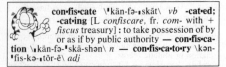

con·fis·cate \ˈkän-fə-ˌskāt\ *vb* **-cat·ed; -cat·ing** [L *confiscare*, fr. *com-* with + *fiscus* treasury] : to take possession of by or as if by public authority — **con·fis·ca·tion** \ˌkän-fə-ˈskā-shən\ *n* — **con·fis·ca·to·ry** \kən-ˈfis-kə-ˌtōr-ē\ *adj*

con·fla·gra·tion \ˌkän-flə-ˈgrā-shən\ *n* : FIRE; *esp* : a large disastrous fire

¹**con·flict** \ˈkän-ˌflikt\ *n* **1** : WAR **2** : a clash between hostile or opposing elements, ideas, or forces

²**con·flict** \kən-ˈflikt\ *vb* : to show opposition or irreconcilability : CLASH

con·flu·ence \ˈkän-ˌflü-əns, kən-ˈflü-\ *n* **1** : a coming together at one point **2** : the meeting or place of meeting of two or more streams — **con·flu·ent** \-ənt\ *adj*

con·flux \ˈkän-ˌfləks\ *n* : CONFLUENCE

con·form \kən-ˈfȯrm\ *vb* **1** : to be similar or identical; *also* : AGREE **2** : to obey customs or standards; *also* : COMPLY — **con·form·able** *adj*

con·for·mance \kən-ˈfȯr-məns\ *n* : CONFORMITY

con·for·ma·tion \ˌkän-fȯr-ˈmä-shən\ *n* : a forming into a whole by arranging parts

con·for·mi·ty \kən-ˈfȯr-mə-tē\ *n*, *pl* **-ties 1** : HARMONY, AGREEMENT **2** : COMPLIANCE, OBEDIENCE

con·found \kən-ˈfau̇nd, kän-\ *vb* **1** : to throw into disorder or confusion **2** : CONFUSE **2 syn** bewilder, puzzle, perplex, befog

con·fra·ter·ni·ty \ˌkän-frə-ˈtər-nə-tē\ *n* : a society devoted esp. to a religious or charitable cause

con·frere \ˈkän-ˌfrer, ˈkōⁿ-\ *n* : COLLEAGUE, COMRADE

con·front \kən-ˈfrənt\ *vb* **1** : to face esp. in challenge : OPPOSE; *also* : to deal unflinchingly with ⟨~ed the issue⟩ **2** : to cause to face or meet — **con·fron·ta·tion** \ˌkän-frən-ˈtā-shən\ *n*

Con·fu·cian \kən-ˈfyü-shən\ *adj* : of or relating to the

Chinese philosopher Confucius or his teachings — **Con·fu·cian·ism** \-shə-ˌni-zəm\ *n*

con·fuse \kən-ˈfyüz\ *vb* **con·fused; con·fus·ing 1** : to make mentally unclear or uncertain; *also* : to disturb the composure of **2** : to mix up : JUMBLE **syn** muddle, befuddle, addle, fluster — **con·fus·ed·ly** \-ˈfyü-zəd-lē\ *adv*

con·fu·sion \-ˈfyü-zhən\ *n* **1** : an act or instance of confusing **2** : the quality or state of being confused

con·fute \kən-ˈfyüt\ *vb* **con·fut·ed; con·fut·ing** : to overwhelm by argument : REFUTE — **con·fu·ta·tion** \ˌkän-fyü-ˈtā-shən\ *n*

cong *abbr* congress; congressional

con·ga \ˈkäŋ-gə\ *n* : a Cuban dance of African origin performed by a group usu. in single file

con·geal \kən-ˈjēl\ *vb* **1** : FREEZE **2** : to make or become hard or thick

con·ge·ner \ˈkän-jə-nər\ *n* : one related to another; *esp* : a plant or animal of the same taxonomic genus as another — **con·ge·ner·ic** \ˌkän-jə-ˈner-ik\ *adj*

con·ge·nial \kən-ˈjē-nyəl\ *adj* **1** : KINDRED, SYMPATHETIC **2** : suited to one's taste or nature : AGREEABLE — **con·ge·ni·al·i·ty** \-ˌjē-nē-ˈa-lə-tē\ *n* — **con·ge·nial·ly** *adv*

con·gen·i·tal \kən-ˈje-nə-tᵊl\ *adj* : existing at or dating from birth **syn** inborn, innate, natural

con·ger eel \ˈkän-gər-\ *n* : a large edible marine eel of the Atlantic

con·ge·ries \ˈkän-jə-(ˌ)rēz\ *n, pl* **congeries** : AGGREGATION, COLLECTION

con·gest \kən-ˈjest\ *vb* **1** : to cause excessive fullness of the blood vessels of (as a lung) **2** : to obstruct by overcrowding — **con·ges·tion** \-ˈjes-chən\ *n* — **con·ges·tive** \-ˈjes-tiv\ *adj*

congestive heart failure *n* : heart failure in which the heart is unable to keep enough blood circulating in the tissues or is unable to pump out the blood returned to it by the veins

¹**con·glom·er·ate** \kən-ˈglä-mə-rət\ *adj* [L *conglomerare* to roll together, fr. *com-* together + *glomerare* to wind into a ball, fr. *glomer-, glomus* ball] : made up of parts from various sources

²**con·glom·er·ate** \-ˌrāt\ *vb* **-at·ed; -at·ing** : to form into a mass — **con·glom·er·a·tion** \-ˌglä-mə-ˈrā-shən\ *n*

³**con·glom·er·ate** \-rət\ *n* **1** : a mass formed of fragments from various sources; *esp* : a rock composed of fragments varying from pebbles to boulders held together by a cementing material **2** : a widely diversified corporation

Con·go·lese \ˌkäŋ-gə-ˈlēz, -ˈlēs\ *n* : a native or inhabitant of Congo — **Congolese** *adj*

con·grat·u·late \kən-ˈgra-chə-ˌlāt\ *vb* **-lat·ed; -lat·ing** : to express sympathetic pleasure to on account of success or good fortune : FELICITATE — **con·grat·u·la·tion** \-ˌgra-chə-ˈlā-shən\ *n* — **con·grat·u·la·to·ry** \-ˈgra-chə-lə-ˌtōr-ē\ *adj*

con·gre·gate \ˈkäŋ-gri-ˌgāt\ *vb* **-gat·ed; -gat·ing** [ME, fr. L *congregatus*, pp. of *congregare*, fr. *com-* together + *greg-, grex* flock] : ASSEMBLE

con·gre·ga·tion \ˌkäŋ-gri-ˈgā-shən\ *n* **1** : an assembly of persons met esp. for worship; *also* : a group that habitually so meets **2** : a religious community or order **3** : the act or an instance of congregating

con·gre·ga·tion·al \-shə-nəl\ *adj* **1** : of or relating to a congregation **2** *cap* : observing the faith and practice of certain Protestant churches which recognize the independence of each congregation in church matters — **con·gre·ga·tion·al·ism** \-nə-ˌli-zəm\ *n, often cap* — **con·gre·ga·tion·al·ist** \-list\ *n, often cap*

con·gress \ˈkäŋ-grəs\ *n* **1** : an assembly esp. of delegates for discussion and usu. action on some question **2** : the body of senators and representatives constituting a nation's legislature — **con·gres·sio·nal** \kən-ˈgre-shə-nəl\ *adj*

con·gress·man \ˈkäŋ-grəs-mən\ *n* : a member of a congress

con·gress·wom·an \-ˌwu̇-mən\ *n* : a female member of a congress

con·gru·ence \kən-ˈgrü-əns, ˈkäŋ-grü-\ *n* : the quality of agreeing or coinciding : CONGRUITY — **con·gru·ent** \kən-ˈgrü-ənt, ˈkäŋ-grü-\ *adj*

con·gru·en·cy \-sē\ *n, pl* **-cies** : CONGRUENCE

con·gru·ity \kän-ˈgrü-ə-tē\ *n, pl* **-ities** : correspondence between things — **con·gru·ous** \ˈkäŋ-grü-əs\ *adj*

con·ic \ˈkä-nik\ *adj* **1** : of or relating to a cone **2** : CONICAL

con·i·cal \ˈkä-ni-kəl\ *adj* : resembling a cone esp. in shape

co·ni·fer \ˈkä-nə-fər, ˈkō-\ *n* : any of an order of shrubs or trees (as the pines) that usu. are evergreen and bear cones — **co·nif·er·ous** \kō-ˈni-fə-rəs\ *adj*

conj *abbr* conjunction

con·jec·ture \kən-ˈjek-chər\ *n* : GUESS, SURMISE — **con·jec·tur·al** \-chə-rəl\ *adj* — **conjecture** *vb*

con·join \kən-ˈjȯin\ *vb* : to join together — **con·joint** \-ˈjȯint\ *adj*

con·ju·gal \ˈkän-ji-gəl\ *adj* : of or relating to marriage : MATRIMONIAL

¹con·ju·gate \ˈkän-ji-gət, -jə-ˌgāt\ *adj* **1** : united esp. in pairs : COUPLED **2** : of kindred origin and meaning ⟨*sing* and *song* are ∼⟩ — **con·ju·gate·ly** *adv*

²con·ju·gate \-jə-ˌgāt\ *vb* **-gat·ed; -gat·ing 1** : INFLECT ⟨∼ a verb⟩ **2** : to join together : COUPLE

con·ju·ga·tion \ˌkän-jə-ˈgā-shən\ *n* **1** : an arrangement of the inflectional forms of a verb **2** : the act of conjugating : the state of being conjugated

con·junct \kän-ˈjəŋkt\ *adj* : JOINED, UNITED

con·junc·tion \kən-ˈjəŋk-shən\ *n* **1** : COMBINATION **2** : occurrence at the same time **3** : a word that joins together sentences, clauses, phrases, or words

con·junc·ti·va \ˌkän-ˌjəŋk-ˈtī-və\ *n, pl* **-vas** *or* **-vae** \-(ˌ)vē\ : the mucous membrane lining the inner surface of the eyelids and continuing over the forepart of the eyeball

con·junc·tive \kən-ˈjəŋk-tiv\ *adj* **1** : CONNECTIVE **2** : CONJUNCT **3** : being or functioning like a conjunction

con·junc·ti·vi·tis \kən-ˌjəŋk-ti-ˈvī-təs\ *n* : inflammation of the conjunctiva

con·junc·ture \kən-ˈjəŋk-chər\ *n* **1** : CONJUNCTION, UNION **2** : JUNCTURE **3**

con·jure \ˈkän-jər, ˈkən- *for 1, 2;* kən-ˈju̇r *for 3*\ *vb* **con·jured; con·jur·ing 1** : to implore earnestly or solemnly **2** : to practice magic; *esp* : to summon (as a devil) by sorcery **3** : to practice sleight of hand — **con·ju·ra·tion** \ˌkän-jü-ˈrā-shən, ˌkən-\ *n* — **con·jur·er** *or* **con·ju·ror** \ˈkän-jər-ər, ˈkən-\ *n*

conk \ˈkäŋk\ *vb* : BREAK DOWN; *esp* : STALL (the motor ∼ed out)

Conn *abbr* Connecticut

con·nect \kə-ˈnekt\ *vb* **1** : JOIN, LINK **2** : to associate in one's mind — **con·nect·able** *adj* — **con·nec·tor** *n*

con·nec·tion \kə-ˈnek-shən\ *n* **1** : JUNCTION, UNION **2** : logical relationship : COHERENCE; *esp* : relation of a word to other words in a sentence **3** : family relationship **4** : BOND, LINK **5** : a person related by blood or marriage **6** : relationship in social affairs or in business **7** : an association of persons; *esp* : a religious denomination

¹con·nec·tive \kə-ˈnek-tiv\ *adj* : serving to connect — **con·nec·tiv·i·ty** \ˌkä-ˌnek-ˈti-və-tē\ *n*

²connective *n* : a word (as a conjunction) that connects words or word groups

con·nex·ion *chiefly Brit var of* CONNECTION

con·ning tower \ˈkä-niŋ-\ *n* : a raised structure on the deck of a submarine

con·nip·tion \kə-ˈnip-shən\ *n* : a fit of rage, hysteria, or alarm

con·nive \kə-ˈnīv\ *vb* **con·nived; con·niv·ing** [F or L; F *conniver,* fr. L *conivēre* to close the eyes, connive] **1** : to pretend ignorance of something one ought to oppose as wrong **2** : to cooperate secretly : give secret aid — **con·niv·ance** *n* — **con·niv·er** *n*

---

con·nois·seur \ˌkä-nə-ˈsər\ *n* : a critical judge in matters of art or taste

---

con·no·ta·tion \ˌkä-nə-ˈtā-shən\ *n* : a meaning in addition to or apart from the thing explicitly named or described by a word

con·no·ta·tive \ˈkä-nə-ˌtā-tiv, kə-ˈnō-tə-\ *adj* **1** : connoting or tending to connote **2** : relating to connotation

con·note \kə-ˈnōt\ *vb* **con·not·ed; con·not·ing** : to suggest or mean as a connotation

con·nu·bi·al \kə-ˈnü-bē-əl, -ˈnyü-\ *adj* : of or relating to marriage : CONJUGAL

con·quer \ˈkäŋ-kər\ *vb* **1** : to gain by force of arms : WIN **2** : to get the better of : OVERCOME **syn** defeat, subjugate, subdue, overthrow, vanquish — **con·quer·or** \-ər\ *n*

con·quest \ˈkän-ˌkwest, ˈkäŋ-\ *n* **1** : an act of conquering : VICTORY **2** : something conquered

con·quis·ta·dor \kȯn-ˈkēs-tə-ˌdȯr, kän-ˈkwis-\ *n, pl* **-do·res** \-ˌkēs-tə-ˈdȯr-ēz, -ˌkwis-\ *or* **-dors** \- : CON-

QUEROR; *esp* : a leader in the Spanish conquest of the Americas in the 16th century

cons *abbr* consonant

con·san·guin·i·ty \ˌkän-ˌsan-ˈgwi-nə-tē, -ˌsaŋ-\ *n, pl* **-ties** : blood relationship — **con·san·guin·e·ous** \-ˈnē-əs\ *adj*

con·science \ˈkän-chəns\ *n* : consciousness of the moral right and wrong of one's own acts or motives — **con·science·less** *adj*

con·sci·en·tious \ˌkän-chē-ˈen-chəs\ *adj* : guided by one's own sense of right and wrong **syn** scrupulous, honorable, honest, upright, just — **con·sci·en·tious·ly** *adv*

conscientious objector *n* : a person who refuses to serve in the armed forces or to bear arms on moral or religious grounds

con·scious \ˈkän-chəs\ *adj* **1** : AWARE **2** : known or felt by one's inner self **3** : mentally awake or alert : not asleep or unconscious **4** : INTENTIONAL — **con·scious·ly** *adv* — **con·scious·ness** *n*

con·script \kən-ˈskript\ *vb* : to enroll by compulsion for military or naval service — **conscript** \ˈkän-ˌskript\ *n* — **con·scrip·tion** \kən-ˈskrip-shən\ *n*

con·se·crate \ˈkän-sə-ˌkrāt\ *vb* **-crat·ed; -crat·ing 1** : to induct (as a bishop) into an office with a religious rite **2** : to make or declare sacred (∼ a church) **3** : to devote solemnly to a purpose — **con·se·cra·tion** \ˌkän-sə-ˈkrā-shən\ *n*

con·sec·u·tive \kən-ˈse-kyə-tiv\ *adj* : following in regular order : SUCCESSIVE — **con·sec·u·tive·ly** *adv*

con·sen·su·al \kən-ˈsen-chə-wəl\ *adj* : involving or based on mutual consent

con·sen·sus \kən-ˈsen-səs\ *n* **1** : agreement in opinion, testimony, or belief **2** : collective opinion

¹con·sent \kən-ˈsent\ *vb* : to give assent or approval

²consent *n* : approval or acceptance of something done or proposed by another

con·se·quence \ˈkän-sə-ˌkwens\ *n* **1** : RESULT **2** : IMPORTANCE **syn** effect, outcome, aftermath, upshot

con·se·quent \-kwənt, -ˌkwent\ *adj* : following as a result or effect

con·se·quen·tial \ˌkän-sə-ˈkwen-chəl\ *adj* **1** : having significant consequences **2** : showing self-importance

con·se·quent·ly \ˈkän-sə-ˌkwent-lē, -kwənt-\ *adv* : as a result : ACCORDINGLY

con·ser·van·cy \kən-ˈsər-vən-sē\ *n, pl* **-cies** : an organization or area designated to conserve natural resources

con·ser·va·tion \ˌkän-sər-ˈvā-shən\ *n* : PRESERVATION; *esp* : planned management of natural resources

con·ser·va·tion·ist \-shə-nist\ *n* : a person who advocates conservation esp. of natural resources

con·ser·va·tism \kən-ˈsər-və-ˌti-zəm\ *n* : disposition to keep to established ways : opposition to change

¹con·ser·va·tive \kən-ˈsər-və-tiv\ *adj* **1** : PRESERVATIVE **2** : disposed to maintain existing views, conditions, or institutions **3** : MODERATE, CAUTIOUS — **con·ser·va·tive·ly** *adv*

²conservative *n* : a person who is conservative esp. in politics

con·ser·va·tor \kən-ˈsər-və-tər, ˈkän-sər-ˌvā-\ *n* **1** : PROTECTOR, GUARDIAN **2** : one named by a court to protect the interests of an incompetent (as a child)

con·ser·va·to·ry \kən-ˈsər-və-ˌtōr-ē\ *n, pl* **-ries 1** : GREENHOUSE **2** : a place of instruction in one of the fine arts (as music)

¹con·serve \kən-ˈsərv\ *vb* **con·served; con·serv·ing** : to keep from losing or wasting : PRESERVE

²con·serve \ˈkän-ˌsərv\ *n* **1** : CONFECTION; *esp* : a candied fruit **2** : PRESERVE; *esp* : one prepared from a mixture of fruits

con·sid·er \kən-ˈsi-dər\ *vb* [ME, fr. MF *considerer*, fr. L *considerare*, fr. *com-* together + *sider-, sidus* heavenly body] **1** : THINK, PONDER **2** : HEED, REGARD **3** : JUDGE, BELIEVE — **con·sid·ered** *adj*

con·sid·er·able \-ˈsi-dər-ə-bəl, -ˈsi-drə-bəl\ *adj* **1** : IM-

PORTANT **2** : large in extent, amount, or degree — **con·sid·er·ably** \-blē\ *adv*

con·sid·er·ate \kən-ˈsi-də-rət\ *adj* : observant of the rights and feelings of others **syn** thoughtful, attentive

con·sid·er·ation \kən-ˌsi-də-ˈrā-shən\ *n* **1** : careful thought : DELIBERATION **2** : a matter taken into account **3** : thoughtful attention **4** : JUDGMENT, OPINION **5** : RECOMPENSE

con·sid·er·ing *prep* : in view of : taking into account

con·sign \kən-ˈsīn\ *vb* **1** : ENTRUST, COMMIT **2** : to deliver formally **3** : to send (goods) to an agent for sale — **con·sign·ee** \ˌkän-sə-ˈnē, -ˌsī-; kən-ˌsī-\ *n* — **con·sign·or** \ˌkän-sə-ˈnòr, -ˌsī-; kən-ˌsī-\ *n*

con·sign·ment \kən-ˈsīn-mənt\ *n* : something consigned esp. in a single shipment

con·sist \kən-ˈsist\ *vb* **1** : to be inherent : LIE — usu. used with *in* **2** : to be composed or made up — usu. used with *of*

con·sis·tence \kən-ˈsis-təns\ *n* : CONSISTENCY

con·sis·ten·cy \-tən-sē\ *n, pl* **-cies 1** : COHESIVENESS, FIRMNESS **2** : agreement or harmony in parts or of different things **3** : UNIFORMITY (∼ of behavior) — **con·sis·tent** \-tənt\ *adj* — **con·sis·tent·ly** *adv*

con·sis·to·ry \kən-ˈsis-tə-rē\ *n, pl* **-ries** : a solemn assembly (as of Roman Catholic cardinals)

consol *abbr* consolidated

¹con·sole \ˈkän-ˌsōl\ *n* **1** : the desklike part of an organ at which the organist sits **2** : the combination of displays and controls of a device or system **3** : a cabinet for a radio or television set resting directly on the floor **4** : a small storage cabinet between bucket seats in an automobile

²con·sole \kən-ˈsōl\ *vb* **con·soled; con·sol·ing** : to soothe the grief of : COMFORT, SOLACE — **con·so·la·tion** \ˌkän-sə-ˈlā-shən\ *n* — **con·so·la·to·ry** \kən-ˈsō-lə-ˌtōr-ē, -ˈsä-\ *adj*

con·sol·i·date \kən-ˈsä-lə-ˌdāt\ *vb* **-dat·ed; -dat·ing 1** : to unite or become united into one whole : COMBINE **2** : to make firm or secure **3** : to form into a compact mass — **con·sol·i·da·tion** \-ˌsä-lə-ˈdā-shən\ *n*

con·som·mé \ˌkän-sə-ˈmā\ *n* [F] : a clear soup made from well-seasoned stock

con·so·nance \ˈkän-sə-nəns\ *n* **1** : AGREEMENT, HARMONY **2** : repetition of consonants esp. as an alternative to rhyme in verse

¹con·so·nant \-nənt\ *adj* : having consonance, harmony, or agreement **syn** consistent, compatible, congruous, congenial, sympathetic — **con·so·nant·ly** *adv*

²consonant *n* **1** : a speech sound (as \p\, \g\, \n\, \l\, \s\, \r\) characterized by constriction or closure at one or more points in the breath channel **2** : a letter other than *a*, *e*, *i*, *o*, and *u* — **con·so·nan·tal** \ˌkän-sə-ˈnant-ᵊl\ *adj*

¹con·sort \ˈkän-ˌsòrt\ *n* **1** : a ship accompanying another **2** : SPOUSE, MATE

²con·sort \kən-ˈsòrt\ *vb* **1** : to keep company **2** : ACCORD, HARMONIZE

con·sor·tium \kən-ˈsòr-shəm; -shē-əm, -tē-\ *n, pl* **-sor·tia** \-shə-; -shē-ə, -tē-\ [L, fellowship] : an agreement or combination (as of companies) formed to undertake a large enterprise

con·spec·tus \kən-ˈspek-təs\ *n* **1** : a brief survey or summary **2** : SUMMARY

con·spic·u·ous \kən-ˈspi-kyə-wəs\ *adj* : attracting attention : PROMINENT, STRIKING **syn** noticeable, remarkable, outstanding — **con·spic·u·ous·ly** *adv*

con·spir·a·cy \kən-ˈspir-ə-sē\ *n, pl* **-cies** : an agreement among conspirators : PLOT

con·spir·a·tor \kən-ˈspir-ə-tər\ *n* : one that conspires — **con·spir·a·to·ri·al** \-ˌspir-ə-ˈtōr-ē-əl\ *adj*

con·spire \kən-ˈspīr\ *vb* **conspired; con·spir·ing** [ME, fr. MF *conspirer*, fr. L *conspirare* to be in harmony, conspire, fr. *com-* with + *spirare* to breathe] : to plan secretly an unlawful act : PLOT

const *abbr* **1** constant **2** constitution; constitutional

con·sta·ble \ˈkän-stə-bəl, ˈkən-\ *n* [ME *conestable*, fr.

OF, fr. LL *comes stabuli*, lit., officer of the stable] : a public officer responsible for keeping the peace

con·stab·u·lary \kən-'sta-byə-ˌler-ē\ *n, pl* **-lar·ies** 1 : the police of a particular district or country 2 : a police force organized like the military

con·stan·cy \'kän-stən-sē\ *n, pl* **-cies** 1 : firmness of mind 2 : STABILITY

¹con·stant \-stənt\ *adj* 1 : STEADFAST, FAITHFUL 2 : FIXED, UNCHANGING 3 : continually recurring : REGULAR — **con·stant·ly** *adv*

²constant *n* : something unchanging

con·stel·la·tion \ˌkän-stə-'lā-shən\ *n* : any of 88 groups of stars forming patterns

con·ster·na·tion \ˌkän-stər-'nā-shən\ *n* : amazed dismay and confusion

con·sti·pa·tion \ˌkän-stə-'pā-shən\ *n* : abnormally difficult or infrequent bowel movements — **con·sti·pate** \'kän-stə-ˌpāt\ *vb*

con·stit·u·en·cy \kən-'sti-chə-wən-sē\ *n, pl* **-cies** : a body of constituents; *also* : an electoral district

¹con·stit·u·ent \-wənt\ *n* 1 : a person entitled to vote for a representative for a district 2 : a component part

²constituent *adj* 1 : COMPONENT 2 : having power to create a government or frame or amend a constitution

con·sti·tute \'kän-stə-ˌtüt, -ˌtyüt\ *vb* **-tut·ed; -tut·ing** 1 : to appoint to an office or duty 2 : SET UP, ESTABLISH ⟨~ a law⟩ 3 : MAKE UP, COMPOSE

con·sti·tu·tion \ˌkän-stə-'tü-shən, -'tyü-\ *n* 1 : an established law or custom 2 : the physical makeup of the individual 3 : the structure, composition, or makeup of something ⟨~ of the sun⟩ 4 : the basic law in a politically organized body; *also* : a document containing such law

¹con·sti·tu·tion·al \-shə-nəl\ *adj* 1 : of or relating to the constitution of body or mind 2 : being in accord with the constitution of a state or society; *also* : of or relating to such a constitution — **con·sti·tu·tion·al·ly** *adv*

²constitutional *n* : an exercise (as a walk) taken for one's health

con·sti·tu·tion·al·i·ty \-ˌtü-shə-'na-lə-tē, -ˌtyü-\ *n* : the quality or state of being constitutional

con·sti·tu·tive \'kän-stə-ˌtü-tiv, -ˌtyü-, kən-'sti-chə-tiv\ *adj* 1 : CONSTRUCTIVE 2 : CONSTITUENT, ESSENTIAL

constr *abbr* construction

con·strain \kən-'strān\ *vb* 1 : COMPEL, FORCE 2 : CONFINE 3 : RESTRAIN

con·straint \-'strānt\ *n* 1 : COMPULSION; *also* : RESTRAINT 2 : repression of one's natural feelings

con·strict \kən-'strikt\ *vb* : to draw together : SQUEEZE — **con·stric·tion** \-'strik-shən\ *n* — **con·stric·tive** \-'strik-tiv\ *adj*

con·stric·tor \kən-'strik-tər\ *n* : a snake that kills its prey by crushing it in its coils

con·struct \kən-'strəkt\ *vb* : BUILD, MAKE — **con·struc·tor** \-'strək-tər\ *n*

con·struc·tion \kən-'strək-shən\ *n* 1 : INTERPRETATION 2 : the art, process, or manner of building; *also* : something built, created, or established : STRUCTURE 3 : syntactical arrangement of words in a sentence — **con·struc·tive** \-tiv\ *adj*

con·struc·tion·ist \-shə-nist\ *n* : a person who construes a legal document (as the U.S. Constitution) in a specific way ⟨a strict ~⟩

con·strue \kən-'strü\ *vb* **con·strued; con·stru·ing** 1 : to analyze the mutual relations of words in a sentence; *also* : TRANSLATE 2 : EXPLAIN, INTERPRET — **con·stru·able** *adj*

con·sub·stan·ti·a·tion \ˌkän-səb-ˌstan-chē-'ā-shən\ *n* : the actual substantial presence and combination of the body and blood of Christ with the eucharistic bread and wine

con·sul \'kän-səl\ *n* 1 : a chief magistrate of the Roman republic 2 : an official appointed by a government to reside in a foreign country to care for the commercial interests of the appointing government's citizens —

con·sul·ar \-sə-lər\ *adj* — **con·sul·ate** \-lət\ *n* — **con·sul·ship** *n*

con·sult \kən-'səlt\ *vb* 1 : to ask the advice or opinion of 2 : CONFER — **con·sul·tant** \-ᵊnt\ *n* — **con·sul·ta·tion** \ˌkän-səl-'tā-shən\ *n*

con·sume \kən-'süm\ *vb* **con·sumed; con·sum·ing** 1 : DESTROY ⟨consumed by fire⟩ 2 : to spend wastefully 3 : to eat up : DEVOUR 4 : to absorb the attention of : ENGROSS — **con·sum·able** *adj* — **con·sum·er** *n*

con·sum·er·ism \kən-'sü-mə-ˌri-zəm\ *n* : the promotion of consumers' interests (as against false advertising)

consumer price index *n* : an index measuring the change in the cost of widely purchased goods and services from the cost in some base period

¹con·sum·mate \'kän-sə-mət, kən-'sə\ *adj* : PERFECT **syn** finished, accomplished

²con·sum·mate \'kän-sə-ˌmāt\ *vb* **-mat·ed; -mat·ing** : to make complete : FINISH, ACHIEVE — **con·sum·ma·tion** \ˌkän-sə-'mā-shən\ *n*

con·sump·tion \kən-'səmp-shən\ *n* 1 : progressive bodily wasting away; *also* : TUBERCULOSIS 2 : the act of consuming or using up 3 : the use of economic goods

¹con·sump·tive \-'səmp-tiv\ *adj* 1 : tending to consume 2 : relating to or affected with consumption

²consumptive *n* : a person who has consumption

cont *abbr* 1 containing 2 contents 3 continent; continental 4 continued 5 control

¹con·tact \'kän-ˌtakt\ *n* 1 : a touching or meeting of bodies 2 : ASSOCIATION, RELATIONSHIP; *also* : CONNECTION, COMMUNICATION 3 : a person serving as a go-between or source of information 4 : CONTACT LENS

²contact *vb* 1 : to come or bring into contact : TOUCH 2 : to get in communication with

contact lens *n* : a thin lens fitting over the cornea usu. to correct vision

con·ta·gion \kən-'tā-jən\ *n* 1 : a contagious disease; *also* : the transmission of such a disease 2 : a disease–producing agent (as a virus) 3 : transmission of an influence on the mind or emotions

con·ta·gious \-jəs\ *adj* 1 : transmitted by contact with an infected person, his or her bodily discharges, or something that has touched either 2 : communicated or transmitted like a contagious disease; *esp* : exciting similar emotion or conduct in others

con·tain \kən-'tān\ *vb* 1 : RESTRAIN 2 : to have within : HOLD 3 : COMPRISE, INCLUDE — **con·tain·ment** *n*

con·tain·er \kən-'tā-nər\ *n* : RECEPTACLE; *esp* : one for shipment of goods

con·tam·i·nant \kən-'ta-mə-nənt\ *n* : something that contaminates

con·tam·i·nate \kən-'ta-mə-ˌnāt\ *vb* **-nat·ed; -nat·ing** : to soil, stain, or infect by contact or association — **con·tam·i·na·tion** \-ˌta-mə-'nā-shən\ *n*

contd *abbr* continued

con·temn \kən-'tem\ *vb* : to view or treat with contempt : DESPISE

con·tem·plate \'kän-təm-ˌplāt\ *vb* **-plat·ed; -plat·ing** [L *contemplari*, fr. *com-* with + *templum* space marked out for observation of auguries] 1 : to view or consider with continued attention 2 : INTEND — **con·tem·pla·tion** \ˌkän-təm-'plā-shən\ *n* — **con·tem·pla·tive** \kən-'tem-plə-tiv, 'kän-təm-ˌplā-\ *adj*

con·tem·po·ra·ne·ous \kən-ˌtem-pə-'rā-nē-əs\ *adj* : CONTEMPORARY 1

con·tem·po·rary \kən-'tem-pə-ˌrer-ē\ *adj* 1 : occurring or existing at the same time 2 : marked by characteristics of the present period — **contemporary** *n*

con·tempt \kən-'tempt\ *n* 1 : the act of despising : the state of mind of one who despises 2 : the state of being despised 3 : disobedience to or open disrespect of a court or legislature

con·tempt·ible \kən-'temp-tə-bəl\ *adj* : deserving contempt : DESPICABLE — **con·tempt·ibly** \-blē\ *adv*

con·temp·tu·ous \-'temp-chə-wəs\ *adj* : feeling or expressing contempt — **con·temp·tu·ous·ly** *adv*

con·tend \kən-'tend\ *vb* **1** : to strive against rivals or difficulties **2** : ARGUE **3** : MAINTAIN, ASSERT — **con·tend·er** *n*

¹con·tent \kən-'tent\ *adj* : SATISFIED

²content *vb* : SATISFY; *esp* : to limit (oneself) in requirements or actions

³content *n* : CONTENTMENT

⁴con·tent \'kän-₁tent\ *n* **1** : something contained ⟨∼s of a room⟩ **2** : subject matter or topics treated (as in a book) **3** : MEANING, SIGNIFICANCE **4** : the amount of material contained

con·tent·ed \kən-'ten-təd\ *adj* : SATISFIED — **con·tent·ed·ly** *adv* — **con·tent·ed·ness** *n*

con·ten·tion \kən-'ten-chən\ *n* **1** : CONTEST, STRIFE **2** : an idea or point for which a person argues — **con·ten·tious** \-chəs\ *adj* — **con·ten·tious·ly** *adv*

con·tent·ment \kən-'tent-mənt\ *n* : ease of mind : SATISFACTION

con·ter·mi·nous \kän-'tər-mə-nəs\ *adj* : having the same or a common boundary — **con·ter·mi·nous·ly** *adv*

¹con·test \kən-'test\ *vb* **1** : to engage in strife : FIGHT **2** : CHALLENGE, DISPUTE — **con·tes·tant** \-'tes-tənt\ *n*

²con·test \'kän-₁test\ *n* : STRUGGLE, COMPETITION

con·text \'kän-₁tekst\ *n* [L *contextus* connection of words, coherence, fr. *contexere* to weave together] : the parts of a discourse that surround a word or passage and help to explain its meaning; *also* : the circumstances surrounding an act or event — **con·tex·tu·al·ly** *adv*

con·tig·u·ous \kən-'ti-gyə-wəs\ *adj* : being in contact : TOUCHING; *also* : NEXT, ADJOINING — **con·ti·gu·i·ty** \₁kän-tə-'gyü-ə-tē\ *n*

con·ti·nence \'känt-ᵊn-əns\ *n* **1** : SELF-RESTRAINT; *esp* : a refraining from sexual intercourse **2** : the ability to retain urine or feces voluntarily

¹con·ti·nent \'känt-ᵊn-ənt\ *adj* : exercising continence

²continent *n* **1** : any of the great divisions of land on the globe **2** *cap* : the continent of Europe

¹con·ti·nen·tal \₁känt-ᵊn-'ent-ᵊl\ *adj* **1** : of or relating to a continent; *esp, often cap* : of or relating to the continent of Europe **2** *often cap* : of or relating to the colonies later forming the U.S. **3** : of or relating to cuisine based on classical European cooking

²continental *n* **1** *often cap* : a soldier in the Continental army **2** : EUROPEAN

continental drift *n* : a hypothetical slow movement of the continents over a fluid layer deep within the earth

continental shelf *n* : a shallow submarine plain forming a border to a continent

continental slope *n* : a usu. steep slope from a continental shelf to the ocean floor

con·tin·gen·cy \kən-'tin-jən-sē\ *n, pl* **-cies** : a chance or possible event

¹con·tin·gent \-jənt\ *adj* **1** : liable but not certain to happen : POSSIBLE **2** : happening by chance : not planned **3** : dependent on something that may or may not occur **4** : CONDITIONAL **syn** accidental, casual, incidental, odd

²contingent *n* : a quota (as of troops) supplied from an area or group

con·tin·u·al \kən-'tin-yə-wəl\ *adj* **1** : CONTINUOUS, UNBROKEN **2** : steadily recurring — **con·tin·u·al·ly** *adv*

con·tin·u·ance \-yə-wəns\ *n* **1** : unbroken succession **2** : the extent of continuing : DURATION **3** : adjournment of legal proceedings

con·tin·u·a·tion \kən-₁tin-yə-'wā-shən\ *n* **1** : extension or prolongation of a state or activity **2** : resumption after an interruption; *also* : something that carries on after a pause or break

con·tin·ue \kən-'tin-yü\ *vb* **-tin·ued; -tinu·ing 1** : to maintain without interruption **2** : ENDURE, LAST **3** : to remain in a place or condition **4** : to resume (as a story) after an intermission **5** : EXTEND; *also* : to per-

sist in **6** : to allow to remain **7** : to keep (a legal case) on the calendar or undecided

con·ti·nu·i·ty \₁kän-tə-'nü-ə-tē, -'nyü-\ *n, pl* **-ties 1** : the state of being continuous **2** : something that has or provides continuity

con·tin·u·ous \kən-'tin-yə-wəs\ *adj* : continuing without interruption — **con·tin·u·ous·ly** *adv*

con·tin·u·um \-yə-wəm\ *n, pl* **-ua** \-yə-wə\ *also* **-u·ums** : something that is the same throughout or consists of a series of variations or of a sequence of things in regular order

con·tort \kən-'tòrt\ *vb* : to twist out of shape — **con·tor·tion** \-'tòr-shən\ *n*

con·tor·tion·ist \-'tòr-shə-nist\ *n* : an acrobat able to twist the body into unusual postures

con·tour \'kän-₁tùr\ *n* [F, fr. It *contorno* fr. *contornare* to round off, sketch in outline, fr. L *com-* together + *tornare* to turn in a lathe, fr. *tornus* lathe] **1** : OUTLINE **2** : SHAPE, FORM — often used in pl. ⟨the ∼s of a statue⟩

contr *abbr* contract; contraction

con·tra·band \'kän-trə-₁band\ *n* : goods legally prohibited in trade; *also* : smuggled goods

con·tra·cep·tion \₁kän-trə-'sep-shən\ *n* : intentional prevention of conception and pregnancy — **con·tra·cep·tive** \-'sep-tive\ *adj or n*

¹con·tract \'kän-₁trakt\ *n* **1** : a binding agreement **2** : an undertaking to win a specified number of tricks in bridge — **con·trac·tu·al** \kän-'trak-chə-wəl\ *adj* — **con·trac·tu·al·ly** *adv*

²con·tract \kən-'trakt, *2 usu* 'kän-₁trakt\ *vb* **1** : to become affected with ⟨∼ a disease⟩ **2** : to establish or undertake by contract **3** : SHRINK, LESSEN; *esp* : to draw together esp. so as to shorten ⟨∼ a muscle⟩ **4** : to shorten (a word) by omitting letters or sounds in the middle — **con·tract·ible** \kən-'trak-tə-bəl, 'kän-₁\ *adj* — **con·trac·tion** \kən-'trak-shən\ *n* — **con·trac·tor** \'kän-₁trak-tər, kən-'trak-\ *n*

con·trac·tile \kən-'trakt-ᵊl\ *adj* : able to contract — **con·trac·til·i·ty** \₁kän-₁trak-'til-ə-tē\ *n*

con·tra·dict \₁kän-trə-'dikt\ *vb* : to assert the contrary of : deny the truth of — **con·tra·dic·tion** \-'dik-shən\ *n* — **con·tra·dic·to·ry** \-'dik-tə-rē\ *adj*

con·tra·dis·tinc·tion \₁kän-trə-dis-'tiŋk-shən\ *n* : distinction by contrast

con·trail \'kän-₁trāl\ *n* : a streak of condensed water vapor created by an airplane or rocket at high altitudes

con·tra·in·di·ca·tion \₁kän-trə-₁in-də-'kā-shən\ *n* : something (as a symptom or condition) that makes a particular treatment or procedure inadvisable

con·tral·to \kən-'tral-tō\ *n, pl* **-tos** : the lowest female voice; *also* : a singer having such a voice

con·trap·tion \kən-'trap-shən\ *n* : CONTRIVANCE, DEVICE

con·tra·pun·tal \₁kän-trə-'pənt-ᵊl\ *adj* : of or relating to counterpoint

con·tra·ri·ety \₁kän-trə-'rī-ə-tē\ *n, pl* **-eties** : the state of being contrary : DISAGREEMENT, INCONSISTENCY

con·trari·wise \'kän-₁trer-ē-₁wīz, kən-'trer-\ *adv* **1** : on the contrary **2** : VICE VERSA

con·trary \'kän-₁trer-ē; *4 often* kən-'trer-ē\ *adj* **1** : opposite in nature or position **2** : COUNTER, OPPOSED **3** : UNFAVORABLE — used of wind or weather **4** : unwilling to accept control or advice — **con·trari·ly** \-₁trer-ə-lē, -'trer-\ *adv* — **con·trary** *n is* 'kän-₁trer-ē, *adv is like adj*\ *n or adv*

¹con·trast \kən-'trast\ *vb* [F *contraster*, fr. MF, to oppose, resist, fr. (assumed) VL *contrastare*, fr. L *contra-* against + *stare* to stand] **1** : to show differences when compared **2** : to compare in such a way as to show differences

²con·trast \'kän-₁trast\ *n* **1** : diversity of adjacent parts in color, emotion, tone, or brightness ⟨the ∼ of a photograph⟩ **2** : unlikeness as shown when things are compared : DIFFERENCE

con•tra•vene \ˌkän-trə-'vēn\ *vb* -vened; -ven•ing 1 : to go or act contrary to ⟨∼ a law⟩ 2 : CONTRADICT

con•tre•temps \'kän-trə-ˌtän, kōⁿ-trə-'täⁿ\ *n, pl* con•tre•temps \-ˌtäⁿ, -ˌtäⁿz\ [F] : an inopportune or embarrassing occurrence

contrib *abbr* contribution; contributor

con•trib•ute \kən-'tri-byət\ *vb* -ut•ed; -ut•ing : to give along with others (as to a fund); *also* : HELP, ASSIST — con•tri•bu•tion \ˌkän-trə-'byü-shən\ *n* — con•trib•u•tor \kən-'tri-byə-tər\ *n* — con•trib•u•to•ry \-byə-ˌtōr-ē\ *adj*

con•trite \'kän-ˌtrīt, kən-'trīt\ *adj* : PENITENT, REPENTANT — con•trite•ly *adv* — con•tri•tion \kən-'tri-shən\ *n*

con•triv•ance \kən-'trī-vəns\ *n* 1 : a mechanical device 2 : SCHEME, PLAN

con•trive \kən-'trīv\ *vb* con•trived; con•triv•ing 1 : PLAN, DEVISE 2 : FRAME, MAKE 3 : to bring about with difficulty — con•triv•er *n*

con•trived \-'trīvd\ *adj* : lacking in natural or spontaneous quality

¹con•trol \kən-'trōl\ *vb* con•trolled; con•trol•ling 1 : to exercise restraining or directing influence over : REGULATE 2 : DOMINATE, RULE

²control *n* 1 : power to direct or regulate 2 : RESERVE, RESTRAINT 3 : a device for regulating a mechanism

con•trol•ler \kən-'trō-lər, 'kän-ˌtrō-lər\ *n* 1 : COMPTROLLER 2 : one that controls

con•tro•ver•sy \'kän-trə-ˌvər-sē\ *n, pl* -sies : a clash of opposing views : DISPUTE — con•tro•ver•sial \ˌkän-trə-ˌvər-shəl, -sē-əl\ *adj*

con•tro•vert \'kän-trə-ˌvərt, ˌkän-trə-'vərt\ *vb* : DENY, CONTRADICT — con•tro•vert•ible *adj*

con•tu•ma•cious \ˌkän-tü-'mā-shəs, -tyü-\ *adj* : stubbornly disobedient syn rebellious, insubordinate, seditious — con•tu•ma•cy \kän-'tü-mə-sē, -'tyü-; 'kän-tyə-\ *n* — con•tu•ma•cious•ly *adv*

con•tu•me•ly \kən-'tü-mə-lē, -'tyü-; 'kän-tə-ˌmē-lē, -tyə-\ *n, pl* -lies : contemptuous treatment : INSULT

con•tu•sion \kən-'tü-zhən, -'tyü-\ *n* : BRUISE — con•tuse \-'tüz, -'tyüz\ *vb*

co•nun•drum \kə-'nən-drəm\ *n* : RIDDLE

conv *abbr* 1 convention 2 convertible

con•va•lesce \ˌkän-və-'les\ *vb* -lesced; -lesc•ing : to recover health gradually — con•va•les•cence \-'ns\ *n* — con•va•les•cent \-'nt\ *adj or n*

con•vec•tion \kən-'vek-shən\ *n* : circulatory motion in a fluid due to warmer portions rising and cooler denser portions sinking; *also* : the transfer of heat by such motion — con•vec•tion•al \-shə-nəl\ *adj* — con•vec•tive \-'vek-tiv\ *adj*

convection oven *n* : an oven with a fan that circulates hot air uniformly and continuously around the food

con•vene \kən-'vēn\ *vb* con•vened; con•ven•ing : ASSEMBLE, MEET

con•ve•nience \kən-'vē-nyəns\ *n* 1 : SUITABLENESS 2 : a laborsaving device 3 : a suitable time ⟨at your ∼⟩ 4 : personal comfort : EASE

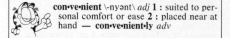

con•ve•nient \-nyənt\ *adj* 1 : suited to personal comfort or ease 2 : placed near at hand — con•ve•nient•ly *adv*

con•vent \'kän-vənt, -ˌvent\ *n* [ME *covent*, fr. OF, fr. ML *conventus*, fr. L, assembly, fr. *convenire* to come together] : a local community or house of a religious order esp. of nuns — con•ven•tu•al \kän-'ven-chə-wəl\ *adj*

con•ven•ti•cle \kən-'ven-ti-kəl\ *n* : MEETING; *esp* : a secret meeting for worship

con•ven•tion \kən-'ven-chən\ *n* 1 : an agreement esp. between states on a matter of common concern 2 : MEETING, ASSEMBLY 3 : an assembly of delegates convened for some purpose 4 : generally accepted custom, practice, or belief

con•ven•tion•al \-chə-nəl\ *adj* 1 : sanctioned by general custom 2 : COMMONPLACE, ORDINARY — con•ven•tion•al•i•ty \-ˌven-chə-'na-lə-tē\ *n* — con•ven•tion•al•ize \-'ven-chə-nə-ˌlīz\ *vb* — con•ven•tion•al•ly *adv*

con•verge \kən-'vərj\ *vb* con•verged; con•verg•ing : to approach one common center or single point — con•ver•gence \kən-'vər-jəns\ *n* — con•ver•gent \-jənt\ *adj*

con•ver•sant \kən-'vərs-ᵊnt\ *adj* : having knowledge and experience — used with *with*

con•ver•sa•tion \ˌkän-vər-'sā-shən\ *n* : an informal talking together — con•ver•sa•tion•al \-shə-nəl\ *adj* — con•ver•sa•tion•al•ly *adv*

con•ver•sa•tion•al•ist \-shə-nᵊl-ist\ *n* : a person who converses a great deal or who excels in conversation

¹con•verse \'kän-ˌvərs\ *n* : CONVERSATION

²con•verse \kən-'vərs\ *vb* con•versed; con•vers•ing : to engage in conversation

³con•verse \'kän-ˌvərs\ *n* : a statement related to another statement by having its hypothesis and conclusion or its subject and predicate reversed or interchanged

⁴con•verse \kən-'vərs, 'kän-ˌvers\ *adj* : reversed in order or relation — con•verse•ly *adv*

con•ver•sion \kən-'vər-zhən\ *n* 1 : a change in nature or form 2 : an experience associated with a decisive adoption of religion

¹con•vert \kən-'vərt\ *vb* 1 : to turn from one belief or party to another 2 : TRANSFORM, CHANGE 3 : MISAPPROPRIATE 4 : EXCHANGE — con•vert•er *or* con•ver•tor \-'vər-tər\ *n*

²con•vert \'kän-ˌvərt\ *n* : a person who has undergone religious conversion

¹con•vert•ible \kən-'vər-tə-bəl\ *adj* : capable of being converted

²convertible *n* : an automobile with a top that may be lowered or removed

con•vex \kän-'veks, 'kän-ˌveks\ *adj* : curved or rounded like the exterior of a sphere or circle — con•vex•i•ty \kän-'vek-sə-tē\ *n*

con•vey \kən-'vā\ *vb* 1 : CARRY, TRANSPORT 2 : TRANSMIT, TRANSFER — con•vey•or *also* con•vey•er \-ər\ *n*

con·vey·ance \-'vā-əns\ n 1 : the act of conveying 2 : a legal paper transferring ownership of property 3 : VEHICLE

¹con·vict \kən-'vikt\ vb : to prove or find guilty

²con·vict \'kän-₁vikt\ n : a person serving a prison sentence

con·vic·tion \kən-'vik-shən\ n 1 : the act of convicting esp. in a court 2 : the state of being convinced : BELIEF

con·vince \kən-'vins\ vb con·vinced; con·vinc·ing : to bring (as by argument) to belief or action — con·vinc·ing adj — con·vinc·ing·ly adv

con·viv·i·al \kən-'vi-vē-əl\ adj [LL convivialis, fr. L convivium banquet, fr. com- together + vivere to live] : enjoying companionship and the pleasures of feasting and drinking : JOVIAL, FESTIVE — con·viv·i·al·i·ty \-₁vi-vē-'a-lə-tē\ n — con·viv·i·al·ly adv

con·vo·ca·tion \₁kän-və-'kā-shən\ n 1 : a ceremonial assembly (as of the clergy) 2 : the act of convoking

con·voke \kən-'vōk\ vb con·voked; con·vok·ing : to call together to a meeting

con·vo·lut·ed \'kän-və-₁lü-təd\ adj 1 : folded in curved or tortuous windings 2 : INVOLVED, INTRICATE

con·vo·lu·tion \₁kän-və-'lü-shən\ n : a tortuous or sinuous structure; esp : one of the ridges of the brain

¹con·voy \'kän-₁vòi, kən-'vòi\ vb : to accompany for protection

²con·voy \'kän-₁vòi\ n 1 : one that convoys; esp : a protective escort (as for ships) 2 : the act of convoying 3 : a group of moving vehicles

con·vulse \kən-'vəls\ vb con·vulsed; con·vuls·ing : to agitate violently

con·vul·sion \kən-'vəl-shən\ n 1 : an abnormal and violent involuntary contraction or series of contractions of muscle 2 : a violent disturbance — con·vul·sive \-siv\ adj — con·vul·sive·ly adv

cony var of CONEY

coo \'kü\ n : a soft low sound made by doves or pigeons; also : a sound like this — coo vb

COO abbr chief operating officer

¹cook \'kuk\ n : a person who prepares food for eating

²cook vb 1 : to prepare food for eating 2 : to subject to heat or fire — cook·er n — cook·ware \-₁war\ n

cook·book \-₁bük\ n : a book of cooking directions and recipes

cook·ery \'ku-kə-rē\ n, pl -er·ies : the art or practice of cooking

cook·ie or cooky \'ku-kē\ n, pl cook·ies : a small sweet flat cake

cook·out \'kuk-₁aut\ n : an outing at which a meal is cooked and served in the open

¹cool \'kül\ adj 1 : moderately cold 2 : not excited : CALM 3 : not friendly 4 : IMPUDENT 5 : protecting from heat 6 slang : very good syn unflappable, composed, collected, unruffled, nonchalant — cool·ly adv — cool·ness n

²cool vb : to make or become cool

³cool n 1 : a cool time or place 2 : INDIFFERENCE; also : SELF-ASSURANCE, COMPOSURE ⟨kept his ∼⟩

cool·ant \'kü-lənt\ n : a usu. fluid cooling agent

cool·er \'kü-lər\ n 1 : a container for keeping food or drink cool 2 : JAIL, PRISON 3 : a tall iced drink

coo·lie \'kü-lē\ n [Hindi kulī] : an unskilled laborer usu. in or from the Far East

coon \'kün\ n : RACCOON

coon·hound \-₁haund\ n : a sporting dog trained to hunt raccoons

coon·skin \-₁skin\ n : the pelt of a raccoon; also : something (as a cap) made of this

¹coop \'küp, 'kup\ n : a small enclosure or building usu. for poultry

²coop vb : to confine in or as if in a coop — usu. used with up

co–op \'kō-₁äp\ n : COOPERATIVE

coo·per \'kü-pər, 'ku-\ n : one who makes or repairs barrels or casks — cooper vb — coo·per·age \-pə-rij\ n

co·op·er·ate \kō-'ä-pə-₁rāt\ vb : to act jointly with another or others — co·op·er·a·tion \-₁ä-pə-'rā-shən\ n — co·op·er·a·tor \-'ä-pə-₁rā-tər\ n

¹co·op·er·a·tive \kō-'ä-prə-tiv, -'ä-pə-₁rā-\ adj 1 : willing to work with others 2 : of or relating to an association formed to enable its members to buy or sell to better advantage by eliminating middlemen's profits

²cooperative n : a cooperative association

co–opt \kō-'äpt\ vb 1 : to choose or elect as a colleague 2 : ABSORB, ASSIMILATE; also : TAKE OVER

¹co·or·di·nate \kō-'òrd-ᵊn-ət\ adj 1 : equal in rank or order 2 : of equal rank in a compound sentence ⟨∼ clause⟩ 3 : joining words or word groups of the same rank — co·or·di·nate·ly adv

²co·or·di·nate \-'òrd-ᵊn-₁āt\ vb -nat·ed; -nat·ing 1 : to make or become coordinate 2 : to work or act together harmoniously — co·or·di·na·tion \-₁òrd-ᵊn-'ā-shən\ n — co·or·di·na·tor \-'òrd-ᵊn-₁ā-tər\ n

³co·or·di·nate \-'òrd-ᵊn-ət\ n 1 : one of a set of numbers used in specifying the location of a point on a surface or in space 2 pl : articles (as of clothing) designed to be used together and to attain their effect through pleasing contrast

coot \'küt\ n 1 : a dark-colored ducklike bird related to the rails 2 : any of several No. American sea ducks 3 : a harmless simple person

coo·tie \'kü-tē\ n : a body louse

cop \'käp\ n : POLICE OFFICER

co–pay·ment \'kō-₁pā-mənt, ₁kō-'\ n : a relatively small fixed fee required of a patient by a health insurer (as an HMO) at the time of each outpatient service or filling of a prescription

¹cope \'kōp\ n : a long cloaklike ecclesiastical vestment

²cope vb coped; cop·ing : to struggle to overcome problems or difficulties

cop·i·er \'kä-pē-ər\ n : one that copies; esp : a machine for making copies

co·pi·lot \'kō-₁pī-lət\ n : an assistant pilot of an aircraft or spacecraft

cop·ing \'kō-piŋ\ n : the top layer of a wall

co·pi·ous \'kō-pē-əs\ adj : LAVISH, ABUNDANT — co·pi·ous·ly adv — co·pi·ous·ness n

cop–out \'käp-₁aut\ n : an excuse for copping out; also : an act of copping out

cop out vb : to back out (as of an unwanted responsibility)

cop·per \'kä-pər\ n 1 : a malleable reddish metallic chemical element that is one of the best conductors of heat and electricity — see ELEMENT table 2 : a coin or token made of copper — cop·pery adj

cop·per·head \'kä-pər-₁hed\ n : a largely coppery brown pit viper esp. of the eastern and central U.S.

cop·pice \'kä-pəs\ n : THICKET

co·pra \'kō-prə\ n : dried coconut meat yielding coconut oil

copse \'käps\ n : THICKET

cop·ter \'käp-tər\ n : HELICOPTER

cop·u·la \'kä-pyə-lə\ n : LINKING VERB — cop·u·la·tive \-lə-tiv, -₁lā-\ adj

cop·u·late \'kä-pyə-₁lāt\ vb -lat·ed; -lat·ing : to engage in sexual intercourse — cop·u·la·tion \₁kä-pyə-'lā-shən\ n — cop·u·la·to·ry \'kä-pyə-lə-₁tòr-ē\ adj

¹copy \'kä-pē\ n, pl cop·ies 1 : an imitation or reproduction of an original work 2 : material to be set in type syn duplicate, reproduction, facsimile, replica

²copy vb cop·ied; copy·ing 1 : to make a copy of 2 : IMITATE — copy·ist n

copy·book \'kä-pē-₁buk\ n : a book formerly used to teach handwriting containing examples to be copied

copy·boy \-₁bòi\ n : a person who carries copy and runs errands (as in a newspaper office)

copy·cat \-₁kat\ n : a slavish imitator

copy·desk \-₁desk\ n : the desk at which newspaper copy is edited

copy editor *n* : one who edits newspaper copy and writes headlines; *also* : one who reads and corrects manuscript copy in a publishing house

copy·read·er \-ˌrē-dər\ *n* : COPY EDITOR

¹**copy·right** \-ˌrīt\ *n* : the sole right to reproduce, publish, and sell a literary or artistic work

²**copyright** *vb* : to secure a copyright on

copy·writ·er \'kä-pē-ˌrī-tər\ *n* : a writer of advertising copy

co·quet *or* **co·quette** \kō-'ket\ *vb* **co·quet·ted; co·quet·ting** : FLIRT — **co·quet·ry** \'kō-kə-trē, kō-'ke-trē\ *n*

co·quette \kō-'ket\ *n* [F, fem. of *coquet*, flirtatious man, dim. of *coq* cock] : FLIRT — **co·quett·ish** *adj*

cor *abbr* corner

Cor *abbr* Corinthians

cor·a·cle \'kòr-ə-kəl\ *n* [W *corwgl*] : a boat made of a frame covered usu. with hide or tarpaulin

cor·al \'kòr-əl\ *n* 1 : a stony or horny material that forms the skeleton of colonies of tiny sea polyps and includes a red form used in jewelry; *also* : a coral-forming polyp or polyp colony 2 : a deep pink color — **coral** *adj*

coral snake *n* : any of several venomous chiefly tropical New World snakes brilliantly banded in red, black, and yellow or white

cor·bel \'kòr-bəl\ *n* : a bracket-shaped architectural member that projects from a wall and supports a weight

¹**cord** \'kòrd\ *n* 1 : a usu. heavy string consisting of several strands woven or twisted together 2 : a long slender anatomical structure (as a tendon or nerve) 3 : a small flexible insulated electrical cable used to connect an appliance with a receptacle 4 : a cubic measure used esp. for firewood and equal to a stack 4×4×8 feet 5 : a rib or ridge on cloth

²**cord** *vb* 1 : to tie or furnish with a cord 2 : to pile (wood) in cords

cord·age \'kòr-dij\ *n* : ROPES, CORDS; *esp* : ropes in the rigging of a ship

¹**cor·dial** \'kòr-jəl\ *adj* [ME, fr. ML *cordialis*, fr. L *cord-, cor* heart] : warmly receptive or welcoming : HEARTFELT, HEARTY — **cor·di·al·i·ty** \ˌkòr-jē-'a-lə-tē, kòr-'ja-\ *n* — **cor·dial·ly** *adv*

²**cordial** *n* 1 : a stimulating medicine or drink 2 : LIQUEUR

cor·dil·le·ra \ˌkòr-dəl-'yer-ə, -də-'ler-\ *n* [Sp] : a series of parallel mountain ranges

cord·less \'kòrd-ləs\ *adj* : having no cord; *esp* : powered by a battery

cor·do·ba \'kòr-də-bə, -və\ *n* — see MONEY table

cor·don \'kòrd-ᵊn\ *n* 1 : an ornamental cord or ribbon 2 : an encircling line (as of troops or police) — **cordon** *vb*

cor·do·van \'kòr-də-vən\ *n* : a soft fine-grained leather

cor·du·roy \'kòr-də-ˌròi\ *n, pl* **-roys** : a heavy ribbed fabric; *also, pl* : trousers of this material

cord·wain·er \'kòrd-ˌwā-nər\ *n* : SHOEMAKER

¹**core** \'kòr\ *n* 1 : the central usu. inedible part of some fruits (as the apple); *also* : an inmost part of something 2 : GIST, ESSENCE

²**core** *vb* **cored; cor·ing** : to take out the core of — **cor·er** *n*

CORE \'kòr\ *abbr* Congress of Racial Equality

co·re·spon·dent \ˌkō-ri-'spän-dənt\ *n* : a person named as guilty of adultery with the defendant in a divorce suit

co·ri·an·der \'kòr-ē-ˌan-dər\ *n* : an herb related to the carrot; *also* : its aromatic dried fruit used as a flavoring

Cor·in·thi·ans \kə-'rin-thē-ənz\ *n* — see BIBLE table

¹**cork** \'kòrk\ *n* 1 : the tough elastic bark of a European oak (**cork oak**) used esp. for stoppers and insulation; *also* : a stopper of this 2 : a tissue of a woody plant making up most of the bark — **corky** *adj*

²**cork** *vb* : to furnish with or stop up with cork or a cork

cork·screw \'kòrk-ˌskrü\ *n* : a device for drawing corks from bottles

corm \'kòrm\ *n* : a solid bulblike underground part of a stem (as of the crocus or gladiolus)

cor·mo·rant \'kòr-mə-rənt, -ˌrant\ *n* [ME *cormeraunt*, fr. MF *cormorant*, fr. OF *cormareng*, fr. *corp* raven + *marenc* of the sea, fr. L *marinus*] : any of a family of dark-colored water birds with a long neck, hooked bill, and distensible throat pouch

¹**corn** \'kòrn\ *n* 1 : the seeds of a cereal grass and esp. of the chief cereal crop of a region (as wheat in Britain and Indian corn in the U.S.); *also* : a cereal grass 2 : sweet corn served as a vegetable

²**corn** *vb* : to salt (as beef) in brine and preservatives

³**corn** *n* : a local hardening and thickening of skin (as on a toe)

¹**corn·ball** \'kòrn-ˌból\ *n* : an unsophisticated person; *also* : something corny

²**cornball** *adj* : CORNY

corn bread *n* : bread made with cornmeal

corn·cob \-ˌkäb\ *n* : the woody core on which the kernels of Indian corn are arranged

corn·crib \-ˌkrib\ *n* : a crib for storing ears of Indian corn

cor·nea \'kòr-nē-ə\ *n* : the transparent part of the coat of the eyeball covering the iris and the pupil — **cor·ne·al** *adj*

corn ear·worm \-'ir-ˌwərm\ *n* : a moth whose larva is destructive esp. to Indian corn

¹**cor·ner** \'kòr-nər\ *n* [ME, fr. OF *cornere*, fr. *corne* horn, corner, fr. L *cornu* horn, point] 1 : the point or angle formed by the meeting of lines, edges, or sides 2 : the place where two streets come together 3 : a quiet secluded place 4 : a position from which retreat or escape is impossible 5 : control of enough of the available supply (as of a commodity) to permit manipulation of the price — **cor·nered** *adj*

²**corner** *vb* 1 : to drive into a corner 2 : to get a corner on (~ the wheat market) 3 : to turn a corner

cor·ner·stone \'kòr-nər-ˌstōn\ *n* 1 : a stone forming part of a corner in a wall; *esp* : such a stone laid at a formal ceremony 2 : something of basic importance

cor·net \kòr-'net\ *n* : a brass band instrument resembling the trumpet

corn flour *n, Brit* : CORNSTARCH

corn·flow·er \'kòrn-ˌflaù(-ə)r\ *n* : BACHELOR'S BUTTON

cor·nice \'kòr-nəs\ *n* : the horizontal projecting part crowning the wall of a building

corn·meal \'kòrn-ˌmēl\ *n* : meal ground from corn

corn·row \-ˌrō\ *n* : a section of hair braided flat to the scalp in rows — **cornrow** *vb*

corn·stalk \-ˌstòk\ *n* : a stalk of Indian corn

corn·starch \-ˌstärch\ *n* : a starch made from corn and used in cookery as a thickening agent

corn syrup *n* : a sweet syrup obtained from cornstarch

cor·nu·co·pia \ˌkòr-nə-'kō-pē-ə, -nyə-\ *n* [LL, fr. L *cornu copiae* horn of plenty] : a horn-shaped container filled with fruits and grain emblematic of abundance

cornucopia

corny \'kòr-nē\ *adj* **corn·i·er; -est** : tiresomely simple or sentimental co·rol·la \kə-'rä-lə, -'rō-\ *n* : the petals of a flower

cor·ol·lary \'kȯr-ə-ˌler-ē\ *n, pl* **-lar·ies 1** : a deduction from a proposition already proved true **2** : CONSEQUENCE, RESULT

co·ro·na \kə-'rō-nə\ *n* **1** : a colored circle often seen around and close to a luminous body (as the sun or moon) **2** : the outermost part of the atmosphere of a star (as the sun) — **co·ro·nal** \'kȯr-ən-ᵊl, kə-'rōn-ᵊl\ *adj*

cor·o·nal \'kȯr-ən-ᵊl\ *n* : a circlet for the head

¹cor·o·nary \'kȯr-ə-ˌner-ē\ *adj* : of or relating to the heart or its blood vessels

²coronary *n, pl* **-nar·ies 1** : a coronary blood vessel **2** : CORONARY THROMBOSIS; *also* : HEART ATTACK

coronary thrombosis *n* : the blocking by a thrombus of one of the arteries supplying the heart tissues

cor·o·na·tion \ˌkȯr-ə-'nā-shən\ *n* : the act or ceremony of crowning a monarch

cor·o·ner \'kȯr-ə-nər\ *n* : a public official who investigates causes of deaths possibly not due to natural causes

cor·o·net \ˌkȯr-ə-'net\ *n* **1** : a small crown **2** : an ornamental band worn around the temples

corp *abbr* **1** corporal **2** corporation

¹cor·po·ral \'kȯr-p(ə-)rəl\ *adj* : of or relating to the body ⟨∼ punishment⟩

²corporal *n* : a noncommissioned officer (as in the army) ranking next below a sergeant

cor·po·rate \'kȯr-p(ə-)rət\ *adj* **1** : INCORPORATED; *also* : belonging to an incorporated body **2** : combined into one body

cor·po·ra·tion \ˌkȯr-pə-'rā-shən\ *n* **1** : the municipal authorities of a town or city **2** : a legal creation authorized to act with the rights and liabilities of a person ⟨a business ∼⟩

cor·po·re·al \kȯr-'pōr-ē-əl\ *adj* **1** : PHYSICAL, MATERIAL **2** *archaic* : BODILY — **cor·po·re·al·i·ty** \kȯr-ˌpōr-ē-'a-lə-tē\ *n* — **cor·po·re·al·ly** *adv*

corps \'kȯr\ *n, pl* **corps** \'kȯrz\ [F, fr. L *corpus* body] **1** : an organized subdivision of a country's military forces **2** : a group acting under common direction

corpse \'kȯrps\ *n* : a dead body

corps·man \'kȯr-mən, 'kȯrz-\ *n* : an enlisted man trained to give first aid

cor·pu·lence \'kȯr-pyə-ləns\ *n* : excessive fatness : OBESITY

cor·pu·lent \-lənt\ *adj* : OBESE

cor·pus \'kȯr-pəs\ *n, pl* **cor·po·ra** \-pə-rə\ [ME, fr. L] **1** : BODY; *esp* : CORPSE **2** : a body of writings or works

cor·pus·cle \'kȯr-pə-səl, -ˌpə-\ *n* **1** : a minute particle **2** : a living cell (as in blood or cartilage) not aggregated into continuous tissues — **cor·pus·cu·lar** \kȯr-'pəs-kyə-lər\ *adj*

cor·pus de·lic·ti \ˌkȯr-pəs-di-'lik-ˌtī, -tē\ *n, pl* **corpora delicti** [NL, lit., body of the crime] **1** : the substantial fact proving that a crime has been committed **2** : the body of a victim of murder

corr *abbr* **1** correct; corrected; correction **2** correspondence; correspondent; corresponding

cor·ral \kə-'ral\ *n* [Sp] : an enclosure for confining or capturing animals; *also* : an enclosure of wagons for defending a camp — **corral** *vb*

¹cor·rect \kə-'rekt\ *vb* **1** : to make right **2** : REPROVE, CHASTISE — **cor·rect·able** \-'rek-tə-bəl\ *adj* — **cor·rec·tion** \-'rek-shən\ *n* — **cor·rec·tion·al** \-'rek-sh(ə-)nəl\ *adj* — **cor·rec·tive** \-'rek-tiv\ *adj*

²correct *adj* **1** : conforming to a conventional standard **2** : agreeing with fact or truth — **cor·rect·ly** *adv* — **cor·rect·ness** *n*

cor·re·late \'kȯr-ə-ˌlāt\ *vb* **-lat·ed; -lat·ing** : to connect in a systematic way : establish the mutual relations of — **cor·re·late** \-lət, -ˌlāt\ *n* — **cor·re·la·tion** \ˌkȯr-ə-'lā-shən\ *n*

cor·rel·a·tive \kə-'re-lə-tiv\ *adj* **1** : reciprocally related **2** : regularly used together (as *either* and *or*) — **correlative** *n* — **cor·rel·a·tive·ly** *adv*

cor·re·spond \ˌkȯr-ə-'spänd\ *vb* **1** : to be in agreement : SUIT, MATCH **2** : to communicate by letter — **cor·re·spond·ing·ly** *adv*

cor·re·spon·dence \-'spän-dəns\ *n* **1** : agreement between particular things **2** : communication by letters; *also* : the letters exchanged

¹cor·re·spon·dent \-dənt\ *adj* **1** : SIMILAR **2** : FITTING, CONFORMING

²correspondent *n* **1** : something that corresponds **2** : a person with whom one communicates by letter **3** : a person employed to contribute news regularly from a place

cor·ri·dor \'kȯr-ə-dər, -ˌdȯr\ *n* **1** : a passageway into which compartments or rooms open (as in a hotel or school) **2** : a narrow strip of land esp. through foreign-held territory **3** : a densely populated strip of land including two or more major cities

cor·ri·gen·dum \ˌkȯr-ə-'jen-dəm\ *n, pl* **-da** \-də\ [L] : an error in a printed work discovered after printing and shown with its correction on a separate sheet

cor·ri·gi·ble \'kȯr-ə-jə-bəl\ *adj* : CORRECTABLE

cor·rob·o·rate \kə-'rä-bə-ˌrāt\ *vb* **-rat·ed; -rat·ing** [L *corroborare*, fr. *robur* strength] : to support with evidence : CONFIRM — **cor·rob·o·ra·tion** \-ˌrä-bə-'rā-shən\ *n* — **cor·rob·o·ra·tive** \-'rä-bə-ˌrā-tiv, -'rä-brə-\ *adj* — **cor·rob·o·ra·to·ry** \-'rä-bə-rə-ˌtȯr-ē\ *adj*

cor·rode \kə-'rōd\ *vb* **cor·rod·ed; cor·rod·ing** : to wear or be worn away gradually (as by chemical action) — **cor·ro·sion** \-'rō-zhən\ *n* — **cor·ro·sive** \-'rō-siv\ *adj or n*

cor·ru·gate \'kȯr-ə-ˌgāt\ *vb* **-gat·ed; -gat·ing** : to form into wrinkles or folds and grooves — **cor·ru·gat·ed** *adj* — **cor·ru·ga·tion** \ˌkȯr-ə-'gā-shən\ *n*

¹cor·rupt \kə-'rəpt\ *vb* **1** : to make evil : DEPRAVE; *esp* : BRIBE **2** : ROT, SPOIL — **cor·rupt·ible** *adj* — **cor·rup·tion** \-'rəp-shən\ *n*

²corrupt *adj* : morally degenerate; *also* : characterized by improper conduct ⟨∼ officials⟩

cor·sage \kȯr-'säzh, -'säj\ *n* [F, bust, bodice, fr. OF. bust, fr. *cors* body, fr. L *corpus*] **1** : the waist or bodice of a dress **2** : a bouquet to be worn or carried

cor·sair \'kȯr-ˌsar\ *n* : PIRATE

cor·set \'kȯr-sət\ *n* : a stiffened undergarment worn for support or to give shape to the waist and hips

cor·tege *also* cor·tège \kȯr-'tezh, 'kȯr-ˌtezh\ *n* [F] : PROCESSION; *esp* : a funeral procession

cor·tex \'kȯr-ˌteks\ *n, pl* **cor·ti·ces** \'kȯr-tə-ˌsēz\ *or* **cor·tex·es** : an outer or covering layer of an organism or one of its parts (the adrenal ∼) (∼ of a plant stem); *esp* : the outer layer of gray matter of the brain — **cor·ti·cal** \'kȯr-ti-kəl\ *adj*

cor·ti·sone \'kȯr-tə-ˌsōn, -ˌzōn\ *n* : an adrenal hormone used in treating rheumatoid arthritis

co·run·dum \kə-'rən-dəm\ *n* : a very hard aluminum-containing mineral used as an abrasive or as a gem

cor·us·cate \'kȯr-ə-ˌskāt\ *vb* **-cat·ed; -cat·ing** : FLASH, SPARKLE — **cor·us·ca·tion** \ˌkȯr-ə-'skā-shən\ *n*

cor·vette \kȯr-'vet\ *n* **1** : a naval sailing ship smaller than a frigate **2** : an armed escort ship smaller than a destroyer

co·ry·za \kə-'rī-zə\ *n* : an inflammatory disorder of the upper respiratory tract; *esp* : COMMON COLD

COS *abbr* **1** cash on shipment **2** chief of staff

co·sig·na·to·ry \kō-'sig-nə-ˌtȯr-ē\ *n* : a joint signer

co·sign·er \'kō-ˌsī-nər\ *n* : COSIGNATORY; *esp* : a joint signer of a promissory note

¹cos·met·ic \käz-'me-tik\ *adj* [Gk *kosmētikos* skilled in adornment, fr. *kosmein* to arrange, adorn, fr. *kosmos* order, ornament, universe] **1** : intended to beautify the hair or complexion **2** : correcting physical defects esp. to improve appearance ⟨∼ dentistry⟩ **3** : SUPERFICIAL

²cosmetic *n* : a cosmetic preparation

cos·me·tol·o·gist \ˌkäz-mə-'tä-lə-jist\ *n* : one who gives beauty treatments — **cos·me·tol·o·gy** \-jē\ *n*

cos·mic \'käz-mik\ *also* cos·mi·cal \-mi-kəl\ *adj* **1** : of

HEY, ODIE. I HAVE AN IDEA

LET'S PUT ON A DISGUISE AND SNEAK UP ON JON'S LUNCH

NICE TRY, GUYS

OH, WELL, AT LEAST WE CAN EAT THE COSTUME

JIM DAVIS 5-25

© 1992 PAWS, INC.

or relating to the cosmos **2** : VAST, GRAND — **cos·mi·cal·ly** *adv*

cosmic ray *n* : a stream of very penetrating atomic nuclei that enter the earth's atmosphere from outer space

cos·mog·o·ny \käz-'mä-gə-nē\ *n*, *pl* **-nies** : the origin or creation of the world or universe

cos·mol·o·gy \-'mä-lə-jē\ *n*, *pl* **-gies** : a branch of astronomy dealing with the origin and structure of the universe — **cos·mo·log·i·cal** \ˌkäz-mə-'lä-ji-kəl\ *adj* — **cos·mol·o·gist** \käz-'mä-lə-jist\ *n*

cos·mo·naut \'käz-mə-ˌnȯt\ *n* : a Soviet or Russian astronaut

cos·mo·pol·i·tan \ˌkäz-mə-'pä-lət-ᵊn\ *adj* : belonging to all the world : not local **syn** universal, global, catholic — **cosmopolitan** *n*

cos·mos \'käz-məs, 1 *also* -ˌmōs, -ˌmäs\ *n* **1** : UNIVERSE **2** : a tall garden herb related to the daisies

co·spon·sor \'kō-ˌspän-sər, -'spän-\ *n* : a joint sponsor — **cosponsor** *vb*

cos·sack \'kä-ˌsak, -sək\ *n* [Pol & Ukrainian *kozak*, of Turkic origin] : a member of a group of frontiersmen of southern Russia organized as cavalry in the czarist army

¹**cost** \'kȯst\ *n* **1** : the amount paid or charged for something : PRICE **2** : the loss or penalty incurred in gaining something **3** *pl* : expenses incurred in a law suit

²**cost** *vb* **cost; cost·ing 1** : to require a specified amount in payment **2** : to cause to pay, suffer, or lose

co–star \'kō-ˌstär\ *n* : one of two leading players in a motion picture or play — **co–star** *vb*

Cos·ta Ri·can \ˌkäs-tə-'rē-kən\ *n* : a native or inhabitant of Costa Rica — **Costa Rican** *adj*

cos·tive \'käs-tiv\ *adj* : affected with or causing constipation

cost·ly \'kȯst-lē\ *adj* **cost·li·er; -est** : of great cost or value : not cheap **syn** dear, valuable, expensive — **cost·li·ness** *n*

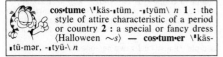

cos·tume \'käs-ˌtüm, -ˌtyüm\ *n* **1** : the style of attire characteristic of a period or country **2** : a special or fancy dress ⟨Halloween ∼s⟩ — **cos·tum·er** \'käs-ˌtü-mər, -ˌtyü-\ *n*

costume jewelry *n* : inexpensive jewelry

co·sy \'kō-zē\ *var of* COZY

¹**cot** \'kät\ *n* : a small house : COTTAGE

²**cot** *n* : a small often collapsible bed

cote \'kōt, 'kät\ *n* : a small shed or coop (as for sheep or doves)

co·te·rie \'kō-tə-ˌrē, ˌkō-tə-'rē\ *n* [F] : an intimate often exclusive group of persons with a common interest

co·ter·mi·nous \ˌkō-'tər-mə-nəs\ *adj* : having the same scope or duration

co·til·lion \kō-'til-yən, kə-\ *n* : a formal ball

cot·tage \'kä-tij\ *n* : a small house — **cot·tag·er** *n*

cottage cheese *n* : a soft uncured cheese made from soured skim milk

cot·ter *or* **cot·tar** \'kä-tər\ *n* : a peasant or farm laborer occupying a cottage and often a small holding

cotter pin *n* : a metal strip bent into a pin whose ends can be spread apart after insertion through a hole or slot

cot·ton \'kät-ᵊn\ *n* [ME *coton*, fr. MF, fr. Ar *quṭun*] **1** : a soft fibrous usu. white substance composed of hairs attached to the seeds of a plant related to the mallow; *also* : this plant **2** : thread or cloth made of cotton — **cot·tony** *adj*

cotton candy *n* : a candy made of spun sugar

cot·ton·mouth \'kät-ᵊn-ˌmau̇th\ *n* : WATER MOCCASIN

cot·ton·seed \-ˌsēd\ *n* : the seed of the cotton plant yielding a protein-rich meal and a fatty oil (**cottonseed oil**) used esp. in cooking

cot·ton·tail \-ˌtāl\ *n* : an American rabbit with a white-tufted tail

cot·ton·wood \-ˌwu̇d\ *n* : a poplar having seeds with cottony hairs

cot·y·le·don \ˌkä-tə-'lēd-ᵊn\ *n* : the first leaf or one of the first pair or whorl of leaves developed by a seed plant

¹**couch** \'kau̇ch\ *vb* **1** : to lie or place on a couch **2** : to phrase in a specified manner

²**couch** *n* : a piece of furniture (as a bed or sofa) that one can sit or lie on

couch·ant \'kau̇-chənt\ *adj* : lying down with the head raised ⟨coat of arms with lion ∼⟩

couch potato *n* : one who spends a great deal of time watching television

cou·gar \'kü-gər\ *n*, *pl* **cougars** *also* **cougar** [F *couguar*, fr. NL *cuguacuarana*, modif. of Tupi (a Brazilian Indian language) *siwasuarána*, fr. *siwasú* deer + *-rana* resembling] : a large powerful tawny brown wild American cat

cough \'kȯf\ *vb* : to force air from the lungs with short sharp noises; *also* : to expel by coughing — **cough** *n*

could \kəd, 'ku̇d\ *past of* CAN — used as an auxiliary in the past or as a polite or less forceful alternative to *can* in the present

cou·lee \'kü-lē\ *n* **1** : a small stream **2** : a dry streambed **3** : GULLY

cou·lomb \'kü-ˌläm, -ˌlōm\ *n* : a unit of electric charge equal to the electricity transferred by a current of one ampere in one second

coun·cil \'kau̇n-səl\ *n* **1** : ASSEMBLY, MEETING **2** : an official body of lawmakers ⟨city ∼⟩ — **coun·cil·lor** *or* **coun·cil·or** \-sə-lər\ *n* — **coun·cil·man** \-səl-mən\ *n* — **coun·cil·wom·an** \-ˌwu̇-mən\ *n*

¹**coun·sel** \'kau̇n-səl\ *n* **1** : ADVICE **2** : a plan of action **3** : deliberation together **4** *pl* **counsel** : LAWYER

²**counsel** *vb* **-seled** *or* **-selled; -sel·ing** *or* **-sel·ling 1** : ADVISE **2** : CONSULT

coun·sel·or *or* **coun·sel·lor** \'kau̇n-sə-lər\ *n* **1** : ADVISER **2** : LAWYER **3** : one who has supervisory duties at a summer camp

¹**count** \'kau̇nt\ *vb* [ME *counten*, fr. MF *compter*, fr. L *computare*, fr. *com-* with + *putare* to consider] **1** : to name or indicate one by one in order to find the total number **2** : to recite numbers in order **3** : CONSIDER,

ACCOUNT **4** : RELY ⟨you can ∼ on me⟩ **5** : to be of value or account — **count·able** adj

²**count** n **1** : the act of counting; also : the total obtained by counting **2** : a particular charge in an indictment or legal declaration

³**count** n [MF comte, fr. LL comes, fr. L, companion, one of the imperial court, fr. com- with + ire to go] : a European nobleman whose rank corresponds to that of a British earl

count·down \'kaunt-ˌdaun\ n : a backward counting in fixed units (as seconds) to indicate the time remaining before an event (as the launching of a rocket) — **count down** vb

¹**coun·te·nance** \'kaunt-ᵊn-ᵊns\ n **1** : the human face **2** : FAVOR, APPROVAL

²**countenance** vb **-nanced; -nanc·ing** : SANCTION, TOLERATE

¹**count·er** \'kaun-tər\ n **1** : a piece (as of metal or plastic) used in reckoning or in games **2** : a level surface over which business is transacted, food is served, or work is conducted

²**count·er** n : a device for recording a number or amount

³**count·er** vb : to act in opposition to

⁴**coun·ter** adv : in an opposite direction : CONTRARY

⁵**coun·ter** n **1** : OPPOSITE, CONTRARY **2** : an answering or offsetting force or blow

⁶**coun·ter** adj : CONTRARY, OPPOSITE

coun·ter·act \ˌkaun-tər-'akt\ vb : to lessen the force of : OFFSET — **coun·ter·ac·tive** \-'ak-tiv\ adj

coun·ter·at·tack \'kaun-tər-ə-ˌtak\ n : an attack made to oppose an enemy's attack — **counterattack** vb

¹**coun·ter·bal·ance** \'kaun-tər-ˌba-ləns\ n : a weight or influence that balances another

²**counterbalance** \ˌkaun-tər-'ba-ləns\ vb : to oppose with equal weight or influence

coun·ter·claim \'kaun-tər-ˌklām\ n : an opposing claim esp. in law

coun·ter·clock·wise \ˌkaun-tər-'kläk-ˌwīz\ adv : in a direction opposite to that in which the hands of a clock rotate — **counterclockwise** adj

coun·ter·cul·ture \'kaun-tər-ˌkəl-chər\ n : a culture esp. of the young with values and mores that run counter to those of established society

coun·ter·es·pi·o·nage \ˌkaun-tər-'es-pē-ə-ˌnäzh, -nij\ n : activities intended to discover and defeat enemy espionage

¹**coun·ter·feit** \'kaun-tər-ˌfit\ adj : SHAM, SPURIOUS; also : FORGED

²**counterfeit** vb **1** : to copy or imitate in order to deceive **2** : PRETEND, FEIGN — **coun·ter·feit·er** n

³**counterfeit** n : something counterfeit : FORGERY syn fraud, sham, fake, imposture, deceit, deception

coun·ter·in·sur·gen·cy \ˌkaun-tər-in-'sər-jən-sē\ n : military activity designed to deal with insurgents

coun·ter·in·tel·li·gence \-in-'te-lə-jəns\ n : organized activities of an intelligence service designed to counter the activities of an enemy's intelligence service

coun·ter·man \'kaun-tər-ˌman, -mən\ n : one who tends a counter

coun·ter·mand \'kaunt-ər-ˌmand\ vb : to withdraw (an order already given) by a contrary order

coun·ter·mea·sure \-ˌme-zhər\ n : an action or device designed to counter another

coun·ter·of·fen·sive \-ə-ˌfen-siv\ n : a large-scale counterattack

coun·ter·pane \-ˌpān\ n : BEDSPREAD

coun·ter·part \-ˌpärt\ n : a person or thing very closely like or corresponding to another person or thing

coun·ter·point \-ˌpoint\ n : music in which one melody is accompanied by one or more other melodies all woven into a harmonious whole

coun·ter·poise \-ˌpoiz\ n : COUNTERBALANCE

coun·ter·rev·o·lu·tion \ˌkaun-tər-ˌre-və-'lü-shən\ n : a revolution opposed to a current or earlier one — **coun·ter·rev·o·lu·tion·ary** \-shə-ˌner-ē\ adj or n

coun·ter·sign \'kaun-tər-ˌsīn\ n **1** : a confirmatory signature added to a writing already signed by another person **2** : a military secret signal that must be given by a person who wishes to pass a guard — **countersign** vb

coun·ter·sink \-ˌsiŋk\ vb **-sunk** \-ˌsəŋk\; **-sink·ing 1** : to form a funnel-shaped enlargement at the outer end of a drilled hole **2** : to set the head of (as a screw) at or below the surface — **countersink** n

coun·ter·spy \-ˌspī\ n : a spy engaged in counterespionage

coun·ter·ten·or \-ˌte-nər\ n : a tenor with an unusually high range

coun·ter·vail \ˌkaun-tər-'vāl\ vb : COUNTERACT

coun·ter·weight \'kaun-tər-ˌwāt\ n : COUNTERBALANCE

count·ess \'kaun-təs\ n **1** : the wife or widow of a count or an earl **2** : a woman holding the rank of a count or an earl in her own right

count·ing·house \'kaun-tiŋ-ˌhaus\ n : a building or office for keeping books and conducting business

count·less \'kaunt-ləs\ adj : INNUMERABLE

coun·tri·fied also **coun·try·fied** \'kən-tri-ˌfīd\ adj **1** : RURAL, RUSTIC **2** : UNSOPHISTICATED **3** : played or sung in the manner of country music

¹**coun·try** \'kən-trē\ n, pl **countries** [ME contree, fr. OF contrée, fr. ML contrata, fr. L contra against, on the opposite side] **1** : REGION, DISTRICT **2** : FATHERLAND **3** : a nation or its territory **4** : rural regions as opposed to towns and cities **5** : COUNTRY MUSIC

²**country** adj **1** : RURAL **2** : of or relating to country music ⟨a ∼ singer⟩

country and western n : COUNTRY MUSIC

country club n : a suburban club for social life and recreation; esp : one having a golf course

coun·try–dance \'kən-trē-ˌdans\ n : an English dance in which partners face each other esp. in rows

coun·try·man \'kən-trē-mən, 2 often -ˌman\ n **1** : an inhabitant of a specified country **2** : COMPATRIOT **3** : one raised or living in the country : RUSTIC

country music n : music derived from or imitating the folk style of the southern U.S. or of the Western cowboy

coun·try·side \'kən-trē-ˌsīd\ n : a rural area or its people

coun·ty \'kaun-tē\ n, pl **counties 1** : the domain of a count **2** : a territorial division of a country or state for purposes of local government

coup \'kü\ n, pl **coups** \'küz\ [F, blow, stroke] **1** : a brilliant sudden stroke or stratagem **2** : COUP D'ÉTAT

coup de grace \ˌkü-də-'gräs\ n, pl **coups de grace** \same\ [F coup de grâce, lit., stroke of mercy] : DEATHBLOW; also : a final decisive stroke or event

coup d'état \ˌkü-də-'tä\ n, pl **coups d'état** \same or -'täz\ [F, lit., stroke of state] : a sudden violent overthrow of a government by a small group

cou·pé or **coupe** \kü-'pā, 2 often 'küp\ n [F coupé, fr. couper to cut] **1** : a closed horse-drawn carriage for two persons inside with an outside seat for the driver **2** usu coupe : a 2-door automobile with an enclosed body

¹**cou·ple** \'kə-pəl\ n **1** : two persons closely associated; esp : a man and a woman married or otherwise paired **2** : PAIR **3** : BOND, TIE **4** : an indefinite small number : FEW ⟨a ∼ of days ago⟩

²**couple** vb **cou·pled; cou·pling** : to link together

cou·plet \'kə-plət\ n : two successive rhyming lines of verse

cou·pling \'kə-pliŋ (usual for 2), -pə-liŋ\ n **1** : CONNECTION **2** : a device for connecting two parts or things

cou·pon \'kü-ˌpän, 'kyü-\ n **1** : a statement attached to a bond showing interest due and designed to be cut off and presented for payment **2** : a form surrendered in order to obtain an article, service, or accommodation **3** : a part of an advertisement to be cut off to use as an order blank or inquiry form or to obtain a discount on merchandise

cour·age \'kər-ij\ *n* : ability to conquer fear or despair
: BRAVERY, VALOR — **cou·ra·geous** \kə-'rā-jəs\ *adj*
— **cou·ra·geous·ly** *adv*

cou·ri·er \'kùr-ē-ər, 'kər-\ *n* : one who bears messages or information esp. for the diplomatic or military services

¹**course** \'kōrs\ *n* **1** : PROGRESS, PASSAGE; *also* : direction of progress **2** : the ground or path over which something moves **3** : method of procedure : CONDUCT, BEHAVIOR **4** : an ordered series of acts or proceedings : sequence of events **5** : a series of instruction periods dealing with a subject **6** : the series of studies leading to graduation from a school or college **7** : the part of a meal served at one time — **of course** : as might be expected

²**course** *vb* **coursed; cours·ing 1** : to hunt with dogs **2** : to run or go speedily

cours·er \'kōrt\ *n* : a swift or spirited horse

¹**court** \'kōrt\ *n* **1** : the residence of a sovereign or similar dignitary **2** : a sovereign's formal assembly of officials and advisers as a governing power **3** : an assembly of the retinue of a sovereign **4** : an open space enclosed by a building or buildings **5** : a space walled or marked off for playing a game (as tennis or basketball) **6** : the place where justice is administered; *also* : a judicial body or a meeting of a judicial body **7** : attention intended to win favor

²**court** *vb* **1** : to try to gain the favor of **2** : WOO **3** : ATTRACT, TEMPT

cour·te·ous \'kər-tē-əs\ *adj* : marked by respect for others : CIVIL, POLITE — **cour·te·ous·ly** *adv*

cour·te·san \'kōr-tə-zən, -ˌzan\ *n* : PROSTITUTE

cour·te·sy \'kər-tə-sē\ *n, pl* **-sies 1** : courteous behavior : POLITENESS **2** : a favor courteously performed

court·house \'kōrt-ˌhaùs\ *n* : a building in which courts of law are held or county offices are located

court·ier \'kōr-tē-ər\ *n* : a person in attendance at a royal court

court·ly \'kōrt-lē\ *adj* **court·li·er; -est** : REFINED, ELEGANT, POLITE **syn** gallant, gracious — **court·li·ness** *n*

court–mar·tial \'kōrt-ˌmär-shəl\ *n, pl* **courts–martial** : a military or naval court for trial of offenses against military or naval law; *also* : a trial by this court — **court–martial** *vb*

court·room \-ˌrüm, -ˌrùm\ *n* : a room in which a court of law is held

court·ship \-ˌship\ *n* : the act of courting : WOOING

court·yard \-ˌyärd\ *n* : an enclosure next to a building

cous·in \'kə-zən\ *n* [ME *cosin*, fr. OF, fr. L *consobrinus*, fr. *com-* with + *sobrinus* second cousin, fr. *soror* sister] : a child of one's uncle or aunt

cou·ture \kü-'tùr, -'tü̇r\ *n* [F] : the business of designing fashionable custom-made women's clothing; *also* : the designers and establishments engaged in this business

cou·tu·ri·er \kü-'tùr-ē-ər, -ē-ˌā\ *n* [F, dressmaker] : the owner of an establishment engaged in couture

cove \'kōv\ *n* : a small sheltered inlet or bay

co·ven \'kə-vən\ *n* : an assembly or band of witches

cov·e·nant \'kə-və-nənt\ *n* : a formal binding agreement : COMPACT — **cov·e·nant** \-nənt, -ˌnant\ *vb*

¹**cov·er** \'kə-vər\ *vb* **1** : to bring or hold within range of a firearm **2** : PROTECT, SHIELD **3** : HIDE, CONCEAL **4** : to place something over or upon **5** : INCLUDE, COMPRISE **6** : to have as one's field of activity (one salesman ~s the state) **7** : to buy (stocks) in order to have them for delivery on a previous short sale

²**cover** *n* **1** : something that protects or shelters **2** : LID, TOP **3** : CASE, BINDING **4** : TABLECLOTH **5** : a cloth used on a bed **6** : SCREEN, DISGUISE **7** : an envelope or wrapper for mail

cov·er·age \'kə-və-rij\ *n* **1** : the act or fact of covering **2** : the total group covered : SCOPE

cov·er·all \'kə-vər-ˌòl\ *n* : a one-piece outer garment worn to protect one's clothes — usu. used in pl.

cover charge *n* : a charge made by a restaurant or nightclub in addition to the charge for food and drink

cover crop *n* : a crop planted to prevent soil erosion and to provide humus

cov·er·let \'kə-vər-lət\ *n* : BEDSPREAD

¹**co·vert** \'kō-ˌvərt, 'kə-vərt\ *adj* **1** : HIDDEN, SECRET **2** : SHELTERED — **co·vert·ly** *adv*

²**co·vert** \'kō-vərt, 'kō-\ *n* **1** : a secret or sheltered place; *esp* : a thicket sheltering game **2** : a feather covering the bases of the quills of the wings and tail of a bird

cov·er–up \'kə-vər-ˌəp\ *n* **1** : a device for masking or concealing **2** : a usu. concerted effort to keep an illegal or unethical act or situation from being made public

cov·et \'kə-vət\ *vb* : to desire enviously (what belongs to another) — **cov·et·ous** *adj* — **cov·et·ous·ness** *n*

cov·ey \'kə-vē\ *n, pl* **coveys** [ME, fr. MF *covee*, fr. OF, fr. *cover* to sit on, brood over, fr. L *cubare* to lie] **1** : a bird with her brood of young **2** : a small flock (as of quail)

¹**cow** \'kaù\ *n* **1** : the mature female of cattle or of an animal (as the moose, elephant, or whale) of which the male is called *bull* **2** : any domestic bovine animal irrespective of sex or age

²**cow** *vb* : INTIMIDATE, DAUNT, OVERAWE

cow·ard \'kaù(-ə)rd\ *n* [ME, fr. OF *coart*, fr. *coe* tail, fr. L *cauda*] : one who lacks courage or shows shameful fear or timidity — **coward** *adj* — **cow·ard·ice** \'kaù-ər-dəs\ *n* — **cow·ard·ly** *adv* or *adj*

cow·bird \'kaù-ˌbərd\ *n* : a small No. American bird that lays its eggs in the nests of other birds

cow·boy \-ˌbòi\ *n* : one (as a mounted ranch hand) who tends cattle or horses

cow·er \'kaù(-ə)r\ *vb* : to shrink or crouch down from fear or cold : QUAIL

cow·girl \'kaù-ˌgərl\ *n* : a girl or woman who tends cattle or horses

cow·hand \'kaù-ˌhand\ *n* : COWBOY

cow·hide \-ˌhīd\ *n* **1** : the hide of a cow; *also* : leather made from it **2** : a coarse whip of braided rawhide

cowl \'kaùl\ *n* : a monk's hood

cow·lick \'kau̇-ˌlik\ n : a turned-up tuft of hair that resists control

cowl·ing \'kau̇-liŋ\ n : a usu. metal covering for the engine or another part of an airplane

cow·man \'kau̇-mən, -ˌman\ n : COWBOY; also : a cattle owner or rancher

co·work·er \'kō-ˌwər-kər\ n : a fellow worker

cow·poke \'kau̇-ˌpōk\ n : COWBOY

cow pony n : a strong and agile horse trained for herding cattle

cow·pox \'kau̇-ˌpäks\ n : a mild disease of the cow that when communicated to humans protects against smallpox

cow·punch·er \-ˌpən-chər\ n : COWBOY

cow·slip \'kau̇-ˌslip\ n 1 : a yellow-flowered European primrose 2 : MARSH MARIGOLD

cox·comb \'käks-ˌkōm\ n : a conceited foolish person : FOP

cox·swain \'käk-sən, -ˌswān\ n : the steersman of a ship's boat or a racing shell

coy \'kȯi\ adj [ME, quiet, shy, fr. MF coi calm, fr. L quietus quiet] 1 : BASHFUL, SHY 2 : marked by artful playfulness : COQUETTISH — **coy·ly** adv — **coy·ness** n

coy·ote \'kī-ˌōt, kī-'ō-tē\ n, pl coyotes or coyote : a mammal of No. America smaller than the related wolves

coyote

coy·pu \'kȯi-pü\ n : NUTRIA 2

coz·en \'kəz-ᵊn\ vb : CHEAT, DEFRAUD — **coz·en·age** \-ij\ n — **coz·en·er** n

¹co·zy \'kō-zē\ adj **co·zi·er; -est** : SNUG, COMFORTABLE — **co·zi·ly** \-zə-lē\ adv — **co·zi·ness** \-zē-nəs\ n

²cozy n, pl **co·zies** : a padded covering for a vessel (as a teapot) to keep the contents hot

cp abbr 1 compare 2 coupon

CP abbr 1 cerebral palsy 2 chemically pure 3 command post 4 communist party

CPA abbr certified public accountant

CPB abbr Corporation for Public Broadcasting

cpd abbr compound

CPI abbr consumer price index

Cpl abbr corporal

CPO abbr chief petty officer

CPOM abbr master chief petty officer

CPOS abbr senior chief petty officer

CPR abbr cardiopulmonary resuscitation

CPT abbr captain

CQ abbr charge of quarters

cr abbr credit; creditor

Cr symbol chromium

¹crab \'krab\ n : any of various crustaceans with a short broad shell and small abdomen

²crab n : an ill-natured person

³crab vb **crabbed; crab·bing** : COMPLAIN, GROUSE

crab apple n : a small often highly colored sour apple; also : a tree that produces crab apples

crab·bed \'kra-bəd\ adj 1 : MOROSE, PEEVISH 2 : CRAMPED, IRREGULAR

crab·by \'kra-bē\ adj **crab·bi·er; -est** : CROSS, ILL-NATURED

crab·grass \'krab-ˌgras\ n : a weedy grass with creeping or sprawling stems that root freely at the nodes

crab louse n : a louse infesting the pubic region in humans

¹crack \'krak\ vb 1 : to break with a sharp sudden sound 2 : to break with or without completely separating into parts 3 : to fail in tone or become harsh ⟨her voice ∼ed⟩ 4 : to subject (as a petroleum oil) to heat for breaking down into lighter products (as gasoline)

²crack n 1 : a sudden sharp noise 2 : a witty or sharp remark 3 : a narrow break or opening : FISSURE 4 : a sharp blow 5 : ATTEMPT, TRY 6 : highly purified cocaine in small chips used illicitly usu. for smoking

³crack adj : extremely proficient

crack·down \'krak-ˌdau̇n\ n : an act or instance of taking positive disciplinary action ⟨a ∼ on gambling⟩ — **crack down** vb

crack·er \'kra-kər\ n 1 : FIRECRACKER 2 : a dry thin crispy baked bread product made of flour and water

crack·er·jack \-ˌjak\ n : something very excellent — **crackerjack** adj

crack·le \'kra-kəl\ vb **crack·led; crack·ling** 1 : to make small sharp snapping noises 2 : to develop fine cracks in a surface — **crackle** n — **crack·ly** \-k(ə-)lē\ adj

crack·pot \'krak-ˌpät\ n : an eccentric person

crack–up \'krak-ˌəp\ n : CRASH, WRECK; also : BREAK-DOWN

crack up vb 1 : PRAISE ⟨isn't all it's cracked up to be⟩ 2 : to laugh or cause to laugh out loud 3 : to crash a vehicle

¹cra·dle \'krād-ᵊl\ n 1 : a baby's bed or cot 2 : a framework or support (as for a telephone receiver) 3 : INFANCY ⟨from ∼ to the grave⟩ 4 : a place of origin

²cradle vb **cra·dled; cra·dling** 1 : to place in or as if in a cradle 2 : SHELTER, REAR

craft \'kraft\ n 1 : ART, SKILL; also : an occupation requiring special skill 2 : CUNNING, GUILE 3 pl usu **craft** : a boat esp. of small size; also : AIRCRAFT, SPACE-CRAFT

crafts·man \'krafts-mən\ n : a skilled artisan — **crafts·man·ship** n

crafty \'kraf-tē\ adj **craft·i·er; -est** : CUNNING, DECEITFUL, SUBTLE — **craft·i·ly** \-tə-lē\ adv — **craft·i·ness** \-tē-nəs\ n

crag \'krag\ n : a steep rugged cliff or rock — **crag·gy** adj

cram \'kram\ vb **crammed; cram·ming** 1 : to pack in tight : JAM 2 : to eat greedily 3 : to study rapidly under pressure for an examination

¹cramp \'kramp\ n 1 : a sudden painful contraction of muscle 2 : sharp abdominal pain — usu. used in pl.

²cramp vb 1 : to affect with a cramp or cramps 2 : to restrain from free action : HAMPER

cran·ber·ry \'kran-ˌber-ē, -bə-rē\ n : the red acid berry of any of several trailing plants related to the heaths; also : one of these plants

¹crane \'krān\ n 1 : any of a family of tall wading birds related to the rails; also : any of several herons 2 : a machine for lifting and carrying heavy objects

²crane vb **craned; cran·ing** : to stretch one's neck to see better

crane fly n : any of numerous long-legged slender dipteran flies that resemble large mosquitoes but do not bite

cranial nerve n : any of the nerves that arise in pairs from the lower surface of the brain and pass through openings in the skull to the periphery of the body

cra·ni·um \'krā-nē-əm\ *n, pl* **-ni·ums** *or* **-nia** \-ə\ : SKULL; *esp* : the part enclosing the brain — **cra·ni·al** \-əl\ *adj*

¹**crank** \'kraŋk\ *n* **1** : a bent part of an axle or shaft or an arm at right angles to the end of a shaft by which circular motion is imparted to or received from it **2** : an eccentric person **3** : a bad-tempered person : GROUCH

²**crank** *vb* : to start or operate by or as if by turning a crank

crank·case \'kraŋk-ˌkās\ *n* : the housing of a crankshaft

crank out *vb* : to produce in a mechanical manner

crank·shaft \'kraŋk-ˌshaft\ *n* : a shaft turning or driven by a crank

cranky \'kraŋ-kē\ *adj* **crank·i·er; -est 1** : IRRITABLE **2** : operating uncertainly or imperfectly

cran·ny \'kra-nē\ *n, pl* **crannies** : CREVICE, CHINK

craps \'kraps\ *n* : a gambling game played with two dice

crap·shoot·er \'krap-ˌshü-tər\ *n* : a person who plays craps

¹**crash** \'krash\ *vb* **1** : to break noisily : SMASH **2** : to damage an airplane in landing **3** : to enter or attend without invitation or without paying ⟨∼ a party⟩

²**crash** *n* **1** : a loud sound (as of things smashing) **2** : an instance of crashing ⟨a plane ∼⟩; *also* : COLLISION **3** : a sudden failure (as of a business)

³**crash** *adj* : marked by concerted effort over the shortest possible time

⁴**crash** *n* : coarse linen fabric used for towels and draperies

crash–land \'krash-ˌland\ *vb* : to land an aircraft or spacecraft under emergency conditions usu. with damage to the craft — **crash landing** *n*

crass \'kras\ *adj* : GROSS, INSENSITIVE — **crass·ly** *adv*

crate \'krāt\ *n* : a container often of wooden slats — **crate** *vb*

cra·ter \'krā-tər\ *n* [L, mixing bowl, crater, fr. Gk *kratēr*, fr. *kerannynai* to mix] **1** : the depression around the opening of a volcano **2** : a depression formed by the impact of a meteorite or by the explosion of a bomb or shell

cra·vat \krə-'vat\ *n* : NECKTIE

crave \'krāv\ *vb* **craved; crav·ing 1** : to ask for earnestly : BEG **2** : to long for : DESIRE

cra·ven \'krā-vən\ *adj* : COWARDLY — **craven** *n*

crav·ing \'krā-viŋ\ *n* : an urgent or abnormal desire

craw·fish \'krò-ˌfish\ *n* **1** : CRAYFISH 1 **2** : SPINY LOBSTER

¹**crawl** \'kròl\ *vb* **1** : to move slowly by drawing the body along the ground **2** : to advance feebly, cautiously, or slowly **3** : to be swarming with or feel as if swarming with creeping things ⟨a place ∼ing with ants⟩ ⟨her flesh ∼ed⟩

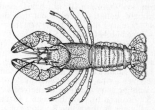

²**crawl** *n* **1** : a very slow pace **2** : a prone speed swimming stroke

cray·fish \'krā-ˌfish\ *n* **1** : any of numerous freshwater crustaceans usu. much smaller than the related lobsters **2** : SPINY LOBSTER

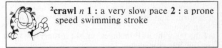

crayfish 1

cray·on \'krā-ˌän, -ən\ *n* : a stick of chalk or wax used for writing, drawing, or coloring; *also* : a drawing made with such material — **crayon** *vb*

¹**craze** \'krāz\ *vb* **crazed; craz·ing** [ME *crasen* to crush, craze, of Scand origin] : to make or become insane

²**craze** *n* : FAD, MANIA

cra·zy \'krā-zē\ *adj* **cra·zi·er; -est 1 :** mentally disordered **:** INSANE **2 :** wildly impractical; *also* **:** ERRATIC — **cra·zi·ly** \-zə-lē\ *adv* — **cra·zi·ness** \-zē-nəs\ *n*

CRC *abbr* Civil Rights Commission

creak \'krēk\ *vb* **:** to make a prolonged squeaking or grating sound — **creak** *n* — **creaky** *adj*

¹cream \'krēm\ *n* **1 :** the yellowish fat-rich part of milk **2 :** a thick smooth sauce, confection, or cosmetic **3 :** the choicest part **4 :** a pale yellow color — **creamy** *adj*

²cream *vb* **1 :** to prepare with a cream sauce **2 :** to beat or blend into creamy consistency **3 :** to defeat decisively

cream cheese *n* **:** a cheese made from whole milk enriched with cream

cream·ery \'krē-mə-rē\ *n, pl* **-er·ies :** an establishment where butter and cheese are made or milk and cream are prepared for sale

crease \'krēs\ *n* **:** a mark or line made by or as if by folding — **crease** *vb*

cre·ate \krē-'āt\ *vb* **cre·at·ed; cre·at·ing :** to bring into being **:** cause to exist **:** MAKE, PRODUCE — **cre·a·tive** \-'ā-tiv\ *adj* — **cre·a·tiv·i·ty** \-kre-(₁)ā-'ti-və-tē\ *n*

cre·a·tion \krē-'ā-shən\ *n* **1 :** the act of creating or producing ⟨∼ of the world⟩ **2 :** something that is created **3 :** all created things **:** WORLD

cre·a·tion·ism \krē-'ā-shə-₁ni-zəm\ *n* **:** a doctrine or theory holding that matter, the various forms of life, and the world were created by God out of nothing — **cre·a·tion·ist** \-nist\ *n or adj*

cre·a·tor \krē-'ā-tər\ *n* **1 :** one that creates **:** MAKER, AUTHOR **2** *cap* **:** GOD 1

crea·ture \'krē-chər\ *n* **:** a lower animal; *also* **:** a human being

crèche \'kresh\ *n* [F, manger, crib] **:** a representation of the Nativity scene

cre·dence \'krēd-²ns\ *n* **:** mental acceptance as true or real

cre·den·tial \kri-'den-chəl\ *n* **:** something that gives a basis for credit or confidence

cre·den·za \kri-'den-zə\ *n* [It., lit., belief, confidence] **:** a sideboard, buffet, or bookcase usu. without legs

cred·i·ble \'kre-də-bəl\ *adj* **:** TRUSTWORTHY, BELIEVABLE — **cred·i·bil·i·ty** \₁kre-də-'bi-lə-tē\ *n*

¹cred·it \'kre-dət\ *vb* **1 :** BELIEVE **2 :** to give credit to

²credit *n* [MF, fr. It *credito*, fr. L *creditum* something entrusted to another, loan, fr. *credere* to believe, entrust] **1 :** the balance (as in a bank) in a person's favor **2 :** time given for payment for goods sold on trust **3 :** an accounting entry of payment received **4 :** BELIEF, FAITH **5 :** financial trustworthiness **6 :** ESTEEM **7 :** a source of honor or distinction **8 :** a unit of academic work

cred·it·able \'kre-də-tə-bəl\ *adj* **:** worthy of esteem or praise — **cred·it·ably** \-blē\ *adv*

credit card *n* **:** a card authorizing purchases on credit

cred·i·tor \'kre-də-tər\ *n* **:** a person to whom money is owed

cre·do \'krē-dō, 'krā-\ *n, pl* **credos** [ME, fr. L, I believe] **:** CREED

cred·u·lous \'kre-jə-ləs\ *adj* **:** inclined to believe esp. on slight evidence — **cre·du·li·ty** \kri-'dü-lə-tē, -'dyü-\ *n*

Cree \'krē\ *n, pl* **Cree** *or* **Crees :** a member of an American Indian people of Canada

creed \'krēd\ *n* [ME *crede*, fr. OE *crēda*, fr. L *credo* I believe, first word of the Apostles' and Nicene Creeds] **:** a statement of the essential beliefs of a religious faith

creek \'krēk, 'krik\ *n* **1** *chiefly Brit* **:** a small inlet **2 :** a stream smaller than a river and larger than a brook

Creek \'krēk\ *n* **:** a member of an American Indian people of Alabama, Georgia, and Florida

creel \'krēl\ *n* **:** a wicker basket esp. for carrying fish

creep \'krēp\ *vb* **crept** \'krept\; **creep·ing 1 :** CRAWL **2 :** to feel as though insects were crawling on the skin

3 : to grow over a surface like ivy — **creep** *n* — **creep·er** *n*

creep·ing \'krē-piŋ\ *adj* **:** developing or advancing by imperceptible degrees

creepy \'krē-pē\ *adj* **creep·i·er; -est :** having or producing a nervous shivery fear

cre·mate \'krē-₁māt\ *vb* **cre·mat·ed; cre·mat·ing :** to reduce (a dead body) to ashes with fire — **cre·ma·tion** \kri-'mā-shən\ *n*

cre·ma·to·ry \'krē-mə-₁tōr-ē, 'kre-\ *n, pl* **-ries :** a furnace for cremating; *also* **:** a structure containing such a furnace

crème \'krem, 'krēm\ *n, pl* **crèmes** *same or* 'kremz, 'krēmz\ [F, lit., cream] **:** a sweet liqueur

cren·el·lat·ed *or* **cren·el·at·ed** \'kren-²l-₁ā-təd\ *adj* **:** having battlements — **cren·el·la·tion** \₁kren-²l-'ā-shən\ *n*

Cre·ole \'krē-₁ōl\ *n* **1 :** a descendant of early French or Spanish settlers of the U.S. Gulf states preserving their speech and culture; *also* **:** a person of mixed French or Spanish and black descent speaking a dialect of French or Spanish **2** *not cap* **:** a language that has evolved from a pidgin but serves as the native language of a speech community

cre·o·sote \'krē-ə-₁sōt\ *n* **:** an oily liquid obtained by distillation of coal tar and used in preserving wood

crepe *or* **crêpe** \'krāp\ *n* **:** a light crinkled fabric of any of various fibers

crêpe su·zette \₁krāp-sù-'zet\ *n, pl* **crêpes suzette** *same or* ₁krāps-\ *or* **crêpe suzettes** \-sù-'zets\ *often cap S* **:** a thin folded or rolled pancake in a hot orangebutter sauce that is sprinkled with a liqueur and set ablaze for serving

cre·pus·cu·lar \kri-'pəs-kyə-lər\ *adj* **1 :** of, relating to, or resembling twilight **2 :** active in the twilight ⟨∼ insects⟩

cre·scen·do \krə-'shen-dō\ *adv or adj* [It] **:** increasing in loudness — used as a direction in music — **crescendo** *n*

cres·cent \'kres-²nt\ *n* [ME *cressant*, fr. MF *croissant*, fr. *creistre* to grow, increase, fr. L *crescere*] **:** the moon at any stage between new moon and first quarter and between last quarter and new moon; *also* **:** something shaped like the figure of the crescent moon with a convex and a concave edge — **cres·cen·tic** \kre-'sen-tik\ *adj*

cress \'kres\ *n* **:** any of several salad plants related to the mustards

¹crest \'krest\ *n* **1 :** a tuft or process on the head of an animal (as a bird) **2 :** a heraldic device **3 :** an upper part, edge, or limit ⟨the ∼ of a hill⟩ — **crest·ed** \'kres-təd\ *adj* — **crest·less** *adj*

²crest *vb* **1 :** CROWN **2 :** to reach the crest of **3 :** to rise to a crest

crest·fall·en \'krest-₁fȯ-lən\ *adj* **:** DISPIRITED, DEJECTED

Cre·ta·ceous \kri-'tā-shəs\ *adj* **:** of, relating to, or being the latest period of the Mesozoic era marked by great increase in flowering plants, diversification of mammals, and extinction of the dinosaurs — **Cretaceous** *n*

cre·tin \'krēt-²n\ *n* [F *crétin*, fr. F dial. *cretin*, lit., wretch, innocent victim, fr. L *christianus* Christian] **1 :** one affected with cretinism **2 :** a stupid person

cre·tin·ism \-i-zəm\ *n* **:** a usu. congenital abnormal condition characterized by physical stunting and mental retardation

cre·tonne \'krē-₁tän\ *n* **:** a strong unglazed cotton cloth for curtains and upholstery

cre·vasse \kri-'vas\ *n* **:** a deep fissure esp. in a glacier

crev·ice \'kre-vəs\ *n* **:** a narrow fissure

¹crew \'krü\ *chiefly Brit past of* CROW

²crew *n* [ME *crue*, lit., reinforcement, fr. MF *creue* increase, fr. *creistre* to grow, fr. L *crescere*] **1 :** a body of people trained to work together for certain purposes **2 :** a group of people who operate a ship, train, aircraft, or spacecraft **3 :** the rowers and coxswain of a

racing shell; *also* : the sport of rowing engaged in by a crew — **crew·man** \-mən\ *n*

crew cut *n* : a very short bristly haircut

crew·el \'krü-əl\ *n* : slackly twisted worsted yarn used for embroidery — **crew·el·work** \-ˌwərk\ *n*

¹**crib** \'krib\ *n* **1** : a manger for feeding animals **2** : a child's bedstead with high sides **3** : a building or bin for storage (as of grain) **4** : something used for cheating in an exam

²**crib** *vb* **cribbed; crib·bing 1** : to put in a crib **2** : STEAL, PLAGIARIZE — **crib·ber** *n*

crib·bage \'kri-bij\ *n* : a card game usu. played by two players and scored on a board (**cribbage board**)

crib death *n* : SUDDEN INFANT DEATH SYNDROME

crick \'krik\ *n* : a painful spasm of muscles (as of the neck)

¹**crick·et** \'kri-kət\ *n* : any of a family of leaping insects related to the grasshoppers and noted for the chirping noises of the male

²**cricket** *n* : a game played with a bat and ball by two teams on a field centering upon two wickets each defended by a batsman

cri·er \'krī(-ə)r\ *n* : one who calls out proclamations and announcements

crime \'krīm\ *n* : a serious offense against the public law

¹**crim·i·nal** \'kri-mən-ᵊl\ *adj* **1** : involving or being a crime **2** : relating to crime or its punishment — **crim·i·nal·i·ty** \ˌkri-mə-'na-lə-tē\ *n* — **crim·i·nal·ly** *adv*

²**criminal** *n* : one who has committed a crime

crim·i·nol·o·gy \ˌkri-mə-'nä-lə-jē\ *n* : the scientific study of crime and criminals — **crim·i·nol·o·gist** \ˌkri-mə-'nä-lə-jist\ *n*

¹**crimp** \'krimp\ *vb* : to cause to become crinkled, wavy, or bent

²**crimp** *n* : something (as a curl in hair) produced by or as if by crimping

¹**crim·son** \'krim-zən\ *n* : a deep purplish red color — **crimson** *adj*

²**crimson** *vb* : to make or become crimson

cringe \'krinj\ *vb* **cringed; cring·ing** : to shrink in fear : WINCE, COWER

crin·kle \'kriŋ-kəl\ *vb* **crin·kled; crin·kling** : to form many short bends or curves; *also* : WRINKLE — **crin·kle** *n* — **crin·kly** \-kə-lē\ *adj*

crin·o·line \'krin-ᵊl-ən\ *n* **1** : an open-weave cloth used for stiffening and lining **2** : a full stiff skirt or underskirt made of crinoline

¹**crip·ple** \'kri-pəl\ *n* : a lame or disabled person — sometimes taken to be offensive

²**cripple** *vb* **crip·pled; crip·pling 1** : to make lame **2** : to make useless or imperfect

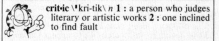

cri·sis \'krī-səs\ *n, pl* **cri·ses** \-ˌsēz\ [L, fr. Gk *krisis*, lit., decision, fr. *krinein* to decide] **1** : the turning point for better or worse in an acute disease or fever **2** : a decisive or critical moment

crisp \'krisp\ *adj* **1** : CURLY, WAVY **2** : BRITTLE **3** : FIRM, FRESH (∼ lettuce) **4** : being sharp and clear **5** : LIVELY, SPARKLING **6** : FROSTY, SNAPPY; *also* : INVIGORATING — **crisp** *vb* — **crisp·ly** *adv* — **crisp·ness** *n* — **crispy** *adj*

¹**criss·cross** \'kris-ˌkròs\ *vb* **1** : to mark with crossed lines **2** : to go or pass back and forth

²**crisscross** *adj* : marked or characterized by crisscrossing — **crisscross** *adv*

³**crisscross** *n* : a pattern formed by crossed lines

crit *abbr* critical; criticism

cri·te·ri·on \krī-'tir-ē-ən\ *n, pl* **-ria** \-ē-ə\ : a standard on which a judgment may be based

crit·ic \'kri-tik\ *n* **1** : a person who judges literary or artistic works **2** : one inclined to find fault

crit·i·cal \'kri-ti-kəl\ *adj* **1** : being or relating to a condition or disease involving danger of death **2** : being a crisis **3** : inclined to criticize **4** : relating to criticism or critics **5** : requiring careful judgment **6** : UNCERTAIN — **crit·i·cal·ly** \-k(ə-)lē\ *adv*

crit·i·cise *Brit var of* CRITICIZE

crit·i·cism \'kri-tə-ˌsi-zəm\ *n* **1** : the act of criticizing; *esp* : CENSURE **2** : a judgment or review **3** : the art of judging works of literature or art

crit·i·cize \'kri-tə-ˌsīz\ *vb* **-cized; -ciz·ing 1** : to judge as a critic : EVALUATE **2** : to find fault : express criticism **syn** blame, censure, condemn

cri·tique \krə-'tēk\ *n* : a critical estimate or discussion

crit·ter \'kri-tər\ *n* : CREATURE

croak \'krōk\ *n* : a hoarse harsh cry (as of a frog) — **croak** *vb*

Croat \'krō-ˌat\ *n* : CROATIAN

Cro·atian \krō-'ā-shən\ *n* : a native or inhabitant of Croatia — **Croatian** *adj*

cro·chet \krō-'shā\ *n* [F, hook, crochet, fr. MF, dim. of *croche* hook] : needlework done with a single thread and hooked needle — **crochet** *vb*

crock \'kräk\ *n* : a thick earthenware pot or jar

crock·ery \'krä-kə-rē\ *n* : EARTHENWARE

croc·o·dile \'krä-kə-ˌdīl\ *n* [ME & L; ME *cocodrille*, fr. OF, fr. ML *cocodrillus*, alter. of L *crocodilus*, fr. Gk *krokodilos* lizard, crocodile, fr. *krokē* shingle, pebble + *drillos* worm] : any of several thick-skinned long-bodied carnivorous reptiles of tropical and subtropical waters

cro·cus \'krō-kəs\ *n*, *pl* **cro·cus·es** *also* **crocus** *or* **cro·ci** \-ˌkī\ : any of a large genus of low herbs related to the irises and having brightly colored flowers borne singly in early spring

crois·sant \krȯ-'sänt, krwä-'säⁿ\ *n*, *pl* **croissants** *same or* -'sänts, -'säⁿz\ : a rich crescent-shaped roll

Cro·Ma·gnon \krō-'mag-nən, -'man-yən\ *n* : any of a tall erect human race known from skeletal remains found chiefly in southern France and usu. classified as the same species as present-day human beings — **Cro–Magnon** *adj*

crone \'krōn\ *n* : HAG

cro·ny \'krō-nē\ *n*, *pl* **cronies** : a close friend esp. of long standing

¹crook \'krůk\ *vb* : to curve or bend sharply

²crook *n* **1** : a bent or curved implement **2** : a bent or curved part; *also* : BEND, CURVE **3** : SWINDLER, THIEF

crook·ed \'krů-kəd\ *adj* **1** : having a crook : BENT, CURVED **2** : DISHONEST — **crook·ed·ly** *adv* — **crook·ed·ness** *n*

croon \'krün\ *vb* : to sing or hum in a gentle murmuring voice — **croon·er** *n*

¹crop \'kräp\ *n* **1** : the handle of a whip; *also* : a short riding whip **2** : a pouch in the throat of many birds and insects where food is received **3** : something that can be harvested; *also* : the yield at harvest

²crop *vb* **cropped; crop·ping 1** : to remove the tips of : cut off short; *also* : TRIM **2** : to feed on by cropping **3** : to devote (land) to crops **4** : to appear unexpectedly

crop·land \-ˌland\ *n* : land devoted to the production of plant crops

crop·per \'krä-pər\ *n* : a raiser of crops; *esp* : SHARE-CROPPER

cro·quet \krō-'kā\ *n* : a game in which mallets are used to drive wooden balls through a series of wickets set out on a lawn

cro·quette \krō-'ket\ *n* [F] : a small often rounded mass of minced meat, fish, or vegetables fried in deep fat

cro·sier \'krō-zhər\ *n* : a staff carried by bishops and abbots

¹cross \'krȯs\ *n* **1** : a structure consisting of an upright beam and a crossbar used esp. by the ancient Romans for execution **2** : a figure of the cross on which Christ was crucified used as a Christian symbol **3** : a hybridizing of unlike individuals or strains; *also* : a product of this **4** : a punch delivered with a circular motion over an opponent's lead

²cross *vb* **1** : to lie or place across; *also* : INTERSECT **2** : to cancel by marking a cross on or by lining through **3** : THWART, OBSTRUCT **4** : to go or extend across : TRAVERSE **5** : HYBRIDIZE **6** : to meet and pass on the way

³cross *adj* **1** : lying across **2** : CONTRARY, OPPOSED **3**

: marked by bad temper **4** : HYBRID — **cross·ly** *adv*

cross·bar \'krȯs-ˌbär\ *n* : a transverse bar or piece

cross·bow \-ˌbō\ *n* : a short bow mounted crosswise at the end of a wooden stock that shoots short arrows

crossbow

cross·breed \'krȯs-ˌbrēd, -'brēd\ *vb* **-bred** \-'bred\: **-breed·ing** : HYBRIDIZE

cross–coun·try \-'kən-trē\ *adj* **1** : extending or moving across a country **2** : proceeding over the countryside (as fields and woods) and not by roads **3** : of or relating to racing or skiing over the countryside instead of over a track or run — **cross–country** *adv*

cross·cur·rent \-'kər-ənt\ *n* **1** : a current running counter to another **2** : a conflicting tendency — usu. used in pl.

¹cross·cut \-ˌkət\ *vb* : to cut or saw crosswise esp. of the grain of wood

²crosscut *adj* **1** : made or used for crosscutting (a ∼ saw) **2** : cut across the grain

³crosscut *n* : something that cuts through transversely

cross–ex·am·ine \ˌkrȯ-sig-'za-mən\ *vb* : to examine with questions to check the answers to previous questions — **cross–ex·am·i·na·tion** \-ˌza-mə-'nā-shən\ *n*

cross–eyed \'krȯ-ˌsīd\ *adj* : having one or both eyes turned inward toward the nose

cross–fer·til·i·za·tion \-ˌfərt-ᵊl-ə-'zā-shən\ *n* **1** : fertilization between sex cells produced by separate individuals or sometimes by individuals of different kinds; *also* : CROSS-POLLINATION **2** : a broadening or productive interchange (as between cultures) — **cross–fer·til·ize** \-'fərt-ᵊl-ˌīz\ *vb*

cross fire *n* **1** : crossing lines of fire in combat **2** : rapid or angry interchange

cross·hair \'krȯs-ˌhar\ *n* : a fine wire or thread in the eyepiece of an optical instrument used as a reference line

cross·hatch \'krȯs-ˌhach\ *vb* : to mark with two series of parallel lines that intersect — **cross–hatch·ing** *n*

cross·ing \'krȯ-siŋ\ *n* **1** : a place or structure for crossing something (as a river) **2** : a point of intersection (as of a street and a railroad track)

cross·over \'krȯs-ˌō-vər\ *n* **1** : CROSSING **2** : a member of a political party who votes in the primary of the other party

cross·piece \'krȯs-ˌpēs\ *n* : a horizontal member

cross–pol·li·na·tion \ˌkrȯs-ˌpä-lə-'nā-shən\ *n* : transfer of pollen from one flower to the stigma of another — **cross–pol·li·nate** \'krȯs-'pä-lə-ˌnāt\ *vb*

cross–pur·pose \'krȯs-'pər-pəs\ *n* : a purpose contrary to another purpose (working at ∼s)

cross–ques·tion \-'kwes-chən\ *vb* : CROSS-EXAMINE — **cross–question** *n*

cross–re·fer \ˌkrȯs-ri-'fər\ *vb* : to refer by a notation or direction from one place to another (as in a book or list) — **cross–ref·er·ence** \'krȯs-'re-frəns\ *n*

cross·road \'krȯs-ˌrōd\ *n* **1** : a road that crosses a main road or runs between main roads **2** : a place where roads meet — usu. used in pl. **3** : a crucial point where a decision must be made

cross section *n* **1** : a section cut across something; *also* : a representation made by or as if by such cutting **2** : a number of persons or things selected from a group that show the general nature of the whole group — **cross–sec·tion·al** *adj*

cross·walk \'kròs-ˌwòk\ *n* : a marked path for pedestrians crossing a street

cross·ways \-ˌwāz\ *adv* : CROSSWISE

cross·wind \-ˌwind\ *n* : a wind not parallel to a course (as of an airplane)

cross·wise \-ˌwīz\ *adv* : so as to cross something : ACROSS, **crosswise** *adj*

cross·word \'kròs-ˌword\ *n* : a puzzle in which words are put into a pattern of numbered squares in answer to clues

crotch \'kräch\ *n* : an angle formed by the parting of two legs, branches, or members

crotch·et \'krä-chət\ *n* : an odd notion : WHIM — **crotch·ety** *adj*

crouch \'kraùch\ *vb* 1 : to stoop or bend low 2 : CRINGE, COWER — **crouch** *n*

croup \'krüp\ *n* : laryngitis esp. of infants marked by a hoarse ringing cough and difficult breathing — **croupy** *adj*

crou·pi·er \'krü-pē-ər, -pē-ˌā\ *n* [F, lit., rider on the rump of a horse, fr. *croupe* rump] : an employee of a gambling casino who collects and pays bets at a gaming table

crou·ton \'krü-ˌtän\ *n* [F *croûton*, dim. of *croûte* crust] : a small cube of bread toasted or fried crisp

¹**crow** \'krō\ *n* 1 : any of various large glossy black birds related to the jays 2 *cap* : a member of an American Indian people of a region in Montana and Wyoming; *also* : the language of the Crow people

²**crow** *vb* 1 : to make the loud shrill sound characteristic of the cock 2 : to utter a sound expressive of pleasure 3 : EXULT, GLOAT; *also* : BRAG, BOAST

³**crow** *n* : the cry of the cock

crow·bar \'krō-ˌbär\ *n* : a metal bar usu. wedge-shaped at the end for use as a pry or lever

¹**crowd** \'kraùd\ *vb* 1 : to press close 2 : to collect in numbers : THRONG 3 : CRAM, STUFF

²**crowd** *n* : a large number of people gathered together at random : THRONG

¹**crown** \'kraùn\ *n* 1 : a mark of victory or honor; *esp* : the title of a champion in a sport 2 : a royal headdress 3 : the top of the head 4 : the highest part (as of a tree or tooth) 5 *often cap* : sovereign power; *also* : MONARCH 6 : a formerly used British silver coin — **crowned** \'kraùnd\ *adj*

²**crown** *vb* 1 : to place a crown on 2 : HONOR 3 : TOP, SURMOUNT 4 : to fit (a tooth) with an artificial crown

crown vetch *n* : a European leguminous herb with umbels of pink-and-white flowers and sharp-angled pods

crow's-foot \'krōz-ˌfùt\ *n*, *pl* **crow's-feet** \-ˌfēt\ : any of the wrinkles around the outer corners of the eyes — usu. used in pl.

crow's nest *n* : a partly enclosed platform high on a ship's mast for use as a lookout

¹**CRT** \ˌsē-(ˌ)är-'tē\ *n*, *pl* **CRTs** *or* **CRT's** : CATHODE-RAY TUBE; *also* : a display device incorporating a cathode-ray tube

²**CRT** *abbr* carrier route

cru·cial \'krü-shəl\ *adj* : DECISIVE; *also* : IMPORTANT, SIGNIFICANT

cru·ci·ble \'krü-sə-bəl\ *n* : a heat-resistant container in which material can be subjected to great heat

cru·ci·fix \'krü-sə-ˌfiks\ *n* : a representation of Christ on the cross

cru·ci·fix·ion \ˌkrü-sə-'fik-shən\ *n* 1 *cap* : the crucifying of Christ 2 : the act of crucifying

cru·ci·form \'krü-sə-ˌfórm\ *adj* : shaped like a cross

cru·ci·fy \'krü-sə-ˌfī\ *vb* **-fied; -fy·ing** 1 : to put to death by nailing or binding the hands and feet to a cross 2 : MORTIFY 1 3 : TORTURE, PERSECUTE

¹**crude** \'krüd\ *adj* **crud·er; crud·est** 1 : not refined : RAW ⟨~ oil⟩ ⟨~ statistics⟩ 2 : lacking grace, taste, tact, or polish : RUDE — **crude·ly** *adv* — **cru·di·ty** \'krü-də-tē\ *n*

²**crude** *n* : unrefined petroleum

cru·el \'krü-əl\ *adj* **cru·el·er** *or* **cru·el·ler; cru·el·est** *or* **cru·el·lest** : causing pain and suffering to others : MERCILESS — **cru·el·ly** *adv* — **cru·el·ty** \-tē\ *n*

cru·et \'krü-ət\ *n* : a small usu. glass bottle for vinegar, oil, or sauce

cruise \'krüz\ *vb* **cruised; cruis·ing** [D *kruisen* to make a cross, cruise] 1 : to sail about touching at a series of ports 2 : to travel for enjoyment 3 : to travel about the streets at random 4 : to travel at the most efficient operating speed ⟨the *cruising* speed of an airplane⟩ — **cruise** *n*

cruis·er \'krü-zər\ *n* 1 : SQUAD CAR 2 : a large fast moderately armored and gunned warship 3 : a motorboat equipped for living aboard

crul·ler \'krə-lər\ *n* 1 : a small sweet cake in the form of a twisted strip fried in deep fat 2 *Northern & Midland* : an unraised doughnut

¹**crumb** \'krəm\ *n* : a small fragment

²**crumb** *vb* 1 : to break into crumbs 2 : to cover with crumbs

crum·ble \'krəm-bəl\ *vb* **crum·bled; crum·bling** : to break into small pieces : DISINTEGRATE — **crum·bly** *adj*

crum·my *also* **crumby** \'krə-mē\ *adj* **crum·mi·er** *also* **crumb·i·er; -est** 1 : MISERABLE, FILTHY 2 : CHEAP, WORTHLESS

crum·pet \'krəm-pət\ *n* : a small round unsweetened bread cooked on a griddle

crum·ple \'krəm-pəl\ *vb* **crum·pled; crum·pling** 1 : to crush together : RUMPLE 2 : COLLAPSE

¹**crunch** \'krənch\ *vb* : to chew with a grinding noise; *also* : to grind or press with a crushing noise

²**crunch** *n* 1 : an act of or a sound made by crunching 2 : a tight or critical situation — **crunchy** *adj*

cru·sade \krü-'sād\ *n* 1 *often cap* : any of the expeditions in the 11th, 12th, and 13th centuries undertaken by Christian countries to take the Holy Land from the Muslims 2 : a reforming enterprise undertaken with zeal — **crusade** *vb* — **cru·sad·er** *n*

cruse \\'krüz, 'krüs\ *n* : a jar for water or oil

¹crush \\'krəsh\ *vb* **1** : to squeeze out of shape **2** : HUG, EMBRACE **3** : to grind or pound to small bits **4** : OVERWHELM, SUPPRESS

²crush *n* **1** : an act of crushing **2** : a violent crowding **3** : INFATUATION

crust \\'krəst\ *n* **1** : the outside part of bread; *also* : a piece of old dry bread **2** : the cover of a pie **3** : a hard surface layer — **crust•al** *adj*

crus•ta•cean \\krəs-'tā-shən\ *n* : any of a large class of mostly aquatic arthropods (as lobsters or crabs) having a firm crustlike shell — **crustacean** *adj*

crusty *adj* **crust•i•er; -est 1** : having or being a crust **2** : CROSS, GRUMPY

crutch \\'krəch\ *n* : a supporting device; *esp* : a support fitting under the armpit for use by the disabled in walking

crux \\'krəks, 'krúks\ *n, pl* **crux•es 1** : a puzzling or difficult problem **2** : a crucial point

¹cry \\'krī\ *vb* **cried; cry•ing 1** : to call out : SHOUT **2** : to proclaim publicly : ADVERTISE **3** : WEEP

²cry *n, pl* **cries 1** : a loud outcry **2** : APPEAL, ENTREATY **3** : a fit of weeping **4** : the characteristic sound uttered by an animal **5** : DISTANCE — usu. used in the phrase *a far cry*

cry•ba•by \\'krī-ˌbā-bē\ *n* : one who cries easily or often

cryo•gen•ic \\ˌkrī-ə-'je-nik\ *adj* : of or relating to the production of very low temperatures; *also* : involving the use of a very low temperature — **cryo•gen•i•cal•ly** \\-ni-k(ə-)lē\ *adv*

cryo•gen•ics \\-niks\ *n* : a branch of physics that relates to the production and effects of very low temperatures

cryo•lite \\'krī-ə-ˌlīt\ *n* : a usu. white mineral used in making aluminum

crypt \\'kript\ *n* : a chamber wholly or partly underground

cryp•tic \\'krip-tik\ *adj* : meant to be puzzling or mysterious

cryp•to•gram \\'krip-tə-ˌgram\ *n* : a communication in cipher or code

cryp•tog•ra•phy \\krip-'tä-grə-fē\ *n* : the coding and decoding of secret messages — **cryp•tog•ra•pher** \\-fər\ *n*

crys•tal \\'krist-ᵊl\ *n* [ME *cristal*, fr. OF, fr. L *crystallum*, fr. Gk *krystallos* ice, crystal] **1** : transparent quartz **2** : something resembling crystal (as in transparency); *esp* : a clear glass used for table articles **3** : a body that is formed by solidification of a substance and has a regular repeating arrangement of atoms and often of external plane faces ⟨a salt ∼⟩ **4** : the transparent cover of a watch dial

crys•tal•line \\'kris-tə-lən\ *adj* **1** : made of or resembling crystal **2** : very clear or sparkling

crys•tal•ise *Brit var of* CRYSTALLIZE

crys•tal•ize \\'kris-tə-ˌlīz\ *vb* **-lized; -liz•ing 1** : to assume or cause to assume a crystalline form **2** : to take or cause to take a definite form — **crys•tal•li•za•tion** \\ˌkris-tə-lə-'zā-shən\ *n*

crys•tal•log•ra•phy \\ˌkris-tə-'lä-grə-fē\ *n* : the science dealing with the forms and structures of crystals — **crys•tal•log•ra•pher** *n*

cs *abbr* case; cases

Cs *symbol* cesium

CS *abbr* **1** civil service **2** county seat

CSA *abbr* Confederate States of America

CSM *abbr* command sergeant major

CST *abbr* central standard time

ct *abbr* **1** carat **2** cent **3** count **4** county **5** court

CT *abbr* **1** central time **2** Connecticut

ctn *abbr* carton

ctr *abbr* **1** center **2** counter

CT scan \\ˌsē-'tē-\ *n* : CAT SCAN

cu *abbr* cubic

Cu *symbol* [L *cuprum*] copper

cub \\'kəb\ *n* : a young individual of some animals (as a fox, bear, or lion)

Cu•ban \\'kyü-bən\ *n* : a native or inhabitant of Cuba — **Cuban** *adj*

cub•by•hole \\'kə-bē-ˌhōl\ *n* : a snug place (as for storing things)

¹cube \\'kyüb\ *n* **1** : a solid having 6 equal square sides **2** : the product obtained by taking a number 3 times as a factor (27 is the ∼ of 3)

²cube *vb* **cubed; cub•ing 1** : to raise to the third power **2** : to form into a cube **3** : to cut into cubes

cube root *n* : a number whose cube is a given number

cu•bic \\'kyü-bik\ *also* **cu•bi•cal** *adj* **1** : having the form of a cube **2** : being the volume of a cube whose edge is a specified unit **3** : having length, width, and height

cu•bi•cle \\'kyü-bi-kəl\ *n* : a small separate space (as for sleeping or studying)

cubic measure *n* : a unit (as cubic inch) for measuring volume — see METRIC SYSTEM table, WEIGHT table

cub•ism \\'kyü-ˌbi-zəm\ *n* : a style of art characterized by the abstraction of natural forms into fragmented geometric shapes — **cub•ist** \\-bist\ *n or adj*

cu•bit \\'kyü-bət\ *n* : an ancient unit of length equal to about 18 inches (46 centimeters)

Cub Scout *n* : a member of the program of the Boy Scouts for boys in the first through fifth grades in school

cuck•old \\'kə-kəld, 'kü-\ *n* : a man whose wife is unfaithful — **cuckold** *vb*

¹cuck•oo \\'kü-kü, 'kú-\ *n, pl* **cuckoos** : a largely grayish brown European bird that lays its eggs in the nests of other birds for them to hatch

²cuckoo *adj* : SILLY, FOOLISH

cu•cum•ber \\'kyü-(ˌ)kəm-bər\ *n* : the long fleshy many-seeded fruit of a vine of the gourd family that is grown as a garden vegetable; *also* : this vine

cud \\'kəd\ *n* : food brought up into the mouth by some animals (as cows) from the rumen to be chewed again

cud·dle \'kəd-əl\ *vb* **cud·dled; cud·dling** : to lie close : SNUGGLE

cud·gel \'kə-jəl\ *n* : a short heavy club — **cudgel** *vb*

¹**cue** \'kyü\ *n* **1** : a word, phrase, or action in a play serving as a signal for the next actor to speak or act **2** : HINT — **cue** *vb*

²**cue** *n* : a tapered rod for striking the balls in billiards or pool

cue ball *n* : the ball a player strikes with a cue in billiards or pool

¹**cuff** \'kəf\ *n* **1** : a part (as of a sleeve or glove) encircling the wrist **2** : the folded hem of a trouser leg

²**cuff** *vb* : to strike esp. with the open hand : SLAP

³**cuff** *n* : a blow with the hand esp. when open

cui·sine \kwi-'zēn\ *n* : style of cooking; *also* : the food prepared

cuke \'kyük\ *n* : CUCUMBER

cul–de–sac \ˌkəl-di-'sak, ˌkul-\ *n*, *pl* **culs–de–sac** *same or* ˌkəlz-, ˌkulz-\ *also* **cul–de–sacs** \ˌkəl-də-'saks, ˌkul-\ [F, lit., bottom of the bag] : a street or passage closed at one end

cu·li·nary \'kə-lə-ˌner-ē, 'kyü-\ *adj* : of or relating to the kitchen or cookery

¹**cull** \'kəl\ *vb* : to pick out from a group

²**cull** *n* : something rejected from a group or lot as worthless or inferior

cul·mi·nate \'kəl-mə-ˌnāt\ *vb* **-nat·ed; -nat·ing** : to reach the highest point — **cul·mi·na·tion** \ˌkəl-mə-'nā-shən\ *n*

cu·lotte \'kü-ˌlät, kyü-, kü-ˌlät, kyü-\ *n* [F, breeches, fr. dim. of *cul* backside] : a divided skirt; *also* : a garment having a divided skirt — often used in pl.

cul·pa·ble \'kəl-pə-bəl\ *adj* : deserving blame — **cul·pa·bil·i·ty** \ˌkəl-pə-'bi-lə-tē\ *n*

cul·prit \'kəl-prət\ *n* [Anglo-French (the French of medieval England) *cul.* (abbr. of *culpable* guilty) + *prest, prit* ready (i.e., to prove it), fr. L *praestus*] : one accused or guilty of a crime

cult \'kəlt\ *n* **1** : formal religious veneration **2** : a religious system; *also* : its adherents **3** : faddish devotion; *also* : a group of persons showing such devotion — **cult·ist** *n*

cul·ti·va·ble \'kəl-tə-və-bəl\ *adj* : capable of being cultivated

cul·ti·vate \'kəl-tə-ˌvāt\ *vb* **-vat·ed; -vat·ing 1** : to prepare for the raising of crops **2** : to foster the growth of by tilling or by labor and care ⟨∼ vegetables⟩ **3** : REFINE, IMPROVE **4** : ENCOURAGE, FURTHER — **cul·ti·va·tion** \ˌkəl-tə-'vā-shən\ *n* — **cul·ti·va·tor** \'kəl-tə-ˌvā-tər\ *n*

cul·ture \'kəl-chər\ *n* **1** : TILLAGE, CULTIVATION **2** : the act of developing by education and training **3** : refinement of intellectual and artistic taste **4** : the customary beliefs, social forms, and material traits of a racial, religious, or social group — **cul·tur·al** \'kəl-chə-rəl\ *adj* — **cul·tur·al·ly** *adv* — **cul·tured** \-chərd\ *adj*

cul·vert \'kəl-vərt\ *n* : a drain crossing under a road or railroad

cum *abbr* cumulative

cum·ber \'kəm-bər\ *vb* : to weigh down : BURDEN, HINDER

cum·ber·some \'kəm-bər-səm\ *adj* : hard to handle or manage because of size or weight

cum·brous \'kəm-brəs\ *adj* : CUMBERSOME — **cum·brous·ly** *adv* — **cum·brous·ness** *n*

cum·in \'kə-mən, 'kyü-\ *n* : a plant of the carrot family cultivated for its aromatic seeds; *also* : the fruit or seed of cumin used as a spice

cum·mer·bund \'kə-mər-ˌbənd, 'kəm-bər-\ *n* [Hindi *kamarband*, fr. Per., fr. *kamar* waist + *band* band] : a broad sash worn as a waistband

cu·mu·la·tive \'kyü-myə-lə-tiv, -ˌlā-\ *adj* : increasing in force or value by successive additions

cu·mu·lo·nim·bus \ˌkyü-myə-lō-'nim-bəs\ *n* : an anvil-shaped cumulus cloud extending to great heights

cu·mu·lus \'kyü-myə-ləs\ *n*, *pl* **-li** \-ˌlī, -ˌlē\ : a massive cloud having a flat base and rounded outlines

cu·ne·i·form \kyü-'nē-ə-ˌfȯrm\ *adj* **1** : wedge-shaped **2** : composed of wedge-shaped characters

cun·ni·lin·gus \ˌkə-ni-'liŋ-gəs\ *also* **cun·ni·linc·tus** \-'liŋk-təs\ *n* : oral stimulation of the vulva or clitoris

¹**cun·ning** \'kə-niŋ\ *adj* **1** : SKILLFUL, DEXTEROUS **2** : marked by wiliness and trickery **3** : CUTE — **cun·ning·ly** *adv*

²**cunning** *n* **1** : SKILL **2** : SLYNESS

¹**cup** \'kəp\ *n* **1** : a small bowl-shaped drinking vessel **2** : the contents of a cup **3** : the consecrated wine of the Communion **4** : something resembling a cup : a small bowl or hollow **5** : a half pint — **cup·ful** *n*

²**cup** *vb* **cupped; cup·ping** : to curve into the shape of a cup

cup·board \'kə-bərd\ *n* : a small closet with shelves for food or dishes

cup·cake \'kəp-ˌkāk\ *n* : a small cake baked in a cuplike mold

cu·pid \'kyü-pəd\ *n* : a winged naked figure of an infant often with a bow and arrow that represents the god Cupid

cu·pid·i·ty \kyü-'pi-də-tē\ *n*, *pl* **-ties** : excessive desire for money

cu·po·la \'kyü-pə-lə, -ˌlō\ *n* : a small structure on top of a roof or building

¹**cur** \'kər\ *n* : a mongrel dog

²**cur** *abbr* **1** currency **2** current

cu·rate \'kyúr-ət\ *n* **1** : a clergyman in charge of a parish **2** : a member of the clergy who assists a rector or vicar — **cu·ra·cy** \-ə-sē\ *n*

cu·ra·tive \-ə-tiv\ *adj* : relating to or used in the cure of diseases — **curative** *n*

cu·ra·tor \'kyúr-ˌā-tər, kyù-'rā-\ *n* : CUSTODIAN; *esp* : one in charge of a place of exhibit (as a museum or zoo)

¹**curb** \'kərb\ *n* **1** : a bit that exerts pressure on a horse's jaws **2** : CHECK, RESTRAINT **3** : a raised edging (as of stone or concrete) along a paved street

²**curb** *vb* : to hold in or back : RESTRAIN

curb·ing \'kər-biŋ\ *n* **1** : the material for a curb **2** : CURB

curd \'kərd\ *n* : the thick protein-rich part of coagulated milk

cur·dle \'kərd-əl\ *vb* **cur·dled; cur·dling** : to form curds; *also* : SPOIL, SOUR

¹**cure** \'kyúr\ *n* **1** : spiritual care **2** : recovery or relief from disease **3** : a curative agent : REMEDY **4** : a course or period of treatment

²**cure** *vb* **cured; cur·ing 1** : to restore to health : HEAL, REMEDY; *also* : to become cured **2** : to process for storage or use ⟨∼ bacon⟩ — **cur·able** *adj*

cu·ré \kyù-'rā\ *n* [F] : a parish priest

cure–all \'kyúr-ˌȯl\ *n* : a remedy for all ills : PANACEA

cu·ret·tage \ˌkyúr-ə-'täzh\ *n* : a surgical scraping or cleaning of a body part (as the uterus)

cur·few \'kər-ˌfyü\ *n* [ME, fr. MF *covrefeu*, signal given to bank the hearth fire, curfew, fr. *covrir* to cover + *feu* fire, fr. L *focus* hearth] : a regulation that specified persons (as children) be off the streets at a set hour of the evening; *also* : the sounding of a signal (as a bell) at this hour

cu·ria \'kyúr-ē-ə, 'kúr-\ *n*, *pl* **cu·ri·ae** \'kyúr-ē-ˌē, 'kúr-ē-ˌī\ *often cap* : the body of congregations, tribunals, and offices through which the pope governs the Roman Catholic Church

cu·rie \'kyúr-ē\ *n* : a unit of radioactivity equal to 37 billion disintegrations per second

cu·rio \'kyúr-ē-ˌō\ *n*, *pl* **cu·ri·os** : an object or article valued because it is strange or rare

cu·ri·ous \'kyúr-ē-əs\ *adj* **1** : having a desire to investigate and learn **2** : STRANGE, UNUSUAL, ODD — **cu·ri·os·i·ty** \ˌkyúr-ē-'ä-sə-tē\ *n* — **cu·ri·ous·ness** *n*

cu·ri·ous·ly *adv* **1** : in a curious manner **2** : as is curious

cu·ri·um \'kyúr-ē-əm\ *n* : a metallic radioactive element produced artificially — see ELEMENT table

¹curl \'kərl\ *vb* **1 :** to form into ringlets **2 :** CURVE, COIL — **curl·er** *n*

²curl *n* **1 :** a lock of hair that coils : RINGLET **2 :** something having a spiral or twisted form — **curly** *adj*

cur·lew \'kər-lü, 'kərl-yü\ *n, pl* **curlews** *or* **curlew** : any of various long-legged brownish birds that have a down-curved bill and are related to the sandpipers and snipes

curli·cue \'kər-li-ˌkyü\ *n* : a fancifully curved or spiral figure

cur·rant \'kər-ənt\ *n* **1 :** a small seedless raisin **2 :** the acid berry of a shrub related to the gooseberry; *also* : this plant

cur·ren·cy \'kər-ən-sē\ *n, pl* **-cies 1 :** general use or acceptance **2 :** something that is in circulation as a medium of exchange : MONEY

¹cur·rent \'kər-ənt\ *adj* **1 :** occurring in or belonging to the present **2 :** used as a medium of exchange **3 :** generally accepted or practiced

²current *n* **1 :** the part of a body of fluid moving continuously in a certain direction; *also* : the swiftest part of a stream **2 :** a flow of electric charge; *also* : the rate of such flow

cur·ric·u·lum \kə-'ri-kyə-ləm\ *n, pl* **-la** \-lə\ *also* **-lums** [L, running, course, fr. *currere* to run] : the courses offered by an educational institution

¹cur·ry \'kər-ē\ *vb* **cur·ried; cur·ry·ing 1 :** to clean the coat of (a horse) with a currycomb **2 :** to treat (tanned leather) esp. by incorporating oil or grease — **curry favor** : to seek to gain favor by flattery or attention

²cur·ry *n, pl* **cur·ries :** a powder of pungent spices used in cooking; *also* : a food seasoned with curry

cur·ry·comb \-ˌkōm\ *n* : a comb used esp. to curry horses — **currycomb** *vb*

¹curse \'kərs\ *n* **1 :** a prayer for harm to come upon one **2 :** something that is cursed **3 :** evil or misfortune coming as if in response to a curse

²curse *vb* **cursed; curs·ing 1 :** to call on divine power to send injury upon **2 :** BLASPHEME **3 :** AFFLICT *syn* execrate, damn, anathematize, objurgate

cur·sive \'kər-siv\ *adj* : written with the strokes of the letters joined together and the angles rounded

cur·sor \'kər-sər\ *n* : a visual cue (as a pointer) on a computer screen that indicates position (as for data entry)

cur·so·ry \'kər-sə-rē\ *adj* : rapidly and often superficially done : HASTY — **cur·so·ri·ly** \-rə-lē\ *adv*

curt \'kərt\ *adj* : rudely short or abrupt — **curt·ly** *adv* — **curt·ness** *n*

cur·tail \(ˌ)kər-'tāl\ *vb* : to cut off the end of : SHORTEN — **cur·tail·ment** *n*

cur·tain \'kərt-ᵊn\ *n* **1 :** a hanging screen that can be drawn back esp. at a window **2 :** the screen between the stage and auditorium of a theater — **curtain** *vb*

curt·sy *or* **curt·sey** \'kərt-sē\ *n, pl* **curtsies** *or* **curtseys** : a courteous bow made by women chiefly by bending the knees — **curtsy** *or* **curtsey** *vb*

cur·va·ceous *also* **cur·va·cious** \ˌkər-'vā-shəs\ *adj* : having curves suggestive of a well-proportioned feminine figure

cur·va·ture \'kər-və-ˌchúr\ *n* : a measure or amount of curving : BEND

¹curve \'kərv\ *vb* **curved; curv·ing :** to bend from a straight line or course

²curve *n* **1 :** a line esp. when curved **2 :** something that bends or curves without angles (a ～ in the road) **3 :** a baseball pitch thrown so that it swerves esp. downward and to one side

cur·vet \(ˌ)kər-'vet\ *n* : a prancing leap of a horse — **curvet** *vb*

¹cush·ion \'kú-shən\ *n* **1 :** a soft pillow or pad to rest on or against **2 :** the springy pad inside the rim of a billiard table **3 :** something soft that prevents discomfort or protects against injury

²cushion *vb* **1 :** to provide (as a seat) with a cushion **2 :** to soften or lessen the force or shock of

cusp \'kəsp\ *n* : a pointed end or part (as of a tooth)

cus·pid \'kəs-pəd\ *n* : a canine tooth

cus·pi·dor \'kəs-pə-ˌdȯr\ *n* : SPITTOON

cus·tard \'kəs-tərd\ *n* : a sweetened cooked mixture of milk and eggs

cus·to·di·al \ˌkəs-'tō-dē-əl\ *adj* : marked by watching and protecting rather than seeking to cure ⟨～ care⟩

cus·to·di·an \ˌkəs-'tō-dē-ən\ *n* : one who has custody (as of a building)

cus·to·dy \'kəs-tə-dē\ *n, pl* **-dies :** immediate charge and control

¹cus·tom \'kəs-təm\ *n* **1 :** habitual course of action : recognized usage **2** *pl* : taxes levied on imports **3 :** business patronage

²custom *adj* **1 :** made to personal order **2 :** doing work only on order

cus·tom·ary \'kəs-tə-ˌmer-ē\ *adj* **1 :** based on or established by custom **2 :** commonly practiced or observed : HABITUAL — **cus·tom·ar·i·ly** *adv*

cus·tom–built \'kəs-təm-'bilt\ *adj* : built to individual order

cus·tom·er \'kəs-tə-mər\ *n* : BUYER, PURCHASER; *esp* : a regular or frequent buyer

cus·tom·house \'kəs-təm-ˌhaús\ *n* : the building where customs are paid

cus·tom·ise *Brit var of* CUSTOMIZE

cus·tom·ize \'kəs-tə-ˌmīz\ *vb* **-ized; -iz·ing :** to build, fit, or alter according to individual specifications

cus·tom–made \'kəs-təm-'mād\ *adj* : made to individual order

¹cut \'kət\ *vb* **cut; cut·ting 1 :** to penetrate or divide with a sharp edge : CLEAVE, GASH; *also* : to experience the growth of (a tooth) through the gum **2 :** to hurt the feelings of **3 :** to strike sharply **4 :** SHORTEN, REDUCE **5 :** to remove by severing or paring **6 :** INTERSECT, CROSS **7 :** to divide into parts **8 :** to go quickly or change direction abruptly **9 :** to cause to stop

²cut *n* **1 :** something made by cutting : GASH, CLEFT **2 :** SHARE **3 :** a segment or section of a meat carcass **4 :** an excavated channel or roadway **5 :** BAND **4 6 :** a sharp stroke or blow **7 :** REDUCTION ⟨～ in wages⟩ **8 :** the shape or manner in which a thing is cut

cut–and–dried \ˌkət-ᵊn-'drīd\ *also* **cut–and–dry** \-'drī\ *adj* : according to a plan, set procedure, or formula

cu·ta·ne·ous \kyú-'tā-nē-əs\ *adj* : of, relating to, or affecting the skin

cut·back \'kət-ˌbak\ *n* **1 :** something cut back **2 :** REDUCTION

cute \'kyüt\ *adj* **cut·er; cut·est** [short for *acute*] **1 :** CLEVER, SHREWD **2 :** daintily attractive : PRETTY

cu·ti·cle \'kyü-ti-kəl\ *n* **1 :** an outer layer (as of skin or a leaf) **2 :** dead or horny epidermis esp. around a fingernail — **cu·tic·u·lar** \kyü-'ti-kyə-lər\ *adj*

cut in *vb* **1 :** to thrust oneself between others **2 :** to interrupt a dancing couple and take one as one's partner

cut·lass \'kət-ləs\ *n* : a short heavy curved sword

cutlass

cut·ler \'kət-lər\ *n* : one who makes, deals in, or repairs cutlery

cut·lery \'kət-lə-rē\ *n* : edged or cutting tools; *esp* : implements for cutting and eating food

cut·let \'kət-lət\ *n* : a slice of meat (as veal) for broiling or frying

cut·off \'kət-ˌȯf\ *n* **1 :** the channel formed when a stream cuts through the neck of an oxbow; *also* : SHORTCUT **2 :** a device for cutting off **3** *pl* : shorts

orig. made from jeans with the legs cut off at the knees or higher

cut·out \'kət-ˌaut\ *n* : something cut out or prepared for cutting out from something else ⟨a page of animal ∼s⟩

cut out *vb* **1** : to be all that one can handle ⟨had her work *cut out* for her⟩ **2** : DISCONNECT **3** : to cease operating ⟨the engine *cut out*⟩ **4** : ELIMINATE ⟨*cut out* unnecessary expense⟩

cut–rate \'kət-'rāt\ *adj* : relating to or dealing in goods sold at reduced rates

cut·ter \'kə-tər\ *n* **1** : a tool or a machine for cutting **2** : a ship's boat for carrying stores and passengers **3** : a small armed vessel in government service **4** : a light sleigh

¹cut·throat \'kət-ˌthrōt\ *n* : MURDERER

²cutthroat *adj* **1** : MURDEROUS, CRUEL : RUTHLESS ⟨∼ competition⟩

cutthroat trout *n* : a large American trout with a red mark under the jaw

¹cut·ting \'kə-tiŋ\ *n* : a piece of a plant able to grow into a new plant

²cutting *adj* **1** : SHARP, EDGED **2** : marked by piercing cold **3** : likely to hurt the feelings : SARCASTIC ⟨a ∼ remark⟩

cut·tle·fish \'kət-ᵊl-ˌfish\ *n* : a 10-armed mollusk related to the squid with an internal shell (**cut·tle·bone** \-ˌbōn\) composed of calcium compounds

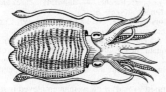

cuttlefish

cut·up \'kət-ˌəp\ *n* : a person who clowns or acts boisterously — **cut up** *vb*

cut·worm \-ˌwərm\ *n* : any of various smooth-bodied moth larvae that feed on plants at night

cw *abbr* clockwise

CWO *abbr* **1** cash with order **2** chief warrant officer

cwt *abbr* hundredweight

-cy \sē\ *n suffix* **1** : action : practice ⟨mendican*cy*⟩ **2** : rank : office ⟨chaplain*cy*⟩ **3** : body : class ⟨constituen*cy*⟩ **4** : state : quality ⟨accura*cy*⟩

cy·an \'sī-ˌan, -ən\ *n* : a greenish blue color

cy·a·nide \'sī-ə-ˌnīd, -nəd\ *n* : a poisonous compound of carbon and nitrogen with another element (as potassium)

cyber– *comb form* : computer : computer network

cy·ber·net·ics \ˌsī-bər-'ne-tiks\ *n* : the science of communication and control theory that is concerned esp. with the comparative study of automatic control systems — **cy·ber·net·ic** *adj*

cy·ber·space \'sī-bər-ˌspās\ *n* : the on-line world of computer networks

cy·cla·men \'sī-klə-mən\ *n* : any of a genus of plants related to the primroses and grown for their showy nodding flowers

¹cy·cle \'sī-kəl\ *n* **1** : a period of time occupied by a series of events that repeat themselves regularly and in the same order **2** : a recurring round of operations or events **3** : one complete occurrence of a periodic process (as a vibration or current alternation) **4** : a circular or spiral arrangement **5** : a long period of time : AGE **6** : BICYCLE **7** : MOTORCYCLE — **cy·clic** \'sī-klik, 'si-\ *or* **cy·cli·cal** \kli-kəl\ *adj* — **cy·cli·cal·ly** \-k(ə-)lē\ *also* **cy·clic·ly** *adv*

²cy·cle \'sī-kəl\ *vb* **cy·cled; cy·cling** : to ride a cycle — **cy·clist** \'sī-klist, -kə-list\ *n*

cy·clone \'sī-ˌklōn\ *n* **1** : a storm or system of winds that rotates about a center of low atmospheric pressure and advances at 20 to 30 miles (about 30 to 50 kilometers) an hour **2** : TORNADO — **cy·clon·ic** \sī-'klä-nik\ *adj*

cy·clo·pe·dia *or* **cy·clo·pae·dia** \ˌsī-klə-'pē-dē-ə\ *n* : ENCYCLOPEDIA

cy·clo·tron \'sī-klə-ˌträn\ *n* : a device for giving high speed to charged particles by magnetic and electric fields

cy·der *Brit var of* CIDER

cyg·net \'sig-nət\ *n* : a young swan

cyl *abbr* cylinder

cyl·in·der \'si-lən-dər\ *n* : the solid figure formed by turning a rectangle about one side as an axis; *also* : a body or space of this form ⟨an engine ∼⟩ ⟨a bullet in the ∼ of a revolver⟩ — **cy·lin·dri·cal** \sə-'lin-dri-kəl\ *adj*

cym·bal \'sim-bəl\ *n* : a concave brass plate that produces a brilliant clashing sound

cyn·ic \'si-nik\ *n* : one who attributes all actions to selfish motives — **cyn·i·cal** \-ni-kəl\ *adj* — **cyn·i·cal·ly** \-k(ə-)lē\ *adv* — **cyn·i·cism** \si-nə-ˌsi-zəm\ *n*

cy·no·sure \'sī-nə-ˌshur, 'si-\ *n* [MF & L; MF, Ursa Minor, guide, fr. L *cynosura* Ursa Minor, fr. Gk *kynosoura*, fr. *kynos oura* dog's tail] : a center of attraction

CYO *abbr* Catholic Youth Organization

cy·pher *chiefly Brit var of* CIPHER

cy·press \'sī-prəs\ *n* **1** : any of a genus of scaly-leaved evergreen trees and shrubs **2** : BALD CYPRESS **3** : the wood of a cypress

Cyp·ri·ot \'si-prē-ət, -ˌät\ *or* **Cyp·ri·ote** \-ˌōt, -ət\ *n* : a native or inhabitant of Cyprus — **Cypriot** *adj*

cyst \'sist\ *n* : an abnormal closed bodily sac usu. containing liquid — **cys·tic** \'sis-tik\ *adj*

cystic fibrosis *n* : a common hereditary disease marked esp. by deficiency of pancreatic enzymes, by respiratory symptoms, and by excessive loss of salt in the sweat

cy·tol·o·gy \sī-'tä-lə-jē\ *n* : a branch of biology dealing with cells — **cy·to·log·i·cal** \ˌsīt-ᵊl-'ä-ji-kəl\ *or* **cy·to·log·ic** \-jik\ *adj* — **cy·tol·o·gist** \sī-'tä-lə-jist\ *n*

cy·to·plasm \'sī-tə-ˌpla-zəm\ *n* : the protoplasm of a cell that lies external to the nucleus — **cy·to·plas·mic** \ˌsī-tə-'plaz-mik\ *adj*

cy·to·sine \'sī-tə-ˌsēn\ *n* : a chemical base that is a pyrimidine coding genetic information in DNA and RNA

CZ *abbr* Canal Zone

czar \'zär, 'tsär\ *n* [NL, fr. Russ *tsar'*, ultim. fr. L

Caesar Caesar] : the ruler of Russia until 1917; *also* : one having great authority — **czar·ist** \-ist\ *n or adj*

cza·ri·na \zä-'rē-nə\ *n* : the wife of a czar

Czech \'chek\ *n* **1** : a native or inhabitant of Czechoslovakia or the Czech Republic **2** : the language of the Czechs — **Czech** *adj*

Czecho·slo·vak \ˌche-kə-'slō-ˌväk, -ˌvak\ *or* **Czecho·slo·va·ki·an** \-slō-'vä-kē-ən, -'va-\ *adj* : of, relating to, or characteristic of Czechoslovakia or its people — **Czechoslovak** *or* **Czechoslovakian** *n*

D

¹d \'dē\ *n, pl* **d's** *or* **ds** \'dēz\ *often cap* **1** : the 4th letter of the English alphabet **2** : a grade rating a student's work as poor

²d *abbr, often cap* **1** date **2** daughter **3** day **4** dead **5** deceased **6** degree **7** Democrat **8** [L *denarius, denarii*] penny; pence **9** depart; departure **10** diameter

D *symbol* deuterium

DA *abbr* **1** deposit account **2** district attorney **3** don't answer

¹dab \'dab\ *n* **1** : a sudden blow or thrust : POKE; *also* : PECK **2** : a gentle touch or stroke : PAT

²dab *vb* **dabbed; dab·bing 1** : to strike or touch gently : PAT **2** : to apply lightly or irregularly : DAUB — **dab·ber** *n*

³dab *n* **1** : DAUB **2** : a small amount

dab·ble \'da-bəl\ *vb* **dab·bled; dab·bling 1** : to wet by splashing : SPATTER **2** : to paddle or play in or as if in water **3** : to work or involve oneself without serious effort — **dab·bler** *n*

da ca·po \dä-'kä-(ˌ)pō\ *adv or adj* [It] : from the beginning — used as a direction in music to repeat

dace \'dās\ *n, pl* **dace** : any of various small No. American freshwater fishes related to the carp

da·cha \'dä-chə\ *n* [Russ] : a Russian country house

dachs·hund \'däks-ˌhunt\ *n, pl* **dachshunds** [G, fr. *Dachs* badger + *Hund* dog] : a small dog of a breed of German origin with a long body, short legs, and long drooping ears

dac·tyl \'dakt-ᵊl\ *n* [ME *dactile*, fr. L *dactylus*, fr. Gk *daktylos*, lit., finger; fr. the fact that the three syllables have the first one longest like the joints of the finger] : a metrical foot of one accented syllable followed by two unaccented syllables — **dac·tyl·ic** \dak-'ti-lik\ *adj or n*

dad \'dad\ *n* : FATHER 1

Da·da \'dä-(ˌ)dä\ *n* : a movement in art and literature based on deliberate irrationality and negation of traditional artistic values — **da·da·ism** \-ˌi-zəm\ *n, often cap* — **da·da·ist** \-ˌist\ *n or adj, often cap*

dad·dy \'da-dē\ *n, pl* **daddies** : FATHER 1

dad·dy long·legs \ˌda-dē-'lòŋ-ˌlegz\ *n, pl* **daddy longlegs** : any of various arachnids resembling the true spiders but having small rounded bodies and long slender legs

dae·mon *var of* DEMON

daf·fo·dil \'da-fə-ˌdil\ *n* : any of a genus of bulbous herbs with usu. large flowers having a trumpetlike center

daf·fy \'da-fē\ *adj* **daf·fi·er; -est** : DAFT

daft \'daft\ *adj* : FOOLISH; *also* : INSANE — **daft·ness** *n*

dag *abbr* dekagram

dag·ger \'da-gər\ *n* **1** : a sharp pointed knife for stabbing **2** : a character † used as a reference mark or to indicate a death date

da·guerre·o·type \də-'ger-(ē-)ə-ˌtīp\ *n* : an early photograph produced on a silver or a silver-covered copper plate

dahl·ia \'dal-yə, 'däl-\ *n* : any of a genus of tuberous herbs related to the daisies and having showy flowers

¹dai·ly \'dā-lē\ *adj* **1** : occurring, done, or used every day or every weekday **2** : of or relating to every day ⟨~ visitors⟩ **3** : computed in terms of one day ⟨~ wages⟩ **syn** diurnal, quotidian — **dai·li·ness** \-lē-nəs\ *n* — **daily** *adv*

²daily *n, pl* **dailies** : a newspaper published every weekday

daily double *n* : a system of betting on races in which the bettor must pick the winners of two stipulated races in order to win

¹dain·ty \'dān-tē\ *n, pl* **dainties** [ME *deinte*, fr. OF *deintié*, fr. L *dignitas* dignity, worth] : something delicious or pleasing to the taste : DELICACY

²dainty *adj* **dain·ti·er; -est 1** : pleasing to the taste **2** : delicately pretty **3** : having or showing delicate taste; *also* : FASTIDIOUS **syn** choice, delicate, exquisite, rare, recherché — **dain·ti·ly** \-ti-lē\ *adv* — **dain·ti·ness** \-tē-nəs\ *n*

dai·qui·ri \'dī-kə-rē, 'da-kə-rē\ *n* [*Daiquirí*, Cuba] : a cocktail made of rum, lime juice, and sugar

dairy \'der-ē\ *n, pl* **dair·ies** [ME *deyerie*, fr. *deye* dairymaid, fr. OE *dǣge* kneader of bread] **1** : CREAMERY **2** : a farm specializing in milk production

dairy·ing \'der-ē-iŋ\ *n* : the business of operating a dairy

dairy·maid \-ˌmād\ *n* : a woman employed in a dairy

dairy·man \-mən, -ˌman\ *n* : a person who operates a dairy farm or works in a dairy

da·is \'dā-əs\ *n* : a raised platform usu. above the floor of a hall or large room

dai·sy \'dā-zē\ *n, pl* **daisies** [ME *dayeseye*, fr. OE *dǣgesēage*, fr. *dǣg* day + *ēage* eye] : any of numerous composite plants having flower heads in which the marginal flowers resemble petals

daisy wheel *n* : a disk with spokes bearing type that serves as the printing element of an electric typewriter or printer; *also* : a printer that uses such a disk

Da·ko·ta \də-'kō-tə\ *n, pl* **Dakotas** *also* **Dakota** : a member of an American Indian people of the northern Mississippi valley; *also* : their language

dal *abbr* dekaliter

da·la·si \dä-'lä-sē\ *n, pl* **dalasi** *or* **dalasis** — see MONEY table

dale \'dāl\ *n* : VALLEY

dal·ly \'da-lē\ *vb* **dal·lied; dal·ly·ing 1** : to act playfully; *esp* : to play amorously **2** : to waste time **3** : LIN-

ger, dawdle **syn** flirt, coquet, toy, trifle — **dal·li·ance**
\-lē-əns\ *n*
dal·ma·tian \dal-'mā-shən\ *n, often cap* : any of a
breed of medium-sized dogs having a white short-
haired coat with black or brown spots

dalmatian

¹**dam** \'dam\ *n* : a female parent — used esp. of a domestic animal
²**dam** *n* : a barrier (as across a stream) to stop the flow
of water — **dam** *vb*
³**dam** *abbr* dekameter

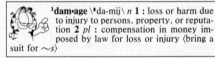
¹**dam·age** \'da-mij\ *n* 1 : loss or harm due
to injury to persons, property, or reputation 2 *pl* : compensation in money imposed by law for loss or injury ⟨bring a
suit for ∼*s*⟩

²**damage** *vb* **dam·aged; dam·ag·ing** : to cause damage
to
dam·a·scene \'da-mə-ˌsēn\ *vb* **-scened; -scen·ing** : to
ornament (as iron or steel) with wavy patterns or with
inlaid work of precious metals
dam·ask \'da-məsk\ *n* 1 : a firm lustrous reversible figured fabric used for household linen 2 : a tough steel
having decorative wavy lines
dame \'dām\ *n* 1 : a woman of rank, station, or authority 2 : an elderly woman 3 : WOMAN

damn \'dam\ *vb* [ME *dampnen*, fr. OF *dampner*, fr. L
damnare, fr. *damnum* damage, loss, fine] 1 : to condemn esp. to hell 2 : CURSE — **damned** *adj*
dam·na·ble \'dam-nə-bəl\ *adj* 1 : liable to or deserving
punishment 2 : DETESTABLE ⟨∼ weather⟩ — **dam-
na·bly** \-blē\ *adv*
dam·na·tion \dam-'nā-shən\ *n* 1 : the act of damning 2
: the state of being damned
¹**damp** \'damp\ *n* 1 : a noxious gas 2 : MOISTURE
²**damp** *vb* : DAMPEN
³**damp** *adj* : MOIST — **damp·ness** *n*
damp·en \'dam-pən\ *vb* 1 : to check or diminish in activity or vigor 2 : to make or become damp
damp·er \'dam-pər\ *n* : one that damps; *esp* : a valve
or movable plate (as in the flue of a stove, furnace, or
fireplace) to regulate the draft
dam·sel \'dam-zəl\ *n* : MAIDEN, GIRL
dam·sel·fly \-ˌflī\ *n* : any of a group of insects that are
closely related to the dragonflies but fold their wings
above the body when at rest
dam·son \'dam-zən\ *n* : a plum with acid purple fruit;
also : its fruit
Dan *abbr* Daniel

¹**dance** \'dans\ *vb* **danced; danc·ing** 1 : to
glide, step, or move through a set series
of movements usu. to music 2 : to move
quickly up and down or about 3 : to perform or take part in as a dancer — **dancer** *n*

²**dance** *n* 1 : an act or instance of dancing 2 : a social
gathering for dancing 3 : a piece of music (as a waltz)
by which dancing may be guided 4 : the art of dancing
D & C *n* [*dilation and* curettage] : a surgical procedure
used to test for cancer of the uterus or to perform an
abortion that involves stretching the opening of the
uterus and scraping the inside walls
dan·de·li·on \'dan-də-ˌlī-ən, -dē-\ *n* [MF *dent de lion*,
lit., lion's tooth] : any of a genus of common yellow-
flowered composite herbs
dan·der \'dan-dər\ *n* : ANGER, TEMPER
dan·di·fy \'dan-di-ˌfī\ *vb* **-fied; -fy·ing** : to cause to resemble a dandy

dandle • database

154

dan·dle \'dand-ᵊl\ *vb* **dan·dled; dan·dling** : to move up and down in one's arms or on one's knee in affectionate play **syn** caress, fondle, love, pet

dan·druff \'dan-drəf\ *n* : a whitish scurf on the scalp that comes off in small scales — **dan·druffy** \-drə-fē\ *adj*

¹**dan·dy** \'dan-dē\ *n, pl* **dandies** 1 : a man unduly attentive to personal appearance 2 : something excellent in its class **syn** fop, coxcomb, popinjay

²**dandy** *adj* **dan·di·er; -est** : very good : FIRST-RATE

Dane \'dān\ *n* 1 : a native or inhabitant of Denmark 2 : GREAT DANE

dan·ger \'dān-jər\ *n* 1 : exposure or liability to injury, harm, or evil 2 : something that may cause injury or harm **syn** peril, hazard, risk, jeopardy

dan·ger·ous \'dān-jə-rəs\ *adj* 1 : HAZARDOUS, PERILOUS 2 : able or likely to inflict injury — **dan·ger·ous·ly** *adv*

dan·gle \'daŋ-gəl\ *vb* **dan·gled; dan·gling** 1 : to hang loosely esp. with a swinging motion : SWING 2 : to be a hanger-on or dependent 3 : to be left without proper grammatical connection in a sentence 4 : to keep hanging uncertainly 5 : to offer as an inducement

Dan·iel \'dan-yəl\ *n* — see BIBLE table

Dan·ish \'dā-nish\ *n* : the language of the Danes — **Danish** *adj*

Danish pastry *n* : a pastry made of a rich yeast-raised dough

dank \'daŋk\ *adj* : disagreeably wet or moist : DAMP — **dank·ness** *n*

dan·seuse \dän-ˈsərz, -ˈsəz; dän-ˈsüz\ *n* [F] : a female ballet dancer

dap·per \'da-pər\ *adj* 1 : SPRUCE, TRIM 2 : being alert and lively in movement and manners : JAUNTY

dap·ple \'da-pəl\ *vb* **dap·pled; dap·pling** : to mark with different-colored spots

DAR *abbr* Daughters of the American Revolution

¹**dare** \'dar\ *vb* **dared; dar·ing** 1 : to have sufficient courage : be bold enough to 2 : CHALLENGE 3 : to confront boldly

²**dare** *n* : an act or instance of daring : CHALLENGE

dare·dev·il \-de-vəl\ *n* : a recklessly bold person

dar·ing \'dar-iŋ\ *n* : venturesome boldness — **daring** *adj* — **dar·ing·ly** *adv*

¹**dark** \'därk\ *adj* 1 : being without light or without much light 2 : not light in color ⟨a ∼ suit⟩ 3 : GLOOMY 4 *often cap* : being a period of stagnation or decline ⟨the *Dark* Ages⟩ 5 : SECRETIVE **syn** dim, dusky, murky, tenebrous — **dark·ly** *adv* — **dark·ness** *n*

²**dark** *n* 1 : absence of light : DARKNESS; *esp* : NIGHT 2 : a dark or deep color — **in the dark** 1 : in secrecy 2 : in ignorance

dark·en \'där-kən\ *vb* 1 : to make or grow dark or darker 2 : DIM 3 : BESMIRCH, TARNISH 4 : to make or become gloomy or forbidding

dark horse *n* : a contestant or a political figure whose abilities and chances as a contender are not known

dark·ling \'där-kliŋ\ *adj* 1 : DARK ⟨a ∼ plain⟩ 2 : MYSTERIOUS

dark·room \'därk-rüm, -rùm\ *n* : a lightproof room in which photographic materials are processed

¹**dar·ling** \'där-liŋ\ *n* 1 : a dearly loved person 2 : FAVORITE

²**darling** *adj* 1 : dearly loved : FAVORITE 2 : very pleasing : CHARMING

¹**darn** \'därn\ *vb* : to mend with interlacing stitches — **darn·er** *n*

²**darn** *or* **darned** \'därnd\ *adv* : VERY, EXTREMELY

darning needle *n* 1 : a needle for darning 2 : DRAGONFLY

¹**dart** \'därt\ *n* 1 : a small missile with a point on one end and feathers on the other; *also, pl* : a game in which darts are thrown at a target 2 : something causing a sudden pain 3 : a stitched tapering fold in a garment 4 : a quick movement

²**dart** *vb* 1 : to throw with a sudden movement 2 : to thrust or move suddenly or rapidly 3 : to shoot with a dart containing a usu. tranquilizing drug

dart·er \'där-tər\ *n* : any of numerous small American freshwater fishes related to the perches

Dar·win·ism \'där-wə-ni-zəm\ *n* : a theory explaining the origin and continued existence of new species of plants and animals by means of natural selection acting on chance variations — **Dar·win·ist** \-nist\ *n or adj*

¹**dash** \'dash\ *vb* 1 : SMASH 2 : to knock, hurl, or thrust violently 3 : SPLASH, SPATTER 4 : RUIN 5 : DEPRESS, SADDEN 6 : to perform or finish hastily 7 : to move with sudden speed

²**dash** *n* 1 : a sudden burst or splash 2 : a stroke of a pen 3 : a punctuation mark — that is used esp. to indicate a break in the thought or structure of a sentence 4 : a small addition ⟨a ∼ of salt⟩ 5 : flashy showiness 6 : animation in style and action 7 : a sudden rush or attempt ⟨made a ∼ for the door⟩ 8 : a short foot race 9 : DASHBOARD

dash·board \-bòrd\ *n* : a panel in an automobile or aircraft below the windshield usu. containing dials and controls

dash·er \'da-shər\ *n* : a device (as in a churn) for agitating something

da·shi·ki \də-ˈshē-kē\ *or* **dai·shi·ki** \dī-\ *n* [modif. of Yoruba (an African language) *dànṣíkí*] : a usu. brightly colored loose-fitting pullover garment

dash·ing \'da-shiŋ\ *adj* 1 : marked by vigorous action 2 : marked by smartness esp. in dress and manners **syn** stylish, chic, fashionable, modish, smart, swank

das·tard \'das-tərd\ *n* 1 : COWARD 2 : a person who acts treacherously — **das·tard·ly** *adj*

dat *abbr* dative

da·ta \'dā-tə, 'da-, 'dä-\ *n sing or pl* [L, pl. of *datum*] : factual information (as measurements or statistics) used as a basis for reasoning, discussion, or calculation

da·ta·base \-bās\ *n* : a usu. large collection of data organized esp. for rapid search and retrieval (as by a computer)

data processing *n* : the action or process of supplying a computer with information and having the computer use it to produce a desired result

¹date \'dāt\ *n* [ME, fr. OF, ultim. fr. L *dactylus*, fr. Gk *daktylos*, lit., finger] : the edible fruit of a tall Old World palm; *also* : this palm

²date *n* [ME, fr. MF, fr. LL *data*, fr. *data* (as in *data Romae* given at Rome), fem. of L *datus*, pp. of *dare* to give] **1** : the day, month, or year of an event **2** : a statement giving the time of execution or making (as of a coin or check) **3** : the period to which something belongs **4** : APPOINTMENT; *esp* : a social engagement between two persons that often has a romantic character **5** : a person with whom one has a usu. romantic date — **to date** : up to the present moment

³date *vb* **dat·ed; dat·ing 1** : to record the date of or on **2** : to determine, mark, or reveal the date, age, or period of **3** : to make or have a date with **4** : ORIGINATE ⟨~s from ancient times⟩ **5** : EXTEND ⟨*dating* back to childhood⟩ **6** : to show qualities typical of a past period

dat·ed \'dā-təd\ *adj* **1** : provided with a date **2** : OLD-FASHIONED **syn** antiquated, archaic, old hat, outdated, outmoded, passé

date·less \'dāt-ləs\ *adj* **1** : ENDLESS **2** : having no date **3** : too ancient to be dated **4** : TIMELESS

date·line \'dāt-₁līn\ *n* : a line in a publication giving the date and place of composition or issue — **dateline** *vb*

da·tive \'dā-tiv\ *adj* : of, relating to, or constituting a grammatical case marking typically the indirect object of a verb — **dative** *n*

da·tum \'dā-təm, 'da-, 'dä-\ *n, pl* **da·ta** \-tə\ *or* **datums** : a single piece of data : FACT

dau *abbr* daughter

¹daub \'dòb\ *vb* **1** : to cover with soft adhesive matter **2** : SMEAR, SMUDGE **3** : to paint crudely — **daub·er** *n*

²daub *n* **1** : something daubed on : SMEAR **2** : a crude picture

daugh·ter \'dò-tər\ *n* **1** : a female offspring esp. of human beings **2** : a human female having a specified ancestor or belonging to a group of common ancestry — **daughter** *adj*

daugh·ter–in–law \'dò-tə-rən-₁lò\ *n, pl* **daugh·ters–in–law** \-tər-zən-\ : the wife of one's son

daunt \'dònt\ *vb* [ME, fr. OF *danter*, alter. of *donter*, fr. L *domitare* to tame] : to lessen the courage of : INTIMIDATE, OVERWHELM

daunt·less \-ləs\ *adj* : FEARLESS, UNDAUNTED **syn** brave, bold, courageous, lionhearted — **daunt·less·ly** *adv*

dau·phin \'dò-fən\ *n, often cap* : the eldest son of a king of France

DAV *abbr* Disabled American Veterans

dav·en·port \'da-vən-₁pòrt\ *n* : a large upholstered sofa

da·vit \'dā-vət, 'da-\ *n* : a small crane on a ship used in pairs esp. to raise or lower boats

daw·dle \'dòd-ᵊl\ *vb* **daw·dled; daw·dling 1** : to spend time wastefully or idly **2** : LOITER — **daw·dler** *n*

¹dawn \'dòn\ *vb* **1** : to begin to grow light as the sun rises **2** : to begin to appear or develop **3** : to begin to be understood ⟨the solution ~ed on him⟩

²dawn *n* **1** : the first appearance of light in the morning **2** : a first appearance : BEGINNING ⟨the ~ of a new era⟩

day \'dā\ *n* **1** : the period of light between one night and the next; *also* : DAYLIGHT **2** : the period of rotation of a planet (as earth) or a moon on its axis **3** : a period of 24 hours beginning at midnight **4** : a specified day or date ⟨wedding ~⟩ **5** : a specified time or period : AGE ⟨in olden ~s⟩ **6** : the conflict or contention of the day **7** : the time set apart by usage or law for work ⟨the 8-hour ~⟩

day·bed \'dā-₁bed\ *n* : a couch that can be converted into a bed

day·book \-₁búk\ *n* : DIARY, JOURNAL

day·break \-₁brāk\ *n* : DAWN

day care *n* : supervision of and care for children or disabled adults provided during the day; *also* : a program offering day care

day·dream \'dā-₁drēm\ *n* : a pleasant reverie — **daydream** *vb*

day·light \'dā-₁līt\ *n* **1** : the light of day **2** : DAYTIME **3** : DAWN **4** : understanding of something that has been obscure **5** *pl* : CONSCIOUSNESS; *also* : WITS **6** : an opening or opportunity esp. for action

daylight saving time *n* : time usu. one hour ahead of standard time

Day of Atonement *n* : YOM KIPPUR

day school *n* : a private school without boarding facilities

day student *n* : a student who attends regular classes at a college or preparatory school but does not live there

day·time \'dā-₁tīm\ *n* : the period of daylight

daze \'dāz\ *vb* **dazed; daz·ing 1** : to stupefy esp. by a blow **2** : DAZZLE — **daze** *n* — **da·zed·ly** \'dā-zəd-lē\ *adv*

daz·zle \'da-zəl\ *vb* **daz·zled; daz·zling 1** : to overpower with light **2** : to impress greatly or confound with brilliance — **dazzle** *n*

dB *abbr* decibel

d/b/a *abbr* doing business as

dbl *or* **dble** *abbr* double

DC *abbr* **1** [It *da capo*] from the beginning **2** direct current **3** District of Columbia **4** doctor of chiropractic

DD *abbr* **1** days after date **2** demand draft **3** dishonorable discharge **4** doctor of divinity

D day *n* [*D*, abbr. for *day*] : a day set for launching an operation (as an invasion)

DDS *abbr* doctor of dental surgery

DDT \₁dē-(₁)dē-'tē\ *n* : a persistent insecticide poisonous to many higher animals

DE *abbr* Delaware

dea·con \'dē-kən\ *n* [ME *dekene*, fr. OE *dēacon*, fr. LL *diaconus*, fr. Gk *diakonos*, lit., servant] : a subordinate officer in a Christian church

dea·con·ess \'dē-kə-nəs\ *n* : a woman chosen to assist in the church ministry

de·ac·ti·vate \dē-'ak-tə-₁vāt\ *vb* : to make inactive or ineffective

¹dead \'ded\ *adj* **1** : LIFELESS **2** : DEATHLIKE, DEADLY ⟨in a ~ faint⟩ **3** : NUMB **4** : very tired **5** : UNRESPONSIVE **6** : EXTINGUISHED ⟨~ coals⟩ **7** : INANIMATE, INERT **8** : no longer active or functioning ⟨a ~ battery⟩ **9** : lacking power, significance, or effect ⟨a ~ custom⟩ **10** : OBSOLETE ⟨a ~ language⟩ **11** : lacking in gaiety or animation ⟨a ~ party⟩ **12** : QUIET, IDLE, UNPRODUCTIVE ⟨~ capital⟩ **13** : lacking elasticity ⟨a ~ tennis ball⟩ **14** : not circulating : STAGNANT ⟨~ air⟩ **15** : lacking warmth, vigor, or taste ⟨~ wine⟩ **16** : absolutely uniform ⟨~ level⟩ **17** : UNERRING, EXACT ⟨a ~ shot⟩ **18** : ABRUPT ⟨a ~ stop⟩ **19** : COMPLETE ⟨a ~ loss⟩

²dead *n, pl* **dead 1** : one that is dead — usu. used collectively ⟨the living and the ~⟩ **2** : the time of greatest quiet ⟨the ~ of the night⟩

³dead *adv* **1** : UTTERLY ⟨~ right⟩ **2** : in a sudden and complete manner ⟨stopped ~⟩ **3** : DIRECTLY ⟨~ ahead⟩

dead·beat \-₁bēt\ *n* : a person who persistently fails to pay personal debts or expenses

dead duck *n* : GONER

dead·en \'ded-ᵊn\ *vb* **1** : to impair in vigor or sensation : BLUNT ⟨~ pain⟩ **2** : to lessen the luster or spirit of **3** : to make (as a wall) soundproof

dead end *n* **1** : an end (as of a street) without an exit **2** : a position, situation, or course of action that leads to nothing further — **dead–end** \₁ded-'end\ *adj*

dead heat *n* : a contest in which two or more contestants tie (as by crossing the finish line simultaneously)

dead letter *n* **1** : something that has lost its force or authority without being formally abolished **2** : a letter that cannot be delivered or returned

dead·line \'ded-ₐlīn\ *n* : a date or time before which something must be done

dead·lock \'ded-ₐläk\ *n* : a stoppage of action because neither faction in a struggle will give in — **deadlock** *vb*

¹dead·ly \'ded-lē\ *adj* **dead·li·er; -est** **1** : likely to cause or capable of causing death **2** : HOSTILE, IMPLACABLE **3** : very accurate : UNERRING **4** : tending to deprive of force or vitality ⟨a ∼ habit⟩ **5** : suggestive of death **6** : very great : EXTREME — **dead·li·ness** *n*

²deadly *adv* **1** : suggesting death ⟨∼ pale⟩ **2** : EXTREMELY ⟨∼ dull⟩

deadly sin *n* : one of seven sins of pride, covetousness, lust, anger, gluttony, envy, and sloth held to be fatal to spiritual progress

¹dead·pan \'ded-ₐpan\ *adj* : marked by an impassive manner or expression — **deadpan** *vb* — **deadpan** *adv*

²deadpan *n* : a completely expressionless face

dead reckoning *n* : the determination of the position of a ship or aircraft solely from the record of the direction and distance of its course

dead·weight \'ded-'wāt\ *n* **1** : the unrelieved weight of an inert mass **2** : a ship's load including the weight of cargo, fuel, crew, and passengers

dead·wood \-ₐwüd\ *n* **1** : wood dead on the tree **2** : useless personnel or material

deaf \'def\ *adj* **1** : unable to hear **2** : unwilling to hear or listen ⟨∼ to all suggestions⟩ — **deaf·ness** *n*

deaf·en \'de-fən\ *vb* : to make deaf

deaf–mute \'def-ₐmyüt\ *n* : a deaf person who has never learned to speak

¹deal \'dēl\ *n* **1** : a usu. large or indefinite quantity or degree ⟨a great ∼ of support⟩ **2** : the act or right of distributing cards to players in a card game; *also* : HAND

²deal *vb* **dealt** \'delt\; **deal·ing** **1** : DISTRIBUTE; *esp* : to distribute playing cards to players in a game **2** : ADMINISTER, DELIVER ⟨dealt him a blow⟩ **3** : to concern itself : TREAT ⟨the book ∼s with crime⟩ **4** : to take action in regard to something ⟨∼ with offenders⟩ **5** : TRADE; *also* : to sell or distribute something as a business ⟨∼ in used cars⟩ **6** : to reach a state of acceptance ⟨∼ with her child's death⟩ — **deal·er** *n*

³deal *n* **1** : BARGAINING, NEGOTIATION; *also* : TRANSACTION **2** : treatment received ⟨a raw ∼⟩ **3** : an often secret agreement or arrangement for mutual advantage **4** : BARGAIN

⁴deal *n* : wood or a board of fir or pine

deal·er·ship \'dē-lər-ₐship\ *n* : an authorized sales agency

deal·ing \'dē-liŋ\ *n* **1** : a way of acting or of doing business **2** *pl* : friendly or business transactions

dean \'dēn\ *n* [ME *deen*, fr. MF *deien*, fr. LL *decanus*, lit., chief of ten, fr. Gk *dekanos*, fr. *deka* ten] **1** : a clergyman who is head of a group of canons or of joint pastors of a church **2** : the head of a division, faculty, college, or school of a university **3** : a college or secondary school administrator in charge of counseling and disciplining students **4** : DOYEN ⟨the ∼ of a diplomatic corps⟩ — **dean·ship** *n*

dean·ery \'dē-nə-rē\ *n, pl* **-er·ies** : the office, jurisdiction, or official residence of a clerical dean

¹dear \'dir\ *adj* **1** : highly valued : PRECIOUS **2** : AFFECTIONATE, FOND **3** : EXPENSIVE **4** : HEARTFELT — **dear·ly** *adv* — **dear·ness** *n*

²dear *n* : a loved one : DARLING

Dear John \-'jän\ *n* : a letter (as to a soldier) in which a woman breaks off a marital or romantic relationship

dearth \'dərth\ *n* : SCARCITY, FAMINE

death \'deth\ *n* **1** : the end of life **2** : the cause of loss

of life **3** : the state of being dead **4** : DESTRUCTION, EXTINCTION **5** : SLAUGHTER — **death·like** *adj*

death·bed \-ₐbed\ *n* **1** : the bed in which a person dies **2** : the last hours of life

death·blow \-ₐblō\ *n* : a destructive or killing stroke or event

death·less \-ləs\ *adj* : IMMORTAL, IMPERISHABLE ⟨∼ fame⟩

death·ly \-lē\ *adj* **1** : FATAL **2** : of, relating to, or suggestive of death ⟨a ∼ pallor⟩ — **deathly** *adv*

death rattle *n* : a sound produced by air passing through mucus in the lungs and air passages of a dying person

death's–head \'deths-ₐhed\ *n* : a human skull emblematic of death

death·watch \'deth-ₐwäch\ *n* : a vigil kept over the dead or dying

deb \'deb\ *n* : DEBUTANTE

de·ba·cle \di-'bä-kəl, -'ba-\ *also* **dé·bâ·cle** \same *or* dā-'bäk\ *n* [F *débâcle*] : DISASTER, FAILURE, ROUT ⟨stock market ∼⟩

de·bar \di-'bär\ *vb* : to bar from having or doing something : PRECLUDE

de·bark \di-'bärk\ *vb* : DISEMBARK — **de·bar·ka·tion** \ₐdē-ₐbär-'kā-shən\ *n*

de·base \di-'bās\ *vb* : to lower in character, quality, or value **syn** degrade, corrupt, deprave — **de·base·ment** *n*

de·bate \di-'bāt\ *vb* **de·bat·ed; de·bat·ing** **1** : to discuss a question by considering opposed arguments **2** : to take part in a debate — **de·bat·able** *adj* — **debate** *n* — **de·bat·er** *n*

de·bauch \di-'bóch\ *vb* : SEDUCE, CORRUPT **syn** debase, demoralize, deprave, pervert — **de·bauch·ery** \-'bò-chə-rē\ *n*

de·ben·ture \di-'ben-chər\ *n* : BOND; *esp* : one secured by the general credit of the issuer rather than a lien on particular assets

de·bil·i·tate \di-'bi-lə-ₐtāt\ *vb* **-tat·ed; -tat·ing** : to impair the health or strength of **syn** weaken, disable, enfeeble, undermine

de·bil·i·ty \di-'bi-lə-tē\ *n, pl* **-ties** : an infirm or weakened state

¹deb·it \'de-bət\ *vb* : to enter as a debit : charge with or as a debit

²debit *n* **1** : an entry in an account showing money paid or owed **2** : DISADVANTAGE, SHORTCOMING

debit card *n* : a card by which money may be withdrawn or the cost of purchases paid directly from the holder's bank account

---

deb·o·nair \ₐde-bə-'nar\ *adj* [ME *debonere*, fr. OF *debonaire*, fr. *de bon aire* of good family or nature] : SUAVE, URBANE; *also* : LIGHTHEARTED

---

de·bouch \di-'baúch, -'büsh\ *vb* [F *déboucher*, fr. *dé-* out of + *bouche* mouth] : to come out into an open area : EMERGE

de·brief \di-'brēf\ *vb* : to question (as a pilot back from a mission) in order to obtain useful information

de·bris \də-'brē, dā-; 'dā-ₐbrē\ *n, pl* **debris** \-'brēz, -ₐbrēz\ **1** : the remains of something broken down or destroyed **2** : an accumulation of rock fragments **3** : RUBBISH

debt \'det\ *n* **1** : SIN, TRESPASS **2** : something owed : OBLIGATION **3** : a condition of owing

debt·or \'de-tər\ *n* **1** : one guilty of neglect or violation of duty **2** : one that owes a debt

de·bug \(ₐ)dē-'bəg\ *vb* : to eliminate errors in

de·bunk \dē-'bəŋk\ *vb* : to expose the sham or falseness of ⟨∼ a legend⟩

¹de·but \'dā-ₐbyü, dā-'byü\ *n* **1** : a first appearance **2** : a formal entrance into society

²debut *vb* : to make a debut; *also* : INTRODUCE

deb·u·tante \ˈde-byu̇-ˌtänt\ n : a young woman making her formal entrance into society

dec abbr 1 deceased 2 decrease

Dec abbr December

de·cade \ˈde-ˌkād, de-ˈkād\ n : a period of 10 years

dec·a·dence \ˈde-kə-dəns, di-ˈkād-ᵊns\ n : DETERIORATION, DECLINE — dec·a·dent \ˈde-kə-dənt, di-ˈkād-ᵊnt\ adj or n

de·caf \ˈdē-ˌkaf\ n : decaffeinated coffee

de·caf·fein·at·ed \(ˌ)dē-ˈka-fə-nā-təd\ adj : having the caffeine removed ⟨∼ coffee⟩

deca·gon \ˈde-kə-ˌgän\ n : a plane polygon of 10 angles and 10 sides

de·cal \ˈdē-ˌkal\ n : a picture, design, or label made to be transferred (as to glass) from specially prepared paper

de·cal·co·ma·nia \di-ˌkal-kə-ˈmā-nē-ə\ n [F décalcomanie, fr. décalquer to copy by tracing (fr. calquer to trace, fr. It calcare, lit., to tread, fr. L) + manie mania, fr. LL mania] : DECAL

Deca·logue \ˈde-kə-ˌlȯg\ n : TEN COMMANDMENTS

de·camp \di-ˈkamp\ vb 1 : to break up a camp 2 : to depart suddenly syn escape, abscond, flee

de·cant \di-ˈkant\ vb : to pour (as wine) gently from one vessel into another

de·cant·er \di-ˈkan-tər\ n : an ornamental glass bottle for serving wine

de·cap·i·tate \di-ˈka-pə-ˌtāt\ vb -tat·ed; -tat·ing : BEHEAD — de·cap·i·ta·tion \-ˌka-pə-ˈtā-shən\ n — de·cap·i·ta·tor \-ˈka-pə-ˌtā-tər\ n

deca·syl·lab·ic \ˌde-kə-sə-ˈla-bik\ adj : having or composed of verses having 10 syllables — decasyllabic n

de·cath·lon \di-ˈkath-lən, -ˌlän\ n : a 10-event athletic contest

de·cay \di-ˈkā\ vb 1 : to decline from a sound or prosperous condition 2 : to cause or undergo decomposition ⟨radium ∼s slowly⟩; esp : to break down while spoiling : ROT — decay n

decd abbr deceased

de·cease \di-ˈsēs\ n : DEATH

¹de·ceased \-ˈsēst\ adj : no longer living; esp : recently dead

²deceased n, pl deceased : a dead person

de·ce·dent \di-ˈsēd-ᵊnt\ n : a deceased person

de·ceit \di-ˈsēt\ n 1 : DECEPTION 2 : TRICK 3 : DECEITFULNESS syn dissimulation, duplicity, guile

de·ceit·ful \-fəl\ adj 1 : practicing or tending to practice deceit 2 : MISLEADING, DECEPTIVE ⟨a ∼ answer⟩ — de·ceit·ful·ly adv — de·ceit·ful·ness n

de·ceive \di-ˈsēv\ vb de·ceived; de·ceiv·ing 1 : to cause to believe an untruth 2 : to use or practice deceit syn beguile, betray, delude, mislead — de·ceiv·er n

de·cel·er·ate \dē-ˈse-lə-ˌrāt\ vb -at·ed; -at·ing : to slow down

De·cem·ber \di-ˈsem-bər\ n [ME Decembre, fr. OF, fr. L December (tenth month), fr. decem ten] : the 12th month of the year

de·cen·cy \ˈdēs-ᵊn-sē\ n, pl -cies 1 : PROPRIETY 2 : conformity to standards of taste, propriety, or quality 3 : standard of propriety — usu. used in pl.

de·cen·ni·al \di-ˈse-nē-əl\ adj 1 : consisting of 10 years 2 : happening every 10 years ⟨∼ census⟩

de·cent \ˈdēs-ᵊnt\ adj 1 : conforming to standards of propriety, good taste, or morality 2 : modestly clothed 3 : free from immodesty or obscenity 4 : ADEQUATE ⟨∼ housing⟩ — de·cent·ly adv

de·cen·tral·i·za·tion \dē-ˌsen-trə-lə-ˈzā-shən\ n 1 : the distribution of powers from a central authority to regional and local authorities 2 : the redistribution of population and industry from urban centers to outlying areas — de·cen·tral·ize \-ˈsen-trə-ˌlīz\ vb

de·cep·tion \di-ˈsep-shən\ n 1 : the act of deceiving 2 : the fact or condition of being deceived 3 : FRAUD, TRICK — de·cep·tive \-ˈsep-tiv\ adj — de·cep·tive·ly adv — de·cep·tive·ness n

deci·bel \ˈde-sə-ˌbel, -bəl\ n : a unit for measuring the relative loudness of sounds

de·cide \di-ˈsīd\ vb de·cid·ed; de·cid·ing [ME, fr. MF decider, fr. L decidere, lit., to cut off, fr. de- off + caedere to cut] 1 : to arrive at a solution that ends uncertainty or dispute about 2 : to bring to a definitive end ⟨one blow decided the fight⟩ 3 : to induce to come to a choice 4 : to make a choice or judgment

de·cid·ed \di-ˈsī-dəd\ adj 1 : UNQUESTIONABLE 2 : FIRM, DETERMINED — de·cid·ed·ly adv

de·cid·u·ous \di-ˈsi-jə-wəs\ adj 1 : falling off or out usu. at the end of a period of growth or function ⟨∼ leaves⟩ ⟨a ∼ tooth⟩ 2 : having deciduous parts ⟨∼ trees⟩

deci·gram \ˈde-sə-ˌgram\ n — see METRIC SYSTEM table

deci·li·ter \-ˈlē-tər\ n — see METRIC SYSTEM table

¹deci·mal \ˈde-sə-məl\ adj : based on the number 10 : reckoning by tens

²decimal n : any number expressed in base 10; esp : DECIMAL FRACTION

decimal fraction n : a fraction (as .25 = $^{25}/_{100}$ or .025 = $^{25}/_{1000}$) or mixed number (as 3.025 = 3 $^{25}/_{1000}$) in which the denominator is a power of 10 usu. expressed by use of the decimal point

decimal point n : a period, centered dot, or in some countries a comma at the left of a decimal fraction (as .678) less than one or between a whole number and a decimal fraction in a mixed number (as 3.678)

deci·mate \ˈde-sə-ˌmāt\ vb -mat·ed; -mat·ing 1 : to take or destroy the 10th part of 2 : to destroy a large part of

deci·me·ter \ˈde-sə-ˌmē-tər\ n — see METRIC SYSTEM table

de·ci·pher \di-ˈsī-fər\ vb 1 : DECODE 2 : to make out the meaning of despite indistinctness — de·ci·pher·able adj

de·ci·sion \di-ˈsi-zhən\ n 1 : the act or result of deciding 2 : promptness and firmness in deciding : DETERMINATION

de·ci·sive \-ˈsī-siv\ adj 1 : having the power to decide ⟨the ∼ vote⟩ 2 : RESOLUTE, DETERMINED 3 : CONCLU-

SIVE ⟨a ∼ victory⟩ — **de·ci·sive·ly** *adv* — **de·ci·sive·ness** *n*

¹deck \'dek\ *n* **1** : a floorlike platform of a ship; *also* : something resembling the deck of a ship **2** : a pack of playing cards

²deck *vb* **1** : ARRAY **2** : DECORATE **3** : to furnish with a deck **4** : KNOCK DOWN, FLOOR

deck·hand \'dek-ˌhand\ *n* : a sailor who performs manual duties

deck·le edge \'dek-əl-\ *n* : the rough untrimmed edge of paper — **deck·le-edged** \-'ejd\ *adj*

de·claim \di-'klām\ *vb* : to speak or deliver in the manner of a formal speech — **dec·la·ma·tion** \ˌde-klə-'mā-shən\ *n* — **de·clam·a·to·ry** \di-'kla-mə-ˌtōr-ē\ *adj*

de·clar·a·tive \di-'klar-ə-tiv\ *adj* : making a declaration ⟨∼ sentence⟩

de·clare \di-'klar\ *vb* **de·clared; de·clar·ing 1** : to make known formally, officially, or explicitly : AN-NOUNCE ⟨∼ war⟩ **2** : to state emphatically : AFFIRM **3** : to make a full statement of **syn** blazon, broadcast, proclaim, publish — **dec·la·ra·tion** \ˌde-klə-'rā-shən\ *n* — **de·clar·a·to·ry** \di-'klar-ə-ˌtōr-ē\ *adj* — **de·clar·er** *n*

de·clas·si·fy \dē-'kla-sə-ˌfī\ *vb* : to remove the security classification of — **de·clas·si·fi·ca·tion** \-ˌkla-sə-fə-'kā-shən\ *n*

de·clen·sion \di-'klen-chən\ *n* **1** : the inflectional forms of a noun, pronoun, or adjective **2** : DECLINE, DETE-RIORATION **3** : DESCENT, SLOPE

¹de·cline \di-'klīn\ *vb* **de·clined; de·clin·ing 1** : to slope downward : DESCEND **2** : DROOP **3** : RECEDE **4** : WANE **5** : to withhold consent; *also* : REFUSE, REJECT **6** : IN-FLECT **2** ⟨∼ a noun⟩ — **de·clin·able** *adj* — **dec·li·na·tion** \ˌde-klə-'nā-shən\ *n*

²decline *n* **1** : a gradual sinking and wasting away **2** : a change to a lower state or level **3** : the time when something is approaching its end **4** : a descending slope

de·cliv·i·ty \di-'kli-və-tē\ *n, pl* **-ties** : a steep downward slope

de·code \dē-'kōd\ *vb* : to convert (a coded message) into ordinary language — **de·cod·er** *n*

dé·col·le·té \dā-ˌkäl-'tā\ *adj* [F] **1** : wearing a strapless or low-necked gown **2** : having a low-cut neckline

de·com·mis·sion \ˌdē-kə-'mi-shən\ *vb* : to remove from service

de·com·pose \ˌdē-kəm-'pōz\ *vb* **1** : to separate into constituent parts **2** : to break down in decay : ROT — **de·com·po·si·tion** \dē-ˌkäm-pə-'zi-shən\ *n*

de·com·press \ˌdē-kəm-'pres\ *vb* : to release from pressure or compression — **de·com·pres·sion** \-'pre-shən\ *n*

de·con·ges·tant \ˌdē-kən-'jes-tənt\ *n* : an agent that re-lieves congestion (as of mucous membranes)

de·con·tam·i·nate \ˌdē-kən-'ta-mə-ˌnāt\ *vb* : to rid of contamination (as radioactive material) — **de·con·tam·i·na·tion** \-ˌta-mə-'nā-shən\ *n*

de·con·trol \ˌdē-kən-'trōl\ *vb* : to end control of ⟨∼ prices⟩ — **decontrol** *n*

de·cor *or* **dé·cor** \dā-'kòr, 'dā-ˌkòr\ *n* : DECORATION; *esp* : the style and layout of interior furnishings

dec·o·rate \'de-kə-ˌrāt\ *vb* **-rat·ed; -rat·ing 1** : to fur-nish with something ornamental ⟨∼ a room⟩ **2** : to award a mark of honor (as a medal) to **syn** adorn, beautify, bedeck, garnish, ornament

dec·o·ra·tion \ˌde-kə-'rā-shən\ *n* **1** : the act or process of decorating **2** : ORNAMENT **3** : a badge of honor

dec·o·ra·tive \'de-kə-rə-tiv\ *adj* : ORNAMENTAL

dec·o·ra·tor \'de-kə-ˌrā-tər\ *n* : one that decorates; *esp* : a person who designs or executes interiors and their furnishings

dec·o·rous \'de-kə-rəs, di-'kòr-əs\ *adj* : PROPER, SEEM-LY, CORRECT

de·co·rum \di-'kòr-əm\ *n* [L] **1** : conformity to accept-ed standards of conduct **2** : ORDERLINESS, PROPRIETY

¹de·coy \'dē-ˌkòi, di-'kòi\ *n* **1** : something that lures or entices; *esp* : an artificial bird used to attract live birds within shot **2** : something used to draw attention away from another

²de·coy \di-'kòi, 'dē-ˌkòi\ *vb* : to lure by or as if by a decoy : ENTICE

¹de·crease \di-'krēs\ *vb* **de·creased; de·creas·ing** : to grow or cause to grow less : DIMINISH

²de·crease \'dē-ˌkrēs\ *n* **1** : the process of decreasing **2** : REDUCTION

¹de·cree \di-'krē\ *n* **1** : ORDER, EDICT **2** : a judicial de-cision

²decree *vb* **de·creed; de·cree·ing 1** : COMMAND **2** : to de-termine or order judicially **syn** dictate, ordain, pre-scribe

dec·re·ment \'de-krə-mənt\ *n* **1** : gradual decrease **2** : the quantity lost by diminution or waste

de·crep·it \di-'kre-pət\ *adj* : broken down with age : WORN-OUT — **de·crep·i·tude** \-pə-ˌtüd, -ˌtyüd\ *n*

de·cre·scen·do \ˌdā-krə-'shen-dō\ *adv or adj* : with a decrease in volume — used as a direction in music

de·crim·i·nal·ize \dē-'kri-mən-ᵊl-ˌīz\ *vb* : to remove or reduce the criminal status of

de·cry \di-'krī\ *vb* : to express strong disapproval of

ded·i·cate \'de-di-ˌkāt\ *vb* **-cat·ed; -cat·ing 1** : to de-vote to the worship of a divine being esp. with sacred rites **2** : to set apart for a definite purpose **3** : to in-scribe or address as a compliment — **ded·i·ca·tion** \ˌde-di-'kā-shən\ *n* — **ded·i·ca·tor** \'de-di-ˌkā-tər\ *n* — **ded·i·ca·to·ry** \-kə-ˌtōr-ē\ *adj*

de·duce \di-'düs, -'dyüs\ *vb* **de·duced; de·duc·ing 1** : to derive by reasoning : INFER **2** : to trace the course of — **de·duc·ible** *adj*

de·duct \di-'dəkt\ *vb* : SUBTRACT — **de·duct·ible** *adj*

de·duc·tion \di-'dək-shən\ *n* **1** : SUBTRACTION **2** : some-thing that is or may be subtracted **3** : the deriving of a conclusion by reasoning : the conclusion so reached — **de·duc·tive** \-'dək-tiv\ *adj* — **de·duc·tive·ly** *adv*

¹deed \'dēd\ *n* **1** : something done **2** : FEAT, EXPLOIT **3** : a document containing some legal transfer, bargain, or contract

²**deed** \vb : to convey or transfer by deed

dee·jay \ˈdē-ˌjā\ n : DISC JOCKEY

deem \ˈdēm\ vb : THINK, JUDGE **syn** consider, account, reckon, regard, view

de–em·pha·size \dē-ˈem-fə-ˌsīz\ vb : to reduce in relative importance; *also* : to attach little importance to — **de–em·pha·sis** \-səs\ n

¹**deep** \ˈdēp\ adj **1** : extending far down, back, within, or outward **2** : having a specified extension downward or backward **3** : difficult to understand; *also* : MYSTERIOUS, OBSCURE ⟨a ~ dark secret⟩ **4** : WISE **5** : ENGROSSED, INVOLVED ⟨~ in thought⟩ **6** : INTENSE, PROFOUND ⟨~ sleep⟩ **7** : dark and rich in color ⟨a ~ red⟩ **8** : having a low musical pitch or range ⟨a ~ voice⟩ **9** : situated well within **10** : covered, enclosed, or filled often to a specified degree — **deep·ly** adv

²**deep** adv **1** : DEEPLY **2** : far on : LATE ⟨~ in the night⟩

³**deep** n **1** : an extremely deep place or part; *esp* : OCEAN **2** : the middle or most intense part ⟨the ~ of winter⟩

deep·en \ˈdē-pən\ vb : to make or become deep or deeper

deep–freeze \ˈdēp-ˈfrēz\ vb **-froze** \-ˈfrōz\; **-fro·zen** \-ˈfrōz-ᵊn\ : QUICK-FREEZE

deep–fry vb : to cook in enough oil to cover the food being fried

deep pocket n **1** : one having substantial financial resources **2** pl : substantial financial resources

deep–root·ed \ˈdēp-ˈrü-təd, -ˈrü-\ adj : deeply implanted or established

deep–sea \ˈdēp-ˈsē\ adj : of, relating to, or occurring in the deeper parts of the sea ⟨~ fishing⟩

deep–seat·ed \ˈdēp-ˈsē-təd\ adj **1** : situated far below the surface **2** : firmly established ⟨~ convictions⟩

deer \ˈdir\ n, pl **deer** [ME, deer, animal, fr. OE *dēor* beast] : any of numerous ruminant mammals with cloven hoofs and usu. antlers esp. in the males

deer·fly \-ˌflī\ n : any of numerous small horseflies

deer·skin \-ˌskin\ n : leather made from the skin of a deer; *also* : a garment of such leather

de·es·ca·late \dē-ˈes-kə-ˌlāt\ vb : to decrease in extent, volume, or scope : LIMIT — **de·es·ca·la·tion** \-ˌes-kə-ˈlā-shən\ n

def abbr **1** defendant **2** definite **3** definition

de·face \di-ˈfās\ vb : to destroy or mar the face or surface of — **de·face·ment** n — **de·fac·er** n

de fac·to \di-ˈfak-tō, dā-\ adj or adv **1** : actually existing ⟨*de facto* segregation⟩ **2** : actually exercising power ⟨*de facto* government⟩

de·fal·ca·tion \di-ˌfal-ˈkā-shən, -ˌfôl-; ˌdē-fəl-\ n : EMBEZZLEMENT

de·fame \di-ˈfām\ vb **de·famed**; **de·fam·ing** : to injure or destroy the reputation of by libel or slander **syn** calumniate, denigrate, libel, malign, slander, vilify — **def·a·ma·tion** \ˌde-fə-ˈmā-shən\ n — **de·fam·a·to·ry** \di-ˈfa-mə-ˌtōr-ē\ adj

de·fault \di-ˈfôlt\ n **1** : failure to do something required by duty or law; *also* : failure to appear for a legal proceeding **2** : failure to compete in or to finish an appointed contest ⟨lose a race by ~⟩ — **default** vb — **de·fault·er** n

¹**de·feat** \di-ˈfēt\ vb **1** : FRUSTRATE, NULLIFY **2** : to win victory over : BEAT

²**defeat** n **1** : FRUSTRATION **2** : an overthrow of an army in battle **3** : loss of a contest

de·feat·ism \-ˈfē-ˌti-zəm\ n : acceptance of or resignation to defeat — **de·feat·ist** \-tist\ n or adj

def·e·cate \ˈde-fi-ˌkāt\ vb **-cat·ed**; **-cat·ing** **1** : to free from impurity or corruption **2** : to discharge feces from the bowels — **def·e·ca·tion** \ˌde-fi-ˈkā-shən\ n

¹**de·fect** \ˈdē-ˌfekt, di-ˈfekt\ n : BLEMISH, FAULT, IMPERFECTION

²**de·fect** \di-ˈfekt\ vb : to desert a cause or party esp. in order to espouse another — **de·fec·tion** \-ˈfek-shən\ n — **de·fec·tor** \-ˈfek-tər\ n

de·fec·tive \di-ˈfek-tiv\ adj : FAULTY, DEFICIENT — **de·fective** n

de·fence chiefly Brit var of DEFENSE

de·fend \di-ˈfend\ vb [ME, fr. OF *defendre*, fr. L *defendere*, fr. *de*- from + *-fendere* to strike] **1** : to repel danger or attack from **2** : to act as attorney for **3** : to oppose the claim of another in a lawsuit : CONTEST **4** : to maintain against opposition ⟨~ an idea⟩ — **de·fend·er** n

de·fen·dant \di-ˈfen-dənt\ n : a person required to make answer in a legal action or suit

de·fense \di-ˈfens\ n **1** : the act of defending : resistance against attack **2** : means, method, or capability of defending **3** : an argument in support **4** : the answer made by the defendant in a legal action **5** : a defending party, group, or team — **de·fense·less** adj — **de·fen·si·ble** adj

defense mechanism n : an often unconscious mental process (as repression) that assists in reaching compromise solutions to personal problems

¹**de·fen·sive** \di-ˈfen-siv\ adj **1** : serving or intended to defend or protect **2** : of or relating to the attempt to keep an opponent from scoring (as in a game) — **de·fen·sive·ly** adv — **de·fen·sive·ness** n

²**defensive** n : a defensive position

¹**de·fer** \di-ˈfər\ vb **de·ferred**; **de·fer·ring** [ME *deferren*, *differren*, fr. MF *differer*, fr. L *differre* to postpone, be different] : POSTPONE, PUT OFF

²**defer** vb **deferred**; **deferring** [ME *deferren*, *differren*, fr. MF *deferer*, *defferer*, fr. LL *deferre*, fr. L, to bring down, bring, fr. *de*- down + *ferre* to carry] : to submit or yield to the opinion or wishes of another

def·er·ence \ˈde-fər-əns\ n : courteous, respectful, or ingratiating regard for another's wishes **syn** honor, homage, obeisance, reverence — **def·er·en·tial** \ˌde-fə-ˈren-chəl\ adj

de·fer·ment \di-ˈfər-mənt\ n : the act of delaying; *esp* : official postponement of military service

de·fi·ance \di-ˈfī-əns\ n **1** : CHALLENGE **2** : disposition to resist or contend

de·fi·ant \-ənt\ adj : full of defiance : BOLD — **de·fi·ant·ly** adv

de·fi·bril·la·tor \dē-'fi-brə-,lā-tər\ n : an electronic device that applies an electric shock to restore the rhythm of a fibrillating heart — **de·fi·bril·late** \-,lāt\ vb — **de·fi·bril·la·tion** \-,fi-brə-'lā-shən\ n

deficiency disease n : a disease (as scurvy or beriberi) caused by a lack of essential dietary elements and esp. a vitamin or mineral

de·fi·cient \di-'fi-shənt\ adj : lacking in something necessary; also : not up to a normal standard — **de·fi·cien·cy** \-shən-sē\ n

def·i·cit \'de-fə-sət\ n : a deficiency in amount; esp : an excess of expenditures over revenue

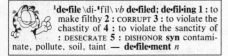 **¹de·file** \di-'fīl\ vb **de·filed; de·fil·ing 1 :** to make filthy **2 :** CORRUPT **3 :** to violate the chastity of **4 :** to violate the sanctity of **:** DESECRATE **5 :** DISHONOR **syn** contaminate, pollute, soil, taint — **de·file·ment** n

²de·file \di-'fīl, 'dē-,fīl\ n : a narrow passage or gorge
de·fine \di-'fīn\ vb **de·fined; de·fin·ing 1 :** to set forth the meaning of ⟨∼ a word⟩ **2 :** to fix or mark the limits of **3 :** to clarify in outline or character — **de·fin·able** adj — **de·fin·er** n
def·i·nite \'de-fə-nət\ adj **1 :** having distinct limits **:** FIXED **2 :** clear in meaning **3 :** typically designating an identified or immediately identifiable person or thing — **def·i·nite·ly** adv — **def·i·nite·ness** n
def·i·ni·tion \,de-fə-'ni-shən\ n **1 :** an act of determining or settling **2 :** a statement of the meaning of a word or word group; also : the action or process of defining **3 :** the action or the power of making definite and clear **:** CLARITY, DISTINCTNESS
de·fin·i·tive \di-'fi-nə-tiv\ adj **1 :** DECISIVE, CONCLUSIVE **2 :** authoritative and apparently exhaustive **3 :** serving to define or specify precisely
de·flate \di-'flāt\ vb **de·flat·ed; de·flat·ing 1 :** to release air or gas from **2 :** to reduce in size, importance, or effectiveness; also : to reduce from a state of inflation **3 :** to become deflated
de·fla·tion \-'flā-shən\ n **1 :** an act or instance of deflating **:** the state of being deflated **2 :** reduction in the volume of available money or credit resulting in a decline of the general price level
de·flect \di-'flekt\ vb : to turn aside — **de·flec·tion** \-'flek-shən\ n
de·flo·ra·tion \,de-flə-'rā-shən\ n : rupture of the hymen
de·flow·er \dē-'flaů(-ə)r\ vb : to deprive of virginity
de·fog \dē-'fóg, -'fäg\ vb : to remove fog or condensed moisture from — **de·fog·ger** n
de·fo·li·ant \dē-'fō-lē-ənt\ n : a chemical spray or dust used to defoliate plants
de·fo·li·ate \-,āt\ vb : to deprive of leaves esp. prematurely — **de·fo·li·a·tion** \dē-,fō-lē-'ā-shən\ n — **de·fo·li·a·tor** \dē-'fō-lē-,ā-tər\ n
de·for·es·ta·tion \dē-,for-ə-'stā-shən\ n : the action or process of clearing an area of forests; also : the state of having been cleared of forests — **de·for·est** \(,)dē-'for-əst, -'fär-\ vb

de·form \di-'fórm\ vb **1 :** DISFIGURE, DEFACE **2 :** to make or become misshapen or changed in shape — **de·for·ma·tion** \,dē-,for-'mā-shən, ,de-fər-\ n
de·for·mi·ty \di-'fór-mə-tē\ n, pl **-ties 1 :** the state of being deformed **2 :** a physical blemish or distortion
de·fraud \di-'fród\ vb : CHEAT
de·fray \di-'frā\ vb : to provide for the payment of **:** PAY — **de·fray·al** n
de·frock \(,)dē-'fräk\ vb : to deprive (as a priest) of the right to exercise the functions of office
de·frost \di-'fróst\ vb **1 :** to thaw out **2 :** to free from ice — **de·frost·er** n
deft \'deft\ adj : quick and neat in action — **deft·ly** adv — **deft·ness** n
de·funct \di-'fəŋkt\ adj : DEAD, EXTINCT
de·fuse \dē-'fyüz\ vb **1 :** to remove the fuse from (a bomb) **2 :** to make less harmful, potent, or tense
de·fy \di-'fī\ vb **de·fied; de·fy·ing** [ME, to renounce faith in, challenge, fr. OF defier, fr. de- from + fier to entrust, ultim. fr. L fidere to trust] **1 :** CHALLENGE, DARE **2 :** to refuse boldly to obey or to yield to **:** DISREGARD ⟨∼ the law⟩ **3 :** WITHSTAND, BAFFLE ⟨a scene that defies description⟩
deg abbr degree
de·gas \dē-'gas\ vb : to remove gas from
de·gen·er·a·cy \di-'je-nə-rə-sē\ n, pl **-cies 1 :** the state of being degenerate **2 :** the process of becoming degenerate **3 :** PERVERSION
¹de·gen·er·ate \di-'je-nə-rət\ adj : fallen or deteriorated from a former, higher, or normal condition — **de·gen·er·a·tion** \-,je-nə-'rā-shən\ n — **de·gen·er·a·tive** \-'je-nə-,rā-tiv\ adj
²de·gen·er·ate \di-'je-nə-,rāt\ vb : to undergo deterioration (as in morality, intelligence, structure, or function)
³de·gen·er·ate \-rət\ n : a degenerate person; esp : a sexual pervert
de·grad·able \di-'grā-də-bəl\ adj : capable of being chemically degraded
de·grade \di-'grād\ vb **1 :** to reduce from a higher to a lower rank or degree **2 :** DEBASE, CORRUPT **3 :** DECOMPOSE — **de·gra·da·tion** \,de-grə-'dā-shən\ n
de·gree \di-'grē\ n [ME, fr. OF degré, fr. (assumed) VL degradus, fr. L de- down + gradus step, grade] **1 :** a step in a series **2 :** a rank or grade of official, ecclesiastical, or social position; also : the civil condition of a person **3 :** the extent, intensity, or scope of something esp. as measured by a graded series **4 :** one of the forms or sets of forms used in the comparison of an adjective or adverb **5 :** a title conferred upon students by a college, university, or professional school on completion of a program of study **6 :** a line or space of the musical staff; also : a note or tone of a musical scale **7 :** a unit of measure for angles that is equal to an angle with its vertex at the center of a circle and its sides cutting off ¹⁄₃₆₀ of the circumference; also : a unit of measure of the arc of a circle equal to the amount of arc cut off by an angle of one degree with its vertex at the center of the circle **8 :** any of various units for measuring temperature

GUESTS ARE A PAIN

FIRST THEY DEFILE MY WATER DISH...

THEN THEY WANT A TOW

JIM DAVIS 11-5

© 1991 PAWS, INC.

de·horn \dē-'hȯrn\ *vb* : to deprive of horns
de·hu·man·ize \dē-'hyü-mə-ˌnīz\ *vb* : to deprive of human qualities, personality, or spirit — **de·hu·man·i·za·tion** \ˌdē-ˌhyü-mə-nə-'zā-shən\ *n*
de·hu·mid·i·fy \ˌdē-hyü-'mi-də-ˌfī\ *vb* : to remove moisture from (as the air) — **de·hu·mid·i·fi·er** *n*
de·hy·drate \dē-'hī-ˌdrāt\ *vb* : to remove water from; *also* : to lose liquid — **de·hy·dra·tion** \ˌdē-hī-'drā-shən\ *n*
de·hy·dro·ge·na·tion \ˌdē-(ˌ)hī-ˌdrä-jə-'nā-shən, -drə-\ *n* : the removal of hydrogen from a chemical compound — **de·hy·dro·ge·nate** \ˌdē-(ˌ)hī-'drä-jə-ˌnāt, dē-'hī-drə-jə-\ *vb*
de·ice \dē-'īs\ *vb* : to keep free or rid of ice — **de·ic·er** *n*
de·i·fy \'dē-ə-ˌfī\ *vb* **-fied; -fy·ing 1** : to make a god of **2** : WORSHIP, GLORIFY — **de·i·fi·ca·tion** \ˌdē-ə-fə-'kā-shən\ *n*
deign \'dān\ *vb* [ME, fr. OF *deignier*, fr. L *dignare, dignari*, fr. *dignus* worthy] : CONDESCEND
de·ion·ize \dē-'ī-ə-ˌnīz\ *vb* : to remove ions from
de·ism \'dē-ˌi-zəm\ *n*, *often cap* : a system of thought advocating natural religion based on human morality and reason rather than divine revelation — **de·ist** \'dē-ist\ *n, often cap* — **de·is·tic** \dē-'is-tik\ *adj*
de·i·ty \'dē-ə-tē, 'dā-\ *n, pl* **-ties 1** : DIVINITY **2 2** *cap* : GOD 1 **3** : a god or goddess
dé·jà vu \ˌdā-ˌzhä-'vü\ *n* [F, adj., already seen] : the feeling that one has seen or heard something before
de·ject·ed \di-'jek-təd\ *adj* : low in spirits : SAD — **de·ject·ed·ly** *adv*
de·jec·tion \di-'jek-shən\ *n* : lowness of spirits
de ju·re \dē-'ju̇r-ē\ *adv or adj* [ML] : by legal right
deka·gram \'de-kə-ˌgram\ *n* — see METRIC SYSTEM table
deka·li·ter \-ˌlē-tər\ *n* — see METRIC SYSTEM table
deka·me·ter \-ˌmē-tər\ *n* — see METRIC SYSTEM table
del *abbr* delegate; delegation
Del *abbr* Delaware
Del·a·ware \'de-lə-ˌwar\ *n, pl* **Delaware** *or* **Delawares** : a member of an American Indian people orig. of the Delaware valley; *also* : their language
¹de·lay \di-'lā\ *n* **1** : the act of delaying : the state of being delayed **2** : the time for which something is delayed
²delay *vb* **1** : POSTPONE, PUT OFF **2** : to stop, detain, or hinder for a time **3** : to move or act slowly
de·lec·ta·ble \di-'lek-tə-bəl\ *adj* **1** : highly pleasing : DELIGHTFUL **2** : DELICIOUS
de·lec·ta·tion \ˌdē-ˌlek-'tā-shən\ *n* : DELIGHT, PLEASURE, DIVERSION
¹del·e·gate \'de-li-gət, -ˌgāt\ *n* **1** : DEPUTY, REPRESENTATIVE **2** : a member of the lower house of the legislature of Maryland, Virginia, or West Virginia
²del·e·gate \-ˌgāt\ *vb* **-gat·ed; -gat·ing 1** : to entrust to another (⟨ authority⟩) **2** : to appoint as one's delegate
del·e·ga·tion \ˌde-li-'gā-shən\ *n* **1** : the act of delegating **2** : one or more persons chosen to represent others
de·lete \di-'lēt\ *vb* **de·let·ed; de·let·ing** [L *delēre* to wipe out, destroy] : to eliminate esp. by blotting out, cutting out, or erasing — **de·le·tion** \-'lē-shən\ *n*
del·e·te·ri·ous \ˌde-lə-'tir-ē-əs\ *adj* : HARMFUL, NOXIOUS
delft \'delft\ *n* **1** : a Dutch pottery with an opaque white glaze and predominantly blue decoration **2** : glazed pottery esp. when blue and white
delft·ware \-ˌwar\ *n* : DELFT
deli \'de-lē\ *n, pl* **del·is** : DELICATESSEN
¹de·lib·er·ate \di-'li-bə-ˌrāt\ *vb* **-at·ed; -at·ing** : to consider carefully — **de·lib·er·a·tion** \-ˌli-bə-'rā-shən\ *n* — **de·lib·er·a·tive** \-'li-bə-ˌrā-tiv, -brə-tiv\ *adj* — **de·lib·er·a·tive·ly** *adv*
²de·lib·er·ate \di-'li-bə-rət, -'li-brət\ *adj* [L *deliberare* to consider carefully, fr. *libra* scale, pound] **1** : determined after careful thought **2** : done or said intention-

ally **3** : UNHURRIED, SLOW — **de·lib·er·ate·ly** *adv* — **de·lib·er·ate·ness** *n*
del·i·ca·cy \'de-li-kə-sē\ *n, pl* **-cies 1** : something pleasing to eat and considered rare or luxurious **2** : FINENESS, DAINTINESS; *also* : FRAILTY **3** : nicety or expressiveness of touch **4** : precise perception and discrimination : SENSITIVITY **5** : sensibility in feeling or conduct; *also* : SQUEAMISHNESS **6** : the quality or state of requiring delicate handling
del·i·cate \'de-li-kət\ *adj* **1** : pleasing to the senses of taste or smell esp. in a mild or subtle way **2** : marked by daintiness or charm : EXQUISITE **3** : FASTIDIOUS, SQUEAMISH, SCRUPULOUS **4** : easily damaged : FRAGILE; *also* : SICKLY **5** : requiring skill or tact **6** : marked by care, skill, or tact **7** : marked by minute precision : very sensitive — **del·i·cate·ly** *adv*
del·i·ca·tes·sen \ˌde-li-kə-'tes-ᵊn\ *n pl* [G, pl. of *Delicatesse* delicacy, fr. F *délicatesse*] **1** : ready-to-eat food products (as cooked meats and prepared salads) **2** *sing, pl* **delicatessens** : a store where delicatessen are sold
de·li·cious \di-'li-shəs\ *adj* : affording great pleasure : DELIGHTFUL; *esp* : very pleasing to the taste or smell — **de·li·cious·ly** *adv* — **de·li·cious·ness** *n*
¹de·light \di-'līt\ *n* **1** : great pleasure or satisfaction : JOY **2** : something that gives great pleasure — **de·light·ful** \-fəl\ *adj* — **de·light·ful·ly** *adv*
²delight *vb* **1** : to take great pleasure **2** : to satisfy greatly : PLEASE
de·light·ed *adj* : highly pleased : GRATIFIED — **de·light·ed·ly** *adv*
de·lim·it \di-'li-mət\ *vb* : to fix the limits of
de·lin·eate \di-'li-nē-ˌāt\ *vb* **-eat·ed; -eat·ing 1** : SKETCH, PORTRAY **2** : to picture in words : DESCRIBE — **de·lin·ea·tion** \-ˌli-nē-'ā-shən\ *n*
de·lin·quen·cy \di-'liŋ-kwən-sē\ *n, pl* **-cies** : the quality or state of being delinquent
¹de·lin·quent \-kwənt\ *n* : a delinquent person
²delinquent *adj* **1** : offending by neglect or violation of duty or of law **2** : being overdue in payment
del·i·quesce \ˌde-li-'kwes\ *vb* **-quesced; -quesc·ing** : MELT, DISSOLVE — **del·i·ques·cent** \-'kwes-ᵊnt\ *adj*
de·lir·i·um \di-'lir-ē-əm\ *n* [L, fr. *delirare* to be crazy, lit., to leave the furrow (in plowing), fr. *de-* from + *lira* furrow] : mental disturbance marked by confusion, disordered speech, and hallucinations; *also* : frenzied excitement — **de·lir·i·ous** \-ē-əs\ *adj* — **de·lir·i·ous·ly** *adv*
delirium tre·mens \-'trē-mənz, -'tre-\ *n* : a violent delirium with tremors that is induced by excessive and prolonged use of alcoholic liquors
de·liv·er \di-'li-vər\ *vb* **-ered; -er·ing 1** : to set free : SAVE **2** : CONVEY, TRANSFER (⟨ a letter⟩) **3** : to assist in giving birth or at the birth of; *also* : to give birth to **4** : UTTER, COMMUNICATE **5** : to send to an intended target or destination — **de·liv·er·ance** *n* — **de·liv·er·er** *n*
de·liv·ery \di-'li-və-rē\ *n, pl* **-er·ies** : the act of delivering something; *also* : something delivered — **de·liv·ery·man** \-ˌman\ *n*
dell \'del\ *n* : a small secluded valley
de·louse \dē-'laus\ *vb* : to remove lice from
del·phin·i·um \del-'fi-nē-əm\ *n* : any of a genus of mostly perennial herbs related to the buttercups with tall branching spikes of irregular flowers
del·ta \'del-tə\ *n* **1** : the 4th letter of the Greek alphabet — Δ or δ **2** : something shaped like a capital Δ; *esp* : the triangular silt-formed land at the mouth of a river — **del·ta·ic** \del-'tā-ik\ *adj*
de·lude \di-'lüd\ *vb* **de·lud·ed; de·lud·ing** : MISLEAD, DECEIVE, TRICK
¹del·uge \'del-ˌyüj\ *n* **1** : a flooding of land by water **2** : a drenching rain **3** : a great amount or number
²deluge *vb* **del·uged; del·ug·ing 1** : INUNDATE, FLOOD **2** : to overwhelm as if with a deluge
de·lu·sion \di-'lü-zhən\ *n* : a deluding or being deluded;

esp : a persistent false psychotic belief — **de·lu·sion·al** \-'lü-zhə-nəl\ *adj* — **de·lu·sive** \-'lü-siv\ *adj*

de·luxe \di-'lüks, -'ləks, -'lüks\ *adj* : notably luxurious or elegant

delve \'delv\ *vb* **delved; delv·ing 1** : DIG **2** : to seek laboriously for information

dely *abbr* delivery

Dem *abbr* Democrat; Democratic

de·mag·ne·tize \dē-'mag-nə-ˌtīz\ *vb* : to cause to lose magnetic properties — **de·mag·ne·ti·za·tion** \dē-ˌmag-nə-tə-'zā-shən\ *n*

dem·a·gogue *or* **dem·a·gog** \'de-mə-ˌgäg\ *n* [Gk *dēmagōgos*, fr. *dēmos* people + *agōgos* leading, fr. *agein* to lead] : a person who appeals to the emotions and prejudices of people esp. in order to gain political power — **dem·a·gogu·ery** \-ˌgä-gə-rē\ *n* — **dem·a·gogy** \-ˌgä-gē, -ˌgä-jē\ *n*

¹de·mand \di-'mand\ *n* **1** : an act of demanding; *also* : something claimed as due or just **2** : the ability and desire to buy goods or services; *also* : the quantity of goods wanted at a stated price **3** : a seeking or being sought after : urgent need **4** : a pressing need or requirement

²demand *vb* **1** : to ask for with authority : claim as due or just **2** : to ask earnestly or in the manner of a command **3** : REQUIRE, NEED

de·mar·cate \di-'mär-ˌkāt, 'dē-ˌmär-\ *vb* **-cat·ed; -cat·ing 1** : DELIMIT **2** : SEPARATE — **de·mar·ca·tion** \ˌdē-ˌmär-'kā-shən\ *n*

dé·marche *or* **de·marche** \dā-'märsh\ *n* : a course of action : MANEUVER

¹de·mean \di-'mēn\ *vb* **de·meaned; de·mean·ing** : to behave or conduct (oneself) usu. in a proper manner

²demean *vb* **de·meaned; de·mean·ing** : DEGRADE, DEBASE

de·mean·or \di-'mē-nər\ *n* : CONDUCT, BEARING

de·mean·our *Brit var of* DEMEANOR

de·ment·ed \di-'men-təd\ *adj* : MAD, INSANE — **de·ment·ed·ly** *adv*

de·men·tia \di-'men-chə\ *n* **1** : mental deterioration **2** : INSANITY

de·mer·it \di-'mer-ət\ *n* **1** : FAULT **2** : a mark placed against a person's record for some fault or offense

de·mesne \di-'mān, -'mēn\ *n* **1** : REALM **2** : manorial land actually possessed by the lord and not held by free tenants **3** : ESTATE **4** : REGION

demi·god \'de-mi-ˌgäd\ *n* : a mythological being with more power than a mortal but less than a god

demi·john \'de-mi-ˌjän\ *n* [F *dame-jeanne*, lit., Lady Jane] : a large narrow-necked bottle usu. enclosed in wickerwork

de·mil·i·ta·rize \dē-'mi-lə-tə-ˌrīz\ *vb* : to strip of military forces, weapons, or fortifications — **de·mil·i·tar·i·za·tion** \dē-ˌmi-lə-tə-rə-'zā-shən\ *n*

demi·mon·daine \ˌde-mi-ˌmän-'dān\ *n* : a woman of the demimonde

demi·monde \'de-mi-ˌmänd\ *n* [F *demi-monde*, fr. *demi-* half + *monde* world] **1** : a class of women on the fringes of respectable society supported by wealthy lovers **2** : a group engaged in activity of doubtful legality or propriety

de·min·er·al·ize \dē-'mi-nə-rə-ˌlīz\ *vb* : to remove the mineral matter from — **de·min·er·al·i·za·tion** \-ˌmi-nə-rə-lə-'zā-shən\ *n*

de·mise \di-'mīz\ *n* **1** : LEASE **2** : transfer of sovereignty to a successor ⟨~ of the crown⟩ **3** : DEATH **4** : loss of status

demi·tasse \'de-mi-ˌtas\ *n* : a small cup of black coffee; *also* : the cup used to serve it

de·mo·bi·lize \di-'mō-bə-ˌlīz, dē-\ *vb* **1** : DISBAND **2** : to discharge from military service — **de·mo·bi·li·za·tion** \di-ˌmō-bə-lə-'zā-shən, dē-\ *n*

de·moc·ra·cy \di-'mä-krə-sē\ *n, pl* **-cies** [MF *democratie*, fr. LL *democratia*, fr. Gk *dēmokratia*, fr. *dēmos* people + *kratos* strength, power] **1** : government by the people; *esp* : rule of the majority **2** : a

government in which the supreme power is held by the people **3** : a political unit that has a democratic government **4** *cap* : the principles and policies of the Democratic party in the U.S. **5** : the common people esp. when constituting the source of political authority **6** : the absence of hereditary or arbitrary class distinctions or privileges

dem·o·crat \'de-mə-ˌkrat\ *n* **1** : one who believes in or practices democracy **2** *cap* : a member of the Democratic party of the U.S.

dem·o·crat·ic \ˌde-mə-'kra-tik\ *adj* **1** : of, relating to, or favoring democracy **2** *often cap* : of or relating to one of the two major political parties in the U.S. associated in modern times with policies of broad social reform and internationalism **3** : relating to or appealing to the common people ⟨~ art⟩ **4** : not snobbish — **dem·o·crat·i·cal·ly** \-ti-k(ə-)lē\ *adv*

de·moc·ra·tize \di-'mä-krə-ˌtīz\ *vb* **-tized; -tiz·ing** : to make democratic

dé·mo·dé \ˌdā-mō-'dā\ *adj* [F] : no longer fashionable : OUT-OF-DATE

de·mo·graph·ics \ˌde-mə-'gra-fiks, ˌdē-\ *n pl* : the statistical characteristics of human populations

de·mog·ra·phy \di-'mä-grə-fē\ *n* : the statistical study of human populations and esp. their size and distribution and the number of births and deaths — **de·mog·ra·pher** \-fər\ *n* — **de·mo·graph·ic** \ˌde-mə-'gra-fik, ˌdē-\ *adj* — **de·mo·graph·i·cal·ly** \-fi-k(ə-)lē\ *adv*

dem·oi·selle \ˌdem-wə-'zel\ *n* [F] : a young woman

de·mol·ish \di-'mä-lish\ *vb* **1** : to destroy by breaking apart : RAZE **2** : SMASH **3** : to put an end to

de·mo·li·tion \ˌde-mə-'li-shən, ˌdē-\ *n* : the act of demolishing; *esp* : destruction by means of explosives

de·mon *or* **dae·mon** \'dē-mən\ *n* **1** : an evil spirit : DEVIL **2** *usu* **daemon** : an attendant power or spirit **3** : one that has unusual drive or effectiveness

de·mon·e·tize \dē-'mä-nə-ˌtīz, -'mə-\ *vb* : to stop using as money or as a monetary standard ⟨~ silver⟩ — **de·mon·e·ti·za·tion** \dē-ˌmä-nə-tə-'zā-shən, -ˌmə-\ *n*

de·mo·ni·ac \di-'mō-nē-ˌak\ *also* **de·mo·ni·a·cal** \ˌdē-mə-'nī-ə-kəl\ *adj* **1** : possessed or influenced by a demon **2** : DEVILISH, FIENDISH

de·mon·ic \di-'mä-nik\ *also* **de·mon·i·cal** \-ni-kəl\ *adj* : DEMONIAC **2**

de·mon·ol·o·gy \ˌdē-mə-'nä-lə-jē\ *n* **1** : the study of demons **2** : belief in demons

de·mon·stra·ble \di-'män-strə-bəl\ *adj* **1** : capable of being demonstrated **2** : APPARENT, EVIDENT — **de·mon·stra·bly** \-blē\ *adv*

dem·on·strate \'de-mən-ˌstrāt\ *vb* **-strat·ed; -strat·ing 1** : to show clearly **2** : to prove or make clear by reasoning or evidence **3** : to explain esp. with many examples **4** : to show publicly ⟨~ a new car⟩ **5** : to make a public display ⟨~ in protest⟩ — **dem·on·stra·tion** \ˌde-mən-'strā-shən\ *n* — **dem·on·stra·tor** \'de-mən-ˌstrā-tər\ *n*

¹de·mon·stra·tive \di-'män-strə-tiv\ *adj* **1** : demonstrating as real or true **2** : characterized by demonstration **3** : pointing out the one referred to and distinguishing it from others of the same class ⟨~ pronoun⟩ **4** : marked by display of feeling : EFFUSIVE — **de·mon·stra·tive·ly** *adv* — **de·mon·stra·tive·ness** *n*

²demonstrative *n* : a demonstrative word and esp. a pronoun

de·mor·al·ize \di-'mȯr-ə-ˌlīz\ *vb* **1** : to corrupt in morals **2** : to weaken in discipline or spirit : DISORGANIZE — **de·mor·al·i·za·tion** \-ˌmȯr-ə-lə-'zā-shən\ *n*

de·mote \di-'mōt\ *vb* **de·mot·ed; de·mot·ing** : to reduce to a lower grade or rank — **de·mo·tion** \-'mō-shən\ *n*

de·mot·ic \di-'mä-tik\ *adj* : COMMON, POPULAR

de·mur \di-'mər\ *vb* **de·murred; de·mur·ring** [ME *demeoren* to linger, fr. OF *demorer*, fr. L *demorari*, fr. *morari* to linger, fr. *mora* delay] : to take exception : OBJECT — **de·mur** *n*

de·mure \di-'myu̇r\ adj 1 : quietly modest : DECOROUS 2 : affectedly modest, reserved, or serious : PRIM syn shy, bashful, coy, difficult, retiring, unassertive — **de·mure·ly** adv
de·mur·rer \di-'mər-ər\ n : a claim by the defendant in a legal action that the plaintiff does not have sufficient grounds to proceed
den \'den\ n 1 : LAIR 2 : HIDEOUT ⟨a robber's ∼⟩; also : a place like a hideout or a center of secret activity ⟨opium ∼⟩ ⟨a ∼ of iniquity⟩ 3 : a cozy private little room
Den abbr Denmark
de·na·ture \dē-'nā-chər\ vb **de·na·tured; de·na·tur·ing** : to remove the natural qualities of; esp : to make (alcohol) unfit for drinking
den·drol·o·gy \den-'drä-lə-jē\ n : the study of trees — **den·drol·o·gist** \-jist\ n
den·gue \'deŋ-gē, -ˌgā\ n [Sp] : an acute infectious disease characterized by headache, severe joint pain, and rash
de·ni·al \di-'nī-əl\ n 1 : rejection of a request 2 : refusal to admit the truth of a statement or charge; also : assertion that something alleged is false 3 : DISAVOWAL 4 : restriction on one's own activity or desires
de·nier \'den-yər\ n : a unit of fineness for yarn
den·i·grate \'de-ni-ˌgrāt\ vb **-grat·ed; -grat·ing** [L denigrare, fr. nigrare to blacken, fr. niger black] : to cast aspersions on : DEFAME — **den·i·gra·tion** \ˌde-ni-'grā-shən\ n
den·im \'de-nəm\ n [F (serge) de Nîmes serge of Nîmes, France] 1 : a firm durable twilled usu. cotton fabric woven with colored warp and white filling threads 2 pl : overalls or trousers of usu. blue denim
den·i·zen \'de-nə-zən\ n : INHABITANT
de·nom·i·nate \di-'nä-mə-ˌnāt\ vb : to give a name to : DESIGNATE
de·nom·i·na·tion \di-ˌnä-mə-'nā-shən\ n 1 : an act of denominating 2 : a value or size of a series of related values (as of money) 3 : NAME, DESIGNATION; esp : a general name for a category 4 : a religious organization uniting local congregations in a single body — **de·nom·i·na·tion·al** \-shə-nəl\ adj
de·nom·i·na·tor \di-'nä-mə-ˌnā-tər\ n : the part of a fraction that is below the line indicating division
de·no·ta·tive \'dē-nō-ˌtā-tiv, di-'nō-tə-tiv\ adj 1 : denoting or tending to denote 2 : relating to denotation
de·note \di-'nōt\ vb 1 : to mark out plainly : INDICATE 2 : to make known 3 : MEAN, NAME — **de·no·ta·tion** \ˌdē-nō-'tā-shən\ n
de·noue·ment \ˌdā-ˌnü-'mäⁿ\ n [F dénouement, lit., untying] : the final outcome of the dramatic complications in a literary work
de·nounce \di-'nau̇ns\ vb **de·nounced; de·nounc·ing** 1 : to pronounce esp. publicly to be blameworthy or evil 2 : to inform against : ACCUSE 3 : to announce formally the termination of (as a treaty) — **de·nounce·ment** n

de no·vo \di-'nō-vō\ adv or adj [L] : over again : ANEW
dense \'dens\ adj **dens·er; dens·est** 1 : marked by compactness or crowding together of parts : THICK ⟨∼ forest⟩ ⟨a ∼ fog⟩ 2 : DULL, STUPID — **dense·ly** adv — **dense·ness** n
den·si·ty \'den-sə-tē\ n, pl **-ties** 1 : the quality or state of being dense 2 : the quantity of something per unit volume, unit area, or unit length
dent \'dent\ n 1 : a small depressed place made by a blow or by pressure 2 : an impression or weakening effect made usu. against resistance 3 : initial progress — **dent** vb
den·tal \'dent-əl\ adj : of or relating to teeth or dentistry — **den·tal·ly** adv
dental floss n : a thread used to clean between the teeth
dental hygienist n : a person licensed to clean and examine teeth
den·tate \'den-ˌtāt\ adj : having pointed projections : NOTCHED
den·ti·frice \'den-tə-frəs\ n [MF, fr. L dentifricium, fr. dent-, dens tooth + fricare to rub] : a powder, paste, or liquid for cleaning the teeth
den·tin \'dent-ᵊn\ or **den·tine** \'den-ˌtēn, den-'tēn\ n : a calcareous material like bone but harder and denser that composes the principal mass of a tooth
den·tist \'den-tist\ n : a person licensed in the care, treatment, and replacement of teeth — **den·tist·ry** n
den·ti·tion \den-'ti-shən\ n : the number, kind, and arrangement of teeth (as of a person or animal); also : TEETH
den·ture \'den-chər\ n : a set of teeth; esp : a partial or complete set of false teeth
de·nude \di-'nüd, -'nyüd\ vb **de·nud·ed; de·nud·ing** : to strip the covering from — **de·nu·da·tion** \ˌdē-nü-'dā-shən, -nyü-\ n
de·nun·ci·a·tion \di-ˌnən-sē-'ā-shən\ n : the act of denouncing; esp : a public condemnation
de·ny \di-'nī\ vb **de·nied; de·ny·ing** 1 : to declare untrue 2 : to refuse to recognize or acknowledge : DISAVOW 3 : to refuse to grant ⟨∼ a request⟩ 4 : to reject as false ⟨∼ a theory⟩
de·o·dar \'dē-ə-ˌdär\ n [Hindi deodār, fr. Skt devadāru, fr. deva god + dāru wood] : an East Indian cedar
de·odor·ant \dē-'ō-də-rənt\ n : a preparation that gets rid of unpleasant odors
de·odor·ize \dē-'ō-də-ˌrīz\ vb : to eliminate the offensive odor of
de·ox·i·dize \dē-'äk-sə-ˌdīz\ vb : to remove oxygen from
de·oxy·ri·bo·nu·cle·ic acid \dē-ˈäk-si-ˌrī-bō-nu̇-ˈklē-ik-, -nyü-\ n : DNA
de·oxy·ri·bose \dē-ˈäk-si-ˈrī-ˌbōs\ n : a sugar with five carbon and four oxygen atoms in each molecule that is part of DNA
dep abbr 1 depart; departure 2 deposit 3 deputy
de·part \di-'pärt\ vb 1 : to go away : go away from : LEAVE 2 : DIE 3 : to turn aside : DEVIATE
de·part·ment \di-'pärt-mənt\ n 1 : a distinct sphere or

category esp. of an activity or attribute **2** : a functional or territorial division (as of a government, business, or college) — **de·part·men·tal** \di-ˌpärt-ˈment-ᵊl, ˌdē-\ *adj*

department store *n* : a store selling a wide variety of goods arranged in several departments

de·par·ture \di-ˈpär-chər\ *n* **1** : the act of going away **2** : a starting out (as on a journey) **3** : DIVERGENCE

de·pend \di-ˈpend\ *vb* **1** : to be determined, based, or contingent ⟨life ~s on food⟩ **2** : TRUST, RELY ⟨you can ~ on me⟩ **3** : to be dependent esp. for financial support **4** : to hang down ⟨a vine ~ing from a tree⟩

de·pend·able \di-ˈpen-də-bəl\ *adj* : TRUSTWORTHY, RELIABLE — **de·pend·abil·i·ty** \-ˌpen-də-ˈbi-lə-tē\ *n*

de·pen·dence *also* **de·pen·dance** \di-ˈpen-dəns\ *n* **1** : the quality or state of being dependent; *esp* : the quality or state of being influenced by or subject to another **2** : RELIANCE, TRUST **3** : something on which one relies **4** : drug addiction; *also* : HABITUATION **2**

de·pen·den·cy \-dən-sē\ *n, pl* **-cies** **1** : DEPENDENCE **2** : a territory under the jurisdiction of a nation but not formally annexed by it

¹**de·pen·dent** \-dənt\ *adj* **1** : hanging down **2** : determined or conditioned by another; *also* : affected with drug dependence **3** : relying on another for support **4** : subject to another's jurisdiction **5** : SUBORDINATE **4**

²**dependent** *also* **de·pen·dant** \-dənt\ *n* : one that is dependent; *esp* : a person who relies on another for support

de·pict \di-ˈpikt\ *vb* **1** : to represent by a picture **2** : to describe in words — **de·pic·tion** \-ˈpik-shən\ *n*

de·pil·a·to·ry \di-ˈpi-lə-ˌtōr-ē\ *n, pl* **-ries** : a preparation for removing hair, wool, or bristles

de·plane \dē-ˈplān\ *vb* : to get out of an airplane

de·plete \di-ˈplēt\ *vb* **de·plet·ed; de·plet·ing** : to exhaust esp. of strength or resources — **de·ple·tion** \-ˈplē-shən\ *n*

de·plor·able \di-ˈplōr-ə-bəl\ *adj* **1** : LAMENTABLE **2** : WRETCHED — **de·plor·ably** *adv*

de·plore \-ˈplōr\ *vb* **de·plored; de·plor·ing** **1** : to feel or express grief for **2** : to regret strongly **3** : to consider unfortunate or deserving of disapproval

de·ploy \di-ˈplȯi\ *vb* : to spread out (as troops or ships) in order for battle — **de·ploy·ment** \-mənt\ *n*

de·po·nent \di-ˈpō-nənt\ *n* : one who gives evidence

de·pop·u·late \dē-ˈpä-pyə-ˌlāt\ *vb* : to reduce greatly the population of — **de·pop·u·la·tion** \-ˌpä-pyə-ˈlā-shən\ *n*

de·port \di-ˈpōrt\ *vb* **1** : CONDUCT, BEHAVE **2** : BANISH, EXILE — **de·por·ta·tion** \ˌdē-ˌpōr-ˈtā-shən\ *n*

de·port·ment \di-ˈpōrt-mənt\ *n* : BEHAVIOR, BEARING

de·pose \di-ˈpōz\ *vb* **de·posed; de·pos·ing** **1** : to remove from high office (as of king) **2** : to testify under oath or by affidavit

¹**de·pos·it** \di-ˈpä-zət\ *vb* **de·pos·it·ed** \-zə-təd\; **de·pos·it·ing** **1** : to place for safekeeping or as a pledge; *esp* : to put money in a bank **2** : to lay down; PLACE **3** : to let fall or sink ⟨silt ~ed by a flood⟩ — **de·pos·i·tor** \-zə-tər\ *n*

²**deposit** *n* **1** : the state of being deposited ⟨money on ~⟩

2 : something placed for safekeeping; *esp* : money deposited in a bank **3** : money given as a pledge **4** : an act of depositing **5** : something laid down ⟨a ~ of silt⟩ **6** : a natural accumulation (as of a mineral)

de·po·si·tion \ˌde-pə-ˈzi-shən, ˌdē-\ *n* **1** : an act of removing from a position of authority **2** : TESTIMONY **3** : the process of depositing **4** : DEPOSIT

de·pos·i·to·ry \di-ˈpä-zə-ˌtōr-ē\ *n, pl* **-ries** : a place where something is deposited esp. for safekeeping

de·pot \ *1, 2 usu* ˈde-ˌpō, *3 usu* ˈdē-\ *n* **1** : STOREHOUSE **2** : a place where military supplies or replacements are kept or assembled **3** : a building for railroad or bus passengers

depr *abbr* depreciation

de·prave \di-ˈprāv\ *vb* **de·praved; de·prav·ing** [ME, fr. MF *depraver*, fr. L *depravare* to pervert, fr. *pravus* crooked, bad] : CORRUPT, PERVERT — **de·praved** *adj* — **de·prav·i·ty** \-ˈpra-və-tē\ *n*

dep·re·cate \ˈde-pri-ˌkāt\ *vb* **-cat·ed; -cat·ing** [L *deprecari* to avert by prayer, fr. *precari* to pray] **1** : to express disapproval of **2** : BELITTLE — **dep·re·ca·tion** \ˌde-pri-ˈkā-shən\ *n*

dep·re·ca·to·ry \ˈde-pri-kə-ˌtōr-ē\ *adj* **1** : APOLOGETIC **2** : serving to deprecate : DISAPPROVING

de·pre·ci·ate \di-ˈprē-shē-ˌāt\ *vb* **-at·ed; -at·ing** [LL *depretiare*, fr. L *pretium* price] **1** : BELITTLE, DISPARAGE **2** : to lessen in price or value — **de·pre·ci·a·tion** \-ˌprē-shē-ˈā-shən\ *n*

dep·re·da·tion \ˌde-prə-ˈdā-shən\ *n* : a laying waste or plundering — **dep·re·date** \ˈde-prə-ˌdāt\ *vb*

de·press \di-ˈpres\ *vb* **1** : to press down : cause to sink to a lower position **2** : to lessen the activity or force of **3** : SADDEN, DISCOURAGE **4** : to lessen in price or value — **de·pres·sor** \-ˈpre-sər\ *n*

de·pres·sant \di-ˈpres-ᵊnt\ *n* : one that depresses; *esp* : a chemical substance (as a drug) that reduces bodily functional activity — **depressant** *adj*

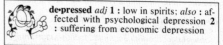 **de·pressed** *adj* **1** : low in spirits; *also* : affected with psychological depression **2** : suffering from economic depression

de·pres·sion \di-ˈpre-shən\ *n* **1** : an act of depressing : a state of being depressed **2** : a pressing down : LOWERING **3** : a state of feeling sad **4** : a psychological disorder marked esp. by sadness, inactivity, difficulty in thinking and concentration, and feelings of dejection **5** : a depressed area or part **6** : a period of low general economic activity with widespread unemployment

¹**de·pres·sive** \di-ˈpre-siv\ *adj* **1** : tending to depress **2** : characterized or affected by psychological depression

²**depressive** *n* : a person affected with or prone to psychological depression

de·pres·sur·ize \(ˌ)dē-ˈpre-shə-ˌrīz\ *vb* : to release pressure from

dep·ri·va·tion \ˌde-prə-ˈvā-shən\ *n* **1** : an act or instance of depriving : LOSS **2** : PRIVATION **2**

de·prive \di-ˈprīv\ *vb* **de·prived; de·priv·ing** **1** : to take something away from **2** : to stop from having something

de·prived *adj* : marked by deprivation esp. of the necessities of life

de·pro·gram \(ˌ)dē-ˈprō-ˌgram, -grəm\ *vb* : to dissuade from convictions usu. of a religious nature often by coercive means

dept *abbr* department

depth \ˈdepth\ *n*, *pl* **depths** \ˈdepths\ **1** : something that is deep; *esp* : the deep part of a body of water **2** : a part that is far from the outside or surface; *also* : the middle or innermost part **3** : ABYSS **4** : a profound or intense state (the ∼s of reflection); *also* : the worst part (during the ∼s of the depression) **5** : a reprehensibly low condition **6** : the distance from top to bottom or from front to back **7** : the quality of being deep **8** : the degree of intensity

depth charge *n* : an explosive device for use underwater esp. against submarines

dep·u·ta·tion \ˌde-pyə-ˈtā-shən\ *n* **1** : the act of appointing a deputy **2** : DELEGATION

de·pute \di-ˈpyüt\ *vb* **de·put·ed**; **de·put·ing** : DELEGATE

dep·u·tize \ˈde-pyə-ˌtīz\ *vb* **-tized**; **-tiz·ing** : to appoint or act as deputy

dep·u·ty \ˈde-pyə-tē\ *n*, *pl* **-ties** **1** : a person appointed to act for or in place of another **2** : an assistant empowered to act as a substitute in the absence of a superior **3** : a member of a lower house of a legislative assembly

der *or* **deriv** *abbr* derivation; derivative

de·rail \di-ˈrāl\ *vb* : to leave or cause to leave the rails — **de·rail·ment** *n*

de·rail·leur \di-ˈrā-lər\ *n* [F *dérailleur*] : a device for shifting gears on a bicycle by moving the chain from one set of exposed gears to another

de·range \di-ˈrānj\ *vb* **de·ranged**; **de·rang·ing** **1** : DISARRANGE, UPSET **2** : to make insane — **de·range·ment** *n*

der·by \ˈdər-bē, *Brit* ˈdär-\ *n*, *pl* **derbies** **1** : a horse race usu. for three-year-olds held annually **2** : a race or contest open to all **3** : a stiff felt hat with dome-shaped crown and narrow brim

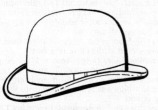

derby 3

de·reg·u·la·tion \(ˌ)dē-ˌre-gyü-ˈlā-shən\ *n* : the act of removing restrictions or regulations — **de·reg·u·late** \-ˈre-gyü-ˌlāt\ *vb*

¹**der·e·lict** \ˈder-ə-ˌlikt\ *adj* **1** : abandoned by the owner or occupant **2** : NEGLIGENT (∼ in his duty)

²**derelict** *n* **1** : something voluntarily abandoned; *esp* : a ship abandoned on the high seas **2** : a destitute homeless social misfit : VAGRANT, BUM

der·e·lic·tion \ˌder-ə-ˈlik-shən\ *n* **1** : the act of abandoning : the state of being abandoned **2** : a failure in duty

de·ride \di-ˈrīd\ *vb* **de·rid·ed**; **de·rid·ing** [L *deridēre*, fr. *ridēre* to laugh] : to laugh at scornfully : RIDICULE

de ri·gueur \də-rē-ˈgər\ *adj* [F] : prescribed or required by fashion, etiquette, or custom : PROPER

de·ri·sion \də-ˈri-zhən\ *n* : RIDICULE — **de·ri·sive** \-ˈrī-siv\ *adj* — **de·ri·sive·ly** *adv* — **de·ri·sive·ness** *n* — **de·ri·so·ry** \-ˈrī-sə-rē\ *adj*

der·i·va·tion \ˌder-ə-ˈvā-shən\ *n* **1** : the formation of a word from an earlier word or root; *also* : an act of as-

certaining or stating the derivation of a word **2** : ETYMOLOGY **3** : SOURCE, ORIGIN; *also* : DESCENT **4** : an act or process of deriving

de·riv·a·tive \di-ˈri-və-tiv\ *n* **1** : a word formed by derivation **2** : something derived — **derivative** *adj*

de·rive \di-ˈrīv\ *vb* **de·rived**; **de·riv·ing** [ME, fr. MF *deriver*, fr. L *derivare*, lit., to draw off (water), fr. *de-* from + *rivus* stream] **1** : to receive or obtain from a source **2** : to obtain from a parent substance **3** : INFER, DEDUCE **4** : to trace the derivation of **5** : to come from a certain source

der·mal \ˈdər-məl\ *adj* : of or relating to the skin : CUTANEOUS

der·ma·ti·tis \ˌdər-mə-ˈtī-təs\ *n* : skin inflammation

der·ma·tol·o·gy \-ˈtä-lə-jē\ *n* : a branch of medical science dealing with the structure, functions, and diseases of the skin — **der·ma·tol·o·gist** \-jist\ *n*

der·mis \ˈdər-məs\ *n* : the sensitive vascular inner layer of the skin

der·o·gate \ˈder-ə-ˌgāt\ *vb* **-gat·ed**; **-gat·ing** **1** : to cause to seem inferior : DISPARAGE **2** : DETRACT — **der·o·ga·tion** \ˌder-ə-ˈgā-shən\ *n* — **de·rog·a·tive** \di-ˈrä-gə-tiv\ *adj*

de·rog·a·to·ry \di-ˈrä-gə-ˌtōr-ē\ *adj* : intended to lower the reputation of a person or thing : DISPARAGING — **de·rog·a·to·ri·ly** \-ˌrä-gə-ˈtōr-ə-lē\ *adv*

der·rick \ˈder-ik\ *n* [obs. *derrick* hangman, gallows, fr. *Derick*, name of 17th cent. Eng. hangman] **1** : a hoisting apparatus : CRANE **2** : a framework over a drill hole (as for oil) for supporting machinery

der·ri·ere *or* **der·ri·ère** \ˌder-ē-ˈer\ *n* : BUTTOCKS

der·ring-do \ˌder-iŋ-ˈdü\ *n* : DARING

der·rin·ger \ˈder-ən-jər\ *n* : a short-barreled pocket pistol

der·vish \ˈdər-vish\ *n* [Turk *derviş*, lit., beggar, fr. Per *darvīsh*] : a member of a Muslim religious order noted for devotional exercises (as bodily movements leading to a trance)

de·sal·i·nate \dē-ˈsa-lə-ˌnāt\ *vb* **-nat·ed**; **-nat·ing** : DESALT — **de·sal·i·na·tion** \-ˌsa-lə-ˈnā-shən\ *n*

de·sal·i·nize \dē-ˈsa-lə-ˌnīz\ *vb* **-nized**; **-niz·ing** : DESALT — **de·sal·i·ni·za·tion** \-ˌsa-lə-nə-ˈzā-shən\ *n*

de·salt \dē-ˈsȯlt\ *vb* : to remove salt from (∼ seawater) — **de·salt·er** *n*

des·cant \ˈdes-ˌkant\ *vb* **1** : to sing or play part music : SING **2** : to discourse or write at length

de·scend \di-ˈsend\ *vb* **1** : to pass from a higher to a lower place or level : pass, move, or climb down or down along **2** : DERIVE (∼ed from royalty) **3** : to pass by inheritance or transmission **4** : to incline, lead, or extend downward **5** : to swoop down or appear suddenly (as in an attack)

¹**de·scen·dant** *or* **de·scen·dent** \di-ˈsen-dənt\ *adj* **1** : DESCENDING **2** : proceeding from an ancestor or source

²**descendant** *or* **descendent** *n* **1** : one descended from another or from a common stock **2** : one deriving directly from a precursor or prototype

de·scent \di-ˈsent\ *n* **1** : ANCESTRY, BIRTH, LINEAGE **2** : the act or process of descending **3** : SLOPE **4** : a descending way (as a downgrade) **5** : a sudden hostile raid or assault **6** : a downward step (as in station or value) : DECLINE

de·scribe \di-ˈskrīb\ *vb* **de·scribed**; **de·scrib·ing** **1** : to represent or give an account of in words **2** : to trace the outline of — **de·scrib·able** *adj*

de·scrip·tion \di-ˈskrip-shən\ *n* **1** : an account of something; *esp* : an account that presents a picture to a person who reads or hears it **2** : KIND, SORT — **de·scrip·tive** \-ˈskrip-tiv\ *adj*

de·scry \di-ˈskrī\ *vb* **de·scried**; **de·scry·ing** **1** : to catch sight of **2** : to discover by observation or investigation

des·e·crate \ˈde-si-ˌkrāt\ *vb* **-crat·ed**; **-crat·ing** : PROFANE — **des·e·cra·tion** \ˌde-si-ˈkrā-shən\ *n*

de·seg·re·gate \dē-ˈse-gri-ˌgāt\ *vb* : to eliminate segregation in; *esp* : to free of any law or practice requiring isolation on the basis of race — **de·seg·re·ga·tion** \-ˌse-gri-ˈgā-shən\ n

de·sen·si·tize \dē-ˈsen-sə-ˌtīz\ vb : to make (a sensitized or hypersensitive individual) insensitive or nonreactive to a sensitizing agent — **de·sen·si·ti·za·tion** \-ˌsen-sə-tə-ˈzā-shən\ n

[1]**des·ert** \ˈde-zərt\ n : dry land with few plants and little rainfall

[2]**des·ert** \ˈde-zərt\ adj : of, relating to, or resembling a desert; esp : being barren and without life ⟨a ∼ island⟩

[3]**de·sert** \di-ˈzərt\ n 1 : the quality or fact of deserving reward or punishment 2 : a just reward or punishment

[4]**de·sert** \di-ˈzərt\ vb 1 : to withdraw from 2 : ABANDON, FORSAKE — **de·sert·er** n — **de·ser·tion** \-ˈzər-shən\ n

de·serve \di-ˈzərv\ vb **de·served; de·serv·ing** : to be worthy of : MERIT — **de·serv·ing** adj

de·served·ly \-ˈzər-vəd-lē\ adv : according to merit : JUSTLY

des·ic·cate \ˈde-si-ˌkāt\ vb **-cat·ed; -cat·ing** : DRY, DEHYDRATE — **des·ic·ca·tion** \ˌde-si-ˈkā-shən\ n — **des·ic·ca·tor** \ˈde-si-ˌkā-tər\ n

de·sid·er·a·tum \di-ˌsi-də-ˈrä-təm, -ˌzi-, -ˈrā-\ n, pl **-ta** \-tä\ [L] : something desired as essential

[1]**de·sign** \di-ˈzīn\ vb 1 : to conceive and plan out in the mind 2 : INTEND 3 : to devise for a specific function or end 4 : to make a pattern or sketch of 5 : to conceive and draw the plans for

[2]**design** n 1 : a particular purpose : deliberate planning 2 : a mental project or scheme : PLAN 3 : a secret project or scheme : PLOT 4 pl : aggressive or evil intent — used with on or against 5 : a preliminary sketch or plan 6 : an underlying scheme that governs functioning, developing, or unfolding : MOTIF 7 : the arrangement of elements or details in a product or a work of art 8 : a decorative pattern 9 : the art of executing designs

[1]**des·ig·nate** \ˈde-zig-ˌnāt, -nət\ adj : chosen but not yet installed ⟨ambassador ∼⟩

[2]**des·ig·nate** \-ˌnāt\ vb **-nat·ed; -nat·ing** 1 : to appoint and set apart for a special purpose 2 : to mark or point out : INDICATE; also : SPECIFY, STIPULATE 3 : to call by a name or title — **des·ig·na·tion** \ˌde-zig-ˈnā-shən\ n

designated hitter n : a baseball player designated at the start of the game to bat in place of the pitcher without causing the pitcher to be removed from the game

de·sign·er \di-ˈzī-nər\ n 1 : one who creates plans for a project or structure 2 : one who designs and manufactures high-fashion clothing — **designer** adj

de·sign·ing \di-ˈzī-niŋ\ adj : CRAFTY, SCHEMING

de·sir·able \di-ˈzī-rə-bəl\ adj 1 : PLEASING, ATTRACTIVE 2 : ADVISABLE ⟨∼ legislation⟩ — **de·sir·abil·i·ty** \-ˌzī-rə-ˈbi-lə-tē\ n — **de·sir·able·ness** n

[1]**de·sire** \di-ˈzīr\ vb **de·sired; de·sir·ing** [ME, fr. OF desirer, fr. L desiderare, fr. sider-, sidus heavenly body] 1 : to long or hope for : exhibit or feel desire for 2 : REQUEST

[2]**desire** n 1 : a strong wish : LONGING, CRAVING 2 : sexual urge or appetite 3 : a usu. formal request for action 4 : something desired

de·sir·ous \di-ˈzīr-əs\ adj : eagerly wishing : DESIRING

de·sist \di-ˈzist, -ˈsist\ vb : to cease to proceed or act

desk \ˈdesk\ n [ME deske, fr. ML desca, fr. OIt desco table, fr. L discus dish, disc] 1 : a table, frame, or case esp. for writing and reading 2 : a counter, stand, or booth at which a person performs duties 3 : a specialized division of an organization (as a newspaper) ⟨city ∼⟩

desk·top publishing \ˈdesk-ˌtäp-\ n : the production of printed matter by means of a microcomputer

[1]**des·o·late** \ˈde-sə-lət, -zə-\ adj 1 : DESERTED, ABANDONED 2 : FORSAKEN, LONELY 3 : DILAPIDATED 4 : BARREN, LIFELESS 5 : CHEERLESS, GLOOMY — **des·o·late·ly** adv — **des·o·late·ness** n

[2]**des·o·late** \-ˌlāt\ vb **-lat·ed; -lat·ing** : to make desolate : lay waste : make wretched

des·o·la·tion \ˌde-sə-ˈlā-shən, -zə-\ n 1 : the action of desolating 2 : GRIEF, SADNESS 3 : LONELINESS 4 : DEVASTATION, RUIN 5 : barren wasteland

des·oxy·ri·bo·nu·cle·ic acid \de-ˌzäk-sē-ˈrī-bō-nü-ˌklē-ik-, -nyü-\ n : DNA

[1]**de·spair** \di-ˈspar\ vb : to lose all hope or confidence — **de·spair·ing·ly** adv

[2]**despair** n 1 : utter loss of hope 2 : a cause of hopelessness

des·patch \dis-ˈpach\ var of DISPATCH

des·per·a·do \ˌdes-pə-ˈrä-dō, -ˈrā-\ n, pl **-does** or **-dos** : a bold or reckless criminal

des·per·ate \ˈdes-pə-rət, -prət\ adj 1 : being beyond or almost beyond hope : causing despair 2 : RASH 3 : extremely intense — **des·per·ate·ly** adv — **des·per·ate·ness** n

des·per·a·tion \ˌdes-pə-ˈrā-shən\ n 1 : a loss of hope and surrender to despair 2 : a state of hopelessness leading to rashness

de·spi·ca·ble \di-ˈspi-kə-bəl, ˈdes-pi-\ adj : deserving to be despised — **de·spi·ca·bly** \-blē\ adv

de·spise \di-ˈspīz\ vb **de·spised; de·spis·ing** 1 : to look down on with contempt or aversion : DISDAIN, DETEST 2 : to regard as negligible, worthless, or distasteful

de·spite \di-ˈspīt\ prep : in spite of

de·spoil \di-ˈspȯil\ vb : to strip of belongings, possessions, or value — **de·spoil·er** n — **de·spoil·ment** n

de·spo·li·a·tion \di-ˌspō-lē-ˈā-shən\ n : the act of plundering : the state of being despoiled

[1]**de·spond** \di-ˈspänd\ vb : to become discouraged or disheartened

[2]**despond** n : DESPONDENCY

de·spon·den·cy \-ˈspän-dən-sē\ n : DEJECTION, HOPELESSNESS — **de·spon·dent** \-dənt\ adj — **de·spon·dent·ly** adv

des·pot \ˈdes-pət, -ˌpät\ n [MF despote, fr. Gk despotēs master, lord, autocrat] 1 : a ruler with absolute power and authority 2 : a person exercising power tyrannically — **des·pot·ic** \des-ˈpä-tik\ adj — **des·po·tism** \ˈdes-pə-ˌti-zəm\ n

des·sert \di-ˈzərt\ n : a course of sweet food, fruit, or cheese served at the close of a meal

des·ti·na·tion \ˌdes-tə-ˈnā-shən\ n 1 : a purpose for which something is destined 2 : an act of appointing, setting aside for a purpose, or predetermining 3 : a place to which one is journeying or to which something is sent

des·tine \ˈdes-tən\ vb **des·tined; des·tin·ing** 1 : to settle in advance 2 : to designate, assign, or dedicate in advance 3 : to direct or set apart for a specific purpose or place

des·ti·ny \ˈdes-tə-nē\ n, pl **-nies** : something to which a person or thing is destined : FATE, FORTUNE 2 : a predetermined course of events

des·ti·tute \ˈdes-tə-ˌtüt, -ˌtyüt\ adj 1 : lacking something needed or desirable 2 : suffering extreme poverty — **des·ti·tu·tion** \ˌdes-tə-ˈtü-shən, -ˈtyü-\ n

de·stroy \di-ˈstrȯi\ vb 1 : to put an end to : RUIN 2 : KILL

de·stroy·er \di-ˈstrȯi-ər\ n 1 : one that destroys 2 : a small speedy warship

de·struc·ti·ble \di-ˈstrək-tə-bəl\ adj : capable of being destroyed — **de·struc·ti·bil·i·ty** \-ˌstrək-tə-ˈbi-lə-tē\ n

de·struc·tion \di-ˈstrək-shən\ n 1 : RUIN 2 : the action

or process of destroying something **3** : a destroying agency

de·struc·tive \di-ˈstrək-tiv\ *adj* **1** : causing destruction : RUINOUS **2** : designed or tending to destroy — **de·struc·tive·ly** *adv* — **de·struc·tive·ness** *n*

de·sue·tude \ˈde-swi-ˌtüd, -ˌtyüd\ *n* : DISUSE

des·ul·to·ry \ˈde-səl-ˌtōr-ē\ *adj* : passing aimlessly from one thing or subject to another : DISCONNECTED

det *abbr* **1** detached; detachment **2** detail

de·tach \di-ˈtach\ *vb* **1** : to separate esp. from a larger mass **2** : DISENGAGE, WITHDRAW — **de·tach·able** *adj*

de·tached \di-ˈtacht\ *adj* **1** : not joined or connected : SEPARATE **2** : ALOOF, IMPARTIAL ⟨a ~ attitude⟩

de·tach·ment \di-ˈtach-mənt\ *n* **1** : SEPARATION **2** : the dispatching of a body of troops or part of a fleet from the main body for special service; *also* : the portion so dispatched **3** : a small permanent military unit of special composition **4** : indifference to worldly concerns : ALOOFNESS **5** : IMPARTIALITY

¹**de·tail** \di-ˈtāl, ˈdē-ˌtāl\ *n* [F *détail*, fr. OF *detail* slice, piece, fr. *detaillier* to cut in pieces, fr. *taillier* to cut] **1** : a dealing with something item by item ⟨go into ~⟩; *also* : ITEM, PARTICULAR ⟨the ~s of a story⟩ **2** : selection (as of soldiers) for special duty; *also* : the persons thus selected

²**detail** *vb* **1** : to report in particulars : SPECIFY **2** : to assign to a special duty

de·tailed \di-ˈtāld, ˈdē-ˌtāld\ *adj* : marked by abundant detail

de·tain \di-ˈtān\ *vb* **1** : to hold in or as if in custody **2** : STOP, DELAY

de·tect \di-ˈtekt\ *vb* : to discover the nature, existence, presence, or fact of — **de·tect·able** *adj* — **de·tec·tion** \-ˈtek-shən\ *n* — **de·tec·tor** \-ˈtek-tər\ *n*

¹**de·tec·tive** \di-ˈtek-tiv\ *adj* **1** : fitted or used for detection **2** : of or relating to detectives

²**detective** *n* : a person employed or engaged in detecting lawbreakers or getting information that is not readily accessible

dé·tente \dā-ˈtänt\ *n* [F] : a relaxation of strained relations or tensions (as between nations)

de·ten·tion \di-ˈten-chən\ *n* **1** : the act or fact of detaining : CONFINEMENT; *esp* : a period of temporary custody prior to disposition by a court **2** : a forced delay

de·ter \di-ˈtər\ *vb* **de·terred; de·ter·ring** [L *deterrēre*, fr. *terrēre* to frighten] **1** : to turn aside, discourage, or prevent from acting (as by fear) **2** : INHIBIT

de·ter·gent \di-ˈtər-jənt\ *n* : a cleansing agent; *esp* : a chemical product similar to soap in its cleaning ability

de·te·ri·o·rate \di-ˈtir-ē-ə-ˌrāt\ *vb* **-rat·ed; -rat·ing** : to make or become worse in quality or condition — **de·te·ri·o·ra·tion** \-ˌtir-ē-ə-ˈrā-shən\ *n*

de·ter·min·able \-ˈtər-mə-nə-bəl\ *adj* : capable of being determined; *esp* : ASCERTAINABLE

de·ter·mi·nant \-mə-nənt\ *n* **1** : something that determines or conditions **2** : GENE

de·ter·mi·nate \di-ˈtər-mə-nət\ *adj* **1** : having fixed limits : DEFINITE **2** : definitely settled — **de·ter·mi·nate·ness** *n*

de·ter·mi·na·tion \di-ˌtər-mə-ˈnā-shən\ *n* **1** : the act of coming to a decision; *also* : the decision or conclusion reached **2** : a fixing of the extent, position, or character of something **3** : accurate measurement (as of length or volume) **4** : firm or fixed purpose

de·ter·mine \di-ˈtər-mən\ *vb* **-mined; -min·ing** **1** : to fix conclusively or authoritatively **2** : to come to a decision : SETTLE, RESOLVE **3** : to fix the form or character of beforehand : ORDAIN; *also* : REGULATE **4** : to find out the limits, nature, dimensions, or scope of ⟨~ a position at sea⟩ **5** : to bring about as a result

de·ter·mined \-ˈtər-mənd\ *adj* **1** : firmly resolved **2** : characterized by or showing determination — **de·ter·mined·ly** \-mənd-lē, -mə-nəd-lē\ *adv* — **de·ter·mined·ness** *n*

de·ter·min·ism \di-ˈtər-mə-ˌni-zəm\ *n* : a doctrine that acts of the will, natural events, or social changes are determined by preceding events or natural causes — **de·ter·min·ist** \-nist\ *n or adj*

de·ter·rence \di-ˈtər-əns\ *n* : the inhibition of criminal behavior by fear esp. of punishment

de·ter·rent \-ənt\ *adj* **1** : serving to deter **2** : relating to deterrence — **deterrent** *n*

de·test \di-ˈtest\ *vb* [L *detestari*, lit., to curse while calling a deity to witness, fr. *de-* from + *testari* to call to witness] : LOATHE, HATE — **de·test·able** *adj* — **de·tes·ta·tion** \ˌdē-tes-ˈtā-shən\ *n*

de·throne \di-ˈthrōn\ *vb* : to remove from a throne : DEPOSE — **de·throne·ment** *n*

det·o·nate \ˈdet-ᵊn-ˌāt\ *vb* **-nat·ed; -nat·ing** : to explode or cause to explode with violence — **det·o·na·tion** \ˌdet-ᵊn-ˈā-shən\ *n*

det·o·na·tor \ˈdet-ᵊn-ˌā-tər\ *n* : a device for detonating an explosive

¹**de·tour** \ˈdē-ˌtür\ *n* : an indirect way replacing part of a route

²**detour** *vb* : to go by detour

de·tox \ˈdē-ˌtäks, di-ˈtäks\ *n* : detoxification from a substance (as alcohol) — **detox** *vb*

de·tox·i·fy \dē-ˈtäk-sə-ˌfī\ *vb* **-fied; -fy·ing** **1** : to remove a poison or toxin or the effect of such from **2** : to free (as a drug user) from an intoxicating or addictive substance or from dependence on it — **de·tox·i·fi·ca·tion** \dē-ˌtäk-sə-fə-ˈkā-shən\ *n*

de·tract \di-ˈtrakt\ *vb* **1** : to take away or diminish the value or effect of something **2** : DIVERT — **de·trac·tion** \-ˈtrak-shən\ *n* — **de·trac·tor** \-ˈtrak-tər\ *n*

de·train \dē-ˈtrān\ *vb* : to leave or cause to leave a railroad train

det·ri·ment \ˈde-trə-mənt\ *n* : INJURY, DAMAGE; *also* : a cause of injury or damage — **det·ri·men·tal** \ˌde-trə-ˈment-ᵊl\ *adj* — **det·ri·men·tal·ly** *adv*

de·tri·tus \di-ˈtrī-təs\ *n, pl* **de·tri·tus** : fragments resulting from disintegration (as of rocks) : DEBRIS

deuce \ˈdüs, ˈdyüs\ *n* **1** : a two in cards or dice **2** : a tie in a tennis game with both sides at 40 **3** : DEVIL — used chiefly as a mild oath

Deut *abbr* Deuteronomy

deu·te·ri·um \dü-'tir-ē-əm, dyü-\ *n* : an isotope of hydrogen that has twice the mass of ordinary hydrogen

Deu·ter·on·o·my \ˌdü-tə-'rä-nə-mē, ˌdyü-\ *n* — see BIBLE table

deut·sche mark \'dòi-chə-ˌmärk\ *n* — see MONEY table

dev *abbr* deviation

de·val·ue \dē-'val-yü\ *vb* : to reduce the international exchange value of ⟨~ a currency⟩ — **de·val·u·a·tion** \-ˌval-yə-'wā-shən\ *n*

dev·as·tate \'de-və-ˌstāt\ *vb* **-tat·ed; -tat·ing 1** : to bring to ruin **2** : to reduce to chaos or helplessness — **dev·as·ta·tion** \ˌde-və-'stā-shən\ *n*

de·vel·op \di-'ve-ləp\ *vb* **1** : to unfold gradually or in detail **2** : to place (exposed photographic material) in chemicals to produce a visible image **3** : to bring out the possibilities of **4** : to make more available or usable ⟨~ land⟩ **5** : to acquire gradually ⟨~ a taste for olives⟩ **6** : to go through a natural process of growth, differentiation, or evolution **7** : to come into being gradually — **de·vel·op·er** *n* — **de·vel·op·ment** *n* — **de·vel·op·men·tal** \-ˌve-ləp-'ment-ᵊl\ *adj*

de·vi·ant \'dē-vē-ənt\ *adj* : deviating esp. from some accepted norm ⟨~ behavior⟩ — **de·vi·ance** \-əns\ *n* — **de·vi·an·cy** \-ən-sē\ *n* — **deviant** *n*

de·vi·ate \'dē-vē-ˌāt\ *vb* **-at·ed; -at·ing** [LL *deviare*, fr. L *de-* from + *via* way] : to turn aside from a course, standard, principle, or topic — **de·vi·ate** \-vē-ət, -vē-ˌāt\ *n* — **de·vi·a·tion** \ˌdē-vē-'ā-shən\ *n*

de·vice \di-'vīs\ *n* **1** : SCHEME, STRATAGEM **2** : a piece of equipment or a mechanism for a special purpose **3** : DESIRE, INCLINATION ⟨left to my own ~s⟩ **4** : an emblematic design

¹dev·il \'de-vəl\ *n* [ME *devel*, fr. OE *dēofol*, fr. LL *diabolus*, fr. Gk *diabolos*, lit., slanderer, fr. *diaballein* to throw across, slander, fr. *dia-* across + *ballein* to throw] **1** *often cap* : the personal supreme spirit of evil **2** : DEMON **3** : a wicked person **4** : an energetic, reckless, or dashing person **5** : FELLOW ⟨poor ~⟩ ⟨lucky ~⟩

²devil *vb* **-iled** *or* **-illed; -il·ing** *or* **-il·ling 1** : to season highly ⟨~ed eggs⟩ **2** : TEASE, ANNOY

dev·il·ish \'de-və-lish\ *adj* **1** : befitting a devil : EVIL; *also* : MISCHIEVOUS **2** : EXTREME — **dev·il·ish·ly** *adv* — **dev·il·ish·ness** *n*

dev·il·ment \'de-vəl-mənt, -ˌment\ *n* : MISCHIEF

dev·il·ry \-rē\ *or* **dev·il·try** \-trē\ *n, pl* **-il·ries** *or* **-il·tries 1** : action performed with the help of the devil **2** : MISCHIEF

de·vi·ous \'dē-vē-əs\ *adj* **1** : deviating from a straight line : ROUNDABOUT **2** : ERRANT **3 3** : TRICKY, CUNNING

¹de·vise \di-'vīz\ *vb* **de·vised; de·vis·ing 1** : INVENT **2** : PLOT **3** : to give (real estate) by will

²devise *n* **1** : a disposing of real property by will **2** : a will or clause of a will disposing of real property **3** : property given by will

de·vi·tal·ize \dē-'vīt-ᵊl-ˌīz\ *vb* : to deprive of life or vitality

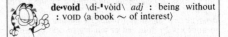

de·void \di-'vòid\ *adj* : being without : VOID ⟨a book ~ of interest⟩

de·voir \də-'vwär\ *n* **1** : DUTY **2** : a formal act of civility or respect

de·volve \di-'välv\ *vb* **de·volved; de·volv·ing** : to pass (as rights or responsibility) from one to another usu. by succession or transmission — **dev·o·lu·tion** \ˌde-və-'lü-shən, ˌdē-\ *n*

De·vo·ni·an \di-'vō-nē-ən\ *adj* : of, relating to, or being the period of the Paleozoic era between the Silurian and the Mississippian — **Devonian** *n*

de·vote \di-'vōt\ *vb* **de·vot·ed; de·vot·ing 1** : to commit to wholly or chiefly **2** : to set apart for a special purpose : DEDICATE

de·vot·ed \-'vō-təd\ *adj* : characterized by loyalty and devotion : FAITHFUL

dev·o·tee \ˌde-və-'tē, -'tā\ *n* : an ardent follower, supporter, or enthusiast

de·vo·tion \di-'vō-shən\ *n* **1** : religious fervor **2** : an act of prayer or private worship — usu. used in pl. **3** : a religious exercise for private use **4** : the fact or state of being dedicated and loyal ⟨~ to music⟩; *also* : the act of devoting — **de·vo·tion·al** \-shə-nəl\ *adj*

de·vour \di-'vaùr\ *vb* **1** : to eat up greedily or ravenously **2** : WASTE, ANNIHILATE **3** : to enjoy avidly ⟨~ a book⟩ — **de·vour·er** *n*

de·vout \di-'vaùt\ *adj* **1** : devoted to religion : PIOUS **2** : expressing devotion or piety **3** : EARNEST, SERIOUS — **de·vout·ly** *adv* — **de·vout·ness** *n*

dew \'dü, 'dyü\ *n* : moisture that condenses on the surfaces of cool bodies at night — **dewy** *adj*

dew·ber·ry \'dü-ˌber-ē, 'dyü-\ *n* : any of several sweet edible berries related to and resembling blackberries; *also* : a trailing bramble bearing these

dew·claw \-ˌklò\ *n* : a digit on the foot of a mammal that does not reach the ground; *also* : its claw or hoof

dew·lap \-ˌlap\ *n* : loose skin hanging under the neck of an animal

dew point *n* : the temperature at which the moisture in the air begins to condense

dex·ter·i·ty \dek-'ster-ə-tē\ *n, pl* **-ties 1** : mental skill or quickness **2** : readiness and grace in physical activity; *esp* : skill and ease in using the hands

dex·ter·ous \'dek-strəs\ *adj* **1** : CLEVER **2** : done with skillfulness **3** : skillful and competent with the hands — **dex·ter·ous·ly** *adv*

dex·trose \'dek-ˌstrōs\ *n* : the naturally occurring form of glucose found in plants and blood

DFC *abbr* Distinguished Flying Cross

dg *abbr* decigram

DG *abbr* **1** [LL *Dei gratia*] by the grace of God **2** director general

DH \ˌdē-'āch\ *n* : DESIGNATED HITTER

dhow \'daù\ *n* : an Arab sailing ship usu. having a long overhang forward and a high poop

DI *abbr* drill instructor

dia *abbr* diameter

di·a·be·tes \ˌdī-ə-'bē-tēz, -təs\ *n* : an abnormal state marked by passage of excessive amounts of urine; *esp* : one (**diabetes mel·li·tus** \-'me-lə-təs\) characterized by deficient insulin, by excess sugar in the blood and urine, and by thrist, hunger, and loss of weight — **di·a·bet·ic** \-'be-tik\ *adj or n*

di·a·bol·ic \ˌdī-ə-'bä-lik\ *or* **di·a·bol·i·cal** \-li-kəl\ *adj* : DEVILISH, FIENDISH — **di·a·bol·i·cal·ly** \-k(ə-)lē\ *adv*

di·a·crit·ic \ˌdī-ə-'kri-tik\ *n* : a mark accompanying a letter and indicating a sound value different from that of the same letter when unmarked — **di·a·crit·i·cal** \-ti-kəl\ *adj*

di·a·dem \'dī-ə-ˌdem\ *n* : CROWN; *esp* : a royal headband

di·aer·e·sis \dī-'er-ə-səs\ *n, pl* **-e·ses** \-ˌsēz\ : a mark placed over a vowel to show that it is pronounced in a separate syllable (as in *naïve*)

diag *abbr* **1** diagonal **2** diagram

di·ag·no·sis \ˌdī-ig-'nō-səs\ *n, pl* **-no·ses** \-ˌsēz\ : the art or act of identifying a disease from its signs and symptoms; *also* : the decision reached by diagnosis — **di·ag·nose** \'dī-ig-ˌnōs\ *vb* — **di·ag·nos·tic** \ˌdī-ig-'näs-tik\ *adj* — **di·ag·nos·ti·cian** \-ˌnäs-'ti-shən\ *n*

¹**di·ag·o·nal** \dī-'a-gə-nəl\ *adj* **1** : extending from one corner to the opposite corner in a 4-sided figure **2** : running in a slanting direction ⟨~ stripes⟩ **3** : having slanting markings or parts ⟨a ~ weave⟩ — **di·ag·o·nal·ly** *adv*

²**diagonal** *n* **1** : a diagonal line **2** : a diagonal row, pattern, or direction **3** : a mark / used esp. to mean "or," "and or," or "per"

¹**di·a·gram** \'dī-ə-ˌgram\ *n* : a design and esp. a drawing that makes something easier to understand — **di·a·gram·ma·ble** \-ˌgra-mə-bəl\ *adj* — **di·a·gram·mat·ic** \ˌdī-ə-grə-'ma-tik\ *adj* — **di·a·gram·mat·i·cal·ly** \-ti-k(ə-)lē\ *adv*

²**diagram** *vb* **-grammed** *or* **-gramed** \-ˌgramd\; **-gram·ming** *or* **-gram·ing** : to represent by a diagram

¹**di·al** \'dī(-ə)l\ *n* [ME *dyal*, fr. ML *dialis* clock wheel revolving daily, fr. L *dies* day] **1** : the face of a sundial **2** : the face of a timepiece **3** : a face with a pointer and numbers that indicate something ⟨the ~ of a gauge⟩ **4** : a device used for making electrical connections or for regulating operation (as of a radio)

²**dial** *vb* **di·aled** *or* **di·alled; di·al·ing** *or* **di·al·ling** **1** : to manipulate a dial so as to operate or select **2** : to make a telephone call or connection

³**dial** *abbr* dialect

di·a·lect \'dī-ə-ˌlekt\ *n* : a regional variety of a language

di·a·lec·tic \ˌdī-ə-'lek-tik\ *n* : the process or art of reasoning by discussion of conflicting ideas; *also* : the tension between opposing elements

di·a·logue \'dī-ə-ˌlòg\ *n* **1** : a conversation between two or more parties **2** : the parts of a literary or dramatic work that represent conversation

di·al·y·sis \dī-'a-lə-səs\ *n, pl* **-y·ses** \-ˌsēz\ **1** : the separation of substances from solution by means of their unequal diffusion through semipermeable membranes **2** : the medical procedure of removing blood from an artery, purifying it by dialysis, and returning it to a vein

diam *abbr* diameter

di·am·e·ter \dī-'a-mə-tər\ *n* [ME *diametre*, fr. MF, fr. L *diametros*, fr. Gk, fr. *dia-* through + *metron* measure] **1** : a straight line passing through the center of a figure or body; *esp* : one that divides a circle in half **2** : the length of a diameter

di·a·met·ric \ˌdī-ə-'me-trik\ *or* **di·a·met·ri·cal** \-tri-kəl\ *adj* **1** : of, relating to, or constituting a diameter **2** : completely opposed or opposite — **di·a·met·ri·cal·ly** \-k(ə-)lē\ *adv*

di·a·mond \'dī-mənd, 'dī-ə-\ *n* **1** : a hard brilliant mineral that consists of crystalline carbon and is used as a gem **2** : a flat figure having four equal sides, two acute angles, and two obtuse angles **3** : any of a suit of playing cards marked with a red diamond **4** : INFIELD; *also* : the entire playing field in baseball

di·a·mond·back rattlesnake \-ˌbak-\ *n* : a large and deadly rattlesnake of the southern U.S.

di·an·thus \dī-'an-thəs\ *n* : ¹PINK 1

di·a·pa·son \ˌdī-ə-'pāz-ᵊn, -'pās-\ *n* **1** : the organ stop governing the flue pipes that form the primary basis of organ tone **2** : the entire range of musical tones

¹**di·a·per** \'dī-pər, 'dī-ə-\ *n* **1** : a cotton or linen fabric woven in a simple geometric pattern **2** : a garment for a baby drawn up between the legs and fastened about the waist

²**diaper** *vb* **1** : to ornament with diaper designs **2** : to put a diaper on

di·aph·a·nous \dī-'a-fə-nəs\ *adj* : of so fine a texture as to be transparent

di·a·pho·ret·ic \ˌdī-ə-fə-'re-tik\ *adj* : having the power to increase perspiration — **diaphoretic** *n*

di·a·phragm \'dī-ə-ˌfram\ *n* **1** : a sheet of muscle between the chest and abdominal cavities of a mammal **2** : a vibrating disk (as in a microphone) **3** : a cup-shaped device usu. of thin rubber fitted over the uterine cervix to act as a mechanical contraceptive barrier — **di·a·phrag·mat·ic** \ˌdī-ə-frag-'ma-tik, -ˌfrag-\ *adj*

di·a·rist \'dī-ə-rist\ *n* : one who keeps a diary

di·ar·rhea \ˌdī-ə-'rē-ə\ *n* : abnormally frequent and watery bowel movements

di·ar·rhoea *chiefly Brit var of* DIARRHEA

di·a·ry \'dī-ə-rē\ *n, pl* **-ries** : a daily record esp. of personal experiences; *also* : a book used as a diary

di·as·to·le \dī-'as-tə-(ˌ)lē\ *n* : the stretching of the chambers of the heart during which they fill with blood — **di·a·stol·ic** \ˌdī-ə-'stä-lik\ *adj*

dia·ther·my \'dī-ə-ˌthər-mē\ *n* : the generation of heat in tissue by electric currents for medical or surgical purposes

di·a·tom \'dī-ə-ˌtäm\ *n* : any of a class of planktonic

one-celled or colonial algae with skeletons of silica

di·atom·ic \ˌdī-ə-ˈtä-mik\ *adj* : having two atoms in the molecule

di·a·tribe \ˈdī-ə-ˌtrīb\ *n* : biting or abusive speech or writing

dib·ble \ˈdi-bəl\ *n* : a pointed hand tool for making holes (as for planting bulbs) in the ground — **dibble** *vb*

¹dice \ˈdīs\ *n, pl* **dice** : DIE 1

²dice *vb* **diced; dic·ing** **1** : to cut into small cubes ⟨∼ carrots⟩ **2** : to play games with dice

di·chot·o·my \dī-ˈkä-tə-mē\ *n, pl* **-mies** : a division or the process of dividing into two esp. mutually exclusive or contradictory groups — **di·chot·o·mous** \-məs\ *adj*

dick·er \ˈdi-kər\ *vb* : BARGAIN, HAGGLE

dick·ey *or* **dicky** \ˈdi-kē\ *n, pl* **dickeys** *or* **dick·ies** : a small fabric insert worn to fill in the neckline

di·cot·y·le·don \ˌdī-ˌkät-ᵊl-ˈēd-ᵊn\ *n* : any of a group of seed plants having an embryo with two cotyledons — **di·cot·y·le·don·ous** *adj*

dict *abbr* dictionary

¹dic·tate \ˈdik-ˌtāt\ *vb* **dic·tat·ed; dic·tat·ing** **1** : to speak or read for a person to transcribe or for a machine to record **2** : COMMAND, ORDER — **dic·ta·tion** \dik-ˈtā-shən\ *n*

²dic·tate \ˈdik-ˌtāt\ *n* : an authoritative rule, prescription, or injunction : COMMAND ⟨the ∼s of conscience⟩

dic·ta·tor \ˈdik-ˌtā-tər\ *n* **1** : a person ruling absolutely and often brutally and oppressively **2** : one that dictates

dic·ta·to·ri·al \ˌdik-tə-ˈtōr-ē-əl\ *adj* : of, relating to, or characteristic of a dictator or a dictatorship

dic·ta·tor·ship \dik-ˈtā-tər-ˌship, ˈdik-ˌtā-\ *n* **1** : the office of a dictator **2** : autocratic rule, control, or leadership **3** : a government or country in which absolute power is held by a dictator or a small clique

dic·tion \ˈdik-shən\ *n* **1** : choice of words esp. with regard to correctness, clearness, or effectiveness : WORDING **2** : ENUNCIATION

dic·tio·nary \ˈdik-shə-ˌner-ē\ *n, pl* **-nar·ies** : a reference book containing words usu. alphabetically arranged along with information about their forms, pronunciations, functions, etymologies, meanings, and syntactical and idiomatic uses

dic·tum \ˈdik-təm\ *n, pl* **dic·ta** \-tə\ *also* **dictums** : a noteworthy, formal, or authoritative statement or observation

did *past of* DO

di·dac·tic \dī-ˈdak-tik\ *adj* **1** : intended to instruct, inform, or teach a moral lesson **2** : making moral observations

di·do \ˈdī-dō\ *n, pl* **didoes** *or* **didos** : a mischievous act : PRANK

¹die \ˈdī\ *vb* **died; dy·ing** \ˈdī-iŋ\ **1** : to stop living : EXPIRE **2** : to pass out of existence ⟨a *dying* race⟩ **3** : SUBSIDE **4** (the wind *died* down) **4** : to long keenly ⟨*dying* to go⟩ **5** : STOP ⟨the motor *died*⟩

²die \ˈdī\ *n* **1** *pl* **dice** \ˈdīs\ : a small cube marked on each face with one to six spots and used usu. in pairs

in games and gambling **2** *pl* **dies** \ˈdīz\ : a device used to shape, finish, or impress an object

die·hard \ˈdī-ˌhärd\ *n* : one who is strongly devoted to or determined

die·sel \ˈdē-zəl, -səl\ *n* **1** : DIESEL ENGINE **2** : a vehicle driven by a diesel engine

diesel engine *n* : an internal combustion engine in whose cylinders air is compressed to a temperature sufficiently high to ignite the fuel

die·sel·ing \ˈdē-zə-liŋ\ *n* : the continued operation of an internal combustion engine after the ignition has been turned off

¹di·et \ˈdī-ət\ *n* [ME *diete*, fr. OF, fr. L *diaeta*, fr. Gk *diaita*, lit., manner of living, fr. *diaitasthai* to lead one's life] **1** : food and drink regularly consumed : FARE **2** : an allowance of food prescribed for a special reason (as to lose weight) — **di·e·tary** \-ə-ˌter-ē\ *adj or n*

²diet *vb* : to eat or cause to eat or drink less or according to a prescribed rule — **di·et·er** *n*

di·e·tet·ics \ˌdī-ə-ˈte-tiks\ *n sing or pl* : the science or art of applying the principles of nutrition to diet — **di·e·tet·ic** *adj*

di·e·ti·tian *or* **di·e·ti·cian** \ˌdī-ə-ˈti-shən\ *n* : a specialist in dietetics

dif *or* **diff** *abbr* difference

dif·fer \ˈdi-fər\ *vb* **dif·fered; dif·fer·ing** **1** : to be unlike **2** : VARY **3** : DISAGREE

dif·fer·ence \ˈdi-frəns, ˈdi-fə-\ *n* **1** : UNLIKENESS ⟨∼ in their looks⟩ **2** : distinction or discrimination in preference **3** : DISAGREEMENT; *also* : an instance or cause of disagreement ⟨unable to settle their ∼s⟩ **4** : the amount by which one number or quantity differs from another

dif·fer·ent \ˈdi-frənt, ˈdi-fə-\ *adj* **1** : unlike in nature or quality **2** : DISTINCT ⟨∼ age groups⟩; *also* : VARIOUS ⟨∼ members of the club⟩ **3** : ANOTHER ⟨try a ∼ channel⟩ **4** : UNUSUAL, SPECIAL — **dif·fer·ent·ly** *adv*

¹dif·fer·en·tial \ˌdi-fə-ˈren-chəl\ *adj* : showing, creating, or relating to a difference

²differential *n* **1** : the amount or degree by which things differ **2** : DIFFERENTIAL GEAR

differential calculus *n* : a branch of mathematics concerned with the study of the rate of change of functions with respect to their variables

differential gear *n* : an arrangement of gears in an automobile that allows one wheel to turn faster than another (as in rounding curves)

dif·fer·en·ti·ate \ˌdi-fə-ˈren-chē-ˌāt\ *vb* **-at·ed; -at·ing** **1** : to make or become different **2** : to recognize or state the difference ⟨∼ between them⟩ — **dif·fer·en·ti·a·tion** \-ˌren-chē-ˈā-shən\ *n*

dif·fi·cult \ˈdi-fi-(ˌ)kəlt\ *adj* **1** : hard to do or make **2** : hard to understand or deal with ⟨∼ reading⟩ ⟨a ∼ child⟩

dif·fi·cul·ty \-(ˌ)kəl-tē\ *n, pl* **-ties 1** : difficult nature ⟨the

∼ of a task⟩ **2** : DISAGREEMENT ⟨settled their *difficulties*⟩ **3** : OBSTACLE ⟨overcome *difficulties*⟩ **4** : TROUBLE ⟨in financial *difficulties*⟩ **syn** hardship, rigor, vicissitude

dif·fi·dent \\'di-fə-dənt\\ *adj* **1** : lacking confidence **2** : RESERVED **1** — **dif·fi·dence** \\-dəns\\ *n* — **dif·fi·dent·ly** *adv*

dif·frac·tion \\di-'frak-shən\\ *n* : the bending or spreading of waves (as of light) esp. when passing through narrow slits

¹dif·fuse \\di-'fyüs\\ *adj* **1** : VERBOSE, WORDY ⟨∼ writing⟩ **2** : not concentrated or localized ⟨∼ light⟩

²dif·fuse \\di-'fyüz\\ *vb* **dif·fused; dif·fus·ing 1** : to pour out or spread widely **2** : to undergo or cause to undergo diffusion **3** : to break up light by diffusion

dif·fu·sion \\di-'fyü-zhən\\ *n* **1** : a diffusing or a being diffused **2** : movement of particles (as of a gas) from a region of high to one of lower concentration **3** : the reflection of light from a rough surface or the passage of light through a translucent material

¹dig \\'dig\\ *vb* **dug** \\'dəg\\; **dig·ging 1** : to turn up the soil (as with a spade) **2** : to hollow out or form by removing earth ⟨∼ a hole⟩ **3** : to uncover or seek by turning up earth ⟨∼ potatoes⟩ **4** : DISCOVER ⟨∼ up information⟩ **5** : POKE, THRUST ⟨∼ a person in the ribs⟩ **6** : to work hard **7** : UNDERSTAND, APPRECIATE; *also* : LIKE, ADMIRE

²dig *n* **1** : THRUST, POKE; *also* : a cutting remark : GIBE **2** *pl* : living accommodations

³dig *abbr* digest

¹di·gest \\'dī-,jest\\ *n* : a summarized or shortened version esp. of a literary work

²di·gest \\di-'jest, də-\\ *vb* **1** : to think over and arrange in the mind **2** : to convert (food) into simpler forms that can be absorbed by the body **3** : to compress into a short summary — **di·gest·ibil·i·ty** \\-,jes-tə-'bi-lə-tē\\ *n* — **di·gest·ible** *adj* — **di·ges·tion** \\-'jes-chən\\ *n* — **di·ges·tive** \\-'jes-tiv\\ *adj*

dig in *vb* **1** : to take a defensive stand esp. by digging trenches **2** : to firmly set to work **3** : to begin eating

dig·it \\'di-jət\\ *n* [ME, fr. L *digitus* finger, toe] **1** : any of the Arabic numerals 1 to 9 and usu. the symbol 0 **2** : FINGER, TOE

dig·i·tal \\'di-jət-ᵊl\\ *adj* **1** : of, relating to, or done with a finger or toe **2** : of, relating to, or using calculation directly with digits rather than through measurable physical quantities ⟨a ∼ computer⟩ **3** : providing a readout in numerical digits ⟨a ∼ watch⟩ — **dig·i·tal·ly** *adv*

dig·i·tal·is \\,di-jə-'ta-ləs\\ *n* : a drug from the common foxglove that is a powerful heart stimulant; *also* : FOXGLOVE

dig·ni·fied \\'dig-nə-,fīd\\ *adj* : showing or expressing dignity

dig·ni·fy \\-,fī\\ *vb* **-fied; -fy·ing** : to give dignity, distinction, or attention to

dig·ni·tary \\'dig-nə-,ter-ē\\ *n, pl* **-tar·ies** : a person of high position or honor

dig·ni·ty \\'dig-nə-tē\\ *n, pl* **-ties 1** : the quality or state of being worthy, honored, or esteemed **2** : high rank,

office, or position **3** : formal reserve of manner, language, or appearance

di·graph \\'dī-,graf\\ *n* : a group of two successive letters whose phonetic value is a single sound (as *ea* in *bread*)

di·gress \\dī-'gres, də-\\ *vb* : to turn aside esp. from the main subject or argument — **di·gres·sion** \\-'gre-shən\\ *n* — **di·gres·sive** \\-'gre-siv\\ *adj*

dike \\'dīk\\ *n* : a bank of earth constructed to control water : LEVEE

dil *abbr* dilute

di·lap·i·dat·ed \\də-'la-pə-,dā-təd\\ *adj* : fallen into partial ruin or decay — **di·lap·i·da·tion** \\-,la-pə-'dā-shən\\ *n*

di·late \\dī-'lāt, 'dī-,lāt\\ *vb* **di·lat·ed; di·lat·ing** : SWELL, DISTEND, EXPAND — **dil·a·ta·tion** \\,di-lə-'tā-shən\\ *n* — **di·la·tion** \\dī-'lā-shən\\ *n*

dil·a·to·ry \\'di-lə-,tōr-ē\\ *adj* **1** : DELAYING **2** : TARDY, SLOW

---

di·lem·ma \\də-'le-mə\\ *n* **1** : a usu. undesirable or unpleasant choice; *also* : a situation involving such a choice **2** : PREDICAMENT

---

dil·et·tante \\,di-lə-'tänt, -'tant\\ *n, pl* **-tantes** *or* **-tan·ti** \\-'tän-tē, -'tan-\\ [It, fr. prp. of *dilettare* to delight, fr. L *dilectare*] : a person having a superficial interest in an art or a branch of knowledge

dil·i·gent \\'di-lə-jənt\\ *adj* : characterized by steady, earnest, and energetic effort : PAINSTAKING — **dil·i·gence** \\-jəns\\ *n* — **dil·i·gent·ly** *adv*

dill \\'dil\\ *n* : an herb related to the carrot with aromatic leaves and seeds used in pickles

dil·ly \\'di-lē\\ *n, pl* **dil·lies** : one that is remarkable or outstanding

dil·ly·dal·ly \\'di-lē-,da-lē\\ *vb* : to waste time by loitering or delaying

¹di·lute \\dī-'lüt, də-\\ *vb* **di·lut·ed; di·lut·ing** : to lessen the consistency or strength of by mixing with something else — **di·lu·tion** \\-'lü-shən\\ *n*

²dilute *adj* : DILUTED, WEAK

¹dim \\'dim\\ *adj* **dim·mer; dim·mest 1** : LUSTERLESS, DULL **2** : not bright or distinct : OBSCURE, FAINT **3** : not seeing or understanding clearly — **dim·ly** *adv* — **dim·ness** *n*

²dim *vb* **dimmed; dim·ming 1** : to make or become dim or lusterless **2** : to reduce the light from

³dim *abbr* **1** dimension **2** diminished **3** diminutive

dime \\'dīm\\ *n* [ME, tenth part, tithe, fr. MF, fr. L *decima*, fr. fem. of *decimus* tenth, fr. *decem* ten] : a U.S. coin worth ¹⁄₁₀ dollar

di·men·sion \\də-'men-chən, dī-\\ *n* **1** : the physical property of length, breadth, or thickness; *also* : a measure of this **2** : EXTENT, SCOPE, PROPORTIONS — usu. used in pl. — **di·men·sion·al** \\-'men-chə-nəl\\ *adj* — **di·men·sion·al·i·ty** \\-,men-chə-'na-lə-tē\\ *n*

di·min·ish \\də-'mi-nish\\ *vb* **1** : to make less or cause to appear less **2** : BELITTLE **3** : DWINDLE **4** : TAPER — **dim·i·nu·tion** \\,di-mə-'nü-shən, -'nyü-\\ *n*

di•min•u•en•do \də-ˌmin-yə-ˈwen-dō\ adv or adj : DE-CRESCENDO

¹di•min•u•tive \də-ˈmin-yə-tiv\ n 1 : a diminutive word or affix 2 : a diminutive individual

²diminutive adj 1 : indicating small size and sometimes the state or quality of being lovable, pitiable, or contemptible ⟨the ~ suffixes -ette and -ling⟩ 2 : extremely small : TINY

dim•i•ty \ˈdi-mə-tē\ n, pl -ties : a thin usu. corded cotton fabric

dim•mer \ˈdi-mər\ n : a device for controlling the amount of light from an electric lighting unit

di•mor•phic \(ˌ)dī-ˈmȯr-fik\ adj : occurring in two distinct forms — di•mor•phism \-ˌfi-zəm\ n

¹dim•ple \ˈdim-pəl\ n : a small depression esp. in the cheek or chin

²dimple vb dim•pled; dim•pling : to form dimples (as in smiling)

din \ˈdin\ n : a loud confused mixture of noises

di•nar \di-ˈnär\ n 1 — see MONEY table 2 — see rial at MONEY table

dine \ˈdīn\ vb dined; din•ing [ME, fr. OF diner, fr. (assumed) VL disjejunare to break one's fast, ultim. fr. L jejunus fasting] 1 : to eat dinner 2 : to give a dinner to

din•er \ˈdī-nər\ n 1 : one that dines 2 : a railroad dining car 3 : a restaurant usu. resembling a dining car

di•nette \dī-ˈnet\ n : an alcove or small room used for dining

din•ghy \ˈdiŋ-ē\ n, pl dinghies 1 : a small boat 2 : LIFE RAFT

din•gle \ˈdiŋ-gəl\ n : a small wooded valley

din•go \ˈdiŋ-gō\ n, pl dingoes : a reddish brown wild dog of Australia

dingo

din•gus \ˈdiŋ-gəs, -əs\ n : DOODAD

din•gy \ˈdin-jē\ adj din•gi•er; -est : DIRTY, DISCOLORED; also : SHABBY — din•gi•ness n

din•ky \ˈdiŋ-kē\ adj din•ki•er; -est : SMALL, INSIGNIFICANT

din•ner \ˈdi-nər\ n : the main meal of the day; also : a formal banquet

din•ner•ware \ˈdi-nər-ˌwar\ n : tableware other than flatware

di•no•fla•gel•late \ˌdī-nō-ˈfla-jə-lət, -ˌlāt\ n : any of an order of planktonic plantlike unicellular flagellates of which some cause red tide

di•no•saur \ˈdī-nə-ˌsȯr\ n [ultim. fr. Gk deinos terrifying + sauros lizard] : any of a group of extinct long-tailed Mesozoic reptiles often of huge size

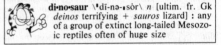

dint \ˈdint\ n 1 : FORCE ⟨by ~ of sheer grit⟩ 2 : DENT

di•o•cese \ˈdī-ə-səs, -ˌsēz, -ˌsēs\ n, pl -ces•es \-sə-səz, -ˌsē-zəz, -ˌsē-səz\ : the territorial jurisdiction of a bishop — di•oc•e•san \dī-ˈä-sə-sən, ˌdī-ə-ˈsēs-ᵊn\ adj or n

di•ode \ˈdī-ˌōd\ n 1 : an electronic device with two electrodes or terminals used esp. as a rectifier

di•ox•in \dī-ˈäk-sən\ n : a hydrocarbon that occurs esp. as a persistent toxic impurity in herbicides (as Agent Orange)

¹dip \ˈdip\ vb dipped; dip•ping 1 : to plunge temporarily or partially under the surface (as of a liquid) 2 : to thrust in a way to suggest immersion 3 : to scoop up or out : LADLE 4 : to lower and then raise quickly ⟨~ a flag in salute⟩ 5 : to drop or slope down esp. suddenly ⟨the moon dipped below the crest⟩ 6 : to decrease moderately and usu. temporarily ⟨prices dipped⟩ 7 : to reach inside or as if inside or below a surface ⟨dipped into their savings⟩ 8 : to delve casually into something; esp : to read superficially ⟨~ into a book⟩

²dip n 1 : an act of dipping; esp : a short swim 2 : inclination downward : DROP 3 : something obtained by or used in dipping 4 : a sauce or soft mixture into which food may be dipped 5 : a liquid into which something may be dipped (as for cleansing or coloring)

diph•the•ria \dif-ˈthir-ē-ə\ n : an acute contagious bacterial disease marked by fever and by coating of the air passages with a membrane that interferes with breathing

diph•thong \ˈdif-ˌthȯŋ\ n : two vowel sounds joined in one syllable to form one speech sound (as ou in out)

dip•loid \ˈdi-ˌplȯid\ adj : having the basic chromosome number doubled — diploid n

di•plo•ma \də-ˈplō-mə\ n, pl diplomas : an official record of graduation from or of a degree conferred by a school

di•plo•ma•cy \də-ˈplō-mə-sē\ n 1 : the art and practice of conducting negotiations between nations 2 : TACT

dip•lo•mat \ˈdi-plə-ˌmat\ n : one employed or skilled in diplomacy — dip•lo•mat•ic \ˌdi-plə-ˈma-tik\ adj

di•plo•ma•tist \də-ˈplō-mə-tist\ n : DIPLOMAT

dip•per \ˈdi-pər\ n 1 : any of a genus of birds that are related to the thrushes and are skilled in diving 2 : something (as a ladle or scoop) that dips or is used for dipping 3 cap : BIG DIPPER 4 cap : LITTLE DIPPER

dip•so•ma•nia \ˌdip-sə-ˈmā-nē-ə\ n : an uncontrollable craving for alcoholic liquors — dip•so•ma•ni•ac \-nē-ˌak\ n

dip•stick \ˈdip-ˌstik\ n : a graduated rod for indicating depth

dip•ter•an \ˈdip-tə-rən\ adj : of, relating to, or being a fly (sense 2) — dipteran n — dip•ter•ous \-rəs\ adj

dir *abbr* **1** direction **2** director

dire \'dīr\ *adj* **dir•er; dir•est 1** : very horrible : DREADFUL **2** : warning of disaster **3** : EXTREME

¹**di•rect** \də-'rekt, dī-\ *vb* **1** : ADDRESS ⟨∼ a letter⟩; *also* : to impart orally : AIM ⟨∼ a remark to the gallery⟩ **2** : to regulate the activities or course of : guide the supervision, organizing, or performance of **3** : to cause to turn, move, or point or to follow a certain course **4** : to point, extend, or project in a specified line or course **5** : to request or instruct with authority **6** : to show or point out the way

²**direct** *adj* **1** : stemming immediately from a source ⟨∼ result⟩ **2** : being or passing in a straight line of descent : LINEAL ⟨∼ ancestor⟩ **3** : leading from one point to another in time or space without turn or stop : STRAIGHT **4** : NATURAL, STRAIGHTFORWARD ⟨a ∼ manner⟩ **5** : operating without an intervening agency or step ⟨∼ action⟩ **6** : effected by the action of the people or the electorate and not by representatives ⟨∼ democracy⟩ **7** : consisting of or reproducing the exact words of a speaker or writer — **direct** *adv* — **di•rect•ly** *adv* — **di•rect•ness** *n*

direct current *n* : an electric current flowing in one direction only

di•rec•tion \də-'rek-shən, dī-\ *n* **1** : MANAGEMENT, GUIDANCE **2** : COMMAND, ORDER, INSTRUCTION **3** : the course or line along which something moves, lies, or points **4** : TENDENCY, TREND — **di•rec•tion•al** \-shə-nəl\ *adj*

di•rec•tive \də-'rek-tiv, dī-\ *n* : something that directs and usu. impels toward an action or goal; *esp* : an order issued by a high-level body or official

direct mail *n* : printed matter used for soliciting business or contributions and mailed direct to individuals

di•rec•tor \də-'rek-tər, dī-\ *n* **1** : one that directs : MANAGER, SUPERVISOR, CONDUCTOR **2** : one of a group of persons who direct the affairs of an organized body or company — **di•rec•to•ri•al** \-,rek-'tōr-ē-əl\ *adj* — **di•rec•tor•ship** *n*

di•rec•tor•ate \-tə-rət\ *n* **1** : the office or position of director **2** : a board of directors; *also* : membership on such a board **3** : an executive staff

di•rec•to•ry \-tə-rē\ *n, pl* **-ries** : an alphabetical or classified list esp. of names and addresses

dire•ful \'dīr-fəl\ *adj* : DREADFUL; *also* : OMINOUS

dirge \'dərj\ *n* : a song of lamentation; *also* : a slow mournful piece of music

dir•ham \'dir-həm\ *n* **1** — see MONEY table **2** — see *dinar, riyal* at MONEY table

di•ri•gi•ble \'dir-ə-jə-bəl, də-'ri-jə-\ *n* : AIRSHIP

dirk \'dərk\ *n* : DAGGER **1**

dirndl \'dərnd-ᵊl\ *n* [short for G *Dirndlkleid,* fr. G dial. *Dirndl* girl + G *Kleid* dress] : a full skirt with a tight waistband

dirt \'dərt\ *n* **1** : a filthy or soiling substance (as mud, dust, or grime) **2** : loose or packed earth : SOIL **3** : moral uncleanness **4** : scandalous gossip **5** : embarrassing or incriminating information

¹**dirty** \'dər-tē\ *adj* **dirt•i•er; -est 1** : SOILED, FILTHY **2** : INDECENT, SMUTTY ⟨∼ jokes⟩ **3** : BASE, UNFAIR ⟨a ∼ trick⟩ **4** : STORMY, FOGGY ⟨∼ weather⟩ **5** : not clear in color : DULL ⟨a ∼ red⟩ — **dirt•i•ness** *n* — **dirty** *adv*

²**dirty** *vb* **dirt•ied; dirty•ing** : to make or become dirty

dis•able \di-'sā-bəl\ *vb* **dis•abled; dis•abling 1** : to disqualify legally **2** : to make unable to perform by or as if by illness, injury, or malfunction — **dis•abil•i•ty** \,di-sə-'bi-lə-tē\ *n*

dis•abled *adj* : incapacitated by illness, injury, or wounds; *also* : physically or mentally impaired

dis•abuse \,di-sə-'byüz\ *vb* : to free from error, fallacy, or misconception

dis•ad•van•tage \,di-səd-'van-tij\ *n* **1** : loss or damage esp. to reputation or finances **2** : an unfavorable, inferior, or prejudicial condition; *also* : HANDICAP — **dis•ad•van•ta•geous** \di-,sad-,van-'tā-jəs, -vən-\ *adj*

dis•ad•van•taged \-tijd\ *adj* : lacking in basic resources or conditions believed necessary for an equal position in society

dis•af•fect \,di-sə-'fekt\ *vb* : to alienate the affection or loyalty of — **dis•af•fec•tion** \-'fek-shən\ *n*

dis•agree \,di-sə-'grē\ *vb* **1** : to fail to agree **2** : to differ in opinion **3** : to cause discomfort or distress ⟨fried foods ∼ with her⟩ — **dis•agree•ment** *n*

dis•agree•able \-ə-bəl\ *adj* **1** : causing discomfort : UNPLEASANT, OFFENSIVE **2** : ILL-TEMPERED, PEEVISH — **dis•agree•able•ness** *n* — **dis•agree•ably** \-blē\ *adv*

dis•al•low \,di-sə-'laù\ *vb* : to refuse to admit or recognize : REJECT ⟨∼ a claim⟩ — **dis•al•low•ance** *n*

dis•ap•pear \,di-sə-'pir\ *vb* **1** : to pass out of sight **2** : to cease to be : become lost — **dis•ap•pear•ance** *n*

dis•ap•point \,di-sə-'point\ *vb* : to fail to fulfill the expectation or hope of — **dis•ap•point•ment** *n*

dis•ap•pro•ba•tion \di-,sa-prə-'bā-shən\ *n* : DISAPPROVAL

dis•ap•prov•al \,di-sə-'prü-vəl\ *n* : adverse judgment : CENSURE

dis•ap•prove \-'prüv\ *vb* **1** : CONDEMN **2** : to feel or express disapproval ⟨∼s of smoking⟩ **3** : REJECT

dis•arm \di-'särm\ *vb* **1** : to take arms or weapons from **2** : to reduce the size and strength of the armed forces of a country **3** : to make harmless, peaceable, or friendly : win over ⟨a ∼ing smile⟩ — **dis•ar•ma•ment** \-'sär-mə-mənt\ *n*

dis•ar•range \,di-sə-'rānj\ *vb* : to disturb the arrangement or order of — **dis•ar•range•ment** *n*

dis•ar•ray \-'rā\ *n* **1** : DISORDER, CONFUSION **2** : disorderly or careless dress

dis•as•sem•ble \,di-sə-'sem-bəl\ *vb* : to take apart

dis•as•so•ci•ate \-'sō-shē-,āt, -sē-\ *vb* : to detach from association

dis•as•ter \di-'zas-tər, -'sas-\ *n* [MF *desastre,* fr. It *disastro,* fr. *astro* star, fr. L *astrum*] : a sudden or great misfortune — **dis•as•trous** \-'zas-trəs\ *adj* — **dis•as•trous•ly** *adv*

dis•avow \,di-sə-'vaù\ *vb* : to deny responsibility for : REPUDIATE — **dis•avow•al** \-'vaù-əl\ *n*

dis•band \dis-'band\ *vb* : to break up the organization of : DISPERSE

dis•bar \dis-'bär\ *vb* : to expel from the legal profession — **dis•bar•ment** *n*

dis•be•lieve \,dis-bə-'lēv\ *vb* **1** : to hold not worthy of belief : not believe **2** : to withhold or reject belief — **dis•be•lief** \-'lēf\ *n* — **dis•be•liev•er** *n*

dis•bur•den \dis-'bərd-ᵊn\ *vb* : to rid of a burden

dis•burse \dis-'bərs\ *vb* **dis•bursed; dis•burs•ing 1** : to pay out : EXPEND **2** : DISTRIBUTE — **dis•burse•ment** *n*

¹**disc** *var of* DISK

²**disc** *abbr* discount

dis•card \dis-'kärd, 'dis-,kärd\ *vb* **1** : to let go a playing card from one's hand; *also* : to play (a card) from a suit other than a trump but different from the one led **2** : to get rid of as unwanted — **dis•card** \'dis-,kärd\ *n*

disc brake *n* : a brake that operates by the friction of a pair of plates pressing against the sides of a rotating disc

dis•cern \di-'sərn, -'zərn\ *vb* **1** : to detect with the eyes : DISTINGUISH **2** : DISCRIMINATE **3** : to come to know or recognize mentally — **dis•cern•ible** *adj* — **dis•cern•ment** *n*

dis•cern•ing *adj* : revealing insight and understanding

¹**dis•charge** \dis-'chärj, 'dis-,chärj\ *vb* **1** : to relieve of a charge, load, or burden : UNLOAD; *esp* : to remove the electrical energy from ⟨∼ a storage battery⟩ **2** : to let or put off ⟨∼ passengers⟩ **3** : SHOOT ⟨∼ an arrow⟩ **4** : to set free ⟨∼ a prisoner⟩ **5** : to dismiss from service or employment ⟨∼ a soldier⟩ **6** : to get rid of by paying or doing ⟨∼ a debt⟩ **7** : to give forth fluid ⟨the river ∼s into the ocean⟩

²**dis•charge** \'dis-,chärj, dis-'chärj\ *n* **1** : the act of discharging, unloading, or releasing **2** : something that

discharges; *esp* : a certification of release or payment **3** : a firing off (as of a gun) **4** : a flowing out (as of blood from a wound); *also* : something that is emitted ⟨a purulent ∽⟩ **5** : release or dismissal esp. from an office or employment; *also* : complete separation from military service **6** : a flow of electricity (as through a gas)

dis·ci·ple \di-'sī-pəl\ *n* **1** : one who accepts and helps to spread the teachings of another; *also* : a convinced adherent **2** *cap* : a member of the Disciples of Christ

dis·ci·pli·nar·i·an \ˌdi-sə-plə-'ner-ē-ən\ *n* : one who enforces order

dis·ci·plin·ary \'di-sə-plə-ˌner-ē\ *adj* : of or relating to discipline; *also* : CORRECTIVE ⟨take ∽ action⟩

[1]**dis·ci·pline** \'di-sə-plən\ *n* **1** : PUNISHMENT **2** : a field of study : SUBJECT **3** : training that corrects, molds, or perfects **4** : control gained by obedience or training : orderly conduct **5** : a system of rules governing conduct

[2]**discipline** *vb* **-plined; -plin·ing 1** : PUNISH **2** : to train or develop by instruction and exercise esp. in self≠control **3** : to bring under control ⟨∽ troops⟩; *also* : to impose order upon

disc jockey *n* : an announcer of a radio show of popular recorded music

dis·claim \dis-'klām\ *vb* : DENY, DISAVOW — **dis·claim·er** *n*

dis·close \dis-'klōz\ *vb* : to expose to view — **dis·clo·sure** \-'klō-zhər\ *n*

dis·co \'dis-kō\ *n, pl* **discos 1** : a nightclub for dancing to live or recorded music **2** : popular dance music characterized by hypnotic rhythm, repetitive lyrics, and electronically produced sounds

dis·col·or \dis-'kə-lər\ *vb* : to alter or change in hue or color esp. for the worse — **dis·col·or·ation** \-ˌkə-lə-'rā-shən\ *n*

dis·com·bob·u·late \ˌdis-kəm-'bä-byü-ˌlāt\ *vb* **-lat·ed; -lat·ing** : UPSET, CONFUSE

dis·com·fit \dis-'kəm-fət, *esp Southern* ˌdis-kəm-'fit\ *vb* : UPSET, FRUSTRATE — **dis·com·fi·ture** \dis-'kəm-fə-ˌchür\ *n*

[1]**dis·com·fort** \dis-'kəm-fərt\ *vb* : to make uncomfortable or uneasy

[2]**discomfort** *n* : mental or physical uneasiness

dis·com·mode \ˌdis-kə-'mōd\ *vb* **-mod·ed; -mod·ing** : INCONVENIENCE, TROUBLE

dis·com·pose \-kəm-'pōz\ *vb* **1** : AGITATE **2** : DISARRANGE — **dis·com·po·sure** \-'pō-zhər\ *n*

dis·con·cert \ˌdis-kən-'sərt\ *vb* : CONFUSE, UPSET

dis·con·nect \ˌdis-kə-'nekt\ *vb* : to undo the connection of — **dis·con·nec·tion** \-'nek-shən\ *n*

dis·con·nect·ed *adj* : not connected; *also* : INCOHERENT — **dis·con·nect·ed·ly** *adv*

dis·con·so·late \dis-'kän-sə-lət\ *adj* **1** : CHEERLESS **2** : hopelessly sad — **dis·con·so·late·ly** *adv*

dis·con·tent \ˌdis-kən-'tent\ *n* : uneasiness of mind : DISSATISFACTION — **dis·con·tent·ed** *adj*

dis·con·tin·ue \ˌdis-kən-'tin-yü\ *vb* **1** : to break the continuity of : cease to operate, use, or take **2** : END — **dis·con·tin·u·ance** \-yə-wəns\ *n* — **dis·con·ti·nu·i·ty** \dis-ˌkän-tə-'nü-ə-tē, -'nyü-\ *n* — **dis·con·tin·u·ous** \ˌdis-kən-'tin-yə-wəs\ *adj*

dis·cord \'dis-ˌkȯrd\ *n* **1** : lack of agreement or harmony : DISSENSION, CONFLICT **2** : a harsh combination of musical sounds **3** : a harsh or unpleasant sound — **dis·cor·dant** \dis-'kȯrd-ᵊnt\ *adj* — **dis·cor·dant·ly** *adv*

dis·co·theque \'dis-kə-ˌtek\ *n* : DISCO 1

[1]**dis·count** \'dis-ˌkaunt\ *n* **1** : a reduction made from a regular or list price **2** : a deduction of interest in advance when lending money

[2]**dis·count** \'dis-ˌkaunt, dis-'kaunt\ *vb* **1** : to deduct from the amount of a bill, debt, or charge usu. for cash or prompt payment; *also* : to sell or offer for sale at a discount **2** : to lend money after deducting the discount ⟨∽ a note⟩ **3** : DISREGARD; *also* : MINIMIZE **4** : to make allowance for bias or exaggeration **5** : to take into account (as a future event) in present calculations — **dis·count·able** *adj* — **dis·count·er** *n*

[3]**dis·count** \'dis-ˌkaunt\ *adj* : selling goods or services at a discount; *also* : sold at or reflecting a discount

dis·coun·te·nance \dis-'kaunt-ᵊn-ənts\ *vb* **1** : EMBARRASS, DISCONCERT **2** : to look with disfavor on

dis·cour·age \dis-'kər-ij\ *vb* **-aged; -ag·ing 1** : to deprive of courage or confidence : DISHEARTEN **2** : to hinder by disfavoring **3** : to attempt to dissuade — **dis·cour·age·ment** *n* — **dis·cour·ag·ing·ly** *adv*

[1]**dis·course** \'dis-ˌkȯrs\ *n* [ME *discours*, fr. ML & LL *discursus*; ML, argument, fr. LL, conversation, fr. L, act of running about, fr. *discurrere* to run about, fr. *currere* to run] **1** : CONVERSATION **2** : formal and usu. extended expression of thought on a subject

[2]**dis·course** \dis-'kȯrs\ *vb* **dis·coursed; dis·cours·ing 1** : to express oneself in esp. oral discourse **2** : TALK, CONVERSE

dis·cour·te·ous \ˌ(ˌ)dis-'kər-tē-əs\ *adj* : lacking courtesy : UNCIVIL, RUDE — **dis·cour·te·ous·ly** *adv*

dis·cour·te·sy \-'kər-tə-sē\ *n* : RUDENESS; *also* : a rude act

dis·cov·er \dis-'kə-vər\ *vb* **1** : to make known or visible **2** : to obtain sight or knowledge of for the first time; *also* : FIND OUT — **dis·cov·er·er** *n*

dis·cov·ery \dis-'kə-və-rē\ *n, pl* **-er·ies 1** : the act or process of discovering **2** : something discovered **3** : the disclosure usu. before a civil trial of pertinent facts or documents

[1]**dis·cred·it** \(ˌ)dis-'kre-dət\ *vb* **1** : DISBELIEVE **2** : to cause disbelief in the accuracy or authority of **3** : DISGRACE — **dis·cred·it·able** *adj*

[2]**discredit** *n* **1** : loss of reputation **2** : lack or loss of belief or confidence

dis·creet \dis-'krēt\ *adj* : showing good judgment; *esp* : capable of observing prudent silence — **dis·creet·ly** *adv*

dis·crep·an·cy \dis-'kre-pən-sē\ *n, pl* **-cies 1** : DIFFER-

ENCE, DISAGREEMENT **2** : an instance of being discrep-
ant

dis·crep·ant \-pənt\ *adj* [ME *discrepaunt*, fr. L *dis-
crepans*, prp. of *discrepare* to sound discordantly, fr.
crepare to rattle, creak] : being at variance : DIS-
AGREEING

dis·crete \dis-ˈkrēt, ˈdis-ˌkrēt\ *adj* **1** : individually distinct **2** : NONCONTINUOUS

dis·cre·tion \dis-ˈkre-shən\ *n* **1** : the quality of being discreet : PRUDENCE **2** : individual choice or judgment **3** : power of
free decision or latitude of choice — **dis-
cre·tion·ary** *adj*

dis·crim·i·nate \dis-ˈkri-mə-ˌnāt\ *vb* **-nat·ed; -nat-
ing 1** : DISTINGUISH, DIFFERENTIATE **2** : to make a difference in treatment on a basis other than individual
merit — **dis·crim·i·na·tion** \-ˌkri-mə-ˈnā-shən\ *n*

dis·crim·i·nat·ing *adj* : marked by discrimination; *esp*
: DISCERNING, JUDICIOUS

dis·crim·i·na·to·ry \dis-ˈkri-mə-nə-ˌtōr-ē\ *adj* : marked
by esp. unjust discrimination ⟨∼ treatment⟩

dis·cur·sive \dis-ˈkər-siv\ *adj* : passing from one topic
to another : RAMBLING — **dis·cur·sive·ly** *adv* — **dis-
cur·sive·ness** *n*

dis·cus \ˈdis-kəs\ *n, pl* **dis·cus·es** : a disk that is hurled
for distance in a track-and-field contest

dis·cuss \di-ˈskəs\ *vb* [ME, fr. L *discussus*, pp. of *dis-
cutere* to disperse, fr. *dis-* apart + *quatere* to shake]
1 : to argue or consider carefully by presenting the
various sides **2** : to talk about — **dis·cus·sion** \-ˈskə-
shən\ *n*

dis·cus·sant \di-ˈskəs-ᵊnt\ *n* : one who takes part in a
formal discussion

¹dis·dain \dis-ˈdān\ *n* : CONTEMPT, SCORN — **dis·dain-
ful** \-fəl\ *adj* — **dis·dain·ful·ly** *adv*

²disdain *vb* **1** : to look on with scorn **2** : to reject or refrain from because of disdain

dis·ease \di-ˈzēz\ *n* : an abnormal bodily condition that
impairs functioning and can usu. be recognized by
signs and symptoms : SICKNESS — **dis·eased** \-ˈzēzd\
adj

dis·em·bark \ˌdi-səm-ˈbärk\ *vb* : to go or put ashore
from a ship — **dis·em·bar·ka·tion** \dis-ˌem-ˌbär-ˈkā-
shən\ *n*

dis·em·body \ˌdi-səm-ˈbä-dē\ *vb* : to deprive of bodily
existence

dis·em·bow·el \-ˈbaü-əl\ *vb* : EVISCERATE 1 — **dis-
em·bow·el·ment** *n*

dis·en·chant \ˌdis-ᵊn-ˈchant\ *vb* : DISILLUSION — **dis-
en·chant·ment** *n*

dis·en·chant·ed \-ˈchan-təd\ *adj* : DISAPPOINTED, DIS-
SATISFIED

dis·en·cum·ber \ˌdis-ᵊn-ˈkəm-bər\ *vb* : to free from
something that burdens

dis·en·fran·chise \ˌdis-ᵊn-ˈfran-ˌchīz\ *vb* : DISFRAN-
CHISE — **dis·en·fran·chise·ment** *n*

dis·en·gage \ˌdis-ᵊn-ˈgāj\ *vb* : RELEASE, EXTRICATE,
DISENTANGLE — **dis·en·gage·ment** *n*

dis·en·tan·gle \ˌdis-ᵊn-ˈtaŋ-gəl\ *vb* : to free from entanglement : UNRAVEL

dis·equi·lib·ri·um \di-ˌsē-kwə-ˈli-brē-əm\ *n* : loss of
lack of equilibrium

dis·es·tab·lish \ˌdi-sə-ˈsta-blish\ *vb* : to end the establishment of; *esp* : to deprive of the status of an established church — **dis·es·tab·lish·ment** *n*

dis·es·teem \ˌdi-sə-ˈstēm\ *n* : lack of esteem : DISFA-
VOR, DISREPUTE

dis·fa·vor \(ˌ)dis-ˈfā-vər\ *n* **1** : DISAPPROVAL, DISLIKE **2**
: the state or fact of being no longer favored

dis·fig·ure \dis-ˈfi-gyər\ *vb* : to spoil the appearance of
⟨*disfigured* by a scar⟩ — **dis·fig·ure·ment** *n*

dis·fran·chise \dis-ˈfran-ˌchīz\ *vb* : to deprive of a
franchise, a legal right, or a privilege; *esp* : to deprive
of the right to vote — **dis·fran·chise·ment** *n*

dis·gorge \-ˈgȯrj\ *vb* : VOMIT; *also* : to discharge forcefully or confusedly

¹dis·grace \-ˈskrās, dis-ˈgrās\ *vb* : to bring reproach
or shame to

²disgrace *n* **1** : SHAME, DISHONOR; *also* : a cause of
shame **2** : the condition of being out of favor : loss of
respect — **dis·grace·ful** \-fəl\ *adj* — **dis·grace·ful-
ly** *adv*

dis·grun·tle \dis-ˈgrənt-ᵊl\ *vb* **dis·grun·tled; dis·grun-
tling** : to put in bad humor

¹dis·guise \dis-ˈgīz\ *vb* **dis·guised; dis·guis·ing 1** : to
change the appearance of to conceal the identity or to
resemble another **2** : HIDE, CONCEAL

²disguise *n* **1** : clothing put on to conceal one's identity
or counterfeit another's **2** : an outward appearance
that hides what something really is

¹dis·gust \dis-ˈgəst\ *n* : AVERSION, REPUGNANCE — **dis-
gust·ful** \-fəl\ *adj*

²disgust *vb* : to provoke to loathing, repugnance, or
aversion : be offensive to — **dis·gust·ed·ly** *adv* —
dis·gust·ing·ly *adv*

¹dish \ˈdish\ *n* [ME, fr. OE *disc* plate, fr. L *discus*
quoit, disk, dish, fr. Gk *diskos*, fr. *dikein* to throw] **1**
: a vessel used for serving food **2** : the food served in
a dish ⟨a ∼ of berries⟩ **3** : food prepared in a particular way **4** : something resembling a dish esp. in being
shallow and concave

²dish *vb* **1** : to put into a dish **2** : to make concave like
a dish

dis·ha·bille \ˌdi-sə-ˈbēl\ *n* [F *déshabillé*] : the state of
being dressed in a casual or careless manner

dis·har·mo·ny \(ˌ)dis-ˈhär-mə-nē\ *n* : lack of harmony
— **dis·har·mo·ni·ous** \-(ˌ)här-ˈmō-nē-əs\ *adj*

dish·cloth \ˈdish-ˌklȯth\ *n* : a cloth for washing dishes

dis·heart·en \dis-ˈhärt-ᵊn\ *vb* : DISCOURAGE, DEJECT

dished \ˈdisht\ *adj* : CONCAVE

di·shev·el \di-ˈshe-vəl\ *vb* **-shev·eled** *or* **-shev·elled;
-shev·el·ing** *or* **-shev·el·ling** [ME *discheveled* with
disordered hair, fr. MF *deschevelé*, fr. pp. of *des-
cheveler* to disarrange the hair, fr. *chevel* hair, fr. L
capillus] : to throw into disorder or disarray — **di-
shev·eled** *or* **di·shev·elled** *adj*

dis·hon·est \di-'sä-nəst\ adj : not honest : UNTRUSTWORTHY, DECEITFUL — **dis·hon·est·ly** adv — **dis·hon·es·ty** \-nə-stē\ n

¹**dis·hon·or** \di-'sä-nər\ vb 1 : DISGRACE 2 : to refuse to accept or pay ⟨~ a check⟩

²**dishonor** n 1 : lack or loss of honor 2 : SHAME, DISGRACE 3 : a cause of disgrace 4 : the act of dishonoring a negotiable instrument when presented for payment — **dis·hon·or·able** \di-'sä-nə-rə-bəl\ adj — **dis·hon·or·ably** \-blē\ adv

dish out vb : to give freely

dish·rag \'dish-₁rag\ n : DISHCLOTH

dish·wash·er \-₁wò-shər, -₁wä-\ n : a person or machine that washes dishes

dish·wa·ter \-₁wò-tər, -₁wä-\ n : water used for washing dishes

dis·il·lu·sion \₁di-sə-'lü-zhən\ vb : to leave without illusion or naive faith and trust — **dis·il·lu·sion·ment** n

dis·il·lu·sioned adj : DISAPPOINTED, DISSATISFIED

dis·in·cli·na·tion \di-₁sin-klə-'nä-shən\ n : a preference for avoiding something : slight aversion

dis·in·cline \₁dis-ᵊn-'klīn\ vb : to make unwilling

dis·in·clined adj : unwilling because of dislike or disapproval

dis·in·fect \₁dis-ᵊn-'fekt\ vb : to cleanse of infectioncausing germs — **dis·in·fec·tant** \-'fek-tənt\ n — **dis·in·fec·tion** \-'fek-shən\ n

dis·in·for·ma·tion \-₁in-fər-'mä-shən\ n : false information deliberately and often covertly spread

dis·in·gen·u·ous \₁dis-ᵊn-'jen-yə-wəs\ adj : lacking in candor; also : giving a false appearance of simple frankness

dis·in·her·it \₁dis-ᵊn-'her-ət\ vb : to deprive of the right to inherit

dis·in·te·grate \di-'sin-tə-₁grāt\ vb 1 : to break or decompose into constituent parts or small particles 2 : to destroy the unity or integrity of — **dis·in·te·gra·tion** \-₁sin-tə-'grā-shən\ n

dis·in·ter \₁dis-ᵊn-'tər\ vb 1 : to take from the grave or tomb 2 : UNEARTH

dis·in·ter·est·ed \(₁)dis-'in-tə-rəs-təd, -₁res-\ adj 1 : not interested 2 : free from selfish motive or interest : UNBIASED — **dis·in·ter·est·ed·ness** n

dis·join \(₁)dis-'jòin\ vb : SEPARATE

dis·joint \(₁)dis-'jòint\ vb : to disturb the orderly arrangement of; also : to separate at the joints

dis·joint·ed adj 1 : DISCONNECTED; esp : INCOHERENT 2 : separated at or as if at the joint

disk or **disc** \'disk\ n 1 : something round and flat; esp : a flat rounded anatomical structure (as the central part of the flower head of a composite plant or a pad of cartilage between vertebrae) 2 usu disc : a phonograph record 3 : a round flat plate coated with a magnetic substance on which data for a computer is stored 4 usu disc : OPTICAL DISK

dis·kette \dis-'ket\ n : FLOPPY DISK

¹**dis·like** \(₁)dis-'līk\ n : a feeling of aversion or disapproval

²**dislike** vb : to regard with dislike : DISAPPROVE

dis·lo·cate \'dis-lō-₁kāt, dis-'lō-\ vb 1 : to put out of place; esp : to displace (a bone or joint) from normal connections ⟨~ a shoulder⟩ 2 : DISRUPT — **dis·lo·ca·tion** \₁dis-(₁)lō-'kā-shən\ n

dis·lodge \(₁)dis-'läj\ vb : to force out of a place esp. of rest, hiding, or defense

dis·loy·al \(₁)dis-'lòi-əl\ adj : lacking in loyalty — **dis·loy·al·ty** n

dis·mal \'diz-məl\ adj [ME, fr. dismal, n., days marked as unlucky in medieval calendars, fr. AF, fr ML dies mali, lit., evil days] 1 : showing or causing gloom or depression 2 : lacking merit — **dis·mal·ly** adv

dis·man·tle \(₁)dis-'mant-ᵊl\ vb **-tled; -tling** 1 : to take apart 2 : to strip of furniture and equipment — **dis·man·tle·ment** n

dis·may \dis-'mā\ vb : to cause to lose courage or resolution from alarm or fear : DAUNT — **dismay** n — **dis·may·ing·ly** adv

dis·mem·ber \dis-'mem-bər\ vb 1 : to cut off or separate the limbs or parts of 2 : to break up or tear into pieces — **dis·mem·ber·ment** n

dis·miss \dis-'mis\ vb 1 : to send away 2 : DISCHARGE 5 3 : to put aside or out of mind 4 : to put out of judicial consideration ⟨~ed all charges⟩ — **dis·miss·al** n

dis·mount \dis-'maùnt\ vb 1 : to get down from something (as a horse or bicycle) 2 : UNHORSE 3 : DISASSEMBLE

dis·obe·di·ence \₁di-sə-'bē-dē-əns\ n : neglect or refusal to obey — **dis·obe·di·ent** \-ənt\ adj

dis·obey \₁di-sə-'bā\ vb : to fail to obey : be disobedient

dis·oblige \₁di-sə-'blīj\ vb 1 : to go counter to the wishes of 2 : INCONVENIENCE

¹**dis·or·der** \di-'sòr-dər\ vb 1 : to disturb the order of 2 : to disturb the regular or normal functions of ⟨a ~ed digestion⟩

²**disorder** n 1 : lack of order : CONFUSION 2 : breach of the peace or public order : TUMULT 3 : an abnormal state of body or mind : AILMENT

dis·or·der·ly \-lē\ adj 1 : offensive to public order : marked by disorder ⟨a ~ desk⟩ — **dis·or·der·li·ness** n

dis·or·ga·nize \di-'sòr-gə-₁nīz\ vb : to break up the regular system of : throw into disorder — **dis·or·ga·ni·za·tion** \di-₁sòr-gə-nə-'zā-shən\ n

dis·ori·ent \di-'sòr-ē-₁ent\ vb : to cause to be confused or lost — **dis·ori·en·ta·tion** \di-₁sòr-ē-ən-'tā-shən\ n

dis·own \di-'sōn\ vb : REPUDIATE, RENOUNCE, DISCLAIM

dis·par·age \di-'spar-ij\ vb **-aged; -ag·ing** [ME to degrade by marriage below one's class, disparage, fr. MF desparagier to marry below one's class, fr. OF, fr. parage extraction, lineage, fr. per peer] 1 : to lower in rank or reputation : DEGRADE **2** : BELITTLE — **dis·par·age·ment** n — **dis·par·ag·ing·ly** adv

dis·pa·rate \ˈdis-pə-rət, dis-ˈpar-ət\ adj : distinct in quality or character — **dis·par·i·ty** \di-ˈspar-ə-tē\ n

dis·pas·sion·ate \(ˌ)dis-ˈpa-shə-nət\ adj : not influenced by strong feeling : CALM, IMPARTIAL — **dis·pas·sion** \-ˈpa-shən\ n — **dis·pas·sion·ate·ly** adv

¹**dis·patch** \di-ˈspach\ vb **1** : to send off or away with promptness or speed esp. on official business **2** : to put to death **3** : to attend to rapidly or efficiently **4** : DEFEAT — **dis·patch·er** n

²**dis·patch** \di-ˈspach, ˈdis-ˌpach\ n **1** : MESSAGE **2** : a news item sent in by a correspondent to a newspaper **3** : the act of dispatching; esp : SHIPMENT **4** : the act of putting to death **5** : promptness and efficiency in performing a task

dis·pel \di-ˈspel\ vb **dis·pelled; dis·pel·ling** : to drive away by scattering : DISSIPATE

dis·pens·able \di-ˈspen-sə-bəl\ adj : capable of being dispensed with

dis·pen·sa·ry \di-ˈspen-sə-rē\ n, pl **-ries** : a place where medicine or medical or dental aid is dispensed

dis·pen·sa·tion \ˌdis-pən-ˈsā-shən\ n **1** : a system of rules for ordering affairs **2** : a particular arrangement or provision esp. of nature **3** : an exemption from a rule or from a vow or oath **4** : the act of dispensing **5** : something dispensed or distributed

dis·pense \di-ˈspens\ vb **dis·pensed; dis·pens·ing 1** : to portion out **2** : ADMINISTER ⟨∼ justice⟩ **3** : EXEMPT **4** : to make up and give out (remedies) — **dis·pens·er** n — **dispense with 1** : SUSPEND **2** : to do without

dis·perse \di-ˈspərs\ vb **dis·persed; dis·pers·ing** : to break up and scatter about : SPREAD — **dis·per·sal** \-ˈspər-səl\ n — **dis·per·sion** \-ˈspər-zhən\ n

dis·pir·it \dis-ˈpir-ət\ vb : DEPRESS, DISCOURAGE, DISHEARTEN

dis·place \dis-ˈplās\ vb **1** : to remove from the usual or proper place; esp : to expel or force to flee from home or native land ⟨displaced persons⟩ **2** : to move out of position ⟨water displaced by a floating object⟩ **3** : to take the place of : REPLACE

dis·place·ment \-mənt\ n **1** : the act of displacing : the state of being displaced **2** : the volume or weight of a fluid (as water) displaced by a floating body (as a ship) **3** : the difference between the initial position of an object and a later position

¹**dis·play** \di-ˈsplā\ vb : to present to view : make evident

²**display** n **1** : a displaying of something **2** : an electronic device (as a cathode-ray tube) that gives information in visual form; also : the visual information

dis·please \(ˌ)dis-ˈplēz\ vb **1** : to arouse the disapproval and dislike of **2** : to be offensive to : give displeasure

dis·plea·sure \-ˈple-zhər\ n : a feeling of dislike and irritation

dis·port \di-ˈspōrt\ vb **1** : DIVERT, AMUSE **2** : FROLIC **3** : DISPLAY

dis·pos·able \di-ˈspō-zə-bəl\ adj **1** : remaining after deduction of taxes ⟨∼ income⟩ **2** : designed to be used once and then thrown away ⟨∼ diapers⟩ — **dispos·able** n

dis·pos·al \di-ˈspō-zəl\ n **1** : CONTROL, COMMAND **2** : an orderly arrangement **3** : a getting rid of **4** : MANAGEMENT, ADMINISTRATION **5** : presenting or bestowing something ⟨∼ of favors⟩ **6** : a device used to reduce waste matter (as by grinding)

dis·pose \di-ˈspōz\ vb **dis·posed; dis·pos·ing 1** : to give a tendency to : INCLINE ⟨disposed to accept⟩ **2** : to put in place : ARRANGE ⟨troops disposed for withdrawal⟩ **3** : SETTLE — **dis·pos·er** n — **dispose of 1** : to transfer to the control of another **2** : to get rid of **3** : to deal with conclusively

dis·po·si·tion \ˌdis-pə-ˈzi-shən\ n **1** : the act or power of disposing : DISPOSAL **2** : RELINQUISHMENT **3** : AR-

RANGEMENT **4** : TENDENCY, INCLINATION **5** : natural attitude toward things ⟨a cheerful ∼⟩

dis·pos·sess \ˌdis-pə-ˈzes\ vb : to put out of possession or occupancy — **dis·pos·ses·sion** \-ˈze-shən\ n

dis·praise \(ˌ)dis-ˈprāz\ vb : DISPARAGE — **dispraise** n — **dis·prais·er** n

dis·pro·por·tion \ˌdis-prə-ˈpōr-shən\ n : lack of proportion, symmetry, or proper relation — **dis·pro·por·tion·ate** \-shə-nət\ adj

dis·prove \(ˌ)dis-ˈprüv\ vb : to prove to be false — **dis·proof** \-ˈprüf\ n

dis·pu·tant \di-ˈspyüt-ᵊnt, ˈdis-pyə-tənt\ n : one that is engaged in a dispute

dis·pu·ta·tion \ˌdis-pyü-ˈtā-shən\ n **1** : DEBATE **2** : an oral defense of an academic thesis

dis·pu·ta·tious \-shəs\ adj : inclined to dispute : ARGUMENTATIVE

¹**dis·pute** \di-ˈspyüt\ vb **dis·put·ed; dis·put·ing 1** : ARGUE, DEBATE **2** : WRANGLE **3** : to deny the truth or rightness of **4** : to struggle against or over : OPPOSE — **dis·put·able** \di-ˈspyü-tə-bəl, ˈdis-pyə-tə-bəl\ adj — **dis·put·er** n

²**dis·pute** n **1** : DEBATE **2** : QUARREL

dis·qual·i·fy \(ˌ)dis-ˈkwä-lə-ˌfī\ vb : to make or declare unfit or not qualified — **dis·qual·i·fi·ca·tion** \-ˌkwä-lə-fə-ˈkā-shən\ n

¹**dis·qui·et** \(ˌ)dis-ˈkwī-ət\ vb : to make uneasy or restless : DISTURB

²**disquiet** n : lack of peace or tranquillity : ANXIETY

dis·qui·etude \(ˌ)dis-ˈkwī-ə-ˌtüd, -ˌtyüd\ n : AGITATION, ANXIETY

dis·qui·si·tion \ˌdis-kwə-ˈzi-shən\ n : a formal inquiry or discussion

¹**dis·re·gard** \ˌdis-ri-ˈgärd\ vb : to pay no attention to : treat as unworthy of notice or regard

²**disregard** n : the act of disregarding : the state of being disregarded : NEGLECT — **dis·re·gard·ful** adj

dis·re·pair \ˌdis-ri-ˈpar\ n : the state of being in need of repair

dis·rep·u·ta·ble \dis-ˈre-pyù-tə-bəl\ adj : having a bad reputation

dis·re·pute \ˌdis-ri-ˈpyüt\ n : lack or decline of reputation : low esteem

dis·re·spect \ˌdis-ri-ˈspekt\ n : DISCOURTESY — **dis·re·spect·ful** adj

dis·robe \dis-ˈrōb\ vb : UNDRESS

dis·rupt \dis-ˈrəpt\ vb **1** : to break apart **2** : to throw into disorder **3** : INTERRUPT — **dis·rup·tion** \-ˈrəp-shən\ n — **dis·rup·tive** \-ˈrəp-tiv\ adj

dis·sat·is·fac·tion \di-ˌsa-təs-ˈfak-shən\ n : DISCONTENT

dis·sat·is·fy \di-ˈsa-təs-ˌfī\ vb : to fail to satisfy : DISPLEASE

dis·sect \di-ˈsekt\ vb **1** : to divide into parts esp. for examination and study **2** : ANALYZE — **dis·sec·tion** \-ˈsek-shən\ n — **dis·sec·tor** \-ˈsek-tər\ n

dis·sect·ed adj : cut deeply into narrow lobes ⟨a ∼ leaf⟩

dis·sem·ble \di-ˈsem-bəl\ vb **-bled; -bling 1** : to hide under or put on a false appearance : conceal facts, intentions, or feelings under some pretense **2** : SIMULATE — **dis·sem·bler** n

dis·sem·i·nate \di-ˈse-mə-ˌnāt\ vb **-nat·ed; -nat·ing** : to spread abroad as if sowing seed ⟨∼ ideas⟩ — **dis·sem·i·na·tion** \-ˌse-mə-ˈnā-shən\ n

dis·sen·sion \di-ˈsen-chən\ n : disagreement in opinion : DISCORD

¹**dis·sent** \di-ˈsent\ vb **1** : to withhold assent **2** : to differ in opinion

²**dissent** n **1** : difference of opinion; esp : religious nonconformity **2** : a written statement in which a justice disagrees with the opinion of the majority

dis·sent·er \di-ˈsen-tər\ n **1** : one that dissents **2** cap : an English Nonconformist

dis·ser·ta·tion \ˌdi-sər-ˈtā-shən\ n : an extended usu. written treatment of a subject; esp : one submitted for a doctorate

dis·ser·vice \di-'sər-vəs\ n : INJURY, HARM, MISCHIEF

dis·sev·er \di-'se-vər\ vb : SEPARATE, DISUNITE

dis·si·dent \'di-sə-dənt\ adj [L dissidens, prp. of dissidēre to sit apart, disagree, fr. dis- apart + sedēre to sit] : disagreeing esp. with an established religious or political system, organization, or belief — **dis·si·dence** \-dəns\ n — **dissident** n

dis·sim·i·lar \di-'si-mə-lər\ adj : UNLIKE — **dis·sim·i·lar·i·ty** \di-si-mə-'lar-ə-tē\ n

dis·sim·u·late \di-'si-myə-ˌlāt\ vb : to hide under a false appearance : DISSEMBLE — **dis·sim·u·la·tion** \di-ˌsi-myə-'lā-shən\ n

dis·si·pate \'di-sə-ˌpāt\ vb **-pat·ed; -pat·ing 1** : to break up and drive off : DISPERSE, SCATTER ⟨the breeze *dissipated* the fog⟩ **2** : SQUANDER **3** : to break up and vanish **4** : to be dissolute; *esp* : to drink alcoholic beverages to excess — **dis·si·pat·ed** adj — **dis·si·pa·tion** \di-sə-'pā-shən\ n

dis·so·ci·ate \di-'sō-shē-ˌāt\ vb **-at·ed; -at·ing** : DISCONNECT, DISUNITE — **dis·so·ci·a·tion** \di-ˌsō-shē-'ā-shən\ n

dis·so·lute \'di-sə-ˌlüt\ adj : loose in morals or conduct — **dis·so·lute·ly** adv — **dis·so·lute·ness** n

dis·so·lu·tion \di-sə-'lü-shən\ n **1** : the action or process of dissolving **2** : separation of a thing into its parts **3** : DECAY; *also* : DEATH **4** : the termination or breaking up of (as an assembly)

dis·solve \di-'zälv\ vb **1** : to separate into component parts **2** : to pass or cause to pass into solution ⟨sugar ~s in water⟩ **3** : TERMINATE, DISPERSE ⟨~ parliament⟩ **4** : to waste or fade away ⟨his courage *dissolved*⟩ **5** : to be overcome emotionally ⟨~ in tears⟩ **6** : to resolve itself as if by dissolution

dis·so·nance \'di-sə-nəns\ n : DISCORD — **dis·so·nant** \-nənt\ adj

dis·suade \di-'swād\ vb **dis·suad·ed; dis·suad·ing** : to advise against a course of action : persuade or try to persuade not to do something — **dis·sua·sion** \-'swā-zhən\ n — **dis·sua·sive** \-'swā-siv\ adj

dist abbr **1** distance **2** district

¹dis·taff \'dis-ˌtaf\ n, pl **distaffs** \-ˌtafs, -ˌtavz\ **1** : a staff for holding the flax, tow, or wool in spinning **2** : a woman's work or domain **3** : the female branch or side of a family

²distaff adj : MATERNAL, FEMALE

dis·tal \'dist-ᵊl\ adj **1** : away from the point of attachment or origin esp. on the body **2** : of, relating to, or being the surface of a tooth that is farthest from the middle of the front of the jaw — **dis·tal·ly** adv

¹dis·tance \'dis-təns\ n **1** : measure of separation in space or time **2** : EXPANSE **3** : the full length ⟨go the ~⟩ **4** : spatial remoteness **5** : COLDNESS, RESERVE **6** : DIFFERENCE, DISPARITY **7** : a distant point

²distance vb **dis·tanced; dis·tanc·ing** : to leave far behind : OUTSTRIP

dis·tant \'dis-tənt\ adj **1** : separate in space : AWAY **2** : FAR-OFF **3** : far apart or behind **4** : not close in relationship ⟨a ~ cousin⟩ **5** : different in kind **6** : RESERVED, ALOOF, COLD ⟨~ politeness⟩ **7** : going a long distance — **dis·tant·ly** adv — **dis·tant·ness** n

dis·taste \(ˌ)dis-'tāst\ n : DISINCLINATION, DISLIKE — **dis·taste·ful** adj

dis·tem·per \(ˌ)dis-'tem-pər\ n : a bodily disorder usu. of a domestic animal; *esp* : a contagious often fatal virus disease of dogs

dis·tend \di-'stend\ vb : EXPAND, SWELL — **dis·ten·si·ble** \-'sten-sə-bəl\ adj — **dis·ten·sion** or **dis·ten·tion** \-chən\ n

dis·tich \'dis-(ˌ)tik\ n : a unit of two lines of poetry

dis·till also **dis·til** \di-'stil\ vb **dis·tilled; dis·till·ing 1** : to fall or let fall in drops **2** : to obtain or purify by distillation — **dis·till·er** n — **dis·till·ery** \-stil-ə-rē\ n

dis·til·late \'dis-tə-ˌlāt, -lət\ n : a liquid product condensed from vapor during distillation

dis·til·la·tion \dis-tə-'lā-shən\ n : the process of puri-

fying a liquid by successive evaporation and condensation

dis·tinct \di-'stiŋkt\ adj **1** : SEPARATE, INDIVIDUAL **2** : presenting a clear unmistakable impression — **dis·tinct·ly** adv — **dis·tinct·ness** n

dis·tinc·tion \di-'stiŋk-shən\ n **1** : the distinguishing of a difference; *also* : the difference distinguished **2** : something that distinguishes **3** : special honor or recognition

dis·tinc·tive \di-'stiŋk-tiv\ adj **1** : serving to distinguish **2** : having or giving style or distinction — **dis·tinc·tive·ly** adv — **dis·tinc·tive·ness** n

dis·tin·guish \di-'stiŋ-gwish\ vb [MF *distinguer*, fr. L *distinguere*, lit., to separate by pricking] **1** : to recognize by some mark or characteristic **2** : to hear or see clearly : DISCERN **3** : to make distinctions ⟨~ between right and wrong⟩ **4** : to give prominence or distinction to; *also* : to take special notice of — **dis·tin·guish·able** adj

dis·tin·guished \-gwisht\ adj **1** : marked by eminence or excellence **2** : befitting an eminent person

dis·tort \di-'stȯrt\ vb **1** : to twist out of the true meaning **2** : to twist out of a natural, normal, or original shape or condition **3** : to cause to be perceived unnaturally — **dis·tor·tion** \-'stȯr-shən\ n

distr abbr distribute; distribution

dis·tract \di-'strakt\ vb **1** : to draw (the attention or mind) to a different object : DIVERT **2** : to stir up or confuse with conflicting emotions or motives — **dis·trac·tion** \-'strak-shən\ n

dis·trait \di-'strā\ adj : DISTRAUGHT 1

dis·traught \di-'strȯt\ adj **1** : agitated with doubt or mental conflict **2** : INSANE

¹dis·tress \di-'stres\ n **1** : suffering of body or mind : PAIN, ANGUISH **2** : TROUBLE, MISFORTUNE **3** : a condition of danger or desperate need — **dis·tress·ful** adj

²distress vb **1** : to subject to great strain or difficulties **2** : UPSET

dis·trib·ute \di-'stri-byüt\ vb **-ut·ed; -ut·ing 1** : to divide among several or many **2** : to spread out : SCATTER; *also* : DELIVER **3** : CLASSIFY — **dis·tri·bu·tion** \dis-trə-'byü-shən\ n

dis·trib·u·tive \di-'stri-byü-tiv\ adj **1** : of or relating to distribution **2** : being or concerned with a mathematical operation (as multiplication in $a(b + c) = ab + ac$) that produces the same result when operating on a whole mathematical expression as when operating on each part and collecting the results — **dis·trib·u·tive·ly** adv

dis·trib·u·tor \di-'stri-byü-tər\ n **1** : one that distributes **2** : one that markets goods **3** : a device for directing current to the spark plugs of an engine

dis·trict \'dis-(ˌ)trikt\ n **1** : a fixed territorial division (as for administrative or electoral purposes) **2** : an area, region, or section with a distinguishing character

district attorney n : the prosecuting attorney of a judicial district

¹dis·trust \dis-'trəst\ n : a lack or absence of trust — **dis·trust·ful** \-fəl\ adj — **dis·trust·ful·ly** adv

²distrust vb : to have no trust or confidence in

dis·turb \di-'stərb\ vb **1** : to interfere with : INTERRUPT **2** : to alter the position or arrangement of; *also* : to upset the natural and esp. the ecological balance of **3** : to destroy the tranquility or composure of : make uneasy **4** : to throw into disorder **5** : INCONVENIENCE — **dis·tur·bance** \-'stər-bəns\ n — **dis·turb·er** n

dis·turbed \-'stərbd\ adj : showing symptoms of emotional illness

dis·unite \dis-yü-'nīt\ vb : DIVIDE, SEPARATE

dis·uni·ty \dis-'yü-nə-tē\ n : lack of unity; *esp* : DISSENSION

dis·use \-'yüs\ n : a cessation of use or practice

¹ditch \'dich\ n : a long narrow channel or trench dug in the earth

²ditch vb **1** : to enclose with a ditch; *also* : to dig a ditch

in **2** : to get rid of : DISCARD **3** : to make a forced land-ing of an airplane on water

dith·er \\'di-<u>th</u>ər\\ *n* : a highly nervous, excited, or ag-itated state

dit·sy *or* **dit·zy** \\'dit-sē\\ *adj* **dits·i·er** *or* **ditz·i·er; -est** : eccentrically silly, giddy, or inane

dit·to \\'di-tō\\ *n, pl* **dittos** [It *ditto, detto,* pp. of *dire* to say, fr. L *dicere*] **1** : a thing mentioned previously or above — used to avoid repeating a word **2** : a mark " or " used as a symbol for the word *ditto*

dit·ty \\'di-tē\\ *n, pl* **ditties** : a short simple song

di·uret·ic \\,dī-yə-'re-tik\\ *adj* : tending to increase urine flow — **diuretic** *n*

di·ur·nal \\dī-'ərn-ᵊl\\ *adj* **1** : DAILY **2** : of, relating to, occurring, or active in the daytime

div *abbr* **1** divided **2** dividend **3** division **4** divorced

di·va \\'dē-və\\ *n, pl* **divas** *or* **di·ve** \\-ˌvā\\ [It, lit., god-dess, fr. L, fem. of *divus* divine, god] : PRIMA DONNA

di·va·gate \\'dī-və-ˌgāt\\ *vb* **-gat·ed; -gat·ing** : to wander or stray from a course or subject : DIVERGE — **di·va·ga·tion** \\,dī-və-'gā-shən\\ *n*

di·van \\'dī-ˌvan, di-'van\\ *n* : COUCH, SOFA

---

¹**dive** \\'dīv\\ *vb* **dived** \\'dīvd\\ *or* **dove** \\'dōv\\; **dived; div·ing 1** : to plunge into water headfirst **2** : SUBMERGE **3** : to come or drop down precipitously **4** : to de-scend in an airplane at a steep angle **5** : to plunge into some matter or activity **6** : DART, LUNGE — **div·er** *n*

²**dive** *n* **1** : the act or an instance of diving **2** : a sharp decline **3** : a disreputable bar or place of amusement

di·verge \\də-'vərj, dī-\\ *vb* **di·verged; di·verg·ing 1** : to move or extend in different directions from a com-mon point : draw apart **2** : to differ in character, form, or opinion **3** : DEVIATE **4** : DEFLECT — **di·ver·gence** \\-'vər-jəns\\ *n* — **di·ver·gent** \\-jənt\\ *adj*

di·vers \\'dī-vərz\\ *adj* : VARIOUS

di·verse \\dī-'vərs, də-, 'dī-ˌvərs\\ *adj* **1** : UNLIKE **2** : composed of distinct forms or qualities — **di·verse·ly** *adv*

di·ver·si·fy \\də-'vər-sə-ˌfī, dī-\\ *vb* **-fied; -fy·ing** : to make different or various in form or quality — **di·ver·si·fi·ca·tion** \\-ˌvər-sə-fə-'kā-shən\\ *n*

di·ver·sion \\də-'vər-zhən, dī-\\ *n* **1** : a turning aside from a course, activity, or use : DEVIATION **2** : some-thing that diverts or amuses : PASTIME

di·ver·si·ty \\də-'vər-sə-tē, dī-\\ *n, pl* **-ties 1** : the condi-tion of being diverse : VARIETY **2** : an instance of be-ing diverse

di·vert \\də-'vərt, dī-\\ *vb* **1** : to turn from a course or purpose : DEFLECT **2** : DISTRACT **3** : ENTERTAIN, AMUSE

di·vest \\dī-'vest, də-\\ *vb* **1** : to deprive or dispossess esp. of property, authority, or rights **2** : to strip esp. of clothing, ornament, or equipment

¹**di·vide** \\də-'vīd\\ *vb* **di·vid·ed; divid·ing 1** : SEPARATE; *also* : CLASSIFY **2** : CLEAVE, PART **3** : DISTRIBUTE, AP-PORTION **4** : to possess or make use of in common

: share in **5** : to cause to be separate, distinct, or apart from one another **6** : to separate into opposing sides or parties **7** : to mark divisions on **8** : to subject to or use in mathematical division; *also* : to be used as a divisor with respect to **9** : to branch out

²**divide** *n* : WATERSHED 1

div·i·dend \\'di-və-ˌdend\\ *n* **1** : an individual share of something distributed **2** : BONUS **3** : a number to be divided **4** : a sum or fund to be divided or distributed

di·vid·er \\də-'vī-dər\\ *n* **1** : one that divides (as a partition) ⟨room ∼⟩ **2** *pl* : COMPASS 5

div·i·na·tion \\,di-və-'nā-shən\\ *n* **1** : the art or practice of using omens or magic powers to foretell the future **2** : unusual insight or intuitive perception

¹**di·vine** \\də-'vīn\\ *adj* **di·vin·er; -est 1** : of, relating to, or being God or a god **2** : supremely good : SUPERB; *also* : HEAVENLY — **di·vine·ly** *adv*

²**divine** *n* **1** : CLERGYMAN **2** : THEOLOGIAN

³**divine** *vb* **di·vined; di·vin·ing 1** : INFER, CONJECTURE **2** : PROPHESY **3** : DOWSE — **di·vin·er** *n*

divining rod *n* : a forked rod believed to reveal the presence of water or minerals by dipping downward when held over a vein

di·vin·i·ty \\də-'vi-nə-tē\\ *n, pl* **-ties 1** : THEOLOGY **2** : the quality or state of being divine **3** : a divine being; *esp* : GOD 1

di·vis·i·ble \\də-'vi-zə-bəl\\ *adj* : capable of being divid-ed — **di·vis·i·bil·i·ty** \\-ˌvi-zə-'bi-lə-tē\\ *n*

di·vi·sion \\də-'vi-zhən\\ *n* **1** : DISTRIBUTION, SEPARA-TION **2** : one of the parts or groupings into which a whole is divided **3** : DISAGREEMENT, DISUNITY **4** : something that divides or separates **5** : the mathe-matical operation of finding how many times one number is contained in another **6** : a large self-contained military unit **7** : an administrative or oper-ating unit of a governmental, business, or educational organization — **di·vi·sion·al** \\-'vi-zhə-nəl\\ *adj*

di·vi·sive \\də-'vī-siv, -'vi-ziv\\ *adj* : creating disunity or dissension — **di·vi·sive·ly** *adv* — **di·vi·sive·ness** *n*

di·vi·sor \\də-'vī-zər\\ *n* : the number by which a divi-dend is divided

di·vorce \\də-'vōrs\\ *n* **1** : an act or instance of legally dissolving a marriage **2** : SEPARATION, SEVERANCE — **divorce** *vb* — **di·vorce·ment** *n*

di·vor·cé \\də-ˌvōr-'sā\\ *n* [F] : a divorced man

di·vor·cée \\də-ˌvōr-'sā, -'sē\\ *n* : a divorced woman

di·vot \\'dī-vət\\ *n* : a piece of turf dug from a golf fair-way in making a stroke

di·vulge \\də-'vəlj, dī-\\ *vb* **di·vulged; di·vulg·ing** : RE-VEAL, DISCLOSE

Dix·ie·land \\'dik-sē-ˌland\\ *n* : jazz music in duple time played in a style developed in New Orleans

diz·zy \\'di-zē\\ *adj* **diz·zi·er; -est** [ME *disy,* fr. OE *dysig* stupid] **1** : FOOLISH, SILLY **2** : having a sensation of whirling : GIDDY **3** : causing or caused by giddiness — **diz·zi·ly** \\-zə-lē\\ *adv* — **diz·zi·ness** \\-zē-nəs\\ *n*

DJ *n, often not cap* : DISC JOCKEY

dk *abbr* **1** dark **2** deck **3** dock

dl *abbr* deciliter

DLitt or **DLit** abbr [NL doctor litterarum] doctor of letters; doctor of literature

DLO abbr dead letter office

dm abbr decimeter

DMD abbr [NL dentariae medicinae doctor] doctor of dental medicine

DMZ abbr demilitarized zone

dn abbr down

DNA \ˌdē-(ˌ)en-ˈā\ n : any of various nucleic acids that are usu. the molecular basis of heredity and are localized esp. in cell nuclei

¹do \ˈdü\ vb **did** \ˈdid\; **done** \ˈdən\; **do·ing**; **does** \ˈdəz\ **1** : to bring to pass : ACCOMPLISH **2** : ACT, BEHAVE ⟨∼ as I say⟩ **3** : to be active or busy ⟨up and ∼ing⟩ **4** : HAPPEN ⟨what's ∼ing?⟩ **5** : to be engaged in the study or practice of : work at ⟨he does tailoring⟩ **6** : COOK ⟨steak done rare⟩ **7** : to put in order (as by cleaning or arranging) ⟨∼ the dishes⟩ **8** : DECORATE ⟨did the hall in blue⟩ **9** : GET ALONG ⟨∼ well in school⟩ **10** : CARRY ON, MANAGE **11** : RENDER ⟨sleep will ∼ you good⟩ **12** : FINISH ⟨when he had done⟩ **13** : EXERT ⟨did my best⟩ **14** : PRODUCE ⟨did a poem⟩ **15** : to play the part of **16** : CHEAT ⟨did him out of his share⟩ **17** : TRAVERSE, TOUR **18** : TRAVEL **19** : to spend or serve out a period of time ⟨did ten years in prison⟩ **20** : SUFFICE, SUIT **21** : to be fitting or proper **22** : USE ⟨doesn't ∼ drugs⟩ **23** — used as an auxiliary verb (1) before the subject in an interrogative sentence ⟨does he work?⟩ and after some adverbs ⟨never did she say so⟩, (2) in a negative statement ⟨I don't know⟩, (3) for emphasis ⟨you ∼ know⟩, and (4) as a substitute for a preceding predicate ⟨he works harder than I ∼⟩ — **do·able** \ˈdü-ə-bəl\ adj — **do away with 1** : to put an end to **2** : DESTROY, KILL — **do by** : to deal with : TREAT ⟨did right by her⟩ — **do for** : to bring about the death or ruin of — **do the trick** : to produce a desired result

²do n **1** : AFFAIR, PARTY **2** : a command or entreaty to do something ⟨list of ∼s and don'ts⟩ **3** : HAIRDO

³do abbr ditto

DOA abbr dead on arrival

DOB abbr date of birth

dob·bin \ˈdä-bən\ n [Dobbin, nickname for Robert] **1** : a farm horse **2** : a quiet plodding horse

Do·ber·man pin·scher \ˈdō-bər-mən-ˈpin-chər\ n : a short-haired medium-sized dog of a breed of German origin

do·bra \ˈdō-brə\ n — see MONEY table

¹doc \ˈdäk\ n : DOCTOR

²doc abbr document

do·cent \ˈdōs-ᵊnt, dōt-ˈsent\ n [obs. G (now Dozent), fr. L docens, prp. of docēre to teach] : TEACHER, LECTURER; also : a person who leads a guided tour

doc·ile \ˈdä-səl\ adj [L docilis, fr. docēre to teach] : easily taught, led, or managed : TRACTABLE — **do·cil·i·ty** \dä-ˈsi-lə-tē\ n

¹dock \ˈdäk\ n : any of a genus of coarse weedy herbs related to buckwheat

²dock vb **1** : to cut off the end of : cut short **2** : to take away a part of : deduct from ⟨∼ a worker's wages⟩

³dock n **1** : an artificial basin to receive ships **2** : ²SLIP 2 **3** : a wharf or platform for loading or unloading materials

⁴dock vb **1** : to bring or come into dock **2** : to join (as two spacecraft) mechanically in space

⁵dock n : the place in a court where a prisoner stands or sits during trial

dock·age \ˈdä-kij\ n : docking facilities

dock·et \ˈdä-kət\ n **1** : a formal abridged record of the proceedings in a legal action; also : a register of such records **2** : a list of legal causes to be tried **3** : a calendar of matters to be acted on : AGENDA **4** : a label attached to a document containing identification or directions — **docket** vb

dock·hand \ˈdäk-ˌhand\ n : LONGSHOREMAN

dock·work·er \-ˌwər-kər\ n : LONGSHOREMAN

dock·yard \-ˌyärd\ n : SHIPYARD

¹doc·tor \ˈdäk-tər\ n [ME doctour teacher, doctor, fr. MF & ML; MF, fr. ML doctor, fr. L, teacher, fr. docēre to teach] **1** : a person holding one of the highest academic degrees (as a PhD) conferred by a university **2** : one skilled in healing arts; esp : an academically and legally qualified physician, surgeon, dentist, or veterinarian **3** : a person who restores or repairs things — **doc·tor·al** \-tə-rəl\ adj

²doctor vb **1** : to give medical treatment to **2** : to practice medicine **3** : REPAIR **4** : to adapt or modify for a desired end **5** : to alter deceptively

doc·tor·ate \ˈdäk-tə-rət\ n : the degree, title, or rank of a doctor

doc·tri·naire \ˌdäk-trə-ˈnar\ n [F] : one who attempts to put an abstract theory into effect without regard to practical difficulties — **doctrinaire** adj

doc·trine \ˈdäk-trən\ n **1** : something that is taught **2** : DOGMA, TENET — **doc·tri·nal** \-trən-ᵊl\ adj

docu·dra·ma \ˈdä-kyə-ˌdrä-mə, -ˌdra-\ n : a drama for television, motion pictures, or theater that deals freely with historical events

doc·u·ment \ˈdä-kyə-mənt\ n : a paper that furnishes information, proof, or support of something else — **doc·u·ment** \-ˌment\ vb — **doc·u·men·ta·tion** \ˌdä-kyə-mən-ˈtā-shən\ n — **doc·u·ment·er** n

doc·u·men·ta·ry \ˌdä-kyə-ˈmen-tə-rē\ adj **1** : consisting of documents; also : being in writing ⟨∼ proof⟩ **2** : giving a factual presentation in artistic form ⟨a ∼ movie⟩ — **documentary** n

DOD abbr Department of Defense

¹dod·der \ˈdä-dər\ n : any of a genus of leafless elongated wiry parasitic herbs deficient in chlorophyll

²dodder vb **dod·dered**; **dod·der·ing 1** : to tremble or shake usu. from age **2** : to progress feebly and unsteadily

¹dodge \ˈdäj\ n **1** : an act of evading by sudden bodily movement **2** : an artful device to evade, deceive, or trick **3** : EXPEDIENT

²dodge vb **dodged**; **dodg·ing 1** : to evade usu. by trickery **2** : to move suddenly aside; also : to avoid or evade by so doing — **dodg·er** n

do·do \ˈdō-dō\ n, pl **dodoes** or **dodos** [Pg doudo, fr. doudo silly, stupid] **1** : an extinct heavy flightless bird of the island of Mauritius related to the pigeons and larger than a turkey **2** : one hopelessly behind the times; also : a stupid person

dodo 1

doe \ˈdō\ n, pl **does** or **doe** : an adult female of various mammals (as a deer, rabbit, or kangaroo) of which the male is called **buck**

DOE abbr Department of Energy

do·er \ˈdü-ər\ n : one that does

does pres 3d sing of DO, pl of DOE

doff \ˈdäf\ vb [ME, fr. don to do + of off] **1** : to take off (the hat) in greeting or as a sign of respect **2** : to rid oneself of

¹dog \ˈdȯg\ n **1** : a flesh-eating domestic mammal relat-

ed to the wolves; *esp* : a male of this animal **2** : a worthless person **3** : FELLOW, CHAP ⟨you lucky ∼⟩ **4** : a mechanical device for holding something **5** : uncharacteristic or affected stylishness or dignity ⟨put on the ∼⟩ **6** *pl* : RUIN ⟨gone to the ∼s⟩

²dog *vb* **dogged; dog•ging 1** : to hunt or track like a hound **2** : to worry as if by pursuit with dogs : PLAGUE

dog•bane \'dòg-ˌbān\ *n* : any of a genus of mostly poisonous herbs with milky juice and often showy flowers

dog•cart \-ˌkärt\ *n* : a light one-horse carriage with two seats back to back

dog•catch•er \-ˌka-chər, -ˌke-\ *n* : a community official assigned to catch and dispose of stray dogs

dog–ear \'dòg-gir\ *n* : the turned-down corner of a leaf of a book — **dog–ear** *vb* — **dog–eared** \-ˌgird\ *adj*

dog•fight \'dòg-ˌfit\ *n* : a fight between fighter planes at close range

dog•fish \-ˌfish\ *n* : any of various small sharks

dog•ged \'dò-gəd\ *adj* : stubbornly determined : TENACIOUS — **dog•ged•ly** *adv* — **dog•ged•ness** *n*

dog•ger•el \'dò-gə-rəl\ *n* : verse that is loosely styled and irregular in measure esp. for comic effect

---

dog•gie bag *or* **doggy bag** \'dò-gē-\ *n* : a container for carrying home leftover food from a restaurant meal

---

¹dog•gy *or* **dog•gie** \'dò-gē\ *n, pl* **doggies** : a small dog

²dog•gy *adj* **dog•gi•er; -est** : of or resembling a dog ⟨a ∼ odor⟩

dog•house \'dòg-ˌhaùs\ *n* : a shelter for a dog — **in the doghouse** : in a state of disfavor

do•gie \'dō-gē\ *n, chiefly West* : a motherless calf in a range herd

dog•leg \'dòg-ˌleg\ *n* : a sharp bend or angle (as in a road) — **dogleg** *vb*

dog•ma \'dòg-ma\ *n, pl* **dogmas** *also* **dog•ma•ta** \-mə-tə\ **1** : a tenet or code of tenets **2** : a doctrine or body of doctrines formally proclaimed by a church

dog•ma•tism \'dòg-mə-ˌti-zəm\ *n* : positiveness in stating matters of opinion esp. when unwarranted or arrogant — **dog•mat•ic** \dòg-'ma-tik\ *adj* — **dog•mat•i•cal•ly** \-ti-k(ə-)lē\ *adv*

do–good•er \'dü-ˌgù-dər\ *n* : an earnest often naive humanitarian or reformer

dog•tooth violet \'dòg-ˌtüth-\ *n* : any of a genus of wild spring-flowering bulbous herbs related to the lilies

dog•trot \'dòg-ˌträt\ *n* : a gentle trot — **dogtrot** *vb*

dog•wood \'dòg-ˌwùd\ *n* : any of a genus of trees and shrubs having heads of small flowers often with showy white, pink, or red bracts

doi•ly \'dòi-lē\ *n, pl* **doilies** : a small often decorative mat

do in *vb* **1** : RUIN **2** : KILL **3** : TIRE, EXHAUST **4** : CHEAT

do•ings \'dü-iŋz\ *n pl* : GOINGS-ON

do–it–yourself *n* : the activity of doing or making something without professional training or help — **do–it–your•self•er** *n*

dogwood

dol *abbr* dollar

dol•drums \'dōl-drəmz, 'däl-\ *n pl* **1** : a spell of listlessness or despondency **2** *often cap* : a part of the ocean near the equator known for calms **3** : a state or period of inactivity, stagnation, or slump

¹dole \'dōl\ *n* **1** : a distribution esp. of food, money, or clothing to the needy; *also* : something so distributed **2** : a grant of government funds to the unemployed

²dole *vb* **doled; dol•ing** : to give or distribute as a charity — usu. used with *out*

dole•ful \'dōl-fəl\ *adj* : full of grief : SAD — **dole•ful•ly** *adv*

dole out *vb* **1** : to give or deliver in small portions **2** : DISH OUT

doll \'däl, 'dòl\ *n* **1** : a small figure of a human being used esp. as a child's plaything **2** : a pretty woman **3** : an attractive person — **doll•ish** \'dä-lish, 'dò-\ *adj*

dol•lar \'dä-lər\ *n* [Dutch or LG *daler*, fr. G *Taler*, short for *Joachimstaler*, fr. Sankt *Joachimsthal*, Bohemia, where talers were first made] **1** : any of various basic monetary units (as in the U.S. and Canada) — see MONEY table **2** : a coin, note, or token representing one dollar **3** : RINGGIT

dol•lop \'dä-ləp\ *n* **1** : LUMP, GLOB **2** : PORTION 1 — **dollop** *vb*

doll up *vb* **1** : to dress elegantly or extravagantly **2** : to make more attractive **3** : to get dolled up

dol•ly \'dä-lē\ *n, pl* **dollies** : a small cart or wheeled platform (as for a television or movie camera)

dol•men \'dōl-mən, 'däl-\ *n* : a prehistoric monument consisting of two or more upright stones supporting a horizontal stone slab

do•lo•mite \'dō-lə-ˌmīt, 'dä-\ *n* : a mineral found in broad layers as a compact limestone

do•lor \'dō-lər, 'dä-\ *n* : mental suffering or anguish : SORROW — **do•lor•ous** *adj* — **do•lor•ous•ly** *adv*

do•lour *chiefly Brit var of* DOLOR

dol•phin \'däl-fən\ *n* **1** : any of various small toothed whales with the snout more or less elongated into a beak **2** : either of two active food fishes of tropical and temperate seas

dolt \'dōlt\ *n* : a stupid person — **dolt•ish** \'dōl-tish\ *adj* — **dolt•ish•ness** *n*

dom *abbr* **1** domestic **2** dominant **3** dominion

-dom *n suffix* **1** : dignity : office ⟨duke*dom*⟩ **2** : realm : jurisdiction ⟨king*dom*⟩ **3** : state or fact of being ⟨free*dom*⟩ **4** : those having a (specified) office, occupation, interest, or character ⟨official*dom*⟩

do·main \dō-'mān\ *n* 1 : complete and absolute ownership of land 2 : land completely owned 3 : a territory over which dominion is exercised 4 : a sphere of knowledge, influence, or activity ⟨the ∼ of science⟩

dome \'dōm\ *n* 1 : a large hemispherical roof or ceiling 2 : a structure or natural formation that resembles the dome of a building 3 : a roofed sports stadium — **dome** *vb*

¹do·mes·tic \də-'mes-tik\ *adj* 1 : living near or about human habitations 2 : TAME, DOMESTICATED 3 : relating and limited to one's own country or the country under consideration 4 : of or relating to the household or the family 5 : devoted to home duties and pleasures 6 : INDIGENOUS — **do·mes·ti·cal·ly** \-ti-k(ə-)lē\ *adv*

²domestic *n* : a household servant

do·mes·ti·cate \də-'mes-ti-ˌkāt\ *vb* **-cat·ed; -cat·ing** : to adapt to life in association with and to the use of humans — **do·mes·ti·ca·tion** \-ˌmes-ti-'kā-shən\ *n*

do·mes·tic·i·ty \ˌdō-ˌmes-'ti-sə-tē, də-\ *n, pl* **-ties** 1 : the quality or state of being domestic or domesticated 2 : domestic activities or life

dom·i·cile \'dä-mə-ˌsil, 'dō-; 'dä-mə-səl\ *n* : a dwelling place : HOME — **domicile** *vb* — **dom·i·cil·i·ary** \ˌdä-mə-'si-lē-ˌer-ē, ˌdō-\ *adj*

dom·i·nance \'dä-mə-nəns\ *n* 1 : AUTHORITY, CONTROL 2 : the property of a genetic dominant that prevents expression of a genetic recessive

¹dom·i·nant \-nənt\ *adj* 1 : controlling or prevailing over all others 2 : overlooking from a high position 3 : producing or being a bodily characteristic that is expressed when a contrasting recessive gene or trait is present

²dominant *n* : a dominant gene or trait

dom·i·nate \'dä-mə-ˌnāt\ *vb* **-nat·ed; -nat·ing** 1 : RULE, CONTROL 2 : to have a commanding position or controlling power over 3 : to rise high above in a position suggesting power to dominate — **dom·i·na·tor** \-ˌnā-tər\ *n*

dom·i·na·tion \ˌdä-mə-'nā-shən\ *n* 1 : supremacy or preeminence over another 2 : exercise of mastery, ruling power, or preponderant influence

dom·i·na·trix \ˌdä-mə-'nā-triks\ *n, pl* **-trices** \-'nā-trə-ˌsēz, -nə-'trī-sēz\ : a woman who dominates and abuses her sexual partner; *also* : a dominating woman

dom·i·neer \ˌdä-mə-'nir\ *vb* 1 : to rule in an arrogant manner 2 : to be overbearing

Do·min·i·can \də-'mi-ni-kən\ *n* : a native or inhabitant of the Dominican Republic — **Dominican** *adj*

do·mi·nie \¹ *usu* 'dä-mə-nē, 2 *usu* 'dō-\ *n* 1 *chiefly Scot* : SCHOOLMASTER 2 : CLERGYMAN

do·min·ion \də-'min-yən\ *n* 1 : DOMAIN 2 : supreme authority : SOVEREIGNTY 3 *often cap* : a self-governing nation of the Commonwealth

dom·i·no \'dä-mə-ˌnō\ *n, pl* **-noes** *or* **-nos** 1 : a long loose hooded cloak usu. worn with a half mask as a masquerade costume 2 : a flat rectangular block used as a piece in a game (**dominoes**)

¹don \'dän\ *vb* **donned; don·ning** [ME, fr. *don* to do + *on*] : to put on (as clothes)

²don *n* [Sp, fr. L *dominus* lord, master] 1 : a Spanish nobleman or gentleman — used as a title prefixed to the Christian name 2 : a head, tutor, or fellow in an English university

do·ña \'dō-nyə\ *n* : a Spanish woman of rank — used as a title prefixed to the Christian name

do·nate \'dō-ˌnāt\ *vb* **do·nat·ed; do·nat·ing** 1 : to make a gift of : CONTRIBUTE 2 : to make a donation

do·na·tion \dō-'nā-shən\ *n* 1 : the making of a gift esp. to a charity 2 : a free contribution : GIFT

¹done \'dən\ *past part of* DO

²done *adj* 1 : doomed to failure, defeat, or death 2 : gone by : OVER ⟨when day is ∼⟩ 3 : cooked sufficiently 4 : conformable to social convention

dong \'dòŋ, 'däŋ\ *n* — see MONEY table

don·key \'däŋ-kē, 'dəŋ-\ *n, pl* **donkeys** 1 : a sturdy and

patient domestic mammal classified with the asses 2 : a stupid or obstinate person

don·ny·brook \'dä-nē-ˌbrúk\ *n, often cap* [*Donnybrook* Fair, annual Irish event once known for its brawls] : an uproarious brawl

do·nor \'dō-nər\ *n* : one that gives, donates, or presents

donut *var of* DOUGHNUT

doo·dad \'dü-ˌdad\ *n* : an often small article whose common name is unknown or forgotten

doo·dle \'düd-əl\ *vb* **doo·dled; doo·dling** : to draw or scribble aimlessly while occupied with something else — **doodle** *n* — **doo·dler** *n*

doom \'düm\ *n* 1 : JUDGMENT; *esp* : a judicial condemnation or sentence 2 : DESTINY 3 : RUIN, DEATH — **doom** *vb*

dooms·day \'dümz-ˌdā\ *n* : JUDGMENT DAY

door \'dòr\ *n* 1 : a barrier by which an entry is closed and opened; *also* : a similar part of a piece of furniture 2 : DOORWAY 3 : a means of access or participation : OPPORTUNITY

door·keep·er \-ˌkē-pər\ *n* : a person who tends a door

door·knob \-ˌnäb\ *n* : a knob that when turned releases a door latch

door·man \-ˌman, -mən\ *n* : a usu. uniformed attendant at the door of a building (as a hotel)

door·mat \-ˌmat\ *n* : a mat placed before or inside a door for wiping dirt from the shoes

door·plate \-ˌplāt\ *n* : a nameplate on a door

door·step \-ˌstep\ *n* : a step or series of steps before an outer door

door·way \-ˌwā\ *n* 1 : the opening that a door closes 2 : DOOR 3

do·pa \'dō-pə\ *n* : a form of an amino acid that is used esp. in the treatment of Parkinson's disease

¹dope \'dōp\ *n* 1 : a preparation for giving a desired quality 2 : a drug esp. when narcotic or addictive and used illegally 3 : a stupid person 4 : INFORMATION

²dope *vb* **doped; dop·ing** 1 : to treat with dope; *esp* : to give a narcotic to 2 : FIGURE OUT — usu. used with *out* 3 : to take dope — **dop·er** *n*

dop·ey *also* **dopy** \'dō-pē\ *adj* **dop·i·er; -est** 1 : dulled by alcohol or a narcotic 2 : SLUGGISH 3 : STUPID — **dop·i·ness** *n*

Dopp·ler effect \'dä-plər-\ *n* : a change in the frequency at which waves (as of sound) reach an observer from a source in motion with respect to the observer

dork \'dòrk\ *n, slang* : NERD; *also* : JERK 2

dorm \'dòrm\ *n* : DORMITORY

dor·mant \'dòr-mənt\ *adj* : INACTIVE; *esp* : not actively growing or functioning ⟨∼ buds⟩ — **dor·man·cy** \-mən-sē\ *n*

dor·mer \'dòr-mər\ *n* [MF *dormeor* dormitory, fr. L *dormitorium*, fr. *dormire* to sleep] : a window built upright in a sloping roof; *also* : the roofed structure containing such a window

dor·mi·to·ry \'dòr-mə-ˌtōr-ē\ *n, pl* **-ries** 1 : a room for sleeping; *esp* : a large room containing a number of beds 2 : a residence hall providing sleeping rooms

dor·mouse \'dòr-ˌmaùs\ *n* : any of numerous Old World squirrellike rodents

dor·sal \'dòr-səl\ *adj* : of, relating to, or located near or on the surface of the body that in humans is the back but in most other animals is the upper surface — **dor·sal·ly** *adv*

do·ry \'dōr-ē\ *n, pl* **dories** : a flat-bottomed boat with high flaring sides and a sharp bow

DOS *abbr* disk operating system

¹dose \'dōs\ *n* [ME, fr. MF, fr. LL *dosis*, fr. Gk, lit., act of giving, fr. *didonai* to give] 1 : a measured quantity

(as of medicine) to be taken or administered at one time **2** : the quantity of radiation administered or absorbed — **dos•age** \'dō-sij\ n

²**dose** vb **dosed; dos•ing 1** : to give in doses **2** : to give medicine to

do•sim•e•ter \dō-'si-mə-tər\ n : a device for measuring doses of X rays or of radioactivity — **do•sim•e•try** \-mə-trē\ n

dos•sier \'dòs-₁yā, 'dò-sē-₁ā\ n [F, bundle of documents labeled on the back, dossier, fr. dos back, fr. L dorsum] : a file containing detailed records on a particular person or subject

¹**dot** \'dät\ n **1** : a small spot : SPECK **2** : a small round mark **3** : a precise point esp. in time ⟨be here on the ∼⟩

²**dot** vb **dot•ted; dot•ting 1** : to mark with a dot ⟨∼ an i⟩ **2** : to cover with or as if with dots — **dot•ter** n

DOT abbr Department of Transportation

dot•age \'dō-tij\ n : feebleness of mind esp. in old age : SENILITY

dot•ard \-tərd\ n : a person in dotage

dote \'dōt\ vb **dot•ed; dot•ing 1** : to be feebleminded esp. from old age **2** : to be lavish or excessive in one's attention, affection, or fondness ⟨doted on her niece⟩

dot matrix n : a rectangular arrangement of dots from which alphanumeric characters can be formed (as by a computer printer)

Dou•ay Version \dü-'ā-\ n : an English translation of the Vulgate used by Roman Catholics

¹**dou•ble** \'də-bəl\ adj **1** : TWOFOLD, DUAL **2** : consisting of two members or parts **3** : being twice as great or as many **4** : folded in two **5** : having more than one whorl of petals ⟨∼ roses⟩

²**double** vb **dou•bled; dou•bling 1** : to make, be, or become twice as great or as many **2** : to make a call in bridge that increases the trick values and penalties of (an opponent's bid) **3** : FOLD **4** : CLENCH **5** : to be or cause to be bent over **6** : to take the place of another **7** : to hit a double **8** : to turn sharply and suddenly; esp : to turn back on one's course

³**double** adv **1** : DOUBLY **2** : two together

⁴**double** n **1** : something twice another in size, strength, speed, quantity, or value **2** : a base hit that enables the batter to reach second base **3** : COUNTERPART, DUPLICATE; esp : a person who closely resembles another **4** : UNDERSTUDY, SUBSTITUTE **5** : a sharp turn : REVERSAL **6** : FOLD **7** : a combined bet placed on two different contests **8** pl : a game between two pairs of players **9** : an act of doubling in a card game

double bond n : a chemical bond in which two atoms in a molecule share two pairs of electrons

double cross n : an act of betraying or cheating esp. an associate — **dou•ble–cross** \₁də-bəl-'kròs\ vb — **dou•ble–cross•er** n

dou•ble–deal•ing \₁də-bəl-'dē-liŋ\ n : DUPLICITY — **dou•ble–deal•er** \-'dē-lər\ n — **double–dealing** adj

dou•ble–deck•er \-'de-kər\ n : something having two decks, levels, or layers — **dou•ble–deck** \-₁dek\ or **dou•ble–decked** \-₁dekt\ adj

dou•ble–dig•it \₁də-bəl-'di-jət\ adj : amounting to 10 percent or more

dou•ble en•ten•dre \₁düb-³l-än-'tänd, ₁də-bəl-, -'tänd-r³\ n, pl **double entendres** \same or -'tän-drəz\ [obs. F, lit., double meaning] : a word or expression capable of two interpretations with one usu. risqué

dou•ble–head•er \₁də-bəl-'he-dər\ n : two games played consecutively on the same day

double helix n : a helix or spiral consisting of two strands (as of DNA) in the surface of a cylinder which coil around its axis

dou•ble–hung \₁də-bəl-'həŋ\ adj, of a window : having an upper and a lower sash that can slide past each other

dou•ble–joint•ed \-'jòin-təd\ adj : having a joint that permits an exceptional degree of freedom of motion of the parts joined ⟨a ∼ finger⟩

double play n : a play in baseball by which two players are put out

dou•blet \'də-blət\ n **1** : a man's close-fitting jacket worn in Europe esp. in the 16th century **2** : one of two similar or identical things

dou•ble take \'də-bəl-₁tāk\ n : a delayed reaction to a surprising or significant situation after an initial failure to notice anything unusual

dou•ble–talk \-₁tòk\ n : language that appears to be meaningful but in fact is a mixture of sense and nonsense

double up vb : to share accommodations for one

double whammy n : a combination of two usu. adverse forces, circumstances, or effects

dou•bloon \₁də-'blün\ n : a former gold coin of Spain and Spanish America

dou•bly \'də-blē\ adv **1** : in a twofold manner **2** : to twice the degree

¹**doubt** \'daút\ vb **1** : to be uncertain about **2** : to lack confidence in : DISTRUST **3** : to consider unlikely — **doubt•able** adj — **doubt•er** n

²**doubt** n **1** : uncertainty of belief or opinion **2** : a condition causing uncertainty, hesitation, or suspense ⟨the outcome was in ∼⟩ **3** : DISTRUST **4** : an inclination not to believe or accept

doubt•ful \'daút-fəl\ adj **1** : QUESTIONABLE **2** : UNDECIDED — **doubt•ful•ly** adv — **doubt•ful•ness** n

¹**doubt•less** \'daút-ləs\ adv **1** : without doubt **2** : PROBABLY

²**doubtless** adj : free from doubt : CERTAIN — **doubt•less•ly** adv

douche \'düsh\ n [F] **1** : a jet of fluid (as water) directed against a part or into a cavity of the body; also : a cleansing with a douche **2** : a device for giving douches — **douche** vb

dough \'dō\ n **1** : a mixture that consists of flour or meal and a liquid (as milk or water) and is stiff enough to knead or roll **2** : something resembling dough esp. in consistency **3** : MONEY — **doughy** \'dō-ē\ adj

dough•boy \-₁bòi\ n : an American infantryman esp. in World War I

dough·nut \-(ˌ)nət\ n : a small usu. ring-shaped cake fried in fat

dough·ty \ˈdau̇-tē\ adj **dough·ti·er; -est** : ABLE, STRONG, VALIANT

Doug·las fir \ˈdə-gləs-\ n : a tall evergreen timber tree of the western U.S.

do up vb **1** : to prepare (as by cleaning) for use **2** : to wrap up **3** : CLOTHE, DECORATE

dour \ˈdau̇r, ˈdu̇r\ adj [ME, fr. L durus hard] **1** : STERN, HARSH **2** : OBSTINATE **3** : SULLEN — **dour·ly** adv

douse \ˈdau̇s, ˈdau̇z\ vb **doused; dous·ing 1** : to plunge into water **2** : DRENCH **3** : EXTINGUISH

¹dove \ˈdəv\ n **1** : any of numerous pigeons; esp : a small wild pigeon **2** : an advocate of peace or of a peaceful policy — **dov·ish** \ˈdə-vish\ adj

²dove \ˈdōv\ past of DIVE

¹dove·tail \ˈdəv-ˌtāl\ n : something that resembles a dove's tail; esp : a flaring tenon and a mortise into which it fits tightly

²dovetail vb **1** : to join by means of dovetails **2** : to fit skillfully together to form a whole ⟨our plans ∼ nicely⟩

dow·a·ger \ˈdau̇-i-jər\ n **1** : a widow owning property or a title from her deceased husband **2** : a dignified elderly woman

dowdy \ˈdau̇-dē\ adj **dowd·i·er; -est** : lacking neatness and charm : SHABBY, UNTIDY; also : lacking smartness

dow·el \ˈdau̇-əl\ n **1** : a pin used for fastening together two pieces of wood **2** : a round rod (as of wood) — **dowel** vb

¹dow·er \ˈdau̇-ər\ n **1** : the part of a deceased husband's real estate which the law gives for life to his widow **2** : DOWRY

²dower vb : to supply with a dower or dowry : ENDOW

dow·itch·er \ˈdau̇-i-chər\ n : any of several long-billed wading birds related to the sandpipers

¹down \ˈdau̇n\ adv **1** : toward or in a lower physical position **2** : to a lying or sitting position **3** : toward or to the ground, floor, or bottom **4** : as a down payment ⟨paid $5 ∼⟩ **5** : on paper ⟨put ∼ what he says⟩ **6** : in a direction that is the opposite of up **7** : SOUTH **8** : to or in a lower or worse condition or status **9** : from a past time **10** : to or in a state of less activity **11** : into defeat ⟨voted the motion ∼⟩

²down prep : down in, on, along, or through : toward the bottom of

³down vb **1** : to go or cause to go or come down **2** : DEFEAT **3** : to cause (a football) to be out of play

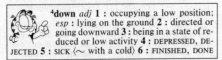

⁴down adj **1** : occupying a low position; esp : lying on the ground **2** : directed or going downward **3** : being in a state of reduced or low activity **4** : DEPRESSED, DEJECTED **5** : SICK ⟨∼ with a cold⟩ **6** : FINISHED, DONE

⁵down n **1** : a low or falling period (as in activity, emo-

tional life, or fortunes) **2** : one of a series of attempts to advance a football

⁶down n : a rolling usu. treeless upland with sparse soil — usu. used in pl.

⁷down n **1** : a covering of soft fluffy feathers; also : such feathers **2** : a downlike covering or material

down·beat \ˈdau̇n-ˌbēt\ n : the downward stroke of a conductor indicating the principally accented note of a measure of music

down·burst \-ˌbərst\ n : a powerful downdraft usu. associated with a thunderstorm that is a hazard for low-flying aircraft; also : MICROBURST

down·cast \-ˌkast\ adj **1** : DEJECTED **2** : directed down ⟨a ∼ glance⟩

down·draft \-ˌdraft\ n : a downward current of gas (as air)

down·er \ˈdau̇-nər\ n **1** : a depressant drug; esp : BARBITURATE **2** : someone or something depressing

down·fall \ˈdau̇n-ˌfȯl\ n **1** : a sudden fall (as from high rank) **2** : something that causes a downfall — **down·fall·en** \-ˌfȯ-lən\ adj

¹down·grade \ˈdau̇n-ˌgrād\ n **1** : a downward slope (as of a road) **2** : a decline toward a worse condition

²downgrade vb : to lower in quality, value, extent, or status

down·heart·ed \-ˈhär-təd\ adj : DEJECTED

down·hill \ˈdau̇n-ˈhil\ adv : toward the bottom of a hill — **downhill** \-ˌhil\ adj

down·load \-ˌlōd\ vb : to transfer (data) from a computer to another device — **down·load·able** \-ˌlō-də-bəl\ adj

down payment n : a part of the full price paid at the time of purchase or delivery with the balance to be paid later

down·pour \ˈdau̇n-ˌpȯr\ n : a heavy rain

down·range \-ˈrānj\ adv : away from a launching site

¹down·right \-ˌrīt\ adv : THOROUGHLY

²downright adj **1** : ABSOLUTE, UTTER ⟨a ∼ lie⟩ **2** : PLAIN, BLUNT ⟨a ∼ man⟩

down·shift \-ˌshift\ vb : to shift an automotive vehicle into a lower gear

down·size \-ˌsīz\ vb : to reduce or undergo reduction in size or numbers

down·spout \-ˌspau̇t\ n : a vertical pipe used to drain rainwater from a roof

Down's syndrome \ˈdau̇nz-\ or **Down syndrome** \ˈdau̇n-\ n : a birth defect characterized by mental retardation, slanting eyes, a broad short skull, broad hands with short fingers, and the presence of an extra chromosome

down·stage \ˈdau̇n-ˈstāj\ adv or adj : toward or at the front of a theatrical stage

down·stairs \-ˈstarz\ adv : on or to a lower floor and esp. the main or ground floor — **down·stairs** \-ˌstarz\ adj or n

down·stream \-ˈstrēm\ adv or adj : in the direction of flow of a stream

down·stroke \-ˌstrōk\ n : a downward stroke

down·swing \-ˌswiŋ\ n 1 : a swing downward 2 : DOWNTURN

down–to–earth adj : PRACTICAL, REALISTIC

down·town \ˈdau̇n-ˌtau̇n\ n : the main business district of a town or city — **downtown** \ˈdau̇n-ˈtau̇n\ adj or adv

down·trod·den \ˈdau̇n-ˈträd-ᵊn\ adj : suffering oppression

down·turn \-ˌtərn\ n : a downward turn esp. in business activity

¹down·ward \ˈdau̇n-wərd\ or **down·wards** \-wərdz\ adv 1 : from a higher to a lower place or condition 2 : from an earlier time 3 : from an ancestor or predecessor

²downward adj : directed toward or situated in a lower place or condition

down·wind \ˈdau̇n-ˈwind\ adv or adj : in the direction that the wind is blowing

downy \ˈdau̇-nē\ adj **down·i·er; -est** : resembling or covered with down

downy mildew n : any of various parasitic fungi producing whitish masses esp. on the underside of plant leaves; also : a plant disease caused by downy mildew

downy woodpecker n : a small black-and-white woodpecker of No. America

dow·ry \ˈdau̇r-ē\ n, pl **dowries** : the property that a woman brings to her husband in marriage

dowse \ˈdau̇z\ vb **dowsed; dows·ing** : to use a divining rod esp. to find water — **dows·er** n

dox·ol·o·gy \däk-ˈsä-lə-jē\ n, pl **-gies** : a usu. short hymn of praise to God

doy·en \ˈdȯi-ən, ˈdwä-yaᵐ\ n : the senior or most experienced person in a group

doy·enne \dȯi-ˈyen, dwä-ˈyen\ n : a woman who is a doyen

doy·ley chiefly Brit var of DOILY

doz abbr dozen

doze \ˈdōz\ vb **dozed; doz·ing** : to sleep lightly — **doze** n

doz·en \ˈdəz-ᵊn\ n, pl **dozens** or **dozen** [ME dozeine, fr. OF dozaine, fr. doze twelve, fr. L duodecim, fr. duo two + decem ten] : a group of twelve — **doz·enth** \-ᵊnth\ adj

¹DP \ˈdē-ˈpē\ n, pl **DP's** or **DPs** : a displaced person

²DP abbr 1 data processing 2 double play

dpt abbr department

DPT abbr diphtheria-pertussis-tetanus (vaccines)

dr abbr 1 debtor 2 dram 3 drive 4 drum

Dr abbr doctor

DR abbr 1 dead reckoning 2 dining room

drab \ˈdrab\ adj **drab·ber; drab·best** 1 : being of a light olive-brown color 2 : DULL, MONOTONOUS, CHEERLESS — **drab·ly** adv — **drab·ness** n

drach·ma \ˈdrak-mə\ n, pl **drach·mas** or **drach·mai** \-ˌmī\ or **drach·mae** \-(ˌ)mē\ — see MONEY table

dra·co·ni·an \drā-ˈkō-nē-ən, drə-\ adj, often cap : CRUEL; also : SEVERE

¹draft \ˈdraft, ˈdråft\ n 1 : the act of drawing or hauling 2 : the act or an instance of drinking or inhaling; also : the portion drunk or inhaled in one such act 3 : DOSE, POTION 4 : DELINEATION, PLAN, DESIGN; also : a preliminary sketch, outline, or version ⟨a rough ~ of a speech⟩ 5 : the act of drawing (as from a cask); also : a portion of liquid so drawn 6 : the depth of water a ship draws esp. when loaded 7 : a system for or act of selecting persons esp. for compulsory military service; also : the persons so selected 8 : an order for the payment of money drawn by one person or bank on another 9 : a heavy demand : STRAIN 10 : a current of air; also : a device to regulate air supply (as in a stove) — **on draft** : ready to be drawn from a receptacle ⟨beer on draft⟩

²draft adj 1 : used or adapted for drawing loads ⟨~ horses⟩ 2 : being or having been on draft ⟨~ beer⟩

³draft vb 1 : to select usu. on a compulsory basis; esp : to conscript for military service 2 : to draw the preliminary sketch, version, or plan of 3 : COMPOSE, PREPARE 4 : to draw off or away — **draft·ee** \draf-ˈtē, dråf-\ n

drafts·man \ˈdraft-smən, ˈdråft-\ n : a person who draws plans (as for buildings or machinery)

drafty \ˈdraf-tē, ˈdråf-\ adj **draft·i·er; -est** : exposed to or abounding in drafts of air

---

¹drag \ˈdrag\ n 1 : a device pulled along under water for detecting or gathering 2 : something (as a harrow or sledge) that is dragged along over a surface 3 : the act or an instance of dragging 4 : something that hinders progress; also : something boring 5 : STREET ⟨the main ~⟩ 6 : clothing typical of one sex worn by a member of the opposite sex

²drag vb **dragged; drag·ging** 1 : HAUL 2 : to move with painful or undue slowness or difficulty 3 : to force into or out of some situation, condition, or course of action 4 : PROTRACT ⟨~ a story out⟩ 5 : to hang or lag behind 6 : to explore, search, or fish with a drag 7 : to trail along on the ground 8 : DRAW, PUFF ⟨~ on a cigarette⟩ — **drag·ger** n

drag·net \-ˌnet\ n 1 : NET, TRAWL 2 : a network of planned actions for pursuing and catching ⟨a police ~⟩

drag·o·man \ˈdra-gə-mən\ n, pl **-mans** or **-men** \-mən\ : an interpreter employed esp. in the Near East

drag·on \ˈdra-gən\ n [ME, fr. OF, fr. L dracon-, draco serpent, dragon, fr. Gk drakōn serpent] : a fabulous animal usu. represented as a huge winged scaly serpent with a crested head and large claws

drag·on·fly \-ˌflī\ n : any of a group of large harmless 4-winged insects that hold the wings horizontal and unfolded in repose

¹dra·goon \drə-ˈgün, dra-\ n [F dragon dragon, dragoon, fr. MF] : a heavily armed mounted soldier

²dragoon vb : to force or attempt to force into submission : COERCE

drag race n : an acceleration contest between vehicles

drag strip n : a site for drag races

¹drain \ˈdrān\ vb 1 : to draw off or flow off gradually or completely 2 : to exhaust physically or emotion-

dragonfly

ally **3** : to make or become gradually dry or empty **4** : to carry away the surface water of : discharge surface or surplus water **5** : EMPTY, EXHAUST — **drain·er** *n*

²drain *n* **1** : a means (as a channel or sewer) of draining **2** : the act of draining **3** : a gradual outflow; *also* : something causing an outflow ⟨a ∼ on our savings⟩

drain·age \'drā-nij\ *n* **1** : the act or process of draining; *also* : something that is drained off **2** : a means for draining : DRAIN, SEWER **3** : an area drained

drain·pipe \'drān-ˌpīp\ *n* : a pipe for drainage

drake \'drāk\ *n* : a male duck

dram \'dram\ *n* **1** — see WEIGHT table **2** : FLUID DRAM **3** : a small drink

dra·ma \'drä-mə, 'dra-\ *n* [LL, fr. Gk, deed, drama, fr. *dran* to do, act] **1** : a literary composition designed for theatrical presentation **2** : dramatic art, literature, or affairs **3** : a series of events involving conflicting forces — **dra·mat·ic** \drə-'ma-tik\ *adj* — **dra·mat·i·cal·ly** \-ti-k(ə-)lē\ *adv* — **dra·ma·tist** \'dra-mə-tist, 'drä-\ *n*

dramatise *Brit var of* DRAMATIZE

dra·ma·tize \'dra-mə-ˌtīz, 'drä-\ *vb* **-tized; -tiz·ing 1** : to adapt for or be suitable for theatrical presentation **2** : to present or represent in a dramatic manner — **dram·a·ti·za·tion** \ˌdra-mə-tə-'zā-shən, ˌdrä-\ *n*

dra·me·dy \'dra-mə-dē, 'drä-\ *n* : a situation comedy having dramatic scenes

drank *past and past part of* DRINK

¹drape \'drāp\ *vb* **draped; drap·ing 1** : to cover or adorn with or as if with folds of cloth **2** : to cause to hang or stretch out loosely or carelessly **3** : to arrange or become arranged in flowing lines or folds

²drape *n* **1** : CURTAIN **2** : arrangement in or of folds **3** : the cut or hang of clothing

drap·er \'drā-pər\ *n, chiefly Brit* : a dealer in cloth and sometimes in clothing and dry goods

drap·ery \'drā-pə-rē\ *n, pl* **-er·ies 1** *Brit* : DRY GOODS **2** : a decorative fabric esp. when hung loosely and in folds; *also* : hangings of heavy fabric used as a curtain

dras·tic \'dras-tik\ *adj* : HARSH, RIGOROUS, SEVERE ⟨∼ punishment⟩ — **dras·ti·cal·ly** \-ti-k(ə-)lē\ *adv*

draught \'draft\, **draughty** \'draf-tē\ *chiefly Brit var of* DRAFT, DRAFTY

draughts \'drafts\ *n, Brit* : CHECKERS

draughts·man *chiefly Brit var of* DRAFTSMAN

¹draw \'drò\ *vb* **drew** \'drü\; **drawn** \'dròn\; **draw·ing 1** : to cause to move toward a force exerted **2** : to cause to go in a certain direction ⟨drew him aside⟩ **3** : to move or go steadily or gradually ⟨night ∼s near⟩ **4** : ATTRACT, ENTICE **5** : PROVOKE, ROUSE ⟨drew enemy fire⟩ **6** : INHALE ⟨∼ a deep breath⟩ **7** : to bring or pull out ⟨drew a gun⟩ **8** : to cause to come out of a container ⟨∼ water for a bath⟩ **9** : EVISCERATE **10** : to require (a specified depth) to float in **11** : ACCUMULATE, GAIN ⟨∼ing interest⟩ **12** : to take money from a place of deposit : WITHDRAW **13** : to receive regularly ⟨∼ a salary⟩ **14** : to take (cards) from a stack or the dealer **15** : to receive or take at random ⟨∼ a winning number⟩ **16** : to bend (a bow) by pulling back the string **17** : WRINKLE, SHRINK **18** : to change shape by or as if by pulling or stretching ⟨a face *drawn* with

sorrow⟩ **19** : to leave (a contest) undecided : TIE **20** : DELINEATE, SKETCH **21** : to write out in due form : DRAFT ⟨∼ up a will⟩ **22** : FORMULATE ⟨∼ comparisons⟩ **23** : INFER ⟨∼ a conclusion⟩ **24** : to spread or elongate (metal) by hammering or by pulling through dies **25** : to produce or allow a draft or current of air ⟨the chimney ∼s well⟩ **26** : to swell out in a wind ⟨all sails ∼ing⟩

²draw *n* **1** : the act, process, or result of drawing **2** : a lot or chance drawn at random **3** : a contest left undecided or deadlocked : TIE **4** : one that draws attention or patronage

draw·back \'drò-ˌbak\ *n* : DISADVANTAGE 2

draw·bridge \-ˌbrij\ *n* : a bridge made to be raised, lowered, or turned to permit or deny passage

draw·er \'dror, 'drò-ər\ *n* **1** : one that draws **2** *pl* : an undergarment for the lower part of the body **3** : a sliding boxlike compartment (as in a table or desk)

draw·ing \'drò-iŋ\ *n* **1** : an act or instance of drawing; *esp* : an occasion when something is decided by drawing lots ⟨tonight's lottery ∼⟩ **2** : the act or art of making a figure, plan, or sketch by means of lines **3** : a representation made by drawing : SKETCH

drawing card *n* : DRAW 4

drawing room *n* : a formal reception room

drawl \'dròl\ *vb* : to speak or utter slowly with vowels greatly prolonged — **drawl** *n*

draw on *vb* : APPROACH ⟨night *draws on*⟩

draw out *vb* **1** : PROLONG **2** : to cause to speak freely

draw·string \'drò-ˌstriŋ\ *n* : a string, cord, or tape for use in closing a bag or controlling fullness in garments or curtains

draw up *vb* **1** : to prepare a draft or version of **2** : to pull oneself erect **3** : to bring or come to a stop

dray \'drā\ *n* : a strong low cart for carrying heavy loads

¹dread \'dred\ *vb* **1** : to fear greatly **2** : to feel extreme reluctance to meet or face

²dread *n* : great fear esp. of some harm to come

³dread *adj* **1** : causing great fear or anxiety **2** : inspiring awe

dread·ful \'dred-fəl\ *adj* **1** : inspiring dread or awe : FRIGHTENING **2** : extremely distasteful, unpleasant, or shocking — **dread·ful·ly** *adv*

dread·locks \'dred-ˌläks\ *n pl* : long braids of hair over the entire head

dread·nought \'dred-ˌnòt\ *n* : BATTLESHIP

¹dream \'drēm\ *n* [ME *dreem*, fr. OE *drēam* noise, joy, and ON *draumr* dream] **1** : a series of thoughts, images, or emotions occurring during sleep **2** : a dreamlike vision : DAYDREAM, REVERIE **3** : something notable for its beauty, excellence, or enjoyable quality **4** : IDEAL — **dreamy** *adj*

²dream \'drēm\ *vb* **dreamed** \'dremt, 'drēmd\ *or* **dreamt** \'dremt\; **dream·ing 1** : to have a dream of **2** : to indulge in daydreams or fantasies : pass (time) in reverie or inaction **3** : IMAGINE — **dream·er** *n*

dream·land \'drēm-ˌland\ *n* : an unreal delightful country that exists in imagination or in dreams

dream up *vb* : INVENT, CONCOCT

dream·world \-ˌwərld\ *n* : a world of illusion or fantasy

drear \'drir\ *adj* : DREARY

drea·ry \'drir-ē\ *adj* **drea·ri·er; -est** [ME *drery*, fr. OE *drēorig* sad, bloody, fr. *drēor* gore] **1** : DOLEFUL, SAD **2** : DISMAL, GLOOMY — **drea·ri·ly** \-ə-lē\ *adv*

¹dredge \'drej\ *vb* **dredged; dredg·ing** : to gather or search with or as if with a dredge — **dredg·er** *n*

²dredge *n* : a machine or barge for removing earth or silt

³dredge *vb* **dredged; dredg·ing** : to coat (food) by sprinkling (as with flour)

dregs \'dregz\ *n pl* **1** : SEDIMENT **1 2** : the most undesirable part ⟨the ∼ of humanity⟩
drench \'drench\ *vb* : to wet thoroughly
¹dress \'dres\ *vb* **1** : to make or set straight : ALIGN **2** : to
prepare for use; *esp* : BUTCHER **3** : TRIM, EMBELLISH
⟨∼ a store window⟩ **4** : to put clothes on : CLOTHE;
also : to put on or wear formal or fancy clothes **5** : to
apply dressings or medicine to **6** : to arrange (the
hair) by combing, brushing, or curling **7** : to apply fertilizer to **8** : SMOOTH, FINISH ⟨∼ leather⟩
²dress *n* **1** : APPAREL, CLOTHING **2** : a garment usu. consisting of a one-piece bodice and skirt — **dress•mak-**
er \-₁mā-kər\ *n* — **dress•mak•ing** \-₁mā-kiŋ\ *n*
³dress *adj* : suitable for a formal occasion; *also* : requiring formal dress
dres•sage \drə-'säzh\ *n* [F] : the execution by a trained
horse of complex movements in response to barely
perceptible signals from its rider
dress down *vb* : to scold severely
¹dress•er \'dre-sər\ *n* : a chest of drawers or bureau
with a mirror
²dresser *n* : one that dresses
dress•ing \'dre-siŋ\ *n* **1** : the act or process of one who
dresses **2** : a sauce for adding to a dish (as a salad) **3**
: a seasoned mixture usu. used as stuffing **4** : material
used to cover an injury
dressing gown *n* : a loose robe worn esp. while dressing or resting
dressy \'dre-sē\ *adj* **dress•i•er; -est 1** : showy in dress
2 : STYLISH, SMART
drew *past of* DRAW
¹drib•ble \'dri-bəl\ *vb* **drib•bled; drib•bling 1** : to fall or
flow in drops : TRICKLE **2** : DROOL **3** : to propel by successive slight taps or bounces
²dribble *n* **1** : a small trickling stream or flow **2** : a driz-
zling shower **3** : the dribbling of a ball or puck
drib•let \'dri-blət\ *n* **1** : a trifling amount **2** : a drop of
liquid
dri•er *or* **dry•er** \'drī-ər\ *n* **1** : a substance that speeds
drying (as of paint or ink) **2** *usu* **dryer** : a device for
drying
¹drift \'drift\ *n* **1** : the motion or course of something
drifting **2** : a mass of matter (as snow or sand) piled
up esp. by wind **3** : earth, gravel, and rock deposited
by a glacier **4** : a general underlying design or tendency : MEANING
²drift *vb* **1** : to float or be driven along by or as if by a
current of water or air **2** : to become piled up by wind
or water
drift•er \'drif-tər\ *n* : a person without aim, ambition,
or initiative
drift net *n* : a fishing net often miles in extent arranged
to drift with the tide or current
drift•wood \'drift-₁wud\ *n* : wood drifted or floated by
water
¹drill \'dril\ *n* **1** : a tool for boring holes **2** : the training
of soldiers in marching and the handling of arms **3** : a
regularly practiced exercise
²drill *vb* **1** : to instruct and exercise by repetition **2** : to

train in or practice military drill **3** : to bore with a drill
— **drill•er** *n*
³drill *n* **1** : a shallow furrow or trench in which seed is
sown **2** : an agricultural implement for making furrows and dropping seed into them
⁴drill *n* : a firm cotton twilled fabric
drill•mas•ter \'dril-₁mas-tər\ *n* : an instructor in military drill
drill press *n* : an upright drilling machine in which the
drill is pressed to the work usu. by a hand lever
drily *var of* DRYLY
¹drink \'driŋk\ *vb* **drank** \'draŋk\; **drunk** \'drəŋk\ *or*
drank; drink•ing 1 : to swallow liquid : IMBIBE **2** : AB-
SORB **3** : to take in through the senses ⟨∼ in the beautiful scenery⟩ **4** : to give or join in a toast **5** : to drink
alcoholic beverages esp. to excess — **drink•able** *adj*
— **drink•er** *n*
²drink *n* **1** : BEVERAGE; *also* : an alcoholic beverage **2**
: a draft or portion of liquid **3** : excessive consumption of alcoholic beverages
¹drip \'drip\ *vb* **dripped; drip•ping 1** : to fall or let fall
in drops **2** : to let fall drops of moisture or liquid ⟨a
dripping faucet⟩ **3** : to overflow with or as if with
moisture
²drip *n* **1** : a falling in drops **2** : liquid that falls, over-
flows, or is extruded in drops **3** : the sound made by
or as if by falling drops
¹drive \'drīv\ *vb* **drove** \'drōv\; **driv•en** \'dri-vən\; **driv-**
ing 1 : to urge, push, or force onward **2** : to carry
through strongly ⟨∼ a bargain⟩ **3** : to set or keep in
motion or operation **4** : to direct the movement or
course of **5** : to convey in a vehicle **6** : to bring into
a specified condition ⟨the noise ∼s me crazy⟩ **7**
: FORCE, COMPEL ⟨*driven* by hunger to steal⟩ **8** : to
project, inject, or impress forcefully ⟨*drove* the lesson
home⟩ **9** : to produce by opening a way ⟨∼ a well⟩ **10**
: to progress with strong momentum ⟨a *driving* rain⟩
11 : to propel an object of play (as a golf ball) by a
hard blow — **driv•er** *n*
²drive *n* **1** : a trip in a carriage or automobile **2** : a driving or collecting of animals ⟨a cattle ∼⟩ **3** : the guiding
of logs downstream to a mill **4** : the act of driving a
ball; *also* : the flight of a ball **5** : DRIVEWAY **6** : a public
road for driving (as in a park) **7** : the state of being
hurried and under pressure **8** : an intensive campaign
⟨membership ∼⟩ **9** : the apparatus by which motion
is imparted to a machine **10** : an offensive or aggressive move **11** : NEED, LONGING **12**
: dynamic quality **13** : a device for reading and writing
on magnetic media (as magnetic tape or disks)
drive–in \'drī-₁vin\ *adj* : accommodating patrons
while they remain in their automobiles — **drive–in** *n*
¹driv•el \'dri-vəl\ *vb* **-eled** *or* **-elled; -el•ing** *or* **-el•ling 1**
: DROOL, SLAVER **2** : to talk or utter stupidly, careless-
ly, or in an infantile way — **driv•el•er** *n*
²drivel *n* : NONSENSE
drive•shaft \'drīv-₁shaft\ *n* : a shaft that transmits mechanical power
drive•way \-₁wā\ *n* : a short private road leading from
the street to a house, garage, or parking lot

¹driz·zle \'dri-zəl\ *n* : a fine misty rain
²drizzle *vb* **driz·zled; driz·zling** : to rain in very small drops
drogue \'drōg\ *n* : a small parachute for slowing down or stabilizing something (as a space capsule)
droll \'drōl\ *adj* [F *drôle,* fr. *drôle* scamp, fr. MF *drolle,* fr. MD, imp] : having a humorous, whimsical, or odd quality ⟨a ~ expression⟩ — **droll·ery** \'drō-lə-rē\ *n* — **drol·ly** *adv*
drom·e·dary \'drä-mə-ˌder-ē\ *n, pl* **-dar·ies** [ME *dromedarie,* fr. MF *dromedaire,* fr. LL *dromedarius,* fr. L *dromad-, dromas,* fr. Gk, running] : CAMEL; *esp* : a domesticated one-humped camel of western Asia and northern Africa
¹drone \'drōn\ *n* 1 : a male honeybee 2 : one that lives on the labors of others : PARASITE 3 : an unmanned aircraft or ship guided by remote control
²drone *vb* **droned; dron·ing** : to sound with a low dull monotonous murmuring sound : speak monotonously
³drone *n* : a deep monotonous sound
drool \'drül\ *vb* 1 : to let liquid flow from the mouth 2 : to talk foolishly
droop \'drüp\ *vb* 1 : to hang or incline downward 2 : to sink gradually 3 : LANGUISH — **droop** *n* — **droopy** *adj*
¹drop \'dräp\ *n* 1 : the quantity of fluid that falls in one spherical mass 2 *pl* : a dose of medicine measured by drops 3 : a small quantity of drink 4 : the smallest practical unit of liquid measure 5 : something (as a pendant or a small round candy) that resembles a liquid drop 6 : FALL 7 : a decline in quantity or quality 8 : a descent by parachute 9 : the distance through which something drops 10 : a slot into which something is to be dropped 11 : something that drops or has dropped
²drop *vb* **dropped; drop·ping** 1 : to fall or let fall in drops 2 : to let fall : LOWER ⟨~ a glove⟩ ⟨*dropped* his voice⟩ 3 : SEND ⟨~ me a note⟩ 4 : to let go : DISMISS ⟨~ the subject⟩ 5 : to knock down : cause to fall 6 : to go lower : become less ⟨prices *dropped*⟩ 7 : to come or go unexpectedly or informally ⟨~ in to call⟩ 8 : to pass from one state into a less active one ⟨~ off to sleep⟩ 9 : to move downward or with a current 10 : QUIT ⟨*dropped* out of the race⟩ — **drop back** : to move toward the rear — **drop behind** : to fail to keep up
drop·kick \-ˈkik\ *n* : a kick made by dropping a ball to the ground and kicking it at the moment it starts to rebound — **drop–kick** *vb*
drop·let \'drä-plət\ *n* : a tiny drop
drop–off \'dräp-ˌòf\ *n* 1 : a steep or perpendicular descent 2 : a marked decline ⟨a ~ in attendance⟩
drop off *vb* : to fall asleep
drop out *vb* : to withdraw from participation or membership; *esp* : to leave school before graduation — **drop·out** \'dräp-ˌaùt\ *n*
drop·per \'drä-pər\ *n* 1 : one that drops 2 : a short glass tube with a rubber bulb used to measure out liquids by drops
drop·pings *n pl* : MANURE, DUNG
drop·sy \'dräp-sē\ *n* [ME *dropesie,* short for *ydropesie,* fr. OF, fr. L *hydropisis,* fr. Gk *hydrōps,* fr. *hydōr* water] : EDEMA — **drop·si·cal** \-si-kəl\ *adj*
dross \'dräs\ *n* 1 : the scum that forms on the surface of a molten metal 2 : waste matter : REFUSE
drought \'draùt\ *also* **drouth** \'draùth\ *n* : a long spell of dry weather
¹drove \'drōv\ *n* 1 : a group of animals driven or moving in a body 2 : a large number : CROWD — usu. used in pl. ⟨tourists arriving in ~s⟩
²drove *past of* DRIVE
drov·er \'drō-vər\ *n* : one that drives domestic animals usu. to market
drown \'draùn\ *vb* **drowned** \'draùnd\; **drown·ing** 1 : to suffocate by submersion esp. in water 2 : to become drowned 3 : to cover with water 4 : to cause to

be muted (as a sound) by a loud noise 5 : OVERPOWER, OVERWHELM
drowse \'draùz\ *vb* **drowsed; drows·ing** : DOZE — **drowse** *n*
drowsy \'draù-zē\ *adj* **drows·i·er; -est** 1 : ready to fall asleep 2 : making one sleepy — **drows·i·ly** \-zə-lē\ *adv* — **drows·i·ness** \-zē-nəs\ *n*
drub \'drəb\ *vb* **drubbed; drub·bing** 1 : to beat severely 2 : to defeat decisively
drudge \'drəj\ *vb* **drudged; drudg·ing** : to do hard, menial, or monotonous work — **drudge** *n* — **drudg·ery** \'drə-jə-rē\ *n*
¹drug \'drəg\ *n* 1 : a substance used as or in medicine 2 : a substance (as heroin or marijuana) that can cause addiction, a marked change in mental status, or psychological dependency
²drug *vb* **drugged; drug·ging** : to affect with or as if with drugs; *esp* : to stupefy with a narcotic
drug·gist \'drə-gist\ *n* : a dealer in drugs and medicines; *also* : PHARMACIST
drug·store \'drəg-ˌstòr\ *n* : a retail shop where medicines and miscellaneous articles are sold
dru·id \'drü-əd\ *n, often cap* : one of an ancient Celtic priesthood appearing in Irish, Welsh, and Christian legends as magicians and wizards
¹drum \'drəm\ *n* 1 : a percussion instrument usu. consisting of a hollow cylinder with a skin or plastic head stretched over one or both ends that is beaten with the hands or with a stick 2 : the sound of a drum; *also* : a similar sound 3 : a drum-shaped object
²drum *vb* **drummed; drum·ming** 1 : to beat a drum 2 : to sound rhythmically : THROB, BEAT 3 : to summon or enlist by or as if by beating a drum ⟨*drummed* into service⟩ 4 : EXPEL — usu. used with *out* 5 : to drive or force by steady effort ⟨~ the facts into memory⟩ 6 : to strike or tap repeatedly so as to produce rhythmic sounds
drum·beat \'drəm-ˌbēt\ *n* : a stroke on a drum or its sound
drum major *n* : the leader of a marching band
drum ma·jor·ette \-ˌmā-jə-ˈret\ *n* : a girl or woman who leads a marching band; *also* : a baton twirler who accompanies a marching band
drum·mer \'drə-mər\ *n* 1 : one that plays a drum 2 : a traveling salesman

drum·stick \'drəm-ˌstik\ *n* 1 : a stick for beating a drum 2 : the lower segment of a fowl's leg

drum up *vb* 1 : to bring about by persistent effort ⟨*drum up* business⟩ 2 : INVENT, ORIGINATE
¹drunk *past part of* DRINK
²drunk \'drəŋk\ *adj* 1 : having the faculties impaired by alcohol ⟨~ drivers⟩ 2 : dominated by an intense feeling ⟨~ with power⟩ 3 : of, relating to, or caused by intoxication
³drunk *n* 1 : a period of excessive drinking 2 : a drunken person
drunk·ard \'drəŋ-kərd\ *n* : one who is habitually drunk
drunk·en \'drəŋ-kən\ *adj* 1 : DRUNK 2 : given to habitual excessive use of alcohol 3 : of, relating to, or resulting from intoxication 4 : unsteady or lurching as if from intoxication — **drunk·en·ly** *adv* — **drunk·en·ness** *n*
drupe \'drüp\ *n* : a partly fleshy one-seeded fruit (as a plum or cherry) that remains closed at maturity
¹dry \'drī\ *adj* **dri·er** \'drī-ər\; **dri·est** \-əst\ 1 : free or freed from water or liquid ⟨~ fruits⟩; *also* : not being in or under water 2 : characterized by lack of water or moisture ⟨~ climate⟩ 3 : lacking freshness : STALE 4 : devoid of natural moisture; *also* : THIRSTY 5 : no longer liquid or sticky ⟨the ink is ~⟩ 6 : not giving

milk ⟨a ∼ cow⟩ **7** : marked by the absence of alcoholic beverages **8** : prohibiting the making or distributing of alcoholic beverages **9** : not sweet ⟨∼ wine⟩ **10** : solid as opposed to liquid ⟨∼ groceries⟩ **11** : containing or employing no liquid **12** : SEVERE; *also* : UNINTERESTING, WEARISOME **13** : not productive **14** : marked by a matter-of-fact, ironic, or terse manner of expression ⟨∼ humor⟩ — **dry·ly** *adv* — **dry·ness** *n*

²**dry** *vb* **dried; dry·ing** : to make or become dry

³**dry** *n, pl* **drys** : PROHIBITIONIST

dry·ad \'drī-əd, -ˌad\ *n* : WOOD NYMPH

dry cell *n* : a battery whose contents are not spillable

dry–clean \'drī-ˌklēn\ *vb* : to clean (fabrics) chiefly with solvents other than water — **dry cleaning** *n*

dry dock \'drī-ˌdäk\ *n* : a dock that can be kept dry during ship construction or repair

dry·er *var of* DRIER

dry farm·ing *n* : farming without irrigation in areas of limited rainfall — **dry–farm** *vb* — **dry farm·er** *n*

dry goods \'drī-ˌgu̇dz\ *n pl* : cloth goods (as fabrics, ribbon, and ready-to-wear clothing)

dry ice *n* : solid carbon dioxide

dry measure *n* : a series of units of capacity for dry commodities — see METRIC SYSTEM table, WEIGHT table

dry run *n* : REHEARSAL, TRIAL

dry·wall \'drī-ˌwȯl\ *n* : PLASTERBOARD

DSC *abbr* **1** Distinguished Service Cross **2** doctor of surgical chiropody

DSM *abbr* Distinguished Service Medal

DST *abbr* daylight saving time

DTP *abbr* diphtheria, tetanus, pertussis (vaccines)

d.t.'s \ˌdē-'tēz\ *n pl, often cap D&T* : DELIRIUM TREMENS

du·al \'dü-əl, 'dyü-\ *adj* **1** : TWOFOLD, DOUBLE **2** : having a double character or nature — **du·al·ism** \-ə-ˌli-zəm\ *n* — **du·al·i·ty** \dü-'a-lə-tē, dyü-\ *n*

¹**dub** \'dəb\ *vb* **dubbed; dub·bing 1** : to confer knighthood upon **2** : NAME, NICKNAME

²**dub** *n* : a clumsy person : DUFFER

³**dub** \'dəb\ *vb* **dubbed; dub·bing** : to add (sound effects) to a motion picture or to a radio or television production

du·bi·ety \dü-'bī-ə-tē, dyü-\ *n, pl* **-eties 1** : UNCERTAINTY **2** : a matter of doubt

du·bi·ous \'dü-bē-əs, 'dyü-\ *adj* **1** : UNCERTAIN **2** : QUESTIONABLE **3** : feeling doubt : UNDECIDED — **du·bi·ous·ly** *adv* — **du·bi·ous·ness** *n*

du·cal \'dü-kəl, 'dyü-\ *adj* : of or relating to a duke or dukedom

duc·at \'də-kət\ *n* : a gold coin formerly used in various European countries

duch·ess \'də-chəs\ *n* **1** : the wife or widow of a duke **2** : a woman holding the rank of duke in her own right

duchy \'də-chē\ *n, pl* **duch·ies** : the territory of a duke or duchess : DUKEDOM

¹**duck** \'dək\ *n, pl* **ducks** : any of various swimming birds related to but smaller than geese and swans

²**duck** *vb* **1** : to thrust or plunge under water **2** : to lower the head or body suddenly : BOW; *also* : DODGE **3** : to

evade a duty, question, or responsibility ⟨∼ the issue⟩

³**duck** *n* **1** : a durable closely woven usu. cotton fabric **2** *pl* : light clothes made of duck

duck·bill \'dək-ˌbil\ *n* : PLATYPUS

duck·ling \-liŋ\ *n* : a young duck

duck·pin \-ˌpin\ *n* **1** : a small bowling pin shorter and wider in the middle than a tenpin **2** *pl but sing in constr* : a bowling game using duckpins

duct \'dəkt\ *n* **1** : a tube or canal for conveying a bodily fluid **2** : a pipe or tube through which a fluid (as air) flows — **duct·less** *adj*

duc·tile \'dək-t⁑l\ *adj* **1** : capable of being drawn out (as into wire) or hammered thin **2** : easily led : DOCILE — **duc·til·i·ty** \ˌdək-'ti-lə-tē\ *n*

ductless gland *n* : an endocrine gland

dud \'dəd\ *n* **1** *pl* : CLOTHING **2** : one that fails completely; *also* : a bomb or missile that fails to explode

dude \'düd, 'dyüd\ *n* **1** : DANDY 1 **2** : a city dweller; *esp* : an Easterner in the West **3** : FELLOW, GUY

dude ranch *n* : a vacation resort offering activities (as horseback riding) typical of western ranches

dud·geon \'də-jən\ *n* : a fit or state of indignation ⟨in high ∼⟩

¹**due** \'dü, 'dyü\ *adj* [ME, fr. MF *deu*, pp. of *devoir* to owe, fr. L *debēre*] **1** : owed or owing as a debt **2** : owed or owing as a right **3** : APPROPRIATE, FITTING **4** : SUFFICIENT, ADEQUATE **5** : REGULAR, LAWFUL ⟨∼ process of law⟩ **6** : ATTRIBUTABLE, ASCRIBABLE ⟨∼ to negligence⟩ **7** : PAYABLE ⟨a bill ∼ today⟩ **8** : SCHEDULED ⟨∼ to arrive soon⟩

²**due** *n* **1** : something that rightfully belongs to one ⟨give everyone their ∼⟩ **2** : DEBT **3** *pl* : FEES, CHARGES

³**due** *adv* : DIRECTLY, EXACTLY ⟨∼ north⟩

du·el \'dü-əl, 'dyü-\ *n* : a combat between two persons; *esp* : one fought with weapons in the presence of witnesses — **duel** *vb* — **du·el·ist** \-ə-list\ *n*

du·en·de \dü-'en-dā\ *n* [Sp dial., charm, fr. Sp, ghost, goblin, fr. *duen de casa*, prob. fr. *dueño de casa* owner of a house] : the power to attract through personal magnetism and charm

du·en·na \dü-'e-nə, dyü-\ *n* **1** : an elderly woman in charge of the younger ladies in a Spanish or Portuguese family **2** : CHAPERON

du·et \dü-'et, dyü-\ *n* : a musical composition for two performers

due to *prep* : BECAUSE OF

duf·fel bag \'də-fəl-\ *n* : a large cylindrical bag for personal belongings

duf·fer \'də-fər\ *n* : an incompetent or clumsy person

dug *past and past part of* DIG

dug·out \'dəg-ˌau̇t\ *n* **1** : a boat made by hollowing out a log **2** : a shelter dug in the ground **3** : a low shelter facing a baseball diamond that contains the players' bench

DUI *abbr* driving under the influence

duke \'dük, 'dyük\ *n* **1** : a sovereign ruler of a continental European duchy **2** : a nobleman of the highest rank; *esp* : a member of the highest grade of the Brit-

ish peerage **3** *slang* : FIST 1 ⟨put up your ∼s⟩ —
duke·dom *n*
dul·cet \'dəl-sət\ *adj* **1** : pleasing to the ear **2** : AGREE-
ABLE, SOOTHING
dul·ci·mer \'dəl-sə-mər\ *n* **1** : a stringed instrument of
trapezoidal shape played with light hammers held in
the hands **2** *or* **dul·ci·more** \-ˌmȯr\ : an American folk
instrument with three or four strings that is held on
the lap and played by plucking or strumming

¹dull \'dəl\ *adj* **1** : mentally slow : STUPID
2 : slow in perception or sensibility **3**
: LISTLESS **4** : slow in action : SLUGGISH ⟨a
∼ market⟩ **5** : lacking intensity; *also* : not
resonant or ringing **6** : BLUNT **7** : lacking brilliance or
luster **8** : low in saturation and lightness ⟨∼ color⟩ **9**
: CLOUDY, OVERCAST **10** : TEDIOUS, UNINTERESTING
— **dull·ness** *or* **dul·ness** *n* — **dul·ly** *adv*

²dull *vb* : to make or become dull
dull·ard \'də-lərd\ *n* : a stupid person
du·ly \'dü-lē, 'dyü-\ *adv* : in a due manner or time
dumb \'dəm\ *adj* **1** : lacking the power of speech **2** : SI-
LENT **3** : STUPID — **dumb·ly** *adv*
dumb·bell \'dəm-ˌbel\ *n* **1** : a bar with weights at the
end used for exercise **2** : one who is stupid
dumb·found *or* **dum·found** \ˌdəm-'faȯnd\ *vb* : ASTON-
ISH, AMAZE
dumb·wait·er \'dəm-ˌwā-tər\ *n* : a small elevator for
conveying food and dishes from one floor to another
dum·my \'də-mē\ *n*, *pl* **dummies 1** : a person who cannot speak; *also* : a stupid person **2** : the exposed hand
in bridge played by the declarer in addition to that
player's own hand; *also* : a bridge player whose hand
is a dummy **3** : an imitative substitute for something;
also : MANNEQUIN **4** : one seeming to act alone but
really acting for another **5** : a mock-up of matter to be
reproduced esp. by printing
¹dump \'dəmp\ *vb* : to let fall in a pile; *also* : to get rid
of carelessly
²dump *n* **1** : a place for dumping something (as refuse)
2 : a reserve supply; *also* : a place where such supplies are kept ⟨an ammunition ∼⟩ **3** : a messy or objectionable place
dump·ing \'dəm-piŋ\ *n* : the selling of goods in quantity at below market price
dump·ling \'dəm-pliŋ\ *n* **1** : a small mass of boiled or
steamed dough **2** : a dessert of fruit baked in biscuit
dough
dumps \'dəmps\ *n pl* : a gloomy state of mind : low
spirits ⟨in the ∼⟩
dump truck *n* : a truck for transporting and dumping
bulk material
dumpy \'dəm-pē\ *adj* **dump·i·er; -est 1** : short and
thick in build **2** : SHABBY
¹dun \'dən\ *n* : a brownish dark gray
²dun *vb* **dunned; dun·ning 1** : to make persistent demands for payment **2** : PLAGUE, PESTER — **dun** *n*
dunce \'dəns\ *n* [John *Duns* Scotus, whose once ac-

cepted writings were ridiculed in the 16th cent.] : a
slow stupid person
dun·der·head \'dən-dər-ˌhed\ *n* : DUNCE, BLOCKHEAD
dune \'dün, 'dyün\ *n* : a hill or ridge of sand piled up
by the wind
dune buggy *n* : a motor vehicle with oversize tires for
use on sand
¹dung \'dəŋ\ *n* : MANURE
²dung *vb* : to dress (land) with dung
dun·ga·ree \ˌdəŋ-gə-'rē\ *n* **1** : a heavy coarse cotton
twill; *esp* : blue denim **2** *pl* : clothes made of blue denim
dun·geon \'dən-jən\ *n* [ME *donjon*, fr. MF, fr.
(assumed) VL *domnion-, domnio* keep, mastery, fr.
L *dominus* lord] : a dark prison commonly underground
dung·hill \'dəŋ-ˌhil\ *n* : a manure pile
dunk \'dəŋk\ *vb* **1** : to dip or submerge temporarily in
liquid **2** : to submerge oneself in water **3** : to shoot a
basketball into the basket from above the rim
duo \'dü-(ˌ)ō, 'dyü-\ *n*, *pl* **du·os 1** : DUET **2** : PAIR **3**
duo·dec·i·mal \ˌdü-ə-'de-sə-məl, ˌdyü-\ *adj* : of, relating to, or being a system of numbers with a base of
12
du·o·de·num \ˌdü-ə-'dē-nəm, ˌdyü-, dù-'äd-ᵊn-əm,
dyü-\ *n*, *pl* **-de·na** \-'dē-nə, -ᵊn-ə\ *or* **-denums** : the
first part of the small intestine extending from the
stomach to the jejunum — **du·o·de·nal** \-'dēn-ᵊl, -ᵊn-
əl\ *adj*
dup *abbr* **1** duplex **2** duplicate
¹dupe \'düp, 'dyüp\ *n* : one who is easily deceived or
cheated : FOOL
²dupe *vb* **duped; dup·ing** : to make a dupe of : DECEIVE,
FOOL
du·ple \'dü-pəl, 'dyü-\ *adj* : having two beats or a multiple of two beats to the measure ⟨∼ time⟩
¹du·plex \'dü-ˌpleks, 'dyü-\ *adj* : DOUBLE
²duplex *n* : something duplex; *esp* : a 2-family house
¹du·pli·cate \'dü-pli-kət, 'dyü-\ *adj* **1** : consisting of or
existing in two corresponding or identical parts or examples **2** : being the same as another
²du·pli·cate \'dü-pli-ˌkāt, 'dyü-\ *vb* **-cat·ed; -cat·ing 1**
: to make double or twofold **2** : to make a copy of —
du·pli·ca·tion \ˌdü-pli-'kā-shən, ˌdyü-\ *n*
³du·pli·cate \-kət\ *n* : a thing that exactly resembles another in appearance, pattern, or content : COPY
du·pli·ca·tor \'dü-pli-ˌkā-tər, 'dyü-\ *n* : COPIER
du·plic·i·ty \dù-'pli-sə-tē, dyü-\ *n*, *pl* **-ties** : the disguising of true intentions by deceptive words or action
du·ra·ble \'dùr-ə-bəl, 'dyùr-\ *adj* : able to exist for a
long time without significant deterioration ⟨∼ goods⟩
— **du·ra·bil·i·ty** \ˌdùr-ə-'bi-lə-tē, ˌdyùr-\ *n*
du·rance \'dùr-əns, 'dyùr-\ *n* : restraint or as if by
physical force ⟨held in ∼ vile⟩
du·ra·tion \dù-'rā-shən, dyü-\ *n* : the time during
which something exists or lasts
du·ress \dù-'res, dyü-\ *n* : compulsion by threat ⟨con-
fession made under ∼⟩
dur·ing \'dùr-iŋ, 'dyùr-\ *prep* **1** : THROUGHOUT ⟨swims

every day ∼ the summer⟩ **2 :** at some point in ⟨broke in ∼ the night⟩

dusk \'dəsk\ *n* **1 :** the darker part of twilight esp. at night **2 :** partial darkness

dusky \'dəs-kē\ *adj* **dusk·i·er; -est 1 :** somewhat dark in color **2 :** SHADOWY — **dusk·i·ness** *n*

¹dust \'dəst\ *n* **1 :** fine particles of matter **2 :** the particles into which something disintegrates **3 :** something worthless **4 :** the surface of the ground — **dustless** *adj* — **dusty** *adj*

²dust *vb* **1 :** to make free of or remove dust **2 :** to sprinkle with fine particles **3 :** to sprinkle in the form of dust

dust bowl *n* **:** a region suffering from long droughts and dust storms

dust devil *n* **:** a small whirlwind containing sand or dust

dust·er \'dəs-tər\ *n* **1 :** one that removes dust **2 :** a dress-length housecoat **3 :** one that scatters fine particles; *esp* **:** a device for applying insecticides to crops

dust·pan \'dəst-ˌpan\ *n* **:** a flat-ended pan for sweepings

dust storm *n* **:** a violent wind carrying dust across a dry region

dutch \'dəch\ *adv, often cap* **:** with each person paying his or her own way ⟨go ∼⟩

Dutch \'dəch\ *n* **1 Dutch** *pl* **:** the people of the Netherlands **2 :** the language of the Netherlands — **Dutch** *adj* — **Dutch·man** \-mən\ *n*

Dutch elm disease *n* **:** a fungous disease of elms characterized by yellowing of the foliage, defoliation, and death

dutch treat *n, often cap D* **:** an entertainment (as a meal) for which each person pays his or her own way — **dutch treat** *adv, often cap D*

du·te·ous \'dü-tē-əs, 'dyü-\ *adj* **:** DUTIFUL, OBEDIENT

du·ti·able \'dü-tē-ə-bəl, 'dyü-\ *adj* **:** subject to a duty ⟨∼ imports⟩

du·ti·ful \'dü-ti-fəl, 'dyü-\ *adj* **1 :** motivated by a sense of duty ⟨a ∼ son⟩ **2 :** coming from or showing a sense of duty ⟨∼ affection⟩ — **du·ti·ful·ly** *adv* — **du·ti·ful·ness** *n*

du·ty \'dü-tē, 'dyü-\ *n, pl* **duties 1 :** conduct or action required by one's occupation or position **2 :** assigned service or business; *esp* **:** active military service **3 :** a moral or legal obligation **4 :** TAX **5 :** the service required (as of a machine) **:** USE ⟨a heavy-*duty* tire⟩

DV *abbr* **1** [L *Deo volente*] God willing **2** Douay Version

DVM *abbr* doctor of veterinary medicine

¹dwarf \'dwȯrf\ *n, pl* **dwarfs** \'dwȯrfs\ *or* **dwarves** \'dwȯrvz\ **:** one that is much below normal size — **dwarf·ish** *adj*

²dwarf *vb* **1 :** to restrict the growth or development of

: STUNT **2 :** to cause to appear smaller ⟨*dwarfed* by comparison⟩

dwell \'dwel\ *vb* **dwelt** \'dwelt\ *or* **dwelled** \'dweld, 'dwelt\; **dwell·ing** [ME, fr. OE *dwellan* to go astray, hinder] **1 :** ABIDE, REMAIN **2 :** RESIDE, EXIST **3 :** to keep the attention directed **4 :** to write or speak insistently — used with *on* or *upon* — **dwell·er** *n*

dwell·ing \'dwe-liŋ\ *n* **:** RESIDENCE

DWI *abbr* driving while intoxicated

dwin·dle \'dwind-ᵊl\ *vb* **dwin·dled; dwin·dling :** to make or become steadily less **:** DIMINISH

dwt *abbr* pennyweight

Dy *symbol* dysprosium

dyb·buk \'di-bək\ *n, pl* **dyb·bu·kim** \ˌdi-bù-'kēm\ *also* **dybbuks :** a wandering soul believed in Jewish folklore to enter and possess a person

¹dye \'dī\ *n* **1 :** color produced by dyeing **2 :** material used for coloring or staining

²dye *vb* **dyed; dye·ing 1 :** to impart a new color to esp. by impregnating with a dye **2 :** to take up or impart color in dyeing

dye·stuff \'dī-ˌstəf\ *n* **:** DYE 2

dying *pres part of* DIE

dyke *chiefly Brit var of* DIKE

dy·nam·ic \dī-'na-mik\ *also* **dy·nam·i·cal** \-mi-kəl\ *adj* **:** of or relating to physical force producing motion **:** ENERGETIC, FORCEFUL

¹dy·na·mite \'dī-nə-ˌmīt\ *n* **:** an explosive made of nitroglycerin absorbed in a porous material; *also* **:** an explosive made without nitroglycerin

²dynamite *vb* **-mit·ed; -mit·ing :** to blow up with dynamite

dy·na·mo \'dī-nə-ˌmō\ *n, pl* **-mos :** an electrical generator

dy·na·mom·e·ter \ˌdī-nə-'mä-mə-tər\ *n* **:** an instrument for measuring mechanical power (as of an engine)

dy·nas·ty \'dī-nəs-tē, -ˌnas-\ *n, pl* **-ties 1 :** a succession of rulers of the same family **2 :** a powerful group or family that maintains its position for a long time — **dy·nas·tic** \dī-'nas-tik\ *adj*

dys·en·tery \'dis-ᵊn-ˌter-ē\ *n, pl* **-ter·ies :** a disease marked by diarrhea with blood and mucus in the feces; *also* **:** DIARRHEA

dys·lex·ia \dis-'lek-sē-ə\ *n* **:** a disturbance of the ability to read or use language — **dys·lex·ic** \-sik\ *adj or n*

dys·pep·sia \dis-'pep-shə, -sē-ə\ *n* **:** INDIGESTION — **dys·pep·tic** \-'pep-tik\ *adj or n*

dys·pro·si·um \dis-'prō-zē-əm\ *n* **:** a metallic chemical element that forms highly magnetic compounds — see ELEMENT table

dys·tro·phy \'dis-trə-fē\ *n, pl* **-phies :** a disorder involving atrophy of muscular tissue; *esp* **:** MUSCULAR DYSTROPHY

dz *abbr* dozen

E

¹e \'ē\ *n, pl* **e's** *or* **es** \'ēz\ *often cap* **1 :** the 5th letter of the English alphabet **2 :** the base of the system of natural logarithms having the approximate value 2.71828 **3 :** a grade rating a student's work as poor or failing

²e *abbr, often cap* **1** east; eastern **2** error **3** excellent

ea *abbr* each

¹each \'ēch\ *adj* **:** being one of the class named ⟨∼ man⟩

²each *pron* **:** every individual one

³each *adv* **:** APIECE ⟨cost five cents ∼⟩

each other *pron* **:** each of two or more in reciprocal action or relation ⟨looked at *each other*⟩

ea·ger \'ē-gər\ *adj* **:** marked by urgent or enthusiastic desire or interest ⟨∼ to learn⟩ **syn** avid, anxious, ardent, keen — **ea·ger·ly** *adv* — **ea·ger·ness** *n*

ea·gle \'ē-gəl\ *n* **1 :** a large bird of prey related to the hawks **2 :** a score of two under par on a hole in golf

ea·glet \'ē-glət\ *n* **:** a young eagle

-ean — see -AN

E and OE *abbr* errors and omissions excepted

¹ear \'ir\ *n* **1 :** the organ of hearing; *also* **:** the outer part of this in a vertebrate **2 :** something resembling a mammal's ear in shape, position, or function **3 :** an ability to understand and appreciate something heard ⟨a good ∼ for music⟩ **4 :** sympathetic attention

²ear *n* **:** the fruiting spike of a cereal (as wheat)

ear·ache \-ˌāk\ *n* **:** an ache or pain in the ear

ear·drum \-ˌdrəm\ *n* **:** a thin membrane that receives and transmits sound waves in the ear

eared \'ird\ *adj* **:** having ears esp. of a specified kind or number ⟨a long-*eared* dog⟩

ear·ful \'ir-ˌfùl\ *n* **:** a verbal outpouring (as of news, gossip, anger, or complaint)

earl \'ərl\ *n* [ME *erl*, fr. OE *eorl* warrior, nobleman] **:** a member of the British peerage ranking below a mar-

quess and above a viscount — **earl·dom** \-dəm\ *n*
ear·lobe \'ir-ˌlōb\ *n* : the pendent part of the ear
[1]**ear·ly** \'ər-lē\ *adv* **ear·li·er; -est** : at an early time (as
in a period or series)
[2]**early** *adj* **ear·li·er; -est 1** : of, relating to, or occurring
near the beginning **2** : ANCIENT, PRIMITIVE **3** : occurring before the usual time ⟨an ∼ breakfast⟩; *also* : occurring in the near future
[1]**ear·mark** \'ir-ˌmärk\ *n* : an identification mark (as on
the ear of an animal); *also* : a distinguishing mark ⟨∼s
of poverty⟩
[2]**earmark** *vb* **1** : to mark with an earmark **2** : to designate for a specific purpose
ear·muff \-ˌməf\ *n* : one of a pair of ear coverings worn
to protect against cold
earn \'ərn\ *vb* **1** : to receive as a return for service **2**
: DESERVE, MERIT **syn** gain, secure, get, obtain, acquire, win — **earn·er** *n*
[1]**ear·nest** \'ər-nəst\ *n* : an intensely serious state of
mind ⟨spoke in ∼⟩
[2]**earnest** *adj* **1** : seriously intent and sober ⟨an ∼ face⟩
⟨an ∼ attempt⟩ **2** : GRAVE, IMPORTANT **syn** solemn,
sedate, staid — **ear·nest·ly** *adv* — **ear·nest·ness** *n*
[3]**earnest** *n* **1** : something of value given by a buyer to
a seller to bind a bargain **2** : PLEDGE
earn·ings \'ər-niŋz\ *n pl* **1** : something (as wages)
earned **2** : the balance of revenue after deduction of
costs and expenses
ear·phone \'ir-ˌfōn\ *n* : a device that reproduces sound
and is worn over or in the ear
ear·plug \-ˌpləg\ *n* : a protective device for insertion
into the opening of the ear
ear·ring \-ˌriŋ\ *n* : an ornament for the earlobe
ear·shot \-ˌshät\ *n* : range of hearing
ear·split·ting \-ˌspli-tiŋ\ *adj* : intolerably loud or shrill
earth \'ərth\ *n* **1** : SOIL, DIRT **2** : LAND, GROUND **3** *often
cap* : the planet on which we live that is 3d in order
from the sun — see PLANET table
earth·en \'ər-thən\ *adj* : made of earth or baked clay
earth·en·ware \-ˌwar\ *n* : slightly porous opaque pottery fired at low heat
earth·ling \'ərth-liŋ\ *n* : an inhabitant of the earth
earth·ly \'ərth-lē\ *adj* : having to do with the earth esp.
as distinguished from heaven — **earth·li·ness** *n*

earth·quake \-ˌkwāk\ *n* : a shaking or
trembling of a portion of the earth

earth science *n* : any of the sciences (as geology or
meteorology) that deal with the earth or one of its
parts
earth·shak·ing \'ərth-ˌshā-kiŋ\ *adj* : of great importance : MOMENTOUS
earth·ward \-wərd\ *also* **earth·wards** \-wərdz\ *adv*
: toward the earth
earth·work \'ərth-ˌwərk\ *n* : an embankment or fortification of earth

earth·worm \-ˌwərm\ *n* : a long segmented worm
found in damp soil
earthy \'ər-thē\ *adj* **earth·i·er; -est 1** : of, relating to,
or consisting of earth; *also* : suggesting earth ⟨∼ fla-
vors⟩ **2** : PRACTICAL **3** : COARSE, GROSS — **earth·i·
ness** *n*
ear·wax \'ir-ˌwaks\ *n* : the yellow waxy secretion from
the ear
ear·wig \-ˌwig\ *n* : any of numerous insects with slender many-jointed antennae and a pair of appendages
resembling forceps at the end of the body
[1]**ease** \'ēz\ *n* **1** : comfort of body or mind **2** : naturalness
of manner **3** : freedom from difficulty or effort **syn** relaxation, rest, repose, leisure
[2]**ease** *vb* **eased; eas·ing 1** : to relieve from distress **2** : to
lessen the pressure or tension of **3** : to make or be-
come less difficult ⟨∼ credit⟩
ea·sel \'ē-zəl\ *n* [Dutch *ezel*, lit., ass] : a frame for supporting something (as an artist's canvas)
[1]**east** \'ēst\ *adv* : to or toward the east
[2]**east** *adj* **1** : situated toward or at the east **2** : coming
from the east
[3]**east** *n* **1** : the general direction of sunrise **2** : the compass point directly opposite to west **3** *cap* : regions or
countries east of a specified or implied point — **east·
er·ly** \'ē-stər-lē\ *adv or adj* — **east·ward** *adv or adj*
— **east·wards** *adv*
Eas·ter \'ē-stər\ *n* : a church feast observed on a Sunday in March or April in commemoration of Christ's
resurrection
east·ern \'ē-stərn\ *adj* **1** *often cap* : of, relating to, or
characteristic of a region designated East **2** *cap* : of,
relating to, or being the Christian churches originating in the Church of the Eastern Roman Empire **3**
: lying toward or coming from the east — **East·ern·
er** *n*
easy \'ē-zē\ *adj* **eas·i·er; -est 1** : marked by ease ⟨an ∼
life⟩; *esp* : not causing distress or difficulty ⟨∼ tasks⟩
2 : MILD, LENIENT ⟨be ∼ on him⟩ **3** : GRADUAL ⟨an ∼
slope⟩ **4** : free from pain, trouble, or worry ⟨rest ∼⟩
5 : LEISURELY ⟨an ∼ pace⟩ **6** : NATURAL ⟨an ∼ man-
ner⟩ **7** : COMFORTABLE ⟨an ∼ chair⟩ — **eas·i·ly** \'ē-zə-
lē\ *adv* — **eas·i·ness** \-zē-nəs\ *n*
easy·go·ing \ˌē-zē-ˈgō-iŋ\ *adj* : relaxed and casual in
style or manner
eat \'ēt\ *vb* **ate** \'āt\; **eat·en** \'ēt-ᵊn\; **eat·ing 1** : to take
in as food **2** : to use up : DEVOUR **3** : COR-
RODE — **eat·able** *adj or n* — **eat·er** *n*
eat·ery \'ē-tə-rē\ *n, pl* **-er·ies** : LUNCHEONETTE, RES-
TAURANT
eaves \'ēvz\ *n pl* : the overhanging lower edge of a roof
eaves·drop \'ēvz-ˌdräp\ *vb* : to listen secretly —
eaves·drop·per *n*
[1]**ebb** \'eb\ *n* **1** : the flowing back from shore of water
brought in by the tide **2** : a point or state of decline
[2]**ebb** *vb* **1** : to recede from the flood **2** : DECLINE ⟨his
fortunes ∼ed⟩
EBCDIC \'eb-sə-ˌdik\ *n* [extended binary coded decimal interchange code] : a computer code for representing alphanumeric information

¹eb·o·ny \'e-bə-nē\ *n, pl* **-nies** : a hard heavy wood of Old World tropical trees related to the persimmon
²ebony *adj* **1** : made of or resembling ebony **2** : BLACK, DARK
ebul·lient \i-'bùl-yənt, -'bəl-\ *adj* **1** : BOILING, AGITATED **2** : EXUBERANT — **ebul·lience** \-yəns\ *n*
EC *abbr* European Community

ec·cen·tric \ik-'sen-trik\ *adj* **1** : deviating from a usual or accepted pattern **2** : deviating from a circular path ⟨∼ orbits⟩ **3** : set with axis or support off center ⟨an ∼ cam⟩; *also* : being off center **syn** erratic, queer, singular, curious, odd — **eccentric** *n* — **ec·cen·tri·cal·ly** \-tri-k(ə-)lē\ *adv* — **ec·cen·tric·i·ty** \ek-ˌsen-'tri-sə-tē\ *n*

Eccles *abbr* Ecclesiastes
Ec·cle·si·as·tes \i-ˌklē-zē-'as-tēz\ *n* — see BIBLE table
ec·cle·si·as·tic \i-ˌklē-zē-'as-tik\ *n* : CLERGYMAN
ec·cle·si·as·ti·cal \-ti-kəl\ *or* **ec·cle·si·as·tic** \-tik\ *adj* : of or relating to a church esp. as an institution ⟨∼ art⟩ — **ec·cle·si·as·ti·cal·ly** \-ti-k(ə-)lē\ *adv*
Ec·cle·si·as·ti·cus \i-ˌklē-zē-'as-ti-kəs\ *n* — see BIBLE table
Ecclus *abbr* Ecclesiasticus
ECG *abbr* electrocardiogram
ech·e·lon \'e-shə-ˌlän\ *n* [F *échelon*, lit., rung of a ladder] **1** : a steplike arrangement (as of troops or airplanes) **2** : a level (as of authority or responsibility) within an organization
echi·no·derm \i-'kī-nə-ˌdərm\ *n* : any of a phylum of marine animals (as starfishes and sea urchins) having similar body parts (as the arms of a starfish) arranged around a central axis and often having a calcium-containing outer skeleton
echo \'e-kō\ *n, pl* **echoes** *also* **echos** : repetition of a sound caused by a reflection of the sound waves; *also* : the reflection of a radar signal by an object — **echo** *vb* — **echo·ic** \e-'kō-ik\ *adj*
echo·lo·ca·tion \ˌe-ko-lō-'kā-shən\ *n* : a process for locating distant or invisible objects by means of sound waves reflected back to the sender (as a bat) by the objects
éclair \ā-'klar\ *n* [F, lit., lightning] : an oblong shell of light pastry with whipped cream or custard filling
éclat \ā-'klä\ *n* [F] **1** : a dazzling effect or success **2** : ACCLAIM
eclec·tic \e-'klek-tik\ *adj* : selecting or made up of what seems best of varied sources — **eclectic** *n*
¹eclipse \i-'klips\ *n* **1** : the total or partial obscuring of one heavenly body by another; *also* : a passing into the shadow of a heavenly body **2** : a falling into obscurity or decline
²eclipse *vb* **eclipsed**; **eclips·ing** : to cause an eclipse of; *also* : SURPASS
eclip·tic \i-'klip-tik\ *n* : the great circle of the celestial sphere that is the apparent path of the sun
ec·logue \'ek-ˌlòg, -ˌläg\ *n* : a pastoral poem
ECM *abbr* European Common Market

ecol *abbr* ecological; ecology
ecol·o·gy \i-'kä-lə-jē, e-\ *n, pl* **-gies** [G *Ökologie,* fr. Gk *oikos* house + *logos* word] **1** : a branch of science concerned with the relationships between organisms and their environment **2** : the pattern of relations between one or more organisms and the environment — **eco·log·i·cal** \ˌē-kə-'lä-ji-kəl, ˌe-\ *also* **eco·log·ic** \-jik\ *adj* — **eco·log·i·cal·ly** \-ji-k(ə-)lē\ *adv* — **ecol·o·gist** \i-'kä-lə-jist, e-\ *n*
econ *abbr* economics; economist; economy
eco·nom·ic \ˌe-kə-'nä-mik, ˌē-\ *adj* : of or relating to the production, distribution, and consumption of goods and services
eco·nom·i·cal \-'nä-mi-kəl\ *adj* **1** : THRIFTY **2** : operating with little waste or at a saving **syn** frugal, sparing, provident — **ec·o·nom·i·cal·ly** \-k(ə-)lē\ *adv*
eco·nom·ics \ˌe-kə-'nä-miks, ˌē-\ *n sing or pl* : a social science dealing with the production, distribution, and consumption of goods and services — **econ·o·mist** \i-'kä-nə-mist\ *n*
econ·o·mise *Brit var of* ECONOMIZE
econ·o·mize \i-'kä-nə-ˌmīz\ *vb* **-mized**; **-miz·ing** : to practice economy : be frugal — **econ·o·miz·er** *n*
¹econ·o·my \i-'kä-nə-mē\ *n, pl* **-mies** [MF *yconomie,* fr. ML *oeconomia,* fr. Gk *oikonomia,* fr. *oikonomos* household manager, fr. *oikos* house + *nemein* to manage] **1** : thrifty and efficient use of resources; *also* : an instance of this **2** : manner of arrangement or functioning : ORGANIZATION **3** : an economic system ⟨a money ∼⟩
²economy *adj* : ECONOMICAL ⟨∼ cars⟩
eco·sys·tem \'ē-kō-ˌsis-təm, 'e-\ *n* : the complex of an ecological community and its environment functioning as a unit in nature
ecru \'e-krü, 'ā-\ *n* [F *écru,* lit., unbleached] : BEIGE — **ecru** *adj*
ec·sta·sy \'ek-stə-sē\ *n, pl* **-sies** : extreme and usu. rapturous emotional excitement — **ec·stat·ic** \ek-'sta-tik, ik-\ *adj* — **ec·stat·i·cal·ly** \-ti-k(ə-)lē\ *adv*
Ecua *abbr* Ecuador
Ec·ua·dor·an \ˌe-kwə-'dòr-ən\ *or* **Ec·ua·dor·ean** *or* **Ec·ua·dor·ian** \-ē-ən\ *n* : a native or inhabitant of Ecuador — **Ecuadorean** *or* **Ecuadorian** *adj*
ec·u·men·i·cal \ˌe-kyù-'me-ni-kəl\ *adj* : general in extent or influence; *esp* : promoting or tending toward worldwide Christian unity — **ec·u·men·i·cal·ly** \-k(ə-)lē\ *adv*
ec·ze·ma \ig-'zē-mə, 'eg-zə-mə, 'ek-sə-\ *n* : an itching skin inflammation with oozing and then crusted lesions — **ec·zem·a·tous** \ig-'ze-mə-təs\ *adj*
ed *abbr* **1** edited; edition; editor **2** education
¹-ed *d after a vowel or* b, g, j, l, m, n, ŋ, r, th, v, z, zh; əd, id *after* d, t; t *after other sounds*\ *vb suffix or adj suffix* **1** — used to form the past participle of regular weak verbs ⟨end*ed*⟩ ⟨fad*ed*⟩ ⟨tri*ed*⟩ ⟨patt*ed*⟩ **2** : having : characterized by ⟨cultur*ed*⟩ ⟨2-legg*ed*⟩; *also* : having the characteristics of ⟨bigot*ed*⟩
²-ed *vb suffix* — used to form the past tense of regular weak verbs ⟨judg*ed*⟩ ⟨deni*ed*⟩ ⟨dropp*ed*⟩

Edam \\'ē-dəm, -ˌdam\ *n* : a yellow Dutch pressed cheese made in balls

ed·dy \\'e-dē\ *n, pl* **eddies** : WHIRLPOOL — **eddy** *vb*

edel·weiss \\'ād-əl-ˌwīs, -ˌvīs\ *n* [G, fr. *edel* noble + *weiss* white] : a small perennial woolly composite herb that grows high in the Alps

ede·ma \i-'dē-mə\ *n* : abnormal accumulation of watery fluid in connective tissue or in a serous cavity — **edem·a·tous** \-'de-mə-təs\ *adj*

Eden \\'ēd-ᵊn\ *n* : PARADISE 2

¹**edge** \\'ej\ *n* **1** : the cutting side of a blade **2** : SHARPNESS; *also* : FORCE, EFFECTIVENESS **3** : the line where something begins or ends; *also* : the area adjoining such an edge **4** : ADVANTAGE — **edged** \\'ejd\ *adj*

²**edge** *vb* **edged; edg·ing 1** : to give or form an edge **2** : to move or force gradually ⟨∼ into a crowd⟩ **3** : to defeat by a small margin ⟨*edged* out her opponent⟩ — **edg·er** *n*

edge·wise \\'ej-ˌwīz\ *adv* : SIDEWAYS

edg·ing \\'e-jiŋ\ *n* : something that forms an edge or border ⟨a lace ∼⟩

edgy \\'e-jē\ *adj* **edg·i·er; -est 1** : SHARP ⟨an ∼ tone⟩ **2** : TENSE, NERVOUS — **edg·i·ness** *n*

ed·i·ble \\'e-də-bəl\ *adj* : fit or safe to be eaten — **ed·i·bil·i·ty** \ˌe-də-'bi-lə-tē\ *n* — **edible** *n*

edict \\'ē-ˌdikt\ *n* : ORDER, DECREE

ed·i·fi·ca·tion \ˌe-də-fə-'kā-shən\ *n* : instruction and improvement esp. in morality — **ed·i·fy** \\'e-də-ˌfī\ *vb*

ed·i·fice \\'e-də-fəs\ *n* : a usu. large building

ed·it \\'e-dət\ *vb* **1** : to revise, assemble, or prepare for publication or release (as a motion picture) **2** : to direct the publication and policies of (as a newspaper) **3** : DELETE — **ed·i·tor** \\'e-də-tər\ *n* — **ed·i·tor·ship** *n* — **ed·i·tress** \-trəs\ *n*

edi·tion \i-'di-shən\ *n* **1** : the form in which a text is published **2** : the total number of copies (as of a book) published at one time **3** : VERSION

¹**ed·i·to·ri·al** \ˌe-də-'tōr-ē-əl\ *adj* **1** : of or relating to an editor or editing **2** : being or resembling an editorial — **ed·i·to·ri·al·ly** *adv*

²**editorial** *n* : an article (as in a newspaper) giving the views of the editors or publishers; *also* : an expression of opinion resembling an editorial ⟨a television ∼⟩

ed·i·to·ri·al·ize \ˌe-də-'tōr-ē-ə-ˌlīz\ *vb* **-ized; -iz·ing 1** : to express an opinion in an editorial **2** : to introduce opinions into factual reporting **3** : to express an opinion — **ed·i·to·ri·al·i·za·tion** \-ˌtōr-ē-ə-lə-'zā-shən\ *n* — **ed·i·to·ri·al·iz·er** *n*

EDP *abbr* electronic data processing

EDT *abbr* Eastern daylight (saving) time

educ *abbr* education; educational

ed·u·ca·ble \\'e-jə-kə-bəl\ *adj* : capable of being educated

ed·u·cate \\'e-jə-ˌkāt\ *vb* **-cat·ed; -cat·ing 1** : to provide with schooling **2** : to develop mentally and morally; *also* : to provide with information **syn** train, discipline, school, instruct, teach — **ed·u·ca·tor** \-ˌkā-tər\ *n*

ed·u·ca·tion \ˌe-jə-'kā-shən\ *n* **1** : the action or process of educating or being educated **2** : a field of study dealing with methods of teaching and learning — **ed·u·ca·tion·al** \-shə-nəl\ *adj*

educational television *n* : PUBLIC TELEVISION

educe \i-'düs, -'dyüs\ *vb* **educed; educ·ing 1** : ELICIT, EVOKE **2** : DEDUCE **syn** extract, evince, extort

ed·u·tain·ment \ˌe-jə-'tān-mənt\ *n* : a form of entertainment that is designed to be educational

¹**-ee** \\'ē, (ˌ)ē\ *n suffix* **1** : one that receives or benefits from (a specified action or thing) ⟨grant*ee*⟩ ⟨patent*ee*⟩ **2** : a person who does (a specified action) ⟨escap*ee*⟩

²**-ee** *n suffix* **1** : a particular esp. small kind of ⟨boot*ee*⟩ **2** : one resembling or suggestive of ⟨goat*ee*⟩

EE *abbr* electrical engineer

EEC *abbr* European Economic Community

EEG *abbr* **1** electroencephalogram **2** electroencephalograph

eel \\'ēl\ *n* : any of numerous snakelike bony fishes with a smooth slimy skin

eel

EEO *abbr* equal employment opportunity

ee·rie *also* **ee·ry** \\'ir-ē\ *adj* **ee·ri·er; -est** : WEIRD, UNCANNY — **ee·ri·ly** \\'ir-ə-lē\ *adv*

eff *abbr* efficiency

ef·face \i-'fās, e-\ *vb* **ef·faced; ef·fac·ing** : to obliterate or obscure by or as if by rubbing out **syn** erase, delete, annul, cancel, expunge — **ef·face·able** *adj* — **ef·face·ment** *n*

¹**ef·fect** \i-'fekt\ *n* **1** : MEANING, INTENT **2** : RESULT **3** : APPEARANCE **4** : INFLUENCE **5** *pl* : GOODS, POSSESSIONS **6** : the quality or state of being operative : OPERATION **syn** consequence, outcome, upshot, aftermath, issue

²**effect** *vb* : to cause to happen ⟨∼ repairs⟩ ⟨∼ changes⟩

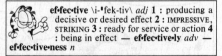

ef·fec·tive \i-'fek-tiv\ *adj* **1** : producing a decisive or desired effect **2** : IMPRESSIVE, STRIKING **3** : ready for service or action **4** : being in effect — **ef·fec·tive·ly** *adv* — **ef·fec·tive·ness** *n*

ef·fec·tu·al \i-'fek-chə-wəl\ *adj* : producing an intended effect : ADEQUATE — **ef·fec·tu·al·ly** *adv*

ef·fec·tu·ate \i-'fek-chə-ˌwāt\ *vb* **-at·ed; -at·ing** : BRING ABOUT, EFFECT

ef·fem·i·nate \ə-'fe-mə-nət\ *adj* : marked by qualities more typical of women than men — **ef·fem·i·na·cy** \-nə-sē\ *n*

ef·fen·di \e-'fen-dē\ *n* [Turk *efendi* master, fr. NGk *aphentēs*, alter. of Gk *authentēs*] : a man of property, authority, or education in an eastern Mediterranean country

ef·fer·ent \'e-fə-rənt\ *adj* : bearing or conducting outward from a more central part ⟨∼ nerves⟩

ef·fer·vesce \ₑe-fər-'ves\ *vb* **-vesced; -vesc·ing** : to bubble and hiss as gas escapes; *also* : to be exhilarated — **ef·fer·ves·cence** \-'ves-ᵊns\ *n* — **ef·fer·ves·cent** \-ᵊnt\ *adj* — **ef·fer·ves·cent·ly** *adv*

ef·fete \e-'fēt\ *adj* **1** : having lost character, vitality, or strength; *also* : DECADENT **2** : EFFEMINATE

ef·fi·ca·cious \ₑe-fə-'kā-shəs\ *adj* : producing an intended effect ⟨∼ remedies⟩ **syn** effectual, effective, efficient — **ef·fi·ca·cy** \'e-fi-kə-sē\ *n*

ef·fi·cient \i-'fi-shənt\ *adj* : productive of desired effects esp. without waste — **ef·fi·cien·cy** \-shən-sē\ *n* — **ef·fi·cient·ly** *adv*

ef·fi·gy \'e-fə-jē\ *n, pl* **-gies** : IMAGE; *esp* : a crude figure of a hated person

ef·flo·res·cence \ₑe-flə-'res-ᵊns\ *n* **1** : the period or state of flowering **2** : the action or process of developing **3** : fullness of development : FLOWERING

ef·flu·ence \'e-ₑflü-əns\ *n* : something that flows out

ef·flu·ent \'e-ₑflü-ənt\ *n* : something that flows out; *esp* : a fluid (as sewage) discharged as waste — **effluent** *adj*

ef·flu·vi·um \e-'flü-vē-əm\ *n, pl* **-via** \-vē-ə\ *or* **-vi·ums** [L, outflow] **1** : a usu. unpleasant emanation **2** : a by-product usu. in the form of waste

ef·fort \'e-fərt\ *n* **1** : EXERTION, ENDEAVOR; *also* : a product of effort **2** : active or applied force — **ef·fort·less** *adj* — **ef·fort·less·ly** *adv*

ef·fron·tery \i-'frən-tə-rē\ *n, pl* **-ter·ies** : shameless boldness : IMPUDENCE **syn** temerity, audacity, brass, gall, nerve, chutzpah

ef·ful·gence \i-'fùl-jəns, -'fəl-\ *n* : radiant splendor : BRILLIANCE — **ef·ful·gent** \-jənt\ *adj*

ef·fu·sion \i-'fyü-zhən, e-\ *n* : a gushing forth; *also* : unrestrained utterance — **ef·fuse** \i-'fyüz, e-\ *vb* — **ef·fu·sive** \i-'fyü-siv, e-\ *adj* — **ef·fu·sive·ly** *adv*

eft \'eft\ *n* : NEWT

EFT *or* **EFTS** *abbr* electronic funds transfer (system)

e.g. *abbr* [L *exempli gratia*] for example

Eg *abbr* Egypt; Egyptian

egal·i·tar·i·an·ism \i-ₑga-lə-'ter-ē-ə-ₑni-zəm\ *n* : a belief in human equality esp. in social, political, and economic affairs — **egal·i·tar·i·an** *adj or n*

¹**egg** \'eg\ *vb* [ME, fr. ON *eggja;* akin to OE *ecg* edge] : to urge to action — usu. used with *on*

²**egg** *n* [ME *egge*, fr. ON *egg;* akin to OE *ǣg* egg, L *ovum*] **1** : a rounded usu. hard-shelled reproductive body esp. of birds and reptiles from which the young hatches; *also* : the egg of the common domestic chicken as an article of food **2** : a germ cell produced by a female

egg·beat·er \'eg-ₑbē-tər\ *n* : a hand-operated kitchen utensil for beating, stirring, or whipping

egg cell *n* : EGG 2

egg·head \-ₑhed\ *n* : INTELLECTUAL, HIGHBROW

egg·nog \-ₑnäg\ *n* : a drink consisting of eggs beaten with sugar, milk or cream, and often alcoholic liquor

egg·plant \-ₑplant\ *n* : the edible usu. large and purplish fruit of a plant related to the potato; *also* : the plant

egg roll *n* : a thin egg-dough casing filled with minced vegetables and often bits of meat and usu. deep-fried

egg·shell \'eg-ₑshel\ *n* : the hard exterior covering of an egg

egis \'ē-jəs\ *var of* AEGIS

eg·lan·tine \'e-glən-ₑtīn, -ₑtēn\ *n* : SWEETBRIER

ego \'ē-gō\ *n, pl* **egos** [L, I] **1** : the self as distinguished from others **2** : the one of the three divisions of the psyche in psychoanalytic theory that is the organized

conscious mediator between the person and reality

ego·cen·tric \ₑē-gō-'sen-trik\ *adj* : concerned or overly concerned with the self; *esp* : SELF-CENTERED

ego·ism \'ē-gō-ₑi-zəm\ *n* **1** : a doctrine holding self-interest to be the motive or the valid end of action **2** : excessive concern for oneself with or without exaggerated feelings of self-importance — **ego·ist** \-ist\ *n* — **ego·is·tic** \ₑē-gō-'is-tik\ *adj* — **ego·is·ti·cal·ly** *adv*

ego·tism \'ē-gə-ₑti-zəm\ *n* **1** : the practice of talking about oneself too much **2** : an exaggerated sense of self-importance : CONCEIT — **ego·tist** \-tist\ *n* — **ego·tis·tic** \ₑē-gə-'tis-tik\ *or* **ego·tis·ti·cal** \-ti-kəl\ *adj* — **ego·tis·ti·cal·ly** *adv*

ego trip *n* : an act that enhances and satisfies one's ego

egre·gious \i-'grē-jəs\ *adj* [L *egregius* outstanding, fr. *ex, e* out of + *greg-, grex* flock, herd] : notably bad : FLAGRANT — **egre·gious·ly** *adv* — **egre·gious·ness** *n*

egress \'ē-ₑgres\ *n* : a way out : EXIT

egret \'ē-grət, i-'gret\ *n* : any of various herons that bear long plumes during the breeding season

Egyp·tian \i-'jip-shən\ *n* **1** : a native or inhabitant of Egypt **2** : the language of the ancient Egyptians from earliest times to about the 3d century A.D. — **Egyptian** *adj*

ei·der \'ī-dər\ *n* : any of several northern sea ducks that yield a soft down

ei·der·down \-ₑdaùn\ *n* **1** : the down of the eider **2** : a quilt filled with eiderdown

ei·do·lon \ī-'dō-lən\ *n, pl* **-lons** *or* **-la** \-lə\ **1** : PHANTOM **2** : IDEAL

eight \'āt\ *n* **1** : one more than seven **2** : the 8th in a set or series **3** : something having eight units — **eight** *adj or pron* — **eighth** \'ātth\ *adj or adv or n*

eight ball *n* : a black pool ball numbered 8 — **behind the eight ball** : in a highly disadvantageous position

eigh·teen \'āt-'tēn\ *n* : one more than 17 — **eighteen** *adj or pron* — **eigh·teenth** \-'tēnth\ *adj or n*

eighty \'ā-tē\ *n, pl* **eight·ies** : eight times 10 — **eight·i·eth** \'ā-tē-əth\ *adj or n* — **eighty** *adj or pron*

ein·stei·ni·um \īn-'stī-nē-əm\ *n* : an artificially produced radioactive element — see ELEMENT table

ei·re·nic *chiefly Brit var of* IRENIC

¹**ei·ther** \'ē-thər, 'ī-\ *adj* **1** : being the one and the other of two : EACH ⟨trees on ∼ side⟩ **2** : being the one or the other of two ⟨take ∼ road⟩

²**either** *pron* : the one or the other

³**either** *conj* — used as a function word before the first of two or more words or word groups of which the last is preceded by *or* to indicate that they represent alternatives ⟨a statement is ∼ true or false⟩

ejac·u·late \i-'ja-kyə-ₑlāt\ *vb* **-lat·ed; -lat·ing 1** : to eject a fluid (as semen) **2** : to utter suddenly : EXCLAIM — **ejac·u·la·tion** \-ₑja-kyə-'lā-shən\ *n* — **ejac·u·la·to·ry** \-'ja-kyə-lə-ₑtōr-ē\ *adj*

eject \i-'jekt\ *vb* : to drive or throw out or off **syn** expel, oust, evict, dismiss — **ejec·tion** \-'jek-shən\ *n*

eke \'ēk\ *vb* **eked; ek·ing** : to gain, supplement, or extend usu. with effort — usu. used with *out* ⟨∼ out a living⟩

EKG *abbr* [G *Elektrokardiogramm*] electrocardiogram; electrocardiograph

el *abbr* elevation

¹**elab·o·rate** \i-'la-bə-rət, -'la-brət\ *adj* **1** : planned or carried out with great care **2** : being complex and usu. ornate — **elab·o·rate·ly** *adv* — **elab·o·rate·ness** *n*

²**elab·o·rate** \i-'la-bə-ₑrāt\ *vb* **-rat·ed; -rat·ing 1** : to build up from simpler ingredients **2** : to work out in detail : develop fully — **elab·o·ra·tion** \-ₑla-bə-'rā-shən\ *n*

élan \ā-'läⁿ\ *n* [F] : ARDOR, SPIRIT

eland \'ē-lənd, -ₑland\ *n, pl* **eland** *also* **elands** [Afrikaans] : either of two large African antelopes with spirally twisted horns in both sexes

elapse \i-'laps\ *vb* **elapsed; elaps·ing** : to slip by : PASS

¹**elas·tic** \i-'las-tik\ *adj* **1** : SPRINGY **2** : FLEXIBLE, PLIABLE **3** : ADAPTABLE **syn** resilient, supple, stretch — **elas·tic·i·ty** \-ˌlas-'ti-sə-tē, ˌē-ˌlas-\ *n*

²**elastic** *n* **1** : elastic material **2** : a rubber band

elate \i-'lāt\ *vb* **elat·ed; elat·ing** : to fill with joy — **ela·tion** \-'lā-shən\ *n*

¹**el·bow** \'el-ˌbō\ *n* **1** : the joint of the arm; *also* : the outer curve of the bent arm **2** : a bend or joint resembling an elbow in shape

²**elbow** *vb* : to push aside with the elbow; *also* : to make one's way by elbowing

el·bow·room \'el-ˌbō-ˌrüm, -ˌrùm\ *n* : enough space for work or operation

¹**el·der** \'el-dər\ *n* **1** : ELDERBERRY 2

²**elder** *adj* **1** : OLDER **2** : EARLIER, FORMER **3** : of higher rank : SENIOR

³**elder** *n* **1** : an older individual : SENIOR **2** : one having authority by reason of age and experience **3** : a church officer

el·der·ber·ry \'el-dər-ˌber-ē\ *n* **1** : the edible black or red fruit of a shrub or tree related to the honeysuckle and bearing flat clusters of small white or pink flowers **2** : a tree or shrub bearing elderberries

el·der·ly \'el-dər-lē\ *adj* **1** : rather old; *esp* : past middle age **2** : of, relating to, or characteristic of later life

el·dest \'el-dəst\ *adj* : of the greatest age

El Do·ra·do \ˌel-də-'rä-dō, -'rä-\ *n* [Sp, lit., the gilded one] : a place of vast riches, abundance, or opportunity

elec *abbr* electric; electrical; electricity

¹**elect** \i-'lekt\ *adj* **1** : CHOSEN, SELECT **2** : elected but not yet installed in office (the president-*elect*)

²**elect** *n, pl* **elect 1** : a selected person **2** *pl* : a select or exclusive group

³**elect** *vb* **1** : to select by vote (as for office or membership) **2** : CHOOSE, PICK

elec·tion \i-'lek-shən\ *n* **1** : an act or process of electing **2** : the fact of being elected

elec·tion·eer \i-ˌlek-shə-'nir\ *vb* : to work for the election of a candidate or party

¹**elec·tive** \i-'lek-tiv\ *adj* **1** : chosen or filled by election **2** : permitting a choice : OPTIONAL

²**elective** *n* : an elective course or subject of study

elec·tor \i-'lek-tər\ *n* **1** : one qualified to vote in an election **2** : one elected to an electoral college — **elec·tor·al** \i-'lek-tə-rəl\ *adj*

electoral college *n* : a body of electors who elect the president and vice president of the U.S.

elec·tor·ate \i-'lek-tə-rət\ *n* : a body of persons entitled to vote

elec·tric \i-'lek-trik\ *adj* [NL *electricus* produced from amber by friction, electric, fr. ML, of amber, fr. L *electrum* amber, fr. Gk *ēlektron*] **1** *or* **elec·tri·cal** \-tri-kəl\ : of, relating to, operated by, or produced by electricity **2** : ELECTRIFYING, THRILLING — **elec·tri·cal·ly** *adv*

electrical storm *n* : THUNDERSTORM

electric chair *n* : a chair used to carry out the death penalty by electrocution

electric eye *n* : PHOTOELECTRIC CELL

elec·tri·cian \i-ˌlek-'tri-shən\ *n* : a person who installs, operates, or repairs electrical equipment

elec·tric·i·ty \i-ˌlek-'tri-sə-tē\ *n, pl* **-ties 1** : a form of energy that occurs in nature and is observable in natural phenomena (as lightning) and that can be produced by friction, chemical reaction, or mechanical effort **2** : electric current

elec·tri·fy \i-'lek-trə-ˌfī\ *vb* **-fied; -fy·ing 1** : to charge with electricity **2** : to equip for use of electric power **3** : THRILL — **elec·tri·fi·ca·tion** \i-ˌlek-trə-fə-'kā-shən\ *n*

elec·tro·car·dio·gram \i-ˌlek-trō-'kär-dē-ə-ˌgram\ *n* : the tracing made by an electrocardiograph

elec·tro·car·dio·graph \-ˌgraf\ *n* : a device for recording the changes of electrical potential occurring during the heartbeat — **elec·tro·car·dio·graph·ic** \-ˌkär-dē-ə-'gra-fik\ *adj* — **elec·tro·car·di·og·ra·phy** \-dē-'ä-grə-fē\ *n*

elec·tro·chem·is·try \-'ke-mə-strē\ *n* : a branch of chemistry that deals with the relation of electricity to chemical changes — **elec·tro·chem·i·cal** \-'ke-mi-kəl\ *adj*

elec·tro·cute \i-'lek-trə-ˌkyüt\ *vb* **-cut·ed; -cut·ing** : to kill by an electric shock; *esp* : to kill (a criminal) in this way — **elec·tro·cu·tion** \-ˌlek-trə-'kyü-shən\ *n*

elec·trode \i-'lek-ˌtrōd\ *n* : a conductor used to establish electrical contact with a nonmetallic part of a circuit

elec·tro·en·ceph·a·lo·gram \i-ˌlek-trō-in-'se-fə-lə-ˌgram\ *n* : the tracing made by an electroencephalograph

elec·tro·en·ceph·a·lo·graph \-ˌgraf\ *n* : an apparatus for detecting and recording brain waves — **elec·tro·en·ceph·a·lo·graph·ic** \-ˌse-fə-lə-'gra-fik\ *adj* — **elec·tro·en·ceph·a·log·ra·phy** \-'lä-grə-fē\ *n*

elec·trol·o·gist \i-ˌlek-'trä-lə-jist\ *n* : one that uses electrical means to remove hair, warts, moles, and birthmarks from the body

elec·trol·y·sis \i-ˌlek-'trä-lə-səs\ *n* **1** : the production of chemical changes by passage of an electric current through an electrolyte **2** : the destruction of hair roots with an electric current — **elec·tro·lyt·ic** \-trə-'li-tik\ *adj*

elec·tro·lyte \i-'lek-trə-ˌlīt\ *n* : a nonmetallic electric conductor in which current is carried by the movement of ions; *also* : a substance whose solution or molten form is such a conductor

elec·tro·mag·net \i-ˌlek-trō-'mag-nət\ *n* : a core of magnetic material surrounded by a coil of wire through which an electric current is passed to magnetize the core

elec·tro·mag·net·ic \-mag-'ne-tik\ *adj* : of, relating to, or produced by electromagnetism — **elec·tro·mag·net·i·cal·ly** *adv*

electromagnetic radiation *n* : a series of electromagnetic waves

electromagnetic wave *n* : a wave (as a radio wave, an X ray, or a wave of visible light) that consists of associated electric and magnetic effects and that travels at the speed of light

elec·tro·mag·ne·tism \i-ˌlek-trō-'mag-nə-ˌti-zəm\ *n* **1** : magnetism developed by a current of electricity **2** : a natural force responsible for interactions between charged particles which result from their charge

elec·tro·mo·tive force \i-ˌlek-trə-'mō-tiv-\ *n* : the potential difference derived from an electrical source per unit quantity of electricity passing through the source

elec·tron \i-'lek-ˌträn\ *n* : a negatively charged elementary particle

elec·tron·ic \i-ˌlek-'trä-nik\ *adj* : of or relating to electrons or electronics — **elec·tron·i·cal·ly** \-ni-k(ə-)lē\ *adv*

electronic mail *n* : messages sent and received electronically

elec·tron·ics \i-ˌlek-'trä-niks\ *n* **1** : the physics of electrons and electronic devices **2** : electronic devices or equipment

electron microscope *n* : an instrument in which a focused beam of electrons is used to produce an enlarged image of a minute object

electron tube *n* : a device in which electrical conduction by electrons takes place within a sealed container and which is used for the controlled flow of electrons

elec·tro·pho·re·sis \i-ˌlek-trə-fə-'rē-səs\ *n* : the movement of suspended particles through a fluid by an electromotive force — **elec·tro·pho·ret·ic** \-'re-tik\ *adj*

elec·tro·plate \i-'lek-trə-ˌplāt\ *vb* : to coat (as with metal) by electrolysis

elec·tro·shock therapy \i-'lek-trō-ˌshäk-\ *n* : the treatment of mental disorder by the induction of coma with an electric current

elec·tro·stat·ics \i-ˌlek-trə-ˈsta-tiks\ *n* : physics dealing with the interactions of stationary electric charges

el·ee·mos·y·nary \ˌe-li-ˈmäs-ᵊn-ˌer-ē\ *adj* : CHARITABLE

el·e·gance \ˈe-li-gəns\ *n* **1** : refined gracefulness; *also* : tasteful richness (as of design) **2** : something marked by elegance — **el·e·gant** \-gənt\ *adj* — **el·e·gant·ly** *adv*

ele·giac \ˌe-lə-ˈjī-ək, -ˌak\ *adj* : of or relating to an elegy

el·e·gy \ˈe-lə-jē\ *n, pl* **-gies** : a song, poem, or speech expressing grief for one who is dead; *also* : a reflective poem usu. melancholy in tone

elem *abbr* elementary

el·e·ment \ˈe-lə-mənt\ *n* **1** *pl* : weather conditions; *esp* : severe weather ⟨boards exposed to the ∼*s*⟩ **2** : natural environment ⟨in her ∼⟩ **3** : a constituent part **4** *pl* : the simplest principles (as of an art or science) : RUDIMENTS **5** : a member of a mathematical set **6** : any of more than 100 fundamental substances that consist of atoms of only one kind **syn** component, ingredient, constituent — **el·e·men·tal** \ˌe-lə-ˈment-ᵊl\ *adj*

CHEMICAL ELEMENTS

ELEMENT	SYMBOL	ATOMIC NUMBER	ATOMIC WEIGHT (C = 12)
actinium	Ac	89	227.0278
aluminum	Al	13	26.98154
americium	Am	95	
antimony	Sb	51	121.75
argon	Ar	18	39.948
arsenic	As	33	74.9216
astatine	At	85	
barium	Ba	56	137.33
berkelium	Bk	97	
beryllium	Be	4	9.01218
bismuth	Bi	83	208.9804
boron	B	5	10.81
bromine	Br	35	79.904
cadmium	Cd	48	112.41
calcium	Ca	20	40.08
californium	Cf	98	
carbon	C	6	12.011
cerium	Ce	58	140.12
cesium	Cs	55	132.9054
chlorine	Cl	17	35.453
chromium	Cr	24	51.996
cobalt	Co	27	58.9332
copper	Cu	29	63.546
curium	Cm	96	
dysprosium	Dy	66	162.50
einsteinium	Es	99	
erbium	Er	68	167.26
europium	Eu	63	151.96
fermium	Fm	100	
fluorine	F	9	18.998403
francium	Fr	87	
gadolinium	Gd	64	157.25
gallium	Ga	31	69.72
germanium	Ge	32	72.59
gold	Au	79	196.9665
hafnium	Hf	72	178.49
helium	He	2	4.00260
holmium	Ho	67	164.9304
hydrogen	H	1	1.0079
indium	In	49	114.82
iodine	I	53	126.9045
iridium	Ir	77	192.22
iron	Fe	26	55.847

ELEMENT	SYMBOL	ATOMIC NUMBER	ATOMIC WEIGHT (C = 12)
krypton	Kr	36	83.80
lanthanum	La	57	138.9055
lawrencium	Lr	103	
lead	Pb	82	207.2
lithium	Li	3	6.941
lutetium	Lu	71	174.967
magnesium	Mg	12	24.305
manganese	Mn	25	54.9380
mendelevium	Md	101	
mercury	Hg	80	200.59
molybdenum	Mo	42	95.94
neodymium	Nd	60	144.24
neon	Ne	10	20.179
neptunium	Np	93	237.0482
nickel	Ni	28	58.69
niobium	Nb	41	92.9064
nitrogen	N	7	14.0067
nobelium	No	102	
osmium	Os	76	190.2
oxygen	O	8	15.9994
palladium	Pd	46	106.42
phosphorus	P	15	30.97376
platinum	Pt	78	195.08
plutonium	Pu	94	
polonium	Po	84	
potassium	K	19	39.0983
praseodymium	Pr	59	140.9077
promethium	Pm	61	
protactinium	Pa	91	231.0359
radium	Ra	88	226.0254
radon	Rn	86	
rhenium	Re	75	186.207
rhodium	Rh	45	102.9055
rubidium	Rb	37	85.4678
ruthenium	Ru	44	101.07
samarium	Sm	62	150.36
scandium	Sc	21	44.9559
selenium	Se	34	78.96
silicon	Si	14	28.0855
silver	Ag	47	107.868
sodium	Na	11	22.98977
strontium	Sr	38	87.62
sulfur	S	16	32.06
tantalum	Ta	73	180.9479
technetium	Tc	43	
tellurium	Te	52	127.60
terbium	Tb	65	158.9254
thallium	Tl	81	204.383
thorium	Th	90	232.0381
thulium	Tm	69	168.9342
tin	Sn	50	118.69
titanium	Ti	22	47.88
tungsten	W	74	183.85
unnilhexium	Unh	106	
unnilpentium	Unp	105	
unnilquadium	Unq	104	
uranium	U	92	238.0289
vanadium	V	23	50.9415
xenon	Xe	54	131.29
ytterbium	Yb	70	173.04
yttrium	Y	39	88.9059
zinc	Zn	30	65.38
zirconium	Zr	40	91.22

el·e·men·ta·ry \ˌe-lə-ˈmen-trē, -tə-rē\ *adj* : SIMPLE, RUDIMENTARY; *also* : of, relating to, or teaching the basic subjects of education

elementary particle *n* : a subatomic particle of matter and energy that does not appear to be made up of other smaller particles

elementary school *n* : a school usu. including the first six or the first eight grades

el·e·phant \'e-lə-fənt\ n, pl **elephants** also **elephant** : any of a family of huge thickset nearly hairless mammals that have the snout lengthened into a trunk and two long curving pointed ivory tusks

elephant

el·e·phan·ti·a·sis \ˌe-lə-fən-'tī-ə-səs\ n, pl **-a·ses** \-ˌsēz\ : enlargement and thickening of tissues in response esp. to infection by minute parasitic worms

el·e·phan·tine \ˌe-lə-'fan-ˌtēn, -ˌtīn, 'e-lə-fən-\ adj **1** : of great size or strength **2** : CLUMSY, PONDEROUS

elev abbr elevation

el·e·vate \'e-lə-ˌvāt\ vb **-vat·ed; -vat·ing 1** : to lift up : RAISE **2** : EXALT, ENNOBLE **3** : ELATE

el·e·va·tion \ˌe-lə-'vā-shən\ n **1** : the height to which something is raised (as above sea level) **2** : a lifting up **3** : something (as a hill or swelling) that is elevated

el·e·va·tor \'e-lə-ˌvā-tər\ n **1** : a cage or platform for conveying people or things from one level to another **2** : a building for storing and discharging grain **3** : a movable surface on an airplane to produce motion up or down

elev·en \i-'le-vən\ n **1** : one more than 10 **2** : the 11th in a set or series **3** : something having 11 units; esp : a football team — **eleven** adj or pron — **eleventh** \-vənth\ adj or n

elf \'elf\ n, pl **elves** \'elvz\ : a mischievous fairy — **elf·ish** \'el-fish\ adj

ELF abbr extremely low frequency

elf·in \'el-fən\ adj : of, relating to, or resembling an elf

elic·it \i-'li-sət\ vb : to draw out or forth syn evoke, educe, extract, extort

elide \i-'līd\ vb **elid·ed; elid·ing** : to suppress or alter by elision

el·i·gi·ble \'e-lə-jə-bəl\ adj : qualified to participate or to be chosen — **el·i·gi·bil·i·ty** \ˌe-lə-jə-'bi-lə-tē\ n — **eligible** n

elim·i·nate \i-'li-mə-ˌnāt\ vb **-nat·ed; -nat·ing** [L eliminatus, pp. of eliminare, fr. limen threshold] **1** : REMOVE, ERADICATE **2** : to pass (wastes) from the body **3** : to leave out : IGNORE — **elim·i·na·tion** \-ˌli-mə-'nā-shən\ n

eli·sion \i-'li-zhən\ n : the omission of a final or initial sound or a word; esp : the omission of an unstressed vowel or syllable in a verse to achieve a uniform rhythm

elite \ā-'lēt, ē-\ n [F élite] **1** : the choice part; also : a superior group **2** : a typewriter type providing 12 characters to the inch — **elite** adj

elit·ism \-'lē-ˌti-zəm\ n : leadership or rule by an elite; also : advocacy of such elitism

elix·ir \i-'lik-sər\ n [ME, fr. ML, fr. Ar al-iksīr the elixir, fr. al the + iksīr elixir] **1** : a substance held capable of prolonging life indefinitely; also : PANACEA **2** : a sweetened alcoholic medicinal solution

Eliz·a·be·than \i-ˌli-zə-'bē-thən\ adj : of, relating to, or characteristic of Elizabeth I of England or her times

elk \'elk\ n, pl **elk** or **elks 1** : MOOSE — used for one of the Old World **2** : a large gregarious deer of No. America, Europe, Asia, and northwestern Africa with curved antlers having many branches

¹ell \'el\ n : a former English cloth measure of 45 inches

²ell n : an extension at right angles to a building

el·lipse \i-'lips, e-\ n : a closed curve of oval shape

el·lip·sis \i-'lip-səs, e-\ n, pl **el·lip·ses** \-ˌsēz\ **1** : omission from an expression of a word clearly implied **2** : marks (as . . .) to show omission

el·lip·soid \i-'lip-ˌsȯid, e-\ n : a surface all plane sections of which are circles or ellipses — **el·lip·soi·dal** \-ˌlip-'sȯid-ᵊl\ also **ellipsoid** adj

el·lip·ti·cal \i-'lip-ti-kəl, e-\ or **el·lip·tic** \-tik\ adj **1** : of, relating to, or shaped like an ellipse **2** : of, relating to, or marked by ellipsis — **el·lip·ti·cal·ly** \-ti-k(ə-)lē\ adv

elm \'elm\ n : any of a genus of large trees that have toothed leaves and nearly circular one-seeded winged fruits and are often grown as shade trees; also : the wood of an elm

el·o·cu·tion \ˌe-lə-'kyü-shən\ n : the art of effective public speaking — **el·o·cu·tion·ist** \-shə-nist\ n

elon·gate \i-'lȯŋ-ˌgāt\ vb **-gat·ed; -gat·ing** : to make or grow longer syn extend, lengthen, prolong, protract — **elon·ga·tion** \ˌ(ˌ)ē-ˌlȯŋ-'gā-shən\ n

elope \i-'lōp\ vb **eloped; elop·ing** : to run away esp. to be married — **elope·ment** n — **elop·er** n

el·o·quent \'e-lə-kwənt\ adj **1** : having or showing clear and forceful expression **2** : clearly showing some feeling or meaning — **el·o·quence** \-kwəns\ n — **el·o·quent·ly** adv

¹else \'els\ adv **1** : in a different or additional manner or place or at a different or additional time (where ~ can we meet) **2** : OTHERWISE (obey or ~ you'll be sorry)

²else adj : OTHER; esp : being in addition (what ~ do you want)

else·where \-ˌhwer\ adv : in or to another place

elu·ci·date \i-'lü-sə-ˌdāt\ vb **-dat·ed; -dat·ing** : to make clear usu. by explanation syn clarify, explain, illuminate — **elu·ci·da·tion** \-ˌlü-sə-'dā-shən\ n

elude \ē-'lüd\ vb **elud·ed; elud·ing 1** : EVADE **2** : to escape the notice of

elu·sive \ē-'lü-siv\ adj : tending to elude : EVASIVE — **elu·sive·ly** adv — **elu·sive·ness** n

el·ver \'el-vər\ n [alter. of eelfare migration of eels] : a young eel

elves pl of ELF

Ely·si·um \i-'li-zhē-əm, -zē-\ n, pl **-si·ums** or **-sia** \-zhē-ə, -zē-\ **1** : PARADISE **2** — **Ely·sian** \-'li-zhən\ adj

em \'em\ n : a length approximately the width of the letter M

EM abbr **1** electromagnetic **2** electron microscope **3** enlisted man

ema·ci·ate \i-'mā-shē-ˌāt\ vb **-at·ed; -at·ing** : to become or cause to become very thin — **ema·ci·a·tion** \-ˌmā-shē-'ā-shən, -sē-\ n

E-mail \'ē-ˌmāl\ n : ELECTRONIC MAIL

emalangeni pl of LILANGENI

em·a·nate \'e-mə-ˌnāt\ vb **-nat·ed; -nat·ing** : to come out from a source syn proceed, spring, rise, arise, originate — **em·a·na·tion** \ˌe-mə-'nā-shən\ n

eman·ci·pate \i-'man-sə-ˌpāt\ vb **-pat·ed; -pat·ing** : to set free syn liberate, release, deliver, discharge — **eman·ci·pa·tion** \-ˌman-sə-'pā-shən\ n — **eman·ci·pa·tor** \-'man-sə-ˌpā-tər\ n

emas·cu·late \i-'mas-kyü-ˌlāt\ vb **-lat·ed; -lat·ing** : CASTRATE, GELD; also : WEAKEN — **emas·cu·la·tion** \-ˌmas-kyü-'lā-shən\ n

em·balm \im-'bäm, -'bälm\ vb : to treat (a corpse) so as to protect from decay — **em·balm·er** n

em·bank·ment \im-'baŋk-mənt\ n : a raised structure (as of earth) to hold back water or carry a roadway

em·bar·go \im-'bär-gō\ n, pl **-goes** [Sp, fr. embargar to bar] : a prohibition on commerce — **embargo** vb

em·bark \im-'bärk\ vb **1** : to put or go on board a ship or airplane **2** : to make a start — **em·bar·ka·tion** \ˌem-ˌbär-'kā-shən\ n

em·bar·rass \im-'bar-əs\ vb **1** : CONFUSE, DISCONCERT **2** : to involve in financial difficulties **3** : to cause to experience self-conscious distress **4** : HINDER, IMPEDE — **em·bar·rass·ing·ly** adv — **em·bar·rass·ment** n

em·bas·sy \'em-bə-sē\ *n, pl* -sies 1 : a group of representatives headed by an ambassador 2 : the function, position, or mission of an ambassador 3 : the official residence and offices of an ambassador

em·bat·tle \im-'bat-ªl\ *vb* : to arrange in order for battle; *also* : FORTIFY

em·bat·tled *adj* 1 : engaged in battle, conflict, or controversy 2 : being a site of battle, conflict, or controversy 3 : characterized by conflict or controversy

em·bed \im-'bed\ *vb* em·bed·ded; em·bed·ding 1 : to enclose closely in a surrounding mass 2 : to make something an integral part of

em·bel·lish \im-'be-lish\ *vb* 1 : ADORN, DECORATE 2 : to add ornamental details to syn beautify, deck, bedeck, garnish, ornament, dress — em·bel·lish·ment *n*

em·ber \'em-bər\ *n* 1 : a glowing or smoldering fragment from a fire 2 *pl* : the smoldering remains of a fire

em·bez·zle \im-'be-zəl\ *vb* -zled; -zling : to steal (as money) by falsifying records — em·bez·zle·ment *n* — em·bez·zler *n*

em·bit·ter \im-'bi-tər\ *vb* 1 : to arouse bitter feelings in 2 : to make bitter

em·bla·zon \-'blāz-ªn\ *vb* 1 : to adorn with heraldic devices 2 : to display conspicuously

em·blem \'em-bləm\ *n* : something (as an object or picture) suggesting another object or an idea : SYMBOL — em·blem·at·ic \.em-blə-'ma-tik\ *also* em·blem·at·i·cal \-ti-kəl\ *adj*

em·body \im-'bä-dē\ *vb* em·bod·ied; em·body·ing 1 : INCARNATE 2 : to express in definite form 3 : to incorporate into a system or body 4 : PERSONIFY syn combine, integrate — em·bodi·ment \-di-mənt\ *n*

em·bold·en \im-'bōl-dən\ *vb* : to inspire with courage

em·bo·lism \'em-bə-.li-zəm\ *n* : the obstruction of a blood vessel by a foreign or abnormal particle

em·bon·point \än-bōn-'pwam\ *n* [F] : plumpness of person : STOUTNESS

em·boss \im-'bäs, -'bȯs\ *vb* : to ornament with raised work

em·bou·chure \'äm-bu̇-.shu̇r, .äm-bu̇-'shu̇r \ *n* [F, ultim. fr. *bouche* mouth] : the position and use of the lips, tongue, and teeth in playing a wind instrument

em·bow·er \im-'bau̇-ər\ *vb* : to shelter or enclose in a bower

¹em·brace \im-'brās\ *vb* em·braced; em·brac·ing 1 : to clasp in the arms; *also* : CHERISH, LOVE 2 : ENCIRCLE 3 : TAKE UP, ADOPT; *also* : WELCOME 4 : INCLUDE 5 : to participate in an embrace syn comprehend, involve, encompass, embody

²embrace *n* : an encircling with the arms

em·bra·sure \im-'brā-zhər\ *n* 1 : an opening in a wall through which a cannon is fired 2 : a recess of a door or window

em·bro·ca·tion \.em-brə-'kā-shən\ *n* : LINIMENT

em·broi·der \im-'brȯi-dər\ *vb* 1 : to ornament with or do needlework 2 : to elaborate with exaggerated detail

em·broi·dery \im-'brȯi-də-rē\ *n, pl* -der·ies 1 : the forming of decorative designs with needlework 2 : something embroidered

em·broil \im-'brȯil\ *vb* 1 : to throw into confusion or disorder 2 : to involve in conflict or difficulties — em·broil·ment *n*

em·bryo \'em-brē-.ō\ *n, pl* embryos : a living thing in its earliest stages of development — em·bry·on·ic \.em-brē-'ä-nik\ *adj*

em·bry·ol·o·gy \.em-brē-'ä-lə-jē\ *n* : a branch of biology dealing with embryos and their development — em·bry·o·log·i·cal \-brē-ə-'lä-ji-kəl\ *adj* — em·bry·ol·o·gist \-brē-'ä-lə-jist\ *n*

em·cee \'em-'sē\ *n* : MASTER OF CEREMONIES — emcee *vb*

emend \ē-'mend\ *vb* : to correct usu. by altering the text of syn rectify, revise, amend — emen·da·tion \.ē-.men-'dā-shən\ *n*

emer *abbr* emeritus

¹em·er·ald \'em-rəld, 'e-mə-\ *n* : a green beryl prized as a gem

²emerald *adj* : brightly or richly green

emerge \i-'mərj\ *vb* emerged; emerg·ing : to rise, come forth, or come out into view — emer·gence \-'mər-jəns\ *n* — emer·gent \-jənt\ *adj*

emer·gen·cy \i-'mər-jən-sē\ *n, pl* -cies : an unforeseen event or condition requiring prompt action syn exigency, contingency, crisis, juncture

emergency room *n* : a hospital room for receiving and treating persons needing immediate medical care

emer·i·ta \i-'mer-ə-tə\ *adj* : EMERITUS — used of a woman

emer·i·tus \i-'mer-ə-təs\ *adj* [L] : retired from active duty ⟨professor ~⟩

em·ery \'e-mə-rē\ *n, pl* em·er·ies : a dark granular corundum used esp. for grinding and polishing

emet·ic \i-'me-tik\ *n* : an agent that induces vomiting — emetic *adj*

emf *n* [*electromotive force*] : POTENTIAL DIFFERENCE

em·i·grate \'e-mə-.grāt\ *vb* -grat·ed; -grat·ing : to leave a place (as a country) to settle elsewhere — em·i·grant \-mi-grənt\ *n* — em·i·gra·tion \.e-mə-'grā-shən\ *n*

émi·gré *also* emi·gré \'e-mi-.grā, .e-mi-'grā\ *n* [F] : a person who emigrates esp. because of political conditions

em·i·nence \'e-mə-nəns\ *n* 1 : high rank or position; *also* : a person of high rank or attainments 2 : a lofty place

em·i·nent \'e-mə-nənt\ *adj* 1 : CONSPICUOUS, EVIDENT 2 : DISTINGUISHED, PROMINENT — em·i·nent·ly *adv*

eminent domain *n* : a right of a government to take private property for public use

emir \i-'mir, ā-\ *n* [Ar *amīr* commander] : a ruler, chief, or commander in Islamic countries — emir·ate \'e-mər-ət\ *n*

em·is·sary \'e-mə-.ser-ē\ *n, pl* -sar·ies : AGENT; *esp* : a secret agent

emis·sion \ē-'mi-shən\ n : something emitted; *esp* : substances discharged into the air

emit \ē-'mit\ vb **emit·ted; emit·ting 1** : to give off or out ⟨∼ light⟩; *also* : EJECT **2** : EXPRESS, UTTER — **emit·ter** n

emol·lient \i-'mäl-yənt\ adj : making soft or supple; *also* : soothing esp. to the skin or mucous membrane — **emol·lient** n

emol·u·ment \i-'mäl-yə-mənt\ n [ME, fr. L *emolumentum* advantage, fr. *emolere* to produce by grinding] : the product (as salary or fees) of an employment

emote \i-'mōt\ vb **emot·ed; emot·ing** : to give expression to emotion in or as if in a play

emo·tion \i-'mō-shən\ n : a usu. intense feeling (as of love, hate, or despair) — **emo·tion·al** \-shə-nəl\ adj — **emo·tion·al·ly** adv

emp abbr emperor; empress

em·pa·thy \'em-pə-thē\ n : the experiencing as one's own of the feelings of another; *also* : the capacity for this — **em·path·ic** \em-'pa-thik\ adj

em·pen·nage \₁äm-pə-'näzh, ₁em-\ n [F] : the tail assembly of an airplane

em·per·or \'em-pər-ər\ n : the sovereign male ruler of an empire

em·pha·sis \'em-fə-səs\ n, pl **-pha·ses** \-₁sēz\ : particular prominence given (as to a syllable in speaking or to a phase of action)

em·pha·sise Brit var of EMPHASIZE

em·pha·size \-₁sīz\ vb **-sized; -siz·ing** : to place emphasis on : STRESS

em·phat·ic \im-'fa-tik, em-\ adj : uttered with emphasis : STRESSED — **em·phat·i·cal·ly** \-'ti-k(ə-)lē\ adv

em·phy·se·ma \₁em-fə-'zē-mə, -'sē-\ n : a condition marked esp. by abnormal expansion of the air spaces of the lungs and often by impairment of heart action

em·pire \'em-₁pīər\ n **1** : a large state or a group of states under a single sovereign who is usu. an emperor; *also* : something resembling a political empire **2** : imperial sovereignty or dominion

em·pir·i·cal \im-'pir-i-kəl\ also **em·pir·ic** \-ik\ adj : based on observation; *also* : subject to verification by observation or experiment ⟨∼ laws⟩ — **em·pir·i·cal·ly** \-i-k(ə-)lē\ adv

em·pir·i·cism \im-'pir-ə-₁si-zəm, em-\ n : the practice of relying on observation and experiment esp. in the natural sciences — **em·pir·i·cist** \-sist\ n

em·place·ment \im-'plās-mənt\ n **1** : a prepared position for weapons or military equipment **2** : PLACEMENT

¹**em·ploy** \im-'plòi\ vb **1** : to make use of **2** : to use the services of **3** : OCCUPY, DEVOTE — **em·ploy·er** n

²**em·ploy** \im-'plòi; 'im-₁plòi, 'em-\ n : EMPLOYMENT

em·ploy·ee or **em·ploye** \im-₁plòi-'ē, ₁em-; im-'plòi-₁ē, em-\ n : a person who works for another

em·ploy·ment \im-'plòi-mənt\ n **1** : OCCUPATION, ACTIVITY **2** : the act of employing : the condition of being employed

em·po·ri·um \im-'pōr-ē-əm, em-\ n, pl **-ri·ums** also **-ria** \-ē-ə\ [L, fr. Gk *emporion*, fr. *emporos* traveler, trader] : a commercial center; *esp* : a store carrying varied articles

em·pow·er \im-'paù-ər\ vb : to give authority or power to; *also* : ENABLE — **em·pow·er·ment** \-mənt\ n

em·press \'em-prəs\ n **1** : the wife or widow of an emperor **2** : a sovereign female ruler of an empire

¹**emp·ty** \'emp-tē\ adj **emp·ti·er; -est 1** : containing nothing **2** : UNOCCUPIED, UNINHABITED **3** : lacking value, force, sense, or purpose **syn** vacant, blank, void, stark, vacuous — **emp·ti·ness** n

²**empty** vb **emp·tied; emp·ty·ing 1** : to make or become empty **2** : to discharge contents; *also* : to remove from what holds or encloses

³**empty** n, pl **empties** : an empty container or vehicle

emp·ty–hand·ed \₁emp-tē-'han-dəd\ adj **1** : having or bringing nothing **2** : having acquired or gained nothing

em·py·re·an \₁em-₁pī-'rē-ən, -pə-\ n **1** : the highest heaven; *also* : FIRMAMENT **2** : an ideal place or state

EMT \₁ē-(₁)em-'tē\ n [emergency medical technician] : a specially trained medical technician licensed to provide basic medical services before and during transportation to a hospital

¹**emu** \'ē-myü, -mü\ n : a swift-running flightless Australian bird smaller than the related ostrich

²**emu** abbr electromagnetic unit

em·u·late \'em-yü-₁lāt\ vb **-lat·ed; -lat·ing** : to strive to equal or excel : IMITATE — **em·u·la·tion** \₁em-yü-'lā-shən\ n — **em·u·lous** \'em-yü-ləs\ adj

emul·si·fi·er \i-'məl-sə-₁fī-ər\ n : a substance (as a soap) that helps to form and stabilize an emulsion

emul·si·fy \-fī\ vb **-fied; -fy·ing** : to disperse (as an oil) in an emulsion — **emul·si·fi·ca·tion** \i-₁məl-sə-fə-'kā-shən\ n

emul·sion \i-'məl-shən\ n **1** : a mixture of mutually insoluble liquids in which one is dispersed in droplets throughout the other ⟨an ∼ of oil in water⟩ **2** : a light-sensitive coating on photographic film or paper

en \'en\ n : a length approximately half the width of the letter M

¹**-en** also **-n** adj suffix : made of : consisting of ⟨earthen⟩

²**-en** vb suffix **1** : become or cause to be ⟨sharpen⟩ **2** : cause or come to have ⟨lengthen⟩

en·able \i-'nā-bəl\ vb **en·abled; en·abling 1** : to make able or feasible **2** : to give legal power, capacity, or sanction to

en·act \i-'nakt\ vb **1** : to make into law **2** : to act out — **en·act·ment** n

enam·el \i-'na-məl\ n **1** : a glasslike substance used to coat the surface of metal or pottery **2** : the hard outer layer of a tooth **3** : a usu. glossy paint that forms a hard coat — **enamel** vb

enam·el·ware \-₁war\ n : metal utensils coated with enamel

en·am·or \i-'na-mər\ vb : to inflame with love

en·am·our chiefly Brit var of ENAMOR

en bloc \än-'bläk\ adv or adj : as a whole : in a mass

enc or **encl** abbr enclosure

en·camp \in-'kamp\ vb : to make camp — **en·camp·ment** n

en·cap·su·late \in-'kap-sə-₁lāt\ vb **-lat·ed; -lat·ing 1** : to encase or become encased in a capsule **2** : SUMMARIZE — **en·cap·su·la·tion** \-₁kap-sə-'lā-shən\ n

en·case \in-'kās\ vb : to enclose in or as if in a case

-ence n suffix **1** : action or process ⟨emergence⟩ : instance of an action or process ⟨reference⟩ **2** : quality or state ⟨dependence⟩

en·ceinte \än-'sant\ adj : PREGNANT

en·ceph·a·li·tis \in-₁se-fə-'lī-təs\ n, pl **-lit·i·des** \-'li-tə-₁dēz\ : inflammation of the brain — **en·ceph·a·lit·ic** \-'li-tik\ adj

en·chain \in-'chān\ vb : FETTER, CHAIN

en·chant \in-'chant\ vb **1** : BEWITCH **2** : ENRAPTURE, FASCINATE — **en·chant·er** n — **en·chant·ing·ly** adv — **en·chant·ment** n — **en·chant·ress** \-'chan-trəs\ n

en·chi·la·da \₁en-chə-'lä-də\ n : a rolled filled tortilla covered with chili sauce and usu. baked

en·ci·pher \in-'sī-fər, en-\ vb : ENCODE

en·cir·cle \in-'sər-kəl\ vb **1** : to pass completely around : SURROUND — **en·cir·cle·ment** n

en·clave \'en-₁klāv; 'än-₁klāv\ n : a distinct territorial, cultural, or social unit enclosed within or as if within foreign territory

en·close \in-'klōz\ vb **1** : to shut up or in; *esp* : to surround with a fence **2** : to include along with something else in a parcel or envelope ⟨∼ a check⟩ — **en·clo·sure** \-'klō-zhər\ n

en·code \in-'kōd, en-\ vb : to convert (a message) into code

en·co·mi·um \en-'kō-mē-əm\ n, pl **-mi·ums** or **-mia** \-mē-ə\ : high or glowing praise

en•com•pass \in-'kəm-pəs\ vb **1** : ENCIRCLE **2** : ENVEL-
OP, INCLUDE

 ¹en•core \'än-ıkōr\ n : a demand for repetition or reappearance; *also* : a further
performance (as of a singer) in response
to such a demand

²encore vb **en•cored; en•cor•ing** : to request an encore
from

¹en•coun•ter \in-'kaùn-tər\ vb **1** : to meet as an enemy
: FIGHT **2** : to meet usu. unexpectedly

²encounter n **1** : a hostile meeting; *esp* : COMBAT **2** : a
chance meeting

en•cour•age \in-'kər-ij\ vb **-aged; -ag•ing 1** : to inspire
with courage and hope **2** : STIMULATE, INCITE **3** : FOS-
TER — **en•cour•age•ment** n — **en•cour•ag•ing•ly** adv

en•croach \in-'krōch\ vb [ME *encrochen* to seize, fr.
MF *encrochier*, fr. OF, fr. *croche* hook] : to enter
gradually or stealthily upon another's property or
rights — **en•croach•ment** n

en•crust \in-'krəst\ vb : to provide with or form a crust

en•crus•ta•tion \(ı)in-ıkrəs-'tā-shən, ıen-\ var of IN-
CRUSTATION

en•cum•ber \in-'kəm-bər\ vb **1** : to weigh down : BUR-
DEN **2** : to hinder the function or activity of — **en•
cum•brance** \-brəns\ n

ency or **encyc** abbr encyclopedia

-en•cy n suffix : quality or state (despond*ency*)

¹en•cyc•li•cal \in-'si-kli-kəl, en-\ adj : addressed to all
the individuals of a group

²encyclical n : an encyclical letter; *esp* : a papal letter
to the bishops of the church

en•cy•clo•pe•dia also **en•cy•clo•pae•dia** \in-ısī-klə-'pē-
dē-ə\ n [ML *encyclopaedia* course of general education, fr. Gk *enkyklios paideia* general education] : a
work treating the various branches of learning — **en•
cy•clo•pe•dic** \-'pē-dik\ adj

en•cyst \in-'sist, en-\ vb : to form or become enclosed
in a cyst — **en•cyst•ment** n

¹end \'end\ n **1** : the part of an area that lies at the
boundary; *also* : a point which marks the extent or
limit of something or at which something ceases to
exist **2** : a ceasing of a course (as of action or activity); *also* : DEATH **3** : the ultimate state; *also* : RESULT,
ISSUE **4** : REMNANT **5** : PURPOSE, OBJECTIVE **6** : a player stationed at the extremity of a line (as in football)
7 : a share, operation, or aspect of an undertaking

²end vb **1** : to bring or come to an end **2** : DESTROY; *also*
: DIE **3** : to form or be at the end of **syn** close, conclude, terminate, finish, complete

en•dan•ger \in-'dān-jər\ vb : to bring into danger; *also*
: to create danger

en•dan•gered adj : being or relating to an endangered
species

endangered species n : a species threatened with extinction

en•dear \in-'dir\ vb : to cause to become beloved or
admired

en•dear•ment \-mənt\ n : a sign of affection : CARESS

en•deav•or \in-'de-vər\ vb : TRY, ATTEMPT — **endeav-
or** n

en•deav•our chiefly Brit var of ENDEAVOR

en•dem•ic \en-'de-mik, in-\ adj : restricted to a particular place (∼ plants) (an ∼ disease) — **endemic** n

end•ing \'en-diŋ\ n : something that forms an end; *esp*
: SUFFIX

en•dive \'en-ıdīv\ n **1** : an herb related to chicory and
grown as a salad plant **2** : the blanched shoot of chicory

end•less \'end-ləs\ adj **1** : having or seeming to have no
end : ETERNAL **2** : united at the ends : CONTINUOUS
(an ∼ belt) **syn** interminable, everlasting, unceasing,
ceaseless, unending — **end•less•ly** adv

end•most \-ımōst\ adj : situated at the very end

end•note \-ınōt\ n : a note placed at the end of a text

en•do•crine \'en-də-krən, -ıkrīn, -ıkrēn\ adj : producing secretions that are distributed by way of the
bloodstream (∼ glands) — **endocrine** n — **en•do•
cri•nol•o•gist** \-kri-'nä-lə-jist\ n — **en•do•cri•nol•o•
gy** \-jē\ n

en•dog•e•nous \en-'dä-jə-nəs\ adj : caused or produced
by factors inside the organism or system (∼ psychic
depression) — **en•dog•e•nous•ly** adv

en•dorse \in-'dòrs\ vb **en•dorsed; en•dors•ing 1** : to
sign one's name on the back of (as a check) **2** : AP-
PROVE, SANCTION — **en•dorse•ment** n

en•do•scope \'en-də-ıskōp\ n : an instrument with
which the interior of a hollow organ (as the rectum)
may be visualized — **en•do•scop•ic** \ıen-də-'skä-pik\
adj — **en•dos•co•py** \en-'däs-kə-pē\ n

en•do•ther•mic \ıen-də-'thər-mik\ adj : characterized
by or formed with absorption of heat

en•dow \in-'daù\ vb **1** : to furnish with funds for support (∼ a school) **2** : to furnish with something freely
or naturally — **en•dow•ment** n

en•due \in-'dü, -'dyü\ vb **en•dued; en•du•ing** : PRO-
VIDE, ENDOW

en•dur•ance \in-'dùr-əns, -'dyùr-\ n **1** : DURATION **2**
: the ability to withstand hardship or stress : FORTI-
TUDE

en•dure \in-'dùr, -'dyùr\ vb **en•dured; en•dur•ing 1**
: LAST, PERSIST **2** : to suffer firmly or patiently : BEAR
3 : TOLERATE — **en•dur•able** adj

end•ways \'end-ıwāz\ adv or adj **1** : LENGTHWISE **2**
: with the end forward **3** : on end

end•wise \-ıwīz\ adv or adj : ENDWAYS

ENE abbr east-northeast

en•e•ma \'e-nə-mə\ n, pl **enemas** also **ene•ma•ta** \ıe-nə-
'mä-tə, 'e-nə-mə-tə\ : injection of liquid into the rectum; *also* : material so injected

en•e•my \'e-nə-mē\ n, pl **-mies** : one that attacks or
tries to harm another : FOE; *esp* : a military opponent

en•er•get•ic \ıe-nər-'je-tik\ adj : marked by energy
: ACTIVE, VIGOROUS **syn** strenuous, lusty, dynamic,
vital — **en•er•get•i•cal•ly** \-ti-k(ə-)lē\ adv

en•er•gise Brit var of ENERGIZE

en•er•gize \'e-nər-ıjīz\ vb **-gized; -giz•ing** : to give energy to

en•er•gy \'e-nər-jē\ n, pl **-gies 1** : vigorous action : EF-

FORT **2** : capacity for action **3** : capacity for performing work **4** : usable power (as heat or electricity); *also* : the resources for producing such power

energy level *n* : one of the stable states of constant energy that may be assumed by a physical system (as the electrons in an atom)

en·er·vate \'e-nər-ˌvāt\ *vb* **-vat·ed; -vat·ing** : to lessen the strength or vigor of : weaken in mind or body — **en·er·va·tion** \ˌe-nər-'vā-shən\ *n*

en·fee·ble \in-'fē-bəl\ *vb* **-bled; -bling** : to make feeble **syn** weaken, debilitate, sap, undermine, cripple — **en·fee·ble·ment** *n*

en·fi·lade \'en-fə-ˌlād, -ˌläd\ *n* : gunfire directed along the length of an enemy battle line — **enfilade** *vb*

en·fold \in-'fōld\ *vb* **1** : ENVELOP **2** : EMBRACE

en·force \in-'fōrs\ *vb* **1** : COMPEL ⟨∼ obedience by threats⟩ **2** : to execute effectively ⟨∼ the law⟩ — **en·force·able** *adj* — **en·force·ment** *n*

en·forc·er \in-'fōr-sər\ *n* : one that enforces; *esp* : an aggressive player (as in ice hockey) known for rough play

en·fran·chise \in-'fran-ˌchīz\ *vb* **-chised; -chis·ing 1** : to set free (as from slavery) **2** : to admit to citizenship; *also* : to grant the vote to — **en·fran·chise·ment** \-ˌchīz-mənt, -chəz-\ *n*

eng *abbr* engine; engineer; engineering

Eng *abbr* England; English

en·gage \in-'gāj\ *vb* **en·gaged; en·gag·ing 1** : PLEDGE; *esp* : to bind by a pledge to marry **2** : EMPLOY, HIRE **3** : to attract and hold esp. by interesting; *also* : to cause to participate **4** : to commence or take part in a venture **5** : to bring or enter into conflict **6** : to connect or interlock with : MESH; *also* : to cause to mesh

en·gage·ment \in-'gāj-mənt\ *n* **1** : APPOINTMENT **2** : EMPLOYMENT **3** : a mutual promise to marry **4** : a hostile encounter

en·gag·ing *adj* : ATTRACTIVE — **en·gag·ing·ly** *adv*

en·gen·der \in-'jen-dər\ *vb* **1** : BEGET **2** : BRING ABOUT, CREATE **syn** generate, breed, occasion, produce

en·gine \'en-jən\ *n* [ME *engin*, fr. OF, fr. L *ingenium* natural disposition, talent] **1** : a mechanical device **2** : a machine for converting energy into mechanical motion **3** : LOCOMOTIVE

¹en·gi·neer \ˌen-jə-'nir\ *n* **1** : a member of a military unit specializing in engineering work **2** : a designer or builder of engines **3** : one trained in engineering **4** : one that operates an engine

²engineer *vb* **1** : to lay out or manage as an engineer **2** : to guide the course of **syn** pilot, lead, steer

en·gi·neer·ing *n* : the practical applications of scientific and mathematical principles

En·glish \'iŋ-glish\ *n* **1** : the language of England, the U.S., and many areas now or formerly under British rule **2 English** *pl* : the people of England **3** : spin imparted to a ball that is driven or rolled — **English** *adj* — **En·glish·man** \-mən\ *n* — **En·glish·wom·an** \-ˌwu̇-mən\ *n*

English horn *n* : a woodwind instrument longer than and having a range lower than the oboe

English setter *n* : any of a breed of bird dogs with a flat silky coat of white or white with color

English sparrow *n* : HOUSE SPARROW

English system *n* : a system of weights and measures in which the foot is the principal unit of length and the pound is the principal unit of weight

engr *abbr* **1** engineer **2** engraved

en·gram \'en-ˌgram\ *n* : a hypothetical change in neural tissue postulated in order to account for persistence of memory

en·grave \in-'grāv\ *vb* **en·graved; en·grav·ing 1** : to produce (as letters or lines) by incising a surface **2** : to cut figures, letters, or designs on for printing; *also* : to print from an engraved plate **3** : PHOTOENGRAVE — **en·grav·er** *n*

en·grav·ing \in-'grā-viŋ\ *n* **1** : the art of one who engraves **2** : an engraved plate; *also* : a print made from it

en·gross \in-'grōs\ *vb* : to take up the whole interest or attention of **syn** monopolize, absorb, consume

en·gulf \in-'gəlf\ *vb* : to flow over and enclose

en·hance \in-'hans\ *vb* **en·hanced; en·hanc·ing** : to increase or improve (as in value or desirability) **syn** heighten, intensify, magnify — **en·hance·ment** *n*

enig·ma \i-'nig-mə\ *n* [L *aenigma*, fr. Gk *ainigma*, fr. *ainissesthai* to speak in riddles, fr. *ainos* fable] : something obscure or hard to understand

enig·mat·ic \ˌen-ig-'ma-tik\ *adj* : resembling an enigma **syn** obscure, cryptic, mystifying — **en·ig·mat·i·cal·ly** \-ti-k(ə-)lē\ *adv*

en·join \in-'jȯin\ *vb* **1** : COMMAND, ORDER **2** : FORBID **syn** direct, bid, charge, command, instruct

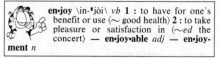

en·joy \in-'jȯi\ *vb* **1** : to have for one's benefit or use ⟨∼ good health⟩ **2** : to take pleasure or satisfaction in ⟨∼ed the concert⟩ — **en·joy·able** *adj* — **en·joy·ment** *n*

enl *abbr* **1** enlarged **2** enlisted

en·large \in-'lärj\ *vb* **en·larged; en·larg·ing 1** : to make or grow larger **2** : ELABORATE **syn** increase, augment, multiply, expand — **en·large·ment** *n*

en·light·en \in-'līt-ᵊn\ *vb* **1** : INSTRUCT, INFORM **2** : to give spiritual insight to — **en·light·en·ment** *n*

en·list \in-'list\ *vb* **1** : to secure the aid or support of **2** : to engage for service in the armed forces — **en·list·ee** \-ˌlis-'tē\ *n* — **en·list·ment** \-'list-mənt\ *n*

en·list·ed \in-'lis-təd\ *adj* : of, relating to, or forming the part of a military force below commissioned or warrant officers

enlisted man *n* : a man or woman in the armed forces ranking below a commissioned or warrant officer

en·liv·en \in-'lī-vən\ *vb* : to give life, action, or spirit to : ANIMATE

en masse \äⁿ-'mas\ *adv* [F] : in a body : as a whole

en·mesh \in-'mesh\ *vb* : to catch or entangle in or as if in meshes

en·mi·ty \'en-mə-tē\ *n*, *pl* **-ties** : ILL WILL; *esp* : mutual hatred **syn** hostility, antipathy, animosity, rancor, antagonism

en·no·ble \i-ˈnō-bəl\ vb **-bled; -bling** : EXALT, ELEVATE; esp : to raise to noble rank — **en·no·ble·ment** n

en·nui \ˌän-ˈwē\ n [F] : BOREDOM

enor·mi·ty \i-ˈnȯr-mə-tē\ n, pl **-ties 1** : an outrageous, vicious, or immoral act **2** : great wickedness **3** : IMMENSITY

enor·mous \i-ˈnȯr-məs\ adj [L enormis, fr. e, ex out of + norma rule] **1** : exceedingly wicked **2** : great in size, number, or degree : HUGE **syn** immense, vast, gigantic, colossal, mammoth, elephantine

¹enough \i-ˈnəf\ adj : SUFFICIENT

²enough adv **1** : SUFFICIENTLY **2** : FULLY, QUITE **3** : TOLERABLY

³enough pron : a sufficient number, quantity, or amount

en·quire \in-ˈkwīr\, **en·qui·ry** \ˈin-ˌkwīr-ē, in-ˈkwīr-; ˈin-kwə-rē, ˈiŋ-\ var of INQUIRE, INQUIRY

en·rage \in-ˈrāj\ vb : to fill with rage

en·rap·ture \in-ˈrap-chər\ vb **en·rap·tured; en·rap·tur·ing** : DELIGHT

en·rich \in-ˈrich\ vb **1** : to make rich or richer **2** : ORNAMENT, ADORN — **en·rich·ment** n

en·roll or **en·rol** \in-ˈrōl\ vb **en·rolled; en·roll·ing 1** : to enter or register on a roll or list **2** : to offer (oneself) for enrolling — **en·roll·ment** n

en route \än-ˈrüt, en-\ adv or adj : on or along the way

ENS abbr ensign

en·sconce \in-ˈskäns\ vb **en·sconced; en·sconc·ing 1** : SHELTER, CONCEAL **2** : to settle snugly or securely **syn** secrete, hide, cache, stash

en·sem·ble \än-ˈsäm-bəl\ n [F, fr. ensemble together, fr. L insimul at the same time] : a group (as of singers, dancers, or players) or a set (as of clothes) producing a single effect

en·sheathe \in-ˈshēth\ vb : to cover with or as if with a sheath

en·shrine \in-ˈshrīn\ vb **1** : to enclose in or as if in a shrine **2** : to cherish as sacred

en·shroud \in-ˈshraúd\ vb : SHROUD, OBSCURE

en·sign \ˈen-sən, 1 also ˈen-ˌsīn\ n **1** : FLAG; also : BADGE, EMBLEM **2** : a commissioned officer in the navy ranking next below a lieutenant junior grade

en·slave \in-ˈslāv\ vb : to make a slave of — **en·slave·ment** n

en·snare \in-ˈsnar\ vb : SNARE, TRAP **syn** entrap, bag, catch, capture

en·sue \in-ˈsü\ vb **en·sued; en·su·ing** : to follow in time or as a result

en·sure \in-ˈshúr\ vb **en·sured; en·sur·ing** : INSURE, GUARANTEE

en·tail \in-ˈtāl\ vb **1** : to limit the inheritance of (property) to the owner's lineal descendants or to a class thereof **2** : to include or involve as a necessary step or result — **en·tail·ment** n

en·tan·gle \in-ˈtaŋ-gəl\ vb : TANGLE, CONFUSE — **en·tan·gle·ment** n

en·tente \än-ˈtänt\ n [F understanding, agreement] : an understanding providing for joint action; also : parties linked by such an entente

en·ter \ˈen-tər\ vb **1** : to go or come in or into **2** : to become a member of : JOIN ⟨∼ the ministry⟩ **3** : BEGIN **4** : to take part in : CONTRIBUTE **5** : to go into or upon and take possession **6** : to set down (as in a list) : REGISTER **7** : to place (a complaint) before a court; also : to put on record ⟨∼ a complaint⟩

en·ter·i·tis \ˌen-tə-ˈrī-təs\ n : intestinal inflammation; also : a disease marked by this

en·ter·prise \ˈen-tər-ˌprīz\ n **1** : UNDERTAKING, PROJECT **2** : readiness for daring action : INITIATIVE **3** : a business organization

en·ter·pris·ing \-ˌprī-ziŋ\ adj : bold and vigorous in action : ENERGETIC

en·ter·tain \ˌen-tər-ˈtān\ vb **1** : to treat or receive as a

guest **2** : AMUSE, DIVERT **3** : to hold in mind **syn** harbor, shelter, lodge, house, billet — **en·ter·tain·er** n — **en·ter·tain·ment** n

en·thrall or **en·thral** \in-ˈthról\ vb **en·thralled; en·thrall·ing 1** : ENSLAVE **2** : to hold spellbound

en·throne \in-ˈthrōn\ vb **1** : to seat on or as if on a throne **2** : EXALT

en·thuse \in-ˈthüz, -ˈthyüz\ vb **en·thused; en·thus·ing 1** : to make enthusiastic **2** : to show enthusiasm

en·thu·si·asm \in-ˈthü-zē-ˌa-zəm, -ˈthyü-\ n [Gk enthousiasmos, fr. enthousiazein to be inspired, irreg. fr. entheos inspired, fr. theos god] **1** : strong warmth of feeling : keen interest : FERVOR **2** : a cause of fervor — **en·thu·si·ast** \-ˌast, -əst\ n — **en·thu·si·as·tic** \in-ˌthü-zē-ˈas-tik, -ˌthyü-\ adj — **en·thu·si·as·ti·cal·ly** \-ti-k(ə-)lē\ adv

en·tice \in-ˈtīs\ vb **en·ticed; en·tic·ing** : ALLURE, TEMPT — **en·tice·ment** n

en·tire \in-ˈtīr\ adj : COMPLETE, WHOLE **syn** sound, perfect, intact, undamaged — **en·tire·ly** adv

en·tire·ty \in-ˈtī-rə-tē, -ˈtīr-tē\ n, pl **-ties 1** : COMPLETENESS **2** : WHOLE, TOTALITY

en·ti·tle \in-ˈtīt-ᵊl\ vb **en·ti·tled; en·ti·tling 1** : NAME, DESIGNATE **2** : to give a right or claim to

en·ti·tle·ment \in-ˈtīt-ᵊl-mənt\ n : a government program providing benefits to members of a specified group

en·ti·ty \ˈen-tə-tē\ n, pl **-ties 1** : EXISTENCE, BEING **2** : something with separate and real existence

en·tomb \in-ˈtüm\ vb : to place in a tomb : BURY — **en·tomb·ment** n

en·to·mol·o·gy \ˌen-tə-ˈmä-lə-jē\ n : a branch of zoology that deals with insects — **en·to·mo·log·i·cal** \-mə-ˈlä-ji-kəl\ adj — **en·to·mol·o·gist** \-jist\ n

en·tou·rage \ˌän-tù-ˈräzh\ n [F] : RETINUE

en·tr'acte \ˈän-ˌtrakt\ n [F] **1** : something (as a dance) performed between two acts of a play **2** : the interval between two acts of a play

en·trails \ˈen-trālz\ n pl : VISCERA; esp : INTESTINES

¹en·trance \ˈen-trəns\ n **1** : permission or right to enter **2** : the act of entering **3** : a means or place of entry

²en·trance \in-ˈtrans\ vb **en·tranced; en·tranc·ing** : CHARM, DELIGHT

en·trant \ˈen-trənt\ n : one that enters esp. as a competitor

en·trap \in-ˈtrap\ vb : ENSNARE, TRAP — **en·trap·ment** n

en·treat \in-ˈtrēt\ vb **1** : to ask urgently : BESEECH **syn** beg, implore, plead, supplicate — **en·treaty** \-ˈtrē-tē\ n

en·trée or **en·tree** \ˈän-ˌtrā\ n [F entrée] **1** : freedom of entry or access **2** : the main course of a meal in the U.S. **syn** admission, admittance, entrance

en·trench \in-ˈtrench\ vb **1** : to place within or surround with a trench esp. for defense; also : to establish solidly ⟨∼ed customs⟩ **2** : ENCROACH, TRESPASS — **en·trench·ment** n

en·tre·pre·neur \ˌän-trə-prə-ˈnər, -ˈnùr, -ˈnyúr\ n [F, fr. OF, fr. entreprendre to undertake] : one who organizes and assumes the risk of a business or enterprise — **en·tre·pre·neur·ial** \-ˈnùr-ē-əl, -ˈnyúr-, -ˈnər-\ adj

en·tro·py \ˈen-trə-pē\ n, pl **-pies 1** : the degree of disorder in a system **2** : an ultimate state of inert uniformity

en·trust \in-ˈtrəst\ vb **1** : to commit something to as a trust **2** : to commit to another with confidence **syn** confide, consign, relegate, commend

en·try \ˈen-trē\ n, pl **entries 1** : ENTRANCE 2, 3; also : VESTIBULE **2** 2 : an entering in a record; also : an item so entered **3** : a headword with its definition or identification; also : VOCABULARY ENTRY **4** : one entered in a contest

en·twine \in-ˈtwīn\ vb : to twine together or around

enu·mer·ate \i-ˈnü-mə-ˌrāt, -ˈnyü-\ vb **-at·ed; -at·ing 1**

: to determine the number of : COUNT **2** : LIST — **enu-mer·a·tion** \-₁nü-mə-'rä-shən, -₁nyü-\ *n*

enun·ci·ate \ē-'nən-sē-₁āt\ *vb* **-at·ed; -at·ing 1** : to state definitely; *also* : ANNOUNCE, PROCLAIM **2** : PRONOUNCE, ARTICULATE — **enun·ci·a·tion** \-₁nən-sē-'ā-shən\ *n*

en·ure·sis \₁en-yū-'rē-səs\ *n* : involuntary discharge of urine : BED-WETTING

env *abbr* envelope

en·vel·op \in-'ve-ləp\ *vb* : to enclose completely with or as if with a covering — **en·vel·op·ment** *n*

en·ve·lope \'en-və-₁lōp, 'än-\ *n* **1** : a usu. paper container for a letter **2** : WRAPPER, COVERING

en·ven·om \in-'ve-nəm\ *vb* **1** : to make poisonous **2** : EMBITTER

en·vi·able \'en-vē-ə-bəl\ *adj* : highly desirable — **en·vi·ably** \-blē\ *adv*

en·vi·ous \'en-vē-əs\ *adj* : feeling or showing envy — **en·vi·ous·ly** *adv* — **en·vi·ous·ness** *n*

en·vi·ron·ment \in-'vī-rən-mənt, -'vīrn-\ *n* **1** : SURROUNDINGS **2** : the whole complex of factors (as soil, climate, and living things) that influence the form and the ability to survive of a plant or animal or ecological community — **en·vi·ron·men·tal** \-₁vī-rən-'ment-ᵊl, -₁vīrn-\ *adj*

en·vi·ron·men·tal·ist \-₁vī-rən-'ment-ᵊl-ist, -₁vīrn-\ *n* : a person concerned about environmental quality esp. with respect to control of pollution

en·vi·rons \in-'vī-rənz\ *n pl* **1** : SUBURBS **2** : SURROUNDINGS; *also* : VICINITY

en·vis·age \in-'vi-zij\ *vb* **-aged; -ag·ing** : to have a mental picture of

en·vi·sion \in-'vi-zhən, en-\ *vb* : to picture to oneself ⟨~s world peace⟩

en·voy \'en-₁vȯi, 'än-\ *n* **1** : a diplomatic agent **2** : REPRESENTATIVE, MESSENGER

¹en·vy \'en-vē\ *n, pl* **envies** [ME *envie,* fr. OF, fr. L *invidia,* fr. *invidus* envious, fr. *invidēre* to look askance at, envy, fr. *vidēre* to see] : painful or resentful awareness of another's advantages; *also* : an object of envy

²envy *vb* **en·vied; en·vy·ing** : to feel envy toward or on account of

en·zyme \'en-₁zīm\ *n* : any of various complex proteins produced by living cells that catalyze specific biochemical reactions at body temperatures — **en·zy·mat·ic** \₁en-zə-'ma-tik\ *adj*

Eo·cene \'ē-ə-₁sēn\ *adj* : of, relating to, or being the epoch of the Tertiary between the Paleocene and the Oligocene — **Eocene** *n*

EOE *abbr* equal opportunity employer

eo·lian \ē-'ō-lē-ən\ *adj* : borne, deposited, or produced by the wind

EOM *abbr* end of month

eon \'ē-ən, 'ē-₁än\ *var of* AEON

EP *abbr* European plan

EPA *abbr* Environmental Protection Agency

ep·au·let *also* **ep·au·lette** \₁e-pə-'let\ *n* [F *épaulette,* dim. of *épaule* shoulder] : a shoulder ornament esp. on a coat or military uniform

épée \'e-₁pā, ā-'pā\ *n* [F] : a fencing or dueling sword

épée

Eph *or* **Ephes** *abbr* Ephesians

ephed·rine \i-'fe-drən\ *n* : a drug used in relieving hay fever, asthma, and nasal congestion

ephem·era \i-'fe-mər-ə\ *n pl* : collectibles (as posters or tickets) not intended to have lasting value

ephem·er·al \i-'fe-mə-rəl\ *adj* [Gk *ephēmeros* lasting a day, daily, fr. *epi-*on *hēmera* day] : SHORT-LIVED, TRANSITORY **syn** passing, fleeting, transient, evanescent

Ephe·sians \i-'fē-zhənz\ *n* — see BIBLE table

ep·ic \'e-pik\ *n* : a long poem in elevated style narrating the deeds of a hero — **epic** *adj*

epi·cen·ter \'e-pi-₁sen-tər\ *n* : the point on the earth's surface directly above the point of origin of an earthquake

epi·cure \'e-pi-₁kyu̇r\ *n* : a person with sensitive and discriminating tastes esp. in food and wine

epi·cu·re·an \₁e-pi-kyu̇-'rē-ən, -'kyu̇r-ē-\ *n* : EPICURE — **epicurean** *adj*

¹ep·i·dem·ic \₁e-pə-'de-mik\ *adj* : affecting many persons at one time ⟨~ disease⟩; *also* : excessively prevalent

²epidemic *n* : an epidemic outbreak esp. of disease

epi·der·mis \₁e-pə-'dər-məs\ *n* : an outer layer esp. of skin — **epi·der·mal** \-məl\ *adj*

epi·glot·tis \₁e-pə-'glä-təs\ *n* : a thin plate of flexible tissue protecting the tracheal opening during swallowing

ep·i·gram \'e-pə-₁gram\ *n* : a short witty poem or saying — **ep·i·gram·mat·ic** \₁e-pə-grə-'ma-tik\ *adj*

ep·i·lep·sy \'e-pə-₁lep-sē\ *n, pl* **-sies** : a disorder typically marked by disturbed electrical rhythms of the central nervous system, by attacks of convulsions, and by loss of consciousness — **ep·i·lep·tic** \₁e-pə-'lep-tik\ *adj or n*

ep·i·logue *also* **ep·i·log** \'e-pə-₁lȯg, -₁läg\ *n* : a speech addressed to the spectators by an actor at the end of a play

epi·neph·rine *also* **epi·neph·rin** \₁e-pə-'ne-frən\ *n* : an adrenal hormone used medicinally esp. as a heart stimulant, a muscle relaxant, and a vasoconstrictor

epiph·a·ny \i-'pi-fə-nē\ *n, pl* **-nies 1** *cap* : January 6 observed as a church festival in commemoration of the coming of the Magi to Jesus at Bethlehem **2** : a sudden striking understanding of something

epis·co·pa·cy \i-'pis-kə-pə-sē\ *n, pl* **-cies 1** : government of a church by bishops **2** : EPISCOPATE

epis·co·pal \i-'pis-kə-pəl\ *adj* **1** : of or relating to a bishop or episcopacy **2** *cap* : of or relating to the Protestant Episcopal Church

Epis·co·pa·lian \i-₁pis-kə-'pāl-yən\ *n* : a member of the Protestant Episcopal Church

epis·co·pate \i-'pis-kə-pət, -₁pāt\ *n* **1** : the rank, office, or term of a bishop **2** : a body of bishops

ep·i·sode \'e-pə-₁sōd\ *n* [Gk *epeisodion,* fr. *epeisodios* coming in besides, fr. *eisodios* coming in, fr. *eis* into + *hodos* road, journey] **1** : a unit of action in a dramatic or literary work **2** : an incident in a course of events : OCCURRENCE ⟨a feverish ~⟩ — **ep·i·sod·ic** \₁e-pə-'sä-dik\ *adj*

epis·tle \i-'pi-səl\ *n* **1** *cap* : one of the letters of the New Testament **2** : LETTER — **epis·to·lary** \i-'pis-tə-₁ler-ē\ *adj*

ep·i·taph \'e-pə-₁taf\ *n* : an inscription in memory of a dead person

ep·i·tha·la·mi·um \₁e-pə-thə-'lā-mē-əm\ *or* **ep·i·tha·la·mi·on** \-mē-ən\ *n, pl* **-mi·ums** *or* **-mia** \-mē-ə\ : a song or poem in honor of a bride and bridegroom

ep·i·the·li·um \₁e-pə-'thē-lē-əm\ *n, pl* **-lia** \-lē-ə\ : a cellular membrane covering a bodily surface or lining a cavity — **ep·i·the·li·al** \-lē-əl\ *adj*

ep·i·thet \'e-pə-₁thet, -thət\ *n* : a characterizing and often abusive word or phrase

epit·o·me \i-'pi-tə-mē\ *n* **1** : ABSTRACT, SUMMARY **2** : EMBODIMENT — **epit·o·mize** \-₁mīz\ *vb*

ep·och \'e-pək, -₁päk\ *n* : a usu. extended period : ERA, AGE — **ep·och·al** \-pə-kəl, -₁pä-\ *adj*

ep·oxy \i-'päk-sē\ *vb* **ep·ox·ied** *or* **ep·oxyed; ep·oxy·ing** : to glue with epoxy resin

epoxy resin *n* : a synthetic resin used in coatings and adhesives

ep·si·lon \'ep-sə-₁län, -lən\ *n* : the 5th letter of the Greek alphabet — E or ε

Ep·som salts \'ep-səm-\ *n* : a bitter colorless or white magnesium salt with cathartic properties

eq *abbr* **1** equal **2** equation

equa·ble \ˈe-kwə-bəl, ˈē-\ *adj* : UNIFORM, EVEN; *esp* : free from unpleasant extremes — **eq·ua·bil·i·ty** \ˌe-kwə-ˈbi-lə-tē, ˌē-\ *n* — **eq·ua·bly** \ˈe-kwə-blē, ˈē-\ *adv*

¹**equal** \ˈē-kwəl\ *adj* **1** : of the same measure, quantity, value, quality, number, degree, or status as another **2** : IMPARTIAL **3** : free from extremes **4** : able to cope with a situation or task — **equal·i·ty** \i-ˈkwä-lə-tē\ *n* — **equal·ly** *adv*

²**equal** *vb* **equaled** *or* **equalled; equal·ing** *or* **equal·ling** : to be or become equal to; *also* : to be identical in value to

³**equal** *n* : one that is equal

equal·ise *Brit var of* EQUALIZE

equal·ize \ˈē-kwə-ˌlīz\ *vb* **-ized; -iz·ing** : to make equal, uniform, or constant — **equal·i·za·tion** \ˌē-kwə-lə-ˈzā-shən\ *n* — **equal·iz·er** *n*

equals sign *or* **equal sign** *n* : a sign = indicating equivalence

equa·nim·i·ty \ˌē-kwə-ˈni-mə-tē, ˌe-\ *n, pl* **-ties** : COMPOSURE

equate \i-ˈkwāt\ *vb* **equat·ed; equat·ing** : to make, treat, or regard as equal or comparable

equa·tion \i-ˈkwā-zhən\ *n* **1** : an act of equating : the state of being equated **2** : a usu. formal statement of equivalence esp. of mathematical expressions

equa·tor \i-ˈkwā-tər, ˈē-\ *n* : an imaginary circle around the earth that is everywhere equally distant from the two poles — **equa·to·ri·al** \ˌē-kwə-ˈtōr-ē-əl, ˌe-\ *adj*

equer·ry \ˈe-kwə-rē, i-ˈkwer-ē\ *n, pl* **-ries 1** : an officer in charge of the horses of a prince or noble **2** : a personal attendant of a member of the British royal family

¹**eques·tri·an** \i-ˈkwes-trē-ən\ *adj* : of or relating to horseback riding; *also* : representing a person on horseback ⟨an ~ statue⟩

²**equestrian** *n* : one who rides a horse

eques·tri·enne \i-ˌkwes-trē-ˈen\ *n* : a female rider on horseback

equi·dis·tant \ˌē-kwə-ˈdis-tənt\ *adj* : equally distant

equi·lat·er·al \ˌē-kwə-ˈla-tə-rəl\ *adj* : having all sides or faces equal ⟨~ triangles⟩

equi·lib·ri·um \ˌē-kwə-ˈli-brē-əm, ˌe-\ *n, pl* **-ri·ums** *or* **-ria** \-brē-ə\ : a state of intellectual or emotional balance; *also* : a state of balance between opposing forces or actions **syn** poise, balance, equipoise

equine \ˈē-ˌkwīn, ˈe-\ *adj* [L *equinus*, fr. *equus* horse] : of or relating to the horse — **equine** *n*

equi·noc·tial \ˌē-kwə-ˈnäk-shəl, ˌe-\ *adj* : relating to an equinox

equi·nox \ˈē-kwə-ˌnäks, ˈe-\ *n* : either of the two times each year when the sun appears directly overhead at the equator and day and night are everywhere of equal length

equip \i-ˈkwip\ *vb* **equipped; equip·ping** : to supply with needed resources

eq·ui·page \ˈe-kwə-pij\ *n* : a horse-drawn carriage usu. with its servants

equip·ment \i-ˈkwip-mənt\ *n* **1** : things used in equipping : SUPPLIES, OUTFIT **2** : the equipping of a person or thing : the state of being equipped

equi·poise \ˈe-kwə-ˌpȯiz, ˈē-\ *n* **1** : BALANCE, EQUILIBRIUM **2** : COUNTERBALANCE

eq·ui·ta·ble \ˈe-kwə-tə-bəl\ *adj* : JUST, FAIR — **eq·ui·ta·bly** \-blē\ *adv*

eq·ui·ta·tion \ˌe-kwə-ˈtā-shən\ *n* : the act or art of riding on horseback

eq·ui·ty \ˈe-kwə-tē\ *n, pl* **-ties 1** : JUSTNESS, IMPARTIALITY **2** : value of a property or of an interest in it in excess of claims against it

equiv *abbr* equivalent

equiv·a·lent \i-ˈkwi-və-lənt\ *adj* : EQUAL; *also* : virtually identical — **equiv·a·lence** \-ləns\ *n* — **equiv·a·lent** *n*

equiv·o·cal \i-ˈkwi-və-kəl\ *adj* **1** : AMBIGUOUS **2** : UNCERTAIN, UNDECIDED **3** : SUSPICIOUS, DUBIOUS ⟨~ behavior⟩ **syn** obscure, dark, vague, enigmatic — **equiv·o·cal·ly** *adv*

equiv·o·cate \i-ˈkwi-və-ˌkāt\ *vb* **-cat·ed; -cat·ing 1** : to use misleading language **2** : to avoid giving a definite answer — **equiv·o·ca·tion** \-ˌkwi-və-ˈkā-shən\ *n*

¹**-er** \ər\ *adj suffix or adv suffix* — used to form the comparative degree of adjectives and adverbs of one or two syllables ⟨hott*er*⟩ ⟨dri*er*⟩ ⟨silli*er*⟩ and sometimes of longer ones

²**-er** \ər\ *also* **-ier** \ē-ər, yər\ *or* **-yer** \yər\ *n suffix* **1** : a person occupationally connected with ⟨hatt*er*⟩ ⟨law-y*er*⟩ **2** : a person or thing belonging to or associated with ⟨old-tim*er*⟩ **3** : a native of : resident of ⟨New Zealand*er*⟩ **4** : one that has ⟨double-deck*er*⟩ **5** : one that produces or yields ⟨pork*er*⟩ **6** : one that does or performs ⟨a specified action⟩ ⟨report*er*⟩ **7** : one that is a suitable object of ⟨a specified action⟩ ⟨broil*er*⟩ **8** : one that is ⟨foreign*er*⟩

Er *symbol* erbium

ER *abbr* emergency room

era \ˈir-ə, ˈer-ə, ˈē-rə\ *n* [LL *aera*, fr. L, counters, pl. of *aes* copper, money] **1** : a chronological order or system of notation reckoned from a given date as basis **2** : a period identified by some special feature **3** : any of the four major divisions of geologic time **syn** age, epoch, period, time

ERA *abbr* Equal Rights Amendment

erad·i·cate \i-ˈra-də-ˌkāt\ *vb* **-cat·ed; -cat·ing** [L *eradicatus*, pp. of *eradicare*, fr. *e-* out + *radix* root] : UPROOT, ELIMINATE **syn** exterminate, annihilate, abolish, extinguish — **erad·i·ca·ble** \-di-kə-bəl\ *adj*

erase \i-ˈrās\ *vb* **erased; eras·ing** : to rub or scratch out ⟨as written words⟩; *also* : OBLITERATE **syn** cancel, efface, delete, expunge — **eras·er** *n* — **era·sure** \i-ˈrā-shər\ *n*

er·bi·um \ˈər-bē-əm\ *n* : a rare metallic element found with yttrium — see ELEMENT table

¹**ere** \ˈer\ *prep* : BEFORE

²**ere** *conj* : BEFORE

¹**erect** \i-ˈrekt\ *adj* **1** : not leaning or lying down : UPRIGHT **2** : being in a state of physiological erection

²**erect** *vb* **1** : BUILD **2** : to fix or set in an upright position **3** : SET UP; *also* : ESTABLISH, DEVELOP

erec·tile \i-ˈrekt-əl, -ˈrek-ˌtīl\ *adj* : capable of becoming erect ⟨~ tissue⟩ ⟨~ feathers of a bird⟩

erec·tion \i-ˈrek-shən\ *n* **1** : the turgid state of a previously flaccid bodily part when it becomes dilated with blood **2** : CONSTRUCTION

ere·long \er-ˈlȯŋ\ *adv* : before long

er·e·mite \ˈer-ə-ˌmīt\ *n* : HERMIT

er·go \ˈer-gō, ˈər-\ *adv* [L] : THEREFORE

er·got \ˈər-gət, -ˌgät\ *n* **1** : a disease of rye and other cereals caused by a fungus; *also* : this fungus **2** : a medicinal compound or preparation derived from an ergot fungus

Er·i·tre·an \ˌer-ə-ˈtrē-ən, -ˈtrā-\ *n* : a native or inhabitant of Eritrea — **Eritrean** *adj*

er·mine \ˈər-mən\ *n, pl* **ermines 1** : any of several weasels with winter fur mostly white; *also* : the white fur of an ermine **2** : a rank or office whose official robe is ornamented with ermine

erode \i-ˈrōd\ *vb* **erod·ed; erod·ing** : to diminish or destroy by degrees; *esp* : to gradually eat into or wear away ⟨soil *eroded* by wind and water⟩ — **erod·ible** \-ˈrō-də-bəl\ *adj*

erog·e·nous \i-ˈrä-jə-nəs\ *adj* **1** : sexually sensitive ⟨~ zones⟩ **2** : of, relating to, or arousing sexual feelings

ero·sion \i-ˈrō-zhən\ *n* : the process or state of being eroded — **ero·sion·al** \-ˈrō-zhə-nəl\ *adj* — **ero·sion·al·ly** *adv*

ero·sive \i-ˈrō-siv\ *adj* : tending to erode — **ero·sive·ness** *n*

erot·ic \i-ˈrä-tik\ *adj* : relating to or dealing with sexual

love : AMATORY — **erot·i·cal·ly** \-ti-k(ə-)lē\ *adv* —
erot·i·cism \-tə-₁si-zəm\ *n*
err \'ər, 'er\ *vb* : to be or do wrong
er·rand \'er-ənd\ *n* : a short trip taken to do something; *also* : the object or purpose of such a trip
er·rant \'er-ənt\ *adj* **1** : WANDERING ⟨an ~ knight⟩ **2** : straying outside proper bounds **3** : deviating from an accepted pattern or standard
er·ra·ta \e-'rä-tə\ *n* : a list of corrigenda
er·rat·ic \i-'ra-tik\ *adj* **1** : having no fixed course **2** : INCONSISTENT; *also* : ECCENTRIC — **er·rat·i·cal·ly** \-ti-k(ə-)lē\ *adv*
er·ra·tum \e-'rä-təm\ *n, pl* **-ta** \-tə\ : CORRIGENDUM
er·ro·ne·ous \i-'rō-nē-əs, e-'rō-\ *adj* : INCORRECT — **er·ro·ne·ous·ly** *adv*
er·ror \'er-ər\ *n* **1** : a usu. ignorant or unintentional deviating from accuracy or truth ⟨made an ~ in adding⟩ **2** : a defensive misplay in baseball **3** : the state of one that errs ⟨to be in ~⟩ **4** : a product of mistake ⟨a typographical ~⟩ — **er·ror·less** *adj*
er·satz \'er-₁zäts\ *adj* [G *ersatz*, fr. *Ersatz*, n., substitute] : being usu. an artificial and inferior substitute
erst \'ərst\ *adv, archaic* : ERSTWHILE
¹erst·while \-₁hwil\ *adv* : in the past : FORMERLY
²erstwhile *adj* : FORMER, PREVIOUS
er·u·di·tion \₁er-ə-'di-shən, ₁er-yə-\ *n* : SCHOLARSHIP, LEARNING — **er·u·dite** \'er-ə-₁dīt, 'er-yə-\ *adj*
erupt \i-'rəpt\ *vb* **1** : to burst forth or cause to burst forth : EXPLODE **2** : to break through a surface ⟨teeth ~*ing* through the gum⟩ **3** : to break out with or as if with a skin rash — **erup·tion** \-'rəp-shən\ *n* — **erup·tive** \-tiv\ *adj*
-ery *n suffix* **1** : qualities collectively : character : -NESS ⟨snobb*ery*⟩ **2** : art : practice ⟨cook*ery*⟩ **3** : place of doing, keeping, producing, or selling ⟨the thing specified⟩ ⟨fish*ery*⟩ ⟨bak*ery*⟩ **4** : collection : aggregate ⟨fin*ery*⟩ **5** : state or condition ⟨slav*ery*⟩
ery·sip·e·las \₁er-ə-'si-pə-ləs, ₁ir-\ *n* : an acute bacterial disease marked by fever and severe skin inflammation
er·y·the·ma \₁er-ə-'thē-mə\ *n* : abnormal redness of the skin due to capillary congestion (as in inflammation)
eryth·ro·cyte \i-'ri-thrə-₁sīt\ *n* : RED BLOOD CELL
Es *symbol* einsteinium
¹-es \əz, iz *after* s, z, sh, ch; z *after* v *or a vowel*\ *n pl suffix* — used to form the plural of most nouns that end in *s* ⟨glass*es*⟩, *z* ⟨fuzz*es*⟩, *sh* ⟨bush*es*⟩, *ch* ⟨peach*es*⟩, or a final *y* that changes to *i* ⟨lad*ies*⟩ and of some nouns ending in *f* that changes to *v* ⟨loav*es*⟩
²-es *vb suffix* — used to form the third person singular present of most verbs that end in *s* ⟨bless*es*⟩, *z* ⟨fizz*es*⟩, *sh* ⟨hush*es*⟩, *ch* ⟨catch*es*⟩, or a final *y* that changes to *i* ⟨defi*es*⟩
es·ca·late \'es-kə-₁lāt\ *vb* **-lat·ed; -lat·ing** : to increase in extent, volume, number, intensity, or scope — **es·ca·la·tion** \₁es-kə-'lā-shən\ *n*
es·ca·la·tor \'es-kə-₁lā-tər\ *n* : a moving set of stairs
es·cal·lop \is-'kä-ləp, -'ka-\ *var of* SCALLOP

es·ca·pade \'es-kə-₁pād\ *n* [F, action of escaping] : a mischievous adventure

¹es·cape \is-'kāp\ *vb* **es·caped; es·cap·ing** [ME, fr. OF *escaper*, fr. (assumed) VL *excappare*, fr. L *ex-* out + LL *cappa* head covering, cloak] **1** : to get free or away **2** : to avoid a threatening evil **3** : AVOID 2 ⟨~ injury⟩ **4** : ELUDE ⟨his name ~*s* me⟩ **5** : to be produced or uttered involuntarily by ⟨let a sob ~ him⟩
²escape *n* **1** : flight from or avoidance of something unpleasant **2** : LEAKAGE **3** : a means of escape
³escape *adj* : providing a means or way of escape
es·cap·ee \is-₁kā-'pē, ₁es-(₁)kā-\ *n* : one that has escaped esp. from prison
escape velocity *n* : the minimum velocity needed by a body (as a rocket) to escape from the gravitational field of a celestial body (as the earth)
es·cap·ism \is-'kā-₁pi-zəm\ *n* : diversion of the mind to imaginative activity as an escape from routine — **es·cap·ist** \-pist\ *adj or n*
es·ca·role \'es-kə-₁rōl\ *n* : ENDIVE 1
es·carp·ment \es-'kärp-mənt\ *n* **1** : a steep slope in front of a fortification **2** : a long cliff
es·chew \is-'chü\ *vb* : SHUN, AVOID
¹es·cort \'es-₁kȯrt\ *n* : one (as a person or warship) accompanying another esp. as a protection or courtesy
²es·cort \is-'kȯrt, es-\ *vb* : to accompany as an escort
es·crow \'es-₁krō\ *n* : something (as a deed or a sum of money) delivered by one person to another to be delivered to a third party only upon the fulfillment of a condition; *also* : a fund or deposit serving as an escrow
es·cu·do \is-'kü-dō\ *n, pl* **-dos 1** — see MONEY table **2** : the peso of Guinea-Bissau
es·cutch·eon \is-'kə-chən\ *n* : the usu. shield-shaped surface on which a coat of arms is shown
Esd *abbr* Esdras
Es·dras \'ez-drəs\ *n* — see BIBLE table
ESE *abbr* east-southeast
Es·ki·mo \'es-kə-₁mō\ *n* **1** : a member of a group of peoples of northern Canada, Greenland, Alaska, and eastern Siberia **2** : any of the languages of the Eskimo peoples
Eskimo dog *n* : a sled dog of American origin
ESL *abbr* English as a second language
esoph·a·gus \i-'sä-fə-gəs\ *n, pl* **-gi** \-₁gī, -₁jī\ : a muscular tube that leads from the cavity behind the mouth to the stomach — **esoph·a·geal** \-₁sä-fə-'jē-əl\ *adj*
es·o·ter·ic \₁e-sə-'ter-ik\ *adj* **1** : designed for or understood only by the specially initiated **2** : PRIVATE, SECRET
esp *abbr* especially
ESP \₁ē-(₁)es-'pē\ *n* : EXTRASENSORY PERCEPTION
es·pa·drille \'es-pə-₁dril\ *n* [F] : a flat sandal usu. having a fabric upper and a flexible sole
es·pal·ier \is-'pal-yər, -₁yā\ *n* : a plant (as a fruit tree) trained to grow flat against a support — **espalier** *vb*

es·pe·cial \is-ˈpe-shəl\ *adj* : SPECIAL, PARTICULAR — **es·pe·cial·ly** *adv*

Es·pe·ran·to \ˌes-pə-ˈran-tō, -ˈrän-\ *n* : an artificial international language based esp. on words common to the chief European languages

es·pi·o·nage \ˈes-pē-ə-ˌnäzh, -nij\ *n* [F *espionnage*] : the practice of spying

es·pla·nade \ˈes-plə-ˌnäd\ *n* : a level open stretch or area; *esp* : one for walking or driving along a shore

es·pous·al \i-ˈspau̇-zəl\ *n* **1** : BETROTHAL; *also* : WEDDING **2** : a taking up (as of a cause) as a supporter — **es·pouse** \-ˈspau̇z\ *vb*

espres·so \e-ˈspre-sō\ *n, pl* **-sos** [It (*caffè*) *espresso*, lit., pressed out coffee] : coffee brewed by forcing steam through finely ground darkly roasted coffee beans

es·prit \i-ˈsprē\ *n* : sprightly wit

es·prit de corps \i-ˌsprē-də-ˈkōr\ *n* [F] : the common spirit existing in the members of a group

es·py \i-ˈspī\ *vb* **es·pied; es·py·ing** : to catch sight of **syn** behold, see, view, descry

Esq *or* **Esqr** *abbr* esquire

es·quire \ˈes-ˌkwīr\ *n* [ME, fr. MF *esquier* squire, fr. LL *scutarius*, fr. L *scutum* shield] **1** : a man of the English gentry ranking next below a knight **2** : a candidate for knighthood serving as attendant to a knight **3** — used as a title of courtesy

-ess \əs, ˌes\ *n suffix* : female (author*ess*)

¹es·say \e-ˈsā, ˈe-ˌsā\ *vb* : ATTEMPT, TRY

²es·say *n* \ˈe-ˌsā, e-ˈsā\ **1** : ATTEMPT **2** \ˈe-ˌsā\ : a literary composition usu. dealing with a subject from a limited or personal point of view — **es·say·ist** \ˈe-ˌsā-ist\ *n*

es·sence \ˈes-ᵊns\ *n* **1** : fundamental nature or quality **2** : a substance distilled or extracted from another substance (as a plant or drug) and having the special qualities of the original substance **3** : PERFUME

¹es·sen·tial \i-ˈsen-chəl\ *adj* **1** : of, relating to, or constituting an essence (voting is an ~ right of citizenship) (~ oils) **2** : of the utmost importance : INDISPENSABLE **syn** imperative, necessary, necessitous — **es·sen·tial·ly** *adv*

²essential *n* : something essential

est *abbr* **1** established **2** estimate; estimated

EST *abbr* eastern standard time

¹-est \əst, ist\ *adj suffix or adv suffix* — used to form the superlative degree of adjectives and adverbs of one or two syllables (fatt*est*) (lat*est*) (lucki*est*) (often*est*) and less often of longer ones

²-est \əst, ist\ *or* **-st** \st\ *vb suffix* — used to form the archaic second person singular of English verbs (with *thou*) (did*st*)

es·tab·lish \i-ˈsta-blish\ *vb* **1** : to institute permanently (~ a law) **2** : FOUND (~ a settlement); *also* : EFFECT **3** : to make firm or stable **4** : to put on a firm basis : SET UP (~ a son in business) **5** : to gain acceptance or recognition of (the movie ~ed her as a star); *also* : PROVE

es·tab·lish·ment \-mənt\ *n* **1** : something established **2** : a place of residence or business with its furnishings and staff **3** : an established ruling or controlling group (the literary ~) **4** : the act or state of establishing or being established

es·tate \i-ˈstāt\ *n* **1** : STATE, CONDITION; *also* : social standing : STATUS **2** : a social or political class (the three ~s of nobility, clergy, and commons) **3** : a person's possessions : FORTUNE **4** : a landed property

¹es·teem \i-ˈstēm\ *n* : high regard

²esteem *vb* **1** : REGARD **2** : to set a high value on **syn** respect, admire, revere

es·ter \ˈes-tər\ *n* : an often fragrant organic compound formed by the reaction of an acid and an alcohol

Esth *abbr* Esther

Es·ther \ˈes-tər\ *n* — see BIBLE table

esthete, esthetic, esthetics *var of* AESTHETE, AESTHETIC, AESTHETICS

es·ti·ma·ble \ˈes-tə-mə-bəl\ *adj* : worthy of esteem

¹es·ti·mate \ˈes-tə-ˌmāt\ *vb* **-mat·ed; -mat·ing 1** : to give or form an approximation (as of value, size, or cost) **2** : JUDGE, CONCLUDE **syn** evaluate, value, rate, appraise, assay, assess — **es·ti·ma·tor** \-ˌmā-tər\ *n*

²es·ti·mate \ˈes-tə-mət\ *n* **1** : OPINION, JUDGMENT **2** : a rough or approximate calculation **3** : a statement of the cost of work to be done

es·ti·ma·tion \ˌes-tə-ˈmā-shən\ *n* **1** : JUDGMENT, OPINION **2** : ESTIMATE **3** : ESTEEM, HONOR

es·ti·vate \ˈes-tə-ˌvāt\ *vb* **-vat·ed; -vat·ing** : to pass the summer in an inactive or resting state — **es·ti·va·tion** \ˌes-tə-ˈvā-shən\ *n*

Es·to·nian \e-ˈstō-nē-ən\ *n* : a native or inhabitant of Estonia — **Estonian** *adj*

es·trange \i-ˈstrānj\ *vb* **es·tranged; es·trang·ing** : to alienate the affections or confidence of — **es·trange·ment** *n*

es·tro·gen \ˈes-trə-jən\ *n* : a substance (as a sex hormone) that tends to cause estrus and the development of female secondary sex characteristics — **es·tro·gen·ic** \ˌes-trə-ˈje-nik\ *adj*

estrous cycle *n* : the cycle of changes in the endocrine and reproductive systems of a female mammal from the beginning of one period of estrus to the beginning of the next

es·trus \ˈes-trəs\ *n* : a periodic state of sexual excitability during which the female of most mammals is willing to mate with the male and is capable of becoming pregnant : HEAT — **es·trous** \-trəs\ *adj*

es·tu·ary \ˈes-chù-ˌwer-ē\ *n, pl* **-ar·ies** : an arm of the sea at the mouth of a river

ET *abbr* eastern time

eta \ˈā-tə\ *n* : the 7th letter of the Greek alphabet — H or η

ETA *abbr* estimated time of arrival

et al \et-ˈal\ *abbr* [L *et alii* (masc.), *et aliae* (fem.), or *et alia* (neut.)] and others

etc *abbr* et cetera

et cet·era \et-ˈse-tə-rə, -ˈse-trə\ [L] : and others esp. of the same kind

etch \ˈech\ *vb* [D *etsen*, fr. G *ätzen* to etch, corrode,

HERE, GARFIELD, TRY THIS COFFEE. IT'S ESPRESSO

WHY THE DINKY CUP?

SLURK!

WELL, WHAT DO YOU THINK?

I'LL LET YOU KNOW AS SOON AS MY BACK TEETH STOP WIGGLING

JIM DAVIS 3-28

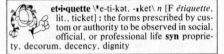

fr. OHG *azzen* to feed] **1** : to produce (as a design) on a hard material by corroding its surface (as by acid) **2** : to delineate clearly — **etch·er** *n*

etch·ing *n* **1** : the action, process, or art of etching **2** : a design produced on or print made from an etched plate

ETD *abbr* estimated time of departure

eter·nal \i-'tərn-ᵊl\ *adj* : EVERLASTING, PERPETUAL — **eter·nal·ly** *adv*

eter·ni·ty \i-'tər-nə-tē\ *n, pl* **-ties 1** : infinite duration **2** : IMMORTALITY

¹-eth \əth, ith\ *or* **-th** \th\ *vb suffix* — used to form the archaic third person singular present of verbs ⟨do*th*⟩

²-eth — see **²-TH**

eth·ane \'e-₁thān\ *n* : a colorless odorless gaseous hydrocarbon found in natural gas and used esp. as a fuel

eth·a·nol \'e-thə-₁nȯl\ *n* : ALCOHOL 1

ether \'ē-thər\ *n* **1** : the upper regions of space; *also* : the gaseous element formerly held to fill these regions **2** : a light flammable liquid used as an anesthetic and solvent

ethe·re·al \i-'thir-ē-əl\ *adj* **1** : CELESTIAL, HEAVENLY **2** : exceptionally delicate : AIRY, DAINTY — **ethe·re·al·ly** *adv* — **ethe·re·al·ness** *n*

eth·i·cal \'e-thi-kəl\ *adj* **1** : of or relating to ethics **2** : conforming to accepted and esp. professional standards of conduct **syn** virtuous, moral, principled — **eth·i·cal·ly** *adv*

eth·ics \'e-thiks\ *n sing or pl* **1** : a discipline dealing with good and evil and with moral duty **2** : moral principles or practice

Ethi·o·pi·an \₁ē-thē-'ō-pē-ən\ *n* : a native or inhabitant of Ethiopia — **Ethiopian** *adj*

¹eth·nic \'eth-nik\ *adj* [ME, heathen, fr. LL *ethnicus*, fr. Gk *ethnikos* national, gentile, fr. *ethnos* nation, people] : of or relating to races or large groups of people classed according to common traits and customs — **eth·ni·cal·ly** *adv*

²ethnic *n* : a member of a minority ethnic group who retains its customs, language, or social views

eth·nol·o·gy \eth-'nä-lə-jē\ *n* : a science dealing with the races of human beings, their origin, distribution, characteristics, and relations — **eth·no·log·i·cal** \₁eth-nə-'lä-ji-kəl\ *adj* — **eth·nol·o·gist** \eth-'nä-lə-jist\ *n*

ethol·o·gy \ē-'thä-lə-jē\ *n* : the scientific and objective study of animal behavior — **etho·log·i·cal** \₁ē-thə-'lä-ji-kəl, ₁e-\ *adj* — **ethol·o·gist** \ē-'thä-lə-jist\ *n*

ethos \'ē-₁thäs\ *n* : the distinguishing character, sentiment, moral nature, or guiding beliefs of a person, group, or institution

ethyl alcohol *n* : ALCOHOL 1

eth·yl·ene \'e-thə-₁lēn\ *n* : a colorless flammable gas found in coal gas or obtained from petroleum

eti·ol·o·gy \₁ē-tē-'ä-lə-jē\ *n* : the causes of a disease or abnormal condition; *also* : a branch of medicine concerned with the causes and origins of diseases — **eti·o·log·ic** \₁ē-tē-ə-'lä-jik\ *or* **eti·o·log·i·cal** \-ji-kəl\ *adj*

et·i·quette \'e-ti-kət, -₁ket\ *n* [F *étiquette*, lit., ticket] : the forms prescribed by custom or authority to be observed in social, official, or professional life **syn** propriety, decorum, decency, dignity

Etrus·can \i-'trəs-kən\ *n* **1** : the language of the Etruscans **2** : an inhabitant of ancient Etruria — **Etruscan** *adj*

et seq *abbr* [L *et sequens*] and the following one; [L *et sequentes* (masc. & fem. pl.) or *et sequentia* (neut. pl.)] and the following ones

-ette \'et, ₁et, ət, it\ *n suffix* **1** : little one ⟨din*ette*⟩ **2** : female (usher*ette*)

étude \'ā-₁tüd, -₁tyüd\ *n* [F, lit., study] : a musical composition for practice to develop technical skill

et·y·mol·o·gy \₁e-tə-'mä-lə-jē\ *n, pl* **-gies 1** : the history of a linguistic form (as a word) shown by tracing its development and relationships **2** : a branch of linguistics dealing with etymologies — **et·y·mo·log·i·cal** \-mə-'lä-ji-kəl\ *adj* — **et·y·mol·o·gist** \-'mä-lə-jist\ *n*

Eu *symbol* europium

eu·ca·lyp·tus \₁yü-kə-'lip-təs\ *n, pl* **-ti** \-₁tī\ *or* **-tus·es** : any of a genus of mostly Australian evergreen trees widely grown for shade or their wood, oils, resins, and gums

Eu·cha·rist \'yü-kə-rəst\ *n* : COMMUNION 2 — **eu·cha·ris·tic** \₁yü-kə-'ris-tik\ *adj, often cap*

¹eu·chre \'yü-kər\ *n* : a card game in which the side naming the trump must take three of five tricks to win

²euchre *vb* **eu·chred; eu·chring** : CHEAT, TRICK

eu·clid·e·an *also* **eu·clid·i·an** \yü-'kli-dē-ən\ *adj, often cap* : of or relating to the geometry of Euclid or a geometry based on similar axioms

eu·gen·ics \yü-'je-niks\ *n* : a science dealing with the improvement (as by selective breeding) of hereditary qualities esp. of human beings — **eu·gen·ic** \-nik\ *adj*

eu·lo·gy \'yü-lə-jē\ *n, pl* **-gies 1** : a speech in praise of some person or thing **2** : high praise — **eu·lo·gis·tic** \₁yü-lə-'jis-tik\ *adj* — **eu·lo·gize** \'yü-lə-₁jīz\ *vb*

eu·nuch \'yü-nək\ *n* : a castrated man

eu·phe·mism \'yü-fə-₁mi-zəm\ *n* [Gk *euphēmismos*, fr. *euphēmos* auspicious, sounding good, fr. *eu-* good + *phēmē* speech] : the substitution of a mild or pleasant expression for one offensive or unpleasant; *also* : the expression substituted — **eu·phe·mis·tic** \₁yü-fə-'mis-tik\ *adj*

eu·pho·ni·ous \yu-'fō-nē-əs\ *adj* : pleasing to the ear — **eu·pho·ni·ous·ly** *adv*

eu·pho·ny \'yü-fə-nē\ *n, pl* **-nies** : the effect produced by words so combined as to please the ear

eu·pho·ria \yu-'fȯr-ē-ə\ *n* : a marked feeling of well‑being or elation — **eu·phor·ic** \-'fȯr-ik\ *adj*

Eur *abbr* Europe; European

Eur·asian \yu-'rā-zhən, -shən\ *adj* **1** : of mixed European and Asian origin **2** : of or relating to Europe and Asia — **Eurasian** *n*

eu·re·ka \yu-'rē-kə\ *interj* [Gk *heurēka* I have found, fr. *heuriskein* to find; fr. the exclamation attributed to

Archimedes on discovering a method for determining the purity of gold] — used to express triumph on a discovery

Eu·ro·bond \\'yùr-ō-ˌbänd\ *n* : a bond of a U.S. corporation that is sold outside the U.S. but that is valued and paid for in dollars and yields interest in dollars

Eu·ro·cur·ren·cy \ˌyùr-ō-ˌkər-ən-sē\ *n* : moneys (as of the U.S. and Japan) held outside their countries of origin and used in the money markets of Europe

Eu·ro·dol·lar \\'yùr-ō-ˌdä-lər\ *n* : a U.S. dollar held as Eurocurrency

Eu·ro·pe·an \ˌyùr-ə-ˈpē-ən\ *n* **1** : a native or inhabitant of Europe **2** : a person of European descent — **European** *adj*

European plan *n* : a hotel plan whereby the daily rates cover only the cost of the room

eu·ro·pi·um \yù-ˈrō-pē-əm\ *n* : a rare metallic chemical element — see ELEMENT table

eu·sta·chian tube \yù-ˈstā-shən-\ *n*, *often cap E* : a tube connecting the inner cavity of the ear with the throat and equalizing air pressure on both sides of the eardrum

eu·tha·na·sia \ˌyü-thə-ˈnā-zhə\ *n* [Gk, easy death, fr. *eu*- good + *thanatos* death] : MERCY KILLING

EVA *abbr* extravehicular activity

evac·u·ate \i-ˈva-kyə-ˌwāt\ *vb* **-at·ed; -at·ing 1** : EMPTY **2** : to discharge wastes from the body **3** : to remove or withdraw from : VACATE — **evac·u·a·tion** \-ˌva-kyə-ˈwā-shən\ *n*

evac·u·ee \i-ˌva-kyə-ˈwē\ *n* : a person removed from a dangerous place

evade \i-ˈvād\ *vb* **evad·ed; evad·ing** : to manage to avoid esp. by dexterity or slyness : ELUDE, ESCAPE

eval·u·ate \i-ˈval-yù-ˌwāt\ *vb* **-at·ed; -at·ing** : APPRAISE, VALUE — **eval·u·a·tion** \-ˌval-yù-ˈwā-shən\ *n*

ev·a·nes·cent \ˌe-və-ˈnes-ᵊnt\ *adj* : tending to vanish like vapor **syn** passing, transient, transitory, momentary — **ev·a·nes·cence** \-ᵊns\ *n*

evan·gel·i·cal \ˌē-ˌvan-ˈje-li-kəl, ˌe-vən-\ *adj* [LL *evangelium* gospel, fr. Gk *evangelion*, fr. *eu*- good + *angelos* messenger] **1** : of or relating to the Christian gospel esp. as presented in the four Gospels **2** : of or relating to certain Protestant churches emphasizing the authority of Scripture and the importance of preaching as contrasted with ritual **3** : ZEALOUS (~ fervor) — **Evangelical** *n* — **Evan·gel·i·cal·ism** \-kə-ˌli-zəm\ *n* — **evan·gel·i·cal·ly** *adv*

evan·ge·lism \i-ˈvan-jə-ˌli-zəm\ *n* **1** : the winning or revival of personal commitments to Christ **2** : militant or crusading zeal — **evan·ge·lis·tic** \-ˌvan-jə-ˈlis-tik\ *adj* — **evan·ge·lis·ti·cal·ly** *adv*

evan·ge·list \i-ˈvan-jə-list\ *n* **1** *often cap* : the writer of any of the four Gospels **2** : a person who evangelizes; *esp* : a Protestant minister or layman who preaches at special services

evan·ge·lize \i-ˈvan-jə-ˌlīz\ *vb* **-lized; -liz·ing 1** : to preach the gospel **2** : to convert to Christianity

evap *abbr* evaporate

evap·o·rate \i-ˈva-pə-ˌrāt\ *vb* **-rat·ed; -rat·ing 1** : to pass off or cause to pass off in vapor **2** : to disappear quickly **3** : to drive out the moisture from (as by heat) — **evap·o·ra·tion** \-ˌva-pə-ˈrā-shən\ *n* — **evap·o·ra·tor** \-ˌrā-tər\ *n*

evap·o·rite \i-ˈva-pə-ˌrīt\ *n* : a sedimentary rock that originates by the evaporation of seawater in an enclosed basin

eva·sion \i-ˈvā-zhən\ *n* **1** : a means of evading **2** : an act or instance of evading — **eva·sive** \i-ˈvā-siv\ *adj* — **eva·sive·ness** *n*

eve \\'ēv\ *n* **1** : EVENING **2** : the period just before some important event

¹even \\'ē-vən\ *adj* **1** : LEVEL, FLAT **2** : REGULAR, SMOOTH **3** : EQUAL, FAIR **4** : BALANCED; *also* : fully revenged **5** : divisible by two **6** : EXACT — **even·ly** *adv* — **even·ness** *n*

²even *adv* **1** : EXACTLY, PRECISELY **2** : FULLY, QUITE **3** : at the very time **4** — used as an intensive to stress identity (~ I know that) **5** — used as an intensive to emphasize something extreme or highly unlikely (so simple ~ a child can do it) **6** — used as an intensive to stress the comparative degree (did ~ better) **7** — used as an intensive to indicate a small or minimum degree (didn't ~ try)

³even *vb* : to make or become even

even·hand·ed \ˌē-vən-ˈhan-dəd\ *adj* : FAIR, IMPARTIAL — **even·hand·ed·ly** *adv*

eve·ning \\'ēv-niŋ\ *n* **1** : the end of the day and early part of the night **2** *chiefly Southern & Midland* : AFTERNOON

evening primrose *n* : a coarse biennial herb with yellow flowers that open in the evening

evening star *n* : a bright planet (as Venus) seen esp. in the western sky at or after sunset

even·song \\'ē-vən-ˌsȯŋ\ *n*, *often cap* **1** : VESPERS **2** : evening prayer esp. when sung

event \i-ˈvent\ *n* [MF or L; MF, fr. L *eventus*, fr. *evenire* to happen, fr. *venire* to come] **1** : OCCURRENCE **2** : a noteworthy happening **3** : CONTINGENCY (in the ~ of rain) **4** : a contest in a program of sports — **event·ful** *adj*

even·tide \\'ē-vən-ˌtīd\ *n* : EVENING

even·tu·al \i-ˈven-chù-wəl\ *adj* : coming at some later time : ULTIMATE — **even·tu·al·ly** *adv*

even·tu·al·i·ty \i-ˌven-chù-ˈwa-lə-tē\ *n*, *pl* **-ties** : a possible event or outcome

even·tu·ate \i-ˈven-chù-ˌwāt\ *vb* **-at·ed; -at·ing** : to result finally

ev·er \\'e-vər\ *adv* **1** : ALWAYS **2** : at any time **3** : in any way : AT ALL

ev·er·glade \\'e-vər-ˌglād\ *n* : a low-lying tract of swampy or marshy land

ev·er·green \-ˌgrēn\ *adj* : having foliage that remains green (most coniferous trees are ~) — **evergreen** *n*

¹ev·er·last·ing \ˌe-vər-ˈlas-tiŋ\ *adj* **1** : enduring forever : ETERNAL **2** : having or being flowers or foliage that retain form or color for a long time when dried — **ev·er·last·ing·ly** *adv*

²everlasting *n* **1** : ETERNITY (from ~) **2** : a plant with everlasting flowers; *also* : its flower

ev·er·more \ˌe-vər-ˈmȯr\ *adv* : FOREVER

ev·ery \\'ev-rē\ *adj* **1** : being each one of a group **2** : all possible (given ~ chance); *also* : COMPLETE (have ~ confidence)

ev·ery·body \\'ev-ri-ˌbä-dē, -bə-\ *pron* : every person

ev·ery·day \\'ev-rē-ˌdā\ *adj* : encountered or used routinely : ORDINARY

ev·ery·one \-(ˌ)wən\ *pron* : EVERYBODY

ev·ery·thing \\'ev-rē-ˌthiŋ\ *pron* **1** : all that exists **2** : all that is relevant

ev·ery·where \\'ev-rē-ˌhwer\ *adv* : in every place or part

evg *abbr* evening

evict \i-ˈvikt\ *vb* **1** : to put (a person) out from a property by legal process **2** : EXPEL **syn** eject, oust, dismiss — **evic·tion** \-ˈvik-shən\ *n*

ev·i·dence \\'e-və-dəns\ *n* **1** : an outward sign **2** : PROOF, TESTIMONY; *esp* : matter submitted in court to determine the truth of alleged facts

ev·i·dent \-dənt\ *adj* : clear to the vision and understanding **syn** manifest, distinct, obvious, apparent, plain

ev·i·dent·ly \\'e-və-dənt-lē, ˌe-və-ˈdent-\ *adv* **1** : in an evident manner **2** : on the basis of available evidence

¹evil \\'ē-vəl\ *adj* **evil·er** *or* **evil·ler; evil·est** *or* **evil·lest 1** : WICKED **2** : causing or threatening distress or harm : PERNICIOUS — **evil·ly** *adv*

²evil *n* **1** : the fact of suffering, misfortune, and wrongdoing **2** : a source of sorrow or distress

evil·do·er \ˌē-vəl-ˈdü-ər\ *n* : one who does evil

evil–mind·ed \-ˈmīn-dəd\ *adj* : having an evil disposition or evil thoughts — **evil–mind·ed·ly** *adv*

evince \i-'vins\ *vb* **evinced; evinc•ing** : SHOW, REVEAL

evis•cer•ate \i-'vi-sə-₁rāt\ *vb* **-at•ed; -at•ing 1** : to remove the entrails of **2** : to deprive of vital content or force — **evis•cer•a•tion** \-₁vi-sə-'rā-shən\ *n*

evoke \i-'vōk\ *vb* **evoked; evok•ing** : to call forth or up — **evo•ca•tion** \₁ē-vō-'kā-shən, ₁e-və-\ *n* — **evoc•a•tive** \i-'vä-kə-tiv\ *adj*

evo•lu•tion \₁e-və-'lü-shən\ *n* **1** : one of a set of prescribed movements (as in a dance) **2** : a process of change in a particular direction **3** : a theory that the various kinds of plants and animals are descended from other kinds that lived in earlier times and that the differences are due to inherited changes that occurred over many generations — **evo•lu•tion•ary** \-shə-₁ner-ē\ *adj* — **evo•lu•tion•ist** \-shə-nist\ *n*

evolve \i-'välv\ *vb* **evolved; evolv•ing** [L *evolvere* to unroll] : to develop or change by or as if by evolution

EW *abbr* enlisted woman

ewe \'yü\ *n* : a female sheep

ew•er \'yü-ər\ *n* : a water pitcher

¹ex \'eks\ *prep* [L] : out of : FROM

²ex *n* : a former spouse

³ex *abbr* **1** example **2** express **3** extra

Ex *abbr* Exodus

ex- \e *also occurs in this prefix where only i is shown below (as in "express") and ks sometimes occurs where only gz is shown (as in "exact")\ prefix* **1** : out of : outside **2** : former ⟨*ex*-president⟩

ex•ac•er•bate \ig-'za-sər-₁bāt\ *vb* **-bat•ed; -bat•ing** : to make more violent, bitter, or severe — **ex•ac•er•ba•tion** \-₁za-sər-'bā-shən\ *n*

¹ex•act \ig-'zakt\ *vb* **1** : to compel to furnish **2** : to call for as suitable or necessary — **ex•ac•tion** \-'zak-shən\ *n*

²exact *adj* : precisely accurate or correct — **ex•act•ly** *adv* — **ex•act•ness** *n*

ex•act•ing \ig-'zak-tiŋ\ *adj* **1** : greatly demanding ⟨an ∼ taskmaster⟩ **2** : requiring close attention and precision

ex•ac•ti•tude \ig-'zak-tə-₁tüd, -₁tyüd\ *n* : the quality or state of being exact

ex•ag•ger•ate \ig-'za-jə-₁rāt\ *vb* **-at•ed; -at•ing** [L *exaggeratus*, pp. of *exaggerare*, lit., to heap up, fr. *agger* heap] : to enlarge (as a statement) beyond normal : OVERSTATE — **ex•ag•ger•at•ed•ly** *adv* — **ex•ag•ger•a•tion** \-₁za-jə-'rā-shən\ *n* — **ex•ag•ger•a•tor** \-'za-jə-₁rā-tər\ *n*

ex•alt \ig-'zȯlt\ *vb* **1** : to raise up esp. in rank, power, or dignity **2** : GLORIFY — **ex•al•ta•tion** \₁eg-₁zȯl-'tā-shən, ₁ek-₁sȯl-\ *n*

ex•am \ig-'zam\ *n* : EXAMINATION

ex•am•ine \ig-'za-mən\ *vb* **ex•am•ined; ex•am•in•ing 1** : to inspect closely **2** : QUESTION; *esp* : to test by questioning **syn** interrogate, query, quiz, catechize — **ex•am•i•na•tion** \-₁za-mə-'nā-shən\ *n*

ex•am•ple \ig-'zam-pəl\ *n* **1** : something forming a model to be followed or avoided **2** : a representative sample **3** : a problem to be solved in order to show the application of some rule

ex•as•per•ate \ig-'zas-pə-₁rāt\ *vb* **-at•ed; -at•ing** : VEX, IRRITATE — **ex•as•per•a•tion** \-₁zas-pə-'rā-shən\ *n*

exc *abbr* **1** excellent **2** except

ex•ca•vate \'ek-skə-₁vāt\ *vb* **-vat•ed; -vat•ing 1** : to hollow out; *also* : to form by hollowing out **2** : to dig out and remove (as earth) **3** : to reveal to view by digging away a covering — **ex•ca•va•tion** \₁ek-skə-'vā-shən\ *n* — **ex•ca•va•tor** \'ek-skə-₁vā-tər\ *n*

ex•ceed \ik-'sēd\ *vb* **1** : to go or be beyond the limit of **2** : SURPASS

ex•ceed•ing•ly \-'sē-diŋ-lē\ *also* **ex•ceed•ing** *adv* : EXTREMELY, VERY

ex•cel \ik-'sel\ *vb* **ex•celled; ex•cel•ling** : SURPASS, OUTDO

ex•cel•lence \'ek-sə-ləns\ *n* **1** : the quality of being excellent **2** : an excellent or valuable quality : VIRTUE **3** : EXCELLENCY **2**

ex•cel•len•cy \-lən-sē\ *n, pl* **-cies 1** : EXCELLENCE **2** — used as a title of honor

ex•cel•lent \-lənt\ *adj* : very good of its kind : FIRST-CLASS — **ex•cel•lent•ly** *adv*

ex•cel•si•or \ik-'sel-sē-ər\ *n* : fine curled wood shavings used esp. for packing fragile items

¹ex•cept \ik-'sept\ *also* **ex•cept•ing** *prep* : with the exclusion or exception of ⟨daily ∼ Sundays⟩

²except *vb* **1** : to take or leave out **2** : OBJECT

³except *also* **excepting** *conj* **1** : UNLESS ⟨∼ you repent⟩ **2** : ONLY ⟨I'd go, ∼ it's too far⟩

ex•cep•tion \ik-'sep-shən\ *n* **1** : the act of excepting **2** : something excepted **3** : OBJECTION

ex•cep•tion•able \ik-'sep-shə-nə-bəl\ *adj* : OBJECTIONABLE

ex•cep•tion•al \ik-'sep-shə-nəl\ *adj* **1** : UNUSUAL **2** : SUPERIOR — **ex•cep•tion•al•ly** *adv*

ex•cerpt \'ek-₁sərpt, 'eg-₁zərpt\ *n* : a passage selected or copied : EXTRACT — **excerpt** \ek-'sərpt, eg-'zərpt; 'ek-₁sərpt, 'eg-₁zərpt\ *vb*

ex•cess \ik-'ses, 'ek-₁ses\ *n* **1** : SUPERFLUITY, SURPLUS **2** : the amount by which one quantity exceeds another **3** : INTEMPERANCE; *also* : an instance of intemperance — **excess** *adj* — **ex•ces•sive** \ik-'se-siv\ *adj* — **ex•ces•sive•ly** *adv*

exch *abbr* exchange; exchanged

¹ex•change \iks-'chānj\ *n* **1** : the giving or taking of one thing in return for another : TRADE **2** : a substituting of one thing for another **3** : interchange of valuables and esp. of bills of exchange or money of different countries **4** : a place where things and services are exchanged; *esp* : a marketplace for securities **5** : a central office in which telephone lines are connected for communication

²exchange *vb* **ex•changed; ex•chang•ing** : to transfer in return for some equivalent : BARTER, SWAP — **ex•change•able** \iks-'chān-jə-bəl\ *adj*

ex•che•quer \'eks-₁che-kər\ *n* [ME *escheker*, fr. OF *eschequier* chessboard, counting table] : TREASURY; *esp* : a national treasury

ex•cise \'ek-₁sīz\ *n* : a tax on the manufacture, sale, or consumption of a commodity

ex•ci•sion \ik-'si-zhən\ *n* : removal by or as if by cutting out esp. by surgical means — **ex•cise** \ik-'sīz\ *vb*

ex•cit•able \ik-'sī-tə-bəl\ *adj* : easily excited — **ex•cit•abil•i•ty** \-₁sī-tə-'bi-lə-tē\ *n*

ex•cite \ik-'sīt\ *vb* **ex•cit•ed; ex•cit•ing 1** : to stir up the emotions of : ROUSE **2** : to increase the activity of : STIMULATE **syn** provoke, pique, quicken — **ex•ci•ta•tion** \₁ek-₁sī-'tā-shən, ₁ek-sə-\ *n* — **ex•cit•ed•ly** *adv* — **ex•cit•ing•ly** *adv*

ex•cite•ment \ik-'sīt-mənt\ *n* : AGITATION, STIR

ex•claim \iks-'klām\ *vb* : to cry out, speak, or utter sharply or vehemently — **ex•cla•ma•tion** \₁eks-klə-'mā-shən\ *n* — **ex•clam•a•to•ry** \iks-'kla-mə-₁tȯr-ē\ *adj*

exclamation point *n* : a punctuation mark ! used esp. after an interjection or exclamation

ex•clude \iks-'klüd\ *vb* **ex•clud•ed; ex•clud•ing 1** : to prevent from using or participating : BAR **2** : to put out : EXPEL — **ex•clu•sion** \-'klü-zhən\ *n*

ex•clu•sive \iks-'klü-siv\ *adj* **1** : reserved for particular persons **2** : snobbishly aloof; *also* : STYLISH **3** : SOLE ⟨∼ rights⟩; *also* : UNDIVIDED **syn** chic, modish, smart, swank, fashionable — **exclusive** *n* — **ex•clu•sive•ly** *adv* — **ex•clu•sive•ness** *n* — **ex•clu•siv•i•ty** \₁eks-₁klü-si-və-tē, iks-, -zi-\ *n*

exclusive of *prep* : not taking into account

ex•cog•i•tate \ek-'skä-jə-₁tāt\ *vb* : to think out : DEVISE

ex•com•mu•ni•cate \₁ek-skə-'myü-nə-₁kāt\ *vb* : to cut off officially from the rites of the church — **ex•com•mu•ni•ca•tion** \-₁myü-nə-'kā-shən\ *n*

ex•co•ri•ate \ek-'skȯr-ē-₁āt\ *vb* **-at•ed; -at•ing** : to criticize severely — **ex•co•ri•a•tion** \(₁)ek-₁skȯr-ē-'ā-shən\ *n*

ex•cre•ment \'ek-skrə-mənt\ *n* : waste discharged from

the body and esp. from the alimentary canal — **ex·cre·men·tal** \ˌek-skrə-ˈment-ᵊl\ adj

ex·cres·cence \ik-ˈskres-ᵊns\ n : OUTGROWTH; esp : an abnormal outgrowth (as a wart)

ex·cre·ta \ik-ˈskrē-tə\ n pl : waste matter separated or eliminated from an organism

ex·crete \ik-ˈskrēt\ vb **ex·cret·ed; ex·cret·ing** : to separate and eliminate wastes from the body esp. in urine or sweat — **ex·cre·tion** \-ˈskrē-shən\ n — **ex·cre·to·ry** \ˈek-skrə-ˌtōr-ē\ adj

ex·cru·ci·at·ing \ik-ˈskrü-shē-ˌā-tiŋ\ adj [L excruciare, fr. cruciare to crucify, fr. crux cross] : intensely painful or distressing syn agonizing, harrowing, torturous — **ex·cru·ci·at·ing·ly** adv

ex·cul·pate \ˈek-(ˌ)skəl-ˌpāt\ vb **-pat·ed; -pat·ing** : to clear from alleged fault or guilt syn absolve, exonerate, acquit, vindicate, clear

ex·cur·sion \ik-ˈskər-zhən\ n 1 : EXPEDITION; esp : a pleasure trip 2 : DIGRESSION — **ex·cur·sion·ist** \-zhə-nist\ n

ex·cur·sive \-ˈskər-siv\ adj : constituting or characterized by digression

¹**ex·cuse** \ik-ˈskyüz\ vb **ex·cused; ex·cus·ing** [ME, fr. OF excuser, fr. L excusare, fr. causa cause, explanation] 1 : to make apology for 2 : PARDON 3 : to release from an obligation 4 : JUSTIFY — **ex·cus·able** adj

²**excuse** \ik-ˈskyüs\ n 1 : an act of excusing 2 : something that excuses or is a reason for excusing : JUSTIFICATION

exec n : EXECUTIVE

ex·e·cra·ble \ˈek-si-krə-bəl\ adj 1 : DETESTABLE 2 : very bad ⟨∼ spelling⟩

ex·e·crate \ˈek-sə-ˌkrāt\ vb **-crat·ed; -crat·ing** [L exsecratus, pp. of exsecrari to put under a curse, fr. ex out of + sacer sacred] : to denounce as evil or detestable; also : DETEST — **ex·e·cra·tion** \ˌek-sə-ˈkrā-shən\ n

ex·e·cute \ˈek-si-ˌkyüt\ vb **-cut·ed; -cut·ing** 1 : to carry out fully : put completely into effect 2 : to do what is called for by (as a law) 3 : to put to death in accordance with a legal sentence 4 : to produce by carrying out a design 5 : to do what is needed to give validity to ⟨∼ a deed⟩ — **ex·e·cu·tion** \ˌek-si-ˈkyü-shən\ n — **ex·e·cu·tion·er** n

¹**ex·ec·u·tive** \ig-ˈze-kyə-tiv\ adj 1 : of or relating to the enforcement of laws and the conduct of affairs 2 : designed for or related to carrying out plans or purposes

²**executive** n 1 : the branch of government with executive duties 2 : one having administrative or managerial responsibility

ex·ec·u·tor \ig-ˈze-kyə-tər\ n : the person named in a will to execute it

ex·ec·u·trix \ig-ˈze-kyə-ˌtriks\ n, pl **ex·ec·u·tri·ces** \-ˌze-kyə-ˈtrī-ˌsēz\ or **ex·ec·u·trix·es** \-ˈze-kyə-ˌtrik-səz\ : a woman who is an executor

ex·e·ge·sis \ˌek-sə-ˈjē-səs\ n, pl **-ge·ses** \-ˈjē-ˌsēz\ : explanation or critical interpretation of a text

ex·e·gete \ˈek-sə-ˌjēt\ n : one who practices exegesis — **ex·e·get·i·cal** \ˌek-sə-ˈje-ti-kəl\ adj

ex·em·plar \ig-ˈzem-ˌplär, -plər\ n 1 : one that serves as a model or example; esp : an ideal model 2 : a typical instance or example

ex·em·pla·ry \ig-ˈzem-plə-rē\ adj : serving as a pattern; also : COMMENDABLE

ex·em·pli·fy \ig-ˈzem-plə-ˌfī\ vb **-fied; -fy·ing** : to illustrate by example : serve as an example of — **ex·em·pli·fi·ca·tion** \-ˌzem-plə-fə-ˈkā-shən\ n

¹**ex·empt** \ig-ˈzempt\ adj : free from some liability to which others are subject

²**exempt** vb : to make exempt : EXCUSE — **ex·emp·tion** \ig-ˈzemp-shən\ n

¹**ex·er·cise** \ˈek-sər-ˌsīz\ n 1 : EMPLOYMENT, USE ⟨∼ of authority⟩ 2 : exertion made for the sake of training or physical fitness 3 : a task or problem done to develop skill 4 pl : a public exhibition or ceremony

²**exercise** vb **-cised; -cis·ing** 1 : EXERT ⟨∼ control⟩ 2 : to train by or engage in exercise 3 : WORRY, DISTRESS — **ex·er·cis·er** n

ex·ert \ig-ˈzert\ vb : to bring or put into action ⟨∼ influence⟩ ⟨∼ed himself⟩ — **ex·er·tion** \-ˈzər-shən\ n

ex·hale \eks-ˈhāl\ vb **ex·haled; ex·hal·ing** 1 : to breathe out 2 : to give up or pass off in the form of vapor — **ex·ha·la·tion** \ˌeks-hə-ˈlā-shən\ n

---

¹**ex·haust** \ig-ˈzȯst\ vb 1 : to use up wholly 2 : to tire or wear out 3 : to draw off or let out completely; also : EMPTY 4 : to develop (a subject) completely

---

²**exhaust** n 1 : the escape of used vapor or gas from an engine; also : the gas that escapes 2 : a system of pipes through which exhaust escapes

ex·haus·tion \ig-ˈzȯs-chən\ n : extreme weariness : FATIGUE

ex·haus·tive \ig-ˈzȯ-stiv\ adj : covering all possibilities : THOROUGH — **ex·haus·tive·ly** adv

¹**ex·hib·it** \ig-ˈzi-bət\ vb 1 : to display esp. publicly 2 : to present to a court in legal form syn display, show, parade, flaunt — **ex·hi·bi·tion** \ˌek-sə-ˈbi-shən\ n — **ex·hib·i·tor** \ig-ˈzi-bə-tər\ n

²**exhibit** n 1 : an act or instance of exhibiting; also : something exhibited 2 : something produced and identified in court for use as evidence

ex·hi·bi·tion·ism \ˌek-sə-ˈbi-shə-ˌni-zəm\ n 1 : a perversion marked by a tendency to indecent exposure 2 : the act or practice of behaving so as to attract attention to oneself — **ex·hi·bi·tion·ist** \-nist\ n or adj

ex·hil·a·rate \ig-ˈzi-lə-ˌrāt\ vb **-rat·ed; -rat·ing** : ENLIVEN, STIMULATE — **ex·hil·a·ra·tion** \-ˌzi-lə-ˈrā-shən\ n

ex·hort \ig-ˈzȯrt\ vb : to urge, advise, or warn earnestly — **ex·hor·ta·tion** \ˌek-ˌsȯr-tā-shən, ˌeg-ˌzȯr-, -zər-\ n

ex·hume \ig-ˈzüm, iks-ˈhyüm\ vb **ex·humed; ex·hum·ing** [F or ML; F exhumer, fr. ML exhumare, fr. L ex out of + humus earth] : DISINTER — **ex·hu·ma·tion** \ˌeks-hyü-ˈmā-shən, ˌeg-zü-\ n

ex·i·gen·cy \ˈek-sə-jən-sē, ig-ˈzi-jən-\ n, pl **-cies** 1 pl

: REQUIREMENTS **2** : urgent need — **ex·i·gent** \'ek-sə-jənt\ *adj*

ex·ig·u·ous \ig-'zi-gyə-wəs\ *adj* : scanty in amount — **ex·i·gu·i·ty** \,eg-zi-'gyü-ə-tē\ *n*

¹ex·ile \'eg-,zīl, 'ek-,sīl\ *n* **1** : BANISHMENT; *also* : voluntary absence from one's country or home **2** : a person driven from his or her native place

²exile *vb* **ex·iled; ex·il·ing** : BANISH, EXPEL **syn** expatriate, deport, ostracize

ex·ist \ig-'zist\ *vb* **1** : to have being **2** : to continue to be : LIVE

ex·is·tence \ig-'zis-təns\ *n* **1** : continuance in living **2** : actual occurrence **3** : something existing — **ex·is·tent** \-tənt\ *adj*

ex·is·ten·tial \,eg-zis-'ten-chəl, ,ek-sis-\ *adj* **1** : of or relating to existence **2** : EMPIRICAL **3** : having being in time and space **4** : of or relating to existentialism or existentialists

ex·is·ten·tial·ism \,eg-zis-'ten-chə-,li-zəm\ *n* : a philosophy centered on individual existence and personal responsibility for acts of free will in the absence of certain knowledge of what is right or wrong — **ex·is·ten·tial·ist** \-list\ *adj or n*

ex·it \'eg-zət, 'ek-sət\ *n* **1** : a departure from a stage **2** : a going out or away; *also* : DEATH **3** : a way out of an enclosed space **4** : a point of departure from an expressway — **exit** *vb*

exo·bi·ol·o·gy \,ek-sō-bī-'ä-lə-jē\ *n* : biology concerned with life originating or existing outside the earth or its atmosphere — **exo·bi·ol·o·gist** \-jist\ *n*

exo·crine gland \'ek-sə-krən-, -,krīn-, -,krēn-\ *n* : a gland (as a salivary gland) that releases a secretion externally by means of a canal or duct

Exod *abbr* Exodus

ex·o·dus \'ek-sə-dəs\ *n* **1** *cap* — see BIBLE table **2** : a mass departure : EMIGRATION

ex of·fi·cio \,ek-sə-'fi-shē-,ō\ *adv or adj* : by virtue of or because of an office (*ex officio* chairman)

ex·og·e·nous \ek-'sä-jə-nəs\ *adj* : caused or produced by factors outside the organism or system — **ex·og·e·nous·ly** *adv*

ex·on·er·ate \ig-'zä-nə-,rāt\ *vb* **-at·ed; -at·ing** [ME, fr. L *exoneratus*, pp. of *exonerare* to unburden, fr. *ex-* out + *onus* load] : to free from blame **syn** acquit, absolve, exculpate, vindicate — **ex·on·er·a·tion** \-,zä-nə-'rā-shən\ *n*

ex·or·bi·tant \ig-'zȯr-bə-tənt\ *adj* : exceeding what is usual or proper

ex·or·cise \'ek-,sȯr-,sīz, -sər-\ *vb* **-cised; -cis·ing 1** : to get rid of by or as if by solemn command **2** : to free of an evil spirit — **ex·or·cism** \-,si-zəm\ *n* — **ex·or·cist** \-,sist\ *n*

exo·sphere \'ek-sō-,sfir\ *n* : the outermost region of the atmosphere

exo·ther·mic \,ek-sō-'thər-mik\ *adj* : characterized by or formed with evolution of heat

ex·ot·ic \ig-'zä-tik\ *adj* **1** : introduced from another country **2** : strikingly, excitingly, or mysteriously different or unusual — **exotic** *n* — **ex·ot·i·cal·ly** \-ti-k(ə-)lē\ *adv* — **ex·ot·i·cism** \-tə-,si-zəm\ *n*

---

exp *abbr* **1** expense **2** experiment **3** export **4** express

ex·pand \ik-'spand\ *vb* **1** : to open up : UNFOLD **2** : ENLARGE **3** : to develop in detail **syn** amplify, swell, distend, inflate, dilate — **ex·pand·er** *n*

ex·panse \ik-'spans\ *n* : a broad extent (as of land or sea)

ex·pan·sion \ik-'span-chən\ *n* **1** : the act or process of expanding **2** : the quality or state of being expanded **3** : an expanded part or thing

ex·pan·sive \ik-'span-siv\ *adj* **1** : tending to expand or to cause expansion **2** : warmly benevolent, generous, or ready to talk **3** : of large extent or scope — **ex·pan·sive·ly** *adv* — **ex·pan·sive·ness** *n*

ex par·te \eks-'pär-tē\ *adv or adj* [ML] : from a one-sided point of view

ex·pa·ti·ate \ek-'spā-shē-,āt\ *vb* **-at·ed; -at·ing** : to talk or write at length — **ex·pa·ti·a·tion** \ek-,spā-shē-'ā-shən\ *n*

¹ex·pa·tri·ate \ek-'spā-trē-,āt\ *vb* **-at·ed; -at·ing** : EXILE — **ex·pa·tri·a·tion** \ek-,spā-trē-'ā-shən\ *n*

²ex·pa·tri·ate \ek-'spā-trē-,āt, -trē-ət\ *adj* : living in a foreign country — **expatriate** *n*

ex·pect \ik-'spekt\ *vb* **1** : SUPPOSE, THINK **2** : to look forward to : ANTICIPATE **3** : to consider reasonable, due, or necessary **4** : to consider to be obliged

ex·pec·tan·cy \-'spek-tən-sē\ *n, pl* **-cies 1** : EXPECTATION **2** : the expected amount (as of years of life)

ex·pec·tant \-tənt\ *adj* : marked by expectation; *esp* : expecting the birth of a child — **ex·pec·tant·ly** *adv*

ex·pec·ta·tion \,ek-,spek-'tā-shən\ *n* **1** : the act or state of expecting **2** : prospect of good or bad fortune — usu. used in pl. **3** : something expected

ex·pec·to·rant \ik-'spek-tə-rənt\ *n* : an agent that promotes the discharge or expulsion of mucus from the respiratory tract — **expectorant** *adj*

ex·pec·to·rate \-,rāt\ *vb* **-rat·ed; -rat·ing** : SPIT — **ex·pec·to·ra·tion** \-,spek-tə-'rā-shən\ *n*

ex·pe·di·ence \ik-'spē-dē-əns\ *n* : EXPEDIENCY

ex·pe·di·en·cy \-ən-sē\ *n, pl* **-cies 1** : fitness to some end **2** : use of expedient means and methods; *also* : something expedient

¹ex·pe·di·ent \-ənt\ *adj* [ME, fr. MF or L; MF, fr. L *expediens*, prp. of *expedire* to extricate, prepare, be useful, fr. *ex-* out + *ped-, pes* foot] **1** : adapted for achieving a particular end **2** : marked by concern with what is advantageous; *esp* : governed by self-interest

²expedient *n* : something expedient; *esp* : a temporary means to an end

ex·pe·dite \'ek-spə-,dīt\ *vb* **-dit·ed; -dit·ing** : to carry out promptly; *also* : to speed up

ex·pe·dit·er \-,dī-tər\ *n* : one that expedites; *esp* : one employed to ensure efficient movement of goods or supplies in a business

ex·pe·di·tion \,ek-spə-'di-shən\ *n* **1** : a journey for a particular purpose; *also* : the persons making it **2** : efficient promptness

ex·pe·di·tion·ary \-'di-shə-ˌner-ē\ *adj* : of, relating to, or constituting an expedition; *also* : sent on military service abroad

ex·pe·di·tious \-'di-shəs\ *adj* : marked by or acting with prompt efficiency **syn** swift, fast, rapid, speedy

ex·pel \ik-'spel\ *vb* **ex·pelled; ex·pel·ling** : to drive or force out : EJECT

ex·pend \-'spend\ *vb* **1** : to pay out : SPEND **2** : UTILIZE; *also* : USE UP — **ex·pend·able** *adj*

ex·pen·di·ture \ik-'spen-di-chər, -ˌchur\ *n* **1** : the act or process of expending **2** : something expended

ex·pense \ik-'spens\ *n* **1** : EXPENDITURE **2** : COST **3** : a cause of expenditure **4** : SACRIFICE

ex·pen·sive \ik-'spen-siv\ *adj* : COSTLY, DEAR — **ex·pen·sive·ly** *adv*

¹ex·pe·ri·ence \ik-'spir-ē-əns\ *n* **1** : observation of or participation in events resulting in or tending toward knowledge **2** : knowledge, practice, or skill derived from observation or participation in events; *also* : the length of such participation **3** : something encountered, undergone, or lived through (as by a person or community)

²experience *vb* **-enced; -enc·ing 1** : FIND OUT, DISCOVER **2** : to have experience of : UNDERGO

ex·pe·ri·enced *adj* : made capable through experience

¹ex·per·i·ment \ik-'sper-ə-mənt\ *n* : a controlled procedure carried out to discover, test, or demonstrate something; *also* : the process of testing — **ex·per·i·men·tal** \-ˌsper-ə-'ment-ᵊl\ *adj*

²ex·per·i·ment \-ˌment\ *vb* : to make experiments — **ex·per·i·men·ta·tion** \ik-ˌsper-ə-mən-'tā-shən\ *n* — **ex·per·i·men·ter** *n*

¹ex·pert \'ek-ˌspərt\ *adj* : showing special skill or knowledge — **ex·pert·ly** *adv* — **ex·pert·ness** *n*

²ex·pert \'ek-ˌspərt\ *n* : an expert person : SPECIALIST

ex·per·tise \ˌek-(ˌ)spər-'tēz\ *n* : the skill of an expert

expert system *n* : computer software that attempts to mimic the reasoning of a human specialist

ex·pi·ate \'ek-spē-ˌāt\ *vb* **-at·ed; -at·ing** : to give satisfaction for : ATONE — **ex·pi·a·tion** \ˌek-spē-'ā-shən\ *n*

ex·pi·a·to·ry \'ek-spē-ə-ˌtōr-ē\ *adj* : serving to expiate

ex·pire \ik-'spīr, ek-\ *vb* **ex·pired; ex·pir·ing 1** : to breathe one's last breath : DIE **2** : to come to an end **3** : to breathe out from or as if from the lungs — **ex·pi·ra·tion** \ˌek-spə-'rā-shən\ *n*

ex·plain \ik-'splān\ *vb* [ME *explanen*, fr. L *explanare*, lit., to make level, fr. *planus* level, flat] **1** : to make clear **2** : to give the reason for — **ex·pla·na·tion** \ˌek-splə-'nā-shən\ *n* — **ex·plan·a·to·ry** \ik-'spla-nə-ˌtōr-ē\ *adj*

ex·ple·tive \'ek-splə-tiv\ *n* : a usu. profane exclamation

ex·pli·ca·ble \ek-'spli-kə-bəl, 'ek-(ˌ)spli-\ *adj* : capable of being explained

ex·pli·cate \'ek-splə-ˌkāt\ *vb* **-cat·ed; -cat·ing** : to give a detailed explanation of — **ex·pli·ca·tion** \ˌek-spli-'kā-shən\ *n*

ex·plic·it \ik-'spli-sət\ *adj* : clearly and precisely expressed — **ex·plic·it·ly** *adv* — **ex·plic·it·ness** *n*

ex·plode \ik-'splōd\ *vb* **ex·plod·ed; ex·plod·ing** [L *explodere* to drive off the stage by clapping, fr. *ex-* out + *plaudere* to clap] **1** : DISCREDIT ⟨∼ a belief⟩ **2** : to burst or cause to burst violently and noisily ⟨∼ a bomb⟩ ⟨the boiler *exploded*⟩ **3** : to undergo a rapid chemical or nuclear reaction with production of heat and violent expansion of gas ⟨dynamite ∼*s*⟩ **4** : to give forth a sudden strong and noisy outburst of emotion **5** : to increase rapidly

ex·plod·ed *adj* : showing the parts separated but in correct relationship to each other ⟨an ∼ view of a carburetor⟩

¹ex·ploit \'ek-ˌsplȯit\ *n* : DEED; *esp* : a notable or heroic act

²ex·ploit \ik-'splȯit\ *vb* **1** : to make productive use of

2 : UTILIZE **2** : to use unfairly for one's own advantage — **ex·ploi·ta·tion** \ˌek-ˌsplȯi-'tā-shən\ *n*

ex·plore \ik-'splȯr\ *vb* **ex·plored; ex·plor·ing 1** : to look into or travel over thoroughly **2** : to examine carefully ⟨∼ a wound⟩ — **ex·plo·ra·tion** \ˌek-splə-'rā-shən\ *n* — **ex·plor·a·to·ry** \ik-'splȯr-ə-ˌtōr-ē\ *adj* — **ex·plor·er** *n*

ex·plo·sion \ik-'splō-zhən\ *n* : the act or an instance of exploding

ex·plo·sive \ik-'splō-siv\ *adj* **1** : relating to or able to cause explosion **2** : tending to explode — **explosive** *n* — **ex·plo·sive·ly** *adv*

ex·po \'ek-spō\ *n, pl* **expos** : EXPOSITION 2

ex·po·nent \ik-'spō-nənt, 'ek-ˌspō-\ *n* **1** : a symbol written above and to the right of a mathematical expression (as ^{3} in a^3) to signify how many times it is to be used as a factor **2** : INTERPRETER, EXPOUNDER **3** : ADVOCATE, CHAMPION — **ex·po·nen·tial** \ˌek-spə-'nen-chəl\ *adj* — **ex·po·nen·tial·ly** *adv*

ex·po·nen·ti·a·tion \ˌek-spə-ˌnen-chē-'ā-shen\ *n* : the mathematical operation of raising a quantity to a power

¹ex·port \ek-'spōrt, 'ek-ˌspōrt\ *vb* : to send (as merchandise) to foreign countries — **ex·por·ta·tion** \ˌek-ˌspōr-'tā-shən, -spər-\ *n* — **ex·port·er** *n*

²ex·port \'ek-ˌspōrt\ *n* **1** : something exported esp. for trade **2** : the act of exporting

ex·pose \ik-'spōz\ *vb* **ex·posed; ex·pos·ing 1** : to deprive of shelter or protection **2** : to submit or subject to an action or influence; *esp* : to subject (as photographic film) to radiant energy (as light) **3** : to bring to light : DISCLOSE **4** : to cause to be open to view

ex·po·sé *or* **ex·po·se** \ˌek-spō-'zā\ *n* : an exposure of something discreditable

ex·po·si·tion \ˌek-spə-'zi-shən\ *n* **1** : a setting forth of the meaning or purpose (as of a writing); *also* : discourse designed to convey information **2** : a public exhibition

ex·pos·i·tor \ik-'spä-zə-tər\ *n* : one who explains : COMMENTATOR

ex post fac·to \ˌeks-'pōst-ˌfak-tō\ *adv or adj* : after the fact

ex·pos·tu·late \ik-'späs-chə-ˌlāt\ *vb* : to reason earnestly with a person esp. in dissuading : REMONSTRATE — **ex·pos·tu·la·tion** \-ˌspäs-chə-'lā-shən\ *n*

ex·po·sure \ik-'spō-zhər\ *n* **1** : the fact or condition of being exposed **2** : the act or an instance of exposing **3** : the length of time for which a film is exposed **4** : a section of a photographic film for one picture

ex·pound \ik-'spaund\ *vb* **1** : STATE **2** : INTERPRET, EXPLAIN — **ex·pound·er** *n*

¹ex·press \ik-'spres\ *adj* **1** : EXPLICIT; *also* : EXACT, PRECISE **2** : SPECIFIC ⟨this ∼ purpose⟩ **3** : traveling at high speed and esp. with few stops ⟨an ∼ train⟩; *also* : adapted to high speed use ⟨∼ roads⟩ — **express·ly** *adv*

²express *adv* : by express ⟨ship it ∼⟩

³express *n* **1** : a system for the prompt transportation of goods; *also* : a company operating such a service or the shipments so transported **2** : an express vehicle

⁴express *vb* **1** : to make known : SHOW, STATE ⟨∼ regret⟩; *also* : SYMBOLIZE **2** : to squeeze out : extract by pressing **3** : to send by express

ex·pres·sion \ik-'spre-shən\ *n* **1** : UTTERANCE **2** : something that represents or symbolizes : SIGN; *esp* : a mathematical symbol or combination of signs and symbols representing a quantity or operation **3** : a significant word or phrase; *also* : manner of expressing (as in writing or music) **4** : facial aspect or vocal intonation indicative of feeling — **ex·pres·sion·less** *adj*

ex·pres·sion·ism \ik-'spre-shə-ˌni-zəm\ *n* : a theory or practice in art of seeking to depict the artist's subjective responses to objects and events — **ex·pres·sion-**

ist \-nist\ *n or adj* — **ex·pres·sion·is·tic** \-ₗspre-shə-ˈnis-tik\ *adj*

ex·pres·sive \ik-ˈspre-siv\ *adj* 1 : of or relating to expression 2 : serving to express — **ex·pres·sive·ly** *adv* — **ex·pres·sive·ness** *n*

ex·press·way \ik-ˈspres-ₗwā\ *n* : a divided superhighway with limited access

ex·pro·pri·ate \ek-ˈsprō-prē-ₗāt\ *vb* **-at·ed; -at·ing** : to deprive of possession or the right to own — **ex·pro·pri·a·tion** \(ₗ)ek-ₗsprō-prē-ˈā-shən\ *n*

expt *abbr* experiment

ex·pul·sion \ik-ˈspəl-shən\ *n* : an expelling or being expelled : EJECTION

ex·punge \ik-ˈspənj\ *vb* **ex·punged; ex·pung·ing** [L *expungere* to mark for deletion by dots, fr. *ex-* out + *pungere* to prick] : OBLITERATE, ERASE

ex·pur·gate \ˈek-spər-ₗgāt\ *vb* **-gat·ed; -gat·ing** : to clear (as a book) of objectionable passages — **ex·pur·ga·tion** \ₗek-spər-ˈgā-shən\ *n*

ex·qui·site \ek-ˈskwi-zət, ˈek-(ₗ)skwi-\ *adj* [ME *exquisit*, fr. L *exquisitus*, pp. of *exquirere* to search out, fr. *ex* out *quaerere* to seek] 1 : marked by flawless form or workmanship 2 : keenly appreciative or sensitive 3 : pleasingly beautiful or delicate 4 : INTENSE

ext *abbr* 1 extension 2 exterior 3 external 4 extra 5 extract

ex·tant \ˈek-stənt; ek-ˈstant\ *adj* : EXISTENT; *esp* : not lost or destroyed

ex·tem·po·ra·ne·ous \ek-ₗstem-pə-ˈrā-nē-əs\ *adj* : not planned beforehand : IMPROMPTU — **ex·tem·po·ra·ne·ous·ly** *adv*

ex·tem·po·rary \ik-ˈstem-pə-ₗrer-ē\ *adj* : EXTEMPORANEOUS

ex·tem·po·re \ik-ˈstem-pə-(ₗ)rē\ *adv* : EXTEMPORANEOUSLY

ex·tem·po·rise *Brit var of* EXTEMPORIZE

ex·tem·po·rize \ik-ˈstem-pə-ₗrīz\ *vb* **-rized; -riz·ing** : to do something extemporaneously

ex·tend \ik-ˈstend\ *vb* 1 : to spread or stretch forth or out (as in reaching) 2 : to exert or cause to exert to full capacity 3 : PROFFER ⟨∼ credit⟩ 4 : PROLONG ⟨∼ a note⟩ 5 : to make greater or broader ⟨∼ knowledge⟩ ⟨∼ a business⟩ 6 : to stretch out or reach across a distance, space, or time *syn* lengthen, elongate, protract — **ex·tend·able** *also* **ex·tend·ible** \-ˈsten-də-bəl\ *adj*

ex·ten·sion \ik-ˈsten-chən\ *n* 1 : an extending or being extended 2 : a program that geographically extends the educational resources of an institution 3 : an additional part; *also* : an extra telephone connected to a line

ex·ten·sive \ik-ˈsten-siv\ *adj* : of considerable extent : FAR-REACHING, BROAD — **ex·ten·sive·ly** *adv*

ex·tent \ik-ˈstent\ *n* 1 : the range or space over which something extends ⟨a property of large ∼⟩ 2 : the point or degree to which something extends ⟨to the fullest ∼ of the law⟩

ex·ten·u·ate \ik-ˈsten-yù-ₗwāt\ *vb* **-at·ed; -at·ing** : to lessen the seriousness of — **ex·ten·u·a·tion** \-ₗsten-yù-ˈwā-shən\ *n*

¹**ex·te·ri·or** \ek-ˈstir-ē-ər\ *adj* 1 : EXTERNAL 2 : suitable for use on an outside surface ⟨∼ paint⟩

²**exterior** *n* : an exterior part or surface

ex·ter·mi·nate \ik-ˈstər-mə-ₗnāt\ *vb* **-nat·ed; -nat·ing** : to get rid of completely usu. by killing off *syn* extirpate, eradicate, abolish, annihilate — **ex·ter·mi·na·tion** \-ₗstər-mə-ˈnā-shən\ *n* — **ex·ter·mi·na·tor** \-ˈstər-mə-ₗnā-tər\ *n*

¹**ex·ter·nal** \ek-ˈstərn-ᵊl\ *adj* 1 : outwardly perceivable; *also* : SUPERFICIAL 2 : of, relating to, or located on the outside or an outer part 3 : arising or acting from without; *also* : FOREIGN ⟨∼ affairs⟩ — **ex·ter·nal·ly** *adv*

²**external** *n* : an external feature

ex·tinct \ik-ˈstiŋkt\ *adj* 1 : EXTINGUISHED; *also* : no

longer active ⟨an ∼ volcano⟩ 2 : no longer existing or in use ⟨dinosaurs are ∼⟩ ⟨∼ languages⟩ — **ex·tinc·tion** \ik-ˈstiŋk-shən\ *n*

ex·tin·guish \ik-ˈstiŋ-gwish\ *vb* : to cause to stop burning; *also* : to bring to an end (as by destroying) — **ex·tin·guish·able** *adj* — **ex·tin·guish·er** *n*

ex·tir·pate \ˈek-stər-ₗpāt\ *vb* **-pat·ed; -pat·ing** [L *exstirpatus*, pp. of *exstirpare*, fr. *ex-* out + *stirps* trunk, root] 1 : to destroy completely 2 : UPROOT *syn* exterminate, eradicate, abolish, annihilate — **ex·tir·pa·tion** \ₗek-stər-ˈpā-shən\ *n*

ex·tol *also* **ex·toll** \ik-ˈstōl\ *vb* **ex·tolled; ex·tol·ling** : to praise highly : GLORIFY

ex·tort \ik-ˈstȯrt\ *vb* [L *extortus*, pp. of *extorquēre* to wrench out, extort, fr. *ex-* out + *torquēre* to twist] : to obtain by force or improper pressure ⟨∼ a bribe⟩ — **ex·tor·tion** \-ˈstȯr-shən\ *n* — **ex·tor·tion·er** *n* — **ex·tor·tion·ist** *n*

ex·tor·tion·ate \ik-ˈstȯr-shə-nət\ *adj* : EXCESSIVE, EXORBITANT — **ex·tor·tion·ate·ly** *adv*

¹**ex·tra** \ˈek-strə\ *adj* 1 : ADDITIONAL 2 : SUPERIOR

²**extra** *n* 1 : a special edition of a newspaper 2 : an added charge 3 : an additional worker or performer (as in a motion picture)

³**extra** *adv* : beyond what is usual

¹**ex·tract** \ik-ˈstrakt, *esp for 3* ˈek-ₗstrakt\ *vb* 1 : to draw out; *esp* : to pull out forcibly ⟨∼ a tooth⟩ 2 : to withdraw (as a juice or a constituent) by a physical or chemical process 3 : to select for citation : QUOTE — **ex·tract·able** *adj* — **ex·trac·tion** \ik-ˈstrak-shən\ *n* — **ex·trac·tor** \-tər\ *n*

²**ex·tract** \ˈek-ₗstrakt\ *n* 1 : EXCERPT, CITATION 2 : a product (as a juice or concentrate) obtained by extracting

ex·tra·cur·ric·u·lar \ₗek-strə-kə-ˈri-kyə-lər\ *adj* : lying outside the regular curriculum; *esp* : of or relating to school-connected activities (as sports) usu. carrying no academic credit

ex·tra·dite \ˈek-strə-ₗdīt\ *vb* **-dit·ed; -dit·ing** : to obtain by or deliver up to extradition

ex·tra·di·tion \ₗek-strə-ˈdi-shən\ *n* : the surrender of an alleged criminal to a different jurisdiction for trial

ex·tra·mar·i·tal \ₗek-strə-ˈmar-ət-ᵊl\ *adj* : of or relating to sexual intercourse by a married person with someone other than his or her spouse

ex·tra·mu·ral \-ˈmyùr-əl\ *adj* : existing or functioning beyond the bounds of an organized unit

ex·tra·ne·ous \ek-ˈstrā-nē-əs\ *adj* 1 : coming from without 2 : not forming a vital part; *also* : IRRELEVANT — **ex·tra·ne·ous·ly** *adv*

ex·traor·di·nary \ik-ˈstrȯrd-ᵊn-ₗer-ē, ₗek-strə-ˈȯrd-\ *adj* 1 : notably unusual or exceptional 2 : employed on special service — **ex·traor·di·nari·ly** \-ₗstrȯrd-ᵊn-ˈer-ə-lē, ₗek-strə-ˈȯrd-\ *adv*

ex·trap·o·late \ik-ˈstra-pə-ₗlāt\ *vb* **-lat·ed; -lat·ing** : to infer (unknown data) from known data — **ex·trap·o·la·tion** \-ₗstra-pə-ˈlā-shən\ *n*

ex·tra·sen·so·ry \ₗek-strə-ˈsen-sə-rē\ *adj* : not acting or occurring through the known senses

extrasensory perception *n* : perception (as in telepathy) of events external to the self not gained through the senses and not deducible from previous experience

ex·tra·ter·res·tri·al \-tə-ˈres-trē-əl\ *adj* : originating or existing outside the earth or its atmosphere ⟨∼ life⟩ — **extraterrestrial** *n*

ex·tra·ter·ri·to·ri·al \-ₗter-ə-ˈtȯr-ē-əl\ *adj* : existing or taking place outside the territorial limits of a jurisdiction

ex·tra·ter·ri·to·ri·al·i·ty \-ₗtȯr-ē-ˈa-lə-tē\ *n* : exemption from the application or jurisdiction of local law or tribunals ⟨diplomats enjoy ∼⟩

ex·trav·a·gant \ik-ˈstra-vi-gənt\ *adj* 1 : EXCESSIVE ⟨∼ claims⟩ 2 : unduly lavish : WASTEFUL 3 : too costly *syn* immoderate, exorbitant, extreme, inordinate, un-

due — **ex·trav·a·gance** \-gəns\ *n* — **ex·trav·a·gant·ly** *adv*

ex·trav·a·gan·za \ik-ₐstra-və-ˈgan-zə\ *n* 1 : a literary or musical work marked by extreme freedom of style and structure 2 : a spectacular show

ex·tra·ve·hic·u·lar \ₐek-strə-vē-ˈhi-kyə-lər\ *adj* : taking place outside a vehicle (as a spacecraft) ⟨∼ activity⟩

¹**ex·treme** \ik-ˈstrēm\ *adj* 1 : very great or intense ⟨∼ cold⟩ 2 : very severe or radical ⟨∼ measures⟩ 3 : going to great lengths or beyond normal limits ⟨politically ∼⟩ 4 : most remote ⟨the ∼ end⟩ 5 : UTMOST; *also* : MAXIMUM — **ex·treme·ly** *adv*

²**extreme** *n* 1 : something located at one end or the other of a range or series 2 : EXTREMITY 4

extremely low frequency *n* : a radio frequency in the lowest range of the radio spectrum

ex·trem·ism \ik-ˈstrē-ₐmi-zəm\ *n* : the quality or state of being extreme; *esp* : advocacy of extreme political measures — **ex·trem·ist** \-mist\ *n or adj*

ex·trem·i·ty \ik-ˈstre-mə-tē\ *n, pl* **-ties** 1 : the most remote part or point 2 : a limb of the body; *esp* : a human hand or foot 3 : the greatest need or danger 4 : the utmost degree; *also* : a drastic or desperate measure

ex·tri·cate \ˈek-strə-ₐkāt\ *vb* **-cat·ed; -cat·ing** [L *extricatus*, pp. of *extricare*, fr. *ex-* out + *tricae* trifles, perplexities] : to free from an entanglement or difficulty **syn** disentangle, untangle, disencumber — **ex·tri·ca·ble** \ik-ˈstri-kə-bəl, ek-; ˈek-(ₐ)stri-\ *adj* — **ex·tri·ca·tion** \ₐek-strə-ˈkā-shən\ *n*

ex·trin·sic \ek-ˈstrin-zik, -sik\ *adj* 1 : not forming part of or belonging to a thing 2 : EXTERNAL — **ex·trin·si·cal·ly** \-zi-k(ə-)lē, -si-\ *adv*

ex·tro·vert *also* **ex·tra·vert** \ˈek-strə-ₐvərt\ *n* : a gregarious and unreserved person — **ex·tro·ver·sion** *or* **ex·tra·ver·sion** \ₐek-strə-ˈvər-zhən\ *n* — **ex·tro·vert·ed** *also* **ex·tra·vert·ed** *adj*

ex·trude \ik-ˈstrüd\ *vb* **ex·trud·ed; ex·trud·ing** 1 : to force, press, or push out 2 : to shape (as plastic) by forcing through a die — **ex·tru·sion** \-ˈstrü-zhən\ *n* — **ex·trud·er** *n*

ex·u·ber·ant \ig-ˈzü-bə-rənt\ *adj* 1 : unrestrained in enthusiasm or style 2 : PROFUSE — **ex·u·ber·ance** \-rəns\ *n* — **ex·u·ber·ant·ly** *adv*

ex·ude \ig-ˈzüd\ *vb* **ex·ud·ed; ex·ud·ing** [L *exsudare*, fr. *ex-* out + *sudare* to sweat] 1 : to discharge slowly through pores or cuts : OOZE 2 : to display conspicuously or abundantly ⟨∼s charm⟩ — **ex·u·date** \ˈek-sù-ₐdāt, -syù-\ *n* — **ex·u·da·tion** \ₐek-sù-ˈdā-shən, -syù-\ *n*

ex·ult \ig-ˈzəlt\ *vb* : REJOICE, GLORY — **ex·ul·tant** \-ˈzəlt-ᵊnt\ *adj* — **ex·ul·tant·ly** *adv* — **ex·ul·ta·tion** \ₐek-(ₐ)səl-ˈtā-shən, ₐeg-(ₐ)zəl-\ *n*

ex·urb \ˈek-ₐsərb, ˈeg-ₐzərb\ *n* : a region outside a city and its suburbs inhabited chiefly by well-to-do families

ex·ur·ban·ite \ek-ˈsər-bə-ₐnīt; eg-ˈzər-\ *n* : one who lives in an exurb

ex·ur·bia \ek-ˈsər-bē-ə, eg-ˈzər-\ *n* : the generalized region of exurbs

-ey — see -Y

¹**eye** \ˈī\ *n* 1 : an organ of sight typically consisting in vertebrates of a globular structure that is located in a socket of the skull, is lined with a sensitive retina, and is normally paired 2 : VISION, PERCEPTION; *also* : faculty of discrimination ⟨an ∼ for bargains⟩ 3 : POINT OF VIEW, JUDGMENT — often used in pl. ⟨in the ∼s of the law⟩ 4 : something suggesting an eye ⟨the ∼ of a needle⟩; *esp* : an undeveloped bud (as on a potato) 5 : the calm center of a cyclone — **eyed** \ˈīd\ *adj*

²**eye** *vb* **eyed; eye·ing** *or* **ey·ing** : to look at : WATCH

eye·ball \ˈī-ₐból\ *n* : the globular capsule of the vertebrate eye

eye·brow \-ₐbraù\ *n* : the ridge over the eye or the hair growing on it

eye·drop·per \-ₐdrä-pər\ *n* : DROPPER 2

eye·glass \-ₐglas\ *n* : a lens worn to aid vision; *also,* pl : GLASSES

eye·lash \-ₐlash\ *n* 1 : the fringe of hair edging the eyelid — usu. used in pl. 2 : a single hair of the eyelashes

eye·let \-lət\ *n* 1 : a small hole intended for ornament or for passage of a cord or lace 2 : a typically metal ring for reinforcing an eyelet : GROMMET

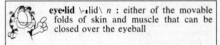
eye·lid \-ₐlid\ *n* : either of the movable folds of skin and muscle that can be closed over the eyeball

eye·lin·er \-ₐlī-nər\ *n* : makeup used to emphasize the contour of the eyes

eye–open·er \-ₐō-pə-nər\ *n* : something startling or surprising — **eye–open·ing** *adj*

eye·piece \-ₐpēs\ *n* : the lens or combination of lenses at the eye end of an optical instrument

eye shadow *n* : a colored cosmetic applied to the eyelids to accent the eyes

eye·sight \-ₐsīt\ *n* : SIGHT, VISION

eye·sore \-ₐsōr\ *n* : something offensive to view

eye·strain \-ₐstrān\ *n* : weariness or a strained state of the eye

eye·tooth \-ˈtüth\ *n* : a canine tooth of the upper jaw

eye·wash \-ˈwȯsh, -ₐwäsh\ *n* 1 : an eye lotion 2 : misleading or deceptive statements, actions, or procedures

eye·wit·ness \-ˈwit-nəs\ *n* : a person who actually sees something happen

ey·rie \ˈir-ē, *or like* AERIE\ *var of* AERIE

ey·rir \ˈā-ₐrir\ *n, pl* **au·rar** \ˈaù-ₐrär\ — see *krona* at MONEY table

Ez *or* **Ezr** *abbr* Ezra

Ezech *abbr* Ezechiel

Eze·chiel \i-ˈzē-kyəl\ *n* — see BIBLE table

Ezek *abbr* Ezekiel

Eze·kiel \i-ˈzē-kyəl\ *n* — see BIBLE table

Ez·ra \ˈez-rə\ *n* — see BIBLE table

F

¹f \\'ef\\ *n, pl* **f's** *or* **fs** \\'efs\\ *often cap* **1** : the 6th letter of the English alphabet **2** : a grade rating a student's work as failing

²f *abbr, often cap* **1** Fahrenheit **2** false **3** family **4** farad **5** female **6** feminine **7** forte **8** French **9** frequency **10** Friday

³f *symbol* focal length

F *symbol* fluorine

FAA *abbr* Federal Aviation Administration

Fa·bi·an \\'fā-bē-ən\\ *adj* : of, relating to, or being a society of socialists organized in England in 1884 to spread socialist principles gradually — **Fabian** *n* — **Fa·bi·an·ism** *n*

fa·ble \\'fā-bəl\\ *n* **1** : a legendary story of supernatural happenings **2** : a narration intended to teach a lesson; *esp* : one in which animals speak and act like people **3** : FALSEHOOD

fa·bled \\'fā-bəld\\ *adj* **1** : FICTITIOUS **2** : told or celebrated in fable

fab·ric \\'fa-brik\\ *n* [MF *fabrique*, fr. L *fabrica* workshop, structure] **1** : STRUCTURE, FRAMEWORK ⟨the ∼ of society⟩ **2** : CLOTH; *also* : a material that resembles cloth

fab·ri·cate \\'fa-bri-ıkāt\\ *vb* **-cat·ed; -cat·ing** **1** : INVENT, CREATE **2** : to make up for the sake of deception **3** : CONSTRUCT, MANUFACTURE — **fab·ri·ca·tion** \\ıfa-bri-'kā-shən\\ *n*

fab·u·lous \\'fa-byə-ləs\\ *adj* **1** : resembling a fable; *also* : INCREDIBLE, MARVELOUS **2** : told in or based on fable — **fab·u·lous·ly** *adv*

fac *abbr* **1** facsimile **2** faculty

fa·cade *also* **fa·çade** \\fə-'säd\\ *n* [F *façade*, fr. It *facciata*, fr. *faccia* face] **1** : the principal face or front of a building **2** : a false, superficial, or artificial appearance ⟨a ∼ of composure⟩ **syn** mask, disguise, front, guise, pretense, veneer

¹face \\'fās\\ *n* **1** : the front part of the head **2** : PRESENCE ⟨in the ∼ of danger⟩ **3** : facial expression : LOOK ⟨put a sad ∼ on⟩ **4** : GRIMACE ⟨made a ∼⟩ **5** : outward appearance ⟨looks easy on the ∼ of it⟩ **6** : CONFIDENCE; *also* : BOLDNESS **7** : DIGNITY, PRESTIGE ⟨afraid to lose ∼⟩ **8** : SURFACE; *esp* : a front, principal, or bounding surface ⟨∼ of a cliff⟩ ⟨the ∼s of a cube⟩ — **faced** \\'fāst, 'fā-səd\\ *adj*

²face *vb* **faced; fac·ing** **1** : to confront brazenly **2** : to line near the edge esp. with a different material; *also* : to cover the front or surface of ⟨∼ a building with marble⟩ **3** : to meet or bring in direct contact or confrontation ⟨*faced* the problem⟩ **4** : to stand or sit with the face toward ⟨∼ the sun⟩ **5** : to have the front oriented toward ⟨a house *facing* the park⟩ **6** : to have as or be a prospect ⟨∼ a grim future⟩ **7** : to turn the face or body in a specified direction — **face the music** : to meet the unpleasant consequences of one's actions

face·down \\ıfās-'daůn\\ *adv* : with the face downward

face·less \\-ləs\\ *n* **1** : lacking a face **2** : lacking character or individuality

face–lift \\'fās-ılift\\ *n* **1** : a cosmetic surgical operation for removal of facial defects (as wrinkles) typical of aging **2** : MODERNIZATION — **face–lift** *vb*

face–off \\'fās-ıôf\\ *n* **1** : a method of beginning play by dropping a puck (as in ice hockey) between two opposing players each of whom attempts to control it **2** : CONFRONTATION

fac·et \\'fa-sət\\ *n* [F *facette*, dim. of *face*] **1** : a small plane surface of a cut gem **2** : ASPECT, PHASE

fa·ce·tious \\fə-'sē-shəs\\ *adj* **1** : joking often inappropriately **2** : JOCULAR, JOCOSE **syn** witty, humorous — **fa·ce·tious·ly** *adv* — **fa·ce·tious·ness** *n*

¹fa·cial \\'fā-shəl\\ *adj* **1** : of or relating to the face **2** : used to improve the appearance of the face

²facial *n* : a facial treatment

fac·ile \\'fa-səl\\ *adj* **1** : easily accomplished, handled, or

attained **2** : SUPERFICIAL **3** : readily manifested and often insincere ⟨∼ prose⟩ **4** : READY, FLUENT ⟨a ∼ writer⟩

fa·cil·i·tate \\fə-'si-lə-ıtāt\\ *vb* **-tat·ed; -tat·ing** : to make easier

fa·cil·i·ty \\fə-'si-lə-tē\\ *n, pl* **-ties** **1** : the quality of being easily performed **2** : ease in performance : APTITUDE **3** : PLIANCY **4** : something that makes easier an action, operation, or course of conduct; *also* : REST ROOM — often used in pl. **5** : something (as a hospital) built or installed for a particular purpose

fac·ing \\'fā-siŋ\\ *n* **1** : a lining at the edge esp. of a garment **2** *pl* : the collar, cuffs, and trimmings of a uniform coat **3** : an ornamental or protective layer **4** : material for facing

fac·sim·i·le \\fak-'si-mə-lē\\ *n* [L *fac simile* make similar] **1** : an exact copy **2** : a system of transmitting and reproducing printed matter or pictures by means of signals sent over telephone lines

fact \\'fakt\\ *n* **1** : DEED; *esp* : CRIME ⟨accessory after the ∼⟩ **2** : the quality of being actual **3** : something that exists or occurs **4** : a piece of information

fac·tion \\'fak-shən\\ *n* : a group or combination (as in a government) acting together within and usu. against a larger body : CLIQUE — **fac·tion·al·ism** \\-shə-nə-ıli-zəm\\ *n*

fac·tious \\'fak-shəs\\ *adj* **1** : of, relating to, or caused by faction **2** : inclined to faction or the formation of factions : causing dissension **syn** insubordinate, contumacious, insurgent, seditious, rebellious

fac·ti·tious \\fak-'ti-shəs\\ *adj* : ARTIFICIAL, SHAM ⟨a ∼ display of grief⟩

fac·toid \\'fak-ıtôid\\ *n* **1** : an invented fact believed to be true because of its appearance in print **2** : a brief and usu. trivial news item

¹fac·tor \\'fak-tər\\ *n* **1** : AGENT **2** : something that actively contributes to a result **3** : GENE **4** : any of the numbers or symbols in mathematics that when multiplied together form a product; *esp* : any of the integers that divide a given integer without a remainder

²factor *vb* **1** : to work as a factor **2** : to find the mathematical factors of and esp. the prime mathematical factors of

¹fac·to·ri·al \\fak-'tŏr-ē-əl\\ *adj* : of, relating to, or being a factor

²factorial *n* : the product of all the positive integers from 1 to a given integer *n*

fac·to·ry \\'fak-trē, -tə-rē\\ *n, pl* **-ries** **1** : a trading post where resident brokers trade **2** : a building or group of buildings used for manufacturing

fac·to·tum \\fak-'tō-təm\\ *n* [NL, lit., do everything, fr. L *fac* do + *totum* everything] : a person (as a servant) having numerous or varied duties

facts of life : the physiological processes and behavior involved in sex and reproduction

fac·tu·al \\'fak-chə-wəl\\ *adj* : of or relating to facts; *also* : based on fact — **fac·tu·al·ly** *adv*

fac·ul·ty \\'fa-kəl-tē\\ *n, pl* **-ties** **1** : ability to act or do : POWER; *also* : natural aptitude **2** : one of the powers of the mind or body ⟨the ∼ of hearing⟩ **3** : the teachers in a school or college or one of its divisions

fad \\'fad\\ *n* : a practice or interest followed for a time with exaggerated zeal : CRAZE — **fad·dish** *adj* — **fad·dist** *n*

fade \\'fād\\ *vb* **fad·ed; fad·ing** **1** : WITHER **2** : to lose or cause to lose freshness or brilliance of color **3** : VANISH **4** : to grow dim or faint

FADM *abbr* fleet admiral

fae·cal, fae·ces *var of* FECAL, FECES

fa·er·ie *also* **fa·ery** \\'fā-rē, 'far-ē\\ *n, pl* **fa·er·ies** **1** : FAIRYLAND **2** : FAIRY

¹fag \\'fag\\ *vb* **fagged; fag·ging** **1** : DRUDGE **2** : to act as a fag **3** : TIRE, EXHAUST

²**fag** *n* 1 : an English public-school boy who acts as servant to another 2 : MENIAL, DRUDGE

³**fag** *n* : CIGARETTE

fag end *n* 1 : REMNANT 2 : the extreme end 3 : the last part or coarser end of a web of cloth 4 : the untwisted end of a rope

fag•ot *or* **fag•got** \'fa-gət\ *n* : a bundle of sticks or twigs

fag•ot•ing *or* **fag•got•ing** *n* : an embroidery produced by tying threads in hourglass-shaped clusters

Fah *or* **Fahr** *abbr* Fahrenheit

Fahr•en•heit \'far-ən-ˌhīt\ *adj* : relating to, conforming to, or having a thermometer scale with the boiling point of water at 212 degrees and the freezing point at 32 degrees above zero

fa•ience *or* **fa•ence** \fä-'äns\ *n* [F] : earthenware decorated with opaque colored glazes

¹**fail** \'fāl\ *vb* 1 : to become feeble; *esp* : to decline in health 2 : to die away 3 : to stop functioning 4 : to fall short ⟨*∼ed* in his duty⟩ 5 : to be or become absent or inadequate 6 : to be unsuccessful 7 : to become bankrupt 8 : DISAPPOINT 9 : NEGLECT

²**fail** *n* : FAILURE (without ∼)

¹**fail•ing** \'fā-liŋ\ *n* : WEAKNESS, SHORTCOMING

²**failing** *prep* : in the absence or lack of

faille \'fīl\ *n* : a somewhat shiny closely woven ribbed fabric (as silk)

fail–safe \'fāl-ˌsāf\ *adj* 1 : incorporating a counteractive feature for a possible source of failure 2 : having no chance of failure

fail•ure \'fāl-yər\ *n* 1 : a failing to do or perform 2 : a state of inability to perform a normal function adequately ⟨heart ∼⟩ 3 : a fracturing or giving way under stress 4 : a lack of success 5 : BANKRUPTCY 6 : DEFICIENCY 7 : DETERIORATION, DECAY 8 : one that has failed

¹**fain** \'fān\ *adj* 1 *archaic* : GLAD; *also* : INCLINED 2 : being obliged or compelled

²**fain** *adv* 1 : with pleasure 2 : by preference

¹**faint** \'fānt\ *adj* [ME *faint, feint,* fr. OF, fr. *faindre, feindre* to feign, shirk] 1 : COWARDLY, SPIRITLESS 2 : weak, dizzy, and likely to faint 3 : lacking vigor or strength : FEEBLE ⟨∼ praise⟩ 4 : INDISTINCT, DIM — **faint•ly** *adv* — **faint•ness** *n*

²**faint** *vb* : to lose consciousness

³**faint** *n* : the action of fainting; *also* : the resulting condition

faint•heart•ed \ˌfānt-'här-təd\ *adj* : lacking courage : TIMID

¹**fair** \'far\ *adj* 1 : pleasing in appearance : BEAUTIFUL 2 : superficially pleasing : SPECIOUS 3 : CLEAN, PURE 4 : CLEAR, LEGIBLE 5 : not stormy or cloudy 6 : JUST 7 : conforming with the rules : ALLOWED; *also* : being within the foul lines ⟨∼ ball⟩ 8 : open to legitimate pursuit or attack ⟨∼ game⟩ 9 : PROMISING, LIKELY ⟨a ∼ chance of winning⟩ 10 : favorable to a ship's course ⟨a ∼ wind⟩ 11 : light in complexion : BLOND 12 : ADEQUATE — **fair•ness** *n*

²**fair** *adv, chiefly Brit* : FAIRLY 4

³**fair** *n* 1 : a gathering of buyers and sellers at a stated time and place for trade 2 : a competitive exhibition (as of farm products) 3 : a sale of assorted articles usu. for a charitable purpose

fair•ground \-ˌgraünd\ *n* : an area where outdoor fairs, circuses, or exhibitions are held

fair•ing \'far-iŋ\ *n* : a structure for producing a smooth outline and reducing drag (as on an airplane)

fair•ly \'far-lē\ *adv* 1 : HANDSOMELY 2 : in a manner of speaking ⟨∼ bursting with pride⟩ 3 : without bias 4 : to a full degree or extent : PLAINLY, DISTINCTLY 5 : SOMEWHAT, RATHER ⟨a ∼ easy job⟩

fair–spo•ken \'far-'spō-kən\ *adj* : pleasant and courteous in speech

fair–trade \-'trād\ *adj* : of, relating to, or being an agreement between a producer and a seller that branded merchandise will be sold at or above a specified price — **fair–trade** *vb*

fair•way \-ˌwā\ *n* : the mowed part of a golf course between tee and green

fairy \'far-ē\ *n, pl* **fair•ies** [ME *fairie* fairyland, fairy people, fr. OF *faerie,* fr. *feie, fee* fairy, fr. L *Fata,* goddess of fate, fr. *fatum* fate] : an imaginary being of folklore and romance usu. having diminutive human form and magic powers — **fairy** *adj*

fairy•land \-ˌland\ *n* 1 : the land of fairies 2 : a beautiful or charming place

fairy tale *n* 1 : a children's story about fairies 2 : FIB

fait ac•com•pli \ˌfāt-ˌa-kōⁿ-'plē\ *n, pl* **faits accomplis** *same or* -'plēz\ [F, accomplished fact] : a thing accomplished and presumably irreversible

faith \'fāth\ *n, pl* **faiths** \'fāths, 'fāt͟hz\ [ME *feith,* fr. OF *feid, foi,* fr. L *fides*] 1 : allegiance to duty or a person : LOYALTY 2 : belief and trust in God 3 : complete trust 4 : a system of religious beliefs — **faith•ful** \-fəl\ *adj* — **faith•ful•ly** *adv* — **faith•ful•ness** *n*

faith•less \'fāth-ləs\ *adj* 1 : DISLOYAL 2 : not to be relied on **syn** false, traitorous, treacherous, unfaithful — **faith•less•ly** *adv* — **faith•less•ness** *n*

fa•ji•ta \fə-'hē-tə\ *n* : a marinated strip usu. of beef or chicken grilled or broiled and served usu. with a flour tortilla and savory fillings — usu. used in pl.

¹**fake** \'fāk\ *adj* : COUNTERFEIT, SHAM

²**fake** *n* 1 : IMITATION, FRAUD; *also* : IMPOSTOR 2 : a simulated move in sports (as a pretended pass)

³**fake** *vb* **faked; fak•ing** 1 : to treat so as to falsify 2 : COUNTERFEIT 3 : to deceive (an opponent) in a sports contest by making a fake — **fak•er** *n*

fa•kir \fə-'kir\ *n* [Ar *faqīr,* lit., poor man] 1 : a Muslim mendicant : DERVISH 2 : a wandering Hindu ascetic

fal•con \'fal-kən, 'fol-\ *n* 1 : a hawk trained for use in falconry 2 : any of various swift long-winged long-tailed hawks having a notched beak and usu. inhabiting open areas

fal•con•ry \'fal-kən-rē, 'fol-\ *n* 1 : the art of training hawks to hunt in cooperation with a person 2 : the sport of hunting with hawks — **fal•con•er** *n*

¹**fall** \'fol\ *vb* **fell** \'fel\; **fall•en** \'fo-lən\; **fall•ing** 1 : to descend freely by the force of gravity 2 : to hang freely 3 : to come or go as if by falling ⟨darkness *fell*⟩ 4 : to become uttered 5 : to lower or become lowered : DROP ⟨her eyes *fell*⟩ 6 : to leave an erect position suddenly and involuntarily 7 : STUMBLE, STRAY 8 : to drop down wounded or dead esp. in battle 9 : to become captured ⟨the city *fell* to the enemy⟩ 10 : to suffer ruin, defeat, or failure 11 : to commit an immoral act 12 : to move or extend in a downward direction 13 : SUBSIDE, ABATE 14 : to decline in quality, activity, quantity, or value 15 : to assume a look of shame or dejection ⟨her face *fell*⟩ 16 : to occur at a certain time 17 : to come by chance 18 : DEVOLVE ⟨the duties *fell* to him⟩ 19 : to have the proper place or station ⟨the accent ∼s on the first syllable⟩ 20 : to come within the scope of something 21 : to pass from one condition to another ⟨*fell* ill⟩ 22 : to set about heartily or actively ⟨∼ to work⟩ — **fall flat** : to produce no response or result — **fall for** 1 : to fall in love with 2 : to become a victim of — **fall foul** : to have a quarrel : CLASH — **fall from grace** : BACKSLIDE — **fall into line** : to comply with a certain course of action — **fall over oneself** *or* **fall over backward** : to display excessive eagerness — **fall short** 1 : to be deficient 2 : to fail to attain

²**fall** *n* 1 : the act of falling 2 : a falling out, off, or away : DROPPING 3 : AUTUMN 4 : a thing or quantity that falls ⟨a light ∼ of snow⟩ 5 : COLLAPSE, DOWNFALL 6 : the surrender or capture of a besieged place 7 : departure from virtue or goodness 8 : SLOPE 9 : WATERFALL — usu. used in pl. 10 : a decrease in size, quantity, degree, or value ⟨a ∼ in price⟩ 11 : the distance which something falls 12 : an act of forcing a wrestler's shoulders to the mat; *also* : a bout of wrestling

fal·la·cious \fə-'lā-shəs\ *adj* 1 : embodying a fallacy (a ∼ argument) 2 : MISLEADING, DECEPTIVE

fal·la·cy \'fa-lə-sē\ *n, pl* **-cies** 1 : a false or mistaken idea 2 : an often plausible argument using false or illogical reasoning

fall back *vb* : RETREAT, RECEDE

fall guy *n* 1 : one that is easily duped 2 : SCAPEGOAT

fal·li·ble \'fa-lə-bəl\ *adj* 1 : liable to be erroneous 2 : capable of making a mistake — **fal·li·bly** \-blē\ *adv*

fall·ing–out \ˌfȯ-liŋ-'aůt\ *n, pl* **fallings–out** *or* **falling–outs** : QUARREL

falling star *n* : METEOR

fal·lo·pi·an tube \fə-'lō-pē-ən-\ *n, often cap F* : either of the pair of anatomical tubes that carry the eggs from the ovary to the uterus

fall·out \'fȯ-ˌlaůt\ *n* 1 : the often radioactive particles that result from a nuclear explosion and descend through the air 2 : a secondary and often lingering effect or result

fall out *vb* : QUARREL

¹**fal·low** \'fa-(ˌ)lō\ *n* : fallow land; *also* : the state or period of being fallow — **fallow** *vb*

²**fallow** *adj* 1 : left without tilling or sowing after plowing 2 : DORMANT, INACTIVE ⟨a writer's ∼ period⟩

false \'fȯls\ *adj* **fals·er; fals·est** 1 : not genuine : ARTIFICIAL 2 : intentionally untrue 3 : adjusted or made so as to deceive ⟨∼ scales⟩ 4 : tending to mislead : DECEPTIVE ⟨∼ promises⟩ 5 : not true ⟨∼ concepts⟩ 6 : not faithful or loyal : TREACHEROUS 7 : not essential or permanent ⟨∼ front⟩ 8 : inaccurate in pitch 9 : based on mistaken ideas — **false·ly** *adv* — **false·ness** *n* — **fal·si·ty** \'fȯl-sə-tē\ *n*

false·hood \'fȯls-ˌhúd\ *n* 1 : LIE 2 : absence of truth or accuracy 3 : the practice of lying

fal·set·to \fȯl-'se-tō\ *n, pl* **-tos** [It, fr. dim. of *falso* false] : an artificially high voice; *esp* : an artificial singing voice that overlaps and extends above the range of the full voice esp. of a tenor

fal·si·fy \'fȯl-sə-ˌfī\ *vb* **-fied; -fy·ing** 1 : to prove to be false 2 : to alter so as to deceive 3 : LIE; *also* : MISREPRESENT — **fal·si·fi·ca·tion** \ˌfȯl-sə-fə-'kā-shən\ *n*

fal·ter \'fȯl-tər\ *vb* 1 : to move unsteadily : STUMBLE, TOTTER 2 : to hesitate in speech : STAMMER 3 : to hesitate in purpose or action : WAVER, FLINCH — **fal·ter·ing·ly** *adv*

fam *abbr* 1 familiar 2 family

fame \'fām\ *n* : public reputation : RENOWN — **famed** \'fāmd\ *adj*

fa·mil·ial \fə-'mil-yəl\ *adj* 1 : of, relating to, or suggestive of a family 2 : tending to occur in more members of a family than expected by chance alone ⟨a ∼ disorder⟩

¹**fa·mil·iar** \fə-'mil-yər\ *n* 1 : COMPANION 2 : a spirit held to attend and serve or guard a person 3 : one who frequents a place

²**familiar** *adj* 1 : closely acquainted : INTIMATE 2 : of or relating to a family 3 : INFORMAL 4 : FORWARD, PRESUMPTUOUS 5 : frequently seen or experienced 6 : of everyday occurrence — **fa·mil·iar·ly** *adv*

fa·mil·iar·ise *Brit var of* FAMILIARIZE

fa·mil·iar·i·ty \fə-ˌmil-'yar-ə-tē, -ˌmi-lē-'ar-\ *n, pl* **-ties** 1 : close friendship : INTIMACY 2 : INFORMALITY 3 : an unduly bold or forward act or expression : IMPROPRIETY 4 : close acquaintance with something

fa·mil·iar·ize \fə-'mil-yə-ˌrīz\ *vb* **-ized; -iz·ing** 1 : to make known or familiar 2 : to make thoroughly acquainted

fam·i·ly \'fam-lē, 'fa-mə-\ *n, pl* **-lies** [ME *familie*, fr. L *familia* household, fr. *famulus* servant] 1 : a group of individuals living under one roof and under one head : HOUSEHOLD 2 : a group of persons of common ancestry : CLAN 3 : a group of things having common characteristics; *esp* : a group of related plants or animals ranking in biological classification above a genus and below an order 4 : a social unit usu. consisting of one or two parents and their children

family planning *n* : planning intended to determine the number and spacing of one's children by using birth control

family tree *n* : GENEALOGY; *also* : a genealogical diagram

fam·ine \'fa-mən\ *n* 1 : an extreme scarcity of food : a great shortage

fam·ish \'fa-mish\ *vb* 1 : STARVE 2 : to suffer for lack of something necessary

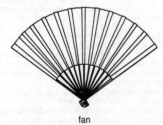

fa·mous \'fā-məs\ *adj* 1 : widely known 2 : honored for achievement 3 : EXCELLENT, FIRST-RATE **syn** renowned, celebrated, noted, notorious, distinguished, eminent, illustrious

fa·mous·ly *adv* : SPLENDIDLY, EXCELLENTLY

¹**fan** \'fan\ *n* : a device (as a hand-waved triangular piece or a mechanism with blades) for producing a current of air

fan

²**fan** *vb* **fanned; fan·ning** 1 : to drive away the chaff from grain by winnowing 2 : to move (air) with or as if with a fan 3 : to direct a current of air upon ⟨∼ a fire⟩ 4 : to stir up to activity : STIMULATE 5 : to spread like a fan 6 : to strike out in baseball

³**fan** *n* : an enthusiastic follower or admirer

fa·nat·ic \fə-'na-tik\ *or* **fa·nat·i·cal** \-ti-kəl\ *adj* [L *fanaticus* inspired by a deity, frenzied, fr. *fanum* temple] : marked by excessive enthusiasm and often intense uncritical devotion — **fanatic** *n* — **fa·nat·i·cism** \-tə-ˌsi-zəm\ *n*

fan·ci·er \'fan-sē-ər\ *n* **1** : one that has a special liking or interest **2** : a person who breeds or grows some kind of animal or plant for points of excellence

fan·ci·ful \'fan-si-fəl\ *adj* **1** : marked by, existing in, or given to unrestrained imagination or whim rather than reason **2** : curiously made or shaped — **fan·ci·ful·ly** *adv*

¹fan·cy \'fan-sē\ *vb* **fan·cied; fan·cy·ing 1** : LIKE **2** : IMAGINE **3** : to believe without evidence or certainty **4** : to visualize or interpret as

²fancy *n, pl* **fancies** [ME *fantasie, fantsy* fantasy, fancy, fr. MF *fantasie*, fr. L *phantasia*, fr. Gk, appearance, imagination] **1** : LIKING, INCLINATION; *also* : LOVE **2** : WHIM, NOTION, IDEA ⟨a passing ∼⟩ **3** : IMAGINATION **4** : TASTE, JUDGMENT **syn** caprice, crotchet, vagary

³fancy *adj* **fan·ci·er; -est 1** : WHIMSICAL **2** : not plain : ORNAMENTAL, POSH **3** : of particular excellence **4** : bred esp. for a showy appearance **5** : EXCESSIVE **6** : executed with technical skill and style — **fan·ci·ly** \'fan-sə-lē\ *adv*

fancy dress *n* : a costume (as for a masquerade) chosen to suit a fancy

fan·cy–free \ˌfan-sē-'frē\ *adj* : free from amorous attachment; *also* : free to imagine

fan·cy·work \'fan-sē-ˌwərk\ *n* : ornamental needlework (as embroidery)

fan·dan·go \fan-'daŋ-gō\ *n, pl* **-gos 1** : a lively Spanish or Spanish-American dance **2** : TOMFOOLERY

fane \'fān\ *n* **1** : TEMPLE **2** : CHURCH

fan·fare \'fan-ˌfär\ *n* **1** : a flourish of trumpets **2** : a showy display

fang \'faŋ\ *n* : a long sharp tooth; *esp* : a grooved or hollow tooth of a venomous snake — **fanged** \'faŋd\ *adj*

fan·light \'fan-ˌlīt\ *n* : a semicircular window with radiating bars like a fan that is set over a door or window

fan·tail \'fan-ˌtāl\ *n* **1** : a fan-shaped tail or end **2** : an overhang at the stern of a ship

fan·ta·sia \fan-'tā-zhə, -zhē-ə, -zē-ə; ˌfan-tə-'zē-ə\ *n* : a musical composition free and fanciful in form

fan·ta·sise *Brit var of* FANTASIZE

fan·ta·size \'fan-tə-ˌsīz\ *vb* **-sized; -siz·ing** : IMAGINE, DAYDREAM

fan·tas·tic \fan-'tas-tik\ *also* **fan·tas·ti·cal** \-ti-kəl\ *adj* **1** : IMAGINARY, UNREAL **2** : conceived by unrestrained fancy **3** : exceedingly or unbelievably great **4** : ECCENTRIC **syn** chimerical, fanciful, imaginary — **fan·tas·ti·cal·ly** \-ti-k(ə-)lē\ *adv*

fan·ta·sy \'fan-tə-sē\ *n, pl* **-sies 1** : IMAGINATION, FANCY **2** : a product of the imagination : ILLUSION **3** : FANTASIA — **fantasy** *vb*

FAQ *abbr* frequently asked question

¹far \'fär\ *adv* **far·ther** \-thər\ *or* **fur·ther** \'fər-\; **far·thest** *or* **fur·thest** \-thəst\ **1** : at or to a considerable distance in space or time ⟨∼ from home⟩ **2** : by a broad interval : WIDELY, MUCH ⟨∼ better⟩ **3** : to or at a definite distance, point, or degree ⟨as ∼ as I know⟩ **4** : to an advanced point or extent ⟨go ∼ in his field⟩ — **by far** : by a considerable margin — **far and away** : DECIDEDLY — **so far** : until now

²far *adj* **farther** *or* **further; farthest** *or* **furthest 1** : remote in space or time **2** : DIFFERENT **3** : LONG ⟨a ∼ journey⟩ **4** : being the more distant of two ⟨on the ∼ side of the lake⟩

far·ad \'far-ˌad, -əd\ *n* : a unit of capacitance equal to the capacitance of a capacitor having a potential difference of one volt between its plates when it is charged with one coulomb of electricity

far·away \'fär-ə-ˌwā\ *adj* **1** : DISTANT, REMOTE **2** : DREAMY

farce \'färs\ *n* **1** : a broadly satirical comedy with an improbable plot **2** : the humor characteristic of farce or pretense **3** : a ridiculous or empty display — **far·ci·cal** \'fär-si-kəl\ *adj*

¹fare \'far\ *vb* **fared; far·ing 1** : GO, TRAVEL **2** : GET ALONG, SUCCEED **3** : EAT, DINE

²fare *n* **1** : range of food : DIET; *also* : material provided for use, consumption, or enjoyment **2** : the price charged to transport a person **2** : a person paying a fare : PASSENGER

¹fare·well \far-'wel\ *vb imper* : get along well — used interjectionally to or by one departing

²farewell *n* **1** : a wish of well-being at parting : GOOD-BYE **2** : LEAVE-TAKING

³fare·well \'far-ˌwel\ *adj* : PARTING, FINAL ⟨a ∼ concert⟩

far–fetched \'fär-'fecht\ *adj* : not easily or naturally deduced or introduced : IMPROBABLE ⟨∼ story⟩

far–flung \-'fləŋ\ *adj* : widely spread or distributed

fa·ri·na \fə-'rē-nə\ *n* [L, meal, flour] : a fine meal (as of wheat) used in puddings or as a breakfast cereal

far·i·na·ceous \ˌfar-ə-'nā-shəs\ *adj* **1** : having a mealy texture or surface **2** : containing or rich in starch

¹farm \'färm\ *n* [ME *ferme* rent, lease, fr. OF, lease, fr. *fermer* to fix, make a contract, fr. L *firmare* to make firm, fr. *firmus* firm] **1** : a tract of land used for raising crops or livestock **2** : a minor-league subsidiary of a major-league baseball team

²farm *vb* : to use (land) as a farm ⟨∼ed 200 acres⟩; *also* : to raise crops or livestock — **farm·er** *n*

farm·hand \'färm-ˌhand\ *n* : a farm laborer

farm·house \-ˌhaùs\ *n* : a dwelling on a farm

farm·ing \'fär-miŋ\ *n* : the occupation or business of a person who farms

farm·land \'färm-ˌland\ *n* : land used or suitable for farming

farm out *vb* : to turn over (as a task) to another

farm·stead \'färm-ˌsted\ *n* : a farm with its buildings

farm·yard \-ˌyärd\ *n* : land around or enclosed by farm buildings

far–off \'fär-'òf\ *adj* : remote in time or space : DISTANT

fa·rouche \fə-'rüsh\ adj [F] **1** : WILD **2** : marked by shyness and lack of polish

far–out \'fär-'aút\ adj : very unconventional ⟨∼ clothes⟩

far·ra·go \fə-'rä-gō, -'rā-\ n, pl **-goes** [L, mixed fodder, mixture] : a confused collection : MIXTURE

far–reach·ing \'fär-'rē-chiŋ\ adj : having a wide range or effect

far·ri·er \'far-ē-ər\ n : a person who shoes horses

¹**far·row** \'far-ō\ vb : to give birth to a litter of pigs

²**farrow** n : a litter of pigs

far·see·ing \'fär-ˌsē-iŋ\ adj : FARSIGHTED 1, 2

far·sight·ed \'fär-ˌsī-təd\ adj **1** : seeing or able to see to a great distance **2** : JUDICIOUS, WISE, SHREWD **3** : affected with an eye condition in which vision is better for distant than near objects — **far·sight·ed·ness** n

¹**far·ther** \'fär-thər\ adv **1** : at or to a greater distance or more advanced point **2** : to a greater degree or extent

²**farther** adj **1** : more distant **2** : ADDITIONAL

far·ther·most \-ˌmōst\ adj : FARTHEST

¹**far·thest** \'fär-thəst\ adj : most distant

²**farthest** adv **1** : to or at the greatest distance : REMOTEST **2** : to the most advanced point **3** : by the greatest degree or extent : MOST

far·thing \'fär-thiŋ\ n **1** : a former British monetary unit equal to ¼ of a penny; also : a coin representing this unit **2** : something of small value

fas·ci·cle \'fa-si-kəl\ n **1** : a small or slender bundle (as of pine needles or nerve fiber) **2** : one of the divisions of a book published in parts — **fas·ci·cled** \-kəld\ adj

fas·ci·nate \'fas-ⁿn-ˌāt\ vb **-nat·ed; -nat·ing** [L fascinare, fr. fascinum evil spell] **1** : to transfix and hold spellbound by an irresistible power **2** : ALLURE **3** : to be irresistibly attractive — **fas·ci·na·tion** \ˌfas-ⁿn-'ā-shən\ n

fas·cism \'fa-ˌshi-zəm\ n, often cap : a political philosophy, movement, or regime that exalts nation and often race and stands for a centralized autocratic often militaristic government — **fas·cist** \-shist\ n or adj, often cap — **fas·cis·tic** \fa-'shis-tik\ adj, often cap

¹**fash·ion** \'fa-shən\ n **1** : the make or form of something **2** : MANNER, WAY **3** : a prevailing custom, usage, or style **4** : the prevailing style (as in dress) syn mode, vogue, rage, trend

²**fashion** vb **1** : MOLD, CONSTRUCT **2** : FIT, ADAPT

fash·ion·able \'fa-shə-nə-bəl\ adj **1** : dressing or behaving according to fashion : STYLISH **2** : of or relating to the world of fashion ⟨∼ resorts⟩ syn chic, modish, smart, swank — **fash·ion·ably** \-blē\ adv

¹**fast** \'fast\ adj **1** : firmly fixed **2** : tightly shut **3** : adhering firmly **4** : STUCK **5** : STAUNCH ⟨∼ friends⟩ **6** : characterized by quick motion, operation, or effect ⟨a ∼ trip⟩ ⟨a ∼ track⟩ **7** : indicating ahead of the correct time ⟨the clock is ∼⟩ **8** : not easily disturbed : SOUND ⟨a ∼ sleep⟩ **9** : permanently dyed; also : being proof against fading ⟨colors ∼ to sunlight⟩ **10** : DISSIPATED, WILD **11** : sexually promiscuous syn rapid, swift, fleet, quick, speedy, hasty

²**fast** adv **1** : in a firm or fixed manner ⟨stuck ∼ in the mud⟩ **2** : SOUNDLY, DEEPLY ⟨∼ asleep⟩ **3** : SWIFTLY **4** : RECKLESSLY

³**fast** vb **1** : to abstain from food **2** : to eat sparingly or abstain from some foods

⁴**fast** n **1** : the act or practice of fasting **2** : a time of fasting

fast·back \'fast-ˌbak\ n : an automobile having a roof with a long slope to the rear

fast·ball \-ˌbȯl\ n : a baseball pitch thrown at full speed

fas·ten \'fas-ⁿn\ vb **1** : to attach or join by or as if by pinning, tying, or nailing **2** : to make fast : fix securely **3** : to become fixed or joined **4** : to focus attention ⟨∼ed onto the newest trends⟩ — **fas·ten·er** n

fas·ten·ing n : something that fastens : FASTENER

fast–food \ˌfast-'füd\ adj : specializing in food that is prepared and served quickly ⟨a ∼ restaurant⟩

fast–for·ward \-'fȯr-wərd\ n **1** : a function of a tape player that advances tape rapidly **2** : a state of rapid advancement — **fast–forward** vb

fas·tid·i·ous \fa-'sti-dē-əs\ adj **1** : overly difficult to please **2** : showing a meticulous or demanding attitude ⟨∼ workmanship⟩ syn nice, finicky, fussy, particular, persnickety, squeamish — **fas·tid·i·ous·ly** adv — **fas·tid·i·ous·ness** n

fast·ness \'fast-nəs\ n **1** : the quality or state of being fast **2** : a fortified or secure place : STRONGHOLD

fast–talk \'fast-ˌtȯk\ vb : to influence by persuasive and usu. deceptive talk

fast–track \'fast-ˌtrak\ vb : to speed up the processing or production of

fast track n : a course leading to rapid advancement or success

¹**fat** \'fat\ adj **fat·ter; fat·test 1** : PLUMP, FLESHY **2** : OILY, GREASY **3** : well filled out : BIG **4** : well stocked : ABUNDANT **5** : richly rewarding — **fat·ness** n

²**fat** n **1** : animal tissue rich in greasy or oily matter **2** : any of numerous energy-rich esters that occur naturally in animal fats and in plants and are soluble in organic solvents (as ether) but not in water **3** : the best or richest portion ⟨lived on the ∼ of the land⟩ **4** : OBESITY **5** : excess matter

fa·tal \'fāt-ᵊl\ adj **1** : FATEFUL ⟨that ∼ day⟩ **2** : causing death or ruin ⟨a ∼ mistake⟩ — **fa·tal·ly** adv

fa·tal·ism \-ᵊ-ˌi-zəm\ n : the belief that events are determined by fate — **fa·tal·ist** \-ist\ n — **fa·tal·is·tic** \ˌfāt-ᵊl-'is-tik\ adj — **fa·tal·is·ti·cal·ly** \-ti-k(ə-)lē\ adv

fa·tal·i·ty \fā-'ta-lə-tē, fə-\ n, pl **-ties 1** : DEADLINESS **2** : FATE **3** : death resulting from a disaster or accident; also : one who suffers such a death

fat·back \'fat-ˌbak\ n : a fatty strip from the back of the hog usu. cured by salting and drying

fat cat n **1** : a wealthy contributor to a political campaign **2** : a wealthy privileged person

fate \'fāt\ n [ME, fr. MF or L; MF, fr. L fatum, lit., what has been spoken, fr. fari to speak] **1** : the cause or will that is held to determine events : DESTINY **2** : LOT, FORTUNE **3** : DISASTER; esp : DEATH **4** : END, OUTCOME **5** cap, pl : the three goddesses of classical mythology who determine the course of human life

fat·ed \'fā-təd\ adj : decreed, controlled, or marked by fate

fate·ful \'fāt-fəl\ adj **1** : OMINOUS, PROPHETIC **2** : IMPORTANT, DECISIVE **3** : DEADLY, DESTRUCTIVE **4** : determined by fate — **fate·ful·ly** adv

fath abbr fathom

fat·head \'fat-ˌhed\ n : a stupid person — **fat·head·ed** \-'he-dəd\ adj

¹**fa·ther** \'fä-thər\ n **1** : a male parent **2** cap : God esp. as the first person of the Trinity **3** : FOREFATHER **4** : one deserving the respect and love given to a father **5** often cap : an early Christian writer accepted by the church as an authoritative witness to its teaching and practice **6** : ORIGINATOR ⟨the ∼ of modern radio⟩; also : SOURCE **7** : PRIEST — used esp. as a title **8** : one of the leading men ⟨city ∼s⟩ — **fa·ther·hood** \-ˌhúd\ n — **fa·ther·less** adj — **fa·ther·ly** adj

²**father** vb **1** : BEGET **2** : to be the founder, producer, or author of **3** : to treat or care for as a father

father–in–law \'fä-thə-rən-ˌlȯ\ n, pl **fathers–in–law** \-thər-zən-\ : the father of one's husband or wife

fa·ther·land \'fä-thər-ˌland\ n **1** : the native land of one's ancestors **2** : one's native land

¹**fath·om** \'fa-thəm\ n [ME fadme, fr. OE fæthm outstretched arms, fathom] : a unit of length equal to 6 feet (about 1.8 meters) used esp. for measuring the depth of water

²**fathom** vb **1** : to measure by a sounding line **2** : PROBE **3** : to penetrate and come to understand — **fath·om·able** \'fa-thə-mə-bəl\ adj

fath·om·less \'fa-thəm-ləs\ adj : incapable of being fathomed

¹**fa·tigue** \fə-'tēg\ n [F] **1** : manual or menial work per-

formed by military personnel **2** *pl* : the uniform or work clothing worn on fatigue and in the field **3** : weariness from labor or stress **4** : the tendency of a material to break under repeated stress

²**fatigue** *vb* **fa·tigued; fa·tigu·ing** : WEARY, TIRE

fat·ten \'fat-ᵊn\ *vb* : to make or grow fat

¹**fat·ty** \'fa-tē\ *adj* **fat·ti·er; -est 1** : containing fat esp. in unusual amounts **2** : GREASY

²**fatty** *n, pl* **fat·ties** : a fat person

fatty acid *n* : any of numerous acids that contain only carbon, hydrogen, and oxygen and that occur naturally in fats and various oils

fa·tu·ity \fə-'tü-ə-tē, -'tyü-\ *n, pl* **-ities** : FOOLISHNESS, STUPIDITY

fat·u·ous \'fa-chù-wəs\ *adj* : FOOLISH, INANE, SILLY — **fat·u·ous·ly** *adv*

fau·bourg \fō-'bùr\ *n* **1** : a suburb esp. of a French city **2** : a city quarter

fau·ces \'fȯ-ˌsēz\ *n pl* [L, throat] : the narrow passage located between the soft palate and the base of the tongue that joins the mouth to the pharynx

fau·cet \'fȯ-sət, 'fä-\ *n* : a fixture for drawing off a liquid (as from a pipe)

¹**fault** \'fȯlt\ *n* **1** : a weakness in character : FAILING **2** : IMPERFECTION, IMPAIRMENT, DEFECT **3** : an error esp. in service in a net or racket game **4** : MISDEMEANOR; *also* : MISTAKE **5** : responsibility for something wrong **6** : a fracture in the earth's crust accompanied by a displacement of one side relative to the other — **fault·i·ly** \'fȯl-tə-lē\ *adv* — **fault·less** *adj* — **fault·less·ly** *adv* — **faulty** *adj*

²**fault** *vb* **1** : to commit a fault : ERR **2** : to fracture so as to produce a geologic fault **3** : to find a fault in

fault·find·er \'fȯlt-ˌfīn-dər\ *n* : a person who tends to find fault or complain **syn** critic, carper, caviler, complainer — **fault·find·ing** *n or adj*

faun \'fȯn\ *n* : a Roman god similar to but gentler than a satyr

fau·na \'fȯ-nə\ *n, pl* **faunas** *also* **fau·nae** \-ˌnē, -ˌnī\ [NL, fr. L *Fauna*, sister of Faunus (the Roman god of animals)] : animals or animal life esp. of a region, period, or environment — **fau·nal** \-nəl\ *adj*

fau·vism \'fō-ˌvi-zəm\ *n, often cap* : a movement in painting characterized by vivid colors, free treatment of form, and a vibrant and decorative effect — **fau·vist** \-vist\ *n, often cap*

faux pas \'fō-ˌpä, fō-'\ *n, pl* **faux pas** *same or* -ˌpäz, -'päz\ [F, lit., false step] : BLUNDER; *esp* : a social blunder

¹**fa·vor** \'fā-vər\ *n* **1** : friendly regard shown toward another esp. by a superior **2** : APPROVAL **3** : PARTIALITY **4** : POPULARITY **5** : gracious kindness; *also* : an act of such kindness **6** *pl* : effort in one's behalf : ATTENTION **7** : a token of love (as a ribbon) usu. worn conspicuously **8** : a small gift or decorative item given out at a party **9** : a special privilege **10** : sexual privileges — usu. used in pl. **11** *archaic* : LETTER **12** : BEHALF, INTEREST

²**favor** *vb* **1** : to regard or treat with favor **2** : OBLIGE **3** : ENDOW ⟨~ed by nature⟩ **4** : to treat gently or care-

fully : SPARE ⟨~ a lame leg⟩ **5** : PREFER **6** : SUPPORT, SUSTAIN **7** : FACILITATE ⟨darkness ~s attack⟩ **8** : RESEMBLE ⟨he ~s his father⟩

fa·vor·able \'fā-və-rə-bəl\ *adj* **1** : APPROVING **2** : HELPFUL, PROMISING, ADVANTAGEOUS ⟨~ weather⟩ — **fa·vor·ably** \-blē\ *adv*

fa·vor·ite \'fā-və-rət, -vrət\ *n* **1** : a person or a thing that is favored above others **2** : a competitor regarded as most likely to win — **favorite** *adj*

favorite son *n* : a candidate supported by the delegates of his state at a presidential nominating convention

fa·vor·it·ism \'fā-və-rə-ˌti-zəm\ *n* : PARTIALITY, BIAS

fa·vour *chiefly Brit var of* FAVOR

¹**fawn** \'fȯn, 'fän\ *vb* **1** : to show affection ⟨a dog ~ing on its master⟩ **2** : to court favor by a cringing or flattering manner **syn** grovel, kowtow, toady, truckle

²**fawn** *n* **1** : a young deer **2** : a light grayish brown

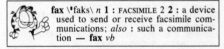

fax \'faks\ *n* **1** : FACSIMILE 2 **2** : a device used to send or receive facsimile communications; *also* : such a communication — **fax** *vb*

fay \'fā\ *n* : FAIRY, ELF — **fay** *adj*

faze \'fāz\ *vb* **fazed; faz·ing** : to disturb the composure or courage of : DAUNT

FBI *abbr* Federal Bureau of Investigation

FCC *abbr* Federal Communications Commission

FD *abbr* fire department

FDA *abbr* Food and Drug Administration

FDIC *abbr* Federal Deposit Insurance Corporation

Fe *symbol* [L *ferrum*] iron

fe·al·ty \'fēl-tē\ *n, pl* **-ties** : LOYALTY, ALLEGIANCE **syn** fidelity, devotion, faithfulness, piety

¹**fear** \'fir\ *vb* **1** : to have a reverent awe of ⟨~ God⟩ **2** : to be afraid of : have fear **3** : to be apprehensive

²**fear** *n* **1** : an unpleasant often strong emotion caused by expectation or awareness of danger; *also* : an instance of or a state marked by this emotion **2** : anxious concern : SOLICITUDE **3** : profound reverence esp. toward God **syn** dread, fright, alarm, panic, terror, trepidation

fear·ful \-fəl\ *adj* **1** : causing fear **2** : filled with fear **3** : showing or caused by fear **4** : extremely bad, intense, or large — **fear·ful·ly** *adv*

fear·less \-ləs\ *adj* : free from fear : BRAVE — **fear·less·ly** *adv* — **fear·less·ness** *n*

fear·some \-səm\ *adj* **1** : causing fear **2** : TIMID

fea·si·ble \'fē-zə-bəl\ *adj* **1** : capable of being done or carried out ⟨a ~ plan⟩ **2** : SUITABLE **3** : REASONABLE, LIKELY **syn** possible, practicable, viable, workable — **fea·si·bil·i·ty** \ˌfē-zə-'bi-lə-tē\ *n* — **fea·si·bly** \'fē-zə-blē\ *adv*

¹**feast** \'fēst\ *n* **1** : an elaborate meal : BANQUET **2** : FESTIVAL 1

²**feast** *vb* **1** : to take part in a feast; *also* : to give a feast for **2** : to enjoy some unusual pleasure or delight **3** : DELIGHT, GRATIFY

feat \'fēt\ *n* : DEED, EXPLOIT, ACHIEVEMENT; *esp* : an act notable for courage, skill, endurance, or ingenuity

¹feath·er \'fe-thər\ *n* **1** : any of the light horny outgrowths that form the external covering of the body of a bird **2** : PLUME **3** : PLUMAGE **4** : KIND, NATURE ⟨birds of a ∼⟩ **5** : ATTIRE, DRESS ⟨in full ∼⟩ **6** : CONDITION, MOOD ⟨in fine ∼⟩ — **feath·ered** \-thərd\ *adj* — **feath·er·less** *àdj* — **feath·ery** *adj* — **a feather in one's cap** : a mark of distinction : HONOR

²feather *vb* **1** : to furnish with a feather ⟨∼ an arrow⟩ **2** : to cover, clothe, line, or adorn with or as if with feathers — **feather one's nest** : to provide for oneself esp. while in a position of trust

feath·er·bed·ding \'fe-thər-₁be-diŋ\ *n* : the requiring of an employer usu. under a union rule or safety statute to employ more workers than are needed

feath·er·edge \-₁ej\ *n* : a very thin sharp edge

feath·er·weight \-₁wāt\ *n* : one that is very light in weight; *esp* : a boxer weighing more than 118 but not over 126 pounds

¹fea·ture \'fē-chər\ *n* **1** : the shape or appearance of the face or its parts **2** : a part of the face : LINEAMENT **3** : a prominent part or characteristic **4** : a special attraction (as in a newspaper) **5** : something offered to the public or advertised as particularly attractive — **fea·ture·less** *adj*

²feature *vb* **1** : to picture in the mind : IMAGINE **2** : to give special prominence to ⟨∼ a story in a newspaper⟩ **3** : to play an important part

feaze \'fēz, 'fāz\ *var of* FAZE

Feb *abbr* February

fe·brile \'fe-₁brīl\ *adj* : FEVERISH

Feb·ru·ary \'fe-b(y)ə-₁wer-ē, 'fe-brə-\ *n* [ME *Februarie*, fr. L *Februarius*, fr. *Februa*, pl., feast of purification] : the 2d month of the year

fe·ces \'fē-₁sēz\ *n pl* : bodily waste discharged from the intestine — **fe·cal** \-kəl\ *adj*

feck·less \'fek-ləs\ *adj* **1** : WEAK, INEFFECTIVE **2** : WORTHLESS, IRRESPONSIBLE

fe·cund \'fe-kənd, 'fē-\ *adj* : FRUITFUL, PROLIFIC — **fe·cun·di·ty** \fi-'kən-də-tē, fe-\ *n*

fe·cun·date \'fe-kən-₁dāt, 'fē-\ *vb* **-dat·ed; -dat·ing 1** : to make fecund **2** : IMPREGNATE — **fe·cun·da·tion** \₁fe-kən-'dā-shən, ₁fē-\ *n*

fed *abbr* federal; federation

fed·er·al \'fe-də-rəl, -drəl\ *adj* **1** : formed by a compact between political units that surrender individual sovereignty to a central authority but retain certain limited powers **2** : of or constituting a form of government in which power is distributed between a central authority and constituent territorial units **3** : of or relating to the central government of a federation **4** *cap* : FEDERALIST **5** *often cap* : of, relating to, or loyal to the federal government or the Union armies of the U.S. in the American Civil War — **fed·er·al·ly** *adv*

Federal *n* : a supporter of the U.S. government in the Civil War; *esp* : a soldier in the federal armies

federal district *n* : a district (as the District of Columbia) set apart as the seat of the central government of a federation

fed·er·al·ism \'fe-də-rə-li-zəm, -drə-\ *n* **1** *often cap* : the distribution of power in an organization (as a government) between a central authority and the constituent units **2** : support or advocacy of federalism **3** *cap* : the principles of the Federalists

fed·er·al·ist \-list\ *n* **1** : an advocate of federalism **2** *often cap* : an advocate of a federal union between the American colonies after the Revolution and of adoption of the U.S. Constitution **3** *cap* : a member of a major political party in the early years of the U.S. favoring a strong centralized national government — **federalist** *adj, often cap*

fed·er·al·ize \'fe-də-rə-₁līz, -drə-\ *vb* **-ized; -iz·ing 1** : to unite in or under a federal system **2** : to bring under the jurisdiction of a federal government

fed·er·ate \'fe-də-₁rāt\ *vb* **-at·ed; -at·ing** : to join in a federation

fed·er·a·tion \₁fe-də-'rā-shən\ *n* **1** : the act of federating; *esp* : the forming of a federal union **2** : a federal government **3** : a union of organizations

fedn *abbr* federation

fe·do·ra \fi-'dōr-ə\ *n* : a low soft felt hat with the crown creased lengthwise

fed up *adj* : utterly sated, tired, or disgusted

fee \'fē\ *n* **1** : an estate in land held from a feudal lord **2** : an inherited or heritable estate in land **3** : a fixed charge; *also* : a charge for a service

fee·ble \'fē-bəl\ *adj* **fee·bler** \-bə-lər\; **fee·blest** \-bə-ləst\ [ME *feble*, fr. OF, fr. L *flebilis* lamentable, wretched, fr. *flēre* to weep] **1** : DECREPIT, FRAIL **2** : INEFFECTIVE, INADEQUATE ⟨a ∼ protest⟩ — **fee·ble·ness** *n* — **fee·bly** \-blē\ *adv*

fee·ble·mind·ed \₁fē-bəl-'mīn-dəd\ *adj* : lacking normal intelligence — **fee·ble·mind·ed·ness** *n*

¹feed \'fēd\ *vb* **fed** \'fed\; **feed·ing 1** : to give food to; *also* : to give as food **2** : EAT 1; *also* : PREY **3** : to furnish what is necessary to the growth or function of — **feed·er** *n*

²feed *n* **1** : a usu. large meal **2** : food for livestock **3** : a mechanism for feeding material to a machine

feed·back \'fēd-₁bak\ *n* **1** : the return to the input of a part of the output of a machine, system, or process **2** : response esp. to one in authority about an activity or policy

feed·lot \'fēd-₁lät\ *n* : land on which cattle are fattened for market

feed·stuff \-₁stəf\ *n* : FEED 2

¹feel \'fēl\ *vb* **felt** \'felt\; **feel·ing 1** : to perceive or examine through physical contact : TOUCH, HANDLE **2** : EXPERIENCE; *also* : to suffer from **3** : to ascertain by cautious trial ⟨∼ out public sentiment⟩ **4** : to be aware of **5** : to be conscious of an inward impression, state of mind, or physical condition **6** : BELIEVE, THINK **7** : to search for something with the fingers : GROPE **8** : SEEM ⟨it ∼s like spring⟩ **9** : to have sympathy or pity

²feel *n* **1** : the sense of touch **2** : SENSATION, FEELING **3** : the quality of a thing as imparted through touch

feel·er \'fē-lər\ *n* **1** : one that feels; *esp* : a tactile organ (as on the head of an insect) **2** : a proposal or remark made to find out the views of other people

feel·ing \'fē-liŋ\ *n* **1** : the sense of touch; *also* : a sensation perceived by this **2** : a state of mind ⟨a ∼ of loneliness⟩ **3** *pl* : general emotional condition : SENSIBILITIES ⟨hurt their ∼s⟩ **4** : OPINION, BELIEF **5** : capacity to respond emotionally

²feeling *adj* **1** : SENSITIVE; *esp* : easily moved emotionally **2** : expressing emotion or sensitivity — **feel·ing·ly** *adv*

feet *pl of* FOOT

feign \'fān\ *vb* **1** : to give a false appearance of : SHAM ⟨∼ illness⟩ **2** : to assert as if true : PRETEND

feint \'fānt\ *n* : something feigned; *esp* : a mock blow or attack intended to distract attention from the real point of attack — **feint** *vb*

feisty \'fī-stē\ *adj* **feist·i·er; -est** : having or showing a lively aggressiveness

feld·spar \'feld-₁spär\ *n* : any of a group of crystalline minerals consisting of silicates of aluminum with another element (as potassium or sodium)

fe·lic·i·tate \fi-'li-sə-₁tāt\ *vb* **-tat·ed; -tat·ing** : CONGRATULATE — **fe·lic·i·ta·tion** \-₁li-sə-'tä-shən\ *n*

fe·lic·i·tous \fi-'li-sə-təs\ *adj* **1** : well chosen : APT **2** : PLEASANT, DELIGHTFUL — **fe·lic·i·tous·ly** *adv*

fe·lic·i·ty \fi-'li-sə-tē\ *n, pl* **-ties 1** : the quality or state of being happy; *esp* : great happiness **2** : something that causes happiness **3** : a pleasing manner or quality esp. in art or language **4** : an apt expression

fe·line \'fē-₁līn\ *adj* [L *felinus*, fr. *felis* cat] **1** : of or relating to cats or their kin **2** : SLY, TREACHEROUS **3** : STEALTHY — **feline** *n*

¹fell \'fel\ *n* : SKIN, HIDE, PELT

²fell *vb* **1** : to cut, beat, or knock down; *also* : KILL **2** : to sew (a seam) by folding one raw edge under the other

³fell *past of* FALL

⁴fell *adj* : CRUEL, FIERCE; *also* : DEADLY

fel·lah \'fe-lə, fə-'lä\ *n, pl* **fel·la·hin** *or* **fel·la·heen** \fe-lə-'hēn\ : a peasant or agricultural laborer in Arab countries (as Egypt or Syria)

fel·la·tio \fə-'lä-shē-ˌō\ *also* **fel·la·tion** \-shən\ *n* : oral stimulation of the penis

fel·low \'fe-lō\ *n* [ME *felawe,* fr. OE *fēolaga,* fr. ON *fēlagi,* fr. *fēlag* partnership, fr. *fē* cattle, money + *lag* act of laying] **1** : COMRADE, ASSOCIATE **2** : EQUAL, PEER **3** : one of a pair : MATE **4** : a member of an incorporated literary or scientific society **5** : MAN, BOY **6** : BOYFRIEND **7** : a person granted a stipend for advanced study

fel·low·man \fe-lō-'man\ *n* : a kindred human being

fel·low·ship \'fe-lō-ˌship\ *n* **1** : the condition of friendly relationship existing among persons : COMRADESHIP **2** : a community of interest or feeling **3** : a group with similar interests **4** : the position of a fellow (as of a university) **5** : the stipend granted a fellow

fellow traveler *n* : a person who sympathizes with and often furthers the ideals and program of an organized group (as the Communist party) without joining it

fel·on \'fe-lən\ *n* **1** : one who has committed a felony **2** : WHITLOW

fel·o·ny \'fe-lə-nē\ *n, pl* **-nies** : a serious crime punishable by a heavy sentence — **fe·lo·ni·ous** \fə-'lō-nē-əs\ *adj*

fel·spar *chiefly Brit var of* FELDSPAR

¹felt \'felt\ *n* **1** : a cloth made of wool and fur often mixed with natural or synthetic fibers **2** : a material resembling felt

²felt *past and past part of* FEEL

fem *abbr* **1** female **2** feminine

fe·male \'fē-ˌmāl\ *adj* [ME, alter. of *femel,* fr. MF *femelle,* fr. ML *femella,* fr. L, girl, dim. of *femina* woman] : of, relating to, or being the sex that bears young; *also* : PISTILLATE **syn** feminine, womanly, womanlike, womanish, effeminate — **female** *n*

¹fem·i·nine \'fe-mə-nən\ *adj* **1** : of the female sex; *also* : characteristic of or appropriate or peculiar to women **2** : of, relating to, or constituting the gender that includes most words or grammatical forms referring to females — **fem·i·nin·i·ty** \ˌfe-mə-'ni-nə-tē\ *n*

²feminine *n* : a noun, pronoun, adjective, or inflectional form or class of the feminine gender; *also* : the feminine gender

fem·i·nism \'fe-mə-ˌni-zəm\ *n* **1** : the theory of the political, economic, and social equality of the sexes **2** : organized activity on behalf of women's rights and interests — **fem·i·nist** \-nist\ *n or adj*

femme fa·tale \ˌfem-fə-'tal\ *n, pl* **femmes fa·tales** \same or -'talz\ [F, lit., disastrous woman] : a seductive woman

fe·mur \'fē-mər\ *n, pl* **fe·murs** *or* **fem·o·ra** \'fe-mə-rə\ : the long leg bone extending from the hip to the knee — **fem·o·ral** \'fe-mə-rəl\ *adj*

¹fen \'fen\ *n* : low swampy land

²fen \'fən\ *n, pl* **fen** — see *yuan* at MONEY table

¹fence \'fens\ *n* [ME *fens,* short for *defens* defense] **1** : a barrier (as of wood or wire) to prevent escape or entry or to mark a boundary **2** : a person who receives stolen goods; *also* : a place where stolen goods are disposed of — **on the fence** : in a position of neutrality or indecision

²fence *vb* **fenced; fenc·ing** **1** : to enclose with a fence **2** : to keep in or out with a fence **3** : to practice fencing **4** : to use tactics of attack and defense esp. in debate — **fenc·er** *n*

fenc·ing *n* **1** : the art or practice of attack and defense with the foil, épée, or saber **2** : the fences of a property or region **3** : material used for building fences

fend \'fend\ *vb* **1** : to keep or ward off : REPEL **2** : SHIFT ⟨~ for yourself⟩

fend·er \'fen-dər\ *n* : a protective device (as a guard over the wheel of an automobile)

fen·es·tra·tion \ˌfe-nə-'strä-shən\ *n* : the arrangement and design of windows and doors in a building

Fe·ni·an \'fē-nē-ən\ *n* : a member of a secret 19th century Irish and Irish-American organization dedicated to overthrowing British rule in Ireland

fen·nel \'fen-əl\ *n* : a garden plant related to the carrot and grown for its aromatic foliage and seeds

FEPC *abbr* Fair Employment Practices Commission

fe·ral \'fir-əl, 'fer-\ *adj* **1** : SAVAGE **2** : WILD 1 **3** : having escaped from domestication and become wild

fer–de–lance \ˌfer-də-'lans\ *n, pl* **fer–de–lance** [F, lit., lance iron, spearhead] : a large venomous pit viper of Central and So. America

¹fer·ment \fər-'ment\ *vb* **1** : to cause or undergo fermentation **2** : to be or cause to be in a state of agitation or intense activity

²fer·ment \'fər-ˌment\ *n* **1** : a living organism (as a yeast) causing fermentation by its enzymes; *also* : ENZYME **2** : AGITATION, TUMULT

fer·men·ta·tion \ˌfər-mən-'tā-shən, -ˌmen-\ *n* **1** : chemical decomposition of an organic substance (as in the souring of milk or the formation of alcohol from sugar) by enzymatic action in the absence of oxygen often with formation of gas **2** : FERMENT 2

fer·mi·um \'fer-mē-əm, 'fər-\ *n* : an artificially produced radioactive metallic chemical element — see ELEMENT table

fern \'fərn\ *n* : any of an order of vascular plants resembling seed plants in having roots, stems, and leaf-like fronds but reproducing by spores instead of by flowers and seeds

fern·ery \'fər-nə-rē\ *n, pl* **-er·ies** **1** : a place for growing ferns **2** : a collection of growing ferns

fe·ro·cious \fə-'rō-shəs\ *adj* **1** : FIERCE, SAVAGE **2** : extremely intense — **fe·ro·cious·ly** *adv* — **fe·ro·cious·ness** *n*

fe·roc·i·ty \fə-'rä-sə-tē\ *n* : the quality or state of being ferocious

¹**fer·ret** \'fer-ət\ *n* : a partially domesticated usu. white European mammal related to the weasels

²**ferret** *vb* **1** : to hunt game with ferrets **2** : to drive out of a hiding place **3** : to find and bring to light by searching ⟨∼ out the truth⟩

fer·ric \'fer-ik\ *adj* : of, relating to, or containing iron

ferric oxide *n* : an oxide of iron found in nature as hematite and as rust and used as a pigment and for polishing

Fer·ris wheel \'fer-əs-\ *n* : an amusement device consisting of a large upright power-driven wheel with seats that remain horizontal around its rim

fer·ro·mag·net·ic \ˌfer-ō-mag-'ne-tik\ *adj* : of or relating to substances that are easily magnetized

fer·rous \'fer-əs\ *adj* : of, relating to, or containing iron

fer·rule \'fer-əl\ *n* : a metal ring or cap around a slender wooden shaft to prevent splitting

¹**fer·ry** \'fer-ē\ *vb* **fer·ried; fer·ry·ing** [ME *ferien*, fr. OE *ferian* to carry, convey] **1** : to carry by boat across a body of water **2** : to cross by a ferry **3** : to convey from one place to another

²**ferry** *n, pl* **ferries** **1** : a place where persons or things are ferried **2** : FERRYBOAT

fer·ry·boat \'fer-ē-ˌbōt\ *n* : a boat used in ferrying

fer·tile \'fərt-ᵊl\ *adj* **1** : producing plentifully : PRODUCTIVE ⟨∼ soils⟩ ⟨a ∼ mind⟩ **2** : capable of developing or reproducing ⟨∼ seed⟩ ⟨a ∼ bull⟩ **syn** fruitful, prolific, fecund, productive — **fer·til·i·ty** \(ˌ)fər-'ti-lə-tē\ *n*

fer·til·ize \'fərt-ᵊl-ˌīz\ *vb* **-ized; -iz·ing** **1** : to unite with in the process of fertilization ⟨a sperm ∼s an egg⟩ **2** : to apply fertilizer to — **fer·til·iza·tion** \ˌfərt-ᵊl-ə-'zā-shən\ *n*

fer·til·iz·er \-ˌī-zər\ *n* : material (as manure or a chemical mixture) for enriching land

fer·ule \'fer-əl\ *n* : a rod or ruler used to punish children

fer·ven·cy \'fər-vən-sē\ *n, pl* **-cies** : FERVOR

fer·vent \'fər-vənt\ *adj* **1** : very hot : GLOWING **2** : marked by great intensity of feeling **syn** impassioned, ardent, fervid, fiery, passionate — **fer·vent·ly** *adv*

fer·vid \-vəd\ *adj* **1** : very hot **2** : ARDENT, ZEALOUS — **fer·vid·ly** *adv*

fer·vor \'fər-vər\ *n* **1** : intense heat **2** : intensity of feeling or expression

fer·vour *chiefly Brit var of* FERVOR

fes·tal \'fest-ᵊl\ *adj* : FESTIVE

fester \'fes-tər\ *vb* **1** : to form pus **2** : PUTREFY, ROT **3** : RANKLE

fes·ti·val \'fes-tə-vəl\ *n* **1** : a time of celebration marked by special observances; *esp* : an occasion marked with religious ceremonies **2** : a periodic season or program of cultural events or entertainment ⟨a dance ∼⟩

fes·tive \'fes-tiv\ *adj* **1** : of, relating to, or suitable for a feast or festival **2** : JOYFUL, GAY — **fes·tive·ly** *adv*

fes·tiv·i·ty \fes-'ti-və-tē\ *n, pl* **-ties** **1** : FESTIVAL 1 **2** : the quality or state of being festive **3** : festive activity

¹**fes·toon** \fes-'tün\ *n* [F *feston*, fr. It *festone*, fr. *festa* festival] **1** : a decorative chain or strip hanging between two points **2** : a carved, molded, or painted ornament representing a decorative chain

²**festoon** *vb* **1** : to hang or form festoons on **2** : to shape into festoons

fe·tal \'fēt-ᵊl\ *adj* : of, relating to, or being a fetus

fetch \'fech\ *vb* **1** : to go or come after and bring or take back ⟨teach a dog to ∼ a stick⟩ **2** : to bring in (as a price) **3** : to cause to come : bring out ⟨∼ed tears from the eyes⟩ **4** : to give by striking ⟨∼ him a blow⟩

fetch·ing *adj* : ATTRACTIVE, PLEASING — **fetch·ing·ly** *adv*

¹**fete** *or* **fête** \'fāt, 'fet\ *n* [F *fête*, fr. OF *feste*] **1** : FESTIVAL **2** : a large elaborate entertainment or party

²**fete** *or* **fête** *vb* **fet·ed** *or* **fêt·ed; fet·ing** *or* **fêt·ing** **1** : to honor or commemorate with a fete **2** : to pay high honor to

fet·id \'fe-təd\ *adj* : having an offensive smell : STINKING

fe·tish *also* **fe·tich** \'fe-tish\ *n* [F & Pg; F *fétiche*, fr. Pg *feitiço*, fr. *feitiço* artificial, false, fr. L *facticius* factitious] **1** : an object (as an idol or image) believed to have magical powers (as in curing disease) **2** : an object of unreasoning devotion or concern **3** : an object whose real or fantasied presence is psychologically necessary for sexual gratification

fe·tish·ism \-ti-ˌshi-zəm\ *n* **1** : belief in or devotion to fetishes **2** : the pathological transfer of sexual interest and gratification to a fetish — **fe·tish·ist** \-shist\ *n* — **fe·tish·is·tic** \ˌfe-ti-'shis-tik\ *adj*

fet·lock \'fet-ˌläk\ *n* : a projection on the back of a horse's leg above the hoof; *also* : a tuft of hair on this

fet·ter \'fe-tər\ *n* **1** : a chain or shackle for the feet **2** : something that confines : RESTRAINT — **fetter** *vb*

fet·tle \'fet-ᵊl\ *n* : a state of fitness or order : CONDITION ⟨in fine ∼⟩

fe·tus \'fē-təs\ *n* : an unborn or unhatched vertebrate esp. after its basic structure is laid down; *esp* : a developing human being in the uterus from usu. three months after pregnancy occurs to birth

feud \'fyüd\ *n* : a prolonged quarrel; *esp* : a lasting conflict between families or clans marked by violent attacks made for revenge — **feud** *vb*

feu·dal \'fyüd-ᵊl\ *adj* **1** : of, relating to, or having the characteristics of a medieval fee **2** : of, relating to, or characteristic of feudalism

feu·dal·ism \'fyüd-ᵊl-ˌi-zəm\ *n* : a system of political organization prevailing in medieval Europe in which a vassal renders service to a lord and receives protection and land in return; *also* : a similar political or social system — **feu·dal·is·tic** \ˌfyüd-ᵊl-'is-tik\ *adj*

¹**feu·da·to·ry** \'fyüd-ə-ˌtōr-ē\ *adj* : owing feudal allegiance

²**feudatory** *n, pl* **-ries** **1** : FIEF **2** : a person who holds lands by feudal law or usage

fe•ver \'fē-vər\ n 1 : a rise in body temperature above the normal; *also* : a disease of which this is a chief symptom 2 : a state of heightened emotion or activity 3 : CRAZE — **fe•ver•ish** *adj* — **fe•ver•ish•ly** *adv*

[1]few \'fyü\ *pron* : not many : a small number

[2]few *adj* 1 : consisting of or amounting to a small number 2 : not many but some ⟨caught a ∼ fish⟩ — **few•ness** *n* — **few and far between** : RARE 3

[3]few *n* 1 : a small number of units or individuals ⟨a ∼ of them⟩ 2 : a special limited number ⟨among the ∼⟩

few•er \'fyü-ər\ *pron* : a smaller number of persons or things

fey \'fā\ *adj* 1 *chiefly Scot* : fated to die; *also* : marked by a foreboding of death or calamity 2 : able to see into the future : VISIONARY 3 : marked by an otherworldly air or attitude 4 : CRAZY, TOUCHED

fez \'fez\ n, pl **fez•zes** *also* **fez•es** : a round red felt hat that has a flat top and a tassel but no brim

fez

ff *abbr* 1 folios 2 [*following*] and the following ones 3 fortissimo

FHA *abbr* Federal Housing Administration

fi•an•cé \ˌfē-ˌän-'sā\ n [F, fr. MF, fr. pp. of *fiancer* to promise, betroth, fr. OF *fiancier*, fr. *fiance* promise, trust, fr. *fier* to trust, ultim. fr. L *fidere*] : a man engaged to be married

fi•an•cée \ˌfē-ˌän-'sā\ n : a woman engaged to be married

fi•as•co \fē-'as-kō\ n, pl **-coes** [F] : a complete failure

fi•at \'fē-ət, -ˌat, -ˌät; 'fī-ət, -ˌat\ n [L, let it be done] : an authoritative and often arbitrary order or decree

[1]fib \'fib\ n : a trivial or childish lie

[2]fib *vb* **fibbed; fib•bing** : to tell a fib — **fib•ber** *n*

fi•ber *or* **fi•bre** \'fī-bər\ n 1 : a threadlike substance or structure (as a muscle cell or fine root); *esp* : a natural (as wool or flax) or artificial (as rayon) filament capable of being spun or woven 2 : indigestible material in human food that stimulates the intestine to move its contents along 3 : an element that gives texture or substance 4 : basic toughness : STRENGTH — **fi•brous** \-brəs\ *adj*

fi•ber•board \'fī-bər-ˌbōrd\ n : a material made by compressing fibers (as of wood) into stiff sheets

fi•ber•fill \-ˌfil\ n : synthetic fibers used as a filling material (as for cushions)

fi•ber•glass \-ˌglas\ n : glass in fibrous form used in making various products (as insulation)

fiber optics n 1 pl : thin transparent fibers of glass or plastic that are enclosed by a less refractive material and that transmit light by internal reflection; *also* : a bundle of such fibers used in an instrument 2 : the technique of the use of fiber optics — **fiber–optic** *adj*

fi•bril \'fī-brəl, 'fi-\ n : a small fiber

fi•bril•la•tion \ˌfi-brə-'lā-shən, ˌfī-\ n : rapid irregular contractions of the heart muscle fibers resulting in a lack of synchronism between heartbeat and pulse — **fib•ril•late** \'fī-brə-ˌlāt, 'fī-\ *vb*

fi•brin \'fī-brən\ n : a white insoluble fibrous protein formed in the clotting of blood

fi•broid \'fī-ˌbròid, 'fi-\ *adj* : resembling, forming, or consisting of fibrous tissue ⟨∼ tumors⟩

fi•bro•sis \fī-'brō-səs\ n : a condition marked by abnormal increase of fiber-containing tissue

fib•u•la \'fi-byə-lə\ n, pl **-lae** \-lē, -ˌlī\ *or* **-las** : the outer and usu. the smaller of the two bones between the knee and ankle — **fib•u•lar** \-lər\ *adj*

FICA *abbr* Federal Insurance Contributions Act

-fication n *comb form* : making : production ⟨simplification⟩

fiche \'fēsh\ n, pl **fiche** : MICROFICHE

fi•chu \'fi-shü\ n [F] : a woman's light triangular scarf draped over the shoulders and fastened in front

fick•le \'fi-kəl\ *adj* : not firm or steadfast in disposition or character : INCONSTANT — **fick•le•ness** *n*

fic•tion \'fik-shən\ n 1 : something (as a story) invented by the imagination 2 : fictitious literature (as novels) — **fic•tion•al** \-shə-nəl\ *adj* — **fic•tion•al•ly** *adv*

fic•ti•tious \fik-'ti-shəs\ *adj* 1 : of, relating to, or characteristic of fiction : IMAGINARY 2 : FEIGNED **syn** chimerical, fanciful, fantastic, unreal

[1]fid•dle \'fid-ᵊl\ n : VIOLIN

[2]fiddle *vb* **fid•dled; fid•dling** 1 : to play on a fiddle 2 : to move the hands or fingers restlessly 3 : PUTTER 4 : MEDDLE, TAMPER — **fid•dler** *n*

fiddler crab n : any of a genus of burrowing crabs with one claw much enlarged in the male

fid•dle•stick \'fid-ᵊl-ˌstik\ n 1 *archaic* : a violin bow 2 pl : NONSENSE — used as an interjection

fi•del•i•ty \fə-'de-lə-tē, fī-\ n, pl **-ties** 1 : the quality or state of being faithful 2 : ACCURACY ⟨∼ in sound reproduction⟩ **syn** allegiance, loyalty, devotion, fealty

[1]fidg•et \'fi-jət\ n 1 pl : uneasiness or restlessness as shown by nervous movements 2 : one that fidgets — **fidg•ety** *adj*

[2]fidget *vb* : to move or cause to move or act restlessly or nervously

fi•du•cia•ry \fə-'dü-shē-ˌer-ē, -'dyü-, -shə-rē\ *adj* 1 : involving a confidence or trust 2 : held or holding in trust for another ⟨∼ accounts⟩ — **fiduciary** *n*

fie \'fī\ *interj* — used to express disgust or disapproval

fief \'fēf\ n : a feudal estate : FEE

[1]field \'fēld\ n 1 : open country 2 : a piece of cleared land for cultivation or pasture 3 : a piece of land yielding some special product 4 : the place where a battle is fought; *also* : BATTLE 5 : an area, division, or sphere of activity ⟨the ∼ of science⟩ ⟨salesmen in the ∼⟩ 6 : an area for military exercises 7 : an area for sports 8 : a background on which something is drawn or projected ⟨a flag with white stars on a ∼ of blue⟩ 9 : a region or space in which a given effect (as magnetism) exists — **field** *adj*

[2]field *vb* 1 : to handle a batted or thrown baseball while on defense 2 : to put into the field 3 : to answer satisfactorily ⟨∼ a tough question⟩ — **field•er** *n*

field day n 1 : a day devoted to outdoor sports and athletic competition 2 : a time of extraordinary pleasure or opportunity

field event n : a track-and-field event (as weight-throwing) other than a race

field glass n : a hand-held binocular telescope — usu. used in pl.

field guide n : a manual for identifying natural objects, plants, or animals

field hockey n : a field game played between two teams of 11 players each whose object is to knock a ball into the opponent's goal with a curved stick

field marshal n : an officer (as in the British army) of the highest rank

field–test \-ˌtest\ *vb* : to test (as a new product) in a natural environment — **field test** *n*

fiend \ˈfēnd\ *n* **1** : DEVIL 1 **2** : DEMON **3** : an extremely wicked or cruel person **4** : a person excessively devoted to a pursuit **5** : ADDICT ⟨dope ∼⟩ — **fiend·ish** *adj* — **fiend·ish·ly** *adv*

fierce \ˈfirs\ *adj* **fierc·er; fierc·est 1** : violently hostile or aggressive in temperament **2** : PUGNACIOUS **3** : INTENSE **4** : furiously active or determined **5** : wild or menacing in appearance **syn** ferocious, barbarous, savage, cruel — **fierce·ly** *adv* — **fierce·ness** *n*

fi·ery \ˈfī-ə-rē\ *adj* **fier·i·er; -est 1** : consisting of fire **2** : BURNING, BLAZING **3** : FLAMMABLE **4** : hot like a fire : INFLAMED, FEVERISH **5** : RED **6** : full of emotion or spirit **7** : IRRITABLE — **fi·eri·ness** \-rē-nəs\ *n*

fi·es·ta \fē-ˈes-tə\ *n* [Sp] : FESTIVAL

fife \ˈfīf\ *n* [G *Pfeife* pipe, fife] : a small flute

FIFO *abbr* first in, first out

fif·teen \fif-ˈtēn\ *n* : one more than 14 — **fifteen** *adj or pron* — **fif·teenth** \-ˈtēnth\ *adj or n*

fifth \ˈfifth\ *n* **1** : one that is number five in a countable series **2** : one of five equal parts of something **3** : a unit of measure for liquor equal to ⅕ U.S. gallon (0.757 liter) — **fifth** *adj or adv*

fifth column *n* : a group of secret supporters of a nation's enemy that engage in espionage or sabotage within the country — **fifth columnist** *n*

fifth wheel *n* : one that is unnecessary and often burdensome

fif·ty \ˈfif-tē\ *n, pl* **fifties** : five times 10 — **fif·ti·eth** \-tē-əth\ *adj or n* — **fifty** *adj or pron*

fif·ty–fif·ty \ˌfif-tē-ˈfif-tē\ *adj* **1** : shared equally ⟨a ∼ proposition⟩ **2** : half favorable and half unfavorable

¹fig \ˈfig\ *n* : a usu. pear-shaped edible fruit of warm regions; *also* : a tree related to the mulberry that bears this fruit

fig: leaves and fruit

²fig *abbr* **1** figurative; figuratively **2** figure

¹fight \ˈfīt\ *vb* **fought** \ˈfȯt\; **fight·ing 1** : to contend against another in battle or physical combat **2** : BOX **3** : to put forth a determined effort **4** : STRUGGLE, CONTEND **5** : to attempt to prevent the success or effectiveness of **6** : WAGE **7** : to gain by struggle

²fight *n* **1** : a hostile encounter : BATTLE **2** : a boxing match **3** : a verbal disagreement **4** : a struggle for a goal or an objective **5** : strength or disposition for fighting ⟨full of ∼⟩

fight·er \ˈfī-tər\ *n* **1** : one that fights; *esp* : WARRIOR **2** : BOXER **3** : a fast maneuverable warplane for destroying enemy aircraft

fig·ment \ˈfig-mənt\ *n* : something imagined or made up

fig·u·ra·tion \ˌfi-gyə-ˈrā-shən, -gə-\ *n* **1** : FORM, OUTLINE **2** : an act or instance of representation in figures and shapes

fig·u·ra·tive \ˈfi-gyə-rə-tiv, -gə-\ *adj* **1** : EMBLEMATIC **2** : SYMBOLIC, METAPHORICAL ⟨∼ language⟩ — **fig·u·ra·tive·ly** *adv*

¹fig·ure \ˈfi-gyər, -gər\ *n* **1** : NUMERAL **2** *pl* : arithmetical calculations **3** : a written or printed character **4** : PRICE, SUM **5** : a combination of points, lines, or surfaces in geometry ⟨a circle is a closed plane ∼⟩ **6** : SHAPE, FORM, OUTLINE **7** : the graphic representation of a form esp. of a person **8** : a diagram or pictorial illustration of textual matter **9** : PATTERN, DESIGN **10** : appearance made or impression produced ⟨they cut quite a ∼⟩ **11** : a series of movements (as in a dance) **12** : PERSONAGE

²figure *vb* **fig·ured; fig·ur·ing 1** : to represent by or as if by a figure or outline **2** : to decorate with a pattern **3** : to indicate or represent by numerals **4** : REGARD, CONSIDER **5** : to be or appear important or conspicuous **6** : COMPUTE, CALCULATE

fig·ure·head \ˈfi-gyər-ˌhed, -gər-\ *n* **1** : a figure on the bow of a ship **2** : a head or chief in name only

figure of speech : a form of expression (as a simile or metaphor) that often compares or identifies one thing with another to convey meaning or heighten effect

figure out *vb* **1** : FIND OUT, DISCOVER **2** : SOLVE

fig·u·rine \ˌfi-gyə-ˈrēn, -gə-\ *n* : a small carved or molded figure

Fi·ji·an \ˈfē-ˌjē-ən, fi-ˈjē-ən\ *n* : a native or inhabitant of the Pacific island country of Fiji — **Fijian** *adj*

fil·a·ment \ˈfi-lə-mənt\ *n* : a fine thread or threadlike object, part, or process — **fil·a·men·tous** \ˌfi-lə-ˈmen-təs\ *adj*

fil·bert \ˈfil-bərt\ *n* : the sweet thick-shelled nut of either of two European hazels; *also* : a shrub or small tree bearing filberts

filch \ˈfilch\ *vb* : to steal furtively

¹file \ˈfī(-ə)l\ *n* : a usu. steel tool with a ridged or toothed surface used esp. for smoothing a hard substance

²file *vb* **filed; fil·ing** : to rub, smooth, or cut away with a file

³file *vb* **filed; fil·ing** [ME, fr. MF *filer* to string documents on a string or wire, fr. *fil* thread, fr. L *filum*] **1** : to arrange in order **2** : to enter or record officially or as prescribed by law ⟨∼ a lawsuit⟩ **3** : to send (copy) to a newspaper

⁴file *n* **1** : a device (as a folder or cabinet) by means of which papers may be kept in order **2** : a collection of papers or publications usu. arranged or classified **3** : a collection of data (as text) treated by a computer as a unit

⁵file *n* : a row of persons, animals, or things arranged one behind the other

⁶file *vb* **filed; fil·ing** : to march or proceed in file

fi·let mi·gnon \fi-(ˌ)lā-mēn-ˈyōⁿ, fi-ˌlā-\ *n, pl* **filets mi·gnons** \-(ˌ)lā-mēn-ˈyōⁿz, -ˌlā-\ [F, lit., dainty fillet] : a thick slice of beef cut from the narrow end of a beef tenderloin

fil·ial \ˈfi-lē-əl, ˈfil-yəl\ *adj* : of, relating to, or befitting a son or daughter

fil·i·bus·ter \ˈfi-lə-ˌbəs-tər\ *n* [Sp *filibustero*, lit., freebooter] **1** : a military adventurer; *esp* : an American engaged in fomenting 19th century Latin American uprisings **2** : the use of delaying tactics (as extremely long speeches) esp. in a legislative assembly; *also* : an instance of this practice — **filibuster** *vb* — **fil·i·bus·ter·er** *n*

fil·i·gree \ˈfi-lə-ˌgrē\ *n* [F *filigrane*] : ornamental openwork (as of fine wire) — **fil·i·greed** \-ˌgrēd\ *adj*

fil·ing \ˈfī-liŋ\ *n* **1** : the act or instance of using a file **2** : a small piece scraped off by a file ⟨iron ∼s⟩

Fil·i·pi·no \ˌfi-lə-ˈpē-nō\ *n, pl* **Filipinos** : a native or inhabitant of the Philippines — **Filipino** *adj*

fill \ˈfil\ *vb* **1** : to make or become full **2** : to stop up : PLUG ⟨∼ a cavity⟩ **3** : FEED, SATIATE **4** : SATISFY, FULFILL ⟨∼ all requirements⟩ **5** : to occupy fully **6** : to spread through ⟨laughter ∼ed the room⟩ **7** : OCCUPY ⟨∼ the office of president⟩ **8** : to put a person in ⟨∼ a vacancy⟩ **9** : to supply as directed ⟨∼ a prescription⟩

²fill *n* **1** : a full supply; *esp* : a quantity that satisfies or satiates **2** : material used esp. for filling a low place

fill·er \ˈfi-lər\ *n* **1** : one that fills **2** : a substance added to another substance (as to increase bulk or weight) **3** : a material used for filling cracks and pores in wood before painting

²fil·ler \ˈfi-ˌler\ *n, pl* **fillers** *or* **filler** — see *forint* at MONEY table

¹fil·let \ˈfi-lət, *in sense 2* fi-ˈlā, ˈfi-(ˌ)lā\ *also* **fi·let** \fi-ˈlā, ˈfi-(ˌ)lā\ *n* [ME *filet*, fr. MF, dim. of *fil* thread] **1** : a narrow band, strip, or ribbon **2** : a piece or slice of boneless meat or fish; *esp* : the tenderloin of beef

²fil·let \ˈfi-lət, *in sense 2 also* fi-ˈlā, ˈfi-(ˌ)lā\ *vb* **1** : to bind or adorn with or as if with a fillet **2** : to cut into fillets

fill in *vb* **1** : to provide necessary or recent information **2** : to serve as a temporary substitute

fill·ing \ˈfi-liŋ\ *n* **1** : material used to fill something ⟨∼ for a tooth⟩ **2** : the yarn interlacing the warp in a fabric **3** : a food mixture used to fill pastry or sandwiches

filling station *n* : SERVICE STATION

fil·lip \ˈfi-ləp\ *n* **1** : a blow or gesture made by a flick or snap of the finger across the thumb **2** : something that serves to arouse or excite — **fillip** *vb*

fill–up \ˈfil-ˌəp\ *n* : an act or instance of filling something

fil·ly \ˈfi-lē\ *n, pl* **fillies** : a young female horse usu. less than four years old

¹film \ˈfilm\ *n* **1** : a thin skin or membrane **2** : a thin coating or layer **3** : a flexible strip of chemically treated material used in taking pictures **4** : MOTION PICTURE — **filmy** *adj*

²film *vb* **1** : to cover with a film **2** : to make a motion picture of

film·dom \ˈfilm-dəm\ *n* : the motion-picture industry

film·og·ra·phy \fil-ˈmä-grə-fē\ *n, pl* **-phies** : a list of motion pictures featuring the work of a film figure or a particular topic

film·strip \ˈfilm-ˌstrip\ *n* : a strip of film bearing a sequence of images for projection as still pictures

fils \ˈfils\ *n, pl* **fils** — see *dinar, dirham, rial* at MONEY table

¹fil·ter \ˈfil-tər\ *n* **1** : a porous material through which a fluid is passed to separate out matter in suspension; *also* : a device containing such material **2** : a device for suppressing waves of certain frequencies; *esp* : one (as for a camera) that absorbs light of certain colors

²filter *vb* **1** : to remove by means of a filter **2** : to pass through a filter — **fil·ter·able** *also* **fil·tra·ble** \-tə-rə-bəl, -trə-\ *adj* — **fil·tra·tion** \fil-ˈtrā-shən\ *n*

filth \ˈfilth\ *n* [ME, fr. OE *fȳlth*, fr. *fūl* foul] **1** : foul matter; *esp* : loathsome dirt or refuse **2** : moral corruption **3** : OBSCENITY — **filth·i·ness** *n* — **filthy** \ˈfil-thē\ *adj*

fil·trate \ˈfil-ˌtrāt\ *n* : fluid that has passed through a filter

¹fin \ˈfin\ *n* **1** : one of the thin external processes by which an aquatic animal (as a fish) moves through water **2** : a fin-shaped part (as on an airplane) **3** : FLIPPER **2** — **finned** \ˈfind\ *adj*

²fin *abbr* **1** finance; financial **2** finish

fi·na·gle \fə-ˈnā-gəl\ *vb* **-gled; -gling 1** : to obtain by indirect or dishonest means : WANGLE **2** : to use devious dishonest methods to achieve one's ends — **fi·na·gler** *n*

¹fi·nal \ˈfīn-ᵊl\ *adj* **1** : not to be altered or undone **2** : ULTIMATE **3** : relating to or occurring at the end or conclusion — **fi·nal·i·ty** \fī-ˈna-lə-tē, fə-\ *n* — **fi·nal·ly** *adv*

²final *n* **1** : a deciding match or game — usu. used in pl. **2** : the last examination in a course — often used in pl.

fi·na·le \fə-ˈna-lē, fi-ˈnä-\ *n* : the close or end of something; *esp* : the last section of a musical composition

fi·nal·ise *Brit var of* FINALIZE

fi·nal·ist \ˈfīn-ᵊl-əst\ *n* : a contestant in the finals of a competition

fi·nal·ize \ˈfīn-ᵊl-ˌīz\ *vb* **-ized; -iz·ing** : to put in final or finished form

¹fi·nance \fə-ˈnans, ˈfī-ˌnans\ *n* [ME, payment, ransom, fr. MF, fr. *finer* to end, pay, fr. *fin* end, fr. L *finis* boundary, end] **1** *pl* : money resources available esp. to a government or business **2** : management of money affairs

²finance *vb* **fi·nanced; fi·nanc·ing 1** : to raise or provide funds for **2** : to furnish with necessary funds **3** : to sell or supply on credit

finance company *n* : a company that makes usu. small short-term loans usu. to individuals

fi·nan·cial \fə-ˈnan-chəl, fī-\ *adj* : relating to finance or financiers — **fi·nan·cial·ly** *adv*

fi·nan·cier \ˌfi-nən-ˈsir, ˌfī-ˌnan-\ *n* **1** : a person skilled in managing public moneys **2** : a person who deals with large-scale finance and investment

finch \ˈfinch\ *n* : any of numerous songbirds with strong conical bills

¹find \ˈfīnd\ *vb* **found** \ˈfaund\; **find·ing 1** : to meet with either by chance or by searching or study : ENCOUNTER, DISCOVER **2** : to obtain by effort or management ⟨∼ time to read⟩ **3** : to arrive at : REACH ⟨the bullet *found* its mark⟩ **4** : EXPERIENCE, FEEL ⟨*found* happiness⟩ **5** : to gain or regain the use of ⟨*found* his voice again⟩ **6** : to determine and make a statement about ⟨∼ a verdict⟩

²find *n* **1** : an act or instance of finding **2** : something found; *esp* : a valuable item of discovery

find·er \ˈfīn-dər\ *n* : one that finds; *esp* : VIEWFINDER

fin de siè·cle \ˌfaⁿ-nan-dē-sē-ˈekl\ *adj* [F, end of century] : of, relating to, or characteristic of the close of the 19th century

find·ing \ˈfīn-diŋ\ *n* **1** : the act of finding **2** : FIND **2 3** : the result of a judicial proceeding or inquiry

find out *vb* : to learn by study, observation, or search : DISCOVER

¹fine \ˈfīn\ *n* : money exacted as a penalty for an offense

²fine *vb* **fined; fin·ing** : to impose a fine on : punish by a fine

³**fine** *adj* **fin·er; fin·est 1** : free from impurity **2** : very thin in gauge or texture **3** : not coarse **4** : SUBTLE, SENSITIVE ⟨a ∼ distinction⟩ **5** : superior in quality or appearance **6** : ELEGANT, REFINED — **fine·ly** *adv* — **fine·ness** *n*

⁴**fine** *adv* **1** : very well **2** — used to express agreement

fine art *n* : art (as painting, sculpture, or music) concerned primarily with the creation of beautiful objects — usu. used in pl.

fin·ery \'fī-nə-rē\ *n, pl* **-er·ies** : ORNAMENT, DECORATION; *esp* : showy clothing and jewels

fine·spun \'fīn-'spən\ *adj* : developed with extremely or excessively fine delicacy or detail

fi·nesse \fə-'nes\ *n* **1** : refinement or delicacy of workmanship, structure, or texture **2** : CUNNING, SUBTLETY — **finesse** *vb*

fine–tune \'fīn-'tün\ *vb* : to adjust so as to bring to the highest level of performance or effectiveness

fin·fish \'fin-₁fish\ *n* : FISH 2

¹**fin·ger** \'fiŋ-gər\ *n* **1** : any of the five divisions at the end of the hand; *esp* : one other than the thumb **2** : something that resembles or does the work of a finger **3** : a part of a glove into which a finger is inserted

²**finger** *vb* **fin·gered; fin·ger·ing 1** : to touch or feel with the fingers : HANDLE **2** : to perform with the fingers or with a certain fingering **3** : to mark the notes of a piece of music as a guide in playing **4** : to point out

fin·ger·board \'fiŋ-gər-₁bōrd\ *n* : the part of a stringed instrument against which the fingers press the strings to vary the pitch

finger bowl *n* : a small water bowl for rinsing the fingers at the table

fin·ger·ing \'fiŋ-gə-riŋ\ *n* **1** : handling or touching with the fingers **2** : the act or method of using the fingers in playing an instrument **3** : the marking of the method of fingering

fin·ger·ling \'fiŋ-gər-liŋ\ *n* : a small fish

fin·ger·nail \'fiŋ-gər-₁nāl\ *n* : the nail of a finger

fin·ger·print \-₁print\ *n* : the pattern of marks made by pressing the tip of a finger or thumb on a surface; *esp* : an ink impression of such a pattern taken for the purpose of identification — **fingerprint** *vb*

fin·ger·tip \-₁tip\ *n* : the tip of a finger

fin·i·al \'fi-nē-əl\ *n* : an ornamental projection or end (as on a spire)

fin·ick·ing \'fi-ni-kiŋ\ *adj* : FINICKY

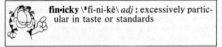

fin·icky \'fi-ni-kē\ *adj* : excessively particular in taste or standards

fi·nis \'fi-nəs\ *n* : END, CONCLUSION

¹**fin·ish** \'fi-nish\ *vb* **1** : TERMINATE **2** : to use or dispose of entirely **3** : to bring to completion : ACCOMPLISH **4** : to put a final coat or surface on **5** : to come to the end of a course or undertaking — **fin·ish·er** *n*

²**finish** *n* **1** : END, CONCLUSION **2** : something that completes or perfects **3** : the final treatment or coating of a surface

fi·nite \'fī-₁nīt\ *adj* **1** : having definite or definable limits; *also* : having a limited nature or existence **2** : being less than some positive integer in number or measure and greater than its negative **3** : showing distinction of grammatical person and number ⟨a ∼ verb⟩

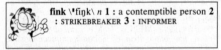

fink \'fiŋk\ *n* **1** : a contemptible person **2** : STRIKEBREAKER **3** : INFORMER

Finn \'fin\ *n* : a native or inhabitant of Finland

fin·nan had·die \₁fi-nən-'ha-dē\ *n* : smoked haddock

¹**Finn·ish** \'fi-nish\ *adj* : of or relating to Finland, the Finns, or Finnish

²**Finnish** *n* : the language of Finland

fin·ny \'fi-nē\ *adj* **1** : having or characterized by fins **2** : relating to or being fish

fiord *var of* FJORD

fir \'fər\ *n* : any of a genus of erect evergreen trees related to the pines; *also* : the light soft wood of a fir

¹**fire** \'fīr\ *n* **1** : the light or heat and esp. the flame of something burning **2** : ENTHUSIASM, ZEAL **3** : fuel that is burning (as in a stove or fireplace) **4** : destructive burning (as of a house) **5** : the firing of weapons — **fire·less** *adj*

²**fire** *vb* **fired; fir·ing 1** : KINDLE, IGNITE ⟨~ a house⟩ **2** : STIR, ENLIVEN ⟨~ the imagination⟩ **3** : to dismiss from employment **4** : SHOOT ⟨~ a gun⟩ ⟨~ an arrow⟩ **5** : BAKE ⟨*firing* pottery in a kiln⟩ **6** : to apply fire or fuel to something ⟨~ a furnace⟩

fire ant *n* : either of two small fiercely stinging South American ants that are pests in the southeastern U.S. esp. in fields used to grow crops

fire·arm \'fīr-ˌärm\ *n* : a weapon (as a pistol) from which a shot is discharged by gunpowder

fire·ball \-ˌbȯl\ *n* **1** : a ball of fire **2** : a very bright meteor **3** : the highly luminous cloud of vapor and dust created by a nuclear explosion **4** : a highly energetic person

fire·boat \-ˌbōt\ *n* : a boat equipped for fighting fires

fire·bomb \-ˌbäm\ *n* : an incendiary bomb — **fire·bomb** *vb*

fire·box \-ˌbäks\ *n* **1** : a chamber (as of a furnace) that contains a fire **2** : a box containing a fire alarm

fire·brand \-ˌbrand\ *n* **1** : a piece of burning wood **2** : a person who creates unrest or strife : AGITATOR

fire·break \-ˌbrāk\ *n* : a barrier of cleared or plowed land intended to check a forest or grass fire

fire·bug \-ˌbəg\ *n* : a person who deliberately sets destructive fires

fire·crack·er \-ˌkra-kər\ *n* : a paper tube containing an explosive and a fuse and set off to make a noise

fire department *n* : an organization for preventing or extinguishing fires; *also* : its members

fire engine *n* : a motor vehicle with equipment for extinguishing fires

fire escape *n* : a stairway or ladder for escape from a burning building

fire·fight·er \'fīr-ˌfī-tər\ *n* : a person who fights fires; *esp* : a member of a fire department

fire·fly \-ˌflī\ *n* : any of various small night-flying beetles that produce flashes of light for courtship purposes

fire·house \-ˌhau̇s\ *n* : FIRE STATION

fire irons *n pl* : tools for tending a fire esp. in a fireplace

fire·man \'fīr-mən\ *n* **1** : STOKER **2** : FIREFIGHTER

fire off *vb* : to write and send

fire·place \-ˌplās\ *n* **1** : a framed opening made in a chimney to hold an open fire **2** : an outdoor structure of brick or stone for an open fire

fire·plug \-ˌpləg\ *n* : HYDRANT

fire·pow·er \-ˌpau̇-ər\ *n* : the ability to deliver gunfire or warheads on a target

¹**fire·proof** \-ˈprüf\ *adj* : resistant to fire

²**fireproof** *vb* : to make fireproof

fire screen *n* : a protective screen before a fireplace

¹**fire·side** \'fīr-ˌsīd\ *n* **1** : a place near the fire or hearth **2** : HOME

²**fireside** *adj* : having an informal or intimate quality

fire station *n* : a building housing fire engines and usu. firefighters

fire·storm \'fīr-ˌstȯrm\ *n* **1** : a large destructive very hot fire **2** : a sudden or violent outburst ⟨~ of criticism⟩

fire tower *n* : a tower (as in a forest) from which a watch for fires is kept

fire·trap \'fīr-ˌtrap\ *n* : a building or place apt to catch on fire or difficult to escape from in case of fire

fire truck *n* : FIRE ENGINE

fire·wa·ter \'fīr-ˌwȯ-tər, -ˌwä-\ *n* : intoxicating liquor

fire·wood \-ˌwu̇d\ *n* : wood used for fuel

fire·work \-ˌwərk\ *n* : a device designed to produce a display of light, noise, and smoke by the burning of explosive or flammable materials

firing line *n* **1** : a line from which fire is delivered against a target **2** : the forefront of an activity

¹**firm** \'fərm\ *adj* **1** : securely fixed in place **2** : SOLID, VIGOROUS ⟨a ~ handshake⟩ **3** : having a compact texture **4** : not subject to change or fluctuation : STEADY ⟨~ prices⟩ **5** : STEADFAST **6** : indicating firm-

ness or resolution — **firm·ly** *adv* — **firm·ness** *n*

²**firm** *vb* : to make or become firm

³**firm** *n* [G *Firma*, fr. It. signature, ultim. fr. L *firmare* to make firm, confirm] **1** : the name under which a company transacts business **2** : a business partnership of two or more persons **3** : a business enterprise

fir·ma·ment \'fər-mə-mənt\ *n* : the arch of the sky : HEAVENS

firm·ware \'firm-ˌwar\ *n* : computer programs contained permanently in a hardware device

¹**first** \'fərst\ *adj* : preceding all others as in time, order, or importance

²**first** *adv* **1** : before any other **2** : for the first time **3** : in preference to something else

³**first** *n* **1** : number one in a countable series **2** : something that is first **3** : the lowest forward gear in an automotive vehicle **4** : the winning or highest place in a competition or examination

first aid *n* : emergency care or treatment given an injured or ill person

first·born \'fərst-ˈbȯrn\ *adj* : ELDEST — **firstborn** *n*

first class *n* : the best or highest group in a classification — **first-class** *adj or adv*

first·hand \'fərst-ˈhand\ *adj* : coming from direct personal observation or experience — **firsthand** *adv*

first lady *n, often cap F&L* : the wife or hostess of the chief executive of a political unit (as a country)

first lieutenant *n* : a commissioned officer (as in the army) ranking next below a captain

first·ling \'fərst-liŋ\ *n* : one that comes or is produced first

first·ly \-lē\ *adv* : in the first place : FIRST

¹**first-rate** \-ˈrāt\ *adj* : of the first order of size, importance, or quality

²**first-rate** *adv* : very well

first sergeant *n* **1** : a noncommissioned officer serving as the chief assistant to the commander of a military unit **2** : a rank in the army below a command sergeant major and in the marine corps below a sergeant major

first strike *n* : a preemptive nuclear attack

first-string \'fərst-ˈstriŋ\ *adj* : being a regular as distinguished from a substitute

firth \'fərth\ *n* [ME, fr. ON *fjǫrthr*] : ESTUARY

fis·cal \'fis-kəl\ *adj* [L *fiscalis*, fr. *fiscus* basket, treasury] **1** : of or relating to taxation, public revenues, or public debt **2** : of or relating to financial matters — **fis·cal·ly** *adv*

¹**fish** \'fish\ *n, pl* **fish** *or* **fish·es 1** : a water-dwelling animal — usu. used in combination ⟨star*fish*⟩ ⟨shell*fish*⟩ **2** : any of numerous cold-blooded water-breathing vertebrates with fins, gills, and usu. scales that include the bony fishes and usu. the cartilaginous and jawless fishes **3** : the flesh of fish used as food

²**fish** *vb* **1** : to attempt to catch fish **2** : to seek something by roundabout means ⟨~ for praise⟩ **3** : to search for something underwater **4** : to engage in a search by groping **5** : to draw forth

fish-and-chips *n pl* : fried fish and french fried potatoes

fish·bowl \'fish-ˌbōl\ *n* **1** : a bowl for the keeping of live fish **2** : a place or condition that affords no privacy

fish·er \'fi-shər\ *n* **1** : one that fishes **2** : a large dark brown No. American arboreal carnivorous mammal related to the weasels

fish·er·man \-mən\ *n* : a person engaged in fishing; *also* : a fishing boat

fish·ery \'fi-shə-rē\ *n, pl* **-er·ies** : the business of catching fish; *also* : a place for catching fish

fish·hook \'fish-ˌhu̇k\ *n* : a usu. barbed hook for catching fish

fish ladder *n* : an arrangement of pools in steps by which fish can pass over a dam

fish·net \'fish-ˌnet\ *n* : netting for catching fish **2** : a coarse open-mesh fabric

fish·tail \-ˌtāl\ *vb* : to have the rear end slide from side to side out of control while moving forward

fish·wife \-ˌwīf\ *n* **1** : a woman who sells fish **2** : a vulgar abusive woman

fishy \ˈfi-shē\ *adj* **fish·i·er; -est 1** : of or resembling fish **2** : QUESTIONABLE

fis·sion \ˈfi-shən, -zhən\ *n* [L *fissio*, fr. *findere* to split] **1** : a cleaving into parts **2** : a method of reproduction in which a living cell or body divides into two or more parts each of which grows into a whole new individual **3** : the splitting of an atomic nucleus resulting in the release of large amounts of energy — **fis·sion·able** \ˈfi-shə-nə-bəl, -zhə-\ *adj*

fis·sure \ˈfi-shər\ *n* : a narrow opening or crack

fist \ˈfist\ *n* **1** : the hand with fingers folded into the palm **2** : INDEX 6

fist·ful \ˈfist-ˌfu̇l\ *n* : HANDFUL

fist·i·cuffs \ˈfis-ti-ˌkəfs\ *n pl* : a fight with usu. bare fists

fis·tu·la \ˈfis-chə-lə\ *n, pl* **-las** *or* **-lae** : an abnormal passage leading from an abscess or hollow organ — **fis·tu·lous** \-ləs\ *adj*

¹fit \ˈfit\ *adj* **fit·ter; fit·test 1** : adapted to a purpose : APPROPRIATE **2** : PROPER, RIGHT **3** : PREPARED, READY **4** : physically and mentally sound — **fit·ly** *adv* — **fit·ness** *n*

²fit *n* **1** : a sudden violent attack (as of bodily disorder) **2** : a sudden outburst

³fit *vb* **fit·ted** *also* **fit; fit·ting 1** : to be suitable for or to **2** : to be correctly adjusted to or shaped for **3** : to insert or adjust until correctly in place **4** : to make a place or room for **5** : to be in agreement or accord with **6** : PREPARE **7** : ADJUST **8** : SUPPLY, EQUIP ⟨*fitted* out with gear⟩ **9** : BELONG — **fit·ter** *n*

⁴fit *n* : the fact, condition, or manner of fitting or being fitted

fit·ful \ˈfit-fəl\ *adj* : not regular : INTERMITTENT ⟨~ sleep⟩ — **fit·ful·ly** *adv*

¹fit·ting \ˈfi-tiŋ\ *adj* : APPROPRIATE, SUITABLE — **fit·ting·ly** *adv*

²fitting *n* **1** : the action or act of one that fits; *esp* : a trying on of clothes being made or altered **2** : a small often standardized part ⟨a plumbing ~⟩

five \ˈfīv\ *n* **1** : one more than four **2** : the 5th in a set or series **3** : something having five units; *esp* : a basketball team **4** : a 5-dollar bill — **five** *adj or pron*

¹fix \ˈfiks\ *vb* **1** : to make firm, stable, or fast **2** : to give a permanent or final form to **3** : AFFIX, ATTACH **4** : to hold or direct steadily ⟨~*es* his eyes on the horizon⟩ **5** : ESTABLISH, SET **6** : ASSIGN ⟨~ the blame⟩ **7** : to set in order : ADJUST **8** : PREPARE **9** : to make whole or sound again **10** : to get even with **11** : to influence by improper or illegal methods ⟨~ a race⟩ — **fix·er** *n*

²fix *n* **1** : PREDICAMENT **2** : a determination of position (as of a ship) **3** : an accurate determination or understanding **4** : an act of improper influence **5** : a supply or dose of something (as an addictive drug) strongly desired or craved **6** : something that fixes or restores

fix·a·tion \fik-ˈsā-shən\ *n* : an obsessive or unhealthy preoccupation or attachment — **fix·ate** \ˈfik-ˌsāt\ *vb*

fix·a·tive \ˈfik-sə-tiv\ *n* : something that stabilizes or sets

fixed \ˈfikst\ *adj* **1** : securely placed or fastened : STATIONARY **2** : not volatile **3** : SETTLED, FINAL **4** : INTENT, CONCENTRATED ⟨a ~ stare⟩ **5** : supplied with a definite amount of something needed (as money) — **fixed·ly** \ˈfik-səd-lē\ *adv* — **fixed·ness** \ˈfik-səd-nəs\ *n*

fix·i·ty \ˈfik-sə-tē\ *n, pl* **-ties** : the quality or state of being fixed or stable

fix·ture \ˈfiks-chər\ *n* **1** : something firmly attached as a permanent part of some other thing **2** : a familiar feature in a particular setting; *esp* : a person associated with a place or activity

¹fizz \ˈfiz\ *vb* : to make a hissing or sputtering sound

²fizz *n* : an effervescent beverage

¹fiz·zle \ˈfi-zəl\ *vb* **fiz·zled; fiz·zling 1** : FIZZ **2** : to fail after a good start — often used with *out*

²fizzle *n* : FAILURE

fjord \fē-ˈȯrd\ *n* [Norw] : a narrow inlet of the sea between cliffs or steep slopes

fjord

fl *abbr* **1** [L *floruit*] flourished **2** fluid

FL *or* **Fla** *abbr* Florida

flab \ˈflab\ *n* : soft flabby body tissue

flab·ber·gast \ˈfla-bər-ˌgast\ *vb* : ASTOUND

flab·by \ˈfla-bē\ *adj* **flab·bi·er; -est** : lacking firmness : FLACCID ⟨~ muscles⟩ — **flab·bi·ness** \-bē-nəs\ *n*

flac·cid \ˈflak-səd\ *adj* : deficient in firmness ⟨~ plant stems⟩

¹flag \ˈflag\ *n* : any of various irises; *esp* : a wild iris

²flag *n* **1** : a usu. rectangular piece of fabric of distinctive design that is used as a symbol (as of a nation) or as a signaling device **2** : something used like a flag to signal or attract attention **3** : one of the cross strokes of a musical note less than a quarter note in value

³flag *vb* **flagged; flag·ging 1** : to signal with or as if with a flag; *esp* : to signal to stop ⟨~ a taxi⟩ **2** : to put a flag on **3** : to call a penalty on

⁴flag *vb* **flagged; flag·ging 1** : to hang loose or limp **2**

: to become unsteady, feeble, or spiritless **3** : to decline in interest or attraction ⟨the topic *flagged*⟩

⁵**flag** *n* : a hard flat stone suitable for paving

flag·el·late \'fla-jə-ˌlāt\ *vb* **-lat·ed; -lat·ing** : to punish by whipping — **flag·el·la·tion** \ˌfla-jə-'lā-shən\ *n*

fla·gel·lum \flə-'je-ləm\ *n, pl* **-la** \-lə\ *also* **-lums** : a long whiplike process that is the primary organ of motion of many microorganisms — **fla·gel·lar** \-lər\ *adj*

fla·geo·let \ˌfla-jə-'let, -'lā\ *n* [F] : a small woodwind instrument belonging to the flute class

fla·gi·tious \flə-'ji-shəs\ *adj* : grossly wicked : VILLAINOUS

flag·on \'fla-gən\ *n* : a container for liquids usu. with a handle, spout, and lid

flag·pole \'flag-ˌpōl\ *n* : a pole on which to raise a flag

fla·grant \'flā-grənt\ *adj* [L *flagrans*, prp. of *flagrare* to burn] : conspicuously bad — **fla·grant·ly** *adv*

fla·gran·te de·lic·to \flə-ˌgran-tē-di-'lik-tō\ *adv or adj* [ML, lit., while the crime is blazing] : in the very act of committing a misdeed; *also* : in the midst of sexual activity

flag·ship \'flag-ˌship\ *n* **1** : the ship that carries the commander of a fleet or subdivision thereof and flies his flag **2** : the most important one of a group

flag·staff \-ˌstaf\ *n* : FLAGPOLE

flag·stone \-ˌstōn\ *n* : ⁵FLAG

¹**flail** \'flāl\ *n* : a tool for threshing grain by hand

²**flail** *vb* : to strike or swing with or as if with a flail

flair \'flar\ *n* [F, lit., sense of smell, fr. OF, odor, fr. *flairier* to give off an odor, fr. (assumed) VL *flagrare*, fr. L *fragrare*] **1** : ability to appreciate or make good use of something : BENT, TALENT **2** : a unique style

flak \'flak\ *n, pl* **flak** [G, fr. *Fliegerabwehrkanonen*, fr. *Flieger* flyer + *Abwehr* defense + *Kanonen* cannons] **1** : antiaircraft guns or bursting shells fired from them **2** : CRITICISM, OPPOSITION

¹**flake** \'flāk\ *n* **1** : a small loose mass or bit **2** : a thin flattened piece or layer : CHIP — **flaky** *adj*

²**flake** *vb* **flaked; flak·ing** : to form or separate into flakes

³**flake** *n* : a markedly eccentric person : ODDBALL — **flak·i·ness** \'flā-kē-nəs\ *n* — **flaky** *adj*

flam·beau \'flam-ˌbō\ *n, pl* **flambeaux** \-ˌbōz\ *or* **flambeaus** [F, fr. MF, fr. *flambe* flame] : a flaming torch

flam·boy·ant \flam-'bȯi-ənt\ *adj* : marked by or given to strikingly elaborate or colorful display or behavior — **flam·boy·ance** \-əns\ *n* — **flam·boy·an·cy** \-ən-sē\ *n* — **flam·boy·ant·ly** *adv*

flame \'flām\ *n* **1** : the glowing gaseous part of a fire **2** : a state of blazing combustion **3** : a flamelike condition **4** : burning zeal or passion **5** : BRILLIANCE **6** : SWEETHEART — **flame** *vb*

fla·men·co \flə-'meŋ-kō\ *n, pl* **-cos** [Sp, fr. *flamenco* of the Gypsies, lit., Flemish, fr. MD *Vlaminc* Fleming] : a vigorous rhythmic dance style of the Spanish Gypsies

flame·throw·er \'flām-ˌthrō-ər\ *n* : a device that expels from a nozzle a burning stream of liquid or semiliquid fuel under pressure

fla·min·go \flə-'miŋ-gō\ *n, pl* **-gos** *also* **-goes** : any of several long-legged long-necked tropical water birds with scarlet wings and a broad bill bent downward

flam·ma·ble \'fla-mə-bəl\ *adj* : easily ignited and quick= burning — **flam·ma·bil·i·ty** \ˌfla-mə-'bi-lə-tē\ *n* — **flammable** *n*

flange \'flanj\ *n* : a rim used for strengthening or guiding something or for attachment to another object

¹**flank** \'flaŋk\ *n* **1** : the fleshy part of the side between the ribs and the hip; *also* : the side of a quadruped **2** : SIDE **3** : the right or left of a formation

²**flank** *vb* **1** : to attack or threaten the flank of **2** : to be situated on the side of : BORDER

flank·er \'flaŋ-kər\ *n* : a football player stationed wide of the formation slightly behind the line of scrimmage as a pass receiver

flan·nel \'flan-əl\ *n* **1** : a soft twilled wool or worsted fabric with a napped surface **2** : a stout cotton fabric napped on one side **3** *pl* : flannel underwear or trousers

¹**flap** \'flap\ *n* **1** : a stroke with something broad : SLAP **2** : something broad, limber, or flat and usu. thin that hangs loose **3** : the motion or sound of something broad and limber as it swings to and fro **4** : a state of excitement or confusion

²**flap** *vb* **flapped; flap·ping 1** : to beat with something broad and flat **2** : FLING **3** : to move (as wings) with a beating motion **4** : to sway loosely usu. with a noise of striking

flap·jack \'flap-ˌjak\ *n* : PANCAKE

flap·per \'fla-pər\ *n* **1** : one that flaps **2** : a young woman of the 1920s who showed freedom from conventions (as in conduct)

¹**flare** \'flar\ *vb* **flared; flar·ing 1** : to flame with a sudden unsteady light **2** : to become suddenly excited or angry ⟨~ up⟩ **3** : to spread outward

²**flare** *n* **1** : an unsteady glaring light **2** : a blaze of light used esp. to signal or illuminate; *also* : a device for producing such a blaze

flare–up \-ˌəp\ *n* : a sudden outburst or intensification

¹**flash** \'flash\ *vb* **1** : to break forth in or like a sudden flame **2** : to appear or pass suddenly or with great speed **3** : to send out in or as if in flashes ⟨~ a message⟩ **4** : to make a sudden display (as of brilliance or feeling) **5** : to gleam or glow intermittently **6** : to fill by a sudden rush of water **7** : to expose to view very briefly ⟨~ a badge⟩ **syn** glance, glint, sparkle, twinkle — **flash·er** *n*

²**flash** *n* **1** : a sudden burst of light **2** : a movement of a flag or light in signaling **3** : a sudden and brilliant burst (as of wit) **4** : a brief time **5** : SHOW, DISPLAY; *esp* : ostentatious display **6** : one that attracts notice; *esp* : an outstanding athlete **7** : GLIMPSE, LOOK **8** : a first brief news report **9** : FLASHLIGHT **10** : a device for producing a brief and very bright flash of light for taking photographs **11** : a quick-spreading flame or momentary intense outburst of radiant heat

³**flash** *adj* **1** : of sudden origin and short duration **2** : involving brief exposure to an intense agent (as heat or cold)

flash·back \'flash-ˌbak\ *n* **1** : interruption of the chronological sequence (as of a film or literary work) by an event of earlier occurrence **2** : a past event remembered vividly

flash back *vb* **1** : to vividly remember a past incident **2** : to employ a flashback

flash·bulb \-ˌbəlb\ *n* : an electric bulb that can be used only once to produce a brief and very bright flash of light for taking photographs

flash card *n* : a card bearing words, numbers, or pictures briefly displayed usu. as a learning aid

flash·cube \'flash-ˌkyüb\ *n* : a cubical device incorporating four flashbulbs

flash·gun \-ˌgən\ *n* : a device for producing a bright flash of light for photography

flash·ing \'fla-shiŋ\ *n* : sheet metal used in waterproofing (as at the angle between a chimney and a roof)

flash·light \'flash-ˌlīt\ *n* : a battery-operated portable electric light

flashy \'fla-shē\ *adj* **flash·i·er; -est 1** : momentarily dazzling ⟨a ~ refusal⟩ **2** : superficially attractive or impressive : SHOWY — **flash·i·ly** \-shə-lē\ *adv* — **flash·i·ness** \-shē-nəs\ *n*

flask \'flask\ *n* : a flattened bottle-shaped container ⟨a whiskey ~⟩

¹**flat** \'flat\ *adj* **flat·ter; flat·test 1** : spread out along a surface; *also* : being or characterized by a horizontal line **2** : having a smooth, level, or even surface **3** : having a broad smooth surface and little thickness **4** : DOWNRIGHT, POSITIVE ⟨a ~ refusal⟩ **5** : FIXED, UNCHANGING ⟨charge a ~ rate⟩ **6** : EXACT, PRECISE ⟨in four minutes ~⟩ **7** : DULL, UNINTERESTING; *also* : IN-

SIPID **8** : DEFLATED **9** : lower than the true pitch; *also* : lower by a half step **10** : free from gloss **11** : lacking depth of characterization — **flat·ly** *adv* — **flat·ness** *n*

²**flat** *n* **1** : a level surface of land : PLAIN **2** : a flat part or surface **3** : a character ♭ that indicates that a specified note is to be lowered by a half step; *also* : the resulting note **4** : something flat **5** : an apartment on one floor **6** : a deflated tire

³**flat** *adv* **1** : FLATLY **2** : COMPLETELY ⟨~ broke⟩ **3** : below the true musical pitch

⁴**flat** *vb* **flat·ted; flat·ting 1** : FLATTEN **2** : to lower in pitch esp. by a half step

flat·bed \'flat-ˌbed\ *n* : a truck or trailer with a body in the form of a platform or shallow box

flat·boat \-ˌbōt\ *n* : a flat-bottomed boat used esp. for carrying bulky freight

flat·car \-ˌkär\ *n* : a railroad freight car without sides or roof

flat·fish \-ˌfish\ *n* : any of an order of flattened marine bony fishes with both eyes on the upper side

flat·foot \-ˌfût, -ˈfût\ *n, pl* **flat·feet** \-ˌfēt, -ˈfēt\ : a condition in which the arch of the foot is flattened so that the entire sole rests upon the ground — **flat–foot·ed** \-ˈfü-təd\ *adj*

Flat·head \-ˌhed\ *n, pl* **Flatheads** *or* **Flathead** : a member of an American Indian people of Montana

flat·iron \-ˌīrn\ *n* : IRON 3

flat·land \-ˌland\ *n* : land lacking significant variation in elevation

flat–out \'flat-ˌaût\ *adj* **1** : being or going at maximum effort or speed **2** : OUT-AND-OUT, DOWNRIGHT ⟨it was a ~ lie⟩

flat out *adv* **1** : BLUNTLY, DIRECTLY **2** : at top speed **3** *usu* **flat–out** : to the greatest degree : COMPLETELY ⟨is just *flat-out* confusing⟩

flat·ten \'flat-ᵊn\ *vb* **1** : to make or become flat

flat·ter \'fla-tər\ *vb* [ME *flateren,* fr. OF *flater* to lick, flatter] **1** : to praise too much or without sincerity **2** : to represent too favorably **3** : to display to advantage **4** : to judge (oneself) favorably or too favorably — **flat·ter·er** *n*

flat·tery \'fla-tə-rē\ *n, pl* **-ter·ies** : flattering speech or attentions : insincere or excessive praise

flat·top \'flat-ˌtäp\ *n* **1** : AIRCRAFT CARRIER **2** : CREW CUT

flat·u·lent \'fla-chə-lənt\ *adj* **1** : full of gas ⟨a ~ stomach⟩ **2** : INFLATED, POMPOUS — **flat·u·lence** \-ləns\ *n*

fla·tus \'flā-təs\ *n* : gas formed in the intestine or stomach

flat·ware \'flat-ˌwar\ *n* : eating and serving utensils

flat·worm \-ˌwürm\ *n* : any of a phylum of flattened mostly parasitic segmented worms (as trematodes and tapeworms)

flaunt \'flônt\ *vb* **1** : to display oneself to public notice **2** : to wave or flutter showily **3** : to display ostentatiously or impudently : PARADE — **flaunt** *n*

flau·tist \'flô-tist, 'flaù-\ *n* [It *flautista*] : FLUTIST

¹**fla·vor** \'flā-vər\ *n* **1** : the quality of something that affects the sense of taste or of taste and smell **2** : a substance that adds flavor **3** : characteristic or predominant quality — **fla·vored** \-vərd\ *adj* — **fla·vor·ful** *adj* — **fla·vor·less** *adj* — **fla·vor·some** *adj*

²**flavor** *vb* : to give or add flavor to

fla·vor·ing *n* : FLAVOR 2

fla·vour *chiefly Brit var of* FLAVOR

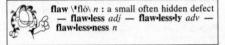

flaw \'flô\ *n* : a small often hidden defect — **flaw·less** *adj* — **flaw·less·ly** *adv* — **flaw·less·ness** *n*

flax \'flaks\ *n* : a fiber that is the source of linen; *also* : a blue-flowered plant grown for this fiber and its oily seeds

flax·en \'flak-sən\ *adj* **1** : made of flax **2** : resembling flax esp. in pale soft straw color

flay \'flā\ *vb* **1** : to strip off the skin or surface of **2** : to criticize harshly

fl dr *abbr* fluid dram

flea \'flē\ *n* : any of an order of small wingless leaping bloodsucking insects

flea·bane \'flē-ˌbān\ *n* : any of various plants of the daisy family once believed to drive away fleas

flea–bit·ten \-ˌbit-ᵊn\ *adj* : bitten by or infested with fleas

flea market *n* : a usu. open-air market for secondhand articles and antiques

¹**fleck** \'flek\ *vb* : STREAK, SPOT

²**fleck** *n* **1** : SPOT, MARK **2** : FLAKE, PARTICLE

fledge \'flej\ *vb* **fledged; fledg·ing** : to develop the feathers necessary for flying

fledg·ling \'flej-liŋ\ *n* **1** : a young bird with flight feathers newly developed **2** : an immature or inexperienced person

flee \'flē\ *vb* **fled** \'fled\; **flee·ing 1** : to run away often from danger or evil **2** : VANISH **3** : to run away from : SHUN

¹**fleece** \'flēs\ *n* **1** : the woolly coat of an animal and esp. a sheep **2** : a soft or woolly covering — **fleecy** *adj*

²**fleece** *vb* **fleeced; fleec·ing 1** : to strip of money or property by fraud or extortion **2** : SHEAR

¹**fleet** \'flēt\ *vb* : to pass rapidly

²**fleet** *n* [ME *flete,* fr. OE *flēot* ship, fr. *flēotan* to float] **1** : a group of warships under one command **2** : a group (as of ships, planes, or trucks) under one management

³**fleet** *adj* **1** : SWIFT, NIMBLE **2** : not enduring : FLEETING — **fleet·ness** *n*

fleet admiral *n* : an admiral of the highest rank in the navy

fleet·ing \'flē-tiŋ\ *adj* : passing swiftly

Flem·ing \'fle-miŋ\ *n* : a member of a Germanic people inhabiting chiefly northern Belgium

Flem·ish \'fle-mish\ *n* **1** : the Dutch language as spoken by the Flemings **2 Flemish** *pl* : FLEMINGS — **Flemish** *adj*

flesh \'flesh\ *n* **1** : the soft parts of an animal's body; *esp* : muscular tissue **2** : MEAT **3** : the physical nature of humans as distinguished from the soul **4** : human beings; *also* : living beings **5** : STOCK, KINDRED **6** : fleshy plant tissue (as fruit pulp) — **fleshed** \'flesht\ *adj*

flesh fly *n* : a dipteran fly whose maggots feed on flesh

flesh•ly \'flesh-lē\ *adj* **1** : CORPOREAL, BODILY **2** : not spiritual : WORLDLY **3** : CARNAL, SENSUAL

flesh out *vb* : to make fuller or more nearly complete

flesh•pot \'flesh-ˌpät\ *n* **1** *pl* : bodily comfort : LUXURY **2** : a place of lascivious entertainment — usu. used in pl.

fleshy \'fle-shē\ *adj* **flesh•i•er; -est 1** : consisting of or resembling animal flesh **2** : PLUMP, FAT

flew *past of* ¹FLY

flex \'fleks\ *vb* : to bend esp. repeatedly — **flex** *n*

flex•i•ble \'flek-sə-bəl\ *adj* **1** : capable of being flexed : PLIANT **2** : yielding to influence : TRACTABLE **3** : readily changed or changing : ADAPTABLE **syn** elastic, supple, resilient, springy — **flex•i•bil•i•ty** \ˌflek-sə-'bi-lə-tē\ *n*

flex•ure \'flek-shər\ *n* : TURN, FOLD

flib•ber•ti•gib•bet \ˌfli-bər-tē-'ji-bət\ *n* : a silly flighty person

¹**flick** \'flik\ *n* **1** : a light sharp jerky stroke or movement **2** : a sound produced by a flick **3** : ²FLICKER **4** : MOVIE — often used in pl.

²**flick** *vb* **1** : to strike lightly with a quick sharp motion **2** : FLUTTER, FLIT

¹**flick•er** \'fli-kər\ *vb* **1** : to move irregularly or unsteadily : FLUTTER **2** : to burn fitfully or with a fluctuating light — **flick•er•ing•ly** *adv*

²**flicker** *n* **1** : an act of flickering **2** : a sudden brief movement ⟨a ∼ of an eyelid⟩ **3** : a momentary stirring ⟨a ∼ of interest⟩ **4** : a slight indication : HINT **5** : a wavering light

³**flicker** *n* : a large barred and spotted No. American woodpecker with a brown back that occurs as an eastern form with yellow on the underside of the wings and tail and a western form with red in these areas

flied *past and past part of* ³FLY

fli•er \'flī-ər\ *n* **1** : one that flies; *esp* : PILOT **2** : a reckless or speculative undertaking **3** *usu* **fly•er** : an advertising circular

¹**flight** \'flīt\ *n* **1** : an act or instance of flying **2** : the ability to fly **3** : a passing through air or space **4** : the distance covered in a flight **5** : swift movement **6** : a trip made by or in an airplane or spacecraft **7** : a group of similar individuals (as birds or airplanes) flying as a unit **8** : a passing (as of the imagination) beyond ordinary limits **9** : a series of stairs from one landing to another — **flight•less** *adj*

²**flight** *n* : an act or instance of running away

flight bag *n* **1** : a lightweight traveling bag with zippered outside pockets **2** : a small canvas satchel

flight line *n* : a parking and servicing area for airplanes

flighty \'flī-tē\ *adj* **flight•i•er; -est 1** : easily upset : VOLATILE **2** : easily excited : SKITTISH **3** : CAPRICIOUS, SILLY — **flight•i•ness** \-tē-nəs\ *n*

flim•flam \'flim-ˌflam\ *n* : DECEPTION, FRAUD — **flim•flam•mery** \-ˌfla-mə-re\ *n*

flim•sy \'flim-zē\ *adj* **flim•si•er; -est 1** : lacking strength or substance **2** : of inferior materials and workmanship **3** : having little worth or plausibility ⟨a ∼ excuse⟩ — **flim•si•ly** \-zə-lē\ *adv* — **flim•si•ness** \-zē-nəs\ *n*

flinch \'flinch\ *vb* [MF *flenchir* to bend] : to shrink from or as if from pain : WINCE — **flinch** *n*

¹**fling** \'fliŋ\ *vb* **flung** \'fləŋ\; **fling•ing 1** : to move hastily, brusquely, or violently ⟨flung out of the room⟩ **2** : to kick or plunge vigorously **3** : to throw with force or recklessness; *also* : to cast as if by throwing **4** : to put suddenly into a state or condition

²**fling** *n* **1** : an act or instance of flinging **2** : a casual try : ATTEMPT **3** : a period of self-indulgence

flint \'flint\ *n* **1** : a hard quartz that produces a spark when struck by steel **2** : an alloy used for producing a spark in lighters — **flinty** *adj*

flint glass *n* : heavy glass containing an oxide of lead and used in lenses and prisms

flint•lock \'flint-ˌläk\ *n* **1** : a lock for a gun using a flint to ignite the charge **2** : a firearm fitted with a flintlock

¹**flip** \'flip\ *vb* **flipped; flip•ping 1** : to turn by tossing ⟨∼ a coin⟩ **2** : to turn over; *also* : to leaf through **3** : FLICK, JERK ⟨∼ a light switch⟩ **4** : to lose self-control — **flip** *n*

²**flip** *adj* : FLIPPANT, IMPERTINENT

flip•pant \'fli-pənt\ *adj* : lacking proper respect or seriousness — **flip•pan•cy** \'fli-pən-sē\ *n*

flip•per \'fli-pər\ *n* **1** : a broad flat limb (as of a seal) adapted for swimming **2** : a paddlelike shoe used in skin diving

flip side *n* : the reverse and usu. less popular side of a phonograph record

¹**flirt** \'flərt\ *vb* **1** : to move erratically : FLIT **2** : to behave amorously without serious intent **3** : to show casual interest ⟨∼ed with the idea⟩; *also* : to come close to ⟨∼ with danger⟩ — **flir•ta•tion** \ˌflər-'tā-shən\ *n* — **flir•ta•tious** \-shəs\ *adj*

²**flirt** *n* **1** : an act or instance of flirting **2** : a person who flirts

flit \'flit\ *vb* **flit•ted; flit•ting** : to pass or move quickly or abruptly from place to place : DART — **flit** *n*

flitch \'flich\ *n* : a side of cured meat; *esp* : a side of bacon

fliv•ver \'fli-vər\ *n* : a small cheap usu. old automobile

¹**float** \'flōt\ *n* **1** : something (as a raft) that floats **2** : a cork buoying up the baited end of a fishing line **3** : a hollow ball that floats at the end of a lever in a cistern or tank and regulates the liquid level **4** : a vehicle with a platform to carry an exhibit **5** : a soft drink with ice cream floating in it

²**float** *vb* **1** : to rest on the surface of or be suspended in a fluid **2** : to move gently on or through a fluid **3** : to cause to float **4** : WANDER **5** : to offer (securities) in order to finance an enterprise **6** : to finance by floating an issue of stocks or bonds **7** : to arrange for ⟨∼ a loan⟩ — **float•er** *n*

¹flock \'fläk\ n **1** : a group of birds or mammals assembled or herded together **2** : a group of people under the guidance of a leader; *esp* : CONGREGATION **3** : a large number

²flock *vb* : to gather or move in a flock

floe \'flō\ n : a flat mass of floating ice

flog \'fläg\ *vb* **flogged; flog·ging 1** : to beat with or as if with a rod or whip **2** : SELL ⟨~ encyclopedias⟩ — **flog·ger** n

¹flood \'fləd\ n **1** : a great flow of water over the land **2** : the flowing in of the tide **3** : an overwhelming volume

²flood *vb* **1** : to cover or become filled with a flood **2** : to fill abundantly or excessively; *esp* : to supply (a carburetor) with too much fuel **3** : to pour forth in a flood — **flood·er** n

flood·gate \'fləd-,gāt\ n : a gate for controlling a body of water : SLUICE

flood·light \-,līt\ n : a lamp that throws a broad beam of light; *also* : the beam itself — **floodlight** *vb*

flood·plain \-,plān\ n : a plain along a river or stream subject to periodic flooding

flood tide n **1** : a rising tide **2** : an overwhelming quantity **3** : a high point

flood·wa·ter \'fləd-,wȯ-tər, -,wä-\ n : the water of a flood

¹floor \'flȯr\ n **1** : the bottom of a room on which one stands **2** : a ground surface **3** : a story of a building **4** : a main level space (as in a legislative chamber) distinguished from a platform or gallery **5** : AUDIENCE **6** : the right to address an assembly **7** : a lower limit ⟨put a ~ under wheat prices⟩ — **floor·ing** n

²floor *vb* **1** : to furnish with a floor **2** : to knock down **3** : AMAZE, DUMBFOUND **4** : to press (a vehicle's accelerator) to the floorboard esp. rapidly

floor·board \-,bȯrd\ n **1** : a board in a floor **2** : the floor of an automobile

floor leader n : a member of a legislative body who has charge of a party's organization and strategy on the floor

floor show n : a series of acts presented in a nightclub

floor·walk·er \'flȯr-,wȯ-kər\ n : a person employed in a retail store to oversee the sales force and aid customers

floo·zy *or* **floo·zie** \'flü-zē\ n, pl **floozies** : a usu. young woman of loose morals

flop \'fläp\ *vb* **flopped; flop·ping 1** : FLAP **2** : to throw oneself down heavily, clumsily, or in a relaxed manner ⟨*flopped* into a chair⟩ **3** : FAIL — **flop** n — **flop** *adv* — **flop·per** n

flop·house \'fläp-,haùs\ n : a cheap hotel

¹flop·py \'flä-pē\ *adj* **flop·pi·er; -est** : tending to flop; *esp* : soft and flexible — **flop·pi·ly** \-pə-lē\ *adv*

²floppy n, pl **floppies** : FLOPPY DISK

floppy disk n : a small flexible disk with a magnetic coating on which computer data can be stored

flo·ra \'flȯr-ə\ n, pl **floras** *also* **flo·rae** \-,ē, -,ī\ [L *Flora*, Roman goddess of flowers] : plants or plant life esp. of a region or period

flo·ral \'flȯr-əl\ *adj* : of or relating to flowers or a flora

flo·res·cence \flō-'res-°ns, flə-\ n : a state or period of being in bloom or flourishing — **flo·res·cent** \-°nt\ *adj*

flor·id \'flȯr-əd\ *adj* **1** : very flowery in style : ORNATE ⟨~ prose⟩ **2** : tinged with red : RUDDY **3** : marked by emotional or sexual fervor

flo·rin \'flȯr-ən\ n **1** : an old gold coin first struck at Florence, Italy, in 1252 **2** : a gold coin of a European country patterned after the florin of Florence **3** : any of several modern silver coins issued in Commonwealth countries **4** : GULDEN

flo·rist \'flȯr-ist\ n : a person who sells flowers or ornamental plants

¹floss \'fläs\ n **1** : soft thread of silk or mercerized cotton for embroidery **2** : DENTAL FLOSS **3** : fluffy fibrous material

²floss *vb* : to use dental floss on (one's teeth) : use dental floss

flossy \'flä-sē\ *adj* **floss·i·er; -est 1** : of, relating to, or having the characteristics of floss **2** : STYLISH, GLAMOROUS — **floss·i·ly** \-sə-lē\ *adv*

flo·ta·tion \flō-'tā-shən\ n : the process or an instance of floating

flo·til·la \flō-'ti-lə\ n [Sp, dim. of *flota* fleet] : a fleet esp. of small ships

flot·sam \'flät-səm\ n : floating wreckage of a ship or its cargo

¹flounce \'flaùns\ *vb* **flounced; flounc·ing 1** : to move with exaggerated jerky or bouncy motions **2** : to go with sudden determination

²flounce n : an act or instance of flouncing — **flouncy** \'flaùn-sē\ *adj*

³flounce n : a strip of fabric attached by one edge; *also* : a wide ruffle

¹floun·der \'flaùn-dər\ n, pl **flounder** *or* **flounders** : FLATFISH; *esp* : any of various important marine food fishes

²flounder *vb* **1** : to struggle to move or obtain footing **2** : to proceed clumsily ⟨~ed through the speech⟩

¹flour \'flaùr\ n : finely ground and sifted meal of a grain (as wheat); *also* : a fine soft powder — **floury** *adj*

²flour *vb* : to coat with or as if with flour

flour·ish \'flər-ish\ *vb* **1** : THRIVE, PROSPER **2** : to be in a state of activity or production ⟨~ed about 1850⟩ **3** : to reach a height of development or influence **4** : to make bold and sweeping gestures **5** : BRANDISH

²flourish n **1** : a florid bit of speech or writing; *also* : an ornamental touch or decorative detail **2** : FANFARE **3** : WAVE ⟨with a ~ of his cane⟩ **4** : showiness in doing something

flout \'flaùt\ *vb* : to treat with contemptuous disregard ⟨~ the law⟩ — **flout·er** n

²flout n : TAUNT

¹flow \'flō\ *vb* **1** : to issue or move in a stream **2** : RISE ⟨the tide ebbs and ~s⟩ **3** : ABOUND **4** : to proceed smoothly and readily **5** : to have a smooth continuity **6** : to hang loose and billowing **7** : COME, ARISE **8** : MENSTRUATE

²flow n **1** : an act of flowing **2** : FLOOD 1, 2 **3** : a smooth uninterrupted movement **4** : STREAM; *also* : a mass of material that has flowed when molten **5** : the quantity that flows in a certain time **6** : MENSTRUATION **7** : a continuous transfer of energy — **flow·age** \'flō-ij\ n

flow·chart \'flō-,chärt\ n : a symbolic diagram showing step-by-step progression through a procedure

flow diagram n : FLOWCHART

¹flow·er \'flaù(-ə)r\ n **1** : a plant shoot modified for reproduction and bearing leaves specialized into floral organs; *esp* : one of a seed plant consisting of a calyx, corolla, stamens, and carpels **2** : a plant cultivated for its blossoms **3** : the best part or example **4** : the finest most vigorous period **5** : a state of blooming or flourishing — **flow·ered** \'flaù(-ə)rd\ *adj* — **flow·er·less** *adj*

²flower *vb* **1** : DEVELOP; *also* : FLOURISH **2** : to produce flowers : BLOOM

flower girl n : a little girl who carries flowers at a wedding

flower head n : a compact cluster of small flowers without stems suggesting a single flower

flowering plant n : any of a major group of vascular plants (as magnolias, grasses, or roses) that produce flowers and fruit and have the seeds enclosed in an ovary

flow·er·pot \'flaù(-ə)r-,pät\ n : a pot in which to grow plants

flow·ery \'flaù(-ə)r-ē\ *adj* **1** : of, relating to, or resembling flowers **2** : full of fine words or phrases — **flow·er·i·ly** \-ə-lē\ *adv* — **flow·er·i·ness** \-ē-nəs\ n

flown \'flōn\ *past part of* ¹FLY

fl oz *abbr* fluid ounce

10-9 JIM DAVIS
© 1985 PAWS, INC.

flu \'flü\ *n* **1** : INFLUENZA **2** : any of several virus diseases marked esp. by respiratory symptoms

flub \'fləb\ *vb* **flubbed; flub·bing** : BOTCH, BLUNDER — **flub** *n*

fluc·tu·ate \'flək-chə-₁wāt\ *vb* **-at·ed; -at·ing 1** : WAVER **2** : to move up and down or back and forth — **fluc·tu·a·tion** \₁flək-chə-'wā-shən\ *n*

flue \'flü\ *n* : a passage (as in a chimney) for directing a current (as of smoke or gases)

flu·ent \'flü-ənt\ *adj* **1** : capable of flowing : FLUID **2** : ready or facile in speech 〈∼ in French〉 **3** : effortlessly smooth and rapid 〈∼ speech〉 — **flu·en·cy** \-ən-sē\ *n* — **flu·ent·ly** *adv*

flue pipe *n* : an organ pipe whose tone is produced by an air current striking the beveled opening of the pipe

¹fluff \'fləf\ *n* **1** : ⁷DOWN 1 〈∼ from a pillow〉 **2** : something fluffy **3** : something inconsequential **4** : BLUNDER; *esp* : an actor's lapse of memory

²fluff *vb* **1** : to make or become fluffy 〈∼ up a pillow〉 **2** : to make a mistake

fluffy \'flə-fē\ *adj* **fluff·i·er; -est 1** : covered with or resembling fluff **2** : being light and soft or airy 〈a ∼ omelet〉 **3** : lacking in meaning or substance — **fluff·i·ly** \-fə-lē\ *adv*

¹flu·id \'flü-əd\ *adj* **1** : capable of flowing **2** : subject to change or movement **3** : showing a smooth easy style 〈∼ movements〉 **4** : available for a different use; *esp* : LIQUID **5** 〈∼ assets〉 — **flu·id·i·ty** \flü-'i-də-tē\ *n* — **flu·id·ly** *adv*

²fluid *n* : a substance (as a liquid or gas) tending to flow or take the shape of its container

fluid dram *or* **flu·i·dram** \₁flü-ə-'dram\ *n* — see WEIGHT table

fluid ounce *n* — see WEIGHT table

¹fluke \'flük\ *n* : any of various trematode flatworms

²fluke *n* **1** : the part of an anchor that fastens in the ground **2** : a lobe of a whale's tail

³fluke *n* : a stroke of luck — **fluky** *also* **fluk·ey** \'flü-kē\ *adj*

flume \'flüm\ *n* **1** : an inclined channel for carrying water **2** : a ravine or gorge with a stream running through it

flung *past and past part of* FLING

flunk \'fləŋk\ *vb* : to fail esp. in an examination or course — **flunk** *n*

flun·ky *or* **flun·key** \'fləŋ-kē\ *n, pl* **flunkies** *or* **flunkeys 1** : a liveried servant; *also* : one performing menial or miscellaneous duties **2** : YES-MAN

fluo·res·cence \flô-'res-ⁿns\ *n* : luminescence caused by radiation absorption that ceases almost immediately after the incident radiation has stopped; *also* : the emitted radiation — **fluo·resce** \-'res\ *vb* — **fluo·res·cent** \-'res-ⁿnt\ *adj*

fluorescent lamp *n* : a tubular electric lamp in which light is produced by the action of ultraviolet light on a fluorescent material that coats the inner surface of the lamp

fluo·ri·date \'flôr-ə-₁dāt\ *vb* **-dat·ed; -dat·ing** : to add a fluoride to (as drinking water) to reduce tooth decay — **fluo·ri·da·tion** \₁flôr-ə-'dā-shən\ *n*

fluo·ride \'flôr-₁īd\ *n* : a compound of fluorine

fluo·ri·nate \'flôr-ə-₁nāt\ *vb* **-nat·ed; -nat·ing** : to treat or cause to combine with fluorine or a compound of fluorine — **fluo·ri·na·tion** \₁flôr-ə-'nā-shən\ *n*

fluo·rine \'flôr-₁ēn, -ən\ *n* : a pale yellowish flammable irritating toxic gaseous chemical element — see ELEMENT table

fluo·rite \'flôr-₁īt\ *n* : a mineral that consists of the fluoride of calcium used as a flux and in making glass

fluo·ro·car·bon \₁flôr-ō-'kär-bən\ *n* : a compound containing fluorine and carbon used chiefly as a lubricant, refrigerant, or nonstick coating; *also* : CHLOROFLUOROCARBON

fluo·ro·scope \'flôr-ə-₁skōp\ *n* : an instrument for observing the internal structure of an opaque object (as the living body) by means of X rays — **fluo·ro·scop·ic** \₁flôr-ə-'skä-pik\ *adj* — **fluo·ros·co·py** \-'ä-skə-pē\ *n*

fluo·ro·sis \flü-'rō-səs, ₁flò-\ *n* : an abnormal condition (as spotting of the teeth) caused by fluorine or its compounds

flur·ry \'flər-ē\ *n, pl* **flurries 1** : a gust of wind **2** : a brief light snowfall **3** : COMMOTION, BUSTLE **4** : a brief outburst of activity 〈a ∼ of trading〉 — **flurry** *vb*

¹flush \'fləsh\ *vb* : to cause (a bird) to take wing suddenly

²flush *n* : a hand of cards all of the same suit

³flush *n* **1** : a sudden flow (as of water) **2** : a surge esp. of emotion 〈a ∼ of triumph〉 **3** : a tinge of red : BLUSH **4** : a fresh and vigorous state (in the ∼ of youth) **5** : a passing sensation of extreme heat

⁴flush *vb* **1** : to flow and spread suddenly and freely **2** : to glow brightly **3** : BLUSH **4** : to wash out with a rush of fluid **5** : INFLAME, EXCITE **6** : to cause to blush

⁵flush *adj* **1** : of a ruddy healthy color **2** : full of life and vigor **3** : filled to overflowing **4** : AFFLUENT **5** : readily available : ABUNDANT **6** : having an unbroken or even surface **7** : directly abutting : immediately adjacent **8** : set even with an edge of a type page or column — **flush·ness** *n*

⁶flush *adv* **1** : in a flush manner **2** : SQUARELY 〈a blow ∼ on the chin〉

⁷flush *vb* : to make flush

flus·ter \'fləs-tər\ *vb* : to put into a state of agitated confusion — **fluster** *n*

flute \'flüt\ *n* **1** : a hollow pipelike musical instrument **2** : a grooved pleat **3** : GROOVE — **flute** *vb* — **flut·ed** *adj*

flut·ing *n* : fluted decoration

flut·ist \'flü-tist\ *n* : a flute player

¹flut·ter \'flə-tər\ *vb* [ME *floteren* to float, flutter, fr. OE *floterian*, fr. *flotian* to float] **1** : to flap the wings rapidly **2** : to move with quick wavering or flapping motions **3** : to vibrate in irregular spasms **4** : to move

flute 1

about or behave in an agitated aimless manner — **flut·tery** \-tə-rē\ *adj*

²flutter *n* **1** : an act of fluttering **2** : a state of nervous confusion **3** : FLURRY

¹flux \'fləks\ *n* **1** : an act of flowing **2** : a state of continuous change **3** : a substance used to aid in fusing metals

²flux *vb* : ¹FUSE

¹fly \'flī\ *vb* **flew** \'flü\; **flown** \'flōn\; **fly·ing 1** : to move in or pass through the air with wings **2** : to move through the air or before the wind **3** : to float or cause to float, wave, or soar in the air **4** : FLEE **5** : to fade and disappear : VANISH **6** : to move or pass swiftly **7** : to become expended or dissipated rapidly **8** : to operate or travel in an aircraft or spacecraft **9** : to journey over by flying **10** : AVOID, SHUN **11** : to transport by flying

²fly *n, pl* **flies 1** : the action or process of flying : FLIGHT **2** *pl* : the space over a theater stage **3** : a garment closing concealed by a fold of cloth **4** : the length of an extended flag from its staff or support **5** : a baseball hit high into the air **6** : the outer canvas of a tent with a double top — **on the fly** : while still in the air

³fly *vb* **flied; fly·ing** : to hit a fly in baseball

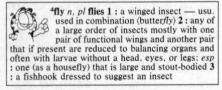

⁴fly *n, pl* **flies 1** : a winged insect — usu. used in combination ⟨butter*fly*⟩ **2** : any of a large order of insects mostly with one pair of functional wings and another pair that if present are reduced to balancing organs and often with larvae without a head, eyes, or legs; *esp* : one (as a housefly) that is large and stout-bodied **3** : a fishhook dressed to suggest an insect

fly·able \'flī-ə-bəl\ *adj* : suitable for flying or being flown

fly ball *n* : ²FLY 5

fly·blown \'flī-ˌblōn\ *adj* : not pure : TAINTED, CORRUPT

fly·by \-ˌbī\ *n, pl* **flybys 1** : a usu. low-altitude flight by an aircraft over a public gathering **2** : a flight of a spacecraft past a heavenly body (as Jupiter) close enough to obtain scientific data

fly–by–night \-bī-ˌnīt\ *adj* **1** : seeking a quick profit usu. by shady acts **2** : TRANSITORY, PASSING

fly casting *n* : the casting of artificial flies in fly-fishing or as a competitive sport

fly·catch·er \-ˌka-chər, -ˌke-\ *n* : any of various passerine birds that feed on insects caught in flight

fly·er *var of* FLIER

fly–fish·ing \'flī-ˌfi-shiŋ\ *n* : a method of fishing in which an artificial fly is used for bait

flying boat *n* : a seaplane with a hull designed for floating

flying buttress *n* : a projecting arched structure to support a wall or building

flying fish *n* : any of numerous sea fishes capable of long gliding flights out of water by spreading their large fins like wings

flying saucer *n* : an unidentified flying object reported to be saucer-shaped or disk-shaped

flying squirrel *n* : any of several No. American squirrels with folds of skin connecting the forelegs and hind legs that enable them to make long gliding leaps

fly·leaf \'flī-ˌlēf\ *n, pl* **fly·leaves** \-ˌlēvz\ : a blank leaf at the beginning or end of a book

fly·pa·per \-ˌpā-pər\ *n* : paper poisoned or coated with a sticky substance for killing or catching flies

fly·speck \-ˌspek\ *n* **1** : a speck of fly dung **2** : something small and insignificant — **flyspeck** *vb*

fly·way \-ˌwā\ *n* : an established air route of migratory birds

fly·wheel \-ˌhwēl\ *n* : a heavy wheel for regulating the speed of machinery

fm *abbr* fathom

Fm *symbol* fermium

FM \'ef-ˌem\ *n* : a broadcasting system using frequency modulation; *also* : a radio receiver of such a system

fn *abbr* footnote

fo *or* **fol** *abbr* folio

FO *abbr* foreign office

foal \'fōl\ *n* : a young horse or related animal; *esp* : one under one year — **foal** *vb*

¹foam \'fōm\ *n* **1** : a mass of bubbles formed on the surface of a liquid : FROTH, SPUME **2** : material (as rubber) in a lightweight cellular form — **foamy** *adj*

²foam *vb* : to form foam : FROTH

fob \'fäb\ *n* **1** : a short strap, ribbon, or chain attached esp. to a pocket watch **2** : a small ornament worn on a fob

FOB *abbr* free on board

fob off *vb* **1** : to put off with a trick, excuse, or inferior substitute **2** : to pass or offer as genuine **3** : to put aside

FOC *abbr* free of charge

focal length *n* : the distance of a focus from a lens or curved mirror

fo·c's·le *var of* FORECASTLE

¹fo·cus \'fō-kəs\ *n, pl* **fo·ci** \-ˌsī\ *also* **fo·cus·es** [NL, fr. L, hearth] **1** : a point at which rays (as of light, heat, or sound) meet or diverge or appear to diverge; *esp* : the point at which an image is formed by a mirror, lens, or optical system **2** : FOCAL LENGTH **3** : adjustment (as of eyes or eyeglasses) that gives clear vision

4 : central point : CENTER — **fo·cal** \'fō-kəl\ *adj* — **fo·cal·ly** *adv*

²focus *vb* **-cused** *also* **-cussed; -cus·ing** *also* **-cus·sing 1** : to bring or come to a focus ⟨~ rays of light⟩ **2** : CENTER ⟨~ attention on a problem⟩ **3** : to adjust the focus of

fod·der \'fä-dər\ *n* : coarse dry food (as cornstalks) for livestock

foe \'fō\ *n* [ME *fo*, fr. OE *fāh*, fr. *fāh* hostile] : ENEMY

FOE *abbr* Fraternal Order of Eagles

foehn *or* **föhn** \'fərn, 'fēn, 'fān\ *n* [G *Föhn*] : a warm dry wind blowing down a mountainside

foe·man \'fō-mən\ *n* : FOE

foe·tal, foe·tus *chiefly Brit var of* FETAL, FETUS

¹fog \'fȯg, 'fäg\ *n* **1** : fine particles of water suspended in the lower atmosphere **2** : mental confusion — **fog·gy** *adj*

²fog *vb* **fogged; fog·ging** : to obscure or be obscured with or as if with fog

fog·horn \'fȯg-ˌhȯrn, 'fäg-\ *n* : a horn sounded in a fog to give warning

fo·gy *also* **fo·gey** \'fō-gē\ *n, pl* **fogies** *also* **fogeys** : a person with old-fashioned ideas ⟨an old ~⟩

foi·ble \'fȯi-bəl\ *n* : a minor failing or weakness in character or behavior

¹foil \'fȯil\ *vb* [ME, to trample, full cloth, fr. MF *fouler*] **1** : to prevent from attaining an end : DEFEAT **2** : to bring to naught : THWART

²foil *n* : a light fencing sword with a flexible blade tapering to a blunt point

³foil *n* [ME, leaf, fr, MF *foille, foil*, fr. L *folium*] **1** : a very thin sheet of metal ⟨aluminum ~⟩ **2** : one that serves as a contrast to another

foist \'fȯist\ *vb* : to pass off (something false or worthless) as genuine

¹fold \'fōld\ *n* **1** : an enclosure for sheep **2** : a group of people with a common faith, belief, or interest

²fold *vb* : to house (sheep) in a fold

³fold *vb* **1** : to lay one part over or against another part **2** : to clasp together **3** : EMBRACE **4** : to bend (as a layer of rock) into folds **5** : to incorporate into a mixture by overturning repeatedly without stirring or beating **6** : to become doubled or pleated **7** : FAIL, COLLAPSE

⁴fold *n* **1** : a doubling or folding over **2** : a part doubled or laid over another part

fold·away \'fōl-də-ˌwā\ *adj* : designed to fold out of the way or out of sight

fold·er \'fōl-dər\ *n* **1** : one that folds **2** : a folded printed circular **3** : a folded cover or large envelope for loose papers

fol·de·rol \'fäl-də-ˌräl\ *n* **1** : a useless trifle **2** : NONSENSE

fold·out \'fōl-ˌdaut\ *n* : a folded leaf (as in a magazine) larger in some dimension than the page

fo·liage \'fō-lē-ij\ *n* : a mass of leaves (as of a plant or forest)

fo·li·at·ed \'fō-lē-ˌā-təd\ *adj* : composed of or separable into layers

fo·lic acid \ˌfō-lik-\ *n* : a vitamin of the vitamin B complex used esp. to treat nutritional anemias

fo·lio \'fō-lē-ˌō\ *n, pl* **fo·li·os 1** : a leaf of a book; *also* : a page number **2** : the size of a piece of paper cut two from a sheet **3** : a book printed on folio pages

¹folk \'fōk\ *n, pl* **folk** *or* **folks 1** : a group of people forming a tribe or nation; *also* : the largest number or most characteristic part of such a group **2** *pl* : PEOPLE, PERSONS ⟨country ~⟩ ⟨old ~s⟩ **3** *folks pl* : the persons of one's own family

²folk *adj* : of, relating to, or originating among the common people ⟨~ music⟩

folk·lore \'fōk-ˌlōr\ *n* : customs, beliefs, stories, and sayings of a people handed down from generation to generation — **folk·lor·ist** \-ist\ *n*

folk mass *n* : a mass in which traditional liturgical music is replaced by folk music

folk·sing·er \'fōk-ˌsiŋ-ər\ *n* : a singer of folk songs — **folk·sing·ing** *n*

folksy \'fōk-sē\ *adj* **folks·i·er; -est 1** : SOCIABLE, FRIENDLY **2** : informal, casual, or familiar in manner or style

folk·way \'fōk-ˌwā\ *n* : a way of thinking, feeling, or acting common to a given group of people; *esp* : a traditional social custom

fol·li·cle \'fä-li-kəl\ *n* **1** : a small anatomical cavity or gland ⟨a hair ~⟩ **2** : a small fluid-filled cavity in the ovary of a mammal enclosing a developing egg

fol·low \'fä-lō\ *vb* **1** : to go or come after **2** : to proceed along **3** : to engage in as a way of life ⟨~ the sea⟩ ⟨~ a profession⟩ **4** : OBEY **5** : PURSUE **6** : to come after in order or rank or natural sequence **7** : to keep one's attention fixed on **8** : to result from **syn** succeed, ensue, supervene — **fol·low·er** *n* — **follow suit 1** : to play a card of the same suit as the card led **2** : to follow an example set

¹fol·low·ing \'fä-lə-wiŋ\ *adj* **1** : next after : SUCCEEDING **2** : that immediately follows

²following *n* : a group of followers, adherents, or partisans

³following *prep* : subsequent to : AFTER

follow–up \'fä-lə-ˌwəp\ *n* : a system or instance of pursuing an initial effort by supplementary action

fol·ly \'fä-lē\ *n, pl* **follies** [ME *folie*, fr. OF, fr. *fol* fool] **1** : lack of good sense **2** : a foolish act or idea : FOOLISHNESS **3** : an excessively costly or unprofitable undertaking

fo·ment \fō-ˈment\ *vb* : INCITE

fo·men·ta·tion \ˌfō-mən-ˈtā-shən, -ˌmen-\ *n* **1** : a hot moist material (as a damp cloth) applied to the body to ease pain **2** : the act of fomenting : INSTIGATION

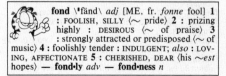

fond \'fänd\ *adj* [ME, fr. *fonne* fool] **1** : FOOLISH, SILLY ⟨~ pride⟩ **2** : prizing highly : DESIROUS ⟨~ of praise⟩ **3** : strongly attracted or predisposed ⟨~ of music⟩ **4** : foolishly tender : INDULGENT; *also* : LOVING, AFFECTIONATE **5** : CHERISHED, DEAR ⟨his ~est hopes⟩ — **fond·ly** *adv* — **fond·ness** *n*

fon·dant \'fän-dənt\ *n* : a creamy preparation of sugar used as a basis for candies or icings

fon·dle \'fänd-ᵊl\ *vb* **fon·dled; fon·dling** : to touch or handle lovingly : CARESS

fon·due *also* **fon·du** \fän-'dü, -'dyü\ *n* [F] : a preparation of melted cheese often flavored with white wine

¹**font** \'fänt\ *n* **1** : a receptacle for baptismal or holy water **2** : FOUNTAIN, SOURCE

²**font** *n* : an assortment of printing type of one size and style

food \'füd\ *n* **1** : material taken into an organism and used for growth, repair, and vital processes and as a source of energy; *also* : organic material produced by green plants and used by them as food **2** : nourishment in solid form **3** : something that nourishes, sustains, or supplies ⟨∼ for thought⟩

food chain *n* : a hierarchical arrangement of organisms in an ecological community such that each uses the next usu. lower member as a food source

food poisoning *n* : a digestive illness caused by bacteria or by chemicals in food

food·stuff \'füd-ˌstəf\ *n* : a substance with food value; *esp* : a specific nutrient (as fat or protein)

¹**fool** \'fül\ *n* [ME, fr. OF *fol*, fr. LL *follis*, fr. L, bellows, bag] **1** : a person who lacks sense or judgment **2** : JESTER **3** : DUPE **4** : IDIOT

²**fool** *vb* **1** : to spend time idly or aimlessly **2** : to meddle or tamper thoughtlessly or ignorantly **3** : JOKE **4** : DECEIVE **5** : FRITTER ⟨∼ed away his time⟩

fool·ery \'fü-lə-rē\ *n, pl* **-er·ies 1** : a foolish act, utterance, or belief **2** : foolish behavior

fool·har·dy \'fül-ˌhär-dē\ *adj* : foolishly daring : RASH — **fool·har·di·ness** \-dē-nəs\ *n*

fool·ish \'fü-lish\ *adj* **1** : showing or arising from folly or lack of judgment **2** : ABSURD, RIDICULOUS **3** : ABASHED — **fool·ish·ly** *adv* — **fool·ish·ness** *n*

fool·proof \'fül-ˌprüf\ *adj* : so simple or reliable as to leave no opportunity for error, misuse, or failure ⟨a ∼ plan⟩

fools·cap \'fül-ˌskap\ *n* [fr. the watermark of a fool's cap formerly applied to such paper] : a size of paper typically 16×13 inches

fool's gold *n* : PYRITE

¹**foot** \'fút\ *n, pl* **feet** \'fēt\ *also* **foot 1** : the end part of a leg below the ankle of a vertebrate animal **2** — see WEIGHT table **3** : a group of syllables forming the basic unit of verse meter **4** : something resembling an animal's foot in position or use **5** : the lowest part : BOTTOM **6** : the part at the opposite end from the head **7** : the part (as of a stocking) that covers the foot

²**foot** *vb* **1** : DANCE **2** : to go on foot **3** : to add up **4** : to pay or provide for paying

foot·age \'fu-tij\ *n* : length expressed in feet

foot·ball \'fut-ˌbol\ *n* **1** : any of several games played by two teams on a rectangular field with goalposts at each end in which the object is to get the ball over the goal line or between goalposts by running, passing, or kicking **2** : the ball used in football

foot·board \-ˌbord\ *n* **1** : a narrow platform on which to stand or brace the feet **2** : a board forming the foot of a bed

foot·bridge \-ˌbrij\ *n* : a bridge for pedestrians

foot·ed \'fu-təd\ *adj* : having a foot or feet of a specified kind or number ⟨flat-*footed*⟩ ⟨four-*footed*⟩

-foot·er \'fu-tər\ *comb form* : one that is a specified number of feet in height, length, or breadth ⟨a six-*footer*⟩

foot·fall \'fut-ˌfol\ *n* : the sound of a footstep

foot·hill \-ˌhil\ *n* : a hill at the foot of higher hills or mountains

foot·hold \-ˌhōld\ *n* **1** : a hold for the feet : FOOTING **2** : a position usable as a base for further advance

foot·ing *n* **1** : the placing of one's feet in a stable position **2** : the act of moving on foot **3** : a place or space for standing : FOOTHOLD **4** : position with respect to one another : STATUS **5** : BASIS

foot·less \'fut-ləs\ *adj* **1** : having no feet **2** : INEPT

foot·lights \-ˌlīts\ *n pl* **1** : a row of lights along the front of a stage floor **2** : the stage as a profession

foo·tling \'füt-liŋ\ *adj* **1** : INEPT **2** : TRIVIAL

foot·lock·er \'fut-ˌlä-kər\ *n* : a small trunk designed to be placed at the foot of a bed (as in a barracks)

foot·loose \-ˌlüs\ *adj* : having no ties : FREE, UNTRAMMELED

foot·man \-mən\ *n* : a male servant who attends a carriage, waits on table, admits visitors, and runs errands

foot·note \-ˌnōt\ *n* **1** : a note of reference, explanation, or comment placed usu. at the bottom of a page **2** : COMMENTARY

foot·pad \-ˌpad\ *n* : a round somewhat flat foot on the leg of a spacecraft for distributing weight to minimize sinking into a surface

foot·path \-ˌpath, -ˌpȧth\ *n* : a narrow path for pedestrians

foot·print \-ˌprint\ *n* **1** : an impression of the foot **2** : the area on a surface covered by something

foot·race \-ˌrās\ *n* : a race run on foot

foot·rest \-ˌrest\ *n* : a support for the feet

foot·sore \-ˌsȯr\ *adj* : having sore or tender feet (as from much walking)

foot·step \-ˌstep\ *n* **1** : the mark of the foot : TRACK **2** : TREAD **3** : distance covered by a step : PACE **4** : a step on which to ascend or descend **5** : a way of life, conduct, or action

foot·stool \-ˌstül\ *n* : a low stool to support the feet

foot·wear \-ˌwar\ *n* : apparel (as shoes or boots) for the feet

foot·work \-ˌwərk\ *n* : the management of the feet (as in boxing)

fop \'fäp\ *n* : DANDY **1** — **fop·pery** \'fä-pə-rē\ *n* — **fop·pish** *adj*

¹**for** \fər, 'fȯr\ *prep* **1** : as a preparation toward ⟨dress ∼ dinner⟩ **2** : toward the purpose or goal of ⟨need time ∼ study⟩ ⟨money ∼ a trip⟩ **3** : so as to reach or attain ⟨run ∼ cover⟩ **4** : as being ⟨took him ∼ a fool⟩ **5** : because of ⟨cry ∼ joy⟩ **6** — used to indicate a recipient ⟨a letter ∼ you⟩ **7** : in support of ⟨fought ∼ his country⟩ **8** : directed at : AFFECTING ⟨a cure ∼ what ails you⟩ **9** — used with a noun or pronoun followed by an infinitive to form the equivalent of a noun clause ⟨∼ you to go would be silly⟩ **10** : in exchange as equal to : so as to return the value of ⟨a lot of trouble ∼ nothing⟩ ⟨pay $10 ∼ a hat⟩ **11** : CONCERNING ⟨a stickler ∼ detail⟩ **12** : CONSIDERING ⟨tall ∼ her age⟩ **13** : through the period of ⟨served ∼ three years⟩ **14** : in honor of

²**for** *conj* : BECAUSE

³**for** *abbr* **1** foreign **2** forestry

fora *pl of* FORUM

¹**for·age** \'fȯr-ij\ *n* **1** : food for animals esp. when taken by browsing or grazing **2** : a search for food or supplies : plies

²**forage** *vb* **for·aged; for·ag·ing 1** : to collect forage from **2** : to search for food or supplies **3** : to get by foraging **4** : to make a search : RUMMAGE

for·ay \'fȯr-ˌā, fȯ-'rā\ *vb* : to raid esp. in search of plunder : PILLAGE — **foray** *n*

¹**for·bear** \fȯr-'bar\ *vb* **-bore** \-'bōr\; **-borne** \-'bȯrn\; **-bear·ing 1** : to refrain from : ABSTAIN **2** : to be patient — **for·bear·ance** \-'bar-əns\ *n*

²**forbear** *var of* FOREBEAR

for·bid \far-'bid\ *vb* **-bade** \-'bad, -'bād\ *or* **-bad** \-'bad\; **-bid·den** \-'bid-ᵊn\; **-bid·ding 1** : to command against : PROHIBIT **2** : HINDER, PREVENT *syn* enjoin, interdict, inhibit, ban

for·bid·ding *adj* : DISAGREEABLE, REPELLENT

for·bode *var of* FOREBODE

¹**force** \'fȯrs\ *n* **1** : strength or energy esp. of an exceptional degree : active power **2** : capacity to persuade or convince **3** : military strength; *also, pl* : the whole military strength (as of a nation) **4** : a body (as of persons or ships) available for a particular purpose **5** : VI-

OLENCE, COMPULSION **6** : an influence (as a push or pull) that causes motion or a change of motion —
force·ful \-fəl\ *adj* — **force·ful·ly** *adv* — **in force 1**
: in great numbers **2** : VALID, OPERATIVE
²**force** *vb* **forced; forc·ing 1** : COMPEL, COERCE **2** : to cause through necessity ⟨*forced* to admit defeat⟩ **3** : to press, attain to, or effect against resistance or inertia ⟨∼ your way through⟩ **4** : to raise or accelerate to the utmost ⟨∼ the pace⟩ **5** : to produce with unnatural or unwilling effort ⟨*forced* a smile⟩ **6** : to hasten (as in growth) by artificial means
for·ceps \ˈfȯr-səps\ *n, pl* **forceps** [L] : a hand‑held instrument for grasping, holding, or pulling objects esp. for delicate operations (as by a surgeon)

forceps

forc·ible \ˈfȯr-sə-bəl\ *adj* **1** : obtained or done by force **2** : showing force or energy : POWERFUL — **forc·i·bly** \-blē\ *adv*
¹**ford** \ˈfȯrd\ *n* : a place where a stream may be crossed by wading
²**ford** *vb* : to cross (a body of water) by wading
¹**fore** \ˈfȯr\ *adv* : in, toward, or adjacent to the front : FORWARD
²**fore** *adj* : being or coming before in time, order, or space
³**fore** *n* : something that occupies a front position

    ⁴**fore** *interj* — used by a golfer to warn anyone within range of the probable line of flight of the ball

fore–and–aft \ˌfȯr-ə-ˈnaft\ *adj* : lying, running, or acting along the length of a structure (as a ship)
¹**fore·arm** \(ˌ)fȯr-ˈärm\ *vb* : to arm in advance : PREPARE
²**fore·arm** \ˈfȯr-ˌärm\ *n* : the part of the arm between the elbow and the wrist
fore·bear \-ˌbar\ *n* : ANCESTOR, FOREFATHER
fore·bode \ˈfȯr-ˈbōd\ *vb* **1** : to have a premonition esp. of misfortune **2** : FORETELL, PREDICT **syn** augur, bode, foreshadow, portend, promise — **fore·bod·ing** *n*
fore·cast \ˈfȯr-ˌkast\ *vb* -**cast** *also* -**cast·ed; -cast·ing 1** : PREDICT, CALCULATE ⟨∼ weather conditions⟩ **2** : to indicate as likely to occur — **forecast** *n* — **fore·cast·er** *n*
fore·cas·tle \ˈfōk-səl\ *n* **1** : the forward part of the upper deck of a ship **2** : the crew's quarters usu. in a ship's bow
fore·close \fȯr-ˈklōz\ *vb* **1** : to shut out : PRECLUDE **2**

: to take legal measures to terminate a mortgage and take possession of the mortgaged property
fore·clo·sure \-ˈklō-zhər\ *n* : the act of foreclosing; *esp* : the legal procedure of foreclosing a mortgage
fore·doom \fōr-ˈdüm\ *vb* : to doom beforehand
fore·fa·ther \ˈfōr-ˌfä-<u>th</u>ər\ *n* **1** : ANCESTOR **2** : a person of an earlier period and common heritage
fore·fend *var of* FORFEND
fore·fin·ger \-ˌfiŋ-gər\ *n* : the finger next to the thumb
fore·foot \-ˌfu̇t\ *n* : either of the front feet of a quadruped; *also* : the front part of the human foot
fore·front \-ˌfrənt\ *n* : the foremost part or place
fore·gath·er *var of* FORGATHER
¹**fore·go** \fōr-ˈgō\ *vb* -**went** \-ˈwent\ -**gone** \-ˈgȯn\ -**go·ing** : PRECEDE
²**forego** *var of* FORGO
fore·go·ing *adj* : PRECEDING
fore·gone \ˈfōr-ˌgȯn\ *adj* : determined in advance ⟨a ∼ conclusion⟩
fore·ground \-ˌgrau̇nd\ *n* **1** : the part of a scene or representation that appears nearest to and in front of the spectator **2** : a position of prominence
fore·hand \-ˌhand\ *n* : a stroke (as in tennis) made with the palm of the hand turned in the direction in which the hand is moving; *also* : the side on which such a stroke is made — **forehand** *adj*

forehand

fore·hand·ed \(ˌ)fōr-ˈhan-dəd\ *adj* : mindful of the future : PRUDENT
fore·head \ˈfȯr-əd, ˈfȯr-ˌhed\ *n* : the part of the face above the eyes
for·eign \ˈfȯr-ən\ *adj* [ME *forein*, fr. OF, fr. LL *foranus* on the outside, fr. L *foris* outside] **1** : situated outside a place or country and esp. one's own country **2** : born in, belonging to, or characteristic of some place or country other than the one under consideration ⟨∼ language⟩ **3** : not connected, pertinent, or characteristically present **4** : related to or dealing with other nations ⟨∼ affairs⟩ **5** : occurring in an abnormal situation in the living body ⟨a ∼ body in the eye⟩
for·eign·er \ˈfȯr-ə-nər\ *n* : a person belonging to or owing allegiance to a foreign country
foreign minister *n* : a governmental minister for foreign affairs

fore·know \fōr-'nō\ *vb* **-knew** \-'nü, -'nyü\; **-known** \-'nōn\; **-know·ing** : to have previous knowledge of — **fore·knowl·edge** \'fōr-ˌnä-lij, fōr-'nä-\ *n*

fore·la·dy \'fōr-ˌlā-dē\ *n* : FOREWOMAN

fore·leg \-ˌleg\ *n* : a front leg

fore·limb \-ˌlim\ *n* : either of an anterior pair of limbs (as wings, arms, or fins)

fore·lock \-ˌläk\ *n* : a lock of hair growing from the front part of the head

fore·man \-mən\ *n* **1** : a spokesperson of a jury **2** : a person in charge of a group of workers

fore·mast \-ˌmast\ *n* : the mast nearest the bow of a ship

fore·most \-ˌmōst\ *adj* : first in time, place, or order : most important : PREEMINENT — **foremost** *adv*

fore·name \-ˌnām\ *n* : a first name

fore·named \-ˌnāmd\ *adj* : previously named : AFORESAID

fore·noon \-ˌnün\ *n* : MORNING

¹fo·ren·sic \fə-'ren-sik\ *adj* [L *forensis* public, forensic, fr. *forum* forum] **1** : belonging to, used in, or suitable to courts of law or to public speaking or debate **2** : relating to the application of scientific knowledge to legal problems ⟨∼ medicine⟩

²forensic *n* **1** : an argumentative exercise **2** *pl* : the art or study of argumentative discourse

fore·or·dain \ˌfōr-òr-'dān\ *vb* : to ordain or decree beforehand : PREDESTINE

fore·part \'fōr-ˌpärt\ *n* **1** : the anterior part of something **2** : the earlier part of a period of time

fore·quar·ter \-ˌkwòr-tər\ *n* : the front half of a lateral half of the body or carcass of a quadruped ⟨a ∼ of beef⟩

fore·run·ner \-ˌrə-nər\ *n* **1** : one that goes before to give notice of the approach of others : HARBINGER **2** : PREDECESSOR, ANCESTOR **syn** precursor, herald

fore·sail \-ˌsāl, -səl\ *n* **1** : the lowest sail on the foremast of a square-rigged ship or schooner **2** : the principal sail forward of the foremast (as of a sloop)

fore·see \fōr-'sē\ *vb* **-saw** \-'sò\; **-seen** \-'sēn\; **-see·ing** : to see or realize beforehand : EXPECT **syn** foreknow, divine, apprehend, anticipate — **fore·see·able** *adj*

fore·shad·ow \-'sha-dō\ *vb* : to give a hint or suggestion of beforehand

fore·short·en \fōr-'shòrt-ᵊn\ *vb* : to shorten (a detail) in a drawing or painting so that it appears to have depth

fore·sight \'fōr-ˌsīt\ *n* **1** : the act or power of foreseeing **2** : care or provision for the future : PRUDENCE **3** : an act of looking forward; *also* : a view forward — **fore·sight·ed** \-ˌsī-təd\ *adj* — **fore·sight·ed·ness** *n*

fore·skin \-ˌskin\ *n* : a fold of skin enclosing the end of the penis

for·est \'fòr-əst\ *n* [ME, fr. OF, fr. LL *forestis* (*silva*) unenclosed (woodland), fr. L *foris* outside] : a large thick growth of trees and underbrush — **for·est·ed** \'fòr-ə-stəd\ *adj* — **for·est·land** \'fòr-əst-ˌland\ *n*

fore·stall \fōr-'stòl, fòr-\ *vb* **1** : to keep out, hinder, or prevent by measures taken in advance **2** : ANTICIPATE

forest ranger *n* : a person in charge of the management and protection of a portion of a forest

for·est·ry \'fòr-ə-strē\ *n* : the science of growing and caring for forests — **for·est·er** \'fòr-ə-stər\ *n*

fore·swear *var of* FORSWEAR

¹fore·taste \'fōr-ˌtāst\ *n* : an advance indication, warning, or notion

²fore·taste \fōr-'tāst\ *vb* : to taste beforehand : ANTICIPATE

fore·tell \fōr-'tel\ *vb* **-told** \-'tōld\; **-tell·ing** : to tell of beforehand : PREDICT **syn** forecast, prophesy, prognosticate

fore·thought \'fōr-ˌthòt\ *n* **1** : PREMEDITATION **2** : consideration for the future

fore·to·ken \fōr-'tō-kən\ *vb* : to indicate in advance

fore·top \'fōr-ˌtäp\ *n* : a platform near the top of a ship's foremast

for·ev·er \fòr-'e-vər\ *adv* **1** : for a limitless time **2** : at all times : ALWAYS

for·ev·er·more \-ˌe-vər-'mòr\ *adv* : FOREVER

fore·warn \fōr-'wòrn\ *vb* : to warn beforehand

forewent *past of* FOREGO

fore·wing \'fōr-ˌwiŋ\ *n* : either of the anterior wings of a 4-winged insect

fore·wom·an \'fōr-ˌwu̇-mən\ *n* : a woman having the responsibilities of a foreman

fore·word \-ˌwərd\ *n* : PREFACE

¹for·feit \'fòr-fət\ *n* **1** : something forfeited : PENALTY, FINE **2** : FORFEITURE **3** : something deposited and then redeemed on payment of a fine **4** *pl* : a game in which forfeits are exacted

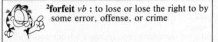

²forfeit *vb* : to lose or lose the right to by some error, offense, or crime

for·fei·ture \'fòr-fə-ˌchu̇r\ *n* **1** : the act of forfeiting **2** : something forfeited : PENALTY

for·fend \fòr-'fend\ *vb* **1** : PREVENT **2** : PROTECT, PRESERVE

for·gath·er \fòr-'ga-thər\ *vb* **1** : to come together : ASSEMBLE **2** : to meet someone usu. by chance

¹forge \'fòrj\ *n* [ME, fr. OF, fr. L *fabrica*, fr. *faber* smith] : a furnace or shop with its furnace where metal is heated and worked

²forge *vb* **forged; forg·ing 1** : to form (metal) by heating and hammering **2** : FASHION, SHAPE ⟨∼ an agreement⟩ **3** : to make or imitate falsely esp. with intent to defraud ⟨∼ a signature⟩ — **forg·er** *n* — **forg·ery** \'fòr-jə-rē\ *n*

³forge *vb* **forged; forg·ing** : to move ahead steadily but gradually

for·get \fər-'get\ *vb* **-got** \-'gät\; **-got·ten** \-'gät-ᵊn\ *or* **-got; -get·ting 1** : to be unable to think of or recall **2** : to fail to become mindful of at the proper time **3** : NEGLECT, DISREGARD — **for·get·ful** \-'get-fəl\ *adj* — **for·get·ful·ly** *adv*

for·get–me–not \fər-'get-mē-ˌnät\ *n* : any of a genus of small herbs with bright blue or white flowers

forg·ing *n* : a piece of forged work

for·give \fər-ˈgiv\ *vb* **-gave** \-ˈgāv\; **-giv·en** \-ˈgi-vən\; **-giv·ing** **1** : to give up resentment of **2** : PARDON, ABSOLVE **3** : to grant relief from payment of — **for·giv·able** *adj* — **for·give·ness** *n*

for·giv·ing *adj* **1** : willing or able to forgive **2** : allowing room for error or weakness

for·go \fȯr-ˈgō\ *vb* **-went** \-ˈwent\; **-gone** \-ˈgȯn\; **-go·ing** : to give up the enjoyment or advantage of : do without

fo·rint \ˈfȯr-int\ *n, pl* **forints** *also* **forint** — see MONEY table

¹fork \ˈfȯrk\ *n* **1** : an implement with two or more prongs for taking up (as in eating), pitching, or digging **2** : a forked part, tool, or piece of equipment **3** : a dividing into branches or a place where something branches; *also* : a branch of such a fork

²fork *vb* **1** : to divide into two or more branches **2** : to give the form of a fork to ⟨~*ing* her fingers⟩ **3** : to raise or pitch with a fork ⟨~ hay⟩ **4** : PAY, CONTRIBUTE — used with *over, out,* or *up*

forked \ˈfȯrkt, ˈfȯr-kəd\ *adj* : having a fork : shaped like a fork ⟨~ lightning⟩

fork·lift \ˈfȯrk-ˌlift\ *n* : a machine for lifting heavy objects by means of steel fingers inserted under the load

for·lorn \fər-ˈlȯrn, fȯr-\ *adj* **1** : sad and lonely because of isolation or desertion **2** : WRETCHED **3** : nearly hopeless — **for·lorn·ly** *adv* — **for·lorn·ness** *n*

¹form \ˈfȯrm\ *n* **1** : SHAPE, STRUCTURE **2** : a body esp. of a person : FIGURE **3** : the essential nature of a thing **4** : established manner of doing or saying something **5** : FORMULA **6** : a document with blank spaces for insertion of information ⟨tax ~⟩ **7** : CEREMONY **8** : manner of performing according to recognized standards **9** : a long seat : BENCH **10** : a model of the human figure used for displaying clothes **11** : MOLD ⟨a ~ for concrete⟩ **12** : type or plates in a frame ready for printing **13** : MODE, KIND, VARIETY ⟨coal is a ~ of carbon⟩ **14** : orderly method of arrangement; *also* : a particular kind or instance of such arrangement ⟨the sonnet ~ in poetry⟩ **15** : the structural element, plan, or design of a work of art **16** : a bounded surface or volume **17** : a grade in a British school or in some American private schools **18** : RACING FORM **19** : known ability to perform; *also* : condition (as of an athlete) suitable for performing **20** : one of the ways in which a word is changed to show difference in use ⟨the plural ~ of a noun⟩ — **form·less** *adj*

²form *vb* **1** : to give form or shape to : FASHION, MAKE **2** : TRAIN, INSTRUCT **3** : CONSTITUTE, COMPOSE **4** : DEVELOP, ACQUIRE ⟨~ a habit⟩ **5** : to arrange in order ⟨~ a battle line⟩ **6** : to take form : ARISE ⟨clouds are ~*ing*⟩ **7** : to take a definite form, shape, or arrangement

¹for·mal \ˈfȯr-məl\ *adj* **1** : according with conventional forms and rules ⟨a ~ dinner party⟩ **2** : done in due or lawful form ⟨a ~ contract⟩ **3** : CEREMONIOUS, PRIM ⟨a ~ manner⟩ **4** : NOMINAL — **for·mal·ly** *adv*

²formal *n* : something (as a social event) formal in character

form·al·de·hyde \fȯr-ˈmal-də-ˌhīd\ *n* : a colorless pungent gas used in water solution as a preservative and disinfectant

for·mal·ise *Brit var of* FORMALIZE

for·mal·ism \ˈfȯr-mə-ˌli-zəm\ *n* : strict adherence to set forms

for·mal·i·ty \fȯr-ˈma-lə-tē\ *n, pl* **-ties** **1** : compliance with formal or conventional rules **2** : the quality or state of being formal **3** : an established form that is required or conventional

for·mal·ize \ˈfȯr-mə-ˌlīz\ *vb* **-ized; -iz·ing** **1** : to give a certain or definite form to **2** : to make formal; *also* : to give formal status or approval to

¹for·mat \ˈfȯr-ˌmat\ *n* **1** : the general composition or style of a publication **2** : the general plan or arrangement of something

²format *vb* **for·mat·ted; for·mat·ting** : to arrange (as material to be printed) in a particular format — **for·mat·ter** *n*

for·ma·tion \fȯr-ˈmā-shən\ *n* **1** : an act of giving form to something : DEVELOPMENT **2** : something that is formed **3** : STRUCTURE, SHAPE **4** : an arrangement of persons or things in a prescribed manner or for a certain purpose

for·ma·tive \ˈfȯr-mə-tiv\ *adj* **1** : giving or capable of giving form : CONSTRUCTIVE **2** : of, relating to, or characterized by important growth or formation ⟨a child's ~ years⟩

for·mer \ˈfȯr-mər\ *adj* **1** : PREVIOUS, EARLIER **2** : FOREGOING **3** : being first mentioned or in order of two or more things

for·mer·ly \-lē\ *adv* : in time past : PREVIOUSLY

form-fit·ting \ˈfȯrm-ˌfi-tiŋ\ *adj* : conforming to the outline of the body

for·mi·da·ble \ˈfȯr-mə-də-bəl, fȯr-ˈmi-\ *adj* **1** : exciting fear, dread, or awe **2** : imposing serious difficulties — **for·mi·da·bly** \-blē\ *adv*

form letter *n* **1** : a letter on a frequently recurring topic that can be sent to different people at different times **2** : a letter for mass circulation sent out in many printed copies

for·mu·la \ˈfȯr-myə-lə\ *n, pl* **-las** *or* **-lae** \-ˌlē, -ˌlī\ **1** : a set form of words for ceremonial use **2** : RECIPE, PRESCRIPTION **3** : a milk mixture or substitute for a baby **4** : a group of symbols or figures joined to express information concisely **5** : a customary or set form or method

for·mu·late \-ˌlāt\ *vb* **-lat·ed; -lat·ing** **1** : to express in a formula **2** : DESIGN, DEVISE ⟨~ a policy⟩ **3** : to prepare according to a formula — **for·mu·la·tion** \ˌfȯr-myə-ˈlā-shən\ *n*

for·ni·ca·tion \ˌfȯr-nə-ˈkā-shən\ *n* : consensual sexual intercourse between two persons not married to each other — **for·ni·cate** \ˈfȯr-nə-ˌkāt\ *vb* — **for·ni·ca·tor** \-ˌkā-tər\ *n*

for·sake \fər-ˈsāk, fȯr-\ *vb* **for·sook** \-ˈsùk\; **for·sak-**

en \-ˈsā-kən\; **for·sak·ing** [ME, fr. OE *forsacan*, fr. *sacan* to dispute] : to renounce or turn away from entirely

for·sooth \fər-ˈsüth\ *adv* : in truth : INDEED

for·swear \fȯr-ˈswar\ *vb* **for·swore** \-ˈswōr\; **for·sworn** \-ˈswōrn\; **for·swear·ing 1** : to swear falsely : commit perjury **2** : to renounce earnestly or under oath **3** : to deny under oath

for·syth·ia \fər-ˈsi-thē-ə\ *n* : any of a genus of shrubs related to the olive and having yellow bell-shaped flowers appearing before the leaves in early spring

fort \ˈfȯrt\ *n* [ME *forte*, fr. MF *fort*, fr. *fort* strong, fr. L *fortis*] **1** : a fortified place **2** : a permanent army post

¹**forte** \ˈfȯrt, ˈfȯr-ˌtā\ *n* [F *fort*, fr. *fort*, adj., strong] : one's strong point

²**for·te** \ˈfȯr-ˌtā\ *adv or adj* [It, fr. *forte* strong] : LOUD — used as a direction in music

forth \ˈfȯrth\ *adv* **1** : FORWARD, ONWARD 〈from that day ∼〉 **2** : out into view 〈put ∼ leaves〉

forth·com·ing \ˌfȯrth-ˈkə-miŋ\ *adj* **1** : coming or available soon 〈the ∼ holidays〉 **2** : marked by openness and candor : OUTGOING

forth·right \ˈfȯrth-ˌrīt\ *adj* : free from ambiguity or evasiveness : going straight to the point 〈a ∼ answer〉 — **forth·right·ly** *adv* — **forth·right·ness** *n*

forth·with \ˌfȯrth-ˈwith\ *adv* : IMMEDIATELY

for·ti·fy \ˈfȯr-tə-ˌfī\ *vb* **-fied; -fy·ing 1** : to strengthen by military defenses **2** : to give physical strength or endurance to **3** : ENCOURAGE **4** : to strengthen or enrich with a material 〈∼ bread with vitamins〉 — **for·ti·fi·ca·tion** \ˌfȯr-tə-fə-ˈkā-shən\ *n*

for·tis·si·mo \fȯr-ˈti-sə-ˌmō\ *adv or adj* : very loud — used as a direction in music

for·ti·tude \ˈfȯr-tə-ˌtüd, -ˌtyüd\ *n* : strength of mind that enables one to meet danger or bear pain or adversity with courage **syn** grit, backbone, pluck, guts

fort·night \ˈfȯrt-ˌnīt\ *n* [ME *fourtenight*, alter. of *fourtene night* fourteen nights] : two weeks — **fort·night·ly** \-lē\ *adj or adv*

for·tress \ˈfȯr-trəs\ *n* : FORT 1

for·tu·itous \fȯr-ˈtü-ə-təs, -ˈtyü-\ *adj* **1** : happening by chance **2** : FORTUNATE

for·tu·ity \-ə-tē\ *n, pl* **-ities 1** : the quality or state of being fortuitous **2** : a chance event or occurrence

for·tu·nate \ˈfȯr-chə-nət\ *adj* **1** : bringing some good thing not foreseen **2** : LUCKY

for·tu·nate·ly \-lē\ *adv* **1** : in a fortunate manner **2** : it is fortunate that

for·tune \ˈfȯr-chən\ *n* **1** : prosperity attained partly through luck; *also* : CHANCE, LUCK **2** : what happens to a person : good or bad luck **3** : FATE, DESTINY **4** : RICHES, WEALTH

fortune hunter *n* : a person who seeks wealth esp. by marriage

for·tune–tell·er \-ˌte-lər\ *n* : a person who professes to tell future events — **for·tune–tell·ing** *n or adj*

for·ty \ˈfȯr-tē\ *n, pl* **forties** : four times 10 — **for·ti·eth** \ˈfȯr-tē-əth\ *adj or n* — **forty** *adj or pron*

for·ty–five \ˌfȯr-tē-ˈfīv\ *n* **1** : a .45 caliber handgun — usu. written .45 **2** : a phonograph record designed to be played at 45 revolutions per minute

for·ty–nin·er \-ˈnī-nər\ *n* : a person in the rush to California for gold in 1849

forty winks *n sing or pl* : a short sleep

fo·rum \ˈfȯr-əm\ *n, pl* **forums** *also* **fo·ra** \-ə\ [L] **1** : the marketplace or central meeting place of an ancient Roman city **2** : a medium (as a publication) of open discussion **3** : COURT **4** : a public assembly, lecture, or program involving audience or panel discussion

¹**for·ward** \ˈfȯr-wərd\ *adj* **1** : being near or at or belonging to the front **2** : EAGER, READY **3** : BRASH, BOLD **4** : notably advanced or developed : PRECOCIOUS **5** : moving, tending, or leading toward a position in front **6** : EXTREME, RADICAL **7** : of, relating to, or getting ready for the future — **for·ward·ness** *n*

²**forward** *adv* : to or toward what is ahead or in front

³**forward** *vb* **1** : to help onward : ADVANCE **2** : to send forward : TRANSMIT **3** : to send or ship onward

⁴**forward** *n* : a player who plays at the front of a team's offensive formation near the opponent's goal

for·ward·er \-wər-dər\ *n* : one that forwards; *esp* : an agent who forwards goods — **for·ward·ing** *n*

for·wards \ˈfȯr-wərdz\ *adv* : FORWARD

¹**fos·sil** \ˈfä-səl\ *adj* [L *fossilis* obtained by digging, fr. *fodere* to dig] **1** : preserved from a past geologic age 〈∼ plants〉 **2** : of or relating to fossil fuels

²**fossil** *n* **1** : a trace or impression or the remains of a plant or animal of a past geologic age preserved in the earth's crust **2** : a person whose ideas are out= of-date — **fos·sil·ize** \ˈfä-sə-ˌlīz\ *vb*

fossil fuel *n* : a fuel (as coal or oil) that is formed in the earth from plant or animal remains

¹**fos·ter** \ˈfȯs-tər\ *adj* [ME, fr. OE *fōstor-*, fr. *fōstor* food, feeding] : affording, receiving, or sharing nourishment or parental care though not related by blood or legal ties 〈∼ parent〉 〈∼ child〉

²**foster** *vb* **1** : to give parental care to : NURTURE **2** : to promote the growth or development of : ENCOURAGE

foster home *n* : a household in which an orphaned, neglected, or delinquent child is placed for care

fos·ter·ling \-tər-liŋ\ *n* : a foster child

Fou·cault pendulum \fü-ˈkō-\ *n* : a device that consists of a heavy weight hung by a long wire and that swings in a constant direction which appears to change showing that the earth rotates

fought *past and past part of* FIGHT

¹**foul** \ˈfau̇l\ *adj* **1** : offensive to the senses : LOATHSOME; *also* : clogged with dirt **2** : ODIOUS, DETESTABLE **3** : OBSCENE, ABUSIVE **4** : DISAGREEABLE, STORMY 〈∼ weather〉 **5** : TREACHEROUS, DISHONORABLE, UNFAIR **6** : marking the bounds of a playing field 〈∼ lines〉; *also* : being outside the foul line 〈∼ ball〉 〈∼ territory〉 **7** : containing marked-up corrections **8** : ENTANGLED — **foul·ly** *adv* — **foul·ness** *n*

²**foul** *n* **1** : an entanglement or collision in fishing or sailing **2** : an infraction of the rules in a game or sport; *also* : a baseball hit outside the foul line

³**foul** *vb* **1** : to make or become foul or filthy **2** : to entangle or become entangled **3** : OBSTRUCT, BLOCK **4** : to collide with **5** : to make or hit a foul

⁴**foul** *adv* : in a foul manner

fou·lard \fü-ˈlärd\ *n* : a lightweight silk of plain or twill weave usu. decorated with a printed pattern

foul–mouthed \ˈfau̇l-ˈmau̇thd, -ˈmau̇tht\ *adj* : given to the use of obscene, profane, or abusive language

foul play *n* : VIOLENCE; *esp* : MURDER

foul–up \ˈfau̇l-ˌəp\ *n* **1** : a state of being fouled up **2** : a mechanical difficulty

foul up *vb* **1** : to spoil by mistakes or poor judgment **2** : to cause a foul-up : BUNGLE

¹**found** \ˈfau̇nd\ *past and past part of* FIND

²**found** *vb* **1** : to take the first steps in building **2** : to set or ground on something solid : BASE **3** : to establish (as an institution) often with provision for future maintenance — **found·er** *n*

foun·da·tion \fau̇n-ˈdā-shən\ *n* **1** : the act of founding **2** : a basis upon which something stands or is supported 〈suspicions without ∼〉 **3** : funds given for the permanent support of an institution : ENDOWMENT; *also* : an institution so endowed **4** : supporting structure : BASE **5** : CORSET — **foun·da·tion·al** \-shə-nəl\ *adj*

foun·der \ˈfau̇n-dər\ *vb* **1** : to make or become lame 〈the horse ∼ed〉 **2** : COLLAPSE **3** : SINK 〈a ∼ing ship〉 **4** : FAIL

found·ling \ˈfau̇nd-liŋ\ *n* : an infant found after its unknown parents have abandoned it

found·ry \ˈfau̇n-drē\ *n, pl* **foundries** : a building or works where metal is cast

fount \ˈfau̇nt\ *n* : SOURCE, FOUNTAIN

foun·tain \ˈfau̇nt-ᵊn\ *n* **1** : a spring of water **2** : SOURCE

3 : an artificial jet of water **4** : a container for liquid that can be drawn off as needed

foun·tain·head \-ˌhed\ *n* : SOURCE

fountain pen *n* : a pen with a reservoir that feeds the writing point with ink

four \'fōr\ *n* **1** : one more than three **2** : the 4th in a set or series **3** : something having four units — **four** *adj or pron*

four–flush \-ˌfləsh\ *vb* : to make a false claim : BLUFF — **four–flush·er** *n*

four·fold \-ˌfōld, -'fōld\ *adj* **1** : being four times as great or as many **2** : having four units or members — **four·fold** \-'fōld\ *adv*

4–H \'fōr-'āch\ *adj* [fr. the fourfold aim of improving the head, heart, hands, and health] : of or relating to a program set up by the U.S. Department of Agriculture to help young people become productive citizens — **4–H'er** *n*

Four Hundred *or* **400** *n* : the exclusive social set of a community — used with *the*

four–in–hand \'fōr-ən-ˌhand\ *n* **1** : a team of four horses driven by one person; *also* : a vehicle drawn by such a team **2** : a necktie tied in a slipknot with long ends overlapping vertically in front

four–o'clock \'fōr-ə-ˌkläk\ *n* : a garden plant with fragrant yellow, red, or white flowers without petals that open late in the afternoon

four–post·er \-'pō-stər\ *n* : a bed with tall corner posts orig. designed to support curtains or a canopy

four·score \'fōr-ˌskōr\ *adj* : being four times twenty : EIGHTY

four·some \'fōr-səm\ *n* **1** : a group of four persons or things **2** : a golf match between two pairs of partners

four·square \-'skwar\ *adj* **1** : SQUARE **2** : marked by boldness and conviction : FORTHRIGHT — **four·square** *adv*

four·teen \fōr-'tēn\ *n* : one more than 13 — **fourteen** *adj or pron* — **four·teenth** \-'tēnth\ *adj or n*

fourth \'fōrth\ *n* **1** : one that is number four in a countable series **2** : one of four equal parts of something — **fourth** *adj or adv*

fourth estate *n, often cap F&E* : the public press

4WD *abbr* four-wheel drive

four–wheel \'fōr-ˌhwēl\ *or* **four·wheeled** \-ˌhwēld\ *adj* : acting on or by means of four wheels of a motor vehicle

¹fowl \'faùl\ *n, pl* **fowl** *or* **fowls 1** : BIRD **2** : a cock or hen of the domestic chicken; *also* : the flesh of these used as food

²fowl *vb* : to hunt wildfowl

¹fox \'fäks\ *n, pl* **fox·es** *also* **fox 1** : any of various flesh-eating mammals related to the wolves but smaller and with shorter legs and a more pointed muzzle; *also* : the fur of a fox **2** : a clever crafty person **3** *cap* : a member of an American Indian people formerly living in what is now Wisconsin

²fox *vb* : TRICK, OUTWIT

fox·glove \'fäks-ˌgləv\ *n* : a common plant related to the snapdragons that is grown for its showy spikes of dotted white or purple tubular flowers and as a source of digitalis

fox·hole \-ˌhōl\ *n* : a pit dug for protection against enemy fire

fox·hound \-ˌhaùnd\ *n* : any of various large swift powerful hounds used in hunting foxes

fox terrier *n* : a small lively terrier that occurs in varieties with smooth dense coats or with harsh wiry coats

fox–trot \'fäks-ˌträt\ *n* **1** : a short broken slow trotting gait **2** : a ballroom dance in duple time

foxy \'fäk-sē\ *adj* **fox·i·er; -est 1** : resembling or suggestive of a fox **2** : WILY **3** : physically attractive

foy·er \'fòi-ər, 'fòi-ˌyā\ *n* [F, lit., fireplace, fr. (assumed) VL *focarium*, fr. L *focus* hearth] : LOBBY; *also* : an entrance hallway

fpm *abbr* feet per minute

FPO *abbr* fleet post office

fps *abbr* feet per second

fr *abbr* **1** father **2** franc **3** friar **4** from

¹Fr *abbr* **1** France; French **2** Friday

²Fr *symbol* francium

fra·cas \'frā-kəs, 'fra-\ *n, pl* **fra·cas·es** \-kə-səz\ [F, din, row, fr. It *fracasso*, fr. *fracassare* to shatter] : BRAWL

frac·tal \'frak-t°l\ *n* : an irregular curve or shape that repeats itself at any scale on which it is examined — **fractal** *adj*

frac·tion \'frak-shən\ *n* **1** : a numerical representation (as ½, ¾, or 3.323) indicating the quotient of two numbers **2** : FRAGMENT **3** : PORTION — **frac·tion·al** \-shə-nəl\ *adj* — **frac·tion·al·ly** *adv*

frac·tious \'frak-shəs\ *adj* **1** : tending to be troublesome : hard to handle or control **2** : QUARRELSOME, IRRITABLE

frac·ture \'frak-chər\ *n* **1** : a breaking of something and esp. a bone **2** : CRACK, CLEFT — **fracture** *vb*

frag·ile \'fra-jəl, -ˌjīl\ *adj* : easily broken : DELICATE — **fra·gil·i·ty** \frə-'ji-lə-tē\ *n*

¹frag·ment \'frag-mənt\ *n* : a part broken off, detached, or incomplete

²frag·ment \-ˌment\ *vb* : to break into fragments — **frag·men·ta·tion** \ˌfrag-mən-'tā-shən, -ˌmən-\ *n*

frag·men·tary \'frag-mən-ˌter-ē\ *adj* : made up of fragments : INCOMPLETE

fra·grant \'frā-grənt\ *adj* : sweet or agreeable in smell — **fra·grance** \-grəns\ *n* — **fra·grant·ly** *adv*

frail \'frāl\ *adj* **1** : morally or physically weak **2** : FRAGILE, DELICATE

frail·ty \'frāl-tē\ *n, pl* **frailties 1** : the quality or state of being frail **2** : a fault due to weakness

¹frame \'frām\ *vb* **framed; fram·ing 1** : PLAN, CONTRIVE **2** : SHAPE, CONSTRUCT **3** : FORMULATE **4** : DRAW UP ⟨~ a constitution⟩ **5** : to make appear guilty **6** : to fit or adjust for a purpose : ARRANGE **7** : to provide with or enclose in a frame — **fram·er** *n*

²frame *n* **1** : something made of parts fitted and joined together **2** : the physical makeup of the body **3** : an arrangement of structural parts that gives form or support **4** : a supporting or enclosing border or open case (as for a window or picture) **5** : one picture of a series (as on a length of film) **6** : FRAME-UP

³frame *adj* : having a wood frame

frame of mind *n* : mental attitude or outlook : MOOD

frame–up \'frā-ˌməp\ *n* **1** : an act or series of actions in which someone is framed **2** : an action that is planned, contrived, or formulated

frame·work \'frām-ˌwərk\ *n* : a basic supporting part or structure

franc \'fraŋk\ *n* — see MONEY table

fran·chise \'fran-ˌchīz\ *n* [ME, fr. MF, fr. *franchir* to free, fr. OF *franc* free] **1** : a special privilege granted to an individual or group ⟨a ~ to operate a ferry⟩ **2** : a constitutional or statutory right or privilege; *esp* : the right to vote

fran·chi·see \ˌfran-chī-'zē, -chə-\ *n* : one granted a franchise

fran·chis·er \'fran-ˌchī-zər\ *n* **1** : FRANCHISEE **2** : FRANCHISOR

fran·chi·sor \ˌfran-chī-'zòr, -chə-\ *n* : one that grants a franchise

fran·ci·um \'fran-sē-əm\ *n* : a radioactive metallic chemical element — see ELEMENT table

Fran·co–Amer·i·can \ˌfraŋ-kō-ə-'mer-ə-kən\ *n* : an American of French or esp. French-Canadian descent — **Franco–American** *adj*

fran·gi·ble \'fran-jə-bəl\ *adj* : BREAKABLE — **fran·gi·bil·i·ty** \ˌfran-jə-'bi-lə-tē\ *n*

¹frank \'fraŋk\ *adj* : marked by free, forthright, and sincere expression — **frank·ness** *n*

²frank *vb* : to mark (a piece of mail) with an official sign so that it can be mailed free; *also* : to mail free

³frank *n* **1** : the signature or mark on a piece of mail

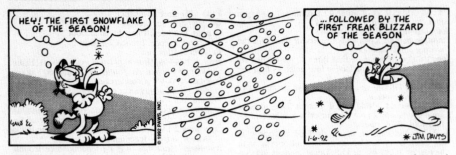

indicating free or paid postage **2** : the privilege of sending mail free

Fran·ken·stein \'fraŋ-kən-₁stīn\ *n* **1** : a monstrous creation that usu. ruins its originator **2** : a monster in the shape of a man

frank·furt·er \'fraŋk-fər-tər, -₁fər-\ *or* **frank·furt** \-fərt\ *n* : a seasoned sausage (as of beef or beef and pork)

frank·in·cense \'fraŋ-kən-₁sens\ *n* : a fragrant resin burned as incense

frank·ly \'fraŋ-klē\ *adv* **1** : in a frank manner **2** : in truth : INDEED

fran·tic \'fran-tik\ *adj* : marked by uncontrolled emotion or disordered anxious activity — **fran·ti·cal·ly** \-ti-k(ə-)lē\ *adv*

frap·pé \fra-'pā\ *or* **frappe** *same or* 'frap\ [F *frappé,* fr. pp. of *frapper* to strike, chill] *n* **1** : an iced or frozen drink **2** : a thick milk shake — **frap·pé** \fra-'pā\ *adj*

fra·ter·nal \frə-'tərn-əl\ *adj* **1** : of, relating to, or involving brothers **2** : of, relating to, or being a fraternity or society **3** : FRIENDLY, BROTHERLY — **fra·ter·nal·ly** *adv*

fra·ter·ni·ty \frə-'tər-nə-tē\ *n, pl* **-ties 1** : a social, honorary, or professional group; *esp* : a men's student organization **2** : BROTHERLINESS, BROTHERHOOD **3** : persons of the same class, profession, or tastes

frat·er·nize \'fra-tər-₁nīz\ *vb* **-nized; -niz·ing 1** : to mingle as friends **2** : to associate on close terms with members of a hostile group — **frat·er·ni·za·tion** \₁fra-tər-nə-'zā-shən\ *n*

frat·ri·cide \'fra-trə-₁sīd\ *n* **1** : one that kills a sibling or countryman **2** : the act of a fratricide — **frat·ri·cid·al** \₁fra-trə-'sīd-əl\ *adj*

fraud \'fròd\ *n* **1** : DECEIT, TRICKERY **2** : TRICK **3** : IMPOSTOR, CHEAT

fraud·u·lent \'frò-jə-lənt\ *adj* : characterized by, based on, or done by fraud : DECEITFUL — **fraud·u·lent·ly** *adv*

fraught \'fròt\ *adj* : full of or accompanied by something specified (∼ with danger)

¹fray \'frā\ *n* **1** : FIGHT, STRUGGLE; *also* : QUARREL, DISPUTE

²fray *vb* **1** : to wear (as an edge of cloth) by rubbing **2** : to separate the threads at the edge of **3** : STRAIN, IRRITATE (∼ed nerves)

fraz·zle \'fra-zəl\ *vb* **fraz·zled; fraz·zling 1** : FRAY **2** : to put in a state of extreme physical or nervous fatigue — **frazzle** *n*

¹freak \'frēk\ *n* **1** : WHIM, CAPRICE **2** : a strange, abnormal, or unusual person or thing **3** *slang* : a person who uses an illicit drug **4** : an ardent enthusiast — **freak·ish** *adj*

²freak *vb* **1** : to experience the effects (as hallucinations) of taking illicit drugs — often used with

out **2** : to distress or become distressed — often used with *out* — **freak–out** \'frē-₁kaút\ *n*

freck·le \'fre-kəl\ *n* : a brownish spot on the skin — **freckle** *vb*

¹free \'frē\ *adj* **fre·er; fre·est 1** : having liberty **2** : enjoying political or personal independence; *also* : not subject to or allowing slavery **3** : made or done voluntarily **4** : SPONTANEOUS **5** : relieved from or lacking something unpleasant **6** : not obstructed : CLEAR **7** : not being used or occupied **8** : not fastened **9** : LAVISH **10** : OPEN, FRANK **11** : given without charge **12** : not literal or exact **13** : not restricted by conventional forms — **free·ly** *adv*

²free *vb* **freed; free·ing 1** : to set free **2** : RELIEVE, RID **3** : DISENTANGLE, CLEAR **syn** release, liberate, discharge, emancipate, loose

³free *adv* **1** : FREELY **2** : without charge

free·base \'frē-₁bās\ *n* : purified cocaine smoked as crack or heated to produce vapors for inhalation — **freebase** *vb*

free·bie *or* **free·bee** \'frē-bē\ *n* : something given without charge

free·board \'frē-₁bòrd\ *n* : the vertical distance between the waterline and the upper edge of the side of a boat

free·boot·er \-₁bü-tər\ *n* [D *vrijbuiter,* fr. *vrijbuit* plunder, fr. *vrij* free + *buit* booty] : PLUNDERER, PIRATE

free·born \'frē-'bòrn\ *adj* **1** : not born in vassalage or slavery **2** : of, relating to, or befitting one that is freeborn

freed·man \'frēd-mən, -₁man\ *n* : a man freed from slavery

free·dom \'frē-dəm\ *n* **1** : the quality or state of being free : INDEPENDENCE **2** : EXEMPTION, RELEASE **3** : EASE, FACILITY **4** : FRANKNESS **5** : unrestricted use **6** : a political right; *also* : FRANCHISE, PRIVILEGE

free enterprise *n* : freedom of private business to operate with little regulation by the government

free–for–all \'frē-fə-₁ròl\ *n* : a competition or fight open to all comers and usu. with no rules : BRAWL — **free–for–all** *adj*

free·hand \-₁hand\ *adj* : done without mechanical aids or devices

free·hold \'frē-₁hōld\ *n* : ownership of an estate for life usu. with the right to bequeath it to one's heirs; *also* : an estate thus owned — **free·hold·er** *n*

free·lance \-₁lans\ *n* : one who pursues a profession (as writing) without a long-term commitment to any one employer — **free·lance** *adj or vb*

free–living \'frē-'li-viŋ\ *adj* **1** : unrestricted in pursuing personal pleasures **2** : being neither parasitic nor symbiotic (∼ organisms)

free·load \'frē-₁lōd\ *vb* : to impose upon another's hospitality — **free·load·er** *n*

free love *n* : the practice of living openly with one of the opposite sex without marriage

free·man \'frē-mən, -₁man\ *n* **1** : one who has civil or political liberty **2** : one having the full rights of a citizen

Free·ma·son \-₁mās-ᵊn\ *n* : a member of a secret fra-

ternal society called Free and Accepted Masons —
Free·ma·son·ry \-rē\ *n*

free·stand·ing \'frē-'stan-diŋ\ *adj* : standing alone or on its own foundation free of support

free·stone \'frē-ıstōn\ *n* 1 : a stone that may be cut freely without splitting 2 : a fruit stone to which the flesh does not cling; *also* : a fruit (as a peach or cherry) having such a stone

free·think·er \-'thiŋ-kər\ *n* : one who forms opinions on the basis of reason independently of authority; *esp* : one who doubts or denies religious dogma — **free·think·ing** *n or adj*

free trade *n* : trade between nations without restrictions (as high taxes on imports)

free verse *n* : verse whose meter is irregular or whose rhythm is not metrical

free·way \'frē-ıwā\ *n* : an expressway without tolls

free·wheel \-'hwēl\ *vb* : to move, live, or play freely or irresponsibly

free·will \'frē-ıwil\ *adj* : VOLUNTARY

free will *n* : voluntary choice or decision

¹**freeze** \'frēz\ *vb* **froze** \'frōz\; **fro·zen** \'frōz-ᵊn\; **freez·ing** 1 : to harden or cause to harden into a solid (as ice) by loss of heat 2 : to withstand freezing 3 : to chill or become chilled with cold 4 : to damage by frost 5 : to adhere solidly by or as if by freezing 6 : to become fixed, motionless, or incapable of speech 7 : to cause to grip tightly 8 : to become clogged with ice 9 : to fix at a certain stage or level

²**freeze** *n* 1 : an act or instance of freezing 2 : the state of being frozen 3 : a state of weather marked by low temperature

freeze–dry \'frēz-'drī\ *vb* : to dry in a frozen state under vacuum esp. for preservation — **freeze–dried** *adj*

freez·er \'frē-zər\ *n* : a compartment, device, or room for freezing food or keeping it frozen

¹**freight** \'frāt\ *n* 1 : payment for carrying goods 2 : CARGO 3 : BURDEN 4 : the carrying of goods by a common carrier 5 : a train that carries freight

²**freight** *vb* 1 : to load with goods for transportation 2 : BURDEN, CHARGE 3 : to ship or transport by freight

freight·er \'frā-tər\ *n* : a ship or airplane used chiefly to carry freight

French \'french\ *n* 1 : the language of France 2 **French** *pl* : the people of France 3 : strong language — **French** *adj* — **French·man** \-mən\ *n* — **French·wom·an** \-ıwù-mən\ *n*

French door *n* : a door with small panes of glass extending the full length

French dressing *n* 1 : a thin salad dressing usu. made of vinegar and oil with spices 2 : a creamy salad dressing flavored with tomatoes

french fry *vb, often cap 1st F* : to fry (as strips of potato) in deep fat until brown — **french fry** *n, often cap 1st F*

French horn *n* : a curved brass instrument with a funnel-shaped mouthpiece and a flaring bell

French toast *n* : bread dipped in a mixture of eggs and milk and fried at a low heat

fre·net·ic \fri-'ne-tik\ *adj* : FRANTIC — **fre·net·i·cal·ly** \-ti-k(ə-)lē\ *adv*

fren·zy \'fren-zē\ *n, pl* **frenzies** 1 : temporary madness or a violently agitated state 2 : intense often disordered activity — **fren·zied** \-zēd\ *adj*

freq *abbr* frequency; frequent; frequently

fre·quen·cy \'frē-kwən-sē\ *n, pl* **-cies** 1 : the fact or condition of occurring frequently 2 : rate of occurrence 3 : the number of cycles per second of an alternating current 4 : the number of waves (as of sound or electromagnetic energy) that pass a fixed point each second

frequency modulation *n* : variation of the frequency of a carrier wave according to another signal; *also* : FM

¹**fre·quent** \frē-'kwent, 'frē-kwənt\ *vb* : to associate

with, be in, or resort to habitually — **fre·quent·er** *n*

²**fre·quent** \'frē-kwənt\ *adj* 1 : happening often or at short intervals 2 : HABITUAL — **fre·quent·ly** *adv*

fres·co \'fres-kō\ *n, pl* **frescoes** [It, fr. *fresco* fresh] : the art of painting on fresh plaster; *also* : a painting done by this method

fresh \'fresh\ *adj* 1 : VIGOROUS, REFRESHED 2 : not containing salt 3 : not altered by processing (as freezing or canning) 4 : free from taint : PURE 5 : fairly strong : BRISK ⟨~ breeze⟩ 6 : not stale, sour, or decayed ⟨~ bread⟩ 7 : not faded 8 : not worn or rumpled 9 : experienced, made, or received newly or anew 10 : ADDITIONAL, ANOTHER ⟨made a ~ start⟩ 11 : ORIGINAL, VIVID 12 : INEXPERIENCED 13 : newly come or arrived ⟨~ from school⟩ 14 : IMPUDENT — **fresh·ly** *adv* — **fresh·ness** *n*

fresh·en \'fre-shən\ *vb* : to make, grow, or become fresh

fresh·et \'fre-shət\ *n* : an overflowing of a stream (as by heavy rains)

fresh·man \'fresh-mən\ *n* 1 : a 1st-year student 2 : BEGINNER, NEWCOMER

fresh·wa·ter \-ıwò-tər, -ıwä-\ *n* : water that is not salty — **freshwater** *adj*

¹**fret** \'fret\ *vb* **fret·ted**; **fret·ting** [ME, to devour, fret, fr. OE *fretan* to devour] 1 : WEAR, CORRODE; *also* : FRAY 2 : RUB, CHAFE 3 : to make by wearing away 4 : to become irritated : WORRY, VEX 5 : GRATE; *also* : AGITATE

²**fret** *n* : an irritated or worried state ⟨in a ~ about the interview⟩

³**fret** *n* : ornamental work esp. of straight lines in symmetrical patterns

⁴**fret** *n* : one of a series of ridges across the fingerboard of a stringed musical instrument — **fret·ted** *adj*

fret·ful \'fret-fəl\ *adj* : IRRITABLE — **fret·ful·ly** *adv* — **fret·ful·ness** *n*

fret·saw \-ısò\ *n* : a narrow-bladed saw used for cutting curved outlines

fret·work \-ıwərk\ *n* 1 : decoration consisting of frets 2 : ornamental openwork or work in relief

Fri *abbr* Friday

fri·a·ble \'frī-ə-bəl\ *adj* : easily crumbled or pulverized ⟨~ soil⟩

fri·ar \'frī-ər\ *n* [ME *frere, fryer*, fr. OF *frere*, lit., brother, fr. L *frater*] : a member of a religious order that orig. lived by alms

fri·ary \'frī-ə-rē\ *n, pl* **-ar·ies** : a monastery of friars

¹**fric·as·see** \'fri-kə-ısē, ıfri-kə-'sē\ *n* : a dish made of meat (as chicken) cut into pieces, stewed in stock, and served in sauce

²**fricassee** *vb* **-seed**; **-see·ing** : to cook as a fricassee

fric·tion \'frik-shən\ *n* 1 : the rubbing of one body against another 2 : the force that resists motion between bodies in contact 3 : clash in opinions between persons or groups : DISAGREEMENT — **fric·tion·al** *adj*

friction tape *n* : a usu. cloth adhesive tape impregnated with insulating material and used esp. to protect and insulate electrical conductors

Fri·day \'frī-dē, -ı)dā\ *n* : the sixth day of the week

fridge \'frij\ *n* : REFRIGERATOR

fried·cake \'frīd-ıkāk\ *n* : DOUGHNUT, CRULLER

friend \'frend\ *n* 1 : one attached to another by respect or affection 2 : ACQUAINTANCE 3 : one who is not hostile 4 : one who supports or favors something ⟨a ~ of art⟩ 5 *cap* : a member of the Society of Friends : QUAKER — **friend·less** *adj* — **friend·li·ness** \-lē-nəs\ *n* — **friend·ly** *adj* — **friend·ship** \-ıship\ *n*

frieze \'frēz\ *n* : an ornamental often sculptured band extending around something (as a building or room)

frig·ate \'fri-gət\ *n* 1 : a square-rigged warship 2 : a warship smaller than a destroyer

fright \'frīt\ *n* 1 : sudden terror : ALARM 2 : something that is ugly or shocking

fright·en \'frīt-ᵊn\ *vb* 1 : to make afraid 2 : to drive

away or out by frightening **3** : to become frightened
— **fright·en·ing·ly** *adv*
fright·ful \\'frīt-fəl\\ *adj* **1** : TERRIFYING **2** : STARTLING **3**
: EXTREME ⟨∼ thirst⟩ — **fright·ful·ly** *adv* — **fright-
ful·ness** *n*
frig·id \\'fri-jəd\\ *adj* **1** : intensely cold **2** : lacking
warmth or ardor : INDIFFERENT **3** : abnormally averse
to or unable to achieve orgasm during sexual intercourse — used esp. of women — **fri·gid·i·ty** \\fri-'ji-
də-tē\\ *n*
frigid zone *n* : the area or region between the arctic
circle and the north pole or between the antarctic circle and the south pole
frill \\'fril\\ *n* **1** : a gathered, pleated, or ruffled edging
2 : something unessential — **frilly** *adj*
fringe \\'frinj\\ *n* **1** : an ornamental border consisting of
short threads or strips hanging from an edge or band
2 : something that resembles a fringe : EDGE **3** : something that is additional or secondary to an activity,
process, or subject — **fringe** *vb*
fringe benefit *n* **1** : an employment benefit paid for by
an employer without affecting basic wage rates **2**
: any additional benefit
frip·pery \\'fri-pə-rē\\ *n, pl* **-per·ies** [MF *friperie*] **1** : FIN-
ERY **2** : pretentious display
frisk \\'frisk\\ *vb* **1** : to leap, skip, or dance in a lively
or playful way : GAMBOL **2** : to search (a person) esp.
for concealed weapons by running the hand rapidly
over the clothing
frisky \\'fris-kē\\ *adj* **frisk·i·er; -est** : PLAYFUL — **frisk-
i·ly** \\-kə-lē\\ *adv* — **frisk·i·ness** \\-kē-nəs\\ *n*
¹frit·ter \\'fri-tər\\ *n* : a small lump of fried batter often
containing fruit or meat
²fritter *vb* **1** : to reduce or waste piecemeal **2** : to break
into small fragments
fritz \\'frits\\ *n* : a state of disorder or disrepair ⟨the car
is on the ∼⟩
friv·o·lous \\'fri-və-ləs\\ *adj* **1** : of little importance
: TRIVIAL **2** : lacking in seriousness — **fri·vol·i·ty** \\fri-
'vä-lə-tē\\ *n* — **friv·o·lous·ly** *adv*
frizz \\'friz\\ *vb* : to form into small tight curls — **frizz**
n — **frizzy** *adj*
¹friz·zle \\'fri-zəl\\ *vb* **friz·zled; friz·zling** : FRIZZ, CURL
— **frizzle** *n*
²frizzle *vb* **friz·zled; friz·zling** **1** : to fry until crisp and
curled **2** : to cook with a sizzling noise
fro \\'frō\\ *adv* : BACK, AWAY — used in the phrase *to
and fro*
frock \\'fräk\\ *n* **1** : an outer garment worn by monks
and friars **2** : an outer garment worn esp. by men **3** : a
woman's or girl's dress
frock coat *n* : a man's usu. double-breasted coat with
knee-length skirts
frog \\'frog, 'fräg\\ *n* **1** : any of various largely aquatic
smooth-skinned tailless leaping amphibians **2** : an ornamental braiding for fastening the front of a garment
by a loop through which a button passes **3** : a condition in the throat causing hoarseness **4** : a small
holder (as of metal, glass, or plastic) with perfora-
tions or spikes that is placed in a bowl or vase to keep
cut flowers in position
frog·man \\'frog-ˌman, 'fräg-, -mən\\ *n* : a swimmer
equipped to work underwater for long periods of time
¹frol·ic \\'frä-lik\\ *vb* **frol·icked; frol·ick·ing** **1** : to make
merry **2** : to play about happily : ROMP
²frolic *n* **1** : a playful or mischievous action **2** : FUN,
MERRIMENT — **frol·ic·some** \\-səm\\ *adj*
from \\'frəm, 'främ\\ *prep* **1** — used to show a starting
point ⟨a letter ∼ home⟩ **2** — used to show removal
or separation ⟨subtract 3 ∼ 9⟩ **3** — used to show a
material, source, or cause ⟨suffering ∼ a cold⟩
frond \\'fränd\\ *n* : a usu. large divided leaf esp. of a fern
or palm tree
¹front \\'frənt\\ *n* **1** : FOREHEAD; *also* : the whole face **2**
: external and often feigned appearance **3** : a region
of active fighting; *also* : a sphere of activity **4** : a po-

litical coalition **5** : the side of a building containing
the main entrance **6** : the forward part or surface **7**
: FRONTAGE **8** : a boundary between two dissimilar air
masses **9** : a position directly before or ahead of
something else **10** : a person, group, or thing used to
mask the identity of the actual controlling agent
²front *vb* **1** : to have the principal side adjacent to something **2** : to serve as a front **3** : CONFRONT
front·age \\'frən-tij\\ *n* **1** : a piece of land lying adjacent
(as to a street or the ocean) **2** : the length of a frontage
3 : the front side of a building
front·al \\'frənt-ᵊl\\ *adj* **1** : of, relating to, or next to the
forehead **2** : of, relating to, or directed at the front ⟨a
∼ attack⟩ — **fron·tal·ly** *adv*
fron·tier \\ˌfrən-'tir\\ *n* **1** : a border between two countries **2** : a region that forms the margin of settled
territory **3** : the outer limits of knowledge or achievement ⟨the ∼s of science⟩ — **fron·tiers·man** \\-'tirz-
mən\\ *n*
fron·tis·piece \\'frən-tə-ˌspēs\\ *n* : an illustration preceding and usu. facing the title page of a book
front man *n* : a person serving as a front or figurehead
front·ward \\'frənt-wərd\\ *or* **front·wards** \\-wərdz\\ *adv*
or adj : toward the front
¹frost \\'frost\\ *n* **1** : freezing temperature **2** : a covering
of tiny ice crystals on a cold surface — **frosty** *adj*
²frost *vb* **1** : to cover with frost **2** : to put icing on (as
a cake) **3** : to produce a slightly roughened surface on
(as glass) **4** : to injure or kill by frost
¹frost·bite \\'frost-ˌbīt\\ *vb* **-bit** \\-ˌbit\\; **-bit·ten** \\-ˌbit-ᵊn\\;
-bit·ing : to injure by frost or frostbite
²frostbite *n* : the freezing or the local effect of a partial
freezing of some part of the body
frost heave *n* : an upthrust of pavement caused by
freezing of moist soil
frost·ing \\'frò-stiŋ\\ *n* **1** : ICING **2** : dull finish on metal
or glass
froth \\'froth\\ *n, pl* **froths** \\'froths, 'frothz\\ **1** : bubbles
formed in or on a liquid **2** : something light or worthless — **frothy** *adj*
frou·frou \\'frü-ˌfrü\\ *n* [F] **1** : a rustling esp. of a woman's skirts **2** : showy or frilly ornamentation
fro·ward \\'frō-wərd\\ *adj* : DISOBEDIENT, WILLFUL
frown \\'fraun\\ *vb* **1** : to wrinkle the forehead (as in displeasure or thought) **2** : to look with disapproval **3** : to
express with a frown — **frown** *n*
frow·sy *or* **frow·zy** \\'frau-zē\\ *adj* **frow·si·er** *or* **frow-
zi·er; -est** : having a slovenly or uncared-for appear-
ance
froze *past of* FREEZE
fro·zen \\'frōz-ᵊn\\ *adj* **1** : treated, affected, or crusted
over by freezing **2** : subject to long and severe cold
3 : incapable of being changed, moved, or undone
: FIXED ⟨∼ wages⟩ **4** : not available for present use ⟨∼
capital⟩ **5** : expressing or characterized by cold un-
friendliness
FRS *abbr* Federal Reserve System
frt *abbr* freight
fruc·ti·fy \\'frək-tə-ˌfī, 'frùk-\\ *vb* **-fied; -fy·ing** **1** : to
bear fruit **2** : to make fruitful or productive
fru·gal \\'frü-gəl\\ *adj* : ECONOMICAL, THRIFTY — **fru-
gal·i·ty** \\frü-'ga-lə-tē\\ *n* — **fru·gal·ly** *adv*
¹fruit \\'früt\\ *n* [ME, fr. OF, fr. L *fructus* fruit, use, fr.
frui to enjoy, have the use of] **1** : a product of plant
growth; *esp* : a usu. edible and sweet reproductive
body (as a strawberry or apple) of a seed plant **2** : a
product of fertilization in a plant; *esp* : the ripe ovary
of a seed plant with its contents and appendages **3**
: CONSEQUENCE, RESULT — **fruit·ed** \\'frü-təd\\ *adj*
²fruit *vb* : to bear or cause to bear fruit
fruit·cake \\'früt-ˌkāk\\ *n* : a rich cake containing nuts,
dried or candied fruits, and spices
fruit fly *n* : any of various small dipteran flies whose
larvae feed on fruit or decaying vegetable matter
fruit·ful \\'früt-fəl\\ *adj* **1** : yielding or producing fruit **2**

: very productive ⟨a ∼ soil⟩; *also* : bringing results ⟨a ∼ idea⟩ — **fruit·ful·ly** *adv* — **fruit·ful·ness** *n*
fru·ition \frü-'i-shən\ *n* **1** : ENJOYMENT **2** : the state of bearing fruit **3** : REALIZATION, ACCOMPLISHMENT
fruit·less \'früt-ləs\ *adj* **1** : not bearing fruit **2** : UNSUC-CESSFUL ⟨a ∼ attempt⟩ — **fruit·less·ly** *adv*
fruity \'frü-tē\ *adj* **fruit·i·er; -est** : resembling a fruit esp. in flavor
frumpy \'frəm-pē\ *adj* **frump·i·er; -est** : DOWDY, DRAB
frus·trate \'frəs-₁trāt\ *vb* **frus·trat·ed; frus·trat·ing 1** : to balk or defeat in an endeavor **2** : to induce feelings of insecurity, discouragement, or dissatisfaction in **3** : to bring to nothing — **frus·trat·ing·ly** *adv* — **frus·tra·tion** \₁frəs-'trā-shən\ *n*
frus·tum \'frəs-təm\ *n, pl* **frustums** *or* **frus·ta** \-tə\ : the part of a cone or pyramid formed by cutting off the top by a plane parallel to the base
frwy *abbr* freeway
¹fry \'frī\ *vb* **fried; fry·ing 1** : to cook in a pan or on a griddle over heat esp. with the use of fat **2** : to undergo frying
²fry *n, pl* **fries 1** : a social gathering where fried food is eaten **2** : a dish of something fried; *esp, pl* : FRENCH FRIES
³fry *n, pl* **fry 1** : recently hatched fishes; *also* : very small adult fishes **2** : members of a group or class ⟨small ∼⟩
fry·er \'frī-ər\ *n* **1** : something (as a young chicken) suitable for frying **2** : a deep utensil for frying foods
FSLIC *abbr* Federal Savings and Loan Insurance Corporation
ft *abbr* **1** feet; foot **2** fort
FTC *abbr* Federal Trade Commission
fuch·sia \'fyü-shə\ *n* **1** : any of a genus of shrubs related to the evening primrose and grown for their showy nodding often red or purple flowers **2** : a vivid reddish purple color
fud·dle \'fəd-ᵊl\ *vb* **fud·dled; fud·dling** : MUDDLE, CON-FUSE
fud·dy–dud·dy \'fə-dē-₁də-dē\ *n, pl* **-dies** : one that is old-fashioned, unimaginative, or conservative
¹fudge \'fəj\ *vb* **fudged; fudg·ing 1** : to exceed the proper bounds of something **2** : CHEAT; *also* : FALSIFY **3** : to fail to come to grips with
²fudge *n* **1** : NONSENSE **2** : a soft candy of milk, sugar, butter, and flavoring
¹fu·el \'fyü-əl, 'fyül\ *n* : a material used to produce heat or power by burning; *also* : a material from which nuclear energy can be liberated
²fuel *vb* **-eled** *or* **-elled; -el·ing** *or* **-el·ling** : to provide with or take in fuel
fuel cell *n* : a device that continuously changes the chemical energy of a fuel directly into electrical energy
¹fu·gi·tive \'fyü-jə-tiv\ *n* **1** : one who flees or tries to escape **2** : something elusive or hard to find
²fugitive *adj* **1** : running away or trying to escape **2** : likely to vanish suddenly : not fixed or lasting
fugue \'fyüg\ *n* **1** : a musical composition in which different parts successively repeat the theme **2** : a disturbed state of consciousness characterized by acts that are not recalled upon recovery
füh·rer *or* **fueh·rer** \'fyúr-ər, 'fir-\ *n* : LEADER; *esp* : TYRANT
¹-ful \fəl\ *adj suffix, sometimes* **-ful·ler;** *sometimes* **-ful·lest 1** : full of ⟨pride*ful*⟩ **2** : characterized by ⟨peace*ful*⟩ **3** : having the qualities of ⟨master*ful*⟩ **4** : tending, given, or liable to ⟨help*ful*⟩
²-ful \₁fül\ *n suffix* : number or quantity that fills or would fill ⟨room*ful*⟩
ful·crum \'fül-krəm, 'fəl-\ *n, pl* **ful·crums** *or* **ful·cra** \-krə\ [LL, fr. L, bedpost] : the support on which a lever turns
ful·fill *or* **ful·fil** \fül-'fil\ *vb* **ful·filled; ful·fill·ing 1** : to put into effect **2** : to bring to an end **3** : SATISFY — **ful·fill·ment** *n*

F fulcrum

¹full \'fül\ *adj* **1** : FILLED **2** : complete esp. in detail, number, or duration **3** : having all the distinguishing characteristics ⟨a ∼ member⟩ **4** : MAXIMUM **5** : rounded in outline ⟨a ∼ figure⟩ **6** : possessing or containing an abundance ⟨∼ of wrinkles⟩ **7** : having an abundance of material ⟨a ∼ skirt⟩ **8** : satisfied esp. with food or drink **9** : having volume or depth of sound **10** : completely occupied with a thought or plan — **full·ness** *also* **ful·ness** *n*
²full *adv* **1** : VERY, EXTREMELY **2** : ENTIRELY **3** : STRAIGHT, SQUARELY ⟨hit him ∼ in the face⟩
³full *n* **1** : the highest or fullest state or degree **2** : the utmost extent **3** : the requisite or complete amount
⁴full *vb* : to shrink and thicken (woolen cloth) by moistening, heating, and pressing — **full·er** *n*
full·back \'fül-₁bak\ *n* : a football back stationed between the halfbacks
full–blood·ed \'fül-'blə-dəd\ *adj* : of unmixed ancestry : PUREBRED
full–blown \-'blōn\ *adj* **1** : being at the height of bloom **2** : fully mature or developed
full–bod·ied \-'bä-dēd\ *adj* : marked by richness and fullness
full dress *n* : the style of dress worn for ceremonial or formal occasions
full–fledged \'fül-'flejd\ *adj* **1** : fully developed **2** : having attained complete status ⟨a ∼ lawyer⟩
full house *n* : a poker hand containing three of a kind and a pair
full moon *n* : the moon with its whole disk illuminated
full–scale \'fül-'skāl\ *adj* **1** : identical to an original in proportion and size ⟨∼ drawing⟩ **2** : involving full use of available resources ⟨a ∼ revolt⟩
full tilt *adv* : at high speed
full–time \'fül-'tīm\ *adj or adv* : involving or working a normal or standard schedule
ful·ly \'fü-lē\ *adv* **1** : in a full manner or degree : COM-PLETELY **2** : at least
ful·mi·nate \'fúl-mə-₁nāt, 'fəl-\ *vb* **-nat·ed; -nat·ing** [ME, fr. ML *fulminare*, fr. L, to strike (of lightning), fr. *fulmen* lightning] : to utter or send out censure or invective : condemn severely — **ful·mi·na·tion** \₁fúl-mə-'nā-shən, ₁fəl-\ *n*
ful·some \'fül-səm\ *adj* **1** : COPIOUS, ABUNDANT ⟨∼ detail⟩ **2** : generous in amount or extent ⟨a ∼ victory⟩ **3** : excessively flattering ⟨∼ praise⟩
fu·ma·role \'fyü-mə-₁rōl\ *n* : a hole in a volcanic region from which hot gases issue
fum·ble \'fəm-bəl\ *vb* **fum·bled; fum·bling 1** : to grope about clumsily **2** : to fail to hold, catch, or handle properly — **fumble** *n*
¹fume \'fyüm\ *n* : a usu. irritating smoke, vapor, or gas
²fume *vb* **fumed; fum·ing 1** : to treat with fumes **2** : to give off fumes **3** : to express anger or annoyance
fu·mi·gant \'fyü-mi-gənt\ *n* : a substance used for fumigation
fu·mi·gate \'fyü-mə-₁gāt\ *vb* **-gat·ed; -gat·ing** : to treat with fumes to disinfect or destroy pests — **fu·mi·ga·tion** \₁fyü-mə-'gā-shən\ *n* — **fu·mi·ga·tor** \'fyü-mə-₁gā-tər\ *n*

¹**fun** \\'fən\ *n* [E dial. *fun* to hoax] **1** : something that provides amusement or enjoyment **2** : ENJOYMENT

²**fun** *adj* : full of fun ⟨a ∼ person⟩ ⟨had a ∼ time⟩

¹**func·tion** \\'fəŋk-shən\ *n* **1** : OCCUPATION **2** : special purpose **3** : the particular purpose for which a person or thing is specially fitted or used or for which a thing exists ⟨the ∼ of a hammer⟩; *also* : the natural or proper action of a bodily part in a living thing ⟨the ∼ of the heart⟩ **4** : a formal ceremony or social affair **5** : a mathematical relationship that assigns to each element of a set one and only one element of the same or another set **6** : a variable (as a quality, trait, or measurement) that depends on and varies with another ⟨height is a ∼ of age in children⟩ — **func·tion·al** \\-shə-nəl\ *adj* — **func·tion·al·ly** *adv*

²**function** *vb* : to have or carry on a function

func·tion·ary \\'fəŋk-shə-ˌner-ē\ *n, pl* **-ar·ies** : one who performs a certain function; *esp* : OFFICIAL

function word *n* : a word (as a preposition, auxiliary verb, or conjunction) expressing the grammatical relationship between other words

¹**fund** \\'fənd\ *n* [L *fundus* bottom, country estate] **1** : a sum of money or resources intended for a special purpose **2** : STORE, SUPPLY **3** *pl* : available money **4** : an organization administering a special fund

²**fund** *vb* **1** : to provide funds for **2** : to convert (a short-term obligation) into a long-term interest-bearing debt

fun·da·men·tal \\ˌfən-də-ˈment-ᵊl\ *adj* **1** : serving as an origin : PRIMARY **2** : BASIC, ESSENTIAL **3** : RADICAL ⟨∼ change⟩ **4** : of central importance : PRINCIPAL — **fundamental** *n* — **fun·da·men·tal·ly** *adv*

fun·da·men·tal·ism \\-ˌi-zəm\ *n*, **1** *often cap* : a Protestant religious movement emphasizing the literal infallibility of the Bible **2** : a movement or attitude stressing strict adherence to a set of basic principles — **fun·da·men·tal·ist** \\-ist\ *adj or n*

¹**fu·ner·al** \\'fyü-nə-rəl\ *adj* **1** : of, relating to, or constituting a funeral **2** : FUNEREAL

²**funeral** *n* : the ceremonies held for a dead person usu. before burial

fu·ner·ary \\'fyü-nə-ˌrer-ē\ *adj* : of, used for, or associated with burial

fu·ne·re·al \\fyü-ˈnir-ē-əl\ *adj* **1** : of or relating to a funeral **2** : suggesting a funeral

fun·gi·cide \\'fən-jə-ˌsīd, 'fəŋ-gə-\ *n* : an agent that kills or checks the growth of fungi — **fun·gi·cid·al** \\ˌfən-jə-ˈsīd-ᵊl, ˌfəŋ-gə-\ *adj*

fun·gus \\'fəŋ-gəs\ *n, pl* **fun·gi** \\'fən-ˌjī, 'fəŋ-ˌgī\ *also* **fun·gus·es** \\'fəŋ-gə-səz\ : any of a major group of organisms (as molds, mildews, and mushrooms) that lack chlorophyll and are usu. classified as plants — **fun·gal** \\-gəl\ *adj* — **fun·gous** \\-gəs\ *adj*

fu·nic·u·lar \\fyü-ˈni-kyə-lər, fə-\ *n* : a cable railway ascending a mountain

funk \\'fəŋk\ *n* : a depressed state of mind

funky \\'fəŋ-kē\ *adj* **funk·i·er; -est 1** : having an earthy unsophisticated style and feeling; *esp* : having the style and feeling of older black American music **2** : odd or quaint in appearance or style

¹**fun·nel** \\'fən-ᵊl\ *n* **1** : a cone-shaped utensil with a tube used for catching and directing a downward flow (as of liquid) **2** : FLUE, SMOKESTACK

²**funnel** *vb* **-neled** *also* **-nelled; -nel·ing** *also* **-nel·ling 1** : to pass through or as if through a funnel **2** : to move to a central point or into a central channel

¹**fun·ny** \\'fə-nē\ *adj* **fun·ni·er; -est 1** : AMUSING **2** : FACETIOUS **3** : PECULIAR **3** **4** : UNDERHANDED — **funny** *adv*

²**funny** *n, pl* **funnies** : a comic strip or a comic section (as of a newspaper)

funny bone *n* : a place at the back of the elbow where a blow easily compresses a nerve and causes a painful tingling sensation

¹**fur** \\'fər\ *n* **1** : an article of clothing made of or with fur **2** : the hairy coat of a mammal esp. when fine, soft, and thick; *also* : this coat dressed for use — **fur** *adj* — **furred** \\'fərd\ *adj*

²**fur** *abbr* furlong

fur·be·low \\'fər-bə-ˌlō\ *n* **1** : FLOUNCE, RUFFLE **2** : showy trimming

fur·bish \\'fər-bish\ *vb* **1** : to make lustrous : POLISH **2** : to give a new look to : RENOVATE

fu·ri·ous \\'fyùr-ē-əs\ *adj* **1** : FIERCE, ANGRY, VIOLENT **2** : BOISTEROUS **3** : INTENSE — **fu·ri·ous·ly** *adv*

furl \\'fərl\ *vb* **1** : to wrap or roll (as a sail or a flag) close to or around something **2** : to curl in furls — **furl** *n*

fur·long \\'fər-ˌlȯŋ\ *n* [ME, fr. OE *furlang*, fr. *furh* furrow + *lang* long] : a unit of distance equal to 220 yards (about 201 meters)

fur·lough \\'fər-lō\ *n* [D *verlof*, lit., permission] : a leave of absence from duty granted esp. to a soldier — **furlough** *vb*

 fur·nace \\'fər-nəs\ *n* : an enclosed structure in which heat is produced

fur·nish \\'fər-nish\ *vb* **1** : to provide with what is needed : EQUIP **2** : SUPPLY, GIVE

fur·nish·ings \\-ni-shiŋz\ *n pl* **1** : articles or accessories of dress **2** : FURNITURE

fur·ni·ture \\'fər-ni-chər\ *n* : equipment that is necessary or desirable; *esp* : movable articles (as chairs or beds) for a room

fu·ror \\'fyùr-ˌȯr\ *n* **1** : ANGER, RAGE **2** : a contagious excitement; *esp* : a fashionable craze **3** : UPROAR

fu·rore \\-ˌȯr\ *n* [It] : FUROR **2, 3**

fur·ri·er \\'fər-ē-ər\ *n* : one who prepares or deals in fur

fur·ring \\'fər-iŋ\ *n* : wood or metal strips applied to a wall or ceiling to form a level surface or an air space

fur·row \\'fər-ō\ *n* **1** : a trench in the earth made by a plow **2** : a narrow groove or wrinkle — **furrow** *vb*

fur•ry \'fər-ē\ *adj* **fur•ri•er; -est 1 :** resembling or consisting of fur **2 :** covered with fur

¹fur•ther \'fər-t͟hər\ *adv* **1 :** FARTHER | **2 :** in addition : MOREOVER **3 :** to a greater extent or degree

²further *vb* : to help forward — **fur•ther•ance** \'fər-thə-rəns\ *n*

³further *adj* **1 :** FARTHER | **2 :** ADDITIONAL

fur•ther•more \'fər-t͟hər-ˌmȯr\ *adv* : in addition to what precedes : BESIDES

fur•ther•most \-ˌmōst\ *adj* : most distant : FARTHEST

fur•thest \'fər-thəst\ *adv or adj* : FARTHEST

fur•tive \'fər-tiv\ *adj* [F or L; F *furtif*, fr. L *furtivus*, fr. *furtum* theft, fr. *fur* thief] : done by stealth : SLY — **fur•tive•ly** *adv* — **fur•tive•ness** *n*

fu•ry \'fyu̇r-ē\ *n, pl* **furies 1 :** intense and often destructive rage **2 :** extreme fierceness or violence **3 :** FRENZY

furze \'fərz\ *n* : GORSE

¹fuse \'fyüz\ *vb* **fused; fus•ing 1 :** MELT **2 :** to unite by or as if by melting together — **fus•ible** *adj*

²fuse *n* : an electrical safety device having a metal wire or strip that melts and interrupts the circuit when the current becomes too strong

³fuse *n* **1 :** a cord or cable that is set afire to ignite an explosive charge **2** *usu* **fuze :** a mechanical or electrical device for setting off the explosive charge of a projectile, bomb, or torpedo

⁴fuse *or* **fuze** \'fyüz\ *vb* **fused** *or* **fuzed; fus•ing** *or* **fuz•ing :** to equip with a fuse

fu•se•lage \'fyü-sə-ˌläzh, -zə-\ *n* : the central body portion of an aircraft

fu•sil•lade \'fyü-sə-ˌläd, -ˌläd\ *n* : a number of shots fired simultaneously or in rapid succession

fu•sion \'fyü-zhən\ *n* **1 :** the act or process of melting or making plastic by heat **2 :** union by or as if by melting **3 :** the union of light atomic nuclei to form heavier nuclei with the release of huge quantities of energy

¹fuss \'fəs\ *n* **1 :** needless bustle or excitement : COMMOTION **2 :** effusive praise **3 :** a state of agitation **4 :** OBJECTION, PROTEST **5 :** DISPUTE

²fuss *vb* : to make a fuss

fuss•bud•get \'fəs-ˌbə-jət\ *n* : one who fusses or is fussy about trifles

fussy \'fə-sē\ *adj* **fuss•i•er; -est 1 :** IRRITABLE **2 :** overly decorated **3 :** requiring or giving close attention or concern to details or niceties — **fuss•i•ly** \-sə-lē\ *adv* — **fuss•i•ness** \-sē-nəs\ *n*

fus•tian \'fəs-chən\ *n* **1 :** a strong usu. cotton fabric **2 :** pretentious writing or speech — **fustian** *adj*

fus•ty \'fəs-tē\ *adj* **fus•ti•er; -est** [ME, fr. *fust* wine cask, fr. MF, club, cask, fr. L *fustis*] **1 :** MUSTY **2 :** OLD-FASHIONED

fut *abbr* future

fu•tile \'fyüt-əl, 'fyü-ˌtīl\ *adj* **1 :** USELESS, VAIN **2 :** FRIVOLOUS, TRIVIAL — **fu•til•i•ty** \fyü-'ti-lə-tē\ *n*

fu•ton \'fü-ˌtän\ *n* [Jp] : a usu. cotton-filled mattress used on the floor or in a frame

¹fu•ture \'fyü-chər\ *adj* **1 :** of, relating to, or constituting a verb tense that expresses time yet to come **2 :** coming after the present

²future *n* **1 :** time that is to come **2 :** what is going to happen **3 :** an expectation of advancement or progressive development **4 :** the future tense; *also* : a verb form in it

fu•tur•ism \'fyü-chə-ˌri-zəm\ *n* : a modern movement in art, music, and literature that tries esp. to express the energy and activity of mechanical processes — **fu•tur•ist** \'fyü-chə-rist\ *n*

fu•tur•is•tic \ˌfyü-chə-'ris-tik\ *adj* : of or relating to the future or to futurism; *also* : very modern

fu•tu•ri•ty \fyu̇-'tùr-ə-tē, -'tyùr-\ *n, pl* **-ties 1 :** FUTURE **2 :** the quality or state of being future **3** *pl* : future events or prospects

fuze *var of* FUSE

fuzz \'fəz\ *n* : fine light particles or fibers (as of down or fluff)

fuzzy \'fə-zē\ *adj* **fuzz•i•er; -est 1 :** having or resembling fuzz **2 :** INDISTINCT — **fuzz•i•ness** \-zē-nəs\ *n*

fwd *abbr* forward

FWD *abbr* front-wheel drive

FY *abbr* fiscal year

-fy *vb suffix* : make : form into ⟨dandi*fy*⟩

FYI *abbr* for your information

G

¹g \'jē\ *n, pl* **g's** *or* **gs** \'jēz\ *often cap* **1 :** the 7th letter of the English alphabet **2 :** a unit of force equal to the force exerted by gravity on a body at rest and used to indicate the force to which a body is subjected when accelerated **3** *slang* : a sum of $1000

²g *abbr, often cap* **1** game **2** gauge **3** good **4** gram **5** gravity

ga *abbr* gauge

¹Ga *abbr* Georgia

²Ga *symbol* gallium

GA *abbr* **1** general assembly **2** general average **3** general of the army **4** Georgia

gab \'gab\ *vb* **gabbed; gab•bing :** to talk in a rapid or thoughtless manner : CHATTER — **gab** *n*

gab•ar•dine \'ga-bər-ˌdēn\ *n* **1 :** GABERDINE 1 **2 :** a firm durable twilled fabric having diagonal ribs and made of various fibers; *also* : a garment of gabardine

gab•ble \'ga-bəl\ *vb* **gab•bled; gab•bling :** JABBER, BABBLE

gab•by \'ga-bē\ *adj* **gab•bi•er; -est :** TALKATIVE, GARRULOUS

gab•er•dine \'ga-bər-ˌdēn\ *n* **1 :** a long loose outer garment worn in medieval times and associated esp. with Jews **2 :** GABARDINE 2

gab·fest \\'gab-ˌfest\\ *n* **1** : an informal gathering for general talk **2** : an extended conversation

ga·ble \\'gā-bəl\\ *n* : the vertical triangular end of a building formed by the sides of the roof sloping from the ridge down to the eaves — **ga·bled** \\-bəld\\ *adj*

Gab·o·nese \\ˌga-bə-'nēz, -'nēs\\ *n* : a native or inhabitant of Gabon — **Gabonese** *adj*

gad \\'gad\\ *vb* **gad·ded; gad·ding** : to be constantly active without specific purpose — usu. used with *about* — **gad·der** *n*

gad·about \\'ga-də-ˌbaût\\ *n* : a person who flits about in social activity

gad·fly \\'gad-ˌflī\\ *n* **1** : a fly that bites or harasses livestock **2** : a person who annoys esp. by persistent criticism

gad·get \\'ga-jət\\ *n* : DEVICE, CONTRIVANCE — **gad·get·ry** \\'ga-jə-trē\\ *n*

gad·o·lin·i·um \\ˌgad-ᵊl-'i-nē-əm\\ *n* : a magnetic metallic chemical element — see ELEMENT table

¹Gael \\'gāl\\ *n* : a Celtic inhabitant of Ireland or Scotland

²Gael *abbr* Gaelic

Gael·ic \\'gā-lik\\ *adj* : of or relating to the Gaels or their languages — **Gaelic** *n*

gaff \\'gaf\\ *n* **1** : a spear used in taking fish or turtles; *also* : a metal hook for holding or lifting heavy fish **2** : the spar supporting the top of a fore-and-aft sail **3** : rough treatment : ABUSE — **gaff** *vb*

gaffe \\'gaf\\ *n* : a social blunder

gaf·fer \\'ga-fər\\ *n* **1** : an old man **2** : a lighting electrician on a motion-picture or television set

¹gag \\'gag\\ *vb* **gagged; gag·ging 1** : to restrict use of the mouth with a gag **2** : to prevent from speaking freely **3** : to retch or cause to retch **4** : OBSTRUCT, CHOKE **5** : BALK **6** : to make quips — **gag·ger** *n*

²gag *n* **1** : something thrust into the mouth esp. to prevent speech or outcry **2** : an official check or restraint on free speech **3** : a laugh-provoking remark or act **4** : PRANK, TRICK

¹gage \\'gāj\\ *n* **1** : a token of defiance; *esp* : a glove or cap cast on the ground as a pledge of combat **2** : SECURITY

²gage *var of* GAUGE

gag·gle \\'ga-gəl\\ *n* [ME *gagyll*, fr. *gagelen* to cackle] **1** : a flock of geese **2** : GROUP, CLUSTER

gai·ety \\'gā-ə-tē\\ *n, pl* **-eties 1** : festive activity : MERRYMAKING **2** : MERRIMENT **3** : FINERY **syn** mirth, festivity, glee, hilarity, jollity

gai·ly \\'gā-lē\\ *adv* : in a gay manner

¹gain \\'gān\\ *n* **1** : PROFIT **2** : ACQUISITION, ACCUMULATION **3** : INCREASE

²gain *vb* **1** : to get possession of : EARN **2** : WIN ⟨∼ a victory⟩ **3** : to increase in ⟨∼ momentum⟩ **4** : PERSUADE **5** : to arrive at **6** : ACHIEVE ⟨∼ strength⟩ **7** : to run fast ⟨the watch ∼s a minute a day⟩ **8** : PROFIT **9**

: INCREASE **10** : to improve in health **syn** accomplish, attain, realize — **gain·er** *n*

gain·ful \\'gān-fəl\\ *adj* : PROFITABLE — **gain·ful·ly** *adv*

gain·say \\ˌgān-'sā\\ *vb* **-said** \\-'sād, -'sed\\; **-say·ing; -says** \\-'sāz, -'sez\\ [ME *gainsayen*, fr. *gain-* against + *-sayen* to say] **1** : DENY, DISPUTE **2** : to speak against **syn** contradict, contravene, impugn, negate — **gain·say·er** *n*

gait \\'gāt\\ *n* : manner of moving on foot; *also* : a particular pattern or style of such moving — **gait·ed** *adj*

gai·ter \\'gā-tər\\ *n* **1** : a leg covering reaching from the instep to ankle, mid-calf, or knee **2** : an overshoe with a fabric upper **3** : an ankle-high shoe with elastic gores in the sides

¹gal \\'gal\\ *n* : GIRL

²gal *abbr* gallon

Gal *abbr* Galatians

ga·la \\'gā-lə, 'ga-, 'gä-\\ *n* : a gay celebration : FESTIVITY — **gala** *adj*

ga·lac·tic \\gə-'lak-tik\\ *adj* : of or relating to a galaxy

Ga·la·tians \\gə-'lā-shənz\\ *n* — see BIBLE table

gal·axy \\'ga-lək-sē\\ *n, pl* **-ax·ies** [ME *galaxie, galaxias,* fr. LL *galaxias,* fr. Gk, fr. *galakt-, gala* milk] **1** *often cap* : MILKY WAY GALAXY — used with *the* **2** : a very large group of stars **3** : an assemblage of brilliant or famous persons or things

gale \\'gāl\\ *n* **1** : a strong wind **2** : an emotional outburst ⟨∼s of laughter⟩

ga·le·na \\gə-'lē-nə\\ *n* : a lustrous bluish gray mineral that consists of the sulfide of lead and is the chief ore of lead

¹gall \\'gól\\ *n* **1** : BILE **2** : something bitter to endure **3** : RANCOR **4** : IMPUDENCE **syn** effrontery, brass, cheek, chutzpah, audacity, presumption

²gall *n* : a skin sore caused by chafing

³gall *vb* **1** : CHAFE; *esp* : to become sore or worn by rubbing **2** : VEX, HARASS

⁴gall *n* : a swelling of plant tissue caused by parasites

¹gal·lant \\gə-'lant, -'länt; 'ga-lənt\\ *n* **1** : a young man of fashion **2** : a man who shows a marked fondness for the company of women and who is esp. attentive to them **3** : SUITOR

²gal·lant \\gə-lənt *(usual for 2, 3, 4)*; gə-'lant, -'länt *(usual for 5)*\\ *adj* **1** : showy in dress or bearing : SMART **2** : SPLENDID, STATELY **3** : SPIRITED, BRAVE **4** : CHIVALROUS, NOBLE **5** : polite and attentive to women — **gal·lant·ly** *adv*

gal·lant·ry \\'ga-lən-trē\\ *n, pl* **-ries 1** *archaic* : gallant appearance **2** : an act of marked courtesy **3** : courteous attention to a woman **4** : conspicuous bravery **syn** heroism, valor, prowess

gall·blad·der \\'gól-ˌbla-dər\\ *n* : a membranous muscular sac attached to the liver and serving to store bile

gal·le·on \\'ga-lē-ən\\ *n* : a large square-rigged sailing ship formerly used esp. by the Spanish

☞ For illustration, see next page.

gal·le·ria \\ˌga-lə-'rē-ə\\ *n* [It] : a roofed and usu. glass-enclosed promenade or court

galleon

gal·lery \'ga-lə-rē\ n, pl **-ler·ies 1** : an outdoor balcony; also : PORCH, VERANDA **2** : a long narrow passage, apartment, or hall **3** : a narrow passage (as one made underground by a miner or through wood by an insect) **4** : a room where works of art are exhibited; also : an organization dealing in works of art **5** : a balcony in a theater, auditorium, or church; esp : the highest one in a theater **6** : the spectators at a tennis or golf match **7** : a photographer's studio — **gal·ler·ied** \-rēd\ adj

gal·ley \'ga-lē\ n, pl **galleys 1** : a long low ship propelled esp. by oars and formerly used esp. in the Mediterranean Sea **2** : the kitchen esp. of a ship or airplane **3** : a proof of typeset matter esp. in a single column

Gal·lic \'ga-lik\ adj : of or relating to Gaul or France

gal·li·mau·fry \ˌga-lə-'mò-frē\ n, pl **-fries** [MF galimafree stew] : HODGEPODGE

gal·li·nule \'ga-lə-ˌnül, -ˌnyül\ n : any of several aquatic birds related to the rails

gal·li·um \'ga-lē-əm\ n : a rare bluish white metallic chemical element — see ELEMENT table

gal·li·vant \'ga-lə-ˌvant\ vb : to travel, roam, or move about for pleasure

gal·lon \'ga-lən\ n — see WEIGHT table

¹gal·lop \'ga-ləp\ vb **1** : to go or cause to go at a gallop **2** : to run fast — **gal·lop·er** n

²gallop n **1** : a bounding gait of a quadruped; esp : a fast 3-beat gait of a horse **2** : a ride or run at a gallop

gal·lows \'ga-lōz\ n, pl **gallows** or **gal·lows·es** : a frame usu. of two upright posts and a crosspiece from which criminals are hanged; also : the punishment of hanging

gall·stone \'gòl-ˌstōn\ n : an abnormal concretion occurring in the gallbladder or bile passages

gal·lus·es \'ga-lə-səz\ n pl : SUSPENDERS

ga·lore \gə-'lòr\ adj [Ir go leor enough] : ABUNDANT, PLENTIFUL

ga·losh \gə-'läsh\ n : a high overshoe

galv abbr galvanized

gal·va·nise Brit var of GALVANIZE

gal·va·nize \'gal-və-ˌnīz\ vb **-nized; -niz·ing 1** : to stimulate as if by an electric shock **2** : to coat (iron or steel) with zinc — **gal·va·ni·za·tion** \ˌgal-və-nə-'zā-shən\ n — **gal·va·niz·er** n

gal·va·nom·e·ter \ˌgal-və-'nä-mə-tər\ n : an instrument for detecting or measuring a small electric current

Gam·bi·an \'gam-bē-ən\ n : a native or inhabitant of Gambia — **Gambian** adj

gam·bit \'gam-bət\ n [It gambetto, lit., act of tripping someone, fr. gamba leg] **1** : a chess opening in which a player risks one or more minor pieces to gain an advantage in position **2** : a calculated move : STRATAGEM syn trick, artifice, gimmick, maneuver, play, ruse

¹gam·ble \'gam-bəl\ vb **gam·bled; gam·bling 1** : to play a game for money or property **2** : BET, WAGER **3** : VENTURE, HAZARD — **gam·bler** n

²gamble n : a risky undertaking

gam·bol \'gam-bəl\ vb **-boled** or **-bolled; -bol·ing** or **-bol·ling** : to skip about in play : FRISK — **gambol** n

gam·brel roof \'gam-brəl-\ n : a roof with a lower

steeper slope and an upper flatter one on each side

¹game \'gām\ n **1** : AMUSEMENT, DIVERSION **2** : SPORT, FUN **3** : SCHEME, PROJECT **4** : a line of work : PROFESSION **5** : CONTEST **6** : animals hunted for sport or food; also : the flesh of a game animal

²game vb **gamed; gam·ing** : to play for a stake : GAMBLE

³game adj : PLUCKY — **game·ly** adv — **game·ness** n

⁴game adj : LAME ⟨a ∼ leg⟩

game·cock \'gām-ˌkäk\ n : a rooster trained for fighting

game fish n : SPORT FISH

game·keep·er \'gām-ˌkē-pər\ n : a person in charge of the breeding and protection of game animals or birds in a private preserve

game·some \'gām-səm\ adj : MERRY syn playful, frolicsome, sportive, antic

game·ster \'gām-stər\ n : GAMBLER

gam·ete \'ga-ˌmēt\ n : a mature germ cell — **ga·met·ic** \gə-'me-tik\ adj

game theory n : the analysis of a situation involving conflicting interests (as in business) in terms of gains and losses among opposing players

gam·in \'ga-mən\ n [F] **1** : a boy who hangs around on the streets **2** : GAMINE 2

ga·mine \ga-'mēn\ n **1** : a girl who hangs around on the streets **2** : a small playfully mischievous girl

gam·ma \'ga-mə\ n : the 3d letter of the Greek alphabet — Γ or γ

gamma globulin n : a blood protein fraction rich in antibodies; also : a solution of this from human blood donors that is given to provide immunity against some infectious diseases (as measles)

gamma ray n : a photon emitted by a radioactive substance; also : a high-energy photon — usu. used in pl.

gam·mer \'ga-mər\ n, archaic : an old woman

gam·mon \'ga-mən\ n, chiefly Brit : a cured ham or side of bacon

gam·ut \'ga-mət\ n : an entire range or series syn scale, spectrum

gamy or **gam·ey** \'gā-mē\ adj **gam·i·er; -est 1** : GAME, PLUCKY **2** : having the flavor of game esp. when near tainting **3** : SCANDALOUS; also : DISREPUTABLE — **gam·i·ness** \-mē-nəs\ n

¹gan·der \'gan-dər\ n : a male goose

²gander n : LOOK, GLANCE

¹gang \'gaŋ\ n **1** : a set of implements or devices arranged to operate together **2** : a group of persons working or associated together; esp : a group of criminals or young delinquents

²gang vb **1** : to attack in a gang — usu. used with up **2** : to form into or move or act as a gang

gang·land \'gaŋ-ˌland\ n : the world of organized crime

gan·gling \'gaŋ-gliŋ\ adj : loosely and awkwardly built : LANKY

gan·gli·on \'gaŋ-glē-ən\ n, pl **-glia** \-ə\ also **-gli·ons** : a mass of nerve cells outside the central nervous system; also : NUCLEUS 3 — **gan·gli·on·ic** \ˌgaŋ-glē-'ä-nik\ adj

gan·gly \'gaŋ-glē\ adj : GANGLING

gang·plank \'gaŋ-ˌplaŋk\ n : a movable bridge from a ship to the shore

gang·plow \-ˌplaü\ n : a plow that turns two or more furrows at one time

gan·grene \'gaŋ-ˌgrēn, gaŋ-'grēn\ n : the death of soft tissues in a local area of the body due to loss of the blood supply — **gangrene** vb — **gan·gre·nous** \'gaŋ-grə-nəs\ adj

gang·ster \'gaŋ-stər\ n : a member of a gang of criminals : RACKETEER

gang·way \'gaŋ-ˌwā\ n **1** : PASSAGEWAY; also : GANGPLANK **2** : clear passage through a crowd

gan·net \'ga-nət\ n, pl **gannets** also **gannet** : any of

several large fish-eating usu. white and black marine birds that breed on offshore islands

gant·let \'gȯnt-lət\ *var of* GAUNTLET

gan·try \'gan-trē\ *n, pl* **gantries** : a frame structure on side supports over or around something

GAO *abbr* General Accounting Office

gaol \'jāl\, **gaol·er** \'jā-lər\ *chiefly Brit var of* JAIL, JAILER

gap \'gap\ *n* **1** : BREACH, CLEFT **2** : a mountain pass **3** : a blank space; *also* : an incomplete or deficient area **4** : a wide difference in character or attitude **5** : a problem caused by a disparity ⟨credibility ∼⟩

gape \'gāp\ *vb* **gaped; gap·ing 1** : to open the mouth wide **2** : to open or part widely **3** : to stare with mouth open **4** : YAWN — **gape** *n*

¹gar \'gär\ *n* : any of several fishes that have a long body resembling that of a pike and long narrow jaws

²gar *abbr* garage

GAR *abbr* Grand Army of the Republic

¹ga·rage \gə-'räzh, -'räj\ *n* [F] : a shelter or repair shop for automobiles

²garage *vb* **ga·raged; ga·rag·ing** : to keep or put in a garage

garage sale *n* : a sale of used household or personal articles held on the seller's own premises

garb \'gärb\ *n* **1** : style of dress **2** : outward form : APPEARANCE — **garb** *vb*

gar·bage \'gär-bij\ *n* **1** : food waste **2** : unwanted or useless material — **gar·bage·man** \-,man\ *n*

gar·ble \'gär-bəl\ *vb* **gar·bled; gar·bling** [ME *garbelen*, fr. It *garbellare* to sift, fr. Ar *gharbala*] : to distort the meaning of ⟨∼ a story⟩

gar·çon \gär-'sōⁿ\ *n, pl* **garçons** *same or* -'sōⁿz\ [F, boy, servant] : WAITER

¹gar·den \'gärd-ⁿn\ *n* **1** : a plot for growing fruits, flowers, or vegetables **2** : a public recreation area; *esp* : one for displaying plants or animals

²garden *vb* : to lay out or work in a garden — **gar·den·er** *n*

gar·de·nia \gär-'dē-nyə\ *n* [NL, genus name, fr. Alexander *Garden* †1791 Scot. naturalist] : the fragrant white or yellow flower of any of a genus of trees or shrubs related to the madder; *also* : one of these trees

garden–variety *adj* : COMMONPLACE, ORDINARY

gar·fish \'gär-,fish\ *n* : GAR

gar·gan·tuan \gär-'gan-chə-wən\ *adj, often cap* : of tremendous size or volume **syn** huge, colossal, gigantic, mammoth, monstrous, titanic

gar·gle \'gär-gəl\ *vb* **gar·gled; gar·gling** : to rinse the throat with liquid agitated by air forced through it from the lungs — **gargle** *n*

gar·goyle \'gär-,gȯil\ *n* **1** : a waterspout in the form of a grotesque human or animal figure projecting from the roof or eaves of a building **2** : a grotesquely carved figure

gar·ish \'gar-ish\ *adj* : FLASHY, GLARING, SHOWY, GAUDY

¹gar·land \'gär-lənd\ *n* : WREATH, CHAPLET

²garland *vb* : to form into or deck with a garland

gar·lic \'gär-lik\ *n* [ME *garlek*, fr. OE *gārlēac*, fr. *gār* spear + *lēac* leek] : an herb related to the lilies and grown for its pungent bulbs used in cooking; *also* : its bulb — **gar·licky** \-li-kē\ *adj*

gar·ment \'gär-mənt\ *n* : an article of clothing

gar·ner \'gär-nər\ *vb* **1** : to gather into storage **2** : to acquire by effort **3** : ACCUMULATE, COLLECT

gar·net \'gär-nət\ *n* [ME *grenat*, fr. MF, fr. *grenat*, adj., red like a pomegranate, fr. *(pomme) grenate* pomegranate] : a transparent deep red mineral sometimes used as a gem

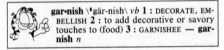

gar·nish \'gär-nish\ *vb* **1** : DECORATE, EMBELLISH **2** : to add decorative or savory touches to (food) **3** : GARNISHEE — **garnish** *n*

gar·nish·ee \,gär-nə-'shē\ *vb* **-eed; -ee·ing 1** : to serve with a garnishment **2** : to take (as a debtor's wages) by legal authority

gar·nish·ment \'gär-nish-mənt\ *n* **1** : GARNISH **2** : a legal warning concerning the attachment of property to satisfy a debt; *also* : the attachment of such property

gar·ni·ture \-ni-chər, -,chür\ *n* : EMBELLISHMENT, TRIMMING

gar·ret \'gar-ət\ *n* [ME *garette* watchtower, fr. MF *garite*] : the part of a house just under the roof : ATTIC

gar·ri·son \'gar-ə-sən\ *n* **1** : a military post; *esp* : a permanent military installation **2** : the troops stationed at a garrison — **garrison** *vb*

garrison state *n* : a state organized on a primarily military basis

gar·rote *or* **ga·rotte** \gə-'rät, -'rōt\ *n* [Sp *garrote*] **1** : a method of execution by strangulation; *also* : the apparatus used **2** : an implement (as a wire with handles) for strangulation — **garrote** *or* **garotte** *vb*

gar·ru·lous \'gar-ə-ləs\ *adj* : TALKATIVE, WORDY — **gar·ru·li·ty** \gə-'rü-lə-tē\ *n* — **gar·ru·lous·ly** *adv* — **gar·ru·lous·ness** *n*

gar·ter \'gär-tər\ *n* : a band or strap worn to hold up a stocking or sock

garter snake *n* : any of numerous harmless American snakes with longitudinal stripes on the back

¹gas \'gas\ *n, pl* **gas·es** *also* **gas·ses** [NL, alter. of L *chaos* space, chaos] **1** : a fluid (as hydrogen or air) that tends to expand indefinitely **2** : a gas or mixture of gases used as a fuel or anesthetic **3** : a substance that can be used to produce a poisonous, asphyxiating, or irritant atmosphere **4** : GASOLINE — **gas·eous** \'ga-sē-əs, -shəs\ *adj*

²gas *vb* **gassed; gas·sing 1** : to treat with gas; *also* : to poison with gas **2** : to fill with gasoline ⟨∼ up the car⟩

gash \'gash\ *n* : a deep long cut — **gash** *vb*

gas·ket \'gas-kət\ *n* : material (as rubber) or a part used to seal a joint

gas·light \'gas-,līt\ *n* **1** : light made by burning illuminating gas **2** : a gas flame; *also* : a gas lighting fixture

gas mask *n* : a mask with a chemical air filter used to protect the face and lungs against poison gas

gas·o·line \'ga-sə-ˌlēn, ˌga-sə-'lēn\ n : a flammable liquid mixture made from petroleum and used esp. as a motor fuel

gasp \'gasp\ vb 1 : to catch the breath audibly (as with shock) 2 : to breathe laboriously : PANT 3 : to utter in a gasping manner — **gasp** n

gas·tric \'gas-trik\ adj : of or relating to the stomach

gastric juice n : the acid digestive secretion of the stomach

gas·tri·tis \gas-'trī-təs\ n : inflammation of the lining of the stomach

gas·tro·en·ter·ol·o·gy \ˌgas-trō-ˌen-tə-'rä-lə-jē\ n : a branch of medicine concerned with the structure, functions, and diseases of the stomach and intestines — **gas·tro·en·ter·ol·o·gist** \-jist\ n

gas·tro·in·tes·ti·nal \ˌgas-trō-in-'tes-tən-ᵊl\ adj : of, relating to, affecting, or including both the stomach and intestine ⟨∼ tract⟩ ⟨∼ distress⟩

gas·tron·o·my \gas-'trä-nə-mē\ n [F gastronomie, fr. Gk Gastronomia, title of a 4th cent. B.C. poem, fr. gastēr belly + -nomia system of laws] : the art of good eating — **gas·tro·nom·ic** \ˌgas-trə-'nä-mik\ also **gas·tro·nom·i·cal** \-mi-kəl\ adj

gas·tro·pod \'gas-trə-ˌpäd\ n : any of a large class of mollusks (as snails and slugs) with a muscular foot and a spiral shell or none — **gastropod** adj

gas·works \'gas-ˌwərks\ n sing or pl : a plant for manufacturing gas

gate \'gāt\ n 1 : an opening for passage in a wall or fence 2 : a city or castle entrance often with defensive structures 3 : the frame or door that closes a gate 4 : a device (as a valve) for controlling the passage of a fluid or signal 5 : the total admission receipts or the number of people at an event

-gate \ˌgāt\ n comb form [Watergate, scandal that resulted in the resignation of President Richard Nixon in 1974] : usu. political scandal often involving the concealment of wrongdoing

gate–crash·er \'gāt-ˌkra-shər\ n : a person who enters without paying admission or attends without invitation

gate·keep·er \-ˌkē-pər\ n : a person who tends or guards a gate

gate·post \-ˌpōst\ n : the post to which a gate is hung or the one against which it closes

gate·way \-ˌwā\ n 1 : an opening for a gate 2 : a means of entrance or exit

¹gath·er \'ga-thər\ vb 1 : to bring together : COLLECT 2 : PICK, HARVEST 3 : to pick up little by little 4 : to gain or win by gradual increase : ACCUMULATE ⟨∼ speed⟩ 5 : to summon up ⟨∼ courage to dive⟩ 6 : to draw about or close to something 7 : to pull (fabric) along a line of stitching into puckers 8 : GUESS, DEDUCE, INFER 9 : ASSEMBLE 10 : to swell out and fill with pus 11 : GROW, INCREASE syn congregate, forgather — **gath·er·er** n

²gather n : a puckering in cloth made by gathering

GATT \'gat\ abbr General Agreement on Tariffs and Trade

gauche \'gōsh\ adj [F, lit., left] 1 : lacking social experience or grace; also : not tactful 2 : crudely made or done syn clumsy, heavy-handed, inept, maladroit

gau·che·rie \ˌgō-shə-'rē\ n : a tactless or awkward action

gau·cho \'gaů-chō\ n, pl **gauchos** : a cowboy of the So. American pampas

gaud \'gôd\ n : ORNAMENT, TRINKET

gaudy \'gô-dē\ adj **gaud·i·er; -est** 1 : ostentatiously or tastelessly ornamented 2 : marked by showiness or extravagance syn garish, flashy, glaring, tawdry — **gaud·i·ly** \-də-lē\ adv — **gaud·i·ness** \-dē-nəs\ n

¹gauge or **gage** \'gāj\ n 1 : measurement according to some standard or system 2 : DIMENSIONS, SIZE 3 usu

gage : an instrument for measuring, testing, or registering

²gauge or **gage** vb **gauged** or **gaged; gaug·ing** or **gag·ing** 1 : MEASURE 2 : to determine the capacity or contents of 3 : ESTIMATE, JUDGE

gaunt \'gônt\ adj 1 : being thin and angular 2 : BARREN, DESOLATE syn bony, lank, lanky, lean, rawboned, skinny — **gaunt·ness** n

¹gaunt·let \'gônt-lət\ n 1 : a protective glove 2 : an open challenge (as to combat) 3 : a dress glove extending above the wrist

²gauntlet n 1 : ORDEAL 2 : a double file of men armed with weapons (as clubs) with which to strike at an individual who is made to run between them

gauze \'gôz\ n : a very thin often transparent fabric used esp. for draperies and surgical dressings — **gauzy** adj

gave past of GIVE

gav·el \'ga-vəl\ n : the mallet of a presiding officer or auctioneer

ga·votte \gə-'vät\ n : a dance of French peasant origin marked by the raising rather than sliding of the feet

gawk \'gôk\ vb : to gape or stare stupidly

gawky \'gô-kē\ adj **gawk·i·er; -est** : AWKWARD, CLUMSY — **gawk·i·ly** \-kə-lē\ adv

gay \'gā\ adj 1 : MERRY 2 : BRIGHT, LIVELY 3 : brilliant in color 4 : given to social pleasures; also : LICENTIOUS 5 : HOMOSEXUAL; also : of, relating to, or used by homosexuals

gay·ety, gay·ly var of GAIETY, GAILY

gaz abbr gazette

gaze \'gāz\ vb **gazed; gaz·ing** : to fix the eyes in a steady intent look syn gape, gawk, glare, goggle, peer, stare — **gaze** n — **gaz·er** n

ga·ze·bo \gə-'zē-bō\ n, pl **-bos** 1 : BELVEDERE 2 : a freestanding roofed structure usu. open on the sides

ga·zelle \gə-'zel\ n, pl **gazelles** also **gazelle** : any of numerous small swift graceful antelopes

gazelle

ga·zette \gə-'zet\ n 1 : NEWSPAPER 2 : an official journal

gaz·et·teer \ˌga-zə-'tir\ n : a geographical dictionary

gaz·pa·cho \gəz-'pä-(ˌ)chō, gə-'spä-\ n, pl **-chos** [Sp] : a spicy soup usu. made from raw vegetables and served cold

GB abbr Great Britain

GCA abbr ground-controlled approach

gd abbr good

Gd symbol gadolinium

GDR abbr German Democratic Republic

Ge symbol germanium

gear \'gir\ n 1 : CLOTHING 2 : movable property : GOODS 3 : EQUIPMENT ⟨fishing ∼⟩ 4 : a mechanism that performs a specific function ⟨steering ∼⟩ 5 : a toothed wheel 6 : working adjustment of gears ⟨in ∼⟩

7 : an adjustment of transmission gears (as of an automobile or bicycle) that determines speed and direction of travel — **gear** *vb*

gear·box \'gir-ˌbäks\ *n* : TRANSMISSION 3

gear·shift \-ˌshift\ *n* : a mechanism by which transmission gears are shifted

gear·wheel \-ˌhwēl\ *n* : GEAR 5

GED *abbr* 1 General Educational Development (tests) 2 general equivalency diploma

geek \'gēk\ *n* : a person often of an intellectual bent who is disapproved of — **geeky** *adj*

geese *pl of* GOOSE

gee·zer \'gē-zər\ *n* : an odd or eccentric person

Gei·ger counter \'gī-gər-\ *n* : an electronic instrument for detecting the presence of cosmic rays or radioactive substances

gei·sha \'gā-shə, 'gē-\ *n, pl* geisha *or* geishas [Jp, fr. *gei* art + *-sha* person] : a Japanese girl or woman who is trained to provide entertaining company for men

gel \'jel\ *n* : a solid jellylike colloid (as gelatin dessert) — **gel** *vb*

gel·a·tin *also* **gel·a·tine** \'je-lət-ᵊn\ *n* : glutinous material and esp. protein obtained from animal tissues by boiling and used as a food, in dyeing, and in photography; *also* : an edible jelly formed with gelatin — **ge·lat·i·nous** \jə-'lat-ᵊn-əs\ *adj*

geld \'geld\ *vb* : CASTRATE

geld·ing *n* : a castrated male horse

gel·id \'je-ləd\ *adj* : extremely cold

gem \'jem\ *n* 1 : JEWEL 2 : a usu. valuable stone cut and polished for ornament 3 : something valued for beauty or perfection

Gem·i·ni \'je-mə-(ˌ)nē, -ˌnī; 'ge-mə-ˌnē\ *n* 1 : a zodiacal constellation between Taurus and Cancer usu. pictured as twins sitting together 2 : the 3d sign of the zodiac in astrology; *also* : one born under this sign

gem·ol·o·gy *or* **gem·mol·o·gy** \je-'mä-lə-jē, jə-\ *n* : the science of gems — **gem·o·log·i·cal** \ˌje-mə-'lä-ji-kəl\ *adj* — **gem·ol·o·gist** *or* **gem·mol·o·gist** \-jist\ *n*

gem·stone \'jem-ˌstōn\ *n* : a mineral or petrified material that when cut and polished can be used in jewelry

gen *abbr* 1 general 2 genitive

Gen *abbr* Genesis

Gen AF *abbr* general of the air force

gen·darme \'zhän-ˌdärm, 'jän-\ *n* [F, intended as sing. of *gensdarmes*, pl. of *gent d'armes*, lit., armed people] : a member of a body of soldiers esp. in France serving as an armed police force

gen·der \'jen-dər\ *n* 1 : any of two or more divisions within a grammatical class that determine agreement with and selection of other words or grammatical forms 2 : SEX 1

gene \'jēn\ *n* : a part of DNA or RNA that contains chemical information needed to make a particular protein (as an enzyme) controlling or influencing an inherited bodily trait (as eye color) or activity or that influences or controls the activity of another gene or genes — **gen·ic** \'jē-nik, 'je-\ *adj*

ge·ne·al·o·gy \ˌjē-nē-'ä-lə-jē, ˌje-, -'a-\ *n, pl* **-gies** : PEDIGREE, LINEAGE; *also* : the study of family pedigrees — **ge·ne·a·log·i·cal** \ˌjē-nē-ə-'lä-ji-kəl, ˌje-\ *adj* — **ge·ne·a·log·i·cal·ly** \-k(ə-)lē\ *adv* — **ge·ne·al·o·gist** \ˌjē-nē-'ä-lə-jist, ˌje-; -'a-\ *n*

genera *pl of* GENUS

¹**gen·er·al** \'je-nə-rəl, 'jen-rəl\ *adj* 1 : of or relating to the whole 2 : taken as a whole 3 : relating to or covering all instances 4 : not special or specialized 5 : common to many ⟨a ∼ custom⟩ 6 : not limited in meaning : not specific 7 : holding superior rank ⟨inspector ∼⟩ **syn** generic, universal

²**general** *n* 1 : something that involves or is applicable to the whole 2 : a commissioned officer ranking next below a general of the army or a general of the air force 3 : a commissioned officer of the highest rank in the marine corps — **in general** : for the most part

general assembly *n* 1 : a legislative assembly; *esp* : a U.S. state legislature 2 *cap* G&A : the supreme deliberative body of the United Nations

gen·er·al·i·sa·tion, gen·er·al·ise *Brit var of* GENERALIZATION, GENERALIZE

gen·er·a·lis·si·mo \ˌje-nə-rə-'li-sə-ˌmō\ *n, pl* **-mos** [It, fr. *generale* general] : the chief commander of an army

gen·er·al·i·ty \ˌje-nə-'ra-lə-tē\ *n, pl* **-ties** 1 : the quality or state of being general 2 : GENERALIZATION 2 3 : a vague or inadequate statement 4 : the greatest part : BULK

gen·er·al·i·za·tion \ˌje-nə-rə-lə-'zā-shən, ˌjen-rə-\ *n* 1 : the act or process of generalizing 2 : a general statement, law, principle, or proposition

gen·er·al·ize \'je-nə-rə-ˌlīz, 'jen-rə-\ *vb* **-ized; -iz·ing** 1 : to make general 2 : to draw general conclusions from 3 : to reach a general conclusion esp. on the basis of particular instances 4 : to extend throughout the body

gen·er·al·ly \'jen-rə-lē, 'jē-nə-\ *adv* 1 : in a general manner 2 : as a rule

general of the air force : a commissioned officer of the highest rank in the air force

general of the army : a commissioned officer of the highest rank in the army

general practitioner *n* : a physician or veterinarian whose practice is not limited to a specialty

gen·er·al·ship \'je-nə-rəl-ˌship, 'jen-rəl-\ *n* 1 : office or tenure of office of a general 2 : LEADERSHIP 3 : military skill as a high commander

general store *n* : a retail store that carries a wide variety of goods but is not divided into departments

gen·er·ate \'je-nə-ˌrāt\ *vb* **-at·ed; -at·ing** : to bring into existence : PRODUCE **syn** create, originate, procreate, spawn

gen·er·a·tion \ˌje-nə-ˈrā-shən\ *n* **1** : a body of living beings constituting a single step in the line of descent from an ancestor; *also* : the average period between generations **2** : PRODUCTION

gen·er·a·tive \ˈje-nə-rə-tiv, -ˌrā-tiv\ *adj* : having the power or function of generating, originating, producing, or reproducing ⟨∼ organs⟩

gen·er·a·tor \ˈje-nə-ˌrā-tər\ *n* : one that generates; *esp* : a machine by which mechanical energy is changed into electrical energy

ge·ner·ic \jə-ˈner-ik\ *adj* **1** : not specific : GENERAL **2** : not protected by a trademark ⟨a ∼ drug⟩ **3** : of or relating to a biological genus — **generic** *n* — **ge·ner·i·cal·ly** \-i-k(ə-)lē\ *adv*

gen·er·ous \ˈje-nə-rəs\ *adj* **1** : free in giving or sharing **2** : HIGH-MINDED, NOBLE **3** : ABUNDANT, AMPLE, COPIOUS syn liberal, bountiful, munificent, openhanded — **gen·er·os·i·ty** \ˌje-nə-ˈrä-sə-tē\ *n* — **gen·er·ous·ly** \ˈje-nə-rəs-lē\ *adv* — **gen·er·ous·ness** *n*

gen·e·sis \ˈje-nə-səs\ *n, pl* **-e·ses** \-ˌsēz\ : the origin or coming into existence of something

Genesis *n* — see BIBLE table

gene–splic·ing \-ˈsplī-siŋ\ *n* : the technique by which recombinant DNA is produced and made to function in an organism

gene therapy *n* : the insertion of normal or altered genes into cells usu. to replace defective genes esp. in the treatment of genetic disorders

ge·net·ic \jə-ˈne-tik\ *adj* : of or relating to the origin, development, or causes of something; *also* : of or relating to genetics — **ge·net·i·cal·ly** \-ti-k(ə-)lē\ *adv*

genetic code *n* : the chemical code that is the basis of genetic inheritance and consists of triplets of three linked chemical groups in DNA and RNA which specify particular amino acids used to make proteins or which start or stop the process of making proteins

genetic engineering *n* : the directed alteration of genetic material by intervention in genetic processes; *esp* : GENE-SPLICING — **genetically engineered** *adj*

ge·net·ics \jə-ˈne-tiks\ *n* : a branch of biology dealing with heredity and variation — **ge·net·i·cist** \-tə-sist\ *n*

ge·nial \ˈjē-nyəl, ˈjē-nē-əl\ *adj* **1** : favorable to growth or comfort ⟨∼ sunshine⟩ **2** : CHEERFUL, KINDLY ⟨a ∼ host⟩ syn affable, congenial, cordial, gracious, sociable — **ge·nial·i·ty** \ˌjē-nē-ˈa-lə-tē, jēn-ˈya-\ *n* — **ge·nial·ly** *adv*

-gen·ic \ˈje-nik\ *adj comb form* **1** : producing : forming **2** : produced by : formed from **3** : suitable for production or reproduction by (such) a medium

ge·nie \ˈjē-nē\ *n, pl* **ge·nies** *also* **ge·nii** \-nē-ˌī\ [F *génie,* fr. Ar *jinnīy*] : a supernatural spirit that often takes human form usu. serving the person who calls on it

gen·i·tal \ˈje-nət-ᵊl\ *adj* **1** : concerned with reproduction ⟨∼ organs⟩ **2** : of, relating to, or characterized by the stage of psychosexual development in psychoanalytic theory in which oral and anal impulses are sub-

ordinated to adaptive interpersonal mechanisms — **gen·i·tal·ly** *adv*

gen·i·ta·lia \ˌje-nə-ˈtāl-yə\ *n pl* : reproductive organs; *esp* : the external genital organs — **gen·i·ta·lic** \-ˈta-lik, -ˈtā-\ *adj*

gen·i·tals \ˈje-nət-ᵊlz\ *n pl* : GENITALIA

gen·i·tive \ˈje-nə-tiv\ *adj* : of, relating to, or constituting a grammatical case marking typically a relationship of possessor or source — **genitive** *n*

gen·i·to·uri·nary \ˌje-nə-tō-ˈyùr-ə-ˌner-ē\ *adj* : of or relating to the genital and urinary organs or functions

ge·nius \ˈjē-nyəs\ *n, pl* **ge·nius·es** *or* **ge·nii** \-nē-ˌī\ [L, tutelary spirit, natural inclinations, fr. *gignere* to beget] **1** *pl* **genii** : an attendant spirit of a person or place; *also* : a person who influences another for good or evil **2** : a strong leaning or inclination **3** : a peculiar or distinctive character or spirit (as of a nation or a language) **4** *pl usu* **genii** : SPIRIT, GENIE **5** *pl usu* **geniuses** : a single strongly marked capacity or aptitude **6** : extraordinary intellectual power; *also* : a person having such power syn gift, faculty, flair, knack, talent

genl *abbr* general

geno·cide \ˈje-nə-ˌsīd\ *n* : the deliberate and systematic destruction of a racial, political, or cultural group

-genous \jə-nəs\ *adj comb form* **1** : producing : yielding ⟨erog*enous*⟩ **2** : having (such) an origin ⟨endog*enous*⟩

genre \ˈzhän-rə, ˈzhän-; ˈzhänᵊr; ˈjän-rə\ *n* **1** : a distinctive type or category esp. of literary composition **2** : a style of painting in which everyday subjects are treated realistically

gens \ˈjenz, ˈgens\ *n, pl* **gen·tes** \ˈjen-ˌtēz, ˈgen-ˌtās\ : a Roman clan embracing the families of the same stock in the male line

gent *n* : GENTLEMAN

gen·teel \jen-ˈtēl\ *adj* **1** : ARISTOCRATIC **2** : ELEGANT, STYLISH **3** : POLITE, REFINED **4** : maintaining the appearance of superior social status **5** : marked by false delicacy, prudery, or affectation — **gen·teel·ly** *adv* — **gen·teel·ness** *n*

gen·tian \ˈjen-chən\ *n* : any of numerous herbs with opposite leaves and showy usu. blue flowers in the fall

gen·tile \ˈjen-ˌtīl\ *n* [LL *gentilis* heathen, pagan, fr. L *gent-, gens* clan, nation] **1** *often cap* : a person who is not Jewish; *esp* : a Christian as distinguished from a Jew **2** : HEATHEN, PAGAN — **gentile** *adj, often cap*

gen·til·i·ty \jen-ˈti-lə-tē\ *n, pl* **-ties** **1** : good birth and family **2** : the qualities characteristic of a well-bred person **3** : good manners **4** : superior social status shown in manners or mode of life

¹gen·tle \ˈjent-ᵊl\ *adj* **gen·tler** \ˈjent-lər, -ᵊl-ər\; **gen·tlest** \ˈjent-ləst, -ᵊl-əst\ **1** : belonging to a family of high social station **2** : of, relating to, or characteristic of a gentleman **3** : KIND, AMIABLE **4** : TRACTABLE, DOCILE **5** : not harsh, stern, or violent **6** : SOFT, DELICATE **7** : MODERATE — **gen·tle·ness** *n* — **gen·tly** *adv*

²gentle *vb* **gen·tled; gen·tling** **1** : to make or become mild, docile, soft, or moderate **2** : MOLLIFY, PLACATE

gen·tle·folk \\'jent-ᵊl-₁fōk\\ *also* **gen·tle·folks** \\-₁fōks\\ *n* : persons of good family and breeding

gen·tle·man \\-mən\\ *n* **1** : a man of good family **2** : a well-bred man **3** : MAN — used in pl. as a form of address — **gen·tle·man·ly** *adj*

gen·tle·wom·an \\-₁wu̇-mən\\ *n* **1** : a woman of good family **2** : a woman attending a lady of rank **3** : a woman with very good manners : LADY

gen·tri·fi·ca·tion \\₁jen-trə-fə-'kā-shən\\ *n* : the process of renewal accompanying the influx of middle-class people into deteriorating areas that often displaces earlier usu. poorer residents — **gen·tri·fy** \\'jen-trə-fī\\ *vb*

gen·try \\'jen-trē\\ *n, pl* **gentries 1** : people of good birth, breeding, and education : ARISTOCRACY **2** : the class of English people between the nobility and the yeomanry **3** : persons of a designated class

gen·u·flect \\'jen-yu̇-₁flekt\\ *vb* : to bend the knee esp. in worship — **gen·u·flec·tion** \\₁jen-yu̇-'flek-shən\\ *n*

gen·u·ine \\'jen-yə-wən\\ *adj* **1** : AUTHENTIC, REAL **2** : SINCERE, HONEST **syn** bona fide, true, veritable — **gen·u·ine·ly** *adv* — **gen·u·ine·ness** *n*

ge·nus \\'jē-nəs\\ *n, pl* **gen·era** \\'je-nə-rə\\ [L, birth, race, kind] : a category of biological classification that ranks between the family and the species and contains related species

geo·cen·tric \\₁jē-ō-'sen-trik\\ *adj* **1** : relating to or measured from the earth's center **2** : having or relating to the earth as a center

geo·chem·is·try \\-'ke-mə-strē\\ *n* : a branch of geology that deals with the chemical composition of and chemical changes in the earth — **geo·chem·i·cal** \\-mi-kəl\\ *adj* — **geo·chem·ist** \\-mist\\ *n*

ge·ode \\'jē-₁ōd\\ *n* : a nodule of stone having a cavity lined with mineral matter

¹geo·de·sic \\₁jē-ə-'de-sik\\ *adj* : made of light straight structural elements ⟨a ~ dome⟩

²geodesic *n* : the shortest line between two points on a surface

geo·det·ic \\₁jē-ə-'de-tik\\ *adj* : of, relating to, or being precise measurement of the earth and its features ⟨a ~ survey⟩

geog *abbr* geographic; geographical; geography

ge·og·ra·phy \\jē-'ä-grə-fē\\ *n, pl* **-phies 1** : a science that deals with the natural features of the earth and the climate, products, and inhabitants **2** : the natural features of a region — **ge·og·ra·pher** \\-fər\\ *n* — **geo·graph·ic** \\₁jē-ə-'gra-fik\\ *or* **geo·graph·i·cal** \\-fi-kəl\\ *adj* — **geo·graph·i·cal·ly** \\-fi-k(ə-)lē\\ *adv*

geol *abbr* geologic; geological; geology

ge·ol·o·gy \\jē-'ä-lə-jē\\ *n, pl* **-gies 1** : a science that deals with the history of the earth and its life esp. as recorded in rocks; *also* : a study of the features of a celestial body (as the moon) **2** : the geologic features of an area — **geo·log·ic** \\₁jē-ə-'lä-jik\\ *or* **geo·log·i·cal** \\-ji-kəl\\ *adj* — **geo·log·i·cal·ly** \\-ji-k(ə-)lē\\ *adv* — **ge·ol·o·gist** \\jē-'ä-lə-jist\\ *n*

geom *abbr* geometric; geometrical; geometry

geo·mag·net·ic \\₁jē-ō-mag-'ne-tik\\ *adj* : of or relating to the magnetism of the earth — **geo·mag·ne·tism** \\-'mag-nə-₁ti-zəm\\ *n*

geometric mean *n* : the *n*th root of the product of *n* numbers; *esp* : a number that is the second term of three consecutive terms of a geometric progression ⟨the *geometric mean* of 9 and 4 is 6⟩

geometric progression *n* : a progression (as 1, ½, ¼) in which the ratio of a term to its predecessor is always the same

ge·om·e·try \\jē-'ä-mə-trē\\ *n, pl* **-tries** [ultim. fr. Gk *geōmetria*, fr. *geōmetrein* to measure the earth, fr. *gē* earth + *metron* measure] : a branch of mathematics dealing with the relations, properties, and measurements of solids, surfaces, lines, points, and angles — **ge·om·e·ter** \\-tər\\ *n* — **geo·met·ric** \\₁jē-ə-'me-trik\\ *or* **geo·met·ri·cal** \\-tri-kəl\\ *adj*

geo·phys·ics \\₁jē-ō-'fi-ziks\\ *n* : the physics of the earth

geo·phys·i·cal \\-zi-kəl\\ *adj* — **geo·phys·i·cist** \\-zə-sist\\ *n*

geo·pol·i·tics \\-'pä-lə-₁tiks\\ *n* : a combination of political and geographic factors relating to a state

Geor·gian \\'jȯr-jən\\ *n* : a native or inhabitant of the Republic of Georgia — **Georgian** *adj*

geo·ther·mal \\₁jē-ō-'thər-məl\\ *adj* : of, relating to, or using the heat of the earth's interior

ger *abbr* gerund

Ger *abbr* German; Germany

ge·ra·ni·um \\jə-'rā-nē-əm\\ *n* [L, fr. Gk *geranion*, fr. *geranos* crane] **1** : any of a genus of herbs with usu. deeply cut leaves and pink, purple, or white flowers followed by long slender dry fruits **2** : any of a genus of herbs of the same family as the geraniums that have clusters of scarlet, pink, or white flowers with the sepals joined at the base into a hollow tube closed at one end

ger·bil *also* **ger·bile** \\'jər-bəl\\ *n* : any of numerous Old World burrowing desert rodents with long hind legs

ge·ri·at·ric \\₁jer-ē-'a-trik\\ *adj* **1** : of or relating to geriatrics or the process of aging **2** : of, relating to, or appropriate for elderly people **3** : OLD

ge·ri·at·rics \\-triks\\ *n* : a branch of medicine dealing with the problems and diseases of old age and aging

germ \\'jərm\\ *n* **1** : a bit of living matter capable of growth and development (as into an organism) **2** : SOURCE, RUDIMENTS **3** : MICROORGANISM; *esp* : one causing disease

Ger·man \\'jər-mən\\ *n* **1** : a native or inhabitant of Germany **2** : the language of Germany, Austria, and parts of Switzerland — **German** *adj* — **Ger·man·ic** \\jər-'ma-nik\\ *adj*

ger·mane \\jər-'mān\\ *adj* [ME *germain*, lit., having the same parents, fr. MF, fr. L *germanus*, fr. *germen* sprout, bud] : RELEVANT, APPROPRIATE **syn** applicable, material, pertinent

ger·ma·ni·um \\jər-'mā-nē-əm\\ *n* : a grayish white hard chemical element used as a semiconductor — see ELEMENT table

German measles *n sing or pl* : an acute contagious virus disease milder than typical measles but damaging to the fetus when occurring early in pregnancy

German shepherd *n* : any of a breed of intelligent responsive working dogs of German origin often used in police work and as guide dogs for the blind

germ cell *n* : an egg or sperm or one of their antecedent cells

ger·mi·cide \\'jər-mə-₁sīd\\ *n* : an agent that destroys germs — **ger·mi·cid·al** \\₁jər-mə-'sīd-ᵊl\\ *adj*

ger·mi·nal \\'jər-mə-nəl\\ *adj* : of or relating to a germ or germ cell; *also* : EMBRYONIC

ger·mi·nate \\'jər-mə-₁nāt\\ *vb* **-nat·ed; -nat·ing 1** : to cause to develop : begin to develop : SPROUT **2** : to come into being : EVOLVE — **ger·mi·na·tion** \\₁jər-mə-'nā-shən\\ *n*

ger·on·tol·o·gy \\₁jer-ən-'tä-lə-jē\\ *n* : a scientific study of aging and the problems of the aged — **ge·ron·to·log·i·cal** \\jə-₁ränt-ᵊl-'ä-ji-kəl\\ *adj* — **ger·on·tol·o·gist** \\₁jer-ən-'tä-lə-jist\\ *n*

ger·ry·man·der \\'jer-ē-₁man-dər\\ *vb* : to divide into election districts so as to give one political party an advantage — **gerrymander** *n*

ger·und \\'jer-ənd\\ *n* : a word having the characteristics of both verb and noun

ge·sta·po \\gə-'stä-pō\\ *n, pl* **-pos** [G, fr. *Geheime Staatspolizei*, lit., secret state police] : a usu. terrorist secret-police organization operating against persons suspected of disloyalty

ges·ta·tion \\je-'stā-shən\\ *n* : PREGNANCY, INCUBATION — **ges·tate** \\'jes-₁tāt\\ *vb*

ges·tic·u·late \\je-'sti-kyə-₁lāt\\ *vb* **-lat·ed; -lat·ing** : to make gestures esp. when speaking — **ges·tic·u·la·tion** \\-₁sti-kyə-'lā-shən\\ *n*

ges·ture \\'jes-chər\\ *n* **1** : a movement usu. of the body or limbs that expresses or emphasizes an idea, sen-

timent, or attitude **2 :** something said or done by way of formality or courtesy, as a symbol or token, or for its effect on the attitudes of others — **ges·tur·al** \-chə-rəl\ *adj* — **gesture** *vb*

ge·sund·heit \gə-'zůnt-ˌhīt\ *interj* [G, lit., health] — used to wish good health esp. to one who has just sneezed

¹**get** \'get\ *vb* **got** \'gät\; **got** *or* **got·ten** \'gät-ᵊn\; **get·ting 1 :** to gain possession of (as by receiving, acquiring, earning, buying, or winning) : PROCURE, OBTAIN, FETCH **2 :** to succeed in coming or going ⟨*got* away to the lake⟩ **3 :** to cause to come or go ⟨*got* the car to the station⟩ **4 :** BEGET **5 :** to cause to be in a certain condition or position ⟨don't ~ wet⟩ **6 :** BECOME ⟨~ sick⟩ **7 :** PREPARE **8 :** SEIZE **9 :** to move emotionally; *also* **:** IRRITATE **10 :** BAFFLE, PUZZLE **11 :** KILL **12 :** HIT **13 :** to be subjected to ⟨~ the measles⟩ **14 :** to receive as punishment **15 :** to find out by calculation **16 :** HEAR; *also* **:** UNDERSTAND **17 :** PERSUADE, INDUCE **18 :** HAVE ⟨he's *got* no money⟩ **19 :** to have as an obligation or necessity ⟨you have *got* to come⟩ **20 :** to establish communication with **21 :** to be able ⟨finally *got* to go to med school⟩ **22 :** to come to be or ⟨*got* talking about old times⟩ **23 :** to leave at once

²**get** \'get\ *n* **:** OFFSPRING, PROGENY

get along *vb* **1 :** GET BY **2 :** to be on friendly terms

get·away \'ge-tə-ˌwā\ *n* **1 :** ESCAPE **2 :** START

get by *vb* **:** to meet one's needs

get–to·geth·er \'get-tə-ˌge-thər\ *n* **:** an informal social gathering

get·up \'get-ˌəp\ *n* **1 :** OUTFIT, COSTUME **2 :** general composition or structure

gew·gaw \'gü-ˌgȯ, 'gyü-\ *n* **:** a showy trifle : BAUBLE, TRINKET

gey·ser \'gī-zər\ *n* [Icelandic *Geysir*, hot spring in Iceland] **:** a spring that intermittently shoots up hot water and steam

Gha·na·ian \gä-'nä-ən\ *n* **:** a native or inhabitant of Ghana — **Ghanaian** *adj*

ghast·ly \'gast-lē\ *adj* **ghast·li·er; -est 1 :** HORRIBLE, SHOCKING **2 :** resembling a ghost : DEATHLIKE, PALE **syn** gruesome, grim, lurid, grisly, macabre

ghat \'gȯt\ *n* [Hindi] **:** a broad flight of steps on an Indian riverbank that provides access to the water

gher·kin \'gər-kən\ *n* **1 :** a small prickly fruit of a vine related to the cucumber used to make pickles **2 :** an immature cucumber

ghet·to \'ge-tō\ *n, pl* **ghettos** *or* **ghettoes :** a quarter of a city in which members of a minority group live because of social, legal, or economic pressure

¹**ghost** \'gōst\ *n* **1 :** the seat of life : SOUL **2 :** a disembodied soul; *esp* **:** the soul of a dead person believed to be an inhabitant of the unseen world or to appear in bodily form to living people **3 :** SPIRIT, DEMON **4 :** a faint trace ⟨a ~ of a smile⟩ **5 :** a false image in a photographic negative or on a television screen — **ghost·ly** *adv*

²**ghost** *vb* **:** GHOSTWRITE

ghost·write \-ˌrīt\ *vb* **-wrote** \-ˌrōt\; **-writ·ten** \-ˌrit-ᵊn\

: to write for and in the name of another — **ghost·writ·er** *n*

ghoul \'gül\ *n* [Ar *ghūl*] **:** a legendary evil being that robs graves and feeds on corpses — **ghoul·ish** *adj*

GHQ *abbr* general headquarters

gi *abbr* gill

¹**GI** \ˌjē-'ī\ *adj* [galvanized iron; fr. abbr. used in listing such articles as garbage cans, but taken as abbr. for *government issue*] **1 :** provided by an official U.S. military supply department ⟨~ shoes⟩ **2 :** of, relating to, or characteristic of U.S. military personnel **3 :** conforming to military regulations or customs ⟨a ~ haircut⟩

²**GI** *n, pl* **GI's** *or* **GIs** \-'īz\ **:** a member or former member of the U.S. armed forces; *esp* **:** an enlisted man

³**GI** *abbr* **1** galvanized iron **2** gastrointestinal **3** general issue **4** government issue

gi·ant \'jī-ənt\ *n* **1 :** a legendary humanlike being of great size and strength **2 :** a living being or thing of extraordinary size or powers — **giant** *adj*

gi·ant·ess \'jī-ən-təs\ *n* **:** a female giant

gib·ber \'ji-bər\ *vb* **:** to speak rapidly, inarticulately, and often foolishly

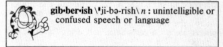

gib·ber·ish \'ji-bə-rish\ *n* **:** unintelligible or confused speech or language

¹**gib·bet** \'ji-bət\ *n* **:** GALLOWS

²**gibbet** *vb* **1 :** to hang on a gibbet **2 :** to expose to public scorn **3 :** to execute by hanging

gib·bon \'gi-bən\ *n* **:** any of several tailless apes of southeastern Asia

gib·bous \'ji-bəs, 'gi-\ *adj* **1 :** rounded like the exterior of a sphere or circle **2 :** seen with more than half but not all of the apparent disk illuminated ⟨~ moon⟩ **3 :** having a hump : HUMPBACKED

gibe \'jīb\ *vb* **gibed; gib·ing :** to utter taunting words **:** SNEER — **gibe** *n*

gib·lets \'jib-ləts\ *n pl* **:** the edible viscera of a fowl

Gib·son girl \'gib-sən-\ *adj* **:** of or relating to a style in women's clothing characterized by high necks, full sleeves, and slender waistlines

gid·dap \'gi-'dap\ *also* **gid·dy·ap** \ˌgi-dē-'ap\ *vb imper* — a command to a horse to go ahead or go faster

gid·dy \'gi-dē\ *adj* **gid·di·er; -est 1 :** DIZZY **2 :** causing dizziness **3 :** not serious : FRIVOLOUS, SILLY — **gid·di·ness** \-dē-nəs\ *n*

gift \'gift\ *n* **1 :** a special ability : TALENT **2 :** something given **:** PRESENT **3 :** the act or power of giving

gift·ed \'gif-təd\ *adj* **:** TALENTED

¹**gig** \'gig\ *n* **1 :** a long light ship's boat **2 :** a light 2-wheeled one-horse carriage

²**gig** *n* **:** a pronged spear for catching fish — **gig** *vb*

³**gig** *n* **:** a job for a specified time; *esp* **:** an entertainer's engagement

⁴**gig** *n* **:** a military demerit — **gig** *vb*

giga·byte \'ji-gə-ˌbīt, 'gi-\ *n* **:** a unit of computer storage capacity approximately equal to one billion bytes

gi·gan·tic \jī-'gan-tik\ *adj* : exceeding the usual (as in size or force)

gig·gle \'gi-gəl\ *vb* **gig·gled; gig·gling** : to laugh with repeated short catches of the breath — **giggle** *n* — **gig·gly** \-gə-lē\ *adj*

GIGO *abbr* garbage in, garbage out

gig·o·lo \'ji-gə-ˌlō\ *n, pl* **-los 1** : a man supported by a woman usu. in return for his attentions **2** : a professional dancing partner or male escort

Gi·la monster \'hē-lə-\ *n* : a large orange and black venomous lizard of the southwestern U.S.

¹gild \'gild\ *vb* **gild·ed** *or* **gilt** \'gilt\; **gild·ing 1** : to overlay with or as if with a thin covering of gold **2** : to give an attractive but often deceptive appearance to

²gild *var of* GUILD

¹gill \'jil\ *n* — see WEIGHT table

²gill \'gil\ *n* : an organ (as of a fish) for obtaining oxygen from water

¹gilt \'gilt\ *adj* : of the color of gold

²gilt *n* : gold or a substance resembling gold laid on the surface of an object

³gilt *n* : a young female swine

gim·crack \'jim-ˌkrak\ *n* : a showy object of little use or value

gim·let \'gim-lət\ *n* : a small tool with screw point and cross handle for boring holes

gim·mick \'gi-mik\ *n* **1** : CONTRIVANCE, GADGET **2** : an important feature that is not immediately apparent : CATCH **3** : a new and ingenious scheme — **gim·micky** \-mi-kē\ *adj*

gim·mick·ry \'gi-mi-krē\ *n, pl* **-ries** : an array of or the use of gimmicks

gimpy \'gim-pē\ *adj* : CRIPPLED, LAME

¹gin \'jin\ *n* [ME *gin*, modif. of OF *engin*] **1** : TRAP, SNARE **2** : a machine to separate seeds from cotton — **gin** *vb*

²gin *n* [by shortening & alter. fr. *geneva*, kind of gin] : a liquor distilled from a grain mash and flavored with juniper berries

gin·ger \'jin-jər\ *n* : the pungent aromatic rootstock of a tropical plant used esp. as a spice and in medicine; *also* : the spice or the plant

ginger ale *n* : a carbonated soft drink flavored with ginger

gin·ger·bread \'jin-jər-ˌbred\ *n* **1** : a cake made with molasses and flavored with ginger **2** : lavish or superfluous ornament

gin·ger·ly \'jin-jər-lē\ *adj* : very cautious or careful — **gingerly** *adv*

gin·ger·snap \-ˌsnap\ *n* : a thin brittle molasses cookie flavored with ginger

ging·ham \'giŋ-əm\ *n* : a clothing fabric usu. of yarn-dyed cotton in plain weave

gin·gi·vi·tis \ˌjin-jə-'vī-təs\ *n* : inflammation of the gums

gink·go *also* **gink·ko** \'giŋ-(ˌ)kō\ *n, pl* **ginkgoes** *or* **ginkgos** : a tree of eastern China with fan-shaped leaves often grown as a shade tree

gin·seng \'jin-ˌseŋ\ *n* : an aromatic root of a Chinese or No. American herb used esp. in Oriental medicine; *also* : one of these herbs

Gip·sy *chiefly Brit var of* GYPSY

gi·raffe \jə-'raf\ *n, pl* **giraffes** [It *giraffa*, fr. Ar *zirāfah*] : an African ruminant mammal with a very long neck and a short coat with dark blotches

gird \'gərd\ *vb* **gird·ed** *or* **girt** \'gərt\; **gird·ing 1** : to encircle or fasten with or as if with a belt ⟨~ on a sword⟩ **2** : to invest esp. with power or authority **3** : PREPARE, BRACE

gird·er \'gər-dər\ *n* : a horizontal main supporting beam

gir·dle \'gərd-ᵊl\ *n* **1** : something (as a belt or sash) that encircles or confines **2** : a woman's supporting undergarment that extends from the waist to below the hips — **girdle** *vb*

girl \'gərl\ *n* **1** : a female child **2** : a young woman **3** : SWEETHEART — **girl·hood** \-ˌhu̇d\ *n* — **girl·ish** *adj*

girl Friday *n* : a female assistant (as in an office) entrusted with a wide variety of tasks

girl·friend \'gərl-ˌfrend\ *n* **1** : a female friend **2** : a frequent or regular female companion of a boy or man

Girl Scout *n* : a member of any of the scouting programs of the Girl Scouts of the United States of America

girth \'gərth\ *n* **1** : a band around an animal by which something (as a saddle) may be fastened on its back **2** : a measure around something

gist \'jist\ *n* [MF, it lies, fr. *gesir* to lie, ultim. fr. L *jacēre*] : the main point or part

¹give \'giv\ *vb* **gave** \'gāv\; **giv·en** \'gi-vən\; **giv·ing 1** : to make a present of **2** : to bestow by formal action **3** : to accord or yield to another **4** : to yield to force, strain, or pressure **5** : to put into the possession or keeping of another **6** : PROFFER **7** : DELIVER ⟨*gave* away the bride⟩ **8** : to present in public performance or to view **9** : PROVIDE ⟨~ a party⟩ **10** : ATTRIBUTE **11** : to make, form, or yield as a product or result ⟨cows ~ milk⟩ **12** : PAY **13** : to deliver by some bodily action ⟨*gave* me a push⟩ **14** : to offer as a pledge ⟨I ~ you my word⟩ **15** : DEVOTE **16** : to cause to have or receive

²give *n* **1** : capacity or tendency to yield to force or strain **2** : the quality or state of being springy

give–and–take \ˌgiv-ən-'tāk\ *n* **1** : COMPROMISE **2** : a usu. good-natured exchange (as of remarks or ideas)

give·away \'gi-və-ˌwā\ *n* **1** : an unintentional revelation or betrayal **2** : something given away free; *esp* : PREMIUM

give in *vb* : SUBMIT, SURRENDER

¹giv·en \'gi-vən\ *adj* **1** : DISPOSED, INCLINED ⟨~ to swearing⟩ **2** : SPECIFIED, PARTICULAR ⟨at a ~ time⟩

²given *prep* : CONSIDERING

given name *n* : a name that precedes one's surname

give out *vb* **1** : EMIT **2** : BREAK DOWN **3** : to become exhausted : COLLAPSE

give up *vb* **1** : SURRENDER **2** : to abandon (oneself) to a feeling, influence, or activity **3** : QUIT

giz·mo *also* **gis·mo** \'giz-mō\ *n, pl* **gizmos** *also* **gismos** : GADGET

giz·zard \'gi-zərd\ *n* : the muscular usu. horny-lined enlargement of the alimentary canal of a bird used for churning and grinding up food

gla·cial \'glā-shəl\ *adj* **1** : extremely cold **2** : of or relating to glaciers **3** : being or relating to a past period of time when a large part of the earth was covered by glaciers **4** *cap* : PLEISTOCENE **5** : very slow ⟨a ~ pace⟩ — **gla·cial·ly** *adv*

gla·ci·ate \'glā-shē-ˌāt\ *vb* **-at·ed; -at·ing 1** : to subject to glacial action **2** : to produce glacial effects in or on — **gla·ci·a·tion** \ˌglā-shē-'ā-shən, -sē-\ *n*

gla·cier \'glā-shər\ *n* : a large body of ice moving slowly down a slope or spreading outward on a land surface

¹glad \'glad\ *adj* **glad·der; glad·dest 1** : experiencing pleasure, joy, or delight **2** : PLEASED **3** : very willing **4** : PLEASANT, JOYFUL **5** : CHEERFUL — **glad·ly** *adv* — **glad·ness** *n*

²glad *n* : GLADIOLUS

glad·den \'glad-ᵊn\ *vb* : to make glad

glade \'glād\ *n* : a grassy open space surrounded by woods

glad·i·a·tor \'gla-dē-ˌā-tər\ *n* **1** : a person engaged in a fight to the death for public entertainment in ancient Rome **2** : a person engaging in a public fight or controversy; *also* : PRIZEFIGHTER — **glad·i·a·to·ri·al** \ˌgla-dē-ə-'tōr-ē-əl\ *adj*

glad·i·o·lus \ˌgla-dē-'ō-ləs\ *n, pl* **-li** \-(ˌ)lē, -ˌlī\ [L, fr. dim. of *gladius* sword] : any of a genus of chiefly African plants related to the irises and having erect sword-shaped leaves and stalks of bright colored flowers

glad·some \'glad-səm\ *adj* : giving or showing joy : CHEERFUL

glad·stone \'glad-ˌstōn\ *n, often cap* : a suitcase with flexible sides on a rigid frame that opens flat into two compartments

glam·or·ise *Brit var of* GLAMORIZE

glam·or·ize *also* **glam·our·ize** \'gla-mə-ˌrīz\ *vb* **-ized; -iz·ing** : to make or look upon as glamorous

glam·our *or* **glam·or** \'gla-mər\ *n* [Sc *glamour* magic spell, alter. of E *grammar;* fr. the popular association of erudition with occult practices] : an exciting and often illusory and romantic attractiveness; *esp* : alluring personal attraction — **glam·or·ous** *also* **glam·our·ous** \-mə-rəs\ *adj*

¹**glance** \'glans\ *vb* **glanced; glanc·ing 1** : to strike and fly off to one side **2** : GLEAM **3** : to give a quick look

²**glance** *n* **1** : a quick intermittent flash or gleam **2** : a deflected impact or blow **3** : a quick look

gland \'gland\ *n* : a cell or group of cells that prepares and secretes a substance (as saliva or sweat) for further use in or discharge from the body

glan·du·lar \'glan-jə-lər\ *adj* : of, relating to, or involving glands

glans \'glanz\ *n, pl* **glan·des** \'glan-ˌdēz\ [L, lit., acorn] : a conical vascular body forming the extremity of the penis or clitoris

¹**glare** \'glar\ *vb* **glared; glar·ing 1** : to shine with a harsh dazzling light **2** : to stare fiercely or angrily

²**glare** *n* **1** : a harsh dazzling light **2** : an angry or fierce stare

glar·ing \'glar-iŋ\ *adj* : very conspicuous ⟨a ~ error⟩ — **glar·ing·ly** *adv*

glass \'glas\ *n* **1** : a hard brittle amorphous usu. transparent or translucent material consisting esp. of silica **2** : something made of glass; *esp* : TUMBLER 2 **3** *pl* : a pair of lenses used to correct defects of vision : SPECTACLES **4** : the quantity held by a glass container — **glass** *adj* — **glass·ful** \-ˌfùl\ *n* — **glassy** *adj*

glass·blow·ing \-ˌblō-iŋ\ *n* : the art of shaping a mass of glass that has been softened by heat by blowing air into it through a tube — **glass·blow·er** *n*

glass·ware \-ˌwar\ *n* : articles made of glass

glau·co·ma \glaù-'kō-mə, glò-\ *n* : a disease of the eye marked by increased pressure within the eyeball resulting in damage to the retina and gradual loss of vision

¹**glaze** \'glāz\ *vb* **glazed; glaz·ing 1** : to furnish (as a window frame) with glass **2** : to apply glaze to

²**glaze** *n* : a glassy coating or surface

gla·zier \'glā-zhər\ *n* : a person who sets glass in window frames

¹**gleam** \'glēm\ *n* **1** : a transient subdued or partly obscured light **2** : GLINT **3** : a faint trace ⟨a ~ of hope⟩

²**gleam** *vb* **1** : to shine with subdued light or moderate brightness **2** : to appear briefly or faintly **syn** flash, glimmer, glisten, glitter, shimmer, sparkle

glean \'glēn\ *vb* **1** : to gather grain left by reapers **2** : to

collect little by little or with patient effort — **glean·able** *adj* — **glean·er** *n*

glean·ings \'glē-niŋz\ *n pl* : things acquired by gleaning

glee \'glē\ *n* [ME, fr. OE *glēo* entertainment, music] **1** : JOY, HILARITY **2** : a part-song for three usu. male voices — **glee·ful** *adj*

glee club *n* : a chorus organized for singing usu. short choral pieces

glen \'glen\ *n* : a narrow hidden valley

glen·gar·ry \glen-'gar-ē\ *n, pl* **-ries** *often cap* : a woolen cap of Scottish origin

glib \'glib\ *adj* **glib·ber; glib·best** : speaking or spoken with careless ease — **glib·ly** *adv*

glide \'glīd\ *vb* **glid·ed; glid·ing 1** : to move smoothly and effortlessly **2** : to descend gradually without engine power ⟨~ in an airplane⟩ — **glide** *n*

glid·er \'glī-dər\ *n* **1** : one that glides **2** : an aircraft resembling an airplane but having no engine **3** : a porch seat suspended from an upright frame

¹**glim·mer** \'gli-mər\ *vb* : to shine faintly or unsteadily

²**glimmer** *n* **1** : a faint unsteady light **2** : INKLING **3** : a small amount : HINT

¹**glimpse** \'glimps\ *vb* **glimpsed; glimps·ing** : to take a brief look : see momentarily or incompletely

²**glimpse** *n* **1** : a faint idea : GLIMMER **2** : a short hurried look

glint \'glint\ *vb* **1** : to shine by reflection : SPARKLE, GLITTER, GLEAM **2** : to appear briefly or faintly — **glint** *n*

glis·san·do \gli-'sän-(ˌ)dō\ *n, pl* **-di** \-(ˌ)dē\ *or* **-dos** : a rapid sliding up or down the musical scale

glis·ten \'glis-ᵊn\ *vb* : to shine by reflection with a soft luster or sparkle

²**glisten** *n* : GLISTER, SPARKLE

glis·ter \'glis-tər\ *vb* : GLITTER

glitch \'glich\ *n* : MALFUNCTION; *also* : SNAG 2

¹**glit·ter** \'gli-tər\ *vb* **1** : to shine with brilliant or metallic luster : SPARKLE **2** : to shine with strong emotion : FLASH ⟨eyes ~*ing* in anger⟩ **3** : to be brilliantly attractive esp. in a superficial way

²**glitter** *n* **1** : sparkling brilliancy, showiness, or attractiveness **2** : small glittering objects used for ornamentation — **glit·tery** \'gli-tə-rē\ *adj*

glitz \'glits\ *n* : extravagant showiness — **glitzy** \'glit-sē\ *adj*

gloam·ing \'glō-miŋ\ *n* : TWILIGHT, DUSK

gloat \'glōt\ *vb* : to think about something with triumphant and often malicious delight

glob \'gläb\ *n* **1** : a small drop **2** : a large rounded mass

glob·al \'glō-bəl\ *adj* **1** : WORLDWIDE **2** : COMPREHENSIVE, GENERAL — **glob·al·ly** *adv*

globe \'glōb\ *n* **1** : BALL, SPHERE **2** : EARTH; *also* : a spherical representation of the earth

globe–trot·ter \'glōb-ˌträ-tər\ *n* : a person who travels widely — **globe–trot·ting** *n or adj*

glob·u·lar \'glä-byə-lər\ *adj* : having the shape of a globe or globule

glob·ule \'glä-(ˌ)byül\ *n* : a tiny globe or ball esp. of a liquid

glob·u·lin \'glä-byə-lən\ *n* : any of a class of simple

proteins insoluble in pure water but soluble in dilute salt solutions that occur widely in plant and animal tissues

glock·en·spiel \'glä-kən-₁shpēl, -₁spēl\ n [G, fr. *Glocke* bell + *Spiel* play] : a percussion musical instrument consisting of a series of metal bars played with two hammers

gloom \'glüm\ n 1 : partial or total darkness 2 : lowness of spirits : DEJECTION 3 : an atmosphere of despondency — **gloom·i·ly** \'glü-mə-lē\ adv — **gloom·i·ness** \-mē-nəs\ n — **gloomy** \'glü-mē\ adj

glop \'gläp\ n : a messy mass or mixture

glo·ri·fy \'glōr-ə-₁fī\ vb **-fied; -fy·ing** 1 : to raise to heavenly glory 2 : to light up brilliantly 3 : EXTOL 4 : to give glory to (as in worship) — **glo·ri·fi·ca·tion** \₁glōr-ə-fə-'kā-shən\ n

glo·ri·ous \'glōr-ē-əs\ adj 1 : possessing or deserving glory : PRAISEWORTHY 2 : conferring glory 3 : RESPLENDENT, MAGNIFICENT 4 : DELIGHTFUL, WONDERFUL — **glo·ri·ous·ly** adv

¹**glo·ry** \'glōr-ē\ n, pl **glories** 1 : RENOWN 2 : honor and praise rendered in worship 3 : something that secures praise or renown 4 : a distinguishing quality or asset 5 : RESPLENDENCE, MAGNIFICENCE 6 : heavenly bliss 7 : a height of prosperity or achievement

²**glory** vb **glo·ried; glo·ry·ing** : to rejoice proudly : EXULT

¹**gloss** \'gläs, 'glòs\ n 1 : LUSTER, SHEEN, BRIGHTNESS 2 : outward show

²**gloss** vb 1 : to give a false appearance of acceptableness to (∼ over inadequacies) 2 : to deal with too lightly or not at all

³**gloss** n [alter. of *gloze*, fr. ME *glose*, fr. MF, fr. ML *glosa, glossa*, fr. Gk *glōssa, glōtta* tongue, language, unusual word] 1 : an explanatory note (as in the margin of a text) 2 : GLOSSARY 3 : an interlinear translation 4 : a continuous commentary accompanying a text

⁴**gloss** vb : to furnish glosses for

glos·sa·ry \'glä-sə-rē, 'glò-\ n, pl **-ries** : a collection of difficult or specialized terms with their meanings — **glos·sar·i·al** \glä-'sar-ē-əl, glò-\ adj

glos·so·la·lia \₁glä-sə-'lā-lē-ə, ₁glò-\ n [Gk *glōssa* tongue, language + *lalia* chatter] : TONGUE 6

¹**glossy** \'glä-sē, 'glò-\ adj **gloss·i·er; -est** : having a surface luster or brightness — **gloss·i·ly** \-sə-lē\ adv — **gloss·i·ness** \-sē-nəs\ n

²**glossy** n, pl **gloss·ies** : a photograph printed on smooth shiny paper

glot·tis \'glä-təs\ n, pl **glot·tis·es** or **glot·ti·des** \-tə-₁dēz\ : the slitlike opening between the vocal cords in the larynx — **glot·tal** \'glät-ᵊl\ adj

glove \'gləv\ n 1 : a covering for the hand having separate sections for each finger 2 : a padded leather covering for the hand for use in a sport

¹**glow** \'glō\ vb 1 : to shine with or as if with intense heat 2 : to have a rich warm usu. ruddy color : FLUSH, BLUSH 3 : to feel hot 4 : to show exuberance or elation ⟨∼ with pride⟩

²**glow** n 1 : brightness or warmth of color; esp : REDNESS

2 : warmth of feeling or emotion 3 : a sensation of warmth 4 : light such as is emitted from a heated substance

glow·er \'glaú-ər\ vb : to stare angrily : SCOWL — **glower** n

glow·worm \'glō-₁wərm\ n : any of various insect larvae or adults that give off light

glox·in·ia \gläk-'si-nē-ə\ n : any of a genus of Brazilian herbs related to the African violets; esp : one with showy bell-shaped or slipper-shaped flowers

gloze \'glōz\ vb **glozed; gloz·ing** : to make appear right or acceptable : GLOSS

glu·cose \'glü-₁kōs\ n 1 : a sugar known in two different forms; esp : DEXTROSE 2 : a sweet light-colored syrup made from cornstarch

glue \'glü\ n : a jellylike protein substance made from animal materials and used for sticking things together; also : any of various other strong adhesives — **glue** vb — **glu·ey** \'glü-ē\ adj

glum \'gləm\ adj **glum·mer; glum·mest** 1 : broodingly morose : SULLEN 2 : DREARY, GLOOMY syn crabbed, dour, saturnine, sulky

¹**glut** \'glət\ vb **glut·ted; glut·ting** 1 : OVERSUPPLY 2 : to fill esp. with food to satiety : SATIATE

²**glut** n : an excessive supply

glu·ten \'glüt-ᵊn\ n : a gluey protein substance that causes dough to be sticky

glu·ti·nous \'glüt-ᵊn-əs\ adj : STICKY

glut·ton \'glət-ᵊn\ n : one that eats to excess — **glut·ton·ous** \'glət-ᵊn-əs\ adj — **glut·tony** \'glət-ᵊn-ē\ n

glyc·er·in or **glyc·er·ine** \'gli-sə-rən\ n : GLYCEROL

glyc·er·ol \'gli-sə-₁ròl, -₁rōl\ n : a sweet syrupy alcohol usu. obtained from fats and used esp. as a solvent

gly·co·gen \'glī-kə-jən\ n : a white tasteless substance that is the chief storage carbohydrate of animals

gm abbr gram

GM abbr 1 general manager 2 guided missile

G–man \'jē-₁man\ n : a special agent of the Federal Bureau of Investigation

GMT abbr Greenwich mean time

gnarled \'närld\ adj 1 : KNOTTY 2 : GLOOMY, SULLEN

gnash \'nash\ vb : to grind (as teeth) together

gnat \'nat\ n : any of various small usu. biting dipteran flies

gnaw \'nò\ vb 1 : to consume, wear away, or make by persistent biting or nibbling 2 : to affect as if by gnawing — **gnaw·er** n

gneiss \'nīs\ n : a layered rock similar in composition to granite

gnome \'nōm\ n : a dwarf of folklore who lives inside the earth and guards precious ore or treasure — **gnom·ish** adj

GNP abbr gross national product

gnu \'nü\ n, pl **gnu** or **gnus** : either of two large African antelopes with an oxlike head and horns and a horselike mane and tail

gnu

¹go \'gō\ *vb* **went** \'went\; **gone** \'gȯn, 'gän\; **go·ing;**
goes \'gōz\ **1** : to move on a course : PROCEED ⟨~
slow⟩ **2** : LEAVE, DEPART **3** : to take a certain course
or follow a certain procedure ⟨reports ~ through department channels⟩ **4** : EXTEND, RUN ⟨his land ~es to
the river⟩; *also* : LEAD ⟨that door ~es to the cellar⟩ **5**
: to be habitually in a certain state ⟨~es armed after
dark⟩ **6** : to become lost, consumed, or spent; *also*
: DIE **7** : ELAPSE, PASS **8** : to pass by sale ⟨went for a
good price⟩ **9** : to become impaired or weakened **10**
: to give way under force or pressure : BREAK **11** : to
move along in a specified manner ⟨it *went* well⟩ **12** : to
be in general or on an average ⟨cheap, as yachts ~⟩
13 : to become esp. as the result of a contest (the decision *went* against him) **14** : to put or subject oneself
⟨~ to great expense⟩ **15** : RESORT ⟨*went* to court to recover damages⟩ **16** : to begin or maintain an action or
motion ⟨here ~es⟩ **17** : to function properly ⟨the
clock doesn't ~⟩ **18** : to be known ⟨~es by an alias⟩
19 : to be or act in accordance ⟨a good rule to ~ by⟩
20 : to come to be applied **21** : to pass by award, assignment, or lot **22** : to contribute to a result ⟨qualities
that ~ to make a hero⟩ **23** : to be about, intending, or
expecting something ⟨is ~ing to leave town⟩ **24** : to
arrive at a certain state or condition ⟨~ to sleep⟩ **25**
: to come to be ⟨the tire *went* flat⟩ **26** : to be capable
of being sung or played ⟨the tune ~es like this⟩ **27** : to
be suitable or becoming : HARMONIZE **28** : to be capable of passing, extending, or being contained or inserted ⟨this coat will ~ in the trunk⟩ **29** : to have a
usual or proper place or position : BELONG ⟨these
books ~ on the top shelf⟩ **30** : to be capable of being
divided ⟨3 ~es into 6 twice⟩ **31** : to have a tendency
⟨that ~es to show that he is honest⟩ **32** : to be acceptable, satisfactory, or adequate **33** : to empty the bladder or bowels **34** : to proceed along or according to
: FOLLOW **35** : TRAVERSE **36** : BET, BID ⟨willing to ~
$50⟩ **37** : to assume the function or obligation of ⟨~
bail for a friend⟩ **38** : to participate to the extent of ⟨~
halves⟩ **39** : WEIGH **40** : ENDURE, TOLERATE **41** : AF-
FORD ⟨can't ~ the price⟩ **42** : SAY — used chiefly in
oral narration of speech **43** : to engage in ⟨don't ~
telling everyone⟩ — **go at 1** : ATTACK, ATTEMPT **2**
: UNDERTAKE — **go back on 1** : ABANDON **2** : BETRAY
3 : FAIL — **go by the board** : to be discarded — **go
down the line** : to give wholehearted support — **go
for 1** : to pass for or serve as **2** : to try to secure **3**
: FAVOR — **go one better** : OUTDO, SURPASS — **go
over 1** : EXAMINE **2** : REPEAT **3** : STUDY, REVIEW —
go places : to be on the way to success — **go steady**
: to date one person exclusively — **go to bat for** : DE-
FEND, CHAMPION — **go to town 1** : to work or act efficiently **2** : to be very successful
²go *n, pl* **goes 1** : the act or manner of going **2** : the
height of fashion ⟨boots are all the ~⟩ **3** : a turn of
affairs : OCCURRENCE **4** : ENERGY, VIGOR **5** : ATTEMPT,
TRY **6** : a spell of activity — **no go** : USELESS, HOPE-
LESS — **on the go** : constantly active
³go *adj* : functioning properly

goad \'gōd\ *n* [ME *gode,* fr. OE *gād* spear, goad] **1** : a
pointed rod used to urge on an animal **2** : something
that urges **syn** stimulus, impetus, incentive, spur,
stimulant — **goad** *vb*
go–ahead \'gō-ə-₁hed\ *n* : authority to proceed
goal \'gōl\ *n* **1** : the mark set as limit to a race; *also* : an
area to be reached safely in children's games **2** : AIM,
PURPOSE **3** : an area or object toward which play is
directed to score; *also* : a successful attempt to score
goal·ie \'gō-lē\ *n* : GOALKEEPER
goal·keep·er \'gōl-₁kē-pər\ *n* : a player who defends
the goal in various games
goal·post \-₁pōst\ *n* : one of the two vertical posts with
a crossbar that constitute the goal in various games
goat \'gōt\ *n, pl* **goats** *or* **goat** : any of various hollow=
horned ruminant mammals related to the sheep that
have backward-curving horns, a short tail, and usu.
straight hair
goa·tee \gō-'tē\ *n* : a small trim pointed or tufted beard
on a man's chin
goat·herd \'gōt-₁hərd\ *n* : a person who tends goats
goat·skin \-₁skin\ *n* : the skin of a goat or a leather
made from it
¹gob \'gäb\ *n* : LUMP, MASS
²gob *n* : SAILOR
gob·bet \'gä-bət\ *n* : LUMP, MASS
¹gob·ble \'gä-bəl\ *vb* **gob·bled; gob·bling 1** : to swallow
or eat greedily **2** : to take eagerly : GRAB
²gobble *vb* **gob·bled; gob·bling** : to make the natural
guttural noise of a male turkey
gob·ble·dy·gook *also* **gob·ble·de·gook** \'gä-bəl-dē-
₁gük, -₁gük\ *n* : generally unintelligible jargon
gob·bler \'gä-blər\ *n* : a male turkey
go–be·tween \'gō-bə-₁twēn\ *n* : an intermediate agent
: BROKER
gob·let \'gä-blət\ *n* : a drinking glass with a foot and
stem
gob·lin \'gä-blən\ *n* : an ugly or grotesque sprite that is
mischievous and sometimes evil and malicious
god \'gäd, 'gȯd\ *n* **1** *cap* : the supreme reality; *esp* : the
Being worshiped as the creator and ruler of the uni-
verse **2** : a being or object believed to have supernatural attributes and powers and to require worship **3**
: a person or thing of supreme value
god·child \'gäd-₁chīld, 'gȯd-\ *n* : a person for whom
another person stands as sponsor at baptism
god·daugh·ter \-₁dȯ-tər\ *n* : a female godchild
god·dess \'gä-dəs, 'gȯ-\ *n* **1** : a female god **2** : a woman
whose charm or beauty arouses adoration
god·fa·ther \'gäd-₁fä-thər, 'gȯd-\ *n* **1** : a man who
sponsors a person at baptism **2** : the leader of an organized crime syndicate
god·head \-₁hed\ *n* **1** : divine nature or essence **2** *cap*
: GOD 1; *also* : the nature of God esp. as existing in
three persons
god·hood \-₁hud\ *n* : DIVINITY
god·less \-ləs\ *adj* : not acknowledging a deity or divine
law — **god·less·ness** *n*
god·like \-₁līk\ *adj* : resembling or having the qualities
of God or a god
god·ly \-lē\ *adj* **god·li·er; -est 1** : DIVINE **2** : PIOUS, DE-
VOUT — **god·li·ness** *n*
god·moth·er \-₁mə-thər\ *n* : a woman who sponsors a
person at baptism
god·par·ent \-₁par-ənt\ *n* : a sponsor at baptism
god·send \-₁send\ *n* : a desirable or needed thing or
event that comes unexpectedly
god·son \-₁sən\ *n* : a male godchild
God·speed \-'spēd\ *n* : a prosperous journey : SUCCESS
(bade him ~)
go·fer \'gō-fər\ *n* [alter. of *go for*] : an employee whose
duties include running errands
go–get·ter \'gō-₁ge-tər\ *n* : an aggressively enterprising person — **go–get·ting** *adj or n*
gog·gle \'gä-gəl\ *vb* **gog·gled; gog·gling** : to stare with
wide or protuberant eyes

gog·gles \'gä-gəlz\ *n pl* : protective glasses set in a flexible frame that fits snugly against the face

go–go \'gō-ˌgō\ *adj* **1** : related to, being, or employed to entertain in a disco ⟨~ dancers⟩ **2** : aggressively enterprising and energetic

go·ings–on \ˌgō-iŋ-ˈzȯn, -ˈzän\ *n pl* : ACTIONS, EVENTS

goi·ter \'gȯi-tər\ *n* : an abnormally enlarged thyroid gland visible as a swelling at the base of the neck — **goi·trous** \-trəs, -tə-rəs\ *adj*

goi·tre *chiefly Brit var of* GOITER

gold \'gōld\ *n* **1** : a malleable yellow metallic chemical element used esp. for coins and jewelry — see ELEMENT table **2** : gold coins; *also* : MONEY **3** : a yellow color

gold·brick \'gōld-ˌbrik\ *n* : a person who shirks assigned work — **goldbrick** *vb*

gold coast *n, often cap G&C* : an exclusive residential district

gold digger *n* : a person who uses charm to extract money or gifts from others

gold·en \'gōl-dən\ *adj* **1** : made of or relating to gold **2** : having the color of gold; *also* : BLOND **3** : SHINING, LUSTROUS **4** : SUPERB **5** : FLOURISHING, PROSPEROUS **6** : radiantly youthful and vigorous **7** : FAVORABLE, ADVANTAGEOUS ⟨a ~ opportunity⟩ **8** : MELLOW, RESONANT

gold·en–ag·er \'gōl-dən-ˈā-jər\ *n* : an elderly and often retired person usu. engaging in club activities

golden hamster *n* : a small tawny hamster often kept as a pet

gold·en·rod \'gōl-dən-ˌräd\ *n* : any of numerous plants related to the daisies but having tall slender stalks with many tiny usu. yellow flower heads

gold·finch \-ˌfinch\ *n* **1** : a small largely red, black, and yellow Old World finch often kept in a cage **2** : any of three small American finches of which the males usu. become bright yellow and black in summer

gold·fish \-ˌfish\ *n* : a small usu. yellow or golden carp often kept as an aquarium or pond fish

gold·smith \-ˌsmith\ *n* : a person who makes or deals in articles of gold

golf \'gälf, 'gȯlf\ *n* : a game played with a small ball and various clubs on a course having 9 or 18 holes — **golf** *vb* — **golf·er** *n*

-gon \ˌgän\ *n comb form* : figure having (so many) angles ⟨hexa*gon*⟩

go·nad \'gō-ˌnad\ *n* : a sperm- or egg-producing gland : OVARY, TESTIS — **go·nad·al** \gō-ˈnad-ᵊl\ *adj*

go·nad·o·trop·ic \gō-ˌna-də-ˈträ-pik\ *also* **go·nad·o·tro·phic** \-ˈtrō-fik,-ˈträf-ik\ *adj* : acting on or stimulating the gonads ⟨~ hormones⟩

go·nad·o·tro·pin \-ˈtrō-pən\ *also* **go·nad·o·tro·phin** \-fən\ *n* : a gonadotropic hormone

gon·do·la \'gän-də-lə *(usual for 1)*, gän-ˈdō-\ *n* **1** : a long narrow boat used on the canals of Venice **2** : a railroad car used for hauling loose freight (as coal) **3** : an enclosure beneath an airship or balloon **4** : an enclosed car suspended from a cable and used esp. for transporting skiers

gondola 1

gon·do·lier \ˌgän-də-ˈlir\ *n* : a person who propels a gondola

¹gone \'gȯn\ *past part of* GO

²gone *adj* **1** : DEAD **2** : LOST, RUINED **3** : SINKING, WEAK **4** : INVOLVED, ABSORBED **5** : INFATUATED **6** : PREGNANT **7** : PAST

gon·er \'gȯ-nər\ *n* : one whose case is hopeless

gong \'gäŋ, 'gȯŋ\ *n* : a metallic disk that produces a resounding tone when struck

gono·coc·cus \ˌgä-nə-ˈkä-kəs\ *n, pl* **-coc·ci** \-ˈkäk-ˌsī, -(ˌ)sē, -ˈkä-ˌkī, -(ˌ)kē\ : a pus-producing bacterium causing gonorrhea — **gono·coc·cal** \-ˈkä-kəl\ *adj*

gon·or·rhea \ˌgä-nə-ˈrē-ə\ *n* : a contagious sexually transmitted inflammation of the genital tract caused by a bacterium — **gon·or·rhe·al** \-ˈrē-əl\ *adj*

goo \'gü\ *n* **1** : a viscid or sticky substance **2** : sentimental tripe — **goo·ey** \-ē\ *adj*

goo·ber \'gü-bər, 'gü-\ *n, Southern & Midland* : PEANUT

¹good \'gu̇d\ *adj* **bet·ter** \'be-tər\; **best** \'best\ **1** : of a favorable character or tendency **2** : BOUNTIFUL, FERTILE **3** : COMELY, ATTRACTIVE **4** : SUITABLE, FIT **5** : SOUND, WHOLE **6** : AGREEABLE, PLEASANT **7** : SALUTARY, WHOLESOME **8** : CONSIDERABLE, AMPLE **9** : FULL **10** : WELL-FOUNDED **11** : TRUE ⟨holds ~ for everybody⟩ **12** : legally valid or effectual **13** : ADEQUATE, SATISFACTORY **14** : conforming to a standard **15** : DISCRIMINATING **16** : COMMENDABLE, VIRTUOUS **17** : KIND **18** : UPPER-CLASS **19** : COMPETENT **20** : LOYAL, CLOSE — **good–heart·ed** \-ˈhär-təd\ *adj* — **good·ish** *adj* — **good–look·ing** \-ˈlu̇-kiŋ\ *adj* — **good–tempered** \-ˈtem-pərd\ *adj*

²good *n* **1** : something good **2** : GOODNESS **3** : BENEFIT, WELFARE ⟨for the ~ of mankind⟩ **4** : something that has economic utility **5** *pl* : personal property **6** *pl* : CLOTH **7** *pl* : WARES, MERCHANDISE **8** : good persons ⟨the ~ die young⟩ **9** *pl* : proof of wrongdoing — **for good** : FOREVER, PERMANENTLY — **to the good** : in a position of net gain or profit ⟨$10 *to the good*⟩

³good *adv* : WELL

good–bye *or* **good–by** \gu̇d-ˈbī, gə-\ *n* : a concluding remark at parting

good–for–noth·ing \'gu̇d-fər-ˌnə-thiŋ\ *n* : an idle worthless person

Good Friday *n* : the Friday before Easter observed as the anniversary of the crucifixion of Christ

good·ly \'gu̇d-lē\ *adj* **good·li·er; -est** **1** : of pleasing appearance **2** : LARGE, CONSIDERABLE

good·man \'gu̇d-mən\ *n, archaic* : MR.

good–na·tured \'gu̇d-ˈnā-chərd\ *adj* : of a cheerful disposition — **good–na·tured·ly** \-chərd-lē\ *adv*

good·ness \-nəs\ *n* : EXCELLENCE, VIRTUE

good·wife \-ˌwīf\ *n, archaic* : MRS.

good·will \-ˈwil\ *n* **1** : BENEVOLENCE **2** : the value of the trade a business has built up over time **3** : cheerful consent **4** : willing effort

goody \'gu̇-dē\ *n, pl* **good·ies** : something that is good esp. to eat

goody–goody \ˌgu̇-dē-ˈgu̇-dē\ *adj* : affectedly good — **goody–goody** *n*

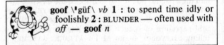

goof \'güf\ *vb* **1** : to spend time idly or foolishly **2** : BLUNDER — often used with *off* — **goof** *n*

---

goof·ball \'güf-ˌbȯl\ *n* **1** *slang* : a barbiturate sleeping pill **2** : a goofy person

go off *vb* **1** : EXPLODE **2** : to follow a course ⟨the party *went off* well⟩

goof–off \'gü-ˌfȯf\ *n* : one who evades work or responsibility

goofy \'gü-fē\ *adj* **goof·i·er; -est** : CRAZY, SILLY — **goof·i·ness** \-fē-nəs\ *n*

goon \'gün\ *n* : a man hired to terrorize or kill opponents

go on *vb* **1** : to continue in a course of action **2** : to take place : HAPPEN

goose \'güs\ *n, pl* **geese** \'gēs\ **1** : any of numerous long-necked web-footed birds related to the swans and ducks; *esp* : a female goose as distinguished from a

gander **2** : a foolish person **3** *pl* **goos·es** : a tailor's smoothing iron

goose·ber·ry \\'güs-₁ber-ē, 'güz-, -bə-rē\\ *n* : the acid berry of any of several shrubs related to the currant and used esp. in jams and pies

goose bumps *n pl* : roughening of the skin caused usu. by cold, fear, or a sudden feeling of excitement

goose·flesh \\-₁flesh\\ *n* : GOOSE BUMPS

goose pimples *n pl* : GOOSE BUMPS

go out *vb* **1** : to become extinguished **2** : to become a candidate ⟨*went out* for the football team⟩

go over *vb* : SUCCEED

GOP *abbr* Grand Old Party (Republican)

go·pher \\'gō-fər\\ *n* **1** : a burrowing American land tortoise **2** : any of a family of No. American burrowing rodents with large cheek pouches opening beside the mouth **3** : any of several small ground squirrels of the prairie region of No. America

¹gore \\'gōr\\ *n* : BLOOD

²gore *n* : a tapering or triangular piece (as of cloth in a skirt)

³gore *vb* **gored; gor·ing** : to pierce or wound with something pointed

¹gorge \\'gòrj\\ *n* **1** : THROAT **2** : a narrow ravine **3** : a mass of matter that chokes up a passage

²gorge *vb* **gorged; gorg·ing** : to eat greedily : stuff to capacity : GLUT

gor·geous \\'gòr-jəs\\ *adj* : resplendently beautiful

Gor·gon·zo·la \\₁gòr-gən-'zō-lə\\ *n* : a blue cheese of Italian origin

go·ril·la \\gə-'ri-lə\\ *n* [NL, fr. Gk *Gorillai*, a tribe of hairy women in an account of a voyage around Africa] : an African anthropoid ape related to but much larger than the chimpanzee

gor·man·dise *chiefly Brit var of* GORMANDIZE

gor·man·dize \\'gòr-mən-₁dīz\\ *vb* **-dized; -diz·ing** : to eat ravenously — **gor·man·diz·er** *n*

gorp \\'gòrp\\ *n* : a snack consisting of high-calorie food (as raisins and nuts)

gorse \\'gòrs\\ *n* : a spiny yellow-flowered Old World evergreen shrub of the legume family

gory \\'gōr-ē\\ *adj* **gor·i·er; -est** **1** : BLOODSTAINED **2** : HORRIBLE, SENSATIONAL

gos·hawk \\'gäs-₁hòk\\ *n* : any of several long-tailed hawks with short rounded wings

gos·ling \\'gäz-liŋ, 'gòz-\\ *n* : a young goose

¹gos·pel \\'gäs-pəl\\ *n* [ME, fr. OE *gōdspel*, fr. *gōd* good + *spell* message, news] **1** : the teachings of Christ and the apostles **2** *cap* : any of the first four books of the New Testament **3** : something accepted as infallible truth

²gospel *adj* **1** : of, relating to, or emphasizing the gospel **2** : relating to or being American religious songs associated with evangelism

gos·sa·mer \\'gä-sə-mər\\ *n* [ME *gossomer*, fr. *gos* goose + *somer* summer] **1** : a film of cobwebs floating in the air **2** : something light, delicate, or tenuous

¹gos·sip \\'gä-səp\\ *n* **1** : a person who habitually reveals personal or sensational facts **2** : rumor or report of an

intimate nature **3** : an informal conversation — **gos·sipy** *adj*

²gossip *vb* : to spread gossip

got *past and past part of* GET

Goth \\'gäth\\ *n* : a member of a Germanic people that early in the Christian era overran the Roman Empire

¹Goth·ic \\'gä-thik\\ *adj* **1** : of or relating to the Goths **2** : of or relating to a style of architecture prevalent in western Europe from the middle 12th to the early 16th century

²Gothic *n* **1** : the Germanic language of the Goths **2** : the Gothic architectural style or decoration

gotten *past part of* GET

Gou·da \\'gü-də\\ *n* : a mild Dutch milk cheese shaped in balls

¹gouge \\'gaůj\\ *n* **1** : a rounded troughlike chisel **2** : a hole or groove made with or as if with a gouge

²gouge *vb* **gouged; goug·ing** **1** : to cut holes or grooves in with or as if with a gouge **2** : DEFRAUD, CHEAT

gou·lash \\'gü-₁läsh, -₁lash\\ *n* [Hungarian *gulyás*] : a stew made with meat, assorted vegetables, and paprika

go under *vb* : to be overwhelmed, defeated, or destroyed : FAIL

gourd \\'gōrd, 'gůrd\\ *n* **1** : any of a family of tendril-bearing vines including the cucumber, squash, and melon **2** : the fruit of a gourd; *esp* : any of various inedible hard-shelled fruits used esp. for ornament or implements

gourde \\'gůrd\\ *n* — see MONEY table

gour·mand \\'gůr-₁mänd\\ *n* **1** : one who is excessively fond of eating and drinking **2** : GOURMET

gour·met \\'gůr-₁mā, gůr-'mā\\ *n* [F, fr. MF, alter. of *gromet* boy servant, vintner's assistant] : a connoisseur of food and drink

gout \\'gaůt\\ *n* : a metabolic disease marked by painful inflammation and swelling of the joints — **gouty** *adj*

gov *abbr* **1** government **2** governor

gov·ern \\'gə-vərn\\ *vb* **1** : to control and direct the making and administration of policy in : RULE **2** : CONTROL, DIRECT, INFLUENCE **3** : DETERMINE, REGULATE **4** : RESTRAIN — **gov·er·nance** \\-vər-nəns\\ *n*

gov·ern·ess \\'gə-vər-nəs\\ *n* : a woman who teaches and trains a child esp. in a private home

gov·ern·ment \\'gə-vərn-mənt\\ *n* **1** : authoritative direction or control : RULE **2** : the making of policy **3** : the organization or agency through which a political unit exercises authority **4** : the complex of institutions, laws, and customs through which a political unit is governed **5** : the governing body — **gov·ern·men·tal** \\₁gə-vərn-'ment-əl\\ *adj*

gov·er·nor \\'gə-vər-nər\\ *n* **1** : one that governs; *esp* : a ruler, chief executive, or head of a political unit (as a state) **2** : an attachment to a machine for automatic control of speed — **gov·er·nor·ship** *n*

govt *abbr* government

gown \\'gaůn\\ *n* **1** : a loose flowing outer garment **2** : an official robe worn esp. by a judge, clergyman, or teacher **3** : a woman's dress ⟨evening ∼s⟩ **4** : a loose robe — **gown** *vb*

gp *abbr* group
GP *abbr* general practitioner
GPO *abbr* 1 general post office 2 Government Printing Office
GQ *abbr* general quarters
gr *abbr* 1 grade 2 grain 3 gram 4 gravity 5 gross
grab \'grab\ *vb* **grabbed; grab·bing** : to take hastily : SNATCH — **grab** *n*
¹**grace** \'grās\ *n* **1** : unmerited help given to people by God (as in overcoming temptation) **2** : freedom from sin through divine grace **3** : a virtue coming from God **4** — used as a title for a duke, a duchess, or an archbishop **5** : a short prayer at a meal **6** : a temporary respite (as from the payment of a debt) **7** : APPROVAL, ACCEPTANCE ⟨in his good ~s⟩ **8** : CHARM **9** : ATTRACTIVENESS, BEAUTY **10** : fitness or proportion of line or expression **11** : ease of movement **12** : a musical trill or ornament — **grace·ful** \-fəl\ *adj* — **grace·ful·ly** *adv* — **grace·ful·ness** *n* — **grace·less** *adj*
²**grace** *vb* **graced; grac·ing** **1** : HONOR **2** : ADORN, EMBELLISH
gra·cious \'grā-shəs\ *adj* **1** : marked by kindness and courtesy **2** : GRACEFUL **3** : characterized by charm and good taste **4** : MERCIFUL — **gra·cious·ly** *adv* — **gra·cious·ness** *n*
grack·le \'gra-kəl\ *n* : any of several American blackbirds with glossy iridescent plumage
grad *abbr* graduate; graduated
gra·da·tion \grā-'dā-shən, grə-\ *n* **1** : a series forming successive stages **2** : a step, degree, or stage in a series **3** : an advance by regular degrees **4** : the act or process of grading
¹**grade** \'grād\ *vb* **grad·ed; grad·ing** **1** : to arrange in grades : SORT **2** : to make level or evenly sloping ⟨~ a highway⟩ **3** : to give a grade to ⟨~ a pupil in history⟩ **4** : to assign to a grade
²**grade** *n* **1** : a degree or stage in a series, order, or ranking **2** : a position in a scale of rank, quality, or order **3** : a class of persons or things of the same rank or quality **4** : a division of the school course representing one year's work; *also* : the pupils in such a division **5** *pl* : the elementary school system **6** : a mark or rating esp. of accomplishment in school **7** : the degree of slope (as of a road); *also* : SLOPE
grad·er \'grā-dər\ *n* : a machine for leveling earth
grade school *n* : ELEMENTARY SCHOOL
gra·di·ent \'grā-dē-ənt\ *n* : SLOPE, GRADE
grad·u·al \'gra-jə-wəl\ *adj* : proceeding or changing by steps or degrees — **grad·u·al·ly** *adv*
grad·u·al·ism \-wə-ˌli-zəm\ *n* : the policy of approaching a desired end gradually
¹**grad·u·ate** \'gra-jə-wət\ *n* **1** : a holder of an academic degree or diploma **2** : a graduated container for measuring contents
²**graduate** *adj* **1** : holding an academic degree or diploma **2** : of or relating to studies beyond the first or bachelor's degree ⟨~ school⟩
³**grad·u·ate** \'gra-jə-ˌwāt\ *vb* **-at·ed; -at·ing** **1** : to grant or receive an academic degree or diploma **2** : to divide into grades, classes, or intervals **3** : to admit to a particular standing or grade
grad·u·a·tion \ˌgra-jə-'wā-shən\ *n* **1** : a mark that graduates something **2** : an act or process of graduating **3** : COMMENCEMENT 2
graf·fi·to \gra-'fē-tō, grə-\ *n*, *pl* **-ti** \-(ˌ)tē\ : an inscription or drawing made on a public surface (as a wall)
¹**graft** \'graft\ *n* **1** : a grafted plant; *also* : the point of union in this **2** : material (as skin) used in grafting **3** : the getting of money or advantage dishonestly; *also* : the money or advantage so gained
²**graft** *vb* **1** : to insert a shoot from one plant into another so that they grow and grow; *also* : to join one thing to another as in plant grafting ⟨~ skin over a burn⟩ **2** : to get (as money) dishonestly — **graft·er** *n*
gra·ham cracker \'grā-əm-, 'gram-\ *n* : a slightly sweet cracker made chiefly of whole wheat flour

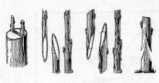

graft 1

Grail \'grāl\ *n* : the cup or platter used according to medieval legend by Christ at the Last Supper and thereafter the object of knightly quests
grain \'grān\ *n* **1** : a seed or fruit of a cereal grass **2** : seeds or fruits of various food plants and esp. cereal grasses; *also* : a plant (as wheat) producing grain **3** : a small hard particle **4** : a unit of weight based on the weight of a grain of wheat — see WEIGHT table **5** : TEXTURE; *also* : the arrangement of fibers in wood **6** : natural disposition — **grained** \'grānd\ *adj*
grain alcohol *n* : ALCOHOL 1
grainy \'grā-nē\ *adj* **grain·i·er; -est** **1** : resembling or having some characteristic of grain : not smooth or fine **2** *of a photograph* : appearing to be composed of grain-like particles
¹**gram** \'gram\ *n* [F *gramme*, fr. LL *gramma*, a small weight, fr. Gk *gramma* letter, writing, a small weight, fr. *graphein* to write] : a metric unit of mass and weight equal to ¹⁄₁₀₀₀ kilogram — see METRIC SYSTEM table
²**gram** *abbr* grammar; grammatical
-gram \ˌgram\ *n comb form* : drawing : writing : record ⟨tele*gram*⟩
gram·mar \'gra-mər\ *n* **1** : the study of the classes of words, their inflections, and their functions and relations in the sentence **2** : a study of what is to be preferred and what avoided in inflection and syntax **3** : speech or writing evaluated according to its conformity to grammatical rules — **gram·mar·i·an** \grə-'mer-ē-ən, -'mar-\ *n* — **gram·mat·i·cal** \-'ma-ti-kəl\ *adj* — **gram·mat·i·cal·ly** \-k(ə-)lē\ *adv*
grammar school *n* **1** : a secondary school emphasizing Latin and Greek in preparation for college; *also* : a British college preparatory school **2** : a school intermediate between the primary grades and high school **3** : ELEMENTARY SCHOOL
gramme \'gram\ *chiefly Brit var of* GRAM
gram·o·phone \'gra-mə-ˌfōn\ *n* : PHONOGRAPH
gra·na·ry \'grā-nə-rē, 'gra-\ *n*, *pl* **-ries** **1** : a storehouse for grain **2** : a region producing grain in abundance

¹**grand** \'grand\ *adj* **1** : higher in rank or importance : FOREMOST, CHIEF **2** : great in size **3** : INCLUSIVE, COMPLETE ⟨a ~ total⟩ **4** : MAGNIFICENT, SPLENDID **5** : showing wealth or high social standing **6** : IMPRESSIVE, STATELY **7** : very good : FINE — **grand·ly** *adv* — **grand·ness** *n*

²**grand** *n*, *slang* : a thousand dollars
gran·dam \'gran-ˌdam, -dəm\ *or* **gran·dame** \-ˌdām, -dəm\ *n* : an old woman
grand·child \'grand-ˌchīld\ *n* : a child of one's son or daughter
grand·daugh·ter \'gran-ˌdȯ-tər\ *n* : a daughter of one's son or daughter
grande dame \'grän-'däm\ *n*, *pl* **grandes dames** : a usu. elderly woman of great prestige or ability
gran·dee \gran-'dē\ *n* : a high-ranking Spanish or Portuguese nobleman
gran·deur \'gran-jər\ *n* **1** : the quality or state of being grand : MAGNIFICENCE **2** : something that is grand
grand·fa·ther \'grand-ˌfä-thər\ *n* : the father of one's father or mother; *also* : ANCESTOR

grandfather clock *n* : a tall clock that stands on the floor

gran·dil·o·quence \gran-'di-lə-kwəns\ *n* : pompous eloquence — **gran·dil·o·quent** \-kwənt\ *adj*

gran·di·ose \'gran-dē-ˌōs, ˌgran-dē-'ōs\ *adj* 1 : IMPRESSIVE, IMPOSING; *also* : affectedly splendid — **gran·di·ose·ly** *adv* — **gran·di·os·i·ty** \ˌgran-dē-'ä-sə-tē\ *n*

grand jury *n* : a jury that examines accusations of crime against persons and makes formal charges on which the persons are later tried

grand mal \'grän-ˌmäl, 'grand-ˌmal\ *n* [F, lit., great illness] : severe epilepsy

grand·moth·er \'grand-ˌmə-thər\ *n* : the mother of one's father or mother; *also* : a female ancestor

grand·par·ent \-ˌpar-ənt\ *n* : a parent of one's father or mother

grand piano *n* : a piano with horizontal frame and strings

grand prix \'grän-'prē\ *n, pl* **grand prix** *same or* -'prēz\ *often cap G&P* : a long-distance auto race over a road course

grand slam *n* 1 : a total victory or success 2 : a home run hit with three runners on base

grand·son \'grand-ˌsən\ *n* : a son of one's son or daughter

grand·stand \-ˌstand\ *n* : a usu. roofed stand for spectators at a racecourse or stadium

grange \'grānj\ *n* 1 : a farm or farmhouse with its various buildings 2 *cap* : one of the lodges of a national association originally made up of farmers; *also* : the association itself — **grang·er** \'grān-jər\ *n*

gran·ite \'gra-nət\ *n* : a hard granular igneous rock used esp. for building — **gra·nit·ic** \gra-'ni-tik\ *adj*

gran·ite·ware \'gra-nət-ˌwar\ *n* : ironware with mottled enamel

gra·no·la \grə-'nō-lə\ *n* : a cereal made of rolled oats and usu. raisins and nuts

¹**grant** \'grant\ *vb* 1 : to consent to : ALLOW, PERMIT 2 : GIVE, BESTOW 3 : to admit as true — **grant·er** *n* — **grant·or** \'gran-tər, -ˌtȯr\ *n*

²**grant** *n* 1 : the act of granting 2 : something granted; *esp* : a gift for a particular purpose ⟨a ∼ for study abroad⟩ 3 : a transfer of property by deed or writing; *also* : the instrument by which such a transfer is made 4 : the property transferred by grant — **grant·ee** \gran-'tē\ *n*

gran·u·lar \'gra-nyə-lər\ *adj* : consisting of or appearing to consist of granules — **gran·u·lar·i·ty** \ˌgra-nyə-'lar-ə-tē\ *n*

gran·u·late \'gra-nyə-ˌlāt\ *vb* **-lat·ed; -lat·ing** : to form into grains or crystals — **gran·u·la·tion** \ˌgra-nyə-'lā-shən\ *n*

gran·ule \'gra-nyül\ *n* : a small grain or particle

grape \'grāp\ *n* [ME, fr. *crape, grape* hook, grape stalk, bunch of grapes, grape] 1 : a smooth-skinned juicy edible greenish white, deep red, or purple berry that is the chief source of wine 2 : any of numerous woody vines widely grown for their bunches of grapes

grape·fruit \'grāp-ˌfrüt\ *n* 1 *pl* **grapefruit** *or* **grape-**fruits : a large edible yellow-skinned citrus fruit 2 : a tree bearing grapefruit

grape hyacinth *n* : any of several small bulbous spring-flowering herbs with clusters of usu. blue flowers that are related to the lilies

grape·shot \'grāp-ˌshät\ *n* : a cluster of small iron balls formerly fired at people from short range by a cannon

grape·vine \-ˌvīn\ *n* 1 : GRAPE 2 2 : RUMOR; *also* : an informal means of circulating information or gossip

graph \'graf\ *n* : a diagram that usu. by means of dots and lines shows change in one variable factor in comparison with one or more other factors — **graph** *vb*

-graph \ˌgraf\ *n comb form* 1 : something written ⟨auto*graph*⟩ 2 : instrument for making or transmitting records ⟨seismo*graph*⟩

¹**graph·ic** \'gra-fik\ *also* **graph·i·cal** \-fi-kəl\ *adj* 1 : being written, drawn, or engraved 2 : vividly described 3 : of or relating to the arts (**graphic arts**) of representation, decoration, and printing on flat surfaces — **graph·i·cal·ly** \-fi-k(ə-)lē\ *adv*

²**graphic** *n* 1 : a picture, map, or graph used for illustration 2 *pl* : a display (as of pictures or graphs) generated by a computer on a screen, printer, or plotter

graph·ics tablet \-fiks-\ *n* : a computer input device for entering pictorial information by drawing or tracing

graph·ite \'gra-ˌfīt\ *n* [G *Graphit*, fr. Gk *graphein* to write] : a soft black form of carbon used esp. for lead pencils and lubricants

grap·nel \'grap-nəl\ *n* : a small anchor with usu. four claws used esp. in dragging or grappling operations

¹**grap·ple** \'gra-pəl\ *n* [MF *grappelle*, dim. of *grape* hook] : the act of grappling

²**grapple** *vb* **grap·pled; grap·pling** 1 : to seize or hold with or as if with a hooked implement 2 : to come to grips with : WRESTLE

¹**grasp** \'grasp\ *vb* 1 : to make the motion of seizing 2 : to take or seize firmly 3 : to enclose and hold with the fingers or arms 4 : COMPREHEND

²**grasp** *n* 1 : HANDLE 2 : EMBRACE 3 : HOLD, CONTROL 4 : the reach of the arms 5 : the power of seizing and holding 6 : COMPREHENSION

grasp·ing *adj* : GREEDY, AVARICIOUS

grass \'gras\ *n* 1 : herbage for grazing animals 2 : any of a large family of plants (as wheat, bamboo, or sugarcane) with jointed stems and narrow leaves 3 : grass-covered land 4 : MARIJUANA — **grassy** *adj*

grass·hop·per \-ˌhä-pər\ *n* : any of numerous leaping plant-eating insects

grass·land \-ˌland\ *n* : land covered naturally or under cultivation with grasses and low-growing herbs

grass roots *n pl* : society at the local level as distinguished from the centers of political leadership

¹**grate** \'grāt\ *vb* **grat·ed; grat·ing** 1 : to pulverize by rubbing against something rough 2 : to grind or rub against with a rasping noise 3 : IRRITATE — **grat·er** *n* — **grat·ing·ly** *adv*

²**grate** *n* 1 : GRATING 2 : a frame of iron bars for holding fuel while it burns

grate·ful \'grāt-fəl\ *adj* 1 : THANKFUL, APPRECIATIVE;

also : expressing gratitude **2** : PLEASING — **grate-ful•ly** *adv* — **grate•ful•ness** *n*

grat•i•fy \'gra-tə-ˌfī\ *vb* **-fied; -fy•ing** : to afford pleasure to — **grat•i•fi•ca•tion** \ˌgra-tə-fə-'kā-shən\ *n*

grat•ing \'grā-tiŋ\ *n* : a framework with parallel bars or crossbars

gra•tis \'gra-təs, 'grā-\ *adv or adj* : without charge or recompense : FREE

grat•i•tude \'gra-tə-ˌtüd, -ˌtyüd\ *n* : THANKFULNESS

gra•tu•itous \grə-'tü-ə-təs, -'tyü-\ *adj* **1** : done or provided without recompense : FREE **2** : UNWARRANTED

gra•tu•ity \-ə-tē\ *n, pl* **-ities** : ¹⁰TIP

gra•va•men \grə-'vā-mən\ *n, pl* **-va•mens** *or* **-vam•i•na** \-'va-mə-nə\ [LL, burden] : the basic or significant part of a grievance or complaint

¹**grave** \'grāv\ *vb* **graved; grav•en** \'grā-vən\ *or* **graved; grav•ing** : SCULPTURE, ENGRAVE

²**grave** *n* : an excavation in the earth as a place of burial; *also* : TOMB

³**grave** \'grāv; 5 *also* 'gräv\ *adj* **1** : IMPORTANT **2** : threatening great harm or danger **3** : DIGNIFIED, SOLEMN **4** : drab in color : SOMBER **5** : of, marked by, or being an accent mark having the form ` — **grave•ly** *adv* — **grave•ness** *n*

grav•el \'gra-vəl\ *n* : pebbles and small pieces of rock larger than grains of sand — **grav•el•ly** *adj*

grave•stone \'grāv-ˌstōn\ *n* : a burial monument

grave•yard \-ˌyärd\ *n* : CEMETERY

grav•id \'gra-vəd\ *adj* [L *gravidus*, fr. *gravis* heavy] : PREGNANT

gra•vim•e•ter \gra-'vi-mə-tər, 'gra-və-ˌmē-\ *n* : a device for measuring variations in a gravitational field

grav•i•tate \'gra-və-ˌtāt\ *vb* **-tat•ed; -tat•ing** : to move or tend to move toward something

grav•i•ta•tion \ˌgra-və-'tā-shən\ *n* **1** : a natural force of attraction that tends to draw bodies together and that occurs because of the mass of the bodies **2** : the action or process of gravitating — **grav•i•ta•tion•al** \-shə-nəl\ *adj* — **grav•i•ta•tion•al•ly** *adv*

grav•i•ty \'gra-və-tē\ *n, pl* **-ties 1** : IMPORTANCE; *esp* : SERIOUSNESS **2** : ²MASS 5 **3** : the gravitational attraction of the mass of a celestial object (as earth) for bodies close to it; *also* : GRAVITATION 1

gra•vure \grə-'vyu̇r\ *n* [F] : PHOTOGRAVURE

gra•vy \'grā-vē\ *n, pl* **gravies 1** : a sauce made from the thickened and seasoned juices of cooked meat **2** : unearned or illicit gain : GRAFT

¹**gray** \'grā\ *adj* **1** : of the color gray; *also* : dull in color **2** : having gray hair **3** : CHEERLESS, DISMAL **4** : intermediate in position or character — **gray•ish** *adj* — **gray•ness** *n*

²**gray** *n* **1** : something of a gray color **2** : a neutral color ranging between black and white

³**gray** *vb* : to make or become gray

gray•beard \'grā-ˌbird\ *n* : an old man

gray•ling \'grā-liŋ\ *n, pl* **grayling** *also* **graylings** : any of several slender freshwater food and sport fishes related to the trouts

gray matter *n* **1** : the grayish part of nervous tissue consisting mostly of nerve cell bodies **2** : INTELLIGENCE

gray wolf *n* : a large wolf of northern No. America and Asia that is usu. gray

¹**graze** \'grāz\ *vb* **grazed; graz•ing 1** : to feed on herbage or pasture **2** : to feed (livestock) on grass or pasture — **graz•er** *n*

²**graze** *vb* **grazed; graz•ing 1** : to touch lightly in passing **2** : SCRATCH, ABRADE

¹**grease** \'grēs\ *n* **1** : rendered animal fat **2** : oily material **3** : a thick lubricant — **greasy** \'grē-sē, -zē\ *adj*

²**grease** \'grēs, 'grēz\ *vb* **greased; greas•ing** : to smear or lubricate with grease

grease•paint \'grēs-ˌpānt\ *n* : theater makeup

great \'grāt\ *adj* **1** : large in size : BIG **2** : ELABORATE, AMPLE **3** : large in number : NUMEROUS **4** : being beyond the average : MIGHTY, INTENSE ⟨a ~ weight⟩ ⟨in

~ pain⟩ **5** : EMINENT, GRAND **6** : long continued ⟨a ~ while⟩ **7** : MAIN, PRINCIPAL **8** : more distant in a family relationship by one generation ⟨a *great*-grandfather⟩ **9** : markedly superior in character, quality, or skill ⟨~ at bridge⟩ **10** : EXCELLENT, FINE ⟨had a ~ time⟩ — **great•ly** *adv* — **great•ness** *n*

great circle *n* : a circle on the surface of a sphere that has the same center as the sphere; *esp* : one on the surface of the earth an arc of which is the shortest travel distance between two points

great•coat \'grāt-ˌkōt\ *n* : a heavy overcoat

Great Dane *n* : any of a breed of tall massive powerful smooth-coated dogs

great•heart•ed \'grāt-'här-təd\ *adj* **1** : COURAGEOUS **2** : MAGNANIMOUS

great power *n, often cap G&P* : one of the nations that figure most decisively in international affairs

great white shark *n* : a large and dangerous shark of warm seas that is light colored below and darker above becoming dirty white in older and larger specimens

grebe \'grēb\ *n* : any of a family of lobe-toed diving birds related to the loons

Gre•cian \'grē-shən\ *adj* : GREEK

greed \'grēd\ *n* : acquisitive or selfish desire beyond reason — **greed•i•ly** \'grē-də-lē\ *adv* — **greed•i•ness** \-dē-nəs\ *n* — **greedy** \'grē-dē\ *adj*

¹**Greek** \'grēk\ *n* **1** : a native or inhabitant of Greece **2** : the ancient or modern language of Greece

²**Greek** *adj* **1** : of, relating to, or characteristic of Greece, the Greeks, or Greek **2** : ORTHODOX 3

¹**green** \'grēn\ *adj* **1** : of the color green **2** : covered with verdure; *also* : consisting of green plants or of the leafy parts of plants ⟨a ~ salad⟩ **3** : UNRIPE; *also* : IMMATURE **4** : having a sickly appearance **5** : not fully processed or treated ⟨~ liquor⟩ ⟨~ hides⟩ **6** : INEXPERIENCED; *also* : NAIVE **7** : concerned with or supporting environmentalism — **green•ish** *adj* — **green•ness** *n*

²**green** *vb* : to make or become green

³**green** *n* **1** : a color between blue and yellow in the spectrum : the color of growing fresh grass or of the emerald **2** : something of a green color **3** : green vegetation; *esp, pl* : leafy herbs or leafy parts of a vegetable ⟨collard ~s⟩ ⟨beet ~s⟩ **4** : a grassy plot; *esp* : a smooth grassy area around the hole into which the ball must be played in golf

green•back \'grēn-ˌbak\ *n* : a U.S. legal-tender note

green bean *n* : a kidney bean that is used as a snap bean when the pods are colored green

green•belt \'grēn-ˌbelt\ *n* : a belt of parks or farmlands around a community

green•ery \'grē-nə-rē\ *n, pl* **-er•ies** : green foliage or plants

green–eyed \'grē-'nīd\ *adj* : JEALOUS

green•gro•cer \'grēn-ˌgrō-sər\ *n* : a retailer of fresh vegetables and fruit

green•horn \-ˌhȯrn\ *n* : an inexperienced person; *also* : NEWCOMER

green•house \-ˌhau̇s\ *n* : a glass structure for the growing of tender plants

greenhouse effect *n* : warming of a planet's atmosphere that occurs when the sun's radiation passes through the atmosphere, is absorbed by the planet, and is reradiated as radiation of longer wavelength that can be absorbed by atmospheric gases

green manure *n* : an herbaceous crop (as clover) plowed under when green to enrich the soil

green onion *n* : a young onion pulled before the bulb has enlarged and used esp. in salads; *also* : SCALLION

green pepper *n* : a sweet pepper before it turns red at maturity

green•room \'grēn-ˌrüm, -ˌru̇m\ *n* : a room in a theater or concert hall where actors or musicians relax before, between, or after appearances

green·sward \-ˌswȯrd\ *n* : turf that is green with growing grass

green thumb *n* : an unusual ability to make plants grow

Green·wich mean time \ˈgri-nij-, ˈgre-, -nich-\ *n* [*Greenwich*, England] : the time of the meridian of Greenwich used as the basis of worldwide standard time

Greenwich time *n* : GREENWICH MEAN TIME

green·wood \ˈgrēn-ˌwu̇d\ *n* : a forest green with foliage

greet \ˈgrēt\ *vb* **1** : to address with expressions of kind wishes **2** : to meet or react to in a specified manner **3** : to be perceived by — **greet·er** *n*

greet·ing *n* **1** : a salutation on meeting **2** *pl* : best wishes : REGARDS

greeting card *n* : a card that bears a message usu. sent on a special occasion

gre·gar·i·ous \gri-ˈgar-ē-əs\ *adj* [L *gregarius* of a flock or herd, fr. *greg-, grex* flock, herd] **1** : SOCIAL, COMPANIONABLE **2** : tending to flock together — **gre·gar·i·ous·ly** *adv* — **gre·gar·i·ous·ness** *n*

grem·lin \ˈgrem-lən\ *n* : a cause of error or equipment malfunction conceived of as a small gnome

gre·nade \grə-ˈnād\ *n* [MF, pomegranate, fr. LL *granata*, fr. L, fem. of *granatus* seedy, fr. *granum* grain] : a small bomb that is thrown by hand or launched (as by a rifle)

gren·a·dier \ˌgre-nə-ˈdir\ *n* : a member of a European regiment formerly armed with grenades

gren·a·dine \ˌgre-nə-ˈdēn, ˈgre-nə-ˌdēn\ *n* : a syrup flavored with pomegranates and used in mixed drinks

grew *past of* GROW

grey *var of* GRAY

grey·hound \ˈgrā-ˌhau̇nd\ *n* : any of a breed of tall slender dogs noted for speed and keen sight

greyhound

grid \ˈgrid\ *n* **1** : GRATING **2** : a network of conductors for distributing electric power **3** : a network of horizontal and perpendicular lines (as for locating points on a map) **4** : GRIDIRON 2; *also* : FOOTBALL

grid·dle \ˈgrid-ᵊl\ *n* : a flat usu. metal surface for cooking food

griddle cake *n* : PANCAKE

grid·iron \ˈgrid-ˌīrn, -ˌī-ərn\ *n* **1** : a grate for broiling food **2** : a football field

grid·lock \-ˌläk\ *n* : a traffic jam in which an intersection is so blocked that vehicles cannot move

grief \ˈgrēf\ *n* **1** : emotional distress caused by or as if by bereavement; *also* : a cause of such distress **2** : MISHAP **3** : DISASTER

griev·ance \ˈgrē-vəns\ *n* **1** : a cause of distress affording reason for complaint or resistance **2** : COMPLAINT

grieve \ˈgrēv\ *vb* **grieved; griev·ing** [ME *greven*, fr. OF *grever*, fr. L *gravare* to burden, fr. *gravis* heavy, grave] **1** : to cause grief or sorrow to : DISTRESS **2** : to feel grief : SORROW

griev·ous \ˈgrē-vəs\ *adj* **1** : causing suffering, grief, or sorrow : SEVERE ⟨a ∼ wound⟩ **2** : OPPRESSIVE, ONEROUS **3** : SERIOUS, GRAVE — **griev·ous·ly** *adv*

¹grill \ˈgril\ *vb* **1** : to broil on a grill; *also* : to fry or toast on a griddle **2** : to question intensely

²grill *n* **1** : a cooking utensil of parallel bars on which food is grilled **2** : an informal restaurant

grille *or* **grill** \ˈgril\ *n* : a grating that forms a barrier or screen

grill·work \ˈgril-ˌwərk\ *n* : work constituting or resembling a grille

grim \ˈgrim\ *adj* **grim·mer; grim·mest** **1** : CRUEL, FIERCE **2** : harsh and forbidding in appearance **3** : ghastly or repellent in character **4** : RELENTLESS — **grim·ly** *adv* — **grim·ness** *n*

gri·mace \ˈgri-məs, gri-ˈmās\ *n* : a facial expression usu. of disgust or disapproval — **grimace** *vb*

grime \ˈgrīm\ *n* : soot, smut, or dirt adhering to or embedded in a surface; *also* : accumulated dirtiness and disorder — **grimy** *adj*

grin \ˈgrin\ *vb* **grinned; grin·ning** : to draw back the lips so as to show the teeth esp. in amusement — **grin** *n*

¹grind \ˈgrīnd\ *vb* **ground** \ˈgrau̇nd\; **grind·ing** **1** : to reduce to small particles **2** : to wear down, polish, or sharpen by friction **3** : OPPRESS **4** : to press with a grating noise : GRIT ⟨∼ the teeth⟩ **5** : to operate or produce by turning a crank **6** : DRUDGE; *esp* : to study hard **7** : to move with difficulty or friction ⟨gears ∼*ing*⟩

²grind *n* **1** : dreary monotonous labor, routine, or study **2** : one who works or studies excessively

grind·er \ˈgrīn-dər\ *n* **1** : MOLAR **2** *pl* : TEETH **3** : one that grinds **4** : SUBMARINE 2

grind·stone \ˈgrīnd-ˌstōn\ *n* : a flat circular stone of natural sandstone that revolves on an axle and is used for grinding, shaping, or smoothing

¹grip \ˈgrip\ *vb* **gripped; grip·ping** **1** : to seize or hold firmly **2** : to hold the interest of strongly

²grip *n* **1** : GRASP; *also* : strength in gripping **2** : a firm tenacious hold **3** : UNDERSTANDING **4** : a device for gripping **5** : TRAVELING BAG

gripe \'grīp\ *vb* **griped; grip·ing 1** : IRRITATE, VEX **2** : to cause or experience spasmodic pains in the bowels **3** : COMPLAIN — **gripe** *n*

grippe \'grip\ *n* : INFLUENZA

gris–gris \'grē-ˌgrē\ *n, pl* **gris–gris** \-ˌgrēz\ [F] : an amulet or incantation used chiefly by people of black African ancestry

gris·ly \'griz-lē\ *adj* **gris·li·er; -est** : HORRIBLE, GRUESOME

grist \'grist\ *n* : grain to be ground or already ground

gris·tle \'gri-səl\ *n* : CARTILAGE — **grist·ly** \'gris-lē\ *adj*

grist·mill \'grist-ˌmil\ *n* : a mill for grinding grain

¹grit \'grit\ *n* **1** : a hard sharp granule (as of sand); *also* : material composed of such granules **2** : unyielding courage — **grit·ty** *adj*

²grit *vb* **grit·ted; grit·ting** : GRIND, GRATE

grits \'grits\ *n pl* : coarsely ground hulled grain (hominy ~)

griz·zled \'gri-zəld\ *adj* : streaked or mixed with gray

griz·zly \'griz-lē\ *adj* **griz·zli·er; -est** : GRIZZLED

grizzly bear *n* : a large pale-coated bear of western No. America

gro *abbr* gross

groan \'grōn\ *vb* **1** : MOAN **2** : to make a harsh sound under sudden or prolonged strain ⟨the chair ~ed under his weight⟩ — **groan** *n*

groat \'grōt\ *n* : an old British coin worth four pennies

gro·cer \'grō-sər\ *n* [ME, fr. MF *grossier* wholesaler, fr. *gros* coarse, wholesale, fr. L *grossus* coarse] : a dealer esp. in staple foodstuffs — **gro·cery** \'grōs-rē, 'grōsh-, 'grōs-ə-\ *n*

grog \'gräg\ *n* [*Old Grog*, nickname of Edward Vernon †1757 Eng. admiral responsible for diluting the sailors' rum] : alcoholic liquor; *esp* : liquor (as rum) mixed with water

grog·gy \'grä-gē\ *adj* **grog·gi·er; -est** : weak and unsteady on the feet or in action — **grog·gi·ly** \-gə-lē\ *adv* — **grog·gi·ness** \-gē-nəs\ *n*

groin \'gróin\ *n* **1** : the juncture of the lower abdomen and inner part of the thigh; *also* : the region of this juncture **2** : the curved line or rib on a ceiling along which two vaults meet

grom·met \'grä-mət, 'grə-\ *n* **1** : a ring of rope **2** : an eyelet of firm material to strengthen or protect an opening

¹groom \'grüm, 'grùm\ *n* **1** : a person responsible for the care of horses **2** : BRIDEGROOM

²groom *vb* **1** : to clean and care for (an animal) **2** : to make neat or attractive **3** : PREPARE

grooms·man \'grümz-mən, 'grùmz-\ *n* : a male friend who attends a bridegroom at his wedding

groove \'grüv\ *n* **1** : a long narrow channel **2** : a fixed routine — **groove** *vb*

groovy \'grü-vē\ *adj* **groov·i·er; -est 1** : EXCELLENT **2** : HIP

grope \'grōp\ *vb* **groped; grop·ing 1** : to feel about or search for blindly or uncertainly ⟨~ for the right word⟩ **2** : to feel one's way by groping

gros·beak \'grōs-ˌbēk\ *n* : any of several finches of Europe or America with large stout conical bills

gro·schen \'grō-shən\ *n, pl* **groschen** — see *schilling* at MONEY table

gros·grain \'grō-ˌgrān\ *n* [F *gros grain* coarse texture] : a silk or rayon fabric with crosswise cotton ribs

¹gross \'grōs\ *adj* **1** : glaringly noticeable **2** : OUT-AND-OUT, UTTER **3** : BIG, BULKY; *esp* : excessively fat **4** : GENERAL, BROAD **5** : consisting of an overall total exclusive of deductions ⟨~ earnings⟩ **6** : CARNAL, EARTHY ⟨~ pleasures⟩ **7** : UNREFINED; *also* : crudely vulgar **8** : lacking knowledge — **gross·ly** *adv* — **gross·ness** *n*

²gross *n* : an overall total exclusive of deductions — **gross** *vb*

³gross *n, pl* **gross** : a total of 12 dozen things ⟨a ~ of pencils⟩

gross national product *n* : the total value of the goods and services produced in a nation during a year

gro·szy \'grō-shē\ *n, pl* **groszy** — see *zloty* at MONEY table

grot \'grät\ *n* : GROTTO

gro·tesque \grō-'tesk\ *adj* **1** : FANCIFUL, BIZARRE **2** : absurdly incongruous **3** : ECCENTRIC — **gro·tesque·ly** *adv*

grot·to \'grä-tō\ *n, pl* **grottoes** *also* **grottos 1** : CAVE **2** : an artificial cavelike structure

grouch \'grauch\ *n* **1** : a fit of bad temper **2** : an habitually irritable or complaining person — **grouch** *vb* — **grouchy** *adj*

¹ground \'graund\ *n* **1** : the bottom of a body of water **2** *pl* : sediment at the bottom of a liquid **3** : a basis for belief, action, or argument **4** : BACKGROUND **5** : the surface of the earth; *also* : SOIL **6** : an area with a particular use ⟨fishing ~s⟩ **7** *pl* : the area about and belonging to a building **8** : a conductor that makes electrical connection with the earth — **ground·less** *adj*

²ground *vb* **1** : to bring to or place on the ground **2** : to run or cause to run aground **3** : to provide a reason or justification for **4** : to furnish with a foundation of knowledge **5** : to connect electrically with a ground **6** : to restrict to the ground; *also* : prohibit from some activity

³ground *past and past part of* GRIND

ground ball *n* : a batted baseball that rolls or bounces along the ground

ground cover *n* : low plants that grow over and cover the soil; *also* : a plant suitable for use as ground cover

ground·er \'graun-dər\ *n* : GROUND BALL

ground·hog \'graund-ˌhòg, -ˌhäg\ *n* : WOODCHUCK

ground·ling \'graund-liŋ\ *n* : a spectator in the pit of an Elizabethan theater

ground rule *n* **1** : a sports rule adopted to modify play on a particular field, court, or course **2** : a rule of procedure

ground squirrel *n* : any of various burrowing rodents of No. America and Eurasia that are related to the squirrels and live in colonies in open areas

ground swell *n* **1** : a broad deep ocean swell caused by an often distant gale or earthquake **2** *usu* **ground-swell** : a rapid spontaneous growth (as of political opinion)

ground·wa·ter \'graund-ˌwò-tər, -ˌwä-\ *n* : water within the earth that supplies wells and springs

ground·work \-ˌwərk\ *n* : FOUNDATION, BASIS

ground zero *n* : the point above, below, or at which a nuclear explosion occurs

¹group \'grüp\ *n* **1** : a number of individuals related by a common factor (as physical association, community of interests, or blood) **2** : a combination of atoms commonly found together in a molecule ⟨a methyl ~⟩

²group *vb* : to associate in groups : CLUSTER, AGGREGATE

grou·per \'grü-pər\ *n, pl* **groupers** *also* **grouper** : any of numerous large solitary bottom fishes of warm seas

group·ie \'grü-pē\ *n* : a fan of a rock group who usu. follows the group around on concert tours; *also* : ENTHUSIAST, FAN

group therapy *n* : therapy in the presence of a therapist in which several patients discuss their personal problems

¹grouse \'graùs\ *n, pl* **grouse** *or* **grouses** : any of numerous ground-dwelling game birds that have feathered legs and are usu. of reddish brown or other protective color

²grouse *vb* **groused; grous·ing** : COMPLAIN, GRUMBLE

grout \'graùt\ *n* : material (as mortar) used for filling spaces — **grout** *vb*

grove \'grōv\ *n* : a small wood usu. without underbrush

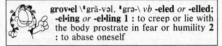

grov·el \'grä-vəl, 'grə-\ *vb* **-eled** *or* **-elled**; **-el·ing** *or* **-el·ling** **1** : to creep or lie with the body prostrate in fear or humility **2** : to abase oneself

grow \'grō\ *vb* **grew** \'grü\; **grown** \'grōn\; **grow·ing** **1** : to spring up and develop to maturity **2** : to be able to grow : THRIVE **3** : to take on some relation through or as if through growth 〈tree limbs *grown* together〉 **4** : INCREASE, EXPAND **5** : to develop from a parent source **6** : BECOME **7** : to have an increasing influence **8** : to cause to grow — **grow·er** *n*

growl \'graùl\ *vb* **1** : RUMBLE **2** : to utter a deep throaty sound **3** : GRUMBLE — **growl** *n*

grown–up \'grō-ˌnəp\ *adj* : not childish : ADULT — **grown–up** *n*

growth \'grōth\ *n* **1** : stage or condition attained in growing **2** : a process of growing esp. through progressive development or increase **3** : a result or product of growing 〈a fine ∼ of hair〉; *also* : an abnormal mass of tissue (as a tumor)

¹**grub** \'grəb\ *vb* **grubbed**; **grub·bing** **1** : to clear or root out by digging **2** : to dig in the ground usu. for a hidden object **3** : to search about

²**grub** *n* **1** : a soft thick wormlike insect larva 〈beetle ∼s〉 **2** : DRUDGE; *also* : a slovenly person **3** : FOOD

grub·by \'grə-bē\ *adj* **grub·bi·er**; **-est** : DIRTY, SLOVENLY — **grub·bi·ness** \-bē-nəs\ *n*

grub·stake \'grəb-ˌstāk\ *n* : supplies or funds furnished a mining prospector in return for a share in his finds

¹**grudge** \'grəj\ *vb* **grudged**; **grudg·ing** **1** : to be reluctant to give : BEGRUDGE

²**grudge** *n* : a feeling of deep-seated resentment or ill will

gru·el \'grü-əl\ *n* : a thin porridge

gru·el·ing *or* **gru·el·ling** \'grü-liŋ, 'grü-ə-\ *adj* : requiring extreme effort : EXHAUSTING

grue·some \'grü-səm\ *adj* [fr. earlier *growsome*, fr. E dial. *grow, grue* to shiver] : inspiring horror or repulsion

gruff \'grəf\ *adj* **1** : rough in speech or manner **2** : being deep and harsh : HOARSE — **gruff·ly** *adv*

grum·ble \'grəm-bəl\ *vb* **grum·bled**; **grum·bling** **1** : to mutter in discontent **2** : GROWL, RUMBLE — **grum·bler** *n*

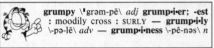

grumpy \'grəm-pē\ *adj* **grump·i·er**; **-est** : moodily cross : SURLY — **grump·i·ly** \-pə-lē\ *adv* — **grump·i·ness** \-pē-nəs\ *n*

grunge \'grənj\ *n* **1** : one that is grungy **2** : heavy metal rock music expressing alienation and discontent **3** : untidy or tattered clothing typically worn by grunge fans

grun·gy \'grən-jē\ *adj* **grun·gi·er**; **-est** : shabby or dirty in character or condition

grun·ion \'grən-yən\ *n* : a fish of the California coast which comes inshore to spawn at nearly full moon

grunt \'grənt\ *n* : a deep throaty sound (as that of a hog) — **grunt** *vb*

GSA *abbr* **1** General Services Administration **2** Girl Scouts of America

G suit *n* [*gravity suit*] : a suit for a pilot or astronaut designed to counteract the physiological effects of acceleration

GSUSA *abbr* Girl Scouts of the United States of America

gt *abbr* great

Gt Brit *abbr* Great Britain

gtd *abbr* guaranteed

GU *abbr* Guam

gua·ca·mo·le \ˌgwä-kə-'mō-lē\ *n* [MexSp] : mashed and seasoned avocado

gua·nine \'gwä-ˌnēn\ *n* : a purine base that codes genetic information in the molecular chain of DNA and RNA

gua·no \'gwä-nō\ *n* [Sp, fr. Quechua (a South American Indian language) *wanu* fertilizer, dung] : a substance composed chiefly of the excrement of seabirds and used as a fertilizer

gua·ra·ni \ˌgwär-ə-'nē\ *n, pl* **guaranies** *also* **guaranis** — see MONEY table

¹**guar·an·tee** \ˌgar-ən-'tē\ *n* **1** : GUARANTOR **2** : GUAR-

ANTY 1 3 : an agreement by which one person undertakes to secure another in the possession or enjoyment of something 4 : an assurance of the quality of or of the length of use to be expected from a product offered for sale 5 : GUARANTY 4

²**guarantee** vb **-teed; -tee·ing 1** : to undertake to answer for the debt, failure to perform, or faulty performance of (another) **2** : to undertake an obligation to establish, perform, or continue **3** : to give security to

guar·an·tor \ˌgar-ən-ˈtòr\ n : one who gives a guarantee

¹**guar·an·ty** \ˈgar-ən-tē\ n, pl **-ties 1** : an undertaking to answer for another's failure to pay a debt or perform a duty **2** : GUARANTEE 3 **3** : GUARANTOR **4** : PLEDGE, SECURITY

²**guaranty** vb **-tied; -ty·ing** : GUARANTEE

¹**guard** \ˈgärd\ n **1** : a person or a body of persons on sentinel duty **2** pl : troops assigned to protect a sovereign **3** : a defensive position (as in boxing) **4** : the act or duty of protecting or defending **5** : PROTECTION **6** : a protective or safety device **7** : a football lineman playing between center and tackle; also : a basketball player stationed toward the rear — **on guard** : WATCHFUL, ALERT

²**guard** vb **1** : PROTECT, DEFEND **2** : to watch over **3** : to be on guard

guard·house \ˈgärd-ˌhaûs\ n **1** : a building occupied by a guard or used as a headquarters by soldiers on guard duty **2** : a military jail

guard·ian \ˈgär-dē-ən\ n **1** : CUSTODIAN **2** : one who has the care of the person or property of another — **guard·ian·ship** n

guard·room \ˈgärd-ˌrüm\ n **1** : a room used by a military guard while on duty **2** : a room where military prisoners are confined

guards·man \ˈgärdz-mən\ n : a member of a military body called guard or guards

Gua·te·ma·lan \ˌgwä-tə-ˈmä-lən\ n : a native or inhabitant of Guatemala — **Guatemalan** adj

gua·va \ˈgwä-və\ n : the sweet yellow or pink acid fruit of a shrubby tropical American tree used esp. for making jam and jelly; also : the tree

gu·ber·na·to·ri·al \ˌgü-bər-nə-ˈtòr-ē-əl\ adj : of or relating to a governor

guer·don \ˈgərd-ᵊn\ n : REWARD, RECOMPENSE

Guern·sey \ˈgərn-zē\ n, pl **Guernseys** : any of a breed of fawn and white dairy cattle that produce rich yellowish milk

guer·ril·la or **gue·ril·la** \gə-ˈri-lə\ n [Sp guerrilla, fr. dim. of guerra war, of Gmc origin] : one who engages in irregular warfare esp. as a member of an independent unit

guess \ˈges\ vb **1** : to form an opinion from little or no evidence **2** : BELIEVE, SUPPOSE **3** : to conjecture correctly about : DISCOVER — **guess** n

guest \ˈgest\ n **1** : a person to whom hospitality (as of a house or a club) is extended **2** : a patron of a commercial establishment (as a hotel) **3** : a person not a regular member of a cast who appears on a program

guf·faw \(ˌ)gə-ˈfò\ n : a loud burst of laughter — **guffaw** vb

guid·ance \ˈgīd-ᵊns\ n **1** : the act or process of guiding **2** : ADVICE, DIRECTION

¹**guide** \ˈgīd\ n **1** : one who leads or directs another's course **2** : one who shows and explains points of interest **3** : something that provides guiding information; also : SIGNPOST **4** : a device to direct the motion of something

²**guide** vb **guid·ed; guid·ing 1** : to act as a guide to **2** : MANAGE, DIRECT **3** : to superintend the training of — **guid·able** \ˈgī-də-bəl\ adj

guide·book \ˈgīd-ˌbùk\ n : a book of information for travelers

guided missile n : a missile whose course may be altered during flight

guide dog n : a dog trained to lead the blind

guide·line \ˈgīd-ˌlīn\ n : an indication or outline of policy or conduct

guide word n : a term at the head of a page of an alphabetical reference work that indicates the alphabetically first or last word on that page

gui·don \ˈgī-ˌdän, ˈgīd-ᵊn\ n : a small flag (as of a military unit)

guild \ˈgild\ n : an association of people with common aims and interests; esp : a medieval association of merchants or craftsmen — **guild·hall** \-ˌhòl\ n

guil·der \ˈgil-dər\ n : GULDEN

guile \ˈgīl\ n : deceitful cunning : DUPLICITY — **guileful** adj — **guile·less·ness** n

guil·lo·tine \ˈgi-lə-ˌtēn, ˌgē-ə-ˈtēn\ n [F, fr. Joseph Guillotin †1814 Fr. physician] : a machine for beheading persons — **guillotine** vb

guilt \ˈgilt\ n **1** : the fact of having committed an offense esp. against the law **2** : BLAMEWORTHINESS **3** : a feeling of responsibility for wrongdoing — **guilt·less** adj

guilty \ˈgil-tē\ adj **guilt·i·er; -est 1** : having committed a breach of conduct or a crime **2** : suggesting or involving guilt **3** : aware of or suffering from guilt — **guilt·i·ly** \-tə-lē\ adv — **guilt·i·ness** \-tē-nəs\ n

guin·ea \ˈgi-nē\ n **1** : a British gold coin no longer issued worth 21 shillings **2** : a unit of value equal to 21 shillings

guinea fowl n : a gray and white spotted West African bird related to the pheasants and widely raised for food; also : any of several related birds

guinea hen n : a female guinea fowl; also : GUINEA FOWL

Guin·ean \ˈgi-nē-ən\ n : a native or inhabitant of Guinea — **Guinean** adj

guinea pig n **1** : a small stocky short-eared and nearly tailless So. American rodent often kept as a pet or used in lab research **2** : a subject of research or testing

guise \'gīz\ *n* **1** : a form or style of dress : COSTUME **2** : external appearance : SEMBLANCE

gui•tar \gi-'tär\ *n* : a musical instrument with usu. six strings plucked with a pick or with the fingers

gulch \'gəlch\ *n* : RAVINE

gul•den \'gül-dən, 'gül-\ *n, pl* **guldens** *or* **gulden** — see MONEY table

gulf \'gəlf\ *n* [ME *goulf*, fr. MF *golfe*, fr. It *golfo*, fr. LL *colpus*, fr. Gk *kolpos* bosom, gulf] **1** : a part of an ocean or sea partly or mostly surrounded by land **2** : ABYSS, CHASM **3** : a wide separation

¹gull \'gəl\ *n* : any of numerous mostly white or gray long-winged web-footed seabirds

²gull *vb* : to make a dupe of : DECEIVE — **gull•ible** \'gə-lə-bəl\ *adj*

³gull *n* : DUPE

gul•let \'gə-lət\ *n* : ESOPHAGUS; *also* : THROAT

gul•ly \'gə-lē\ *n, pl* **gullies** : a trench worn in the earth by and often filled with running water after rains

gulp \'gəlp\ *vb* **1** : to swallow hurriedly or greedily **2** : SUPPRESS ⟨~ down a sob⟩ **3** : to catch the breath as if in taking a long drink — **gulp** *n*

¹gum \'gəm\ *n* : the oral tissue that surrounds the necks of the teeth

²gum *n* **1** : a sticky plant exudate; *esp* : one that hardens on drying **2** : a sticky substance **3** : a preparation usu. of a plant gum sweetened and flavored and used for chewing — **gum•my** *adj*

gum arabic *n* : a water-soluble gum obtained from several acacias and used esp. in making inks, adhesives, confections, and pharmaceuticals

gum•bo \'gəm-bō\ *n* [AmerF *gombo*, of Bantu origin] : a rich thick soup usu. thickened with okra

gum•drop \'gəm-ɪdräp\ *n* : a candy made usu. from corn syrup with gelatin and coated with sugar crystals

gump•tion \'gəmp-shən\ *n* **1** : shrewd common sense **2** : ENTERPRISE, INITIATIVE

gum•shoe \'gəm-ɪshü\ *n* : DETECTIVE — **gumshoe** *vb*

¹gun \'gən\ *n* **1** : CANNON **2** : a portable firearm **3** : a discharge of a gun **4** : something suggesting a gun in shape or function **5** : THROTTLE — **gunned** \'gənd\ *adj*

²gun *vb* **gunned; gun•ning 1** : to hunt with a gun **2** : SHOOT **3** : to open up the throttle of so as to increase speed

gun•boat \'gən-ɪbōt\ *n* : a small lightly armed ship for use in shallow waters

gun•fight \-ɪfīt\ *n* : a duel with guns — **gun•fight•er** *n*

gun•fire \-ɪfīr\ *n* : the firing of guns

gung ho \'gəŋ-'hō\ *adj* [*Gung ho!*, motto (taken to mean "work together") adopted by certain U.S. marines in World War II, fr. Chin *gōnghé*, short for *Zhōngguó Gōngyè Hézuò Shè* Chinese Industrial Cooperatives Society] : extremely zealous or enthusiastic

gun•man \-mən\ *n* : a man armed with a gun; *esp* : a professional killer

gun•ner \'gə-nər\ *n* **1** : a soldier or airman who oper-

ates or aims a gun **2** : one who hunts with a gun

gun•nery \'gə-nə-rē\ *n* : the use of guns; *esp* : the science of the flight of projectiles and effective use of guns

gunnery sergeant *n* : a noncommissioned officer in the marine corps ranking next below a first sergeant

gun•ny•sack \'gə-nē-ɪsak\ *n* : a sack made of a coarse heavy fabric (as burlap)

gun•point \'gən-ɪpòint\ *n* : the muzzle of a gun — **at gunpoint** : under a threat of death by being shot

gun•pow•der \-ɪpaù-dər\ *n* : an explosive powder used in guns and blasting

gun•shot \-ɪshät\ *n* **1** : shot fired from a gun **2** : the range of a gun ⟨within ~⟩

gun•shy \-ɪshī\ *adj* **1** : afraid of a loud noise **2** : markedly distrustful

gun•sling•er \-ɪsliŋ-ər\ *n* : a skilled gunman esp. in the old West

gun•smith \-ɪsmith\ *n* : one who designs, makes, or repairs firearms

gun•wale *also* **gun•nel** \'gən-ᵊl\ *n* : the upper edge of a ship's or boat's side

gup•py \'gə-pē\ *n, pl* **guppies** [R.J.L. *Guppy* †1916 Trinidadian naturalist] : a small brightly colored tropical fish

gur•gle \'gər-gəl\ *vb* **gur•gled; gur•gling** : to make a sound like that of an irregularly flowing or gently splashing liquid — **gurgle** *n*

Gur•kha \'gùr-kə, 'gər-\ *n* : a soldier from Nepal in the British or Indian army

gur•ney \'gər-nē\ *n, pl* **gurneys** : a wheeled cot or stretcher

gu•ru \'gùr-ü\ *n, pl* **gurus** [Hindi *gurū*, fr. Sanskrit *guru*, fr. *guru*, adj., heavy, venerable] **1** : a personal religious and spiritual teacher in Hinduism **2** : a teacher in matters of fundamental concern **3** : EXPERT ⟨a fitness ~⟩

gush \'gəsh\ *vb* **1** : to issue or pour forth copiously or violently : SPOUT **2** : to make an effusive display of affection or enthusiasm

gush•er \'gə-shər\ *n* : one that gushes; *esp* : an oil well with a large natural flow

gushy \'gə-shē\ *adj* **gush•i•er; -est** : marked by effusive sentimentality

gus•set \'gə-sət\ *n* : a triangular insert (as in a seam of a sleeve) to give width or strength — **gusset** *vb*

gus•sy up \'gə-sē-\ *vb* : to dress up

¹gust \'gəst\ *n* **1** : a sudden brief rush of wind **2** : a sudden outburst : SURGE — **gusty** *adj*

²gust *vb* : to blow in gusts

gus•ta•to•ry \'gəs-tə-ɪtōr-ē\ *adj* : relating to or associated with the sense of taste

gus•to \'gəs-tō\ *n, pl* **gustoes** : enthusiastic enjoyment; *also* : VITALITY 4

¹gut \'gət\ *n* **1** *pl* : BOWELS, ENTRAILS **2** : the alimentary canal or a part of it (as the intestine); *also* : BELLY,

ABDOMEN **3** *pl* : the inner essential parts **4** *pl* : COURAGE, PLUCK

²**gut** *vb* **gut·ted; gut·ting 1** : EVISCERATE **2** : to destroy the inside of

gutsy \'gət-sē\ *adj* **guts·i·er; -est** : marked by courage and determination

gut·ter \'gə-tər\ *n* : a groove or channel for carrying off esp. rainwater

gut·ter·snipe \-ˌsnīp\ *n* : a street urchin

gut·tur·al \'gə-tə-rəl\ *adj* **1** : sounded in the throat **2** : being or marked by an utterance that is strange, unpleasant, or disagreeable — **guttural** *n*

gut·ty \'gə-tē\ *adj* **gut·ti·er; -est 1** : GUTSY **2** : having a vigorous challenging quality

gut–wrench·ing \'gət-ˌren-chiŋ\ *adj* : causing emotional anguish

¹**guy** \'gī\ *n* : a rope, chain, or rod attached to something as a brace or guide

²**guy** *vb* : to steady or reinforce with a guy

³**guy** *n* : MAN, FELLOW; *also, pl* : PERSONS ⟨all the ∼s came⟩

⁴**guy** *vb* : to make fun of : RIDICULE

Guy·a·nese \ˌgī-ə-ˈnēz\ *n, pl* **Guyanese** : a native or inhabitant of Guyana — **Guyanese** *adj*

guz·zle \'gə-zəl\ *vb* **guz·zled; guz·zling** : to drink greedily

gym \'jim\ *n* : GYMNASIUM

gym·kha·na \jim-ˈkä-nə\ *n* : a meet featuring sports contests; *esp* : a contest of automobile-driving skill

gym·na·si·um *for 1* jim-ˈnä-zē-əm, -zhəm, *for 2* gim-ˈnä-zē-əm\ *n, pl* **-na·si·ums** *or* **-na·sia** \-ˈnä-zē-ə, -ˈnä-zhə; -ˈnä-zē-ə\ [L, exercise ground, school, fr. Gk *gymnasion*, fr. *gymnazein* to exercise naked, fr. *gymnos* naked] **1** : a room or building for indoor sports **2** : a European secondary school that prepares students for the university

gym·nas·tics \ jim-ˈnas-tiks\ *n* : a competitive sport developed from physical exercises designed to demonstrate strength, balance, and body control — **gym·nast** \'jim-ˌnast\ *n* — **gym·nas·tic** *adj*

gym·no·sperm \'jim-nə-ˌspərm\ *n* : any of a class or subdivision of woody vascular seed plants (as conifers) that produce naked seeds not enclosed in an ovary

gyn *or* **gynecol** *abbr* gynecology

gy·nae·col·o·gy *chiefly Brit var of* GYNECOLOGY

gy·ne·col·o·gy \ˌgī-nə-ˈkä-lə-jē\ *n* : a branch of medicine dealing with the diseases and hygiene of women — **gy·ne·co·log·ic** \-ni-kə-ˈlä-jik\ *or* **gy·ne·co·log·i·cal** \-ji-kəl\ *adj* — **gy·ne·col·o·gist** \-nə-ˈkä-lə-jist\ *n*

gyp \'jip\ *n* **1** : CHEAT, SWINDLER **2** : FRAUD, SWINDLE — **gyp** *vb*

gyp·sum \'jip-səm\ *n* : a calcium-containing mineral used in making plaster of paris

Gyp·sy \'jip-sē\ *n, pl* **Gypsies** [by shortening & alter. fr. *Egyptian*] : a member of a traditionally traveling people coming orig. from India and living chiefly in Europe, Asia, and No. America; *also* : the language of the Gypsies

gypsy moth *n* : an Old World moth that was introduced into the U.S. where its caterpillar is a destructive defoliator of many trees

gy·rate \'jī-ˌrāt\ *vb* **gy·rat·ed; gy·rat·ing 1** : to revolve around a point or axis **2** : to oscillate with or as if with a circular or spiral motion — **gy·ra·tion** \jī-ˈrā-shən\ *n*

gyr·fal·con \'jər-ˌfal-kən, -ˌfȯl-\ *n* : an arctic falcon with several color forms that is the largest of all falcons

gy·ro \'jī-rō\ *n, pl* **gyros** : GYROSCOPE

gy·ro·scope \'jī-rō-ˌskōp\ *n* : a wheel or disk mounted to spin rapidly about an axis that is free to turn in various directions

Gy Sgt *abbr* gunnery sergeant

gyve \'jīv, 'gīv\ *n* : FETTER — **gyve** *vb*

H

¹**h** \'āch\ *n, pl* **h's** *or* **hs** \'ā-chəz\ *often cap* : the 8th letter of the English alphabet

²**h** *abbr, often cap* **1** hard; hardness **2** heroin **3** hit **4** husband

H *symbol* hydrogen

¹**ha** \'hä\ *interj* — used esp. to express surprise or joy

²**ha** *abbr* hectare

Hab *abbr* Habacuc; Habakkuk

Ha·ba·cuc \'ha-bə-ˌkək, hə-ˈba-kək\ *n* : HABAKKUK

Ha·bak·kuk \'ha-bə-ˌkək, hə-ˈba-kək\ *n* — see BIBLE table

ha·ba·ne·ra \ˌhä-bə-ˈner-ə\ *n* [Sp *(danza) habanera*, lit., dance of Havana] : a Cuban dance in slow time; *also* : the music for this dance

ha·be·as cor·pus \'hä-bē-əs-ˈkȯr-pəs\ *n* [ME, fr. ML, lit., you should have the body (the opening words of the writ)] : a writ issued to bring a party before a court

hab·er·dash·er \'ha-bər-ˌda-shər\ *n* : a dealer in men's clothing and accessories

hab·er·dash·ery \-ˌda-shə-rē\ *n, pl* **-er·ies 1** : goods sold by a haberdasher **2** : a haberdasher's shop

ha·bil·i·ment \hə-ˈbi-lə-mənt\ *n* **1** *pl* : TRAPPINGS, EQUIPMENT **2** : DRESS; *esp* : the dress characteristic of an occupation or occasion — usu. used in pl.

hab·it \'ha-bət\ *n* **1** : DRESS, GARB **2** : BEARING, CONDUCT **3** : PHYSIQUE **4** : mental makeup **5** : a usual manner of behavior : CUSTOM **6** : a behavior pattern acquired by frequent repetition **7** : ADDICTION **8** : mode of growth or occurrence ⟨trees with a spreading ∼⟩

hab·it·able \'ha-bə-tə-bəl\ *adj* : capable of being lived in — **hab·it·abil·i·ty** \ˌha-bə-tə-ˈbi-lə-tē\ *n*

hab·i·tat \'ha-bə-ˌtat\ *n* [L, it inhabits] : the place or environment where a plant or animal naturally occurs

hab·i·ta·tion \ˌha-bə-ˈtā-shən\ *n* **1** : OCCUPANCY **2** : a dwelling place : RESIDENCE **3** : SETTLEMENT

hab·it–form·ing \'ha-bət-ˌfȯr-miŋ\ *adj* : causing addiction : ADDICTIVE

ha·bit·u·al \hə-ˈbi-chə-wəl\ *adj* **1** : CUSTOMARY **2** : doing, practicing, or acting by force of habit **3** : inherent in an individual — **ha·bit·u·al·ly** *adv* — **ha·bit·u·al·ness** *n*

ha·bit·u·ate \hə-ˈbi-chə-ˌwāt\ *vb* **-at·ed; -at·ing 1** : ACCUSTOM **2** : to cause or undergo habituation

ha·bit·u·a·tion \hə-ˌbi-chə-ˈwā-shən\ *n* **1** : the process of making habitual **2** : psychological dependence on a drug after a period of use

ha·bi·tué *also* **ha·bi·tue** \hə-ˈbi-chə-ˌwā\ *n* [F] : one who may be regularly found in or at (as a place of entertainment)

ha·ci·en·da \ˌhä-sē-ˈen-də\ *n* **1** : a large estate in a Spanish-speaking country **2** : the main building of a farm or ranch

¹**hack** \'hak\ *vb* **1** : to cut or sever with repeated irregular blows **2** : to cough in a short dry manner **3** : to manage successfully; *also* : TOLERATE

²**hack** *n* **1** : an implement for hacking **2** : a short dry cough **3** : a hacking blow

³**hack** *n* **1** : a horse hired or used for varied work **2** : a horse worn out in service **3** : a light easy often 3-gaited saddle horse **4** : HACKNEY, TAXICAB **5** : a person who works solely for mercenary reasons; *esp* : a writer working solely for commercial success — **hack** *adj*

⁴**hack** *vb* : to operate a taxicab

hack•er \\'ha-kər\ *n* **1** : one that hacks; *also* : a person unskilled at something **2** : an expert at using a computer **3** : a person who illegally gains access to and sometimes tampers with information in a computer system

hack•ie \\'ha-kē\ *n* : a taxicab driver

hack•le \\'ha-kəl\ *n* **1** : one of the long feathers on the neck or back of a bird **2** *pl* : hairs (as on a dog's neck) that can be erected **3** *pl* : TEMPER, DANDER

hack•man \\'hak-mən\ *n* : HACKIE

¹**hack•ney** \\'hak-nē\ *n, pl* **hackneys 1** : a horse for riding or driving **2** : a carriage or automobile kept for hire

²**hackney** *vb* : to make trite

hack•neyed \\'hak-nēd\ *adj* : lacking in freshness or originality

hack•saw \\'hak-ˌsȯ\ *n* : a fine-tooth saw in a frame for cutting metal

hack•work \-ˌwərk\ *n* : work done on order usu. according to a formula

had *past and past part of* HAVE

had•dock \\'ha-dək\ *n, pl* **haddock** *also* **haddocks** : an Atlantic food fish usu. smaller than the related cod

Ha•des \\'hā-(ˌ)dēz\ *n* **1** : the abode of the dead in Greek mythology **2** *often not cap* : HELL

haem *chiefly Brit var of* HEME

hae•ma•tite *Brit var of* HEMATITE

haf•ni•um \\'haf-nē-əm\ *n* : a gray metallic chemical element — see ELEMENT table

haft \\'haft\ *n* : the handle of a weapon or tool

hag \\'hag\ *n* **1** : an ugly or evil-looking old woman **2** : WITCH 1

Hag *abbr* Haggai

Hag•gai \\'ha-gē-ˌī, 'ha-ˌgī\ *n* — see BIBLE table

hag•gard \\'ha-gərd\ *adj* : having a worn or emaciated appearance **syn** careworn, wasted, drawn — **hag•gard•ly** *adv* — **hag•gard•ness** *n*

hag•gis \\'ha-gəs\ *n* : a traditionally Scottish dish made of the heart, liver, and lungs of a sheep or a calf minced with suet, onions, oatmeal, and seasonings

hag•gle \\'ha-gəl\ *vb* **hag•gled; hag•gling** : to argue in bargaining — **hag•gler** *n*

Ha•gi•og•ra•pha \ˌha-gē-'ä-grə-fə, ˌhä-jē-\ *n pl* — see BIBLE table

ha•gi•og•ra•phy \ˌha-gē-'ä-grə-fē, ˌhä-jē-\ *n* **1** : biography of saints or venerated persons **2** : idealizing or idolizing biography — **ha•gi•og•ra•pher** \-fər\ *n*

hai•ku \\'hī-(ˌ)kü\ *n, pl* **haiku** : an unrhymed Japanese verse form of three lines containing usu. 5, 7, and 5 syllables respectively; *also* : a poem in this form

¹**hail** \\'hāl\ *n* **1** : precipitation in the form of small lumps of ice **2** : something that gives the effect of falling hail

²**hail** *vb* **1** : to precipitate hail **2** : to pour down and strike like hail

³**hail** *interj* [ME, fr. ON *heill*, fr. *heill* healthy] — used to express acclamation

⁴**hail** *vb* **1** : SALUTE, GREET **2** : SUMMON

⁵**hail** *n* **1** : an expression of greeting, approval, or praise **2** : hearing distance

Hail Mary *n* : a salutation and prayer to the Virgin Mary

hail•stone \\'hāl-ˌstōn\ *n* : a pellet of hail

hail•storm \-ˌstȯrm\ *n* : a storm accompanied by hail

hair \\'har\ *n* : a threadlike outgrowth esp. from the skin of a mammal; *also* : a covering or growth of hairs of an animal or a body part — **haired** \\'hard\ *adj* — **hair•less** *adj*

hair•breadth \\'har-ˌbredth\ *or* **hairs•breadth** \\'harz-\ *n* : a very small distance or margin

hair•brush \-ˌbrəsh\ *n* : a brush for the hair

hair•cloth \-ˌklȯth\ *n* : a stiff wiry fabric used esp. for upholstery

hair•cut \-ˌkət\ *n* : the act, process, or style of cutting and shaping the hair

hair•do \-ˌdü\ *n, pl* **hairdos** : a way of wearing the hair

hair•dress•er \-ˌdre-sər\ *n* : one who dresses or cuts hair — **hair•dress•ing** *n*

hair•line \-ˌlīn\ *n* **1** : a very thin line **2** : the outline of the hair on the head

hair•piece \-ˌpēs\ *n* **1** : supplementary hair (as a switch) used in some women's hairdos **2** : TOUPEE

hair•pin \-ˌpin\ *n* **1** : a U-shaped pin to hold the hair in place **2** : a sharp U-shaped turn in a road — **hairpin** *adj*

hair–rais•ing \\'har-ˌrā-ziŋ\ *adj* : causing terror or astonishment

hair•split•ter \-ˌspli-tər\ *n* : a person who makes excessively fine distinctions in reasoning — **hair•split•ting** \-ˌspli-tiŋ\ *adj or n*

hair•style \-ˌstīl\ *n* : HAIRDO — **hair•styl•ing** *n*

hair•styl•ist \-ˌstī-list\ *n* : HAIRDRESSER

hair–trigger *adj* : immediately responsive to the slightest stimulus

hairy \\'har-ē\ *adj* **hair•i•er; -est 1** : covered with or as if with hair **2** : tending to cause nervous tension (a few ~ moments) — **hair•i•ness** \-ē-nəs\ *n*

hairy woodpecker *n* : a common No. American woodpecker with a white back that is larger than the similarly marked downy woodpecker

Hai•tian \\'hā-shən\ *n* : a native or inhabitant of Haiti — **Haitian** *adj*

hajj \\'haj\ *n* : the Islamic religious pilgrimage to Mecca

hajji \\'ha-jē\ *n* : one who has made a pilgrimage to Mecca — often used as a title

hake \\'hāk\ *n* : any of several marine food fishes related to the cod

ha•la•la \hə-'lä-lə\ *n, pl* **halala** *or* **halalas** — see *riyal* at MONEY table

hal•berd \\'hal-bərd, 'hȯl-\ *also* **hal•bert** \-bərt\ *n* : a weapon esp. of the 15th and 16th centuries consisting of a battle-ax and pike on a long handle

hal•cy•on \\'hal-sē-ən\ *adj* [Gk *halkyōn*, a mythical bird believed to nest at sea and to calm the waves] : CALM, PEACEFUL

¹**hale** \\'hāl\ *adj* : free from defect, disease, or infirmity **syn** healthy, sound, robust, well

²**hale** *vb* **haled; hal•ing 1** : HAUL, PULL **2** : to compel to go

ha·ler \\'hä-lər\ *n, pl* **ha·le·ru** \\'hä-lə-ˌrü\ — see *koruna* at MONEY table

¹half \\'haf, 'håf\ *n, pl* **halves** \\'havz, 'håvz\ **1 :** either of two equal parts into which something is divisible **2 :** one of a pair

²half *adj* **1 :** being one of two equal parts **2 :** amounting to nearly half **3 :** PARTIAL, INCOMPLETE — **half** *adv*

half–and–half \ˌhaf-ᵊn-'haf, ˌhåf-ᵊn-'håf\ *n* : something that is half one thing and half another

half·back \\'haf-ˌbak, 'håf-\ *n* **1 :** a football back stationed on or near the flank **2 :** a player stationed immediately behind the forward line

half–baked \-'bākt\ *adj* **1 :** not thoroughly baked **2 :** poorly planned; *also* : lacking common sense

half–breed \-ˌbrēd\ *n* : one of mixed racial descent — often used disparagingly — **half–breed** *adj*

half brother *n* : a brother related through one parent only

half–caste \\'haf-ˌkast, 'håf-\ *n* : HALF-BREED — **half–caste** *adj*

half–dol·lar \-'dä-lər\ *n* **1 :** a coin representing one half of a dollar **2 :** the sum of fifty cents

half–heart·ed \-'här-təd\ *adj* : lacking spirit or interest — **half·heart·ed·ly** *adv* — **half·heart·ed·ness** *n*

half–life \-ˌlīf\ *n* : the time required for half of something (as atoms or a drug) to undergo a process

half–mast \-'mast\ *n* : a point about halfway down from the top of a mast or staff

half note *n* : a musical note equal in time to one half of a whole note

half·pen·ny \\'häp-nē\ *n, pl* **half·pence** \\'hā-pəns\ or **halfpennies** : a formerly used British coin representing one half of a penny

half–pint \\'haf-ˌpīnt, 'håf-\ *adj* : of less than average size — **half–pint** *n*

half sister *n* : a sister related through one parent only

half sole *n* : a shoe sole extending from the shank forward — **half–sole** *vb*

half–staff \\'haf-'staf, 'håf-\ *n* : HALF-MAST

half step *n* : a musical interval equivalent to one twelfth of an octave

half·time \\'haf-ˌtīm, 'håf-\ *n* : an intermission between halves of a game

half–track \-ˌtrak\ *n* : a motor vehicle propelled by an endless chain-track drive system; *esp* : such a vehicle lightly armored for military use

half–truth \-ˌtrüth\ *n* : a statement that is only partially true; *esp* : one that deliberately mixes truth and falsehood

half·way \-'wā\ *adj* **1 :** midway between two points **2 :** PARTIAL 1 — **halfway** *adv*

half–wit \-ˌwit\ *n* : a foolish or imbecilic person — **half–wit·ted** \-'wi-təd\ *adj* — **half–wit·ted·ness** *n*

hal·i·but \\'ha-lə-bət\ *n, pl* **halibut** *also* **halibuts** [ME *halybutte*, fr. *haly, holy* holy + *butte* flatfish; fr. its being eaten on holy days] : a large edible marine flatfish

ha·lite \\'ha-ˌlīt, 'hā-\ *n* : ROCK SALT

hal·i·to·sis \ˌha-lə-'tō-səs\ *n* : the condition of having fetid breath

hall \\'hòl\ *n* **1 :** the residence of a medieval king or noble; *also* : the house of a landed proprietor **2 :** a large public building **3 :** a college or university building; *also* : DORMITORY **4 :** LOBBY; *also* : CORRIDOR **5 :** AUDITORIUM

hal·le·lu·jah \ˌha-lə-'lü-yə\ *interj* [Heb *hallĕlūyāh* praise (ye) the Lord] — used to express praise, joy, or thanks

hall·mark \\'hòl-ˌmärk\ *n* **1 :** a mark put on an article to indicate origin, purity, or genuineness **2 :** a distinguishing characteristic

hal·low \\'ha-lō\ *vb* **1 :** CONSECRATE **2 :** REVERE — **hallowed** \-lōd, -lə-wəd\ *adj*

Hal·low·een *also* **Hal·low·e'en** \ˌha-lə-'wēn, ˌhä-\ *n* : the evening of October 31 observed esp. by children in merrymaking and masquerading

hal·lu·ci·nate \hə-'lüs-ᵊn-ˌāt\ *vb* **-nat·ed; -nat·ing :** to have hallucinations or experience as a hallucination

---

 **hal·lu·ci·na·tion** \hə-ˌlüs-ᵊn-'ā-shən\ *n* : perception of objects with no reality due usu. to use of drugs or to disorder of the nervous system; *also* : something so perceived **syn** delusion, illusion, mirage — **hal·lu·ci·na·to·ry** \-ᵊn-ə-ˌtōr-ē\ *adj*

---

hal·lu·ci·no·gen \hə-'lüs-ᵊn-ə-jən\ *n* : a substance that induces hallucinations — **hal·lu·ci·no·gen·ic** \-ˌlüs-ᵊn-ə-'je-nik\ *adj or n*

hall·way \\'hòl-ˌwä\ *n* **1 :** an entrance hall **2 :** CORRIDOR

ha·lo \\'hā-lo\ *n, pl* **halos** *or* **haloes** [L *halos*, fr. Gk *halōs* threshing floor, disk, halo] **1 :** a circle of light appearing to surround a shining body (as the sun) **2 :** the aura of glory surrounding an idealized person or thing

hal·o·gen \\'ha-lə-jən\ *n* : any of the five elements fluorine, chlorine, bromine, iodine, and astatine

¹halt \\'hòlt\ *adj* : LAME

²halt *n* : STOP

³halt *vb* **1 :** to stop marching or traveling **2 :** DISCONTINUE, END

¹hal·ter \\'hòl-tər\ *n* **1 :** a rope or strap for leading or tying an animal; *also* : HEADSTALL **2 :** NOOSE **3 :** a brief blouse held in place by straps around the neck and across the back

²halter *vb* **hal·tered; hal·ter·ing 1 :** to catch with or as if with a halter; *also* : to put a halter on (as a horse) **2 :** HANG; IMPEDE, RESTRAIN

halt·ing \\'hòl-tiŋ\ *adj* : UNCERTAIN, FALTERING — **halt·ing·ly** *adv*

halve \\'hav, 'håv\ *vb* **halved; halv·ing 1 :** to divide into two equal parts **2 :** to reduce to one half

halv·ers \\'ha-vərz, 'hà-\ *n pl* : half shares : HALVES

halves *pl of* HALF

hal·yard \\'hal-yərd\ *n* : a rope or tackle for hoisting and lowering (as sails)

¹ham \\'ham\ *n* **1 :** a buttock with its associated thigh — usu. used in pl. **2 :** a cut of meat and esp. pork from the thigh **3 :** a showy performer **4 :** an operator of an amateur radio station — **ham** *adj*

²ham *vb* **hammed; ham•ming** : to overplay a part : OVERACT

ham•burg•er \\'ham-₁bər-gər\\ *or* **ham•burg** \\-₁bərg\\ *n* [G *Hamburger* of Hamburg, Germany] **1** : ground beef **2** : a sandwich consisting of a ground-beef patty in a round roll

ham•let \\'ham-lət\\ *n* : a small village

¹ham•mer \\'ha-mər\\ *n* **1** : a hand tool used for pounding; *also* : something resembling a hammer in form or function **2** : the part of a gun whose striking action causes explosion of the charge **3** : a metal sphere hurled for distance in a track-and-field event **(hammer throw) 4** : ACCELERATOR 2

²hammer *vb* **1** : to beat, drive, or shape with repeated blows of a hammer : POUND **2** : to produce or bring about as if by repeated blows — usu. used with *out*

ham•mer•head \\'ha-mər-₁hed\\ *n* **1** : the striking part of a hammer **2** : any of a family of medium-sized sharks with eyes at the ends of lateral extensions of the flattened head

hammerhead 2

ham•mer•lock \\-₁läk\\ *n* : a wrestling hold in which an opponent's arm is held bent behind the back

ham•mer•toe \\-₁tō\\ *n* : a toe deformed by having one or more joints permanently flexed

¹ham•mock \\'ha-mək\\ *n* [Sp *hamaca*, of AmerInd origin] : a swinging couch hung by cords at each end

²hammock *n* : a fertile elevated area of the southern U.S. and esp. Florida with hardwood vegetation and soil rich in humus

¹ham•per \\'ham-pər\\ *vb* : IMPEDE; *also* : RESTRAIN **syn** trammel, clog, fetter, shackle

²hamper *n* : a large basket

ham•ster \\'ham-stər\\ *n* [G, fr. OHG *hamustro*, of Slavic origin] : any of a subfamily of small Old World rodents with large cheek pouches

¹ham•string \\'ham-₁striŋ\\ *n* : any of several muscles at the back of the thigh or tendons at the back of the knee

²hamstring *vb* **-strung** \\-₁strəŋ\\; **-string•ing 1** : to cripple by cutting the leg tendons **2** : to make ineffective or powerless

¹hand \\'hand\\ *n* **1** : the end of a front limb when modified (as in humans) for grasping **2** : an indicator or pointer on a dial **3** : personal possession — usu. used in pl.; *also* : CONTROL **4** : SIDE 5 **5** : a pledge esp. of betrothal **6** : HANDWRITING **7** : SKILL, ABILITY; *also* : a significant part **8** : ASSISTANCE; *also* : PARTICIPATION **9** : an outburst of applause **10** : a single round in a card game; *also* : the cards held by a player after a deal **11** : WORKER, EMPLOYEE; *also* : a member of a ship's crew — **hand•less** *adj* — **at hand** : near in time or place — **on hand** : in present possession or readily available

²hand *vb* **1** : to lead, guide, or assist with the hand **2** : to give, pass, or transmit with the hand

hand•bag \\'hand-₁bag\\ *n* : a bag for carrying small personal articles and money

hand•ball \\-₁bȯl\\ *n* : a game played by striking a small rubber ball against a wall with the hand

hand•bill \\-₁bil\\ *n* : a small printed sheet for distribution by hand

hand•book \\-₁bu̇k\\ *n* : a concise reference book : MANUAL

hand•car \\-₁kär\\ *n* : a small 4-wheeled railroad car propelled by hand or by a small motor

hand•clasp \\-₁klasp\\ *n* : HANDSHAKE

hand•craft \\-₁kraft\\ *vb* : to fashion by manual skill

¹hand•cuff \\-₁kəf\\ *n* : a metal fastening that can be locked around a wrist and is usu. connected with another such fastening — usu. used in pl.

²handcuff *vb* : MANACLE

hand•ful \\-₁fu̇l\\ *n*, *pl* **hand•fuls** \\-₁fu̇lz\\ *also* **hands•ful** \\'handz-₁fu̇l\\ **1** : as much or as many as the hand will grasp **2** : a small number **3** : as much as one can manage

hand•gun \\-₁gən\\ *n* : a firearm held and fired with one hand

¹hand•i•cap \\'han-di-₁kap\\ *n* [obs. E *handicap*, a game in which forfeits were held in a cap, fr. *hand in cap*] **1** : a contest in which an artificial advantage is given or disadvantage imposed on a contestant to equalize chances of winning; *also* : the advantage given or disadvantage imposed **2** : a disadvantage that makes achievement difficult

²handicap *vb* **-capped; -cap•ping 1** : to give a handicap to **2** : to put at a disadvantage

hand•i•capped *adj* : having a physical or mental disability that limits activity

hand•i•cap•per \\-₁ka-pər\\ *n* : a person who predicts the winners in a horse race usu. for a publication

hand•i•craft \\'han-di-₁kraft\\ *n* **1** : manual skill **2** : an occupation requiring manual skill **3** : the articles fashioned by those engaged in handicraft — **hand•i•craft•er** \\-₁kraf-tər\\ *n* — **hand•i•crafts•man** \\-₁krafts-mən\\ *n*

hand in glove *or* **hand and glove** *adv* : in an extremely close relationship

hand•i•work \\'han-di-₁wərk\\ *n* : work done personally or by the hands

hand•ker•chief \\'haŋ-kər-chəf, -₁chēf \\ *n*, *pl* **-chiefs** \\-chəfs, -₁chēfs\\ *also* **-chieves** \\-₁chēvz\\ : a small piece of cloth used for various personal purposes (as the wiping of the face)

¹han•dle \\'hand-ᵊl\\ *n* : a part (as of a tool) designed to be grasped by the hand — **han•dled** \\-ᵊld\\ *adj* — **off the handle** : into a state of sudden and violent anger — usu. used with *fly*

²handle *vb* **han•dled; han•dling 1** : to touch, hold, or manage with the hands **2** : to have responsibility for **3** : to deal or trade in **4** : to behave in a certain way when managed or directed ⟨a car that ∼*s* well⟩ — **han•dler** *n*

han•dle•bar \\'hand-ᵊl-₁bär\\ *n* : a usu. bent bar with a grip at each end (as for steering a bicycle) — usu. used in pl.

hand•made \\'hand-'mād\\ *adj* : made by hand or by a hand process

hand•maid•en \\-₁mād-ᵊn\\ *also* **hand•maid** \\-₁mād\\ *n* : a female attendant

hand–me–down \\-me-₁dau̇n\\ *adj* : used by one person after having been used by another — **hand–me–down** *n*

hand•out \\'han-₁dau̇t\\ *n* **1** : a portion (as of food) given to a beggar **2** : a piece of printed information for free distribution; *also* : a prepared statement released to the press

hand•pick \\'hand-'pik\\ *vb* : to select personally ⟨a ∼*ed* candidate⟩

hand•rail \\-₁rāl\\ *n* : a narrow rail for grasping as a support

hand•saw \\-₁sȯ\\ *n* : a saw designed to be used with one hand

hands down *adv* **1** : with little effort **2** : without question

hand•sel \'han-səl\ *n* **1** : a gift made as a token of good luck **2** : a first installment : earnest money

hand•set \'hand-ˌset\ *n* : a combined telephone transmitter and receiver mounted on a handle

hand•shake \-ˌshāk\ *n* : a clasping usu. of right hands by two people

hands–off \'handz-'òf\ *adj* : characterized by noninterference

hand•some \'han-səm\ *adj* hand•som•er; -est [ME *handsom* easy to manipulate] **1** : SIZABLE, AMPLE **2** : GENEROUS, LIBERAL **3** : pleasing and usu. impressive in appearance **syn** beautiful, lovely, pretty, comely, fair — hand•some•ly *adv* — hand•some•ness *n*

hands–on \'handz-'òn, -'än\ *adj* **1** : being or providing direct practical experience in the operation of something **2** : characterized by active personal involvement ⟨∼ management⟩

hand•spring \'hand-ˌspriŋ\ *n* : an acrobatic feat in which the body turns in a full circle from a standing position and lands first on the hands and then on the feet

hand•stand \-ˌstand\ *n* : an act of supporting the body on the hands with the trunk and legs balanced in the air

hand–to–hand *adj* : involving physical contact or very close range ⟨∼ fighting⟩ — hand to hand *adv*

hand–to–mouth *adj* : having or providing nothing to spare

hand•wo•ven \'hand-ˌwō-vən\ *adj* : produced on a hand-operated loom

hand•writ•ing \-ˌrī-tiŋ\ *n* : writing done by hand; *also* : the form of writing peculiar to a person — hand•writ•ten \-ˌrit-°n\ *adj*

handy \'han-dē\ *adj* hand•i•er; -est **1** : conveniently near **2** : easily used **3** : DEXTEROUS — hand•i•ly \-də-lē\ *adv* — hand•i•ness \-dē-nəs\ *n*

handy•man \-ˌman\ *n* **1** : one who does odd jobs **2** : one competent in a variety of small skills or repair work

¹hang \'haŋ\ *vb* hung \'həŋ\ *also* hanged; hang•ing **1** : to fasten or remain fastened to an elevated point without support from below; *also* : to fasten or be fastened so as to allow free motion on the point of suspension ⟨∼ a door⟩ **2** : to suspend by the neck until dead; *also* : to die by hanging **3** : DROOP ⟨*hung* his head in shame⟩ **4** : to fasten to a wall ⟨∼ wallpaper⟩ **5** : to prevent (a jury) from coming to a decision **6** : to display (pictures) in a gallery **7** : to remain stationary in the air **8** : to be imminent **9** : DEPEND **10** : to take hold for support **11** : to be burdensome **12** : to undergo delay **13** : to incline downward; *also* : to fit or fall from the figure in easy lines **14** : to be raptly attentive **15** : LINGER, LOITER — hang•er *n*

²hang *n* **1** : the manner in which a thing hangs **2** : an understanding of something

han•gar \'haŋ-ər\ *n* [F] : a covered and usu. enclosed area for housing and repairing aircraft

hang•dog \'haŋ-ˌdòg\ *adj* **1** : ASHAMED, GUILTY **2** : ABJECT, COWED

hang•er–on \'haŋ-ər-'òn, -'än\ *n, pl* hangers–on : one who hangs around a person or place esp. for personal gain

hang in *vb* : to persist tenaciously

hang•ing *n* **1** : an execution by strangling or snapping the neck by a suspended noose **2** : something hung

hang•man \'haŋ-mən\ *n* : a public executioner

hang•nail \-ˌnāl\ *n* : a bit of skin hanging loose at the edge of a fingernail

hang on *vb* **1** : HANG IN **2** : to keep a telephone connection open

hang•out \'haŋ-ˌaút\ *n* : a favorite place for spending time

hang•over \-ˌō-vər\ *n* **1** : something that remains from what is past **2** : disagreeable physical effects following heavy drinking

hang–up \'haŋ-ˌəp\ *n* : a source of mental or emotional difficulty

hang up *vb* **1** : to place on a hook or hanger **2** : to end a telephone conversation by replacing the receiver on the cradle **3** : to keep delayed or suspended

hank \'haŋk\ *n* : COIL, LOOP

han•ker \'haŋ-kər\ *vb* : to desire strongly or persistently — han•ker•ing *n*

han•kie *or* han•ky \'haŋ-kē\ *n, pl* hankies : HANDKERCHIEF

han•ky–pan•ky \ˌhaŋ-kē-'paŋ-kē\ *n* **1** : questionable or underhanded activity **2** : sexual dalliance

han•sel *var of* HANDSEL

han•som \'han-səm\ *n* : a 2-wheeled covered carriage with the driver's seat elevated at the rear

Ha•nuk•kah \'kä-nə-kə, 'hä-\ *n* [Heb *ḥănukkāh* dedication] : an 8-day Jewish holiday commemorating the rededication of the Temple of Jerusalem after its defilement by Antiochus of Syria

hap \'hap\ *n* **1** : HAPPENING **2** : CHANCE, FORTUNE

¹hap•haz•ard \hap-'ha-zərd\ *n* : CHANCE

²haphazard *adj* : marked by lack of plan or order — hap•haz•ard•ly *adv* — hap•haz•ard•ness *n*

hap•less \'hap-ləs\ *adj* : UNFORTUNATE — hap•less•ly *adv* — hap•less•ness *n*

hap•loid \'hap-ˌlòid\ *adj* : having the number of chromosomes characteristic of gametic cells — haploid *n*

hap•ly \'hap-lē\ *adv* : by chance

hap•pen \'ha-pən\ *vb* **1** : to occur by chance **2** : to take place **3** : CHANCE **2**

hap•pen•ing *n* **1** : OCCURRENCE **2** : an event that is especially interesting, entertaining, or important

hap•pi•ly \'ha-pə-lē\ *adv* **1** : LUCKILY **2** : in a happy manner or state ⟨lived ∼ ever after⟩ **3** : APTLY, SUCCESSFULLY

hap•pi•ness \'ha-pē-nəs\ *n* **1** : a state of well=being and contentment; *also* : a pleasurable satisfaction **2** : APTNESS

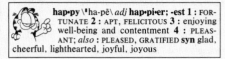

hap·py \'ha-pē\ *adj* **hap·pi·er; -est 1** : FORTUNATE **2** : APT, FELICITOUS **3** : enjoying well-being and contentment **4** : PLEASANT; *also* : PLEASED, GRATIFIED **syn** glad, cheerful, lighthearted, joyful, joyous

hap·py–go–lucky \ˌha-pē-gō-'lə-kē\ *adj* : CAREFREE

happy hour *n* : a period of time when the price of drinks at a bar is reduced

hara-kiri \ˌhar-i-'kir-ē, -'kar-ē\ *n* [Jp *harakiri,* fr. *hara* belly + *kiri* cutting] : ritual suicide by disembowelment

ha·rangue \hə-'raŋ\ *n* **1** : a ranting speech or writing **2** : LECTURE — **harangue** *vb* — **ha·rangu·er** *n*

ha·rass \hə-'ras, 'har-əs\ *vb* [F *harasser,* fr. MF, fr. *harer* to set a dog on, fr. OF *hare,* interj. used to incite dogs, of Gmc origin] **1** : EXHAUST, FATIGUE **2** : to worry and impede by repeated raids **3** : to annoy continually **syn** harry, plague, pester, tease, bedevil — **ha·rass·ment** *n*

har·bin·ger \'här-bən-jər\ *n* : one that announces or foreshadows what is coming : PRECURSOR; *also* : PORTENT

¹**har·bor** \'här-bər\ *n* **1** : a place of security and comfort **2** : a part of a body of water protected and deep enough to furnish anchorage : PORT

²**harbor** *vb* **1** : to give or take refuge : SHELTER **2** : to be the home or habitat of; *also* : LIVE **3** : to hold a thought or feeling ⟨∼ a grudge⟩

har·bor·age \'här-bə-rij\ *n* : HARBOR

har·bour *chiefly Brit var of* HARBOR

hard \'härd\ *adj* **1** : not easily penetrated : not easily yielding to pressure **2** : high in alcoholic content **3** : containing salts that prevent lathering with soap ⟨∼ water⟩ **4** : stable in value ⟨∼ currency⟩ **5** : physically fit **6** : FIRM, DEFINITE ⟨∼ agreement⟩; *also* : based on clear fact ⟨∼ evidence⟩ **7** : CLOSE, SEARCHING ⟨∼ look⟩ **8** : REALISTIC ⟨good ∼ sense⟩ **9** : OBDURATE, UNFEELING ⟨∼ heart⟩ **10** : difficult to bear ⟨∼ times⟩; *also* : HARSH, SEVERE **11** : RESENTFUL ⟨∼ feelings⟩ **12** : STRICT, UNRELENTING ⟨∼ bargain⟩ **13** : INCLEMENT ⟨∼ winter⟩ **14** : intense in force or manner ⟨∼ blow⟩ **15** : ARDUOUS, STRENUOUS ⟨∼ work⟩ **16** : sounding as in *arcing* and *geese* respectively — used of *c* and *g* **17** : TROUBLESOME ⟨∼ problem⟩ **18** : having difficulty in doing something ⟨∼ of hearing⟩ **19** : addictive and gravely detrimental to health ⟨∼ drugs⟩ **20** : of or relating to the natural sciences and esp. the physical sciences — **hard** *adv* — **hard·ness** *n*

hard–and–fast *adj* : rigidly binding : STRICT ⟨a ∼ rule⟩

hard·back \'härd-ˌbak\ *n* : a hardcover book

hard·ball \-ˌbȯl\ *n* **1** : BASEBALL **2** : forceful uncompromising methods

hard–bit·ten \-'bit-ᵊn\ *adj* : SEASONED, TOUGH ⟨∼ campaigners⟩

hard·board \-ˌbȯrd\ *n* : a very dense fiberboard

hard–boiled \-'bȯild\ *adj* **1** *of an egg* : boiled until both white and yolk have solidified **2** : lacking sentiment : TOUGH; *also* : HARDHEADED **2**

hard·bound \-ˌbaȯnd\ *adj* : HARDCOVER

hard copy *n* : copy of textual or graphic information (as from computer storage) produced on paper

hard–core \'härd-'kȯr\ *adj* **1** : extremely resistant to solution or improvement **2** : being the most determined or dedicated members of a specified group **3** : containing explicit depictions of sex acts — **hard core** *n*

hard–cov·er \-'kə-vər\ *adj* : having rigid boards on the sides covered in cloth or paper ⟨∼ books⟩

hard disk *n* : a sealed rigid metal disk used as a computer storage device

hard·en \'härd-ᵊn\ *vb* **1** : to make or become hard or harder **2** : to confirm or become confirmed in disposition or action — **hard·en·er** *n*

hard·hack \'härd-ˌhak\ *n* : an American spirea with dense clusters of pink or white flowers and leaves having a hairy rusty yellow underside

hard hat *n* **1** : a protective hat worn esp. by construction workers **2** : a construction worker

hard·head·ed \'härd-'he-dəd\ *adj* **1** : STUBBORN, WILLFUL **2** : SOBER, REALISTIC — **hard·head·ed·ly** *adv* — **hard·head·ed·ness** *n*

hard–heart·ed \-'här-təd\ *adj* : PITILESS, CRUEL — **hard–heart·ed·ly** *adv* — **hard–heart·ed·ness** *n*

har·di·hood \'här-dē-ˌhu̇d\ *n* **1** : resolute courage and fortitude **2** : VIGOR, ROBUSTNESS

hard–line \'härd-'līn\ *adj* : advocating or involving a rigidly uncompromising course of action — **hard–lin·er** \-'lī-nər\ *n*

hard·ly \'härd-lē\ *adv* **1** : with force **2** : SEVERELY **3** : with difficulty **4** : only just : BARELY **5** : certainly not

hard–nosed \'härd-'nōzd\ *adj* : TOUGH, UNCOMPROMISING; *also* : HARDHEADED **2**

hard palate *n* : the bony anterior part of the palate forming the roof of the mouth

hard·pan \'härd-ˌpan\ *n* : a compact layer in soil that is impenetrable by roots

hard–pressed \-'prest\ *adj* : HARD PUT; *esp* : being under financial strain

hard put *adj* **1** : barely able **2** : faced with difficulty or perplexity

hard rock *n* : rock music marked by a heavy beat, high amplification, and usu. frenzied performances

hard–shell \'härd-ˌshel\ *adj* : HIDEBOUND, UNCOMPROMISING ⟨a ∼ conservative⟩

hard·ship \-ˌship\ *n* **1** : SUFFERING, PRIVATION **2** : something that causes suffering or privation

hard·tack \-ˌtak\ *n* : a saltless hard biscuit, bread, or cracker

hard·top \-ˌtäp\ *n* : an automobile having a permanent rigid top

hard·ware \-ˌwar\ *n* **1** : ware (as cutlery or tools) made of metal **2** : the physical components (as electronic devices) of a vehicle (as a spacecraft) or an apparatus (as a computer)

hard·wood \-ˌwu̇d\ *n* : the wood of a broad-leaved usu. deciduous tree as distinguished from that of a conifer; *also* : such a tree — **hardwood** *adj*

hard·work·ing \-'wər-kiŋ\ *adj* : INDUSTRIOUS

har·dy \ˈhär-dē\ adj **har·di·er; -est 1** : BOLD, BRAVE **2** : AUDACIOUS, BRAZEN **3** : ROBUST; also : able to withstand adverse conditions (as of weather) (∼ shrubs) — **har·di·ly** \-də-lē\ adv — **har·di·ness** \-dē-nəs\ n

hare \ˈhar\ n, pl **hare** or **hares** : any of various swift timid long-eared mammals like the related rabbits but born with open eyes and fur

hare·bell \ˈhar-ˌbel\ n : a slender herb with bright blue bell-shaped flowers

hare·brained \-ˈbränd\ adj : FOOLISH

hare·lip \-ˈlip\ n : a birth defect in which the upper lip is vertically split — **hare·lipped** \-ˈlipt\ adj

ha·rem \ˈhar-əm\ n [Ar ḥarīm, lit., something forbidden & ḥaram, lit., sanctuary] **1** : a house or part of a house allotted to women in a Muslim household **2** : the women and servants occupying a harem **3** : a group of females associated with one male

hark \ˈhärk\ vb : LISTEN

harken var of HEARKEN

har·le·quin \ˈhär-li-kən, -kwən\ n **1** cap : a character (as in comedy) with a shaved head, masked face, variegated tights, and wooden sword **2** : CLOWN 2

har·lot \ˈhär-lət\ n : PROSTITUTE

¹harm \ˈhärm\ n **1** : physical or mental damage : INJURY **2** : MISCHIEF, HURT — **harm·ful** \-fəl\ adj — **harm·ful·ly** adv — **harm·ful·ness** n — **harm·less** adj — **harm·less·ly** adv — **harm·less·ness** n

²harm vb : to cause harm to : INJURE

¹har·mon·ic \här-ˈmä-nik\ adj **1** : of or relating to musical harmony or harmonics **2** : pleasing to the ear — **har·mon·i·cal·ly** \-ni-k(ə-)lē\ adv

²harmonic n : a musical overtone

har·mon·i·ca \här-ˈmä-ni-kə\ n : a small wind instrument in which the sound is produced by metal reeds

har·mo·ni·ous \här-ˈmō-nē-əs\ adj **1** : musically concordant **2** : CONGRUOUS **3** : marked by accord in sentiment or action — **har·mo·ni·ous·ly** adv — **har·mo·ni·ous·ness** n

har·mo·nise Brit var of HARMONIZE

har·mo·ni·um \här-ˈmō-nē-əm\ n : a keyboard wind instrument in which the wind acts on a set of metal reeds

har·mo·nize \ˈhär-mə-ˌnīz\ vb **-nized; -niz·ing 1** : to play or sing in harmony **2** : to be in harmony **3** : to bring into consonance or accord — **har·mo·ni·za·tion** \ˌhär-mə-nə-ˈzā-shən\ n

har·mo·ny \ˈhär-mə-nē\ n, pl **-nies 1** : musical agreement of sounds; esp : the combination of tones into chords and progressions of chords **2** : a pleasing arrangement of parts; also : ACCORD **3** : internal calm

¹har·ness \ˈhär-nəs\ n **1** : the gear other than a yoke of a draft animal **2** : something that resembles a harness

²harness vb **1** : to put a harness on; also : YOKE **2** : UTILIZE

¹harp \ˈhärp\ n : a musical instrument consisting of a triangular frame set with strings plucked by the fingers — **harp·ist** \ˈhär-pist\ n

²harp vb **1** : to play on a harp **2** : to dwell on a subject tiresomely — **harp·er** n

har·poon \här-ˈpün\ n : a barbed spear used esp. in hunting whales — **harpoon** vb — **har·poon·er** n

harp·si·chord \ˈhärp-si-ˌkȯrd\ n : a keyboard instrument producing tones by the plucking of its strings with quills or with leather or plastic points

har·py \ˈhär-pē\ n, pl **harpies** [L Harpyia, a mythical predatory monster having a woman's head and a bird's body, fr. Gk] **1** : a predatory person : LEECH 2 **2** : a shrewish woman

har·ri·dan \ˈhar-əd-ᵊn\ n : SHREW 2

¹har·ri·er \ˈhar-ē-ər\ n **1** : any of a breed of medium-sized foxhounds **2** : a runner on a cross-country team

²harrier n : a slender long-legged hawk

¹har·row \ˈhar-ō\ n : a cultivating tool that has spikes, spring teeth, or disks and is used esp. to pulverize and smooth the soil

²harrow vb **1** : to cultivate with a harrow **2** : TORMENT, VEX

har·ry \ˈhar-ē\ vb **har·ried; har·ry·ing 1** : RAID, PILLAGE **2** : to torment by or as if by constant attack syn worry, annoy, plague, pester

harsh \ˈhärsh\ adj **1** : disagreeably rough **2** : causing discomfort or pain **3** : unduly exacting : SEVERE — **harsh·ly** adv — **harsh·ness** n

hart \ˈhärt\ n, chiefly Brit : STAG

har·um-scar·um \ˌhar-əm-ˈskar-əm\ adj : RECKLESS, IRRESPONSIBLE

¹har·vest \ˈhär-vəst\ n **1** : the season for gathering in crops; also : the act of gathering in a crop **2** : a mature crop **3** : the product or reward of effort

²harvest vb **1** : to gather in a crop : REAP **2** : to gather, hunt, or kill (as deer) for human use or population control — **har·vest·er** n

has pres 3d sing of HAVE

has-been \ˈhaz-ˌbin\ n : one that has passed the peak of ability, power, effectiveness, or popularity

¹hash \ˈhash\ vb [F hacher, fr. OF hachier, fr. hache battle-ax, of Gmc origin] **1** : to chop into small pieces **2** : to talk about

²hash n **1** : chopped meat mixed with potatoes and browned **2** : HODGEPODGE, JUMBLE

³hash n : HASHISH

hash browns n pl : boiled potatoes that are diced, mixed with chopped onions and shortening, and fried

hash·ish \ˈha-ˌshēsh, ha-ˈshēsh\ [Ar ḥashīsh] n : the concentrated resin from the flowering tops of the female hemp plant

hasp \ˈhasp\ n : a fastener (as for a door) consisting of a hinged metal strap that fits over a staple and is secured by a pin or padlock

hasp

has·sle \ˈha-səl\ n **1** : WRANGLE; also : FIGHT **2** : an annoying or troublesome concern — **hassle** vb

has·sock \ˈha-sək\ n **1** : a cushion that serves as a seat or leg rest; also : a cushion to kneel on in prayer

haste \ˈhāst\ n **1** : rapidity of motion or action : SPEED **2** : rash or headlong action **3** : excessive eagerness — **hast·i·ly** \ˈhā-stə-lē\ adv — **hast·i·ness** \-stē-nəs\ n — **hasty** \ˈhā-stē\ adj

has·ten \ˈhās-ᵊn\ vb **1** : to urge on **2** : to move or act quickly : HURRY syn speed, accelerate, quicken

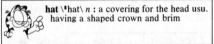

hat \ˈhat\ n : a covering for the head usu. having a shaped crown and brim

hat·box \ˈhat-ˌbäks\ n : a round piece of luggage esp. for carrying hats

¹hatch \ˈhach\ n **1** : a small door or opening **2** : a door or cover for access down into a compartment of a ship

²hatch vb **1** : to produce by incubation; also : INCUBATE **2** : to emerge from an egg or pupa; also : to give forth young **3** : ORIGINATE — **hatch·ery** \ˈha-chə-rē\ n

hatch·back \ˈhach-ˌbak\ n : an automobile with a rear hatch that opens upward

hatch·et \ˈha-chət\ n **1** : a short-handled ax with a hammerlike part opposite the blade **2** : TOMAHAWK

hatchet man *n* : a person hired for murder, coercion, or unscrupulous attack

hatch·ing \\'ha-chiŋ\ *n* : the engraving or drawing of closely spaced fine lines chiefly to give an effect of shading; *also* : the pattern so created

hatch·way \\'hach-ˌwā\ *n* : a hatch giving access usu. by a ladder or stairs

¹**hate** \\'hāt\ *n* **1** : intense hostility and aversion **2** : an object of hatred — **hate·ful** \-fəl\ *adj* — **hate·ful·ly** *adv* — **hate·ful·ness** *n*

²**hate** *vb* **hat·ed; hat·ing 1** : to express or feel extreme enmity **2** : to find distasteful *syn* detest, abhor, abominate, loathe — **hat·er** *n*

ha·tred \\'hā-trəd\ *n* : HATE; *also* : prejudiced hostility or animosity

hat·ter \\'ha-tər\ *n* : one that makes, sells, or cleans and repairs hats

hau·berk \\'hȯ-bərk\ *n* : a coat of mail

haugh·ty \\'hȯ-tē\ *adj* **haugh·ti·er; -est** [obs. *haught,* fr. ME *haute,* fr. MF *haut,* lit., high, fr. L *altus*] : disdainfully proud *syn* insolent, lordly, overbearing, arrogant — **haugh·ti·ly** \-tə-lē\ *adv* — **haugh·ti·ness** \-tē-nəs\ *n*

¹**haul** \\'hȯl\ *vb* **1** : to exert traction on : DRAW, PULL **2** : to furnish transportation : CART — **haul·er** *n*

²**haul** *n* **1** : PULL, TUG **2** : the result of an effort to obtain, collect, or win **3** : the length or course of a transportation route; *also* : LOAD

haul·age \\'hȯ-lij\ *n* **1** : the act or process of hauling **2** : a charge for hauling

haunch \\'hȯnch\ *n* **1** : ²HIP **1 2** : HINDQUARTER 2 — usu. used in pl. **3** : HINDQUARTER 1

¹**haunt** \\'hȯnt\ *vb* **1** : to visit often : FREQUENT **2** : to recur constantly and spontaneously to; *also* : to reappear continually in **3** : to visit or inhabit as a ghost — **haunt·er** *n* — **haunt·ing·ly** *adv*

²**haunt** \\'hȯnt, 2 is usu\ 'hant\ *n* **1** : a place habitually frequented **2** *chiefly dial* : GHOST

haute cou·ture \ˌōt-kü-'tu̇r\ *n* [F] : the establishments or designers that create exclusive and often trend-setting fashions for women; *also* : the fashions created

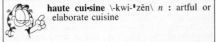

haute cui·sine \-kwi-'zēn\ *n* : artful or elaborate cuisine

hau·teur \hȯ-'tər, ō-, hō-\ *n* : ARROGANCE, HAUGHTINESS

¹**have** \\'hav, həv, v; *in sense 2 before "to" usu* 'haf\ *vb* **had** \\'had, həd\; **hav·ing; has** \\'haz, həz, *in sense 2 before "to" usu* 'has\ **1** : to hold in possession; *also* : to hold in one's use, service, or regard **2** : to be compelled or forced ⟨~ to go now⟩ **3** : to stand in relationship to ⟨*has* many enemies⟩ **4** : OBTAIN; *also* : RECEIVE, ACCEPT **5** : to be marked by **6** : SHOW; *also* : USE, EXERCISE **7** : EXPERIENCE; *also* : TAKE ⟨~ a look⟩ **8** : to entertain in the mind ⟨~ an idea⟩ **9** : to cause to **10** : ALLOW **11** : to be competent in **12** : to hold in a disadvantageous position; *also* : TRICK **13** : BEGET **14** : to partake of **15** — used as an auxiliary with the past participle to form the present perfect, past perfect, or future perfect — **have at** : ATTACK — **have coming** : DESERVE — **have done with** : to be finished with — **have had it** : to have endured all one will permit or can stand — **have to do with** : to have in the way of relation with or effect on

²**have** \\'hav\ *n* : one that has material wealth

ha·ven \\'hā-vən\ *n* **1** : HARBOR, PORT **2** : a place of safety **3** : a place offering favorable conditions ⟨a tourist's ~⟩

have–not \\'hav-ˌnät, -'nät\ *n* : one that is poor in material wealth

hav·er·sack \\'ha-vər-ˌsak\ *n* [F *havresac,* fr. G *Habersack* bag for oats] : a bag similar to a knapsack but worn over one shoulder

hav·oc \\'ha-vək\ *n* **1** : wide and general destruction **2** : great confusion and disorder

haw \\'hȯ\ *n* : a hawthorn berry; *also* : HAWTHORN

Ha·wai·ian \hə-'wä-yən\ *n* : the Polynesian language of Hawaii

¹**hawk** \\'hȯk\ *n* **1** : any of numerous mostly small or medium-sized day-flying birds of prey (as a falcon or kite) **2** : a supporter of a war or a warlike policy — **hawk·ish** *adj*

²**hawk** vb : to offer goods for sale by calling out in the street — **hawk•er** n

³**hawk** vb : to make a harsh coughing sound in or as if in clearing the throat; also : to raise by hawking

hawk•weed \'hòk-ˌwēd\ n : any of several plants related to the daisies usu. having red or orange flower heads

haw•ser \'hò-zər\ n : a large rope for towing, mooring, or securing a ship

haw•thorn \'hò-ˌthòrn\ n : any of a genus of spiny spring-flowering shrubs or trees related to the apple

¹**hay** \'hā\ n 1 : herbage (as grass) mowed and cured for fodder 2 : REWARD 3 slang : BED ⟨hit the ~⟩ 4 : a small amount of money

²**hay** vb : to cut, cure, and store for hay

hay•cock \'hā-ˌkäk\ n : a small conical pile of hay

hay fever n : an acute allergic reaction esp. to plant pollen that resembles a cold

hay•loft \'hā-ˌlòft\ n : a loft for hay

hay•mow \-ˌmaú\ n : a mow of or for hay

hay•rick \-ˌrik\ n : a large sometimes thatched outdoor stack of hay

hay•seed \-ˌsēd\ n, pl hayseed or hayseeds 1 : clinging bits of straw or chaff from hay 2 : BUMPKIN, YOKEL

hay•stack \-ˌstak\ n : a stack of hay

hay•wire \-ˌwīr\ adj : being out of order or control 2 : CRAZY

¹**haz•ard** \'ha-zərd\ n [ME, a dice game, fr. MF hasard, fr. Ar az-zahr the die] 1 : a source of danger 2 : CHANCE; also : ACCIDENT 3 : an obstacle on a golf course — **haz•ard•ous** adj

²**hazard** vb : VENTURE, RISK

¹**haze** \'hāz\ n 1 : fine dust, smoke, or light vapor causing lack of transparency in the air 2 : vagueness of mind or perception

²**haze** vb hazed; haz•ing : to harass by abusive and humiliating tricks usu. by way of initiation

ha•zel \'hā-zəl\ n 1 : any of a genus of shrubs or small trees related to the birches and bearing edible nuts (**ha•zel•nuts** \-ˌnəts\) 2 : a light brown color

hazy \'hā-zē\ adj haz•i•er; -est 1 : obscured or darkened by haze 2 : VAGUE, INDEFINITE — **haz•i•ly** \-zə-lē\ adv — **haz•i•ness** \-zē-nəs\ n

Hb abbr hemoglobin

HBM abbr Her Britannic Majesty; His Britannic Majesty

H–bomb \'āch-ˌbäm\ n : HYDROGEN BOMB

HC abbr 1 Holy Communion 2 House of Commons

hd abbr head

HD abbr heavy-duty

hdbk abbr handbook

hdkf abbr handkerchief

HDL \ˌāch-(ˌ)dē-ˈel\ n [high-density lipoprotein] : a cholesterol-poor protein-rich lipoprotein of blood plasma correlated with reduced risk of atherosclerosis

hdwe abbr hardware

he \'hē\ pron 1 : that male one 2 : a person : the person ⟨~ who hesitates is lost⟩

He symbol helium

HE abbr 1 Her Excellency 2 His Eminence 3 His Excellency

¹**head** \'hed\ n 1 : the front or upper part of the body containing the brain, the chief sense organs, and the mouth 2 : MIND; also : natural aptitude 3 : POISE 4 : the obverse of a coin 5 : INDIVIDUAL; also, pl head : one of a number (as of cattle) 6 : the end that is upper or higher or opposite the foot; also : either end of something (as a drum) whose two ends need not be distinguished 7 : the source of a stream 8 : DIRECTOR, LEADER; also : a leading element (as of a procession) 9 : a projecting part; also : the striking part of a weapon 10 : the place of leadership or honor 11 : a separate part or topic 12 : the foam on a fermenting or effervescing liquid 13 : CRISIS — **head•ed** \'he-dəd\ adj — **head•less** adj

²**head** adj : PRINCIPAL, CHIEF

³**head** vb 1 : to provide with or form a head; also : to form the head of 2 : LEAD, CONDUCT 3 : to get in front of esp. so as to stop; also : SURPASS 4 : to put or stand at the head of 5 : to point or proceed in a certain direction

head•ache \'he-ˌdāk\ n 1 : pain in the head 2 : a baffling situation or problem

head•band \'hed-ˌband\ n : a band worn on or around the head

head•board \-ˌbòrd\ n : a board forming the head (as of a bed)

head cold n : a common cold centered in the nasal passages and adjacent mucous tissues

head•dress \'hed-ˌdres\ n : an often elaborate covering for the head

head•first \-ˈfərst\ adv : HEADLONG 1 — **headfirst** adj

head•gear \-ˌgir\ n : a covering or protective device for the head

head•hunt•ing \-ˌhən-tiŋ\ n : the practice of seeking out and decapitating enemies and preserving their heads as trophies — **head•hunt•er** \-tər\ n

head•ing \'he-diŋ\ n 1 : the compass direction in which the longitudinal axis of a ship or airplane points 2 : something that forms or serves as a head

head•land \'hed-lənd, -ˌland\ n : PROMONTORY

head•light \-ˌlīt\ n : a light mounted on the front of a vehicle to illuminate the road ahead

head•line \-ˌlīn\ n : a head of a newspaper story or article usu. printed in large type

head•lock \-ˌläk\ n : a wrestling hold in which one encircles the opponent's head with one arm

¹**head•long** \-ˈlòŋ\ adv 1 : with the head foremost 2 : RECKLESSLY 3 : without delay

²**head•long** \-ˌlòŋ\ adj 1 : PRECIPITATE, RASH 2 : plunging with the head foremost

head•man \'hed-ˈman, -ˌman\ n : one who is a leader : CHIEF

head•mas•ter \-ˌmas-tər\ n : a man who is head of a private school

head·mis·tress \-ˌmis-trəs\ n : a woman who is head of a private school

head–on \'hed-'ȯn, -'än\ adj : having the front facing in the direction of initial contact or line of sight ⟨∼ collision⟩ — **head–on** adv

head·phone \-ˌfōn\ n : an earphone held on by a band over the head

head·piece \-ˌpēs\ n : a covering for the head

head·pin \-ˌpin\ n : a bowling pin that stands foremost in the arrangement of pins

head·quar·ters \-ˌkwȯr-tərz\ n sing or pl 1 : a place from which a commander exercises command 2 : the administrative center of an enterprise

head·rest \-ˌrest\ n 1 : a support for the head 2 : a pad at the top of the back of an automobile seat

head·room \-ˌrüm, -ˌru̇m\ n : vertical space in which to stand, sit, or move

head·set \-ˌset\ n : a pair of headphones

head·ship \-ˌship\ n : the position, office, or dignity of a head

heads·man \'hedz-mən\ n : EXECUTIONER

head·stall \'hed-ˌstȯl\ n : a part of a bridle or halter that encircles the head

head·stone \-ˌstōn\ n : a memorial stone at the head of a grave

head·strong \-ˌstrȯŋ\ adj 1 : not easily restrained 2 : directed by ungovernable will syn unruly, intractable, willful, pertinacious, refractory, stubborn

head·wait·er \-'wā-tər\ n : the head of the dining-room staff of a restaurant or hotel

head·wa·ter \-ˌwȯ-tər, -ˌwä-\ n : the source of a stream — usu. used in pl.

head·way \-ˌwā\ n : forward motion; also : PROGRESS

head wind n : a wind blowing in a direction opposite to a course esp. of a ship or aircraft

head·word \'hed-ˌwərd\ n 1 : a word or term placed at the beginning 2 : a word qualified by a modifier

head·work \-ˌwərk\ n : mental work or effort : THINKING

heady \'he-dē\ adj **head·i·er; -est** 1 : WILLFUL, RASH; also : IMPETUOUS 2 : INTOXICATING 3 : SHREWD

heal \'hēl\ vb 1 : to make or become healthy, sound, or whole 2 : CURE, REMEDY — **heal·er** n

health \'helth\ n 1 : sound physical or mental condition; also : overall condition of the body ⟨in poor ∼⟩ 2 : WELL-BEING 3 : a toast to someone's health or prosperity

health·ful \'helth-fəl\ adj 1 : beneficial to health 2 : HEALTHY — **health·ful·ly** adv — **health·ful·ness** n

health maintenance organization n : HMO

healthy \'hel-thē\ adj **health·i·er; -est** 1 : enjoying or typical of good health : WELL 2 : evincing or conducive to health 3 : PROSPEROUS; also : CONSIDERABLE — **health·i·ly** \-thə-lē\ adv — **health·i·ness** \-thē-nəs\ n

¹heap \'hēp\ n : PILE; also : LOT

²heap vb 1 : to throw or lay in a heap 2 : to give in large quantities; also : to load heavily

hear \'hir\ vb **heard** \'hərd\; **hear·ing** 1 : to perceive by the ear 2 : to gain knowledge of by hearing : LEARN 3 : HEED; also : ATTEND 4 : to give a legal hearing to or take testimony from — **hear·er** n

hear·ing n 1 : the process, function, or power of perceiving sound; esp : the special sense by which noises and tones are received as stimuli 2 : EARSHOT 3 : opportunity to be heard 4 : a listening to arguments (as in a court); also : a session of (as of a legislative committee) in which testimony is taken from witnesses

hear·ken \'här-kən\ vb : to give attention : LISTEN syn hear, hark, heed

hear·say \'hir-ˌsā\ n : RUMOR

hearse \'hərs\ n : a vehicle for carrying the dead to the grave

heart \'härt\ n 1 : a hollow muscular organ that by rhythmic contraction keeps up the circulation of the blood in the body; also : something resembling a heart in shape 2 : any of a suit of playing cards marked with a red figure of a heart; also, pl : a card game in which the object is to avoid taking tricks containing hearts 3 : the whole personality; also : the emotional or moral as distinguished from the intellectual nature 4 : COURAGE 5 : one's innermost being 6 : CENTER; also : the essential part 7 : the younger central part of a compact leafy cluster (as of lettuce) — **heart·ed** \'här-təd\ adj — **by heart** : by rote or from memory

heart·ache \-ˌāk\ n : anguish of mind

heart attack n : an acute episode of heart disease due to insufficient blood supply to the heart muscle

heart·beat \'härt-ˌbēt\ n : one complete pulsation of the heart

heart·break \-ˌbrāk\ n : crushing grief

heart·break·ing \-ˌbrā-kiŋ\ adj : causing extreme sorrow or distress — **heart·break·er** \-ˌbrā-kər\ n

heart·bro·ken \-ˌbrō-kən\ adj : overcome by sorrow

heart·burn \-ˌbərn\ n : a burning distress in the area of the heart usu. due to spasms of the esophagus or upper stomach

heart disease n : an abnormal organic condition of the heart or of the heart and circulation

heart·en \'härt-ⁿn\ vb : ENCOURAGE, CHEER

heart·felt \'härt-ˌfelt\ adj : deeply felt : SINCERE

hearth \'härth\ n 1 : an area (as of brick) in front of a fireplace; also : the floor of a fireplace 2 : HOME

hearth·stone \'härth-ˌstōn\ n 1 : stone forming a hearth 2 : HOME

heart·less \'härt-ləs\ adj : CRUEL

heart·rend·ing \-ˌren-diŋ\ adj : HEARTBREAKING

heart·sick \-ˌsik\ adj : very despondent — **heart·sick·ness** n

heart·strings \-ˌstriŋz\ n pl : the deepest emotions or affections

heart·throb \-ˌthräb\ n 1 : the throb of a heart 2 : sentimental emotion 3 : SWEETHEART

heart–to–heart adj : SINCERE, FRANK

heart·warm·ing \'härt-ˌwȯr-miŋ\ adj : inspiring sympathetic feeling

heart·wood \-ˌwu̇d\ n : the older harder nonliving and usu. darker wood of the central part of a tree trunk

¹hearty \'här-tē\ adj **heart·i·er; -est** 1 : giving full support; also : JOVIAL 2 : vigorously healthy 3 : ABUNDANT; also : NOURISHING syn sincere, wholehearted, unfeigned, heartfelt — **heart·i·ly** \-tə-lē\ adv — **heart·i·ness** \-tē-nəs\ n

²hearty n, pl **heart·ies** : an enthusiastic jovial fellow; also : SAILOR

¹heat \'hēt\ vb 1 : to make or become warm or hot 2 : EXCITE — **heat·ed·ly** adv — **heat·er** n

²heat n 1 : a condition of being hot : WARMTH 2 : a form of energy that when added to a body causes the body to rise in temperature, to fuse, to evaporate, or to expand 3 : high temperature 4 : intensity of feeling; also : sexual excitement esp. in a female mammal 5 : a preliminary race for narrowing the competition 6 : pungency of flavor 7 slang : POLICE 8 : PRESSURE, COERCION; also : ABUSE, CRITICISM

heat exchanger n : a device (as an automobile radiator) for transferring heat from one fluid to another without allowing them to mix

heat exhaustion n : a condition marked by weakness, nausea, dizziness, and profuse sweating resulting from physical exertion in a hot environment

heath \'hēth\ n 1 : any of a large family of often evergreen shrubby plants (as a blueberry or heather) of wet acid soils 2 : a tract of wasteland — **heathy** adj

hea·then \'hē-thən\ n, pl **heathens** or **heathen** 1 : an unconverted member of a people or nation that does not acknowledge the God of the Bible 2 : an uncivilized or irreligious person — **heathen** adj — **hea·then·dom** n — **hea·then·ish** adj — **hea·then·ism** n

heath·er \'he-thər\ n : a northern and alpine evergreen

heath with usu. lavender flowers — **heath•ery** adj
heat lightning n : flashes of light without thunder ascribed to distant lightning reflected by high clouds
heat•stroke \'hēt-ˌstrōk\ n : a disorder marked esp. by
high body temperature without sweating and by collapse that follows prolonged exposure to excessive
heat
¹**heave** \'hēv\ vb **heaved** or **hove** \'hōv\; **heav•ing 1** :
rise or lift upward **2** : THROW **3** : to rise and fall rhythmically; also : PANT **4** : RETCH **5** : PULL, PUSH —
heav•er n
²**heave** n **1** : an effort to lift or raise **2** : THROW, CAST **3**
: an upward motion **4** pl : a chronic lung disease of
horses marked by difficult breathing and persistent
cough

heav•en \'he-vən\ n **1** : FIRMAMENT —
usu. used in pl. **2** often cap : the abode of
the Deity and of the blessed dead; also
: a spiritual state of everlasting commun-
ion with God **3** cap : GOD **1 4** : a place of supreme
happiness — **heav•en•ly** adj — **heav•en•ward** adv
or adj

¹**heavy** \'he-vē\ adj **heav•i•er; -est 1** : having great
weight **2** : hard to bear **3** : SERIOUS **4** : DEEP, PRO-
FOUND **5** : burdened with something oppressive; also
: PREGNANT **6** : SLUGGISH **7** : DRAB; also : DOLEFUL **8**
: DROWSY **9** : greater than the average of its kind or
class **10** : very rich and hard to digest; also : not properly raised or leavened **11** : producing goods (as steel)
used in the production of other goods — **heavi•ly**
\-və-lē\ adv — **heavi•ness** \-vē-nəs\ n
²**heavy** n, pl **heav•ies** : a theatrical role representing a
dignified or imposing person; also : a villain esp. in a
story
heavy–du•ty \ˌhe-vē-'dü-tē, -'dyü-\ adj : able to withstand unusual strain
heavy–hand•ed \-'han-dəd\ adj **1** : CLUMSY **2** : OPPRES-
SIVE, HARSH
heavy•heart•ed \-'här-təd\ adj : SADDENED, DESPON-
DENT
heavy metal n : energetic and highly amplified electronic rock music
heavy•set \ˌhe-vē-'set\ adj : stocky and compact in
build
heavy water n : water enriched in deuterium
heavy•weight \'he-vē-ˌwāt\ n : one above average in
weight; esp : a boxer weighing over 175 pounds
Heb abbr Hebrews
He•bra•ism \'hē-brā-ˌi-zəm\ n : the thought, spirit, or
practice characteristic of the Hebrews — **He•bra•
ic** \hi-'brā-ik\ adj
He•bra•ist \'hē-ˌbrā-ist\ n : a specialist in Hebrew and
Hebraic studies
He•brew \'hē-brü\ n **1** : the language of the Hebrews
2 : a member of or descendant from a group of Semitic peoples; esp : ISRAELITE — **Hebrew** adj
He•brews \'hē-(ˌ)brüz\ n — see BIBLE table

hec•a•tomb \'he-kə-ˌtōm\ n : an ancient Greek and Roman sacrifice of 100 oxen or cattle
heck•le \'he-kəl\ vb **heck•led; heck•ling** : to harass
with questions or gibes : BADGER — **heck•ler** n
hect•are \'hek-ˌtar\ n — see METRIC SYSTEM table
hec•tic \'hek-tik\ adj **1** : being hot and flushed **2** : filled
with excitement, activity, or confusion — **hec•ti•cal-
ly** \-ti-k(ə-)lē\ adv
hec•to•gram \'hek-tə-ˌgram\ n — see METRIC SYSTEM
table
hec•to•li•ter \'hek-tə-ˌlē-tər\ n — see METRIC SYSTEM
table
hec•to•me•ter \'hek-tə-ˌmē-tər, hek-'tä-mə-tər\ n —
see METRIC SYSTEM table
hec•tor \'hek-tər\ vb [hector bully, fr. Hector, champion of Troy in Greek legend] **1** : SWAGGER **2** : to intimidate by bluster or personal pressure
¹**hedge** \'hej\ n **1** : a fence or boundary formed of
shrubs or small trees **2** : BARRIER **3** : a means of protection (as against financial loss)
²**hedge** vb **hedged; hedg•ing 1** : ENCIRCLE **2** : HINDER **3**
: to protect oneself financially by a counterbalancing
action **4** : to evade the risk of commitment — **hedg•
er** n
hedge•hog \'hej-ˌhȯg, -ˌhäg\ n : a small Old World
insect-eating mammal covered with spines; also
: PORCUPINE

hedgehog

hedge•hop \-ˌhäp\ vb : to fly an airplane very close to
the ground
hedge•row \-ˌrō\ n : a row of shrubs or trees bounding
or separating fields
he•do•nism \'hēd-ᵊn-ˌi-zəm\ n [Gk hēdonē pleasure]
: the doctrine that pleasure is the chief good in life;
also : a way of life based on this — **he•do•nist** \-ist\
n — **he•do•nis•tic** \ˌhēd-ᵊn-'i-stik\ adj
¹**heed** \'hēd\ vb : to pay attention
²**heed** n : ATTENTION, NOTICE — **heed•ful** \-fəl\ adj —
heed•ful•ly adv — **heed•ful•ness** n — **heed•less** adj
— **heed•less•ly** adv — **heed•less•ness** n
¹**heel** \'hēl\ n **1** : the hind part of the foot **2** : one of the
crusty ends of a loaf of bread **3** : a solid attachment
forming the back of the sole of a shoe **4** : a rear, low,
or bottom part **5** : a contemptible person
²**heel** vb : to tilt to one side : LIST
¹**heft** \'heft\ n : WEIGHT, HEAVINESS

²**heft** vb : to test the weight of by lifting

hefty \'hef-tē\ adj **heft•i•er; -est 1** : marked by bigness, bulk, and usu. strength **2** : impressively large

he•ge•mo•ny \hi-'je-mə-nē\ n : preponderant influence or authority over others — DOMINATION

he•gi•ra \hi-'jī-rə\ n [the Hegira, flight of Muhammad from Mecca in A.D. 622, fr. ML, fr. Ar hijrah, lit., flight] : a journey esp. when undertaken to escape a dangerous or undesirable environment

heif•er \'he-fər\ n : a young cow; esp : one that has not had a calf

height \'hīt\ n **1** : the highest part or point **2** : the distance from the bottom to the top of something standing upright **3** : ALTITUDE

height•en \'hīt-ᵊn\ vb **1** : to increase in amount or degree **2** : to make or become high or higher **syn** enhance, intensify, aggravate, magnify

Heim•lich maneuver \'hīm-lik-\ n [Henry J. Heimlich b1920 Am. surgeon] : the manual application of sudden upward pressure on the upper abdomen of a choking victim to force a foreign object from the windpipe

hei•nous \'hā-nəs\ adj [ME, fr. MF haineus, fr. haine hate, fr. hair to hate] : hatefully or shockingly evil — **hei•nous•ly** adv — **hei•nous•ness** n

heir \'ar\ n : one who inherits or is entitled to inherit property, rank, title, or office — **heir•ship** n

heir apparent n, pl **heirs apparent** : an heir whose right to succeed (as to a title) cannot be taken away if he or she survives the present holder

heir•ess \'ar-əs\ n : a female heir esp. to great wealth

heir•loom \'ar-ˌlüm\ n **1** : a piece of personal property that descends by inheritance **2** : something handed on from one generation to another

heir presumptive n, pl **heirs presumptive** : an heir whose present right to inherit could be lost through the birth of a nearer relative

heist \'hīst\ vb, slang : to commit armed robbery on; also : STEAL — **heist** n, slang

held past and past part of HOLD

he•li•cal \'he-li-kəl, 'hē-\ adj : SPIRAL

he•li•cop•ter \'he-lə-ˌkäp-tər, 'hē-\ n [F hélicoptère, fr. Gk helix spiral + pteron wing] : an aircraft that is supported in the air by one or more rotors revolving on substantially vertical axes

he•lio•cen•tric \ˌhē-lē-ō-'sen-trik\ adj : having or relating to the sun as center

he•lio•trope \'hē-lē-ə-ˌtrōp\ n [L heliotropium, fr. Gk hēliotropion, fr. hēlios sun + tropos turn; fr. its flowers' turning toward the sun] : any of a genus of herbs or shrubs related to the forget-me-not that have small white or purple flowers

he•li•port \'he-lə-ˌpōrt\ n : a landing and takeoff place for a helicopter

he•li•um \'hē-lē-əm\ n [NL, fr. Gk hēlios sun] : a very light nonflammable gaseous chemical element occurring in various natural gases — see ELEMENT table

he•lix \'hē-liks\ n, pl **he•li•ces** \'he-lə-ˌsēz, 'hē-\ also **he•lix•es** \'hē-lik-səz\ : something spiral in form

hell \'hel\ n **1** : a nether world in which the dead continue to exist **2** : the realm of the devil in which the damned suffer everlasting punishment **3** : a place or state of torment or destruction — **hell•ish** adj

hell–bent \'hel-ˌbent\ adj : stubbornly determined

hell•cat \-ˌkat\ n **1** : WITCH 2 **2** : a violently temperamental person; esp : an ill-tempered woman

hel•le•bore \'he-lə-ˌbōr\ n **1** : any of a genus of poisonous herbs related to the buttercups; also : the dried root of a hellebore **2** : a poisonous plant related to the lilies; also : its dried roots used in medicine and insecticides

Hel•lene \'he-ˌlēn\ n : GREEK

Hel•le•nism \'he-lə-ˌni-zəm\ n : a body of humanistic and classical ideals associated with ancient Greece — **Hel•len•ic** \he-'le-nik\ adj — **Hel•le•nist** \'he-lə-nist\ n

Hel•le•nis•tic \ˌhe-lə-'nis-tik\ adj : of or relating to Greek history, culture, or art after Alexander the Great

hell–for–leather adv : at full speed

hell•gram•mite \'hel-grə-ˌmīt\ n : an aquatic insect larva that is used as bait in fishing

hell•hole \'hel-ˌhōl\ n : a place of extreme misery or squalor

hell•ion \'hel-yən\ n : a troublesome or mischievous person

hel•lo \hə-'lō, he-\ n, pl **hellos** : an expression of greeting — used interjectionally

helm \'helm\ n **1** : a lever or wheel for steering a ship **2** : a position of control

hel•met \'hel-mət\ n : a protective covering for the head

helms•man \'helmz-mən\ n : the person at the helm : STEERSMAN

hel•ot \'he-lət\ n : SLAVE, SERF

¹**help** \'help\ vb **1** : AID, ASSIST **2** : IMPROVE, RELIEVE **3** : to be of use; also : PROMOTE **4** : to change for the better **5** : to refrain from; also : PREVENT **6** : to serve with food or drink ⟨∼ yourself⟩ — **help•er** n

²**help** n **1** : AID, ASSISTANCE; also : a source of aid **2** : REMEDY, RELIEF **3** : one who assists another **4** : EMPLOYEE — **help•ful** \-fəl\ adj — **help•ful•ly** adv — **help•ful•ness** n — **help•less** adj — **help•less•ly** adv — **help•less•ness** n

helper T cell n : a T cell of the immune system that has a protein on its surface to which HIV attaches and that is reduced to 20 percent or less of normal numbers in AIDS

help•ing n : a portion of food

help•mate \'help-ˌmāt\ n **1** : HELPER **2** : WIFE

help•meet \-ˌmēt\ n : HELPMATE

hel•ter–skel•ter \ˌhel-tər-'skel-tər\ adv **1** : in undue haste or disorder **2** : HAPHAZARDLY

helve \'helv\ n : a handle of a tool or weapon

Hel•ve•tian \hel-'vē-shən\ adj : SWISS — **Helvetian** n

¹**hem** \'hem\ n **1** : a border of an article (as of cloth) doubled back and stitched down **2** : RIM, MARGIN

²**hem** *vb* **hemmed; hem·ming 1** : to make a hem in sewing; *also* : BORDER, EDGE **2** : to surround restrictively
he–man \'hē-₁man\ *n* : a strong virile man
he·ma·tite \'hē-mə-₁tīt\ *n* : a mineral that consists of an oxide of iron and that constitutes an important iron ore
he·ma·tol·o·gy \₁hē-mə-'tä-lə-jē\ *n* : a branch of biology that deals with the blood and blood-forming organs — **he·ma·to·log·ic** \-tə-'lä-jik\ *also* **he·ma·to·log·i·cal** \-ji-kəl\ *adj* — **he·ma·tol·o·gist** \-'tä-lə-jist\ *n*
heme \'hēm\ *n* : the deep red iron-containing part of hemoglobin
hemi·sphere \'he-mə-₁sfir\ *n* **1** : one of the halves of the earth as divided by the equator into northern and southern parts (**northern hemisphere, southern hemisphere**) or by a meridian into two parts so that one half (**eastern hemisphere**) to the east of the Atlantic ocean includes Europe, Asia, and Africa and the half (**western hemisphere**) to the west includes No. and So. America and surrounding waters **2** : either of two half spheres formed by a plane through the sphere's center — **hemi·spher·ic** \₁he-mə-'sfir-ik, -'sfer-\ *or* **hemi·spher·i·cal** \-'sfir-i-kəl, -'sfer-\ *adj*
hem·line \'hem-₁līn\ *n* : the line formed by the lower edge of a garment
hem·lock \'hem-₁läk\ *n* **1** : any of several poisonous herbs related to the carrot **2** : an evergreen tree related to the pines; *also* : its soft light wood
he·mo·glo·bin \'hē-mə-₁glō-bən\ *n* : an iron-containing compound found in red blood cells that carries oxygen from the lungs to the body tissues
he·mo·phil·ia \₁hē-mə-'fi-lē-ə\ *n* : a hereditary blood defect usu. of males that slows blood clotting with resulting difficulty in stopping bleeding — **he·mo·phil·i·ac** \-lē-₁ak\ *adj or n*
hem·or·rhage \'hem-rij, 'he-mə-\ *n* : a large discharge of blood from the blood vessels — **hemorrhage** *vb* — **hem·or·rhag·ic** \₁he-mə-'ra-jik\ *adj*
hem·or·rhoid \'hem-₁ròid, 'he-mə-\ *n* : a swollen mass of dilated veins at or just within the anus — usu. used in pl.
hemp \'hemp\ *n* : a tall widely grown Asian herb related to the mulberry that is the source of a tough fiber used in rope and of marijuana and hashish from its flowers and leaves; *also* : the fiber — **hemp·en** \'hem-pən\ *adj*
hem·stitch \'hem-₁stich\ *vb* : to embroider (fabric) by drawing out parallel threads and stitching the exposed threads in groups to form designs
hen \'hen\ *n* : a female chicken esp. over a year old; *also* : a female bird
hence \'hens\ *adv* **1** : AWAY **2** : from this time **3** : CONSEQUENTLY **4** : from this source or origin
hence·forth \'hens-₁fòrth\ *adv* : from this point on
hence·for·ward \-'fòr-wərd\ *adv* : HENCEFORTH
hench·man \'hench-mən\ *n* [ME *hengestman* groom, fr. *hengest* stallion] : a trusted follower or supporter
hen·na \'he-nə\ *n* **1** : an Old World tropical shrub with fragrant white flowers; *also* : a reddish brown dye obtained from its leaves and used esp. on hair **2** : the color of henna dye
hen·peck \'hen-₁pek\ *vb* : to nag and boss one's husband
hep \'hep\ *adj* : HIP
hep·a·rin \'he-pə-rən\ *n* : a compound found esp. in liver that slows the clotting of blood and is used medically
he·pat·ic \hi-'pa-tik\ *adj* : of, relating to, or associated with the liver
he·pat·i·ca \hi-'pa-ti-kə\ *n* : any of a genus of herbs related to the buttercups that have lobed leaves and delicate white, pink, or bluish flowers
hep·a·ti·tis \₁he-pə-'tī-təs\ *n, pl* **-tit·i·des** \-'ti-tə-₁dēz\ : inflammation of the liver; *also* : a virus disease of which this is a feature
hep·tam·e·ter \hep-'ta-mə-tər\ *n* : a line of verse containing seven metrical feet
¹**her** \'hər\ *adj* : of or relating to her or herself
²**her** *pron, objective case of* SHE
¹**her·ald** \'her-əld\ *n* **1** : an official crier or messenger **2** : HARBINGER **3** : ANNOUNCER **4** : ADVOCATE

²**herald** *vb* **1** : to give notice of **2** : HAIL, GREET; *also* : PUBLICIZE

he·ral·dic \he-'ral-dik, hə-\ *adj* : of or relating to heralds or heraldry
her·ald·ry \'her-əl-drē\ *n, pl* **-ries 1** : the practice of devising and granting armorial insignia and of tracing genealogies **2** : INSIGNIA **3** : PAGEANTRY
herb \'ərb, 'hərb\ *n* **1** : a seed plant that lacks woody tissue and dies to the ground at the end of a growing season **2** : a plant or plant part valued for medicinal or savory qualities — **her·ba·ceous** \₁ər-'bā-shəs, ₁hər-\ *adj*
herb·age \'ər-bij, 'hər-\ *n* : green plants esp. when used or fit for grazing
herb·al·ist \'ər-bə-list, 'hər-\ *n* **1** : one who practices healing by the use of herbs **2** : one who collects or grows herbs
her·bar·i·um \₁ər-'bar-ē-əm, ₁hər-\ *n, pl* **-ia** \-ē-ə\ **1** : a collection of dried plant specimens **2** : a place that houses an herbarium
her·bi·cide \'ər-bə-₁sīd, 'hər-\ *n* : an agent used to destroy or inhibit plant growth — **her·bi·cid·al** \₁ər-bə-'sīd-əl, ₁hər-\ *adj*
her·biv·o·rous \₁ər-'bi-və-rəs, ₁hər-\ *adj* : feeding on plants — **her·bi·vore** \'ər-bə-₁vòr, 'hər-\ *n*
her·cu·le·an \₁hər-kyə-'lē-ən, ₁hər-'kyü-lē-\ *adj, often cap* [*Hercules*, hero of Greek myth renowned for his strength] : of extraordinary power, size, or difficulty
¹**herd** \'hərd\ *n* **1** : a group of animals of one kind kept or living together **2** : a group of people with a common bond **3** : MOB
²**herd** *vb* : to assemble or move in a herd — **herd·er** *n*

herds·man \'hərdz-mən\ n : one who manages, breeds, or tends livestock

¹**here** \'hir\ adv 1 : in or at this place; also : NOW 2 : at or in this point, particular, or case 3 : in the present life or state 4 : to this place

²**here** n : this place (get away from ∼)

here·abouts \'hir-ə-ˌbaůts\ or **here·about** \-ˌbaůt\ adv : in this vicinity

¹**here·af·ter** \hir-¹af-tər\ adv 1 : after this in sequence or in time 2 : in some future time or state

²**hereafter** n, often cap 1 : FUTURE 2 : an existence beyond earthly life

here·by \hir-¹bī\ adv : by means of this

he·red·i·tary \hə-¹re-də-ˌter-ē\ adj 1 : genetically passed or passable from parent to offspring 2 : passing by inheritance; also : having title or possession through inheritance 3 : of a kind established by tradition

he·red·i·ty \-də-tē\ n : the qualities and potentialities genetically derived from one's ancestors; also : the passing of these from ancestor to descendant

Her·e·ford \'hər-fərd\ n : any of a breed of red‑coated beef cattle with white faces and markings

here·in \hir-¹in\ adv : in this

here·of \-¹əv, -¹äv\ adv : of this

here·on \-¹ȯn, -¹än\ adv : on this

her·e·sy \'her-ə-sē\ n, pl **-sies** [ME heresie, fr. OF, fr. LL haeresis, fr. LGk hairesis, fr. Gk, action of taking, choice, sect, fr. hairein to take] 1 : adherence to a religious opinion contrary to church dogma 2 : an opinion or doctrine contrary to church dogma 3 : dissent from a dominant theory, opinion, or practice — **her·e·tic** \-ˌtik\ n — **he·ret·i·cal** \hə-¹re-ti-kəl\ adj

here·to \hir-¹tü\ adv : to this document

here·to·fore \'hir-tə-ˌfȯr\ adv : up to this time

here·un·der \hir-¹ən-dər\ adv : under this or according to this writing

here·un·to \hir-¹ən-tü\ adv : to this

here·upon \'hir-ə-ˌpȯn, -ˌpän\ adv : on this or immediately after this

here·with \'hir-¹with, -¹with\ adv 1 : with this 2 : HEREBY

her·i·ta·ble \'her-ə-tə-bəl\ adj : capable of being inherited

her·i·tage \'her-ə-tij\ n 1 : property that descends to an heir 2 : LEGACY 3 : BIRTHRIGHT

her·maph·ro·dite \(ˌ)hər-¹ma-frə-ˌdīt\ n : an animal or plant having both male and female reproductive organs — **hermaphrodite** adj — **her·maph·ro·dit·ic** \(ˌ)hər-ˌma-frə-¹di-tik\ adj

her·met·ic \hər-¹me-tik\ also **her·met·i·cal** \-ti-kəl\ adj : AIRTIGHT — **her·met·i·cal·ly** \-ti-k(ə-)lē\ adv

her·mit \'hər-mət\ n [ME eremite, fr. OF, fr. LL eremita, fr. LGk erēmitēs, fr. Gk, adj., living in the desert, fr. erēmia desert, fr. erēmos desolate] : one who lives in solitude esp. for religious reasons

her·mit·age \-mə-tij\ n 1 : the dwelling of a hermit 2 : a secluded dwelling

her·nia \'hər-nē-ə\ n, pl **-ni·as** or **-ni·ae** \-nē-ˌē, -nē-ˌī\ : a protrusion of a bodily part (as a loop of intestine) into a pouch of the weakened wall of a cavity in which it is normally enclosed — **her·ni·ate** \-nē-ˌāt\ vb — **her·ni·a·tion** \ˌhər-nē-¹ā-shən\ n

he·ro \'hē-rō\ n, pl **heroes** 1 : a mythological or legendary figure of great strength or ability 2 : a man admired for his achievements and qualities 3 : the chief male character in a literary or dramatic work 4 pl usu **heros** : SUBMARINE 2 — **he·ro·ic** \hi-¹rō-ik\ adj — **he·ro·i·cal·ly** \-i-k(ə-)lē\ adv

heroic couplet n : a rhyming couplet in iambic pentameter

he·ro·ics \hi-¹rō-iks\ n pl : heroic or showy behavior

her·o·in \'her-ə-wən\ n : an illicit addictive narcotic drug made from morphine

her·o·ine \'her-ə-wən\ n 1 : a woman admired for her achievements and qualities 2 : the chief female character in a literary or dramatic work

her·o·ism \'her-ə-ˌwi-zəm\ n 1 : heroic conduct 2 : the qualities of a hero syn valor, prowess, gallantry

her·on \'her-ən\ n, pl **herons** also **heron** : any of various long-legged long-billed wading birds with soft plumage

her·pes \'hər-pēz\ n : any of several virus diseases characterized by the formation of blisters on the skin or mucous membranes

herpes sim·plex \-¹sim-ˌpleks\ n : either of two virus diseases marked in one by watery blisters above the waist (as on the mouth and lips) and in the other on the sex organs

herpes zos·ter \-¹zäs-tər\ n : SHINGLES

her·pe·tol·o·gy \ˌhər-pə-¹tä-lə-jē\ n : a branch of zoology dealing with reptiles and amphibians — **her·pe·tol·o·gist** \ˌhər-pə-¹tä-lə-jist\ n

her·ring \'her-iŋ\ n, pl **herring** or **herrings** : a valuable narrow-bodied food fish of the north Atlantic; also : a related fish of the north Pacific harvested esp. for its roe

her·ring·bone \'her-iŋ-ˌbōn\ n : a pattern made up of rows of parallel lines with adjacent rows slanting in reverse directions; also : a twilled fabric with this pattern

hers \'hərz\ pron : one or the ones belonging to her

her·self \hər-¹self\ pron : SHE, HER — used reflexively, for emphasis, or in absolute constructions

hertz \'hərts, 'herts\ n, pl **hertz** : a unit of frequency equal to one cycle per second

hes·i·tant \'he-zə-tənt\ adj : tending to hesitate — **hes·i·tance** \-təns\ n — **hes·i·tan·cy** \-tən-sē\ n — **hes·i·tant·ly** adv

hes·i·tate \'he-zə-ˌtāt\ vb **-tat·ed; -tat·ing** 1 : to hold back (as in doubt) 2 : PAUSE syn waver, vacillate, falter, shilly-shally — **hes·i·ta·tion** \ˌhe-zə-¹tā-shən\ n

het·ero·dox \'he-tə-rə-ˌdäks\ adj 1 : differing from an

YOU KNOW, GARFIELD, EXERCISE REALLY PAYS

NOT ENOUGH

KNOW WHAT I GOT FROM LIFTING WEIGHTS?

A HERNIA?

RIPPLING BICEPS!

THAT REMINDS ME. HOW ABOUT SPAGHETTI FOR DINNER?

© 1988 PAWS, INC.   JIM DAVIS   8-10

acknowledged standard **2** : holding unorthodox opinions — **het·er·o·doxy** \-ˌdäk-sē\ *n*

het·er·o·ge·neous \ˌhe-tə-rə-ˈjē-nē-əs, -nyəs\ *adj* : consisting of dissimilar ingredients or constituents : MIXED — **het·er·o·ge·ne·ity** \-jə-ˈnē-ə-tē\ *n* — **het·er·o·ge·neous·ly** *adv*

het·ero·sex·u·al \ˌhe-tə-rō-ˈsek-shə-wəl\ *adj* **1** : of, relating to, or marked by sexual interest in the opposite sex; *also* : of, relating to, or involving sexual intercourse between members of opposite sex **2** : of or relating to different sexes — **heterosexual** *n* — **het·ero·sex·u·al·i·ty** \-ˌsek-shə-ˈwa-lə-tē\ *n*

hew \ˈhyü\ *vb* **hewed; hewed** *or* **hewn** \ˈhyün\; **hewing 1** : to cut or fell with blows (as of an ax) **2** : to give shape to with or as if with an ax **3** : to conform strictly — **hew·er** *n*

HEW *abbr* Department of Health, Education, and Welfare

¹hex \ˈheks\ *vb* **1** : to practice witchcraft **2** : JINX

²hex *n* : SPELL, JINX

³hex *adj* : HEXAGONAL

⁴hex *abbr* hexagon

hexa·gon \ˈhek-sə-ˌgän\ *n* : a polygon having six angles and six sides — **hex·ag·o·nal** \hek-ˈsa-gən-ᵊl\ *adj*

hex·am·e·ter \hek-ˈsa-mə-tər\ *n* : a line of verse containing six metrical feet

hey·day \ˈhā-ˌdā\ *n* : a period of greatest strength, vigor, or prosperity

hf *abbr* half

Hf *symbol* hafnium

HF *abbr* high frequency

hg *abbr* hectogram

Hg *symbol* [NL *hydrargyrum*, lit., water silver] mercury

hgt *abbr* height

hgwy *abbr* highway

HH *abbr* **1** Her Highness **2** His Highness **3** His Holiness

HHS *abbr* Department of Health and Human Services

HI *abbr* **1** Hawaii **2** humidity index

hi·a·tus \hī-ˈā-təs\ *n* [L, fr. *hiare* to yawn] **1** : a break in an object : GAP **2** : a lapse in continuity

hi·ba·chi \hi-ˈbä-chē\ *n* [Jp] : a charcoal brazier

hi·ber·nate \ˈhī-bər-ˌnāt\ *vb* **-nat·ed; -nat·ing** : to pass the winter in a torpid or resting state — **hi·ber·na·tion** \ˌhī-bər-ˈnā-shən\ *n* — **hi·ber·na·tor** \ˈhī-bər-ˌnā-tər\ *n*

hi·bis·cus \hī-ˈbis-kəs, hə-\ *n* : any of a genus of herbs, shrubs, and trees related to the mallows and noted for large showy flowers

hic·cup *also* **hic·cough** \ˈhi-(ˌ)kəp\ *n* : a spasmodic breathing movement checked by sudden closing of the glottis accompanied by a peculiar sound; *also, pl* : an attack of hiccuping — **hiccup** *vb*

hick \ˈhik\ *n* [*Hick*, nickname for *Richard*] : an awkward provincial person — **hick** *adj*

hick·o·ry \ˈhi-kə-rē\ *n, pl* **-ries** : any of a genus of No. American hardwood trees related to the walnuts; *also* : the wood of a hickory — **hickory** *adj*

hi·dal·go \hi-ˈdal-gō\ *n, pl* **-gos** *often cap* [Sp, fr. earlier *fijo dalgo*, lit., son of something] : a member of the lower nobility of Spain

hidden tax *n* **1** : a tax ultimately paid by someone other than the person on whom it is formally levied **2** : an economic injustice that reduces one's income or buying power

¹hide \ˈhīd\ *vb* **hid** \ˈhid\; **hid·den** \ˈhid-ᵊn\ *or* **hid; hiding 1** : to put or remain out of sight **2** : to conceal for shelter or protection; *also* : to seek protection **3** : to keep secret **4** : to turn away in shame or anger — **hid·er** *n*

²hide *n* : the skin of an animal

hide–and–seek \ˌhīd-ᵊn-ˈsēk\ *n* : a children's game in which everyone hides from one player who tries to find them

hide·away \ˈhī-də-ˌwā\ *n* : HIDEOUT

hide·bound \ˈhīd-ˌbau̇nd\ *adj* : being inflexible or conservative

hid·eous \ˈhi-dē-əs\ *adj* [ME *hidous*, fr. OF, fr. *hisde, hide* terror] **1** : offensive to one of the senses : UGLY **2** : morally offensive : SHOCKING **syn** ghastly, grisly, gruesome, horrible, lurid, macabre — **hid·eous·ly** *adv* — **hid·eous·ness** *n*

hide·out \ˈhī-ˌdau̇t\ *n* : a place of refuge or concealment

hie \ˈhī\ *vb* **hied; hy·ing** *or* **hie·ing** : HASTEN

hi·er·ar·chy \ˈhī-ə-ˌrär-kē\ *n, pl* **-chies 1** : a ruling body of clergy organized into ranks **2** : persons or things arranged in a graded series — **hi·er·ar·chi·cal** \ˌhī-ə-ˈrär-ki-kəl\ *adj* — **hi·er·ar·chi·cal·ly** \-k(ə-)lē\ *adv*

hi·er·o·glyph·ic \ˌhī-ə-rə-ˈgli-fik\ *n* [MF *hieroglyphique*, adj., ultim. fr. Gk *hieroglyphikos*, fr. *hieros* sacred + *glyphein* to carve] **1** : a character in a system of picture writing (as of the ancient Egyptians) **2** : a symbol or sign difficult to decipher

hieroglyphic 1

hi–fi \ˈhī-ˈfī\ *n* **1** : HIGH FIDELITY **2** : equipment for reproduction of sound with high fidelity

hig·gle·dy–pig·gle·dy \ˌhi-gəl-dē-ˈpi-gəl-dē\ *adv* : in confusion

¹high \ˈhī\ *adj* **1** : ELEVATED; *also* : TALL **2** : advanced toward fullness or culmination; *also* : slightly tainted **3** : advanced esp. in complexity ⟨∼*er* mathematics⟩ **4** : long past **5** : SHRILL, SHARP **6** : far from the equator ⟨∼ latitudes⟩ **7** : exalted in character **8** : of greater degree, size, or amount than average ⟨∼ in cholesterol⟩ **9** : of relatively great importance **10** : FORCIBLE, STRONG ⟨∼ winds⟩ **11** : showing elation or excitement **12** : INTOXICATED; *also* : excited or stupefied by or as if by a drug — **high·ly** *adv*

²high *adv* **1** : at or to a high place or degree **2** : LUXURIOUSLY ⟨living ∼⟩

³high *n* **1** : an elevated place **2** : a region of high barometric pressure **3** : a high point or level **4** : the gear of a vehicle giving the highest speed **5** : an excited or stupefied state produced by or as if by a drug

high·ball \ˈhī-ˌbȯl\ *n* : a usu. tall drink of liquor mixed with water or a carbonated beverage

high beam *n* : the long-range focus of a vehicle headlight

high·born \ˈhī-ˈbȯrn\ *adj* : of noble birth

high·boy \-ˌbȯi\ *n* : a high chest of drawers mounted on a base with legs

high·bred \-ˈbred\ *adj* : coming from superior stock

high·brow \-ˈbrau̇\ *n* : a person of superior learning or culture — **highbrow** *adj* — **high·brow·ism** \-ˌbrau̇-ˌi-zəm\ *n*

high–density li·po·pro·tein \-ˌlī-pō-ˈprō-tēn, -ˌli-\ *n* : HDL

high·er–up \ˌhī-ər-ˈəp\ *n* : a superior officer or official

high·fa·lu·tin \ˌhī-fə-ˈlüt-ᵊn\ *adj* : PRETENTIOUS, POMPOUS

high fashion *n* **1** : HIGH STYLE **2** : HAUTE COUTURE

high fidelity *n* : the reproduction of sound or image with a high degree of faithfulness to the original

high five *n* : a slapping of upraised right hands by two people (as in celebration) — **high–five** *vb*

high–flown \ˈhī-ˈflōn\ *adj* **1** : EXALTED **2** : BOMBASTIC

high frequency *n* : a radio frequency between 3 and 30 megahertz

high gear *n* **1** : HIGH 4 **2** : a state of intense or maximum activity

high–hand·ed \ˈhī-ˈhan-dəd\ *adj* : OVERBEARING — **high–hand·ed·ly** *adv* — **high–hand·ed·ness** *n*

high–hat \-ˈhat\ *adj* : SUPERCILIOUS, SNOBBISH — **high–hat** *vb*

high·land \'hī-lənd\ *n* : elevated or mountainous land
high·land·er \-lən-dər\ *n* **1** : an inhabitant of a highland **2** *cap* : an inhabitant of the Scottish Highlands
¹**high·light** \-ₗlīt\ *n* : an event or detail of major importance
²**highlight** *vb* **1** : EMPHASIZE **2** : to constitute a highlight of
high–mind·ed \-'mīn-dəd\ *adj* : marked by elevated principles and feelings — **high·mind·ed·ness** *n*
high·ness \'hī-nəs\ *n* **1** : the quality or state of being high **2** — used as a title (as for kings)
high–pres·sure \-'pre-shər\ *adj* : using or involving aggressive and insistent sales techniques
high–rise \-'rīz\ *adj* : having several stories and being equipped with elevators ⟨~ apartments⟩; *also* : of or relating to high-rise buildings
high road *n* : HIGHWAY
high school *n* : a school usu. including grades 9 to 12 or 10 to 12
high sea *n* : the open sea outside territorial waters — usu. used in pl.
high–sound·ing \'hī-'saun-diŋ\ *adj* : POMPOUS, IMPOSING
high–spir·it·ed \-'spir-ə-təd\ *adj* : characterized by a bold or energetic spirit
high–strung \-'strəŋ\ *adj* : having an extremely nervous or sensitive temperament
high style *n* : the newest in fashion or design
high·tail \'hī-ₗtāl\ *vb* : to retreat at full speed
high tech \-'tek\ *n* : HIGH TECHNOLOGY
high technology *n* : technology involving the use of advanced devices
high–ten·sion \'hī-'ten-chən\ *adj* : having or using a high voltage
high–test \-'test\ *adj* : having a high octane number
high–toned \-'tōnd\ *adj* **1** : high in social, moral, or intellectual quality **2** : PRETENTIOUS, POMPOUS
high·way \'hī-ₗwā\ *n* : a main direct road
high·way·man \'hī-ₗwā-mən\ *n* : a person who robs travelers on a road
hi·jack *also* **high·jack** \'hī-ₗjak\ *vb* : to steal esp. by stopping a vehicle on the highway; *also* : to commandeer a flying airplane — **hijack** *n* — **hi·jack·er** *n*
¹**hike** \'hīk\ *vb* **hiked; hik·ing 1** : to move or raise with a sudden motion **2** : to take a long walk — **hik·er** *n*
²**hike** *n* **1** : a long walk **2** : RISE, INCREASE
hi·lar·i·ous \hi-'lar-ē-əs, hī-\ *adj* : marked by or providing boisterous merriment — **hi·lar·i·ous·ly** *adv* — **hi·lar·i·ty** \-ə-tē\ *n*
hill \'hil\ *n* **1** : a usu. rounded elevation of land **2** : a little heap or mound (as of earth) — **hilly** *adj*
hill·bil·ly \'hil-ₗbi-lē\ *n, pl* **-lies** : a person from a backwoods area
hill·ock \'hi-lək\ *n* : a small hill
hill·side \'hil-ₗsīd\ *n* : the part of a hill between the summit and the foot
hill·top \-ₗtäp\ *n* : the top of a hill
hilt \'hilt\ *n* : a handle esp. of a sword or dagger
him \'him\ *pron, objective case of* HE
Hi·ma·la·yan \ₗhi-mə-'lā-ən, hi-'mäl-yən\ *adj* : of, re-

lating to, or characteristic of the Himalaya mountains or the people living there
him·self \him-'self\ *pron* : HE, HIM — used reflexively, for emphasis, or in absolute constructions
¹**hind** \'hīnd\ *n, pl* **hinds** *also* **hind** : a female of a common Eurasian deer
²**hind** *adj* : REAR
¹**hin·der** \'hin-dər\ *vb* **1** : to impede the progress of **2** : to hold back **syn** obstruct, block, bar, impede
²**hind·er** \'hīn-dər\ *adj* : HIND
Hin·di \'hin-dē\ *n* : a literary and official language of northern India
hind·most \'hīnd-ₗmōst\ *adj* : farthest to the rear
hind·quar·ter \-ₗkwȯr-tər\ *n* **1** : one side of the back half of the carcass of a quadruped **2** *pl* : the part of the body of a quadruped behind the junction of hind limbs and trunk
hin·drance \'hin-drəns\ *n* **1** : the state of being hindered; *also* : the action of hindering **2** : IMPEDIMENT 1
hind·sight \'hīnd-ₗsīt\ *n* : understanding of an event after it has happened
Hindu–Arabic *adj* : relating to, being, or composed of Arabic numerals
Hin·du·ism \'hin-dü-ₗi-zəm\ *n* : a body of religious beliefs and practices native to India — **Hin·du** *n or adj*
hind wing *n* : either of the posterior wings of a 4-winged insect
¹**hinge** \'hinj\ *n* : a jointed device on which a swinging part (as a door, gate, or lid) turns
²**hinge** *vb* **hinged; hing·ing 1** : to attach by or furnish with hinges **2** : to be contingent on a single consideration
hint \'hint\ *n* **1** : an indirect or summary suggestion **2** : CLUE **3** : a very small amount **syn** dash, soupçon, suspicion, tincture, touch — **hint** *vb*
hin·ter·land \'hin-tər-ₗland\ *n* **1** : a region behind a coast **2** : a region remote from cities
¹**hip** \'hip\ *n* : the fruit of a rose
²**hip** *n* **1** : the part of the body on either side below the waist consisting of the side of the pelvis and the upper thigh **2** : HIP JOINT

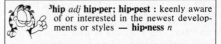

³**hip** *adj* **hip·per; hip·pest** : keenly aware of or interested in the newest developments or styles — **hip·ness** *n*

⁴**hip** *vb* **hipped; hip·ping** : TELL, INFORM
hip·bone \'hip-'bōn, -ₗbōn\ *n* : the large flaring bone that makes a lateral half of the pelvis in mammals
hip joint *n* : the articulation between the femur and the hipbone
hipped \'hipt\ *adj* : having hips esp. of a specified kind ⟨broad-*hipped*⟩
hip·pie *or* **hip·py** \'hi-pē\ *n, pl* **hippies** : a usu. young person who rejects established mores, advocates nonviolence, and often uses psychedelic drugs or

marijuana; *also* : a long-haired unconventionally dressed young person

hip•po \'hi-pō\ *n, pl* **hippos** : HIPPOPOTAMUS

hip•po•drome \'hi-pə-ˌdrōm\ *n* : an arena for equestrian performances

hip•po•pot•a•mus \ˌhi-pə-'pä-tə-məs\ *n, pl* **-mus•es** *or* **-mi** \-ˌmī\ [L, fr. Gk *hippopotamos*, alter. of *hippos* *potamios*, lit., river horse] : a large thick-skinned river mammal of sub-Saharan Africa that is related to the swine

¹**hire** \'hīr\ *n* 1 : payment for labor or personal services : WAGES 2 : EMPLOYMENT 3 : one who is hired

²**hire** *vb* **hired; hir•ing** 1 : to employ for pay 2 : to engage the temporary use of for pay 3 : to take employment

hire•ling \'hīr-liŋ\ *n* : a hired person; *esp* : one with mercenary motives

hir•sute \'hər-ˌsüt, 'hir-\ *adj* : HAIRY

¹**his** \'hiz\ *adj* : of or relating to him or himself

²**his** *pron* : one or the ones belonging to him

His•pan•ic \hi-'spa-nik\ *adj* : of, relating to, or being a person of Latin-American descent living in the U.S. — **Hispanic** *n*

hiss \'his\ *vb* : to make a sharp sibilant sound; *also* : to express disapproval of by hissing — **hiss** *n*

hist *abbr* historian; historical; history

his•ta•mine \'his-tə-ˌmēn, -mən\ *n* : a compound widespread in animal tissues that plays a major role in allergic reactions (as hay fever)

his•to•gram \'his-tə-ˌgram\ *n* : a representation of statistical data by rectangles whose widths represent class intervals and whose heights usu. represent corresponding frequencies

his•to•ri•an \hi-'stōr-ē-ən\ *n* : a student or writer of history

his•to•ric•i•ty \ˌhis-tə-'ri-sə-tē\ *n* : historical actuality

his•to•ri•og•ra•pher \hi-ˌstōr-ē-'ä-grə-fər\ *n* : HISTORIAN

his•to•ry \'his-tə-rē\ *n, pl* **-ries** [L *historia*, fr. Gk, inquiry, history, fr. *histōr, istōr* knowing, learned] 1 : a chronological record of significant events often with an explanation of their causes 2 : a branch of knowledge that records and explains past events 3 : events that form the subject matter of history 4 : an established record ⟨a convict's ∼ of violence⟩ — **his•tor•ic** \hi-'stȯr-ik\ *adj* — **his•tor•i•cal** \-i-kəl\ *adj* — **his•tor•i•cal•ly** \-k(ə-)lē\ *adv*

his•tri•on•ic \ˌhis-trē-'ä-nik\ *adj* [LL *histrionicus*, fr. L *histrio* actor] 1 : deliberately affected 2 : of or relating to actors, acting, or the theater — **his•tri•on•i•cal•ly** \-ni-k(ə-)lē\ *adv*

his•tri•on•ics \-niks\ *n pl* 1 : theatrical performances 2 : deliberate display of emotion for effect

¹**hit** \'hit\ *vb* **hit; hit•ting** 1 : to reach with a blow : STRIKE; *also* : to arrive with a force like a blow ⟨the storm ∼⟩ 2 : to make or bring into contact : COLLIDE 3 : to affect detrimentally ⟨was ∼ by the flu⟩ 4 : to make a request of 5 : to come upon 6 : to accord with : SUIT 7 : REACH, ATTAIN 8 : to indulge in often to excess — **hit•ter** *n*

²**hit** *n* 1 : an act or instance of hitting or being hit 2 : a great success 3 : BASE HIT 4 : a dose of an illegal drug 5 : a murder committed by a gangster

¹**hitch** \'hich\ *vb* 1 : to move by jerks 2 : to catch or fasten esp. by a hook or knot 3 : HITCHHIKE

²**hitch** *n* 1 : JERK, PULL 2 : a sudden halt 3 : a connection between something towed and its mover 4 : KNOT

hitch•hike \'hich-ˌhīk\ *vb* : to travel by securing free rides from passing vehicles — **hitch•hik•er** *n*

¹**hith•er** \'hi-t͟hər\ *adv* : to this place

²**hither** *adj* : being on the near or adjacent side

hith•er•to \-ˌtü\ *adv* : up to this time

HIV \ˌāch-(ˌ)ī-'vē\ *n* [*human immunodeficiency virus*] : any of several retroviruses that infect and destroy helper T cells causing the great reduction in their numbers diagnostic of AIDS

hive \'hīv\ *n* 1 : a container for housing honeybees 2 : a colony of bees 3 : a place swarming with busy occupants — **hive** *vb*

hives \'hīvz\ *n sing or pl* : an allergic disorder marked by raised itching patches on the skin or mucous membranes

hl *abbr* hectoliter

HL *abbr* House of Lords

hm *abbr* hectometer

HM *abbr* 1 Her Majesty; Her Majesty's 2 His Majesty; His Majesty's

HMO \ˌāch-(ˌ)em-'ō\ *n* [*health maintenance organization*] : a comprehensive health-care organization financed by periodic fixed payments by voluntarily enrolled individuals and families

HMS *abbr* 1 Her Majesty's ship 2 His Majesty's ship

Ho *symbol* holmium

hoa•gie *also* **hoa•gy** \'hō-gē\ *n, pl* **hoagies** : SUBMARINE 2

hoard \'hōrd\ *n* : a hidden accumulation — **hoard** *vb* — **hoard•er** *n*

hoar•frost \'hȯr-ˌfrȯst\ *n* : FROST 2

hoarse \'hȯrs\ *adj* **hoars•er; hoars•est** 1 : rough and harsh in sound 2 : having a grating voice — **hoarse•ly** *adv* — **hoarse•ness** *n*

hoary \'hȯr-ē\ *adj* **hoar•i•er; -est** 1 : gray or white with or as if with age 2 : ANCIENT — **hoar•i•ness** \'hȯr-ē-nəs\ *n*

hoax \'hōks\ *n* : an act intended to trick or dupe; *also* : something accepted or established by fraud — **hoax** *vb* — **hoax•er** *n*

hob \'häb\ *n* : MISCHIEF, TROUBLE

¹**hob•ble** \'hä-bəl\ *vb* **hob•bled, hob•bling** 1 : to limp along; *also* : to make lame 2 : FETTER

²**hobble** *n* 1 : a hobbling movement 2 : something used to hobble an animal

hob•by \'hä-bē\ *n, pl* **hobbies** : a pursuit or interest engaged in for relaxation — **hob•by•ist** \-ist\ *n*

hob•by•horse \'hä-bē-ˌhȯrs\ *n* 1 : a stick with a horse's head on which children pretend to ride 2 : a toy horse mounted on rockers 3 : a topic to which one constantly reverts

hob•gob•lin \'häb-ˌgäb-lən\ *n* 1 : a mischievous goblin 2 : BOGEY 1

hob•nail \-ˌnāl\ *n* : a short large-headed nail for studding shoe soles — **hob•nailed** \-ˌnāld\ *adj*

hob•nob \-ˌnäb\ *vb* **hob•nobbed; hob•nob•bing** : to associate familiarly

ho•bo \'hō-bō\ *n, pl* **hoboes** *also* **hobos** : TRAMP 2

¹**hock** \'häk\ *n* : a joint or region in the hind limb of a quadruped just above the foot and corresponding to the human ankle

²**hock** *n* [D *hok* pen, prison] : PAWN; *also* : DEBT 3 — **hock** *vb*

hock•ey \'hä-kē\ *n* 1 : FIELD HOCKEY 2 : ICE HOCKEY

ho•cus-po•cus \ˌhō-kəs-'pō-kəs\ *n* 1 : SLEIGHT OF HAND 2 : nonsense or sham used to conceal deception

hod \'häd\ *n* : a long-handled carrier for mortar or bricks

hodge•podge \'häj-ˌpäj\ *n* : a heterogeneous mixture : JUMBLE

hoe \'hō\ *n* : a long-handled implement with a thin flat blade used esp. for cultivating, weeding, or loosening the earth around plants — **hoe** *vb*

hoe•cake \'hō-ˌkāk\ *n* : a small cornmeal cake

hoe•down \-ˌdaȯn\ *n* 1 : SQUARE DANCE 2 : a gathering featuring hoedowns

¹**hog** \'hȯg, 'häg\ *n, pl* **hogs** *also* **hog** 1 : a domestic swine esp. when grown 2 : a selfish, gluttonous, or filthy person — **hog•gish** *adj*

²**hog** *vb* **hogged; hog•ging** : to take or hold selfishly

ho•gan \'hō-ˌgän\ *n* : a Navajo Indian dwelling usu. made of logs and mud

hog•back \'hȯg-ˌbak, 'häg-\ *n* : a ridge with a sharp summit and steep sides

hog•nose snake \'hȯg-ˌnōz-, 'häg-\ *or* **hog•nosed**

hogan

snake \-ₙnōzd-\ *n* : any of a genus of rather small harmless stout-bodied No. American snakes that seldom bite but hiss wildly and often play dead when disturbed

hogs•head \'hȯgz-ₙhed, 'hägz-\ *n* **1** : a large cask or barrel **2** : a liquid measure equal to 63 U.S. gallons

hog–tie \'hȯg-ₙtī, 'häg-\ *vb* **1** : to tie together the feet of (∼ a calf) **2** : to make helpless

hog•wash \-ₙwȯsh, -ₙwäsh\ *n* **1** : SWILL, SLOP **2** : NONSENSE, BALONEY

hog–wild \-'wīld\ *adj* : lacking in restraint

hoi pol•loi \ₙhȯi-pə-'lȯi\ *n pl* [Gk, the many] : the general populace

¹**hoist** \'hȯist\ *vb* : RAISE, LIFT

²**hoist** *n* **1** : LIFT **2** : an apparatus for hoisting

hoke \'hōk\ *vb* **hoked; hok•ing** : FAKE — usu. used with *up*

hok•ey \'hō-kē\ *adj* **hok•i•er; -est** : CORNY; *also* : PHONY

ho•kum \'hō-kəm\ *n* : NONSENSE

¹**hold** \'hōld\ *vb* **held** \'held\; **hold•ing 1** : POSSESS; *also* : KEEP **2** : RESTRAIN **3** : to have a grasp on **4** : to support, remain, or keep in a particular situation or position **5** : SUSTAIN; *also* : RESERVE **6** : BEAR, COMPORT **7** : to maintain in being or action : PERSIST **8** : CONTAIN, ACCOMMODATE **9** : HARBOR, ENTERTAIN; *also* : CONSIDER, REGARD **10** : to carry on by concerted action; *also* : CONVOKE **11** : to occupy esp. by appointment or election **12** : to be valid **13** : HALT, PAUSE — **hold•er** *n* — **hold forth** : to speak at length — **hold to** : to adhere to : MAINTAIN — **hold with** : to agree with or approve of

²**hold** *n* **1** : STRONGHOLD **2** : CONFINEMENT; *also* : PRISON **3** : the act or manner of holding : GRIP **4** : a restraining, dominating, or controlling influence **5** : something that may be grasped as a support **6** : an order or indication that something is to be reserved or delayed — **on hold** : in a temporary state of waiting (as during a phone call); *also* : in a state of postponement ⟨plans *on hold*⟩

³**hold** *n* **1** : the interior of a ship below decks; *esp* : a ship's cargo deck **2** : an airplane's cargo compartment

hold•ing *n* **1** : land or other property owned **2** : a ruling of a court esp. on an issue of law

holding pattern *n* : a course flown by an aircraft waiting to land

hold out *vb* **1** : to continue to fight or work **2** : to refuse to come to an agreement — **hold•out** \'hōl-ₙdaut\ *n*

hold•over \'hōl-ₙdō-vər\ *n* : one that is held over

hold•up \'hōl-ₙdəp\ *n* **1** : DELAY **2** : robbery at the point of a gun

hole \'hōl\ *n* **1** : an opening into or through something **2** : a hollow place (as a pit or cave) **3** : DEN, BURROW **4** : a wretched or dingy place **5** : a unit of play from tee to cup in golf **6** : an awkward position — **hole** *vb*

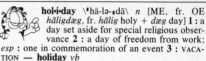

hol•i•day \'hä-lə-ₙdā\ *n* [ME, fr. OE *hāligdæg*, fr. *hālig* holy + *dæg* day] **1** : a day set aside for special religious observance **2** : a day of freedom from work; *esp* : one in commemoration of an event **3** : VACATION — **holiday** *vb*

ho•li•ness \'hō-lē-nəs\ *n* : the quality or state of being holy — used as a title for various high religious officials

ho•lis•tic \hō-'lis-tik\ *adj* : relating to or concerned with integrated wholes or complete systems rather than with the analysis or treatment of separate parts ⟨∼ medicine⟩ ⟨∼ ecology⟩

hol•ler \'hä-lər\ *vb* : to cry out : SHOUT — **holler** *n*

¹**hol•low** \'hä-lō\ *n* **1** : CAVITY, HOLE **2** : a surface depression

²**hollow** *adj* **hol•low•er** \'hä-lə-wər\; **hol•low•est** \-lə-wəst\ **1** : CONCAVE, SUNKEN **2** : having a cavity within **3** : lacking in real value, sincerity, or substance; *also* : FALSE **4** : MUFFLED ⟨a ∼ sound⟩ — **hol•low•ness** *n*

³**hollow** *vb* : to make or become hollow

hol•low•ware *or* **hol•lo•ware** \'hä-lə-ₙwar\ *n* : vessels (as bowls or cups) with a significant depth and volume

hol•ly \'hä-lē\ *n, pl* **hollies** : either of two trees or shrubs with branches of usu. evergreen glossy spiny-margined leaves and red berries

hol•ly•hock \'hä-lē-ₙhäk, -ₙhȯk\ *n* [ME *holihoc*, fr. *holi* holy + *hoc* mallow] : a perennial Chinese herb related to the mallows that is widely grown for its tall stalks of showy flowers

hol•mi•um \'hōl-mē-əm\ *n* : a metallic chemical element — see ELEMENT table

ho•lo•caust \'hä-lə-ₙkȯst, 'hō-\ *n* **1** : a thorough destruction esp. by fire **2** *often cap* : the killing of European Jews by the Nazis during World War II; *also* : GENOCIDE

Ho•lo•cene \'hō-lə-ₙsēn\ *adj* : of, relating to, or being the present geologic epoch — **Holocene** *n*

ho•lo•gram \'hō-lə-ₙgram, 'hä-\ *n* : a three-dimensional image produced by an interference pattern of light (as laser light)

ho•lo•graph \'hō-lə-ₙgraf, 'hä-\ *n* : a document wholly in the handwriting of its author

ho•log•ra•phy \hō-'lä-grə-fē\ *n* : the process of making a hologram — **ho•lo•graph•ic** \ₙhō-lə-'gra-fik, ₙhä-\ *adj*

Hol·stein \'hōl-₁stēn, -₁stīn\ *n* : any of a breed of large black-and-white dairy cattle that produce large quantities of comparatively low-fat milk

Hol·stein–Frie·sian \-'frē-zhən\ *n* : HOLSTEIN

hol·ster \'hōl-stər\ *n* [D] : a usu. leather case for a firearm

ho·ly \'hō-lē\ *adj* **ho·li·er; -est 1** : worthy of absolute devotion **2** : SACRED **3** : having a divine quality **syn** hallowed, blessed, sanctified, consecrated — **ho·li·ly** \-lə-lē\ *adv*

Holy Spirit *n* : the third person of the Christian Trinity

ho·ly·stone \'hō-lē-₁stōn\ *n* : a soft sandstone used to scrub a ship's decks — **holystone** *vb*

hom·age \'ä-mij, 'hä-\ *n* [ME, fr. OF *hommage*, fr. *homme* man, vassal, fr. L *homo* human being] : expression of high regard; *also* : TRIBUTE 3

hom·bre \'äm-brē, 'əm-, -₁brā\ *n* : GUY, FELLOW

hom·burg \'häm-₁bərg\ *n* [*Homburg*, Germany] : a man's felt hat with a stiff curled brim and a high crown creased lengthwise

¹**home** \'hōm\ *n* **1** : one's residence; *also* : HOUSE **2** : the social unit formed by a family living together **3** : a congenial environment; *also* : HABITAT **4** : a place of origin **5** : the objective in various games

²**home** *vb* **homed; hom·ing 1** : to go or return home **2** : to proceed to or toward a source of radiated energy used as a guide

home·body \'hōm-₁bä-dē\ *n* : one whose life centers in the home

home·boy \-₁bȯi\ *n* **1** : a boy or man from one's neighborhood, hometown, or region **2** : a fellow member of a youth gang

home·bred \-'bred\ *adj* : produced at home : INDIGENOUS

home·com·ing \-₁kə-miŋ\ *n* **1** : a return home **2** : the return of a group of people esp. on a special occasion to a place formerly frequented

home computer *n* : a small inexpensive microcomputer

home economics *n* : the theory and practice of homemaking

home·grown \'hōm-'grōn\ *adj* **1** : grown domestically **2** : LOCAL, INDIGENOUS

home·land \-₁land\ *n* **1** : native land **2** : an area set aside to be a state for a people of a particular national, cultural, or racial origin

¹**home·less** \-ləs\ *adj* : having no home or permanent residence

²**homeless** *n pl* : persons esp. in urban areas that have no home

home·ly \'hōm-lē\ *adj* **home·li·er; -est 1** : FAMILIAR **2** : unaffectedly natural **3** : lacking beauty or proportion — **home·li·ness** \-lē-nəs\ *n*

home·made \'hōm-₁mād\ *adj* : made in the home, on the premises, or by one's own efforts

home·mak·er \-₁mā-kər\ *n* : one who manages a household esp. as a wife and mother — **home·mak·ing** \-kiŋ\ *n*

ho·me·op·a·thy \₁hō-mē-'ä-pə-thē\ *n* : a system of medical practice that treats disease esp. with minute doses of a remedy that would in healthy persons produce symptoms similar to those of the disease treated — **ho·meo·path** \'hō-mē-ə-₁path\ *n* — **ho·meo·path·ic** \₁hō-mē-ə-'pa-thik\ *adj*

ho·meo·sta·sis \₁hō-mē-ō-'stā-səs\ *n* : the maintence of a relatively stable state of equilibrium between interrelated physiological, psychological, or social factors characteristic of an individual or group — **ho·meo·stat·ic** \-'sta-tik\ *adj*

home plate *n* : a slab at the apex of a baseball diamond that a base runner must touch in order to score

hom·er \'hō-mər\ *n* : HOME RUN — **homer** *vb*

home·room \'hōm-₁rüm, -₁rüm\ *n* : a classroom where pupils report at the beginning of each school day

home run *n* : a hit in baseball that enables the batter to go around all the bases and score a run

home·school \'hōm-₁skül\ *vb* : to teach school subjects to one's children at home — **home·school·er** \-₁skü-lər\ *n*

home·sick \'hōm-₁sik\ *adj* : longing for home and family while absent from them — **home·sick·ness** *n*

home·spun \-₁spən\ *adj* **1** : spun or made at home; *also* : made of a loosely woven usu. woolen or linen fabric **2** : SIMPLE, HOMELY

¹**home·stead** \-₁sted\ *n* : the home and land occupied by a family

²**homestead** *vb* : to acquire or settle on public land — **home·stead·er** *n*

home·stretch \-'strech\ *n* **1** : the part of a racecourse between the last curve and the winning post **2** : a final stage (as of a project)

¹**home·ward** \-wərd\ *or* **home·wards** \-wərdz\ *adv* : toward home

²**homeward** *adj* : being or going toward home

home·work \-₁wərk\ *n* **1** : an assignment given a student to be completed outside the classroom **2** : preparatory reading or research

hom·ey \'hō-mē\ *adj* **hom·i·er; -est** : characteristic of home

ho·mi·cide \'hä-mə-₁sīd, 'hō-\ *n* [L *homicida* murderer & *homicidium* manslaughter; both fr. *homo* human being + *caedere* to cut, kill] **1** : a person who kills another **2** : a killing of one human being by another — **hom·i·cid·al** \₁hä-mə-'sīd-ᵊl\ *adj*

hom·i·ly \'hä-mə-lē\ *n, pl* **-lies** : SERMON — **hom·i·let·ic** \₁hä-mə-'le-tik\ *adj*

homing pigeon *n* : a racing pigeon trained to return home

hom·i·nid \'hä-mə-nəd, -₁nid\ *n* : any of a family of primate mammals that comprise all living humans and extinct ancestral and related forms — **hominid** *adj*

hom·i·ny \'hä-mə-nē\ *n* : hulled corn with the germ removed

ho·mo·ge·neous \₁hō-mə-'jē-nē-əs, -nyəs\ *adj* : of the same or a similar kind; *also* : of uniform structure — **ho·mo·ge·ne·ity** \-jə-'nē-ə-tē\ *n* — **ho·mo·ge·neous·ly** *adv*

ho·mog·e·nise *Brit var of* HOMOGENIZE
ho·mog·e·nize \hō-ˈmä-jə-ˌnīz, hə-\ *vb* **-nized; -niz·ing 1 :** to make homogeneous **2 :** to reduce the particles in (as milk) to uniform size and distribute them evenly throughout the liquid — **ho·mog·e·ni·za·tion** \-ˌmä-jə-nə-ˈzā-shən\ *n* — **ho·mog·e·niz·er** *n*
ho·mo·graph \ˈhä-mə-ˌgraf, ˈhō-\ *n :* one of two or more words spelled alike but different in origin, meaning, or pronunciation (as the *bow* of a ship, a *bow* and arrow)
ho·mol·o·gy \hō-ˈmä-lə-jē, hə-\ *n, pl* **-gies 1 :** structural likeness between corresponding parts of different plants or animals due to evolution from a common ancestor **2 :** structural likeness between different parts of the same individual — **ho·mol·o·gous** \-ˈmä-lə-gəs\ *adj*
hom·onym \ˈhä-mə-ˌnim, ˈhō-\ *n* **1 :** HOMOPHONE, HOMOGRAPH **2 :** one of two or more words spelled and pronounced alike but different in meaning (as *pool* of water and *pool* the game)
ho·mo·pho·bia \ˌhō-mə-ˈfō-bē-ə\ *n :* irrational fear of, aversion to, or discrimination against homosexuality or homosexuals — **ho·mo·pho·bic** \-ˈfō-bik\ *adj*
ho·mo·phone \ˈhä-mə-ˌfōn, ˈhō-\ *n :* one of two or more words (as *to, too, two*) pronounced alike but different in meaning or derivation or spelling
Ho·mo sa·pi·ens \ˌhō-mō-ˈsä-pē-ənz, -ˈsa-\ *n :* HUMANKIND
ho·mo·sex·u·al \ˌhō-mō-ˈsek-shə-wəl\ *adj :* of, relating to, or marked by sexual interst in the same sex as oneself; *also :* of, relating to, or involving sexual intercouse between members of the same sex — **homosexual** *n* — **ho·mo·sex·u·al·i·ty** \-ˌsek-shə-ˈwa-lə-tē\ *n*
hon *abbr* honor; honorable; honorary
Hon·du·ran \hän-ˈdùr-ən\ *or* **Hon·du·ra·ne·an** *or* **Hon·du·ra·ni·an** \ˌhan-dù-ˈrā-nē-ən, -dyù-\ *n :* a native or inhabitant of Honduras — **Honduran** *or* **Honduranean** *or* **Honduranian** *adj*
hone \ˈhōn\ *n :* WHETSTONE — **hone** *vb* — **hon·er** *n*
hone in *vb :* to move toward or direct attention to an objective
¹hon·est \ˈä-nəst\ *adj* **1 :** free from deception : TRUTHFUL; *also :* GENUINE, REAL **2 :** REPUTABLE **3 :** CREDITABLE **4 :** marked by integrity **5 :** FRANK *syn* upright, just, conscientious, honorable — **hon·est·ly** *adv* — **hon·es·ty** \-nə-stē\ *n*
²honest *adv :* HONESTLY; *also :* with all sincerity ⟨I didn't do it, ~⟩
hon·ey \ˈhə-nē\ *n, pl* **honeys :** a sweet sticky substance made by honeybees from the nectar of flowers
hon·ey·bee \ˈhə-nē-ˌbē\ *n :* a social and colonial 4≠ winged insect often kept in hives for the honey it produces
¹hon·ey·comb \-ˌkōm\ *n :* a mass of 6-sided wax cells built by honeybees; *also :* something of similar structure or appearance
²honeycomb *vb :* to make or become full of cavities like a honeycomb
hon·ey·dew \-ˌdü, -ˌdyü\ *n :* a sweetish deposit secreted on plants by aphids, scale insects, or fungi
honeydew melon *n :* a smooth-skinned muskmelon with sweet green flesh
honey locust *n :* a tall usu. spiny No. American leguminous tree with hard durable wood and long twisted pods
hon·ey·moon \ˈhə-nē-ˌmün\ *n* **1 :** a period of harmony esp. just after marriage **2 :** a holiday taken by a newly married couple — **honeymoon** *vb*
hon·ey·suck·le \ˈhə-nē-ˌsə-kəl\ *n :* any of a genus of shrubs or vines with tube-shaped flowers rich in nectar
honk \ˈhäŋk, ˈhòŋk\ *n :* the cry of a goose; *also :* a similar sound (as of a horn) — **honk** *vb* — **honk·er** *n*
hon·ky–tonk \ˈhäŋ-kē-ˌtäŋk, ˈhòŋ-kē-ˌtòŋk\ *n :* a taw-

dry nightclub or dance hall — **honky–tonk** *adj*
¹hon·or \ˈä-nər\ *n* **1 :** good name : REPUTATION; *also :* outward respect **2 :** PRIVILEGE **3 :** a person of superior standing — used esp. as a title **4 :** one who brings respect or fame **5 :** an evidence or symbol of distinction **6 :** CHASTITY, PURITY **7 :** INTEGRITY *syn* homage, reverence, deference, obeisance
²honor *vb* **1 :** to regard or treat with honor **2 :** to confer honor on **3 :** to fulfill the terms of; *also :* to accept as payment — **hon·or·ee** \ˌä-nə-ˈrē\ *n* — **hon·or·er** *n*
hon·or·able \ˈä-nə-rə-bəl\ *adj* **1 :** deserving of honor **2 :** of great renown **3 :** accompanied with marks of honor **4 :** doing credit to the possessor **5 :** characterized by integrity — **hon·or·able·ness** *n* — **hon·or·ably** \-blē\ *adv*
hon·o·rar·i·um \ˌä-nə-ˈrer-ē-əm\ *n, pl* **-ia** \-ē-ə\ *also* **-iums :** a reward usu. for services on which custom or propriety forbids a price to be set
hon·or·ary \ˈä-nə-ˌrer-ē\ *adj* **1 :** having or conferring distinction **2 :** conferred in recognition of achievement without the usual prerequisites ⟨~ degree⟩ **3 :** UNPAID, VOLUNTARY — **hon·or·ari·ly** \ˌä-nə-ˈrer-ə-lē\ *adv*
hon·or·if·ic \ˌä-nə-ˈri-fik\ *adj :* conferring or conveying honor ⟨~ titles⟩
hon·our, hon·our·able *chiefly Brit var of* HONOR, HONORABLE
¹hood \ˈhùd\ *n* **1 :** a covering for the head and neck and sometimes the face **2 :** an ornamental fold (as at the back of an ecclesiastical vestment) **3 :** a cover for parts of mechanisms; *esp :* the covering over an automobile engine — **hood·ed** \ˈhù-dəd\ *adj*
²hood \ˈhùd, ˈhüd\ *n :* HOODLUM
³hood \ˈhùd\ *n :* NEIGHBORHOOD 4
-hood \ˌhùd\ *n suffix* **1 :** state : condition : quality : character ⟨boy*hood*⟩ ⟨hardi*hood*⟩ **2 :** instance of a (specified) state or quality ⟨false*hood*⟩ **3 :** individuals sharing a (specified) state or character ⟨brother*hood*⟩
hood·lum \ˈhüd-ləm, ˈhùd-\ *n* **1 :** THUG **2 :** a young ruffian
hoo·doo \ˈhü-dü\ *n, pl* **hoodoos 1 :** a body of magical practices traditional esp. among blacks in the southern U.S. **2 :** something that brings bad luck — **hoodoo** *vb*
hood·wink \ˈhùd-ˌwiŋk\ *vb :* to deceive by false appearance
hoo·ey \ˈhü-ē\ *n :* NONSENSE
hoof \ˈhùf, ˈhüf\ *n, pl* **hooves** \ˈhùvz, ˈhüvz\ *or* **hoofs :** a horny covering that protects the ends of the toes of ungulate mammals (as horses or cattle); *also :* a hoofed foot — **hoofed** \ˈhùft, ˈhüft\ *adj*
¹hook \ˈhùk\ *n* **1 :** a curved or bent device for catching, holding, or pulling **2 :** something curved or bent like a hook **3 :** a flight of a ball (as in golf) that curves in a direction opposite to the dominant hand of the player propelling it **4 :** a short punch delivered with a circular motion and with the elbow bent and rigid
²hook *vb* **1 :** CURVE, CROOK **2 :** to seize or make fast with a hook **3 :** STEAL **4 :** to work as a prostitute
hoo·kah \ˈhù-kə, ˈhü-\ *n* [Ar *ḥuqqah* bottle of a water pipe] : WATER PIPE
hook·er \ˈhù-kər\ *n* **1 :** one that hooks **2 :** PROSTITUTE
hook·up \ˈhù-ˌkəp\ *n :* an assemblage (as of apparatus or circuits) used for a specific purpose (as in radio)
hook·worm \ˈhùk-ˌwərm\ *n :* any of several parasitic intestinal nematode worms having hooks or plates around the mouth; *also :* infestation with or disease caused by hookworms
hoo·li·gan \ˈhü-li-gən\ *n :* RUFFIAN, HOODLUM
hoop \ˈhùp, ˈhüp\ *n* **1 :** a circular strip used esp. for holding together the staves of a barrel **2 :** a circular figure or object : RING **3 :** a circle of flexible material for expanding a woman's skirt **4 :** BASKETBALL — usu. used in pl.
hoop·la \ˈhüp-ˌlä, ˈhùp-\ *n* [F *houp-là*, interj.] : TO-DO; *also :* BALLYHOO

hoose·gow \'hüs-₁gaů\ *n* [Sp *juzgado* panel of judges, courtroom] : JAIL

¹hoot \'hüt\ *vb* **1** : to shout or laugh usu. in contempt **2** : to make the natural throat noise of an owl — **hoot·er** *n*

²hoot *n* **1** : a sound of hooting **2** : the least bit ⟨don't give a ∼⟩ **3** : something or someone amusing ⟨the play is a real ∼⟩

¹hop \'häp\ *vb* **hopped; hop·ping 1** : to move by quick springy leaps **2** : to make a quick trip **3** : to ride on esp. surreptitiously and without authorization

²hop *n* **1** : a short brisk leap esp. on one leg **2** : DANCE **3** : a short trip by air

³hop *n* : a vine related to the mulberry whose ripe dried pistillate catkins are used esp. in flavoring malt liquors; *also, pl* : its pistillate catkins

¹hope \'hōp\ *vb* **hoped; hop·ing** : to desire with expectation of fulfillment

²hope *n* **1** : TRUST, RELIANCE **2** : desire accompanied by expectation of fulfillment; *also* : something hoped for **3** : one that gives promise for the future — **hope·ful** \-fəl\ *adj* — **hope·ful·ness** *n* — **hope·less** *adj* — **hope·less·ly** *adv* — **hope·less·ness** *n*

HOPE *abbr* Health Opportunity for People Everywhere

hope·ful·ly \'hōp-fə-lē\ *adv* **1** : in a hopeful manner **2** : it is hoped

Ho·pi \'hō-pē\ *n, pl* **Hopi** *also* **Hopis** : a member of an American Indian people of Arizona; *also* : the language of the Hopi people

hopped–up \'häpt-'əp\ *adj* **1** : being under the influence of a narcotic; *also* : full of enthusiasm or excitement **2** : having more power than usual ⟨a ∼ engine⟩

hop·per \'hä-pər\ *n* **1** : a usu. immature hopping insect (as a grasshopper) **2** : a usu. funnel-shaped container for delivering material (as grain) **3** : a freight car with hinged doors in a sloping bottom **4** : a box into which a bill to be considered by a legislative body is dropped **5** : a tank holding a liquid and having a device for releasing its contents through a pipe

hop·scotch \'häp-₁skäch\ *n* : a child's game in which a player tosses an object (as a stone) into areas of a figure drawn on the ground and hops through the figure to pick up the object

hor *abbr* horizontal

horde \'hôrd\ *n* : THRONG, SWARM

ho·ri·zon \hə-'rīz-°n\ *n* [Gk *horizont-, horizōn,* fr. prp. of *horizein* to bound, fr. *horos* limit, boundary] **1** : the apparent junction of earth and sky **2** : range of outlook or experience

hor·i·zon·tal \₁hôr-ə-'zänt-°l\ *adj* : parallel to the horizon : LEVEL — **horizontal** *n* — **hor·i·zon·tal·ly** *adv*

hor·mon·al \hôr-'mōn-°l\ *adj* : of, relating to, or effected by hormones

hor·mone \'hôr-₁mōn\ *n* [Gk *hormōn,* prp. of *horman* to stir up, fr. *hormē* impulse, assault] : a product of living cells that circulates in body fluids and has a specific effect on the activity of cells remote from its point of origin

horn \'hôrn\ *n* **1** : one of the hard projections of bone or keratin on the head of many hoofed mammals **2** : something resembling or suggesting a horn **3** : a brass wind instrument **4** : a usu. electrical device that makes a noise ⟨automobile ∼⟩ — **horned** \'hôrnd\ *adj* — **horn·less** *adj*

horn·book \'hôrn-₁bůk\ *n* **1** : a child's primer consisting of a sheet of parchment or paper protected by a sheet of transparent horn **2** : a rudimentary treatise

horned toad *n* : any of several small harmless insect= eating lizards with spines on the head resembling horns and spiny scales on the body

hor·net \'hôr-nət\ *n* : any of the larger social wasps

horn in *vb* : to participate without invitation : INTRUDE

horn·pipe \'hôrn-₁pīp\ *n* : a lively folk dance of the British Isles

horny \'hôr-nē\ *adj* **horn·i·er; -est 1** : of or made of horn; *also* : HARD, CALLOUS **2** : having horns **3** : desiring sexual gratification; *also* : excited sexually

ho·rol·o·gy \hə-'rä-lə-jē\ *n* : the science of measuring time or constructing time-indicating instruments — **hor·o·log·ic** \₁hôr-ə-'lä-jik\ *adj* — **ho·rol·o·gist** \hə-'rä-lə-jist\ *n*

horo·scope \'hôr-ə-₁skōp\ *n* [ME *oruscope,* fr. MF *horoscope,* fr. L *horoscopus,* fr. Gk *hōroskopos,* fr. *hōra* hour + *skopos* watcher] **1** : a diagram of the relative positions of planets and signs of the zodiac at a particular time for use by astrologers to foretell events of a person's life **2** : an astrological forecast

hor·ren·dous \hò-'ren-dəs\ *adj* : DREADFUL, HORRIBLE

hor·ri·ble \'hôr-ə-bəl\ *adj* **1** : marked by or conducive to horror **2** : highly disagreeable — **hor·ri·ble·ness** *n* — **hor·ri·bly** \-blē\ *adv*

hor·rid \'hôr-əd\ *adj* **1** : HIDEOUS **2** : REPULSIVE — **hor·rid·ly** *adv*

hor·ri·fy \'hôr-ə-₁fī\ *vb* **-fied; -fy·ing** : to cause to feel horror **syn** appall, daunt, dismay

hor·ror \'hôr-ər\ *n* **1** : painful and intense fear, dread, or dismay **2** : intense repugnance **3** : something that horrifies

hors de com·bat \₁òr-də-kōⁿ-'bä\ *adv or adj* : in a disabled condition

hors d'oeuvre \òr-'dərv\ *n, pl* **hors d'oeuvres** *same or* -'dərvz\ *also* **hors d'oeuvre** [F *hors-d'oeuvre,* lit., outside of the work] : any of various savory foods usu. served as appetizers

horse \'hôrs\ *n, pl* **hors·es** *also* **horse 1** : a large solid= hoofed herbivorous mammal domesticated as a draft and saddle animal **2** : a supporting framework usu. with legs — **horse·less** *adj*

¹horse·back \'hôrs-₁bak\ *n* : the back of a horse

²horseback *adv* : on horseback

horse chestnut *n* : a large Asian tree with palmate

leaves, erect conical clusters of showy flowers, and large glossy brown seeds enclosed in a prickly bur; *also* : its seed

horse·flesh \'hòrs-₁flesh\ *n* : horses for riding, driving, or racing

horse·fly \-₁flī\ *n* : any of a family of large dipteran flies with bloodsucking females

horse·hair \-₁har\ *n* **1** : the hair of a horse esp. from the mane or tail **2** : cloth made from horsehair

horse·hide \-₁hīd\ *n* **1** : the dressed or raw hide of a horse **2** : the ball used in baseball

horse latitudes *n pl* : either of two calm regions near 30°N and 30°S latitude

horse·laugh \'hòrs-₁laf, -₁làf\ *n* : a loud boisterous laugh

horse·man \-mən\ *n* **1** : one who rides horseback; *also* : one skilled in managing horses **2** : a breeder or raiser of horses — **horse·man·ship** *n*

horse·play \-₁plā\ *n* : rough boisterous play

horse·play·er \-ər\ *n* : a bettor on horse races

horse·pow·er \'hòrs-₁paù-ər\ *n* : a unit of power equal in the U.S. to 746 watts

horse·rad·ish \-₁ra-dish\ *n* : a tall white-flowered herb related to the mustards whose pungent root is used as a condiment; *also* : the pungent condiment

horse·shoe \'hòrs-₁shü\ *n* **1** : a usu. U-shaped protective metal plate fitted to the rim of a horse's hoof **2** *pl* : a game in which horseshoes are pitched at a fixed object — **horse·shoe** *vb* — **horse·sho·er** *n*

horseshoe crab *n* : any of several marine arthropods with a broad crescent-shaped combined head and thorax

horse·tail \'hòrs-₁tāl\ *n* : any of a genus of primitive spore-producing plants with hollow jointed stems and leaves reduced to sheaths about the joints

horse·whip \-₁hwip\ *vb* : to flog with a whip made to be used on a horse

horse·wom·an \-₁wù-mən\ *n* : a woman skilled in riding horseback or in caring for or managing horses; *also* : a woman who breeds or raises horses

hors·ey *or* **horsy** \'hòr-sē\ *adj* **hors·i·er; -est 1** : of, relating to, or suggesting a horse **2** : having to do with horses or horse racing

hort *abbr* horticultural; horticulture

hor·ta·tive \'hòr-tə-tiv\ *adj* : giving exhortation

hor·ta·to·ry \'hòr-tə-₁tòr-ē\ *adj* : HORTATIVE

hor·ti·cul·ture \'hòr-tə-₁kəl-chər\ *n* : the science and art of growing fruits, vegetables, flowers, and ornamental plants — **hor·ti·cul·tur·al** \₁hòr-tə-'kəl-chə-rəl\ *adj* — **hor·ti·cul·tur·ist** \-rist\ *n*

Hos *abbr* Hosea

ho·san·na \hō-'za-nə, -'zä-\ *interj* [Gk *hōsanna*, fr. Heb *hōshīʿāh-nnā* pray, save (us)!] — used as a cry of acclamation and adoration — **hosanna** *n*

¹hose \'hōz\ *n, pl* **hose** *or* **hos·es 1** *pl* **hose** : STOCKING, SOCK; *also* : a close-fitting garment covering the legs and waist **2** : a flexible tube for conveying fluids (as from a faucet)

²hose *vb* **hosed; hos·ing** : to spray, water, or wash with a hose

Ho·sea \hō-'zā-ə, -'zē-\ *n* — see BIBLE table

ho·siery \'hō-zhə-rē, -zə-\ *n* : STOCKINGS, SOCKS

hosp *abbr* hospital

hos·pice \'häs-pəs\ *n* **1** : a lodging for travelers or for young persons or the underprivileged **2** : a facility or program for caring for dying persons

hos·pi·ta·ble \hä-'spi-tə-bəl, 'häs-(₁)pi-\ *adj* **1** : given to generous and cordial reception of guests **2** : readily receptive — **hos·pi·ta·bly** \-blē\ *adv*

hos·pi·tal \'häs-₁pit-ᵊl\ *n* [ME, fr. OF, fr. ML *hospitale* hospice, guest house, fr. neut. of L *hospitalis* of a guest, fr. *hospit-, hospes* guest, host] : an institution where the sick or injured receive medical or surgical care

hos·pi·tal·ise *Brit var of* HOSPITALIZE

hos·pi·tal·i·ty \₁häs-pə-'ta-lə-tē\ *n, pl* **-ties** : hospitable treatment, reception, or disposition

hos·pi·tal·ize \'häs-₁pit-ᵊl-₁īz\ *vb* **-ized; -iz·ing** : to place in a hospital as a patient — **hos·pi·tal·i·za·tion** \₁häs-₁pit-ᵊl-ə-'zā-shən\ *n*

¹host \'hōst\ *n* [ME, fr. OF, fr. LL *hostis*, fr. L, stranger, enemy] **1** : ARMY **2** : MULTITUDE

²host *n* [ME *hoste* host, guest, fr. OF, fr. L *hospit-, hospes*] **1** : one who receives or entertains guests **2** : an animal or plant on or in which a parasite lives — **host** *vb*

³host *n, often cap* [ultim. fr. L *hostia* sacrifice] : the eucharistic bread

hos·tage \'häs-tij\ *n* **1** : a person kept as a pledge pending the fulfillment of an agreement **2** : a person taken by force to secure the taker's demands

hos·tel \'häst-ᵊl\ *n* [ME, fr. OF, fr. ML *hospitale* hospice] **1** : INN **2** : a supervised lodging for youth — **hos·tel·er** *n*

hos·tel·ry \-rē\ *n, pl* **-ries** : INN, HOTEL

host·ess \'hō-stəs\ *n* : a woman who acts as host

hos·tile \'häst-ᵊl, 'häs-₁tīl\ *adj* : marked by usu. overt antagonism : UNFRIENDLY — **hostile** *n* — **hos·tile·ly** *adv*

hos·til·i·ty \hä-'sti-lə-tē\ *n, pl* **-ties 1** : an unfriendly state or action **2** *pl* : overt acts of war

hos·tler \'häs-lər, 'äs-\ *n* : one who takes care of horses or mules

hot \'hät\ *adj* **hot·ter; hot·test 1** : marked by a high temperature or an uncomfortable degree of body heat **2** : giving a sensation of heat or of burning **3** : ARDENT, FIERY **4** : sexually excited **5** : EAGER **6** : newly made or received **7** : PUNGENT **8** : unusually lucky or favorable ⟨~ dice⟩ **9** : recently and illegally obtained ⟨~ jewels⟩ — **hot** *adv* — **hot·ly** *adv* — **hot·ness** *n*

hot·bed \-₁bed\ *n* **1** : a glass-covered bed of soil heated (as by fermenting manure) and used esp. for raising seedlings **2** : an environment that favors rapid growth or development

hot–blood·ed \-'blə-dəd\ *adj* : easily roused or excited

hot·box \-₁bäks\ *n* : a bearing (as of a railroad car) overheated by friction

hot button *n* : an emotional issue or concern that triggers immediate intense reaction

hot·cake \-₁kāk\ *n* : PANCAKE

hot dog n : a cooked frankfurter usu. served in a long split roll

ho•tel \hō-'tel\ n [F hôtel, fr. OF hostel, fr. ML hospitale hospice] : a building where lodging and usu. meals, entertainment, and various personal services are provided for the public

hot flash n : a sudden brief flushing and sensation of heat usu. associated with menopausal endocrine imbalance

hot•head•ed \'hät-'he-dəd\ adj : FIERY, IMPETUOUS — hot•head \-₁hed\ n — hot•head•ed•ly adv — hot•head•ed•ness n

hot•house \-₁haùs\ n : a heated greenhouse esp. for raising tropical plants

hot line n : a telephone line for emergency use (as between governments or to a counseling service)

hot plate n : a simple portable appliance for heating or for cooking

hot potato n : an embarrassing or controversial issue

hot rod n : an automobile modified for high speed and fast acceleration — hot–rod•der \-'rä-dər\ n

hots \'häts\ n pl : strong sexual desire — usu. used with the

hot seat n : a position of anxiety or embarrassment

hot•shot \'hät-₁shät\ n : a showily skillful person

hot tub n : a large wooden tub of hot water in which bathers soak and usu. socialize

hot water n : TROUBLE, DIFFICULTY

hot–wire \'hät-₁wīr\ vb : to start (an automobile) by short-circuiting the ignition system

¹hound \'haùnd\ n 1 : any of various long-eared hunting dogs that track prey by scent 2 : FAN, ADDICT

²hound vb : to pursue relentlessly

hour \'aùr\ n 1 : the 24th part of a day : 60 minutes 2 : the time of day 3 : a particular or customary time 4 : a class session — hour•ly adv or adj

hour•glass \'aùr-₁glas\ n : a glass vessel for measuring time in which sand runs from an upper compartment to a lower compartment in an hour

hou•ri \'hùr-ē\ n [F, fr. Per hūri, fr. Ar ḥūrīyah] : one of the beautiful maidens of the Muslim paradise

¹house \'haùs\ n, pl hous•es \'haù-zəz\ 1 : a building for human habitation 2 : an animal shelter (as a den or nest) 3 : a building in which something is stored 4 : HOUSEHOLD; also : FAMILY 5 : a residence for a religious community or for students; also : those in residence 6 : a legislative body 7 : a place of business or entertainment 8 : a business organization 9 : the audience in a theater or concert hall — house•ful n

²house \'haùz\ vb housed; hous•ing 1 : to provide with or take shelter : LODGE 2 : STORE

house•boat \'haùs-₁bōt\ n : a pleasure boat fitted for use as a dwelling or for leisurely cruising

house•boy \-₁bòi\ n : a boy or man hired to act as a household servant

house•break \-₁brāk\ vb house•broke; house•bro•ken; house•break•ing : to train in excretory habits acceptable in indoor living

house•break•ing \-₁brā-kiŋ\ n : the act of breaking into a dwelling with the intent of committing a felony

house•clean \-₁klēn\ vb : to clean a house and its furniture — house•clean•ing n

house•coat \-₁kōt\ n : a woman's often long-skirted informal garment for wear around the house

house•fly \-₁flī\ n : a dipteran fly that is common about human habitations

¹house•hold \-₁hōld\ n : those who dwell as a family under the same roof — house•hold•er n

²household adj 1 : DOMESTIC 2 : FAMILIAR, COMMON ⟨a ~ name⟩

house•keep•er \-₁kē-pər\ n : a woman employed to take care of a house

house•keep•ing \-₁kē-piŋ\ n : the care and management of a house or institutional property

house•lights \-₁līts\ n pl : the lights that illuminate the auditorium of a theater

house•maid \-₁mād\ n : a female servant employed to do housework

house•moth•er \-₁mə-thər\ n : a woman acting as hostess, chaperon, and often housekeeper in a group residence

house•plant \-₁plant\ n : a plant grown or kept indoors

house sparrow n : a Eurasian sparrow widely introduced in urban and agricultural areas

house•top \'haùs-₁täp\ n : ROOF

house•wares \-₁warz\ n pl : small articles of household equipment

house•warm•ing \-₁wòr-miŋ\ n : a party to celebrate the taking possession of a house or premises

house•wife \-₁wīf\ n : a married woman in charge of a household — house•wife•ly adj — house•wif•ery \-₁wī-fə-rē\ n

house•work \-₁wərk\ n : the work of housekeeping

¹hous•ing \'haù-ziŋ\ n 1 : SHELTER; also : dwellings provided for people 2 : something that covers or protects

²housing n : CAPARISON 1

HOV abbr high-occupancy vehicle

hove past and past part of HEAVE

hov•el \'hə-vəl, 'hä-\ n : a small, wretched, and often dirty house : HUT

hov•er \'hə-vər, 'hä-\ vb hov•ered; hov•er•ing 1 : FLUTTER; also : to move to and fro 2 : to be in an uncertain state

hov•er•craft \-₁kraft\ n : a vehicle that rides on a cushion of air over a surface

¹how \'haù\ adv 1 : in what way or manner ⟨~ was it done⟩ 2 : with what meaning ⟨~ do we interpret such behavior⟩ 3 : for what reason ⟨~ could you have done such a thing⟩ 4 : to what extent or degree ⟨~ deep is it⟩ 5 : in what state or condition ⟨~ are you⟩ — how about : what do you say to or think of ⟨how about coming with me⟩ — how come : why is it that

²how conj 1 : the way or manner in which ⟨remember ~ they fought⟩ 2 : HOWEVER ⟨do it ~ you like⟩

¹how•be•it \haù-'bē-ət\ conj : ALTHOUGH

²howbeit adv : NEVERTHELESS

how·dah \'haù-də\ *n* [Hindi *hauda*] : a seat or covered pavilion on the back of an elephant or camel

¹how·ev·er \haù-'e-vər\ *conj* : in whatever manner that

²however *adv* 1 : to whatever degree; *also* : in whatever manner 2 : in spite of that

how·it·zer \'haù-ət-sər\ *n* : a short cannon that shoots shells at a high angle

howl \'haùl\ *vb* 1 : to emit a loud long doleful sound characteristic of dogs 2 : to cry loudly — **howl** *n*

howl·er \'haù-lər\ *n* 1 : one that howls 2 : a humorous and ridiculous blunder

howl·ing *adj* 1 : DESOLATE, WILD 2 : very great ⟨a ~ success⟩

how·so·ev·er \ˌhaù-sə-'we-vər\ *adv* : HOWEVER 1

hoy·den \'hòid-ᵊn\ *n* : a girl or woman of saucy, boisterous, or carefree behavior — **hoy·den·ish** *adj*

hp *abbr* horsepower

HP *abbr* high pressure

HPF *abbr* highest possible frequency

HQ *abbr* headquarters

hr *abbr* 1 here 2 hour

HR *abbr* House of Representatives

HRH *abbr* 1 Her Royal Highness 2 His Royal Highness

hrzn *abbr* horizon

HS *abbr* high school

HST *abbr* Hawaiian standard time

ht *abbr* height

HT *abbr* 1 Hawaii time 2 high-tension

http *abbr* hypertext transfer protocol

hua·ra·che \wə-'rä-chē\ *n* [MexSp] : a sandal with an upper made of interwoven leather strips

hub \'həb\ *n* 1 : the central part of a circular object (as a wheel) 2 : a center of activity; *esp* : an airport or city with heavy air traffic

hub·bub \'hə-bəb\ *n* : UPROAR; *also* : TURMOIL

hub·cap \'həb-ˌkap\ *n* : a removable metal cap over the end of an axle

hu·bris \'hyü-brəs\ *n* : exaggerated pride or self-confidence

huck·le·ber·ry \'hə-kəl-ˌber-ē\ *n* 1 : an American shrub related to the blueberry; *also* : its edible dark blue berry 2 : BLUEBERRY

huck·ster \'hək-stər\ *n* : PEDDLER, HAWKER — **huckster** *vb*

HUD *abbr* Department of Housing and Urban Development

¹hud·dle \'həd-ᵊl\ *vb* **hud·dled; hud·dling** 1 : to crowd together 2 : CONFER

²huddle *n* 1 : a closely packed group 2 : MEETING, CONFERENCE

hue \'hyü\ *n* 1 : COLOR; *also* : gradation of color 2 : the attribute of colors that permits them to be classed as red, yellow, green, blue, or an intermediate color — **hued** \'hyüd\ *adj*

hue and cry *n* : a clamor of pursuit or protest

huff \'həf\ *n* : a fit of anger or pique — **huff** *vb* — **huffy** *adj*

hug \'həg\ *vb* **hugged; hug·ging** 1 : EMBRACE 2 : to stay close to — **hug** *n*

huge \'hyüj\ *adj* **hug·er; hug·est** : very large or extensive — **huge·ly** *adv* — **huge·ness** *n*

hug·ger–mug·ger \'hə-gər-ˌmə-gər\ *n* 1 : SECRECY 2 : CONFUSION, MUDDLE

Hu·gue·not \'hyü-gə-ˌnät\ *n* : a French Protestant of the 16th and 17th centuries

hu·la \'hü-lə\ *n* : a sinuous Polynesian dance usu. accompanied by chants

hulk \'həlk\ *n* 1 : a heavy clumsy ship 2 : an old ship unfit for service 3 : a bulky or unwieldy person or thing

hulk·ing \'həl-kiŋ\ *adj* : BURLY, MASSIVE

¹hull \'həl\ *n* 1 : the outer covering of a fruit or seed 2 : the frame or body esp. of a ship or boat

²hull *vb* : to remove the hulls of — **hull·er** *n*

hul·la·ba·loo \'hə-lə-bə-ˌlü\ *n, pl* **-loos** : a confused noise : UPROAR

hul·lo \ˌhə-'lō\ *chiefly Brit var of* HELLO

hum \'həm\ *vb* **hummed; hum·ming** 1 : to utter a sound like that of the speech sound \m\ prolonged 2 : DRONE 3 : to be busily active 4 : to run smoothly 5 : to sing with closed lips — **hum** *n* — **hum·mer** *n*

¹hu·man \'hyü-mən, 'yü-\ *adj* 1 : of, relating to, being, or characteristic of humans 2 : having human form or attributes — **hu·man·ly** *adv* — **hu·man·ness** *n*

²human *n* : any of a species of primate mammals comprising all living persons and their recent ancestors; *also* : HOMINID

hu·mane \hyü-'mān, yü-\ *adj* 1 : marked by compassion, sympathy, or consideration for others 2 : HUMANISTIC — **hu·mane·ly** *adv* — **hu·mane·ness** *n*

human immunodeficiency virus *n* : HIV

hu·man·ism \'hyü-mə-ˌni-zəm, 'yü-\ *n* 1 : devotion to the humanities; *also* : the revival of classical letters characteristic of the Renaissance 2 : a doctrine or way of life centered on human interests or values — **hu·man·ist** \-nist\ *n or adj* — **hu·man·is·tic** \ˌhyü-mə-'nis-tik, ˌyü-\ *adj*

hu·man·i·tar·i·an \hyü-ˌma-nə-'ter-ē-ən, yü-\ *n* : one who practices philanthropy — **humanitarian** *adj* — **hu·man·i·tar·i·an·ism** *n*

hu·man·i·ty \hyü-'ma-nə-tē, yü-\ *n, pl* **-ties** 1 : the quality or state of being human or humane 2 *pl* : the branches of learning dealing with human concerns (as philosophy) as opposed to natural processes (as physics) 3 : the human race

hu·man·ize \'hyü-mə-ˌnīz, 'yü-\ *vb* **-ized; -iz·ing** : to make human or humane — **hu·man·iza·tion** \ˌhyü-mə-nə-'zā-shən, ˌyü-\ *n* — **hu·man·iz·er** *n*

hu·man·kind \'hyü-mən-ˌkīnd, 'yü-\ *n* : the human race

hu·man·oid \'hyü-mə-ˌnòid, 'yü-\ *adj* : having human form or characteristics — **humanoid** *n*

¹hum·ble \'həm-bəl\ *adj* **hum·bler** \-bə-lər\; **hum·blest** \-bə-ləst\ [ME, fr. OF, fr. L *humilis* low, humble, fr. *humus* earth] 1 : not proud or haughty 2 : not pretentious : UNASSUMING 3 : INSIGNIFICANT **syn** meek, modest, lowly — **hum·ble·ness** *n* — **hum·bly** *adv*

²humble *vb* **hum·bled; hum·bling** 1 : to make humble 2 : to destroy the power or prestige of — **hum·bler** *n*

¹hum·bug \'həm-ˌbəg\ *n* 1 : HOAX, FRAUD 2 : NONSENSE

²humbug *vb* **hum·bugged; hum·bug·ging** : DECEIVE

hum·ding·er \'həm-'diŋ-ər\ *n* : a person or thing of striking excellence

hum·drum \'həm-ˌdrəm\ *adj* : MONOTONOUS, DULL — **humdrum** *n*

hu·mer·us \'hyü-mə-rəs\ *n, pl* **hu·meri** \'hyü-mə-ˌrī, -ˌrē\ : the long bone extending from shoulder to elbow

hu·mid \'hyü-məd, 'yü-\ *adj* : containing or characterized by perceptible moisture : DAMP — **hu·mid·ly** *adv*

hu·mid·i·fy \hyü-'mi-də-ˌfī\ *vb* **-fied; -fy·ing** : to make humid — **hu·mid·i·fi·ca·tion** \-ˌmi-də-fə-'kā-shən\ *n* — **hu·mid·i·fi·er** \-'mi-də-ˌfī-ər\ *n*

hu·mid·i·ty \hyü-'mi-də-tē, yü-\ *n, pl* **-ties** : the amount of atmospheric moisture

hu·mi·dor \'hyü-mə-ˌdòr, 'yü-\ *n* : a case (as for storing cigars) in which the air is kept properly humidified

hu·mil·i·ate \hyü-'mi-lē-ˌāt, yü-\ *vb* **-at·ed; -at·ing** : to injure the self-respect of : MORTIFY — **hu·mil·i·at·ing·ly** *adv* — **hu·mil·i·a·tion** \-ˌmi-lē-'ā-shən\ *n*

hu·mil·i·ty \hyü-'mi-lə-tē, yü-\ *n* : the quality or state of being humble

hum·ming·bird \'hə-miŋ-ˌbərd\ *n* : any of a family of tiny American birds related to the swifts

hum·mock \'hə-mək\ *n* : a rounded mound : KNOLL — **hum·mocky** \-mə-kē\ *adj*

hu·mon·gous \hyü-'məŋ-gəs, -'mäŋ-\ *adj* [perh. alter. of *huge* + *monstrous*] : extremely large

¹hu·mor \'hyü-mər, 'yü-\ *n* **1** : TEMPERAMENT **2** : MOOD **3** : WHIM **4** : a quality that appeals to a sense of the ludicrous or incongruous; *also* : a keen perception of the ludicrous or incongruous **5** : comical or amusing entertainment — **hu·mor·ist** \'hyü-mə-rist, 'yü-\ *n* — **hu·mor·less** \'hyü-mər-ləs, 'yü-\ *adj* — **hu·mor·less·ly** *adv* — **hu·mor·less·ness** *n* — **hu·mor·ous** \'hyü-mə-rəs, 'yü-\ *adj* — **hu·mor·ous·ly** *adv* — **hu·mor·ous·ness** *n*

²**humor** *vb* : to comply with the wishes or mood of

hu·mour *chiefly Brit var of* HUMOR

hump \'həmp\ *n* **1** : a rounded protuberance (as on the back of a camel) **2** : a difficult phase or obstacle (over the ∼) — **humped** *adj*

hump·back \'həmp-ıbak; *1 also* -ıbak\ *n* **1** : HUNCH-BACK **2** : HUMPBACK WHALE — **hump·backed** *adj*

humpback whale *n* : a large baleen whale having very long flippers

hu·mus \'hyü-məs, 'yü-\ *n* : the dark organic part of soil formed from decaying matter

Hun \'hən\ *n* : a member of an Asian people that invaded Europe about A.D. 450

¹**hunch** \'hənch\ *vb* **1** : to thrust oneself forward **2** : to assume or cause to assume a bent or crooked posture

²**hunch** *n* **1** : PUSH **2** : a strong intuitive feeling about what will happen

hunch·back \'hənch-ıbak\ *n* : a person with a crooked back; *also* : a back with a hump — **hunch·backed** *adj*

hun·dred \'hən-drəd\ *n, pl* **hundreds** *or* **hundred** : 10 times 10 — **hundred** *adj* — **hun·dredth** \-drədth\ *adj or n*

hun·dred·weight \-ıwāt\ *n, pl* **hundredweight** *or* **hundredweights** — see WEIGHT table

¹**hung** *past and past part of* HANG

²**hung** *adj* : unable to reach a decision or verdict ⟨a ∼ jury⟩

Hung *abbr* Hungarian; Hungary

Hun·gar·i·an \ıhəŋ-'ger-ē-ən\ *n* **1** : a native or inhabitant of Hungary **2** : the language of the Hungarians — **Hungarian** *adj*

hun·ger \'həŋ-gər\ *n* **1** : a craving or urgent need for food **2** : a strong desire — **hunger** *vb* — **hun·gri·ly** *adv* — **hun·gry** *adj*

hung·over \'həŋ-'ō-vər\ *adj* : having a hangover

hung up *adj* **1** : DELAYED **2** : ENTHUSIASTIC; *also* : PREOCCUPIED

hunk \'həŋk\ *n* **1** : a large piece **2** : an attractive well-built man — **hunky** *adj*

hun·ker \'həŋ-kər\ *vb* **1** : CROUCH, SQUAT — usu. used with *down* **2** : to settle in for a sustained period — used with *down*

hun·ky–do·ry \ıhəŋ-kē-'dōr-ē\ *adj* : quite satisfactory : FINE

¹**hunt** \'hənt\ *vb* **1** : to pursue for food or in sport; *also* : to take part in a hunt **2** : to try to find : SEEK **3** : to drive or chase esp. by harrying **4** : to traverse in search of prey — **hunt·er** *n*

²**hunt** *n* : an act, practice, or instance of hunting

hunt·ress \'hən-trəs\ *n* : a woman who hunts game

hunts·man \'hənts-mən\ *n* **1** : HUNTER **2** : a person who manages a hunt and looks after the hounds

hur·dle \'hərd-ə l\ *n* **1** : a barrier to leap over in a race **2** : OBSTACLE — **hurdle** *vb* — **hur·dler** *n*

hur·dy–gur·dy \ıhər-dē-'gər-dē, 'hər-dē-ıgər-dē\ *n, pl* **-gur·dies** : a musical instrument in which the sound is produced by turning a crank

hurl \'hərl\ *vb* **1** : to move or cause to move vigorously **2** : to throw down with violence **3** : FLING; *also* : PITCH — **hurl** *n* — **hurl·er** *n*

hur·ly–bur·ly \ıhər-lē-'bər-lē\ *n* : UPROAR, TUMULT

Hu·ron \'hyur-ən, 'hyur-ıän\ *n, pl* **Hurons** *or* **Huron** : a member of a confederacy of American Indian peoples formerly living between Georgian Bay and Lake Ontario

hur·rah \hu-'rò, -'rä\ *also* **hur·ray** \hu-'rä\ *interj* — used to express joy, approval, or encouragement

hur·ri·cane \'hər-ə-ıkān\ *n* [Sp *huracán*, of AmerInd origin] : a tropical cyclone with winds of 74 miles (118 kilometers) per hour or greater that is usu. accompanied by rain, thunder, and lightning

¹**hur·ry** \'hər-ē\ *vb* **hur·ried; hur·ry·ing 1** : to carry or cause to go with haste **2** : to impel to a greater speed **3** : to move or act with haste — **hur·ried·ly** *adv* — **hur·ried·ness** *n*

²**hurry** *n* : extreme haste or eagerness

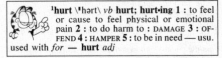

¹**hurt** \'hərt\ *vb* **hurt; hurt·ing 1** : to feel or cause to feel physical or emotional pain **2** : to do harm to : DAMAGE **3** : OFFEND **4** : HAMPER **5** : to be in need — usu. used with *for* — **hurt** *adj*

²**hurt** *n* **1** : a bodily injury or wound **2** : SUFFERING **3** : HARM, WRONG — **hurt·ful** *adj* — **hurt·ful·ness** *n*

hur·tle \'hərt-ə l\ *vb* **hur·tled; hur·tling 1** : to move rapidly or forcefully **2** : HURL, FLING

¹**hus·band** \'həz-bənd\ *n* [ME *husbonde*, fr. OE *hūsbonda* master of a house, fr. ON *hūsbōndi*, fr. *hūs* house + *bōndi* householder] : a male partner in a marriage

²**husband** *vb* : to manage prudently

hus·band·man \'həz-bənd-mən\ *n* : FARMER

hus·band·ry \'həz-bən-drē\ *n* **1** : the control or judicious use of resources **2** : AGRICULTURE

¹**hush** \'həsh\ *vb* **1** : to make or become quiet or calm **2** : SUPPRESS

²**hush** *n* : SILENCE, QUIET

hush–hush \'həsh-ıhəsh\ *adj* : SECRET, CONFIDENTIAL

¹**husk** \'həsk\ *n* **1** : a usu. thin dry outer covering of a seed or fruit **2** : an outer layer : SHELL

²**husk** *vb* : to strip the husk from — **husk·er** *n*

¹**husky** \'həs-kē\ *adj* **hus·ki·er; -est** : HOARSE — **hus·ki·ly** \-kə-lē\ *adv* — **hus·ki·ness** \-kē-nəs\ *n*

²**husky** *adj* **1** : BURLY, ROBUST **2** : LARGE

³**husky** *n, pl* **huskies** : a heavy-coated working dog of the New World arctic

hus·sar \(ı)hə-'zär\ *n* [Hung *huszár*] : a member of any of various European cavalry units

hus·sy \\ˈhə-zē, -sē\ *n, pl* **hussies** [alter. of *housewife*]
1 : a lewd or brazen woman **2** : a pert or mischievous
girl
hus·tings \\ˈhəs-tiŋz\ *n pl* : a place where political campaign speeches are made; *also* : the proceedings in an
election campaign
hus·tle \\ˈhə-səl\ *vb* **hus·tled; hus·tling 1** : JOSTLE,
SHOVE **2** : HASTEN, HURRY **3** : to work energetically
— **hustle** *n* — **hus·tler** \\ˈhəs-lər\ *n*
hut \\ˈhət\ *n* : a small and often temporary dwelling
: SHACK
hutch \\ˈhəch\ *n* **1** : a chest or compartment for storage
2 : a cupboard usu. surmounted with open shelves **3**
: a pen or coop for an animal **4** : HUT
huz·zah *or* **huz·za** \(ˌ)hə-ˈzä\ *n* : a shout of acclaim —
often used interjectionally to express joy or approba-
tion
HV *abbr* **1** high velocity **2** high voltage
HVAC *abbr* heating, ventilating and air-conditioning
hvy *abbr* heavy
HW *abbr* hot water
hwy *abbr* highway
hy·a·cinth \\ˈhī-ə-(ˌ)sinth\ *n* : a bulbous Mediterranean
herb related to the lilies that is widely grown for its
spikes of fragrant bell-shaped flowers
hy·ae·na *var of* HYENA
hy·brid \\ˈhī-brəd\ *n* **1** : an offspring of genetically differing parents (as members of different breeds or
species) **2** : one of mixed origin or composition —
hybrid *adj* — **hy·brid·i·za·tion** \ˌhī-brə-də-ˈzā-shən\
n — **hy·brid·ize** \\ˈhī-brə-ˌdīz\ *vb* — **hy·brid·iz·er** *n*
hy·dra \\ˈhī-drə\ *n* : any of numerous small tubular
freshwater coelenterates that are polyps having at
one end a mouth surrounded by tentacles
hy·dran·gea \hī-ˈdrän-jə\ *n* : any of a genus of shrubs
related to the currants and grown for their showy
clusters of white or tinted flowers

hy·drant \\ˈhī-drənt\ *n* : a pipe with a valve
and spout at which water may be drawn
from a main pipe

hy·drate \\ˈhī-ˌdrāt\ *n* : a compound formed by union of
water with some other substance — **hydrate** *vb*
hy·drau·lic \hī-ˈdrò-lik\ *adj* **1** : operated, moved, or effected by means of water **2** : of or relating to hydrau-
lics **3** : operated by the resistance offered or the
pressure transmitted when a quantity of liquid is
forced through a small orifice or through a tube **4**
: hardening or setting under water
hy·drau·lics \-liks\ *n* : a science that deals with practical applications of liquid (as water) in motion
hydro \\ˈhī-drō\ *n* : HYDROPOWER
hy·dro·car·bon \\ˈhī-drō-ˌkär-bən\ *n* : an organic compound containing only carbon and hydrogen
hy·dro·ceph·a·lus \ˌhī-drō-ˈse-fə-ləs\ *n* : abnormal increase in the amount of fluid in the cranial cavity ac-

companied by enlargement of the skull and atrophy
of the brain
hy·dro·chlo·ric acid \ˌhī-drə-ˈklōr-ik-\ *n* : a sharp-
smelling corrosive acid used in the laboratory and in
industry and present in dilute form in gastric juice
hy·dro·dy·nam·ics \ˌhī-drō-dī-ˈna-miks\ *n* : a science
that deals with the motion of fluids and the forces acting on moving bodies immersed in fluids — **hy·dro·**
dy·nam·ic *adj*
hy·dro·elec·tric \ˌhī-drō-i-ˈlek-trik\ *adj* : of or relating
to production of electricity by waterpower — **hy·**
dro·elec·tric·i·ty \-ˌlek-ˈtri-sə-tē\ *n*
hy·dro·foil \\ˈhī-drə-ˌfòil\ *n* : a boat that has fins attached to the bottom by struts for lifting the hull clear
of the water to allow faster speeds
hy·dro·gen \\ˈhī-drə-jən\ *n* [F *hydrogène,* fr. Gk *hydōr*
water + *-genēs* born; fr. the fact that water is generated by its combustion] : a gaseous colorless odorless highly flammable chemical element that is the
lightest of the elements — **hy·drog·e·nous** \hī-ˈdrä-
jə-nəs\ *adj* — see ELEMENT table
hy·dro·ge·nate \hī-ˈdrä-jə-ˌnāt, ˈhī-drə-\ *vb* **-nat·ed;**
-nat·ing : to combine or treat with hydrogen; *esp* : to
add hydrogen to the molecule of — **hy·dro·ge·na·**
tion \hī-ˌdrä-jə-ˈnā-shən, ˌhī-drə-\ *n*
hydrogen bomb *n* : a bomb whose violent explosive
power is due to the sudden release of atomic energy
resulting from the fusion of light nuclei (as of hydrogen atoms)
hydrogen peroxide *n* : an unstable compound of hydrogen and oxygen used esp. as an oxidizing and
bleaching agent, an antiseptic, and a propellant
hy·dro·graph·ic \ˌhī-drə-ˈgra-fik\ *adj* : of or relating to
the description and study of bodies of water — **hy·**
drog·ra·pher *n* — **hy·drog·ra·phy** \hī-ˈdrä-grə-fē\ *n*
hy·drol·o·gy \hī-ˈdrä-lə-jē\ *n* : a science dealing with
the properties, distribution, and circulation of water
— **hy·dro·log·ic** \ˌhī-drə-ˈlä-jik\ *or* **hy·dro·log·i·cal**
\-ji-kəl\ *adj* — **hy·drol·o·gist** \hī-ˈdrä-lə-jist\ *n*
hy·dro·ly·sis \hī-ˈdrä-lə-səs\ *n* : a chemical decomposition involving the addition of the elements of water
hy·drom·e·ter \hī-ˈdrä-mə-tər\ *n* : a floating instrument for determining specific gravities of liquids and
hence the strength (as of alcoholic liquors)
hy·dro·pho·bia \ˌhī-drə-ˈfō-bē-ə\ *n* [LL, fr. Gk, fr. *hy-*
dōr water + *phobos* fear] : RABIES
hy·dro·phone \\ˈhī-drə-ˌfōn\ *n* : an underwater listening
device
¹hy·dro·plane \\ˈhī-drə-ˌplān\ *n* **1** : a powerboat designed for racing that skims the surface of the water
2 : SEAPLANE
²hydroplane *vb* : to skid on a wet road due to loss of
contact between the tires and road
hy·dro·pon·ics \ˌhī-drə-ˈpä-niks\ *n* : the growing of
plants in nutrient solutions — **hy·dro·pon·ic** *adj*
hy·dro·pow·er \\ˈhī-drə-ˌpaú-ər\ *n* : hydroelectric power
hy·dro·sphere \\ˈhī-drə-ˌsfir\ *n* : the water (as vapor or
lakes) of the earth
hy·dro·stat·ic \ˌhī-drə-ˈsta-tik\ *adj* : of or relating to

fluids at rest or to the pressures they exert or transmit
hy·dro·ther·a·py \ˌhī-drə-ˈther-ə-pē\ n : the use of water esp. externally in the treatment of disease or disability
hy·dro·ther·mal \ˌhī-drə-ˈthər-məl\ adj : of or relating to hot water
hy·drous \ˈhī-drəs\ adj : containing water
hy·drox·ide \hī-ˈdräk-ˌsīd\ n 1 : a negatively charged ion consisting of one atom of oxygen and one atom of hydrogen 2 : a compound of hydroxide with an element or group
hy·e·na \hī-ˈē-nə\ n [L hyaena, fr. Gk hyaina, fr. hys hog] : any of several large nocturnal carnivorous mammals of Asia and Africa
hy·giene \ˈhī-ˌjēn\ n 1 : a science concerned with establishing and maintaining good health 2 : conditions or practices conducive to health — hy·gien·ic \hī-ˈjenik, -ˈjē-\ adj — hy·gien·i·cal·ly \-ni-k(ə-)lē\ adv — hy·gien·ist \hī-ˈjē-nist, ˈhī-ˌjē-, hī-ˈje-\ n
hy·grom·e·ter \hī-ˈgrä-mə-tər\ n : any of several instruments for measuring the humidity of the atmosphere
hy·gro·scop·ic \ˌhī-grə-ˈskä-pik\ adj : readily taking up and retaining moisture
hying pres part of HIE
hy·men \ˈhī-mən\ n : a fold of mucous membrane partly closing the opening of the vagina
hy·me·ne·al \ˌhī-mə-ˈnē-əl\ adj : NUPTIAL
hymn \ˈhim\ n : a song of praise esp. to God — hymn vb
hym·nal \ˈhim-nəl\ n : a book of hymns
hyp abbr hypothesis; hypothetical
¹hype \ˈhīp\ vb hyped; hyp·ing 1 : STIMULATE — usu. used with up 2 : INCREASE — hyped–up adj
²hype vb hyped; hyp·ing 1 : DECEIVE 2 : PUBLICIZE
³hype n 1 : DECEPTION, PUT-ON 2 : PUBLICITY
hy·per \ˈhī-pər\ adj 1 : HIGH-STRUNG, EXCITABLE 2 : extremely active
hy·per·acid·i·ty \ˌhī-pər-ə-ˈsi-də-tē\ n : the condition of containing excessive acid esp. in the stomach — hy·per·acid \-ˈa-səd\ adj
hy·per·ac·tive \-ˈak-tiv\ adj : excessively or pathologically active — hy·per·ac·tiv·i·ty \-ˌak-ˈti-və-tē\ n
hy·per·bar·ic \ˌhī-pər-ˈbar-ik\ adj : of, relating to, or utilizing greater than normal pressure (as of oxygen)
hy·per·bo·la \hī-ˈpər-bə-lə\ n, pl -las or -lae \-(ˌ)lē\ : a curve formed by the intersection of a double right circular cone with a plane that cuts both halves of the cone — hy·per·bol·ic \ˌhī-pər-ˈbä-lik\ adj
hy·per·bo·le \hī-ˈpər-bə-(ˌ)lē\ n : extravagant exaggeration used as a figure of speech
hy·per·crit·i·cal \ˌhī-pər-ˈkri-ti-kəl\ adj : excessively critical — hy·per·crit·i·cal·ly \-k(ə-)lē\ adv
hy·per·opia \ˌhī-pə-ˈrō-pē-ə\ n : a condition in which visual images come to focus behind the retina resulting esp. in defective vision for near objects — hy·per·opic \-ˈrō-pik, -ˈrä-\ adj
hy·per·sen·si·tive \-ˈsen-sə-tiv\ adj 1 : excessively or abnormally sensitive 2 : abnormally susceptible physiologically to a specific agent (as a drug) — hy·per·sen·si·tive·ness n — hy·per·sen·si·tiv·i·ty \-ˌsen-sə-ˈti-və-tē\ n
hy·per·ten·sion \ˈhī-pər-ˌten-chən\ n : high blood pressure — hy·per·ten·sive \ˌhī-pər-ˈten-siv\ adj or n
hy·per·text \ˈhī-pər-ˌtekst\ n : a database format in which information related to that on display can be accessed directly from the display
hy·per·thy·roid·ism \ˌhī-pər-ˈthī-ˌrȯi-ˌdi-zəm\ n : excessive activity of the thyroid gland; also : the resulting bodily condition — hy·per·thy·roid \-ˈthī-ˌrȯid\ adj
hy·per·tro·phy \hī-ˈpər-trə-fē\ n, pl -phies : excessive development of a body part — hy·per·tro·phic \ˌhī-pər-ˈtrō-fik\ adj — hypertrophy vb
hy·per·ven·ti·late \ˌhī-pər-ˈven-tə-ˌlāt\ vb : to breathe rapidly and deeply esp. to the point of losing an ab-

normal amount of carbon dioxide from the blood — hy·per·ven·ti·la·tion \-ˌven-tə-ˈlā-shən\ n
hy·phen \ˈhī-fən\ n : a punctuation mark - used esp. to divide or to compound words or word parts — hyphen vb
hy·phen·ate \ˈhī-fə-ˌnāt\ vb -at·ed; -at·ing : to connect or divide with a hyphen — hy·phen·ation \ˌhī-fə-ˈnāshən\ n
hyp·no·sis \hip-ˈnō-səs\ n, pl -no·ses \-ˌsēz\ : an induced state that resembles sleep and in which the subject is responsive to suggestions of the inducer (hyp·no·tist \ˈhip-nə-tist\) — hyp·no·tism \ˈhip-nəˌti-zəm\ n — hyp·no·tiz·able \ˈhip-nə-ˌtī-zə-bəl\ adj — hyp·no·tize \-ˌtīz\ vb
¹hyp·not·ic \hip-ˈnä-tik\ adj 1 : inducing sleep : SOPORIFIC 2 : of or relating to hypnosis or hypnotism 3 : readily holding the attention — hyp·not·i·cal·ly \-ti-k(ə-)lē\ adv
²hypnotic n : a sleep-inducing drug
hy·po \ˈhī-pō\ n, pl hypos : SODIUM THIOSULFATE
hy·po·cen·ter \ˈhī-pə-ˌsen-tər\ n : the point of origin of an earthquake
hy·po·chon·dria \ˌhī-pə-ˈkän-drē-ə\ n [NL, fr. LL, pl., upper abdomen (formerly regarded as the seat of hypochondria), fr. Gk, lit., the parts under the cartilage (of the breastbone), fr. hypo- under + chondros cartilage] : depression of mind often centered on imaginary physical ailments — hy·po·chon·dri·ac \-drē-ˌak\ adj or n
hy·poc·ri·sy \hi-ˈpä-krə-sē\ n, pl -sies : a feigning to be what one is not or to believe what one does not; esp : the false assumption of an appearance of virtue or religion — hyp·o·crite \ˈhi-pə-ˌkrit\ n — hyp·o·crit·i·cal \ˌhi-pə-ˈkri-ti-kəl\ adj — hyp·o·crit·i·cal·ly \-k(ə-)lē\ adv
¹hy·po·der·mic \ˌhī-pə-ˈdər-mik\ adj : administered by or used in making an injection beneath the skin
²hypodermic n : HYPODERMIC SYRINGE; also : an injection made with this
hypodermic needle n : NEEDLE 3; also : HYPODERMIC SYRINGE
hypodermic syringe n : a small syringe with a hollow needle for injecting material into or through the skin
hy·po·gly·ce·mia \ˌhī-pō-glī-ˈsē-mē-ə\ n : abnormal decrease of sugar in the blood — hy·po·gly·ce·mic \-mik\ adj
hy·pot·e·nuse \hī-ˈpät-ᵊn-ˌüs, -ˌyüs, -ˌüz, -ˌyüz\ n : the side of a triangle having a right angle that is opposite the right angle; also : its length
hy·poth·e·sis \hī-ˈpä-thə-səs\ n, pl -e·ses \-ˌsēz\ : an assumption made esp. in order to test its logical or empirical consequences — hy·po·thet·i·cal \ˌhī-pə-ˈtheti-kəl\ adj — hy·po·thet·i·cal·ly \-k(ə-)lē\ adv
hy·poth·e·size \-ˌsīz\ vb -sized; -siz·ing : to adopt as a hypothesis
hy·po·thy·roid·ism \ˌhī-pō-ˈthī-ˌrȯi-ˌdi-zəm\ n : deficient activity of the thyroid gland; also : a resultant lowered metabolic rate and general loss of vigor — hy·po·thy·roid adj
hys·sop \ˈhi-səp\ n : a European mint sometimes used as a potherb
hys·ter·ec·to·my \ˌhis-tə-ˈrek-tə-mē\ n, pl -mies : surgical removal of the uterus
hys·te·ria \hi-ˈster-ē-ə, -ˈstir-\ n [NL, fr. E hysteric, adj., fr. L hystericus, fr. Gk hysterikos, fr. hystera womb; fr. the Greek notion that hysteria was peculiar to women and caused by disturbances in the uterus] 1 : a nervous disorder marked esp. by defective emotional control 2 : unmanageable fear or outburst of emotion — hys·ter·ic \-ˈster-ik\ n — hys·ter·i·cal \-ˈster-i-kəl\ also hysteric adj — hys·ter·i·cal·ly \-k(ə-)lē\ adv
hys·ter·ics \-ˈster-iks\ n pl : a fit of uncontrollable laughter or crying
Hz abbr hertz

I

¹i \'ī\ *n, pl* i's *or* is \'īz\ *often cap* : the 9th letter of the English alphabet

²i *abbr, often cap* island; isle

¹I \'ī, ə\ *pron* : the one speaking or writing

²I *abbr* interstate

³I *symbol* iodine

Ia *or* IA *abbr* Iowa

-ial *adj suffix* : ¹-AL ⟨manor*ial*⟩

iamb \'ī-ˌam\ *or* iam•bus \ī-'am-bəs\ *n, pl* iambs \'ī-ˌamz\ *or* iam•bus•es : a metrical foot of one unaccented syllable followed by one accented syllable — iam•bic \ī-'am-bik\ *adj or n*

-ian — see -AN

-i•at•ric \ē-'a-trik\ *also* -i•at•ri•cal \-tri-kəl\ *adj comb form* : of or relating to (such) medical treatment or healing ⟨pedi*atric*⟩

-i•at•rics \ē-'a-triks\ *n pl comb form* : medical treatment ⟨pedi*atrics*⟩

ib *or* ibid *abbr* ibidem

ibex \'ī-ˌbeks\ *n, pl* ibex *or* ibex•es [L] : any of several Old World wild goats with large curved horns

ibi•dem \'i-bə-ˌdem, i-'bī-dəm\ *adv* [L] : in the same place

-ibility — see -ABILITY

ibis \'ī-bəs\ *n, pl* ibis *or* ibis•es [L, fr. Gk, fr. Egypt *hb*] : any of various wading birds related to the herons but having a downwardly curved bill

-ible — see -ABLE

ibu•pro•fen \ˌī-byü-'prō-fən\ *n* : a nonsteroidal anti= inflammatory drug used to relieve pain and fever

IC \ˌī-'sē\ *n* : INTEGRATED CIRCUIT

¹-ic \ik\ *adj suffix* 1 : of, relating to, or having the form of : being ⟨panoram*ic*⟩ 2 : related to, derived from, or containing ⟨alcohol*ic*⟩ 3 : in the manner of : like that of : characteristic of 4 : associated or dealing with : utilizing ⟨electron*ic*⟩ 5 : characterized by : exhibiting ⟨nostalg*ic*⟩ : affected with ⟨allerg*ic*⟩ 6 : caused by 7 : tending to produce ⟨analges*ic*⟩

²-ic *n suffix* : one having the character or nature of : one belonging to or associated with : one exhibiting or affected by : one that produces

-i•cal \i-kəl\ *adj suffix* : -IC ⟨symmetr*ical*⟩ ⟨geolog*ical*⟩ — -i•cal•ly \i-kə-lē, -klē\ *adv suffix*

ICBM \ˌī-ˌsē-(ˌ)bē-'em\ *n, pl* ICBM's *or* ICBMs \-'emz\ : an intercontinental ballistic missile

ICC *abbr* Interstate Commerce Commission

¹ice \'īs\ *n* 1 : frozen water 2 : a substance resembling ice 3 : a state of coldness (as from formality or reserve) 4 : a flavored frozen dessert; *esp* : one containing nomilk or cream

²ice *vb* iced; ic•ing 1 : FREEZE 2 : CHILL 3 : to cover with or as if with icing

ice age *n* : a time of widespread glaciation

ice bag *n* : a waterproof bag to hold ice for local application of cold to the body

ice•berg \'īs-ˌbərg\ *n* : a large floating mass of ice broken off from a glacier

iceberg lettuce *n* : any of various crisp light green lettuces that form a compact head like a cabbage

ice•boat \'īs-ˌbōt\ *n* : a boatlike frame on runners propelled on ice by sails

ice•bound \-ˌbau̇nd\ *adj* : surrounded, obstructed, or covered by ice

ice•box \-ˌbäks\ *n* : REFRIGERATOR

ice•break•er \-ˌbrā-kər\ *n* : a ship equipped to make a channel through ice

ice cap *n* : a glacier forming on relatively level land and flowing outward from its center

ice cream *n* : a frozen food containing sweetened or flavored cream or butterfat

ice hockey *n* : a game in which two teams of ice= skating players try to shoot a puck into the opponent's goal

ice•house \'īs-ˌhau̇s\ *n* : a building in which ice is made or stored

Ice•land•er \-ˌlan-dər, -lən-\ *n* : a native or inhabitant of Iceland

¹Ice•lan•dic \īs-'lan-dik\ *adj* : of, relating to, or characteristic of Iceland, the Icelanders, or their language

²Icelandic *n* : the language of Iceland

ice•man \'īs-ˌman\ *n* : one who sells or delivers ice

ice milk *n* : a sweetened frozen food made of skim milk

ice pick *n* : a hand tool ending in a spike for chipping ice

ice storm *n* : a storm in which falling rain freezes on contact

ice water *n* : chilled or iced water esp. for drinking

ich•thy•ol•o•gy \ˌik-thē-'ä-lə-jē\ *n* : a branch of zoology dealing with fishes — ich•thy•ol•o•gist \-jist\ *n*

ici•cle \'ī-ˌsi-kəl\ *n* : a hanging mass of ice formed by the freezing of dripping water

ic•ing \'ī-siŋ\ *n* : a sweet usu. creamy mixture used to coat baked goods

ICJ *abbr* International Court of Justice

icky \'i-kē\ *adj* ick•i•er; -est : OFFENSIVE, DISTASTEFUL — ick•i•ness *n*

icon \'ī-ˌkän\ *n* 1 : IMAGE; *esp* : a religious image painted on a wood panel 2 : a small picture on a computer display that suggests the purpose of an available function

icon•o•clasm \ī-'kä-nə-ˌkla-zəm\ *n* : the doctrine, practice, or attitude of an iconoclast

icon•o•clast \-ˌklast\ *n* [ML *iconoclastes*, fr. MGk *eikonoklastēs*, lit., image destroyer, fr. Gk *eikōn* image + *klan* to break] 1 : one who destroys religious images or opposes their veneration 2 : one who attacks cherished beliefs or institutions

-ics \iks\ *n sing or pl suffix* 1 : study : knowledge : skill : practice ⟨linguist*ics*⟩ ⟨electron*ics*⟩ 2 : characteristic actions or activities ⟨acrobat*ics*⟩ 3 : characteristic qualities, operations, or phenomena ⟨mechan*ics*⟩

ic•tus \'ik-təs\ *n* : the recurring stress or beat in a rhythmic or metrical series of sounds

ICU *abbr* intensive care unit

icy \'ī-sē\ *adj* ic•i•er; -est 1 : covered with, abounding in, or consisting of ice 2 : intensely cold 3 : being cold and unfriendly — ic•i•ly \'ī-sə-lē\ *adv* — ic•i•ness \-sē-nəs\ *n*

¹id \'id\ *n* [L, it] : the part of the psyche in psychoanalytic theory that is completely unconscious and concerned with instinctual needs and drives

²id *abbr* idem

ID *abbr* 1 Idaho 2 identification

idea \ī-'dē-ə\ *n* 1 : a plan for action : DESIGN 2 : something imagined or pictured in the mind 3 : a central meaning or purpose syn concept, conception, notion, impression

¹ide•al \ī-'dēl\ *adj* 1 : existing only in the mind : IMAGINARY; *also* : lacking practicality 2 : of or relating to an ideal or to perfection : PERFECT

²ideal *n* 1 : a standard of excellence 2 : one regarded as a model worthy of imitation 3 : GOAL syn archetype, example, exemplar, paradigm, pattern

ide•al•ise Brit var of IDEALIZE

ide•al•ism \ī-'dē-ə-ˌli-zəm\ *n* : the practice of forming ideals or living under their influence; *also* : an idealized representation — ide•al•ist \-list\ *n* — ide•al•is•tic \ī-ˌdē-ə-'lis-tik\ *adj* — ide•al•is•ti•cal•ly \-ti-k(ə-)lē\ *adv*

ide•al•ize \ī-'dē-ə-ˌlīz\ *vb* -ized; -iz•ing : to think of or represent as ideal — ide•al•i•za•tion \-ˌdē-ə-lə-'zā-shən\ *n*

ide•al•ly \ī-'dē-lē, -'dē-ə-lē\ *adv* 1 : in idea or imagina-

tion : MENTALLY **2** : in agreement with an ideal : PER-
FECTLY

ide·a·tion \ˌī-dē-ˈā-shən\ *n* : the forming of ideas —
ide·ate \ˈī-dē-ˌāt\ *vb* — **ide·a·tion·al** \ˌī-dē-ˈā-shə-
nəl\ *adj*

idem \ˈī-ˌdem, ˈē-, ˈi-\ *pron* [L, same] : something previously mentioned

iden·ti·cal \ī-ˈden-ti-kəl\ *adj* **1** : being the same **2** : essentially alike **syn** equivalent, equal, tantamount

iden·ti·fi·ca·tion \ī-ˌden-tə-fə-ˈkā-shən\ *n* **1** : an act of
identifying : the state of being identified **2** : evidence
of identity **3** : an unconscious psychological process
by which an individual models thoughts, feelings, and
actions after another person or an object

iden·ti·fy \ī-ˈden-tə-ˌfī\ *vb* **-fied; -fy·ing 1** : to regard
as identical **2** : ASSOCIATE **3** : to establish the identity
of **4** : to practice psychological identification —
iden·ti·fi·able \-ˌden-tə-ˈfī-ə-bəl\ *adj* — **iden·ti·fi·
ably** \-blē\ *adv* — **iden·ti·fi·er** \-ˌfī-(-ə)r\ *n*

iden·ti·ty \ī-ˈden-tə-tē\ *n, pl* **-ties 1** : sameness of essential character **2** : INDIVIDUALITY **3** : the fact of being the same person or thing as claimed

identity crisis *n* : psychological conflict esp. in adolescence involving confusion about one's social role and
one's personality

ideo·gram \ˈī-dē-ə-ˌgram, ˈi-\ *n* **1** : a picture or symbol
used in a system of writing to represent a thing or an
idea **2** : a character or symbol used in a system of
writing to represent an entire word

ide·ol·o·gy \ˌī-dē-ˈä-lə-jē, ˌi-\ *also* **ide·al·o·gy** \-ˈä-lə-jē,
-ˈa-\ *n, pl* **-gies 1** : the body of ideas characteristic of
a particular individual, group, or culture **2** : the as-
sertions, theories, and aims that constitute a political,
social, and economic program — **ide·o·log·i·cal** \ˌī-
dē-ə-ˈlä-ji-kəl, ˌi-\ *adj* — **ide·ol·o·gist** \-dē-ˈä-lə-jist\ *n*

ides \ˈīdz\ *n sing or pl* : the 15th day of March, May,
July, or October or the 13th day of any other month
in the ancient Roman calendar

id·i·o·cy \ˈi-dē-ə-sē\ *n, pl* **-cies 1** : extreme mental retardation **2** : something notably stupid or foolish

id·i·om \ˈi-dē-əm\ *n* **1** : the language peculiar to a person or group **2** : the characteristic form or structure
of a language **3** : an expression that cannot be understood from the meanings of its separate words (as
give way) — **id·i·o·mat·ic** \ˌi-dē-ə-ˈma-tik\ *adj* — **id·
i·o·mat·i·cal·ly** \-ti-k(ə-)lē\ *adv*

id·i·o·path·ic \ˌi-dē-ə-ˈpa-thik\ *adj* : arising spontaneously or from an obscure or unknown cause (an ∼
disease)

id·i·o·syn·cra·sy \ˌi-dē-ə-ˈsiŋ-krə-sē\ *n, pl* **-sies** : personal peculiarity — **id·i·o·syn·crat·ic** \ˌi-dē-ō-sin-
ˈkra-tik\ *adj* — **id·i·o·syn·crat·i·cal·ly** \-ˈkra-ti-k(ə-)lē\
adv

id·i·ot \ˈi-dē-ət\ *n* [ME, fr. L *idiota* ignorant person, fr.
Gk *idiōtēs* one in a private station, ignorant person,
fr. *idios* one's own, private] **1** : a mentally retarded
person requiring complete custodial care **2** : a foolish
or stupid person — **id·i·ot·ic** \ˌi-dē-ˈä-tik\ *adj* — **id·
i·ot·i·cal·ly** \-ti-k(ə-)lē\ *adv*

¹**idle** \ˈīd-ᵊl\ *adj* **idler** \ˈī-də-lər\; **idlest** \ˈī-də-ləst\ **1**
: GROUNDLESS, WORTHLESS, USELESS (∼ talk) **2** : not
occupied or employed : INACTIVE **3** : LAZY — **idle·
ness** *n* — **idly** \ˈīd-lē\ *adv*

²**idle** *vb* **idled; idling 1** : to spend time doing nothing **2**
: to make idle **3** : to run without being connected so
that power is not used for useful work — **idler** *n*

idol \ˈīd-ᵊl\ *n* **1** : an image worshiped as a god; *also* : a
false god **2** : an object of passionate devotion

idol·a·ter *or* **idol·a·tor** \ī-ˈdä-lə-tər\ *n* : a worshiper of
idols

idol·a·try \-trē\ *n, pl* **-tries 1** : the worship of a physical
object as a god **2** : excessive devotion — **idol·a·trous**
\-trəs\ *adj*

idol·ize \ˈīd-ᵊl-ˌīz\ *vb* **-ized; -iz·ing** : to make an idol of
— **idol·i·za·tion** \ˌīd-ᵊl-ə-ˈzā-shən\ *n*

idyll \ˈīd-ᵊl\ *n* **1** : a simple work of writing or poetry

that describes country life or suggests a peaceful setting **2** : a fit subject for an idyll — **idyl·lic** \ī-ˈdi-lik\
adj

i.e. \ˈī-ˈē\ *abbr* [L *id est*] that is

IE *abbr* industrial engineer

-ier — see -ER

if \ˈif \ *conj* **1** : in the event that (∼ he stays, I leave)
2 : WHETHER (ask ∼ he left) **3** — used as a function
word to introduce an exclamation expressing a wish
(∼ it would only rain) **4** : even though (an interesting
∼ untenable argument)

IF *abbr* intermediate frequency

if·fy \ˈi-fē\ *adj* : full of contingencies or unknown conditions

-i·fy \ə-ˌfī\ *vb suffix* : -FY

IG *abbr* inspector general

ig·loo \ˈi-glü\ *n, pl* **igloos** [Inuit (an Eskimo language)
iglu house] : an Eskimo house or hut often made of
snow blocks and in the shape of a dome

ig·ne·ous \ˈig-nē-əs\ *adj* **1** : FIERY **2** : formed by solidification of molten rock

ig·nite \ig-ˈnīt\ *vb* **ig·nit·ed; ig·nit·ing** : to set afire or
catch fire — **ig·nit·able** \-ˈnī-tə-bəl\ *adj*

ig·ni·tion \ig-ˈni-shən\ *n* **1** : a setting on fire **2** : the process or means (as an electric spark) of igniting the
fuel mixture in an engine

ig·no·ble \ig-ˈnō-bəl\ *adj* **1** : of common birth **2** : not
honorable : BASE, MEAN **syn** despicable, scurvy, sordid, vile, wretched — **ig·no·bly** *adv*

ig·no·min·i·ous \ˌig-nə-ˈmi-nē-əs\ *adj* **1** : DISHONOR-
ABLE **2** : DESPICABLE **3** : HUMILIATING, DEGRADING
syn disreputable, discreditable, disgraceful, inglor-
ious — **ig·no·min·i·ous·ly** *adv* — **ig·no·mi·ny** \ˈig-nə-
ˌmi-nē, ig-ˈnä-mə-nē\ *n*

ig·no·ra·mus \ˌig-nə-ˈrā-məs\ *n* [*Ignoramus*, ignorant
lawyer in *Ignoramus* (1615), play by George Ruggle]
: an utterly ignorant person

ig·no·rance \ˈig-nə-rəns\ *n* : the state of being ignorant

ig·no·rant \ˈig-nə-rənt\ *adj* **1** : lacking knowledge **2**
: resulting from or showing lack of knowledge or intelligence **3** : UNAWARE, UNINFORMED **syn** benighted,
illiterate, uneducated, unlettered, untutored — **ig·
no·rant·ly** *adv*

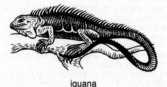

ig·nore \ig-ˈnōr\ *vb* **ig·nored; ig·nor·ing**
: to refuse to take notice of **syn** overlook,
slight, neglect

---

igua·na \i-ˈgwä-nə\ *n* : any of various large tropical
American lizards

iguana

ihp *abbr* indicated horsepower

IHS \ˌī-ˌäch-ˈes\ [LL, part transliteration of Gk IHΣ,
abbreviation for IHΣΟΥΣ *Iēsous* Jesus] — used as a
Christian symbol and monogram for *Jesus*

ikon *var of* ICON

IL *abbr* Illinois

il·e·itis \ˌi-lē-ˈī-təs\ *n* : inflammation of the ileum

il·e·um \ˈi-lē-əm\ *n, pl* **il·ea** \-lē-ə\ : the part of the small
intestine between the jejunum and the large intestine

il·i·ac \ˈi-lē-ˌak\ *adj* : of, relating to, or located near the
ilium

il·i·um \ˈi-lē-əm\ *n* : the uppermost and largest of the
three bones making up either side of the pelvis

ilk \'ilk\ *n* : SORT, KIND

¹ill \'il\ *adj* **worse** \'wərs\; **worst** \'wərst\ **1** : attended or caused by an evil intent ⟨∼ deeds⟩ **2** : not normal or sound ⟨∼ health⟩; *also* : not in good health : SICK **3** : BAD, UNLUCKY ⟨∼ omen⟩ **4** : not right or proper ⟨∼ manners⟩ **5** : UNFRIENDLY, HOSTILE ⟨∼ feeling⟩

²ill *adv* **worse; worst 1** : with displeasure **2** : in a harsh manner **3** : HARDLY, SCARCELY ⟨can ∼ afford it⟩ **4** : BADLY, UNLUCKILY **5** : in a faulty way

³ill *n* **1** : EVIL **2** : MISFORTUNE, DISTRESS **3** : AILMENT, SICKNESS; *also* : TROUBLE

⁴ill *abbr* illustrated; illustration; illustrator

Ill *abbr* Illinois

ill–ad·vised \ˌil-əd-'vīzd\ *adj* : not well counseled ⟨∼ efforts⟩ — **ill–ad·vis·ed·ly** \-'vī-zəd-lē\ *adv*

ill–bred \-'bred\ *adj* : badly brought up : IMPOLITE

il·le·gal \il-'lē-gəl\ *adj* : not lawful; *also* : not sanctioned by official rules **syn** unlawful, criminal, illegitimate, illicit, wrongful — **il·le·gal·i·ty** \ˌil-i-'ga-lə-tē\ *n* — **il·le·gal·ly** *adv*

il·leg·i·ble \il-'le-jə-bəl\ *adj* : not legible — **il·leg·i·bil·i·ty** \il-ˌle-jə-'bi-lə-tē\ *n* — **il·leg·i·bly** \il-'le-jə-blē\ *adv*

il·le·git·i·mate \ˌil-i-'ji-tə-mət\ *adj* **1** : born of unmarried parents **2** : ILLOGICAL **3** : ILLEGAL — **il·le·git·i·ma·cy** \-'ji-tə-mə-sē\ *n* — **il·le·git·i·mate·ly** *adv*

ill–fat·ed \'il-'fā-təd\ *adj* : UNFORTUNATE

ill–fa·vored \-'fā-vərd\ *adj* : UGLY, UNATTRACTIVE

ill–got·ten \-'gät-ᵊn\ *adj* : acquired by improper means ⟨∼ gains⟩

ill–hu·mored \-'hyü-mərd, -'yü-\ *adj* : SURLY, IRRITABLE

il·lib·er·al \il-'li-bə-rəl\ *adj* : not liberal : NARROW, BIGOTED

il·lic·it \il-'li-sət\ *adj* : not permitted : UNLAWFUL — **il·lic·it·ly** *adv*

il·lim·it·able \il-'li-mə-tə-bəl\ *adj* : BOUNDLESS, MEASURELESS — **il·lim·it·ably** \-blē\ *adv*

Il·li·nois \ˌi-lə-'nói *also* -'nóiz\ *n, pl* **Illinois** : a member of an American Indian people of Illinois, Iowa, and Wisconsin

il·lit·er·ate \il-'li-tə-rət\ *adj* **1** : having little or no education; *esp* : unable to read or write **2** : showing a lack of familiarity with the fundamentals of a particular field of knowledge — **il·lit·er·a·cy** \-'li-tə-rə-sē\ *n* — **illiterate** *n*

ill–man·nered \'il-'ma-nərd\ *adj* : marked by bad manners : RUDE

ill–na·tured \-'nā-chərd\ *adj* : CROSS, SURLY — **ill–na·tured·ly** *adv*

ill·ness \'il-nəs\ *n* : SICKNESS

il·log·i·cal \il-'lä-ji-kəl\ *adj* : lacking sound reasoning; *also* : SENSELESS — **il·log·i·cal·ly** \-ji-k(ə-)lē\ *adv*

ill–starred \'il-'stärd\ *adj* : UNLUCKY **1**

ill–tem·pered \-'tem-pərd\ *adj* : CROSS

ill–treat \-'trēt\ *vb* : to treat cruelly or improperly : MALTREAT — **ill–treat·ment** *n*

il·lu·mi·nate \il-'lü-mə-ˌnāt\ *vb* **-nat·ed; -nat·ing 1** : to supply or brighten with light : light up **2** : to make clear : ELUCIDATE **3** : to decorate (as a manuscript) with designs or pictures in gold or colors — **il·lu·mi·nat·ing·ly** *adv* — **il·lu·mi·na·tion** \-ˌlü-mə-'nā-shən\ *n* — **il·lu·mi·na·tor** \-'lü-mə-ˌnā-tər\ *n*

il·lu·mine \i-'lü-mən\ *vb* **-mined; -min·ing** : ILLUMINATE

ill–us·age \'il-'yü-sij\ *n* : harsh, unkind, or abusive treatment

ill–use \-'yüz\ *vb* : MALTREAT, ABUSE

il·lu·sion \i-'lü-zhən\ *n* [ME, fr. MF, fr. LL *illusio*, fr. L, action of mocking, fr. *illudere* to mock at, fr. *ludere* to play, mock] **1** : a mistaken idea : MISCONCEPTION **2** : a misleading visual image; *also* : HALLUCINATION

il·lu·sion·ist \i-'lü-zhə-nist\ *n* : one that produces illusions; *esp* : a sleight-of-hand performer

il·lu·sive \i-'lü-siv\ *adj* : DECEPTIVE

il·lu·so·ry \i-'lü-sə-rē, -zə-\ *adj* : DECEPTIVE

illust *or* **illus** *abbr* illustrated; illustration

il·lus·trate \'i-ləs-ˌtrāt\ *vb* **-trat·ed; -trat·ing** [L *illustrare*, fr. *lustrare* to purify, make bright] **1** : to explain by use of examples : CLARIFY; *also* : DEMONSTRATE **2** : to provide with pictures or figures that explain or decorate **3** : to serve to explain or decorate — **il·lus·tra·tor** \'i-lə-ˌstrā-tər\ *n*

il·lus·tra·tion \ˌi-lə-'strā-shən\ *n* **1** : the act of illustrating : the condition of being illustrated **2** : an example or instance that helps make something clear **3** : a picture or diagram that explains or decorates

il·lus·tra·tive \i-'ləs-trə-tiv, 'i-lə-ˌstrā-\ *adj* : serving, tending, or designed to illustrate — **il·lus·tra·tive·ly** *adv*

il·lus·tri·ous \i-'ləs-trē-əs\ *adj* : notably outstanding because of rank or achievement **syn** distinguished, eminent, famous, great, notable, prominent — **il·lus·tri·ous·ness** *n*

ill will *n* : unfriendly feeling

ILS *abbr* instrument landing system

¹im·age \'i-mij\ *n* **1** : a likeness or imitation of a person or thing; *esp* : STATUE **2** : a picture of an object formed by a device (as a mirror or lens) **3** : a person strikingly like another person ⟨he is the ∼ of his father⟩ **4** : a mental picture or conception : IMPRESSION, IDEA, CONCEPT **5** : a vivid representation or description

²image *vb* **im·aged; im·ag·ing 1** : to call up a mental picture of **2** : to describe or portray in words **3** : to create a representation of **4** : REFLECT, MIRROR **5** : to make appear : PROJECT

im·ag·ery \'i-mij-rē\ *n* **1** : IMAGES; *also* : the art of making images **2** : figurative language **3** : mental images; *esp* : the products of imagination

imag·in·able \i-'ma-jə-nə-bəl\ *adj* : capable of being imagined : CONCEIVABLE — **imag·in·ably** *adv*

imag·i·nary \i-'ma-jə-ˌner-ē\ *adj* **1** : existing only in the imagination **2** : containing or relating to a quantity (**imaginary unit**) that is the positive square root of minus 1 ($\sqrt{-1}$)

imaginary number *n* : a complex number (as $2 + 3i$) with a nonzero term (**imaginary part**) containing the imaginary unit as a factor

imag·i·na·tion \i-ˌma-jə-ˈnā-shən\ n 1 : the act or power of forming a mental image of something not present to the senses or not previously known or experienced 2 : creative ability 3 : RESOURCEFULNESS 4 : a mental image : a creation of the mind — **imag·i·na·tive** \i-ˈma-jə-nə-tiv, -ˌnā-\ adj — **imag·i·na·tive·ly** adv

imag·ine \i-ˈma-jən\ vb **imag·ined; imag·in·ing** 1 : to form a mental picture of something not present 2 : THINK, GUESS ⟨I ∼ it will rain⟩

im·ag·ism \ˈi-mi-ˌji-zəm\ n, often cap : a movement in poetry advocating free verse and the expression of ideas and emotions through clear precise images — **im·ag·ist** \-jist\ n

ima·go \i-ˈmā-gō, -ˈmä-\ n, pl **imagoes** or **ima·gi·nes** \-ˈmā-gə-ˌnēz, -ˈmä-\ [NL, fr. L, image] : an insect in its final adult stage — **ima·gi·nal** \i-ˈmä-gən-ᵊl, -ˈmä-\ adj

im·bal·ance \ˈim-ˈba-ləns\ n : lack of balance : the state of being out of equilibrium or out of proportion

im·be·cile \ˈim-bə-səl, -ˌsil\ n 1 : a mentally retarded person who needs help in routine personal care 2 : FOOL, IDIOT — **imbecile** or **im·be·cil·ic** \ˌim-bə-ˈsi-lik\ adj — **im·be·cil·i·ty** \ˌim-bə-ˈsi-lə-tē\ n

imbed var of EMBED

im·bibe \im-ˈbīb\ vb **im·bibed; im·bib·ing** 1 : to receive and retain in the mind 2 : DRINK 3 : to take in or up : ABSORB — **im·bib·er** n

im·bri·ca·tion \ˌim-brə-ˈkā-shən\ n 1 : an overlapping of edges (as of tiles) 2 : a pattern showing imbrication — **im·bri·cate** \ˈim-bri-kət\ adj

im·bro·glio \im-ˈbrōl-yō\ n, pl **-glios** [It, fr. imbrogliare to entangle] 1 : a confused mass 2 : a complicated situation; also : a serious or embarrassing misunderstanding

im·brue \im-ˈbrü\ vb **im·brued; im·bru·ing** : STAIN ⟨hands imbrued with blood⟩

im·bue \-ˈbyü\ vb **im·bued; im·bu·ing** 1 : to permeate or influence as if by dyeing 2 : to tinge or dye deeply

IMF abbr International Monetary Fund

imit abbr imitative

im·i·ta·ble \ˈi-mə-tə-bəl\ adj : capable or worthy of being imitated or copied

im·i·tate \ˈi-mə-ˌtāt\ vb **-tat·ed; -tat·ing** 1 : to follow as a model : COPY 2 : RESEMBLE 3 : REPRODUCE 4 : MIMIC, COUNTERFEIT — **im·i·ta·tor** \-ˌtā-tər\ n

im·i·ta·tion \ˌi-mə-ˈtā-shən\ n 1 : an act of imitating 2 : COPY, COUNTERFEIT 3 : a literary work that reproduces the style of another author — **imitation** adj

im·i·ta·tive \ˈi-mə-ˌtā-tiv\ adj 1 : marked by imitation 2 : inclined to imitate 3 : COUNTERFEIT

im·mac·u·late \i-ˈma-kyə-lət\ adj 1 : being without stain or blemish : PURE 2 : spotlessly clean ⟨∼ linen⟩ — **im·mac·u·late·ly** adv

im·ma·nent \ˈi-mə-nənt\ adj : having existence only in the mind — **im·ma·nence** \-nəns\ n — **im·ma·nen·cy** \-nən-sē\ n

im·ma·te·ri·al \ˌi-mə-ˈtir-ē-əl\ adj 1 : not consisting of matter : SPIRITUAL 2 : UNIMPORTANT, TRIFLING **syn** bodiless, disembodied, incorporeal, insubstantial, nonphysical — **im·ma·te·ri·al·i·ty** \-ˌtir-ē-ˈa-lə-tē\ n

im·ma·ture \ˌi-mə-ˈtùr, -ˈtyùr\ adj : lacking complete development : not yet mature — **im·ma·tu·ri·ty** \-ˈtùr-ə-tē, -ˈtyùr-\ n

im·mea·sur·able \(ˌ)i-ˈme-zhə-rə-bəl\ adj : not capable of being measured : indefinitely extensive : ILLIMITABLE — **im·mea·sur·ably** \-blē\ adv

im·me·di·a·cy \i-ˈmē-dē-ə-sē\ n, pl **-cies** 1 : the quality or state of being immediate 2 : something that is of immediate importance

im·me·di·ate \i-ˈmē-dē-ət\ adj 1 : acting directly and alone : DIRECT ⟨the ∼ cause of death⟩ 2 : being next in line or relation ⟨members of the ∼ family⟩ 3 : not distant : CLOSE 4 : made or done at once ⟨an ∼ response⟩ 5 : near to or related to the present time ⟨the ∼ future⟩ — **im·me·di·ate·ly** adv

im·me·mo·ri·al \ˌi-mə-ˈmòr-ē-əl\ adj : extending beyond the reach of memory, record, or tradition

im·mense \i-ˈmens\ adj [MF, fr. L immensus immeasurable, fr. mensus, pp. of metiri to measure] 1 : very great in size or degree : VAST, HUGE 2 : EXCELLENT — **im·mense·ly** adv — **im·men·si·ty** \-ˈmen-sə-tē\ n

im·merse \i-ˈmərs\ vb **im·mersed; im·mers·ing** 1 : to plunge or dip esp. into a fluid 2 : ENGROSS, ABSORB 3 : to baptize by immersing — **im·mer·sion** \-ˈmər-zhən\ n

im·mi·grant \ˈi-mi-grənt\ n 1 : a person who immigrates 2 : a plant or animal that becomes established where it did not previously occur

im·mi·grate \ˈi-mə-ˌgrāt\ vb **-grat·ed; -grat·ing** : to come into a foreign country and take up residence — **im·mi·gra·tion** \ˌi-mə-ˈgrā-shən\ n

im·mi·nent \ˈi-mə-nənt\ adj : ready to take place; esp : hanging threateningly over one's head — **im·mi·nence** \-nəns\ n — **im·mi·nent·ly** adv

im·mis·ci·ble \(ˌ)i-ˈmi-sə-bəl\ adj : incapable of mixing — **im·mis·ci·bil·i·ty** \-ˌmi-sə-ˈbi-lə-tē\ n

im·mo·bile \(ˌ)i-ˈmō-bəl\ adj : incapable of being moved : IMMOVABLE, FIXED — **im·mo·bil·i·ty** \ˌi-mō-ˈbi-lə-tē\ n

im·mo·bi·lize \i-ˈmō-bə-ˌlīz\ vb : to make immobile — **im·mo·bi·li·za·tion** \ˌi-ˌmō-bə-lə-ˈzā-shən\ n

im·mod·er·ate \(ˌ)i-ˈmä-də-rət\ adj : lacking in moderation : EXCESSIVE — **im·mod·er·a·cy** \-rə-sē\ n — **im·mod·er·ate·ly** adv

im·mod·est \(ˌ)i-ˈmä-dəst\ adj : not modest : BRAZEN, INDECENT ⟨an ∼ dress⟩ ⟨∼ conduct⟩ — **im·mod·est·ly** adv — **im·mod·es·ty** \-də-stē\ n

im·mo·late \ˈi-mə-ˌlāt\ vb **-lat·ed; -lat·ing** [L immolare, fr. mola grits; fr. the custom of sprinkling victims with sacrificial meal] : to offer in sacrifice; esp : to kill as a sacrificial victim — **im·mo·la·tion** \ˌi-mə-ˈlā-shən\ n

im·mor·al \(ˌ)i-ˈmòr-əl\ adj : not moral — **im·mor·al·ly** adv

im·mo·ral·i·ty \ˌi-mò-ˈra-lə-tē, ˌi-mə-\ n 1 : WICKEDNESS; esp : UNCHASTITY 2 : an immoral act or practice

¹im·mor·tal \(ˌ)i-ˈmòrt-ᵊl\ adj 1 : not mortal : exempt from death ⟨∼ gods⟩ 2 : destined to be remembered forever ⟨those ∼ words⟩ — **im·mor·tal·ly** adv

²immortal n 1 : one exempt from death 2 pl, often cap : the gods in Greek and Roman mythology 3 : a person whose fame is lasting ⟨an ∼ of baseball⟩

im·mor·tal·ise Brit var of IMMORTALIZE

im·mor·tal·i·ty \ˌi-mòr-ˈta-lə-tē\ n : the quality or state of being immortal; esp : unending existence

im·mor·tal·ize \i-ˈmòrt-ᵊl-ˌīz\ vb **-ized; -iz·ing** : to make immortal

im·mov·able \(ˌ)i-ˈmü-və-bəl\ adj 1 : firmly fixed, settled, or fastened : FAST, STATIONARY ⟨∼ mountains⟩ 2 : STEADFAST, UNYIELDING 3 : IMPASSIVE — **im·mov·abil·i·ty** \-ˌmü-və-ˈbi-lə-tē\ n — **im·mov·ably** \-blē\ adv

im·mune \i-ˈmyün\ adj 1 : EXEMPT 2 : having a special capacity for resistance (as to a disease) 3 : containing or producing antibodies — **im·mu·ni·ty** \-ˈmyü-nə-tē\ n

immune response n : a response of the body to an antigen resulting in the formation of antibodies and cells designed to react with the antigen and render it harmless

immune system n : the bodily system that protects the body from foreign substances, cells, and tissues by producing the immune response and that includes esp. the thymus, spleen, lymph nodes, and lymphocytes

im·mu·nize \ˈi-myə-ˌnīz\ vb **-nized; -niz·ing** : to make immune — **im·mu·ni·za·tion** \ˌi-myə-nə-ˈzā-shən\ n

im·mu·no·de·fi·cien·cy \ˌi-myə-nō-di-ˈfi-shən-sē\ n : inability to produce the normal number of antibodies or immunologically sensitized cells esp. in response to specific antigens — **im·mu·no·de·fi·cient** \-ˈfi-shənt\ *adj*

im·mu·no·glob·u·lin \ˌi-myə-nō-ˈglä-byə-lən\ *n* : ANTI-BODY

im·mu·nol·o·gy \ˌi-myə-ˈnä-lə-jē\ *n* : a science that deals with the immune system, immunity, and the immune response — **im·mu·no·log·ic** \-nə-ˈlä-jik\ *or* **im·mu·no·log·i·cal** \-ji-kəl\ *adj* — **im·mu·no·log·i·cal·ly** \-ji-k(ə-)lē\ *adv* — **im·mu·nol·o·gist** \-ˈnä-lə-jist\ *n*

im·mu·no·sup·pres·sion \ˌi-myə-nō-sə-ˈpre-shən\ *n* : suppression (as by drugs) of natural immune responses — **im·mu·no·sup·press** \-ˈpres\ *vb* — **im·mu·no·sup·pres·sive** \-ˈpre-siv\ *adj*

im·mu·no·ther·a·py \-ˈther-ə-pē\ *n* : treatment or prevention of disease by attempting to induce immunity

im·mure \i-ˈmyu̇r\ *vb* **im·mured; im·mur·ing 1** : to enclose within or as if within walls **2** : to build into a wall; *esp* : to entomb in a wall

im·mu·ta·ble \(ˌ)i-ˈmyü-tə-bəl\ *adj* : UNCHANGEABLE, UNCHANGING — **im·mu·ta·bil·i·ty** \-ˌmyü-tə-ˈbi-lə-tē\ *n* — **im·mu·ta·bly** \-ˈmyü-tə-blē\ *adv*

¹**imp** \ˈimp\ *n* **1** : a small demon : FIEND **2** : a mischievous child

²**imp** *abbr* **1** imperative **2** imperfect **3** imperial **4** import; imported

¹**im·pact** \im-ˈpakt\ *vb* **1** : to press together **2** : to have an impact on

²**im·pact** \ˈim-ˌpakt\ *n* **1** : a forceful contact, collision, or onset; *also* : the impetus communicated in or as if in a collision **2** : EFFECT

im·pact·ed \im-ˈpak-təd\ *adj* **1** : packed or wedged in **2** : wedged between the jawbone and another tooth

im·pair \im-ˈpar\ *vb* : to diminish in quantity, value, excellence, or strength : DAMAGE, LESSEN — **im·pair·ment** *n*

im·paired \-ˈpard\ *adj* : being in a less than perfect or whole condition; *esp* : handicapped or functionally defective — often used in combination ⟨hearing*impaired*⟩

im·pa·la \im-ˈpa-lə\ *n*, *pl* **impalas** *or* **impala** : a large brownish African antelope that in the male has slender curving horns

im·pale \im-ˈpāl\ *vb* **im·paled; im·pal·ing** : to pierce with or as if with something pointed — **im·pale·ment** *n*

im·pal·pa·ble \(ˌ)im-ˈpal-pə-bəl\ *adj* **1** : unable to be felt by touch : INTANGIBLE **2** : not easily seen or understood — **im·pal·pa·bly** \-blē\ *adv*

im·pan·el \im-ˈpan-ᵊl\ *vb* : to enter in or on a panel : ENROLL ⟨∼ a jury⟩

im·part \im-ˈpärt\ *vb* **1** : to give from one's store or abundance ⟨the sun ∼*s* warmth⟩ **2** : to make known

im·par·tial \(ˌ)im-ˈpär-shəl\ *adj* : not partial : UNBIASED, JUST — **im·par·tial·i·ty** \-ˌpär-shē-ˈa-lə-tē\ *n* — **im·par·tial·ly** *adv*

im·pass·able \(ˌ)im-ˈpa-sə-bəl\ *adj* : incapable of being passed, traversed, or crossed ⟨∼ roads⟩ — **im·pass·ably** \-blē\ *adv*

im·passe \ˈim-ˌpas\ *n* **1** : an impassable road or way **2** : a predicament from which there is no obvious escape

im·pas·si·ble \(ˌ)im-ˈpa-sə-bəl\ *adj* : incapable of feeling : IMPASSIVE

im·pas·sioned \im-ˈpa-shənd\ *adj* : filled with passion or zeal : showing great warmth or intensity of feeling **syn** passionate, ardent, fervent, fervid

im·pas·sive \(ˌ)im-ˈpa-siv\ *adj* : showing no signs of feeling, emotion, or interest : EXPRESSIONLESS, INDIFFERENT **syn** stoic, phlegmatic, apathetic, stolid — **im·pas·sive·ly** *adv* — **im·pas·siv·i·ty** \ˌim-ˌpa-ˈsi-və-tē\ *n*

im·pas·to \im-ˈpas-tō, -ˈpäs-\ *n* : the thick application of a pigment to a canvas or panel in painting; *also* : the body of pigment so applied

im·pa·tiens \im-ˈpā-shənz, -shəns\ *n* : any of a genus of

annual herbs with usu. spurred flowers and seed capsules that readily split open

im·pa·tient \(ˌ)im-ˈpā-shənt\ *adj* **1** : not patient : restless or short of temper esp. under irritation, delay, or opposition **2** : INTOLERANT ⟨∼ of poverty⟩ **3** : prompted or marked by impatience **4** : ANXIOUS — **im·pa·tience** \-shəns\ *n* — **im·pa·tient·ly** *adv*

im·peach \im-ˈpēch\ *vb* [ME *empechen* to accuse, fr. MF *empeechier* to hinder, fr. LL *impedicare* to fetter, fr. L *pedica* fetter, fr. *ped-*, *pes* foot] **1** : to charge (a public official) before an authorized tribunal with misconduct in office **2** : to challenge the credibility or validity of **3** : to remove from public office for misconduct — **im·peach·ment** *n*

im·pec·ca·ble \(ˌ)im-ˈpe-kə-bəl\ *adj* **1** : not capable of sinning or wrongdoing **2** : FAULTLESS, IRREPROACHABLE ⟨a man of ∼ character⟩ — **im·pec·ca·bil·i·ty** \-ˌpe-kə-ˈbi-lə-tē\ *n* — **im·pec·ca·bly** \-ˈpe-kə-blē\ *adv*

im·pe·cu·nious \ˌim-pi-ˈkyü-nyəs, -nē-əs\ *adj* : having little or no money — **im·pe·cu·nious·ness** *n*

im·ped·ance \im-ˈpēd-ᵊns\ *n* : the opposition in an electrical circuit to the flow of an alternating current

im·pede \im-ˈpēd\ *vb* **im·ped·ed; im·ped·ing** [L *impedire*, fr. *ped-*, *pes* foot] : to interfere with the progress of

im·ped·i·ment \im-ˈpe-də-mənt\ *n* **1** : something that impedes, hinders, or obstructs **2** : a speech defect

im·ped·i·men·ta \im-ˌpe-də-ˈmen-tə\ *n pl* : things that impede

im·pel \im-ˈpel\ *vb* **im·pelled; im·pel·ling** : to urge or drive forward or on : FORCE; *also* : PROPEL

im·pel·ler *also* **im·pel·lor** \im-ˈpe-lər\ *n* : a rotor esp. in a pump

im·pend \im-ˈpend\ *vb* **1** : to hover or hang over threateningly : MENACE **2** : to be about to occur

im·pen·e·tra·ble \(ˌ)im-ˈpe-nə-trə-bəl\ *adj* **1** : incapable of being penetrated or pierced ⟨an ∼ jungle⟩ **2** : incapable of being comprehended : INSCRUTABLE ⟨an ∼ mystery⟩ — **im·pen·e·tra·bil·i·ty** \-ˌpe-nə-trə-ˈbi-lə-tē\ *n* — **im·pen·e·tra·bly** \-ˈpe-nə-trə-blē\ *adv*

im·pen·i·tent \(ˌ)im-ˈpe-nə-tənt\ *adj* : not penitent : not repenting of sin — **im·pen·i·tence** \-təns\ *n*

im·per·a·tive \im-ˈper-ə-tiv\ *adj* **1** : expressing a command, request, or encouragement ⟨∼ sentence⟩ **2** : having power to restrain, control, or direct **3** : NECESSARY — **imperative** *n* — **im·per·a·tive·ly** *adv*

im·per·cep·ti·ble \ˌim-pər-ˈsep-tə-bəl\ *adj* : not perceptible; *esp* : too slight to be perceived ⟨∼ changes⟩ — **im·per·cep·ti·bly** \-blē\ *adv*

im·per·cep·tive \ˌim-pər-ˈsep-tiv\ *adj* : not perceptive

imperf *abbr* imperfect

¹**im·per·fect** \(ˌ)im-ˈpər-fikt\ *adj* **1** : not perfect : DEFECTIVE, INCOMPLETE **2** : of, relating to, or being a verb tense used to designate a continuing state or an incomplete action esp. in the past — **im·per·fect·ly** *adv*

²**imperfect** *n* : the imperfect tense; *also* : a verb form in it

im·per·fec·tion \ˌim-pər-ˈfek-shən\ *n* : the quality or state of being imperfect; *also* : FAULT, BLEMISH

im·pe·ri·al \im-ˈpir-ē-əl\ *adj* **1** : of, relating to, or befitting an empire or an emperor; *also* : of or relating to the United Kingdom or to the Commonwealth or British Empire **2** : ROYAL, SOVEREIGN; *also* : REGAL, IMPERIOUS **3** : of unusual size or excellence

im·pe·ri·al·ism \im-ˈpir-ē-ə-ˌli-zəm\ *n* : the policy of seeking to extend the power, dominion, or territories of a nation — **im·pe·ri·al·ist** \-list\ *n or adj* — **im·pe·ri·al·is·tic** \-ˌpir-ē-ə-ˈlis-tik\ *adj* — **im·pe·ri·al·is·ti·cal·ly** \-ti-k(ə-)lē\ *adv*

im·per·il \im-ˈper-əl\ *vb* **-iled** *or* **-illed; -il·ing** *or* **-il·ling** : ENDANGER

im·pe·ri·ous \im-ˈpir-ē-əs\ *adj* **1** : COMMANDING, LORDLY **2** : ARROGANT, DOMINEERING **3** : IMPERATIVE, URGENT — **im·pe·ri·ous·ly** *adv*

im·per·ish·able \(ˌ)im-ˈper-i-shə-bəl\ *adj* : not perishable or subject to decay

im·per·ma·nent \(ˌ)im-ˈpər-mə-nənt\ *adj* : not permanent : TRANSIENT — **im·per·ma·nent·ly** *adv*

im·per·me·able \(ˌ)im-ˈpər-mē-ə-bəl\ *adj* : not permitting passage (as of a fluid) through its substance

im·per·mis·si·ble \ˌim-pər-ˈmi-sə-bəl\ *adj* : not permissible

im·per·son·al \(ˌ)im-ˈpər-sə-nəl\ *adj* 1 : not referring to any particular person or thing 2 : not involving human emotions — **im·per·son·al·i·ty** \-ˌpər-sə-ˈna-lə-tē\ *n* — **im·per·son·al·ly** *adv*

im·per·son·ate \im-ˈpər-sə-ˌnāt\ *vb* -at·ed; -at·ing : to assume or act the character of — **im·per·son·a·tion** \-ˌpər-sə-ˈnā-shən\ *n* — **im·per·son·a·tor** \-ˈpər-sə-ˌnā-tər\ *n*

im·per·ti·nent \(ˌ)im-ˈpərt-ᵊn-ənt\ *adj* 1 : IRRELEVANT 2 : not restrained within due or proper bounds : RUDE, INSOLENT, SAUCY — **im·per·ti·nence** \-əns\ *n* — **im·per·ti·nent·ly** *adv*

im·per·turb·able \ˌim-pər-ˈtər-bə-bəl\ *adj* : marked by extreme calm, impassivity, and steadiness : SERENE — **im·per·turb·ably** *adv*

im·per·vi·ous \(ˌ)im-ˈpər-vē-əs\ *adj* 1 : incapable of being penetrated (as by moisture) 2 : not capable of being affected or disturbed ⟨~ to criticism⟩

im·pe·ti·go \ˌim-pə-ˈtē-gō, -ˈtī-\ *n* : a contagious skin disease characterized by vesicles, pustules, and yellowish crusts

im·pet·u·ous \im-ˈpe-chə-wəs\ *adj* 1 : marked by impulsive vehemence ⟨~ temper⟩ 2 : marked by force and violence ⟨with ~ speed⟩ — **im·pet·u·os·i·ty** \(ˌ)im-ˌpe-chə-ˈwä-sə-tē\ *n* — **im·pet·u·ous·ly** *adv*

im·pe·tus \ˈim-pə-təs\ *n* [L, assault, impetus, fr. *impetere* to attack, fr. *petere* to go to, seek] 1 : a driving force : IMPULSE; *also* : INCENTIVE 2 : MOMENTUM

im·pi·e·ty \(ˌ)im-ˈpī-ə-tē\ *n, pl* -ties 1 : the quality or state of being impious 2 : an impious act

im·pinge \im-ˈpinj\ *vb* **im·pinged; im·ping·ing** 1 : to strike or dash esp. with a sharp collision 2 : ENCROACH, INFRINGE — **im·pinge·ment** *n*

im·pi·ous \ˈim-pē-əs, (ˌ)im-ˈpī-\ *adj* : not pious : IRREVERENT, PROFANE

imp·ish \ˈim-pish\ *adj* : of, relating to, or befitting an imp; *esp* : MISCHIEVOUS — **imp·ish·ly** *adv* — **imp·ish·ness** *n*

im·pla·ca·ble \(ˌ)im-ˈpla-kə-bəl, -ˈplā-\ *adj* : not capable of being appeased, pacified, mitigated, or changed ⟨an ~ enemy⟩ — **im·pla·ca·bil·i·ty** \-ˌpla-kə-ˈbi-lə-tē, -ˌplā-\ *n* — **im·pla·ca·bly** \-ˈpla-kə-blē\ *adv*

im·plant \im-ˈplant\ *vb* 1 : to set firmly or deeply 2 : to fix in the mind or spirit 3 : to insert in a living site for growth or absorption — **im·plant** \ˈim-ˌplant\ *n* — **im·plan·ta·tion** \ˌim-ˌplan-ˈtā-shən\ *n*

im·plau·si·ble \(ˌ)im-ˈplȯ-zə-bəl\ *adj* : not plausible — **im·plau·si·bil·i·ty** \-ˌplȯ-zə-ˈbi-lə-tē\ *n* — **im·plau·si·bly** \-ˈplȯ-zə-blē\ *adv*

¹**im·ple·ment** \ˈim-plə-mənt\ *n* [ME, fr. LL *implementum* action of filling up, fr. L *implēre* to fill up] : TOOL, UTENSIL, INSTRUMENT

²**im·ple·ment** \-ˌment\ *vb* 1 : CARRY OUT; *esp* : to put into practice 2 : to provide implements for — **im·ple·men·ta·tion** \ˌim-plə-mən-ˈtā-shən\ *n*

im·pli·cate \ˈim-plə-ˌkāt\ *vb* -cat·ed; -cat·ing 1 : IMPLY 2 : INVOLVE — **im·pli·ca·tion** \ˌim-plə-ˈkā-shən\ *n*

im·plic·it \im-ˈpli-sət\ *adj* : understood though not directly stated or expressed : IMPLIED; *also* : POTENTIAL 2 : COMPLETE, UNQUESTIONING, ABSOLUTE ⟨~ faith⟩ — **im·plic·it·ly** *adv*

im·plode \im-ˈplōd\ *vb* **im·plod·ed; im·plod·ing** : to burst or collapse inward — **im·plo·sion** \-ˈplō-zhən\ *n* — **im·plo·sive** \-siv\ *adj*

im·plore \im-ˈplȯr\ *vb* **im·plored; im·plor·ing** : BESEECH, ENTREAT **syn** supplicate, beg, importune, plead

im·ply \im-ˈplī\ *vb* **im·plied; im·ply·ing** 1 : to involve or indicate by inference, association, or necessary

consequence rather than by direct statement ⟨war *implies* fighting⟩ 2 : to express indirectly : hint at : SUGGEST

im·po·lite \ˌim-pə-ˈlīt\ *adj* : not polite : RUDE, DISCOURTEOUS

im·pol·i·tic \(ˌ)im-ˈpä-lə-ˌtik\ *adj* : not politic : RASH

im·pon·der·a·ble \(ˌ)im-ˈpän-də-rə-bəl\ *adj* : incapable of being weighed or evaluated with exactness — **imponderable** *n*

¹**im·port** \im-ˈpȯrt\ *vb* 1 : MEAN, SIGNIFY 2 : to bring (as merchandise) into a place or country from a foreign or external source — **im·port·er** *n*

²**im·port** \ˈim-ˌpȯrt\ *n* 1 : IMPORTANCE, SIGNIFICANCE 2 : MEANING, SIGNIFICATION 3 : something (as merchandise) brought in from another country

im·por·tance \im-ˈpȯrt-ᵊns\ *n* : the quality or state of being important : MOMENT, SIGNIFICANCE **syn** consequence, import, weight

im·por·tant \im-ˈpȯrt-ᵊnt\ *adj* 1 : marked by importance : SIGNIFICANT 2 : giving an impression of importance — **im·por·tant·ly** *adv*

im·por·ta·tion \ˌim-ˌpȯr-ˈtā-shən, -pər-\ *n* 1 : the act or practice of importing 2 : something imported

im·por·tu·nate \im-ˈpȯr-chə-nət\ *adj* 1 : troublesomely urgent or persistent 2 : BURDENSOME, TROUBLESOME

im·por·tune \ˌim-pər-ˈtün, -ˈtyün; im-ˈpȯr-chən\ *vb* -tuned; -tun·ing : to urge or beg with troublesome persistence — **im·por·tu·ni·ty** \ˌim-pər-ˈtü-nə-tē, -ˈtyü-\ *n*

im·pose \im-ˈpōz\ *vb* **im·posed; im·pos·ing** 1 : to establish or apply by authority ⟨~ a tax⟩; *also* : to establish by force ⟨*imposed* a government⟩ 2 : OBTRUDE ⟨*imposed* herself on others⟩ 3 : to take unwarranted advantage of something ⟨~ on her good nature⟩ — **im·po·si·tion** \ˌim-pə-ˈzi-shən\ *n*

im·pos·ing *adj* : impressive because of size, bearing, dignity, or grandeur — **im·pos·ing·ly** *adv*

im·pos·si·ble \(ˌ)im-ˈpä-sə-bəl\ *adj* 1 : incapable of being or of occurring 2 : enormously difficult 3 : extremely undesirable : UNACCEPTABLE — **im·pos·si·bil·i·ty** \-ˌpä-sə-ˈbi-lə-tē\ *n* — **im·pos·si·bly** \-ˈpä-sə-blē\ *adv*

¹**im·post** \ˈim-ˌpōst\ *n* : TAX, DUTY

²**impost** *n* : a block, capital, or molding from which an arch springs

im·pos·tor *or* **im·pos·ter** \im-ˈpäs-tər\ *n* : one that assumes an identity or title not one's own in order to deceive

im·pos·ture \im-ˈpäs-chər\ *n* : DECEPTION; *esp* : fraudulent impersonation

im·po·tent \ˈim-pə-tənt\ *adj* 1 : lacking in power or strength : HELPLESS 2 : unable to copulate; *also* : STERILE — **im·po·tence** \-təns\ *n* — **im·po·ten·cy** \-tən-sē\ *n* — **im·po·tent·ly** *adv*

im·pound \im-ˈpaúnd\ *vb* 1 : CONFINE, ENCLOSE ⟨~ stray dogs⟩ 2 : to seize and hold in legal custody 3 : to collect in a reservoir ⟨~ water⟩ — **im·pound·ment** *n*

im·pov·er·ish \im-ˈpä-və-rish\ *vb* : to make poor; *also* : to deprive of strength, richness, or fertility — **im·pov·er·ish·ment** *n*

im·prac·ti·ca·ble \(ˌ)im-ˈprak-ti-kə-bəl\ *adj* : not practicable : incapable of being put into practice or use

im·prac·ti·cal \(ˌ)im-ˈprak-ti-kəl\ *adj* 1 : not practical 2 : IMPRACTICABLE

im·pre·cate \ˈim-pri-ˌkāt\ *vb* -cat·ed; -cat·ing : CURSE — **im·pre·ca·tion** \ˌim-pri-ˈkā-shən\ *n*

im·pre·cise \ˌim-pri-ˈsīs\ *adj* : not precise — **im·pre·cise·ly** *adv* — **im·pre·cise·ness** *n* — **im·pre·ci·sion** \-ˈsi-zhən\ *n*

¹**im·preg·na·ble** \im-ˈpreg-nə-bəl\ *adj* : incapable of being taken by assault : UNCONQUERABLE, UNASSAILABLE — **im·preg·na·bil·i·ty** \(ˌ)im-ˌpreg-nə-ˈbi-lə-tē\ *n*

im·preg·nate \im-ˈpreg-ˌnāt\ *vb* -nat·ed; -nat·ing 1 : to fertilize or make pregnant 2 : to cause to be filled,

permeated, or saturated — **im·preg·na·tion** \ˌim-ˌpreg-ˈnā-shən\ n

im·pre·sa·rio \ˌim-prə-ˈsär-ē-ˌō\ n, pl **-ri·os** [It, fr. impresa undertaking, fr. imprendere to undertake] **1** : the manager or conductor of an opera or concert company **2** : one who puts on an entertainment **3** : MANAGER, PRODUCER

¹**im·press** \im-ˈpres\ vb **1** : to apply with or produce (as a mark) by pressure : IMPRINT **2** : to press, stamp, or print in or upon **3** : to produce a vivid impression of **4** : to affect esp. forcibly or deeply — **im·press·ible** adj

²**im·press** \ˈim-ˌpres\ n **1** : a characteristic or distinctive mark **2** : IMPRESSION, EFFECT **3** : IMPRESSION 2 **4** : an image of something formed by or as if by pressure; esp : SEAL **5** : a product of pressure or influence

³**im·press** \im-ˈpres\ vb **1** : to force into naval service **2** : to get the aid or services of by forcible argument or persuasion — **im·press·ment** n

im·pres·sion \im-ˈpre-shən\ n **1** : a characteristic trait or feature resulting from influence : IMPRESS **2** : a stamp, form, or figure made by impressing : IMPRINT **3** : an esp. marked influence or effect on feeling, sense, or mind **4** : a single print or copy (as from type or from an engraved plate or book) **5** : all the copies of a publication (as a book) printed for one issue : PRINTING **6** : a usu. vague notion or remembrance **7** : an imitation in caricature of a noted personality as a form of entertainment

im·pres·sion·able \im-ˈpre-shə-nə-bəl\ adj : capable of being easily impressed : easily molded or influenced

im·pres·sion·ism \im-ˈpre-shə-ˌni-zəm\ n, often cap : a theory or practice in modern art of depicting the natural appearances of objects by dabs or strokes of primary unmixed colors in order to simulate actual reflected light — **im·pres·sion·is·tic** \-ˌpre-shə-ˈnis-tik\ adj

im·pres·sion·ist \im-ˈpre-shə-nist\ n **1** often cap : a painter who practices impressionism **2** : an entertainer who does impressions

im·pres·sive \im-ˈpre-siv\ adj : making or tending to make a marked impression ⟨an ~ speech⟩ — **im·pres·sive·ly** adv — **im·pres·sive·ness** n

im·pri·ma·tur \ˌim-prə-ˈmä-ˌtùr\ n [NL, let it be printed] **1** : a license to print or publish; also : official approval of a publication by a censor **2** : SANCTION, APPROVAL

¹**im·print** \im-ˈprint, ˈim-ˌprint\ vb **1** : to stamp or mark by or as if by pressure : IMPRESS **2** : to fix firmly (as on the memory)

²**im·print** \ˈim-ˌprint\ n **1** : something imprinted or printed **2** : a publisher's name printed at the foot of a title page **3** : an indelible distinguishing effect or influence

im·pris·on \im-ˈpriz-ᵊn\ vb : to put in or as if in prison : CONFINE — **im·pris·on·ment** n

im·prob·a·ble \(ˌ)im-ˈprä-bə-bəl\ adj : unlikely to be true or to occur — **im·prob·a·bil·i·ty** \-ˌprä-bə-ˈbi-lə-tē\ n — **im·prob·a·bly** \-ˈprä-bə-blē\ adv

im·promp·tu \im-ˈprämp-tü, -tyü\ adj [F, fr. impromptu extemporaneously, fr. L in promptu in readiness] **1** : made or done on or as if on the spur of the moment **2** : EXTEMPORANEOUS, UNREHEARSED — **impromptu** adv or n

im·prop·er \(ˌ)im-ˈprä-pər\ adj **1** : not proper, fit, or suitable **2** : INCORRECT, INACCURATE **3** : not in accord with propriety, modesty, or good manners — **im·prop·er·ly** adv

improper fraction n : a fraction whose numerator is equal to or larger than the denominator

im·pro·pri·e·ty \ˌim-prə-ˈprī-ə-tē\ n, pl **-ties 1** : an improper act or remark; esp : an unacceptable use of a word or of language **2** : the quality or state of being improper

im·prove \im-ˈprüv\ vb **im·proved; im·prov·ing 1** : to enhance or increase in value or quality **2** : to grow or become better ⟨your work is improving⟩ **3** : to make good use of ⟨~ the time by reading⟩ — **im·prov·able** \-ˈprü-və-bəl\ adj

im·prove·ment \im-ˈprüv-mənt\ n **1** : the act or process of improving **2** : increased value or excellence of something **3** : something that adds to the value or appearance of a thing

im·prov·i·dent \(ˌ)im-ˈprä-və-dənt\ adj : not providing for the future — **im·prov·i·dence** \-dəns\ n

im·pro·vise \ˈim-prə-ˌvīz\ vb **-vised; -vis·ing** [F improviser, fr. It improvvisare, fr. improvviso sudden, fr. L improvisus, lit., unforeseen] **1** : to compose, recite, play, or sing on the spur of the moment : EXTEMPORIZE ⟨~ on the piano⟩ **2** : to make, invent, or arrange offhand ⟨~ a sail out of shirts⟩ — **im·pro·vi·sa·tion** \im-ˌprä-və-ˈzā-shən, ˌim-prə-və-\ n — **im·pro·vis·er** or **im·pro·vi·sor** \ˈim-prə-ˈvī-zər, ˈim-prə-ˌvī-\ n

im·pru·dent \(ˌ)im-ˈprüd-ᵊnt\ adj : not prudent : lacking discretion — **im·pru·dence** \-ᵊns\ n

im·pu·dent \ˈim-pyù-dənt\ adj : marked by contemptuous boldness or disregard of others — **im·pu·dence** \-dəns\ n — **im·pu·dent·ly** adv

im·pugn \im-ˈpyün\ vb [ME, to assail, ultim. fr. L impugnare, fr. pugnare to fight] : to attack by words or arguments : oppose or attack as false or as lacking integrity

im·puis·sance \im-ˈpwis-ᵊns, -ˈpyü-ə-səns\ n [ME, fr. MF] : the quality or state of being powerless : WEAKNESS

im·pulse \ˈim-ˌpəls\ n **1** : a force that starts a body into motion; also : the motion produced by such a force **2** : an arousing of the mind and spirit to some usu. unpremeditated action **3** : NERVE IMPULSE

im·pul·sion \im-ˈpəl-shən\ n **1** : the act of impelling : the state of being impelled **2** : a force that impels **3** : IMPULSE 2; also : COMPULSION 3

im·pul·sive \im-ˈpəl-siv\ adj **1** : having the power of or actually driving or impelling **2** : acting or prone to act on impulse ⟨~ buying⟩ — **im·pul·sive·ly** adv — **im·pul·sive·ness** n

im·pu·ni·ty \im-'pyü-nə-tē\ *n* [MF or L; MF *impunité*, fr. L *impunitas*, fr. *impune* without punishment, fr. *poena* penalty, punishment] : exemption from punishment, harm, or loss

im·pure \(ₐ)im-'pyùr\ *adj* **1** : not pure : UNCHASTE, OBSCENE **2** : DIRTY, FOUL **3** : ADULTERATED, MIXED — im·pu·ri·ty \-'pyùr-ə-tē\ *n*

im·pute \im-'pyüt\ *vb* im·put·ed; im·put·ing **1** : to lay the responsibility or blame for often falsely or unjustly **2** : to credit to a person or a cause : ATTRIBUTE — im·put·able \-'pyü-tə-bəl\ *adj* — im·pu·ta·tion \ₐim-pyù-'tā-shən\ *n*

¹in \'in\ *prep* **1** — used to indicate physical surroundings ⟨swim ~ the lake⟩ **2** : INTO 1 ⟨ran ~ the house⟩ **3** : DURING ⟨~ the summer⟩ **4** : WITH ⟨written ~ pencil⟩ **5** — used to indicate one's situation or state of being ⟨~ luck⟩ ⟨~ love⟩ **6** — used to indicate manner or purpose ⟨~ a hurry⟩ ⟨said ~ reply⟩ **7** : INTO 2 ⟨broke ~ pieces⟩

²in *adv* **1** : to or toward the inside ⟨come ~⟩; *also* : to or toward some destination or place ⟨flew ~ from the South⟩ **2** : at close quarters : NEAR ⟨the enemy closed ~⟩ **3** : into the midst of something ⟨mix ~ the flour⟩ **4** : to or at its proper place ⟨fit a piece ~⟩ **5** : WITHIN ⟨locked ~⟩ **6** : in vogue or season **7** : in one's presence, possession, or control ⟨the results are ~⟩

³in *adj* **1** : located inside or within **2** : that is in position, operation, or power ⟨the ~ party⟩ **3** : directed inward : INCOMING ⟨the ~ train⟩ **4** : keenly aware of and responsive to what is new and smart ⟨the ~ crowd⟩; *also* : extremely fashionable ⟨the ~ thing to do⟩

⁴in *n* **1** : one who is in office or power or on the inside **2** : INFLUENCE, PULL ⟨he has an ~ with the owner⟩

⁵in *abbr* **1** inch **2** inlet

In *symbol* indium

IN *abbr* Indiana

in- \(ₐ)in\ *prefix* : not : absence of : NON-, UN-

inaccessibility	inauthentic
inaccessible	incautious
inaccuracy	incombustible
inaccurate	incomprehension
inaction	inconclusive
inactive	incongruent
inactivity	inconsistency
inadmissibility	inconsistent
inadmissible	incoordination
inadvisability	incurious
inadvisable	indecipherable
inapparent	indemonstrable
inapplicable	indestructible
inapposite	indeterminable
inapproachable	indiscernible
inappropriate	indistinguishable
inaptitude	inedible
inarguable	ineducable
inartistic	ineffaceable
inattentive	inefficacious
inaudible	inefficacy
inaudibly	inelastic
inauspicious	inelasticity

inequitable	inhospitable
inequity	injudicious
ineradicable	inoffensive
inerrant	insanitary
inexpedient	insensitive
inexpensive	insensitivity
inexpressive	insignificance
inextinguishable	insignificant
infeasible	insolvable
inharmonious	insusceptible

in·abil·i·ty \ₐi-nə-'bi-lə-tē\ *n* : the quality or state of being unable

in ab·sen·tia \ₐin-ab-'sen-chə, -chē-ə\ *adv* : in one's absence

in·ac·ti·vate \(ₐ)i-'nak-tə-ₐvāt\ *vb* : to make inactive — in·ac·ti·va·tion \(ₐ)i-ₐnak-tə-'vā-shən\ *n*

in·ad·e·quate \(ₐ)i-'na-di-kwət\ *adj* : not adequate : INSUFFICIENT — in·ad·e·qua·cy \-kwə-sē\ *n* — in·ad·e·quate·ly *adv* — in·ad·e·quate·ness *n*

in·ad·ver·tent \ₐi-nəd-'vərt-ᵊnt\ *adj* **1** : HEEDLESS, INATTENTIVE **2** : UNINTENTIONAL — in·ad·ver·tence \-ᵊns\ *n* — in·ad·ver·ten·cy \-ᵊn-sē\ *n* — in·ad·ver·tent·ly *adv*

in·alien·able \(ₐ)i-'nāl-yə-nə-bəl, -'nā-lē-ə-\ *adj* : incapable of being alienated, surrendered, or transferred ⟨~ rights⟩ — in·alien·abil·i·ty \(ₐ)i-ₐnāl-yə-nə-'bi-lə-tē, -ₐnā-lē-ə-\ *n* — in·alien·ably *adv*

in·amo·ra·ta \i-ₐnä-mə-'rä-tə\ *n* : a woman with whom one is in love

inane \i-'nān\ *adj* inan·er; -est : EMPTY, INSUBSTANTIAL; *also* : SHALLOW, SILLY — inan·i·ty \i-'na-nə-tē\ *n*

in·an·i·mate \(ₐ)i-'na-nə-mət\ *adj* : not animate or animated : lacking the qualities of living things — in·an·i·mate·ly *adv* — in·an·i·mate·ness *n*

in·ap·pre·cia·ble \ₐi-nə-'prē-shə-bəl\ *adj* : too small to be perceived — in·ap·pre·cia·bly \-blē\ *adv*

in·apt \(ₐ)i-'napt\ *adj* **1** : not suitable **2** : INEPT — in·apt·ly *adv* — in·apt·ness *n*

in·ar·tic·u·late \ₐi-när-'ti-kyə-lət\ *adj* **1** : not understandable as spoken words **2** : MUTE **3** : incapable of being expressed by speech; *also* : UNSPOKEN **4** : not having the power of distinct utterance or effective expression — in·ar·tic·u·late·ly *adv*

in·as·much as \ₐi-nəz-'məch-\ *conj* : seeing that : SINCE

in·at·ten·tion \ₐi-nə-'ten-chən\ *n* : failure to pay attention : DISREGARD

¹in·au·gu·ral \i-'nò-gyə-rəl, -gə-\ *adj* **1** : of or relating to an inauguration **2** : marking a beginning

²inaugural *n* **1** : an inaugural address **2** : INAUGURATION

in·au·gu·rate \i-'nò-gyə-ₐrāt, -gə-\ *vb* -rat·ed; -rat·ing **1** : to introduce into an office with suitable ceremonies : INSTALL **2** : to dedicate ceremoniously **3** : BEGIN, INITIATE — in·au·gu·ra·tion \-ₐnò-gyə-'rā-shən, -gə-\ *n*

in·board \'in-ˌbȯrd\ *adv* **1** : inside the hull of a ship **2** : close or closest to the center line of a vehicle or craft — **inboard** *adj*

in·born \'in-'bȯrn\ *adj* **1** : present from or as if from birth **2** : HEREDITARY, INHERITED **syn** innate, congenital, native

in·bound \'in-ˌbau̇nd\ *adj* : inward bound ⟨∼ traffic⟩

in·bred \'in-'bred\ *adj* **1** : ingrained in one's nature as deeply as if by heredity **2** : subjected to or produced by inbreeding

in·breed·ing \'in-ˌbrē-diŋ\ *n* **1** : the interbreeding of closely related individuals esp. to preserve and fix desirable characters of and to eliminate unfavorable characters from a stock **2** : confinement to a narrow range or a local or limited field of choice — **in·breed** \-'bred\ *vb*

inc *abbr* **1** incomplete **2** incorporated **3** increase

In·ca \'iŋ-kə\ *n* [Sp, fr. Quechua (a So. American Indian language) *inka* ruler of the Inca empire] **1** : a noble or a member of the ruling family of an Indian empire of Peru, Bolivia, and Ecuador until the Spanish conquest **2** : a member of any people under Inca influence

in·cal·cu·la·ble \(ˌ)in-'kal-kyə-lə-bəl\ *adj* : not capable of being calculated; *esp* : too large or numerous to be calculated — **in·cal·cu·la·bly** \-blē\ *adv*

in·can·des·cent \ˌin-kən-'des-ᵊnt\ *adj* **1** : glowing with heat **2** : SHINING, BRILLIANT — **in·can·des·cence** \-ᵊns\ *n*

incandescent lamp *n* : a lamp in which an electrically heated filament emits light

in·can·ta·tion \ˌin-ˌkan-'tā-shən\ *n* : a use of spells or verbal charms spoken or sung as a part of a ritual of magic; *also* : a formula of words used in or as if in such a ritual

in·ca·pa·ble \(ˌ)in-'kā-pə-bəl\ *adj* : lacking ability or qualification for a particular purpose; *also* : UNQUALIFIED — **in·ca·pa·bil·i·ty** \ˌkā-pə-'bi-lə-tē\ *n*

in·ca·pac·i·tate \ˌin-kə-'pa-sə-ˌtāt\ *vb* **-tat·ed; -tat·ing** : to make incapable or unfit : DISQUALIFY, DISABLE

in·ca·pac·i·ty \ˌin-kə-'pa-sə-tē\ *n, pl* **-ties** : the quality or state of being incapable

in·car·cer·ate \in-'kär-sə-ˌrāt\ *vb* **-at·ed; -at·ing** : IMPRISON, CONFINE — **in·car·cer·a·tion** \(ˌ)in-ˌkär-sə-'rā-shən\ *n*

in·car·na·dine \in-'kär-nə-ˌdīn, -ˌdēn\ *vb* **-dined; -din·ing** : REDDEN

in·car·nate \in-'kär-nət, -ˌnāt\ *adj* **1** : having bodily and esp. human form and substance **2** : PERSONIFIED — **in·car·nate** \-ˌnāt\ *vb*

in·car·na·tion \ˌin-ˌkär-'nā-shən\ *n* **1** : the embodiment of a deity or spirit in an earthly form **2** *cap* : the union of divine and human natures in Jesus Christ **3** : a person showing a trait or typical character to a marked degree **4** : the act of incarnating : the state of being incarnate

incase *var of* ENCASE

in·cen·di·ary \in-'sen-dē-ˌer-ē\ *adj* **1** : of or relating to a deliberate burning of property **2** : tending to excite or inflame **3** : designed to start fires ⟨an ∼ bomb⟩ — **incendiary** *n*

¹in·cense \'in-ˌsens\ *n* **1** : material used to produce a fragrant odor when burned **2** : the perfume or smoke from some spices and gums when burned

²in·cense \in-'sens\ *vb* **in·censed; in·cens·ing** : to make extremely angry

in·cen·tive \in-'sen-tiv\ *n* [ME, fr. LL *incentivum*, fr. *incentivus* stimulating, fr. L, setting the tune, fr. *incinere* to set the tune, fr. *canere* to sing] : something that incites or is likely to incite to determination or action

in·cep·tion \in-'sep-shən\ *n* : BEGINNING, COMMENCEMENT

in·cer·ti·tude \(ˌ)in-'sər-tə-ˌtüd, -ˌtyüd\ *n* **1** : UNCER-

TAINTY, DOUBT, INDECISION **2** : INSECURITY, INSTABILITY

in·ces·sant \(ˌ)in-'ses-ᵊnt\ *adj* : continuing or flowing without interruption ⟨∼ rains⟩ — **in·ces·sant·ly** *adv*

in·cest \'in-ˌsest\ *n* [ME, fr. L *incestus* sexual impurity, fr. *incestus* impure, fr. *castus* pure] : sexual intercourse between persons so closely related that marriage is illegal — **in·ces·tu·ous** \in-'ses-chù-wəs\ *adj*

¹inch \'inch\ *n* [ME, fr. OE *ynce*, fr. L *uncia* twelfth part, inch, ounce] — see WEIGHT table

²inch *vb* : to move by small degrees

in·cho·ate \in-'kō-ət, 'in-kə-ˌwāt\ *adj* : being only partly in existence or operation : INCOMPLETE, INCIPIENT

inch·worm \'inch-ˌwərm\ *n* : LOOPER

in·ci·dence \'in-sə-dəns\ *n* : rate of occurrence or effect

¹in·ci·dent \-dənt\ *n* **1** : OCCURRENCE, HAPPENING **2** : an action likely to lead to grave consequences esp. in diplomatic matters

²incident *adj* **1** : occurring or likely to occur esp. in connection with some other happening **2** : falling or striking on something ⟨∼ light rays⟩

¹in·ci·den·tal \ˌin-sə-'dent-ᵊl\ *adj* **1** : subordinate, nonessential, or attendant in position or significance ⟨∼ expenses⟩ **2** : CASUAL, CHANCE

²incidental *n* **1** *pl* : minor items (as of expense) that are not individually accounted for **2** : something incidental

in·ci·den·tal·ly \ˌin-sə-'den-tə-lē, -'dent-lē\ *adv* **1** : in an incidental manner **2** : by the way

in·cin·er·ate \in-'si-nə-ˌrāt\ *vb* **-at·ed; -at·ing** : to burn to ashes

in·cin·er·a·tor \in-'si-nə-ˌrā-tər\ *n* : a furnace for burning waste

in·cip·i·ent \in-'si-pē-ənt\ *adj* : beginning to be or become apparent

in·cise \in-'sīz\ *vb* **in·cised; in·cis·ing** **1** : to cut into **2** : CARVE, ENGRAVE

in·ci·sion \in-'si-zhən\ *n* : CUT, GASH; *esp* : a surgical cut

in·ci·sive \in-'sī-siv\ *adj* : impressively direct and decisive — **in·ci·sive·ly** *adv*

in·ci·sor \in-'sī-zər\ *n* : a front tooth typically adapted for cutting

in·cite \in-'sīt\ *vb* **in·cit·ed; in·cit·ing** : to arouse to action : stir up — **in·cite·ment** *n* — **in·cit·er** *n*

in·ci·vil·i·ty \ˌin-sə-'vi-lə-tē\ *n* **1** : RUDENESS, DISCOURTESY **2** : a rude or discourteous act

incl *abbr* include; included; including; inclusive

in·clem·ent \(ˌ)in-'kle-mənt\ *adj* : SEVERE, STORMY ⟨∼ weather⟩ — **in·clem·en·cy** \-mən-sē\ *n*

in·cli·na·tion \ˌin-klə-'nā-shən\ *n* **1** : PROPENSITY, BENT; *esp* : LIKING **2** : BOW, NOD ⟨an ∼ of the head⟩ **3** : a tilting of something **4** : SLANT, SLOPE

¹in·cline \in-'klīn\ *vb* **in·clined; in·clin·ing** **1** : BOW, BEND **2** : to be drawn toward an opinion or course of action **3** : to deviate from the vertical or horizontal : SLOPE **4** : INFLUENCE, PERSUADE — **in·clin·er** *n*

²in·cline \'in-ˌklīn\ *n* : SLOPE

inclose, inclosure *var of* ENCLOSE, ENCLOSURE

in·clude \in-'klüd\ *vb* **in·clud·ed; in·clud·ing** : to take in or comprise as a part of a whole ⟨the price ∼s tax⟩ — **in·clu·sion** \in-'klü-zhən\ *n* — **in·clu·sive** \-'klü-siv\ *adj*

incog *abbr* incognito

¹in·cog·ni·to \ˌin-ˌkäg-'nē-tō, in-'käg-nə-ˌtō\ *n, pl* **-tos** **1** : one appearing or living incognito **2** : the state or disguise of an incognito

²incognito *adv or adj* [It, fr. L *incognitus* unknown, fr. *cognoscere* to know] : with one's identity concealed

in·co·her·ent \ˌin-kō-'hir-ənt, -'her-\ *adj* **1** : not sticking closely or compactly together **2** : not clearly or logically connected : RAMBLING — **in·co·her·ence** \-əns\ *n* — **in·co·her·ent·ly** *adv*

in·come \'in-ˌkəm\ *n* : a gain usu. measured in money that derives from labor, business, or property

income tax *n* : a tax on the net income of an individual or business concern

in·com·ing \'in-ˌkə-miŋ\ *adj* : coming in ⟨the ∼ tide⟩ ⟨∼ freshmen⟩

in·com·men·su·rate \ˌin-kə-'men-sə-rət, -'men-chə-\ *adj* : not commensurate; *esp* : INADEQUATE

in·com·mode \ˌin-kə-'mōd\ *vb* **-mod·ed; -mod·ing** : INCONVENIENCE, DISTURB

in·com·mu·ni·ca·ble \ˌin-kə-'myü-ni-kə-bəl\ *adj* : not communicable : not capable of being communicated or imparted; *also* : UNCOMMUNICATIVE

in·com·mu·ni·ca·do \ˌin-kə-ˌmyü-nə-'kä-dō\ *adv or adj* : without means of communication; *also* : in solitary confinement ⟨a prisoner held ∼⟩

in·com·pa·ra·ble \(ˌ)in-'käm-pə-rə-bəl, -prə-\ *adj* **1** : eminent beyond comparison : MATCHLESS **2** : not suitable for comparison — **in·com·pa·ra·bly** \-blē\ *adv*

in·com·pat·i·ble \ˌin-kəm-'pa-tə-bəl\ *adj* : incapable of or unsuitable for association or use together ⟨∼ colors⟩ ⟨temperamentally ∼⟩ — **in·com·pat·i·bil·i·ty** \ˌin-kəm-ˌpa-tə-°bi-lə-tē\ *n*

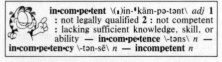

in·com·pe·tent \(ˌ)in-'käm-pə-tənt\ *adj* **1** : not legally qualified **2** : not competent : lacking sufficient knowledge, skill, or ability — **in·com·pe·tence** \-təns\ *n* — **in·com·pe·ten·cy** \-tən-sē\ *n* — **incompetent** *n*

in·com·plete \ˌin-kəm-'plēt\ *adj* : lacking a part or parts : UNFINISHED, IMPERFECT — **in·com·plete·ly** *adv* — **in·com·plete·ness** *n*

in·com·pre·hen·si·ble \ˌin-ˌkäm-prē-'hen-sə-bəl\ *adj* : impossible to comprehend : UNINTELLIGIBLE

in·con·ceiv·able \ˌin-kən-'sē-və-bəl\ *adj* **1** : impossible to comprehend **2** : UNBELIEVABLE

in·con·gru·ous \(ˌ)in-'käŋ-grü-wəs\ *adj* : not consistent with or suitable to the surroundings or associations — **in·con·gru·i·ty** \ˌin-kən-'grü-ə-tē, -ˌkän-\ *n* — **in·con·gru·ous·ly** *adv*

in·con·se·quen·tial \ˌin-ˌkän-sə-'kwen-chəl\ *adj* **1** : ILLOGICAL; *also* : IRRELEVANT **2** : of no significance : UNIMPORTANT — **in·con·se·quence** \(ˌ)in-'kän-sə-ˌkwens\ *n* — **in·con·se·quen·tial·ly** *adv*

in·con·sid·er·able \ˌin-kən-'si-də-rə-bəl\ *adj* : SLIGHT, TRIVIAL

in·con·sid·er·ate \ˌin-kən-'si-də-rət\ *adj* : HEEDLESS, THOUGHTLESS; *esp* : not respecting the rights or feelings of others — **in·con·sid·er·ate·ly** *adv* — **in·con·sid·er·ate·ness** *n*

in·con·sol·able \ˌin-kən-'sō-lə-bəl\ *adj* : incapable of being consoled — **in·con·sol·ably** \-blē\ *adv*

in·con·spic·u·ous \ˌin-kən-'spi-kyə-wəs\ *adj* : not readily noticeable — **in·con·spic·u·ous·ly** *adv*

in·con·stant \(ˌ)in-'kän-stənt\ *adj* : not constant : CHANGEABLE **syn** fickle, capricious, mercurial, unstable, volatile — **in·con·stan·cy** \-stən-sē\ *n* — **in·con·stant·ly** *adv*

in·con·test·able \ˌin-kən-'tes-tə-bəl\ *adj* : not contestable : INDISPUTABLE — **in·con·test·ably** \-'tes-tə-blē\ *adv*

in·con·ti·nent \(ˌ)in-'känt-°n-ənt\ *adj* **1** : lacking self-restraint **2** : unable to retain a bodily discharge (as urine) voluntarily — **in·con·ti·nence** \-əns\ *n*

in·con·tro·vert·ible \ˌin-ˌkän-trə-'vər-tə-bəl\ *adj* : not open to question : INDISPUTABLE ⟨∼ evidence⟩ — **in·con·tro·vert·ibly** \-blē\ *adv*

¹in·con·ve·nience \ˌin-kən-'vē-nyəns\ *n* **1** : something that is inconvenient **2** : the quality or state of being inconvenient

²inconvenience *vb* : to subject to inconvenience

in·con·ve·nient \ˌin-kən-'vē-nyənt\ *adj* : not convenient : causing trouble or annoyance : INOPPORTUNE — **in·con·ve·nient·ly** *adv*

in·cor·po·rate \in-'kȯr-pə-ˌrāt\ *vb* **-rat·ed; -rat·ing 1** : to unite closely or so as to form one body : BLEND **2** : to form, form into, or become a corporation **3** : to give material form to : EMBODY — **in·cor·po·ra·tion** \-ˌkȯr-pə-'rā-shən\ *n*

in·cor·po·re·al \ˌin-kȯr-'pōr-ē-əl\ *adj* : having no material body or form

in·cor·rect \ˌin-kə-'rekt\ *adj* **1** : INACCURATE, FAULTY

2 : not true : WRONG 3 : UNBECOMING, IMPROPER —
in·cor·rect·ly adv — **in·cor·rect·ness** n
in·cor·ri·gi·ble \(₁)in-ˈkȯr-ə-jə-bəl\ adj : incapable of
being corrected, amended, or reformed — **in·cor·ri·gi·bil·i·ty** \(₁)in-ˌkȯr-ə-jə-ˈbi-lə-tē\ n — **in·cor·ri·gi·bly** \-ˈkȯr-ə-jə-blē\ adv
in·cor·rupt·ible \ˌin-kə-ˈrəp-tə-bəl\ adj 1 : not subject
to decay or dissolution 2 : incapable of being bribed
or morally corrupted — **in·cor·rupt·ibil·i·ty** \-ˌrəp-tə-ˈbi-lə-tē\ n — **in·cor·rupt·ibly** \-ˈrəp-tə-blē\ adv
incr abbr increase; increased
¹**in·crease** \in-ˈkrēs, ˈin-ˌkrēs\ vb **in·creased; in·creas·ing** 1 : to become greater : GROW 2 : to multiply by
the production of young ⟨rabbits ∼ rapidly⟩ 3 : to
make greater — **in·creas·ing·ly** \-ˈkrē-siŋ-lē\ adv
²**in·crease** \ˈin-ˌkrēs, in-ˈkrēs\ n 1 : addition or enlargement in size, extent, or quantity : GROWTH 2 : something that is added to an original stock or amount (as
by growth)
in·cred·i·ble \(₁)in-ˈkre-də-bəl\ adj : too extraordinary
and improbable to be believed; also : hard to believe
— **in·cred·i·bil·i·ty** \(₁)in-ˌkre-də-ˈbi-lə-tē\ n — **in·cred·i·bly** \-ˈkre-də-blē\ adv
in·cred·u·lous \-ˈkre-jə-ləs\ adj 1 : SKEPTICAL 2 : ex-
pressing disbelief — **in·cre·du·li·ty** \ˌin-kri-ˈdü-lə-tē,
-ˈdyü-\ n — **in·cred·u·lous·ly** adv
in·cre·ment \ˈiŋ-krə-mənt, ˈin-\ n 1 : the action or process of increasing esp. in quantity or value : EN-
LARGEMENT; also : QUANTITY 2 : something gained or
added; esp : one of a series of regular consecutive additions — **in·cre·men·tal** \ˌiŋ-krə-ˈment-ᵊl, ˌin-\
— **in·cre·men·tal·ly** adv
in·crim·i·nate \in-ˈkri-mə-ˌnāt\ vb **-nat·ed; -nat·ing**
: to charge with or prove involvement in a crime or
fault : ACCUSE — **in·crim·i·na·tion** \-ˌkri-mə-ˈnā-shən\ n — **in·crim·i·na·to·ry** \-ˈkri-mə-nə-ˌtȯr-ē\ adj
incrust var of ENCRUST
in·crus·ta·tion \ˌin-ˌkrəs-ˈtā-shən\ n 1 : CRUST; also
: something resembling a crust ⟨∼ of habits⟩ 2 : the
act of encrusting : the state of being encrusted
in·cu·bate \ˈiŋ-kyu-ˌbāt, ˈin-\ vb **-bat·ed; -bat·ing** : to
sit on (eggs) to hatch by the warmth of the body; also
: to keep (as an embryo) under conditions favorable
for development — **in·cu·ba·tion** \ˌiŋ-kyu-ˈbā-shən,
ˌin-\ n
in·cu·ba·tor \ˈiŋ-kyu-ˌbāt-ər, ˈin-\ n : one that incu-
bates; esp : an apparatus providing suitable conditions (as of warmth and moisture) for incubating
something (as a premature baby)
in·cu·bus \ˈiŋ-kyə-bəs, ˈin-\ n, pl **-bi** \-ˌbī, -ˌbē\ also
-bus·es [ME, fr. LL, fr. L incubare to lie on] 1 : a
spirit supposed to work evil on persons in their sleep
2 : NIGHTMARE 1 3 : one that oppresses like a nightmare
in·cul·cate \in-ˈkəl-ˌkāt, ˈin-(ˌ)kəl-\ vb **-cat·ed; -cat·ing** [L inculcare, lit., to tread on, fr. calcare to trample, fr. calx heel] : to teach and impress by frequent
repetitions or admonitions — **in·cul·ca·tion** \ˌin-(ˌ)kəl-ˈkā-shən\ n
in·cul·pa·ble \(₁)in-ˈkəl-pə-bəl\ adj : free from guilt
: INNOCENT
in·cul·pate \in-ˈkəl-ˌpāt, ˈin-(ˌ)kəl-\ vb **-pat·ed; -pat·ing** : INCRIMINATE
in·cum·ben·cy \in-ˈkəm-bən-sē\ n, pl **-cies** 1 : some-
thing that is incumbent 2 : the quality or state of being
incumbent 3 : the office or period of office of an incumbent
¹**in·cum·bent** \in-ˈkəm-bənt\ n : the holder of an office
or position
²**incumbent** adj 1 : imposed as a duty 2 : occupying a
specified office 3 : lying or resting on something else
in·cun·ab·u·lum \ˌin-kyə-ˈna-byə-ləm, ˌiŋ-\ n, pl **-la**
\-lə\ [NL, fr. L incunabula, pl., bands holding the
baby in a cradle, fr. cunae cradle] : a book printed before 1501

in·cur \in-ˈkər\ vb **in·curred; in·cur·ring** : to become
liable or subject to : bring down upon oneself
in·cur·able \(₁)in-ˈkyur-ə-bəl\ adj 1 : not subject to
cure 2 : not likely to be changed — **incurable** n —
in·cur·ably \(₁)in-ˈkyur-ə-blē\ adv
in·cur·sion \in-ˈkər-zhən\ n 1 : a sudden hostile invasion : RAID 2 : an entering in or into (as an activity)
in·cus \ˈiŋ-kəs\ n, pl **in·cu·des** \iŋ-ˈkyü-(ˌ)dēz\ [NL, fr.
L, anvil] : the middle bone of a chain of three small
bones in the ear of a mammal
ind abbr 1 independent 2 index 3 industrial; industry
Ind abbr 1 Indian 2 Indiana
in·debt·ed \in-ˈde-təd\ adj 1 : owing gratitude or recognition to another 2 : owing money — **in·debt·ed·ness** n
in·de·cent \(₁)in-ˈdēs-ᵊnt\ adj : not decent; esp : mor-
ally offensive — **in·de·cen·cy** \-ᵊn-sē\ n — **in·de·cent·ly** adv
in·de·ci·sion \ˌin-di-ˈsi-zhən\ n : a wavering between
two or more possible courses of action : IRRESOLU-
TION
in·de·ci·sive \ˌin-di-ˈsī-siv\ adj 1 : INCONCLUSIVE 2
: marked by or prone to indecision 3 : INDEFINITE —
in·de·ci·sive·ly adv — **in·de·ci·sive·ness** n
in·de·co·rous \(₁)in-ˈde-kə-rəs, ˌin-di-ˈkȯr-əs\ adj : not
decorous **syn** improper, unseemly, indecent, unbe-
coming, indelicate — **in·de·co·rous·ly** adv — **in·de·co·rous·ness** n
in·deed \in-ˈdēd\ adv 1 : without any question : TRULY
— often used interjectionally to express irony, disbelief, or surprise 2 : in reality 3 : all things considered
indef abbr indefinite
in·de·fat·i·ga·ble \ˌin-di-ˈfa-ti-gə-bəl\ adj : UNTIRING
— **in·de·fat·i·ga·bly** \-blē\ adv
in·de·fea·si·ble \-ˈfē-zə-bəl\ adj : not capable of being
annulled or voided — **in·de·fea·si·bly** \-blē\ adv
in·de·fen·si·ble \-ˈfen-sə-bəl\ adj 1 : incapable of being
maintained as right or valid 2 : INEXCUSABLE 3 : incapable of being protected against physical attack
in·de·fin·able \-ˈfī-nə-bəl\ adj : incapable of being precisely described or analyzed — **in·de·fin·ably** \-blē\
adv
in·def·i·nite \(₁)in-ˈde-fə-nət\ adj 1 : not defining or
identifying ⟨an is an ∼ article⟩ 2 : not precise : VAGUE
3 : having no fixed limit — **in·def·i·nite·ly** adv — **in·def·i·nite·ness** n
in·del·i·ble \in-ˈde-lə-bəl\ adj [ME, fr. ML indelibilis,
alter. of L indelebilis, fr. delēre to delete, destroy] 1
: not capable of being removed or erased 2 : making
marks that cannot be erased 3 : LASTING, UNFORGET-
TABLE — **in·del·i·bly** \-ˈde-lə-blē\ adv
in·del·i·cate \(₁)in-ˈde-li-kət\ adj : not delicate; esp
: IMPROPER, COARSE, TACTLESS **syn** indecent, unseemly, indecorous, unbecoming — **in·del·i·ca·cy** \-ˈde-lə-kə-sē\ n
in·dem·ni·fy \in-ˈdem-nə-ˌfī\ vb **-fied; -fy·ing** [L in-
demnis unharmed, fr. in- not + damnum damage] 1
: to secure against hurt, loss, or damage 2 : to make
compensation to for hurt, loss, or damage — **in·dem·ni·fi·ca·tion** \-ˌdem-nə-fə-ˈkā-shən\ n
in·dem·ni·ty \in-ˈdem-nə-tē\ n, pl **-ties** 1 : security
against hurt, loss, or damage; also : exemption from
incurred penalties or liabilities 2 : something that in-
demnifies
¹**in·dent** \in-ˈdent\ vb [ME, fr. MF endenter, fr. OF, fr.
dent tooth, fr. L dent-, dens] 1 : to notch the edge of
2 : INDENTURE 3 : to set (as a line of a paragraph) in
from the margin
²**indent** vb 1 : to force inward so as to form a depression
2 : to form a dent in
in·den·ta·tion \ˌin-ˌden-ˈtā-shən\ n 1 : NOTCH; also: a
usu. deep recess (as in a coastline) 2 : the action of
indenting : the condition of being indented 3 : DENT
4 : INDENTION 2

in·den·tion \in-ˈden-chən\ *n* **1** : INDENTATION 2 **2** : the blank space produced by indenting

¹**in·den·ture** \in-ˈden-chər\ *n* **1** : a written certificate or agreement; *esp* : a contract binding one person (as an apprentice) to work for another for a given period of time — usu. used in pl. **2** : INDENTATION 1 **3** : DENT

²**indenture** *vb* **in·den·tured; in·den·tur·ing** : to bind (as an apprentice) by indentures

in·de·pen·dence \ˌin-də-ˈpen-dəns\ *n* : the quality or state of being independent : FREEDOM

Independence Day *n* : July 4 observed as a legal holiday in commemoration of the adoption of the Declaration of Independence in 1776

in·de·pen·dent \ˌin-də-ˈpen-dənt\ *adj* **1** : SELF-GOVERNING; *also* : not affiliated with a larger controlling unit **2** : not requiring or relying on something else or somebody else ⟨an ~ conclusion⟩ ⟨~ of her parents⟩ **3** : not easily influenced : showing self-reliance and personal freedom ⟨an ~ mind⟩ **4** : not committed to a political party ⟨an ~ voter⟩ **5** : MAIN ⟨an ~ clause⟩ — **independent** *n* — **in·de·pen·dent·ly** *adv*

in·de·scrib·able \ˌin-di-ˈskrī-bə-bəl\ *adj* **1** : that cannot be described **2** : being too intense or great for description — **in·de·scrib·ably** \-blē\ *adv*

in·de·ter·mi·nate \ˌin-di-ˈtər-mə-nət\ *adj* **1** : VAGUE; *also* : not known in advance **2** : not limited in advance; *also* : not leading to a definite end or result — **in·de·ter·mi·na·cy** \-nə-sē\ *n* — **in·de·ter·mi·nate·ly** *adv*

¹**in·dex** \ˈin-ˌdeks\ *n, pl* **in·dex·es** *or* **in·di·ces** \-də-ˌsēz\ **1** : POINTER **2** : SIGN, INDICATION ⟨an ~ of character⟩ **3** : a guide for facilitating references; *esp* : an alphabetical list of items treated in a printed work with the page number where each item may be found **4** : a list of restricted or prohibited material **5** *pl usu* **indices** : a number or symbol or expression (as an exponent) associated with another to indicate a mathematical operation or use or position in an arrangement or expansion **6** : a character ☞ used to direct attention (as to a note) **7** : INDEX NUMBER

²**index** *vb* **1** : to provide with or put into an index **2** : to serve as an index of **3** : to regulate by indexation

in·dex·ation \ˌin-ˌdek-ˈsā-shən\ *n* : a system of economic control in which a body of variables (as wages and interest) rise or fall at the same rate as an index of the cost of living

index finger *n* : FOREFINGER

in·dex·ing *n* : INDEXATION

index number *n* : a number used to indicate change in magnitude (as of cost) as compared with the magnitude at some specified time usu. taken as 100

index of refraction : the ratio of the speed of radiation in one medium to that in another medium

in·dia ink \ˈin-dē-ə-\ *n, often cap 1st I* **1** : a solid black pigment used in drawing **2** : a fluid made from india ink

In·di·an \ˈin-dē-ən\ *n* **1** : a native or inhabitant of the subcontinent of India **2** : a person of Indian descent **3** : AMERICAN INDIAN — **Indian** *adj*

Indian corn *n* : a tall widely grown American cereal grass bearing seeds on long ears; *also* : its ears or seeds

Indian meal *n* : CORNMEAL

Indian paintbrush *n* : any of a genus of herbaceous plants related to the snapdragon that have brightly colored bracts

Indian pipe *n* : a waxy white leafless saprophytic herb of Asia and the U.S.

Indian summer *n* : a period of mild weather in late autumn or early winter

In·dia paper \ˈin-dē-ə-\ *n* **1** : a thin absorbent paper used esp. for taking impressions (as of steel engravings) **2** : a thin tough opaque printing paper

indic *abbr* indicative

in·di·cate \ˈin-də-ˌkāt\ *vb* **-cat·ed; -cat·ing 1** : to point out or to **2** : to show indirectly **3** : to state briefly —

in·di·ca·tion \ˌin-də-ˈkā-shən\ *n* — **in·di·ca·tor** \ˈin-də-ˌkā-tər\ *n*

¹**in·dic·a·tive** \in-ˈdi-kə-tiv\ *adj* **1** : of, relating to, or being a verb form that represents an act or state as a fact ⟨~ mood⟩ **2** : serving to indicate ⟨actions ~ of fear⟩

²**indicative** *n* **1** : the indicative mood of a language **2** : a form in the indicative mood

in·di·cia \in-ˈdi-shə, -shē-ə\ *n pl* **1** : distinctive marks **2** : postal markings often imprinted on mail or mailing labels

in·dict \in-ˈdīt\ *vb* [alter. of earlier *indite*, fr. ME, fr. OF *enditer*, lit., to write down] **1** : to charge with a fault or offense **2** : to charge with a crime by the finding of a jury — **in·dict·able** *adj* — **in·dict·ment** *n*

in·dif·fer·ent \in-ˈdi-frənt, -fə-rənt\ *adj* **1** : UNBIASED, UNPREJUDICED **2** : of no importance one way or the other **3** : marked by no special liking for or dislike of something **4** : being neither excessive nor inadequate **5** : PASSABLE, MEDIOCRE **6** : being neither right nor wrong — **in·dif·fer·ence** \-frəns, -fə-rəns\ *n* — **in·dif·fer·ent·ly** *adv*

in·dig·e·nous \in-ˈdi-jə-nəs\ *adj* : produced, growing, or living naturally in a particular region

in·di·gent \ˈin-di-jənt\ *adj* : IMPOVERISHED, NEEDY — **in·di·gence** \-jəns\ *n*

in·di·gest·ible \ˌin-dī-ˈjes-tə-bəl, -də-\ *adj* : not readily digested

in·di·ges·tion \-ˈjes-chən\ *n* : inadequate or difficult digestion : DYSPEPSIA

in·dig·nant \in-ˈdig-nənt\ *adj* : filled with or marked by indignation — **in·dig·nant·ly** *adv*

in·dig·na·tion \ˌin-dig-ˈnā-shən\ *n* : anger aroused by something unjust, unworthy, or mean

in·dig·ni·ty \in-ˈdig-nə-tē\ *n, pl* **-ties** : an offense against personal dignity or self-respect; *also* : humiliating treatment

in·di·go \ˈin-di-ˌgō\ *n, pl* **-gos** *or* **-goes** [It dial., fr. L *indicum*, fr. Gk *indikon*, fr. *indikos* Indic, fr. *Indos* India] **1** : a blue dye obtained from plants or synthesized **2** : a deep reddish blue color

in·di·rect \ˌin-də-ˈrekt, -dī-\ *adj* **1** : not straight ⟨an ~ route⟩ **2** : not straightforward and open ⟨~ methods⟩ **3** : not having a plainly seen connection ⟨an ~ cause⟩ **4** : not directly to the point ⟨an ~ answer⟩ — **in·di·rec·tion** \-ˈrek-shən\ *n* — **in·di·rect·ly** *adv* — **in·di·rect·ness** *n*

in·dis·creet \ˌin-di-ˈskrēt\ *adj* : not discreet : IMPRUDENT — **in·dis·creet·ly** *adv*

in·dis·cre·tion \ˌin-di-ˈskre-shən\ *n* **1** : IMPRUDENCE **2** : something marked by lack of discretion; *esp* : an act deviating from accepted morality

in·dis·crim·i·nate \ˌin-di-ˈskri-mə-nət\ *adj* **1** : not marked by discrimination or careful distinction **2** : HAPHAZARD, RANDOM **3** : UNRESTRAINED **4** : MOTLEY — **in·dis·crim·i·nate·ly** *adv*

in·dis·pens·able \ˌin-di-ˈspen-sə-bəl\ *adj* : absolutely essential : REQUISITE — **in·dis·pens·abil·i·ty** \-ˌspen-sə-ˈbi-lə-tē\ *n* — **indispensable** *n* — **in·dis·pens·ably** \-ˈspen-sə-blē\ *adv*

in·dis·posed \-ˈspōzd\ *adj* **1** : slightly ill **2** : AVERSE — **in·dis·po·si·tion** \(ˌ)in-ˌdis-pə-ˈzi-shən\ *n*

in·dis·put·able \ˌin-di-ˈspyü-tə-bəl, (ˌ)in-ˈdis-pyə-\ *adj* : not disputable : UNQUESTIONABLE ⟨~ proof⟩ — **in·dis·put·ably** \-blē\ *adv*

in·dis·sol·u·ble \ˌin-di-ˈsäl-yə-bəl\ *adj* : not capable of being dissolved, undone, or broken : PERMANENT

in·dis·tinct \ˌin-di-ˈstiŋkt\ *adj* **1** : not sharply outlined or separable : BLURRED, FAINT, DIM **2** : not readily distinguishable : UNCERTAIN — **in·dis·tinct·ly** *adv* — **in·dis·tinct·ness** *n*

in·dite \in-ˈdīt\ *vb* **in·dit·ed; in·dit·ing** : COMPOSE ⟨~ a poem⟩; *also* : to put in writing ⟨~ a letter⟩

THE MOST IMPORTANT PART OF WRITING A BOOK IS PICKING A GOOD TITLE. I THINK I'LL CALL MINE "NIGHTS OF INDISCRETION"

NO, NO. A WRITER MUST WRITE SOMETHING HE KNOWS ABOUT

THAT'S IT! I'LL CALL IT "NIGHTS OF INDIGESTION"

© 1988 PAWS, INC.   JIM DAVIS 2-10

in·di·um \'in-dē-əm\ *n* : a malleable silvery metallic chemical element — see ELEMENT table

indiv *abbr* individual

¹in·di·vid·u·al \₁in-də-'vi-jə-wəl\ *adj* **1** : of, relating to, or associated with an individual ⟨∼ traits⟩ **2** : being an individual : existing as an indivisible whole **3** : intended for one person **4** : SEPARATE ⟨∼ copies⟩ **5** : having marked individuality ⟨an ∼ style⟩ — **in·di·vid·u·al·ly** *adv*

²individual *n* **1** : a single member of a category : a particular person, animal, or thing **2** : PERSON ⟨a disagreeable ∼⟩

in·di·vid·u·al·ise *Brit var of* INDIVIDUALIZE

in·di·vid·u·al·ism \₁in-də-'vi-jə-wə-₁li-zəm\ *n* **1** : a doctrine that the interests of the individual are primary **2** : a doctrine holding that the individual has political or economic rights with which the state must not interfere **3** : INDIVIDUALITY

in·di·vid·u·al·ist \-list\ *n* **1** : one that pursues a markedly independent course in thought or action **2** : one that advocates or practices individualism — **individualist** *or* **in·di·vid·u·al·is·tic** \-₁vi-jə-wə-'lis-tik\ *adj*

in·di·vid·u·al·i·ty \-₁vi-jə-'wa-lə-tē\ *n, pl* **-ties** **1** : the sum of qualities that characterize and distinguish an individual from all others; *also* : PERSONALITY **2** : separate or distinct existence **3** : INDIVIDUAL, PERSON

in·di·vid·u·al·ize \-'vi-jə-wə-₁līz\ *vb* **-ized; -iz·ing** **1** : to make individual in character **2** : to treat or notice individually : PARTICULARIZE **3** : to adapt to the needs of an individual

individual retirement account *n* : IRA

in·di·vid·u·ate \₁in-də-'vi-jə-₁wāt\ *vb* **-at·ed; -at·ing** : to give individuality to : form into an individual — **in·di·vid·u·a·tion** \-₁vi-jə-'wā-shən\ *n*

in·di·vis·i·ble \₁in-də-'vi-zə-bəl\ *adj* : impossible to divide or separate — **in·di·vis·i·bil·i·ty** \-₁vi-zə-'bi-lə-tē\ *n* — **in·di·vis·i·bly** *adv*

in·doc·tri·nate \in-'däk-trə-₁nāt\ *vb* **-nat·ed; -nat·ing** **1** : to instruct esp. in fundamentals or rudiments : TEACH **2** : to teach the beliefs and doctrines of a particular group — **in·doc·tri·na·tion** \(₁)in-₁däk-trə-'nā-shən\ *n* — **in·doc·tri·na·tor** *n*

In·do-Eu·ro·pe·an \₁in-dō-₁yùr-ə-'pē-ən\ *adj* : of, relating to, or constituting a family of languages comprising those spoken in most of Europe and in the parts of the world colonized by Europeans since 1500 and also in Persia, the subcontinent of India, and some other parts of Asia

in·do·lent \'in-də-lənt\ *adj* [LL *indolens* insensitive to pain, fr. L *dolēre* to feel pain] **1** : slow to develop or heal ⟨∼ ulcers⟩ **2** : LAZY — **in·do·lence** \-ləns\ *n* — **in·do·lent·ly** *adv*

in·dom·i·ta·ble \in-'dä-mə-tə-bəl\ *adj* : UNCONQUERABLE ⟨∼ courage⟩ — **in·dom·i·ta·bly** \-blē\ *adv*

In·do·ne·sian \₁in-də-'nē-zhən\ *n* : a native or inhabitant of the Republic of Indonesia — **Indonesian** *adj*

in·door \'in-₁dȯr\ *adj* **1** : of or relating to the inside of a building **2** : living, located, or carried on within a building

in·doors \in-'dȯrz\ *adv* : in or into a building

indorse *var of* ENDORSE

in·du·bi·ta·ble \(₁)in-'dü-bə-tə-bəl, -'dyü-\ *adj* : UNQUESTIONABLE — **in·du·bi·ta·bly** \-blē\ *adv*

in·duce \in-'düs, -'dyüs\ *vb* **in·duced; in·duc·ing** **1** : PERSUADE, INFLUENCE **2** : BRING ABOUT **3** : to produce (as an electric current) by induction **4** : to determine by induction; *esp* : to infer from particulars — **in·duc·er** *n*

in·duce·ment \-mənt\ *n* **1** : something that induces : MOTIVE **2** : the act or process of inducing

in·duct \in-'dəkt\ *vb* **1** : to place in office **2** : to admit as a member **3** : to enroll for military training or service — **in·duct·ee** \-₁dək-'tē\ *n*

in·duc·tance \in-'dək-təns\ *n* : a property of an electric circuit by which a varying current produces an electromotive force in that circuit or in a nearby circuit; *also* : the measure of this property

in·duc·tion \in-'dək-shən\ *n* **1** : the act or process of inducting; *also* : INITIATION **2** : the formality by which a civilian is inducted into military service **3** : inference of a generalized conclusion from particular instances; *also* : a conclusion so reached **4** : the act of causing or bringing on or about **5** : the process by which an electric current, an electric charge, or magnetism is produced in a body by the proximity of an electric or magnetic field

in·duc·tive \in-'dək-tiv\ *adj* : of, relating to, or employing induction

in·duc·tor \in-'dək-tər\ *n* : an electrical component that acts upon another or is itself acted upon by induction

in·dulge \in-'dəlj\ *vb* **in·dulged; in·dulg·ing** **1** : to give free rein to : GRATIFY **2** : HUMOR **3** : to gratify one's taste or desire for ⟨∼ in alcohol⟩

in·dul·gence \in-'dəl-jəns\ *n* **1** : remission of temporal punishment due in Roman Catholic doctrine for sins whose eternal punishment has been remitted by reception of the sacrifice of penance **2** : the act of indulging : the state of being indulgent **3** : an indulgent act **4** : the thing indulged in **5** : SELF-INDULGENCE — **in·dul·gent** \-jənt\ *adj* — **in·dul·gent·ly** *adv*

in·du·rat·ed \'in-dyù-₁rā-təd, -dù-\ *adj* : physically or emotionally hardened — **in·du·ra·tion** \₁in-dyù-'rā-shən, -dù-\ *n*

in·dus·tri·al \in-'dəs-trē-əl\ *adj* **1** : of or relating to industry; *also* : HEAVY-DUTY **2** : characterized by highly developed industries — **in·dus·tri·al·ly** *adv*

in·dus·tri·al·ise *Brit var of* INDUSTRIALIZE

in·dus·tri·al·ist \-ə-list\ *n* : a person owning or engaged in the management of an industry

in·dus·tri·al·ize \in-'dəs-trē-ə-₁līz\ *vb* **-ized; -iz·ing** : to make or become industrial — **in·dus·tri·al·i·za·tion** \-₁dəs-trē-ə-lə-'zā-shən\ *n*

in·dus·tri·ous \in-'dəs-trē-əs\ *adj* : DILIGENT, BUSY — **in·dus·tri·ous·ly** *adv* — **in·dus·tri·ous·ness** *n*

in·dus·try \'in-(₁)dəs-trē\ *n, pl* **-tries** **1** : DILIGENCE **2** : a department or branch of a craft, art, business, or manufacture; *esp* : one that employs a large personnel and capital **3** : a distinct group of productive enterprises **4** : manufacturing activity as a whole

in·dwell \(ˌ)in-ˈdwel\ *vb* : to exist within as an activating spirit or force

¹**in·e·bri·ate** \i-ˈnē-brē-ˌāt\ *vb* **-at·ed; -at·ing** : to make drunk : INTOXICATE — **in·e·bri·a·tion** \-ˌnē-brē-ˈā-shən\ *n*

²**in·e·bri·ate** \-ət\ *n* : one that is drunk; *esp* : DRUNKARD

in·ef·fa·ble \(ˌ)in-ˈe-fə-bəl\ *adj* **1** : incapable of being expressed in words : INDESCRIBABLE ⟨∼ joy⟩ **2** : UNSPEAKABLE ⟨∼ disgust⟩ **3** : not to be uttered : TABOO — **in·ef·fa·bly** \-blē\ *adv*

in·ef·fec·tive \ˌi-nə-ˈfek-tiv\ *adj* **1** : INEFFECTUAL **2** : not able to perform efficiently or as expected : INCAPABLE — **in·ef·fec·tive·ly** *adv* — **in·ef·fec·tive·ness** *n*

in·ef·fec·tu·al \-ˈfek-chə-wəl\ *adj* **1** : not producing the proper or usual effect **2** : INEFFECTIVE 2 — **in·ef·fec·tu·al·ly** *adv*

in·ef·fi·cient \ˌi-nə-ˈfi-shənt\ *adj* **1** : not producing the desired effect **2** : wasteful of time or energy **3** : INCAPABLE, INCOMPETENT — **in·ef·fi·cien·cy** \-ˈfi-shən-sē\ *n* — **in·ef·fi·cient·ly** *adv*

in·el·e·gant \(ˌ)i-ˈne-li-gənt\ *adj* : lacking in refinement, grace, or good taste — **in·el·e·gance** \-gəns\ *n* — **in·el·e·gant·ly** *adv*

in·el·i·gi·ble \(ˌ)i-ˈne-lə-jə-bəl\ *adj* : not qualified for an office or position — **in·el·i·gi·bil·i·ty** \(ˌ)i-ˌne-lə-jə-ˈbi-lə-tē\ *n*

in·eluc·ta·ble \ˌi-ni-ˈlək-tə-bəl\ *adj* : not to be avoided, changed, or resisted — **in·eluc·ta·bly** \-blē\ *adv*

in·ept \i-ˈnept\ *adj* **1** : lacking in fitness or aptitude : UNFIT **2** : FOOLISH **3** : being out of place : INAPPROPRIATE **4** : generally incompetent : BUNGLING — **inept·ly** *adv* — **in·ept·ness** *n*

in·ep·ti·tude \(ˌ)i-ˈnep-ti-ˌtüd, -ˌtyüd\ *n* : the quality or state of being inept; *esp* : INCOMPETENCE

in·equal·i·ty \ˌi-ni-ˈkwä-lə-tē\ *n* **1** : the quality of being unequal or uneven; *esp* : UNEVENNESS, DISPARITY **2** : an instance of being unequal

in·ert \i-ˈnərt\ *adj* [L *inert-, iners* unskilled, idle, fr. *art-, ars* skill] **1** : powerless to move **2** : SLUGGISH **3** : lacking in active properties ⟨chemically ∼⟩ — **inert·ly** *adv* — **in·ert·ness** *n*

in·er·tia \i-ˈnər-shə, -shē-ə\ *n* **1** : a property of matter whereby it remains at rest or continues in uniform motion unless acted upon by some outside force **2** : INERTNESS, SLUGGISHNESS — **in·er·tial** \-shəl\ *adj*

in·es·cap·able \ˌi-nə-ˈskä-pə-bəl\ *adj* : incapable of being escaped : INEVITABLE — **in·es·cap·ably** \-blē\ *adv*

in·es·ti·ma·ble \(ˌ)i-ˈnes-tə-mə-bəl\ *adj* **1** : incapable of being estimated or computed ⟨∼ errors⟩ **2** : too valuable or excellent to be fully appreciated — **in·es·ti·ma·bly** \-blē\ *adv*

in·ev·i·ta·ble \i-ˈne-və-tə-bəl\ *adj* : incapable of being avoided or evaded : bound to happen — **in·ev·i·ta·bil·i·ty** \(ˌ)i-ˌne-və-tə-ˈbi-lə-tē\ *n*

in·ev·i·ta·bly \-blē\ *adv* **1** : in an inevitable way **2** : as is to be expected

in·ex·act \ˌi-nig-ˈzakt\ *adj* **1** : not precisely correct or true : INACCURATE **2** : not rigorous and careful — **in·ex·act·ly** *adv* — **in·ex·act·ness** *n*

in·ex·cus·able \ˌi-nik-ˈskyü-zə-bəl\ *adj* : being without excuse or justification — **in·ex·cus·ably** \-blē\ *adv*

in·ex·haust·ible \ˌi-nig-ˈzò-stə-bəl\ *adj* **1** : incapable of being used up ⟨an ∼ supply⟩ **2** : UNTIRING — **in·ex·haust·ibly** \-blē\ *adv*

in·ex·o·ra·ble \(ˌ)i-ˈnek-sə-rə-bəl\ *adj* : not to be moved by entreaty : RELENTLESS — **in·ex·o·ra·bly** *adv*

in·ex·pe·ri·ence \ˌi-nik-ˈspir-ē-əns\ *n* : lack of experience or of knowledge gained by experience — **in·ex·pe·ri·enced** \-ənst\ *adj*

in·ex·pert \(ˌ)i-ˈnek-ˌspərt\ *adj* : not expert : UNSKILLED — **in·ex·pert·ly** *adv*

in·ex·pi·a·ble \(ˌ)i-ˈnek-spē-ə-bəl\ *adj* : not capable of being atoned for

in·ex·pli·ca·ble \ˌi-nik-ˈspli-kə-bəl, (ˌ)i-ˈnek-(ˌ)spli-\ *adj* : incapable of being explained or accounted for — **in·ex·pli·ca·bly** \-blē\ *adv*

in·ex·press·ible \-ˈspre-sə-bəl\ *adj* : not capable of being expressed — **in·ex·press·ibly** \-blē\ *adv*

in ex·tre·mis \ˌin-ik-ˈstrā-məs, -ˈstrē-\ *adv* : in extreme circumstances; *esp* : at the point of death

in·ex·tri·ca·ble \ˌi-nik-ˈstri-kə-bəl, (ˌ)i-ˈnek-(ˌ)stri-\ *adj* **1** : forming a maze or tangle from which it is impossible to get free **2** : incapable of being disentangled or untied — **in·ex·tri·ca·bly** \-blē\ *adv*

inf *abbr* **1** infantry **2** infinitive

in·fal·li·ble \(ˌ)in-ˈfa-lə-bəl\ *adj* **1** : incapable of error : UNERRING **2** : SURE, CERTAIN ⟨an ∼ remedy⟩ — **in·fal·li·bil·i·ty** \(ˌ)in-ˌfa-lə-ˈbi-lə-tē\ *n* — **in·fal·li·bly** \(ˌ)in-ˈfa-lə-blē\ *adv*

in·fa·mous \ˈin-fə-məs\ *adj* **1** : having a reputation of the worst kind **2** : DISGRACEFUL — **in·fa·mous·ly** *adv*

in·fa·my \-mē\ *n, pl* **-mies** **1** : evil reputation brought about by something grossly criminal, shocking, or brutal **2** : an extreme and publicly known criminal or evil act **3** : the state of being infamous

in·fan·cy \ˈin-fən-sē\ *n, pl* **-cies** **1** : early childhood **2** : a beginning or early period of existence

in·fant \ˈin-fənt\ *n* [ME *enfaunt*, fr. MF *enfant*, fr. L *infant-, infans*, adj., incapable of speech, young, fr. *fant-, fans*, prp. of *fari* to speak] : BABY; *also* : a person who is a legal minor

in·fan·ti·cide \in-ˈfan-tə-ˌsīd\ *n* : the killing of an infant

in·fan·tile \ˈin-fən-ˌtīl, -tᵊl, -ˌtēl\ *adj* : of or relating to infants; *also* : CHILDISH

infantile paralysis *n* : POLIOMYELITIS

in·fan·try \ˈin-fən-trē\ *n, pl* **-tries** [MF & It; MF *infanterie*, fr. It *infanteria*, fr. *infante* boy, foot soldier] : soldiers trained, armed, and equipped to fight on foot — **in·fan·try·man** \-mən\ *n*

in·farct \ˈin-ˌfärkt\ *n* [L *infarctus*, pp. of *infarcire* to stuff] : an area of dead tissue (as of the heart wall) caused by blocking of local blood circulation — **in·farc·tion** \in-ˈfärk-shən\ *n*

in·fat·u·ate \in-ˈfa-chə-ˌwāt\ *vb* **-at·ed; -at·ing** : to inspire with a foolish or extravagant love or admiration — **in·fat·u·a·tion** \-ˌfa-chə-ˈwā-shən\ *n*

in·fect \in-ˈfekt\ *vb* **1** : to contaminate with disease-producing matter **2** : to communicate a germ or disease to **3** : to cause to share one's feelings

in·fec·tion \in-ˈfek-shən\ *n* **1** : a disease or condition caused by a germ or parasite; *also* : such a germ or parasite **2** : an act or process of infecting — **in·fec·tious** \-shəs\ *adj* — **in·fec·tive** \-ˈfek-tiv\ *adj*

infectious mononucleosis *n* : an acute infectious disease characterized by fever, swelling of lymph glands, and increased numbers of lymph cells in the blood

in·fe·lic·i·tous \ˌin-fi-ˈli-sə-təs\ *adj* : not appropriate in application or expression — **in·fe·lic·i·ty** \-sə-tē\ *n*

in·fer \in-ˈfər\ *vb* **in·ferred; in·fer·ring** **1** : to derive as a conclusion from facts or premises **2** : GUESS, SURMISE **3** : to lead to as a conclusion or consequence **4** : HINT, SUGGEST **syn** deduce, conclude, judge, gather — **in·fer·ence** \ˈin-frəns, -fə-rəns\ *n* — **in·fer·en·tial** \ˌin-fə-ˈren-chəl\ *adj*

in·fe·ri·or \in-ˈfir-ē-ər\ *adj* **1** : situated lower down **2** : of low or lower degree or rank **3** : of lesser quality **4** : of little or less importance, value, or merit — **inferior** *n* — **in·fe·ri·or·i·ty** \(ˌ)in-ˌfir-ē-ˈòr-ə-tē\ *n*

in·fer·nal \in-ˈfərn-ᵊl\ *adj* **1** : of or relating to hell **2** : HELLISH, FIENDISH ⟨∼ schemes⟩ **3** : DAMNABLE ⟨an ∼ pest⟩ — **in·fer·nal·ly** *adv*

in·fer·no \in-ˈfər-nō\ *n, pl* **-nos** [It, hell, fr. LL *infernus* hell, fr. L, lower] : a place or a state that resembles or suggests hell; *also* : intense heat

in·fer·tile \(ˌ)in-ˈfərt-ᵊl\ *adj* : not fertile or productive : BARREN — **in·fer·til·i·ty** \ˌin-fər-ˈti-lə-tē\ *n*

in·fest \in-ˈfest\ *vb* : to trouble by spreading or swarming in or over; *also* : to live in or on as a parasite — **in·fes·ta·tion** \ˌin-ˌfes-ˈtā-shən\ *n*

in·fi·del \'in-fəd-ºl, -fə-ˌdel\ *n* **1** : one who is not a Christian or opposes Christianity **2** : an unbeliever esp. with respect to a particular religion

in·fi·del·i·ty \ˌin-fə-'de-lə-tē, -fī-\ *n, pl* **-ties 1** : lack of belief in a religion **2** : UNFAITHFULNESS, DISLOYALTY **3** : marital unfaithfulness or an instance of it

in·field \'in-ˌfēld\ *n* : the part of a baseball field inside the baselines — **in·field·er** *n*

in·fight·ing \'in-ˌfī-tiŋ\ *n* **1** : fighting at close quarters **2** : dissension or rivalry among members of a group

in·fil·trate \in-'fil-ˌtrāt, 'in-(ˌ)fil-\ *vb* **-trat·ed; -trat·ing 1** : to enter or filter into or through something **2** : to pass into or through by or as if by filtering or permeating — **in·fil·tra·tion** \ˌin-(ˌ)fil-'trā-shən\ *n* — **in·fil·tra·tor** *n*

in·fi·nite \'in-fə-nət\ *adj* **1** : LIMITLESS, BOUNDLESS, ENDLESS ⟨~ space⟩ **2** : VAST, IMMENSE; *also* : INEXHAUSTIBLE ⟨~ wealth⟩ **3** : greater than any preassigned finite value however large ⟨~ number of positive integers⟩; *also* : extending to infinity ⟨~ plane surface⟩ — **infinite** *n* — **in·fi·nite·ly** *adv*

in·fin·i·tes·i·mal \(ˌ)in-ˌfi-nə-'te-sə-məl\ *adj* : immeasurably or incalculably small — **in·fin·i·tes·i·mal·ly** *adv*

in·fin·i·tive \in-'fi-nə-tiv\ *n* : a verb form having the characteristics of both verb and noun and in English usu. being used with *to*

in·fin·i·tude \in-'fi-nə-ˌtüd, -ˌtyüd\ *n* **1** : the quality or state of being infinite **2** : something that is infinite esp. in extent

in·fin·i·ty \in-'fi-nə-tē\ *n, pl* **-ties 1** : the quality of being infinite **2** : unlimited extent of time, space, or quantity : BOUNDLESSNESS **3** : an indefinitely great number or amount

in·firm \in-'fərm\ *adj* **1** : deficient in vitality; *esp* : feeble from age **2** : weak of mind, will, or character : IRRESOLUTE **3** : not solid or stable : INSECURE

in·fir·ma·ry \in-'fər-mə-rē\ *n, pl* **-ries** : a place for the care of the infirm or sick

in·fir·mi·ty \in-'fər-mə-tē\ *n, pl* **-ties 1** : FEEBLENESS **2** : DISEASE, AILMENT **3** : a personal failing : FOIBLE

infl *abbr* influenced

in·flame \in-'flām\ *vb* **in·flamed; in·flam·ing 1** : KINDLE **2** : to excite to excessive or uncontrollable action or feeling; *also* : INTENSIFY **3** : to affect or become affected with inflammation

in·flam·ma·ble \in-'fla-mə-bəl\ *adj* **1** : FLAMMABLE **2** : easily inflamed, excited, or angered : IRASCIBLE

in·flam·ma·tion \ˌin-flə-'mā-shən\ *n* : a bodily response to injury in which an affected area becomes red, hot, and painful and congested with blood

in·flam·ma·to·ry \in-'fla-mə-ˌtōr-ē\ *adj* **1** : tending to excite the senses or to arouse anger, disorder, or tumult : SEDITIOUS **2** : causing or accompanied by inflammation ⟨an ~ disease⟩

in·flate \in-'flāt\ *vb* **in·flat·ed; in·flat·ing 1** : to swell with air or gas ⟨~ a balloon⟩ **2** : to puff up : ELATE **3** : to expand or increase abnormally ⟨~ prices⟩ — **in·flat·able** *adj*

in·fla·tion \in-'flā-shən\ *n* **1** : an act of inflating : the state of being inflated **2** : empty pretentiousness : POMPOSITY **3** : an increase in the volume of money and credit resulting in a continuing rise in the general price level

in·fla·tion·ary \-shə-ˌner-ē\ *adj* : of, characterized by, or productive of inflation

in·flect \in-'flekt\ *vb* **1** : to turn from a direct line or course : CURVE **2** : to vary a word by inflection **3** : to change or vary the pitch of the voice

in·flec·tion \in-'flek-shən\ *n* **1** : the act or result of curving or bending **2** : a change in pitch or loudness of the voice **3** : the change of form that words undergo to mark case, gender, number, tense, person, mood, or voice — **in·flec·tion·al** \-shə-nəl\ *adj*

in·flex·i·ble \(ˌ)in-'flek-sə-bəl\ *adj* **1** : UNYIELDING **2** : RIGID **3** : incapable of change — **in·flex·i·bil·i·ty**

\-ˌflek-sə-'bi-lə-tē\ *n* — **in·flex·i·bly** \-'flek-sə-blē\ *adv*

in·flex·ion \in-'flek-shən\ *chiefly Brit var of* INFLECTION

in·flict \in-'flikt\ *vb* : AFFLICT; *also* : to give by or as if by striking — **in·flic·tion** \-'flik-shən\ *n*

in·flo·res·cence \ˌin-flə-'res-ºns\ *n* : the manner of development and arrangement of flowers on a stem; *also* : a flowering stem with its appendages : a flower cluster

in·flow \'in-ˌflō\ *n* : a flowing in

¹in·flu·ence \'in-ˌflü-əns\ *n* **1** : the act or power of producing an effect without apparent force or direct authority **2** : the power or capacity of causing an effect in indirect or intangible ways ⟨under the ~ of liquor⟩ **3** : a person or thing that exerts influence — **in·flu·en·tial** \ˌin-flü-'en-chəl\ *adj*

²influence *vb* **-enced; -enc·ing 1** : to affect or alter by influence : SWAY **2** : to have an effect on the condition or development of : MODIFY

in·flu·en·za \ˌin-flü-'en-zə\ *n* [It, lit., influence, fr. ML *influentia;* fr. the belief that epidemics were due to the influence of the stars] : an acute and very contagious virus disease marked by fever, prostration, aches and pains, and respiratory inflammation; *also* : any of various feverish usu. virus diseases typically with respiratory symptoms

in·flux \'in-ˌfləks\ *n* : a coming in

in·fo \'in-(ˌ)fō\ *n* : INFORMATION

in·fold \in-'fōld\ *vb* **1** : ENFOLD **2** : to fold inward or toward one another

in·fo·mer·cial \'in-fō-ˌmər-shəl\ *n* : a television program that is an extended advertisement often including a discussion or demonstration

in·form \in-'fôrm\ *vb* **1** : to communicate knowledge to : TELL **2** : to give information or knowledge **3** : to act as an informer **syn** acquaint, apprise, advise, notify

in·for·mal \(ˌ)in-'fôr-məl\ *adj* **1** : conducted or carried out without formality or ceremony ⟨an ~ party⟩ **2** : characteristic of or appropriate to ordinary, casual, or familiar use ⟨~ clothes⟩ — **in·for·mal·i·ty** \ˌin-fôr-'ma-lə-tē, -fər-\ *n* — **in·for·mal·ly** \(ˌ)in-'fôr-mə-lē\ *adv*

in·for·mant \in-'fôr-mənt\ *n* : a person who gives information : INFORMER

in·for·ma·tion \ˌin-fər-'mā-shən\ *n* **1** : the communication or reception of knowledge or intelligence **2** : knowledge obtained from investigation, study, or instruction : FACTS, DATA — **in·for·ma·tion·al** \-shə-nəl\ *adj*

in·for·ma·tive \in-'fôr-mə-tiv\ *adj* : imparting knowledge : INSTRUCTIVE

in·formed \in-'fôrmd\ *adj* **1** : having or based on information **2** : EDUCATED, KNOWLEDGEABLE

informed consent *n* : consent to a medical procedure by someone who understands what is involved

in·form·er \-'for-mər\ *n* : one that informs; *esp* : a person who informs against others for illegalities esp. for financial gain

in·fo·tain·ment \ˌin-fō-'tān-mənt\ *n* : a television program that presents information (as news) in a manner intended to be entertaining

in·frac·tion \in-'frak-shən\ *n* [ME, fr. ML *infractio,* fr. L, subduing, fr. *infringere* to break, crush] : the act of infringing : VIOLATION

in·fra dig \ˌin-frə-'dig\ *adj* [short for L *infra dignitatem*] : being beneath one's dignity

in·fra·red \ˌin-frə-'red\ *adj* : being, relating to, or using radiation having wavelengths longer than those of red light — **infrared** *n*

in·fra·struc·ture \'in-frə-ˌstrək-chər\ *n* **1** : the underlying foundation or basic framework (as of a system or organization) **2** : the system of public works of a country, state, or region; *also* : the resources (as buildings or equipment) required for an activity

in·fre·quent \(¡)in-ˈfrē-kwənt\ adj 1 : seldom happening : RARE 2 : placed or occurring at wide intervals in space or time syn uncommon, scarce, sporadic — in·fre·quent·ly adv

in·fringe \in-ˈfrinj\ vb in·fringed; in·fring·ing 1 : VIOLATE, TRANSGRESS ⟨∼ a patent⟩ 2 : ENCROACH, TRESPASS — in·fringe·ment n

in·fu·ri·ate \in-ˈfyùr-ē-ˌāt\ vb -at·ed; -at·ing : to make furious : ENRAGE — in·fu·ri·at·ing·ly adv

in·fuse \in-ˈfyüz\ vb in·fused; in·fus·ing 1 : to instill a principle or quality in : INTRODUCE 2 : INSPIRE, ANIMATE 3 : to steep (as tea) without boiling — in·fu·sion \-ˈfyü-zhən\ n

¹-ing \iŋ\ n suffix 1 : action or process ⟨sleeping⟩ : instance of an action or process ⟨a meeting⟩ 2 : product or result of an action or process ⟨an engraving⟩ ⟨earnings⟩ 3 : something used in an action or process ⟨a bed covering⟩ 4 : something connected with, consisting of, or used in making ⟨a specified thing⟩ ⟨scaffolding⟩ 5 : something related to ⟨a specified concept⟩ ⟨offing⟩

²-ing n suffix : one of a (specified) kind

³-ing vb suffix or adj suffix — used to form the present participle ⟨sailing⟩ and sometimes to form an adjective resembling a present participle but not derived from a verb ⟨swashbuckling⟩

in·ga·ther \ˈin-ˌga-thər\ vb : to gather in : ASSEMBLE

in·ge·nious \in-ˈjēn-yəs\ adj 1 : marked by special aptitude at discovering, inventing, or contriving 2 : marked by originality, resourcefulness, and cleverness in conception or execution — in·ge·nious·ly adv — in·ge·nious·ness n

in·ge·nue or in·gé·nue \ˈan-jə-ˌnü, ˈän-; ˈaⁿ-zhə-, ˈäⁿ-\ n : a naive girl or young woman; esp : an actress portraying such a person

in·ge·nu·i·ty \ˌin-jə-ˈnü-ə-tē, -ˈnyü-\ n, pl -ties : skill or cleverness in planning or inventing : INVENTIVENESS

in·gen·u·ous \in-ˈjen-yə-wəs\ adj [L ingenuus native, freeborn, fr. gignere to beget] 1 : STRAIGHTFORWARD, FRANK 2 : NAIVE — in·gen·u·ous·ly adv — in·gen·u·ous·ness n

in·gest \in-ˈjest\ vb : to take in for or as if for digestion — in·ges·tion \-ˈjes-chən\ n

in·gle·nook \ˈiŋ-gəl-ˌnùk\ n : a nook by a large open fireplace; also : a bench occupying this nook

in·glo·ri·ous \(¡)in-ˈglōr-ē-əs\ adj 1 : SHAMEFUL 2 : not glorious : lacking fame or honor — in·glo·ri·ous·ly adv

in·got \ˈiŋ-gət\ n : a mass of metal cast in a form convenient for storage or transportation

¹in·grain \(¡)in-ˈgrān\ vb : to work indelibly into the natural texture or mental or moral constitution — in·grained adj

²in·grain \ˈin-ˌgrān\ adj 1 : made of fiber that is dyed before being spun into yarn 2 : made of yarn that is dyed before being woven or knitted 3 : INNATE — in·grain n

in·grate \ˈin-ˌgrāt\ n : an ungrateful person

in·gra·ti·ate \in-ˈgrā-shē-ˌāt\ vb -at·ed; -at·ing : to gain favor by deliberate effort

in·gra·ti·at·ing adj 1 : capable of winning favor

: PLEASING ⟨an ∼ smile⟩ 2 : FLATTERING ⟨an ∼ manner⟩

in·grat·i·tude \(¡)in-ˈgra-tə-ˌtüd, -ˌtyüd\ n : lack of gratitude : UNGRATEFULNESS

in·gre·di·ent \in-ˈgrē-dē-ənt\ n : one of the substances that make up a mixture or compound : CONSTITUENT

in·gress \ˈin-ˌgres\ n : ENTRANCE, ACCESS — in·gres·sion \in-ˈgre-shən\ n

in·grow·ing \ˈin-ˌgrō-iŋ\ adj : growing or tending inward

in·grown \-ˌgrōn\ adj : grown in; esp : having the free tip or edge embedded in the flesh ⟨∼ toenail⟩

in·gui·nal \ˈiŋ-gwən-ᵊl\ adj : of, relating to, or situated in or near the region of the groin

in·hab·it \in-ˈha-bət\ vb : to live or dwell in — in·hab·it·able adj

in·hab·i·tant \in-ˈha-bə-tənt\ n : a permanent resident in a place

in·hal·ant \in-ˈhā-lənt\ n : something (as a medicine) that is inhaled

in·ha·la·tor \ˈin-hə-ˌlā-tər\ n : a device that provides a mixture of carbon dioxide and oxygen for breathing

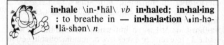

in·hale \in-ˈhāl\ vb in·haled; in·hal·ing : to breathe in — in·ha·la·tion \ˌin-hə-ˈlā-shən\ n

in·hal·er \in-ˈhā-lər\ n : a device by means of which medicinal material is inhaled

in·here \in-ˈhir\ vb in·hered; in·her·ing : to be inherent

in·her·ent \in-ˈhir-ənt, -ˈher-\ adj : established as an essential part of something : INTRINSIC — in·her·ent·ly adv

in·her·it \in-ˈher-ət\ vb : to receive esp. from one's ancestors — in·her·it·able \-ə-tə-bəl\ adj — in·her·i·tance \-ə-təns\ n — in·her·i·tor \-ə-tər\ n

in·hib·it \in-ˈhi-bət\ vb 1 : PROHIBIT, FORBID 2 : to hold in check : RESTRAIN

in·hi·bi·tion \ˌin-hə-ˈbi-shən\ n 1 : PROHIBITION, RESTRAINT 2 : a usu. inner check on free activity, expression, or functioning

in–house \ˈin-ˌhaùs, -ˈhaùs\ adj : existing, originating, or carried on within a group or organization

in·hu·man \(¡)in-ˈhyü-mən, -ˈyü-\ adj 1 : lacking pity, kindness, or mercy : SAVAGE 2 : COLD, IMPERSONAL 3 : not worthy of or conforming to the needs of human beings 4 : of or suggesting a nonhuman class of beings — in·hu·man·ly adv — in·hu·man·ness n

in·hu·mane \ˌin-hyü-ˈmān, -yü-\ adj : not humane : INHUMAN 1

in·hu·man·i·ty \-ˈma-nə-tē\ n, pl -ties 1 : the quality or state of being cruel or barbarous 2 : a cruel or barbarous act

in·im·i·cal \i-ˈni-mi-kəl\ adj 1 : being adverse often by reason of hostility 2 : HOSTILE, UNFRIENDLY — in·im·i·cal·ly adv

in·im·i·ta·ble \(ˌ)i-ˈni-mə-tə-bəl\ *adj* : not capable of being imitated

in·iq·ui·ty \i-ˈni-kwə-tē\ *n, pl* **-ties** [ME *iniquite*, fr. MF *iniquité*, fr. L *iniquitas*, fr. *iniquus* uneven, fr. *aequus* equal] **1** : WICKEDNESS **2** : a wicked act — **in·iq·ui·tous** \-təs\ *adj*

¹ini·tial \i-ˈni-shəl\ *adj* **1** : of or relating to the beginning : INCIPIENT **2** : FIRST — **ini·tial·ly** *adv*

²initial *n* : the first letter of a word or name

³initial *vb* **-tialed** *or* **-tialled; -tial·ing** *or* **-tial·ling** : to affix an initial to

¹ini·ti·ate \i-ˈni-shē-ˌāt\ *vb* **-at·ed; -at·ing 1** : START, BEGIN **2** : to induct into membership by or as if by special ceremonies **3** : to instruct in the rudiments or principles of something — **ini·ti·a·tion** \-ˌni-shē-ˈā-shən\ *n*

²ini·tiate \i-ˈni-shē-ət\ *n* **1** : a person who is undergoing or has passed an initiation **2** : a person who is instructed or adept in some special field

ini·tia·tive \i-ˈni-shə-tiv\ *n* **1** : an introductory step **2** : self-reliant enterprise ⟨showed great ∼⟩ **3** : a process by which laws may be introduced or enacted directly by vote of the people

ini·tia·to·ry \i-ˈni-shē-ə-ˌtōr-ē\ *adj* **1** : INTRODUCTORY **2** : tending or serving to initiate ⟨∼ rites⟩

in·ject \in-ˈjekt\ *vb* **1** : to force into something ⟨∼ serum with a needle⟩ **2** : to introduce as an element into some situation or subject ⟨∼ a note of suspicion⟩ — **in·jec·tion** \-ˈjek-shən\ *n*

in·junc·tion \in-ˈjəŋk-shən\ *n* **1** : ORDER, ADMONITION **2** : a court writ whereby one is required to do or to refrain from doing a specified act

in·jure \ˈin-jər\ *vb* **in·jured; in·jur·ing** : WRONG, DAMAGE, HURT **syn** harm, impair, mar, spoil

in·ju·ry \ˈin-jə-rē\ *n, pl* **-ries 1** : an act that damages or hurts : WRONG **2** : hurt, damage, or loss sustained — **in·ju·ri·ous** \in-ˈjùr-ē-əs\ *adj*

in·jus·tice \(ˌ)in-ˈjəs-təs\ *n* **1** : violation of a person's rights : UNFAIRNESS **2** : an unjust act or deed : WRONG

¹ink \ˈiŋk\ *n* [ME *enke*, fr. OF, fr. LL *encaustum*, fr. L *encaustus* burned in, fr. Gk *enkaustos*, fr. *enkaiein* to burn in] : a usu. liquid and colored material for writing and printing — **inky** *adj*

²ink *vb* : to put ink on; *esp* : SIGN

ink·blot test \ˈiŋk-ˌblät-\ *n* : any of several psychological tests based on the interpretation of irregular figures

ink·horn \-ˌhòrn\ *n* : a small bottle (as of horn) for holding ink

in–kind \ˈin-ˈkīnd\ *adj* : consisting of something (as goods) other than money

in·kling \ˈiŋ-kliŋ\ *n* **1** : HINT, INTIMATION **2** : a vague idea

ink·stand \ˈiŋk-ˌstand\ *n* : INKWELL; *also* : a pen and ink stand

ink·well \-ˌwel\ *n* : a container for ink

in·laid \ˈin-ˈlād\ *adj* : decorated with material set into a surface

¹in·land \ˈin-ˌland, -lənd\ *adj* **1** *chiefly Brit* : not foreign : DOMESTIC ⟨∼ revenue⟩ **2** : of or relating to the interior of a country

²inland *n* : the interior of a country

³inland *adv* : into or toward the interior

in–law \ˈin-ˌlò\ *n* : a relative by marriage

¹in·lay \(ˌ)in-ˈlā, ˈin-ˌlā\ *vb* **in·laid** \-ˈlād\; **in·lay·ing** : to set (a material) into a surface or ground material esp. for decoration

²in·lay \ˈin-ˌlā\ *n* **1** : inlaid work **2** : a shaped filling cemented into a tooth

in·let \ˈin-ˌlet, -lət\ *n* **1** : a small or narrow bay **2** : an opening for intake esp. of a fluid

in–line skate *n* : a roller skate whose four wheels are set in a straight line

in·mate \ˈin-ˌmāt\ *n* : any of a group occupying a single place of residence; *esp* : a person confined (as in a hospital or prison)

in me·di·as res \in-ˌmā-dē-əs-ˈrās\ *adv* [L, lit., into the midst of things] : in or into the middle of a narrative or plot

in me·mo·ri·am \ˌin-mə-ˈmōr-ē-əm\ *prep* [L] : in memory of

in·most \ˈin-ˌmōst\ *adj* : deepest within : INNERMOST

inn \ˈin\ *n* : HOTEL, TAVERN

in·nards \ˈi-nərdz\ *n pl* **1** : the internal organs of a human being or animal; *esp* : VISCERA **2** : the internal parts of a structure or mechanism

in·nate \i-ˈnāt\ *adj* **1** : existing in, belonging to, or determined by factors present in an individual from birth : NATIVE **2** : INHERENT, INTRINSIC — **in·nate·ly** *adv*

in·ner \ˈi-nər\ *adj* **1** : situated farther in ⟨the ∼ bark⟩ **2** : near a center esp. of influence ⟨the ∼ circle⟩ **3** : of or relating to the mind or spirit

inner city *n* : the usu. older, poorer, and more densely populated section of a city — **inner–city** *adj*

in·ner–di·rect·ed \ˌi-nər-də-ˈrek-təd, -(ˌ)dī-\ *adj* : directed in thought and action by one's own scale of values as opposed to external norms

inner ear *n* : the part of the ear that is most important for hearing, is located in a cavity in the temporal bone, and contains sense organs of hearing and of awareness of position in space

in·ner·most \ˈi-nər-ˌmōst\ *adj* : farthest inward : INMOST

in·ner·sole \ˈi-nər-ˈsōl\ *n* : INSOLE

in·ner·spring \ˈi-nər-ˈspriŋ\ *adj* : having coil springs inside a padded casing

inner tube *n* : an airtight rubber tube inside a tire to hold air under pressure

in·ning \ˈi-niŋ\ *n* **1** *sing or pl* : a division of a cricket match **2** : a baseball team's turn at bat; *also* : a division of a baseball game consisting of a turn at bat for each team

inn·keep·er \ˈin-ˌkē-pər\ *n* **1** : a proprietor of an inn **2** : a hotel manager

in·no·cence \ˈi-nə-səns\ *n* **1** : BLAMELESSNESS; *also*

| I, THE CAPED AVENGER, SHALL SEEK OUT INJUSTICE WHEREVER IT MAY LURK... | AND WITH ONE SWIFT MOTION OF MY MIGHTY HAND, I WILL GO... | NAUGHTY, NAUGHTY, NAUGHTY! |

: freedom from legal guilt **2** : GUILELESSNESS, SIMPLIC-
ITY; *also* : IGNORANCE
in·no·cent \-sənt\ *adj* [ME, fr. MF, fr. L *innocens*, fr.
nocens wicked, fr. *nocēre* to harm] **1** : free from guilt
or sin : BLAMELESS **2** : harmless in effect or intention;
also : CANDID **3** : free from legal guilt or fault : LAW-
FUL **4** : INGENUOUS **5** : UNAWARE — **innocent** *n* —
in·no·cent·ly *adv*
in·noc·u·ous \i-'nä-kyə-wəs\ *adj* **1** : HARMLESS **2** : not
offensive; *also* : INSIPID
in·nom·i·nate \i-'nä-mə-nət\ *adj* : having no name;
also : ANONYMOUS
in·no·vate \'i-nə-ˌvāt\ *vb* **-vat·ed; -vat·ing** : to introduce as or as if new : make changes — **in·no·va·
tive** \-ˌvā-tiv\ *adj* — **in·no·va·tor** \-ˌvā-tər\ *n*
in·no·va·tion \ˌi-nə-'vā-shən\ *n* **1** : the introduction of
something new **2** : a new idea, method, or device
in·nu·en·do \ˌin-yə-'wen-dō\ *n, pl* **-dos** *or* **-does** [L, by
hinting, fr. *innuere* to hint, fr. *nuere* to nod] : HINT,
INSINUATION; *esp* : a veiled reflection on character or
reputation
in·nu·mer·a·ble \i-'nü-mə-rə-bəl, -'nyü-\ *adj* : too
many to be numbered
in·oc·u·late \i-'nä-kyə-ˌlāt\ *vb* **-lat·ed; -lat·ing** [ME, to
insert a bud in a plant, fr. L *inoculare*, fr. *oculus* eye,
bud] : to introduce something into; *esp* : to introduce
a serum or antibody into (an organism) to treat or prevent a disease — **in·oc·u·la·tion** \-ˌnä-kyə-'lā-shən\ *n*
in·op·er·a·ble \(ˌ)i-'nä-pə-rə-bəl\ *adj* **1** : not suitable
for surgery **2** : not operable
in·op·er·a·tive \-'nä-pə-rə-tiv, -'nä-pə-ˌrā-\ *adj* : not
functioning
in·op·por·tune \(ˌ)i-ˌnä-pər-'tün, -'tyün\ *adj* : INCON-
VENIENT, INAPPROPRIATE — **in·op·por·tune·ly** *adv*
in·or·di·nate \i-'nȯrd-ᵊn-ət\ *adj* : exceeding reasonable
limits : IMMODERATE ⟨an ~ curiosity⟩ — **in·or·di·
nate·ly** *adv*
in·or·gan·ic \ˌi-ˌnȯr-'ga-nik\ *adj* : being or composed
of matter of other than plant or animal origin : MIN-
ERAL
in·pa·tient \'in-ˌpā-shənt\ *n* : a hospital patient who receives lodging and food as well as treatment
in·put \'in-ˌpu̇t\ *n* **1** : something put in **2** : power or energy put into a machine or system **3** : information fed
into a computer or data processing system **4** : AD-
VICE, OPINION — **input** *vb*
in·quest \'in-ˌkwest\ *n* **1** : an official inquiry or examination esp. before a jury **2** : INQUIRY, INVESTIGATION
in·qui·e·tude \(ˌ)in-'kwī-ə-ˌtüd, -ˌtyüd\ *n* : UNEASI-
NESS, RESTLESSNESS
in·quire \in-'kwīr\ *vb* **in·quired; in·quir·ing 1** : to ask
about : ASK **2** : INVESTIGATE, EXAMINE — **in·quir-
er** *n* — **in·quir·ing·ly** *adv*
in·qui·ry \'in-ˌkwīr-ē, in-'kwīr-ē; 'in-kwə-rē, 'iŋ-\ *n,
pl* **-ries** **1** : a request for information; *also* : RESEARCH
2 : a systematic investigation of a matter of public interest
in·qui·si·tion \ˌin-kwə-'zi-shən, ˌiŋ-\ *n* **1** : a judicial or
official inquiry usu. before a jury **2** *cap* : a former Roman Catholic tribunal for the discovery and punishment of heresy **3** : a severe questioning — **in·quis-
i·tor** \in-'kwi-zə-tər\ *n* — **in·quis·i·to·ri·al** \-ˌkwi-zə-
'tȯr-ē-əl\ *adj*
in·quis·i·tive \in-'kwi-zə-tiv\ *adj* **1** : given to examination or investigation ⟨an ~ mind⟩ **2** : unduly curious
— **in·quis·i·tive·ly** *adv* — **in·quis·i·tive·ness** *n*
in re \in-'rā, -'rē\ *prep* : in the matter of
INRI *abbr* [L *Iesus Nazarenus Rex Iudaeorum*] Jesus
of Nazareth, King of the Jews
in·road \'in-ˌrōd\ *n* **1** : INVASION, RAID **2** : ENCROACH-
MENT
in·rush \'in-ˌrəsh\ *n* : a crowding or flooding in
ins *abbr* **1** inches **2** insurance
INS *abbr* Immigration and Naturalization Service
in·sa·lu·bri·ous \ˌin-sə-'lü-brē-əs\ *adj* : UNWHOLE-
SOME, NOXIOUS

ins and outs *n pl* **1** : characteristic peculiarities **2**
: RAMIFICATIONS
in·sane \(ˌ)in-'sān\ *adj* **1** : exhibiting serious and debil-
itating mental disorder; *also* : used by or for the insane **2** : ABSURD — **in·sane·ly** *adv* — **in·san·i·ty** \in-
'sa-nə-tē\ *n*
in·sa·tia·ble \(ˌ)in-'sā-shə-bəl\ *adj* : incapable of being
satisfied — **in·sa·tia·bil·i·ty** \(ˌ)in-ˌsā-shə-'bi-lə-tē\ *n*
— **in·sa·tia·bly** *adv*
in·sa·tiate \(ˌ)in-'sā-shē-ət, -shət\ *adj* : INSATIABLE —
in·sa·tiate·ly *adv*
in·scribe \in-'skrīb\ *vb* **1** : to write, engrave, or print as
a lasting record **2** : ENROLL **3** : to write, engrave, or
print characters upon **4** : to dedicate to someone **5** : to
draw within a figure so as to touch in as many places
as possible — **in·scrip·tion** \-'skrip-shən\ *n*
in·scru·ta·ble \in-'skrü-tə-bəl\ *adj* : not readily com-
prehensible : MYSTERIOUS — **in·scru·ta·bly** \-blē\ *adv*
in·seam \'in-ˌsēm\ *n* : the seam on the inside of the leg
of a pair of pants; *also* : the length of this seam
in·sect \'in-ˌsekt\ *n* [L *insectum*, fr. *insectus*, pp. of *in-
secare* to cut into, fr. *secare* to cut] : any of a class
of small usu. winged arthropod animals (as flies,
bees, beetles, and moths) with usu. three pairs of legs
as adults
in·sec·ti·cide \in-'sek-tə-ˌsīd\ *n* : a preparation for destroying insects — **in·sec·ti·cid·al** \(ˌ)in-ˌsek-tə-'sīd-
ᵊl\ *adj*
in·sec·tiv·o·rous \ˌin-ˌsek-'ti-və-rəs\ *adj* : depending
on insects as food
in·se·cure \ˌin-si-'kyu̇r\ *adj* **1** : UNCERTAIN **2** : not protected : UNSAFE **3** : LOOSE, SHAKY **4** : not highly stable; *also* : lacking assurance : ANXIOUS, FEARFUL —
in·se·cure·ly *adv* — **in·se·cu·ri·ty** \-'kyu̇r-ə-tē\ *n*
in·sem·i·nate \in-'se-mə-ˌnāt\ *vb* **-nat·ed; -nat·ing** : to
introduce semen into the genital tract of (a female) —
in·sem·i·na·tion \-ˌse-mə-'nā-shən\ *n*
in·sen·sate \(ˌ)in-'sen-ˌsāt, -sət\ *adj* **1** : lacking sense
or understanding; *also* : FOOLISH **2** : INANIMATE **3**
: BRUTAL, INHUMAN ⟨~ rage⟩
in·sen·si·ble \(ˌ)in-'sen-sə-bəl\ *adj* **1** : IMPERCEPTIBLE;
also : SLIGHT, GRADUAL **2** : INANIMATE **3** : UNCON-
SCIOUS **4** : lacking sensory perception or ability to react ⟨~ to pain⟩ **5** : APATHETIC, INDIFFERENT; *also*
: UNAWARE ⟨~ of their danger⟩ **6** : MEANINGLESS **7**
: lacking delicacy or refinement — **in·sen·si·bil·i·ty**
\-ˌsen-sə-'bi-lə-tē\ *n* — **in·sen·si·bly** \-'sen-sə-blē\
adv
in·sen·tient \(ˌ)in-'sen-chē-ənt\ *adj* : lacking percep-
tion, consciousness, or animation — **in·sen·tience**
\-chē-əns\ *n*
in·sep·a·ra·ble \(ˌ)in-'se-prə-bəl, -pə-rə-\ *adj* : incapa-
ble of being separated or disjoined — **in·sep·a·ra·
bil·i·ty** \-ˌse-prə-'bi-lə-tē, -pə-rə-\ *n* — **inseparable**
— **in·sep·a·ra·bly** \-'se-prə-blē, -pə-rə-\ *adv*
¹in·sert \in-'sərt\ *vb* **1** : to put or thrust in ⟨~ a key in
a lock⟩ ⟨~ a comma⟩ **2** : INTERPOLATE **3** : to set in (as
a piece of fabric) and make fast
²in·sert \'in-ˌsərt\ *n* : something that is inserted or is for
insertion; *esp* : written or printed material inserted
(as between the leaves of a book)
in·ser·tion \in-'sər-shən\ *n* **1** : something that is inserted **2** : the act or process of inserting
in·set \'in-ˌset\ *vb* **inset** *or* **in·set·ted; in·set·ting** : to set
in : INSERT — **inset** *n*
¹in·shore \'in-'shȯr\ *adj* **1** : situated, living, or carried
on near shore **2** : moving toward shore
²inshore *adv* : to or toward shore
¹in·side \in-'sīd, 'in-ˌsīd\ *n* **1** : an inner side or surface
: INTERIOR **2** : inward nature, thoughts, or feeling **3** *pl*
: VISCERA, ENTRAILS **4** : a position of power, trust, or
familiarity — **inside** *adj*
²inside *adv* **1** : on the inner side **2** : in or into the interior
³inside *prep* **1** : in or into the inside of **2** : WITHIN ⟨~
an hour⟩
inside of *prep* : INSIDE

in·sid·er \in-ˈsī-dər\ n : a person who is in a position of power or has access to confidential information

in·sid·i·ous \in-ˈsi-dē-əs\ adj [L insidiosus, fr. insidiae ambush, fr. insidēre to sit in, sit on, fr. sedēre to sit] 1 : SLY, TREACHEROUS 2 : SEDUCTIVE 3 : having a gradual and cumulative effect : SUBTLE — **in·sid·i·ous·ly** adv — **in·sid·i·ous·ness** n

in·sight \ˈin-ˌsīt\ n : the power, act, or result of seeing into a situation : UNDERSTANDING, PENETRATION — **in·sight·ful** \ˈin-ˌsīt-fəl, in-ˈsīt-\ adj

in·sig·nia \in-ˈsig-nē-ə\ or **in·sig·ne** \-(ˌ)nē\ n, pl **-nia** or **-ni·as** : a distinguishing mark esp. of authority or honor : BADGE

in·sin·cere \ˌin-sin-ˈsir\ adj : not sincere : HYPOCRITICAL — **in·sin·cere·ly** adv — **in·sin·cer·i·ty** \-ˈser-ə-tē\ n

in·sin·u·ate \in-ˈsin-yə-ˌwāt\ vb **-at·ed; -at·ing** [L insinuare, fr. sinuare to bend, curve, fr. sinus curve] 1 : to introduce gradually or in a subtle, indirect, or artful way 2 : to imply in a subtle or devious way — **in·sin·u·a·tion** \(ˌ)in-ˌsin-yə-ˈwā-shən\ n

in·sin·u·at·ing adj 1 : winning favor and confidence by imperceptible degrees 2 : tending gradually to cause doubt, distrust, or change of outlook

in·sip·id \in-ˈsi-pəd\ adj 1 : lacking taste or savor 2 : DULL, FLAT — **in·si·pid·i·ty** \ˌin-sə-ˈpi-də-tē\ n

in·sist \in-ˈsist\ vb [MF or L; MF insister, fr. L insistere to stand upon, persist, fr. sistere to take a stand] : to take a resolute stand

in·sis·tence \in-ˈsis-təns\ n : the act of insisting; also : an insistent attitude or quality : URGENCY

in·sis·tent \in-ˈsis-tənt\ adj : disposed to insist — **in·sis·tent·ly** adv

in si·tu \in-ˈsī-tü, -ˈsē-\ adv or adj [L, in position] : in the natural or original position

in·so·far as \ˌin-sə-ˈfär-\ conj : to the extent or degree that

insol abbr insoluble

in·so·la·tion \ˌin-(ˌ)sō-ˈlā-shən\ n : solar radiation that has been received

in·sole \ˈin-ˌsōl\ n 1 : an inside sole of a shoe 2 : a loose thin strip placed inside a shoe for warmth or comfort

in·so·lent \ˈin-sə-lənt\ adj : contemptuous, rude, disrespectful, or bold in behavior or language — **in·so·lence** \-ləns\ n

in·sol·u·ble \(ˌ)in-ˈsäl-yə-bəl\ adj 1 : having or admitting of no solution or explanation 2 : difficult or impossible to dissolve — **in·sol·u·bil·i·ty** \-ˌsäl-yə-ˈbi-lə-tē\ n

in·sol·vent \(ˌ)in-ˈsäl-vənt\ adj 1 : unable or insufficient to pay all debts ⟨an ∼ estate⟩ 2 : IMPOVERISHED, DEFICIENT — **in·sol·ven·cy** \-vən-sē\ n

in·som·nia \in-ˈsäm-nē-ə\ n : prolonged and usu. abnormal sleeplessness

in·so·much as \ˌin-sə-ˈməch-\ conj : INASMUCH AS

insomuch that conj : to such a degree that : SO

in·sou·ci·ance \in-ˈsü-sē-əns, aⁿ-süs-ˈyäⁿs\ n [F] : lighthearted unconcern — **in·sou·ci·ant** \in-ˈsü-sē-ənt, aⁿ-süs-ˈyäⁿ\ adj

insp abbr inspector

in·spect \in-ˈspekt\ vb : to view closely and critically : EXAMINE — **in·spec·tion** \-ˈspek-shən\ n — **in·spec·tor** \-tər\ n

inspector general n : the head of a system of inspection (as of an army)

in·spi·ra·tion \ˌin-spə-ˈrā-shən\ n 1 : the act or power of moving the intellect or emotions 2 : INHALATION 3 : the quality or state of being inspired; also : something that is inspired 4 : an inspiring agent or influence — **in·spi·ra·tion·al** \-shə-nəl\ adj

in·spire \in-ˈspīr\ vb **in·spired; in·spir·ing** 1 : to influence, move, or guide by divine or supernatural inspiration 2 : exert an animating, enlivening, or exalting influence upon; also : AFFECT 3 : to communicate to an agent supernaturally; also : bring out or about 4 : INHALE 5 : INCITE 6 : to spread by indirect means — **in·spir·er** n

in·spir·it \in-ˈspir-ət\ vb : ENCOURAGE, HEARTEN

inst abbr 1 instant 2 institute; institution; institutional

in·sta·bil·i·ty \ˌin-stə-ˈbi-lə-tē\ n : lack of steadiness; esp : lack of emotional or mental stability

in·stall or **in·stal** \in-ˈstól\ vb **in·stalled; in·stall·ing** 1 : to place formally in office : induct into an office, rank, or order 2 : to establish in an indicated place, condition, or status 3 : to set up for use or service — **in·stal·la·tion** \ˌin-stə-ˈlā-shən\ n

¹**in·stall·ment** also **in·stal·ment** \in-ˈstól-mənt\ n : INSTALLATION

²**installment** also **instalment** n 1 : one of the parts into which a debt or sum is divided for payment 2 : one of several parts presented at intervals

¹**in·stance** \ˈin-stəns\ n 1 : INSTIGATION, REQUEST 2 : EXAMPLE ⟨for ∼⟩ 3 : an event or step that is part of a process or series **syn** case, illustration, sample, specimen

²**instance** vb **in·stanced; in·stanc·ing** : to mention as a case or example

¹**in·stant** \ˈin-stənt\ n 1 : MOMENT ⟨the ∼ we met⟩ 2 : the present or current month

²**instant** adj 1 : URGENT 2 : PRESENT, CURRENT 3 : IMMEDIATE ⟨∼ relief⟩ 4 : premixed or precooked for easy final preparation ⟨∼ cake mix⟩; also : immediately soluble in water ⟨∼ coffee⟩

in·stan·ta·neous \ˌin-stən-ˈtā-nē-əs\ adj : done or occurring in an instant or without delay — **in·stan·ta·neous·ly** adv

in·stan·ter \in-ˈstan-tər\ adv : at once

in·stan·ti·ate \in-ˈstan-chē-ˌāt\ vb **-at·ed; -at·ing** : to represent (an abstraction) by a concrete example — **in·stan·ti·a·tion** \-ˌstan-chē-ˈā-shən\ n

in·stant·ly \ˈin-stənt-lē\ adv : at once : IMMEDIATELY

in·state \in-ˈstāt\ vb : to establish in a rank or office : INSTALL

in·stead \in-ˈsted\ adv 1 : as a substitute or equivalent 2 : as an alternative : RATHER

instead of *prep* : as a substitute for or alternative to
in·step \'in-₁step\ *n* : the arched part of the human foot in front of the ankle joint; *esp* : its upper surface

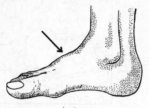

instep

in·sti·gate \'in-stə-₁gāt\ *vb* **-gat·ed; -gat·ing** : to goad or urge forward : PROVOKE, INCITE ⟨∼ a revolt⟩ — **in·sti·ga·tion** \₁in-stə-'gā-shən\ *n* — **in·sti·ga·tor** \'in-stə-₁gā-tər\ *n*
in·still *also* **in·stil** \in-'stil\ *vb* **in·stilled; in·still·ing 1** : to cause to enter drop by drop **2** : to impart gradually
¹**in·stinct** \'in-₁stiŋkt\ *n* **1** : a natural aptitude **2** : a largely inheritable and unalterable tendency of an organism to make a complex and specific response to environmental stimuli without involving reason; *also* : behavior originating below the conscious level — **in·stinc·tive** \in-'stiŋk-tiv\ *adj* — **in·stinc·tive·ly** *adv*
²**in·stinct** \in-'stiŋkt, 'in-₁stiŋkt\ *adj* : IMBUED, INFUSED
in·stinc·tu·al \in-'stiŋk-chə-wəl\ *adj* : of, relating to, or based on instinct
¹**in·sti·tute** \'in-stə-₁tüt, -₁tyüt\ *vb* **-tut·ed; -tut·ing 1** : to establish in a position or office **2** : ORGANIZE **3** : INAUGURATE, INITIATE
²**institute** *n* **1** : an elementary principle recognized as authoritative; *also, pl* : a collection of such principles and precepts **2** : an organization for the promotion of a cause : ASSOCIATION : an educational institution **4** : a brief course of instruction on a particular field
in·sti·tu·tion \₁in-stə-'tü-shən, -'tyü-\ *n* **1** : an act of originating, setting up, or founding **2** : an established practice, law, or custom **3** : a society or corporation esp. of a public character ⟨a charitable ∼⟩; *also* : ASYLUM **3** — **in·sti·tu·tion·al** \-'tü-shə-nəl, -'tyü-\ *adj* — **in·sti·tu·tion·al·ize** \-nə-₁līz\ *vb* — **in·sti·tu·tion·al·ly** *adv*
instr *abbr* **1** instructor **2** instrument; instrumental
in·struct \in-'strəkt\ *vb* [ME, fr. L *instructus*, pp. of *instruere*, fr. *struere* to build] **1** : TEACH **2** : INFORM **3** : to give an order or a command to
in·struc·tion \in-'strək-shən\ *n* **1** : LESSON, PRECEPT **2** : COMMAND, ORDER **3** *pl* : DIRECTIONS **4** : the action, practice, or profession of a teacher — **in·struc·tion·al** \-shə-nəl\ *adj*
in·struc·tive \in-'strək-tiv\ *adj* : carrying a lesson : ENLIGHTENING
in·struc·tor \in-'strək-tər\ *n* : one that instructs; *esp* : a

college teacher below professorial rank — **in·struc·tor·ship** *n*

in·stru·ment \'in-strə-mənt\ *n* **1** : a device used to produce music **2** : a means by which something is done **3** : a device for doing work and esp. precision work **4** : a legal document (as a deed) **5** : a device used in navigating an airplane — **in·stru·ment** \-₁ment\ *vb*

in·stru·men·tal \₁in-strə-'ment-ºl\ *adj* **1** : acting as an agent or means **2** : of, relating to, or done with an instrument **3** : relating to, composed for, or performed on a musical instrument
in·stru·men·tal·ist \-'men-tə-list\ *n* : a player on a musical instrument
in·stru·men·tal·i·ty \₁in-strə-mən-'ta-lə-tē, -₁men-\ *n, pl* **-ties 1** : the quality or state of being instrumental **2** : MEANS, AGENCY
in·stru·men·ta·tion \₁in-strə-mən-'tā-shən, -₁men-\ *n* **1** : ORCHESTRATION **2** : instruments for a particular purpose
instrument panel *n* : DASHBOARD
in·sub·or·di·nate \₁in-sə-'bord-ºn-ət\ *adj* : disobedient to authority — **in·sub·or·di·na·tion** \-₁bord-ºn-'ā-shən\ *n*
in·sub·stan·tial \₁in-səb-'stan-chəl\ *adj* **1** : lacking substance or reality **2** : lacking firmness or solidity
in·suf·fer·able \(₁)in-'sə-fə-rə-bəl\ *adj* : not to be endured : INTOLERABLE ⟨an ∼ bore⟩ — **in·suf·fer·ably** \-blē\ *adv*
in·suf·fi·cient \₁in-sə-'fi-shənt\ *adj* : not sufficient; *also* : INCOMPETENT — **in·suf·fi·cien·cy** \-shən-sē\ *n* — **in·suf·fi·cient·ly** *adv*
in·su·lar \'in-sə-lər, -syə-\ *adj* **1** : of, relating to, or forming an island **2** : dwelling or situated on an island **3** : NARROW-MINDED — **in·su·lar·i·ty** \₁in-sə-'lar-ə-tē, -syə-\ *n*
in·su·late \'in-sə-₁lāt\ *vb* **-lat·ed; -lat·ing** [L *insula* island] : ISOLATE; *esp* : to separate a conductor of electricity, heat, or sound from other conducting bodies by means of a nonconductor — **in·su·la·tion** \₁in-sə-'lā-shən\ *n* — **in·su·la·tor** \'in-sə-₁lā-tər\ *n*
in·su·lin \'in-sə-lən\ *n* : a pancreatic hormone essential esp. for the metabolism of carbohydrates and used in the control of diabetes mellitus
¹**in·sult** \in-'səlt\ *vb* [MF or L; MF *insulter*, fr. L *insultare*, lit., to spring upon, fr. *saltare* to leap] : to treat with insolence or contempt : AFFRONT — **in·sult·ing·ly** *adv*
²**in·sult** \'in-₁səlt\ *n* : a gross indignity
in·su·per·a·ble \(₁)in-'sü-pə-rə-bəl\ *adj* : incapable of being surmounted, overcome, passed over, or solved — **in·su·per·a·bly** \-blē\ *adv*
in·sup·port·able \₁in-sə-'pōr-tə-bəl\ *adj* **1** : UNENDURABLE **2** : UNJUSTIFIABLE
in·sur·able \in-'shù-rə-bəl\ *adj* : capable of being or proper to be insured
in·sur·ance \in-'shùr-əns\ *n* **1** : the business of insuring

persons or property **2** : coverage by contract whereby one party agrees to guarantee another against a specified loss **3** : the sum for which something is insured **4** : a means of guaranteeing protection or safety

in·sure \in-'shŭr\ *vb* **in·sured; in·sur·ing 1** : to provide or obtain insurance on or for : UNDERWRITE **2** : to make certain : ENSURE

in·sured \in-'shŭrd\ *n* : a person whose life or property is insured

in·sur·er \in-'shŭr-ər\ *n* : one that insures; *esp* : an insurance company

in·sur·gent \in-'sər-jənt\ *n* **1** : a person who revolts against civil authority or an established government : REBEL **2** : a member of a political party who rebels against it — **in·sur·gence** \-jəns\ *n* — **in·sur·gen·cy** \-jən-sē\ *n* — **insurgent** *adj*

in·sur·mount·able \ˌin-sər-maŭn-tə-bəl\ *adj* : INSUPERABLE — **in·sur·mount·ably** \-blē\ *adv*

in·sur·rec·tion \ˌin-sə-'rek-shən\ *n* : an act or instance of revolting against civil authority or an established government — **in·sur·rec·tion·ist** \-shə-nist\ *n*

int *abbr* **1** interest **2** interior **3** intermediate **4** internal **5** international **6** intransitive

in·tact \in-'takt\ *adj* : untouched esp. by anything that harms or diminishes

in·ta·glio \in-'tal-yō\ *n, pl* **-glios** [It] : an engraving cut deeply into the surface of a hard material (as stone)

in·take \'in-ˌtāk\ *n* **1** : an opening through which fluid enters **2** : the act of taking in **3** : something taken in

in·tan·gi·ble \(ˌ)in-'tan-jə-bəl\ *adj* : incapable of being touched : IMPALPABLE — **intangible** *n* — **in·tan·gi·bly** \-blē\ *adv*

in·te·ger \'in-ti-jər\ *n* [L, adj., whole, entire] : a number (as 1, 2, 3, 12, 432) that is not a fraction and does not include a fraction, is the negative of such a number, or is 0

in·te·gral \'in-ti-grəl\ *adj* **1** : essential to completeness **2** : formed as a unit with another part **3** : composed of parts that make up a whole **4** : ENTIRE

integral calculus *n* : calculus concerned esp. with advanced methods of finding lengths, areas, and volumes

in·te·grate \'in-tə-ˌgrāt\ *vb* **-grat·ed; -grat·ing 1** : to form, coordinate, or blend into a functioning whole : UNITE **2** : to incorporate into a larger unit **3** : to end the segregation of and bring into equal membership in society or an organization; *also* : DESEGREGATE — **in·te·gra·tion** \ˌin-tə-'grā-shən\ *n*

integrated circuit *n* : a group of tiny electronic components and their connections that is produced in or on a small slice of material (as silicon)

in·teg·ri·ty \in-'te-grə-tē\ *n* **1** : adherence to a code of values : INCORRUPTIBILITY **2** : SOUNDNESS **3** : COMPLETENESS

in·teg·u·ment \in-'te-gyə-mənt\ *n* : a covering layer (as a skin or cuticle) of an organism

in·tel·lect \'int-əl-ˌekt\ *n* **1** : the power of knowing : the capacity for knowledge **2** : the capacity for rational or intelligent thought esp. when highly developed **3** : a person with great intellectual powers

in·tel·lec·tu·al \ˌint-əl-'ek-chə-wəl\ *adj* **1** : of, relating to, or performed by the intellect : RATIONAL **2** : given to study, reflection, and speculation **3** : engaged in activity requiring the creative use of the intellect — **intellectual** *n* — **in·tel·lec·tu·al·ly** *adv*

in·tel·lec·tu·al·ism \-chə-wə-ˌli-zəm\ *n* : devotion to the exercise of intellect or to intellectual pursuits

in·tel·li·gence \in-'te-lə-jəns\ *n* **1** : ability to learn and understand or to deal with new or trying situations **2** : mental acuteness **3** : INFORMATION, NEWS **4** : an agency engaged in obtaining information esp. concerning an enemy or possible enemy; *also* : the information so gained

intelligence quotient *n* : a number often used as a measure of a person's intelligence

in·tel·li·gent \in-'te-lə-jənt\ *adj* [L *intelligens*, fr. *intel-*

ligere to understand, fr. *inter* between + *legere* to select] : having or showing intelligence or intellect — **in·tel·li·gent·ly** *adv*

in·tel·li·gen·tsia \in-ˌte-lə-'jent-sē-ə, -'gent-\ *n* [Russ *intelligentsiya*, fr. L *intelligentia* intelligence] : intellectuals forming a vanguard or elite

in·tel·li·gi·ble \in-'te-lə-jə-bəl\ *adj* : capable of being understood or comprehended — **in·tel·li·gi·bil·i·ty** \-ˌte-lə-jə-'bi-lə-tē\ *n* — **in·tel·li·gi·bly** \-'te-lə-jə-blē\ *adv*

in·tem·per·ance \(ˌ)in-'tem-pə-rəns\ *n* : lack of moderation; *esp* : habitual or excessive drinking of intoxicants — **in·tem·per·ate** \-pə-rət\ *adj* — **in·tem·per·ate·ness** *n*

in·tend \in-'tend\ *vb* [ME *entenden, intenden*, fr. MF *entendre* to purpose, fr. L *intendere* to stretch out, aim at, fr. *tendere* to stretch] **1** : to have in mind as a purpose or aim **2** : to design for a specified use or future

in·ten·dant \in-'ten-dənt\ *n* : an official (as a governor) esp. under the French, Spanish, or Portuguese monarchies

¹**in·tend·ed** *adj* **1** : expected to be such in the future; *esp* : BETROTHED **2** : INTENTIONAL

²**intended** *n* : an engaged person

in·tense \in-'tens\ *adj* **1** : existing in an extreme degree **2** : marked by great zeal, energy, or eagerness **3** : showing strong feeling; *also* : deeply felt — **in·tense·ly** *adv*

in·ten·si·fy \in-'ten-sə-ˌfī\ *vb* **-fied; -fy·ing 1** : to make or become intense or more intensive **2** : to make more acute : SHARPEN **syn** aggravate, heighten, enhance, magnify — **in·ten·si·fi·ca·tion** \-ˌten-sə-fə-'kā-shən\ *n*

in·ten·si·ty \in-'ten-sə-tē\ *n, pl* **-ties 1** : the quality or state of being intense; *esp* : degree of strength, energy, or force

¹**in·ten·sive** \in-'ten-siv\ *adj* **1** : highly concentrated **2** : serving to give emphasis — **in·ten·sive·ly** *adv*

²**intensive** *n* : an intensive word, particle, or prefix

intensive care *n* : special medical equipment and services for taking care of seriously ill patients ⟨an *intensive care* unit⟩

¹**in·tent** \in-'tent\ *n* **1** : the state of mind with which an act is done : VOLITION **2** : PURPOSE, AIM **3** : MEANING, SIGNIFICANCE

²**intent** *adj* **1** : directed with keen attention ⟨an ∼ gaze⟩ **2** : ENGROSSED; *also* : DETERMINED — **in·tent·ly** *adv* — **in·tent·ness** *n*

in·ten·tion \in-'ten-chən\ *n* **1** : a determination to act in a certain way **2** : PURPOSE, AIM, END **syn** intent, design, object, objective, goal

in·ten·tion·al \in-'ten-chə-nəl\ *adj* : done by intention or design : INTENDED — **in·ten·tion·al·ly** *adv*

in·ter \in-'tər\ *vb* **-terred; -ter·ring** : BURY

in·ter·ac·tion \ˌin-tər-'ak-shən\ *n* : mutual or reciprocal action or influence — **in·ter·act** \-'akt\ *vb*

in·ter·ac·tive \-'ak-tiv\ *adj* **1** : mutually or reciprocally active **2** : allowing two-way electronic communications (as between a person and a computer) — **in·ter·ac·tive·ly** *adv*

in·ter alia \ˌin-tər-'ä-lē-ə, -'ä-\ *adv* : among other things

in·ter·atom·ic \ˌin-tər-ə-'tä-mik\ *adj* : existing or acting between atoms

in·ter·breed \-'brēd\ *vb* **-bred** \-'bred\; **-breed·ing** : to breed together

in·ter·ca·la·ry \in-'tər-kə-ˌler-ē\ *adj* **1** : INTERCALATED ⟨February 29 is an ∼ day⟩ **2** : INTERPOLATED

in·ter·ca·late \-ˌlāt\ *vb* **-lat·ed; -lat·ing 1** : to insert (as a day) in a calendar **2** : to insert between or among existing elements or layers — **in·ter·ca·la·tion** \-ˌtər-kə-'lā-shən\ *n*

in·ter·cede \ˌin-tər-'sēd\ *vb* **-ced·ed; -ced·ing** : to act between parties with a view to reconciling differences

¹**in·ter·cept** \ˌin-tər-ˈsept\ *vb* **1** : to stop or interrupt the progress or course of **2** : to include (as part of a curve or solid) between two points, curves, or surfaces **3** : to gain possession of (an opponent's pass in football) — **in·ter·cep·tion** \-ˈsep-shən\ *n*

²**in·ter·cept** \ˈin-tər-ˌsept\ *n* : INTERCEPTION; *esp* : the interception of a target by an interceptor or missile

in·ter·cep·tor \ˌin-tər-ˈsep-tər\ *n* : a fighter plane designed for defense against attacking bombers

in·ter·ces·sion \ˌin-tər-ˈse-shən\ *n* **1** : MEDIATION **2** : prayer or petition in favor of another — **in·ter·ces·sor** \-ˈse-sər\ *n* — **in·ter·ces·so·ry** \-ˈse-sə-rē\ *adj*

¹**in·ter·change** \ˌin-tər-ˈchānj\ *vb* **1** : to put each in the place of the other **2** : EXCHANGE **3** : to change places mutually — **in·ter·change·able** \-ˈchān-jə-bəl\ *adj* — **in·ter·change·ably** \-blē\ *adv*

²**in·ter·change** \ˈin-tər-ˌchānj\ *n* **1** : EXCHANGE **2** : a highway junction that by separated levels permits passage between highways without crossing traffic streams

in·ter·col·le·giate \ˌin-tər-kə-ˈlē-jət\ *adj* : existing or carried on between colleges

in·ter·com \ˈin-tər-ˌkäm\ *n* : a two-way system for localized communication

in·ter·con·ti·nen·tal \ˌin-tər-ˌkänt-ᵊn-ˈent-ᵊl\ *adj* **1** : extending among or carried on between continents ⟨~ trade⟩ **2** : capable of traveling between continents ⟨~ ballistic missiles⟩

in·ter·course \ˈin-tər-ˌkōrs\ *n* **1** : connection or dealings between persons or nations **2** : physical sexual contact between individuals that involves the genitalia of at least one person ⟨oral ~⟩; *esp* : SEXUAL INTERCOURSE

in·ter·de·nom·i·na·tion·al \ˌin-tər-di-ˌnä-mə-ˈnä-shə-nəl\ *adj* : involving different denominations

in·ter·de·part·men·tal \ˌin-tər-di-ˌpärt-ˈment-ᵊl, -ˌdē-\ *adj* : carried on between or involving different departments (as of a college)

in·ter·de·pen·dent \ˌin-tər-di-ˈpen-dənt\ *adj* : dependent upon one another — **in·ter·de·pen·dence** \-dəns\ *n*

in·ter·dict \ˌin-tər-ˈdikt\ *vb* **1** : to prohibit by decree **2** : to destroy, cut off, or damage (as an enemy line of supply) — **in·ter·dic·tion** \-ˈdik-shən\ *n*

in·ter·dis·ci·plin·ary \-ˈdi-sə-plə-ˌner-ē\ *adj* : involving two or more academic, scientific, or artistic disciplines

¹**in·ter·est** \ˈin-trəst; ˈin-tə-rəst, -ˌrest\ *n* **1** : right, title, or legal share in something **2** : a charge for borrowed money that is generally a percentage of the amount borrowed; *also* : the return received by capital on its investment **3** : WELFARE, BENEFIT; *also* : SELF-INTEREST **4** : CURIOSITY, CONCERN **5** : readiness to be concerned with or moved by an object or class of objects **6** : a quality in a thing that arouses interest

²**interest** *vb* **1** : to persuade to participate or engage **2** : to engage the attention of

in·ter·est·ing *adj* : holding the attention — **in·ter·est·ing·ly** *adv*

¹**in·ter·face** \ˈin-tər-ˌfās\ *n* **1** : a surface forming a common boundary of two bodies, spaces, or phases ⟨an oil-water ~⟩ **2** : the place at which two independent systems meet and act on or communicate with each other ⟨the man-machine ~⟩ **3** : the means by which interaction or communication is achieved at an interface — **in·ter·fa·cial** \ˌin-tər-ˈfā-shəl\ *adj*

²**interface** *vb* **-faced; -fac·ing 1** : to connect by means of an interface **2** : to serve as an interface

in·ter·faith \ˌin-tər-ˈfāth\ *adj* : involving persons of different religious faiths

in·ter·fere \ˌin-tər-ˈfir\ *vb* **-fered; -fer·ing** [MF *(s')* *entreferir* to strike one another, fr. OF, fr. *entre* between, among + *ferir* to strike, fr. L *ferire*] **1** : to come in collision or be in opposition : CLASH **2** : to enter into the affairs of others **3** : to affect one another

in·ter·fer·ence \-ˈfir-əns\ *n* **1** : the act or process of interfering **2** : something that interferes : OBSTRUCTION **3** : the mutual effect on meeting of two waves resulting in areas of increased and decreased amplitude **4** : the blocking of an opponent in football to make way for the ballcarrier **5** : the illegal hindering of an opponent in sports

in·ter·fer·om·e·ter \ˌin-tər-fə-ˈrä-mə-tər\ *n* : a device that uses the interference of waves (as of light) for making precise measurements — **in·ter·fer·om·e·try** \-fə-ˈrä-mə-trē\ *n*

in·ter·fer·on \ˌin-tər-ˈfir-ˌän\ *n* : any of a group of antiviral proteins of low molecular weight produced usu. by animal cells in response to a virus, a parasite in the cell, or a chemical

in·ter·ga·lac·tic \ˌin-tər-gə-ˈlak-tik\ *adj* : relating to or situated in the spaces between galaxies

in·ter·gla·cial \-ˈglā-shəl\ *n* : a warm period between successive glaciations

in·ter·gov·ern·men·tal \-ˌgə-vərn-ˈment-ᵊl\ *adj* : existing or occurring between two governments or levels of government

in·ter·im \ˈin-tə-rəm\ *n* [L, adv., meanwhile, fr. *inter* between] : a time intervening : INTERVAL — **interim** *adj*

¹**in·te·ri·or** \in-ˈtir-ē-ər\ *adj* **1** : lying, occurring, or functioning within the limiting boundaries : INSIDE, INNER **2** : remote from the surface, border, or shore : INLAND

²**interior** *n* **1** : the inland part (as of a country) **2** : INSIDE **3** : the internal affairs of a state or nation **4** : a scene or view of the interior of a building

interior decoration *n* : INTERIOR DESIGN — **interior decorator** *n*

interior design *n* : the art or practice of planning and supervising the design and execution of architectural interiors and their furnishings — **interior designer** *n*

interj *abbr* interjection

in·ter·ject \ˌin-tər-ˈjekt\ *vb* : to throw in between or among other things

in·ter·jec·tion \ˌin-tər-ˈjek-shən\ *n* : an exclamatory word (as *ouch*) — **in·ter·jec·tion·al·ly** \-shə-nə-lē\ *adv*

in·ter·lace \ˌin-tər-ˈlās\ *vb* **1** : to unite by or as if by lacing together : INTERWEAVE **2** : INTERSPERSE

in·ter·lard \ˌin-tər-ˈlärd\ *vb* : to vary by inserting or interjecting something

in·ter·leave \ˌin-tər-ˈlēv\ *vb* **-leaved; -leav·ing** : to arrange in alternate layers

in·ter·leu·kin \ˌin-tər-ˈlü-kən\ *n* : any of several proteins of low molecular weight that are produced by cells of the body and regulate the immune system and immune responses

¹**in·ter·line** \ˌin-tər-ˈlīn\ *vb* : to insert between lines already written or printed

²**interline** *vb* : to provide (as a coat) with an interlining

in·ter·lin·ear \ˌin-tər-ˈli-nē-ər\ *adj* : inserted between lines already written or printed ⟨an ~ translation of a text⟩

in·ter·lin·ing \ˈin-tər-ˌlī-niŋ\ *n* : a lining (as of a coat) between the ordinary lining and the outside fabric

in·ter·link \ˌin-tər-ˈliŋk\ *vb* : to link together

in·ter·lock \ˌin-tər-ˈläk\ *vb* **1** : to engage or interlace together : lock together : UNITE **2** : to connect so that action of one part affects action of another part — **in·ter·lock** \ˈin-tər-ˌläk\ *n*

in·ter·loc·u·tor \ˌin-tər-ˈlä-kyə-tər\ *n* : one who takes part in dialogue or conversation

in·ter·loc·u·to·ry \-ˌtōr-ē\ *adj* : pronounced during the progress of a legal action and having only provisional force ⟨an ~ decree⟩

in·ter·lope \ˌin-tər-ˈlōp\ *vb* **-loped; -lop·ing 1** : to encroach on the rights (as in trade) of others **2** : INTRUDE, INTERFERE — **in·ter·lop·er** *n*

in·ter·lude \ˈin-tər-ˌlüd\ *n* **1** : a usu. short simple play or dramatic entertainment **2** : an intervening period,

space, or event **3** : a piece of music inserted between the parts of a longer composition or a religious service
in·ter·mar·riage \ₐin-tər-ˈmar-ij\ *n* **1** : marriage within one's own group as required by custom **2** : marriage between members of different groups
in·ter·mar·ry \-ˈmar-ē\ *vb* **1** : to marry each other **2** : to marry within a group **3** : to become connected by intermarriage
¹**in·ter·me·di·ary** \ₐin-tər-ˈmē-dē-ₐer-ē\ *adj* **1** : INTERMEDIATE **2** : acting as a mediator
²**intermediary** *n, pl* **-ar·ies** : MEDIATOR, GO-BETWEEN
¹**in·ter·me·di·ate** \ₐin-tər-ˈmē-dē-ət\ *adj* : being or occurring at the middle place or degree or between extremes
²**intermediate** *n* **1** : one that is intermediate **2** : INTERMEDIARY
intermediate school *n* **1** : JUNIOR HIGH SCHOOL **2** : a school usu. comprising grades 4 – 6
in·ter·ment \in-ˈtər-mənt\ *n* : BURIAL
in·ter·mezzo \ₐin-tər-ˈmet-sō, -ˈmed-zō\ *n, pl* **-zi** \-sē, -zē\ *or* **-zos** [It, ultim. fr. L *intermedius* intermediate] : a short movement connecting major sections of an extended musical work (as a symphony); *also* : a short independent instrumental composition
in·ter·mi·na·ble \(ₐ)in-ˈtər-mə-nə-bəl\ *adj* : ENDLESS; *esp* : wearisomely protracted — **in·ter·mi·na·bly** \-blē\ *adv*
in·ter·min·gle \ₐin-tər-ˈmiŋ-gəl\ *vb* : to mingle or mix together
in·ter·mis·sion \ₐin-tər-ˈmi-shən\ *n* **1** : INTERRUPTION, BREAK **2** : a temporary halt esp. in a public performance
in·ter·mit \-ˈmit\ *vb* **-mit·ted; -mit·ting** : DISCONTINUE; *also* : to be intermittent
in·ter·mit·tent \-ˈmit-ᵊnt\ *adj* : coming and going at intervals *syn* recurrent, periodic, alternate — **in·ter·mit·tent·ly** *adv*
in·ter·mix \ₐin-tər-ˈmiks\ *vb* : to mix together : INTERMINGLE — **in·ter·mix·ture** \-ˈmiks-chər\ *n*
in·ter·mo·lec·u·lar \-mə-ˈle-kyə-lər\ *adj* : existing or acting between molecules
in·ter·mon·tane \ₐin-tər-ˈmän-ₐtān\ *adj* : situated between mountains
¹**in·tern** \ˈin-ₐtərn, in-ˈtərn\ *vb* : to confine or impound esp. during a war — **in·tern·ee** \(ₐ)in-ₐtər-ˈnē\ *n* — **in·tern·ment** \-ˈtərn-mənt\ *n*
²**in·tern** *also* **in·terne** \ˈin-ₐtərn\ *n* : an advanced student or recent graduate (as in medicine) gaining supervised practical experience — **in·tern·ship** *n*
³**in·tern** \ˈin-ₐtərn\ *vb* : to act as an intern
in·ter·nal \in-ˈtərn-ᵊl\ *adj* **1** : INWARD, INTERIOR **2** : relating to or located in the inside of the body ⟨∼ pain⟩ **3** : of, relating to, or occurring within the confines of an organized structure ⟨∼ affairs⟩ **4** : of, relating to, or existing within the mind **5** : INTRINSIC, INHERENT — **in·ter·nal·ly** *adv*
internal combustion engine *n* : an engine in which the fuel is ignited within the engine cylinder
internal medicine *n* : a branch of medicine that deals with the diagnosis and treatment of diseases not requiring surgery
¹**in·ter·na·tion·al** \ₐin-tər-ˈna-shə-nəl\ *adj* **1** : common to or affecting two or more nations ⟨∼ trade⟩ **2** : of, relating to, or constituting a group having members in two or more nations — **in·ter·na·tion·al·ly** *adv*
²**international** *n* : one that is international; *esp* : an organization of international scope
in·ter·na·tion·al·ise *Brit var of* INTERNATIONALIZE
in·ter·na·tion·al·ism \-ˈna-shə-nə-ₐli-zəm\ *n* : a policy of cooperation among nations; *also* : an attitude favoring such a policy
in·ter·na·tion·al·ize \-ˈna-shə-nə-ₐlīz\ *vb* : to make international; *esp* : to place under international control
in·ter·ne·cine \ₐin-tər-ˈne-ₐsēn, -ˈnē-ₐsīn\ *adj* [L *internecinus*, fr. *internecare* to destroy, kill, fr. *necare*

to kill, fr. *nec-, nex* violent death] **1** : DEADLY; *esp* : mutually destructive **2** : of, relating to, or involving conflict within a group ⟨∼ feuds⟩
In·ter·net \ˈin-tər-ₐnet\ *n* : an electronic communications network that connects computer networks worldwide
in·ter·nist \ˈin-ₐtər-nist\ *n* : a physician who specializes in internal medicine
in·ter·nun·cio \ₐin-tər-ˈnən-sē-ₐō, -ˈnún-\ *n* [It *internunzio*] : a papal legate of lower rank than a nuncio
in·ter·of·fice \-ˈò-fəs\ *adj* : functioning or communicating between the offices of an organization
in·ter·per·son·al \-ˈpərs-ᵊn-əl\ *adj* : being, relating to, or involving relations between persons — **in·ter·per·son·al·ly** *adv*
in·ter·plan·e·tary \ₐin-tər-ˈpla-nə-ₐter-ē\ *adj* : existing, carried on, or operating between planets ⟨∼ space⟩
in·ter·play \ˈin-tər-ₐplā\ *n* : INTERACTION
in·ter·po·late \in-ˈtər-pə-ₐlāt\ *vb* **-lat·ed; -lat·ing 1** : to change (as a text) by inserting new or foreign matter **2** : to insert (as words) into a text or into a conversation **3** : to estimate values of (a function) between two known values — **in·ter·po·la·tion** \-ₐtər-pə-ˈlā-shən\ *n*
in·ter·pose \ₐin-tər-ˈpōz\ *vb* **-posed; -pos·ing 1** : to place between **2** : to thrust in : INTRUDE, INTERRUPT **3** : to inject between parts of a conversation or argument **4** : to come or be between *syn* interfere, intercede, intermediate, intervene — **in·ter·po·si·tion** \-pə-ˈzi-shən\ *n*
in·ter·pret \in-ˈtər-prət\ *vb* **1** : to explain the meaning of; *also* : to act as an interpreter : TRANSLATE **2** : to understand according to individual belief, judgment, or interest **3** : to represent artistically — **in·ter·pret·er** *n* — **in·ter·pre·tive** \-ˈtər-prə-tiv\ *adj*
in·ter·pre·ta·tion \in-ₐtər-prə-ˈtā-shən\ *n* **1** : EXPLANATION **2** : an instance of artistic interpretation in performance or adaptation — **in·ter·pre·ta·tive** \-ˈtər-prə-ₐtā-tiv\ *adj*
in·ter·ra·cial \-ˈrā-shəl\ *adj* : of, involving, or designed for members of different races
in·ter·reg·num \ₐin-tə-ˈreg-nəm\ *n, pl* **-nums** *or* **-na** \-nə\ **1** : the time during which a throne is vacant between two successive reigns or regimes **2** : a pause in a continuous series
in·ter·re·late \ₐin-tər-ri-ˈlāt\ *vb* : to bring into or have a mutual relationship — **in·ter·re·lat·ed·ness** \-ˈlā-təd-nəs\ *n* — **in·ter·re·la·tion** \-ˈlā-shən\ *n* — **in·ter·re·la·tion·ship** *n*
interrog *abbr* interrogative
in·ter·ro·gate \in-ˈter-ə-ₐgāt\ *vb* **-gat·ed; -gat·ing** : to question esp. formally and systematically : ASK — **in·ter·ro·ga·tion** \-ₐter-ə-ˈgā-shən\ *n* — **in·ter·ro·ga·tor** \-ˈter-ə-ₐgā-tər\ *n*
in·ter·rog·a·tive \ₐin-tə-ˈrä-gə-tiv\ *adj* : asking a question ⟨∼ sentence⟩ — **interrogative** *n* — **in·ter·rog·a·tive·ly** *adv*
in·ter·rog·a·to·ry \ₐin-tə-ˈrä-gə-ₐtōr-ē\ *adj* : INTERROGATIVE
in·ter·rupt \ₐin-tə-ˈrəpt\ *vb* **1** : to stop or hinder by breaking in **2** : to break the uniformity or continuity of **3** : to break in by speaking while another is speaking — **in·ter·rupt·er** *n* — **in·ter·rup·tion** \-ˈrəp-shən\ *n* — **in·ter·rup·tive** \-ˈrəp-tiv\ *adj*
in·ter·scho·las·tic \ₐin-tər-skə-ˈlas-tik\ *adj* : existing or carried on between schools
in·ter·sect \ₐin-tər-ˈsekt\ *vb* **1** : to divide by passing through or across **2** : to meet and cross (as at a point); *also* : OVERLAP — **in·ter·sec·tion** \-ˈsek-shən\ *n*
in·ter·sperse \ₐin-tər-ˈspərs\ *vb* **-spersed; -spers·ing 1** : to place something at intervals in or among **2** : to insert at intervals among other things — **in·ter·sper·sion** \-ˈspər-zhən\ *n*
¹**in·ter·state** \ₐin-tər-ˈstāt\ *adj* : relating to, including, or connecting two or more states esp. of the U.S.
²**in·ter·state** \ˈin-tər-ₐstāt\ *n* : an interstate highway

in·ter·stel·lar \ˌin-tər-ˈste-lər\ adj : located or taking place among the stars

in·ter·stice \in-ˈtər-stəs\ n, pl **-stic·es** \-stə-ˌsēz, -stə-səz\ : a space that intervenes between things : CHINK — **in·ter·sti·tial** \ˌin-tər-ˈsti-shəl\ adj

in·ter·tid·al \ˌin-tər-ˈtīd-ᵊl\ adj : of, relating to, or being the area that is above low-tide mark but exposed to tidal flooding ⟨life in the ~ mud⟩

in·ter·twine \-ˈtwīn\ vb : to twine or cause to twine about one another : INTERLACE — **in·ter·twine·ment** n

in·ter·twist \-ˈtwist\ vb : INTERTWINE

in·ter·ur·ban \-ˈər-bən\ adj : connecting cities or towns

in·ter·val \ˈin-tər-vəl\ n [ME intervalle, fr. MF, fr. L intervallum space between ramparts, interval, fr. inter- between + vallum rampart] 1 : a space of time between events or states : PAUSE 2 : a space between objects, units, or states 3 : the difference in pitch between two tones

in·ter·vene \ˌin-tər-ˈvēn\ vb **-vened; -ven·ing** 1 : to occur, fall, or come between points of time or events 2 : to enter or appear as an unrelated feature or circumstance ⟨rain intervened and we postponed the trip⟩ 3 : to come in or between in order to stop, settle, or modify ⟨~ in a quarrel⟩ 4 : to occur or lie between two things — **in·ter·ven·tion** \-ˈven-chən\ n

in·ter·ven·tion·ism \-ˈven-chə-ˌni-zəm\ n : interference by one country in the political affairs of another — **in·ter·ven·tion·ist** \-ˈven-chə-nist\ n or adj

in·ter·view \ˈin-tər-ˌvyü\ n 1 : a formal consultation usu. to evaluate qualifications 2 : a meeting at which a writer or reporter obtains information from a person; also : the recorded or written account of such a meeting — **interview** vb — **in·ter·view·ee** \ˌin-tər-(ˌ)vyü-ˈē\ n — **in·ter·view·er** n

in·ter·vo·cal·ic \ˌin-tər-vō-ˈka-lik\ adj : immediately preceded and immediately followed by a vowel

in·ter·weave \ˌin-tər-ˈwēv\ vb **-wove** \-ˈwōv\ also **-weaved; -wo·ven** \-ˈwō-vən\ also **-weaved; -weav·ing** : to weave or blend together : INTERTWINE, INTERMINGLE — **interwoven** adj

in·tes·tate \in-ˈtes-ˌtāt, -tət\ adj 1 : having made no valid will ⟨died ~⟩ 2 : not disposed of by will ⟨~ estate⟩

in·tes·tine \in-ˈtes-tən\ n : the tubular part of the alimentary canal that extends from stomach to anus and consists of a long narrow upper part (**small intestine**) followed by a broader shorter lower part (**large intestine**) — **in·tes·ti·nal** \-tən-ᵊl\ adj

¹in·ti·mate \ˈin-tə-ˌmāt\ vb **-mat·ed; -mat·ing** 1 : ANNOUNCE, NOTIFY 2 : to communicate indirectly : HINT — **in·ti·ma·tion** \ˌin-tə-mā-shən\ n

²in·ti·mate \ˈin-tə-mət\ adj 1 : INTRINSIC; also : INNERMOST 2 : marked by very close association, contact, or familiarity 3 : marked by a warm friendship 4 : suggesting informal warmth or privacy 5 : of a very personal or private nature — **in·ti·ma·cy** \ˈin-tə-mə-sē\ n — **in·ti·mate·ly** adv

³in·ti·mate \ˈin-tə-mət\ n : an intimate friend, associate, or confidant

in·tim·i·date \in-ˈti-mə-ˌdāt\ vb **-dat·ed; -dat·ing** : to make timid or fearful : FRIGHTEN; esp : to compel or deter by or as if by threats syn cow, bulldoze, bully, browbeat — **in·tim·i·dat·ing·ly** adv — **in·tim·i·da·tion** \-ˌti-mə-ˈdā-shən\ n

intl or **intnl** abbr international

in·to \ˈin-tü\ prep 1 : to the inside of ⟨ran ~ the house⟩ 2 : to the state, condition, or form of ⟨got ~ trouble⟩ 3 : AGAINST ⟨ran ~ a wall⟩

in·tol·er·a·ble \(ˌ)in-ˈtä-lə-rə-bəl\ adj 1 : UNBEARABLE 2 : EXCESSIVE — **in·tol·er·a·bly** \-blē\ adv

in·tol·er·ant \(ˌ)in-ˈtä-lə-rənt\ adj 1 : unable or unwilling to endure 2 : unwilling to grant equality, freedom, or other social rights : BIGOTED — **in·tol·er·ance** \-rəns\ n

in·to·na·tion \ˌin-tō-ˈnä-shən\ n 1 : the act of intoning and esp. of chanting 2 : something that is intoned 3 : the manner of singing, playing, or uttering tones 4 : the rise and fall in pitch of the voice in speech

in·tone \in-ˈtōn\ vb **in·toned; in·ton·ing** : to utter in musical or prolonged tones : CHANT

in to·to \in-ˈtō-tō\ adv [L, on the whole] : TOTALLY, ENTIRELY

in·tox·i·cant \in-ˈtäk-si-kənt\ n : something that intoxicates; esp : an alcoholic drink — **intoxicant** adj

in·tox·i·cate \-sə-ˌkāt\ vb **-cat·ed; -cat·ing** 1 : to affect by a drug (as alcohol or cocaine) esp. to the point of physical or mental impairment 2 : to excite to enthusiasm or frenzy — **in·tox·i·ca·tion** \-ˌtäk-sə-ˈkā-shən\ n

in·trac·ta·ble \(ˌ)in-ˈtrak-tə-bəl\ adj : not easily controlled : OBSTINATE

in·tra·mu·ral \-ˈmyür-əl\ adj : being or occurring within the walls or limits (as of a city or college) ⟨~ sports⟩

in·tra·mus·cu·lar \-ˈməs-kyə-lər\ adj : situated within, occurring in, or administered by entering a muscle — **in·tra·mus·cu·lar·ly** adv

intrans abbr intransitive

in·tran·si·gent \-jənt\ adj : UNCOMPROMISING; also : IRRECONCILABLE — **in·tran·si·gence** \-jəns\ n — **intransigent** n

in·tran·si·tive \(ˌ)in-ˈtran-sə-tiv, -zə-\ adj : not transitive; esp : not having or containing an object ⟨an ~ verb⟩ — **in·tran·si·tive·ly** adv — **in·tran·si·tive·ness** n

in·tra·state \ˌin-trə-ˈstāt\ adj : existing or occurring within a state

in·tra·uter·ine device \-ˈyü-tə-rən-, -ˌrīn-\ n : a device (as a spiral of plastic) inserted and left in the uterus to prevent pregnancy

in·tra·ve·nous \ˌin-trə-ˈvē-nəs\ adj : being within or entering by way of the veins; also : used in or using intravenous procedures — **in·tra·ve·nous·ly** adv

intrench var of ENTRENCH

in·trep·id \in-ˈtre-pəd\ adj : characterized by resolute fearlessness, fortitude, and endurance — **in·tre·pid·i·ty** \ˌin-trə-ˈpi-də-tē\ n

in·tri·cate \ˈin-tri-kət\ adj [ME, fr. L intricatus, pp. of intricare to entangle, fr. tricae trifles, complications] 1 : having many complexly interrelated parts : COMPLICATED 2 : difficult to follow, understand, or solve — **in·tri·ca·cy** \-tri-kə-sē\ n — **in·tri·cate·ly** adv

¹in·trigue \in-ˈtrēg\ vb **in·trigued; in·trigu·ing** 1 : to accomplish by intrigue 2 : to carry on an intrigue; esp : PLOT, SCHEME 3 : to arouse the interest, desire, or curiosity of — **in·trigu·ing·ly** adv

²in·trigue \ˈin-ˌtrēg, in-ˈtrēg\ n 1 : a secret scheme : MACHINATION 2 : a clandestine love affair

in·trin·sic \in-ˈtrin-zik, -sik\ adj : belonging to the essential nature or constitution of a thing — **in·trin·si·cal·ly** \-zi-k(ə-)lē, -si-\ adv

introd abbr introduction

in·tro·duce \ˌin-trə-ˈdüs, -ˈdyüs\ vb **-duced; -duc·ing** 1 : to lead or bring in esp. for the first time 2 : to bring into practice or use 3 : to cause to be acquainted 4 : to present for discussion 5 : PLACE, INSERT syn insinuate, interpolate, interpose, interject — **in·tro·duc·tion** \-ˈdək-shən\ n — **in·tro·duc·to·ry** \-ˈdək-tə-rē\ adj

in·troit \ˈin-ˌtrȯit, -ˌtrō-ət\ n often cap : the first part of the traditional proper of the Mass 2 : a piece of music sung or played at the beginning of a worship service

in·tro·spec·tion \-ˈspek-shən\ n : a reflective looking inward : an examination of one's own thoughts or feelings — **in·tro·spect** \ˌin-trə-ˈspekt\ vb — **in·tro·spec·tive** \-ˈspek-tiv\ adj — **in·tro·spec·tive·ly** adv

in·tro·vert \ˈin-trə-ˌvərt\ n : a reserved or shy person — **in·tro·ver·sion** \ˌin-trə-ˈvər-zhən\ n — **introvert** adj — **in·tro·vert·ed** \ˈin-trə-ˌvər-təd\ adj

in•trude \in-ˈtrüd\ *vb* **in•trud•ed; in•trud•ing 1** : to thrust, enter, or force in or upon **2** : ENCROACH, TRESPASS — **in•trud•er** *n* — **in•tru•sion** \-ˈtrü-zhən\ *n* — **in•tru•sive** \-ˈtrü-siv\ *adj* — **in•tru•sive•ness** *n*

intrust *var of* ENTRUST

in•tu•it \in-ˈtü-ət, -ˈtyü-\ *vb* : to apprehend by intuition

in•tu•ition \ˌin-tù-ˈwi-shən, -tyù-\ *n* **1** : quick and ready insight **2** : the power or faculty of knowing things without conscious reasoning — **in•tu•i•tive** \in-ˈtü-ə-tiv, -ˈtyü-\ *adj* — **in•tu•i•tive•ly** *adv*

In•u•it \ˈi-nù-wət, ˈi-nyù-\ *n* [Inuit *inuit*, pl. of *inuk* person] **1** : a member of the Eskimo people of No. America and Greenland **2** : the language of the Inuit people

in•un•date \ˈi-nən-ˌdāt\ *vb* **-dat•ed; -dat•ing** : to cover with or as if with a flood : OVERFLOW — **in•un•da•tion** \ˌi-nən-ˈdā-shən\ *n*

in•ure \i-ˈnür, -ˈnyür\ *vb* **in•ured; in•ur•ing** [ME *enuren*, fr. en- in + *ure*, n., use, custom, fr. MF *uevre* work, practice, fr. L *opera* work] **1** : to accustom to accept something undesirable **2** : to become of advantage

inv *abbr* **1** inventor **2** invoice

in vac•uo \in-ˈva-kyù-ˌwō\ *adv* [L] : in a vacuum

in•vade \in-ˈvād\ *vb* **in•vad•ed; in•vad•ing 1** : to enter for conquest or plunder **2** : to encroach upon **3** : to spread through and usu. harm ⟨germs ∼ the tissues⟩ — **in•vad•er** *n*

¹in•va•lid \(ˌ)in-ˈva-ləd\ *adj* : being without foundation or force in fact, reason, or law — **in•va•lid•i•ty** \ˌin-və-ˈli-də-tē\ *n* — **in•val•id•ly** *adv*

²in•va•lid \ˈin-və-ləd\ *adj* : being in ill health : SICKLY

³invalid \ˈin-və-ləd\ *n* : a person in usu. chronic ill health — **in•va•lid•ism** \-lə-ˌdi-zəm\ *n*

⁴in•va•lid \ˈin-və-ləd, -ˌlid\ *vb* **1** : to remove from active duty by reason of sickness or disability **2** : to make sickly or disabled

in•val•i•date \(ˌ)in-ˈva-lə-ˌdāt\ *vb* : to make invalid; *esp* : to weaken or make valueless — **in•val•i•da•tion** \in-ˌva-lə-ˈdā-shən\ *n*

in•valu•able \-ˈval-yə-bəl, -yə-wə-bəl\ *adj* : valuable beyond estimation

in•vari•able \-ˈver-ē-ə-bəl\ *adj* : not changing or capable of change : CONSTANT — **in•vari•ably** \-blē\ *adv*

in•va•sion \in-ˈvā-zhən\ *n* : an act or instance of invading; *esp* : entry of an army into a country for conquest

in•va•sive \in-ˈvā-siv, -ziv\ *adj* **1** : tending to spread ⟨∼ cancer cells⟩ **2** : involving entry into the living body (as by surgery) ⟨∼ therapy⟩

in•vec•tive \in-ˈvek-tiv\ *n* **1** : an abusive expression or speech **2** : abusive language — **invective** *adj*

in•veigh \in-ˈvā\ *vb* : to protest or complain bitterly or vehemently : RAIL

in•vei•gle \in-ˈvā-gəl, -ˈvē-\ *vb* **in•vei•gled; in•vei•gling** [modif. of MF *aveugler* to blind, hoodwink] **1** : to win over by flattery : ENTICE **2** : to acquire by ingenuity or flattery

in•vent \in-ˈvent\ *vb* **1** : to think up **2** : to create or produce for the first time — **in•ven•tor** \-ˈven-tər\ *n*

in•ven•tion \in-ˈven-chən\ *n* **1** : INVENTIVENESS **2** : a creation of the imagination; *esp* : a false conception

3 : a device, contrivance, or process originated after study and experiment **4** : the act or process of inventing

in•ven•tive \in-ˈven-tiv\ *adj* **1** : CREATIVE, INGENIOUS ⟨an ∼ composer⟩ **2** : characterized by invention ⟨an ∼ turn of mind⟩ — **in•ven•tive•ness** *n*

---

in•ven•to•ry \ˈin-vən-ˌtōr-ē\ *n, pl* **-ries 1** : an itemized list of current goods or assets **2** : SURVEY, SUMMARY **3** : STOCK, SUPPLY **4** : the act or process of taking an inventory — **inventory** *vb*

---

¹in•verse \(ˌ)in-ˈvərs, ˈin-ˌvərs\ *adj* : opposite in order, nature, or effect : REVERSED — **in•verse•ly** *adv*

²inverse *n* : something inverse or resulting in or from inversion : OPPOSITE

in•ver•sion \in-ˈvər-zhən\ *n* **1** : a reversal of position, order, or relationship; *esp* : an increase of temperature with altitude through a layer of air **2** : the act or process of inverting

in•vert \in-ˈvərt\ *vb* **1** : to reverse in position, order, or relationship **2** : to turn upside down or inside out **3** : to turn inward

¹in•ver•te•brate \(ˌ)in-ˈvər-tə-brət, -ˌbrēt\ *adj* : lacking a backbone; *also* : of or relating to invertebrates

²invertebrate *n* : an invertebrate animal (as a jellyfish, insect, or worm)

¹in•vest \in-ˈvest\ *vb* **1** : to install formally in an office or honor **2** : to furnish with power or authority : VEST **3** : to cover completely : ENVELOP **4** : CLOTHE, ADORN **5** : BESIEGE **6** : to endow with a quality or characteristic

²invest *vb* **1** : to commit (money) in order to earn a financial return **2** : to expend for future benefits or advantages **3** : to make an investment — **in•ves•tor** \-ˈves-tər\ *n*

in•ves•ti•gate \in-ˈves-tə-ˌgāt\ *vb* **-gat•ed; -gat•ing** [L *investigare* to track, investigate, fr. *vestigium* footprint, track] : to study by close examination and systematic inquiry — **in•ves•ti•ga•tion** \-ˌves-tə-ˈgā-shən\ *n* — **in•ves•ti•ga•tive** \-ˈves-tə-ˌgā-tiv\ *adj* — **in•ves•ti•ga•tor** \-ˌgā-tər\ *n*

in•ves•ti•ture \in-ˈves-tə-ˌchùr, -chər\ *n* **1** : the act of ratifying or establishing in office **2** : something that covers or adorns

¹in•vest•ment \in-ˈvest-mənt\ *n* **1** : an outer layer : ENVELOPE **2** : INVESTITURE 1 **3** : BLOCKADE, SIEGE

²investment *n* : the outlay of money for income or profit; *also* : the sum invested or the property purchased

in•vet•er•ate \in-ˈve-tə-rət\ *adj* **1** : firmly established by age or long persistence **2** : confirmed in a habit

in•vi•a•ble \(ˌ)in-ˈvī-ə-bəl\ *adj* : incapable of surviving

in•vid•i•ous \in-ˈvi-dē-əs\ *adj* **1** : tending to cause discontent, animosity, or envy **2** : ENVIOUS **3** : OBNOXIOUS — **in•vid•i•ous•ly** *adv*

in•vig•o•rate \in-ˈvi-gə-ˌrāt\ *vb* **-rat•ed; -rat•ing** : to give life and energy to : ANIMATE — **in•vig•o•ra•tion** \-ˌvi-gə-ˈrā-shən\ *n*

in•vin•ci•ble \(ˌ)in-ˈvin-sə-bəl\ *adj* : incapable of being conquered, overcome, or subdued — **in·vin·ci·bil·i·ty** \-ˌvin-sə-ˈbi-lə-tē\ *n* — **in·vin·ci·bly** \-ˈvin-sə-blē\ *adv*

in·vi·o·la·ble \-ˈvī-ə-lə-bəl\ *adj* 1 : safe from violation or profanation 2 : UNASSAILABLE — **in·vi·o·la·bil·i·ty** \-ˌvī-ə-lə-ˈbi-lə-tē\ *n*

in·vi·o·late \-ˈvī-ə-lət\ *adj* : not violated or profaned : PURE

in·vis·i·ble \-ˈvi-zə-bəl\ *adj* 1 : incapable of being seen ⟨∼ to the naked eye⟩ 2 : HIDDEN 3 : IMPERCEPTIBLE, INCONSPICUOUS — **in·vis·i·bil·i·ty** \-ˌvi-zə-ˈbi-lə-tē\ *n* — **in·vis·i·bly** \-ˈvi-zə-blē\ *adv*

in·vi·ta·tion·al \ˌin-və-ˈtā-shə-nəl\ *adj* : limited to invited participants ⟨an ∼ tournament⟩ — **invitational** *n*

in·vite \in-ˈvīt\ *vb* **in·vit·ed; in·vit·ing** 1 : ENTICE, TEMPT 2 : to increase the likelihood of 3 : to request the presence or participation of : ASK 4 : to request formally 5 : ENCOURAGE — **in·vi·ta·tion** \ˌin-və-ˈtā-shən\ *n*

in·vit·ing *adj* : ATTRACTIVE, TEMPTING

in vi·tro \in-ˈvē-trō, -ˈvī-, -ˈvi-\ *adv or adj* [NL, lit., in glass] : outside the living body and in an artificial environment ⟨*in vitro* fertilization⟩

in·vo·ca·tion \ˌin-və-ˈkā-shən\ *n* 1 : SUPPLICATION; *esp* : a prayer at the beginning of a service 2 : a formula for conjuring : INCANTATION

¹**in·voice** \ˈin-ˌvȯis\ *n* [modif. of MF *envois*, pl. of *envoi* message] : an itemized list of goods shipped usu. specifying the price and the terms of sale : BILL

²**invoice** *vb* **in·voiced; in·voic·ing** : to send an invoice to or for : BILL

in·voke \in-ˈvōk\ *vb* **in·voked; in·vok·ing** 1 : to petition for help or support 2 : to appeal to or cite as authority ⟨∼ a law⟩ 3 : to call forth by incantation : CONJURE ⟨∼ spirits⟩ 4 : to make an earnest request for : SOLICIT 5 : to put into effect or operation 6 : to bring about : CAUSE

in·vol·un·tary \(ˌ)in-ˈvä-lən-ˌter-ē\ *adj* 1 : done contrary to or without choice 2 : COMPULSORY 3 : not controlled by the will : REFLEX ⟨∼ contractions⟩ — **in·vol·un·tari·ly** \-ˌvä-lən-ˈter-ə-lē\ *adv*

in·vo·lute \ˈin-və-ˌlüt\ *adj* : INVOLVED, INTRICATE

in·vo·lu·tion \ˌin-və-ˈlü-shən\ *n* 1 : the act or an instance of enfolding or entangling 2 : COMPLEXITY, INTRICACY

in·volve \in-ˈvälv\ *vb* **in·volved; in·volv·ing** 1 : to draw in as a participant 2 : ENVELOP 3 : to occupy (as oneself) absorbingly; *esp* : to commit oneself emotionally 4 : to relate closely : CONNECT 5 : to have as part of itself : INCLUDE 6 : ENTAIL, IMPLY 7 : to have an effect on — **in·volve·ment** *n*

in·volved \-ˈvälvd\ *adj* : INTRICATE, COMPLEX ⟨an ∼ plot⟩

in·vul·ner·a·ble \(ˌ)in-ˈvəl-nə-rə-bəl\ *adj* 1 : incapable of being wounded, injured, or damaged 2 : immune to or proof against attack — **in·vul·ner·a·bil·i·ty** \-ˌvəl-nə-rə-ˈbi-lə-tē\ *n* — **in·vul·ner·a·bly** \-ˈvəl-nə-rə-blē\ *adv*

¹**in·ward** \ˈin-wərd\ *adj* 1 : situated on the inside 2 : MENTAL; *also* : SPIRITUAL 3 : directed toward the interior

²**inward** *or* **in·wards** \-wərdz\ *adv* 1 : toward the inside, center, or interior 2 : toward the inner being

in·ward·ly \ˈin-wərd-lē\ *adv* 1 : MENTALLY, SPIRITUALLY 2 : INTERNALLY ⟨bled ∼⟩ 3 : to oneself ⟨cursed ∼⟩

IOC *abbr* International Olympic Committee

io·dide \ˈī-ə-ˌdīd\ *n* : a compound of iodine with another element or group

io·dine \ˈī-ə-ˌdīn, -əd-ᵊn\ *n* 1 : a nonmetallic chemical element used esp. in medicine and photography — see ELEMENT table 2 : a solution of iodine used as a local antiseptic

io·dise *Brit var of* IODIZE

io·dize \ˈī-ə-ˌdīz\ *vb* **io·dized; io·diz·ing** : to treat with iodine or an iodide

ion \ˈī-ən, ˈī-ˌän\ *n* [Gk, neut. of *iōn*, prp. of *ienai* to

go; so called because in electrolysis it goes to one of the two poles] : an electrically charged particle, atom, or group of atoms — **ion·ic** \ī-ˈä-nik\ *adj*

-ion *n suffix* : act, process, state, or condition (validation)

ion·ise *Brit var of* IONIZE

ion·ize \ˈī-ə-ˌnīz\ *vb* **ion·ized; ion·iz·ing** 1 : to convert wholly or partly into ions 2 : to become ionized — **ion·iz·able** \ˌī-ə-ˈnī-zə-bəl\ *adj* — **ion·iza·tion** \ˌī-ə-nə-ˈzā-shən\ *n* — **ion·iz·er** \ˈī-ə-ˌnī-zər\ *n*

ion·o·sphere \ī-ˈä-nə-ˌsfir\ *n* : the part of the earth's atmosphere extending from about 30 miles (50 kilometers) to the exosphere that contains ionized atmospheric gases — **ion·o·spher·ic** \ī-ˌä-nə-ˈsfir-ik, -ˈsfer-\ *adj*

IOOF *abbr* Independent Order of Odd Fellows

io·ta \ī-ˈō-tə\ *n* [L, fr. Gk *iōta*] 1 : the 9th letter of the Greek alphabet — I or ι 2 : a very small quantity : JOT

IOU \ˌī-(ˌ)ō-ˈyü\ *n* : an acknowledgement of a debt

IP *abbr* innings pitched

ip·e·cac \ˈi-pi-ˌkak\ *n* [Pg *ipecacuanha*] : an emetic and expectorant drug used esp. as a syrup in treating accidental poisoning; *also* : either of two So. American plants or their rhizomes and roots used to make ipecac

ip·so fac·to \ˌip-sō-ˈfak-tō\ *adv* [NL, lit., by the fact itself] : by the very nature of the case

iq *abbr* [L *idem quod*] the same as

IQ \ˈī-ˈkyü\ *n* : INTELLIGENCE QUOTIENT

¹**Ir** *abbr* Irish

²**Ir** *symbol* iridium

IR *abbr* infrared

¹**IRA** \ˌī-(ˌ)är-ˈā; ˈī-rə\ *n* [individual retirement account] : a savings account in which a person may make tax deductible deposits up to a stipulated amount each year with deposits and interest taxable after the person's retirement

²**IRA** *abbr* Irish Republican Army

Ira·ni·an \i-ˈrä-nē-ən *also* -ˈrā-\ *n* : a native or inhabitant of Iran — **Iranian** *adj*

Iraqi \i-ˈra-kē, -ˈrä-\ *n* : a native or inhabitant of Iraq — **Iraqi** *adj*

iras·ci·ble \i-ˈra-sə-bəl\ *adj* : marked by hot temper and easily provoked anger **syn** choleric, testy, touchy, cranky, cross — **iras·ci·bil·i·ty** \-ˌra-sə-ˈbi-lə-tē\ *n*

irate \ī-ˈrāt\ *adj* 1 : roused to ire 2 : arising from anger — **irate·ly** *adv*

ire \ˈīr\ *n* : ANGER, WRATH — **ire·ful** *adj*

Ire *abbr* Ireland

iren·ic \ī-ˈre-nik\ *adj* : favoring, conducive to, or operating toward peace or conciliation

ir·i·des·cence \ˌir-ə-ˈdes-ᵊns\ *n* : a rainbowlike play of colors — **ir·i·des·cent** \-ᵊnt\ *adj*

irid·i·um \ir-ˈi-dē-əm\ *n* : a hard brittle heavy metallic chemical element — see ELEMENT table

iris \ˈī-rəs\ *n, pl* **iris·es** *or* **iri·des** \ˈī-rə-ˌdēz, ˈir-ə-\ [ME, fr. L *iris* rainbow, iris plant, fr. Gk, rainbow, iris plant, iris of the eye] 1 : the colored part around the pupil of the eye 2 : any of a large genus of plants with linear basal leaves and large showy flowers

Irish \ˈīr-ish\ *n* 1 **Irish** *pl* : the people of Ireland 2 : the Celtic language of Ireland — **Irish** *adj* — **Irish·man** \-mən\ *n* — **Irish·wom·an** \-ˌwu̇-mən\ *n*

Irish bull *n* : an incongruous statement (as "it was hereditary in his family to have no children")

Irish coffee *n* : hot sugared coffee with Irish whiskey and whipped cream

Irish moss *n* : the dried and bleached plants of two red algae; *also* : either of these red algae

Irish setter *n* : any of a breed of bird dogs with a mahogany-red coat

irk \ˈərk\ *vb* : to make weary, irritated, or bored : ANNOY

irk·some \'ərk-səm\ *adj* : tending to irk : ANNOYING — **irk·some·ly** *adv*

¹iron \'īrn, 'ī-ərn\ *n* **1** : a heavy malleable magnetic metallic chemical element that rusts easily and is vital to biological processes — see ELEMENT table **2** : something made of metal and esp. iron; *also* : something (as handcuffs) used to bind or restrain ⟨put them in ∼s⟩ **3** : a household device with a flat base that is heated and used for pressing cloth **4** : STRENGTH, HARDNESS

²iron *vb* **1** : to press or smooth with or as if with a heated iron **2** : to remove (as wrinkles) by ironing — **iron·er** *n*

¹iron·clad \-'klad\ *adj* **1** : sheathed in iron armor **2** : so firm or secure as to be unbreakable

²iron·clad \-'klad\ *n* : an armored naval vessel esp. of the 19th century

iron curtain *n* : a political, military, and ideological barrier that isolates an area; *esp, often cap* : one isolating an area under Soviet control

iron·ic \ī-'rä-nik\ *or* **iron·i·cal** \-ni-kəl\ *adj* **1** : of, relating to, or marked by irony **2** : given to irony

iron·i·cal·ly \-ni-k(ə-)lē\ *adv* **1** : in an ironic manner **2** : it is ironic

iron·ing *n* : clothes ironed or to be ironed

iron lung *n* : a device for artificial respiration that encloses the chest in a chamber in which changes of pressure force air into and out of the lungs

iron out *vb* : to remove or lessen difficulties in or extremes of

iron oxide *n* : FERRIC OXIDE

iron·stone \'īrn-ˌstōn, 'ī-ərn-\ *n* **1** : a hard iron-rich sedimentary rock **2** : a hard heavy durable pottery developed in England in the 19th century

iron·ware \-ˌwar\ *n* : articles made of iron

iron·weed \-ˌwēd\ *n* : any of several mostly weedy American plants related to the asters that have terminal heads of red or purple flowers

iron·wood \-ˌwu̇d\ *n* : any of numerous trees or shrubs with exceptionally hard wood; *also* : the wood

iron·work \-ˌwərk\ *n* **1** : work in iron **2** *pl* : a mill or building where iron or steel is smelted or heavy iron or steel products are made — **iron·work·er** *n*

iro·ny \'ī-rə-nē\ *n, pl* **-nies** [L *ironia,* fr. Gk *eirōnia,* fr. *eirōn* dissembler] **1** : the use of words to express the opposite of what one really means **2** : incongruity between the actual result of a sequence of events and the expected result

Iro·quois \'ir-ə-ˌkwȯi\ *n, pl* **Iroquois** *same or* -ˌkwȯiz\ **1** *pl* : an American Indian confederacy of New York that consisted of the Cayuga, Mohawk, Oneida, Onondaga, and Seneca and later included the Tuscarora **2** : a member of any of the Iroquois peoples

ir·ra·di·ate \i-'rā-dē-ˌāt\ *vb* **-at·ed; -at·ing 1** : ILLUMINATE **2** : ENLIGHTEN **3** : to treat by exposure to radiation **4** : RADIATE — **ir·ra·di·a·tion** \-ˌrā-dē-'ā-shən\ *n*

ir·ra·tio·nal \(ˌ)i-'ra-shə-nəl\ *adj* **1** : incapable of reasoning ⟨∼ beasts⟩; *also* : defective in mental power ⟨∼ with fever⟩ **2** : not based on reason ⟨∼ fears⟩ **3** : being or numerically equal to an irrational number — **ir·ra·tio·nal·i·ty** \(ˌ)i-ˌra-shə-'na-lə-tē\ *n* — **ir·ra·tio·nal·ly** *adv*

²irrational *n* : IRRATIONAL NUMBER

irrational number *n* : a real number that cannot be expressed as the quotient of two integers

ir·rec·on·cil·able \(ˌ)i-ˌre-kən-'sī-lə-bəl, -ˈre-kən-ˌsī-\ *adj* : impossible to reconcile, adjust, or harmonize — **ir·rec·on·cil·abil·i·ty** \(ˌ)i-ˌre-kən-ˌsī-lə-'bi-lə-tē\ *n*

ir·re·cov·er·able \ˌir-i-'kə-və-rə-bəl\ *adj* : not capable of being recovered or rectified : IRREPARABLE — **ir·re·cov·er·ably** \-blē\ *adv*

ir·re·deem·able \ˌir-i-'dē-mə-bəl\ *adj* **1** : not redeemable; *esp* : not terminable by payment of the principal ⟨an ∼ bond⟩ **2** : not convertible into gold or silver at the will of the holder **3** : being beyond remedy : HOPELESS

ir·re·den·tism \-'den-ˌti-zəm\ *n* : a principle or policy directed toward the incorporation of a territory historically or ethnically part of another into that other — **ir·re·den·tist** \-tist\ *n or adj*

ir·re·duc·ible \ˌir-i-'dü-sə-bəl, -'dyü-\ *adj* : not reducible — **ir·re·duc·ibly** \-blē\ *adv*

ir·re·fut·able \ˌir-i-'fyü-tə-bəl, (ˌ)i-'re-fyət-\ *adj* : impossible to refute

irreg *abbr* irregular

ir·reg·u·lar \(ˌ)i-'re-gyə-lər\ *adj* **1** : not regular : not natural or uniform **2** : not conforming to the normal or usual manner of inflection ⟨∼ verbs⟩ **3** : not belonging to a regular or organized army ⟨∼ troops⟩ — **irregular** *n* — **ir·reg·u·lar·ly** *adv*

ir·reg·u·lar·i·ty \ˌi-ˌre-gyə-'lar-ə-tē\ *n, pl* **-ties 1** : something that is irregular **2** : the quality or state of being irregular **3** : occasional constipation

ir·rel·e·vant \(ˌ)i-'re-lə-vənt\ *adj* : not relevant — **ir·rel·e·vance** \-vəns\ *n*

ir·re·li·gious \ˌir-i-'li-jəs\ *adj* : lacking religious emotions, doctrines, or practices

ir·re·me·di·a·ble \ˌir-i-'mē-dē-ə-bəl\ *adj* : impossible to remedy or correct

ir·re·mov·able \-'mü-və-bəl\ *adj* : not removable

ir·rep·a·ra·ble \(ˌ)i-'re-pə-rə-bəl\ *adj* : impossible to make good, undo, repair, or remedy ⟨∼ damage⟩

ir·re·place·able \ˌir-i-'plā-sə-bəl\ *adj* : not replaceable

ir·re·press·ible \-'pre-sə-bəl\ *adj* : impossible to repress or control

ir·re·proach·able \-'prō-chə-bəl\ *adj* : not reproachable : BLAMELESS

ir·re·sist·ible \ˌir-i-'zis-tə-bəl\ *adj* : impossible to successfully resist — **ir·re·sist·ibly** \-blē\ *adv*

ir·res·o·lute \(ˌ)i-'re-zə-ˌlüt\ *adj* : uncertain how to act or proceed : VACILLATING — **ir·res·o·lute·ly** \-ˌlüt-lē, (ˌ)i-ˌre-zə-'lüt-\ *adv* — **ir·res·o·lu·tion** \(ˌ)i-ˌre-zə-'lü-shən\ *n*

ir·re·spec·tive of \ˌir-i-ˈspek-tiv-\ prep : without regard to

ir·re·spon·si·ble \-ˈspän-sə-bəl\ adj : not responsible — ir·re·spon·si·bil·i·ty \-ˌspän-sə-ˈbi-lə-tē\ n — ir·re·spon·si·bly \-ˈspän-sə-blē\ adv

ir·re·triev·able \ˌir-i-ˈtrē-və-bəl\ adj : not retrievable : IRRECOVERABLE

ir·rev·er·ence \(ˌ)i-ˈre-və-rəns\ n 1 : lack of reverence 2 : an irreverent act or utterance — ir·rev·er·ent \-rənt\ adj

ir·re·vers·ible \ˌir-i-ˈvər-sə-bəl\ adj : incapable of being reversed

ir·rev·o·ca·ble \(ˌ)i-ˈre-və-kə-bəl\ adj : incapable of being revoked or recalled — ir·rev·o·ca·bly \-blē\ adv

ir·ri·gate \ˈir-ə-ˌgāt\ vb -gat·ed; -gat·ing 1 : to supply (as land) with water by artificial means; also : to flush with liquid — ir·ri·ga·tion \ˌir-ə-ˈgā-shən\ n

ir·ri·ta·bil·i·ty \ˌir-ə-tə-ˈbi-lə-tē\ n 1 : the property of living things and of protoplasm that enables reaction to stimuli 2 : the quality or state of being irritable; esp : readiness to become annoyed or angry

ir·ri·ta·ble \ˈir-ə-tə-bəl\ adj : capable of being irritated; esp : readily or easily irritated — ir·ri·ta·bly \-blē\ adv

ir·ri·tate \ˈir-ə-ˌtāt\ vb -tat·ed; -tat·ing 1 : to excite to anger : EXASPERATE 2 : to make sore or inflamed — ir·ri·tant \ˈir-ə-tənt\ adj or n — ir·ri·tat·ing·ly adv — ir·ri·ta·tion \ˌir-ə-ˈtā-shən\ n

ir·rupt \(ˌ)i-ˈrəpt\ vb 1 : to rush in forcibly or violently 2 : to increase suddenly in numbers (rabbits ~ in cycles) — ir·rup·tion \-ˈrəp-shən\ n

IRS abbr Internal Revenue Service

is pres 3d sing of BE

Isa or Is abbr Isaiah

Isa·iah \ī-ˈzā-ə\ n — see BIBLE table

Isa·ias \ī-ˈzā-əs\ n : ISAIAH

ISBN abbr International Standard Book Number

-ish \ish\ adj suffix 1 : of, relating to, or being ⟨Finnish⟩ 2 : characteristic of ⟨boyish⟩ ⟨mulish⟩ 3 : inclined or liable to ⟨bookish⟩ 4 : having a touch or trace of : somewhat ⟨purplish⟩ 5 : having the approximate age of ⟨fortyish⟩

isin·glass \ˈīz-ᵊn-ˌglas, ˈī-ziŋ-\ n 1 : a gelatin obtained from various fish 2 : mica esp. in thin sheets

isl abbr island

Is·lam \is-ˈläm, iz-, -ˈlam, ˈis-ˌ, ˈiz-ˌ\ n [Ar islām submission (to the will of God)] : the religious faith of Muslims; also : the civilization built on this faith — Is·lam·ic \is-ˈlä-mik, iz-, -ˈla-\ adj

is·land \ˈī-lənd\ n 1 : a body of land smaller than a continent surrounded by water 2 : something resembling an island in its isolation

is·land·er \ˈī-lən-dər\ n : a native or inhabitant of an island

isle \ˈīl\ n : ISLAND; esp : a small island

is·let \ˈī-lət\ n : a small island

ism \ˈi-zəm\ n : a distinctive doctrine, cause, or theory

-ism \ˌi-zəm\ n suffix 1 : act : practice : process ⟨criticism⟩ 2 : manner of action or behavior characteristic of a (specified) person or thing ⟨fanaticism⟩ 3 : state : condition : property ⟨dualism⟩ 4 : abnormal state or condition ⟨alcoholism⟩ 5 : doctrine : theory : cult ⟨Buddhism⟩ 6 : adherence to a set of principles ⟨stoicism⟩ 7 : prejudice or discrimination on the basis of a (specified) attribute ⟨racism⟩ ⟨sexism⟩ 8 : characteristic or peculiar feature or trait ⟨colloquialism⟩

iso·bar \ˈī-sə-ˌbär\ n : a line on a map connecting places of equal barometric pressure — iso·bar·ic \ˌī-sə-ˈbär-ik, -ˈbar-\ adj

iso·late \ˈī-sə-ˌlāt\ vb -lat·ed; -lat·ing [fr. isolated set apart, fr. F isolé, fr. It isolato, fr. isola island, fr. L insula] : to place or keep by itself : separate from others — iso·la·tion \ˌī-sə-ˈlā-shən\ n

iso·lat·ed adj 1 : occurring alone or once : UNIQUE 2 : SPORADIC

iso·la·tion·ism \ˌī-sə-ˈlā-shə-ˌni-zəm\ n : a policy of national isolation by abstention from international political and economic relations — iso·la·tion·ist \-shə-nist\ n or adj

iso·mer \ˈī-sə-mər\ n : any of two or more chemical compounds that contain the same numbers of atoms of the same elements but differ in structural arrangement and properties — iso·mer·ic \ˌī-sə-ˈmer-ik\ adj — iso·mer·ism \ī-ˈsä-mə-ˌri-zəm\ n

iso·met·rics \ˌī-sə-ˈme-triks\ n sing or pl : exercise involving a series of brief and intense contractions of muscles against each other or against an immovable resistance — iso·met·ric adj

iso·prene \ˈī-sə-ˌprēn\ n : a hydrocarbon used esp. in making synthetic rubber

isos·ce·les \ī-ˈsä-sə-ˌlēz\ adj : having two equal sides ⟨an ~ triangle⟩

iso·therm \ˈī-sə-ˌthərm\ n : a line on a map connecting points having the same temperature

iso·ther·mal \ˌī-sə-ˈthər-məl\ adj : of, relating to, or marked by equality of temperature

iso·tope \ˈī-sə-ˌtōp\ n [Gk isos equal + topos place] : any of the forms of a chemical element that differ chiefly in the number of neutrons in an atom — iso·to·pic \ˌī-sə-ˈtä-pik, -ˈtō-\ adj — iso·to·pi·cal·ly \-ˈtä-pi-k(ə-)lē, -ˈtō-\ adv

Isr abbr Israel; Israeli

Is·rae·li \iz-ˈrā-lē\ n, pl Israelis also Israeli : a native or inhabitant of Israel — Israeli adj

Is·ra·el·ite \ˈiz-rē-ə-ˌlīt\ n : a member of the Hebrew people descended from Jacob

is·su·ance \ˈi-shü-wəns\ n : the act of issuing or giving out esp. officially

¹is·sue \ˈi-shü\ n 1 : the action of going, coming, or flowing out : EGRESS, EMERGENCE 2 : EXIT, OUTLET, VENT 3 : OFFSPRING, PROGENY 4 : OUTCOME, RESULT 5 : a point of debate or controversy; also : the point at which an unsettled matter is ready for a decision 6 : a discharge (as of blood) from the body 7 : something coming forth from a specified source 8 : the act of officially giving out or printing : PUBLICATION; also : the quantity of things given out at one time

²**issue** *vb* **is·sued; is·su·ing 1 :** to go, come, or flow out **2 :** to come forth or cause to come forth : EMERGE, DISCHARGE, EMIT **3 :** ACCRUE **4 :** to descend from a specified parent or ancestor **5 :** to result in **6 :** to put forth or distribute officially **7 :** PUBLISH **8 :** EMANATE, RESULT — **is·su·er** *n*

¹**-ist** \ist\ *n suffix* **1 :** one that performs a (specified) action ⟨cyc*list*⟩ : one that makes or produces ⟨novel*ist*⟩ **2 :** one that plays a (specified) musical instrument ⟨harp*ist*⟩ **3 :** one that operates a (specified) mechanical instrument or contrivance ⟨machin*ist*⟩ **4 :** one that specializes in a (specified) art or science or skill ⟨geolog*ist*⟩ **5 :** one that adheres to or advocates a (specified) doctrine or system or code of behavior ⟨social*ist*⟩ or that of a (specified) individual ⟨Darwin*ist*⟩

²**-ist** *adj suffix* : -ISTIC

isth·mi·an \'is-mē-ən\ *adj* : of, relating to, or situated in or near an isthmus

isth·mus \'is-məs\ *n* : a narrow strip of land connecting two larger portions of land

-is·tic \'is-tik\ *or* **-is·ti·cal** \'is-ti-kəl\ *adj suffix* : of, relating to, or characteristic of ⟨altru*istic*⟩

¹**it** \'it\ *pron* **1 :** that one — used of a lifeless thing, a plant, a person or animal, or an abstract entity ⟨∼'s a big building⟩ ⟨∼'s a shade tree⟩ ⟨who is ∼⟩ ⟨beauty is everywhere and ∼ is a source of joy⟩ **2 :** — used as a subject of an impersonal verb that expresses a condition or action without reference to an agent ⟨∼ is raining⟩ **3 :** — used as an anticipatory subject or object ⟨∼'s good to see you⟩

²**it** \'it\ *n* : the player in a game who performs the principal action of the game (as trying to find others in hide-and-seek)

It *abbr* Italian; Italy
ital *abbr* italic; italicized
Ital *abbr* Italian
Ital·ian \i-'tal-yən\ *n* **1 :** a native or inhabitant of Italy **2 :** the language of Italy — **Italian** *adj*
ital·ic \i-'ta-lik, ī-\ *adj* : relating to type in which the letters slope up toward the right (as in *"italic"*) — **italic** *n*
ital·i·cise *Brit var of* ITALICIZE
ital·i·cize \i-'ta-lə-ˌsīz, ī-\ *vb* **-cized; -ciz·ing :** to print in italics
itch \'ich\ *n* **1 :** an uneasy irritating skin sensation prob. related to sensing pain **2 :** a skin disorder ac-

companied by an itch **3 :** a persistent desire — **itch** *vb* — **itchy** *adj*

-ite \ˌīt\ *n suffix* **1 :** native : resident ⟨suburban*ite*⟩ **2 :** adherent : follower ⟨Lenin*ite*⟩ **3 :** product ⟨metabo*lite*⟩ **4 :** mineral : rock ⟨quartz*ite*⟩

item \'ī-təm\ *n* [L, likewise, also] **1 :** a separate particular in a list, account, or series : ARTICLE **2 :** a separate piece of news (as in a newspaper)

item·ise *Brit var of* ITEMIZE

item·ize \'ī-tə-ˌmīz\ *vb* **-ized; -iz·ing :** to set down in detail : LIST — **item·i·za·tion** \ˌī-tə-mə-'zā-shən\ *n*

it·er·ate \'i-tə-ˌrāt\ *vb* **-at·ed; -at·ing :** REITERATE, REPEAT

it·er·a·tion \ˌi-tə-'rā-shən\ *n* **1 :** REPETITION; *esp* : a computational process in which a series of operations is repeated until a condition is met **2 :** one repetition of the series of operations in iteration

itin·er·ant \ī-'ti-nə-rənt, ə-\ *adj* : traveling from place to place; *esp* : covering a circuit ⟨an ∼ preacher⟩

itin·er·ary \ī-'ti-nə-ˌrer-ē, ə-\ *n, pl* **-ar·ies 1 :** the route of a journey or the proposed outline of one **2 :** a travel diary **3 :** GUIDEBOOK

its \'its\ *adj* : of or relating to it or itself

it·self \it-'self\ *pron* : that identical one — used reflexively, for emphasis, or in absolute constructions

-ity \ə-tē\ *n suffix* : quality : state : degree ⟨alkalin*ity*⟩

IUD \ˌī-(ˌ)yü-'dē\ *n* : INTRAUTERINE DEVICE

IV \ˌī-'vē\ *n* [*intravenous*] : an apparatus used to give an intravenous injection or feeding; *also* : such an injection or feeding

-ive \iv\ *adj suffix* : that performs or tends toward an (indicated) action ⟨correct*ive*⟩

ivo·ry \'ī-vrē, -və-rē\ *n, pl* **-ries** [ME *ivorie*, fr. OF *ivoire*, fr. L *eboreus* of ivory, fr. *ebur* ivory] **1 :** the hard creamy-white material composing the tusks of an elephant or walrus **2 :** a pale yellow color **3 :** something made of ivory or of a similar substance

ivory tower *n* **1 :** an impractical lack of concern with urgent problems **2 :** a place of learning

ivy \'ī-vē\ *n, pl* **ivies :** a trailing woody evergreen vine with small black berries that is related to ginseng

IWW *abbr* Industrial Workers of the World

-ize \ˌīz\ *vb suffix* **1 :** cause to be or conform to or resemble ⟨American*ize*⟩ : cause to be formed into ⟨union*ize*⟩ **2 :** subject to a (specified) action ⟨satir*ize*⟩ **3 :** saturate, treat, or combine with ⟨macadam*ize*⟩ **4 :** treat like ⟨idol*ize*⟩ **5 :** become : become like ⟨crystal*lize*⟩ **6 :** be productive in or of : engage in a (specified) activity ⟨philosoph*ize*⟩ **7 :** adopt or spread the manner of activity or the teaching of ⟨Christian*ize*⟩

J

¹j \'jā\ *n, pl* **j's** *or* **js** \'jāz\ *often cap* : the 10th letter of the English alphabet

²j *abbr, often cap* **1** jack **2** journal **3** judge **4** justice

¹jab \'jab\ *vb* **jabbed; jab·bing** : to thrust quickly or abruptly : POKE

²jab *n* : a usu. short straight punch

jab·ber \'ja-bər\ *vb* : to talk rapidly, indistinctly, or unintelligibly : CHATTER — **jabber** *n* — **jab·ber·er** *n*

jab·ber·wocky \'ja-bər-ˌwä-kē\ *n* : meaningless speech or writing

ja·bot \zha-'bō, 'ja-ˌbō\ *n* : a ruffle worn down the front of a dress or shirt

jac·a·ran·da \ˌja-kə-'ran-də\ *n* : any of a genus of pinnate-leaved tropical American trees with clusters of showy blue flowers

¹jack \'jak\ *n* **1** : a mechanical device; *esp* : one used to raise a heavy body a short distance **2** : a male donkey **3** : a small target ball in lawn bowling **4** : a small national flag flown by a ship **5** : a small 6-pointed metal object used in a game (**jacks**) **6** : a playing card bearing the figure of a soldier or servant **7** : a socket into which a plug is inserted for connecting electric circuits

²jack *vb* **1** : to raise by means of a jack **2** : INCREASE ⟨~ up prices⟩

jack·al \'ja-kəl\ *n* [Turk *çakal*, fr. Per *shagāl*] : any of several mammals of Asia and Africa related to the wolves

jack·a·napes \'ja-kə-ˌnāps\ *n* **1** : MONKEY, APE **2** : an impudent or conceited person

jack·ass \'jak-ˌas\ *n* **1** : DONKEY; *esp* : a male donkey **2** : a stupid person : FOOL

jack·boot \-ˌbüt\ *n* **1** : a heavy military boot of glossy black leather extending above the knee **2** : a laceless military boot reaching to the calf

jack·daw \'jak-ˌdȯ\ *n* : a black and gray Old World crowlike bird

jack·et \'ja-kət\ *n* [ME *jaket*, fr. MF *jaquet*, dim. of *jaque* short jacket, fr. *jacque* peasant, fr. the name *Jacques* James] **1** : a garment for the upper body usu. having a front opening, collar, and sleeves **2** : an outer covering or casing ⟨a book ~⟩

Jack Frost *n* : frost or frosty weather personified

jack·ham·mer \'jak-ˌha-mər\ *n* : a pneumatic percussion tool for drilling rock or breaking pavement

jack–in–the–box *n, pl* **jack–in–the–boxes** *or* **jacks–in–the–box** : a toy consisting of a small box out of which a figure springs when the lid is raised

jack–in–the–pulpit *n, pl* **jack–in–the–pulpits** *or* **jacks–in–the–pulpit** : an American spring-flowering woodland herb having an upright club-shaped spadix arched over by a green and purple spathe

¹jack·knife \-ˌnīf\ *n* **1** : a large pocketknife **2** : a dive in which the diver bends from the waist and touches the ankles before straightening out

²jackknife *vb* : to fold like a jackknife ⟨the trailer truck *jackknifed*⟩

jack·leg \'jak-ˌleg\ *adj* **1** : lacking skill or training **2** : MAKESHIFT

jack–of–all–trades *n, pl* **jacks–of–all–trades** : one who is able to do passable work at various tasks

jack–o'–lan·tern \'ja-kə-ˌlan-tərn\ *n* : a lantern made of a pumpkin cut to look like a human face

jack·pot \'jak-ˌpät\ *n* **1** : a large sum of money formed by the accumulation of stakes from previous play (as in poker) **2** : an impressive and often unexpected success or reward

jack·rab·bit \-ˌra-bət\ *n* : any of several large hares of western No. America with very long ears and hind legs

jack·straw \-ˌstrȯ\ *n* **1** *pl* : a game in which straws or thin sticks are let fall in a heap and each player in turn tries to remove them one at a time without disturbing

the rest **2** : one of the straws or sticks in jackstraws

jack–tar \-'tär\ *n, often cap* : SAILOR

Ja·cob's ladder \'jā-kəbz-\ *n* : any of several perennial herbs related to phlox that have pinnate leaves and blue or white bell-shaped flowers

jac·quard \'ja-ˌkärd\ *n, often cap* : a fabric of intricate variegated weave or pattern

¹jade \'jād\ *n* **1** : a broken-down, vicious, or worthless horse **2** : a disreputable woman

²jade *vb* **jad·ed; jad·ing** **1** : to wear out by overwork or abuse **2** : to become weary **syn** exhaust, fatigue, tire

³jade *n* [F, fr. obs. Sp (*piedra de la*) *ijada*, lit., loin stone; fr. the belief that jade cures renal colic] : a usu. green gemstone that takes a high polish

jad·ed *adj* : dulled by a surfeit or excess

¹jag \'jag\ *n* : a sharp projecting part

²jag *n* : SPREE

jag·ged \'ja-gəd\ *adj* : sharply notched

jag·uar \'ja-ˌgwär\ *n* : a black-spotted tropical American cat that is larger and stockier than the Old World leopard

jaguar

jai alai \'hī-ˌlī\ *n* [Sp, fr. Basque, fr. *jai* festival + *alai* merry] : a court game played by usu. two or four players with a ball and a curved wicker basket strapped to the wrist

jail \'jāl\ *n* [ME *jaiole*, fr. OF, fr. LL *caveola*, dim. of L *cavea* cage] : PRISON; *esp* : one for persons held in lawful custody — **jail** *vb*

jail·bird \-ˌbərd\ *n* : an habitual criminal

jail·break \-ˌbrāk\ *n* : a forcible escape from jail

jail·er *or* **jail·or** \'jā-lər\ *n* : a keeper of a jail

jal·ap \'ja-ləp, 'jä-\ *n* : a powdered purgative drug from the root of a Mexican plant related to the morning glory; *also* : this root or plant

ja·la·pe·ño \ˌhä-lə-'pān-(ˌ)yō\ *n* : a Mexican hot pepper

ja·lopy \jə-'lä-pē\ *n, pl* **ja·lop·ies** : a dilapidated vehicle (as an automobile)

jal·ou·sie \'ja-lə-sē\ *n* [F, lit., jealousy] : a blind, window, or door with adjustable horizontal slats or louvers

¹jam \'jam\ *vb* **jammed; jam·ming** **1** : to press into a close or tight position **2** : to cause to become wedged so as to be unworkable; *also* : to make or become unworkable through the jamming of a movable part **3** : to push forcibly ⟨~ on the brakes⟩ **4** : CRUSH, BRUISE **5** : to make unintelligible by sending out interfering signals or messages **6** : to take part in a jam session — **jam·mer** *n*

²jam *n* **1** : a crowded mass that impedes or blocks ⟨traffic ~⟩ **2** : a difficult state of affairs

³jam *n* : a food made by boiling fruit and sugar to a thick consistency

Jam *abbr* Jamaica

Ja·mai·can \jə-'mā-kən\ *n* : a native or inhabitant of Jamaica — **Jamaican** *adj*

jamb \'jam\ *n* [ME *jambe*, fr. MF, lit., leg] : an upright piece forming the side of an opening (as of a door)

jam·ba·laya \ˌjəm-bə-'lī-ə\ *n* [LaF] : rice cooked with

ham, sausage, chicken, shrimp, or oysters and seasoned with herbs

jam•bo•ree \ˌjam-bə-ˈrē\ n : a large festive gathering

James \ˈjāmz\ n — see BIBLE table

jam–pack \ˈjam-ˈpak\ vb : to pack tightly or to excess

jam session n : an impromptu performance esp. by
jazz musicians

Jan abbr January

jan•gle \ˈjaŋ-gəl\ vb **jan•gled; jan•gling** : to make a
harsh or discordant sound — **jangle** n

jan•i•tor \ˈja-nə-tər\ n [L, fr. janua door] : a person
who has the care of a building — **jan•i•to•ri•al** \ˌja-
nə-ˈtōr-ē-əl\ adj

Jan•u•ary \ˈja-nyə-ˌwer-ē\ n [ME Januarie, fr. L Jan-
uarius, first month of the ancient Roman year, fr. Ja-
nus, two-faced god of gates and beginnings] : the 1st
month of the year

¹ja•pan \jə-ˈpan\ n : a varnish giving a hard brilliant finish

²japan vb **ja•panned; ja•pan•ning** : to cover with a coat
of japan

Jap•a•nese \ˌja-pə-ˈnēz, -ˈnēs\ n, pl **Japanese 1** : a native or inhabitant of Japan **2** : the language of Japan
— **Japanese** adj

Japanese beetle n : a small metallic green and brown
scarab beetle introduced from Japan that is a pest on
the roots of grasses as a grub and on foliage and fruits
as an adult

¹jape \ˈjāp\ vb **japed; jap•ing 1** : JOKE **2** : MOCK

²jape n : JEST, GIBE

¹jar \ˈjär\ vb **jarred; jar•ring 1** : to make a harsh or discordant sound **2** : to have a harsh or disagreeable effect **3** : VIBRATE, SHAKE

²jar n **1** : a state of conflict **2** : a harsh discordant sound
3 : JOLT **4** : a painful effect : SHOCK

³jar n : a widemouthed container usu. of glass or earthenware

jar•di•niere \ˌjärd-ᵊn-ˈir\ n : an ornamental stand for
plants or flowers

jar•gon \ˈjär-gən\ n **1** : confused unintelligible language
2 : the special vocabulary of a particular group or activity **3** : obscure and often pretentious language

Jas abbr James

jas•mine \ˈjaz-mən\ n [F jasmin, fr. Ar yāsamīn] : any
of various climbing shrubs with fragrant flowers

jas•per \ˈjas-pər\ n : a usu. red, yellow, or brown
opaque quartz

jaun•dice \ˈjȯn-dəs\ n : yellowish discoloration of skin,
tissues, and body fluids by bile pigments; also : an
abnormal condition marked by jaundice

jaun•diced \-dəst\ adj **1** : affected with or as if with
jaundice **2** : exhibiting envy, distaste, or hostility

jaunt \ˈjȯnt\ n : a short trip usu. for pleasure

jaun•ty \ˈjȯn-tē\ adj **jaun•ti•er; -est** : sprightly in manner or appearance : LIVELY — **jaun•ti•ly** \-tə-lē\ adv
— **jaun•ti•ness** \-tē-nəs\ n

Ja•va•nese \ˌja-və-ˈnēz, ˌjä-, -ˈnēs\ n : a native or inhabitant of the Indonesian island of Java

jav•e•lin \ˈja-və-lən\ n **1** : a light spear **2** : a slender
shaft thrown for distance in a track-and-field contest

¹jaw \ˈjȯ\ n **1** : either of the bony or cartilaginous structures that support the soft tissues enclosing the
mouth and that usu. bear teeth **2** : the parts forming
the walls of the mouth and serving to open and close
it — usu. used in pl. **3** : one of a pair of movable parts
for holding or crushing something — **jawed** \ˈjȯd\
adj

²jaw vb : to talk abusively, indignantly, or at length

jaw•bone \-ˌbōn\ n : JAW 1

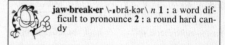

jaw•break•er \-ˌbrā-kər\ n **1** : a word difficult to pronounce **2** : a round hard candy

jay \ˈjā\ n : any of various noisy brightly colored often
largely blue birds smaller than the related crows

jay•bird \ˈjā-ˌbərd\ n : JAY

jay•vee \ˈjā-ˈvē\ n **1** : JUNIOR VARSITY **2** : a member of
a junior varsity team

jay•walk \ˈjā-ˌwȯk\ vb : to cross a street carelessly
without regard for traffic regulations — **jay•walk-
er** n

¹jazz \ˈjaz\ n **1** : American music characterized by improvisation, syncopated rhythms, and contrapuntal
ensemble playing **2** : empty talk **3** : similar but unspecified things : STUFF

²jazz vb : ENLIVEN ⟨∼ things up⟩

jazzy \ˈja-zē\ adj **jazz•i•er; -est 1** : having the characteristics of jazz **2** : marked by unrestraint, animation,
or flashiness

JCS abbr joint chiefs of staff

jct abbr junction

JD abbr **1** [L juris doctor] doctor of jurisprudence;
doctor of law **2** [L jurum doctor] doctor of laws **3** justice department **4** juvenile delinquent

jeal•ous \ˈje-ləs\ adj **1** : demanding complete devotion
2 : suspicious of a rival or of one believed to enjoy an
advantage **3** : VIGILANT — **jeal•ous•ly** adv — **jeal-
ou•sy** \-lə-sē\ n

jeans \ˈjēnz\ n pl [pl. of jean twilled cloth, short for
jean fustian, fr. ME Gene Genoa, Italy] : pants made
of durable twilled cotton cloth

jeep \ˈjēp\ n [prob. fr. g.p. (abbr. of general purpose)]
: a small four-wheel drive general-purpose motor vehicle used in World War II

¹jeer \ˈjir\ vb : to speak or cry out in derision : MOCK

²jeer n : TAUNT

Je•ho•vah \ji-ˈhō-və\ n : GOD 1

je•hu \ˈjē-hü, -hyü\ n : a driver of a coach or cab

je•june \ji-ˈjün\ adj [L jejunus empty of food, hungry,
meager] : lacking interest or significance : DULL

je•ju•num \ji-ˈjü-nəm\ n [L] : the section of the small
intestine between the duodenum and the ileum — **je-
ju•nal** \-ˈjün-ᵊl\ adj

jell \ˈjel\ vb **1** : to come to the consistency of jelly **2** : to
take shape

jel•ly \ˈje-lē\ n, pl **jellies 1** : a food with a soft elastic
consistency due usu. to the presence of gelatin or
pectin; esp : a fruit product made by boiling sugar and

the juice of a fruit **2** : a substance resembling jelly — **jelly** *vb*

jelly bean *n* : a bean-shaped candy

jel·ly·fish \'je-lē-ˌfish\ *n* : a coelenterate with a saucer-shaped jellylike body

jen·net \'je-nət\ *n* **1** : a small Spanish horse **2** : a female donkey

jen·ny \'je-nē\ *n, pl* **jennies** : a female bird or donkey

jeop·ar·dy \'je-pər-dē\ *n* [ME *jeopardie*, fr. OF *jeu parti* alternative, lit., divided game] : exposure to death, loss, or injury ⟨*syn* peril, hazard, risk, danger — **jeop·ar·dize** \-ˌdīz\ *vb*

Jer *abbr* Jeremiah; Jeremias

jer·e·mi·ad \ˌjer-ə-ˈmī-əd, -ˌad\ *n* : a prolonged lamentation or complaint; *also* : a cautionary or angry harangue

Jer·e·mi·ah \ˌjer-ə-ˈmī-ə\ *n* — see BIBLE table

Jer·e·mi·as \ˌjer-ə-ˈmī-əs\ *n* : JEREMIAH

¹jerk \'jərk\ *n* **1** : a short quick pull or twist : TWITCH **2** : an annoyingly stupid or foolish person — **jerk·i·ly** \'jər-kə-lē\ *adv* — **jerky** \'jər-kē\ *adj*

²jerk *vb* **1** : to give a sharp quick push, pull, or twist **2** : to move in short abrupt motions

jer·kin \'jər-kən\ *n* : a close-fitting usu. sleeveless jacket

jerk·wa·ter \'jərk-ˌwȯ-tər, -ˌwä-\ *adj* [fr. *jerkwater* rural train] : of minor importance : INSIGNIFICANT ⟨~ towns⟩

jer·ry–built \'jer-ē-ˌbilt\ *adj* : built cheaply and flimsily

jer·sey \'jər-zē\ *n, pl* **jerseys** [*Jersey*, one of the Channel islands] **1** : a plain weft-knitted fabric **2** : a close-fitting knitted shirt **3** *often cap* : any of a breed of small usu. fawn-colored dairy cattle

jess \'jes\ *n* : a leg strap by which a captive bird of prey may be controlled

jes·sa·mine \'je-sə-mən\ *var of* JASMINE

jest \'jest\ *n* **1** : an act intended to provoke laughter **2** : a witty remark **3** : a frivolous mood ⟨said in ~⟩ — **jest** *vb*

jest·er \'jes-tər\ *n* : a retainer formerly kept to provide casual entertainment

¹jet \'jet\ *n* : a velvet-black coal that takes a good polish and is often used for jewelry

²jet *vb* **jet·ted; jet·ting** : to spout or emit in a stream

³jet *n* **1** : a forceful rush (as of liquid or gas) through a narrow opening; *also* : a nozzle for a jet of fluid **2** : a jet-propelled airplane

⁴jet *vb* **jet·ted; jet·ting** : to travel by jet

jet lag *n* : a condition that is marked esp. by fatigue and irritability and occurs following a long flight through several time zones — **jet–lagged** *adj*

jet·lin·er \'jet-ˌlī-nər\ *n* : a jet-propelled airliner

jet·port \-ˌpȯrt\ *n* : an airport designed to handle jets

jet–pro·pelled \ˌjet-prə-ˈpeld\ *adj* : driven by an engine (**jet engine**) that produces propulsion (**jet propulsion**) by the rearward discharge of a jet of fluid (as heated air and exhaust gases)

jet·sam \'jet-səm\ *n* : jettisoned goods; *esp* : such goods washed ashore

jet set *n* : an international group of wealthy people who frequent fashionable resorts

jet stream *n* : a long narrow high-altitude current of high-speed winds blowing generally from the west

jet·ti·son \'je-tə-sən\ *vb* **1** : to throw (goods) overboard to lighten a ship or aircraft in distress **2** : DISCARD — **jettison** *n*

jet·ty \'je-tē\ *n, pl* **jetties 1** : a pier built to influence the current or to protect a harbor **2** : a landing wharf

jeu d'es·prit \zhœ̄-des-ˈprē\ *n, pl* **jeux d'esprit** *same*\ [F, lit., play of the mind] : a witty comment or composition

Jew \'jü\ *n* **1** : ISRAELITE **2** : one whose religion is Judaism — **Jew·ish** *adj*

¹jew·el \'jü-əl\ *n* [ME *juel*, fr. OF, prob. dim. of *jeu* game, play, fr. L *jocus* game, joke] **1** : an ornament of precious metal **2** : GEMSTONE, GEM

²jewel *vb* **-eled** *or* **-elled; -el·ing** *or* **-el·ling** : to adorn or equip with jewels

jew·el·er *or* **jew·el·ler** \'jü-ə-lər\ *n* : a person who makes or deals in jewelry and related articles

jew·el·lery *chiefly Brit var of* JEWELRY

jew·el·ry \'jü-əl-rē\ *n* : JEWELS; *esp* : objects of precious metal set with gems and worn for personal adornment

Jew·ry \'jür-ē, 'jú-ər-ē, 'jü-rē\ *n* : the Jewish people

jg *abbr* junior grade

¹jib \'jib\ *n* : a triangular sail set on a line running from the bow to the mast

²jib *vb* **jibbed; jib·bing** : to refuse to proceed further

jibe \'jīb\ *vb* **jibed; jib·ing** : to be in accord : AGREE

jif·fy \'ji-fē\ *n, pl* **jiffies** : MOMENT, INSTANT ⟨I'll be ready in a ~⟩

¹jig \'jig\ *n* **1** : a lively dance in triple rhythm **2** : TRICK, GAME ⟨the ~ is up⟩ **3** : a device used to hold work during manufacture or assembly

²jig *vb* **jigged; jig·ging** : to dance a jig

jig·ger \'ji-gər\ *n* : a measure usu. holding 1 to 2 ounces (30 to 60 milliliters) used in mixing drinks

jig·gle \'ji-gəl\ *vb* **jig·gled; jig·gling** : to move with quick little jerks — **jiggle** *n*

jig·saw \'jig-ˌsȯ\ *n* : a machine saw with a narrow vertically reciprocating blade for cutting curved lines

jigsaw puzzle *n* : a puzzle consisting of small irregularly cut pieces to be fitted together to form a picture

ji·had \ji-ˈhäd, -ˈhad\ *n* **1** : a Muslim holy war **2** : CRUSADE 2

¹jilt \'jilt\ *vb* : to drop (a lover) capriciously or unfeelingly

jilt *n* : one who jilts a lover

jim crow \'jim-ˈkrō\ *n, often cap J&C* : discrimination against blacks esp. by legal enforcement or traditional sanctions — **jim crow** *adj, often cap J&C* — **jim crow·ism** \-ˈkrō-ˌi-zəm\ *n, often cap J&C*

jim–dan·dy \'jim-ˈdan-dē\ *n* : something excellent of its kind

I WORKED ON A JIGSAW PUZZLE FOR EIGHT HOURS

AS IT TURNED OUT, THERE WAS A PIECE MISSING

SMALL WORLD

I WORKED ON A PUZZLE FOR EIGHT HOURS, AND THERE WERE 499 PIECES MISSING

JIM DAVIS 5-17

jim·mies \'ji-mēz\ *n pl* : tiny rod-shaped bits of usu. chocolate-flavored candy often sprinkled on ice cream

¹**jim·my** \'ji-mē\ *n, pl* **jimmies** : a small crowbar

²**jimmy** *vb* **jim·mied; jim·my·ing** : to force open with a jimmy

jim·son·weed \'jim-sən-ˌwēd\ *n, often cap* : a coarse poisonous weed related to the tomato that has large trumpet-shaped white or violet flowers

¹**jin·gle** \'jiŋ-gəl\ *vb* **jin·gled; jin·gling** : to make a light clinking or tinkling sound

²**jingle** *n* **1** : a light clinking or tinkling sound **2** : a short verse or song with catchy repetition

jin·go·ism \'jiŋ-gō-ˌi-zəm\ *n* : extreme chauvinism or nationalism marked esp. by a belligerent foreign policy — **jin·go·ist** \-ist\ *n* — **jin·go·is·tic** \ˌjiŋ-gō-'is-tik\ *adj*

jin·rik·sha \jin-'rik-ˌshô\ *n* : RICKSHA

¹**jinx** \'jiŋks\ *n* : one that brings bad luck

²**jinx** *vb* : to foredoom to failure or misfortune

jit·ney \'jit-nē\ *n, pl* **jitneys** : a small bus that serves a regular route on a flexible schedule

jit·ter·bug \'ji-tər-ˌbəg\ *n* : a dance in which couples two-step, balance, and twirl vigorously in standardized patterns — **jitterbug** *vb*

jit·ters \'ji-tərz\ *n pl* : extreme nervousness — **jit·tery** \-tə-rē\ *adj*

¹**jive** \'jīv\ *n* **1** : swing music or dancing performed to it **2** : glib, deceptive, or foolish talk **3** : the jargon of jazz enthusiasts

²**jive** *vb* **jived; jiv·ing 1** : KID, TEASE **2** : to dance to or play jive

Jn *or* **Jno** *abbr* John

Jo *abbr* Joel

¹**job** \'jäb\ *n* **1** : a piece of work **2** : something that has to be done : TASK **3** : a regular remunerative position — **job·less** *adj*

²**job** *vb* **jobbed; job·bing 1** : to do occasional pieces of work for hire **2** : to hire or let by the job

Job \'jōb\ *n* — see BIBLE table

job action *n* : a protest action by workers to force compliance with demands

job·ber \'jä-bər\ *n* **1** : a person who buys goods and then sells them to other dealers : MIDDLEMAN **2** : a person who does work by the job

job·hold·er \'jäb-ˌhōl-dər\ *n* : one having a regular job

jock \'jäk\ *n* [*jockstrap*] : ATHLETE; *esp* : a college athlete

¹**jock·ey** \'jä-kē\ *n, pl* **jockeys** : one who rides a horse esp. as a professional in a race

²**jockey** *vb* **jock·eyed; jock·ey·ing** : to maneuver or manipulate by adroit or devious means

jock·strap \'jäk-ˌstrap\ *n* [E slang *jock* penis] : ATHLETIC SUPPORTER

jo·cose \jō-'kōs\ *adj* : MERRY, HUMOROUS **syn** jocular, facetious, witty

joc·u·lar \'jä-kyə-lər\ *adj* : marked by jesting : PLAYFUL — **joc·u·lar·i·ty** \ˌjäk-yə-'lar-ə-tē\ *n* — **joc·u·lar·ly** *adv*

jo·cund \'jä-kənd\ *adj* : marked by mirth or cheerfulness

jodh·pur \'jäd-pər\ *n* **1** *pl* : riding breeches loose above the knee and tight-fitting below **2** : an ankle-high boot fastened with a strap

Jo·el \'jō-əl\ *n* — see BIBLE table

¹**jog** \'jäg\ *vb* **jogged; jog·ging 1** : to give a slight shake or push to **2** : to go at a slow monotonous pace **3** : to run or ride at a slow trot — **jog·ger** *n*

²**jog** *n* **1** : a slight shake **2** : a jogging movement or pace

³**jog** *n* **1** : a projecting or retreating part of a line or surface **2** : a brief abrupt change in direction

jog·gle \'jä-gəl\ *vb* **jog·gled; jog·gling** : to shake slightly — **joggle** *n*

john \'jän\ *n* **1** : TOILET **2** : a prostitute's client

John \'jän\ *n* — see BIBLE table

john·ny \'jä-nē\ *n, pl* **johnnies** : a short-sleeved gown opening in the back that is worn by hospital patients

John·ny–jump–up \ˌjä-nē-'jəmp-ˌəp\ *n* : any of various small-flowered cultivated pansies

joie de vi·vre \ˌzhwä-də-'vēvrᵊ\ *n* [F] : keen enjoyment of life

join \'jòin\ *vb* **1** : to come or bring together so as to form a unit **2** : to come or bring into close association **3** : to become a member of **4** : ADJOIN **5** : to take part in a collective activity

join·er \'jòi-nər\ *n* **1** : a worker who constructs articles by joining pieces of wood **2** : a gregarious person who joins many organizations

¹**joint** \'jòint\ *n* **1** : the point of contact between bones of an animal skeleton with the parts that surround and support it **2** : a cut of meat suitable for roasting **3** : a place where two things or parts are connected **4** : ESTABLISHMENT; *esp* : a shabby or disreputable establishment **5** : a marijuana cigarette — **joint·ed** *adj*

²**joint** *adj* **1** : UNITED **2** : common to two or more — **joint·ly** *adv*

³**joint** *vb* **1** : to unite by or provide with a joint **2** : to separate the joints of

joist \'jòist\ *n* : any of the small beams ranged parallel from wall to wall in a building to support a floor or ceiling

¹**joke** \'jōk\ *n* : something said or done to provoke laughter; *esp* : a brief narrative with a humorous climax

²**joke** *vb* **joked; jok·ing** : to make jokes — **jok·ing·ly** *adv*

jok·er \'jō-kər\ *n* **1** : a person who jokes **2** : an extra card used in some card games **3** : a misleading part of an agreement that works to one party's disadvantage

jol·li·fi·ca·tion \ˌjä-li-fə-'kā-shən\ *n* : a festive celebration

jol·li·ty \'jä-lə-tē\ *n, pl* **-ties** : GAIETY, MERRIMENT

jol·ly \'jä-lē\ *adj* **jol·li·er; -est** : full of high spirits : MERRY

¹**jolt** \'jōlt\ *vb* **1** : to give a quick hard knock or blow to **2** : to move with a sudden jerky motion — **jolt·er** *n*

²**jolt** *n* **1** : an abrupt jerky blow or movement **2** : a sudden shock

Jon *abbr* Jonah; Jonas

Jo·nah \'jō-nə\ *n* — see BIBLE table

Jo·nas \'jō-nəs\ *n* : JONAH

jon·gleur \zhōⁿ-'glər\ *n* : an itinerant medieval minstrel

jon·quil \'jän-kwəl\ *n* [F *jonquille*, fr. Sp *junquillo*, dim. of *junco* reed, fr. L *juncus*] : a narcissus with fragrant clustered white or yellow flowers

Jor·da·ni·an \jòr-'dā-nē-ən\ *n* : a native or inhabitant of Jordan — **Jordanian** *adj*

josh \'jäsh\ *vb* : TEASE, JOKE

Josh *abbr* Joshua

Josh·ua \'jä-shü-ə\ *n* — see BIBLE table

Joshua tree *n* : a tall branched yucca of the southwestern U.S.

jos·tle \'jä-səl\ *vb* **jos·tled; jos·tling 1** : to come in contact or into collision **2** : to make one's way by pushing and shoving

Jos·ue \'jä-shü-ē\ *n* : JOSHUA

¹**jot** \'jät\ *n* : the least bit : IOTA

²**jot** *vb* **jot·ted; jot·ting** : to write briefly and hurriedly

jot·ting \'jä-tiŋ\ *n* : a brief note

joule \'jül\ *n* : a unit of work or energy equal to the work done by a force of one newton acting through a distance of one meter

jounce \'jaúns\ *vb* **jounced; jounc·ing** : JOLT — **jounce** *n*

jour *abbr* **1** journal **2** journeyman

jour·nal \'jərn-ᵊl\ *n* [ME, service book containing the day hours, fr. MF, fr. *journal* daily, fr. L *diurnalis*, fr. *dies* day] **1** : a brief account of daily events **2** : a record of proceedings (as of a legislative body) **3** : a periodical (as a newspaper) dealing esp. with current

events **4** : the part of a rotating axle or spindle that turns in a bearing

jour·nal·ese \ˌjər-nə-ˈlēz, -ˈlēs\ *n* : a style of writing held to be characteristic of newspapers

jour·nal·ism \ˈjər-nə-ˌli-zəm\ *n* **1** : the business of writing for, editing, or publishing periodicals (as newspapers) **2** : writing designed for or characteristic of newspapers — **jour·nal·ist** \-list\ *n* — **jour·nal·is·tic** \ˌjər-nə-ˈlis-tik\ *adj*

¹jour·ney \ˈjər-nē\ *n, pl* **journeys** [ME, fr. OF *journee* day's journey, fr. *jour* day] : a traveling from one place to another

²journey *vb* **jour·neyed; jour·ney·ing** : to go on a journey : TRAVEL

jour·ney·man \-mən\ *n* **1** : a worker who has learned a trade and works for another person **2** : an experienced reliable worker

¹joust \ˈjau̇st\ *vb* : to engage in a joust

²joust *n* : a combat on horseback between two knights with lances esp. as part of a tournament

jo·vial \ˈjō-vē-əl\ *adj* : marked by good humor — **jo·vi·al·i·ty** \ˌjō-vē-ˈa-lə-tē\ *n* — **jo·vi·al·ly** *adv*

¹jowl \ˈjau̇l\ *n* : loose flesh about the lower jaw or throat

²jowl *n* **1** : the lower jaw **2** : CHEEK

¹joy \ˈjȯi\ *n* [ME, fr. OF *joie*, fr. L *gaudia*] **1** : a feeling of happiness that comes from success, good fortune, or a sense of well-being **2** : a source of happiness syn bliss, delight, enjoyment, pleasure — **joy·less** *adj*

²joy *vb* : REJOICE

joy·ful \-fəl\ *adj* : experiencing, causing, or showing joy — **joy·ful·ly** *adv*

joy·ous \ˈjȯi-əs\ *adj* : JOYFUL — **joy·ous·ly** *adv* — **joy·ous·ness** *n*

joy·ride \ˈjȯi-ˌrīd\ *n* : a ride for pleasure often marked by reckless driving — **joyride** *vb* — **joy·rid·er** *n* — **joy·rid·ing** *n*

joy·stick \-ˌstik\ *n* : a control device (as for a computer display) consisting of a lever capable of motion in two or more directions

JP *abbr* **1** jet propulsion **2** justice of the peace

Jr *abbr* junior

jt *or* **jnt** *abbr* joint

ju·bi·lant \ˈjü-bə-lənt\ *adj* [L *jubilans*, prp. of *jubilare* to rejoice] : EXULTANT — **ju·bi·lant·ly** *adv*

ju·bi·la·tion \ˌjü-bə-ˈlā-shən\ *n* : EXULTATION

ju·bi·lee \ˈjü-bə-ˌlē, ˌjü-bə-ˈlē\ *n* [ME, fr. MF & LL; MF *jubilé*, fr. LL *jubilaeus*, fr. LGk *iōbēlaios*, fr. Heb *yōbhēl* ram's horn, trumpet, jubilee] **1** : a 50th anniversary **2** : a season or occasion of celebration

Jud *abbr* Judith

Ju·da·ic \jü-ˈdā-ik\ *also* **Ju·da·ical** \-ˈdā-ə-kəl\ *adj* : of, relating to, or characteristic of Jews or Judaism

Ju·da·ism \ˈjü-də-ˌi-zəm, -ˌdā-, -dē-\ *n* : a religion developed among the ancient Hebrews and marked by belief in one God and by the moral and ceremonial laws of the Old Testament and the rabbinic tradition

Jude \ˈjüd\ *n* — see BIBLE table

Judg *abbr* Judges

¹judge \ˈjəj\ *vb* **judged; judg·ing** **1** : to form an authoritative opinion **2** : to decide as a judge : TRY **3** : to form an estimate or evaluation about something : THINK syn conclude, deduce, gather, infer

²judge *n* **1** : a public official authorized to decide questions brought before a court **2** : UMPIRE **3** : one who gives an authoritative opinion : CRITIC — **judge·ship** *n*

Judges *n* — see BIBLE table

judg·ment *or* **judge·ment** \ˈjəj-mənt\ *n* **1** : a decision or opinion given after judging ; *esp* : a formal decision given by a court **2** *cap* : the final judging of mankind by God **3** : the process of forming an opinion by discerning and comparing **4** : the capacity for judging : DISCERNMENT

judg·men·tal \ˌjəj-ˈmen-təl\ *adj* **1** : of, relating to, or involving judgment **2** : characterized by a tendency to judge harshly — **judg·men·tal·ly** *adv*

Judgment Day *n* : the day of the final judging of all human beings by God

ju·di·ca·ture \ˈjü-di-kə-ˌchu̇r\ *n* **1** : the administration of justice **2** : JUDICIARY 1

ju·di·cial \jü-ˈdi-shəl\ *adj* **1** : of or relating to the administration of justice or the judiciary **2** : ordered or enforced by a court **3** : CRITICAL — **ju·di·cial·ly** *adv*

ju·di·cia·ry \jü-ˈdi-shē-ˌer-ē, -shə-rē\ *n* **1** : a system of courts of law; *also* : the judges of these courts **2** : a branch of government in which judicial power is vested — **judiciary** *adj*

ju·di·cious \jü-ˈdi-shəs\ *adj* : having, exercising, or characterized by sound judgment syn prudent, sage, sane, sensible, wise — **ju·di·cious·ly** *adv*

Ju·dith \ˈjü-dəth\ *n* — see BIBLE table

ju·do \ˈjü-dō\ *n* [Jp, fr. *jū* weakness + *dō* art] : a sport derived from jujitsu that emphasizes the use of quick movement and leverage to throw an opponent — **ju·do·ist** \-ist\ *n*

¹jug \ˈjəg\ *n* **1** : a large deep container with a narrow mouth and a handle **2** : JAIL, PRISON

²jug *vb* **jugged; jug·ging** : JAIL, IMPRISON

jug·ger·naut \ˈjə-gər-ˌnȯt\ *n* [Hindi *Jagannāth*, title of Vishnu (a Hindu god), lit., lord of the world] : a massive inexorable force or object that crushes everything in its path

jug·gle \ˈjə-gəl\ *vb* **jug·gled; jug·gling** **1** : to keep several objects in motion in the air at the same time **2** : to manipulate esp. in order to achieve a desired and often fraudulent end — **jug·gler** \ˈjə-glər\ *n*

jug·u·lar \ˈjə-gyə-lər\ *adj* : of, relating to, or situated in or on the throat or neck ⟨the ~ veins⟩

juice \ˈjüs\ *n* **1** : the extractable fluid contents of cells or tissues **2** *pl* : the natural fluids of an animal body **3** : something that supplies power; *esp* : ELECTRICITY 2

juic·er \ˈjü-sər\ *n* : an appliance for extracting juice (as from fruit)

juice up *vb* : to give life, energy, or spirit to

juicy \'jü-sē\ *adj* **juic·i·er; -est 1** : SUCCULENT **2** : rich in interest; *also* : RACY — **juic·i·ly** \-sə-lē\ *adv* — **juic·i·ness** \-sē-nəs\ *n*

ju·jit·su *or* **ju·jut·su** \jü-'jit-sü\ *n* [Jp *jūjutsu*, fr. *jū* weakness + *jutsu* art, skill] : an art of fighting employing holds, throws, and paralyzing blows

ju·jube \'jü-ıjüb, 'jü-jù-ıbē\ *n* : a fruit-flavored gumdrop or lozenge

juke·box \'jük-ıbäks\ *n* : a coin-operated machine that automatically plays selected recordings

Jul *abbr* July

ju·lep \'jü-ləp\ *n* [ME, sweetened water, fr. MF, fr. Ar *julāb*, fr. Per *gulāb*, fr. *gul* rose + *āb* water] : a drink made of bourbon, sugar, and mint served over crushed ice

Ju·ly \jù-'lī\ *n* [ME *Julie*, fr. OE *Julius*, fr. L, fr. Gaius *Julius* Caesar] : the 7th month of the year

¹jum·ble \'jəm-bəl\ *vb* **jum·bled; jum·bling** : to mix in a confused mass

²jumble *n* : a disorderly mass or pile

jum·bo \'jəm-bō\ *n, pl* **jumbos** [*Jumbo*, a huge elephant exhibited by P.T. Barnum] : a very large specimen of its kind — **jumbo** *adj*

¹jump \'jəmp\ *vb* **1** : to spring into the air : leap over **2** : to give a start **3** : to rise or increase suddenly or sharply **4** : to make a sudden attack **5** : ANTICIPATE ⟨∼ the gun⟩ **6** : to leave hurriedly and often furtively ⟨∼ town⟩ **7** : to act or move before (as a signal) — **jump bail** : to abscond after being released from custody on bail — **jump ship 1** : to leave the company of a ship without authority **2** : to desert a cause

²jump *n* **1** : a spring into the air; *esp* : one made for height or distance in a track meet **2** : a sharp sudden increase **3** : an initial advantage

¹jump·er \'jəm-pər\ *n* : one that jumps

²jumper *n* **1** : a loose blouse **2** : a sleeveless one-piece dress worn usu. with a blouse **3** *pl* : a child's sleeveless coverall

jumping bean *n* : a seed of any of several Mexican shrubs that tumbles about because of the movements of a small moth larva inside it

jumping-off place *n* **1** : a remote or isolated place **2** : a place from which an enterprise is launched

jump-start \'jəmp-ıstärt\ *vb* : to start (an engine or vehicle) by connection to an external power source

jump·suit \'jəmp-ısüt\ *n* **1** : a coverall worn by parachutists in jumping **2** : a one-piece garment consisting of a blouse or shirt with attached trousers or shorts

jumpy \'jəm-pē\ *adj* **jump·i·er; -est** : NERVOUS, JITTERY

jun *abbr* junior

Jun *abbr* June

junc *abbr* junction

jun·co \'jəŋ-kō\ *n, pl* **juncos** *or* **juncoes** : any of a genus of small common pink-billed American finches that are largely gray with conspicuous white feathers in the tail

junc·tion \'jəŋk-shən\ *n* **1** : an act of joining **2** : a place or point of meeting

junc·ture \'jeŋk-chər\ *n* **1** : JOINT, CONNECTION **2** : UNION **3** : a critical time or state of affairs

June \'jün\ *n* [ME, fr. L *Junius*] : the 6th month of the year

jun·gle \'jəŋ-gəl\ *n* **1** : a thick tangled mass of tropical vegetation; *also* : a tract overgrown with vegetation **2** : a place of ruthless struggle for survival

¹ju·nior \'jü-nyər\ *adj* **1** : YOUNGER **2** : lower in rank **3** : of or relating to juniors

²junior *n* **1** : a person who is younger or of lower rank than another **2** : a student in the next-to-last year before graduating

junior college *n* : a school that offers studies corresponding to those of the 1st two years of college

junior high school *n* : a school usu. including grades 7–9

junior varsity *n* : a team whose members lack the experience or qualifications required for the varsity

ju·ni·per \'jü-nə-pər\ *n* : any of numerous coniferous shrubs or trees with leaves like needles or scales and female cones like berries

¹junk \'jəŋk\ *n* **1** : old iron, glass, paper, or waste; *also* : discarded articles **2** : a shoddy product **3** *slang* : NARCOTICS; *esp* : HEROIN — **junky** *adj*

²junk *vb* : DISCARD, SCRAP

³junk *n* : a ship of eastern Asia with a high stern and 4-cornered sails

junk

junk·er \'jəŋ-kər\ *n* : something (as an old automobile) ready for scrapping

Jun·ker \'yuŋ-kər\ *n* [G] : a member of the Prussian landed aristocracy

junk·et \'jəŋ-kət\ *n* **1** : a pudding of sweetened flavored milk set by rennet **2** : a trip made by an official at public expense

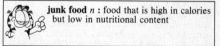

junk food *n* : food that is high in calories but low in nutritional content

junk·ie *also* **junky** \'jəŋ-kē\ *n, pl* **junkies 1** *slang* : a narcotics peddler or addict **2** : one that derives inordinate pleasure from or is dependent on something ⟨sugar ∼⟩

HERE I AM, TRAPPED IN A BALL OF YARN

MY WHOLE LIFE JUST FLASHED BEFORE MY EYES

AND IT LOOKED LIKE A JUNK FOOD COMMERCIAL

JIM DAVIS 8-2

jun·ta \'hün-tə, 'jən-, 'hən-\ *n* [Sp, fr. *junto* joined, fr. L *junctus*, pp. of *jungere* to join] : a group of persons controlling a government esp. after a revolutionary seizure of power

Ju·pi·ter \'jü-pə-tər\ *n* : the largest of the planets and the one 5th in order of distance from the sun — see PLANET table

Ju·ras·sic \ju-'ra-sik\ *adj* : of, relating to, or being the period of the Mesozoic era between the Triassic and the Cretaceous that is marked esp. by the presence of dinosaurs — **Jurassic** *n*

ju·rid·i·cal \ju-'ri-di-kəl\ *or* **ju·rid·ic** \-dik\ *adj* **1** : of or relating to the administration of justice **2** : LEGAL — **ju·rid·i·cal·ly** \-di-k(ə-)lē\ *adv*

ju·ris·dic·tion \ˌjür-əs-'dik-shən\ *n* **1** : the power, right, or authority to interpret and apply the law **2** : the authority of a sovereign power **3** : the limits or territory within which authority may be exercised — **ju·ris·dic·tion·al** \-shə-nəl\ *adj*

ju·ris·pru·dence \-'prüd-ᵊns\ *n* **1** : a system of laws **2** : the science or philosophy of law

ju·rist \'jür-ist\ *n* : one having a thorough knowledge of law; *esp* : JUDGE

ju·ris·tic \ju-'ris-tik\ *adj* **1** : of or relating to a jurist or jurisprudence **2** : of, relating to, or recognized in law

ju·ror \'jür-ər, -ˌȯr\ *n* : a member of a jury

¹ju·ry \'jür-ē\ *n, pl* **juries** **1** : a body of persons sworn to inquire into a matter submitted to them and to give their verdict **2** : a committee for judging and awarding prizes

²jury *adj* : improvised for temporary use esp. in an emergency ⟨a ~ mast⟩

jury–rig \'jür-ē-ˌrig\ *vb* : to construct or arrange in a makeshift fashion

¹just \'jəst\ *adj* **1** : having a basis in or conforming to fact or reason : REASONABLE ⟨~ comment⟩ **2** : CORRECT, PROPER ⟨~ proportions⟩ **3** : morally or legally right ⟨a ~ title⟩ **4** : DESERVED, MERITED ⟨~ punish-

ment⟩ **syn** upright, honorable, conscientious, honest — **just·ly** *adv* — **just·ness** *n*

²just \'jəst, 'jist\ *adv* **1** : EXACTLY ⟨~ right⟩ **2** : very recently ⟨has ~ left⟩ **3** : BARELY ⟨~ too late⟩ **4** : DIRECTLY ⟨~ west of here⟩ **5** : ONLY ⟨~ last year⟩ **6** : QUITE ⟨~ wonderful⟩ **7** : POSSIBLY ⟨it ~ might work⟩

jus·tice \'jəs-təs\ *n* **1** : the administration of what is just (as by assigning merited rewards or punishments) **2** : JUDGE **3** : the administration of law **4** : FAIRNESS; *also* : RIGHTEOUSNESS

justice of the peace : a local magistrate empowered chiefly to try minor cases, to administer oaths, and to perform marriages

jus·ti·fy \'jəs-tə-ˌfī\ *vb* **-fied; -fy·ing** **1** : to prove to be just, right, or reasonable **2** : to pronounce free from guilt or blame **3** : to adjust spaces in a line of printed text so the margins are even — **jus·ti·fi·able** *adj* — **jus·ti·fi·ca·tion** \ˌjəs-tə-fə-'kā-shən\ *n*

jut \'jət\ *vb* **jut·ted; jut·ting** : PROJECT, PROTRUDE

jute \'jüt\ *n* : a strong glossy fiber from either of two tropical plants used esp. for making sacks and twine

juv *abbr* juvenile

¹ju·ve·nile \'jü-və-ˌnīl, -nəl\ *adj* **1** : showing incomplete development **2** : of, relating to, or characteristic of children or young people

²juvenile *n* **1** : a young person; *esp* : one below the legally established age of adulthood **2** : a young animal (as a fish or bird) or plant **3** : an actor or actress who plays youthful parts

juvenile delinquency *n* : violation of the law or antisocial behavior by a juvenile — **juvenile delinquent** *n*

jux·ta·pose \'jək-stə-ˌpōz\ *vb* **-posed; -pos·ing** : to place side by side — **jux·ta·po·si·tion** \ˌjək-stə-pə-'zi-shən\ *n*

JV *abbr* junior varsity

K

¹k \'kā\ *n, pl* **k's** *or* **ks** \'kāz\ **1** *often cap* : the 11th letter of the English alphabet **2** *cap* : STRIKEOUT

²k *abbr* **1** karat **2** kitchen **3** knit **4** kosher — often enclosed in a circle

¹K *abbr* Kelvin

²K *symbol* [NL *kalium*] potassium

ka·bob \kə-'bäb, 'kä-ˌbäb\ *n* : cubes of meat cooked with vegetables usu. on a skewer

Ka·bu·ki \kə-'bü-kē\ *n* : traditional Japanese popular drama with highly stylized singing and dancing

kad·dish \'kä-dish\ *n, often cap* : a Jewish prayer recited in the daily synagogue ritual and by mourners at public services after the death of a close relative

kaf·fee·klatsch \'kȯ-fē-ˌklach, 'kä-\ *n, often cap* [G]

: an informal social gathering for coffee and conversation

kai·ser \'kī-zər\ *n* : EMPEROR; *esp* : the ruler of Germany from 1871 to 1918

kale \'kāl\ *n* : a hardy cabbage with curled leaves that do not form a head

ka·lei·do·scope \kə-'lī-də-ˌskōp\ *n* : a tube containing loose bits of colored material (as glass) and two mirrors at one end that shows many different patterns as it is turned — **ka·lei·do·scop·ic** \-ˌlī-də-'skä-pik\ *adj* — **ka·lei·do·scop·i·cal·ly** \-pi-k(ə-)lē\ *adv*

ka·ma·ai·na \ˌkä-mə-'ī-nə\ *n* [Hawaiian *kama'āina*, fr. *kama* child + *'āina* land] : one who has lived in Hawaii for a long time

kame \'kām\ *n* [Sc, lit., comb] : a short ridge or mound of material deposited by water from a melting glacier

ka·mi·ka·ze \ˌkä-mi-ˈkä-zē\ *n* [Jp, lit., divine wind] : a member of a corps of Japanese pilots assigned to make a suicidal crash on a target; *also* : an airplane flown in such an attack

Kan *or* **Kans** *abbr* Kansas

kan·ga·roo \ˌkaŋ-gə-ˈrü\ *n, pl* **-roos** : any of various large leaping marsupial mammals of Australia and adjacent islands with powerful hind legs and a long thick tail

kangaroo court *n* : a court or an illegal self-appointed tribunal characterized by irresponsible, perverted, or irregular procedures

ka·o·lin \ˈkä-ə-lən\ *n* : a fine usu. white clay used in ceramics and refractories and for the treatment of diarrhea

ka·pok \ˈkä-ˌpäk\ *n* : silky fiber from the seeds of a tropical tree used esp. as a filling (as for life preservers)

Kap·o·si's sar·co·ma \ˈka-pə-sēz-sär-ˈkō-mə\ *n* : a neoplastic disease associated esp. with AIDS that affects esp. the skin and mucous membranes and is characterized usu. by the formation of pink to reddish-brown or bluish plaques

kap·pa \ˈka-pə\ *n* : the 10th letter of the Greek alphabet — K or κ

ka·put *also* **ka·putt** \kä-ˈpùt, kə-, -ˈpüt\ *adj* [G, fr. F *capot* not having made a trick at piquet] **1** : utterly defeated or destroyed **2** : unable to function : USELESS

kar·a·kul \ˈkar-ə-kəl\ *n* : the dark tightly curled pelt of the newborn lamb of a hardy Asian breed of sheep

kar·a·o·ke \ˌkar-ē-ˈō-kē\ *n* [Jp] : a device that plays instrumental accompaniments for songs to which the user sings along

kar·at \ˈkar-ət\ *n* : a unit for expressing proportion of gold in an alloy equal to ¹⁄₂₄ part of pure gold

ka·ra·te \kə-ˈrä-tē\ *n* [Jp, lit., empty hand] : an art of self-defense in which an attacker is disabled by crippling kicks and punches

kar·ma \ˈkär-mə\ *n, often cap* [Skt] : the force generated by a person's actions held in Hinduism and Buddhism to perpetuate reincarnation and to determine the nature of the person's next existence — **karmic** \-mik\ *adj*

karst \ˈkärst\ *n* [G] : an irregular limestone region with sinks, underground streams, and caverns

ka·ty·did \ˈkä-tē-ˌdid\ *n* : any of several large green tree-dwelling American grasshoppers with long antennae

kay·ak \ˈkī-ˌak\ *n* : an Eskimo canoe made of a skin-covered frame with a small opening and propelled by a double-bladed paddle; *also* : a similar portable boat

kayo \(ˌ)kā-ˈō, ˈkä-ō\ *n* : KNOCKOUT — **kayo** *vb*

ka·zoo \kə-ˈzü\ *n, pl* **kazoos** : a toy musical instrument consisting of a tube with a membrane sealing one end and a side hole to sing or hum into

KB *abbr* kilobyte

kc *abbr* kilocycle

KC *abbr* **1** Kansas City **2** King's Counsel **3** Knights of Columbus

kc/s *abbr* kilocycles per second

KD *abbr* knocked down

ke·bab *or* **ke·bob** \kə-ˈbäb\ *var of* KABOB

kedge \ˈkej\ *n* : a small anchor

¹keel \ˈkēl\ *n* **1** : the chief structural member of a ship running lengthwise along the center of its bottom **2** : something (as a bird's breastbone) like a ship's keel in form or use — **keeled** \ˈkēld\ *adj*

²keel *vb* : FAINT, SWOON — usu. used with *over*

keel·boat \ˈkēl-ˌbōt\ *n* : a shallow covered keeled riverboat for freight that is usu. rowed, poled, or towed

keel·haul \-ˌhȯl\ *vb* : to haul under the keel of a ship as punishment

¹keen \ˈkēn\ *adj* **1** : SHARP ⟨a ~ knife⟩ **2** : SEVERE ⟨a ~ wind⟩ **3** : ENTHUSIASTIC ⟨~ about swimming⟩ **4** : mentally alert ⟨a ~ mind⟩ **5** : STRONG, ACUTE ⟨~ eyesight⟩

6 : WONDERFUL, EXCELLENT — **keen·ly** *adv* — **keen·ness** *n*

²keen *n* : a lamentation for the dead uttered in a loud wailing voice or in a wordless cry — **keen** *vb*

¹keep \ˈkēp\ *vb* **kept** \ˈkept\; **keep·ing 1** : FULFILL, OBSERVE ⟨~ a promise⟩ ⟨~ a holiday⟩ **2** : GUARD ⟨~ us from harm⟩; *also* : to take care of ⟨~ a neighbor's children⟩ **3** : MAINTAIN ⟨~ silence⟩ **4** : to have in one's service or at one's disposal ⟨~ a horse⟩ **5** : to preserve a record in ⟨~ a diary⟩ **6** : to have in stock for sale **7** : to retain in one's possession ⟨~ what you find⟩ **8** : to carry on (as a business) : CONDUCT **9** : HOLD, DETAIN ⟨~ him in jail⟩ **10** : to refrain from revealing ⟨~ a secret⟩ **11** : to continue in good condition ⟨meat will ~ in a freezer⟩ **12** : ABSTAIN, REFRAIN — **keep·er** *n*

²keep *n* **1** : FORTRESS **2** : the means or provisions by which one is kept — **for keeps 1** : with the provision that one keep what one has won ⟨play marbles *for keeps*⟩ **2** : PERMANENTLY

keep·ing *n* : CONFORMITY ⟨in ~ with good taste⟩

keep·sake \ˈkēp-ˌsāk\ *n* : MEMENTO

keep up *vb* **1** : to persevere in **2** : MAINTAIN, SUSTAIN **3** : to keep informed **4** : to continue without interruption

keg \ˈkeg\ *n* : a small cask or barrel

keg·ler \ˈke-glər\ *n* : ¹BOWLER

kelp \ˈkelp\ *n* : any of various coarse brown seaweeds; *also* : a mass of these or their ashes often used as fertilizer

Kelt \ˈkelt\ *var of* CELT

kel·vin \ˈkel-vən\ *n* : a unit of temperature equal to ¹⁄₂₇₃.₁₆ of the Kelvin scale temperature of the triple point of water and equal to the Celsius degree

Kelvin *adj* : relating to, conforming to, or being a temperature scale according to which absolute zero is 0 K, the equivalent of −273.15°C

ken \ˈken\ *n* **1** : range of vision : SIGHT **2** : range of understanding

ken·nel \ˈken-ᵊl\ *n* : a shelter for a dog or cat; *also* : an establishment for the breeding or boarding of dogs or cats — **kennel** *vb*

ke·no \ˈkē-nō\ *n* : a game resembling bingo

Ken·tucky bluegrass \kən-ˈtə-kē-\ *n* : a valuable pasture and meadow grass of both Europe and America

Ke·nyan \ˈke-nyən, ˈkē-\ *n* : a native or inhabitant of Kenya — **Kenyan** *adj*

Ke·ogh plan \ˈkē-(ˌ)ō-\ *n* [Eugene James *Keogh* †1989 Am. politician] : an individual retirement account for the self-employed

ke·pi \ˈkā-pē, ˈke-\ *n* [F] : a military cap with a round flat top and a visor

ker·a·tin \ˈker-ət-ᵊn\ *n* : any of various sulfur-containing proteins that make up hair and horny tissues

kerb \ˈkərb\ *n, Brit* : CURB 3

ker·chief \ˈkər-chəf, -ˌchēf\ *n, pl* **kerchiefs** \-chəfs, -ˌchēfs\ *also* **kerchieves** \-ˌchēvz\ [ME *courchef*, fr. OF *cuevrechief*, fr. *covrir* to cover + *chief* head] **1** : a square of cloth worn by women esp. as a head covering **2** : HANDKERCHIEF

kerf \ˈkərf\ *n* : a slit or notch made by a saw or cutting torch

ker·nel \ˈkərn-ᵊl\ *n* **1** : the inner softer part of a seed, fruit stone, or nut **2** : a whole seed of a cereal ⟨a ~ of corn⟩ **3** : a central or essential part : CORE

ker·o·sene *or* **ker·o·sine** \ˈker-ə-ˌsēn, ˌker-ə-ˈsēn\ *n* : a flammable oil produced from petroleum and used esp. for a fuel and as a solvent

ketch \ˈkech\ *n* : a large fore-and-aft rigged boat with two masts

ketch·up \ˈke-chəp, ˈka-\ *n* : a seasoned tomato puree

ket·tle \ˈket-ᵊl\ *n* : a metallic vessel for boiling liquids

ket·tle·drum \-ˌdrəm\ *n* : a brass, copper, or fiberglass drum with calfskin or plastic stretched across the top

¹key \\'kē\ *n* **1** : a usu. metal instrument by which the bolt of a lock is turned; *also* : a device having the form or function of a key **2** : a means of gaining or preventing entrance, possession, or control **3** : EXPLANATION, SOLUTION **4** : one of the levers pressed by a finger in operating or playing an instrument **5** : a leading individual or principle **6** : a system of seven tones based on their relationship to a tonic; *also* : the tone or pitch of a voice **7** : a small switch for opening or closing an electric circuit ⟨a telegraph ∼⟩

²key *vb* **1** : SECURE, FASTEN **2** : to regulate the musical pitch of **3** : to bring into harmony or conformity **4** : to make nervous — usu. used with *up*

³key *adj* : BASIC, CENTRAL ⟨∼ issues⟩

⁴key *n* : a low island or reef (as off the southern coast of Florida)

⁵key *n, slang* : a kilogram esp. of marijuana or heroin

key·board \-ˌbȯrd\ *n* **1** : a row of keys (as on a piano) **2** : an assemblage of keys for operating a machine

key club *n* : a private club serving liquor and providing entertainment

key·hole \\'kē-ˌhōl\ *n* : a hole for receiving a key

¹key·note \-ˌnōt\ *n* **1** : the first and harmonically fundamental tone of a scale **2** : the central fact, idea, or mood

²keynote *vb* **1** : to set the keynote of **2** : to deliver the major address (as at a convention) — **key·not·er** *n*

key·punch \\'kē-ˌpənch\ *n* : a machine with a keyboard used to cut holes or notches in punch cards — **key·punch** *vb* — **key·punch·er** *n*

key·stone \-ˌstōn\ *n* : the wedge-shaped piece at the crown of an arch that locks the other pieces in place

key·stroke \-ˌstrōk\ *n* : an act or instance of depressing a key on a keyboard

key word *n* : a word that is a key; *esp, usu* **key·word** : a significant word used as an indication of the content of or in searching (as a document or database)

kg *abbr* kilogram

KGB *abbr* [Russ *Komitet gosudarstvennoĭ bezopasnosti*] (Soviet) State Security Committee

kha·ki \\'ka-kē, 'kä-\ *n* [Hindi *khaki* dust-colored, fr. *khāk* dust, fr. Per] **1** : a light yellowish brown color **2** : a khaki-colored cloth; *also* : a military uniform of this cloth

khan \\'kän, 'kan\ *n* : a Mongol leader; *esp* : a successor of Genghis Khan

khe·dive \kə-'dēv\ *n* : a ruler of Egypt from 1867 to 1914 governing as a viceroy of the sultan of Turkey

khoum \\'küm\ *n* — see *ouguiya* at MONEY table

kHz *abbr* kilohertz

KIA *abbr* killed in action

kib·ble \\'ki-bəl\ *vb* **kib·bled; kib·bling** : to grind coarsely — **kibble** *n*

kib·butz \ki-'bu̇ts, -'büts\ *n, pl* **kib·but·zim** \-ˌbu̇t-'sēm, -ˌbüt-\ [NHeb *qibbūṣ*] : a communal farm or settlement in Israel

ki·bitz·er \\'ki-bət-sər, kə-'bit-\ *n* : one who looks on and usu. offers unwanted advice esp. at a card game — **kib·itz** \\'ki-bəts\ *vb*

ki·bosh \\'kī-ˌbäsh\ *n* : something that serves as a check or stop ⟨put the ∼ on his plan⟩

¹kick \\'kik\ *vb* **1** : to strike out or hit with the foot; *also* : to score by kicking a ball **2** : to object strongly **3** : to recoil when fired — **kick·er** *n*

²kick *n* **1** : a blow or thrust with the foot; *esp* : a propelling of a ball with the foot **2** : the recoil of a gun **3** : a feeling or expression of objection **4** : stimulating effect esp. of pleasure

kick·back \\'kik-ˌbak\ *n* **1** : a sharp violent reaction **2** : a secret return of a part of a sum received

kick·box·ing \\'kik-ˌbäk-siŋ\ *n* : boxing in which boxers are permitted to kick with bare feet

kick in *vb* **1** : CONTRIBUTE **2** *slang* : DIE

kick·off \\'kik-ˌȯf\ *n* **1** : a kick that puts the ball in play (as in football) **2** : COMMENCEMENT

kick off *vb* **1** : to start or resume play with a placekick **2** : to begin proceedings **3** *slang* : DIE

kick over *vb* : to begin or cause to begin to fire — used of an internal combustion engine

kick·shaw \\'kik-ˌshȯ\ *n* [modif. of F *quelque chose* something] **1** : DELICACY **2** : TRINKET

kick·stand \\'kik-ˌstand\ *n* : a swiveling metal bar attached to a 2-wheeled vehicle for holding it up when not in use

kicky \\'ki-kē\ *adj* : providing a kick or thrill : EXCITING

¹kid \\'kid\ *n* **1** : a young goat **2** : the flesh, fur, or skin of a young goat; *also* : something made of kid **3** : CHILD, YOUNGSTER — **kid·dish** *adj*

²kid *vb* **kid·ded; kid·ding 1** : FOOL **2** : TEASE — **kid·der** *n* — **kid·ding·ly** *adv*

kid·nap \\'kid-ˌnap\ *vb* **kid·napped** *or* **kid·naped** \-ˌnapt\; **kid·nap·ping** *or* **kid·nap·ing** \-ˌna-piŋ\ : to hold or carry a person away by unlawful force or by fraud and against one's will — **kid·nap·per** *or* **kid·nap·er** \-ˌna-pər\ *n*

kid·ney \\'kid-nē\ *n, pl* **kidneys** : either of a pair of organs lying near the backbone that excrete waste products of the body in the form of urine

kidney bean *n* **1** : an edible seed of the common cultivated bean; *esp* : one that is large and dark red **2** : a plant bearing kidney beans

kid·skin \\'kid-ˌskin\ *n* : the skin of a young goat used for leather

kiel·ba·sa \kēl-'bä-sə, kil-\ *n, pl* **-basas** *also* **-ba·sy** \-'bä-sē\ [Pol *kiełbasa*] : a smoked sausage of Polish origin

¹kill \\'kil\ *vb* **1** : to deprive of life **2** : to put an end to ⟨∼ competition⟩; *also* : DEFEAT ⟨∼ a proposed amendment⟩ **3** : USE UP ⟨∼ time⟩ **4** : to mark for omission **syn** slay, murder, assassinate, execute — **kill·er** *n*

LET'S SEE... WE HAVE EVERYTHING FOR THE BEACH EXCEPT A BEACH BALL

HEY, GARFIELD! BRING SOMETHING WE CAN KICK AROUND IN THE SURF!

WITHOUT EVEN LOOKING AROUND I KNOW I SHOULD HAVE REPHRASED THAT

JIM DAVIS

© 1986 PAWS, INC.

10-29

²kill *n* **1** : an act of killing **2** : an animal or animals killed (as in a hunt); *also* : an aircraft, ship, or vehicle destroyed by military action

kill·deer \'kil-₁dir\ *n, pl* **killdeers** *or* **killdeer** [imit.] : an American plover with a plaintive penetrating cry

killdeer

killer bee *n* : AFRICANIZED BEE

killer whale *n* : a small gregarious black and white flesh-eating whale with a white oval patch behind each eye

kill·ing *n* : a sudden notable gain or profit

kill·joy \'kil-₁jȯi\ *n* : one who spoils the pleasures of others

kiln \'kil, 'kiln\ *n* : a heated enclosure (as an oven) for processing a substance by burning, firing, or drying — **kiln** *vb*

ki·lo \'kē-lō\ *n, pl* **kilos** : KILOGRAM

ki·lo·byte \'ki-lə-₁bīt, 'kē-\ *n* : 1024 bytes

kilo·cy·cle \'ki-lə-₁sī-kəl\ *n* : KILOHERTZ

ki·lo·gram \'kē-lə-₁gram, 'ki-\ *n* **1** : the basic metric unit of mass that is nearly equal to the mass of 1000 cubic centimeters of water at its maximum density — see METRIC SYSTEM table **2** : the weight of a kilogram mass under earth's gravity

ki·lo·hertz \'ki-lə-₁hərts, 'kē-, -₁herts\ *n* : 1000 hertz

kilo·li·ter \'ki-lə-₁lē-tər\ *n* — see METRIC SYSTEM table

ki·lo·me·ter \ki-'lä-mə-tər, 'ki-lə-₁mē-\ *n* — see METRIC SYSTEM table

ki·lo·ton \'ki-lə-₁tən, 'kē-lō-\ *n* **1** : 1000 tons **2** : an explosive force equivalent to that of 1000 tons of TNT

ki·lo·volt \-₁vōlt\ *n* : 1000 volts

kilo·watt \'ki-lə-₁wät\ *n* : 1000 watts

kilowatt–hour *n* : a unit of energy equal to that expended by one kilowatt in one hour

kilt \'kilt\ *n* : a knee-length pleated skirt usu. of tartan worn by men in Scotland

kil·ter \'kil-tər\ *n* : proper condition ⟨out of ∼⟩

ki·mo·no \kə-'mō-nə\ *n, pl* **-nos 1** : a loose robe with wide sleeves traditionally worn with a wide sash as an outer garment by the Japanese **2** : a loose dressing gown or jacket

kin \'kin\ *n* **1** : an individual's relatives **2** : KINSMAN

ki·na \'kē-nə\ *n* — see MONEY table

¹kind \'kīnd\ *n* **1** : essential quality or character **2** : a group united by common traits or interests : CATEGORY; *also* : VARIETY **3** : goods or commodities as distinguished from money

²kind *adj* **1** : of a sympathetic, forbearing, or pleasant nature **2** : arising from sympathy or forbearance ⟨∼ deeds⟩ **syn** benevolent, benign, benignant, kindly — **kind·ness** *n*

kin·der·gar·ten \'kin-dər-₁gärt-ᵊn\ *n* [G, lit., children's garden] : a school or class for children usu. from four to six years old

kin·der·gart·ner \-₁gärt-nər\ *n* **1** : a kindergarten pupil **2** : a kindergarten teacher

kind·heart·ed \₁kīnd-'här-təd\ *adj* : marked by a sympathetic nature

kin·dle \'kind-ᵊl\ *vb* **kin·dled; kin·dling 1** : to set on fire : start burning **2** : to stir up : AROUSE **3** : ILLUMINATE, GLOW

kin·dling \'kind-liŋ, 'kin-lən\ *n* : easily combustible material for starting a fire

¹kind·ly \'kīnd-lē\ *adj* **kind·li·er; -est 1** : of an agreeable or beneficial nature **2** : of a sympathetic or generous nature — **kind·li·ness** *n*

²kindly *adv* **1** : READILY ⟨does not take ∼ to criticism⟩ **2** : SYMPATHETICALLY **3** : COURTEOUSLY, OBLIGINGLY

kind of *adv* : to a moderate degree ⟨it's *kind of* late to begin⟩

¹kin·dred \'kin-drəd\ *n* **1** : a group of related individuals **2** : one's relatives

²kindred *adj* : of a like nature or character

kine \'kīn\ *archaic pl of* COW

kin·e·ma \'ki-nə-mə\ *Brit var of* CINEMA

ki·ne·mat·ics \₁ki-nə-'ma-tiks\ *n* : a science that deals with motion apart from considerations of mass and force — **ki·ne·mat·ic** \-tik\ *or* **ki·ne·mat·i·cal** \-ti-kəl\ *adj*

kin·es·the·sia \₁ki-nəs-'thē-zhə, -zhē-ə\ *or* **kin·es·the·sis** \-'thē-səs\ *n, pl* **-the·sias** *or* **-the·ses** \-₁sēz\ : a sense that perceives bodily movement, position, and weight and is mediated by nervous elements in tendons, muscles, and joints; *also* : sensory experience derived from this sense — **kin·es·thet·ic** \-'the-tik\ *adj*

ki·net·ic \kə-'ne-tik\ *adj* : of or relating to the motion of material bodies and the forces and energy (**kinetic energy**) associated with them

ki·net·ics \-tiks\ *n sing or pl* : a science that deals with the effects of forces upon the motions of material bodies or with changes in a physical or chemical system

kin·folk \'kin-₁fōk\ *or* **kinfolks** *n pl* : RELATIVES

king \'kiŋ\ *n* **1** : a male sovereign **2** : a chief among competitors ⟨home-run ∼⟩ **3** : the principal piece in the game of chess **4** : a playing card bearing the figure of a king **5** : a checker that has been crowned — **king·less** *adj* — **king·ly** *adj* — **king·ship** *n*

king crab *n* **1** : HORSESHOE CRAB **2** : a large crab of the north Pacific caught commercially for food

king·dom \'kiŋ-dəm\ *n* **1** : a country whose head is a king or queen **2** : a realm or region in which something or someone is dominant ⟨a cattle ∼⟩ **3** : one of

the three primary divisions of lifeless material, plants, and animals into which natural objects are grouped; *also* : a biological category that ranks above the phylum

king·fish·er \-₁fi-shər\ *n* : any of numerous usu. bright≈ colored crested birds that feed chiefly on fish

king·pin \'kiŋ-₁pin\ *n* **1** : HEADPIN **2** : the leader in a group or undertaking

Kings *n* — see BIBLE table

king–size \'kiŋ-₁sīz\ *or* **king–sized** \-₁sīzd\ *adj* **1** : longer than the regular or standard size **2** : unusually large **3** : having dimensions of about 76 by 80 inches (1.9 by 2.0 meters) ⟨a ∼ bed⟩; *also* : of a size that fits a king-size bed

kink \'kiŋk\ *n* **1** : a short tight twist or curl **2** : a mental peculiarity : QUIRK **3** : CRAMP ⟨a ∼ in the back⟩ **4** : an imperfection likely to cause difficulties in operation — **kinky** *adj*

kin·ship \'kin-₁ship\ *n* : RELATIONSHIP

kins·man \'kinz-mən\ *n* : RELATIVE; *esp* : a male relative

kins·wom·an \-₁wu̇-mən\ *n* : a female relative

ki·osk \'kē-₁äsk\ *n* : a small structure with one or more open sides

Ki·o·wa \'kī-ə-₁wȯ, -₁wä, -₁wä\ *n, pl* **Kiowa** *or* **Kiowas** : a member of an American Indian people of Colorado, Kansas, New Mexico, Oklahoma, and Texas

kip \'kip, 'gip\ *n, pl* **kip** *or* **kips** — see MONEY table

kip·per \'ki-pər\ *n* : a fish (as a herring) preserved by salting and drying or smoking — **kipper** *vb*

kirk \'kərk, 'kirk\ *n, chiefly Scot* : CHURCH

kir·tle \'kərt-ᵊl\ *n* : a long gown or dress worn by women

kis·met \'kiz-₁met, -mət\ *n, often cap* [Turk, fr. Ar *qismah* portion, lot] : FATE

¹kiss \'kis\ *vb* **1** : to touch or caress with the lips as a mark of affection or greeting **2** : to touch gently or lightly

²kiss *n* **1** : a caress with the lips **2** : a gentle touch or contact **3** : a bite-size candy

kiss·er \'ki-sər\ *n* **1** : one that kisses **2** *slang* : MOUTH **3** *slang* : FACE

kit \'kit\ *n* **1** : a set of articles for personal use; *also* : a set of tools or implements or of parts to be assembled **2** : a container (as a case) for a kit

kitch·en \'ki-chən\ *n* **1** : a room with cooking facilities **2** : the personnel that prepares, cooks, and serves food

kitch·en·ette \₁ki-chə-'net\ *n* : a small kitchen or an alcove containing cooking facilities

kitchen police *n* **1** : KP **2** : the work of KPs

kitch·en·ware \'ki-chən-₁war\ *n* : utensils and appliances for kitchen use

kite \'kīt\ *n* **1** : any of various long-winged hawks often with deeply forked tails **2** : a light frame covered with paper or cloth and designed to be flown in the air at the end of a long string

kith \'kith\ *n* [ME, fr. OE *cȳthth*, fr. *cūth* known] : familiar friends, neighbors, or relatives ⟨∼ and kin⟩

kitsch \'kich\ *n* [G] : shoddy or cheap artistic or literary material — **kitschy** *adj*

kit·ten \'kit-ᵊn\ *n* : a young cat — **kit·ten·ish** *adj*

¹kit·ty \'ki-tē\ *n, pl* **kitties** : CAT; *esp* : KITTEN

²kitty *n, pl* **kitties** : a fund in a poker game made up of contributions from each pot; *also* : POOL

kit·ty–cor·ner *or* **kit·ty–cornered** *var of* CATER-CORNER

ki·wi \'kē-(₁)wē\ *n* : any of a small genus of flightless New Zealand birds

kiwi

ki·wi·fruit \-₁früt\ *n* : a brownish hairy egg-shaped fruit of a subtropical vine that has sweet bright green flesh and small edible black seeds

KJV *abbr* King James Version

KKK *abbr* Ku Klux Klan

kl *abbr* kiloliter

klatch *or* **klatsch** \'klach\ *n* [G *Klatsch* gossip] : a gathering marked by informal conversation

klep·to·ma·nia \₁klep-tə-'mā-nē-ə\ *n* : a persistent neurotic impulse to steal esp. without economic motive — **klep·to·ma·ni·ac** \-nē-₁ak\ *n*

klieg light *or* **kleig light** \'klēg-\ *n* : a very bright lamp used in making motion pictures

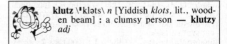 **klutz** \'kləts\ *n* [Yiddish *klots*, lit., wooden beam] : a clumsy person — **klutzy** *adj*

km *abbr* kilometer

kn *abbr* knot

knack \'nak\ *n* **1** : a clever way of doing something **2** : natural aptitude

knap·sack \'nap-₁sak\ *n* : a bag (as of canvas) strapped on the back and used esp. for carrying supplies

knave \'nāv\ *n* **1** : ROGUE **2** : JACK 6 — **knav·ery** \'nā-və-rē\ *n* — **knav·ish** \'nā-vish\ *adj*

knead \'nēd\ *vb* : to work and press into a mass with the hands; *also* : MASSAGE — **knead·er** *n*

knee \'nē\ *n* : the joint in the middle part of the leg — **kneed** \'nēd\ *adj*

knee·cap \'nē-₁kap\ *n* : a thick flat movable bone forming the front of the knee

knee·hole \-ˌhōl\ *n* : a space (as under a desk) for the knees

kneel \ˈnēl\ *vb* **knelt** \ˈnelt\ *or* **kneeled; kneel·ing** : to bend the knee : fall or rest on the knees

¹knell \ˈnel\ *vb* **1** : to ring esp. for a death or disaster **2** : to summon, announce, or proclaim by a knell

²knell *n* **1** : a stroke of a bell esp. when tolled (as for a funeral) **2** : an indication of the end or failure of something

knew *past of* KNOW

knick·ers \ˈni-kərz\ *n pl* : loose-fitting short pants gathered at the knee

knick·knack \ˈnik-ˌnak\ *n* : a small trivial article intended for ornament

¹knife \ˈnīf\ *n, pl* **knives** \ˈnīvz\ **1** : a cutting instrument consisting of a sharp blade fastened to a handle **2** : a sharp cutting tool in a machine

²knife *vb* **knifed; knif·ing** : to stab, slash, or wound with a knife

¹knight \ˈnīt\ *n* **1** : a mounted warrior of feudal times serving a king **2** : a man honored by a sovereign for merit and in Great Britain ranking below a baronet **3** : a man devoted to the service of a lady **4** : a member of an order or society **5** : a chess piece having an L-shaped move — **knight·ly** *adj*

²knight *vb* : to make a knight of

knight·hood \ˈnīt-ˌhủd\ *n* **1** : the rank, dignity, or profession of a knight **2** : CHIVALRY **3** : knights as a class or body

knish \kə-ˈnish\ *n* [Yiddish] : a small round or square of dough stuffed with a filling (as of meat or fruit) and baked or fried

¹knit \ˈnit\ *vb* **knit** *or* **knit·ted; knit·ting 1** : to link firmly or closely **2** : WRINKLE ⟨∼ her brows⟩ **3** : to form a fabric by interlacing yarn or thread in connected loops with needles **4** : to grow together — **knit·ter** *n*

²knit *n* **1** : a basic knitting stitch **2** : a knitted garment or fabric

knit·wear \-ˌwar\ *n* : knitted clothing

knob \ˈnäb\ *n* **1** : a rounded protuberance; *also* : a small rounded ornament or handle **2** : a rounded usu. isolated hill — **knobbed** \ˈnäbd\ *adj* — **knob·by** \ˈnä-bē\ *adj*

¹knock \ˈnäk\ *vb* **1** : to strike with a sharp blow **2** : BUMP, COLLIDE **3** : to make a pounding noise; *esp* : to have engine knock **4** : to find fault with

²knock *n* **1** : a sharp blow **2** : a pounding noise; *esp* : one caused by abnormal ignition in an automobile engine

knock·down \ˈnäk-ˌdaủn\ *n* **1** : the action of knocking down **2** : something (as a blow) that knocks down **3** : something that can be easily assembled or disassembled

knock down *vb* **1** : to strike to the ground with or as if with as sharp blow **2** : to take apart : DISASSEMBLE **3** : to receive as income or salary : EARN **4** : to make a reduction in

knock·er \ˈnä-kər\ *n* : one that knocks; *esp* : a device hinged to a door for use in knocking

knock–knee \ˈnäk-ˌnē\ *n* : a condition in which the legs curve inward at the knees — **knock–kneed** \-ˌnēd\ *adj*

knock·off \ˈnäk-ˌòf\ *n* : a copy or imitation of someone or something popular

knock off *vb* **1** : to stop doing something **2** : to do quickly, carelessly, or routinely **3** : to deduct from a price **4** : KILL **5** : ROB **6** : COPY, IMITATE

knock·out \ˈnäk-ˌaủt\ *n* **1** : a blow that fells and immobilizes an opponent (as in boxing) **2** : something sensationally striking or attractive

knock out *vb* **1** : to defeat by a knockout **2** : to make unconscious or inoperative **3** : to tire out : EXHAUST

knock·wurst *or* **knack·wurst** \ˈnäk-ˌwərst, -ˌvủrst\ *n* : a short thick heavily seasoned sausage

knoll \ˈnōl\ *n* : a small round hill

¹knot \ˈnät\ *n* **1** : an interlacing (as of string) forming a lump or knob and often used for fastening or tying together **2** : PROBLEM **3** : a bond of union; *esp* : the marriage bond **4** : a protuberant lump or swelling in tissue **5** : a rounded cross-grained area in lumber that is a section through the junction of a tree branch with the trunk; *also* : the woody tissue forming this junction in a tree **6** : GROUP, CLUSTER **7** : an ornamental bow of ribbon **8** : one nautical mile per hour; *also* : one nautical mile — **knot·ty** *adj*

²knot *vb* **knot·ted; knot·ting 1** : to tie in or with a knot **2** : ENTANGLE

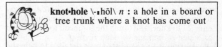

knot·hole \-ˌhōl\ *n* : a hole in a board or tree trunk where a knot has come out

knout \ˈnaủt, ˈnüt\ *n* : a whip used for flogging

know \ˈnō\ *vb* **knew** \ˈnü, ˈnyü\; **known** \ˈnōn\; **know·ing 1** : to perceive directly : have understanding or direct cognition of; *also* : to recognize the nature of **2** : to be acquainted or familiar with **3** : to be aware of the truth of **4** : to have a practical understanding of — **know·able** *adj* — **know·er** *n* — **in the know** : possessing confidential information

know–how \ˈnō-ˌhaủ\ *n* : knowledge of how to do something smoothly and efficiently

know·ing *adj* **1** : having or reflecting knowledge, intelligence, or information **2** : shrewdly and keenly alert **3** : DELIBERATE, INTENTIONAL **syn** clever, bright, smart — **know·ing·ly** *adv*

knowl·edge \ˈnä-lij\ *n* **1** : understanding gained by actual experience ⟨a ∼ of carpentry⟩ **2** : range of information ⟨to the best of my ∼⟩ **3** : clear perception of truth **4** : something learned and kept in the mind

knowl·edge·able \ˈnä-li-jə-bəl\ *adj* : having or showing knowledge or intelligence

knuck·le \ˈnə-kəl\ *n* : the rounded knob at a joint and esp. at a finger joint

knuckle down *vb* : to apply oneself earnestly

knuckle under *vb* : SUBMIT, SURRENDER

knurl \ˈnərl\ *n* **1** : KNOB **2** : one of a series of small ridges on a metal surface to aid in gripping — **knurled** \ˈnərld\ *adj* — **knurly** *adj*

HEY, DOG! I LAUGH AT YOUR LOOKS! I SPIT ON YOUR FEET!

I LIKE PICKING ON THE DOG NEXT DOOR AS LONG AS THERE IS A STURDY FENCE BETWEEN US

KNOTHOLES! I FORGOT ABOUT THE KNOTHOLES!

5-30

© 1988 PAWS, INC.

JIM DAVIS

¹KO \(ₗ)kā-ˈō, ˈkā-ō\ n : KNOCKOUT

²KO vb KO'd; KO'•ing : to knock out in boxing

ko•ala \kō-ˈä-lə\ n : a gray furry Australian marsupial with large hairy ears that feeds on eucalyptus leaves

ko•bo \ˈkō-(ₗ)bō\ n, pl kobo — see naira at MONEY table

K of C abbr Knights of Columbus

kohl•ra•bi \kōl-ˈrä-bē\ n, pl -bies [G, fr. It cavolo rapa, lit., cabbage turnip] : a cabbage that forms no head but has a swollen fleshy edible stem

ko•lin•sky \kə-ˈlin-skē\ n, pl -skies : the fur of various Asian minks

kook \ˈkük\ n : SCREWBALL 2

kooky also kook•ie \ˈkü-kē\ adj kook•i•er; -est : having the characteristics of a kook : CRAZY, ECCENTRIC — kook•i•ness n

ko•peck or ko•pek \ˈkō-ₗpek\ n [Russ kopeĭka] — see ruble at MONEY table

Ko•ran \kə-ˈran, -ˈrän\ n [Ar qurʾān] : a sacred book of Islam that contains revelations made to Muhammad by Allah

Ko•re•an \kə-ˈrē-ən\ n : a native or inhabitant of Korea — Korean adj

ko•ru•na \ˈkòr-ə-ₗnä\ n, pl ko•ru•ny \-ə-nē\ or korunas or ko•rum \ˈkòr-əm\ — see MONEY table

ko•sher \ˈkō-shər\ adj [Yiddish, fr. Heb kāshēr fit, proper] 1 : ritually fit for use according to Jewish law 2 : selling or serving kosher food

kow•tow \kaù-ˈtaù, ˈkaù-ₗtaù\ vb [Chin kòutóu, fr. kòu to knock + tóu head] 1 : to show obsequious deference 2 : to kneel and touch the forehead to the ground as a sign of homage or deep respect

KP \ₗkā-ˈpē\ n 1 : an enlisted man detailed to help the cooks in a military mess 2 : the work of KPs

kph abbr kilometers per hour

Kr symbol krypton

kraal \ˈkräl, ˈkròl\ n 1 : a native village in southern Africa 2 : an enclosure for domestic animals in southern Africa

kraut \ˈkraùt\ n : SAUERKRAUT

Krem•lin \ˈkrem-lən\ n : the Russian or Soviet government

Krem•lin•ol•o•gist \ₗkrem-lə-ˈnä-lə-jist\ n : a specialist in the policies and practices of the Soviet government

¹kro•na \ˈkrō-nə\ n, pl kro•nor \-ₗnòr\ [Sw] — see MONEY table

²kro•na \ˈkrō-nə\ n, pl kro•nur \-nər\ [Icel] — see MONEY table

kro•ne \ˈkrō-nə\ n, pl kro•ner \-nər\ — see MONEY table

Kru•ger•rand \ˈkrü-gər-ₗrand, -ₗränd\ n : a 1-ounce gold coin of the Republic of South Africa

kryp•ton \ˈkrip-ₗtän\ n : a gaseous chemical element used esp. in electric lamps — see ELEMENT table

KS abbr Kansas

kt abbr 1 karat 2 knight

ku•do \ˈkü-dō, ˈkyü-\ n, pl kudos [fr. kudos (taken as pl.)] 1 : AWARD, HONOR 2 : COMPLIMENT, PRAISE

ku•dos \ˈkü-ₗdäs, ˈkyü-\ n : fame and renown resulting from achievement

kud•zu \ˈkùd-zü, ˈkəd-\ n [Jp kuzu] : a creeping leguminous vine used for hay, forage, and erosion control

ku•lak \ˈkü-ˈlak, kyü-, -ˈläk\ n [Russ, lit., fist] 1 : a wealthy peasant farmer in 19th century Russia 2 : a farmer characterized by Communists as too wealthy

kum•quat \ˈkəm-ₗkwät\ n : any of several small citrus fruits with sweet spongy rind and acid pulp

kung fu \ₗkəŋ-ˈfü, ₗkùŋ-\ n : a Chinese art of self-defense resembling karate

ku•rus \kə-ˈrüsh\ n, pl kurus — see lira at MONEY table

Ku•waiti \kù-ˈwä-tē\ n : a native or inhabitant of Kuwait — Kuwaiti adj

kV abbr kilovolt

kvetch \ˈkvech, ˈkfech\ vb : to complain habitually — kvetch n

kW abbr kilowatt

kwa•cha \ˈkwä-chə\ n, pl kwacha — see MONEY table

kwan•za \ˈkwän-zə\ n, pl kwanzas or kwanza — see MONEY table

kwash•i•or•kor \ₗkwä-shē-ˈòr-kòr, -òr-ˈkòr\ n : a disease of young children caused by deficient intake of protein

kWh abbr kilowatt-hour

Ky or KY abbr Kentucky

kyat \ˈchät\ n — see MONEY table

ky•bosh chiefly Brit var of KIBOSH

L

¹l \ˈel\ n, pl l's or ls \ˈelz\ often cap : the 12th letter of the English alphabet

²l abbr, often cap 1 lake 2 large 3 left 4 [L libra] pound 5 line 6 liter

¹La abbr Louisiana

²La symbol lanthanum

LA abbr 1 law agent 2 Los Angeles 3 Louisiana

lab \ˈlab\ n : LABORATORY

Lab n : LABRADOR RETRIEVER

¹la•bel \ˈlā-bəl\ n 1 : a slip attached to something for identification or description 2 : a descriptive or identifying word or phrase 3 : BRAND 3

²label vb -beled or -belled; -bel•ing or -bel•ling 1 : to affix a label to 2 : to describe or name with a label

la•bi•al \ˈlā-bē-əl\ adj : of or relating to the lips or labia

la•bia ma•jo•ra \ˈlā-bē-ə-mə-ˈjòr-ə\ n pl : the outer fatty folds of the vulva

labia mi•no•ra \-mə-ˈnòr-ə\ n pl : the inner highly vascular folds of the vulva

la•bile \ˈlā-ₗbīl, -bəl\ adj 1 : UNSTABLE 2 : ADAPTABLE

la•bi•um \ˈlā-bē-əm\ n, pl la•bia \-ə\ [NL, fr. L, lip] : any of the folds at the margin of the vulva

¹la•bor \ˈlā-bər\ n 1 : physical or mental effort; also : human activity that provides the goods or services in an economy 2 : the physical efforts of giving birth; also : the period of such labor 3 : TASK 4 : those who do manual labor or work for wages; also : labor unions or their officials

²labor vb 1 : WORK 2 : to move with great effort 3 : to be in the labor of giving birth 4 : to suffer from some disadvantage or distress ⟨∼ under a delusion⟩ 5 : to treat or work out laboriously — la•bor•er n

lab•o•ra•to•ry \ˈla-brə-ₗtòr-ē, -bə-rə-\ n, pl -ries : a place equipped for making scientific experiments or tests

Labor Day n : the 1st Monday in September observed as a legal holiday in recognition of the working people

la•bored \ˈlā-bərd\ adj : not freely or easily done ⟨∼ breathing⟩

la•bo•ri•ous \lə-ˈbōr-ē-əs\ adj 1 : INDUSTRIOUS 2 : requiring great effort — la•bo•ri•ous•ly adv

la•bor•sav•ing \ˈlā-bər-ₗsā-viŋ\ adj : designed to replace or decrease labor

labor union n : an organization of workers formed to advance its members' interest in respect to wages and working conditions

la•bour chiefly Brit var of LABOR

lab•ra•dor•ite \ˈla-brə-ₗdòr-ₗīt\ n : an iridescent feldspar used in jewelry

Lab•ra•dor retriever \ˈla-brə-ₗdòr-\ n : a strongly built retriever having a short dense black, yellow, or chocolate coat

la•bur•num \lə-ˈbər-nəm\ n : a leguminous shrub or

tree with hanging clusters of yellow flowers

lab·y·rinth \'la-bə-,rinth\ n : a place constructed of or filled with confusing intricate passageways : MAZE

lab·y·rin·thine \,la-bə-'rin-thən, -,thīn, -,thēn\ adj : INTRICATE, INVOLVED

lac \'lak\ n : a resinous substance secreted by a scale insect and used chiefly in the form of shellac

¹lace \'lās\ vb **laced; lac·ing 1** : TIE **2** : to adorn with lace **3** : INTERTWINE **4** : BEAT, LASH **5** : to add to something to impart zest or savor to

²lace n [ME, fr. OF las, fr. L laqueus snare, noose] **1** : a cord or string used for drawing together two edges **2** : an ornamental braid **3** : a fine openwork usu. figured fabric made of thread — **lacy** \'lā-sē\ adj

lac·er·ate \'la-sə-,rāt\ vb **-at·ed; -at·ing** : to tear roughly — **lac·er·a·tion** \,la-sə-'rā-shən\ n

lace·wing \'lās-,wiŋ\ n : any of various insects with delicate wing veins, long antennae, and often brilliant eyes

lach·ry·mal or **lac·ri·mal** \'la-krə-məl\ adj **1** usu lacrimal : of, relating to, or being glands that produce tears **2** : of, relating to, or marked by tears

lach·ry·mose \'la-krə-,mōs\ adj **1** : TEARFUL **2** : MOURNFUL

¹lack \'lak\ vb **1** : to be wanting or missing **2** : to be deficient in

²lack n : the fact or state of being wanting or deficient : NEED

lack·a·dai·si·cal \,la-kə-'dā-zi-kəl\ adj : lacking life, spirit, or zest — **lack·a·dai·si·cal·ly** \-k(ə-)lē\ adv

lack·ey \'la-kē\ n, pl **lackeys 1** : FOOTMAN, SERVANT **2** : TOADY

lack·lus·ter \'lak-,ləs-tər\ adj : DULL

la·con·ic \lə-'kä-nik\ adj [L laconicus Spartan, fr. Gk lakōnikos; fr. the Spartan reputation for terseness of speech] : sparing of words : TERSE syn concise, curt, short, succinct, brusque — **la·con·i·cal·ly** \-ni-k(ə-)lē\ adv

lac·quer \'la-kər\ n : a clear or colored usu. glossy and quick-drying surface coating — **lacquer** vb

lac·ri·ma·tion \,la-krə-'mā-shən\ n : secretion of tears

la·crosse \lə-'krȯs\ n [CanF la crosse, lit., the crosier] : a goal game in which players use a long-handled triangular-headed stick having a mesh pouch for catching, carrying, and throwing the ball

lac·tate \'lak-,tāt\ vb **lac·tat·ed; lac·tat·ing** : to secrete milk — **lac·ta·tion** \lak-'tā-shən\ n

lac·tic \'lak-tik\ adj **1** : of or relating to milk **2** : obtained from sour milk or whey

lactic acid n : a syrupy acid present in blood and muscle tissue and used in food and medicine

lac·tose \'lak-,tōs\ n : a sugar present in milk

la·cu·na \lə-'kü-nə, -'kyü-\ n, pl **la·cu·nae** \-,nē\ or **la·cu·nas** [L, pool, pit, gap, fr. lacus lake] : a blank space or missing part : GAP

lad \'lad\ n : YOUTH; also : FELLOW

lad·der \'la-dər\ n : a structure for climbing that consists of two parallel sidepieces joined at intervals by crosspieces

lad·die \'la-dē\ n : a young lad

lad·en \'lād-ᵊn\ adj : LOADED, BURDENED

lad·ing \'lā-diŋ\ n : CARGO, FREIGHT

la·dle \'lād-ᵊl\ n : a deep-bowled long-handled spoon used in taking up and conveying liquids — **ladle** vb

la·dy \'lā-dē\ n, pl **ladies** [ME, fr. OE hlǣfdīge, fr. hlāf bread + -dīge (akin to dǣge kneader of bread)] **1** : a woman of property, rank, or authority; also : a woman of superior social position or of refinement **2** : WOMAN **3** : WIFE

lady beetle n : LADYBUG

la·dy·bird \'lā-dē-,bərd\ n : LADYBUG

la·dy·bug \-,bəg\ n : any of various small nearly hemispherical and usu. brightly colored beetles that feed mostly on other insects

la·dy·fin·ger \-,fiŋ-gər\ n : a small finger-shaped sponge cake

lady–in–waiting n, pl **ladies–in–waiting** : a lady appointed to attend or wait on a queen or princess

la·dy·like \'lā-dē-,līk\ adj : WELL-BRED

la·dy·ship \-,ship\ n : the condition of being a lady : rank of lady

lady's slipper or **lady slipper** n : any of several No. American orchids with slipper-shaped flowers

¹lag \'lag\ n **1** : a slowing up or falling behind; also : the amount by which one lags **2** : INTERVAL

²lag vb **lagged; lag·ging 1** : to fail to keep up : stay behind **2** : to slacken gradually syn dawdle, dally, tarry, loiter

la·ger \'lä-gər\ n : a light-colored usu. dry beer

lag·gard \'la-gərd\ adj : tending to lag — **laggard** n — **lag·gard·ly** adv or adj — **lag·gard·ness** n

la·gniappe \'lan-,yap\ n : something given free esp. with a purchase

la·goon \lə-'gün\ n : a shallow sound, channel, or pond near or connected to a larger body of water

laid past and past part of LAY

laid–back \'lād-'bak\ adj : having a relaxed style or character ⟨~ music⟩

lain past part of ¹LIE

lair \'lar\ n : the resting or living place of a wild animal : DEN

laird \'lard\ n, Scot : a landed proprietor

lais·ser–faire chiefly Brit var of LAISSEZ-FAIRE

lais·sez–faire \,le-sā-'far, ,lā-, -,zā-\ n [F laissez faire let do] : a doctrine opposing governmental control of economic affairs beyond that necessary to maintain peace and property rights

la·ity \'lā-ə-tē\ n **1** : the people of a religious faith as distinct from its clergy **2** : the mass of people as distinct from those of a particular field

lake \'lāk\ n : an inland body of standing water of considerable size; also : a pool of liquid (as lava or pitch)

¹lam \'lam\ vb **lammed; lam·ming** : to flee hastily — **lam** n

²lam abbr laminated

Lam abbr Lamentations

la·ma \'lä-mə\ n : a Buddhist monk of Tibet or Mongolia

la·ma·sery \'lä-mə-,ser-ē\ n, pl **-ser·ies** : a monastery for lamas

¹lamb \'lam\ n **1** : a young sheep; also : its flesh used as food **2** : an innocent or gentle person

²lamb vb : to bring forth a lamb

lam·baste or **lam·bast** \lam-'bāst, -'bast\ vb **1** : BEAT **2** : EXCORIATE syn castigate, flay, lash

lamb·da \'lam-də\ n : the 11th letter of the Greek alphabet — Λ or λ

lam·bent \'lam-bənt\ adj [L lambens, prp. of lambere to lick] **1** : FLICKERING **2** : softly radiant ⟨~ eyes⟩ **3** : marked by lightness or brilliance ⟨~ humor⟩ syn effulgent, incandescent, lucent, luminous — **lam·ben·cy** \-bən-sē\ n — **lam·bent·ly** adv

lamb·skin \'lam-,skin\ n : a lamb's skin or a small fine-grade sheepskin or the leather made from either

¹lame \'lām\ adj **lam·er; lam·est 1** : having a body part and esp. a limb so disabled as to impair freedom of movement; also : marked by stiffness and soreness **2** : lacking substance : WEAK — **lame·ly** adv — **lame·ness** n

²lame vb **lamed; lam·ing** : to make lame : CRIPPLE, DISABLE

la·mé \lä-'mā, la-\ n [F] : a brocaded clothing fabric with tinsel filling threads (as of gold or silver)

lame·brain \'lām-,brān\ n : DOLT

lame duck n : an elected official continuing to hold office between an election and the inauguration of a successor — **lame–duck** adj

¹la·ment \lə-'ment\ vb **1** : to mourn aloud : WAIL **2** : to express sorrow or regret for : BEWAIL — **lam·en·ta·ble** \'la-mən-tə-bəl, lə-'men-tə-\ adj — **lam·en·ta·bly** \-blē\ adv — **lam·en·ta·tion** \,la-mən-'tā-shən\ n

²**lament** *n* **1** : a crying out in grief : WAIL **2** : DIRGE, ELEGY **3** : COMPLAINT

Lamentations *n* — see BIBLE table

la·mia \'lā-mē-ə\ *n* : a female demon

lam·i·na \'la-mə-nə\ *n, pl* **-nae** \-ₗnē\ *or* **-nas** : a thin plate or scale

¹**lam·i·nate** \'la-mə-ₗnāt\ *vb* **-nat·ed; -nat·ing** : to make by uniting layers of one or more materials — **lam·i·na·tion** \ₗla-mə-'nā-shən\ *n*

²**lam·i·nate** \-nət\ *n* : a product manufactured by laminating

lamp \'lamp\ *n* **1** : a vessel with a wick for burning a flammable liquid (as oil) to produce light **2** : a device for producing light or heat

lamp·black \-ₗblak\ *n* : black soot used esp. as a pigment

lamp·light·er \-ₗlī-tər\ *n* : one that lights a lamp

lam·poon \lam-'pün\ *n* : SATIRE; *esp* : a harsh satire directed against an individual — **lampoon** *vb*

lam·prey \'lam-prē\ *n, pl* **lampreys** : any of a family of eel-shaped jawless fishes that have well-developed eyes and a large disk-shaped sucking mouth armed with horny teeth

la·nai \lə-'nī\ *n* [Hawaiian *lānai*] : PORCH, VERANDA

¹**lance** \'lans\ *n* **1** : a spear carried by mounted soldiers **2** : any of various sharp-pointed implements; *esp* : LANCET

²**lance** *vb* **lanced; lanc·ing** : to pierce or open with a lance ⟨∼ a boil⟩

lance corporal *n* : an enlisted man in the marine corps ranking above a private first class and below a corporal

lanc·er \'lan-sər\ *n* : a cavalryman of a unit formerly armed with lances

lan·cet \'lan-sət\ *n* : a sharp-pointed and usu. 2-edged surgical instrument

¹**land** \'land\ *n* **1** : the solid part of the surface of the earth; *also* : a part of the earth's surface ⟨fenced ∼⟩ ⟨marshy ∼⟩ **2** : NATION **3** : REALM, DOMAIN — **land·less** *adj*

²**land** *vb* **1** : DISEMBARK; *also* : to touch at a place on shore **2** : to alight or cause to alight on a surface **3** : to bring to or arrive at a destination **4** : to catch and bring in ⟨∼ a fish⟩; *also* : GAIN, SECURE ⟨∼ a job⟩

lan·dau \'lan-ₗdaù\ *n* : a 4-wheeled carriage with a top divided into two sections that can be lowered, thrown back, or removed

land·ed *adj* : having an estate in land ⟨∼ gentry⟩

land·er \'lan-dər\ *n* : a space vehicle designed to land on a celestial body

land·fall \'land-ₗfȯl\ *n* : a sighting or making of land (as after a voyage); *also* : the land first sighted

land·fill \-ₗfil\ *n* : a low-lying area on which refuse is buried between layers of earth

land·form \-ₗfȯrm\ *n* : a natural feature of a land surface

land·hold·er \-ₗhōl-dər\ *n* : a holder or owner of land — **land·hold·ing** \-diŋ\ *adj or n*

land·ing \'lan-diŋ\ *n* **1** : the action of one that lands **2** : a place for discharging or taking on passengers and cargo **3** : a level part of a staircase

landing gear *n* : the part that supports the weight of an aircraft when it is on the ground

land·la·dy \'land-ₗlā-dē\ *n* : a woman who is a landlord

land·locked \-ₗläkt\ *adj* **1** : enclosed or nearly enclosed by land ⟨a ∼ country⟩ **2** : confined to fresh water by some barrier ⟨∼ salmon⟩

land·lord \-ₗlȯrd\ *n* **1** : the owner of property leased or rented to another **2** : a person who rents lodgings : INNKEEPER

land·lub·ber \-ₗlə-bər\ *n* : one who knows little of the sea or seamanship

land·mark \-ₗmärk\ *n* **1** : an object that marks a course or boundary or serves as a guide **2** : an event that marks a turning point **3** : a structure of unusual historical and usu. aesthetic interest

land·mass \-ₗmas\ *n* : a large area of land

land mine *n* **1** : a mine placed on or just below the surface of the ground and designed to be exploded by the weight of someone or something passing over it **2** : a trap for the unwary

land·own·er \-ₗō-nər\ *n* : an owner of land

¹**land·scape** \-ₗskāp\ *n* **1** : a picture of natural inland scenery **2** : a portion of land that can be seen in one glance

²**landscape** *vb* **land·scaped; land·scap·ing** : to modify (a natural landscape) by grading, clearing, or decorative planting

land·slide \-ₗslīd\ *n* **1** : the slipping down of a mass of rocks or earth on a steep slope; *also* : the mass of material that slides **2** : an overwhelming victory esp. in a political contest

lands·man \'landz-mən\ *n* : a person who lives on land; *esp* : LANDLUBBER

land·ward \'land-wərd\ *adv or adj* : to or toward the land

lane \'lān\ *n* **1** : a narrow passageway (as between fences) **2** : a relatively narrow way or track ⟨traffic ∼⟩

lang *abbr* language

lan·guage \'laŋ-gwij\ *n* [ME, fr. OF, fr. *langue* tongue, language, fr. L *lingua*] **1** : the words, their pronunciation, and the methods of combining them used and understood by a community **2** : form or style of verbal expression **3** : a system of signs and symbols and rules for using them that is used to carry information

lan·guid \'laŋ-gwəd\ *adj* **1** : WEAK **2** : sluggish in character or disposition : LISTLESS **3** : SLOW — **lan·guid·ly** *adv* — **lan·guid·ness** *n*

lan·guish \'laŋ-gwish\ *vb* **1** : to become languid **2** : to become dispirited : PINE **3** : to appeal for sympathy by assuming an expression of grief

lan·guor \'laŋ-gər\ *n* **1** : a languid feeling **2** : listless indolence or inertia **syn** lethargy, lassitude, torpidity, torpor — **lan·guor·ous** *adj* — **lan·guor·ous·ly** *adv*

lank \'laŋk\ *adj* **1** : not well filled out **2** : hanging straight and limp

lanky \'laŋ-kē\ *adj* **lank·i·er; -est** : ungracefully tall and thin

lan·o·lin \'lan-ᵊl-ən\ *n* : the fatty coating of sheep's wool esp. when refined for use in ointments and cosmetics

lan·ta·na \lan-'tä-nə\ *n* : any of a genus of tropical shrubs related to the vervains with showy heads of small bright flowers

lan·tern \'lan-tərn\ *n* **1** : a usu. portable light with a protective covering **2** : the chamber in a lighthouse containing the light **3** : a projector for slides

lan·tha·num \'lan-thə-nəm\ *n* : a soft malleable metallic chemical element — see ELEMENT table

lan·yard \'lan-yərd\ *n* **1** : a piece of rope for fastening something in ships; *also* : any of various cords

Lao·tian \lā-'ō-shən, 'laů-shən\ *n* : a native or inhabitant of Laos — **Laotian** *adj*

¹**lap** \'lap\ *n* **1** : a loose panel of a garment **2** : the clothing that lies on the knees, thighs, and lower part of the trunk when one sits; *also* : the front part of the lower trunk and thighs of a seated person **3** : an environment of nurture ⟨the ~ of luxury⟩ **4** : CHARGE, CONTROL ⟨in the ~ of the gods⟩

²**lap** *vb* **lapped; lap·ping 1** : FOLD **2** : WRAP **3** : to lay over or near so as to partly cover

³**lap** *n* **1** : the amount by which an object overlaps another; *also* : the part of an object that overlaps another **2** : an act or instance of going over a course (as a track or swimming pool)

⁴**lap** *vb* **lapped; lap·ping 1** : to scoop up food or drink with the tip of the tongue; *also* : DEVOUR — usu. used with *up* **2** : to splash gently ⟨*lapping* waves⟩

⁵**lap** *n* **1** : an act or instance of lapping **2** : a gentle splashing sound

lap·dog \'lap-ˌdȯg\ *n* : a small dog that may be held in the lap

la·pel \lə-'pel\ *n* : the fold of the front of a coat that is usu. a continuation of the collar

¹**lap·i·dary** \'la-pə-ˌder-ē\ *n, pl* **-dar·ies** : a person who cuts, polishes, or engraves precious stones

²**lapidary** *adj* **1** : of, relating to, or suitable for engraved inscriptions **2** : of or relating to precious stones or the art of cutting them

lap·in \'la-pən\ *n* : rabbit fur usu. sheared and dyed

la·pis la·zu·li \ˌla-pəs-'la-zə-lē, -zhə-\ *n* : a usu. blue semiprecious stone often having sparkling bits of pyrite

Lapp \'lap\ *n* : a member of a people of northern Scandinavia, Finland, and the Kola peninsula of Russia

lap·pet \'la-pət\ *n* : a fold or flap on a garment

¹**lapse** \'laps\ *n* [L *lapsus,* fr. *labi* to slip] **1** : a slight error **2** : a fall from a higher to a lower state **3** : the termination of a right or privilege through failure to meet requirements **4** : INTERRUPTION **5** : APOSTASY **6** : a passage of time; *also* : INTERVAL **syn** blooper, blunder, boner, goof, mistake, slip

²**lapse** *vb* **lapsed; laps·ing 1** : to commit apostasy **2** : to sink or slip gradually : SUBSIDE **3** : CEASE

lap·top \'lap-ˌtäp\ *adj* : of a size that can be used conveniently on one's lap ⟨a ~ computer⟩ — **laptop** *n*

lap·wing \'lap-ˌwiŋ\ *n* : an Old World crested plover

lar·board \'lär-bərd\ *n* : ⁵PORT

lar·ce·ny \'lär-sə-nē\ *n, pl* **-nies** [ME, fr. MF *larcin* theft, fr. L *latrocinium* robbery, fr. *latro* mercenary soldier] : THEFT — **lar·ce·nous** \-nəs\ *adj*

larch \'lärch\ *n* : any of a genus of trees related to the pines that shed their needles in the fall

¹**lard** \'lärd\ *vb* **1** : to insert strips of usu. pork fat into (meat) before cooking; *also* : GREASE **2** *obs* : ENRICH

²**lard** *n* : a soft white fat obtained by rendering fatty tissue of the hog

lar·der \'lär-dər\ *n* : a place where foods (as meat) are kept

lar·es and pe·na·tes \'lar-ēz . . . pə-'nä-tēz\ *n pl* **1** : household gods **2** : personal or household effects

large \'lärj\ *adj* **larg·er; larg·est 1** : having more than usual power, capacity, or scope **2** : exceeding most other things of like kind in quantity or size **syn** big, great, oversize — **large·ness** *n* — **at large 1** : UNCONFINED **2** : as a whole

large·ly \'lärj-lē\ *adv* : to a large extent

lar·gesse *or* **lar·gess** \lär-'zhes, -'jes\ *n* **1** : liberal giving **2** : a generous gift

¹**lar·go** \'lär-gō\ *adv or adj* [It, slow, broad, fr. L *largus* abundant] : at a very slow tempo — used as a direction in music

²**largo** *n, pl* **largos** : a largo movement

lar·i·at \'lar-ē-ət\ *n* [AmerSp *la reata* the lasso, fr. Sp *la* the + AmerSp *reata* lasso, fr. Sp *reatar* to tie again] : a long rope used to catch or tether livestock : LASSO

¹**lark** \'lärk\ *n* : any of a family of small songbirds; *esp* : SKYLARK

²**lark** *n* : something done solely for fun or adventure

³**lark** *vb* : to engage in harmless fun or mischief — often used with *about*

lark·spur \'lärk-ˌspər\ *n* : DELPHINIUM; *esp* : any of the cultivated annual delphiniums

lar·va \'lär-və\ *n, pl* **lar·vae** \-(ˌ)vē\ *also* **larvas** [L, specter, mask] : the wingless often wormlike form in which insects hatch from the egg; *also* : any young animal (as a tadpole) that is fundamentally unlike its parent — **lar·val** \-vəl\ *adj*

lar·yn·gi·tis \ˌlar-ən-'jī-təs\ *n* : inflammation of the larynx

lar·ynx \'lar-iŋks\ *n, pl* **la·ryn·ges** \lə-'rin-ˌjēz\ *or* **lar·ynx·es** : the upper part of the trachea containing the vocal cords — **la·ryn·ge·al** \lə-'rin-jəl\ *adj*

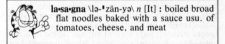

la·sa·gna \lə-'zän-yə\ *n* [It] : boiled broad flat noodles baked with a sauce usu. of tomatoes, cheese, and meat

las·car \'las-kər\ *n* : an Indian sailor

las·civ·i·ous \lə-'si-vē-əs\ *adj* : LUSTFUL, LEWD **syn** licentious, lecherous, libidinous, salacious — **las·civ·i·ous·ness** *n*

la·ser \'lā-zər\ *n* [*l*ight *a*mplification by *s*timulated *e*mission of *r*adiation] : a device that produces an intense monochromatic beam of light

laser disc *n* : an optical disk on which programs are recorded for playback on a television set

¹**lash** \'lash\ *vb* **1** : to move violently or suddenly **2** : WHIP **3** : to attack verbally

²**lash** *n* **1** : a stroke esp. with a whip; *also* : WHIP **2** : a stinging rebuke **3** : EYELASH

³**lash** *vb* : to bind with or as if with a line

lass \'las\ *n* : GIRL

lass·ie \'la-sē\ *n* : LASS

las·si·tude \'la-sə-ˌtüd, -ˌtyüd\ *n* : WEARINESS, FATIGUE **2** : LANGUOR

las·so \'la-sō, la-'sü\ *n, pl* **lassos** *or* **lassoes** [Sp *lazo*] : a rope or long leather thong with a noose used for catching livestock — **lasso** *vb*

¹**last** \'last\ *vb* **1** : to continue in existence or operation **2** : to remain fresh or unimpaired : ENDURE **3** : to manage to continue **4** : to be enough for the needs of

²**last** *n* : a foot-shaped form on which a shoe is shaped or repaired

³**last** *vb* : to shape with a last

⁴**last** *adv* **1** : at the end **2** : most recently **3** : in conclusion

⁵**last** *adj* **1** : following all the rest : FINAL **2** : next before the present **3** : most up-to-date **4** : farthest from a specified quality, attitude, or likelihood ⟨the ∼ thing we want⟩ **4** : CONCLUSIVE; *also* : SUPREME — **last·ly** *adv*

⁶**last** *n* : something that is last — **at last** : FINALLY

Last Supper *n* : the supper eaten by Jesus and his disciples on the night of his betrayal

lat *abbr* latitude

Lat *abbr* Latin

¹**latch** \'lach\ *vb* : to catch or get hold

²**latch** *n* : a catch that holds a door or gate closed

³**latch** *vb* : to make fast with a latch

latch·et \'la-chət\ *n* : a strap, thong, or lace for fastening a shoe or sandal

latch·key \'lach-ˌkē\ *n* : a key for opening a door latch esp. from the outside

latch·string \-ˌstriŋ\ *n* : a string on a latch that may be left hanging outside the door for raising the latch

¹**late** \'lāt\ *adj* **lat·er; lat·est** **1** : coming or remaining after the due, usual, or proper time **2** : far advanced toward the close or end **3** : recently deceased **4** : made, appearing, or happening just previous to the present : RECENT — **late·ly** *adv* — **late·ness** *n*

²**late** *adv* **lat·er; lat·est** **1** : after the usual or proper time; *also* : at or to an advanced point in time **2** : RECENTLY

late·com·er \'lāt-ˌkə-mər\ *n* : one who arrives late

la·teen \la-'tēn\ *adj* : relating to or being a triangular sail extended by a long spar slung to a low mast

la·tent \'lāt-ᵊnt\ *adj* : present but not visible or active **syn** dormant, quiescent, potential — **la·ten·cy** \-ᵊn-sē\ *n*

¹**lat·er·al** \'la-tə-rəl\ *adj* : situated on, directed toward, or coming from the side — **lat·er·al·ly** *adv*

²**lateral** *n* **1** : a branch from the main part **2** : a football pass thrown parallel to the line of scrimmage or away from the opponent's goal

la·tex \'lā-ˌteks\ *n, pl* **la·ti·ces** \'lā-tə-ˌsēz, 'la-\ *or* **la·tex·es** **1** : a milky juice produced by various plant cells (as of milkweeds, poppies, and the rubber tree) **2** : a water emulsion of a synthetic rubber or plastic used esp. in paint

lath \'lath, 'lath\ *n, pl* **laths** *or* **lath** : a thin narrow strip of wood used esp. as a base for plaster; *also* : a building material in sheets used for the same purpose — **lath** *vb*

lathe \'lāth\ *n* : a machine in which a piece of material is held and turned while being shaped by a tool

¹**lath·er** \'la-thər\ *n* **1** : a foam or froth formed when a detergent is agitated in water; *also* : foam from profuse sweating (as by a horse) **2** : DITHER

²**lather** *vb* : to spread lather over; *also* : to form a lather

Lat·in \'lat-ᵊn\ *n* **1** : the language of ancient Rome **2** : a member of any of the peoples whose languages derive from Latin — **Latin** *adj*

Latin American *n* : a native or inhabitant of any of the countries of No., Central, or So. America whose official language is Spanish or Portuguese — **Latin–American** *adj*

La·ti·no \lə-'tē-nō\ *n, pl* **-nos** : a native or inhabitant of Latin America; *also* : a person of Latin-American origin living in the U.S. — **Latino** *adj*

lat·i·tude \'la-tə-ˌtüd, -ˌtyüd\ *n* **1** : angular distance north or south from the earth's equator measured in degrees **2** : a region marked by its latitude **3** : freedom of action or choice

lat·i·tu·di·nar·i·an \ˌla-tə-ˌtü-də-'ner-ē-ən, -ˌtyü-\ *n* : a person who is liberal in religious belief and conduct

la·trine \lə-'trēn\ *n* : TOILET

lat·ter \'la-tər\ *adj* **1** : more recent; *also* : FINAL **2** : relating to, or being the second of two things referred to

lat·ter–day *adj* **1** : of present or recent times **2** : of a later or subsequent time

Latter–day Saint *n* : a member of a religious body founded by Joseph Smith in 1830 and accepting the Book of Mormon as divine revelation : MORMON

lat·ter·ly \'la-tər-lē\ *adv* **1** : LATER **2** : of late : RECENTLY

lat·tice \'la-təs\ *n* **1** : a framework of crossed wood or metal strips; *also* : a window, door, or gate having a lattice **2** : a regular geometrical arrangement

lat·tice·work \-ˌwərk\ *n* : LATTICE; *also* : work made of lattices

Lat·vi·an \'lat-vē-ən\ *n* : a native or inhabitant of Latvia — **Latvian** *adj*

¹**laud** \'lȯd\ *n* : PRAISE, ACCLAIM

²**laud** *vb* : PRAISE, EXTOL **syn** celebrate, eulogize, glorify, magnify — **laud·able** *adj* — **laud·ably** *adv*

lau·da·num \'lȯd-ᵊn-əm\ *n* : a tincture of opium

lau·da·to·ry \'lȯ-də-ˌtȯr-ē\ *adj* : of, relating to, or expressive of praise

¹**laugh** \'laf, 'làf\ *vb* : to show mirth, joy, or scorn with a smile and chuckle or explosive sound; *also* : to become amused or derisive — **laugh·able** *adj* — **laugh·ing·ly** *adv*

²**laugh** *n* **1** : the act of laughing **2** : JOKE; *also* : JEER **3** *pl* : SPORT **1**

laugh·ing·stock \'la-fiŋ-ˌstäk, 'là-\ *n* : an object of ridicule

laugh·ter \'laf-tər, 'làf-\ *n* : the action or sound of laughing

¹**launch** \'lȯnch\ *vb* [ME, fr. OF *lancher*, fr. LL *lanceare* to wield a lance] **1** : THROW, HURL; *also* : to send off ⟨∼ a rocket⟩ **2** : to set afloat **3** : to set in operation : START — **launch·er** *n*

²**launch** *n* : an act or instance of launching

³**launch** *n* : a small open or half-decked motorboat

launch·pad \'lȯnch-ˌpad\ *n* : a platform from which a rocket is launched

laun·der \'lȯn-dər\ *vb* **1** : to wash or wash and iron clothing and household linens **2** : to transfer (as money of an illegal origin) through an outside party to conceal the true source — **laun·der·er** *n*

laun·dress \'lȯn-drəs\ *n* : a woman who is a laundry worker

laun·dry \'lȯn-drē\ *n, pl* **laundries** [fr. obs. *launder* launderer, fr. MF *lavandier*, fr. ML *lavandarius*, fr. L *lavandus* needing to be washed, fr. *lavare* to wash] **1** : a place where laundering is done **2** : clothes or linens that have been or are to be laundered — **laun·dry·man** \-mən\ *n*

lau·re·ate \'lȯr-ē-ət\ *n* : the recipient of honor for achievement in an art or science — **lau·re·ate·ship** *n*

lau·rel \'lȯ-rəl\ *n* **1** : any of a genus of evergreen trees related to the sassafras and cinnamon; *esp* : a small tree of southern Europe **2** : MOUNTAIN LAUREL **3** : a crown of laurel : HONOR — usu. used in pl.

lav *abbr* lavatory

la·va \'lä-və, 'la-\ *n* [It] : melted rock coming from a volcano; *also* : such rock that has cooled and hardened

la·vage \lə-'väzh\ *n* [F] : WASHING; *esp* : the washing out (as of an organ) esp. for medicinal reasons

lav·a·to·ry \'la-və-ˌtōr-ē\ *n, pl* **-ries 1** : a fixed washbowl with running water and drainpipe **2** : BATHROOM

lave \'läv\ *vb* **laved; lav·ing** : WASH

lav·en·der \'la-vən-dər\ *n* **1** : a Mediterranean mint or its dried leaves and flowers used to perfume clothing and bed linen **2** : a pale purple color

¹lav·ish \'la-vish\ *adj* [ME *lavas* abundance, fr. MF *lavasse* downpour, fr. *laver* to wash] **1** : expending or bestowing profusely **2** : expended or produced in abundance **3** : marked by excess — **lav·ish·ly** *adv* — **lav·ish·ness** *n*

²lavish *vb* : to expend or give freely

law \'lȯ\ *n* **1** : a rule of conduct or action established by custom or laid down and enforced by a governing authority; *also* : the whole body of such rules **2** : the control brought about by enforcing rules **3** *cap* : the revelation of the divine will set forth in the Old Testament; *also* : the first part of the Jewish scriptures — see BIBLE table **4** : a rule or principle of construction or procedure **5** : the science that deals with laws and their interpretation and application **6** : the profession of a lawyer **7** : a rule or principle stating something that always works in the same way under the same conditions

law·break·er \'lȯ-ˌbrā-kər\ *n* : one who violates the law

law·ful \'lȯ-fəl\ *adj* **1** : permitted by law **2** : RIGHTFUL — **law·ful·ly** *adv*

law·giv·er \-ˌgi-vər\ *n* : LEGISLATOR

law·less \'lȯ-ləs\ *adj* **1** : having no laws **2** : UNRULY, DISORDERLY ⟨a ~ mob⟩ — **law·less·ly** *adv* — **law·less·ness** *n*

law·mak·er \-ˌmā-kər\ *n* : LEGISLATOR

law·man \'lȯ-mən\ *n* : a law enforcement official (as a sheriff or marshal)

¹lawn \'lȯn\ *n* : ground (as around a house) covered with mowed grass

²lawn *n* : a fine sheer linen or cotton fabric

lawn bowling *n* : a bowling game played on a green with wooden balls which are rolled at a jack

law·ren·ci·um \lȯ-'ren-sē-əm\ *n* : a short-lived radioactive element — see ELEMENT table

law·suit \'lȯ-ˌsüt\ *n* : a suit in law

law·yer \'lȯ-yər\ *n* : one who conducts lawsuits for clients or advises as to legal rights and obligations in other matters — **law·yer·ly** *adj*

lax \'laks\ *adj* **1** : not strict ⟨~ discipline⟩ **2** : not tense or rigid **syn** remiss, negligent, neglectful, delinquent, derelict — **lax·i·ty** \'lak-sə-tē\ *n* — **lax·ly** *adv* — **lax·ness** *n*

¹lax·a·tive \'lak-sə-tiv\ *adj* : relieving constipation

²laxative *n* : a usu. mild laxative drug

¹lay \'lā\ *vb* **laid** \'lād\; **lay·ing 1** : to beat or strike down **2** : to put on or set down : PLACE **3** : to produce and deposit eggs **4** : SETTLE; *also* : ALLAY **5** : SPREAD **6** : PREPARE, CONTRIVE **7** : WAGER **8** : to impose esp. as a duty or burden **9** : to set in order or position **10** : to bring to a specified condition **11** : to put forward : SUBMIT

²lay *n* : the way in which something lies or is laid in relation to something else

³lay *past of* ¹LIE

⁴lay *n* **1** : a simple narrative poem **2** : SONG

⁵lay *adj* **1** : of or relating to the laity **2** : not of a particular profession; *also* : lacking extensive knowledge of a particular subject

lay·away \'lā-ə-ˌwā\ *n* : a purchasing agreement by which a retailer agrees to hold merchandise secured by a deposit until the price is paid in full

lay·er \'lā-ər\ *n* **1** : one that lays **2** : one thickness, course, or fold laid or lying over or under another

lay·ette \lā-'et\ *n* [F, fr. MF, dim. of *laye* box] : an outfit of clothing and equipment for a newborn infant

lay·man \'lā-mən\ *n* : a person who is a member of the laity

lay·off \'lā-ˌȯf\ *n* **1** : a period of inactivity **2** : the act of dismissing an employee usu. temporarily

lay·out \'lā-ˌaùt\ *n* : the final arrangement, plan, or design of something

lay·over \-ˌō-vər\ *n* : STOPOVER

lay·per·son \-ˌpər-sən\ *n* : a member of the laity

lay·wom·an \'lā-ˌwù-mən\ *n* : a woman who is a member of the laity

la·zar \'la-zər, 'lā-\ *n* : LEPER

laze \'lāz\ *vb* **lazed; laz·ing** : to pass time in idleness or relaxation

la·zy \'lā-zē\ *adj* **la·zi·er; -est 1** : disliking activity or exertion **2** : encouraging idleness **3** : SLUGGISH **4** : DROOPY, LAX **5** : not rigorous or strict — **la·zi·ly** \-zə-lē\ *adv* — **la·zi·ness** \-zē-nəs\ *n*

la·zy·bones \-ˌbōnz\ *n sing or pl* : a lazy person

lazy Su·san \ˌlā-zē-'süz-ᵊn\ *n* : a revolving tray used for serving food

lb *abbr* [L *libra*] pound

lc *abbr* lowercase

LC *abbr* Library of Congress

¹LCD \ˌel-(ˌ)sē-'dē\ *n* [*liquid crystal display*] : a display (as of the time in a watch) that consists of segments of a liquid crystal whose reflectivity varies with the voltage applied to them

²LCD *abbr* least common denominator; lowest common denominator

LCDR *abbr* lieutenant commander

LCM *abbr* least common multiple; lowest common multiple

LCpl *abbr* lance corporal

LCS *abbr* League Championship Series

ld *abbr* **1** load **2** lord

LD *abbr* learning disabled; learning disability

LDC *abbr* less developed country

ldg *abbr* **1** landing **2** loading

LDL \ˌel-(ˌ)dē-ˈel\ *n* [*low-density lipoprotein*] : a cholesterol-rich protein-poor lipoprotein of blood plasma correlated with increased risk of atherosclerosis

L-do·pa \ˈel-ˈdō-pə\ *n* : an isomer of dopa used esp. in the treatment of Parkinson's disease

LDS *abbr* Latter-day Saints

lea \ˈlē, ˈlā\ *n* : PASTURE, MEADOW

leach \ˈlēch\ *vb* : to pass a liquid (as water) through to carry off the soluble components; *also* : to dissolve out by such means ⟨∼ alkali from ashes⟩

¹lead \ˈlēd\ *vb* **led** \ˈled\; **lead·ing 1** : to guide on a way **2** : LIVE ⟨∼ a quiet life⟩ **3** : to direct the operations, activity, or performance of ⟨∼ an orchestra⟩ **4** : to go at the head of : be first ⟨∼ a parade⟩ **5** : to begin play with; *also* : BEGIN, OPEN **6** : to tend toward a definite result ⟨study ∼*ing* to a degree⟩ — **lead·er** *n* — **lead·er·less** *adj* — **lead·er·ship** *n*

²lead \ˈlēd\ *n* **1** : a position at the front; *also* : a margin by which one leads **2** : the privilege of leading in cards; *also* : the card or suit led **3** : EXAMPLE **4** : one that leads **5** : a principal role (as in a play); *also* : one who plays such a role **6** : INDICATION, CLUE **7** : an insulated electrical conductor

³lead \ˈled\ *n* **1** : a heavy malleable bluish white chemical element —see ELEMENT table **2** : an article made of lead; *esp* : a weight for sounding at sea **3** : a thin strip of metal used to separate lines of type in printing **4** : a thin stick of marking substance in or for a pencil

⁴lead \ˈled\ *vb* **1** : to cover, line, or weight with lead **2** : to fix (glass) in position with lead **3** : to treat or mix with lead or a lead compound

lead·en \ˈled-ᵊn\ *adj* **1** : made of lead; *also* : of the color of lead **2** : SLUGGISH, DULL

lead off *vb* : OPEN, BEGIN; *esp* : to bat first in an inning — **lead·off** \ˈlēd-ˌof\ *n or adj*

¹leaf \ˈlēf\ *n, pl* **leaves** \ˈlēvz\ **1** : a usu. flat and green outgrowth of a plant stem that is a unit of foliage and functions esp. in photosynthesis; *also* : FOLIAGE **2** : something that is suggestive of a leaf — **leaf·less** *adj* — **leafy** *adj*

²leaf *vb* **1** : to produce leaves **2** : to turn the pages of a book

leaf·age \ˈlē-fij\ *n* : FOLIAGE

leafed \ˈlēft\ *adj* : LEAVED

leaf·hop·per \ˈlēf-ˌhä-pər\ *n* : any of a family of small leaping insects related to the cicadas that suck the juices of plants

leaf·let \ˈlē-flət\ *n* **1** : a division of a compound leaf **2** : PAMPHLET, FOLDER

leaf mold *n* : a compost or layer composed chiefly of decayed vegetable matter

leaf·stalk \ˈlēf-ˌstok\ *n* : PETIOLE

¹league \ˈlēg\ *n* : a unit of distance equal to about three miles (five kilometers)

²league *n* **1** : an association or alliance for a common purpose **2** : CLASS, CATEGORY — **league** *vb* — **leagu·er** \ˈlē-gər\ *n*

¹leak \ˈlēk\ *vb* **1** : to enter or escape through a leak **2** : to let a substance in or out through an opening **3** : to become or make known

²leak *n* **1** : a crack or hole that accidentally admits a fluid or light or lets it escape; *also* : something that secretly or accidentally permits the admission or escape of something else **2** : LEAKAGE — **leaky** *adj*

leak·age \ˈlē-kij\ *n* **1** : the act of leaking **2** : the thing or amount that leaks

¹lean \ˈlēn\ *vb* **1** : to bend from a vertical position : INCLINE **2** : to cast one's weight to one side for support **3** : to rely on for support **4** : to incline in opinion, taste, or desire — **lean** *n*

²lean *adj* **1** : lacking or deficient in flesh and esp. in fat **2** : lacking richness or productiveness **3** : low in fuel content — **lean·ness** *n*

leant \ˈlent\ *chiefly Brit past of* LEAN

lean-to \ˈlēn-ˌtü\ *n, pl* **lean-tos** \-ˌtüz\ : a wing or extension of a building having a roof of only one slope; *also* : a rough shed or shelter with a similar roof

¹leap \ˈlēp\ *vb* **leapt** \ˈlēpt, ˈlept\ *or* **leaped; leap·ing** : to spring free from a surface or over an obstacle : JUMP

²leap *n* : JUMP

leap·frog \ˈlēp-ˌfrog, -ˌfräg\ *n* : a game in which a player bends down and is vaulted over by another — **leapfrog** *vb*

leap year *n* : a year containing 366 days with February 29 as the extra day

learn \ˈlərn\ *vb* **learned** \ˈlərnd, ˈlərnt\; **learn·ing 1** : to gain knowledge, understanding, or skill by study or experience; *also* : MEMORIZE **2** : to find out : ASCERTAIN — **learn·er** *n*

learn·ed \ˈlər-nəd\ *adj* : SCHOLARLY, ERUDITE — **learn·ed·ly** *adv* — **learn·ed·ness** *n*

learn·ing \ˈlər-niŋ\ *n* : KNOWLEDGE, ERUDITION

learning disabled *adj* : having difficulty in learning a basic scholastic skill because of a disorder (as dyslexia) that interferes with the learning process — **learning disability** *n*

learnt \ˈlərnt\ *chiefly Brit past and past part of* LEARN

¹lease \ˈlēs\ *n* : a contract transferring real estate for a term of years or at will usu. for a specified rent

²lease *vb* **leased; leas·ing 1** : to grant by lease **2** : to hold under a lease syn let, charter, hire, rent

lease·hold \ˈlēs-ˌhōld\ *n* **1** : a tenure by lease **2** : land held by lease — **lease·hold·er** *n*

leash \ˈlēsh\ *n* [ME *lees, leshe,* fr. OF *laisse,* fr. *laissier* to let go, fr. L *laxare* to loosen, fr. *laxus* slack] : a line for leading or restraining an animal — **leash** *vb*

¹least \ˈlēst\ *adj* **1** : lowest in importance or position **2** : smallest in size or degree **3** : SLIGHTEST

²least *n* : one that is least

³least *adv* : in the smallest or lowest degree

least common denominator *n* : the least common multiple of two or more denominators

least common multiple *n* : the smallest common multiple of two or more numbers

least·wise \ˈlēst-ˌwīz\ *adv* : at least

leath·er \ˈle-thər\ *n* : animal skin dressed for use — **leath·ern** \-thərn\ *adj* — **leath·ery** *adj*

leath·er·neck \-ˌnek\ *n* : MARINE

¹leave \ˈlēv\ *vb* **left** \ˈleft\; **leav·ing 1** : to allow or cause to remain behind **2** : to have as a remainder **3** : BEQUEATH **4** : to let stay without interference **5** : to go away : depart from **6** : GIVE UP, ABANDON

²leave *n* **1** : PERMISSION; *also* : authorized absence from duty **2** : DEPARTURE

³leave *vb* **leaved; leav·ing** : LEAF

leaved \ˈlēvd\ *adj* : having leaves

¹leav·en \ˈle-vən\ *n* **1** : a substance (as yeast) used to produce fermentation (as in dough) **2** : something that modifies or lightens

²leaven *vb* : to raise (dough) with a leaven; *also* : to permeate with a modifying or vivifying element

leav·en·ing *n* : LEAVEN

leaves *pl of* LEAF

leave–tak·ing \ˈlēv-ˌtā-kiŋ\ *n* : DEPARTURE, FAREWELL

leav·ings \ˈlē-viŋz\ *n pl* : REMNANT, RESIDUE

Leb·a·nese \ˌle-bə-ˈnēz, -ˈnēs\ *n* : a native or inhabitant of Lebanon — **Lebanese** *adj*

lech·ery \ˈle-chə-rē\ *n* : inordinate indulgence in sexual activity — **lech·er** \ˈle-chər\ *n* — **lech·er·ous** \ˈle-chə-rəs\ *adj* — **lech·er·ous·ly** *adv* — **lech·er·ous·ness** *n*

lec·i·thin \ˈle-sə-thən\ *n* : any of several waxy phosphorus-containing substances that are common in animals and plants, form colloidal solutions in water, and have emulsifying and wetting properties

lect *abbr* lecture; lecturer

lec·tern \ˈlek-tərn\ *n* : a stand to support a book for a standing reader

lec·tor \-tər\ *n* : one whose chief duty is to read the lessons in a church service

lec·ture \'lek-chər\ *n* **1** : a discourse given before an audience esp. for instruction **2** : REPRIMAND — **lecture** *vb* — **lec·tur·er** *n* — **lec·ture·ship** *n*

led *past and past part of* LEAD

LED \¡el-(¡)ē-'dē\ *n* [*l*ight-*e*mitting *d*iode] : a semiconductor diode that emits light when a voltage is applied to it and is used esp. for electronic displays

le·der·ho·sen \'lā-dər-¡hōz-ᵊn\ *n pl* : leather shorts often with suspenders worn esp. in Bavaria

ledge \'lej\ *n* [ME *legge* bar of a gate] **1** : a shelflike projection from a top or an edge **2** : REEF

led·ger \'le-jər\ *n* : a book containing accounts to which debits and credits are transferred in final form

lee \'lē\ *n* **1** : a protecting shelter **2** : the side (as of a ship) that is sheltered from the wind — **lee** *adj*

leech \'lēch\ *n* **1** : any of various segmented usu. freshwater worms that are related to the earthworms and have a sucker at each end **2** : a hanger-on who seeks gain

leek \'lēk\ *n* : an onionlike herb grown for its mildly pungent leaves and stalk

leer \'lir\ *n* : a suggestive, knowing, or malicious look — **leer** *vb*

leery \'lir-ē\ *adj* : SUSPICIOUS, WARY

lees \'lēz\ *n pl* : DREGS

¹lee·ward \'lē-wərd, 'lü-ərd\ *n* : the lee side

²leeward *adj* : situated away from the wind

lee·way \'lē-¡wā\ *n* **1** : lateral movement of a ship when under way **2** : an allowable margin of freedom or variation

¹left \'left\ *adj* [ME, fr. OE, weak; fr. the left hand's being the weaker in most individuals] **1** : of, relating to, or being the side of the body in which the heart is mostly located; *also* : located nearer to this side than to the right **2** *often cap* : of, adhering to, or constituted by the political Left — **left** *adv*

²left *n* **1** : the left hand; *also* : the side or part that is on or toward the left side **2** *cap* : those professing political views marked by desire to reform the established order and usu. to give greater freedom to the common man

³left *past and past part of* LEAVE

left–hand *adj* **1** : situated on the left **2** : LEFT-HANDED

left–hand·ed \'left-'han-dəd\ *adj* **1** : using the left hand habitually or more easily than the right **2** : designed for or done with the left hand **3** : INSINCERE, BACK-HANDED ⟨a ~ compliment⟩ **4** : COUNTERCLOCKWISE — **left–handed** *adv*

left·ism \'lef-¡ti-zəm\ *n* **1** : the principles and views of the Left **2** : advocacy of the doctrines of the Left — **left·ist** \-tist\ *n or adj*

left·over \'left-¡ō-vər\ *n* : something that remains unused or unconsumed

¹leg \'leg\ *n* **1** : a limb of an animal used esp. for sup-

porting the body and in walking; *also* : the part of the vertebrate leg between knee and foot **2** : something resembling or analogous to an animal leg (table ~) **3** : the part of an article of clothing that covers the leg **4** : a portion of a trip — **leg·ged** \'le-gəd\ *adj* — **leg·less** *adj*

²leg *vb* **legged; leg·ging** : to use the legs in walking or esp. in running

³leg *abbr* **1** legal **2** legislative; legislature

leg·a·cy \'le-gə-sē\ *n, pl* **-cies** : INHERITANCE; *also* : something that has come from a predecessor or the past

le·gal \'lē-gəl\ *adj* **1** : of or relating to law or lawyers **2** : LAWFUL; *also* : STATUTORY **3** : enforced in courts of law — **le·gal·i·ty** \li-'ga-lə-tē\ *n* — **le·gal·ize** \'lē-gə-¡līz\ *vb* — **le·gal·ly** *adv*

le·gal·ism \'lē-gə-¡li-zəm\ *n* **1** : strict, literal, or excessive conformity to the law or to a religious or moral code **2** : a legal term — **le·gal·is·tic** \¡lē-gə-'lis-tik\ *adj*

leg·ate \'le-gət\ *n* : an official representative

leg·a·tee \¡le-gə-'tē\ *n* : a person to whom a legacy is bequeathed

le·ga·tion \li-'gā-shən\ *n* **1** : a diplomatic mission headed by a minister **2** : the official residence and office of a minister in a foreign country

le·ga·to \li-'gä-tō\ *adv or adj* [It, lit., tied] : in a smooth and connected manner (as of music)

leg·end \'le-jənd\ *n* [ME *legende*, fr. MF & ML; MF *legende*, fr. ML *legenda*, fr. L *legere* to read] **1** : a story coming down from the past; *esp* : one popularly accepted as historical though not verifiable **2** : an inscription on an object; *also* : CAPTION **3** : an explanatory list of the symbols on a map or chart

leg·end·ary \'le-jən-¡der-ē\ *adj* **1** : of, relating to, or characteristic of a legend **2** : FAMOUS — **leg·en·dari·ly** \-¡der-ə-lē\ *adv*

leg·er·de·main \¡le-jər-də-'mān\ *n* [ME, fr. MF *leger de main* light of hand] : SLEIGHT OF HAND

leg·ging *or* **leg·gin** \'le-gən, -gin\ *n* : a covering for the leg; *also* : TIGHTS

leg·gy \'le-gē\ *adj* **leg·gi·er; -est** **1** : having unusually long legs **2** : having long and attractive legs **3** : SPINDLY — used of a plant

leg·horn \'leg-¡hôrn, 'le-gərn\ *n* **1** : a fine plaited straw; *also* : a hat made of this straw **2** : any of a Mediterranean breed of small hardy fowls

leg·i·ble \'le-jə-bəl\ *adj* : capable of being read : CLEAR — **leg·i·bil·i·ty** \¡le-jə-'bi-lə-tē\ *n* — **leg·i·bly** \'le-jə-blē\ *adv*

¹le·gion \'lē-jən\ *n* **1** : a unit of the Roman army comprising 3000 to 6000 soldiers **2** : MULTITUDE **3** : an association of ex-servicemen — **le·gion·ary** \-jə-¡ner-ē\ *n* — **le·gion·naire** \¡lē-jə-'nar\ *n*

²legion *adj* : MANY, NUMEROUS

legis *abbr* legislation; legislative; legislature

leg·is·late \'le-jəs-¡lāt\ *vb* **-lat·ed; -lat·ing** : to make or enact laws; *also* : to bring about by legislation — **leg·is·la·tor** \-¡lā-tər\ *n*

leg·is·la·tion \ˌle-jəs-ˈlā-shən\ *n* **1** : the action of legislating **2** : laws made by a legislative body

leg·is·la·tive \ˈle-jəs-ˌlā-tiv\ *adj* **1** : having the power of legislating **2** : of or relating to a legislature or legislation

leg·is·la·ture \ˈle-jəs-ˌlā-chər\ *n* : an organized body of persons having the authority to make laws

leg·it \li-ˈjit\ *adj, slang* : LEGITIMATE

¹le·git·i·mate \li-ˈji-tə-mət\ *adj* **1** : lawfully begotten **2** : GENUINE **3** : LAWFUL **4** : conforming to recognized principles or accepted rules or standards — le·git·i·ma·cy \-mə-sē\ *n* — le·git·i·mate·ly *adv*

²le·git·i·mate \-ˌmāt\ *vb* : to make legitimate

leg·it·i·mise *Brit var of* LEGITIMIZE

le·git·i·mize \li-ˈji-tə-ˌmīz\ *vb* **-mized; -miz·ing** : LEGITIMATE

leg·man \ˈleg-ˌman\ *n* **1** : a reporter assigned usu. to gather information **2** : an assistant who gathers information and runs errands

le·gume \ˈle-ˌgyüm, li-ˈgyüm\ *n* [F] **1** : any of a large family of plants having fruits that are dry pods and split when ripe and including important food and forage plants (as beans and clover); *also* : the part (as seeds or pods) of a legume used as food **2** : the pod of a legume — le·gu·mi·nous \li-ˈgyü-mə-nəs\ *adj*

¹lei \ˈlā, ˈlā-ē\ *n* : a wreath or necklace usu. of flowers

²lei \ˈlā\ *pl of* LEU

lei·sure \ˈlē-zhər, ˈle-, ˈlā-\ *n* **1** : time free from work or duties **2** : EASE; *also* : CONVENIENCE **syn** relaxation, rest, repose — lei·sure·ly *adj or adv*

leit·mo·tiv *or* leit·mo·tif \ˈlīt-mō-ˌtēf\ *n* [G *Leitmotiv*, fr. *leiten* to lead + *Motiv* motive] : a dominant recurring theme

lek \ˈlek\ *n, pl* leks *or* le·ke *also* lek *or* le·ku — see MONEY table

lem·ming \ˈle-miŋ\ *n* [Norw] : any of various short-tailed northern rodents; *esp* : one of Europe noted for recurrent mass migrations

lem·on \ˈle-mən\ *n* **1** : an acid yellow usu. nearly oblong citrus fruit; *also* : a citrus tree that bears lemons **2** : something (as an automobile) unsatisfactory or defective — lem·ony *adj*

lem·on·ade \ˌle-mə-ˈnād\ *n* : a beverage of lemon juice, sugar, and water

lem·pi·ra \lem-ˈpir-ə\ *n* — see MONEY table

le·mur \ˈlē-mər\ *n* : any of various arboreal mammals largely of Madagascar that are related to the monkeys and have large eyes, very soft woolly fur, and a long furry tail

lend \ˈlend\ *vb* lent \ˈlent\; lend·ing **1** : to give for temporary use on condition that the same or its equivalent be returned **2** : AFFORD, FURNISH **3** : ACCOMMODATE — lend·er *n*

lend–lease \-ˈlēs\ *n* : the transfer of goods and services to an ally to aid in a common cause with payment made by a return of the items or their use in the cause

lemur

or by a similar transfer of other goods and services

length \ˈleŋth\ *n* **1** : the longer or longest dimension of an object; *also* : a measured distance **2** : duration or extent in time or space **3** : the length of something taken as a unit of measure **4** : a single piece of a series of pieces that may be joined together ⟨a ∼ of pipe⟩ — at length **1** : in full **2** : FINALLY

length·en \ˈleŋ-thən\ *vb* : to make or become longer **syn** extend, elongate, prolong, protract

length·wise \ˈleŋth-ˌwīz\ *adv* : in the direction of the length — lengthwise *adj*

lengthy \ˈleŋ-thē\ *adj* length·i·er; -est **1** : protracted excessively **2** : EXTENDED, LONG

le·nient \ˈlē-nē-ənt, -nyənt\ *adj* : of mild and tolerant disposition or effect **syn** indulgent, forbearing, merciful, tolerant — le·ni·en·cy \ˈlē-nē-ən-sē, -nyən-sē\ *n* — le·ni·ent·ly *adv*

len·i·tive \ˈle-nə-tiv\ *adj* : alleviating pain or harshness

len·i·ty \ˈle-nə-tē\ *n* : LENIENCY

lens \ˈlenz\ *n* [L *lent-, lens* lentil; so called fr. the shape of a convex lens] **1** : a curved piece of glass or plastic used singly or combined in an optical instrument for forming an image; *also* : a device for focusing radiation other than light **2** : a transparent body in the eye that focuses light rays on receptors at the back of the eye

Lent \ˈlent\ *n* : a 40-day period of penitence and fasting observed from Ash Wednesday to Easter by many churches — Lent·en \-ᵊn\ *adj*

len·til \ˈlent-ᵊl\ *n* : a Eurasian annual legume grown for its flat edible seeds and for fodder; *also* : its seed

Leo \ˈlē-ō\ *n* [L, lit., lion] **1** : a zodiacal constellation between Cancer and Virgo usu. pictured as a lion **2** : the 5th sign of the zodiac in astrology; *also* : one born under this sign

le·one \lē-ˈōn\ *n, pl* leones *or* leone — see MONEY table

le·o·nine \ˈlē-ə-ˌnīn\ *adj* : of, relating to, or resembling a lion

leop·ard \'le-pərd\ *n* : a large usu. tawny and black-spotted cat of southern Asia and Africa

le·o·tard \'lē-ə-ˌtärd\ *n* : a close-fitting garment worn esp. by dancers and for exercise

lep·er \'le-pər\ *n* **1** : a person affected with leprosy **2** : OUTCAST

lep·re·chaun \'le-prə-ˌkän\ *n* : a mischievous elf of Irish folklore

lep·ro·sy \'le-prə-sē\ *n* : a chronic bacterial disease marked esp. if not treated by slow-growing swellings with deformity and loss of sensation of affected parts — **lep·rous** \-prəs\ *adj*

lep·ton \lep-'tän\ *n, pl* **lep·ta** \-'tä\ — see *drachma* at MONEY table

les·bi·an \'lez-bē-ən\ *n, often cap* [fr. the reputed homosexual group associated with the poet Sappho of Lesbos] : a female homosexual — **lesbian** *adj, often cap* — **les·bi·an·ism** \-ə-ˌni-zəm\ *n*

lèse ma·jes·té *or* **lese maj·es·ty** \'läz-ˌma-jə-stē, 'lez-, 'lēz-\ *n* [MF *lese majesté,* fr. L *laesa majestas,* lit., injured majesty] : an offense violating the dignity of a sovereign

le·sion \'lē-zhən\ *n* : an abnormal structural change in the body due to injury or disease; *esp* : one clearly marked off from healthy tissue around it

¹less \'les\ *adj, comparative of* ¹LITTLE **1** : FEWER ⟨∼ than six⟩ **2** : of lower rank, degree, or importance **3** : SMALLER; *also* : more limited in quantity

²less *adv, comparative of* ²LITTLE : to a lesser extent or degree

³less *n, pl* **less 1** : a smaller portion **2** : something of less importance

⁴less *prep* : diminished by : MINUS

-less \ləs\ *adj suffix* **1** : destitute of : not having ⟨child*less*⟩ **2** : unable to be acted on or to act (in a specified way) ⟨daunt*less*⟩

les·see \le-'sē\ *n* : a tenant under a lease

less·en \'les-ᵊn\ *vb* : to make or become less **syn** decrease, diminish, dwindle, abate

less·er \'le-sər\ *adj, comparative of* ¹LITTLE : of less size, quality, or significance

les·son \'les-ᵊn\ *n* **1** : a passage from sacred writings read in a service of worship **2** : a reading or exercise to be studied by a pupil; *also* : something learned **3** : a period of instruction **4** : an instructive example

les·sor \'le-ˌsòr, le-'sòr\ *n* : one who conveys property by a lease

lest \ˌlest\ *conj* : for fear that

¹let \'let\ *n* [ME *lette,* fr. *letten* to delay, hinder, fr. OE *lettan*] **1** : HINDRANCE, OBSTACLE **2** : a shot or point in racket games that does not count

²let *vb* **let; let·ting** [ME *leten,* fr. OE *lǣtan*] **1** : to cause to : MAKE ⟨∼ it be known⟩ **2** : RENT, LEASE; *also* : to assign esp. after bids **3** : ALLOW, PERMIT ⟨∼ me go⟩

-let \lət\ *n suffix* **1** : small one ⟨book*let*⟩ **2** : article worn on ⟨wrist*let*⟩

let·down \'let-ˌdaùn\ *n* **1** : DISAPPOINTMENT **2** : a slackening of effort

le·thal \'lē-thəl\ *adj* : DEADLY, FATAL — **le·thal·ly** *adv*

leth·ar·gy \'le-thər-jē\ *n* **1** : abnormal drowsiness **2** : the quality or state of being lazy or indifferent **syn** languor, lassitude, torpor — **le·thar·gic** \li-'thär-jik\ *adj*

let on *vb* **1** : REVEAL **1 2** : PRETEND

¹let·ter \'le-tər\ *n* **1** : a symbol that stands for a speech sound and constitutes a unit of an alphabet **2** : a written or printed communication **3** *pl* : LITERATURE; *also* : LEARNING **4** : the literal meaning ⟨the ∼ of the law⟩ **5** : a single piece of type

²letter *vb* : to mark with letters : INSCRIBE — **let·ter·er** *n*

let·ter·boxed \'le-tər-ˌbäkst\ *adj* : being a video recording formatted so as to display the full frame of a wide-screen motion picture

let·ter·head \'le-tər-ˌhed\ *n* : stationery with a printed or engraved heading; *also* : the heading itself

let·ter–per·fect \ˌle-tər-'pər-fikt\ *adj* : correct to the smallest detail

let·ter·press \'le-tər-ˌpres\ *n* : printing done directly by impressing the paper on an inked raised surface

letters of marque \-'märk\ : a license granted to a private person by a government to fit out an armed ship to capture enemy shipping

letters patent *n pl* : a written grant from a government to a person in a form readily open for inspection by all

let·tuce \'le-təs\ *n* [ME *letuse,* fr. MF *laitues,* pl. of *laitue,* fr. L *lactuca,* fr. *lac* milk; fr. its milky juice] : a garden composite plant with crisp leaves used esp. in salads

let·up \'let-ˌəp\ *n* : a lessening of effort

leu \'leù\ *n, pl* **lei** \'lā\ — see MONEY table

leu·kae·mia *chiefly Brit var of* LEUKEMIA

leu·ke·mia \lü-'kē-mē-ə\ *n* : a disease in which white blood cells increase greatly — **leu·ke·mic** \-mik\ *adj or n*

leu·ko·cyte \'lü-kə-ˌsīt\ *n* : any of the white or colorless cells with a nucleus found in bodily tissues and esp. blood

lev \'lef\ *n, pl* **le·va** \'le-və\ — see MONEY table

Lev *or* **Levit** *abbr* Leviticus

¹le·vee \'le-vē; le-'vē, -'vā\ *n* [F *lever* act of arising] : a reception held by or for a person of distinction

²lev·ee \'le-vē\ *n* : an embankment to prevent or confine flooding; *also* : a river landing place

¹lev·el \'le-vəl\ *n* **1** : a device for establishing a horizontal line or plane **2** : horizontal condition **3** : a horizontal position, line, or surface often taken as an index of altitude; *also* : a flat area of ground **4** : height, position, rank, or size in a scale

²level *vb* **-eled** *or* **-elled; -el·ing** *or* **-el·ling 1** : to make flat or level; *also* : to come to a level **2** : AIM, DIRECT **3** : EQUALIZE **4** : RAZE — **lev·el·er** *n*

³level *adj* **1** : having a flat even surface **2** : HORIZONTAL **3** : of the same height or rank; *also* : UNIFORM **4**

: steady and cool in judgment — **lev·el·ly** *adv* — **lev·el·ness** *n*

lev·el·head·ed \ˌle-vəl-ˈhe-dəd\ *adj* : having sound judgment : SENSIBLE

le·ver \ˈle-vər, ˈlē-\ *n* **1** : a bar used for prying or dislodging something; *also* : a means for achieving one's purpose **2** : a rigid piece turning about an axis and used for transmitting and changing force and motion

le·ver·age \ˈle-vrij, ˈlē-, -və-rij\ *n* : the action or mechanical effect of a lever

le·vi·a·than \li-ˈvī-ə-thən\ *n* **1** : a large sea animal **2** : something large or formidable

lev·i·tate \ˈle-və-ˌtāt\ *vb* **-tat·ed; -tat·ing** : to rise or cause to rise in the air in seeming defiance of gravitation — **lev·i·ta·tion** \ˌle-və-ˈtā-shən\ *n*

Le·vit·i·cus \li-ˈvi-tə-kəs\ *n* — see BIBLE table

lev·i·ty \ˈle-və-tē\ *n* : lack of seriousness **syn** lightness, flippancy, frivolity

¹levy \ˈle-vē\ *n*, *pl* **lev·ies 1** : the imposition or collection of an assessment; *also* : an amount levied **2** : the enlistment or conscription of men for military service; *also* : troops raised by levy

²levy *vb* **lev·ied; levy·ing 1** : to impose or collect by legal authority **2** : to enlist for military service **3** : WAGE (~ war) **4** : to seize property

lewd \ˈlüd\ *adj* [ME *lewed* vulgar, fr. OE *lǣwede* lay, ignorant] **1** : sexually unchaste **2** : OBSCENE, VULGAR — **lewd·ly** *adv* — **lewd·ness** *n*

lex·i·cog·ra·phy \ˌlek-sə-ˈkä-grə-fē\ *n* **1** : the editing or making of a dictionary **2** : the principles and practices of dictionary making — **lex·i·cog·ra·pher** \-fər\ *n* — **lex·i·co·graph·i·cal** \-kō-ˈgra-fi-kəl\ *or* **lex·i·co·graph·ic** \-fik\ *adj*

lex·i·con \ˈlek-sə-ˌkän\ *n*, *pl* **lex·i·ca** \-si-kə\ *or* **lexicons 1** : DICTIONARY **2** : the vocabulary of a language, speaker, or subject

lg *abbr* **1** large **2** long

LH *abbr* **1** left hand **2** lower half

li *abbr* link

Li *symbol* lithium

LI *abbr* Long Island

li·a·bil·i·ty \ˌlī-ə-ˈbi-lə-tē\ *n*, *pl* **-ties 1** : the quality or state of being liable **2** *pl* : DEBTS **3** : DISADVANTAGE

li·a·ble \ˈlī-ə-bəl\ *adj* **1** : legally obligated : RESPONSIBLE **2** : LIKELY, APT (~ to fall) **3** : SUSCEPTIBLE

li·ai·son \ˈlē-ə-ˌzän, lē-ˈā-\ *n* [F] **1** : a close bond : INTERRELATIONSHIP **2** : an illicit sexual relationship **3** : communication for mutual understanding (as between parts of an armed force); *also* : one that carries on a liaison

li·ar \ˈlī-ər\ *n* : a person who lies

¹lib \ˈlib\ *n* : LIBERATION

²lib *abbr* **1** liberal **2** librarian; library

li·ba·tion \lī-ˈbā-shən\ *n* **1** : an act of pouring a liquid as a sacrifice (as to a god); *also* : the liquid poured **2** : DRINK

¹li·bel \ˈlī-bəl\ *n* [ME, written declaration, fr. MF, fr. L *libellus*, dim. of *liber* book] **1** : a spoken or written statement or a representation that gives an unjustly unfavorable impression of a person or thing **2** : the action or crime of publishing a libel — **li·bel·ous** *or* **li·bel·lous** \-bə-ləs\ *adj*

²libel *vb* **-beled** *or* **-belled; -bel·ing** *or* **-bel·ling** : to make or publish a libel — **li·bel·er** *n* — **li·bel·ist** *n*

¹lib·er·al \ˈli-brəl, -bə-rəl\ *adj* [ME, fr. MF, fr. L *liberalis* suitable for a freeman, generous, fr. *liber* free] **1** : of, relating to, or based on the liberal arts **2** : GENEROUS, BOUNTIFUL **3** : not literal **4** : not narrow in opinion or judgment : TOLERANT; *also* : not orthodox **5** : not conservative — **lib·er·al·i·ty** \ˌli-bə-ˈra-lə-tē\ *n* — **lib·er·al·ize** \ˈli-brə-ˌlīz, -bə-rə-\ *vb* — **lib·er·al·ly** *adv*

²liberal *n* : a person who holds liberal views

liberal arts *n pl* : the studies (as language, philosophy, history, literature, or abstract science) in a college or university intended to provide chiefly general knowl-

edge and to develop the general intellectual capacities

lib·er·al·ism \ˈli-brə-ˌli-zəm, -bə-rə-\ *n* : liberal principles and theories

lib·er·ate \ˈli-bə-ˌrāt\ *vb* **-at·ed; -at·ing 1** : to free from bondage or restraint; *also* : to raise to equal rights and status **2** : to free (as a gas) from combination — **lib·er·a·tion** \ˌli-bə-ˈrā-shən\ *n* — **lib·er·a·tor** \ˈli-bə-ˌrā-tər\ *n*

lib·er·at·ed *adj* : freed from or opposed to traditional social and sexual attitudes or roles (a ~ marriage)

Li·be·ri·an \lī-ˈbir-ē-ən\ *n* : a native or inhabitant of Liberia — **Liberian** *adj*

lib·er·tar·i·an \ˌli-bər-ˈter-ē-ən\ *n* **1** : an advocate of the doctrine of free will **2** : one who upholds the principles of unrestricted liberty

lib·er·tine \ˈli-bər-ˌtēn\ *n* : a person who leads a dissolute life

lib·er·ty \ˈli-bər-tē\ *n*, *pl* **-ties 1** : FREEDOM **2** : an action going beyond normal limits; *esp* : FAMILIARITY **3** : a short leave from naval duty

li·bid·i·nous \lə-ˈbid-ᵊn-əs\ *adj* **1** : LASCIVIOUS **2** : LIBIDINAL

li·bi·do \lə-ˈbē-dō, -ˈbī-\ *n*, *pl* **-dos** [NL, fr. L, desire, lust] **1** : psychic energy derived from basic biological urges **2** : sexual drive — **li·bid·i·nal** \lə-ˈbid-ᵊn-əl\ *adj*

Li·bra \ˈlē-brə\ *n* [L, lit., scales] **1** : a zodiacal constellation between Virgo and Scorpio usu. pictured as a balance scale **2** : the 7th sign of the zodiac in astrology; *also* : one born under this sign

li·brar·i·an \lī-ˈbrer-ē-ən\ *n* : a specialist in the management of a library

li·brary \ˈlī-ˌbrer-ē\ *n*, *pl* **-brar·ies 1** : a place in which books and related materials are kept for use but not for sale **2** : a collection of books

li·bret·to \lə-ˈbre-tō\ *n*, *pl* **-tos** *or* **-ti** \-tē\ [It, dim. of *libro* book, fr. L *liber*] : the text esp. of an opera — **li·bret·tist** \-tist\ *n*

Lib·y·an \ˈli-bē-ən\ *n* : a native or inhabitant of Libya — **Libyan** *adj*

lice *pl of* LOUSE

li·cense *or* **li·cence** \ˈlīs-ᵊns\ *n* **1** : permission to act **2** : a permission granted by authority to engage in an activity **3** : a document, plate, or tag providing proof of a license **4** : freedom used irresponsibly — **license** *vb*

licensed practical nurse *n* : a specially trained person who is licensed (as by a state) to provide routine care for the sick

licensed vocational nurse *n* : a licensed practical nurse licensed to practice in the states of California and Texas

li·cens·ee \ˌlīs-ᵊn-ˈsē\ *n* : a licensed person

licente *pl of* SENTE

li·cen·ti·ate \lī-ˈsen-chē-ət\ *n* : one licensed to practice a profession

li·cen·tious \lī-ˈsen-chəs\ *adj* : LEWD, LASCIVIOUS — **li·cen·tious·ly** *adv* — **li·cen·tious·ness** *n*

li·chee *var of* LITCHI

li·chen \ˈlī-kən\ *n* : any of various complex lower plants made up of an alga and a fungus growing as a unit on a solid surface — **li·chen·ous** *adj*

lic·it \ˈli-sət\ *adj* : LAWFUL

¹lick \ˈlik\ *vb* **1** : to draw the tongue over; *also* : to flicker over like a tongue **2** : THRASH; *also* : DEFEAT

²lick *n* **1** : a stroke of the tongue **2** : a small amount **3** : a hasty careless effort **4** : BLOW **5** : a natural deposit of salt that animals lick

lick·e·ty-split \ˌli-kə-tē-ˈsplit\ *adv* : at great speed

lick·spit·tle \ˈlik-ˌspit-ᵊl\ *n* : a fawning subordinate : TOADY

lic·o·rice \ˈli-kə-rish, -rəs\ *n* [ME *licorice*, fr. OF, fr. LL *liquiritia*, alter. of L *glycyrrhiza*, fr. Gk *glykyrrhiza*, fr. *glykys* sweet + *rhiza* root] **1** : the dried root of a European leguminous plant; *also* : an extract from it used esp. as a flavoring and in medicine **2** : a candy flavored with licorice **3** : a plant yielding licorice

lid \\'lid\ *n* **1** : a movable cover **2** : EYELID **3** : something that confines or suppresses — **lid•ded** \\'li-dəd\ *adj*

li•do \\'lē-dō\ *n, pl* **lidos** : a fashionable beach resort

¹lie \\'lī\ *vb* **lay** \\'lā\; **lain** \\'lān\; **ly•ing** \\'lī-iŋ\ **1** : to be in, stay at rest in, or assume a horizontal position; *also* : to be in a helpless or defenseless state **2** : EXTEND **3** : to occupy a certain relative position **4** : to have an effect esp. through mere presence

²lie *n* : the position in which something lies

³lie *vb* **lied; ly•ing** \\'lī-iŋ\ : to tell a lie

⁴lie *n* : an untrue statement made with intent to deceive

lied \\'lēt\ *n, pl* **lie•der** \\'lē-dər\ [G] : a German song esp. of the 19th century

lie detector *n* : an instrument for detecting physiological evidence of the tension that accompanies lying

lief \\'lēv, 'lēf\ *adv* : GLADLY, WILLINGLY

¹liege \\'lēj\ *adj* : LOYAL, FAITHFUL

²liege *n* **1** : VASSAL **2** : a feudal superior

lien \\'lēn, 'lē-ən\ *n* : a legal claim on the property of another for the satisfaction of a debt or duty

lieu \\'lü\ *n, archaic* : PLACE, STEAD — **in lieu of** : in the place of

lieut *abbr* lieutenant

lieu•ten•ant \lü-'te-nənt\ *n* [ME, fr. MF, fr. *lieu* place + *tenant* holding, fr. *tenir* to hold, fr. L *tenēre*] **1** : a representative of another in the performance of duty **2** : FIRST LIEUTENANT; *also* : SECOND LIEUTENANT **3** : a commissioned officer in the navy ranking next below a lieutenant commander — **lieu•ten•an•cy** \-nən-sē\ *n*

lieutenant colonel *n* : a commissioned officer (as in the army) ranking next below a colonel

lieutenant commander *n* : a commissioned officer in the navy ranking next below a commander

lieutenant general *n* : a commissioned officer (as in the army) ranking next below a general

lieutenant governor *n* : a deputy or subordinate governor

lieutenant junior grade *n, pl* **lieutenants junior grade** : a commissioned officer in the navy ranking next below a lieutenant

life \\'līf\ *n, pl* **lives** \\'līvz\ **1** : the quality that distinguishes a vital and functional being from a dead body or inanimate matter; *also* : a state of an organism characterized esp. by capacity for metabolism, growth, reaction to stimuli, and reproduction **2** : the physical and mental experiences of an individual **3** : BIOGRAPHY **4** : a specific phase or period ⟨adult ∼⟩ **5** : the period from birth to death; *also* : a sentence of imprisonment for the remainder of a person's life **6** : a way of living **7** : PERSON **8** : ANIMATION, SPIRIT; *also* : LIVELINESS **9** : living beings ⟨forest ∼⟩ **10** : animate activity ⟨signs of ∼⟩ **11** : one providing interest and vigor ⟨∼ of the party⟩ — **life•less** *adj* — **life•like** *adj*

life•blood \\'līf-ˌbləd\ *n* : a basic source of strength and vitality

life•boat \-ˌbōt\ *n* : a sturdy boat designed for use in saving lives at sea

life•guard \-ˌgärd\ *n* : a usu. expert swimmer employed to safeguard bathers

life•line \-ˌlīn\ *n* **1** : a line to which persons may cling for safety **2** : something considered vital for survival

life•long \-ˌlȯŋ\ *adj* : continuing through life

life preserver *n* : a buoyant device designed to save a person from drowning

lif•er \\'lī-fər\ *n* **1** : a person sentenced to life imprisonment **2** : a person who makes a career in the armed forces

life raft *n* : a raft for use by people forced into the water

life•sav•ing \\'līf-ˌsā-viŋ\ *n* : the skill or practice of saving or protecting lives esp. of drowning persons — **life•sav•er** \-ˌsā-vər\ *n*

life science *n* : a branch of science (as biology, medicine, anthropology, or sociology) that deals with living organisms and life processes — usu. used in pl. — **life scientist** *n*

life•style \\'līf-ˌstīl\ *n* : a way of living

life•time \-ˌtīm\ *n* : the duration of an individual's existence

life•work \-'wərk\ *n* : the entire or principal work of one's lifetime; *also* : a work extending over a lifetime

LIFO *abbr* last in, first out

¹lift \\'lift\ *vb* **1** : RAISE, ELEVATE; *also* : RISE, ASCEND **2** : to put an end to : STOP **3** : to pay off ⟨∼ a mortgage⟩ — **lift•er** *n*

²lift *n* **1** : LOAD **2** : the action or an instance of lifting **3** : HELP; *also* : a ride along one's way **4** : RISE, ADVANCE **5** *chiefly Brit* : ELEVATOR **6** : an elevation of the spirits **7** : the upward force that is developed by a moving airfoil and that opposes the pull of gravity

lift•off \\'lift-ˌtȯf\ *n* : a vertical takeoff (as by a rocket)

lift truck *n* : a small truck for lifting and transporting loads

lig•a•ment \\'li-gə-mənt\ *n* : a band of tough tissue that holds bones together or supports an organ in place

li•gate \\'lī-ˌgāt\ *vb* **li•gat•ed; li•gat•ing** : to tie with a ligature — **li•ga•tion** \lī-'gā-shən\ *n*

lig•a•ture \\'li-gə-ˌchùr, -chər\ *n* **1** : something that binds or ties; *also* : a thread used in surgery esp. for tying blood vessels **2** : a printed or written character consisting of two or more letters or characters (as æ) united

¹light \\'līt\ *n* **1** : something that makes vision possible : electromagnetic radiation visible to the human eye; *also* : the sensation aroused by stimulation of the visual sense organs **2** : DAYLIGHT **3** : a source of light (as a candle) **4** : ENLIGHTENMENT; *also* : TRUTH **5** : public knowledge ⟨facts brought to ∼⟩ **6** : a particular aspect presented to view ⟨saw the matter in a different ∼⟩ **7** : WINDOW **8** *pl* : STANDARDS ⟨according to his ∼s⟩ **9** : CELEBRITY **10** : LIGHTHOUSE, BEACON; *also* : TRAFFIC LIGHT **11** : a flame for lighting something

²light *adj* : having light : BRIGHT **2** : PALE 2 ⟨∼ blue⟩ — **light•ness** *n*

³light *vb* **lit** \\'lit\ *or* **light•ed; light•ing** **1** : to make or become light **2** : to cause to burn : BURN **3** : to conduct with a light **4** : ILLUMINATE

⁴light *adj* **1** : not heavy **2** : not serious ⟨∼ reading⟩ **3** : SCANTY ⟨∼ rain⟩ **4** : easily disturbed ⟨a ∼ sleeper⟩ **5** : GENTLE ⟨a ∼ blow⟩ **6** : easily endurable ⟨a ∼ cold⟩; *also* : requiring little effort ⟨∼ exercise⟩ **7** : SWIFT, NIMBLE **8** : FRIVOLOUS **9** : DIZZY **10** : made with lower calorie content or less of some ingredient than usual ⟨∼ salad dressing⟩ **11** : producing goods for direct consumption by the consumer ⟨∼ industry⟩ — **light•ly** *adv* — **light•ness** *n*

⁵light *adv* **1** : LIGHTLY **2** : with little baggage ⟨travel ∼⟩

⁶light *vb* **lit** \\'lit\ *or* **light•ed; light•ing** **1** : SETTLE, ALIGHT **2** : to fall unexpectedly **3** : HAPPEN

light–emitting diode *n* : LED

¹light•en \\'lī-ᵊn\ *vb* **1** : ILLUMINATE, BRIGHTEN **2** : to give out flashes of lightning

²lighten *vb* **1** : to relieve of a burden **2** : GLADDEN **3** : to become lighter

lighten up *vb* : to take things less seriously

¹ligh•ter \\'lī-tər\ *n* : a barge used esp. in loading or unloading ships

²lighter \\'lī-tər\ *n* : one that lights; *esp* : a device for lighting

light•face \\'līt-ˌfās\ *n* : a type having light thin lines — **light•faced** \-ˌfāst\ *adj*

light–head•ed \\'līt-ˌhe-dəd\ *adj* **1** : feeling confused or dizzy **2** : lacking maturity or seriousness

light•heart•ed \-ˌhär-təd\ *adj* : free from worry — **light•heart•ed•ly** *adv* — **light•heart•ed•ness** *n*

light•house \-ˌhaùs\ *n* : a structure with a powerful light for guiding sailors

light meter *n* : a usu. hand-held device for indicating correct photographic exposure

¹**light·ning** \'līt-niŋ\ *n* : the flashing of light produced by a discharge of atmospheric electricity; *also* : the discharge itself

²**lightning** *adj* : extremely fast

lightning bug *n* : FIREFLY

lightning rod *n* : a grounded metallic rod set up on a structure to protect it from lightning

light out *vb* : to leave in a hurry

light·proof \'līt-ˌprüf\ *adj* : impenetrable by light

lights \'līts\ *n pl* : the lungs esp. of a slaughtered animal

light·ship \'līt-ˌship\ *n* : a ship with a powerful light moored at a place dangerous to navigation

light show *n* : a kaleidoscopic display (as of colored lights)

light·some \'līt-səm\ *adj* 1 : free from care 2 : NIMBLE

¹**light·weight** \'līt-ˌwāt\ *n* : one of less than average weight; *esp* : a boxer weighing more than 126 but not over 135 pounds

²**lightweight** *adj* 1 : INCONSEQUENTIAL 2 : of less than average weight

light-year \'līt-ˌyir\ *n* 1 : an astronomical unit of distance equal to the distance that light travels in one year in a vacuum or about 5.88 trillion miles (9.46 trillion kilometers) 2 : an extremely large measure of comparison ⟨saw it ∼s ago⟩

lig·nin \'lig-nən\ *n* : a substance related to cellulose that occurs in the woody cell walls of plants and in the cementing material between them

lig·nite \'lig-ˌnīt\ *n* : brownish black soft coal

¹**like** \'līk\ *vb* **liked; lik·ing** 1 : ENJOY ⟨∼s baseball⟩ 2 : WANT 3 : CHOOSE ⟨does as she ∼s⟩ — **lik·able** *or* **like·able** \'lī-kə-bəl\ *adj*

²**like** *n* : PREFERENCE

³**like** *adj* : SIMILAR **syn** alike, analogous, comparable, parallel, uniform

⁴**like** *prep* 1 : similar or similarly to ⟨it's ∼ when we were kids⟩ 2 : typical of 3 : comparable to 4 : as though there would be ⟨looks ∼ rain⟩ 5 : such as ⟨a subject ∼ physics⟩

⁵**like** *n* 1 : COUNTERPART 2 : one that is similar to another — **and the like** : ET CETERA

⁶**like** *conj* : in the same way that

-like \ˌlīk\ *adj comb form* : resembling or characteristic of ⟨lady*like*⟩ ⟨life*like*⟩

like·li·hood \'lī-klē-ˌhůd\ *n* : PROBABILITY

¹**like·ly** \'lī-klē\ *adj* **like·li·er; -est** 1 : very probable 2 : BELIEVABLE 3 : PROMISING ⟨a ∼ place to fish⟩

²**likely** *adv* : in all probability

lik·en \'lī-kən\ *vb* : COMPARE

like·ness \'līk-nəs\ *n* 1 : COPY, PORTRAIT 2 : SEMBLANCE 3 : RESEMBLANCE

like·wise \-ˌwīz\ *adv* 1 : in like manner 2 : in addition : ALSO

lik·ing \'lī-kiŋ\ *n* : favorable regard; *also* : TASTE

li·ku·ta \li-'kü-tə\ *n, pl* **ma·ku·ta** \mä-\ — see *zaire* at MONEY table

li·lac \'lī-lək, -ˌlak, -ˌläk\ *n* [obs. F (now *lilas*), fr. Ar *līlak*, fr. Per *nīlak* bluish, fr. *nīl* blue, fr. Skt *nīla* dark blue] 1 : a shrub related to the olive that produces large clusters of fragrant grayish pink, purple, or white flowers 2 : a moderate purple color

lil·an·ge·ni \ˌli-lən-'ge-nē\ *n, pl* **em·a·lan·ge·ni** \ˌe-mə-lən-'ge-nē\ — see MONEY table

lil·li·pu·tian \ˌli-lə-'pyü-shən\ *adj, often cap* 1 : SMALL, MINIATURE 2 : PETTY

lilt \'lilt\ *n* 1 : a cheerful lively song or tune 2 : a rhythmical swing or flow

lily \'li-lē\ *n, pl* **lil·ies** : any of a genus of tall bulbous herbs with leafy stems and usu. funnel-shaped flowers; *also* : any of various related plants

lily of the valley : a low perennial herb related to the lilies that produces a raceme of fragrant nodding bell= shaped white flowers

li·ma bean \'lī-mə-\ *n* : a bushy or tall-growing bean widely cultivated for its flat edible usu. pale green or whitish seeds; *also* : the seed

limb \'lim\ *n* 1 : one of the projecting paired appendages (as legs, arms, or wings) used by an animal esp. in moving or grasping 2 : a large branch of a tree : BOUGH — **limb·less** *adj*

¹**lim·ber** \'lim-bər\ *adj* 1 : FLEXIBLE, SUPPLE 2 : LITHE, NIMBLE

²**limber** *vb* : to make or become limber

¹**lim·bo** \'lim-bō\ *n, pl* **limbos** [ME, fr. ML, abl. of *limbus* limbo, fr. L, border] 1 *often cap* : an abode of souls barred from heaven through no fault of their own 2 : a place or state of confinement, oblivion, or uncertainty

²**limbo** *n, pl* **limbos** : a West Indian acrobatic dance orig. for men

Lim·burg·er \'lim-ˌbər-gər\ *n* : a pungent semisoft surface-ripened cheese

¹**lime** \'līm\ *n* : a caustic powdery white solid that consists of calcium and oxygen, is obtained from limestone or shells, and is used in making cement and in fertilizer — **lime** *vb* — **limy** \'lī-mē\ *adj*

²**lime** *n* : a small yellowish green citrus fruit with juicy acid pulp

lime·ade \ˌlīm-'ād, 'lī-ˌmād\ *n* : a beverage of lime juice, sugar, and water

lime·light \'līm-ˌlīt\ *n* 1 : a device in which flame is directed against a cylinder of lime formerly used in the theater to cast a strong white light on the stage 2 : the center of public attention

lim·er·ick \'li-mə-rik\ *n* : a light or humorous poem of 5 lines

lime·stone \'līm-ˌstōn\ *n* : a rock that is formed by accumulation of organic remains (as shells), is used in building, and yields lime when burned

¹**lim·it** \'li-mət\ *n* 1 : something that restrains or confines; *also* : the utmost extent 2 : BOUNDARY; *also, pl* : BOUNDS 3 : a prescribed maximum or minimum — **lim·it·less** *adj* — **lim·it·less·ness** *n*

²**limit** *vb* 1 : to set limits to 2 : to reduce in quantity or extent — **lim·i·ta·tion** \ˌli-mə-'tā-shən\ *n*

lim·it·ed *adj* 1 : confined within limits 2 : offering faster service esp. by making fewer stops

limn \'lim\ *vb* **limned; limn·ing** \'li-miŋ, 'lim-niŋ\ 1 : DRAW; *also* : PAINT 2 : DELINEATE 3 : DESCRIBE

limo \'li-(ˌ)mō\ *n, pl* **limos** : LIMOUSINE

li·mo·nite \'lī-mə-ˌnīt\ *n* : a ferric oxide that is a major ore of iron — **li·mo·nit·ic** \ˌlī-mə-'ni-tik\ *adj*

lim·ou·sine \'li-mə-ˌzēn, ˌli-mə-'zēn\ *n* [F] 1 : a large luxurious often chauffeur-driven sedan 2 : a large vehicle for transporting passengers to and from an airport

¹**limp** \'limp\ *vb* : to walk lamely; *also* : to proceed with difficulty

²**limp** *n* : a limping movement or gait

³**limp** *adj* 1 : having no defined shape; *also* : not stiff or rigid 2 : lacking in strength or firmness — **limp·ly** *adv* — **limp·ness** *n*

lim·pet \'lim-pət\ *n* : any of numerous gastropod sea mollusks with a conical shell that clings to rocks or timbers

lim·pid \'lim-pəd\ *adj* : CLEAR, TRANSPARENT

lin *abbr* 1 lineal 2 linear

lin·age \'lī-nij\ *n* : the number of lines of written or printed matter

linch·pin \'linch-ˌpin\ *n* : a locking pin inserted crosswise (as through the end of an axle)

lin·den \'lin-dən\ *n* : any of a genus of trees with large heart-shaped leaves and clustered yellowish flowers rich in nectar

¹**line** \'līn\ *n* 1 : CORD, ROPE, WIRE; *also* : a length of material used in measuring and leveling 2 : pipes for conveying a fluid ⟨a gas ∼⟩ 3 : a horizontal row of written or printed characters; *also* : VERSE 4 : NOTE 5 : the words making up a part in a drama — usu. used in

pl. **6 :** something distinct, long, and narrow; *also* **: ROUTE 7 :** a state of agreement **8 :** a course of conduct, action, or thought; *also* **: OCCUPATION 9 : LIMIT 10 :** an arrangement of persons or objects of one kind in an orderly series ⟨waiting in ∼⟩ **11 :** a transportation system **12 :** the football players who are stationed on the line of scrimmage **13 :** a long narrow mark; *also* **: EQUATOR 14 :** a geometric element that is the path of a moving point **15 : CONTOUR 16 :** a general plan **17 :** an indication based on insight or investigation

²**line** *vb* **lined; lin·ing 1 :** to mark with a line **2 :** to place or form a line along **3 : ALIGN**

³**line** *vb* **lined; lin·ing :** to cover the inner surface of

lin·eage \ˈli-nē-ij\ *n* **:** lineal descent from a common progenitor; *also* **: FAMILY**

lin·eal \ˈli-nē-əl\ *adj* **1 : LINEAR 2 :** consisting of or being in a direct line of ancestry; *also* **: HEREDITARY**

lin·ea·ment \ˈli-nē-ə-mənt\ *n* **:** an outline, feature, or contour of a body and esp. of a face — usu. used in pl.

lin·ear \ˈli-nē-ər\ *adj* **1 :** of, relating to, resembling, or having a graph that is a line and esp. a straight line **: STRAIGHT 2 :** composed of simply drawn lines with little attempt at pictorial representation ⟨∼ script⟩ **3 :** being long and uniformly narrow

line·back·er \ˈlīn-ˌba-kər\ *n* **:** a defensive football player who lines up just behind the line of scrimmage

line drive *n* **:** a batted baseball hit in a flatter path than a fly ball

line·man \ˈlīn-mən\ *n* **1 :** a person who sets up or repairs communication or power lines **2 :** a player in the line in football

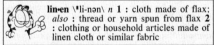

lin·en \ˈli-nən\ *n* **1 :** cloth made of flax; *also* **:** thread or yarn spun from flax **2 :** clothing or household articles made of linen cloth or similar fabric

line of scrimmage : an imaginary line in football parallel to the goal lines and tangent to the nose of the ball laid on the ground before a play

¹**lin·er** \ˈlī-nər\ *n* **:** a ship or airplane of a regular transportation line

²**liner** *n* **:** one that lines or is used as a lining — **lin·er·less** *adj*

line score *n* **:** a score of a baseball game giving the runs, hits, and errors made by each team

lines·man \ˈlīnz-mən\ *n* **1 : LINEMAN 1 2 :** an official who assists a referee

line·up \ˈlī-ˌnəp\ *n* **1 :** a list of players taking part in a game (as of baseball) **2 :** a line of persons arranged esp. for identification by police

ling \ˈliŋ\ *n* **:** any of various fishes related to the cod

-ling \liŋ\ *n suffix* **1 :** one associated with ⟨nest*ling*⟩ **2 :** young, small, or minor one ⟨duck*ling*⟩

lin·ger \ˈliŋ-gər\ *vb* **: TARRY;** *also* **: PROCRASTINATE** — **lin·ger·er** *n*

lin·ge·rie \ˌlän-jə-ˈrā, ˌlaⁿ-zhə-, -ˈrē\ *n* [F, fr. MF, fr.

linge linen, fr. L *lineus* made of linen, fr. *linum* flax, linen] **:** women's intimate apparel

lin·go \ˈliŋ-gō\ *n, pl* **lingoes :** a usu. strange or incomprehensible language

lin·gua fran·ca \ˌliŋ-gwə-ˈfraŋ-kə\ *n, pl* **lingua francas** *or* **lin·guae fran·cae** \-gwē-ˈfraŋ-ˌkē\ [It] **1** *often cap* **:** a common language consisting of Italian mixed with French, Spanish, Greek, and Arabic that was formerly spoken in Mediterranean ports **2 :** a common or commercial tongue among speakers of different languages

lin·gual \ˈliŋ-gwəl\ *adj* **:** of, relating to, or produced by the tongue

lin·guist \ˈliŋ-gwist\ *n* **1 :** a person skilled in languages **2 :** a person who specializes in linguistics

lin·guis·tics \liŋ-ˈgwis-tiks\ *n* **:** the study of human speech including the units, nature, structure, and modification of language — **lin·guis·tic** \-tik\ *adj*

lin·i·ment \ˈli-nə-mənt\ *n* **:** a liquid preparation rubbed on the skin esp. to relieve pain

lin·ing \ˈlī-niŋ\ *n* **:** material used to line esp. an inner surface

link \ˈliŋk\ *n* **1 :** a connecting structure; *esp* **:** a single ring of a chain **2 : BOND, TIE** — **link** *vb* — **link·er** *n*

link·age \ˈliŋ-kij\ *n* **1 :** the manner or style of being united **2 :** the quality or state of being linked **3 :** a system of links

linking verb *n* **:** a word or expression (as a form of *be, become, feel,* or *seem*) that links a subject with its predicate

links \ˈliŋks\ *n pl* **:** a golf course

link·up \ˈliŋ-ˌkəp\ *n* **1 : MEETING 2 :** something that serves as a linking device or factor

lin·net \ˈli-nət\ *n* **:** an Old World finch

li·no·leum \lə-ˈnō-lē-əm\ *n* [L *linum* flax + *oleum* oil] **:** a floor covering with a canvas back and a surface of hardened linseed oil and a filler

lin·seed \ˈlin-ˌsēd\ *n* **:** the seeds of flax yielding a yellowish oil (**linseed oil**) used esp. in paints and linoleum

lin·sey-wool·sey \ˌlin-zē-ˈwu̇l-zē\ *n* **:** a coarse sturdy fabric of wool and linen or cotton

lint \ˈlint\ *n* **1 :** linen made into a soft fleecy substance **2 :** fine ravels and short fibers of yarn or fabric **3 :** the fibers that surround cotton seeds and form the cotton staple

lin·tel \ˈlint-ᵊl\ *n* **:** a horizontal piece across the top of an opening (as of a door) that carries the weight of the structure above it

li·on \ˈlī-ən\ *n, pl* **lions :** a large heavily-built cat of Africa and southern Asia with a shaggy mane in the male

li·on·ess \ˈlī-ə-nəs\ *n* **:** a female lion

li·on·heart·ed \ˌlī-ən-ˈhär-təd\ *adj* **: COURAGEOUS, BRAVE**

li·on·ise *Brit var of* LIONIZE

li·on·ize \ˈlī-ə-ˌnīz\ *vb* **-ized; -iz·ing :** to treat as an object of great interest or importance — **li·on·i·za·tion** \ˌlī-ə-nə-ˈzā-shən\ *n*

lip \'lip\ n 1 : either of the two fleshy folds that surround the mouth; also : the margin of the human lip 2 : a part or projection suggesting a lip 3 : the edge of a hollow vessel or cavity — **lipped** \'lipt\ adj

lip·id \'li-pəd\ n : any of various substances (as fats and waxes) that with proteins and carbohydrates make up the principal structural parts of living cells

li·po·pro·tein \,lī-pō-'prō-,tēn, ,li-\ n : a protein that is a complex of protein and lipid

li·po·suc·tion \'li-pə-,sək-shən, 'lī-\ n : surgical removal of local fat deposits (as in the thighs) esp. for cosmetic purposes

lip·read·ing \'lip-,rē-diŋ\ n : the interpreting of a speaker's words by watching lip and facial movements without hearing the voice

lip service n : an avowal of allegiance that is only verbal

lip·stick \'lip-,stik\ n : a waxy solid colored cosmetic in stick form for the lips — **lip·sticked** \-,stikt\ adj

liq abbr 1 liquid 2 liquor

liq·ue·fy also liq·ui·fy \'li-kwə-,fī\ vb -fied; -fy·ing : to make or become liquid — **liq·ue·fi·er** \-,fī-ər\ n

li·queur \li-'kər\ n [F] : a distilled alcoholic liquor flavored with aromatic substances and usu. sweetened

¹liq·uid \'li-kwəd\ adj 1 : flowing freely like water 2 : neither solid nor gaseous 3 : shining and clear (large ∼ eyes) 4 : smooth and musical in tone; also : smooth and unconstrained in movement 5 : consisting of or capable of ready conversion into cash (∼ assets) — **li·quid·i·ty** \li-'kwi-də-tē\ n

²liquid n : a liquid substance

liq·ui·date \'li-kwə-,dāt\ vb -dat·ed; -dat·ing 1 : to settle the accounts and distribute the assets of (as a business) 2 : to pay off (∼ a debt) 3 : to get rid of; esp : KILL — **liq·ui·da·tion** \,li-kwə-'dā-shən\ n

liquid crystal n : an organic liquid that resembles a crystal in having ordered molecular arrays

liquid crystal display n : LCD

liquid measure n : a unit or series of units for measuring liquid capacity — see METRIC SYSTEM table, WEIGHT table

li·quor \'li-kər\ n : a liquid substance; esp : a distilled alcoholic beverage

li·quo·rice chiefly Brit var of LICORICE

li·ra \'lir-ə, 'lē-rə\ n — see MONEY table

lisente pl of SENTE

lisle \'līl\ n : a smooth tightly twisted thread usu. made of long-staple cotton

lisp \'lisp\ vb : to pronounce \s\ and \z\ imperfectly esp. by turning them into \th\ and \th\; also : to speak childishly — **lisp** n — **lisp·er** n

lis·some also lis·som \'li-səm\ adj 1 : easily flexed 2 : LITHE 2 3 : NIMBLE — **lis·some·ly** adv

¹list \'list\ vb, archaic : PLEASE; also : WISH

²list vb, archaic : LISTEN

³list n 1 : a simple series of words or numerals; also : an official roster 2 : CATALOG, CHECKLIST

⁴list vb : to make a list of; also : to include on a list — **list·ee** \li-'stē\ n

⁵list vb : TILT

⁶list n : a leaning to one side : TILT

lis·ten \'lis-ᵊn\ vb 1 : to pay attention in order to hear 2 : HEED — **lis·ten·er** n

lis·ten·er·ship \'lis-ᵊn-ər-,ship\ n : the audience for a radio program or recording

list·ing \'lis-tiŋ\ n 1 : an act or instance of making or including in a list 2 : something that is listed

list·less \'list-ləs\ adj : SPIRITLESS, LANGUID — **list·less·ly** adv — **list·less·ness** n

list price n : the price of an item as published in a catalog, price list, or advertisement before being discounted

lists \'lists\ n pl : an arena for combat (as jousting)

¹lit \'lit\ past and past part of LIGHT

²lit abbr 1 liter 2 literal; literally 3 literary 4 literature

lit·a·ny \'lit-ᵊn-ē\ n, pl -nies [ME letanie, fr. OF, fr. LL litania, fr. LGk litaneia, fr. Gk, entreaty, fr. litanos suppliant] 1 : a prayer consisting of a series of supplications and responses said alternately by a leader and a group 2 : a lengthy recitation (a ∼ of complaints)

li·tchi \'lē-chē, 'lī-\ n [Chin (Beijing dialect) lìzhī] 1 : an oval fruit with a hard scaly outer covering, a small hard seed, and edible flesh 2 : an Asian tree bearing litchis

lite var of ³LIGHT 10

li·ter \'lē-tər\ n — see METRIC SYSTEM table

lit·er·al \'li-tə-rəl\ adj 1 : adhering to fact or to the ordinary or usual meaning (as of a word) 2 : UNADORNED; also : PROSAIC 3 : VERBATIM

lit·er·al·ism \-rə-,li-zəm\ n 1 : adherence to the explicit substance (as of an idea) 2 : fidelity to observable fact — **lit·er·al·ist** \-list\ n — **lit·er·al·is·tic** \,li-tə-rə-'lis-tik\ adj

lit·er·al·ly \'li-tə-rə-lē, 'li-trə-\ adv 1 : ACTUALLY (was ∼ insane) 2 : VIRTUALLY (∼ poured out new ideas)

lit·er·ary \'li-tə-,rer-ē\ adj 1 : of or relating to literature 2 : WELL-READ

lit·er·ate \'li-trət, -tə-rət\ adj 1 : EDUCATED; also : able to read and write 2 : LITERARY; also : POLISHED, LUCID — **lit·er·a·cy** \'li-trə-sē, -tə-rə-\ n — **literate** n

li·te·ra·ti \,li-tə-'rä-tē\ n pl 1 : the educated class 2 : persons interested in literature or the arts

lit·er·a·ture \'li-trə-,chùr, -tə-rə-, -chər\ n 1 : the production of written works having excellence of form or expression and dealing with ideas of permanent interest 2 : the written works produced in a particular language, country, or age

lithe \'līth, 'līth\ adj 1 : SUPPLE 2 : characterized by effortless grace; also : athletically slim

lithe·some \'līth-səm, 'līth-\ adj : LISSOME

lith·i·um \'li-thē-əm\ n : a light silver-white metallic chemical element — see ELEMENT table

li·thog·ra·phy \li-'thä-grə-fē\ n : the process of printing from a plane surface (as a smooth stone or metal plate) on which the image to be printed is ink-receptive and the blank area ink-repellent — **lith-**

o·graph \'li-thə-ˌgraf\ vb — **lithograph** n — **li·thog·ra·pher** \li-'thä-grə-fər, 'li-thə-ˌgra-fər\ n — **lith·o·graph·ic** \ˌli-thə-'gra-fik\ adj — **lith·o·graph·i·cal·ly** \-fi-k(ə-)lē\ adv

li·thol·o·gy \li-'thä-lə-jē\ n, pl **-gies** : the study of rocks — **lith·o·log·ic** \ˌli-thə-'lä-jik\ or **lith·o·log·i·cal** \-ji-kəl\ adj

lith·o·sphere \'li-thə-ˌsfir\ n : the outer part of the solid earth

Lith·u·a·nian \ˌli-thù-'wā-nē-ən, -thyù-\ n **1** : a native or inhabitant of Lithuania **2** : the language of the Lithuanians — **Lithuanian** adj

lit·i·gant \'li-ti-gənt\ n : a party to a lawsuit — **litigant** adj

lit·i·gate \-ˌgāt\ vb **-gat·ed; -gat·ing** : to carry on a legal contest by judicial process; also : to contest at law — **lit·i·ga·tion** \ˌli-tə-'gā-shən\ n

li·ti·gious \lə-'ti-jəs\ adj **1** : CONTENTIOUS **2** : prone to engage in lawsuits **3** : of or relating to litigation — **li·ti·gious·ly** adv — **li·ti·gious·ness** n

lit·mus \'lit-məs\ n : a coloring matter from lichens that turns red in acid solutions and blue in alkaline

litmus test n : a test in which a single factor (as an attitude) is decisive

Litt D or **Lit D** abbr [ML litterarum doctor] : doctor of letters; doctor of literature

¹**lit·ter** \'li-tər\ n [ME, fr. OF litiere, fr. lit bed, fr. L lectus] **1** : a covered and curtained couch with shafts that is used to carry a single passenger; also : a device (as a stretcher) for carrying a sick or injured person **2** : material used as bedding for animals; also : material used to absorb the urine and feces of animals **3** : the offspring of an animal at one birth **4** : RUBBISH

litter 1

²**litter** vb **1** : to give birth to young **2** : to strew or mark with scattered objects

lit·ter·bug \'li-tər-ˌbəg\ n : one who litters a public area

¹**lit·tle** \'lit-ᵊl\ adj **lit·tler** \'lit-ᵊl-ər\ or **less** \'les\ or **less·er** \'le-sər\; **lit·tlest** \'lit-ᵊl-əst\ or **least** \'lēst\ **1** : not big; also : YOUNG **2** : not important **3** : PETTY **3 4** : not much — **lit·tle·ness** n

²**little** adv **less** \'les\; **least** \'lēst\ **1** : SLIGHTLY; also : not at all **2** : INFREQUENTLY

³**little** n **1** : a small amount or quantity **2** : a short time or distance

Little Dipper n : the seven bright stars of Ursa Minor arranged in a form resembling a dipper

little theater n : a small theater for low-cost dramatic productions designed for a limited audience

lit·to·ral \'li-tə-rəl; ˌli-tə-'ral\ adj : of, relating to, or growing on or near a shore esp. of the sea — **littoral** n

lit·ur·gy \'li-tər-jē\ n, pl **-gies** : a rite or body of rites prescribed for public worship — **li·tur·gi·cal** \lə-'tər-ji-kəl\ adj — **li·tur·gi·cal·ly** \-k(ə-)lē\ adv — **lit·ur·gist** \'li-tər-jist\ n

liv·able also **live·able** \'li-və-bəl\ adj **1** : suitable for living in or with **2** : ENDURABLE — **liv·a·bil·i·ty** \ˌli-və-'bi-lə-tē\ n

¹**live** \'liv\ vb **lived; liv·ing 1** : to be or continue alive **2** : SUBSIST **3** : RESIDE **4** : to conduct one's life **5** : to remain in human memory or record

²**live** \'līv\ adj **1** : having life **2** : BURNING, GLOWING ⟨a ∼ cigar⟩ **3** : connected to electric power ⟨a ∼ wire⟩ **4** : UNEXPLODED ⟨a ∼ bomb⟩ **5** : of continuing interest ⟨a ∼ issue⟩ **6** : of or involving the actual presence of real people ⟨∼ audience⟩; also : broadcast directly at the time of production ⟨a ∼ radio program⟩ **7** : being in play ⟨a ∼ ball⟩

lived–in \'livd-ˌin\ adj : of or suggesting long-term human habitation or use

live down vb : to live so as to wipe out the memory or effects of

live in vb : to live in one's place of employment — used of a servant — **live–in** \'liv-ˌin\ adj

live·li·hood \'līv-lē-ˌhùd\ n : means of support or subsistence

live·long \'liv-ˌlòn\ adj [ME lef long, fr. lef dear + long long] : WHOLE, ENTIRE ⟨the ∼ day⟩

live·ly \'līv-lē\ adj **live·li·er; -est 1** : ANIMATED ⟨∼ debate⟩ **2** : KEEN, VIVID ⟨∼ interest⟩ **3** : showing activity or vigor ⟨a ∼ manner⟩ **4** : quick to rebound ⟨a ∼ ball⟩ **5** : full of life **syn** vivacious, sprightly, gay, spirited — **live·li·ness** n — **live·ly** adv

liv·en \'lī-vən\ vb : ENLIVEN

¹**liv·er** \'li-vər\ n **1** : a large glandular organ of vertebrates that secretes bile and is a center of metabolic activity **2** : the liver of an animal (as a calf or chicken) eaten as food

²**liver** n : one that lives esp. in a specified way ⟨a fast ∼⟩

liv·er·ish \'li-və-rish\ adj **1** : resembling liver esp. in color **2** : BILIOUS **3** : PEEVISH — **liv·er·ish·ness** adj

liv·er·wort \'li-vər-ˌwərt\ n : any of a class of flowerless plants resembling the related mosses

liv·er·wurst \-ˌwərst, -ˌwùrst\ n [part trans. of G Leberwurst, fr. Leber liver + Wurst sausage] : a sausage consisting chiefly of liver

liv·ery \'li-və-rē\ n, pl **-er·ies 1** : a servant's uniform; also : distinctive dress **2** : the feeding, care, and stabling of horses for pay; also : an establishment (as a stable or business) keeping horses or vehicles for hire — **liv·er·ied** \-rēd\ adj

liv·ery·man \-mən\ n : the keeper of a livery

lives pl of LIFE

live·stock \'līv-ˌstäk\ n : farm animals kept for use and profit

live wire n : an alert, active, or aggressive person

liv·id \'li-vəd\ adj [F livide, fr. L lividus, fr. livēre to be blue] **1** : discolored by bruising **2** : ASHEN, PALLID **3** : REDDISH **4** : ENRAGED — **li·vid·i·ty** \li-'vi-də-tē\ n

¹**liv·ing** \'li-vin\ adj **1** : having life **2** : NATURAL **3** : full of life and vigor; also : VIVID

²**living** n **1** : the condition of being alive **2** : LIVELIHOOD **3** : manner of life

living room n : a room in a residence used for the common social activities of the occupants

living wage n : a wage sufficient to provide an acceptable standard of living

living will n : a document requesting that the signer not be kept alive by artificial means unless there is a reasonable expectation of recovery

livre \'lēvrᵊ\ n : the pound of Lebanon

liz·ard \'li-zərd\ n : any of a group of 4-legged reptiles with long tapering tails

Lk abbr Luke

ll abbr lines

lla·ma \'lä-mə\ n [Sp] : any of a genus of wild or domesticated So. American mammals related to the camels but smaller and without a hump

lla·no \'lä-nō\ n, pl **llanos** : an open grassy plain esp. of Latin America

LLD abbr [NL legum doctor] doctor of laws

LNG abbr liquefied natural gas

¹**load** \'lōd\ n **1** : PACK; also : CARGO **2** : a mass of weight

supported by something **3** : something that burdens the mind or spirits **4** : a large quantity — usu. used in pl. **5** : a standard, expected, or authorized burden
²load *vb* **1** : to put a load in or on; *also* : to receive a load **2** : to encumber with an obligation or something heavy or disheartening **3** : to increase the weight of by adding something **4** : to supply abundantly **5** : to put a charge in (as a firearm)
load·ed *adj* **1** *slang* : HIGH 12 **2** : having a large amount of money
load·stone *var of* LODESTONE
¹loaf \'lōf\ *n*, *pl* **loaves** \'lōvz\ : a shaped or molded mass esp. of bread
²loaf *vb* : to spend time in idleness : LOUNGE — **loaf·er** *n*
loam \'lōm, 'lüm\ *n* : SOIL; *esp* : a loose soil of mixed clay, sand, and silt — **loamy** *adj*
¹loan \'lōn\ *n* **1** : money lent at interest; *also* : something lent for the borrower's temporary use **2** : the grant of temporary use
²loan *vb* : LEND
loan shark *n* : a person who lends money at excessive rates of interest — **loan·shark·ing** \'lōn-ˌshär-kiŋ\ *n*
loan·word \'lōn-ˌwərd\ *n* : a word taken from another language and at least partly naturalized
loath \'lōth, 'lōth\ *also* **loathe** \'lōth, lōth\ *adj* : RELUCTANT

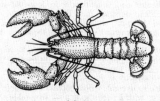

loathe \'lōth\ *vb* **loathed; loath·ing** : to dislike greatly **syn** abominate, abhor, detest, hate

loath·ing \'lō-thiŋ\ *n* : extreme disgust
loath·some \'lōth-səm, 'lōth-\ *adj* : exciting loathing : REPULSIVE
lob \'läb\ *vb* **lobbed; lob·bing** : to throw, hit, or propel something in a high arc — **lob** *n*
¹lob·by \'lä-bē\ *n*, *pl* **lobbies 1** : a corridor used esp. as a passageway or waiting room **2** : a group of persons engaged in lobbying
²lobby *vb* **lob·bied; lob·by·ing** : to try to influence public officials and esp. legislators — **lob·by·ist** *n*
lobe \'lōb\ *n* : a curved or rounded part esp. of a bodily organ — **lo·bar** \'lō-bər\ *adj* — **lobed** \'lōbd\ *adj*
lo·bot·o·my \lō-'bä-tə-mē\ *n*, *pl* **-mies** : surgical severance of certain nerve fibers in the brain for the relief of some mental disorders
lob·ster \'läb-stər\ *n* [ME, fr. OE *loppestre*, fr. *loppe* spider] : any of a family of edible marine crustaceans with two large pincerlike claws and four other pairs of legs; *also* : SPINY LOBSTER
¹lo·cal \'lō-kəl\ *adj* **1** : of, relating to, or occupying a particular place **2** : serving a particular limited district; *also* : making all stops ⟨a ~ train⟩ **3** : affecting a small part of the body ⟨~ infection⟩ — **lo·cal·ly** *adv*
²local *n* : one that is local
lo·cale \lō-'kal\ *n* : a place that is the setting for a particular event
lo·cal·ise *Brit var of* LOCALIZE

lo·cal·i·ty \lō-'ka-lə-tē\ *n*, *pl* **-ties** : a particular spot, situation, or location
lo·cal·ize \'lō-kə-ˌlīz\ *vb* **-ized; -iz·ing** : to fix in or confine to a definite place or locality — **lo·cal·i·za·tion** \ˌlō-kə-lə-'zā-shən\ *n*
lo·cate \'lō-ˌkāt, lō-'kāt\ *vb* **lo·cat·ed; lo·cat·ing 1** : STATION, SETTLE **2** : to determine the site of **3** : to find or fix the place of in a sequence
lo·ca·tion \lō-'kā-shən\ *n* **1** : SITUATION, PLACE **2** : the process of locating **3** : a place outside a studio where a motion picture is filmed
loc cit *abbr* [L *loco citato*] in the place cited
loch \'läk, 'läk\ *n, Scot* : LAKE; *also* : a bay or arm of the sea esp. when nearly landlocked
¹lock \'läk\ *n* : a tuft, strand, or ringlet of hair; *also* : a cohering bunch (as of wool or flax)
²lock *n* **1** : a fastening in which a bolt is operated **2** : the mechanism of a firearm by which the charge is exploded **3** : an enclosure (as in a canal) used in raising or lowering boats from level to level **4** : AIR LOCK **5** : a wrestling hold
³lock *vb* **1** : to fasten the lock of; *also* : to make fast with a lock **2** : to confine or exclude by means of a lock **3** : INTERLOCK **4** : to make or become motionless by the interlocking of parts
lock·er \'lä-kər\ *n* **1** : a drawer, cupboard, or compartment for individual storage use **2** : an insulated compartment for storing frozen food
lock·et \'lä-kət\ *n* : a small usu. metal case for a memento worn suspended from a chain or necklace
lock·jaw \'läk-ˌjò\ *n* : a symptom of tetanus marked by spasms of the jaw muscles and inability to open the jaws; *also* : TETANUS
lock·nut \-ˌnət\ *n* **1** : a nut screwed tight on another to prevent it from slacking back **2** : a nut designed to lock itself when screwed tight
lock·out \-ˌaut\ *n* : the suspension of work by an employer during a labor dispute in order to make employees accept the terms being offered
lock·smith \-ˌsmith\ *n* : one who makes or repairs locks
lock·step \-ˌstep\ *n* : a mode of marching in step by a body of men moving in a very close single file
lock·up \-ˌəp\ *n* : JAIL
lo·co \'lō-kō\ *adj* [Sp] *slang* : CRAZY, FRENZIED
lo·co·mo·tion \ˌlō-kə-'mō-shən\ *n* **1** : the act or power of moving from place to place **2** : TRAVEL

lobster

¹lo·co·mo·tive \ˌlō-kə-ˈmō-tiv\ *adj* : of or relating to locomotion or a locomotive

²locomotive *n* : a self-propelled vehicle used to move railroad cars

lo·co·mo·tor \ˌlō-kə-ˈmō-tər\ *adj* : of or relating to locomotion or organs used in locomotion

lo·co·weed \ˈlō-kō-ˌwēd\ *n* : any of several leguminous plants of western N. America that are poisonous to livestock

lo·cus \ˈlō-kəs\ *n, pl* **lo·ci** \ˈlō-ˌsī\ [L] **1** : PLACE, LOCALITY **2** : the set of all points whose location is determined by stated conditions

lo·cust \ˈlō-kəst\ *n* **1** : a usu. destructive migratory grasshopper **2** : CICADA **3** : any of various leguminous trees; *also* : the wood of a locust

lo·cu·tion \lō-ˈkyü-shən\ *n* : a particular form of expression; *also* : PHRASEOLOGY

lode \ˈlōd\ *n* : an ore deposit

lode·stone \-ˌstōn\ *n* : an iron-containing rock with magnetic properties

¹lodge \ˈläj\ *vb* **lodged; lodg·ing 1** : to provide quarters for; *also* : to settle in a place **2** : CONTAIN **3** : to come to a rest and remain **4** : to deposit for safekeeping **5** : to vest (as authority) in an agent **6** : FILE ⟨~ a complaint⟩

²lodge *n* **1** : a house set apart for residence in a special season or by an employee on an estate; *also* : INN **2** : a den or lair esp. of gregarious animals **3** : the meeting place of a branch of a fraternal organization; *also* : the members of such a branch

lodg·er \ˈlä-jər\ *n* : a person who occupies a rented room in another's house

lodg·ing \ˈlä-jiŋ\ *n* **1** : DWELLING **2** : a room or suite of rooms in another's house rented as a dwelling place — usu. used in pl.

lodg·ment *or* **lodge·ment** \ˈläj-mənt\ *n* **1** : a lodging place **2** : the act or manner of lodging **3** : DEPOSIT

loess \ˈles, ˈləs\ *n* : a usu. yellowish brown loamy deposit believed to be chiefly deposited by the wind

¹loft \ˈlȯft\ *n* [ME, fr. OE, air, sky, fr. ON *lopt*] **1** : ATTIC **2** : GALLERY ⟨organ ~⟩ **3** : an upper floor (as in a warehouse or barn) esp. when not partitioned **4** : the thickness of a fabric or insulated material (as of a sleeping bag)

²loft *vb* : to strike or throw a ball so that it rises high in the air

lofty \ˈlȯf-tē\ *adj* **loft·i·er; -est 1** : NOBLE; *also* : SUPERIOR **2** : extremely proud **3** : HIGH, TALL — **loft·i·ly** \ˈlȯf-tə-lē\ *adv* — **loft·i·ness** \-tē-nəs\ *n*

¹log \ˈlȯg, ˈläg\ *n* **1** : a bulky piece of unshaped timber **2** : an apparatus for measuring a ship's speed **3** : the daily record of a ship's progress; *also* : a regularly kept record of performance (as of an airplane)

²log *vb* **logged; log·ging 1** : to cut (trees) for lumber; *also* : to clear (land) of trees in lumbering **2** : to enter in a log **3** : to sail a ship or fly an airplane for (an indicated distance or period of time) **4** : to have (an indicated record) to one's credit : ACHIEVE — **log·ger** \ˈlȯ-gər, ˈlä-\ *n*

³log *n* : LOGARITHM

lo·gan·ber·ry \ˈlō-gən-ˌber-ē\ *n* : a red-fruited upright-growing dewberry; *also* : its fruit

log·a·rithm \ˈlȯ-gə-ˌri-thəm, ˈlä-\ *n* : the exponent that indicates the power to which a base is raised to produce a given number ⟨the ~ of 100 to base 10 is 2 since $10^2 = 100$⟩ — **log·a·rith·mic** \ˌlȯ-gə-ˈrith-mik, ˌlä-\ *adj*

loge \ˈlōzh\ *n* **1** : a small compartment; *also* : a box in a theater **2** : a small partitioned area; *also* : the forward section of a theater mezzanine

log·ger·head \ˈlȯ-gər-ˌhed, ˈlä-\ *n* : a large sea turtle of subtropical and temperate waters — **at loggerheads** : in a state of quarrelsome disagreement

log·gia \ˈlō-jē-ə, ˈlȯ-jä\ *n, pl* **loggias** \ˈlō-jē-əz, ˈlȯ-jäz\ : a roofed open gallery

log·ic \ˈlä-jik\ *n* **1** : a science that deals with the rules

and tests of sound thinking and proof by reasoning **2** : sound reasoning **3** : the arrangement of circuit elements for arithmetical computation in a computer — **log·i·cal** \-ji-kəl\ *adj* — **log·i·cal·ly** \-jik(ə-)lē\ *adv* — **lo·gi·cian** \lō-ˈji-shən\ *n*

lo·gis·tics \lō-ˈjis-tiks\ *n sing or pl* : the procurement, maintenance, and transportation of matériel, facilities, and personnel — **lo·gis·tic** \-tik\ *adj*

log·jam \ˈlȯg-ˌjam, ˈläg-\ *n* **1** : a deadlocked jumble of logs in a watercourse **2** : DEADLOCK

logo \ˈlȯ-gō\ *n, pl* **log·os** \-gōz\ : an identifying symbol (as for advertising)

logo·type \ˈlȯ-gə-ˌtīp, ˈlä-\ *n* : LOGO

log·roll·ing \-ˌrō-liŋ\ *n* : the trading of votes by legislators to secure favorable action on projects of individual interest

lo·gy \ˈlō-gē\ *also* **log·gy** \ˈlȯ-gē, ˈlä-\ *adj* **lo·gi·er; -est** : deficient in vitality : SLUGGISH

loin \ˈlȯin\ *n* **1** : the part of the body on each side of the spinal column and between the hip and the lower ribs; *also* : a cut of meat from this part of an animal **2** *pl* : the pubic region; *also* : the organs of reproduction

loin·cloth \-ˌklȯth\ *n* : a cloth worn about the loins often as the sole article of clothing in warm climates

loi·ter \ˈlȯi-tər\ *vb* **1** : LINGER **2** : to hang around idly **syn** dawdle, dally, procrastinate, lag, tarry — **loi·ter·er** *n*

loll \ˈläl\ *vb* **1** : DROOP, DANGLE **2** : LOUNGE

lol·li·pop *or* **lol·ly·pop** \ˈlä-li-ˌpäp\ *n* : a lump of hard candy on a stick

lol·ly·gag \ˈlä-lē-ˌgag\ *vb* **-gagged; -gag·ging** : DAWDLE

Lond *abbr* London

lone \ˈlōn\ *adj* **1** : SOLITARY ⟨a ~ sentinel⟩ **2** : SOLE, ONLY ⟨the ~ theater in town⟩ **3** : ISOLATED ⟨a ~ tree⟩

lone·ly \ˈlōn-lē\ *adj* **lone·li·er; -est 1** : being without company **2** : UNFREQUENTED ⟨a ~ spot⟩ **3** : LONESOME — **lone·li·ness** *n*

lon·er \ˈlō-nər\ *n* : one that avoids others

lone·some \ˈlōn-səm\ *adj* **1** : sad from lack of companionship **2** : REMOTE; *also* : SOLITARY — **lone·some·ly** *adv* — **lone·some·ness** *n*

¹long \ˈlȯŋ\ *adj* **lon·ger** \ˈlȯŋ-gər\; **lon·gest** \ˈlȯŋ-gəst\ **1** : extending for a considerable distance; *also* : TALL, ELONGATED **2** : having a specified length **3** : extending over a considerable time; *also* : TEDIOUS **4** : containing many items in a series **5** : being a syllable or speech sound of relatively great duration **6** : extending far into the future **7** : well furnished with something — used with *on*

²long *adv* : for or during a long time

³long *n* : a long period of time

⁴long *vb* **longed; long·ing** \ˈlȯŋ-iŋ\ : to feel a strong desire or wish **syn** yearn, hanker, pine, hunger, thirst

⁵long *abbr* longitude

long·boat \ˈlȯŋ-ˌbōt\ *n* : a large boat usu. carried by a merchant sailing ship

long·bow \-ˌbō\ *n* : a wooden bow drawn by hand and used esp. by medieval English archers

lon·gev·i·ty \län-ˈje-və-tē\ *n* [LL *longaevitas*, fr. L *longaevus* long-lived, fr. *longus* long + *aevum* age] : a long duration of individual life; *also* : length of life

long·hair \ˈlȯŋ-ˌhar\ *n* **1** : a lover of classical music **2** : HIPPIE **3** : a domestic cat having long outer fur — **long·haired** \-ˈhard\ *or* **long·hair** *adj*

long·hand \-ˌhand\ *n* : HANDWRITING

long·horn \-ˌhȯrn\ *n* : any of the cattle with long horns formerly common in the southwestern U.S.

long hundredweight *n, Brit* — see WEIGHT table

long·ing \ˈlȯŋ-iŋ\ *n* : a strong desire esp. for something unattainable — **long·ing·ly** *adv*

lon·gi·tude \ˈlän-jə-ˌtüd, -ˌtyüd\ *n* : angular distance expressed usu. in degrees east or west from the prime meridian through Greenwich, England

lon·gi·tu·di·nal \ˌlän-jə-ˈtüd-ᵊn-əl, -ˈtyüd-\ *adj* **1** : ex-

SOME PEOPLE LOSE WEIGHT

I JUST GIVE IT A TEMPORARY LEAVE OF ABSENCE

JIM DAVIS 12-4

© 1986 PAWS, INC.

tending lengthwise **2** : of or relating to length — **lon·gi·tu·di·nal·ly** \-ē\ *adv*

long·shore·man \'lȯŋ-ˌshȯr-mən\ *n* : a laborer at a wharf who loads and unloads cargo

long–suf·fer·ing \-'sə-friŋ, -fə-riŋ\ *n* : long and patient endurance of offense

long–term \'lȯŋ-'tərm\ *adj* **1** : extending over or involving a long period of time **2** : constituting a financial obligation based on a term usu. of more than 10 years ⟨∼ bonds⟩

long·time \'lȯŋ-'tīm\ *adj* : of long duration ⟨∼ friends⟩

long ton *n* — see WEIGHT table

lon·gueur \lōⁿ-'gœr\ *n, pl* **longueurs** *same or* -'gœrz\ [F, lit., length] : a dull tedious passage or section

long–wind·ed \ˌlȯŋ-'win-dəd\ *adj* : tediously long in speaking or writing

loo·fah \'lü-fə\ *n* : a sponge consisting of the fibrous skeleton of a gourd

¹look \'lu̇k\ *vb* **1** : to exercise the power of vision : SEE **2** : EXPECT **3** : to have an appearance that befits ⟨∼s the part⟩ **4** : SEEM ⟨∼s thin⟩ **5** : to direct one's attention : HEED **6** : POINT, FACE **7** : to show a tendency — **look after** : to take care of — **look for** : EXPECT

²look *n* **1** : the action of looking : GLANCE **2** : EXPRESSION; *also* : physical appearance **3** : ASPECT

look down *vb* : to regard with contempt — used with *on* or *upon*

looking glass *n* : MIRROR

look·out \'lu̇k-ˌau̇t\ *n* **1** : a person assigned to watch (as on a ship) **2** : a careful watch **3** : VIEW **4** : a matter of concern

look up *vb* **1** : IMPROVE ⟨business is *looking up*⟩ **2** : to search for in or as if in a reference work **3** : to seek out esp. for a brief visit

¹loom \'lüm\ *n* : a frame or machine for weaving together threads or yarns into cloth

²loom *vb* **1** : to come into sight in an unnaturally large, indistinct, or distorted form **2** : to appear in an impressively exaggerated form

loon \'lün\ *n* : any of several web-footed blackand-white fish-eating diving birds

loo·ny *or* **loo·ney** \'lü-nē\ *adj* **loo·ni·er; -est** : CRAZY, FOOLISH

loony bin *n* : an insane asylum

loop \'lüp\ *n* **1** : a fold or doubling of a line through which another line or hook can be passed; *also* : a loop-shaped figure or course ⟨a ∼ in a river⟩ **2** : a circular airplane maneuver executed in the vertical plane **3** : a piece of film or magnetic tape whose ends are spliced together to project or play continuously — **loop** *vb*

loop·er \'lü-pər\ *n* : any of numerous rather small hairless moth caterpillars that move with a looping movement

loop·hole \'lüp-ˌhōl\ *n* **1** : a small opening in a wall through which firearms may be discharged **2** : a means of escape; *esp* : an ambiguity or omission that allows one to evade the intent of a law or contract

¹loose \'lüs\ *adj* **loos·er; loos·est 1** : not rigidly fastened **2** : free from restraint or obligation **3** : not dense or compact in structure **4** : not chaste : LEWD **5** : SLACK **6** : not precise or exact — **loose·ly** *adv* — **loose·ness** *n*

²loose *vb* **loosed; loos·ing 1** : RELEASE **2** : UNTIE **3** : DETACH **4** : DISCHARGE **5** : RELAX, SLACKEN

³loose *adv* : LOOSELY

loos·en \'lüs-ᵊn\ *vb* **1** : FREE **2** : to make or become loose **3** : to relax the severity of

loot \'lüt\ *n* [Hindi *lūṭ*; akin to Skt *luṇṭati* he plunders] : goods taken in war or by robbery : PLUNDER — **loot** *vb* — **loot·er** *n*

¹lop \'läp\ *vb* **lopped; lop·ping** : to cut branches or twigs from : TRIM; *also* : to cut off

²lop *vb* **lopped; lop·ping** : to hang downward; *also* : to flop or sway loosely

lope \'lōp\ *n* : an easy bounding gait — **lope** *vb*

lop·sid·ed \'läp-'sī-dəd\ *adj* **1** : leaning to one side **2** : UNSYMMETRICAL — **lop·sid·ed·ly** *adv* — **lop·sid·ed·ness** *n*

lo·qua·cious \lō-'kwā-shəs\ *adj* : excessively talkative — **lo·quac·i·ty** \-'kwa-sə-tē\ *n*

¹lord \'lȯrd\ *n* [ME *loverd, lord,* fr. OE *hlāford,* fr. *hlāf* loaf + *weard* keeper] **1** : one having power and authority over others; *esp* : a person from whom a feudal fee or estate is held **2** : a man of rank or high position; *esp* : a British nobleman **3** *pl, cap* : the upper house of the British parliament **4** : a person of great power in some field

²lord *vb* : to act like a lord; *esp* : to put on airs — usu. used with *it*

lord chancellor *n, pl* **lords chancellor** : a British officer of state who presides over the House of Lords, serves as head of the British judiciary, and is usu. a leading member of the cabinet

lord·ly \-lē\ *adj* **lord·li·er; -est 1** : DIGNIFIED; *also* : NOBLE **2** : HAUGHTY

lord·ship \-ˌship\ *n* **1** : the rank or dignity of a lord — used as a title **2** : the authority or territory of a lord

Lord's Supper *n* : COMMUNION

lore \'lōr\ *n* : KNOWLEDGE; *esp* : traditional knowledge or belief

lor·gnette \lȯrn-'yet\ *n* [F, fr. *lorgner* to take a sidelong look at, fr. MF, fr. *lorgne* squinting] : a pair of eyeglasses or opera glasses with a handle

lorn \'lȯrn\ *adj* : FORSAKEN, DESOLATE

lor·ry \'lȯr-ē\ *n, pl* **lorries** *chiefly Brit* : MOTORTRUCK

lose \'lüz\ *vb* **lost** \'lȯst\; **los·ing** \'lü-ziŋ\ **1** : DESTROY **2** : to miss from a customary place : MISLAY **3** : to suffer deprivation of **4** : to fail to use : WASTE **5** : to fail to win or obtain ⟨∼ the game⟩ **6** : to fail to keep or maintain ⟨∼ his balance⟩ **7** : to wander from ⟨∼ her way⟩ **8** : to get rid of — **los·er** *n*

loss \'lȯs\ *n* **1** : RUIN **2** : the harm resulting from losing **3** : something that is lost **4** *pl* : killed, wounded, or captured soldiers **5** : failure to win **6** : an amount by

which the cost exceeds the selling price **7** : decrease in amount or degree

loss leader *n* : an article sold at a loss in order to draw customers

lost \\'lòst\\ *adj* **1** : not used, won, or claimed **2** : no longer possessed or known **3** : ruined or destroyed physically or morally **4** : DENIED; *also* : HARDENED **5** : unable to find the way; *also* : HELPLESS **6** : ABSORBED, RAPT **7** : not appreciated or understood ⟨his jokes were ∼ on me⟩

lot \\'lät\\ *n* **1** : an object used in deciding something by chance; *also* : the use of lots to decide something **2** : SHARE, PORTION; *also* : FORTUNE, FATE **3** : a plot of land **4** : a group of individuals : SET **5** : a considerable quantity

loth \\'lòth, 'lōth\\ *var of* LOATH

lo·ti \\'lō-tē\\ *n, pl* **ma·lo·ti** \\mä-'lō-tē\\ — see MONEY table

lo·tion \\'lō-shən\\ *n* : a liquid preparation for cosmetic and external medicinal use

lot·tery \\'lä-tə-rē\\ *n, pl* **-ter·ies 1** : a drawing of lots in which prizes are given to the winning names or numbers **2** : a matter determined by chance

lo·tus \\'lō-təs\\ *n* **1** : a fruit held in Greek legend to cause dreamy contentment and forgetfulness **2** : any of various water lilies represented esp. in ancient Egyptian and Hindu art **3** : any of several leguminous forage plants

loud \\'laùd\\ *adj* **1** : marked by intensity or volume of sound **2** : CLAMOROUS, NOISY **3** : obtrusive or offensive in color or pattern ⟨a ∼ suit⟩ — **loud** *adv* — **loud·ly** *adv* — **loud·ness** *n*

loud-mouthed \\-ˌmaùtht, -ˌmaùthd\\ *adj* : given to loud offensive talk

loud·speak·er \\-ˌspē-kər\\ *n* : a device that changes electrical signals into sound

¹lounge \\'laùnj\\ *vb* **lounged; loung·ing** : to act or move lazily or listlessly

²lounge *n* **1** : a room with comfortable furniture; *also* : a room (as in a theater) with lounging, smoking, and toilet facilities **2** : a long couch

lour \\'laùr\\, **loury** \\'laùr-ē\\ *var of* LOWER, LOWERY

louse \\'laùs\\ *n, pl* **lice** \\'līs\\ **1** : any of various small wingless usu. flattened insects parasitic on warm-blooded animals **2** : a plant pest (as an aphid) **3** : a contemptible person

lousy \\'laù-zē\\ *adj* **lous·i·er; -est 1** : infested with lice **2** : POOR, INFERIOR **3** : amply supplied ⟨∼ with money⟩ — **lous·i·ly** \\-zə-lē\\ *adv* — **lous·i·ness** \\-zē-nəs\\ *n*

lout \\'laùt\\ *n* : a stupid awkward fellow — **lout·ish** *adj* — **lout·ish·ly** *adv*

lou·ver *or* **lou·vre** \\'lü-vər\\ *n* **1** : an opening having parallel slanted slats to allow flow of air but to exclude rain or sun or to provide privacy; *also* : a slat in such an opening **2** : a device with movable slats for controlling the flow of air or light

¹love \\'ləv\\ *n* **1** : strong affection **2** : warm attachment ⟨∼ of the sea⟩ **3** : attraction based on sexual desire **4**: a beloved person **5** : unselfish loyal and benevolent concern for others **6** : a score of zero in tennis — **love·less** *adj*

²love *vb* **loved; lov·ing 1** : CHERISH **2** : to feel a passion, devotion, or tenderness for **3** : CARESS **4** : to take pleasure in ⟨∼s to play bridge⟩ — **lov·able** \\'lə-və-bəl\\ *adj* — **lov·er** *n*

love·bird \\'ləv-ˌbərd\\ *n* : any of various small usu. gray or green parrots that seem to show caring behavior for their mates

love·lorn \\-ˌlòrn\\ *adj* : deprived of love or of a lover

love·ly \\'ləv-lē\\ *adj* **love·li·er; -est** : BEAUTIFUL — **love·li·ly** \\'ləv-lə-lē\\ *adv* — **love·li·ness** *n* — **lovely** *adv*

love·mak·ing \\-ˌmā-kiŋ\\ *n* **1** : COURTSHIP **2** : sexual activity; *esp* : COPULATION

love·sick \\-ˌsik\\ *adj* **1** : YEARNING **2** : expressing a lover's longing — **love·sick·ness** *n*

lov·ing \\'lə-viŋ\\ *adj* **1** : AFFECTIONATE **2** : PAINSTAKING — **lov·ing·ly** *adv*

¹low \\'lō\\ *vb* : MOO

²low *n* : MOO

³low *adj* **low·er** \\'lō-ər\\; **low·est** \\'lō-əst\\ **1** : not high or tall ⟨∼ wall⟩; *also* : DÉCOLLETÉ **2** : situated or passing below the normal level or surface ⟨∼ ground⟩; *also* : marking a nadir **3** : not loud ⟨∼ voice⟩ **4** : being near the equator **5** : humble in status **6** : WEAK; *also* : DEPRESSED **7** : STRICKEN, PROSTRATE **8** : less than usual in number, amount, or value; *also* : of lesser degree than average **9** : falling short of a standard **10** : UNFAVORABLE — **low** *adv* — **low·ness** *n*

⁴low *n* **1** : something that is low **2** : a region of low barometric pressure **3** : the arrangement of gears in an automobile transmission that gives the slowest speed and greatest power

low beam *n* : the short-range focus of a vehicle headlight

low blow *n* : an unprincipled attack

low·brow \\'lō-ˌbraù\\ *n* : a person with little taste or intellectual interest

low–density lipoprotein *n* : LDL

low·down \\-ˌdaùn\\ *n* : pertinent and esp. guarded information

low–down \\-ˌdaùn\\ *adj* **1** : MEAN, CONTEMPTIBLE **2** : deeply emotional

low–end \\-ˌend\\ *adj* : of, relating to, or being the lowest-priced merchandise in a manufacturer's line

¹low·er \\'laù-ər\\ *vb* **1** : FROWN **2** : to become dark, gloomy, and threatening

²low·er \\'lō-ər\\ *adj* **1** : relatively low (as in rank) **2** : situated beneath the earth's surface **3** : constituting the popular and more representative branch of a bicameral legislative body

³**low•er** \'lō-ər\ *vb* **1** : DROP; *also* : DIMINISH **2** : to let descend by its own weight; *also* : to reduce the height of **3** : to reduce in value, number, or amount **4** : DEGRADE; *also* : HUMBLE

low•er•case \ˌlō-ər-ˈkās\ *adj* : being a letter that belongs to or conforms to the series a, b, c, etc., rather than A, B, C, etc. — **lowercase** *n*

lower class *n* : a social class occupying a position below the middle class and having the lowest status in a society — **lower–class** \-ˈklas\ *adj*

low•er•most \'lō-ər-ˌmōst\ *adj* : LOWEST

low•ery \'laú-ə-rē\ *adj* : GLOOMY, LOWERING

lowest common denominator *n* **1** : LEAST COMMON DENOMINATOR **2** : something designed to appeal to a lowbrow audience; *also* : such an audience

lowest common multiple *n* : LEAST COMMON MULTIPLE

low–key \'lō-ˈkē\ *also* **low–keyed** \-ˈkēd\ *adj* : of low intensity : RESTRAINED

low•land \'lō-lənd, -ˌland\ *n* : low and usu. level country

low•life \'lō-ˌlīf\ *n, pl* **low•lifes** \-ˌlīfs\ *also* **low•lives** \-ˌlīvz\ : a person of low social status or moral character

low•ly \'lō-lē\ *adj* **low•li•er; -est 1** : HUMBLE, MEEK **2** : ranking low in some hierarchy — **low•li•ness** *n*

low–rise \'lō-ˈrīz\ *adj* **1** : having few stories and not equipped with elevators (a ~ building) **2** : of, relating to, or characterized by low-rise buildings

low–tech \'lō-ˈtek\ *adj* : technologically simple or unsophisticated

¹**lox** \'läks\ *n* : liquid oxygen

²**lox** *n, pl* **lox** *or* **lox•es** : smoked salmon

loy•al \'lȯi-əl\ *adj* [MF, fr. OF *leial, leel*, fr. L *legalis* legal] **1** : faithful in allegiance to one's government **2** : faithful esp. to a cause or ideal : CONSTANT — **loy•al•ly** \'lȯi-ə-lē\ *adv* — **loy•al•ty** \'lȯi-əl-tē\ *n*

loy•al•ist \'lȯi-ə-list\ *n* : one who is or remains loyal to a political party, government, or sovereign

loz•enge \'lä-zənj\ *n* **1** : a diamond-shaped figure **2** : a small flat often medicated candy

LP *abbr* low pressure

LPG *abbr* liquefied petroleum gas

LPGA *abbr* Ladies Professional Golf Association

LPN \ˌel-ˈpē-ˈen\ *n* : LICENSED PRACTICAL NURSE

Lr *symbol* Lawrencium

LSD \ˌel-(ˌ)es-ˈdē\ *n* [G *Lysergsäure-Diäthylamid* lysergic acid diethylamide] : an illicit drug that causes psychotic symptoms similar to those of schizophrenia

lt *abbr* light

Lt *abbr* lieutenant

LT *abbr* long ton

LTC *or* **Lt Col** *abbr* lieutenant colonel

Lt Comdr *abbr* lieutenant commander

ltd *abbr* limited

LTG *or* **Lt Gen** *abbr* lieutenant general

LTJG *abbr* lieutenant, junior grade

ltr *abbr* letter

Lu *symbol* lutetium

lu•au \'lü-ˌaú\ *n* : a Hawaiian feast

lub *abbr* lubricant; lubricating

lub•ber \'lə-bər\ *n* **1** : LOUT **2** : an unskilled seaman — **lub•ber•ly** *adj*

lube \'lüb\ *n* : LUBRICANT; *also* : an application of a lubricant

lu•bri•cant \'lü-bri-kənt\ *n* : a material capable of reducing friction when applied between moving parts

lu•bri•cate \'lü-brə-ˌkāt\ *vb* **-cat•ed; -cat•ing** : to apply a lubricant to — **lu•bri•ca•tion** \ˌlü-brə-ˈkā-shən\ *n* — **lu•bri•ca•tor** \'lü-brə-ˌkā-tər\ *n*

lu•bri•cious \lü-ˈbri-shəs\ *or* **lu•bri•cous** \'lü-bri-kəs\ *adj* **1** : SMOOTH, SLIPPERY **2** : LECHEROUS; *also* : SALACIOUS — **lu•bric•i•ty** \lü-ˈbri-sə-tē\ *n*

lu•cent \'lüs-ᵊnt\ *adj* **1** : LUMINOUS **2** : CLEAR, LUCID — **lu•cent•ly** *adv*

lu•cerne \lü-ˈsərn\ *n, chiefly Brit* : ALFALFA

lu•cid \'lü-səd\ *adj* **1** : SHINING **2** : mentally sound **3** : easily understood — **lu•cid•i•ty** \lü-ˈsi-də-tē\ *n* — **lu•cid•ly** *adv* — **lu•cid•ness** *n*

Lu•ci•fer \'lü-sə-fər\ *n* [ME, the morning star, a fallen rebel archangel, the Devil, fr. OE, fr. L, the morning star, fr. *lucifer* light-bearing] : DEVIL, SATAN

¹**luck** \'lək\ *n* **1** : CHANCE, FORTUNE **2** : good fortune — **luck•less** *adj*

²**luck** *vb* **1** : to prosper or succeed esp. through chance or good fortune — usu. used with *out* **2** : to come upon something desirable by chance — usu. used with *out, on, onto,* or *into*

luck•i•ly \'lə-kə-lē\ *adv* **1** : in a lucky manner **2** : FORTUNATELY **2**

lucky \'lə-kē\ *adj* **luck•i•er; -est 1** : favored by luck : FORTUNATE **2** : FORTUITOUS **3** : seeming to bring good luck — **luck•i•ness** *n*

lu•cra•tive \'lü-krə-tiv\ *adj* : PROFITABLE — **lu•cra•tive•ly** *adv* — **lu•cra•tive•ness** *n*

lu•cre \'lü-kər\ *n* [ME, fr. L *lucrum*] : PROFIT; *also* : MONEY

lu•cu•bra•tion \ˌlü-kyə-ˈbrā-shən, -kə-\ *n* : laborious study : MEDITATION

lu•di•crous \'lü-də-krəs\ *adj* : LAUGHABLE, RIDICULOUS — **lu•di•crous•ly** *adv* — **lu•di•crous•ness** *n*

luff \'ləf\ *vb* : to turn the head of a ship toward the wind

¹**lug** \'ləg\ *vb* **lugged; lug•ging 1** : DRAG, PULL **2** : to carry laboriously

²**lug** *n* **1** : a projecting piece (as for fastening, support, or traction) **2** : a nut securing a wheel on an automobile

lug•gage \'lə-gij\ *n* : containers (as suitcases) for carrying personal belongings : BAGGAGE

lu•gu•bri•ous \lu-ˈgü-brē-əs\ *adj* : mournful often to an exaggerated degree — **lu•gu•bri•ous•ly** *adv* — **lu•gu•bri•ous•ness** *n*

Luke \'lük\ *n* — see BIBLE table

luke•warm \'lük-ˈwȯrm\ *adj* **1** : moderately warm : TEPID **2** : not enthusiastic — **luke•warm•ly** *adv*

¹**lull** \'ləl\ *vb* **1** : SOOTHE, CALM **2** : to cause to relax vigilance

²**lull** *n* **1** : a temporary calm (as during a storm) **2** : a temporary drop in activity

lul•la•by \'lə-lə-ˌbī\ *n, pl* **-bies** : a song to lull children to sleep

lum•ba•go \ˌləm-ˈbā-gō\ *n* : rheumatic pain in the lower back and loins

lum•bar \'ləm-bər, -ˌbär\ *adj* : of, relating to, or constituting the loins or the vertebrae between the thoracic vertebrae and sacrum (~ region)

¹**lum•ber** \'ləm-bər\ *vb* : to move heavily or clumsily

²**lumber** *n* **1** : surplus or disused articles that are stored away **2** : timber or logs esp. when dressed for use

³**lumber** *vb* : to cut logs; *also* : to saw logs into lumber — **lum•ber•man** \-mən\ *n*

lum•ber•jack \-ˌjak\ *n* : LOGGER

lum•ber•yard \-ˌyärd\ *n* : a place where lumber is kept for sale

lu•mi•nary \'lü-mə-ˌner-ē\ *n, pl* **-nar•ies 1** : a very famous person **2** : a source of light; *esp* : a celestial body

lu•mi•nes•cence \ˌlü-mə-ˈnes-ᵊns\ *n* : the low-temperature emission of light (as by a chemical or physiological process); *also* : such light — **lu•mi•nes•cent** \-ᵊnt\ *adj*

lu•mi•nous \'lü-mə-nəs\ *adj* **1** : emitting light; *also* : LIGHTED **2** : CLEAR, INTELLIGIBLE — **lu•mi•nance** \-nəns\ *n* — **lu•mi•nos•i•ty** \ˌlü-mə-ˈnä-sə-tē\ *n* — **lu•mi•nous•ly** *adv*

lum•mox \'lə-məks\ *n* : a clumsy person

¹**lump** \'ləmp\ *n* **1** : a piece or mass of indefinite size and shape **2** : AGGREGATE, TOTALITY **3** : a usu. abnormal swelling — **lump•ish** *adj* — **lumpy** *adj*

²**lump** *vb* **1** : to heap together in a lump **2** : to form into lumps

³**lump** *adj* : not divided into parts ⟨a ~ sum⟩

lu·na·cy \ˈlü-nə-sē\ *n, pl* **-cies** 1 : INSANITY 2 : extreme folly

lu·nar \ˈlü-nər\ *adj* : of or relating to the moon

lu·na·tic \ˈlü-nə-ˌtik\ *adj* [ME *lunatik*, fr. LL *lunaticus*, fr. L *luna* moon; fr. the belief that lunacy fluctuated with the phases of the moon] 1 : INSANE; *also* : used for insane persons 2 : extremely foolish — **lunatic** *n*

¹**lunch** \ˈlənch\ *n* 1 : a light meal usu. eaten in the middle of the day 2 : the food prepared for a lunch

²**lunch** *vb* : to eat lunch

lun·cheon \ˈlən-chən\ *n* : a usu. formal lunch

lun·cheon·ette \ˌlən-chə-ˈnet\ *n* : a small restaurant serving light lunches

lunch·room \ˈlənch-ˌrüm, -ˌrum\ *n* 1 : LUNCHEONETTE 2 : a room (as in a school) where lunches are sold and eaten or lunches brought from home may be eaten

lu·nette \lü-ˈnet\ *n* : something shaped like a crescent

lung \ˈləŋ\ *n* 1 : one of the usu. paired baglike breathing organs in the chest of an air-breathing vertebrate 2 : a mechanical device to promote breathing and make it easier — **lunged** \ˈləŋd\ *adj*

lunge \ˈlənj\ *n* 1 : a sudden thrust or pass (as with a sword) 2 : a sudden forward stride or leap — **lunge** *vb*

lu·pine \ˈlü-pən\ *n* : any of a genus of leguminous plants with long upright clusters of pealike flowers

lu·pus \ˈlü-pəs\ *n* [ML, fr. L, wolf] : any of several diseases characterized by skin lesions; *esp* : SYSTEMIC LUPUS ERYTHEMATOSUS

lurch \ˈlərch\ *n* : a sudden swaying or tipping movement — **lurch** *vb*

¹**lure** \ˈlu̇r\ *n* 1 : ENTICEMENT; *also* : APPEAL 2 : an artificial bait for catching fish

²**lure** *vb* **lured; lur·ing** : to draw on with a promise of pleasure or gain

lu·rid \ˈlu̇r-əd\ *adj* 1 : wan and ghostly pale in appearance 2 : shining with the red glow of fire seen through smoke or cloud 3 : GRUESOME; *also* : SENSATIONAL **syn** ghastly, grisly, grim, horrible, macabre — **luridly** *adv*

lurk \ˈlərk\ *vb* 1 : to move furtively : SNEAK 2 : to lie concealed

lus·cious \ˈlə-shəs\ *adj* 1 : having a pleasingly sweet taste or smell 2 : sensually appealing — **lusciously** *adv* — **lus·cious·ness** *n*

¹**lush** \ˈləsh\ *adj* : having or covered with abundant growth ⟨~ pastures⟩

²**lush** *n* : an habitual heavy drinker

lust \ˈləst\ *n* 1 : usu. intense or unbridled sexual desire : LASCIVIOUSNESS 2 : an intense longing — **lust** *vb* — **lust·ful** *adj*

lus·ter *or* **lus·tre** \ˈləs-tər\ *n* 1 : a shine or sheen esp. from reflected light 2 : BRIGHTNESS, GLITTER 3 : GLO-

RY, SPLENDOR — **lus·ter·less** *adj* — **lus·trous** \-trəs\ *adj*

lus·tral \ˈləs-trəl\ *adj* : PURIFICATORY

lusty \ˈləs-tē\ *adj* **lust·i·er; -est** : full of vitality : ROBUST — **lust·i·ly** \ˈləs-tə-lē\ *adv* — **lust·i·ness** \-tē-nəs\ *n*

lute \ˈlüt\ *n* : a stringed musical instrument with a large pear-shaped body and a fretted fingerboard — **lu·te·nist** *or* **lu·ta·nist** \ˈlüt-ᵊn-ist\ *n*

lu·te·tium *also* **lu·te·cium** \lü-ˈtē-shē-əm, -shəm\ *n* : a metallic chemical element — see ELEMENT table

Lu·ther·an \ˈlü-thə-rən\ *n* : a member of a Protestant denomination adhering to the doctrines of Martin Luther — **Lu·ther·an·ism** \-rə-ˌni-zəm\ *n*

lux·u·ri·ant \ˌləg-ˈzhu̇r-ē-ənt, ˌlək-ˈshu̇r-\ *adj* 1 : yielding or growing abundantly : LUSH, PRODUCTIVE 2 : abundantly rich and varied; *also* : FLORID **syn** exuberant, lavish, opulent, prodigal, profuse, riotous — **lux·u·ri·ance** \-ē-əns\ *n* — **lux·u·ri·ant·ly** *adv*

lux·u·ri·ate \-ē-ˌāt\ *vb* **-at·ed; -at·ing** 1 : to grow profusely 2 : REVEL

lux·u·ry \ˈlək-shə-rē, ˈləg-zhə-\ *n, pl* **-ries** 1 : great ease and comfort 2 : something adding to pleasure or comfort but not absolutely necessary — **lux·u·ri·ous** \ˌləg-ˈzhu̇r-ē-əs, ˌlək-ˈshu̇r-\ *adj* — **lux·u·ri·ous·ly** *adv*

lv *abbr* leave

LVN *n* : LICENSED VOCATIONAL NURSE

lwei \lə-ˈwā\ *n, pl* **lwei** — see *kwanza* at MONEY table

LWV *abbr* League of Women Voters

¹**-ly** \lē\ *adj suffix* 1 : like in appearance, manner, or nature ⟨queen*ly*⟩ 2 : characterized by regular recurrence in (specified) units of time : every ⟨hour*ly*⟩

²**-ly** *adv suffix* 1 : in a (specified) manner ⟨slow*ly*⟩ 2 : from a (specified) point of view ⟨grammatical*ly*⟩

ly·ce·um \lī-ˈsē-əm, ˈlī-sē-\ *n* 1 : a hall for public lectures 2 : an association providing public lectures, concerts, and entertainments

lye \ˈlī\ *n* : a corrosive alkaline substance used esp. in making soap

ly·ing \ˈlī-iŋ\ *adj* : UNTRUTHFUL, FALSE

ly·ing-in \ˌlī-iŋ-ˈin\ *n, pl* **lyings-in** *or* **lying-ins** : the state during and consequent to childbirth : CONFINEMENT

Lyme disease \ˈlīm-\ *n* [*Lyme*, Connecticut, where it was first reported] : an acute inflammatory disease that is caused by a spirochete transmitted by ticks, is characterized esp. by chills and fever, and if left untreated may result in joint pain, arthritis, and cardiac and neurological disorders

lymph \ˈlimf\ *n* : a pale liquid consisting chiefly of blood plasma and white blood cells, circulating in thin-walled tubes (**lymphatic vessels**), and bathing the body tissues — **lym·phat·ic** \lim-ˈfa-tik\ *adj*

lymph·ade·nop·a·thy \ˌlim-ˌfad-ᵊn-ˈä-pə-thē\ *n, pl* **-thies** : abnormal enlargement of the lymph nodes

lymph node *n* : any of the rounded masses of lymphoid tissue surrounded by a capsule

lym·pho·cyte \ˈlim-fə-ˌsīt\ *n* : any of the weakly motile leukocytes produced in lymphoid tissue that are the

typical cells in lymph and include the cellular mediators (as a B cell or a T cell) of immunity

lym·phoid \'lim-ˌfȯid\ *adj* **1** : of, relating to, or being
tissue (as of the lymph nodes) containing lymphocytes **2** : of, relating to, or resembling lymph

lym·pho·ma \lim-'fō-mə\ *n, pl* **-mas** *or* **-ma·ta** \-mə-tə\
: a tumor of lymphoid tissue

lynch \'linch\ *vb* : to put to death by mob action without legal sanction or due process of law — **lynch·
er** *n*

lynx \'links\ *n, pl* **lynx** *or* **lynx·es** : any of several wildcats with a short tail, long legs, and usu. tufted ears

lyre \'līr\ *n* : a stringed musical instrument of the harp
class used by the ancient Greeks

¹lyr·ic \'lir-ik\ *n* **1** : a lyric poem **2** *pl* : the words of a
popular song — **lyr·i·cal** \-i-kəl\ *adj*

lynx

²lyric *adj* **1** : suitable for singing : MELODIC **2** : expressing direct and usu. intense personal emotion

ly·ser·gic acid di·eth·yl·am·ide \lə-'sər-jik . . . ˌdī-ˌe-
thə-'la-ˌmīd, lī-, -'la-məd\ *n* : LSD

LZ *abbr* landing zone

M

¹m \'em\ *n, pl* **m's** *or* **ms** \'emz\ *often cap* : the 13th
letter of the English alphabet

²m *abbr, often cap* **1** Mach **2** male **3** married **4** masculine **5** medium **6** [L *meridies*] noon **7** meter **8** mile **9**
[L *mille*] thousand **10** minute **11** month **12** moon

ma \'mä, 'mȯ\ *n* : MOTHER

MA *abbr* **1** [ML *magister artium*] master of arts **2**
Massachusetts **3** mental age

ma'am \'mam, *after "yes" often* əm\ *n* : MADAM

Mac *abbr* Machabees

Mac *or* **Macc** *abbr* Maccabees

ma·ca·bre \mə-'käb; 'kä-brə, -bər\ *adj* [F] **1** : having
death as a subject **2** : GRUESOME **3** : HORRIBLE

mac·ad·am \mə-'ka-dəm\ *n* : a roadway or pavement
of small closely packed broken stone — **mac·ad·am·
ize** \-də-ˌmīz\ *vb*

ma·caque \mə-'kak, -'käk\ *n* : any of a genus of short-
tailed chiefly Asian monkeys

mac·a·ro·ni \ˌma-kə-'rō-nē\ *n* **1** : pasta made chiefly of
wheat flour and shaped in the form of slender tubes
2 *pl* **-nis** *or* **-nies** : FOP, DANDY

mac·a·roon \ˌma-kə-'rün\ *n* : a small cookie made
chiefly of egg whites, sugar, and ground almonds or
coconut

ma·caw \mə-'kȯ\ *n* : any of numerous parrots of Central and So. America

Mac·ca·bees \'ma-kə-ˌbēz\ *n* — see BIBLE table

¹mace \'mās\ *n* : a spice made from the fibrous coating
of the nutmeg

²mace *n* **1** : a heavy often spiked club used as a weapon
esp. in the Middle Ages **2** : an ornamental staff carried as a symbol of authority

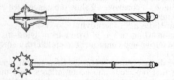

mace 1

Mac·e·do·nian \ˌma-sə-'dō-nyən, -nē-ən\ *n* : a native
or inhabitant of Macedonia — **Macedonian** *adj*

mac·er·ate \'ma-sə-ˌrāt\ *vb* **-at·ed; -at·ing** **1** : to cause
to waste away **2** : to soften by steeping or soaking so
as to separate the parts — **mac·er·a·tion** \ˌma-sə-'rā-
shən\ *n*

mach *abbr* machine; machinery; machinist

Mach \'mäk\ *n* : a speed expressed by a Mach number

Mach·a·bees \'ma-kə-ˌbēz\ *n* : MACCABEES

ma·chete \mə-'she-tē\ *n* : a large heavy knife used for
cutting sugarcane and underbrush and as a weapon

Ma·chi·a·vel·lian \ˌma-kē-ə-'ve-lē-ən\ *adj* [Niccolò
Machiavelli, †1527 Ital. political philosopher]
: characterized by cunning, duplicity, and bad faith
— **Ma·chi·a·vel·lian·ism** *n*

mach·i·na·tion \ˌma-kə-'nā-shən, ˌma-shə-\ *n* : an act
of planning esp. to do harm; *esp* : PLOT — **mach·
i·nate** \'ma-kə-ˌnāt, 'ma-shə-\ *vb*

¹ma·chine \mə-'shēn\ *n* **1** : CONVEYANCE, VEHICLE; *esp*
: AUTOMOBILE **2** : a combination of mechanical parts
that transmit forces, motion, and energy one to another **3** : an instrument (as a lever) for transmitting or
modifying force or motion **4** : an electrical, electronic, or mechanical device for performing a task ⟨a sewing ∼⟩ **5** : a highly organized political group under the
leadership of a boss or small clique

²machine *vb* **ma·chined; ma·chin·ing** : to shape or finish by machine-operated tools — **ma·chin·able**
\-'shē-nə-bəl\ *adj*

machine gun *n* : an automatic gun capable of rapid
continuous firing — **machine–gun** *vb* — **machine
gunner** *n*

machine language *n* : the set of symbolic instruction
codes used to represent operations and data in a machine (as a computer)

machine–readable *adj* : directly usable by a computer

ma·chin·ery \mə-'shē-nə-rē\ *n, pl* **-er·ies** **1** : MACHINES;
also : the working parts of a machine **2** : the means
by which something is done

ma·chin·ist \mə-'shē-nist\ *n* : a person who makes or
works on machines

ma·chis·mo \mä-'chēz-(ˌ)mō, -'chiz-\ *n* : a strong or
exaggerated pride in one's masculinity

Mach number \'mäk-\ *n* : a number representing the
ratio of the speed of a body to the speed of sound in
the surrounding atmosphere

ma·cho \'mä-chō\ *adj* [Sp, lit., male, fr. L *masculus*]
: characterized by machismo

mack·er·el \'ma-kə-rəl\ *n, pl* **mackerel** *or* **mackerels**
: a No. Atlantic food fish greenish above and silvery
below

mack·i·naw \'ma-kə-ˌnȯ\ *n* : a short heavy plaid coat

mack·in·tosh *also* **mac·in·tosh** \'ma-kən-ˌtäsh\ *n* **1**
chiefly Brit : RAINCOAT **2** : a lightweight waterproof
fabric

mac·ra·mé *also* **mac·ra·me** \'ma-krə-ˌmā\ *n* [ultim. fr.
Ar *miqramah* coverlet] : a coarse lace or fringe made
by knotting threads or cords in a geometrical pattern

mac·ro \'ma-(ˌ)krō\ *adj* : very large; *also* : involving
large quantities or being on a large scale

mac·ro·bi·ot·ic \ˌma-krō-bī-'ä-tik, -bē-\ *adj* : relating to
or being a very restricted diet (as one containing
chiefly whole grains)

mac·ro·cosm \'ma-krə-ˌkä-zəm\ *n* : the great
world: UNIVERSE

ma·cron \'mā-ˌkrän, 'ma-\ *n* : a mark ˉ placed over a vowel (as in \'māk\) to show that the vowel is long

mac·ro·scop·ic \ˌma-krə-'skä-pik\ *adj* : visible to the naked eye — **mac·ro·scop·i·cal·ly** \-pi-k(ə-)lē\ *adv*

mad \'mad\ *adj* **mad·der; mad·dest 1** : disordered in mind : INSANE **2** : being rash and foolish **3** : FURIOUS, ENRAGED **4** : carried away with enthusiasm **5** : RABID **6** : marked by wild gaiety and merriment **7** : FRANTIC — **mad·ly** *adv* — **mad·ness** *n*

Mad·a·gas·can \ˌma-də-'gas-kən\ *n* : a native or inhabitant of Madagascar

mad·am \'ma-dəm\ *n* **1** *pl* **mes·dames** \mā-'däm\ — used as a form of polite address to a woman **2** *pl* **mad·ams** : the female head of a house of prostitution

ma·dame \mə-'dam, *before a surname also* 'ma-dəm\ *n, pl* **mes·dames** \mā-'däm\ — MISTRESS — used as a title equivalent to *Mrs.* for a married woman not of English-speaking nationality

mad·cap \'mad-ˌkap\ *adj* : WILD, RECKLESS — **mad·cap** *n*

mad·den \'mad-ᵊn\ *vb* : to make mad — **mad·den·ing·ly** *adv*

mad·der \'ma-dər\ *n* : a Eurasian herb with yellow flowers and fleshy red roots; *also* : its root or a dye prepared from it

made *past and past part of* MAKE

Ma·dei·ra \mə-'dir-ə\ *n* : an amber-colored dessert wine

ma·de·moi·selle \ˌma-də-mə-'zel, -mwə-, mam-'zel\ *n, pl* **ma·de·moi·selles** \-'zelz\ *or* **mes·de·moi·selles** \ˌmā-də-me-'zel, -mwe-\ : an unmarried girl or woman — used as a title for an unmarried woman not of English-speaking nationality

made–up \'mā-'dəp\ *adj* **1** : fancifully conceived or falsely devised **2** : marked by the use of makeup

mad·house \'mad-ˌhaús\ *n* **1** : a place for the detention and care of the insane **2** : a place of great uproar

mad·man \'mad-ˌman, -mən\ *n* : LUNATIC

Ma·don·na \mə-'dä-nə\ *n* : a representation (as a picture or statue) of the Virgin Mary

ma·dras \'ma-drəs, ˌma-'dras, -'dräs\ *n* [*Madras,* India] : a fine usu. cotton fabric with various designs (as plaid)

mad·ri·gal \'ma-dri-gəl\ *n* [It *madrigale*] **1** : a short lyrical poem in a strict poetic form **2** : an elaborate part-song esp. of the 16th and 17th centuries

mad·wom·an \'mad-ˌwú-mən\ *n* : a woman who is insane

mael·strom \'māl-strəm\ *n* **1** : a violent whirlpool **2** : TUMULT

mae·stro \'mī-strō\ *n, pl* **maestros** *or* **mae·stri** \-ˌstrē\ [It] : a master in an art; *esp* : an eminent composer, conductor, or teacher of music

Ma·fia \'mä-fē-ə\ *n* [It] : a secret criminal society of Sicily or Italy; *also* : a similar organization elsewhere

ma·fi·o·so \ˌmä-fē-'ō-(ˌ)sō\ *n, pl* **-si** \-(ˌ)sē\ : a member of the Mafia

---

¹**mag** \'mag\ *n* : MAGAZINE

²**mag** *abbr* **1** magnetism **2** magneto **3** magnitude

mag·a·zine \'ma-gə-ˌzēn\ *n* **1** : a storehouse esp. for military supplies **2** : a place for keeping gunpowder in a fort or ship **3** : a publication usu. containing stories, articles, or poems and issued periodically **4** : a container in a gun for holding cartridges; *also* : a chamber (as on a camera) for film

ma·gen·ta \mə-'jen-tə\ *n* : a deep purplish red color

mag·got \'ma-gət\ *n* : the legless wormlike larva of a dipteran fly — **mag·goty** *adj*

ma·gi \'mā-ˌjī\ *n pl, often cap* : the three wise men from the East who paid homage to the infant Jesus

mag·ic \'ma-jik\ *n* **1** : the use of means (as charms or spells) believed to have supernatural power over natural forces **2** : an extraordinary power or influence seemingly from a supernatural force **3** : SLEIGHT OF HAND — **magic** *adj* — **mag·i·cal** \-ji-kəl\ *adj* — **mag·i·cal·ly** \-ji-k(ə-)lē\ *adv*

ma·gi·cian \mə-'ji-shən\ *n* : one skilled in magic

mag·is·te·ri·al \ˌma-jə-'stir-ē-əl\ *adj* **1** : AUTHORITA-TIVE **2** : of or relating to a magistrate or a magistrate's office or duties

mag·is·tral \'ma-jə-strəl\ *adj* : AUTHORITATIVE

mag·is·trate \'ma-jə-ˌstrāt\ *n* : an official entrusted with administration of the laws — **mag·is·tra·cy** \-strə-sē\ *n*

mag·ma \'mag-mə\ *n* : molten rock material within the earth — **mag·mat·ic** \mag-'ma-tik\ *adj*

mag·nan·i·mous \mag-'na-nə-məs\ *adj* **1** : showing or suggesting a lofty and courageous spirit **2** : NOBLE, GENEROUS — **mag·na·nim·i·ty** \ˌmag-nə-'ni-mə-tē\ *n* — **mag·nan·i·mous·ly** *adv* — **mag·nan·i·mous·ness** *n*

mag·nate \'mag-ˌnāt\ *n* : a person of rank, influence, or distinction

mag·ne·sia \mag-'nē-shə, -zhə\ *n* [NL, fr. *magnes carneus,* a white earth, lit., flesh magnet] : a light white oxide of magnesium used as a laxative

mag·ne·sium \mag-'nē-zē-əm, -zhəm\ *n* : a silvery white light malleable metallic chemical element — see ELEMENT table

mag·net \'mag-nət\ *n* **1** : LODESTONE **2** : a body that is able to attract iron **3** : something that attracts

mag·net·ic \mag-'ne-tik\ *adj* **1** : having an unusual ability to attract ⟨a ∼ leader⟩ **2** : of or relating to a magnet or magnetism **3** : magnetized or capable of being magnetized — **mag·net·i·cal·ly** \-ti-k(ə-)lē\ *adv*

magnetic disk *n* : DISK 3

magnetic north *n* : the northerly direction in the earth's magnetic field indicated by the north-seeking pole of a compass needle

magnetic resonance imaging *n* : a noninvasive diagnostic technique that produces computerized images of internal body tissues based on electromagnetically induced activity of atoms within the body

magnetic tape *n* : a ribbon coated with a magnetic material on which information (as sound) may be stored

mag·ne·tise *Brit var of* MAGNETIZE

mag·ne·tism \'mag-nə-ˌti-zəm\ *n* **1** : the power (as of

a magnet) to attract iron **2** : the science that deals
with magnetic phenomena **3** : an ability to attract
mag·ne·tite \'mag-nə-ˌtīt\ *n* : a black mineral that is an
important iron ore
mag·ne·tize \'mag-nə-ˌtīz\ *vb* **-tized; -tiz·ing 1** : to induce magnetic properties in **2** : to attract like a magnet : CHARM — **mag·ne·tiz·able** *adj* — **mag·ne·ti-
za·tion** \ˌmag-nə-tə-'zā-shən\ *n* — **mag·ne·tiz·er** *n*
mag·ne·to \mag-'nē-tō\ *n, pl* **-tos** : a generator used to
produce sparks in an internal combustion engine
mag·ne·tom·e·ter \ˌmag-nə-'tä-mə-tər\ *n* : an instrument for measuring the strength of a magnetic field
mag·ne·to·sphere \mag-'nē-tə-ˌsfir, -'ne-\ *n* : a region
around a celestial object (as the earth) in which
charged particles are trapped by its magnetic field —
mag·ne·to·spher·ic \-ˌnē-tə-'sfir-ik, -'sfer-\ *adj*
mag·ni·fi·ca·tion \ˌmag-nə-fə-'kā-shən\ *n* **1** : the act of
magnifying **2** : the amount by which an optical lens or
instrument magnifies
mag·nif·i·cent \mag-'ni-fə-sənt\ *adj* **1** : characterized
by grandeur or beauty : SPLENDID **2** : EXALTED, NOBLE
syn imposing, stately, grand, majestic — **mag·nif-
i·cence** \-səns\ *n* — **mag·nif·i·cent·ly** *adv*
mag·nif·i·co \mag-'ni-fi-ˌkō\ *n, pl* **-coes** *or* **-cos 1** : a nobleman of Venice **2** : a person of high position
mag·ni·fy \'mag-nə-ˌfī\ *vb* **-fied; -fy·ing 1** : EXTOL,
LAUD; *also* : to cause to be held in greater esteem **2**
: INTENSIFY; *also* : to enlarge in fact or in appearance ⟨a microscope *magnifies* an object⟩
— **mag·ni·fi·er** \'mag-nə-ˌfī-ər\ *n*
mag·nil·o·quent \mag-'ni-lə-kwənt\ *adj* : characterized
by an exalted and often bombastic style or manner
— **mag·nil·o·quence** \-kwəns\ *n*
mag·ni·tude \'mag-nə-ˌtüd, -ˌtyüd\ *n* **1** : greatness of
size or extent **2** : SIZE **3** : QUANTITY **4** : a number representing the brightness of a celestial body
mag·no·lia \mag-'nōl-yə\ *n* : any of a genus of usu.
spring-flowering shrubs and trees with large often fragrant flowers
mag·num opus \'mag-nəm-'ō-pəs\ *n* [L] : the greatest
achievement of an artist or writer
mag·pie \'mag-ˌpī\ *n* : any of various long-tailed often
black-and-white birds related to the jays
Mag·yar \'mag-ˌyär, 'mäg-; 'mä-ˌjär\ *n* : a member of
the dominant people of Hungary — **Magyar** *adj*
ma·ha·ra·ja *or* **ma·ha·ra·jah** \ˌmä-hə-'rä-jə\ *n* : a Hindu prince ranking above a raja
ma·ha·ra·ni *or* **ma·ha·ra·nee** \-'rä-nē\ *n* **1** : the wife of
a maharaja **2** : a Hindu princess ranking above a rani
ma·ha·ri·shi \ˌmä-hə-'rē-shē\ *n* : a Hindu teacher of
mystical knowledge
ma·hat·ma \mə-'hät-mə, -'hat-\ *n* [Skt *mahātman*, fr.
mahātman great-souled, fr. *mahat* great + *ātman*
soul] : a person revered for high-mindedness, wisdom, and selflessness
Ma·hi·can \mə-'hē-kən\ *n, pl* **Mahican** *or* **Mahicans**
: a member of an American Indian people of the upper Hudson River valley
ma·hog·a·ny \mə-'hä-gə-nē\ *n, pl* **-nies** : the reddish
wood of any of various chiefly tropical trees that is

used in furniture; *also* : a tree yielding this wood
ma·hout \mə-'haût\ *n* [Hindi *mahāut*] : a keeper and
driver of an elephant
maid \'mād\ *n* **1** : an unmarried girl or young woman
2 : MAIDSERVANT
¹maid·en \'mād-ᵊn\ *n* : MAID 1 — **maid·en·ly** *adj*
²maiden *adj* **1** : UNMARRIED; *also* : VIRGIN **2** : of, relating to, or befitting a maiden **3** : FIRST ⟨~ voyage⟩
maid·en·hair fern \-ˌhar-\ *n* : any of a genus of ferns
with delicate feathery fronds
maid·en·head \'mād-ᵊn-ˌhed\ *n* **1** : VIRGINITY **2** : HY-
MEN
maid·en·hood \-ˌhùd\ *n* : the condition or time of being
a maiden
maid–in–waiting *n, pl* **maids–in–waiting** : a young
woman appointed to attend a queen or princess
maid of honor : a bride's principal unmarried wedding
attendant
maid·ser·vant \'mād-ˌsər-vənt\ *n* : a girl or woman
who is a servant
¹mail \'māl\ *n* [ME *male* bag, fr. OF] **1** : something sent
or carried in the postal system **2** : a nation's postal
system — often used in pl.
²mail *vb* : to send by mail
³mail *n* [ME *maille*, fr. MF, fr. L *macula* spot, mesh]
: armor made of metal links or plates

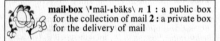

mail·box \'māl-ˌbäks\ *n* **1** : a public box
for the collection of mail **2** : a private box
for the delivery of mail

mail·man \-ˌman\ *n* : a man who delivers mail
maim \'mām\ *vb* : to mutilate, disfigure, or wound seriously : CRIPPLE
¹main \'mān\ *n* **1** : FORCE ⟨with might and ~⟩ **2** : MAIN-
LAND; *also* : HIGH SEA **3** : the chief part **4** : a principal
pipe, duct, or circuit of a utility system
²main *adj* **1** : CHIEF, PRINCIPAL **2** : fully exerted ⟨~
force⟩ **3** : expressing the chief predication in a complex sentence ⟨the ~ clause⟩ — **main·ly** *adv*
main·frame \'mān-ˌfrām\ *n* : a large fast computer
main·land \-ˌland, -lənd\ *n* : a continuous body of land
constituting the chief part of a country or continent
main·line \-ˌlīn\ *vb, slang* : to inject a narcotic drug
into a vein
main line *n* : a principal highway or railroad line
main·mast \'mān-ˌmast, -məst\ *n* : the principal mast
on a sailing ship
main·sail \-ˌsāl, -səl\ *n* : the largest sail on the mainmast
main·spring \-ˌspriŋ\ *n* **1** : the chief spring in a mechanism (as of a watch) **2** : the chief motive, agent, or
cause
main·stay \-ˌstā\ *n* **1** : a stay running from the head of
the mainmast to the foot of the foremast **2** : a chief
support
main·stream \-ˌstrēm\ *n* : a prevailing current or direction of activity or influence — **mainstream** *adj*
main·tain \mān-'tān\ *vb* [ME *mainteinen*, fr. OF

maintenir, fr. ML *manutenēre,* fr. L *manu tenēre* to hold in the hand] **1 :** to keep in an existing state (as of repair) **2 :** to sustain against opposition or danger **3 :** to continue in : CARRY ON **4 :** to provide for : SUPPORT **5 :** ASSERT — **main·tain·abil·i·ty** \-ˌtā-nə-ˈbi-lə-tē\ *n* — **main·tain·able** \-ˈtā-nə-bəl\ *adj* — **main·te·nance** \ˈmānt-ᵊn-əns\ *n*

main·top \ˈmān-ˌtäp\ *n* **:** a platform at the head of the mainmast of a square-rigged ship

mai·son·ette \ˌmāz-ᵊn-ˈet\ *n* **1 :** a small house **2 :** an apartment often on two floors

maître d' *or* **maî·tre d'** \ˌmā-trə-ˈdē, ˌme-\ *n, pl* **maître d's** *or* **maitre d's** \-ˈdēz\ **:** MAÎTRE D'HÔTEL

maî·tre d'hô·tel \ˌmā-trə-dō-ˈtel, ˌme-\ *n, pl* **maîtres d'hôtel** *same*\ [F, lit., master of house] **1 :** MAJORDOMO **2 :** HEADWAITER

maize \ˈmāz\ *n* **:** INDIAN CORN

Maj *abbr* major

maj·es·ty \ˈma-jə-stē\ *n, pl* **-ties 1 :** sovereign power, authority, or dignity; *also* **:** the person of a sovereign — used as a title **2 :** GRANDEUR, SPLENDOR — **ma·jes·tic** \mə-ˈjes-tik\ *adj* — **ma·jes·ti·cal·ly** \-ti-k(ə-)lē\ *adv*

Maj Gen *abbr* Major General

ma·jol·i·ca \mə-ˈjä-li-kə\ *also* **ma·iol·i·ca** \-ˈyä-\ *n* **:** any of several faiences; *esp* **:** an Italian tin-glazed pottery

¹**ma·jor** \ˈmā-jər\ *adj* **1 :** greater in number, extent, or importance ⟨a ~ poet⟩ **2 :** notable or conspicuous in effect or scope ⟨a ~ improvement⟩ **3 :** SERIOUS ⟨a ~ illness⟩ **4 :** having half steps between the 3d and 4th and the 7th and 8th degrees ⟨~ scale⟩; *also* **:** based on a major scale ⟨~ key⟩ ⟨~ chord⟩

²**major** *n* **1 :** a commissioned officer (as in the army) ranking next below a lieutenant colonel **2 :** an academic subject chosen as a field of specialization; *also* **:** a student specializing in such a field

³**major** *vb* **:** to pursue an academic major

ma·jor·do·mo \ˌmā-jər-ˈdō-mō\ *n, pl* **-mos** [Sp *mayordomo* or obs. It *maiordomo,* fr. ML *major domus,* lit., chief of the house] **1 :** a head steward **2 :** BUTLER

ma·jor·ette \ˌmā-jə-ˈret\ *n* **:** DRUM MAJORETTE

major general *n* **:** a commissioned officer (as in the army) ranking next below a lieutenant general

ma·jor·i·ty \mə-ˈjòr-ə-tē\ *n, pl* **-ties 1 :** the age at which full civil rights are accorded; *also* **:** the status of one who has attained this age **2 :** a number greater than half of a total; *also* **:** the excess of this greater number over the remainder **3 :** the rank of a major

ma·jus·cule \ˈma-jəs-ˌkyül, mə-ˈjəs-\ *n* **:** a large letter (as a capital)

¹**make** \ˈmāk\ *vb* **made** \ˈmād\; **mak·ing 1 :** to cause to exist, occur, or appear; *also* **:** DESTINE ⟨was made to be an actor⟩ **2 :** FASHION ⟨~ a dress⟩; *also* **:** COMPOSE **3 :** to formulate in the mind ⟨~ plans⟩ **4 :** CONSTITUTE ⟨house *made* of stone⟩ **5 :** to compute to be **6 :** to set in order : PREPARE ⟨~ a bed⟩ **7 :** to cause to be or become; *also* **:** APPOINT **8 :** ENACT; *also* **:** EXECUTE ⟨~ a will⟩ **9 :** CONCLUDE (didn't know what to ~ of it) **10 :** CARRY OUT, PERFORM ⟨~ a gesture⟩ **11 :** COMPEL **12 :** to assure the success of ⟨will ~ us or break us⟩ **13 :** to amount to in significance ⟨~s no difference⟩ **14 :** to be capable of developing or being fashioned into **15 :** REACH, ATTAIN; *also* **:** GAIN **16 :** to start out : GO **17 :** to have weight or effect (courtesy ~s for safer driving) **syn** form, shape, fabricate, manufacture — **mak·er** *n* — **make believe :** PRETEND — **make do :** to manage with the means at hand — **make fun of :** RIDICULE, MOCK — **make good 1 :** INDEMNIFY ⟨*make good* the loss⟩; *also* **:** to carry out successfully ⟨*make good* his promise⟩ **2 :** SUCCEED — **make way 1 :** to give room for passing, entering, or occupying **2 :** to make progress

²**make** *n* **1 :** the manner or style of construction; *also* **:** BRAND **3 2 :** MAKEUP **3 :** the action of manufacturing — **on the make :** in search of wealth, social status, or sexual adventure

¹**make–be·lieve** \ˈmāk-bə-ˌlēv\ *n* **:** a pretending to believe : PRETENSE

²**make–believe** *adj* **:** IMAGINED, PRETENDED

make–do \-ˌdü\ *adj* **:** MAKESHIFT

make out *vb* **1 :** to draw up in writing ⟨*make out* a list⟩ **2 :** to find or grasp the meaning of ⟨can you *make* that *out*⟩ **3 :** to represent as being **4 :** to pretend to be true **5 :** DISCERN ⟨*make out* a ship in the fog⟩ **6 :** GET ALONG, FARE ⟨*make out* well in life⟩ **7 :** to engage in amorous kissing and caressing

make over *vb* **:** REMAKE, REMODEL — **make·over** \ˈmā-ˌkō-vər\ *n*

make·shift \ˈmāk-ˌshift\ *n* **:** a temporary expedient — **makeshift** *adj*

make·up \ˈmā-ˌkəp\ *n* **1 :** the way in which something is put together; *also* **:** physical, mental, and moral constitution **2 :** cosmetics esp. for the face; *also* **:** materials (as wigs and cosmetics) used in making up

make up *vb* **1 :** FORM, COMPOSE **2 :** to compensate for a deficiency **3 :** SETTLE ⟨*made up* my mind⟩ **4 :** INVENT, IMPROVISE **5 :** to become reconciled **6 :** to put on makeup (as for a play)

make–work \ˈmāk-ˌwərk\ *n* **:** BUSYWORK

mak·ings \ˈmā-kiŋz\ *n pl* **:** the material from which something is made

makuta *pl of* LIKUTA

Mal *abbr* Malachi

Mal·a·chi \ˈma-lə-ˌkī\ *n* — see BIBLE table

Mal·a·chi·as \ˌma-lə-ˈkī-əs\ *n* **:** MALACHI

mal·a·chite \ˈma-lə-ˌkīt\ *n* **:** a mineral that is a green carbonate of copper used for making ornamental objects

mal·adapt·ed \ˌma-lə-ˈdap-təd\ *adj* **:** poorly suited to a particular use, purpose, or situation

mal·ad·just·ed \ˌma-lə-ˈjəs-təd\ *adj* **:** poorly or inadequately adjusted (as to one's environment) — **mal·ad·just·ment** \-ˈjəst-mənt\ *n*

mal·adroit \ˌma-lə-ˈdròit\ *adj* **:** not adroit : INEPT

mal·a·dy \ˈma-lə-dē\ *n, pl* **-dies :** a disease or disorder of body or mind

mal·aise \mə-ˈlāz, ma-\ *n* [F] **:** a hazy feeling of not being well

mal·a·mute \ˈma-lə-ˌmyüt\ *n* **:** a dog often used to draw sleds esp. in northern No. America

mal·a·prop·ism \ˈma-lə-ˌprä-ˌpi-zəm\ *n* **:** a usu. humorous misuse of a word

mal·ap·ro·pos \ˌma-ˌla-prə-ˈpō, ma-ˈla-prə-ˌpō\ *adv* **:** in an inappropriate or inopportune way — **malapropos** *adj*

ma·lar·ia \mə-ˈler-ē-ə\ *n* [It, fr. *mala aria* bad air] **:** a disease marked by recurring chills and fever and caused by a protozoan parasite of the blood that is transmitted by anopheles mosquitoes — **ma·lar·i·al** \-əl\ *adj*

mal·ar·key \mə-ˈlär-kē\ *n* **:** insincere or foolish talk

mal·a·thi·on \ˌma-lə-ˈthī-ən, -ˌän\ *n* **:** an insecticide with a relatively low toxicity for mammals

Ma·la·wi·an \mə-ˈlä-wē-ən\ *n* **:** a native or inhabitant of Malawi — **Malawian** *adj*

Ma·lay \mə-ˈlā, ˈmā-ˌlā\ *n* **1 :** a member of a people of the Malay Peninsula and Archipelago **2 :** the language of the Malays — **Malay** *adj* — **Ma·lay·an** \mə-ˈlā-ən, ˈmā-ˌlā-\ *n or adj*

Ma·lay·sian \mə-ˈlā-zhən, -shən\ *n* **:** a native or inhabitant of Malaysia — **Malaysian** *adj*

mal·con·tent \ˌmal-kən-ˈtent\ *adj* **:** marked by a dissatisfaction with the existing state of affairs : DISCONTENTED — **malcontent** *n*

mal de mer \ˌmal-də-ˈmer\ *n* [F] **:** SEASICKNESS

¹**male** \ˈmāl\ *adj* **1 :** of, relating to, or being the sex that produces germ cells which fertilize the eggs of a female; *also* **:** STAMINATE **2 :** MASCULINE — **male·ness** *n*

²**male** *n* **:** a male individual

male·dic·tion \ˌma-lə-ˈdik-shən\ *n* **:** CURSE, EXECRATION

male·fac·tor \'ma-lə-ˌfak-tər\ *n* : EVILDOER; *esp* : one who commits an offense against the law — **mal·e·fac·tion** \ˌma-lə-'fak-shən\ *n*

ma·lef·ic \mə-'le-fik\ *adj* **1** : BALEFUL **2** : MALICIOUS

ma·lef·i·cent \-fə-sənt\ *adj* : working or productive of harm or evil

ma·lev·o·lent \mə-'le-və-lənt\ *adj* : having, showing, or arising from ill will, spite, or hatred **syn** malignant, malign, malicious, spiteful — **ma·lev·o·lence** \-ləns\ *n*

mal·fea·sance \mal-'fēz-ᵊns\ *n* : wrongful conduct esp. by a public official

mal·for·ma·tion \ˌmal-fòr-'mā-shən\ *n* : irregular or faulty formation or structure; *also* : an instance of this — **mal·formed** \mal-'fòrmd\ *adj*

mal·func·tion \mal-'fəŋk-shən\ *vb* : to fail to operate normally — **malfunction** *n*

Ma·li·an \'mä-lē-ən\ *n* : a native or inhabitant of Mali — **Malian** *adj*

mal·ice \'ma-ləs\ *n* : desire to cause injury or distress to another — **ma·li·cious** \mə-'li-shəs\ *adj* — **ma·li·cious·ly** *adv*

¹ma·lign \mə-'līn\ *adj* **1** : evil in nature, influence, or effect; *also* : MALIGNANT **2** **2** : moved by ill will

²malign *vb* : to speak evil of : DEFAME

ma·lig·nant \mə-'lig-nənt\ *adj* **1** : INJURIOUS, MALIGN **2** : tending to produce death or deterioration ⟨a ∼ tumor⟩ — **ma·lig·nan·cy** \-nən-sē\ *n* — **ma·lig·nant·ly** *adv* — **ma·lig·ni·ty** \-nə-tē\ *n*

ma·lin·ger \mə-'liŋ-gər\ *vb* [F *malingre* sickly] : to pretend illness so as to avoid duty — **ma·lin·ger·er** *n*

mal·i·son \'ma-lə-sən, -zən\ *n* : CURSE

mall \'mòl, 'mal\ *n* **1** : a shaded walk : PROMENADE **2** : an urban shopping area featuring a variety of shops surrounding a concourse **3** : a usu. large enclosed suburban shopping area containing various shops

mal·lard \'ma-lərd\ *n*, *pl* **mallard** *or* **mallards** : a common wild duck that is the source of domestic ducks

mallard

mal·lea·ble \'ma-lē-ə-bəl\ *adj* **1** : capable of being extended or shaped by beating with a hammer or by the pressure of rollers **2** : ADAPTABLE, PLIABLE **syn** plastic, pliant, ductile, supple — **mal·le·a·bil·i·ty** \ˌma-lē-ə-'bi-lə-tē\ *n*

mal·let \'ma-lət\ *n* **1** : a tool with a large head for driving another tool or for striking a surface without mar-

ring it **2** : a long-handled hammerlike implement for striking a ball (as in croquet)

mal·le·us \'ma-lē-əs\ *n*, *pl* **mal·lei** \-lē-ˌī, -lē-ˌē\ [NL, fr. L, hammer] : the outermost of the three small bones of the mammalian middle ear

mal·low \'ma-lō\ *n* : any of a genus of herbs with lobed leaves, usu. showy flowers, and a disk-shaped fruit

malm·sey \'mälm-zē\ *n*, *often cap* : the sweetest variety of Madeira

mal·nour·ished \mal-'nər-isht\ *adj* : UNDERNOURISHED

mal·nu·tri·tion \ˌmal-nü-'tri-shən, -nyü-\ *n* : faulty and esp. inadequate nutrition

mal·oc·clu·sion \ˌma-lə-'klü-zhən\ *n* : faulty coming together of teeth in biting

mal·odor·ous \ma-'lō-də-rəs\ *adj* : ill-smelling — **mal·odor·ous·ly** *adv* — **mal·odor·ous·ness** *n*

ma·lo·ti \mə-'lō-tē\ *pl of* LOTI

mal·prac·tice \mal-'prak-təs\ *n* : a dereliction of professional duty or a failure of professional skill that results in injury, loss, or damage

malt \'mòlt\ *n* **1** : grain and esp. barley steeped in water until it has sprouted and used in brewing and distilling **2** : liquor made with malt — **malty** *adj*

malted milk \'mòl-təd-\ *n* : a powder prepared from dried milk and an extract from malt; *also* : a beverage of this powder in milk or other liquid

Mal·thu·sian \mal-'thü-zhən, -'thyü-\ *adj* : of or relating to a theory that population unless checked (as by war) tends to increase faster than its means of subsistence — **Malthusian** *n* — **Mal·thu·sian·ism** \-zhə-ˌni-zəm\ *n*

malt·ose \'mòl-ˌtōs\ *n* : a sugar formed esp. from starch by the action of enzymes

mal·treat \mal-'trēt\ *vb* : to treat cruelly or roughly : ABUSE — **mal·treat·ment** *n*

ma·ma *or* **mam·ma** \'mä-mə\ *n* : MOTHER

mam·bo \'mäm-bō\ *n*, *pl* **mambos** : a dance of Cuban origin related to the rumba — **mambo** *vb*

mam·mal \'ma-məl\ *n* : any of a class of warm-blooded vertebrates that includes humans and all other animals which nourish their young with milk and have the skin more or less covered with hair — **mam·ma·li·an** \mə-'mā-lē-ən, ma-\ *adj or n*

mam·ma·ry \'ma-mə-rē\ *adj* : of, relating to, or being the glands (**mammary glands**) that in female mammals secrete milk

mam·mo·gram \'ma-mə-ˌgram\ *n* : an X-ray photograph of the breasts

mam·mog·ra·phy \ma-'mä-grə-fē\ *n* : X-ray examination of the breasts (as for early detection of cancer)

mam·mon \'ma-mən\ *n*, *often cap* : material wealth having a debasing influence

¹mam·moth \'ma-məth\ *n* : any of a genus of large hairy extinct elephants

²mammoth *adj* : of very great size : GIGANTIC **syn** colossal, enormous, immense, vast, elephantine

¹man \'man\ *n*, *pl* **men** \'men\ **1** : a human being; *esp* : an adult male **2** : the human race : MANKIND **3** : one possessing in high degree the qualities considered distinctive of manhood **4** : an adult male servant or employee **5** : the individual who can fulfill one's requirements ⟨he's your ∼⟩ **6** : one of the pieces with which various games (as chess) are played; *also* : one of the players on a team **7** *often cap* : white society or people

²**man** *vb* **manned; man·ning 1** : to supply with men ⟨∼ a fleet⟩ **2** : FORTIFY, BRACE

³**man** *abbr* manual

Man *abbr* Manitoba

man–about–town *n, pl* **men–about–town** : a worldly and socially active man

man·a·cle \'ma-ni-kəl\ *n* **1** : a shackle for the hand or wrist **2** : something used as a restraint

man·age \'ma-nij\ *vb* **man·aged; man·ag·ing 1** : HANDLE, CONTROL; *also* : to direct or carry on business or affairs **2** : to make and keep compliant **3** : to treat with care : HUSBAND **4** : to achieve one's purpose : CONTRIVE — **man·age·abil·i·ty** \ıma-ni-jə-'bi-lə-tē\ *n* — **man·age·able** \'ma-ni-jə-bəl\ *adj* — **man·age·able·ness** *n* — **man·age·ably** \-blē\ *adv*

man·age·ment \'ma-nij-mənt\ *n* **1** : the act or art of managing : CONTROL **2** : judicious use of means to accomplish an end **3** : the group of those who manage or direct an enterprise

man·ag·er \'ma-ni-jər\ *n* : one that manages — **man·a·ge·ri·al** \ıma-nə-'jir-ē-əl\ *adj*

ma·ña·na \mən-'yä-nə\ [Sp, lit., tomorrow] *n* : an indefinite time in the future

man–at–arms *n, pl* **men–at–arms** : SOLDIER; *esp* : one who is heavily armed and mounted

man·a·tee \'ma-nə-ıtē\ *n* : any of a genus of chiefly tropical plant-eating aquatic mammals having a broad rounded tail

Man·chu·ri·an \man-'chu̇r-ē-ən\ *n* : a native or inhabitant of Manchuria, China — **Manchurian** *adj*

man·ci·ple \'man-sə-pəl\ *n* : a steward or purveyor esp. for a college or monastery

man·da·mus \man-'dā-məs\ *n* [L, we enjoin] : a writ issued by a superior court commanding that an official act or duty be performed

man·da·rin \'man-də-rən\ *n* **1** : a public official of high rank under the Chinese Empire **2** *cap* : the chief dialect group of China **3** : a yellow to reddish orange loose-skinned citrus fruit; *also* : a tree that bears mandarins

man·date \'man-ıdāt\ *n* **1** : an authoritative command **2** : an authorization to act given to a representative **3** : a commission granted by the League of Nations to a member nation for governing conquered territory; *also* : a territory so governed

man·da·to·ry \'man-də-ıtōr-ē\ *adj* **1** : containing or constituting a command : OBLIGATORY **2** : of or relating to a League of Nations mandate

man·di·ble \'man-də-bəl\ *n* **1** : JAW; *esp* : a lower jaw **2** : either segment of a bird's bill — **man·dib·u·lar** \man-'di-byə-lər\ *adj*

man·do·lin \ıman-də-'lin, 'mand-ə̇l-ən\ *n* : a stringed musical instrument with a pear-shaped body and a fretted neck

man·drake \'man-ıdrāk\ *n* **1** : an Old World herb of the nightshade family or its large forked root superstitiously credited with human and medicinal attributes **2** : MAYAPPLE

man·drel *also* **man·dril** \'man-drəl\ *n* **1** : an axle or spindle inserted into a hole in a piece of work to support it during machining **2** : a metal bar used as a core around which material may be cast, shaped, or molded

man·drill \'man-drəl\ *n* : a large baboon of western central Africa

mane \'mān\ *n* : long heavy hair growing about the neck of some mammals (as a horse) — **maned** \'mānd\ *adj*

man–eat·er \'man-ıē-tər\ *n* : one (as a shark or cannibal) that has or is thought to have an appetite for human flesh — **man–eat·ing** *adj*

ma·nège \ma-'nezh, mə-\ *n* : the art of horsemanship or of training horses

ma·nes \'mä-ınäs, 'mā-ınēz\ *n pl, often cap* : the spirits of the dead and gods of the lower world in ancient Roman belief

ma·neu·ver \mə-'nü-vər, -'nyü-\ *n* [F *manœuvre*, fr. OF *maneuvre* work done by hand, fr. ML *manuopera*, fr. L *manu operare* to work by hand] **1** : a military or naval movement; *also* : an armed forces' training exercise — often used in pl. **2** : a procedure involving expert physical movement **3** : an evasive' movement or shift of tactics; *also* : an action taken to gain a tactical end — **maneuver** *vb* — **ma·neu·ver·abil·i·ty** \-ınü-və-rə-'bi-lə-tē, -ınyü-\ *n* — **ma·neu·ver·able** \-'nü-və-rə-bəl, -'nyü-\ *adj*

man Friday *n* : an efficient and devoted aide or employee

man·ful \'man-fəl\ *adj* : having or showing courage and resolution — **man·ful·ly** *adv*

man·ga·nese \'maŋ-gə-ınēz, -ınēs\ *n* : a metallic chemical element resembling iron but not magnetic — see ELEMENT table

mange \'mānj\ *n* : any of several contagious itchy skin diseases esp. of domestic animals — **mangy** \'mān-jē\ *adj*

man·ger \'mān-jər\ *n* : a trough or open box for livestock feed or fodder

¹**man·gle** \'maŋ-gəl\ *vb* **man·gled; man·gling 1** : to cut, bruise, or hack with repeated blows **2** : to spoil or injure esp. through ineptitude — **man·gler** *n*

²**mangle** *n* : a machine with heated rollers for ironing laundry

man·go \'maŋ-gō\ *n, pl* **mangoes** *also* **mangos** [Pg *manga*] : a usu. yellowish red slightly acid juicy tropical fruit borne by an evergreen tree related to the sumacs; *also* : this tree

man·grove \'man-ıgrōv\ *n* : any of a genus of tropical maritime trees that send out many prop roots and form dense thickets important in coastal land building

man·han·dle \'man-ıhand-ə̇l\ *vb* : to handle roughly

man·hat·tan \man-'hat-ə̇n\ *n, often cap* : a cocktail made of whiskey and vermouth

man·hole \'man-ıhōl\ *n* : a hole through which a person may go esp. to gain access to an underground or enclosed structure

man·hood \-ıhu̇d\ *n* **1** : the condition of being an adult male **2** : manly qualities : COURAGE **3** : MEN ⟨the nation's ∼⟩

man–hour \-'au̇r\ *n* : a unit of one hour's work by one person

man·hunt \-ıhənt\ *n* : an organized hunt for a person esp. for one charged with a crime

ma·nia \'mā-nē-ə, -nyə\ *n* **1** : excitement of psychotic proportions accompanied by disorganized behavior and elevated mood **2** : excessive enthusiasm

ma·ni·ac \'mā-nē-ıak\ *n* : LUNATIC, MADMAN

ma·ni·a·cal \mə-'nī-ə-kəl\ *also* **ma·ni·ac** \'mā-nē-ak\ *adj* **1** : affected with or suggestive of madness **2** : FRANTIC

man·ic \'ma-nik\ *adj* : affected with, relating to, or resembling mania — **manic** *n* — **man·i·cal·ly** \-ni-k(ə-)lē\ *adv*

man·ic–de·pres·sive \ıma-nik-di-'pre-siv\ *adj* : characterized by mania or by psychotic depression or by alternating mania and depression — **manic–depressive** *n*

¹**man·i·cure** \'ma-nə-ıkyu̇r\ *n* **1** : MANICURIST **2** : a treatment for the care of the hands and nails

²**manicure** *vb* **-cured; -cur·ing 1** : to do manicure work on **2** : to trim closely and evenly

man·i·cur·ist \-ıkyu̇r-ist\ *n* : a person who gives manicure treatments

¹**man·i·fest** \'ma-nə-ıfest\ *adj* [ME, fr. MF or L; MF *manifeste*, fr. L *manifestus*, caught in the act, flagrant, perh. fr. *manus* hand + *-festus* (akin to L *infestus* hostile)] **1** : readily perceived by the senses

and esp. by the sight **2** : easily understood : OBVIOUS — **man·i·fest·ly** adv

²manifest vb : to make evident or certain by showing or displaying syn evince, demonstrate, exhibit

³manifest n : a list of passengers or an invoice of cargo for a ship or plane

man·i·fes·ta·tion \ˌma-nə-fə-'stā-shən\ n : DISPLAY, DEMONSTRATION

man·i·fes·to \ˌma-nə-'fes-tō\ n, pl **-tos** or **-toes** : a public declaration of intentions, motives, or views

¹man·i·fold \'ma-nə-ˌfōld\ adj **1** : marked by diversity or variety **2** : consisting of or operating many of one kind combined

²manifold n : a pipe fitting with several lateral outlets for connecting it with other pipes

³manifold vb **1** : MULTIPLY **2** : to make a number of copies of (as a letter)

man·i·kin or **man·ni·kin** \'ma-ni-kən\ n **1** : MANNEQUIN **2** : a little man : DWARF

Ma·nila hemp \mə-'ni-lə-\ n : a tough fiber from a Philippine plant related to the banana that is used for cordage

manila paper n, often cap M : a tough brownish paper made orig. from Manila hemp

man·i·oc \'ma-nē-ˌäk\ n : CASSAVA

ma·nip·u·late \mə-'ni-pyə-ˌlāt\ vb **-lat·ed; -lat·ing 1** : to treat or operate manually or mechanically esp. with skill **2** : to manage or use skillfully **3** : to influence esp. with intent to deceive — **ma·nip·u·la·tion** \mə-ˌni-pyə-'lā-shən\ n — **ma·nip·u·la·tive** \-'ni-pyə-ˌlā-tiv\ adj — **ma·nip·u·la·tor** \-ˌlā-tər\ n

man·kind n **1** \'man-'kīnd\ : the human race **2** \-ˌkīnd\ : men as distinguished from women

¹man·ly \'man-lē\ adj **man·li·er; -est** : having qualities appropriate to or generally associated with a man : BOLD, RESOLUTE — **man·li·ness** n

²manly adv : in a manly manner

man–made \'man-'mād\ adj : made by humans rather than nature ⟨∼ systems⟩; esp : SYNTHETIC ⟨∼ fibers⟩

man·na \'ma-nə\ n **1** : food miraculously supplied to the Israelites in the wilderness **2** : something of value that comes unexpectedly : WINDFALL

manned \'mand\ adj : carrying or performed by a person ⟨∼ spaceflight⟩

man·ne·quin \'ma-ni-kən\ n **1** : a form representing the human figure used esp. for displaying clothes **2** : a person employed to model clothing

man·ner \'ma-nər\ n **1** : KIND, SORT **2** : a way of acting or proceeding ⟨worked in a brisk ∼⟩; also : normal behavior ⟨spoke bluntly as was his ∼⟩ **3** : a method of artistic execution **4** pl : social conduct; also : BEARING **5** pl : BEHAVIOR ⟨taught the child good ∼s⟩

man·nered \'ma-nərd\ adj **1** : having manners of a specified kind ⟨well-*mannered*⟩ **2** : having an artificial character ⟨a highly ∼ style⟩

man·ner·ism \'ma-nə-ˌri-zəm\ n **1** : ARTIFICIALITY, PRECIOSITY **2** : a peculiarity of action, bearing, or treatment syn pose, air, affectation

man·ner·ly \'ma-nər-lē\ adj : showing good manners : POLITE — **man·ner·li·ness** n — **mannerly** adv

man·nish \'ma-nish\ adj **1** : resembling or suggesting a man rather than a woman **2** : generally associated with or characteristic of a man — **man·nish·ly** adv — **man·nish·ness** n

ma·noeu·vre \mə-'nü-vər, -'nyü-\ chiefly Brit var of MANEUVER

man–of–war \ˌman-əv-'wòr\ n, pl **men–of–war** \ˌmen-\ : WARSHIP

ma·nom·e·ter \mə-'nä-mə-tər\ n : an instrument for measuring the pressure of gases and vapors — **mano·met·ric** \ˌma-nə-'me-trik\ adj

man·or \'ma-nər\ n **1** : the house or hall of an estate; also : a landed estate **2** : an English estate of a feudal lord — **ma·no·ri·al** \mə-'nòr-ē-əl\ adj — **ma·no·ri·al·ism** \-ə-ˌli-zəm\ n

man power n **1** : power available from or supplied by

the physical effort of human beings **2** usu **man·pow·er** : the total supply of persons available and fitted for service

man·qué \mäⁿ-'kā\ adj [F, fr. pp. of *manquer* to lack, fail] : short of or frustrated in the fulfillment of one's aspirations or talents ⟨a poet ∼⟩

man·sard \'man-ˌsärd, -sərd\ n : a roof having two slopes on all sides with the lower slope steeper than the upper one

manse \'mans\ n : the residence esp. of a Presbyterian minister

man·ser·vant \'man-ˌsər-vənt\ n, pl **men·ser·vants** \'men-ˌsər-vənts\ : a male servant

man·sion \'man-chən\ n : a large imposing residence; also : a separate apartment in a large structure

man–size \'man-ˌsīz\ or **man–sized** \-ˌsīzd\ adj : suitable for or requiring a man

man·slaugh·ter \-ˌslò-tər\ n : the unlawful killing of a human being without express or implied malice

man·ta \'man-tə\ n : a square piece of cloth or blanket used in southwestern U.S. and Latin America as a cloak or shawl

man·teau \man-'tō\ n : a loose cloak, coat, or robe

man·tel \'mant-ᵊl\ n : a beam, stone, or arch serving as a lintel to support the masonry above a fireplace; also : a shelf above a fireplace

man·tel·piece \'mant-ᵊl-ˌpēs\ n : the shelf of a mantel

man·til·la \man-'tē-yə, -'ti-lə\ n : a light scarf worn over the head and shoulders esp. by Spanish and Latin-American women

man·tis \'man-təs\ n, pl **man·tis·es** or **man·tes** \-ˌtēz\ [NL, fr. Gk, lit., diviner, prophet] : any of a group of large usu. green insect-eating insects that hold their prey in forelimbs folded as if in prayer

man·tis·sa \man-'ti-sə\ n : the part of a logarithm to the right of the decimal point

¹man·tle \'mant-ᵊl\ n **1** : a loose sleeveless garment worn over other clothes **2** : something that covers, enfolds, or envelopes **3** : a lacy sheath that gives light by incandescence when placed over a flame **4** : the portion of the earth lying between the crust and the core **5** : MANTEL

²mantle vb **man·tled; man·tling 1** : to cover with a mantle **2** : BLUSH

man·tra \'man-trə\ n : a mystical formula of invocation or incantation (as in Hinduism)

¹man·u·al \'man-yə-wəl\ adj **1** : of, relating to, or involving the hands; also : worked by hand ⟨a ∼ pump⟩ **2** : requiring or using physical skill and energy — **man·u·al·ly** adv

²manual n **1** : a small book; esp : HANDBOOK **2** : the prescribed movements in the handling of a military item and esp. a weapon during a drill or ceremony ⟨the ∼ of arms⟩ **3** : a keyboard esp. of an organ

man·u·fac·to·ry \ˌman-yə-'fak-tə-rē\ n : FACTORY

¹man·u·fac·ture \ˌman-yə-'fak-chər\ n [MF, fr. ML *manufactura*, L manu *factus* made by hand] **1** : something made from raw materials **2** : the process of making wares by hand or by machinery; also : a productive industry using machinery

²manufacture vb **-tured; -tur·ing 1** : to make from raw materials by hand or by machinery; also : to engage in manufacture **2** : INVENT, FABRICATE; also : CREATE — **man·u·fac·tur·er** n

man·u·mit \ˌman-yə-'mit\ vb **-mit·ted; -mit·ting** : to free from slavery — **man·u·mis·sion** \-'mi-shən\ n

¹ma·nure \mə-'nùr, -'nyùr\ vb **ma·nured; ma·nur·ing** : to fertilize land with manure

²manure n : FERTILIZER; esp : refuse from stables and barnyards — **ma·nu·ri·al** \-'nùr-ē-əl, -'nyùr-\ adj

man·u·script \'man-yə-ˌskript\ n [L manu *scriptus* written by hand] **1** : a written or typewritten compo-

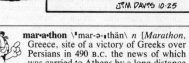

sition or document; *also* : a document submitted for publication **2** : writing as opposed to print

Manx \'maŋks\ *n pl* : the people of the Isle of Man — **Manx** *adj*

¹**many** \'me-nē\ *adj* **more** \'mōr\; **most** \'mōst\ : consisting of or amounting to a large but indefinite number ⟨∼ years ago⟩

²**many** *pron* : a large number ⟨∼ are called⟩

³**many** *n* : a large but indefinite number ⟨a good ∼ of them⟩

many·fold \ˌme-nē-'fōld\ *adv* : by many times

many–sid·ed \-'sī-dəd\ *adj* **1** : having many sides or aspects **2** : VERSATILE

Mao·ism \'mau̇-ˌi-zəm\ *n* : the theory and practice of Communism developed in China chiefly by Mao Tse=tung — **Mao·ist** \'mau̇-ist\ *n or adj*

Mao·ri \'mau̇r-ē\ *n, pl* **Maori** *or* **Maoris** : a member of a Polynesian people native to New Zealand

¹**map** \'map\ *n* [ML *mappa*, fr. L, napkin, towel] **1** : a representation usu. on a flat surface of the whole or part of an area **2** : a representation of the celestial sphere or part of it

²**map** *vb* **mapped; map·ping 1** : to make a map of **2** : to plan in detail ⟨∼ out a program⟩ — **map·pa·ble** \'ma-pə-bəl\ *adj* — **map·per** *n*

MAP *abbr* modified American plan

ma·ple \'mā-pəl\ *n* : any of a genus of trees or shrubs with 2-winged dry fruit and opposite leaves; *also* : the hard light-colored wood of a maple used esp. for floors and furniture

maple sugar *n* : sugar made by boiling maple syrup

maple syrup *n* : syrup made by concentrating the sap of maple trees esp. the sugar maple

mar \'mär\ *vb* **marred; mar·ring** : to detract from the wholeness or perfection of : SPOIL **syn** injure, hurt, harm, damage, impair, blemish

Mar *abbr* March

ma·ra·ca \mə-'rä-kə, -'ra-\ *n* [Pg *maracá*] : a rattle usu. made from a gourd and used as a percussion instrument

mar·a·schi·no cherry \ˌmar-ə-'skē-nō-, -'shē-\ *n, often cap M* : a cherry preserved in a sweet liqueur made from the juice of a bitter wild cherry

mar·a·thon \'mar-ə-ˌthän\ *n* [*Marathon,* Greece, site of a victory of Greeks over Persians in 490 B.C. the news of which was carried to Athens by a long-distance runner] **1** : a long-distance race esp. on foot **2** : an endurance contest

mar·a·thon·er \'mar-ə-ˌthä-nər\ *n* : a person who takes part in a marathon — **mar·a·thon·ing** *n*

ma·raud \mə-'rȯd\ *vb* : to roam about and raid in search of plunder : PILLAGE — **ma·raud·er** *n*

mar·ble \'mär-bəl\ *n* **1** : a limestone that can be polished and used in fine building work **2** : something resembling marble (as in coldness) **3** : a small ball (as of glass) used in various games; *also, pl* : a children's game played with these small balls — **marble** *adj*

mar·bling \-bə-liŋ, -bliŋ\ *n* : an intermixture of fat through the lean of a cut of meat

mar·cel \mär-'sel\ *n* : a deep soft wave made in the hair by the use of a heated curling iron — **marcel** *vb*

¹**march** \'märch\ *n* : a border region : FRONTIER

²**march** *vb* **1** : to move along in or as if in military formation **2** : to walk in a direct purposeful manner; *also* : PROGRESS, ADVANCE **3** : TRAVERSE ⟨∼ed 10 miles⟩ — **march·er** *n*

³**march** *n* **1** : the action of marching; *also* : the distance covered (as by a military unit) in a march **2** : a regular measured stride or rhythmic step used in marching **3** : forward movement **4** : a piece of music with marked rhythm suitable for marching to

March *n* [ME, fr. OF, fr. L *martius,* fr. *martius* of Mars, fr. *Mart-, Mars,* Roman god of war] : the 3d month of the year

mar·chio·ness \'mär-shə-nəs\ *n* **1** : the wife or widow of a marquess **2** : a woman holding the rank of a marquess in her own right

Mar·di Gras \'mär-dē-ˌgrä\ *n* [F, lit., fat Tuesday] : the Tuesday before Ash Wednesday often observed with parades and merrymaking

¹**mare** \'mar\ *n* : an adult female of the horse or a related mammal

²**ma·re** \'mär-(ˌ)ā\ *n, pl* **ma·ria** \'mär-ē-ə\ : any of sev-

eral large dark areas on the surface of the moon or Mars

mar·ga·rine \'mär-jə-rən\ *n* : a food product made usu. from vegetable oils churned with skimmed milk and used as a substitute for butter

mar·gin \'mär-jən\ *n* **1** : the part of a page outside the main body of printed or written matter **2** : EDGE **3** : a spare amount, measure, or degree allowed for use if needed **4** : measure or degree of difference ⟨a one≠ vote ∼⟩

mar·gin·al \-jə-nəl\ *adj* **1** : written or printed in the margin **2** : of, relating to, or situated at a margin or border **3** : close to the lower limit of quality or acceptability **4** : excluded from or existing outside the mainstream of society or a group — **mar·gin·al·ly** *adv*

mar·gi·na·lia \ˌmär-jə-ˈnā-lē-ə\ *n pl* : marginal notes

mar·grave \'mär-ˌgrāv\ *n* : the military governor esp. of a medieval German border province

ma·ri·a·chi \ˌmär-ē-ˈä-chē, ˌmar-\ *n* : a Mexican street band; *also* : a member of or the music of such a band

mari·gold \'mar-ə-ˌgōld, 'mer-\ *n* : any of a genus of tropical American herbs related to the daisies that are grown for their double yellow, orange, or reddish flower heads

mar·i·jua·na *also* **mar·i·hua·na** \ˌmar-ə-ˈwä-nə, -ˈhwä-\ *n* [MexSp *marihuana*] : the dried leaves and flowering tops of the female hemp plant smoked usu. illegally for their intoxicating effect; *also* : HEMP

ma·rim·ba \mə-ˈrim-bə\ *n* : a xylophone of southern Africa and Central America; *also* : a modern version of it

ma·ri·na \mə-ˈrē-nə\ *n* : a dock or basin providing secure moorings for pleasure boats

mar·i·na·ra \ˌmar-ə-ˈnar-ə\ *adj* [It (*alla*) *marinara*, lit., in sailor style] : made with tomatoes, onions, garlic, and spices; *also* : served with marinara sauce

mar·i·nate \'mar-ə-ˌnāt\ *vb* **-nat·ed; -nat·ing** : to steep (as meat or fish) in a brine or pickle

¹ma·rine \mə-ˈrēn\ *adj* **1** : of or relating to the sea or its navigation or commerce **2** : of or relating to marines

²marine *n* **1** : the mercantile and naval shipping of a country **2** : any of a class of soldiers serving on shipboard or with a naval force

mar·i·ner \'mar-ə-nər\ *n* : SAILOR

mar·i·o·nette \ˌmar-ē-ə-ˈnet, ˌmer-\ *n* : a puppet moved by strings or by hand

mar·i·tal \'mar-ət-ᵊl\ *adj* : of or relating to marriage : CONJUGAL **syn** matrimonial, connubial, nuptial

mar·i·time \'mar-ə-ˌtīm\ *adj* **1** : of, relating to, or bordering on the sea **2** : of or relating to navigation or commerce of the sea

mar·jo·ram \'mär-jə-rəm\ *n* : any of various fragrant mints often used in cookery

¹mark \'märk\ *n* **1** : something (as a line or fixed object) designed to record position; *also* : the starting line or position in a track event **2** : TARGET; *also* : GOAL, OBJECT **3** : an object of abuse or ridicule **4** : the question under discussion **5** : NORM (not up to the ∼) **6** : a visible sign : INDICATION; *also* : CHARACTERISTIC **7** : a written or printed symbol **8** : GRADE (a ∼ of B+) **9** : IMPORTANCE, DISTINCTION **10** : a lasting impression ⟨made his ∼ in the world⟩; *also* : a damaging impression left on a surface

²mark *vb* **1** : to set apart by a line or boundary **2** : to designate by a mark or make a mark on **3** : CHARACTERIZE (the vehemence that ∼s his speeches); *also* : SIGNALIZE (this year ∼s our 50th anniversary) **4** : to take notice of : OBSERVE — **mark·er** *n*

³mark *n* — see MONEY table

Mark \'märk\ *n* — see BIBLE table

mark·down \'märk-ˌdaún\ *n* **1** : a lowering of price **2** : the amount by which an original price is reduced

mark down *vb* : to put a lower price on

marked \'märkt\ *adj* : NOTICEABLE — **mark·ed·ly** \'mär-kəd-lē\ *adv*

¹mar·ket \'mär-kət\ *n* **1** : a meeting together of people for trade by purchase and sale; *also* : a public place where such a meeting is held **2** : the rate or price offered for a commodity or security **3** : a geographical area of demand for commodities; *also* : extent of demand **4** : a retail establishment usu. of a specific kind

²market *vb* : to go to a market to buy or sell; *also* : SELL — **mar·ket·able** *adj*

mar·ket·place \'mär-kət-ˌplās\ *n* **1** : an open square in a town where markets are held **2** : the world of trade or economic activity

mark·ka \'mär-ˌkä\ *n, pl* **mark·kaa** \'mär-ˌkä\ *or* **markkas** \-ˌkäz\ — see MONEY table

marks·man \'märks-mən\ *n* : a person skillful at hitting a target — **marks·man·ship** *n*

mark·up \'mär-ˌkəp\ *n* **1** : a raising of price **2** : an amount added to the cost price of an article to determine the selling price

mark up *vb* : to put a higher price on

marl \'märl\ *n* : an earthy deposit rich in lime used esp. as fertilizer — **marly** \'mär-lē\ *adj*

mar·lin \'mär-lən\ *n* : any of several large oceanic sport fishes related to sailfishes

mar·line·spike *also* **mar·lin·spike** \'mär-lən-ˌspīk\ *n* : a pointed iron tool used to separate strands of rope or wire (as in splicing)

mar·ma·lade \'mär-mə-ˌlād\ *n* : a clear jelly holding in suspension pieces of fruit and fruit rind

mar·mo·re·al \ˌmär-ˈmōr-ē-əl\ *adj* : of, relating to, or suggestive of marble

mar·mo·set \'mär-mə-ˌset\ *n* : any of numerous small bushy-tailed tropical American monkeys

mar·mot \'mär-mət\ *n* : any of a genus of stout short≠ legged burrowing No. American rodents

marmot

¹ma·roon \mə-ˈrün\ *vb* **1** : to put ashore (as on a desolate island) and leave to one's fate **2** : to leave in isolation and without hope of escape

²maroon *n* : a dark red color

mar·quee \mär-ˈkē\ *n* [modif. of F *marquise*, lit., marchioness] **1** : a large tent set up (as for an outdoor party) **2** : a usu. metal and glass canopy over an entrance (as of a theater)

mar·quess \'mär-kwəs\ *n* **1** : a nobleman of hereditary rank in Europe and Japan **2** : a member of the British peerage ranking below a duke and above an earl

mar·que·try \'mär-kə-trē\ *n* : inlaid work of wood, shell, or ivory (as on a table or cabinet)

mar·quis \'mär-kwəs, mär-ˈkē\ *n* : MARQUESS

mar·quise \mär-ˈkēz\ *n, pl* **mar·quises** *same or* -ˈkē-zəz\ : MARCHIONESS

mar·riage \'mar-ij\ *n* **1** : the state of being married **2** : a wedding ceremony and attendant festivities **3** : a close union — **mar·riage·able** *adj*

mar·row \'mar-ō\ *n* : a soft vascular tissue that fills the cavities of most bones

mar·row·bone \'mar-ə-ˌbōn, 'mar-ō-\ *n* : a bone (as a shinbone) rich in marrow

mar·ry \'mar-ē\ *vb* **mar·ried; mar·ry·ing 1 :** to join as husband and wife according to law or custom **2 :** to take as husband or wife : WED **3 :** to enter into a close union — **mar·ried** *adj or n*

Mars \'märz\ *n* : the planet 4th from the sun and conspicuous for its red color — see PLANET table

marsh \'märsh\ *n* : a tract of soft wet land — **marshy** *adj*

¹mar·shal \'mär-shəl\ *n* **1 :** a high official in a medieval household; *also* : a person in charge of the ceremonial aspects of a gathering **2 :** a general officer of the highest military rank **3 :** an administrative officer (as of a U.S. judicial district) having duties similar to a sheriff's **4 :** the administrative head of a city police or fire department

²marshal *vb* **mar·shaled** *or* **mar·shalled; mar·shal·ing** *or* **mar·shal·ling 1 :** to arrange in order, rank, or position **2 :** to bring together **3 :** to lead with ceremony : USHER

marsh gas *n* : METHANE

marsh·mal·low \'märsh-ˌmel-ō, -ˌma-\ *n* : a light creamy confection made from corn syrup, sugar, albumen, and gelatin

marsh marigold *n* : a swamp herb related to the buttercups that has bright yellow flowers

mar·su·pi·al \mär-'sü-pē-əl\ *n* : any of an order of primitive mammals (as opossums, kangaroos, or wombats) that bear very immature young which is nourished in a pouch on the abdomen of the female — **marsupial** *adj*

mart \'märt\ *n* : MARKET

mar·ten \'märt-ᵊn\ *n, pl* **marten** *or* **martens** : a slender weasellike mammal with fine gray or brown fur; *also* : this fur

mar·tial \'mär-shəl\ *adj* [L *martialis* of Mars, fr. *Mart-, Mars* Mars, Roman god of war] **1 :** of, relating to, or suited for war or a warrior ⟨~ music⟩ **2 :** of or relating to an army or military life **3 :** WARLIKE

martial law *n* **1 :** the law applied in occupied territory by the occupying military forces **2 :** the established law of a country administered by military forces in an emergency when civilian law enforcement agencies are unable to maintain public order and safety

mar·tian \'mär-shən\ *adj, often cap* : of or relating to the planet Mars or its hypothetical inhabitants — **martian** *n, often cap*

mar·tin \'märt-ᵊn\ *n* : any of several small swallows and flycatchers

mar·ti·net \ˌmärt-ᵊn-'et\ *n* : a strict disciplinarian

mar·tin·gale \'märt-ᵊn-ˌgāl\ *n* : a strap connecting a horse's girth to the bit or reins so as to hold down its head

mar·ti·ni \mär-'tē-nē\ *n* : a cocktail made of gin or vodka and dry vermouth

¹mar·tyr \'mär-tər\ *n* [ME, fr. OE, fr. LL, fr. Gk *martyr-, martys,* lit., witness] **1 :** a person who dies rather than renounce a religion; *also* : a person who makes a great sacrifice for the sake of principle **2 :** a great or constant sufferer

²martyr *vb* **1 :** to put to death for adhering to a belief **2 :** TORTURE

mar·tyr·dom \'mär-tər-dəm\ *n* **1 :** the suffering and death of a martyr **2 :** TORTURE

¹mar·vel \'mär-vəl\ *n* **1 :** something that causes wonder or astonishment **2 :** intense surprise or interest

²marvel *vb* **mar·veled** *or* **mar·velled; mar·vel·ing** *or* **mar·vel·ling** : to feel surprise, wonder, or amazed curiosity

mar·vel·ous *or* **mar·vel·lous** \'mär-və-ləs\ *adj* **1 :** causing wonder **2 :** of the highest kind or quality — **mar·vel·ous·ly** *adv* — **mar·vel·ous·ness** *n*

Marx·ism \'märk-ˌsi-zəm\ *n* : the political, economic, and social principles and policies advocated by Karl Marx — **Marx·ist** \-sist\ *n or adj*

mar·zi·pan \'märt-sə-ˌpän, -ˌpan; 'mär-zə-ˌpan\ *n* [G] : a confection of almond paste, sugar, and egg whites

masc *abbr* masculine

mas·cara \mas-'kar-ə\ *n* : a cosmetic esp. for coloring the eyelashes

mas·car·po·ne \ˌmas-kär-'pō-nā\ *n* : an Italian cream cheese

mas·cot \'mas-ˌkät, -kət\ *n* [F *mascotte,* fr. Provençal *mascoto,* fr. *masco* witch, fr. ML *masca*] : a person, animal, or object believed to bring good luck

¹mas·cu·line \'mas-kyə-lən\ *adj* **1 :** MALE; *also* : MANLY **2 :** of, relating to, or constituting the gender that includes most words or grammatical forms referring to males — **mas·cu·lin·i·ty** \ˌmas-kyə-'li-nə-tē\ *n*

²masculine *n* : a noun, pronoun, adjective, or inflectional form or class of the masculine gender; *also* : the masculine gender

¹mash \'mash\ *n* **1 :** a mixture of ground feeds for livestock **2 :** crushed malt or grain steeped in hot water to make wort **3 :** a soft pulpy mass

²mash *vb* **1 :** to reduce to a soft pulpy state **2 :** CRUSH, SMASH ⟨~ a finger⟩ — **mash·er** *n*

MASH *abbr* mobile army surgical hospital

¹mask \'mask\ *n* **1 :** a cover for the face usu. for disguise or protection **2 :** MASQUE **3 :** a figure of a head worn on the stage in antiquity **4 :** a copy of a face made by means of a mold ⟨death ~⟩ **5 :** something that conceals or disguises **6 :** the face of an animal

²mask *vb* **1 :** to conceal from view : DISGUISE **2 :** to cover for protection

mask·er \'mas-kər\ *n* : a participant in a masquerade

mas·och·ism \'ma-sə-ˌki-zəm, 'ma-zə-\ *n* **1 :** a sexual perversion characterized by pleasure in being subjected to pain or humiliation **2 :** pleasure in being abused or dominated — **mas·och·ist** \-kist\ *n* — **mas·och·is·tic** \ˌma-sə-'kis-tik, ˌma-zə-\ *adj*

ma·son \'mās-ᵊn\ *n* **1 :** a skilled worker who builds with stone, brick, or concrete **2 *cap* :** FREEMASON

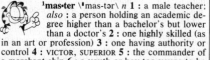

Ma·son·ic \mə-'sä-nik\ adj : of or relating to Freemasons or Freemasonry

ma·son·ry \'mās-ᵊn-rē\ n, pl **-ries** **1** : something constructed of materials used by masons **2** : the art, trade, or work of a mason **3** cap : FREEMASONRY

masque \'mask\ n **1** : MASQUERADE **2** : a short allegorical dramatic performance (as of the 17th century)

¹mas·quer·ade \ˌmas-kə-'rād\ n **1** : a social gathering of persons wearing masks; also : a costume for wear at such a gathering **2** : DISGUISE

²masquerade vb **-ad·ed; -ad·ing** **1** : to disguise oneself : POSE **2** : to take part in a masquerade — **mas·quer·ad·er** n

¹mass \'mas\ n **1** cap : a sequence of prayers and ceremonies forming the eucharistic service of the Roman Catholic Church **2** often cap : a celebration of the Eucharist **3** : a musical setting for parts of the Mass

²mass n **1** : a quantity or aggregate of matter usu. of considerable size **2** : EXPANSE, BULK; also : MASSIVENESS **3** : the principal part **4** : AGGREGATE, WHOLE **5** : the quantity of matter that a body possesses as measured by its inertia **6** : a large quantity, amount, or number **7** : the great body of people — usu. used in pl. — **massy** adj

³mass vb : to form or collect into a mass

Mass abbr Massachusetts

mas·sa·cre \'ma-si-kər\ n **1** : the killing of many persons under cruel or atrocious circumstances **2** : a wholesale slaughter — **massacre** vb

¹mas·sage \mə-'säzh, -'säj\ n : manipulation of tissues (as by rubbing and kneading) esp. for therapeutic purposes

²massage vb **mas·saged; mas·sag·ing** **1** : to subject to massage **2** : to treat flatteringly; also : MANIPULATE, DOCTOR ⟨∼ data⟩

mas·seur \ma-'sər\ n : a man who practices massage

mas·seuse \-'sərz, -'süz\ n : a woman who practices massage

mas·sif \ma-'sēf\ n : a principal mountain mass

mas·sive \'ma-siv\ adj **1** : forming or consisting of a large mass **2** : large in structure, scope, or degree — **mas·sive·ly** adv — **mas·sive·ness** n

mass·less \'mas-ləs\ adj : having no mass ⟨∼ particles⟩

mass medium n, pl **mass media** : a medium of communication (as the newspapers or television) that is designed to reach the mass of the people

mass-pro·duce \ˌmas-prə-'düs, -'dyüs\ vb : to produce in quantity usu. by machinery — **mass production** n

¹mast \'mast\ n **1** : a long pole or spar rising from the keel or deck of a ship and supporting the yards, booms, and rigging **2** : a slender vertical structure — **mast·ed** \'mas-təd\ adj

²mast n : nuts (as acorns) accumulated on the forest floor and often serving as food for animals (as hogs)

mas·tec·to·my \ma-'stek-tə-mē\ n, pl **-mies** : surgical removal of the breast

¹mas·ter \'mas-tər\ n **1** : a male teacher; also : a person holding an academic degree higher than a bachelor's but lower than a doctor's **2** : one highly skilled (as in an art or profession) **3** : one having authority or control **4** : VICTOR, SUPERIOR **5** : the commander of a merchant ship **6** : a youth or boy too young to be called mister — used as a title **7** : an original from which copies are made

²master vb **1** : to become master of : OVERCOME **2** : to become skilled or proficient in **3** : to produce a master recording of (as a musical performance)

master chief petty officer n : a petty officer of the highest rank in the navy

mas·ter·ful \'mas-tər-fəl\ adj **1** : inclined and usu. competent to act as a master **2** : having or reflecting the skill of a master — **mas·ter·ful·ly** adv — **mas·ter·ful·ness** n

master gunnery sergeant n : a noncommissioned officer in the marine corps ranking above a master sergeant

master key n : a key designed to open several different locks

mas·ter·ly \'mas-tər-lē\ adj : indicating thorough knowledge or superior skill ⟨∼ performance⟩ — **mas·ter·ly** adv

mas·ter·mind \-ˌmīnd\ n : a person who provides the directing or creative intelligence for a project — **mastermind** vb

master of ceremonies : a person who acts as host at a formal event or a program of entertainment

mas·ter·piece \'mas-tər-ˌpēs\ n : a work done with extraordinary skill

master plan n : an overall plan

master's \'mas-tərz\ n : a master's degree

master sergeant n **1** : a noncommissioned officer in the army ranking next below a sergeant major **2** : a noncommissioned officer in the air force ranking next below a senior master sergeant **3** : a noncommissioned officer in the marine corps ranking next below a master gunnery sergeant

mas·ter·stroke \'mas-tər-ˌstrōk\ n : a masterly performance or move

mas·ter·work \-ˌwərk\ n : MASTERPIECE

mas·tery \'mas-tə-rē\ n **1** : DOMINION; also : SUPERIORITY **2** : possession or display of great skill or knowledge

mast·head \'mast-ˌhed\ n **1** : the top of a mast **2** : the printed matter in a newspaper or periodical giving the title and details of ownership and rates of subscription or advertising

mas·tic \'mas-tik\ n : a pasty material used as a coating or cement

mas·ti·cate \'mas-tə-ˌkāt\ vb **-cat·ed; -cat·ing** : CHEW — **mas·ti·ca·tion** \ˌmas-tə-'kā-shən\ n

mas·tiff \'mas-təf\ n : any of a breed of large smooth-coated dogs used esp. as guard dogs

mast·odon \'mas-tə-ˌdän\ *n* [NL, fr. Gk *mastos* breast + *odōn, odous* tooth] : any of numerous huge extinct mammals related to the mammoths

mas·toid \'mas-ˌtȯid\ *n* : a bony prominence behind the ear — **mastoid** *adj*

mas·tur·ba·tion \ˌmas-tər-'bā-shən\ *n* : stimulation of the genital organs apart from sexual intercourse, usu. to orgasm, and esp. by use of one's own hand — **mas·tur·bate** \'mas-tər-ˌbāt\ *vb* — **mas·tur·ba·to·ry** \'mas-tər-bə-ˌtȯr-ē\ *adj*

¹**mat** \'mat\ *n* 1 : a piece of coarse woven or plaited fabric 2 : something made up of many intertwined strands 3 : a large thick pad used as a surface for wrestling and gymnastics

²**mat** *vb* **mat·ted; mat·ting** 1 : to provide with a mat 2 : to form into a tangled mass

³**mat** *vb* **mat·ted; mat·ting** 1 : to make (as a color) matte 2 : to provide (a picture) with a mat

⁴**mat** *var of* ²MATTE

⁵**mat** *or* **matt** *or* **matte** *n* : a border going around a picture between picture and frame or serving as the frame

mat·a·dor \'ma-tə-ˌdȯr\ *n* [Sp, fr. *matar* to kill] : a bullfighter whose role is to kill the bull in a bullfight

¹**match** \'mach\ *n* 1 : a person or thing equal or similar to another; *also* : one able to cope with another : RIVAL 2 : a suitable pairing of persons or objects 3 : a contest or game between two or more individuals 4 : a marriage union; *also* : a prospective marriage partner — **match·less** *adj*

²**match** *vb* 1 : to meet as an antagonist; *also* : PIT 2 : to provide with a worthy competitor; *also* : to set in comparison with 3 : MARRY 4 : to combine suitably or congenially; *also* : ADAPT, SUIT 5 : to provide with a counterpart

³**match** *n* : a short slender piece of flammable material (as wood) tipped with a combustible mixture that ignites through friction

match·book \'mach-ˌbu̇k\ *n* : a small folder containing rows of paper matches

match·lock \-ˌläk\ *n* : a musket with a slow-burning cord lowered over a hole in the breech to ignite the charge

match·mak·er \-ˌmā-kər\ *n* : one who arranges a match and esp. a marriage

match·wood \-ˌwu̇d\ *n* : small pieces of wood

¹**mate** \'māt\ *vb* **mat·ed; mat·ing** : CHECKMATE — **mate** *n*

²**mate** *n* 1 : ASSOCIATE, COMPANION; *also* : HELPER 2 : a deck officer on a merchant ship ranking below the captain 3 : one of a pair; *esp* : either member of a married couple or a breeding pair of animals

³**mate** *vb* **mat·ed; mat·ing** 1 : to join or fit together 2 : to come or bring together as mates 3 : COPULATE

¹**ma·te·ri·al** \mə-'tir-ē-əl\ *adj* 1 : PHYSICAL ⟨~ world⟩; *also* : BODILY ⟨~ needs⟩ 2 : of or relating to matter rather than form ⟨~ cause⟩; *also* : EMPIRICAL ⟨~ knowledge⟩ 3 : highly important : SIGNIFICANT 4 : of a physical or worldly nature ⟨~ progress⟩ — **ma·te·ri·al·ly** *adv*

²**material** *n* 1 : the elements or substance of which something is composed or made 2 : apparatus necessary for doing or making something

ma·te·ri·al·ise *Brit var of* MATERIALIZE

ma·te·ri·al·ism \mə-'tir-ē-ə-ˌli-zəm\ *n* 1 : a theory that everything can be explained as being or coming from matter 2 : a preoccupation with material rather than intellectual or spiritual things — **ma·te·ri·al·ist** \-list\ *n or adj* — **ma·te·ri·al·is·tic** \-ˌtir-ē-ə-'lis-tik\ *adj* — **ma·te·ri·al·is·ti·cal·ly** \-ti-k(ə-)lē\ *adv*

ma·te·ri·al·ize \mə-'tir-ē-ə-ˌlīz\ *vb* **-ized; -iz·ing** 1 : to give material form to; *also* : to assume bodily form 2 : to make an often unexpected appearance — **ma·te·ri·al·i·za·tion** \mə-ˌtir-ē-ə-lə-'zā-shən\ *n*

ma·té·ri·el *or* **ma·te·ri·el** \mə-ˌtir-ē-'el\ *n* [F *matériel*] : equipment, apparatus, and supplies used by an organization

ma·ter·nal \mə-'tərn-ᵊl\ *adj* 1 : MOTHERLY 2 : related through or inherited or derived from a female parent — **ma·ter·nal·ly** *adv*

¹**ma·ter·ni·ty** \mə-'tər-nə-tē\ *n, pl* **-ties** 1 : the quality or state of being a mother; *also* : MOTHERLINESS 2 : a hospital facility for the care of women before and during childbirth and for newborn babies

²**maternity** *adj* 1 : designed for wear during pregnancy ⟨a ~ dress⟩ 2 : effective for the period close to and including childbirth ⟨~ leave⟩

¹**math** \'math\ *n* : MATHEMATICS

²**math** *abbr* mathematical; mathematician

math·e·mat·ics \ˌma-thə-'ma-tiks\ *n* : the science of numbers and their properties, operations, and relations and with shapes in space and their structure and measurement — **math·e·mat·i·cal** \-'ma-ti-kəl\ *adj* — **math·e·mat·i·cal·ly** \-ti-k(ə-)lē\ *adv* — **math·e·ma·ti·cian** \ˌma-thə-mə-'ti-shən\ *n*

mat·i·nee *or* **mat·i·née** \ˌmat-ᵊn-'ā\ *n* [F *matinée*, lit., morning, fr. OF, fr. *matin* morning, fr. L *matutinum*, fr. neut. of *matutinus* of the morning, fr. *Matuta*, goddess of morning] : a musical or dramatic performance in the daytime and esp. the afternoon

mat·ins \'mat-ᵊnz\ *n pl, often cap* 1 : special prayers said between midnight and 4 a.m. 2 : a morning service of liturgical prayer in Anglican churches

ma·tri·arch \'mā-trē-ˌärk\ *n* : a female who rules or dominates a family, group, or state — **ma·tri·ar·chal** \ˌmā-trē-'är-kəl\ *adj* — **ma·tri·ar·chy** \'mā-trē-ˌär-kē\ *n*

ma·tri·cide \'ma-trə-ˌsīd, 'mā-\ *n* : the murder of a mother by her child — **ma·tri·cid·al** \ˌma-trə-'sīd-ᵊl, ˌmā-\ *adj*

ma·tric·u·late \mə-'tri-kyə-ˌlāt\ *vb* **-lat·ed; -lat·ing** : to enroll as a member of a body and esp. of a college or university — **ma·tric·u·la·tion** \-ˌtri-kyə-'lā-shən\ *n*

mat·ri·mo·ny \'ma-trə-ˌmō-nē\ *n* [ME, fr. MF *matremoine*, fr. L *matrimonium*, fr. *mater* mother, matron] : MARRIAGE — **mat·ri·mo·ni·al** \ˌma-trə-'mō-nē-əl\ *adj* — **mat·ri·mo·ni·al·ly** *adv*

ma·trix \'mā-triks\ *n, pl* **ma·tri·ces** \'mā-trə-ˌsēz, 'ma-\ *or* **ma·trix·es** \'mā-trik-səz\ **1** : something within or from which something else originates, develops, or takes form **2** : a mold from which a relief surface (as a piece of type) is made

ma·tron \'mā-trən\ *n* **1** : a married woman usu. of dignified maturity or social distinction **2** : a woman supervisor (as in a school or police station) — **ma·tron·ly** *adj*

Matt *abbr* Matthew

¹matte *or* **matt** \'mat\ *var of* ³MAT

²matte *also* **matt** \'mat\ *adj* : not shiny : DULL

¹mat·ter \'ma-tər\ *n* **1** : a subject of interest or concern **2** *pl* : events or circumstances of a particular situation **3** : the subject of a discourse or writing **4** : TROUBLE, DIFFICULTY ⟨what's the ∼⟩ **5** : the substance of which a physical object is composed **6** : PUS **7** : an indefinite amount or quantity ⟨a ∼ of a few days⟩ **8** : something written or printed **9** : MAIL

²matter *vb* : to be of importance

mat·ter–of–fact \ˌma-tə-rəv-'fakt\ *adj* : adhering to fact; *also* : being plain, straightforward, or unemotional — **mat·ter–of–fact·ly** *adv* — **mat·ter–of–fact·ness** *n*

Mat·thew \'ma-thyü\ *n* — see BIBLE table

mat·tins *often cap, chiefly Brit var of* MATINS

mat·tock \'ma-tək\ *n* : a digging and grubbing tool with features of an adze and an ax or pick

mat·tress \'ma-trəs\ *n* **1** : a fabric case filled with resilient material used as or for a bed **2** : an inflatable airtight sack for use as a mattress

mat·u·rate \'ma-chə-ˌrāt\ *vb* **-rat·ed; -rat·ing** : MATURE

mat·u·ra·tion \ˌma-chə-'rā-shən\ *n* **1** : the process of becoming mature **2** : the emergence of personal and behavioral characteristics through growth processes — **mat·u·ra·tion·al** \-shə-nəl\ *adj*

¹ma·ture \mə-'tur, -'tyur\ *adj* **ma·tur·er; -est 1** : based on slow careful consideration **2** : having attained a final or desired state **3** : of or relating to a condition of full development **4** : due for payment — **ma·ture·ly** *adv*

²mature *vb* **ma·tured; ma·tur·ing** : to reach or bring to maturity or completion

ma·tu·ri·ty \mə-'tur-ə-tē, -'tyur-\ *n* **1** : the quality or state of being mature; *esp* : full development **2** : the date when a note becomes due for payment

ma·tu·ti·nal \ˌma-chü-'tīn-ᵊl; mə-'tüt-ᵊn-əl, -'tyüt-\ *adj* : of, relating to, or occurring in the morning : EARLY

mat·zo \'mät-sə\ *n, pl* **mat·zoth** \-ˌsōt, -ˌsōth, -sōs\ *or* **mat·zos** [Yiddish *matse*, fr. Heb *maṣṣāh*] : unleavened bread eaten esp. at the Passover

maud·lin \'mȯd-lən\ *adj* [alter. of Mary *Magdalene;* fr. her depiction as a weeping, penitent sinner] **1** : drunk enough to be silly **2** : weakly and effusively sentimental

¹maul \'mȯl\ *n* : a heavy hammer often with a wooden head used esp. for driving wedges

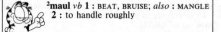

²maul *vb* **1** : BEAT, BRUISE; *also* : MANGLE **2** : to handle roughly

maun·der \'mȯn-dər\ *vb* **1** : to wander slowly and idly **2** : to speak indistinctly or disconnectedly

mau·so·le·um \ˌmȯ-sə-'lē-əm, ˌmȯ-zə-\ *n, pl* **-leums** *or* **-lea** \-'lē-ə\ [L, fr. Gk *mausōleion*, fr. *Mausōlos* Mausolus † *ab* 353 B.C. ruler of Caria whose tomb was one of the seven wonders of the ancient world] : a large tomb; *esp* : a usu. stone building for entombment of the dead above ground

mauve \'mōv, 'mȯv\ *n* : a moderate purple, violet, or lilac color

ma·ven *or* **ma·vin** \'mā-vən\ *n* [Yiddish *meyvn*, fr. LHeb *mēbhīn*] : EXPERT

mav·er·ick \'ma-vrik, -və-rik\ *n* [perh. fr. Samuel A. *Maverick* † 1870 Am. pioneer who did not brand his calves] **1** : an unbranded range animal **2** : NONCONFORMIST

maw \'mȯ\ *n* **1** : STOMACH; *also* : the crop of a bird **2** : the throat, gullet, or jaws esp. of a voracious animal

mawk·ish \'mȯ-kish\ *adj* : sickly sentimental — **mawk·ish·ly** *adv* — **mawk·ish·ness** *n*

max *abbr* maximum

maxi \'mak-sē\ *n, pl* **max·is** : a long skirt, dress, or coat

maxi- *comb form* **1** : extra long ⟨*maxi*-kilt⟩ **2** : extra large ⟨*maxi*-problems⟩

max·il·la \mak-'si-lə\ *n, pl* **max·il·lae** \-'si-(ˌ)lē\ *or* **maxillas** : JAW **1**; *esp* : an upper jaw — **max·il·lary** \'mak-sə-ˌler-ē\ *adj*

max·im \'mak-səm\ *n* : a proverbial saying

max·i·mal \'mak-sə-məl\ *adj* : MAXIMUM — **max·i·mal·ly** *adv*

max·i·mise *Brit var of* MAXIMIZE

max·i·mize \'mak-sə-ˌmīz\ *vb* **-mized; -miz·ing 1** : to increase to a maximum **2** : to make the most of — **max·i·mi·za·tion** \ˌmak-sə-mə-'zā-shən\ *n*

max·i·mum \'mak-sə-məm\ *n, pl* **-ma** \-mə\ *or* **-mums 1** : the greatest quantity, value, or degree **2** : an upper limit allowed by authority **3** : the largest of a set of numbers — **maximum** *adj*

may \'mā\ *verbal auxiliary, past* **might** \'mīt\; *pres sing & pl* **may 1** : have permission or liberty to ⟨∼ go now⟩ **2** : be in some degree likely to ⟨you ∼ be right⟩ **3** — used as an auxiliary to express a wish, purpose, contingency, or concession

May \'mā\ *n* [ME, fr. OF *mai*, fr. L *Maius*, fr. *Maia*, Roman goddess] : the 5th month of the year

Ma·ya \'mī-ə\ *n, pl* **Maya** *or* **Mayas** : a member of a group of peoples of Yucatán, Guatemala, and adjacent areas — **Ma·yan** \'mī-ən\ *n or adj*

may·ap·ple \'mā-ˌa-pəl\ *n* : a No. American woodland herb related to the barberry that has a poisonous root, one or two large leaves, and an edible but insipid yellow fruit

may·be \'mā-bē, 'me-\ *adv* : PERHAPS

May Day \'mā-ˌdā\ n : May 1 celebrated as a spring-time festival and in some countries as Labor Day

may·flow·er \'mā-ˌflaů-ər\ n : any of several spring blooming herbs (as the trailing arbutus or an anemone)

may·fly \'mā-ˌflī\ n : any of an order of insects with an aquatic nymph and a short-lived fragile adult having membranous wings

may·hem \'mā-ˌhem, 'mā-əm\ n 1 : willful and permanent crippling, mutilation, or disfigurement of a person 2 : needless or willful damage

may·on·naise \'mā-ə-ˌnāz\ n [F] : a dressing made of egg yolks, vegetable oil, and vinegar or lemon juice

may·or \'mā-ər\ n : an official elected to act as chief executive or nominal head of a city or borough — **may·or·al** \-əl\ adj — **may·or·al·ty** \-əl-tē\ n

may·pole \'mā-ˌpōl\ n, often cap : a tall flower-wreathed pole forming a center for May Day sports and dances

maze \'māz\ n : a confusing intricate network of passages — **mazy** adj

ma·zur·ka \mə-'zər-kə\ n : a Polish dance in moderate triple measure

MB abbr Manitoba

MBA abbr master of business administration

mc abbr megacycle

¹MC n : MASTER OF CEREMONIES

²MC abbr member of Congress

Mc·Coy \mə-'kòi\ n : something that is neither imitation nor substitute ⟨the real ∼⟩

MCPO abbr master chief petty officer

¹Md abbr Maryland

²Md symbol mendelevium

MD abbr 1 [NL medicinae doctor] doctor of medicine 2 Maryland 3 muscular dystrophy

mdnt abbr midnight

mdse abbr merchandise

MDT abbr mountain daylight (saving) time

me \'mē\ pron, objective case of I

Me abbr Maine

ME abbr 1 Maine 2 mechanical engineer 3 medical examiner

¹mead \'mēd\ n : an alcoholic beverage brewed from water and honey, malt, and yeast

²mead n, archaic : MEADOW

mead·ow \'me-dō\ n : land in or mainly in grass; esp : a tract of moist low-lying usu. level grassland — **mead·ow·land** \-ˌland\ n — **mead·owy** \'me-də-wē\ adj

mead·ow·lark \'me-dō-ˌlärk\ n : any of several No. American songbirds related to the orioles that are streaked brown above and in northernmost forms have a yellow breast marked with a black crescent

mead·ow·sweet \-ˌswēt\ n : a No. American native or naturalized spirea

mea·ger or **mea·gre** \'mē-gər\ adj 1 : THIN 2 : lacking richness, fertility, or strength; also : POOR syn scanty, scant, spare, sparse — **mea·ger·ly** adv — **mea·ger·ness** n

¹meal \'mēl\ n 1 : an act or the time of eating a portion of food 2 : the portion of food eaten at a meal

²meal n 1 : usu. coarsely ground seeds of a cereal 2 : a product resembling seed meal — **mealy** adj

meal·time \'mēl-ˌtīm\ n : the usual time at which a meal is served

mealy·bug \'mē-lē-ˌbəg\ n : any of a family of scale insects with a white powdery covering that are destructive pests esp. of fruit trees

mealy-mouthed \'mē-lē-ˌmaůthd, -ˌmaůtht\ adj : not plain and straightforward : DEVIOUS

¹mean \'mēn\ vb meant \'ment\; **mean·ing** 1 : to have in the mind as a purpose 2 : to serve to convey, show, or indicate : SIGNIFY 3 : to have importance to the degree of 4 : to direct to a particular individual

²mean adj 1 : HUMBLE 2 : lacking acumen : DULL 3 : SHABBY, CONTEMPTIBLE 4 : IGNOBLE, BASE 5 : STIN-

GY 6 : pettily selfish or malicious 7 : VEXATIOUS 8 : EXCELLENT — **mean·ly** adv — **mean·ness** n

³mean adj 1 : occupying a middle position (as in space, order, or time) 2 : being a mean : AVERAGE ⟨a ∼ value⟩

⁴mean n 1 : a middle point between extremes 2 pl : something helpful in achieving a desired end 3 pl : material resources affording a secure life 4 : ARITHMETIC MEAN

¹me·an·der \mē-'an-dər\ n [L maeander, fr. Gk maiandros, fr. Maiandros (now Menderes), river in Asia Minor] 1 : a winding course 2 : a winding of a stream — **me·an·drous** \-drəs\ adj

²meander vb 1 : to follow a winding course 2 : to wander aimlessly or casually

mean·ing n 1 : the thing one intends to convey esp. by language; also : the thing that is thus conveyed 2 : AIM 3 : SIGNIFICANCE; esp : implication of a hidden significance 4 : CONNOTATION; also : DENOTATION — **mean·ing·ful** \-fəl\ adj — **mean·ing·ful·ly** adv — **mean·ing·less** adj

¹mean·time \'mēn-ˌtīm\ n : the intervening time

²meantime adv : MEANWHILE

¹mean·while \-ˌhwīl\ n : MEANTIME

²meanwhile adv 1 : during the intervening time 2 : at the same time

meas abbr measure

mea·sles \'mē-zəlz\ n sing or pl : an acute virus disease marked by fever and an eruption of distinct circular red spots

mea·sly \'mēz-lē, -zə-lē\ adj **mea·sli·er; -est** : contemptibly small or insignificant

¹mea·sure \'me-zhər, 'mā-\ n 1 : an adequate or moderate portion; also : a suitable limit 2 : the dimensions, capacity, or amount of something ascertained by measuring; also : an instrument for measuring 3 : a unit of measurement; also : a system of such units 4 : the act or process of measuring 5 : rhythmic structure or movement 6 : the part of a musical staff between two bars 7 : CRITERION 8 : a means to an end 9 : a legislative bill — **mea·sure·less** adj

²measure vb **mea·sured; mea·sur·ing** 1 : to mark or fix in multiples of a specific unit ⟨∼ off five centimeters⟩ 2 : to find out the size, extent, or amount of 3 : to bring into comparison or competition 4 : to serve as a means of measuring 5 : to have a specified measurement — **mea·sur·able** \'me-zhə-rə-bəl, 'mā-\ adj — **mea·sur·ably** \-blē\ adv — **mea·sur·er** n

mea·sure·ment \'me-zhər-mənt, 'mā-\ n 1 : the act or process of measuring 2 : a figure, extent, or amount obtained by measuring

measure up vb 1 : to have necessary or fitting qualifications 2 : to equal esp. in ability

meat \'mēt\ n 1 : FOOD; esp : solid food as distinguished from drink 2 : animal and esp. mammal flesh considered as food 3 : the edible part inside a covering (as a shell or rind) — **meaty** adj

meat·ball \-ˌbòl\ n : a small ball of chopped or ground meat

meat loaf n : a dish of ground meat seasoned and baked in the form of a loaf

mec·ca \'me-kə\ n, often cap [Mecca, Saudi Arabia, a destination of pilgrims in the Islamic world] : a center of activity sought as a goal by people sharing a common interest

mech abbr mechanical; mechanics

¹me·chan·ic \mi-'ka-nik\ adj : of or relating to manual work or skill

²mechanic n 1 : a manual worker 2 : MACHINIST; esp : one who repairs cars

me·chan·i·cal \mi-'ka-ni-kəl\ adj 1 : of or relating to machinery, to manual operations, or to mechanics 2 : done as if by a machine : AUTOMATIC syn instinctive, impulsive, spontaneous — **me·chan·i·cal·ly** \-k(ə-)lē\ adv

mechanical drawing *n* : drawing done with the aid of instruments

me·chan·ics \mi-'ka-niks\ *n sing or pl* **1** : a branch of physics that deals with energy and forces and their effect on bodies **2** : the practical application of mechanics (as to the operation of machines) **3** : mechanical or functional details

mech·a·nism \'me-kə-ˌni-zəm\ *n* **1** : a piece of machinery; *also* : a process or technique for achieving a result **2** : mechanical operation or action **3** : the fundamental processes involved in or responsible for a natural phenomenon ⟨the visual ∼⟩

mech·a·nis·tic \ˌme-kə-'nis-tik\ *adj* **1** : mechanically determined ⟨∼ universe⟩ **2** : MECHANICAL — **mech·a·nis·ti·cal·ly** \-ti-k(ə-)lē\ *adv*

mech·a·nize \'me-kə-ˌnīz\ *vb* **-nized; -niz·ing 1** : to make mechanical **2** : to equip with machinery esp. in order to replace human or animal labor **3** : to equip with armed and armored motor vehicles — **mech·a·ni·za·tion** \ˌme-kə-nə-'zā-shən\ *n* — **mech·a·niz·er** *n*

med *abbr* **1** medical; medicine **2** medieval **3** medium

MEd *abbr* master of education

med·al \'med-ᵊl\ *n* [MF *medaille*, fr. OIt *medaglia* coin worth half a denarius, medal, fr. (assumed) VL *medalis* half, alter. of LL *medialis* middle, fr. L *medius*] **1** : a small usu. metal object bearing a religious emblem or picture **2** : a piece of metal issued to commemorate a person or event or to award excellence or achievement

med·al·ist *or* **med·al·list** \'med-ᵊl-ist\ *n* **1** : a designer or maker of medals **2** : a recipient of a medal as an award

me·dal·lion \mə-'dal-yən\ *n* **1** : a large medal **2** : a tablet or panel bearing a portrait or an ornament

med·dle \'med-ᵊl\ *vb* **med·dled; med·dling** : to interfere without right or propriety — **med·dler** \'med-ᵊl-ər\ *n*

med·dle·some \'med-ᵊl-səm\ *adj* : inclined to meddle

me·dia \'mē-dē-ə\ *n, pl* **me·di·as** : MEDIUM 4

me·di·al \'mē-dē-əl\ *adj* : occurring in or extending toward the middle

¹me·di·an \'mē-dē-ən\ *n* **1** : a value in an ordered set of values below and above which there are an equal number of values **2** : MEDIAN STRIP

²median *adj* **1** : being in the middle or in an intermediate position **2** : relating to or constituting a statistical median

median strip *n* : a strip dividing a highway into lanes according to the direction of travel

me·di·ate \'mē-dē-ˌāt\ *vb* **-at·ed; -at·ing 1** : to act as an intermediary; *esp* : to work with opposing sides in order to resolve (as a dispute) or bring about (as a settlement) **2** : to bring about, influence, or transmit (as a physical process or effect) by acting as an intermediate or controlling agent or mechanism **syn** intercede, intervene, interpose, interfere — **me·di·a·tion** \ˌmē-dē-'ā-shən\ *n* — **me·di·a·tor** \'mē-dē-ˌā-tər\ *n*

med·ic \'me-dik\ *n* : one engaged in medical work; *esp* : CORPSMAN

med·i·ca·ble \'me-di-kə-bəl\ *adj* : CURABLE

med·ic·aid \'me-di-ˌkād\ *n, often cap* : a program of financial assistance for medical care designed for those unable to afford regular medical service and financed jointly by the state and federal governments

med·i·cal \'me-di-kəl\ *adj* : of or relating to the science or practice of medicine or the treatment of disease — **med·i·cal·ly** \-k(ə-)lē\ *adv*

medical examiner *n* : a public officer who performs autopsies on bodies to find the cause of death

me·di·ca·ment \mi-'di-kə-mənt, 'me-di-kə-\ *n* : a substance used in therapy

medi·care \'me-di-ˌker\ *n, often cap* : a government program of financial assistance for medical care esp. for the aged

med·i·cate \'me-də-ˌkāt\ *vb* **-cat·ed; -cat·ing** : to treat with medicine

med·i·ca·tion \ˌme-də-'kā-shən\ *n* **1** : the act or process of medicating **2** : MEDICINE 1

me·dic·i·nal \mə-'dis-ᵊn-əl\ *adj* : tending or used to cure disease or relieve pain — **me·dic·i·nal·ly** *adv*

med·i·cine \'me-də-sən\ *n* **1** : a substance or preparation used in treating disease **2** : a science and art dealing with the prevention and cure of disease

medicine ball *n* : a heavy stuffed leather ball used for conditioning exercises

medicine man *n* : a priestly healer or sorcerer esp. among the American Indians : SHAMAN

med·i·co \'me-di-ˌkō\ *n, pl* **-cos** : a medical practitioner or student

me·di·e·val *or* **me·di·ae·val** \ˌmē-dē-'ē-vəl, ˌme-, ˌmē-'dē-vəl\ *adj* **1** : of, relating to, or characteristic of the Middle Ages **2** : extremely outmoded or antiquated — **me·di·e·val·ism** \-və-ˌli-zəm\ *n* — **me·di·e·val·ist** \-list\ *n*

me·di·o·cre \ˌmē-dē-'ō-kər\ *adj* [ME, fr. MF, fr. L *mediocris*, fr. *medius* middle + *ocris* stony mountain] : of moderate or low quality : ORDINARY — **me·di·oc·ri·ty** \-'ä-krə-tē\ *n*

med·i·tate \'me-də-ˌtāt\ *vb* **-tat·ed; -tat·ing 1** : to muse over : CONTEMPLATE, PONDER **2** : INTEND, PLAN — **med·i·ta·tion** \ˌme-də-'tā-shən\ *n* — **med·i·ta·tive** \'me-də-ˌtā-tiv\ *adj* — **med·i·ta·tive·ly** *adv*

Med·i·ter·ra·nean \ˌme-də-tə-'rā-nē-ən, -'rā-nyən\ *adj* : of or relating to the Mediterranean Sea or to the lands or people around it

¹me·di·um \'mē-dē-əm\ *n, pl* **mediums** *or* **me·dia** \-dē-ə\ [L] **1** : something in a middle position; *also* : a middle position or degree **2** : a means of effecting or conveying something **3** : a surrounding or enveloping substance **4** : a channel or system of communication, information, or entertainment **5** : a mode of artistic expression **6** : an individual held to be a channel of communication between the earthly world and a world of spirits **7** : a condition or environment in which something may function or flourish

²medium *adj* : intermediate in amount, quality, position, or degree

me·di·um·is·tic \ˌmē-dē-ə-'mis-tik\ *adj* : of, relating to, or being a spiritualistic medium

med·ley \'med-lē\ *n, pl* **medleys 1** : HODGEPODGE **2** : a musical composition made up esp. of a series of songs

me·dul·la \mə-'də-lə\ *n, pl* **-las** *or* **-lae** \-(ˌ)lē, -ˌlī\ : an inner or deep anatomical part; *also* : the posterior part (**medulla ob·lon·ga·ta** \-ˌä-ˌblȯŋ-'gä-tə\) of the vertebrate brain that is continuous with the spinal cord

meed \'mēd\ *n* : a fitting return

meek \'mēk\ *adj* **1** : characterized by patience and long-suffering **2** : deficient in spirit and courage **3** : MODERATE — **meek·ly** *adv* — **meek·ness** *n*

meer·schaum \'mir-shəm, -ˌshȯm\ *n* [G, fr. *Meer* sea + *Schaum* foam] : a tobacco pipe made of a light white clayey mineral

¹meet \'mēt\ *vb* **met** \'met\; **meet·ing 1** : to come upon : FIND **2** : JOIN, INTERSECT **3** : to appear to the perception of **4** : OPPOSE, FIGHT **5** : to join in conversation or discussion; *also* : ASSEMBLE **6** : to conform to **7** : to pay fully **8** : to cope with **9** : to provide for **10** : to be introduced to

²meet *n* : an assembling esp. for a hunt or for competitive sports

³meet *adj* : SUITABLE, PROPER

meet·ing \'mē-tiŋ\ *n* **1** : an act of coming together : ASSEMBLY **2** : JUNCTION, INTERSECTION

meet·ing·house \-ˌhaùs\ *n* : a building for public assembly and esp. for Protestant worship

mega- *or* **meg-** *comb form* **1** : great : large ⟨*mega*hit⟩ **2** : million : multiplied by one million ⟨*mega*hertz⟩

mega·byte \'me-gə-ˌbīt\ *n* : a unit of computer storage capacity equal to 1,048,576 bytes

mega·cy·cle \-ˌsī-kəl\ *n* : MEGAHERTZ

mega·death \-ˌdeth\ *n* : one million deaths — used as a unit in reference to nuclear warfare

mega·hertz \ˈme-gə-ˌhərts, -ˌherts\ *n* : a unit of frequency equal to one million hertz

mega·lith \ˈme-gə-ˌlith\ *n* : a large stone used in prehistoric monuments — **mega·lith·ic** \ˌme-gə-ˈli-thik\ *adj*

meg·a·lo·ma·nia \ˌme-gə-lō-ˈmā-nē-ə, -nyə\ *n* : a mental disorder marked by feelings of personal omnipotence and grandeur — **meg·a·lo·ma·ni·ac** \-ˈmā-nē-ˌak\ *adj or n*

meg·a·lop·o·lis \ˌme-gə-ˈlä-pə-ləs\ *n* : a very large urban unit

mega·phone \ˈme-gə-ˌfōn\ *n* : a cone-shaped device used to intensify or direct the voice — **megaphone** *vb*

mega·ton \-ˌtən\ *n* : an explosive force equivalent to that of one million tons of TNT

mega·vi·ta·min \-ˌvī-tə-mən\ *adj* : relating to or consisting of very large doses of vitamins — **mega·vi·ta·mins** *n pl*

mei·o·sis \mī-ˈō-səs\ *n* : a process of cell division in gamete-producing cells in which the number of chromosomes is reduced to one half — **mei·ot·ic** \mī-ˈä-tik\ *adj*

mel·an·cho·lia \ˌme-lən-ˈkō-lē-ə\ *n* : a mental disorder marked by extreme depression often with delusions

mel·an·chol·ic \ˌme-lən-ˈkä-lik\ *adj* 1 : DEPRESSED 2 : of or relating to melancholia

mel·an·choly \ˈme-lən-ˌkä-lē\ *n, pl* **-chol·ies** [ME *malencolie*, fr. MF *melancolie*, fr. LL *melancholia*, fr. Gk. fr. *melan-, melas* black + *cholē* bile; so called fr. the former belief that it was caused by an excess of black bile, a substance supposedly secreted by the kidneys or spleen] : depression of spirits : DEJECTION — **melancholy** *adj*

Mel·a·ne·sian \ˌme-lə-ˈnē-zhən\ *n* : a member of the dominant native group of the Pacific island grouping of Melanesia — **Melanesian** *adj*

mé·lange \mā-ˈläⁿzh, -ˈlänj\ *n* : a mixture esp. of incongruous elements

mel·a·nin \ˈme-lə-nən\ *n* : a dark brown or black animal or plant pigment

mel·a·nism \ˈme-lə-ˌni-zəm\ *n* : an increased amount of black or nearly black pigmentation

mel·a·no·ma \ˌme-lə-ˈnō-mə\ *n, pl* **-mas** *also* **-ma·ta** \-mə-tə\ : a usu. malignant tumor containing dark pigment

¹meld \ˈmeld\ *vb* : to show or announce for a score in a card game

²meld *n* : a card or combination of cards that is or can be melded

me·lee \ˈmā-ˌlā, mā-ˈlā\ *n* [F *mêlée*] : a confused struggle **syn** fracas, row, brawl, donnybrook

me·lio·rate \ˈmēl-yə-ˌrāt, ˈmē-lē-ə-\ *vb* **-rat·ed; -rat·ing** : AMELIORATE — **me·lio·ra·tion** \ˌmēl-yə-ˈrā-shən, ˌmē-lē-ə-\ *n* — **me·lio·ra·tive** \ˈmēl-yə-ˌrā-tiv, ˈmē-lē-ə-\ *adj*

mel·lif·lu·ous \me-ˈli-flə-wəs, mə-\ *adj* [LL *mellifluus*, fr. L *mel* honey + *fluere* to flow] : sweetly flowing — **mel·lif·lu·ous·ly** *adv* — **mel·lif·lu·ous·ness** *n*

¹mel·low \ˈme-lō\ *adj* 1 : soft and sweet because of ripeness; *also* : well aged and pleasingly mild ⟨~ wine⟩ 2 : made gentle by age or experience 3 : being rich and full but not garish or strident ⟨~ colors⟩ 4 : of soft loamy consistency ⟨~ soil⟩ — **mel·low·ness** *n*

²mellow *vb* : to make or become mellow

me·lo·di·ous \mə-ˈlō-dē-əs\ *adj* : pleasing to the ear — **me·lo·di·ous·ly** *adv* — **me·lo·di·ous·ness** *n*

melo·dra·ma \ˈme-lə-ˌdrä-mə, -ˌdra-\ *n* : an extravagantly theatrical play in which action and plot predominate over characterization — **melo·dra·mat·ic** \ˌme-lə-drə-ˈma-tik\ *adj* — **melo·dra·mat·i·cal·ly** \-ti-k(ə-)lē\ *adv* — **melo·dra·ma·tist** \ˌme-lə-ˈdra-mə-tist, -ˈdrä-\ *n*

mel·o·dy \ˈme-lə-dē\ *n, pl* **-dies** 1 : sweet or agreeable sound 2 : a particular succession of notes : TUNE, AIR — **me·lod·ic** \mə-ˈlä-dik\ *adj* — **me·lod·i·cal·ly** \-di-k(ə-)lē\ *adv*

mel·on \ˈme-lən\ *n* : any of various fruits (as a muskmelon or watermelon) of the gourd family usu. eaten raw

---

¹melt \ˈmelt\ *vb* 1 : to change from a solid to a liquid state usu. by heat 2 : DISSOLVE, DISINTEGRATE; *also* : to cause to disperse or disappear 3 : to make or become tender or gentle

---

²melt *n* : a melted substance

melt·down \ˈmelt-ˌdaůn\ *n* : the melting of the core of a nuclear reactor

melt·wa·ter \-ˌwȯ-tər, -ˌwä-\ *n* : water derived from the melting of ice and snow

mem *abbr* 1 member 2 memoir 3 memorial

mem·ber \ˈmem-bər\ *n* 1 : a part (as an arm, leg, leaf, or branch) of an animal or plant 2 : one of the individuals composing a group 3 : a constituent part of a whole

mem·ber·ship \-ˌship\ *n* 1 : the state or status of being a member 2 : the body of members

mem·brane \ˈmem-ˌbrān\ *n* : a thin pliable layer esp. of animal or plant origin — **mem·bra·nous** \-brə-nəs\ *adj*

me·men·to \mə-ˈmen-tō\ *n, pl* **-tos** *or* **-toes** [ME, fr. L, remember] : something that serves to warn or remind; *also* : SOUVENIR

memo \ˈme-mō\ *n, pl* **mem·os** : MEMORANDUM

mem·oir \ˈmem-ˌwär\ *n* 1 : MEMORANDUM 2 : AUTOBIOGRAPHY — usu. used in pl. 3 : an account of something noteworthy; *also, pl* : the record of the proceedings of a learned society

mem·o·ra·bil·ia \ˌme-mə-rə-ˈbi-lē-ə, -ˈbil-yə\ *n pl* [L] : things worthy of remembrance; *also* : MEMENTOS

mem·o·ra·ble \ˈme-mə-rə-bəl\ *adj* : worth remembering : NOTABLE — **mem·o·ra·bil·i·ty** \ˌme-mə-rə-ˈbi-lə-tē\ *n* — **mem·o·ra·ble·ness** *n* — **mem·o·ra·bly** \-blē\ *adv*

mem·o·ran·dum \ˌme-mə-ˈran-dəm\ *n, pl* **-dums** *or*

-da \-də\ **1** : an informal record; *also* : a written reminder **2** : an informal written note

¹me·mo·ri·al \mə-'mōr-ē-əl\ *adj* : serving to preserve remembrance

²memorial *n* **1** : something designed to keep remembrance alive; *esp* : MONUMENT **2** : a statement of facts often accompanied with a petition — **me·mo·ri·al·ize** *vb*

Memorial Day *n* : the last Monday in May or formerly May 30 observed as a legal holiday in honor of those who died in war

mem·o·rise *Brit var of* MEMORIZE

mem·o·rize \'me-mə-ˌrīz\ *vb* **-rized; -riz·ing** : to learn by heart — **mem·o·ri·za·tion** \ˌme-mə-rə-'zā-shən\ *n* — **mem·o·riz·er** *n*

mem·o·ry \'me-mə-rē\ *n, pl* **-ries** **1** : the power or process of remembering **2** : the store of things remembered **3** : COMMEMORATION **4** : something remembered **5** : the time within which past events are remembered **6** : a device (as in a computer) in which information can be stored **syn** remembrance, recollection, reminiscence

men *pl of* MAN

¹men·ace \'me-nəs\ *n* **1** : THREAT **2** : DANGER; *also* : NUISANCE

²menace *vb* **men·aced; men·ac·ing** **1** : THREATEN **2** : ENDANGER — **men·ac·ing·ly** *adv*

mé·nage \mā-'näzh\ *n* [F] : HOUSEHOLD

me·nag·er·ie \mə-'na-jə-rē\ *n* : a collection of wild animals esp. for exhibition

¹mend \'mend\ *vb* **1** : to improve in manners or morals **2** : to put into good shape : REPAIR **3** : to improve in or restore to health : HEAL — **mend·er** *n*

²mend *n* **1** : an act of mending **2** : a mended place

men·da·cious \men-'dā-shəs\ *adj* : given to deception or falsehood : UNTRUTHFUL **syn** dishonest, deceitful — **men·da·cious·ly** *adv* — **men·dac·i·ty** \-'da-sə-tē\ *n*

men·de·le·vi·um \ˌmen-də-'lē-vē-əm, -'lā-\ *n* : a radioactive chemical element artificially produced — see ELEMENT table

men·di·cant \'men-di-kənt\ *n* **1** : BEGGAR **2** *often cap* : FRIAR — **men·di·can·cy** \-kən-sē\ *n* — **mendicant** *adj*

men·folk \'men-ˌfōk\ *or* **men·folks** \-ˌfōks\ *n pl* **1** : men in general **2** : the men of a family or community

men·ha·den \men-'hād-ᵊn, mən-\ *n, pl* **-den** *also* **-dens** : a marine fish related to the herring that is abundant along the Atlantic coast of the U.S.

¹me·nial \'mē-nē-əl, -nyəl\ *adj* **1** : of or relating to servants **2** : HUMBLE; *also* : SERVILE — **me·ni·al·ly** *adv*

²menial *n* : a domestic servant

men·in·gi·tis \ˌme-nən-'jī-təs\ *n, pl* **-git·i·des** \-'ji-tə-ˌdēz\ : inflammation of the membranes enclosing the brain and spinal cord; *also* : a usu. bacterial disease marked by this

me·ninx \'mē-niŋks, 'me-\ *n, pl* **me·nin·ges** \mə-'nin-(ˌ)jēz\ : any of the three membranes that envelop the brain and spinal cord — **men·in·ge·al** \ˌme-nən-'jē-əl\ *adj*

me·nis·cus \mə-'nis-kəs\ *n, pl* **me·nis·ci** \-'nis-ˌkī, -ˌkē\ *also* **me·nis·cus·es** **1** : CRESCENT **2** : the curved upper surface of a column of liquid

men·o·pause \'me-nə-ˌpȯz\ *n* : the period of life when menstruation stops naturally — **men·o·paus·al** \ˌme-nə-'pȯ-zəl\ *adj*

me·no·rah \mə-'nȯr-ə\ *n* [Heb *měnōrāh* candlestick] : a candelabrum that is used in Jewish worship

men·ses \'men-ˌsēz\ *n pl* : the menstrual flow

men·stru·a·tion \ˌmen-strə-'wā-shən, men-'strā-\ *n* : a discharging of bloody matter at approximately monthly intervals from the uterus of breeding-age nonpregnant primate females; *also* : PERIOD 6 — **men·stru·al** \'men-strə-wəl\ *adj* — **men·stru·ate** \'men-strə-ˌwāt, -ˌstrāt\ *vb*

men·su·ra·ble \'men-sə-rə-bəl, '-chə-\ *adj* : MEASURABLE

men·su·ra·tion \ˌmen-sə-'rā-shən, ˌmen-chə-\ *n* : MEASUREMENT

-ment \mənt\ *n suffix* **1** : concrete result, object, or agent of a (specified) action ⟨embank*ment*⟩ ⟨entangle*ment*⟩ **2** : concrete means or instrument of a (specified) action ⟨entertain*ment*⟩ **3** : action : process ⟨encircle*ment*⟩ ⟨develop*ment*⟩ **4** : place of a (specified) action ⟨encamp*ment*⟩ **5** : state : condition ⟨amaze*ment*⟩

men·tal \'ment-ᵊl\ *adj* **1** : of or relating to the mind **2** : of, relating to, or affected with a disorder of the mind ⟨∼ illness⟩ — **men·tal·ly** *adv*

mental age *n* : a measure of a child's mental development in terms of the number of years it takes an average child to reach the same level

mental deficiency *n* : MENTAL RETARDATION

men·tal·i·ty \men-'ta-lə-tē\ *n, pl* **-ties** **1** : mental power or capacity **2** : mode or way of thought

mental retardation *n* : subaverage intellectual ability present from infancy that is characterized by an IQ of 70 or less and problems in development, learning, and social adjustment

men·thol \'men-ˌthȯl, -ˌthōl\ *n* : an alcohol occurring esp. in mint oils that has the odor and cooling properties of peppermint — **men·tho·lat·ed** \-thə-ˌlā-təd\ *adj*

¹men·tion \'men-chən\ *n* **1** : a brief or casual reference **2** : a formal citation for outstanding achievement

²mention *vb* **1** : to refer to : CITE **2** : to cite for superior achievement — **not to mention** : to say nothing of

men·tor \'men-ˌtȯr, -tər\ *n* : a trusted counselor or guide; *also* : TUTOR, COACH

menu \'men-yü, 'mān-\ *n, pl* **menus** [F, fr. *menu* small, detailed, fr. L *minutus* minute (adj.)] **1** : a list of the dishes available (as in a restaurant) for a meal; *also* : the dishes served **2** : a list of offerings or options

me·ow \mē-'aù\ *vb* : to make the characteristic cry of a cat — **meow** *n*

mer *abbr* meridian

mer·can·tile \'mər-kən-ˌtēl, -ˌtīl\ *adj* : of or relating to merchants or trading

¹mer·ce·nary \'mərs-ᵊn-ˌer-ē\ *n, pl* **-nar·ies** : a person who serves merely for wages; *esp* : a soldier hired into foreign service

²mercenary *adj* **1** : serving merely for pay or gain **2** : hired for service in a foreign army

mer·cer \'mər-sər\ *n, Brit* : a dealer in usu. expensive fabrics

mer·cer·ise *Brit var of* MERCERIZE

mer·cer·ize \'mər-sə-ˌrīz\ *vb* **-ized; -iz·ing** : to treat cotton yarn or cloth with alkali so that it looks silky or takes a better dye

¹mer·chan·dise \'mər-chən-ˌdīz, -ˌdīs\ *n* : the commodities or goods that are bought and sold in business

²mer·chan·dise \-ˌdīz\ *vb* **-dised; -dis·ing** : to buy and sell in business : TRADE — **mer·chan·dis·er** *n*

mer·chant \'mər-chənt\ *n* **1** : a buyer and seller of commodities for profit **2** : STOREKEEPER

mer·chant·able \'mər-chən-tə-bəl\ *adj* : acceptable to buyers : MARKETABLE

mer·chant·man \'mər-chənt-mən\ *n* : a ship used in commerce

merchant marine *n* : the commercial ships of a nation

merchant ship *n* : MERCHANTMAN

mer·ci·ful·ly \'mər-si-fə-lē\ *adv* **1** : in a merciful manner **2** : FORTUNATELY 2

mer·cu·ri·al \ˌmər-'kyur-ē-əl\ *adj* **1** : unpredictably changeable **2** : MERCURIC — **mer·cu·ri·al·ly** *adv* — **mer·cu·ri·al·ness** *n*

mer·cu·ric \ˌmər-'kyur-ik\ *adj* : of, relating to, or containing mercury

mercuric chloride *n* : a poisonous compound of mercury and chlorine used as an antiseptic and fungicide

mer·cu·ry \'mər-kyə-rē\ *n, pl* **-ries 1** : a heavy silver-white liquid metallic chemical element used esp. in scientific instruments — see ELEMENT table **2** *cap* : the planet nearest the sun — see PLANET table

mer·cy \'mər-sē\ *n, pl* **mercies** [ME, fr. OF *merci,* fr. ML *merced-, merces,* fr. L, price paid, wages, fr. *merc-, merx* merchandise] **1** : compassion shown to an offender; *also* : imprisonment rather than death for first-degree murder **2** : a blessing resulting from divine favor or compassion; *also* : a fortunate circumstance **3** : compassion shown to victims of misfortune — **mer·ci·ful** \-si-fəl\ *adj* — **mer·ci·less** \-si-ləs\ *adj* — **mer·ci·less·ly** *adv* — **mercy** *adj*

mercy killing *n* : the act or practice of killing or permitting the death of hopelessly sick or injured persons or animals with as little pain as possible for reasons of mercy

¹mere \'mir\ *n* : LAKE, POOL

²mere *adj, superlative* **mer·est 1** : being nothing more than ⟨a ～ child⟩ **2** : not diluted : PURE — **mere·ly** *adv*

mer·e·tri·cious \ˌmer-ə-'tri-shəs\ *adj* [L *meretricius,* fr. *meretrix* prostitute, fr. *merēre* to earn] : tawdrily attractive; *also* : SPECIOUS — **mer·e·tri·cious·ly** *adv* — **mer·e·tri·cious·ness** *n*

mer·gan·ser \(ˌ)mər-'gan-sər\ *n* : any of various fish-eating wild ducks with a usu. crested head and a slender bill hooked at the end and serrated along the margins

merge \'mərj\ *vb* **merged; merg·ing 1** : to blend gradually **2** : to combine, unite, or coalesce into one **syn** mingle, amalgamate, fuse, interfuse, intermingle

merg·er \'mər-jər\ *n* **1** : the act or process of merging **2** : absorption by a corporation of one or more others

me·rid·i·an \mə-'ri-dē-ən\ *n* [ME, fr. MF *meridien,* fr. L *meridianus,* fr. *meridies* noon, south, irreg. fr. *medius* mid + *dies* day] **1** : the highest point : CULMINATION **2** : any of the imaginary circles on the earth's surface passing through the north and south poles — **meridian** *adj*

me·ringue \mə-'raŋ\ *n* [F] : a baked dessert topping of stiffly beaten egg whites and powdered sugar

me·ri·no \mə-'rē-nō\ *n, pl* **-nos** [Sp] **1** : any of a breed of sheep noted for fine soft wool **2** : a fine soft fabric or yarn of wool or wool and cotton

¹mer·it \'mer-ət\ *n* **1** : laudable or blameworthy traits or actions **2** : a praiseworthy quality; *also* : character or conduct deserving reward or honor **3** *pl* : the intrinsic nature of a legal case; *also* : legal significance

²merit *vb* : EARN, DESERVE

mer·i·toc·ra·cy \ˌmer-ə-'tä-krə-sē\ *n, pl* **-cies** : a system in which the talented are chosen and moved ahead based on their achievement; *also* : leadership by the talented

mer·i·to·ri·ous \ˌmer-ə-'tōr-ē-əs\ *adj* : deserving honor or esteem — **mer·i·to·ri·ous·ly** *adv* — **mer·i·to·ri·ous·ness** *n*

mer·maid \'mər-ˌmād\ *n* : a legendary sea creature with a woman's upper body and a fish's tail

mer·man \-ˌman, -mən\ *n* : a legendary sea creature with a man's upper body and a fish's tail

mer·ri·ment \'mer-i-mənt\ *n* **1** : HILARITY **2** : FESTIVITY

mer·ry \'mer-ē\ *adj* **mer·ri·er; -est 1** : full of gaiety or high spirits **2** : marked by festivity **3** : BRISK ⟨a ～ pace⟩ **syn** blithe, jocund, jovial, jolly, mirthful — **mer·ri·ly** \'mer-ə-lē\ *adv*

merry-go-round \'mer-ē-gō-ˌraùnd\ *n* **1** : a circular revolving platform with benches and figures of animals on which people sit for a ride **2** : a busy round of activities

mer·ry·mak·ing \'mer-ē-ˌmā-kiŋ\ *n* **1** : jovial or festive activity **2** : a festive occasion — **mer·ry·mak·er** \-ˌmā-kər\ *n*

me·sa \'mā-sə\ *n* [Sp, lit., table, fr. L *mensa*] : a flat-topped hill with steep sides

mes·cal \me-'skal, mə-\ *n* **1** : a small cactus that is the source of a stimulant used esp. by Mexican Indians **2** : a usu. colorless liquor distilled from the leaves of an agave; *also* : this agave

mes·ca·line \'mes-kə-lən, -ˌlēn\ *n* : a hallucinatory alkaloid from the mescal cactus

mesdames *pl of* MADAM *or of* MADAME *or of* MRS.

mesdemoiselles *pl of* MADEMOISELLE

¹mesh \'mesh\ *n* **1** : one of the openings between the threads or cords of a net; *also* : one of the similar spaces in a network **2** : the fabric of a net **3** : NETWORK **4** : working contact (as of the teeth of gears) ⟨in ～⟩ — **meshed** \'mesht\ *adj*

²mesh *vb* **1** : to catch in or as if in a mesh **2** : to be in or come into mesh : ENGAGE **3** : to fit together properly

mesh·work \'mesh-ˌwərk\ *n* : NETWORK

me·si·al \'mē-zē-əl, -sē-\ *adj* : of, relating to, or being the surface of a tooth that is closest to the middle of the front of the jaw

mes·mer·ise *Brit var of* MESMERIZE

mes·mer·ize \'mez-mə-ˌrīz\ *vb* **-ized; -iz·ing** : HYPNOTIZE — **mes·mer·ic** \mez-'mer-ik\ *adj* — **mes·mer·ism** \'mez-mə-ˌri-zəm\ *n*

Me·so·lith·ic \ˌme-zə-'li-thik\ *adj* : of, relating to, or being a transitional period of the Stone Age between the Paleolithic and the Neolithic periods

me·so·sphere \'me-zə-ˌsfir\ *n* : a layer of the atmosphere between the stratosphere and the thermosphere

Me·so·zo·ic \ˌme-zə-'zō-ik, ˌmē-\ *adj* : of, relating to, or being the era of geologic history between the Paleozoic and the Cenozoic and extending from about 245 million years ago to about 65 million years ago — **Mesozoic** *n*

mes·quite \mə-'skēt, me-\ *n* : any of several spiny leguminous trees and shrubs chiefly of the southwestern U.S. with sugar-rich pods important as fodder; *also* : mesquite wood used esp. in grilling food

¹mess \'mes\ *n* **1** : a quantity of food; *also* : enough food of a specified kind for a dish or meal ⟨a ～ of beans⟩ **2** : a group of persons who regularly eat together;

also : a meal eaten by such a group **3** : a place where meals are regularly served to a group **4** : a confused, dirty, or offensive state — **messy** *adj*

²**mess** *vb* **1** : to supply with meals; *also* : to take meals with a mess **2** : to make dirty or untidy; *also* : BUNGLE **3** : INTERFERE, MEDDLE **4** : PUTTER, TRIFLE

mes·sage \'me-sij\ *n* : a communication sent by one person to another

messeigneurs *pl of* MONSEIGNEUR

mes·sen·ger \'mes-ᵊn-jər\ *n* : one who carries a message or does an errand

messenger RNA *n* : an RNA that carries the code for a particular protein from DNA in the nucleus to a ribosome in the cytoplasm and acts as a template for the formation of that protein

Mes·si·ah \mə-'sī-ə\ *n* **1** : the expected king and deliverer of the Jews **2** : Jesus **3** *not cap* : a professed or accepted leader of a cause — **mes·si·an·ic** \₁me-sē-'a-nik\ *adj*

messieurs *pl of* MONSIEUR

mess·mate \'mes-₁māt\ *n* : a member of a group who eat regularly together

Messrs. \'me-sərz\ *pl of* MR.

mes·ti·zo \me-'stē-zō\ *n, pl* **-zos** [Sp, fr. *mestizo* mixed, fr. LL *mixticius*, fr. L *mixtus*, pp. of *miscēre* to mix] : a person of mixed blood

¹**met** *past and past part of* MEET

²**met** *abbr* metropolitan

me·tab·o·lism \mə-'ta-bə-₁li-zəm\ *n* : the processes by which the substance of plants and animals incidental to life is built up and broken down; *also* : the processes by which a substance is handled in the body ⟨∼ of sugar⟩ — **met·a·bol·ic** \₁me-tə-'bä-lik\ *adj* — **me·tab·o·lize** \-'ta-bə-₁līz\ *vb*

me·tab·o·lite \-₁līt\ *n* **1** : a product of metabolism **2** : a substance essential to the metabolism of a particular organism or to a metabolic process

meta·car·pal \₁me-tə-'kär-pəl\ *n* : any of usu. five more or less elongated bones of the part of the hand or forefoot that connect the wrist and the bones of the digits — **metacarpal** *adj*

meta·car·pus \-'kär-pəs\ *n* : the part of the hand or forefoot that contains the metacarpus

met·al \'met-ᵊl\ *n* **1** : any of various opaque, fusible, ductile, and typically lustrous substances that are good conductors of electricity and heat **2** : METTLE; *also* : the material out of which a person or thing is made — **me·tal·lic** \mə-'ta-lik\ *adj*

met·al·lur·gy \'met-ᵊl-₁ər-jē\ *n* : the science and technology of metals — **met·al·lur·gi·cal** \₁met-ᵊl-'ər-ji-kəl\ *adj* — **met·al·lur·gist** \'met-ᵊl-₁ər-jist\ *n*

met·al·ware \'met-ᵊl-₁war\ *n* : metal utensils for household use

met·al·work \-₁wərk\ *n* : work and esp. artistic work made of metal — **met·al·work·er** \-₁wər-kər\ *n* — **met·al·work·ing** *n*

meta·mor·phism \₁me-tə-'mòr-₁fi-zəm\ *n* : a change in the structure of rock; *esp* : a change to a more compact and more highly crystalline form produced by pressure, heat, and water — **meta·mor·phic** \-'mòr-fik\ *adj*

meta·mor·pho·sis \₁me-tə-'mòr-fə-səs\ *n, pl* **-pho·ses** \-₁sēz\ **1** : a change of physical form, structure, or substance esp. by supernatural means; *also* : a striking alteration (as in appearance or character) **2** : a fundamental change in form and often habits of an animal accompanying the transformation of a larva into an adult — **meta·mor·phose** \-₁fōz, -₁fōs\ *vb*

met·a·phor \'me-tə-₁fòr\ *n* : a figure of speech in which a word for one idea or thing is used in place of another to suggest a likeness between them (as in "the ship plows the sea") — **met·a·phor·i·cal** \₁me-tə-'fòr-i-kəl\ *adj*

meta·phys·ics \₁me-tə-'fi-ziks\ *n* [ML *Metaphysica*, title of Aristotle's treatise on the subject, fr. Gk (*ta*) *meta* (*ta*) *physika*, lit., the (works) after the physical

(works); fr. its position in his collected works] : the philosophical study of the ultimate causes and underlying nature of things — **meta·phys·i·cal** \-'fi-zi-kəl\ *adj* — **meta·phy·si·cian** \-fə-'zi-shən\ *n*

me·tas·ta·sis \mə-'tas-tə-səs\ *n, pl* **-ta·ses** \-₁sēz\ : transfer of a health-impairing agency (as cancer cells) to a new site in the body; *also* : a secondary growth of a malignant tumor — **me·tas·ta·size** \-tə-₁sīz\ *vb* — **met·a·stat·ic** \₁me-tə-'sta-tik\ *adj*

meta·tar·sal \₁me-tə-'tär-səl\ *n* : any of the bones of the foot between the tarsus and the bones of the digits that in humans include five more or less elongated bones — **metatarsal** *adj*

meta·tar·sus \-'tär-səs\ *n* : the part of the human foot or the hind foot in quadrupeds that contains the metatarsals

¹**mete** \'mēt\ *vb* **met·ed; met·ing 1** *archaic* : MEASURE **2** : ALLOT

²**mete** *n* : BOUNDARY ⟨∼s and bounds⟩

me·te·or \'mē-tē-ər, -₁òr\ *n* **1** : a small particle of matter in the solar system directly observable only by its glow from frictional heating on falling into the earth's atmosphere **2** : the streak of light produced by a meteor

me·te·or·ic \₁mē-tē-'òr-ik\ *adj* **1** : of, relating to, or resembling a meteor **2** : transiently brilliant ⟨a ∼ career⟩ — **me·te·or·i·cal·ly** \-i-k(ə-)lē\ *adv*

me·te·or·ite \'mē-tē-ə-₁rīt\ *n* : a meteor that reaches the surface of the earth

me·te·or·oid \'mē-tē-ə-₁ròid\ *n* : a small particle of matter in the solar system

me·te·o·rol·o·gy \₁mē-tē-ə-'rä-lə-jē\ *n* : a science that deals with the atmosphere and its phenomena and esp. with weather forecasting — **me·te·o·ro·log·ic** \₁mē-tē-₁òr-ə-'lä-jik\ *or* **me·te·o·ro·log·i·cal** \-'lä-ji-kəl\ *adj* — **me·te·o·rol·o·gist** \₁mē-tē-ə-'rä-lə-jist\ *n*

¹**me·ter** \'mē-tər\ *n* : rhythm in verse or music

²**meter** *n* : the basic metric unit of length — see METRIC SYSTEM table

³**meter** *n* : a measuring and sometimes recording instrument

⁴**meter** *vb* **1** : to measure by means of a meter **2** : to print postal indicia on by means of a postage meter ⟨∼ed mail⟩

meter–kilogram–second *adj* : of, relating to, or being a system of units based on the meter, the kilogram, and the second

meter maid *n* : a policewoman assigned to write tickets for parking violations

meth·a·done \'me-thə-₁dōn\ *also* **meth·a·don** \-₁dän\ *n* : a synthetic addictive narcotic drug used esp. as a substitute narcotic in the treatment of heroin addiction

meth·am·phet·amine \₁me-tham-'fe-tə-₁mēn, -thəm-, -mən\ *n* : a drug used medically in the form of its hydrochloride in the treatment of obesity and often illicitly as a stimulant

meth·ane \'me-₁thān\ *n* : a colorless odorless flammable gas produced by decomposition of organic matter or from coal and used esp. as a fuel

meth·a·nol \'me-thə-₁nòl, -₁nōl\ *n* : a volatile flammable poisonous liquid alcohol used esp. as a solvent and as an antifreeze

meth·aqua·lone \me-'tha-kwə-₁lōn\ *n* : a sedative and hypnotic habit-forming drug that is not a barbiturate

meth·od \'me-thəd\ *n* [MF *methode*, fr. L *methodus*, fr. Gk *methodos*, fr. *meta* with + *hodos* way] **1** : a procedure or process for achieving an end **2** : orderly arrangement : PLAN **syn** mode, manner, way, fashion, system — **me·thod·i·cal** \mə-'thä-di-kəl\ *adj* — **me·thod·i·cal·ly** \-k(ə-)lē\ *adv* — **me·thod·i·cal·ness** *n*

meth·od·ise *Brit var of* METHODIZE

Meth·od·ist \'me-thə-dist\ *n* : a member of a Protestant denomination adhering to the doctrines of John Wesley — **Meth·od·ism** \-₁di-zəm\ *n*

meth·od·ize \'me-thə-ˌdīz\ vb **-ized; -iz·ing** : SYSTEMATIZE

meth·od·ol·o·gy \ˌme-thə-'dä-lə-jē\ n, pl **-gies 1** : a body of methods and rules followed in a science or discipline **2** : the study of the principles or procedures of inquiry in a particular field

meth·yl \'me-thəl\ n : a chemical group consisting of carbon and hydrogen

methyl alcohol n : METHANOL

meth·yl·mer·cury \ˌme-thəl-'mər-kyə-rē\ n : any of various toxic compounds of mercury that often occur as pollutants which accumulate in animals esp. at the top of a food chain

met·i·cal \'me-ti-kəl\ n — see MONEY table

me·tic·u·lous \mə-'ti-kyə-ləs\ adj [L meticulosus fearful, fr. metus fear] : extremely careful in attending to details — **me·tic·u·lous·ly** adv — **me·tic·u·lous·ness** n

mé·tier \'me-ˌtyā, me-'tyā\ n : an area of activity in which one is expert or successful

me·tre \'mē-tər\ chiefly Brit var of METER

met·ric \'me-trik\ adj **1** : of or relating to measurement; esp : of or relating to the metric system **2** : METRICAL 1

met·ri·cal \'me-tri-kəl\ adj **1** : of, relating to, or composed in meter **2** : METRIC 1 — **met·ri·cal·ly** \-k(ə-)lē\ adv

met·ri·ca·tion \ˌme-tri-'kā-shən\ n : the act or process of converting into or expressing in the metric system

met·ri·cize \'me-trə-ˌsīz\ vb **-cized; -ciz·ing** : to change into or express in the metric system

metric system n : a decimal system of weights and measures based on the meter and on the kilogram

metric ton n — see METRIC SYSTEM table

¹met·ro \'me-trō\ n, pl **metros** : SUBWAY

²metro adj : of, relating to, or characteristic of a metropolis and sometimes including its suburbs

met·ro·nome \'me-trə-ˌnōm\ n : an instrument for marking exact time by a regularly repeated tick

me·trop·o·lis \mə-'trä-pə-ləs\ n [ME, fr. LL, fr. Gk mētropolis, fr. mētēr mother + polis city] : the chief or capital city of a country, state, or region — **met·ro·pol·i·tan** \ˌme-trə-'pä-lət-ᵊn\ adj

met·tle \'met-ᵊl\ n **1** : SPIRIT, COURAGE **2** : quality of temperament

met·tle·some \'met-ᵊl-səm\ adj : full of mettle : COURAGEOUS

MeV abbr million electron volts

¹mew \'myü\ vb : MEOW — **mew** n

²mew vb : CONFINE

mews \'myüz\ n pl, chiefly Brit : stables usu. with living quarters built around a court; also : a narrow street with dwellings converted from stables

Mex abbr Mexican; Mexico

Mex·i·can \'mek-si-kən\ n : a native or inhabitant of Mexico — **Mexican** adj

mez·za·nine \'mez-ᵊn-ˌēn, ˌmez-ᵊn-'ēn\ n **1** : a low-ceilinged story between two main stories of a building **2** : the lowest balcony in a theater; also : the first few rows of such a balcony

mez·zo for·te \ˌmet-(ˌ)sō-'fȯr-ˌtā, ˌmed-(ˌ)zō-, -tē\ adj or adv [It] : moderately loud — used as a direction in music

mez·zo pia·no \-pē-'ä-(ˌ)nō\ adj or adv [It] : moderately soft — used as a direction in music

mez·zo–so·pra·no \-sə-'pra-nō, -'prä-\ n : a woman's voice having a range between that of the soprano and contralto; also : a singer having such a voice

MFA abbr master of fine arts

mfr abbr manufacture; manufacturer

mg abbr milligram

Mg symbol magnesium

MG abbr **1** machine gun **2** major general **3** military government

mgr abbr **1** manager **2** monseigneur **3** monsignor

mgt or **mgmt** abbr management

MGy Sgt abbr master gunnery sergeant

MHz abbr megahertz

mi abbr **1** mile; mileage **2** mill

MI abbr **1** Michigan **2** military intelligence

MIA \ˌem-(ˌ)ī-'ā\ n [missing in action] : a member of the armed forces whose whereabouts following a combat mission are unknown

Mi·ami \mī-'a-mē, -mə\ n, pl **Miami** or **Mi·am·is** : a member of an American Indian people orig. of Wisconsin and Indiana

mi·as·ma \mī-'az-mə, mē-\ n, pl **-mas** also **-ma·ta** \-mə-tə\ **1** : a vapor from a swamp formerly believed to cause disease **2** : a harmful influence or atmosphere — **mi·as·mal** \-məl\ adj — **mi·as·mic** \-mik\ adj

Mic abbr Micah

mi·ca \'mī-kə\ n [NL, fr. L, grain, crumb] : any of various mineral silicates readily separable into thin transparent sheets

Mi·cah \'mī-kə\ n — see BIBLE table

mice pl of MOUSE

Mich abbr Michigan

Mi·che·as \'mī-kē-əs, mī-'kē-əs\ n : MICAH

Mic·mac \'mik-ˌmak\ n, pl **Micmac** or **Micmacs** : a member of an American Indian people of eastern Canada

micr- or **micro-** comb form **1** : small : minute ⟨microcapsule⟩ **2** : one millionth part of a specified unit ⟨microsecond⟩

¹mi·cro \'mī-krō\ adj **1** : very small; esp : MICROSCOPIC **2** : involving minute quantities or variations

²micro n : MICROCOMPUTER

mi·crobe \'mī-ˌkrōb\ n : MICROORGANISM; esp : one causing disease — **mi·cro·bi·al** \mī-'krō-bē-əl\ adj

mi·cro·bi·ol·o·gy \ˌmī-krō-bī-'ä-lə-jē\ n : a branch of biology dealing esp. with microscopic forms of life — **mi·cro·bi·o·log·i·cal** \-bī-ə-'lä-ji-kəl\ adj — **mi·cro·bi·ol·o·gist** \-bī-'ä-lə-jist\ n

mi·cro·brew·ery \'mī-krō-ˌbrü-ə-rē\ n : a small brewery making specialty beer in limited quantities

mi·cro·burst \-ˌbərst\ n : a violent short-lived localized downdraft that creates extreme wind shears at low altitudes

mi·cro·cap·sule \'mī-krō-ˌkap-səl, -ˌsül\ n : a tiny capsule containing material (as a medicine) released when the capsule is broken, melted, or dissolved

mi·cro·chip \-ˌchip\ n : INTEGRATED CIRCUIT

mi·cro·cir·cuit \-ˌsər-kət\ n : a compact electronic circuit

mi·cro·com·put·er \-kəm-ˌpyü-tər\ n : a very small computer that uses a microprocessor

mi·cro·cosm \'mī-krə-ˌkä-zəm\ n : an individual or community thought of as a miniature world or universe

mi·cro·elec·tron·ics \ˌmī-krō-i-ˌlek-'trä-niks\ n : a branch of electronics that deals with the miniaturization of electronic circuits and components — **mi·cro·elec·tron·ic** \-nik\ adj

mi·cro·en·cap·su·late \ˌmī-krō-in-'kap-sə-ˌlāt\ vb : to enclose (as a drug) in a microcapsule — **mi·cro·en·cap·su·la·tion** \-in-ˌkap-sə-'lā-shən\ n

mi·cro·fiche \'mī-krō-ˌfēsh, -ˌfish\ n, pl **-fiche** or **-fiches** \same or -ˌfē-shəz, -ˌfi-\ : a sheet of microfilm containing rows of images of pages of printed matter

mi·cro·film \-ˌfilm\ n : a film bearing a photographic record (as of print) on a reduced scale — **microfilm** vb

mi·cro·graph \'mī-krə-ˌgraf\ n : a graphic reproduction of the image of an object formed by a microscope

mi·cro·me·te·or·ite \ˌmī-krō-'mē-tē-ə-ˌrīt\ n : a very small particle in interplanetary space

mi·crom·e·ter \mī-'krä-mə-tər\ n : an instrument used with a telescope or microscope for measuring minute distances

mi·cro·min·ia·tur·iza·tion \ˌmī-kro-ˌmi-nē-ə-ˌchùr-ə-'zā-shən, -ˌmi-ni-ˌchùr-, -chər-\ n : the process of

METRIC SYSTEM[1]

		LENGTH	
unit	abbreviation	number of meters	approximate U.S. equivalent
kilometer	km	1,000	0.62 mile
hectometer	hm	100	328.08 feet
dekameter	dam	10	32.81 feet
meter	m	1	39.37 inches
decimeter	dm	0.1	3.94 inches
centimeter	cm	0.01	0.39 inch
millimeter	mm	0.001	0.039 inch

		AREA	
unit	abbreviation	number of square meters	approximate U.S. equivalent
square kilometer	sq km or km2	1,000,000	0.3861 square mile
hectare	ha	10,000	2.47 acres
are	a	100	119.60 square yards
square centimeter	sq cm or cm2	0.0001	0.155 square inch

		VOLUME	
unit	abbreviation	number of cubic meters	approximate U.S. equivalent
cubic meter	m3	1	1.307 cubic yards
cubic decimeter	dm3	0.001	61.023 cubic inches
cubic centimeter	cu cm or cm3 also cc	0.000001	0.061 cubic inch

		CAPACITY			
unit	abbreviation	number of liters	approximate U.S. equivalent		
			cubic	dry	liquid
kiloliter	kl	1,000	1.31 cubic yards		
hectoliter	hl	100	3.53 cubic feet	2.84 bushels	
dekaliter	dal	10	0.35 cubic foot	1.14 pecks	2.64 gallons
liter	l	1	61.02 cubic inches	0.908 quart	1.057 quarts
deciliter	dl	0.1	6.1 cubic inches	0.18 pint	0.21 pint
centiliter	cl	0.01	0.61 cubic inch		0.338 fluid ounce
milliliter	ml	0.001	0.061 cubic inch		0.27 fluid dram

		MASS AND WEIGHT	
unit	abbreviation	number of grams	approximate U.S. equivalent
metric ton	t	1,000,000	1.102 short tons
kilogram	kg	1,000	2.2046 pounds
hectogram	hg	100	3.527 ounces
dekagram	dag	10	0.353 ounce
gram	g	1	0.035 ounce
decigram	dg	0.1	1.543 grains
centigram	cg	0.01	0.154 grain
milligram	mg	0.001	0.015 grain

[1]For metric equivalents of U.S. units see Weights and Measures table

producing things in a very small size and esp. in a size smaller than one considered miniature — **mi•cro•min•ia•tur•ized** \-'mi-nē-ə-chə-ˌrīzd, -'mi-ni-chə-\ *adj*
mi•cron \'mī-ˌkrän\ *n,* : one millionth of a meter
mi•cro•or•gan•ism \ˌmī-krō-'ȯr-gə-ˌni-zəm\ *n* : an organism (as a bacterium) too tiny to be seen by the unaided eye
mi•cro•phone \'mī-krə-ˌfōn\ *n* : an instrument for converting sound waves into variations of an electric current for transmitting or recording sound
mi•cro•pho•to•graph \ˌmī-krə-'fō-tə-ˌgraf \ *n* : PHOTOMICROGRAPH
mi•cro•pro•ces•sor \ˌmī-krō-'prä-ˌse-sər\ *n* : a computer processor contained on a microchip
mi•cro•scope \'mī-krə-ˌskōp\ *n* : an instrument for making magnified images of minute objects usu. using light — **mi•cros•co•py** \mī-'kräs-kə-pē\ *n*
mi•cro•scop•ic \ˌmī-krə-'skä-pik\ *also* **mi•cro•scop•i•cal** \-pi-kəl\ *adj* 1 : of, relating to, or involving the use of the microscope 2 : too tiny to be seen without the use of a microscope : very small — **mi•cro•scop•i•cal•ly** \-pi-k(ə-)lē\ *adv*
mi•cro•sec•ond \'mī-krō-ˌse-kənd\ *n* : one millionth of a second
mi•cro•sur•gery \ˌmī-krō-'sər-jə-rē\ *n* : minute dissection or manipulation (as by a laser beam) of living structures or tissue — **mi•cro•sur•gi•cal** \-'sər-ji-kəl\ *adj*

¹mi•cro•wave \'mī-krə-ˌwāv\ *n* 1 : a radio wave between one millimeter and one meter in wavelength 2 : MICROWAVE OVEN
²microwave *vb* : to heat or cook in a microwave oven — **mi•cro•wav•able** *or* **mi•cro•wave•able** \ˌmī-krə-'wā-və-bəl\ *adj*
microwave oven *n* : an oven in which food is cooked by the absorption of microwave energy by water molecules in the food
¹mid \'mid\ *adj* : MIDDLE
²mid *abbr* middle
mid•air \'mid-'ar\ *n* : a point or region in the air well above the ground
mid•day \'mid-ˌdā, -'dā\ *n* : NOON
mid•den \'mid-ᵊn\ *n* : a refuse heap
¹mid•dle \'mid-ᵊl\ *adj* 1 : equally distant from the extremes : MEDIAL, CENTRAL 2 : being at neither extreme : INTERMEDIATE 3 *cap* : constituting an intermediate period
²middle *n* 1 : a middle part, point, or position 2 : WAIST
middle age *n* : the period of life from about 40 to about 60 — **mid•dle–aged** \ˌmid-ᵊl-'ājd\ *adj*
Middle Ages *n pl* : the period of European history from about A.D. 500 to about 1500
mid•dle•brow \'mid-ᵊl-ˌbraȯ\ *n* : a person who is moderately but not highly cultivated — **middlebrow** *adj*
middle class *n* : a social class holding a position be-

tween the upper class and the lower class — **middle–class** *adj*

middle ear *n* : a small membrane-lined cavity of the ear through which sound waves are transmitted by a chain of tiny bones

middle finger *n* : the midmost of the five digits of the hand

mid·dle·man \'mid-ᵊl-ˌman\ *n* : INTERMEDIARY; *esp* : one intermediate between the producer of goods and the retailer or consumer

middle–of–the–road *adj* : standing for or following a course of action midway between extremes; *esp* : being neither liberal nor conservative in politics — **mid·dle–of–the–road·er** \-'rō-dər\ *n* — **mid·dle–of–the–road·ism** \-'rō-ˌdi-zəm\ *n*

middle school *n* : a school usu. including grades 5 to 8 or 6 to 8

mid·dle·weight \'mid-ᵊl-ˌwāt\ *n* : one of average weight; *esp* : a boxer weighing more than 147 but not over 160 pounds

mid·dling \'mid-liŋ, -lən\ *adj* **1** : of middle, medium, or moderate size, degree, or quality **2** : MEDIOCRE

mid·dy \'mi-dē\ *n, pl* **middies** : MIDSHIPMAN

midge \'mij\ *n* : a very small fly : GNAT

midg·et \'mi-jət\ *n* **1** : a very small person **2** : something (as an animal) very small for its kind

midi \'mi-dē\ *n* : a calf-length dress, coat, or skirt

mid·land \'mid-lənd, -ˌland\ *n* : the interior or central region of a country

mid·life \'mid-'līf\ *n* : MIDDLE AGE

midlife crisis *n* : a period of emotional turmoil in middle age characterized esp. by a strong desire for change

mid·most \-ˌmōst\ *adj* : being in or near the exact middle — **midmost** *adv*

mid·night \-ˌnīt\ *n* : 12 o'clock at night

mid·point \'mid-ˌpȯint, -'pȯint\ *n* : a point at or near the center or middle

mid·riff \'mi-ˌdrif\ *n* [ME *midrif*, fr. OE *midhrif*, fr. *midde* mid + *hrif* belly] **1** : DIAPHRAGM 1 **2** : the mid≠ region of the human torso

mid·sec·tion \-ˌsek-shən\ *n* : a section midway between the extremes; *esp* : MIDRIFF 2

mid·ship·man \'mid-ˌship-mən, (ˌ)mid-'ship-\ *n* : a student in a naval academy

mid·ships \-ˌships\ *adv* : AMIDSHIPS

midst \'midst\ *n* **1** : the interior or central part or point **2** : a position of proximity to the members of a group ⟨in our ∼⟩ **3** : the condition of being surrounded or beset — **midst** *prep*

mid·stream \'mid-'strēm, -ˌstrēm\ *n* : the middle of a stream

mid·sum·mer \-'sə-mər, -ˌsə-\ *n* **1** : the middle of summer **2** : the summer solstice

mid·town \'mid-ˌtaun, -'taun\ *n* : a central section of a city; *esp* : one situated between sections called *downtown* and *uptown* — **midtown** *adj*

¹mid·way \'mid-ˌwā, -'wā\ *adv* : in the middle of the way or distance

²mid·way \-ˌwā\ *n* : an avenue (as at a carnival) for concessions and amusements

mid·week \-ˌwēk\ *n* : the middle of the week — **mid·week·ly** \-ˌwē-klē, -'wē-\ *adj or adv*

mid·wife \'mid-ˌwīf\ *n* : a person who helps women in childbirth — **mid·wife·ry** \-ˌwī-fə-rē\ *n*

mid·win·ter \'mid-'win-tər, -ˌwin-\ *n* **1** : the winter solstice **2** : the middle of winter

mid·year \-ˌyir\ *n* **1** : the middle of a year **2** : a midyear examination — **midyear** *adj*

mien \'mēn\ *n* **1** : air or bearing esp. as expressive of mood or personality : DEMEANOR **2** : APPEARANCE, ASPECT

miff \'mif\ *vb* : to put into an ill humor

¹might \'mīt\ *past of* MAY — used as an auxiliary to express permission or possibility in the past, a present condition contrary to fact, less probability or possi-

bility than *may*, or as a polite alternative to *may*, *ought*, or *should*

²might *n* : the power, authority, or resources of an individual or a group

mighty \'mī-tē\ *adj* **might·i·er; -est** **1** : very strong : POWERFUL **2** : GREAT, NOTABLE — **might·i·ly** \'mī-tə-lē\ *adv* — **might·i·ness** \-tē-nəs\ *n* — **mighty** *adv*

mi·gnon·ette \ˌmin-yə-'net\ *n* : an annual garden herb with spikes of tiny fragrant flowers

mi·graine \'mī-ˌgrān\ *n* [F, fr. LL *hemicrania* pain in one side of the head, fr. Gk *hēmikrania*, fr. *hēmi-* half + *kranion* cranium] : a condition marked by recurrent severe headache and often nausea; *also* : an attack of migraine

mi·grant \'mī-grənt\ *n* : one that migrates; *esp* : a person who moves in order to find work (as picking crops) — **migrant** *adj*

mi·grate \'mī-ˌgrāt\ *vb* **mi·grat·ed; mi·grat·ing** **1** : to move from one country or place to another **2** : to pass usu. periodically from one region or climate to another for feeding or breeding — **mi·gra·tion** \mī-'grā-shən\ *n* — **mi·gra·to·ry** \'mī-grə-ˌtōr-ē\ *adj*

mi·ka·do \mə-'kä-dō\ *n, pl* **-dos** : an emperor of Japan

mike \'mīk\ *n* : MICROPHONE

¹mil \'mil\ *n* : a unit of length equal to ¹⁄₁₀₀₀ inch

²mil *abbr* military

milch \'milk, 'milch\ *adj* : giving milk ⟨∼ cow⟩

mild \'mīld\ *adj* **1** : gentle in nature or behavior **2** : moderate in action or effect **3** : TEMPERATE **syn** easy, complaisant, amiable, lenient — **mild·ly** *adv* — **mild·ness** *n*

mil·dew \'mil-ˌdü, -ˌdyü\ *n* : a superficial usu. whitish growth produced on organic matter and on plants by a fungus; *also* : a fungus producing this growth — **mildew** *vb*

mile \'mīl\ *n* [ME, fr. OE *mīl*, fr. L *milia* miles, fr. *milia passuum*, lit., thousands of paces] **1** — see WEIGHT table **2** : NAUTICAL MILE

mile·age \'mī-lij\ *n* **1** : an allowance for traveling expenses at a certain rate per mile **2** : distance in miles traveled (as in a day) **3** : the amount of service yielded (as by a tire) expressed in terms of miles of travel **4** : the average number of miles a car will travel on a gallon of gasoline

mile·post \'mīl-ˌpōst\ *n* : a post indicating the distance in miles from a given point

mile·stone \-ˌstōn\ *n* **1** : a stone serving as a milepost **2** : a significant point in development

mi·lieu \mēl-'yər, -'yü, -'yœ\ *n, pl* **mi·lieus** *or* **mi·lieux** \same *or* -'yərz, -'yüz, -'yœz\ [F] : ENVIRONMENT, SETTING

mil·i·tant \'mi-lə-tənt\ *adj* **1** : engaged in warfare **2** : aggressively active esp. in a cause — **mil·i·tance** \-təns\ *n* — **mil·i·tan·cy** \-tən-sē\ *n* — **militant** *n* — **mil·i·tant·ly** *adv*

mil·i·ta·rise *Brit var of* MILITARIZE

mil·i·ta·rism \'mi-lə-tə-ˌri-zəm\ *n* **1** : predominance of the military class or its ideals **2** : a policy of aggressive military preparedness — **mil·i·ta·rist** \-rist\ *n* — **mil·i·ta·ris·tic** \ˌmi-lə-tə-'ris-tik\ *adj*

mil·i·ta·rize \'mi-lə-tə-ˌrīz\ *vb* **-rized; -riz·ing** **1** : to equip with military forces and defenses **2** : to give a military character to

¹mil·i·tary \'mi-lə-ˌter-ē\ *adj* **1** : of or relating to soldiers, arms, war, or the army **2** : performed by armed forces; *also* : supported by armed force **syn** martial, warlike — **mil·i·tar·i·ly** \ˌmi-lə-'ter-ə-lē\ *adv*

²military *n, pl* **military** *also* **mil·i·tar·ies** **1** : the military, naval, and air forces of a nation **2** : military persons

mil·i·tate \'mi-lə-ˌtāt\ *vb* **-tat·ed; -tat·ing** : to have weight or effect

mi·li·tia \mə-'li-shə\ *n* : a part of the organized armed forces of a country liable to call only in emergency — **mi·li·tia·man** \-mən\ *n*

¹milk \'milk\ *n* **1** : a nutritive usu. whitish fluid secreted

by female mammals for feeding their young **2** : a milk-like liquid (as a plant juice) — **milk·i·ness** \'mil-kē-nəs\ *n* — **milky** *adj*

²milk *vb* **1** : to draw off the milk of ⟨∼ a cow⟩ **2** : to draw something from as if by milking

milk·maid \'milk-ˌmād\ *n* : DAIRYMAID

milk·man \-ˌman, -mən\ *n* : a person who sells or delivers milk

milk of magnesia : a milk-white mixture of hydroxide of magnesium and water used as an antacid and laxative

milk shake *n* : a thoroughly blended drink made of milk, a flavoring syrup, and often ice cream

milk·sop \'milk-ˌsäp\ *n* : an unmanly man

milk·weed \-ˌwēd\ *n* : any of a genus of herbs with milky juice and clustered flowers

Milky Way *n* **1** : a broad irregular band of light that stretches across the sky and is caused by the light of a very great number of faint stars **2** : MILKY WAY GALAXY

Milky Way galaxy *n* : the galaxy of which the sun is a member and which includes the stars that comprise the Milky Way

¹mill \'mil\ *n* **1** : a building with machinery for grinding grain into flour **2** : a machine used in processing (as by grinding, stamping, cutting, or finishing) raw material **3** : FACTORY

²mill *vb* **1** : to process in a mill **2** : to move in a circle or in an eddying mass

³mill *n* : one tenth of a cent

mill·age \'mi-lij\ *n* : a rate (as of taxation) expressed in mills

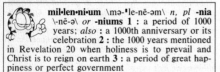

mil·len·ni·um \mə-'le-nē-əm\ *n, pl* **-nia** \-nē-ə\ *or* **-niums 1** : a period of 1000 years; *also* : a 1000th anniversary or its celebration **2** : the 1000 years mentioned in Revelation 20 when holiness is to prevail and Christ is to reign on earth **3** : a period of great happiness or perfect government

mill·er \'mi-lər\ *n* **1** : one that operates a mill and esp. a flour mill **2** : any of various moths having powdery wings

mil·let \'mi-lət\ *n* : any of several small-seeded cereal and forage grasses cultivated for grain or hay; *also* : the grain of a millet

mil·li·am·pere \ˌmi-lē-'am-ˌpir\ *n* : one thousandth of an ampere

mil·liard \'mil-ˌyärd, 'mi-lē-ärd\ *n, Brit* : a thousand millions

mil·li·bar \'mi-lə-ˌbär\ *n* : a unit of atmospheric pressure

mil·li·gram \-ˌgram\ *n* — see METRIC SYSTEM table

mil·li·li·ter \-ˌlē-tər\ *n* — see METRIC SYSTEM table

mil·lime \mə-'lēm\ *n* — see *dinar* at MONEY table

mil·li·me·ter \'mi-lə-ˌmē-tər\ *n* — see METRIC SYSTEM table

mil·li·ner \'mi-lə-nər\ *n* [irreg. fr. *Milan*, Italy; fr. the importation of women's finery from Italy in the 16th century] : a person who designs, makes, trims, or sells women's hats

mil·li·nery \'mi-lə-ˌner-ē\ *n* **1** : women's apparel for the head **2** : the business or work of a milliner

mill·ing \'mi-liŋ\ *n* : a corrugated edge on a coin

mil·lion \'mil-yən\ *n, pl* **millions** *or* **million** : a thousand thousands — **million** *adj* — **mil·lionth** \-yənth\ *adj or n*

mil·lion·aire \ˌmil-yə-'ner, 'mil-yə-ˌner\ *n* : one whose wealth is estimated at a million or more (as of dollars or pounds)

mil·li·pede \'mi-lə-ˌpēd\ *n* : any of a class of arthropods related to the centipedes and having a long segmented body with a hard covering, two pairs of legs on most segments, and no poison fangs

mil·li·sec·ond \-se-kənd\ *n* : one thousandth of a second

mil·li·volt \-ˌvōlt\ *n* : one thousandth of a volt

mill·pond \'mil-ˌpänd\ *n* : a pond made by damming a stream to produce a fall of water for operating a mill

mill·race \-ˌrās\ *n* : a canal in which water flows to and from a mill wheel

mill·stone \-ˌstōn\ *n* : either of two round flat stones used for grinding grain

mill·stream \-ˌstrēm\ *n* : a stream whose flow is used to run a mill; *also* : the stream in a millrace

mill wheel *n* : a waterwheel that drives a mill

mill·wright \'mil-ˌrit\ *n* : a person who builds mills or sets up or maintains their machinery

milt \'milt\ *n* : the sperm-containing fluid of a male fish

mime \'mīm\ *n* **1** : MIMIC **2** : PANTOMIME — **mime** *vb*

mim·eo·graph \'mi-mē-ə-ˌgraf\ *n* : a machine for making many copies by means of a stencil through which ink is pressed — **mimeograph** *vb*

mi·me·sis \mə-'mē-səs, mī-\ *n* : IMITATION, MIMICRY

mi·met·ic \-'me-tik\ *adj* **1** : IMITATIVE **2** : relating to, characterized by, or exhibiting mimicry

¹mim·ic \'mi-mik\ *n* : one that mimics

²mimic *vb* **mim·icked** \-mikt\; **mim·ick·ing 1** : to imitate closely **2** : to ridicule by imitation **3** : to resemble by biological mimicry

mim·ic·ry \'mi-mi-krē\ *n, pl* **-ries 1** : an instance of mimicking **2** : a superficial resemblance of one organism to another or to natural objects among which it lives that gives it an advantage (as protection from predation)

mi·mo·sa \mə-'mō-sə, mī-, -zə\ *n* : any of a genus of leguminous trees, shrubs, and herbs of warm regions with ball-shaped heads of small white or pink flowers

min *abbr* **1** minim **2** minimum **3** mining **4** minister **5** minor **6** minute

min·a·ret \ˌmi-nə-'ret\ *n* [F, fr. Turk *minare*, fr. Ar *manārah* lighthouse] : a tall slender tower of a mosque from which a muezzin calls the faithful to prayer

mi·na·to·ry \'mi-nə-ˌtōr-ē, 'mī-\ *adj* : THREATENING, MENACING

mince \'mins\ *vb* **minced; minc·ing 1** : to cut into very small pieces **2** : to restrain (words) within the bounds of decorum **3** : to walk in a prim affected manner

mince·meat \'mins-ˌmēt\ *n* : a finely chopped mixture

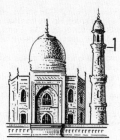

1 minaret

esp. of raisins, apples, spices, and often meat used as a filling for a pie

¹**mind** \'mīnd\ *n* **1 :** MEMORY **2 :** the part of an individual that feels, perceives, thinks, wills, and esp. reasons **3 :** INTENTION, DESIRE **4 :** normal mental condition **5 :** OPINION, VIEW **6 :** MOOD **7 :** mental qualities of a person or group **8 :** intellectual ability

²**mind** *vb* **1** *chiefly dial* **:** REMEMBER **2 :** to attend to closely **3 :** HEED, OBEY **4 :** to be concerned about; *also* **:** DISLIKE **5 :** to be careful or cautious **6 :** to take charge of **7 :** to regard with attention

mind–bend·ing \'mīnd-₁ben-diŋ\ *adj* **:** MIND-BLOWING

mind–blow·ing \-₁blō-iŋ\ *adj* **:** PSYCHEDELIC 1; *also* **:** MIND-BOGGLING

mind–bog·gling \-₁bä-gə-liŋ\ *adj* **:** mentally or emotionally exciting or overwhelming

mind·ed \'mīn-dəd\ *adj* **1 :** INCLINED, DISPOSED **2 :** having a mind of a specified kind or concerned with a specific thing — usu. used in combination 〈narrow*minded*〉

mind·ful \'mīnd-fəl\ *adj* **:** bearing in mind **:** AWARE — **mind·ful·ly** *adv* — **mind·ful·ness** *n*

mind·less \-ləs\ *adj* **1 :** marked by a lack of mind or consciousness; *esp* **:** marked by no use of the intellect **2 :** not mindful **:** HEEDLESS — **mind·less·ly** *adv* — **mind·less·ness** *n*

¹**mine** \'mīn\ *pron* **:** that which belongs to me

²**mine** *n* **1 :** an excavation in the earth from which minerals are taken; *also* **:** an ore deposit **2 :** an underground passage beneath an enemy position **3 :** an explosive device for destroying enemy personnel, vehicles, or ships **4 :** a rich source of supply

³**mine** *vb* **mined; min·ing 1 :** to dig a mine **2 :** UNDERMINE **3 :** to get ore from the earth **4 :** to place military mines in — **min·er** *n*

mine·field \'mīn-₁fēld\ *n* **1 :** an area set with mines **2 :** something resembling a minefield esp. in having many dangers

mine·lay·er \-₁lā-ər\ *n* **:** a naval vessel for laying underwater mines

min·er·al \'mi-nə-rəl\ *n* **1 :** a crystalline substance (as diamond or quartz) of inorganic origin **2 :** a naturally occurring substance (as coal, salt, or water) obtained usu. from the ground — **mineral** *adj*

min·er·al·ise *Brit var of* MINERALIZE

min·er·al·ize \'mi-nə-rə-₁līz\ *vb* **-ized; -iz·ing 1 :** to impregnate or supply with minerals **2 :** to change into mineral form — **min·er·al·i·za·tion** \-rə-lə-'zā-shən\ *n*

min·er·al·o·gy \₁mi-nə-'rä-lə-jē, -'ra-\ *n* **:** a science dealing with minerals — **min·er·al·og·i·cal** \₁mi-nə-rə-'lä-ji-kəl\ *adj* — **min·er·al·o·gist** \₁mi-nə-'rä-lə-jist, -'ra-\ *n*

mineral oil *n* **:** an oil of mineral origin; *esp* **:** a refined petroleum oil used as a laxative

mineral water *n* **:** water infused with mineral salts or gases

min·e·stro·ne \₁mi-nə-'strō-nē, -'strön\ *n* [It, fr. *minestra*, fr. *minestrare* to serve, dish up, fr. L *ministrare*, fr. *minister* servant] **:** a rich thick vegetable soup

mine·sweep·er \'mīn-₁swē-pər\ *n* **:** a warship designed for removing or neutralizing underwater mines

min·gle \'miŋ-gəl\ *vb* **min·gled; min·gling 1 :** to bring or combine together **:** MIX **2 :** ASSOCIATE; *also* **:** to move about (as in a group)

ming tree \'miŋ-\ *n* **:** a dwarfed usu. evergreen tree grown as bonsai; *also* **:** an artificial plant resembling this

mini \'mi-nē\ *n, pl* **min·is :** something small of its kind — **mini** *adj*

mini- *comb form* **:** smaller or briefer than usual, normal, or standard

min·ia·ture \'mi-nē-ə-₁chùr, 'mi-ni-₁chùr, -chər\ *n* [It *miniatura* art of illuminating a manuscript, fr. ML, fr. L *miniare* to color with red lead, fr. *minium* red lead] **1 :** a copy on a much reduced scale; *also* **:** something small of its kind **2 :** a small painting (as on ivory or metal) — **miniature** *adj* — **min·ia·tur·ist** \-₁chùr-ist, -chər-\ *n*

min·ia·tur·ize \'mi-nē-ə-₁chə-₁rīz, 'mi-ni-\ *vb* **-ized; -iz·ing :** to design or construct in small size — **min·ia·tur·i·za·tion** \₁mi-nē-ə-₁chùr-ə-¹zā-shən, ₁mi-ni-, -chər-\ *n*

mini·bar \'mi-nē-₁bär\ *n* **:** a small refrigerator in a hotel room that is stocked with beverages and snacks

mini·bike \'mi-nē-₁bīk\ *n* **:** a small one-passenger motorcycle

mini·bus \-₁bəs\ *n* **:** a small bus or van

mini·com·put·er \-kəm-₁pyü-tər\ *n* **:** a computer between a mainframe and a microcomputer in size and speed

min·im \'mi-nəm\ *n* — see WEIGHT table

min·i·mal \'mi-nə-məl\ *adj* **1 :** relating to or being a

minimum : LEAST **2** : of or relating to minimalism or minimal art — **min·i·mal·ly** *adv*

minimal art *n* : abstract art consisting primarily of simple geometric forms executed in an impersonal style — **minimal artist** *n*

min·i·mal·ism \\'mi-nə-mə-₁li-zəm\\ *n* : MINIMAL ART; *also* : a style (as in music or literature) marked by extreme spareness or simplicity — **min·i·mal·ist** \\-list\\ *n*

min·i·mise *Brit var of* MINIMIZE

min·i·mize \\'mi-nə-₁mīz\\ *vb* **-mized; -miz·ing 1** : to reduce or keep to a minimum **2** : to underestimate intentionally; *also* : BELITTLE **syn** depreciate, decry, disparage

min·i·mum \\'mi-nə-məm\\ *n, pl* **-ma** \\-mə\\ *or* **-mums 1** : the least quantity assignable, admissible, or possible **2** : the least of a set of numbers **3** : the lowest degree or amount of variation (as of temperature) reached or recorded — **minimum** *adj*

min·ion \\'min-yən\\ *n* [MF *mignon* darling] **1** : a servile dependent, follower, or underling **2** : one highly favored **3** : a subordinate official

min·is·cule \\'mi-nəs-₁kyül\\ *var of* MINUSCULE

mini·se·ries \\'mi-nē-₁sir-ēz\\ *n* : a television story presented in sequential episodes

mini·skirt \\-₁skərt\\ *n* : a skirt with the hemline several inches above the knee

¹min·is·ter \\'mi-nə-stər\\ *n* **1** : AGENT **2** : a member of the clergy esp. of a Protestant communion **3** : a high officer of state who heads a division of governmental activities **4** : a diplomatic representative to a foreign state — **min·is·te·ri·al** \\₁mi-nə-'stir-ē-əl\\ *adj*

²minister *vb* **1** : to perform the functions of a minister of religion **2** : to give aid or service — **min·is·tra·tion** \\₁mi-nə-'strā-shən\\ *n*

¹min·is·trant \\'mi-nə-strənt\\ *adj, archaic* : performing service as a minister

²ministrant *n* : one that ministers

min·is·try \\'mi-nə-strē\\ *n, pl* **-tries 1** : MINISTRATION **2** : the office, duties, or functions of a minister; *also* : the period of service or office **3** : CLERGY **4** : AGENCY **5** *often cap* : the body of ministers governing a nation or state; *also* : a government department headed by a minister

mini·van \\'mi-nē-₁van\\ *n* : a small van

mink \\'miŋk\\ *n, pl* **mink** *or* **minks** : either of two slender mammals resembling the related weasels; *also* : the soft lustrous typically dark brown fur of a mink

mink

Minn *abbr* Minnesota

min·ne·sing·er \\'mi-ni-₁siŋ-ər, -₁ziŋ-\\ *n* [G, fr. Middle High German, fr. *minne* love + *singer* singer] : any of a class of German lyric poets and musicians of the 12th to the 14th centuries

min·now \\'mi-nō\\ *n, pl* **minnows** *also* **minnow** : any of numerous small freshwater fishes

¹mi·nor \\'mī-nər\\ *adj* **1** : inferior in importance, size, or degree **2** : not having reached majority **3** : having the third, sixth, and sometimes the seventh degrees lowered by a half step (~ scale); *also* : based on a minor scale (~ key) **4** : not serious (~ illness)

²minor *n* **1** : a person who has not attained majority **2** : a subject of academic study chosen as a secondary field of specialization

³minor *vb* : to pursue an academic minor

mi·nor·i·ty \\mə-'nòr-ə-tē, mī-\\ *n, pl* **-ties 1** : the period

or state of being a minor **2** : the smaller in number of two groups; *esp* : a group having less than the number of votes necessary for control **3** : a part of a population differing from others (as in race); *also* : a member of a minority

mi·nox·i·dil \\mə-'näk-sə-₁dil\\ *n* : a drug used orally to treat hypertension and topically in solution to promote hair regrowth in some forms of baldness

min·ster \\'min-stər\\ *n* : a large or important church

min·strel \\'min-strəl\\ *n* **1** : a medieval singer of verses; *also* : MUSICIAN, POET **2** : any of a group of performers usu. with blackened faces in a program of black American songs, jokes, and impersonations (a ~ show)

min·strel·sy \\-sē\\ *n* : the singing and playing of a minstrel; *also* : a body of minstrels

¹mint \\'mint\\ *n* **1** : any of a large family of square-stemmed herbs and shrubs; *esp* : one (as spearmint) that is fragrant and is the source of a flavoring oil **2** : a mint-flavored piece of candy — **minty** *adj*

²mint *n* **1** : a place where coins are made **2** : a vast sum — **mint** *vb* — **mint·age** \\-ij\\ *n* — **mint·er** *n*

³mint *adj* : unmarred as if fresh from a mint (in ~ condition)

min·u·end \\'min-yə-₁wend\\ *n* : a number from which another is to be subtracted

min·u·et \\₁min-yə-'wet\\ *n* : a slow graceful dance

¹mi·nus \\'mī-nəs\\ *prep* **1** : diminished by : LESS (7 ~ 3 equals 4) **2** : LACKING, WITHOUT (~ his hat)

²minus *n* : a negative quantity or quality

³minus *adj* **1** : algebraically negative (~ quantity) **2** : having negative qualities

mi·nus·cule \\'mi-nəs-₁kyül\\ *n* : a lowercase letter

²minuscule *adj* : very small

minus sign *n* : a sign — used in mathematics to indicate subtraction or a negative quantity

¹min·ute \\'mi-nət\\ *n* **1** : a 60th part of an hour or of a degree : 60 seconds **2** : a short space of time **3** *pl* : the official record of the proceedings of a meeting

²mi·nute \\mī-'nüt, mə-, -'nyüt\\ *adj* **mi·nut·er; -est 1** : very small **2** : of little importance : TRIFLING **3** : marked by close attention to details **syn** diminutive, tiny, miniature, wee — **mi·nute·ly** *adv* — **mi·nute·ness** *n*

min·ute·man \\'mi-nət-₁man\\ *n* : a member of a group of armed men pledged to take the field at a minute's notice during and immediately before the American Revolution

mi·nu·tia \\mə-'nü-shə, -'nyü-, -shē-ə\\ *n, pl* **-ti·ae** \\-shē-₁ē\\ [L] : a minute or minor detail — usu. used in pl.

minx \\'miŋks\\ *n* : a pert girl

Mio·cene \\'mī-ə-₁sēn\\ *adj* : of, relating to, or being the epoch of the Tertiary between the Oligocene and the Pliocene — **Miocene** *n*

mir·a·cle \\'mir-i-kəl\\ *n* **1** : an extraordinary event manifesting divine intervention in human affairs **2** : an unusual event, thing, or accomplishment : WONDER, MARVEL — **mi·rac·u·lous** \\mə-'ra-kyə-ləs\\ *adj* — **mi·rac·u·lous·ly** *adv*

miracle drug *n* : a usu. newly discovered drug that elicits a dramatic response in a patient's condition

mi·rage \\mə-'räzh\\ *n* **1** : an illusion that often appears as a pool of water or a mirror in which distant objects are seen inverted, is sometimes seen at sea, in the desert, or over a hot pavement, and results from atmospheric conditions **2** : something illusory and unattainable

¹mire \\'mīr\\ *n* : heavy and often deep mud or slush — **miry** *adj*

²mire *vb* **mired; mir·ing** : to stick or sink in or as if in mire

¹mir·ror \\'mir-ər\\ *n* **1** : a polished or smooth surface (as of glass) that forms images by reflection **2** : a true representation

²mirror *vb* : to reflect in or as if in a mirror

mirth \\'mərth\\ *n* : gladness or gaiety accompanied

with laughter *syn* glee, jollity, hilarity, merriment — **mirth·ful** \-fəl\ *adj* — **mirth·ful·ly** *adv* — **mirth·ful·ness** *n* — **mirth·less** *adj*

MIRV \ˈmərv\ *n* [*multiple independently targeted reentry vehicle*] : an ICBM with multiple warheads that have different targets — **MIRV** *vb*

mis·ad·ven·ture \ˌmi-səd-ˈven-chər\ *n* : MISFORTUNE, MISHAP

mis·aligned \ˌmi-sə-ˈlīnd\ *adj* : not properly aligned — **mis·align·ment** \-ˈlīn-mənt\ *n*

mis·al·li·ance \ˌmi-sə-ˈlī-əns\ *n* : an improper or unsuitable marriage

mis·al·lo·ca·tion \ˌmi-ˌsa-lə-ˈkā-shən\ *n* : faulty or improper allocation

mis·an·thrope \ˈmis-ən-ˌthrōp\ *n* : one who hates mankind — **mis·an·throp·ic** \ˌmis-ən-ˈthrä-pik\ *adj* — **mis·an·throp·i·cal·ly** \-pi-k(ə-)lē\ *adv* — **mis·an·thro·py** \mi-ˈsan-thrə-pē\ *n*

mis·ap·ply \ˌmi-sə-ˈplī\ *vb* : to apply wrongly — **mis·ap·pli·ca·tion** \ˌmi-ˌsa-plə-ˈkā-shən\ *n*

mis·ap·pre·hend \ˌmi-ˌsa-pri-ˈhend\ *vb* : MISUNDERSTAND — **mis·ap·pre·hen·sion** \-ˈhen-chən\ *n*

mis·ap·pro·pri·ate \ˌmi-sə-ˈprō-prē-ˌāt\ *vb* : to appropriate wrongly (as by embezzlement) — **mis·ap·pro·pri·a·tion** \-ˌprō-prē-ˈā-shən\ *n*

mis·be·got·ten \-bi-ˈgät-ən\ *adj* : ILLEGITIMATE; *also* : ill-conceived

mis·be·have \ˌmis-bi-ˈhāv\ *vb* : to behave improperly — **mis·be·hav·er** *n* — **mis·be·hav·ior** \-ˈhā-vyər\ *n*

mis·be·liev·er \-bə-ˈlē-vər\ *n* : one who holds a false or unorthodox belief

mis·brand \mis-ˈbrand\ *vb* : to brand falsely or in a misleading manner

misc *abbr* miscellaneous

mis·cal·cu·late \mis-ˈkal-kyə-ˌlāt\ *vb* : to calculate wrongly — **mis·cal·cu·la·tion** \ˌmis-ˌkal-kyə-ˈlā-shən\ *n*

mis·call \mis-ˈkȯl\ *vb* : MISNAME

mis·car·riage \-ˈkar-ij\ *n* 1 : failure in the administration of justice 2 : spontaneous expulsion of a fetus before it is capable of independent life

mis·car·ry \-ˈkar-ē\ *vb* 1 : to have a miscarriage of a fetus 2 : to go wrong; *also* : to be unsuccessful

mis·ce·ge·na·tion \mi-se-jə-ˈnā-shən, ˌmi-si-jə-ˈnā-\ *n* [L *miscēre* to mix + *genus* race] : marriage or cohabitation between persons of different races

mis·cel·la·neous \ˌmi-sə-ˈlā-nē-əs\ *adj* 1 : consisting of diverse things or members 2 : having various traits; *also* : dealing with or interested in diverse subjects — **mis·cel·la·neous·ly** *adv* — **mis·cel·la·neous·ness** *n*

mis·cel·la·ny \ˈmi-sə-ˌlā-nē\ *n, pl* **-nies** 1 : a collection of writings on various subjects 2 : HODGEPODGE

mis·chance \mis-ˈchans\ *n* : bad luck; *also* : MISHAP

mis·chief \ˈmis-chəf\ *n* 1 : injury caused by a particular agent 2 : a source of harm or irritation 3 : action that annoys; *also* : MISCHIEVOUSNESS

mis·chie·vous \ˈmis-chə-vəs\ *adj* 1 : HARMFUL, INJURIOUS 2 : causing annoyance or minor injury 3 : irresponsibly playful — **mis·chie·vous·ly** *adv* — **mis·chie·vous·ness** *n*

mis·ci·ble \ˈmi-sə-bəl\ *adj* : capable of being mixed

mis·com·mu·ni·ca·tion \ˌmis-kə-ˌmyü-nə-ˈkā-shən\ *n* : failure to communicate clearly

mis·con·ceive \ˌmis-kən-ˈsēv\ *vb* : to interpret incorrectly — **mis·con·cep·tion** \-ˈsep-shən\ *n*

mis·con·duct \mis-ˈkän-(ˌ)dəkt\ *n* 1 : MISMANAGEMENT 2 : intentional wrongdoing 3 : improper behavior

mis·con·strue \ˌmis-kən-ˈstrü\ *vb* : MISINTERPRET — **mis·con·struc·tion** \-ˈstrək-shən\ *n*

mis·count \mis-ˈkau̇nt\ *vb* : to count incorrectly : MISCALCULATE

mis·cre·ant \ˈmis-krē-ənt\ *n* : one who behaves criminally or viciously — **miscreant** *adj*

mis·cue \mis-ˈkyü\ *n* : MISTAKE, ERROR — **miscue** *vb*

mis·deed \mis-ˈdēd\ *n* : a wrong deed

mis·de·mean·or \ˌmis-di-ˈmē-nər\ *n* 1 : a crime less serious than a felony 2 : MISDEED

mis·di·rect \ˌmis-də-ˈrekt, -dī-\ *vb* : to give a wrong direction to — **mis·di·rec·tion** \-ˈrek-shən\ *n*

mis·do·ing \mis-ˈdü-iŋ\ *n* : WRONGDOING — **mis·do** \-ˈdü\ *vb* — **mis·do·er** \-ˈdü-ər\ *n*

mise–en–scène \ˌmē-ˌzän-ˈsen, -ˈsän\ *n, pl* **mise–en–scènes** *same or* -ˈsenz, -ˈsänz\ [F] 1 : the arrangement of the scenery, property, and actors on a stage 2 : SETTING; *also* : ENVIRONMENT

mi·ser \ˈmī-zər\ *n* [L *miser* miserable] : a person who hoards and is stingy with money — **mi·ser·li·ness** \-lē-nəs\ *n* — **mi·ser·ly** *adj*

mis·er·a·ble \ˈmi-zə-rə-bəl, ˈmiz-rə-\ *adj* 1 : wretchedly deficient; *also* : causing extreme discomfort 2 : being in a state of distress 3 : SHAMEFUL — **mis·er·a·ble·ness** *n* — **mis·er·a·bly** \-blē\ *adv*

mis·ery \ˈmi-zə-rē\ *n, pl* **-er·ies** 1 : suffering and want caused by poverty or affliction 2 : a cause of suffering or discomfort 3 : emotional distress

mis·fea·sance \mis-ˈfēz-əns\ *n* : the performance of a lawful action in an illegal or improper manner

mis·file \-ˈfīl\ *vb* : to file in the wrong place

mis·fire \-ˈfīr\ *vb* 1 : to fail to fire 2 : to miss an intended effect — **misfire** *n*

mis·fit \ˈmis-ˌfit, *sense 1 also* mis-ˈfit\ *n* 1 : something that fits badly 2 : one who is poorly adjusted to a situation or environment

mis·for·tune \mis-ˈfȯr-chən\ *n* 1 : bad luck 2 : an unfortunate condition or event

mis·giv·ing \-ˈgi-viŋ\ *n* : a feeling of doubt or suspicion esp. concerning a future event

mis·gov·ern \-ˈgə-vərn\ *vb* : to govern badly — **mis·gov·ern·ment** *n*

mis·guid·ance \mis-ˈgīd-əns\ *n* : faulty guidance — **mis·guide** \-ˈgīd\ *vb*

mis·guid·ed \-ˈgī-dəd\ *adj* : led or prompted by wrong or inappropriate motives or ideals — **mis·guid·ed·ly** *adv*

mis·han·dle \-ˈhand-əl\ *vb* 1 : MALTREAT 2 : to manage wrongly

mis·hap \ˈmis-ˌhap\ *n* : an unfortunate accident

mish·mash \ˈmish-ˌmash, -ˌmäsh\ *n* : HODGEPODGE, JUMBLE

mis·in·form \ˌmis-ən-ˈfȯrm\ *vb* : to give false or misleading information to — **mis·in·for·ma·tion** \ˌmi-ˌsin-fər-ˈmā-shən\ *n*

mis·in·ter·pret \ˌmis-ən-ˈtər-prət\ *vb* : to understand or explain wrongly — **mis·in·ter·pre·ta·tion** \-ˌtər-prə-ˈtā- shən\ *n*

mis·judge \mis-ˈjəj\ *vb* 1 : to estimate wrongly 2 : to have an unjust opinion of — **mis·judg·ment** \mis-ˈjəj-mənt\ *n*

mis·la·bel \-ˈlā-bəl\ *vb* : to label incorrectly or falsely

mis·lay \mis-ˈlā\ *vb* **-laid** \-ˈlād\; **-lay·ing** : MISPLACE, LOSE

mis·lead \mis-ˈlēd\ *vb* **-led** \-ˈled\; **-lead·ing** : to lead in a wrong direction or into a mistaken action or belief — **mis·lead·ing·ly** *adv*

mis·like \-ˈlīk\ *vb* : DISLIKE — **mislike** *n*

mis·man·age \-ˈma-nij\ *vb* : to manage badly — **mis·man·age·ment** *n*

mis·match \-ˈmach\ *vb* : to match unsuitably or badly — **mismatch** \mis-ˈmach, ˈmis-ˌmach\ *n*

mis·name \-ˈnām\ *vb* : to name incorrectly : MISCALL

mis·no·mer \mis-ˈnō-mər\ *n* : a wrong name or designation

mi·sog·y·ny \mə-ˈsä-jə-nē\ *n* [Gk *misogynia*, fr. *misein* to hate + *gynē* woman] : a hatred of women — **mi·sog·y·nist** \-nist\ *n or adj* — **mi·sog·y·nis·tic** \mə-ˌsä-jə-ˈnis-tik\ *adj*

mis·ori·ent \mi-ˈsȯr-ē-ˌent\ *vb* : to orient improperly or incorrectly — **mis·ori·en·ta·tion** \mi-ˌsȯr-ē-ən-ˈtā-shən\ *n*

mis·place \mis-ˈplās\ *vb* 1 : to put in a wrong or un-

remembered place **2** : to set on a wrong object ⟨~ trust⟩

mis·play \-ˈplā\ *n* : a wrong or unskillful play — **mis·play** \mis-ˈplā, ˈmis-ˌplā\ *vb*

mis·print \ˈmis-ˌprint\ *n* : a mistake in printed matter — **mis·print** \mis-ˈprint\ *vb*

mis·pro·nounce \ˌmis-prə-ˈnaůns\ *vb* : to pronounce incorrectly — **mis·pro·nun·ci·a·tion** \-prə-ˌnən-sē-ˈā-shən\ *n*

mis·quote \mis-ˈkwōt\ *vb* : to quote incorrectly — **mis·quo·ta·tion** \ˌmis-kwō-ˈtā-shən\ *n*

mis·read \-ˈrēd\ *vb* **-read** \-ˈred\; **-read·ing** \-ˈrē-diŋ\ : to read or interpret incorrectly

mis·rep·re·sent \ˌmis-ˌre-pri-ˈzent\ *vb* : to represent falsely or unfairly — **mis·rep·re·sen·ta·tion** \-ˌzen-ˈtā-shən\ *n*

¹**mis·rule** \mis-ˈrül\ *vb* : MISGOVERN

²**misrule** *n* **1** : MISGOVERNMENT **2** : DISORDER

¹**miss** \ˈmis\ *vb* **1** : to fail to hit, reach, or contact **2** : to feel the absence of **3** : to fail to obtain **4** : AVOID ⟨just ~ed hitting the other car⟩ **5** : OMIT **6** : to fail to understand **7** : to fail to perform or attend; *also* : MISFIRE

²**miss** *n* **1** : a failure to hit or to attain a result **2** : MISFIRE

³**miss** *n* **1** *cap* — used as a title prefixed to the name of an unmarried woman or girl **2** : a young unmarried woman or girl

Miss *abbr* Mississippi

mis·sal \ˈmi-səl\ *n* : a book containing all that is said or sung at mass during the entire year

mis·send \mis-ˈsend\ *vb* : to send incorrectly ⟨missent mail⟩

mis·shap·en \-ˈshā-pən\ *adj* : badly shaped : having an ugly shape

mis·sile \ˈmi-səl\ *n* [L, fr. neut. of *missilis* capable of being thrown, fr. *mittere* to let go, send] : an object (as a stone, bullet, or rocket) thrown or projected usu. so as to strike a target

miss·ing \ˈmi-siŋ\ *adj* : ABSENT; *also* : LOST ⟨~ in action⟩

mis·sion \ˈmi-shən\ *n* **1** : a group of missionaries; *also* : a place where missionaries work **2** : a group of envoys to a foreign country; *also* : a team of specialists or cultural leaders sent to a foreign country **3** : TASK

¹**mis·sion·ary** \ˈmi-shə-ˌner-ē\ *adj* : of, relating to, or engaged in missions

²**missionary** *n, pl* **-ar·ies** : a person commissioned by a church to spread its faith or carry on humanitarian work

mis·sion·er \ˈmi-shə-nər\ *n* : MISSIONARY

Mis·sis·sip·pi·an \ˌmi-sə-ˈsi-pē-ən\ *adj* : of, relating to, or being the period of the Paleozoic era between the Devonian and the Pennsylvanian — **Mississippian** *n*

mis·sive \ˈmi-siv\ *n* : LETTER

mis·speak \mis-ˈspēk\ *vb* : to say imperfectly or incorrectly

mis·spell \-ˈspel\ *vb* : to spell incorrectly — **mis·spell·ing** *n*

mis·spend \-ˈspend\ *vb* **-spent** \-ˈspent\; **-spend·ing** : WASTE, SQUANDER ⟨my *misspent* youth⟩

mis·state \mis-ˈstāt\ *vb* : to state incorrectly — **mis·state·ment** *n*

mis·step \-ˈstep\ *n* **1** : a wrong step **2** : MISTAKE, BLUNDER

mist \ˈmist\ *n* **1** : water in the form of particles suspended or falling in the air **2** : something that obscures understanding — **mist** *vb*

mis·tak·able \mə-ˈstā-kə-bəl\ *adj* : capable of being misunderstood or mistaken

¹**mis·take** \mi-ˈstāk\ *vb* **-took** \-ˈtůk\; **-tak·en** \-ˈstā-kən\; **-tak·ing** **1** : to blunder in the choice of **2** : MISINTERPRET **3** : to make a wrong judgment of the character or ability of **4** : to confuse with another — **mis·tak·en·ly** *adv* — **mis·tak·er** *n*

²**mistake** *n* **1** : a wrong judgment : MISUNDERSTANDING **2** : a wrong action or statement : ERROR

¹**mis·ter** \ˈmis-tər\ *n* **1** *cap* — used sometimes instead of *Mr.* **2** : SIR — used without a name in addressing a man

²**mist·er** \ˈmis-tər\ *n* : a device for spraying mist

mis·tle·toe \ˈmi-səl-ˌtō\ *n* : a European parasitic green shrub with yellowish flowers and waxy white berries that grows on trees

mis·tral \ˈmis-trəl, mi-ˈsträl\ *n* [F, fr. Provençal, fr. *mistral* masterful, fr. LL *magistralis* of a teacher, fr. L *magister* master] : a strong cold dry northerly wind of southern France

mis·treat \mis-ˈtrēt\ *vb* : to treat badly : ABUSE — **mis·treat·ment** *n*

mis·tress \ˈmis-trəs\ *n* **1** : a woman who has power, authority, or ownership ⟨~ of the house⟩ **2** : something personified as female that rules or dominates ⟨when Rome was ~ of the world⟩ **3** : a woman other than his wife with whom a married man has sexual relations; *also, archaic* : SWEETHEART **4** — used archaically as a title prefixed to the name of a married or unmarried woman

mis·tri·al \ˈmis-ˌtrīl\ *n* : a trial that has no legal effect

¹**mis·trust** \mis-ˈtrəst\ *n* : a lack of confidence : DISTRUST — **mis·trust·ful** \-fəl\ *adj* — **mis·trust·ful·ly** *adv* — **mis·trust·ful·ness** *n*

²**mistrust** *vb* : to have no trust or confidence in : SUSPECT

misty \ˈmis-tē\ *adj* **mist·i·er; -est** **1** : obscured by or as if by mist : INDISTINCT **2** : TEARFUL — **mist·i·ly** \-tə-lē\ *adv* — **mist·i·ness** \-tē-nəs\ *n*

mis·un·der·stand \ˌmi-sən-dər-ˈstand\ *vb* **-stood** \-ˈstůd\; **-stand·ing** **1** : to fail to understand **2** : to interpret incorrectly

mis·un·der·stand·ing \-ˈstan-diŋ\ *n* **1** : MISINTERPRETATION **2** : DISAGREEMENT, QUARREL

mis·us·age \mis-ˈyü-sij\ *n* **1** : bad treatment : ABUSE **2** : wrong or improper use

mis·use \mis-ˈyüz\ *vb* **1** : to use incorrectly **2** : ABUSE, MISTREAT — **mis·use** \-ˈyüs\ *n*

mite \ˈmīt\ *n* **1** : any of numerous tiny arthropod animals related to the spiders that often live and feed on animals or plants **2** : a small coin or sum of money **3** : a small amount : BIT

¹mi·ter or **mi·tre** \'mī-tər\ n [ME mitre, fr. MF, fr. L mitra headband, turban, fr. Gk] **1** : a headdress worn by bishops and abbots **2** : MITER JOINT

²miter or **mitre** vb **mi·tered** or **mi·tred; mi·ter·ing** or **mi·tring** \'mī-tə-riŋ\ **1** : to match or fit together in a miter joint **2** : to bevel the ends of for making a miter joint

miter joint n : a joint made by fitting together two parts with the ends cut at an angle

mit·i·gate \'mi-tə-ˌgāt\ vb **-gat·ed; -gat·ing 1** : to make less harsh or hostile **2** : to make less severe or painful — **mit·i·ga·tion** \ˌmi-tə-'gā-shən\ n — **mit·i·ga·tive** \'mi-tə-ˌgā-tiv\ adj

mi·to·sis \mī-'tō-səs\ n, pl **-to·ses** \-ˌsēz\ : a process that takes place in the nucleus of a dividing cell and results in the formation of two new nuclei each of which has the same number of chromosomes as the parent nucleus; also : cell division in which mitosis occurs — **mi·tot·ic** \-'tä-tik\ adj

mitt \'mit\ n **1** : a baseball catcher's or first baseman's glove 2 slang : HAND

mit·ten \'mit-ᵊn\ n : a covering for the hand having a separate section for the thumb only

¹mix \'miks\ vb **1** : to combine into one mass **2** : ASSOCIATE **3** : to form by mingling components **4** : to produce (a recording) by electronically combining sounds from different sources **5** : HYBRIDIZE **6** : CONFUSE ⟨~es up the facts⟩ **7** : to become involved **syn** blend, merge, coalesce, amalgamate, fuse — **mix·able** adj — **mix·er** n

²mix n : a product of mixing; esp : a commercially prepared mixture of food ingredients

mixed number n : a number (as 5⅔) composed of an integer and a fraction

mixed–up \'mikst-'əp\ adj : CONFUSED

mixt abbr mixture

mix·ture \'miks-chər\ n **1** : the act or process of mixing; also : the state of being mixed **2** : a product of mixing

mix–up \'miks-ˌəp\ n **1** : an instance of confusion **2** : CONFLICT, FIGHT

miz·zen also **miz·en** \'miz-ᵊn\ n **1** : a fore-and-aft sail set on the mizzenmast **2** : MIZZENMAST — **mizzen** also **mizen** adj

miz·zen·mast \-ˌmast, -məst\ n : the mast aft or next aft of the mainmast

mk abbr **1** mark **2** markka

Mk abbr Mark

mks abbr meter-kilogram-second

mkt abbr market

mktg abbr marketing

ml abbr milliliter

Mlle abbr [F] mademoiselle

Mlles abbr [F] mesdemoiselles

mm abbr millimeter

MM abbr [F] messieurs

Mme abbr [F] madame

Mmes abbr mesdames

Mn symbol manganese

MN abbr Minnesota

mne·mon·ic \nə-'mä-nik\ adj : assisting or designed to assist memory; also : of or relating to memory

mo abbr month

¹Mo abbr **1** Missouri **2** Monday

²Mo symbol molybdenum

MO abbr **1** mail order **2** medical officer **3** Missouri **4** modus operandi **5** money order

moan \'mōn\ n : a low prolonged sound indicative of pain or grief — **moan** vb

moat \'mōt\ n : a deep wide usu. water-filled trench around a castle

¹mob \'mäb\ n [L mobile vulgus vacillating crowd] **1**

: MASSES, RABBLE **2** : a disorderly crowd **3** : a criminal gang

²mob vb **mobbed; mob·bing 1** : to crowd about and attack or annoy **2** : to crowd into or around ⟨shoppers mobbed the stores⟩

¹mo·bile \'mō-bəl, -ˌbīl, -ˌbēl\ adj **1** : capable of moving or being moved **2** : changeable in appearance, mood, or purpose; also : ADAPTABLE **3** : having the opportunity for or undergoing a shift in social status **4** : using vehicles for transportation ⟨~ warfare⟩ — **mo·bil·i·ty** \mō-'bi-lə-tē\ n

²mo·bile \'mō-ˌbēl\ n : a construction or sculpture (as of wire and sheet metal) with parts that can be set in motion by air currents; also : a similar structure suspended so that it is moved by a current of air

mobile home n : a trailer used as a permanent dwelling

mo·bi·lise chiefly Brit var of MOBILIZE

mo·bi·lize \'mō-bə-ˌlīz\ vb **-lized; -liz·ing 1** : to put into movement or circulation **2** : to assemble and make ready for action ⟨~ army reserves⟩ — **mo·bi·li·za·tion** \ˌmō-bə-lə-'zā-shən\ n — **mo·bi·liz·er** \'mō-bə-ˌlī-zər\ n

mob·ster \'mäb-stər\ n : a member of a criminal gang

moc·ca·sin \'mä-kə-sən\ n **1** : a soft leather heelless shoe **2** : WATER MOCCASIN

mo·cha \'mō-kə\ n [Mocha, port in Yemen] **1** : choice coffee grown in Arabia **2** : a mixture of coffee and chocolate or cocoa **3** : a dark chocolate-brown color

¹mock \'mäk, 'mȯk\ vb **1** : to treat with contempt or ridicule **2** : DELUDE **3** : DEFY **4** : to mimic in sport or derision — **mock·er** n — **mock·ery** \'mä-kə-rē, 'mȯ-\ n — **mock·ing·ly** adv

²mock adj : SHAM, PSEUDO

mock–he·ro·ic \ˌmäk-hi-'rō-ik, ˌmȯk-\ adj : ridiculing or burlesquing heroic style, character, or action ⟨a ~ poem⟩

mock·ing·bird \'mä-kiŋ-ˌbərd, 'mȯ-\ n : a grayish No. American songbird related to the catbirds and thrashers that mimics the calls of other birds

mock–up \'mä-ˌkəp, 'mȯ-\ n : a full-sized structural model built for study, testing, or display ⟨a ~ of a car⟩

¹mod \'mäd\ adj **1** : of, relating to, or being the style of the 1960s British youth culture **2** : HIP, TRENDY

²mod abbr **1** moderate **2** modern **3** modification; modified

mode \'mōd\ n **1** : a particular form or variety of something; also : STYLE **2** : a manner of doing something **3** : the most frequent value of a set of data — **mod·al** \'mōd-ᵊl\ adj

¹mod·el \'mäd-ᵊl\ n **1** : structural design **2** : a miniature representation; also : a pattern of something to be made **3** : an example for imitation or emulation **4** : one who poses for an artist; also : MANNEQUIN **5** : TYPE, DESIGN

²model vb **mod·eled** or **mod·elled; mod·el·ing** or **mod·el·ling 1** : SHAPE, FASHION, CONSTRUCT **2** : to work as a fashion model

³model adj **1** : serving as or worthy of being a pattern ⟨a ~ student⟩ **2** : being a miniature representation of something ⟨a ~ airplane⟩

mo·dem \'mō-dəm, -ˌdem\ n : a device that converts signals from one device (as a computer) to a form compatible with another (as a telephone)

¹mod·er·ate \'mä-də-rət\ adj **1** : avoiding extremes; also : TEMPERATE **2** : AVERAGE; also : MEDIOCRE **3** : limited in scope or effect **4** : not expensive — **mod·erate** n — **mod·er·ate·ly** adv — **mod·er·ate·ness** n

²mod·er·ate \'mä-də-ˌrāt\ vb **-at·ed; -at·ing 1** : to lessen the intensity of : TEMPER **2** : to act as a moderator — **mod·er·a·tion** \ˌmä-də-'rā-shən\ n

mod·er·a·tor \'mä-də-ˌrā-tər\ n **1** : MEDIATOR **2** : one who presides over an assembly, meeting, or discussion

mod·ern \'mä-dərn\ adj [LL modernus, fr. L modo just now, fr. modus measure] : of, relating to, or char-

acteristic of the present or the immediate past : CON-
TEMPORARY — **modern** n — **mo·der·ni·ty** \mə-'dər-
nə-tē\ n — **mod·ern·ly** adv — **mod·ern·ness** n
mod·ern·ise Brit var of MODERNIZE
mod·ern·ism \'mä-dər-ˌni-zəm\ n : a practice, movement, or belief peculiar to modern times
mod·ern·ize \'mä-dər-ˌnīz\ vb **-ized; -iz·ing** : to make
or become modern — **mod·ern·i·za·tion** \ˌmä-dər-nə-
'zā-shən\ n — **mod·ern·iz·er** n
mod·est \'mä-dəst\ adj **1** : having a moderate estimate
of oneself; also : DIFFIDENT **2** : observing the proprieties of dress and behavior **3** : limited in size,
amount, or scope — **mod·est·ly** adv — **mod·es·ty**
\-də-stē\ n
mod·i·cum \'mä-di-kəm\ n : a small amount
modif abbr modification
mod·i·fy \'mä-də-ˌfī\ vb **-fied; -fy·ing 1** : MODERATE **2**
: to limit the meaning of esp. in a grammatical construction **3** : CHANGE, ALTER — **mod·i·fi·ca·tion**
\ˌmä-də-fə-'kā-shən\ n — **mod·i·fi·er** \'mä-də-ˌfī-ər\
n
mod·ish \'mō-dish\ adj : FASHIONABLE, STYLISH —
mod·ish·ly adv — **mod·ish·ness** n
mo·diste \mō-'dēst\ n : a maker of fashionable dresses
and hats
mod·u·lar \'mä-jə-lər\ adj : constructed with standardized units
mod·u·lar·ized \'mä-jə-lə-ˌrīzd\ adj : containing or
consisting of modules
mod·u·late \'mä-jə-ˌlāt\ vb **-lat·ed; -lat·ing 1** : to tune
to a key or pitch **2** : to keep in proper measure or proportion : TEMPER **3** : to vary the amplitude or frequency of a carrier wave for the transmission of
intelligence (as in radio or television) — **mod·u·la·
tion** \ˌmä-jə-'lā-shən\ n — **mod·u·la·tor** \'mä-jə-ˌlā-
tər\ n — **mod·u·la·to·ry** \-lə-ˌtōr-ē\ adj
mod·ule \'mä-jül\ n **1** : any in a series of standardized
units for use together **2** : an assembly of wired electronic parts for use with other such assemblies **3** : an
independent unit that constitutes a part of the total
structure of a space vehicle (a propulsion ∼)
mo·dus op·er·an·di \ˌmō-dəs-ˌä-pə-'ran-dē, -ˌdī\ n, pl
mo·di operandi \'mō-ˌdē-ä-, 'mō-ˌdī-\ [NL] : a
method of procedure
¹**mo·gul** \'mō-gəl, mō-'gəl\ n [fr. Mogul, member of a
Muslim dynasty ruling northern India] : an important
person : MAGNATE
²**mogul** \'mō-gəl\ n : a bump in a ski run
mo·hair \'mō-ˌhar\ n [modif. of obs. It mocaiarro, fr.
Ar mukhayyar, lit., choice] : a fabric or yarn made
wholly or in part from the long silky hair of the Angora goat; also : this goat hair
Mo·ham·med·an var of MUHAMMADAN
Mo·hawk \'mō-ˌhök\ n, pl **Mohawk** or **Mohawks** : a
member of an American Indian people of the Mohawk River valley, New York; also : the language of
the Mohawk people
Mo·he·gan \mō-'hē-gən, mə-\ or **Mo·hi·can** \-'hē-kən\
n, pl **Mohegan** or **Mohegans** or **Mohican** or **Mohi-
cans** : a member of an American Indian people of
southeastern Connecticut
Mo·hi·can \mō-'hē-kən, mə-\ var of MAHICAN
moi·e·ty \'mòi-ə-tē\ n, pl **-ties** : one of two equal or approximately equal parts
moil \'mòil\ vb : to work hard : DRUDGE — **moil** n —
moil·er n
moi·ré \mò-'rā, mwä-\ or **moire** \same or 'mòir,
'mwär\ n : a fabric (as silk) having a watered appearance
moist \'mòist\ adj : slightly or moderately wet —
moist·ly adv — **moist·ness** n
moist·en \'mòis-ᵊn\ vb : to make or become moist —
moist·en·er n
mois·ture \'mòis-chər\ n : the small amount of liquid
that causes dampness
mois·tur·ise Brit var of MOISTURIZE

mois·tur·ize \'mòis-chə-ˌrīz\ vb **-ized; -iz·ing** : to add
moisture to — **mois·tur·iz·er** n
mol abbr molecular; molecule
mo·lar \'mō-lər\ n [ME molares, pl., fr. L molaris, fr.
molaris of a mill, fr. mola millstone] : any of the
broad teeth adapted to grinding food and located in
the back of the jaw — **molar** adj
mo·las·ses \mə-'la-səz\ n : the thick brown syrup that
is separated from raw sugar in sugar manufacture
¹**mold** \'mōld\ n : crumbly soil rich in organic matter
²**mold** n **1** : distinctive nature or character **2** : the frame
on or around which something is constructed **3** : a
cavity in which something is shaped; also : an object
so shaped **4** : MOLDING
³**mold** vb **1** : to shape in or as if in a mold **2** : to ornament with molding — **mold·er** n
⁴**mold** n : a surface growth of fungus esp. on damp or
decaying matter; also : a fungus that forms molds —
mold·i·ness \'mōl-dē-nəs\ n — **moldy** adj
⁵**mold** vb : to become moldy
mold·board \'mōld-ˌbörd\ n : a curved iron plate attached above the plowshare to lift and turn the soil
mold·er \'mōl-dər\ vb : to crumble into small pieces
mold·ing \'mōl-diŋ\ n **1** : an act or process of shaping
in a mold; also : an object so shaped **2** : a decorative
surface, plane, or curved strip
¹**mole** \'mōl\ n : a small often pigmented spot or protuberance on the skin
²**mole** n : any of numerous small burrowing insect-
eating mammals related to the shrews and hedgehogs
³**mole** n : a massive breakwater or jetty
molecular biology n : a branch of biology dealing with
the ultimate physical and chemical organization of
living matter and esp. with the molecular basis of inheritance and protein synthesis — **molecular biologist** n
molecular weight n : the mass of a molecule that is
equal to the sum of the masses of all atoms contained
in the molecule's formula
mol·e·cule \'mä-li-ˌkyül\ n : the smallest particle of
matter that is the same chemically as the whole mass
— **mo·lec·u·lar** \mə-'le-kyə-lər\ adj
mole·hill \'mōl-ˌhil\ n : a little ridge of earth thrown up
by a mole
mole·skin \-ˌskin\ n **1** : the skin of the mole used as fur
2 : a heavy durable cotton fabric
mo·lest \mə-'lest\ vb **1** : ANNOY, DISTURB **2** : to make
annoying sexual advances to; esp : to force physical
and usu. sexual contact on — **mo·les·ta·tion** \ˌmō-
ˌles-'tā-shən\ n — **mo·lest·er** n
moll \'mäl\ n : a gangster's girlfriend
mol·li·fy \'mä-lə-ˌfī\ vb **-fied; -fy·ing 1** : to soothe in
temper : APPEASE **2** : SOFTEN **3** : to reduce in intensity
: ASSUAGE — **mol·li·fi·ca·tion** \ˌmä-lə-fə-'kā-shən\ n
mol·lusk or **mol·lusc** \'mä-ləsk\ n : any of a large phylum of usu. shelled and aquatic invertebrate animals
(as snails, clams, and squids) — **mol·lus·can** also
mol·lus·kan \mə-'ləs-kən\ adj
¹**mol·ly·cod·dle** \'mä-lē-ˌkäd-ᵊl\ n : a pampered man or
boy
²**mollycoddle** vb **mol·ly·cod·dled; mol·ly·cod·dling**
: PAMPER
Mo·lo·tov cocktail \'mä-lə-ˌtöf-, 'mò-\ n [Vyacheslav
M. Molotov †1986 Soviet foreign minister] : a crude
bomb made of a bottle filled usu. with gasoline and
fitted with a wick (as a saturated rag) that is ignited
just prior to hurling
¹**molt** \'mōlt\ vb : to shed hair, feathers, outer skin, or
horns periodically with the cast-off parts being replaced by new growth — **molt·er** n
²**molt** n : the act or process of molting
mol·ten \'mōlt-ᵊn\ adj **1** : fused or liquefied by heat **2**
: GLOWING
mo·ly \'mō-lē\ n : a mythical herb with black root,
white flowers, and magic powers
mo·lyb·de·num \mə-'lib-də-nəm\ n : a metallic chem-

ical element used in strengthening and hardening steel — see ELEMENT table

mom \\'mäm, 'məm\ *n* : MOTHER

mom–and–pop *adj* : being a small owner-operated business

mo·ment \\'mō-mənt\ *n* **1** : a minute portion of time : INSTANT **2** : a time of excellence ⟨he has his ∼*s*⟩ **3** : IMPORTANCE **syn** consequence, significance, weight, import

mo·men·tari·ly \\ˌmō-mən-'ter-ə-lē\ *adv* **1** : for a moment **2** *archaic* : INSTANTLY **3** : at any moment : SOON

mo·men·tary \\'mō-mən-ˌter-ē\ *adj* **1** : continuing only a moment; *also* : EPHEMERAL **2** : recurring at every moment — **mo·men·tar·i·ness** \-ˌter-ē-nəs\ *n*

mo·men·tous \mō-'men-təs\ *adj* : very important — **mo·men·tous·ly** *adv* — **mo·men·tous·ness** *n*

mo·men·tum \mō-'men-təm\ *n, pl* **mo·men·ta** \-'men-tə\ *or* **momentums** : a property that a moving body has due to its mass and motion; *also* : IMPETUS

mom·my \\'mä-mē, 'mə-\ *n, pl* **mom·mies** : MOTHER

Mon *abbr* Monday

mon·arch \\'mä-nərk, -ˌnärk\ *n* **1** : a person who reigns over a kingdom or an empire **2** : one holding preeminent position or power **3** : MONARCH BUTTERFLY — **mo·nar·chi·cal** \mə-'när-ki-kəl\ *also* **mo·nar·chic** \-'när-kik\ *adj*

monarch butterfly *n* : a large orange and black migratory American butterfly whose larva feeds on milkweed

monarch butterfly

mon·ar·chist \\'mä-nər-kist\ *n* : a believer in monarchical government — **mon·ar·chism** \-ˌki-zəm\ *n*

mon·ar·chy \\'mä-nər-kē\ *n, pl* **-chies** : a nation or state governed by a monarch

mon·as·tery \\'mä-nə-ˌster-ē\ *n, pl* **-ter·ies** : a house for persons under religious vows (as monks)

mo·nas·tic \mə-'nas-tik\ *adj* : of or relating to monasteries or to monks or nuns — **monastic** *n* — **mo·nas·ti·cal·ly** \-ti-k(ə-)lē\ *adv* — **mo·nas·ti·cism** \-tə-ˌsi-zəm\ *n*

mon·au·ral \mä-'nòr-əl\ *adj* : MONOPHONIC — **mon·au·ral·ly** *adv*

Mon·day \\'mən-dē, -ˌdā\ *n* : the second day of the week

mon·e·tary \\'mä-nə-ˌter-ē, 'mə-\ *adj* : of or relating to money or to the mechanisms by which it is supplied and circulated in the economy

mon·ey \\'mə-nē\ *n, pl* **moneys** *or* **mon·ies** \\'mə-nēz\ **1** : something (as metal currency) accepted as a medium of exchange **2** : wealth reckoned in monetary terms **3** : the 1st, 2d, and 3d places in a horse or dog race

MONEY

NAME	SUBDIVISIONS	COUNTRY
afghani	100 puls	Afghanistan
baht *or* tical	100 satang	Thailand
balboa	100 centesimos	Panama
birr	100 cents	Ethiopia

NAME	SUBDIVISIONS	COUNTRY
bolivar	100 centimos	Venezuela
boliviano	100 centavos	Bolivia
cedi	100 pesewas	Ghana
colón	100 centimos	Costa Rica
colón	100 centavos	El Salvador
cordoba	100 centavos	Nicaragua
dalasi	100 bututs	Gambia
deutsche mark	100 pfennig	Germany
dinar	100 centimes	Algeria
dinar	1000 fils	Bahrain
dinar	1000 fils	Iraq
dinar	1000 fils	Jordan
dinar	1000 fils	Kuwait
dinar	1000 dirhams	Libya
dinar	1000 millimes	Tunisia
dinar	100 paras	Yugoslavia
dirham	100 centimes	Morocco
dirham	100 fils	United Arab Emirates
dobra	100 centimos	São Tomé and Príncipe
dollar[1]	100 cents	Antigua and Barbuda, Dominica, Grenada, St. Kitts-Nevis, St. Lucia, St. Vincent and the Grenadines
dollar	100 cents	Australia
dollar	100 cents	Bahamas
dollar	100 cents	Barbados
dollar	100 cents	Belize
dollar	100 cents	Bermuda
dollar	100 sen *or* cents	Brunei
dollar	100 cents	Canada
dollar	100 cents	China (Taiwan)
or yuan		
dollar	100 cents	Fiji
dollar	100 cents	Guyana
dollar	100 cents	Jamaica
dollar	100 cents	Liberia
dollar	100 cents	New Zealand
dollar	100 cents	Singapore
dollar	100 cents	Trinidad and Tobago
dollar	100 cents	United States
dollar	100 cents	Zimbabwe
dollar—see RINGGIT, below		
dong	100 xu	Vietnam
drachma	100 lepta	Greece
escudo	100 centavos	Cape Verde
escudo	100 centavos	Portugal
florin—see GULDEN, below		
forint	100 filler	Hungary
franc	100 centimes	Belgium
franc[2]	100 centimes	Benin, Burkina Faso, Cameroon, Central African Republic, Chad, Congo, Equatorial Guinea, Gabon, Ivory Coast, Mali, Niger, Senegal, Togo
franc	100 centimes	Burundi
franc	100 centimes	Djibouti
franc	100 centimes	France
franc	100 centimes	Guinea
franc	100 centimes	Luxembourg
franc	100 centimes	Madagascar
franc	100 centimes[3]	Rwanda
franc	100 centimes *or* rappen	Switzerland
gourde	100 centimes	Haiti
guarani	100 centimos	Paraguay

NAME	SUBDIVISIONS	COUNTRY
gulden *or* guilder *or* florin	100 cents	Netherlands
gulden *or* guilder *or* florin	100 cents	Suriname
kina	100 toea	Papua New Guinea
kip	100 at	Laos
koruna	100 haleru	Czech Republic
krona	100 aurar (*sing* eyrir)	Iceland
krona	100 ore	Sweden
krone	100 ore	Denmark
krone	100 ore	Norway
kwacha	100 tambala	Malawi
kwacha	100 ngwee	Zambia
kwanza	100 lwei	Angola
kyat	100 pyas	Myanmar
lek	100 qindarka	Albania
lempira	100 centavos	Honduras
leone	100 cents	Sierra Leone
leu	100 bani	Romania
lev	100 stotinki	Bulgaria
lilangeni (*pl* emalangeni)	100 cents	Swaziland
lira	100 centesimi[3]	Italy
lira *or* pound	100 cents	Malta
lira	100 kurus	Turkey
livre — see POUND, below		
loti (*pl* maloti)	100 licente *or* lisente (*sing* sente)	Lesotho
mark — see DEUTSCHE MARK, above		
markka	100 pennia	Finland
metical	100 centavos	Mozambique
naira	100 kobo	Nigeria
ngultrum	100 chetrums	Bhutan
ouguiya	5 khoums	Mauritania
pa'anga	100 seniti	Tonga
pataca	100 avos	Macao
peseta	100 centimos[3]	Spain
peso		Argentina
peso	100 centavos	Chile
peso	100 centavos	Colombia
peso	100 centavos	Cuba
peso	100 centavos	Dominican Republic
peso	100 centavos	Guinea-Bissau
peso	100 centavos	Mexico
peso *or* piso	100 sentimos *or* centavos	Philippines
peso	100 centesimos	Uruguay
pound	100 cents	Cyprus
pound	100 piastres	Egypt
pound	100 pence	Ireland
pound *or* livre	100 piastres	Lebanon
pound	100 piastres	Sudan
pound	100 piastres	Syria
pound	100 pence	United Kingdom
pound — see LIRA, above		
pula	100 thebe	Botswana
quetzal	100 centavos	Guatemala
rand	100 cents	South Africa
real	100 centavos	Brazil
rial	100 dinars	Iran
rial	1000 baiza	Oman
rial	100 fils	Yemen
riel	100 sen	Cambodia
ringgit *or* dollar	100 sen	Malaysia
riyal	100 dirhams	Qatar
riyal	100 halala	Saudi Arabia
ruble	100 kopecks	Russia
rupee	100 paise	India
rupee	100 cents	Mauritius

NAME	SUBDIVISIONS	COUNTRY
rupee	100 paisa	Nepal
rupee	100 paisa	Pakistan
rupee	100 cents	Seychelles
rupee	100 cents	Sri Lanka
rupiah	100 sen	Indonesia
schilling	100 groschen	Austria
shekel *or* sheqel	100 agorot	Israel
shilling	100 cents	Kenya
shilling	100 cents	Somalia
shilling	100 cents	Tanzania
shilling	100 cents	Uganda
sol	100 centavos	Peru
sucre	100 centavos	Ecuador
taka	100 paisa *or* poisha	Bangladesh
tala	100 sene	Samoa
tical — see BAHT, above		
tugrik	100 mongo	Mongolia
won	100 chon	North Korea
won	100 chon	South Korea
yen	100 sen[3]	Japan
yuan	100 fen	China (mainland)
yuan — see DOLLAR, above		
zaire	100 makuta (*sing* likuta)	Democratic Republic of Congo
zloty	100 groszy	Poland

[1] Dollars issued by the Eastern Caribbean Central Bank, established to promote economic cooperation among the member nations.
[2] Francs issued by the African Financial Community, established to promote economic cooperation among the member nations.
[3] No longer minted; a subdivision in name only.

mon•eyed \'mə-nēd\ *adj* **1** : having money : WEALTHY **2** : consisting in or derived from money
mon•ey•lend•er \'mə-nē-ˌlen-dər\ *n* : one (as a bank or pawnbroker) whose business is lending money
money market *n* : the trade in short-term negotiable financial instruments
money of account : a denominator of value or basis of exchange used in keeping accounts
money order *n* : an order purchased at a post office, bank, or telegraph office directing another office to pay a sum of money to a party named on it
mon•ger \'məŋ-gər, 'mäŋ-\ *n* **1** : DEALER **2** : one who tries to stir up or spread something
mon•go \'mäŋ-(ˌ)gō\ *n, pl* **mongo** — see *tugrik* at MONEY table
Mon•gol \'mäŋ-gəl, 'män-ˌgōl\ *n* : a member of any of several traditionally pastoral peoples of Mongolia — **Mongol** *adj*
Mon•go•lian \män-'gōl-yən, mäŋ-, -'gō-lē-ən\ *n* **1** : a native or inhabitant of Mongolia **2** : a member of the Mongoloid racial stock — **Mongolian** *adj*
mon•gol•ism \'mäŋ-gə-ˌli-zəm\ *n* : DOWN'S SYNDROME
Mon•gol•oid \'mäŋ-gə-ˌlòid\ *adj* **1** : of or relating to a major racial stock native to Asia that includes peoples of northern and eastern Asia, Malaysians, Eskimos, and often American Indians **2** *often not cap* : of, relating to, or affected with Down's syndrome — **Mongoloid** *n*
mon•goose \'män-ˌgüs, 'mäŋ-\ *n, pl* **mon•goos•es** *also* **mon•geese** \-ˌgēs\ : any of a group of small agile Old World mammals that are related to the civet cats and feed on small animals and fruits
mon•grel \'mäŋ-grəl, 'məŋ-\ *n* : an offspring of parents of different breeds; *esp* : one of uncertain ancestry
mo•nism \'mō-ˌni-zəm, 'mä-\ *n* : a view that reality is basically one unitary organic whole — **mo•nist** \'mō-nist, 'mä-\ *n*
mo•ni•tion \mō-'ni-shən, mə-\ *n* : WARNING, CAUTION
¹mon•i•tor \'mä-nə-tər\ *n* **1** : a student appointed to assist a teacher **2** : one that monitors; *esp* : a video display screen (as for a computer)

²**monitor** *vb* : to watch, check, or observe for a special purpose

mon·i·to·ry \'mä-nə-ˌtōr-ē\ *adj* : giving admonition : WARNING

¹**monk** \'məŋk\ *n* [ME, fr. OE *munuc*, fr. LL *monachus*, fr. LGk *monachos*, fr. Gk, adj., single, fr. *monos* single, alone] : a man belonging to a religious order and living in a monastery — **monk·ish** *adj*

²**monk** *n* : MONKEY

¹**mon·key** \'məŋ-kē\ *n, pl* **monkeys** : a nonhuman primate mammal; *esp* : one of the smaller, longer-tailed, and usu. more arboreal primates as contrasted with the apes

²**monkey** *vb* **mon·keyed; mon·key·ing 1** : FOOL, TRIFLE **2** : TAMPER

monkey bars *n pl* : a framework of bars on which children can play

mon·key·shine \'mən-kē-ˌshīn\ *n* : PRANK — usu. used in pl.

monkey wrench *n* : a wrench with one fixed and one adjustable jaw at right angles to a handle

monks·hood \'məŋks-ˌhùd\ *n* : any of a genus of poisonous plants related to the buttercups; *esp* : a tall Old World plant with usu. purplish flowers

¹**mono** \'mä-nō\ *adj* : MONOPHONIC

²**mono** *n* : INFECTIOUS MONONUCLEOSIS

mono·chro·mat·ic \ˌmä-nə-krō-'ma-tik\ *adj* **1** : having or consisting of one color **2** : consisting of radiation (as light) of a single wavelength

mono·chrome \'mä-nə-ˌkrōm\ *adj* : involving or producing visual images in a single color or in varying tones of a single color ⟨~ television⟩

mon·o·cle \'mä-ni-kəl\ *n* : an eyeglass for one eye

mono·clo·nal \ˌmä-nə-'klō-nəl\ *adj* : produced by, being, or composed of cells derived from a single cell ⟨~ antibodies⟩

mono·cot·y·le·don \ˌmä-nə-ˌkät-ᵊl-'ēd-ᵊn\ *n* : any of a class or subclass of chiefly herbaceous seed plants having an embryo with a single cotyledon and usu. parallel-veined leaves

mon·o·dy \'mä-nə-dē\ *n, pl* **-dies** : ELEGY, DIRGE — **mo·nod·ic** \mə-'nä-dik\ *or* **mo·nod·i·cal** \-di-kəl\ *adj* — **mon·o·dist** \'mä-nə-dist\ *n*

mo·nog·a·my \mə-'nä-gə-mē\ *n* **1** : marriage with but one person at a time **2** : the practice of having a single mate during a period of time — **mo·nog·a·mist** \-mist\ *n* — **mo·nog·a·mous** \-məs\ *adj*

mono·gram \'mä-nə-ˌgram\ *n* : a sign of identity composed of the combined initials of a name — **monogram** *vb*

mono·graph \'mä-nə-ˌgraf\ *n* : a learned treatise on a small area of learning

mono·lin·gual \ˌmä-nō-'liŋ-gwəl\ *adj* : knowing or using only one language

mono·lith \'män-ᵊl-ˌith\ *n* **1** : a single great stone often in the form of a monument or column **2** : something large and powerful that acts as a single unified force — **mono·lith·ic** \ˌmän-ᵊl-'i-thik\ *adj*

mono·logue *also* **mono·log** \'män-ᵊl-ˌòg\ *n* **1** : a dramatic soliloquy; *also* : a long speech monopolizing conversation **2** : the routine of a stand-up comic — **mono·logu·ist** \-ˌòg-ist\ *or* **mo·no·lo·gist** \mə-'nä-lə-jist; 'män-ᵊl-ˌò-gist\ *n*

mono·ma·nia \ˌmä-nə-'mä-nē-ə, -nyə\ *n* **1** : mental disorder limited in expression to one area of thought **2** : excessive concentration on a single object or idea — **mono·ma·ni·ac** \-nē-ˌak\ *n or adj*

mono·mer \'mä-nə-mər\ *n* : a simple chemical compound that can be polymerized

mono·nu·cle·o·sis \ˌmä-nō-ˌnü-klē-'ō-səs, -ˌnyü-\ *n* : INFECTIOUS MONONUCLEOSIS

mono·phon·ic \ˌmä-nə-'fä-nik\ *adj* : of or relating to sound recording or reproduction involving a single transmission path

mono·plane \'mä-nə-ˌplān\ *n* : an airplane with only one set of wings

mo·nop·o·ly \mə-'nä-pə-lē\ *n, pl* **-lies** [L *monopolium*, fr. Gk *monopōlion*, fr. *monos* alone, single + *pōlein* to sell] **1** : exclusive ownership (as through command of supply) **2** : a commodity controlled by one party **3** : one that has a monopoly — **mo·nop·o·list** \-list\ *n* — **mo·nop·o·lis·tic** \mə-ˌnä-pə-'lis-tik\ *adj* — **mo·nop·o·li·za·tion** \-lə-'zā-shən\ *n* — **mo·nop·o·lize** \mə-'nä-pə-ˌlīz\ *vb*

mono·rail \'mä-nə-ˌrāl\ *n* : a single rail serving as a track for a vehicle; *also* : a vehicle traveling on such a track

mono·so·di·um glu·ta·mate \ˌmä-nə-ˌsō-dē-əm-'glütə-ˌmāt\ *n* : a crystalline salt used to enhance the flavor of food

mono·syl·la·ble \'mä-nə-ˌsi-lə-bəl\ *n* : a word of one syllable — **mono·syl·lab·ic** \ˌmä-nə-sə-'la-bik\ *adj* — **mono·syl·lab·i·cal·ly** \-bi-k(ə-)lē\ *adv*

mono·the·ism \'mä-nə-(ˌ)thē-ˌi-zəm\ *n* : a doctrine or belief that there is only one deity — **mono·the·ist** \-ˌthē-ist\ *n* — **mono·the·is·tic** \-thē-'is-tik\ *adj*

mono·tone \'mä-nə-ˌtōn\ *n* : a succession of syllables, words, or sentences in one unvaried key or pitch

mo·not·o·nous \mə-'nät-ᵊn-əs\ *adj* **1** : uttered or sounded in one unvarying tone **2** : tediously uniform — **mo·not·o·nous·ly** *adv* — **mo·not·o·nous·ness** *n*

mo·not·o·ny \mə-'nät-ᵊn-ē\ *n* : tedious sameness or uniformity

mono·un·sat·u·rat·ed \ˌmä-nō-ˌən-'sa-chə-ˌrā-təd\ *adj* : containing one double or triple bond per molecule — used esp. of an oil or fatty acid

mon·ox·ide \mə-'näk-ˌsīd\ *n* : an oxide containing one atom of oxygen in a molecule

mon·sei·gneur \ˌmōⁿ-sān-'yər\ *n, pl* **mes·sei·gneurs** \ˌmā-sān-'yər, -'yərz\ : a French dignitary — used as a title

mon·sieur \məs-'yər, mə-'shər, *Fr* mə-'syœ̄\ *n, pl* **mes·sieurs** *same or* -'yərz, -'shərz\ : a Frenchman of high rank or station — used as a title equivalent to *Mister*

mon·si·gnor \män-'sē-nyər\ *n, pl* **monsignors** *or* **mon·si·gno·ri** \ˌmän-ˌsēn-'yōr-ē\ [It *monsignore*] : a Roman Catholic prelate — used as a title

mon·soon \män-'sün\ *n* [obs. Dutch *monssoen*, fr. Pg *monção*, fr. Ar *mawsim* time, season] **1** : a periodic wind esp. in the Indian Ocean and southern Asia **2** : the season of the southwest monsoon esp. in India **3** : rainfall associated with the monsoon

¹**mon·ster** \'män-stər\ *n* **1** : an abnormally developed plant or animal **2** : an animal of strange or terrifying shape; *also* : one unusually large of its kind **3** : an extremely ugly, wicked, or cruel person — **mon·stros·i·ty** \män-'strä-sə-tē\ *n* — **mon·strous** \'män-strəs\ *adj* — **mon·strous·ly** *adv*

²**monster** *adj* : very large : ENORMOUS

mon·strance \'män-strəns\ *n* : a vessel in which the consecrated Host is exposed for the adoration of the faithful

Mont *abbr* Montana

mon·tage \män-'täzh\ *n* [F] **1** : a composite photograph made by combining several separate pictures **2** : an artistic composition made up of several different kinds of elements **3** : a varied mixture : JUMBLE

month \'mənth\ *n, pl* **months** \'məns, 'mənths\ : one of the 12 parts into which the year is divided — **month·ly** *adv or adj or n*

month·long \'mənth-'lòŋ\ *adj* : lasting a month

mon·u·ment \'män-yə-mənt\ *n* **1** : a lasting reminder; *esp* : a structure erected in remembrance of a person or event **2** : NATIONAL MONUMENT

mon·u·men·tal \ˌmän-yə-'ment-ᵊl\ *adj* **1** : of or relating to a monument **2** : MASSIVE; *also* : OUTSTANDING **3** : very great — **mon·u·men·tal·ly** *adv*

moo \'mü\ *vb* : to make the natural throat noise of a cow — **moo** *n*

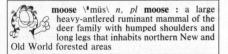

¹**mood** \'müd\ *n* **1** : a conscious state of mind or predominant emotion : FEELING **2** : a prevailing attitude : DISPOSITION **3** : a distinctive atmosphere

²**mood** *n* : distinction of form of a verb to express whether its action or state is conceived as fact or in some other manner (as wish)

moody \'mü-dē\ *adj* **mood·i·er; -est 1** : GLOOMY **2** : subject to moods : TEMPERAMENTAL — **mood·i·ly** \-də-lē\ *adv* — **mood·i·ness** \-dē-nəs\ *n*

¹**moon** \'mün\ *n* **1** : the earth's natural satellite **2** : SATELLITE 2

²**moon** *vb* : to engage in idle reverie

moon·beam \'mün-ˌbēm\ *n* : a ray of light from the moon

¹**moon·light** \-ˌlīt\ *n* : the light of the moon — **moonlit** \-ˌlit\ *adj*

²**moonlight** *vb* **moon·light·ed; moon·light·ing** : to hold a second job in addition to a regular one — **moonlight·er** *n*

moon·scape \-ˌskāp\ *n* : the surface of the moon as seen or as pictured

moon·shine \-ˌshīn\ *n* **1** : MOONLIGHT **2** : empty talk **3** : intoxicating liquor usu. illegally distilled

moon·stone \-ˌstōn\ *n* : a transparent or translucent feldspar of pearly luster used as a gem

moon·struck \-ˌstrək\ *adj* **1** : mentally unbalanced **2** : romantically sentimental **3** : lost in fantasy

¹**moor** \'mùr\ *n* **1** *chiefly Brit* : an expanse of open rolling infertile land **2** : a boggy area; *esp* : one that is peaty and dominated by grasses and sedges

²**moor** *vb* : to make fast with or as if with cables, lines, or anchors

Moor \'mùr\ *n* : one of the Arab and Berber conquerors of Spain — **Moor·ish** *adj*

moor·ing \'mùr-iŋ\ *n* **1** : a place where or an object to which a craft can be made fast **2** : an established practice or stabilizing influence — usu. used in pl.

moor·land \-lənd, -ˌland\ *n* : land consisting of moors

moose \'müs\ *n, pl* **moose** : a large heavy-antlered ruminant mammal of the deer family with humped shoulders and long legs that inhabits northern New and Old World forested areas

¹**moot** \'müt\ *vb* : to bring up for discussion; *also* : DEBATE

²**moot** *adj* **1** : open to question; *also* : DISPUTED **2** : having no practical significance

¹**mop** \'mäp\ *n* : an implement made of absorbent material fastened to a handle and used esp. for cleaning floors

²**mop** *vb* **mopped; mop·ping** : to use a mop on : clean with a mop

mope \'mōp\ *vb* **moped; mop·ing 1** : to become dull, dejected, or listless **2** : DAWDLE

mo·ped \'mō-ˌped\ *n* : a light low-powered motorbike that can be pedaled

mop·pet \'mä-pət\ *n* [obs. E *mop* fool, child] : CHILD

mo·raine \mə-'rān\ *n* : an accumulation of earth and stones left by a glacier

¹**mor·al** \'mòr-əl\ *adj* **1** : of or relating to principles of right and wrong **2** : conforming to a standard of right behavior; *also* : capable of right and wrong action **3** : probable but not proved ⟨a ∼ certainty⟩ **4** : having the effects of such on the mind, confidence, or will ⟨a ∼ victory⟩ **syn** virtuous, righteous, noble, ethical, principled — **mor·al·ly** *adv*

²**moral** *n* **1** : the practical meaning (as of a story) **2** *pl* : moral practices or teachings

mo·rale \mə-'ral\ *n* **1** : MORALITY **2** : the mental and emotional attitudes of an individual to the tasks at hand; *also* : ESPRIT DE CORPS

mor·al·ise *Brit var of* MORALIZE

mor·al·ist \'mòr-ə-list\ *n* **1** : one who leads a moral life **2** : a thinker or writer concerned with morals **3** : one concerned with regulating the morals of others — **mor·al·is·tic** \ˌmòr-ə-'lis-tik\ *adj* — **mor·al·is·ti·cal·ly** \-ti-k(ə-)lē\ *adv*

mo·ral·i·ty \mə-'ra-lə-tē\ *n, pl* **-ties** : moral conduct : VIRTUE

mor·al·ize \'mòr-ə-ˌlīz\ *vb* **-ized; -iz·ing** : to make moral reflections — **mor·al·i·za·tion** \ˌmòr-ə-lə-'zā-shən\ *n* — **mor·al·iz·er** \'mòr-ə-ˌlī-zər\ *n*

mo·rass \mə-'ras\ *n* : SWAMP; *also* : something that entangles, impedes, or confuses

mor·a·to·ri·um \ˌmòr-ə-'tōr-ē-əm\ *n, pl* **-ri·ums** *or* **-ria** \-ē-ə\ [ultim. fr. L *mora* delay] : a suspension of activity

mo·ray \mə-'rā, 'mòr-ˌā\ *n* : any of numerous often brightly colored biting eels of warm seas

mor·bid \'mòr-bəd\ *adj* **1** : of, relating to, or typical of disease; *also* : DISEASED, SICKLY **2** : characterized by gloomy or unwholesome ideas or feelings **3** : GRISLY, GRUESOME ⟨∼ details⟩ — **mor·bid·i·ty** \mòr-'bi-də-tē\ *n* — **mor·bid·ly** *adv* — **mor·bid·ness** *n*

mor·dant \'mòrd-ənt\ *adj* **1** : biting or caustic in manner or style **2** : BURNING, PUNGENT — **mor·dant·ly** *adv*

¹**more** \'mōr\ *adj* **1** : GREATER **2** : ADDITIONAL

²**more** *adv* **1** : in addition **2** : to a greater or higher degree

³**more** *n* **1** : a greater quantity, number, or amount ⟨the ∼ the merrier⟩ **2** : an additional amount ⟨costs a little ∼⟩

⁴**more** *pron* : additional persons or things or a greater amount

mo·rel \mə-'rel\ *n* : any of several pitted edible fungi

more·over \mōr-'ō-vər\ *adv* : in addition : FURTHER

mo·res \'mòr-ˌāz\ *n pl* [L, pl. of *mor-, mos* custom] **1** : the fixed morally binding customs of a group **2** : HABITS, MANNERS

Mor·gan \'mòr-gən\ *n* : any of an American breed of lightly built horses

morgue \'mòrg\ *n* : a place where the bodies of dead persons are kept until released for burial

mor·i·bund \'mòr-ə-(ˌ)bənd\ *adj* : being in a dying condition

Mor·mon \'mòr-mən\ *n* : a member of the Church of Jesus Christ of Latter-day Saints — **Mor·mon·ism** \-mə-ˌni-zəm\ *n*

morn \'mòrn\ *n* : MORNING

morn·ing \'mòr-niŋ\ *n* **1** : the early part of the day; *esp* : the time from the sunrise to noon **2** : BEGINNING

morning glory *n* : any of various twining plants related to the sweet potato that have often showy bell-shaped or funnel-shaped flowers

morning sickness *n* : nausea and vomiting that occur in the morning esp. during early pregnancy

morning star *n* : a bright planet (as Venus) seen in the eastern sky before or at sunrise

Mo·roc·can \mə-'rä-kən\ *n* : a native or inhabitant of Morocco

mo·roc·co \mə-'rä-kō\ *n* : a fine leather made of goatskins tanned with sumac

mo·ron \'mòr-ˌän\ *n* **1** : a mentally retarded person having a potential mental age of between 8 and 12 years and capable of doing routine work under supervision **2** : a very stupid person — **mo·ron·ic** \mə-'rä-nik\ *adj* — **mo·ron·i·cal·ly** \-ni-k(ə-)lē\ *adv*

mo·rose \mə-'rōs\ *adj* [L *morosus* hard to please, exacting, fr. *mor-, mos* custom, disposition] : having a sullen disposition; *also* : GLOOMY — **mo·rose·ly** *adv* — **mo·rose·ness** *n*

morph \'mòrf\ *vb* : to change in form or character : TRANSFORM

mor·pheme \'mòr-ˌfēm\ *n* : a meaningful linguistic unit that contains no smaller meaningful parts — **mor·phe·mic** \mòr-'fē-mik\ *adj*

mor·phia \'mòr-fē-ə\ *n* : MORPHINE

mor·phine \'mòr-ˌfēn\ *n* [F, fr. Gk *Morpheus*, Greek god of dreams] : an addictive drug obtained from opium and used to ease pain or induce sleep

mor·phol·o·gy \mòr-'fä-lə-jē\ *n* **1** : a branch of biology dealing with the form and structure of organisms **2** : a study and description of word formation in a language — **mor·pho·log·i·cal** \ˌmòr-fə-'lä-ji-kəl\ *adj* — **mor·phol·o·gist** \mòr-'fä-lə-jist\ *n*

mor·ris \'mòr-əs\ *n* : a vigorous English dance traditionally performed by men wearing costumes and bells

mor·row \'mär-ō\ *n* : the next day

Morse code \'mòrs-\ *n* : either of two codes consisting of dots and dashes or long and short sounds used for transmitting messages

mor·sel \'mòr-səl\ *n* [ME, fr. OF, dim. of *mors* bite, fr. L *morsus*, fr. *mordēre* to bite] **1** : a small piece of food or quantity **2** : a tasty dish

mor·tal \'mòrt-ᵊl\ *adj* **1** : causing death : FATAL; *also* : leading to eternal punishment ⟨~ sin⟩ **2** : subject to death ⟨~ man⟩ **3** : implacably hostile ⟨~ foe⟩ **4** : very great : EXTREME ⟨~ fear⟩ **5** : HUMAN ⟨~ limitations⟩ — **mortal** *n* — **mor·tal·i·ty** \mòr-'ta-lə-tē\ *n* — **mor·tal·ly** \'mòrt-ᵊl-ē\ *adv*

¹mor·tar \'mòr-tər\ *n* **1** : a strong bowl in which substances are pounded or crushed with a pestle **2** : a short-barreled cannon used to fire shells at high angles

²mortar *n* : a building material (as a mixture of lime and cement with sand and water) that is spread between bricks or stones to bind them together as it hardens — **mortar** *vb*

mor·tar·board \'mòr-tər-ˌbòrd\ *n* **1** : a square board for holding mortar **2** : an academic cap with a flat square top

mort·gage \'mòr-gij\ *n* [ME *morgage*, fr. MF, fr. OF, fr. *mort* dead + *gage* gage] : a transfer of rights to a piece of property usu. as security for the payment of a loan or debt that becomes void when the debt is paid — **mortgage** *vb* — **mort·gag·ee** \ˌmòr-gi-'jē\ *n* — **mort·gag·or** \ˌmòr-gi-'jòr\ *n*

mor·ti·cian \mòr-'ti-shən\ *n* [L *mort-, mors* death + E *-ician* (as in *physician*)] : UNDERTAKER

mor·ti·fy \'mòr-tə-ˌfī\ *vb* **-fied; -fy·ing 1** : to subdue (as the body) esp. by abstinence or self-inflicted pain **2** : HUMILIATE **3** : to become necrotic or gangrenous — **mor·ti·fi·ca·tion** \ˌmòr-tə-fə-'kä-shən\ *n*

mor·tise *also* **mor·tice** \'mòr-təs\ *n* : a hole cut in a piece of wood into which another piece fits to form a joint

mor·tu·ary \'mòr-chə-ˌwer-ē\ *n, pl* **-ar·ies** : a place in which dead bodies are kept until burial

mos *abbr* months

mo·sa·ic \mō-'zā-ik\ *n* : a surface decoration made by inlaying small pieces (as of colored glass or stone) to form figures or patterns; *also* : a design made in mosaic — **mosaic** *adj*

mo·sey \'mō-zē\ *vb* **mo·seyed; mo·sey·ing** : SAUNTER

mosh \'mäsh\ *vb* : to engage in various uninhibited often frenzied activities with others near the stage at a rock concert

Mos·lem \'mäz-ləm\ *var of* MUSLIM

mosque \'mäsk\ *n* : a building used for public worship by Muslims

mos·qui·to \mə-'skē-tō\ *n, pl* **-toes** *also* **-tos** : any of a family of dipteran flies the female of which sucks the blood of animals

mosquito net *n* : a net or screen for keeping out mosquitoes

moss \'mòs\ *n* : any of a class of green plants that lack flowers but have small leafy stems and often grow in clumps — **mossy** *adj*

moss·back \'mòs-ˌbak\ *n* : an extremely conservative person : FOGY

¹most \'mōst\ *adj* **1** : GREATEST ⟨the ~ ability⟩ **2** : the majority of ⟨~ people⟩

²most *adv* **1** : to the greatest or highest degree ⟨~ beautiful⟩ **2** : to a very great degree ⟨a ~ careful driver⟩

³most *n* : the greatest amount ⟨the ~ I can do⟩

⁴most *pron* : the greatest number or part ⟨~ became discouraged⟩

-most \ˌmōst\ *adj suffix* : most ⟨inner*most*⟩ : most toward ⟨end*most*⟩

most·ly \'mōst-lē\ *adv* : MAINLY

mot \'mō\ *n, pl* **mots** *same or* 'mōz\ [F, word, saying, fr. LL *muttum* grunt] : a witty saying

mote \'mōt\ n : a small particle

mo·tel \mō-'tel\ n [blend of *motor* and *hotel*] : a hotel in which the rooms are accessible from the parking area

mo·tet \mō-'tet\ n : a choral work on a sacred text for several voices usu. without instrumental accompaniment

moth \'mȯth\ n, pl **moths** \'mȯthz, 'mȯths\ : any of various insects belonging to the same order as the butterflies but usu. night-flying and with a stouter body and smaller wings

moth·ball \'mȯth-ˌbȯl\ n 1 : a ball (as of naphthalene) used to keep moths out of clothing 2 pl : protective storage

¹**moth·er** \'mə-thər\ n 1 : a female parent 2 : the superior of a religious community of women 3 : SOURCE, ORIGIN — **moth·er·hood** \-ˌhu̇d\ n — **moth·er·less** adj — **moth·er·li·ness** \-lē-nəs\ n — **moth·er·ly** adj

²**mother** vb 1 : to give birth to; *also* : PRODUCE 2 : to care for or protect like a mother

moth·er·board \'mə-thər-ˌbȯrd\ n : the main circuit board esp. of a microcomputer

moth·er-in-law \'mə-thər-ən-ˌlȯ\ n, pl **mothers-in-law** \'mə-thərz-\ : the mother of one's spouse

moth·er·land \'mə-thər-ˌland\ n 1 : the land of origin of something 2 : the native land of one's ancestors

moth·er-of-pearl \ˌmə-thər-əv-'pərl\ n : the hard pearly matter forming the inner layer of a mollusk shell

mo·tif \mō-'tēf\ n [F, motive, motif] : a dominant idea or central theme (as in a work of art)

mo·tile \'mōt-ᵊl, 'mō-ˌtīl\ adj : capable of spontaneous movement — **mo·til·i·ty** \mō-'ti-lə-tē\ n

¹**mo·tion** \'mō-shən\ n 1 : an act, process, or instance of moving 2 : a proposal for action (as by a deliberative body) 3 pl : ACTIVITIES, MOVEMENTS — **mo·tion·less** adj — **mo·tion·less·ly** adv — **mo·tion·less·ness** n

²**motion** vb : to direct or signal by a movement

motion picture n : a series of pictures projected on a screen so rapidly that they produce a continuous picture in which persons and objects seem to move

motion sickness n : sickness induced by motion and characterized by nausea

mo·ti·vate \'mō-tə-ˌvāt\ vb **-vat·ed; -vat·ing** : to provide with a motive : IMPEL — **mo·ti·va·tion** \ˌmō-tə-'vā-shən\ n — **mo·ti·va·tion·al** \-shə-nəl\ adj — **mo·ti·va·tor** \'mō-tə-ˌvā-tər\ n

¹**mo·tive** \'mō-tiv, 2 also mō-'tēv\ n 1 : something (as a need or desire) that causes a person to act 2 : a recurrent theme in a musical composition 3 : MOTIF — **mo·tive·less** adj

²**mo·tive** \'mō-tiv\ adj 1 : moving to action 2 : of or relating to motion

mot·ley \'mät-lē\ adj 1 : variegated in color 2 : made up of diverse often incongruous elements **syn** heterogeneous, miscellaneous, assorted, mixed, varied

¹**mo·tor** \'mō-tər\ n 1 : one that imparts motion 2 : a machine that produces motion or power for doing work 3 : AUTOMOBILE

²**motor** vb : to travel or transport by automobile : DRIVE — **mo·tor·ist** n

mo·tor·bike \'mō-tər-ˌbīk\ n : a small lightweight motorcycle

mo·tor·boat \-ˌbōt\ n : a boat propelled by a motor

mo·tor·cade \-ˌkād\ n : a procession of motor vehicles

mo·tor·car \-ˌkär\ n : AUTOMOBILE

mo·tor·cy·cle \'mō-tər-ˌsī-kəl\ n : a 2-wheeled automotive vehicle — **mo·tor·cy·clist** \-k(ə-)list\ n

motor home n : a large motor vehicle equipped as living quarters

motor inn n : MOTEL

mo·tor·ise Brit var of MOTORIZE

mo·tor·ize \'mō-tə-ˌrīz\ vb **-ized; -iz·ing** 1 : to equip with a motor 2 : to equip with automobiles

mo·tor·man \'mō-tər-mən\ n : an operator of a motor-driven vehicle (as a streetcar or subway train)

motor scooter n : a low 2- or 3-wheeled automotive vehicle resembling a child's scooter but having a seat

mo·tor·truck \'mō-tər-ˌtrək\ n : an automotive truck

motor vehicle n : an automotive vehicle (as an automobile) not operated on rails

mot·tle \'mät-ᵊl\ vb **mot·tled; mot·tling** : to mark with spots of different color : BLOTCH

mot·to \'mä-tō\ n, pl **mottoes** also **mottos** [It, fr. LL *muttum* grunt, fr. L *muttire* to mutter] 1 : a sentence, phrase, or word inscribed on something to indicate its character or use 2 : a short expression of a guiding rule of conduct

moue \'mü\ n : a little grimace

mould \'mōld\ var of MOLD

moult \'mōlt\ var of MOLT

mound \'mau̇nd\ n 1 : an artificial bank or hill of earth or stones 2 : KNOLL 3 : HEAP, PILE

¹**mount** \'mau̇nt\ n : a high hill

²**mount** vb 1 : to increase in amount or extent; *also* : RISE, ASCEND 2 : to get up on something; *esp* : to seat oneself on (as a horse) for riding 3 : to put in position (~ artillery) 4 : to set on something that elevates 5 : to attach to a support 6 : to prepare esp. for examination or display — **mount·able** adj — **mount·er** n

³**mount** n 1 : FRAME, SUPPORT 2 : a means of conveyance; *esp* : SADDLE HORSE

moun·tain \'mau̇nt-ᵊn\ n : a landmass higher than a hill — **moun·tain·ous** \-ᵊn-əs\ adj — **moun·tainy** \-ᵊn-ē\ adj

mountain ash n : any of various trees related to the roses that have pinnate leaves and red or orange-red fruits

mountain bike n : a bicycle with wide knobby tires, straight handlebars, and 18 or 21 gears that is designed to operate esp. over unpaved terrain

moun·tain·eer \ˌmau̇nt-ᵊn-'ir\ n 1 : a native or inhabitant of a mountainous region 2 : one who climbs mountains for sport

mountain goat n : a ruminant mammal of mountainous northwestern No. America that resembles a goat

mountain goat

mountain laurel *n* : a No. American evergreen shrub or small tree of the heath family with glossy leaves and clusters of rose-colored or white flowers

mountain lion *n* : COUGAR

moun·tain·side \'maunt-ᵊn-ˌsīd\ *n* : the side of a mountain

moun·tain·top \-ˌtäp\ *n* : the summit of a mountain

moun·te·bank \'maunt-i-ˌbaŋk\ *n* [It *montimbanco*, fr. *montare* to mount + *in* in, on + *banco, banca* bench] : QUACK, CHARLATAN

Moun·tie \'maun-tē\ *n* : a member of the Royal Canadian Mounted Police

mount·ing \'maun-tiŋ\ *n* : something that serves as a frame or support

mourn \'mōrn\ *vb* : to feel or express grief or sorrow — **mourn·er** *n*

mourn·ful \-fəl\ *adj* : expressing, feeling, or causing sorrow — **mourn·ful·ly** *adv* — **mourn·ful·ness** *n*

mourn·ing \'mōr-niŋ\ *n* 1 : an outward sign (as black clothes) of grief for a person's death 2 : a period of time during which signs of grief are shown

mouse \'maus\ *n, pl* **mice** \'mīs\ 1 : any of numerous small rodents with pointed snout, long body, and slender tail 2 : a small manual device that controls cursor movement on a computer display

mous·er \'mau-sər\ *n* : a cat proficient at catching mice

mouse·trap \'maus-ˌtrap\ *n* 1 : a trap for catching mice 2 : a stratagem that lures one to defeat or destruction — **mousetrap** *vb*

mousse \'müs\ *n* [F, lit., froth] 1 : a molded chilled dessert made with sweetened and flavored whipped cream or egg whites and gelatin 2 : a foamy preparation used in styling hair — **mousse** *vb*

mous·tache \'məs-ˌtash, (ˌ)məs-'tash\ *var of* MUSTACHE

mousy *or* **mous·ey** \'mau-sē, -zē\ *adj* **mous·i·er; -est** 1

: QUIET, STEALTHY 2 : TIMID 3 : grayish brown — **mous·i·ness** \'mau-sē-nəs, -zē-\ *n*

¹**mouth** \'mauth\ *n, pl* **mouths** \'mauthz, 'mauths\ 1 : the opening through which an animal takes in food; *also* : the cavity that encloses the tongue, lips, and teeth in the typical vertebrate 2 : something resembling a mouth (as in affording entrance) — **mouthed** \'mauthd, 'mautht\ *adj* — **mouth·ful** *n*

²**mouth** \'mauth\ *vb* 1 : SPEAK; *also* : DECLAIM 2 : to repeat without comprehension or sincerity 3 : to form soundlessly with the lips

mouth·part \'mauth-ˌpärt\ *n* : a structure or appendage near the mouth (as of an insect) esp. when adapted for eating

mouth·piece \-ˌpēs\ *n* 1 : a part (as of a musical instrument) that goes in the mouth or to which the mouth is applied 2 : SPOKESMAN

mouth·wash \-ˌwosh, -ˌwäsh\ *n* : a usu. antiseptic liquid preparation for cleaning the mouth and teeth

mou·ton \'mü-ˌtän\ *n* : processed sheepskin that has been sheared or dyed to resemble beaver or seal

¹**move** \'müv\ *vb* **moved; mov·ing** 1 : to change or cause to change position or posture 2 : to go or cause to go from one point to another; *also* : DEPART 3 : to take or cause to take action 4 : to show marked activity 5 : to stir the emotions 6 : to make a formal request, application, or appeal 7 : to change one's residence 8 : EVACUATE 2 — **mov·able** *or* **move·able** \'mü-və-bəl\ *adj*

²**move** *n* 1 : an act of moving 2 : a calculated step taken to gain an objective 3 : a change of location 4 : an agile action esp. in sports

move·ment \'müv-mənt\ *n* 1 : the act or process of moving : MOVE 2 : a series of organized activities working toward an objective 3 : the moving parts of a mechanism (as of a watch) 4 : RHYTHM 5 : a section of an extended musical composition 6 : an act of voiding the bowels; *also* : STOOL 4

mov·er \'mü-vər\ *n* : one that moves; *esp* : one that moves the belongings of others from one location to another

mov·ie \'mü-vē\ *n* 1 : MOTION PICTURE 2 *pl* : a showing of a motion picture 3 *pl* : the motion-picture industry

¹**mow** \'mau\ *n* : the part of a barn where hay or straw is stored

²**mow** \'mō\ *vb* **mowed; mowed** *or* **mown** \'mōn\; **mow·ing** 1 : to cut (as grass) with a scythe or machine 2 : to cut the standing herbage of (∼ the lawn) — **mow·er** *n*

Mo·zam·bi·can \ˌmō-zəm-'bē-kən\ *n* : a native or inhabitant of Mozambique

moz·za·rel·la \ˌmät-sə-'re-lə\ *n* [It] : a moist white unsalted unripened mild cheese of a smooth rubbery texture

MP *abbr* 1 melting point 2 member of parliament 3 metropolitan police 4 military police; military policeman

mpg *abbr* miles per gallon

mph *abbr* miles per hour

Mr. \'mis-tər\ *n, pl* **Messrs.** \'me-sərz\ — used as a

conventional title of courtesy before a man's surname or his title of office

MRI *abbr* magnetic resonance imaging

Mrs. \'mi-səz, -səs, *esp Southern* 'mi-zəz, -zəs\ *n, pl* **Mes·dames** \mā-'däm, -'dam\ — used as a conventional title of courtesy before a married woman's surname

Ms. \'miz\ *n, pl* **Mss.** *or* **Mses.** \'mi-zez\ — used instead of *Miss* or *Mrs.*

MS *abbr* 1 manuscript 2 master of science 3 military science 4 Mississippi 5 motor ship 6 multiple sclerosis

msec *abbr* millisecond

msg *abbr* message

MSG *abbr* 1 master sergeant 2 monosodium glutamate

msgr *abbr* 1 monseigneur 2 monsignor

MSgt *abbr* master sergeant

MSS *abbr* manuscripts

MST *abbr* mountain standard time

mt *abbr* mount; mountain

Mt *abbr* Matthew

MT *abbr* 1 metric ton 2 Montana 3 mountain time

mtg *abbr* 1 meeting 2 mortgage

mtge *abbr* mortgage

mu \'myü, 'mü\ *n* : the 12th letter of the Greek alphabet — M or μ

¹much \'məch\ *adj* **more** \'mōr\; **most** \'mōst\ : great in quantity, amount, extent, or degree (∼ money)

²much *adv* **more**; **most** 1 : to a great degree or extent (∼ happier) 2 : ALMOST, NEARLY (looks ∼ as he did before)

³much *n* 1 : a great quantity, amount, extent, or degree 2 : something considerable or impressive

mu·ci·lage \'myü-sə-lij\ *n* : a watery sticky solution (as of a gum) used esp. as an adhesive — **mu·ci·lag·i·nous** \ₘyü-sə-'la-jə-nəs\ *adj*

muck \'mək\ *n* 1 : soft moist barnyard manure 2 : FILTH, DIRT 3 : a dark richly organic soil; *also* : MUD, MIRE — **mucky** *adj*

muck·rake \-ₘrāk\ *vb* : to expose publicly real or apparent misconduct of a prominent individual or business — **muck·rak·er** *n*

mu·cus \'myü-kəs\ *n* : a slimy slippery protective secretion of membranes (**mucous membranes**) lining some body cavities — **mu·cous** \-kəs\ *adj*

mud \'məd\ *n* : soft wet earth : MIRE — **mud·di·ly** \'mə-də-lē\ *adv* — **mud·di·ness** \-dē-nəs\ *n* — **mud·dy** \'mə-dē\ *adj or vb*

mud·dle \'məd-əl\ *vb* **mud·dled; mud·dling** 1 : to make muddy 2 : to confuse esp. with liquor 3 : to mix up or make a mess of 4 : to think or act in a confused way

mud·dle·head·ed \ₘməd-əl-'he-dəd\ *adj* 1 : mentally confused 2 : INEPT

mud·flat \'məd-ₘflat\ *n* : a level tract alternately covered and left bare by the tide

mud·guard \'məd-ₘgärd\ *n* : a guard over or a flap be-

hind a wheel of a vehicle to catch or deflect mud

mud·room \-ₘrüm, -ₘrüm\ *n* : a room in a house for removing dirty or wet footwear and clothing

mud·sling·er \-ₘsliŋ-ər\ *n* : one who uses invective esp. against a political opponent — **mud·sling·ing** \-ₘsliŋ-iŋ\ *n*

Muen·ster \'mən-stər, 'mün-, 'mùn-\ *n* : a semisoft bland cheese

mu·ez·zin \mü-'ez-ᵊn, myü-\ *n* : a Muslim crier who calls the hour of daily prayer

¹muff \'məf\ *n* : a warm tubular covering for the hands

²muff *n* : a bungling performance; *esp* : a failure to hold a ball in attempting a catch — **muff** *vb*

muf·fin \'mə-fən\ *n* : a small soft cake baked in a cup-shaped container

muf·fle \'mə-fəl\ *vb* **muf·fled; muf·fling** 1 : to wrap up so as to conceal or protect 2 : to wrap or pad with something to dull the sound of 3 : to keep down : SUPPRESS

muf·fler \'mə-flər\ *n* 1 : a scarf worn around the neck 2 : a device (as on a car's exhaust) to deaden noise

muf·ti \'məf-tē\ *n* : civilian clothes

¹mug \'məg\ *n* : a usu. metal or earthenware cylindrical drinking cup

²mug *vb* **mugged; mug·ging** 1 : to pose or make faces esp. to attract attention or for a camera 2 : PHOTOGRAPH

³mug *vb* **mugged; mug·ging** : to assault usu. with intent to rob — **mug·ger** *n*

mug·gy \'mə-gē\ *adj* **mug·gi·er; -est** : being warm and humid — **mug·gi·ness** \-gē-nəs\ *n*

mug·wump \'məg-ₘwəmp\ *n* [obs. slang *mugwump* kingpin, fr. Massachuset (a No. American Indian language) *mugquomp* war leader] : an independent in politics

Mu·ham·mad·an \mō-'ha-mə-dən, -'hä-; mü-\ *n* : MUSLIM — **Mu·ham·mad·an·ism** \-də-ₙni-zəm\ *n*

mu·ja·hid·een *or* **mu·ja·hed·in** \mü-ₙja-hi-'dēn, -jä-\ *pl* [Ar *mujāhidīn*, pl. of *mujāhid*, lit., person who wages jihad] : Islamic guerrilla fighters esp. in the Middle East

muk·luk \'mək-ₗlək\ *n* 1 : an Eskimo boot of sealskin or reindeer skin 2 : a boot with a soft leather sole worn over several pairs of socks

mu·lat·to \mù-'la-tō, myü-, -'lä-\ *n, pl* **-toes** *or* **-tos** [Sp *mulato*, fr. *mulo* mule, fr. L *mulus*] : a first-generation offspring of a black person and a white person; *also* : a person of mixed white and black ancestry

mul·ber·ry \'məl-ₗber-ē\ *n* : any of a genus of trees with edible berrylike fruit and leaves used as food for silkworms; *also* : the fruit

mulch \'məlch\ *n* : a protective covering (as of straw or leaves) spread on the ground esp. to reduce evaporation or control weeds — **mulch** *vb*

¹mulct \'məlkt\ *n* : FINE, PENALTY

²mulct *vb* 1 : FINE 2 : CHEAT, DEFRAUD

¹mule \'myül\ *n* 1 : a hybrid offspring of a male donkey and a female horse 2 : a very stubborn person —

mul·ish \'myü-lish\ *adj* — **mul·ish·ly** *adv* — **mulish·ness** *n*

²**mule** *n* : a slipper whose upper does not extend around the heel of the foot

mule deer *n* : a long-eared deer of western No. America

mu·le·teer \,myü-lə-'tir\ *n* : one who drives mules

¹**mull** \'məl\ *vb* : PONDER, MEDITATE

²**mull** *vb* : to heat, sweeten, and flavor (as wine) with spices

mul·lein \'mə-lən\ *n* : a tall herb related to the snapdragons that has coarse woolly leaves and flowers in spikes

mul·let \'mə-lət\ *n, pl* **mullet** *or* **mullets** : any of a family of largely gray chiefly marine bony fishes including valuable food fishes

mul·li·gan stew \'mə-li-gən-\ *n* : a stew made from whatever ingredients are available

mul·li·ga·taw·ny \,mə-li-gə-'tò-nē\ *n* : a soup usu. of chicken stock seasoned with curry

mul·lion \'məl-yən\ *n* : a vertical strip separating windowpanes

multi- *comb form* **1** : many : multiple ⟨*multi*unit⟩ **2** : many times over ⟨*multi*millionaire⟩

mul·ti·col·ored \,məl-ti-'kə-lərd\ *adj* : having many colors

mul·ti·cul·tur·al \,məl-tē-'kəl-chə-rəl, -,tī-\ *adj* : of, relating to, reflecting, or adapted to diverse cultures ⟨a ∼ society⟩

mul·ti·di·men·sion·al \-ti-də-'men-chə-nəl, -,tī-, -dī-\ *adj* : of, relating to, or having many facets or dimensions ⟨a ∼ problem⟩ ⟨∼ space⟩

mul·ti·fac·et·ed \-'fa-sə-təd\ *adj* : having several distinct facets

mul·ti·fam·i·ly \-'fam-lē, -'fa-mə-\ *adj* : designed for use by several families

mul·ti·far·i·ous \,məl-tə-'far-ē-əs\ *adj* : having great variety : DIVERSE — **mul·ti·far·i·ous·ness** *n*

mul·ti·form \'məl-ti-,fòrm\ *adj* : having many forms or appearances — **mul·ti·for·mi·ty** \,məl-ti-'fòr-mə-tē\ *n*

mul·ti·lat·er·al \,məl-ti-'la-tə-rəl, -,tī-, -'la-trəl\ *adj* : having many sides or participants ⟨∼ treaty⟩ — **mul·ti·lat·er·al·ism** \-'la-tə-rə-,li-zəm\ *n*

mul·ti·lev·el \-'le-vəl\ *adj* : having several levels

mul·ti·lin·gual \-'liŋ-gwəl\ *adj* : knowing or using several languages — **mul·ti·lin·gual·ism** \-gwə-,li-zəm\ *n*

mul·ti·me·dia \-'mē-dē-ə\ *adj* : using, involving, or encompassing several media ⟨a ∼ advertising campaign⟩

mul·ti·mil·lion·aire \,məl-ti-,mil-yə-'nar, -,tī-, -'mil-yə-,nar\ *n* : a person worth several million dollars

mul·ti·na·tion·al \-'na-shə-nəl\ *adj* **1** : of or relating to several nationalities **2** : relating to or involving several nations **3** : having divisions in several countries ⟨a ∼ corporation⟩ — **multinational** *n*

¹**mul·ti·ple** \'məl-tə-pəl\ *adj* **1** : more than one; *also* : MANY **2** : VARIOUS

²**multiple** *n* : the product of a quantity by an integer ⟨35 is a ∼ of 7⟩

multiple–choice *adj* : having several answers given from which the correct one is to be chosen ⟨a ∼ question⟩

multiple personality *n* : a mental and emotional disorder which is a neurosis and in which the personality becomes separated into two or more parts each of which controls behavior part of the time

multiple sclerosis *n* : a disease marked by patches of hardened tissue in the brain or spinal cord and associated esp. with partial or complete paralysis and muscular tremor

mul·ti·plex \'məl-tə-,pleks\ *n* : CINEPLEX

mul·ti·pli·cand \,məl-tə-pli-'kand\ *n* : the number that is to be multiplied by another

mul·ti·pli·ca·tion \,məl-tə-plə-'kā-shən\ *n* **1** : INCREASE **2** : a short method of finding the result of adding a

figure the number of times indicated by another figure

multiplication sign *n* **1** : TIMES SIGN **2** : a centered dot indicating multiplication

mul·ti·plic·i·ty \,məl-tə-'pli-sə-tē\ *n, pl* **-ties** : a great number or variety

mul·ti·pli·er \'məl-tə-,plī-ər\ *n* : one that multiplies; *esp* : a number by which another number is multiplied

mul·ti·ply \'məl-tə-,plī\ *vb* **-plied; -ply·ing 1** : to increase in number (as by breeding) **2** : to find the product of by multiplication; *also* : to perform multiplication

mul·ti·pur·pose \,məl-ti-'pər-pəs, -,tī-\ *adj* : having or serving several purposes

mul·ti·ra·cial \-'rā-shəl\ *adj* : composed of, involving, or representing various races

mul·ti·sense \-,sens\ *adj* : having several meanings ⟨∼ words⟩

mul·ti·sto·ry \-,stòr-ē\ *adj* : having several stories ⟨∼ buildings⟩

mul·ti·tude \'məl-tə-,tüd, -,tyüd\ *n* : a great number — **mul·ti·tu·di·nous** \,məl-tə-'tüd-ᵊn-əs, -'tyüd-\ *adj*

mul·ti·unit \,məl-ti-'yü-nət, -,tī-\ *adj* : having several units

mul·ti·vi·ta·min \-'vī-tə-mən\ *adj* : containing several vitamins and esp. all known to be essential to health

¹**mum** \'məm\ *adj* : SILENT

²**mum** *n* : CHRYSANTHEMUM

³**mum** *chiefly Brit var of* MOM

mum·ble \'məm-bəl\ *vb* **mum·bled; mum·bling** : to speak in a low indistinct manner — **mumble** *n* — **mum·bler** *n* — **mum·bly** *adj*

mum·ble·ty–peg \'məm-bəl-tē-,peg\ *also* **mum·ble-the–peg** \'məm-bəl-thə-\ *n* : a game in which the players try to flip a knife from various positions so that the blade will stick into the ground

mum·bo jum·bo \,məm-bō-'jəm-bō\ *n* **1** : a complicated ritual with elaborate trappings **2** : GIBBERISH, NONSENSE

mum·mer \'mə-mər\ *n* **1** : an actor esp. in a pantomime **2** : a person who goes merrymaking in disguise during festivals — **mum·mery** *n*

mum·my \'mə-mē\ *n, pl* **mummies** [ME *mummie* powdered parts of a mummified body used as a drug, fr. MF *momie*, fr. ML *mumia*, fr. Ar *mūmiyah* bitumen, mummy, fr. Per *mūm* wax] : a body embalmed for burial in the manner of the ancient Egyptians — **mum·mi·fi·ca·tion** \,mə-mi-fə-'kā-shən\ *n* — **mum·mi·fy** \'mə-mi-,fī\ *vb*

mumps \'məmps\ *n sing or pl* [fr. pl. of obs. *mump* grimace] : a virus disease marked by fever and swelling esp. of the salivary glands

mun *or* **munic** *abbr* municipal

munch \'mənch\ *vb* : to eat with a chewing action; *also* : to snack on

munch·ies \'mən-chēz\ *n pl* **1** : hunger pangs **2** : light snack foods

mun·dane \,mən-'dān, 'mən-,dān\ *adj* **1** : of or relating to the world **2** : concerned with the practical details of everyday life — **mun·dane·ly** *adv*

mu·nic·i·pal \myù-'ni-sə-pəl\ *adj* **1** : of, relating to, or characteristic of a municipality **2** : restricted to one locality — **mu·nic·i·pal·ly** *adv*

mu·nic·i·pal·i·ty \myù-,ni-sə-'pa-lə-tē\ *n, pl* **-ties** : an urban political unit with corporate status and usu. powers of self-government

mu·nif·i·cent \myù-'ni-fə-sənt\ *adj* : liberal in giving : GENEROUS — **mu·nif·i·cence** \-səns\ *n*

mu·ni·tion \myù-'ni-shən\ *n* : ARMAMENT, AMMUNITION

¹**mu·ral** \'myùr-əl\ *adj* **1** : of or relating to a wall **2** : applied to and made part of a wall or ceiling surface

²**mural** *n* : a mural painting — **mu·ral·ist** *n*

¹**mur·der** \'mər-dər\ *n* **1** : the crime of unlawfully killing a person esp. with malice aforethought **2** : something unusually difficult or dangerous

IT'S FUN TO LIE HERE AND MUSE ON THE MEANING OF LIFE,

AND MUSE ON THE MYRIAD OF SOLUTIONS TO THE WORLD'S WOES,

AND TO COUNT THE CRACKS IN THE CEILING

JIM DAVIS 1-28

© 1986 PAWS, INC.

²murder *vb* **1 :** to commit a murder; *also* : to kill brutally **2 :** to put an end to **3 :** to spoil by performing poorly ⟨∼ a song⟩ — **mur•der•er** *n*

mur•der•ess \'mər-də-rəs\ *n* : a woman who murders

mur•der•ous \'mər-də-rəs\ *adj* **1 :** having or appearing to have the purpose of murder **2 :** marked by or causing murder or bloodshed ⟨∼ gunfire⟩ — **mur•der•ous•ly** *adv*

murk \'mərk\ *n* : DARKNESS, GLOOM — **murk•i•ly** \'mər-kə-lē\ *adv* — **murk•i•ness** \-kē-nəs\ *n* — **murky** *adj*

mur•mur \'mər-mər\ *n* **1 :** a muttered complaint **2 :** a low indistinct often continuous sound — **murmur** *vb* — **mur•mur•er** *n* — **mur•mur•ous** *adj*

mus *abbr* **1** museum **2** music; musician

mus•ca•tel \ˌməs-kə-'tel\ *n* : a sweet fortified wine

¹mus•cle \'mə-səl\ *n* [ME, fr. MF, fr. L *musculus*, fr. dim. of *mus* mouse] **1 :** a body tissue consisting of long cells that contract when stimulated and produce motion; *also* : an organ consisting of this tissue and functioning in moving a body part **2 :** STRENGTH, BRAWN — **mus•cled** \'mə-səld\ *adj* — **mus•cu•lar** \'məs-kyə-lər\ *adj* — **mus•cu•lar•i•ty** \ˌməs-kyə-'lar-ə-tē\ *n*

²muscle *vb* **mus•cled; mus•cling :** to force one's way

mus•cle–bound \'mə-səl-ˌbaund\ *adj* : having some of the muscles abnormally enlarged and lacking in elasticity (as from excessive exercise)

muscular dystrophy *n* : any of a group of diseases characterized by progressive wasting of muscles

mus•cu•la•ture \'məs-kyə-lə-ˌchŭr\ *n* : the muscles of the body or its parts

¹muse \'myüz\ *vb* **mused; mus•ing** [ME, fr. MF *muser* to gape, idle, muse, fr. *muse* mouth of an animal, fr. ML *musus*] : to become absorbed in thought — **mus•ing•ly** *adv*

²muse *n* [fr. *Muse* any of the nine sister goddesses of learning and the arts in Greek myth, fr. ME, fr. MF, fr. L *Musa*, fr. Gk *Mousa*] : a source of inspiration

mu•se•um \myü-'zē-əm\ *n* : an institution devoted to the procurement, care, and display of objects of lasting interest or value

¹mush \'məsh\ *n* **1 :** cornmeal boiled in water **2 :** sentimental drivel

²mush *vb* : to travel esp. over snow with a sled drawn by dogs

¹mush•room \'məsh-ˌrüm, -ˌrum\ *n* : the fleshy usu. caplike spore-bearing organ of various fungi esp. when edible; *also* : such a fungus

²mushroom *vb* **1 :** to collect wild mushrooms **2 :** to spread out : EXPAND **3 :** to grow rapidly

mushy \'mə-shē\ *adj* **mush•i•er; -est :** soft like mush **2 :** excessively sentimental

mu•sic \'myü-zik\ *n* **1 :** the science or art of combining tones into a composition having structure and continuity; *also* : vocal or instrumental sounds having rhythm, melody, or harmony **2 :** an agreeable sound

¹mu•si•cal \'myü-zi-kəl\ *adj* **1 :** of or relating to music or musicians **2 :** having the pleasing tonal qualities of music **3 :** fond of or gifted in music — **mu•si•cal•ly** \-k(ə-)lē\ *adv*

²musical *n* : a film or theatrical production consisting of musical numbers and dialogue based on a unifying plot

mu•si•cale \ˌmyü-zi-'kal\ *n* : a usu. private social gathering featuring music

mu•si•cian \myü-'zi-shən\ *n* : a composer, conductor, or performer of music — **mu•si•cian•ly** *adj* — **mu•si•cian•ship** *n*

mu•si•col•o•gy \ˌmyü-zi-'kä-lə-jē\ *n* : the study of music as a field of knowledge or research — **mu•si•co•log•i•cal** \-kə-'lä-ji-kəl\ *adj* — **mu•si•col•o•gist** \-'kä-lə-jist\ *n*

musk \'məsk\ *n* : a substance obtained esp. from a small Asian deer (**musk deer**) and used as a perfume fixative — **musk•i•ness** \'məs-kē-nəs\ *n* — **musky** *adj*

musk•keg \'məs-ˌkeg\ *n* : BOG; *esp* : a mossy bog in northern No. America

musk•kel•lunge \'məs-kə-ˌlənj\ *n, pl* **muskellunge :** a large No. American pike that is a valuable sport fish

mus•ket \'məs-kət\ *n* [MF *mousquet*, fr. It *moschetto* arrow for a crossbow, musket, fr. dim. of *mosca* fly, fr. L *musca*] : a heavy large-caliber muzzle-loading shoulder firearm — **mus•ke•teer** \ˌməs-kə-'tir\ *n*

mus•ket•ry \'məs-kə-trē\ *n* **1 :** MUSKETS **2 :** MUSKETEERS **3 :** musket fire

musk•mel•on \'məsk-ˌme-lən\ *n* : a small round to oval melon that has usu. a sweet edible green or orange flesh

musk ox *n* : a heavyset shaggy-coated wild ox of Greenland and the arctic tundra of northern No. America

musk•rat \'məs-ˌkrat\ *n, pl* **muskrat** *or* **muskrats :** a large No. American aquatic rodent with webbed feet and dark brown fur; *also* : its fur

Mus•lim \'məz-ləm\ *n* : an adherent of Islam — **Muslim** *adj*

mus•lin \'məz-lən\ *n* : a plain-woven sheer to coarse cotton fabric

¹muss \'məs\ *n* : a state of disorder — **muss•i•ly** \'mə-sə-lē\ *adv* — **muss•i•ness** \-sē-nəs\ *n* — **mussy** *adj*

²muss *vb* : to make untidy : DISARRANGE

mus•sel \'mə-səl\ *n* **1 :** a dark edible saltwater bivalve mollusk **2 :** any of various freshwater bivalve mollusks of the central U.S. having shells with a pearly lining

must \'məst\ *vb* — used as an auxiliary esp. to express a command, requirement, or necessity

²must *n* **1 :** an imperative duty **2 :** an indispensable item

mus•tache \'məs-ˌtash, (ˌ)məs-'tash\ *n* : the hair growing on the human upper lip — **mus•tached** \-'tasht, -'tasht\ *adj*

mus•tang \'məs-ˌtaŋ\ *n* [MexSp *mestengo*, fr. Sp, stray, fr. *mesteño* strayed, fr. *mesta* annual roundup of cattle that disposed of strays, fr. ML (*animalia*) *mixta* mixed animals] : a small hardy naturalized horse of the western plains of America; *also* : BRONC

mus·tard \'məs-tərd\ *n* **1** : a pungent yellow powder of the seeds of an herb related to the cabbage and used as a condiment or in medicine **2** : a plant that yields mustard; *also* : a closely related plant — **mustardy** *adj*

mustard gas *n* : a poison gas used in warfare that has violent irritating and blistering effects

¹mus·ter \'məs-tər\ *n* **1** : an act of assembling (as for military inspection); *also* : critical examination **2** : an assembled group

²muster *vb* [ME *mustren* to show, muster, fr. OF *monstrer*, fr. L *monstrare* to show, fr. *monstrum* evil omen, monster] **1** : CONVENE, ASSEMBLE; *also* : to call the roll of **2** : ACCUMULATE **3** : to call forth : ROUSE **4** : to amount to : COMPRISE

muster out *vb* : to discharge from military service

musty \'məs-tē\ *adj* **mus·ti·er; -est** : MOLDY, STALE; *also* : tasting or smelling of damp or decay — **must·i·ly** \-tə-lē\ *adv* — **must·i·ness** \-tē-nəs\ *n*

mu·ta·ble \'myü-tə-bəl\ *adj* **1** : prone to change : FICKLE **2** : capable of or liable to mutation : VARIABLE — **mu·ta·bil·i·ty** \ˌmyü-tə-'bi-lə-tē\ *n*

mu·tant \'myüt-ᵊnt\ *adj* : of, relating to, or produced by mutation — **mu·tant** *n*

mu·tate \'myü-ˌtāt\ *vb* **mu·tat·ed; mu·tat·ing** : to undergo or cause to undergo mutation — **mu·ta·tive** \'myü-ˌtā-tiv, -tə-tiv\ *adj*

mu·ta·tion \myü-'tā-shən\ *n* **1** : CHANGE **2** : an inherited physical or biochemical change in genetic material; *also* : the process of producing a mutation **3** : an individual, strain, or trait resulting from mutation — **mu·ta·tion·al** *adj*

¹mute \'myüt\ *adj* **mut·er; mut·est 1** : unable to speak : DUMB **2** : SILENT — **mute·ly** *adv* — **mute·ness** *n*

²mute *n* **1** : a person who cannot or does not speak **2** : a device on a musical instrument that reduces, softens, or muffles the tone

³mute *vb* **mut·ed; mut·ing** : to muffle, reduce, or eliminate the sound of

mu·ti·late \'myüt-ᵊl-ˌāt\ *vb* **-lat·ed; -lat·ing 1** : to cut up or alter radically so as to make imperfect **2** : MAIM, CRIPPLE — **mu·ti·la·tion** \ˌmyüt-ᵊl-'ā-shən\ *n* — **mu·ti·la·tor** \'myüt-ᵊl-ˌā-tər\ *n*

mu·ti·ny \'myüt-ᵊn-ē\ *n, pl* **-nies** : willful refusal to obey constituted authority; *esp* : revolt against a superior officer — **mu·ti·neer** \ˌmyüt-ᵊn-'ir\ *n* — **mu·ti·nous** \'myüt-ᵊn-əs\ *adj* — **mu·ti·nous·ly** *adv* — **mutiny** *vb*

mutt \'mət\ *n* : MONGREL, CUR

mut·ter \'mət-ər\ *vb* **1** : to speak indistinctly or with a low voice and lips partly closed **2** : GRUMBLE — **mutter** *n*

mut·ton \'mət-ᵊn\ *n* [ME *motoun*, fr. OF *moton* ram] : the flesh of a mature sheep used for food — **mut·tony** *adj*

mut·ton·chops \'mət-ᵊn-ˌchäps\ *n pl* : whiskers on the side of the face that are narrow at the temple and broad and round by the lower jaws

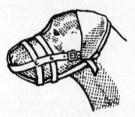

mu·tu·al \'myü-chə-wəl\ *adj* **1** : given and received in equal amount ⟨∼ trust⟩ **2** : having the same feelings one for the other ⟨∼ enemies⟩ **3** : COMMON, JOINT ⟨a ∼ friend⟩ — **mu·tu·al·ly** *adv*

mutual fund *n* : an investment company that invests money of its shareholders in a usu. diversified group of securities of other corporations

muu-muu \'mü-ˌmü\ *n* : a loose dress of Hawaiian origin

¹muz·zle \'mə-zəl\ *n* **1** : the nose and jaws of an animal; *also* : a covering for the muzzle to prevent biting or eating **2** : the mouth of a gun

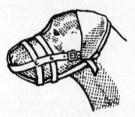

muzzle 1

²muzzle *vb* **muz·zled; muz·zling 1** : to put a muzzle on **2** : to restrain from expression : GAG

mV *abbr* millivolt

MV *abbr* motor vessel

MVP *abbr* most valuable player

MW *abbr* megawatt

my \'mī\ *adj* **1** : of or relating to me or myself **2** — used interjectionally esp. to express surprise

my·col·o·gy \mī-'kä-lə-jē\ *n* : a branch of biology dealing with fungi — **my·co·log·i·cal** \ˌmī-kə-'lä-ji-kəl\ *adj* — **my·col·o·gist** \mī-'kä-lə-jist\ *n*

my·elo·ma \ˌmī-ə-'lō-mə\ *n, pl* **-mas** *or* **-ma·ta** \-mə-tə\ : a primary tumor of the bone marrow

my·nah *or* **my·na** \'mī-nə\ *n* : any of several Asian starlings; *esp* : a dark brown slightly crested bird sometimes taught to mimic speech

my·o·pia \mī-'ō-pē-ə\ *n* : a condition in which visual images come to a focus in front of the retina resulting esp. in defective vision of distant objects — **my·o·pic** \-'ō-pik, -'ä-\ *adj* — **my·o·pi·cal·ly** \-pi-k(ə-)lē\ *adv*

¹myr·i·ad \'mir-ē-əd\ *n* [Gk *myriad-, myrias,* fr. *myrioi* countless, ten thousand] : an indefinitely large number

²myriad *adj* : consisting of a very great but indefinite number

myr·mi·don \'mər-mə-ˌdän\ *n* : a loyal follower; *esp* : one who executes orders without protest or pity

I HATE SNOW

WOOOOOOSSSH

AND THE FEELING IS MUTUAL

JIM DAVIS 2-5

© 1997 PAWS, INC./Distributed by Universal Press Syndicate

myrrh \\'mər\ *n* : a fragrant aromatic plant gum used in perfumes and formerly for incense

myr·tle \\'mərt-ᵊl\ *n* : an evergreen shrub of southern Europe with shiny leaves, fragrant flowers, and black berries; *also* : PERIWINKLE

my·self \mī-'self, mə-\ *pron* : I, ME — used reflexively, for emphasis, or in absolute constructions ⟨I hurt ∼⟩ ⟨I ∼ did it⟩ ⟨∼ busy, I sent him instead⟩

mys·tery \\'mis-tə-rē\ *n*, *pl* **-ter·ies** 1 : a religious truth known by revelation alone 2 : something not understood or beyond understanding 3 : enigmatic quality or character 4 : a work of fiction dealing with the solution of a mysterious crime — **mys·te·ri·ous** \mis-'tir-ē-əs\ *adj* — **mys·te·ri·ous·ly** *adv* — **mys·te·ri·ous·ness** *n*

¹**mys·tic** \\'mis-tik\ *adj* 1 : of or relating to mystics or mysticism 2 : MYSTERIOUS; *also* : MYSTIFYING

²**mystic** *n* : a person who follows, advocates, or experiences mysticism

mys·ti·cal \\'mis-ti-kəl\ *adj* 1 : SPIRITUAL, SYMBOLIC 2 : of or relating to an intimate knowledge of or direct communion with God (as through contemplation or visions)

mys·ti·cism \\'mis-tə-ˌsi-zəm\ *n* : the belief that direct knowledge of God or ultimate reality is attainable through immediate intuition or insight

mys·ti·fy \\'mis-tə-ˌfī\ *vb* **-fied; -fy·ing** 1 : to perplex the mind of 2 : to make mysterious — **mys·ti·fi·ca·tion** \ˌmis-tə-fə-'kā-shən\ *n*

mys·tique \mi-'stēk\ *n* [F] 1 : an air or attitude of mystery and reverence developing around something or someone 2 : the special esoteric skill essential in a calling or activity

myth \\'mith\ *n* 1 : a usu. legendary narrative that presents part of the beliefs of a people or explains a practice or natural phenomenon 2 : an imaginary or unverifiable person or thing — **myth·i·cal** \\'mi-thi-kəl\ *adj*

my·thol·o·gy \mi-'thä-lə-jē\ *n*, *pl* **-gies** : a body of myths and esp. of those dealing with the gods and heroes of a people — **myth·o·log·i·cal** \ˌmi-thə-'lä-ji-kəl\ *adj* — **my·thol·o·gist** \mi-'thä-lə-jist\ *n*

N

¹**n** \\'en\ *n*, *pl* **n's** *or* **ns** \\'enz\ *often cap* 1 : the 14th letter of the English alphabet 2 : an unspecified quantity

²**n** *abbr*, *often cap* 1 net 2 neuter 3 noon 4 normal 5 north; northern 6 note 7 noun 8 number

N *symbol* nitrogen

-n — see -EN

Na *symbol* [NL *natrium*] sodium

NA *abbr* 1 no account 2 North America 3 not applicable 4 not available

NAACP \ˌen-ˌdə-bəl-ˌā-ˌsē-'pē, ˌen-ˌā-ˌā-ˌsē-\ *abbr* National Association for the Advancement of Colored People

nab \\'nab\ *vb* **nabbed; nab·bing** : SEIZE; *esp* : ARREST

NAB *abbr* New American Bible

na·bob \\'nā-ˌbäb\ *n* [Urdu *nawwāb*, provincial governor (in the Mogul empire), fr. Ar *nuwwāb*, pl. of *nā'ib* governor] : a man of great wealth or prominence

na·celle \nə-'sel\ *n* : an enclosure (as for an engine) on an aircraft

na·cho \\'nä-chō\ *n*, *pl* **nachos** [AmerSp] : a tortilla chip topped with melted cheese and often additional savory toppings

na·cre \\'nā-kər\ *n* : MOTHER-OF-PEARL

na·dir \\'nā-ˌdir, -dər\ *n* [ME, fr. MF, fr. Ar *naẓīr* opposite] 1 : the point of the celestial sphere that is directly opposite the zenith and directly beneath the observer 2 : the lowest point

¹**nag** \\'nag\ *n* : HORSE; *esp* : an old or decrepit horse

²**nag** *vb* **nagged; nag·ging** 1 : to find fault incessantly : COMPLAIN 2 : to irritate by constant scolding or urging 3 : to be a continuing source of annoyance ⟨a *nagging* backache⟩

³**nag** *n* : one who nags habitually

Nah *abbr* Nahum

Na·huatl \\'nä-ˌwät-ᵊl\ *n* : a group of American Indian languages of central and southern Mexico

Na·hum \\'nä-həm, -əm\ *n* — see BIBLE table

NAIA *abbr* National Association of Intercollegiate Athletes

na·iad \\'nā-əd, 'nī-, -ˌad\ *n*, *pl* **naiads** *or* **na·ia·des** \-ə-ˌdēz\ 1 : one of the nymphs in ancient mythology living in lakes, rivers, springs, and fountains 2 : an aquatic young of some insects (as a dragonfly)

¹**na·if** *or* **na·if** \nä-'ēf\ *adj* : NAIVE

²**naïf** *or* **naif** *n* : a naive person

¹**nail** \\'nāl\ *n* 1 : a horny sheath protecting the end of each finger and toe in humans and related primates 2 : a slender pointed fastener with a head designed to be pounded in

²**nail** *vb* : to fasten with or as if with a nail — **nail·er** *n*

nail down *vb* : to settle or establish clearly and unmistakably

nain·sook \\'nān-ˌsu̇k\ *n* [Hindi *nainsukh*, fr. *nain* eye + *sukh* delight] : a soft lightweight muslin

nai·ra \\'nī-rə\ *n* — see MONEY table

na·ive *or* **na·ïve** \nä-'ēv\ *adj* **na·iv·er; -est** [F *naïve*, fem. of *naïf*, fr. OF, inborn, natural, fr. L *nativus* native] 1 : marked by unaffected simplicity : ARTLESS, INGENUOUS 2 : CREDULOUS **syn** natural, innocent, simple, unaffected, unsophisticated, unstudied — **na·ive·ly** *adv* — **na·ive·ness** *n*

na·ïve·té *also* **na·ive·té** *or* **na·ive·te** \ˌnä-ē-və-'tā, nä-'ē-və-ˌtā\ *n* 1 : a naive remark or action 2 : the quality or state of being naive

na·ive·ty *also* **na·ïve·ty** \nä-'ē-və-tē\ *n*, *pl* **-ties** : NA·ÏVETÉ

na·ked \\'nā-kəd\ *adj* 1 : having no clothes on : NUDE 2 : UNSHEATHED ⟨a ∼ sword⟩ 3 : lacking a usual or natural covering ⟨as of foliage or feathers⟩ 4 : PLAIN, UNADORNED ⟨the ∼ truth⟩ 5 : not aided by artificial means ⟨seen by the ∼ eye⟩ — **na·ked·ly** *adv* — **na·ked·ness** *n*

nam·by–pam·by \ˌnam-bē-'pam-bē\ *adj* 1 : INSIPID 2 : WEAK, INDECISIVE **syn** bland, flat, inane, jejune, vapid, wishy-washy

¹**name** \\'nām\ *n* 1 : a word or words by which a person or thing is known 2 : a disparaging epithet ⟨call him ∼s⟩ 3 : REPUTATION; *esp* : distinguished reputation ⟨made a ∼ for herself⟩ 4 : FAMILY, CLAN ⟨was a disgrace to their ∼⟩ 5 : appearance as opposed to reality ⟨a friend in ∼ only⟩

²**name** *vb* **named; nam·ing** 1 : to give a name to : CALL 2 : to mention or identify by name 3 : NOMINATE, APPOINT 4 : to decide on : CHOOSE 5 : to mention explicitly : SPECIFY ⟨∼ a price⟩ — **name·able** *adj*

³**name** *adj* 1 : of, relating to, or bearing a name ⟨∼ tag⟩ 2 : having an established reputation ⟨∼ brands⟩

name day *n* : the church feast day of the saint after whom one is named

name·less \\'nām-ləs\ *adj* 1 : having no name 2 : not marked with a name ⟨a ∼ grave⟩ 3 : not known by name ⟨a ∼ hero⟩ 4 : too distressing to be described ⟨∼ fears⟩ — **name·less·ly** *adv*

name·ly \-lē\ *adv* : that is to say : AS ⟨the cat family, ∼, lions, tigers, and similar animals⟩

name·plate \-ˌplāt\ *n* : a plate or plaque bearing a name (as of a resident)

name·sake \-ˌsāk\ *n* : one that has the same name as another; *esp* : one named after another

Na·mib·ian \nə-ˈmi-bē-ən, -byən\ *n* : a native or inhabitant of Namibia — **Namibian** *adj*

nan·keen \nan-ˈkēn\ *n* : a durable brownish yellow cotton fabric orig. woven by hand in China

nan·ny goat \ˈna-nē-\ *n* : a female domestic goat

nano·me·ter \ˈna-nə-ˌmē-tər\ *n* : one billionth of a meter

nano·sec·ond \-ˌse-kənd\ *n* : one billionth of a second

¹**nap** \ˈnap\ *vb* **napped; nap·ping 1** : to sleep briefly esp. during the day : DOZE **2** : to be off guard ⟨was caught *napping*⟩

²**nap** *n* : a short sleep esp. during the day

³**nap** *n* : a soft downy fibrous surface (as on yarn and cloth) — **nap·less** *adj* — **napped** \ˈnapt\ *adj*

na·palm \ˈnā-ˌpälm, -ˌpäm\ *n* [*naphth*alene + *palm*itate, salt of a fatty acid] **1** : a thickener used in jelling gasoline (as for incendiary bombs) **2** : fuel jelled with napalm

nape \ˈnāp, ˈnap\ *n* : the back of the neck

na·pery \ˈnā-pə-rē\ *n* : household linen esp. for the table

naph·tha \ˈnaf-thə, ˈnap-\ *n* : any of various liquid hydrocarbon mixtures used chiefly as solvents

naph·tha·lene \-ˌlēn\ *n* : a crystalline substance used esp. in organic synthesis and as a moth repellent

nap·kin \ˈnap-kən\ *n* **1** : a piece of material (as cloth) used at table to wipe the lips or fingers and protect the clothes **2** : a small cloth or towel

na·po·leon \nə-ˈpōl-yən, -ˈpō-lē-ən\ *n* : an oblong pastry with a filling of cream, custard, or jelly

Na·po·le·on·ic \nə-ˌpō-lē-ˈä-nik\ *adj* : of, relating to, or characteristic of Napoleon I or his family

narc *also* **nark** \ˈnärk\ *n, slang* : a person (as a government agent) who investigates narcotics violations

nar·cis·sism \ˈnär-sə-ˌsi-zəm\ *n* [G *Narzissismus,* fr. *Narziss* Narcissus, beautiful youth of Greek mythology who fell in love with his own image] **1** : undue dwelling on one's own self or attainments **2** : love of or sexual desire for one's own body — **nar·cis·sist** \-sist\ *n or adj* — **nar·cis·sis·tic** \ˌnär-sə-ˈsis-tik\ *adj*

nar·cis·sus \när-ˈsi-səs\ *n, pl* **-cis·sus** *or* **-cis·sus·es** *or* **-cis·si** \-ˌsī, -ˌsē\ : DAFFODIL; *esp* : one with short-tubed flowers usu. borne separately

nar·co·sis \när-ˈkō-səs\ *n, pl* **-co·ses** \-ˌsēz\ : a state of stupor, unconsciousness, or arrested activity produced by the influence of chemicals (as narcotics)

nar·cot·ic \när-ˈkä-tik\ *n* [ME *narkotik,* fr. MF *narcotique,* fr. *narcotique,* adj., fr. ML *narcoticus,* fr. Gk *narkōtikos,* fr. *narkoun* to benumb, fr. *narkē* numbness] : a drug (as opium) that dulls the senses and induces sleep — **narcotic** *adj*

nar·co·tize \ˈnär-kə-ˌtīz\ *vb* **-tized; -tiz·ing 1** : to treat with or subject to a narcotic; *also* : to put into a state

of narcosis **2** : to soothe to unconsciousness or unawareness

nard \ˈnärd\ *n* : a fragrant ointment of the ancients

na·res \ˈnar-(ˌ)ēz\ *n pl* [L] : the pair of openings of the nose

Nar·ra·gan·set \ˌnar-ə-ˈgan-sət\ *n, pl* **Narraganset** *or* **Narragansets** : a member of an American Indian people of Rhode Island

nar·rate \ˈnar-ˌāt\ *vb* **nar·rat·ed; nar·rat·ing** : to recite the details of (as a story) : RELATE, TELL — **nar·ra·tion** \na-ˈrā-shən\ *n* — **nar·ra·tor** \ˈnar-ˌā-tər\ *n*

nar·ra·tive \ˈnar-ə-tiv\ *n* **1** : something that is narrated : STORY **2** : the art or practice of narrating

¹**nar·row** \ˈnar-ō\ *adj* **1** : of slender or less than standard width **2** : limited in size or scope : RESTRICTED **3** : not liberal in views : PREJUDICED **4** : interpreted or interpreting strictly **5** : CLOSE ⟨won by a ~ margin⟩; *also* : barely successful ⟨a ~ escape⟩ — **nar·row·ly** *adv* — **nar·row·ness** *n*

²**narrow** *n* : a narrow passage : STRAIT — usu. used in pl.

³**narrow** *vb* : to lessen in width or extent

nar·row-mind·ed \ˌnar-ō-ˈmīn-dəd\ *adj* : not liberal or broad-minded **syn** illiberal, bigoted, hidebound, intolerant

nar·whal \ˈnär-ˌhwäl, ˈnär-wəl\ *n* : an arctic sea mammal about 20 feet (6 meters) long that is related to the dolphins and in the male has a long twisted ivory tusk

narwhal

NAS *abbr* naval air station

NASA \ˈna-sə\ *abbr* National Aeronautics and Space Administration

¹**na·sal** \ˈnā-zəl\ *n* **1** : a nasal part **2** : a nasal consonant or vowel

²**nasal** *adj* **1** : of or relating to the nose **2** : uttered through the nose — **na·sal·ly** *adv*

na·sal·ize \ˈnā-zə-ˌlīz\ *vb* **-ized; -iz·ing** : to make nasal or pronounce as a nasal sound — **na·sal·i·za·tion** \ˌnā-zə-lə-ˈzā-shən\ *n*

na·scent \ˈnas-ᵊnt, ˈnās-\ *adj* : coming into existence : beginning to grow or develop — **na·scence** \-ᵊns\ *n*

nas·tur·tium \nə-ˈstər-shəm, na-\ *n* : either of two widely cultivated watery-stemmed herbs with showy spurred flowers and pungent seeds

nas·ty \ˈnas-tē\ *adj* **nas·ti·er; -est 1** : FILTHY **2** : INDECENT, OBSCENE **3** : HARMFUL, DANGEROUS ⟨took a ~ fall⟩ **4** : DISAGREEABLE ⟨~ weather⟩ **5** : MEAN, ILL-NATURED ⟨a ~ temper⟩ **6** : DIFFICULT, VEXATIOUS ⟨a ~ problem⟩ **7** : UNFAIR, DIRTY ⟨a ~ trick⟩ — **nas·ti·ly** \ˈnas-tə-lē\ *adv* — **nas·ti·ness** \-tē-nəs\ *n*

nat *abbr* **1** national **2** native **3** natural

na·tal \ˈnāt-ᵊl\ *adj* **1** : NATIVE **2** : of, relating to, or present at birth

na·ta·to·ri·um \ˌnā-tə-ˈtōr-ē-əm, ˌna-\ *n* : a swimming pool esp. indoors

na·tion \ˈnā-shən\ *n* [ME *nacioun*, fr. MF *nation*, fr. L *nation-, natio* birth, race, nation, fr. *nasci* to be born] **1** : NATIONALITY 5; *also* : a politically organized nationality **2** : a community of people composed of one or more nationalities with its own territory and government **3** : the territory of a nation **4** : a federation of tribes (as of American Indians) — **na·tion·hood** *n*

¹**na·tion·al** \ˈna-shə-nəl\ *adj* **1** : of or relating to a nation **2** : comprising or characteristic of a nationality **3** : FEDERAL **3** — **na·tion·al·ly** *adv*

²**national** *n* **1** : one who owes allegiance to a nation **2** : a competition that is national in scope — usu. used in pl.

National Guard *n* **1** : a militia force recruited by each state of the U.S., equipped by the federal government, and jointly maintained subject to the call of either **2** *often not cap* : a military force serving as a national constabulary and defense force

na·tion·al·ise *chiefly Brit var of* NATIONALIZE

na·tion·al·ism \ˈna-shə-nə-ˌli-zəm\ *n* : devotion to national interests, unity, and independence

na·tion·al·ist \-list\ *n* **1** : an advocate of or believer in nationalism **2** *cap* : a member of a political party or group advocating national independence or strong national government — **nationalist** *adj, often cap* — **na·tion·al·is·tic** \ˌna-shə-nə-ˈlis-tik\ *adj*

na·tion·al·i·ty \ˌna-shə-ˈna-lə-tē\ *n, pl* **-ties 1** : national character **2** : a legal relationship involving allegiance of an individual and protection on the part of the state **3** : membership in a particular nation **4** : political independence or existence as a separate nation **5** : a people having a common origin, tradition, and language and capable of forming a state **6** : an ethnic group within a larger unit (as a nation)

na·tion·al·ize \ˈna-shə-nə-ˌlīz\ *vb* **-ized; -iz·ing 1** : to make national : make a nation of **2** : to remove from private ownership and place under government control — **na·tion·al·i·za·tion** \ˌna-shə-nə-lə-ˈzā-shən\ *n*

national monument *n* : a place of historic, scenic, or scientific interest set aside for preservation usu. by presidential proclamation

national park *n* : an area of special scenic, historical, or scientific importance set aside and maintained by a national government esp. for recreation or study

national seashore *n* : a recreational area adjacent to a seacoast and maintained by the federal government

na·tion·wide \ˌnā-shən-ˈwīd\ *adj* : extending throughout a nation

¹**na·tive** \ˈnā-tiv\ *adj* **1** : INBORN, NATURAL **2** : born in a particular place or country **3** : belonging to a person because of the place or circumstances of birth ⟨her ∼ language⟩ **4** : grown, produced, or originating in a particular place : INDIGENOUS **syn** aboriginal, autochthonous, endemic

²**native** *n* : one that is native; *esp* : a person who belongs to a particular country by birth

Native American *n* : AMERICAN INDIAN

na·tiv·ism \ˈnā-ti-ˌvi-zəm\ *n* **1** : a policy of favoring native inhabitants over immigrants **2** : the revival or perpetuation of a native culture esp. in opposition to acculturation

na·tiv·i·ty \nə-ˈti-və-tē, nā-\ *n, pl* **-ties 1** : the process or circumstances of being born : BIRTH **2** *cap* : the birth of Christ

natl *abbr* national

NATO \ˈnā-(ˌ)tō\ *abbr* North Atlantic Treaty Organization

nat·ty \ˈna-tē\ *adj* **nat·ti·er; -est** : trimly neat and tidy : SMART — **nat·ti·ly** \-tə-lē\ *adv* — **nat·ti·ness** \-tē-nəs\ *n*

¹**nat·u·ral** \ˈna-chə-rəl\ *adj* **1** : determined by nature : INBORN, INNATE ⟨∼ ability⟩ **2** : BORN ⟨a ∼ fool⟩ **3** : ILLEGITIMATE **4** : HUMAN **5** : of or relating to nature **6** : not artificial **7** : being simple and sincere : not affected **8** : LIFELIKE **9** : being neither sharp nor flat **syn** ingenuous, naive, unsophisticated, artless, guileless — **nat·u·ral·ness** *n*

²**natural** *n* **1** : IDIOT **2** : a character ♮ placed on a line or space of the musical staff to nullify the effect of a preceding sharp or flat **3** : one obviously suitable for a purpose **4** : AFRO

natural childbirth *n* : a system of managing childbirth in which the mother prepares to remain conscious and assist in delivery with little or no use of drugs

natural gas *n* : a combustible gaseous mixture of hydrocarbons coming from the earth's crust and used chiefly as a fuel and raw material

natural history *n* **1** : a treatise on some aspect of nature **2** : the study of natural objects esp. from an amateur or popular point of view

nat·u·ral·ise *Brit var of* NATURALIZE

nat·u·ral·ism \ˈna-chə-rə-ˌli-zəm\ *n* **1** : action or thought based only on natural desires and instincts **2** : a doctrine that denies a supernatural explanation of the origin or development of the universe and holds that scientific laws account for all of nature **3** : realism in art and literature — **nat·u·ral·is·tic** \ˌna-chə-rə-ˈlis-tik\ *adj*

nat·u·ral·ist \-list\ *n* **1** : one that advocates or practices naturalism **2** : a student of animals or plants esp. in the field

nat·u·ral·ize \-ˌlīz\ *vb* **-ized; -iz·ing 1** : to become or cause to become established as if native ⟨∼ new forage crops⟩ **2** : to confer the rights of a citizen on — **nat·u·ral·iza·tion** \ˌna-chə-rə-lə-ˈzā-shən\ *n*

nat·u·ral·ly \ˈna-chə-rə-lē, ˈnach-rə-\ *adv* **1** : by nature : by natural character or ability **2** : as might be expected **3** : without artificial aid; *also* : without affectation **4** : REALISTICALLY

natural science *n* : a science (as physics, chemistry, or biology) that deals with matter, energy, and their interrelations and transformations or with objectively measurable phenomena — **natural scientist** *n*

natural selection *n* : the natural process that results in the survival of individuals or groups best adjusted to their environment

na·ture \ˈnā-chər\ *n* [ME, fr. MF, fr. L *natura*, fr. *natus*, pp. of *nasci* to be born] **1** : the inherent quality or basic constitution of a person or thing **2** : KIND, SORT **3** : DISPOSITION, TEMPERAMENT **4** : the physical universe **5** : one's natural instincts or way of life ⟨quirks of human ∼⟩; *also* : primitive state ⟨a return to ∼⟩ **6** : natural scenery or environment ⟨beauties of ∼⟩

naught \ˈnȯt, ˈnät\ *n* **1** : NOTHING **2** : the arithmetical symbol 0 : ZERO

naugh·ty \ˈnȯ-tē, ˈnä-\ *adj* **naugh·ti·er; -est 1** : guilty of disobedience or misbehavior **2** : lacking in taste or propriety — **naugh·ti·ly** \-tə-lē\ *adv* — **naugh·ti·ness** \-tē-nəs\ *n*

nau·sea \ˈnȯ-zē-ə, -sē-; ˈnȯ-zhə, -shə\ *n* [L, seasickness, nausea, fr. Gk *nautia, nausia*, fr. *nautēs* sailor] **1** : sickness of the stomach with a desire to vomit **2** : extreme disgust

nau·se·ate \ˈnȯ-zē-ˌāt, -sē-, -zhē-, -shē-\ *vb* **-at·ed; -at·ing** : to affect or become affected with nausea — **nau·se·at·ing·ly** *adv*

nau·seous \ˈnȯ-shəs, -zē-əs\ *adj* **1** : causing nausea or disgust **2** : affected with nausea or disgust

naut *abbr* nautical

nau·ti·cal \ˈnȯ-ti-kəl\ *adj* : of or relating to sailors, navigation, or ships — **nau·ti·cal·ly** \-k(ə-)lē\ *adv*

nautical mile *n* : a unit of distance equal to about 6080 feet (1852 meters)

nau·ti·lus \ˈnȯt-ᵊl-əs\ *n, pl* **-lus·es** *or* **-li** \-ᵊl-ˌī, -ˌē\ : any of a genus of sea mollusks related to the octopuses but having a spiral chambered shell

nav *abbr* **1** naval **2** navigable; navigation

Na·va·jo *also* **Na·va·ho** \'na-və-ıhō, 'nä-\ *n, pl* **-jo** *or* **-jos** *also* **-ho** *or* **-hos** : a member of an American Indian people of northern New Mexico and Arizona; *also* : their language

na·val \'nā-vəl\ *adj* : of, relating to, or possessing a navy

naval stores *n pl* : products (as pitch, turpentine, or rosin) obtained from resinous conifers (as pines)

nave \'nāv\ *n* [ML *navis*, fr. L, ship] : the central part of a church running lengthwise

na·vel \'nā-vəl\ *n* : a depression in the middle of the abdomen that marks the point of attachment of fetus and mother

navel orange *n* : a seedless orange having a pit at the blossom end where the fruit encloses a small secondary fruit

nav·i·ga·ble \'na-vi-gə-bəl\ *adj* **1** : capable of being navigated ⟨a ∼ river⟩ **2** : capable of being steered — **nav·i·ga·bil·i·ty** \ına-vi-gə-'bi-lə-tē\ *n*

nav·i·gate \'na-və-ıgāt\ *vb* **-gat·ed; -gat·ing 1** : to sail on or through ⟨∼ the Atlantic Ocean⟩ **2** : to steer or direct the course of a ship or aircraft **3** : MOVE; *esp* : WALK ⟨could hardly ∼⟩ — **nav·i·ga·tion** \ına-və-'gā-shən\ *n* — **nav·i·ga·tor** \'na-və-ıgā-tər\ *n*

na·vy \'nā-vē\ *n, pl* **navies 1** : FLEET; *also* : the warships belonging to a nation **2** *often cap* : a nation's organization for naval warfare

navy yard *n* : a yard where naval vessels are built or repaired

¹nay \'nā\ *adv* **1** : NO

²nay *n* : a negative vote; *also* : a person casting such a vote

³nay *conj* : not merely this but also : not only so but ⟨he was happy, ∼, ecstatic⟩

nay·say·er \'nā-ısā-ər\ *n* : one who denies, refuses, or opposes something

Na·zi \'nät-sē, 'nat-\ *n* [G, fr. *Nationalsozialist*, lit., national socialist] : a member of a German fascist party controlling Germany from 1933 to 1945 under Adolf Hitler — **Nazi** *adj* — **Na·zism** \'nät-ısi-zəm, 'nat-\ *or* **Na·zi·ism** \-sē-ıi-zəm\ *n*

Nb *symbol* niobium

NB *abbr* **1** New Brunswick **2** nota bene

NBA *abbr* **1** National Basketball Association **2** National Boxing Association

NBC *abbr* National Broadcasting Company

NBS *abbr* National Bureau of Standards

NC *abbr* **1** no charge **2** North Carolina

NCAA *abbr* National Collegiate Athletic Association

NCE *abbr* New Catholic Edition

NCO \ıen-ısē-'ō\ *n* : NONCOMMISSIONED OFFICER

nd *abbr* no date

Nd *symbol* neodymium

ND *abbr* North Dakota

N Dak *abbr* North Dakota

Ne *symbol* neon

NE *abbr* **1** Nebraska **2** New England **3** northeast

Ne·an·der·thal \nē-'an-dər-ıthôl, nā-'än-dər-ıtäl\ *adj* : of, relating to, or being an extinct Old World human; *also* : suggestive of a caveman — **Neanderthal** *n*

neap tide \'nēp-\ *n* : a tide of minimum range occurring at the first and third quarters of the moon

¹near \'nir\ *adv* **1** : at, within, or to a short distance or time **2** : ALMOST

²near *prep* : close to

³near *adj* **1** : closely related or associated; *also* : INTIMATE **2** : not far away; *also* : being the closer or left• hand member of a pair **3** : barely avoided ⟨a ∼ accident⟩ **4** : DIRECT, SHORT ⟨by the ∼est route⟩ **5** : STINGY **6** : not real but very like ⟨∼ silk⟩ — **near·ly** *adv* — **near·ness** *n*

⁴near *vb* : APPROACH

near beer *n* : any of various malt liquors low in alcohol

near·by \nir-'bī, 'nir-ıbī\ *adv or adj* : close at hand

near·sight·ed \'nir-'sī-təd\ *adj* : able to see near things more clearly than distant ones : MYOPIC — **near·sight·ed·ly** *adv* — **near·sight·ed·ness** *n*

neat \'nēt\ *adj* [MF *net*, fr. L *nitidus* bright, neat, fr. *nitēre* to shine] **1** : being orderly and clean **2** : not mixed or diluted ⟨∼ brandy⟩ **3** : marked by tasteful simplicity **4** : PRECISE, SYSTEMATIC **5** : SKILLFUL, ADROIT **6** : FINE, ADMIRABLE **syn** shipshape, tidy, trig, trim — **neat** *adv* — **neat·ly** *adv* — **neat·ness** *n*

neath \'nēth\ *prep, dial* : BENEATH

neat's–foot oil \'nēts-ıfůt-\ *n* [*neat* ox or cow] : a pale yellow fatty oil made esp. from the bones of cattle and used chiefly as a leather dressing

neb \'neb\ *n* **1** : the beak of a bird or tortoise; *also* : NOSE, SNOUT **2** : NIB

Neb *or* **Nebr** *abbr* Nebraska

NEB *abbr* New English Bible

neb·u·la \'ne-byə-lə\ *n, pl* **-lae** \-ılē, -ılī\ *also* **-las** [NL, fr. L, mist, cloud] **1** : any of numerous clouds of gas or dust in interstellar space **2** : GALAXY — **neb·u·lar** \-lər\ *adj*

neb·u·liz·er \'ne-byə-ılī-zər\ *n* : ATOMIZER

neb·u·lous \'ne-byə-ləs\ *adj* **1** : of or relating to a nebula **2** : HAZY, INDISTINCT

¹nec·es·sary \'ne-sə-ıser-ē\ *n, pl* **-saries** : an indispensable item

²necessary *adj* **1** : INEVITABLE, INESCAPABLE; *also* : CERTAIN **2** : PREDETERMINED **3** : COMPULSORY **4** : positively needed : INDISPENSABLE **syn** imperative, necessitous, essential — **nec·es·sar·i·ly** \ıne-sə-'ser-ə-lē\ *adv*

ne·ces·si·tate \ni-'se-sə-ıtāt\ *vb* **-tat·ed; -tat·ing** : to make necessary

ne·ces·si·tous \ni-'se-sə-təs\ *adj* **1** : NEEDY, IMPOVERISHED **2** : URGENT **3** : NECESSARY

ne·ces·si·ty \ni-'se-sə-tē\ *n, pl* **-ties 1** : conditions that cannot be changed **2** : WANT, POVERTY **3** : something that is necessary **4** : very great need

¹neck \'nek\ *n* **1** : the part of the body connecting the head and the trunk **2** : the part of a garment covering or near to the neck **3** : a relatively narrow part suggestive of a neck ⟨∼ of a bottle⟩ ⟨∼ of land⟩ **4** : a narrow margin esp. of victory ⟨won by a ∼⟩ — **necked** \'nekt\ *adj*

²neck *vb* : to kiss and caress amorously

neck and neck *adv or adj* : very close (as in a race)

neck·er·chief \'ne-kər-chəf, -ıchēf\ *n, pl* **-chiefs** \-chəfs, -ıchēfs\ *also* **-chieves** \-ıchēvz\ : a square of cloth worn folded about the neck like a scarf

neck·lace \'ne-kləs\ *n* : an ornament worn around the neck

neck·line \'nek-ılīn\ *n* : the outline of the neck opening of a garment

neck·tie \-ıtī\ *n* : a strip of cloth worn around the neck and tied in front

ne·crol·o·gy \nə-'krä-lə-jē\ *n, pl* **-gies 1** : OBITUARY **2** : a list of the recently dead

nec·ro·man·cy \'ne-krə-ıman-sē\ *n* **1** : the art or practice of conjuring up the spirits of the dead for purposes of magically revealing the future **2** : MAGIC, SORCERY — **nec·ro·man·cer** \-sər\ *n*

ne·crop·o·lis \nə-'krä-pə-ləs, ne-\ *n, pl* **-lis·es** *or* **-les** \-ılēz\ *or* **-leis** \-ılās\ *or* **-li** \-ılī, -ılē\ : CEMETERY; *esp* : a large elaborate cemetery of an ancient city

ne·cro·sis \nə-'krō-səs, ne-\ *n, pl* **ne·cro·ses** \-ısēz\ : usu. local death of body tissue — **ne·crot·ic** \-'krä-tik\ *adj*

nec·tar \'nek-tər\ *n* **1** : the drink of the Greek and Roman gods; *also* : any delicious drink **2** : a sweet plant secretion that is the raw material of honey

nec·tar·ine \ınek-tə-'rēn\ *n* : a smooth-skinned peach

née *or* **nee** \'nā\ *adj* [F, lit., born] — used to identify a woman by her maiden family name

¹need \'nēd\ *n* **1** : OBLIGATION ⟨no ∼ to hurry⟩ **2** : a lack of something requisite, desirable, or useful **3** : a con-

dition requiring supply or relief ⟨when the ∼ arises⟩ **4** : POVERTY **syn** necessity, exigency

²**need** *vb* **1** : to be in want **2** : to have cause or occasion for : REQUIRE ⟨he ∼s advice⟩ **3** : to be under obligation or necessity ⟨we ∼ to know the truth⟩

need•ful \ˈnēd-fəl\ *adj* : NECESSARY, REQUISITE

¹**nee•dle** \ˈnēd-ᵊl\ *n* **1** : a slender pointed usu. steel implement used in sewing **2** : a slender rod (as for knitting, controlling a small opening, or transmitting vibrations to or from a recording) ⟨a phonograph ∼⟩ **3** : a slender hollow instrument by which material is introduced into or withdrawn from the body **4** : a slender indicator on a dial **5** : a needle-shaped leaf (as of a pine)

²**needle** *vb* **nee•dled; nee•dling** : PROD, GOAD; *esp* : to incite to action by repeated gibes

nee•dle•point \ˈnēd-ᵊl-ˌpȯint\ *n* **1** : lace worked with a needle over a paper pattern **2** : embroidery done on canvas across counted threads — **needlepoint** *adj*

need•less \ˈnēd-ləs\ *adj* : UNNECESSARY — **need•less•ly** *adv* — **need•less•ness** *n*

nee•dle•wom•an \ˈnēd-ᵊl-ˌwu̇-mən\ *n* : a woman who does needlework; *esp* : SEAMSTRESS

nee•dle•work \-ˌwərk\ *n* : work done with a needle; *esp* : work (as embroidery) other than plain sewing

needs \ˈnēdz\ *adv* : of necessity : NECESSARILY ⟨must ∼ be recognized⟩

needy \ˈnē-dē\ *adj* **need•i•er; -est** : being in want : POVERTY-STRICKEN

ne'er \ˈner\ *adv* : NEVER

ne'er–do–well \ˈner-dü-ˌwel\ *n* : an idle worthless person — **ne'er–do–well** *adj*

ne•far•i•ous \ni-ˈfar-ē-əs\ *adj* [L *nefarius*, fr. *nefas* crime, fr. *ne-* not + *fas* right, divine law] : very wicked : EVIL **syn** bad, immoral, iniquitous, sinful, vicious — **ne•far•i•ous•ly** *adv*

neg *abbr* negative

ne•gate \ni-ˈgāt\ *vb* **ne•gat•ed; ne•gat•ing 1** : to deny the existence or truth of **2** : to cause to be ineffective or invalid : NULLIFY

ne•ga•tion \ni-ˈgā-shən\ *n* **1** : the action or operation of negating or making negative **2** : a negative doctrine or statement

¹**neg•a•tive** \ˈne-gə-tiv\ *adj* **1** : marked by denial, prohibition, or refusal ⟨a ∼ reply⟩ **2** : not positive or constructive; *esp* : not affirming the presence of what is sought or suspected to be present ⟨test results were ∼⟩ **3** : less than zero ⟨a ∼ number⟩ **4** : being, relating to, or charged with electricity of which the electron is the elementary unit **5** : having the light and dark parts opposite to what they were in the original photographic subject — **neg•a•tive•ly** *adv* — **neg•a•tive•ness** *n* — **neg•a•tiv•i•ty** \ˌne-gə-ˈti-və-tē\ *n*

²**negative** *n* **1** : a negative word or statement **2** : a negative vote or reply; *also* : REFUSAL **3** : something that is the opposite or negation of something else **4** : the side that votes or argues for the opposition (as in a debate) **5** : a negative number **6** : a negative photographic image on transparent material

³**negative** *vb* **-tived; -tiv•ing 1** : to refuse to accept or approve **2** : to vote against **3** : DISPROVE

negative income tax *n* : a system of federal subsidy payments to families with incomes below a stipulated level

neg•a•tiv•ism \ˈne-gə-ti-ˌvi-zəm\ *n* : an attitude of skepticism and denial of nearly everything affirmed or suggested by others

¹**ne•glect** \ni-ˈglekt\ *vb* [L *neglegere, neclegere,* fr. *nec-* not + *legere* to gather] **1** : DISREGARD **2** : to leave undone or unattended to esp. through carelessness **syn** omit, ignore, over-look, slight, forget, miss

²**neglect** *n* **1** : an act or instance of neglecting something **2** : the condition of being neglected — **ne•glect•ful** *adj*

neg•li•gee *also* **neg•li•gé** \ˌne-glə-ˈzhā\ *n* : a woman's long flowing dressing gown

neg•li•gent \ˈne-gli-jənt\ *adj* : marked by neglect **syn** neglectful, remiss, delinquent, derelict — **neg•li•gence** \-jəns\ *n* — **neg•li•gent•ly** *adv*

neg•li•gi•ble \ˈne-gli-jə-bəl\ *adj* : so small as to be neglected or disregarded

ne•go•ti•ant \ni-ˈgō-shē-ənt\ *n* : NEGOTIATOR

ne•go•ti•ate \ni-ˈgō-shē-ˌāt\ *vb* **-at•ed; -at•ing** [L *negotiari* to carry on business, fr. *negotium* business, fr. *neg-* not + *otium* leisure] **1** : to confer with another so as to arrive at the settlement of some matter; *also* : to arrange for or bring about by such conferences ⟨∼ a treaty⟩ **2** : to transfer to another by delivery or endorsement in return for equivalent value ⟨∼ a check⟩ **3** : to get through, around, or over successfully ⟨∼ a turn⟩ — **ne•go•tia•ble** \-shə-bəl, -shē-ə-\ *adj* — **ne•go•ti•a•tion** \ni-ˌgō-sē-ˈā-shən, -shē-\ *n* — **ne•go•ti•a•tor** \-ˈgō-shē-ˌā-tər\ *n*

ne•gri•tude \ˈne-grə-ˌtüd, -ˌtyüd, ˈnē-\ *n* : a consciousness of and pride in one's African heritage

Ne•gro \ˈnē-grō\ *n, pl* **Negroes** [Sp or Pg, fr. *negro* black] : a member of the black race — **Negro** *adj* — **Ne•groid** \ˈnē-ˌgrȯid\ *n or adj, often not cap*

Neh *abbr* Nehemiah

Ne•he•mi•ah \ˌnē-ə-ˈmī-ə\ *n* — see BIBLE table

neigh \ˈnā\ *n* : a loud prolonged cry of a horse — **neigh** *vb*

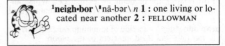

¹**neigh•bor** \ˈnā-bər\ *n* **1** : one living or located near another **2** : FELLOWMAN

²**neighbor** *vb* : to be next to or near to : border on

neigh•bor•hood \ˈnā-bər-ˌhu̇d\ *n* **1** : NEARNESS **2** : a place or region near : VICINITY; *also* : a number or amount near ⟨costs in the ∼ of $10⟩ **3** : the people living near one another **4** : a section lived in by neighbors and usu. having distinguishing characteristics

neigh•bor•ly \-lē\ *adj* : befitting congenial neighbors; *esp* : FRIENDLY — **neigh•bor•li•ness** *n*

neigh•bour *chiefly Brit var of* NEIGHBOR

¹**nei•ther** \ˈnē-thər, ˈnī-\ *pron* : neither one : not the one and not the other ⟨∼ of the two⟩

²**nei·ther** *conj* **1** : not either ⟨∼ good nor bad⟩ **2** : NOR ⟨∼ did I⟩

³**nei·ther** *adj* : not either ⟨∼ hand⟩

nel·son \'nel-sən\ *n* : a wrestling hold in which one applies leverage against an opponent's arm, neck, and head

nem·a·tode \'ne-mə-ˌtōd\ *n* : any of a phylum of elongated cylindrical worms parasitic in animals or plants or free-living in soil or water

nem·e·sis \'ne-mə-səs\ *n, pl* **-e·ses** \-ˌsēz\ [L *Nemesis*, goddess of divine retribution, fr. Gk] **1** : one that inflicts retribution or vengeance **2** : a formidable and usu. victorious rival **3** : an act or effect of retribution; *also* : CURSE

neo·clas·sic \nē-ō-'kla-sik\ *or* **neo·clas·si·cal** \-si-kəl\ *adj* : of or relating to a revival or adaptation of the classical style esp. in literature, art, or music

neo·co·lo·nial·ism \ˌnē-ō-kə-'lō-nē-ə-ˌli-zəm\ *n* : the economic and political policies by which a nation indirectly maintains or extends its influence over other areas or peoples — **neo·co·lo·nial** *adj* — **neo·co·lo·nial·ist** \-list\ *n or adj*

neo·con·ser·va·tive \-kən-'sər-və-tiv\ *n* : a former liberal espousing political conservatism — **neo·con·ser·va·tism** \-və-ˌti-zəm\ *n* — **neoconservative** *adj*

neo·dym·i·um \ˌnē-ō-'di-mē-əm\ *n* : a yellow metallic chemical element — see ELEMENT table

neo·im·pres·sion·ism \ˌnē-ō-im-'pre-shə-ˌni-zəm\ *n, often cap N&I* : a late 19th century French art movement that attempted to make impressionism more precise and to use a pointillist painting technique

Neo·lith·ic \ˌnē-ə-'li-thik\ *adj* : of or relating to the latest period of the Stone Age characterized by polished stone implements

ne·ol·o·gism \nē-'ä-lə-ˌji-zəm\ *n* : a new word or expression

ne·on \'nē-ˌän\ *n* [Gk, neut. of *neos* new] **1** : a gaseous colorless chemical element used in electric lamps — see ELEMENT table **2** : a lamp in which a discharge through neon gives a reddish glow — **neon** *adj*

neo·na·tal \nē-ō-'nāt-əl\ *adj* : of, relating to, or affecting the newborn — **neo·na·tal·ly** *adv*

ne·o·nate \'nē-ə-ˌnāt\ *n* : a newborn child

neo·phyte \'nē-ə-ˌfīt\ *n* **1** : a new convert : PROSELYTE **2** : NOVICE **3** : BEGINNER *syn* apprentice, freshman, newcomer, rookie, tenderfoot, tyro

neo·plasm \'nē-ə-ˌpla-zəm\ *n* : a new growth of tissue serving no useful purpose in the body : TUMOR — **neo·plas·tic** \ˌnē-ə-'plas-tik\ *adj*

neo·prene \'nē-ə-ˌprēn\ *n* : a synthetic rubber used esp. for special-purpose clothing (as wet suits)

Ne·pali \nə-'pȯ-lē, -'pä-\ *n, pl* **Nepali** : a native or inhabitant of Nepal — **Nepali** *adj*

ne·pen·the \nə-'pen-thē\ *n* **1** : a potion used by the ancients to dull pain and sorrow **2** : something capable of making one forget grief or suffering

neph·ew \'ne-fyü, *chiefly Brit* -vyü\ *n* : a son of one's brother, sister, brother-in-law, or sister-in-law

ne·phrit·ic \ni-'fri-tik\ *adj* **1** : RENAL **2** : of, relating to, or affected with nephritis

ne·phri·tis \ni-'frī-təs\ *n, pl* **ne·phrit·i·des** \-'fri-tə-ˌdēz\ : kidney inflammation

ne plus ul·tra \ˌnē-ˌpləs-'əl-trə\ *n* [NL, (go) no more beyond] : the highest point capable of being attained

nep·o·tism \'ne-pə-ˌti-zəm\ *n* [F *népotisme*, fr. It *nepotismo*, fr. *nepote* nephew, fr. L *nepot-*, *nepos* grandson, nephew] : favoritism shown to a relative (as in the granting of jobs)

Nep·tune \'nep-ˌtün, -ˌtyün\ *n* : the planet 8th in order from the sun — see PLANET table — **Nep·tu·ni·an** \nep-'tü-nē-ən, -'tyü-\ *adj*

nep·tu·ni·um \nep-'tü-nē-əm, -'tyü-\ *n* : a short-lived radioactive element — see ELEMENT table

nerd \'nərd\ *n* : an unstylish or socially inept person;

esp : one slavishly devoted to intellectual pursuits — **nerdy** *adj*

Ne·re·id \'nir-ē-əd\ *n* : a sea nymph in Greek mythology

¹**nerve** \'nərv\ *n* **1** : SINEW, TENDON ⟨strain every ∼⟩ **2** : any of the strands of nervous tissue that carry nerve impulses between the brain and spinal cord and every part of the body **3** : power of endurance or control : FORTITUDE; *also* : BOLDNESS, DARING **4** *pl* : NERVOUSNESS **5** : a vein of a leaf or insect wing — **nerved** \'nərvd\ *adj* — **nerve·less** *adj*

²**nerve** *vb* **nerved; nerv·ing** : to give strength or courage to

nerve cell *n* : NEURON; *also* : the nucleus-containing central part of a neuron exclusive of its processes

nerve gas *n* : a chemical weapon damaging esp. to the nervous and respiratory systems

nerve impulse *n* : a physical and chemical change that moves along a process of a neuron after stimulation and carries a record of sensation or an instruction to act

nerve–rack·ing *or* **nerve–wrack·ing** \'nərv-ˌra-kiŋ\ *adj* : extremely trying on the nerves

ner·vous \'nər-vəs\ *adj* **1** : FORCIBLE, SPIRITED **2** : of, relating to, or made up of nerve cells or nerves **3** : easily excited or annoyed : JUMPY **4** : TIMID, APPREHENSIVE ⟨a ∼ smile⟩ **5** : UNEASY, UNSTEADY — **nervous·ly** *adv* — **ner·vous·ness** *n*

nervous breakdown *n* : an attack of mental or emotional disorder of sufficient severity to be incapacitating esp. when requiring hospitalization

nervous system *n* : a bodily system that in vertebrates is made up of the brain and spinal cord, nerves, ganglia, and parts of the sense organs and that receives and interprets stimuli and transmits nerve impulses

nervy \'nər-vē\ *adj* **nerv·i·er; -est 1** : showing calm courage **2** : marked by impudence or presumption ⟨a ∼ salesperson⟩ **3** : EXCITABLE, NERVOUS *syn* bold, cheeky, forward, fresh, impudent, saucy

-ness \nəs\ *n suffix* : state : condition : quality : degree ⟨good*ness*⟩

¹**nest** \'nest\ *n* **1** : the shelter prepared by a bird for its eggs and young **2** : a place where eggs (as of insects or fish) are laid and hatched **3** : a place of rest, retreat, or lodging **4** : DEN, HANGOUT ⟨a ∼ of thieves⟩ **5** : the occupants of a nest **6** : a series of objects (as bowls or tables) fitting inside or under one another

²**nest** *vb* **1** : to build or occupy a nest **2** : to fit compactly together or within one another

nest egg *n* : a fund of money accumulated as a reserve

nes·tle \'ne-səl\ *vb* **nes·tled; nes·tling 1** : to settle snugly or comfortably **2** : to press closely and affectionately : CUDDLE **3** : to settle, shelter, or house as if in a nest

nest·ling \'nest-liŋ\ *n* : a bird too young to leave its nest

¹**net** \'net\ *n* **1** : a meshed fabric twisted, knotted, or woven together at regular intervals **2** : a device made all or partly of net and used esp. to catch birds, fish, or insects **3** : something made of net used esp. for protecting, confining, carrying, or dividing ⟨a tennis ∼⟩ **4** : SNARE, TRAP

²**net** *vb* **net·ted; net·ting 1** : to cover or enclose with or as if with a net **2** : to catch in or as if in a net

³**net** *adj* : free from all charges or deductions ⟨∼ profit⟩ ⟨∼ weight⟩

⁴**net** *vb* **net·ted; net·ting** : to gain or produce as profit : CLEAR, YIELD ⟨his business *netted* $50,000 a year⟩

⁵**net** *n* : a net amount, profit, weight, or price

Neth *abbr* Netherlands

neth·er \'ne-thər\ *adj* : situated down or below ⟨the ∼ regions of the earth⟩

Neth·er·land·er \'ne-thər-ˌlan-dər\ *n* : a native or inhabitant of the Netherlands

neth·er·most \-₁mōst\ adj : LOWEST

neth·er·world \-₁wərld\ n 1 : the world of the dead 2 : UNDERWORLD

nett Brit var of NET

net·ting n 1 : NETWORK 2 : the act or process of making a net or network

¹**net·tle** \'net-ᵊl\ n : any of a genus of coarse herbs with stinging hairs

²**nettle** vb **net·tled; net·tling** : PROVOKE, VEX, IRRITATE

net·tle·some \'net-ᵊl-səm\ adj : causing vexation : IRRITATING

net·work \'net-₁wərk\ n 1 : NET 2 : a system of elements (as lines or channels) that cross in the manner of the threads in a net 3 : a group or system of related or connected parts; esp : a chain of radio or television stations

net·work·ing \'net-₁wər-kiŋ\ n : the exchange of information or services among individuals, groups, or institutions

neu·ral \'nùr-əl, 'nyùr-\ adj : of, relating to, or involving a nerve or the nervous system

neu·ral·gia \nù-'ral-jə, nyù-\ n : acute pain that follows the course of a nerve — **neu·ral·gic** \-jik\ adj

neur·as·then·ic \₁nùr-əs-'the-nik, ₁nyùr-, -thē-\ adj : affected with or suggestive of mental disorder characterized esp. by fatiguing easily, lack of motivation, feelings of inadequacy, and psychosomatic symptoms — **neur·as·then·ia** \-'thē-nē-ə\ n — **neurasthenic** n

neu·ri·tis \-'rī-təs\ n, pl **-rit·i·des** \-'ri-tə-₁dēz\ or **-ri·tis·es** : inflammation of a nerve — **neu·rit·ic** \-'ri-tik\ adj or n

neu·rol·o·gy \nù-'rä-lə-jē, nyù-\ n : the scientific study of the nervous system — **neu·ro·log·i·cal** \₁nùr-ə-'lä-ji-kəl, ₁nyùr-\ or **neu·ro·log·ic** \-jik\ adj — **neuro·log·i·cal·ly** \-ji-k(ə-)lē\ adv — **neu·rol·o·gist** \nù-'rä-lə-jist, nyù-\ n

neu·ron \'nü-₁rän, 'nyü-\ also **neu·rone** \-₁rōn\ n : a cell with specialized processes that is the fundamental functional unit of nervous tissue

neu·ro·sci·ence \₁nùr-ō-'sī-əns, ₁nyùr-\ n : a branch of the life sciences that deals with the anatomy, physiology, biochemistry, or molecular biology of nerves and nervous tissue and with their relation to behavior and learning — **neu·ro·sci·en·tist** \-ən-tist\ n

neu·ro·sis \nù-'rō-səs, nyù-\ n, pl **-ro·ses** \-₁sēz\ : a mental and emotional disorder that is less serious than a psychosis, is not characterized by disturbance of the use of language, and is accompanied by various bodily and mental disturbances (as visceral symptoms, anxieties, or phobias)

neu·ro·sur·gery \nùr-ō-'sər-jə-rē, ₁nyùr-\ n : surgery of nervous structures (as nerves, the brain, or the spinal cord) — **neu·ro·sur·geon** \-'sər-jən\ n

¹**neu·rot·ic** \nù-'rä-tik, nyù-\ adj : of, relating to, being, or affected with a neurosis; also : NERVOUS — **neu·rot·i·cal·ly** \-ti-k(ə-)lē\ adv

²**neurotic** n : an emotionally unstable or neurotic person

neu·ro·trans·mit·ter \₁nùr-ō-trans-'mi-tər, ₁nyùr-, -tranz-\ n : a substance (as acetylcholine) that transmits nerve impulses across the gap between neurons

neut abbr neuter

¹**neu·ter** \'nü-tər, 'nyü-\ adj [ME neutre, fr. MF & L: MF neutre, fr. L neuter, lit., neither, fr. ne- not + uter which of two] 1 : of, relating to, or constituting the gender that includes most words or grammatical forms referring to things classed as neither masculine nor feminine 2 : having imperfectly developed or no sex organs

²**neuter** n 1 : a noun, pronoun, adjective, or inflectional form or class of the neuter gender; also : the neuter gender 2 : WORKER 2; also : a spayed or castrated animal

³**neuter** vb : CASTRATE, SPAY

¹**neu·tral** \'nü-trəl, 'nyü-\ n 1 : one that is neutral 2 : a neutral color 3 : a position of disengagement (as of gears)

²**neutral** adj 1 : not favoring either side in a quarrel, contest, or war 2 : of or relating to a neutral state or power 3 : MIDDLING, INDIFFERENT 4 : having no hue : GRAY; also : not decided in color 5 : neither acid nor basic (a ~ solution) 6 : not electrically charged

neu·tral·ise Brit var of NEUTRALIZE

neu·tral·ism \'nü-trə-₁li-zəm, 'nyü-\ n : a policy or the advocacy of neutrality esp. in international affairs

neu·tral·i·ty \nü-'tra-lə-tē, nyü-\ n : the quality or state of being neutral; esp : refusal to take part in a war between other powers

neu·tral·ize \'nü-trə-₁līz, 'nyü-\ vb **-ized; -iz·ing** : to make neutral; esp : COUNTERACT — **neu·tral·i·za·tion** \₁nü-trə-lə-'zā-shən, ₁nyü-\ n

neu·tri·no \nü-'trē-nō, nyü-\ n, pl **-nos** : an uncharged elementary particle held to be massless or very light

neu·tron \'nü-₁trän, 'nyü-\ n : an uncharged atomic particle that is nearly equal in mass to the proton

neutron bomb n : a nuclear bomb designed to produce lethal neutrons but less blast and fire damage than other nuclear bombs

neutron star n : a hypothetical dense celestial object that results from the collapse of a large star

Nev abbr Nevada

nev·er \'ne-vər\ adv 1 : not ever 2 : not in any degree, way, or condition

nev·er·more \₁ne-vər-'mōr\ adv : never again

nev·er–nev·er land \₁ne-vər-'ne-vər-\ n : an ideal or imaginary place

nev·er·the·less \₁ne-vər-thə-'les\ adv : in spite of that : HOWEVER

ne·vus \'nē-vəs\ n, pl **ne·vi** \-₁vī\ : a usu. pigmented birthmark

¹**new** \'nü, 'nyü\ adj 1 : not old : RECENT, MODERN 2 : recently discovered, recognized, or learned about ⟨~ drugs⟩ 3 : UNFAMILIAR 4 : different from the former 5 : not accustomed ⟨~ to the work⟩ 6 : beginning as a repetition of a previous act or thing ⟨a ~ year⟩ 7 : REFRESHED, REGENERATED ⟨rest made a ~ man of him⟩ 8 : being in a position or place for the first time ⟨a ~ member⟩ 9 cap : having been in use after medieval times : MODERN ⟨New Latin⟩ syn novel, newfangled, fresh — **new·ish** adj — **new·ness** n

²**new** adv : NEWLY ⟨new-mown hay⟩

New Age adj 1 : of, relating to, or being a late 20th century social movement incorporating various untraditional concepts and practices relating esp. to spiritual, emotional, and physical well-being 2 : of, relating to, or being a soft soothing form of instrumental music

¹**new·born** \-₁bòrn\ adj 1 : recently born 2 : born anew ⟨~ hope⟩

²**newborn** n, pl **newborn** or **newborns** : a newborn individual

new·com·er \-₁kə-mər\ n 1 : one recently arrived 2 : BEGINNER

New Deal n : the legislative and administrative program of President F. D. Roosevelt to promote economic recovery and social reform during the 1930s — **New Dealer** n

new·el \'nü-əl, 'nyü-\ n : a post about which the steps of a circular staircase wind; also : a post at the foot of a stairway or one at a landing

new·fan·gled \'nü-'faŋ-gəld, 'nyü-\ adj 1 : attracted to novelty 2 : of the newest style : NOVEL

new–fash·ioned \-'fa-shənd\ adj 1 : made in a new fashion or form 2 : UP-TO-DATE

new·found \-'faùnd\ adj : newly found

New Left n : a radical political movement originating in the 1960s

new·ly \'nü-lē, 'nyü-\ adv 1 : LATELY, RECENTLY 2 : ANEW, AFRESH

new·ly·wed \-ˌwed\ *n* : one recently married

new moon *n* : the phase of the moon with its dark side toward the earth; *also* : the thin crescent moon seen for a few days after the new moon phase

news \ˈnüz, ˈnyüz\ *n* **1** : a report of recent events : TIDINGS **2** : material reported in a newspaper or news periodical or on a newscast

news·boy \ˈnüz-ˌbȯi, ˈnyüz-\ *n* : one who delivers or sells newspapers

news·cast \-ˌkast\ *n* : a radio or television broadcast of news — **news·cast·er** \-ˌkas-tər\ *n*

news·let·ter \-ˌle-tər\ *n* : a small newspaper containing news or information of interest chiefly to a special group

news·mag·a·zine \-ˌma-gə-ˌzēn\ *n* : a usu. weekly magazine devoted chiefly to summarizing and analyzing news

news·man \-mən, -ˌman\ *n* : one who gathers, reports, or comments on the news : REPORTER

news·pa·per \-ˌpā-pər\ *n* : a paper that is published at regular intervals and contains news, articles of opinion, features, and advertising

news·pa·per·man \-ˌpā-pər-ˌman\ *n* : one who owns or is employed by a newspaper

news·print \-ˌprint\ *n* : paper made chiefly from wood pulp and used mostly for newspapers

news·reel \-ˌrēl\ *n* : a short motion picture portraying current events

news·stand \-ˌstand\ *n* : a place where newspapers and periodicals are sold

news·week·ly \-ˌwēk-lē\ *n* : a weekly newspaper or newsmagazine

news·wom·an \-ˌwu̇-mən\ *n* : a woman who gathers, reports, or comments on the news : REPORTER

news·wor·thy \-ˌwər-thē\ *adj* : sufficiently interesting to the general public to warrant reporting (as in a newspaper)

newsy \ˈnü-zē, ˈnyü-\ *adj* **news·i·er; -est** : filled with news; *esp* : TALKATIVE

newt \ˈnüt, ˈnyüt\ *n* : any of various small chiefly aquatic salamanders

New Testament *n* : the second of the two chief divisions of the Bible — see BIBLE table

new·ton \ˈnüt-ᵊn, ˈnyüt-\ *n* : the unit of force in the metric system equal to the force required to impart an acceleration of one meter per second per second to a mass of one kilogram

new wave *n, often cap N&W* : the latest and esp. the most outrageous style — **new–wave** *adj*

New World *n* : the western hemisphere; *esp* : the continental landmass of No. and So. America

New Year *n* **1** : NEW YEAR'S DAY; *also* : the first days of the year **2** : ROSH HASHANAH

New Year's Day *n* : January 1 observed as a legal holiday

New Zea·land·er \nü-ˈzē-lən-dər, nyü-\ *n* : a native or inhabitant of New Zealand

¹next \ˈnekst\ *adj* : immediately preceding or following : NEAREST

²next *prep* : nearest or adjacent to

³next *adv* **1** : in the time, place, or order nearest or immediately succeeding **2** : on the first occasion to come

nex·us \ˈnek-səs\ *n, pl* **nex·us·es** \-sə-səz\ *or* **nex·us** \-səs, -ˌsüs\ : CONNECTION, LINK

Nez Percé \ˈnez-ˈpərs, *F* nā-per-sā\ *n* : a member of an American Indian people of Idaho, Washington, and Oregon; *also* : the language of the Nez Percé

NF *abbr* Newfoundland

NFC *abbr* National Football Conference

NFL *abbr* National Football League

Nfld *abbr* Newfoundland

NG *abbr* **1** National Guard **2** no good

ngul·trum \eŋ-ˈgül-trəm\ *n* — see MONEY table

ngwee \eŋ-ˈgwē\ *n, pl* **ngwee** — see *kwacha* at MONEY table

NH *abbr* New Hampshire

NHL *abbr* National Hockey League

Ni *symbol* nickel

ni·a·cin \ˈnī-ə-sən\ *n* : NICOTINIC ACID

nib \ˈnib\ *n* : POINT; *esp* : a pen point

¹nib·ble \ˈni-bəl\ *vb* **nib·bled; nib·bling** : to bite gently or bit by bit

²nibble *n* : a small or cautious bite

ni·cad \ˈnī-ˌkad\ *n* : a rechargeable dry cell that has a nickel cathode and a cadmium anode

Nic·a·ra·guan \ˌni-kə-ˈrä-gwən\ *n* : a native or inhabitant of Nicaragua — **Nicaraguan** *adj*

nice \ˈnīs\ *adj* **nic·er; nic·est** [ME, foolish, wanton, fr. OF, fr. L *nescius* ignorant, fr. *nescire* to not know] **1** : FASTIDIOUS, DISCRIMINATING **2** : marked by delicate discrimination or treatment **3** : PLEASING, AGREEABLE; *also* : well-executed **4** : WELL-BRED ⟨~ people⟩ **5** : VIRTUOUS, RESPECTABLE **syn** choosy, finicky, particular, persnickety, picky — **nice·ly** *adv* — **nice·ness** *n*

nice–nel·ly \ˈnīs-ˈne-lē\ *adj, often cap 2d N* **1** : marked by euphemism **2** : PRUDISH — **nice nelly** *n, often cap 2d N* — **nice–nel·ly·ism** \-ˌi-zəm\ *n, often cap 2d N*

nice·ty \ˈnī-sə-tē\ *n, pl* **-ties 1** : a dainty, delicate, or elegant thing ⟨enjoy the *niceties* of life⟩ **2** : a fine point or distinction ⟨*niceties* of workmanship⟩ **3** : EXACTNESS, PRECISION, ACCURACY

niche \ˈnich\ *n* [F] **1** : a recess in a wall esp. for a statue **2** : a place, employment, or activity for which a person or thing is best fitted **3** : the living space or role of an organism in an ecological community esp. with regard to food consumption

¹nick \ˈnik\ *n* **1** : a small notch or groove **2** : the final critical moment ⟨in the ~ of time⟩

²nick *vb* : NOTCH, CHIP

nick·el \ˈni-kəl\ *n* **1** : a hard silver-white metallic chemical element capable of a high polish and used in alloys — see ELEMENT table **2** : the U.S. 5-cent piece made of copper and nickel; *also* : the Canadian 5-cent piece

nick·el·ode·on \ˌni-kə-ˈlō-dē-ən\ *n* **1** : an early movie

theater to which admission cost five cents **2** : JUKE-
BOX

nick·er \'ni-kər\ vb : NEIGH, WHINNY — **nicker** n

nick·name \'nik-ₘnām\ n [ME nekename additional
name, alter. (from misdivision of an ekename) of
ekename, fr. eke also + name] **1** : a usu. descriptive
name given instead of or in addition to the one belonging to a person, place, or thing **2** : a familiar form
of a proper name — **nickname** vb

nic·o·tine \'ni-kə-ₘtēn\ n : a poisonous and addictive
substance in tobacco that is used as an insecticide

nic·o·tin·ic acid \ₘni-kə-ˈtē-nik-, -ˈti-\ n : an organic
acid of the vitamin B complex found in plants and animals and used against pellagra

niece \'nēs\ n : a daughter of one's brother, sister,
brother-in-law, or sister-in-law

nif·ty \'nif-tē\ adj **nif·ti·er; -est** : very good : very attractive

Ni·ge·ri·an \nī-ˈjir-ē-ən\ n : a native or inhabitant of
Nigeria — **Nigerian** adj

nig·gard \'ni-gərd\ n : a stingy person : MISER — **nig-
gard·li·ness** \-lē-nəs\ n — **nig·gard·ly** adj or adv

nig·gling \'ni-gə-liŋ\ adj **1** : PETTY **2** : bothersome in a
petty way **syn** inconsequential, measly, picayune,
piddling, trifling, trivial

¹nigh \'nī\ adv **1** : near in place, time, or relationship **2**
: NEARLY, ALMOST

²nigh adj : CLOSE, NEAR

³nigh prep : NEAR

night \'nīt\ n **1** : the period between dusk and dawn **2**
: the darkness of night **3** : a period of misery or unhappiness **4** : NIGHTFALL — **night** adj

night blindness n : reduced visual capacity in faint
light (as at night)

night·cap \'nīt-ₘkap\ n **1** : a cloth cap worn with night-
clothes **2** : a usu. alcoholic drink taken at bedtime

night·clothes \-ₘklōthz, -ₘklōz\ n pl : garments worn in
bed

night·club \-ₘkləb\ n : a place of entertainment open at
night usu. serving food and liquor and providing music for dancing

night crawl·er \-ₘkrö-lər\ n : EARTHWORM; esp : a large
earthworm found on the soil surface at night

night·dress \'nīt-ₘdres\ n : NIGHTGOWN

night·fall \-ₘföl\ n : the coming of night

night·gown \-ₘgaún\ n : a loose garment for wear in bed

night·hawk \-ₘhök\ n : any of a genus of American
birds related to and resembling the whippoorwill

night·in·gale \'nīt-ªn-ₘgāl, 'nī-tiŋ-\ n [ME, fr. OE
nihtegale, fr. niht night + galan to sing] : any of several Old World thrushes noted for the sweet usu. nocturnal song of the male

night·life \'nīt-ₘlīf\ n : the activity of pleasure⹀
seekers at night

night·ly \'nīt-lē\ adj **1** : happening, done, or produced
by night or every night **2** : of or relating to the night
or every night — **nightly** adv

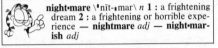

night·mare \'nīt-ₘmar\ n **1** : a frightening
dream **2** : a frightening or horrible experience — **nightmare** adj — **night·mar-
ish** adj

night rider n : a member of a secret band who ride
masked at night doing violence to punish or terrorize

night·shade \'nīt-ₘshād\ n : any of a large genus of
herbs, shrubs, and trees that include poisonous forms
(as belladonna) and important food plants (as the potato, tomato, and eggplant)

night·shirt \-ₘshərt\ n : a nightgown resembling a shirt

night soil n : human excrement used esp. for fertilizing
the soil

night·stick \'nīt-ₘstik\ n : a police officer's club

night·time \-ₘtīm\ n : the time from dusk to dawn

night·walk·er \-ₘwò-kər\ n : a person who roves about
at night esp. with criminal or immoral intent

ni·hil·ism \'nī-ə-ₘli-zəm, 'nē-hə-\ n **1** : a viewpoint that
traditional values and beliefs are unfounded and that
existence is senseless and useless **2** : ANARCHISM
: TERRORISM — **ni·hil·ist** \-list\ n or adj — **ni·hil·is-
tic** \ₘnī-ə-ˈlis-tik, ₘnē-hə-\ adj

nil \'nil\ n : ZERO, NOTHING

nim·ble \'nim-bəl\ adj **nim·bler; nim·blest** [ME nimel,
fr. OE numol holding much, fr. niman to take] **1**
: quick and light in motion : AGILE (a ∼ dancer) **2**
: quick in understanding and learning : CLEVER (a ∼
mind) **syn** active, brisk, sprightly, spry, zippy —
nim·ble·ness n — **nim·bly** \-blē\ adv

nim·bus \'nim-bəs\ n, pl **nim·bi** \-ₘbī, -bē\ or **nim·
bus·es 1** : a figure (as a disk) in an art work suggesting
radiant light about the head of a divinity, saint, or
sovereign **2** : a rain cloud; also : THUNDERHEAD

NIMBY \'nim-bē\ abbr not in my backyard

nim·rod \'nim-ₘräd\ n : HUNTER

nin·com·poop \'nin-kəm-ₘpüp\ n : FOOL, SIMPLETON

nine \'nīn\ n **1** : one more than eight **2** : the 9th in a set
or series **3** : something having nine units; esp : a baseball team — **nine** adj or pron — **ninth** \'nīnth\ adj
or adv or n

nine days' wonder n : something that creates a short⹀
lived sensation

nine·pins \'nīn-ₘpinz\ n : tenpins played without the
headpin

nine·teen \nīn-ˈtēn\ n : one more than 18 — **nineteen**
adj or pron — **nine·teenth** \-ˈtēnth\ adj or n

nine·ty \'nīn-tē\ n, pl **nineties** : nine times 10 — **nine-
ti·eth** \-tē-əth\ adj or n — **ninety** adj or pron

nin·ja \'nin-jə, -(ₘ)jä\ n, pl **ninja** or **ninjas**
[Jp] : a person trained in ancient Japa-
nese martial arts and employed esp. for
espionage and assassinations

nin·ny \'ni-nē\ n, pl **ninnies** : FOOL

ni·o·bi·um \nī-ˈō-bē-əm\ n : a gray metallic chemical
element used in alloys — see ELEMENT table

¹nip \'nip\ vb **nipped; nip·ping 1** : to catch hold of and

squeeze tightly between two surfaces, edges, or
points **2** : ³CLIP **3** : to destroy the growth, progress,
or fulfillment of ⟨*nipped* in the bud⟩ **4** : to injure or
make numb with cold : CHILL **5** : SNATCH, STEAL
²**nip** *n* **1** : a sharp stinging cold **2** : a biting or pungent
flavor **3** : PINCH, BITE **4** : a small portion : BIT
³**nip** *n* : a small quantity of liquor : SIP
⁴**nip** *vb* **nipped; nip•ping** : to take liquor in nips : TIPPLE
nip and tuck *adj or adv* : so close that the lead shifts
rapidly from one contestant to another
nip•per \ˈni-pər\ *n* **1** : one that nips **2** *pl* : PINCERS **3**
: CHILD; *esp* : a small boy
nip•ple \ˈni-pəl\ *n* : the protuberance of a mammary
gland through which milk is drawn off : TEAT; *also*
: something resembling a nipple
nip•py \ˈni-pē\ *adj* **nip•pi•er; -est 1** : PUNGENT, SHARP
2 : CHILLY
nir•va•na \nir-ˈvä-nə\ *n, often cap* [Skt *nirvāṇa*, lit.,
act of extinguishing, fr. *nis-* out + *vāti* it blows] **1**
: the final freeing of a soul from all that enslaves it;
esp : the supreme happiness that according to Buddhism comes when all passion, hatred, and delusion
die out and the soul is released from the necessity of
further purification **2** : OBLIVION; *also* : PARADISE
ni•sei \nē-ˈsā, ˈnē-ˌsā\ *n, pl* **nisei** *also* **niseis** : a son or
daughter of immigrant Japanese parents who is born
and educated in America
ni•si \ˈnī-ˌsī\ *adj* [L, unless, fr. *ne-* not + *si* if] : taking
effect at a specified time unless previously modified
or voided ⟨a divorce decree ∼⟩
nit \ˈnit\ *n* : the egg of a parasitic insect (as a louse);
also : the young insect
nite *var of* NIGHT
ni•ter \ˈnī-tər\ *n* : POTASSIUM NITRATE
nit–pick•ing \ˈnit-ˌpi-kiŋ\ *n* : minute and usu. unjustified criticism — **nit•pick•er** *n*
¹**ni•trate** \ˈnī-ˌtrāt, -trət\ *n* **1** : a salt or ester of nitric
acid **2** : sodium nitrate or potassium nitrate used as a
fertilizer
²**ni•trate** \-ˌtrāt\ *vb* **ni•trat•ed; ni•trat•ing** : to treat or
combine with nitric acid or a nitrate — **ni•tra•tion**
\nī-ˈtrā-shən\ *n*
ni•tre *chiefly Brit var of* NITER
ni•tric acid \ˈnī-trik-\ *n* : a corrosive liquid acid used
esp. in making dyes, explosives, and fertilizers
ni•tri•fi•ca•tion \ˌnī-trə-fə-ˈkā-shən\ *n* : the oxidation
(as by bacteria) of ammonium salts to nitrites and
then to nitrates — **ni•tri•fy•ing** \ˈnī-trə-fī-iŋ\ *adj*
ni•trite \ˈnī-ˌtrīt\ *n* : a salt of nitrous acid
ni•tro \ˈnī-trō\ *n, pl* **nitros** : any of various nitrated
products; *esp* : NITROGLYCERIN
ni•tro•gen \ˈnī-trə-jən\ *n* : a tasteless odorless gaseous
chemical element constituting 78 percent of the atmosphere by volume — see ELEMENT table — **ni-
trog•e•nous** \nī-ˈträ-jə-nəs\ *adj*
nitrogen narcosis *n* : a state of euphoria and exhila-
ration caused by nitrogen forced into a diver's bloodstream from atmospheric air under pressure
ni•tro•glyc•er•in *or* **ni•tro•glyc•er•ine** \ˌnī-trə-ˈgli-sə-
rən\ *n* : a heavy oily explosive liquid used to make

dynamite and in medicine to dilate blood vessels
ni•trous acid \ˈnī-trəs-\ *n* : an unstable nitrogen-
containing acid known only in solution or in the form
of its salts
nitrous oxide *n* : a colorless gas used esp. as an anesthetic in dentistry
nit•ty–grit•ty \ˈni-tē-ˌgri-tē, ˌni-tē-ˈgri-tē\ *n* : what is
essential and basic : specific practical details
nit•wit \ˈnit-ˌwit\ *n* : a scatterbrained or stupid person
¹**nix** \ˈniks\ *n* : NOTHING
²**nix** *vb* : VETO, REJECT
³**nix** *adv* : NO
NJ *abbr* New Jersey
NL *abbr* National League
NLRB *abbr* National Labor Relations Board
NM *abbr* **1** nautical mile **2** New Mexico
N Mex *abbr* New Mexico
NMI *abbr* no middle initial
NNE *abbr* north-northeast
NNW *abbr* north-northwest
¹**no** \ˈnō\ *adv* **1** — used to express the negative of an
alternative ⟨shall we continue or ∼⟩ **2** : in no respect
or degree ⟨he is ∼ better than the others⟩ **3** : not so
⟨∼, I'm not ready⟩ **4** — used with an adjective to imply a meaning opposite to the positive statement ⟨in
∼ uncertain terms⟩ **5** — used to introduce a more
emphatic or explicit statement ⟨has the right, ∼, the
duty to continue⟩ **6** — used as an interjection to express surprise or doubt ⟨∼—you don't say⟩ **7** —
used in combination with a verb to form a compound
adjective ⟨*no*-bake pie⟩
²**no** *adj* **1** : not any; *also* : hardly any **2** : not a ⟨she's ∼
expert⟩
³**no** \ˈnō\ *n, pl* **noes** *or* **nos** \ˈnōz\ **1** : REFUSAL, DENIAL
2 : a negative vote or decision; *also, pl* : persons voting in the negative
⁴**no** *abbr* **1** north; northern **2** [L *numero*, abl. of *numer-
us*] number
¹**No** *or* **Noh** \ˈnō\ *n, pl* **No** *or* **Noh** : classic Japanese
dance-drama having a heroic theme, a chorus, and
highly stylized action, costuming, and scenery
²**No** *symbol* nobelium
No•bel•ist \nō-ˈbe-list\ *n* : a winner of a Nobel prize
no•bel•i•um \nō-ˈbe-lē-əm\ *n* : a radioactive chemical
element produced artificially — see ELEMENT table
No•bel prize \nō-ˈbel-, ˈnō-ˌbel-\ *n* : any of various annual prizes (as in peace, literature, or medicine) established by the will of Alfred Nobel for the
encouragement of persons who work for the interests
of humanity
no•bil•i•ty \nō-ˈbi-lə-tē\ *n* **1** : the quality or state of being noble **2** : nobles considered as forming a class
¹**no•ble** \ˈnō-bəl\ *adj* **no•bler; no•blest** [ME, fr. OF, fr.
L *nobilis* well known, noble, fr. *noscere* to come to
know] **1** : ILLUSTRIOUS; *also* : FAMOUS, NOTABLE **2** : of
high birth, rank, or station : ARISTOCRATIC **3** : EXCEL-
LENT **4** : STATELY, IMPOSING ⟨a ∼ edifice⟩ **5** : of a superior nature **syn** august, baronial, grand, grandiose,
magnificent, majestic — **no•ble•ness** *n* — **no•bly**
\-blē\ *adv*

²**no·ble** *n* : a person of noble rank or birth

no·ble·man \'nō-bəl-mən\ *n* : a member of the nobility : PEER

no·blesse oblige \nō-ıbles-ə-'blēzh\ *n* [F, lit., nobility obligates] : the obligation of honorable, generous, and responsible behavior associated with high rank or birth

no·ble·wom·an \'nō-bəl-ıwu̇-mən\ *n* : a woman of noble rank : PEERESS

¹**no·body** \'nō-ıbä-dē, -bə-\ *pron* : no person

²**nobody** *n, pl* **no·bod·ies** : a person of no influence or importance

no–brain·er \'nō-'brā-nər\ *n* : something that requires a minimum of thought

noc·tur·nal \näk-'tərn-ᵊl\ *adj* **1** : of, relating to, or occurring in the night **2** : active at night ⟨a ∼ bird⟩

noc·turne \'näk-ıtərn\ *n* : a work of art dealing with night; *esp* : a dreamy pensive composition for the piano

noc·u·ous \'nä-kyə-wəs\ *adj* : HARMFUL — **noc·u·ous·ly** *adv*

nod \'näd\ *vb* **nod·ded; nod·ding 1** : to bend the head downward or forward (as in bowing, going to sleep, or giving assent) **2** : to move up and down ⟨tulips *nodding* in the breeze⟩ **3** : to show by a nod of the head ⟨∼ agreement⟩ **4** : to make a slip or error in a moment of abstraction — **nod** *n*

nod·dle \'näd-ᵊl\ *n* : HEAD

nod·dy \'nä-dē\ *n, pl* **noddies 1** : FOOL **2** : a stout-bodied tropical tern

node \'nōd\ *n* : a thickened, swollen, or differentiated area (as of tissue); *esp* : the part of a stem from which a leaf arises — **nod·al** \-ᵊl\ *adj*

nod·ule \'nä-jül\ *n* : a small lump or swelling — **nod·u·lar** \'nä-jə-lər\ *adj*

no·el \nō-'el\ *n* [F *noël* Christmas, carol, fr. L *natalis* birthday] **1** : a Christmas carol **2** *cap* : the Christmas season

noes *pl of* NO

no–fault \'nō-'fȯlt\ *adj* **1** : of, relating to, or being a motor vehicle insurance plan under which someone involved in an accident is compensated usu. up to a stipulated limit for actual losses by that person's own insurance company regardless of who is responsible **2** : of, relating to, or being a divorce law under which neither party is held responsible for the breakup of the marriage

nog·gin \'nä-gən\ *n* **1** : a small mug or cup; *also* : a small quantity of drink **2** : a person's head

no–good \'nō-'gu̇d\ *adj* : having no worth, virtue, use, or chance of success — **no–good** \'nō-ıgu̇d\ *n*

Noh *var of* NO

no–hit·ter \(ı)nō-'hi-tər\ *n* : a baseball game or part of a game in which a pitcher allows no base hits

no·how \'nō-ıhau̇\ *adv* : in no manner

¹**noise** \'nȯiz\ *n* [ME, fr. OF, strife, quarrel, noise, fr. L *nausea* nausea] **1** : loud, confused, or senseless shouting or outcry **2** : SOUND; *esp* : one that lacks agreeable musical quality or is noticeably unpleasant **3** : unwanted electronic signal or disturbance — **noise·less** *adj* — **noise·less·ly** *adv*

²**noise** *vb* **noised; nois·ing** : to spread by rumor or report ⟨the story was *noised* abroad⟩

noise·mak·er \'nȯiz-ımā-kər\ *n* : one that makes noise; *esp* : a device used to make noise at parties

noise pollution *n* : annoying or harmful noise in an environment

noi·some \'nȯi-səm\ *adj* **1** : HARMFUL, UNWHOLESOME **2** : offensive to the senses (as smell) : DISGUSTING **syn** insalubrious, noxious, sickly, unhealthful, unhealthy

noisy \'nȯi-zē\ *adj* **nois·i·er; -est 1** : making loud noises **2** : full of noises : LOUD — **nois·i·ly** \-zə-lē\ *adv* — **nois·i·ness** \-zē-nəs\ *n*

nol·le pro·se·qui \ınä-lē-'prä-sə-ıkwī\ *n* [L, to be unwilling to pursue] : an entry on the record of a legal action that the prosecutor or plaintiff will proceed no further in an action or suit or in some aspect of it

no·lo con·ten·de·re \ınō-lō-kən-'ten-də-rē\ *n* [L, I do not wish to contend] : a plea in a criminal prosecution that subjects the defendant to conviction but does not admit guilt or preclude denying the charges in another proceeding

nol–pros \'näl-'präs\ *vb* **nol–prossed; nol–pros·sing** : to discontinue by entering a nolle prosequi

nom *abbr* nominative

no·mad \'nō-ımad\ *n* **1** : a member of a people who have no fixed residence but move from place to place **2** : an individual who roams about aimlessly — **no·mad** *adj* — **no·mad·ic** \nō-'ma-dik\ *adj*

no–man's–land \'nō-ımanz-ıland\ *n* **1** : an area of unowned, unclaimed, or uninhabited land **2** : an unoccupied area between opposing troops

nom de guerre \ınäm-di-'ger\ *n, pl* **noms de guerre** *same or* ınämz-\ [F, lit., war name] : PSEUDONYM

nom de plume \-'plüm\ *n, pl* **noms de plume** *same or* ınämz-\ [F, pen name; prob. coined in E] : PEN NAME

no·men·cla·ture \'nō-mən-ıklā-chər\ *n* **1** : NAME, DESIGNATION **2** : a system of terms used in a science or art

nom·i·nal \'nä-mən-ᵊl\ *adj* **1** : being something in name or form only ⟨∼ head of a party⟩ **2** : TRIFLING ⟨a ∼ price⟩ — **nom·i·nal·ly** *adv*

nom·i·nate \'nä-mə-ınāt\ *vb* **-nat·ed; -nat·ing** : to choose as a candidate for election, appointment, or honor **syn** appoint, designate, name, tap — **nom·i·na·tion** \ınä-mə-'nā-shən\ *n*

nom·i·na·tive \'nä-mə-nə-tiv\ *adj* : of, relating to, or constituting a grammatical case marking typically the subject of a verb — **nominative** *n*

nom·i·nee \ınä-mə-'nē\ *n* : a person nominated for an office, duty, or position

non- \(')nän *or* ınän *before stressed syllables;* ınän *elsewhere*\ *prefix* **1** : not : reverse of : absence of **2** : having no importance

nonabrasive	noncontagious
nonabsorbent	noncontinuous
nonacademic	noncorroding
nonacceptance	noncorrosive
nonacid	noncritical
nonactivated	noncrystalline
nonadaptive	nondeductible
nonaddictive	nondelivery
nonadhesive	nondemocratic
nonadjacent	nondenominational
nonadjustable	nondepartmental
nonaggression	nondestructive
nonalcoholic	nondevelopment
nonappearance	nondiscrimination
nonaromatic	nondiscriminatory
nonathletic	nondistinctive
nonattendance	nondurable
nonbeliever	noneconomic
nonbelligerent	noneducational
nonbreakable	nonelastic
noncancerous	nonelection
noncandidate	nonelective
noncellular	nonelectric
nonclerical	nonelectrical
noncoital	nonemotional
noncombat	nonenforcement
noncombustible	nonessential
noncommercial	nonethical
noncommunist	non-euclidean
noncompeting	nonexclusive
noncompetitive	nonexempt
noncompliance	nonexistence
noncomplying	nonexistent
nonconducting	nonexplosive
nonconflicting	nonfarm
nonconformance	nonfatal
nonconforming	nonfattening
nonconstructive	nonfederated

nonferrous
nonfiction
nonfictional
nonfilamentous
nonfilterable
nonflammable
nonflowering
nonfood
nonfreezing
nonfulfillment
nonfunctional
nongraded
nonhereditary
nonhomogeneous
nonhomologous
nonhuman
nonidentical
nonimportation
nonindustrial
noninfectious
noninflammable
nonintellectual
nonintercourse
noninterference
nonintoxicant
nonintoxicating
noninvasive
nonionizing
nonirritating
nonlegal
nonlethal
nonlife
nonlinear
nonliterary
nonliving
nonlogical
nonmagnetic
nonmalignant
nonmaterial
nonmember
nonmembership
nonmigratory
nonmilitary
nonmoral
nonmotile
nonmoving
nonnegotiable
nonobservance
nonoccurrence
nonofficial
nonoily
nonorthodox
nonparallel
nonparasitic
nonparticipant
nonparticipating
nonpathogenic
nonpaying
nonpayment
nonperformance
nonperishable
nonphysical
nonpoisonous
nonpolar
nonpolitical

nonporous
nonpregnant
nonproductive
nonprofessional
nonprotein
nonradioactive
nonrandom
nonreactive
nonreciprocal
nonrecognition
nonrecurrent
nonrecurring
nonrefillable
nonreligious
nonrenewable
nonresidential
nonrestricted
nonreturnable
nonreversible
nonruminant
nonsalable
nonscientific
nonscientist
nonseasonal
nonsectarian
nonsegregated
nonselective
non-self-governing
nonexist
nonsexual
nonshrinkable
nonsinkable
nonsmoker
nonsmoking
nonsocial
nonspeaking
nonspecialist
nonspecific
nonsteroidal
nonsuccess
nonsurgical
nontaxable
nonteaching
nontechnical
nontemporal
nontenured
nontheistic
nonthreatening
nontoxic
nontraditional
nontransferable
nontypical
nonuniform
nonvascular
nonvenomous
nonverbal
nonviable
nonvisual
nonvocal
nonvolatile
nonvoter
nonvoting
nonworker
nonworking
nonzero

non·age \'nä-nij, 'nō-\ n 1 : legal minority 2 : a period of youth 3 : IMMATURITY

no·na·ge·nar·i·an \,nō-nə-jə-'ner-ē-ən, ,nä-\ n : a person whose age is in the nineties

non·aligned \,nän-ə-'līnd\ adj : not allied with other nations

non·book \'nän-,bùk\ n : a book of little literary merit that is often a compilation (as of pictures or speeches)

¹**nonce** \'näns\ n : the one, particular, or present occasion or purpose ⟨for the ∼⟩

²**nonce** adj : occurring, used, or made only once or for a special occasion ⟨a ∼ word⟩

non·cha·lant \,nän-shə-'länt\ adj [F, fr. OF, fr. prp. of nonchaloir to disregard, fr. non- not + chaloir to concern, fr. L calēre to be warm] : giving an effect of unconcern or indifference **syn** collected, composed, cool, imperturbable, unflappable, unruffled — **non·cha·lance** \-'läns\ n — **non·cha·lant·ly** adv

non·com \'nän-,käm\ n : NONCOMMISSIONED OFFICER

non·com·ba·tant \,nän-kəm-'bat-ənt, nän-'käm-bə-tənt\ n : a member (as a chaplain) of the armed forces whose duties do not include fighting; also : CIVILIAN — **noncombatant** adj

non·com·mis·sioned officer \,nän-kə-'mi-shənd-\ n : a subordinate officer in the armed forces appointed from enlisted personnel

non·com·mit·tal \,nän-kə-'mit-əl\ adj : indicating neither consent nor dissent

non com·pos men·tis \,nän-,käm-pəs-'men-təs\ adj : not of sound mind

non·con·duc·tor \,nän-kən-'dək-tər\ n : a substance that is a very poor conductor of heat, electricity, or sound

non·con·form·ist \-kən-'fòr-mist\ n 1 often cap : a person who does not conform to an established church and esp. the Church of England 2 : a person who does not conform to a generally accepted pattern of thought or action **syn** dissenter, dissident, heretic, schismatic, sectary, separatist — **non·con·for·mi·ty** \-'fòr-mə-tē\ n

non·co·op·er·a·tion \,nän-kō-,ä-pə-'rā-shən\ n : failure or refusal to cooperate; esp : refusal through civil disobedience of a people to cooperate with the government of a country

non·cred·it \(,)nän-'kre-dət\ adj : not offering credit toward a degree

non·cus·to·di·al \,nän-kə-'stō-dē-əl\ adj : of or being a parent who does not have legal custody of a child

non·dairy \'nän-'der-ē\ adj : containing no milk or milk products

non·de·script \,nän-di-'skript\ adj 1 : not belonging to any particular class or kind 2 : lacking distinctive qualities

non·drink·er \-'driŋ-kər\ n : a person who abstains from alcohol

¹**none** \'nən\ pron 1 : not any ⟨∼ of them went⟩ 2 : not one ⟨∼ of the family⟩ 3 : not any such thing or person ⟨half a loaf is better than ∼⟩

²**none** adj, archaic : not any : NO

³**none** adv : by no means : not at all ⟨he got there ∼ too soon⟩

non·en·ti·ty \,nän-'en-tə-tē\ n 1 : something that does not exist or exists only in the imagination 2 : one of no consequence or significance **syn** nobody, nothing, whippersnapper

nones \'nōnz\ n sing or pl : the 7th day of March, May, July, or October or the 5th day of any other month in the ancient Roman calendar

none·such \'nən-,səch\ n : one without an equal — **nonesuch** adj

none·the·less \,nən-thə-'les\ adv : NEVERTHELESS

non·event \'nän-i-,vent\ n 1 : an event that fails to take place or to satisfy expectations 2 : a highly promoted event of little intrinsic interest

non·fat \-'fat\ adj : lacking fat solids : having fat solids removed ⟨∼ milk⟩

non·gono·coc·cal \,nän-,gä-nə-'kä-kəl\ adj : not caused by a gonococcus

non·he·ro \'nän-'hē-rō\ n : ANTIHERO

non·in·ter·ven·tion \,nän-,in-tər-'ven-chən\ n : refusal or failure to intervene (as in the affairs of other countries)

non·met·al \'nän-'met-əl\ n : a chemical element (as carbon) that lacks the characteristics of a metal — **non·me·tal·lic** \,nän-mə-'ta-lik\ adj

non·neg·a·tive \-'ne-gə-tiv\ *adj* : not negative : being either positive or zero

non·nu·cle·ar \'nän-'nü-klē-ər\ *adj* **1** : not nuclear **2** : not having, using, or involving nuclear weapons

non·ob·jec·tive \nän-əb-'jek-tiv\ *adj* **1** : not objective **2** : representing no natural or actual object, figure, or scene ⟨~ art⟩

¹non·pa·reil \-pə-'rel\ *adj* : having no equal : PEERLESS

²nonpareil *n* **1** : an individual of unequaled excellence : PARAGON **2** : a small flat disk of chocolate covered with white sugar pellets

non·par·ti·san \'nän-'pär-tə-zən\ *adj* : not partisan; *esp* : not influenced by political party spirit or interests

non·per·son \-'pərs-ᵊn\ *n* **1** : UNPERSON **2** : a person having no social or legal status

non·plus \'nän-'pləs\ *vb* **-plussed** *also* **-plused** \-'pləst\; **-plus·sing** *also* **-plus·ing** : PUZZLE, PERPLEX

non·pre·scrip·tion \nän-pri-'skrip-shən\ *adj* : available for sale legally without a doctor's prescription

non·prof·it \'nän-'prä-fət\ *adj* : not conducted or maintained for the purpose of making a profit ⟨a ~ organization⟩

non·pro·lif·er·a·tion \nän-prə-li-fə-'rä-shən\ *adj* : providing for the stoppage of proliferation (as of nuclear arms) ⟨a ~ treaty⟩

non·read·er \'nän-'rē-dər\ *n* : one who does not read

non·rep·re·sen·ta·tion·al \nän-re-pri-zen-'tä-shə-nəl\ *adj* : NONOBJECTIVE 2

non·res·i·dent \'nän-'re-zə-dənt\ *adj* : not living in a particular place — **non·res·i·dence** \-dəns\ *n* — **nonresident** *n*

non·re·sis·tance \nän-ri-'zis-təns\ *n* : the principles or practice of passive submission to authority even when unjust or oppressive

non·re·stric·tive \-ri-'strik-tiv\ *adj* **1** : not serving or tending to restrict **2** : not limiting the reference of the word or phrase modified ⟨a ~ clause⟩

non·rig·id \nän-'ri-jəd\ *adj* : maintaining form by pressure of contained gas ⟨a ~ airship⟩

non·sched·uled \'nän-'ske-jüld\ *adj* : licensed to carry passengers or freight by air without a regular schedule

non·sense \'nän-sens, -səns\ *n* **1** : foolish or meaningless words or actions **2** : things of no importance or value — **non·sen·si·cal** \nän-'sen-si-kəl\ *adj* — **non·sen·si·cal·ly** \-k(ə-)lē\ *adv*

non se·qui·tur \nän-'se-kwə-tər\ *n* [L, it does not follow] : an inference that does not follow from the premises

non·sked \'nän-'sked\ *n* : a nonscheduled transport plane or airline

non·skid \'nän-'skid\ *adj* : designed to prevent skidding

non·slip \-'slip\ *adj* : designed to prevent slipping

non·stan·dard \nän-'stan-dərd\ *adj* **1** : not standard **2** : not conforming to the usage characteristic of educated native speakers of a language

non·start·er \'nän-'stär-tər\ *n* **1** : one that does not start **2** : one that is not productive or effective

non·stick \-'stik\ *adj* : allowing easy removal of cooked food particles

non·stop \-'stäp\ *adj* : done or made without a stop — **nonstop** *adv*

non·sup·port \nän-sə-'pōrt\ *n* : failure to support; *esp* : failure on the part of one under obligation to provide maintenance

non–U \'nän-'yü\ *adj* : not characteristic of the upper classes

non·union \-'yü-nyən\ *adj* **1** : not belonging to a trade union ⟨~ carpenters⟩ **2** : not recognizing or favoring trade unions or their members ⟨~ employers⟩

non·us·er \-'yü-zər\ *n* : one who does not make use of something (as drugs)

non·vi·o·lence \'nän-'vī-ə-ləns\ *n* **1** : abstention from violence as a matter of principle **2** : avoidance of violence **3** : nonviolent political demonstrations — **non·vi·o·lent** \-lənt\ *adj*

non·white \nän-'hwīt, -'wīt\ *n* : a person whose features and esp. skin color are different from those of peoples of northwestern Europe — **nonwhite** *adj*

non·wo·ven \'nän-'wō-vən\ *adj* : made of fibers held together by interlocking or bonding (as by chemical or thermal means) — **nonwoven** *n*

noo·dle \'nüd-ᵊl\ *n* [G *Nudel*] : a food paste made with egg and shaped typically in ribbon form

nook \'nu̇k\ *n* **1** : an interior angle or corner formed usu. by two walls ⟨a chimney ~⟩ **2** : a sheltered or hidden place ⟨searched every ~ and cranny⟩

noon \'nün\ *n* : the middle of the day : 12 o'clock in the daytime — **noon** *adj*

noon·day \'nün-dā\ *n* : NOON, MIDDAY

no one *pron* : NOBODY

noon·tide \'nün-tīd\ *n* : NOON

noon·time \-tīm\ *n* : NOON

noose \'nüs\ *n* : a loop with a running knot (as in a lasso) that binds closer the more it is drawn

nope \'nōp\ *adv* : NO

nor \'nȯr\ *conj* : and not ⟨not for you ~ for me⟩ — used esp. to introduce and negate the second member and each later member of a series of items preceded by *neither* ⟨neither here ~ there⟩

Nor *abbr* Norway; Norwegian

Nor·dic \'nȯr-dik\ *adj* **1** : of or relating to the Germanic peoples of northern Europe and esp. of Scandinavia **2** : of or relating to competitive ski events involving cross-country racing, ski jumping, or biathlon — **Nordic** *n*

nor·epi·neph·rine \nȯr-e-pə-'ne-frən\ *n* : a nitrogen-containing neurotransmitter in parts of the sympathetic and central nervous systems

norm \'nȯrm\ *n* [L *norma*, lit., carpenter's square] **1** : an authoritative standard or model; *esp* : a set standard of development or achievement usu. derived from the average or median achievement of a large

normal • noteworthy

group **2** : a typical or widespread practice, procedure, or custom **syn** average, mean, median, par

¹**nor·mal** \'nȯr-məl\ *adj* **1** : REGULAR, STANDARD, NATURAL **2** : of average intelligence; *also* : sound in mind and body — **nor·mal·cy** \-sē\ *n* — **nor·mal·i·ty** \nȯr-'ma-lə-tē\ *n* — **nor·mal·ly** *adv*

²**normal** *n* **1** : one that is normal **2** : the usual condition, level, or quantity

nor·mal·ise *Brit var of* NORMALIZE

nor·mal·ize \'nȯr-mə-ˌlīz\ *vb* **-ized; -iz·ing** : to make or restore to normal — **nor·mal·i·za·tion** \ˌnȯr-mə-lə-'zā-shən\ *n*

Nor·man \'nȯr-mən\ *n* **1** : a native or inhabitant of Normandy **2** : one of the 10th century Scandinavian conquerors of Normandy **3** : one of the Norman-French conquerors of England in 1066 — **Norman** *adj*

nor·ma·tive \'nȯr-mə-tiv\ *adj* : of, relating to, or determining norms — **nor·ma·tive·ly** *adv* — **nor·ma·tive·ness** *n*

Norse \'nȯrs\ *n, pl* **Norse 1** : NORWEGIAN; *also* : any of the western Scandinavian dialects or languages **2** *pl* : SCANDINAVIANS; *also* : NORWEGIANS

Norse·man \-mən\ *n* : any of the ancient Scandinavians

¹**north** \'nȯrth\ *adv* : to, toward, or in the north

²**north** *adj* **1** : situated toward or at the north **2** : coming from the north

³**north** *n* **1** : the direction to the left of one facing east **2** : the compass point directly opposite to south **3** *cap* : regions or countries north of a specified or implied point — **north·er·ly** \'nȯr-thər-lē\ *adv or adj* — **north·ern** \-thərn\ *adj* — **North·ern·er** \-thər-nər\ *n* — **north·ern·most** \-thərn-ˌmōst\ *adj* — **north·ward** \'nȯrth-wərd\ *adv or adj* — **north·wards** \-wərdz\ *adv*

north·east \nȯr-'thēst\ *n* **1** : the general direction between north and east **2** : the compass point midway between north and east **3** *cap* : regions or countries northeast of a specified or implied point — **northeast** *adj or adv* — **north·east·er·ly** \-'thē-stər-lē\ *adv or adj* — **north·east·ern** \-stərn\ *adj*

north·east·er \-'thēs-tər\ *n* **1** : a strong northeast wind **2** : a storm with northeast winds

north·er \'nȯr-thər\ *n* **1** : a strong north wind **2** : a storm with north winds

northern lights *n pl* : AURORA BOREALIS

north pole *n, often cap N&P* : the northernmost point of the earth

North Star *n* : the star toward which the northern end of the earth's axis points

north·west \nȯrth-'west\ *n* **1** : the general direction between north and west **2** : the compass point midway between north and west **3** *cap* : regions or countries northwest of a specified or implied point — **north·west** *adj or adv* — **north·west·ern** \-'we-stər-lē\ *adv or adj* — **north·west·ern** \-'we-stərn\ *adj*

Norw *abbr* Norway; Norwegian

Nor·we·gian \nȯr-'wē-jən\ *n* **1** : a native or inhabitant of Norway **2** : the language of Norway — **Norwegian** *adj*

nos *abbr* numbers

¹**nose** \'nōz\ *n* **1** : the part of the face or head containing the nostrils and covering the front of the nasal cavity **2** : the sense of smell **3** : something (as a point, edge, or projecting front part) that resembles a nose (the ~ of a plane) — **nosed** \'nōzd\ *adj*

²**nose** *vb* **nosed; nos·ing 1** : to detect by or as if by smell : SCENT **2** : to push or move with the nose **3** : to touch or rub with the nose : NUZZLE **4** : PRY **5** : to move ahead slowly (the ship *nosed* into her berth)

nose·bleed \'nōz-ˌblēd\ *n* : a bleeding from the nose

nose cone *n* : a protective cone constituting the forward end of an aerospace vehicle

nose dive *n* **1** : a downward nose-first plunge (as of an airplane) **2** : a sudden extreme drop (as in prices)

nose·gay \'nōz-ˌgā\ *n* : a small bunch of flowers : POSY

nose out *vb* **1** : to discover often by prying **2** : to defeat by a narrow margin

nose·piece \-ˌpēs\ *n* **1** : a fitting at the lower end of a microscope tube to which the objectives are attached **2** : the bridge of a pair of eyeglasses

no–show \'nō-ˌshō\ *n* : a person who reserves space (as on an airplane or at a concert) but neither uses nor cancels the reservation

nos·tal·gia \nä-'stal-jə\ *n* [NL, fr. Gk *nostos* return home + *algos* pain, grief] **1** : HOMESICKNESS **2** : a wistful yearning for something past or irrecoverable — **nos·tal·gic** \-jik\ *adj*

nos·tril \'näs-trəl\ *n* [ME *nosethirl*, fr. OE *nosthyrl*, fr. *nosu* nose + *thyrel* hole] **1** : either of the nares usu. with the adjoining nasal wall and passage **2** : either fleshy lateral wall of the nose

nos·trum \'näs-trəm\ *n* [L, neut. of *noster* our, ours, fr. *nos* we] : a questionable medicine or remedy

nosy *or* **nos·ey** \'nō-zē\ *adj* **nos·i·er; -est** : INQUISITIVE, PRYING

not \'nät\ *adv* **1** — used to make negative a group of words or a word (the boys are ~ here) **2** — used to stand for the negative of a preceding group of words (sometimes hard to see and sometimes ~)

no·ta be·ne \nō-tə-'bē-nē, -'be-\ [L, mark well] — used to call attention to something important

no·ta·bil·i·ty \ˌnō-tə-'bi-lə-tē\ *n, pl* **-ties 1** : the quality or state of being notable **2** : NOTABLE

¹**no·ta·ble** \'nō-tə-bəl\ *adj* **1** : NOTEWORTHY, REMARKABLE (a ~ achievement) **2** : DISTINGUISHED, PROMINENT (two ~ politicians made speeches)

²**notable** *n* : a person of note **syn** bigwig, eminence, nabob, personage, somebody, VIP

no·ta·bly \'nō-tə-blē\ *adv* **1** : in a notable manner **2** : ESPECIALLY, PARTICULARLY

no·tar·i·al \nō-'ter-ē-əl\ *adj* : of, relating to, or done by a notary public

no·ta·rize \'nō-tə-ˌrīz\ *vb* **-rized; -riz·ing** : to acknowledge or make legally authentic as a notary public

no·ta·ry public \'nō-tə-rē-\ *n, pl* **notaries public** *or* **notary publics** : a public official who attests or certifies writings (as deeds) to make them legally authentic

no·ta·tion \nō-'tā-shən\ *n* **1** : ANNOTATION, NOTE **2** : the act, process, or method of representing data by marks, signs, figures, or characters; *also* : a system of symbols (as letters, numerals, or musical notes) used in such notation

¹**notch** \'näch\ *n* **1** : a V-shaped hollow in an edge or surface **2** : a narrow pass between two mountains

²**notch** *vb* **1** : to cut or make notches in **2** : to score or record by or as if by cutting a series of notches (~ed 20 points for the team)

notch·back \'näch-ˌbak\ *n* : an automobile with a trunk whose lid forms a distinct deck

¹**note** \'nōt\ *vb* **not·ed; not·ing 1** : to notice or observe with care; *also* : to record or preserve in writing **2** : to make special mention of : REMARK

²**note** *n* **1** : a musical sound **2** : a cry, call, or sound esp. of a bird **3** : a special tone in a person's words or voice (a ~ of fear) **4** : a character in music used to indicate duration of a tone by its shape and pitch by its position on the staff **5** : a characteristic feature : MOOD, QUALITY (a ~ of optimism) **6** : MEMORANDUM **7** : a brief and informal record; *also* : a written or printed comment or explanation **8** : a written promise to pay a debt **9** : a piece of paper money **10** : a short informal letter **11** : a formal diplomatic or official communication **12** : DISTINCTION, REPUTATION (an artist of ~) **13** : OBSERVATION, NOTICE, HEED (take ~ of the time)

note·book \'nōt-ˌbuk\ *n* : a book for notes or memoranda

not·ed \'nō-təd\ *adj* : well known by reputation : EMINENT, CELEBRATED

note·wor·thy \'nōt-ˌwər-the\ *adj* : worthy of note : REMARKABLE

¹**noth•ing** \'nə-thiŋ\ *pron* **1** : no thing ⟨leaves ∼ to the imagination⟩ **2** : no part **3** : one of no interest, value, or importance ⟨she's ∼ to me⟩

²**nothing** *adv* : not at all : in no degree

³**nothing** *n* **1** : something that does not exist **2** : ZERO **3** : a person or thing of little or no value or importance

⁴**nothing** *adj* : of no account : worthless

noth•ing•ness \'nə-thiŋ-nəs\ *n* **1** : the quality or state of being nothing **2** : NONEXISTENCE; *also* : utter insignificance **3** : something insignificant or valueless

¹**no•tice** \'nō-təs\ *n* **1** : WARNING, ANNOUNCEMENT **2** : notification of the termination of an agreement or contract at a specified time **3** : ATTENTION, HEED ⟨bring the matter to my ∼⟩ **4** : a written or printed announcement **5** : a short critical account or examination (as of a play) : REVIEW

²**notice** *vb* **no•ticed; no•tic•ing 1** : to make mention of : remark on : NOTE **2** : to take notice of : OBSERVE, MARK

no•tice•able \'nō-tə-sə-bəl\ *adj* **1** : worthy of notice **2** : capable of being or likely to be noticed — **no•tice•ably** \-blē\ *adv*

no•ti•fy \'nō-tə-ˌfī\ *vb* **-fied; -fy•ing 1** : to give notice of : report the occurrence of **2** : to give notice to — **no•ti•fi•ca•tion** \ˌnō-tə-fə-'kā-shən\ *n*

no•tion \'nō-shən\ *n* **1** : IDEA, CONCEPTION ⟨have a ∼ of what he means⟩ **2** : a belief held : OPINION, VIEW **3** : WHIM, FANCY ⟨a sudden ∼ to go⟩ **4** *pl* : small useful articles (as pins, needles, or thread)

no•tion•al \'nō-shə-nəl\ *adj* **1** : existing in the mind only : IMAGINARY, UNREAL **2** : given to foolish or fanciful moods or ideas : WHIMSICAL

no•to•ri•ous \nō-'tōr-ē-əs\ *adj* : generally known and talked of; *esp* : widely and unfavorably known — **no•to•ri•ety** \ˌnō-tə-'rī-ə-tē\ *n* — **no•to•ri•ous•ly** \nō-'tōr-ē-əs-lē\ *adv*

¹**not•with•stand•ing** \ˌnät-with-'stan-diŋ, -with-\ *prep* : in spite of

²**notwithstanding** *adv* : NEVERTHELESS

³**notwithstanding** *conj* : ALTHOUGH

nou•gat \'nü-gət\ *n* [F, fr. Provençal, fr. Old Provençal nogat, fr. *noga* nut, ultim. fr. L *nuc-, nux*] : a confection of nuts or fruit pieces in a sugar paste

nought \'nȯt, 'nät\ *var of* NAUGHT

noun \'naun\ *n* : a word that is the name of a subject of discourse (as a person or place)

nour•ish \'nər-ish\ *vb* : to promote the growth or development of

nour•ish•ing *adj* : giving nourishment

nour•ish•ment \'nər-ish-mənt\ *n* **1** : FOOD, NUTRIENT **2** : the action or process of nourishing

nou•veau riche \ˌnü-ˌvō-'rēsh\ *n, pl* **nou•veaux riches** *same* \ [F] : a person newly rich : PARVENU

Nov *abbr* November

no•va \'nō-və\ *n, pl* **novas** *or* **no•vae** \-(ˌ)vē, -ˌvī\ [NL, fem. of L *novus* new] : a star that suddenly increases greatly in brightness and then within a few months or years grows dim again

¹**nov•el** \'nä-vəl\ *adj* **1** : having no precedent : NEW **2** : STRANGE, UNUSUAL

²**novel** *n* : a long invented prose narrative dealing with human experience through a connected sequence of events — **nov•el•ist** \-və-list\ *n*

nov•el•ette \ˌnä-və-'let\ *n* : a brief novel or long short story

nov•el•ize \'nä-və-ˌlīz\ *vb* **-ized; -iz•ing** : to convert into the form of a novel — **nov•el•i•za•tion** \ˌnä-və-lə-'zā-shən\ *n*

no•vel•la \nō-'ve-lə\ *n, pl* **novellas** *or* **no•vel•le** \-'ve-lē\ : NOVELETTE

nov•el•ty \'nä-vəl-tē\ *n, pl* **-ties 1** : something new or unusual **2** : NEWNESS **3** : a small manufactured article intended mainly for personal or household adornment — usu. used in pl.

No•vem•ber \nō-'vem-bər\ *n* [ME *Novembre*, fr. OF, fr. L *November* (ninth month), fr. *novem* nine] : the 11th month of the year

no•ve•na \nō-'vē-nə\ *n* : a Roman Catholic nine-day period of prayer

nov•ice \'nä-vəs\ *n* **1** : a new member of a religious or-

der who is preparing to take the vows of religion **2** : one who is inexperienced or untrained

no·vi·tiate \nō-¹vi-shət\ *n* **1** : the period or state of being a novice **2** : a house where novices are trained **3** : NOVICE

¹now \¹naů\ *adv* **1** : at the present time or moment **2** : in the time immediately before the present **3** : IMMEDIATELY, FORTHWITH **4** — used with the sense of present time weakened or lost (as to express command, introduce an important point, or indicate a transition) ⟨∼ hear this⟩ **5** : SOMETIMES ⟨∼ one and ∼ another⟩ **6** : under the present circumstances **7** : at the time referred to

²now *conj* : in view of the fact ⟨∼ that you're here, we'll start⟩

³now *n* : the present time or moment : PRESENT

⁴now *adj* **1** : of or relating to the present time ⟨the ∼ president⟩ **2** : excitingly new ⟨∼ clothes⟩; *also* : constantly aware of what is new ⟨∼ people⟩

NOW *abbr* **1** National Organization for Women **2** negotiable order of withdrawal

now·a·days \¹naů-ə-₁dāz\ *adv* : at the present time

no·way \¹nō-₁wā\ *or* **no·ways** \-₁wāz\ *adv* : NOWISE

no·where \-₁hwer\ *adv* : not anywhere — **nowhere** *n*

nowhere near *adv* : not nearly

no·wise \¹nō-₁wīz\ *adv* : in no way

nox·ious \¹näk-shəs\ *adj* : harmful esp. to health or morals

noz·zle \¹nä-zəl\ *n* : a short tube constricted in the middle or at one end and used (as on a hose) to speed up or direct a flow of fluid

np *abbr* **1** no pagination **2** no place (of publication)

Np *symbol* neptunium

NP *abbr* notary public

NR *abbr* not rated

NRA *abbr* National Rifle Association

NS *abbr* **1** not specified **2** Nova Scotia

NSA *abbr* National Security Agency

NSC *abbr* National Security Council

NSF *abbr* **1** National Science Foundation **2** not sufficient funds

NSW *abbr* New South Wales

NT *abbr* **1** New Testament **2** Northern Territory **3** Northwest Territories

nth \¹enth\ *adj* **1** : numbered with an unspecified or indefinitely large ordinal number (for the ∼ time) **2** : EXTREME, UTMOST ⟨to the ∼ degree⟩

NTP *abbr* normal temperature and pressure

nt wt *or* **n wt** *abbr* net weight

nu \¹nü, ¹nyü\ *n* : the 13th letter of the Greek alphabet— N or ν

NU *abbr* name unknown

nu·ance \¹nü-₁äns, ¹nyü-, nü-¹äns, nyü-\ *n* [F] : a shade of difference : a delicate variation (as in tone or meaning)

nub \¹nəb\ *n* **1** : KNOB, LUMP **2** : GIST, POINT ⟨the ∼ of the story⟩

nub·bin \¹nə-bən\ *n* **1** : something (as an ear of Indian corn) that is small for its kind, stunted, undeveloped, or imperfect **2** : a small projecting bit

nu·bile \¹nü-₁bīl, ¹nyü-, -bil\ *adj* **1** : of marriageable condition or age **2** : sexually attractive ⟨∼ young women⟩

nu·cle·ar \¹nü-klē-ər, ¹nyü-\ *adj* **1** : of, relating to, or constituting a nucleus **2** : of, relating to, or using the atomic nucleus or energy derived from it **3** : of, relating to, or being a weapon whose destructive power results from an uncontrolled nuclear reaction

nu·cle·ate \¹nü-klē-₁āt, ¹nyü-\ *vb* **-at·ed; -at·ing** : to form, act as, or have a nucleus — **nu·cle·ation** \₁nü-klē-¹ā-shən, ₁nyü-\ *n*

nu·cle·ic acid \nú-¹klē-ik-, nyú-, -¹klā-\ *n* : any of various complex organic acids (as DNA) found esp. in cell nuclei

nu·cle·us \¹nü-klē-əs, ¹nyü-\ *n, pl* **nu·clei** \-klē-₁ī\ *also* **nu·cle·us·es** [NL, fr. L, kernel, dim. of *nuc-, nux* nut]

1 : a central mass or part about which matter gathers or is collected : CORE **2** : a cell part that is characteristic of all living things except viruses, bacteria, and certain algae, that is necessary for heredity and for making proteins, that contains the chromosomes with their genes, and that is enclosed in a membrane **3** : a mass of gray matter or group of nerve cells in the central nervous system **4** : the central part of an atom that comprises nearly all of the atomic mass

¹nude \¹nüd, ¹nyüd\ *adj* **nud·er; nud·est** : BARE, NAKED, UNCLOTHED — **nu·di·ty** \¹nü-də-tē, ¹nyü-\ *n*

²nude *n* **1** : a nude human figure esp. as depicted in art **2** : the condition of being nude ⟨in the ∼⟩

nudge \¹nəj\ *vb* **nudged; nudg·ing** : to touch or push gently (as with the elbow) usu. in order to seek attention — **nudge** *n*

nud·ism \¹nü-₁di-zəm, ¹nyü-\ *n* : the practice of going nude esp. in mixed groups at specially secluded places — **nud·ist** \-dist\ *n*

nu·ga·to·ry \-gə-₁tōr-ē\ *adj* **1** : INCONSEQUENTIAL, WORTHLESS **2** : having no force : INEFFECTUAL

nug·get \¹nə-gət\ *n* : a lump of precious metal (as gold)

nui·sance \¹nüs-ᵊns, ¹nyüs-\ *n* : an annoying or troublesome person or thing

nuisance tax *n* : an excise tax collected in small amounts directly from the consumer

¹nuke \¹nük, ¹nyük\ *n* **1** : a nuclear weapon **2** : a nuclear power plant

²nuke *vb* **nuked; nuk·ing** **1** : to attack with nuclear weapons **2** : MICROWAVE

null \¹nəl\ *adj* **1** : having no legal or binding force : INVALID, VOID **2** : amounting to nothing **2** : INSIGNIFICANT — **nul·li·ty** \¹nə-lə-tē\ *n*

null and void *adj* : having no force, binding power, or validity

nul·li·fy \¹nə-lə-₁fī\ *vb* **-fied; -fy·ing** : to make null or valueless; *also* : ANNUL — **nul·li·fi·ca·tion** \₁nə-lə-fə-¹kā-shən\ *n*

num *abbr* numeral

Num *or* **Numb** *abbr* Numbers

numb \¹nəm\ *adj* : lacking sensation or emotion : BENUMBED — **numb** *vb* — **numb·ly** *adv* — **numb·ness** *n*

¹num·ber \¹nəm-bər\ *n* **1** : the total of individuals or units taken together **2** : an indefinite total (a small ∼ of tickets remain unsold) **3** : an ascertainable total ⟨the sands of the desert are without ∼⟩ **4** : a distinction of word form to denote reference to one or more than one **5** : a unit belonging to a mathematical system and subject to its laws; *also, pl* : ARITHMETIC **6** : a symbol used to represent a mathematical number; *also* : such a number used to identify or designate ⟨a phone ∼⟩ **7** : one in a series ⟨the best ∼ on the program⟩

☞　For table, see next page.

²number *vb* **1** : COUNT, ENUMERATE **2** : to include with or be one of a group **3** : to restrict to a small or definite number **4** : to assign a number to **5** : to comprise in number : TOTAL

num·ber·less \-ləs\ *adj* : INNUMERABLE, COUNTLESS

Numbers *n* — see BIBLE table

nu·mer·al \¹nü-mə-rəl, ¹nyü-\ *n* : conventional symbol representing a number — **numeral** *adj*

nu·mer·ate \¹nü-mə-₁rāt, ¹nyü-\ *vb* **-at·ed; -at·ing** : ENUMERATE

nu·mer·a·tor \-₁rā-tər\ *n* : the part of a fraction above the line

nu·mer·ic \nú-¹mer-ik, nyú-\ *adj* : NUMERICAL; *esp* : denoting a number or a system of numbers

nu·mer·i·cal \-¹mer-i-kəl\ *adj* **1** : of or relating to numbers **2** : expressed in or involving numbers — **nu·mer·i·cal·ly** \-k(ə-)lē\ *adv*

nu·mer·ol·o·gy \₁nü-mə-¹rä-lə-jē, ₁nyü-\ *n* : the study of the occult significance of numbers — **nu·mer·ol·o·gist** \-jist\ *n*

TABLE OF NUMBERS

| CARDINAL NUMBERS[1] | | | ORDINAL NUMBERS[4] | |
NAME[2]	SYMBOL		NAME[5]	SYMBOL
	Hindu-Arabic	Roman[3]		
zero *or* naught *or* cipher	0		first	1st
one	1	I	second	2d *or* 2nd
two	2	II	third	3d *or* 3rd
three	3	III	fourth	4th
four	4	IV	fifth	5th
five	5	V	sixth	6th
six	6	VI	seventh	7th
seven	7	VII	eighth	8th
eight	8	VIII	ninth	9th
nine	9	IX	tenth	10th
ten	10	X	eleventh	11th
eleven	11	XI	twelfth	12th
twelve	12	XII	thirteenth	13th
thirteen	13	XIII	fourteenth	14th
fourteen	14	XIV	fifteenth	15th
fifteen	15	XV	sixteenth	16th
sixteen	16	XVI	seventeenth	17th
seventeen	17	XVII	eighteenth	18th
eighteen	18	XVIII	nineteenth	19th
nineteen	19	XIX	twentieth	20th
twenty	20	XX	twenty-first	21st
twenty-one	21	XXI	twenty-second	22d *or* 22nd
twenty-two	22	XXII	twenty-third	23d *or* 23rd
twenty-three	23	XXIII	twenty-fourth	24th
twenty-four	24	XXIV	twenty-fifth	25th
twenty-five	25	XXV	twenty-sixth	26th
twenty-six	26	XXVI	twenty-seventh	27th
twenty-seven	27	XXVII	twenty-eighth	28th
twenty-eight	28	XXVIII	twenty-ninth	29th
twenty-nine	29	XXIX	thirtieth	30th
thirty	30	XXX	thirty-first *etc*	31st
thirty-one *etc*	31	XXXI	fortieth	40th
forty	40	XL	fiftieth	50th
fifty	50	L	sixtieth	60th
sixty	60	LX	seventieth	70th
seventy	70	LXX	eightieth	80th
eighty	80	LXXX	ninetieth	90th
ninety	90	XC	hundredth *or* one hundredth	100th
one hundred	100	C		
one hundred one *or* one hundred and one *etc*	101	CI	hundred and first *or* one hundred and first *etc*	101st
two hundred	200	CC	two hundredth	200th
three hundred	300	CCC	three hundredth	300th
four hundred	400	CD	four hundredth	400th
five hundred	500	D	five hundredth	500th
six hundred	600	DC	six hundredth	600th
seven hundred	700	DCC	seven hundredth	700th
eight hundred	800	DCCC	eight hundredth	800th
nine hundred	900	CM	nine hundredth	900th
one thousand *or* ten hundred *etc*	1,000	M	thousandth *or* one thousandth	1,000th
two thousand *etc*	2,000	MM	two thousandth *etc*	2,000th
five thousand	5,000	$\overline{V}$	five thousandth	5,000th
ten thousand	10,000	$\overline{X}$	ten thousandth	10,000th
one hundred thousand	100,000	$\overline{C}$	hundred thousandth *or* one hundred thousandth	100,000th
one million	1,000,000	$\overline{M}$	millionth *or* one millionth	1,000,000th

[1]The cardinal numbers are used in simple counting or in answer to "how many?" The words for these numbers may be used as nouns (I counted to *ten*), as pronouns (*ten* were found), or as adjectives (*ten* cows).

[2]In formal writing the numbers one to one hundred and in less formal writing the numbers one to nine are commonly written out, while larger numbers are given in numerals. A number occurring at the beginning of a sentence is usually written out. Except in very formal writing numerals are used for dates. Hindu-Arabic numerals from 1,000 to 9,999 are often written without commas (1000; 9999). Year numbers are always written without commas (1783).

[3]The Roman numerals are written either in capitals or in lowercase letters.

[4]The ordinal numbers are used to show the order in which such items as names, objects, and periods of time are considered (the *twelfth* month; the *fourth* row of seats; the *18th* century).

[5]Each of the names of the ordinal numbers except *first* and *second* is used for one of the equal parts into which a whole may be divided (a *fourth*; a *sixth*; a *tenth*) and also as the denominator in fractions (*one fourth*; *three fifths*). Fractions used as nouns are usually written as two words, but fractions used as adjectives are usually hyphenated (a *two-thirds* majority). When a two-word ordinal number is used as a noun to name a denominator, a hyphen is usually used to make sure that there is only one meaning (*six hundred ten-thousandths* means only 600/10,000 and not 610/1000). When fractions are written in numerals, the cardinal symbols are used (¼, ⅗, ⅚).

nu•mer•ous \'nü-mə-rəs, 'nyü-\ *adj* : consisting of, including, or relating to a great number : MANY

nu•mis•mat•ics \ˌnü-məz-'ma-tiks, ˌnyü-\ *n* : the study or collection of monetary objects — **nu•mis•mat•ic** \-tik\ *adj* — **nu•mis•ma•tist** \nü-'miz-mə-tist, nyü-\ *n*

num•skull \'nəm-ˌskəl\ *n* : a stupid person : DUNCE

nun \'nən\ *n* : a woman belonging to a religious order; *esp* : one under solemn vows of poverty, chastity, and obedience

nun•cio \'nən-sē-ˌō, 'nün-\ *n*, *pl* **-ci•os** [It, fr. L *nuntius* messenger] : a permanent high-ranking papal representative to a civil government

nun•nery \'nə-nə-rē\ *n*, *pl* **-ner•ies** : a convent of nuns

¹nup•tial \'nəp-shəl\ *adj* : of or relating to marriage or a wedding

²nuptial *n* : MARRIAGE, WEDDING — usu. used in pl.

¹nurse \'nərs\ *n* [ME, fr. OF *nurice*, fr. LL *nutricia*, fr. L, fem. of *nutricius* nourishing] **1** : a girl or woman employed to take care of children **2** : a person trained to care for sick people

²nurse *vb* **nursed; nurs•ing 1** : SUCKLE **2** : to take charge of and watch over **3** : TEND ⟨∼ an invalid⟩ **4** : to treat with special care ⟨∼ a headache⟩ **5** : to hold in one's mind or consideration ⟨∼ a grudge⟩ **6** : to act or serve as a nurse

nurse•maid \'nərs-ˌmād\ *n* : NURSE 1

nurse–prac•ti•tion•er \-prak-'ti-shə-nər\ *n* : a registered nurse who is qualified to assume some of the duties formerly assumed only by a physician

nurs•ery \'nər-sə-rē\ *n*, *pl* **-er•ies 1** : a room for children **2** : a place where children are temporarily cared for in their parents' absence **3** : a place where young plants are grown usu. for transplanting

nurs•ery•man \-mən\ *n* : a man who keeps or works in a plant nursery

nursery school *n* : a school for children under kindergarten age

nursing home *n* : a private establishment providing care for persons (as the aged or the chronically ill) who are unable to care for themselves

nurs•ling \'nərs-liŋ\ *n* **1** : one that is solicitously cared for **2** : a nursing child

¹nur•ture \'nər-chər\ *n* **1** : TRAINING, UPBRINGING; *also* : the influences that modify the expression of an individual's heredity **2** : FOOD, NOURISHMENT

²nurture *vb* **nur•tured; nur•tur•ing 1** : to care for : FEED, NOURISH **2** : EDUCATE, TRAIN **3** : FOSTER

nut \'nət\ *n* **1** : a dry fruit or seed with a hard shell and a firm inner kernel; *also* : its kernel **2** : a metal block with a hole through it that is fastened to a bolt or screw by means of a screw thread within the hole **3** : the ridge on the upper end of the fingerboard in a stringed musical instrument over which the strings pass **4** : a foolish, eccentric, or crazy person **5** : ENTHUSIAST

nut•crack•er \'nət-ˌkra-kər\ *n* : an instrument for cracking nuts

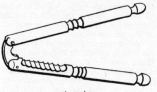

nutcracker

nut•hatch \-ˌhach\ *n* : any of various small tree-climbing chiefly insect-eating birds

nut•meg \-ˌmeg, -ˌmäg\ *n* [ME *notemuge*, ultim. fr. Old Provençal *noz muscada*, lit., musky nut] : a spice made by grinding the nutlike aromatic seed of a tropical tree; *also* : the seed or tree

nu•tria \'nü-trē-ə, 'nyü-\ *n* [Sp] **1** : the durable usu. light brown fur of a nutria **2** : a So. American aquatic rodent with webbed hind feet

¹nu•tri•ent \'nü-trē-ənt, 'nyü-\ *adj* : NOURISHING

²nutrient *n* : a nutritive substance or ingredient

nu•tri•ment \-trə-mənt\ *n* : NUTRIENT

nu•tri•tion \nü-'tri-shən, nyü-\ *n* : the act or process of nourishing; *esp* : the processes by which an individual takes in and utilizes food material — **nu•tri•tion•al** \-shə-nəl\ *adj* — **nu•tri•tious** \-shəs\ *adj* — **nu•tri•tive** \'nü-trə-tiv, 'nyü-\ *adj*

nuts \'nəts\ *adj* **1** : ENTHUSIASTIC, KEEN **2** : CRAZY, DEMENTED

nut•shell \'nət-ˌshel\ *n* : the shell of a nut — **in a nutshell** : in a few words ⟨that's the story *in a nutshell*⟩

nut•ty \'nə-tē\ *adj* **nut•ti•er; -est 1** : containing or suggesting nuts ⟨a ∼ flavor⟩ **2** : mentally unbalanced

nuz•zle \'nə-zəl\ *vb* **nuz•zled; nuz•zling 1** : to root around, push, or touch with or as if with the nose **2** : NESTLE, SNUGGLE

NV *abbr* Nevada

NW *abbr* northwest

NWT *abbr* Northwest Territories

NY *abbr* New York

NYC *abbr* New York City

ny•lon \'nī-ˌlän\ *n* **1** : any of numerous strong tough elastic synthetic materials used esp. in textiles and plastics **2** *pl* : stockings made of nylon

nymph \'nimf\ *n* **1** : any of the lesser goddesses in ancient mythology represented as maidens living in the mountains, forests, meadows, and waters **2** : GIRL **3** : an immature insect resembling the adult but smaller, less differentiated, and usu. lacking wings

nym•pho•ma•nia \ˌnim-fə-'mā-nē-ə, -nyə\ *n* : excessive sexual desire by a female — **nym•pho•ma•ni•ac** \-nē-ˌak\ *n or adj*

NZ *abbr* New Zealand

O

¹o \'ō\ *n*, *pl* **o's** *or* **os** \'ōz\ *often cap* **1** : the 15th letter of the English alphabet **2** : ZERO

²o *abbr*, *often cap* **1** ocean **2** Ohio **3** ohm

¹O \'ō\ *var of* OH

²O *symbol* oxygen

o/a *abbr* on or about

oaf \'ōf\ *n* : a stupid or awkward person — **oaf•ish** *adj*

oak \'ōk\ *n*, *pl* **oaks** *or* **oak** : any of a genus of trees or shrubs related to the beech and chestnut and bearing a rounded thin-shelled nut surrounded at the base by a hardened cup; *also* : the usu. tough hard durable wood of an oak — **oak•en** \'ō-kən\ *adj*

oa•kum \'ō-kəm\ *n* : loosely twisted hemp or jute fiber impregnated with tar and used esp. in caulking ships

oar \'ōr\ *n* : a long pole with a broad blade at one end used for propelling or steering a boat

oar•lock \'ōr-ˌläk\ *n* : a U-shaped device for holding an oar in place

oars•man \'ōrz-mən\ *n* : one who rows esp. in a racing crew

OAS *abbr* Organization of American States

oa•sis \ō-'ā-səs\ *n*, *pl* **oa•ses** \-ˌsēz\ : a fertile or green area in an arid region

oat \'ōt\ *n* : a cereal grass widely grown for its edible seed; *also* : this seed — **oat•en** \-ᵊn\ *adj*

oat•cake \'ōt-ˌkāk\ *n* : a thin flat oatmeal cake

oath \'ōth\ *n, pl* **oaths** \'ōthz, 'ōths\ **1** : a solemn appeal to God to witness to the truth of a statement or the sacredness of a promise **2** : an irreverent or careless use of a sacred name

oat·meal \'ōt-ˌmēl\ *n* **1** : ground or rolled oats **2** : porridge made from ground or rolled oats

Ob *or* **Obad** *abbr* Obadiah

Oba·di·ah \ˌō-bə-'dī-ə\ *n* — see BIBLE table

ob·bli·ga·to \ˌä-blə-'gä-tō\ *n, pl* **-tos** *also* **-ti** \-'gä-tē\ [It] : an accompanying part usu. played by a solo instrument

ob·du·rate \'äb-də-rət, -dyə-\ *adj* : stubbornly resistant : UNYIELDING **syn** inflexible, adamant, rigid, uncompromising — **ob·du·ra·cy** \-rə-sē\ *n*

obe·di·ent \ō-'bē-dē-ənt\ *adj* : submissive to the restraint or command of authority **syn** docile, tractable, amenable, biddable — **obe·di·ence** \-əns\ *n* — **obe·di·ent·ly** *adv*

obei·sance \ō-'bē-səns, -'bā-\ *n* : a bow made to show respect or submission; *also* : DEFERENCE, HOMAGE

ob·e·lisk \'ä-bə-ˌlisk\ *n* [MF *obelisque,* fr. L *obeliscus,* fr. Gk *obeliskos,* fr. dim. of *obelos* spit, pointed pillar] : a 4-sided pillar that tapers toward the top and ends in a pyramid

obese \ō-'bēs\ *adj* [L *obesus,* fr. *ob-* against + *esus,* pp. of *edere* to eat] : excessively fat **syn** corpulent, fleshy, gross, overweight, portly, stout — **obe·si·ty** \-'bē-sə-tē\ *n*

obey \ō-'bā\ *vb* **obeyed; obey·ing 1** : to follow the commands or guidance of : behave obediently **2** : to comply with ⟨∼ orders⟩ **syn** conform, keep, mind, observe

ob·fus·cate \'äb-fə-ˌskāt\ *vb* **-cat·ed; -cat·ing 1** : to make dark or obscure **2** : CONFUSE — **ob·fus·ca·tion** \ˌäb-fəs-'kā-shən\ *n*

OB–GYN *abbr* obstetrician gynecologist; obstetrics gynecology

obi \'ō-bē\ *n* [Jp] : a broad sash worn esp. with a Japanese kimono

obit \ō-'bit, 'ō-bət\ *n* : OBITUARY

obi·ter dic·tum \ˌō-bə-tər-'dik-təm\ *n, pl* **obiter dic·ta** \-tə\ [LL, lit., something said in passing] : an incidental remark or observation

obit·u·ary \ə-'bi-chə-ˌwer-ē\ *n, pl* **-ar·ies** : a notice of a person's death usu. with a short biographical account

obj *abbr* object; objective

¹ob·ject \'äb-jikt\ *n* **1** : something that may be seen or felt; *also* : something that may be perceived or examined mentally **2** : something that arouses an emotional response (as of affection or pity) **3** : AIM, PURPOSE **4** : a word or word group denoting that on or toward which the action of a verb is directed; *also* : a noun or noun equivalent in a prepositional phrase

²ob·ject \əb-'jekt\ *vb* **1** : to offer in opposition **2** : to oppose something; *also* : DISAPPROVE **syn** protest, remonstrate, expostulate — **ob·jec·tor** \-'jek-tər\ *n*

ob·jec·ti·fy \əb-'jek-tə-ˌfī\ *vb* **-fied; -fy·ing** : to make objective

ob·jec·tion \əb-'jek-shən\ *n* **1** : the act of objecting **2** : a reason for or a feeling of disapproval

ob·jec·tion·able \əb-'jek-shə-nə-bəl\ *adj* : UNDESIRABLE, OFFENSIVE — **ob·jec·tion·ably** \-blē\ *adv*

¹ob·jec·tive \əb-'jek-tiv\ *adj* **1** : of or relating to an object or end **2** : existing outside and independent of the mind **3** : of, relating to, or constituting a grammatical case marking typically the object of a verb or preposition **4** : treating or dealing with facts without distortion by personal feelings or prejudices — **ob·jec·tive·ly** *adv* — **ob·jec·tive·ness** *n* — **ob·jec·tiv·i·ty** \ˌäb-ˌjek-'ti-və-tē\ *n*

²objective *n* **1** : the lens (as in a microscope) nearest the object and forming an image of it **2** : an aim, goal, or end of action

ob·jet d'art \ˌōb-ˌzhā-'där\ *n, pl* **ob·jets d'art** *same*\ [F] : an article of artistic worth; *also* : CURIO **syn** knickknack, bauble, bibelot, gewgaw, novelty, trinket

ob·jet trou·vé \ˌòb-ˌzhā-trü-'vā\ *n, pl* **objets trouvés** *same*\ [F, lit., found object] : a found natural object (as a piece of driftwood) held to have aesthetic value; *also* : an artifact not orig. intended as art but displayed as a work of art

ob·jur·ga·tion \ˌäb-jər-'gā-shən\ *n* : a harsh rebuke — **ob·jur·gate** \'äb-jər-ˌgāt\ *vb*

obl *abbr* **1** oblique **2** oblong

ob·late \ä-'blāt\ *adj* : flattened or depressed at the poles ⟨an ∼ spheroid⟩

ob·la·tion \ə-'blā-shən\ *n* : a religious offering

ob·li·gate \'ä-blə-ˌgāt\ *vb* **-gat·ed; -gat·ing** : to bind legally or morally

ob·li·ga·tion \ˌä-blə-'gā-shən\ *n* **1** : an act of obligating oneself to a course of action **2** : something (as a promise or a contract) that binds one to a course of action **3** : INDEBTEDNESS; *also* : LIABILITY **4** : DUTY — **oblig·a·to·ry** \ə-'bli-gə-ˌtòr-ē\ *adj*

oblige \ə-'blīj\ *vb* **obliged; oblig·ing** [ME, fr. OF *obliger,* fr. L *obligare,* lit., to bind to, fr. *ob-* toward + *ligare* to bind] **1** : FORCE, COMPEL **2** : to bind by a favor; *also* : to do a favor for or do something as a favor

oblig·ing *adj* : willing to do favors — **oblig·ing·ly** *adv*

oblique \ō-'blēk\ *adj* **1** : neither perpendicular nor parallel : SLANTING **2** : not straightforward : INDIRECT — **oblique·ly** *adv* — **oblique·ness** *n* — **obliq·ui·ty** \-'bli-kwə-tē\ *n*

oblit·er·ate \ə-'bli-tə-ˌrāt\ *vb* **-at·ed; -at·ing** [L *oblitterare,* fr. *ob* in the way of + *littera* letter] **1** : to make undecipherable by wiping out or covering over **2** : to remove from recognition or memory **3** : CANCEL — **oblit·er·a·tion** \-ˌbli-tə-'rā-shən\ *n*

obliv·i·on \ə-'bli-vē-ən\ *n* **1** : the condition of being oblivious **2** : the condition or state of being forgotten

obliv·i·ous \ə-'bli-vē-əs\ *adj* **1** : lacking memory or mindful attention **2** : UNAWARE — **obliv·i·ous·ly** *adv* — **obliv·i·ous·ness** *n*

ob·long \'ä-ˌblòŋ\ *adj* : deviating from a square, circular, or spherical form by elongation in one dimension — **oblong** *n*

ob·lo·quy \'ä-blə-kwē\ *n, pl* **-quies 1** : strongly condemnatory utterance or language **2** : bad repute : DISGRACE **syn** dishonor, shame, infamy, disrepute, ignominy

ob·nox·ious \äb-'näk-shəs\ *adj* : REPUGNANT, OFFENSIVE — **ob·nox·ious·ly** *adv* — **ob·nox·ious·ness** *n*

oboe \'ō-bō\ *n* [It, fr. F *hautbois,* fr. *haut* high + *bois* wood] : a woodwind instrument with a slender conical tube and a double reed mouthpiece — **obo·ist** \'ō-ˌbō-ist\ *n*

oboe

ob·scene \äb-'sēn\ *adj* **1** : REPULSIVE **2** : deeply offensive to morality or decency; *esp* : designed to incite to lust or depravity **syn** gross, vulgar, coarse, crude, indecent — **ob·scene·ly** *adv* — **ob·scen·i·ty** \-'se-nə-tē\ *n*

ob·scu·ran·tism \äb-'skyur-ən-ˌti-zəm, ˌäb-skyù-'ran-\ *n* **1** : opposition to the spread of knowledge **2**

: deliberate vagueness or abstruseness — **ob·scu·ran·tist** \-tist\ *n or adj*

¹**ob·scure** \äb-ʹskyu̇r\ *adj* **1** : DIM, GLOOMY **2** : not readily understood : VAGUE **3** : REMOTE; *also* : HUMBLE **syn** dark, dusky, murky, tenebrous — **ob·scure·ly** *adv* — **ob·scu·ri·ty** \-ʹskyu̇r-ə-tē\ *n*

²**obscure** *vb* **ob·scured; ob·scur·ing 1** : to make dark, dim, or indistinct **2** : to conceal or hide by or as if by covering

ob·se·qui·ous \əb-ʹsē-kwē-əs\ *adj* : humbly or excessively attentive (as to a person in authority) : FAWNING, SYCOPHANTIC **syn** menial, servile, slavish, subservient — **ob·se·qui·ous·ly** *adv* — **ob·se·qui·ous·ness** *n*

ob·se·quy \ʹäb-sə-kwē\ *n, pl* **-quies** : a funeral or burial rite — usu. used in pl.

ob·serv·able \əb-ʹzər-və-bəl\ *adj* **1** : NOTEWORTHY **2** : capable of being observed — **ob·serv·abil·ity** \-ʹbil-ə-tē\ *n*

ob·ser·vance \əb-ʹzər-vəns\ *n* **1** : a customary practice or ceremony **2** : an act or instance of following a custom, rule, or law **3** : OBSERVATION

ob·ser·vant \-vənt\ *adj* **1** : WATCHFUL (⟨∼ spectators) **2** : KEEN, PERCEPTIVE **3** : MINDFUL (⟨∼ of the amenities)

ob·ser·va·tion \ˌäb-sər-ʹvā-shən, -zər-\ *n* **1** : an act or instance of observing **2** : the gathering of information (as for scientific studies) by noting facts or occurrences **3** : a conclusion drawn from observing; *also* : REMARK, STATEMENT **4** : the fact of being observed

ob·ser·va·to·ry \əb-ʹzər-və-ˌtōr-ē\ *n, pl* **-ries** : a place or institution equipped for observation of natural phenomena (as in astronomy)

ob·serve \əb-ʹzərv\ *vb* **ob·served; ob·serv·ing 1** : to conform one's action or practice to **2** : CELEBRATE **3** : to make a scientific observation of **4** : to see or sense esp. through careful attention **5** : to come to realize esp. through consideration of noted facts **6** : REMARK — **ob·serv·er** *n*

ob·sess \əb-ʹses\ *vb* : to preoccupy intensely or abnormally

ob·ses·sion \äb-ʹse-shən\ *n* : a persistent disturbing preoccupation with an idea or feeling; *also* : an emotion or idea causing such a preoccupation — **ob·ses·sive** \-ʹse-siv\ *adj or n* — **ob·ses·sive·ly** *adv*

ob·sid·i·an \äb-ʹsi-dē-ən\ *n* : a dark natural glass formed by the cooling of molten lava

ob·so·les·cent \ˌäb-sə-ʹles-ᵊnt\ *adj* : going out of use : becoming obsolete — **ob·so·les·cence** \-ᵊns\ *n*

ob·so·lete \ˌäb-sə-ʹlēt, ʹäb-sə-ˌlēt\ *adj* : no longer in use; *also* : OLD-FASHIONED **syn** extinct, outworn, passé, superseded

ob·sta·cle \ʹäb-sti-kəl\ *n* : something that stands in the way or opposes

ob·stet·rics \əb-ʹste-triks\ *n sing or pl* : a branch of medicine that deals with birth and with its antecedents and sequels — **ob·stet·ric** \-trik\ *or* **ob·stet·ri·cal** \-tri-kəl\ *adj* — **ob·ste·tri·cian** \ˌäb-stə-ʹtri-shən\ *n*

ob·sti·nate \ʹäb-stə-nət\ *adj* : fixed and unyielding (as

in an opinion or course) despite reason or persuasion : STUBBORN — **ob·sti·na·cy** \-nə-sē\ *n* — **ob·sti·nate·ly** *adv*

ob·strep·er·ous \əb-ʹstre-pə-rəs\ *adj* **1** : uncontrollably noisy **2** : stubbornly resistant to control : UNRULY — **ob·strep·er·ous·ness** *n*

ob·struct \əb-ʹstrəkt\ *vb* **1** : to block by an obstacle **2** : to impede the passage, action, or operation of **3** : to cut off from sight — **ob·struc·tive** \-ʹstrək-tiv\ *adj* — **ob·struc·tor** \-tər\ *n*

ob·struc·tion \əb-ʹstrək-shən\ *n* **1** : an act of obstructing : the state of being obstructed **2** : something that obstructs : HINDRANCE

ob·struc·tion·ist \-shə-nist\ *n* : a person who hinders progress or business esp. in a legislative body — **ob·struc·tion·ism** \-shə-ˌni-zəm\ *n*

ob·tain \əb-ʹtān\ *vb* **1** : to gain or attain usu. by planning or effort **2** : to be generally recognized or established **syn** procure, secure, win, earn, acquire — **ob·tain·able** *adj*

ob·trude \əb-ʹtrüd\ *vb* **ob·trud·ed; ob·trud·ing 1** : to thrust out **2** : to thrust forward without warrant or request **3** : INTRUDE — **ob·tru·sion** \-ʹtrü-zhən\ *n* — **ob·tru·sive** \-ʹtrü-siv\ *adj* — **ob·tru·sive·ly** *adv* — **ob·tru·sive·ness** *n*

ob·tuse \äb-ʹtüs, -ʹtyüs\ *adj* **ob·tus·er; -est 1** : exceeding 90 degrees but less than 180 degrees (⟨∼ angle) **2** : not pointed or acute : BLUNT **3** : not sharp or quick of wit — **ob·tuse·ly** *adv* — **ob·tuse·ness** *n*

obv *abbr* obverse

¹**ob·verse** \ʹäb-vərs, ʹäb-ˌvərs\ *adj* **1** : facing the observer or opponent **2** : being a counterpart or complement — **ob·verse·ly** *adv*

²**ob·verse** \ʹäb-ˌvərs, äb-ʹvərs\ *n* **1** : the side (as of a coin) bearing the principal design and lettering **2** : a front or principal surface **3** : a counterpart having the opposite orientation or force

ob·vi·ate \ʹäb-vē-ˌāt\ *vb* **-at·ed; -at·ing** : to anticipate and prevent (as a situation) or make unnecessary (as an action) **syn** prevent, avert, forestall, forfend, preclude — **ob·vi·a·tion** \ˌäb-vē-ʹā-shən\ *n*

ob·vi·ous \ʹäb-vē-əs\ *adj* [L *obvius,* fr. *obviam* in the way, fr. *ob* in the way of + *viam,* acc. of *via* way] : easily found, seen, or understood : PLAIN **syn** evident, manifest, patent, clear — **ob·vi·ous·ly** *adv* — **ob·vi·ous·ness** *n*

OC *abbr* officer candidate

oc·a·ri·na \ˌä-kə-ʹrē-nə\ *n* [It] : a wind instrument typically having an oval body with finger holes and a projecting mouthpiece

occas *abbr* occasionally

¹**oc·ca·sion** \ə-ʹkā-zhən\ *n* **1** : a favorable opportunity **2** : a direct or indirect cause **3** : the time of an event **4** : EXIGENCY **5** *pl* : AFFAIRS, BUSINESS **6** : a special event : CELEBRATION

²**occasion** *vb* : BRING ABOUT, CAUSE

oc·ca·sion·al \ə-ʹkā-zhə-nəl\ *adj* **1** : happening or met with now and then (⟨∼ visits) **2** : used or designed for

a special occasion ⟨∼ verse⟩ **syn** infrequent, rare, sporadic — **oc·ca·sion·al·ly** *adv*

oc·ci·den·tal \ˌäk-sə-ˈdent-ᵊl\ *adj, often cap* [fr. *Occident* West, fr. ME, fr. L *occident-, occidens,* fr. prp. of *occidere* to fall, set (of the sun)] : WESTERN — **Occidental** *n*

oc·clude \ə-ˈklüd\ *vb* **oc·clud·ed; oc·clud·ing 1** : OBSTRUCT ⟨an *occluded* artery⟩ **2** : to come together with opposing surfaces in contact — used of teeth — **oc·clu·sion** \-ˈklü-zhən\ *n* — **oc·clu·sive** \-ˈklü-siv\ *adj*

¹**oc·cult** \ə-ˈkəlt\ *adj* **1** : not revealed : SECRET **2** : ABSTRUSE, MYSTERIOUS **3** : of or relating to supernatural agencies, their effects, or knowledge of them — **oc·cult·ism** \-ˈkəl-ˌti-zəm\ *n* — **oc·cult·ist** \-tist\ *n*

²**occult** *n* : occult matters — used with *the*

oc·cu·pan·cy \ˈä-kyə-pən-sē\ *n, pl* **-cies 1** : the act of occupying : the state of being occupied **2** : an occupied building or part of a building

oc·cu·pant \-pənt\ *n* : one who occupies something; *esp* : RESIDENT

oc·cu·pa·tion \ˌä-kyə-ˈpā-shən\ *n* **1** : an activity in which one engages; *esp* : VOCATION **2** : the taking possession of property; *also* : the taking possession of an area by a foreign military force — **oc·cu·pa·tion·al** \-shə-nəl\ *adj* — **oc·cu·pa·tion·al·ly** *adv*

occupational therapy *n* : therapy by means of activity; *esp* : creative activity prescribed for its effect in promoting recovery or rehabilitation — **occupational therapist** *n*

oc·cu·py \ˈä-kyə-ˌpī\ *vb* **-pied; -py·ing 1** : to engage the attention or energies of **2** : to fill up (an extent in space or time) **3** : to take or hold possession of **4** : to reside in as owner or tenant — **oc·cu·pi·er** *n*

oc·cur \ə-ˈkər\ *vb* **oc·curred; oc·cur·ring** [L *occurrere,* fr. *ob-* in the way + *currere* to run] **1** : to be found or met with : APPEAR **2** : HAPPEN **3** : to come to mind

oc·cur·rence \ə-ˈkər-əns\ *n* **1** : something that takes place **2** : the action or process of occurring

ocean \ˈō-shən\ *n* **1** : the whole body of salt water that covers nearly three fourths of the surface of the earth **2** : any of the large bodies of water into which the great ocean is divided — **ocean·ic** \ˌō-shē-ˈa-nik\ *adj*

ocean·ar·i·um \ˌō-shə-ˈnar-ē-əm\ *n, pl* **-iums** *or* **-ia** \-ē-ə\ : a large marine aquarium

ocean·front \ˈō-shən-ˌfrənt\ *n* : a shore area on the ocean

ocean·go·ing \-ˌgō-iŋ\ *adj* : of, relating to, or suitable for travel on the ocean

ocean·og·ra·phy \ˌō-shə-ˈnä-grə-fē\ *n* : a science dealing with the ocean and its phenomena — **ocean·og·ra·pher** \-fər\ *n* — **ocean·o·graph·ic** \-nə-ˈgra-fik\ *adj*

oce·lot \ˈä-sə-ˌlät, ˈō-\ *n* : a medium-sized American wildcat ranging southward from Texas to northern Argentina and having a tawny yellow or gray coat with black markings

ocher *or* **ochre** \ˈō-kər\ *n* : an earthy usu. red or yellow iron ore used as a pigment; *also* : the color esp. of yellow ocher

o'·clock \ə-ˈkläk\ *adv* : according to the clock

OCR *abbr* optical character reader; optical character recognition

OCS *abbr* officer candidate school

oct *abbr* octavo

Oct *abbr* October

oc·ta·gon \ˈäk-tə-ˌgän\ *n* : a polygon of eight angles and eight sides — **oc·tag·o·nal** \äk-ˈta-gən-ᵊl\ *adj*

oc·tane \ˈäk-ˌtān\ *n* : OCTANE NUMBER

octane number *n* : a number used to measure the antiknock properties of gasoline that increases as the likelihood of knocking decreases

oc·tave \ˈäk-tiv\ *n* **1** : a musical interval embracing eight degrees; *also* : a tone or note at this interval or the whole series of notes, tones, or keys within this interval **2** : a group of eight

oc·ta·vo \äk-ˈtā-vō, -ˈtä-\ *n, pl* **-vos 1** : the size of a piece of paper cut eight from a sheet **2** : a book printed on octavo pages

oc·tet \äk-ˈtet\ *n* **1** : a musical composition for eight voices or eight instruments; *also* : the performers of such a composition **2** : a group or set of eight

Oc·to·ber \äk-ˈtō-bər\ *n* [ME *Octobre,* fr. OF, fr. L *October* (eighth month), fr. *octo* eight] : the 10th month of the year

oc·to·ge·nar·i·an \ˌäk-tə-jə-ˈner-ē-ən\ *n* : a person whose age is in the eighties

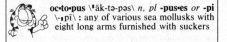

oc·to·pus \ˈäk-tə-pəs\ *n, pl* **-pus·es** *or* **-pi** \-ˌpī\ : any of various sea mollusks with eight long arms furnished with suckers

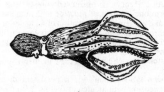

octopus

oc·to·syl·lab·ic \ˌäk-tə-sə-ˈla-bik\ *adj* : composed of verses having eight syllables — **octosyllabic** *n*

¹**oc·u·lar** \ˈä-kyə-lər\ *adj* **1** : VISUAL **2** : of or relating to the eye or the eyesight

²**ocular** *n* : EYEPIECE

oc·u·list \ˈä-kyə-list\ *n* **1** : OPHTHALMOLOGIST **2** : OPTOMETRIST

¹**OD** \ˌō-ˈdē\ *n* : an overdose of a drug and esp. a narcotic

²**OD** *vb* **OD'd** *or* **ODed; OD'ing** : to become ill or die from an OD

³**OD** *abbr* **1** doctor of optometry **2** [L *oculus dexter*] right eye **3** officer of the day **4** olive drab **5** overdraft **6** overdrawn

odd \ˈäd\ *adj* [ME *odde,* fr. ON *oddi* point of land, triangle, odd number] **1** : being only one of a pair or set ⟨an ∼ shoe⟩ **2** : somewhat more than the number mentioned ⟨forty ∼ years ago⟩ **3** : being an integer (as 1, 3, or 5) not divisible by two without leaving a remainder **4** : additional to what is usual ⟨∼ jobs⟩ **5** : STRANGE ⟨an ∼ way of behaving⟩ — **odd•ness** *n*

odd•ball \'äd-ˌbȯl\ *n* : one that is eccentric — **oddball** *adj*

odd•i•ty \'ä-də-tē\ *n, pl* **-ties 1** : one that is odd **2** : the quality or state of being odd

odd•ly \'äd-lē\ *adv* **1** : in an odd manner **2** : it is odd that

odd•ment \'äd-mənt\ *n* : something left over : REMNANT

odds \'ädz\ *n pl* **1** : a difference by which one thing is favored over another **2** : DISAGREEMENT — usu. used with *at* **3** : the ratio between the amount to be paid for a winning bet and the amount of the bet ⟨the horse went off at ∼ of 6–1⟩

odds and ends *n pl* : miscellaneous things or matters

odds–on \'ädz-ˌȯn, -ˌän\ *adj* : having a better than even chance to win

ode \'ōd\ *n* : a lyric poem that expresses a noble feeling with dignity

odi•ous \'ō-dē-əs\ *adj* : causing or deserving hatred or repugnance — **odi•ous•ly** *adv* — **odi•ous•ness** *n*

odi•um \'ō-dē-əm\ *n* **1** : merited loathing : HATRED **2** : DISGRACE

odom•e•ter \ō-'dä-mə-tər\ *n* [F *odomètre,* fr. Gk *hodometron,* fr. *hodos* way, road + *metron* measure] : an instrument for measuring distance traveled (as by a vehicle)

odor \'ō-dər\ *n* **1** : the quality of something that stimulates the sense of smell; *also* : a sensation resulting from such stimulation **2** : REPUTE, ESTIMATION — **odored** \'ō-dərd\ *adj* — **odor•less** *adj* — **odor•ous** *adj*

odour *chiefly Brit var of* ODOR

od•ys•sey \'ä-də-sē\ *n, pl* **-seys** [the *Odyssey,* epic poem attributed to Homer recounting the long wanderings of Odysseus] : a long wandering marked usu. by many changes of fortune

oe•cu•men•i•cal \ˌesp Brit ˌē-\ *var of* ECUMENICAL

OED *abbr* Oxford English Dictionary

oe•de•ma *chiefly Brit var of* EDEMA

oe•di•pal \'e-də-pəl, 'ē-\ *adj, often cap* : of, relating to, or resulting from the Oedipus complex

Oe•di•pus complex \-pəs-\ *n* : the positive sexual feelings of a child toward the parent of the opposite sex and hostile or jealous feelings toward the parent of the same sex that may be a source of adult personality disorder when unresolved

OEO *abbr* Office of Economic Opportunity

o'er \'ȯr\ *adv or prep* : OVER

OES *abbr* Order of the Eastern Star

oe•soph•a•gus *chiefly Brit var of* ESOPHAGUS

oeu•vre \œvrᵊ\ *n, pl* **oeuvres** \same \ : a substantial body of work constituting the lifework of a writer, an artist, or a composer

of \'əv, 'äv\ *prep* **1** : FROM ⟨a man ∼ the West⟩ **2** : having as a significant background or character element ⟨a man ∼ noble birth⟩ ⟨a woman ∼ ability⟩ **3** : owing to ⟨died ∼ flu⟩ **4** : BY ⟨the plays ∼ Shakespeare⟩ **5** : having as component parts or material, contents, or members ⟨a house ∼ brick⟩ ⟨a glass ∼ water⟩ ⟨a pack ∼ fools⟩ **6** : belonging to or included by ⟨the front ∼ the house⟩ ⟨a time ∼ life⟩ ⟨one ∼ you⟩ ⟨the best ∼ its kind⟩ ⟨the son ∼ a doctor⟩ **7** : ABOUT ⟨tales ∼ the West⟩ **8** : connected with : OVER ⟨the queen ∼ England⟩ **9** : that is : signified as ⟨the city ∼ Rome⟩ **10** — used to indicate apposition of the words it joins ⟨that fool ∼ a husband⟩ **11** : as concerns : FOR ⟨love ∼ nature⟩ **12** — used to indicate the application of an adjective ⟨fond ∼ candy⟩ **13** : BEFORE ⟨quarter ∼ ten⟩

OF *abbr* outfield

¹off \'ȯf\ *adv* **1** : from a place or position ⟨drove ∼ in a new car⟩; *also* : ASIDE ⟨turned ∼ into a side road⟩ **2** : at a distance in time or space ⟨stood ∼ a few yards⟩ ⟨several years ∼⟩ **3** : so as to be unattached or removed ⟨the lid blew ∼⟩ **4** : to a state of discontinuance, exhaustion, or completion ⟨shut the radio ∼⟩ **5** : away from regular work ⟨took time ∼ for lunch⟩

²off *prep* **1** : away from ⟨just ∼ the highway⟩ ⟨take it ∼ the table⟩ **2** : to seaward of ⟨two miles ∼ the coast⟩ **3** : FROM ⟨borrowed a dollar ∼ me⟩ **4** : at the expense of ⟨lives ∼ his parents⟩ **5** : not now engaged in ⟨∼ duty⟩ **6** : abstaining from ⟨∼ liquor⟩ **7** : below the usual level of ⟨∼ his game⟩

³off *adj* **1** : more removed or distant **2** : started on the way **3** : not operating **4** : not correct **5** : REMOTE, SLIGHT **6** : INFERIOR **7** : provided for ⟨well ∼⟩

⁴off *abbr* office; officer; official

of•fal \'ȯ-fəl\ *n* : the waste or by-product of a process; *esp* : the viscera and trimmings of a butchered animal removed in dressing

off and on *adv* : INTERMITTENTLY

¹off•beat \'ȯf-ˌbēt\ *n* : the unaccented part of a musical measure

²offbeat *adj* : ECCENTRIC, UNCONVENTIONAL

off–col•or \'ȯf-'kə-lər\ *or* **off–col•ored** \-lərd\ *adj* **1** : not having the right or standard color **2** : of doubtful propriety : verging on indecency ⟨∼ stories⟩

of•fend \ə-'fend\ *vb* **1** : SIN, TRANSGRESS **2** : to cause discomfort or pain : HURT **3** : to cause dislike or vexation : ANNOY **syn** affront, insult, outrage — **of•fend•er** *n*

of•fense *or* **of•fence** \ə-'fens, *esp for 2 & 3* 'ä-ˌfens\ *n* **1** : something that outrages the senses **2** : ATTACK, ASSAULT **3** : the offensive team or members of a team playing offensive positions **4** : DISPLEASURE **5** : SIN, MISDEED **6** : an infraction of law : CRIME

¹of•fen•sive \ə-'fen-siv *esp for 1 & 2* 'ä-ˌfen-\ *adj* **1** : AGGRESSIVE **2** : of or relating to an attempt to score in a game; *also* : of or relating to a team in possession of the ball or puck **3** : OBNOXIOUS **4** : INSULTING — **of•fen•sive•ly** *adv* — **of•fen•sive•ness** *n*

²offensive *n* : ATTACK

¹of•fer \'ȯ-fər\ *vb* **of•fered; of•fer•ing 1** : SACRIFICE **2** : to present for acceptance : TENDER; *also* : to propose as payment **3** : PROPOSE, SUGGEST; *also* : to declare one's readiness **4** : to try or begin to exert ⟨∼ resistance⟩ **5** : to place on sale — **of•fer•ing** *n*

²offer *n* **1** : PROPOSAL **2** : BID **3** : TRY

of•fer•to•ry \'ȯ-fər-ˌtȯr-ē\ *n, pl* **-ries** : the presentation of offerings at a church service; *also* : the musical accompaniment during it

off•hand \'ȯf-'hand\ *adv or adj* : without previous thought or preparation

off–hour \-ˌau̇(-ə)r\ *n* : a period of time other than a rush hour; *also* : a period of time other than business hours

of•fice \'ȯ-fəs\ *n* **1** : a special duty or position; *esp* : a position of authority in government ⟨run for ∼⟩ **2** : a prescribed form or service of worship; *also* : RITE **3** : an assigned or assumed duty or role **4** : a place where a business is transacted or a service is supplied

of•fice•hold•er \'ȯ-fəs-ˌhōl-dər\ *n* : one holding a public office

of•fi•cer \'ȯ-fə-sər\ *n* **1** : one charged with the enforcement of law **2** : one who holds an office of trust or authority **3** : a person who holds a position of authority or command in the armed forces; *esp* : COMMISSIONED OFFICER

¹of•fi•cial \ə-'fi-shəl\ *n* : OFFICER 2

²official *adj* **1** : of or relating to an office or to officers **2** : AUTHORIZED, AUTHORITATIVE **3** : befitting or characteristic of a person in office — **of•fi•cial•ly** *adv*

of•fi•cial•dom \ə-'fi-shəl-dəm\ *n* : officials as a class

of•fi•cial•ism \ə-'fi-shə-ˌli-zəm\ *n* : lack of flexibility and initiative combined with excessive adherence to regulations

of·fi·ci·ant \ə-'fi-shē-ənt\ *n* : one (as a priest) who officiates at a religious rite

of·fi·ci·ate \ə-'fi-shē-ˌāt\ *vb* **-at·ed; -at·ing 1** : to perform a ceremony, function, or duty **2** : to act in an official capacity

of·fi·cious \ə-'fi-shəs\ *adj* : volunteering one's services where they are neither asked for nor needed — **of·fi·cious·ly** *adv* — **of·fi·cious·ness** *n*

off·ing \'ȯ-fiŋ\ *n* : the near or foreseeable future

off–line \'ȯf-'līn\ *adj or adv* : not connected to or controlled directly by a computer

off of *prep* : OFF

off·print \'ȯf-ˌprint\ *n* : a separately printed excerpt (as from a magazine)

off–road \-'rōd\ *adj* : of, relating to, or being a vehicle designed for use away from public roads

off–sea·son \-ˌsēz-ᵊn\ *n* : a time of suspended or reduced activity

¹off·set \-ˌset\ *n* **1** : a sharp bend (as in a pipe) by which one part is turned aside out of line **2** : a printing process in which an inked impression is first made on a rubber-blanketed cylinder and then transferred to the paper

²off·set *vb* **off·set; off·set·ting 1** : to place over against : BALANCE **2** : to compensate for **3** : to form an offset in (as a wall)

off·shoot \'ȯf-ˌshüt\ *n* **1** : a collateral or derived branch, descendant, or member **2** : a branch of a main stem (as of a plant)

¹off·shore \'ȯf-'shōr\ *adv* **1** : at a distance from the shore **2** : outside the country : ABROAD

²off·shore \'ȯf-ˌshōr\ *adj* **1** : moving away from the shore **2** : situated off the shore but within waters under a country's control

off·side \-'sīd\ *adv or adj* : illegally in advance of the ball or puck

off·spring \-ˌspriŋ\ *n, pl* **offspring** *also* **offsprings** : PROGENY, YOUNG

off·stage \'ȯf-ˌstāj, -ˌstāj\ *adv or adj* **1** : off or away from the stage **2** : out of the public view ⟨deals made ∼⟩

off–the–record *adj* : given or made in confidence and not for publication

off–the–shelf *adj* : available as a stock item : not specially designed or made

off–the–wall *adj* : highly unusual : BIZARRE

off·track \'ȯf-'trak\ *adv or adj* : away from a racetrack

off–white \'ȯf-'hwīt\ *n* : a yellowish or grayish white color

off year *n* **1** : a year in which no major election is held **2** : a year of diminished activity or production

oft \'ȯft\ *adv* : OFTEN

of·ten \'ȯ-fən\ *adv* : many times : FREQUENTLY

of·ten·times \-ˌtīmz\ *or* **oft·times** \'ȯf-ˌtīmz, 'ȯft-\ *adv* : OFTEN

ogle \'ō-gəl\ *vb* **ogled; ogling** : to look at in a flirtatious way — **ogle** *n* — **ogler** *n*

ogre \'ō-gər\ *n* **1** : a monster of fairy tales and folklore that eats people **2** : a dreaded person or object

ogress \'ō-grəs\ *n* : a female ogre

oh \'ō\ *interj* **1** — used to express an emotion or in response to physical stimuli **2** — used in direct address

OH *abbr* Ohio

ohm \'ōm\ *n* : a unit of electrical resistance equal to the resistance of a circuit in which a potential difference of one volt produces a current of one ampere — **ohm·ic** \'ō-mik\ *adj*

ohm·me·ter \'ōm-ˌmē-tər\ *n* : an instrument for indicating resistance in ohms directly

¹oil \'ȯil\ *n* [ME *oile*, fr. OF, fr. L *oleum* olive oil, fr. Gk *elaion*, fr. *elaia* olive] **1** : any of numerous fatty or greasy liquid substances obtained from plants, animals, or minerals and used for fuel, food, medicines, and manufacturing **2** : PETROLEUM **3** : artists' colors made with oil; *also* : a painting in such colors — **oil·i·ness** \'ȯi-lē-nəs\ *n* — **oily** \'ȯi-lē\ *adj*

²oil *vb* : to put oil in or on — **oil·er** *n*

oil·cloth \'ȯil-ˌklȯth\ *n* : cloth treated with oil or paint and used for table and shelf coverings

oil pan *n* : the lower section of a crankcase used as an oil reservoir

oil shale *n* : a rock (as shale) from which oil can be recovered

oil·skin \'ȯil-ˌskin\ *n* **1** : an oiled waterproof cloth **2** : an oilskin raincoat **3** *pl* : an oilskin coat and trousers

oink \'ȯiŋk\ *n* : the natural noise of a hog — **oink** *vb*

oint·ment \'ȯint-mənt\ *n* : a salve for use on the skin

OJ *abbr* orange juice

Ojib·wa *or* **Ojib·way** \ō-'jib-ˌwā\ *n, pl* **Ojibwa** *or* **Ojibwas** *or* **Ojibway** *or* **Ojibways** : a member of an American Indian people of the region around Lake Superior and westward

OJT *abbr* on-the-job training

¹OK *or* **okay** \ō-'kā\ *adv or adj* : all right

²OK *or* **okay** *vb* **OK'd** *or* **okayed; OK'·ing** *or* **okay·ing** : APPROVE, AUTHORIZE — **OK** *or* **okay** *n*

³OK *abbr* Oklahoma

Okla *abbr* Oklahoma

okra \'ō-krə\ *n* : a tall annual plant related to the hollyhocks that has edible green pods; *also* : these pods

¹old \'ōld\ *adj* **1** : ANCIENT; *also* : of long standing **2** *cap* : belonging to an early period ⟨*Old* Irish⟩ **3** : having existed for a specified period of time **4** : of or relating to a past era **5** : advanced in years **6** : showing the effects of age or use **7** : no longer in use — **old·ish** \'ōl-dish\ *adj*

²old *n* : old or earlier time ⟨days of ∼⟩

old·en \'ōl-dən\ *adj* : of or relating to a bygone era

¹old–fash·ioned \'ōld-'fa-shənd\ *adj* **1** : OUT-OF-DATE, ANTIQUATED **2** : CONSERVATIVE

²old–fashioned *n* : a cocktail usu. made with whiskey, bitters, sugar, a twist of lemon peel, and water or soda water

old guard *n, often cap O&G* : the conservative members of an organization

old hat *adj* **1** : OLD-FASHIONED **2** : STALE, TRITE

old·ie \\'ōl-dē\ *n* : something old; *esp* : a popular song from the past

old–line \\'ōld-'līn\ *adj* **1** : ORIGINAL, ESTABLISHED ⟨an ~ business⟩ **2** : adhering to old policies or practices

old maid *n* **1** : SPINSTER **2** : a prim fussy person — **old–maid·ish** \\'ōld-'mā-dish\ *adj*

old man *n* **1** : HUSBAND **2** : FATHER

old·ster \\'ōld-stər\ *n* : an old or elderly person

Old Testament *n* : the first of the two chief divisions of the Bible — see BIBLE table

old–time \\'ōld-'tīm\ *adj* **1** : of, relating to, or characteristic of an earlier period **2** : of long standing

old–tim·er \-'tī-mər\ *n* VETERAN; *also* : OLDSTER

old–world \-'wərld\ *adj* : having old-fashioned charm

Old World *n* : the eastern hemisphere exclusive of Australia; *esp* : continental Europe

ole·ag·i·nous \ō-lē-'a-jə-nəs\ *adj* : OILY

ole·an·der \\'ō-lē-ˌan-dər\ *n* : a poisonous evergreen shrub often grown for its fragrant white to red flowers

oleo \\'ō-lē-ˌō\ *n, pl* **oleos** : MARGARINE

oleo·mar·ga·rine \ˌō-lē-ō-'mär-jə-rən\ *n* : MARGARINE

ol·fac·to·ry \äl-'fak-tə-rē, ōl-\ *adj* : of or relating to the sense of smell

oli·gar·chy \\'ä-lə-ˌgär-kē, 'ō-\ *n, pl* **-chies 1** : a government in which power is in the hands of a few **2** : a state having an oligarchy; *also* : the group holding power in such a state — **oli·garch** \-ˌgärk\ *n* — **oli·gar·chic** \ˌä-lə-'gär-kik, ˌō-\ *or* **oli·gar·chi·cal** \-ki-kəl\ *adj*

Oli·go·cene \\'ä-li-gō-ˌsēn, ə-'li-gə-ˌsēn\ *adj* : of, relating to, or being the epoch of the Tertiary between the Eocene and the Miocene — **Oligocene** *n*

olio \\'ō-lē-ˌō\ *n, pl* **olios** : HODGEPODGE, MEDLEY

ol·ive \\'ä-liv\ *n* **1** : an Old World evergreen tree grown in warm regions for its fruit that is a food and the source of an edible oil (**olive oil**) **2** : a dull yellow to yellowish green color

olive drab *n* **1** : a grayish olive color **2** : an olive drab wool or cotton fabric; *also* : a uniform of this fabric

ol·iv·ine \\'ä-lə-ˌvēn\ *n* : a usu. greenish mineral that is a complex silicate of magnesium and iron

Olym·pic Games \ō-'lim-pik-\ *n pl* : a modified revival of an ancient Greek festival consisting of international athletic contests that are held at separate winter and summer gatherings at four-year intervals

om \\'ōm\ *n* : a mantra consisting of the sound "om" used in contemplating ultimate reality

Oma·ha \\'ō-mə-ˌhä, -ˌhȯ\ *n, pl* **Omaha** *or* **Omahas** : a member of an American Indian people of northeastern Nebraska

om·buds·man \\'äm-ˌbu̇dz-mən, äm-'bu̇dz-\ *n, pl* **-men** \-mən\ **1** : a government official appointed to investigate complaints made by individuals against abuses or capricious acts of public officials **2** : one that investigates reported complaints (as from students or consumers)

ome·ga \ō-'mā-gə\ *n* : the 24th and last letter of the Greek alphabet — Ω or ω

om·elet *or* **om·elette** \\'äm-lət, 'ä-mə-\ *n* [F *omelette*,

alter. of MF *alumelle*, lit., knife blade, modif. of L *lamella*, dim. of *lamina* thin plate] : eggs beaten with milk or water, cooked without stirring until set, and folded over

omen \\'ō-mən\ *n* : an event or phenomenon believed to be a sign or warning of a future occurrence

om·i·cron \\'ä-mə-ˌkrän, 'ō-\ *n* : the 15th letter of the Greek alphabet — O or ο

om·i·nous \\'ä-mə-nəs\ *adj* : foretelling evil : THREATENING — **om·i·nous·ly** *adv* — **om·i·nous·ness** *n*

omis·si·ble \ō-'mi-sə-bəl\ *adj* : that may be omitted

omis·sion \ō-'mi-shən\ *n* **1** : something neglected or left undone **2** : the act of omitting : the state of being omitted

omit \ō-'mit\ *vb* **omit·ted; omit·ting 1** : to leave out or leave unmentioned **2** : to fail to perform : NEGLECT

¹om·ni·bus \\'äm-ni-(ˌ)bəs\ *n* : BUS

²omnibus *adj* : of, relating to, or providing for many things at once ⟨an ~ bill⟩

om·nip·o·tent \äm-'ni-pə-tənt\ *adj* : having unlimited authority or influence : ALMIGHTY — **om·nip·o·tence** \-əns\ *n* — **om·nip·o·tent·ly** *adv*

om·ni·pres·ent \ˌäm-ni-'prez-ᵊnt\ *adj* : present in all places at all times — **om·ni·pres·ence** \-ᵊns\ *n*

om·ni·scient \äm-'ni-shənt\ *adj* : having infinite awareness, understanding, and insight — **om·ni·science** \-shəns\ *n* — **om·ni·scient·ly** *adv*

---

om·ni·um–gath·er·um \ˌäm-nē-əm-'ga-thə-rəm\ *n, pl* **omnium–gatherums** : a miscellaneous collection

om·niv·o·rous \äm-'ni-və-rəs\ *adj* : feeding on both animal and vegetable substances; *also* : AVID ⟨an ~ reader⟩ — **om·niv·o·rous·ly** *adv*

¹on \\'ȯn, 'än\ *prep* **1** : in or to a position over and in contact with ⟨jumped ~ his horse⟩ **2** : touching the surface of ⟨shadows ~ the wall⟩ **3** : AT, TO ⟨~ the right were the mountains⟩ **4** : IN, ABOARD ⟨went ~ the train⟩ **5** : during or at the time of ⟨came ~ Monday⟩ ⟨every hour ~ the hour⟩ **6** : through the agency of ⟨was cut ~ a tin can⟩ **7** : in a state or process of ⟨~ fire⟩ ⟨~ the wane⟩ **8** : connected with as a member or participant ⟨~ a committee⟩ ⟨~ tour⟩ **9** — used to indicate a basis, source, or standard of computation ⟨has it ~ good authority⟩ ⟨10 cents ~ the dollar⟩ **10** : with regard to ⟨a monopoly ~ wheat⟩ **11** : at or toward as an object ⟨crept up ~ her⟩ **12** : ABOUT, CONCERNING ⟨a book ~ minerals⟩

²on *adv* **1** : in or into a position of contact with or attachment to a surface **2** : FORWARD **3** : into operation

³on *adj* : being in operation or in progress

ON *abbr* Ontario

¹once \\'wəns\ *adv* **1** : one time only **2** : at any one time **3** : FORMERLY **4** : by one degree of relationship

²once *n* : one single time — **at once 1** : at the same time **2** : IMMEDIATELY

³once *adj* : FORMER

⁴once *conj* : AS SOON AS

once–over \'wəns-ˌō-vər\ n : a swift examination or survey

on•com•ing \'òn-ˌkə-miŋ, 'än-\ adj : APPROACHING ⟨∼ traffic⟩

¹one \'wən\ adj 1 : being a single unit or thing ⟨∼ person went⟩ 2 : being one in particular ⟨early ∼ morning⟩ 3 : being the same in kind or quality ⟨members of ∼ race⟩; also : UNITED 4 : being not specified or fixed ⟨∼ day soon⟩

²one n 1 : the number denoting unity 2 : the 1st in a set or series 3 : a single person or thing — one•ness \'wən-nəs\ n

³one pron 1 : a certain indefinitely indicated person or thing ⟨saw ∼ of his friends⟩ 2 : a person in general ⟨∼ never knows⟩ 3 — used in place of a first-person pronoun

Onei•da \ō-'nī-də\ n, pl Oneida or Oneidas : a member of an American Indian people orig. of New York

oner•ous \'ä-nə-rəs, 'ō-\ adj : imposing or constituting a burden : TROUBLESOME syn oppressive, exacting, burdensome, weighty

one•self \(ˌ)wən-'self\ also one's self pron : one's own self — usu. used reflexively or for emphasis

one–sid•ed \'wən-'sī-dəd\ adj 1 : having or occurring on one side only; also : having one side prominent or more developed 2 : PARTIAL ⟨a ∼ interpretation⟩

one•time \-ˌtīm\ adj : FORMER

one–to–one \ˌwən-tə-'wən\ adj : pairing each element of a set uniquely with an element of another set

one up adj : being in a position of advantage ⟨was one up on the others⟩

one–way adj : moving, allowing movement, or functioning in only one direction ⟨∼ streets⟩

on•go•ing \'òn-ˌgō-iŋ, 'än-\ adj : continuously moving forward

on•ion \'ən-yən\ n : the pungent edible bulb of a cultivated plant related to the lilies; also : this plant

on•ion•skin \-ˌskin\ n : a thin strong translucent paper of very light weight

on–line adj or adv : connected to or controlled directly by a computer

on•look•er \'òn-ˌlù-kər, 'än-\ n : SPECTATOR

¹on•ly \'ōn-lē\ adj 1 : unquestionably the best 2 : SOLE

²only adv 1 : MERELY, JUST ⟨∼ $2⟩ 2 : SOLELY ⟨known ∼ to me⟩ 3 : at the very least ⟨was ∼ too true⟩ 4 : as a final result ⟨will ∼ make you sick⟩

³only conj : except that

on•o•mato•poe•ia \ˌä-nə-ˌmä-tə-'pē-ə\ n 1 : formation of words in imitation of natural sounds ⟨as buzz or hiss⟩ 2 : the use of words whose sound suggests the sense — on•o•mato•poe•ic \-ˈpē-ik\ or on•o•mato•po•et•ic \-ˌpō-ˈe-tik\ adj — on•o•mato•poe•i•cal•ly \-ˈpē-ə-k(ə-)lē\ or on•o•mato•po•et•i•cal•ly \-ˌpō-ˈe-ti-k(ə-)lē\ adv

On•on•da•ga \ˌä-nən-'dò-gə, -ˈdä-, -ˈdä-\ n, pl -ga or -gas : a member of an American Indian people of New York and Canada

on•rush \'òn-ˌrəsh, 'än-\ n : a rushing onward — on•rush•ing adj

on•set \-ˌset\ n 1 : ATTACK 2 : BEGINNING

on•shore \-ˌshōr\ adj 1 : moving toward the shore 2 : situated on or near the shore — on•shore \-'shōr\ adv

on•slaught \'òn-ˌslòt, 'än-\ n : a fierce attack; also : something resembling such an attack ⟨an ∼ of questions⟩

Ont abbr Ontario

on•to \'òn-tü, 'än-\ prep : to a position or point on

onus \'ō-nəs\ n 1 : BURDEN 2 : OBLIGATION 3 : BLAME

¹on•ward \'òn-wərd, 'än-\ also on•wards \-wərdz\ adv : FORWARD

²onward adj : directed or moving onward : FORWARD

on•yx \'ä-niks\ n [ME onix, fr. MF & L; MF, fr. L onyx, fr. Gk, lit., claw, nail] : a translucent chalcedony in parallel layers of different colors

oo•dles \'üd-ᵊlz\ n pl : a great quantity

oo•lite \'ō-ə-ˌlīt\ n : a rock consisting of small round grains cemented together — oo•lit•ic \ˌō-ə-'li-tik\ adj

¹ooze \'üz\ n 1 : a soft deposit (as of mud) on the bottom of a body of water 2 : soft wet ground : MUD — oozy \'ü-zē\ adj

²ooze vb oozed; ooz•ing 1 : to flow or leak out slowly or imperceptibly 2 : EXUDE

³ooze n : something that oozes

op abbr 1 operation; operative; operator 2 opportunity 3 opus

OP abbr 1 observation post 2 out of print

opac•i•ty \ō-'pa-sə-tē\ n, pl -ties 1 : the quality or state of being opaque 2 : obscurity of meaning 3 : mental dullness 4 : an opaque spot in a normally transparent structure

opal \'ō-pəl\ n : a mineral with iridescent colors that is used as a gem

opal•es•cent \ˌō-pə-'les-ᵊnt\ adj : IRIDESCENT — opal•es•cence \-ᵊns\ n

opaque \ō-'pāk\ adj 1 : blocking the passage of radiant energy and esp. light 2 : not easily understood 3 : OBTUSE — opaque•ly adv — opaque•ness n

op art \'äp-\ n : OPTICAL ART — op artist n

op cit abbr [L opere citato] in the work cited

ope \'ōp\ vb oped; op•ing archaic : OPEN

OPEC abbr Organization of Petroleum Exporting Countries

¹open \'ō-pən\ adj open•er; open•est 1 : not shut or shut up ⟨an ∼ door⟩ 2 : not secret or hidden; also : FRANK 3 : not enclosed or covered ⟨an ∼ fire⟩; also : not protected 4 : free to be entered or used ⟨an ∼ tournament⟩ 5 : easy to get through or see ⟨∼ country⟩ 6 : spread out : EXTENDED 7 : not decided ⟨an ∼ question⟩ 8 : readily accessible and cooperative; also : GENEROUS 9 : having components separated by a space in writing and printing ⟨the name Spanish moss is an ∼ compound⟩ 10 : having openings, interruptions, or spaces ⟨an ∼ mesh⟩ 11 : ready to operate ⟨stores are ∼⟩ 12 : free from restraints or controls ⟨∼ season⟩ — open•ly adv — open•ness n

²open \ˈō-pən\ *vb* **opened; open·ing 1 :** to change or move from a shut position; *also* : to make open by clearing away obstacles **2 :** to make accessible **3 :** to make openings in **4 :** to make or become functional ⟨~ a store⟩ **5 :** REVEAL; *also* : ENLIGHTEN **6 :** BEGIN — **open·er** *n*

³open *n* **1 :** OUTDOORS **2 :** a contest or tournament open to all

open–air *adj* : OUTDOOR ⟨~ theaters⟩

open·hand·ed \ˌō-pən-ˈhan-dəd\ *adj* : GENEROUS — **open·hand·ed·ly** *adv*

open–heart *adj* : of, relating to, or performed on a heart temporarily relieved of circulatory function and laid open for inspection and treatment

open–hearth *adj* : of, relating to, or being a process of making steel in a furnace that reflects the heat from the roof onto the material

open·ing *n* **1 :** an act or instance of making or becoming open **2 :** BEGINNING **3 :** something that is open **4 :** OCCASION; *also* : an opportunity for employment

open–mind·ed \ˌō-pən-ˈmīn-dəd\ *adj* : free from rigidly fixed preconceptions

open sentence *n* : a statement (as in mathematics) containing at least one blank or unknown so that when the blank is filled or a quantity substituted for the unknown the statement becomes a complete statement that is either true or false

open shop *n* : an establishment having members and nonmembers of a labor union on the payroll

open·work \ˈō-pən-ˌwərk\ *n* : work so made as to show openings through its substance ⟨a railing of wrought-iron ~⟩ — **open–worked** \-ˌwərkt\ *adj*

¹opera *pl of* OPUS

²op·era \ˈä-prə, -pə-rə\ *n* : a drama set to music — **op·er·at·ic** \ˌä-pə-ˈra-tik\ *adj*

op·er·a·ble \ˈä-pə-rə-bəl\ *adj* **1 :** fit, possible, or desirable to use **2 :** likely to result in a favorable outcome upon surgical treatment

opera glasses *n pl* : small binoculars for use in a theater

op·er·ate \ˈä-pə-ˌrāt\ *vb* **-at·ed; -at·ing 1 :** to perform work ; FUNCTION **2 :** to produce an effect **3 :** to put or keep in operation **4 :** to perform or subject to an operation — **op·er·a·tor** \-ˌrā-tər\ *n*

operating system *n* : software that controls the operation of a computer

op·er·a·tion \ˌä-pə-ˈrā-shən\ *n* **1 :** a doing or performing of a practical work **2 :** an exertion of power or influence; *also* : method or manner of functioning **3 :** a surgical procedure **4 :** a process of deriving one mathematical expression from others according to a rule **5 :** a military action or mission — **op·er·a·tion·al** \-shə-nəl\ *adj*

¹op·er·a·tive \ˈä-pə-rə-tiv, -ˌrā-\ *adj* **1 :** producing an appropriate effect **2 :** OPERATING ⟨an ~ force⟩ **3 :** having to do with physical operations; *also* : WORKING ⟨an ~ craftsman⟩ **4 :** based on or consisting of an operation ⟨~ dentistry⟩

²operative *n* : OPERATOR; *esp* : a secret agent

op·er·et·ta \ˌä-pə-ˈre-tə\ *n* [It, dim. of *opera* opera] : a

light musical-dramatic work with a romantic plot, spoken dialogue, and dancing scenes

oph·thal·mic \äf-ˈthal-mik, äp-\ *adj* [Gk *ophthalmikos*, fr. *ophthalmos* eye] : of, relating to, or located near the eye

oph·thal·mol·o·gy \ˌäf-ˌthal-ˈmä-lə-jē, ˌäp-\ *n* : a branch of medicine dealing with the structure, functions, and diseases of the eye — **oph·thal·mol·o·gist** \-jist\ *n*

oph·thal·mo·scope \äf-ˈthal-mə-ˌskōp, äp-\ *n* : an instrument for use in viewing the interior of the eye and esp. the retina

opi·ate \ˈō-pē-ət, -pē-ˌāt\ *n* : a preparation or derivative of opium; *also* : a narcotic or a substance with similar activity — **opiate** *adj*

opine \ō-ˈpīn\ *vb* **opined; opin·ing :** to express an opinion : STATE

opin·ion \ə-ˈpin-yən\ *n* **1 :** a belief stronger than impression and less strong than positive knowledge **2 :** JUDGMENT **3 :** a formal statement by an expert after careful study

opin·ion·at·ed \ə-ˈpin-yə-ˌnā-təd\ *adj* : obstinately adhering to personal opinions

opi·um \ˈō-pē-əm\ *n* [ME, fr. L, fr. Gk *opion*, fr. dim. of *opos* sap] : an addictive narcotic drug that is the dried juice of a poppy

opos·sum \ə-ˈpä-səm\ *n, pl* **opossums** *also* **opossum :** a common omnivorous tree-dwelling marsupial mammal of the eastern U.S. that is active esp. at night

opp *abbr* opposite

op·po·nent \ə-ˈpō-nənt\ *n* : one that opposes : ADVERSARY

op·por·tune \ˌä-pər-ˈtün, -ˈtyün\ *adj* [ME, fr. MF *opportun*, fr. L *opportunus*, fr. *ob-* toward + *portus* port, harbor] : SUITABLE — **op·por·tune·ly** *adv*

op·por·tun·ism \ˌä-pər-ˈtü-ˌni-zəm, -ˈtyü-\ *n* : a taking advantage of opportunities or circumstances esp. with little regard for principles or ultimate consequences — **op·por·tun·ist** \-nist\ *n* — **op·por·tu·nis·tic** \-tü-ˈnis-tik, -tyü-\ *adj*

op·por·tu·ni·ty \ˌä-pər-ˈtü-nə-tē, -ˈtyü-\ *n, pl* **-ties 1 :** a favorable combination of circumstances, time, and place **2 :** a chance for advancement

op·pose \ə-ˈpōz\ *vb* **op·posed; op·pos·ing 1 :** to place opposite or against something (as to provide resistance or contrast) **2 :** to strive against : RESIST — **op·po·si·tion** \ˌä-pə-ˈzi-shən\ *n*

¹op·po·site \ˈä-pə-zət\ *adj* **1 :** set over against something that is at the other end or side **2 :** OPPOSED, HOSTILE; *also* : contrarily turned or moving — **op·po·site·ly** *adv* — **op·po·site·ness** *n*

²opposite *n* : one that is opposed or contrary

³opposite *adv* : on or to an opposite side

⁴opposite *prep* : across from and usu. facing ⟨the house ~ ours⟩

op·press \ə-ˈpres\ *vb* **1 :** to crush by abuse of power or authority **2 :** to weigh down : BURDEN *syn* aggrieve, wrong, persecute — **op·pres·sive** \-'pre-siv\ adj — **op·pres·sive·ly** adv — **op·pres·sor** \-'pre-sər\ n

op·pres·sion \ə-'pre-shən\ n 1 : unjust or cruel exercise of power or authority 2 : DEPRESSION

op·pro·bri·ous \ə-'prō-brē-əs\ adj : expressing or deserving opprobrium — **op·pro·bri·ous·ly** adv

op·pro·bri·um \-brē-əm\ n 1 : something that brings disgrace 2 : INFAMY

¹opt \'äpt\ vb : to make a choice; esp : to decide in favor of something

²opt abbr 1 optical; optician; optics 2 option; optional

op·tic \'äp-tik\ adj : of or relating to vision or the eye

op·ti·cal \'äp-ti-kəl\ adj 1 : relating to optics 2 : OPTIC 3 : of, relating to, or using light

optical art n : nonobjective art characterized by the use of geometric patterns often for an illusory effect

optical disk n : a disk on which information has been recorded digitally and which is read using a laser

optical fiber n : a single fiber-optic strand

op·ti·cian \äp-'ti-shən\ n 1 : a maker of or dealer in optical items and instruments 2 : a person who makes or orders eyeglass and contact lenses to prescription and sells glasses

op·tics \'äp-tiks\ n pl : a science that deals with the nature and properties of light

op·ti·mal \'äp-tə-məl\ adj : most desirable or satisfactory — **op·ti·mal·ly** adv

op·ti·mism \'äp-tə-ˌmi-zəm\ n [F optimisme, fr. L optimum, n., best, fr. neut. of optimus best] 1 : a doctrine that this world is the best possible world 2 : an inclination to anticipate the best possible outcome of actions or events — **op·ti·mist** \-mist\ n — **op·ti·mis·tic** \ˌäp-tə-'mis-tik\ adj — **op·ti·mis·ti·cal·ly** \-ti-k(ə-)lē\ adv

op·ti·mum \'äp-tə-məm\ n, pl **-ma** \-mə\ also **-mums** [L] : the amount or degree of something most favorable to an end; also : greatest degree attained under implied or specified conditions

option \'äp-shən\ n 1 : the power or right to choose 2 : a right to buy or sell something at a specified price during a specified period 3 : something offered for choice — **op·tion·al** \-shə-nəl\ adj

op·tom·e·try \äp-'tä-mə-trē\ n : the art or profession of examining the eyes for defects of vision and of prescribing corrective lenses or exercises — **op·tom·e·trist** \-trist\ n

opt out vb : to choose not to participate

op·u·lence \'ä-pyə-ləns\ n 1 : WEALTH 2 : ABUNDANCE

op·u·lent \'ä-pyə-lənt\ adj 1 : WEALTHY 2 : richly abundant — **op·u·lent·ly** adv

opus \'ō-pəs\ n, pl **opera** \'ō-pə-rə, 'ä-\ also **opuses** \'ō-pə-səz\ : WORK; esp : a musical composition

or \'òr\ conj — used as a function word to indicate an alternative ⟨sink ∼ swim⟩

OR abbr 1 operating room 2 Oregon

-or \ər\ n suffix : one that does a (specified) thing ⟨calculator⟩

or·a·cle \'òr-ə-kəl\ n 1 : one held to give divinely inspired answers or revelations 2 : an authoritative or wise utterance; also : a person of great authority or wisdom — **orac·u·lar** \ò-'ra-kyə-lər\ adj

¹oral \'òr-əl\ adj 1 : SPOKEN 2 : of or relating to the mouth 3 : of, relating to, or characterized by the first stage of psychosexual development in psychoanalytic theory in which libidinal gratification is derived from intake (as of food), by sucking, and later by biting 4 : relating to or characterized by personality traits of passive dependency and aggressiveness — **oral·ly** adv

²oral n : an oral examination — usu. used in pl.

orang \ə-'raŋ\ n : ORANGUTAN

or·ange \'òr-inj\ n 1 : a juicy citrus fruit with reddish yellow rind; also : an evergreen tree with fragrant white flowers that bears this fruit 2 : a color between red and yellow

or·ange·ade \ˌòr-in-'jād\ n : a beverage of orange juice, sugar, and water

orange hawkweed n : a weedy herb related to the daisies with bright orange-red flower heads

or·an·gery \'òr-inj-rē\ n, pl **-ries** : a protected place (as a greenhouse) for raising oranges in cool climates

orang·utan \ə-'raŋ-ə-ˌtaŋ, -ˌtan\ n [Bazaar Malay (Malay-based pidgin), fr. Malay orang man + hutan forest] : a large reddish brown tree-living anthropoid ape of Borneo and Sumatra

orate \ò-'rāt\ vb **orat·ed; orat·ing** : to speak in a declamatory manner

ora·tion \ə-'rā-shən\ n : an elaborate discourse delivered in a formal and dignified manner

or·a·tor \'òr-ə-tər\ n : one noted for skill and power as a public speaker

or·a·tor·i·cal \ˌòr-ə-'tòr-i-kəl\ adj : of, relating to, or characteristic of an orator or oratory — **or·a·tor·i·cal·ly** \-'tòr-i-k(ə-)lē\ adv

or·a·to·rio \ˌòr-ə-'tòr-ē-ˌō\ n, pl **-rios** : a lengthy choral work usu. on a scriptural subject

¹or·a·to·ry \'òr-ə-ˌtòr-ē\ n, pl **-ries** : a private or institutional chapel

²oratory n : the art of speaking eloquently and effectively using **syn** rhetoric, elocution

orb \'òrb\ n : a spherical body; also : EYE

¹or·bit \'òr-bət\ n [L orbita, lit., path, rut] 1 : a path described by one body in its revolution about another 2 : range or sphere of activity — **or·bit·al** \-ᵊl\ adj

²orbit vb 1 : CIRCLE 2 : to send up and make revolve in an orbit ⟨∼ a satellite⟩ — **or·bit·er** n

orch abbr orchestra

or·chard \'òr-chərd\ n [ME, fr. OE ortgeard, fr. ort- (fr. L hortus garden) + geard yard] : a place where fruit trees, sugar maples, or nut trees are grown; also : the trees of such a place — **or·chard·ist** \-chər-dist\ n

or·ches·tra \'òr-kə-strə\ n 1 : the front section of seats on the main floor of a theater 2 : a group of instrumentalists organized to perform ensemble music — **or·ches·tral** \òr-'kes-trəl\ adj — **or·ches·tral·ly** adv

or·ches·trate \'òr-kə-ˌsträt\ vb **-trat·ed; -trat·ing** 1 : to compose or arrange for an orchestra 2 : to arrange so as to achieve a desired effect — **or·ches·tra·tion** \ˌòr-kə-'strā-shən\ n

or·chid \'òr-kəd\ n : any of a large family of plants having often showy flowers with three petals of which the middle one is enlarged into a lip; also : a flower of an orchid

or·dain \òr-'dān\ vb 1 : to admit to the ministry or priesthood by the ritual of a church 2 : DECREE, ENACT; also : DESTINE — **or·dain·ment** n

or·deal \òr-'dēl, 'òr-ˌdēl\ n : a severe trial or experience

¹or·der \'òr-dər\ vb 1 : ARRANGE, REGULATE 2 : COMMAND 3 : to place an order

²order n 1 : a group of people formally united; also : a badge or medal of such a group 2 : any of the several grades of the Christian ministry; also, pl : ORDINATION 3 : a rank, class, or special group of persons or things 4 : a category of biological classification ranking above the family and below the class 5 : ARRANGEMENT, SEQUENCE; also : the prevailing state of things 6 : a customary mode of procedure; also : the rule of law or proper authority 7 : a specific rule, regulation, or authoritative direction 8 : a style of building; also : an architectural column forming the unit of a style 9 : condition esp. with regard to repair 10 : a written direction to pay money or to buy or sell goods; also : goods bought or sold

¹or·der·ly \'òr-dər-lē\ adj 1 : arranged according to

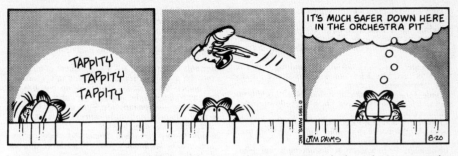

IT'S MUCH SAFER DOWN HERE IN THE ORCHESTRA PIT

TAPPITY TAPPITY TAPPITY

some order; *also* : NEAT, TIDY **2** : well behaved ⟨an ∼ crowd⟩ **syn** methodical, systematic, regular — **or-der-li-ness** *n*

²or-der-ly *n, pl* **-lies 1** : a soldier who attends a superior officer **2** : a hospital attendant who does general work

¹or-di-nal \'òrd-ᵊn-əl\ *n* : an ordinal number

²ordinal *adj* : indicating order or rank (as sixth) in a series

or-di-nance \'òrd-ᵊn-əns\ *n* : an authoritative decree or law; *esp* : a municipal regulation

or-di-nary \'òrd-ᵊn-ˌer-ē\ *adj* **1** : to be expected : USUAL **2** : of common quality, rank, or ability; *also* : POOR, INFERIOR **syn** customary, routine, normal, everyday — **or-di-nar-i-ly** \ˌòrd-ᵊn-ˈer-ə-lē\ *adv* — **or-di-nar-i-ness** \'òrd-ᵊn-ˌer-ē-nəs\ *n*

or-di-nate \'òrd-ᵊn-ət, -ˌāt\ *n* : the coordinate of a point in a plane coordinate system that is the distance of the point from the horizontal axis found by measuring along a line parallel to the vertical axis

or-di-na-tion \ˌòrd-ᵊn-ˈā-shən\ *n* : the act or ceremony by which a person is ordained

ord-nance \'òrd-nəns\ *n* **1** : military supplies **2** : CANNON, ARTILLERY

Or-do-vi-cian \ˌòr-də-ˈvi-shən\ *adj* : of, relating to, or being the period of the Paleozoic era between the Cambrian and the Silurian — **Ordovician** *n*

or-dure \'òr-jər\ *n* : EXCREMENT

¹ore \'ōr\ *n* : a mineral mined to obtain a substance that it contains

²ore \'ər-ə\ *n, pl* **ore** — see *krona, krone* at MONEY table

Ore *or* **Oreg** *abbr* Oregon

oreg-a-no \ə-ˈre-gə-ˌnō\ *n* : a bushy perennial mint used as a seasoning and a source of oil

org *abbr* organization; organized

or-gan \'òr-gən\ *n* **1** : a musical instrument having sets of pipes sounded by compressed air and controlled by keyboards; *also* : an instrument in which the sounds of the pipe organ are approximated by electronic devices **2** : a differentiated animal or plant structure (as a heart or a leaf) made up of cells and tissues and performing some bodily function **3** : a group that performs a specialized function ⟨the various ∼s of government⟩ **4** : PERIODICAL

or-gan-dy *also* **or-gan-die** \'òr-gən-dē\ *n, pl* **-dies** [F *organdi*] : a fine transparent muslin with a stiff finish

or-gan-elle \ˌòr-gə-ˈnel\ *n* : a specialized cell part that resembles an organ in having a special function

or-gan-ic \òr-ˈga-nik\ *adj* **1** : of, relating to, or arising in a bodily organ **2** : of, relating to, or derived from living things **3** : of, relating to, or containing carbon compounds **4** : of or relating to a branch of chemistry dealing with carbon compounds **5** : involving, producing, or dealing in foods produced without the use of laboratory-made fertilizers, growth substances, antibiotics, or pesticides **6** : ORGANIZED ⟨an ∼ whole⟩ — **or-gan-i-cal-ly** \-ni-k(ə-)lē\ *adv*

or-ga-nise *Brit var of* ORGANIZE

or-gan-ism \'òr-gə-ˌni-zəm\ *n* : an individual living

thing (as a person, animal, or plant) — **or-gan-is-mic** \ˌòr-gə-ˈniz-mik\ *adj*

or-gan-ist \'òr-gə-nist\ *n* : a person who plays an organ

or-ga-ni-za-tion \ˌòr-gə-nə-ˈzā-shən\ *n* **1** : the act or process of organizing or of being organized; *also* : the condition or manner of being organized **2** : ASSOCIATION, SOCIETY **3** : an administrative structure (as a business or a political party) — **or-ga-ni-za-tion-al** \-shə-nəl\ *adj*

or-ga-nize \'òr-gə-ˌnīz\ *vb* **-nized; -niz-ing 1** : to develop an organic structure **2** : to form into a complete and functioning whole **3** : to set up an administrative structure for **4** : to arrange by systematic planning and united effort **5** : to join in a union; *also* : UNIONIZE **syn** institute, found, establish, constitute — **or-ga-niz-er** *n*

or-gano-chlo-rine \òr-ˌga-nə-ˈklōr-ˌēn\ *adj* : of or relating to the chlorinated hydrocarbon pesticides (as DDT) — **organochlorine** *n*

or-gano-phos-phate \-ˈfäs-ˌfāt\ *n* : an organophosphorus pesticide — **organophosphate** *adj*

or-gano-phos-pho-rus \-ˈfäs-fə-rəs\ *also* **or-gano-phos-pho-rous** \-fäs-ˈfōr-əs\ *adj* : of, relating to, or being a phosphorus-containing organic pesticide (as malathion)

or-gan-za \òr-ˈgan-zə\ *n* : a sheer dress fabric resembling organdy and usu. made of silk, rayon, or nylon

or-gasm \'òr-ˌga-zəm\ *n* : the climax of sexual excitement — **or-gas-mic** \òr-ˈgaz-mik\ *adj*

or-gi-as-tic \ˌòr-jē-ˈas-tik\ *adj* : of, relating to, or marked by orgies

or-gu-lous \'òr-gyə-ləs, -gə-\ *adj* : PROUD

or-gy \'òr-jē\ *n, pl* **orgies** : a gathering marked by unrestrained indulgence (as in sexual activity, alcohol, or drugs)

ori-el \'ōr-ē-əl\ *n* : a window built out from a wall and usu. supported by a bracket

ori-ent \'ōr-ē-ˌent\ *vb* **1** : to set in a definite position esp. in relation to the points of the compass **2** : to acquaint with an existing situation or environment **3** : to direct toward the interests of a particular group — **ori-en-ta-tion** \ˌōr-ē-ən-ˈtā-shən\ *n*

Orient *n* : EAST **3**; *esp* : the countries of eastern Asia

ori-en-tal \ˌōr-ē-ˈent-ᵊl\ *adj* [fr. *Orient* East, fr. ME, fr. MF, fr. L *orient-, oriens,* fr. prp. of *oriri* to rise] *often cap* : of or situated in the Orient — **Oriental** *n*

ori-en-tate \'ōr-ē-ən-ˌtāt\ *vb* **-tat-ed; -tat-ing 1** : ORIENT **2** : to face east

ori-fice \'òr-ə-fəs\ *n* : OPENING, MOUTH

ori-flamme \'òr-ə-ˌflam\ *n* : a brightly colored banner used as a standard or ensign in battle

orig *abbr* original; originally

ori-ga-mi \ˌòr-ə-ˈgä-mē\ *n* : the art or process of Japanese paper folding

or-i-gin \'òr-ə-jən\ *n* **1** : ANCESTRY **2** : rise, beginning, or derivation from a source; *also* : CAUSE **3** : the intersection of coordinate axes

¹orig-i-nal \ə-ˈri-jə-nəl\ *n* : something from which a

copy, reproduction, or translation is made : PROTO-
TYPE

²orig·i·nal *adj* 1 : FIRST, INITIAL 2 : not copied from
something else : FRESH 3 : INVENTIVE — orig·i·nal·i·ty \-ˌri-jə-ˈna-lə-tē\ *n* — orig·i·nal·ly \-ˈri-jən-ᵊl-ē\
adv

orig·i·nate \ə-ˈri-jə-ˌnāt\ *vb* -nat·ed; -nat·ing 1 : to give
rise to : INITIATE 2 : to come into existence : BEGIN
— orig·i·na·tor \-ˌnā-tər\ *n*

ori·ole \ˈȯr-ē-ˌōl\ *n* : any of various New World birds
of which the males are usu. black and yellow or black
and orange

or·i·son \ˈȯr-ə-sən\ *n* : PRAYER

or·mo·lu \ˈȯr-mə-ˌlü\ *n* : a golden or gilded brass used
for decorative purposes

¹or·na·ment \ˈȯr-nə-mənt\ *n* : something that lends
grace or beauty — or·na·men·tal \ˌȯr-nə-ˈment-ᵊl\
adj

²or·na·ment \-ˌment\ *vb* : to provide with ornament
: ADORN — or·na·men·ta·tion \ˌȯr-nə-mən-ˈtā-shən\
n

or·nate \ȯr-ˈnāt\ *adj* : elaborately decorated — or·nate·ly *adv* — or·nate·ness *n*

or·nery \ˈȯr-nə-rē, ˈä-nə-\ *adj* : having an irritable disposition

or·ni·thol·o·gy \ˌȯr-nə-ˈthä-lə-jē\ *n, pl* -gies : a branch
of zoology dealing with birds — or·ni·tho·log·i·cal
\-thə-ˈlä-ji-kəl\ *adj* — or·ni·thol·o·gist \-ˈthä-lə-jist\ *n*

oro·tund \ˈȯr-ə-ˌtənd\ *adj* 1 : SONOROUS 2 : POMPOUS
— oro·tun·di·ty \ȯr-ə-ˈtən-di-tē\ *n*

or·phan \ˈȯr-fən\ *n* : a child deprived by death of one
or usu. both parents — orphan *vb*

or·phan·age \ˈȯr-fə-nij\ *n* : an institution for the care of
orphans

or·tho·don·tia \ˌȯr-thə-ˈdän-chə, -chē-ə\ *n* : ORTHO-
DONTICS

or·tho·don·tics \ˌȯr-thə-ˈdän-tiks\ *n* : a branch of dentistry concerned with the correction of faults in the
arrangement and placing of the teeth — or·tho·don·tist \-ˈdän-tist\ *n*

or·tho·dox \ˈȯr-thə-ˌdäks\ *adj* [MF or LL; MF *ortho-
doxe*, fr. LL *orthodoxus*, fr. LGk *orthodoxos*, fr. Gk
orthos right + *doxa* opinion] 1 : conforming to established doctrine esp. in religion 2 : CONVENTIONAL 3
cap : of or relating to a Christian church originating
in the church of the Eastern Roman Empire — or·tho·doxy \-ˌdäk-sē\ *n*

or·thog·ra·phy \ȯr-ˈthä-grə-fē\ *n* : SPELLING — or·tho·graph·ic \ˌȯr-thə-ˈgra-fik\ *adj*

or·tho·pe·dics \ˌȯr-thə-ˈpē-diks\ *n sing or pl* : a branch
of medicine concerned with the correction or prevention of skeletal deformities — or·tho·pe·dic \-dik\ *adj*
— or·tho·pe·dist \-dist\ *n*

-ory \ˌȯr-ē, ə-rē\ *adj suffix* 1 : of, relating to, or
characterized by ⟨anticipat*ory*⟩ 2 : serving for, producing, or maintaining ⟨illus*ory*⟩

Os *symbol* osmium

OS *abbr* 1 [L *oculus sinister*] left eye 2 ordinary seaman 3 out of stock

Osage \ō-ˈsāj\ *n, pl* Osag·es *or* Osage : a member of an
American Indian people orig. of Missouri

os·cil·late \ˈä-sə-ˌlāt\ *vb* -lat·ed; -lat·ing 1 : to swing
backward and forward like a pendulum 2 : to move or
travel back and forth between two points 3 : VARY,
FLUCTUATE — os·cil·la·tion \ˌä-sə-ˈlā-shən\ *n* — os·cil·la·tor \ˈä-sə-ˌlā-tər\ *n* — os·cil·la·to·ry \ˈä-sə-lə-ˌtȯr-ē\ *adj*

os·cil·lo·scope \ä-ˈsi-lə-ˌskōp\ *n* : an instrument in
which variations in current or voltage appear as a visible wave form on a fluorescent screen

os·cu·late \ˈäs-kyə-ˌlāt\ *vb* -lat·ed; -lat·ing : KISS —
os·cu·la·tion \ˌäs-kyə-ˈlā-shən\ *n* — os·cu·la·to·ry
\ˈäs-kyə-lə-ˌtȯr-ē\ *adj*

Osee \ˈō-ˌzē, ō-ˈzā-ə\ *n* : HOSEA

OSHA \ˈō-shə\ *abbr* Occupational Safety and Health
Administration

osier \ˈō-zhər\ *n* : any of various willows with pliable
twigs used esp. in making baskets and furniture; *also*
: a twig from an osier

os·mi·um \ˈäz-mē-əm\ *n* : a heavy hard brittle metallic
chemical element used esp. as a catalyst and in alloys
— see ELEMENT table

os·mo·sis \äz-ˈmō-səs, äs-\ *n* : movement of a solvent
through a semipermeable membrane into a solution
of higher concentration that tends to equalize the
concentrations of the solutions on either side of the
membrane — os·mot·ic \-ˈmä-tik\ *adj*

os·prey \ˈäs-prē, -ˌprā\ *n, pl* ospreys : a large brown
and white fish-eating hawk

os·si·fy \ˈä-sə-ˌfī\ *vb* -fied; -fy·ing : to make or become
hardened or set in one's ways — os·si·fi·ca·tion \ˌä-sə-fə-ˈkā-shən\ *n*

os·su·ary \ˈä-shə-ˌwer-ē, -syə-\ *n, pl* -ar·ies : a depository for the bones of the dead

os·ten·si·ble \ä-ˈsten-sə-bəl\ *adj* : shown outwardly
: PROFESSED, APPARENT — os·ten·si·bly \-blē\ *adv*

os·ten·ta·tion \ˌäs-tən-ˈtā-shən\ *n* : pretentious or excessive display — os·ten·ta·tious \-shəs\ *adj* — os·ten·ta·tious·ly *adv*

os·teo·path \ˈäs-tē-ə-ˌpath\ *n* : a practitioner of osteop-
athy

os·te·op·a·thy \ˌäs-tē-ˈä-pə-thē\ *n* : a system of treating
diseases emphasizing manipulation (as of joints) but
not excluding other agencies (as the use of medicine
and surgery) — os·teo·path·ic \ˌäs-tē-ə-ˈpa-thik\ *adj*

os·teo·po·ro·sis \ˌäs-tē-ō-pə-ˈrō-səs\ *n, pl* -ro·ses
\-ˌsēz\ : a condition affecting esp. older women and
characterized by fragile and porous bones

os·tra·cise *Brit var of* OSTRACIZE

os·tra·cize \ˈäs-trə-ˌsīz\ *vb* -cized; -ciz·ing [Gk *ostrak-
izein* to banish by voting with potsherds, fr. *ostrakon*
shell, potsherd] : to exclude from a group by common
consent — os·tra·cism \-ˌsi-zəm\ *n*

os·trich \ˈäs-trich, ˈȯs-\ *n* : a very large swift-
footed flightless bird of Africa and Arabia

Os·we·go tea \ä-ˈswē-gō-\ *n* : a No. American mint
with showy scarlet flowers

OT *abbr* 1 occupational therapy 2 Old Testament 3
overtime

¹oth·er \ˈə-thər\ *adj* 1 : being the one left; *also* : being
the ones distinct from those first mentioned 2 : AL-
TERNATE ⟨every ∼ day⟩ 3 : DIFFERENT 4 : ADDITIONAL
5 : recently past ⟨the ∼ night⟩

²other *pron* 1 : remaining one or ones 2 : a different or
additional one ⟨something or ∼⟩

oth·er·wise \ˈə-thər-ˌwīz\ *adv* 1 : in a different way 2
: in different circumstances 3 : in other respects 4 : if
not 5 : NOT — otherwise *adj*

oth·er·world \-ˌwərld\ *n* : a world beyond death or beyond present reality

oth·er·world·ly \ˌə-thər-ˈwərld-lē\ *adj* : not worldly
: concerned with spiritual, intellectual, or imaginative
matters

oti·ose \ˈō-shē-ˌōs, ˈō-tē-\ *adj* 1 : FUTILE 2 : IDLE 3
: USELESS

oto·lar·yn·gol·o·gy \ˌō-tō-ˌlar-ən-ˈgä-lə-jē\ *n* : a medical specialty concerned esp. with the ear, nose, and
throat — oto·lar·yn·gol·o·gist \-jist\ *n*

oto·rhi·no·lar·yn·gol·o·gy \ˌō-tō-ˌrī-nō-ˌlar-ən-ˈgä-lə-
jē\ *n* : OTOLARYNGOLOGY — oto·rhi·no·lar·yn·gol·o·gist \-jist\ *n*

OTS *abbr* officers' training school

Ot·ta·wa \ˈä-tə-wə, -ˌwä, -ˌwȯ\ *n, pl* Ottawas *or* Ot·tawa : a member of an American Indian people of
Michigan and southern Ontario

ot·ter \ˈä-tər\ *n, pl* otters *also* otter : any of various
web-footed fish-eating mammals with dark brown fur
that are related to the weasels; *also* : the fur

ot·to·man \ˈä-tə-mən\ *n* : an upholstered seat or couch
usu. without a back; *also* : an overstuffed footstool

ou·bli·ette \ˌü-blē-ˈet\ *n* [F, fr. MF, fr. *oublier* to for-

otter

get, ultim. fr. L *oblivisci*] : a dungeon with an opening at the top

ought \'ȯt\ *verbal auxiliary* — used to express moral obligation, advisability, natural expectation, or logical consequence

ou·gui·ya \ü-'gwē-ə, -'gē\ *n, pl* **ouguiya** — see MONEY table

ounce \'au̇ns\ *n* [ME, fr. MF *unce,* fr. L *uncia* twelfth part, ounce, fr. *unus* one] **1** : a unit of avoirdupois, troy, and apothecaries' weight — see WEIGHT table **2** : FLUID OUNCE

our \är, 'au̇r\ *adj* : of or relating to us or ourselves

ours \'au̇rz, 'ärz\ *pron* : that which belongs to us

our·selves \är-'selvz, au̇r-\ *pron* : our own selves — used reflexively, for emphasis, or in absolute constructions ⟨we pleased ∼⟩ ⟨we'll do it ∼⟩ ⟨we were tourists ∼⟩

-ous \əs\ *adj suffix* : full of : abounding in : having : possessing the qualities of ⟨clamor*ous*⟩ ⟨poison*ous*⟩

oust \'au̇st\ *vb* : to eject from or deprive of property or position : EXPEL **syn** evict, dismiss, banish, deport

oust·er \'au̇s-tər\ *n* : EXPULSION

¹out \'au̇t\ *adv* **1** : in a direction away from the inside or center **2** : beyond control **3** : to extinction, exhaustion, or completion **4** : in or into the open **5** : so as to retire a batter or base runner; *also* : so as to be retired

²out *vb* : to become known ⟨the truth will ∼⟩

³out *prep* **1** : out through ⟨looked ∼ the window⟩ **2** : outward on or along ⟨drive ∼ the river road⟩

⁴out *adj* **1** : situated outside or at a distance **2** : not in : ABSENT; *also* : not being in power **3** : not successful in reaching base **4** : not being in vogue or fashion : not up-to-date

⁵out *n* **1** : one who is out of office **2** : the retiring of a batter or base runner

out·age \'au̇-tij\ *n* : a period or instance of interruption esp. of electricity

out–and–out *adj* : COMPLETE, THOROUGHGOING ⟨an ∼ fraud⟩

out·bid \au̇t-'bid\ *vb* : to make a higher bid than

¹out·board \'au̇t-ˌbōrd\ *adj* **1** : situated outboard **2** : having or using an outboard motor

²outboard *adv* **1** : outside a ship's hull : away from the long axis of a ship **2** : in a position closer to the wing tip of an airplane

outboard motor *n* : a small internal combustion engine

with propeller attached for mounting at the stern of a small boat

out·bound \'au̇t-ˌbau̇nd\ *adj* : outward bound ⟨∼ traffic⟩

out·break \-ˌbrāk\ *n* **1** : a sudden increase in activity, incidence, or numbers **2** : INSURRECTION, REVOLT

out·build·ing \-ˌbil-diŋ\ *n* : a building separate from but accessory to a main house

out·burst \-ˌbərst\ *n* : ERUPTION; *esp* : a violent expression of feeling

out·cast \-ˌkast\ *n* : one that is cast out by society

out·class \au̇t-'klas\ *vb* : SURPASS

out·come \'au̇t-ˌkəm\ *n* : a final consequence : RESULT

out·crop \-ˌkräp\ *n* : a coming out of bedrock to the surface of the ground; *also* : the part of a rock formation that thus appears — **outcrop** *vb*

out·cry \-ˌkrī\ *n* : a loud cry : CLAMOR

out·dat·ed \au̇t-'dā-təd\ *adj* : OUTMODED

out·dis·tance \-'dis-təns\ *vb* : to go far ahead of (as in a race) : OUTSTRIP

out·do \-'dü\ *vb* **-did** \-'did\; **-done** \-'dən\; **-do·ing; -does** \-'dəz\ : to go beyond in action or performance

out·door \'au̇t-ˌdōr, -'dōr\ *also* **out·doors** \-'dōrz, -'dȯrz\ *adj* **1** : of or relating to the outdoors **2** : performed outdoors **3** : not enclosed (as by a roof)

¹out·doors \'au̇t-'dōrz, -'dȯrz\ *adv* : in or into the open air

²outdoors *n* **1** : the open air **2** : the world away from human habitation

out·draw \au̇t-'drȯ\ *vb* **-drew** \-'drü\; **-drawn** \-'drȯn\; **-draw·ing 1** : to attract a larger audience than **2** : to draw a handgun more quickly than

out·er \'au̇-tər\ *adj* **1** : EXTERNAL **2** : situated farther out; *also* : being away from a center

out·er·most \-ˌmōst\ *adj* : farthest out

outer space *n* : SPACE 5

out·face \au̇t-'fās\ *vb* **1** : to cause to waver or submit **2** : DEFY

out·field \'au̇t-ˌfēld\ *n* : the part of a baseball field beyond the infield and within the foul lines; *also* : players in the outfield — **out·field·er** \-ˌfēl-dər\ *n*

out·fight \au̇t-'fīt\ *vb* : to surpass in fighting : DEFEAT

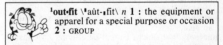

¹out·fit \'au̇t-ˌfit\ *n* **1** : the equipment or apparel for a special purpose or occasion **2** : GROUP

²outfit *vb* **out·fit·ted; out·fit·ting** : EQUIP — **out·fit·ter** *n*

out·flank \au̇t-'flaŋk\ *vb* : to get around the flank of (an opposing force)

out·flow \'au̇t-ˌflō\ *n* **1** : a flowing out **2** : something that flows out

out·fox \au̇t-'fäks\ *vb* : OUTWIT

out·go \'au̇t-ˌgō\ *n, pl* **outgoes** : EXPENDITURES, OUTLAY

out·go·ing \-ˌgō-iŋ\ *adj* **1** : going out ⟨∼ tide⟩ **2** : retiring from a place or position **3** : FRIENDLY

out·grow \au̇t-'grō\ *vb* **-grew** \-'grü\; **-grown** \-'grōn\;

-grow·ing 1 : to grow faster than 2 : to grow too large for

out·growth \'aut-ıgrōth\ n : a product of growing out : OFFSHOOT; also : CONSEQUENCE, RESULT

out·guess \aut-'ges\ vb : OUTWIT

out·gun \-'gən\ vb : to surpass in firepower

out·house \'aut-ıhaus\ n : OUTBUILDING; esp : an outdoor toilet

out·ing \'au-tiŋ\ n : a brief stay or trip in the open

out·land·ish \aut-'lan-dish\ adj 1 : of foreign appearance or manner; also : BIZARRE 2 : remote from civilization — out·land·ish·ly adv

out·last \-'last\ vb : to last longer than

¹out·law \'aut-ılo\ n 1 : a person excluded from the protection of the law 2 : a lawless person

²outlaw vb 1 : to deprive of the protection of the law 2 : to make illegal — out·law·ry \'aut-ılor-ē\ n

out·lay \'aut-ılā\ n 1 : the act of spending 2 : EXPENDITURE

out·let \'aut-ılet, -lət\ n 1 : EXIT, VENT 2 : a means of release (as for an emotion) 3 : a market for a commodity 4 : a receptacle for the plug of an electrical device

¹out·line \'aut-ılīn\ n 1 : a line marking the outer limits of an object or figure 2 : a drawing in which only contours are marked 3 : SUMMARY, SYNOPSIS 4 : PLAN

²outline vb 1 : to draw the outline of 2 : to indicate the chief features or parts of

out·live \aut-'liv\ vb : to live longer than syn outlast, survive

out·look \'aut-ıluk\ n 1 : a place offering a view; also : VIEW 2 : STANDPOINT 3 : the prospect for the future

out·ly·ing \-ılī-iŋ\ adj : distant from a center or main body

out·ma·neu·ver \ıaut-mə-'nü-vər, -'nyü-\ vb : to defeat by more skillful maneuvering

out·mod·ed \aut-'mō-dəd\ adj 1 : no longer in style 2 : no longer acceptable or current

out·num·ber \-'nəm-bər\ vb : to exceed in number

out of prep 1 : out from within or behind ⟨walk out of the room⟩ ⟨look out of the window⟩ 2 : from a state of ⟨wake up out of a deep sleep⟩ 3 : beyond the limits of ⟨out of sight⟩ 4 : BECAUSE OF ⟨came out of curiosity⟩ 5 : FROM, WITH ⟨built it out of scrap⟩ 6 : in or into a state of loss or not having ⟨cheated him out of $5000⟩ ⟨we're out of matches⟩ 7 : from among ⟨one out of four⟩ — out of it : SQUARE, OLD-FASHIONED

out-of-bounds adv or adj : outside the prescribed boundaries or limits

out-of-date adj : no longer in fashion or in use : OUTMODED

out-of-door or out-of-doors adj : OUTDOOR

out-of-the-way adj 1 : UNUSUAL 2 : being off the beaten track

out·pa·tient \'aut-ıpā-shənt\ n : a patient who visits a hospital or clinic for diagnosis or treatment without staying overnight

out·per·form \ıaut-pər-'form\ vb : to perform better than

out·play \aut-'plā\ vb : to play more skillfully than

out·point \-'point\ vb : to win more points than

out·post \'aut-ıpōst\ n 1 : a security detachment dispatched by a main body of troops to protect it from enemy surprise; also : a military base established (as by treaty) in a foreign country 2 : an outlying or frontier settlement

out·pour·ing \-ıpōr-iŋ\ n : something that pours out or is poured out

out·pull \aut-'pul\ vb : OUTDRAW 1

¹out·put \'aut-ıput\ n 1 : the amount produced (as by a machine or factory) : PRODUCTION 2 : the information produced by a computer

²output vb out·put·ted or output; out·put·ting : to produce as output

¹out·rage \'aut-ırāj\ n [ME, fr. MF, excess, outrage, fr. outre beyond, in excess, fr. L ultra] 1 : a violent or shameful act 2 : INJURY, INSULT 3 : the anger or resentment aroused by an outrage

²outrage vb out·raged; out·rag·ing 1 : RAPE 2 : to subject to violent injury or gross insult 3 : to arouse to extreme resentment

out·ra·geous \aut-'rā-jəs\ adj : extremely offensive, insulting, or shameful : SHOCKING — out·ra·geous·ly adv

out·rank \-'raŋk\ vb : to rank higher than

ou·tré \ü-'trā\ adj [F] : violating convention or propriety : BIZARRE

¹out·reach \aut-'rēch\ vb 1 : to surpass in reach 2 : to get the better of by trickery

²out·reach \'aut-ırēch\ n 1 : the act of reaching out 2 : the extent of reach 3 : the extending of services beyond usual limits

out·rid·er \-ırī-dər\ n : a mounted attendant

out·rig·ger \-ıri-gər\ n 1 : a frame that extends from the side of a canoe or boat to prevent upsetting 2 : a craft equipped with an outrigger

¹out·right \aut-'rīt\ adv 1 : COMPLETELY 2 : INSTANTANEOUSLY

²out·right \'aut-ırīt\ adj 1 : being exactly what is stated ⟨an ~ lie⟩ 2 : given or made without reservation or encumbrance ⟨~ sale⟩

out·run \aut-'rən\ vb -ran \-'ran\; -run; -run·ning : to run faster than; also : EXCEED

out·sell \-'sel\ vb -sold \-'sōld\; -sell·ing : to exceed in sales

out·set \'aut-ıset\ n : BEGINNING, START

out·shine \aut-'shīn\ vb -shone \-'shōn\ or -shined; -shin·ing 1 : to shine brighter than 2 : SURPASS

¹out·side \aut-'sīd, 'aut-ısīd\ n 1 : a place or region beyond an enclosure or boundary 2 : EXTERIOR 3 : the utmost limit or extent

²outside adj 1 : OUTER 2 : coming from without ⟨~ influences⟩ 3 : being apart from one's regular duties ⟨~ activities⟩ 4 : REMOTE ⟨an ~ chance⟩

³outside adv : on or to the outside

⁴outside *prep* **1** : on or to the outside of **2** : beyond the limits of **3** : EXCEPT

outside of *prep* **1** : OUTSIDE **2** : BESIDES

out·sid·er \aút-'sī-dər\ *n* : a person who does not belong to a group

out·size \'aút-ˌsīz\ *also* **out·sized** \-ˌsīzd\ *adj* : unusually large : extravagant in size or degree

out·skirts \-ˌskərts\ *n pl* : the outlying parts (as of a city) : BORDERS

out·smart \aút-'smärt\ *vb* : OUTWIT

out·sourc·ing \'aút-ˌsōr-siŋ\ *n* : the subcontracting of manufacturing work to outside and esp. foreign and nonunion companies

out·spend \-'spend\ *vb* **1** : to exceed the limits of in spending ⟨∼s his income⟩ **2** : to spend more than

out·spo·ken \aút-'spō-kən\ *adj* : direct and open in speech or expression — **out·spo·ken·ly** *adv* — **out·spo·ken·ness** *n*

out·spread \-'spred\ *vb* **-spread; -spread·ing** : to spread out

out·stand·ing \-'stan-diŋ\ *adj* **1** : PROJECTING **2** : UNPAID; *also* : UNRESOLVED **3** : publicly issued and sold **4** : CONSPICUOUS; *also* : DISTINGUISHED — **out·stand·ing·ly** *adv*

out·stay \-'stā\ *vb* **1** : OVERSTAY **2** : to surpass in endurance

out·stretched \-'strecht\ *adj* : stretched out : EXTENDED

out·strip \-'strip\ *vb* **1** : to go faster than **2** : EXCEL, SURPASS

out·take \'aút-ˌtāk\ *n* : something taken out; *esp* : a take that is not used in an edited version of a film or videotape

out·vote \-'vōt\ *vb* : to defeat by a majority of votes

¹out·ward \'aút-wərd\ *adj* **1** : moving or directed toward the outside **2** : showing outwardly

²outward *or* **out·wards** \-wərdz\ *adv* : toward the outside

out·ward·ly \-wərd-lē\ *adv* : on the outside : EXTERNALLY

out·wear \aút-'war\ *vb* **-wore** \-'wōr\; **-worn** \-'wōrn\; **-wear·ing** : to wear longer than : OUTLAST

out·weigh \-'wā\ *vb* : to exceed in weight, value, or importance

out·wit \-'wit\ *vb* : to get the better of by superior cleverness

¹out·work \-'wərk\ *vb* : to outdo in working

²out·work \'aút-ˌwərk\ *n* : a minor defensive position outside a fortified area

out·worn \aút-'wōrn\ *adj* : OUTMODED

ou·zo \'ü-(ˌ)zō\ *n* : a colorless anise-flavored unsweetened Greek liqueur

ova *pl of* OVUM

oval \'ō-vəl\ *adj* [ML *ovalis*, fr. LL, of an egg, fr. L *ovum*] : egg-shaped; *also* : broadly elliptical — **oval** *n*

ova·ry \'ō-və-rē\ *n, pl* **-ries 1** : one of the usu. paired female reproductive organs producing eggs and in vertebrates sex hormones **2** : the part of a flower in which seeds are produced — **ovar·i·an** \ō-'var-ē-ən, -'ver-\ *adj*

ovate \'ō-ˌvāt\ *adj* : egg-shaped

ova·tion \ō-'vā-shən\ *n* [L *ovation-, ovatio*, fr. *ovare* to exult] : an enthusiastic popular tribute

ov·en \'ə-vən\ *n* : a chamber (as in a stove) for baking, heating, or drying

oven·bird \-ˌbərd\ *n* : a large olive-green American warbler that builds its dome-shaped nest on the ground

¹over \'ō-vər\ *adv* **1** : across a barrier or intervening space **2** : across the brim ⟨boil ∼⟩ **3** : so as to bring the underside up **4** : out of a vertical position **5** : beyond some quantity, limit, or norm **6** : ABOVE **7** : at an end **8** : THROUGH; *also* : THOROUGHLY **9** : AGAIN ⟨do it ∼⟩

²over *prep* **1** : above in position, authority, or scope ⟨towered ∼ her⟩ ⟨obeyed those ∼ him⟩ **2** : more than

⟨cost ∼ $100⟩ **3** : ON, UPON ⟨a cape ∼ her shoulders⟩ **4** : along the length of ⟨∼ the road⟩ **5** : through the medium of : ON ⟨spoke ∼ TV⟩ **6** : all through ⟨showed me ∼ the house⟩ **7** : on or to the other side or beyond ⟨jump ∼ a ditch⟩ **8** : DURING ⟨∼ the past 25 years⟩ **9** : on account of ⟨trouble ∼ money⟩

³over *adj* **1** : UPPER, HIGHER **2** : REMAINING **3** : ENDED

over- *prefix* **1** : so as to exceed or surpass **2** : excessive; excessively

overabundance	overgraze
overabundant	overhasty
overactive	overheat
overaggressive	overindulge
overambitious	overindulgence
overanxious	overindulgent
overbid	overlarge
overbold	overlearn
overbuild	overload
overburden	overlong
overbuy	overmodest
overcapacity	overnice
overcapitalize	overoptimism
overcareful	overoptimistic
overcautious	overpay
overcompensation	overpraise
overconfidence	overproduce
overconfident	overproduction
overconscientious	overprotect
overcook	overprotective
overcritical	overrate
overcrowd	overreact
overdecorated	overreaction
overdependence	overrefinement
overdetermined	overrepresented
overdevelop	overripe
overdress	oversensitive
overeager	oversensitiveness
overeat	oversimple
overeducated	oversimplification
overemphasis	oversimplify
overemphasize	overspecialization
overenthusiastic	overspecialize
overestimate	overspend
overexcite	overstimulation
overexcited	overstock
overexert	oversubtle
overexertion	oversupply
overextend	overtax
overfatigued	overtired
overfeed	overtrain
overfill	overuse
overgeneralization	overvalue
overgeneralize	overzealous
overgenerous	

over·act \ˌō-vər-'akt\ *vb* : to exaggerate in acting

¹over·age \ˌō-vər-'āj\ *adj* **1** : too old to be useful **2** : older than is normal for one's position, function, or grade

²over·age \'ō-və-rij\ *n* : SURPLUS

over·all \ˌō-vər-'ól\ *adj* : including everything ⟨∼ expenses⟩

over·alls \'ō-vər-ˌólz\ *n pl* : trousers of strong material usu. with a piece extending up to cover the chest

over·arm \-ˌärm\ *adj* : done with the arm raised above the shoulder

over·awe \ˌō-vər-'ó\ *vb* : to restrain or subdue by awe

over·bal·ance \-'ba-ləns\ *vb* **1** : OUTWEIGH **2** : to cause to lose balance

over·bear·ing \-'bar-iŋ\ *adj* : ARROGANT, DOMINEERING

over·blown \-'blōn\ *adj* **1** : PORTLY **2** : INFLATED, PRETENTIOUS

over·board \'ō-vər-ˌbōrd\ *adv* **1** : over the side of a ship into the water **2** : to extremes of enthusiasm

¹over·cast \'ō-vər-ˌkast\ *adj* : clouded over : GLOOMY

²overcast *n* : COVERING; *esp* : a covering of clouds

over·charge \ˌō-vər-'chärj\ *vb* **1** : to charge too much

2 : to fill or load too full — **over·charge** \'ō-vər-ˌchärj\ *n*

over·coat \'ō-vər-ˌkōt\ *n* : a warm coat worn over indoor clothing

over·come \ˌō-vər-'kəm\ *vb* **-came** \-'kām\; **-come**; **-com·ing** 1 : CONQUER 2 : to make helpless or exhausted

over·do \ˌō-vər-'dü\ *vb* **-did** \-'did\; **-done** \-'dən\; **-do·ing**; **-does** \-'dəz\ 1 : to do too much; *also* : to tire oneself 2 : EXAGGERATE 3 : to cook too long

over·dose \'ō-vər-ˌdōs\ *n* : too great a dose (as of medicine); *also* : a lethal or toxic amount (as of a drug) — **over·dose** \ˌō-vər-'dōs\ *vb*

over·draft \'ō-vər-ˌdraft, -ˌdraft\ *n* : an overdrawing of a bank account; *also* : the sum overdrawn

over·draw \ˌō-vər-'dro\ *vb* **-drew** \-'drü\; **-drawn** \-'dron\; **-draw·ing** 1 : to draw checks on a bank account for more than the balance 2 : EXAGGERATE

over·drive \'ō-vər-ˌdrīv\ *n* : an automotive transmission gear that transmits to the driveshaft a speed greater than the engine speed

over·dub \ˌō-vər-'dəb\ *vb* : to transfer (recorded sound) onto an earlier recording for a combined effect — **over·dub** \'ō-vər-ˌdəb\ *n*

over·due \-'dü, -'dyü\ *adj* 1 : unpaid when due; *also* : not appearing or presented on time 2 : more than ready

over·ex·pose \ˌō-vər-ik-'spōz\ *vb* : to expose (as film) for more time than is needed — **over·ex·po·sure** \-'spō-zhər\ *n*

¹**over·flow** \-'flō\ *vb* 1 : INUNDATE; *also* : to pour forth in a flood 2 : to flow over the brim or top of

²**over·flow** \'ō-vər-ˌflō\ *n* 1 : FLOOD; *also* : SURPLUS 2 : an outlet for surplus liquid

over·fly \ˌō-vər-'flī\ *vb* **-flew** \-'flü\; **-flown** \-'flōn\; **-fly·ing** : to fly over in an airplane or spacecraft — **over·flight** \'ō-vər-ˌflīt\ *n*

over·grow \ˌō-vər-'grō\ *vb* **-grew** \-'grü\; **-grown** \-'grōn\; **-grow·ing** 1 : to grow over so as to cover 2 : OUTGROW 3 : to grow excessively

over·hand \'ō-vər-ˌhand\ *adj* : made with the hand brought down from above — **overhand** *adv* — **over·hand·ed** \-ˌhan-dəd\ *adv or adj*

¹**over·hang** \'ō-vər-ˌhaŋ, ˌō-vər-'haŋ\ *vb* **-hung** \-ˌhəŋ, -'həŋ\; **-hang·ing** 1 : to project over : jut out 2 : to hang over threateningly

²**over·hang** \'ō-vər-ˌhaŋ\ *n* : a part (as of a roof) that overhangs

over·haul \ˌō-vər-'hol\ *vb* 1 : to examine thoroughly and make necessary repairs and adjustments 2 : OVERTAKE

¹**over·head** \ˌō-vər-'hed\ *adv* : ALOFT

²**over·head** \'ō-vər-ˌhed\ *adj* : operating or lying above ⟨~ door⟩

³**over·head** \'ō-vər-ˌhed\ *n* : business expenses not chargeable to a particular part of the work

over·hear \ˌō-vər-'hir\ *vb* **-heard** \-'hərd\; **-hear·ing** : to hear without the speaker's knowledge or intention

over·joyed \ˌō-vər-'joid\ *adj* : filled with great joy

over·kill \'ō-vər-ˌkil\ *n* 1 : destructive capacity greatly exceeding that required for a target 2 : a large excess

over·land \'ō-vər-ˌland, -lənd\ *adv or adj* : by, on, or across land

over·lap \ˌō-vər-'lap\ *vb* 1 : to lap over 2 : to have something in common — **over·lap** \'ō-vər-ˌlap\ *n*

over·lay \ˌō-vər-'lā\ *vb* **-laid** \-'lād\; **-lay·ing** : to lay or spread over or across — **over·lay** \'ō-vər-ˌlā\ *n*

over·leap \ˌō-vər-'lēp\ *vb* **-leaped** *or* **-leapt** \-'lēpt, -'lept\; **-leap·ing** 1 : to leap over or across 2 : to defeat (oneself) by going too far

over·lie \ˌō-vər-'lī\ *vb* **-lay** \-'lā\; **-lain** \-'lān\; **-ly·ing** : to lie over or upon

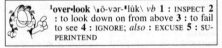

¹**over·look** \ˌō-vər-'luk\ *vb* 1 : INSPECT 2 : to look down on from above 3 : to fail to see 4 : IGNORE; *also* : EXCUSE 5 : SUPERINTEND

²**over·look** \'ō-vər-ˌluk\ *n* : a place from which to look upon a scene below

over·lord \-ˌlord\ *n* : a lord who has supremacy over other lords

over·ly \'ō-vər-lē\ *adv* : EXCESSIVELY

over·match \ˌō-vər-'mach\ *vb* : to be more than a match for : DEFEAT

over·much \-'məch\ *adj or adv* : too much

¹**over·night** \-'nīt\ *adv* 1 : on or during the night 2 : SUDDENLY (became famous ~)

²**overnight** *adj* : of, lasting, or staying the night ⟨~ guests⟩

over·pass \'ō-vər-ˌpas\ *n* 1 : a crossing (as of two highways) at different levels by means of a bridge 2 : the upper level of an overpass

over·play \ˌō-vər-'plā\ *vb* 1 : EXAGGERATE; *also* : OVEREMPHASIZE 2 : to rely too much on the strength of

over·pop·u·la·tion \ˌō-vər-ˌpä-pyə-'lā-shən\ *n* : the condition of having a population so dense as to cause a decline in population or in living conditions — **over·pop·u·lat·ed** \-'pä-pyə-ˌlā-təd\ *adj*

over·pow·er \-'paú-ər\ *vb* : to overcome by superior force

over·price \ˌō-vər-'prīs\ *vb* : to price too high

over·print \-'print\ *vb* : to print over with something additional — **over·print** \'ō-vər-ˌprint\ *n*

over·qual·i·fied \-'kwä-lə-ˌfīd\ *adj* : having more education, training, or experience than a job calls for

over·reach \ˌō-vər-'rēch\ *vb* : to defeat (oneself) by too great an effort

over·ride \-'rīd\ *vb* **-rode** \-'rōd\; **-rid·den** \-'rid-ᵊn\; **-rid·ing** 1 : to ride over or across 2 : to prevail over; *also* : to set aside ⟨~ a veto⟩

over·rule \-'rül\ *vb* 1 : to prevail over 2 : to rule against 3 : to set aside

¹**over·run** \-'rən\ *vb* **-ran** \-'ran\; **-run·ning** 1 : to defeat and occupy the positions of 2 : OVERSPREAD; *also* : INFEST 3 : to go beyond 4 : to flow over

²**over·run** \'ō-vər-ˌrən\ *n* 1 : an act or instance of over-

running; *esp* : an exceeding of estimated costs **2** : the amount by which something overruns

over·sea \ˌō-vər-ˈsē, ˈō-vər-ˌsē\ *adj or adv* : OVERSEAS

over·seas \ˌō-vər-ˈsēz, -ˌsēz\ *adv or adj* : beyond or across the sea : ABROAD

over·see \ˌō-vər-ˈsē\ *vb* **-saw** \-ˈsȯ\; **-seen** \-ˈsēn\; **-seeing** **1** : OVERLOOK **2** : INSPECT; *also* : SUPERVISE — **over·seer** \ˈō-vər-ˌsir\ *n*

over·sell \ˌō-vər-ˈsel\ *vb* **-sold**; **-sel·ling** : to sell too much to or too much of

over·sexed \ˌō-vər-ˈsekst\ *adj* : exhibiting excessive sexual drive or interest

over·shad·ow \-ˈsha-dō\ *vb* **1** : to cast a shadow over **2** : to exceed in importance

over·shoe \ˈō-vər-ˌshü\ *n* : a protective outer shoe; *esp* : GALOSH

over·shoot \ˌō-vər-ˈshüt\ *vb* **-shot** \-ˈshät\; **-shooting** **1** : to pass swiftly beyond **2** : to shoot over or beyond

over·sight \ˈō-vər-ˌsīt\ *n* **1** : SUPERVISION **2** : an inadvertent omission or error

over·size \ˌō-vər-ˈsīz\ *or* **over·sized** \-ˈsīzd\ *adj* : of more than ordinary size

over·sleep \ˌō-vər-ˈslēp\ *vb* **-slept** \-ˈslept\; **-sleeping** : to sleep beyond the time for waking

over·spread \-ˈspred\ *vb* **-spread**; **-spread·ing** : to spread over or above

over·state \-ˈstāt\ *vb* : EXAGGERATE — **over·statement** *n*

over·stay \-ˈstā\ *vb* : to stay beyond the time or limits of

over·step \-ˈstep\ *vb* : EXCEED

over·sub·scribe \-səb-ˈskrīb\ *vb* : to subscribe for more of than is available, asked for, or offered for sale

overt \ō-ˈvərt, ˈō-ˌvərt\ *adj* [ME, fr. MF *ouvert, overt*, fr. pp. of *ouvrir* to open] : not secret — **overt·ly** *adv*

over·take \ˌō-vər-ˈtāk\ *vb* **-took** \-ˈtu̇k\; **-tak·en** \-ˈtākən\; **-tak·ing** : to catch up with; *also* : to catch up with and pass by

over–the–counter *adj* : sold lawfully without a prescription ⟨∼ drugs⟩

over·throw \ˌō-vər-ˈthrō\ *vb* **-threw** \-ˈthrü\; **-thrown** \-ˈthrōn\; **-throw·ing** **1** : UPSET **2** : to bring down : DEFEAT ⟨∼ a government⟩ **3** : to throw over or past — **over·throw** \ˈō-vər-ˌthrō\ *n*

over·time \ˈō-vər-ˌtīm\ *n* : time beyond a set limit; *esp* : working time in excess of a standard day or week — **overtime** *adv*

over·tone \-ˌtōn\ *n* **1** : one of the higher tones in a complex musical tone **2** : IMPLICATION, SUGGESTION

over·trick \ˈō-vər-ˌtrik\ *n* : a card trick won in excess of the number bid

over·ture \ˈō-vər-ˌchu̇r, -chər\ *n* [ME, lit., opening, fr. MF, fr. (assumed) VL *opertura*, alter. of L *apertura*] **1** : an opening offer **2** : an orchestral introduction to a musical dramatic work

over·turn \ˌō-vər-ˈtərn\ *vb* **1** : to turn over : UPSET **2** : INVALIDATE

over·view \ˈō-vər-ˌvyü\ *n* : a general survey : SUMMARY

over·ween·ing \ˌō-vər-ˈwē-niŋ\ *adj* **1** : ARROGANT **2** : IMMODERATE

over·weight \ˈō-vər-ˌwāt\ *n* **1** : weight above what is required or allowed **2** : bodily weight greater than normal — **overweight** *adj*

over·whelm \ˌō-vər-ˈhwelm\ *vb* **1** : OVERTHROW **2** : SUBMERGE **3** : to overcome completely

over·whelm·ing *adj* : EXTREME, GREAT ⟨∼ joy⟩ — **over·whelm·ing·ly** *adv*

over·win·ter \-ˈwin-tər\ *vb* : to survive the winter

over·work \-ˈwərk\ *vb* **1** : to work or cause to work too hard or long **2** : to use too much — **overwork** *n*

over·wrought \ˌō-vər-ˈrȯt\ *adj* **1** : extremely excited **2** : elaborated to excess

ovi·duct \ˈō-və-ˌdəkt\ *n* : a tube that serves for the passage of eggs from an ovary

ovip·a·rous \ō-ˈvi-pə-rəs\ *adj* : reproducing by eggs that hatch outside the parent's body

ovoid \ˈō-ˌvȯid\ *or* **ovoi·dal** \ō-ˈvȯid-ᵊl\ *adj* : egg-shaped : OVAL

ovu·la·tion \ˌäv-yə-ˈlā-shən, ˌōv-\ *n* : the discharge of a mature egg from the ovary — **ovu·late** \ˈäv-yə-ˌlāt, ˈōv-\ *vb*

ovule \ˈäv-yül, ˈōv-\ *n* : any of the bodies in a plant ovary that after fertilization become seeds

ovum \ˈō-vəm\ *n, pl* **ova** \-və\ : EGG 2

ow \ˈau̇\ *interj* — used esp. to express sudden pain

owe \ˈō\ *vb* **owed; ow·ing 1** : to be under obligation to pay or render **2** : to be indebted to or for; *also* : to be in debt

owing to *prep* : BECAUSE OF

owl \ˈau̇l\ *n* : any of an order of chiefly nocturnal birds of prey with a large head and eyes and strong talons — **owl·ish** *adj* — **owl·ish·ly** *adv*

owl·et \ˈau̇-lət\ *n* : a young or small owl

¹own \ˈōn\ *adj* : belonging to oneself — used as an intensive after a possessive adjective ⟨her ∼ car⟩

²own *vb* **1** : to have or hold as property **2** : ACKNOWLEDGE; *also* : CONFESS — **owner** *n* — **own·er·ship** *n*

³own *pron* : one or ones belonging to oneself

ox \ˈäks\ *n, pl* **ox·en** \ˈäk-sən\ *also* **ox** : any of the common large domestic cattle kept for milk, draft, and meat; *esp* : an adult castrated male ox

ox·blood \ˈäks-ˌbləd\ *n* : a moderate reddish brown

ox·bow \-ˌbō\ *n* **1** : a U-shaped collar worn by a draft ox **2** : a U-shaped bend in a river — **oxbow** *adj*

ox·ford \ˈäks-fərd\ *n* : a low shoe laced or tied over the instep

ox·i·dant \ˈäk-sə-dənt\ *n* : OXIDIZING AGENT — **oxidant** *adj*

ox·i·da·tion \ˌäk-sə-ˈdā-shən\ *n* : the act or process of oxidizing; *also* : the condition of being oxidized — **ox·i·da·tive** \ˈäk-sə-ˌdā-tiv\ *adj*

ox·ide \\'äk-ₗsīd\\ *n* : a compound of oxygen with another element or group

ox·i·dize \\'äk-sə-ₗdīz\\ *vb* **-dized; -diz·ing** : to combine with oxygen (iron rusts because it is *oxidized* by exposure to the air) — **ox·i·diz·er** *n*

oxidizing agent *n* : a substance (as oxygen or nitric acid) that oxidizes by taking up electrons

ox·y·gen \\'äk-si-jən\\ *n* [F *oxygène*, fr. Gk *oxys* acidic, lit., sharp + *-genēs* giving rise to; so called because it was once thought to be an essential element of all acids] : a colorless odorless gaseous chemical element that is found in the air, is essential to life, and is involved in combustion — see ELEMENT table

ox·y·gen·ate \\'äk-si-jə-ₗnāt\\ *vb* **-at·ed; -at·ing** : to impregnate, combine, or supply with oxygen — **ox·y·gen·a·tion** \\ₗäk-si-jə-'nā-shən\\ *n*

oxygen mask *n* : a device worn over the nose and mouth through which oxygen is supplied

oxygen tent *n* : a canopy which can be placed over a bedridden person and within which a flow of oxygen can be maintained

ox·y·mo·ron \\ₗäk-sē-'mōr-ₗän\\ *n* : a combination of contradictory words (as *cruel kindness*)

oys·ter \\'òi-stər\\ *n* : any of various marine mollusks with an irregular 2-valved shell that include commercially important edible shellfish and pearl producers — **oys·ter·ing** *n* — **oys·ter·man** \\'òi-stər-mən\\ *n*

oz *abbr* [obs. It *onza* (now *oncia*)] ounce; ounces

ozone \\'ō-ₗzōn\\ *n* **1** : a bluish gaseous reactive form of oxygen that is formed naturally in the atmosphere and is used for disinfecting, deodorizing, and bleaching **2** : pure and refreshing air

ozone layer *n* : an atmospheric layer at heights of about 25 miles (40 kilometers) with high ozone content which blocks most solar ultraviolet radiation

P

¹p \\'pē\\ *n, pl* **p's** *or* **ps** \\'pēz\\ *often cap* : the 16th letter of the English alphabet

²p *abbr, often cap* **1** page **2** participle **3** past **4** pawn **5** pence; penny **6** per **7** petite **8** pint **9** pressure **10** purl

P *symbol* phosphorus

pa \\'pä, 'pò\\ *n* : FATHER

¹Pa *abbr* **1** pascal **2** Pennsylvania

²Pa *symbol* protactinium

¹PA \\(ₗ)pē-'ā\\ *n* : PHYSICIAN'S ASSISTANT

²PA *abbr* **1** Pennsylvania **2** per annum **3** power of attorney **4** press agent **5** private account **6** professional association **7** public address **8** purchasing agent

pa·'an·ga \\pä-'äŋ-gə\\ *n* — see MONEY table

pab·u·lum \\'pa-byə-ləm\\ *n* [L, food, fodder] : usu. soft digestible food

Pac *abbr* Pacific

PAC *abbr* political action committee

¹pace \\'pās\\ *n* **1** : rate of movement or progress (as in walking or working) **2** : a step in walking; *also* : a measure of length based on such a step **3** : GAIT; *esp* : a horse's gait in which the legs on the same side move together

²pace *vb* **paced; pac·ing 1** : to go or cover at a pace or with slow steps **2** : to measure off by paces **3** : to set or regulate the pace of

³pa·ce \\'pā-sē; 'pä-ₗkā, -ₗchā\\ *prep* : contrary to the opinion of

pace·mak·er \\'pās-ₗmā-kər\\ *n* **1** : one that sets the pace for another **2** : a body part (as of the heart) that serves to establish and maintain a rhythmic activity **3** : an electrical device for stimulating or steadying the heartbeat

pac·er \\'pā-sər\\ *n* **1** : a horse that paces **2** : PACEMAKER

pachy·derm \\'pa-ki-ₗdərm\\ *n* [F *pachyderme*, fr. Gk *pachydermos* thick-skinned, fr. *pachys* thick + *derma* skin] : any of various thick-skinned hoofed mammals (as an elephant)

pach·ys·an·dra \\ₗpa-ki-'san-drə\\ *n* : any of a genus of low shrubby evergreen plants used as a ground cover

pa·cif·ic \\pə-'si-fik\\ *adj* **1** : tending to lessen conflict **2** : CALM, PEACEFUL

pac·i·fi·er \\'pa-sə-ₗfī-ər\\ *n* : one that pacifies; *esp* : a device for a baby to chew or suck on

pac·i·fism \\'pa-sə-ₗfi-zəm\\ *n* : opposition to war or violence as a means of settling disputes — **pac·i·fist** \\-fist\\ *n or adj* — **pac·i·fis·tic** \\ₗpa-sə-'fis-tik\\ *adj*

pac·i·fy \\'pa-sə-ₗfī\\ *vb* **-fied; -fy·ing 1** : to allay anger or agitation in : SOOTHE **2** : SETTLE; *also* : SUBDUE — **pac·i·fi·ca·tion** \\ₗpa-sə-fə-'kā-shən\\ *n*

¹pack \\'pak\\ *n* **1** : a compact bundle; *also* : a flexible container for carrying a bundle esp. on the back **2** : a large amount : HEAP **3** : a set of playing cards **4** : a

group or band of people or animals **5** : wet absorbent material for application to the body

²pack *vb* **1** : to stow goods in for transportation **2** : to fill in or surround so as to prevent passage of air, steam, or water **3** : to put into a protective container **4** : to load with a pack ⟨~ a mule⟩ **5** : to crowd in **6** : to make into a pack **7** : to cause to go without ceremony ⟨~ them off to school⟩ **8** : WEAR, CARRY ⟨~ a gun⟩

³pack *vb* : to make up fraudulently so as to secure a desired result ⟨~ a jury⟩

¹pack·age \\'pa-kij\\ *n* **1** : BUNDLE, PARCEL **2** : a group of related things offered as a whole

²package *vb* **pack·aged; pack·ag·ing** : to make into or enclose in a package

package deal *n* : an offer containing several items all or none of which must be accepted

package store *n* : a store that sells alcoholic beverages in sealed containers for consumption off the premises

pack·er \\'pa-kər\\ *n* : one that packs; *esp* : a wholesale food dealer

pack·et \\'pa-kət\\ *n* **1** : a small bundle or package **2** : a passenger boat carrying mail and cargo on a regular schedule

pack·horse \\'pak-ₗhòrs\\ *n* : a horse used to carry goods or supplies

pack·ing \\'pa-kiŋ\\ *n* : material used to pack something

pack·ing·house \\-ₗhaùs\\ *n* : an establishment for processing and packing food and esp. meat and its by=products

pack rat *n* : a bushy-tailed rodent of the Rocky Mountain area that hoards food and miscellaneous objects

pack·sad·dle \\'pak-ₗsad-ᵊl\\ *n* : a saddle for supporting loads on the back of an animal

pack·thread \\-ₗthred\\ *n* : strong thread for tying

pact \\'pakt\\ *n* : AGREEMENT, TREATY

¹pad \\'pad\\ *n* **1** : a cushioning part or thing : CUSHION **2** : the cushioned underside of the foot or toes of some mammals **3** : the floating leaf of a water plant **4** : a writing tablet **5** : LAUNCHPAD **6** : living quarters; *also* : BED

²pad *vb* **pad·ded; pad·ding 1** : to furnish with a pad or padding **2** : to expand with needless or fraudulent matter

pad·ding *n* : the material with which something is padded

¹pad·dle \\'pad-ᵊl\\ *vb* **pad·dled; pad·dling** : to move the hands and feet about in shallow water

²paddle *n* **1** : an implement with a flat blade used in propelling and steering a small craft (as a canoe) **2** : an implement used for stirring, mixing, or beating **3** : a broad board on the outer rim of a waterwheel or a paddle wheel

³**paddle** *vb* **pad·dled; pad·dling 1 :** to move on or through water by or as if by using a paddle **2 :** to beat or stir with a paddle

paddle wheel *n* : a wheel with paddles around its outer edge used to move a boat

paddle wheeler *n* : a steam-driven vessel propelled by a paddle wheel

pad·dock \'pa-dək\ *n* **1 :** a usu. enclosed area for pasturing or exercising animals; *esp* : one where racehorses are saddled and paraded before a race **2 :** an area at a racecourse where racing cars are parked

pad·dy \'pa-dē\ *n, pl* **paddies :** wet land where rice is grown

paddy wagon *n* : an enclosed motortruck for carrying prisoners

pad·lock \'pad-ˌläk\ *n* : a removable lock with a curved piece that snaps into a catch — **padlock** *vb*

pa·dre \'pä-drā\ *n* [Sp or It or Pg, lit., father, fr. L *pater*] **1 :** PRIEST **2 :** a military chaplain

pae·an \'pē-ən\ *n* : an exultant song of praise or thanksgiving

pae·di·at·ric, pae·di·a·tri·cian, pae·di·at·rics *chiefly Brit var of* PEDIATRIC, PEDIATRICIAN, PEDIATRICS

pa·gan \'pā-gən\ *n* [ME, fr. LL *paganus* fr. L, country dweller, fr. *pagus* country district] : HEATHEN — **pagan** *adj* — **pa·gan·ism** \-gə-ˌni-zəm\ *n*

¹**page** \'pāj\ *n* : ATTENDANT; *esp* : one employed to deliver messages

²**page** *vb* **paged; pag·ing :** to summon by repeatedly calling out the name of

³**page** *n* : a single leaf (as of a book); *also* : a single side of such a leaf

⁴**page** *vb* **paged; pag·ing :** to mark or number the pages of

pag·eant \'pa-jənt\ *n* [ME *pagyn, padgeant,* lit., scene of a play, fr. ML *pagina,* perh. fr. L, page] : an elaborate spectacle, show, or procession esp. with tableaux or floats — **pag·eant·ry** \-jən-trē\ *n*

page·boy \'pāj-ˌbȯi\ *n* [¹*page*] : an often shoulder-length hairdo with the ends of the hair turned smoothly under

pag·er \'pā-jər\ *n* : one that pages; *esp* : BEEPER

pag·i·nate \'pa-jə-ˌnāt\ *vb* **-nat·ed; -nat·ing :** ⁴PAGE

pag·i·na·tion \ˌpa-jə-'nā-shən\ *n* **1 :** the paging of written or printed matter **2 :** the number and arrangement of pages (as of a book)

pa·go·da \pə-'gō-də\ *n* : a tower with roofs curving upward at the division of each of several stories

paid *past and past part of* PAY

pail \'pāl\ *n* : a usu. cylindrical vessel with a handle — **pail·ful** \-ˌfu̇l\ *n*

¹**pain** \'pān\ *n* **1 :** PUNISHMENT, PENALTY **2 :** suffering or distress of body or mind; *also* : a basic bodily sensation marked by discomfort (as throbbing or aching) **3** *pl* : great care **4 :** one that irks or annoys — **pain·ful** \-fəl\ *adj* — **pain·ful·ly** *adv* — **pain·less** *adj* — **pain·less·ly** *adv*

²**pain** *vb* : to cause or experience pain

pain·kill·er \'pān-ˌki-lər\ *n* : something (as a drug) that relieves pain — **pain·kill·ing** *adj*

pains·tak·ing \'pān-ˌstā-kiŋ\ *adj* : taking pains : showing care — **pains·taking** *n* — **pains·tak·ing·ly** *adv*

¹**paint** \'pānt\ *vb* **1 :** to apply color, pigment, or paint to **2 :** to produce or portray in lines or colors on a surface; *also* : to practice the art of painting **3 :** to decorate with colors **4 :** to use cosmetics **5 :** to describe vividly **6 :** SWAB — **paint·er** *n*

²**paint** *n* **1 :** something produced by painting **2 :** MAKEUP **3 :** a mixture of a pigment and a liquid that forms a thin adherent coating when spread on a surface; *also* : the dry pigment used in making this mixture **4 :** an applied coating of paint

paint·brush \'pānt-ˌbrəsh\ *n* : a brush for applying paint

painting *n* **1 :** a work (as a picture) produced by painting **2 :** the art or occupation of painting

¹**pair** \'par\ *n, pl* **pairs** *also* **pair** [ME *paire,* fr. OF, fr. L *paria* equal things, fr. neut. pl. of *par* equal] **1 :** two things of a kind designed for use together **2 :** something made up of two corresponding pieces ⟨a ∼ of trousers⟩ **3 :** a set of two people or animals

²**pair** *vb* **1 :** to arrange in pairs **2 :** to form a pair : MATCH **3 :** to become associated with another

pai·sa \pī-'sä\ *n, pl* **paisa** *or* **pai·se** \-'sä\ — *see rupee, taka* at MONEY table

pais·ley \'pāz-lē\ *adj, often cap* : decorated with colorful curved abstract figures ⟨a ∼ shawl⟩

Pai·ute \'pī-ˌüt, -ˌyüt\ *n* : a member of an American Indian people orig. of Utah, Arizona, Nevada, and California

pa·ja·mas \pə-'jä-məz, -'ja-\ *n pl* : a loose suit for sleeping or lounging

Pak·i·stani \ˌpa-ki-'sta-nē, ˌpä-ki-'stä-nē\ *n* : a native or inhabitant of Pakistan — **Pak·i·stani** *adj*

pal \'pal\ *n* : a close friend

pal·ace \'pa-ləs\ *n* [ME *palais,* fr. OF, fr. L *palatium,* fr. *Palatium,* the Palatine Hill in Rome where the emperors' residences were built] **1 :** the official residence of a chief of state **2 :** MANSION

pal·a·din \'pa-lə-dən\ *n* **1 :** a trusted military leader (as for a medieval prince) **2 :** a leading champion of a cause

pa·laes·tra \pə-'les-trə\ *n, pl* **-trae** \-(ˌ)trē\ : a school in ancient Greece or Rome for sports (as wrestling)

pa·lan·quin \ˌpa-lən-'kēn\ *n* : an enclosed couch for one person borne on the shoulders of men by means of poles

pal·at·able \'pa-lə-tə-bəl\ *adj* : agreeable to the taste **syn** appetizing, savory, tasty, toothsome

pal·a·tal \'pa-lət-əl\ *adj* **1 :** of or relating to the palate **2 :** pronounced with some part of the tongue near or touching the hard palate ⟨the \y\ in *yeast* and the \sh\ in *she* are ∼ sounds⟩

pal·a·tal·ize \'pa-lət-əl-ˌīz\ *vb* **-ized; -iz·ing :** to pronounce or change into a palatal sound — **pal·a·tal·iza·tion** \ˌpa-lət-əl-ə-'zā-shən\ *n*

pal·ate \'pa-lət\ *n* **1 :** the roof of the mouth separating the mouth from the nasal cavity **2 :** TASTE

pa·la·tial \pə-'lā-shəl\ *adj* **1 :** of, relating to, or being a palace **2 :** MAGNIFICENT

pa·lat·i·nate \pə-'lat-ᵊn-ət\ *n* : the territory of a palatine

¹**pal·a·tine** \'pa-lə-ˌtīn\ *adj* **1 :** possessing royal privileges; *also* : of or relating to a palatine or a palatinate **2 :** of or relating to a palace : PALATIAL

²**palatine** *n* **1 :** a feudal lord having sovereign power within his domains **2 :** a high officer of an imperial palace

pa·la·ver \pə-'la-vər, -'lä-\ *n* [Pg *palavra* word, speech, fr. LL *parabola* parable, speech] **1 :** a long parley **2 :** idle talk — **palaver** *vb*

¹**pale** \'pāl\ *n* **1 :** a stake or picket of a fence **2 :** an enclosed place; *also* : a district or territory within certain bounds or under a particular jurisdiction **3 :** LIMITS, BOUNDS ⟨conduct beyond the ∼⟩

²**pale** *vb* **paled; pal·ing :** to enclose with or as if with pales : FENCE

³**pale** *adj* **pal·er; pal·est 1 :** deficient in color or intensity : WAN ⟨∼ face⟩ **2 :** lacking in brightness : DIM ⟨∼ star⟩ **3 :** not dark or intense in hue ⟨∼ blue⟩ — **pale·ness** *n*

⁴**pale** *vb* **paled; pal·ing :** to make or become pale

pale·face \'pāl-ˌfās\ *n* : a white person

Pa·leo·cene \'pā-lē-ə-ˌsēn\ *adj* : of, relating to, or being the earliest epoch of the Tertiary — **Paleocene** *n*

pa·le·og·ra·phy \ˌpā-lē-'ä-grə-fē\ *n* [NL *palaeographia,* fr. Gk *palaios* ancient + *graphein* to write] : the study of ancient writings and inscriptions — **pa·le·og·ra·pher** *n*

Pa·leo·lith·ic \ˌpā-lē-ə-'li-thik\ *adj* : of or relating to the earliest period of the Stone Age characterized by rough or chipped stone implements

pa·le·on·tol·o·gy \ˌpā-lē-ˌän-ˈtä-lə-jē\ *n* : a science dealing with the life of past geologic periods as known from fossil remains — **pa·le·on·tol·o·gist** \-ˌän-ˈtä-lə-jist, -ən-\ *n*

Pa·leo·zo·ic \ˌpā-lē-ə-ˈzō-ik\ *adj* : of, relating to, or being the era of geologic history extending from about 570 million years ago to about 245 million years ago — **Paleozoic** *n*

pal·ette \ˈpa-lət\ *n* : a thin often oval board that a painter holds and mixes colors on; *also* : the colors on a palette

pal·frey \ˈpȯl-frē\ *n, pl* **palfreys** *archaic* : a saddle horse that is not a warhorse; *esp* : one suitable for a woman

pa·limp·sest \ˈpa-ləmp-ˌsest\ *n* [L *palimpsestus*, fr. Gk *palimpsēstos* scraped again] : writing material (as a parchment) used after the erasure of earlier writing

pal·in·drome \ˈpa-lən-ˌdrōm\ *n* : a word, verse, or sentence (as "Able was I ere I saw Elba") or a number (as 1881) that reads the same backward or forward

pal·ing \ˈpā-liŋ\ *n* **1** : a fence of pales **2** : material for pales **3** : PALE, PICKET

pal·i·sade \ˌpa-lə-ˈsād\ *n* **1** : a high fence of stakes esp. for defense **2** : a line of steep cliffs

¹pall \ˈpȯl\ *vb* **1** : to lose in interest or attraction **2** : SATIATE, CLOY

²pall *n* **1** : a heavy cloth draped over a coffin **2** : something that produces a gloomy atmosphere

pal·la·di·um \pə-ˈlā-dē-əm\ *n* : a silver-white metallic chemical element used esp. as a catalyst and in alloys — see ELEMENT table

pall·bear·er \ˈpȯl-ˌbar-ər\ *n* : a person who attends the coffin at a funeral

¹pal·let \ˈpa-lət\ *n* : a small, hard, or makeshift bed

²pallet *n* : a portable platform for transporting and storing materials

pal·li·ate \ˈpa-lē-ˌāt\ *vb* **-at·ed; -at·ing 1** : to ease (as a disease) without curing **2** : to cover by excuses and apologies — **pal·li·a·tion** \ˌpa-lē-ˈā-shən\ *n* — **pal·li·a·tive** \ˈpa-lē-ˌā-tiv\ *adj or n*

pal·lid \ˈpa-ləd\ *adj* : PALE, WAN

pal·lor \ˈpa-lər\ *n* : PALENESS

¹palm \ˈpäm, ˈpälm\ *n* [ME, fr. OE, fr. L *palma* palm of the hand, palm tree; fr. the resemblance of the tree's leaves to the outstretched hand] **1** : any of a family of mostly tropical trees, shrubs, or vines usu. with a tall unbranched stem topped by a crown of large leaves **2** : a symbol of victory; *also* : VICTORY

²palm *n* : the underpart of the hand between the fingers and the wrist

³palm *vb* **1** : to conceal in or with the hand ⟨~ a card⟩ **2** : to impose by fraud

pal·mate \ˈpal-ˌmāt, ˈpäl-\ *also* **pal·mat·ed** \-ˌmā-təd\ *adj* : resembling a hand with the fingers spread

pal·met·to \pal-ˈme-tō\ *n, pl* **-tos** *or* **-toes** : any of several usu. small palms with fan-shaped leaves

palm·ist·ry \ˈpä-mə-strē, ˈpäl-\ *n* : the practice of reading a person's character or future from the markings on the palms — **palm·ist** \ˈpä-mist, ˈpäl-\ *n*

Palm Sunday *n* : the Sunday preceding Easter and commemorating Christ's triumphal entry into Jerusalem

palmy \ˈpä-mē, ˈpäl-\ *adj* **palm·i·er; -est 1** : abounding in or bearing palms **2** : FLOURISHING, PROSPEROUS

pal·o·mi·no \ˌpa-lə-ˈmē-nō\ *n, pl* **-nos** [AmerSp, fr. Sp, like a dove, fr. L *palumbinus*, fr. *palumbes*, a species of dove] : a horse with a pale cream to golden coat and cream or white mane and tail

pal·pa·ble \ˈpal-pə-bəl\ *adj* **1** : capable of being touched or felt : TANGIBLE **2** : OBVIOUS, PLAIN **syn** perceptible, sensible, appreciable, tangible, detectable — **pal·pa·bly** \-blē\ *adv*

pal·pate \ˈpal-ˌpāt\ *vb* **pal·pat·ed; pal·pat·ing** : to examine by touch esp. medically — **pal·pa·tion** \pal-ˈpā-shən\ *n*

pal·pi·tate \ˈpal-pə-ˌtāt\ *vb* **-tat·ed; -tat·ing** : to beat rapidly and strongly : THROB — **pal·pi·ta·tion** \ˌpal-pə-ˈtā-shən\ *n*

pal·sy \ˈpȯl-zē\ *n, pl* **palsies 1** : PARALYSIS **2** : a condition marked by tremor — **pal·sied** \-zēd\ *adj*

pal·ter \ˈpȯl-tər\ *vb* **pal·tered; pal·ter·ing 1** : to act insincerely : EQUIVOCATE **2** : HAGGLE

pal·try \ˈpȯl-trē\ *adj* **pal·tri·er; -est 1** : TRASHY ⟨a ~ pamphlet⟩ **2** : MEAN, DESPICABLE ⟨a ~ trick⟩ **3** : TRIVIAL ⟨~ excuses⟩ **4** : MEAGER, MEASLY ⟨a ~ sum⟩

pam *abbr* pamphlet

pam·pas \ˈpam-pəz, ˈpäm-, -pəs\ *n pl* : wide grassy So. American plains

pam·per \ˈpam-pər\ *vb* : to treat with excessive attention : INDULGE **syn** coddle, humor, baby, spoil

pam·phlet \ˈpam-flət\ *n* [ME *pamflet* unbound booklet, fr. *Pamphilus seu De Amore* Pamphilus or On Love, popular Latin love poem of the 12th cent.] : an unbound printed publication

pam·phle·teer \ˌpam-flə-ˈtir\ *n* : a writer of pamphlets attacking something or urging a cause

¹pan \ˈpan\ *n* **1** : a usu. broad, shallow, and open container for domestic use; *also* : something resembling such a container **2** : a basin or depression in land **3** : HARDPAN

²pan *vb* **panned; pan·ning 1** : to wash earth or gravel in a pan in searching for gold **2** : to criticize severely

Pan *abbr* Panama

pan·a·cea \ˌpa-nə-ˈsē-ə\ *n* : a remedy for all ills or difficulties : CURE-ALL

pa·nache \pə-ˈnash, -ˈnäsh\ *n* [MF *pennache*, ultim. fr. LL *pinnaculum* small wing] **1** : an ornamental tuft (as of feathers) esp. on a helmet **2** : dash or flamboyance in style and action

pan·a·ma \ˈpa-nə-ˌmä, -ˌmȯ\ *n, often cap* : a handmade hat braided from strips of the leaves from a tropical American tree

Pan·a·ma·ni·an \ˌpa-nə-ˈmā-nē-ən\ *n* : a native or inhabitant of Panama — **Panamanian** *adj*

pan·a·tela \ˌpa-nə-ˈte-lə\ *n* [Sp, fr. AmerSp, a long thin biscuit, ultim. fr. L *panis* bread] **:** a long slender cigar with straight sides

pan•cake \\'pan-ˌkāk\ *n* **:** a flat cake made of thin batter and fried on both sides

pan•chro•mat•ic \ˌpan-krō-'ma-tik\ *adj* **:** sensitive to all colors of visible light ⟨∼ film⟩

pan•cre•as \'paŋ-krē-əs, 'pan-\ *n* **:** a large compound gland of vertebrates that produces insulin and discharges enzymes into the intestine — **pan•cre•at•ic** \ˌpaŋ-krē-'a-tik, ˌpan-\ *adj*

pan•da \'pan-də\ *n* **1 :** a long-tailed Himalayan mammal related to and resembling the racoon **2 :** a large black-and-white mammal of western China usu. classified with the bears

panda: *A* panda 1, *B* panda 2

pan•dem•ic \pan-'de-mik\ *n* **:** a widespread outbreak of disease — **pandemic** *adj*

pan•de•mo•ni•um \ˌpan-də-'mō-nē-əm\ *n* **:** a wild uproar : TUMULT

¹pan•der \'pan-dər\ *n* **1 :** a go-between in love intrigues **2 :** PIMP **3 :** someone who caters to or exploits others' desires or weaknesses

²pander *vb* **:** to act as a pander

P & I *abbr* principal and interest

P & L *abbr* profit and loss

pan•dow•dy \pan-'daů-dē\ *n, pl* **-dies :** a deep≈ dish apple dessert spiced, sweetened, and covered with a crust

pane \'pān\ *n* **:** a sheet of glass (as in a door or window)

pan•e•gyr•ic \ˌpa-nə-'jir-ik\ *n* **:** a eulogistic oration or writing — **pan•e•gyr•ist** \-'jir-ist\ *n*

¹pan•el \'pan-əl\ *n* **1 :** a list of persons appointed for special duty ⟨a jury ∼⟩; *also* **:** a group of people taking part in a discussion or quiz program **2 :** a section of something (as a wall or door) often sunk below the level of the frame; *also* **:** a flat piece of construction material **3 :** a flat piece of wood on which a picture is painted **4 :** a mount for controls or dials

²panel *vb* **-eled** *or* **-elled; -el•ing** *or* **-el•ling :** to decorate with panels

paneling *n* **:** decorative panels

pan•el•ist \'pan-əl-ist\ *n* **:** a member of a discussion or quiz panel

panel truck *n* **:** a small motortruck with a fully enclosed body

pang \'paŋ\ *n* **:** a sudden sharp spasm (as of pain) or attack (as of remorse)

¹pan•han•dle \'pan-ˌhand-əl\ *n* **:** a narrow projection of a larger territory (as a state) ⟨the Texas ∼⟩

²panhandle *vb* **-dled; -dling :** to ask for money on the street — **pan•han•dler** *n*

¹pan•ic \'pa-nik\ *n* **:** a sudden overpowering fright **syn** terror, consternation, dismay, alarm, dread, fear — **pan•icky** \-ni-kē\ *adj*

²panic *vb* **pan•icked** \-nikt\; **pan•ick•ing :** to affect or be affected with panic

pan•i•cle \'pa-ni-kəl\ *n* **:** a branched flower cluster (as of a lilac) in which each branch from the main stem has one or more flowers

pan•jan•drum \pan-'jan-drəm\ *n, pl* **-drums** *also* **-dra** \-drə\ **:** a powerful personage or pretentious official

pan•nier *also* **pan•ier** \'pan-yər\ *n* **:** a large basket esp. for bearing on the back

pan•o•ply \'pa-nə-plē\ *n, pl* **-plies 1 :** a full suit of armor **2 :** a protective covering **3 :** an impressive array

pan•ora•ma \ˌpa-nə-'ra-mə, -'rä-\ *n* **1 :** a picture unrolled before one's eyes **2 :** a complete view in every direction — **pan•oram•ic** \-'ra-mik\ *adj*

pan out *vb* **:** TURN OUT; *esp* **:** SUCCEED

pan•sy \'pan-zē\ *n, pl* **pansies** [ME *pensee*, fr. MF *pensée*, fr. *pensée* thought, fr. *penser* to think, fr. L *pensare* to ponder] **:** a low-growing garden herb related to the violet; *also* **:** its showy flower

¹pant \'pant\ *vb* [ME, fr. MF *pantaisier*, fr. (assumed) VL *phantasiare* to have hallucinations, fr. Gk *phantasioun*, fr. *phantasia* appearance, imagination] **1 :** to breathe in a labored manner **2 :** YEARN **3 :** THROB

²pant *n* **:** a panting breath or sound

³pant *n* **1 :** an outer garment covering each leg separately and usu. extending from the waist to the ankle — usu. used in pl. **2** *pl* **:** PANTIE

pan•ta•loons \ˌpan-tə-'lünz\ *n pl* **1 :** close-fitting trousers of the 19th century usu. having straps passing under the instep **2 :** loose-fitting usu. shorter than ankle-length trousers

pan•the•ism \'pan-thē-ˌi-zəm\ *n* **:** a doctrine that equates God with the forces and laws of the universe — **pan•the•ist** \-ist\ *n* — **pan•the•is•tic** \ˌpan-thē-'is-tik\ *adj*

pan•the•on \'pan-thē-ˌän, -ən\ *n* **1 :** a temple dedicated to all the gods; *also* **:** the gods of a people **2 :** a group of illustrious people

pan•ther \'pan-thər\ *n, pl* **panthers** *also* **panther 1** **:** LEOPARD; *esp* **:** a black one **2 :** COUGAR **3 :** JAGUAR

pant•ie *or* **panty** \'pan-tē\ *n, pl* **pant•ies :** a woman's or child's short underpants — usu. used in pl.

pan•to•mime \'pan-tə-ˌmīm\ *n* **1 :** a play in which the actors use no words **2 :** expression of something by bodily or facial movements only — **pantomime** *vb* — **pan•to•mim•ic** \ˌpan-tə-'mi-mik\ *adj*

pan•try \'pan-trē\ *n, pl* **pantries :** a storage room for food or dishes

pant•suit \'pant-ˌsüt\ *n* **:** a woman's outfit consisting usu. of a long jacket and pants of the same material

panty hose *n pl* **:** a one-piece undergarment for women consisting of hosiery combined with a pantie

panty•waist \'pan-tē-ˌwāst\ *n* **:** SISSY

pap \'pap\ *n* **:** soft food for infants or invalids

pa•pa \'pä-pə\ *n* **:** FATHER

pa•pa•cy \'pä-pə-sē\ *n, pl* **-cies 1 :** the office of pope **2** **:** a succession of popes **3 :** the term of a pope's reign **4** *cap* **:** the system of government of the Roman Catholic Church

pa•pa•in \pə-'pä-ən, -'pī-ən\ *n* **:** an enzyme in papaya juice used esp. as a meat tenderizer and in medicine

pa•pal \'pä-pəl\ *adj* **:** of or relating to the pope or to the Roman Catholic Church

pa•paw *n* **1** \pə-'pò\: PAPAYA **2** \'pä-ˌpò\: a No. American tree with yellow edible fruit; *also* **:** its fruit

pa•pa•ya \pə-'pī-ə\ *n* **:** a tropical American tree with large yellow black-seeded edible fruit; *also* **:** its fruit

pa•per \'pä-pər\ *n* [ME *papir*, fr. MF *papier*, fr. L *papyrus* papyrus, paper, fr. Gk *papyros* papyrus] **1 :** a pliable substance made usu. of vegetable matter and used to write or print on, to wrap things in, or to cover walls; *also* **:** a single sheet of this substance **2 :** a printed or written document **3 :** NEWSPAPER **4 :** WALLPAPER — **paper** *adj or vb* — **pa•pery** \'pä-pə-rē\ *adj*

pa•per•back \-ˌbak\ *n* **:** a paper-covered book

pa•per•board \-ˌbòrd\ *n* **:** a material made from cellu-

lose fiber (as wood pulp) like paper but usu. thicker
pa·per·hang·er \'pā-pər-₁haŋ-ər\ n : one that applies wallpaper — **pa·per·hang·ing** n
pa·per·weight \-₁wāt\ n : an object used to hold down loose papers by its weight
pa·pier–mâché \₁pā-pər-mə-'shā, ₁pa-₁pyä-mə-, -ma-\ n [F, lit., chewed paper] : a molding material of wastepaper and additives (as glue) — **papier–mâché** adj
pa·pil·la \pə-'pi-lə\ n, pl **-lae** \-(₁)lē, -₁lī\ [L, nipple] : a small projecting bodily part (as one of the nubs on the surface of the tongue) that resembles a tiny nipple in form — **pap·il·lary** \'pa-pə-₁ler-ē, pə-'pi-lə-rē\ adj
pa·poose \pa-'püs, pə-\ n : a young child of No. American Indian parents
pa·pri·ka \pə-'prē-kə, pa-\ n [Hung] : a mild red spice made from the fruit of various cultivated sweet peppers
Pap smear \'pap-\ n : a method for the early detection of cancer esp. of the uterine cervix
Pap test n : PAP SMEAR
pap·ule \'pa-pyül\ n : a small solid usu. conical lesion of the skin — **pap·u·lar** \-pyə-lər\ adj
pa·py·rus \pə-'pī-rəs\ n, pl **-rus·es** or **-ri** \-(₁)rē, -₁rī\ : a tall grassy sedge of the Nile valley 2 : paper made from papyrus pith
¹par \'pär\ n 1 : a stated value (as of a security) 2 : a common level : EQUALITY 3 : an accepted standard or normal condition 4 : the score standard set for each hole of a golf course — **par** adj
²par abbr 1 paragraph 2 parallel 3 parish
pa·ra \'pär-ə\ n, pl **paras** or **para** — see dinar at MONEY table
par·a·ble \'par-ə-bəl\ n : a simple story told to illustrate a moral truth
pa·rab·o·la \pə-'ra-bə-lə\ n : a plane curve formed by the intersection of a cone with a plane parallel to a straight line in its surface — **par·a·bol·ic** \₁par-ə-'bä-lik\ adj
para·chute \'par-ə-₁shüt\ n [F, fr. para- (as in parasol) + chute fall] : a device for slowing the descent of a person or object through the air that consists of a usu. hemispherical canopy beneath which the person or object is suspended — **parachute** vb — **para·chut·ist** \-'shü-tist\ n

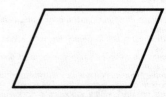

¹pa·rade \pə-'rād\ n 1 : a pompous display : EXHIBITION 2 : MARCH, PROCESSION; esp : a ceremonial formation and march 3 : a place for strolling

²parade vb **pa·rad·ed; pa·rad·ing** 1 : to march in a parade 2 : PROMENADE 3 : SHOW OFF 4 : MASQUERADE
par·a·digm \'par-ə-₁dīm, -₁dim\ n 1 : MODEL, PATTERN 2 : a systematic inflection of a verb or noun showing a complete conjugation or declension — **par·a·dig·mat·ic** \₁par-ə-dig-'ma-tik\ adj
par·a·dise \'par-ə-₁dīs, -₁dīz\ n [ME paradis, fr. OF, fr. LL paradisus, fr. Gk paradeisos, lit., enclosed

park, of Iranian origin] 1 : HEAVEN 2 : a place or state of bliss
par·a·di·si·a·cal \₁par-ə-də-'sī-ə-kəl\ or **par·a·dis·i·ac** \-'di-zē-₁ak, -sē-\ adj : of, relating to, or resembling paradise
par·a·dox \'par-ə-₁däks\ n : a statement that seems contrary to common sense and yet is perhaps true — **par·a·dox·i·cal** \₁par-ə-'däk-si-kəl\ adj — **par·a·dox·i·cal·ly** \-k(ə-)lē\ adv
par·af·fin \'par-ə-fən\ n : a waxy substance used esp. for making candles and sealing foods
par·a·gon \'par-ə-₁gän, -gən\ n : a model of perfection : PATTERN
¹para·graph \'par-ə-₁graf\ n : a subdivision of a written composition that deals with one point or gives the words of one speaker; also : a character (as ¶) marking the beginning of a paragraph
²paragraph vb : to divide into paragraphs
Par·a·guay·an \₁par-ə-'gwī-ən, -'gwä-\ n : a native or inhabitant of Paraguay — **Paraguayan** adj
par·a·keet \'par-ə-₁kēt\ n : any of numerous usu. small slender parrots with a long graduated tail
para·le·gal \₁par-ə-'lē-gəl\ adj : of, relating to, or being a paraprofessional who assists a lawyer — **paralegal** n
Par·a·li·pom·e·non \₁par-ə-lə-'pä-mə-₁nän\ n : CHRONICLES
par·al·lax \'par-ə-₁laks\ n : the difference in apparent direction of an object as seen from two different points
¹par·al·lel \'par-ə-₁lel\ adj [L parallelus, fr. Gk parallēlos, fr. para beside + allēlōn of one another, fr. allos . . . allos one . . . another, fr. allos other] 1 : lying or moving in the same direction but always the same distance apart 2 : similar in essential parts — **par·al·lel·ism** \-₁le-₁li-zəm\ n
²parallel n 1 : a parallel line, curve, or surface 2 : one of the imaginary circles on the earth's surface that parallel the equator and mark the latitude 3 : something essentially similar to another 4 : SIMILARITY, LIKENESS
³parallel vb 1 : COMPARE 2 : to correspond to 3 : to extend in a parallel direction with
par·al·lel·o·gram \₁par-ə-'le-lə-₁gram\ n : a 4-sided geometric figure with opposite sides equal and parallel

parallelogram

par·a·lyse Brit var of PARALYZE
pa·ral·y·sis \pə-'ra-lə-səs\ n, pl **-y·ses** \-₁sēz\ : loss of

function and esp. of feeling or the power of voluntary motion — **par·a·lyt·ic** \\par-ə-'li-tik\ *adj or n*

par·a·lyze \'par-ə-₁līz\ *vb* **-lyzed; -lyz·ing 1** : to affect with paralysis **2** : to make powerless or inactive — **par·a·lyz·ing·ly** *adv*

par·a·me·cium \₁par-ə-'mē-shəm, -shē-əm, -sē-əm\ *n, pl* **-cia** \-shə, -shē-ə, -sē-ə\ *also* **-ciums** : any of a genus of slipper-shaped protozoans that move by cilia

para·med·ic \₁par-ə-'me-dik\ *also* **para·med·i·cal** \-di-kəl\ *n* **1** : a person who assists a physician in a paramedical capacity **2** : a specially trained medical technician licensed to provide a wide range of emergency services before or during transportation to a hospital

para·med·i·cal \₁par-ə-'me-di-kəl\ *also* **para·med·ic** \-'me-dik\ *adj* : concerned with supplementing the work of trained medical professionals

pa·ram·e·ter \pə-'ra-mə-tər\ *n* **1** : a quantity whose value characterizes a statistical population or a member of a system (as a family of curves) **2** : a physical property whose value determines the characteristics or behavior of a system **3** : a characteristic element : FACTOR — **para·met·ric** \₁par-ə-'me-trik\ *adj*

para·mil·i·tary \₁par-ə-'mi-lə-₁ter-ē\ *adj* : formed on a military pattern esp. as an auxiliary military force

par·a·mount \'par-ə-₁maùnt\ *adj* : superior to all others : SUPREME **syn** preponderant, predominant, dominant, chief, sovereign

par·amour \'par-ə-₁mùr\ *n* : an illicit lover

para·noia \₁par-ə-'nòi-ə\ *n* : a psychosis marked by delusions and irrational suspicion usu. without hallucinations — **par·a·noid** \'par-ə-₁nòid\ *adj or n*

par·a·pet \'par-ə-pət, -₁pet\ *n* **1** : a protecting rampart **2** : a low wall or railing (as at the edge of a bridge)

par·a·pher·na·lia \₁par-ə-fə-'nāl-yə, -fər-\ *n sing or pl* **1** : personal belongings **2** : EQUIPMENT, APPARATUS

para·phrase \'par-ə-₁frāz\ *n* : a restatement of a text giving the meaning in different words — **paraphrase** *vb*

para·ple·gia \₁par-ə-'plē-jə, -jē-ə\ *n* : paralysis of the lower trunk and legs — **para·ple·gic** \-jik\ *adj or n*

para·pro·fes·sion·al \₁-prə-'fe-shə-nəl\ *n* : a trained aide who assists a professional — **paraprofessional** *adj*

para·psy·chol·o·gy \₁par-ə-sī-'kä-lə-jē\ *n* : a field of study concerned with investigating telepathy and related subjects — **para·psy·chol·o·gist** \-jist\ *n*

par·a·site \'par-ə-₁sīt\ *n* [MF, fr. L *parasitus*, fr. Gk *parasitos*, fr. *para-* beside + *sitos* grain, food] **1** : a plant or animal living in, with, or on another organism usu. to its harm **2** : one depending on another and not making adequate return — **par·a·sit·ic** \₁par-ə-'si-tik\ *adj* — **par·a·sit·ism** \'par-ə-sə-₁ti-zəm, -₁sī-₁ti-\ *n* — **par·a·sit·ize** \-sə-₁tīz\ *vb*

par·a·si·tol·o·gy \₁par-ə-sə-'tä-lə-jē\ *n* : a branch of biology dealing with parasites and parasitism esp. among animals — **par·a·si·tol·o·gist** \-jist\ *n*

para·sol \'par-ə-₁sòl\ *n* [F, fr. It *parasole*, fr. *parare* to

shield + *sole* sun, fr. L *sol*] : a lightweight umbrella used as a shield against the sun

para·sym·pa·thet·ic nervous system \₁par-ə-₁sim-pə-'the-tik-\ *n* : the part of the autonomic nervous system that tends to induce secretion, to increase the tone and contractility of smooth muscle, and to slow heart rate

para·thi·on \₁par-ə-'thī-ən, -₁än\ *n* : an extremely toxic insecticide

para·thy·roid \-'thī-₁ròid\ *n* : PARATHYROID GLAND — **parathyroid** *adj*

parathyroid gland *n* : any of usu. four small endocrine glands adjacent to or embedded in the thyroid gland that produce a hormone (**parathyroid hormone**) concerned with calcium and phosphorus metabolism

para·troop·er \'par-ə-₁trü-pər\ *n* : a member of the paratroops

para·troops \-₁trüps\ *n pl* : troops trained to parachute from an airplane

para·ty·phoid \₁par-ə-'tī-₁fòid\ *n* : a bacterial food poisoning resembling typhoid fever

par·boil \'pär-₁bòil\ *vb* : to boil briefly

¹**par·cel** \'pär-səl\ *n* **1** : a tract or plot of land **2** : COLLECTION, LOT **3** : a wrapped bundle : PACKAGE

²**parcel** *vb* **-celed** *or* **-celled; -cel·ing** *or* **-cel·ling** : to divide into portions

parcel post *n* **1** : a mail service handling parcels **2** : packages handled by parcel post

parch \'pärch\ *vb* **1** : to toast under dry heat **2** : to shrivel with heat

parch·ment \'pärch-mənt\ *n* : the skin of an animal prepared for writing on; *also* : a writing on such material

pard \'pärd\ *n* : LEOPARD

¹**par·don** \'pärd-ᵊn\ *n* : excuse of an offense without penalty; *esp* : an official release from legal punishment

²**pardon** *vb* : to free from penalty : EXCUSE, FORGIVE — **par·don·able** \'pärd-ᵊn-ə-bəl\ *adj*

par·don·er \'pärd-ᵊn-ər\ *n* **1** : a medieval preacher delegated to raise money for religious works by soliciting offerings and granting indulgences **2** : one that pardons

pare \'par\ *vb* **pared; par·ing 1** : to trim off an outside part (as the skin or rind) of **2** : to reduce as if by paring ⟨~ expenses⟩ — **par·er** *n*

par·e·gor·ic \₁par-ə-'gòr-ik\ *n* : an alcoholic preparation of opium and camphor used esp. to relieve pain

par·ent \'par-ənt\ *n* **1** : one that begets or brings forth offspring : FATHER, MOTHER **2** : one who brings up and cares for another **3** : SOURCE, ORIGIN — **par·ent·age** \-ən-tij\ *n* — **pa·ren·tal** \pə-'rent-ᵊl\ *adj* — **par·ent·hood** *n*

par·en·the·sis \pə-'ren-thə-səs\ *n, pl* **-the·ses** \-₁sēz\ **1** : a word, phrase, or sentence inserted in a passage to explain or modify the thought **2** : one of a pair of punctuation marks ( ) used esp. to enclose parenthetic matter — **par·en·thet·ic** \₁par-ən-'the-tik\ *or* **par·en·thet·i·cal** \-ti-kəl\ *adj* — **par·en·thet·i·cal·ly** \-k(ə-)lē\ *adv*

pa·ren·the·size \pə-'ren-thə-ısīz\ *vb* **-sized; -siz·ing** : to make a parenthesis of

par·ent·ing \'par-ən-tiŋ, 'per-\ *n* : the raising of a child by its parents

pa·re·sis \pə-'rē-səs, 'par-ə-\ *n, pl* **pa·re·ses** \-ısēz\ : a usu. incomplete paralysis; *also* : insanity caused by syphilitic alteration of the brain that leads to dementia and paralysis

par ex·cel·lence \ıpär-ıek-sə-'läⁿs\ *adj* [F, lit., by excellence] : being the best of a kind : PREEMINENT

par·fait \pär-'fä\ *n* [F, lit., something perfect] : a cold dessert made of layers of fruit, syrup, ice cream, and whipped cream

pa·ri·ah \pə-'rī-ə\ *n* : OUTCAST

pa·ri·etal \pə-'rī-ət-ᵊl\ *adj* **1** : of, relating to, or forming the walls of an anatomical structure **2** : of or relating to college living or its regulation

pari–mu·tu·el \ıpar-i-'myü-chə-wəl\ *n* : a betting system in which winners share the total stakes minus a percentage for the management

par·ing \'par-iŋ\ *n* : a pared-off piece

pa·ri pas·su \ıpar-i-'pa-sü\ *adv or adj* [L, with equal step] : at an equal rate or pace

par·ish \'par-ish\ *n* **1** : a church district in the care of one pastor; *also* : the residents of such an area **2** : a local church community **3** : a civil division of the state of Louisiana : COUNTY

pa·rish·io·ner \pə-'ri-shə-nər\ *n* : a member or resident of a parish

par·i·ty \'par-ə-tē\ *n, pl* **-ties** : EQUALITY, EQUIVALENCE

¹park \'pärk\ *n* **1** : a tract of ground kept as a game preserve or recreation area **2** : a place where vehicles (as automobiles) are parked **3** : an enclosed stadium used esp. for ball games

²park *vb* **1** : to leave a vehicle temporarily (as in a parking lot or garage) **2** : to set and leave temporarily

par·ka \'pär-kə\ *n* : a very warm jacket with a hood

Par·kin·son's disease \'pär-kən-sənz-\ *n* : a chronic progressive nervous disease chiefly of later life marked by tremor and weakness of resting muscles and by a shuffling gait

Parkinson's law *n* : an observation in office organization: work expands so as to fill the time available for its completion

park·way \'pärk-ıwä\ *n* : a broad landscaped thoroughfare

par·lance \'pär-ləns\ *n* **1** : SPEECH **2** : manner of speaking ⟨military ∼⟩

¹par·lay \'pär-ılā, -lē\ *vb* : to increase or change into something of much greater value

²parlay *n* : a series of bets in which the original stake plus its winnings are risked on successive wagers

par·ley \'pär-lē\ *n, pl* **parleys** : a conference usu. over matters in dispute : DISCUSSION — **parley** *vb*

par·lia·ment \'pär-lə-mənt\ *n* [ME, fr. OF *parlement*, fr. *parler* to speak, fr. ML *parabolare*, fr. LL *parabola* speech, parable] **1** : a formal governmental conference **2** *cap* : an assembly that constitutes the supreme legislative body of a country (as the United Kingdom) — **par·lia·men·ta·ry** \ıpär-lə-'men-tə-rē\ *adj*

par·lia·men·tar·i·an \ıpär-lə-ımen-'ter-ē-ən\ *n* **1** *often cap* : an adherent of the parliament during the English Civil War **2** : an expert in parliamentary procedure

par·lor \'pär-lər\ *n* **1** : a room for conversation or the reception of guests **2** : a place of business ⟨beauty ∼⟩

par·lour \'pär-lər\ *chiefly Brit var of* PARLOR

par·lous \'pär-ləs\ *adj* : full of danger or risk : PRECARIOUS — **par·lous·ly** *adv*

Par·me·san \'pär-mə-ızän, -ızän, -ızan\ *n* : a hard dry cheese with a sharp flavor

par·mi·gia·na \ıpär-mi-'jä-nə, ıpär-mi-'zhän\ *or* **par·mi·gia·no** \-'jä-(ı)nō\ *adj* : made or covered with Parmesan cheese ⟨veal ∼⟩

pa·ro·chi·al \pə-'rō-kē-əl\ *adj* **1** : of or relating to a church parish **2** : limited in scope : NARROW, PROVINCIAL — **pa·ro·chi·al·ism** \-ə-ıli-zəm\ *n*

parochial school *n* : a school maintained by a religious body

par·o·dy \'par-ə-dē\ *n, pl* **-dies** [L *parodia*, fr. Gk *parōidia*, fr. *para-* beside + *aidein* to sing] : a humorous or satirical imitation — **parody** *vb*

pa·role \pə-'rōl\ *n* : a conditional release of a prisoner whose sentence has not expired — **parole** *vb* — **pa·rol·ee** \-ırō-'lē, -'rō-ılē\ *n*

par·ox·ysm \'par-ək-ısi-zəm, pə-'räk-\ *n* : a sudden sharp attack (as of pain or coughing) : CONVULSION — **par·ox·ys·mal** \ıpar-ək-'si-məl, pə-ıräk-\ *adj*

par·quet \'pär-ıkā, pär-'kā\ *n* [F] **1** : a flooring of parquetry **2** : the lower floor of a theater; *esp* : the forward part of the orchestra

par·que·try \'pär-kə-trē\ *n, pl* **-tries** : fine woodwork inlaid in patterns

par·ra·keet *var of* PARAKEET

par·ri·cide \'par-ə-ısīd\ *n* **1** : one that murders a parent or a close relative **2** : the act of a parricide

par·rot \'par-ət\ *n* : any of numerous bright-colored tropical birds that have a stout hooked bill

parrot fever *n* : an infectious disease of birds marked by diarrhea and wasting and transmissible to humans

par·ry \'par-ē\ *vb* **par·ried; par·ry·ing 1** : to ward off a weapon or blow **2** : to evade esp. by an adroit answer — **parry** *n*

parse \'pärs *also* 'pärz\ *vb* **parsed; pars·ing** : to give a grammatical description of a word or a group of words

par·sec \'pär-ısek\ *n* : a unit of measure for interstellar space equal to 3.26 light-years

par·si·mo·ny \'pär-sə-ımō-nē\ *n* : extreme or excessive frugality — **par·si·mo·ni·ous** \ıpär-sə-'mō-nē-əs\ *adj* — **par·si·mo·ni·ous·ly** *adv*

pars·ley \'pär-slē\ *n* : a garden plant related to the carrot that has finely divided leaves used as a seasoning or garnish

pars·nip \'pär-snəp\ *n* : a garden plant related to the carrot that has a long edible usu. whitish root; *also* : this root

par·son \'pärs-ᵊn\ *n* [ME *persone*, fr. OF, fr. ML *persona*, lit., person, fr. L] : MINISTER 2, PASTOR

par·son·age \'pärs-ᵊn-ij\ *n* : a house provided by a church for its pastor

¹part \'pärt\ *n* **1** : a division or portion of a whole **2** : the melody or score for a particular voice or instrument **3** : a spare piece for a machine **4** : DUTY, FUNCTION **5** : one of the sides in a dispute **6** : ROLE; *also* : an actor's lines in a play **7** *pl* : TALENTS, ABILITY **8** : the line where one's hair divides (as in combing)

²part *vb* **1** : to take leave of someone **2** : to divide or break into parts : SEPARATE **3** : to go away : DEPART; *also* : DIE **4** : to give up possession ⟨∼ed with her jewels⟩ **5** : APPORTION, SHARE

³part *abbr* **1** participial; participle **2** particular

par·take \pär-'tāk\ *vb* **-took** \-'tuk\; **-tak·en** \-'tā-kən\; **-tak·ing 1** : to have a share or part **2** : to take a portion (as of food) — **par·tak·er** *n*

par·terre \pär-'ter\ *n* [F, fr. MF, fr. *par terre* on the ground] **1** : an ornamental garden with paths between the flower beds **2** : the part of a theater floor behind the orchestra

par·the·no·gen·e·sis \ıpär-thə-nō-'je-nə-səs\ *n* [NL, fr. Gk *parthenos* virgin + L *genesis* genesis] : development of a new individual from an unfertilized egg, female sex cell — **par·the·no·ge·net·ic** \-jə-'ne-tik\ *adj*

par·tial \'pär-shəl\ *adj* **1** : not total or general : affecting a part only **2** : favoring one party over the other : BIASED **3** : markedly fond — used with *to* — **par·tial·i·ty** \ıpär-shē-'a-lə-tē\ *n* — **par·tial·ly** *adv*

par·tic·i·pate \pär-'ti-sə-ıpāt\ *vb* **-pat·ed; -pat·ing 1** : to take part in something ⟨∼ in a game⟩ **2** : SHARE — **par·tic·i·pant** \-pənt\ *adj or n* — **par·tic·i·pa·tion**

\-ˌti-sə-ˈpā-shən\ n — **par·tic·i·pa·tor** \-ˈti-sə-ˌpā-tər\ n — **par·tic·i·pa·to·ry** \-ˈti-sə-pə-ˌtōr-ē\ adj
par·ti·ci·ple \ˈpär-tə-ˌsi-pəl\ n : a word having the characteristics of both verb and adjective — **par·ti·cip·i·al** \ˌpär-tə-ˈsi-pē-əl\ adj
par·ti·cle \ˈpär-ti-kəl\ n 1 : a very small bit of matter 2 : a unit of speech (as an article, preposition, or conjunction) expressing some general aspect of meaning or some connective or limiting relation
par·ti·cle·board \-ˌbōrd\ n : a board made of very small pieces of wood bonded together
par·ti·col·or \ˌpär-tē-ˈkə-lər\ or **par·ti·col·ored** \-lərd\ adj : showing different colors or tints; esp : having one main color broken by patches of one or more other colors
[1]**par·tic·u·lar** \pər-ˈti-kyə-lər\ adj 1 : of or relating to a specific person or thing (the laws of a ~ state) 2 : DISTINCTIVE, SPECIAL (the ~ point of his talk) 3 : SEPARATE, INDIVIDUAL (each ~ hair) 4 : attentive to details : PRECISE 5 : hard to please : EXACTING — **par·tic·u·lar·i·ty** \-ˌti-kyə-ˈlar-ə-tē\ n — **par·tic·u·lar·ly** adv
[2]**particular** n : an individual fact or detail
par·tic·u·lar·ise Brit var of PARTICULARIZE
par·tic·u·lar·ize \pər-ˈti-kyə-lə-ˌrīz\ vb **-ized; -iz·ing** 1 : to state in detail : SPECIFY 2 : to go into details
par·tic·u·late \pər-ˈti-kyə-lət, pär-, -ˌlāt\ adj : relating to or existing as minute separate particles — **particulate** n
[1]**part·ing** n : a place or point of separation or divergence
[2]**parting** adj : given, taken, or performed at parting (a ~ kiss)
par·ti·san also **par·ti·zan** \ˈpär-tə-zən, -sən\ n 1 : one that takes the part of another : ADHERENT 2 : GUERRILLA — **partisan** adj — **par·ti·san·ship** n
par·tite \ˈpär-ˌtīt\ adj : divided into a usu. specified number of parts
par·ti·tion \pär-ˈti-shən\ n 1 : DIVISION 2 : something that divides or separates; esp : an interior dividing wall — **partition** vb
par·ti·tive \ˈpär-tə-tiv\ adj : of, relating to, or denoting a part
part·ly \ˈpärt-lē\ adv : in part : in some measure or degree
part·ner \ˈpärt-nər\ n 1 : ASSOCIATE, COLLEAGUE 2 : either of two persons who dance together 3 : one who plays on the same team with another 4 : SPOUSE 5 : one of two or more persons contractually associated as joint principals in a business — **part·ner·ship** n
part of speech : a class of words (as nouns or verbs) distinguished according to the kind of idea denoted and the function performed in a sentence
par·tridge \ˈpär-trij\ n, pl **partridge** or **par·tridg·es** : any of various stout-bodied game birds
part–song \ˈpärt-ˌsȯŋ\ n : a song with two or more voice parts
part–time \-ˈtīm\ adj or adv : involving or working less than a full or regular schedule — **part–tim·er** \-ˌtī-mər\ n
par·tu·ri·tion \ˌpär-tə-ˈri-shən, ˌpär-chə-, ˌpär-tyü-\ n : CHILDBIRTH
part·way \ˈpärt-ˈwā\ adv : to some extent : PARTLY
par·ty \ˈpär-tē\ n, pl **parties** 1 : a person or group taking one side of a question; esp : a group of persons organized for the purpose of directing the policies of a government 2 : a person or group concerned in an action or affair : PARTICIPANT 3 : a group of persons detailed for a common task 4 : a social gathering
par·ve·nu \ˈpär-və-ˌnü, -ˌnyü\ n [F, fr. pp. of parvenir to arrive, fr. L pervenire, fr. per through + venire to come] : one who has recently or suddenly risen to wealth or power but has not yet secured the social position associated with it
pas \ˈpä\ n, pl **pas** \same or ˈpäz\ : a dance step or combination of steps

pas·cal \pas-ˈkal\ n : a unit of pressure in the metric system equal to one newton per square meter
pas·chal \ˈpas-kəl\ adj : of, relating to, appropriate for, or used during Passover or Easter ceremonies
pa·sha \ˈpä-shə, ˈpa-; pə-ˈshä\ n : a man (as formerly a governor in Turkey) of high rank
[1]**pass** \ˈpas\ vb 1 : MOVE, PROCEED 2 : to go away; also : DIE 3 : to move past, beyond, or over 4 : to allow to elapse : SPEND 5 : to go or make way through 6 : to go or allow to go unchallenged 7 : to undergo transfer 8 : to render a legal judgment 9 : OCCUR 10 : to secure the approval of (as a legislature) 11 : to go or cause to go through an inspection, test, or course of study successfully 12 : to be regarded 13 : CIRCULATE 14 : VOID 2 15 : to transfer the ball or puck to another player 16 : to decline to bid or bet on one's hand in a card game 17 : to give a base on balls to — **pass·er** n
[2]**pass** n : a gap in a mountain range
[3]**pass** n 1 : the act or an instance of passing 2 : REALIZATION, ACCOMPLISHMENT 3 : a state of affairs 4 : a written authorization to leave, enter, or move about freely 5 : a transfer of a ball or puck from one player to another 6 : BASE ON BALLS 7 : EFFORT, TRY 8 : a sexually inviting gesture or approach
[4]**pass** abbr 1 passenger 2 passive
pass·able \ˈpa-sə-bəl\ adj 1 : capable of being passed or traveled on 2 : just good enough : TOLERABLE — **pass·ably** \-blē\ adv
pas·sage \ˈpa-sij\ n 1 : a means (as a road or corridor) of passing 2 : the action or process of passing 3 : a voyage esp. by sea or air 4 : a right or permission to pass 5 : ENACTMENT 6 : a usu. brief portion or section (as of a book)
pas·sage·way \-ˌwā\ n : a way that allows passage
pass·book \ˈpas-ˌbu̇k\ n : BANKBOOK
pas·sé \pa-ˈsā\ adj 1 : past one's prime 2 : not up-to-date : OUTMODED
pas·sel \ˈpa-səl\ n : a large number
pas·sen·ger \ˈpas-ᵊn-jər\ n : a traveler in a public or private conveyance
pass·er·by \ˈpa-sər-ˌbī\ n, pl **pass·ers·by** : one who passes by
pas·ser·ine \ˈpa-sə-ˌrīn\ adj : of or relating to the large order of birds comprising singing birds that perch
pas·sim \ˈpa-səm\ adv [L, fr. passus scattered, fr. pp. of pandere to spread] : here and there : THROUGHOUT
pass·ing n : the act of one that passes or causes to pass; esp : DEATH
pas·sion \ˈpa-shən\ n 1 often cap : the sufferings of Christ between the night of the Last Supper and his death 2 : strong feeling; also, pl : the emotions as distinguished from reason 3 : RAGE, ANGER 4 : LOVE; also : an object of affection or enthusiasm 5 : sexual desire — **pas·sion·ate** \ˈpa-shə-nət\ adj — **pas·sion·ate·ly** adv — **pas·sion·less** adj
pas·sion·flow·er \ˈpa-shən-ˌflau̇-ər\ n [fr. the fancied resemblance of parts of the flower to the instruments of Christ's crucifixion] : any of a genus of chiefly tropical woody climbing vines or erect herbs with showy flowers and pulpy often edible berries (**passion fruit**)
pas·sive \ˈpa-siv\ adj 1 : not active : acted upon 2 : asserting that the grammatical subject is subjected to or affected by the action represented by the verb (~ voice)3 : making use of the sun's heat usu. without the aid of mechanical devices 4 : SUBMISSIVE, PATIENT — **passive** n — **pas·sive·ly** adv — **pas·siv·i·ty** \pa-ˈsi-və-tē\ n
pass·key \ˈpas-ˌkē\ n : a key for opening two or more locks
pass out vb : to lose consciousness
Pass·over \ˈpas-ˌō-vər\ n [fr. the exemption of the Israelites from the slaughter of the firstborn in Egypt (Exod 12:23–27)] : a Jewish holiday celebrated in

March or April in commemoration of the Hebrews' liberation from slavery in Egypt

pass·port \'pas-ˌpōrt\ n : an official document issued by a country upon request to a citizen requesting protection during travel abroad

pass up vb : DECLINE, REJECT

pass·word \'pas-ˌwərd\ n 1 : a word or phrase that must be spoken by a person before being allowed to pass a guard 2 : a sequence of characters required for access to a computer system

¹**past** \'past\ adj 1 : AGO ⟨10 years ∼⟩ 2 : just gone or elapsed ⟨the ∼ month⟩ 3 : having existed or taken place in a period before the present : BYGONE 4 : of, relating to, or constituting a verb tense that expresses time gone by

²**past** prep or adv : BEYOND

³**past** n 1 : time gone by 2 : something that happened or was done in a former time 3 : the past tense; also : a verb form in it 4 : a secret past life

pas·ta \'päs-tə\ n [It] 1 : a paste in processed form (as spaghetti) or in the form of fresh dough (as ravioli) 2 : a dish of cooked pasta

¹**paste** \'pāst\ n 1 : DOUGH 2 : a smooth food product made by evaporation or grinding (tomato ∼) 3 : a shaped dough (as spaghetti or ravioli) 4 : a preparation (as of flour and water) for sticking things together 5 : a brilliant glass used for artificial gems

²**paste** vb past·ed; past·ing : to cause to adhere by paste : STICK

paste·board \'pāst-ˌbōrd\ n : PAPERBOARD

¹**pas·tel** \pas-'tel\ n 1 : a paste made of powdered pigment; also : a crayon of such paste 2 : a drawing in pastel 3 : a pale or light color

²**pastel** adj 1 : of or relating to a pastel 2 : pale in color

pas·tern \'pas-tərn\ n : the part of a horse's foot extending from the fetlock to the top of the hoof

pas·teur·iza·tion \ˌpas-chə-rə-'zā-shən, ˌpas-tə-\ n : partial sterilization of a substance (as milk) by heat or radiation — **pas·teur·ize** \'pas-chə-ˌrīz, 'pas-tə-\ vb — **pas·teur·iz·er** n

pas·tiche \pas-'tēsh\ n : a composition (as in literature or music) made up of selections from different works

pas·tille \pas-'tēl\ n : an aromatic or medicated lozenge

pas·time \'pas-ˌtīm\ n : DIVERSION; esp : something that serves to make time pass agreeably

pas·tor \'pas-tər\ n [ME pastour, fr. OF, fr. L pastor, herdsman, fr. pascere to feed, pasture, nurture] : a minister or priest serving a local church or parish — **pas·tor·ate** \-tə-rət\ n

¹**pas·to·ral** \'pas-tə-rəl\ adj 1 : of or relating to shepherds or to rural life 2 : of or relating to spiritual guidance esp. of a congregation 3 : of or relating to the pastor of a church

²**pastoral** n : a literary work dealing with shepherds or rural life

pas·to·rale \ˌpas-tə-'räl, -'ral\ n [It] : a musical composition having a pastoral theme

past participle n : a participle that typically expresses completed action, that is one of the principal parts of the verb, and that is used in the formation of perfect tenses in the active voice and of all tenses in the passive voice

pas·tra·mi \pə-'strä-mē\ n [Yiddish pastrame] : a highly seasoned smoked beef prepared esp. from shoulder cuts

pas·try \'pā-strē\ n, pl **pastries** : sweet baked goods made of dough or with a crust made of enriched dough

pas·tur·age \'pas-chə-rij\ n : PASTURE

¹**pas·ture** \'pas-chər\ n 1 : plants (as grass) for the feeding esp. of grazing livestock 2 : land or a plot of land used for grazing

²**pasture** vb pas·tured; pas·tur·ing 1 : GRAZE 2 : to use as pasture

pasty \'pā-stē\ adj past·i·er; -est : resembling paste; esp : pallid and unhealthy in appearance

¹**pat** \'pat\ n 1 : a light tap esp. with the hand or a flat instrument; also : the sound made by it 2 : something (as butter) shaped into a small flat usu. square individual portion

²**pat** adv : in a pat manner : PERFECTLY

³**pat** vb pat·ted; pat·ting 1 : to strike lightly with a flat instrument 2 : to flatten, smooth, or put into place or shape with a pat 3 : to tap gently or lovingly with the hand

⁴**pat** adj 1 : exactly suited to the occasion : APT 2 : memorized exactly 3 : UNYIELDING

PAT abbr point after touchdown

pa·ta·ca \pə-'tä-kə\ n — see MONEY table

¹**patch** \'pach\ n 1 : a piece used to cover a torn or worn place; also : one worn on a garment as an ornament or insignia 2 : a small area distinct from that about it 3 : a shield worn over the socket of an injured or missing eye

²**patch** vb 1 : to mend or cover with a patch 2 : to make of fragments 3 : to repair usu. in hasty fashion

patch test n : a test for allergic sensitivity made by applying to the unbroken skin small pads soaked with the allergen to be tested

patch·work \'pach-ˌwərk\ n : something made of pieces of different materials, shapes, or colors

patchy \'pa-chē\ adj patch·i·er; -est : marked by or consisting of patches; also : irregular in appearance or quality — **patch·i·ness** \-chē-nəs\ n

pate \'pāt\ n : HEAD; esp : the crown of the head

pâ·té also **pate** \pä-'tā\ n [F] 1 : a meat or fish pie or patty 2 : a spread of finely chopped or pureed seasoned meat

pa·tel·la \pə-'te-lə\ n, pl **-lae** \-'te-(ˌ)lē, -ˌlī\ or **-las** [L] : KNEECAP

pat·en \'pat-ᵊn\ n 1 : PLATE; esp : one of precious metal for the eucharistic bread 2 : a thin disk

¹**pa·tent** \1 & 4 are 'pat-ᵊnt, Brit also 'pāt-, 2 & 3 are 'pat-ᵊnt, 'pāt-\ adj 1 : open to public inspection — used chiefly in the phrase letters patent 2 : free from

obstruction **3** : EVIDENT, OBVIOUS **4** : protected by a patent **syn** manifest, distinct, apparent, palpable, plain, clear — **pat·ent·ly** adv

²pat·ent \'pat-ᵊnt, Brit also 'pāt-\ n **1** : an official document conferring a right or privilege **2** : a document securing to an inventor for a term of years exclusive right to his or her invention **3** : something patented

³pat·ent vb : to secure by patent

pat·en·tee \,pat-ᵊn-'tē, Brit also ,pāt-\ n : one to whom a grant is made or a privilege secured by patent

patent medicine \'pat-ᵊnt-\ n : a packaged nonprescription drug protected by a trademark; also : any proprietary drug

pa·ter·fa·mil·i·as \,pā-tər-fə-'mil-ē-əs\ n, pl **pa·tres·fa·mil·i·as** \,pā-,trēz-\ [L] : the father of a family : the male head of a household

pa·ter·nal \pə-'tərn-ᵊl\ adj **1** : FATHERLY **2** : related through or inherited or derived from a father — **pa·ter·nal·ly** adv

pa·ter·nal·ism \-,i-zəm\ n : a system under which an authority treats those under its control paternally (as by regulating their conduct and supplying their needs)

pa·ter·ni·ty \pə-'tər-nə-tē\ n **1** : FATHERHOOD **2** : descent from a father

¹path \'path, 'pàth\ n, pl **paths** \'pathz, 'paths, 'pàthz, 'pàths\ **1** : a trodden way **2** : ROUTE, COURSE — **path·less** adj

²path or **pathol** abbr pathology

path·break·ing \'path-,brā-kiŋ\ adj : TRAILBLAZING

pa·thet·ic \pə-'thet-ik\ adj : evoking tenderness, pity, or sorrow **syn** pitiful, piteous, pitiable, poor — **pa·thet·i·cal·ly** \-ti-k(ə-)lē\ adv

path·find·er \'path-,fīn-dər, 'pàth-\ n : one that discovers a way; esp : one that explores untraveled regions to mark out a new route

patho·gen \'pa-thə-jən\ n : a specific agent (as a bacterium) causing disease — **patho·gen·ic** \,pa-thə-'je-nik\ adj — **patho·ge·nic·i·ty** \-jə-'ni-sə-tē\ n

pa·thol·o·gy \pə-'thä-lə-jē\ n, pl **-gies 1** : the study of the essential nature of disease **2** : the abnormality of structure and function characteristic of a disease — **path·o·log·i·cal** \,pa-thə-'lä-ji-kəl\ adj — **pa·thol·o·gist** \pə-'thä-lə-jist\ n

pa·thos \'pā-,thäs, -,thōs\ n : an element in experience or artistic representation evoking pity or compassion

path·way \'path-,wā, 'pàth-\ n : PATH

pa·tience \'pā-shəns\ n **1** : the capacity, habit, or fact of being patient **2** chiefly Brit : SOLITAIRE 2

¹pa·tient \'pā-shənt\ adj **1** : bearing pain or trials without complaint **2** : showing self-control : CALM **3** : STEADFAST, PERSEVERING — **pa·tient·ly** adv

²patient n : one under medical care

pa·ti·na \pə-'tē-nə, pa-tē-,nä; 'pa-tē-\ n, pl **pa·ti·nas** \-nəz\ or **pa·ti·nae** \'pa-tə-,nē, -,nī\ **1** : a green film formed on copper and bronze by exposure to moist air **2** : a superficial covering or exterior

pa·tio \'pa-tē-,ō, 'pä-\ n, pl **pa·ti·os 1** : COURTYARD **2**

: an often paved area near a dwelling used esp. for outdoor dining

pa·tois \'pa-,twä\ n, pl **pa·tois** \-,twäz\ [F] **1** : a dialect other than the standard dialect; esp : uneducated or provincial speech **2** : JARGON 2

pa·tri·arch \'pā-trē-,ärk\ n **1** : a man revered as father or founder (as of a tribe) **2** : a venerable old man **3** : an ecclesiastical dignitary (as the bishop of an Eastern Orthodox see) — **pa·tri·ar·chal** \,pā-trē-'är-kəl\ adj — **pa·tri·arch·ate** \'pā-trē-,är-kət, -,kät\ n — **pa·tri·ar·chy** \-,är-kē\ n

pa·tri·cian \pə-'tri-shən\ n : a person of high birth : ARISTOCRAT — **patrician** adj

pat·ri·cide \'pa-trə-,sīd\ n **1** : one who murders his or her own father **2** : the murder of one's own father

pat·ri·mo·ny \'pa-trə-,mō-nē\ n : something (as an estate) inherited or derived esp. from one's father : HERITAGE — **pat·ri·mo·ni·al** \,pa-trə-'mō-nē-əl\ adj

pa·tri·ot \'pā-trē-ət, -,ät\ n [MF patriote compatriot, fr. LL patriota, fr. Gk patriōtēs, fr. patria lineage, fr. patr-, patēr father] : one who loves his or her country — **pa·tri·ot·ic** \,pā-trē-'ä-tik\ adj — **pa·tri·ot·i·cal·ly** \-ti-k(ə-)lē\ adv — **pa·tri·o·tism** \'pā-trē-ə-,ti-zəm\ n

pa·tris·tic \pə-'tris-tik\ adj : of or relating to the church fathers or their writings

¹pa·trol \pə-'trōl\ n **1** : the action of going the rounds (as of an area) for observation or the maintenance of security; also : a person or group performing such an action

²patrol vb **pa·trolled; pa·trol·ling** : to carry out a patrol

patrol car n : SQUAD CAR

pa·trol·man \pə-'trōl-mən\ n : a police officer assigned to a beat

patrol wagon n : PADDY WAGON

pa·tron \'pā-trən\ n [ME, fr. MF, fr. ML & L; ML patronus patron saint, patron of a benefice, pattern, fr. L, defender, fr. patr-, pater father] **1** : a person chosen or named as special protector **2** : a wealthy or influential supporter (∼ of poets); also : BENEFACTOR **3** : a regular client or customer

pa·tron·age \'pa-trə-nij, 'pā-\ n **1** : the support or influence of a patron **2** : the trade of customers **3** : control of appointment to government jobs

pa·tron·ess \'pā-trə-nəs\ n : a woman who is a patron

pa·tron·ise Brit var of PATRONIZE

pa·tron·ize \'pā-trə-,nīz, 'pa-\ vb **-ized; -iz·ing 1** : to be a customer of **2** : to treat condescendingly, haughtily, or coolly

pat·ro·nym·ic \,pa-trə-'ni-mik\ n : a name derived from the name of one's father or a paternal ancestor usu. by the addition of an affix

pa·troon \pə-'trün\ n : the proprietor of a manorial estate esp. in New York under Dutch rule

pat·sy \'pat-sē\ n, pl **pat·sies** : a person who is easily duped or victimized

¹pat·ter \'pa-tər\ vb : to talk glibly or mechanically **syn** chatter, prate, chat, prattle, babble

²patter n **1** : a specialized lingo **2** : extremely rapid talk (a comedian's ∼)

HELP!

YOU ARE PATHETIC

JIM DAVIS 9-14

³**patter** vb : to strike, pat, or tap rapidly
⁴**patter** n : a quick succession of taps or pats ⟨the ∼ of rain⟩
¹**pat·tern** \'pa-tərn\ n [ME patron, fr. MF, fr. ML patronus, fr. L, defender, fr. patr-, pater father] 1 : an ideal model for something 2 : something used as a model for making things ⟨a dressmaker's ∼⟩ 3 : SAMPLE 4 : an artistic design 5 : CONFIGURATION
²**pattern** vb : to form according to a pattern
pat·ty also **pat·tie** \'pa-tē\ n, pl **patties** 1 : a little pie 2 : a small flat cake esp. of chopped food
pau·ci·ty \'pò-sə-tē\ n : smallness of number or quantity
paunch \'pònch\ n : a usu. large belly : POTBELLY — **paunchy** adj
pau·per \'pò-pər\ n : a person without means of support except from charity — **pau·per·ism** \-pə-ri-zəm\ n — **pau·per·ize** \-pə-rīz\ vb
¹**pause** \'pòz\ n 1 : a temporary stop; also : a period of inaction 2 : a brief suspension of the voice 3 : a sign ⌒ or ⌣ above or below a musical note or rest to show it is to be prolonged 4 : a reason for pausing
²**pause** vb **paused; paus·ing** : to stop, rest, or linger for a time
pave \'pāv\ vb **paved; pav·ing** : to cover (as a road) with hard material in order to smooth or firm the surface
pave·ment \'pāv-mənt\ n 1 : a paved surface 2 : the material with which something is paved
pa·vil·ion \pə-'vil-yən\ n [ME pavilon, fr. OF paveillon, fr. L papilion-, papilio butterfly] 1 : a large tent 2 : a light structure (as in a park) used for entertainment or shelter
pav·ing \'pā-viŋ\ n : PAVEMENT
¹**paw** \'pò\ n : the foot of a quadruped (as a dog or lion) having claws
²**paw** vb 1 : to touch or strike with a paw; also : to scrape with a hoof 2 : to feel or handle clumsily or rudely 3 : to flail about or grab with the hands
pawl \'pòl\ n : a pivoted tongue or sliding bolt designed to fall into notches on another machine part to permit motion in one direction only
¹**pawn** \'pòn\ n [ME pown, fr. MF poon, fr. ML pedon-, pedo foot soldier, fr. LL, one with broad feet, fr. L ped-, pes foot] : a chess piece of the least value
²**pawn** n 1 : something deposited as security for a loan; also : HOSTAGE 2 : the state of being pledged
³**pawn** vb : to deposit as a pledge
pawn·bro·ker \'pòn-brō-kər\ n : one who lends money on goods pledged
Paw·nee \pò-'nē\ n, pl **Pawnee** or **Pawnees** : a member of an American Indian people orig. of Kansas and Nebraska
pawn·shop \'pòn-shäp\ n : a pawnbroker's place of business
paw·paw var of PAPAW
¹**pay** \'pā\ vb **paid** \'pād\ also in sense 7 **payed; pay·ing** [ME, fr. OF paier, fr. L pacare to pacify, fr. pac-, pax peace] 1 : to make due return to for goods or services 2 : to discharge indebtedness for : SETTLE ⟨∼ a bill⟩ 3 : to give in forfeit ⟨∼ the penalty⟩ 4 : REQUITE 5 : to give, offer, or make freely or as fitting ⟨∼ attention⟩ 6 : to be profitable to : RETURN 7 : to make slack and allow to run out ⟨∼ out a rope⟩ — **pay·able** adj — **pay·ee** \pā-'ē\ n — **pay·er** n
²**pay** n 1 : something paid; esp : WAGES 2 : the status of being paid by an employer : EMPLOY
³**pay** adj 1 : containing something valuable (as gold) ⟨∼ dirt⟩ 2 : equipped to receive a fee for use ⟨∼ telephone⟩ 3 : requiring payment
pay·check \'pā-chek\ n 1 : a check in payment of wages or salary 2 : WAGES, SALARY
pay·load \-lōd\ n : the load carried by a vehicle in addition to what is necessary for its operation; also : the weight of such a load

pay·mas·ter \-mas-tər\ n : one who distributes the payroll
pay·ment \'pā-mənt\ n 1 : the act of paying 2 : something paid
pay·off \-ȯf\ n 1 : PROFIT, REWARD; also : RETRIBUTION 2 : the climax of an incident or enterprise ⟨the ∼ of a story⟩
pay–per–view n : a cable television service by which customers can order access to a single airing of a TV feature
pay·roll \-rōl\ n : a list of persons entitled to receive pay; also : the money to pay those on such a list
payt abbr payment
pay up vb : to pay what is due; also : to pay in full
Pb symbol [L plumbum] lead
PBS abbr Public Broadcasting Service
PBX \pē-(.)bē-'eks\ n [private branch exchange] : a private telephone switchboard
¹**PC** \pē-'sē\ n, pl **PCs** or **PC's** [personal computer] : MICROCOMPUTER
²**PC** abbr 1 Peace Corps 2 percent; percentage 3 politically correct 4 postcard 5 [L post cibum] after meals 6 professional corporation
PCB \pē-sē-'bē\ n : POLYCHLORINATED BIPHENYL
PCP \pē-sē-'pē\ n : PHENCYCLIDINE
pct abbr percent; percentage
pd abbr paid
Pd symbol palladium
PD abbr 1 per diem 2 police department 3 potential difference
PDQ \pē-dē-'kyü\ adv, often not cap [abbr. of pretty damned quick] : IMMEDIATELY
PDT abbr Pacific daylight (saving) time
PE abbr 1 physical education 2 printer's error 3 professional engineer
pea \'pē\ n, pl **peas** also **pease** \'pēz\ 1 : the round edible protein-rich seed borne in the pod of a widely grown leguminous vine; also : this vine 2 : any of various plants resembling or related to the pea
peace \'pēs\ n 1 : a state of calm and quiet; esp : public security under law 2 : freedom from disturbing thoughts or emotions 3 : a state of concord (as between persons or governments); also : an agreement to end hostilities — **peace·able** \'pē-sə-bəl\ adj — **peace·ably** \-blē\ adv — **peace·ful** adj — **peace·ful·ly** adv
peace·keep·ing \'pēs-kē-piŋ\ n : the preserving of peace; esp : international enforcement and supervision of a truce — **peace·keep·er** n
peace·mak·er \-mā-kər\ n : one who settles an argument or stops a fight
peace·time \-tīm\ n : a time when a nation is not at war
peach \'pēch\ n [ME peche, fr. MF, fr. LL persica, fr. L (malum) Persicum, lit., Persian fruit] : a sweet juicy fruit of a low tree with pink blossoms related to the cherry and plums; also : this tree
pea·cock \'pē-käk\ n [ME pecok, fr. pe- (fr. OE pēa peafowl, fr. L pavo peacock) + cok cock] : the male peafowl that can spread its long tail feathers to make a colorful display
pea·fowl \-faùl\ n : either of two large domesticated Asian pheasants
pea·hen \-hen\ n : the female peafowl
¹**peak** \'pēk\ n 1 : a pointed or projecting part 2 : the top of a hill or mountain; also : MOUNTAIN 3 : the front projecting part of a cap 4 : the narrow part of a ship's bow or stern 5 : the highest level or greatest degree — **peak** adj
²**peak** vb : to bring to or reach a maximum
peaked \'pē-kəd\ adj : THIN, SICKLY
¹**peal** \'pēl\ n 1 : the loud ringing of bells 2 : a set of tuned bells 3 : a loud sound or succession of sounds
²**peal** vb : to give out peals : RESOUND
pea·nut \'pē-(.)nət\ n 1 : an annual herb related to the pea but having pods that ripen underground; also

peafowl: *A* female, *B* male

: this pod or one of the edible seeds it bears **2** *pl* : a very small amount

pear \\'par\ *n* : the fleshy fruit of a tree related to the apple; *also* : this tree

pearl \\'pərl\ *n* **1** : a small hard often lustrous body formed within the shell of some mollusks and used as a gem **2** : one that is choice or precious ⟨∼s of wisdom⟩ **3** : a slightly bluish medium gray color — **pearly** \\'pər-lē\ *adj*

peas·ant \\'pez-ᵊnt\ *n* **1** : any of a class of small landowners or laborers tilling the soil **2** : a usu. uneducated person of low social status — **peas·ant·ry** \-ᵊn-trē\ *n*

pea·shoot·er \\'pē-ₐshü-tər\ *n* : a toy blowgun for shooting peas

peat \\'pēt\ *n* : a dark substance formed by partial decay of plants (as mosses) in water — **peaty** *adj*

peat moss *n* : SPHAGNUM

¹peb·ble \\'pe-bəl\ *n* : a small usu. round stone — **peb·bly** \-b(ə-)lē\ *adj*

²pebble *vb* **peb·bled; peb·bling** : to produce a rough surface texture in ⟨∼ leather⟩

pec \\'pek\ *n* : PECTORAL MUSCLE

pe·can \pi-'kän, -'kan; 'pē-ₐkan\ *n* : the smooth-shelled edible nut of a large American hickory; *also* : this tree

pec·ca·dil·lo \ₐpe-kə-'di-lō\ *n*, *pl* **-loes** *or* **-los** : a slight offense

pec·ca·ry \\'pe-kə-rē\ *n*, *pl* **-ries** : any of several American chiefly tropical mammals resembling but smaller than the related pigs

peccary

pec·ca·vi \pe-'kä-ₐvē\ *n* [L, I have sinned, fr. *peccare* to sin] : an acknowledgment of sin

¹peck \\'pek\ *n* — see WEIGHT table

²peck *vb* **1** : to strike or pierce with or as if with the bill **2** : to make (as a hole) by pecking **3** : to pick up with or as if with the bill

³peck *n* **1** : an impression made by pecking **2** : a quick sharp stroke

pecking order *also* **peck order** *n* : a basic pattern of social organization within a flock of poultry in which

each bird pecks another lower in the scale without being pecked in return and submits to pecking by one of higher rank; *also* : a social hierarchy

pec·tin \\'pek-tən\ *n* : any of various water-soluble plant substances that cause fruit jellies to set — **pec·tic** \-tik\ *adj*

pec·to·ral \\'pek-tə-rəl\ *adj* : of or relating to the breast or chest

pectoral muscle *n* : either of two muscles on each side of the body which connect the front walls of the chest with the bones of the upper arm and shoulder

pe·cu·liar \pi-'kyül-yər\ *adj* [ME *peculier*, fr. L *peculiaris* of private property, special, fr. *peculium* private property, fr. *pecus* cattle] **1** : belonging exclusively to one person or group **2** : CHARACTERISTIC, DISTINCTIVE **3** : QUEER, ODD **syn** idiosyncratic, eccentric, singular, strange, weird — **pe·cu·liar·i·ty** \-ₐkyül-'yar-ə-tē, -ₐkyü-lē-'ar-\ *n* — **pe·cu·liar·ly** *adv*

pe·cu·ni·ary \pi-'kyü-nē-ₐer-ē\ *adj* : of or relating to money : MONETARY

ped·a·gogue *also* **ped·a·gog** \\'pe-də-ₐgäg\ *n* : TEACHER, SCHOOLMASTER

ped·a·go·gy \\'pe-də-ₐgō-jē, -ₐgä-\ *n* : the art or profession of teaching; *esp* : EDUCATION **2** — **ped·a·gog·ic** \ₐpe-də-'gä-jik, -'gō-\ *or* **ped·a·gog·i·cal** \-ji-kəl\ *adj*

¹ped·al \\'ped-ᵊl\ *n* : a lever worked by the foot

²pedal *adj* : of or relating to the foot

³ped·al \\'ped-ᵊl\ *vb* **ped·aled** *also* **ped·alled; ped·al·ing** *also* **ped·al·ling 1** : to use or work a pedal (as of a piano or bicycle) **2** : to ride a bicycle

ped·ant \\'ped-ᵊnt\ *n* **1** : a person who makes a show of knowledge **2** : a formal uninspired teacher — **pe·dan·tic** \pi-'dan-tik\ *adj* — **ped·ant·ry** \\'ped-ᵊn-trē\ *n*

ped·dle \\'ped-ᵊl\ *vb* **ped·dled; ped·dling** : to sell or offer for sale from place to place — **ped·dler** *also* **ped·lar** \\'ped-lər\ *n*

ped·er·ast \\'pe-də-ₐrast\ *n* [Gk *paiderastēs*, lit., lover of boys] : one that practices anal intercourse esp. with a boy — **ped·er·as·ty** \\'pe-də-ₐras-tē\ *n*

ped·es·tal \\'pe-dəst-ᵊl\ *n* **1** : the support or foot of something (as a column, statue, or vase) that is upright **2** : a position of high regard

¹pe·des·tri·an \pə-'des-trē-ən\ *adj* **1** : ORDINARY **2** : going on foot

²pedestrian *n* : WALKER

pe·di·at·rics \ₐpē-dē-'a-triks\ *n* : a branch of medicine dealing with the development, care, and diseases of children — **pe·di·at·ric** \-trik\ *adj* — **pe·di·a·tri·cian** \ₐpē-dē-ə-'tri-shən\ *n*

pedi·cab \\'pe-di-ₐkab\ *n* : a pedal-driven tricycle with seats for a driver and two passengers

ped·i·cure \\'pe-di-ₐkyúr\ *n* : care of the feet, toes, and nails; *also* : a single treatment of these parts — **ped·i·cur·ist** \-ₐkyúr-ist\ *n*

ped·i·gree \\'pe-də-ₐgrē\ *n* [ME *pedegru*, fr. MF *pie de grue* crane's foot; fr. the shape made by the lines of a genealogical chart] **1** : a record of a line of ancestors **2** : an ancestral line — **ped·i·greed** \-ₐgrēd\ *adj*

ped·i·ment \\'pe-də-mənt\ *n* : a low triangular gablelike decoration (as over a door or window) on a building

pe·dom·e·ter \pi-'dä-mə-tər\ *n* : an instrument that measures the distance one walks

pe·dun·cle \\'pē-ₐdəŋ-kəl\ *n* : a narrow supporting stalk

peek \\'pēk\ *vb* **1** : to look furtively **2** : to peer from a place of concealment **3** : GLANCE — **peek** *n*

¹peel \\'pēl\ *vb* [ME *pelen*, fr. MF *peler*, fr. L *pilare* to remove the hair from, fr. *pilus* hair] **1** : to strip the skin, bark, or rind from **2** : to strip off (as a coat); *also* : to come off **3** : to lose the skin, bark, or rind

²peel *n* : a skin or rind esp. of a fruit

peel·ing \\'pē-liŋ\ *n* : a peeled-off piece or strip (as of skin or rind)

peen \\'pēn\ *n* : the usu. hemispherical or wedge-shaped end of the head of a hammer opposite the face

¹**peep** \'pēp\ *vb* : to utter a feeble shrill sound or the slightest sound

²**peep** *n* : a feeble shrill sound

³**peep** *vb* **1** : to look slyly esp. through an aperture : PEEK **2** : to begin to emerge — **peep·er** *n*

⁴**peep** *n* **1** : a first faint appearance **2** : a brief or furtive look

peep·hole \'pēp-ˌhōl\ *n* : a hole to peep through

¹**peer** \'pir\ *n* **1** : one of equal standing with another : EQUAL **2** : NOBLE — **peer·age** \-ij\ *n*

²**peer** *vb* **1** : to look intently or curiously **2** : to come slightly into view

peer·ess \'pir-əs\ *n* : a woman who is a peer

peer·less \'pir-ləs\ *adj* : having no equal : MATCHLESS **syn** supreme, unequalled, unparalleled, incomparable

¹**peeve** \'pēv\ *vb* **peeved; peev·ing** : to make resentful : ANNOY

²**peeve** *n* **1** : a feeling or mood of resentment **2** : a particular grievance

pee·vish \'pē-vish\ *adj* : querulous in temperament : FRETFUL **syn** irritable, petulant, huffy — **pee·vish·ly** *adv* — **pee·vish·ness** *n*

pee·wee \'pē-(ˌ)wē\ *n* : one that is diminutive or tiny

¹**peg** \'peg\ *n* **1** : a small pointed piece (as of wood) used to pin down or fasten things or to fit into holes **2** : a projecting piece used as a support or boundary marker **3** : SUPPORT, PRETEXT **4** : STEP, DEGREE **5** : THROW

²**peg** *vb* **pegged; peg·ging 1** : to put a peg into : fasten, pin down, or attach with or as if with pegs **2** : to work hard and steadily : PLUG **3** : HUSTLE **4** : to mark by pegs **5** : to hold (as prices) at a set level or rate **6** : IDENTIFY **7** : THROW

PEI *abbr* Prince Edward Island

pei·gnoir \pān-'wär, pen-\ *n* [F, lit., garment worn while combing the hair, fr. MF, fr. *peigner* to comb the hair, fr. L *pectinare*, fr. *pectin-, pecten* comb] : NEGLIGEE

¹**pe·jo·ra·tive** \pi-'jòr-ə-tiv\ *n* : a pejorative word or phrase

²**pejorative** *adj* : having negative connotations : DISPARAGING — **pe·jo·ra·tive·ly** *adv*

peke \'pēk\ *n, often cap* : PEKINGESE

Pe·king·ese *or* **Pe·kin·ese** \ˌpē-kə-'nēz, -'nēs; -kiŋ-'ēz, -'ēs\ *n, pl* **Pekingese** *or* **Pekinese** : any of a breed of Chinese origin of small short-legged long-haired dogs

pe·koe \'pē-(ˌ)kō\ *n* : a black tea made from young tea leaves

pel·age \'pel-ij\ *n* : the hairy covering of a mammal

pe·lag·ic \pə-'la-jik\ *adj* : OCEANIC

pelf \'pelf\ *n* : MONEY, RICHES

pel·i·can \'pe-li-kən\ *n* : any of a genus of large web-footed birds having a pouched lower bill used to scoop in fish

pel·la·gra \pə-'la-grə, -'lä-\ *n* : a disease caused by a diet with too little nicotinic acid and protein and marked by a skin rash, disease of the digestive system, and nervous symptoms

pel·let \'pe-lət\ *n* **1** : a little ball (as of medicine) **2** : BULLET — **pel·let·al** \-lə-təl\ *adj* — **pel·let·ize** \-ˌtīz\ *vb*

pell–mell \ˌpel-'mel\ *adv* **1** : in mingled confusion **2** : HEADLONG

pel·lu·cid \pə-'lü-səd\ *adj* : extremely clear : LIMPID, TRANSPARENT **syn** translucent, lucid, lucent

¹**pelt** \'pelt\ *n* : a skin esp. of a fur-bearing animal

²**pelt** *vb* : to strike with a succession of blows or missiles

pel·vis \'pel-vəs\ *n, pl* **pel·vis·es** \-və-səz\ *or* **pel·ves** \-ˌvēz\ : a basin-shaped part of the vertebrate skeleton consisting of the large bone of each hip and the nearby bones of the spine — **pel·vic** \-vik\ *adj*

pem·mi·can *also* **pem·i·can** \'pe-mi-kən\ *n* : dried meat pounded fine and mixed with melted fat

¹**pen** \'pen\ *vb* **penned; pen·ning** : to shut in or as if in a pen

²**pen** *n* **1** : a small enclosure for animals **2** : a small place of confinement or storage

³**pen** *n* **1** : an implement for writing or drawing with ink or a similar fluid **2** : a writing instrument regarded as a means of expression

⁴**pen** *vb* **penned; pen·ning** : WRITE

⁵**pen** *n* : PENITENTIARY

⁶**pen** *abbr* peninsula

PEN *abbr* International Association of Poets, Playwrights, Editors, Essayists and Novelists

pe·nal \'pēn-ᵊl\ *adj* : of or relating to punishment

pe·nal·ise *Brit var of* PENALIZE

pe·nal·ize \'pēn-ᵊl-ˌīz, 'pen-\ *vb* **-ized; -iz·ing** : to put a penalty on

pen·al·ty \'pen-ᵊl-tē\ *n, pl* **-ties 1** : punishment for crime or offense **2** : something forfeited when a person fails to do something agreed to **3** : disadvantage, loss, or hardship due to some action

pen·ance \'pe-nəns\ *n* **1** : an act performed to show sorrow or repentance for sin **2** : a sacrament (as in the Roman Catholic Church) consisting of confession, absolution, and a penance directed by the confessor

pence \'pens\ *pl of* PENNY

pen·chant \'pen-chənt\ *n* [F, fr. prp. of *pencher* to incline, fr. (assumed) VL *pendicare*, fr. L *pendere* to weigh] : a strong inclination : LIKING **syn** leaning, propensity, predilection, predisposition

¹**pen·cil** \'pen-səl\ *n* : a writing or drawing tool consisting of or containing a slender cylinder of a solid marking substance

²**pencil** *vb* **-ciled** *or* **-cilled; -cil·ing** *or* **-cil·ling** : to draw or write with a pencil

pen·dant *also* **pen·dent** \'pen-dənt\ *n* : a hanging ornament (as an earring)

pen·dent *or* **pen·dant** \'pen-dənt\ *adj* : SUSPENDED, OVERHANGING

pend·ing \'pen-diŋ\ *prep* **1** : DURING **2** : while awaiting

pending *adj* **1** : not yet decided **2** : IMMINENT

pen·du·lous \'pen-jə-ləs, -də-\ *adj* : hanging loosely : DROOPING

pen·du·lum \-ləm\ *n* : a body that swings freely from a fixed point

pe·ne·plain *also* **pe·ne·plane** \'pē-ni-ˌplān\ *n* : a large almost flat land surface shaped by erosion

pen·e·trate \'pe-nə-ˌtrāt\ *vb* **-trat·ed; -trat·ing 1** : to enter into : PIERCE **2** : PERMEATE **3** : to see into : UNDERSTAND **4** : to affect deeply — **pen·e·tra·ble** \-trə-bəl\ *adj* — **pen·e·tra·tion** \ˌpe-nə-'trā-shən\ *n* — **pen·e·tra·tive** \'pe-nə-ˌtrā-tiv\ *adj*

pen·e·trat·ing *adj* **1** : having the power of entering, piercing, or pervading ⟨a ~ shriek⟩ ⟨a ~ odor⟩ **2** : ACUTE, DISCERNING ⟨a ~ look⟩

pen·guin \'pen-gwən, 'peŋ-\ *n* : any of various erect short-legged flightless seabirds of the southern hemisphere

pen·i·cil·lin \ˌpe-nə-'si-lən\ *n* : any of several antibiotics produced by molds or synthetically and used against various bacteria

pen·in·su·la \pə-'nin-sə-lə\ *n* [L *paeninsula*, fr. *paene* almost + *insula* island] : a long narrow portion of land extending out into the water — **pen·in·su·lar** \-lər\ *adj*

pe·nis \'pē-nəs\ *n, pl* **pe·nes** \-ˌnēz\ *or* **pe·nis·es** : a male organ of copulation that in the human male also functions as the channel by which urine leaves the body

¹**pen·i·tent** \'pe-nə-tənt\ *adj* : feeling sorrow for sins or offenses : REPENTANT — **pen·i·tence** \-təns\ *n* — **pen·i·ten·tial** \ˌpe-nə-'ten-chəl\ *adj*

²**penitent** *n* : a penitent person

¹**pen·i·ten·tia·ry** \ˌpe-nə-'ten-chə-rē\ *n, pl* **-ries** : a state or federal prison

²**penitentiary** *adj* : of, relating to, or incurring confinement in a penitentiary

pen·knife \'pen-ˌnīf\ *n* : a small pocketknife

pen·light *or* **pen·lite** \-ˌlīt\ *n* : a small flashlight resembling a fountain pen in size or shape

pen·man \'pen-mən\ *n* **1** : COPYIST **2** : one skilled in penmanship **3** : AUTHOR

pen·man·ship \-ˌship\ *n* : the art or practice of writing with the pen

Penn *or* **Penna** *abbr* Pennsylvania

pen name *n* : an author's pseudonym

pen·nant \'pe-nənt\ *n* **1** : a tapering flag used esp. for signaling **2** : a flag symbolic of championship

pen·ni \'pe-nē\ *n, pl* **pen·nia** \-nē-ə\ *or* **pen·nis** \-nēz\ — see *markka* at MONEY table

pen·non \'pe-nən\ *n* **1** : a long narrow ribbonlike flag borne on a lance **2** : WING

Penn·syl·va·nian \ˌpen-səl-'vā-nyən\ *adj* : of, relating to, or being the period of the Paleozoic era between the Mississippian and the Permian — **Pennsylvanian** *n*

pen·ny \'pe-nē\ *n, pl* **pennies** \-nēz\ *or* **pence** \'pens\ **1** : a British monetary unit formerly equal to ¹/₁₂ shilling but now equal to ¹/₁₀₀ pound; *also* : a coin of this value — see *pound* at MONEY table **2** *pl* **pennies** : a cent of the U.S. or Canada — **pen·ni·less** \'pe-ni-ləs\ *adj*

pen·ny-pinch·ing \'pe-nē-ˌpin-chiŋ\ *n* : PARSIMONY — **pen·ny-pinch·er** *n* — **penny-pinching** *adj*

pen·ny·weight \-ˌwāt\ *n* — see WEIGHT table

pen·ny-wise \-ˌwīz\ *adj* : wise or prudent only in small matters

pe·nol·o·gy \pi-'nä-lə-jē\ *n* : a branch of criminology dealing with prisons and the treatment of offenders

¹pen·sion \'pen-chən\ *n* : a fixed sum paid regularly esp. to a person retired from service

²pension *vb* : to pay a pension to — **pen·sion·er** *n*

pen·sive \'pen-siv\ *adj* : musingly, dreamily, or sadly thoughtful **syn** reflective, speculative, contemplative, meditative — **pen·sive·ly** *adv*

pen·stock \'pen-ˌstäk\ *n* **1** : a sluice or gate for regulating a flow **2** : a pipe for carrying water

pent \'pent\ *adj* : shut up : CONFINED

pen·ta·gon \'pen-tə-ˌgän\ *n* : a polygon of five angles and five sides — **pen·tag·o·nal** \pen-'ta-gən-ᵊl\ *adj*

pen·tam·e·ter \pen-'ta-mə-tər\ *n* : a line of verse containing five metrical feet

Pen·te·cost \'pen-ti-ˌkȯst\ *n* : the 7th Sunday after Easter observed as a church festival commemorating the descent of the Holy Spirit on the apostles — **Pen·te·cos·tal** \ˌpen-ti-'käst-ᵊl\ *adj*

Pentecostal *n* : a member of a Christian religious body that stresses expressive worship, evangelism, and spiritual gifts — **Pen·te·cos·tal·ism** \ˌpen-ti-'käst-ᵊl-ˌi-zəm\ *n*

---

pent·house \'pent-ˌhaůs\ *n* [alter. of ME *pentis*, fr. MF *appentiz*, fr. *apent*, pp. of *apendre* to attach, hang against] **1** : a shed or sloping roof attached to a wall or building **2** : an apartment built on the roof of a building

pen·ul·ti·mate \pi-'nəl-tə-mət\ *adj* : next to the last ⟨∼ syllable⟩

pen·um·bra \pə-'nəm-brə\ *n, pl* **-brae** \-(ˌ)brē\ *or* **-bras** : the partial shadow surrounding a complete shadow (as in an eclipse)

pe·nu·ri·ous \pə-'nur-ē-əs, -'nyur-\ *adj* **1** : marked by penury **2** : MISERLY **syn** stingy, close, tightfisted, parsimonious

pen·u·ry \'pe-nyə-rē\ *n* **1** : extreme poverty **2** : extreme frugality

pe·on \'pē-ˌän, -ən\ *n, pl* **peons** *or* **pe·o·nes** \pā-'ō-nēz\ **1** : a member of the landless laboring class in Spanish America **2** : one bound to service for payment of a debt — **pe·on·age** \-ə-nij\ *n*

pe·o·ny \'pē-ə-nē\ *n, pl* **-nies** : any of a genus of chiefly Eurasian plants with large often double red, pink, or white flowers; *also* : the flower

¹peo·ple \'pē-pəl\ *n, pl* **people** [ME *peple*, fr. OF *peuple*, fr. L *populus*] **1** *pl* : human beings making up a group or linked by a common characteristic or interest **2** *pl* : human beings — often used in compounds instead of *persons* ⟨sales*people*⟩ **3** *pl* : the mass of persons in a community : POPULACE; *also* : ELECTORATE ⟨the ∼'s choice⟩ **4** *pl* **peoples** : a body of persons (as a tribe, nation, or race) united by a common culture, sense of kinship, or political organization

²people *vb* **peo·pled; peo·pling** : to supply or fill with or as if with people

¹pep \'pep\ *n* : brisk energy or initiative — **pep·py** *adj*

²pep *vb* **pepped; pep·ping** : to put pep into : STIMULATE

¹pep·per \'pe-pər\ *n* **1** : either of two pungent condiments from the berry (**pep·per·corn** \-ˌkȯrn\) of an East Indian climbing plant; *also* : this plant **2** : a plant related to the tomato and widely grown for its hot or mild sweet fruit; *also* : this fruit

²pepper *vb* **pep·pered; pep·per·ing** **1** : to sprinkle or season with or as if with pepper **2** : to shower with missiles or rapid blows

pep·per·mint \-ˌmint, -mənt\ *n* : a pungent aromatic mint; *also* : candy flavored with its oil

pep·per·o·ni \ˌpe-pə-'rō-nē\ *n* : a highly seasoned beef and pork sausage

pep·pery \'pe-pə-rē\ *adj* **1** : having the qualities of pepper : PUNGENT, HOT **2** : having a hot temper **3** : FIERY

pep·sin \'pep-sən\ *n* : an enzyme of the stomach that promotes digestion by breaking down proteins; *also* : a preparation of this used medicinally

pep·tic \'pep-tik\ *adj* **1** : relating to or promoting digestion **2** : caused by digestive juices ⟨a ∼ ulcer⟩

Pe·quot \'pē-ˌkwät\ *n* : a member of an American Indian people of eastern Connecticut

¹per \'pər\ *prep* **1** : by means of **2** : to or for each **3** : ACCORDING TO

²per *adv* : for each : APIECE

³per *abbr* **1** period **2** person

¹per·ad·ven·ture \'pər-əd-ˌven-chər\ *adv, archaic* : PERHAPS

²peradventure *n* **1** : DOUBT **2** : CHANCE **4**

per·am·bu·late \pə-'ram-byə-ˌlāt\ *vb* **-lat·ed; -lat·ing** : to travel over esp. on foot — **per·am·bu·la·tion** \-ˌram-byə-'lā-shən\ *n* per·am·bu·la·tor \pə-'ram-byə-₁lā-tər\ n, chiefly Brit : a baby carriage

per an·num \(₁)pər-'a-nəm\ adv [ML] : in or for each year : ANNUALLY

per·cale \(₁)pər-'kāl, 'pər-₁; (₁)pər-'kal\ n : a fine woven cotton cloth

per cap·i·ta \(₁)pər-'ka-pə-tə\ adv or adj [ML, by heads] : by or for each person

per·ceive \pər-'sēv\ vb per·ceived; per·ceiv·ing 1 : to attain awareness : REALIZE 2 : to become aware of through the senses — per·ceiv·able adj

¹per·cent \pər-'sent\ adv [per + L centum hundred] : in each hundred

²percent n, pl percent or percents 1 : one part in a hundred : HUNDREDTH 2 : PERCENTAGE

per·cent·age \pər-'sen-tij\ n 1 : a part of a whole expressed in hundredths 2 : the result obtained by multiplying a number by a percent 3 : ADVANTAGE, PROFIT 4 : PROBABILITY; also : favorable odds

per·cen·tile \pər-'sen-₁tīl\ n : a value on a scale of one hundred indicating the standing of a score or grade in terms of the percentage of scores or grades falling with or below it

per·cept \'pər-₁sept\ n : an impression of an object obtained by use of the senses

per·cep·ti·ble \pər-'sep-tə-bəl\ adj : capable of being perceived — per·cep·ti·bly \-blē\ adv

per·cep·tion \pər-'sep-shən\ n 1 : an act or result of perceiving 2 : awareness of one's environment through physical sensation 3 : ability to understand : INSIGHT, COMPREHENSION syn penetration, discernment, discrimination

per·cep·tive \pər-'sep-tiv\ adj : capable of or exhibiting keen perception : OBSERVANT — per·cep·tive·ly adv

per·cep·tu·al \pər-'sep-chə-wəl\ adj : of, relating to, or involving sensory stimulus as opposed to abstract concept — per·cep·tu·al·ly adv

¹perch \'pərch\ n 1 : a roost for a bird 2 : a high station or vantage point

²perch vb : ROOST

³perch n, pl perch or perch·es : either of two small freshwater bony fishes used for food; also : any of various fishes resembling or related to these

per·chance \pər-'chans\ adv : PERHAPS

per·cip·i·ent \pər-'si-pē-ənt\ adj : capable of or characterized by perception — per·cip·i·ence \-əns\ n

per·co·late \'pər-kə-₁lāt\ vb -lat·ed; -lat·ing 1 : to trickle or filter through a permeable substance 2 : to filter hot water through to extract the essence ⟨∼ coffee⟩ — per·co·la·tor \-₁lā-tər\ n

per con·tra \(₁)pər-'kän-trə\ adv [It, by the opposite side (of the ledger)] 1 : on the contrary 2 : by way of contrast

per·cus·sion \pər-'kə-shən\ n 1 : a sharp blow : IMPACT; esp : a blow upon a cap (percussion cap) designed to explode the charge in a firearm 2 : the beating or striking of a musical instrument; also : instruments sounded by striking, shaking, or scraping

per di·em \pər-'dē-əm, -'dī-\ adv [ML] : by the day — per diem adj or n

per·di·tion \pər-'di-shən\ n 1 : eternal damnation 2 : HELL

per·du·ra·ble \(₁)pər-'dùr-ə-bəl, -'dyùr-\ adj : very durable — per·du·ra·bil·i·ty \-₁dùr-ə-'bi-lə-tē, -₁dyùr-\ n

per·e·gri·na·tion \₁per-ə-grə-'nā-shən\ n : a traveling about esp. on foot

per·e·grine \'per-ə-grən, -₁grēn\ n : a swift nearly cosmopolitan falcon that often nests in cities and is used in falconry

pe·remp·to·ry \pə-'remp-tə-rē\ adj 1 : barring a right of action or delay 2 : expressive of urgency or command : IMPERATIVE 3 : marked by arrogant self-

assurance syn imperious, masterful, domineering, magisterial — pe·remp·to·ri·ly \-tə-rə-lē\ adv

¹pe·ren·ni·al \pə-'re-nē-əl\ adj 1 : present at all seasons of the year ⟨∼ streams⟩ 2 : continuing to live from year to year ⟨∼ plants⟩ 3 : recurring regularly : PERMANENT ⟨∼ problems⟩ syn lasting, perpetual, enduring, everlasting — pe·ren·ni·al·ly adv

²perennial n : a perennial plant

perf abbr 1 perfect 2 perforated

¹per·fect \'pər-fikt\ adj 1 : being without fault or defect 2 : EXACT, PRECISE 3 : COMPLETE 4 : relating to or being a verb tense that expresses an action or state completed at the time of speaking or at a time spoken of — per·fect·ly adv — per·fect·ness n

²per·fect \pər-'fekt\ vb : to make perfect

³per·fect \'pər-fikt\ n : the perfect tense; also : a verb form in it

per·fect·ible \pər-'fek-tə-bəl, 'pər-fik-\ adj : capable of improvement or perfection — per·fect·ibil·i·ty \pər-₁fek-tə-'bi-lə-tē, ₁pər-fik-\ n

per·fec·tion \pər-'fek-shən\ n 1 : the quality or state of being perfect 2 : the highest degree of excellence 3 : the act or process of perfecting

per·fec·tion·ist \-shə-nist\ n : a person who will not accept or be content with anything less than perfection

per·fec·to \pər-'fek-tō\ n, pl -tos : a cigar that is thick in the middle and tapers almost to a point at each end

per·fi·dy \'pər-fə-dē\ n, pl -dies [L perfidia, fr. perfidus faithless, fr. per- detrimental to + fides faith] : violation of faith or loyalty : TREACHERY — per·fid·i·ous \pər-'fi-dē-əs\ adj — per·fid·i·ous·ly adv

per·fo·rate \'pər-fə-₁rāt\ vb -rat·ed; -rat·ing : to bore through : PIERCE; esp : to make a line of holes in to facilitate separation — per·fo·ra·tion \₁pər-fə-'rā-shən\ n

per·force \pər-'fōrs\ adv : of necessity

per·form \pər-'fòrm\ vb 1 : FULFILL 2 : CARRY OUT, DO 3 : FUNCTION 4 : to do in a set manner 5 : to give a performance — per·form·er n

per·for·mance \pər-'fòr-₁məns\ n 1 : the act or process of performing 2 : DEED, FEAT 3 : a public presentation

¹per·fume \pər-'fyüm, 'pər-₁fyüm\ n 1 : a usu. pleasant odor : FRAGRANCE 2 : a preparation used for scenting

²per·fume \pər-'fyüm, 'pər-₁fyüm\ vb per·fumed; per·fum·ing : SCENT

per·fum·ery \pər-'fyü-mə-rē\ n : PERFUMES

per·func·to·ry \pər-'fəŋk-tə-rē\ adj : done merely as a duty — per·func·to·ri·ly adv

per·go·la \'pər-gə-lə\ n [It] : a structure consisting of posts supporting an open roof in the form of a trellis

perh abbr perhaps

per·haps \pər-'haps\ adv : possibly but not certainly

per·i·gee \'per-ə-₁jē\ n [MF, fr. NL perigeum, fr. Gk perigeion, fr. peri around, near + gē earth] : the point at which an orbiting object is nearest the body (as the earth) being orbited

peri·he·lion \₁per-ə-'hēl-yən\ n, pl -he·lia \-'hēl-yə\ : the point in the path of a celestial body (as a planet) that is nearest to the sun

per·il \'per-əl\ n : DANGER; also : a source of danger : RISK — per·il·ous adj — per·il·ous·ly adv

pe·rim·e·ter \pə-'ri-mə-tər\ n 1 : the boundary of a closed plane figure; also : its length 2 : a line bounding or protecting an area

¹pe·ri·od \'pir-ē-əd\ n 1 : SENTENCE; also : the full pause closing the utterance of a sentence 2 : END, STOP 3 : a punctuation mark . used esp. to mark the end of a declarative sentence or an abbreviation 4 : an extent of time; esp : one regarded as a stage or division in a process or development 5 : a portion of time in which a recurring phenomenon completes one cycle and is ready to begin again 6 : a single cyclic occurrence of menstruation

²period adj : of or relating to a particular historical period ⟨∼ furniture⟩

per·i·od·ic \₁pir-ē-'ä-dik\ adj 1 : occurring at regular intervals of time **2** : happening repeatedly **3** : of or relating to a sentence that has no trailing elements following full grammatical statement of the essential idea

¹pe·ri·od·i·cal \ˌpir-ē-'ä-di-kəl\ *adj* **1** : PERIODIC **2** : published at regular intervals **3** : of or relating to a periodical — **pe·ri·od·i·cal·ly** \-k(ə-)lē\ *adv*

²periodical *n* : a periodical publication

periodic table *n* : an arrangement of chemical elements based on their atomic structure and on their properties

peri·odon·tal \ˌper-ē-ō-'dänt-ᵊl\ *adj* **1** : surrounding a tooth **2** : of or affecting periodontal tissues or regions ⟨∼ disease⟩

per·i·pa·tet·ic \ˌper-ə-pə-'te-tik\ *adj* : performed or performing while moving about : ITINERANT

pe·riph·er·al \pə-'ri-fər-əl\ *n* : a device connected to a computer to provide communication or auxiliary functions

peripheral nervous system *n* : the part of the nervous system that is outside the central nervous system and comprises the spinal nerves, the cranial nerves except the one supplying the retina, and the autonomic nervous system

pe·riph·ery \pə-'ri-fə-rē\ *n, pl* **-er·ies 1** : the boundary of a rounded figure **2** : outward bounds : border area — **pe·riph·er·al** \-fə-rəl\ *adj*

pe·riph·ra·sis \pə-'ri-frə-səs\ *n, pl* **-ra·ses** \-ˌsēz\ : CIRCUMLOCUTION

peri·scope \'per-ə-ˌskōp\ *n* : a tubular optical instrument enabling an observer to see an otherwise blocked field of view

per·ish \'per-ish\ *vb* : to become destroyed or ruined : DIE

per·ish·able \'per-i-shə-bəl\ *adj* : easily spoiled ⟨∼ foods⟩ — **perishable** *n*

peri·stal·sis \ˌper-ə-'stȯl-səs, -'stal-\ *n, pl* **-stal·ses** : waves of contraction passing along the walls of a hollow muscular organ and esp. the intestine and forcing its contents onward — **per·i·stal·tic** \-'stȯl-tik, -'stal-\ *adj*

peri·style \'per-ə-ˌstīl\ *n* : a row of columns surrounding a building or court

peri·to·ne·um \ˌper-ə-tə-'nē-əm\ *n, pl* **-ne·ums** *or* **-nea** : the smooth transparent serous membrane that lines the cavity of the abdomen — **peri·to·ne·al** \-'nē-əl\ *adj*

peri·to·ni·tis \ˌper-ə-tə-'nī-təs\ *n* : inflammation of the peritoneum

peri·wig \'per-i-ˌwig\ *n* : WIG

¹per·i·win·kle \'per-i-ˌwiŋ-kəl\ *n* : a usu. blue= flowered creeping plant cultivated as a ground cover

²periwinkle *n* : any of various small edible seashore snails

per·ju·ry \'pər-jə-rē\ *n* : the voluntary violation of an oath to tell the truth : lying under oath — **per·jure** \'pər-jər\ *vb* — **per·jur·er** *n*

¹perk \'pərk\ *vb* **1** : to thrust (as the head) up impudently or jauntily **2** : to regain vigor or spirit **3** : to make trim or brisk : FRESHEN — **perky** *adj*

²perk *vb* : PERCOLATE

³perk *n* : PERQUISITE — usu. used in pl.

per·lite \'pər-ˌlīt\ *n* : volcanic glass that when expanded by heat forms a lightweight material used esp. in concrete and plaster and for potting plants

¹perm \'pərm\ *n* : PERMANENT

²perm *vb* : to give (hair) a permanent

³perm *abbr* permanent

per·ma·frost \'pər-mə-ˌfrȯst\ *n* : a permanently frozen layer below the surface in frigid regions of a planet

¹per·ma·nent \'pər-mə-nənt\ *adj* : LASTING, STABLE — **per·ma·nence** \-nəns\ *n* — **per·ma·nen·cy** \-nən-sē\ *n* — **per·ma·nent·ly** *adv*

²permanent *n* : a long-lasting hair wave or straightening

permanent press *n* : the process of treating fabrics

with chemicals (as resin) and heat for setting the shape and for aiding wrinkle resistance

per·me·able \'pər-mē-ə-bəl\ *adj* : having small openings that permit liquids or gases to seep through — **per·me·a·bil·i·ty** \ˌpər-mē-ə-'bi-lə-tē\ *n*

per·me·ate \'pər-mē-ˌāt\ *vb* **-at·ed; -at·ing 1** : PERVADE **2** : to seep through the pores of : PENETRATE — **per·me·ation** \ˌpər-mē-'ā-shən\ *n*

Perm·ian \'pər-mē-ən\ *adj* : of, relating to, or being the latest period of the Paleozoic era — **Permian** *n*

per·mis·si·ble \pər-'mi-sə-bəl\ *adj* : that may be permitted : ALLOWABLE

per·mis·sion \pər-'mi-shən\ *n* : formal consent : AUTHORIZATION

per·mis·sive \pər-'mi-siv\ *adj* : granting permission; *esp* : INDULGENT — **per·mis·sive·ly** *adv* — **per·mis·sive·ness** *n*

¹per·mit \pər-'mit\ *vb* **per·mit·ted; per·mit·ting 1** : to consent to : ALLOW **2** : to make possible

²per·mit \'pər-ˌmit, pər-'mit\ *n* : a written permission : LICENSE

per·mu·ta·tion \ˌpər-myū-'tā-shən\ *n* **1** : a major or fundamental change **2** : the act or process of changing the order of an ordered set of objects **syn** innovation, mutation, vicissitude

per·ni·cious \pər-'ni-shəs\ *adj* [ME, fr. MF *pernicieus*, fr. L *perniciosus*, fr. *pernicies* destruction, fr. *per-* through + *nec-, nex* violent death] : very destructive or injurious — **per·ni·cious·ly** *adv*

per·ora·tion \'per-ə-ˌrā-shən, 'pər-\ *n* : the concluding part of a speech

¹per·ox·ide \pə-'räk-ˌsīd\ *n* : an oxide containing a large proportion of oxygen; *esp* : HYDROGEN PEROXIDE

²peroxide *vb* **-id·ed; -id·ing** : to bleach with hydrogen peroxide

perp *abbr* **1** perpendicular **2** perpetrator

per·pen·dic·u·lar \ˌpər-pən-'di-kyə-lər\ *adj* **1** : standing at right angles to the plane of the horizon **2** : forming a right angle with each other or with a given line or plane — **perpendicular** *n* — **per·pen·dic·u·lar·i·ty** \-ˌdi-kyə-'lar-ə-tē\ *n* — **per·pen·dic·u·lar·ly** *adv*

per·pe·trate \'pər-pə-ˌtrāt\ *vb* **-trat·ed; -trat·ing** : to be guilty of : COMMIT — **per·pe·tra·tion** \ˌpər-pə-'trā-shən\ *n* — **per·pe·tra·tor** \'pər-pə-ˌtrā-tər\ *n*

per·pet·u·al \pər-'pe-chə-wəl\ *adj* **1** : continuing forever : EVERLASTING **2** : occurring continually : CONSTANT ⟨∼ annoyance⟩ **syn** ceaseless, unceasing, continual, continuous, incessant, unremitting — **per·pet·u·al·ly** *adv*

per·pet·u·ate \pər-'pe-chə-ˌwāt\ *vb* **-at·ed; -at·ing** : to make perpetual : cause to last indefinitely — **per·pet·u·a·tion** \-ˌpe-chə-'wā-shən\ *n*

per·pe·tu·ity \ˌpər-pə-'tü-ə-tē, -'tyü-\ *n, pl* **-ties 1** : ETERNITY 1 **2** : the quality or state of being perpetual

per·plex \pər-'pleks\ *vb* : to disturb mentally; *esp* : CONFUSE — **per·plex·i·ty** \-'plek-sə-tē\ *n*

per·plexed \-'plekst\ *adj* **1** : filled with uncertainty : PUZZLED **2** : full of difficulty : COMPLICATED — **per·plexed·ly** \-'plek-səd-lē\ *adv*

per·qui·site \'pər-kwə-zət\ *n* : a privilege or profit beyond regular pay

pers *abbr* person; personal

per se \(ˌ)pər-'sā\ *adv* [L] : by, of, or in itself : as such

per·se·cute \'pər-si-ˌkyüt\ *vb* **-cut·ed; -cut·ing** : to pursue in such a way as to injure or afflict : HARASS; *esp* : to cause to suffer because of belief — **per·se·cu·tion** \ˌpər-si-'kyü-shən\ *n* — **per·se·cu·tor** \'pər-si-ˌkyü-tər\ *n*

per·se·vere \ˌpər-sə-'vir\ *vb* **-vered; -ver·ing** : to persist (as in an undertaking) in spite of difficulties — **per·se·ver·ance** \-'vir-əns\ *n*

Per·sian \'pər-zhən\ *n* **1** : a native or inhabitant of ancient Persia **2** : a member of one of the peoples of modern Iran **3** : the language of the Persians

Persian cat *n* : any of a breed of stocky round=

headed domestic cats that have a long silky coat

Persian lamb *n* : a pelt that is obtained from lambs that are older than those yielding broadtail and that has very silky tightly curled fur

per•si•flage \'pər-si-ˌfläzh, 'per-\ *n* [F, fr. *persifler* to banter, fr. *per-* thoroughly + *siffler* to whistle, hiss, boo, ultim. fr. L *sibilare*] : lightly jesting or mocking talk

per•sim•mon \pər-'si-mən\ *n* : either of two trees related to the ebony; *also* : the edible orange-red plumlike fruit of a persimmon

per•sist \pər-'sist, -'zist\ *vb* 1 : to go on resolutely or stubbornly in spite of difficulties 2 : to continue to exist — **per•sis•tence** \-'sis-təns, -'zis-\ *n* — **per•sis•ten•cy** \-tən-sē\ *n* — **per•sis•tent** \-tənt\ *adj* — **per•sis•tent•ly** *adv*

per•snick•e•ty \pər-'sni-kə-tē\ *adj* : fussy about small details

per•son \'pər-sən\ *n* [ME, fr. OF *persone*, fr. L *persona* actor's mask, character in a play, person, prob. fr. Etruscan *phersu* mask, fr. Gk *prosōpa*, pl. of *prosōpon* face, mask] 1 : a human being : INDIVIDUAL — used in combination esp. by those who prefer to avoid *man* in compounds applicable to both sexes ⟨chair*person*⟩ 2 : one of the three modes of being in the Godhead as understood by Trinitarians 3 : the body of a human being 4 : the individual personality of a human being : SELF 5 : reference of a segment of discourse to the speaker, to one spoken to, or to one spoken of esp. as indicated by certain pronouns

per•son•able \'pər-sə-nə-bəl\ *adj* : pleasant in person : ATTRACTIVE

per•son•age \'pər-sə-nij\ *n* : a person of rank, note, or distinction

¹per•son•al \'pər-sə-nəl\ *adj* 1 : of, relating to, or affecting a person : PRIVATE ⟨~ correspondence⟩ 2 : done in person ⟨a ~ inquiry⟩ 3 : relating to the person or body ⟨~ injuries⟩ 4 : relating to an individual esp. in an offensive way ⟨resented such ~ remarks⟩ 5 : of or relating to temporary or movable property as distinguished from real estate 6 : denoting grammatical person

²personal *n* 1 : a short newspaper paragraph relating to a person or group or to personal matters 2 : a short personal or private communication in the classified ads section of a newspaper

personal computer *n* : MICROCOMPUTER

per•son•al•ise *Brit var of* PERSONALIZE

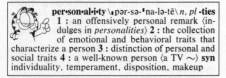

per•son•al•i•ty \ˌpər-sə-'na-lə-tē\ *n, pl* **-ties** 1 : an offensively personal remark ⟨indulges in *personalities*⟩ 2 : the collection of emotional and behavioral traits that characterize a person 3 : distinction of personal and social traits 4 : a well-known person ⟨a TV ~⟩ **syn** individuality, temperament, disposition, makeup

per•son•al•ize \'pər-sə-nə-ˌlīz\ *vb* **-ized; -iz•ing** : to make personal or individual; *esp* : to mark as belonging to a particular person

per•son•al•ly \-nə-lē\ *adv* 1 : in person 2 : as a person 3 : as far as oneself is concerned

per•son•al•ty \'pər-sə-nəl-tē\ *n, pl* **-ties** : personal property

per•so•na non gra•ta \pər-'sō-nə-ˌnän-'gra-tə, -'grä-\ *adj* [L] : being personally unacceptable or unwelcome

per•son•ate \'pər-sə-ˌnāt\ *vb* **-at•ed; -at•ing** : IMPERSONATE, REPRESENT

per•son•i•fy \pər-'sä-nə-ˌfī\ *vb* **-fied; -fy•ing** 1 : to think of or represent as a person 2 : to be the embodiment of : INCARNATE ⟨~ the law⟩ — **per•son•i•fi•ca•tion** \-ˌsä-nə-fə-'kā-shən\ *n*

per•son•nel \ˌpər-sə-'nel\ *n* : a body of persons employed

per•spec•tive \pər-'spek-tiv\ *n* 1 : the science of painting and drawing so that objects represented have apparent depth and distance 2 : the aspect in which a subject or its parts are mentally viewed; *esp* : a view of things (as objects or events) in their true relationship or relative importance

per•spi•ca•cious \ˌpər-spə-'kā-shəs\ *adj* : having or showing keen understanding or discernment — **per•spi•cac•i•ty** \-'ka-sə-tē\ *n*

per•spic•u•ous \pər-'spi-kyə-wəs\ *adj* : plain to the understanding — **per•spi•cu•i•ty** \ˌpər-spə-'kyü-ə-tē\ *n*

per•spire \pər-'spīr\ *vb* **per•spired; per•spir•ing** : SWEAT — **per•spi•ra•tion** \ˌpər-spə-'rā-shən\ *n*

per•suade \pər-'swād\ *vb* **per•suad•ed; per•suad•ing** : to win over to a belief or course of action by argument or entreaty — **per•sua•sive** \-'swā-siv, -ziv\ *adj* — **per•sua•sive•ly** *adv* — **per•sua•sive•ness** *n*

per•sua•sion \pər-'swā-zhən\ *n* 1 : the act or process of persuading 2 : a system of religious beliefs; *also* : a group holding such beliefs

¹pert \'pərt\ *adj* [ME, open, bold, pert, modif. of OF *apert*, fr. L *apertus* open, fr. pp. of *aperire* to open] 1 : saucily free and forward : IMPUDENT 2 : stylishly trim : JAUNTY 3 : LIVELY

²pert *abbr* pertaining

per•tain \pər-'tān\ *vb* 1 : to belong to as a part, quality, or function ⟨duties ~ing to the office⟩ 2 : to have reference : RELATE ⟨books ~ing to birds⟩

per•ti•na•cious \ˌpər-tə-'nā-shəs\ *adj* 1 : holding resolutely to an opinion or purpose 2 : obstinately persistent ⟨a ~ bill collector⟩ **syn** dogged, mulish, headstrong, perverse — **per•ti•nac•i•ty** \-'na-sə-tē\ *n*

per•ti•nent \'pərt-ᵊn-ənt\ *adj* : relating to the matter under consideration **syn** relevant, germane, applicable, apropos — **per•ti•nence** \-əns\ *n*

per•turb \pər-'tərb\ *vb* : to disturb greatly esp. in mind : UPSET — **per•tur•ba•tion** \ˌpər-tər-'bā-shən\ *n*

per•tus•sis \pər-'tə-səs\ *n* : WHOOPING COUGH

pe•ruke \pə-'rük\ *n* : WIG

pe•ruse \pə-'rüz\ *vb* **pe•rused; pe•rus•ing** : READ; *esp* : to read over attentively or leisurely — **pe•rus•al** \-'rü-zəl\ *n*

Pe•ru•vi•an \pə-'rü-vē-ən\ *n* : a native or inhabitant of Peru

per•vade \pər-'vād\ *vb* **per•vad•ed; per•vad•ing** : to spread through every part of : PERMEATE, PENETRATE — **per·va·sive** \-'vā-siv, -ziv\ *adj*

per·verse \pər-'vərs\ *adj* **1** : turned away from what is right or good : CORRUPT **2** : obstinate in opposing what is reasonable or accepted — **per·verse·ly** *adv* — **per·verse·ness** *n* — **per·ver·si·ty** \-'vər-sə-tē\ *n*

per·ver·sion \pər-'vər-zhən\ *n* **1** : the action of perverting : the condition of being perverted **2** : a perverted form of something; *esp* : aberrant sexual behavior

¹**per·vert** \pər-'vərt\ *vb* **1** : to lead astray : CORRUPT ⟨∼ the young⟩ **2** : to divert to a wrong purpose : MISAPPLY ⟨∼ evidence⟩ **syn** deprave, debase, debauch, demoralize — **per·ver·ter** *n*

²**per·vert** \'pər-ˌvərt\ *n* : one that is perverted; *esp* : one given to sexual perversion

pe·se·ta \pə-'sā-tə\ *n* — see MONEY table

pe·se·wa \pə-'sā-wə\ *n* — see cedi at MONEY table

pes·ky \'pes-kē\ *adj* **pes·ki·er; -est** : causing annoyance : TROUBLESOME

pe·so \'pā-sō\ *n*, *pl* pesos — see MONEY table

pes·si·mism \'pe-sə-ˌmi-zəm\ *n* [F *pessimisme*, fr. L *pessimus* worst] : an inclination to take the least favorable view (as of events) or to expect the worst — **pes·si·mist** \-mist\ *n* — **pes·si·mis·tic** \ˌpe-sə-'mis-tik\ *adj*

pest \'pest\ *n* **1** : a destructive epidemic disease : PLAGUE **2** : a plant or animal detrimental to humans **3** : one that pesters : NUISANCE — **pesty** *adj*

pes·ter \'pes-tər\ *vb* : to harass with petty irritations : ANNOY

pes·ti·cide \'pes-tə-ˌsīd\ *n* : an agent used to destroy pests

pes·tif·er·ous \pes-'ti-fə-rəs\ *adj* **1** : PESTILENT **2** : ANNOYING

pes·ti·lence \'pes-tə-ləns\ *n* : a destructive infectious swiftly spreading disease; *esp* : BUBONIC PLAGUE

pes·ti·lent \-lənt\ *adj* **1** : dangerous to life : DEADLY **2** : PERNICIOUS, HARMFUL **3** : TROUBLESOME **4** : INFECTIOUS, CONTAGIOUS

pes·ti·len·tial \ˌpes-tə-'len-chəl\ *adj* **1** : causing or tending to cause pestilence : DEADLY **2** : morally harmful

pes·tle \'pes-əl, 'pest-ᵊl\ *n* : an implement for grinding substances in a mortar — **pestle** *vb*

¹**pet** \'pet\ *n* **1** : FAVORITE, DARLING **2** : a domesticated animal kept for pleasure rather than utility

²**pet** *adj* **1** : kept or treated as a pet ⟨∼ dog⟩ **2** : expressing fondness ⟨∼ name⟩ **3** : particularly liked or favored

³**pet** *vb* **pet·ted; pet·ting 1** : to stroke gently or lovingly **2** : to make a pet of : PAMPER **3** : to engage in amorous kissing and caressing

⁴**pet** *n* : a fit of peevishness, sulkiness, or anger — **pettish** *adj*

Pet *abbr* Peter

pet·al \'pet-ᵊl\ *n* : one of the modified leaves of a flower's corolla

pe·tard \pə-'tärd, -'tär\ *n* : a case containing an explosive to break down a door or gate or breach a wall

pe·ter \'pē-tər\ *vb* : to diminish gradually and come to an end ⟨his energy ∼ed out⟩

Pe·ter \'pē-tər\ *n* — see BIBLE table

pet·i·ole \'pe-tē-ˌōl\ *n* : a slender stem that supports a leaf

pe·tite \pə-'tēt\ *adj* [F] : small and trim of figure ⟨a ∼ woman⟩ — **petite** *n*

petit four \ˌpe-tē-'fȯr\ *n*, *pl* petits fours *or* petit fours \-'fȯrz\ [F, lit., small oven] : a small cake cut from pound or sponge cake and frosted

¹**pe·ti·tion** \pə-'ti-shən\ *n* : an earnest request : ENTREATY; *esp* : a formal written request made to an authority

²**petition** *vb* : to make a request to or for — **pe·ti·tion·er** *n*

pe·trel \'pe-trəl\ *n* : any of numerous seabirds that fly far from land

pet·ri·fy \'pe-trə-ˌfī\ *vb* **-fied; -fy·ing 1** : to convert (organic matter) into stone or stony material **2** : to make rigid or inactive (as from fear or awe) — **pet·ri·fac·tion** \ˌpe-trə-'fak-shən\ *n*

pet·ro·chem·i·cal \ˌpe-trō-'ke-mi-kəl\ *n* : a chemical isolated or derived from petroleum or natural gas — **pet·ro·chem·is·try** \-'ke-mə-strē\ *n*

pet·rol \'pe-trəl\ *n*, *Brit* : GASOLINE

pet·ro·la·tum \ˌpe-trə-'lā-təm\ *n* : PETROLEUM JELLY

pe·tro·leum \pə-'trō-lē-əm\ *n* [ML, fr. Gk *petra* rock + L *oleum* oil] : an oily flammable liquid obtained from wells drilled in the ground and refined into gasoline, fuel oils, and other products

petroleum jelly *n* : a tasteless, odorless, and oily or greasy substance from petroleum that is used esp. in ointments and dressings

¹**pet·ti·coat** \'pe-tē-ˌkōt\ *n* **1** : a skirt worn under a dress **2** : an outer skirt

²**petticoat** *adj* : of, relating to, or exercised by women : FEMALE

pet·ti·fog \'pe-tē-ˌfȯg, -ˌfäg\ *vb* **-fogged; -fog·ging 1** : to engage in legal trickery **2** : to quibble over insignificant details — **pet·ti·fog·ger** *n*

pet·ty \'pe-tē\ *adj* **pet·ti·er; -est** [ME *pety* small, minor, alter. of *petit*, fr. MF, small] **1** : having secondary rank : MINOR ⟨∼ prince⟩ **2** : of little importance : TRIFLING ⟨∼ faults⟩ **3** : marked by narrowness or meanness — **pet·ti·ly** \'pe-tə-lē\ *adv* — **pet·ti·ness** \-tē-nəs\ *n*

petty officer *n* : a subordinate officer in the navy or coast guard appointed from among the enlisted men

petty officer first class *n* : a petty officer ranking below a chief petty officer

petty officer second class *n* : a petty officer ranking below a petty officer first class

petty officer third class *n* : a petty officer ranking below a petty officer second class

pet·u·lant \'pe-chə-lənt\ *adj* : marked by capricious ill humor **syn** irritable, peevish, fretful, fractious, querulous — **pet·u·lance** \-ləns\ *n* — **pet·u·lant·ly** *adv*

pe·tu·nia \pi-'tün-yə, -'tyün-\ *n* : any of a genus of tropical American herbs related to the potato and having bright funnel-shaped flowers

pew \'pyü\ *n* [ME *pewe*, fr. MF *puie* balustrade, fr. L *podia*, pl. of *podium* parapet, podium, fr. Gk *podion* base, dim. of *pod-*, *pous* foot] : any of the benches with backs fixed in rows in a church

pe·wee \'pē-(ˌ)wē\ *n* : any of various small flycatchers

pew·ter \'pyü-tər\ *n* **1** : an alloy of tin used esp. for household utensils **2** : a bluish gray color — **pewter** *adj* — **pew·ter·er** *n*

pey·o·te \pā-'ō-tē\ *also* **pey·otl** \-'ōt-ᵊl\ *n* : a stimulant drug derived from an American cactus; *also* : this cactus

pf *abbr* **1** pfennig **2** preferred

PFC *or* **Pfc** *abbr* private first class

pfd *abbr* preferred

pfen·nig \'fe-nig\ *n*, *pl* pfennig *also* pfennigs *or* pfen·ni·ge \'fe-ni-gə\ — see deutsche mark at MONEY table

pg *abbr* page

PG *abbr* postgraduate

PGA *abbr* Professional Golfers' Association

pH \(ˌ)pē-'āch\ *n* : a value used to express acidity and alkalinity; *also* : the condition represented by such a value

PH *abbr* **1** pinch hit **2** public health

pha·eton \'fā-ət-ᵊn\ *n* [F *phaéton*, fr. Gk *Phaethōn*, son of the sun god who persuaded his father to let him drive the chariot of the sun but who lost control of the horses with disastrous consequences] **1** : a light 4-wheeled horse-drawn vehicle **2** : an open automobile with two cross seats

☞ For illustration, see next page.

phage \'fāj\ *n* : BACTERIOPHAGE

phaeton 1

pha·lanx \'fā-₁laŋks\ n, pl **pha·lanx·es** or **pha·lan·ges** \fə-'lan-₁jēz\ 1 : a group or body (as of troops) in compact formation 2 pl phalanges : one of the digital bones of the hand or foot of a vertebrate

phal·a·rope \'fa-lə-₁rōp\ n, pl **-ropes** also **-rope** : any of a genus of small shorebirds related to sandpipers

phal·lic \'fa-lik\ adj 1 : of, relating to, or resembling a phallus 2 : relating to or being the stage of psychosexual development in psychoanalytic theory during which children become interested in their own sexual organs

phal·lus \'fa-ləs\ n, pl **phal·li** \'fa-₁lī\ or **phal·lus·es** : PENIS; also : a symbolic representation of the penis

Phan·er·o·zo·ic \₁fa-nə-rə-'zō-ik\ adj : of, relating to, or being an eon of geologic history comprising the Paleozoic, Mesozoic, and Cenozoic

phan·tasm \'fan-₁ta-zəm\ n : a product of the imagination : ILLUSION — **phan·tas·mal** \fan-'taz-məl\ adj

phan·tas·ma·go·ria \fan-₁taz-mə-'gōr-ē-ə\ n : a constantly shifting complex succession of things seen or imagined; also : a scene that constantly changes or fluctuates

phantasy var of FANTASY

phan·tom \'fan-təm\ n 1 : something (as a specter) that is apparent to sense but has no substantial existence 2 : a mere show : SHADOW — **phantom** adj

pha·raoh \'fer-ō, 'fā-rō\ n, often cap : a ruler of ancient Egypt

phar·i·sa·ical \₁far-ə-'sā-ə-kəl\ adj : hypocritically self-righteous

phar·i·see \'far-ə-₁sē\ n 1 cap : a member of an ancient Jewish sect noted for strict observance of rites and ceremonies of the traditional law 2 : a self-righteous or hypocritical person — **phar·i·sa·ic** \₁far-ə-'sā-ik\ adj

pharm abbr pharmaceutical; pharmacist; pharmacy

phar·ma·ceu·ti·cal \₁fär-mə-'sü-ti-kəl\ adj : of, relating to, or engaged in pharmacy or the manufacture and sale of medicinal drugs — **pharmaceutical** n

phar·ma·col·o·gy \₁fär-mə-'kä-lə-jē\ n 1 : the science of drugs esp. as related to medicinal uses 2 : the reactions and properties of one or more drugs — **phar·ma·co·log·i·cal** \-kə-'lä-ji-kəl\ also **phar·ma·co·log·ic** \-kə-'lä-jik\ adj — **phar·ma·col·o·gist** \-'kä-lə-jist\ n

phar·ma·co·poe·ia also **phar·ma·co·pe·ia** \-kə-'pē-ə\ n 1 : a book describing drugs and medicinal preparations 2 : a stock of drugs

phar·ma·cy \'fär-mə-sē\ n, pl **-cies** 1 : the art, practice, or profession of preparing and dispensing medical drugs 2 : DRUGSTORE — **phar·ma·cist** \-sist\ n

phar·ynx \'far-iŋks\ n, pl **pha·ryn·ges** \fə-'rin-₁jēz\ also **phar·ynx·es** : the space just back of the mouth into which the nostrils, esophagus, and trachea open — **pha·ryn·ge·al** \fə-'rin-jəl, ₁far-ən-'jē-əl\ adj

phase \'fāz\ n 1 : a particular appearance in a recurring series of changes (∼s of the moon) 2 : a stage or interval in a process or cycle (first ∼ of an experiment) 3 : an aspect or part under consideration — **pha·sic** \'fā-zik\ adj

phase in vb : to introduce in stages

phase·out \'fā-₁zau̇t\ n : a gradual stopping of operations or production

phase out vb : to stop production or use of in stages

PhD abbr [L philosophiae doctor] doctor of philosophy

pheas·ant \'fez-ᵊnt\ n, pl **pheasant** or **pheasants** : any of numerous long-tailed brilliantly colored game birds related to the domestic chicken

pheasant

phen·cy·cli·dine \₁fen-'sī-klə-₁dēn\ n : a drug used esp. as a veterinary anesthetic and sometimes illicitly to induce vivid mental imagery

phe·no·bar·bi·tal \₁fē-nō-'bär-bə-₁tȯl\ n : a crystalline drug used as a hypnotic and sedative

phe·nol \'fē-₁nȯl\ n : a corrosive poisonous acidic compound present in coal and wood tars and used in solution as a disinfectant

phe·nom·e·non \fi-'nä-mə-₁nän, -nən\ n, pl **-na** \-nə\ or **-nons** [LL phaenomenon, fr. Gk phainomenon, fr. neut. of phainomenos, prp. of phainesthai to appear] 1 pl **-na** : an observable fact or event 2 : an outward sign of the working of a law of nature 3 pl **-nons** : an extraordinary person or thing : PRODIGY — **phe·nom·e·nal** \-'nä-mən-ᵊl\ adj — **phe·nom·e·non·al·ly** adv

pher·o·mone \'fer-ə-₁mōn\ n : a chemical substance that is produced by an animal and serves to stimulate a behavioral response in other individuals of the same species — **pher·o·mon·al** \₁fer-ə-'mōn-ᵊl\ adj

phi \'fī\ n : the 21st letter of the Greek alphabet — Φ or φ

phi·al \'fī-əl\ n : VIAL

Phil abbr Philippians

phi·lan·der \fə-'lan-dər\ vb 1 : to make love without serious intent 2 : to have many love affairs — **phi·lan·der·er** n

phi·lan·thro·py \fə-'lan-thrə-pē\ n, pl **-pies** 1 : goodwill toward all people; esp : effort to promote human welfare 2 : a charitable act or gift; also : an organization that distributes or is supported by donated funds — **phil·an·throp·ic** \₁fi-lən-'thrä-pik\ adj — **phil·an·throp·i·cal·ly** \-pi-k(ə-)lē\ adv — **phi·lan·thro·pist** \fə-'lan-thrə-pist\ n

phi·lat·e·ly \fə-'lat-ᵊl-ē\ n : the collection and study of postage and imprinted stamps — **phil·a·tel·ic** \₁fi-lə-'te-lik\ adj — **phi·lat·e·list** \fə-'lat-ᵊl-ist\ n

Phi·le·mon \fə-'lē-mən, fī-\ n — see BIBLE table

Phi·lip·pi·ans \fə-'li-pē-ənz\ n — see BIBLE table

phi·lip·pic \fə-'li-pik\ n : TIRADE

phi·lis·tine \'fi-lə-₁stēn; fə-'lis-tən\ n, often cap [Philistine, inhabitant of ancient Philistia (Palestine)] : a person who is smugly insensitive or indifferent to intellectual or artistic values — **philistine** adj, often cap

Phil·lips \'fi-ləps\ adj : of, relating to, or being a screw having a head with a cross slot or its corresponding screwdriver

philo·den·dron \₁fi-lə-'den-drən\ n, pl **-drons** or **-dra** \-drə\ [NL, fr. Gk, neut. of philodendros loving trees, fr. philos dear, friendly + dendron tree] : any of various plants of the arum family grown for their showy foliage

phi·lol·o·gy \fə-'lä-lə-jē\ n 1 : the study of literature and relevant fields 2 : LINGUISTICS; esp : historical

and comparative linguistics — **phil·o·log·i·cal** \ˌfi-lə-ˈlä-ji-kəl\ *adj* — **phi·lol·o·gist** \fə-ˈlä-lə-jist\ *n*

philos *abbr* philosopher; philosophy

phi·los·o·pher \fə-ˈlä-sə-fər\ *n* **1** : a reflective thinker : SCHOLAR **2** : a student of or specialist in philosophy **3** : a person whose philosophical perspective makes it possible to meet trouble calmly

phi·los·o·phise *Brit var of* PHILOSOPHIZE

phi·los·o·phize \fə-ˈlä-sə-ˌfīz\ *vb* **-phized; -phiz·ing 1** : to reason like a philosopher : THEORIZE **2** : to expound a philosophy esp. superficially

phi·los·o·phy \fə-ˈlä-sə-fē\ *n, pl* **-phies 1** : sciences and liberal arts exclusive of medicine, law, and theology ⟨doctor of ∼⟩ **2** : a critical study of fundamental beliefs and the grounds for them **3** : a system of philosophical concepts ⟨Aristotelian ∼⟩ **4** : a basic theory concerning a particular subject or sphere of activity **5** : the sum of the ideas and convictions of an individual or group ⟨her ∼ of life⟩ **6** : calmness of temper and judgment — **phil·o·soph·ic** \ˌfi-lə-ˈsä-fik\ *or* **phil·o·soph·i·cal** \-fi-kəl\ *adj* — **phil·o·soph·i·cal·ly** \-k(ə-)lē\ *adv*

phil·ter *or* **phil·tre** \ˈfil-tər\ *n* **1** : a potion, drug, or charm held to arouse sexual passion **2** : a magic potion

phle·bi·tis \fli-ˈbī-təs\ *n* : inflammation of a vein

phle·bot·o·my \fli-ˈbä-tə-mē\ *n, pl* **-mies** : the opening of a vein esp. for removing or releasing blood

phlegm \ˈflem\ *n* : thick mucus secreted in abnormal quantity esp. in the nose and throat

phleg·mat·ic \fleg-ˈma-tik\ *adj* : having or showing a slow and stolid temperament **syn** impassive, apathetic, stoic

phlo·em \ˈflō-ˌem\ *n* : a vascular plant tissue external to the xylem that carries dissolved food material and functions in support and storage

phlox \ˈfläks\ *n, pl* **phlox** *or* **phlox·es** : any of a genus of American herbs that have tall stalks with showy spreading terminal clusters of flowers

pho·bia \ˈfō-bē-ə\ *n* : an irrational persistent fear or dread

phoe·be \ˈfē-(ˌ)bē\ *n* : a flycatcher of the eastern U.S. that has a slight crest and is grayish brown above and yellowish white below

phoe·nix \ˈfē-niks\ *n* : a legendary bird held to live for centuries and then to burn itself to death and rise fresh and young from its ashes

phon *abbr* phonetics

¹**phone** \ˈfōn\ *n* **1** : TELEPHONE **2** : EARPHONE

²**phone** *vb* **phoned; phon·ing** : TELEPHONE

pho·neme \ˈfō-ˌnēm\ *n* : one of the elementary units of speech that distinguish one utterance from another — **pho·ne·mic** \fō-ˈnē-mik\ *adj*

pho·net·ics \fə-ˈne-tiks\ *n* : the study and systematic classification of the sounds made in spoken utterance

— **pho·net·ic** \-tik\ *adj* — **pho·ne·ti·cian** \ˌfō-nə-ˈti-shən\ *n*

pho·nic \ˈfä-nik\ *adj* **1** : of, relating to, or producing sound **2** : of or relating to the sounds of speech or to phonics — **pho·ni·cal·ly** \-ni-k(ə-)lē\ *adv*

pho·nics \ˈfä-niks\ *n* : a method of teaching people to read and pronounce words by learning the phonetic value of letters, letter groups, and esp. syllables

pho·no·graph \ˈfō-nə-ˌgraf\ *n* : an instrument for reproducing sounds by means of the vibration of a needle following a spiral groove on a revolving disc

pho·nol·o·gy \fə-ˈnä-lə-jē\ *n* : a study and description of the sound changes in a language — **pho·no·log·i·cal** \ˌfō-nə-ˈlä-ji-kəl\ *adj* — **pho·nol·o·gist** \fə-ˈnä-lə-jist\ *n*

pho·ny *or* **pho·ney** \ˈfō-nē\ *adj* **pho·ni·er; -est** : marked by empty pretension : FAKE — **phony** *n*

phos·phate \ˈfäs-ˌfāt\ *n* : a salt of a phosphoric acid — **phos·phat·ic** \fäs-ˈfa-tik\ *adj*

phos·phor \ˈfäs-fər\ *n* : a phosphorescent substance

phos·pho·res·cence \ˌfäs-fə-ˈres-ᵊns\ *n* **1** : luminescence caused by radiation absorption followed by emission that continues after the incident radiation stops **2** : an enduring luminescence without sensible heat — **phos·pho·res·cent** \-ᵊnt\ *adj* — **phos·pho·res·cent·ly** *adv*

phosphoric acid \ˌfäs-ˈfòr-ik-, -ˈfär-\ *n* : any of several oxygen-containing acids of phosphorus

phos·pho·rus \ˈfäs-fə-rəs\ *n* [NL, fr. Gk *phōsphoros* light-bearing, fr. *phōs* light + *pherein* to carry, bring] : a nonmetallic chemical element that has characteristics similar to nitrogen and occurs widely esp. as phosphates — see ELEMENT table — **phos·phor·ic** \fäs-ˈfòr-ik, -ˈfär-\ *adj* — **phos·pho·rous** \ˈfäs-fə-rəs; fäs-ˈfòr-əs, -ˈfòr-\ *adj*

phot- *or* **photo-** *comb form* **1** : light ⟨*photo*graphy⟩ **2** : photograph : photographic ⟨*photo*engraving⟩ **3** : photoelectric ⟨*photo*cell⟩

pho·to \ˈfō-tō\ *n, pl* **photos** : PHOTOGRAPH — **photo** *vb or adj*

pho·to·cell \ˈfō-tə-ˌsel\ *n* : PHOTOELECTRIC CELL

pho·to·chem·i·cal \ˌfō-tō-ˈke-mi-kəl\ *adj* : of, relating to, or resulting from the chemical action of radiant energy

pho·to·com·pose \-kəm-ˈpōz\ *vb* : to compose reading matter for reproduction by means of characters photographed on film — **pho·to·com·po·si·tion** \-ˌkäm-pə-ˈzi-shən\ *n*

pho·to·copy \ˈfō-tə-ˌkä-pē\ *n* : a photographic reproduction of graphic matter — **photocopy** *vb*

pho·to·elec·tric \ˌfō-tō-i-ˈlek-trik\ *adj* : relating to an electrical effect due to the interaction of light with matter — **pho·to·elec·tri·cal·ly** \-tri-k(ə-)lē\ *adv*

photoelectric cell *n* : a device whose electrical properties are modified by the action of light

pho·to·en·grave \ˌfō-tō-in-ˈgrāv\ *vb* : to make a photoengraving of

pho·to·en·grav·ing *n* : a process by which an etched printing plate is made from a photograph or drawing; *also* : a print made from such a plate

photo finish *n* : a race finish so close that a photograph of the finish is used to determine the winner

¹**pho·tog** \fə-'täg\ *n* : PHOTOGRAPHER

²**photog** *abbr* photographic; photography

pho·to·gen·ic \ˌfō-tə-'je-nik\ *adj* : eminently suitable esp. aesthetically for being photographed

pho·to·graph \'fō-tə-ˌgraf\ *n* : a picture taken by photography — **photograph** *vb* — **pho·tog·ra·pher** \fə-'tä-grə-fər\ *n*

pho·tog·ra·phy \fə-'tä-grə-fē\ *n* : the art or process of producing images on a sensitized surface (as film in a camera) by the action of light — **pho·to·graph·ic** \ˌfō-tə-'gra-fik\ *adj* — **pho·to·graph·i·cal·ly** \-fi-k(ə-)lē\ *adv*

pho·to·gra·vure \ˌfō-tə-grə-'vyùr\ *n* : a process for making prints from an intaglio plate prepared by photographic methods

pho·to·li·thog·ra·phy \ˌfō-tō-li-'thä-grə-fē\ *n* : the process of photographically transferring a pattern to a surface for etching (as in making an integrated circuit)

pho·tom·e·ter \fō-'tä-mə-tər\ *n* : an instrument for measuring the intensity of light — **pho·to·met·ric** \ˌfō-tə-'me-trik\ *adj* — **pho·tom·e·try** \fō-'tä-mə-trē\ *n*

pho·to·mi·cro·graph \ˌfō-tə-'mī-krə-ˌgraf\ *n* : a photograph of a microscope image — **pho·to·mi·crog·ra·phy** \-mī-'krä-grə-fē\ *n*

pho·ton \'fō-ˌtän\ *n* : a quantum of electromagnetic radiation

pho·to·play \'fō-tō-ˌplā\ *n* : MOTION PICTURE

pho·to·sen·si·tive \ˌfō-tə-'sen-sə-tiv\ *adj* : sensitive or sensitized to the action of radiant energy

pho·to·sphere \'fō-tə-ˌsfir\ *n* : the luminous surface of a star — **pho·to·spher·ic** \ˌfō-tə-'sfir-ik, -'sfer-\ *adj*

pho·to·syn·the·sis \ˌfō-tō-'sin-thə-səs\ *n* : the process by which chlorophyll-containing plants make carbohydrates from water and from carbon dioxide in the air in the presence of light — **pho·to·syn·the·size** \-ˌsīz\ *vb* — **pho·to·syn·thet·ic** \-sin-'the-tik\ *adj*

phr *abbr* phrase

¹**phrase** \'frāz\ *n* 1 : a brief expression 2 : a group of two or more grammatically related words that form a sense unit expressing a thought

²**phrase** *vb* **phrased; phras·ing** : to express in words

phrase·ol·o·gy \ˌfrā-zē-'ä-lə-jē\ *n, pl* **-gies** : a manner of phrasing : STYLE

phras·ing *n* : style of expression

phre·net·ic \fri-'ne-tik\ *adj* : FRENETIC

phren·ic \'fre-nik\ *adj* : of or relating to the diaphragm ⟨~ nerves⟩

phre·nol·o·gy \fri-'nä-lə-jē\ *n* : the study of the conformation of the skull based on the belief that it indicates mental faculties and character traits

phy·lac·tery \fə-'lak-tə-rē\ *n, pl* **-ter·ies** 1 : one of two small square leather boxes containing slips inscribed with scripture passages and traditionally worn on the left arm and forehead by Jewish men during morning weekday prayers 2 : AMULET

phy·lum \'fī-ləm\ *n, pl* **phy·la** \-lə\ [NL, fr. Gk *phylon* tribe, race] : a major division of the animal and in some classifications the plant kingdom; *also* : a group (as of people) apparently of common origin

phys *abbr* 1 physical 2 physics

¹**phys·ic** \'fi-zik\ *n* 1 : the profession of medicine 2 : MEDICINE; *esp* : PURGATIVE

²**physic** *vb* **phys·icked; phys·ick·ing** : PURGE 2

¹**phys·i·cal** \'fi-zi-kəl\ *adj* 1 : of or relating to nature or the laws of nature 2 : material as opposed to mental or spiritual 3 : of, relating to, or produced by the forces and operations of physics 4 : of or relating to the body — **phys·i·cal·ly** \-k(ə-)lē\ *adv*

²**physical** *n* : PHYSICAL EXAMINATION

physical education *n* : instruction in the development and care of the body ranging from simple calisthenics

to training in hygiene, gymnastics, and the performance and management of athletic games

physical examination *n* : an examination of the bodily functions and condition of an individual

physical science *n* : any of the sciences (as physics and astronomy) that deal primarily with nonliving materials — **physical scientist** *n*

physical therapy *n* : the treatment of disease by physical and mechanical means (as massage, exercise, water, or heat) — **physical therapist** *n*

phy·si·cian \fə-'zi-shən\ *n* : a doctor of medicine

physician's assistant *n* : a person certified to provide basic medical care usu. under a licensed physician's supervision

phys·i·cist \'fi-zə-sist\ *n* : a scientist who specializes in physics

phys·ics \'fi-ziks\ *n* [L *physica,* pl., natural sciences, fr. Gk *physika,* fr. *physis* growth, nature, fr. *phyein* to bring forth] 1 : the science of matter and energy and their interactions 2 : the physical properties and composition of something

phys·i·og·no·my \ˌfi-zē-'äg-nə-mē\ *n, pl* **-mies** : facial appearance esp. as a reflection of inner character

phys·i·og·ra·phy \ˌfi-zē-'ä-grə-fē\ *n* : geography dealing with physical features of the earth — **phys·io·graph·ic** \ˌfi-zē-ō-'gra-fik\ *adj*

phys·i·ol·o·gy \ˌfi-zē-'ä-lə-jē\ *n* 1 : a branch of biology dealing with the functions and functioning of living matter and organisms 2 : functional processes in an organism or any of its parts — **phys·i·o·log·i·cal** \-zē-ə-'lä-ji-kəl\ *or* **phys·i·o·log·ic** \-jik\ *adj* — **phys·i·o·log·i·cal·ly** \-ji-k(ə-)lē\ *adv* — **phys·i·ol·o·gist** \-zē-'ä-lə-jist\ *n*

phys·io·ther·a·py \ˌfi-zē-ō-'ther-ə-pē\ *n* : PHYSICAL THERAPY — **phys·io·ther·a·pist** \-pist\ *n*

phy·sique \fə-'zēk\ *n* : the build of a person's body : bodily constitution

phy·to·plank·ton \ˌfī-tō-ˌplaŋk-tən\ *n* : plant life of the plankton

pi \'pī\ *n, pl* **pis** \'pīz\ 1 : the 16th letter of the Greek alphabet — Π or π 2 : the symbol π denoting the ratio of the circumference of a circle to its diameter; *also* : the ratio itself equal to approximately 3.1416

PI *abbr* private investigator

pi·a·nis·si·mo \ˌpē-ə-'ni-sə-ˌmō\ *adv or adj* : very softly — used as a direction in music

pi·a·nist \pē-'a-nist, 'pē-ə-\ *n* : one who plays the piano

¹**pi·a·no** \pē-'ä-nō\ *adv or adj* : SOFTLY — used as a direction in music

²**piano** \pē-'a-nō\ *n, pl* **pianos** [It, short for *pianoforte,* fr. *gravicembalo col piano e forte,* lit., harpsichord with soft and loud; fr. the fact that its tones could be varied in loudness] : a musical instrument having steel strings sounded by felt-covered hammers operated from a keyboard

pi·ano·forte \pē-ˌa-nō-'fòr-ˌtā, -tē; pē-'a-nə-ˌfòrt\ *n* : PIANO

pi·as·tre *also* **pi·as·ter** \pē-'as-tər\ *n* — see *pound* at MONEY table

pi·az·za \pē-'a-zə, *esp for 1* -'at-sə\ *n, pl* **piazzas** *or* **pi·az·ze** \-'at-(ˌ)sä, -'ät-\ [It, fr. L *platea* broad street] 1 : an open square esp. in an Italian town 2 : a long hall with an arched roof 3 *dial* : VERANDA, PORCH

pi·broch \'pē-ˌbräk\ *n* : a set of variations for the bagpipe

pic \'pik\ *n, pl* **pics** *or* **pix** \'piks\ 1 : PHOTOGRAPH 2 : MOTION PICTURE

pi·ca \'pī-kə\ *n* : a typewriter type with 10 characters to the inch

pic·a·resque \ˌpi-kə-'resk, ˌpē-\ *adj* : of or relating to rogues ⟨~ fiction⟩

pic·a·yune \ˌpi-kē-'yün\ *adj* : of little value : TRIVIAL; *also* : PETTY

pic·ca·lil·li \ˌpi-kə-'li-lē\ *n* : a relish of chopped vegetables and spices

pic·co·lo \ˈpi-kə-ˌlō\ *n, pl* **-los** [It, short for *piccolo flauto* small flute] : a small shrill flute pitched an octave higher than the ordinary flute

pice \ˈpīs\ *n, pl* **pice** : PAISA

¹**pick** \ˈpik\ *vb* **1** : to pierce or break up with a pointed instrument **2** : to remove bit by bit; *also* : to remove covering matter from **3** : to gather by plucking ⟨∼ apples⟩ **4** : CULL, SELECT **5** : ROB ⟨∼ a pocket⟩ **6** : PROVOKE ⟨∼ a quarrel⟩ **7** : to dig into or pull lightly at **8** : to pluck with fingers or a pick **9** : to loosen or pull apart with a sharp point ⟨∼ wool⟩ **10** : to unlock with a wire **11** : to eat sparingly — **pick·er** *n* — **pick on** : to single out for criticism, teasing, or bullying

²**pick** *n* **1** : the act or privilege of choosing **2** : the best or choicest one **3** : the part of a crop gathered at one time

³**pick** *n* **1** : a heavy wooden-handled tool pointed at one or both ends **2** : a pointed implement used for picking **3** : a small thin piece (as of plastic) used to pluck the strings of a stringed instrument

pick·a·back \ˈpi-gē-ˌbak, ˈpi-kə-\ *var of* PIGGYBACK

pick·ax \ˈpik-ˌaks\ *n* : ³PICK 1

pick·er·el \ˈpi-kə-rəl\ *n, pl* **pickerel** *or* **pickerels** : either of two bony fishes related to the pikes; *also* : WALLEYE 2

pickerel

pick·er·el·weed \-ˌwēd\ *n* : an American shallow-water herb that bears spikes of blue flowers

¹**pick·et** \ˈpi-kət\ *n* **1** : a pointed stake (as for a fence) **2** : a detached body of soldiers on outpost duty; *also* : SENTINEL **3** : a person posted by a labor union where workers are on strike; *also* : a person posted for a protest

²**picket** *vb* **1** : to guard with pickets **2** : TETHER **3** : to post pickets at ⟨∼ a factory⟩ **4** : to serve as a picket

pick·ings \ˈpi-kiŋz, -kənz\ *n pl* **1** : gleanable or eatable fragments : SCRAPS **2** : yield for effort expended : RETURN

pick·le \ˈpi-kəl\ *n* **1** : a brine or vinegar solution for preserving foods; *also* : a food (as a cucumber) preserved in a pickle **2** : a difficult situation : PLIGHT — **pickle** *vb*

pick·lock \ˈpik-ˌläk\ *n* **1** : BURGLAR, THIEF **2** : a tool for picking locks

pick·pock·et \ˈpik-ˌpä-kət\ *n* : one who steals from pockets

pick·up \ˈpik-ˌəp\ *n* **1** : a hitchhiker who is given a ride **2** : a temporary chance acquaintance **3** : a picking up **4** : revival of business activity **5** : ACCELERATION **6**

: the conversion of mechanical movements into electrical impulses in the reproduction of sound; *also* : a device for making such conversion **7** : a light truck having an enclosed cab and an open body with low sides and a tailgate

pick up *vb* **1** : to take hold of and lift **2** : IMPROVE **3** : to put in order

picky \ˈpi-kē\ *adj* **pick·i·er; -est** : FUSSY, FINICKY

¹**pic·nic** \ˈpik-nik\ *n* : an outing with food usu. provided by members of the group and eaten in the open

²**picnic** *vb* **pic·nicked; pic·nick·ing** : to go on a picnic : eat in picnic fashion

pi·cot \ˈpē-ˌkō\ *n* : one of a series of small loops forming an edging on ribbon or lace

pic·to·ri·al \pik-ˈtōr-ē-əl\ *adj* : of, relating to, or consisting of pictures

¹**pic·ture** \ˈpik-chər\ *n* **1** : a representation made by painting, drawing, or photography **2** : a vivid description in words **3** : IMAGE, COPY **4** : a transitory visual image (as on a TV screen) **5** : MOTION PICTURE **6** : SITUATION

²**picture** *vb* **pic·tured; pic·tur·ing** **1** : to paint or draw a picture of **2** : to describe vividly in words **3** : to form a mental image of

pic·tur·esque \ˌpik-chə-ˈresk\ *adj* **1** : resembling a picture ⟨a ∼ landscape⟩ **2** : CHARMING, QUAINT ⟨a ∼ character⟩ **3** : GRAPHIC, VIVID ⟨a ∼ account⟩ — **pic·tur·esque·ness** *n*

picture tube *n* : a cathode-ray tube on which the picture in a television set appears

pid·dle \ˈpid-ᵊl\ *vb* **pid·dled; pid·dling** : to act or work idly : DAWDLE

pid·dling \ˈpid-ᵊl-əŋ, -iŋ\ *adj* : TRIVIAL, PALTRY

pid·gin \ˈpi-jən\ *n* [fr. *pidgin English*, fr. Chinese Pidgin English *pidgin* business] : a simplified speech used for communication between people with different languages

pie \ˈpī\ *n* : a dish consisting of a pastry crust and a filling (as of fruit or meat)

¹**pie·bald** \ˈpī-ˌbȯld\ *adj* : of different colors; *esp* : blotched with white and black ⟨a ∼ horse⟩

²**piebald** *n* : a piebald animal

¹**piece** \ˈpēs\ *n* **1** : a part of a whole : FRAGMENT **2** : one of a group, set, or mass ⟨chess ∼⟩; *also* : a single item ⟨a ∼ of news⟩ **3** : a length, weight, or size in which something is made or sold **4** : a product (as an essay) of creative work **5** : FIREARM **6** : COIN

²**piece** *vb* **pieced; piec·ing** **1** : to repair or complete by adding pieces : PATCH **2** : to join into a whole

pièce de ré·sis·tance \pē-ˌes-də-rā-ˌzē-ˈstäns\ *n, pl* **pièces de ré·sis·tance** *same*\ [F] **1** : the chief dish of a meal **2** : an outstanding item

piece·meal \ˈpēs-ˌmēl\ *adv or adj* : one piece at a time : GRADUALLY

piece·work \-ˌwərk\ *n* : work done and paid for by the piece — **piece·work·er** *n*

pie chart *n* : a circular chart that shows quantities or frequencies by parts of a circle shaped like pieces of pie

pied \\'pīd\\ *adj* : of two or more colors in blotches : VARIEGATED

pied-à-terre \\pē-ˌä-də-'ter\\ *n, pl* **pieds-à-terre** \\same\\ [F. lit., foot to the ground] : a temporary or second lodging

pier \\'pir\\ *n* 1 : a support for a bridge span 2 : a structure built out into the water for use as a landing place or a promenade or to protect or form a harbor 3 : an upright supporting part (as a pillar) of a building or structure

pierce \\'pirs\\ *vb* **pierced; pierc·ing** 1 : to enter or thrust into sharply or painfully : STAB 2 : to make a hole in or through : PERFORATE 3 : to force or make a way into or through : PENETRATE 4 : to see through : DISCERN

pies *pl of* PI *or of* PIE

pi·ety \\'pī-ə-tē\\ *n, pl* **pi·et·ies** 1 : fidelity to natural obligations (as to parents) 2 : dutifulness in religion : DEVOUTNESS 3 : a pious act

pif·fle \\'pi-fəl\\ *n* : trifling talk or action

pig \\'pig\\ *n* 1 : SWINE; *esp* : a young swine 2 : PORK 3 : one that resembles a pig (as in dirtiness or greed) 4 : a crude casting of metal (as iron)

pi·geon \\'pi-jən\\ *n* : any of numerous stout-bodied short-legged birds with smooth thick plumage

¹pi·geon·hole \\'pi-jən-ˌhōl\\ *n* : a small open compartment (as in a desk) for keeping letters or documents

²pigeonhole *vb* 1 : to place in or as if in a pigeonhole : FILE 2 : to lay aside 3 : CLASSIFY

pi·geon-toed \\-ˌtōd\\ *adj* : having the toes turned in

pig·gish \\'pi-gish\\ *adj* 1 : GREEDY 2 : STUBBORN

pig·gy·back \\'pi-gē-ˌbak\\ *adv or adj* 1 : up on the back and shoulders 2 : on a railroad flatcar

pig·head·ed \\'pig-'he-dəd\\ *adj* : OBSTINATE, STUBBORN

pig latin *n, often cap L* : a jargon that is made by systematic alteration of English

pig·let \\'pi-glət\\ *n* : a small usu. young swine

pig·ment \\'pig-mənt\\ *n* 1 : coloring matter 2 : a powder mixed with a liquid to give color (as in paints)

pig·men·ta·tion \\ˌpig-mən-'tā-shən\\ *n* : coloration with or deposition of pigment; *esp* : an excessive deposition of bodily pigment

pig·my *var of* PYGMY

pig·nut \\'pig-ˌnət\\ *n* : the bitter nut of any of several hickory trees; *also* : any of these trees

pig·pen \\-ˌpen\\ *n* 1 : a pen for pigs 2 : a dirty place

pig·skin \\-ˌskin\\ *n* 1 : the skin of a swine or leather made of it 2 : FOOTBALL 2

pig·sty \\-ˌstī\\ *n* : PIGPEN

pig·tail \\-ˌtāl\\ *n* : a tight braid of hair

pi·ka \\'pī-kə\\ *n* : any of various small short-eared mammals related to the rabbits and occurring in rocky uplands of Asia and western No. America

¹pike \\'pīk\\ *n* : a sharp point or spike

²pike *n, pl* **pike** *or* **pikes** : a large slender long-snouted freshwater bony fish valued for food; *also* : any of various related fishes

³pike *n* : a long wooden shaft with a pointed steel head formerly used as a foot soldier's weapon

⁴pike *n* : TURNPIKE

pik·er \\'pī-kər\\ *n* 1 : one who does things in a small way or on a small scale 2 : TIGHTWAD, CHEAPSKATE

pike·staff \\'pīk-ˌstaf\\ *n* : the staff of a foot soldier's pike

pi·laf *or* **pi·laff** \\pi-'läf, 'pē-ˌläf\\ *or* **pi·lau** \\pi-'lō, -'lȯ, 'pē-lō, -lȯ\\ *n* : a dish of seasoned rice often with meat

pi·las·ter \\'pi-ˌlas-tər, 'pī-ˌlas-tər\\ *n* : an architectural support that looks like a rectangular column and projects slightly from a wall

pil·chard \\'pil-chərd\\ *n* : any of several fishes related to the herrings and often packed as sardines

¹pile \\'pīl\\ *n* : a long slender column (as of wood or steel) driven into the ground to support a vertical load

²pile *n* 1 : a quantity of things heaped together 2 : PYRE 3 : a great number or quantity : LOT

³pile *vb* **piled; pil·ing** 1 : to lay in a pile : STACK 2 : to heap up : ACCUMULATE 3 : to press forward in a mass : CROWD

⁴pile *n* : a velvety surface of fine short hairs or threads (as on cloth) — **piled** \\'pīld\\ *adj* — **pile·less** *adj*

piles \\'pīlz\\ *n pl* : HEMORRHOIDS

pil·fer \\'pil-fər\\ *vb* : to steal in small quantities

pil·grim \\'pil-grəm\\ *n* [ME, fr. OF *peligrin*, fr. LL *pelegrinus*, alter. of L *peregrinus* foreigner, fr. *peregrinus* foreign, fr. *peregri* abroad, fr. *per* through + *ager* land] 1 : one who journeys in foreign lands : WAYFARER 2 : one who travels to a shrine or holy place as an act of devotion 3 *cap* : one of the English settlers founding Plymouth colony in 1620

pil·grim·age \\-grə-mij\\ *n* : a journey of a pilgrim esp. to a shrine or holy place

pil·ing \\'pī-liŋ\\ *n* : a structure of piles

pill \\'pil\\ *n* 1 : a medicine in a small rounded mass to be swallowed whole 2 : a disagreeable or tiresome person 3 *often cap* : an oral contraceptive — usu. used with *the*

pil·lage \\'pi-lij\\ *vb* **pil·laged; pil·lag·ing** : to take booty : LOOT, PLUNDER — **pillage** *n* — **pil·lag·er** *n*

pil·lar \\'pi-lər\\ *n* 1 : a strong upright support (as for a roof) 2 : a column or shaft standing alone esp. as a monument — **pil·lared** \\-lərd\\ *adj*

pill·box \\'pil-ˌbäks\\ *n* 1 : a shallow round box for pills 2 : a low concrete emplacement esp. for machine guns

pil·lion \\'pil-yən\\ *n* 1 : a pad or cushion placed behind a saddle for an extra rider 2 *chiefly Brit* : a motorcycle or bicycle saddle for a passenger

¹pil·lo·ry \\'pi-lə-rē\\ *n, pl* **-ries** : a wooden frame for public punishment having holes in which the head and hands can be locked

²pillory *vb* **-ried; -ry·ing** 1 : to set in a pillory 2 : to expose to public scorn

¹pil·low \\'pi-lō\\ *n* : a case filled with springy material (as feathers) and used to support the head of a resting person

²pillow *vb* : to rest or place on or as if on a pillow; *also* : to serve as a pillow for

pil·low·case \\-ˌkās\\ *n* : a removable covering for a pillow

¹pi·lot \\'pī-lət\\ *n* 1 : HELMSMAN, STEERSMAN 2 : a person qualified and licensed to take ships into and out of a port 3 : GUIDE, LEADER 4 : one that flies an aircraft or spacecraft 5 : a television show filmed or taped as a sample of a proposed series — **pi·lot·less** *adj*

²pilot *vb* : CONDUCT, GUIDE; *esp* : to act as pilot of

³pilot *adj* : serving as a guiding or activating device or as a testing or trial unit ⟨a ~ light⟩ ⟨a ~ factory⟩

pi·lot·house \\'pī-lət-ˌhaůs\\ *n* : a shelter on the upper deck of a ship for the steering gear and the helmsman

pil·sner *also* **pil·sen·er** \\'pilz-nər, 'pil-zə-\\ *n* [G, lit., of Pilsen (Plzeň), city in the Czech Republic] 1 : a light beer with a strong flavor of hops 2 : a tall slender footed glass for beer

pi·men·to \\pə-'men-tō\\ *n, pl* **pimentos** *or* **pimento** [Sp *pimienta* allspice, pepper, fr. LL *pigmenta*, pl. of *pigmentum* plant juice, fr. L, pigment] 1 : ALLSPICE 2 : PIMIENTO

pi·mien·to \\pə-'men-tō\\ *n, pl* **-tos** : any of various mild red sweet pepper fruits used esp. to stuff olives and to make paprika

pimp \\'pimp\\ *n* : a man who solicits clients for a prostitute — **pimp** *vb*

pim·per·nel \\'pim-pər-ˌnel, -nəl\\ *n* : any of a genus of herbs related to the primroses

pim·ple \\'pim-pəl\\ *n* : a small inflamed swelling on the skin often containing pus — **pim·ply** \\-p(ə-)lē\\ *adj*

¹pin \\'pin\\ *n* 1 : a piece of wood or metal used esp. for fastening articles together or as a support by which one article may be suspended from another; *esp* : a small pointed piece of wire with a head used for fastening clothes or attaching papers 2 : an ornament or emblem fastened to clothing with a pin **3** : one of the wooden pieces constituting the target (as in bowling); *also* : the staff of the flag marking a hole on a golf course **4** : LEG

²**pin** *vb* **pinned; pin·ning 1** : to fasten, join, or secure with a pin **2** : to hold fast or immobile **3** : ATTACH, HANG 〈*pinned* their hopes on one man〉 **4** : to assign the blame for 〈~ a crime on someone〉 **5** : to define clearly : ESTABLISH 〈~ down an idea〉

PIN *abbr* personal identification number

pi·ña co·la·da \ˌpēn-yə-kō-ˈlä-də, ˌpē-nə-\ *n* [Sp, lit., strained pineapple] : a tall drink made of rum, cream of coconut, and pineapple juice mixed with ice

pin·afore \ˈpi-nə-ˌfȯr\ *n* : a sleeveless dress or apron fastened at the back

pince–nez \paⁿs-ˈnā\ *n, pl* **pince–nez** *same or* -ˈnāz\ [F, lit., pinch-nose] : eyeglasses clipped to the nose by a spring

pin·cer \ˈpin-sər\ *n* **1** *pl* : a gripping instrument with two handles and two grasping jaws **2** : a claw (as of a lobster) resembling pincers

¹**pinch** \ˈpinch\ *vb* **1** : to squeeze between the finger and thumb or between the jaws of an instrument **2** : to compress painfully **3** : CONTRACT, SHRIVEL **4** : to be miserly; *also* : to subject to strict economy **5** : to confine or limit narrowly **6** : STEAL **7** : ARREST

²**pinch** *n* **1** : a critical point : EMERGENCY **2** : painful effect **3** : an act of pinching **4** : a very small quantity **5** : ARREST

³**pinch** *adj* : SUBSTITUTE 〈a ~ runner〉

pinch–hit \ˌpinch-ˈhit\ *vb* **1** : to bat in the place of another player esp. when a hit is particularly needed **2** : to act or serve in place of another — **pinch hit** *n* — **pinch hitter** *n*

pin curl *n* : a curl made usu. by dampening a strand of hair, coiling it, and securing it by a hairpin or clip

pin·cush·ion \ˈpin-ˌku̇-shən\ *n* : a cushion for pins not in use

¹**pine** \ˈpīn\ *n* : any of a genus of evergreen cone=bearing trees; *also* : the light durable resinous wood of a pine

²**pine** *vb* **pined; pin·ing 1** : to lose vigor or health through distress **2** : to long for something intensely

pi·ne·al \ˈpī-nē-əl, pī-ˈnē-əl\ *adj* : PINEAL GLAND — **pineal** *adj*

pineal gland *n* : a small usu. conical appendage of the brain of all vertebrates with a cranium that functions primarily as an endocrine organ

pine·ap·ple \ˈpīn-ˌa-pəl\ *n* : a tropical plant bearing an edible juicy fruit; *also* : its fruit

pin·feath·er \ˈpin-ˌfe-thər\ *n* : a new feather just coming through the skin

ping \ˈpiŋ\ *n* **1** : a sharp sound like that of a bullet striking **2** : engine knock

pin·hole \ˈpin-ˌhōl\ *n* : a small hole made by, for, or as if by a pin

¹**pin·ion** \ˈpin-yən\ *n* : the end section of a bird's wing; *also* : WING

²**pinion** *vb* : to restrain by binding the arms; *also* : SHACKLE

³**pinion** *n* : a gear with a small number of teeth designed to mesh with a larger wheel or rack

¹**pink** \ˈpiŋk\ *n* **1** : any of a genus of plants with narrow leaves often grown for their showy flowers **2** : the highest degree : HEIGHT 〈the ~ of condition〉

²**pink** *n* : a light tint of red

³**pink** *adj* **1** : of the color pink **2** : holding socialistic views — **pink·ish** *adj*

⁴**pink** *vb* **1** : to perforate in an ornamental pattern **2** : PIERCE, STAB **3** : to cut a saw-toothed edge on

pink elephants *n pl* : hallucinations arising esp. from heavy drinking or use of narcotics

pink·eye \ˈpiŋk-ˌī\ *n* : an acute contagious eye inflammation

pin·kie *or* **pin·ky** \ˈpiŋ-kē\ *n, pl* **pinkies** : the smallest finger of the hand

pin·nace \ˈpi-nəs\ *n* **1** : a light sailing ship **2** : a ship's boat

pin·na·cle \ˈpi-ni-kəl\ *n* [ME *pinacle*, fr. MF, fr. LL *pinnaculum* small wing, gable, fr. L *pinna* wing, battlement] **1** : a turret ending in a small spire **2** : a lofty peak **3** : ACME

pin·nate \ˈpi-ˌnāt\ *adj* : resembling a feather esp. in having similar parts arranged on each side of an axis 〈a ~ leaf〉 — **pin·nate·ly** *adv*

pi·noch·le \ˈpē-ˌnə-kəl\ *n* : a card game played with a 48-card deck

pi·ñon *or* **pin·yon** \ˈpin-ˌyōn, -ˌyän\ *n, pl* **pi·ñons** *or* **pin·yons** *or* **pi·ño·nes** \pin-ˈyō-nēz\ [AmerSp *piñón*] : any of various low-growing pines of western No. America with edible seeds; *also* : the edible seed of a piñon

pin·point \ˈpin-ˌpȯint\ *vb* : to locate, hit, or aim with great precision

pin·prick \ˈpin-ˌprik\ *n* **1** : a small puncture made by or as if by a pin **2** : a petty irritation or annoyance

pins and needles *n pl* : a pricking tingling sensation in a limb growing numb or recovering from numbness — **on pins and needles** : in a nervous or jumpy state of anticipation

pin·stripe \ˈpin-ˌstrīp\ *n* : a narrow stripe on a fabric; *also* : a suit with such stripes — **pin–striped** \-ˌstrīpt\ *adj*

pint \ˈpīnt\ *n* — see WEIGHT table

pin·to \ˈpin-ˌtō\ *n, pl* **pintos** *also* **pintoes** : a spotted horse or pony

pinto bean *n* : a spotted seed produced by a kind of kidney bean and used for food

pin·up \ˈpin-ˌəp\ *adj* : suitable or designed for hanging on a wall; *also* : suited (as by beauty) to be the subject of a pinup photograph

pin·wheel \-ˌhwēl, -ˌwēl\ *n* **1** : a fireworks device in the form of a revolving wheel of colored fire **2** : a toy consisting of lightweight vanes that revolve at the end of a stick

pin·worm \-ˌwərm\ *n* : a nematode worm parasitic in the human intestine

pin·yin \ˈpin-ˈyin\ *n, often cap* : a system for writing Chinese ideograms by using Roman letters to represent the sounds

¹**pi·o·neer** \ˌpī-ə-ˈnir\ *n* **1** : one that originates or helps open up a new line of thought or activity **2** : an early settler in a territory

²**pioneer** *vb* **1** : to act as a pioneer **2** : to open or prepare for others to follow; *also* : SETTLE

pi·ous \ˈpī-əs\ *adj* **1** : marked by reverence for deity : DEVOUT **2** : excessively or affectedly religious **3** : SACRED, DEVOTIONAL **4** : showing loyal reverence for a person or thing : DUTIFUL **5** : marked by sham or hypocrisy — **pi·ous·ly** *adv*

¹**pip** \ˈpip\ *n* : one of the dots used on dice and dominoes to indicate numerical value

²**pip** *n* : a small fruit seed (as of an apple)

¹**pipe** \ˈpīp\ *n* **1** : a tubular musical instrument played by forcing air through it **2** : BAGPIPE **3** : a tube designed to conduct something (as water, steam, or oil) **4** : a device for smoking having a tube with a bowl at one end and a mouthpiece at the other

²**pipe** *vb* **piped; pip·ing 1** : to play on a pipe **2** : to speak in a high or shrill voice **3** : to convey by or as if by pipes — **pip·er** *n*

pipe down *vb* : to stop talking or making noise

pipe dream *n* : an illusory or fantastic hope

pipe·line \ˈpīp-ˌlīn\ *n* **1** : a line of pipe with pumps, valves, and control devices for conveying fluids **2** : a channel for information

pi·pette *or* **pi·pet** \pī-ˈpet\ *n* : a device for measuring and transferring small volumes of liquid

pipe up *vb* : to speak loudly and distinctly; *also* : to express an opinion freely

pip·ing \ˈpī-piŋ\ *n* **1** : the music of pipes **2** : a narrow fold of material used to decorate edges or seams

piping hot *adj* : very hot

pip·pin \'pi-pən\ *n* : any of several yellowish apples

pip–squeak \'pip-ˌskwēk\ *n* : one that is small or insignificant

pi·quant \'pē-kənt\ *adj* **1** : pleasantly savory : PUNGENT **2** : engagingly provocative; *also* : having a lively charm — **piquan·cy** \-kən-sē\ *n*

¹pique \'pēk\ *n* [F] : a passing feeling of wounded vanity : RESENTMENT

²pique *vb* **piqued; piqu·ing 1** : IRRITATE 1 **2** : to arouse by a provocation or challenge : GOAD

pi·qué *or* **pi·que** \pi-'kā\ *n* : a durable ribbed clothing fabric

pi·quet \pi-'kā\ *n* : a 2-handed card game played with 32 cards

pi·ra·cy \'pī-rə-sē\ *n, pl* **-cies 1** : robbery on the high seas; *also* : an act resembling such robbery **2** : the unauthorized use of another's production or invention

pi·ra·nha \pə-'rän-ə, -'rän-yə\ *n* [Pg. fr. Tupi (So. American Indian language) *piráya*, fr. *pira* fish + *áya* tooth] : any of various usu. small So. American fishes with sharp teeth that include some known to attack humans and large animals

pi·rate \'pī-rət\ *n* [ME, fr. MF or L; MF, fr. L *pirata*, fr. Gk *peiratēs*, fr. *peiran* to attempt, test] : one who commits piracy — **pirate** *vb* — **pi·rat·i·cal** \pə-'rati-kəl, pī-\ *adj*

pir·ou·ette \ˌpir-ə-'wet\ *n* [F] : a rapid whirling about of the body; *esp* : a full turn on the toe or ball of one foot in ballet — **pirouette** *vb*

pis *pl of* PI

pis·ca·to·ri·al \ˌpis-kə-'tōr-ē-əl\ *adj* : of or relating to fishing

Pi·sces \'pī-sēz\ *n* [ME, fr. L, lit., fishes] **1** : a zodiacal constellation between Aquarius and Aries usu. pictured as a fish **2** : the 12th sign of the zodiac in astrology; *also* : one born under this sign

pis·mire \'pis-ˌmīr\ *n* : ANT

pi·so \'pē-(ˌ)sō\ *n* : the peso of the Philippines

pis·ta·chio \pə-'sta-shē-ˌō, -'stä-\ *n, pl* **-chios** : the greenish edible seed of a small Asian tree related to the sumacs; *also* : the tree

pis·til \'pist-ᵊl\ *n* : the female reproductive organ in a flower — **pis·til·late** \'pis-tə-ˌlāt\ *adj*

pis·tol \'pist-ᵊl\ *n* : a handgun whose chamber is integral with the barrel

pis·tol–whip \-ˌhwip\ *vb* : to beat with a pistol

pis·ton \'pis-tən\ *n* : a sliding piece that receives and transmits motion and that usu. consists of a short cylinder inside a large cylinder

¹pit \'pit\ *n* **1** : a hole, shaft, or cavity in the ground **2** : an often sunken area designed for a particular use; *also* : an enclosed place (as for cockfights) **3** : HELL; *also, pl* : WORST ⟨it's the ~s⟩ **4** : a natural hollow or indentation in a surface **5** : a small indented mark or scar (as from disease or corrosion) **6** : an area beside a racecourse where cars are fueled and repaired during a race

²pit *vb* **pit·ted; pit·ting 1** : to form pits in or become marred with pits **2** : to match for fighting

---

³pit *n* : the stony seed of some fruits (as the cherry, peach, and date)

---

⁴pit *vb* **pit·ted; pit·ting** : to remove the pit from

pi·ta \'pē-tə\ *n* [NGk] : a thin flat bread

pit–a–pat \ˌpi-ti-'pat\ *n* : PITTER-PATTER — **pit–a–pat** *adv or adj*

pit bull *n* : a powerful compact short-haired dog developed for fighting

¹pitch \'pich\ *n* **1** : a dark sticky substance left over esp. from distilling tar or petroleum **2** : resin from various conifers — **pitchy** *adj*

²pitch *vb* **1** : to erect and fix firmly in place ⟨~ a tent⟩ **2** : THROW, FLING **3** : to deliver a baseball to a batter **4** : to toss (as coins) toward a mark **5** : to set at a particular level ⟨~ the voice low⟩ **6** : to fall headlong **7** : to have the front end (as of a ship) alternately plunge and rise **8** : to incline downward : SLOPE

³pitch *n* **1** : the action or a manner of pitching **2** : degree of slope ⟨~ of a roof⟩ **3** : the relative level of some quality or state ⟨a high ~ of excitement⟩ **4** : highness

or lowness of sound; *also* : a standard frequency for tuning instruments **5** : an often high-pressure sales talk **6** : the delivery of a baseball to a batter; *also* : the baseball delivered

pitch·blende \'pich-ˌblend\ *n* : a dark mineral that is the chief source of uranium

¹**pitch·er** \'pi-chər\ *n* : a container for liquids that usu. has a lip and a handle

²**pitcher** *n* : one that pitches esp. in a baseball game

pitcher plant *n* : any of various plants with leaves modified to resemble pitchers in which insects are trapped and digested

pitch·fork \'pich-ˌfȯrk\ *n* : a long-handled fork used esp. in pitching hay

pitch in *vb* **1** : to begin to work **2** : to contribute to a common effort

pitch·man \'pich-mən\ *n* : SALESMAN; *esp* : one who sells merchandise on the streets or from a concession

pit·e·ous \'pi-tē-əs\ *adj* : arousing pity : PITIFUL — **pit·e·ous·ly** *adv*

pit·fall \'pit-ˌfȯl\ *n* **1** : TRAP, SNARE; *esp* : a covered pit used for capturing animals **2** : a hidden danger or difficulty

pith \'pith\ *n* **1** : loose spongy tissue esp. in the center of the stem of vascular plants **2** : the essential part : CORE

pithy \'pi-thē\ *adj* **pith·i·er; -est 1** : consisting of or filled with pith **2** : having substance and point : CONCISE

piti·able \'pi-tē-ə-bəl\ *adj* : PITIFUL

piti·ful \'pi-ti-fəl\ *adj* **1** : arousing or deserving pity ⟨a ∼ sight⟩ **2** : MEAN, MEAGER — **piti·ful·ly** *adv*

piti·less \'pi-ti-ləs\ *adj* : devoid of pity : MERCILESS — **pit·i·less·ly** *adv*

pi·ton \'pē-ˌtän\ *n* [F] : a spike, wedge, or peg that can be driven into a rock or ice surface as a support

pit·tance \'pit-ᵊns\ *n* : a small portion, amount, or allowance

pit·ted \'pi-təd\ *adj* : marked with pits

pit·ter–pat·ter \'pi-tər-ˌpa-tər, 'pi-tē-\ *n* : a rapid succession of light taps or sounds — **pitter–patter** \ˌpi-tər-'pa-tər, ˌpi-tē-\ *adv or adj* — **pitter–patter** *same as adv*\ *vb*

pi·tu·i·tary \pə-'tü-ə-ˌter-ē, -'tyü-\ *n, pl* **-itar·ies** : PITUITARY GLAND — **pituitary** *adj*

pituitary gland *n* : a small oval endocrine gland attached to the brain which produces various hormones that affect most basic bodily functions

pit viper *n* : any of various mostly New World venomous snakes with a sensory pit on each side of the head and hollow perforated fangs

pity \'pi-tē\ *n, pl* **pit·ies** [ME *pite*, fr. OF *pité*, fr. L *pietas* piety, pity, fr. *pius* pious] **1** : sympathetic sorrow : COMPASSION **2** : something to be regretted

²**pity** *vb* **pit·ied; pity·ing** : to feel pity for

¹**piv·ot** \'pi-vət\ *n* : a fixed pin on which something turns — **pivot** *adj* — **piv·ot·al** \'pi-vət-ᵊl\ *adj*

²**pivot** *vb* : to turn on or as if on a pivot

pix *pl of* PIC

pix·el \'pik-səl, -ˌsel\ *n* : any of the small elements that together make up an image (as on a television screen)

pix·ie *or* **pixy** \'pik-sē\ *n, pl* **pix·ies** : FAIRY; *esp* : a mischievous sprite

piz·za \'pēt-sə\ *n* [It] : an open pie made of rolled bread dough spread with a spiced mixture (as of tomatoes, cheese, and ground meat) and baked

piz·zazz *or* **pi·zazz** \pə-'zaz\ *n* **1** : GLAMOUR **2** : VITALITY

piz·ze·ria \ˌpēt-sə-'rē-ə\ *n* : an establishment where pizzas are made and sold

piz·zi·ca·to \ˌpit-si-'kä-tō\ *adv or adj* [It] : by means of plucking instead of bowing — used as a direction in music

pj's \'pē-ˌjāz\ *n pl* : PAJAMAS

pk *abbr* **1** park **2** peak **3** peck **4** pike

pkg *abbr* package

pkt *abbr* **1** packet **2** pocket

pkwy *abbr* parkway

pl *abbr* **1** place **2** plate **3** plural

¹**plac·ard** \'pla-kərd, -ˌkärd\ *n* : a notice posted in a public place : POSTER

²**plac·ard** \-ˌkärd, -kərd\ *vb* **1** : to cover with or as if with placards **2** : to announce by or as if by posting

pla·cate \'plā-ˌkāt, 'pla-\ *vb* **pla·cat·ed; pla·cat·ing** : to soothe esp. by concessions : APPEASE — **pla·ca·ble** \'pla-kə-bəl, 'plā-\ *adj*

¹**place** \'plās\ *n* [ME, fr. OF, open space, fr. L *platea* broad street, fr. Gk *plateia* (*hodos*), fr. fem. of *platys* broad, flat] **1** : SPACE, ROOM **2** : an indefinite region : AREA **3** : a building or locality used for a special purpose **4** : a center of population **5** : a particular part of a surface : SPOT **6** : relative position in a scale or sequence; *also* : position at the end of a competition ⟨last ∼⟩ **7** : ACCOMMODATION; *esp* : SEAT **8** : the position of a figure within a numeral (12 is a two ∼ number) **9** : JOB; *esp* : public office **10** : a public square **11** : 2d place at the finish (as of a horse race)

²**place** *vb* **placed; plac·ing 1** : to put in a particular place : SET **2** : to distribute in an orderly manner : ARRANGE **3** : IDENTIFY **4** : to give an order for ⟨∼ a bet⟩ **5** : to earn a given spot in a competition; *esp* : to come in 2d

pla·ce·bo \plə-'sē-bō\ *n, pl* **-bos** [L, I shall please] : an inert medication used for its psychological effect or for purposes of comparison in an experiment

place·hold·er \'plās-ˌhōl-dər\ *n* : a symbol that in a mathematical or logical expression that may be replaced by the name of any element of a set

place·kick \-ˌkik\ *n* : the kicking of a ball placed or held on the ground — **placekick** *vb* — **place·kick·er** *n*

place·ment \'plās-mənt\ *n* : an act or instance of placing

place–name \-ˌnām\ *n* : the name of a geographical locality

pla·cen·ta \plə-'sen-tə\ *n, pl* **-tas** *or* **-tae** \-(ˌ)tē\ [NL, fr. L, flat cake] : the organ in most mammals by which the fetus is joined to the maternal uterus and is nourished — **pla·cen·tal** \-'sent-ᵊl\ *adj*

plac·er \'pla-sər\ *n* : a deposit of sand or gravel containing particles of valuable mineral (as gold)

plac·id \'pla-səd\ *adj* : UNDISTURBED, PEACEFUL **syn** tranquil, serene, calm — **pla·cid·i·ty** \pla-'si-də-tē\ *n* — **plac·id·ly** *adv*

plack·et \'pla-kət\ *n* : a slit in a garment

pla·gia·rise *Brit var of* PLAGIARIZE

pla·gia·rize \'plā-jə-ˌrīz\ *vb* **-rized; -riz·ing** : to present the ideas or words of another as one's own — **pla·gia·rism** \-ˌri-zəm\ *n* — **pla·gia·rist** \-rist\ *n*

¹**plague** \'plāg\ *n* **1** : a disastrous evil or influx; *also* : NUISANCE **2** : PESTILENCE; *esp* : a destructive contagious bacterial disease (as bubonic plague)

²**plague** *vb* **plagued; plagu·ing 1** : to afflict with or as if with disease or disaster **2** : TEASE, TORMENT, HARASS

plaid \'plad\ *n* **1** : a rectangular length of tartan worn esp. over the left shoulder as part of the Scottish national costume **2** : a twilled woolen fabric with a tartan pattern **3** : a pattern of unevenly spaced repeated stripes crossing at right angles — **plaid** *adj*

¹**plain** \'plān\ *n* : an extensive area of level or rolling treeless country

²**plain** *adj* **1** : lacking ornament ⟨a ∼ dress⟩ **2** : free of extraneous matter **3** : OPEN, UNOBSTRUCTED ⟨∼ view⟩ **4** : EVIDENT, OBVIOUS **5** : easily understood : CLEAR **6** : CANDID, BLUNT **7** : SIMPLE, UNCOMPLICATED ⟨∼ cooking⟩ **8** : lacking beauty or ugliness — **plain·ly** *adv* — **plain·ness** *n*

plain·clothes·man \'plān-'klōthz-mən, -'klōz-, -ˌman\

PLANETS

SYMBOL	NAME	MEAN DISTANCE FROM THE SUN		PERIOD OF REVOLUTION IN DAYS OR YEARS	EQUATORIAL DIAMETER IN MILES
		astronomical units	million miles		
☿	Mercury	0.387	36.0	87.97 d.	3,032
♀	Venus	0.723	67.2	224.70 d.	7,523
⊕	Earth	1.000	92.9	365.26 d.	7,928
♂	Mars	1.524	141.5	686.98 d.	4,218
♃	Jupiter	5.203	483.4	11.86 y.	88,900
♄	Saturn	9.522	884.6	29.46 y.	74,900
♅	Uranus	19.201	1783.8	84.01 y.	31,800
♆	Neptune	30.074	2793.9	164.79 y.	30,800
♇	Pluto	39.725	3690.5	247.69 y.	1,400

n : a police officer who wears civilian clothes instead of a uniform while on duty : DETECTIVE

plain·spo·ken \-'spō-kən\ *adj* : FRANK

plaint \'plānt\ *n* **1** : LAMENTATION, WAIL **2** : PROTEST, COMPLAINT

plain·tiff \'plān-təf\ *n* : the complaining party in a lawsuit

plain·tive \'plān-tiv\ *adj* : expressive of suffering or woe : MELANCHOLY — **plain·tive·ly** *adv*

plait \'plāt, 'plat\ *n* **1** : PLEAT **2** : a braid esp. of hair or straw — **plait** *vb*

¹plan \'plan\ *n* **1** : a drawing or diagram showing the parts or details of something **2** : a method for accomplishing an objective; *also* : GOAL, AIM

²plan *vb* **planned; plan·ning 1** : to form a plan of ⟨~ a new city⟩ **2** : INTEND ⟨*planned* to go⟩ — **plan·ner** *n*

¹plane \'plān\ *vb* **planed; plan·ing** : to smooth or level off with or as if with a plane — **plan·er** *n*

²plane *n* : PLANE TREE

³plane *n* : a tool for smoothing or shaping a wood surface

⁴plane *n* **1** : a level or flat surface **2** : a level of existence, consciousness, or development **3** : AIRPLANE

⁵plane *adj* **1** : FLAT, LEVEL **2** : dealing with flat surfaces or figures ⟨~ geometry⟩

plane·load \'plān-,lōd\ *n* : a load that fills an airplane

plan·et \'pla-nət\ *n* [ME *planete*, fr. OF, fr. LL *planeta*, modif. of Gk *planēt-, planēs*, lit., wanderer, fr. *planasthai* to wander] : any of the large bodies in the solar system that revolve around the sun — **plan·e·tary** \-nə-,ter-ē\ *adj*

plan·e·tar·i·um \,pla-nə-'ter-ē-əm\ *n, pl* **-i·ums** *or* **-ia** \-ē-ə\ : a building or room housing a device to project images of celestial bodies

plan·e·tes·i·mal \,pla-nə-'tes-ə-məl\ *n* : any of numerous small solid celestial bodies which may have existed during the formation of the solar system

plan·e·toid \'pla-nə-,tòid\ *n* : a body resembling a planet; *esp* : ASTEROID

plane tree *n* : any of a genus of trees (as a sycamore) with large lobed leaves and globe-shaped fruit

plan·gent \'plan-jənt\ *adj* **1** : having a loud reverberating sound **2** : having an expressive esp. plaintive quality — **plan·gen·cy** \-jən-sē\ *n*

¹plank \'plaŋk\ *n* **1** : a heavy thick board **2** : an article in the platform of a political party

²plank *vb* **1** : to cover with planks **2** : to set or lay down forcibly **3** : to cook and serve on a board

plank·ing \'plaŋ-kiŋ\ *n* : a quantity or covering of planks

plank·ton \'plaŋk-tən\ *n* [G, fr. Gk, neut. of *planktos* drifting] : the passively floating or weakly swimming animal and plant life of a body of water — **plank·ton·ic** \plaŋk-'tä-nik\ *adj*

¹plant \'plant\ *vb* **1** : to set in the ground to grow **2** : ES-

TABLISH, SETTLE **3** : to stock or provide with something **4** : to place firmly or forcibly **5** : to hide or arrange with intent to deceive

²plant *n* **1** : any of a kingdom of living things that usu. have no locomotor ability or obvious sense organs and have cellulose cell walls and usu. capacity for indefinite growth **2** : the land, buildings, and machinery used in carrying on a trade or business

¹plan·tain \'plant-ᵊn\ *n* [ME, fr. OF, fr. L *plantagin-, plantago*, fr. *planta* sole of the foot; fr. its broad leaves] : any of a genus of short-stemmed weedy herbs with spikes of tiny greenish flowers

²plantain *n* [Sp *plántano, plátano* plane tree, banana tree, fr. ML *plantanus* plane tree, alter. of L *platanus*] : a banana plant with starchy greenish fruit that are eaten cooked; *also* : its fruit

plan·tar \'plant-tər, -,tär\ *adj* : of or relating to the sole of the foot

plan·ta·tion \plan-'tā-shən\ *n* **1** : a large group of plants and esp. trees under cultivation **2** : an agricultural estate usu. worked by resident laborers

plant·er \'plant-tər\ *n* **1** : one that plants or sows; *esp* : an owner or operator of a plantation **2** : a container for plants

plant louse *n* : APHID

plaque \'plak\ *n* [F] **1** : an ornamental brooch **2** : a flat thin piece (as of metal) used for decoration; *also* : a commemorative tablet **3** : a bacteria-containing film on a tooth

plash \'plash\ *n* : SPLASH — **plash** *vb*

plas·ma \'plaz-mə\ *n* **1** : the fluid part of blood, lymph, or milk **2** : a gas composed of ionized particles — **plas·mat·ic** \plaz-'ma-tik\ *adj*

¹plas·ter \'plas-tər\ *n* **1** : a dressing consisting of a backing spread with an often medicated substance that clings to the skin ⟨adhesive ~⟩ **2** : a paste that hardens as it dries and is used for coating walls and ceilings

²plaster *vb* : to cover with or as if with plaster — **plas·ter·er** *n*

plas·ter·board \'plas-tər-,bōrd\ *n* : a wallboard consisting of fiberboard, paper, or felt over a plaster core

plaster of par·is \-'par-əs\ *often cap 2d P* : a white powder made from gypsum and used as a quicksetting paste with water for casts and molds

¹plas·tic \'plas-tik\ *adj* [L *plasticus* of molding, fr. Gk *plastikos*, fr. *plassein* to mold, form] **1** : capable of being molded ⟨~ clay⟩ **2** : characterized by or using modeling ⟨~ arts⟩ **3** : made or consisting of a plastic **syn** pliable, pliant, ductile, malleable, adaptable — **plas·tic·i·ty** \plas-'ti-sə-tē\ *n*

²plastic *n* : a plastic substance; *esp* : a synthetic or processed material that can be formed into rigid objects or into films or filaments

plastic surgery *n* : surgery to repair, restore, or improve lost, injured, defective, or misshapen body parts — **plastic surgeon** *n*

¹plat \'plat\ *n* **1** : a small plot of ground **2** : a plan of a piece of land with actual or proposed features (as lots)

²plat *vb* **plat·ted; plat·ting** : to make a plat of

¹plate \'plāt\ *n* **1** : a flat thin piece of material **2** : domestic hollowware made of or plated with gold, silver, or base metals **3** : DISH **4** : HOME PLATE **5** : the molded metal or plastic cast of a page of type to be printed from **6** : a sheet of glass coated with a chemical sensitive to light and used in photography **7** : the part of a denture that fits to the mouth; *also* : DENTURE **8** : something printed from an engraving **9** : a huge mobile segment of the earth's crust

²plate *vb* **plat·ed; plat·ing 1** : to overlay with metal (as gold or silver) **2** : to make a printing plate of

pla·teau \pla-'tō\ *n*, *pl* **plateaus** *or* **pla·teaux** \-'tōz\ [F] : a large level area of high land

plate glass *n* : rolled, ground, and polished sheet glass

plat·en \'plat-ᵊn\ *n* **1** : a flat plate; *esp* : one that exerts or receives pressure (as in a printing press) **2** : the roller of a typewriter or printer

plate tectonics *n* : a theory in geology that the lithosphere is divided into plates at the boundaries of which much of earth's seismic activity occurs

plat·form \'plat-ˌfȯrm\ *n* **1** : a raised flooring or stage for speakers, performers, or workers **2** : a declaration of the principles on which a group of persons (as a political party) stands

plat·ing \'plā-tiŋ\ *n* : a coating of metal plates or plate (the ~ of a ship)

plat·i·num \'plat-ᵊn-əm\ *n* : a heavy grayish white metallic chemical element — see ELEMENT table

plat·i·tude \'pla-tə-ˌtüd, -ˌtyüd\ *n* : a flat or trite remark — **plat·i·tu·di·nous** \-'tüd-ᵊn-əs, -'tyüd-\ *adj*

pla·ton·ic love \plə-'tä-nik-, plā-\ *n*, *often cap P* : a close relationship between two persons without sexual desire

pla·toon \plə-'tün\ *n* [F *peloton* small detachment, lit., ball, fr. *pelote* little ball] **1** : a subdivision of a company-size military unit usu. consisting of two or more squads or sections **2** : a group of football players trained either for offense or for defense and sent into the game as a body

platoon sergeant *n* : a noncommissioned officer in the army ranking below a first sergeant

plat·ter \'pla-tər\ *n* **1** : a large serving plate **2** : a phonograph record

platy \'pla-tē\ *n*, *pl* **platy** *or* **plat·ys** *or* **plat·ies** : either of two small stocky often brilliantly colored bony fishes that are popular for tropical aquariums

platy·pus \'pla-ti-pəs\ *n*, *pl* **platy·pus·es** *also* **platy·pi** \-ˌpī\ [NL, fr. Gk *platypous* flat-footed, fr. *platys* broad, flat + *pous* foot] : a small aquatic egg-laying marsupial mammal of Australia with webbed feet and a fleshy bill like a duck's

platypus

plau·dit \'plȯ-dət\ *n* : an act of applause

plau·si·ble \'plȯ-zə-bəl\ *adj* [L *plausibilis* worthy of applause, fr. *plausus*, pp. of *plaudere* to applaud] : seemingly worthy of belief — **plau·si·bil·i·ty** \ˌplȯ-zə-'bi-lə-tē\ *n* — **plau·si·bly** \'plȯ-zə-blē\ *adv*

¹play \'plā\ *n* **1** : brisk handling of something (as a weapon) **2** : the course of a game; *also* : a particular act or maneuver in a game **3** : recreational activity; *esp* : the spontaneous activity of children **4** : JEST ⟨said in ~⟩ **5** : the act or an instance of punning **6** : GAMBLING **7** : OPERATION ⟨bring extra force into ~⟩ **8** : a brisk or light movement **9** : free motion (as of part of a machine) **10** : scope for action **11** : PUBLICITY **12** : an effort to arouse liking ⟨made a ~ for her⟩ **13** : a stage representation of a drama; *also* : a dramatic composition — **play·ful** \-fəl\ *adj* — **play·ful·ly** *adv* — **play·ful·ness** *n* — **in play** : in condition or position to be played

²play *vb* **1** : to engage in recreation : FROLIC **2** : to handle or behave lightly or absentmindedly **3** : to make a pun ⟨~ on words⟩ **4** : to take advantage ⟨~ on fears⟩ **5** : to move or operate in a brisk or irregular manner ⟨a flashlight ~ed over the wall⟩ **6** : to perform music ⟨~ on a violin⟩; *also* : to perform (music) on an instrument ⟨~ a waltz⟩ **7** : to perform music upon ⟨~ the piano⟩; *also* : to sound in performance ⟨the organ is ~ing⟩ **8** : to cause to emit sounds ⟨~ a radio⟩ **9** : to act in a dramatic medium; *also* : to act in the character of ⟨~ the hero⟩ **10** : GAMBLE **11** : to behave in a specified way ⟨~ safe⟩; *also* : COOPERATE ⟨~ along with him⟩ **12** : to deal with; *also* : EMPHASIZE ⟨~ up her good qualities⟩ **13** : to perform for amusement ⟨~ a trick⟩ **14** : WREAK **15** : to contend with in a game; *also* : to fill (a certain position) on a team **16** : to make wagers on ⟨~ the races⟩ **17** : WIELD, PLY **18** : to keep in action — **play·er** *n*

play·act·ing \'plā-ˌak-tiŋ\ *n* **1** : performance in theatrical productions **2** : insincere or artificial behavior

play·back \-ˌbak\ *n* : an act of reproducing recorded sound or pictures — **play back** *vb*

play·bill \-ˌbil\ *n* : a poster advertising the performance of a play

play·book \-ˌbu̇k\ *n* : a notebook containing diagrammed football plays

play·boy \-ˌbȯi\ *n* : a man whose chief interest is the pursuit of pleasure

play·go·er \-ˌgō-ər\ *n* : a person who frequently attends plays

play·ground \-ˌgrau̇nd\ *n* : an area used for games and play esp. by children

play·house \-ˌhau̇s\ *n* **1** : THEATER **2** : a small house for children to play in

playing card *n* : any of a set of 24 to 78 cards marked to show its rank and suit and used to play a game of cards

play·let \ˈplā-lət\ *n* : a short play

play·mate \-ˌmāt\ *n* : a companion in play

play-off \-ˌȯf\ *n* : a contest or series of contests to break a tie or determine a championship

play·pen \-ˌpen\ *n* : a portable enclosure in which a young child may play

play·suit \-ˌsüt\ *n* : a sports and play outfit for women and children

play·thing \-ˌthiŋ\ *n* : TOY

play·wright \-ˌrīt\ *n* : a writer of plays

pla·za \ˈpla-zə, ˈplä-\ *n* [Sp, fr. L *platea* broad street] **1** : a public square in a city or town **2** : a shopping center

PLC *abbr, Brit* public limited company

plea \ˈplē\ *n* **1** : a defendant's answer in law to a charge or indictment **2** : something alleged as an excuse **3** : ENTREATY, APPEAL

plead \ˈplēd\ *vb* **plead·ed** *or* **pled** \ˈpled\; **plead·ing 1** : to argue before a court or authority ⟨∼ a case⟩ **2** : to answer to a charge or indictment ⟨∼ guilty⟩ **3** : to argue for or against something ⟨∼ for acquittal⟩ **4** : to appeal earnestly ⟨∼s for help⟩ **5** : to offer as a plea (as in defense) ⟨∼ed illness⟩ — **plead·er** *n*

pleas·ant \ˈplez-ᵊnt\ *adj* **1** : giving pleasure : AGREEABLE ⟨a ∼ experience⟩ **2** : marked by pleasing behavior or appearance ⟨a ∼ person⟩ — **pleas·ant·ly** *adv* — **pleas·ant·ness** *n*

pleas·ant·ry \-ᵊn-trē\ *n, pl* **-ries** : a pleasant and casual act or speech

¹please \ˈplēz\ *vb* **pleased; pleas·ing 1** : to give pleasure or satisfaction to **2** : LIKE ⟨do as you ∼⟩ **3** : to be the will or pleasure of ⟨may it ∼ his Majesty⟩

²please *adv* — used as a function word to express politeness or emphasis in a request ⟨∼ come in⟩

pleas·ing *adj* : giving pleasure — **pleas·ing·ly** *adv*

plea·sur·able \ˈple-zhə-rə-bəl\ *adj* : PLEASANT, GRATIFYING — **plea·sur·ably** \-blē\ *adv*

plea·sure \ˈple-zhər\ *n* **1** : DESIRE, INCLINATION ⟨await your ∼⟩ **2** : a state of gratification : ENJOYMENT **3** : a source of delight or joy

¹pleat \ˈplēt\ *vb* **1** : FOLD; *esp* : to arrange in pleats **2** : BRAID

²pleat *n* : a fold (as in cloth) made by doubling material over on itself

plebe \ˈplēb\ *n* : a freshman at a military or naval academy

¹ple·be·ian \pli-ˈbē-ən\ *n* **1** : a member of the Roman plebs **2** : one of the common people

²plebeian *adj* **1** : of or relating to plebeians **2** : COMMON, VULGAR

pleb·i·scite \ˈple-bə-ˌsīt, -sət\ *n* : a vote of the people (as of a country) on a proposal submitted to them

plebs \ˈplebz\ *n, pl* **ple·bes** \ˈplē-bēz\ **1** : the general populace **2** : the common people of ancient Rome

plec·trum \ˈplek-trəm\ *n, pl* **plec·tra** \-trə\ *or* **plectrums** [L] : ³PICK 3

¹pledge \ˈplej\ *n* **1** : something given as security for the performance of an act **2** : the state of being held as a security or guaranty **3** : TOAST 3 **4** : PROMISE, VOW

²pledge *vb* **pledged; pledg·ing 1** : to deposit as a pledge **2** : TOAST 3 : to bind by a pledge : PLIGHT **4** : PROMISE

Pleis·to·cene \ˈplī-stə-ˌsēn\ *adj* : of, relating to, or being the earlier epoch of the Quaternary — **Pleistocene** *n*

ple·na·ry \ˈplē-nə-rē, ˈple-\ *adj* **1** : FULL ⟨∼ power⟩ **2** : including all entitled to attend ⟨∼ session⟩

pleni·po·ten·tia·ry \ˌple-nə-pə-ˈten-chə-rē, -ˌten-chē-ˌer-ē\ *n, pl* **-ries** : a diplomatic agent having full authority — **plenipotentiary** *adj*

plen·i·tude \ˈple-nə-ˌtüd, -ˌtyüd\ *n* **1** : COMPLETENESS **2** : ABUNDANCE

plen·te·ous \ˈplen-tē-əs\ *adj* **1** : FRUITFUL **2** : existing in plenty

plen·ti·ful \ˈplen-ti-fəl\ *adj* **1** : containing or yielding plenty **2** : ABUNDANT — **plen·ti·ful·ly** *adv*

plen·ty \ˈplen-tē\ *n* : a more than adequate number or amount

ple·num \ˈple-nəm, ˈplē-\ *n, pl* **-nums** *or* **-na** \-nə\ : a general assembly of all members esp. of a legislative body

pleth·o·ra \ˈple-thə-rə\ *n* : an excessive quantity or fullness; *also* : PROFUSION

pleu·ri·sy \ˈplu̇r-ə-sē\ *n* : inflammation of the membrane that lines the chest and covers the lungs

plex·us \ˈplek-səs\ *n, pl* **plex·us·es** \-sə-səz\ : an interlacing network esp. of blood vessels or nerves

pli·able \ˈplī-ə-bəl\ *adj* **1** : FLEXIBLE **2** : yielding easily to others **syn** plastic, pliant, ductile, malleable, adaptable — **pli·abil·i·ty** \ˌplī-ə-ˈbi-lə-tē\ *n*

pli·ant \ˈplī-ənt\ *adj* **1** : FLEXIBLE **2** : easily influenced : PLIABLE — **pli·an·cy** \-ən-sē\ *n*

pli·ers \ˈplī-ərz\ *n pl* : small pincers for bending or cutting wire or handling small objects

¹plight \ˈplīt\ *vb* : to put or give in pledge : ENGAGE

²plight *n* : an unfortunate, difficult, or precarious situation

plinth \ˈplinth\ *n* : the lowest part of the base of an architectural column

Plio·cene \ˈplī-ə-ˌsēn\ *adj* : of, relating to, or being the latest epoch of the Tertiary — **Pliocene** *n*

PLO *abbr* Palestine Liberation Organization

plod \ˈpläd\ *vb* **plod·ded; plod·ding 1** : to walk heavily or slowly : TRUDGE **2** : to work laboriously and monotonously : DRUDGE — **plod·der** *n* — **plod·dingly** *adv*

plop \ˈpläp\ *vb* **plopped; plop·ping 1** : to fall or move with a sound like that of something dropping into water **2** : to set, drop, or throw heavily — **plop** *n*

¹plot \ˈplät\ *n* **1** : a small area of ground **2** : a ground plan (as of an area) **3** : the main story (as of a book or movie) **4** : a secret scheme : INTRIGUE

²plot *vb* **plot·ted; plot·ting 1** : to make a plot or plan of **2** : to mark on or as if on a chart **3** : to plan or contrive esp. secretly — **plot·ter** *n*

plo·ver \ˈplə-vər, ˈplō-\ *n, pl* **plover** *or* **plovers** : any of a family of shore-inhabiting birds that differ from the sandpipers in having shorter stouter bills

¹plow *or* **plough** \ˈplau̇\ *n* **1** : an implement used to cut, lift, turn over, and partly break up soil **2** : a device (as a snowplow) operating like a plow

²plow *or* **plough** *vb* **1** : to open, break up, or work with a plow **2** : to move through like a plow ⟨a ship ∼ing the waves⟩ **3** : to proceed laboriously — **plow·able** *adj* — **plow·er** *n*

plow·boy \ˈplau̇-ˌbȯi\ *n* : a boy who leads the horse drawing a plow

plow·man \-mən, -ˌman\ *n* **1** : a man who guides a plow **2** : a farm laborer

plow·share \-ˌsher\ *n* : a part of a plow that cuts the earth

ploy \ˈplȯi\ *n* : a tactic intended to embarrass or frustrate an opponent

¹pluck \ˈplək\ *vb* **1** : to pull off or out : PICK; *also* : to

pull something from **2** : to play (an instrument) by pulling the strings **3** : TUG, TWITCH

²pluck *n* **1** : an act or instance of plucking **2** : SPIRIT, COURAGE

plucky \'plə-kē\ *adj* **pluck·i·er; -est** : COURAGEOUS, SPIRITED

¹plug \'pləg\ *n* **1** : STOPPER; *also* : an obstructing mass **2** : a cake of tobacco **3** : a poor or worn-out horse **4** : SPARK PLUG **5** : a lure with several hooks used in fishing **6** : a device on the end of a cord for making an electrical connection **7** : a piece of favorable publicity

²plug *vb* **plugged; plug·ging 1** : to stop, make tight, or secure by inserting a plug **2** : HIT, SHOOT **3** : to publicize insistently **4** : PLOD, DRUDGE

plum \'pləm\ *n* [ME, fr. OE *plūme*, modif. of L *prunum* plum, fr. Gk *proumnon*] **1** : a smooth-skinned juicy fruit borne by trees related to the peach and cherry; *also* : a tree bearing plums **2** : a raisin when used in desserts (as puddings) **3** : something excellent; *esp* : something desirable given in return for a favor

plum·age \'plü-mij\ *n* : the feathers of a bird — **plumaged** \-mijd\ *adj*

¹plumb \'pləm\ *n* : a weight on the end of a line (**plumb line**) used esp. by builders to show vertical direction

²plumb *adv* **1** : VERTICALLY **2** : COMPLETELY **3** : EXACTLY; *also* : IMMEDIATELY

³plumb *vb* : to sound, adjust, or test with a plumb ⟨∼ the depth of a well⟩

⁴plumb *adj* **1** : VERTICAL **2** : COMPLETE

plumb·er \'plə-mər\ *n* : a worker who fits or repairs pipes and fixtures

plumb·ing \'plə-miŋ\ *n* : a system of pipes in a building for supplying and carrying off water

¹plume \'plüm\ *n* : FEATHER; *esp* : a large, conspicuous, or showy feather — **plumed** \'plümd\ *adj* — **plumy** \'plü-mē\ *adj*

²plume *vb* **plumed; plum·ing 1** : to provide or deck with feathers **2** : to indulge (oneself) in pride

¹plum·met \'plə-mət\ *n* : PLUMB; *also* : PLUMB LINE

²plummet *vb* : to drop or plunge straight down

¹plump \'pləmp\ *vb* **1** : to drop or fall suddenly or heavily **2** : to favor something strongly ⟨∼ing for change⟩

²plump *n* : a sudden heavy fall or blow; *also* : the sound made by it

³plump *adv* **1** : straight down; *also* : straight ahead **2** : UNQUALIFIEDLY

⁴plump *adj* : having a full rounded usu. pleasing form **syn** fleshy, stout, roly-poly, rotund — **plump·ness** *n*

¹plun·der \'plən-dər\ *vb* : to take the goods of by force or wrongfully : PILLAGE — **plun·der·er** *n*

²plunder *n* : something taken by force or theft : LOOT

¹plunge \'plənj\ *vb* **plunged; plung·ing 1** : IMMERSE, SUBMERGE **2** : to enter or cause to enter a state or course of action suddenly or violently ⟨∼ into war⟩ **3** : to cast oneself into or as if into water **4** : to gamble heavily and recklessly **5** : to descend suddenly

²plunge *n* : a sudden dive, leap, or rush

plung·er \'plən-jər\ *n* **1** : one that plunges **2** : a sliding piece driven by or against fluid pressure : PISTON **3** : a rubber cup on a handle pushed against an opening to free a waste outlet of an obstruction

plunk \'pləŋk\ *vb* **1** : to make or cause to make a hollow metallic sound **2** : to drop heavily or suddenly — **plunk** *n*

plu·per·fect \(ˌ)plü-'pər-fikt\ *adj* [ME *pluperfyth*, modif. of LL *plusquamperfectus*, lit., more than perfect] : of, relating to, or constituting a verb tense that denotes an action or state as completed at or before a past time spoken of — **pluperfect** *n*

plu·ral \'plùr-əl\ *adj* [ME, fr. MF & L; MF *plurel*, fr. L *pluralis*, fr. *plur-, plus* more] : of, relating to, or constituting a word form used to denote more than one — **plural** *n*

plu·ral·i·ty \plù-'ra-lə-tē\ *n*, *pl* **-ties 1** : the state of being plural **2** : an excess of votes over those cast for an opposing candidate **3** : the greatest number of votes cast when not a majority

plu·ral·ize \'plùr-ə-ˌlīz\ *vb* **-ized; -iz·ing** : to make plural or express in the plural form — **plu·ral·i·za·tion** \ˌplùr-ə-lə-'zā-shən\ *n*

¹plus \'pləs\ *adj* [L, more] **1** : mathematically positive **2** : having or being in addition to what is anticipated **3** : falling high in a specified range ⟨a grade of B ∼⟩

²plus *n*, *pl* **plus·es** \'plə-səz\ *also* **plus·ses 1** : a sign +

(**plus sign**) used in mathematics to indicate addition or a positive quantity **2** : an added quantity; *also* : a positive quality **3** : SURPLUS

³**plus** *prep* **1** : increased by : with the addition of ⟨3 ∼ 4⟩ **2** : BESIDES

⁴**plus** *conj* : AND ⟨soup ∼ salad and bread⟩

¹**plush** \'pləsh\ *n* : a fabric with a pile longer and less dense than velvet pile — **plushy** *adj*

²**plush** *adj* : notably luxurious — **plush·ly** *adv* — **plush·ness** *n*

Plu·to \'plü-tō\ *n* : the planet farthest from the sun — see PLANET table

plu·toc·ra·cy \plü-'tä-krə-sē\ *n, pl* **-cies 1** : government by the wealthy **2** : a controlling class of the wealthy — **plu·to·crat** \'plü-tə-ˌkrat\ *n* — **plu·to·crat·ic** \ˌplü-tə-'kra-tik\ *adj*

plu·to·ni·um \plü-'tō-nē-əm\ *n* : a radioactive chemical element formed by the decay of neptunium — see ELEMENT table

plu·vi·al \'plü-vē-əl\ *adj* **1** : of or relating to rain **2** : characterized by abundant rain

¹**ply** \'plī\ *vb* **plied; ply·ing 1** : to use, practice, or work diligently ⟨∼ a trade⟩ **2** : to keep supplying something to ⟨plied them with liquor⟩ **3** : to go or travel regularly esp. by sea

²**ply** *n, pl* **plies** : one of the folds, thicknesses, or strands of which something (as plywood or yarn) is made

³**ply** *vb* **plied; ply·ing** : to twist together ⟨∼ yarns⟩

Plym·outh Rock \'pli-məth-\ *n* : any of an American breed of medium-sized single-combed domestic fowls

ply·wood \'plī-ˌwu̇d\ *n* : material made of thin sheets of wood glued and pressed together

pm *abbr* premium

Pm *symbol* promethium

PM *abbr* **1** paymaster **2** police magistrate **3** postmaster **4** post meridiem — often not cap. and often punctuated **5** postmortem **6** prime minister **7** provost marshal

pmk *abbr* postmark

PMS *abbr* premenstrual syndrome

pmt *abbr* payment

pneu·mat·ic \nu̇-'ma-tik, nyu̇-\ *adj* **1** : of, relating to, or using air or wind **2** : moved by air pressure **3** : filled with compressed air — **pneu·mat·i·cal·ly** \-ti-k(ə-)lē\ *adv*

pneu·mo·co·ni·o·sis \ˌnü-mō-ˌkō-nē-'ō-səs, ˌnyü-\ *n* : a disease of the lungs caused by habitual inhalation of irritant mineral or metallic particles

pneu·mo·nia \nu̇-'mō-nyə, nyu̇-\ *n* : an inflammatory disease of the lungs

Po *symbol* polonium

PO *abbr* **1** petty officer **2** post office

¹**poach** \'pōch\ *vb* [ME *pochen*, fr. MF *pocher*, fr. OF *pochier*, lit., to put into a bag, fr. *poche* bag, pocket, of Gmc origin] : to cook (as an egg or fish) in simmering liquid

²**poach** *vb* : to hunt or fish unlawfully — **poach·er** *n*

POB *abbr* post office box

pock \'päk\ *n* : a small swelling on the skin (as in smallpox); *also* : a spot suggesting this

¹**pock·et** \'pä-kət\ *n* **1** : a small bag open at the top or side inserted in a garment **2** : supply of money : MEANS **3** : RECEPTACLE, CONTAINER **4** : a small isolated area or group **5** : a small body of ore — **pock·et·ful** *n*

²**pocket** *vb* **1** : to put in or as if in a pocket **2** : STEAL

³**pocket** *adj* **1** : small enough to fit in a pocket; *also* : SMALL, MINIATURE **2** : carried in or paid from one's own pocket

¹**pock·et·book** \-ˌbu̇k\ *n* **1** : PURSE; *also* : HANDBAG **2** : financial resources

²**pocketbook** *adj* : relating to money

pocket gopher *n* : GOPHER 2

pock·et·knife \'pä-kət-ˌnīf\ *n* : a knife with a folding blade to be carried in the pocket

pocket veto *n* : an indirect veto of a legislative bill by

an executive through retention of the bill unsigned until after adjournment of the legislature

pock·mark \'päk-ˌmärk\ *n* : a pit or scar caused by smallpox or acne — **pock·marked** \-ˌmärkt\ *adj*

po·co \'pō-kō, ˌpō-\ *adv* [It, little, fr. L *paucus*] : SOMEWHAT — used to qualify a direction in music ⟨∼ allegro⟩

po·co a po·co \ˌpō-kō-ä-'pō-kō, ˌpò-kō-ä-'pò-\ *adv* : little by little : GRADUALLY — used as a direction in music

pod \'päd\ *n* **1** : a dry fruit (as of a pea) that splits open when ripe **2** : an external streamlined compartment (as for a jet engine) on an airplane **3** : a compartment (as for personnel, a power unit, or an instrument) on a ship or craft

POD *abbr* pay on delivery

po·di·a·try \pə-'dī-ə-trē, pō-\ *n* : the medical care and treatment of the human foot — **po·di·a·trist** \pə-'dī-ə-trist, pō-\ *n*

po·di·um \'pō-dē-əm\ *n, pl* **podiums** *or* **po·dia** \-dē-ə\ **1** : a dais esp. for an orchestral conductor **2** : LECTERN

POE *abbr* port of entry

po·em \'pō-əm\ *n* : a composition in verse

po·esy \'pō-ə-zē\ *n* : POETRY

po·et \'pō-ət\ *n* [ME, fr. OF *poete*, fr. L *poeta*, fr. Gk *poiētēs* maker, poet, fr. *poiein* to make] : a writer of poetry; *also* : a creative artist of great sensitivity

po·et·as·ter \'pō-ə-ˌtas-tər\ *n* : an inferior poet

po·et·ess \'pō-ə-təs\ *n* : a girl or woman who is a poet

poetic justice *n* : an outcome in which vice is punished and virtue rewarded usu. in a manner peculiarly or ironically appropriate

po·et·ry \'pō-ə-trē\ *n* **1** : metrical writing **2** : POEMS — **po·et·ic** \pō-'e-tik\ *or* **po·et·i·cal** \-ti-kəl\ *adj*

po·grom \'pō-grəm, pō-'gräm\ *n* [Yiddish, fr. Russ, lit., devastation] : an organized massacre of helpless people and esp. of Jews

poi \'pȯi\ *n, pl* **poi** *or* **pois** : a Hawaiian food of taro root cooked, pounded, and kneaded to a paste and often allowed to ferment

poi·gnant \'pȯi-nyənt\ *adj* **1** : painfully affecting the feelings ⟨∼ grief⟩ **2** : deeply moving ⟨∼ scene⟩ — **poi·gnan·cy** \-nyən-sē\ *n*

poin·ci·ana \ˌpȯin-sē-'a-nə\ *n* : any of several ornamental tropical leguminous trees or shrubs with bright orange or red flowers

poin·set·tia \pȯin-'se-tē-ə\ *n* : any of several showy tropical American spurges with usu. scarlet bracts around their small greenish flowers

¹**point** \'pȯint\ *n* **1** : an individual detail; *also* : the most important essential **2** : PURPOSE **3** : a geometric element that has position but no size **4** : a particular place : LOCALITY **5** : a particular stage or degree **6** : a sharp end : TIP **7** : a projecting piece of land **8** : a punctuation mark; *esp* : PERIOD **9** : DECIMAL POINT **10** : one of the divisions of the compass **11** : a unit of counting (as in a game score) — **point·less** *adj* — **pointy** *adj* — **beside the point** : IRRELEVANT — **to the point** : RELEVANT, PERTINENT

²**point** *vb* **1** : to furnish with a point : SHARPEN **2** : PUNCTUATE **3** : to separate (a decimal fraction) from an integer by a decimal point — usu. used with *off* **4** : to indicate the position of esp. by extending a finger **5** : to direct attention to ⟨∼ out an error⟩ **6** : AIM, DIRECT **7** : to lie extended, aimed, or turned in a particular direction : FACE, LOOK

point–blank \'pȯint-'blaŋk\ *adj* **1** : so close to the target that a missile fired will travel in a straight line to the mark **2** : DIRECT, BLUNT — **point–blank** *adv*

point·ed \'pȯin-təd\ *adj* **1** : having a point **2** : being to the point : DIRECT **3** : aimed at a particular person or group; *also* : CONSPICUOUS, MARKED — **point·ed·ly** *adv*

point·er \'pȯin-tər\ *n* **1** : one that points out : INDICATOR **2** : a large short-haired hunting dog **3** : HINT, TIP

poin·til·lism \'pwan-tē-ˌyi-zəm, 'pȯint-əl-ˌi-zəm\ *n* [F

pointillisme, fr. *pointiller* to stipple, fr. *point* point]
: the theory or practice in painting of applying small
strokes or dots of color to a surface so that from a distance they blend together — **poin·til·list** *also* **poin-
til·liste** \ˌpwaⁿ-tē-ˈyēst, ˈpȯint-ᵊl-ist\ *n or adj*
point of no return : a critical point at which turning
back or reversal is not possible
point of view : a position from which something is considered or evaluated

 ¹poise \ˈpȯiz\ *n* **1** : BALANCE **2** : self-possessed calmness; *also* : a particular way
of carrying oneself

²poise *vb* **poised; pois·ing** : BALANCE
poi·sha \ˈpȯi-shə\ *n, pl* **poisha** : the paisa of Bangladesh
¹poi·son \ˈpȯiz-ᵊn\ *n* [ME, fr. OF, drink, poisonous
drink, poison, fr. L *potion-, potio* drink] : a substance
that through its chemical action can injure or kill —
poi·son·ous \-ᵊn-əs\ *adj*
²poison *vb* **1** : to injure or kill with poison **2** : to treat
or taint with poison **3** : to affect destructively : COR-
RUPT (∼*ed* her mind) — **poi·son·er** *n*
poison hemlock *n* : a large branching poisonous herb
with finely divided leaves and white flowers that is
related to the carrot
poison ivy *n* **1** : a usu. climbing plant related to the
sumacs that has leaves composed of three shiny leaflets and produces an irritating oil causing a usu. intensely itching skin rash; *also* : any of several related
plants **2** : a skin rash caused by poison ivy

poison ivy 1

poison oak *n* : any of several shrubby plants closely
related to poison ivy and having similar properties
poison sumac *n* : a smooth American swamp shrub
with pinnate leaves, greenish flowers, greenish white
berries, and irritating properties like the related poison ivy
¹poke \ˈpōk\ *n* : BAG, SACK
²poke *vb* **poked; pok·ing** **1** : PROD; *also* : to stir up by

prodding **2** : to make a prodding or jabbing movement
esp. repeatedly **3** : HIT, PUNCH **4** : to thrust forward
obtrusively **5** : RUMMAGE **6** : MEDDLE, PRY **7** : DAWDLE
— **poke fun at** : RIDICULE, MOCK
³poke *n* : a quick thrust; *also* : PUNCH
¹pok·er \ˈpō-kər\ *n* : a metal rod for stirring a fire
²po·ker \ˈpō-kər\ *n* : any of several card games in which
the player with the highest hand at the end of the betting wins

poker: hands in descending value: *1* five of a kind,
2 royal flush, *3* straight flush, *4* four of a kind, *5* full
house, *6* flush, *7* straight, *8* three of a kind, *9* two
pairs, *10* one pair

poke·weed \ˈpōk-ˌwēd\ *n* : a coarse American perennial herb with clusters of white flowers and dark purple juicy berries
poky *or* **pok·ey** \ˈpō-kē\ *adj* **pok·i·er; -est** **1** : small and
cramped **2** : SHABBY, DULL **3** : annoyingly slow
pol \ˈpäl\ *n* : POLITICIAN
po·lar \ˈpō-lər\ *adj* **1** : of or relating to a geographical
pole **2** : of or relating to a pole (as of a magnet)
polar bear *n* : a large creamy-white bear that inhabits
arctic regions

polar bear

Po·lar·is \pə-ˈlar-əs\ *n* : NORTH STAR
po·lar·ise *Brit var of* POLARIZE
po·lar·i·ty \pō-ˈlar-ə-tē\ *n, pl* **-ties** : the condition of
having poles and esp. magnetic or electrical poles
po·lar·i·za·tion \ˌpō-lə-rə-ˈzā-shən\ *n* **1** : the action of
polarizing : the state of being polarized **2** : concentration about opposing extremes
po·lar·ize \ˈpō-lə-ˌrīz\ *vb* **-ized; -iz·ing** **1** : to cause
(light waves) to vibrate in a definite way **2** : to give

physical polarity to **3** : to break up into opposing groups

pol·der \'pōl-dər, 'päl-\ *n* [D] : a tract of low land reclaimed from the sea

¹**pole** \'pōl\ *n* : a long slender piece of wood or metal ⟨telephone ∼⟩

²**pole** *vb* **poled; pol·ing** : to impel or push with a pole

³**pole** *n* **1** : either end of an axis esp. of the earth **2** : either of the terminals of an electric device (as a battery or generator) **3** : one of two or more regions in a magnetized body at which the magnetism is concentrated — **pole·ward** \'pōl-wərd\ *adj or adv*

Pole \'pōl\ *n* : a native or inhabitant of Poland

¹**pole·ax** \'pō-ˌaks\ *n* : a battle-ax with a short handle

²**poleax** *vb* : to attack or fell with or as if with a poleax

pole·cat \'pōl-ˌkat\ *n, pl* **polecats** *or* **polecat 1** : a European carnivorous mammal of which the ferret is considered a domesticated variety **2** : SKUNK

po·lem·ic \pə-'le-mik\ *n* : the art or practice of disputation — usu. used in pl. — **po·lem·i·cal** \-mi-kəl\ *also* **po·lem·ic** \-mik\ *adj* — **po·lem·i·cist** \-sist\ *n*

pole·star \'pōl-ˌstär\ *n* **1** : NORTH STAR **2** : a directing principle : GUIDE

pole vault *n* : a field contest in which each contestant uses a pole to vault for height over a crossbar — **pole–vault** *vb* — **pole–vault·er** *n*

¹**po·lice** \pə-'lēs\ *vb* **po·liced; po·lic·ing 1** : to control, regulate, or keep in order esp. by use of police ⟨∼ a highway⟩ **2** : to make clean and put in order

²**police** *n, pl* **police** [MF, government, fr. LL *politia*, fr. Gk *politeia*, fr. *politēs* citizen, fr. *polis* city, state] **1** : the department of government that keeps public order and safety and enforces the laws; *also* : the members of this department **2** : a private organization resembling a police force; *also* : its members **3** : military personnel detailed to clean and put in order

po·lice·man \-mən\ *n* : POLICE OFFICER

police officer *n* : a member of a police force

police state *n* : a state characterized by repressive, arbitrary, totalitarian rule by means of secret police

po·lice·wom·an \pə-'lēs-ˌwu̇-mən\ *n* : a woman who is a police officer

¹**pol·i·cy** \'pä-lə-sē\ *n, pl* **-cies** : a definite course or method of action selected to guide and determine present and future decisions

²**policy** *n, pl* **-cies** : a writing whereby a contract of insurance is made

pol·i·cy·hold·er \'pä-lə-sē-ˌhōl-dər\ *n* : one granted an insurance policy

po·lio \'pō-lē-ˌō\ *n, pl* **polios** : POLIOMYELITIS — **polio** *adj*

po·lio·my·eli·tis \-ˌmī-ə-'lī-təs\ *n* : an acute virus disease marked by inflammation of the nerve cells of the spinal cord

¹**pol·ish** \'pä-lish\ *vb* **1** : to make smooth and glossy usu. by rubbing **2** : to refine or improve in manners, condition, or style

²**polish** *n* **1** : a smooth glossy surface : LUSTER **2** : REFINEMENT, CULTURE **3** : the action or process of polishing **4** : a preparation used to produce a gloss

Pol·ish \'pō-lish\ *n* : the Slavic language of the Poles — **Polish** *adj*

polit *abbr* political; politician

po·lit·bu·ro \'pä-lət-ˌbyu̇r-ō, 'pō-, pə-'lit-\ *n* [Russ *politbyuro*] : the principal policy-making committee of a Communist party

po·lite \pə-'līt\ *adj* **po·lit·er; -est 1** : REFINED, CULTIVATED ⟨∼ society⟩ **2** : marked by correct social conduct : COURTEOUS; *also* : CONSIDERATE, TACTFUL — **po·lite·ly** *adv* — **po·lite·ness** *n*

po·li·tesse \ˌpä-li-'tes\ *n* [F] : formal politeness

pol·i·tic \'pä-lə-ˌtik\ *adj* **1** : wise in promoting a policy ⟨a ∼ statesman⟩ **2** : shrewdly tactful ⟨a ∼ move⟩

po·lit·i·cal \pə-'li-ti-kəl\ *adj* **1** : of or relating to government or politics **2** : involving or charged or concerned with acts against a government or a political system ⟨∼ prisoners⟩ — **po·lit·i·cal·ly** \-k(ə-)lē\ *adv*

politically correct *adj* : conforming to a belief that language and practices which could offend sensibilities (as in matters of sex or race) should be eliminated

pol·i·ti·cian \ˌpä-lə-'ti-shən\ *n* : a person actively engaged in government or politics

pol·i·tick \'pä-lə-ˌtik\ *vb* : to engage in political discussion or activity

po·lit·i·co \pə-'li-ti-ˌkō\ *n, pl* **-cos** *also* **-coes** : POLITICIAN

pol·i·tics \'pä-lə-ˌtiks\ *n sing or pl* **1** : the art or science of government, of guiding or influencing governmental policy, or of winning and holding control over a government **2** : political affairs or business; *esp* : competition between groups or individuals for power and leadership **3** : political opinions

pol·i·ty \'pä-lə-tē\ *n, pl* **-ties** : a politically organized unit; *also* : the form or constitution of such a unit

pol·ka \'pōl-kə, 'pō-kə\ *n* [Czech, fr. *Polka* Polish woman, fem. of *Polák* Pole] : a lively couple dance of Bohemian origin; *also* : music for this dance — **polka** *vb*

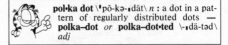

pol·ka dot \'pō-kə-ˌdät\ *n* : a dot in a pattern of regularly distributed dots — **polka–dot** *or* **polka–dot·ted** \-ˌdä-təd\ *adj*

¹**poll** \'pōl\ *n* **1** : HEAD **2** : the casting and recording of votes; *also* : the total vote cast **3** : the place where votes are cast — usu. used in pl. **4** : a questioning of persons to obtain information or opinions to be analyzed

²**poll** *vb* **1** : to cut off or shorten a growth or part of : CLIP, SHEAR **2** : to receive and record the votes of **3** : to receive (as votes) in an election **4** : to question in a poll

pol·lack *or* **pol·lock** \'pä-lək\ *n, pl* **pollack** *or* **pollock** : an important Atlantic food fish that is related to the cods; *also* : a related food fish of the north Pacific

pol·len \'pä-lən\ *n* [NL, fr. L, fine flour] : a mass of male spores of a seed plant usu. appearing as a yellow dust

pol·li·na·tion \ˌpä-lə-'nā-shən\ *n* : the carrying of pollen to the female part of a plant to fertilize the seed — **pol·li·nate** \'pä-lə-ˌnāt\ *vb* — **pol·li·na·tor** \-ˌnā-tər\ *n*

poll·ster \'pōl-stər\ *n* : one that conducts a poll or compiles data obtained by a poll

poll tax *n* : a tax of a fixed amount per person levied on adults

pol·lute \pə-'lüt\ *vb* **pol·lut·ed; pol·lut·ing** : to make impure; *esp* : to contaminate (an environment) esp. with man-made waste — **pol·lut·ant** \-'lüt-ᵊnt\ *n* — **pol·lut·er** *n* — **pol·lu·tion** \-'lü-shən\ *n*

pol·ly·wog *or* **pol·li·wog** \'pä-lē-ˌwäg\ *n* : TADPOLE

po·lo \'pō-lō\ *n* : a game played by two teams on horseback using long-handled mallets to drive a wooden ball

po·lo·ni·um \pə-'lō-nē-əm\ *n* [NL, fr. ML *Polonia* Poland, birthplace of its discoverer, Mme. Curie] : a radioactive metallic chemical element — see ELEMENT table

pol·ter·geist \'pōl-tər-ˌgīst\ *n* [G, fr. *poltern* to knock + *Geist* spirit] : a noisy usu. mischievous ghost held to be responsible for unexplained noises

pol·troon \päl-'trün\ *n* : COWARD

poly- *comb form* **1** : many : several ⟨*poly*syllabic⟩ **2** : polymeric ⟨*poly*ester⟩

poly·chlo·ri·nat·ed bi·phe·nyl \ˌpä-li-'klōr-ə-ˌnā-təd-ˌbī-'fen-ᵊl, -'fēn-\ *n* : any of several industrial compounds that are poisonous environmental pollutants

poly·clin·ic \ˌpä-li-'kli-nik\ *n* : a clinic or hospital treating diseases of many sorts

poly·es·ter \'pä-lē-ˌes-tər\ *n* : a polymer composed of ester groups used esp. in making fibers or plastics

poly·eth·yl·ene \ˌpä-lē-'e-thə-ˌlēn\ *n* : a lightweight plastic resistant to chemicals and moisture and used chiefly in packaging

po·lyg·a·my \pə-'li-gə-mē\ *n* : the practice of having more than one wife or husband at one time — **po·lyg·a·mist** \-mist\ *n* — **po·lyg·a·mous** \-məs\ *adj*

poly·glot \'pä-li-ˌglät\ *adj* **1** : speaking or writing several languages **2** : containing or made up of several languages — **polyglot** *n*

poly·gon \'pä-li-ˌgän\ *n* : a closed plane figure bounded by straight lines — **po·lyg·o·nal** \pə-'li-gən-ᵊl\ *adj*

poly·graph \'pä-li-ˌgraf\ *n* : an instrument for recording variations of several bodily functions (as blood pressure) simultaneously — **po·lyg·ra·pher** \pə-'li-grə-fər, 'pä-li-ˌgra-fər\ *n*

poly·he·dron \ˌpä-li-'hē-drən\ *n* : a solid formed by plane faces that are polygons — **poly·he·dral** \-drəl\ *adj*

poly·math \'pä-li-ˌmath\ *n* : a person of encyclopedic learning

poly·mer \'pä-lə-mər\ *n* : a chemical compound formed by union of small molecules and usu. consisting of repeating structural units — **poly·mer·ic** \ˌpä-lə-'mer-ik\ *adj*

po·lym·er·i·za·tion \pə-ˌli-mə-rə-'zā-shən\ *n* : a chemical reaction in which two or more small molecules combine to form polymers — **po·lym·er·ize** \pə-'li-mə-ˌrīz\ *vb*

Poly·ne·sian \ˌpä-lə-'nē-zhən\ *n* **1** : a member of any of the indigenous peoples of Polynesia **2** : a group of Austronesian languages spoken in Polynesia — **Polynesian** *adj*

poly·no·mi·al \ˌpä-lə-'nō-mē-əl\ *n* : an algebraic expression having one or more terms each of which consists of a constant multiplied by one or more variables raised to a nonnegative integral power — **polynomial** *adj*

pol·yp \'pä-ləp\ *n* **1** : an invertebrate animal (as a coral) that is a coelenterate having a hollow cylindrical body closed at one end **2** : a projecting mass of swollen and hypertrophied or tumorous membrane ⟨a rectal ∼⟩

po·lyph·o·ny \pə-'li-fə-nē\ *n* : music consisting of two

or more melodically independent but harmonizing voice parts — **poly·phon·ic** \ˌpä-li-'fä-nik\ *adj*

poly·pro·pyl·ene \ˌpä-lē-'prō-pə-ˌlēn\ *n* : any of various polymer plastics or fibers

poly·sty·rene \ˌpä-li-'stīr-ˌēn\ *n* : a rigid transparent nonconducting thermoplastic used esp. in molded products and foams

poly·syl·lab·ic \-sə-'la-bik\ *adj* **1** : having more than three syllables **2** : characterized by polysyllabic words

poly·syl·la·ble \ˌpä-li-ˌsi-lə-bəl\ *n* : a polysyllabic word

poly·tech·nic \ˌpä-li-'tek-nik\ *adj* : of, relating to, or instructing in many technical arts or applied sciences

poly·the·ism \'pä-li-thē-ˌi-zəm\ *n* : belief in or worship of many gods — **poly·the·ist** \-ˌthē-ist\ *adj or n* — **poly·the·is·tic** \ˌpä-li-thē-'is-tik\ *adj*

poly·un·sat·u·rat·ed \ˌpä-lē-ˌən-'sa-chə-ˌrā-təd\ *adj* : having many double or triple bonds in a molecule — used esp. of an oil or fatty acid

poly·ure·thane \ˌpä-lē-'yur-ə-ˌthān\ *n* : any of various polymers used esp. in foams and in resins (as for coatings)

poly·vi·nyl \ˌpä-li-'vīn-ᵊl\ *adj* : of, relating to, or being a polymerized vinyl compound, resin, or plastic — often used in combination

pome·gran·ate \'pä-mə-ˌgra-nət\ *n* [ME *poumgrenet*, fr. MF *pomme grenate*, lit., seedy apple] : a tropical reddish fruit with many seeds and an edible crimson pulp; *also* : the tree that bears it

¹**pom·mel** \'pə-məl, 'pä-\ *n* **1** : the knob on the hilt of a sword **2** : the knoblike bulge at the front and top of a saddlebow

²**pom·mel** \'pə-məl\ *vb* **-meled** *or* **-melled; -mel·ing** *or* **-mel·ling** : PUMMEL

pomp \'pämp\ *n* **1** : brilliant display : SPLENDOR **2** : OSTENTATION

pom·pa·dour \'päm-pə-ˌdōr\ *n* : a style of dressing the hair high over the forehead

pom·pa·no \'päm-pə-ˌnō, 'päm-\ *n, pl* **-no** *or* **-nos** : a New World fish esp. of warmer Atlantic coasts

pom–pom \'päm-ˌpäm\ *n* **1** : an ornamental ball or tuft used on a cap or costume **2** : a fluffy ball flourished by cheerleaders

pom·pon \'päm-ˌpän\ *n* **1** : POM-POM **2** : a chrysanthemum or dahlia with small rounded flower heads

pomp·ous \'päm-pəs\ *adj* **1** : suggestive of pomp; *esp* : OSTENTATIOUS **2** : pretentiously dignified **3** : excessively elevated or ornate **syn** arrogant, magisterial, self-important — **pom·pos·i·ty** \päm-'pä-sə-tē\ *n* — **pomp·ous·ly** *adv*

pon·cho \'pän-chō\ *n, pl* **ponchos** [AmerSp, fr. Araucanian (American Indian language of Chile)] **1** : a blanket with a slit in the middle for the head so that it can be worn as a garment **2** : a waterproof garment resembling a poncho

pond \'pänd\ *n* : a small body of water

pon·der \'pän-dər\ *vb* **pon·dered; pon·der·ing 1** : to weigh in the mind **2** : to consider carefully

pon·der·o·sa pine \'pän-də-ˌrō-sə-, -zə-\ *n* : a tall pine of western No. America with long needles; *also* : its strong reddish wood

pon·der·ous \'pän-də-rəs\ *adj* **1** : of very great weight **2** : UNWIELDY, CLUMSY ⟨a ∼ weapon⟩ **3** : oppressively dull ⟨a ∼ speech⟩ **syn** cumbrous, cumbersome, weighty

pone \'pōn\ *n, Southern & Midland* : an oval-shaped cornmeal cake; *also* : corn bread in the form of pones

pon·iard \'pän-yərd\ *n* : DAGGER

pon·tiff \'pän-təf\ *n* : POPE — **pon·tif·i·cal** \pän-'ti-fi-kəl\ *adj*

¹**pon·tif·i·cate** \pän-'ti-fi-kət, -fə-ˌkāt\ *n* : the state, office, or term of office of a pontiff

²**pon·tif·i·cate** \pän-'ti-fə-ˌkāt\ *vb* **-cat·ed; -cat·ing** : to deliver dogmatic opinions

pon·toon \pän-'tün\ *n* **1** : a flat-bottomed boat **2** : a

boat or float used in building a floating temporary bridge **3** : a float of a seaplane

po·ny \'pō-nē\ *n, pl* **ponies** : a small horse

po·ny·tail \-ˌtāl\ *n* : a style of arranging hair to resemble the tail of a pony

pooch \'püch\ *n* : DOG

poo·dle \'püd-ᵊl\ *n* [G *Pudel*, short for *Pudelhund*, fr. *pudeln* to splash + *Hund* dog] : a dog of any of three breeds of active intelligent heavy-coated solid-colored dogs

pooh–pooh \'pü-'pü\ *also* **pooh** \'pü\ *vb* **1** : to express contempt or impatience **2** : DERIDE, SCORN

¹pool \'pül\ *n* **1** : a small deep body of usu. fresh water **2** : a small body of standing liquid **3** : SWIMMING POOL

²pool *vb* : to form a pool

³pool *n* **1** : all the money bet on the result of a particular event **2** : any of several games of billiards played on a table having six pockets **3** : the amount contributed by the participants in a joint venture **4** : a combination between competing firms for mutual profit **5** : a readily available supply

⁴pool *vb* : to combine (as resources) in a common fund or effort

¹poop \'püp\ *n* : an enclosed superstructure at the stern of a ship

²poop *n, slang* : INFORMATION

poop deck *n* : a partial deck above a ship's main afterdeck

poor \'pùr\ *adj* **1** : lacking material possessions ⟨~ people⟩ **2** : less than adequate : MEAGER ⟨~ crop⟩ **3** : arousing pity ⟨you ~ thing⟩ **4** : inferior in quality or value **5** : UNPRODUCTIVE, BARREN ⟨~ soil⟩ **6** : fairly unsatisfactory ⟨~ prospects⟩; *also* : UNFAVORABLE ⟨~ opinion⟩ — **poor·ly** *adv*

poor boy \'pō-ˌbói, 'pōr-\ *n* : SUBMARINE 2

poor·house \'pùr-ˌhaùs\ *n* : a publicly supported home for needy or dependent persons

poor–mouth \-ˌmaùth, -ˌmaùth\ *vb* : to plead poverty as a defense or excuse

¹pop \'päp\ *vb* **popped; pop·ping** **1** : to go, come, enter, or issue forth suddenly or quickly ⟨~ into bed⟩ **2** : to put or thrust suddenly ⟨~ questions⟩ **3** : to burst or cause to burst with a sharp sound; *also* : to make a sharp sound **4** : to protrude from the sockets **5** : SHOOT **6** : to hit a pop-up

²pop *n* **1** : a sharp explosive sound **2** : SHOT **3** : SODA POP

³pop *n* : FATHER

⁴pop *adj* **1** : POPULAR ⟨~ music⟩ **2** : of or relating to pop music ⟨~ singer⟩ **3** : of or relating to the popular culture disseminated through the mass media ⟨~ psychology⟩ **4** : of, relating to, or imitating pop art ⟨~ painter⟩

⁵pop *n* : pop music or culture; *also* : POP ART

⁶pop *adj* : popular population

pop art *n* : art in which commonplace objects (as comic strips or soup cans) are used as subject matter — **pop artist** *n*

pop·corn \'päp-ˌkòrn\ *n* : an Indian corn whose kernels burst open into a white starchy mass when heated; *also* : the burst kernels

pope \'pōp\ *n, often cap* : the head of the Roman Catholic Church

pop–eyed \'päp-ˌīd\ *adj* : having eyes that bulge (as from disease)

pop fly *n* : POP-UP

pop·gun \'päp-ˌgən\ *n* : a toy gun for shooting pellets with compressed air

pop·in·jay \'pä-pən-ˌjā\ *n* [ME *papejay* parrot, fr. MF *papegai, papejai*, fr. Ar *babghā'*] : a strutting supercilious person

pop·lar \'pä-plər\ *n* **1** : any of a genus of slender quick-growing trees (as a cottonwood) related to the willows **2** : the wood of a poplar

pop·lin \'pä-plən\ *n* : a strong plain-woven fabric with crosswise ribs

pop·over \'päp-ˌō-vər\ *n* : a hollow muffin from a thin batter rich in egg

pop·per \'pä-pər\ *n* : a utensil for popping corn

pop·py \'pä-pē\ *n, pl* **poppies** : any of a genus of herbs with showy flowers including one that yields opium

pop·py·cock \-ˌkäk\ *n* : empty talk or writing : NONSENSE

pop·u·lace \'pä-pyə-ləs\ *n* **1** : the common people **2** : POPULATION

pop·u·lar \'pä-pyə-lər\ *adj* **1** : of or relating to the general public ⟨~ government⟩ **2** : suited to the tastes of the general public ⟨~ style⟩ **3** : INEXPENSIVE ⟨~ rates⟩ **4** : frequently encountered or widely accepted ⟨~ notion⟩ **5** : commonly liked or approved ⟨~ teacher⟩ — **pop·u·lar·i·ty** \ˌpä-pyə-'lar-ə-tē\ *n* — **pop·u·lar·ize** \'pä-pyə-lə-ˌrīz\ *vb* — **pop·u·lar·ly** *adv*

pop·u·late \'pä-pyə-ˌlāt\ *vb* **-lat·ed; -lat·ing** **1** : to have a place in : INHABIT **2** : PEOPLE

pop·u·la·tion \ˌpä-pyə-'lā-shən\ *n* **1** : the people or number of people in an area **2** : the organisms inhabiting a particular locality **3** : a group of individuals or items from which samples are taken for statistical measurement

population explosion *n* : a pyramiding of numbers of a biological population; *esp* : the recent great increase in human numbers resulting from increased survival and exponential population growth

pop·u·list \'pä-pyə-list\ *n* : a believer in or advocate of the rights, wisdom, or virtues of the common people — **pop·u·lism** \-ˌli-zəm\ *n*

pop·u·lous \'pä-pyə-ləs\ *adj* **1** : densely populated; *also* : having a large population **2** : CROWDED — **pop·u·lous·ness** *n*

pop–up \'päp-ˌəp\ *n* : a short high fly in baseball

por·ce·lain \'pōr-sə-lən\ *n* : a fine-grained translucent ceramic ware

porch \'pōrch\ *n* : a covered entrance usu. with a separate roof

por·cine \'pȯr-ˌsīn\ *adj* : of, relating to, or suggesting swine

por·cu·pine \'pȯr-kyə-ˌpīn\ *n* [ME *porkepin,* fr. MF *porc espin,* fr. It *porcospino,* fr. L *porcus* pig + *spina* spine, prickle] : any of various mammals having stiff sharp spines mingled with their hair

¹**pore** \'pȯr\ *vb* **pored; por·ing 1** : to read studiously or attentively ⟨∼ over a book⟩ **2** : PONDER, REFLECT

²**pore** *n* : a tiny hole or space (as in the skin or soil) — **pored** \'pȯrd\ *adj*

pork \'pȯrk\ *n* : the flesh of swine dressed for use as food

pork barrel *n* : government projects or appropriations yielding rich patronage benefits

pork·er \'pȯr-kər\ *n* : HOG; *esp* : a young pig suitable for use as fresh pork

por·nog·ra·phy \pȯr-'nä-grə-fē\ *n* : the depiction of erotic behavior intended to cause sexual excitement — **por·no·graph·ic** \ˌpȯr-nə-'gra-fik\ *adj*

po·rous \'pȯr-əs\ *adj* **1** : full of pores **2** : permeable to fluids : ABSORPTIVE — **po·ros·i·ty** \pə-'rä-sə-tē\ *n*

por·phy·ry \'pȯr-fə-rē\ *n, pl* **-ries** : a rock consisting of feldspar crystals embedded in a compact fine-grained base material — **por·phy·rit·ic** \ˌpȯr-fə-'ri-tik\ *adj*

por·poise \'pȯr-pəs\ *n* [ME *porpoys,* fr. MF *porpois,* fr. ML *porcopiscis,* fr. L *porcus* pig + *piscis* fish] : any of a family of small gregarious toothed whales; *also* : DOLPHIN 1

por·ridge \'pȯr-ij\ *n* : a soft food made by boiling meal of grains or legumes in milk or water

por·rin·ger \'pȯr-ən-jər\ *n* : a low one-handled metal bowl or cup

¹**port** \'pȯrt\ *n* **1** : HARBOR **2** : a city with a harbor **3** : AIRPORT

²**port** *n* **1** : an inlet or outlet (as in an engine) for a fluid **2** : PORTHOLE

³**port** *vb* : to turn or put a helm to the left

⁴**port** *n* : the left side of a ship or airplane looking forward — **port** *adj*

⁵**port** *n* : a sweet fortified wine

por·ta·ble \'pȯr-tə-bəl\ *adj* : capable of being carried — **portable** *n*

¹**por·tage** \'pȯr-tij, pȯr-'täzh\ *n* [ME, fr. MF, fr. *porter* to carry] : the carrying of boats and goods overland between navigable bodies of water; *also* : a route for such carrying

²**portage** *vb* **por·taged; por·tag·ing** : to carry gear over a portage

por·tal \'pȯrt-ᵊl\ *n* : DOOR, ENTRANCE; *esp* : a grand or imposing one

portal–to–portal *adj* : of or relating to the time spent by a worker in traveling from the entrance to an employer's property to the worker's actual job site (as in a mine)

port·cul·lis \pȯrt-'kə-ləs\ *n* : a grating at the gateway of a castle or fortress that can be let down to stop entrance

porte co·chere \ˌpȯrt-kō-'sher\ *n* [F *porte cochère,* lit., coach door] : a roofed structure extending from the entrance of a building over an adjacent driveway and sheltering those getting in or out of vehicles

por·tend \pȯr-'tend\ *vb* **1** : to give a sign or warning of beforehand **2** : INDICATE, SIGNIFY **syn** augur, prognosticate, foretell, predict, forecast, prophesy

por·tent \'pȯr-ˌtent\ *n* **1** : something that foreshadows a coming event : OMEN **2** : MARVEL, PRODIGY

por·ten·tous \pȯr-'ten-təs\ *adj* **1** : of, relating to, or constituting a portent **2** : PRODIGIOUS **3** : self-consciously solemn : POMPOUS

¹**por·ter** \'pȯr-tər\ *n, chiefly Brit* : DOORKEEPER

²**porter** *n* **1** : a person who carries burdens; *esp* : one employed (as at a terminal) to carry baggage **2** : an attendant in a railroad car **3** : a dark heavy ale

por·ter·house \'pȯr-tər-ˌhau̇s\ *n* : a choice beefsteak with a large tenderloin

port·fo·lio \pȯrt-'fō-lē-ˌō\ *n, pl* **-li·os 1** : a portable case for papers or drawings **2** : the office and functions of a minister of state **3** : the securities held by an investor

port·hole \'pȯrt-ˌhōl\ *n* : an opening (as a window) in the side of a ship or aircraft

por·ti·co \'pȯr-ti-ˌkō\ *n, pl* **-coes** *or* **-cos** [It] : a row of columns supporting a roof around or at the entrance of a building

¹**por·tion** \'pȯr-shən\ *n* **1** : one's part or share ⟨a ∼ of food⟩ **2** : DOWRY **3** : an individual's lot **4** : a part of a whole ⟨a ∼ of the sky⟩

²**portion** *vb* **1** : to divide into portions **2** : to allot to as a portion

port·land cement \'pȯrt-lənd-\ *n* : a cement made by calcining and grinding a mixture of clay and limestone

port·ly \'pȯrt-lē\ *adj* **port·li·er; -est** : somewhat stout

port·man·teau \pȯrt-'man-ˌtō\ *n, pl* **-teaus** *or* **-teaux** \-ˌtōz\ [MF *portemanteau,* fr. *porter* to carry + *manteau* mantle, fr. L *mantellum*] : a large traveling bag

port of call : an intermediate port where ships customarily stop for supplies, repairs, or transshipment of cargo

port of entry 1 : a place where foreign goods may be cleared through a customhouse **2** : a place where an alien may enter a country

por·trait \'pȯr-trət, -ˌtrāt\ *n* : a picture (as a painting or photograph) of a person usu. showing the face

por·trait·ist \-trə-tist\ *n* : a maker of portraits

por·trai·ture \'pȯr-trə-ˌchu̇r\ *n* : the practice or art of making portraits

por·tray \pȯr-'trā\ *vb* **1** : to make a picture of : DEPICT **2** : to describe in words **3** : to play the role of — **por·tray·al** *n*

Por·tu·guese \'pȯr-chə-ˌgēz, -ˌgēs; ˌpȯr-chə-'gēz, -'gēs\ *n, pl* **Portuguese 1** : a native or inhabitant of Portugal **2** : the language of Portugal and Brazil — **Portuguese** *adj*

Portuguese man–of–war *n* : any of several large colonial marine invertebrate animals related to the jellyfishes and having a large sac by which the colony floats at the surface

por·tu·laca \ˌpȯr-chə-'la-kə\ *n* : a tropical succulent herb cultivated for its showy flowers

pos *abbr* **1** position **2** positive

¹**pose** \'pōz\ *vb* **posed; pos·ing 1** : to assume or cause to assume a posture usu. for artistic purposes **2** : to set forth : PROPOSE ⟨∼ a question⟩ **3** : to affect an attitude or character

²**pose** *n* **1** : a sustained posture; *esp* : one assumed by a model **2** : an attitude assumed for effect : PRETENSE

¹**pos·er** \'pō-zər\ *n* : a puzzling question

²**poser** *n* : a person who poses

po·seur \pō-'zər\ *n* [F, lit., poser] : an affected or insincere person

posh \'päsh\ *adj* : FASHIONABLE

pos·it \'pä-zət\ *vb* : to assume the existence of : POSTULATE

po·si·tion \pə-'zi-shən\ *n* **1** : an arranging in order **2** : the stand taken on a question **3** : the point or area occupied by something : SITUATION **4** : a certain arrangement of bodily parts ⟨exercise in a sitting ∼⟩ **5** : RANK, STATUS **6** : EMPLOYMENT, JOB — **position** *vb*

¹**pos·i·tive** \'pä-zə-tiv\ *adj* **1** : expressed definitely ⟨her answer was a ∼ no⟩ **2** : CONFIDENT, CERTAIN **3** : of, relating to, or constituting the degree of grammatical comparison that denotes no increase in quality, quantity, or relation **4** : not fictitious : REAL **5** : active and effective in function ⟨∼ leadership⟩ **6** : having the light and shade as existing in the original subject ⟨a ∼ photograph⟩ **7** : numerically greater than zero ⟨a ∼ number⟩ **8** : being, relating to, or charged with electricity of which the proton is the elementary unit **9** : AFFIRMATIVE ⟨a ∼ response⟩ — **pos·i·tive·ly** *adv* — **pos·i·tive·ness** *n*

²positive *n* **1** : the positive degree or a positive form in a language **2** : a positive photograph

pos·i·tron \\'pä-zə-ˌträn\\ *n* : a positively charged particle having the same mass and magnitude of charge as the electron

poss *abbr* possessive

pos·se \\'pä-sē\\ *n* [ML *posse comitatus*, lit., power or authority of the county] : a body of persons organized to assist a sheriff in an emergency

pos·sess \pə-'zes\ *vb* **1** : to have as property : OWN **2** : to have as an attribute, knowledge, or skill **3** : to enter into and control firmly ⟨~ed by a devil⟩ — **pos·ses·sor** \-'ze-sər\ *n*

pos·ses·sion \-'ze-shən\ *n* **1** : control or occupancy of property **2** : OWNERSHIP **3** : something owned : PROPERTY **4** : domination by something (as an evil spirit, a passion, or an idea) **5** : SELF-CONTROL

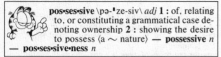

pos·ses·sive \pə-'ze-siv\ *adj* **1** : of, relating to, or constituting a grammatical case denoting ownership **2** : showing the desire to possess ⟨a ~ nature⟩ — **possessive** *n* — **pos·ses·sive·ness** *n*

pos·si·ble \\'pä-sə-bəl\\ *adj* **1** : being within the limits of ability, capacity, or realization **2** : being something that may or may not occur ⟨~ dangers⟩ **3** : able or fitted to become ⟨a ~ site for a bridge⟩ — **pos·si·bil·i·ty** \ˌpä-sə-'bi-lə-tē\ *n* — **pos·si·bly** \\'pä-sə-blē\\ *adv*

pos·sum \\'pä-səm\\ *n* : OPOSSUM

¹post \\'pōst\\ *n* **1** : an upright piece of timber or metal serving esp. as a support : PILLAR **2** : a pole or stake set up as a mark or indicator

²post *vb* **1** : to affix to a usual place (as a wall) for public notices **2** : to publish or announce by or as if by a public notice ⟨~ grades⟩ **3** : to forbid (property) to trespassers by putting up a notice **4** : SCORE 4

³post *n* **1** *obs* : COURIER **2** *chiefly Brit* : ¹MAIL; *also* : POST OFFICE

⁴post *vb* **1** : to ride or travel with haste : HURRY **2** : MAIL ⟨~ a letter⟩ **3** : to enter in a ledger **4** : INFORM ⟨kept him ~ed on new developments⟩

⁵post *n* **1** : the place at which a soldier is stationed; *esp* : a sentry's beat or station **2** : a station or task to which a person is assigned **3** : the place at which a body of troops is stationed : CAMP **4** : OFFICE, POSITION **5** : a trading settlement or station

⁶post *vb* **1** : to station in a given place **2** : to put up (as bond)

post·age \\'pōs-tij\\ *n* : the fee for postal service; *also* : stamps representing this fee

post·al \\'pōst-əl\\ *adj* : of or relating to the mails or the post office

postal card *n* : POSTCARD

postal service *n* : a government agency or department handling the transmission of mail

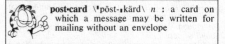

post·card \\'pōst-ˌkärd\\ *n* : a card on which a message may be written for mailing without an envelope

post chaise *n* : a 4-wheeled closed carriage for two to four persons

post·date \ˌpōst-'dāt\ *vb* : to date with a date later than that of execution ⟨~ a check⟩

post·doc·tor·al \-'däk-tə-rəl\ *also* **post·doc·tor·ate** \-tə-rət\ *adj* : of, relating to, or engaged in advanced academic or professional work beyond a doctor's degree

post·er \\'pō-stər\\ *n* : a bill or placard for posting often in a public place

¹pos·te·ri·or \pō-'stir-ē-ər, pä-\ *adj* **1** : later in time **2** : situated behind

²pos·te·ri·or \pä-'stir-ē-ər, pō-\ *n* : the hinder bodily parts; *esp* : BUTTOCKS

pos·ter·i·ty \pä-'ster-ə-tē\ *n* **1** : the descendants from one ancestor **2** : all future generations

pos·tern \\'pōs-tərn, 'päs-\\ *n* **1** : a back door or gate **2** : a private or side entrance

post exchange *n* : a store at a military post that sells to military personnel and authorized civilians

post·grad·u·ate \ˌpōst-'gra-jə-wət\ *adj* : of or relating to studies beyond the bachelor's degree — **postgraduate** *n*

post·haste \\'pōst-'hāst\\ *adv* : with all possible speed

post·hole \-ˌhōl\ *n* : a hole for a post and esp. a fence post

post·hu·mous \'päs-chə-məs\ *adj* **1** : born after the death of the father **2** : published after the death of the author — **post·hu·mous·ly** *adv*

post·hyp·not·ic \ˌpōst-hip-'nä-tik\ *adj* : of, relating to, or characteristic of the period following a hypnotic trance

pos·til·ion *or* **pos·til·lion** \pō-'stil-yən\ *n* : a rider on the left-hand horse of a pair drawing a coach

Post·im·pres·sion·ism \ˌpōst-im-'pre-shə-ˌni-zəm\ *n* : a late 19th century French theory or practice of art that stresses variously volume, picture structure, or expressionism

post·lude \'pōst-ˌlüd\ *n* : an organ solo played at the end of a church service

post·man \-mən, -ˌman\ *n* : MAILMAN

post·mark \-ˌmärk\ *n* : an official postal marking on a piece of mail; *esp* : the mark canceling the postage stamp — **postmark** *vb*

post·mas·ter \-ˌmas-tər\ *n* : a person who has charge of a post office

postmaster general *n, pl* **postmasters general** : an official in charge of a national postal service

post me·ri·di·em \ˌpōst-mə-'ri-dē-əm\ *adj* [L] : being after noon

post·mis·tress \'pōst-ˌmis-trəs\ *n* : a woman in charge of a post office

¹post·mor·tem \ˌpōst-'mòr-təm\ *adj* [L *post mortem* after death] **1** : done, occurring, or collected after death **2** : following the event

²postmortem *n* **1** : an analysis or discussion of an event after it is over **2** : AUTOPSY

post·na·sal drip \'pōst-ˌnā-zəl-\ *n* : flow of mucous secretion from the posterior part of the nasal cavity onto the wall of the pharynx

post·na·tal \(ˌ)pōst-'nāt-ᵊl\ *adj* : occurring or being after birth; *esp* : of or relating to a newborn infant

post office *n* **1** : POSTAL SERVICE **2** : a local branch of a post office department

post·op·er·a·tive \(ˌ)pōst-'ä-prə-tiv, -pə-ˌrā-\ *adj* : following or having undergone a surgical operation ⟨∼ care⟩

post·paid \'pōst-'pād\ *adv* : with the postage paid by the sender and not chargeable to the receiver

post·par·tum \(ˌ)pōst-'pär-təm\ *adj* [NL *post partum* after birth] : following parturition — **postpartum** *adv*

post·pone \pōst-'pōn\ *vb* **post·poned; post·pon·ing** : to put off to a later time — **post·pone·ment** *n*

post road *n* : a road over which mail is carried

post·script \'pōst-ˌskript\ *n* : a note added esp. to a completed letter

post time *n* : the designated time for the start of a horse race

pos·tu·lant \'päs-chə-lənt\ *n* : a probationary candidate for membership in a religious order

¹pos·tu·late \'päs-chə-ˌlāt\ *vb* **-lat·ed; -lat·ing** : to assume as true

²pos·tu·late \'päs-chə-lət, -ˌlāt\ *n* : a proposition taken for granted as true esp. as a basis for a chain of reasoning

¹pos·ture \'päs-chər\ *n* **1** : the position or bearing of the body or one of its parts **2** : STATE, CONDITION **3** : ATTITUDE

²posture *vb* **pos·tured; pos·tur·ing** : to strike a pose esp. for effect

post·war \'pōst-'wòr\ *adj* : of or relating to the period after a war

po·sy \'pō-zē\ *n, pl* **posies 1** : a brief sentiment : MOTTO **2** : a bunch of flowers; *also* : FLOWER

¹pot \'pät\ *n* **1** : a rounded container used chiefly for domestic purposes **2** : the total of the bets at stake at one time **3** : RUIN ⟨go to ∼⟩ — **pot·ful** *n*

²pot *vb* **pot·ted; pot·ting 1** : to preserve or place in a pot **2** : SHOOT

³pot *n* : MARIJUANA

po·ta·ble \'pō-tə-bəl\ *adj* : suitable for drinking — **po·ta·bil·i·ty** \ˌpō-tə-'bi-lə-tē\ *n*

po·tage \pō-'täzh\ *n* : a thick soup

pot·ash \'pät-ˌash\ *n* [sing. of *pot ashes*] : potassium or any of its various compounds esp. as used in agriculture

po·tas·si·um \pə-'ta-sē-əm\ *n* : a silver-white soft metallic chemical element that occurs abundantly in nature — see ELEMENT table

potassium bromide *n* : a crystalline salt used as a sedative and in photography

potassium carbonate *n* : a white salt used in making glass and soap

potassium nitrate *n* : a soluble salt used in making gunpowder, as a fertilizer, and in medicine

po·ta·tion \pō-'tā-shən\ *n* : a usu. alcoholic drink; *also* : the act of drinking

po·ta·to \pə-'tā-tō\ *n, pl* **-toes** : the edible starchy tuber of a plant related to the tomato; *also* : this plant

potato beetle *n* : COLORADO POTATO BEETLE

potato bug *n* : COLORADO POTATO BEETLE

pot·bel·ly \'pät-ˌbe-lē\ *n* : a protruding abdomen — **pot·bel·lied** \-lēd\ *adj*

pot·boil·er \-ˌbòi-lər\ *n* : a usu. inferior work of art or literature produced chiefly for profit

po·tent \'pōt-ᵊnt\ *adj* **1** : having authority or influence : POWERFUL **2** : chemically or medicinally effective **3** : able to copulate — used esp. of the male **syn** forceful, forcible, mighty, puissant — **po·ten·cy** \-ᵊn-sē\ *n*

po·ten·tate \'pōt-ᵊn-ˌtāt\ *n* : one who wields controlling power : RULER

¹po·ten·tial \pə-'ten-chəl\ *adj* : existing in possibility : capable of becoming actual ⟨a ∼ champion⟩ **syn** dormant, latent, quiescent — **po·ten·ti·al·i·ty** \pə-ˌten-chē-'a-lə-tē\ *n* — **po·ten·tial·ly** \-'ten-chə-lē\ *adv*

²potential *n* **1** : something that can develop or become actual ⟨a ∼ for violence⟩ **2** : the work required to move a unit positive charge from infinity to a point in question; *also* : POTENTIAL DIFFERENCE

potential difference *n* : the difference in potential between two points that represents the work involved in the transfer of a unit quantity of electricity from one point to the other

potential energy *n* : the energy an object has because of its position or the arrangement of its parts

po·ten·ti·ate \pə-'ten-chē-ˌāt\ *vb* **-at·ed; -at·ing** : to make potent; *esp* : to augment the activity of (as a drug) synergistically — **po·ten·ti·a·tion** \-ˌten-chē-'ā-shən\ *n*

pot·head \'pät-ˌhed\ *n* : a person who smokes marijuana

poth·er \'pä-thər\ *n* : a noisy disturbance; *also* : FUSS

pot·herb \'pät-ˌərb, -ˌhərb\ *n* : an herb whose leaves or stems are boiled for greens or used to season food

pot·hole \'pät-ˌhōl\ *n* : a large pit or hole (as in a road surface)

pot·hook \-ˌhùk\ *n* : an S-shaped hook for hanging pots and kettles over an open fire

po·tion \'pō-shən\ *n* : a mixture of liquids (as liquor or medicine)

pot·luck \'pät-'lək\ *n* : the regular meal available to a guest for whom no special preparations have been made

pot·pie \-'pī\ *n* : pastry-covered meat and vegetables cooked in a deep dish

pot·pour·ri \ˌpō-pù-'rē\ *n* [F *pot pourri*, lit., rotten pot] **1** : a mixture of flowers, herbs, and spices used for scent **2** : a miscellaneous collection

pot·sherd \'pät-ˌshərd\ *n* : a pottery fragment

pot·shot \-ˌshät\ *n* **1** : a shot taken from ambush or at a random or easy target **2** : a critical remark made in a random or sporadic manner

pot·tage \'pä-tij\ *n* : a thick soup of vegetables and often meat

¹pot·ter \'pä-tər\ *n* : one that makes pottery

²potter *vb* : PUTTER

pot·tery \'pä-tə-rē\ n, pl -ter·ies 1 : a place where earthen pots and dishes are made 2 : the art of the potter 3 : dishes, pots, and vases made from clay

¹pouch \'pau̇ch\ n 1 : a small bag (as for tobacco) carried on the person 2 : a bag for storing or transporting goods ⟨mail ∼⟩ ⟨diplomatic ∼⟩ 3 : an anatomical sac; esp : one for carrying the young on the abdomen of a female marsupial (as a kangaroo)

²pouch vb : to put or form into or as if into a pouch

poult \'pōlt\ n : a young fowl; esp : a young turkey

poul·ter·er \'pōl-tər-ər\ n : one that deals in poultry

poul·tice \'pōl-təs\ n : a soft usu. heated and medicated mass spread on cloth and applied to a sore or injury — poultice vb

poul·try \'pōl-trē\ n : domesticated birds kept for eggs or meat — poul·try·man \-mən\ n

pounce \'pau̇ns\ vb pounced; pounc·ing : to spring or swoop upon and seize something

¹pound \'pau̇nd\ n, pl pounds also pound 1 : a unit of avoirdupois, troy, and apothecaries' weight — see WEIGHT table 2 — see MONEY table

²pound n : a public enclosure where stray animals are kept

³pound vb 1 : to crush to a powder or pulp by beating 2 : to strike or beat heavily or repeatedly 3 : DRILL 1 4 : to move or move along heavily

pound·age \'pau̇n-dij\ n : POUNDS; also : weight in pounds

pound cake n : a rich cake made with a large proportion of eggs and shortening

pound–fool·ish \'pau̇nd-'fü-lish\ adj : imprudent in dealing with large sums or large matters

pour \'pōr\ vb 1 : to flow or cause to flow in a stream or flood 2 : to rain hard 3 : to supply freely and copiously

pour·boire \pu̇r-'bwär\ n [F, fr. pour boire for drinking] : TIP, GRATUITY

pout \'pau̇t\ vb : to show displeasure by thrusting out the lips; also : to look sullen — pout n

pov·er·ty \'pä-vər-tē\ n [ME poverte, fr. OF poverté, fr. L paupertat-, paupertas, fr. pauper poor] 1 : lack of money or material possessions : WANT 2 : poor quality (as of soil)

poverty line n : a level of personal or family income below which one is classified as poor according to government standards

pov·er·ty–strick·en \'pä-vər-tē-ˌstri-kən\ adj : very poor : DESTITUTE

POW \ˌpē-(ˌ)ō-'də-bəl-(ˌ)yü\ n : PRISONER OF WAR

¹pow·der \'pau̇-dər\ n [ME poudre, fr. OF, fr. L pulver-, pulvis dust] 1 : dry material made up of fine particles; also : a usu. medicinal or cosmetic preparation in this form 2 : a solid explosive (as gunpowder) — pow·dery adj

²powder vb 1 : to sprinkle or cover with or as if with powder 2 : to reduce to powder

powder room n : a rest room for women

¹pow·er \'pau̇-ər\ n 1 : the ability to act or produce an effect 2 : a position of ascendancy over others : AUTHORITY 3 : one that has control or authority; esp : a sovereign state 4 : physical might; also : mental or moral vigor 5 : the number of times as indicated by an exponent a number is to be multiplied by itself; also : the product itself 6 : force or energy used to do work; also : the time rate at which work is done or energy transferred 7 : MAGNIFICATION 2 — pow·er·ful \-fəl\ adj — pow·er·ful·ly adv — pow·er·less adj

²power vb : to supply with power and esp. motive power

pow·er·boat \-ˌbōt\ n : MOTORBOAT

pow·er·house \'pau̇-ər-ˌhau̇s\ n 1 : POWER PLANT 1 2 : one having great drive, energy, or ability

power plant n 1 : a building in which electric power is generated 2 : an engine and related parts supplying the motive power of a self-propelled vehicle

pow·wow \'pau̇-ˌwau̇\ n 1 : a No. American Indian ceremony (as for victory in war) 2 : a meeting for discussion : CONFERENCE

pox \'päks\ n, pl pox or pox·es : any of various diseases (as smallpox or syphilis) marked by a rash on the skin

pp abbr 1 pages 2 pianissimo

PP abbr 1 parcel post 2 past participle 3 postpaid 4 prepaid

ppd abbr 1 postpaid 2 prepaid

PPS abbr [L post postscriptum] an additional postscript

ppt abbr precipitate

PQ abbr Province of Quebec

pr abbr 1 pair 2 price

Pr symbol praseodymium

PR abbr 1 payroll 2 public relations 3 Puerto Rico

prac·ti·ca·ble \'prak-ti-kə-bəl\ adj : capable of being put into practice, done, or accomplished — prac·ti·ca·bil·i·ty \ˌprak-ti-kə-'bi-lə-tē\ n

prac·ti·cal \'prak-ti-kəl\ adj 1 : of, relating to, or shown in practice ⟨∼ questions⟩ 2 : VIRTUAL ⟨∼ control⟩ 3 : capable of being put to use ⟨a ∼ knowledge of French⟩ 4 : inclined to action as opposed to speculation ⟨a ∼ person⟩ 5 : qualified by practice ⟨a good ∼ mechanic⟩ — prac·ti·cal·i·ty \ˌprak-ti-'ka-lə-tē\ n — prac·ti·cal·ly \-k(ə-)lē\ adv

practical joke n : a prank intended to trick or embarrass someone or cause physical discomfort

practical nurse n : a professional nurse without all of the qualifications of a registered nurse; esp : LICENSED PRACTICAL NURSE

¹prac·tice or prac·tise \'prak-təs\ vb prac·ticed or prac·tised; prac·tic·ing or prac·tis·ing 1 : CARRY OUT, APPLY ⟨∼ what you preach⟩ 2 : to perform or work at repeatedly so as to become proficient ⟨∼ tennis strokes⟩ 3 : to do or perform customarily ⟨∼ politeness⟩ 4 : to be professionally engaged in ⟨∼ law⟩

²practice also practise n 1 : actual performance or application 2 : customary action 3 : HABIT 3 : systematic exercise for proficiency 4 : the exercise of a profession; also : a professional business

prac·ti·tion·er \prak-ˈti-shə-nər\ *n* : one who practices a profession

prae·tor \ˈprē-tər\ *n* : an ancient Roman magistrate ranking below a consul — **prae·to·ri·an** \prē-ˈtōr-ē-ən, -ˈtȯr-\ *adj*

prag·mat·ic \prag-ˈma-tik\ *also* **prag·mat·i·cal** \-ti-kəl\ *adj* **1** : of or relating to practical affairs **2** : concerned with the practical consequences of actions or beliefs — **pragmatic** *n* — **prag·mat·i·cal·ly** \-ti-k(ə-)lē\ *adv*

prag·ma·tism \ˈprag-mə-ˌti-zəm\ *n* : a practical approach to problems and affairs

prai·rie \ˈprer-ē\ *n* : a broad tract of level or rolling grassland

prairie dog *n* : an American burrowing black‑tailed rodent related to the squirrels and living in colonies

prairie schooner *n* : a covered wagon used by pioneers in cross-country travel

praise \ˈprāz\ *vb* **praised; prais·ing 1** : to express approval of : COMMEND **2** : to glorify (a divinity or a saint) esp. in song — **praise** *n*

praise·wor·thy \-ˌwər-thē\ *adj* : LAUDABLE

pra·line \ˈprä-ˌlēn, ˈprä-\ *n* [F] : a confection of nuts and sugar

pram \ˈpram\ *n, chiefly Brit* : PERAMBULATOR

prance \ˈprans\ *vb* **pranced; pranc·ing 1** : to spring from the hind legs ⟨a *prancing* horse⟩ **2** : SWAGGER; *also* : CAPER — **prance** *n* — **pranc·er** *n*

prank \ˈpraŋk\ *n* : a playful or mildly mischievous act : TRICK

prank·ster \ˈpraŋk-stər\ *n* : a person who plays pranks

pra·seo·dym·i·um \ˌprā-zē-ō-ˈdi-mē-əm\ *n* : a yellow-ish white metallic chemical element — see ELEMENT table

prate \ˈprāt\ *vb* **prat·ed; prat·ing** : to talk long and idly : chatter foolishly

prat·fall \ˈprat-ˌfȯl\ *n* **1** : a fall on the buttocks **2** : a humiliating blunder

¹prat·tle \ˈprat-ᵊl\ *vb* **prat·tled; prat·tling** : PRATE, BABBLE

²prattle *n* : trifling or childish talk

prawn \ˈprȯn\ *n* : any of numerous edible shrimplike crustaceans; *also* : SHRIMP 1

pray \ˈprā\ *vb* **1** : ENTREAT, IMPLORE **2** : to ask earnestly for something **3** : to address God or a god esp. with supplication

prayer \ˈprar\ *n* **1** : a supplication or expression addressed to God or a god; *also* : a set order of words used in praying **2** : an earnest request or wish **3** : the act or practice of praying to God or a god **4** : a religious service consisting chiefly of prayers — often used in pl. **5** : something prayed for **6** : a slight chance

prayer book *n* : a book containing prayers and often directions for worship

prayer·ful \ˈprar-fəl\ *adj* **1** : DEVOUT **2** : EARNEST — **prayer·ful·ly** *adv*

praying mantis *n* : MANTIS

PRC *abbr* People's Republic of China

preach \ˈprēch\ *vb* **1** : to deliver a sermon **2** : to set forth in a sermon **3** : to advocate earnestly — **preach·er** *n* — **preach·ment** *n*

pre·ad·o·les·cence \ˈprē-ˌad-ᵊl-ˈes-ᵊns\ *n* : the period of human development just preceding adolescence — **pre·ad·o·les·cent** \-ᵊnt\ *adj or n*

pre·am·ble \ˈprē-ˌam-bəl\ *n* [ME, fr. MF *preambule*, fr. ML *preambulum*, fr. LL, neut. of *praeambulus* walking in front of, fr. L *prae* in front of + *ambulare* to walk] : an introductory part ⟨the ∼ to a constitution⟩

pre·ar·range \ˌprē-ə-ˈrānj\ *vb* : to arrange beforehand — **pre·ar·range·ment** *n*

pre·as·signed \ˌprē-ə-ˈsīnd\ *adj* : assigned beforehand

prec *abbr* preceding

Pre·cam·bri·an \ˈprē-ˈkam-brē-ən, -ˈkām-\ *adj* : of, relating to, or being the era that is earliest in geologic history and is characterized esp. by the appearance of single-celled organisms — **Precambrian** *n*

pre·can·cel \ˌprē-ˈkan-səl\ *vb* : to cancel (a postage stamp) in advance of use — **precancel** *n* — **pre·can·cel·la·tion** \ˌprē-ˌkan-sə-ˈlā-shən\ *n* :

pre·can·cer·ous \ˌprē-ˈkan-sə-rəs\ *adj* : likely to become cancerous

pre·car·i·ous \pri-ˈkar-ē-əs\ *adj* : dependent on uncertain conditions : dangerously insecure : UNSTABLE ⟨a ∼ foothold⟩ ⟨∼ prosperity⟩ **syn** delicate, sensitive, ticklish, touchy, tricky — **pre·car·i·ous·ly** *adv* — **pre·car·i·ous·ness** *n*

pre·cau·tion \pri-ˈkȯ-shən\ *n* : a measure taken beforehand to prevent harm or secure good — **pre·cau·tion·ary** \-shə-ˌner-ē\ *adj*

pre·cede \pri-ˈsēd\ *vb* **pre·ced·ed; pre·ced·ing** : to be, go, or come ahead or in front of (as in rank or time)

prec·e·dence \ˈpre-sə-dəns, pri-ˈsēd-ᵊns\ *n* **1** : the act or fact of preceding **2** : consideration based on order of importance : PRIORITY

¹prec·e·dent \pri-ˈsēd-ᵊnt, ˈpre-sə-dənt\ *adj* : prior in time, order, or significance

²prec·e·dent \ˈpre-sə-dənt\ *n* : something said or done that may serve to authorize or justify further words or acts of the same or a similar kind

pre·ced·ing \pri-ˈsē-diŋ\ *adj* : that precedes **syn** antecedent, foregoing, prior, former, anterior

pre·cen·tor \pri-ˈsen-tər\ *n* : a leader of the singing of a choir or congregation

pre·cept \ˈprē-ˌsept\ *n* : a command or principle intended as a general rule of action or conduct

pre·cep·tor \pri-ˈsep-tər, ˈprē-ˌsep-\ *n* : TUTOR

pre·ces·sion \prē-ˈse-shən\ *n* : a slow gyration of the rotation axis of a spinning body (as the earth) — **pre·cess** \prē-ˈses\ *vb* — **pre·ces·sion·al** \-ˈsə-shə-nəl\ *adj*

pre·cinct \ˈprē-ˌsiŋkt\ *n* **1** : an administrative subdivision (as of a city) : DISTRICT ⟨police ∼⟩ ⟨electoral ∼⟩ **2** : an enclosure bounded by the limits of a building or place — often used in pl. **3** *pl* : ENVIRONS

pre·ci·os·i·ty \ˌpre-shē-ˈä-sə-tē\ *n, pl* **-ties** : fastidious refinement

pre·cious \ˈpre-shəs\ *adj* **1** : of great value ⟨∼ jewels⟩ **2** : greatly cherished : DEAR ⟨∼ memories⟩ **3** : AFFECTED ⟨∼ language⟩

prec·i·pice \ˈpre-sə-pəs\ *n* : a steep cliff

pre·cip·i·tan·cy \pri-ˈsi-pə-tən-sē\ *n* : undue hastiness or suddenness

¹pre·cip·i·tate \pri-ˈsi-pə-ˌtāt\ *vb* **-tat·ed; -tat·ing** [L *praecipitare*, fr. *praecipit-, praeceps* headlong, fr. *prae* in front of + *caput* head] **1** : to throw violently **2** : to throw down **3** : to cause to happen quickly or abruptly ⟨∼ a quarrel⟩ **4** : to cause to separate from solution or suspension **5** : to fall as rain, snow, or hail **syn** speed, accelerate, quicken, hasten, hurry

²pre·cip·i·tate \pri-ˈsi-pə-tət, -ˌtāt\ *n* : the solid matter that separates from a solution or suspension

³pre·cip·i·tate \pri-ˈsi-pə-tət\ *adj* **1** : showing extreme or unwise haste : RASH **2** : falling with steep descent; *also* : PRECIPITOUS — **pre·cip·i·tate·ly** *adv* — **pre·cip·i·tate·ness** *n*

pre·cip·i·ta·tion \pri-ˌsi-pə-ˈtā-shən\ *n* **1** : rash haste **2** : the process of precipitating or forming a precipitate **3** : water that falls to earth esp. as rain or snow; *also* : the quantity of this water

pre·cip·i·tous \pri-ˈsi-pə-təs\ *adj* **1** : PRECIPITATE **2** : having the character of a precipice : very steep ⟨a ∼ slope⟩; *also* : containing precipices ⟨∼ trails⟩ — **pre·cip·i·tous·ly** *adv*

pré·cis \prā-ˈsē\ *n, pl* **pré·cis** \-ˈsēz\ [F] : a concise summary of essentials

pre·cise \pri-ˈsīs\ *adj* **1** : exactly defined or stated : DEFINITE **2** : highly accurate : EXACT **3** : conforming strictly to a standard : SCRUPULOUS — **pre·cise·ly** *adv* — **pre·cise·ness** *n*

pre·ci·sion \pri-ˈsi-zhən\ *n* : the quality or state of being precise

pre·clude \pri-ˈklüd\ *vb* **pre·clud·ed; pre·clud·ing** : to make impossible : BAR, PREVENT

pre·co·cious \pri-ˈkō-shəs\ *adj* [L *praecoc-, praecox,* lit., ripening early, fr. *prae-* ahead + *coquere* to cook] : early in development and esp. in mental development — **pre·co·cious·ly** *adv* — **pre·coc·i·ty** \pri-ˈkä-sə-tē\ *n*

pre·con·ceive \ˌprē-kən-ˈsēv\ *vb* : to form an opinion of beforehand — **pre·con·cep·tion** \-ˈsep-shən\ *n*

pre·con·cert·ed \-ˈsər-təd\ *adj* : arranged or agreed on in advance

pre·con·di·tion \-ˈdi-shən\ *vb* : to put in proper or desired condition or frame of mind in advance

pre·cook \ˌprē-ˈkůk\ *vb* : to cook partially or entirely before final cooking or reheating

pre·cur·sor \pri-ˈkər-sər\ *n* : one that precedes and indicates the approach of another : FORERUNNER

pred *abbr* predicate

pre·da·ceous *or* **pre·da·cious** \pri-ˈdā-shəs\ *adj* : living by preying on others : PREDATORY

pre·date \ˈprē-ˈdāt\ *vb* : ANTEDATE

pre·da·tion \pri-ˈdā-shən\ *n* **1** : the act of preying or plundering **2** : a mode of life in which food is primarily obtained by killing and consuming animals

pred·a·tor \ˈpre-də-tər\ *n* : an animal that lives by predation

pred·a·to·ry \ˈpre-də-ˌtōr-ē\ *adj* **1** : of or relating to plunder ⟨∼ warfare⟩ **2** : disposed to exploit others **3** : preying upon other animals

pre·de·cease \ˌprē-di-ˈsēs\ *vb* **-ceased; -ceas·ing** : to die before another person

pre·de·ces·sor \ˈpre-də-ˌse-sər, ˈprē-\ *n* : a previous holder of a position to which another has succeeded

pre·des·ig·nate \(ˌ)prē-ˈde-zig-ˌnāt\ *vb* : to designate beforehand

pre·des·ti·na·tion \ˌprē-ˌdes-tə-ˈnā-shən\ *n* : the act of foreordaining to an earthly lot or eternal destiny by divine decree; *also* : the state of being so foreordained — **pre·des·ti·nate** \prē-ˈdes-tə-ˌnāt\ *vb*

pre·des·tine \prē-ˈdes-tən\ *vb* : to settle beforehand : FOREORDAIN

pre·de·ter·mine \ˌprē-di-ˈtər-mən\ *vb* : to determine beforehand

pred·i·ca·ble \ˈpre-di-kə-bəl\ *adj* : capable of being predicated or affirmed

pre·dic·a·ment \pri-ˈdi-kə-mənt\ *n* : a difficult or trying situation **syn** dilemma, pickle, quagmire, jam

¹pred·i·cate \ˈpre-di-kət\ *n* : the part of a sentence or clause that expresses what is said of the subject

²pred·i·cate \ˈpre-də-ˌkāt\ *vb* **-cat·ed; -cat·ing 1** : AFFIRM **2** : to assert to be a quality or attribute **3** : FOUND, BASE — **pred·i·ca·tion** \ˌpre-də-ˈkā-shən\ *n*

pre·dict \pri-ˈdikt\ *vb* : to declare in advance — **pre·dict·abil·i·ty** \-ˌdik-tə-ˈbi-lə-tē\ *n* — **pre·dict·able** \-ˈdik-tə-bəl\ *adj* — **pre·dict·ably** \-blē\ *adv* — **pre·dic·tion** \-ˈdik-shən\ *n*

pre·di·gest \ˌprē-dī-ˈjest\ *vb* : to simplify for easy use; *also* : to subject to artificial or natural partial digestion

pre·di·lec·tion \ˌpre-də-ˈlek-shən, ˌprē-\ *n* : an established preference for something

pre·dis·pose \ˌprē-di-ˈspōz\ *vb* : to incline in advance : make susceptible — **pre·dis·po·si·tion** \ˌprē-ˌdis-pə-ˈzi-shən\ *n*

pre·dom·i·nant \pri-ˈdä-mə-nənt\ *adj* : greater in importance, strength, influence, or authority — **pre·dom·i·nance** \-nəns\ *n*

pre·dom·i·nant·ly \-nənt-lē\ *adv* : for the most part : MAINLY

pre·dom·i·nate \pri-ˈdä-mə-ˌnāt\ *vb* : to be superior esp. in power or numbers : PREVAIL

pree·mie \ˈprē-mē\ *n* : a premature baby

pre·em·i·nent \prē-ˈe-mə-nənt\ *adj* : having highest rank : OUTSTANDING — **pre·em·i·nence** \-nəns\ *n* — **pre·em·i·nent·ly** *adv*

pre·empt \prē-ˈempt\ *vb* **1** : to settle upon (public land) with the right to purchase before others; *also* : to take by such right **2** : to seize upon before someone else can **3** : to take the place of **syn** usurp, confiscate, appropriate, expropriate — **pre·emp·tion** \-ˈemp-shən\ *n*

pre·emp·tive \prē-ˈemp-tiv\ *adj* : marked by the seizing of the initiative : initiated by oneself ⟨∼ attack⟩

preen \ˈprēn\ *vb* **1** : to dress or smooth up : PRIMP **2** : to trim or dress with the bill — used of a bird **3** : to pride (oneself) for achievement

pre·ex·ist \ˌprē-ig-ˈzist\ *vb* : to exist before — **pre·ex·is·tence** \-ˈzis-təns\ *n* — **pre·ex·is·tent** \-tənt\ *adj*

pref *abbr* **1** preface **2** preference **3** preferred **4** prefix

pre·fab \(ˌ)prē-ˈfab, ˈprē-ˌfab\ *n* : a prefabricated structure

pre·fab·ri·cate \(ˌ)prē-ˈfa-brə-ˌkāt\ *vb* : to manufacture the parts of (a structure) beforehand for later assembly — **pre·fab·ri·ca·tion** \ˌprē-ˌfa-bri-ˈkā-shən\ *n*

¹pref·ace \ˈpre-fəs\ *n* : the introductory remarks of a speaker or writer — **pref·a·to·ry** \ˈpre-fə-ˌtōr-ē\ *adj*

²preface *vb* **pref·aced; pref·ac·ing** : to introduce with a preface

pre·fect \ˈprē-ˌfekt\ *n* **1** : a high official; *esp* : a chief officer or magistrate **2** : a student monitor

pre·fec·ture \ˈprē-ˌfek-chər\ *n* : the office, term, or residence of a prefect

pre·fer \pri-ˈfər\ *vb* **pre·ferred; pre·fer·ring 1** : PROMOTE **2** : to like better **3** : to bring (as a charge) against a person — **pref·er·a·ble** \ˈpre-fə-rə-bəl\ *adj* — **pref·er·a·bly** \-blē\ *adv*

pref·er·ence \ˈpre-frəns, -fə-rəns\ *n* **1** : a special liking for one thing over another **2** : CHOICE, SELECTION — **pref·er·en·tial** \ˌpre-fə-ˈren-chəl\ *adj*

pref·er·ment \pri-ˈfər-mənt\ *n* : PROMOTION, ADVANCEMENT

pre·fig·ure \prē-ˈfi-gyər\ *vb* **1** : FORESHADOW **2** : to imagine beforehand

¹pre·fix \ˈprē-ˌfiks, prē-ˈfiks\ *vb* : to place before ⟨∼ a title to a name⟩

²**pre·fix** \'prē-ˌfiks\ n : an affix occurring at the beginning of a word

pre·flight \ˌprē-'flīt\ adj : preparing for or preliminary to flight

pre·form \(ˌ)prē-'fȯrm, 'prē-ˌfȯrm\ vb : to form or shape beforehand

preg·na·ble \'preg-nə-bəl\ adj : vulnerable to capture ⟨a ~ fort⟩

preg·nant \'preg-nənt\ adj 1 : containing unborn young within the body 2 : rich in significance : MEANINGFUL — **preg·nan·cy** \-nən-sē\ n

pre·heat \ˌprē-'hēt\ vb : to heat beforehand; esp : to heat (an oven) to a designated temperature before using

pre·hen·sile \prē-'hen-səl, -ˌsīl\ adj : adapted for grasping esp. by wrapping around ⟨a monkey with a ~ tail⟩

pre·his·tor·ic \ˌprē-his-'tȯr-ik\ or **pre·his·tor·i·cal** \-i-kəl\ adj : of, relating to, or existing in the period before written history began

pre·judge \(ˌ)prē-'jəj\ vb : to judge before full hearing or examination

¹**prej·u·dice** \'pre-jə-dəs\ n 1 : DAMAGE; esp : detriment to one's rights or claims 2 : an opinion made without adequate basis — **prej·u·di·cial** \ˌpre-jə-'di-shəl\ adj

²**prejudice** vb **-diced; -dic·ing** 1 : to damage by a judgment or action esp. at law 2 : to cause to have prejudice

prel·ate \'pre-lət\ n : an ecclesiastic (as a bishop) of high rank — **prel·a·cy** \-lə-sē\ n

pre·launch \'prē-'lȯnch\ adj : preparing for or preliminary to launch

pre·lim \'prē-ˌlim, pri-'lim\ n or adj : PRELIMINARY

¹**pre·lim·i·nary** \pri-'li-mə-ˌner-ē\ n, pl **-nar·ies** : something that precedes or introduces the main business or event

²**preliminary** adj : preceding the main discourse or business

pre·lude \'prel-ˌyüd; 'pre-ˌlüd, 'prā-\ n 1 : an introductory performance or event 2 : a musical section or movement introducing the main theme; also : an organ solo played at the beginning of a church service

prem abbr premium

pre·mar·i·tal \(ˌ)prē-'mar-ət-ᵊl\ adj : existing or occurring before marriage

pre·ma·ture \ˌprē-mə-'tu̇r, -'tyu̇r, -'chu̇r\ adj : happening, coming, born, or done before the usual or proper time — **pre·ma·ture·ly** adv

¹**pre·med** \ˌprē-'med\ n : a premedical student or course of study

²**premed** adj : PREMEDICAL

pre·med·i·cal \(ˌ)prē-'me-di-kəl\ adj : preceding and preparing for the professional study of medicine

pre·med·i·tate \pri-'me-də-ˌtāt\ vb : to consider and plan beforehand — **pre·med·i·ta·tion** \-ˌme-də-'tā-shən\ n

pre·men·stru·al \(ˌ)prē-'men-strə-wəl\ adj : of, relating to, or occurring in the period just before menstruation

premenstrual syndrome n : a varying group of symptoms manifested by some women prior to menstruation

pre·mie var of PREEMIE

¹**pre·mier** \pri-'mir, -'myir, 'prē-mē-ər\ adj [ME primier, fr. MF premier first, chief, fr. L primarius first of the first rank] : first in rank or importance : CHIEF; also : first in time : EARLIEST

²**premier** n : PRIME MINISTER — **pre·mier·ship** n

¹**pre·miere** \pri-'myer, -'mir\ n : a first performance

²**premiere** or **pre·mier** \same as ¹PREMIERE\ vb **-miered; -mier·ing** : to give or receive a first public performance

prem·ise \'pre-məs\ n 1 : a statement of fact or a supposition made or implied as a basis of argument 2 pl : a piece of land with the structures on it; also : the place of business of an enterprise

pre·mi·um \'prē-mē-əm\ n [L praemium booty, reward, fr. prae before + emere to take, buy] 1 : REWARD, PRIZE 2 : a sum over and above the stated value 3 : something paid over and above a fixed wage or price 4 : something given with a purchase 5 : the sum paid for a contract of insurance 6 : an unusually high value

pre·mix \prē-'miks\ vb : to mix before use

¹**pre·mo·lar** \(ˌ)prē-'mō-lər\ adj : situated in front of or preceding the molar teeth

²**premolar** n : any of the double-pointed grinding teeth which are located between the canines and the true molars and of which there are two on each side of each human jaw

pre·mo·ni·tion \ˌprē-mə-'ni-shən, ˌpre-\ n 1 : previous warning 2 : PRESENTIMENT — **pre·mon·i·to·ry** \pri-'mä-nə-ˌtȯr-ē\ adj

pre·na·tal \'prē-'nāt-ᵊl\ adj : occurring, existing, or taking place before birth

pre·oc·cu·pa·tion \prē-ˌä-kyə-'pā-shən\ n : complete absorption of the mind or interests; also : something that causes such absorption

pre·oc·cu·pied \prē-'ä-kyə-ˌpīd\ adj 1 : lost in thought; also : absorbed in some preoccupation 2 : already occupied **syn** abstracted, absent, absentminded

pre·oc·cu·py \-ˌpī\ vb 1 : to occupy the attention of beforehand 2 : to take possession of before another

pre·op·er·a·tive \(ˌ)prē-'ä-prə-tiv, -pə-ˌrā-\ adj : occurring before a surgical operation

pre·or·dain \ˌprē-ȯr-'dān\ vb : FOREORDAIN

pre–owned \(ˌ)prē-'ōnd\ adj : SECONDHAND

prep abbr 1 preparatory 2 preposition

pre·pack·age \(ˌ)prē-'pa-kij\ vb : to package (as food) before offering for sale to the customer

preparatory school n 1 : a usu. private school preparing students primarily for college 2 Brit : a private elementary school preparing students primarily for public schools

pre·pare \pri-'par\ vb **pre·pared; pre·par·ing** 1 : to make or get ready ⟨~ dinner⟩ ⟨~ a student for college⟩ 2 : to get ready beforehand 3 : to put together : COMPOUND ⟨~ a prescription⟩ — **prep·a·ra·tion** \ˌpre-pə-'rā-shən\ n — **pre·pa·ra·to·ry** \pri-'par-ə-ˌtȯr-ē\ adj

pre·pared·ness \pri-'par-əd-nəs\ n : a state of adequate preparation

pre·pay \(ˌ)prē-'pā\ vb **-paid** \-'pād\; **-pay·ing** : to pay or pay the charge on in advance

pre·pon·der·ant \pri-'pän-də-rənt\ adj : having greater weight, force, influence, or frequency — **pre·pon·der·ance** \-rəns\ n — **pre·pon·der·ant·ly** adv

pre·pon·der·ate \pri-'pän-də-ˌrāt\ vb **-at·ed; -at·ing** [L praeponderare, fr. prae- ahead + ponder-, pondus weight] : to exceed in weight, force, influence, or frequency : PREDOMINATE

prep·o·si·tion \ˌpre-pə-'zi-shən\ n : a word that combines with a noun or pronoun to form a phrase — **prep·o·si·tion·al** \-'zi-shə-nəl\ adj

pre·pos·sess \ˌprē-pə-'zes\ vb 1 : to cause to be preoccupied 2 : to influence beforehand esp. favorably

pre·pos·sess·ing adj : tending to create a favorable impression ⟨a ~ manner⟩

pre·pos·ses·sion \-'ze-shən\ n 1 : PREJUDICE 2 : an exclusive concern with one idea or object

pre·pos·ter·ous \pri-'päs-tə-rəs\ adj : contrary to nature or reason : ABSURD

prep·py or **prep·pie** \'pre-pē\ n, pl **preppies** 1 : a student at or a graduate of a preparatory school 2 : a person deemed to dress or behave like a preppy

pre·puce \'prē-ˌpyüs\ n : FORESKIN

pre·quel \'prē-kwəl\ n : a literary or dramatic work whose story precedes that of an earlier work

pre·re·cord·ed \(ˌ)prē-ri-'kȯr-dəd\ adj : recorded for later broadcast

pre·req·ui·site \prē-'re-kwə-zət\ n : something required beforehand or for the end in view — **prereq·uisite** *adj*

pre·rog·a·tive \pri-ˈrä-gə-tiv\ *n* : an exclusive or special right, power, or privilege

pres *abbr* **1** present **2** president

¹**pres·age** \ˈpre-sij\ *n* **1** : something that foreshadows a future event : OMEN **2** : FOREBODING

²**pres·age** \ˈpre-sij, pri-ˈsāj\ *vb* **pre·saged; pre·sag·ing 1** : to give an omen or warning of : FORESHADOW **2** : FORETELL, PREDICT

pres·by·o·pia \ˌprez-bē-ˈō-pē-ə\ *n* : a visual condition in which loss of elasticity of the lens of the eye causes defective accommodation and inability to focus sharply for near vision — **pres·by·o·pic** \-ˈō-pik, -ˈä-\ *adj or n*

pres·by·ter \ˈprez-bə-tər\ *n* **1** : PRIEST, MINISTER **2** : an elder in a Presbyterian church

¹**Pres·by·te·ri·an** \ˌprez-bə-ˈtir-ē-ən\ *n* : a member of a Presbyterian church

²**Presbyterian** *adj* **1** *often not cap* : characterized by a graded system of representative ecclesiastical bodies (as presbyteries) exercising legislative and judicial powers **2** : of or relating to a group of Protestant Christian bodies that are presbyterian in government — **Pres·by·te·ri·an·ism** \-ə-ˌni-zəm\ *n*

pres·by·tery \ˈprez-bə-ˌter-ē\ *n, pl* **-ter·ies 1** : the part of a church reserved for the officiating clergy **2** : a ruling body in Presbyterian churches consisting of the ministers and representative elders of a district

¹**pre·school** \ˈprē-ˌskül\ *adj* : of or relating to the period in a child's life from infancy to the age of five or six — **pre·school·er** \-ˌskü-lər\ *n*

²**preschool** *n* : NURSERY SCHOOL

pre·science \ˈpre-shəns, ˈprē-\ *n* : foreknowledge of events; *also* : FORESIGHT — **pre·scient** \-shənt, -shē-ənt\ *adj*

pre·scribe \pri-ˈskrīb\ *vb* **pre·scribed; pre·scrib·ing 1** : to lay down as a guide or rule of action **2** : to direct the use of (as a medicine) as a remedy

pre·scrip·tion \pri-ˈskrip-shən\ *n* **1** : the action of prescribing rules or directions **2** : a written direction for the preparation and use of a medicine; *also* : a medicine prescribed

pres·ence \ˈprez-ᵊns\ *n* **1** : the fact or condition of being present **2** : the space immediately around a person **3** : one that is present **4** : the bearing of a person; *esp* : stately bearing

¹**pres·ent** \ˈprez-ᵊnt\ *n* : something presented : GIFT

²**pre·sent** \pri-ˈzent\ *vb* **1** : to bring into the presence or acquaintance of : INTRODUCE **2** : to bring before the public (~ a play) **3** : to make a gift to **4** : to give formally **5** : to lay (as a charge) before a court for inquiry **6** : to aim or direct (as a weapon) so as to face in a particular direction — **pre·sent·able** *adj* — **pre·sen·ta·tion** \ˌpre-ˌzen-ˈtā-shən, ˌprez-ᵊn-\ *n* — **pre·sent·ment** \pri-ˈzent-mənt\ *n*

³**pres·ent** \ˈprez-ᵊnt\ *adj* **1** : now existing or in progress (~ conditions) **2** : being in view or at hand (~ at the meeting) **3** : under consideration (the ~ problem) **4** : of, relating to, or constituting a verb tense that expresses present time or the time of speaking

⁴**pres·ent** \ˈprez-ᵊnt\ *n* **1** *pl* : the present legal document **2** : the present tense; *also* : a verb form in it **3** : the present time

pres·ent–day \ˈprez-ᵊnt-ˈdā\ *adj* : now existing or occurring : CURRENT

pre·sen·ti·ment \pri-ˈzen-tə-mənt\ *n* : a feeling that something is about to happen : PREMONITION

pres·ent·ly \ˈprez-ᵊnt-lē\ *adv* **1** : SOON **2** : NOW

present participle *n* : a participle that typically expresses present action and that in English is formed with the suffix *-ing* and is used in the formation of the progressive tenses

¹**pre·serve** \pri-ˈzərv\ *vb* **pre·served; pre·serv·ing 1** : to keep safe : GUARD, PROTECT **2** : to keep from decaying; *esp* : to process food (as by canning or pickling)

to prevent spoilage **3** : MAINTAIN (~ silence) — **pres·er·va·tion** \ˌpre-zər-ˈvā-shən\ *n* — **pre·ser·va·tive** \pri-ˈzər-və-tiv\ *adj or n* — **pre·serv·er** *n*

²**preserve** *n* **1** : preserved fruit — often used in pl. **2** : an area for the protection of natural resources (as animals)

pre·set \(ˌ)prē-ˈset\ *vb* **-set; -set·ting** : to set beforehand

pre·shrunk \-ˈshrəŋk\ *adj* : subjected to a shrinking process during manufacture usu. to reduce later shrinking

pre·side \pri-ˈzīd\ *vb* **pre·sid·ed; pre·sid·ing** [L *praesidēre* to guard, preside over, fr. *prae* in front of + *sedēre* to sit] **1** : to exercise guidance or control **2** : to occupy the place of authority; *esp* : to act as chairman

pres·i·dent \ˈprez-zə-dənt\ *n* **1** : one chosen to preside (~ of the assembly) **2** : the chief officer of an organization (as a corporation or society) **3** : an elected official serving as both chief of state and chief political executive; *also* : a chief of state often with only minimal political powers — **pres·i·den·cy** \-dən-sē\ *n* — **pres·i·den·tial** \ˌpre-zə-ˈden-chəl\ *adj*

pre·si·dio \pri-ˈsē-dē-ˌō, -ˈsi-\ *n, pl* **-di·os** [Sp] : a military post or fortified settlement in areas currently or orig. under Spanish control

pre·sid·i·um \pri-ˈsi-dē-əm\ *n, pl* **-ia** \-dē-ə\ *or* **-iums** [Russ *prezidium*, fr. L *praesidium* garrison] : a permanent executive committee that acts for a larger body in a Communist country

¹**pre·soak** \(ˌ)prē-ˈsōk\ *vb* : to soak beforehand

²**pre·soak** \ˈprē-ˌsōk\ *n* **1** : an instance of presoaking **2** : a preparation used in presoaking clothes

pre·sort \(ˌ)prē-ˈsòrt\ *vb* : to sort (mail) by zip code usu. before delivery to a post office

¹**press** \ˈpres\ *n* **1** : a crowded condition : THRONG **2** : a machine for exerting pressure **3** : CLOSET, CUPBOARD **4** : PRESSURE **5** : the properly creased condition of a freshly pressed garment **6** : PRINTING PRESS; *also* : the act or the process of printing **7** : a printing or publishing establishment **8** : the media (as newspapers and magazines) of public news and comment; *also* : persons (as reporters) employed in these media **9** : comment in newspapers and periodicals

²**press** *vb* **1** : to bear down upon : push steadily against **2** : ASSAIL, COMPEL **3** : to squeeze out the juice or contents of (~ grapes) **4** : to squeeze to a desired density, shape, or smoothness; *esp* : IRON **5** : to try hard to persuade : URGE **6** : to follow through : PROSECUTE **7** : CROWD **8** : to force one's way **9** : to require haste or speed in action — **press·er** *n*

press agent *n* : an agent employed to establish and maintain good public relations through publicity

press·ing *adj* : URGENT

press·man \ˈpres-mən, -ˌman\ *n* : the operator of a press and esp. a printing press

press·room \-ˌrüm, -ˌrüm\ *n* **1** : a room in a printing plant containing the printing presses **2** : a room for the use of reporters

¹**pres·sure** \ˈpre-shər\ *n* **1** : the burden of physical or mental distress **2** : the action of pressing; *esp* : the application of force to something by something else in direct contact with it **3** : the force exerted over a surface divided by its area **4** : the stress or urgency of matters demanding attention

²**pressure** *vb* **pres·sured; pres·sur·ing** : to apply pressure to

pressure group *n* : a group that seeks to influence governmental policy but not to elect candidates to office

pressure suit *n* : an inflatable suit for high-altitude flight or spaceflight to protect the body from low pressure

pres·sur·ise *Brit var of* PRESSURIZE

pres·sur·ize \ˈpre-shə-ˌrīz\ *vb* **-ized; -iz·ing 1** : to maintain higher pressure within than without; *esp* : to maintain normal atmospheric pressure within (as an

airplane cabin) during high-altitude flight or space-flight **2 :** to apply pressure to **3 :** to design to withstand pressure — **pres·sur·i·za·tion** \ˌpre-shə-rə-ˈzā-shən\ n

pres·ti·dig·i·ta·tion   \ˌpres-tə-ˌdi-jə-ˈtā-shən\   n : SLEIGHT OF HAND

pres·tige \pres-ˈtēzh, -ˈtēj\ n [F, fr. MF, conjuror's trick, illusion, fr. LL *praestigium*, fr. L *praestigiae*, pl., conjuror's tricks, fr. *praestringere* to graze, blunt, constrict, fr. *prae-* in front of + *stringere* to bind tight] **:** standing or estimation in the eyes of people **:** REPUTATION **syn** influence, authority, weight, cachet — **pres·ti·gious** \-ˈti-jəs, -ˈtē-\ *adj*

pres·to \ˈpres-tō\ *adv or adj* [It] **1 :** suddenly as if by magic **:** IMMEDIATELY **2 :** at a rapid tempo — used as a direction in music

pre·stress \(ˌ)prē-ˈstres\ *vb* **:** to introduce internal stresses into (as a structural beam) to counteract later load stresses

pre·sum·ably \pri-ˈzü-mə-blē\ *adv* **:** by reasonable assumption

pre·sume \pri-ˈzüm\ *vb* **pre·sumed; pre·sum·ing 1 :** to take upon oneself without leave or warrant **:** DARE **2 :** to take for granted **:** ASSUME **3 :** to act or behave with undue boldness — **pre·sum·able** \-ˈzü-mə-bəl\ *adj*

pre·sump·tion \pri-ˈzəmp-shən\ n **1 :** presumptuous attitude or conduct **:** AUDACITY **2 :** an attitude or belief dictated by probability; *also* **:** the grounds lending probability to a belief — **pre·sump·tive** \-tiv\ *adj*

pre·sump·tu·ous \pri-ˈzəmp-chə-wəs\ *adj* **:** overstepping due bounds **:** taking liberties — **pre·sump·tu·ous·ly** *adv*

pre·sup·pose \ˌprē-sə-ˈpōz\ *vb* **1 :** to suppose beforehand **2 :** to require beforehand as a necessary condition — **pre·sup·po·si·tion** \(ˌ)prē-ˌsə-pə-ˈzi-shən\ n

pre·teen \ˈprē-ˈtēn\ n **:** a boy or girl not yet 13 years old — **preteen** *adj*

pre·tend \pri-ˈtend\ *vb* **1 :** PROFESS (doesn't ∼ to be scientific) **2 :** FEIGN (∼ to be angry) **3 :** to lay claim (∼ to a throne) — **pre·tend·er** n

pre·tense *or* **pre·tence** \ˈprē-ˌtens, pri-ˈtens\ n **1 :** CLAIM; *esp* **:** one not supported by fact **2 :** mere display **:** SHOW **3 :** an attempt to attain a certain condition (made a ∼ at discipline) **4 :** false show **:** PRETEXT — **pre·ten·sion** \pri-ˈten-chən\ n

pre·ten·tious \pri-ˈten-chəs\ *adj* **1 :** making or possessing usu. unjustified claims (as to excellence) (a ∼ literary style) **2 :** making demands on one's ability or means **:** AMBITIOUS (too ∼ an undertaking) — **pre·ten·tious·ly** *adv* — **pre·ten·tious·ness** n

pret·er·it *or* **pret·er·ite** \ˈpre-tə-rət\ *adj* **:** PAST **3** — **preterit** n

pre·ter·nat·u·ral \ˌprē-tər-ˈna-chə-rəl\ *adj* **1 :** exceeding what is natural **2 :** inexplicable by ordinary means — **pre·ter·nat·u·ral·ly** *adv*

pre·text \ˈprē-ˌtekst\ n **:** a purpose stated or assumed to cloak the real intention or state of affairs

pret·ti·fy \ˈpri-ti-ˌfī\ *vb* **-fied; -fy·ing :** to make pretty — **pret·ti·fi·ca·tion** \ˌpri-ti-fə-ˈkā-shən\ n

¹pret·ty \ˈpri-tē\ *adj* **pret·ti·er; -est** [ME *praty, prety,* fr. OE *prættig* tricky, fr. *prætt* trick] **1 :** pleasing by delicacy or grace **:** having conventionally accepted elements of beauty (∼ flowers) **2 :** MISERABLE, TERRIBLE (a ∼ state of affairs) **3 :** moderately large (a ∼ profit) **syn** comely, fair, beautiful, attractive, lovely — **pret·ti·ly** \-tə-lē\ *adv* — **pret·ti·ness** \-tē-nəs\ n

²pretty *adv* **:** in some degree **:** MODERATELY

³pretty *vb* **pret·tied; pret·ty·ing :** to make pretty

pret·zel \ˈpret-səl\ n [G *Brezel,* ultim. fr. L *brachiatus* having branches like arms, fr. *brachium* arm] **:** a brittle or chewy glazed usu. salted slender bread often shaped like a loose knot

prev *abbr* previous; previously

pre·vail \pri-ˈvāl\ *vb* **1 :** to win mastery **:** TRIUMPH **2 :** to be or become effective **:** SUCCEED **3 :** to urge successfully (∼ed upon her to sing) **4 :** to be frequent **:** PREDOMINATE — **pre·vail·ing·ly** *adv*

prev·a·lent \ˈpre-və-lənt\ *adj* **:** generally or widely existent **:** WIDESPREAD — **prev·a·lence** \-ləns\ n

pre·var·i·cate \pri-ˈvar-ə-ˌkāt\ *vb* **-cat·ed; -cat·ing :** to deviate from the truth **:** EQUIVOCATE — **pre·var·i·ca·tion** \-ˌvar-ə-ˈkā-shən\ n — **pre·var·i·ca·tor** \-ˈvar-ə-ˌkā-tər\ n

pre·vent \pri-ˈvent\ *vb* **1 :** to keep from happening or existing (steps to ∼ war) **2 :** to hold back **:** HINDER, STOP (∼ us from going) — **pre·vent·able** *also* **pre·vent·ible** \-ˈven-tə-bəl\ *adj* — **pre·ven·tion** \-ˈven-chən\ n — **pre·ven·tive** \-ˈven-tiv\ *adj or n* — **pre·ven·ta·tive** \-ˈven-tə-tiv\ *adj or n*

pre·ver·bal \ˌprē-ˈvər-bəl\ *adj* **:** having not yet acquired the faculty of speech

¹pre·view \ˈprē-ˌvyü\ *vb* **:** to see or discuss beforehand; *esp* **:** to view or show in advance of public presentation

²preview n **1 :** an advance showing or viewing **2** *also* **pre·vue** \-ˌvyü\ **:** a showing of snatches from a motion picture advertised for future appearance **3 :** FORETASTE

pre·vi·ous \ˈprē-vē-əs\ *adj* **:** going before **:** EARLIER, FORMER **syn** foregoing, prior, preceding, antecedent — **pre·vi·ous·ly** *adv*

pre·vi·sion \prē-ˈvi-zhən\ n **1 :** FORESIGHT, PRESCIENCE **2 :** FORECAST, PREDICTION

pre·war \ˈprē-ˈwȯr\ *adj* **:** occurring or existing before a war

¹prey \ˈprā\ n, *pl* **prey** *also* **preys 1 :** an animal taken for food by a predator; *also* **:** VICTIM **2 :** the act or habit of preying

²prey *vb* **1 :** to raid for booty **2 :** to seize and devour prey **3 :** to have a harmful or wearing effect

prf *abbr* proof

¹price \ˈprīs\ n **1** *archaic* **:** VALUE **2 :** the amount of money paid or asked for the sale of a specified thing; *also* **:** the cost at which something is obtained

²price *vb* **priced; pric·ing 1 :** to set a price on **2 :** to ask the price of **3** : to drive by raising prices ⟨*priced* themselves out of the market⟩

price–fix·ing \'prīs-₁fik-siŋ\ *n* : the setting of prices artificially (as by producers or government)

price·less \-ləs\ *adj* : having a value beyond any price : INVALUABLE **syn** precious, costly, expensive

price support *n* : artificial maintenance of prices of a commodity at a level usu. fixed through government action

price war *n* : a period of commercial competition in which prices are repeatedly cut by the competitors

pric·ey *also* **pric·y** \'prī-sē\ *adj* **pric·i·er; -est** : EXPENSIVE

¹**prick** \'prik\ *n* **1** : a mark or small wound made by a pointed instrument **2** : something sharp or pointed **3** : an instance of pricking; *also* : a sensation of being pricked

²**prick** *vb* **1** : to pierce slightly with a sharp point; *also* : to have or cause a pricking sensation **2** : to affect with anguish or remorse ⟨∼*s* his conscience⟩ **3** : to outline with punctures ⟨∼ out a pattern⟩ **4** : to stand or cause to stand erect ⟨the dog's ears ∼*ed* up at the sound⟩ **syn** punch, puncture, perforate, bore, drill

prick·er \'pri-kər\ *n* : BRIAR; *also* : THORN

¹**prick·le** \'pri-kəl\ *n* **1** : a small sharp process (as on a plant) **2** : a slight stinging pain — **prick·ly** \'pri-klē\ *adj*

²**prickle** *vb* **prick·led; prick·ling 1** : to prick lightly **2** : TINGLE

prickly heat *n* : a red cutaneous eruption with intense itching and tingling caused by inflammation around the ducts of the sweat glands

prickly pear *n* : any of numerous cacti with usu. yellow flowers and prickly flat or rounded joints; *also* : the sweet pulpy pear-shaped edible fruit of various prickly pears

¹**pride** \'prīd\ *n* **1** : CONCEIT **2** : justifiable self-respect **3** : elation over an act or possession **4** : haughty behavior : DISDAIN **5** : ostentatious display — **pride·ful** *adj*

²**pride** *vb* **prid·ed; prid·ing** : to indulge (as oneself) in pride

priest \'prēst\ *n* [ME *preist*, fr. OE *prēost*, ultim. fr. LL *presbyter* elder, priest, fr. Gk *presbyteros*, fr. compar. of *presbys* old man, elder] : a person having authority to perform the sacred rites of a religion; *esp* : a member of the Anglican, Eastern, or Roman Catholic clergy ranking below a bishop and above a deacon — **priest·hood** *n* — **priest·li·ness** *n* — **priest·ly** *adj*

priest·ess \'prēs-təs\ *n* : a woman authorized to perform the sacred rites of a religion

prig \'prig\ *n* : one who irritates by rigid or pointed observance of proprieties — **prig·gish** \'pri-gish\ *adj* — **prig·gish·ly** *adv*

¹**prim** \'prim\ *adj* **prim·mer; prim·mest** : stiffly formal and precise — **prim·ly** *adv* — **prim·ness** *n*

²**prim** *abbr* **1** primary **2** primitive

pri·ma·cy \'prī-mə-sē\ *n* **1** : the state of being first (as in rank) **2** : the office, rank, or character of an ecclesiastical primate

pri·ma don·na \₁pri-mə-'dä-nə\ *n, pl* **prima donnas** [It, lit., first lady] **1** : a principal female singer (as in an opera company) **2** : an extremely sensitive, vain, or undisciplined person

pri·ma fa·cie \₁prī-mə-'fā-shə, -sē, -shē\ *adj or adv* [L, at first view] **1** : based on immediate impression : APPARENT **2** : SELF-EVIDENT

pri·mal \'prī-məl\ *adj* **1** : ORIGINAL, PRIMITIVE **2** : first in importance

pri·mar·i·ly \prī-'mer-ə-lē\ *adv* **1** : FUNDAMENTALLY **2** : ORIGINALLY

¹**pri·ma·ry** \'prī-₁mer-ē, -mə-rē\ *adj* **1** : first in order of time or development; *also* : PREPARATORY **2** : of first rank or importance; *also* : FUNDAMENTAL **3** : not derived from or dependent on something else ⟨∼ sources⟩

²**primary** *n, pl* **-ries** : a preliminary election in which voters nominate or express a preference among candidates usu. of their own party

primary color *n* : any of a set of colors from which all other colors may be derived

primary school *n* **1** : a school usu. including grades 1-3 and sometimes kindergarten **2** : ELEMENTARY SCHOOL

pri·mate \'prī-₁māt *or esp for 1* -mət\ *n* **1** *often cap* : the highest-ranking bishop of a province or nation **2** : any of an order of mammals including humans, apes, and monkeys

¹**prime** \'prīm\ *n* **1** : the earliest stage of something; *esp* : SPRINGTIME **2** : the most active, thriving, or successful stage or period (as of one's life) **3** : the best individual; *also* : the best part of something **4** : any integer other than 0, + 1, or −1 that is not divisible without remainder by any integer except + 1, −1, and plus or minus itself; *esp* : any such integer that is positive

²**prime** *adj* **1** : standing first (as in time, rank, significance, or quality) ⟨∼ requisite⟩ **2** : of, relating to, or being a number that is prime

³**prime** *vb* **primed; prim·ing 1** : FILL, LOAD **2** : to lay a preparatory coating upon (as in painting) **3** : to put in working condition **4** : to instruct beforehand : COACH

prime meridian *n* : the meridian of 0° longitude which runs through Greenwich, England, and from which other longitudes are reckoned east and west

prime minister *n* **1** : the chief minister of a ruler or state **2** : the chief executive of a parliamentary government

¹**prim·er** \'pri-mər\ *n* **1** : a small book for teaching children to read **2** : a small introductory book on a subject

²**prim·er** \'prī-mər\ *n* **1** : one that primes **2** : a device for igniting an explosive **3** : material for priming a surface

prime rate *n* : an interest rate announced by a bank to be the lowest available to its most credit-worthy customers

prime time *n* **1** : the time period when the television or radio audience is largest; *also* : prime-time television **2** : the choicest or busiest time

pri·me·val \prī-'mē-vəl\ *adj* : of or relating to the earliest ages : PRIMITIVE

¹**prim·i·tive** \'pri-mə-tiv\ *adj* **1** : ORIGINAL, PRIMARY **2** : of, relating to, or characteristic of an early stage of development **3** : ELEMENTAL, NATURAL **4** : of, relating to, or produced by a tribal people or culture **5** : SELF-TAUGHT; *also* : produced by a self-taught artist — **prim·i·tive·ly** *adv* — **prim·i·tive·ness** *n* — **prim·i·tiv·i·ty** \₁pri-mə-'ti-və-tē\ *n*

²**primitive** *n* **1** : something primitive **2** : a primitive artist **3** : a member of a primitive people

prim·i·tiv·ism \'pri-mə-ti-₁vi-zəm\ *n* **1** : belief in the superiority of a simple way of life close to nature **2** : the style of art of primitive peoples or primitive artists

pri·mo·gen·i·tor \₁prī-mō-'je-nə-tər\ *n* : ANCESTOR, FOREFATHER

pri·mo·gen·i·ture \-'je-nə-₁chùr\ *n* **1** : the state of being the firstborn of a family **2** : an exclusive right of inheritance belonging to the eldest son

pri·mor·di·al \prī-'mòr-dē-əl\ *adj* : first created or developed : existing in its original state : PRIMEVAL

primp \'primp\ *vb* : to dress in a careful or finicky manner

prim·rose \'prim-₁rōz\ *n* : any of a genus of perennial herbs with large leaves arranged at the base of the stem and clusters of showy flowers on leafless stalks

prin *abbr* **1** principal **2** principle

prince \'prins\ *n* [ME, fr. OF, fr. L *princeps* leader, initiator, fr. *primus* first + *capere* to take] **1** : MONARCH, KING **2** : a male member of a royal family; *esp* : a son of the monarch **3** : a person of high standing

(as in a class) — **prince·dom** \-dəm\ *n* — **prince·ly** *adj*
prince·ling \-liŋ\ *n* : a petty prince
prin·cess \'prin-səs, -ˌses\ *n* **1** : a female member of a royal family **2** : the consort of a prince
¹prin·ci·pal \'prin-sə-pəl\ *adj* : most important — **prin·ci·pal·ly** *adv*
²principal *n* **1** : a leading person (as in a play) **2** : the chief officer of an educational institution **3** : the person from whom an agent's authority derives **4** : a capital sum placed at interest or used as a fund
prin·ci·pal·i·ty \ˌprin-sə-'pa-lə-tē\ *n, pl* **-ties** : the position, territory, or jurisdiction of a prince
principal parts *n pl* : the inflected forms of a verb
prin·ci·ple \'prin-sə-pəl\ *n* **1** : a general or fundamental law, doctrine, or assumption **2** : a rule or code of conduct; *also* : devotion to such a code **3** : the laws or facts of nature underlying the working of an artificial device **4** : a primary source : ORIGIN; *also* : an underlying faculty or endowment **5** : the active part (as of a drug)
prin·ci·pled \-pəld\ *adj* : exhibiting, based on, or characterized by principle ⟨high-*principled*⟩
prink \'priŋk\ *vb* : PRIMP
¹print \'print\ *n* **1** : a mark made by pressure **2** : something stamped with an impression **3** : printed state or form **4** : printed matter **5** : a copy made by printing **6** : cloth with a pattern applied by printing
²print *vb* **1** : to stamp (as a mark) in or on something **2** : to produce impressions of (as from type) **3** : to write in letters like those of printer's type **4** : to make (a positive picture) from a photographic negative
print·able \'prin-tə-bəl\ *adj* **1** : capable of being printed or of being printed from **2** : worthy or fit to be published
print·er \'prin-tər\ *n* : one that prints; *esp* : a device that produces printout
print·ing *n* **1** : reproduction in printed form **2** : the art, practice, or business of a printer **3** : IMPRESSION 5
printing press *n* : a machine that produces printed copies
print·out \'print-ˌaút\ *n* : a printed output produced by a computer — **print out** *vb*
¹pri·or \'prī-ər\ *n* : the superior ranking next to the abbot or abbess of a religious house
²prior *adj* **1** : earlier in time or order **2** : taking precedence logically or in importance — **pri·or·i·ty** \prī-'òr-ə-tē\ *n*
pri·or·ess \'prī-ə-rəs\ *n* : a nun corresponding in rank to a prior
pri·or·i·tize \prī-'òr-ə-ˌtīz, 'prī-ə-rə-ˌtīz\ *vb* **-tized; -tiz·ing** : to list or rate in order of priority
prior to *prep* : in advance of : BEFORE
pri·o·ry \'prī-ə-rē\ *n, pl* **-ries** : a religious house under a prior or prioress
prise *chiefly Brit var of* ⁵PRIZE
prism \'pri-zəm\ *n* [LL *prisma*, fr. Gk, lit., anything sawed, fr. *priein* to saw] **1** : a solid whose sides are parallelograms and whose ends are parallel and alike in shape and size **2** : a usu. 3-sided transparent object

that refracts light so that it breaks up into rainbow colors — **pris·mat·ic** \priz-'ma-tik\ *adj*
pris·on \'priz-ᵊn\ *n* : a place or state of confinement esp. for criminals

pris·on·er \'priz-ᵊn-ər\ *n* : a person deprived of liberty; *esp* : one on trial or in prison

prisoner of war : a person captured in war
pris·sy \'pri-sē\ *adj* **pris·si·er; -est** : being overly prim and precise : PRIGGISH — **pris·si·ness** \-sē-nəs\ *n*
pris·tine \'pris-ˌtēn, pri-'stēn\ *adj* **1** : PRIMITIVE **2** : having the purity of its original state : UNSPOILED
prith·ee \'pri-thē\ *interj, archaic* — used to express a wish or request
pri·va·cy \'prī-və-sē\ *n, pl* **-cies** **1** : the quality or state of being apart from others **2** : SECRECY
¹pri·vate \'prī-vət\ *adj* **1** : belonging to or intended for a particular individual or group ⟨~ property⟩ **2** : restricted to the individual : PERSONAL ⟨~ opinion⟩ **3** : carried on by the individual independently ⟨~ study⟩ **4** : not holding public office ⟨a ~ citizen⟩ **5** : withdrawn from company or observation ⟨a ~ place⟩ **6** : not known publicly — **pri·vate·ly** *adv*
²private *n* : an enlisted man of the lowest rank in the marine corps or of one of the two lowest ranks in the army — **in private** : not openly or in public
pri·va·teer \ˌprī-və-'tir\ *n* : an armed private ship licensed to attack enemy shipping; *also* : a sailor on such a ship
private first class *n* : an enlisted man ranking next below a corporal in the army and next below a lance corporal in the marine corps
pri·va·tion \prī-'vā-shən\ *n* **1** : DEPRIVATION 1 **2** : the state of being deprived; *esp* : lack of what is needed for existence
priv·et \'pri-vət\ *n* : a nearly evergreen shrub related to the olive and widely used for hedges
¹priv·i·lege \'priv-lij, 'pri-və-\ *n* [ME, fr. OF, fr. L *privilegium* law for or against a private person, fr. *privus* private + *leg-, lex* law] : a right or immunity granted as an advantage or favor esp. to some and not others
²privilege *vb* **-leged; -leg·ing** : to grant a privilege to
priv·i·leged *adj* **1** : having or enjoying one or more privileges ⟨~ classes⟩ **2** : not subject to disclosure in a court of law ⟨a ~ communication⟩
¹priv·y \'pri-vē\ *adj* **1** : PERSONAL, PRIVATE **2** : SECRET **3** : admitted as one sharing in a secret ⟨~ to the conspiracy⟩ — **priv·i·ly** \'pri-və-lē\ *adv*
²privy *n, pl* **priv·ies** : TOILET; *esp* : OUTHOUSE
¹prize \'prīz\ *n* **1** : something offered or striven for in competition or in contests of chance **2** : something exceptionally desirable
²prize *adj* **1** : awarded or worthy of a prize ⟨a ~ essay⟩; *also* : awarded as a prize ⟨a ~ medal⟩ **2** : OUTSTANDING
³prize *vb* **prized; priz·ing** : to value highly : ESTEEM

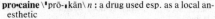

⁴prize *n* : property (as a ship) lawfully captured in time of war

⁵prize *vb* **prized; priz·ing** : PRY

prize·fight \'prīz-ˌfīt\ *n* : a professional boxing match — **prize·fight·er** *n* — **prize·fight·ing** *n*

prize·win·ner \-ˌwi-nər\ *n* : a winner of a prize — **prize·win·ning** *adj*

¹pro \'prō\ *n, pl* **pros** : a favorable argument, person, or position

²pro *adv* : in favor : FOR

³pro *n or adj* : PROFESSIONAL

PRO *abbr* public relations officer

prob *abbr* **1** probable; probably **2** problem

prob·a·bil·i·ty \ˌprä-bə-'bi-lə-tē\ *n, pl* **-ties 1** : the quality or state of being probable **2** : something probable **3** : a measure of how often a particular event will occur if something (as tossing a coin) is done repeatedly which results in any of a number of possible events

prob·a·ble \'prä-bə-bəl\ *adj* **1** : apparently or presumably true ⟨a ~ hypothesis⟩ **2** : likely to be or become true or real ⟨a ~ result⟩ — **prob·a·bly** \-bə-blē\ *adv*

¹pro·bate \'prō-ˌbāt\ *n* : the judicial determination of the validity of a will

²pro·bate *vb* **pro·bat·ed; pro·bat·ing** : to establish (a will) by probate as genuine and valid

pro·ba·tion \prō-'bā-shən\ *n* **1** : subjection of an individual to a period of testing and trial to ascertain fitness (as for a job) **2** : the action of giving a convicted offender freedom during good behavior under the supervision of a probation officer — **pro·ba·tion·ary** \-shə-ˌner-ē\ *adj*

pro·ba·tion·er \-shə-nər\ *n* **1** : a person (as a newly admitted student nurse) whose fitness is being tested during a trial period **2** : a convicted offender on probation

pro·ba·tive \'prō-bə-tiv\ *adj* **1** : serving to test or try **2** : serving to prove

¹probe \'prōb\ *n* **1** : a slender instrument for examining a cavity (as a wound) **2** : an information-gathering device sent into outer space **3** : a penetrating investigation **syn** inquiry, inquest, research, inquisition

²probe *vb* **probed; prob·ing 1** : to examine with a probe **2** : to investigate thoroughly

pro·bi·ty \'prō-bə-tē\ *n* : UPRIGHTNESS, HONESTY

prob·lem \'prä-bləm\ *n* **1** : a question raised for consideration or solution **2** : an intricate unsettled question **3** : a source of perplexity or vexation — **problem** *adj*

prob·lem·at·ic \ˌprä-blə-'ma-tik\ *or* **prob·lem·at·i·cal** \-ti-kəl\ *adj* **1** : difficult to solve or decide : PUZZLING **2** : DUBIOUS, QUESTIONABLE

pro·bos·cis \prə-'bä-səs, -'bäs-kəs\ *n, pl* **-bos·cis·es** *also* **-bos·ci·des** \-'bäs-ə-ˌdēz\ [L, fr. Gk *proboskis*, fr. *pro-* before + *boskein* to feed] : a long flexible snout (as the trunk of an elephant)

proc *abbr* proceedings

pro·caine \'prō-ˌkān\ *n* : a drug used esp. as a local anesthetic

pro·ce·dure \prə-'sē-jər\ *n* **1** : a particular way of doing something ⟨democratic ~⟩ **2** : a series of steps followed in a regular order ⟨surgical ~⟩ — **pro·ce·dur·al** \-'sē-jə-rəl\ *adj*

pro·ceed \prō-'sēd\ *vb* **1** : to come forth : ISSUE **2** : to go on in an orderly way; *also* : CONTINUE **3** : to begin and carry on an action **4** : to take legal action **5** : to go forward : ADVANCE

pro·ceed·ing *n* **1** : PROCEDURE **2** *pl* : DOINGS **3** *pl* : legal action **4** : TRANSACTION **5** *pl* : an official record of things said or done

pro·ceeds \'prō-ˌsēdz\ *n pl* : the total amount or the profit arising from a business deal

¹pro·cess \'prä-ˌses, 'prō-\ *n, pl* **pro·cess·es** \-ˌse-səz, -sə-səz, -sə-ˌsēz\ **1** : PROGRESS, ADVANCE **2** : something going on : PROCEEDING **3** : a natural phenomenon marked by gradual changes that lead toward a particular result ⟨the ~ of growth⟩ **4** : a series of actions or operations directed toward a particular result ⟨a manufacturing ~⟩ **5** : legal action **6** : a mandate issued by a court; *esp* : SUMMONS **7** : a projecting part of an organism or organic structure

²process *vb* : to subject to a special process

pro·ces·sion \prə-'se-shən\ *n* : a group of individuals moving along in an orderly often ceremonial way

pro·ces·sion·al \-'se-shə-nəl\ *n* **1** : music for a procession **2** : a ceremonial procession

pro·ces·sor \'prä-ˌse-sər, 'prō-\ *n* **1** : one that processes **2** : the part of a computer that operates on data

pro–choice \(ˌ)prō-'chȯis\ *adj* : favoring the legalization of abortion

pro·claim \prō-'klām\ *vb* : to make known publicly : DECLARE

proc·la·ma·tion \ˌprä-klə-'mā-shən\ *n* : an official public announcement

pro·cliv·i·ty \prō-'kli-və-tē\ *n, pl* **-ties** : an inherent inclination esp. toward something objectionable

pro·con·sul \-'kän-səl\ *n* **1** : a governor or military commander of an ancient Roman province **2** : an administrator in a modern colony or occupied area — **pro·con·su·lar** \-sə-lər\ *adj*

pro·cras·ti·nate \prə-'kras-tə-ˌnāt, prō-\ *vb* **-nat·ed; -nat·ing** [L *procrastinare*, fr. *pro-* forward + *crastinus* of tomorrow, fr. *cras* tomorrow] : to put off usu. habitually doing something that should be done **syn** dawdle, delay — **pro·cras·ti·na·tion** \-ˌkras-tə-'nā-shən\ *n* — **pro·cras·ti·na·tor** \-'kras-tə-ˌnā-tər\ *n*

pro·cre·ate \'prō-krē-ˌāt\ *vb* **-at·ed; -at·ing** : to beget or bring forth offspring **syn** reproduce, breed, generate, propagate — **pro·cre·ation** \ˌprō-krē-'ā-shən\ *n* — **pro·cre·ative** \'prō-krē-ˌā-tiv\ *adj* — **pro·cre·ator** \-ˌā-tər\ *n*

pro·crus·te·an \prə-'krəs-tē-ən\ *adj, often cap* [fr. *Procrustes*, villain of Greek mythology who made victims fit his bed by stretching them or cutting off their legs] : marked by arbitrary often ruthless disregard of individual differences or special circumstances

proc·tor \'präk-tər\ *n* : one appointed to supervise students (as at an examination) — **proctor** *vb* — **proc·to·ri·al** \präk-ˈtōr-ē-əl\ *adj*

proc·u·ra·tor \ˈprä-kyə-ˌrā-tər\ *n* : a Roman provincial administrator

pro·cure \prə-ˈkyu̇r\ *vb* **pro·cured; pro·cur·ing 1** : to get possession of : OBTAIN **2** : to make women available for promiscuous sexual intercourse **3** : ACHIEVE *syn* secure, acquire, gain, win, earn — **pro·cur·able** \-ˈkyu̇r-ə-bəl\ *adj* — **pro·cure·ment** *n* — **pro·cur·er** *n*

¹**prod** \ˈpräd\ *vb* **prod·ded; prod·ding 1** : to thrust a pointed instrument into : GOAD **2** : INCITE, STIR — **prod** *n*

²**prod** *abbr* product; production

prod·i·gal \ˈprä-di-gəl\ *adj* **1** : recklessly extravagant; *also* : LUXURIANT **2** : WASTEFUL, LAVISH *syn* profuse, lush, opulent — **prodigal** *n* — **prod·i·gal·i·ty** \ˌprä-də-ˈga-lə-tē\ *n*

pro·di·gious \prə-ˈdi-jəs\ *adj* **1** : exciting wonder **2** : extraordinary in size or degree : ENORMOUS *syn* monstrous, tremendous, stupendous, monumental — **pro·di·gious·ly** *adv*

prod·i·gy \ˈprä-də-jē\ *n, pl* **-gies 1** : something extraordinary : WONDER **2** : a highly talented child

¹**pro·duce** \prə-ˈdüs, -ˈdyüs\ *vb* **pro·duced; pro·duc·ing 1** : to present to view : EXHIBIT **2** : to give birth or rise to : YIELD **3** : EXTEND, PROLONG **4** : to give being or form to : BRING ABOUT, MAKE; *esp* : MANUFACTURE **5** : to cause to accrue ⟨∼ a profit⟩ — **pro·duc·er** *n*

²**pro·duce** \ˈprä-(ˌ)düs, ˈprō- *also* -(ˌ)dyüs\ *n* : PRODUCT 2; *also* : agricultural products and esp. fresh fruits and vegetables

prod·uct \ˈprä-(ˌ)dəkt\ *n* **1** : the number resulting from multiplication **2** : something produced

pro·duc·tion \prə-ˈdək-shən\ *n* **1** : something produced : PRODUCT **2** : the act or process of producing — **pro·duc·tive** \-ˈdək-tiv\ *adj* — **pro·duc·tive·ness** *n* — **pro·duc·tiv·i·ty** \(ˌ)prō-ˌdək-ˈti-və-tē, ˌprä-(ˌ)dək-\ *n*

pro·em \ˈprō-ˌem\ *n* **1** : preliminary comment : PREFACE **2** : PRELUDE

prof *abbr* **1** professional **2** professor

¹**pro·fane** \prō-ˈfān\ *vb* **pro·faned; pro·fan·ing 1** : to treat (something sacred) with irreverence or contempt **2** : to debase by an unworthy use — **prof·a·na·tion** \ˌprä-fə-ˈnā-shən\ *n*

²**pro·fane** *adj* [ME *prophane*, fr. MF, fr. L *profanus*, fr. *pro-* before + *fanum* temple] **1** : not concerned with religion : SECULAR **2** : not holy because unconsecrated, impure, or defiled **3** : serving to debase what is holy : IRREVERENT ⟨∼ language⟩ — **pro·fane·ly** *adv* — **pro·fane·ness** *n*

pro·fan·i·ty \prō-ˈfa-nə-tē\ *n, pl* **-ties 1** : the quality or state of being profane **2** : the use of profane language **3** : profane language

pro·fess \prə-ˈfes\ *vb* **1** : to declare or admit openly : AFFIRM **2** : to declare in words only : PRETEND **3** : to confess one's faith in **4** : to practice or claim to be versed in (a calling or occupation) — **pro·fess·ed·ly** \-ˈfe-səd-lē\ *adv*

pro·fes·sion \prə-ˈfe-shən\ *n* **1** : an open declaration or avowal of a belief or opinion **2** : a calling requiring specialized knowledge and often long academic preparation **3** : the whole body of persons engaged in a calling

¹**pro·fes·sion·al** \prə-ˈfe-shə-nəl\ *adj* **1** : of, relating to, or characteristic of a profession **2** : engaged in one of the professions **3** : participating for gain in an activity often engaged in by amateurs — **pro·fes·sion·al·ly** *adv*

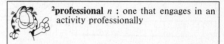

²**professional** *n* : one that engages in an activity professionally

pro·fes·sion·al·ism \-nə-ˌli-zəm\ *n* **1** : the conduct, aims, or qualities that characterize or mark a profession or a professional person **2** : the following of a profession (as athletics) for gain or livelihood

pro·fes·sion·al·ize \-nə-ˌlīz\ *vb* **-ized; -iz·ing** : to give a professional nature to

pro·fes·sor \prə-ˈfe-sər\ *n* : a teacher at a university or college; *esp* : a faculty member of the highest academic rank — **pro·fes·so·ri·al** \ˌprō-fə-ˈsōr-ē-əl, ˌprä-\ *adj* — **pro·fes·sor·ship** *n*

prof·fer \ˈprä-fər\ *vb* **prof·fered; prof·fer·ing** : to present for acceptance : OFFER — **proffer** *n*

pro·fi·cient \prə-ˈfi-shənt\ *adj* : well advanced in an art, occupation, or branch of knowledge *syn* adept, skillful, expert, masterful, masterly — **pro·fi·cien·cy** \-shən-sē\ *n* — **proficient** *n* — **pro·fi·cient·ly** *adv*

¹**pro·file** \ˈprō-ˌfīl\ *n* [It *profilo*, fr. *profilare* to draw in outline, fr. *pro-* forward (fr. L) + *filare* to spin, fr. LL, fr. L *filum* thread] **1** : a representation of something in outline; *esp* : a human head seen in side view **2** : a concise biographical sketch **3** : degree or level of public exposure ⟨keep a low ∼⟩

²**profile** *vb* **pro·filed; pro·fil·ing** : to write or draw a profile of

¹**prof·it** \ˈprä-fət\ *n* **1** : a valuable return : GAIN **2** : the excess of the selling price of goods over their cost — **prof·it·less** *adj*

²**profit** *vb* **1** : to be of use : BENEFIT **2** : to derive benefit : GAIN — **prof·it·able** \ˈprä-fə-tə-bəl\ *adj* — **prof·it·ably** \-blē\ *adv*

prof·i·teer \ˌprä-fə-ˈtir\ *n* : one who makes what is considered an unreasonable profit — **profiteer** *vb*

prof·li·gate \ˈprä-fli-gət, -flə-ˌgāt\ *adj* **1** : completely given up to dissipation and licentiousness **2** : wildly extravagant — **prof·li·ga·cy** \-gə-sē\ *n* — **profligate** *n* — **prof·li·gate·ly** *adv*

pro for·ma \(ˌ)prō-ˈfȯr-mə\ *adj* : done or existing as a matter of form

pro·found \prə-ˈfau̇nd, prō-\ *adj* **1** : marked by intellectual depth or insight ⟨a ∼ thought⟩ **2** : coming from or reaching to a depth ⟨a ∼ sigh⟩ **3** : deeply felt : INTENSE ⟨∼ sympathy⟩ — **pro·found·ly** *adv* — **pro·fun·di·ty** \-ˈfən-də-tē\ *n*

pro·fuse \prə-ˈfyüs, prō-\ *adj* : pouring forth liberally

: ABUNDANT **syn** lavish, prodigal, luxuriant, exuberant — **pro·fuse·ly** *adv* — **pro·fu·sion** \-ˈfyü-zhən\ *n*

prog *abbr* program

pro·gen·i·tor \prō-ˈje-nə-tər\ *n* 1 : a direct ancestor : FOREFATHER 2 : ORIGINATOR, PRECURSOR

prog·e·ny \ˈprä-jə-nē\ *n, pl* **-nies** : OFFSPRING, CHILDREN, DESCENDANTS

pro·ges·ter·one \prō-ˈjes-tə-ˌrōn\ *n* : a female hormone that causes the uterus to undergo changes so as to provide a suitable environment for a fertilized egg

prog·na·thous \ˈpräg-nə-thəs\ *adj* : having the jaws projecting beyond the upper part of the face

prog·no·sis \präg-ˈnō-səs\ *n, pl* **-no·ses** \-ˌsēz\ 1 : the prospect of recovery from disease 2 : FORECAST

¹**prog·nos·tic** \präg-ˈnäs-tik\ *n* 1 : PORTENT 2 : PROPHECY

²**prognostic** *adj* : of, relating to, or serving as ground for prognostication or a prognosis

prog·nos·ti·cate \präg-ˈnäs-tə-ˌkāt\ *vb* **-cat·ed; -cat·ing** : to foretell from signs or symptoms — **prog·nos·ti·ca·tion** \-ˌnäs-tə-ˈkā-shən\ *n* — **prog·nos·ti·ca·tor** \-ˈnäs-tə-ˌkā-tər\ *n*

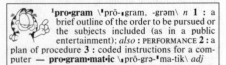

¹**pro·gram** \ˈprō-ˌgram, -grəm\ *n* 1 : a brief outline of the order to be pursued or the subjects included (as in a public entertainment); *also* : PERFORMANCE 2 : a plan of procedure 3 : coded instructions for a computer — **pro·gram·mat·ic** \ˌprō-grə-ˈma-tik\ *adj*

²**program** *also* **programme** *vb* **-grammed** *or* **-gramed; -gram·ming** *or* **-gram·ing** 1 : to arrange or furnish a program of or for 2 : to enter in a program 3 : to provide (as a computer) with a program — **pro·gram·ma·bil·i·ty** \(ˌ)prō-ˌgra-mə-ˈbi-lə-tē\ *n* — **pro·gram·ma·ble** \ˈprō-ˌgra-mə-bəl\ *adj* — **pro·gram·mer** *also* **pro·gram·er** \ˈprō-ˌgra-mər, -grə-\ *n*

programme *chiefly Brit var of* PROGRAM

programmed instruction *n* : instruction through information given in small steps with each requiring a correct response by the learner before going on to the next step

pro·gram·ming *or* **pro·gram·ing** *n* 1 : the planning, scheduling, or performing of a program 2 : the process of instructing or learning by means of an instruction program 3 : the process of preparing an instruction program

¹**prog·ress** \ˈprä-grəs, -ˌgres\ *n* 1 : a forward movement : ADVANCE 2 : a gradual betterment

²**pro·gress** \prə-ˈgres\ *vb* 1 : to move forward : PROCEED 2 : to develop to a more advanced stage : IMPROVE

pro·gres·sion \prə-ˈgre-shən\ *n* 1 : an act of progressing : ADVANCE 2 : a continuous and connected series

¹**pro·gres·sive** \prə-ˈgre-siv\ *adj* 1 : of, relating to, or characterized by progress ⟨a ~ city⟩ 2 : moving forward or onward : ADVANCING 3 : increasing in extent or severity ⟨a ~ disease⟩ 4 *often cap* : of or relating to political Progressives 5 : of, relating to, or constituting a verb form that expresses action in progress at the time of speaking or a time spoken of — **pro·gres·sive·ly** *adv*

²**progressive** *n* 1 : one that is progressive 2 : a person believing in moderate political change and social improvement by government action; *esp, cap* : a member of a Progressive Party in the U.S.

pro·hib·it \prō-ˈhi-bət\ *vb* 1 : to forbid by authority 2 : to prevent from doing something

pro·hi·bi·tion \ˌprō-ə-ˈbi-shən\ *n* 1 : the act of prohibiting 2 : the forbidding by law of the sale or manufacture of alcoholic beverages — **pro·hi·bi·tion·ist** \-ˈbi-shə-nist\ *n* — **pro·hib·i·tive** \prō-ˈhi-bə-tiv\ *adj* — **pro·hib·i·tive·ly** *adv* — **pro·hib·i·to·ry** \-ˈhi-bə-ˌtōr-ē\ *adj*

¹**proj·ect** \ˈprä-ˌjekt, -jikt\ *n* 1 : a specific plan or design : SCHEME 2 : a planned undertaking ⟨a research ~⟩

²**pro·ject** \prə-ˈjekt\ *vb* 1 : to devise in the mind : DESIGN 2 : to throw forward 3 : PROTRUDE 4 : to cause (light or shadow) to fall into space or (an image) to fall on a surface ⟨~ a beam of light⟩ 5 : to attribute (a thought, feeling, or personal characteristic) to a person, group, or object — **pro·jec·tion** \-ˈjek-shən\ *n*

pro·jec·tile \prə-ˈjekt-əl, -ˈjek-ˌtīl\ *n* 1 : a body hurled or projected by external force; *esp* : a missile for a firearm 2 : a self-propelling weapon

pro·jec·tion·ist \prə-ˈjek-shə-nist\ *n* : one that operates a motion-picture projector or television equipment

pro·jec·tor \-ˈjek-tər\ *n* : one that projects; *esp* : a device for projecting pictures on a screen

pro·le·gom·e·non \ˌprō-li-ˈgä-mə-ˌnän, -nən\ *n, pl* **-e·na** \-nə\ : prefatory remarks

pro·le·tar·i·an \ˌprō-lə-ˈter-ē-ən\ *n* : a member of the proletariat — **proletarian** *adj*

pro·le·tar·i·at \-ē-ət\ *n* : the laboring class; *esp* : industrial workers who sell their labor to live

pro-life \(ˌ)prō-ˈlīf\ *n* : ANTIABORTION

pro·lif·er·ate \prə-ˈli-fə-ˌrāt\ *vb* **-at·ed; -at·ing** : to grow or increase by rapid production of new units (as cells or offspring) — **pro·lif·er·a·tion** \-ˌli-fə-ˈrā-shən\ *n*

pro·lif·ic \prə-ˈli-fik\ *adj* 1 : producing young or fruit abundantly 2 : marked by abundant inventiveness or productivity ⟨a ~ writer⟩ — **pro·lif·i·cal·ly** \-fi-k(ə-)lē\ *adv*

pro·lix \prō-ˈliks, ˈprō-ˌliks\ *adj* : VERBOSE **syn** wordy, diffuse, redundant — **pro·lix·i·ty** \prō-ˈlik-sə-tē\ *n*

pro·logue *also* **pro·log** \ˈprō-ˌlȯg, -ˌläg\ *n* : PREFACE ⟨~ of a play⟩

pro·long \prə-ˈlȯŋ\ *vb* 1 : to lengthen in time : CONTINUE ⟨~ a meeting⟩ 2 : to lengthen in extent or range **syn** protract, extend, elongate, stretch — **pro·lon·ga·tion** \ˌprō-ˌlȯŋ-ˈgā-shən\ *n*

prom \ˈpräm\ *n* : a formal dance given by a high school or college class

¹**prom·e·nade** \ˌprä-mə-ˈnād, -ˈnäd\ *vb* **-nad·ed; -nad·ing** 1 : to take a promenade 2 : to walk about in or on

²**promenade** *n* [F, fr. *promener* to take for a walk, fr. L *prominare* to drive forward] 1 : a place for strolling 2 : a leisurely walk for pleasure or display 3 : an opening grand march at a formal ball

pro·me·thi·um \prə-'mē-thē-əm\ *n* : a metallic chemical element obtained from uranium or neodymium — see ELEMENT table

prom·i·nence \'prä-mə-nəns\ *n* **1** : something prominent **2** : the quality, state, or fact of being prominent or conspicuous **3** : a mass of cloudlike gas that arises from the sun's chromosphere

prom·i·nent \-nənt\ *adj* **1** : jutting out : PROJECTING **2** : readily noticeable : CONSPICUOUS **3** : DISTINGUISHED, EMINENT **syn** remarkable, outstanding, striking, salient — **prom·i·nent·ly** *adv*

pro·mis·cu·ous \prə-'mis-kyə-wəs\ *adj* **1** : consisting of various sorts and kinds : MIXED **2** : not restricted to one class or person **3** : having a number of sexual partners **syn** miscellaneous, assorted, heterogeneous, motley, varied — **pro·mis·cu·i·ty** \,prä-mis-'kyü-ə-tē, ,prō-,mis-\ *n* — **pro·mis·cu·ous·ly** *adv* — **pro·mis·cu·ous·ness** *n*

¹**prom·ise** \'prä-məs\ *n* **1** : a pledge to do or not to do something specified **2** : ground for expectation of success or improvement **3** : something promised

²**promise** *vb* **prom·ised; prom·is·ing 1** : to engage to do, bring about, or provide ⟨~ help⟩ **2** : to suggest beforehand ⟨dark clouds ~ rain⟩ **3** : to give ground for expectation ⟨it ~s to be a good game⟩

prom·is·ing *adj* : likely to succeed or yield good results — **prom·is·ing·ly** *adv*

prom·is·so·ry \'prä-mə-,sōr-ē\ *adj* : containing a promise

prom·on·to·ry \'prä-mən-,tōr-ē\ *n*, *pl* **-ries** : a point of land jutting into the sea : HEADLAND

pro·mote \prə-'mōt\ *vb* **pro·mot·ed; pro·mot·ing 1** : to advance in station, rank, or honor **2** : to contribute to the growth or prosperity of : FURTHER **3** : LAUNCH — **pro·mo·tion** \-'mō-shən\ *n* — **pro·mo·tion·al** \-shə-nəl\ *adj*

pro·mot·er \-'mō-tər\ *n* : one that promotes; *esp* : one that assumes the financial responsibilities of a sports event

¹**prompt** \'prämpt\ *vb* **1** : INCITE **2** : to assist (one acting or reciting) by suggesting the next words **3** : INSPIRE, URGE — **prompt·er** *n*

²**prompt** *adj* **1** : being ready and quick to act; *also* : PUNCTUAL **2** : performed readily or immediately ⟨~ service⟩ — **prompt·ly** *adv* — **prompt·ness** *n*

prompt·book \-,búk\ *n* : a copy of a play with directions for performance used by a theater prompter

promp·ti·tude \'prämp-tə-,tüd, -,tyüd\ *n* : the quality or habit of being prompt : PROMPTNESS

pro·mul·gate \'prä-məl-,gāt; prō-'məl-\ *vb* **-gat·ed; -gat·ing** : to make known or put into force by open declaration — **prom·ul·ga·tion** \,prä-məl-'gā-shən, ,prō-(,)məl-\ *n*

pron *abbr* **1** pronoun **2** pronounced **3** pronunciation

prone \'prōn\ *adj* **1** : having a tendency or inclination : DISPOSED **2** : lying face downward; *also* : lying flat or prostrate **syn** subject, exposed, open, liable, susceptible — **prone·ness** *n*

prong \'pròng\ *n* : one of the sharp points of a fork : TINE; *also* : a slender projecting part (as of an antler) — **pronged** \'pròngd\ *adj*

prong·horn \'pròng-,hòrn\ *n*, *pl* **pronghorn** *also* **pronghorns** : a ruminant mammal of treeless parts of western No. America that resembles an antelope

pro·noun \'prō-,naún\ *n* : a word used as a substitute for a noun

pro·nounce \prə-'naúns\ *vb* **pro·nounced; pro·nounc·ing 1** : to utter officially or as an opinion ⟨~ sentence⟩ **2** : to employ the organs of speech in order to produce ⟨~ a word⟩; *esp* : to say or speak correctly ⟨she can't ~ his name⟩ — **pro·nounce·able** *adj* — **pro·nun·ci·a·tion** \-,nən-sē-'ā-shən\ *n*

pro·nounced *adj* : strongly marked : DECIDED

pro·nounce·ment \prə-'naúns-mənt\ *n* : a formal declaration of opinion; *also* : ANNOUNCEMENT

pronghorn

pron·to \'prän-,tō\ *adv* [Sp, fr. L *promptus* prompt] : QUICKLY

pro·nu·clear \'prō-'nü-klē-ər, -'nyü-\ *adj* : supporting the use of nuclear-powered electric generating stations

pro·nun·ci·a·men·to \prō-,nən-sē-ə-'men-tō\ *n*, *pl* **-tos** *or* **-toes** : PROCLAMATION, MANIFESTO

¹**proof** \'prüf\ *n* **1** : the evidence that compels acceptance by the mind of a truth or fact **2** : a process or operation that establishes validity or truth : TEST **3** : a trial impression (as from type) **4** : a trial print from a photographic negative **5** : alcoholic content (as of a beverage) indicated by a number that is twice the percent by volume of alcohol present ⟨whiskey of 90 ~ is 45% alcohol⟩

²**proof** *adj* **1** : successful in resisting or repelling ⟨~ against tampering⟩ ⟨water*proof*⟩ **2** : of standard strength or quality or alcoholic content

proof·read \-,rēd\ *vb* : to read and mark corrections in — **proof·read·er** *n*

¹**prop** \'präp\ *n* : something that props

²**prop** *vb* **propped; prop·ping 1** : to support by placing something under or against **2** : SUSTAIN, STRENGTHEN

³**prop** *n* : PROPERTY 4

⁴**prop** *n* : PROPELLER

⁵**prop** *abbr* **1** property **2** proposition **3** proprietor

pro·pa·gan·da \,prä-pə-'gan-də, ,prō-\ *n* [NL, fr. *Congregatio de propaganda fide* Congregation for propagating the faith, organization established by Pope Gregory XV] : the spreading of ideas or information to further or damage a cause; *also* : ideas or allegations spread for such a purpose — **pro·pa·gan·dist** \-dist\ *n*

pro·pa·gan·dize \-,dīz\ *vb* **-dized; -diz·ing** : to subject to or carry on propaganda

prop·a·gate \'prä-pə-,gāt\ *vb* **-gat·ed; -gat·ing 1** : to reproduce or cause to reproduce biologically : MULTIPLY **2** : to cause to spread — **prop·a·ga·tion** \,prä-pə-'gā-shən\ *n*

pro·pane \'prō-,pān\ *n* : a heavy flammable gas found in petroleum and natural gas and used esp. as a fuel

pro·pel \prə-'pel\ *vb* **pro·pelled; pro·pel·ling** : to drive forward or onward **syn** push, shove, thrust

pro·pel·lant *also* **pro·pel·lent** \-'pe-lənt\ *n* : something (as a fuel) that propels — **propellant** *or* **propellent** *adj*

pro·pel·ler \prə-'pe-lər\ *n* : a device consisting of a hub fitted with blades that is used to propel a vehicle (as a motorboat or an airplane)

pro·pen·si·ty \prə-'pen-sə-tē\ *n*, *pl* **-ties** : an often intense natural inclination or preference

¹**prop·er** \'prä-pər\ *adj* **1** : referring to one individual only ⟨~ noun⟩ **2** : belonging characteristically to a species or individual : PECULIAR **3** : very satisfactory : EXCELLENT **4** : strictly limited to a specified thing ⟨the city ~⟩ **5** : CORRECT ⟨the ~ way to proceed⟩ **6** : strictly decorous : GENTEEL **7** : marked by suitability or rightness ⟨~ punishment⟩ **syn** meet, appropriate, fitting, seemly — **prop·er·ly** *adv*

²**proper** *n* : the parts of the Mass that vary according to the liturgical calendar

prop·er·tied \'prä-pǝr-tēd\ *adj* : owning property and esp. much property

prop·er·ty \'prä-pǝr-tē\ *n, pl* **-ties 1** : a quality peculiar to an individual or thing **2** : something owned; *esp* : a piece of real estate **3** : OWNERSHIP **4** : an article or object used in a play or motion picture other than painted scenery and actor's costumes

proph·e·cy *also* **proph·e·sy** \'prä-fǝ-sē\ *n, pl* **-cies** *also* **-sies 1** : an inspired utterance of a prophet **2** : PREDICTION

proph·e·sy \-ˌsī\ *vb* **-sied; -sy·ing 1** : to speak or utter by divine inspiration **2** : PREDICT — **proph·e·si·er** *n*

proph·et \'prä-fǝt\ *n* [ME *prophete,* fr. OF, fr. L *propheta,* fr. Gk *prophētēs,* fr. *pro* for + *phanai* to speak] **1** : one who utters divinely inspired revelations **2** : one who foretells future events

proph·et·ess \'prä-fǝ-tǝs\ *n* : a woman who is a prophet

pro·phet·ic \prǝ-'fe-tik\ *or* **pro·phet·i·cal** \-ti-kǝl\ *adj* : of, relating to, or characteristic of a prophet or prophecy — **pro·phet·i·cal·ly** \-ti-k(ǝ-)lē\ *adv*

Proph·ets \'prä-fǝts\ *n pl* — see BIBLE table

¹**pro·phy·lac·tic** \ˌprō-fǝ-'lak-tik, ˌprä-\ *adj* **1** : preventing or guarding from disease **2** : PREVENTIVE

²**prophylactic** *n* : something prophylactic; *esp* : a device (as a condom) for preventing venereal infection or conception

pro·phy·lax·is \-'lak-sǝs\ *n, pl* **-lax·es** \-'lak-ˌsēz\ : measures designed to preserve health and prevent the spread of disease

pro·pin·qui·ty \prǝ-'piŋ-kwǝ-tē\ *n* **1** : KINSHIP **2** : nearness in place or time : PROXIMITY

pro·pi·ti·ate \prō-'pi-shē-ˌāt\ *vb* **-at·ed; -at·ing** : to gain or regain the favor of : APPEASE — **pro·pi·ti·a·tion** \-ˌpi-shē-'ā-shǝn\ *n* — **pro·pi·ti·a·to·ry** \-'pi-shē-ǝ-ˌtōr-ē\ *adj*

pro·pi·tious \prǝ-'pi-shǝs\ *adj* **1** : favorably disposed ⟨~ deities⟩ **2** : being of good omen ⟨~ circumstances⟩

prop·man \'präp-ˌman\ *n* : one who is in charge of stage properties

pro·po·nent \prǝ-'pō-nǝnt\ *n* : one who argues in favor of something

¹**pro·por·tion** \prǝ-'pōr-shǝn\ *n* **1** : BALANCE, SYMMETRY **2** : SHARE, QUOTA **3** : the relation of one part to another or to the whole with respect to magnitude, quantity, or degree : RATIO **4** : SIZE, DEGREE — **in proportion** : PROPORTIONAL

²**proportion** *vb* **-tioned; -tion·ing 1** : to adjust (a part or thing) in size relative to other parts or things **2** : to make the parts of harmonious

pro·por·tion·al \prǝ-'pōr-shǝ-nǝl\ *adj* : corresponding in size, degree, or intensity; *also* : having the same or a constant ratio — **pro·por·tion·al·ly** *adv*

pro·por·tion·ate \prǝ-'pōr-shǝ-nǝt\ *adj* : PROPORTIONAL — **pro·por·tion·ate·ly** *adv*

pro·pose \prǝ-'pōz\ *vb* **pro·posed; pro·pos·ing 1** : PLAN, INTEND ⟨~s to buy a house⟩ **2** : to make an offer of marriage **3** : to offer for consideration : SUGGEST ⟨~ a policy⟩ — **pro·pos·al** \-'pō-zǝl\ *n* — **pro·pos·er** *n*

¹**prop·o·si·tion** \ˌprä-pǝ-'zi-shǝn\ *n* **1** : something proposed for consideration : PROPOSAL **2** : a request for sexual intercourse **3** : a statement of something to be discussed, proved, or explained **4** : SITUATION, AFFAIR ⟨a tough ~⟩ — **prop·o·si·tion·al** \-'zi-shǝ-nǝl\ *adj*

²**proposition** *vb* **-tioned; -tion·ing** : to make a proposal to; *esp* : to suggest sexual intercourse to

pro·pound \prǝ-'paúnd\ *vb* : to set forth for consideration ⟨~ a doctrine⟩

pro·pri·e·tary \prǝ-'prī-ǝ-ˌter-ē\ *adj* **1** : of, relating to, or characteristic of a proprietor ⟨~ rights⟩ **2** : made and sold by one with the sole right to do so ⟨~ medicines⟩

pro·pri·e·tor \prǝ-'prī-ǝ-tǝr\ *n* : OWNER — **pro·pri·e·tor·ship** *n*

pro·pri·e·tress \-'prī-ǝ-trǝs\ *n* : a woman who is a proprietor

pro·pri·e·ty \prǝ-'prī-ǝ-tē\ *n, pl* **-ties 1** : the standard of what is socially acceptable in conduct or speech **2** *pl* : the customs of polite society

pro·pul·sion \prǝ-'pǝl-shǝn\ *n* **1** : the action or process of propelling **2** : something that propels — **pro·pul·sive** \-siv\ *adj*

pro ra·ta \(ˌ)prō-'rä-tǝ, -'rä-\ *adv* : in proportion to the share of each : PROPORTIONATELY

pro·rate \(ˌ)prō-'rāt\ *vb* **pro·rat·ed; pro·rat·ing** : to divide, distribute, or assess proportionately

pro·rogue \prǝ-'rōg\ *vb* **pro·rogued; pro·rogu·ing** : to suspend or end a session of (a legislative body) — **pro·ro·ga·tion** \ˌprō-rō-'gä-shǝn\ *n*

pros *pl of* PRO

pro·sa·ic \prō-'zā-ik\ *adj* : lacking imagination or excitement : DULL

pro·sce·ni·um \prō-'sē-nē-ǝm\ *n* **1** : the part of a stage in front of the curtain **2** : the wall containing the arch that frames the stage

pro·scribe \prō-'skrīb\ *vb* **pro·scribed; pro·scrib·ing 1** : OUTLAW **2** : to condemn or forbid as harmful — **pro·scrip·tion** \-'skrip-shǝn\ *n*

prose \'prōz\ *n* [ME, fr. MF, fr. L *prosa,* fr. fem. of *prorsus, prosus,* straightforward, being in prose, alter. of *proversus,* pp. of *provertere* to turn forward] : the ordinary language people use in speaking or writing

pros·e·cute \'prä-si-ˌkyüt\ *vb* **-cut·ed; -cut·ing 1** : to follow to the end ⟨~ an investigation⟩ **2** : to seek legal punishment of ⟨~ a forger⟩ — **pros·e·cu·tion** \ˌprä-si-'kyü-shǝn\ *n* — **pros·e·cu·tor** \'prä-si-ˌkyü-tǝr\ *n*

¹**pros·e·lyte** \'prä-sǝ-ˌlīt\ *n* : a new convert to a religion, belief, or party — **pros·e·ly·tism** \-ˌlī-ˌti-zǝm\ *n*

²**proselyte** *vb* **-lyt·ed; -lyt·ing** : PROSELYTIZE

pros·e·ly·tise *Brit var of* PROSELYTIZE

pros·e·ly·tize \'prä-sǝ-lǝ-ˌtīz\ *vb* **-tized; -tiz·ing 1** : to induce someone to convert to one's faith **2** : to recruit someone to join one's party, institution, or cause

pros·o·dy \'prä-sǝ-dē, -zǝ-\ *n, adj* **-dies** : the study of versification and esp. of metrical structure

¹**pros·pect** \'prä-ˌspekt\ *n* **1** : an extensive view; *also* : OUTLOOK **2** : the act of looking forward **3** : a mental vision of something to come **4** : something that is awaited or expected : POSSIBILITY **5** : a potential buyer or customer; *also* : a likely candidate — **pro·spec·tive** \prǝ-'spek-tiv, 'prä-ˌspek-\ *adj* — **pro·spec·tive·ly** *adv*

²**pros·pect** \'prä-ˌspekt\ *vb* : to explore esp. for mineral deposits — **pros·pec·tor** \-ˌspek-tǝr, prä-'spek-\ *n*

pro·spec·tus \prǝ-'spek-tǝs\ *n* : a preliminary statement that describes an enterprise and is distributed to prospective buyers or participants

pros·per \'präs-pǝr\ *vb* **pros·pered; pros·per·ing** : SUCCEED; *esp* : to achieve economic success

pros·per·i·ty \präs-'per-ǝ-tē\ *n* : thriving condition : SUCCESS; *esp* : economic well-being

pros·per·ous \'präs-pǝ-rǝs\ *adj* **1** : FAVORABLE ⟨~ winds⟩ **2** : marked by success or economic well-being ⟨a ~ business⟩

pros·tate \'präs-ˌtāt\ *n* : PROSTATE GLAND — **pros·tat·ic** \prä-'sta-tik\ *adj*

prostate gland *n* : a glandular body about the base of the male urethra that produces a secretion which is a major part of the fluid ejaculated during an orgasm

pros·ta·ti·tis \ˌpräs-tǝ-'tī-tǝs\ *n* : inflammation of the prostate gland

pros·the·sis \präs-'thē-sǝs, 'präs-thǝ-\ *n, pl* **-the·ses**

\-ˌsēz\ : an artificial replacement for a missing body part — **pros·thet·ic** \präs-ˈthe-tik\ adj

pros·thet·ics \-ˈthe-tiks\ n pl : the surgical or dental specialty concerned with the design, construction, and fitting of prostheses

¹pros·ti·tute \ˈpräs-tə-ˌtüt, -ˌtyüt\ vb **-tut·ed; -tut·ing 1** : to offer indiscriminately for sexual activity esp. for money **2** : to devote to corrupt or unworthy purposes — **pros·ti·tu·tion** \ˌpräs-tə-ˈtü-shən, -ˈtyü-\ n

²prostitute n : one who engages in sexual activities for money

¹pros·trate \ˈprä-ˌsträt\ adj **1** : stretched out with face on the ground in adoration or submission **2** : lying flat **3** : completely overcome ⟨~ with a cold⟩

²prostrate vb **pros·trat·ed; pros·trat·ing 1** : to throw or put into a prostrate position **2** : to reduce to a weak or powerless condition — **pros·tra·tion** \prä-ˈstrā-shən\ n

prosy \ˈprō-zē\ adj **pros·i·er; -est 1** : PROSAIC **2** : TEDIOUS

Prot abbr Protestant

prot·ac·tin·i·um \ˌprō-ˌtak-ˈti-nē-əm\ n : a metallic radioactive chemical element of relatively short life — see ELEMENT table

pro·tag·o·nist \prō-ˈta-gə-nist\ n **1** : the principal character in a drama or story **2** : a leader or supporter of a cause

pro·te·an \ˈprō-tē-ən\ adj : able to assume different shapes or roles

pro·tect \prə-ˈtekt\ vb : to shield from injury : GUARD

pro·tec·tion \prə-ˈtek-shən\ n **1** : the act of protecting : the state of being protected **2** : one that protects ⟨wear a helmet as a ~⟩ **3** : the supervision or support of one that is smaller and weaker **4** : the freeing of producers from foreign competition in their home market by high duties on foreign competitive goods — **pro·tec·tive** \-ˈtek-tiv\ adj

pro·tec·tion·ist \-shə-nist\ n : an advocate of government economic protection for domestic producers through restrictions on foreign competitors — **pro·tec·tion·ism** \-shə-ˌni-zəm\ n

pro·tec·tor \prə-ˈtek-tər\ n **1** : one that protects : GUARDIAN **2** : a device used to prevent injury : GUARD **3** : REGENT 1

pro·tec·tor·ate \-tə-rət\ n **1** : government by a protector **2** : the relationship of superior authority assumed by one state over a dependent one; also : the dependent political unit in such a relationship

pro·té·gé \ˈprō-tə-ˌzhā\ n [F] : one who is protected, trained, or guided by an influential person

pro·tein \ˈprō-ˌtēn\ n [F protéine, fr. LGk prōteios primary, fr. Gk prōtos first] : any of numerous complex nitrogen-containing substances that consist of chains of amino acids, are present in all living cells, and are an essential part of the human diet

pro tem \prō-ˈtem\ adv : PRO TEMPORE

pro tem·po·re \prō-ˈtem-pə-rē\ adv [L] : for the time being

Pro·te·ro·zo·ic \ˌprä-tə-rə-ˈzō-ik, ˌprō-\ adj : of, relating to, or being the eon of geologic history between the Archean and the Phanerozoic — **Proterozoic** n

¹pro·test \ˈprō-ˌtest\ n **1** : the act of protesting; esp : an organized public demonstration of disapproval **2** : a complaint or objection against an idea, an act, or a course of action

²pro·test \prō-ˈtest\ vb **1** : to assert positively : make solemn declaration of ⟨~s his innocence⟩ **2** : to object strongly : make a protest against ⟨~ a ruling⟩ — **pro·tes·ta·tion** \ˌprä-təs-ˈtā-shən\ n — **pro·test·er** or **pro·tes·tor** \-tər\ n

Prot·es·tant \ˈprä-təs-tənt, 3 also prə-ˈtes-\ n **1** : a member or adherent of one of the Christian churches deriving from the Reformation **2** : a Christian not of a Catholic or Orthodox church **3** not cap : one who makes a protest — **Prot·es·tant·ism** \ˈprä-təs-tən-ˌti-zəm\ n

pro·tha·la·mi·on \ˌprō-thə-ˈlā-mē-ən\ or **pro·tha·la·mi·um** \-mē-əm\ n, pl **-mia** \-mē-ə\ : a song in celebration of a marriage

pro·to·col \ˈprō-tə-ˌkòl\ n [MF prothocole, fr. ML protocollum, fr. LGk prōtokollon first sheet of a papyrus roll bearing date of manufacture, fr. Gk prōtos first + kollan to glue together, fr. kolla glue] **1** : an original draft or record **2** : a preliminary memorandum of diplomatic negotiation **3** : a code of diplomatic or military etiquette **4** : a set of conventions for formatting data in an electronic communications system

pro·ton \ˈprō-ˌtän\ n [Gk prōton, neut. of prōtos first] : a positively charged atomic particle present in all atomic nuclei — **pro·ton·ic** \-ˈtä-nik\ adj

pro·to·plasm \ˈprō-tə-ˌpla-zəm\ n : the complex colloidal largely protein substance of living plant and animal cells — **pro·to·plas·mic** \ˌprō-tə-ˈplaz-mik\ adj

pro·to·type \ˈprō-tə-ˌtīp\ n : an original model : ARCHETYPE

pro·to·zo·an \ˌprō-tə-ˈzō-ən\ n : any of a phylum or subkingdom of unicellular lower invertebrate animals that include some pathogenic parasites of humans and domestic animals — **protozoan** adj

pro·tract \prō-ˈtrakt\ vb : to prolong in time or space syn extend, lengthen, elongate, stretch

pro·trac·tor \-ˈtrak-tər\ n : an instrument for drawing and measuring angles

pro·trude \prō-ˈtrüd\ vb **pro·trud·ed; pro·trud·ing** : to stick out or cause to stick out : jut out — **pro·tru·sion** \-ˈtrü-zhən\ n

pro·tu·ber·ance \prō-ˈtü-bə-rəns, -ˈtyü-\ n : something that protrudes

pro·tu·ber·ant \-rənt\ adj : extending beyond the surrounding surface in a bulge

proud \ˈpraud\ adj **1** : having or showing excessive self-esteem : HAUGHTY **2** : highly pleased : EXULTANT **3** : having proper self-respect ⟨too ~ to beg⟩ **4** : GLORIOUS ⟨a ~ occasion⟩ **5** : SPIRITED ⟨a ~ steed⟩ syn arrogant, insolent, overbearing, disdainful — **proud·ly** adv

prov abbr **1** province; provincial **2** provisional

Prov abbr Proverbs

prove \ˈprüv\ vb **proved; proved** or **prov·en** \ˈprü-vən\; **prov·ing 1** : to test by experiment or by a stan-

dard **2** : to establish the truth of by argument or evidence **3** : to show to be correct, valid, or genuine **4** : to turn out esp. after trial or test (the car *proved* to be a good choice) — **prov•able** \'prü-və-bəl\ *adj*

prov•e•nance \'prä-və-nəns\ *n* : ORIGIN, SOURCE

Pro•ven•çal \ˌprō-ˌvän-'säl, ˌprä-vən-\ *n* **1** : a native or inhabitant of Provence **2** : a Romance language spoken in southern France — **Provençal** *adj*

prov•en•der \'prä-vən-dər\ *n* **1** : dry food for domestic animals : FEED **2** : FOOD, VICTUALS

pro•ve•nience \prə-'vē-nyəns\ *n* : ORIGIN, SOURCE

prov•erb \'prä-ˌvərb\ *n* : a pithy popular saying : ADAGE

pro•ver•bi•al \prə-'vər-bē-əl\ *adj* **1** : of, relating to, or resembling a proverb **2** : commonly spoken of **Proverbs** *n* — see BIBLE table

pro•vide \prə-'vīd\ *vb* **pro•vid•ed; pro•vid•ing** [ME, fr. L *providēre*, lit., to see ahead, fr. *pro-* forward + *vidēre* to see] **1** : to take measures beforehand (∼ against inflation) **2** : to make a proviso or stipulation **3** : to supply what is needed (∼ for a family) **4** : EQUIP **5** : to supply for use : YIELD — **pro•vid•er** *n*

pro•vid•ed *conj* : on condition that : IF

prov•i•dence \'prä-və-dəns\ *n* **1** *often cap* : divine guidance or care **2** *cap* : GOD **|** **3** : the quality or state of being provident

prov•i•dent \-dənt\ *adj* **1** : making provision for the future : PRUDENT **2** : FRUGAL — **prov•i•dent•ly** *adv*

prov•i•den•tial \ˌprä-və-'den-chəl\ *adj* **1** : of, relating to, or determined by Providence **2** : OPPORTUNE, LUCKY

pro•vid•ing *conj* : PROVIDED

prov•ince \'prä-vəns\ *n* **1** : an administrative district or division of a country **2** *pl* : all of a country except the metropolises **3** : proper business or scope : SPHERE

pro•vin•cial \prə-'vin-chəl\ *adj* **1** : of or relating to a province **2** : limited in outlook : NARROW (∼ ideas) — **pro•vin•cial•ism** \-chə-ˌli-zəm\ *n*

proving ground *n* : a place for scientific experimentation or testing

¹pro•vi•sion \prə-'vi-zhən\ *n* **1** : the act or process of providing; *also* : a measure taken beforehand **2** : a stock of needed supplies; *esp* : a stock of food — usu. used in pl. **3** : PROVISO

²provision *vb* : to supply with provisions

pro•vi•sion•al \-'vi-zhə-nəl\ *adj* : provided for a temporary need : CONDITIONAL — **pro•vi•sion•al•ly** *adv*

pro•vi•so \prə-'vī-zō\ *n, pl* **-sos** *or* **-soes** [ME, fr. ML *proviso quod* provided that] : an article or clause that introduces a condition : STIPULATION

prov•o•ca•tion \ˌprä-və-'kā-shən\ *n* **1** : the act of provoking **2** : something that provokes

pro•voc•a•tive \prə-'vä-kə-tiv\ *adj* : serving to provoke or excite

pro•voke \prə-'vōk\ *vb* **pro•voked; pro•vok•ing 1** : to incite to anger : INCENSE **2** : to call forth : EVOKE (a remark that *provoked* laughter) **3** : to stir up on purpose (∼ an argument) **syn** irritate, exasperate, aggravate, inflame, rile, pique — **pro•vok•er** *n*

pro•vo•lo•ne \ˌprō-və-'lō-nē\ *n* : a usu. firm pliant often smoked Italian cheese

pro•vost \'prō-ˌvōst, 'prä-vəst\ *n* : a high official : DIGNITARY; *esp* : a high-ranking university administrative officer

pro•vost mar•shal \'prō-ˌvō-'mär-shəl\ *n* : an officer who supervises the military police of a command

prow \'praú\ *n* : the bow of a ship

prow•ess \'praú-əs\ *n* **1** : military valor and skill **2** : extraordinary ability

prowl \'praúl\ *vb* : to roam about stealthily — **prowl** *n* — **prowl•er** *n*

prox•i•mal \'präk-sə-məl\ *adj* **1** : next to or nearest the point of attachment or origin; *esp* : located toward the center of the body **2** : of, relating to, or being the mesial and distal surfaces of a tooth — **prox•i•mal•ly** *adv*

prox•i•mate \'präk-sə-mət\ *adj* **1** : DIRECT (the ∼ cause) **2** : very near

prox•im•i•ty \präk-'si-mə-tē\ *n* : NEARNESS

prox•i•mo \'präk-sə-ˌmō\ *adj* [L *proximo mense* in the next month] : of or occurring in the next month after the present

proxy \'präk-sē\ *n, pl* **prox•ies** : the authority or power to act for another; *also* : a document giving such authorization — **proxy** *adj*

prude \'prüd\ *n* : a person who shows or affects extreme modesty — **prud•ery** \'prü-də-rē\ *n* — **prud•ish** *adj* — **prud•ish•ly** *adv*

pru•dent \'prüd-ᵊnt\ *adj* **1** : shrewd in the management of practical affairs **2** : CAUTIOUS, DISCREET **3** : PROVIDENT, FRUGAL **syn** judicious, foresighted, sensible, sane — **pru•dence** \-ᵊns\ *n* — **pru•den•tial** \prü-'den-chəl\ *adj* — **pru•dent•ly** *adv*

¹prune \'prün\ *n* : a dried plum

²prune *vb* **pruned; prun•ing** : to cut off unwanted parts (as of a tree)

pru•ri•ent \'prúr-ē-ənt\ *adj* : LASCIVIOUS; *also* : exciting to lasciviousness — **pru•ri•ence** \-ē-əns\ *n*

¹pry \'prī\ *vb* **pried; pry•ing** : to look closely or inquisitively; *esp* : SNOOP

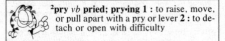

²pry *vb* **pried; pry•ing 1** : to raise, move, or pull apart with a pry or lever **2** : to detach or open with difficulty

³pry *n* : a tool for prying

Ps *or* **Psa** *abbr* Psalms

PS *abbr* **1** [L *postscriptum*] postscript **2** public school

PSA *abbr* public service announcement

psalm \'säm, 'sälm\ *n, often cap* [ME, fr. OE *psealm*, fr. LL *psalmus*, fr. Gk *psalmos*, lit., twanging of a harp, fr. *psallein* to pluck, play a stringed instrument] : a sacred song or poem; *esp* : one of the hymns collected in the Book of Psalms — **psalm•ist** *n*

psalm•o•dy \'sä-mə-dē, 'säl-\ *n* : the singing of psalms in worship

Psalms *n* — see BIBLE table

Psal•ter \'sòl-tər\ *n* : the Book of Psalms; *also* : a collection of the Psalms arranged for devotional use

pseud *abbr* pseudonym; pseudonymous

pseu·do \'sü-dō\ *adj* : SPURIOUS, SHAM

pseu·do·nym \'sü-də-ˌnim\ *n* : a fictitious name — **pseu·don·y·mous** \sü-'dä-nə-məs\ *adj*

PSG *abbr* platoon sergeant

¹**psi** \'sī, 'psī\ *n* : the 23d letter of the Greek alphabet — Ψ or ψ

²**psi** *abbr* pounds per square inch

pso·ri·a·sis \sə-'rī-ə-səs\ *n* : a chronic skin disease characterized by red patches covered with white scales

PST *abbr* Pacific standard time

¹**psych** *also* **psyche** \'sīk\ *vb* **psyched; psych·ing 1** : OUTWIT, OUTGUESS; *also* : to analyze beforehand **2** : INTIMIDATE; *also* : to prepare oneself psychologically ⟨get *psyched* up for the game⟩

²**psych** *abbr* psychology

psy·che \'sī-kē\ *n* : SOUL, SELF; *also* : MIND

psy·che·del·ic \ˌsī-kə-'de-lik\ *adj* **1** : of, relating to, or causing abnormal psychic effects ⟨~ drugs⟩ **2** : relating to the taking of psychedelic drugs ⟨~ experience⟩ **3** : imitating, suggestive of, or reproducing the effects of psychedelic drugs ⟨~ art⟩ ⟨~ colors⟩ — **psy·che·del·i·cal·ly** \-li-k(ə-)lē\ *adv*

psy·chi·a·try \sə-'kī-ə-trē, sī-\ *n* : a branch of medicine dealing with mental, emotional, and behavioral disorders — **psy·chi·at·ric** \ˌsī-kē-'a-trik\ *adj* — **psy·chi·a·trist** \-trist, sī-\ *n*

¹**psy·chic** \'sī-kik\ *also* **psy·chi·cal** \-ki-kəl\ *adj* **1** : of or relating to the psyche **2** : lying outside the sphere of physical science **3** : sensitive to nonphysical or supernatural forces — **psy·chi·cal·ly** \-k(ə-)lē\ *adv*

²**psychic** *n* : a person apparently sensitive to nonphysical forces; *also* : MEDIUM 6

psy·cho \'sī-kō\ *n, pl* **psychos** : a mentally disturbed person — **psycho** *adj*

psy·cho·ac·tive \ˌsī-kō-'ak-tiv\ *adj* : affecting the mind or behavior

psy·cho·anal·y·sis \ˌsī-kō-ə-'na-lə-səs\ *n* : a method of dealing with psychic disorders by having the patient talk freely about personal experiences and esp. about early childhood and dreams — **psy·cho·an·a·lyst** \-'an-əl-ist\ *n* — **psy·cho·an·a·lyt·ic** \-ˌan-əl-'i-tik\ *adj* — **psy·cho·an·a·lyze** \-'an-əl-ˌīz\ *vb*

psy·cho·dra·ma \ˌsī-kə-'drä-mə, -'dra-\ *n* **1** : an extemporized dramatization designed to afford catharsis for one or more of the participants from whose life the plot is taken **2** : a dramatic event or story with psychological overtones

psy·cho·gen·ic \-'je-nik\ *adj* : originating in the mind or in mental or emotional conflict

psychol *abbr* psychologist; psychology

psy·chol·o·gy \sī-'kä-lə-jē\ *n, pl* **-gies 1** : the science of mind and behavior **2** : the mental and behavioral characteristics of an individual or group — **psy·cho·log·i·cal** \ˌsī-kə-'lä-ji-kəl\ *adj* — **psy·cho·log·i·cal·ly** \-ji-k(ə-)lē\ *adv* — **psy·chol·o·gist** \sī-'kä-lə-jist\ *n*

psy·cho·path \'sī-kō-ˌpath\ *n* : a mentally ill or unstable person; *esp* : one who has not lost contact with reality but who engages in abnormally aggressive and seriously irresponsible behavior with little or no feeling of guilt — **psy·cho·path·ic** \ˌsī-kə-'pa-thik\ *adj*

psy·cho·sex·u·al \ˌsī-kō-'sek-shə-wəl\ *adj* **1** : of or relating to the mental, emotional, and behavioral aspects of sexual development **2** : of or relating to the physiological psychology of sex

psy·cho·sis \sī-'kō-səs\ *n, pl* **-cho·ses** \-ˌsēz\ : a serious mental illness (as schizophrenia) marked by loss of or greatly lessened ability to test whether what one is thinking and feeling about the real world is really true

psy·cho·so·mat·ic \ˌsī-kō-sə-'ma-tik\ *adj* : of, relating to, involving, or concerned with bodily symptoms caused by mental or emotional disturbance

psy·cho·ther·a·py \ˌsī-kō-'ther-ə-pē\ *n* : treatment of mental or emotional disorder or of related bodily ills

by psychological means — **psy·cho·ther·a·pist** \-pist\ *n*

psy·chot·ic \sī-'kä-tik\ *adj* : of or relating to psychosis ⟨~ behavior⟩ — **psychotic** *n*

psy·cho·tro·pic \ˌsī-kə-'trō-pik\ *adj* : acting on the mind ⟨~ drugs⟩

pt *abbr* **1** part **2** payment **3** pint **4** point **5** port

Pt *symbol* platinum

PT *abbr* **1** Pacific time **2** part-time **3** physical therapy **4** physical training

PTA *abbr* Parent-Teacher Association

ptar·mi·gan \'tär-mi-gən\ *n, pl* **-gan** *or* **-gans** : any of various grouses of northern regions with completely feathered feet

PT boat \(ˌ)pē-'tē-\ *n* [*patrol* torpedo] : a small fast patrol craft usu. armed with torpedos

pte *abbr, Brit* private

ptg *abbr* printing

PTO *abbr* **1** Parent-Teacher Organization **2** please turn over

pto·maine \'tō-ˌmān\ *n* : any of various chemical substances formed by bacteria in decaying matter (as meat) and including a few poisonous ones

PTV *abbr* public television

Pu *symbol* plutonium

¹**pub** \'pəb\ *n, chiefly Brit* **1** : PUBLIC HOUSE 2 **2** : TAVERN

²**pub** *abbr* **1** public **2** publication **3** published; publisher; publishing

pu·ber·ty \'pyü-bər-tē\ *n* : the condition of being or period of becoming first capable of reproducing sexually — **pu·ber·tal** \-bərt-ᵊl\ *adj*

pu·bes \'pyü-bēz\ *n, pl* **pubes 1** : the hair that appears upon the lower middle region of the abdomen at puberty **2** : the pubic region

pu·bes·cence \pyü-'bes-ᵊns\ *n* **1** : the quality or state of being pubescent **2** : a pubescent covering or surface

pu·bes·cent \-ᵊnt\ *adj* **1** : arriving at or having reached puberty **2** : covered with fine soft short hairs

pu·bic \'pyü-bik\ *adj* : of, relating to, or situated near the pubes or the pubis

pu·bis \'pyü-bəs\ *n, pl* **pu·bes** \-bēz\ : the ventral and anterior of the three principal bones composing either half of the pelvis

publ *abbr* **1** publication **2** published; publisher

¹**pub·lic** \'pə-blik\ *adj* **1** : exposed to general view ⟨the story became ~⟩ **2** : of, relating to, or affecting the people as a whole ⟨~ opinion⟩ **3** : CIVIC, GOVERNMENTAL ⟨~ expenditures⟩ **4** : of, relating to, or serving the community ⟨~ officials⟩ **5** : not private : SOCIAL ⟨~ morality⟩ **6** : open to all ⟨~ library⟩ : well known : PROMINENT ⟨~ figures⟩ — **pub·lic·ly** *adv*

²**public** *n* **1** : the people as a whole : POPULACE **2** : a group of people having common interests

pub·li·can \'pə-bli-kən\ *n* **1** : a Jewish tax collector for the ancient Romans **2** *chiefly Brit* : the licensee of a pub

pub·li·ca·tion \ˌpə-blə-'kā-shən\ *n* **1** : the act or process of publishing **2** : a published work

public house *n* **1** : INN **2** *chiefly Brit* : a licensed saloon or bar

pub·li·cise *Brit var of* PUBLICIZE

pub·li·cist \'pə-blə-sist\ *n* : one that publicizes; *esp* : PRESS AGENT

pub·lic·i·ty \(ˌ)pə-'bli-sə-tē\ *n* **1** : information with news value issued to gain public attention or support **2** : public attention or acclaim

pub·li·cize \'pə-blə-ˌsīz\ *vb* **-cized; -ciz·ing** : to bring to public attention : ADVERTISE

public relations *n sing or pl* : the business of fostering public goodwill toward a person, firm, or institution; *also* : the degree of goodwill and understanding achieved

public school *n* **1** : an endowed secondary boarding school in Great Britain offering a classical curriculum

and preparation for the universities or public service
2 : a free tax-supported school controlled by a local
governmental authority

public–spirited *adj* : motivated by devotion to the general or national welfare

public television *n* : television supported by public funds and private contributions rather than by commercials

public works *n pl* : works (as schools or highways) constructed with public funds for public use

pub·lish \'pə-blish\ *vb* **1** : to make generally known : announce publicly **2** : to produce or release literature, information, musical scores or sometimes recordings, or art for sale to the public — **pub·lish·er** *n*

¹**puck** \'pək\ *n* : a mischievous sprite — **puck·ish** *adj* — **puck·ish·ly** *adv*

²**puck** *n* : a disk used in ice hockey

¹**puck·er** \'pə-kər\ *vb* **puck·ered; puck·er·ing** : to contract into folds or wrinkles

²**pucker** *n* : FOLD, WRINKLE

pud·ding \'pu-diŋ\ *n* : a soft, spongy, or thick creamy dessert

pud·dle \'pəd-ᵊl\ *n* : a very small pool of usu. dirty or muddy water

pu·den·dum \pyü-'den-dəm\ *n, pl* **-da** \-də\ [NL, fr. L *pudēre* to be ashamed] : the human external genital organs esp. of a woman

pudgy \'pə-jē\ *adj* **pudg·i·er; -est** : being short and plump : CHUBBY

pueb·lo \'pwe-blō, pü-'e-\ *n, pl* **-los** [Sp, village, lit., people, fr. L *populus*] **1** : an American Indian village of Arizona or New Mexico that consists of flat-roofed stone or adobe houses joined in groups sometimes several stories high **2** *cap* : a member of a group of American Indian peoples of the southwestern U.S.

pu·er·ile \'pyu̇-ə-rəl\ *adj* : CHILDISH, SILLY — **pu·er·il·i·ty** \,pyü-ə-'ri-lə-tē\ *n*

pu·er·per·al \pyü-'ər-pə-rəl\ *adj* : of, relating to, or occurring during childbirth or the period immediately following ⟨∼ infection⟩ ⟨∼ depression⟩

puerperal fever *n* : an abnormal condition that results from infection of the placental site following childbirth or abortion

Puer·to Ri·can \,pȯr-tə-'rē-kən, ,pwer-\ *n* : a native or inhabitant of Puerto Rico — **Puerto Rican** *adj*

¹**puff** \'pəf\ *vb* **1** : to blow in short gusts **2** : PANT **3** : to emit small whiffs or clouds **4** : BLUSTER, BRAG **5** : INFLATE, SWELL **6** : to make proud or conceited **7** : to praise extravagantly

²**puff** *n* **1** : a short discharge (as of air or smoke); *also* : a slight explosive sound accompanying it **2** : a light fluffy pastry **3** : a slight swelling **4** : a fluffy mass; *also* : a small pad for applying cosmetic powder **5** : a laudatory notice or review — **puffy** *adj*

puff·ball \'pəf-,bȯl\ *n* : any of various globe-shaped and often edible fungi

puf·fin \'pə-fən\ *n* : any of several seabirds having a short neck and a deep grooved parti-colored bill

¹**pug** \'pəg\ *n* **1** : any of a breed of small stocky short-haired dogs with a wrinkled face **2** : a close coil of hair

²**pug** *n* : ¹BOXER

pu·gi·lism \'pyü-jə-,li-zəm\ *n* : BOXING — **pu·gi·list** \-list\ *n* — **pu·gi·lis·tic** \,pyü-jə-'lis-tik\ *adj*

pug·na·cious \,pəg-'nā-shəs\ *adj* : having a quarrelsome or combative nature **syn** belligerent, bellicose, contentious, truculent — **pug·nac·i·ty** \-'na-sə-tē\ *n*

puis·sance \'pwi-səns, 'pyü-ə-\ *n* : POWER, STRENGTH — **puis·sant** \-sənt\ *adj*

puke \'pyük\ *vb* **puked; puk·ing** : VOMIT — **puke** *n*

puk·ka \'pə-kə\ *adj* [Hindi *pakkā* cooked, ripe, solid, fr. Skt *pakva*] : GENUINE, AUTHENTIC; *also* : FIRST-CLASS, COMPLETE

pul \'pül\ *n, pl* **puls** \'pülz\ *or* **pul** — see *afghani* at MONEY table

pug

pu·la \'pü-lə, 'pyü-\ *n, pl* **pula** — see MONEY table

pul·chri·tude \'pəl-krə-,tüd, -,työd\ *n* : BEAUTY — **pul·chri·tu·di·nous** \,pəl-krə-'tüd-ᵊn-əs, -'työd-\ *adj*

pule \'pyül\ *vb* **puled; pul·ing** : WHINE, WHIMPER

¹**pull** \'pu̇l\ *vb* **1** : to exert force so as to draw (something) toward the force; *also* : MOVE ⟨∼ out of a driveway⟩ **2** : PLUCK; *also* : EXTRACT ⟨∼ a tooth⟩ **3** : STRETCH, STRAIN ⟨∼ a tendon⟩ **4** : to draw apart : TEAR **5** : to make (as a proof) by printing **6** : REMOVE **7** : DRAW ⟨∼ a gun⟩ **8** : to carry out esp. with daring ⟨∼ a robbery⟩ **9** : PERPETRATE, COMMIT **10** : ATTRACT **11** : to express strong sympathy — **pull·er** *n*

²**pull** *n* **1** : the act or an instance of pulling **2** : the effort expended in moving **3** : ADVANTAGE; *esp* : special influence **4** : a device for pulling something or for operating by pulling **5** : a force that attracts or compels **6** : an injury from abnormal straining or stretching ⟨a muscle ∼⟩

pull·back \'pu̇l-,bak\ *n* : an orderly withdrawal of troops

pul·let \'pu̇l-ət\ *n* : a young hen esp. of the domestic chicken when less than a year old

pul·ley \'pu̇-lē\ *n, pl* **pulleys** : a wheel used to transmit power by means of a belt, rope, or chain; *esp* : one with a grooved rim that forms part of a tackle for hoisting or for changing the direction of a force

Pull·man \'pu̇l-mən\ *n* : a railroad passenger car with comfortable furnishings esp. for night travel

pull off *vb* : to accomplish successfully

pull·out \'pu̇l-,au̇t\ *n* : PULLBACK

pull·over \'pu̇l-,ō-vər\ *adj* : put on by being pulled over the head ⟨∼ sweater⟩ — **pull·over** *n*

pull–up \'pu̇l-,əp\ *n* : CHIN-UP

pull up *vb* : to bring or come to an often abrupt halt : STOP

pul·mo·nary \'pu̇l-mə-,ner-ē, 'pəl-\ *adj* : of, relating to, or carried on by the lungs ⟨the ∼ circulation⟩

pulp \'pəlp\ *n* **1** : the soft juicy or fleshy part of a fruit or vegetable **2** : a soft moist mass **3** : the soft sensitive tissue that fills the central cavity of a tooth **4** : a material (as from wood) used in making paper **5** : a magazine using cheap paper and often dealing with sensational material — **pulpy** *adj*

pul·pit \'pu̇l-,pit\ *n* : a raised platform or high reading desk used in preaching or conducting a worship service

pulp·wood \'pəlp-,wu̇d\ *n* : wood used in making pulp for paper

pul·sar \'pəl-,sär\ *n* : a celestial source of pulsating electromagnetic radiation (as radio waves)

pul·sate \'pəl-,sāt\ *vb* **pul·sat·ed; pul·sat·ing** : to expand and contract rhythmically : BEAT — **pul·sa·tion** \,pəl-'sā-shən\ *n*

pulse \'pəls\ *n* **1** : the regular throbbing in the arteries caused by the contractions of the heart **2** : rhythmical beating, vibrating, or sounding **3** : a brief change in electrical current or voltage — **pulse** *vb*

pul·ver·ise *Brit var of* PULVERIZE

pul·ver·ize \\'pəl-və-ˌrīz\\ *vb* **-ized; -iz·ing 1** : to reduce (as by crushing or grinding) or be reduced to very small particles **2** : DEMOLISH

pu·ma \\'pü-mə, 'pyü-\\ *n, pl* **pumas** *also* **puma** : COUGAR

pum·ice \\'pə-məs\\ *n* : a light porous volcanic glass used esp. for smoothing and polishing

pum·mel \\'pə-məl\\ *vb* **-meled** *also* **-melled; -mel·ing** *also* **-mel·ling** : POUND, BEAT

¹**pump** \\'pəmp\\ *n* : a device for raising, transferring, or compressing fluids esp. by suction or pressure

²**pump** *vb* **1** : to raise (as water) with a pump **2** : to draw fluid from with a pump; *also* : to fill by means of a pump ⟨∼ up a tire⟩ **3** : to force or propel in the manner of a pump — **pump·er** *n*

³**pump** *n* : a low shoe that grips the foot chiefly at the toe and heel

pum·per·nick·el \\'pəm-pər-ˌni-kəl\\ *n* : a dark rye bread

pump·kin \\'pəmp-kən, 'pəŋ-kən\\ *n* : the large usu. orange fruit of a vine of the gourd family that is widely used as food; *also* : this vine

pun \\'pən\\ *n* : the humorous use of a word in a way that suggests two or more interpretations — **pun** *vb*

¹**punch** \\'pənch\\ *vb* **1** : PROD, POKE; *also* : DRIVE, HERD ⟨∼ing cattle⟩ **2** : to strike with the fist **3** : to emboss, perforate, or make with a punch **4** : to operate, produce, or enter (as data) by or as if by punching — **punch·er** *n*

²**punch** *n* **1** : a quick blow with or as if with the fist **2** : effective energy or forcefulness

³**punch** *n* : a tool for piercing, stamping, cutting, or forming

⁴**punch** *n* [perh. fr. Hindi *pāc* five, fr. Skt *pañca;* fr. the number of ingredients] : a drink usu. composed of wine or alcoholic liquor and nonalcoholic beverages; *also* : a drink composed of nonalcoholic beverages

punched card \\'pəncht-\\ *n* : a card with holes punched in particular positions to represent data

pun·cheon \\'pən-chən\\ *n* : a large cask

punch line *n* : the sentence or phrase in a joke that makes the point

punchy \\'pən-chē\\ *adj* **punch·i·er; -est 1** : having punch : FORCEFUL **2** : DAZED, CONFUSED

punc·til·io \\ˌpəŋk-'ti-lē-ˌō\\ *n, pl* **-i·os 1** : a nice detail of conduct in a ceremony or in observance of a code **2** : careful observance of forms (as in social conduct)

punc·til·i·ous \\ˌpəŋk-'ti-lē-əs\\ *adj* : marked by precise accordance with codes or conventions **syn** meticulous, scrupulous, careful, punctual

punc·tu·al \\'pəŋk-chə-wəl\\ *adj* : being on time : PROMPT — **punc·tu·al·i·ty** \\ˌpəŋk-chə-'wa-lə-tē\\ *n* — **punc·tu·al·ly** *adv*

punc·tu·ate \\'pəŋk-chə-ˌwāt\\ *vb* **-at·ed; -at·ing 1** : to mark or divide (written matter) with punctuation marks **2** : to break into at intervals **3** : EMPHASIZE

punc·tu·a·tion \\ˌpəŋk-chə-'wā-shən\\ *n* : the act, practice, or system of inserting standardized marks in written matter to clarify the meaning and separate structural units

¹**punc·ture** \\'pəŋk-chər\\ *n* **1** : an act of puncturing **2** : a small hole or wound made by puncturing

²**puncture** *vb* **punc·tured; punc·tur·ing 1** : to make a hole in : PIERCE **2** : to make useless as if by a puncture

pun·dit \\'pən-dət\\ *n* **1** : a learned person : TEACHER **2** : AUTHORITY, CRITIC

pun·gent \\'pən-jənt\\ *adj* **1** : having a sharp incisive quality : CAUSTIC ⟨a ∼ editorial⟩ **2** : causing a sharp or irritating sensation; *esp* : ACRID ⟨∼ smell of burning leaves⟩ — **pun·gen·cy** \\-jən-sē\\ *n* — **pun·gent·ly** *adv*

pun·ish \\'pə-nish\\ *vb* **1** : to impose a penalty on for a fault or crime ⟨∼ an offender⟩ **2** : to inflict a penalty for ⟨∼ treason with death⟩ **3** : to inflict injury on : HURT **syn** chastise, castigate, chasten, discipline, correct — **pun·ish·able** *adj*

pun·ish·ment *n* **1** : retributive suffering, pain, or loss : PENALTY **2** : rough treatment

pu·ni·tive \\'pyü-nə-tiv\\ *adj* : inflicting, involving, or aiming at punishment

¹**punk** \\'pəŋk\\ *n* **1** : a young inexperienced person **2** : a petty hoodlum

²**punk** *adj* : very poor : INFERIOR

³**punk** *n* : dry crumbly wood useful for tinder; *also* : a substance made from fungi for use as tinder

pun·kin \\'pəŋ-kən\\ *var of* PUMPKIN

pun·ster \\'pən-stər\\ *n* : one who is given to punning

¹**punt** \\'pənt\\ *n* : a long narrow flat-bottomed boat with square ends

²**punt** *vb* : to propel (as a punt) with a pole

³**punt** *vb* : to kick a football or soccer ball dropped from the hands before it touches the ground

⁴**punt** *n* : the act or an instance of punting a ball

pu·ny \\'pyü-nē\\ *adj* [MF *puisné* younger, lit., born afterward, fr. *puis* afterward (fr. L *post*) + *né* born, fr. L *natus*] : slight in power, size, or importance : WEAK

pup \\'pəp\\ *n* : a young dog; *also* : one of the young of some other animals

pu·pa \\'pyü-pə\\ *n, pl* **pu·pae** \\-(ˌ)pē\\ *or* **pupas** [NL, fr. L *pupa* doll] : a form of some insects (as a bee, moth, or beetle) between the larva and the adult that usu. has a protective covering (as a cocoon) — **pu·pal** \\-pəl\\ *adj*

¹**pu·pil** \\'pyü-pəl\\ *n* **1** : a child or young person in school or in the charge of a tutor **2** : DISCIPLE

²**pupil** *n* : the dark central opening of the iris of the eye

pup·pet \\'pə-pət\\ *n* [ME *popet*, fr. MF *poupette*, ultim. fr. L *pupa* doll] **1** : a small figure of a person or animal moved by hand or by strings or wires **2** : DOLL **3** : one whose acts are controlled by an outside force or influence

pup·pe·teer \\ˌpə-pə-'tir\\ *n* : one who manipulates puppets

pup·py \\'pə-pē\\ *n, pl* **puppies** : a young domestic dog

pur·blind \\'pər-ˌblīnd\\ *adj* **1** : partly blind **2** : lacking in insight : OBTUSE

¹**pur·chase** \\'pər-chəs\\ *vb* **pur·chased; pur·chas·ing** : to obtain by paying money or its equivalent : BUY — **pur·chas·able** \\-chə-sə-bəl\\ *adj* — **pur·chas·er** *n*

²**purchase** *n* **1** : an act or instance of purchasing **2** : something purchased **3** : a secure hold or grasp; *also* : advantageous leverage

pur·dah \\'pər-də\\ *n* : seclusion of women from public observation among Muslims and some Hindus esp. in India; *also* : a state of seclusion

pure \\'pyu̇r\\ *adj* **pur·er; pur·est 1** : unmixed with any other matter : free from taint ⟨∼ gold⟩ ⟨∼ water⟩ **2** : SHEER, ABSOLUTE ⟨∼ nonsense⟩ **3** : ABSTRACT, THEORETICAL ⟨∼ mathematics⟩ **4** : free from what vitiates, weakens, or pollutes ⟨speaks a ∼ French⟩ **5** : free from moral fault : INNOCENT **6** : CHASTE, CONTINENT — **pure·ly** *adv*

pure–blood·ed \\-ˌblə-dəd\\ *or* **pure–blood** \\-ˌbləd\\ *adj* : FULL-BLOODED — **pure·blood** *n*

pure·bred \\-'bred\\ *adj* : bred from members of a recognized breed, strain, or kind without crossbreeding over many generations — **pure·bred** \\-ˌbred\\ *n*

¹**pu·ree** \\pyu̇-'rā, -'rē\\ *n* [F *purée*, fr. MF, fr. fem. of *puré*, pp. of *purer* to purify, strain, fr. L *purare* to purify] : a paste or thick liquid suspension usu. made from finely ground cooked food; *also* : a thick soup made of pureed vegetables

²**puree** *vb* **pu·reed; pu·ree·ing** : to make a puree of

pur·ga·tion \\ˌpər-'gā-shən\\ *n* : the act or result of purging

¹**pur·ga·tive** \\'pər-gə-tiv\\ *adj* : purging or tending to purge

²**purgative** *n* : a strong laxative : CATHARTIC

pur·ga·to·ry \\'pər-gə-ˌtȯr-ē\\ *n, pl* **-ries 1** : an intermediate state after death for expiatory purification **2** : a place or state of temporary punishment — **pur·ga·tor·i·al** \ˌpər-gə-ˈtōr-ē-əl\ adj

¹**purge** \ˈpərj\ vb **purged; purg·ing 1** : to cleanse or purify esp. from sin **2** : to have or cause strong and usu. repeated emptying of the bowels **3** : to get rid of ⟨the leaders had been purged⟩

²**purge** n **1** : something that purges; esp : PURGATIVE **2** : an act or result of purging; esp : a ridding of persons regarded as treacherous or disloyal

pu·ri·fy \ˈpyùr-ə-ˌfī\ vb **-fied; -fy·ing** : to make or become pure — **pu·ri·fi·ca·tion** \ˌpyùr-ə-fə-ˈkā-shən\ — **pu·ri·fi·ca·to·ry** \pyù-ˈri-fi-kə-ˌtōr-ē\ adj — **pu·ri·fi·er** n

Pu·rim \ˈpùr-(ˌ)im\ n : a Jewish holiday celebrated in February or March in commemoration of the deliverance of the Jews from the massacre plotted by Haman

pu·rine \ˈpyùr-ˌēn\ n : any of a group of bases including several (as adenine or guanine) that are constituents of DNA or RNA

pur·ism \ˈpyùr-ˌi-zəm\ n : rigid adherence to or insistence on purity or nicety esp. in use of words — **pur·ist** \-ist\ n — **pu·ris·tic** \pyù-ˈris-tik\ adj

pu·ri·tan \ˈpyùr-ət-ᵊn\ n **1** cap : a member of a 16th and 17th century Protestant group in England and New England opposing the ceremonies and government of the Church of England **2** : one who practices or preaches a stricter or professedly purer moral code than that which prevails — **pu·ri·tan·i·cal** \ˌpyùr-ə-ˈta-ni-kəl\ adj — **pu·ri·tan·i·cal·ly** adv

pu·ri·ty \ˈpyùr-ə-tē\ n : the quality or state of being pure

¹**purl** \ˈpərl\ vb : to knit in purl stitch

²**purl** n : a stitch in knitting

³**purl** n : a gentle murmur or movement (as of purling water)

⁴**purl** vb **1** : EDDY, SWIRL **2** : to make a soft murmuring sound

pur·lieu \ˈpər-lü, ˈpərl-yü\ n **1** : an outlying district : SUBURB **2** pl : ENVIRONS

pur·loin \(ˌ)pər-ˈlòin, ˈpər-ˌlòin\ vb : STEAL, FILCH

¹**pur·ple** \ˈpər-pəl\ adj **pur·pler; pur·plest 1** : of the color purple **2** : highly rhetorical ⟨a ~ passage⟩ **3** : PROFANE ⟨~ language⟩ — **pur·plish** adj

²**purple** n **1** : a bluish red color **2** : a purple robe emblematic esp. of regal rank or authority

¹**pur·port** \ˈpər-ˌpōrt\ n : meaning conveyed or implied; also : GIST

²**pur·port** \(ˌ)pər-ˈpōrt\ vb : to convey or profess outwardly as the meaning or intention : CLAIM — **pur·port·ed·ly** \-ˈpōr-təd-lē\ adv

¹**pur·pose** \ˈpər-pəs\ n **1** : an object or result aimed at : INTENTION **2** : RESOLUTION, DETERMINATION — **pur·pose·ful** \-fəl\ adj — **pur·pose·ful·ly** adv — **pur·pose·less** adj — **pur·pose·ly** adv

²**purpose** vb **pur·posed; pur·pos·ing** : to propose as an aim to oneself

purr \ˈpər\ n : a low murmur typical of a contented cat — **purr** vb

¹**purse** \ˈpərs\ n **1** : a receptacle (as a pouch) to carry money and often other small objects in **2** : RESOURCES **3** : a sum of money offered as a prize or present

²**purse** vb **pursed; purs·ing** : PUCKER

purs·er \ˈpər-sər\ n : an official on a ship who keeps accounts and attends to the comfort of passengers

purs·lane \ˈpər-slən, -ˌslān\ n : a fleshy-leaved weedy trailing plant with tiny yellow flowers that is sometimes used in salads

pur·su·ance \pər-ˈsü-əns\ n : the act of carrying out or into effect

pur·su·ant to \-ˈsü-ənt-\ prep : in carrying out : ACCORDING TO

pur·sue \pər-ˈsü\ vb **pur·sued; pur·su·ing 1** : to follow in order to overtake or overcome : CHASE **2** : to seek to accomplish ⟨~ a goal⟩ **3** : to proceed along ⟨~ a course⟩ **4** : to engage in ⟨~ a career⟩ — **pur·su·er** n

pur·suit \pər-ˈsüt\ n **1** : the act of pursuing **2** : OCCUPATION, BUSINESS

pu·ru·lent \ˈpyùr-ə-lənt, -yə-\ adj : containing or accompanied by pus ⟨a ~ discharge⟩ — **pu·ru·lence** \-ləns\ n

pur·vey \(ˌ)pər-ˈvā\ vb **pur·veyed; pur·vey·ing** : to supply (as provisions) usu. as a business — **pur·vey·ance** \-əns\ n — **pur·vey·or** \-ər\ n

pur·view \ˈpər-ˌvyü\ n **1** : the range or limit esp. of authority, responsibility, or intention **2** : range of vision, understanding, or cognizance

pus \ˈpəs\ n : thick yellowish white fluid matter (as in a boil) formed at a place of inflammation and infection (as an abscess) and containing germs, blood cells, and tissue debris

¹**push** \ˈpùsh\ vb [ME pusshen, fr. OF poulser to beat, push, fr. L pulsare, fr. pellere to drive, strike] **1** : to press against with force in order to drive or impel **2** : to thrust forward, downward, or outward **3** : to urge on : press forward **4** : to cause to increase ⟨~ prices to record levels⟩ **5** : to urge or press the advancement, adoption, or practice of; esp : to make aggressive efforts to sell **6** : to engage in the illicit sale of narcotics

²**push** n **1** : a vigorous effort : DRIVE **2** : an act of pushing : SHOVE **3** : vigorous enterprise : ENERGY

push–button adj **1** : operated or done by means of push buttons **2** : using or dependent on complex and more or less automatic mechanisms ⟨~ warfare⟩

push button n : a small button or knob that when pushed operates something esp. by closing an electric circuit

push·cart \ˈpùsh-ˌkärt\ n : a cart or barrow pushed by hand

push·er \ˈpù-shər\ n : one that pushes; esp : one that pushes illegal drugs

push·over \-ˌō-vər\ n **1** : an opponent easy to defeat **2** : SUCKER **3** : something easily accomplished

push–up \-ˌəp\ n : a conditioning exercise performed in a prone position by raising and lowering the body with the straightening and bending of the arms while keeping the back straight and supporting the body on the hands and toes

pushy \ˈpù-shē\ adj **push·i·er; -est** : aggressive often to an objectionable degree

pu·sil·lan·i·mous \ˌpyü-sə-ˈla-nə-məs\ adj [LL pusillanimis, fr. L pusillus very small (dim. of pusus boy) + animus spirit] : contemptibly timid : COWARDLY — **pu·sil·la·nim·i·ty** \ˌpyü-sə-lə-ˈni-mə-tē\ n

¹**puss** \ˈpùs\ n : CAT

²**puss** n : FACE

¹**pussy** \ˈpù-sē\ n, pl **puss·ies** : CAT

²**pus·sy** \ˈpə-sē\ adj **pus·si·er; -est** : full of or resembling pus

pussy·cat \ˈpù-sē-ˌkat\ n : CAT

pussy·foot \-ˌfùt\ vb **1** : to tread or move warily or stealthily **2** : to refrain from committing oneself

pussy willow \ˈpù-sē-\ n : a willow having large silky catkins

pus·tule \ˈpəs-chül\ n : a pus-filled pimple

put \ˈpùt\ vb **put; put·ting 1** : to bring into a specified position : PLACE ⟨~ the book on the table⟩ **2** : SEND, THRUST : to throw with an upward pushing motion ⟨~ the shot⟩ **4** : to bring into a specified state ⟨~ the plan into effect⟩ **5** : SUBJECT ⟨~ traitors to death⟩ **6** : IMPOSE **7** : to set before one for decision ⟨~ the question⟩ **8** : EXPRESS, STATE **9** : TRANSLATE, ADAPT **10** : APPLY, ASSIGN ⟨~ them to work⟩ **11** : ESTIMATE ⟨~ the number at 20⟩ **12** : ATTACH, ATTRIBUTE ⟨~ a high value on it⟩ **13** : to take a specified course ⟨the ship ~ out to sea⟩

pu·ta·tive \'pyü-tə-tiv\ *adj* **1** : commonly accepted **2** : assumed to exist or to have existed

put–down \'pùt-ˌdaùn\ *n* : a belittling remark

put in *vb* **1** : to come in with : INTERPOSE ⟨*put in* a good word for me⟩ **2** : to spend time at some occupation or job ⟨*put in* eight hours at the office⟩

put off *vb* : POSTPONE, DELAY

¹put–on \'pùt-ˌon, -ˌän\ *adj* : PRETENDED, ASSUMED

²put–on *n* **1** : a deliberate act of misleading someone **2** : PARODY, SPOOF

put·out \'pùt-ˌaùt\ *n* : the retiring of a base runner or batter in baseball

put out *vb* **1** : EXTINGUISH **2** : ANNOY; *also* : INCONVENIENCE **3** : to cause to be out (as in baseball)

pu·tre·fy \'pyü-trə-ˌfī\ *vb* **-fied; -fy·ing** : to make or become putrid : ROT — **pu·tre·fac·tion** \ˌpyü-trə-'fak-shən\ *n* — **pu·tre·fac·tive** \-tiv\ *adj*

pu·tres·cent \pyü-'tres-ᵊnt\ *adj* : becoming putrid : ROTTING — **pu·tres·cence** \-ᵊns\ *n*

pu·trid \'pyü-trəd\ *adj* **1** : ROTTEN, DECAYED **2** : VILE, CORRUPT — **pu·trid·i·ty** \pyü-'tri-də-tē\ *n*

putsch \'pùch\ *n* [G] : a secretly plotted and suddenly executed attempt to overthrow a government

putt \'pət\ *n* : a golf stroke made on the green to cause the ball to roll into the hole — **putt** *vb*

put·tee \ˌpə-'tē, 'pə-tē\ *n* [Hindi *paṭṭī* strip of cloth] **1** : a cloth strip wrapped around the lower leg **2** : a leather legging

¹put·ter \'pù-tər\ *n* : one that puts

²putt·er \'pə-tər\ *n* **1** : a golf club used in putting **2** : one that putts

³put·ter \'pə-tər\ *vb* **1** : to move or act aimlessly or idly **2** : TINKER

put·ty \'pə-tē\ *n, pl* **putties** [F *potée* potter's glaze, lit., potful, fr. OF, fr. *pot* pot] **1** : a doughlike cement used esp. to fasten glass in sashes **2** : one who is easily manipulated — **putty** *vb*

put up *vb* **1** : SHEATHE **2** : to prepare so as to preserve for later use **3** : to offer for public sale ⟨*put* the house *up* for auction⟩ **4** : ACCOMMODATE, LODGE **5** : BUILD **6** : to engage in ⟨*put up* a struggle⟩ **7** : CONTRIBUTE, PAY — **put up with** : TOLERATE **2**

¹puz·zle \'pə-zəl\ *vb* **puz·zled; puz·zling 1** : to bewilder mentally : PERPLEX **2** : to solve with difficulty or ingenuity ⟨∼ out a riddle⟩ **3** : to be in a quandary ⟨∼ over what to do⟩ **4** : to attempt a solution of a puzzle ⟨∼ over a person's words⟩ **syn** mystify, bewilder, nonplus, confound — **puz·zle·ment** *n* — **puz·zler** *n*

²puzzle *n* **1** : something that puzzles **2** : a question, problem, or contrivance designed for testing ingenuity

PVC *abbr* polyvinyl chloride

pvt *abbr* private

PW *abbr* prisoner of war

pwt *abbr* pennyweight

PX *abbr* post exchange

pya \pē-'ä\ *n* — see *kyat* at MONEY table

pyg·my \'pig-mē\ *n, pl* **pygmies** [ME *pigmei*, fr. L *pygmaeus* of a pygmy, dwarfish, fr. Gk *pygmaios*, fr. *pygmē* fist, measure of length] **1** *cap* : any of a small people of equatorial Africa **2** : DWARF — **pygmy** *adj*

py·ja·mas \pə-'jà-məz\ *chiefly Brit var of* PAJAMAS

py·lon \'pī-ˌlän, -lən\ *n* **1** : a usu. massive gateway; *esp* : an Egyptian one flanked by flat-topped pyramids **2** : a tower that supports wires over a long span **3** : a post or tower marking the course in an airplane race

py·or·rhea \ˌpī-ə-'rē-ə\ *n* : an inflammation with pus of the sockets of the teeth

¹pyr·a·mid \'pir-ə-ˌmid\ *n* **1** : a massive structure with a square base and four triangular faces meeting at a point **2** : a geometrical solid having a polygon for its base and three or more triangles for its sides that meet at a point to form the top — **py·ra·mi·dal** \pə-'ra-məd-ᵊl, ˌpir-ə-'mid-\ *adj*

²pyramid *vb* **1** : to build up in the form of a pyramid : heap up **2** : to increase rapidly on a broadening base

pyre \'pīr\ *n* : a combustible heap for burning a dead body as a funeral rite

py·re·thrum \pī-'rē-thrəm\ *n* : an insecticide made from the dried heads of any of several Old World chrysanthemums

py·rim·i·dine \pī-'ri-mə-ˌdēn\ *n* : any of a group of bases including several (as cytosine, thymine, or uracil) that are constituents of DNA or RNA

py·rite \'pī-ˌrīt\ *n* : a mineral containing sulfur and iron that is brass-yellow in color

py·rol·y·sis \pī-'rä-lə-səs\ *n* : chemical change caused by the action of heat

py·ro·ma·nia \ˌpī-rō-'mā-nē-ə\ *n* : an irresistible impulse to start fires — **py·ro·ma·ni·ac** \-nē-ˌak\ *n*

py·ro·tech·nics \ˌpī-rə-'tek-niks\ *n pl* **1** : a display of fireworks **2** : a spectacular display (as of extreme virtuosity) — **py·ro·tech·nic** \-nik\ *also* **py·ro·tech·ni·cal** \-ni-kəl\ *adj*

Pyr·rhic \'pir-ik\ *adj* : achieved at excessive cost ⟨a ∼ victory⟩; *also* : costly to the point of outweighing expected benefits

Py·thag·o·re·an theorem \pī-ˌtha-gə-'rē-ən-\ *n* : a theorem in geometry: the square of the length of the hypotenuse of a right triangle equals the sum of the squares of the lengths of the other two sides

py·thon \'pī-ˌthän, -thən\ *n* [L, monstrous serpent killed by the god Apollo, fr. Gk *Pythōn*] : a large snake (as a boa) that squeezes and suffocates its prey; *esp* : any of the large Old World snakes that include the largest snakes living at the present time

pyx \'piks\ *n* : a small case used to carry the Eucharist

Q

¹**q** \'kyü\ *n, pl* **q's** *or* **qs** \'kyüz\ *often cap* : the 17th letter of the English alphabet

²**q** *abbr, often cap* **1** quart **2** quarto **3** queen **4** query **5** question

QB *abbr* quarterback

QED *abbr* [L *quod erat demonstrandum*] which was to be demonstrated

qin·tar \kin-'tär\ *n, pl* **qin·dar·ka** \kin-'där-kə\ *or* **qintar** — see *lek* at MONEY table

qi·vi·ut \'kē-vē-ıüt\ *n* [Inuit] : the wool of the undercoat of the musk ox

Qld *abbr* Queensland

QM *abbr* quartermaster

QMC *abbr* quartermaster corps

QMG *abbr* quartermaster general

qq v *abbr* [L *quae vide*] which (*pl*) see

qr *abbr* quarter

qt *abbr* **1** quantity **2** quart

q.t. \ıkyü-'tē\ *n, often cap Q&T* : QUIET — usu. used in the phrase *on the q.t.*

qto *abbr* quarto

qty *abbr* quantity

qu *or* **ques** *abbr* question

¹**quack** \'kwak\ *vb* : to make the characteristic cry of a duck

²**quack** *n* : a sound made by quacking

³**quack** *n* **1** : CHARLATAN **2** : a pretender to medical skill **syn** faker, impostor, mountebank — **quack** *adj* — **quack·ery** \'kwa-kə-rē\ *n* — **quack·ish** *adj*

¹**quad** \'kwäd\ *n* : QUADRANGLE

²**quad** *n* : QUADRUPLET

³**quad** *abbr* quadrant

quad·ran·gle \'kwä-ıdraŋ-gəl\ *n* **1** : QUADRILATERAL **2** : a 4-sided courtyard or enclosure — **quad·ran·gu·lar** \kwä-'draŋ-gyə-lər\ *adj*

quad·rant \'kwä-drənt\ *n* **1** : one quarter of a circle : an arc of 90° **2** : any of the four quarters into which something is divided by two lines intersecting each other at right angles

qua·drat·ic \kwä-'dra-tik\ *adj* : having or being a term in which the variable (as *x*) is squared but containing no term in which the variable is raised to a higher power than a square ⟨a ∼ equation⟩ — **quadratic** *n*

qua·dren·ni·al \kwä-'dre-nē-əl\ *adj* **1** : consisting of or lasting for four years **2** : occurring every four years

qua·dren·ni·um \-nē-əm\ *n, pl* **-niums** *or* **-nia** \-nē-ə\ : a period of four years

¹**quad·ri·lat·er·al** \ıkwä-drə-'la-tə-rəl\ *n* : a polygon of four sides

²**quadrilateral** *adj* : having four sides

qua·drille \kwä-'dril, kə-\ *n* : a square dance made up of five or six figures in various rhythms

quad·ri·par·tite \ıkwä-drə-'pär-ıtīt\ *adj* **1** : consisting of four parts **2** : shared by four parties or persons

qua·driv·i·um \kwä-'dri-vē-əm\ *n* : the four liberal arts of arithmetic, music, geometry, and astronomy in a medieval university

quad·ru·ped \'kwä-drə-ıped\ *n* : an animal having four feet — **qua·dru·pe·dal** \kwä-'drü-pəd-əl, ıkwä-drə-'ped-ᵊl\ *adj*

¹**qua·dru·ple** \kwä-'drü-pəl, -'drə-; 'kwä-drə-\ *vb* **qua·dru·pled; qua·dru·pling** : to make or become four times as great or as many

²**quadruple** *adj* : FOURFOLD

qua·dru·plet \kwä-'drə-plət, -'drü-; 'kwä-drə-\ *n* **1** : one of four offspring born at one birth **2** : a group of four of a kind

¹**qua·dru·pli·cate** \kwä-'drü-pli-kət\ *adj* **1** : repeated four times **2** : FOURTH

²**qua·dru·pli·cate** \-plə-ıkāt\ *vb* **-cat·ed; -cat·ing** **1** : QUADRUPLE **2** : to prepare in quadruplicate — **qua·dru·pli·ca·tion** \-ıdrü-plə-'kā-shən\ *n*

³**qua·dru·pli·cate** \-'drü-pli-kət\ *n* **1** : four copies all alike ⟨typed in ∼⟩ **2** : one of four like things

quaff \'kwäf, 'kwaf\ *vb* : to drink deeply or repeatedly — **quaff** *n*

quag·mire \'kwag-ımīr, 'kwäg-\ *n* **1** : soft miry land that yields under the foot **2** : PREDICAMENT

qua·hog \'kō-ıhog, 'kwo-, 'kwō-, -ıhäg\ *n* : a round thick-shelled edible No. American clam

quai \'kā\ *n* : QUAY

¹**quail** \'kwāl\ *n, pl* **quail** *or* **quails** [ME *quaille*, fr. MF, fr. ML *quaccula*, of imit. origin] : any of numerous small short-winged plump game birds (as a bobwhite) related to the domestic chicken

²**quail** *vb* [ME, to grow feeble, fr. MD *quelen*] : to lose heart : COWER **syn** recoil, shrink, flinch, wince, blanch

quaint \'kwānt\ *adj* : unusual or different in character or appearance; *esp* : pleasingly old-fashioned or unfamiliar **syn** odd, queer, curious, strange — **quaint·ly** *adv* — **quaint·ness** *n*

¹**quake** \'kwāk\ *vb* **quaked; quak·ing** **1** : to shake usu. from shock or instability **2** : to tremble usu. from cold or fear

²**quake** *n* : a shaking or trembling; *esp* : EARTHQUAKE

Quak·er \'kwā-kər\ *n* : FRIEND 5

qual *abbr* quality

qual·i·fi·ca·tion \ıkwä-lə-fə-'kā-shən\ *n* **1** : LIMITATION, MODIFICATION **2** : a special skill that fits a person for some work or position **3** : REQUIREMENT

qual·i·fied \'kwä-lə-ıfīd\ *adj* **1** : fitted for a given purpose or job **2** : limited in some way

qual·i·fi·er \'kwä-lə-ıfī-ər\ *n* **1** : one that satisfies requirements **2** : a word or word group that limits the meaning of another word or word group

qual·i·fy \'kwä-lə-ıfī\ *vb* **-fied; -fy·ing** **1** : to reduce from a general to a particular form : MODIFY **2** : to make less harsh **3** : to limit the meaning of (as a noun) **4** : to fit by skill or training for some purpose **5** : to give or have a legal right to do something **6** : to demonstrate the necessary ability ⟨∼ for the finals⟩ **syn** moderate, temper

qual·i·ta·tive \'kwä-lə-ıtā-tiv\ *adj* : of, relating to, or involving quality — **qual·i·ta·tive·ly** *adv*

¹**qual·i·ty** \'kwä-lə-tē\ *n, pl* **-ties** **1** : peculiar and essential character : NATURE **2** : degree of excellence **3** : high social status **4** : a distinguishing attribute

²**quality** *adj* : being of high quality

qualm \'kwäm, 'kwälm\ *n* **1** : a sudden attack (as of nausea) **2** : a sudden feeling of doubt, fear, or uneasiness esp. in not following one's conscience or better judgment

qualm·ish \'kwä-mish, 'kwäl-\ *adj* **1** : feeling qualms : NAUSEATED **2** : overly scrupulous : SQUEAMISH **3** : of, relating to, or producing qualms

quan·da·ry \'kwän-drē\ *n, pl* **-ries** : a state of perplexity or doubt

quan·ti·ta·tive \'kwän-tə-ıta-tiv\ *adj* : of, relating to, or involving quantity — **quan·ti·ta·tive·ly** *adv*

quan·ti·ty \'kwän-tə-tē\ *n, pl* **-ties** **1** : AMOUNT, NUMBER **2** : a considerable amount

quan·tize \'kwän-ıtīz\ *vb* **quan·tized; quan·tiz·ing** : to subdivide (as energy) into small units

quan·tum \'kwän-təm\ *n, pl* **quan·ta** \-tə\ [L, neut. of *quantus* how much] **1** : QUANTITY, AMOUNT **2** : an elemental unit of energy

quantum mechanics *n sing or pl* : a theory of matter based on the concept of possession of wave properties by elementary particles — **quantum mechanical** *adj* — **quantum mechanically** *adv*

quantum theory *n* : a theory in physics based on the idea that radiant energy (as light) is composed of small separate packets of energy

quar *abbr* quarterly

quar·an·tine \'kwòr-ən-ˌtēn\ n [modif. of It *quarantena*, lit., period of forty days, fr. *quaranta* forty, fr. L *quadraginta*] **1** : a period during which a ship suspected of carrying contagious disease is forbidden contact with the shore **2** : a restraint on the movements of persons or goods to prevent the spread of pests or disease **3** : a place or period of quarantine **4** : a state of enforced isolation — **quarantine** vb

quark \'kwȯrk, 'kwärk\ n : a hypothetical elementary particle that carries a fractional charge and is held to be a constituent of heavier particles (as protons and neutrons)

¹quar·rel \'kwȯr-əl\ n **1** : a ground of dispute **2** : a verbal clash : CONFLICT — **quar·rel·some** \-səm\ adj

²quarrel vb **-reled** or **-relled; -rel·ing** or **-rel·ling 1** : to find fault **2** : to dispute angrily : WRANGLE

¹quar·ry \'kwȯr-ē\ n, pl **quarries** [ME *querre* entrails of game given to the hounds, fr. MF *cuiree*] **1** : game hunted with hawks **2** : PREY

²quarry n, pl **quarries** [ME *quarey*, alter. of *quarrere*, fr. MF *quarriere*, fr. (assumed) OF *quarre* squared stone, fr. L *quadrum* square] : an open excavation usu. for obtaining building stone or limestone — **quarry** vb

quart \'kwȯrt\ n — see WEIGHT table

¹quar·ter \'kwȯr-tər\ n **1** : one of four equal parts **2** : a fourth of a dollar; *also* : a coin of this value **3** : a district of a city **4** pl : LODGINGS ⟨moved into new ∼s⟩ **5** : MERCY, CLEMENCY ⟨gave no ∼⟩ **6** : a fourth part of the moon's period

²quarter vb **1** : to divide into four equal parts **2** : to provide with shelter

¹quar·ter·back \-ˌbak\ n : a football player who calls the signals and directs the offensive play for the team

²quarterback vb **1** : to direct the offensive play of a football team **2** : LEAD, BOSS

quar·ter·deck \-ˌdek\ n : the stern area of a ship's upper deck

quarter horse n : any of a breed of compact muscular saddle horses characterized by great endurance and by high speed for short distances

quarter horse

¹quar·ter·ly \'kwȯr-tər-lē\ adv : at 3-month intervals

²quarterly adj : occurring, issued, or payable at 3-month intervals

³quarterly n, pl **-lies** : a periodical published four times a year

quar·ter·mas·ter \-ˌmas-tər\ n **1** : a petty officer who attends to a ship's helm, binnacle, and signals **2** : an army officer who provides clothing and subsistence for troops

quar·ter·staff \-ˌstaf\ n, pl **-staves** \-ˌstavz, -ˌstāvz\ : a long stout staff formerly used as a weapon

quar·tet also **quar·tette** \kwȯr-'tet\ n **1** : a musical composition for four instruments or voices **2** : a group of four and esp. of four musicians

quar·to \'kwȯr-tō\ n, pl **quartos 1** : the size of a piece of paper cut four from a sheet **2** : a book printed on quarto pages

quartz \'kwȯrts\ n : a common often transparent crystalline mineral that is a form of silica

quartz·ite \'kwȯrt-ˌsīt\ n : a compact granular rock composed of quartz and derived from sandstone

qua·sar \'kwā-ˌzär, -ˌsär\ n : any of a class of extremely distant starlike celestial objects

¹quash \'kwäsh, 'kwȯsh\ vb : to suppress or extinguish summarily and completely : QUELL

²quash vb : to set aside by judicial action

qua·si \'kwā-ˌzī, -ˌsī; 'kwä-zē, -sē\ adj : being in some sense or degree ⟨a ∼ corporation⟩

quasi- comb form [L, as if, as it were, approximately, fr. *quam* as + *si* if] : in some sense or degree ⟨*quasi*historical⟩

Qua·ter·na·ry \'kwä-tər-ˌner-ē, kwə-'tər-nə-rē\ adj : of, relating to, or being the geologic period from the end of the Tertiary to the present — **Quaternary** n

qua·train \'kwä-ˌtrān\ n : a unit of four lines of verse

qua·tre·foil \'ka-tər-ˌfȯil, 'ka-trə-\ n : a stylized figure often of a flower with four petals

qua·ver \'kwā-vər\ vb **1** : TREMBLE, SHAKE **2** : TRILL **3** : to speak in tremulous tones syn shudder, quake, twitter, quiver, shiver — **quaver** n

quay \'kē, 'kwā, 'kā\ n : WHARF

Que abbr Quebec

quean \'kwēn\ n : PROSTITUTE

quea·sy \'kwē-zē\ adj **quea·si·er; -est** : NAUSEATED — **quea·si·ly** \-zə-lē\ adv — **quea·si·ness** \-zē-nəs\ n

queen \'kwēn\ n **1** : the wife or widow of a king **2** : a female monarch **3** : a woman notable for rank, power, or attractiveness **4** : the most powerful piece in the game of chess **5** : a playing card bearing the figure of a queen **6** : a fertile female of a social insect (as a bee or termite) — **queen·ly** adj

Queen Anne's lace \-'anz-\ n : a widely naturalized Eurasian herb from which the cultivated carrot originated

queen consort n, pl **queens consort** : the wife of a reigning king

queen mother n : a dowager queen who is mother of the reigning sovereign

queen–size adj : having dimensions of approximately 60 inches by 80 inches ⟨∼ bed⟩; *also* : of a size that fits a queen-size bed

¹queer \'kwir\ adj **1** : differing from the usual or normal : PECULIAR, STRANGE **2** : COUNTERFEIT syn weird, bizarre, eccentric, curious — **queer** n — **queer·ly** adv — **queer·ness** n

²queer vb : to spoil the effect of : DISRUPT ⟨∼ed our plans⟩

quell \'kwel\ vb **1** : to put an end to by force ⟨∼ a riot⟩ **2** : CALM, PACIFY

quench \'kwench\ vb **1** : PUT OUT, EXTINGUISH **2** : SUBDUE **3** : SLAKE, SATISFY ⟨∼ed his thirst⟩ — **quench·able** adj — **quench·er** n — **quench·less** adj

quer·u·lous \'kwer-ə-ləs, -yə-ləs\ adj **1** : constantly complaining **2** : FRETFUL, WHINING syn petulant, pettish, irritable, peevish, huffy — **quer·u·lous·ly** adv — **quer·u·lous·ness** n

que·ry \'kwir-ē, 'kwer-\ n, pl **queries** : QUESTION — **query** vb

quest \'kwest\ n : SEARCH — **quest** vb

¹ques·tion \'kwes-chən\ n **1** : an interrogative expression : QUERY **2** : a subject for debate; *also* : a proposition to be voted on **3** : INQUIRY **4** : DISPUTE

²question vb **1** : to ask questions **2** : DOUBT, DISPUTE **3** : to subject to analysis : EXAMINE syn interrogate, quiz, query — **ques·tion·er** n

ques·tion·able \'kwes-chə-nə-bəl\ adj **1** : not certain or exact : DOUBTFUL **2** : not believed to be true, sound, or moral syn dubious, problematical, moot, debatable — **ques·tion·ably** \-blē\ adv

question mark n : a punctuation mark ? used esp. at the end of a sentence to indicate a direct question

ques·tion·naire \ˌkwes-chə-'nar\ n : a set of questions for obtaining information

quet·zal \ket-'säl, -'sal\ *n, pl* **quetzals** *or* **quet·za·les** \-'sä-läs, -'sa-\ **1 :** a Central American bird with brilliant plumage **2** *pl quetzales* — see MONEY table

¹queue \'kyü\ *n* [F, lit., tail, fr. L *cauda, coda*] **1 :** a braid of hair usu. worn hanging at the back of the head **2 :** a waiting line (as of persons)

²queue *vb* **queued; queu·ing** *or* **queue·ing :** to line up in a queue

quib·ble \'kwi-bəl\ *n* **1 :** an evasion of or shifting from the point at issue **2 :** a minor objection or criticism — **quibble** *vb* — **quib·bler** *n*

¹quick \'kwik\ *adj* **1 :** LIVING **2 :** RAPID, SPEEDY ⟨∼ steps⟩ **3 :** prompt to understand, think, or perceive **:** ALERT **4 :** easily aroused ⟨a ∼ temper⟩ **5 :** turning or bending sharply ⟨a ∼ turn in the road⟩ **syn** fleet, fast, hasty, expeditious — **quick** *adv* — **quick·ly** *adv* — **quick·ness** *n*

²quick *n* **1 :** a sensitive area of living flesh **2 :** a vital part **:** HEART

quick bread *n* **:** a bread made with a leavening agent that permits immediate baking of the dough or batter

quick·en \'kwi-kən\ *vb* **1 :** to come to life **:** REVIVE **2 :** AROUSE, STIMULATE **3 :** to increase in speed **:** HASTEN **4 :** to show vitality (as by growing or moving) **syn** animate, enliven, liven, vivify

quick–freeze \'kwik-'frēz\ *vb* **-froze** \-'frōz\; **-fro·zen** \-'frō-zᵊn\; **-freez·ing :** to freeze (food) for preservation so rapidly that the natural juices and flavor are not lost

quick·ie \'kwi-kē\ *n* **:** something hurriedly done or made

quick·lime \'kwik-ₗlīm\ *n* **:** ¹LIME

quick·sand \-ₗsand\ *n* **:** a deep mass of loose sand mixed with water

quick·sil·ver \-ₗsil-vər\ *n* **:** MERCURY 1

quick·step \-ₗstep\ *n* **:** a spirited march tune or dance

quick–wit·ted \'kwik-'wi-təd\ *adj* **:** mentally alert **syn** clever, bright, smart, intelligent

quid \'kwid\ *n* **:** a lump of something chewable ⟨a ∼ of tobacco⟩

quid pro quo \ₗkwid-ₗprō-'kwō\ *n* [NL, something for something] **:** something given or received for something else

qui·es·cent \kwī-'es-ᵊnt\ *adj* **:** being at rest **:** QUIET **syn** latent, dormant, potential — **qui·es·cence** \-ᵊns\ *n*

¹qui·et \'kwī-ət\ *n* **:** REPOSE

²quiet *adj* **1 :** marked by little motion or activity **:** CALM **2 :** GENTLE, MILD ⟨a ∼ disposition⟩ **3 :** enjoyed in peace and relaxation ⟨a ∼ cup of tea⟩ **4 :** free from noise or uproar **5 :** not showy **:** MODEST ⟨∼ clothes⟩ **6 :** SECLUDED ⟨a ∼ nook⟩ — **quiet** *adv* — **qui·et·ly** *adv* — **qui·et·ness** *n*

³quiet *vb* **1 :** CALM, PACIFY **2 :** to become quiet ⟨∼ down⟩

qui·etude \'kwī-ə-ₗtüd, -ₗtyüd\ *n* **:** QUIETNESS, REPOSE

qui·etus \kwī-'ē-təs\ *n* [ME *quietus est*, fr. ML, he is

quit, formula of discharge from obligation] **1 :** final settlement (as of a debt) **2 :** DEATH

quill \'kwil\ *n* **1 :** a large stiff feather; *also* **:** the hollow tubular part of a feather **2 :** one of the hollow sharp spines of a hedgehog or porcupine **3 :** a pen made from a feather

¹quilt \'kwilt\ *n* **:** a padded bed coverlet

²quilt *vb* **1 :** to fill, pad, or line like a quilt **2 :** to stitch or sew in layers with padding in between **3 :** to make quilts

quince \'kwins\ *n* **:** a hard yellow applelike fruit; *also* **:** a tree related to the roses that bears this fruit

qui·nine \'kwī-ₗnīn\ *n* **:** a bitter white drug obtained from cinchona bark and used esp. in treating malaria

quint \'kwint\ *n* **:** QUINTUPLET

quin·tal \'kwint-ᵊl, 'kant-\ *n* **:** HUNDREDWEIGHT

quin·tes·sence \kwin-'tes-ᵊns\ *n* **1 :** the purest essence of something **2 :** the most typical example — **quin·tes·sen·tial** \ₗkwin-tə-'sen-chəl\ *adj* — **quin·tes·sen·tial·ly** *adv*

quin·tet *also* **quin·tette** \kwin-'tet\ *n* **1 :** a musical composition for five instruments or voices **2 :** a group of five and esp. of five musicians

¹quin·tu·ple \kwin-'tü-pəl, -'tyü-, -'tə-\ *adj* **1 :** having five units or members **2 :** being five times as great or as many — **quintuple** *n*

²quintuple *vb* **quin·tu·pled; quin·tu·pling :** to make or become five times as great or as many

quin·tu·plet \kwin-'tə-plət, -'tü-, -'tyü-\ *n* **1 :** a group of five of a kind **2 :** one of five offspring born at one birth

¹quin·tu·pli·cate \kwin-'tü-pli-kət, -'tyü-\ *adj* **1 :** repeated five times **2 :** FIFTH

²quintuplicate *n* **1 :** one of five like things **2 :** five copies all alike ⟨typed in ∼⟩

³quin·tu·pli·cate \-plə-ₗkāt\ *vb* **-cat·ed; -cat·ing 1 :** QUINTUPLE **2 :** to provide in quintuplicate

¹quip \'kwip\ *n* **:** a clever remark **:** GIBE

²quip *vb* **quipped; quip·ping 1 :** to make quips **:** GIBE **2 :** to jest or gibe at

quire \'kwīr\ *n* **:** a set of 24 or sometimes 25 sheets of paper of the same size and quality

quirk \'kwərk\ *n* **:** a peculiarity of action or behavior — **quirky** *adj*

quirt \'kwərt\ *n* **:** a riding whip with a short handle and a rawhide lash

quis·ling \'kwiz-liŋ\ *n* [Vidkun *Quisling* †1945 Norw. politician who collaborated with the Nazis] **:** one who helps the invaders of one's own country

quit \'kwit\ *vb* **quit** *also* **quit·ted; quit·ting 1 :** CONDUCT, BEHAVE ⟨∼ themselves well⟩ **2 :** to depart from **:** LEAVE; *also* **:** to bring to an end **3 :** to give up for good ⟨∼ smoking⟩ ⟨∼ my job⟩ **syn** acquit, comport, deport, demean — **quit·ter** *n*

quite \'kwit\ *adv* **1 :** COMPLETELY, WHOLLY **2 :** to an extreme **:** POSITIVELY **3 :** to a considerable extent **:** RATHER

quits \'kwits\ *adj* **:** even or equal with another ⟨call it ∼⟩

quit·tance \'kwit-ᵊns\ *n* **:** REQUITAL

¹quiv·er \'kwi-vər\ *n* : a case for carrying arrows
²quiver *vb* **quiv·ered; quiv·er·ing** : to shake with a slight trembling motion **syn** shiver, shudder, quaver, quake, tremble — **quiv·er·ing·ly** *adv*
³quiver *n* : the act or action of quivering : TREMOR
qui vive \kē-'vēv\ *n* [F *qui-vive,* fr. *qui vive?* long live who?, challenge of a French sentry] : ALERT ⟨on the *qui vive* for prowlers⟩
quix·ot·ic \kwik-'sä-tik\ *adj* [fr. Don *Quixote,* hero of the novel *Don Quixote de la Mancha* by Cervantes] : foolishly impractical esp. in the pursuit of ideals — **quix·ot·i·cal·ly** \-ti-kə-lē\ *adv*
¹quiz \'kwiz\ *n, pl* **quiz·zes 1** : an eccentric person **2** : PRACTICAL JOKE **3** : a short oral or written test
²quiz *vb* **quizzed; quiz·zing 1** : MOCK **2** : to look at inquisitively **3** : to question closely **syn** ask, interrogate, query
quiz·zi·cal \'kwi-zi-kəl\ *adj* **1** : comically quaint **2** : mildly teasing or mocking **3** : expressive of puzzlement, curiosity, or disbelief
quoit \'kwät, 'kwȯit, 'kȯit\ *n* **1** : a flattened ring of iron or circle of rope used in a throwing game **2** *pl* : a game in which quoits are thrown at an upright pin in an attempt to ring the pin
quon·dam \'kwän-dəm, -ˌdam\ *adj* [L, at one time, formerly, fr. *quom, cum* when] : FORMER
quo·rum \'kwȯr-əm\ *n* : the number of members required to be present for business to be legally transacted
quot *abbr* quotation

quo·ta \'kwō-tə\ *n* : a proportional part esp. when assigned : SHARE
quot·able \'kwō-tə-bəl\ *adj* : fit for or worth quoting — **quot·abil·i·ty** \-'bi-lə-tē\ *n*
quo·ta·tion \kwō-'tā-shən\ *n* **1** : the act or process of quoting **2** : the price currently bid or offered for something **3** : something that is quoted
quotation mark *n* : one of a pair of punctuation marks " " or ' ' used esp. to indicate the beginning and end of a quotation in which exact phraseology is directly cited
quote \'kwōt\ *vb* **quot·ed; quot·ing** [ML *quotare* to mark the number of, number references, fr. L *quotus* of what number or quantity, fr. *quot* how many, (as) many as] **1** : to speak or write a passage from another usu. with acknowledgment; *also* : to repeat a passage in substantiation or illustration **2** : to state the market price of a commodity, stock, or bond **3** : to inform a hearer or reader that matter following is quoted — **quote** *n*
quoth \'kwōth\ *vb past* [ME, past of *quethen* to say, fr. OE *cwethan*] *archaic* : SAID — usu. used in the 1st and 3d persons with the subject following
quo·tid·i·an \kwō-'ti-dē-ən\ *adj* **1** : DAILY **2** : COMMONPLACE, ORDINARY
quo·tient \'kwō-shənt\ *n* : the number obtained by dividing one number by another
qv *abbr* [L *quod vide*] which see
qy *abbr* query

R

¹r \'är\ *n, pl* **r's** *or* **rs** \'ärz\ *often cap* : the 18th letter of the English alphabet
²r *abbr, often cap* **1** rabbi **2** radius **3** rare **4** Republican **5** rerun **6** resistance **7** right **8** river **9** roentgen **10** rook **11** run
Ra *symbol* radium
RA *abbr* **1** regular army **2** Royal Academy
¹rab·bet \'ra-bət\ *n* : a groove in the edge or face of a surface (as a board) esp. to receive another piece
²rabbet *vb* : to cut a rabbet in; *also* : to join by means of a rabbet
rab·bi \'ra-ˌbī\ *n* [LL, fr. Gk *rhabbi,* fr. Heb *rabbī* my master, fr. *rabh* master + *-ī* my] **1** : MASTER, TEACHER — used by Jews as a term of address **2** : a Jew trained and ordained for professional religious leadership — **rab·bin·ic** \rə-'bi-nik\ *or* **rab·bin·i·cal** \-ni-kəl\ *adj*
rab·bin·ate \'ra-bə-nət, -ˌnāt\ *n* **1** : the office of a rabbi **2** : the whole body of rabbis
rab·bit \'ra-bət\ *n, pl* **rabbit** *or* **rabbits** : any of various long-eared burrowing mammals distinguished from the related hares by being blind, naked, and helpless at birth; *also* : the pelt of a rabbit
rabbit ears *n* : an indoor V-shaped television antenna

rab·ble \'ra-bəl\ *n* **1** : MOB **2 2** : the lowest class of people
rab·ble–rous·er \'ra-bəl-ˌraü-zər\ *n* : one that stirs up (as to hatred or violence) the masses of the people

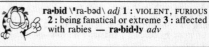

ra·bid \'ra-bəd\ *adj* **1** : VIOLENT, FURIOUS **2** : being fanatical or extreme **3** : affected with rabies — **ra·bid·ly** *adv*
ra·bies \'rā-bēz\ *n, pl* **rabies** [NL, fr. L, madness] : an acute deadly virus disease of the nervous system transmitted by the bite of an affected animal
rac·coon \ra-'kün\ *n, pl* **raccoon** *or* **raccoons** : a gray No. American chiefly tree-dwelling mammal with a black mask, a bushy ringed tail, and nocturnal habits; *also* : its pelt
¹race \'rās\ *n* **1** : a strong current of running water; *also* : its channel **2** : an onward course (as of time or life) **3** : a contest of speed **4** : a contest for a desired end (as election to office)
²race *vb* **raced; rac·ing 1** : to run in a race **2** : to run swiftly : RUSH **3** : to engage in a race with **4** : to drive or ride at high speed — **rac·er** *n*
³race *n* **1** : a family, tribe, people, or nation of the same

stock; *also* : MANKIND **2** : a group of individuals within a biological species able to breed together — **racial** \'rā-shəl\ *adj* — **ra·cial·ly** *adv*

race·course \'rās-ˌkōrs\ *n* : a course for racing

race·horse \-ˌhȯrs\ *n* : a horse bred or kept for racing

ra·ceme \rā-'sēm\ *n* [L *racemus* bunch of grapes] : a flower cluster with flowers borne along a stem and blooming from the base toward the tip — **rac·e·mose** \'ra-sə-ˌmōs\ *adj*

race·track \'rās-ˌtrak\ *n* : a usu. oval course on which races are run

race·way \-ˌwā\ *n* **1** : a channel for a current of water **2** : RACECOURSE

ra·cial·ism \'rā-shə-ˌli-zəm\ *n* : RACISM — **ra·cial·ist** \-list\ *n* — **ra·cial·is·tic** \ˌrā-shə-'lis-tik\ *adj*

racing form *n* : a paper giving data about racehorses for use by bettors

rac·ism \'rā-ˌsi-zəm\ *n* : a belief that some races are by nature superior to others; *also* : discrimination based on such belief — **rac·ist** \-sist\ *n*

¹**rack** \'rak\ *n* **1** : an instrument of torture on which a body is stretched **2** : a framework on or in which something may be placed (as for display or storage) **3** : a bar with teeth on one side to mesh with a pinion or worm gear

²**rack** *vb* **1** : to torture on or as if on a rack **2** : to stretch or strain by force **3** : TORMENT **4** : to place on or in a rack

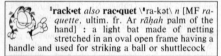
¹**rack·et** *also* **rac·quet** \'ra-kət\ *n* [MF *raquette*, ultim. fr. Ar *rāḥah* palm of the hand] : a light bat made of netting stretched in an oval open frame having a handle and used for striking a ball or shuttlecock

²**racket** *n* **1** : confused noise : DIN **2** : a fraudulent or dishonest scheme or activity

³**racket** *vb* : to make a racket

rack·e·teer \ˌra-kə-'tir\ *n* : a person who obtains money by an illegal enterprise usu. involving intimidation — **rack·e·teer·ing** *n*

rack up *vb* : ACCUMULATE, GAIN

ra·con·teur \ˌra-ˌkän-'tər\ *n* : one good at telling anecdotes

racy \'rā-sē\ *adj* **rac·i·er**; **-est 1** : full of zest **2** : PUNGENT, SPICY **3** : RISQUÉ, SUGGESTIVE — **rac·i·ly** \'rā-sə-lē\ *adv* — **rac·i·ness** \-sē-nəs\ *n*

rad *abbr* **1** radical **2** radio **3** radius

ra·dar \'rā-ˌdär\ *n* [*radio detecting and ranging*] : a device that emits radio waves for detecting and locating an object by the reflection of the radio waves and that may use this reflection to determine the object's direction and speed

ra·dar·scope \'rā-ˌdär-ˌskōp\ *n* : a visual display on a radar receiver

¹**ra·di·al** \'rā-dē-əl\ *adj* : arranged or having parts arranged like rays around a common center (the ~ form of a starfish) — **ra·di·al·ly** *adv*

²**radial** *n* : a pneumatic tire with cords laid perpendicular to the center line

radial engine *n* : an internal combustion engine with cylinders arranged radially like the spokes of a wheel

ra·di·ant \'rā-dē-ənt\ *adj* **1** : SHINING, GLOWING **2** : beaming with happiness **3** : transmitted by radiation **syn** brilliant, bright, luminous, lustrous — **ra·di·ance** \-əns\ *n* — **ra·di·ant·ly** *adv*

radiant energy *n* : energy traveling as electromagnetic waves

ra·di·ate \'rā-dē-ˌāt\ *vb* **-at·ed; -at·ing 1** : to send out rays : SHINE, GLOW **2** : to issue in or as if in rays ⟨light ~s⟩ **3** : to spread around as from a center — **ra·di·a·tion** \ˌrā-dē-'ā-shən\ *n*

radiation sickness *n* : sickness that results from exposure to radiation and is commonly marked by fatigue, nausea, vomiting, loss of teeth and hair, and in more severe cases by damage to blood-forming tissue

ra·di·a·tor \'rā-dē-ˌā-tər\ *n* : any of various devices (as a set of pipes or tubes) for transferring heat from a fluid within to an area or object outside

¹**rad·i·cal** \'ra-di-kəl\ *adj* [ME, fr. LL *radicalis*, fr. L *radic-*, *radix* root] **1** : FUNDAMENTAL, EXTREME, THOROUGHGOING **2** : of or relating to radicals in politics — **rad·i·cal·ism** \-kə-ˌli-zəm\ *n* — **rad·i·cal·ly** *adv*

²**radical** *n* **1** : a person who favors rapid and sweeping changes in laws and methods of government **2** : a group of atoms considered as a unit that remains unchanged during reactions **3** : a mathematical expression indicating a root by means of a radical sign; *also* : RADICAL SIGN

rad·i·cal·ise *Brit var of* RADICALIZE

rad·i·cal·ize \-kə-ˌlīz\ *vb* **-ized; -iz·ing** : to make radical esp. in politics — **rad·i·cal·i·za·tion** \ˌra-di-kə-lə-'zā-shən\ *n*

radical sign *n* : the sign $\sqrt{}$ placed before a mathematical expression to indicate that its root is to be taken

radii *pl of* RADIUS

¹**ra·dio** \'rā-dē-ˌō\ *n*, *pl* **ra·di·os 1** : the wireless transmission or reception of signals using electromagnetic waves **2** : a radio receiving set **3** : the radio broadcasting industry — **radio** *adj*

²**radio** *vb* : to communicate or send a message to by radio

ra·dio·ac·tiv·i·ty \ˌrā-dē-ō-ˌak-'ti-və-tē\ *n* : the property that some elements or isotopes have of spontaneously emitting energetic particles by the disintegration of their atomic nuclei — **ra·dio·ac·tive** \-'ak-tiv\ *adj*

radio astronomy *n* : astronomy dealing with radio waves received from outside the earth's atmosphere

ra·dio·car·bon \ˌrā-dē-ō-'kär-bən\ *n* : CARBON 14

radio frequency *n* : an electromagnetic wave frequency intermediate between audio frequencies and infrared frequencies used esp. in radio and television transmission

ra·dio·gram \'rā-dē-ō-ˌgram\ *n* : a message transmitted by radio

ra·dio·graph \-ˌgraf\ *n* : a photograph made by some form of radiation other than light; *esp* : an X=

ray photograph — **radiograph** vb — **ra·dio·graph·ic** \ˌrā-dē-ō-ˈgra-fik\ adj — **ra·dio·graph·i·cal·ly** \-fi-k(ə-)lē\ adv — **ra·di·og·ra·phy** \ˌrā-dē-ˈä-grə-fē\ n

ra·dio·iso·tope \ˌrā-dē-ō-ˈī-sə-ˌtōp\ n : a radioactive isotope

ra·di·ol·o·gy \ˌrā-dē-ˈä-lə-jē\ n : the use of radiant energy (as X rays and radium radiations) in medicine — **ra·di·ol·o·gist** \-jist\ n

ra·dio·man \ˈrā-dē-ō-ˌman\ n : a radio operator or technician

ra·di·om·e·ter \ˌrā-dē-ˈä-mə-tər\ n : an instrument for measuring the intensity of radiant energy — **ra·dio·met·ric** \ˌrā-dē-ō-ˈme-trik\ adj — **ra·di·om·e·try** \-mə-trē\ n

ra·dio·phone \ˈrā-dē-ə-ˌfōn\ n : RADIOTELEPHONE

ra·dio·sonde \ˈrā-dē-ō-ˌsänd\ n : a small radio transmitter carried aloft (as by balloon) and used to transmit meteorological data

ra·dio·tele·phone \ˌrā-dē-ō-ˈte-lə-ˌfōn\ n : a telephone that uses radio waves wholly or partly instead of connecting wires — **ra·dio·te·le·pho·ny** \-tə-ˈle-fə-nē, -ˈte-lə-ˌfō-nē\ n

radio telescope n : a radio receiver-antenna combination used for observation in radio astronomy

ra·dio·ther·a·py \ˌrā-dē-ō-ˈther-ə-pē\ n : the treatment of disease by means of radiation (as X rays) — **ra·dio·ther·a·pist** \-pist\ n

rad·ish \ˈra-dish\ n [ME, alter. of OE rædic, fr. L radic-, radix root, radish] : a pungent fleshy root usu. eaten raw; also : a plant related to the mustards that produces this root

ra·di·um \ˈrā-dē-əm\ n : a very radioactive metallic chemical element that is used in the treatment of cancer — see ELEMENT table

ra·di·us \ˈrā-dē-əs\ n, pl **ra·dii** \-ē-ˌī\ also **ra·di·us·es** 1 : a straight line extending from the center of a circle or a sphere to the circumference or surface; also : the length of a radius 2 : the bone on the thumb side of the human forearm 3 : a circular area defined by the length of its radius syn range, reach, scope, compass

RADM abbr rear admiral

ra·don \ˈrā-ˌdän\ n : a heavy radioactive gaseous chemical element — see ELEMENT table

RAF abbr Royal Air Force

raf·fia \ˈra-fē-ə\ n : fiber used esp. for making baskets and hats that is obtained from the stalks of the leaves of a Madagascar palm (**raffia palm**)

raff·ish \ˈra-fish\ adj : jaunty or sporty esp. in a flashy or vulgar manner — **raff·ish·ly** adv — **raff·ish·ness** n

¹**raf·fle** \ˈra-fəl\ vb **raf·fled; raf·fling** : to dispose of by a raffle

²**raffle** n : a lottery in which the prize is won by one of a number of persons buying chances

¹**raft** \ˈraft\ n 1 : a number of logs or timbers fastened together to form a float 2 : a flat structure for support or transportation on water

²**raft** vb 1 : to travel or transport by raft 2 : to make into a raft

³**raft** n : a large amount or number

raf·ter \ˈraf-tər\ n : any of the parallel beams that support a roof

¹**rag** \ˈrag\ n 1 : a waste piece of cloth 2 : NEWSPAPER

²**rag** n : a composition in ragtime

ra·ga \ˈrä-gə\ n 1 : a traditional melodic pattern or mode in Indian music 2 : an improvisation based on a raga

rag·a·muf·fin \ˈra-gə-ˌmə-fən\ n [ME Ragamuffyn, name for a ragged, oafish person] : a ragged dirty person

¹**rage** \ˈrāj\ n 1 : violent and uncontrolled anger 2 : VOGUE, FASHION

²**rage** vb **raged; rag·ing** 1 : to be furiously angry : RAVE 2 : to continue out of control (the fire raged)

rag·ged \ˈra-gəd\ adj 1 : TORN, TATTERED; also : wearing tattered clothes 2 : done in an uneven way (a ~ performance) — **rag·ged·ly** adv — **rag·ged·ness** n

rag·lan \ˈra-glən\ n : an overcoat with sleeves (**raglan sleeves**) sewn in with seams slanting from neck to underarm

ra·gout \ra-ˈgü\ n [F ragoût, fr. ragoûter to revive the taste, fr. re- + a- to (fr. L ad-) + goût taste, fr. L gustus] : a highly seasoned meat stew with vegetables

rag·pick·er \ˈrag-ˌpi-kər\ n : one who collects rags and refuse for a living

rag·time \-ˌtīm\ n : music in which there is more or less continuous syncopation in the melody

rag·top \ˈrag-ˌtäp\ n : CONVERTIBLE

rag·weed \-ˌwēd\ n : any of several chiefly No. American weedy composite herbs with allergenic pollen

¹**raid** \ˈrād\ n : a sudden usu. surprise attack or invasion : FORAY

²**raid** vb : to make a raid on — **raid·er** n

¹**rail** \ˈrāl\ n [ME raile, fr. MF reille ruler, bar, fr. L regula ruler, fr. regere to keep straight, direct, rule] 1 : a bar extending from one support to another as a guard or barrier 2 : a bar of steel forming a track for wheeled vehicles 3 : RAILROAD

²**rail** vb : to provide with a railing

³**rail** n, pl rail or rails : any of numerous small wading birds often hunted as game birds

⁴**rail** vb [ME, fr. MF railler to mock, fr. OProv ralhar to babble, joke] : to complain angrily : SCOLD, REVILE — **rail·er** n

rail·ing \ˈrā-liŋ\ n : a barrier of rails

rail·lery \ˈrā-lə-rē\ n, pl **-ler·ies** : good-natured ridicule : BANTER

¹**rail·road** \ˈrāl-ˌrōd\ n : a permanent road with rails fixed to ties providing a track for cars; also : such a road and its assets constituting a property

²**railroad** vb 1 : to put through (as a law) too hastily 2 : to convict hastily or with insufficient or improper evidence 3 : to send by rail 4 : to work on a railroad — **rail·road·er** n — **rail·road·ing** n

rail·way \-ˌwā\ n : RAILROAD

rai·ment \ˈrā-mənt\ n : CLOTHING

¹**rain** \ˈrān\ n 1 : water falling in drops from the clouds 2 : a shower of objects (a ~ of bullets) — **rainy** adj

²**rain** vb 1 : to send down rain 2 : to fall as or like rain 3 : to pour down

rain·bow \-ˌbō\ n : an arc or circle of colors formed by the refraction and reflection of the sun's rays in rain, spray, or mist

rainbow trout n : a large stout-bodied fish of western No. America closely related to the salmons of the Pacific and usu. having red or pink stripes with black dots along its sides

rain check n 1 : a ticket stub good for a later performance when the scheduled one is rained out 2 : an assurance of a deferred extension of an offer

rain·coat \ˈrān-ˌkōt\ n : a waterproof or water-repellent coat

rain·drop \-ˌdräp\ n : a drop of rain

rain·fall \-ˌfȯl\ n 1 : amount of precipitation measured by depth 2 : a fall of rain

rain forest n : a tropical woodland having an annual rainfall of at least 100 inches (254 centimeters) and marked by lofty broad-leaved evergreen trees forming a continuous canopy

rain·mak·ing \ˈrān-ˌmā-kiŋ\ n : the action or process of producing or attempting to produce rain by artificial means — **rain·mak·er** n

rain out vb : to interrupt or prevent by rain

rain·storm \ˈrān-ˌstȯrm\ n : a storm of or with rain

rain·wa·ter \-ˌwȯ-tər, -ˌwä-\ n : water fallen as rain

¹**raise** \ˈrāz\ vb **raised; rais·ing** 1 : to cause or help to rise : LIFT (~ a window) 2 : AWAKEN, AROUSE (enough to ~ the dead) 3 : BUILD, ERECT (~ a monument) 4 : PROMOTE (was raised to captain) 5 : END (~ a siege) 6 : COLLECT (~ money) 7 : BREED, GROW (~ cattle) (~ corn); also : BRING UP (~ a family) 8

: PROVOKE ⟨~ a laugh⟩ **9** : to bring to notice ⟨~ an objection⟩ **10** : INCREASE ⟨~ prices⟩; *also* : to bet more than **11** : to make light and spongy ⟨~ dough⟩ **12** : to multiply a quantity by itself a specified number of times **13** : to cause to form ⟨~ a blister⟩ *syn* lift, hoist, boost, elevate — **rais•er** *n*

²raise *n* : an increase in amount (as of a bid or bet); *also* : an increase in pay

rai•sin \'rāz-ᵊn\ *n* [ME, fr. MF, grape, fr. L *racemus* cluster of grapes or berries] : a grape dried for food

rai•son d'être \ˌrā-ˌzōⁿ-'detrᵊ\ *n* : reason or justification for existence

ra•ja *or* **ra•jah** \'rä-jə\ *n* [Hindi *rājā*, fr. Skt *rājan* king] : an Indian prince

¹rake \'rāk\ *n* : a long-handled garden tool having a crossbar with prongs

²rake *vb* **raked; rak•ing 1** : to gather, loosen, or smooth with or as if with a rake **2** : to sweep the length of (as a trench or ship) with gunfire

³rake *n* : inclination from either perpendicular or horizontal : SLANT

⁴rake *n* : a dissolute man : LIBERTINE

rake–off \'rāk-ˌȯf\ *n* : a percentage or cut taken

¹rak•ish \'rā-kish\ *adj* : DISSOLUTE — **rak•ish•ly** *adv* — **rak•ish•ness** *n*

²rakish *adj* **1** : having a trim appearance indicative of speed ⟨a ~ sloop⟩ **2** : JAUNTY, SPORTY ⟨~ clothes⟩ — **rak•ish•ly** *adv* — **rak•ish•ness** *n*

¹ral•ly \'ra-lē\ *vb* **ral•lied; ral•ly•ing 1** : to bring together for a common purpose; *also* : to bring back to order ⟨a leader ~*ing* his forces⟩ **2** : to arouse to activity or from depression or weakness **3** : to make a comeback *syn* stir, rouse, awaken, waken, kindle

²rally *n*, *pl* **rallies 1** : an act of rallying **2** : a mass meeting to arouse enthusiasm **3** : a competitive automobile event run over public roads

³rally *vb* **ral•lied; ral•ly•ing** : BANTER

¹ram \'ram\ *n* **1** : a male sheep **2** : BATTERING RAM

²ram *vb* **rammed; ram•ming 1** : to force or drive in or through **2** : CRAM, CROWD **3** : to strike against violently

RAM \'ram\ *n* : RANDOM-ACCESS MEMORY

¹ram•ble \'ram-bəl\ *vb* **ram•bled; ram•bling** : to go about aimlessly : ROAM, WANDER

²ramble *n* : a leisurely excursion; *esp* : an aimless walk

ram•bler \'ram-blər\ *n* **1** : a person who rambles **2** : any of various climbing roses with large clusters of small often double flowers

ram•bunc•tious \ram-'bəŋk-shəs\ *adj* : UNRULY

ra•mie \'rā-mē, 'ra-\ *n* : a strong lustrous bast fiber from an Asian nettle

ram•i•fi•ca•tion \ˌra-mə-fə-'kā-shən\ *n* **1** : the act or process of branching **2** : CONSEQUENCE, OUTGROWTH

ram•i•fy \'ra-mə-ˌfī\ *vb* **-fied; -fy•ing** : to branch out

ramp \'ramp\ *n* : a sloping passage or roadway connecting different levels

¹ram•page \'ram-ˌpāj, (ˌ)ram-'pāj\ *vb* **ram•paged; ram•pag•ing** : to rush about wildly

²ram•page \'ram-ˌpāj\ *n* : a course of violent or riotous action or behavior — **ram•pa•geous** \ram-'pā-jəs\ *adj*

ram•pant \'ram-pənt\ *adj* : unchecked in growth or spread : RIFE ⟨fear was ~ in the town⟩ — **ram•pan•cy** \-pən-sē\ *n* — **ram•pant•ly** *adv*

ram•part \'ram-ˌpärt\ *n* **1** : a protective barrier **2** : a broad embankment raised as a fortification

¹ram•rod \'ram-ˌräd\ *n* **1** : a rod used to ram a charge into a muzzle-loading gun **2** : a cleaning rod for small arms **3** : BOSS, OVERSEER

²ramrod *adj* : marked by rigidity or severity

³ramrod *vb* : to direct, supervise, and control

ram•shack•le \'ram-ˌsha-kəl\ *adj* : RICKETY, TUMBLE-DOWN

ran *past of* RUN

¹ranch \'ranch\ *n* [MexSp *rancho* small ranch, fr. Sp, camp, hut & Sp dial., small farm, fr. Old Spanish

ranchear (*se*) to take up quarters, fr. MF (*se*) *ranger* to take up a position, fr. *ranger* to set in a row] **1** : an establishment for the raising and grazing of livestock (as cattle, sheep, or horses) **2** : a large farm devoted to a specialty **3** : RANCH HOUSE 2

²ranch *vb* : to live or work on a ranch — **ranch•er** *n*

ranch house *n* **1** : the main house on a ranch **2** : a one-story house typically with a low-pitched roof

ran•cho \'ran-chō, 'rän-\ *n*, *pl* **ranchos** : RANCH 1

ran•cid \'ran-səd\ *adj* **1** : having a rank smell or taste **2** : ROTTEN, SPOILED — **ran•cid•i•ty** \ran-'si-də-tē\ *n*

ran•cor \'raŋ-kər\ *n* : bitter deep-seated ill will *syn* antagonism, animosity, antipathy, enmity, hostility — **ran•cor•ous** *adj*

ran•cour *Brit var of* RANCOR

rand \'rand, 'ränd, 'ränt\ *n*, *pl* **rand** — see MONEY table

R & B *abbr* rhythm and blues

R and D *n* : research and development

ran•dom \'ran-dəm\ *adj* : CHANCE, HAPHAZARD — **ran•dom•ly** *adv* — **ran•dom•ness** *n*

random–access *adj* : allowing access to stored data in any order the user desires

random–access memory *n* : a computer memory that provides the main internal storage for programs and data

ran•dom•ize \'ran-də-ˌmīz\ *vb* **-ized; -iz•ing** : to select, assign, or arrange in a random way — **ran•dom•i•za•tion** \ˌran-də-mə-'zā-shən\ *n*

R and R *abbr* rest and recreation; rest and recuperation

rang *past of* RING

¹range \'rānj\ *n* **1** : a series of things in a row **2** : a cooking stove having an oven and a flat top with burners **3** : open land where animals (as livestock) may roam and graze **4** : the act of ranging about **5** : the distance a weapon will shoot or is to be shot **6** : a place where shooting is practiced **7** : the space or extent included, covered, or used : SCOPE **8** : a variation within limits *syn* reach, compass, radius, circle

²range *vb* **ranged; rang•ing 1** : to set in a row or in proper order **2** : to set in place among others of the same kind **3** : to roam over or through : EXPLORE **4** : to roam at large or freely **5** : to correspond in direction or line **6** : to vary within limits **7** : to find the range of an object by instrument (as radar)

rang•er \'rān-jər\ *n* **1** : FOREST RANGER **2** : a member of a body of troops who range over a region **3** : an expert in close-range fighting and raiding tactics

rangy \'rān-jē\ *adj* **rang•i•er; -est** : being long-limbed and slender — **rang•i•ness** \'rān-jē-nəs\ *n*

ra•ni *or* **ra•nee** \rä-'nē, 'rä-ˌnē\ *n* : a raja's wife

¹rank \'raŋk\ *adj* **1** : strong and vigorous and usu. coarse in growth ⟨~ weeds⟩ **2** : unpleasantly strong-smelling — **rank•ly** *adv* — **rank•ness** *n*

²rank *n* **1** : ROW **2** : a line of soldiers ranged side by side **3** *pl* : the body of enlisted personnel ⟨rose from the ~s⟩ **4** : an orderly arrangement **5** : CLASS, DIVISION **6** : a grade of official standing (as in an army) **7** : position in a group **8** : superior position

³rank *vb* **1** : to arrange in lines or in regular formation **2** : RATE **3** : to rate above (as in official standing) **4** : to take or have a relative position

rank and file *n* : the general membership of a body as contrasted with its leaders

rank•ing \'raŋ-kiŋ\ *adj* **1** : having a high position : FOREMOST **2** : being next to the chairman in seniority

ran•kle \'raŋ-kəl\ *vb* **ran•kled; ran•kling** [ME *ranclen* to fester, fr. MF *rancler*, fr. OF *draoncler*, *raoncler*, fr. *draoncle*, *raoncle* festering sore, fr. (assumed) VL *dracunculus*, fr. L, dim. of *draco* serpent] : to cause anger, irritation, or bitterness

ran•sack \'ran-ˌsak\ *vb* : to search thoroughly; *esp* : to search through and rob

ran•som \'ran-səm\ *n* [ME *ransoun*, fr. OF *rançon*, fr. L *redemption-*, *redemptio* act of buying back, fr. *red-*

imere to buy back, redeem] **1** : something paid or demanded for the freedom of a captive **2** : the act of ransoming

²**ransom** *vb* : to free from captivity or punishment by paying a price — **ran•som•er** *n*

rant \'rant\ *vb* **1** : to talk loudly and wildly **2** : to scold violently — **rant•er** *n* — **rant•ing•ly** *adv*

¹**rap** \'rap\ *n* **1** : a sharp blow **2** : a sharp rebuke **3** : a negative often undeserved reputation ⟨a bum ∼⟩ **4** : responsibility for or consequences of an action ⟨take the ∼⟩

²**rap** *vb* **rapped; rap•ping 1** : to strike sharply : KNOCK **2** : to utter sharply **3** : to criticize sharply

³**rap** *vb* **rapped; rap•ping 1** : to talk freely and frankly **2** : to perform rap music

⁴**rap** *n* **1** : TALK, CONVERSATION **2** : a rhythmic chanting of usu. rhymed couplets to a musical accompaniment; *also* : a piece so performed

ra•pa•cious \rə-'pā-shəs\ *adj* **1** : excessively greedy or covetous **2** : living on prey **3** : RAVENOUS 2 — **ra•pa•cious•ly** *adv* — **ra•pa•cious•ness** *n* — **ra•pac•i•ty** \-'pa-sə-tē\ *n*

¹**rape** \'rāp\ *n* : a European herb related to the mustards that is grown as a forage crop and for its seeds (**rape•seed** \-ₐsēd\)

²**rape** *vb* **raped; rap•ing** : to commit rape on — **rap•er** *n* — **rap•ist** \'rā-pist\ *n*

³**rape** *n* **1** : a carrying away by force **2** : sexual intercourse by a man with a woman without her consent and chiefly by force or deception; *also* : unlawful sexual intercourse of any kind by force or threat

¹**rap•id** \'ra-pəd\ *adj* [L *rapidus* strong-flowing, rapid, fr. *rapere* to seize, carry away] : very fast : SWIFT **syn** fleet, quick, speedy — **ra•pid•i•ty** \rə-'pi-də-tē\ *n* — **rap•id•ly** *adv*

²**rapid** *n* : a place in a stream where the current flows very fast usu. over obstructions — usu. used in pl.

rapid eye movement *n* : rapid conjugate movement of the eyes associated with REM sleep

rapid transit *n* : fast passenger transportation (as by subway) in cities

ra•pi•er \'rā-pē-ər\ *n* : a straight 2-edged sword with a narrow pointed blade

rapier

rap•ine \'ra-pən, -pīn\ *n* : PILLAGE, PLUNDER

rap•pel \ra-'pel, ra-\ *vb* **-pelled; -pel•ling** : to descend (as from a cliff) by sliding down a rope

rap•pen \'rä-pən\ *n*, *pl* **rappen** : the centime of Switzerland

rap•port \ra-'pōr\ *n* : RELATION; *esp* : relation characterized by harmony

rap•proche•ment \ra-ₐprōsh-'mäⁿ, ra-'prōsh-ₐmäⁿ\ *n* : the establishment of or a state of having cordial relations

rap•scal•lion \rap-'skal-yən\ *n* : RASCAL, SCAMP

rapt \'rapt\ *adj* **1** : carried away with emotion **2** : ABSORBED, ENGROSSED — **rapt•ly** \'rapt-lē\ *adv* — **rapt•ness** *n*

rap•ture \'rap-chər\ *n* : spiritual or emotional ecstasy — **rap•tur•ous** \-chə-rəs\ *adj* — **rap•tur•ous•ly** *adv*

rapture of the deep : NITROGEN NARCOSIS

ra•ra avis \ₐrar-ə-'ā-vəs\ *n* [L, rare bird] : a rare person or thing : RARITY

¹**rare** \'rar\ *adj* **rar•er; rar•est 1** : not thick or dense : THIN ⟨∼ air⟩ **2** : unusually fine : EXCELLENT, SPLENDID **3** : seldom met with — **rare•ly** *adv* — **rare•ness** *n* — **rar•i•ty** \'rar-ə-tē\ *n*

²**rare** *adj* **rar•er; rar•est** : cooked so that the inside is still red ⟨∼ beef⟩

rare•bit \'rar-bət\ *n* : WELSH RABBIT

rar•efac•tion \ₐrar-ə-'fak-shən\ *n* **1** : the action or process of rarefying **2** : the state of being rarefied

rar•efy *also* **rar•i•fy** \'rar-ə-ₐfī\ *vb* **-fied; -fy•ing** : to make or become rare, thin, or less dense

rar•ing \'rar-ən, -iŋ\ *adj* : full of enthusiasm or eagerness ⟨∼ to go⟩

ras•cal \'ras-kəl\ *n* **1** : a mean or dishonest person **2** : a mischievous person — **ras•cal•i•ty** \ras-'ka-lə-tē\ *n* — **ras•cal•ly** \'ras-kə-lē\ *adj*

¹**rash** \'rash\ *adj* : having or showing little regard for consequences : too hasty in decision, action, or speech : RECKLESS **syn** daring, foolhardy, adventurous, venturesome — **rash•ly** *adv* — **rash•ness** *n*

²**rash** *n* : an eruption on the body

rash•er \'ra-shər\ *n* : a thin slice of bacon or ham broiled or fried; *also* : a portion consisting of several such slices

¹**rasp** \'rasp\ *vb* **1** : to rub with or as if with a rough file **2** : to grate harshly on (as one's nerves) **3** : to speak in a grating tone

²**rasp** *n* : a coarse file with cutting points instead of ridges

rasp•ber•ry \'raz-ₐber-ē, -bə-rē\ *n* **1** : any of various edible usu. black or red berries produced by some brambles; *also* : such a bramble **2** : a sound of contempt made by protruding the tongue through the lips and expelling air forcibly

¹**rat** \'rat\ *n* **1** : any of numerous rodents larger than the related mice **2** : a contemptible person; *esp* : one that betrays friends or associates

²**rat** *vb* **rat•ted; rat•ting 1** : to betray or inform on one's associates **2** : to hunt or catch rats

rat cheese *n* : CHEDDAR

ratch•et \'ra-chət\ *n* : a device that consists of a bar or wheel having slanted teeth into which a pawl drops so as to allow motion in only one direction

ratchet wheel *n* : a toothed wheel held in position or turned by a pawl

¹**rate** \'rāt\ *vb* **rat•ed; rat•ing** : to scold violently

²**rate** *n* **1** : quantity, amount, or degree measured by some standard **2** : an amount (as of payment) measured by its relation to some other amount (as of time) **3** : a charge, payment, or price fixed according to a ratio, scale, or standard ⟨tax ∼⟩ **4** : RANK, CLASS

³**rate** *vb* **rat•ed; rat•ing 1** : ESTIMATE **2** : CONSIDER, REGARD **3** : to settle the relative rank or class of **4** : to be classed : RANK **5** : to have a right to : DESERVE **6** : to be of consequence — **rat•er** *n*

rath•er \'ra-thər, 'rä-, 'rə-\ *adv* [ME, fr. OE *hrathor*, compar. of *hrathe* quickly] **1** : more properly **2** : PREFERABLY **3** : more correctly speaking **4** : to the contrary : INSTEAD **5** : SOMEWHAT

raths•kel•ler \'rät-ₐske-lər, 'rat-\ *n* [obs. G (now *Ratskeller*), city-hall basement restaurant, fr. *Rat* council + *Keller* cellar] : a usu. basement tavern or restaurant

rat•i•fy \'ra-tə-ₐfī\ *vb* **-fied; -fy•ing** : to approve and accept formally — **rat•i•fi•ca•tion** \ₐra-tə-fə-'kā-shən\ *n*

rat•ing \'rā-tiŋ\ *n* **1** : a classification according to grade : RANK **2** *Brit* : a naval enlisted man **3** : an estimate of the credit standing and business responsibility of a person or firm

ra•tio \'rā-shō, -shē-ō\ *n*, *pl* **ra•tios 1** : the indicated quotient of two numbers or mathematical expressions **2** : the relationship in number, quantity, or degree between two or more things

ra•ti•o•ci•na•tion \ₐra-tē-ₐōs-ᵊn-'ā-shən, -shē-, -ₐäs-\ *n*

: exact thinking : REASONING — **ra·ti·o·ci·nate** \-'ōs-ᵊn-ˌāt, -'äs-\ *vb* — **ra·ti·o·ci·na·tive** \-'ōs-ᵊn-ˌā-tiv, -'äs-\ *adj* — **ra·ti·o·ci·na·tor** \-'ōs-ᵊn-ˌā-tər, -'äs-\ *n*

¹ra·tion \'ra-shən, 'rā-\ *n* **1** : a food allowance for one day **2** : FOOD, PROVISIONS, DIET — usu. used in pl. **3** : SHARE, ALLOTMENT

²ration *vb* **1** : to supply with or allot as rations **2** : to use or allot sparingly **syn** apportion, portion, prorate, parcel

¹ra·tio·nal \'ra-shə-nəl\ *adj* **1** : having reason or understanding **2** : of or relating to reason **3** : relating to, consisting of, or being one or more rational numbers — **ra·tio·nal·ly** *adv*

²rational *n* : RATIONAL NUMBER

ra·tio·nale \ˌra-shə-'nal\ *n* **1** : an explanation of principles controlling belief or practice **2** : an underlying reason

ra·tio·nal·ise *Brit var of* RATIONALIZE

ra·tio·nal·ism \'ra-shə-nə-ˌli-zəm\ *n* : the practice of guiding one's actions and opinions solely by what seems reasonable — **ra·tio·nal·ist** \-list\ *n* — **rationalist** *or* **ra·tio·nal·is·tic** \ˌra-shə-nə-'lis-tik\ *adj*

ra·tio·nal·i·ty \ˌra-shə-'na-lə-tē\ *n, pl* **-ties** : the quality or state of being rational

ra·tio·nal·ize \'ra-shə-nə-ˌlīz\ *vb* **-ized; -iz·ing 1** : to make (something irrational) appear rational or reasonable **2** : to provide a natural explanation of (as a myth) **3** : to justify (as one's behavior or weaknesses) esp. to oneself **4** : to find plausible but untrue reasons for conduct — **ra·tio·nal·i·za·tion** \ˌra-shə-nə-lə-'zā-shən\ *n*

rational number *n* : an integer or the quotient of an integer divided by a nonzero integer

rat race *n* : strenuous, tiresome, and usu. competitive activity or rush

rat·tan \ra-'tan, rə-\ *n* : a cane or switch made from one of the long stems of an Asian climbing palm; *also* : this palm

rat·ter \'ra-tər\ *n* : a rat-catching dog or cat

¹rat·tle \'rat-ᵊl\ *vb* **rat·tled; rat·tling 1** : to make or cause to make a series of clattering sounds **2** : to move with a clattering sound **3** : to say or do in a brisk lively fashion ⟨~ off the answers⟩ **4** : CONFUSE, UPSET ⟨~ a witness⟩

²rattle *n* **1** : a toy that produces a rattle when shaken **2** : a series of clattering and knocking sounds **3** : a rattling organ at the end of a rattlesnake's tail

rat·tler \'rat-lər\ *n* : RATTLESNAKE

rat·tle·snake \'rat-ᵊl-ˌsnāk\ *n* : any of various American pit vipers with a rattle at the end of the tail

rattlesnake

rat·tle·trap \'rat-ᵊl-ˌtrap\ *n* : something (as an old car) rickety and full of rattles

rat·tling \'rat-liŋ\ *adj* **1** : LIVELY, BRISK **2** : FIRST-RATE, SPLENDID

rat·trap \'rat-ˌtrap\ *n* **1** : a trap for rats **2** : a dilapidated building

rat·ty \'ra-tē\ *adj* **rat·ti·er; -est 1** : infested with rats **2** : of, relating to, or suggestive of rats **3** : SHABBY

rau·cous \'rȯ-kəs\ *adj* **1** : HARSH, HOARSE, STRIDENT **2** : boisterously disorderly — **rau·cous·ly** *adv* — **rau·cous·ness** *n*

raun·chy \'rȯn-chē, 'rän-\ *adj* **raun·chi·er; -est 1**

: SLOVENLY, DIRTY **2** : OBSCENE, SMUTTY — **raun·chi·ness** \-chē-nəs\ *n*

¹rav·age \'ra-vij\ *n* [F] : an act or result of ravaging : DEVASTATION

²ravage *vb* **rav·aged; rav·ag·ing** : to lay waste : DEVASTATE — **rav·ag·er** *n*

¹rave \'rāv\ *vb* **raved; rav·ing** [ME *raven*] **1** : to talk wildly in or as if in delirium : STORM, RAGE **2** : to talk with extreme enthusiasm

²rave *n* **1** : an act or instance of raving **2** : an extravagantly favorable criticism

¹rav·el \'ra-vəl\ *vb* **-eled** *or* **-elled; -el·ing** *or* **-el·ling 1** : UNRAVEL, UNTWIST **2** : TANGLE, CONFUSE

²ravel *n* **1** : something tangled **2** : something raveled out; *esp* : a loose thread

¹ra·ven \'rā-vən\ *n* : a large black bird related to the crow

²raven *adj* : black and glossy like a raven's feathers

³rav·en \'ra-vən\ *vb* **rav·ened; rav·en·ing 1** : to devour greedily **2** : DESPOIL, PLUNDER **3** : PREY

rav·en·ous \'ra-və-nəs\ *adj* **1** : RAPACIOUS, VORACIOUS **2** : eager for food : very hungry — **rav·en·ous·ly** *adv* — **rav·en·ous·ness** *n*

ra·vine \rə-'vēn\ *n* : a small narrow steep-sided valley larger than a gully

ra·vi·o·li \ˌra-vē-'ō-lē\ *n* [It, fr. It dial., pl. of *raviolo*, lit., little turnip, dim. of *rava* turnip, fr. L *rapa*] : small cases of dough with a savory filling (as of meat or cheese)

rav·ish \'ra-vish\ *vb* **1** : to seize and take away by violence **2** : to overcome with emotion and esp. with joy or delight **3** : RAPE — **rav·ish·er** *n* — **rav·ish·ment** *n*

¹raw \'rȯ\ *adj* **raw·er** \'rȯ-ər\; **raw·est** \'rȯ-əst\ **1** : not cooked **2** : changed little from the original form : not processed ⟨~ materials⟩ **3** : having the surface abraded or irritated ⟨a ~ sore⟩ **4** : not trained or experienced ⟨~ recruits⟩ **5** : VULGAR, COARSE **6** : disagreeably cold and damp ⟨a ~ day⟩ **7** : UNFAIR ⟨~ deal⟩ — **raw·ness** *n*

²raw *n* : a raw place or state; *esp* : NUDITY

raw·boned \'rȯ-'bōnd\ *adj* **1** : LEAN, GAUNT **2** : having a heavy frame that seems to have little flesh

raw·hide \'rȯ-ˌhīd\ *n* : the untanned skin of cattle; *also* : a whip made of this

¹ray \'rā\ *n* : any of an order of large flat cartilaginous fishes that have the eyes on the upper surface and the hind end of the body slender and taillike

²ray *n* [ME, fr. MF *rai*, fr. L *radius* rod, ray] **1** : any of the lines of light that appear to radiate from a bright object **2** : a thin beam of radiant energy (as light) **3** : light from a beam **4** : a thin line like a beam of light **5** : an animal or plant structure resembling a ray **6** : a tiny bit : PARTICLE ⟨a ~ of hope⟩

ray·on \'rā-ˌän\ *n* : a fiber made from cellulose; *also* : yarn, thread, or fabric made from such fibers

raze \'rāz\ *vb* **razed; raz·ing 1** : to scrape, cut, or shave off **2** : to destroy to the ground : DEMOLISH

ra·zor \'rā-zər\ *n* : a sharp cutting instrument used to shave off hair

ra·zor–backed \'rā-zər-ˌbakt\ *or* **ra·zor·back** \-ˌbak\ *adj* : having a sharp narrow back ⟨~ horse⟩

razor clam *n* : any of a family of marine bivalve mollusks having a long narrow curved thin shell

¹razz \'raz\ *n* : RASPBERRY 2

²razz *vb* : RIDICULE, TEASE

Rb *symbol* rubidium

RBC *abbr* red blood cells; red blood count

RBI \ˌär-(ˌ)bē-'ī, 'ri-bē\ *n, pl* **RBIs** *or* **RBI** [*run batted in*] : a run in baseball that is driven in by a batter

RC *abbr* **1** Red Cross **2** Roman Catholic

RCAF *abbr* Royal Canadian Air Force

RCMP *abbr* Royal Canadian Mounted Police

RCN *abbr* Royal Canadian Navy

rct *abbr* recruit

rd *abbr* **1** road **2** rod **3** round

RD *abbr* rural delivery

RDA *abbr* recommended daily allowance; recommended dietary allowance

re *rā, *****rē\ *prep* : with regard to

Re *symbol* rhenium

re- \rē, ˌrē, *****rē\ *prefix* **1** : again : for a second time **2** : anew : in a new or different form **3** : back : backward

reabsorb	rechristen	reenact
reacquire	reclassification	reenactment
reactivate	reclassify	reenergize
reactivation	recoin	reenlist
readdress	recolonization	reenlistment
readjust	recolonize	reenter
readjustment	recolor	reequip
readmission	recombine	reestablish
readmit	recommence	reestablishment
reaffirm	recommission	reevaluate
reaffirmation	recommit	reevaluation
realign	recompile	reexamination
realignment	recompose	reexamine
reallocate	recomputation	reexport
reallocation	recompute	refashion
reanalysis	reconceive	refight
reanalyze	reconcentrate	refigure
reanimate	reconception	refinish
reanimation	recondensation	refit
reannex	recondense	refix
reannexation	reconfirm	refloat
reappear	reconfirmation	refold
reappearance	reconnect	reforge
reapplication	reconquer	reformulate
reapply	reconquest	reformulation
reappoint	reconsecrate	refortify
reappointment	reconsecration	refound
reapportion	recontact	refreeze
reapportionment	recontaminate	refuel
reappraisal	recontamination	refurnish
reappraise	reconvene	regain
rearm	reconvert	regather
rearmament	recook	regild
rearouse	recopy	regive
rearrange	recross	regrade
rearrangement	recrystallize	regrind
rearrest	recut	regrow
reascend	redecorate	regrowth
reassemble	redecoration	rehandle
reassembly	rededicate	rehear
reassert	rededication	reheat
reassess	redefine	rehouse
reassessment	redefinition	reimpose
reassign	redeposit	reimposition
reassignment	redesign	reincorporate
reassume	redetermination	reinsert
reattach	redetermine	reinsertion
reattachment	redevelop	reintegrate
reattain	redevelopment	reinterpret
reattempt	redirect	reinterpretation
reauthorization	rediscount	reintroduce
reauthorize	rediscover	reintroduction
reawaken	rediscovery	reinvention
rebaptism	redissolve	reinvest
rebaptize	redistill	reinvestment
rebid	redistillation	reinvigorate
rebind	redraft	reinvigoration
reboil	redraw	reissue
rebroadcast	reecho	rejudge
reburial	reedit	rekindle
rebury	reelect	reknit
recalculate	reelection	relaunch
recalculation	reemerge	relearn
rechannel	reemergence	relight
recharge	reemphasis	reline
rechargeable	reemphasize	reload
recharter	reemploy	remanufacture
recheck	reemployment	remap

renegotiate	
renegotiation	
renominate	
renomination	
renumber	
reoccupy	
reoccur	
reopen	
reorder	
reorganization	
reorganize	
reorient	
reorientation	
repack	
repaint	
repass	
repeople	
rephotograph	
rephrase	
replant	
repopulate	
reprice	
reprocess	
reprogram	
republication	
republish	
repurchase	
reradiate	
reread	
rereading	
rerecord	
reroute	
reschedule	
rescore	
rescreen	
reseal	
reseed	
resell	
reset	
resettle	
resettlement	
resew	
reshow	
resocialization	
resow	
respell	
restaff	
restart	
restate	
restatement	
restock	
restrengthen	
restructure	
restudy	
restuff	
restyle	
resubmit	
resummon	
resupply	
resurface	
resurvey	
resynthesis	
resynthesize	
retaste	
retell	
retest	
retool	
retrain	
retransmission	
retransmit	
retrial	
reunification	
reunify	
reunite	
reusable	
reuse	

remarriage
remarry
rematch
remelt
remigration
remix
remold
rename

revaluate
revaluation
revalue
revisit
rewarm
rewash

reweave
rewed
reweigh
rewire
rezone

¹reach \'rēch\ vb 1 : to stretch out 2 : to touch or attempt to touch or seize 3 : to extend to 4 : to communicate with 5 : to arrive at **syn** gain, realize, achieve, attain — **reach•able** adj — **reach•er** n

²reach n 1 : an unbroken stretch of a river 2 : the act of reaching 3 : a reachable distance; also : ability to reach 4 : a range of knowledge or comprehension

re•act \rē-'akt\ vb 1 : to exert a return or counteracting influence 2 : to have or show a reaction 3 : to act in opposition to a force or influence 4 : to move or tend in a reverse direction 5 : to undergo chemical reaction

re•ac•tant \rē-'ak-tənt\ n : a chemically reacting substance

re•ac•tion \rē-'ak-shən\ n 1 : the act or process of reacting 2 : a counter tendency; esp : a tendency toward a former esp. outmoded political or social order or policy 3 : bodily, mental, or emotional response to a stimulus 4 : chemical change 5 : a process involving change in atomic nuclei

re•ac•tion•ary \rē-'ak-shə-₁ner-ē\ adj : relating to, marked by, or favoring esp. political reaction — **re•actionary** n

re•ac•tive \rē-'ak-tiv\ adj : reacting or tending to react

re•ac•tor \rē-'ak-tər\ n 1 : one that reacts 2 : a device for the controlled release of nuclear energy

¹read \'rēd\ vb read \'red\; read•ing 1 : to understand language by interpreting written symbols for speech sounds 2 : to utter aloud written or printed words 3 : to learn by observing ⟨~ nature's signs⟩ 4 : to study by a course of reading ⟨~s law⟩ 5 : to discover the meaning of ⟨~ the clues⟩ 6 : to recognize or interpret as if by reading 7 : to attribute (a meaning) to something ⟨~ guilt in his manner⟩ 8 : INDICATE ⟨thermometer ~s 10°⟩ 9 : to consist in phrasing or meaning ⟨the two versions ~ differently⟩ — **read•abil•i•ty** \₁rē-də-'bi-lə-tē\ n — **read•able** \'rē-də-bəl\ adj — **read•ably** \-blē\ adv — **read•er** n

²read \'red\ adj : informed by reading ⟨widely ~⟩

read•er•ship \'rē-dər-₁ship\ n : the mass or a particular group of readers

read•ing n 1 : something read or for reading 2 : a particular version 3 : data indicated by an instrument ⟨thermometer ~⟩ 4 : a particular interpretation (as of a law) 5 : a particular performance (as of a musical work) 6 : an indication of a certain state of affairs

read–only memory n : a computer memory that contains special-purpose information (as a program) which cannot be altered

read•out \'rēd-₁aut\ n : the process of removing information from an automatic device (as a computer) and displaying it in an understandable form; also : the information removed from such a device

read out vb 1 : to read aloud 2 : to expel from an organization

¹ready \'re-dē\ adj read•i•er; -est 1 : prepared for use or action 2 : likely to do something indicated; also : willingly disposed : INCLINED 3 : spontaneously prompt ⟨her ~ wit⟩ 4 : immediately available ⟨~ cash⟩ — **read•i•ly** \'re-də-lē\ adv — **read•i•ness** \-dē-nəs\ n — **at the ready** : ready for immediate use

²ready vb read•ied; ready•ing : to make ready : PREPARE

ready–made \₁re-dē-'mād\ adj : already made up for general sale : not specially made — **ready–made** n

ready room n : a room in which pilots are briefed and await orders

re•agent \rē-'ā-jənt\ n : a substance that takes part in or brings about a particular chemical reaction

¹re•al \'rēl\ adj [ME, real, relating to things (in law), fr. MF, fr. ML & LL; ML realis relating to things (in law), fr. LL, real, fr. L res thing, fact] 1 : of or relating to fixed or immovable things (as land) ⟨~ property⟩ 2 : not artificial : GENUINE; also : not imaginary — **re•al•ness** n — **for real** 1 : in earnest 2 : GENUINE

²real adv : VERY

³real \rā-'äl\ n — see MONEY table

real estate n : property in buildings and land

re•al•ism \'rē-ə-₁li-zəm\ n 1 : the disposition to face facts and to deal with them practically 2 : true and faithful portrayal of nature and of people in art or literature — **re•al•ist** \-list\ adj or n — **re•al•is•tic** \₁rē-ə-'lis-tik\ adj — **re•al•is•ti•cal•ly** \-ti-k(ə-)lē\ adv

re•al•i•ty \rē-'a-lə-tē\ n, pl -ties 1 : the quality or state of being real 2 : something real 3 : the totality of real things and events

re•al•ize \'rē-ə-₁līz\ vb -ized; -iz•ing 1 : to make actual : ACCOMPLISH 2 : to convert into money ⟨~ assets⟩ 3 : OBTAIN, GAIN ⟨~ a profit⟩ 4 : to be aware of : UNDERSTAND — **re•al•iz•able** adj — **re•al•i•za•tion** \₁rē-ə-lə-'zā-shən\ n

re•al•ly \'rē-lē, 'ri-\ adv : in truth : in fact : ACTUALLY

realm \'relm\ n 1 : KINGDOM 2 : SPHERE, DOMAIN

real number n : any of the numbers (as −2, 3, ⅞, .25, π) that are rational or irrational

re•al•po•li•tik \rā-'äl-₁pō-li-₁tēk\ n [G] : politics based on practical and material factors rather than on theoretical or ethical objectives

real time n : the actual time during which something takes place — **real–time** adj

re•al•ty \'rēl-tē\ n : REAL ESTATE

¹ream \'rēm\ n [ME reme, fr. MF raime, fr. Ar rizmah, lit., bundle] : a quantity of paper that is variously 480, 500, or 516 sheets

²ream vb : to enlarge, shape, or clear with a reamer

ream·er \'rē-mər\ *n* : a tool with cutting edges that is used to enlarge or shape a hole

reap \'rēp\ *vb* **1** : to cut or clear with a scythe, sickle, or machine **2** : to gather by or as if by cutting : HARVEST ⟨∼ a reward⟩ — **reap·er** *n*

¹rear \'rir\ *vb* **1** : to erect by building **2** : to set or raise upright **3** : to breed and raise for use or market ⟨∼ livestock⟩ **4** : BRING UP, FOSTER **5** : to lift or rise up; *esp* : to rise on the hind legs

²rear *n* **1** : the unit (as of an army) or area farthest from the enemy **2** : BACK; *also* : the position at the back of something

³rear *adj* : being at the back

rear admiral *n* : a commissioned officer in the navy or coast guard ranking next below a vice admiral

¹rear·ward \'rir-wərd\ *adj* **1** : being at or toward the rear **2** : directed toward the rear

²rear·ward *also* **rear·wards** \-wərdz\ *adv* : at or toward the rear

reas *abbr* reasonable

¹rea·son \'rēz-ᵊn\ *n* [ME *resoun*, fr. OF *raison*, fr. L *ration-, ratio* reason, computation] **1** : a statement offered in explanation or justification **2** : GROUND, CAUSE **3** : the power to think : INTELLECT **4** : a sane or sound mind **5** : due exercise of the faculty of logical thought

²reason *vb* **1** : to talk with another to cause a change of mind **2** : to use the faculty of reason : THINK **3** : to discover or formulate by the use of reason — **rea·son·er** *n* — **rea·son·ing** *n*

rea·son·able \'rēz-ᵊn-ə-bəl\ *adj* **1** : being within the bounds of reason : not extreme **2** : INEXPENSIVE **3** : able to reason : RATIONAL — **rea·son·able·ness** *n* — **rea·son·ably** \-blē\ *adv*

re·as·sure \rē-ə-'shùr\ *vb* **1** : to assure again **2** : to restore confidence to : free from fear — **re·as·sur·ance** \-'shùr-əns\ *n* — **re·as·sur·ing·ly** *adv*

¹re·bate \'rē-ˌbāt\ *vb* **re·bat·ed; re·bat·ing** : to make or give a rebate

²rebate *n* : a return of part of a payment **syn** deduction, abatement, discount

³re·bate \'ra-bət, 'rē-ˌbāt\ *chiefly Brit var of* RABBET

¹reb·el \'re-bəl\ *adj* [ME, fr. OF *rebelle*, fr. L *rebellis*, fr. *re- + bellum* war] : of or relating to rebels

²rebel *n* : one that rebels against authority

³re·bel \ri-'bel\ *vb* **re·belled; re·bel·ling 1** : to resist the authority of one's government **2** : to act in or show disobedience **3** : to feel or exhibit anger or revulsion

re·bel·lion \ri-'bel-yən\ *n* : resistance to authority; *esp* : defiance against a government through uprising or revolt

re·bel·lious \-yəs\ *adj* **1** : given to or engaged in rebellion **2** : inclined to resist authority — **re·bel·lious·ly** *adv* — **re·bel·lious·ness** *n*

re·birth \ˌrē-'bərth\ *n* **1** : a new or 2d birth **2** : RENAISSANCE, REVIVAL

re·born \-'bòrn\ *adj* : born again : REGENERATED, REVIVED

¹re·bound \ˌrē-'baùnd, 'rē-ˌbaùnd\ *vb* **1** : to spring back on or as if on striking another body **2** : to recover from a setback or frustration

²re·bound \'rē-ˌbaùnd\ *n* **1** : the action of rebounding **2** : a rebounding ball **3** : a reaction to setback or frustration

re·buff \ri-'bəf\ *vb* : to reject or criticize sharply : SNUB — **rebuff** *n*

re·build \(ˌ)rē-'bild\ *vb* **-built** \-'bilt\; **-build·ing 1** : REPAIR, RECONSTRUCT; *also* : REMODEL **2** : to build again

¹re·buke \ri-'byük\ *vb* **re·buked; re·buk·ing** : to reprimand sharply : REPROVE

²rebuke *n* : a sharp reprimand

re·bus \'rē-bəs\ *n* [L, by things, abl. pl. of *res* thing] : a representation of syllables or words by means of pictures; *also* : a riddle composed of such pictures

re·but \ri-'bət\ *vb* **re·but·ted; re·but·ting** : to refute esp. formally (as in debate) by evidence and arguments **syn** disprove, controvert, confute — **re·but·ter** *n*

re·but·tal \ri-'bət-ᵊl\ *n* : the act of rebutting

rec *abbr* **1** receipt **2** record; recording **3** recreation

re·cal·ci·trant \ri-'kal-sə-trənt\ *adj* [LL *recalcitrant-, recalcitrans*, prp. of *recalcitrare* to be stubbornly disobedient, fr. L, to kick back, fr. *re-* back, again + *calcitrare* to kick, fr. *calc-, calx* heel] **1** : stubbornly resisting authority **2** : resistant to handling or treatment **syn** refractory, headstrong, willful, unruly, ungovernable — **re·cal·ci·trance** \-trəns\ *n*

¹re·call \ri-'kòl\ *vb* **1** : to call back **2** : REMEMBER, RECOLLECT **3** : REVOKE, CANCEL

²re·call \ri-'kòl, 'rē-ˌkòl\ *n* **1** : a summons to return **2** : the procedure of removing an official by popular vote **3** : remembrance of things learned or experienced **4** : the act of revoking **5** : a call by a manufacturer for the return of a product that may be defective or contaminated

re·cant \ri-'kant\ *vb* : to take back (something one has said) publicly : make an open confession of error — **re·can·ta·tion** \ˌrē-ˌkan-'tā-shən\ *n*

¹re·cap \'rē-ˌkap, rē-'kap\ *vb* **re·capped; re·cap·ping** : RECAPITULATE — **recap** \'rē-ˌkap\ *n*

²recap *vb* **re·capped; re·cap·ping** : RETREAD — **re·cap** \'rē-ˌkap\ *n*

re·ca·pit·u·late \ˌrē-kə-'pi-chə-ˌlāt\ *vb* **-lat·ed; -lat·ing** : to restate briefly : SUMMARIZE — **re·ca·pit·u·la·tion** \-ˌpi-chə-'lā-shən\ *n*

re·cap·ture \(ˌ)rē-'kap-chər\ *vb* **1** : to capture again **2** : to experience again ⟨∼ happy times⟩

re·cast \(ˌ)rē-'kast\ *vb* **1** : to cast again **2** : REVISE, REMODEL ⟨∼ a sentence⟩

recd *abbr* received

re·cede \ri-'sēd\ *vb* **re·ced·ed; re·ced·ing 1** : to move back or away **2** : to slant backward **3** : DIMINISH, CONTRACT

¹re·ceipt \ri-'sēt\ *n* **1** : RECIPE **2** : the act of receiving **3** : something received — usu. used in pl. **4** : a written acknowledgment of something received

²**re·ceipt** *vb* **1** : to give a receipt for **2** : to mark as paid

re·ceiv·able \ri-'sē-və-bəl\ *adj* **1** : capable of being received: *esp* : acceptable as legal ⟨~ certificates⟩ : subject to call for payment ⟨notes ~⟩

re·ceive \ri-'sēv\ *vb* **re·ceived; re·ceiv·ing 1** : to take in or accept (as something sent or paid) : come into possession of : GET **2** : CONTAIN, HOLD **3** : to permit to enter : GREET, WELCOME **4** : to be at home to visitors **5** : to accept as true or authoritative **6** : to be the subject of : UNDERGO, EXPERIENCE ⟨~ a shock⟩ **7** : to change incoming radio waves into sounds or pictures

re·ceiv·er \ri-'sē-vər\ *n* **1** : one that receives **2** : a person legally appointed to receive and have charge of property or money involved in a lawsuit **3** : a device for converting electromagnetic waves or signals into audio or visual form ⟨telephone ~⟩

re·ceiv·er·ship \-,ship\ *n* **1** : the office or function of a receiver **2** : the condition of being in the hands of a receiver

re·cen·cy \'rēs-ᵊn-sē\ *n* : RECENTNESS

re·cent \'rēs-ᵊnt\ *adj* **1** : of the present time or time just past ⟨~ history⟩ **2** : having lately come into existence : NEW, FRESH **3** *cap* : HOLOCENE — **re·cent·ly** *adv* — **re·cent·ness** *n*

re·cep·ta·cle \ri-'sep-ti-kəl\ *n* **1** : something used to receive and hold something else : CONTAINER **2** : the enlarged end of a flower stalk upon which the parts of the flower grow **3** : an electrical fitting containing the live parts of a circuit

re·cep·tion \ri-'sep-shən\ *n* **1** : the act of receiving **2** : a social gathering at which guests are formally welcomed

re·cep·tion·ist \ri-'sep-shə-nist\ *n* : a person employed to greet callers

re·cep·tive \ri-'sep-tiv\ *adj* : able or inclined to receive; *esp* : open and responsive to ideas, impressions, or suggestions — **re·cep·tive·ly** *adv* — **re·cep·tive·ness** *n* — **re·cep·tiv·i·ty** \,rē-,sep-'ti-və-tē\ *n*

re·cep·tor \ri-'sep-tər\ *n* **1** : one that receives; *esp* : SENSE ORGAN **2** : a chemical group or molecule in the outer cell membrane or in the cell interior that has an affinity for a specific chemical group, molecule, or virus

¹**re·cess** \'rē-,ses, ri-'ses\ *n* **1** : a secret or secluded place **2** : an indentation in a line or surface (as an alcove in a room) **3** : a suspension of business or procedure for rest or relaxation

²**recess** *vb* **1** : to put into a recess **2** : to make a recess in **3** : to interrupt for a recess **4** : to take a recess

re·ces·sion \ri-'se-shən\ *n* **1** : the act of receding : WITHDRAWAL **2** : a departing procession (as at the end of a church service) **3** : a period of reduced economic activity

re·ces·sion·al \ri-'se-shə-nəl\ *n* **1** : a hymn or musical piece at the conclusion of a service or program **2** : RECESSION 2

¹**re·ces·sive** \ri-'se-siv\ *adj* **1** : tending to recede **2** : producing or being a bodily characteristic that is masked or not expressed when a contrasting dominant gene or trait is present ⟨~ genes⟩ ⟨~ traits⟩

²**recessive** *n* : a recessive characteristic or gene; *also* : an individual that has one or more recessive characteristics

re·cher·ché \rə-,sher-'shā, -'sheər-,shā\ *adj* [F] **1** : CHOICE, RARE **2** : excessively refined

re·cid·i·vism \ri-'si-də-,vi-zəm\ *n* : a tendency to relapse into a previous condition; *esp* : relapse into criminal behavior — **re·cid·i·vist** \-vist\ *n*

recip *abbr* reciprocal; reciprocity

re·ci·pe \'re-sə-(,)pē\ *n* [L, take, imperative of *recipere* to take, receive, fr. *re-* back + *capere* to take] **1** : a set of instructions for making something from various ingredients **2** : a method of procedure : FORMULA

re·cip·i·ent \ri-'si-pē-ənt\ *n* : one that receives

¹**re·cip·ro·cal** \ri-'si-prə-kəl\ *adj* **1** : inversely related **2** : MUTUAL, SHARED **3** : serving to reciprocate **4** : mutually corresponding — **re·cip·ro·cal·ly** *adv*

²**reciprocal** *n* **1** : something in a reciprocal relationship to another **2** : one of a pair of numbers (as ⅔, 3⁄2) whose product is one

re·cip·ro·cate \-,kāt\ *vb* **-cat·ed; -cat·ing 1** : to move backward and forward alternately **2** : to give and take mutually **3** : to make a return for something done or given — **re·cip·ro·ca·tion** \-,si-prə-'kā-shən\ *n*

rec·i·proc·i·ty \,re-sə-'prä-sə-tē\ *n, pl* **-ties 1** : the quality or state of being reciprocal **2** : mutual exchange of privileges (as trade advantages between countries)

re·cit·al \ri-'sīt-ᵊl\ *n* **1** : an act or instance of reciting : ACCOUNT **2** : a public reading or recitation ⟨a poetry ~⟩ **3** : a concert given by a musician, dancer, or dance troupe **4** : a public exhibition of skill given by music or dance pupils — **re·cit·al·ist** \-ᵊl-ist\ *n*

rec·i·ta·tion \,re-sə-'tā-shən\ *n* **1** : RECITING, RECITAL **2** : delivery before an audience usu. of something memorized **3** : a classroom exercise in which pupils answer questions on a lesson they have studied

re·cite \ri-'sīt\ *vb* **re·cit·ed; re·cit·ing 1** : to repeat verbatim (as something memorized) **2** : to recount in some detail : RELATE **3** : to reply to a teacher's questions on a lesson — **re·cit·er** *n*

reck·less \'re-kləs\ *adj* : lacking caution : RASH **syn** hasty, brash, hotheaded, thoughtless — **reck·less·ly** *adv* — **reck·less·ness** *n*

reck·on \'re-kən\ *vb* **1** : COUNT, CALCULATE, COMPUTE **2** : CONSIDER, REGARD **3** *chiefly dial* : THINK, SUPPOSE, GUESS

reck·on·ing *n* **1** : an act or instance of reckoning **2** : a settling of accounts ⟨day of ~⟩

re·claim \ri-'klām\ *vb* **1** : to recall from wrong conduct : REFORM **2** : to change from an undesirable to a desired condition ⟨~ marshy land⟩ **3** : to obtain from a waste product or by-product **4** : to demand or obtain the return of — **re·claim·able** *adj* — **rec·la·ma·tion** \,re-klə-'mā-shən\ *n*

re·cline \ri-'klīn\ *vb* **re·clined; re·clin·ing 1** : to lean or incline backward **2** : to lie down : REST

re·clin·er \ri-'klī-nər\ *n* : a chair with an adjustable back and footrest

re·cluse \'re-,klüs, ri-'klüs\ *n* : a person who leads a secluded or solitary life : HERMIT

rec·og·nise *chiefly Brit var of* RECOGNIZE

rec·og·ni·tion \,re-kəg-'ni-shən\ *n* **1** : the act of recognizing : the state of being recognized : ACKNOWLEDGMENT **2** : special notice or attention

re·cog·ni·zance \ri-'käg-nə-zəns\ *n* : a promise recorded before a court or magistrate to do something (as to appear in court or to keep the peace) usu. under penalty of a money forfeiture

rec·og·nize \'re-kəg-,nīz\ *vb* **-nized; -niz·ing 1** : to acknowledge (as a speaker in a meeting) as one entitled to be heard at the time **2** : to acknowledge the existence or the independence of (a country or government) **3** : to take notice of **4** : to acknowledge with appreciation **5** : to acknowledge acquaintance with **6** : to identify as previously known **7** : to perceive clearly : REALIZE — **rec·og·niz·able** \'re-kəg-,nī-zə-bəl\ *adj* — **rec·og·niz·ably** \-blē\ *adv*

¹**re·coil** \ri-'kȯil\ *vb* **1** : to draw back : RETREAT **2** : to spring back to or as if to a starting point **syn** shrink, flinch, wince, quail, blanch

²**re·coil** \'rē-,kȯil, ri-'kȯil\ *n* : the action of recoiling (as by a gun or spring)

re·coil·less \-,kȯil-ləs, -'kȯil-ləs\ *adj* : venting expanding propellant gas before recoil is produced ⟨~ gun⟩

rec·ol·lect \,re-kə-'lekt\ *vb* : to recall to mind : REMEMBER **syn** recall, remind, reminisce, bethink

I WONDER HOW YOU MAKE THESE SEATS RECLINE

MAYBE THIS LITTLE BUTTON DOES THE TRICK

NOPE. THAT'S NOT IT

rec·ol·lec·tion \ˌre-kə-ˈlek-shən\ *n* **1** : the act or power of recollecting **2** : something recollected

re·com·bi·nant DNA \(ˌ)rē-ˈkäm-bə-nənt-\ *n* : genetically engineered DNA prepared in vitro by joining together DNA fragments usu. from more than one species of organism

rec·om·mend \ˌre-kə-ˈmend\ *vb* **1** : to present as deserving of acceptance or trial **2** : to give in charge : COMMIT **3** : to make acceptable **4** : ADVISE, COUNSEL — **rec·om·mend·able** \-ˈmen-də-bəl\ *adj*

rec·om·men·da·tion \ˌre-kə-mən-ˈdā-shən\ *n* **1** : the act of recommending **2** : something recommended **3** : something that recommends

¹rec·om·pense \ˈre-kəm-ˌpens\ *vb* **-pensed; -pens·ing 1** : to give compensation to : pay for **2** : to return in kind : REQUITE **syn** reimburse, indemnify, repay, compensate

²recompense *n* : COMPENSATION

rec·on·cile \ˈre-kən-ˌsīl\ *vb* **-ciled; -cil·ing 1** : to cause to be friendly or harmonious again **2** : ADJUST, SETTLE ⟨~ differences⟩ **3** : to bring to submission or acceptance **syn** conform, accommodate, harmonize, coordinate — **rec·on·cil·able** *adj* — **rec·on·cile·ment** *n* — **rec·on·cil·er** *n*

rec·on·cil·i·a·tion \ˌre-kən-ˌsi-lē-ˈā-shən\ *n* **1** : the action of reconciling **2** : the Roman Catholic sacrament of penance

re·con·dite \ˈre-kən-ˌdīt\ *adj* **1** : hard to understand : PROFOUND, ABSTRUSE **2** : little known : OBSCURE

re·con·di·tion \ˌrē-kən-ˈdi-shən\ *vb* **1** : to restore to good condition (as by replacing parts) **2** : to condition anew

re·con·nais·sance \ri-ˈkä-nə-zəns, -səns\ *n* [F, lit., recognition] : a preliminary survey of an area; *esp* : an exploratory military survey of enemy territory

re·con·noi·ter *or* **re·con·noi·tre** \ˌrē-kə-ˈnȯi-tər, ˌre-\ *vb* **-noi·tered** *or* **-noi·tred; -noi·ter·ing** *or* **-noi·tring** : to make a reconnaissance of : engage in reconnaissance

re·con·sid·er \ˌrē-kən-ˈsi-dər\ *vb* : to consider again with a view to changing or reversing — **re·con·sid·er·a·tion** \-ˌsi-də-ˈrā-shən\ *n*

re·con·sti·tute \ˌrē-ˈkän-stə-ˌtüt, -ˌtyüt\ *vb* : to restore to a former condition by adding water ⟨~ powdered milk⟩

re·con·struct \ˌrē-kən-ˈstrəkt\ *vb* : to construct again : REBUILD

re·con·struc·tion \ˌrē-kən-ˈstrək-shən\ *n* **1** : the action of reconstructing : the state of being reconstructed **2** *often cap* : the reorganization and reestablishment of the seceded states in the Union after the American Civil War **3** : something reconstructed

¹re·cord \ri-ˈkȯrd\ *vb* **1** : to set down in writing **2** : to register permanently **3** : INDICATE, READ **4** : to give evidence of **5** : to cause (as sound or visual images) to be registered (as on magnetic tape) in a form that permits reproduction

²rec·ord \ˈre-kərd\ *n* **1** : the act of being recorded **2** : a written account of proceedings **3** : known facts about a person; *also* : a collection of items of information (as in a database) treated as a unit **4** : an attested top performance **5** : something on which sound or visual images have been recorded

re·cord·er \ri-ˈkȯr-dər\ *n* **1** : a judge in some city courts **2** : one who records transactions officially **3** : a recording device **4** : a wind instrument with a whistle mouthpiece and eight fingerholes

re·cord·ing *n* : RECORD 5

re·cord·ist \ri-ˈkȯr-dist\ *n* : one who records sound esp. on film

¹re·count \ri-ˈkau̇nt\ *vb* : to relate in detail : TELL **syn** recite, rehearse, narrate, describe, state, report

²re·count \ˈrē-ˌkau̇nt, (ˌ)rē-ˈkau̇nt\ *vb* : to count again

³re·count \ˈrē-ˌkau̇nt, (ˌ)rē-ˈkau̇nt\ *n* : a second or fresh count

re·coup \ri-ˈküp\ *vb* : to get an equivalent or compensation for : make up for something lost

re·course \ˈrē-ˌkȯrs, ri-ˈkȯrs\ *n* **1** : a turning to someone or something for assistance or protection **2** : a source of aid : RESORT

re·cov·er \ri-ˈkə-vər\ *vb* **-ered; -er·ing 1** : to get back again : REGAIN, RETRIEVE **2** : to regain normal health, poise, or status **3** : to make up for : RECOUP ⟨~ed all his losses⟩ **4** : RECLAIM ⟨~ land from the sea⟩ **5** : to obtain a legal judgment in one's favor — **re·cov·er·able** *adj* — **re·cov·ery** \-ˈkə-və-rē\ *n*

re·cov·er \ˌrē-ˈkə-vər\ *vb* : to cover again

¹rec·re·ant \ˈre-krē-ənt\ *adj* [ME, fr. MF, fr. prp. of *recroire* to renounce one's cause in a trial by battle, fr. *re-* back + *croire* to believe, fr. L *credere*] **1** : COWARDLY **2** : UNFAITHFUL

²recreant *n* **1** : COWARD **2** : DESERTER

rec·re·ate \ˈre-krē-ˌāt\ *vb* **-at·ed; -at·ing 1** : to give new life or freshness to **2** : to take recreation — **rec·re·ative** \-ˌā-tiv\ *adj*

re·cre·ate \ˌrē-krē-ˈāt\ *vb* : to create again — **re·cre·ation** \-ˈā-shən\ *n* — **re·cre·ative** \-ˈā-tiv\ *adj*

rec·re·ation \ˌre-krē-ˈā-shən\ *n* : a refreshing of strength or spirits after work; *also* : a means of refreshment **syn** diversion, entertainment, amusement — **rec·re·ation·al** \-shə-nəl\ *adj*

recreational vehicle *n* : a vehicle designed for recreational use (as camping)

re·crim·i·na·tion \ri-ˌkri-mə-ˈnā-shən\ *n* : a retaliatory accusation — **re·crim·i·nate** \-ˈkri-mə-ˌnāt\ *vb* — **re·crim·i·na·tory** \-ˈkri-mə-nə-ˌtȯr-ē\ *adj*

re·cru·des·cence \ˌrē-krü-ˈdes-ᵊns\ *n* : a renewal or breaking out again esp. of something unhealthful or dangerous

¹re·cruit \ri-ˈkrüt\ *vb* **1** : to form or strengthen with new members ⟨~ an army⟩ **2** : to enlist as a member of an armed service **3** : to secure the services of **4** : to seek to enroll **5** : to restore or increase in health or vigor ⟨resting to ~ his strength⟩ — **re·cruit·er** *n* — **re·cruit·ment** *n*

²recruit *n* [F *recrute, recrue* fresh growth, new levy of soldiers, fr. MF, fr. *recroistre* to grow up again, fr. L *recrescere*] : a newcomer to an activity or field; *esp* : a newly enlisted member of the armed forces

rec sec *abbr* recording secretary

rect *abbr* **1** receipt **2** rectangle; rectangular **3** rectified

rec·tal \'rekt-ᵊl\ *adj* : of or relating to the rectum — **rec·tal·ly** *adv*

rect·an·gle \'rek-ˌtaŋ-gəl\ *n* : a 4-sided figure with four right angles; *esp* : one with adjacent sides of unequal length — **rect·an·gu·lar** \rek-'taŋ-gyə-lər\ *adj*

rec·ti·fi·er \'rek-tə-ˌfī-ər\ *n* : one that rectifies; *esp* : a device for converting alternating current into direct current

rec·ti·fy \'rek-tə-ˌfī\ *vb* **-fied; -fy·ing** : to make or set right : CORRECT **syn** emend, amend, mend, right — **rec·ti·fi·ca·tion** \ˌrek-tə-fə-'kā-shən\ *n*

rec·ti·lin·ear \ˌrek-tə-'li-nē-ər\ *adj* **1** : moving in a straight line ⟨∼ motion⟩ **2** : characterized by straight lines

rec·ti·tude \'rek-tə-ˌtüd, -ˌtyüd\ *n* **1** : moral integrity **2** : correctness of procedure **syn** virtue, goodness, morality, probity

rec·to \'rek-tō\ *n, pl* **rectos** : a right-hand page

rec·tor \'rek-tər\ *n* **1** : a priest or minister in charge of a parish **2** : the head of a university or school — **rec·to·ri·al** \rek-'tōr-ē-əl\ *adj*

rec·to·ry \'rek-tə-rē\ *n, pl* **-ries** : the residence of a rector or a parish priest

rec·tum \'rek-təm\ *n, pl* **rectums** *or* **rec·ta** \-tə\ [ME, fr. ML, fr. *rectum intestinum*, lit., straight intestine] : the last part of the intestine joining the colon and anus

re·cum·bent \ri-'kəm-bənt\ *adj* : lying down : RECLINING

re·cu·per·ate \ri-'kü-pə-ˌrāt-, -'kyü-\ *vb* **-at·ed; -at·ing** : to get back (as health or strength) : RECOVER — **re·cu·per·a·tion** \-ˌkü-pə-'rā-shən, -ˌkyü-\ *n* — **re·cu·per·a·tive** \-'kü-pə-ˌrā-tiv, -ˌkyü-\ *adj*

re·cur \ri-'kər\ *vb* **re·curred; re·cur·ring** **1** : to go or come back in thought or discussion **2** : to occur or appear again esp. after an interval : occur time after time — **re·cur·rence** \-'kər-əns\ *n* — **re·cur·rent** \-ənt\ *adj*

re·cy·cle \rē-'sī-kəl\ *vb* **1** : to pass again through a cycle of changes or treatment **2** : to process (as liquid body waste, glass, or cans) in order to regain materials for human use — **re·cy·cla·ble** \-k(ə)lə-bəl\ *adj* — **recycle** *n*

¹red \'red\ *adj* **red·der; red·dest** **1** : of the color red **2** : endorsing radical social or political change esp. by force **3** *often cap* : of or relating to the former U.S.S.R. or its allies — **red·ly** *adv* — **red·ness** *n*

²red *n* **1** : the color of blood or of the ruby **2** : a revolutionary in politics **3** *cap* : COMMUNIST **4** : the condition of showing a loss (in the ∼)

re·dact \ri-'dakt\ *vb* **1** : to put in writing : FRAME **2** : EDIT — **re·dac·tor** \-'dak-tər\ *n*

re·dac·tion \-'dak-shən\ *n* **1** : an act or instance of redacting **2** : EDITION

red alga *n* : any of a group of reddish usu. marine algae

red blood cell *n* : any of the hemoglobin-containing cells that carry oxygen from the lungs to the tissues and are responsible for the red color of vertebrate blood

red·breast \'red-ˌbrest\ *n* : ROBIN

red–carpet *adj* : marked by red-carpet courtesy

red cedar *n* : an American juniper with fragrant close-grained red wood; *also* : its wood

red clover *n* : a Eurasian clover with globe-shaped heads of reddish flowers widely cultivated for hay and forage

red·coat \'red-ˌkōt\ *n* : a British soldier esp. during the Revolutionary War

red·den \'red-ᵊn\ *vb* : to make or become red or reddish : FLUSH, BLUSH

red·dish \'re-dish\ *adj* : tinged with red — **red·dish·ness** *n*

re·deem \ri-'dēm\ *vb* [ME *redemen*, modif. of MF *redimer*, fr. L *redimere*, fr. *re-*, *red-* re- + *emere* to take,

buy] **1** : to recover (property) by discharging an obligation **2** : to ransom, free, or rescue by paying a price **3** : to free from the consequences of sin **4** : to remove the obligation of by payment ⟨the government ∼s savings bonds⟩; *also* : to convert into something of value **5** : to make good (a promise) by performing : FULFILL **6** : to atone for — **re·deem·able** *adj* — **re·deem·er** *n*

re·demp·tion \ri-'demp-shən\ *n* : the act of redeeming : the state of being redeemed — **re·demp·tive** \-tiv\ *adj* — **re·demp·to·ry** \-tə-rē\ *adj*

re·de·ploy \ˌrē-di-'plȯi\ *vb* **1** : to transfer from one area or activity to another **2** : to relocate men or equipment — **re·de·ploy·ment** *n*

red–eye \'red-ˌī\ *n* **1** : cheap whiskey **2** : a late night or overnight flight

red fox *n* : a fox with orange-red to reddish brown fur

red fox

red giant *n* : a very large star with a relatively low surface temperature

red–hand·ed \'red-'han-dəd\ *adv or adj* : in the act of committing a misdeed

red·head \-ˌhed\ *n* : a person having red hair — **red·head·ed** \-ˌhe-dəd\ *adj*

red herring *n* : a diversion intended to distract attention from the real issue

red–hot \'red-'hät\ *adj* **1** : extremely hot; *esp* : glowing with heat **2** : EXCITED, FURIOUS **3** : very new ⟨∼ news⟩

re·dial \'rē-ˌdīl\ *n* : a telephone function that automatically repeats the dialing of the last number called — **redial** *vb*

re·dis·trib·ute \ˌrē-də-'stri-byüt\ *vb* **1** : to alter the distribution of **2** : to spread to other areas — **re·dis·tri·bu·tion** \(ˌ)rē-ˌdis-trə-'byü-shən\ *n*

re·dis·trict \ˌrē-'dis-(ˌ)trikt\ *vb* : to organize into new territorial and esp. political divisions

red–let·ter \'red-ˌle-tər\ *adj* : of special significance : MEMORABLE

red–light district *n* : a district with many houses of prostitution

re·do \(ˌ)rē-'dü\ *vb* : to do over or again; *esp* : REDECORATE

red oak *n* : any of numerous American oaks with leaves usu. having spiny-tipped lobes and acorns that take two years to mature; *also* : the wood of a red oak

red·o·lent \'red-ᵊl-ənt\ *adj* **1** : FRAGRANT, AROMATIC **2** : having a specified fragrance ⟨a room ∼ of cooked cabbage⟩ **3** : REMINISCENT, SUGGESTIVE — **red·o·lence** \-əns\ *n* — **red·o·lent·ly** *adv*

re·dou·ble \(ˌ)rē-'də-bəl\ *vb* : to make twice as great in size or amount; *also* : INTENSIFY

re·doubt \ri-'daut\ *n* [F *redoute*, fr. It *ridotto*, fr. ML *reductus* secret place, fr. L, withdrawn, fr. *reducere* to lead back, fr. *re-* back + *ducere* to lead] : a small usu. temporary fortification

re·doubt·able \ri-'daù-tə-bəl\ *adj* [ME *redoutable*, fr. MF, fr. *redouter* to dread, fr. *re-* re- + *douter* to doubt] : arousing dread or fear : FORMIDABLE

re·dound \ri-'daund\ *vb* **1** : to have an effect **2** : to become added or transferred : ACCRUE

red pepper *n* : CAYENNE PEPPER

¹re·dress \ri-'dres\ *vb* **1** : to set right : REMEDY **2** : COMPENSATE **3** : to remove the cause of (a grievance) **4** : AVENGE

²**re·dress** *n* **1** : relief from distress **2** : means or possibility of seeking a remedy **3** : compensation for loss or injury **4** : an act or instance of redressing

red·shift \'red-ˌshift\ *n* : displacement of the spectrum of a heavenly body toward longer wavelength

red snapper *n* : any of various reddish fishes including several food fishes

red spider *n* : SPIDER MITE

red squirrel *n* : a common American squirrel with the upper parts chiefly red

red–tailed hawk \'red-ˌtāld-\ *n* : a common rodent≠eating hawk of eastern No. America with a rather short typically reddish tail

red tape *n* [fr. the red tape formerly used to bind legal documents in England] : official routine or procedure marked by excessive complexity which results in delay or inaction

red tide *n* : seawater discolored by the presence of large numbers of dinoflagellates which produce a toxin that renders infected shellfish poisonous

re·duce \ri-'düs, -'dyüs\ *vb* **re·duced; re·duc·ing 1** : LESSEN **2** : to bring to a specified state or condition ⟨*reduced* them to tears⟩ **3** : to put in a lower rank or grade **4** : CONQUER ⟨∼ a fort⟩ **5** : to bring into a certain order or classification **6** : to correct (as a fracture) by restoration of displaced parts **7** : to lessen one's weight *syn* decrease, diminish, abate, dwindle, recede — **re·duc·er** *n* — **re·duc·ible** \-'dü-sə-bəl, -'dyü-\ *adj*

re·duc·tion \ri-'dək-shən\ *n* **1** : the act of reducing : the state of being reduced **2** : something made by reducing **3** : the amount taken off in reducing something

re·dun·dan·cy \ri-'dən-dən-sē\ *n, pl* **-cies 1** : the quality or state of being redundant : SUPERFLUITY **2** : something redundant or in excess **3** : the use of surplus words

re·dun·dant \-dənt\ *adj* : exceeding what is needed or normal : SUPERFLUOUS; *esp* : using more words than necessary — **re·dun·dant·ly** *adv*

red–winged blackbird \'red-ˌwiŋd-\ *n* : a No. American blackbird of which the adult male is black with a patch of bright scarlet on the wings

red·wood \'red-ˌwüd\ *n* : a tall coniferous timber tree esp. of coastal California; *also* : its durable wood

reed \'rēd\ *n* **1** : any of various tall slender grasses of wet areas; *also* : a stem or growth of reed **2** : a musical instrument made from the hollow stem of a reed **3** : an elastic tongue of cane, wood, or metal by which tones are produced in organ pipes and certain other wind instruments — **reedy** *adj*

re·ed·u·cate \(ˌ)rē-'e-jə-ˌkāt\ *vb* : to train again; *esp* : to rehabilitate through education — **re·ed·u·ca·tion** *n*

¹**reef** \'rēf\ *n* **1** : a part of a sail taken in or let out in regulating the sail's size **2** : reduction in sail area by reefing

²**reef** *vb* : to reduce the area of a sail by rolling or folding part of it

³**reef** *n* : a ridge of rocks, sand or coral at or near the surface of the water

reef·er \'rē-fər\ *n* : a marijuana cigarette

¹**reek** \'rēk\ *n* : a strong or disagreeable fume or odor

²**reek** *vb* **1** : to give off or become permeated with a strong or offensive odor **2** : to give a strong impression of some constituent quality ⟨an excuse that ∼*ed* of falsehood⟩ — **reek·er** *n* — **reeky** \'rē-kē\ *adj*

¹**reel** \'rēl\ *n* : a revolvable device on which something flexible (as film or tape) is wound; *also* : a quantity of something wound on such a device

²**reel** *vb* **1** : to wind on or as if on a reel **2** : to pull or draw (as a fish) by reeling a line — **reel·able** *adj* — **reel·er** *n*

³**reel** *vb* **1** : WHIRL; *also* : to be giddy **2** : to waver or fall back (as from a blow) **3** : to walk or move unsteadily

⁴**reel** *n* : a reeling motion

⁵**reel** *n* : a lively Scottish dance or its music

reel off *vb* : to tell or recite rapidly and easily ⟨*reeled off* the right answers⟩

re·en·try \rē-'en-trē\ *n* **1** : a second or new entry **2** : the action of reentering the earth's atmosphere from space

reeve \'rēv\ *vb* **rove** \'rōv\ *or* **reeved; reev·ing** : to pass (as a rope) through a hole in a block or cleat

¹**ref** \'ref\ *n* : REFEREE **2**

²**ref** *abbr* **1** reference **2** referred **3** reformed **4** refunding

re·fec·tion \ri-'fek-shən\ *n* **1** : refreshment esp. after hunger or fatigue **2** : food and drink together : REPAST

re·fec·to·ry \ri-'fek-tə-rē\ *n, pl* **-ries** : a dining hall (as in a monastery or college)

re·fer \ri-'fər\ *vb* **re·ferred; re·fer·ring 1** : to assign to a certain source, cause, or relationship **2** : to direct or send to some person or place (as for information or help) **3** : to submit to someone else for consideration or action **4** : to have recourse (as for information or aid) **5** : to have connection : RELATE **6** : to direct attention : speak of : MENTION, ALLUDE *syn* recur, repair, resort, apply, go, turn — **re·fer·able** \'re-fə-rə-bəl, ri-'fər-ə-\ *adj*

¹**ref·er·ee** \ˌre-fə-'rē\ *n* **1** : a person to whom an issue esp. in law is referred for investigation or settlement **2** : an umpire in certain games

²**referee** *vb* **-eed; -ee·ing** : to act as referee

ref·er·ence \'re-frəns, -fə-rəns\ *n* **1** : the act of referring **2** : RELATION, RESPECT **3** : ALLUSION, MENTION **4** : something that refers a reader to another passage or book **5** : consultation esp. for obtaining information ⟨books for ∼⟩ **6** : a person of whom inquiries as to character or ability can be made **7** : a written recommendation of a person for employment

ref·er·en·dum \ˌre-fə-'ren-dəm\ *n, pl* **-da** \-də\ *or* **-dums** : the submitting of legislative measures to the voters for approval or rejection; *also* : a vote on a measure so submitted

ref·er·ent \'re-frənt, -fə-rənt\ *n* : one that refers or is referred to; *esp* : the thing a word stands for — **referent** *adj*

re·fer·ral \ri-'fər-əl\ *n* **1** : the act or an instance of referring **2** : one that is referred

¹**re·fill** \rē-'fil\ *vb* : to fill again : REPLENISH — **re·fill·able** *adj*

²**re·fill** \'rē-ˌfil\ *n* : a new or fresh supply of something

re·fi·nance \ˌrē-fə-'nans, (ˌ)rē-'fī-nans\ *vb* : to renew or reorganize the financing of

re·fine \ri-'fīn\ *vb* **re·fined; re·fin·ing 1** : to free from impurities or waste matter **2** : IMPROVE, PERFECT **3** : to free or become free of what is coarse or uncouth **4** : to make improvements by introducing subtle changes — **re·fin·er** *n*

re·fined \ri-'fīnd\ *adj* **1** : freed from impurities **2** : CULTURED, CULTIVATED **3** : SUBTLE

re·fine·ment \ri-'fīn-mənt\ *n* **1** : the action of refining **2** : the quality or state of being refined **3** : a refined feature or method; *also* : something intended to improve or perfect

re·fin·ery \ri-'fī-nə-rē\ *n, pl* **-er·ies** : a building and equipment for refining metals, oil, or sugar

refl *abbr* reflex; reflexive

re·flect \ri-'flekt\ *vb* [ME, fr. L *reflectere* to bend back, fr. *re-* back + *flectere* to bend] **1** : to bend or cast back (as light, heat, or sound) **2** : to give back a likeness or image of as a mirror does **3** : to bring as a result ⟨∼*ed* credit on him⟩ **4** : to cast reproach or blame ⟨their bad conduct ∼*ed* on their training⟩ **5** : PONDER, MEDITATE — **re·flec·tion** \-'flek-shən\ *n* — **re·flec·tive** \-tiv\ *adj* — **re·flec·tiv·i·ty** \(ˌ)rē-ˌflek-'ti-və-tē\ *n*

re·flec·tor \ri-'flek-tər\ *n* : one that reflects; *esp* : a polished surface for reflecting radiation (as light)

¹**re•flex** \'rē-₁fleks\ n 1 : an automatic and usu. inborn response to a stimulus not involving higher mental centers 2 pl : the power of acting or responding with enough speed ⟨an athlete with great ∼es⟩

²**reflex** adj 1 : bent or directed back 2 : of, relating to, or produced by a reflex — **re•flex•ly** adv

re•flex•ion chiefly Brit var of REFLECTION

¹**re•flex•ive** \ri-'flek-siv\ adj : of or relating to an action directed back upon the doer or the grammatical subject ⟨a ∼ verb⟩ ⟨the ∼ pronoun himself⟩ — **re•flex•ive•ly** adv — **re•flex•ive•ness** n

²**reflexive** n : a reflexive verb or pronoun

re•fo•cus \(₁)rē-'fō-kəs\ vb 1 : to focus again 2 : to change the emphasis or direction of ⟨∼ed her life⟩

re•for•es•ta•tion \₁rē-₁fôr-ə-'stā-shən\ n : the action of renewing forest cover by planting seeds or young trees — **re•for•est** \rē-'fôr-əst\ vb

¹**re•form** \ri-'fôrm\ vb 1 : to make better or improve by removal of faults 2 : to correct or improve one's own character or habits syn correct, rectify, emend, remedy, redress, revise — **re•form•able** adj — **re•for•ma•tive** \-'fôr-mə-tiv\ adj

²**reform** n : improvement or correction of what is corrupt or defective

re–form \rē-'fôrm\ vb : to form again

ref•or•ma•tion \₁re-fər-'mā-shən\ n 1 : the act of reforming : the state of being reformed 2 cap : a 16th century religious movement marked by the establishment of the Protestant churches

¹**re•for•ma•to•ry** \ri-'fôr-mə-₁tôr-ē\ adj : aiming at or tending toward reformation : REFORMATIVE

²**reformatory** n, pl -ries : a penal institution for reforming esp. young or first offenders

re•form•er \ri-'fôr-mər\ n 1 : one that works for or urges reform 2 cap : a leader of the Protestant Reformation

refr abbr refraction

re•fract \ri-'frakt\ vb [L refractus, pp. of refringere to break open, break up, fr. re- back + frangere to break] : to subject to refraction

re•frac•tion \ri-'frak-shən\ n : the bending of a ray (as of light) when it passes obliquely from one medium into another in which its speed is different — **re•frac•tive** \-tiv\ adj

re•frac•to•ry \ri-'frak-tə-rē\ adj 1 : OBSTINATE, STUBBORN, UNMANAGEABLE 2 : capable of enduring high temperature ⟨∼ bricks⟩ syn recalcitrant, intractable, ungovernable, unruly, headstrong, willful — **re•frac•to•ri•ness** \ri-'frak-tə-rē-nəs\ n — **refractory** n

¹**re•frain** \ri-'frān\ vb : to hold oneself back : FORBEAR — **re•frain•ment** n

²**refrain** n : a phrase or verse recurring regularly in a poem or song

re•fresh \ri-'fresh\ vb 1 : to make or become fresh or fresher 2 : to revive by or as if by renewal of supplies ⟨∼ one's memory⟩ 3 : to freshen up 4 : to supply or take refreshment syn restore, rejuvenate, renovate,

refurbish — **re•fresh•er** n — **re•fresh•ing•ly** adv

re•fresh•ment \-mənt\ n 1 : the act of refreshing : the state of being refreshed 2 : something that refreshes 3 pl : a light meal; also : assorted light foods

re•fried beans \'rē-₁frīd-\ n pl : beans cooked with seasonings, fried, then mashed and fried again

refrig abbr refrigerating; refrigeration

re•frig•er•ate \ri-'frij-ə-₁rāt\ vb -at•ed; -at•ing : to make cool; esp : to chill or freeze (food) for preservation — **re•frig•er•ant** \-jə-rənt\ adj or n — **re•frig•er•a•tion** \-₁fri-jə-'rā-shən\ n — **re•frig•er•a•tor** \-'fri-jə-₁rā-tər\ n

ref•uge \'re-₁fyüj\ n 1 : shelter or protection from danger or distress 2 : a place that provides protection

ref•u•gee \₁re-fyü-'jē\ n : one who flees for safety esp. to a foreign country

re•ful•gence \ri-'ful-jəns, -'fəl-\ n : a radiant or resplendent quality or state — **re•ful•gent** \-jənt\ adj

¹**re•fund** \ri-'fənd, 'rē-₁fənd\ vb : to give or put back (money) : REPAY — **re•fund•able** adj

²**refund** \'rē-₁fənd\ n 1 : the act of refunding 2 : a sum refunded

re•fur•bish \ri-'fər-bish\ vb : to brighten or freshen up : RENOVATE

¹**re•fuse** \ri-'fyüz\ vb **re•fused; re•fus•ing** 1 : to decline to accept : REJECT 2 : to decline to do, give, or grant : DENY — **re•fus•al** \-'fyü-zəl\ n

²**ref•use** \'re-₁fyüs, -₁fyüz\ n : rejected or worthless matter : RUBBISH, TRASH

re•fute \ri-'fyüt\ vb **re•fut•ed; re•fut•ing** [L refutare to check, suppress, refute] : to prove to be false by argument or evidence — **ref•u•ta•tion** \₁re-fyü-'tā-shən\ n — **re•fut•er** n

¹**reg** \'reg\ n : REGULATION

²**reg** abbr 1 region 2 register; registered; registration 3 regular

re•gal \'rē-gəl\ adj 1 : of, relating to, or befitting a king : ROYAL 2 : STATELY, SPLENDID — **re•gal•ly** adv

re•gale \ri-'gāl\ vb **re•galed; re•gal•ing** 1 : to entertain richly or agreeably 2 : to give pleasure or amusement to syn gratify, delight, please, rejoice, gladden

re•ga•lia \ri-'gāl-yə\ n pl 1 : the emblems, symbols, or paraphernalia of royalty (as the crown and scepter) 2 : the insignia of an office or order 3 : special costume : FINERY

¹**re•gard** \ri-'gärd\ n 1 : CONSIDERATION, HEED; also : CARE, CONCERN 2 : GAZE, GLANCE, LOOK 3 : RESPECT, ESTEEM 4 pl : friendly greetings implying respect and esteem 5 : an aspect to be considered : PARTICULAR — **re•gard•ful** adj — **re•gard•less** adj

²**regard** vb 1 : to think of : CONSIDER 2 : to pay attention to 3 : to show respect for : HEED 4 : to hold in high esteem : care for 5 : to look at : gaze upon 6 archaic : to relate to

re•gard•ing prep : CONCERNING

regardless of \ri-'gärd-ləs-\ prep : in spite of

re•gat•ta \ri-'gä-tə, -'ga-\ n : a boat race or a series of boat races

regd abbr registered

re•gen•cy \'rē-jən-sē\ n, pl -cies 1 : the office or government of a regent or body of regents **2** : a body of regents **3** : the period during which a regent governs

re·gen·er·a·cy \ri-ˈje-nə-rə-sē\ *n* : the state of being regenerated

¹re·gen·er·ate \ri-ˈje-nə-rət\ *adj* **1** : formed or created again **2** : spiritually reborn or converted

²re·gen·er·ate \ri-ˈje-nə-ˌrāt\ *vb* **1** : to subject to spiritual renewal **2** : to reform completely **3** : to replace (a body part) by a new growth of tissue **4** : to give new life to : REVIVE — **re·gen·er·a·tion** \-ˌje-nə-ˈrā-shən\ *n* — **re·gen·er·a·tive** \-ˈje-nə-ˌrā-tiv\ *adj* — **re·gen·er·a·tor** \-ˌrā-tər\ *n*

re·gent \ˈrē-jənt\ *n* **1** : a person who rules during the childhood, absence, or incapacity of the sovereign **2** : a member of a governing board (as of a state university) — **regent** *adj*

reg·gae \ˈre-ˌgā\ *n* : popular music of Jamaican origin that combines native styles with elements of rock and soul music

reg·i·cide \ˈre-jə-ˌsīd\ *n* **1** : one who murders a king **2** : murder of a king

re·gime *also* **ré·gime** \rā-ˈzhēm, ri-\ *n* **1** : REGIMEN **2** : a form or system of government **3** : a government in power; *also* : a period of rule

reg·i·men \ˈre-jə-mən\ *n* **1** : a systematic course of treatment or training ⟨a strict dietary ∼⟩ **2** : GOVERNMENT

¹reg·i·ment \ˈre-jə-mənt\ *n* : a military unit consisting usu. of a number of battalions — **reg·i·men·tal** \ˌre-jə-ˈment-təl\ *adj*

²reg·i·ment \ˈre-jə-ˌment\ *vb* : to organize rigidly esp. for regulation or central control; *also* : to subject to order or uniformity — **reg·i·men·ta·tion** \ˌre-jə-mən-ˈtā-shən\ *n*

reg·i·men·tals \ˌre-jə-ˈmen-təlz\ *n pl* **1** : a regimental uniform **2** : military dress

re·gion \ˈrē-jən\ *n* [ME, fr. MF, fr. L *region-, regio*, fr. *regere* to rule] : an often indefinitely defined part or area

re·gion·al \ˈrē-jə-nəl\ *adj* **1** : affecting a particular region : LOCALIZED **2** : of, relating to, characteristic of, or serving a region — **re·gion·al·ly** *adv*

¹reg·is·ter \ˈre-jə-stər\ *n* **1** : a record of items or details; *also* : a book or system for keeping such a record **2** : the range of a voice or instrument **3** : a device to regulate ventilation or heating **4** : an automatic device recording a number or quantity

²register *vb* **-tered; -ter·ing 1** : to enter in a register (as in a list of guests) **2** : to record automatically **3** : to secure special care for (mail matter) by paying additional postage **4** : to convey an impression of : EXPRESS **5** : to make or adjust so as to correspond exactly

registered nurse *n* : a graduate trained nurse who has been licensed to practice by a state authority after passing qualifying examinations

reg·is·trant \ˈre-jə-strənt\ *n* : one that registers or is registered

reg·is·trar \-ˌsträr\ *n* : an official recorder or keeper of records (as at an educational institution)

reg·is·tra·tion \ˌre-jə-ˈstrā-shən\ *n* **1** : the act of registering **2** : an entry in a register **3** : the number of persons registered : ENROLLMENT **4** : a document certifying an act of registering

reg·is·try \ˈre-jə-strē\ *n, pl* **-tries 1** : ENROLLMENT, REGISTRATION **2** : a place of registration **3** : an official record book or an entry in one

reg·nant \ˈreg-nənt\ *adj* **1** : REIGNING **2** : DOMINANT **3** : of common or widespread occurrence

¹re·gress \ˈrē-ˌgres\ *n* **1** : an act or the privilege of going or coming back **2** : RETROGRESSION

²re·gress \ri-ˈgres\ *vb* : to go or cause to go back or to a lower level — **re·gres·sive** *adj* — **re·gres·sor** \-ˈgre-sər\ *n*

re·gres·sion \ri-ˈgre-shən\ *n* : the act or an instance of

regressing; *esp* : reversion to an earlier mental or behavioral level

¹re·gret \ri-ˈgret\ *vb* **re·gret·ted; re·gret·ting 1** : to mourn the loss or death of **2** : to be very sorry for **3** : to experience regret — **re·gret·ta·ble** \-ˈgre-tə-bəl\ *adj* — **re·gret·ter** *n*

²regret *n* **1** : sorrow caused by something beyond one's power to remedy **2** : an expression of sorrow **3** *pl* : a note politely declining an invitation — **re·gret·ful** \-fəl\ *adj* — **re·gret·ful·ly** *adv*

re·gret·ta·bly \-ˈgre-tə-blē\ *adv* **1** : to a regrettable extent **2** : it is to be regretted

re·group \(ˌ)rē-ˈgrüp\ *vb* : to form into a new grouping

regt *abbr* regiment

¹reg·u·lar \ˈre-gyə-lər\ *adj* [ME *reguler*, fr. MF, fr. LL *regularis* regular, fr L, of a bar, fr. *regula* rule, straightedge, fr. *regere* to keep straight, rule] **1** : belonging to a religious order **2** : made, built, or arranged according to a rule, standard, or type; *also* : even or symmetrical in form or structure **3** : ORDERLY, METHODICAL ⟨∼ habits⟩; *also* : not varying : STEADY ⟨a ∼ pace⟩ **4** : made, selected, or conducted according to rule or custom **5** : properly qualified (not a ∼ lawyer⟩ **6** : conforming to the normal or usual manner or inflection **7** : of, relating to, or constituting the permanent standing military force of a state — **reg·u·lar·i·ty** \ˌre-gyə-ˈlar-ə-tē\ *n* — **reg·u·lar·ize** \ˈre-gyə-lə-ˌrīz\ *vb* — **reg·u·lar·ly** *adv*

²regular *n* **1** : one that is regular (as in attendance) **2** : a member of the regular clergy **3** : a soldier in a regular army **4** : a player on an athletic team who is usu. in the starting lineup

reg·u·late \ˈre-gyə-ˌlāt\ *vb* **-lat·ed; -lat·ing 1** : to govern or direct according to rule : CONTROL **2** : to bring under the control of law or authority **3** : to put in good order **4** : to fix or adjust the time, amount, degree, or rate of — **reg·u·la·tive** \-ˌlā-tiv\ *adj* — **reg·u·la·tor** \-ˌlā-tər\ *n* — **reg·u·la·to·ry** \-lə-ˌtōr-ē\ *adj*

reg·u·la·tion \ˌre-gyə-ˈlā-shən\ *n* **1** : the act of regulating; the state of being regulated **2** : a rule dealing with details of procedure **3** : an order issued by an executive authority of a government and having the force of law

re·gur·gi·tate \rē-ˈgər-jə-ˌtāt\ *vb* **-tat·ed; -tat·ing** [ML *regurgitare*, fr. L *re-* re- + LL *gurgitare* to engulf, fr. L *gurgit-, gurges* whirlpool] : to throw or be thrown back, up, or out ⟨∼ food⟩ — **re·gur·gi·ta·tion** \-ˌgər-jə-ˈtā-shən\ *n*

re·hab \ˈrē-ˌhab\ *n* **1** : REHABILITATION **2** : a rehabilitated building — **rehab** *vb*

re·ha·bil·i·tate \ˌrē-hə-ˈbi-lə-ˌtāt, ˌrē-ə-\ *vb* **-tat·ed; -tat·ing 1** : to restore to a former capacity, rank, or right : REINSTATE **2** : to restore to good condition or health — **re·ha·bil·i·ta·tion** \-ˌbi-lə-ˈtā-shən\ *n* — **re·ha·bil·i·ta·tive** \-ˌtā-tiv\ *adj*

re·hash \ˈrē-ˈhash\ *vb* : to present again in another form without real change or improvement — **rehash** *n*

re·hear·ing \ˈrē-ˈhir-iŋ\ *n* : a second or new hearing by the same tribunal

re·hears·al \ri-ˈhər-səl\ *n* **1** : something told again : RECITAL **2** : a private performance or practice session preparatory to a public appearance

re·hearse \ri-ˈhərs\ *vb* **re·hearsed; re·hears·ing 1** : to say again : REPEAT **2** : to recount in order : ENUMERATE; *also* : RELATE 1 **3** : to give a rehearsal of **4** : to train by rehearsal **5** : to engage in a rehearsal — **re·hears·er** *n*

¹reign \ˈrān\ *n* **1** : the authority or rule of a sovereign **2** : the time during which a sovereign rules

²reign *vb* **1** : to rule as a sovereign **2** : to be predominant or prevalent

re·im·burse \ˌrē-əm-ˈbərs\ *vb* **-bursed; -burs·ing** [*re-* + obs. E *imburse* to put in the pocket, pay, fr. ML *imbursare* to put into a purse, fr. L *in-* in + ML *bursa* purse, fr. LL, hide of an ox, fr. Gk *byrsa*] : to pay back : make restitution : REPAY **syn** indemnify, recompense, requite, compensate — **re·im·burs·able** *adj* — **re·im·burse·ment** *n*

¹**rein** \\ˈrān\\ *n* **1** : a strap fastened to a bit by which a rider or driver controls an animal **2** : a restraining influence : CHECK **3** : controlling or guiding power **4** : complete freedom — usu. used in the phrase *give rein to*

²**rein** *vb* : to check or direct by reins

re·in·car·na·tion \\ˌrē-(ˌ)in-(ˌ)kär-ˈnā-shən\\ *n* : rebirth of the soul in a new body — **re·in·car·nate** \\ˌrē-in-ˈkär-ˌnāt\\ *vb*

rein·deer \\ˈrān-ˌdir\\ *n* [ME *reindere*, fr. ON *hreinn* reindeer + ME *deer*] : CARIBOU — used esp. for the Old World caribou

reindeer moss *n* : a gray, erect, tufted, and much-branched edible lichen of northern regions that is an important food of reindeer

re·in·fec·tion \\ˌrē-in-ˈfek-shən\\ *n* : infection following another infection of the same type

re·in·force \\ˌrē-ən-ˈfōrs\\ *vb* **1** : to strengthen with additional forces ⟨∼ our troops⟩ **2** : to strengthen with new force, aid, material, or support — **re·in·force·ment** *n* — **re·in·forc·er** *n*

re·in·state \\ˌrē-in-ˈstāt\\ *vb* **-stat·ed; -stat·ing** : to restore to a former position, condition, or capacity — **re·in·state·ment** *n*

re·in·vent \\ˌrē-in-ˈvent\\ *vb* **1** : to make as if for the first time something already invented ⟨∼ the wheel⟩ **2** : to remake completely

re·it·er·ate \\rē-ˈi-tə-ˌrāt\\ *vb* **-at·ed; -at·ing** : to state or do over again or repeatedly — **re·it·er·a·tion** \\-ˌi-tə-ˈrā-shən\\ *n*

¹**re·ject** \\ri-ˈjekt\\ *vb* **1** : to refuse to accept, consider, use, or submit to **2** : to refuse to hear, receive, or admit : REPEL **3** : to rebuff or withhold love from **4** : to throw out esp. as useless or unsatisfactory **5** : to subject to the immunological process of sloughing off (foreign tissue) — **re·jec·tion** \\-ˈjek-shən\\ *n*

²**re·ject** \\ˈrē-ˌjekt\\ *n* : a rejected person or thing

re·joice \\ri-ˈjȯis\\ *vb* **re·joiced; re·joic·ing 1** : to give joy to : GLADDEN **2** : to feel joy or great delight — **re·joic·er** *n*

re·join \\(ˌ)rē-ˈjȯin *for 1,* ri-*for 2*\\ *vb* **1** : to join again **2** : to say in answer (as to a plaintiff's plea in court) : REPLY

re·join·der \\ri-ˈjȯin-dər\\ *n* : REPLY; *esp* : an answer to a reply

re·ju·ve·nate \\ri-ˈjü-və-ˌnāt\\ *vb* **-nat·ed; -nat·ing** : to make young or youthful again : give new vigor to **syn** renew, refresh, renovate, restore — **re·ju·ve·na·tion** \\-ˌjü-və-ˈnā-shən\\ *n*

rel *abbr* **1** relating; relative **2** religion; religious

¹**re·lapse** \\ri-ˈlaps, ˈrē-ˌlaps\\ *n* **1** : the act or process of backsliding or worsening **2** : a recurrence of illness after a period of improvement

²**re·lapse** \\ri-ˈlaps\\ *vb* **re·lapsed; re·laps·ing** : to slip or fall back into a former worse state (as of illness)

re·late \\ri-ˈlāt\\ *vb* **re·lat·ed; re·lat·ing 1** : to give an account of : TELL, NARRATE **2** : to show or establish

logical or causal connection between **3** : to have relationship or connection **4** : to have or establish relationship ⟨the way a child ∼s to a teacher⟩ **5** : to respond favorably — **re·lat·able** *adj* — **re·lat·er** *or* **re·la·tor** \\-ˈlā-tər\\ *n*

re·lat·ed *adj* **1** : connected by some understood relationship **2** : connected through membership in the same family — **re·lat·ed·ness** *n*

re·la·tion \\ri-ˈlā-shən\\ *n* **1** : NARRATION, ACCOUNT **2** : CONNECTION, RELATIONSHIP **3** : connection by blood or marriage : KINSHIP; *also* : RELATIVE **4** : REFERENCE, RESPECT (in ∼ to) **5** : the state of being mutually interested or involved (as in social or commercial matters) **6** *pl* : DEALINGS, AFFAIRS **7** *pl* : SEXUAL INTERCOURSE — **re·la·tion·al** \\-shə-nəl\\ *adj*

re·la·tion·ship \\-ˌship\\ *n* : the state of being related or interrelated

¹**rel·a·tive** \\ˈre-lə-tiv\\ *n* **1** : a word referring grammatically to an antecedent **2** : a thing having a relation to or a dependence upon another thing **3** : a person connected with another by blood or marriage

²**relative** *adj* **1** : introducing a subordinate clause qualifying an expressed or implied antecedent ⟨∼ pronoun⟩; *also* : introduced by such a connective ⟨∼ clause⟩ **2** : PERTINENT, RELEVANT **3** : not absolute or independent : COMPARATIVE **4** : expressed as the ratio of the specified quantity to the total magnitude or to the mean of all quantities involved **syn** dependent, contingent, conditional — **rel·a·tive·ly** *adv* — **rel·a·tive·ness** *n*

relative humidity *n* : the ratio of the amount of water vapor actually present in the air to the greatest amount possible at the same temperature

rel·a·tiv·is·tic \\ˌre-lə-ti-ˈvis-tik\\ *adj* **1** : of, relating to, or characterized by relativity **2** : moving at a velocity that is a significant fraction of the speed of light so that effects predicted by the theory of relativity become evident ⟨a ∼ electron⟩ — **rel·a·tiv·is·ti·cal·ly** \\-ti-k(ə-)lē\\ *adv*

rel·a·tiv·i·ty \\ˌre-lə-ˈti-və-tē\\ *n, pl* **-ties 1** : the quality or state of being relative **2** : a theory in physics that considers mass and energy to be equivalent and that predicts changes in mass, dimension, and time which are related to speed but are noticeable esp. at speeds approaching that of light

re·lax \\ri-ˈlaks\\ *vb* **1** : to make or become less firm, tense, or rigid **2** : to make less severe or strict **3** : to seek rest or recreation — **re·lax·er** *n*

¹**re·lax·ant** \\ri-ˈlak-sənt\\ *adj* : of, relating to, or producing relaxation

²**relaxant** *n* : a relaxing agent; *esp* : a drug that induces muscular relaxation

re·lax·ation \\ˌrē-ˌlak-ˈsā-shən\\ *n* **1** : the act of relaxing or state of being relaxed : a lessening of tension **2** : DIVERSION, RECREATION

¹**re·lay** \\ˈrē-ˌlā\\ *n* **1** : a fresh supply (as of horses or men) arranged beforehand to relieve others **2** : a race

between teams in which each team member covers a specified part of a course **3** : an electromagnetic device in which the opening or closing of one circuit activates another device (as a switch in another circuit) **4** : the act of passing along by stages

²re·lay \'rē-ˌlā, ri-'lā\ *vb* **re·layed; re·lay·ing 1** : to place in or provide with relays **2** : to pass along by relays **3** : to control or operate by a relay

³re·lay \(ˌ)rē-'lā\ *vb* **-laid** \-'lād\; **-lay·ing** : to lay again

¹re·lease \ri-'lēs\ *vb* **re·leased; re·leas·ing 1** : to set free from confinement or restraint; *also* : DISMISS **2** : to relieve from something that oppresses, confines, or burdens **3** : RELINQUISH ⟨∼ a claim⟩ **4** : to permit publication, performance, exhibition, or sale of; *also* : to make available to the public **syn** emancipate, discharge, free, liberate

²release *n* **1** : relief or deliverance from sorrow, suffering, or trouble **2** : discharge from an obligation or responsibility **3** : an act of setting free : the state of being freed **4** : a document effecting a legal release **5** : a releasing for performance or publication; *also* : the matter released (as to the press) **6** : a device for holding or releasing a mechanism as required

rel·e·gate \'re-lə-ˌgāt\ *vb* **-gat·ed; -gat·ing 1** : to send into exile : BANISH **2** : to remove or dismiss to some less prominent position **3** : to assign to a particular class or sphere **4** : to submit to someone or something for appropriate action : DELEGATE **syn** commit, entrust, consign, commend — **rel·e·ga·tion** \ˌre-lə-'gā-shən\ *n*

re·lent \ri-'lent\ *vb* **1** : to become less stern, severe, or harsh **2** : SLACKEN

re·lent·less \-ləs\ *adj* : showing or promising no abatement of severity, intensity, or pace ⟨∼ pressure⟩ — **re·lent·less·ly** *adv* — **re·lent·less·ness** *n*

rel·e·vance \'re-lə-vəns\ *n* : relation to the matter at hand; *also* : practical and esp. social applicability

rel·e·van·cy \-vən-sē\ *n* : RELEVANCE

rel·e·vant \'re-lə-vənt\ *adj* : bearing on the matter at hand : PERTINENT **syn** germane, material, applicable, apropos — **rel·e·vant·ly** *adv*

re·li·able \ri-'lī-ə-bəl\ *adj* : fit to be trusted or relied on : DEPENDABLE, TRUSTWORTHY — **re·li·abil·i·ty** \-ˌlī-ə-'bi-lə-tē\ *n* — **re·li·able·ness** *n* — **re·li·ably** \-'lī-ə-blē\ *adv*

re·li·ance \ri-'lī-əns\ *n* **1** : the act of relying **2** : the state of being reliant **3** : one relied on

re·li·ant \ri-'lī-ənt\ *adj* : having reliance on someone or something : DEPENDENT

rel·ic \'re-lik\ *n* **1** : an object venerated because of its association with a saint or martyr **2** : SOUVENIR, MEMENTO **3** *pl* : REMAINS, RUINS **4** : a remaining trace : VESTIGE

rel·ict \'re-likt\ *n* : WIDOW

re·lief \ri-'lēf\ *n* **1** : removal or lightening of something oppressive, painful, or distressing **2** : WELFARE 2 **3** : military assistance to an endangered post or force **4** : release from a post or from performance of a duty; *also* : one that takes the place of another on duty **5** : legal remedy or redress **6** : projection of figures or ornaments from the background (as in sculpture) **7** : the elevations of a land surface

relief pitcher *n* : a baseball pitcher who takes over for another during a game

re·lieve \ri-'lēv\ *vb* **re·lieved; re·liev·ing 1** : to free partly or wholly from a burden or from distress **2** : to bring about the removal or alleviation of : MITIGATE **3** : to release from a post or duty; *also* : to take the place of **4** : to break the monotony of **5** : to discharge the bladder or bowels of (oneself) **syn** alleviate, lighten, assuage, allay — **re·liev·er** *n*

relig *abbr* religion

re·li·gion \ri-'li-jən\ *n* **1** : the service and worship of God or the supernatural **2** : devotion to a religious faith **3** : a personal set or institutionalized system of religious beliefs, attitudes, and practices **4** : a cause,

principle, or belief held to with faith and ardor — **re·li·gion·ist** *n*

¹re·li·gious \ri-'li-jəs\ *adj* **1** : relating or devoted to an acknowledged ultimate reality or deity **2** : of or relating to religious beliefs or observances **3** : scrupulously and conscientiously faithful **4** : FERVENT, ZEALOUS — **re·li·gious·ly** *adv*

²religious *n*, *pl* **religious** : a member of a religious order under monastic vows

re·lin·quish \ri-'liŋ-kwish, -'lin-\ *vb* **1** : to withdraw or retreat from : ABANDON, QUIT **2** : GIVE UP ⟨∼ a title⟩ **3** : to let go of : RELEASE **syn** yield, leave, resign, surrender, cede, waive — **re·lin·quish·ment** *n*

rel·i·quary \'re-lə-ˌkwer-ē\ *n*, *pl* **-quar·ies** : a container for religious relics

¹rel·ish \'re-lish\ *n* [ME *reles* taste, fr. OF, something left behind, release, fr. *relessier* to relax, release, fr. L *relaxare*] **1** : characteristic flavor : SAVOR **2** : keen enjoyment or delight in something : GUSTO **3** : APPETITE, INCLINATION **4** : a highly seasoned sauce (as of pickles) eaten with other food to add flavor

²relish *vb* **1** : to add relish to **2** : to take pleasure in : ENJOY **3** : to eat with pleasure — **rel·ish·able** *adj*

re·live \rē-'liv\ *vb* : to live again or over again; *esp* : to experience again in the imagination

re·lo·cate \(ˌ)rē-'lō-ˌkāt, ˌrē-lō-'kāt\ *vb* **1** : to locate again **2** : to move to a new location — **re·lo·ca·tion** \ˌrē-lō-'kā-shən\ *n*

re·luc·tant \ri-'lək-tənt\ *adj* : feeling or showing aversion, hesitation or unwillingness ⟨∼ to get involved⟩ **syn** disinclined, indisposed, hesitant, loath, averse — **re·luc·tance** \-təns\ *n* — **re·luc·tant·ly** *adv*

re·ly \ri-'lī\ *vb* **re·lied; re·ly·ing** [ME *relien* to rally, fr. MF *relier* to connect, rally, fr. L *religare* to tie back, fr. *re-* back + *ligare* to tie] : to place faith or confidence in : DEPEND

REM \'rem\ *n* : RAPID EYE MOVEMENT

re·main \ri-'mān\ *vb* **1** : to be left after others have been removed, subtracted, or destroyed **2** : to be something yet to be shown, done, or treated (it ∼ s to be seen) **3** : to stay after others have gone **4** : to continue unchanged

re·main·der \ri-'mān-dər\ *n* **1** : that which is left over : a remaining group, part, or trace **2** : the number left after a subtraction **3** : the number that is left over from the dividend after division and that is less than the divisor **4** : a book sold at a reduced price by the publisher after sales have slowed **syn** leavings, rest, balance, remnant, residue

re·mains \-'mānz\ *n pl* **1** : a remaining part or trace ⟨the ∼ of a meal⟩ **2** : a dead body

¹re·make \(ˌ)rē-'māk\ *vb* **-made** \-'mād\; **-mak·ing** : to make anew or in a different form

²re·make \'rē-ˌmāk\ *n* : one that is remade; *esp* : a new version of a motion picture

re·mand \ri-'mand\ *vb* : to order back; *esp* : to return to custody pending trial or for further detention

¹re·mark \ri-'märk\ *n* **1** : the act of remarking : OBSERVATION, NOTICE **2** : a passing observation or comment

²remark *vb* **1** : to take notice of : OBSERVE **2** : to express as an observation or comment : SAY

re·mark·able \ri-'mär-kə-bəl\ *adj* : worthy of being or likely to be noticed : UNUSUAL, EXTRAORDINARY, NOTEWORTHY — **re·mark·able·ness** *n*

re·mark·ably \ri-'mär-kə-blē\ *adv* **1** : in a remarkable manner **2** : as is remarkable

re·me·di·a·ble \ri-'mē-dē-ə-bəl\ *adj* : capable of being remedied

re·me·di·al \ri-'mē-dē-əl\ *adj* : intended to remedy or improve

¹rem·e·dy \'re-mə-dē\ *n*, *pl* **-dies 1** : a medicine or treatment that cures or relieves a disease or condition **2** : something that corrects or counteracts an evil or compensates for a loss

²**remedy** *vb* **-died; -dy·ing** : to provide or serve as a remedy for

re·mem·ber \ri-'mem-bər\ *vb* **-bered; -ber·ing** **1** : to bring to mind or think of again : RECOLLECT **2** : to keep from forgetting : keep in mind **3** : to convey greetings from **4** : COMMEMORATE

re·mem·brance \-brəns\ *n* **1** : an act of remembering : RECOLLECTION **2** : the ability to remember : MEMORY **3** : the period over which one's memory extends **4** : a memory of a person, thing, or event **5** : something that serves to bring to mind : REMINDER **6** : a greeting or gift recalling or expressing friendship or affection

re·mind \ri-'mīnd\ *vb* : to put in mind of something : cause to remember — **re·mind·er** *n*

rem·i·nisce \₁re-mə-'nis\ *vb* **-nisced; -nisc·ing** : to indulge in reminiscence

rem·i·nis·cence \-'nis-ᵊns\ *n* **1** : a recalling or telling of a past experience **2** : an account of a memorable experience

rem·i·nis·cent \-ᵊnt\ *adj* **1** : of or relating to reminiscence **2** : marked by or given to reminiscence **3** : serving to remind : SUGGESTIVE — **rem·i·nis·cent·ly** *adv*

re·miss \ri-'mis\ *adj* **1** : negligent or careless in the performance of work or duty **2** : showing neglect or inattention **syn** lax, neglectful, delinquent, derelict — **re·miss·ly** *adv* — **re·miss·ness** *n*

re·mis·sion \ri-'mi-shən\ *n* **1** : the act or process of remitting **2** : a state or period during which something is remitted

re·mit \ri-'mit\ *vb* **re·mit·ted; re·mit·ting** **1** : FORGIVE, PARDON **2** : to give or gain relief from (as pain) **3** : to refer for consideration, report, or decision **4** : to refrain from exacting or enforcing (as a penalty) **5** : to send (money) in payment of a bill

re·mit·tal \ri-'mit-ᵊl\ *n* : REMISSION

re·mit·tance \ri-'mit-ᵊns\ *n* **1** : a sum of money remitted **2** : transmittal of money (as to a distant place)

rem·nant \'rem-nənt\ *n* **1** : a usu. small part or trace remaining **2** : an unsold or unused end of fabrics that are sold by the yard

re·mod·el \₁rē-'mäd-ᵊl\ *vb* : to alter the structure of : MAKE OVER

re·mon·strance \ri-'män-strəns\ *n* : an act or instance of remonstrating

re·mon·strant \-strənt\ *adj* : vigorously objecting or opposing — **remonstrant** *n* — **re·mon·strant·ly** *adv*

re·mon·strate \ri-'män-₁strāt\ *vb* **-strat·ed; -strat·ing** : to plead in opposition to something : speak in protest or reproof **syn** expostulate, object, protest — **re·mon·stra·tion** \ri-₁män-'strā-shən, ₁re-mən-\ *n* — **re·mon·stra·tor** \ri-'män-₁strā-tər\ *n*

rem·o·ra \'re-mə-rə\ *n* : any of a family of marine bony fishes with sucking organs on the head by which they cling esp. to other fishes

re·morse \ri-'mòrs\ *n* [ME, fr. MF *remors*, fr. ML *morsus*, fr. LL, act of biting again, fr. L *remordēre* to bite again, fr. *re-* again + *mordēre* to bite] : a gnawing distress arising from a sense of guilt for past wrongs **syn** penitence, repentance, contrition — **re·morse·ful** *adj*

re·morse·less \-ləs\ *adj* **1** : MERCILESS **2** : PERSISTENT, RELENTLESS

¹**re·mote** \ri-'mōt\ *adj* **re·mot·er; -est** **1** : far off in place or time : not near **2** : not closely related : DISTANT **3** : located out of the way : SECLUDED **4** : acting, acted on, or controlled indirectly or from a distance **5** : small in degree : SLIGHT ⟨a ∼ chance⟩ **6** : distant in manner — **re·mote·ly** *adv* — **re·mote·ness** *n*

²**remote** *n* **1** : a radio or television program or a portion of a program originating outside the studio **2** : REMOTE CONTROL 2

remote control *n* **1** : control (as by radio signal) of operation from a point at some distance removed **2** : a device or mechanism for controlling something from a distance

¹**re·mount** \(₁)rē-'maùnt\ *vb* **1** : to mount again **2** : to furnish remounts to

²**re·mount** \'rē-₁maùnt\ *n* : a fresh horse to replace one disabled or exhausted

¹**re·move** \ri-'müv\ *vb* **re·moved; re·mov·ing** **1** : to move from one place to another : TRANSFER **2** : to move by lifting or taking off or away **3** : DISMISS, DISCHARGE **4** : to get rid of : ELIMINATE ⟨∼ a fire hazard⟩ **5** : to change one's residence or location **6** : to go away : DEPART **7** : to be capable of being removed — **re·mov·able** *adj* — **re·mov·al** \-'mü-vəl\ *n* — **re·mov·er** *n*

²**remove** *n* **1** : a transfer from one location to another : MOVE **2** : a degree or stage of separation

REM sleep *n* : a state of sleep associated esp. with rapid eye movements and dreaming and occurring approximately at 90-minute intervals

re·mu·ner·ate \ri-'myü-nə-₁rāt\ *vb* **-at·ed; -at·ing** : to pay an equivalent for or to : RECOMPENSE — **re·mu·ner·a·tor** \-₁rā-tər\ *n*

re·mu·ner·a·tion \ri-₁myü-nə-'rā-shən\ *n* : COMPENSATION, PAYMENT

re·mu·ner·a·tive \ri-'myü-nə-rə-tiv, -₁rā-\ *adj* : serving to remunerate : GAINFUL

re·nais·sance \₁re-nə-'säns, -'zäns\ *n* **1** *cap* : the cultural revival and beginnings of modern science in Europe in the 14th-17th centuries; *also* : the period of the Renaissance **2** *often cap* : a movement or period of vigorous artistic and intellectual activity **3** : REBIRTH, REVIVAL

re·nal \'rēn-ᵊl\ *adj* : of, relating to, or located in or near the kidneys

re·nas·cence \ri-'nas-ᵊns, -'nās-\ *n, often cap* : RENAISSANCE

rend \'rend\ *vb* **rent** \'rent\; **rend·ing** **1** : to remove by violence : WREST **2** : to tear forcibly apart : SPLIT

ren·der \'ren-dər\ *vb* **1** : to extract (as lard) by heating **2** : to give to another; *also* : YIELD **3** : to give in return **4** : to do (a service) for another ⟨∼ aid⟩ **5** : to cause to be or become : MAKE **6** : to reproduce or represent by artistic or verbal means **7** : TRANSLATE ⟨∼ into English⟩

¹**ren·dez·vous** \'rän-di-₁vü, -dā-\ *n, pl* **ren·dez·vous** \-₁vüz\ [MF, fr. *rendez vous* present yourselves] **1** : a place appointed for a meeting; *also* : a meeting at an appointed place **2** : a place of popular resort **3** : the process of bringing two spacecraft together

²**rendezvous** *vb* **-voused** \-₁vüd\; **-vous·ing** \-₁vü-iŋ\; **-vouses** \-₁vüz\ : to come or bring together at a rendezvous

ren·di·tion \ren-'di-shən\ *n* : an act or a result of rendering ⟨first ∼ of the work into English⟩

ren·e·gade \'re-ni-₁gād\ *n* [Sp *renegado*, fr. ML *renegatus*, fr. pp. of *renegare* to deny, fr. L *re-* re- + *negare* to deny] : a deserter from one faith, cause, principle, or party for another

re·nege \ri-'nig, -'neg, -'nēg, -'nāg\ *vb* **re·neged; re·neg·ing** **1** : to go back on a promise or commitment **2** : to fail to follow suit when able in a card game in violation of the rules — **re·neg·er** *n*

re·new \ri-'nü, -'nyü\ *vb* **1** : to make or become new, fresh, or strong again **2** : to restore to existence : RECREATE, REVIVE **3** : to make or do again : REPEAT ⟨∼ a complaint⟩ **4** : to begin again : RESUME ⟨∼ed his efforts⟩ **5** : REPLACE ⟨∼ the lining of a coat⟩ **6** : to grant or obtain an extension of or on ⟨∼ a lease⟩ ⟨∼ a subscription⟩ — **re·new·er** *n*

re·new·able \ri-'nü-ə-bəl, -'nyü-\ *adj* **1** : capable of being renewed **2** : capable of being replaced by natural ecological cycles or sound management procedures ⟨∼ resources⟩

re·new·al \ri-'nü-əl, -'nyü-\ *n* **1** : the act of renewing : the state of being renewed **2** : something renewed

ren·net \'re-nət\ *n* **1** : the contents of the stomach of an unweaned animal (as a calf) or the lining membrane of the stomach used for curdling milk **2** : rennin or a substitute used to curdle milk

ren·nin \\'re-nən\ *n* : a stomach enzyme that coagulates casein and is used commercially to curdle milk in the making of cheese

re·nounce \ri-'naůns\ *vb* **re·nounced; re·nounc·ing 1** : to give up, refuse, or resign usu. by formal declaration **2** : to refuse further to follow, obey, or recognize : REPUDIATE — **re·nounce·ment** *n*

ren·o·vate \'re-nə-ˌvāt\ *vb* **-vat·ed; -vat·ing 1** : to make like new again : put in good condition : REPAIR **2** : to restore to vigor or activity — **ren·o·va·tion** \ˌre-nə-'vā-shən\ *n* — **ren·o·va·tor** \'re-nə-ˌvā-tər\ *n*

re·nown \ri-'naůn\ *n* : a state of being widely acclaimed and honored : FAME, CELEBRITY **syn** honor, glory, reputation, repute — **re·nowned** \-'naůnd\ *adj*

¹rent \'rent\ *n* **1** : money or the amount of money paid or due at intervals for the use of another's property **2** : property rented or for rent

²rent *vb* **1** : to give possession and use of in return for rent **2** : to take and hold under an agreement to pay rent **3** : to be for rent ⟨∼s for $100 a month⟩ — **rent·er** *n*

³rent *n* **1** : a tear in cloth **2** : a split in a party or organized group : SCHISM

¹rent·al \'ren-təl\ *n* **1** : an amount paid or collected as rent **2** : something that is rented **3** : an act of renting

²rental *adj* : of or relating to rent

re·nun·ci·a·tion \ri-ˌnən-sē-'ā-shən\ *n* : the act of renouncing : REPUDIATION

rep *abbr* **1** repair **2** repeat **3** report; reporter **4** representative **5** republic

Rep *abbr* Republican

re·pack·age \(ˌ)rē-'pa-kij\ *vb* : to package again or anew; *esp* : to put into a more attractive form

¹re·pair \ri-'par\ *vb* [ME, fr. MF *repairier* to go back to one's country, fr. LL *repatriare*, fr. L *re-* re- + *patria* native country] : to make one's way : GO ⟨∼ed to the drawing room⟩

²repair *vb* [ME, fr. MF *reparer*, fr. L *reparare*, fr. *re-* re- + *parare* to prepare] **1** : to restore to good condition : FIX **2** : to restore to a healthy state **3** : REMEDY ⟨∼ a wrong⟩ — **re·pair·er** *n* — **re·pair·man** \-ˌman\ *n*

³repair *n* **1** : a result of repairing **2** : an act of repairing **3** : condition with respect to need of repairing ⟨in bad ∼⟩

rep·a·ra·tion \ˌre-pə-'rā-shən\ *n* **1** : the act of making amends for a wrong **2** : amends made for a wrong; *esp* : money paid by a defeated nation in compensation for damages caused during hostilities — usu. used in pl. **syn** redress, restitution, indemnity

re·par·a·tive \ri-'par-ə-tiv\ *adj* **1** : of, relating to, or effecting repairs **2** : serving to make amends

rep·ar·tee \ˌre-pər-'tē\ *n* **1** : a witty reply **2** : a succession of clever replies; *also* : skill in making such replies

re·past \ri-'past, 'rē-ˌpast\ *n* : a supply of food and drink served as a meal

re·pa·tri·ate \rē-'pā-trē-ˌāt\ *vb* **-at·ed; -at·ing** : to send or bring back to the country of origin or citizenship ⟨∼ prisoners of war⟩ — **re·pa·tri·ate** \-trē-ət, -trē-ˌāt\ *n* — **re·pa·tri·a·tion** \-ˌpā-trē-'ā-shən\ *n*

re·pay \rē-'pā\ *vb* **-paid** \-'pād\; **-pay·ing 1** : to pay back : REFUND **2** : to give or do in return or requital **3** : to make a return payment to : RECOMPENSE, REQUITE **syn** remunerate, compensate, reimburse, indemnify — **re·pay·able** *adj* — **re·pay·ment** *n*

re·peal \ri-'pēl\ *vb* : to annul by authoritative and esp. legislative action — **repeal** *n* — **re·peal·er** *n*

¹re·peat \ri-'pēt\ *vb* **1** : to say again **2** : to do again **3** : to say over from memory — **re·peat·able** *adj* — **re·peat·er** *n*

²re·peat \ri-'pēt, 'rē-ˌpēt\ *n* **1** : the act of repeating **2** : something repeated or to be repeated (as a radio or television program)

re·peat·ed \ri-'pē-təd\ *adj* : done or recurring again and again : FREQUENT — **re·peat·ed·ly** *adv*

re·pel \ri-'pel\ *vb* **re·pelled; re·pel·ling 1** : to drive away : REPULSE **2** : to fight against : RESIST **3** : to turn away : REJECT **4** : to cause aversion in : DISGUST

¹re·pel·lent *also* **re·pel·lant** \ri-'pe-lənt\ *adj* **1** : tending to drive away ⟨a mosquito-*repellent* spray⟩ **2** : causing disgust

²repellent *also* **repellant** *n* : something that repels; *esp* : a substance that repels insects

re·pent \ri-'pent\ *vb* **1** : to turn from sin and resolve to reform one's life **2** : to feel sorry for (something done) : REGRET — **re·pen·tance** \ri-'pent-ᵊns\ *n* — **re·pen·tant** \-ᵊnt\ *adj*

re·per·cus·sion \ˌrē-pər-'kə-shən, ˌre-\ *n* **1** : REVERBERATION **2** : a reciprocal action or effect **3** : a widespread, indirect, or unforeseen effect of something done or said

rep·er·toire \'re-pər-ˌtwär\ *n* [F] **1** : a list of plays, operas, pieces, or parts which a company or performer is prepared to present **2** : a list of the skills or devices possessed by a person or needed in his occupation

rep·er·to·ry \'re-pər-ˌtōr-ē\ *n, pl* **-ries 1** : REPOSITORY **2** : REPERTOIRE **3** : a company that presents its repertoire in the course of one season at one theater

rep·e·ti·tion \ˌre-pə-'ti-shən\ *n* **1** : the act or an instance of repeating **2** : the fact of being repeated

rep·e·ti·tious \-'ti-shəs\ *adj* : marked by repetition; *esp* : tediously repeating — **rep·e·ti·tious·ly** *adv* — **rep·e·ti·tious·ness** *n*

re·pet·i·tive \ri-'pe-ti-tiv\ *adj* : REPETITIOUS — **re·pet·i·tive·ly** *adv* — **re·pet·i·tive·ness** *n*

re·pine \ri-'pīn\ *vb* **re·pined; re·pin·ing 1** : to feel or express discontent or dejection **2** : to long for something

repl *abbr* replace; replacement

re·place \ri-'plās\ *vb* **1** : to restore to a former place or position **2** : to take the place of : SUPPLANT **3** : to put something new in the place of — **re·place·able** *adj* — **re·plac·er** *n*

re·place·ment \ri-'plās-mənt\ *n* **1** : the act of replacing : the state of being replaced **2** : one that replaces another esp. in a job or function

¹re·play \(ˌ)rē-'plā\ *vb* : to play again or over

²re·play \'rē-ˌplā\ *n* **1** : an act or instance of replaying **2** : the playing of a tape (as a videotape)

re·plen·ish \ri-'ple-nish\ *vb* : to fill or build up again : stock or supply anew — **re·plen·ish·ment** *n*

re·plete \ri-'plēt\ *adj* **1** : fully provided **2** : FULL; *esp* : full of food — **re·plete·ness** *n*

re·ple·tion \ri-'plē-shən\ *n* : the state of being replete

rep·li·ca \'re-pli-kə\ *n* [It, repetition, fr. *replicare* to repeat, fr. LL, fr. L to fold back, fr. *re-* back + *plicare* to fold] **1** : an exact reproduction (as of a painting) executed by the original artist **2** : a copy exact in all details : DUPLICATE

¹rep·li·cate \'re-plə-ˌkāt\ *vb* **-cat·ed; -cat·ing** : DUPLICATE, REPEAT

²rep·li·cate \-kət\ *n* : one of several identical experiments or procedures

rep·li·ca·tion \ˌre-plə-'kā-shən\ *n* **1** : ANSWER, REPLY **2** : precise copying or reproduction; *also* : an act or process of this

¹re·ply \ri-'plī\ *vb* **re·plied; re·ply·ing** : to say or do in answer : RESPOND

²reply *n, pl* **replies** : ANSWER, RESPONSE

¹re·port \ri-'pōrt\ *n* [ME, fr. MF, fr. OF, fr. *reporter* to report, fr. L *reportare*, fr. *re-* back + *portare* to carry] **1** : common talk : RUMOR **2** : FAME, REPUTATION **3** : a usu. detailed account or statement **4** : an explosive noise

²report *vb* **1** : to give an account of : RELATE, TELL **2** : to serve as carrier of (a message) **3** : to prepare or present (as an account of an event) for a newspaper or a broadcast **4** : to make a charge of misconduct against **5** : to present oneself (as for work) **6** : to make

Panel 1: HERE'S MY SIXTH-GRADE REPORT CARD!

Panel 2: MY PARENTS WERE SO PROUD

Panel 3: "JON HAS NOT SHOVED ANY CRAYONS UP HIS NOSE THIS TERM"

JIM DAViES 3-11

known to the authorities ⟨∼ a fire⟩ **7** : to return or present (as a matter referred to a committee) with conclusions and recommendations — **re·port·able** *adj*

re·port·age \ri-'pȯr-tij, *esp for 2* ˌre-pər-'täzh, ˌre-ˌpȯr-'\ *n* [F] **1** : the act or process of reporting news **2** : writing intended to give an account of observed or documented events

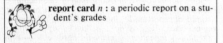 **report card** *n* : a periodic report on a student's grades

re·port·ed·ly \ri-'pȯr-təd-lē\ *adv* : according to report
re·port·er \ri-'pȯr-tər\ *n* : one that reports; *esp* : a person who gathers and reports news for a news medium — **re·por·to·ri·al** \ˌre-pər-'tȯr-ē-əl\ *adj*
¹**re·pose** \ri-'pōz\ *vb* **re·posed; re·pos·ing 1** : to lay at rest **2** : to lie at rest **3** : to lie dead **4** : to take a rest **5** : to rest for support : LIE
²**repose** *n* **1** : a state of resting (as after exertion); *esp* : SLEEP **2** : eternal or heavenly rest **3** : CALM, PEACE **4** : cessation or absence of activity, movement, or animation **5** : composure of manner : POISE — **re·pose·ful** *adj*
³**repose** *vb* **re·posed; re·pos·ing 1** : to place (as trust) in someone or something **2** : to place for control, management, or use
re·pos·i·to·ry \ri-'pä-zə-ˌtȯr-ē\ *n, pl* **-ries 1** : a place where something is deposited or stored **2** : a person to whom something is entrusted
re·pos·sess \ˌrē-pə-'zes\ *vb* **1** : to regain possession of **2** : to take possession in default of the payment of installments due — **re·pos·ses·sion** \-'ze-shən\ *n*
rep·re·hend \ˌre-pri-'hend\ *vb* : to express disapproval of : CENSURE **syn** criticize, condemn, denounce, blame, pan — **rep·re·hen·sion** \-'hen-chən\ *n*
rep·re·hen·si·ble \-'hen-sə-bəl\ *adj* : deserving blame or censure : CULPABLE — **rep·re·hen·si·bly** \-blē\ *adv*
rep·re·sent \ˌre-pri-'zent\ *vb* **1** : to present a picture or a likeness of : PORTRAY, DEPICT **2** : to serve as a sign or symbol of **3** : to act the role of **4** : to stand in the place of : act or speak for **5** : to be a member or example of : TYPIFY **6** : to serve as an elected representative of **7** : to describe as having a specified quality or character **8** : to state with the purpose of affecting judgment or action
rep·re·sen·ta·tion \ˌre-pri-zen-'tā-shən\ *n* **1** : the act of representing **2** : one (as a picture or image) that represents something else **3** : the state of being represented in a legislative body; *also* : the body of persons representing a constituency **4** : a usu. formal statement made to effect a change
¹**rep·re·sen·ta·tive** \ˌre-pri-'zen-tə-tiv\ *adj* **1** : serving to represent **2** : standing or acting for another **3** : founded on the principle of representation : carried on by elected representatives ⟨∼ government⟩ — **rep·re·sen·ta·tive·ly** *adv* — **rep·re·sen·ta·tive·ness** *n*
²**representative** *n* **1** : a typical example of a group,

class, or quality **2** : one that represents another; *esp* : one representing a district in a legislative body usu. as a member of a lower house
re·press \ri-'pres\ *vb* **1** : CURB, SUBDUE **2** : RESTRAIN, SUPPRESS **3** : to exclude from consciousness — **re·pres·sion** \-'pre-shən\ *n* — **re·pres·sive** \-'pre-siv\ *adj*
¹**re·prieve** \ri-'prēv\ *vb* **re·prieved; re·priev·ing 1** : to delay the punishment or execution of **2** : to give temporary relief to
²**reprieve** *n* **1** : the act of reprieving : the state of being reprieved **2** : a formal temporary suspension of a sentence esp. of death **3** : a temporary respite
¹**rep·ri·mand** \'re-prə-ˌmand\ *n* : a severe or formal reproof
²**reprimand** *vb* : to reprove severely or formally
¹**re·print** \(ˌ)rē-'print\ *vb* : to print again
²**re·print** \'rē-ˌprint\ *n* : a reproduction of printed matter
re·pri·sal \ri-'prī-zəl\ *n* : an act in retaliation for something done by another
re·prise \ri-'prēz\ *n* : a recurrence, renewal, or resumption of an action; *also* : a musical repetition
¹**re·proach** \ri-'prōch\ *n* **1** : an expression of disapproval **2** : DISGRACE, DISCREDIT **3** : the act of reproaching : REBUKE **4** : a cause or occasion of blame or disgrace — **re·proach·ful** \-fəl\ *adj* — **re·proach·ful·ly** *adv* — **re·proach·ful·ness** *n*
²**reproach** *vb* **1** : CENSURE, REBUKE **2** : to cast discredit on **syn** chide, admonish, reprove, reprimand — **re·proach·able** *adj*
rep·ro·bate \'re-prə-ˌbāt\ *n* **1** : a person foreordained to damnation **2** : a thoroughly bad person : SCOUNDREL — **reprobate** *adj*
rep·ro·ba·tion \ˌre-prə-'bā-shən\ *n* : strong disapproval : CONDEMNATION
re·pro·duce \ˌrē-prə-'düs, -'dyüs\ *vb* **1** : to produce again or anew **2** : to produce offspring — **re·pro·duc·ible** \-'dü-sə-bəl, -'dyü-\ *adj* — **re·pro·duc·tion** \-'dək-shən\ *n* — **re·pro·duc·tive** \-'dək-tiv\ *adj*
re·proof \ri-'prüf\ *n* : blame or censure for a fault
re·prove \ri-'prüv\ *vb* **re·proved; re·prov·ing 1** : to administer a rebuke to **2** : to express disapproval of **syn** reprimand, admonish, reproach, chide — **re·prov·er** *n*
rept *abbr* report
rep·tile \'rep-təl, -ˌtīl\ *n* [ME *reptil*, fr. MF or LL; MF *reptile*, fr. LL *reptile*, fr. L *repere* to crawl] : any of a large class of air-breathing scaly vertebrates including snakes, lizards, alligators, turtles, and extinct related forms (as dinosaurs) — **rep·til·i·an** \rep-'ti-lē-ən\ *adj or n*
re·pub·lic \ri-'pə-blik\ *n* [F *république*, fr. MF *republique*, fr. L *respublica*, fr. *res* thing, wealth + *publica*, fem. of *publicus* public] **1** : a government having a chief of state who is not a monarch and is usu. a president; *also* : a nation or other political unit having such a government **2** : a government in which supreme power is held by the citizens entitled to vote and is exercised by elected officers and representa-

tives governing according to law; *also* **:** a nation or other political unit having such a form of government **3 :** a constituent political and territorial unit of the former nations of Czechoslovakia, the U.S.S.R., or Yugoslavia

¹**re·pub·li·can** \-bli-kən\ *adj* **1 :** of, relating to, or resembling a republic **2 :** favoring or supporting a republic **3** *cap* **:** of, relating to, or constituting one of the two major political parties in the U.S. evolving in the mid-19th century — **re·pub·li·can·ism** *n, often cap*

²**republican** *n* **1 :** one that favors or supports a republican form of government **2** *cap* **:** a member of a republican party and esp. of the Republican party of the U.S.

re·pu·di·ate \ri-ˈpyü-dē-ˌāt\ *vb* **-at·ed; -at·ing** [L *repudiare* to cast off, divorce, fr. *repudium* divorce] **1 :** to cast off **: DISOWN 2 :** to refuse to have anything to do with **:** refuse to acknowledge, accept, or pay ⟨∼ a charge⟩ ⟨∼ a debt⟩ **syn** spurn, reject, decline — **re·pu·di·a·tion** \-ˌpyü-dē-ˈā-shən\ *n* — **re·pu·di·a·tor** \-ˈpyü-dē-ˌā-tər\ *n*

re·pug·nance \ri-ˈpəg-nəns\ *n* **1 :** the quality or fact of being contradictory or inconsistent **2 :** strong dislike, distaste, or antagonism

re·pug·nant \-nənt\ *adj* **1 :** marked by repugnance **2 :** contrary to a person's tastes or principles **:** exciting distaste or aversion **syn** repellent, abhorrent, distasteful, obnoxious, revolting, loathsome — **re·pug·nant·ly** *adv*

¹**re·pulse** \ri-ˈpəls\ *vb* **re·pulsed; re·puls·ing 1 :** to drive or beat back **: REPEL 2 :** to repel by discourtesy or denial **: REBUFF 3 :** to cause a feeling of repulsion in **: DISGUST**

²**repulse** *n* **1 : REBUFF, REJECTION 2 :** the action of repelling an attacker **:** the fact of being repelled

re·pul·sion \ri-ˈpəl-shən\ *n* **1 :** the action of repulsing **:** the state of being repulsed **2 :** the force with which bodies, particles, or like forces repel one another **3 :** a feeling of aversion

re·pul·sive \-siv\ *adj* **1 :** serving or tending to repel or reject **2 :** arousing aversion or disgust **syn** repugnant, revolting, loathsome, noisome — **re·pul·sive·ly** *adv* — **re·pul·sive·ness** *n*

rep·u·ta·ble \ˈre-pyə-tə-bəl\ *adj* **:** having a good reputation **: ESTIMABLE** — **rep·u·ta·bly** \-blē\ *adv*

rep·u·ta·tion \ˌre-pyü-ˈtā-shən\ *n* **1 :** overall quality or character as seen or judged by people in general **2 :** place in public esteem or regard

¹**re·pute** \ri-ˈpyüt\ *vb* **re·put·ed; re·put·ing : BELIEVE, CONSIDER**

²**repute** *n* **1 : REPUTATION 2 :** the state of being favorably known or spoken of

re·put·ed \ri-ˈpyü-təd\ *adj* **1 : REPUTABLE 2 :** according to reputation **: SUPPOSED** — **re·put·ed·ly** *adv*

req *abbr* **1** request **2** require; required **3** requisition

¹**re·quest** \ri-ˈkwest\ *n* **1 :** an act or instance of asking for something **2 :** a thing asked for **3 :** the condition of being asked for ⟨available on ∼⟩

²**request** *vb* **1 :** to make a request to or of **2 :** to ask for — **re·quest·er** *n*

re·qui·em \ˈre-kwē-əm, ˈrā-\ *n* [ME, fr. L (first word of the requiem mass), acc. of *requies* rest, fr. *quies* quiet, rest] **1 :** a mass for a dead person; *also* **:** a musical setting for this **2 :** a musical service or hymn in honor of the dead

re·quire \ri-ˈkwīr\ *vb* **re·quired; re·quir·ing 1 :** to demand as necessary or essential **2 : COMMAND, ORDER**

re·quire·ment \-mənt\ *n* **1 :** something (as a condition or quality) required ⟨entrance ∼s⟩ **2 : NECESSITY**

req·ui·site \ˈre-kwə-zət\ *adj* **: REQUIRED, NECESSARY** — **requisite** *n*

req·ui·si·tion \ˌre-kwə-ˈzi-shən\ *n* **1 :** formal application or demand (as for supplies) **2 :** the state of being in demand or use — **requisition** *vb*

re·quite \ri-ˈkwīt\ *vb* **re·quit·ed; re·quit·ing 1 :** to make return for **: REPAY 2 :** to make retaliation for **: AVENGE 3 :** to make return to — **re·quit·al** \-ˈkwīt-ᵊl\ *n*

rere·dos \ˈrer-ə-ˌdäs\ *n* **:** a usu. ornamental wood or stone screen or partition wall behind an altar

re·run \ˈrē-ˌrən, (ˌ)rē-ˈrən\ *n* **:** the act or an instance of running again or anew; *esp* **:** a showing of a motion picture or television program after its first run — **re·run** \(ˌ)rē-ˈrən\ *vb*

res *abbr* **1** research **2** reservation; reserve **3** reservoir **4** residence; resident **5** resolution

re·sale \ˈrē-ˌsāl, (ˌ)rē-ˈsāl\ *n* **:** the act of selling again usu. to a new party — **re·sal·able** \(ˌ)rē-ˈsā-lə-bəl\ *adj*

re·scind \ri-ˈsind\ *vb* **: REPEAL, CANCEL, ANNUL** — **re·scis·sion** \-ˈsi-zhən\ *n*

re·script \ˈrē-ˌskript\ *n* **:** an official or authoritative order or decree

res·cue \ˈres-kyü\ *vb* **res·cued; res·cu·ing** [ME, fr. MF *rescourre*, fr. OF, fr. *re-* re- + *escourre* to shake out, fr. L *excutere*] **:** to free from danger, harm, or confinement — **rescue** *n* — **res·cu·er** *n*

re·search \ri-ˈsərch, ˈrē-ˌsərch\ *n* **1 :** careful or diligent search **2 :** studious inquiry or examination aimed at the discovery and interpretation of new knowledge **3 :** the collecting of information about a particular subject — **research** *vb* — **re·search·er** *n*

re·sec·tion \ri-ˈsek-shən\ *n* **:** the surgical removal of part of an organ or structure

re·sem·blance \ri-ˈzem-bləns\ *n* **:** the quality or state of resembling

re·sem·ble \ri-ˈzem-bəl\ *vb* **-bled; -bling :** to be like or similar to

re·sent \ri-ˈzent\ *vb* **:** to feel or exhibit annoyance or indignation at — **re·sent·ful** \-fəl\ *adj* — **re·sent·ful·ly** *adv* — **re·sent·ment** *n*

re·ser·pine \ri-ˈsər-ˌpēn, -pən\ *n* **:** a drug used in treating high blood pressure and nervous tension

res·er·va·tion \ˌre-zər-ˈvā-shən\ *n* **1 :** an act of reserving **2 :** something (as a room in a hotel) arranged for in advance **3 :** something reserved; *esp* **:** a tract of public land set aside for special use **4** : a limiting condition

¹re·serve \ri-ˈzərv\ *vb* **re·served; re·serv·ing 1** : to store for future or special use **2** : to hold back for oneself **3** : to set aside or arrange to have set aside or held for special use

²reserve *n* **1** : something reserved : STOCK, STORE **2** : a military force withheld from action for later use — usu. used in pl. **3** : the military forces of a country not part of the regular services; *also* : RESERVIST **4** : a tract set apart : RESERVATION **5** : an act of reserving **6** : restraint or caution in one's words or bearing **7** : money or its equivalent kept in hand or set apart to meet liabilities

re·served \ri-ˈzərvd\ *adj* **1** : restrained in words and actions **2** : set aside for future or special use — **re·serv·ed·ly** \-ˈzər-vəd-lē\ *adv* — **re·serv·ed·ness** \-vəd-nəs\ *n*

re·serv·ist \ri-ˈzər-vist\ *n* : a member of a military reserve

res·er·voir \ˈre-zə-ˌvwär, -zər-, -ˌvwȯr\ *n* [F] : a place where something is kept in store; *esp* : an artificial lake where water is collected as a water supply

re·shuf·fle \rē-ˈshə-fəl\ *vb* **1** : to shuffle again **2** : to reorganize usu. by redistribution of existing elements — **reshuffle** *n*

re·side \ri-ˈzīd\ *vb* **re·sid·ed; re·sid·ing 1** : to make one's home : DWELL **2** : to be present as a quality or vested as a right

res·i·dence \ˈre-zə-dəns\ *n* **1** : the act or fact of residing in a place as a dweller or in discharge of a duty or an obligation **2** : the place where one actually lives **3** : a building used as a home : DWELLING **4** : the period of living in a place

res·i·den·cy \ˈre-zə-dən-sē\ *n, pl* **-cies 1** : the residence of or the territory under a diplomatic resident **2** : a period of advanced training in a medical specialty

¹res·i·dent \-dənt\ *adj* **1** : RESIDING **2** : being in residence **3** : not migratory

²resident *n* **1** : one who resides in a place **2** : a diplomatic representative with governing powers (as in a protectorate) **3** : a physician serving a residency

res·i·den·tial \ˌre-zə-ˈden-chəl\ *adj* **1** : used as a residence or by residents **2** : occupied by or restricted to residences — **res·i·den·tial·ly** *adv*

¹re·sid·u·al \ri-ˈzi-jə-wəl\ *adj* : being a residue or remainder

²residual *n* **1** : a residual product or substance **2** : a payment (as to an actor or writer) for each rerun after an initial showing (as of a taped TV show)

re·sid·u·ary \ri-ˈzi-jə-ˌwer-ē\ *adj* : of, relating to, or constituting a residue esp. of an estate

res·i·due \ˈre-zə-ˌdü, -ˌdyü\ *n* : a part remaining after another part has been taken away : REMAINDER

re·sid·u·um \ri-ˈzi-jə-wəm\ *n, pl* **re·sid·ua** \-jə-wə\ [L] **1** : something remaining or residual after certain deductions are made **2** : a residual product

re·sign \ri-ˈzīn\ *vb* [ME, fr. MF *resigner*, fr. L *resignare*, lit., to unseal, cancel, fr. *signare* to sign, seal] **1** : to give up deliberately (as one's position) esp. by a formal act **2** : to give (oneself) over (as to grief or despair) without resistance — **re·sign·ed·ly** \-ˈzī-nəd-lē\ *adv*

re–sign \ˌ)rē-ˈsīn\ *vb* : to sign again

res·ig·na·tion \ˌre-zig-ˈnā-shən\ *n* **1** : an act or instance of resigning; *also* : a formal notification of such an act **2** : the quality or state of being resigned

re·sil·ience \ri-ˈzil-yəns\ *n* **1** : the ability of a body to regain its original size and shape after being compressed, bent, or stretched **2** : an ability to recover from or adjust easily to change or misfortune

re·sil·ien·cy \-yən-sē\ *n* : RESILIENCE

re·sil·ient \-yənt\ *adj* : marked by resilience

res·in \ˈrez-ᵊn\ *n* : any of various substances obtained from the gum or sap of some trees and used esp. in varnishes, plastics, and medicine; *also* : a comparable synthetic product — **res·in·ous** *adj*

¹re·sist \ri-ˈzist\ *vb* **1** : to fight against : OPPOSE ⟨∼ aggression⟩ **2** : to withstand the force or effect of ⟨∼ disease⟩ **syn** combat, repel — **re·sist·ible** \-ˈzis-tə-bəl\ *adj* — **re·sist·less** *adj*

²resist *n* : something (as a coating) that resists or prevents a particular action

re·sis·tance \ri-ˈzis-təns\ *n* **1** : the act or an instance of resisting : OPPOSITION **2** : the power or capacity to resist; *esp* : the inherent ability of an organism to resist harmful influences (as disease or infection) **3** : the opposition offered by a body to the passage through it of a steady electric current

re·sis·tant \-tənt\ *adj* : giving or capable of resistance

re·sis·tor \ri-ˈzis-tər\ *n* : a device used to provide resistance to the flow of an electric current in a circuit

res·o·lute \ˈre-zə-ˌlüt\ *adj* : firmly determined in purpose : RESOLVED **syn** steadfast, staunch, faithful, true, loyal — **res·o·lute·ly** *adv* — **res·o·lute·ness** *n*

res·o·lu·tion \ˌre-zə-ˈlü-shən\ *n* **1** : the act or process of resolving **2** : the action of solving; *also* : SOLUTION **3** : the quality of being resolute : FIRMNESS, DETERMINATION **4** : a formal statement expressing the opinion, will, or intent of a body of persons

¹re·solve \ri-ˈzälv\ *vb* **re·solved; re·solv·ing 1** : to break up into constituent parts : ANALYZE **2** : to distinguish between or make visible adjacent parts of **3** : to find an answer to : SOLVE **4** : DETERMINE, DECIDE **5** : to make or pass a formal resolution — **re·solv·able** *adj*

²resolve *n* **1** : fixity of purpose **2** : something resolved

res·o·nance \ˈre-zə-nəns\ *n* **1** : the quality or state of being resonant **2** : a reinforcement of sound in a vibrating body caused by waves from another body vibrating at nearly the same rate

res·o·nant \-nənt\ *adj* **1** : continuing to sound : RESOUNDING **2** : relating to or exhibiting resonance **3** : intensified and enriched by or as if by resonance — **res·o·nant·ly** *adv*

res·o·nate \-ˌnāt\ *vb* **-nat·ed; -nat·ing 1** : to produce or exhibit resonance **2** : REVERBERATE, RESOUND

res·o·na·tor \-ˌnā-tər\ *n* : something that resounds or exhibits resonance

re·sorp·tion \rē-ˈsȯrp-shən, -ˈzȯrp-\ *n* : the action or process of breaking down and assimilating something (as a tooth or an embryo)

¹re·sort \ri-ˈzȯrt\ *n* [ME, fr. MF, resource, recourse, fr. *resortir* to rebound, resort, fr. OF, fr. *sortir* to escape, sally] **1** : one looked to for help : REFUGE **2** : RECOURSE **3** : frequent or general visiting ⟨place of ∼⟩ : a frequently visited place : HAUNT **5** : a place providing recreation esp. to vacationers

²resort *vb* **1** : to go often or habitually **2** : to have recourse ⟨∼ed to violence⟩

re·sound \ri-ˈzaůnd\ *vb* **1** : to become filled with sound : REVERBERATE, RING **2** : to sound loudly

re·sound·ing *adj* **1** : RESONATING, RESONANT **2** : impressively sonorous ⟨∼ name⟩ **3** : EMPHATIC, UNEQUIVOCAL ⟨a ∼ success⟩ — **re·sound·ing·ly** *adv*

re·source \ˈrē-ˌsȯrs, ri-ˈsȯrs\ *n* [F *ressource*, fr. OF *ressourse* relief, resource, fr. *resourdre* to relieve, lit., to rise again, fr. L *resurgere*, fr. *re-* again + *surgere* to rise] **1** : a source of supply or support — usu. used in pl. **2** *pl* : available funds **3** : a possibility of relief or recovery **4** : a means of spending leisure time **5** : ability to meet and handle situations — **re·source·ful** \ri-ˈsȯrs-fəl\ *adj* — **re·source·ful·ness** *n*

resp *abbr* respective; respectively

¹re·spect \ri-ˈspekt\ *n* **1** : relation to something usu. specified : REGARD ⟨in ∼ to⟩ **2** : high or special regard : ESTEEM **3** *pl* : an expression of respect or deference **4** : DETAIL, PARTICULAR — **re·spect·ful** \-fəl\ *adj* — **re·spect·ful·ly** *adv* — **re·spect·ful·ness** *n*

²respect *vb* **1** : to consider deserving of high regard : ESTEEM **2** : to refrain from interfering with ⟨∼ another's

privacy⟩ **3** : to have reference to : CONCERN — **re·spect·er** *n*

re·spect·able \ri-'spek-tə-bəl\ *adj* **1** : worthy of respect : ESTIMABLE **2** : decent or correct in conduct : PROPER **3** : fair in size, quantity, or quality : MODERATE, TOLERABLE **4** : fit to be seen : PRESENTABLE — **re·spect·a·bil·i·ty** \-ɪspek-tə-'bi-lə-tē\ *n* — **re·spect·ably** \-'spek-tə-blē\ *adv*

re·spect·ing *prep* : with regard to

re·spec·tive \-tiv\ *adj* : PARTICULAR, SEPARATE ⟨returned to their ~ homes⟩

re·spec·tive·ly \-lē\ *adv* **1** : as relating to each **2** : each in the order given

res·pi·ra·tion \ɪres-pə-'rā-shən\ *n* **1** : an act or the process of breathing **2** : the physical and chemical processes (as breathing and oxidation) by which a living thing obtains oxygen and eliminates waste gases (as carbon dioxide) — **re·spi·ra·to·ry** \'res-pə-rə-ɪtōr-ē, ri-'spī-rə-\ *adj* — **re·spire** \ri-'spīr\ *vb*

res·pi·ra·tor \'res-pə-ɪrā-tər\ *n* **1** : a device covering the mouth or nose esp. to prevent inhaling harmful vapors **2** : a device for artificial respiration

re·spite \'res-pət\ *n* **1** : a temporary delay **2** : an interval of rest or relief

re·splen·dent \ri-'splen-dənt\ *adj* : shining brilliantly : gloriously bright : SPLENDID — **re·splen·dence** \-dəns\ *n* — **re·splen·dent·ly** *adv*

re·spond \ri-'spänd\ *vb* **1** : ANSWER, REPLY **2** : REACT ⟨~ed to a call for help⟩ **3** : to show favorable reaction ⟨~ to medication⟩ — **re·spond·er** *n*

re·spon·dent \ri-'spän-dənt\ *n* : one who responds; *esp* : one who answers in various legal proceedings — **respondent** *adj*

re·sponse \ri-'späns\ *n* **1** : an act of responding **2** : something constituting a reply or a reaction

re·spon·si·bil·i·ty \ri-ɪspän-sə-'bi-lə-tē\ *n, pl* **-ties 1** : the quality or state of being responsible **2** : something for which one is responsible

re·spon·si·ble \ri-'spän-sə-bəl\ *adj* **1** : liable to be called upon to answer for one's acts or decisions : ANSWERABLE **2** : able to fulfill one's obligations : RELIABLE, TRUSTWORTHY **3** : able to choose for oneself between right and wrong **4** : involving accountability or important duties ⟨~ position⟩ — **re·spon·si·ble·ness** *n* — **re·spon·si·bly** \-blē\ *adv*

re·spon·sive \-siv\ *adj* **1** : RESPONDING **2** : quick to respond : SENSITIVE **3** : using responses ⟨~ readings⟩ — **re·spon·sive·ly** *adv* — **re·spon·sive·ness** *n*

¹**rest** \'rest\ *n* **1** : REPOSE, SLEEP **2** : freedom from work or activity **3** : a state of motionlessness or inactivity **4** : a place of shelter or lodging **5** : a silence in music equivalent in duration to a note of the same value; *also* : a character indicating this **6** : something used as a support — **rest·ful** \-fəl\ *adj* — **rest·ful·ly** *adv*

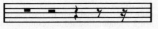

rest 5

²**rest** *vb* **1** : to get rest by lying down; *esp* : SLEEP **2** : to cease from action or motion **3** : to give rest to : set at rest **4** : to sit or lie fixed or supported **5** : to place on or against a support **6** : to remain based or founded **7** : to cause to be firmly fixed : GROUND **8** : to remain for action : DEPEND

³**rest** *n* : something left over

res·tau·rant \'res-trənt, -tə-ɪränt\ *n* [F, fr. prp. of *restaurer* to restore, fr. L *restaurare*] : a public eating place

res·tau·ra·teur \ɪres-tə-rə-'tər\ *also* **res·tau·ran·teur** \-ɪrän-\ *n* : the operator or proprietor of a restaurant

rest home *n* : an establishment that gives care for the aged or convalescent

res·ti·tu·tion \ɪres-tə-'tü-shən, -'tyü-\ *n* : the act of restoring : the state of being restored; *esp* : restoration of something to its rightful owner **syn** amends, redress, reparation, indemnity, compensation

res·tive \'res-tiv\ *adj* [ME, fr. MF *restif*, fr. *rester* to stop behind, remain, fr. L *restare*, fr. *re-* back + *stare* to stand] **1** : BALKY **2** : UNEASY, FIDGETY **syn** restless, impatient, nervous — **res·tive·ly** *adv* — **res·tive·ness** *n*

rest·less \'rest-ləs\ *adj* **1** : lacking or denying rest ⟨a ~ night⟩ **2** : never resting or settled : always moving ⟨the ~ sea⟩ **3** : marked by or showing unrest esp. of mind ⟨~ pacing back and forth⟩ **syn** restive, impatient, nervous, fidgety — **rest·less·ly** *adv* — **rest·less·ness** *n*

re·stor·able \ri-'stōr-ə-bəl\ *adj* : fit for restoring or reclaiming

res·to·ra·tion \ɪres-tə-'rā-shən\ *n* **1** : an act of restoring : the state of being restored **2** : something (as a building) that has been restored

re·stor·ative \ri-'stōr-ə-tiv\ *n* : something that restores esp. to consciousness or health — **restorative** *adj*

re·store \ri-'stōr\ *vb* **re·stored; re·stor·ing 1** : to give back : RETURN **2** : to put back into use or service **3** : to put or bring back into a former or original state **4** : to put again in possession of something — **re·stor·er** *n*

re·strain \ri-'strān\ *vb* **1** : to prevent from doing something **2** : to limit, restrict, or keep under control : CURB **3** : to place under restraint or arrest — **re·strain·able** *adj* — **re·strain·er** *n*

re·strained \ri-'strānd\ *adj* : marked by restraint : DISCIPLINED — **re·strain·ed·ly** \-'strā-nəd-lē\ *adv*

restraining order *n* : a legal order directing one person to stay away from another

re·straint \ri-'strānt\ *n* **1** : an act of restraining : the state of being restrained **2** : a restraining force, agency, or device **3** : deprivation or limitation of liberty : CONFINEMENT **4** : control over one's feelings : RESERVE

re·strict \ri-'strikt\ *vb* **1** : to confine within bounds

: LIMIT **2** : to place under restriction as to use — **re·stric·tive** *adj* — **re·stric·tive·ly** *adv*

re·stric·tion \ri-'strik-shən\ *n* **1** : something (as a law or rule) that restricts **2** : an act of restricting : the state of being restricted

rest room *n* : a room or suite of rooms that includes sinks and toilets

¹**re·sult** \ri-'zəlt\ *vb* [ME, fr. ML *resultare*, fr. L, to rebound, fr. *re-* re- + *saltare* to leap] : to come about as an effect or consequence — **re·sul·tant** \-'zəlt-ᵊnt\ *adj or n*

²**result** *n* **1** : something that results : EFFECT, CONSEQUENCE **2** : beneficial or discernible effect **3** : something obtained by calculation or investigation

re·sume \ri-'züm\ *vb* **re·sumed; re·sum·ing 1** : to take or assume again **2** : to return to or begin again after interruption **3** : to take back to oneself — **re·sump·tion** \-'zəmp-shən\ *n*

ré·su·mé *or* **re·su·me** *or* **re·su·mé** \'re-zə-ˌmā, ˌre-zə-'mā\ *n* [F *résumé*] : SUMMARY; *esp* : a short account of one's career and qualifications usu. prepared by a job applicant

re·sur·gence \ri-'sər-jəns\ *n* : a rising again into life, activity, or prominence — **re·sur·gent** \-jənt\ *adj*

res·ur·rect \ˌre-zə-'rekt\ *vb* **1** : to raise from the dead **2** : to bring to attention or use again

res·ur·rec·tion \ˌre-zə-'rek-shən\ *n* **1** *cap* : the rising of Christ from the dead **2** *often cap* : the rising to life of all human dead before the final judgment **3** : REVIVAL

re·sus·ci·tate \ri-'sə-sə-ˌtāt\ *vb* **-tat·ed; -tat·ing** : to revive from apparent death or unconsciousness; *also* : REVITALIZE — **re·sus·ci·ta·tion** \ri-ˌsə-sə-'tā-shən, ˌrē-\ *n* — **re·sus·ci·ta·tor** \-'tā-tər\ *n*

ret *abbr* **1** retain **2** retired **3** return

¹**re·tail** \'rē-ˌtāl, *esp for 2 also* ri-'tāl\ *vb* **1** : to sell in small quantities directly to the ultimate consumer **2** : to tell in detail or to one person after another — **re·tail·er** *n*

²**re·tail** \'rē-ˌtāl\ *n* : the sale of goods in small amounts to ultimate consumers — **retail** *adj or adv*

re·tain \ri-'tān\ *vb* **1** : to hold in possession or use **2** : to engage (as a lawyer) by paying a fee in advance **3** : to keep in a fixed place or position **syn** detain, withhold, reserve

¹**re·tain·er** \ri-'tā-nər\ *n* **1** : one that retains **2** : a servant in a wealthy household; *also* : EMPLOYEE

²**retainer** *n* : a fee paid to secure services (as of a lawyer)

¹**re·take** \(ˌ)rē-'tāk\ *vb* **-took** \-'tùk\; **-tak·en** \-'tā-kən\; **-tak·ing 1** : to take or seize again **2** : to photograph again

²**re·take** \'rē-ˌtāk\ *n* : a second photographing of a motion-picture scene

re·tal·i·ate \ri-'ta-lē-ˌāt\ *vb* **-at·ed; -at·ing** : to return like for like; *esp* : to get revenge — **re·tal·i·a·tion** \-ˌta-lē-'ā-shən\ *n* — **re·tal·ia·to·ry** \-'tal-yə-ˌtōr-ē\ *adj*

re·tard \ri-'tärd\ *vb* : to hold back : delay the progress of **syn** slow, slacken, detain — **re·tar·da·tion** \ˌrē-ˌtär-'dā-shən, ri-\ *n* — **re·tard·er** *n*

re·tard·ed *adj* : slow or limited in intellectual, emotional, or academic progress ⟨a ~ child⟩

retch \'rech\ *vb* : to try to vomit; *also* : VOMIT

re·ten·tion \ri-'ten-chən\ *n* **1** : the act of retaining : the state of being retained **2** : the power of retaining esp. in the mind : RETENTIVENESS

re·ten·tive \-'ten-tiv\ *adj* : having the power of retaining; *esp* : retaining knowledge easily — **re·ten·tive·ness** *n*

re·think \(ˌ)rē-'think\ *vb* **-thought** \-'thȯt\; **-think·ing** : to think about again : RECONSIDER

ret·i·cent \'re-tə-sənt\ *adj* : tending not to talk or give out information **2** : RELUCTANT **syn** reserved, taciturn, closemouthed — **ret·i·cence** \-səns\ *n* — **ret·i·cent·ly** *adv*

ret·i·na \'ret-ᵊn-ə\ *n, pl* **retinas** *or* **ret·i·nae** \-ᵊn-ˌē\ : the sensory membrane lining the eye that receives the image formed by the lens — **ret·i·nal** \'ret-ᵊn-əl\ *adj*

ret·i·nue \'ret-ᵊn-ˌü, -ˌyü\ *n* : the body of attendants or followers of a distinguished person

re·tire \ri-'tīr\ *vb* **re·tired; re·tir·ing 1** : RETREAT **2** : to withdraw esp. for privacy **3** : to withdraw from one's occupation or position : conclude one's career **4** : to go to bed **5** : to cause to be out in baseball — **re·tire·ment** *n*

re·tired \ri-'tīrd\ *adj* **1** : SECLUDED, QUIET **2** : withdrawn from active duty or from one's career

re·tir·ee \ri-ˌtī-'rē\ *n* : a person who has retired from a career

re·tir·ing *adj* : SHY, RESERVED

¹**re·tort** \ri-'tȯrt\ *vb* [L *retortus*, pp. of *retorquēre*, lit., to twist back, hurl back, fr. *re-* back + *torquēre* to twist] **1** : to say in reply : answer back usu. sharply **2** : to answer (an argument) by a counter argument **3** : RETALIATE

²**retort** *n* : a quick, witty, or cutting reply

³**re·tort** \ri-'tȯrt, 'rē-ˌtȯrt\ *n* [MF *retorte*, fr. ML *retorta*, fr. L, fem. of *retortus*, pp. of *retorquēre* to twist back; fr. its shape] : a vessel in which substances are distilled or broken up by heat

re·touch \(ˌ)rē-'təch\ *vb* : TOUCH UP; *esp* : to change (as a photographic negative) in order to produce a more desirable appearance

re·trace \(ˌ)rē-'trās\ *vb* : to go over again or in a reverse direction ⟨*retraced* his steps⟩

re·tract \ri-'trakt\ *vb* **1** : to draw back or in **2** : to withdraw (as a charge or promise) : DISAVOW — **re·tract·able** *adj* — **re·trac·tion** \-'trak-shən\ *n*

re·trac·tile \ri-'trakt-ᵊl, -'trak-ˌtīl\ *adj* : capable of being drawn back or in ⟨~ claws⟩

¹**re·tread** \(ˌ)rē-'tred\ *vb* **re·tread·ed; re·tread·ing** : to put a new tread on (a worn tire)

²**re·tread** \'rē-ˌtred\ *n* **1** : a retreaded tire **2** : one pressed into service again; *also* : REMAKE

¹**re·treat** \ri-'trēt\ *n* **1** : an act of withdrawing esp. from something dangerous, difficult, or disagreeable **2** : a military signal for withdrawal; *also* : a military flag-lowering ceremony **3** : a place of privacy or safety : REFUGE **4** : a period of group withdrawal for prayer, meditation, and study

²**retreat** *vb* **1** : to make a retreat : WITHDRAW **2** : to slope backward

re·trench \ri-'trench\ *vb* [obs. F *retrencher* (now *retrancher*), fr. MF *retrenchier*, fr. *re-* + *trenchier* to cut] **1** : to cut down or pare away : REDUCE, CURTAIL **2** : to cut down expenses : ECONOMIZE — **re·trench·ment** *n*

ret·ri·bu·tion \ˌre-trə-'byü-shən\ *n* : something administered or exacted in recompense; *esp* : PUNISHMENT **syn** reprisal, vengeance, revenge, retaliation — **re·trib·u·tive** \ri-'tri-byə-tiv\ *adj* — **re·trib·u·to·ry** \-byə-ˌtōr-ē\ *adj*

re·trieve \ri-'trēv\ *vb* **re·trieved; re·triev·ing 1** : to search about for and bring in (killed or wounded game) **2** : RECOVER, RESTORE — **re·triev·able** *adj* — **re·triev·al** \-'trē-vəl\ *n*

re·triev·er \ri-'trē-vər\ *n* : one that retrieves; *esp* : a dog of any of several breeds used esp. for retrieving game

ret·ro·ac·tive \ˌre-trō-'ak-tiv\ *adj* : made effective as of a date prior to enactment ⟨a ~ pay raise⟩ — **ret·ro·ac·tive·ly** *adv*

ret·ro·fit \'re-trō-ˌfit, ˌre-trō-'fit\ *vb* : to furnish (as an aircraft) with newly available equipment — **ret·ro·fit** \'re-trō-ˌfit\ *n*

¹**ret·ro·grade** \'re-trə-ˌgrād\ *adj* **1** : moving or tending backward **2** : tending toward or resulting in a worse condition

²**ret·ro·grade** *vb* **1** : RETREAT **2** : DETERIORATE, DEGEN-
ERATE

ret·ro·gres·sion \,re-trə-'gre-shən\ *n* : return to a former and less complex level of development or organization — **ret·ro·gress** \,re-trə-'gres\ *vb* — **ret·ro·**
gres·sive \,re-trə-'gre-siv\ *adj*

ret·ro·rock·et \'re-trō-,rä-kət\ *n* : an auxiliary rocket
engine (as on a spacecraft) used to slow forward motion

ret·ro·spect \'re-trə-,spekt\ *n* : a review of past events
— **ret·ro·spec·tion** \,re-trə-'spek-shən\ *n* — **ret·ro·**
spec·tive \-'spek-tiv\ *adj* — **ret·ro·spec·tive·ly** *adv*

ret·ro·vi·rus \'re-trō-,vī-rəs\ *n* : any of a group of RNA-
containing viruses (as HIV) that make DNA using
RNA instead of the reverse

¹**re·turn** \ri-'tərn\ *vb* **1** : to go or come back **2** : to pass,
give, or send back to an earlier possessor **3** : to put
back to or in a former place or state **4** : REPLY, AN-
SWER **5** : to report esp. officially **6** : to elect to office
7 : to bring in (as profit) : YIELD **8** : to give or perform
in return — **re·turn·er** *n*

²**return** *n* **1** : an act of coming or going back to or from
a former place or state **2** : RECURRENCE **3** : a report
of the results of balloting **4** : a formal statement of
taxable income **5** : the profit from labor, investment,
or business : YIELD **6** : the act of returning something
7 : something that returns or is returned; *also* : a
means for conveying something (as water) back to its
starting point **8** : something given in repayment or re-
ciprocation; *also* : ANSWER, RETORT **9** : an answering
play — **return** *adj*

¹**re·turn·able** \ri-'tər-nə-bəl\ *adj* : capable of being re-
turned (as for reuse or recycling); *also* : permitted to
be returned

²**returnable** *n* : a returnable beverage container

re·turn·ee \ri-,tər-'nē\ *n* : one who returns

re·union \rē-'yü-nyən\ *n* **1** : an act of reuniting : the
state of being reunited **2** : a meeting of persons after
separation

¹**rev** \'rev\ *n* : a revolution of a motor

²**rev** *vb* **revved; rev·ving** : to increase the revolutions
per minute of (a motor)

³**rev** *abbr* **1** revenue **2** reverse **3** review; reviewed **4** re-
vised; revision **5** revolution

Rev *abbr* **1** Revelation **2** Reverend

re·vamp \(,)rē-'vamp\ *vb* : RECONSTRUCT, REVISE; *also*
: RENOVATE

re·vanche \rə-'väⁿsh\ *n* [F] : REVENGE; *esp* : a usu. political policy designed to recover lost territory or status

re·veal \ri-'vēl\ *vb* **1** : to make known **2** : to show plainly : open up to view

re·veil·le \'re-və-lē\ *n* [modif. of F *réveillez,* imper. pl.
of *réveiller* to awaken, fr. *eveiller* to awaken, fr.
(assumed) VL *exvigilare,* fr. L *vigilare* to keep
watch, stay awake] : a military signal sounded at
about sunrise

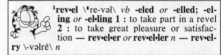

¹**rev·el** \'re-vəl\ *vb* **-eled** *or* **-elled; -el-**
ing *or* **-el·ling** **1** : to take part in a revel
2 : to take great pleasure or satisfac-
tion — **rev·el·er** *or* **rev·el·ler** *n* — **rev·el-**
ry \-vəlrē\ *n*

²**revel** *n* : a usu. wild party or celebration

rev·e·la·tion \,re-və-'lā-shən\ *n* **1** : an act of revealing
2 : something revealed; *esp* : an enlightening or astonishing disclosure

Revelation *n* — see BIBLE table

¹**re·venge** \ri-'venj\ *vb* **re·venged; re·veng·ing** : to in-
flict harm or injury in return for (a wrong) : AVENGE
— **re·veng·er** *n*

²**revenge** *n* **1** : a desire for revenge **2** : an act or instance
of retaliation to get even **3** : an opportunity for getting
satisfaction **syn** vengeance, retribution, reprisal —
re·venge·ful *adj*

rev·e·nue \'re-və-,nü, -,nyü\ *n* [ME, fr. MF, fr. *revenir*
to return, fr. L *revenire,* fr. *re-* back + *venire* to
come] **1** : investment income **2** : money collected by
a government (as through taxes)

rev·e·nu·er \'re-və-,nü-ər, -,nyü-\ *n* : a revenue officer
or boat

re·verb \ri-'vərb, 'rē-,vərb\ *n* : an electronically produced echo effect in recorded music; *also* : a device
for producing reverb

re·ver·ber·ate \ri-'vər-bə-,rāt\ *vb* **-at·ed; -at·ing 1** : RE-
FLECT ⟨~ light or heat⟩ **2** : to resound in or as if in a
series of echoes — **re·ver·ber·a·tion** \-,vər-bə-'rā-
shən\ *n*

re·vere \ri-'vir\ *vb* **re·vered; re·ver·ing** : to show hon-
or and devotion to : VENERATE **syn** reverence, worship, adore

¹**rev·er·ence** \'re-vrəns, -və-rəns\ *n* **1** : honor or respect
felt or shown **2** : a gesture (as a bow or curtsy) of respect

²**reverence** *vb* **-enced; -enc·ing** : to regard or treat with
reverence

¹**rev·er·end** \'re-vrənd, -və-rənd\ *adj* **1** : worthy of rev-
erence : REVERED **2** : being a member of the clergy —
used as a title

²**reverend** *n* : a member of the clergy

rev·er·ent \'re-vrənt, -və-rənt\ *adj* : expressing reverence — **rev·er·ent·ly** *adv*

rev·er·en·tial \,re-və-'ren-chəl\ *adj* : REVERENT

rev·er·ie *also* **rev·ery** \'re-və-rē\ *n, pl* **-er·ies 1** : DAY-
DREAM **2** : the state of being lost in thought

re·ver·sal \ri-'vər-səl\ *n* : an act or process of reversing

¹**re·verse** \ri-'vərs\ *adj* **1** : opposite to a previous or nor-
mal condition (in ~ order) **2** : acting or working in a
manner opposite the usual **3** : bringing about reverse
movement ⟨~ gear⟩ — **re·verse·ly** *adv*

²**reverse** *vb* **re·versed; re·vers·ing 1** : to turn upside
down or completely about in position or direction **2**
: to set aside or change (as a legal decision) **3** : to
change to the contrary ⟨~ a policy⟩ **4** : to go or cause
to go in the opposite direction **5** : to put (as a car) in
reverse — **re·vers·ible** \-'vər-sə-bəl\ *adj*

³**reverse** *n* **1** : something contrary to something else : OPPOSITE **2** : an act or instance of reversing; *esp* : a change for the worse **3** : the back of something **4** : a gear that reverses something

re·ver·sion \ri-'vər-zhən\ *n* **1** : the right of succession or future possession (as to a title or property) **2** : return toward some former or ancestral condition; *also* : a product of this — **re·ver·sion·ary** \-zhə-₁ner-ē\ *adj*

re·vert \ri-'vərt\ *vb* **1** : to come or go back ⟨∼ed to savagery⟩ **2** : to return to a proprietor or his or her heirs **3** : to return to an ancestral type

¹**re·view** \ri-'vyü\ *n* **1** : an act of revising **2** : a formal military inspection **3** : a general survey **4** : INSPECTION, EXAMINATION; *esp* : REEXAMINATION **5** : a critical evaluation (as of a book) **6** : a magazine devoted to reviews and essays **7** : a renewed study of previously studied material **8** : REVUE

²**re·view** \ri-'vyü, *1 also* 'rē-\ *vb* **1** : to examine or study again; *esp* : to reexamine judicially **2** : to hold a review of ⟨∼ troops⟩ **3** : to write a critical examination of ⟨∼ a novel⟩ **4** : to look back over ⟨∼ed her accomplishments⟩ **5** : to study material again

re·view·er \ri-'vyü-ər\ *n* : one that reviews; *esp* : a writer of critical reviews

re·vile \ri-'vīl\ *vb* **re·viled; re·vil·ing** : to abuse verbally : rail at syn vituperate, berate, rate, upbraid, scold — **re·vile·ment** *n* — **re·vil·er** *n*

re·vise \ri-'vīz\ *vb* **re·vised; re·vis·ing 1** : to look over something written in order to correct or improve **2** : to make a new version of — **re·vis·able** *adj* — **re·vise** *n* — **re·vis·er** *or* **re·vi·sor** \-'vī-zər\ *n* — **re·vi·sion** \-'vi-zhən\ *n*

re·vi·tal·ise *Brit var of* REVITALIZE

re·vi·tal·ize \₁rē-'vīt-ᵊl-₁īz\ *vb* **-ized; -iz·ing** : to give new life or vigor to — **re·vi·tal·i·za·tion** \(₁)rē-₁vīt-ᵊl-ə-'zā-shən\ *n*

re·viv·al \ri-'vī-vəl\ *n* **1** : an act of reviving : the state of being revived **2** : a new publication or presentation (as of a book or play) **3** : an evangelistic meeting or series of meetings

re·vive \ri-'vīv\ *vb* **re·vived; re·viv·ing 1** : to bring back to life consciousness, or activity : make or become fresh or strong again **2** : to bring back into use — **re·viv·er** *n*

re·viv·i·fy \rē-'vi-və-₁fī\ *vb* : REVIVE — **re·viv·i·fi·ca·tion** \-₁vi-və-fə-'kā-shən\ *n*

re·vo·ca·ble \'re-və-kə-bəl\ *also* ri-'vō-kə-bəl\ *adj* : capable of being revoked

re·vo·ca·tion \₁re-və-'kā-shən\ *n* : an act or instance of revoking

re·voke \ri-'vōk\ *vb* **re·voked; re·vok·ing 1** : to annul by recalling or taking back : REPEAL, RESCIND **2** : RENEGE **2** — **re·vok·er** *n*

¹**re·volt** \ri-'vōlt\ *vb* **1** : to throw off allegiance to a ruler or government : REBEL **2** : to experience disgust or shock **3** : to turn or cause to turn away with disgust or abhorrence — **re·volt·er** *n*

²**revolt** *n* : REBELLION, INSURRECTION

re·volt·ing *adj* : extremely offensive — **re·volt·ing·ly** *adv*

rev·o·lu·tion \₁re-və-'lü-shən\ *n* **1** : the action by a heavenly body of going round in an orbit **2** : ROTATION **3** : a sudden, radical, or complete change; *esp* : the overthrow or renunciation of one ruler or government and substitution of another by the governed

¹**rev·o·lu·tion·ary** \-shə-₁ner-ē\ *adj* **1** : of or relating to revolution **2** : tending to or promoting revolution **3** : constituting or bringing about a major change

²**revolutionary** *n, pl* **-ar·ies** : one who takes part in a revolution or who advocates revolutionary doctrines

rev·o·lu·tion·ise *Brit var of* REVOLUTIONIZE

rev·o·lu·tion·ist \₁re-və-'lü-shə-nist\ *n* : REVOLUTIONARY — **revolutionist** *adj*

rev·o·lu·tion·ize \-₁nīz\ *vb* **-ized; -iz·ing** : to change fundamentally or completely : make revolutionary — **rev·o·lu·tion·iz·er** *n*

re·volve \ri-'välv\ *vb* **re·volved; re·volv·ing 1** : to turn over in the mind : reflect upon : PONDER **2** : to move in an orbit; *also* : ROTATE — **re·volv·able** *adj*

re·volv·er \ri-'väl-vər\ *n* : a pistol with a revolving cylinder of several chambers

re·vue \ri-'vyü\ *n* : a theatrical production consisting typically of brief often satirical sketches and songs

re·vul·sion \ri-'vəl-shən\ *n* **1** : a strong sudden reaction or change of feeling **2** : a feeling of complete distaste or repugnance

revved *past and past part of* REV

revving *pres part of* REV

¹**re·ward** \ri-'wȯrd\ *vb* **1** : to give a reward to or for **2** : RECOMPENSE

²**reward** *n* **1** : something given in return for good or evil done or received; *esp* : something given or offered for some service or attainment **2** : a stimulus that is administered to an organism after a response and that increases the probability of occurrence of the response syn premium, prize, award

¹**re·wind** \(₁)rē-'wīnd\ *vb* **-wound; -wind·ing 1** : to wind again **2** : to reverse the winding of (as film)

²**re·wind** \'rē-₁wīnd\ *n* **1** : something that rewinds **2** : an act of rewinding

re·work \(₁)rē-'wərk\ *vb* **1** : REVISE **2** : to reprocess for further use

¹**re·write** \(₁)rē-'rīt\ *vb* **-wrote; -writ·ten; -writ·ing** : to make a revision of : REVISE

²**re·write** \'rē-₁rīt\ *n* : an instance or a piece of rewriting

RF *abbr* radio frequency

RFD *abbr* rural free delivery

Rh *symbol* rhodium

RH *abbr* right hand

rhap·so·dy \'rap-sə-dē\ *n, pl* **-dies** [L *rhapsodia* portion of an epic poem adapted for recitation, fr. Gk *rhapsōidia* recitation of selections from epic poetry, fr. *rhaptein* to sew, stitch together + *aidein* to sing] **1** : an expression of extravagant praise or ecstasy **2** : an instrumental composition of irregular form —

rhap•sod•ic \rap-'sä-dik\ *adj* — **rhap•sod•i•cal•ly** \-di-k(ə-)lē\ *adv* — **rhap•so•dize** \'rap-sə-₁dīz\ *vb*

rhea \'rē-ə\ *n* : either of two large flightless 3-toed So. American birds that resemble but are smaller than the African ostrich

rhe•ni•um \'rē-nē-əm\ *n* : a rare heavy hard metallic chemical element — see ELEMENT table

rheo•stat \'rē-ə-₁stat\ *n* : a resistor for regulating an electric current by means of variable resistances — **rheo•stat•ic** \₁rē-ə-'sta-tik\ *adj*

rhe•sus monkey \'rē-səs-\ *n* : a pale brown Indian monkey often used in medical research

rhet•o•ric \'re-tə-rik\ *n* [ME *rethorik*, fr. MF *rethorique*, fr. L *rhetorica*, fr. Gk *rhētorikē*, lit., art of oratory, fr. *rhētōr* public speaker, fr. *eirein* to speak] : the art of speaking or writing effectively — **rhe•tor•i•cal** \ri-'tòr-i-kəl\ *adj* — **rhet•o•ri•cian** \₁re-tə-'ri-shən\ *n*

rheum \'rüm\ *n* : a watery discharge from the mucous membranes esp. of the eyes or nose — **rheumy** *adj*

rheu•mat•ic fever \rü-'ma-tik-\ *n* : an acute disease chiefly of children and young adults that is characterized by fever, by inflammation and pain in and around the joints, and by inflammation of the membranes surrounding the heart and the heart valves

rheu•ma•tism \'rü-mə-₁ti-zəm, 'rù-\ *n* : any of various conditions marked by stiffness, pain, or swelling in muscles or joints — **rheu•mat•ic** \rù-'ma-tik\ *adj*

rheu•ma•toid arthritis \-₁tòid-\ *n* : a progressive constitutional disease characterized by inflammation and swelling of joint structures

Rh factor \¦är-'āch-\ *n* [*rh*esus monkey (in which it was first detected)] : any of one or more inherited substances in red blood cells that may cause dangerous reactions in some infants or in transfusions

rhine•stone \'rīn-₁stōn\ *n* : a colorless imitation stone of high luster made of glass, paste, or gem quartz

rhi•no \'rī-nō\ *n*, *pl* **rhino** *or* **rhinos** : RHINOCEROS

rhi•noc•er•os \rī-'nä-sə-rəs\ *n*, *pl* **-noc•er•os•es** *or* **-noc•er•os** *or* **-noc•eri** \-'nä-sə-₁rī\ [ME *rinoceros*, fr. L *rhinoceros*, fr. Gk *rhinokerōs*, fr. *rhin-, rhis* nose + *keras* horn] : any of a family of large thick-skinned mammals of Africa and Asia with one or two upright horns of keratin on the snout and three toes on each foot

rhi•zome \'rī-₁zōm\ *n* : a fleshy, rootlike, and usu. horizontal underground plant stem that forms shoots above and roots below — **rhi•zom•a•tous** \rī-'zä-mə-təs\ *adj*

Rh–neg•a•tive \₁är-₁āch-'ne-gə-tiv\ *adj* : lacking Rh factors in the red blood cells

rho \'rō\ *n* : the 17th letter of the Greek alphabet — P or ρ

rho•di•um \'rō-dē-əm\ *n* : a hard ductile metallic chemical element — see ELEMENT table

rho•do•den•dron \₁rō-də-'den-drən\ *n* : any of a genus of shrubs or trees of the heath family with clusters of large bright flowers

rhom•boid \'räm-₁bòid\ *n* : a parallelogram with unequal adjacent sides and angles that are not right angles — **rhomboid** *or* **rhom•boi•dal** \räm-'bòid-əl\ *adj*

rhom•bus \'räm-bəs\ *n*, *pl* **rhom•bus•es** *or* **rhom•bi** \-₁bī\ : a parallelogram having all four sides equal

Rh–pos•i•tive \₁är-₁āch-'pä-zə-tiv\ *adj* : containing one or more Rh factors in the red blood cells

rhu•barb \'rü-₁bärb\ *n* [ME *rubarbe*, fr. MF *reubarbe*, fr. ML *reubarbarum*, alter. of *rha barbarum*, lit., barbarian rhubarb] : a garden plant related to the buckwheat having leaves with thick juicy edible pink and red stems

¹rhyme \'rīm\ *n* **1** : a composition in verse that rhymes; *also* : POETRY **2** : correspondence in terminal sounds (as of two lines of verse)

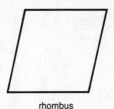

rhombus

²rhyme *vb* **rhymed; rhym•ing 1** : to make rhymes; *also* : to write poetry **2** : to have rhymes : be in rhyme

rhythm \'ri-thəm\ *n* **1** : regular rise and fall in the flow of sound in speech **2** : a movement or activity in which some action or element recurs regularly — **rhyth•mic** \'rith-mik\ *or* **rhyth•mi•cal** \-mi-kəl\ *adj* — **rhyth•mi•cal•ly** \-k(ə-)lē\ *adv*

rhythm and blues *n* : popular music based on blues and black folk music

rhythm method *n* : birth control by refraining from sexual intercourse during the time when ovulation is most likely to occur

RI *abbr* Rhode Island

ri•al \rē-'òl, -'äl\ *n* — see MONEY table

¹rib \'rib\ *n* **1** : any of the series of curved bones of the chest of most vertebrates that are joined to the backbone in pairs and help to support the body wall and protect the organs inside **2** : something resembling a rib in shape or function **3** : any of the parallel ridges in a knitted or woven fabric

²rib *vb* **ribbed; rib•bing 1** : to furnish or strengthen with ribs **2** : to form ridges in knitting or weaving

³rib *vb* **ribbed; rib•bing** : to poke fun at : TEASE — **rib•ber** *n*

rib•ald \'ri-bəld\ *adj* : coarse or indecent esp. in language ⟨∼ jokes⟩ — **rib•ald•ry** \-bəl-drē\ *n*

rib•and \'ri-bənd\ *n* : RIBBON

rib•bon \'ri-bən\ *n* **1** : a narrow fabric typically of silk or velvet used for trimming and for badges **2** : a strip of inked cloth (as in a typewriter) **3** : TATTER, SHRED ⟨torn to ∼s⟩

ri•bo•fla•vin \₁rī-bə-'flā-vən, 'rī-bə-₁flā-vən\ *n* : a growth-promoting vitamin of the vitamin B complex occurring in milk and liver

ri•bo•nu•cle•ic acid \₁rī-bō-nù-₁klē-ik-, -nyù-, -₁klä-\ *n* : RNA

ri•bose \'rī-₁bōs\ *n* : a sugar with five carbon atoms and five oxygen atoms in each molecule that is part of RNA

ri•bo•some \'rī-bə-₁sōm\ *n* : any of the RNA= rich cytoplasmic granules in a cell that are sites of protein synthesis — **ri•bo•som•al** \₁rī-bə-'sō-məl\ *adj*

rice \'rīs\ *n* : the starchy seeds of an annual grass that are cooked and used for food; *also* : this widely cultivated grass of warm wet areas

rich \'rich\ *adj* **1** : possessing or controlling great wealth : WEALTHY **2** : COSTLY, VALUABLE **3** : deep and pleasing in color or tone **4** : ABUNDANT **5** : containing much sugar, fat, or seasoning; *also* : high in combustible content **6** : FRUITFUL, FERTILE — **rich•ly** *adv* — **rich•ness** *n*

rich•es \'ri-chəz\ *n pl* [ME, sing. or pl., fr. *richesse*, lit., richness, fr. OF, fr. *riche* rich] : things that make one rich : WEALTH

Rich•ter scale \'rik-tər-\ *n* : a scale for expressing the magnitude of a seismic disturbance (as an earthquake) in terms of the energy dissipated in it

rick \'rik\ *n* : a large stack (as of hay) in the open air

rick•ets \'ri-kəts\ *n* : a childhood deficiency disease marked esp. by soft deformed bones and caused by inadequate sunlight or inadequate vitamin D

rick•ett•sia \ri-'ket-sē-ə\ *n*, *pl* **-si•as** *or* **-si•ae** \-sē-₁ē\

: any of a group of rod-shaped bacteria that cause various diseases (as typhus)

rick•ety \\'ri-kə-tē\\ *adj* **1** : affected with rickets **2** : SHAKY; *also* : in unsound physical condition

rick•sha *or* **rick•shaw** \\'rik-₁shȯ\\ *n* : a small covered 2-wheeled carriage pulled by one person and used orig. in Japan

¹ric•o•chet \\'ri-kə-₁shā, *Brit also* -₁shet\\ *n* : a bouncing off at an angle (as of a bullet off a wall); *also* : an object that ricochets

²ricochet *vb* **-cheted** \-₁shād\ *or* **-chet•ted** \-₁she-təd\; **-chet•ing** \-₁shā-iŋ\ *or* **-chet•ting** \-₁she-tiŋ\ : to skip with or as if with glancing rebounds

rid \\'rid\\ *vb* **rid** *also* **rid•ded; rid•ding** : to make free : CLEAR, RELIEVE — **rid•dance** \\'rid-ᵊns\\ *n*

rid•den \\'rid-ᵊn\\ *adj* **1** : harassed, oppressed, or obsessed by ⟨debt-*ridden*⟩ **2** : excessively full of or supplied with ⟨slum-*ridden*⟩

¹rid•dle \\'rid-ᵊl\\ *n* : a puzzling question to be solved or answered by guessing

²riddle *vb* **rid•dled; rid•dling** **1** : EXPLAIN, SOLVE **2** : to speak in riddles

³riddle *n* : a coarse sieve

⁴riddle *vb* **rid•dled; rid•dling** **1** : to sift with a riddle **2** : to pierce with many holes **3** : PERMEATE

¹ride \\'rīd\\ *vb* **rode** \\'rōd\\; **rid•den** \\'rid-ᵊn\\; **rid•ing** **1** : to go on an animal's back or in a conveyance (as a boat, car, or airplane); *also* : to sit on and control so as to be carried along ⟨~ a bicycle⟩ **2** : to float or move on water ⟨~ at anchor⟩; *also* : to move like a floating object **3** : to bear along : CARRY ⟨*rode* her on their shoulders⟩ **4** : to travel over a surface ⟨car ~s well⟩ **5** : to proceed over on horseback **6** : to torment by nagging or teasing

²ride *n* **1** : an act of riding; *esp* : a trip on horseback or by vehicle **2** : a way (as a road or path) suitable for riding **3** : a mechanical device (as a merry-go-round) for riding on **4** : a means of transportation

rid•er \\'rī-dər\\ *n* **1** : one that rides **2** : an addition to a document often attached on a separate piece of paper **3** : a clause dealing with an unrelated matter attached to a legislative bill during passage — **rid•er•less** *adj*

¹ridge \\'rij\\ *n* **1** : a range of hills **2** : a raised line or strip **3** : the line made where two sloping surfaces (as of a roof) meet — **ridgy** *adj*

²ridge *vb* **ridged; ridg•ing** **1** : to form into a ridge **2** : to extend in ridges

¹rid•i•cule \\'ri-də-₁kyül\\ *n* : the act of exposing to laughter : DERISION

²ridicule *vb* **-culed; -cul•ing** : to laugh at or make fun of mockingly or contemptuously **syn** deride, taunt, twit, mock

ri•dic•u•lous \rə-'di-kyə-ləs\ *adj* : arousing or deserving ridicule : ABSURD, PREPOSTEROUS **syn** laughable, ludicrous, farcical, risible — **ri•dic•u•lous•ly** *adv* — **ri•dic•u•lous•ness** *n*

ri•el \rē-'el\ *n* — see MONEY table

RIF *abbr* reduction in force

rife \\'rīf\\ *adj* : WIDESPREAD, PREVALENT, ABOUNDING — **rife** *adv* — **rife•ly** *adv*

riff \\'rif\\ *n* : a repeated phrase in jazz typically supporting a solo improvisation; *also* : a piece based on such a phrase — **riff** *vb*

riff•raff \\'rif-₁raf\\ *n* [ME *riffe raffe*, fr. *rif and raf* every single one, fr. MF *rif et raf* completely] **1** : RABBLE **2** : REFUSE, RUBBISH

¹ri•fle \\'rī-fəl\\ *vb* **ri•fled; ri•fling** : to ransack esp. with the intent to steal — **ri•fler** *n*

²rifle *vb* **ri•fled; ri•fling** : to cut spiral grooves into the bore of ⟨*rifled* pipe⟩ — **rifling** *n*

³rifle *n* **1** : a shoulder weapon with a rifled bore **2** *pl* : soldiers armed with rifles — **ri•fle•man** \-fəl-mən\ *n*

rift \\'rift\\ *n* **1** : CLEFT, FISSURE **2** : FAULT **6** **3** : ESTRANGEMENT, SEPARATION — **rift** *vb*

¹rig \\'rig\\ *vb* **rigged; rig•ging** **1** : to fit out (as a ship) with rigging **2** : CLOTHE, DRESS **3** : EQUIP **4** : to set up esp. as a makeshift ⟨~ up a shelter⟩

²rig *n* **1** : the distinctive shape, number, and arrangement of sails and masts of a ship **2** : a carriage with its horse **3** : CLOTHING, DRESS **4** : EQUIPMENT

³rig *vb* **rigged; rig•ging** **1** : to manipulate or control esp. by deceptive or dishonest means **2** : to fix in advance for a desired result — **rig•ger** *n*

rig•ging \\'ri-giŋ, -gən\\ *n* **1** : the ropes and chains that hold and move masts, sails, and spars of a ship **2** : a network (as in theater scenery) used for support and manipulation

¹right \\'rīt\\ *adj* **1** : RIGHTEOUS, UPRIGHT **2** : JUST, PROPER **3** : conforming to truth or fact : CORRECT **4** : APPROPRIATE, SUITABLE **5** : STRAIGHT ⟨a ~ line⟩ **6** : GENUINE, REAL **7** : of, relating to, or being the side of the body which is away from the heart and on which the hand is stronger and more skilled in most persons **8** : located nearer to the right hand; *esp* : being on the right when facing in the same direction as the observer **9** : made to be placed or worn outward ⟨~ side of a rug⟩ **10** : NORMAL, SOUND (not in her ~ mind) **syn** correct, accurate, exact, precise, nice — **right•ness** *n*

²right *n* **1** : qualities that constitute what is correct, just, proper, or honorable **2** : something (as a power or privilege) to which one has a just or lawful claim **3** : just action or decision : the cause of justice **4** : the side or part that is on or toward the right side **5** *cap* : political conservatives **6** *often cap* : a conservative position — **right•ward** \-wərd\ *adj*

³right *adv* **1** : according to what is right ⟨live ~⟩ **2** : EXACTLY, PRECISELY ⟨~ here and now⟩ **3** : DIRECTLY ⟨went ~ home⟩ **4** : according to fact or truth ⟨guess ~⟩ **5** : all the way : COMPLETELY ⟨~ to the end⟩ **6** : IMMEDIATELY ⟨~ after lunch⟩ **7** : QUITE, VERY ⟨~ nice weather⟩ **8** : on or to the right ⟨looked ~ and left⟩

⁴right *vb* **1** : to relieve from wrong **2** : to adjust or restore to a proper state or position **3** : to bring or restore to an upright position **4** : to become upright — **right•er** *n*

right angle *n* : an angle whose measure is 90° : an angle

whose sides are perpendicular to each other —
right–an·gled \'rīt-ˌaŋ-gəld\ *or* **right–an·gle** \-gəl\
adj
right circular cone *n* : CONE 2
righ·teous \'rī-chəs\ *adj* : acting or being in accordance
with what is just, honorable, and free from guilt or
wrong : UPRIGHT **syn** virtuous, noble, moral, ethical
— **righ·teous·ly** *adv* — **righ·teous·ness** *n*
right·ful \'rīt-fəl\ *adj* **1** : JUST; *also* : FITTING **2** : having
or held by a legally just claim — **right·ful·ly** *adv* —
right·ful·ness *n*
right–hand \'rīt-ˌhand\ *adj* **1** : situated on the right **2**
: RIGHT-HANDED **3** : chiefly relied on ⟨his ∼ man⟩
right–hand·ed \-'han-dəd\ *adj* **1** : using the right hand
habitually or better than the left **2** : designed for or
done with the right hand **3** : CLOCKWISE ⟨a ∼ twist⟩
— **right–handed** *adv* — **right–hand·ed·ly** *adv* —
right–hand·ed·ness *n*
right·ly \'rīt-lē\ *adv* **1** : FAIRLY, JUSTLY **2** : PROPERLY **3**
: CORRECTLY, EXACTLY
right–of–way *n, pl* **rights–of–way 1** : a legal right of
passage over another person's ground **2** : the area
over which a right-of-way exists **3** : the land on which
a public road is built **4** : the land occupied by a railroad **5** : the land used by a public utility **6** : the right
of traffic to take precedence over other traffic
right on *interj* — used to express agreement or give
encouragement
right–to–life *adj* : ANTIABORTION — **right–to–lifer** *n*
right triangle *n* : a triangle having one right angle
rig·id \'ri-jəd\ *adj* **1** : lacking flexibility **2** : strictly observed **syn** severe, stern, rigorous, stringent — **ri-
gid·i·ty** \rə-'ji-də-tē\ *n* — **rig·id·ly** *adv*
rig·ma·role \'ri-gə-mə-ˌrōl\ *n* [alter. of obs. *ragman
roll* long list, catalog] **1** : confused or senseless talk **2**
: a complex and ritualistic procedure
rig·or \'ri-gər\ *n* **1** : the quality of being inflexible or
unyielding : STRICTNESS **2** : HARSHNESS, SEVERITY **3** : a
tremor caused by a chill **4** : strict precision : EXACT-
NESS — **rig·or·ous** *adj* — **rig·or·ous·ly** *adv*
rig·or mor·tis \ˌri-gər-'mòr-təs\ *n* [NL, stiffness of
death] : temporary rigidity of muscles occurring after
death
rig·our *chiefly Brit var of* RIGOR
rile \'rī(ə)l\ *vb* **riled; ril·ing 1** : to make angry **2** : ROIL 1
rill \'ril\ *n* : a very small brook
¹rim \'rim\ *n* **1** : the outer part of a wheel **2** : an outer
edge esp. of something curved : BORDER, MARGIN
²rim *vb* **rimmed; rim·ming 1** : to serve as a rim for
: BORDER **2** : to run around the rim of
¹rime \'rīm\ *n* : FROST **2** — **rimy** \'rī-mē\ *adj*
²rime *var of* RHYME
rind \'rīnd\ *n* : a usu. hard or tough outer layer (lemon
∼)
¹ring \'riŋ\ *n* **1** : a circular band worn as an ornament
or token or used for holding or fastening ⟨wedding ∼⟩
⟨key ∼⟩ **2** : something circular in shape ⟨smoke ∼⟩ **3**
: a place for contest or display ⟨boxing ∼⟩; *also*
: PRIZEFIGHTING **4** : ANNUAL RING **5** : a group of people who work together for selfish or dishonest purposes — **ringed** *adj* — **ring·like** \'riŋ-ˌlik\ *adj*
²ring *vb* **ringed; ring·ing** \'riŋ-iŋ\ **1** : ENCIRCLE **2** : to
throw a ring over (a mark) in a game (as quoits) **3** : to
move in a ring or spirally
³ring *vb* **rang** \'raŋ\; **rung** \'rəŋ\; **ring·ing** \'riŋ-iŋ\ **1** : to
sound resonantly when struck; *also* : to feel as if
filled with such sound **2** : to cause to make a clear metallic sound by striking **3** : to announce or call by or
as if by striking a bell ⟨∼ an alarm⟩ **4** : to repeat loudly and persistently **5** : to summon esp. by a bell ⟨∼
for the butler⟩
⁴ring *n* **1** : a set of bells **2** : the clear resonant sound of
vibrating metal **3** : resonant tone : SONORITY **4** : a
sound or character expressive of a particular quality
5 : an act or instance of ringing; *esp* : a telephone call
ring·er \'riŋ-ər\ *n* **1** : one that sounds by ringing **2** : one

that enters a competition under false representations
3 : one that closely resembles another
²ringer *n* : one that encircles or puts a ring around
ring finger *n* : the third finger of the left hand counting
the forefinger as one
ring·git \'riŋ-git\ *n* — see MONEY table
ring·lead·er \'riŋ-ˌlē-dər\ *n* : a leader esp. of a group
of troublemakers
ring·let \-lət\ *n* : a long curl
ring·mas·ter \-ˌmas-tər\ *n* : one in charge of performances in a circus ring
ring up *vb* **1** : to total and record esp. by means of a
cash register **2** : ACHIEVE ⟨rang up many triumphs⟩
ring·worm \'riŋ-ˌwərm\ *n* : any of several contagious
skin diseases caused by fungi and marked by ring-
shaped discolored patches
rink \'riŋk\ *n* : a level extent of ice marked off for skating or various games; *also* : a similar surface (as of
wood) marked off or enclosed for a sport or game
⟨roller-skating ∼⟩
¹rinse \'rins\ *vb* **rinsed; rins·ing** [ME *rincen,* fr. MF
rincer, fr. (assumed) VL *recentiare,* fr. L *recent-, re-
cens* fresh, recent] **1** : to wash lightly or in water only
2 : to cleanse (as of soap) with clear water **3** : to treat
(hair) with a rinse — **rins·er** *n*
²rinse *n* **1** : an act of rinsing **2** : a liquid used for rinsing
3 : a solution that temporarily tints hair
ri·ot \'rī-ət\ *n* **1** *archaic* : disorderly behavior **2** : disturbance of the public peace; *esp* : a violent public
disorder **3** : random or disorderly profusion ⟨a ∼ of
color⟩ **4** : one that is wildly amusing ⟨the comedy is
a ∼⟩ — **riot** *vb* — **ri·ot·er** *n* — **ri·ot·ous** *adj*
¹rip \'rip\ *vb* **ripped; rip·ping 1** : to cut or tear open **2**
: to saw or split (wood) with the grain — **rip·per** *n*
²rip *n* : a rent made by ripping
RIP *abbr* [L *requiescat in pace*] may he rest in peace,
may she rest in peace; [L *requiescant in pace*] may
they rest in peace
ri·par·i·an \rə-'per-ē-ən\ *adj* : of or relating to the bank
of a stream, river, or lake
rip cord *n* : a cord that is pulled to release the pilot
parachute which lifts a main parachute out of its container
ripe \'rīp\ *adj* **rip·er; rip·est 1** : fully grown and developed : MATURE ⟨∼ fruit⟩ **2** : fully prepared for some
use or object : READY — **ripe·ly** *adv* — **ripe·ness** *n*
rip·en \'rī-pən\ *vb* **rip·ened; rip·en·ing 1** : to grow or
make ripe **2** : to bring to completeness or perfection;
also : to age or cure (cheese) to develop characteristic flavor, odor, body, texture, and color
rip–off \'rip-ˌof\ *n* **1** : an act of stealing : THEFT **2** : a
cheap imitation — **rip off** *vb*
ri·poste \ri-'pōst\ *n* [F, modif. of It *risposta,* lit., an-
swer] **1** : a fencer's return thrust after a parry **2** : a
retaliatory maneuver or response; *esp* : a quick retort
— **riposte** *vb*
rip·ple \'ri-pəl\ *vb* **rip·pled; rip·pling 1** : to become
lightly ruffled on the surface **2** : to make a sound like
that of rippling water — **ripple** *n*
rip·saw \'rip-ˌsò\ *n* : a coarse-toothed saw used to cut
wood in the direction of the grain
rip·stop \-ˌstäp\ *adj* : being a fabric woven in such a
way that small tears do not spread ⟨∼ nylon⟩ — **rip-
stop** *n*
¹rise \'rīz\ *vb* **rose** \'rōz\; **ris·en** \'riz-ən\; **ris·ing 1** : to
get up from sitting, kneeling, or lying **2** : to get up
from sleep or from one's bed **3** : to return from death
4 : to take up arms **5** : to end a session : ADJOURN **6**
: to appear above the horizon **7** : to move upward
: ASCEND **8** : to extend above other objects **9** : to attain a higher level or rank **10** : to increase in quantity
or in intensity **11** : to come into being : HAPPEN, BE-
GIN, ORIGINATE
²rise *n* **1** : a spot higher than surrounding ground **2** : an
upward slope **3** : an act of rising : a state of being ris-
en **4** : BEGINNING, ORIGIN **5** : the elevation of one

point above another **6** : an increase in amount, number, or volume **7** : an angry reaction

ris•er \'rī-zər\ *n* **1** : one that rises **2** : the upright part between stair treads

ris•i•bil•i•ty \,ri-zə-'bi-lə-tē\ *n, pl* **-ties** : the ability or inclination to laugh — often used in pl.

ris•i•ble \'ri-zə-bəl\ *adj* **1** : able or inclined to laugh **2** : arousing laughter; *esp* : amusingly ridiculous

¹risk \'risk\ *n* : exposure to possible loss or injury : DANGER, PERIL — **risk•i•ness** \'ris-kē-nəs\ *n* — **risky** *adj*

²risk *vb* **1** : to expose to danger ⟨∼ed his life⟩ **2** : to incur the danger of

ris•qué \ris-'kā\ *adj* [F] : verging on impropriety or indecency

ri•tard \ri-'tärd\ *adv or adj* : with a gradual slackening in tempo — used as a direction in music

rite \'rīt\ *n* **1** : a set form for conducting a ceremony **2** : the liturgy of a church **3** : a ceremonial act or action

rit•u•al \'ri-chə-wəl\ *n* **1** : the established form esp. for a religious ceremony **2** : a system of rites **3** : a ceremonial act or action **4** : a customarily repeated act or series of acts — **ritual** *adj* — **rit•u•al•ism** \-wə-,li-zəm\ *n* — **rit•u•al•is•tic** \,ri-chə-wə-'lis-tik\ *adj* — **rit•u•al•is•ti•cal•ly** \-ti-k(ə-)lē\ *adv* — **rit•u•al•ly** *adv*

riv *abbr* river

¹ri•val \'rī-vəl\ *n* [MF or L; MF, fr. L *rivalis* one using the same stream as another, rival in love, fr. *rivalis* of a stream, fr. *rivus* stream] **1** : one of two or more trying to get what only one can have **2** : one striving for competitive advantage **3** : one that equals another esp. in desired qualities : MATCH, PEER

²rival *adj* : COMPETING

³rival *vb* **-valed** *or* **-valled; -val•ing** *or* **-val•ling** **1** : to be in competition with **2** : to try to equal or excel **3** : to have qualities that approach or equal another's

ri•val•ry \'rī-vəl-rē\ *n, pl* **-ries** : COMPETITION

rive \'riv\ *vb* **rived** \'rīvd\; **riv•en** \'ri-vən\ *also* **rived; riv•ing** **1** : SPLIT, REND **2** : SHATTER

riv•er \'ri-vər\ *n* **1** : a natural stream larger than a brook **2** : a large stream or flow

riv•er•bank \-,baŋk\ *n* : the bank of a river

riv•er•bed \-,bed\ *n* : the channel occupied by a river

riv•er•boat \-,bōt\ *n* : a boat for use on a river

riv•er•front \-,frənt\ *n* : the land or area along a river

riv•er•side \-,sīd\ *n* : the side or bank of a river

¹riv•et \'ri-vət\ *n* : a metal bolt with a head at one end used to join parts by being put through holes in them and then being flattened on the plain end to make another head

²rivet *vb* : to fasten with or as if with a rivet — **riv•et•er** *n*

riv•u•let \'ri-vyə-lət, -və-\ *n* : a small stream

ri•yal \rē-'äl, -'al\ *n* — see MONEY table

rm *abbr* **1** ream **2** room

Rn *symbol* radon

¹RN \,är-'en\ *n* : REGISTERED NURSE

²RN *abbr* Royal Navy

RNA \,är-(,)en-'ā\ *n* : any of various nucleic acids (as messenger RNA) that are found esp. in the cytoplasm of cells, have ribose as the 5-carbon sugar, and are associated with the control of cellular chemical activities

rnd *abbr* round

¹roach \'rōch\ *n, pl* **roach** *also* **roach•es** : any of various bony fishes related to the carp; *also* : any of various sunfishes

²roach *n* **1** : COCKROACH **2** : the butt of a marijuana cigarette

road \'rōd\ *n* **1** : ROADSTEAD — often used in pl. **2** : an open way for vehicles, persons, and animals : HIGHWAY **3** : ROUTE, PATH **4** : a series of scheduled visits (as games or performances) in several locations or the travel necessary to make these visits ⟨the team is on the ∼⟩

road•bed \'rōd-,bed\ *n* **1** : the foundation of a road or railroad **2** : the part of the surface of a road on which vehicles travel

road•block \-,bläk\ *n* **1** : a barricade on the road ⟨a police ∼⟩ **2** : an obstruction to progress

road•ie \'rō-dē\ *n* : one who works for traveling entertainers

road•kill \'rōd-,kil\ *n* : an animal that has been killed on a road by a motor vehicle

road•run•ner \-,rə-nər\ *n* : a largely terrestrial bird of the southwestern U.S. and Mexico that is a speedy runner

road•side \'rōd-,sīd\ *n* : the strip of land along a road — **roadside** *adj*

road•stead \-,sted\ *n* : an anchorage for ships usu. less sheltered than a harbor

road•ster \'rōd-stər\ *n* **1** : a driving horse **2** : an open automobile that seats two

road•way \-,wā\ *n* : ROAD; *esp* : ROADBED

road•work \-,wərk\ *n* **1** : work done in constructing or repairing roads **2** : conditioning for an athletic contest (as a boxing match) consisting mainly of long runs

roam \'rōm\ *vb* **1** : WANDER, ROVE **2** : to range or wander over or about

¹roan \'rōn\ *adj* : of dark color (as black, red, or brown) sprinkled with white ⟨a ∼ horse⟩

²roan *n* : an animal (as a horse) with a roan coat; *also* : its color

¹roar \'rōr\ *vb* **1** : to utter a full loud prolonged sound **2** : to make a loud confused sound (as of wind or waves) — **roar•er** *n*

²roar *n* : a sound of roaring

¹roast \'rōst\ *vb* **1** : to cook by dry heat (as before a fire or in an oven) **2** : to criticize severely or kiddingly

²roast *n* **1** : a piece of meat suitable for roasting **2** : an outing at which food is roasted ⟨corn ∼⟩ **3** : severe criticism or kidding

³roast *adj* : ROASTED

roast•er \'rō-stər\ *n* **1** : one that roasts **2** : a device for roasting **3** : something suitable for roasting

rob \'räb\ *vb* **robbed; rob•bing** **1** : to steal from **2** : to deprive of something due or expected **3** : to commit robbery — **rob·ber** *n*

robber fly *n* : any of a family of predaceous flies

rob·bery \\'rä-bə-rē\\ *n, pl* **-ber·ies** : the act or practice of robbing; *esp* : theft of something from a person by use of violence or threat

¹**robe** \\'rōb\\ *n* **1** : a long flowing outer garment; *esp* : one used for ceremonial occasions **2** : a wrap or covering for the lower body (as for sitting outdoors)

²**robe** *vb* **robed; rob·ing 1** : to clothe with or as if with a robe **2** : DRESS

rob·in \\'rä-bən\\ *n* **1** : a small chiefly European thrush with a somewhat orange face and breast **2** : a large No. American thrush with a grayish back, a streaked throat, and a chiefly dull reddish breast

---

ro·bot \\'rō-ıbät, -bət\\ *n* [Czech, fr. *robota* compulsory labor] **1** : a machine that looks and acts like a human being **2** : an efficient but insensitive person **3** : a device that automatically performs esp. repetitive tasks **4** : something guided by automatic controls — **ro·bot·ic** \\rō-'bä-tik\\ *adj*

ro·bot·ics \\rō-'bä-tiks\\ *n* : technology dealing with the design, construction, and operation of robots

ro·bust \\rō-'bəst, 'rō-(ı)bəst\\ *adj* [L *robustus* oaken, strong, fr. *robur* oak, strength] : strong and vigorously healthy — **ro·bust·ly** *adv* — **ro·bust·ness** *n*

ROC *abbr* Republic of China (Taiwan)

¹**rock** \\'räk\\ *vb* **1** : to move back and forth in or as if in a cradle **2** : to sway or cause to sway back and forth

²**rock** *n* **1** : a rocking movement **2** : popular music usu. played on electric instruments and characterized by a strong beat and much repetition

³**rock** *n* **1** : a mass of stony material; *also* : broken pieces of stone **2** : solid mineral deposits **3** : something like a rock in firmness **4** : GEM; *esp* : DIAMOND — **rock** *adj* — **rock·like** *adj* — **rocky** *adj*

rock and roll *n* : ²ROCK 2

rock·bound \\'räk-ıbaùnd\\ *adj* : fringed or covered with rocks

rock·er \\'rä-kər\\ *n* **1** : one of the curved pieces on which something (as a chair or cradle) rocks **2** : a chair that rocks on rockers **3** : a device that works with a rocking motion **4** : a rock performer, song, or enthusiast

¹**rock·et** \\'rä-kət\\ *n* [It *rocchetta*, lit., small distaff] **1** : a firework that is propelled through the air by the discharge of gases produced by a burning substance **2** : a jet engine that operates on the same principle as a firework rocket but carries the oxygen needed for burning its fuel **3** : a rocket-propelled bomb or missile

²**rocket** *vb* **1** : to convey by means of a rocket **2** : to rise abruptly and rapidly

rock·et·ry \\'rä-kə-trē\\ *n* : the study or use of rockets

rocket ship *n* : a rocket-propelled spacecraft

rock·fall \\'räk-ıfòl\\ *n* : a mass of falling or fallen rocks

rock·fish \\-ıfish\\ *n* : any of various market bony fishes that live among rocks or on rocky bottoms

rock salt *n* : common salt in rocklike masses or large crystals

Rocky Mountain sheep *n* : BIGHORN

ro·co·co \\rə-'kō-kō\\ *adj* [F, irreg. fr. *rocaille* style of ornament, lit., stone debris] : of or relating to an artistic style esp. of the 18th century marked by fanciful curved forms and elaborate ornamentation — **rococo** *n*

rod \\'räd\\ *n* **1** : a straight slender stick **2** : a stick or bundle of twigs used in punishing a person; *also* : PUNISHMENT **3** : a staff borne to show rank **4** — see WEIGHT table **5** : any of the rod-shaped receptor cells of the retina that are sensitive to faint light **6** *slang* : HANDGUN

rode *past of* RIDE

ro·dent \\'rōd-ᵊnt\\ *n* [ultim. fr. L *rodent-, rodens*, prp. of *rodere* to gnaw] : any of an order of relatively small mammals (as mice, squirrels, and beavers) with sharp front teeth used for gnawing

ro·deo \\'rō-dē-ıō, rə-'dā-ō\\ *n, pl* **ro·de·os** [Sp, fr. *rodear* to surround, fr. *rueda* wheel, fr. L *rota*] **1** : ROUNDUP 1 **2** : a public performance featuring cowboy skills (as riding and roping)

¹**roe** \\'rō\\ *n, pl* **roe** *or* **roes** : DOE

²**roe** *n* : the eggs of a fish esp. while bound together in a mass

roe·buck \\'rō-ıbək\\ *n, pl* **roebuck** *or* **roebucks** : a male roe deer

roe deer *n* : either of two small nimble European or Asian deers

roe deer

roent·gen \\'rent-gən, 'rənt-, -jən\\ *n* : the international unit of measurement for X rays and gamma rays

rog·er \\'rä-jər\\ *interj* — used esp. in radio and signaling to indicate that a message has been received and understood

rogue \\'rōg\\ *n* **1** : a dishonest person : SCOUNDREL **2** : a mischievous person : SCAMP — **rogu·ery** \\'rō-gə-rē\\ *n* — **rogu·ish** *adj* — **rogu·ish·ly** *adv* — **rogu·ish·ness** *n*

roil \\'ròil, *for 2 also* 'rīl\\ *vb* **1** : to make cloudy or mud-

---

dy by stirring up **2** : RILE 1 — **roily** \ˈrȯi-lē\ *adj*
rois·ter \ˈrȯi-stər\ *vb* **rois·tered; rois·ter·ing** : to engage in noisy revelry : CAROUSE — **rois·ter·er** *n* — **rois·ter·ous** \-stə-rəs\ *adj*
ROK *abbr* Republic of Korea (South Korea)
role *also* **rôle** \ˈrōl\ *n* **1** : an assigned or assumed character; *also* : a part played (as by an actor) **2** : FUNCTION
role model *n* : a person whose behavior in a particular role is imitated by others
¹**roll** \ˈrōl\ *n* **1** : a document containing an official record **2** : an official list of names **3** : something (as a bun) that is rolled up or rounded as if rolled **4** : something that rolls : ROLLER
²**roll** *vb* **1** : to move by turning over and over **2** : to press with a roller **3** : to move on wheels **4** : to sound with a full reverberating tone **5** : to make a continuous beating sound (as on a drum) **6** : to utter with a trill **7** : to move onward as if by completing a revolution ⟨years ~ed by⟩ **8** : to flow or seem to flow in a continuous stream or with a rising and falling motion (the river ~ed on) **9** : to swing or sway from side to side **10** : to shape or become shaped in rounded form
³**roll** *n* **1** : a sound produced by rapid strokes on a drum **2** : a heavy reverberating sound **3** : a rolling movement or action **4** : a swaying movement (as of a ship) **5** : SOMERSAULT
roll·back \ˈrōl-ˌbak\ *n* : the act or an instance of rolling back
roll back *vb* **1** : to reduce (as a commodity price) on a national scale **2** : to cause to withdraw : push back
roll bar *n* : an overhead metal bar on an automobile designed to protect riders in case the automobile overturns
roll call *n* : the act or an instance of calling off a list of names (as of soldiers); *also* : a time for a roll call
roll·er \ˈrō-lər\ *n* **1** : a revolving cylinder used for moving, pressing, shaping, applying, or smoothing something **2** : a rod on which something is rolled up **3** : a long heavy ocean wave
roll·er coast·er \ˈrō-lər-ˌkō-stər\ *n* : an amusement ride consisting of an elevated railway having sharp curves and steep slopes

roller skate *n* : a skate with wheels instead of a runner — **roller-skate** *vb* — **roller skater** *n*

rol·lick \ˈrä-lik\ *vb* : ROMP, FROLIC
rol·lick·ing *adj* : full of fun and good spirits
roly-poly \ˌrō-lē-ˈpō-lē\ *adj* : ROTUND
Rom *abbr* **1** Roman **2** Romance **3** Romania; Romanian **4** Romans
ROM \ˈräm\ *n* : READ-ONLY MEMORY
ro·maine \rō-ˈmān\ *n* [F, lit., Roman] : a garden lettuce with a tall loose head of long crisp leaves
¹**Ro·man** \ˈrō-mən\ *n* **1** : a native or resident of Rome **2** *not cap* : roman letters or type

²**Roman** *adj* **1** : of or relating to Rome or the Romans and esp. the ancient Romans **2** *not cap* : relating to type in which the letters are upright (as in this definition) **3** : of or relating to the Roman Catholic Church
Roman candle *n* : a cylindrical firework that discharges balls of fire
Roman Catholic *adj* : of, relating to, or being a Christian church led by the pope and having a liturgy centered in the Mass — **Roman Catholicism** *n*
¹**ro·mance** \rō-ˈmans, ˈrō-ˌmans\ *n* [ME *romauns*, fr. OF *romans* French, something written in French, tale in verse, fr. ML *Romanice* in a vernacular language, ultim. fr. L *Romanus* Roman] **1** : a medieval tale of knightly adventure **2** : a prose narrative dealing with heroic or mysterious events set in a remote time or place **3** : a love story **4** : a romantic attachment or episode between lovers — **ro·manc·er** *n*
²**romance** *vb* **ro·manced; ro·manc·ing 1** : to exaggerate or invent detail or incident **2** : to have romantic fancies **3** : to carry on a romantic episode with
Romance \rō-ˈmans, ˈrō-ˌmans\ *adj* : of or relating to any of several languages developed from Latin
Ro·ma·nian \rù-ˈmā-nē-ən, rō-, -nyən\ *n* **1** : a native or inhabitant of Romania **2** : the language of the Romanians
Roman numeral *n* : a numeral in a system of notation that is based on the ancient Roman system
Ro·ma·no \rō-ˈmä-nō\ *n* : a hard Italian cheese that is sharper than Parmesan
Ro·mans \ˈrō-mənz\ *n* — see BIBLE table
¹**ro·man·tic** \rō-ˈman-tik\ *n* : a romantic person; *esp* : a romantic writer, composer, or artist
²**romantic** *adj* **1** : IMAGINARY **2** : VISIONARY **3** : having an imaginative or emotional appeal **4** : of, relating to, or having the characteristics of romanticism — **ro·man·ti·cal·ly** \-ti-k(ə-)lē\ *adv*
ro·man·ti·cism \rō-ˈman-tə-ˌsi-zəm\ *n, often cap* : a literary movement (as in early 19th century England) marked esp. by emphasis on the imagination and the emotions and by the use of autobiographical material — **ro·man·ti·cist** \-sist\ *n, often cap*
romp \ˈrämp\ *vb* **1** : to play actively and noisily **2** : to win a contest easily — **romp** *n*
romp·er \ˈräm-pər\ *n* **1** : one that romps **2** : a child's one-piece garment with the lower part shaped like bloomers — usu. used in pl.
rood \ˈrüd\ *n* : CROSS, CRUCIFIX
¹**roof** \ˈrüf, ˈrùf\ *n, pl* **roofs** \ˈrüfs, ˈrùfs; ˈrüvz, ˈrùvz\ **1** : the upper covering part of a building **2** : something suggesting a roof of a building — **roofed** \ˈrüft, ˈrùft\ *adj* — **roof·ing** *n* — **roof·less** *adj*
²**roof** *vb* : to cover with a roof
roof·top \-ˌtäp\ *n* : a roof esp. of a house
¹**rook** \ˈrùk\ *n* : a common Old World bird resembling the related crow
²**rook** *vb* : CHEAT, SWINDLE
³**rook** *n* : a chess piece that can move parallel to the sides of the board across any number of unoccupied squares

rook•ery \'rù-kə-rē\ n, pl **-er•ies** : a breeding ground or haunt of gregarious birds or mammals; *also* : a colony of such birds or mammals

rook•ie \'rù-kē\ n : BEGINNER, RECRUIT; *esp* : a first-year player in a professional sport

¹**room** \'rüm, 'rùm\ n 1 : an extent of space occupied by or sufficient or available for something 2 : a partitioned part of a building : CHAMBER; *also* : the people in a room 3 : OPPORTUNITY, CHANCE ⟨∼ to develop his talents⟩ — **room•ful** n — **roomy** adj

²**room** vb : to occupy lodgings : LODGE — **room•er** n

room•ette \rü-'met, rú-\ n : a small private room on a railroad sleeping car

room•mate \'rüm-ₐmāt, 'rùm-\ n : one of two or more persons sharing the same room or dwelling

¹**roost** \'rüst\ n : a support on which or a place where birds perch

²**roost** vb : to settle on or as if on a roost

roost•er \'rüs-tər, 'rùs-\ n : an adult male domestic chicken : COCK

¹**root** \'rüt, 'rút\ n 1 : the leafless usu. underground part of a seed plant that functions in absorption, aeration, and storage or as a means of anchorage; *also* : an underground plant part esp. when fleshy and edible 2 : something (as the basal part of a tooth or hair) resembling a root 3 : SOURCE, ORIGIN 4 : the essential core : HEART ⟨get to the ∼ of the matter⟩ 5 : a number that when taken as a factor an indicated number of times gives a specified number 6 : the lower part — **root•less** adj — **root•like** adj

²**root** vb 1 : to form roots 2 : to fix or become fixed by or as if by roots : ESTABLISH 3 : UPROOT

³**root** vb 1 : to turn up or dig with the snout ⟨pigs ∼ing⟩ 2 : to poke or dig around (as in search of something)

⁴**root** \'rüt\ vb 1 : to applaud or encourage noisily : CHEER 2 : to wish success or lend support to — **root•er** n

root beer n : a sweetened carbonated beverage flavored with extracts of roots and herbs

root•let \'rüt-lət, 'rùt-\ n : a small root

root•stock \-ₐstäk\ n : an underground part of a plant that resembles a rhizome

¹**rope** \'rōp\ n 1 : a large strong cord made of strands of fiber 2 : a hangman's noose 3 : a thick string (as of pearls) made by twisting or braiding

²**rope** vb **roped; rop•ing** 1 : to bind, tie, or fasten together with a rope 2 : to separate or divide by means of a rope 3 : LASSO

Ror•schach test \'ror-ₐshäk-\ n : a psychological test in which a subject interprets ink-blot designs in terms that reveal intellectual and emotional factors

ro•sa•ry \'rō-zə-rē\ n, pl **-ries** 1 *often cap* : a Roman Catholic devotion consisting of meditation on sacred mysteries during recitation of Hail Marys 2 : a string of beads used in praying

¹**rose** past of RISE

²**rose** \'rōz\ n 1 : any of a genus of usu. prickly often climbing shrubs with divided leaves and bright often fragrant flowers; *also* : one of these flowers 2 : something resembling a rose in form 3 : a moderate purplish red color — **rose** adj

ro•sé \rō-'zā\ n [F] : a light pink wine

ro•se•ate \'rō-zē-ət, -zē-ₐāt\ adj 1 : resembling a rose esp. in color 2 : OPTIMISTIC ⟨a ∼ view of the future⟩

rose•bud \'rōz-ₐbəd\ n : the flower of a rose when it is at most partly open

rose•bush \-ₐbùsh\ n : a shrubby rose

rose•mary \'rōz-ₐmer-ē\ n, pl **-mar•ies** [ME rosmarine, fr. L rosmarinus, fr. ros dew + marinus of the sea, fr. mare sea] : a fragrant shrubby Old World mint; *also* : its leaves used as a seasoning

ro•sette \rō-'zet\ n [F] 1 : a usu. small badge or ornament of ribbon gathered in the shape of a rose 2 : a circular ornament filled with representations of leaves

rose•wa•ter \'rōz-ₐwò-tər, -ₐwä-\ n : a watery solution of the fragrant constituents of the rose used as a perfume

rose•wood \-ₐwúd\ n : any of various tropical trees with dark red wood streaked with black; *also* : this wood

Rosh Ha•sha•nah \ₐräsh-hə-'shä-nə, ₐrōsh-, -'shō-\ n [Heb rōsh hashshānāh, lit., beginning of the year] : the Jewish New Year observed as a religious holiday in September or October

ros•in \'räz-ᵊn\ n : a brittle resin obtained esp. from pine trees and used esp. in varnishes and on violin bows

ros•ter \'räs-tər\ n 1 : a list of personnel; *also* : the persons listed on a roster 2 : an itemized list

ros•trum \'räs-trəm\ n, pl **rostrums** or **ros•tra** \-trə\ [L Rostra, pl., a platform for speakers in the Roman Forum decorated with the beaks of captured ships, fr. pl. of rostrum beak, ship's beak, fr. rodere to gnaw] : a stage or platform for public speaking

rosy \'rō-zē\ adj **ros•i•er; -est** 1 : of the color rose 2 : HOPEFUL, PROMISING — **ros•i•ly** \'rō-zə-lē\ adv — **ros•i•ness** \-zē-nəs\ n

¹**rot** \'rät\ vb **rot•ted; rot•ting** : to undergo decomposition : DECAY

²**rot** n 1 : DECAY 2 : any of various diseases of plants or animals in which tissue breaks down 3 : NONSENSE

¹**ro•ta•ry** \'rō-tə-rē\ adj 1 : turning on an axis like a wheel 2 : having a rotating part

²**rotary** n, pl **-ries** 1 : a rotary machine 2 : a one-way circular road junction

ro•tate \'rō-ₐtāt\ vb **ro•tat•ed; ro•tat•ing** 1 : to turn or cause to turn about an axis or a center : REVOLVE 2 : to alternate in a series **syn** turn, circle, spin, whirl, twirl — **ro•ta•tion** \rō-'tā-shən\ n — **ro•ta•tor** \'rō-ₐtā-tər\ n — **ro•ta•to•ry** \'rō-tə-ₐtōr-ē\ adj

ROTC abbr Reserve Officers' Training Corps

rote \'rōt\ n 1 : repetition from memory often without attention to meaning 2 : fixed routine or repetition — **rote** adj

ro•tis•ser•ie \rō-'ti-sə-rē\ n [F] 1 : a restaurant specializing in broiled and barbecued meats **2** : an appliance fitted with a spit on which food is rotated before or over a source of heat

ro·to·gra·vure \ˌrō-tə-grə-ˈvyur\ *n* : PHOTOGRAVURE

ro·tor \ˈrō-tər\ *n* **1** : a part that rotates; *esp* : the rotating part of an electrical machine **2** : a system of rotating horizontal blades for supporting a helicopter

ro·to·till·er \ˈrō-tō-ˌti-lər\ *n* : an engine-powered machine with rotating blades used to lift and turn over soil

rot·ten \ˈrät-ᵊn\ *adj* **1** : having rotted **2** : CORRUPT **3** : extremely unpleasant or inferior — **rot·ten·ness** *n*

rot·ten·stone \ˈrät-ᵊn-ˌstōn\ *n* : a decomposed siliceous limestone used for polishing

ro·tund \rō-ˈtənd\ *adj* : rounded out **syn** plump, chubby, portly, stout — **ro·tun·di·ty** \-ˈtən-də-tē\ *n*

ro·tun·da \rō-ˈtən-də\ *n* **1** : a round building; *esp* : one covered by a dome **2** : a large round room

rou·ble \ˈrü-bəl\ *var of* RUBLE

roué \rü-ˈā\ *n* [F, lit., broken on the wheel, fr. pp. of *rouer* to break on the wheel, fr. ML *rotare*, fr. L, to rotate; fr. the feeling that such a person deserves this punishment] : a man devoted to a life of sensual pleasure : RAKE

rouge \ˈrüzh, ˈrüj\ *n* [F, lit., red] : a cosmetic used to give a red color to cheeks and lips — **rouge** *vb*

¹rough \ˈrəf\ *adj* **rough·er**; **rough·est 1** : uneven in surface : not smooth **2** : SHAGGY **3** : not calm : TURBULENT, TEMPESTUOUS **4** : marked by harshness or violence **5** : DIFFICULT, TRYING **6** : coarse or rugged in character or appearance **7** : marked by lack of refinement **8** : CRUDE, UNFINISHED **9** : done or made hastily or tentatively — **rough·ly** *adv* — **rough·ness** *n*

²rough *n* **1** : uneven ground covered with high grass esp. along a golf fairway **2** : a crude, unfinished, or preliminary state; *also* : something in such a state **3** : ROWDY, TOUGH

³rough *vb* **1** : ROUGHEN **2** : MANHANDLE **3** : to make or shape roughly esp. in a preliminary way — **rough·er** *n*

rough·age \ˈrə-fij\ *n* : FIBER 2; *also* : food containing much indigestible material acting as fiber

rough–and–ready \ˌrə-fən-ˈre-dē\ *adj* : rude or unpolished in nature, method, or manner but effective in action or use

rough–and–tum·ble \-ˈtəm-bəl\ *n* : rough unrestrained fighting or struggling — **rough–and–tumble** *adj*

rough·en \ˈrə-fən\ *vb* **rough·ened**; **rough·en·ing** : to make or become rough

rough–hewn \ˈrəf-ˈhyün\ *adj* **1** : being rough and unfinished (∼ beams) **2** : lacking smooth manners or social grace — **rough–hew** \-ˈhyü\ *vb*

rough·house \ˈrəf-ˌhaus\ *vb* **rough·housed**; **rough·hous·ing** : to participate in rough noisy behavior — **roughhouse** *n*

rough·neck \ˈrəf-ˌnek\ *n* **1** : ROWDY, TOUGH **2** : a worker on a crew drilling oil wells

rough·shod \ˈrəf-ˌshäd\ *adv* : with no consideration for the wishes or feelings of others ⟨rode ∼ over the opposition⟩

rou·lette \rü-ˈlet\ *n* [F, lit., small wheel] **1** : a gambling game in which a whirling wheel is used **2** : a wheel or disk with teeth around the outside

¹round \ˈraund\ *adj* **1** : having every part of the surface or circumference the same distance from the center **2** : CYLINDRICAL **3** : COMPLETE, FULL **4** : approximately correct; *esp* : exact only to a specific decimal or place ⟨∼ numbers⟩ **5** : liberal or ample in size or amount **6** : BLUNT, OUTSPOKEN **7** : moving in or forming a circle **8** : having curves rather than angles — **round·ish** *adj* — **round·ness** *n*

²round *prep or adv* : AROUND

³round *n* **1** : something round (as a circle, globe, or ring) **2** : a curved or rounded part (as a rung of a ladder) **3** : an indirect path or course; *also* : a regu-

larly covered route (as of a security guard) **4** : a series or cycle of recurring actions or events **5** : one shot fired by a soldier or a gun; *also* : ammunition for one shot **6** : a period of time or a unit of play in a game or contest **7** : a cut of meat (as beef) esp. between the rump and the lower leg — **in the round 1** : FREESTANDING **2** : with a center stage surrounded by an audience ⟨theater *in the round*⟩

⁴round *vb* **1** : to make or become round **2** : to go or pass around or part way around **3** : COMPLETE, FINISH **4** : to become plump or shapely **5** : to express as a round number — often used with *off* **6** : to follow a winding course : BEND

¹round·about \ˈraun-də-ˌbaut\ *adj* : INDIRECT, CIRCUITOUS

²roundabout *n, Brit* : MERRY-GO-ROUND

roun·de·lay \ˈraun-də-ˌlā\ *n* **1** : a simple song with a refrain **2** : a poem with a recurring refrain

round·house \ˈraund-ˌhaus\ *n* **1** : a circular building for housing and repairing locomotives **2** : a blow with the hand made with a wide swing

round·ly \ˈraund-lē\ *adv* **1** : in a complete manner; *also* : WIDELY **2** : in a blunt way **3** : with vigor

round–shoul·dered \-ˌshōl-dərd\ *adj* : having the shoulders stooping or rounded

round–trip *n* : a trip to a place and back

round·up \ˈraun-ˌdəp\ *n* **1** : the gathering together of cattle on the range by riding around them and driving them in; *also* : the ranch hands and horses engaged in a roundup **2** : a gathering in of scattered persons or things **3** : SUMMARY ⟨news ∼⟩ — **round up** *vb*

round·worm \-ˌwərm\ *n* : NEMATODE

rouse \ˈrauz\ *vb* **roused**; **rous·ing 1** : to excite to activity : stir up **2** : to wake from sleep — **rous·er** *n*

roust·about \ˈraus-tə-ˌbaut\ *n* : one who does heavy unskilled labor (as on a dock or in an oil field)

¹rout \ˈraut\ *n* **1** : MOB 1, 2 **2** : DISTURBANCE **3** : a fashionable gathering

²rout *vb* **1** : RUMMAGE **2** : to gouge out **3** : to expel by force

³rout *n* **1** : a state of wild confusion or disorderly retreat **2** : a disastrous defeat

⁴rout *vb* **1** : to put to flight **2** : to defeat decisively

¹route \ˈrüt, ˈraut\ *n* **1** : a traveled way **2** : CHANNEL **3** : a line of travel

²route *vb* **rout·ed**; **rout·ing** : to send by a selected route : DIRECT

route·man \-mən, -ˌman\ *n* : one who sells and makes deliveries on an assigned route

rout·er \ˈrau-tər\ *n* : a machine with a revolving spindle and cutter for shaping a surface (as of wood)

rou·tine \rü-ˈtēn\ *n* [F, fr. MF, fr. *route* traveled way] **1** : a regular course of procedure **2** : an often repeated speech or formula **3** : a part fully worked out ⟨a comedy ∼⟩ **4** : a set of computer instructions that will perform a certain task — **routine** *adj* — **rou·tine·ly** *adv* — **rou·tin·ize** \-ˈtē-ˌnīz\ *vb*

¹rove \ˈrōv\ *vb* **roved**; **rov·ing** : to wander over or through — **rov·er** *n*

²rove *past and past part of* REEVE

¹row \ˈrō\ *vb* **1** : to propel a boat with oars **2** : to transport in a rowboat **3** : to pull an oar in a crew — **row·er** \ˈrō-ər\ *n*

²row *n* : an act or instance of rowing

³row *n* **1** : a number of objects in an orderly sequence **2** : WAY, STREET

⁴row \ˈrau\ *n* : a noisy quarrel

⁵row \ˈrau\ *vb* : to engage in a row

row·boat \ˈrō-ˌbōt\ *n* : a small boat designed to be rowed

row·dy \ˈrau-dē\ *adj* **row·di·er**; **-est** : coarse or boisterous in behavior : ROUGH — **row·di·ness** \ˈrau-dē-nəs\ *n* — **rowdy** *n* — **row·dy·ish** *adj* — **row·dy·ism** *n*

row·el \ˈrau-əl\ *n* : a small pointed wheel on a rider's spur — **rowel** *vb*

¹**roy·al** \ˈròi-əl\ *adj* **1** : of or relating to a sovereign : RE-GAL **2** : fit for a king or queen ⟨a ∼ welcome⟩ — **roy·al·ly** *adv*

²**royal** *n* : a person of royal blood

royal flush *n* : a straight flush having an ace as the highest card

roy·al·ist \ˈròi-ə-list\ *n* : an adherent of a king or of monarchical government

roy·al·ty \ˈròi-əl-tē\ *n, pl* **-ties 1** : the state of being royal **2** : royal persons **3** : a share of a profit or profit (as of a mine or oil well) claimed by the owner for allowing another person to use the property **4** : a payment made to an author or composer for each copy of a work sold or to an inventor for each article sold under a patent

RP *abbr* **1** relief pitcher **2** Republic of the Philippines

rpm *abbr* revolutions per minute

rps *abbr* revolutions per second

rpt *abbr* **1** repeat **2** report

RR *abbr* **1** railroad **2** rural route

RS *abbr* **1** recording secretary **2** revised statutes **3** right side **4** Royal Society

RSV *abbr* Revised Standard Version

RSVP *abbr* [F *répondez s'il vous plaît*] please reply

rt *abbr* **1** right **2** route

RT *abbr* **1** radiotelephone **2** round-trip

rte *abbr* route

Ru *symbol* ruthenium

¹**rub** \ˈrəb\ *vb* **rubbed; rub·bing 1** : to use pressure and friction on a body or object **2** : to fret or chafe with friction **3** : to scour, polish, erase, or smear by pressure and friction

²**rub** *n* **1** : DIFFICULTY, OBSTRUCTION **2** : something grating to the feelings

¹**rub·ber** \ˈrə-bər\ *n* **1** : one that rubs **2** : ERASER **3** : a flexible waterproof elastic substance made from the milky juice esp. of a So. American tropical tree or made synthetically; *also* : something made of this material — **rubber** *adj* — **rub·ber·ize** \ˈrə-bə-ˌrīz\ *vb* — **rub·bery** *adj*

²**rubber** *n* **1** : a contest that consists of an odd number of games and is won by the side that takes a majority

2 : an extra game played to decide a tie

¹**rub·ber·neck** \-ˌnek\ *n* **1** : an idly or overly inquisitive person **2** : a person on a guided tour

²**rubberneck** *vb* : to look about, stare, or listen with excessive curiosity — **rub·ber·neck·er** *n*

rub·bish \ˈrə-bish\ *n* **1** : useless waste or rejected matter : TRASH **2** : something worthless or nonsensical

rub·ble \ˈrə-bəl\ *n* : broken fragments esp. of a destroyed building

ru·bel·la \rü-ˈbe-lə\ *n* : GERMAN MEASLES

ru·bi·cund \ˈrü-bi-(ˌ)kənd\ *adj* : RED, RUDDY

ru·bid·i·um \rü-ˈbi-dē-əm\ *n* : a soft silvery metallic chemical element — see ELEMENT table

ru·ble \ˈrü-bəl\ *n* — see MONEY table

ru·bric \ˈrü-brik\ *n* [ME *rubrike* red ocher, heading in red letters of part of a book, fr. MF *rubrique*, fr. L *rubrica*, fr. *ruber* red] **1** : HEADING, TITLE; *also* : CLASS, CATEGORY **2** : a rule esp. for the conduct of a religious service

ru·by \ˈrü-bē\ *n, pl* **rubies** : a clear red precious stone — **ruby** *adj*

ru·by–throat·ed hummingbird \ˈrü-bē-ˌthrō-təd-\ *n* : a bright green and whitish hummingbird of eastern No. America with a red throat in the male

ruck·us \ˈrə-kəs\ *n* : ROW, DISTURBANCE

rud·der \ˈrə-dər\ *n* : a movable flat piece attached vertically at the rear of a ship or aircraft for steering

rud·dy \ˈrə-dē\ *adj* **rud·di·er; -est** : REDDISH; *esp* : of a healthy reddish complexion — **rud·di·ness** \ˈrə-dē-nəs\ *n*

rude \ˈrüd\ *adj* **rud·er; rud·est 1** : roughly made : CRUDE **2** : UNDEVELOPED, PRIMITIVE **3** : IMPOLITE **4** : UNSKILLED — **rude·ly** *adv* — **rude·ness** *n*

ru·di·ment \ˈrü-də-mənt\ *n* **1** : an elementary principle or basic skill — usu. used in pl. **2** : something not fully developed — usu. used in pl. — **ru·di·men·ta·ry** \ˌrü-də-ˈmen-tə-rē\ *adj*

¹**rue** \ˈrü\ *n* : REGRET, SORROW — **rue·ful** \-fəl\ *adj* — **rue·ful·ly** *adv* — **rue·ful·ness** *n*

²**rue** \'rü\ *vb* **rued; ru·ing** : to feel regret, remorse, or penitence for

³**rue** *n* : a European strong-scented woody herb with bitter-tasting leaves

ruff \'rəf\ *n* **1** : a large round pleated collar worn about 1600 **2** : a fringe of long hair or feathers around the neck of an animal — **ruffed** \'rəft\ *adj*

ruf·fi·an \'rə-fē-ən\ *n* : a brutal person — **ruf·fi·an·ly** *adj*

¹**ruf·fle** \'rə-fəl\ *vb* **ruf·fled; ruf·fling 1** : to roughen the surface of **2** : IRRITATE, VEX **3** : to erect (as hair or feathers) in or like a ruff **4** : to flip through (as pages) **5** : to draw into or provide with plaits or folds

²**ruffle** *n* **1** : a strip of fabric gathered or pleated on one edge **2** : RUFF 2 **3** : RIPPLE — **ruf·fly** \'rə-fə-lē, -flē\ *adj*

RU 486 \'är-,yü-,fôr-,ā-tē-'siks\ *n* : a drug taken orally to induce abortion esp. early in pregnancy

rug \'rəg\ *n* **1** : a covering for the legs, lap, and feet **2** : a piece of heavy fabric usu. with a nap or pile used as a floor covering

rug·by \'rəg-bē\ *n, often cap* [*Rugby* School, Rugby, England, where it was first played] : a football game in which play is continuous and interference and forward passing are not permitted

rug·ged \'rə-gəd\ *adj* **1** : having a rough uneven surface **2** : TURBULENT, STORMY **3** : HARSH, STERN **4** : ROBUST, STURDY — **rug·ged·ize** \'rə-gə-,dīz\ *vb* — **rug·ged·ly** *adv* — **rug·ged·ness** *n*

¹**ru·in** \'rü-ən\ *n* **1** : complete collapse or destruction **2** : the remains of something destroyed — usu. used in pl. **3** : a cause of destruction **4** : the action of destroying

²**ruin** *vb* **1** : DESTROY **2** : to damage beyond repair **3** : BANKRUPT

ru·in·ation \,rü-ə-'nā-shən\ *n* : RUIN, DESTRUCTION

ru·in·ous \'rü-ə-nəs\ *adj* **1** : RUINED, DILAPIDATED **2** : causing ruin — **ru·in·ous·ly** *adv*

¹**rule** \'rül\ *n* **1** : a guide or principle for governing action : REGULATION **2** : the usual way of doing something **3** : the exercise of authority or control : GOVERNMENT **4** : RULER 2

²**rule** *vb* **ruled; rul·ing 1** : CONTROL; *also* : GOVERN **2** : to be supreme or outstanding in **3** : to give or state as a considered decision **4** : to mark on paper with or as if with a ruler

rul·er \'rü-lər\ *n* **1** : SOVEREIGN **2** : a straight strip of material (as wood or metal) marked off in units and used for measuring or as a straightedge

rum \'rəm\ *n* **1** : an alcoholic liquor made from molasses or sugarcane **2** : alcoholic liquor

Ru·ma·nian \rü-'mā-nē-ən, -nyən\ *n* : ROMANIAN — **Rumanian** *adj*

rum·ba \'rəm-bə, 'rùm-\ *n* : a dance of Cuban origin marked by strong rhythmic movements

¹**rum·ble** \'rəm-bəl\ *vb* **rum·bled; rum·bling** : to make

a low heavy rolling sound; *also* : to move along with such a sound — **rum·bler** *n*

²**rumble** *n* **1** : a low heavy rolling sound **2** : a street fight esp. among gangs

rumble seat *n* : a folding seat in the back of an automobile that is not covered by the top

rum·bling \'rəm-bliŋ\ *n* **1** : RUMBLE **2** : widespread talk or complaints — usu. used in pl.

ru·men \'rü-mən\ *n, pl* **ru·mi·na** \-mə-nə\ *or* **rumens** : the large first compartment of the stomach of a ruminant (as a cow)

¹**ru·mi·nant** \'rü-mə-nənt\ *n* : a ruminant mammal

²**ruminant** *adj* **1** : chewing the cud; *also* : of or relating to a group of hoofed mammals (as cattle, deer, and camels) that chew the cud and have a complex usu. 4-chambered stomach **2** : MEDITATIVE

ru·mi·nate \'rü-mə-,nāt\ *vb* **-nat·ed; -nat·ing** [L *ruminari* to chew the cud, muse upon, fr. *rumin-, rumen* first stomach chamber of a ruminant] **1** : MEDITATE, MUSE **2** : to chew the cud — **ru·mi·na·tion** \,rü-mə-'nā-shən\ *n*

¹**rum·mage** \'rə-mij\ *vb* **rum·maged; rum·mag·ing** : to search thoroughly — **rum·mag·er** *n*

²**rummage** *n* **1** : a miscellaneous collection **2** : an act of rummaging

rum·my \'rə-mē\ *n* : any of several card games for two or more players

ru·mor \'rü-mər\ *n* **1** : common talk **2** : a statement or report current but not authenticated — **rumor** *vb*

ru·mour *chiefly Brit var of* RUMOR

rump \'rəmp\ *n* **1** : the rear part of an animal; *also* : a cut of meat (as beef) behind the upper sirloin **2** : a small or inferior remnant (as of a group)

rum·ple \'rəm-pəl\ *vb* **rum·pled; rum·pling** : TOUSLE, MUSS, WRINKLE — **rumple** *n* — **rum·ply** \'rəm-pə-lē\ *adj*

rum·pus \'rəm-pəs\ *n* : DISTURBANCE, RUCKUS

rumpus room *n* : a room usu. in the basement of a home that is used for games, parties, and recreation

¹**run** \'rən\ *vb* **ran** \'ran\; **run; run·ning 1** : to go faster than a walk **2** : to take to flight : FLEE **3** : to go without restraint ⟨let chickens ∼ loose⟩ **4** : to go rapidly or hurriedly : HASTEN, RUSH **5** : to make a quick or casual trip or visit **6** : to contend in a race; *esp* : to enter an election **7** : to put forward as a candidate for office **8** : to move on or as if on wheels : pass or slide freely **9** : to go back and forth : PLY **10** : to move in large numbers esp. to a spawning ground ⟨shad are *running*⟩ **11** : FUNCTION, OPERATE ⟨left the motor *running*⟩ **12** : to continue in force ⟨two years to ∼⟩ **13** : to flow rapidly or under pressure : MELT, FUSE, DISSOLVE; *also* : DISCHARGE 7 ⟨my nose is *running*⟩ **14** : to tend to produce or to recur ⟨family ∼s to blonds⟩ **15** : to take a certain direction **16** : to be worded or written **17** : to be current ⟨rumors *running* wild⟩ **18** : to cause to run **19** : TRACE ⟨∼ down a rumor⟩ **20** : to perform or bring about by running **21** : to cause to pass ⟨∼ a wire from the antenna⟩ **22** : to cause to collide **23** : SMUGGLE **24** : MANAGE, CONDUCT, OPERATE ⟨∼

a business) **25** : INCUR ⟨~ a risk⟩ **26** : to permit to accumulate before settling ⟨~ up a bill⟩

²run n **1** : an act or the action of running **2** : a migration of fish; also : the migrating fish **3** : a score in baseball **4** : BROOK, CREEK **5** : a continuous series esp. of similar things **6** : persistent heavy demands from depositors, creditors, or customers **7** : the quantity of work turned out in a continuous operation; also : a period of operation (as of a machine or plant) **8** : the usual or normal kind ⟨the ordinary ~ of students⟩ **9** : the distance covered in continuous travel or sailing **10** : a regular course or trip **11** : freedom of movement in a place or area ⟨has the ~ of the house⟩ **12** : an enclosure for animals **13** : an inclined course (as for skiing) **14** : a lengthwise ravel (as in a stocking) — **run·less** adj

run·about \'rə-nə-ˌbaut\ n : a light wagon, automobile, or motorboat

run·a·gate \'rə-nə-ˌgāt\ n **1** : VAGABOND **2** : FUGITIVE

run·around \'rə-nə-ˌraund\ n : evasive or delaying action esp. in response to a request

¹run·away \'rə-nə-ˌwā\ n **1** : one that runs away : FUGITIVE **2** : the act of running away out of control; also : something (as a horse) that is running out of control

²runaway adj **1** : FUGITIVE **2** : won by a long lead; also : extremely successful **3** : subject to uncontrolled changes ⟨~ inflation⟩ **4** : operating out of control ⟨a ~ locomotive⟩

run·down \'rən-ˌdaun\ n : an item-by-item report or review : SUMMARY

run–down \'rən-ˈdaun\ adj **1** : EXHAUSTED, WORN-OUT ⟨that ~ feeling⟩ **2** : being in poor repair ⟨a ~ farm⟩

run down vb **1** : to collide with and knock down **2** : to chase until exhausted or captured **3** : to find by search **4** : DISPARAGE **5** : to cease to operate for lack of motive power **6** : to decline in physical condition

rune \'rün\ n **1** : any of the characters of any of several alphabets formerly used by the Germanic peoples **2** : MYSTERY, MAGIC **3** : a poem esp. in Finnish or Old Norse — **ru·nic** \'rü-nik\ adj

¹rung past part of RING

²rung \'rəŋ\ n **1** : a rounded crosspiece between the legs of a chair **2** : one of the crosspieces of a ladder

run–in \'rən-ˌin\ n **1** : ALTERCATION, QUARREL **2** : something run in

run in vb **1** : to insert as additional matter **2** : to arrest esp. for a minor offense **3** : to pay a casual visit

run·nel \'rən-əl\ n : BROOK, STREAMLET

run·ner \'rə-nər\ n **1** : one that runs **2** : BASE RUNNER **3** : BALLCARRIER **4** : a thin piece or part on which something (as a sled or an ice skate) slides **5** : the support of a drawer or a sliding door **6** : a horizontal branch from the base of a plant that produces new plants **7** : a plant producing runners **8** : a long narrow carpet **9** : a narrow decorative cloth cover for a table or dresser top

run·ner-up \'rə-nər-ˌəp\ n, pl **runners-up** also **runner-ups** : the competitor in a contest who finishes second

¹run·ning adj **1** : FLOWING **2** : FLUID, RUNNY **3** : CON-

TINUOUS, INCESSANT **4** : measured in a straight line ⟨cost per ~ foot⟩ **5** : of or relating to an act of running **6** : made or trained for running ⟨~ horse⟩ ⟨~ shoes⟩

²running adv : in succession

running light n : any of the lights carried by a vehicle (as a ship) at night

run·ny \'rə-nē\ adj : having a tendency to run ⟨a ~ dough⟩ ⟨a ~ nose⟩

run·off \'rən-ˌof\ n : a final contest (as an election) to a previous indecisive contest

run–of–the–mill adj : not outstanding : AVERAGE

run on vb **1** : to talk at length **2** : to continue (matter in type) without a break or a new paragraph **3** : to place or add (as an entry in a dictionary) at the end of a paragraphed item — **run–on** \'rən-ˌon, -ˌän\ n

runt \'rənt\ n : an unusually small person or animal : DWARF — **runty** adj

run·way \'rən-ˌwā\ n **1** : a beaten path made by animals; also : a passage for animals **2** : a paved strip of ground for the landing and takeoff of aircraft **3** : a narrow platform from a stage into an auditorium **4** : a support (as a track) on which something runs

ru·pee \rü-ˈpē, 'rü-ˌpē\ n — see MONEY table

ru·pi·ah \rü-ˈpē-ə\ n, pl **rupiah** or **rupiahs** — see MONEY table

¹rup·ture \'rəp-chər\ n : a breaking or tearing apart; also : HERNIA

²rupture vb **rup·tured; rup·tur·ing** : to cause or undergo rupture

ru·ral \'rur-əl\ adj : of or relating to the country, country people, or agriculture

---

ruse \'rüs, 'rüz\ n : a wily subterfuge : TRICK, ARTIFICE

---

¹rush \'rəsh\ n : any of various often tufted and hollow-stemmed grasslike marsh plants — **rushy** adj

²rush vb [ME rysshen, fr. MF ruser to put to flight, deceive, fr. L recusare to refuse] **1** : to move forward or act with too great haste or eagerness or without preparation **2** : to perform in a short time or at high speed **3** : ATTACK, CHARGE — **rush·er** n

³rush n **1** : a violent forward motion **2** : unusual demand or activity **3** : a crowding of people to one place **4** : a running play in football **5** : a sudden feeling of pleasure

⁴rush adj : requiring or marked by special speed or urgency ⟨~ orders⟩

rush hour n : a time when the amount of traffic or business is at a peak

rusk \'rəsk\ n : a sweet or plain bread baked, sliced, and baked again until dry and crisp

Russ abbr Russia; Russian

rus·set \'rə-sət\ n **1** : a coarse reddish brown cloth **2** : a reddish brown or yellowish brown color **3** : a baking potato — **russet** adj

Rus·sian \'rə-shən\ n **1** : a native or inhabitant of Rus-

sia **2** : a Slavic language of the Russian people —
Russian *adj*
rust **'**rəst\ *n* **1** : a reddish coating formed on iron when
it is exposed to esp. moist air **2** : any of numerous
plant diseases characterized by usu. reddish spots;
also : a fungus causing rust **3** : a reddish brown color
— **rust** *vb* — **rusty** *adj*
¹rus•tic **'**rəs-tik\ *adj* : of, relating to, or suitable for the
country or country people — **rus•ti•cal•ly** \-ti-k(ə-)lē\
adv — **rus•tic•i•ty** \\ʌrəs-**'**ti-sə-tē\ *n*
²rustic *n* : a rustic person
rus•ti•cate **'**rəs-ti-ʌkāt\ *vb* **-cat•ed; -cat•ing** : to go into
or reside in the country — **rus•ti•ca•tion** \\ʌrəs-ti-**'**kā-
shən\ *n*
¹rus•tle **'**rə-səl\ *vb* **rus•tled; rus•tling 1** : to make or
cause a rustle **2** : to cause to rustle (〜 a newspaper)
3 : to act or move with energy or speed; *also* : to procure in this way **4** : to forage food **5** : to steal cattle
from the range — **rus•tler** *n*
²rustle *n* : a quick series of small sounds (〜 of leaves)
¹rut **'**rət\ *n* : state or period of sexual excitement esp.
in male deer — **rut** *vb*

²rut *n* **1** : a track worn by wheels or by habitual passage
of something **2** : a usual or fixed routine
ru•ta•ba•ga \\ʌrü-tə-**'**bā-gə, ʌrü-\ *n* : a turnip with a large
yellowish root
Ruth **'**rüth\ *n* — see BIBLE table
ru•the•ni•um \\rü-**'**thē-nē-əm\ *n* : a hard brittle metallic
chemical element — see ELEMENT table
ruth•less **'**rüth-ləs\ *adj* [fr. *ruth* compassion, pity, fr.
ME *ruthe*, fr. *ruen* to rue, fr. OE *hrēowan*] : having
no pity : MERCILESS, CRUEL — **ruth•less•ly** *adv* —
ruth•less•ness *n*
¹RV \\ʌär-**'**vē\ *n* : RECREATIONAL VEHICLE
²RV *abbr* Revised Version
R–value **'**är-ʌval-yü\ *n* : a measure of resistance to the
flow of heat through a substance (as insulation)
RW *abbr* **1** right worshipful **2** right worthy
rwy *or* **ry** *abbr* railway
-ry \rē\ *n suffix* : -ERY 〈bigot*ry*〉
rye **'**rī\ *n* **1** : a hardy annual grass grown for grain or
as a cover crop; *also* : its seed **2** : a whiskey distilled
from a rye mash

S

¹s **'**es\ *n, pl* **s's** *or* **ss** **'**e-səz\ *often cap* : the 19th letter
of the English alphabet
²s *abbr, often cap* **1** saint **2** second **3** senate **4** series **5**
shilling **6** singular **7** small **8** son **9** south; southern
¹-s \s *after sounds* f, k, k̲, p, t, th; əz *after sounds* ch,
j, s, sh, z, zh; z *after other sounds*\ *n pl suffix* — used
to form the plural of most nouns that do not end in *s*,
z, *sh*, or *ch* or in *y* following a consonant 〈head*s*〉
〈book*s*〉 〈boy*s*〉 〈belief*s*〉, to form the plural of proper
nouns that end in *y* following a consonant 〈Mary*s*〉,
and with or without a preceding apostrophe to form
the plural of abbreviations, numbers, letters, and
symbols used as nouns 〈MC*s*〉 〈4*s*〉 〈 + #*s*〉 〈B's〉
²-s *adv suffix* — used to form adverbs denoting usual
or repeated action or state 〈works night*s*〉
³-s *vb suffix* — used to form the third person singular present of most verbs that do not end in *s*, *z*, *sh*,
or *ch* or in *y* followng a consonant 〈fall*s*〉 〈take*s*〉
〈play*s*〉
S *symbol* sulfur
SA *abbr* **1** Salvation Army **2** seaman apprentice **3** sex
appeal **4** [L *sine anno* without year] without date **5**
South Africa **6** South America **7** subject to approval
Sab•bath **'**sa-bəth\ *n* [ME *sabat*, fr. OF & OE, fr. L
sabbatum, fr. Gk *sabbaton*, fr. Heb *shabbāth*, lit.,
rest] **1** : the 7th day of the week observed as a day of
worship by Jews and some Christians **2** : Sunday observed among Christians as a day of worship
sab•bat•i•cal \sə-**'**ba-ti-kəl\ *n* : a leave often with pay
granted (as to a college professor) usu. every 7th year
for rest, travel, or research
sa•ber *or* **sa•bre** **'**sā-bər\ *n* [F *sabre*] : a cavalry sword
with a curved blade and thick back
saber saw *n* : a portable electric saw with a pointed reciprocating blade
sa•ble **'**sā-bəl\ *n, pl* **sables 1** : the color black **2** *pl*
: mourning garments **3** : a dark brown mammal chief-
ly of northern Asia related to the weasels; *also* : its
fur or pelt
¹sab•o•tage **'**sa-bə-ʌtäzh\ *n* [F] **1** : deliberate destruction of an employer's property or hindering of production by workers **2** : destructive or hampering
action by enemy agents or sympathizers in time of
war
²sabotage *vb* **-taged; -tag•ing** : to practice sabotage on
: WRECK
sab•o•teur \\ʌsa-bə-**'**tər\ *n* : a person who practices sabotage

sac **'**sak\ *n* : a pouch in an animal or plant often containing a fluid
SAC *abbr* Strategic Air Command
sac•cha•rin **'**sa-kə-rən\ *n* : a white crystalline compound used as an artificial calorie-free sweetener
sac•cha•rine **'**sa-kə-rən\ *adj* : nauseatingly sweet 〈〜
poetry〉
sac•er•do•tal \\ʌsa-sər-**'**dōt-ᵊl, -kər-\ *adj* : PRIESTLY
sac•er•do•tal•ism \-ᵊl-ʌi-zəm\ *n* : a religious belief emphasizing the powers of priests as essential mediators
between God and man
sa•chem **'**sā-chəm\ *n* : a No. American Indian chief
sa•chet \sa-**'**shā\ *n* [F, fr. OF, dim. of *sac* bag] : a small
bag filled with perfumed powder for scenting clothes
¹sack **'**sak\ *n* **1** : a usu. rectangular-shaped bag (as of
paper or burlap) **2** : a loose jacket or short coat
²sack *vb* : DISMISS, FIRE
³sack *n* [modif. of MF *sec* dry, fr. L *siccus*] : a white
wine popular in England in the 16th and 17th centuries
⁴sack *vb* : to plunder a captured town
sack•cloth \-ʌklȯth\ *n* : a rough garment worn as a sign
of penitence
sac•ra•ment **'**sa-krə-mənt\ *n* **1** : a formal religious act
or rite; *esp* : one (as baptism or the Eucharist) held to
have been instituted by Christ **2** : the elements of the
Eucharist — **sac•ra•men•tal** \\ʌsa-krə-**'**ment-ᵊl\ *adj*
sa•cred **'**sā-krəd\ *adj* **1** : set apart for the service or
worship of deity **2** : devoted exclusively to one service or use **3** : worthy of veneration or reverence **4**
: of or relating to religion : RELIGIOUS **syn** blessed, divine, hallowed, holy, sanctified — **sa•cred•ly** *adv* —
sa•cred•ness *n*
sacred cow *n* : one that is often unreasonably immune
from criticism
¹sac•ri•fice **'**sa-krə-ʌfīs\ *n* **1** : the offering of something
precious to deity **2** : something offered in sacrifice **3**
: LOSS, DEPRIVATION **4** : a bunt allowing a base runner
to advance while the batter is put out; *also* : a fly ball
allowing a runner to score after the catch — **sac-
ri•fi•cial** \\ʌsa-krə-**'**fi-shəl\ *adj* — **sac•ri•fi•cial•ly** *adv*
²sac•ri•fice *vb* **-ficed; -fic•ing 1** : to offer up or kill as a
sacrifice **2** : to accept the loss or destruction of for an
end, cause, or ideal **3** : to make a sacrifice in baseball
sac•ri•lege **'**sa-krə-lij\ *n* [ME, fr. OF, fr. L *sacri-
legium*, fr. *sacrilegus* one who steals sacred things,
fr. *sacr-, sacer* sacred + *legere* to gather, steal] **1** : violation of something consecrated to God **2** : gross ir-

reverence toward a hallowed person, place, or thing
— **sac·ri·le·gious** \ˌsa-krə-ˈli-jəs, -ˈlē-\ *adj* — **sac·ri·le·gious·ly** *adv*
sac·ris·tan \ˈsa-krə-stən\ *n* 1 : a church officer in charge of the sacristy 2 : SEXTON
sac·ris·ty \ˈsa-krə-stē\ *n*, *pl* -ties : VESTRY
sac·ro·il·i·ac \ˌsa-krō-ˈi-lē-ˌak\ *n* : the joint between the upper part of the hipbone and the sacrum
sac·ro·sanct \ˈsa-krō-ˌsaŋkt\ *adj* : SACRED, INVIOLABLE
sa·crum \ˈsa-krəm, ˈsā-\ *n*, *pl* **sa·cra** \ˈsa-krə, ˈsā-\ : the part of the vertebral column that is directly connected with or forms a part of the pelvis and in humans consists of five fused vertebrae
sad \ˈsad\ *adj* **sad·der; sad·dest** 1 : GRIEVING, MOURNFUL, DOWNCAST 2 : causing sorrow 3 : DULL, SOMBER — **sad·ly** *adv* — **sad·ness** *n*
sad·den \ˈsad-ᵊn\ *vb* : to make sad
¹**sad·dle** \ˈsad-ᵊl\ *n* 1 : a usu. padded leather-covered seat (as for a rider on horseback) 2 : the upper back portion of a carcass (as of mutton)

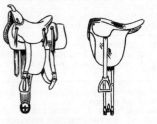

saddle 1

²**saddle** *vb* **sad·dled; sad·dling** 1 : to put a saddle on 2 : OPPRESS, BURDEN
sad·dle·bow \ˈsad-ᵊl-ˌbō\ *n* : the arch in the front of a saddle
saddle horse *n* : a horse suited for or trained for riding
Sad·du·cee \ˈsa-jə-ˌsē, ˈsa-dyə-\ *n* : a member of an ancient Jewish sect consisting of a ruling class of priests and rejecting certain doctrines — **Sad·du·ce·an** \ˌsa-jə-ˈsē-ən, ˌsa-dyə-\ *adj*
sad·iron \ˈsa-ˌdi-ərn\ *n* : a flatiron with a removable handle
sa·dism \ˈsā-ˌdi-zəm, ˈsa-\ *n* : a sexual perversion in which gratification is obtained by inflicting physical or mental pain on others — **sa·dist** \ˈsā-dist, ˈsa-\ *n* — **sa·dis·tic** \sə-ˈdis-tik\ *adj* — **sa·dis·ti·cal·ly** \-ti-k(ə-)lē\ *adv*
SAE *abbr* 1 self-addressed envelope 2 Society of Automotive Engineers 3 stamped addressed envelope
sa·fa·ri \sə-ˈfär-ē, -ˈfar-\ *n* [Ar *safarīy* of a trip] 1 : a hunting expedition esp. in eastern Africa 2 : JOURNEY, TRIP
¹**safe** \ˈsāf\ *adj* **saf·er; saf·est** 1 : free from harm or risk 2 : affording safety; *also* : secure from danger or loss 3 : RELIABLE — **safe·ly** *adv*
²**safe** *n* : a container for keeping articles (as valuables) safe
safe–con·duct \-ˈkän-(ˌ)dəkt\ *n* : a pass permitting a person to go through enemy lines
¹**safe·guard** \-ˌgärd\ *n* : a measure or device for preventing accident
²**safeguard** *vb* : to provide a safeguard for : PROTECT
safe·keep·ing \ˈsāf-ˈkē-piŋ\ *n* : a keeping or being kept in safety
safe sex *n* : sexual activity and esp. sexual intercourse in which various measures (as the use of latex condoms) are taken to avoid disease (as AIDS) transmitted by sexual contact
safe·ty \ˈsāf-tē\ *n*, *pl* **safeties** 1 : freedom from danger : SECURITY 2 : a protective device 3 : a football play in which the ball is downed by the offensive team be-

hind its own goal line 4 : a defensive football back in the deepest position — **safety** *adj*
safety glass *n* : shatter-resistant material formed of two sheets of glass with a sheet of clear plastic between them
safety match *n* : a match that ignites only when struck on a special surface
saf·flow·er \ˈsa-ˌflaü-ər\ *n* : a widely grown Old World herb related to the daisies that has large orange or red flower heads yielding a dyestuff and seeds rich in edible oil
saf·fron \ˈsa-frən\ *n* : a deep orange powder from the flower of a crocus used to color and flavor foods
sag \ˈsag\ *vb* **sagged; sag·ging** 1 : to droop or settle from or as if from pressure 2 : to lose firmness or vigor — **sag** *n*
sa·ga \ˈsä-gə\ *n* [ON] : a narrative of heroic deeds; *esp* : one recorded in Iceland in the 12th and 13th centuries
sa·ga·cious \sə-ˈgā-shəs\ *adj* : of keen mind : SHREWD — **sa·gac·i·ty** \-ˈga-sə-tē\ *n*
sag·a·more \ˈsa-gə-ˌmōr\ *n* : a subordinate No. American Indian chief
¹**sage** \ˈsāj\ *adj* [ME, fr. OF, fr. (assumed) VL *sapius*, fr. L *sapere* to taste, have good taste, be wise] : WISE, PRUDENT — **sage·ly** *adv*
²**sage** *n* : one who is distinguished for wisdom
³**sage** *n* [ME, fr. MF *sauge*, fr. L *salvia*, fr. *salvus* healthy; fr. its use as a medicinal herb] 1 : a mint with leaves used in flavoring 2 : SAGEBRUSH
sage·brush \ˈsāj-ˌbrəsh\ *n* : any of several low shrubby No. American composite plants; *esp* : one of the western U.S. with a sagelike odor
Sag·it·tar·i·us \ˌsa-jə-ˈter-ē-əs\ *n* [L, lit., archer] 1 : a zodiacal constellation between Scorpio and Capricorn usu. pictured as a centaur archer 2 : the 9th sign of the zodiac in astrology; *also* : one born under this sign
sa·go \ˈsā-gō\ *n*, *pl* **sagos** : a dry granulated starch esp. from the pith of various tropical palms (**sago palm**)
sa·gua·ro \sə-ˈwär-ə, -ˈgwär-, -ō\ *n*, *pl* -ros [MexSp] : a desert cactus of the southwestern U.S. and Mexico with a tall columnar simple or sparsely branched trunk of up to 60 feet (18 meters)
said *past and past part of* SAY
¹**sail** \ˈsāl\ *n* 1 : a piece of fabric by means of which the wind is used to propel a ship 2 : a sailing ship 3 : something resembling a sail 4 : a trip on a sailboat
²**sail** *vb* 1 : to travel on a sailing ship 2 : to pass over in a ship 3 : to manage or direct the course of a ship 4 : to move with ease, grace, or nonchalance
sail·board \ˈsāl-ˌbōrd\ *n* : a modified surfboard having a mast and sailed by a standing person
sail·boat \-ˌbōt\ *n* : a boat propelled primarily by sail
sail·cloth \-ˌklòth\ *n* : a heavy canvas used for sails, tents, or upholstery
sail·fish \-ˌfish\ *n* : any of a genus of large marine bony fishes with a large dorsal fin that are related to marlins
sail·ing *n* : the sport of handling or riding in a sailboat
sail·or \ˈsā-lər\ *n* : one that sails; *esp* : a member of a ship's crew
sail·plane \ˈsāl-ˌplān\ *n* : a glider designed to rise in an upward air current
saint \ˈsānt, *before a name* (ˌ)sānt *or* sənt\ *n* 1 : one officially recognized as preeminent for holiness 2 : one of the spirits of the departed in heaven 3 : a holy or godly person — **saint·ed** \ˈsān-təd\ *adj* — **saint·hood** \-ˌhủd\ *n*
Saint Ber·nard \-bər-ˈnärd\ *n* : any of a Swiss alpine breed of tall powerful working dogs used esp. formerly in aiding lost travelers
☞ For illustration, see next page.
saint·ly \ˈsānt-lē\ *adj* : relating to, resembling, or befitting a saint — **saint·li·ness** \-lē-nəs\ *n*
Saint Val·en·tine's Day \-ˈva-lən-ˌtīnz-\ *n* : February

Saint Bernard

14 observed in honor of St. Valentine and as a time for exchanging valentines

¹sake \'sāk\ *n* **1** : END, PURPOSE **2** : personal or social welfare, safety, or well-being

²sa·ke *or* **sa·ki** \'sä-kē\ *n* : a Japanese alcoholic beverage of fermented rice

sa·laam \sə-'läm\ *n* [Ar *salām*, lit., peace] **1** : a salutation or ceremonial greeting in the East **2** : an obeisance performed by bowing very low and placing the right palm on the forehead — **salaam** *vb*

sa·la·cious \sə-'lā-shəs\ *adj* **1** : arousing sexual desire or imagination **2** : LUSTFUL — **sa·la·cious·ly** *adv* — **sa·la·cious·ness** *n*

sal·ad \'sa-ləd\ *n* : a cold dish (as of lettuce, vegetables, fish, eggs, or fruit) served with dressing

sal·a·man·der \'sa-lə-ˌman-dər\ *n* : any of numerous amphibians that look like lizards but have scaleless usu. smooth moist skin

sa·la·mi \sə-'lä-mē\ *n* [It] : a highly seasoned sausage of pork and beef

sal·a·ry \'sa-lə-rē\ *n, pl* **-ries** [ME *salarie*, fr. L *salarium* pension, salary, fr. neut. of *salarius* of salt, fr. *sal* salt] : payment made at regular intervals for services

sale \'sāl\ *n* **1** : transfer of ownership of property from one person to another in return for money **2** : ready market : DEMAND **3** : AUCTION **4** : a selling of goods at bargain prices — **sal·able** *or* **sale·able** \'sā-lə-bəl\ *adj*

sales·girl \'sālz-ˌgərl\ *n* : SALESWOMAN

sales·man \-mən\ *n* : a person who sells in a store or to outside customers — **sales·man·ship** *n*

sales·per·son \-ˌpər-sən\ *n* : a salesman or saleswoman

sales·wom·an \-ˌwu̇-mən\ *n* : a woman who sells merchandise

sal·i·cyl·ic acid \ˌsa-lə-'si-lik-\ *n* : a crystalline organic acid used in the form of its salts and other derivatives to relieve pain and fever

¹sa·lient \'sāl-yənt, 'sā-lē-ənt\ *adj* : jutting forward beyond a line; *also* : PROMINENT **syn** conspicuous, striking, noticeable

²salient *n* : a projecting part in a line of defense

¹sa·line \'sā-ˌlēn, -ˌlīn\ *adj* : consisting of or containing salt : SALTY — **sa·lin·i·ty** \sā-'li-nə-tē, sə-\ *n*

²saline *n* **1** : a metallic salt esp. with a purgative action **2** : a saline solution

sa·li·va \sə-'lī-və\ *n* : a liquid secreted into the mouth that helps digestion — **sal·i·vary** \'sa-lə-ˌver-ē\ *adj*

sal·i·vate \'sa-lə-ˌvāt\ *vb* **-vat·ed; -vat·ing** : to produce saliva esp. in excess — **sal·i·va·tion** \ˌsa-lə-'vā-shən\ *n*

sal·low \'sa-lō\ *adj* : of a yellowish sickly color ⟨a ∼ face⟩

sal·ly \'sa-lē\ *n, pl* **sallies 1** : a rushing attack on besiegers by troops of a besieged place **2** : a witty remark or retort **3** : a brief excursion — **sally** *vb*

salm·on \'sa-mən\ *n, pl* **salmon** *also* **salmons 1** : any of several bony fishes with pinkish flesh used for food that are related to the trouts **2** : a strong yellowish pink color

sal·mo·nel·la \ˌsal-mə-'ne-lə\ *n, pl* **-nel·lae** \-'ne-(ˌ)lē, -ˌlī\ *or* **-nellas** *or* **-nella** : any of a genus of rod-shaped bacteria that cause various illnesses (as food poisoning)

sa·lon \sə-'län, 'sa-ˌlän, sa-'lōⁿ\ *n* [F] : an elegant drawing room; *also* : a fashionable shop ⟨beauty ∼⟩

sa·loon \sə-'lün\ *n* **1** : a large public cabin on a ship **2** : a place where liquors are sold and drunk : BARROOM **3** *Brit* : SEDAN **2**

---

sal·sa \'sȯl-sə, 'säl-\ *n* : a spicy sauce of tomatoes, onions, and hot peppers

sal soda \'sal-'sō-də\ *n* : SODIUM CARBONATE

¹salt \'sȯlt\ *n* **1** : a white crystalline substance that consists of sodium and chlorine and is used in seasoning foods **2** : a saltlike cathartic substance (as Epsom salts) **3** : a compound formed usu. by action of an acid on metal **4** : SAILOR — **salt·i·ness** \'sȯl-tē-nəs\ *n* — **salty** \'sȯl-tē\ *adj*

²salt *vb* : to preserve, season, or feed with salt

³salt *adj* : preserved or treated with salt; *also* : SALTY

SALT *abbr* Strategic Arms Limitation Talks

salt away *vb* : to lay away safely : SAVE

salt·box \'sȯlt-ˌbäks\ *n* : a frame dwelling with two stories in front and one behind and a long sloping roof

salt·cel·lar \-ˌse-lər\ *n* : a small container for holding salt at the table

---

sal·tine \sȯl-'tēn\ *n* : a thin crisp cracker sprinkled with salt

---

salt lick *n* : LICK **5**

salt·pe·ter \'sȯlt-'pē-tər\ *n* [ME *salt petre*, alter. of *salpetre*, fr. MF, fr. ML *sal petrae*, lit., salt of the rock] **1** : POTASSIUM NITRATE **2** : SODIUM NITRATE

salt·wa·ter \-ˌwȯ-tər, -ˌwä-\ *adj* : of, relating to, or living in salt water

sa·lu·bri·ous \sə-'lü-brē-əs\ *adj* : favorable to health

sal·u·tary \'sal-yə-ˌter-ē\ *adj* : health-giving; *also* : BENEFICIAL

sal·u·ta·tion \ˌsal-yə-'tā-shən\ *n* : an expression of greeting, goodwill, or courtesy usu. by word or gesture

sa·lu·ta·to·ri·an \sə-ˌlü-tə-'tōr-ē-ən\ *n* : the student having the 2nd highest rank in a graduating class who delivers the salutatory address

sa·lu·ta·to·ry \sə-'lü-tə-ˌtōr-ē\ *adj* : relating to or being the welcoming oration delivered at an academic commencement

¹sa·lute \sə-'lüt\ *vb* **sa·lut·ed; sa·lut·ing** 1 : GREET 2 : to honor by special ceremonies 3 : to show respect to (a superior officer) by a formal position of hand, rifle, or sword

²salute *n* 1 : GREETING 2 : the formal position assumed in saluting a superior

¹sal·vage \'sal-vij\ *n* 1 : money paid for saving a ship, its cargo, or passengers when the ship is wrecked or in danger 2 : the saving of a ship 3 : the saving of possessions in danger of being lost 4 : things saved from loss or destruction (as by a wreck or fire)

²salvage *vb* **sal·vaged; sal·vag·ing** : to rescue from destruction

sal·va·tion \sal-'vā-shən\ *n* 1 : the saving of a person from sin or its consequences esp. in the life after death 2 : the saving from danger, difficulty, or evil 3 : something that saves

¹salve \'sav, 'sàv\ *n* 1 : a medicinal substance applied to the skin 2 : a soothing influence

²salve *vb* **salved; salv·ing** : EASE, SOOTHE

sal·ver \'sal-vər\ *n* [F *salve*, fr. Sp *salva* sampling of food to detect poison, tray, fr. *salvar* to save, sample food to detect poison, fr. LL *salvare* to save, fr. L *salvus* safe] : a small serving tray

sal·vo \'sal-vō\ *n, pl* **salvos** *or* **salvoes** : a simultaneous discharge of guns

Sam *or* **Saml** *abbr* Samuel

SAM \'sam, ˌes-ˌā-'em\ *n* [surface-to-*air* *m*issile] : a guided missile for use against aircraft by ground units

sa·mar·i·um \sə-'mer-ē-əm\ *n* : a gray lustrous metallic chemical element — see ELEMENT table

¹same \'sām\ *adj* 1 : being the one referred to : not different 2 : SIMILAR — **same·ness** *n*

²same *pron* : the same one or ones

³same *adv* : in the same manner

Sa·mo·an \sə-'mō-ən\ *n* : a native or inhabitant of Samoa — **Samoan** *adj*

sam·o·var \'sa-mə-ˌvär\ *n* [Russ, fr. *samo-* self + *varit'* to boil] : an urn with a spigot at the base used esp. in Russia to boil water for tea

sam·pan \'sam-ˌpan\ *n* : a flat-bottomed skiff of the Far East usu. propelled by two short oars

¹sam·ple \'sam-pəl\ *n* : a representative piece, item, or set of individuals that shows the quality or nature of the whole from which it was taken : EXAMPLE, SPECIMEN

²sample *vb* **sam·pled; sam·pling** : to judge the quality of by a sample

sam·pler \'sam-plər\ *n* : a piece of needlework; *esp* : one testing skill in embroidering

Sam·u·el \'sam-yə-wəl\ *n* — see BIBLE table

sam·u·rai \'sa-mə-ˌrī, 'sam-yə-\ *n, pl* **samurai** : a member of a Japanese feudal warrior class practicing a chivalric code

san·a·to·ri·um \ˌsa-nə-'tōr-ē-əm\ *n, pl* **-riums** *or* **-ria** \-ē-ə\ 1 : a health resort 2 : an establishment for the care esp. of convalescents or the chronically ill

sanc·ti·fy \'saŋk-tə-ˌfī\ *vb* **-fied; -fy·ing** 1 : to make holy : CONSECRATE 2 : to free from sin — **sanc·ti·fi·ca·tion** \ˌsaŋk-tə-fə-'kā-shən\ *n*

sanc·ti·mo·nious \ˌsaŋk-tə-'mō-nē-əs\ *adj* : hypocritically pious — **sanc·ti·mo·nious·ly** *adv*

¹sanc·tion \'saŋk-shən\ *n* 1 : authoritative approval 2 : a measure (as a threat or fine) designed to enforce a law or standard (economic ∼s)

²sanction *vb* : to give approval to : RATIFY **syn** endorse, accredit, certify, approve

sanc·ti·ty \'saŋk-tə-tē\ *n, pl* **-ties** 1 : GODLINESS 2 : SACREDNESS

sanc·tu·ary \'saŋk-chə-ˌwer-ē\ *n, pl* **-ar·ies** 1 : a consecrated place (as the part of a church in which the altar is placed) 2 : a place of refuge (bird ∼)

sanc·tum \'saŋk-təm\ *n, pl* **sanctums** *also* **sanc·ta** \-tə\ : a private office or study : DEN (an editor's ∼)

¹sand \'sand\ *n* : loose particles of hard broken rock — **sandy** *adj*

²sand *vb* 1 : to cover or fill with sand 2 : to scour, smooth, or polish with an abrasive (as sandpaper) — **sand·er** *n*

san·dal \'sand-ᵊl\ *n* : a shoe consisting of a sole strapped to the foot; *also* : a low or open slipper or rubber overshoe

san·dal·wood \-ˌwüd\ *n* : the fragrant yellowish heartwood of a parasitic tree of southern Asia that is much used in ornamental carving and cabinetwork; *also* : the tree

sand·bag \'sand-ˌbag\ *n* : a bag filled with sand and used in fortifications, as ballast, or as a weapon

sand·bank \-ˌbaŋk\ *n* : a deposit of sand (as in a bar or shoal)

sand·bar \-ˌbär\ *n* : a ridge of sand formed in water by tides or currents

sand·blast \-ˌblast\ *vb* : to treat with a stream of sand blown (as for cleaning stone) by compressed air — **sand·blast·er** *n*

sand dollar *n* : any of numerous flat circular sea urchins chiefly of sandy bottoms in shallow water

S & H *abbr* shipping and handling

sand·hog \'sand-ˌhòg, -ˌhäg\ *n* : a laborer who builds underwater tunnels

sand·lot \-ˌlät\ *n* : a vacant lot esp. when used for the unorganized sports of children — **sand·lot** *adj* — **sand·lot·ter** *n*

sand·man \-ˌman\ *n* : the genie of folklore who makes children sleepy

sand·pa·per \-ˌpā-pər\ *n* : paper with abrasive (as sand) glued on one side used in smoothing and polishing surfaces — **sandpaper** *vb*

sand·pip·er \-ˌpī-pər\ *n* : any of numerous shorebirds with a soft-tipped bill longer than that of the related plovers

sand·stone \-ˌstōn\ *n* : rock made of sand united by a natural cement

sand·storm \-ˌstȯrm\ *n* : a windstorm that drives clouds of sand

sand trap *n* : a hazard on a golf course consisting of a hollow containing sand

¹**sand·wich** \ˈsand-(ˌ)wich\ *n* [after John Montagu, 4th Earl of *Sandwich* †1792 Eng. diplomat] **1** : two or more slices of bread with a layer (as of meat or cheese) spread between them **2** : something resembling a sandwich

²**sandwich** *vb* : to squeeze or crowd in

sane \ˈsān\ *adj* **san·er; san·est** : mentally sound and healthy; *also* : SENSIBLE, RATIONAL — **sane·ly** *adv*

sang *past of* SING

sang·froid \ˈsän-ˈfrwä\ *n* [F *sang-froid*, lit., cold blood] : self-possession or an imperturbable state esp. under strain

san·gui·nary \ˈsaŋ-gwə-ˌner-ē\ *adj* : BLOODY ⟨~ battle⟩

san·guine \ˈsaŋ-gwən\ *adj* **1** : RUDDY **2** : CHEERFUL, HOPEFUL

sanit *abbr* sanitary; sanitation

san·i·tar·i·an \ˌsa-nə-ˈter-ē-ən\ *n* : a specialist in sanitation and public health

san·i·tar·i·um \ˌsa-nə-ˈter-ē-əm\ *n*, *pl* **-i·ums** *or* **-ia** \-ē-ə\ : SANATORIUM

san·i·tary \ˈsa-nə-ˌter-ē\ *adj* **1** : of or relating to health : HYGIENIC **2** : free from filth or infective matter

sanitary napkin *n* : a disposable absorbent pad used to absorb uterine flow (as during menstruation)

san·i·ta·tion \ˌsa-nə-ˈtā-shən\ *n* : the act or process of making sanitary; *also* : protection of health by maintenance of sanitary conditions

san·i·tize \ˈsa-nə-ˌtīz\ *vb* **-tized; -tiz·ing 1** : to make sanitary **2** : to make more acceptable by removing unpleasant features

san·i·ty \ˈsa-nə-tē\ *n* : soundness of mind

sank *past of* SINK

sans \ˈsanz\ *prep* : WITHOUT

San·skrit \ˈsan-ˌskrit\ *n* : an ancient language that is the classical language of India and of Hinduism — **Sanskrit** *adj*

San·ta Ana \ˌsan-tə-ˈa-nə\ *n* [*Santa Ana* Mountains in southern Calif.] : a hot dry wind from the north, northeast, or east in southern California

¹**sap** \ˈsap\ *n* **1** : a vital fluid; *esp* : a watery fluid that circulates through a vascular plant **2** : a foolish gullible person — **sap·less** *adj*

²**sap** *vb* **sapped; sap·ping 1** : UNDERMINE **2** : to weaken gradually

sap·id \ˈsa-pəd\ *adj* : FLAVORFUL

sa·pi·ent \ˈsā-pē-ənt, ˈsa-\ *adj* : WISE, DISCERNING — **sa·pi·ence** \-əns\ *n*

sa·pling \ˈsa-pliŋ\ *n* : a young tree

sap·phire \ˈsa-ˌfīr\ *n* : a hard transparent usu. rich blue gem

sap·py \ˈsa-pē\ *adj* **sap·pi·er; -est 1** : full of sap **2** : overly sentimental **3** : SILLY, FOOLISH

sap·ro·phyte \ˈsa-prə-ˌfīt\ *n* : a living thing and esp. a plant living on dead or decaying organic matter — **sap·ro·phyt·ic** \ˌsa-prə-ˈfi-tik\ *adj*

sap·suck·er \ˈsap-ˌsə-kər\ *n* : any of a genus of small No. American woodpeckers

sap·wood \-ˌwu̇d\ *n* : the younger active and usu. lighter and softer outer layer of wood (as of a tree trunk)

sar·casm \ˈsär-ˌka-zəm\ *n* **1** : a cutting or contemptuous remark **2** : ironic criticism or reproach — **sar·cas·tic** \sär-ˈkas-tik\ *adj* — **sar·cas·ti·cal·ly** \-ti-k(ə-)lē\ *adv*

sar·co·ma \sär-ˈkō-mə\ *n*, *pl* **-mas** *also* **-ma·ta** \-mə-tə\ : a malignant tumor esp. of connective tissue, bone, cartilage, or striated muscle

sar·coph·a·gus \sär-ˈkä-fə-gəs\ *n*, *pl* **-gi** \-ˌgī, -ˌjī\ *also* **-gus·es** [L *sarcophagus* (*lapis*) limestone used for coffins, fr. Gk (*lithos*) *sarkophagos*, lit., flesh-eating stone, fr. *sark-*, *sarx* flesh + *phagein* to eat] : a large stone coffin

sar·dine \sär-ˈdēn\ *n*, *pl* **sardines** *also* **sardine** : a young or small fish preserved for use as food

sar·don·ic \sär-ˈdä-nik\ *adj* : disdainfully or skeptically humorous : derisively mocking **syn** ironic, satiric, sarcastic — **sar·don·i·cal·ly** \-ni-k(ə-)lē\ *adv*

sa·ri *also* **sa·ree** \ˈsär-ē\ *n* [Hindi *sārī*] : a garment worn by women in southern Asia that consists of a long cloth draped around the body and head or shoulder

sa·rong \sə-ˈrȯŋ, -ˈräŋ\ *n* : a loose garment wrapped around the body and worn by men and women of the Malay Archipelago and the Pacific islands

sar·sa·pa·ril·la \ˌsas-ə-pə-ˈri-lə, ˌsärs-\ *n* **1** : the dried roots of a tropical American smilax used esp. for flavoring; *also* : the plant **2** : a sweetened carbonated beverage flavored with sassafras and an oil from a birch

sar·to·ri·al \sär-ˈtȯr-ē-əl\ *adj* : of or relating to a tailor or tailored clothes — **sar·to·ri·al·ly** *adv*

SASE *abbr* self-addressed stamped envelope

¹**sash** \ˈsash\ *n* : a broad band worn around the waist or over the shoulder

²**sash** *n*, *pl* **sash** *also* **sash·es** : a frame for panes of glass in a door or window; *also* : the movable part of a window

sa·shay \sa-ˈshā\ *vb* **1** : WALK, GLIDE, GO **2** : to strut or move about in an ostentatious manner **3** : to proceed in a diagonal or sideways manner

Sask *abbr* Saskatchewan

Sas·quatch \ˈsas-ˌkwach, -ˌkwäch\ *n* [Halkomelem (American Indian language of British Columbia) *sésq̓əc*] : a large hairy humanlike creature reported to exist in the northwestest U.S. and western Canada

sas·sa·fras \ˈsa-sə-ˌfras\ *n* [Sp *sasafrás*] : a No. American tree related to the laurel; *also* : its carcinogenic dried root bark

sassy \'sa-sē\ adj **sass•i•er; -est** : SAUCY

[1]sat past and past part of SIT

[2]sat abbr saturate; saturated; saturation

Sat abbr Saturday

Sa•tan \'sāt-ᵊn\ n : DEVIL

sa•tang \sə-'täŋ\ n, pl **satang** or **satangs** — see baht at MONEY table

sa•tan•ic \sə-'ta-nik, sā-\ adj **1** : of or characteristic of Satan **2** : extremely malicious or wicked — **sa•tan•i•cal•ly** \-ni-k(ə-)lē\ adv

satch•el \'sa-chəl\ n : SUITCASE

sate \'sāt\ vb **sat•ed; sat•ing** : to satisfy to the full; also : SURFEIT, GLUT

sa•teen \sa-'tēn, sə-\ n : a cotton cloth finished to resemble satin

sat•el•lite \'sat-ᵊl-ˌīt\ n [F, fr. L satelles attendant] **1** : an obsequious follower of a distinguished person : TOADY **2** : a celestial body that orbits a larger body **3** : a manufactured object that orbits a celestial body

sa•ti•ate \'sā-shē-ˌāt\ vb **-at•ed; -at•ing** : to satisfy fully or to excess

sa•ti•ety \sə-'tī-ə-tē\ n : fullness to the point of excess

sat•in \'sat-ᵊn\ n : a fabric (as of silk) with a glossy surface — **sat•iny** adj

sat•in•wood \'sat-ᵊn-ˌwùd\ n : a hard yellowish brown wood of satiny luster; also : a tree yielding this wood

sat•ire \'sa-ˌtīr\ n : biting wit, irony, or sarcasm used to expose vice or folly; also : a literary work having these qualities — **sa•tir•ic** \sə-'tir-ik\ or **sa•tir•i•cal** \-i-kəl\ adj — **sa•tir•i•cal•ly** adv — **sat•i•rist** \'sa-tə-rist\ n — **sat•i•rize** \-tə-ˌrīz\ vb

sat•is•fac•tion \ˌsa-təs-'fak-shən\ n **1** : payment through penance of punishment incurred by sin **2** : CONTENTMENT, GRATIFICATION **3** : reparation for an insult **4** : settlement of a claim

sat•is•fac•to•ry \-'fak-tə-rē\ adj : giving satisfaction : ADEQUATE — **sat•is•fac•to•ri•ly** \-'fak-tə-rə-lē\ adv

sat•is•fy \'sa-təs-ˌfī\ vb **-fied; -fy•ing 1** : to answer or discharge (a claim) in full **2** : to make happy : GRATIFY **3** : to pay what is due to **4** : CONVINCE **5** : to meet the requirements of — **sat•is•fy•ing•ly** adv

sa•trap \'sā-ˌtrap, 'sa-\ n [ME, fr. L satrapes, fr. Gk satrapēs, fr. OPer khshathrapāvan, lit., protector of the dominion] : a petty prince : a subordinate ruler

sat•u•rate \'sa-chə-ˌrāt\ vb **-rat•ed; -rat•ing 1** : to soak thoroughly **2** : to treat or charge with something to the point where no more can be absorbed, dissolved, or retained — **sat•u•ra•ble** \'sa-chə-rə-bəl\ adj — **sat•u•ra•tion** \ˌsa-chə-'rā-shən\ n

Sat•ur•day \'sa-tər-dē, -ˌdā\ n : the 7th day of the week

Saturday night special n : a cheap easily concealed handgun

Sat•urn \'sa-tərn\ n : the planet 6th in order from the sun — see PLANET table

sat•ur•nine \'sa-tər-ˌnīn\ adj : SULLEN, SARDONIC

sa•tyr \'sā-tər\ n **1** often cap : a woodland deity in Greek mythology having certain characteristics of a horse or goat **2** : a lecherous man

[1]sauce \'sòs, 3 usu 'sas\ n **1** : a fluid dressing or topping for food **2** : stewed fruit **3** : IMPUDENCE

[2]sauce \'sòs, 2 usu 'sas\ vb **sauced; sauc•ing 1** : to put sauce on; also : to add zest to **2** : to be impudent to

sauce•pan \'sòs-ˌpan\ n : a small deep cooking pan with a handle

sau•cer \'sò-sər\ n : a rounded shallow dish for use under a cup

saucy \'sa-sē, 'sò-\ adj **sauc•i•er; -est** : IMPUDENT, PERT — **sauc•i•ly** \-sə-lē\ adv — **sauc•i•ness** \-sē-nəs\ n

Sau•di \'saü-dē, 'sò-; sä-'ü-dē\ n : SAUDI ARABIAN — **Saudi** adj

Saudi Arabian n : a native or inhabitant of Saudi Arabia — **Saudi Arabian** adj

sau•er•kraut \'saù-ər-ˌkraùt\ n [G, fr. sauer sour + Kraut greens] : finely cut cabbage fermented in brine

sau•na \'saù-nə\ n **1** : a Finnish steam bath in which the

steam is provided by water thrown on hot stones **2** : a dry heat bath; also : a room or cabinet used for such a bath

saun•ter \'sòn-tər, 'sän-\ vb : STROLL

sau•ro•pod \'sòr-ə-ˌpäd\ n : any of a suborder of plant‑eating dinosaurs (as a brontosaurus) with a long neck and tail and a small head — **sauropod** adj

sau•sage \'sò-sij\ n [ultim. fr. LL salsicia, fr. L salsus salted] : minced and highly seasoned meat (as pork) usu. enclosed in a tubular casing

S Aust abbr South Australia

sau•té \sò-'tā, sō-\ vb **sau•téed** or **sau•téd; sau•té•ing** [F] : to fry lightly in a little fat — **sauté** n

sau•terne \sō-'tərn, sò-\ n, often cap : a usu. semisweet American white wine

[1]sav•age \'sa-vij\ adj [ME sauvage, fr. MF, fr. ML salvaticus, alter. of L silvaticus of the woods, wild, fr. silva wood, forest] **1** : WILD, UNTAMED **2** : UNCIVILIZED, BARBAROUS **3** : CRUEL, FIERCE — **sav•age•ly** adv — **sav•age•ness** n — **sav•age•ry** \-rē\ n

[2]savage n **1** : a member of a primitive human society **2** : a rude, unmannerly, or brutal person

sa•van•na or **sa•van•nah** \sə-'va-nə\ n [Sp zavana] : grassland containing scattered trees

sa•vant \sa-'vänt, sə-, 'sa-vənt\ n : a learned person : SCHOLAR

[1]save \'sāv\ vb **saved; sav•ing 1** : to redeem from sin **2** : to rescue from danger **3** : to preserve or guard from destruction or loss **4** : to put aside as a store or reserve — **sav•er** n

[2]save n : a play that prevents an opponent from scoring or winning

[3]save prep : EXCEPT

[4]save conj : BUT

savings and loan association n : a cooperative association that holds savings of members in the form of dividend-bearing shares and that invests chiefly in mortgage loans

savings bank n : a bank that holds funds of individual depositors in interest-bearing accounts and makes long-term investments (as mortgage loans)

savings bond n : a registered U.S. bond issued in denominations of $50 to $10,000

sav•ior or **sav•iour** \'sāv-yər\ n **1** : one who saves **2** cap : Jesus Christ

sa•voir faire \ˌsav-ˌwär-'far\ n [F savoir-faire, lit., knowing how to do] : sureness in social behavior

[1]sa•vor also **sa•vour** \'sā-vər\ n **1** : the taste and odor of something **2** : a special flavor or quality — **sa•vory** adj

[2]savor also **savour** vb **1** : to have a specified taste, smell, or quality **2** : to taste with pleasure

sa•vo•ry \'sā-və-rē\ n, pl **-ries** : either of two aromatic mints used in cooking

[1]savvy \'sa-vē\ vb **sav•vied; sav•vy•ing** : UNDERSTAND, COMPREHEND

[2]savvy n : practical know-how ⟨political ∼⟩ — **savvy** adj

[1]saw past of SEE

[2]saw \'sò\ n : a cutting tool with a blade having a line of teeth along its edge

[3]saw vb **sawed** \'sòd\; **sawed** or **sawn** \'sòn\; **saw•ing** : to cut or shape with or as if with a saw

[4]saw n : a common saying : MAXIM

saw•dust \'sò-(ˌ)dəst\ n : fine particles made by a saw in cutting

saw•fly \-ˌflī\ n : any of numerous insects belonging to the same order as bees and wasps and including many whose larvae are plant-feeding pests

saw•horse \-ˌhòrs\ n : a rack on which wood is rested while being sawed by hand

saw•mill \-ˌmil\ n : a mill for sawing logs

saw palmetto n : any of several shrubby palms with spiny-toothed petioles

saw•yer \'sò-yər\ n : a person who saws timber

sax \'saks\ n : SAXOPHONE

sax·i·frage \'sak-sə-frij, -ˌfrāj\ *n* [ME, fr. MF, fr. LL *saxifraga*, fr. L, fem. of *saxifragus*, breaking rocks] : any of a genus of plants with showy flowers and usu. with leaves growing in tufts close to the ground

sax·o·phone \'sak-sə-ˌfōn\ *n* : a musical instrument having a conical metal tube with a reed mouthpiece and finger keys — **sax·o·phon·ist** \-ˌfō-nist\ *n*

¹**say** \'sā\ *vb* **said** \'sed\; **say·ing; says** \'sez\ **1** : to express in words ⟨~ what you mean⟩ **2** : to state as opinion or belief **3** : PRONOUNCE; *also* : RECITE, REPEAT ⟨~ your prayers⟩ **4** : INDICATE ⟨the clock ~*s* noon⟩

²**say** *n, pl* **says** \'sāz\ **1** : an expression of opinion **2** : power of decision

say·ing *n* : a commonly repeated statement

say–so \'sā-(ˌ)sō\ *n* : an esp. authoritative assertion or decision; *also* : the right to decide

sb *abbr* substantive

Sb *symbol* [L *stibium*] antimony

SB *abbr* [NL *scientiae baccalaureus*] bachelor of science

SBA *abbr* Small Business Administration

sc *abbr* **1** scale **2** scene **3** science

Sc *symbol* scandium

SC *abbr* **1** South Carolina **2** supreme court

¹**scab** \'skab\ *n* **1** : scabies of domestic animals **2** : a protective crust over a sore or wound **3** : a worker who replaces a striker or works under conditions not authorized by a union **4** : any of various bacterial or fungus plant diseases marked by crusted spots on stems or leaves — **scab·by** *adj*

²**scab** *vb* **scabbed; scab·bing 1** : to become covered with a scab **2** : to work as a scab

scab·bard \'ska-bərd\ *n* : a sheath for the blade of a weapon (as a sword)

sca·bies \'skā-bēz\ *n* [L] : contagious itch or mange caused by mites living as parasites under the skin

sca·brous \'ska-brəs, 'skā-\ *adj* **1** : DIFFICULT, KNOTTY **2** : rough to the touch : SCALY, SCURFY ⟨a ~ leaf⟩ **3** : dealing with suggestive, indecent, or scandalous themes; *also* : SQUALID

scad \'skad\ *n* : a large number or quantity — usu. used in pl.

scaf·fold \'ska-fəld, -ˌfōld\ *n* **1** : a raised platform for workers to sit or stand on **2** : a platform on which a criminal is executed (as by hanging)

scaf·fold·ing *n* : a system of scaffolds; *also* : materials for scaffolds

scal·a·wag \'ska-li-ˌwag\ *n* : RASCAL

¹**scald** \'skȯld\ *vb* **1** : to burn with or as if with hot liquid or steam **2** : to heat to just below the boiling point

²**scald** *n* : a burn caused by scalding

¹**scale** \'skāl\ *n* **1** : either pan of a balance **2** : BALANCE — usu. used in pl. **3** : a weighing instrument

²**scale** *vb* **scaled; scal·ing** : WEIGH

³**scale** *n* **1** : one of the small thin plates that cover the body esp. of a fish or reptile **2** : a thin plate or flake **3** : a thin coating, layer, or incrustation **4** : SCALE INSECT — **scaled** \'skāld\ *adj* — **scale·less** \'skāl-ləs\ *adj* — **scaly** *adj*

⁴**scale** *vb* **scaled; scal·ing** : to strip of scales

⁵**scale** *n* [ME, fr. LL *scala* ladder, staircase, fr. L *scalae*, pl., stairs, rungs, ladder] **1** : something divided into regular spaces as a help in drawing or measuring **2** : a graduated series **3** : the size of a sample (as a model) in proportion to the size of the actual thing **4** : a standard of estimation or judgment **5** : a series of musical tones going up or down in pitch according to a specified scheme

⁶**scale** *vb* **scaled; scal·ing 1** : to climb by or as if by a ladder **2** : to arrange in a graded series

scale insect *n* : any of numerous small insects with wingless scale-covered females that are related to aphids and live and are often pests on plants

scale·pan \'skāl-ˌpan\ *n* : ¹SCALE 1

scal·lion \'skal-yən\ *n* [ultim. fr. L *ascalonia* (*caepa*) onion of Ascalon (seaport in Palestine)] : an onion without an enlarged bulb

¹**scal·lop** \'skä-ləp, 'ska-\ *n* **1** : any of numerous marine bivalve mollusks with radially ridged shells; *also* : a large edible muscle of this mollusk **2** : one of a continuous series of rounded projections forming an edge

²**scallop** *vb* **1** : to bake in a casserole ⟨~*ed* potatoes⟩ **2** : to shape, cut, or finish in scallops ⟨~*ed* edges⟩

¹**scalp** \'skalp\ *n* : the part of the skin and flesh of the head usu. covered with hair

²**scalp** *vb* **1** : to remove the scalp from **2** : to resell at greatly increased prices ⟨~ tickets⟩ — **scalp·er** *n*

scal·pel \'skal-pəl\ *n* : a small straight knife with a thin blade used esp. in surgery

scam \'skam\ *n* : a fraudulent or deceptive act or operation

scamp \'skamp\ *n* : RASCAL

scam·per \'skam-pər\ *vb* : to run nimbly and playfully — **scamper** *n*

scam·pi \'skam-pē\ *n, pl* **scampi** [It] : SHRIMP; *esp* : large shrimp prepared with a garlic-flavored sauce

¹**scan** \'skan\ *vb* **scanned; scan·ning 1** : to read (verses) so as to show metrical structure **2** : to examine closely **3** : to examine with a sensing device esp. to obtain information **4** : to make a scan of (as the human body) — **scan·ner** *n*

²**scan** *n* **1** : the act or process of scanning **2** : a picture of the distribution of radioactive material in something; *also* : an image of a bodily part produced (as by computer) by combining radiographic data obtained from several angles or sections

Scand *abbr* Scandinavia; Scandinavian

scan·dal \'skand-ᵊl\ *n* [ME, fr. LL *scandalum* stumbling block, offense, fr. Gk *skandalon*] **1** : DISGRACE, DISHONOR **2** : malicious gossip : SLANDER — **scan·dal·ize** *vb* — **scan·dal·ous** *adj* — **scan·dal·ous·ly** *adv*

scan·dal·mon·ger \-ˌmən-gər, -ˌmän-\ *n* : a person who circulates scandal

Scan·di·na·vian \ˌskan-də-ˈnā-vē-ən\ *n* : a native or inhabitant of Scandinavia — **Scandinavian** *adj*

scan·di·um \'skan-dē-əm\ *n* : a white metallic chemical element — see ELEMENT table

¹scant \'skant\ *adj* **1** : barely sufficient **2** : having scarcely enough **syn** scanty, skimpy, meager, sparse, exiguous

²scant *vb* **1** : SKIMP **2** : STINT

scant·ling \'skant-liŋ\ *n* : a small piece of lumber (as an upright in a house)

scanty \'skan-tē\ *adj* **scant·i·er; -est** : barely sufficient : SCANT — **scant·i·ly** \'skan-tə-lē\ *adv* — **scant·i·ness** \-tē-nəs\ *n*

scape·goat \'skāp-ˌgōt\ *n* : one that bears the blame for others

scape·grace \-ˌgrās\ *n* [*scape* (escape)] : an incorrigible rascal

scap·u·la \'ska-pyə-lə\ *n, pl* **-lae** \-ˌlē\ *or* **-las** [L] : SHOULDER BLADE

scap·u·lar \-lər\ *n* : a pair of small cloth squares worn on the breast and back under the clothing esp. for religious purposes

scar \'skär\ *n* : a mark left after injured tissue has healed — **scar** *vb*

scar·ab \'skar-əb\ *n* [MF *scarabee*, fr. L *scarabaeus*] : any of a family of large stout beetles; *also* : an ornament (as a gem) representing such a beetle

scarce \'skers\ *adj* **scarc·er; scarc·est** **1** : deficient in quantity or number : not plentiful **2** : intentionally absent (made himself ∼ at inspection time) — **scar·ci·ty** \'sker-sə-tē\ *n*

scarce·ly \-lē\ *adv* **1** : BARELY **2** : almost not **3** : very probably not

¹scare \'sker\ *vb* **scared; scar·ing** : FRIGHTEN, STARTLE

²scare *n* : FRIGHT — **scary** *adj*

scare·crow \'sker-ˌkrō\ *n* : a crude figure set up to scare birds away from crops

¹scarf \'skärf\ *n, pl* **scarves** \'skärvz\ *or* **scarfs** **1** : a broad band (as of cloth) worn about the shoulders, around the neck, over the head, or about the waist **2** : a long narrow cloth cover for a table or dresser top

²scarf *vb* [alter. of earlier *scoff* eat greedily] : to eat greedily

scar·i·fy \'skar-ə-ˌfī\ *vb* **-fied; -fy·ing** **1** : to make scratches or small cuts in (∼ skin for vaccination) (∼ seeds to help them germinate) **2** : to lacerate the feelings of **3** : to break up and loosen the surface of (as a road) — **scar·i·fi·ca·tion** \ˌskar-ə-fə-ˈkā-shən\ *n*

scar·let \'skär-lət\ *n* : a bright red color — **scarlet** *adj*

scarlet fever *n* : an acute contagious disease marked by fever, sore throat, and red rash and caused by certain streptococci

scarp \'skärp\ *n* : a line of cliffs produced by faulting or erosion

scath·ing \'skā-thiŋ\ *adj* : bitterly severe (a ∼ condemnation)

scat·o·log·i·cal \ˌska-tə-ˈlä-ji-kəl\ *adj* : concerned with obscene matters

scat·ter \'ska-tər\ *vb* **1** : to distribute or strew about irregularly **2** : DISPERSE

scat·ter·brain \'ska-tər-ˌbrān\ *n* : a silly careless person — **scat·ter·brained** \-ˌbrānd\ *adj*

scav·enge \'ska-vənj\ *vb* **scav·enged; scav·eng·ing** : to work or function as a scavenger

scav·en·ger \'ska-vən-jər\ *n* [alter. of earlier *scavager*, fr. ME *skawager* customs collector, fr. *skawage* customs, fr. OF *escauwage* inspection] : a person or animal that collects, eats, or disposes of refuse or waste

sce·nar·io \sə-ˈnar-ē-ˌō\ *n, pl* **-i·os** : the plot or outline of a dramatic work; *also* : an account of a possible action

scene \'sēn\ *n* [MF, stage, fr. L *scena, scaena* stage, scene, prob. fr. Etruscan, fr. Gk *skēnē* temporary shelter, tent, building forming the background for a dramatic performance, stage] **1** : a division of one act of a play **2** : a single situation or sequence in a play or motion picture **3** : a stage setting **4** : VIEW, PROSPECT **5** : the place of an occurrence or action **6** : a display of strong feeling and esp. anger **7** : a sphere of activity (the fashion ∼) — **sce·nic** \'sē-nik\ *adj*

scen·ery \'sē-nə-rē\ *n, pl* **-er·ies** **1** : the painted scenes or hangings and accessories used on a theater stage **2** : a picturesque view or landscape

¹scent \'sent\ *n* **1** : ODOR, SMELL **2** : sense of smell **3** : course of pursuit : TRACK **4** : PERFUME **2** — **scent·ed** \'sen-təd\ *adj* — **scent·less** *adj*

²scent *vb* **1** : SMELL **2** : to imbue or fill with odor

scep·ter \'sep-tər\ *n* : a staff borne by a sovereign as an emblem of authority

scep·tic \'skep-tik\ *var of* SKEPTIC

scep·tre *Brit var of* SCEPTER

sch *abbr* school

¹sched·ule \'ske-jül, *esp Brit* **ˈ**she-dyül\ *n* **1** : a list of items or details **2** : TIMETABLE

²schedule *vb* **sched·uled; sched·ul·ing** **1** : to make a schedule of; *also* : to enter on a schedule **2** : to appoint, assign, or designate for a fixed time

sche·mat·ic \ski-ˈma-tik\ *adj* : of or relating to a scheme or diagram : DIAGRAMMATIC — **schematic** *n* — **sche·mat·i·cal·ly** \-ti-k(ə-)lē\ *adv*

¹scheme \'skēm\ *n* **1** : a plan for doing something; *esp* : a crafty plot **2** : a systematic design

²scheme *vb* **schemed; schem·ing** : to form a plot : INTRIGUE — **schem·er** *n*

Schick test \'shik-\ *n* : a serological test for susceptibility to diphtheria

schil·ling \'shi-liŋ\ *n* — see MONEY table

schism \'si-zəm, 'ski-\ *n* **1** : DIVISION, SPLIT; *also* : DISCORD, DISSENSION **2** : a formal division in or separation from a religious body

schis·mat·ic \siz-ˈma-tik, ski-\ *n* : one who creates or takes part in schism — **schismatic** *adj*

schist \'shist\ *n* : a metamorphic crystalline rock

schizo·phre·nia \ˌskit-sə-ˈfrē-nē-ə\ *n* [NL, fr. Gk *schizein* to split + *phrēn* diaphragm, mind] : a psychotic mental illness that is characterized by a twisted view of the real world, by a greatly reduced ability to carry out one's daily tasks, and by abnormal ways

JIM DAVIS 7-17

© 1987 PAWS, INC.

of thinking, feeling, and behaving — **schiz·oid** \'skit-ˌsȯid\ *adj or n* — **schizo·phren·ic** \ˌskit-sə-'fre-nik\ *adj or n*

schle·miel \shlə-'mēl\ *n* : an unlucky bungler : CHUMP

schlepp *or* **schlep** \'shlep\ *vb* [Yiddish *shlepn*] **1** : DRAG, HAUL **2** : to move slowly or awkwardly

schlock \'shläk\ *or* **schlocky** \'shlä-kē\ *adj* : of low quality or value — **schlock** *n*

schmaltz *also* **schmalz** \'shmȯlts, 'shmälts\ *n* [Yiddish *shmalts*, lit., rendered fat] : sentimental or florid music or art — **schmaltzy** *adj*

schnau·zer \'shnaut-sər, 'shnaù-zər\ *n* [G, fr. *Schnauze* snout] : a dog of any of three breeds that are characterized by a wiry coat, long head, small ears, heavy eyebrows, and long hair on the muzzle

schol·ar \'skä-lər\ *n* **1** : STUDENT, PUPIL **2** : a learned person : SAVANT — **schol·ar·ly** *adj*

schol·ar·ship \-ˌship\ *n* **1** : the qualities or learning of a scholar **2** : money awarded to a student to help pay for further education

scho·las·tic \skə-'las-tik\ *adj* : of or relating to schools, scholars, or scholarship

¹school \'skül\ *n* **1** : an institution for teaching and learning; *also* : the pupils in attendance **2** : a body of persons of like opinions or beliefs ⟨the radical ∼⟩

²school *vb* : TEACH, TRAIN, DRILL

³school *n* : a large number of one kind of water animal swimming and feeding together

school·boy \-ˌbȯi\ *n* : a boy attending school

school·fel·low \-ˌfe-lō\ *n* : SCHOOLMATE

school·girl \-ˌgərl\ *n* : a girl attending school

school·house \-ˌhaùs\ *n* : a building used as a school

school·marm \-ˌmärm\ *or* **school·ma'am** \-ˌmäm, -ˌmam\ *n* **1** : a woman schoolteacher **2** : a person who exhibits characteristics popularly attributed to schoolteachers

school·mas·ter \-ˌmas-tər\ *n* : a male schoolteacher

school·mate \-ˌmāt\ *n* : a school companion

school·mis·tress \-ˌmis-trəs\ *n* : a woman schoolteacher

school·room \-ˌrüm, -ˌrum\ *n* : CLASSROOM

school·teach·er \-ˌtē-chər\ *n* : one who teaches in a school

schoo·ner \'skü-nər\ *n* : a fore-and-aft rigged sailing ship

schuss \'shùs, 'shüs\ *vb* [G *Schuss*, n., lit., shot] : to ski down a slope at high speed — **schuss** *n*

sci *abbr* science; scientific

sci·at·i·ca \sī-'a-ti-kə\ *n* : pain in the region of the hips or along the course of the nerve at the back of the thigh

sci·ence \'sī-əns\ *n* [ME, fr. MF, fr. L *scientia*, fr. *scient-, sciens* having knowledge, fr. prp. of *scire* to know] **1** : an area of knowledge that is an object of study; *esp* : NATURAL SCIENCE **2** : knowledge covering general truths or the operation of general laws especially as obtained and tested through the scientific method — **sci·en·tif·ic** \ˌsī-ən-'ti-fik\ *adj* — **sci·en·tif·i·cal·ly** \-fi-k(ə-)lē\ *adv* — **sci·en·tist** \'sī-ən-tist\ *n*

schooner

science fiction *n* : fiction dealing principally with the impact of actual or imagined science on society or individuals

scientific method *n* : the rules and methods for the pursuit of knowledge involving the finding and stating of a problem, the collection of facts through observation and experiment, and the making and testing of ideas that need to be proven right or wrong

scim·i·tar \'si-mə-tər\ *n* : a curved sword used chiefly by Arabs and Turks

scin·til·la \sin-'ti-lə\ *n* : SPARK, TRACE

scin·til·late \'sint-ᵊl-ˌāt\ *vb* **-lat·ed; -lat·ing** : SPARKLE, GLEAM — **scin·til·la·tion** \ˌsint-ᵊl-'ā-shən\ *n*

sci·on \'sī-ən\ *n* **1** : a shoot of a plant joined to a stock in grafting **2** : DESCENDANT

scis·sors \'si-zərz\ *n pl* : a cutting instrument like shears but usu. smaller

scissors kick *n* : a swimming kick in which the legs move like scissors

scle·ro·sis \sklə-'rō-səs\ *n* : abnormal hardening of tissue (as of an artery); *also* : a disease characterized by this — **scle·rot·ic** \-'rä-tik\ *adj*

scoff \'skäf\ *vb* : MOCK, JEER — **scoff·er** *n*

scoff·law \-ˌlȯ\ *n* : a contemptuous law violator

¹scold \'skōld\ *n* : a person who scolds

²scold *vb* : to censure severely or angrily

sconce \'skäns\ *n* : a candlestick or an electric light fixture fastened to a wall

scone \'skōn, 'skän\ *n* : a biscuit (as of oatmeal) baked on a griddle

¹scoop \'sküp\ *n* **1** : a large shovel; *also* : a utensil with a shovellike or rounded end **2** : an act of scooping **3** : information of immediate interest

²scoop *vb* **1** : to take out or up or empty with or as if with a scoop **2** : to make hollow **3** : to report a news item in advance of

scoot \'sküt\ *vb* : to move swiftly

scoot·er \'skü-tər\ *n* **1** : a child's vehicle consisting of

a narrow board mounted between two wheels tandem with an upright steering handle attached to the front wheel **2 :** MOTOR SCOOTER

¹scope \'skōp\ *n* [It *scopo* purpose, goal, fr. Gk *skopos*] **1 :** space or opportunity for action or thought **2 :** extent covered **:** RANGE

²scope *n* **:** an instrument (as a microscope or radarscope) for viewing

scorch \'skȯrch\ *vb* **:** to burn the surface of; *also* **:** to dry or shrivel with heat ⟨∼ed lawns⟩

¹score \'skōr\ *n, pl* **scores 1** *or pl* **score :** TWENTY **2 :** CUT, SCRATCH, SLASH **3 :** a record of points made (as in a game) **4 :** DEBT **5 :** REASON, GROUND **6 :** the music of a composition or arrangement with different parts indicated **7 :** success in obtaining something (as drugs) esp. illegally

²score *vb* **scored; scor•ing 1 :** RECORD **2 :** to keep score in a game **3 :** to mark with lines, grooves, scratches, or notches **4 :** to gain or tally in or as if in a game ⟨*scored* a point⟩ **5 :** to assign a grade or score to ⟨∼ the tests⟩ **6 :** to compose a score for **7 :** SUCCEED — **score•less** *adj* — **scor•er** *n*

¹scorn \'skȯrn\ *n* **:** an emotion involving both anger and disgust **:** CONTEMPT — **scorn•ful** \-fəl\ *adj* — **scorn•ful•ly** *adv*

²scorn *vb* **:** to hold in contempt **:** DISDAIN — **scorn•er** *n*

Scor•pio \'skȯr-pē-ˌō\ *n* [L, lit., scorpion] **1 :** a zodiacal constellation between Libra and Sagittarius usu. pictured as a scorpion **2 :** the 8th sign of the zodiac in astrology; *also* **:** one born under this sign

scor•pi•on \'skȯr-pē-ən\ *n* **:** any of an order of arthropods related to the spiders that have a poisonous stinger at the tip of a long jointed tail

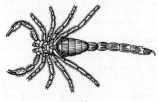

scorpion

¹Scot \'skät\ *n* **:** a native or inhabitant of Scotland

²Scot *abbr* Scotland; Scottish

Scotch \'skäch\ *n* **1 :** SCOTS **2 Scotch** *pl* **:** the people of Scotland **3 :** a whiskey distilled in Scotland esp. from malted barley — **Scotch** *adj* — **Scotch•man** \-mən\ *n* — **Scotch•wom•an** \-ˌwu̇-mən\ *n*

Scotch pine *n* **:** a pine that is naturalized in the U.S. from northern Europe and Asia and is a valuable timber tree

Scotch terrier *n* **:** SCOTTISH TERRIER

scot–free \'skät-'frē\ *adj* **:** free from obligation, harm, or penalty

Scots \'skäts\ *n* **:** the English language of Scotland

Scots•man \'skäts-mən\ *n* **:** SCOT

Scots•wom•an \-ˌwu̇-mən\ *n* **:** a woman who is a Scot

Scot•tie \'skä-tē\ *n* **:** SCOTTISH TERRIER

Scot•tish \'skä-tish\ *adj* **:** of, relating to, or characteristic of Scotland, Scots, or the Scots

Scottish terrier *n* **:** any of an old Scottish breed of terrier with short legs, a large head with small erect ears, a broad deep chest, and a thick rough coat

scoun•drel \'skau̇n-drəl\ *n* **:** a disreputable person **:** VILLAIN

¹scour \'skau̇r\ *vb* **1 :** to rub (as with a gritty substance) in order to clean **2 :** to cleanse by or as if by rubbing

²scour *vb* **1 :** to move rapidly through **:** RUSH **2 :** to examine thoroughly

¹scourge \'skərj\ *n* **1 :** LASH, WHIP **2 :** PUNISHMENT; *also* **:** a cause of affliction (as a plague)

²scourge *vb* **scourged; scourg•ing 1 :** LASH, FLOG **2 :** to punish severely

¹scout \'skau̇t\ *vb* [ME, fr. MF *escouter* to listen, fr. L *auscultare*] **1 :** to look around **:** RECONNOITER **2 :** to inspect or observe to get information

²scout *n* **1 :** a person sent out to get information; *also* **:** a soldier, airplane, or ship sent out to reconnoiter **2 :** BOY SCOUT **3 :** GIRL SCOUT — **scout•mas•ter** \-ˌmas-tər\ *n*

³scout *vb* **:** SCORN, SCOFF

scow \'skau̇\ *n* **:** a large flat-bottomed boat with square ends

scowl \'skau̇l\ *vb* **:** to make a frowning expression of displeasure — **scowl** *n*

SCPO *abbr* senior chief petty officer

scrab•ble \'skra-bəl\ *vb* **scrab•bled; scrab•bling 1 :** SCRAPE, SCRATCH **2 :** CLAMBER, SCRAMBLE **3 :** to work hard and long **4 :** SCRIBBLE — **scrabble** *n* — **scrab•bler** *n*

scrag•gly \'skra-glē\ *adj* **:** IRREGULAR; *also* **:** RAGGED, UNKEMPT

scram \'skram\ *vb* **scrammed; scram•ming :** to go away at once

scram•ble \'skram-bəl\ *vb* **scram•bled; scram•bling 1 :** to clamber clumsily around **2 :** to struggle for or as if for possession of something **3 :** to spread irregularly **4 :** to mix together **5 :** to cook (eggs) by stirring during frying — **scramble** *n*

¹scrap \'skrap\ *n* **1 :** FRAGMENT, PIECE **2 :** discarded material **:** REFUSE

²scrap *vb* **scrapped; scrap•ping 1 :** to make into scrap ⟨∼ a battleship⟩ **2 :** to get rid of as useless

³scrap *n* **:** FIGHT

⁴scrap *vb* **scrapped; scrap•ping :** FIGHT, QUARREL — **scrap•per** *n*

scrap•book \'skrap-ˌbu̇k\ *n* **:** a blank book in which mementos are kept

¹scrape \'skrāp\ *vb* **scraped; scrap•ing 1 :** to remove by drawing a knife over; *also* **:** to clean or smooth by rubbing off the covering **2 :** to damage or injure the surface of by contact with something rough **3 :** to draw across a surface with a grating sound **4 :** to get

together (money) by strict economy **5** : to get along with difficulty — **scrap•er** *n*

²**scrape** *n* **1** : the act or the effect of scraping **2** : a bow accompanied by a drawing back of the foot **3** : an unpleasant predicament

¹**scrap•py** \'skra-pē\ *adj* **scrap•pi•er; -est** : DISCONNECTED, FRAGMENTARY

²**scrappy** *adj* **scrap•pi•er; -est 1** : QUARRELSOME **2** : having an aggressive and determined spirit

¹**scratch** \'skrach\ *vb* **1** : to scrape, dig, or rub with or as if with claws or nails ⟨a dog ∼*ing* at the door⟩ ⟨∼*ed* my arm⟩ **2** : SCRAPE **3** ⟨∼*ed* his nails across the blackboard⟩ **3** : SCRAPE 4 **4** : to cancel or erase by or as if by drawing a line through **5** : to withdraw from a contest — **scratchy** *adj*

²**scratch** *n* **1** : a mark or injury made by or as if by scratching; *also* : a sound so made **2** : the starting line in a race **3** : a point at the beginning of a project at which nothing has been done ahead of time ⟨built from ∼⟩

³**scratch** *adj* **1** : made as or used for a trial attempt ⟨∼ paper⟩ **2** : made or done by chance ⟨a ∼ hit⟩

scrawl \'skrȯl\ *vb* : to write hastily and carelessly — **scrawl** *n*

scraw•ny \'skrȯ-nē\ *adj* **scraw•ni•er; -est** : very thin : SKINNY

¹**scream** \'skrēm\ *vb* : to cry out loudly and shrilly

²**scream** *n* : a loud shrill cry

scream•ing *adj* : so striking as to attract notice as if by screaming ⟨∼ headlines⟩

screech \'skrēch\ *vb* : SHRIEK — **screech** *n* — **screechy** \'skrē-chē\ *adj*

¹**screen** \'skrēn\ *n* **1** : a device or partition used to hide, restrain, protect, or decorate ⟨a window ∼⟩; *also* : something that shelters, protects, or conceals **2** : a sieve or perforated material for separating finer from coarser parts (as of sand) **3** : a surface on which an image is made to appear (as in television) **4** : the motion-picture industry

²**screen** *vb* **1** : to shield with or as if with a screen **2** : to separate with or as if with a screen **3** : to present (as a motion picture) on the screen

screen•ing \'skrē-niŋ\ *n* **1** : metal or plastic mesh (as for window screens) **2** : a showing of a motion picture

¹**screw** \'skrü\ *n* [ME, fr. MF *escroe* female screw, nut, fr. ML *scrofa*, fr. L, sow] **1** : a machine consisting of a solid cylinder with a spiral groove around it and a corresponding hollow cylinder into which it fits **2** : a naillike metal piece with a spiral groove and a head with a slot that is inserted into material by rotating and is used to fasten pieces of solid material together **3** : PROPELLER

²**screw** *vb* **1** : to fasten or close by means of a screw **2** : to operate or adjust by means of a screw **3** : to move

or cause to move spirally; *also* : to close or set in position by such an action

screw•ball \'skrü-,bȯl\ *n* **1** : a baseball pitch breaking in a direction opposite to a curve **2** : a whimsical, eccentric, or crazy person

screw•driv•er \-,drī-vər\ *n* **1** : a tool for turning screws **2** : a drink made of vodka and orange juice

screw•worm \'skrü-,wərm\ *n* : an American blowfly of warm regions whose larva matures in wounds or sores of mammals and may cause disease or death; *esp* : its larva

screwy \'skrü-ē\ *adj* **screw•i•er; -est 1** : crazily absurd, eccentric, or unusual **2** : CRAZY, INSANE

scrib•ble \'skri-bəl\ *vb* **scrib•bled; scrib•bling** : to write hastily or carelessly — **scribble** *n* — **scrib•bler** *n*

scribe \'skrīb\ *n* **1** : a scholar of Jewish law in New Testament times **2** : a person whose business is the copying of writing **3** : JOURNALIST

scrim \'skrim\ *n* : a light loosely woven cotton or linen cloth

scrim•mage \'skri-mij\ *n* : the play between two football teams beginning with the snap of the ball; *also* : practice play between two teams — **scrimmage** *vb*

scrimp \'skrimp\ *vb* : to economize greatly ⟨∼ and save⟩

scrim•shaw \'skrim-,shȯ\ *n* : carved or engraved articles made orig. by American whalers usu. from baleen or whale ivory — **scrimshaw** *vb*

scrip \'skrip\ *n* **1** : a certificate showing its holder is entitled to something (as stock or land) **2** : paper money issued for temporary use in an emergency

¹**script** \'skript\ *n* **1** : written matter (as lines for a play or broadcast) **2** : HANDWRITING

²**script** *abbr* scripture

scrip•ture \'skrip-chər\ *n* **1** *cap* : the books of the Bible — often used in pl. **2** : the sacred writings of a religion — **scrip•tur•al** \'skrip-chə-rəl\ *adj* — **scrip•tur•al•ly** *adv*

scriv•en•er \'skri-və-nər\ *n* : SCRIBE, COPYIST, WRITER

scrod \'skräd\ *n* : a young fish (as a cod or haddock); *esp* : one split and boned for cooking

scrof•u•la \'skrȯ-fyə-lə\ *n* : tuberculosis of lymph nodes esp. in the neck

¹**scroll** \'skrōl\ *n* : a roll of paper or parchment for writing a document; *also* : a spiral or coiled ornamental form suggesting a loosely or partly rolled scroll

²**scroll** *vb* : to move or cause to move text or graphics up, down, or across a display screen

scroll saw *n* : JIGSAW

scro•tum \'skrō-təm\ *n, pl* **scro•ta** \-tə\ *or* **scrotums** [L] : a pouch that in most male mammals contains the testes

scrounge \'skraúnj\ *vb* **scrounged; scroung•ing** : to collect by or as if by foraging

¹**scrub** \'skrəb\ *n* **1** : a thick growth of stunted trees or shrubs; *also* : an area of land covered with scrub **2** : an inferior domestic animal **3** : a person of insignificant size or standing **4** : a player not on the first team — **scrub** *adj* — **scrub•by** *adj*

²**scrub** vb **scrubbed; scrub·bing 1 :** to clean or wash by rubbing 〈~ clothes〉 〈~ out a spot〉 **2 :** CANCEL

³**scrub** n **:** an act or instance of scrubbing 〈gave the clothes a good ~〉

scrub·ber \'skrə-bər\ n **:** one that scrubs; *esp* **:** an apparatus for removing impurities esp. from gases

scruff \'skrəf\ n **:** the loose skin of the back of the neck **:** NAPE

scruffy \'skrə-fē\ adj **scruff·i·er; -est :** UNKEMPT, SLOVENLY

scrump·tious \'skrəmp-shəs\ adj **:** DELIGHTFUL, EXCELLENT; *esp* **:** DELICIOUS — **scrump·tious·ly** adv

¹**scru·ple** \'skrü-pəl\ n [ME *scrupul*, MF *scrupule*, fr. L *scrupulus*, dim. of *scrupus* source of uneasiness, lit., sharp stone] **1 :** a point of conscience or honor **2 :** hesitation due to ethical considerations

²**scruple** vb **scru·pled; scru·pling :** to be reluctant on grounds of conscience **:** HESITATE

scru·pu·lous \'skrü-pyə-ləs\ adj **1 :** having moral integrity **2 :** PAINSTAKING — **scru·pu·lous·ly** adv — **scru·pu·lous·ness** n

scru·ti·nise *Brit var of* SCRUTINIZE

scru·ti·nize \'skrüt-ə-ˌnīz\ vb **-nized; -niz·ing :** to examine closely

scru·ti·ny \'skrüt-ᵊn-ē\ n, pl **-nies** [L *scrutinium*, fr. *scrutari* to search, examine, prob. fr. *scruta* trash] **:** a careful looking over **syn** inspection, examination, analysis

scu·ba \'skü-bə\ n [*self-contained underwater breathing apparatus*] **:** an apparatus for breathing while swimming underwater

scuba diver n **:** one who swims underwater with the aid of scuba gear

¹**scud** \'skəd\ vb **scud·ded; scud·ding :** to move speedily

²**scud** n **:** light clouds driven by the wind

¹**scuff** \'skəf\ vb **1 :** to scrape the feet while walking **:** SHUFFLE **2 :** to scratch or become scratched or worn away

²**scuff** n **1 :** a mark or injury caused by scuffing **2 :** a flat-soled slipper without heel strap

scuf·fle \'skə-fəl\ vb **scuf·fled; scuf·fling 1 :** to struggle confusedly at close quarters **2 :** to shuffle one's feet — **scuffle** n

¹**scull** \'skəl\ n **1 :** an oar for use in sculling; *also* **:** one of a pair of short oars for a single oarsman **2 :** a racing shell propelled by one or two persons using sculls

²**scull** vb **:** to propel (a boat) by an oar over the stern

scul·lery \'skə-lə-rē\ n, pl **-ler·ies** [ME, department of household in charge of dishes, fr. MF *escuelerie*, fr. *escuelle* bowl, fr. L *scutella* drinking bowl] **:** a small room near the kitchen used for cleaning dishes, cooking utensils, and vegetables

scul·lion \'skəl-yən\ n [ME *sculion*, fr. MF *escouillon* dishcloth, alter. of *escouvillon*, fr. *escouve* broom, fr. L *scopae*, lit., twigs bound together] **:** a kitchen helper

sculpt \'skəlpt\ vb **:** CARVE, SCULPTURE

sculp·tor \'skəlp-tər\ n **:** a person who produces works of sculpture

¹**sculp·ture** \'skəlp-chər\ n **:** the act, process, or art of carving or molding material (as stone, wood, or plastic); *also* **:** work produced this way — **sculp·tur·al** \'skəlp-chə-rəl\ adj

²**sculpture** vb **sculp·tured; sculp·tur·ing :** to form or alter as or as if a work of sculpture

scum \'skəm\ n **1 :** a slimy or filmy covering on the surface of a liquid **2 :** waste matter **3 :** RABBLE

scup·per \'skə-pər\ n **:** an opening in the side of a ship through which water on deck is drained overboard

scurf \'skərf\ n **:** thin dry scales of skin (as dandruff); *also* **:** a scaly deposit or covering — **scurfy** \'skər-fē\ adj

scur·ri·lous \'skər-ə-ləs\ adj **:** coarsely jesting **:** OBSCENE, VULGAR

scur·ry \'skər-ē\ vb **scur·ried; scur·ry·ing :** SCAMPER

¹**scur·vy** \'skər-vē\ n **:** a disease marked by spongy gums, loosened teeth, and bleeding under the skin and caused by lack of vitamin C

²**scurvy** adj **:** MEAN, CONTEMPTIBLE — **scur·vi·ly** \'skər-və-lē\ adv

scutch·eon \'skə-chən\ n **:** ESCUTCHEON

¹**scut·tle** \'skət-ᵊl\ n **:** a pail for carrying coal

²**scuttle** n **:** a small opening with a lid esp. in the deck, side, or bottom of a ship

³**scuttle** vb **scut·tled; scut·tling :** to cut a hole in the deck, side, or bottom of (a ship) in order to sink

⁴**scuttle** vb **scut·tled; scut·tling :** SCURRY, SCAMPER

scut·tle·butt \'skət-ᵊl-ˌbət\ n **:** GOSSIP

scythe \'sīth\ n **:** an implement for mowing (as grass or grain) by hand — **scythe** vb

SD abbr **1** South Dakota **2** special delivery

S Dak abbr South Dakota

SDI abbr Strategic Defense Initiative

Se symbol selenium

SE abbr southeast

sea \'sē\ n **1 :** a large body of salt water **2 :** OCEAN **3 :** rough water; *also* **:** a large wave **4 :** something likened to the sea esp. in vastness — **sea** adj — **at sea :** LOST, BEWILDERED

sea anemone n **:** any of numerous coelenterate polyps whose form, bright and varied colors, and cluster of tentacles superficially resemble a flower

sea·bird \'sē-ˌbərd\ n **:** a bird (as a gull) frequenting the open ocean

sea·board \-ˌbōrd\ n **:** SEACOAST; *also* **:** the land bordering a coast

sea·coast \-ˌkōst\ n **:** the shore of the sea

sea·far·er \-ˌfar-ər\ n **:** SEAMAN

sea·far·ing \-ˌfar-iŋ\ n **:** the use of the sea for travel or transportation — **seafaring** adj

sea·food \-ˌfüd\ n **:** edible marine fish and shellfish

sea·go·ing \-ˌgō-iŋ\ adj **:** OCEANGOING

sea horse n **:** any of a genus of small marine fishes with

I BOUGHT YOU A SEAFOOD LUNCH, GARFIELD

THEY HAD A SPECIAL ON UGLY FISH

QUICK, I'M LOSING MY APPETITE

JIM DAVIS 6-21

the head and forepart of the body sharply flexed like the head and neck of a horse

¹seal \'sēl\ *n, pl* **seals** *also* **seal 1** : any of numerous large carnivorous sea mammals occurring chiefly in cold regions and having limbs adapted for swimming **2** : the pelt of a seal

²seal *vb* : to hunt seals

³seal *n* **1** : GUARANTEE, PLEDGE **2** : a device having a raised design that can be stamped on clay or wax; *also* : the impression made by stamping with such a device **3** : something that seals or closes up ⟨safety ∼⟩

⁴seal *vb* **1** : to affix a seal to; *also* : AUTHENTICATE **2** : to fasten with or as if with a seal to prevent tampering **3** : to close or make secure against access, leakage, or passage **4** : to determine irrevocably ⟨∼ed his fate⟩

sea–lane \'sē-₁lān\ *n* : an established sea route

seal·ant \'sē-lənt\ *n* : a sealing agent

seal·er \'sē-lər\ *n* : a coat applied to prevent subsequent coats of paint or varnish from sinking in

sea level *n* : the level of the surface of the sea esp. at its mean midway between mean high and low water

sea lion *n* : any of several large Pacific seals with external ears

seal·skin \'sēl-₁skin\ *n* **1** : ¹SEAL 2 **2** : a garment of sealskin

¹seam \'sēm\ *n* **1** : the line of junction of two edges and esp. of edges of fabric sewn together **2** : a layer of mineral matter **3** : WRINKLE — **seam·less** *adj*

²seam *vb* **1** : to join by or as if by sewing **2** : WRINKLE, FURROW

sea·man \'sē-mən\ *n* **1** : one who assists in the handling of ships : MARINER **2** : an enlisted man in the navy ranking next below a petty officer third class

seaman apprentice *n* : an enlisted man in the navy ranking next below a seaman

seaman recruit *n* : an enlisted man of the lowest rank in the navy

sea·man·ship \'sē-mən-₁ship\ *n* : the art or skill of handling a ship

sea·mount \'sē-₁maunt\ *n* : an underwater mountain

seam·stress \'sēm-strəs\ *n* : a woman who does sewing

seamy \'sē-mē\ *adj* **seam·i·er; -est 1** : UNPLEASANT **2** : DEGRADED, SORDID

sé·ance \'sā-₁äns\ *n* [F] : a meeting to receive communications from spirits

sea·plane \'sē-₁plān\ *n* : an airplane that can take off from and land on water

sea·port \-₁pōrt\ *n* : a port for oceangoing ships

sear \'sir\ *vb* **1** : WITHER **2** : to burn or scorch esp. on the surface; *also* : BRAND — **sear** *n*

¹search \'sərch\ *vb* [ME *cerchen*, fr. MF *cerchier* to go about, survey, search, fr. LL *circare* to go about, fr. L *circum* round about] **1** : to look through in trying to find something **2** : SEEK **3** : PROBE — **search·er** *n*

²search *n* : the act of searching

search·light \-₁līt\ *n* : an apparatus for projecting a powerful beam of light; *also* : the light projected

sea·scape \'sē-₁skāp\ *n* **1** : a view of the sea **2** : a picture representing a scene at or of the sea

sea·shell \'sē-₁shel\ *n* : the shell of a marine animal and esp. a mollusk

sea·shore \-₁shōr\ *n* : the shore of a sea

sea·sick \-₁sik\ *adj* : nauseated by or as if by the motion of a ship — **sea·sick·ness** *n*

sea·side \'sē-₁sīd\ *n* : SEASHORE

¹sea·son \'sē-zən\ *n* [ME, fr. OF *saison*, fr. L *sation-, satio* action of sowing, fr. *serere* to sow] **1** : one of the divisions of the year (as spring or summer) **2** : a special period ⟨the Easter ∼⟩ — **sea·son·al** \-zə-nəl\ *adj* — **sea·son·al·ly** *adv*

²season *vb* **1** : to make pleasant to the taste by use of salt, pepper, or spices **2** : to make (as by aging or drying) suitable for use **3** : to accustom or habituate to something (as hardship) **syn** harden, inure, acclimatize, toughen — **sea·son·er** *n*

sea·son·able \'sē-zə-nə-bəl\ *adj* : occurring at a good or proper time **syn** timely, propitious, opportune — **sea·son·ably** \-blē\ *adv*

sea·son·ing *n* : something that seasons : CONDIMENT

¹seat \'sēt\ *n* **1** : a chair, bench, or stool for sitting on **2** : a place which serves as a capital or center

²seat *vb* **1** : to place in or on a seat **2** : to provide seats for

seat belt *n* : straps designed to hold a person in a seat

SEATO \'sē-₁tō\ *abbr* Southeast Asia Treaty Organization

seat–of–the–pants *adj* : employing or based on personal experience, judgment, and effort rather than technological aids ⟨∼ navigation⟩

sea urchin *n* : any of numerous spiny marine echinoderms having thin brittle globular shells

sea·wall \'sē-₁wòl\ *n* : an embankment to protect the shore from erosion

¹sea·ward \'sē-wərd\ *n* : the direction or side away from land and toward the open sea

²seaward *also* **sea·wards** \-wərdz\ *adv* : toward the sea

³seaward *adj* **1** : directed or situated toward the sea **2** : coming from the sea

sea·wa·ter \'sē-₁wò-tər, -₁wä-\ *n* : water in or from the sea

sea·way \-₁wā\ *n* : an inland waterway that admits ocean shipping

sea·weed \-₁wēd\ *n* : a marine alga (as a kelp); *also* : a mass of marine algae

sea·wor·thy \-₁wər-thē\ *adj* : fit for a sea voyage ⟨a ∼ ship⟩

se·ba·ceous \si-'bā-shəs\ *adj* : of, relating to, or secreting fatty material

sec *abbr* **1** second; secondary **2** secretary **3** section **4** [L *secundum*] according to

SEC *abbr* Securities and Exchange Commission

se·cede \si-'sēd\ *vb* **se·ced·ed; se·ced·ing** : to withdraw from an organized body and esp. from a political body

se·ces·sion \si-'se-shən\ *n* : the act of seceding — **se·ces·sion·ist** *n*

se·clude \si-'klüd\ *vb* **se·clud·ed; se·clud·ing** : to keep or shut away from others

se·clu·sion \si-'klü-zhən\ *n* : the act of secluding : the state of being secluded — **se·clu·sive** \-siv\ *adj*

¹sec·ond \'se-kənd\ *adj* [ME, fr. OF, fr. L *secundus* second, following, favorable, fr. *sequi* to follow] **1** : being number two in a countable series **2** : next after the first **3** : ALTERNATE ⟨every ∼ year⟩ — **second** *or* **sec·ond·ly** *adv*

²second *n* **1** : one that is second **2** : one who assists another (as in a duel) **3** : an inferior or flawed article (as of merchandise) **4** : the second forward gear in a motor vehicle

³second *n* [ME *secunde*, fr. ML *secunda*, fr. L, fem. of *secundus* second; fr. its being the second division of a unit into 60 parts, as a minute is the first] **1** : the 60th part of a minute of time or angular measure **2** : an instant of time

⁴second *vb* **1** : to encourage or give support to **2** : to act as a second to **3** : to support (a motion) by adding one's voice to that of a proposer

¹sec·ond·ary \'se-kən-₁der-ē\ *adj* **1** : second in rank, value, or occurrence : LESSER **2** : belonging to a second or later stage of development **3** : coming after the primary or elementary ⟨∼ schools⟩ **syn** subordinate, collateral, dependent

²secondary *n, pl* **-ar·ies** : the defensive backfield of a football team

secondary sex characteristic *n* : a physical characteristic that appears in members of one sex at puberty or in seasonal breeders at breeding season and is not directly concerned with reproduction

second fiddle *n* : one that plays a supporting or subservient role

sec·ond–guess \₁se-kənd-'ges\ *vb* **1** : to think out other strategies or explanations for after the event **2** : to seek to anticipate or predict

sec·ond·hand \-ˈhand\ *adj* **1** : not original **2** : not new : USED 〈∼ clothes〉 **3** : dealing in used goods

second lieutenant *n* : a commissioned officer (as in the army) ranking next below a first lieutenant

sec·ond–rate \ˌse-kənd-ˈrāt\ *adj* : INFERIOR

second–story man *n* : a burglar who enters by an upstairs window

sec·ond–string \ˈse-kənd-ˈstriŋ\ *adj* : being a substitute (as on a team)

se·cre·cy \ˈsē-krə-sē\ *n, pl* **-cies 1** : the habit or practice of being secretive **2** : the condition of being hidden or concealed

¹**se·cret** \ˈsē-krət\ *adj* **1** : HIDDEN, CONCEALED 〈a ∼ staircase〉 **2** : COVERT, STEALTHY; *also* : engaged in detecting or spying 〈a ∼ agent〉 **3** : kept from general knowledge — **se·cret·ly** *adv*

²**secret** *n* **1** : MYSTERY **2** : something kept from the knowledge of others

sec·re·tar·i·at \ˌse-krə-ˈter-ē-ət\ *n* **1** : the office of a secretary **2** : the secretarial staff in an office **3** : the administrative department of a governmental organization 〈the UN ∼〉

sec·re·tary \ˈse-krə-ˌter-ē\ *n, pl* **-tar·ies 1** : a person employed to handle records, correspondence, and routine work for another person **2** : an officer of a corporation or business who is in charge of correspondence and records **3** : an official at the head of a department of government **4** : a writing desk — **sec·re·tar·i·al** \ˌse-krə-ˈter-ē-əl\ *adj* — **sec·re·tary·ship** \ˈse-krə-ˌter-ē-ˌship\ *n*

¹**se·crete** \si-ˈkrēt\ *vb* **se·cret·ed; se·cret·ing** : to form and give off (a secretion)

²**se·crete** \si-ˈkrēt, ˈsē-krət\ *vb* **se·cret·ed; se·cret·ing** : HIDE, CONCEAL

se·cre·tion \si-ˈkrē-shən\ *n* **1** : the process of secreting something **2** : a product of glandular activity; *esp* : one (as a hormone) useful in the organism **3** : the act of hiding something — **se·cre·to·ry** \ˈsē-krə-ˌtōr-ē\ *adj*

se·cre·tive \ˈsē-krə-tiv, si-ˈkrē-\ *adj* : tending to keep secrets or to act secretly — **se·cre·tive·ly** *adv* — **se·cre·tive·ness** *n*

sect \ˈsekt\ *n* **1** : a dissenting religious body **2** : a religious denomination **3** : a group adhering to a distinctive doctrine or to a leader

²**sect** *abbr* section; sectional

¹**sec·tar·i·an** \sek-ˈter-ē-ən\ *adj* **1** : of or relating to a sect or sectarian **2** : limited in character or scope — **sec·tar·i·an·ism** *n*

²**sectarian** *n* **1** : an adherent of a sect **2** : a narrow or bigoted person

sec·ta·ry \ˈsek-tə-rē\ *n, pl* **-ries** : a member of a sect

¹**sec·tion** \ˈsek-shən\ *n* **1** : a part cut off or separated **2** : a distinct part **3** : the appearance that a thing has or would have if cut straight through

²**section** *vb* **1** : to separate or become separated into sections **2** : to represent in sections

sec·tion·al \ˈsek-shə-nəl\ *adj* **1** : of, relating to, or characteristic of a section **2** : local or regional rather than general in character **3** : divided into sections — **sec·tion·al·ism** *n*

sec·tor \ˈsek-tər\ *n* **1** : a part of a circle between two radii **2** : an area assigned to a military leader to defend **3** : a subdivision of society

sec·u·lar \ˈse-kyə-lər\ *adj* **1** : not sacred or ecclesiastical **2** : not bound by monastic vows 〈a ∼ priest〉

sec·u·lar·ise *Brit var of* SECULARIZE

sec·u·lar·ism \ˈse-kyə-lə-ˌri-zəm\ *n* : indifference to or exclusion of religion — **sec·u·lar·ist** \-rist\ *n* — **secularist** *or* **sec·u·lar·is·tic** \ˌse-kyə-lə-ˈris-tik\ *adj*

sec·u·lar·ize \ˈse-kyə-lə-ˌrīz\ *vb* **-ized; -iz·ing 1** : to make secular **2** : to transfer from ecclesiastical to civil or lay use, possession, or control — **sec·u·lar·i-**

za·tion \ˌse-kyə-lə-rə-ˈzā-shən\ *n* — **sec·u·lar·iz·er** \ˈse-kyə-lə-ˌrī-zər\ *n*

¹**se·cure** \si-ˈkyu̇r\ *adj* **se·cur·er; -est** [L *securus* safe, secure, fr. *se* without + *cura* care] **1** : easy in mind : free from fear **2** : free from danger or risk of loss : SAFE **3** : CERTAIN, SURE — **se·cure·ly** *adv*

²**secure** *vb* **se·cured; se·cur·ing 1** : to make safe : GUARD **2** : to assure payment of by giving a pledge or collateral **3** : to fasten safely 〈∼ a door〉 **4** : GET, ACQUIRE

se·cu·ri·ty \si-ˈkyu̇r-ə-tē\ *n, pl* **-ties 1** : SAFETY **2** : freedom from worry **3** : something given as pledge of payment 〈a ∼ deposit〉 **4** *pl* : bond or stock certificates **5** : PROTECTION

secy *abbr* secretary

se·dan \si-ˈdan\ *n* **1** : a covered chair borne on poles by two men **2** : an automobile seating four or more people and usu. having a permanent top

¹**se·date** \si-ˈdāt\ *adj* : quiet and dignified in behavior **syn** staid, sober, serious, solemn — **se·date·ly** *adv*

²**sedate** *vb* **se·dat·ed; se·dat·ing** : to dose with sedatives — **se·da·tion** \si-ˈdā-shən\ *n*

¹**sed·a·tive** \ˈse-də-tiv\ *adj* : serving or tending to relieve tension

²**sedative** *n* : a sedative drug

sed·en·tary \ˈsed-ᵊn-ˌter-ē\ *adj* : characterized by or requiring much sitting

sedge \ˈsej\ *n* : any of a family of plants esp. of marshy areas that differ from the related grasses esp. in having solid stems — **sedgy** \ˈse-jē\ *adj*

sed·i·ment \ˈse-də-mənt\ *n* **1** : the material that settles to the bottom of a liquid **2** : material (as stones and sand) deposited by water, wind, or a glacier — **sed·i·men·ta·ry** \ˌse-də-ˈmen-tə-rē\ *adj* — **sed·i·men·ta·tion** \-mən-ˈtā-shən, -ˌmen-\ *n*

se·di·tion \si-ˈdi-shən\ *n* : the causing of discontent, insurrection, or resistance against a government — **se·di·tious** \-shəs\ *adj*

se·duce \si-ˈdüs, -ˈdyüs\ *vb* **se·duced; se·duc·ing 1** : to persuade to disobedience or disloyalty **2** : to lead astray **3** : to entice to sexual intercourse **syn** tempt, entice, inveigle, lure — **se·duc·er** *n* — **se·duc·tion** \-ˈdək-shən\ *n* — **se·duc·tive** \-tiv\ *adj*

sed·u·lous \ˈse-jə-ləs\ *adj* [L *sedulus*, fr. *sedulo* sincerely, diligently, fr. *se* without + *dolus* guile] : DILIGENT, PAINSTAKING

¹**see** \ˈsē\ *vb* **saw** \ˈsȯ\; **seen** \ˈsēn\; **see·ing 1** : to perceive by the eye; *also* : to have the power of sight **2** : EXPERIENCE **3** : UNDERSTAND **4** : to make sure 〈∼ that order is kept〉 **5** : to meet with **6** : to keep company with esp. in dating **7** : ACCOMPANY, ESCORT **syn** behold, descry, espy, view, observe, note, discern

²**see** *n* : the authority or jurisdiction of a bishop

¹**seed** \ˈsēd\ *n, pl* **seed** *or* **seeds 1** : the grains of plants used for sowing **2** : a ripened ovule of a flowering plant that may develop into a new plant; *also* : a plant structure (as a spore or small dry fruit) capable of producing a new plant **3** : DESCENDANTS **4** : SOURCE, ORIGIN — **seed·less** *adj* — **go to seed** *or* **run to seed 1** : to develop seed **2** : DECAY

²**seed** *vb* **1** : SOW, PLANT 〈∼ land to grass〉 **2** : to bear or shed seeds **3** : to remove seeds from — **seed·er** *n*

seed·bed \-ˌbed\ *n* : soil or a bed of soil prepared for planting seed

seed·ling \ˈsēd-liŋ\ *n* **1** : a young plant grown from seed **2** : a young tree before it becomes a sapling

seed·time \ˈsēd-ˌtīm\ *n* : the season for sowing

seedy \ˈsē-dē\ *adj* **seed·i·er; -est 1** : containing or full of seeds **2** : SHABBY

seek \ˈsēk\ *vb* **sought** \ˈsȯt\; **seek·ing 1** : to search for **2** : to try to reach or obtain **3** : ATTEMPT — **seek·er** *n*

seem \ˈsēm\ *vb* **1** : to appear to the observation or understanding **2** : to give the impression of being : APPEAR

seem·ing *adj* : outwardly apparent — **seem·ing·ly** *adv*
seem·ly \'sēm-lē\ *adj* **seem·li·er; -est 1** : conventionally proper **2** : FIT
seep \'sēp\ *vb* : to flow or pass slowly through fine pores or cracks — **seep·age** \'sē-pij\ *n*
seer \'sir\ *n* : a person who foresees or predicts events : PROPHET
seer·suck·er \'sir-ˌsə-kər\ *n* [Hindi *śīrśaker,* fr. Per *shīr-o-shakar,* lit., milk and sugar] : a light fabric of linen, cotton, or rayon usu. striped and slightly puckered
see·saw \'sē-ˌsò\ *n* **1** : a contest in which now one side now the other has the lead **2** : a children's sport of riding up and down on the ends of a plank supported in the middle; *also* : the plank so used — **seesaw** *vb*
seethe \'sēth\ *vb* **seethed; seeth·ing** [archaic *seethe* boil] : to become violently agitated
seg·ment \'seg-mənt\ *n* **1** : a division of a thing : SECTION **2** : a part cut off from a geometrical figure (as a circle) by one or more points, lines, or planes — **seg·ment·ed** \-ˌmen-təd\ *adj*
seg·re·gate \'se-gri-ˌgāt\ *vb* **-gat·ed; -gat·ing** [L *segregare,* fr. *se-* apart + *greg-, grex* herd, flock] : to cut off from others; *esp* : to separate by races — **seg·re·ga·tion** \ˌse-gri-'gā-shən\ *n*
seg·re·ga·tion·ist \ˌse-gri-'gā-shə-nist\ *n* : one who believes in or practices the segregation of races
sei·gneur \sān-'yər\ *n, often cap* [MF, fr. ML *senior,* fr. L, adj., elder] : a feudal lord
¹seine \'sān\ *n* : a large weighted fishing net
²seine *vb* **seined; sein·ing** : to fish or catch with a seine — **sein·er** *n*
seis·mic \'sīz-mik, 'sīs-\ *adj* : of, relating to, resembling, or caused by an earthquake — **seis·mi·cal·ly** \-mi(ə-)lē\ *adv* — **seis·mic·i·ty** \sīz-'mi-sə-tē, sīs-\ *n*
seis·mo·gram \'sīz-mə-ˌgram, 'sīs-\ *n* : the record of an earth tremor made by a seismograph
seis·mo·graph \-ˌgraf\ *n* : an apparatus to measure and record seismic vibrations — **seis·mo·graph·ic** \ˌsīz-mə-'gra-fik, ˌsīs-\ *adj* — **seis·mog·ra·phy** \sīz-'mä-grə-fē, sīs-\ *n*
seis·mol·o·gy \sīz-'mä-lə-jē, sīs-\ *n* : a science that deals with earthquakes — **seis·mo·log·i·cal** \ˌsīz-mə-'lä-ji-kəl, ˌsīs-\ *adj* — **seis·mol·o·gist** \sīz-'mä-lə-jist, sīs-\ *n*
seis·mom·e·ter \sīz-'mä-mə-tər, sīs-\ *n* : a seismograph measuring the actual movement of the ground
seize \'sēz\ *vb* **seized; seiz·ing 1** : to lay hold of or take possession of by force **2** : ARREST **3** : UNDERSTAND **4** : to attack or overwhelm physically : AFFLICT **syn** take, grasp, clutch, snatch, grab
sei·zure \'sē-zhər\ *n* **1** : the act of seizing : the state of being seized **2** : a sudden attack (as of disease)
sel *abbr* select; selected; selection
sel·dom \'sel-dəm\ *adv* : not often : RARELY
¹se·lect \sə-'lekt\ *adj* **1** : CHOSEN, PICKED; *also* : CHOICE **2** : judicious or restrictive in choice : DISCRIMINATING
²select *vb* : to choose from a number or group : pick out
se·lec·tion \sə-'lek-shən\ *n* **1** : the act or process of selecting **2** : something selected : CHOICE **3** : a natural or artificial process that tends to favor the survival and reproduction of individuals with certain traits but not those with others
se·lec·tive \sə-'lek-tiv\ *adj* : of or relating to selection : selecting or tending to select (~ shoppers)
selective service *n* : a system for calling men up for military service : DRAFT
se·lect·man \si-'lekt-ˌman, -mən\ *n* : one of a board of officials elected in towns of most New England states to administer town affairs
se·le·ni·um \sə-'lē-nē-əm\ *n* : a nonmetallic chemical element — see ELEMENT table
self \'self\ *n, pl* **selves** \'selvz\ **1** : the essential person distinct from all other persons in identity **2** : a particular side of a person's character **3** : personal interest : SELFISHNESS

self- *comb form* **1** : oneself : itself **2** : of oneself or itself **3** : by oneself or itself; *also* : automatic **4** : to, for, or toward oneself

self-abasement	self-forgetful
self-absorbed	self-giving
self-absorption	self-governing
self-accusation	self-government
self-acting	self-hate
self-addressed	self-help
self-adjusting	self-hypnosis
self-administer	self-identity
self-advancement	self-image
self-aggrandizement	self-importance
self-aggrandizing	self-important
self-analysis	self-imposed
self-appointed	self-improvement
self-asserting	self-incrimination
self-assertion	self-induced
self-assertive	self-indulgence
self-assurance	self-indulgent
self-assured	self-inflicted
self-awareness	self-interest
self-betrayal	self-knowledge
self-closing	self-limiting
self-conceit	self-love
self-concern	self-lubricating
self-condemned	self-luminous
self-confessed	self-operating
self-confidence	self-perception
self-confident	self-perpetuating
self-congratulation	self-pity
self-congratulatory	self-portrait
self-constituted	self-possessed
self-contradiction	self-possession
self-contradictory	self-preservation
self-control	self-proclaimed
self-correcting	self-propelled
self-created	self-propelling
self-criticism	self-protection
self-cultivation	self-realization
self-deceit	self-referential
self-deception	self-regard
self-defeating	self-reliance
self-definition	self-reliant
self-delusion	self-reproach
self-denial	self-respect
self-denying	self-respecting
self-deprecating	self-restraint
self-deprecation	self-revelation
self-depreciation	self-rule
self-despair	self-sacrifice
self-destruct	self-sacrificing
self-destruction	self-satisfaction
self-destructive	self-satisfied
self-determination	self-service
self-discipline	self-serving
self-distrust	self-starting
self-doubt	self-styled
self-educated	self-sufficiency
self-employed	self-sufficient
self-employment	self-supporting
self-esteem	self-sustaining
self-examination	self-taught
self-explaining	self-torment
self-explanatory	self-winding
self-expression	self-worth

self–cen·tered \'self-'sen-tərd\ *adj* : concerned only with one's own self — **self–cen·tered·ness** *n*
self–com·posed \ˌself-kəm-'pōzd\ *adj* : having control over one's emotions
self–con·scious \'self-'kän-chəs\ *adj* : uncomfortably conscious of oneself as an object of observation by others — **self–con·scious·ly** *adv* — **self–con·scious·ness** *n*
self–con·tained \ˌself-kən-'tānd\ *adj* **1** : complete in it-

self 2 : showing self-control; *also* : reserved in manner

self-de·fense \'self-di-'fens\ *n* 1 : a plea of justification for the use of force or for homicide 2 : the act of defending oneself, one's property, or a close relative

self-ef·fac·ing \-ə-'fā-siŋ\ *adj* : RETIRING, SHY

self-ev·i·dent \ˌself-'e-və-dənt\ *adj* : evident without proof or reasoning

self-fer·til·iza·tion \ˌself-ˌfərt-ᵊl-ə-'zā-shən\ *n* : fertilization of a plant or animal by its own pollen or sperm

self-ful·fill·ing \ˌself-fül-'fi-liŋ\ *adj* : becoming real or true by virtue of having been predicted or expected ⟨a ∼ prophecy⟩

self·ish \'sel-fish\ *adj* : concerned with one's own welfare excessively or without regard for others — **self·ish·ly** *adv* — **self·ish·ness** *n*

self·less \'self-ləs\ *adj* : UNSELFISH — **self·less·ness** *n*

self-made \'self-'mād\ *adj* : having achieved success or prominence by one's own efforts ⟨a ∼ man⟩

self-pol·li·na·tion \ˌself-ˌpä-lə-'nā-shən\ *n* : pollination of a flower by its own pollen or sometimes by pollen from another flower on the same plant

self-reg·u·lat·ing \'self-'re-gyə-ˌlā-tiŋ\ *adj* : AUTOMATIC

self-righ·teous \-'rī-chəs\ *adj* : strongly convinced of one's own righteousness — **self-righ·teous·ly** *adv*

self·same \'self-ˌsām\ *adj* : precisely the same : IDENTICAL

self-seal·ing \'self-'sē-liŋ\ *adj* : capable of sealing itself (as after puncture)

self-seek·ing \'self-'sē-kiŋ\ *adj* : seeking only to further one's own interests — **self-seeking** *n*

self-start·er \-'stär-tər\ *n* : a person who has initiative

self-will \'self-'wil\ *n* : OBSTINACY

sell \'sel\ *vb* **sold** \'sōld\; **sell·ing** 1 : to transfer (property) in return for money or something else of value 2 : to deal in as a business 3 : to be sold ⟨cars are ∼*ing* well⟩ — **sell·er** *n*

sell out *vb* 1 : to dispose of entirely by sale; *esp* : to sell one's business 2 : BETRAY — **sell·out** \'sel-ˌaŭt\ *n*

selt·zer \'selt-sər\ *n* [modif. of G *Selterser (Wasser)* water of Selters, fr. Nieder *Selters*, Germany] : artificially carbonated water

sel·vage *or* **sel·vedge** \'sel-vij\ *n* : the edge of a woven fabric so formed as to prevent raveling

selves *pl of* SELF

sem *abbr* 1 semicolon 2 seminar 3 seminary

se·man·tic \si-'man-tik\ *also* **se·man·ti·cal** \-ti-kəl\ *adj* : of or relating to meaning in language

se·man·tics \si-'man-tiks\ *n sing or pl* : the study of meanings in language

sema·phore \'se-mə-ˌfȯr\ *n* 1 : a visual signaling apparatus with movable arms 2 : signaling by hand-held flags

semaphore 2: alphabet; 3 positions following Z: error, end of word, numerals follow; numerals 1,2,3,4,5,6,7,8,9,0 same as A through J

sem·blance \'sem-bləns\ *n* 1 : outward appearance 2 : IMAGE, LIKENESS

se·men \'sē-mən\ *n* [NL, fr. L, seed] : a sticky whitish fluid of the male reproductive tract that contains the sperm

se·mes·ter \sə-'mes-tər\ *n* [G, fr. L *semestris* half-yearly, fr. *sex* six + *mensis* month] 1 : half a year 2 : one of the two terms into which many colleges divide the school year

semi- \'se-mi, -ˌmī\ *prefix* 1 : precisely half of 2 : half in quantity or value; *also* : half of or occurring halfway through a specified period 3 : partly : incompletely 4 : partial : incomplete 5 : having some of the characteristics of

semiannual	semiofficial
semiarid	semipermanent
semicentennial	semipolitical
semicircle	semiprecious
semicircular	semiprivate
semicivilized	semiprofessional
semiclassical	semireligious
semiconscious	semiretired
semidarkness	semiskilled
semidivine	semisoft
semiformal	semisolid
semigloss	semisweet
semi–independent	semitransparent
semiliquid	semiweekly
semiliterate	semiyearly
semimonthly	

semi \'se-ˌmī\ *n, pl* **sem·is** : SEMITRAILER

semi·au·to·mat·ic \ˌse-mē-ˌȯ-tə-'ma-tik\ *adj, of a firearm* : reloading by mechanical means but requiring release and another press of the trigger to fire again

semi·co·lon \'se-mi-ˌkō-lən\ *n* : a punctuation mark ; used esp. to separate major sentence elements

semi·con·duc·tor \ˌse-mi-kən-'dək-tər\ *n* : a substance whose electrical conductivity is between that of a conductor and an insulator — **semi·con·duct·ing** *adj*

¹semi·fi·nal \ˌse-mi-'fīn-ᵊl\ *adj* : being next to the last in an elimination tournament

²semi·fi·nal \'se-mi-ˌfīn-ᵊl\ *n* : a semifinal round or match — **semi·fi·nal·ist** \-ist\ *n*

semi·lu·nar \-'lü-nər\ *adj* : shaped like a crescent

sem·i·nal \'se-mən-ᵊl\ *adj* 1 : of, relating to, or consisting of seed or semen 2 : containing or contributing the seeds of later development : CREATIVE, ORIGINAL — **sem·i·nal·ly** *adv*

sem·i·nar \'se-mə-ˌnär\ *n* 1 : a course of study pursued by a group of advanced students doing original research under a professor 2 : CONFERENCE

sem·i·nary \'se-mə-ˌner-ē\ *n, pl* **-nar·ies** [ME, seedbed, nursery, fr. L *seminarium*, fr. *semen* seed] : an educational institution; *esp* : one that gives theological training — **sem·i·nar·i·an** \ˌse-mə-'ner-ē-ən\ *n*

Sem·i·nole \'se-mə-ˌnōl\ *n, pl* **Semi·noles** *or* **Seminole** : a member of an American Indian people of Florida

semi·per·me·able \ˌse-mi-'pər-mē-ə-bəl\ *adj* : partially but not freely or wholly permeable; *esp* : permeable to some usu. small molecules but not to other usu. larger particles ⟨a ∼ membrane⟩ — **semi·per·me·abil·i·ty** \-ˌpər-mē-ə-'bi-lə-tē\ *n*

Sem·ite \'se-ˌmīt\ *n* : a member of any of a group of peoples (as the Hebrews or Arabs) of southwest Asia — **Se·mit·ic** \sə-'mi-tik\ *adj*

semi·trail·er \'se-mi-ˌtrā-lər, -ˌmī-\ *n* : a freight trailer that when attached is supported at its forward end by the truck tractor; *also* : a semitrailer with attached tractor

semp·stress \'semp-strəs\ *var of* SEAMSTRESS

¹sen \'sen\ *n, pl* **sen** — see *yen* at MONEY table

²sen *n, pl* **sen** — see *dollar, ringgit, rupiah* at MONEY table

© 1996 PAWS, INC./Distributed by Universal Press Syndicate

³**sen** n, pl **sen** — see *riel* at MONEY table

⁴**sen** abbr **1** senate; senator **2** senior

sen•ate \'se-nət\ n : the second of two chambers of a legislature

sen•a•tor \'se-nə-tər\ n : a member of a senate — **sen•a•to•ri•al** \ı se-nə-'tōr-ē-əl\ adj

send \'send\ vb **sent** \'sent\; **send•ing 1** : to cause to go **2** : EMIT **3** : to propel or drive esp. with force **4** : to put or bring into a certain condition — **send•er** n

send–off \'send-ı òf\ n : a demonstration of goodwill and enthusiasm at the start of a new venture (as a trip)

se•ne \'sā-(ı)nā\ n, pl **sene** — see *tala* at MONEY table

Sen•e•ca \'se-ni-kə\ n, pl **Seneca** or **Senecas** : a member of an American Indian people of western New York

Sen•e•ga•lese \ı se-ni-gə-'lēz, -'lēs\ n, pl **Senegalese** : a native or inhabitant of Senegal — **Senegalese** adj

se•nes•cence \si-'nes-əns\ n : the state of being old; *also* : the process of becoming old — **se•nes•cent** \-ənt\ adj

se•nile \'sē-ı nīl, 'se-\ adj : OLD, AGED; *esp* : exhibiting a loss of mental ability associated with old age — **se•nil•i•ty** \si-'ni-lə-tē\ n

¹**se•nior** \'sē-nyər\ n **1** : a person older or of higher rank than another **2** : a member of the graduating class of a high school or college

²**senior** adj [ME, fr. L, older, elder, compar. of *senex* old] **1** : ELDER **2** : more advanced in dignity or rank **3** : belonging to the final year of a school or college course

senior chief petty officer n : a petty officer in the navy or coast guard ranking next below a master chief petty officer

senior citizen n : an elderly person; *esp* : one who has retired

senior high school n : a school usu. including grades 10 to 12

se•nior•i•ty \sēn-'yòr-ə-tē\ n **1** : the quality or state of being senior **2** : a privileged status owing to length of continuous service

senior master sergeant n : a noncommissioned officer in the air force ranking next below a chief master sergeant

sen•i•ti \'se-nə-tē\ n, pl **seniti** — see *pa'anga* at MONEY table

sen•na \'se-nə\ n **1** : CASSIA 2; *esp* : one used medicinally **2** : the dried leaflets or pods of a cassia used as a purgative

sen•sa•tion \sen-'sā-shən\ n **1** : awareness (as of noise or heat) or a mental process (as seeing or hearing) due to stimulation of a sense organ; *also* : an indefinite bodily feeling **2** : a condition of excitement; *also* : the thing that causes this condition

sen•sa•tion•al \-shə-nəl\ adj **1** : of or relating to sensation or the senses **2** : arousing an intense and usu. superficial interest or emotional reaction — **sen•sa•tion•al•ly** adv

sen•sa•tion•al•ise Brit var of SENSATIONALIZE

sen•sa•tion•al•ism \-nə-ı li-zəm\ n : the use or effect of sensational subject matter or treatment — **sen•sa•tion•al•ist** \-nə-list\ adj or n — **sen•sa•tion•al•is•tic** \-ı sā-shənə-'lis-tik\ adj

sen•sa•tion•al•ize \-nə-ı līz\ vb **-ized; -iz•ing** : to present in a sensational manner

¹**sense** \'sens\ n **1** : semantic content : MEANING **2** : the faculty of perceiving by means of sense organs; *also* : a bodily function or mechanism (as sight, hearing, or smell) basically involving a stimulus and a sense organ **3** : SENSATION, AWARENESS **4** : INTELLIGENCE, JUDGMENT **5** : OPINION ⟨the ∼ of the meeting⟩ — **sense•less** adj — **sense•less•ly** adv

²**sense** vb **sensed; sens•ing 1** : to be or become aware of ⟨∼ danger⟩; *also* : to perceive by the senses **2** : to detect (as radiation) automatically

sense organ n : a bodily structure (as an eye or ear) that receives stimuli (as heat or light) which excite nerve cells to send information to the brain

sen•si•bil•i•ty \ı sen-sə-'bi-lə-tē\ n, pl **-ties** : delicacy of feeling : SENSITIVITY

sen•si•ble \'sen-sə-bəl\ adj **1** : capable of being perceived by the senses or the mind; *also* : capable of receiving sense impressions **2** : AWARE, CONSCIOUS **3** : REASONABLE, RATIONAL — **sen•si•bly** \-blē\ adv

sen•si•tise Brit var of SENSITIZE

sen•si•tive \'sen-sə-tiv\ adj **1** : subject to excitation by or responsive to stimuli **2** : having power of feeling **3** : of such a nature as to be easily affected **4** : TOUCHY ⟨a ∼ issue⟩ — **sen•si•tive•ness** n — **sen•si•tiv•i•ty** \ı sen-sə-'ti-və-tē\ n

sensitive plant n : any of several mimosas with leaves that fold or droop when touched

sen•si•tize \'sen-sə-ı tīz\ vb **-tized; -tiz•ing** : to make or become sensitive or hypersensitive — **sen•si•ti•za•tion** \ı sen-sə-tə-'zā-shən\ n

sen•sor \'sen-ı sòr, -sər\ n : a device that responds to a physical stimulus

sen•so•ry \'sen-sə-rē\ adj : of or relating to sensation or the senses

sen•su•al \'sen-shə-wəl\ adj **1** : relating to gratification of the senses **2** : devoted to the pleasures of the senses — **sen•su•al•ist** n — **sen•su•al•i•ty** \ı sen-shə-'wa-lə-tē\ n — **sen•su•al•ly** adv

sen•su•ous \'sen-shə-wəs\ adj **1** : relating to the senses or to things that can be perceived by the senses **2** : VOLUPTUOUS — **sen•su•ous•ly** adv — **sen•su•ous•ness** n

sent past and past part of SEND

sen•te \sen-'tē\ n, pl **li•cen•te** or **li•sen•te** \li-'sen-tē\ — see *loti* at MONEY table

¹**sen•tence** \'sent-ᵊns, -ᵊnz\ n [ME, fr. MF, fr. L *sententia*, lit., feeling, opinion, fr. *sentire* to feel] **1** : the punishment set by a court **2** : a grammatically self-contained speech unit that expresses an assertion, a question, a command, a wish, or an exclamation

²**sentence** *vb* **sen·tenced; sen·tenc·ing** : to impose a sentence on

sen·ten·tious \sen-ˈten-chəs\ *adj* : using wise sayings or proverbs; *also* : using pompous language

sen·tient \ˈsen-chənt, -chē-ənt\ *adj* : capable of feeling : having perception

sen·ti·ment \ˈsen-tə-mənt\ *n* **1** : FEELING; *also* : thought and judgment influenced by feeling : emotional attitude **2** : OPINION, NOTION

sen·ti·men·tal \ˌsen-tə-ˈment-ᵊl\ *adj* **1** : influenced by tender feelings **2** : affecting the emotions **syn** bathetic, maudlin, mawkish, mushy — **sen·ti·men·tal·ism** *n* — **sen·ti·men·tal·ist** *n* — **sen·ti·men·tal·i·ty** \-ˌmen-ˈta-lə-tē, -mən-\ *n* — **sen·ti·men·tal·ly** *adv*

sen·ti·men·tal·ise *Brit var of* SENTIMENTALIZE

sen·ti·men·tal·ize \-ˈment-ᵊl-ˌīz\ *vb* **-ized; -iz·ing 1** : to indulge in sentiment **2** : to look upon or imbue with sentiment — **sen·ti·men·tal·i·za·tion** \-ˌment-ᵊl-ə-ˈzā-shən\ *n*

sen·ti·mo \sen-ˈtē-(ˌ)mō\ *n, pl* **-mos** — see *peso* at MONEY table

sen·ti·nel \ˈsent-ᵊn-əl\ *n* [MF *sentinelle*, fr. It *sentinella*, fr. *sentina* vigilance, fr. *sentire* to perceive, fr. L] : one that watches or guards

sen·try \ˈsen-trē\ *n, pl* **sentries** : SENTINEL, GUARD

sep *abbr* separate, separated

Sep *abbr* September

SEP *abbr* simplified employee pension

se·pal \ˈsē-pəl, ˈse-\ *n* : one of the modified leaves comprising a flower calyx

sep·a·ra·ble \ˈse-pə-rə-bəl\ *adj* : capable of being separated

¹**sep·a·rate** \ˈse-pə-ˌrāt\ *vb* **-rat·ed; -rat·ing 1** : to set or keep apart : DISCONNECT, SEVER **2** : to keep apart by something intervening **3** : to cease to be together : PART

²**sep·a·rate** \ˈse-prət, -pə-rət\ *adj* **1** : not connected **2** : divided from each other **3** : SINGLE, PARTICULAR (the ~ pieces of the puzzle) — **sep·a·rate·ly** *adv*

³**sep·a·rate** *n* : an article of dress designed to be worn interchangeably with others to form various combinations

sep·a·ra·tion \ˌse-pə-ˈrā-shən\ *n* **1** : the act or process of separating : the state of being separated **2** : a point, line, means, or area of division **3** : a formal separating of a married couple by agreement but without divorce

sep·a·rat·ist \ˈse-prə-tist, ˈse-pə-ˌrā-\ *n* : an advocate of separation (as from a political body) — **sep·a·rat·ism** \ˈse-prə-ˌti-zəm\ *n*

sep·a·ra·tive \ˈse-pə-ˌrā-tiv, ˈse-prə-tiv\ *adj* : tending toward, causing, or expressing separation

sep·a·ra·tor \ˈse-pə-ˌrā-tər\ *n* : one that separates; *esp* : a device for separating cream from milk

se·pia \ˈsē-pē-ə\ *n* : a brownish gray to dark brown color

sep·sis \ˈsep-səs\ *n, pl* **sep·ses** \ˈsep-ˌsēz\ : a toxic condition due to spread of bacteria or their products in the body

Sept *abbr* September

Sep·tem·ber \sep-ˈtem-bər\ *n* [ME *Septembre*, fr. OF & OE, both fr. L *September* (seventh month), fr. *septem* seven] : the 9th month of the year having 30 days

sep·tic \ˈsep-tik\ *adj* **1** : PUTREFACTIVE **2** : relating to or characteristic of sepsis

sep·ti·ce·mia \ˌsep-tə-ˈsē-mē-ə\ *n* : BLOOD POISONING

septic tank *n* : a tank in which sewage is disintegrated by bacteria

sep·tu·a·ge·nar·i·an \ˌsep-tü-ə-jə-ˈner-ē-ən, -ˌtyü-\ *n* : a person whose age is in the seventies — **septua·genarian** *adj*

Sep·tu·a·gint \sep-ˈtü-ə-jənt, -ˈtyü-\ *n* : a Greek version of the Old Testament prepared in the 3d and 2d centuries B.C. by Jewish scholars

sep·tum \ˈsep-təm\ *n, pl* **sep·ta** \-tə\ : a dividing wall or membrane esp. between bodily spaces or masses of soft tissue

se·pul·chral \sə-ˈpəl-krəl\ *adj* **1** : relating to burial or the grave **2** : GLOOMY

¹**sep·ul·chre** *or* **sep·ul·cher** \ˈse-pəl-kər\ *n* : a burial vault : TOMB

²**sepulchre** *or* **sepulcher** *vb* **-chred** *or* **-chered; -chring** *or* **-cher·ing** : BURY, ENTOMB

sep·ul·ture \ˈse-pəl-ˌchŭr\ *n* **1** : BURIAL **2** : SEPULCHRE

seq *abbr* [L *sequens, sequentes, sequentia*] the following

seqq *abbr* [L *sequentia*] the following ones

se·quel \ˈsē-kwəl\ *n* **1** : logical consequence **2** : a literary or cinematic work continuing a story begun in a preceding one

se·quence \ˈsē-kwəns\ *n* **1** : SERIES **2** : chronological order of events **3** : RESULT, SEQUEL **syn** succession, chain, progression, train — **se·quen·tial** \si-ˈkwen-chəl\ *adj* — **se·quen·tial·ly** *adv*

se·quent \ˈsē-kwənt\ *adj* **1** : SUCCEEDING, CONSECUTIVE **2** : RESULTANT

se·ques·ter \si-ˈkwes-tər\ *vb* : to set apart : SEGREGATE

se·ques·trate \ˈsē-kwəs-ˌtrāt, si-ˈkwes-\ *vb* **-trat·ed; -trat·ing** : SEQUESTER — **se·ques·tra·tion** \ˌsē-kwəs-ˈtrā-shən, ˌse-\ *n*

se·quin \ˈsē-kwən\ *n* **1** : an old gold coin of Turkey and Italy **2** : a small metal or plastic plate used for ornamentation esp. on clothing

se·quoia \si-ˈkwȯi-ə\ *n* : either of two huge California coniferous trees

ser *abbr* **1** serial **2** series

sera *pl of* SERUM

se·ra·glio \sə-ˈral-yō\ *n, pl* **-glios** [It *serraglio*] : HAREM

se·ra·pe \sə-ˈrä-pē\ *n* : a colorful woolen shawl worn over the shoulders esp. by Mexican men

ser·aph \ˈser-əf\ *n, pl* **ser·a·phim** \-ə-ˌfim, -ˌfēm\ *or* **seraphs** : one of the 6-winged angels standing in the presence of God

ser·a·phim \ˈser-ə-ˌfim, -ˌfēm\ *n pl* **1** : the highest order of angels **2** *sing, pl* **seraphim** : SERAPH — **se·raph·ic** \sə-ˈra-fik\ *adj*

Serb \ˈsərb\ *n* : a native or inhabitant of Serbia

Ser·bo-Cro·a·tian \ˌsər-(ˌ)bō-krō-ˈā-shən\ *n* : a Slavic language spoken in Croatia, Bosnia and Herzegovina, Serbia, and Montenegro

sere \ˈsir\ *adj* : DRY, WITHERED

¹**ser·e·nade** \ˌser-ə-ˈnād\ *n* [F, fr. It *serenata*, fr. *sereno* clear, calm (of weather)] : music sung or played as a compliment esp. outdoors at night for a woman being courted

²**serenade** *vb* **-nad·ed; -nad·ing** : to entertain with or perform a serenade

ser·en·dip·i·ty \ˌser-ən-ˈdi-pə-tē\ *n* [fr. its possession by the heroes of the Persian fairy tale *The Three Princes of Serendip*] : the gift of finding valuable or agreeable things not sought for — **ser·en·dip·i·tous** \-təs\ *adj*

se·rene \sə-ˈrēn\ *adj* **1** : CLEAR (~ skies) **2** : QUIET, CALM **syn** tranquil, peaceful, placid — **se·rene·ly** *adv* — **se·ren·i·ty** \sə-ˈre-nə-tē\ *n*

serf \ˈsərf\ *n* : a member of a servile class bound to the land and subject to the will of the landowner — **serf·dom** \-dəm\ *n*

serg *or* **sergt** *abbr* sergeant

serge \ˈsərj\ *n* : a twilled woolen cloth

ser·geant \ˈsär-jənt\ *n* [ME, servant, attendant, sergeant, fr. OF *sergent, serjant*, fr. L *servient-, serviens*, prp. of *servire* to serve] **1** : a noncommissioned officer (as in the army) ranking next below a staff sergeant **2** : an officer in a police force

sergeant first class *n* : a noncommissioned officer in the army ranking next below a master sergeant

sergeant major *n, pl* **sergeants major** *or* **sergeant majors 1** : a senior staff noncommissioned officer in the army or marine corps serving as advisor in matters related to enlisted personnel **2** : a noncommissioned officer in the marine corps ranking above a first sergeant

¹**se•ri•al** \'sir-ē-əl\ *adj* **1** : appearing in parts that follow regularly ⟨a ∼ story⟩ **2** : effecting a series of similar acts over a period of time ⟨a ∼ killer⟩; *also* : occurring in such a series — **se•ri•al•ly** *adv*

²**serial** *n* : a serial story or other writing — **se•ri•al•ist** \-ə-list\ *n*

se•ries \'sir-ēz\ *n, pl* **series** : a number of things or events arranged in order and connected by being alike in some way **syn** succession, progression, sequence, chain, train, string

seri•graph \'ser-ə-ˌgraf\ *n* : an original silk-screen print — **se•rig•ra•pher** \sə-'ri-grə-fər\ *n* — **se•rig•ra•phy** \-fē\ *n*

se•ri•ous \'sir-ē-əs\ *adj* **1** : thoughtful or subdued in appearance or manner : SOBER **2** : requiring much thought or work **3** : EARNEST, DEVOTED **4** : DANGEROUS, HARMFUL **5** : excessive or impressive in quantity or degree ⟨making ∼ money⟩ **syn** grave, sedate, staid — **se•ri•ous•ly** *adv* — **se•ri•ous•ness** *n*

ser•mon \'sər-mən\ *n* [ME, fr. OF, fr. ML *sermon, sermo,* fr. L, speech, conversation, fr. *serere* to link together] **1** : a religious discourse esp. as part of a worship service **2** : a lecture on conduct or duty

se•rol•o•gy \sə-'rä-lə-jē\ *n* : a science dealing with serums and esp. their reactions and properties — **se•ro•log•i•cal** \ˌsir-ə-'lä-ji-kəl\ *or* **se•ro•log•ic** \-jik\ *adj*

se•rous \'sir-əs\ *adj* : of, relating to, resembling, or producing serum; *esp* : of thin watery constitution

ser•pent \'sər-pənt\ *n* : SNAKE

¹**ser•pen•tine** \'sər-pən-ˌtēn, -ˌtīn\ *adj* **1** : SLY, CRAFTY **2** : WINDING, TURNING

²**ser•pen•tine** \-ˌtēn\ *n* : a dull-green mineral having a mottled appearance

ser•rate \'ser-ˌāt\ *adj* : having a saw-toothed edge ⟨a ∼ leaf⟩

ser•ried \'ser-ēd\ *adj* : DENSE

se•rum \'sir-əm\ *n, pl* **serums** *or* **se•ra** \-ə\ [L, whey, wheylike fluid] : the clear yellowish antibody-containing fluid that can be separated from blood when it clots; *also* : a preparation of animal serum containing specific antibodies and used to prevent or cure disease

serv *abbr* service

ser•vant \'sər-vənt\ *n* : one that serves others; *esp* : a person employed for domestic or personal work

¹**serve** \'sərv\ *vb* **served; serv•ing 1** : to work as a servant **2** : to render obedience and worship to (God) **3** : to comply with the commands or demands of **4** : to work through or perform a term of service (as in the army) **5** : PUT IN ⟨*served* five years in jail⟩ **6** : to be of use : ANSWER ⟨pine boughs *served* for a bed⟩ **7** : BENEFIT **8** : to prove adequate or satisfactory for ⟨a pie that ∼*s* eight people⟩ **9** : to make ready and pass out ⟨∼ drinks⟩ **10** : to furnish or supply with something ⟨one power company *serving* the whole state⟩ **11** : to wait on ⟨∼ a customer⟩ **12** : to treat or act toward in a specified way **13** : to put the ball in play (as in tennis) — **serv•er** *n*

²**serve** *n* : the act of serving a ball (as in tennis)

¹**ser•vice** \'sər-vəs\ *n* **1** : the occupation of a servant **2** : HELP, BENEFIT **3** : a meeting for worship; *also* : a form followed in worship or in a ceremony ⟨burial ∼⟩ **4** : the act, fact, or means of serving **5** : performance of official or professional duties **6** : SERVE **7** : a set of dishes or silverware **8** : a branch of public employment; *also* : the persons in it ⟨civil ∼⟩ **9** : military or naval duty

²**service** *vb* **ser•viced; ser•vic•ing** : to do maintenance or repair work on or for

ser•vice•able \'sər-və-sə-bəl\ *adj* : prepared for service : USEFUL, USABLE

ser•vice•man \'sər-vəs-ˌman, -mən\ *n* **1** : a male member of the armed forces **2** : a man employed to repair or maintain equipment

service station *n* : a retail station for servicing motor vehicles

ser•vice•wom•an \'sər-vəs-ˌwu̇-mən\ *n* : a female member of the armed forces

ser•vile \'sər-vəl, -ˌvīl\ *adj* **1** : befitting a slave or servant **2** : behaving like a slave : SUBMISSIVE — **ser•vil•i•ty** \ˌsər-'vi-lə-tē\ *n*

serv•ing \'sər-viŋ\ *n* : HELPING

ser•vi•tor \'sər-və-tər\ *n* : a male servant

ser•vi•tude \'sər-və-ˌtüd, -ˌtyüd\ *n* : SLAVERY, BONDAGE

ser•vo \'sər-vō\ *n, pl* **servos 1** : SERVOMOTOR **2** : SERVOMECHANISM

ser•vo•mech•a•nism \'sər-vō-ˌme-kə-ˌni-zəm\ *n* : a device for automatically correcting the performance of a mechanism

ser•vo•mo•tor \-ˌmō-tər\ *n* : a mechanism that supplements a primary control

ses•a•me \'se-sə-mē\ *n* : a widely cultivated annual herb of warm regions; *also* : its seeds that yield an edible oil (sesame oil) and are used in flavoring

ses•qui•cen•ten•ni•al \ˌses-kwi-sen-'te-nē-əl\ *n* [L *sesqui-* one and a half, half again] : a 150th anniversary or its celebration — **sesquicentennial** *adj*

ses•qui•pe•da•lian \ˌses-kwə-pə-'dāl-yən\ *adj* **1** : having many syllables : LONG **2** : using long words

ses•sile \'se-sil, -səl\ *adj* : permanently attached and not free to move about

ses•sion \'se-shən\ *n* **1** : a meeting or series of meetings of a body (as a court or legislature) for the transaction of business **2** : a meeting or period devoted to a particular activity

¹**set** \'set\ *vb* **set; set•ting 1** : to cause to sit **2** : PLACE **3** : ARRANGE, ADJUST **4** : to cause to be or do **5** : SETTLE, DECREE **6** : to fix in a frame **7** : to fix at a certain amount **8** : WAGER, STAKE **9** : to make or become fast or rigid **10** : to adapt (as words) to something (as music) **11** : to become fixed or firm or solid **12** : to be suitable : FIT **13** : BROOD **14** : to have a certain direction **15** : to pass below the horizon **16** : to defeat in bridge — **set about** : to begin to do — **set forth** : to begin a trip — **set off 1** : to start out on a course or a trip **2** : to cause to explode — **set out** : to begin a

trip or undertaking — **set sail** : to begin a voyage — **set upon** : to attack usu. with violence

²set *n* **1** : a setting or a being set **2** : DIRECTION, COURSE; *also* : TENDENCY **3** : FORM, BUILD **4** : the fit of something (as a coat) **5** : an artificial setting for the scene of a play or motion picture **6** : a group of tennis games in which one side wins at least six **7** : a group of persons or things of the same kind or having a common characteristic usu. classed together **8** : a collection of things and esp. of mathematical elements (as numbers or points) **9** : an electronic apparatus ⟨a television ∼⟩

³set *adj* **1** : DELIBERATE, INTENT **2** : fixed by authority or custom **3** : RIGID **4** : PERSISTENT

set·back \'set-₁bak\ *n* : a temporary defeat : REVERSE

set back *vb* **1** : HINDER, DELAY; *also* : REVERSE **2** : COST

set piece 1 : a composition (as in literature or music) executed in fixed or ideal form often with brilliant effect **2** : a scene, depiction, speech, or event obviously designed to have an imposing effect

set·screw \'set-₁skrü\ *n* : a screw screwed through one part tightly upon or into another part to prevent relative movement

set·tee \se-'tē\ *n* : a bench or sofa with a back and arms

set·ter \'se-tər\ *n* : a large long-coated hunting dog

set·ting \'se-tiŋ\ *n* **1** : the frame in which a gem is set **2** : the time, place, and circumstances in which something occurs or develops; *also* : SCENERY **3** : music written for a text (as of a poem) **4** : the eggs that a fowl sits on for hatching at one time

set·tle \'set-ᵊl\ *vb* **set·tled; set·tling** [ME *settlen* to seat, bring to rest, come to rest, fr. OE *setlan*, fr. *setl* seat] **1** : to place so as to stay **2** : to establish in residence; *also* : COLONIZE **3** : to make compact **4** : QUIET, CALM **5** : to establish or secure permanently **6** : to direct one's efforts **7** : to fix by agreement **8** : to give legally **9** : ADJUST, ARRANGE **10** : DECIDE, DETERMINE **11** : to make a final disposition of ⟨∼ an account⟩ **12** : to come to rest **13** : to reach an agreement on **14** : to sink gradually to a lower level **15** : to become clear by depositing sediment — **set·tler** *n*

set·tle·ment \'set-ᵊl-mənt\ *n* **1** : the act or process of settling **2** : BESTOWAL ⟨a marriage ∼⟩ **3** : payment or adjustment of an account **4** : COLONY **5** : a small village **6** : an institution providing various community services esp. to large city populations **7** : adjustment of doubts and differences

set–to \'set-₁tü\ *n, pl* **set–tos** : FIGHT

set·up \'set-₁əp\ *n* **1** : the manner or act of arranging **2** : glass, ice, and nonalcoholic beverage for mixing served to patrons who supply their own liquor **3** : something (as a plot) that has been constructed or contrived; *also* : FRAME-UP

set up *vb* **1** : to place in position; *also* : ASSEMBLE **2** : CAUSE **3** : FOUND, ESTABLISH **4** : FRAME **5**

sev·en \'se-vən\ *n* **1** : one more than six **2** : the 7th in a set or series **3** : something having seven units — **seven** *adj or pron* — **sev·enth** \-vənth\ *adj or adv or n*

sev·en·teen \₁se-vən-'tēn\ *n* : one more than 16 — **sev·enteen** *adj or pron* — **sev·en·teenth** \-'tēnth\ *adj or n*

seventeen–year locust *n* : a cicada of the U.S. that has in the North a life of 17 years and in the South of 13 years of which most is spent underground as a nymph and only a few weeks as a winged adult

sev·en·ty \'se-vən-tē\ *n, pl* **-ties** : seven times 10 — **sev·en·ti·eth** \-tē-əth\ *adj or n* — **seventy** *adj or pron*

sev·en·ty–eight \₁se-vən-tē-'āt\ *n* : a phonograph record designed to be played at 78 revolutions per minute

sev·er \'se-vər\ *vb* **sev·ered; sev·er·ing** : DIVIDE; *esp* : to separate by or as if by cutting — **sev·er·ance** \'sev-rəns, 'se-və-\ *n*

sev·er·al \'sev-rəl, 'se-və-\ *adj* [ME, fr. MF, fr. ML *separalis*, fr. L *separ* separate, fr. *separare* to sepa-

rate] **1** : INDIVIDUAL, DISTINCT ⟨federal union of the ∼ states⟩ **2** : consisting of an indefinite number but yet not very many — **sev·er·al·ly** *adv*

severance pay *n* : extra pay given an employee upon termination of employment

se·vere \sə-'vir\ *adj* **se·ver·er; -est 1** : marked by strictness or sternness : AUSTERE **2** : strict in discipline **3** : causing distress and esp. physical discomfort or pain ⟨∼ weather⟩ ⟨a ∼ wound⟩ **4** : hard to endure ⟨∼ trials⟩ **5** : SERIOUS ⟨∼ depression⟩ **syn** stern, ascetic, astringent — **se·vere·ly** *adv* — **se·ver·i·ty** \-'ver-ə-tē\ *n*

sew \'sō\ *vb* **sewed; sewn** \'sōn\ *or* **sewed; sew·ing 1** : to unite or fasten by stitches **2** : to engage in sewing

sew·age \'sü-ij\ *n* : waste materials carried off by sewers

¹sew·er \'sō-ər\ *n* : one that sews

²sew·er \'sü-ər\ *n* : an artificial pipe or channel to carry off waste matter

sew·er·age \'sü-ə-rij\ *n* **1** : a system of sewers **2** : SEWAGE

sew·ing *n* **1** : the activity of one who sews **2** : material that has been or is to be sewed

sex \'seks\ *n* **1** : either of the two major forms that occur in many living things and are designated male or female according to their role in reproduction; *also* : the qualities by which these sexes are differentiated and which directly or indirectly function in reproduction involving two parents **2** : sexual activity or behavior; *also* : SEXUAL INTERCOURSE — **sexed** \'sekst\ *adj* — **sex·less** *adj*

sex·a·ge·nar·i·an \₁sek-sə-jə-'ner-ē-ən\ *n* : a person whose age is in the sixties — **sexagenarian** *adj*

sex cell *n* : an egg cell or sperm cell

sex chromosome *n* : one of usu. a pair of chromosomes that are usu. similar in one sex but different in the other sex and are concerned with the inheritance of sex

sex hormone *n* : a hormone (as from the gonads or adrenal cortex) that affects the growth or function of the reproductive organs or the development of secondary sex characteristics

sex·ism \'sek-₁si-zəm\ *n* : prejudice or discrimination based on sex; *esp* : discrimination against women — **sex·ist** \'sek-sist\ *adj or n*

sex·pot \'seks-₁pät\ *n* : a conspicuously sexy woman

sex symbol *n* : a usu. renowned person (as an entertainer) noted and admired for conspicuous attractiveness

sex·tant \'sek-stənt\ *n* [NL *sextant-, sextans* sixth part of a circle, fr. L, sixth part, fr. *sextus* sixth] : a navigational instrument for determining latitude

sex·tet \sek-'stet\ *n* **1** : a musical composition for six voices or instruments; *also* : the performers of such a composition **2** : a group or set of six

sex·ton \'sek-stən\ *n* : one who takes care of church property

sex·u·al \'sek-shə-wəl\ *adj* : of, relating to, or involving sex or the sexes ⟨a ∼ spore⟩ ⟨∼ relations⟩ — **sex·u·al·i·ty** \₁sek-shə-'wa-lə-tē\ *n* — **sex·u·al·ly** \'sek-shə-wə-lē\ *adv*

sexual intercourse *n* **1** : intercourse between a male and a female in which the penis is inserted into the vagina **2** : intercourse between individuals involving genital contact other than insertion of the penis into the vagina

sexually transmitted disease *n* : a disease (as syphilis, gonorrhea, AIDS, or the genital form of herpes simplex) that is caused by a microorganism or virus usu. or often transmitted by direct sexual contact

sexual relations *n pl* : SEXUAL INTERCOURSE

sexy \'sek-sē\ *adj* **sex·i·er; -est** : sexually suggestive or stimulating : EROTIC

SF *abbr* **1** sacrifice fly **2** science fiction

SFC *abbr* sergeant first class

SG *abbr* **1** senior grade **2** sergeant **3** solicitor general **4** surgeon general

sgd *abbr* signed

Sgt *abbr* sergeant

Sgt Maj *abbr* sergeant major

sh *abbr* share

shab·by \'sha-bē\ *adj* **shab·bi·er; -est 1** : dressed in worn clothes **2** : threadbare and faded from wear **3** : DESPICABLE, MEAN; *also* : UNFAIR ⟨∼ treatment⟩ — **shab·bi·ly** \'sha-bə-lē\ *adv* — **shab·bi·ness** \-bē-nəs\ *n*

shack \'shak\ *n* : HUT, SHANTY

¹**shack·le** \'sha-kəl\ *n* **1** : something (as a manacle or fetter) that confines the legs or arms **2** : a check on free action made as if by fetters **3** : a device for making something fast or secure

²**shackle** *vb* **shack·led; shack·ling** : to bind or fasten with shackles

shad \'shad\ *n, pl* **shad** : any of several sea fishes related to the herrings that swim up rivers to spawn and include some important food fishes

¹**shade** \'shād\ *n* **1** : partial obscurity **2** : space sheltered from the light esp. of the sun **3** : PHANTOM **4** : something that shelters from or intercepts light or heat; *also, pl* : SUNGLASSES **5** : a dark color or a variety of a color **6** : a small difference

²**shade** *vb* **shad·ed; shad·ing 1** : to shelter from light and heat **2** : DARKEN, OBSCURE **3** : to mark with degrees of light or color **4** : to show slight differences esp. in color or meaning

shad·ing *n* : the color and lines representing darkness or shadow in a drawing or painting

¹**shad·ow** \'sha-dō\ *n* **1** : partial darkness in a space from which light rays are cut off **2** : SHELTER **3** : shade cast upon a surface by something intercepting rays from a light ⟨the ∼ of a tree⟩ **4** : PHANTOM **5** : a shaded portion of a picture **6** : a small portion or degree : TRACE ⟨a ∼ of doubt⟩ **7** : a source of gloom or unhappiness — **shad·owy** *adj*

²**shadow** *vb* **1** : to cast a shadow on **2** : to represent faintly or vaguely **3** : to follow and watch closely : TRAIL

shad·ow·box \'sha-dō-ˌbäks\ *vb* : to box with an imaginary opponent esp. for training

shady \'shā-dē\ *adj* **shad·i·er; -est 1** : affording shade **2** : of questionable honesty or reputation

¹**shaft** \'shaft\ *n, pl* **shafts 1** : the long handle of a spear or lance **2** : SPEAR, LANCE **3** *or pl* **shaves** \'shavz\ : POLE; *esp* : one of two poles between which a horse is hitched to pull a vehicle **4** : something (as a column) long and slender **5** : a bar to support a rotating piece or to transmit power by rotation **6** : an inclined opening in the ground (as for finding or mining ore) **7** : a vertical opening (as for an elevator) through the floors of a building **8** : harsh or unfair treatment — usu. used with *the*

²**shaft** *vb* **1** : to fit with a shaft **2** : to treat unfairly or harshly

shag \'shag\ *n* : a shaggy tangled mass or covering (as of wool) : long coarse or matted fiber, nap, or pile

shag·gy \'sha-gē\ *adj* **shag·gi·er; -est 1** : rough with or as if with long hair or wool **2** : tangled or rough in surface

shah \'shä, 'shò\ *n, often cap* : a sovereign of Iran until 1979

Shak *abbr* Shakespeare

¹**shake** \'shāk\ *vb* **shook** \'shůk\; **shak·en** \'shā-kən\; **shak·ing 1** : to move or cause to move jerkily or irregularly **2** : BRANDISH, WAVE ⟨*shaking* his fist⟩ **3** : to disturb emotionally ⟨*shaken* by her death⟩ **4** : WEAKEN ⟨*shook* his faith⟩ **5** : to bring or come into a certain position, condition, or arrangement by or as if by moving jerkily **6** : to clasp (hands) in greeting or as a sign of goodwill or agreement **syn** tremble, quake, quaver, shiver, quiver — **shak·able** \'shā-kə-bəl\ *adj*

²**shake** *n* **1** : the act or a result of shaking **2** : DEAL, TREATMENT ⟨a fair ∼⟩

shake·down \'shāk-ˌdaůn\ *n* **1** : an improvised bed **2** : EXTORTION **3** : a process or period of adjustment **4** : a test (as of a new ship or airplane) under operating conditions

shake down *vb* **1** : to take up temporary quarters **2** : to occupy a makeshift bed **3** : to become accustomed esp. to new surroundings or duties **4** : to settle down **5** : to give a shakedown test to **6** : to obtain money from in a deceitful or illegal manner **7** : to bring about a reduction of

shak·er \'shā-kər\ *n* **1** : one that shakes ⟨pepper ∼⟩ **2** *cap* : a member of a religious sect founded in England in 1747

shake-up \'shāk-ˌəp\ *n* : an extensive often drastic reorganization

shaky \'shā-kē\ *adj* **shak·i·er; -est** : UNSOUND, WEAK — **shak·i·ly** \'shā-kə-lē\ *adv* — **shak·i·ness** \-kē-nəs\ *n*

shale \'shāl\ *n* : a finely layered rock formed from clay, mud, or silt

shall \shəl, 'shal\ *vb, past* **should** \shəd, 'shůd\; *pres sing & pl* **shall** — used as an auxiliary to express a command, what seems inevitable or likely in the future, simple futurity, or determination

shal·lop \'sha-ləp\ *n* : a light open boat

shal·lot \shə-'lät, 'sha-lət\ *n* [modif. of F *échalote*] **1** : a small clustered bulb that is used in seasoning and is produced by a perennial herb belonging to a subspecies of the onion; *also* : this herb **2** : GREEN ONION

¹**shal·low** \'sha-lō\ *adj* **1** : not deep **2** : not intellectually profound

²**shallow** *n* : a shallow place in a body of water — usu. used in pl.

¹**sham** \'sham\ *n* **1** : an ornamental covering for a pillow **2** : COUNTERFEIT, IMITATION **3** : a person who shams

²**sham** *vb* **shammed; sham·ming** : FEIGN, PRETEND — **sham·mer** *n*

³**sham** *adj* : not genuine : FALSE, FEIGNED

sha·man \'shä-mən, 'shā-\ *n* [ultim. fr. Evenki (a language of Siberia) *šamān*] : a priest or priestess who uses magic to cure the sick, to divine the hidden, and to control events

sham·ble \'sham-bəl\ *vb* **sham·bled; sham·bling** : to shuffle along — **shamble** *n*

sham·bles \'sham-bəlz\ *n* **1** : a scene of great slaughter **2** : a scene or state of great destruction or disorder; *also* : MESS

¹**shame** \'shām\ *n* **1** : a painful sense of having done something wrong, improper, or immodest **2** : DISGRACE, DISHONOR **3** : a cause of feeling shame **4** : something to be regretted ⟨it's a ∼ you'll miss the party⟩ — **shame·ful** \-fəl\ *adj* — **shame·ful·ly** *adv* — **shame·less** *adj* — **shame·less·ly** *adv*

²**shame** *vb* **shamed; sham·ing 1** : DISGRACE **2** : to make ashamed

shame·faced \'shām-ˌfāst\ *adj* : ASHAMED, ABASHED — **shame·faced·ly** \-ˌfā-səd-lē, -ˌfāst-lē\ *adv*

¹**sham·poo** \sham-'pü\ *vb* [Hindi *cāpo*, imper. of *cāpnā* to press, shampoo] : to wash (as the hair) with soap and water or with a special preparation; *also* : to clean (as a rug) similarly

²**shampoo** *n, pl* **shampoos 1** : the act or an instance of shampooing **2** : a preparation for use in shampooing

sham·rock \'sham-ˌräk\ *n* [Ir *seamróg*, dim. of *seamar* clover] : a plant of folk legend with leaves composed of three leaflets that is associated with St. Patrick and Ireland

shang·hai \shaŋ-'hī\ *vb* **shang·haied; shang·hai·ing** [*Shanghai*, China] : to force aboard a ship for service

as a sailor; *also* : to trick or force into an undesirable position

Shan·gri–la \ˌshaŋ-gri-ˈlä\ *n* [*Shangri-La,* imaginary land depicted in the novel *Lost Horizon* (1933) by James Hilton] : a remote idyllic hideaway

shank \ˈshaŋk\ *n* **1** : the part of the leg between the knee and the human ankle or a corresponding part of a quadruped **2** : a cut of meat from the leg **3** : the narrow part of the sole of a shoe beneath the instep **4** : the part of a tool or instrument (as a key or anchor) connecting the functioning part with a part by which it is held or moved

shan·tung \ˌshan-ˈtəŋ\ *n* : a fabric in plain weave having a slightly irregular surface

shan·ty \ˈshan-tē\ *n, pl* **shanties** [prob. fr. CanF *chantier* lumber camp, hut, fr. F, gantry, fr. L *cantherius* rafter, trellis] : a small roughly built shelter or dwelling

¹shape \ˈshāp\ *vb* **shaped; shap·ing 1** : to form esp. in a particular shape **2** : DESIGN **3** : ADAPT, ADJUST **4** : REGULATE **syn** make, fashion, fabricate, manufacture, frame, mold

²shape *n* **1** : APPEARANCE **2** : surface configuration : FORM **3** : bodily contour apart from the head and face : FIGURE **4** : PHANTOM **5** : CONDITION — **shaped** \ˈshāpt\ *adj*

shape·less \ˈshā-pləs\ *adj* **1** : having no definite shape **2** : not shapely — **shape·less·ly** *adv* — **shape·less·ness** *n*

shape·ly \ˈshā-plē\ *adj* **shape·li·er; -est** : having a pleasing shape — **shape·li·ness** *n*

shard \ˈshärd\ *also* **sherd** \ˈshərd\ *n* : a broken piece : FRAGMENT

¹share \ˈshar\ *n* : PLOWSHARE

²share *n* **1** : a portion belonging to one person or group **2** : any of the equal interests into which the capital stock of a corporation is divided

³share *vb* **shared; shar·ing 1** : APPORTION **2** : to use or enjoy with others **3** : PARTICIPATE — **shar·er** *n*

share·crop·per \-ˌkrä-pər\ *n* : a farmer who works another's land in return for a share of the crop — **share·crop** *vb*

share·hold·er \-ˌhōl-dər\ *n* : STOCKHOLDER

¹shark \ˈshärk\ *n* : any of various active, usu. predaceous, and mostly large marine cartilaginous fishes

²shark *n* : a greedy crafty person

shark·skin \-ˌskin\ *n* **1** : the hide of a shark or leather made from it **2** : a fabric (as of cotton or rayon) woven from strands of many fine threads and having a sleek appearance and silky feel

¹sharp \ˈshärp\ *adj* **1** : having a thin cutting edge or fine point : not dull or blunt **2** : COLD, NIPPING ⟨a ~ wind⟩ **3** : keen in intellect, perception, or attention **4** : BRISK, ENERGETIC **5** : IRRITABLE ⟨a ~ temper⟩ **6** : causing intense distress ⟨a ~ pain⟩ **7** : HARSH, CUTTING ⟨a ~ rebuke⟩ **8** : affecting the senses as if cutting or piercing ⟨a ~ sound⟩ ⟨a ~ smell⟩ **9** : not smooth or rounded ⟨~ features⟩ **10** : involving an abrupt or extreme change ⟨a ~ turn⟩ **11** : CLEAR, DISTINCT ⟨mountains in ~ relief⟩; *also* : easy to perceive ⟨a ~

contrast⟩ **12** : higher than the true pitch; *also* : raised by a half step **13** : STYLISH ⟨a ~ dresser⟩ **syn** keen, acute, quick-witted, penetrative — **sharp·ly** *adv* — **sharp·ness** *n*

²sharp *adv* **1** : in a sharp manner **2** : EXACTLY, PRECISELY ⟨left at 8 ~⟩

³sharp *n* **1** : a sharp edge or point **2** : a character ♯ which indicates that a specified note is to be raised by a half step; *also* : the resulting note **3** : SHARPER

⁴sharp *vb* : to raise in pitch by a half step

sharp·en \ˈshär-pən\ *vb* : to make or become sharp — **sharp·en·er** *n*

sharp·er \ˈshär-pər\ *n* : SWINDLER; *esp* : a cheating gambler

sharp·ie *or* **sharpy** \ˈshär-pē\ *n, pl* **sharp·ies 1** : SHARPER **2** : a person who is exceptionally keen or alert

sharp·shoot·er \ˈshärp-ˌshü-tər\ *n* : a good marksman — **sharp·shoot·ing** *n*

shat·ter \ˈsha-tər\ *vb* : to dash or burst into fragments — **shat·ter·proof** \ˈsha-tər-ˌprüf\ *adj*

¹shave \ˈshāv\ *vb* **shaved; shaved** *or* **shav·en** \ˈshā-vən\; **shav·ing 1** : to slice in thin pieces **2** : to make bare or smooth by cutting the hair from **3** : to cut or pare off by the sliding movement of a razor **4** : to skim along or near the surface of

²shave *n* **1** : any of various tools for cutting thin slices **2** : an act or process of shaving

shav·er \ˈshā-vər\ *n* **1** : an electric razor **2** : BOY, YOUNGSTER

shaves *pl of* SHAFT

shav·ing *n* **1** : the act of one that shaves **2** : something shaved off

shawl \ˈshȯl\ *n* : a square or oblong piece of fabric used esp. by women as a loose covering for the head or shoulders

Shaw·nee \shȯ-ˈnē, shä-\ *n, pl* **Shawnee** *or* **Shawnees** : a member of an American Indian people orig. of the central Ohio valley; *also* : their language

shd *abbr* should

she \ˈshē\ *pron* : that female one ⟨who is ~⟩; *also* : that one regarded as feminine ⟨~'s a fine ship⟩

sheaf \ˈshēf\ *n, pl* **sheaves** \ˈshēvz\ **1** : a bundle of stalks and ears of grain **2** : a group of things bound together

¹shear \ˈshir\ *vb* **sheared; sheared** *or* **shorn** \ˈshȯrn\; **shear·ing 1** : to cut the hair or wool from : CLIP, TRIM **2** : to deprive by or as if by cutting **3** : to cut or break sharply

²shear *n* **1** : any of various cutting tools that consist of two blades fastened together so that the edges slide one by the other — usu. used in pl. **2** *chiefly Brit* : the act, an instance, or the result of shearing **3** : an action or stress caused by applied forces that causes two parts of a body to slide on each other

sheath \ˈshēth\ *n, pl* **sheaths** \ˈshēthz, ˈshēths\ **1** : a case for a blade (as of a knife); *also* : an anatomical covering suggesting such a case **2** : a close-fitting dress usu. worn without a belt

sheathe \ˈshēth\ *also* **sheath** \ˈshēth\ *vb* **sheathed;**

sheath·ing 1 : to put into a sheath **2** : to cover with something that guards or protects

sheath·ing \'shē-<u>th</u>iŋ, -thiŋ\ *n* : material used to sheathe something; *esp* : the first covering of boards or of waterproof material on the outside wall of a frame house or on a timber roof

sheave \'shiv, 'shēv\ *n* : a grooved wheel or pulley (as on a pulley block)

she·bang \shi-'baŋ\ *n* : CONTRIVANCE, AFFAIR, CONCERN (sold the whole ∼)

¹shed \'shed\ *vb* **shed; shed·ding 1** : to cause to flow from a cut or wound ⟨∼ blood⟩ **2** : to pour down in drops ⟨∼ tears⟩ **3** : to give out (as light) : DIFFUSE **4** : to throw off (as a natural covering) : DISCARD

²shed *n* : a slight structure built for shelter or storage

sheen \'shēn\ *n* : a subdued luster

sheep \'shēp\ *n, pl* **sheep 1** : any of various cud=chewing mammals that are stockier than the related goats and lack a beard in the male; *esp* : one raised for meat or for its wool or skin **2** : a timid or defenseless person **3** : SHEEPSKIN

sheep dog *n* : a dog used to tend, drive, or guard sheep

sheep·fold \'shēp-₁fōld\ *n* : a pen or shelter for sheep

sheep·herd·er \-₁hər-dər\ *n* : a worker in charge of sheep esp. on open range — **sheep·herd·ing** *n*

sheep·ish \'shē-pish\ *adj* : BASHFUL, TIMID; *esp* : embarrassed by consciousness of a fault — **sheep·ish·ly** *adv*

sheep·skin \'shēp-₁skin\ *n* **1** : the hide of a sheep or leather prepared from it; *also* : PARCHMENT **2** : DIPLOMA

¹sheer \'shir\ *vb* : to turn from a course

²sheer *adj* **1** : very thin or transparent **2** : UNQUALIFIED ⟨∼ folly⟩ **3** : very steep **syn** pure, simple, absolute, unadulterated, unmitigated — **sheer** *adv*

¹sheet \'shēt\ *n* **1** : a broad piece of cloth (as for a bed); *also* : SAIL **2** : a single piece of paper **3** : a broad flat surface ⟨a ∼ of ice⟩ **4** : something broad and long and relatively thin

²sheet *n* : a rope used to trim a sail

sheet·ing \'shē-tiŋ\ *n* : material in the form of sheets or suitable for forming into sheets

sheikh *or* **sheik** \'shēk, 'shāk\ *n* : an Arab chief — **sheikh·dom** *or* **sheik·dom** \-dəm\ *n*

shek·el \'she-kəl\ *n* — see MONEY table

shelf \'shelf\ *n, pl* **shelves** \'shelvz\ **1** : a thin flat usu. long and narrow structure fastened horizontally (as on a wall) above the floor to hold things **2** : something (as a sandbar) that suggests a shelf

shelf life *n* : the period of storage time during which a material will remain useful

¹shell \'shel\ *n* **1** : a hard or tough often thin outer covering of an animal (as a beetle, turtle, or mollusk) or of an egg or a seed or fruit (as a nut); *also* : something that resembles a shell ⟨a pastry ∼⟩ **2** : a light narrow racing boat propelled by oarsmen **3** : a case holding an explosive and designed to be fired from a cannon; *also* : a case holding the charge of powder and shot or bullet for small arms **4** : a plain usu. sleeveless blouse or sweater — **shelled** \'sheld\ *adj* — **shelly** \'she-lē\ *adj*

²shell *vb* **1** : to remove from a shell or husk **2** : BOMBARD — **shell·er** *n*

¹shel·lac \shə-'lak\ *n* **1** : a purified lac **2** : lac dissolved in alcohol and used as a wood filler or finish

²shellac *vb* **shel·lacked; shel·lack·ing 1** : to coat or treat with shellac **2** : to defeat decisively

shel·lack·ing *n* : a sound drubbing

shell bean *n* : a bean grown esp. for its edible seeds; *also* : its edible seed

shell·fish \-₁fish\ *n* : an invertebrate water animal (as an oyster or lobster) with a shell

shell out *vb* : PAY

shell shock *n* : a psychological and nervous disorder of soldiers resulting from traumatic experience in combat — **shell–shocked** \'shel-₁shäkt\ *adj*

¹shel·ter \'shel-tər\ *n* : something that gives protection : REFUGE

²shelter *vb* **shel·tered; shel·ter·ing** : to give protection or refuge to

shelve \'shelv\ *vb* **shelved; shelv·ing 1** : to slope gradually **2** : to store on shelves **3** : to dismiss from service or use **4** : to put aside : DEFER ⟨∼ a proposal⟩

shelv·ing \'shel-viŋ\ *n* : material for shelves; *also* : SHELVES

she·nan·i·gan \shə-'na-ni-gən\ *n* **1** : an underhand trick **2** : questionable conduct — usu. used in pl. **3** : high-spirited or mischievous activity — usu. used in pl.

¹shep·herd \'she-pərd\ *n* **1** : one who tends sheep **2** : GERMAN SHEPHERD

²shepherd *vb* : to tend as or in the manner of a shepherd

shep·herd·ess \'she-pər-dəs\ *n* : a woman who tends sheep

sheq·el \'she-kəl\ *n, pl* **sheq·a·lim** \she-'kä-lim\ *var of* SHEKEL

sher·bet \'shər-bət\ *n* [Turk *şerbet,* fr. Per *sharbat,* fr. Ar *sharbah* drink] **1** : a drink of sweetened diluted fruit juice **2** *or* **sher·bert** \-bərt\ : a frozen dessert of fruit juices, sugar, milk or water, and egg whites or gelatin

sherd *var of* SHARD

sher·iff \'sher-əf\ *n* [ME *shirreve,* fr. OE *scīrgerēfa,* lit., shire reeve (local official)] : a county officer charged with the execution of the law and the preservation of order

sher·ry \'sher-ē\ *n, pl* **sherries** [alter. of earlier *sherris* (taken as pl.), fr. *Xeres* (now *Jerez*), Spain] : a fortified wine with a nutty flavor

Shet·land pony \'shet-lənd-\ *n* : any of a breed of small stocky shaggy hardy ponies

shew \'shō\ *Brit var of* SHOW

shi·at·su *also* **shi·at·zu** \shē-'ät-sü\ *n* [short for Jp *shiatsuryōhō*] : a finger massage of those bodily areas used in acupuncture

shib·bo·leth \'shi-bə-ləth\ *n* [Heb *shibbōleth* stream; fr. the use of this word as a test to distinguish the men of Gilead from members of the tribe of Ephraim, who pronounced it *sibbōleth* (Judges 12:5, 6)] **1** : CATCHWORD 2 **2** : language that is a criterion for distinguishing members of a group

¹shield \'shēld\ *n* **1** : a broad piece of defensive armor carried on the arm **2** : something that protects or hides

²shield *vb* : to protect or hide with a shield **syn** protect, guard, safeguard

shier *comparative of* SHY

shiest *superlative of* SHY

¹shift \'shift\ *vb* **1** : EXCHANGE, REPLACE **2** : to change place, position, or direction : MOVE; *also* : to change gears **3** : GET BY, MANAGE

²shift *n* **1** : SCHEME, TRICK **2** : a woman's slip or loose-fitting dress **3** : a change in direction, emphasis, or attitude **4** : a group working together alternating with other groups **5** : TRANSFER **6** : GEARSHIFT

shift·less \'shift-ləs\ *adj* : LAZY, INEFFICIENT — **shift·less·ness** *n*

shifty \'shif-tē\ *adj* **shift·i·er; -est 1** : TRICKY; *also* : ELUSIVE **2** : indicative of a tricky nature ⟨∼ eyes⟩

shih tzu \'shēd-'zü, 'shēt-'sü\ *n, pl* **shih tzus** *also* **shih tzu** *often cap S&T* : any of a breed of small short-legged dogs of Chinese origin that have a short muzzle and a long dense coat

shill \'shil\ *n* : one who acts as a decoy (as for a pitchman) — **shill** *vb*

shil·le·lagh *also* **shil·la·lah** \shə-'lā-lē\ *n* [*Shillelagh,* town in Ireland] : CUDGEL, CLUB

shil·ling \'shi-liŋ\ *n* — see MONEY TABLE

shil·ly–shal·ly \'shi-lē-₁sha-lē\ *vb* **shil·ly–shal·lied; shil·ly–shal·ly·ing 1** : to show hesitation or lack of decisiveness **2** : to waste time

shim \'shim\ *n* : a thin often tapered piece of wood, metal, or stone used (as in leveling) to fill in space

shim•mer \'shi-mər\ *vb* : to shine waveringly or tremulously : GLIMMER **syn** flash, gleam, glint, sparkle, glitter — **shimmer** *n* — **shim•mery** *adj*
shim•my \'shi-mē\ *n, pl* **shimmies** : an abnormal vibration esp. in the front wheels of a motor vehicle — **shimmy** *vb*
¹**shin** \'shin\ *n* : the front part of the leg below the knee
²**shin** *vb* **shinned; shin•ning** : to climb (as a pole) by gripping alternately with arms or hands and legs
shin•bone \'shin-ˌbōn\ *n* : TIBIA
¹**shine** \'shīn\ *vb* **shone** \'shōn\ *or* **shined; shin•ing 1** : to give or cause to give light **2** : GLEAM, GLITTER **3** : to be eminent, conspicuous, or distinguished ⟨gave her a chance to ∼⟩ **4** : POLISH ⟨∼ your shoes⟩
²**shine** *n* **1** : BRIGHTNESS, RADIANCE **2** : LUSTER, BRILLIANCE **3** : fair weather ⟨rain or ∼⟩ **4** : LIKING, FANCY ⟨took a ∼ to them⟩ **5** : a polish given to shoes
shin•er \'shī-nər\ *n* **1** : a small silvery fish; *esp* : any of numerous small freshwater American fishes related to the carp **2** : a discoloration of the skin around the eye due to bruising
¹**shin•gle** \'shiŋ-gəl\ *n* **1** : a small thin piece of building material used in overlapping rows for covering a roof or outside wall **2** : a small sign
²**shingle** *vb* **shin•gled; shin•gling** : to cover with shingles
³**shingle** *n* : a beach strewn with gravel; *also* : coarse gravel (as on a beach)
shin•gles \'shiŋ-gəlz\ *n* : an acute inflammation of the spinal and cranial nerves caused by reactivation of the chicken pox virus and associated with eruptions and pain along the course of the affected nerves
shin•ny \'shi-nē\ *vb* **shin•nied; shin•ny•ing** : SHIN
shin•splints \'shin-ˌsplints\ *n sing or pl* : a condition marked by pain and sometimes tenderness and swelling in the shin caused by repeated small injuries to muscles and associated tissue esp. from running
Shin•to \'shin-ˌtō\ *n* : the indigenous religion of Japan consisting esp. in reverence of the spirits of natural forces and imperial ancestors — **Shin•to•ism** *n* — **Shin•to•ist** *n or adj*
shiny \'shī-nē\ *adj* **shin•i•er; -est** : BRIGHT, RADIANT; *also* : POLISHED
¹**ship** \'ship\ *n* **1** : a large oceangoing boat **2** : a ship's officers and crew **3** : AIRSHIP, AIRCRAFT, SPACECRAFT
²**ship** *vb* **shipped; ship•ping 1** : to put or receive on board a ship for transportation **2** : to have transported by a carrier **3** : to take or draw into a boat ⟨∼ oars⟩ ⟨∼ water⟩ **4** : to engage to serve on a ship — **ship•per** *n*
-ship \ˌship\ *n suffix* **1** : state : condition : quality ⟨friend*ship*⟩ **2** : office : dignity : profession ⟨lord*ship*⟩ ⟨clerk*ship*⟩ **3** : art : skill ⟨horseman*ship*⟩ **4** : something showing, exhibiting, or embodying a quality or state ⟨town*ship*⟩ **5** : one entitled to a (specified) rank, title, or appellation ⟨his Lord*ship*⟩ **6** : the body of persons engaged in a specified activity ⟨reader*ship*⟩
ship•board \'ship-ˌbōrd\ *n* : SHIP
ship•build•er \-ˌbil-dər\ *n* : one who designs or builds ships
ship•fit•ter \-ˌfi-tər\ *n* **1** : one who constructs ships **2** : a naval enlisted man who works as a plumber
ship•mate \-ˌmāt\ *n* : a fellow sailor
ship•ment \-mənt\ *n* : the process of shipping; *also* : the goods shipped
ship•ping *n* **1** : SHIPS; *esp* : ships in one port or belonging to one country **2** : transportation of goods
ship•shape \'ship-ˌshāp\ *adj* : TRIM, TIDY
ship•worm \-ˌwərm\ *n* : any of various wormlike marine clams that burrow in wood and damage wooden ships and wharves
¹**ship•wreck** \-ˌrek\ *n* **1** : a wrecked ship **2** : destruction or loss of a ship **3** : total loss or failure : RUIN
²**shipwreck** *vb* : to cause or meet disaster at sea through destruction or foundering

ship•wright \'ship-ˌrīt\ *n* : a carpenter skilled in ship construction and repair
ship•yard \-ˌyärd\ *n* : a place where ships are built or repaired
shire \'shīr, *in place-name compounds* ˌshir, shər\ *n* : a county in Great Britain
shirk \'shərk\ *vb* : to avoid performing (duty or work) — **shirk•er** *n*
shirr \'shər\ *vb* **1** : to make shirring in **2** : to bake (eggs removed from the shell) until set
shirr•ing \'shər-iŋ\ *n* : a decorative gathering in cloth made by drawing up parallel lines of stitches

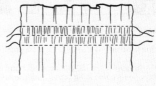

shirring

shirt \'shərt\ *n* **1** : a loose cloth garment usu. having a collar, sleeves, a front opening, and a tail long enough to be tucked inside trousers or a skirt **2** : UNDERSHIRT — **shirt•less** *adj*
shirt•ing \'shir-tiŋ\ *n* : cloth suitable for making shirts
shish ke•bab \'shish-kə-ˌbäb\ *n* [Turk *şiş kebabı,* fr. *şiş* spit + *kebap* roast meat] : kabob cooked on skewers
shiv \'shiv\ *n, slang* : KNIFE
¹**shiv•er** \'shi-vər\ *vb* : TREMBLE, QUIVER **syn** shudder, quaver, shake, quake
²**shiver** *n* : an instance of shivering — **shiv•ery** *adj*
¹**shoal** \'shōl\ *n* **1** : SHALLOW **2** : a sandbank or bar creating a shallow
²**shoal** *n* : a large group (as of fish)
shoat \'shōt\ *n* : a weaned young pig
¹**shock** \'shäk\ *n* **1** : a pile of sheaves of grain or cornstalks set up in a field
²**shock** *n* [MF *choc,* fr. *choquer* to strike against] **1** : a sharp impact or violent shake or jar **2** : a sudden violent mental or emotional disturbance **3** : a state of bodily collapse caused esp. by crushing wounds, blood loss, or burns **4** : the effect of a charge of electricity passing through the body **5** : an attack of stroke or heart disease **6** : SHOCK ABSORBER — **shock•proof** \-ˌprüf\ *adj*
³**shock** *vb* **1** : to strike with surprise, horror, or disgust **2** : to subject to the action of an electrical discharge
⁴**shock** *n* : a thick bushy mass (as of hair)
shock absorber *n* : any of several devices for absorbing the energy of sudden shocks in machinery
shock•er \'shä-kər\ *n* : one that shocks; *esp* : a sensational work of fiction or drama
shock•ing *adj* : extremely startling and offensive — **shock•ing•ly** *adv*
shock therapy *n* : the treatment of mental disorder by induction of coma or convulsions by drugs or electricity
shock wave *n* : a wave formed by the sudden violent compression of the medium through which it travels
¹**shod•dy** \'shä-dē\ *n* **1** : wool reclaimed from old rags; *also* : a fabric made from it **2** : inferior or imitation material
²**shoddy** *adj* **shod•di•er; -est 1** : made of shoddy **2** : poorly done or made — **shod•di•ly** \'shä-də-lē\ *adv* — **shod•di•ness** \-dē-nəs\ *n*
¹**shoe** \'shü\ *n* **1** : a covering for the human foot **2** : HORSESHOE **3** : the part of a brake that presses on the wheel
²**shoe** *vb* **shod** \'shäd\ *also* **shoed** \'shüd\; **shoe•ing** : to put a shoe or shoes on
shoe•lace \'shü-ˌlās\ *n* : a lace or string for fastening a shoe

shoe·mak·er \-ₗmā-kər\ n : one who makes or repairs shoes

shoe·string \-ₗstriŋ\ n 1 : SHOELACE 2 : a small sum of money

sho·gun \'shō-gən\ n [Jp shōgun general] : any of a line of military governors ruling Japan until the revolution of 1867–68

shone past and past part of SHINE

shook past of SHAKE

shook–up \(ₗ)shŭk-'əp\ adj : nervously upset : AGITATED

¹shoot \'shüt\ vb shot \'shät\; shoot·ing 1 : to drive (as an arrow or bullet) forward quickly or forcibly 2 : to hit, kill, or wound with a missile 3 : to cause a missile to be driven forth or forth from ⟨∼ a gun⟩ 4 : to send forth (as a ray of light) 5 : to thrust forward or out 6 : to pass rapidly along ⟨∼ the rapids⟩ 7 : PHOTOGRAPH, FILM 8 : to move swiftly : DART 9 : to grow by or as if by sending out shoots; also : MATURE, DEVELOP — shoot·er n

²shoot n 1 : a plant stem with its leaves and branches esp. when not yet mature 2 : an act of shooting 3 : a shooting match

shooting iron n : FIREARM

shooting star n : METEOR 2

shoot up vb : to inject a narcotic into a vein

¹shop \'shäp\ n [ME shoppe, fr. OE sceoppa booth] 1 : a place where things are made or worked on : FACTORY, MILL 2 : a retail store ⟨dress ∼⟩

²shop vb shopped; shop·ping : to visit stores for purchasing or examining goods — shop·per n

shop·keep·er \'shäp-ₗkē-pər\ n : a retail merchant

shop·lift \-ₗlift\ vb : to steal goods on display from a store — shop·lift·er n

shop·talk \-ₗtȯk\ n : talk about one's business or special interests

shop·worn \-ₗwȯrn\ adj : soiled or frayed from much handling in a store

¹shore \'shȯr\ n : land along the edge of a body of water — shore·less adj

²shore vb shored; shor·ing : to give support to : BRACE

³shore n : ¹PROP

shore·bird \-ₗbərd\ n : any of a suborder of birds (as the plovers and sandpipers) mostly found along the seashore

shore patrol n : a branch of a navy that exercises guard and police functions

shor·ing \'shȯr-iŋ\ n : a group of things that shore something up

shorn past part of SHEAR

¹short \'shȯrt\ adj 1 : not long or tall 2 : not great in distance 3 : brief in time 4 : not coming up to standard or to an expected amount 5 : CURT, ABRUPT 6 : insufficiently supplied 7 : made with shortening : FLAKY 8 : consisting of or relating to a sale of securities or commodities that the seller does not possess or has

not contracted for at the time of the sale ⟨∼ sale⟩ — short·ness n

²short adv 1 : ABRUPTLY, CURTLY 2 : at some point before a goal aimed at

³short n 1 : something shorter than normal or standard 2 pl : drawers or trousers of less than knee length 3 : SHORT CIRCUIT

⁴short vb : SHORT-CIRCUIT

short·age \'shȯr-tij\ n : LACK, DEFICIT

short·cake \'shȯrt-ₗkāk\ n : a dessert consisting of short biscuit spread with sweetened fruit

short·change \-'chānj\ vb : to cheat esp. by giving less than the correct amount of change

short circuit n : a connection made between points in an electric circuit where current is not intended to flow — short–circuit vb

short·com·ing \'shȯrt-ₗkə-miŋ\ n : FAULT 1, FAILING

short·cut \-ₗkət\ n 1 : a route more direct than that usu. taken 2 : a quicker way of doing something

short·en \'shȯrt-ᵊn\ vb : to make or become short syn curtail, abbreviate, abridge, retrench

short·en·ing \'shȯrt-ᵊn-iŋ\ n : a substance (as lard or butter) that makes pastry tender and flaky

short·hand \'shȯrt-ₗhand\ n : a method of writing rapidly by using symbols and abbreviations for letters, words, or phrases : STENOGRAPHY

short·hand·ed \ₗshȯrt-'han-dəd\ adj : short of the needed number of people

short·horn \'shȯrt-ₗhȯrn\ n, often cap : any of a breed of red, roan, or white cattle of English origin

short hundredweight n — see WEIGHT table

short–lived \'shȯrt-'livd, -'līvd\ adj : of short life or duration

short·ly \'shȯrt-lē\ adv 1 : in a few words 2 : in a short time : SOON

short order n : an order for food that can be quickly cooked

short shrift n 1 : a brief respite from death 2 : little consideration

short·sight·ed \'shȯrt-ₗsī-təd\ adj 1 : NEARSIGHTED 2 : lacking foresight — short·sight·ed·ness n

short·stop \-ₗstäp\ n : a baseball player defending the area between second and third base

short story n : a short work of fiction usu. dealing with a few characters and a single event

short–tem·pered \ₗshȯrt-'tem-pərd\ adj : having a quick temper

short–term \'shȯrt-ₗtərm\ adj 1 : occurring over or involving a relatively short period of time 2 : of or relating to a financial transaction based on a term usu. of less than a year

short ton n — see WEIGHT table

short·wave \'shȯrt-ₗwāv\ n : a radio wave with a wavelength between 10 and 100 meters

Sho·sho·ne or Sho·sho·ni \shə-'shō-nē\ n, pl Shoshones or Shoshoni : a member of an American Indian people orig. ranging through California, Idaho, Nevada, Utah, and Wyoming

¹shot \'shät\ n 1 : an act of shooting 2 : a stroke or throw in some games 3 : something that is shot : MIS-

SILE, PROJECTILE; *esp* : small pellets forming a charge for a shotgun **4** : a metal sphere that is thrown for distance in the shot put **5** : RANGE, REACH **6** : MARKSMAN **7** : a single photographic exposure **8** : a single sequence of a motion picture or a television program made by one camera **9** : an injection (as of medicine) into the body **10** : a small serving of undiluted liquor

²**shot** *past and past part of* SHOOT

shot·gun \'shät-ˌgən\ *n* : a gun with a smooth bore used to fire shot at short range

shot put *n* : a field event in which a shot is heaved for distance

should \'shd, shəd\ *past of* SHALL — used as an auxiliary to express condition, obligation or propriety, probability, or futurity from a point of view in the past

¹**shoul·der** \'shōl-dər\ *n* **1** : the part of the body of a person or animal where the arm or foreleg joins the body **2** : either edge of a roadway **3** : a rounded or sloping part (as of a bottle) where the neck joins the body

²**shoulder** *vb* **1** : to push or thrust with the shoulder **2** : to bear on the shoulder **3** : to take the responsibility of

shoulder belt *n* : an automobile safety belt worn across the torso and over the shoulder

shoulder blade *n* : a flat triangular bone at the back of each shoulder

shout \'shaut\ *vb* : to utter a sudden loud cry — **shout** *n*

shove \'shəv\ *vb* **shoved; shov·ing** : to push along, aside, or away — **shove** *n*

¹**shov·el** \'shə-vəl\ *n* **1** : a broad long-handled scoop used to lift and throw material **2** : the amount a shovel will hold

²**shovel** *vb* **-eled** *or* **-elled; -el·ing** *or* **-el·ling 1** : to take up and throw with a shovel **2** : to dig or clean out with a shovel

¹**show** \'shō\ *vb* **showed** \'shōd\; **shown** \'shōn\ *or* **showed; show·ing 1** : to cause or permit to be seen : EXHIBIT ⟨∼ anger⟩ **2** : CONFER, BESTOW ⟨∼ mercy⟩ **3** : REVEAL, DISCLOSE ⟨∼ed courage in battle⟩ **4** : INSTRUCT ⟨∼ me how⟩ **5** : PROVE ⟨∼s he was guilty⟩ **6** : APPEAR **7** : to be noticeable **8** : to be third in a horse race

²**show** *n* **1** : a demonstrative display **2** : outward appearance ⟨a ∼ of resistance⟩ **3** : SPECTACLE **4** : a theatrical presentation **5** : a radio or television program **6** : third place in a horse race

¹**show·case** \'shō-ˌkās\ *n* : a cabinet for displaying items (as in a store)

²**showcase** *vb* **show·cased; show·cas·ing** : EXHIBIT

show·down \'shō-ˌdaun\ *n* : a decisive confrontation or contest; *esp* : the showing of poker hands to determine the winner of a pot

¹**show·er** \'shau-ər\ *n* **1** : a brief fall of rain **2** : a party given by friends who bring gifts **3** : a bath in which water is showered on the person; *also* : a facility (as a stall) for such a bath — **show·ery** *adj*

²**shower** *vb* **1** : to rain or fall in a shower **2** : to bathe in a shower

show·man \'shō-mən\ *n* : one having a gift for dramatization and visual effectiveness — **show·man·ship** *n*

show-off \'shō-ˌof\ *n* : one that seeks to attract attention by conspicuous behavior

show off *vb* **1** : to display proudly **2** : to act as a show≠ off

show·piece \'shō-ˌpēs\ *n* : an outstanding example used for exhibition

show·place \-ˌplās\ *n* : an estate or building that is a showpiece

show up *vb* : ARRIVE

showy \'shō-ē\ *adj* **show·i·er; -est** : superficially impressive or striking — **show·i·ly** \'shō-ə-lē\ *adv* — **show·i·ness** \-ē-nəs\ *n*

shpt *abbr* shipment

shrap·nel \'shrap-nəl\ *n, pl* **shrapnel** : bomb, mine, or shell fragments

¹**shred** \'shred\ *n* : a narrow strip cut or torn off : a small fragment

²**shred** *vb* **shred·ded; shred·ding** : to cut or tear into shreds

shrew \'shrü\ *n* **1** : any of a family of very small mammals with velvety fur that are related to the moles **2** : a scolding woman

shrewd \'shrüd\ *adj* : CLEVER, ASTUTE — **shrewd·ly** *adv* — **shrewd·ness** *n*

shrew·ish \'shrü-ish\ *adj* : having an irritable disposition : ILL-TEMPERED

shriek \'shrēk\ *n* : a shrill cry : SCREAM, YELL — **shriek** *vb*

shrift \'shrift\ *n, archaic* : the act of shriving

shrike \'shrīk\ *n* : any of numerous usu. largely grayish or brownish birds that often impale their usu. insect prey upon thorns before devouring it

¹**shrill** \'shril\ *vb* : to make a high-pitched piercing sound

²**shrill** *adj* : high-pitched : PIERCING ⟨∼ whistle⟩ — **shril·ly** *adv*

shrimp \'shrimp\ *n, pl* **shrimps** *or* **shrimp 1** : any of various small marine crustaceans related to the lobsters **2** : a small or puny person

shrine \'shrīn\ *n* [ME, receptacle for the relics of a saint, fr. OE *scrīn*, fr. L *scrinium* case, chest] **1** : the tomb of a saint; *also* : a place where devotion is paid to a saint or deity **2** : a place or object hallowed by its associations

¹**shrink** \'shriŋk\ *vb* **shrank** \'shraŋk\ *also* **shrunk** \'shrəŋk\; **shrunk** *or* **shrunk·en** \'shrəŋ-kən\; **shrink·ing 1** : to draw back or away **2** : to become smaller or more compact **3** : to lessen in value **syn** contract, constrict, compress, condense — **shrink·able** *adj*

²**shrink** *n* : a clinical psychiatrist or psychologist

shrink·age \'shriŋ-kij\ *n* **1** : the act of shrinking **2** : the amount lost by shrinkage

shrive \'shrīv\ *vb* **shrived** *or* **shrove** \'shrōv\; **shriv·en** \'shri-vən\ *or* **shrived** [ME, fr. OE *scrīfan* to prescribe, allot, shrive, fr. L *scribere* to write] : to minister the sacrament of penance to

shriv·el \'shri-vəl\ *vb* **-eled** *or* **-elled; -el·ing** *or* **-el·ling** : to shrink and draw into wrinkles : DWINDLE

¹**shroud** \'shraud\ *n* **1** : something that covers or screens **2** : a cloth placed over a dead body **3** : any of the ropes leading from the masthead of a ship to the side to support the mast

²**shroud** *vb* : to veil or screen from view

shrub \'shrəb\ *n* : a low usu. several-stemmed woody plant — **shrub·by** *adj*

shrub·bery \'shrə-bə-rē\ *n, pl* **-ber·ies** : a planting or growth of shrubs

shrug \'shrəg\ *vb* **shrugged; shrug·ging** : to hunch (the shoulders) up to express aloofness, indifference, or uncertainty — **shrug** *n*

shrug off *vb* **1** : to brush aside : MINIMIZE **2** : to shake off **3** : to remove (a garment) by wriggling out

¹**shuck** \'shək\ *n* : SHELL, HUSK

²**shuck** *vb* : to strip of shucks

shud·der \'shə-dər\ *vb* : TREMBLE, QUAKE — **shudder** *n*

shuf·fle \'shə-fəl\ *vb* **shuf·fled; shuf·fling 1** : to mix in a disorderly mass **2** : to rearrange the order of (cards in a pack) by mixing two parts of the pack together **3** : to shift from place to place **4** : to move with a sliding or dragging gait **5** : to dance in a slow lagging manner — **shuffle** *n*

shuf·fle·board \'shə-fəl-ˌbōrd\ *n* : a game in which players use long-handled cues to shove disks into scoring areas marked on a smooth surface

shun \'shən\ *vb* **shunned; shun·ning** : to avoid deliberately or habitually **syn** evade, elude, escape, duck

¹**shunt** \'shənt\ *vb* [ME, to flinch] : to turn off to one

side; *esp* : to switch (a train) from one track to another

²**shunt** *n* 1 : a method or device for turning or thrusting aside 2 : a conductor joining two points in an electrical circuit forming an alternate path through which a portion of the current may pass

shut \'shət\ *vb* **shut; shut·ting** 1 : CLOSE 2 : to forbid entrance into 3 : to lock up 4 : to fold together ⟨~ a penknife⟩ 5 : to cease or suspend activity ⟨~ down an assembly line⟩

shut·down \-ˌdaün\ *n* : a temporary cessation of activity (as in a factory)

shut–in \'shət-ˌin\ *n* : an invalid confined to home, a room, or bed

shut·out \'shət-ˌaüt\ *n* : a game or contest in which one side fails to score

shut out *vb* 1 : EXCLUDE 2 : to prevent (an opponent) from scoring in a game or contest

shut·ter \'shə-tər\ *n* 1 : a movable cover for a door or window : BLIND 2 : the part of a camera that opens and closes to expose the film

shut·ter·bug \'shə-tər-ˌbəg\ *n* : a photography enthusiast

¹**shut·tle** \'shət-ᵊl\ *n* 1 : an instrument used in weaving for passing the horizontal threads between the vertical threads 2 : a vehicle traveling back and forth over a short route ⟨a ~ bus⟩ 3 : SPACE SHUTTLE

²**shuttle** *vb* **shut·tled; shut·tling** : to move frequently back and forth

shut·tle·cock \'shət-ᵊl-ˌkäk\ *n* : a light conical object (as of cork or plastic) used in badminton

shut up *vb* : to cease or cause to cease talking

¹**shy** \'shī\ *adj* **shi·er** *or* **shy·er** \'shī-ər\; **shi·est** *or* **shy·est** \'shī-əst\ 1 : easily frightened : TIMID 2 : WARY 3 : BASHFUL 4 : DEFICIENT, LACKING — **shy·ly** *adv* — **shy·ness** *n*

²**shy** *vb* **shied; shy·ing** 1 : to show a dislike : RECOIL 2 : to start suddenly aside through fright ⟨the horse *shied*⟩

shy·ster \'shīs-tər\ *n* : an unscrupulous lawyer or politician

Si *symbol* silicon

Si·a·mese \ˌsī-ə-ˈmēz, -ˈmēs\ *n, pl* **Sia·mese** : THAI — **Siamese** *adj*

Siamese twin *n* [fr. Chang †1874 and Eng †1874 twins born in Siam with bodies united] : one of a pair of twins with bodies joined together at birth

¹**sib·i·lant** \'si-bə-lənt\ *adj* : having, containing, or producing the sound of or a sound resembling that of the *s* or the *sh* in *sash* — **sib·i·lant·ly** *adv*

²**sibilant** *n* : a sibilant speech sound (as English \s\, \z\, \sh\, \zh\, \ch (=tsh)\, or \j (=dzh)\)

sib·ling \'si-bliŋ\ *n* : a brother or sister considered irrespective of sex; *also* : one of two or more offspring having one common parent

sib·yl \'si-bəl\ *n, often cap* : PROPHETESS — **sib·yl·line** \-bə-ˌlīn, -ˌlēn\ *adj*

sic \'sik, 'sēk\ *adv* : intentionally so written — used after a printed word or passage to indicate that it exactly reproduces an original ⟨said he seed [~] it all⟩

sick \'sik\ *adj* 1 : not in good health : ILL; *also* : of, relating to, or intended for use in sickness ⟨~ pay⟩ 2 : NAUSEATED 3 : DISGUSTED 4 : PINING 5 : MACABRE, SADISTIC ⟨~ jokes⟩ — **sick·ly** *adj*

sick·bed \'sik-ˌbed\ *n* : a bed on which one lies sick

sick·en \'si-kən\ *vb* : to make or become sick — **sick·en·ing·ly** *adv*

sick·le \'si-kəl\ *n* : a cutting tool consisting of a curved metal blade with a short handle

sickle–cell anemia *n* : an inherited anemia in which red blood cells tend to become crescent-shaped and cannot carry oxygen properly and which occurs esp. in individuals of African, Mediterranean, or southwest Asian ancestry

sick·ness \'sik-nəs\ *n* 1 : ill health; *also* : a specific disease 2 : NAUSEA

side \'sīd\ *n* 1 : the right or left part of the trunk of a body 2 : a place away from a central point or line 3 : a border of an object; *esp* : one of the longer borders as contrasted with an end 4 : an outer surface of an object 5 : a position regarded as opposite to another 6 : a body of contestants — **side** *adj*

side·arm \-ˌärm\ *adj* : made with a sideways sweep of the arm — **sidearm** *adv*

side arm *n* : a weapon worn at the side or in the belt

side·bar \'sīd-ˌbär\ *n* : a short news story accompanying a major story and presenting related information

side·board \-ˌbōrd\ *n* : a piece of dining-room furniture for holding articles of table service

side·burns \-ˌbərnz\ *n pl* : whiskers on the side of the face in front of the ears

side by side *adv* 1 : beside one another 2 : in the same place, time, or circumstance — **side–by–side** *adj*

side·car \-ˌkär\ *n* : a one-wheeled passenger car attached to the side of a motorcycle

side effect *n* : a secondary and usu. adverse effect (as of a drug)

side·kick \'sīd-ˌkik\ *n* : PAL, PARTNER

¹**side·long** \'sīd-ˌlȯŋ\ *adv* : in the direction of or along the side : OBLIQUELY

²**sidelong** *adj* : directed to one side ⟨~ look⟩

side·man \'sīd-ˌman\ *n* : a member of a jazz or swing orchestra

side·piece \-ˌpēs\ *n* : a piece forming or contained in the side of something

si·de·re·al \sī-ˈdir-ē-əl, sə-\ *adj* [L *sidereus*, fr. *sider-*, *sidas* star, constellation] 1 : of or relating to the stars 2 : measured by the apparent motion of the stars

side·sad·dle \'sīd-ˌsad-ᵊl\ *n* : a saddle for women on which the rider sits with both legs on the same side of the horse — **sidesaddle** *adv*

side·show \'sīd-ˌshō\ *n* 1 : a minor show offered in addition to a main exhibition (as of a circus) 2 : an incidental diversion

side·step \-ˌstep\ *vb* 1 : to step aside 2 : AVOID, EVADE

side·stroke \-ˌstrōk\ *n* : a swimming stroke which is executed on the side and in which the arms are swept backward and downward and the legs do a scissors kick

side·swipe \-ˌswīp\ *vb* : to strike with a glancing blow along the side — **sideswipe** *n*

¹side·track \-ˌtrak\ *n* : SIDING 1

²sidetrack *vb* 1 : to switch from a main railroad line to a siding 2 : to turn aside from a purpose

side·walk \'sīd-ˌwȯk\ *n* : a paved walk at the side of a road or street

side·wall \-ˌwȯl\ *n* 1 : a wall forming the side of something 2 : the side of an automobile tire

side·ways \-ˌwāz\ *adv or adj* 1 : from the side 2 : with one side to the front 3 : to, toward, or at one side

side·wind·er \-ˌwīn-dər\ *n* : a small pale-colored desert rattlesnake of the southwestern U.S.

sid·ing \'sī-diŋ\ *n* 1 : a short railroad track connected with the main track 2 : material (as boards) covering the outside of frame buildings

si·dle \'sīd-ᵊl\ *vb* **si·dled; si·dling** : to move sideways or with one side foremost

SIDS *abbr* sudden infant death syndrome

siege \'sēj\ *n* 1 : the placing of an army around or before a fortified place to force its surrender 2 : a persistent attack (as of illness)

sie·mens \'sē-mənz, 'zē-\ *n* : a unit of conductance equivalent to one ampere per volt

si·er·ra \sē-'er-ə\ *n* [Sp, lit., saw, fr. L *serra*] : a range of mountains esp. with jagged peaks

si·es·ta \sē-'es-tə\ *n* [Sp, fr. L *sexta (hora)* noon, lit., sixth hour] : a midday rest or nap

sieve \'siv\ *n* : a utensil with meshes or holes to separate finer particles from coarser or solids from liquids

sift \'sift\ *vb* 1 : to pass through a sieve 2 : to separate with or as if with a sieve 3 : to examine carefully 4 : to scatter by or as if by passing through a sieve — **sift·er** *n*

sig *abbr* 1 signal 2 signature

sigh \'sī\ *vb* 1 : to let out a deep audible breath (as in weariness or sorrow) 2 : GRIEVE, YEARN — **sigh** *n*

¹sight \'sīt\ *n* 1 : something seen or worth seeing 2 : the process or power of seeing; *esp* : the sense of which the eye is the receptor and by which qualities of appearance (as position, shape, and color) are perceived 3 : INSPECTION 4 : a device (as a small bead on a gun barrel) that aids the eye in aiming 5 : VIEW, GLIMPSE 6 : the range of vision — **sight·less** *adj*

²sight *vb* 1 : to get sight of 2 : to aim by means of a sight

sight·ed \'sī-təd\ *adj* : having sight

sight·ly \-lē\ *adj* : pleasing to the sight

sight-see·ing \'sīt-ˌsē-iŋ\ *adj* : engaged in or used for seeing sights of interest — **sight·seer** \-ˌsē-ər\ *n*

sig·ma \'sig-mə\ *n* : the 18th letter of the Greek alphabet — Σ or σ or ς

¹sign \'sīn\ *n* 1 : a gesture expressing a command, wish, or thought 2 : SYMBOL 3 : a notice publicly displayed for advertising purposes or for giving direction or warning 4 : OMEN, PORTENT 5 : TRACE, VESTIGE

²sign *vb* 1 : to mark with a sign 2 : to represent by a sign 3 : to make a sign or signal 4 : to write one's name in token of assent or obligation 5 : to assign legally 6 : to use sign language — **sign·er** *n*

¹sig·nal \'sig-nəl\ *n* 1 : a sign agreed on as the start of some joint action 2 : a sign giving warning or notice of something 3 : the message, sound, or image transmitted in electronic communication (as radio)

²signal *vb* **-naled** *or* **-nalled; -nal·ing** *or* **-nal·ling** 1 : to notify by a signal 2 : to communicate by signals

³signal *adj* : DISTINGUISHED ⟨a ∼ honor⟩ — **sig·nal·ly** *adv*

sig·nal·ise *Brit var of* SIGNALIZE

sig·nal·ize \'sig-nə-ˌlīz\ *vb* **-ized; -iz·ing** : to point out or make conspicuous — **sig·nal·i·za·tion** \ˌsig-nə-lə-'zā-shən\ *n*

sig·nal·man \'sig-nəl-mən, -ˌman\ *n* : a person who signals or works with signals

sig·na·to·ry \'sig-nə-ˌtȯr-ē\ *n, pl* **-ries** : a person or government that signs jointly with others — **signatory** *adj*

sig·na·ture \'sig-nə-ˌchu̇r\ *n* 1 : the name of a person written by himself or herself 2 : the sign placed after the clef to indicate the key or the meter of a piece of music

sign·board \'sīn-ˌbȯrd\ *n* : a board bearing a sign or notice

sig·net \'sig-nət\ *n* : a small intaglio seal (as in a ring)

sig·nif·i·cance \sig-'ni-fi-kəns\ *n* 1 : something signified : MEANING 2 : SUGGESTIVENESS 3 : CONSEQUENCE, IMPORTANCE

sig·nif·i·cant \-kənt\ *adj* 1 : having meaning; *esp* : having a hidden or special meaning 2 : having or likely to have considerable influence or effect : IMPORTANT — **sig·nif·i·cant·ly** *adv*

sig·ni·fy \'sig-nə-ˌfī\ *vb* **-fied; -fy·ing** 1 : to show by a sign 2 : MEAN, IMPORT 3 : to have significance — **sig·ni·fi·ca·tion** \ˌsig-nə-fə-'kā-shən\ *n*

sign in *vb* : to make a record of arrival (as by signing a register)

sign language *n* : a formal system of hand gestures used for communication (as by the deaf)

sign off *vb* : to announce the end (as of a program or broadcast)

sign of the cross : a gesture of the hand forming a cross (as to invoke divine blessing)

sign on *vb* 1 : ENLIST 2 : to announce the start of broadcasting for the day

sign out *vb* : to make a record of departure (as by signing a register)

sign·post \'sīn-ˌpōst\ *n* : a post bearing a sign

Sikh \'sēk\ *n* : an adherent of a religion of India marked by rejection of caste — **Sikh·ism** *n*

si·lage \'sī-lij\ *n* : fodder fermented (as in a silo) to produce a rich moist animal feed

¹si·lence \'sī-ləns\ *n* 1 : the state of being silent 2 : STILLNESS 3 : SECRECY

²silence *vb* **si·lenced; si·lenc·ing** 1 : to reduce to silence : STILL 2 : to cause to cease hostile firing or criticism

si·lenc·er \'sī-lən-sər\ *n* : a device for muffling the noise of a gunshot

si·lent \'sī-lənt\ *adj* 1 : not speaking : MUTE; *also* : TACITURN 2 : STILL, QUIET 3 : performed or borne without utterance **syn** reticent, reserved, closemouthed, close — **si·lent·ly** *adv*

¹sil·hou·ette \ˌsi-lə-'wet\ *n* [F] 1 : a representation of the outlines of an object filled in with black or some other uniform color 2 : OUTLINE ⟨∼ of a ship⟩

²silhouette *vb* **-ett·ed; -ett·ing** : to represent by a silhouette; *also* : to show against a light background

sil·i·ca \'si-li-kə\ *n* : a mineral that consists of silicon and oxygen

sil·i·cate \'si-lə-ˌkāt, 'si-li-kət\ *n* : a chemical salt that consists of a metal combined with silicon and oxygen

si·li·ceous *or* **si·li·cious** \sə-'li-shəs\ *adj* : of, relating to, or containing silica or a silicate

sil·i·con \'si-li-kən, 'si-lə-ˌkän\ *n* : a nonmetallic chemical element that occurs in combination as the most abundant element next to oxygen in the earth's crust and is used esp. in electronics — see ELEMENT table

sil·i·cone \'si-lə-ˌkōn\ *n* : an organic silicon compound used esp. for lubricants and varnishes

sil·i·co·sis \ˌsi-lə-'kō-səs\ *n* : a lung disease caused by prolonged inhaling of silica dusts

silk \'silk\ *n* 1 : a fine strong lustrous protein fiber produced by insect larvae usu. for their cocoons; *esp* : one from moth larvae (**silk·worms** \-ˌwərmz\) used for cloth 2 : thread or cloth made from silk — **silk·en** \'sil-kən\ *adj* — **silky** *adj*

silk screen *n* : a stencil process in which coloring matter is forced through the meshes of a prepared silk or

organdy screen; *also* : a print made by this process
— **silk–screen** *vb*

sill \\'sil\ *n* : a heavy crosspiece (as of wood or stone)
that forms the bottom member of a window frame or
a doorway; *also* : a horizontal supporting piece at the
base of a structure

sil•ly \\'si-lē\ *adj* **sil•li•er; -est** [ME *sely, silly* happy, innocent, pitiable, feeble, fr. OE *sǣlig*] : FOOLISH, AB-
SURD, STUPID — **sil•li•ness** *n*

si•lo \\'sī-lō\ *n, pl* **silos** [Sp] **1** : a trench, pit,
or esp. a tall cylinder for making and
storing silage **2** : an underground structure for housing a guided missile

¹**silt** \\'silt\ *n* **1** : fine earth; *esp* : particles of such soil
floating in rivers, ponds, or lakes **2** : a deposit (as by
a river) of silt — **silty** *adj*

²**silt** *vb* : to obstruct or cover with silt — **silt•ation** \sil-
'tā-shən\ *n*

Si•lu•ri•an \sī-'lùr-ē-ən\ *adj* : of, relating to, or being
the period of the Paleozoic era between the Ordovician and the Devonian marked by the appearance of
the first land plants — **Silurian** *n*

¹**sil•ver** \\'sil-vər\ *n* **1** : a white ductile metallic chemical
element that takes a high polish and is a better conductor of heat and electricity than any other substance — see ELEMENT table **2** : coin made of silver
3 : FLATWARE **4** : a grayish white color — **sil•very** *adj*

²**silver** *adj* **1** : relating to, made of, or coated with silver
2 : SILVERY

³**silver** *vb* **sil•vered; sil•ver•ing** : to coat with or as if
with silver — **sil•ver•er** *n*

silver bromide *n* : a light-sensitive compound used
esp. in photography

sil•ver•fish \\'sil-vər-ˌfish\ *n* : any of various small
wingless insects found in houses and sometimes injurious esp. to sized paper and starched clothes

silver iodide *n* : a light-sensitive compound used in
photography, rainmaking, and medicine

silver maple *n* : a No. American maple with deeply cut
leaves that are green above and silvery white below

silver nitrate *n* : a soluble compound used in photography and as an antiseptic

sil•ver•ware \\'sil-vər-ˌwar\ *n* : FLATWARE

sim•i•an \\'si-mē-ən\ *n* : MONKEY, APE — **simian** *adj*

sim•i•lar \\'si-mə-lər\ *adj* : marked by correspondence
or resemblance **syn** alike, akin, comparable, parallel
— **sim•i•lar•i•ty** \ˌsi-mə-'lar-ə-tē\ *n* — **sim•i•lar•ly**
adv

sim•i•le \\'si-mə-(ˌ)lē\ *n* [ME, fr. L, likeness, comparison, fr. neut. of *similis* like, similar] : a figure of
speech in which two dissimilar things are compared
by the use of *like* or *as* (as in "cheeks like roses")

si•mil•i•tude \sə-'mi-lə-ˌtüd, -ˌtyüd\ *n* : LIKENESS, RE-
SEMBLANCE

sim•mer \\'si-mər\ *vb* **sim•mered; sim•mer•ing 1** : to
stew at or just below the boiling point **2** : to be on the
point of bursting out with violence or emotional disturbance — **simmer** *n*

si•mo•nize \\'sī-mə-ˌnīz\ *vb* **-nized; -niz•ing** : to polish
with or as if with wax

si•mo•ny \\'sī-mə-nē, 'si-\ *n* [ME *symonie,* fr. LL *simo-
nia,* fr. *Simon* Magus sorcerer of Samaria in Acts 8:9–
24] : the buying or selling of a church office

sim•pa•ti•co \sim-'pä-ti-ˌkō, -'pa-\ *adj* : CONGENIAL,
LIKABLE

sim•per \\'sim-pər\ *vb* : to smile in a silly manner —
simper *n*

sim•ple \\'sim-pəl\ *adj* **sim•pler** \-pə-lər\; **sim•plest** \-pə-
ləst\ [ME, fr. OF, plain, uncomplicated, artless, fr. L
simplus, simplex, lit., single; L *simplus* fr. *sim-* one
+ *-plus* multiplied by; L *simplex* fr. *sim-* + *-plex*
-fold] **1** : free from dishonesty or vanity : INNOCENT
2 : free from ostentation **3** : of humble origin or modest position **4** : STUPID **5** : not complex : PLAIN ⟨a ∼
melody⟩ ⟨∼ directions⟩ **6** : lacking education, experience, or intelligence **7** : developing from a single
ovary ⟨a ∼ fruit⟩ **syn** easy, facile, light, effortless —
sim•ple•ness *n* — **sim•ply** *adv*

simple interest *n* : interest paid or computed on the
original principal only of a loan or on the amount of
an account

sim•ple•ton \\'sim-pəl-tən\ *n* : FOOL

sim•plic•i•ty \sim-'pli-sə-tē\ *n* **1** : lack of complication
: CLEARNESS **2** : CANDOR, ARTLESSNESS **3** : plainness in
manners or way of life **4** : SILLINESS, FOLLY

sim•pli•fy \\'sim-plə-ˌfī\ *vb* **-fied; -fy•ing** : to make less
complex — **sim•pli•fi•ca•tion** \ˌsim-plə-fə-'kā-shən\
n

sim•plis•tic \sim-'plis-tik\ *adj* : excessively simple
: tending to overlook complexities ⟨a ∼ solution⟩

sim•u•late \\'sim-yə-ˌlāt\ *vb* **-lat•ed; -lat•ing** : to give or
create the effect or appearance of : IMITATE; *also* : to
make a simulation of — **sim•u•la•tor** \\'sim-yə-ˌlā-tər\
n

sim•u•la•tion \ˌsim-yə-'lā-shən\ *n* **1** : the act or process
of simulating **2** : an object that is not genuine **3** : the
imitation by one system or process of the way in
which another system or process works

si•mul•ta•ne•ous \ˌsī-məl-'tā-nē-əs, ˌsi-\ *adj* : occurring
or operating at the same time — **si•mul•ta•ne•ous•-
ly** *adv* — **si•mul•ta•ne•ous•ness** *n*

¹**sin** \\'sin\ *n* **1** : an offense esp. against God **2** : FAULT
3 : a weakened state of human nature in which the
self is estranged from God — **sin•less** *adj*

²**sin** *vb* **sinned; sin•ning** : to commit a sin — **sin•ner** *n*

¹**since** \\'sins\ *adv* **1** : from a past time until now **2** : backward in time : AGO **3** : after a time in the past

²**since** *conj* **1** : from the time when **2** : seeing that : BE-
CAUSE

³**since** *prep* **1** : in the period after ⟨changes made ∼ the
war⟩ **2** : continuously from ⟨has been here ∼ 1980⟩

sin•cere \sin-'sir\ *adj* **sin•cer•er; sin•cer•est 1** : free
from hypocrisy : HONEST **2** : GENUINE, REAL — **sin•-
cere•ly** *adv* — **sin•cer•i•ty** \-'ser-ə-tē\ *n*

si•ne•cure \\'sī-ni-ˌkyür, 'si-\ *n* : a paying job that requires little or no work

si•ne die \ˌsī-ni-'dī-ˌē, ˌsi-nā-'dē-ˌā\ *adv* [L, without
day] : INDEFINITELY

si•ne qua non \ˌsi-ni-ˌkwä-ˈnän, -ˈnōn\ n, pl sine qua nons also sine qui•bus non \-ˈkwi-(ˌ)bùs-\ [LL, without which not] : something indispensable or essential

sin•ew \ˈsin-yü\ n 1 : TENDON 2 : physical strength — sin•ewy adj

sin•ful \ˈsin-fəl\ adj : marked by or full of sin : WICKED — sin•ful•ly adv — sin•ful•ness n

¹sing \ˈsiŋ\ vb sang \ˈsaŋ\ or sung \ˈsəŋ\; sung; sing•ing 1 : to produce musical tones with the voice; also : to utter with musical tones 2 : to make a prolonged shrill sound ⟨locusts ~ing⟩ 3 : to produce harmonious sustained sounds ⟨birds ~ing⟩ 4 : CHANT, INTONE 5 : to write poetry; also : to celebrate in song or verse 6 : to give information or evidence — sing•er n

²sing abbr singular

Sin•ga•por•ean \ˌsiŋ-ə-ˈpōr-ē-ən\ n : a native or inhabitant of Singapore — Singaporean adj

singe \ˈsinj\ vb singed; singe•ing : to scorch lightly the outside of; esp : to remove the hair or down from (a plucked fowl) with flame

¹sin•gle \ˈsiŋ-gəl\ adj 1 : UNMARRIED 2 : being alone : being the only one 3 : having only one feature or part 4 : made for one person syn sole, unique, lone, solitary, separate, particular — sin•gle•ness n — sin•gly adv

²single vb sin•gled; sin•gling 1 : to select (one) from a group 2 : to hit a single

³single n 1 : a separate person or thing; also : an unmarried person 2 : a hit in baseball that enables the batter to reach first base 3 pl : a tennis match with one player on each side

single bond n : a chemical bond in which one pair of electrons is shared by two atoms in a molecule

single–lens reflex n : a camera having a single lens that forms an image which is reflected to the viewfinder or recorded on film

sin•gle•tree \-ˌtrē\ n : WHIFFLETREE

sin•gu•lar \ˈsiŋ-gyə-lər\ adj 1 : of, relating to, or constituting a word form denoting one person, thing, or instance 2 : OUTSTANDING, EXCEPTIONAL 3 : of unusual quality 4 : ODD, PECULIAR — singular n — sin•gu•lar•i•ty \ˌsiŋ-gyə-ˈlar-ə-tē\ n — sin•gu•lar•ly adv

sin•is•ter \ˈsi-nəs-tər\ adj [ME, fr. L, on the left side, inauspicious] 1 : singularly evil or productive of evil 2 : accompanied by or leading to disaster syn baleful, malign, malefic, maleficent

¹sink \ˈsiŋk\ vb sank \ˈsaŋk\ or sunk \ˈsəŋk\; sunk; sink•ing 1 : SUBMERGE 2 : to descend lower and lower 3 : to grow less in volume or height 4 : to slope downward 5 : to penetrate downward 6 : to fail in health or strength 7 : LAPSE, DEGENERATE 8 : to cause (a ship) to descend to the bottom 9 : to make (a hole or shaft) by digging, boring, or cutting 10 : INVEST — sink•able adj

²sink n 1 : DRAIN, SEWER 2 : a basin connected with a drain 3 : an extensive depression in the land surface

sink•er \ˈsiŋ-kər\ n : a weight for sinking a fishing line or net

sink•hole \ˈsiŋk-ˌhōl\ n : a hollow place in which drainage collects

sin tax n : a tax on substances or activities considered sinful or harmful

sin•u•ous \ˈsin-yə-wəs\ adj : bending in and out : WINDING — sin•u•os•i•ty \ˌsin-yə-ˈwä-sə-tē\ n

si•nus \ˈsī-nəs\ n [ME, fr. ML, fr. L, curve, hollow] 1 : any of several cavities of the skull usu. connecting with the nostrils 2 : a space forming a channel (as for the passage of blood)

si•nus•itis \ˌsī-nə-ˈsī-təs\ n : inflammation of a sinus of the skull

Sioux \ˈsü\ n, pl Sioux \same or ˈsüz\ [F] : DAKOTA

sip \ˈsip\ vb sipped; sip•ping : to drink in small quantities — sip n

¹si•phon \ˈsī-fən\ n 1 : a bent tube through which a liquid can be transferred by means of air pressure up and over the edge of one container and into another container placed at a lower level 2 usu sy•phon : a bottle that ejects soda water through a tube when a valve is opened

siphon 1

²siphon vb si•phoned; si•phon•ing : to draw off by means of a siphon

sir \ˈsər\ n [ME sire sire, fr. OF, fr. L senior, compar. of senex old, old man] 1 : a man of rank or position — used as a title before the given name of a knight or baronet 2 — used as a usu. respectful form of address

Si•rach \ˈsī-rak, sə-ˈräk\ n — see BIBLE table

¹sire \ˈsīr\ n 1 : FATHER; also, archaic : FOREFATHER 2 archaic : LORD — used as a form of address and a title 3 : the male parent of an animal (as a horse or dog)

²sire vb sired; sir•ing : BEGET

si•ren \ˈsī-rən\ n 1 : a seductive or alluring woman 2 : an electrically operated device for producing a loud shrill warning signal — siren adj

sir•loin \ˈsər-ˌlòin\ n [alter. of earlier surloin, modif. of MF surlonge, fr. sur over (fr. L super) + longe loin] : a cut of beef taken from the part in front of the round

sirup var of SYRUP

si·sal \'sī-səl, -zəl\ *n* : a strong cordage fiber from an agave; *also* : this agave

sis·sy \'si-sē\ *n, pl* **sissies** : an effeminate boy or man; *also* : a timid or cowardly person

sis·ter \'sis-tər\ *n* 1 : a female having one or both parents in common with another individual 2 : a member of a religious order of women : NUN 3 *chiefly Brit* : NURSE 4 : a woman regarded as a comrade — **sis·ter·ly** *adj*

sis·ter·hood \-,hùd\ *n* 1 : the state of being a sister 2 : a community or society of sisters 3 : the solidarity of women based on shared conditions

sis·ter–in–law \'sis-tə-rən-,lò\ *n, pl* **sisters–in–law** : the sister of one's spouse; *also* : the wife of one's brother

sit \'sit\ *vb* **sat** \'sat\; **sit·ting** 1 : to rest upon the buttocks or haunches 2 : ROOST, PERCH 3 : to occupy a seat 4 : to hold a session 5 : to cover eggs for hatching : BROOD 6 : to pose for a portrait 7 : to remain quiet or inactive 8 : FIT 9 : to cause (oneself) to be seated 10 : to place in position 11 : to keep one's seat on ⟨∼ a horse⟩ 12 : BABY-SIT — **sit·ter** *n*

si·tar \si-'tär\ *n* [Hindi *sitār*] : an Indian lute with a long neck and a varying number of strings

sit·com \'sit-,käm\ *n* : SITUATION COMEDY

site \'sīt\ *n* : LOCATION

sit–in \'sit-,in\ *n* : an act of sitting in the seats or on the floor of an establishment as a means of organized protest

sit·u·at·ed \'si-chə-,wā-təd\ *adj* : LOCATED, PLACED

sit·u·a·tion \,si-chə-'wā-shən\ *n* 1 : LOCATION, SITE 2 : JOB 3 : CONDITION, CIRCUMSTANCES

situation comedy *n* : a radio or television comedy series that involves a continuing cast of characters in a succession of episodes

sit–up \'sit-,əp\ *n* : an exercise performed from a supine position by raising the trunk to a sitting position without lifting the feet and returning to the original position

six \'siks\ *n* 1 : one more than five 2 : the 6th in a set or series 3 : something having six units — **six** *adj or pron* — **sixth** \'siksth\ *adj or adv or n*

six–gun \'siks-,gən\ *n* : a 6-chambered revolver

six–pack \-,pak\ *n* : six bottles or cans (as of beer) packaged and purchased together; *also* : the contents of a six-pack

six·pence \-pəns, *US also* -,pens\ *n* : the sum of six pence; *also* : an English silver coin of this value

six–shoot·er \'siks-,shü-tər\ *n* : SIX-GUN

six·teen \,siks-'tēn\ *n* : one more than 15 — **sixteen** *adj or pron* — **six·teenth** \-'tēnth\ *adj or n*

six·ty \'siks-tē\ *n, pl* **sixties** : six times 10 — **six·ti·eth** \'siks-tē-əth\ *adj or n* — **sixty** *adj or pron*

siz·able *or* **size·able** \'sī-zə-bəl\ *adj* : quite large — **siz·ably** \-blē\ *adv*

¹size \'sīz\ *n* : physical extent or bulk : DIMENSIONS; *also* : considerable proportions — **sized** \'sīzd\ *adj*

²size *vb* **sized; siz·ing** 1 : to grade or classify according to size 2 : to form a judgment of ⟨∼ up the situation⟩

³size *n* : a gluey material used for filling the pores in paper, plaster, or textiles — **siz·ing** *n*

⁴size *vb* **sized; siz·ing** : to cover, stiffen, or glaze with size

siz·zle \'si-zəl\ *vb* **siz·zled; siz·zling** : to fry or shrivel up with a hissing sound — **sizzle** *n*

SJ *abbr* Society of Jesus

SK *abbr* Saskatchewan

ska \'skä\ *n* : popular music of Jamaican origin combining traditional Caribbean rhythms and jazz

¹skate \'skāt\ *n, pl* **skates** *also* **skate** : any of a family of rays with thick broad winglike fins

²skate *n* 1 : a metal frame and runner attached to a shoe and used for gliding over ice 2 : ROLLER SKATE — **skate** *vb* — **skat·er** *n*

skate·board \'skāt-,bòrd\ *n* : a short board mounted on small wheels — **skate·board·er** *n* — **skate·board·ing** *n*

skeet \'skēt\ *n* : trapshooting in which clay targets are thrown in such a way that their angle of flight simulates that of a flushed game bird

skein \'skān\ *n* : a loosely twisted quantity of yarn or thread wound on a reel

skel·e·ton \'ske-lət-ᵊn\ *n* 1 : a usu. bony supporting framework of an animal body 2 : a bare minimum 3 : FRAMEWORK — **skel·e·tal** \-lət-ᵊl\ *adj*

skep·tic \'skep-tik\ *n* 1 : one who believes in skepticism 2 : a person disposed to skepticism esp. regarding religion — **skep·ti·cal** \-ti-kəl\ *adj*

skep·ti·cism \'skep-tə-,si-zəm\ *n* 1 : a doubting state of mind 2 : a doctrine that certainty of knowledge cannot be attained 3 : doubt concerning religion

sketch \'skech\ *n* 1 : a rough drawing or outline 2 : a short or light literary composition (as a story or essay); *also* : a short comedy piece — **sketch** *vb* — **sketchy** *adj*

¹skew \'skyü\ *vb* : TWIST, SWERVE

²skew *n* : SLANT

skew·er \'skyü-ər\ *n* : a long pin for holding small pieces of meat and vegetables for broiling — **skewer** *vb*

¹ski \'skē\ *n, pl* **skis** [Norw. fr. ON *skīth* stick of wood, ski] : one of a pair of long strips (as of wood, metal or plastic) curving upward in front that are used for gliding over snow or water

²ski *vb* **skied** \'skēd\; **ski·ing** : to glide on skis — **ski·er** *n*

¹skid \'skid\ *n* 1 : a plank for supporting something above the ground 2 : a device placed under a wheel to prevent turning 3 : a timber or rail over or on which something is slid or rolled 4 : the act of skidding 5 : a runner on the landing gear of an aircraft 6 : ²PALLET

²skid *vb* **skid·ded; skid·ding** 1 : to slide without rotating ⟨a *skidding* wheel⟩ 2 : to slide sideways on the road ⟨the car *skidded* on ice⟩ 3 : SLIDE, SLIP

skid row *n* : a district of cheap saloons frequented by vagrants and alcoholics

skiff \'skif\ *n* : a small boat

ski jump *n* : a jump made by a person wearing skis; *also* : a course or track prepared for such jumping — **ski jump** *vb* — **ski jumper** *n*

skil·ful *chiefly Brit var of* SKILLFUL

ski lift *n* : a mechanical device (as a chairlift) for carrying skiers up a long slope

skill \'skil\ *n* 1 : ability to use one's knowledge effectively in doing something 2 : developed or acquired ability **syn** art, craft, cunning, dexterity, expertise, know-how — **skilled** \'skild\ *adj*

skil·let \'skil-lət\ *n* : a frying pan

skill·ful \'skil-fəl\ *adj* 1 : having or displaying skill : EXPERT 2 : accomplished with skill — **skill·ful·ly** *adv* — **skill·ful·ness** *n*

¹skim \'skim\ *vb* **skimmed; skim·ming** 1 : to take off from the top of a liquid; *also* : to remove (scum or cream) from ⟨∼ milk⟩ 2 : to read rapidly and superficially 3 : to pass swiftly over — **skim·mer** *n*

²skim *adj* : having the cream removed

skimp \'skimp\ *vb* : to give insufficient attention, effort, or funds; *also* : to save by skimping

skimpy \'skim-pē\ *adj* **skimp·i·er; -est** : deficient in supply or execution

¹skin \'skin\ *n* 1 : the outer limiting layer of an animal body; *also* : the usu. thin tough tissue of which this is made 2 : an outer or surface layer (as a rind or peel) — **skin·less** *adj* — **skinned** *adj*

²skin *vb* **skinned; skin·ning** : to free from skin : remove the skin of

³skin *adj* : devoted to showing nudes ⟨∼ magazines⟩

skin diving *n* : the sport of swimming under water with a face mask and flippers and esp. without a portable breathing device — **skin–dive** *vb* — **skin diver** *n*

skin·flint \'skin-,flint\ *n* : a very stingy person

skin graft *n* : a piece of skin taken from one area to

replace skin in another area — **skin grafting** *n*
¹**skin•ny** \'ski-nē\ *adj* **skin•ni•er; -est 1 :** resembling skin
2 : very thin
²**skinny** *n* **:** inside information
skin•ny–dip•ping \-ˌdi-piŋ\ *n* **:** swimming in the nude
skin•tight \'skin-'tīt\ *adj* **:** closely fitted to the figure
¹**skip** \'skip\ *vb* **skipped; skip•ping 1 :** to move with leaps
and bounds **2 :** to leap lightly over **3 :** to pass from
point to point (as in reading) disregarding what is in
between **4 :** to pass over without notice or mention
²**skip** *n* **:** a light bouncing step; *also* **:** a gait of alternate
hops and steps
skip•jack \'skip-ˌjak\ *n* **:** a small sailboat with vertical
sides and a bottom similar to a flat V
skip•per \'ski-pər\ *n* [ME, fr. MD *schipper*, fr. *schip*
ship] **:** the master of a ship; *also* **:** the manager of a
baseball team — **skipper** *vb*
skir•mish \'skər-mish\ *n* **:** a minor engagement in war;
also **:** a minor dispute or contest — **skirmish** *vb*
¹**skirt** \'skərt\ *n* **:** a free-hanging garment or part of a
garment extending from the waist down
²**skirt** *vb* **1 :** to pass around the outer edge of **2 :** BORDER
3 : EVADE
skit \'skit\ *n* **:** a brief dramatic sketch
ski tow *n* **:** SKI LIFT
skit•ter \'ski-tər\ *vb* **:** to glide or skip lightly or quickly
: skim along a surface
skit•tish \'ski-tish\ *adj* **1 :** CAPRICIOUS **2 :** easily frightened ⟨a ∼ horse⟩; *also* **:** WARY
ski•wear \'skē-ˌwar\ *n* **:** clothing suitable for wear
while skiing
skosh \'skōsh\ *n* [Jp *sukoshi*] **:** a small amount **:** BIT
skul•dug•gery *or* **skull•dug•gery** \ˌskəl-'də-gə-rē\ *n, pl*
-ger•ries : underhanded or unscrupulous behavior
skulk \'skəlk\ *vb* **:** to move furtively **:** SNEAK, LURK —
skulk•er *n*
skull \'skəl\ *n* **:** the skeleton of the head of a vertebrate
that protects the brain and supports the jaws
skull and crossbones *n, pl* **skulls and crossbones :** a
depiction of a human skull over crossbones usu. indicating a danger
skull•cap \'skəl-ˌkap\ *n* **:** a close-fitting brimless cap
¹**skunk** \'skəŋk\ *n, pl* **skunks** *also* **skunk 1 :** any of various New World mammals related to the weasels that
can forcibly eject an ill-smelling fluid when startled **2**
: a contemptible person
²**skunk** *vb* **:** to defeat decisively; *esp* **:** to shut out in a
game
skunk cabbage *n* **:** either of two No. American perennial herbs related to the arums that occur in shaded
wet to swampy areas and have a fetid odor suggestive
of a skunk
sky \'skī\ *n, pl* **skies 1 :** the upper air **2 :** HEAVEN —
sky•ey \'skī-ē\ *adj*
sky•cap \-ˌkap\ *n* **:** a person employed to carry luggage
at an airport
sky•div•ing \-ˌdī-viŋ\ *n* **:** the sport of jumping from an
airplane and executing various body maneuvers before opening a parachute — **sky diver** *n*
sky•jack \-ˌjak\ *vb* **:** to commandeer an airplane in
flight by threat of violence — **sky•jack•er** *n* — **sky-
jack•ing** *n*
¹**sky•lark** \-ˌlärk\ *n* **:** a European lark noted for singing
in steep upward flight
²**skylark** *vb* **:** FROLIC, SPORT
sky•light \'skī-ˌlīt\ *n* **:** a window in a roof or ceiling —
sky•light•ed \-ˌlī-təd\ *adj*
sky•line \-ˌlīn\ *n* **1 :** HORIZON **2 :** an outline against the
sky
¹**sky•rock•et** \-ˌrä-kət\ *n* **:** ROCKET 1
²**skyrocket** *vb* **:** ROCKET 2
sky•scrap•er \-ˌskrā-pər\ *n* **:** a very tall building
sky•walk \-ˌwȯk\ *n* **:** an aerial walkway connecting two
buildings
sky•ward \-wərd\ *adv* **:** toward the sky
sky•writ•ing \-ˌrī-tiŋ\ *n* **:** writing in the sky formed by

smoke emitted from an airplane — **sky•writ•er** *n*
slab \'slab\ *n* **:** a thick flat piece or slice
¹**slack** \'slak\ *adj* **1 :** CARELESS, NEGLIGENT **2 :** SLUG-
GISH, LISTLESS **3 :** not taut **:** LOOSE **4 :** not busy or active **syn** lax, remiss, neglectful, delinquent, derelict
— **slack•ly** *adv* — **slack•ness** *n*
²**slack** *vb* **1 :** to make or become slack **:** LOOSEN, RELAX
2 : SLAKE 2
³**slack** *n* **1 :** cessation of movement or flow **:** LETUP **2 :** a
part that hangs loose without strain ⟨∼ of a rope⟩ **3**
: trousers esp. for casual wear — usu. used in pl.
slack•en \'sla-kən\ *vb* **:** to make or become slack
slack•er \'sla-kər\ *n* **:** one that shirks work or evades
military duty
slag \'slag\ *n* **:** the waste left after the melting of ores
and the separation of metal from them
slain *past part of* SLAY
slake \'slāk, *for 2 also* 'slak\ *vb* **slaked; slak•ing 1 :** to
relieve or satisfy with or as if with refreshing drink
⟨∼ thirst⟩ **2 :** to cause (lime) to crumble by mixture
with water
sla•lom \'slä-ləm\ *n* [Norw *slalåm*, lit., sloping track]
: skiing in a zigzag course between obstacles
¹**slam** \'slam\ *n* **:** the winning of every trick or of all
tricks but one in bridge
²**slam** *n* **:** a heavy jarring impact **:** BANG
³**slam** *vb* **slammed; slam•ming 1 :** to shut violently and
noisily **2 :** to throw or strike with a loud impact
slam•mer \'sla-mər\ *n* **:** JAIL, PRISON
¹**slan•der** \'slan-dər\ *vb* **:** to utter slander against **:** DE-
FAME — **slan•der•er** *n*
²**slander** *n* [ME *sclaundre, slaundre*, fr. OF *esclandre*,
fr. LL *scandalum* stumbling block, offense] **:** a false
report maliciously uttered and tending to injure the
reputation of a person — **slan•der•ous** *adj*
slang \'slaŋ\ *n* **:** an informal nonstandard vocabulary
composed typically of invented words, arbitrarily
changed words, and extravagant figures of speech —
slangy *adj*
¹**slant** \'slant\ *n* **1 :** a sloping direction, line, or plane **2**
: a particular or personal viewpoint — **slant** *adj* —
slant•wise \-ˌwīz\ *adv or adj*
²**slant** *vb* **1 :** SLOPE **2 :** to interpret or present in accordance with a special viewpoint or bias **syn** incline,
lean, list, tilt, heel — **slant•ing•ly** *adv*
slap \'slap\ *vb* **slapped; slap•ping 1 :** to strike sharply
with the open hand **2 :** REBUFF, INSULT — **slap** *n*
slap•stick \-ˌstik\ *n* **:** comedy stressing horseplay
¹**slash** \'slash\ *vb* **1 :** to cut with sweeping strokes **2 :** to
cut slits in (a garment) **3 :** to reduce sharply
²**slash** *n* **1 :** GASH **2 :** an ornamental slit in a garment
slat \'slat\ *n* **:** a thin narrow flat strip
¹**slate** \'slāt\ *n* **1 :** a dense fine-grained rock that splits
into thin layers **2 :** a roofing tile or a writing tablet
made from this rock **3 :** a written or unwritten record
⟨start with a clean ∼⟩ **4 :** a list of candidates for election
²**slate** *vb* **slat•ed; slat•ing 1 :** to cover with slate **2 :** to
designate for action or appointment
slath•er \'sla-thər\ *vb* **:** to spread with or on thickly or
lavishly
slat•tern \'sla-tərn\ *n* **:** a slovenly woman — **slat-
tern•ly** *adj*
¹**slaugh•ter** \'slȯ-tər\ *n* **1 :** the butchering of livestock
for market **2 :** great destruction of lives esp. in battle
²**slaughter** *vb* **1 :** to kill (animals) for food **:** BUTCHER **2**
: to kill in large numbers or in a bloody way **:** MAS-
SACRE
slaugh•ter•house \-ˌhaus\ *n* **:** an establishment where
animals are butchered
Slav \'släv, 'slav\ *n* **:** a person speaking a Slavic language
¹**slave** \'slāv\ *n* [ME *sclave*, fr. OF or ML; OF *esclave*,
fr. ML *sclavus*, fr. *Sclavus* Slav; fr. the enslavement
of Slavs in eastern Europe in the Middle Ages] **1 :** a
person held in servitude as property **2 :** a device (as

the printer of a computer) that is directly responsive to another — **slave** *adj*
²**slave** *vb* **slaved; slav·ing** : to work like a slave : DRUDGE
¹**sla·ver** \'sla-vər, 'slä-\ *n* : SLOBBER — **slaver** *vb*
²**slav·er** \'slä-vər\ *n* : a ship or a person engaged in transporting slaves
slav·ery \'slāv-rē, 'slä-və-\ *n* **1** : wearisome drudgery **2** : the condition of being a slave **3** : the practice of owning slaves **syn** servitude, bondage, enslavement
¹**Slav·ic** \'sla-vik, 'slä-\ *n* : a branch of the Indo≈European language family including various languages (as Russian or Polish) of eastern Europe
²**Slavic** *adj* : of or relating to the Slavs or their languages
slav·ish \'slä-vish\ *adj* **1** : SERVILE **2** : obeying or imitating with no freedom of judgment or choice — **slav·ish·ly** *adv*
slaw \'slò\ *n* : COLESLAW
slay \'slā\ *vb* **slew** \'slü\; **slain** \'slān\; **slay·ing** : KILL — **slay·er** *n*
sleaze \'slēz\ *n* : a sleazy quality, appearance, or behavior
slea·zy \'slē-zē\ *adj* **slea·zi·er; -est 1** : FLIMSY, SHODDY **2** : marked by cheapness of character or quality
¹**sled** \'sled\ *n* : a vehicle usu. on runners adapted esp. for sliding on snow
²**sled** *vb* **sled·ded, sled·ding** : to ride or carry on a sled
¹**sledge** \'slej\ *n* : SLEDGEHAMMER
²**sledge** *n* : a strong heavy sled
sledge·ham·mer \'slej-₁ha-mər\ *n* : a large heavy hammer wielded with both hands — **sledgehammer** *adj* or *vb*
¹**sleek** \'slēk\ *vb* **1** : to make smooth or glossy **2** : to gloss over
²**sleek** *adj* : having a smooth well-groomed look
¹**sleep** \'slēp\ *n* **1** : the natural periodic suspension of consciousness during which bodily powers are restored **2** : a state (as death or coma) suggesting sleep — **sleep·less** *adj* — **sleep·less·ness** *n*
²**sleep** *vb* **slept** \'slept\; **sleep·ing 1** : to rest or be in a state of sleep; *also* : to spend in sleep **2** : to have sexual intercourse — usu. used with *with* **3** : to provide sleeping space for
sleep·er \'slē-pər\ *n* **1** : one that sleeps **2** : a horizontal beam to support something on or near ground level **3** : SLEEPING CAR **4** : someone or something unpromising or unnoticed that suddenly attains prominence or value
sleeping bag *n* : a warmly lined bag for sleeping esp. outdoors
sleeping car *n* : a railroad car with berths for sleeping
sleeping pill *n* : a drug in tablet or capsule form taken to induce sleep
sleeping sickness *n* : a serious disease of tropical Africa that is marked by fever, lethargy, tremors, and loss of weight and is caused by protozoans transmitted by the tsetse fly
sleep·over \'slēp-₁ō-vər\ *n* : an overnight stay (as at another's home)
sleep·walk·er \'slēp-₁wò-kər\ *n* : one that walks while or as if while asleep — **sleep·walk** \-₁wòk\ *vb*
sleepy \'slē-pē\ *adj* **sleep·i·er; -est 1** : ready for sleep **2** : quietly inactive — **sleep·i·ly** \'slē-pə-lē\ *adv* — **sleep·i·ness** \-pē-nəs\ *n*
sleet \'slēt\ *n* : frozen or partly frozen rain — **sleet** *vb* — **sleety** *adj*
sleeve \'slēv\ *n* **1** : a part of a garment covering an arm **2** : a tubular part designed to fit over another part — **sleeved** *adj* — **sleeve·less** *adj*
¹**sleigh** \'slā\ *n* : an open usu. horse-drawn vehicle on runners for use on snow or ice
²**sleigh** *vb* : to drive or travel in a sleigh
sleight \'slīt\ *n* **1** : TRICK **2** : DEXTERITY
sleight of hand : a trick requiring skillful manual manipulation

slen·der \'slen-dər\ *adj* **1** : SLIM, THIN **2** : WEAK, SLIGHT **3** : MEAGER, INADEQUATE
slen·der·ize \-də-₁rīz\ *vb* **-ized; -iz·ing** : to make slender
sleuth \'slüth\ *n* [short for *sleuthhound* bloodhound, fr. ME, fr. *sleuth* track of an animal or person, fr. ON *slōth*] : DETECTIVE
¹**slew** \'slü\ *past of* SLAY
²**slew** *vb* : TURN, VEER, SKID
¹**slice** \'slīs\ *vb* **sliced; slic·ing 1** : to cut a slice from; *also* : to cut into slices **2** : to hit (a ball) so that a slice results
²**slice** *n* **1** : a thin flat piece cut from something **2** : a flight of a ball (as in golf) that curves in the direction of the dominant hand of the player hitting it
¹**slick** \'slik\ *vb* : to make smooth or sleek
²**slick** *adj* **1** : very smooth : SLIPPERY **2** : CLEVER, SMART
³**slick** *n* : a smooth patch of water covered with a film of oil **2** : a popular magazine printed on coated paper
slick·er \'sli-kər\ *n* **1** : a long loose raincoat **2** : a slick tricky person **3** : a city dweller esp. of natty appearance or sophisticated mannerisms
¹**slide** \'slīd\ *vb* **slid** \'slid\; **slid·ing** \'slī-diŋ\ **1** : to move smoothly along a surface **2** : to fall by a loss of support **3** : to pass unobtrusively **4** : to move or pass smoothly; *also* : to pass unnoticed ⟨let it ∼ by⟩ **5** : to fall or dive toward a base in baseball
²**slide** *n* **1** : an act or instance of sliding **2** : something (as a cover or fastener) that operates by sliding **3** : a fall of a mass of earth or snow down a hillside **4** : a surface on which something slides **5** : a glass plate on which a specimen is mounted for examination under a microscope **6** : a small transparent photograph that can be projected on a screen
²**slid·er** \'slī-dər\ *n* **1** : one that slides **2** : a baseball pitch that looks like a fastball but curves slightly
slide rule *n* : a manual device for calculation consisting of a ruler and a movable middle piece graduated with logarithmic scales
slier *comparative of* SLY
sliest *superlative of* SLY
¹**slight** \'slīt\ *adj* **1** : SLENDER; *also* : FRAIL **2** : UNIMPORTANT **3** : SCANTY, MEAGER — **slight·ly** *adv*
²**slight** *vb* **1** : to treat as unimportant **2** : to ignore discourteously **3** : to perform or attend to carelessly
³**slight** *n* : a humiliating discourtesy
¹**slim** \'slim\ *adj* **slim·mer; slim·mest** [D, bad, inferior, fr. MD, *slimp* crooked, bad] **1** : SLENDER, SLIGHT, THIN **2** : SCANTY, MEAGER
²**slim** *vb* **slimmed; slim·ming** : to make or become slender
slime \'slīm\ *n* **1** : sticky mud **2** : a slippery substance (as on the skin of a slug or catfish) — **slimy** *adj*
¹**sling** \'sliŋ\ *vb* **slung** \'sləŋ\; **sling·ing 1** : to throw forcibly : FLING **2** : to hurl with or as if with a sling
²**sling** *n* **1** : a short strap with strings attached for hurling stones or shot **2** : something (as a rope or chain) used to hoist, lower, support, or carry; *esp* : a bandage hanging from the neck to support an arm or hand
sling·shot \'sliŋ-₁shät\ *n* : a forked stick with elastic bands for throwing small stones or shot
slink \'sliŋk\ *vb* **slunk** \'sləŋk\ *also* **slinked** \'sliŋkt\; **slink·ing 1** : to move stealthily or furtively **2** : to move sinuously — **slinky** *adj*
¹**slip** \'slip\ *vb* **slipped; slip·ping 1** : to escape quietly or secretly **2** : to slide along or cause to slide along smoothly **3** : to make a mistake **4** : to pass unnoticed or undone **5** : to fall off from a standard or level
²**slip** *n* **1** : a ramp for repairing ships **2** : a ship's berth between two piers **3** : secret or hurried departure, escape, or evasion **4** : BLUNDER **5** : a sudden mishap **6** : a woman's one-piece garment worn under a dress **7** : PILLOWCASE
³**slip** *n* **1** : a shoot or twig from a plant for planting or grafting **2** : a long narrow strip; *esp* : one of paper used for a record ⟨deposit ∼⟩

⁴slip *vb* **slipped; slip•ping** : to take slips from (a plant)
slip•knot \'slip-ˌnät\ *n* : a knot that slips along the rope around which it is made
slipped disk *n* : a protrusion of one of the disks of cartilage between vertebrae with pressure on spinal nerves resulting esp. in low back pain

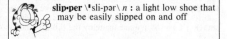

slip•per \'sli-pər\ *n* : a light low shoe that may be easily slipped on and off

slip•pery \'sli-pə-rē\ *adj* **slip•per•i•er; -est 1** : icy, wet, smooth, or greasy enough to cause one to fall or lose one's hold **2** : not to be trusted : TRICKY — **slip•per•i•ness** *n*
slip•shod \'slip-'shäd\ *adj* : SLOVENLY, CARELESS ⟨∼ work⟩
slip•stream \'slip-ˌstrēm\ *n* : a stream (as of air) driven aft by a propeller
slip•up \'slip-ˌəp\ *n* **1** : MISTAKE **2** : ACCIDENT
¹slit \'slit\ *vb* **slit; slit•ting 1** : SLASH **2** : to cut off or away
²slit *n* : a long narrow cut or opening
slith•er \'sli-thər\ *vb* : to slip or glide along like a snake — **slith•ery** *adj*
sliv•er \'sli-vər\ *n* : SPLINTER

slob \'släb\ *n* : a slovenly or boorish person

slob•ber \'slä-bər\ *vb* **slob•bered; slob•ber•ing** : to dribble saliva — **slobber** *n*
sloe \'slō\ *n* : the fruit of the blackthorn
slog \'släg\ *vb* **slogged; slog•ging 1** : to hit hard : BEAT **2** : to work hard and steadily
slo•gan \'slō-gən\ *n* [alter. of earlier *slogorn*, fr. ScGael *sluagh-ghairm*, fr. *sluagh* army, host + *gairm* cry] : a word or phrase expressing the spirit or aim of a party, group, or cause
sloop \'slüp\ *n* : a single-masted sailboat with a jib and a fore-and-aft mainsail

¹slop \'släp\ *n* **1** : thin tasteless drink or liquid food — usu. used in pl. **2** : food waste for animal feed : SWILL **3** : excreted body waste — usu. used in pl.
²slop *vb* **slopped; slop•ping 1** : SPILL **2** : to feed with slop ⟨∼ hogs⟩
¹slope \'slōp\ *vb* **sloped; slop•ing** : SLANT, INCLINE
²slope *n* **1** : upward or downward slant or degree of slant **2** : ground that forms an incline **3** : the part of a landmass draining into a particular ocean
slop•py \'slä-pē\ *adj* **slop•pi•er; -est 1** : MUDDY, SLUSHY **2** : SLOVENLY, MESSY
slosh \'släsh\ *vb* **1** : to flounder through or splash about in or with water, mud, or slush **2** : to move with a splashing motion
slot \'slät\ *n* **1** : a long narrow opening or groove **2** : a position in a sequence
slot car *n* : an electric toy racing car that runs on a grooved track
sloth \'slȯth\ *n, pl* **sloths** \'slȯths, 'slȯthz\ **1** : LAZINESS, INDOLENCE **2** : any of several slow-moving plant-eating arboreal mammals of So. and Central America — **sloth•ful** *adj*

sloth 2

slot machine *n* **1** : a machine whose operation is begun by dropping a coin into a slot **2** : a coin-operated gam-

bling machine that pays off according to the matching of symbols on wheels spun by a handle

¹slouch \'slaůch\ *n* **1** : a lazy or incompetent person **2** : a loose or drooping gait or posture

²slouch *vb* : to walk, stand, or sit with a slouch : SLUMP

¹slough \'slü, *2 usu* 'slaů\ *n* **1** : a wet and marshy or muddy place (as a swamp) **2** : a discouraged state of mind

²slough \'sləf\ *also* **sluff** *n* : something that has been or may be shed or cast off

³slough \'sləf\ *also* **sluff** *vb* : to cast off

Slo·vak \'slō-ˌväk, -ˌvak\ *n* : a member of a Slavic people of Slovakia — **Slovak** *adj* — **Slo·va·ki·an** \slō-'vä-kē-ən, -'va-\ *adj or n*

slov·en \'slə-vən\ *n* [ME *sloveyn* rascal, perh. fr. D dial. *sloovin* woman of low character] : an untidy person

Slo·vene \'slō-ˌvēn\ *n* : a member of a Slavic people living largely in Slovenia — **Slovene** *adj* — **Slo·ve·nian** \slō-'vē-nē-ən\ *adj or n*

slov·en·ly \'slə-vən-lē\ *adj* **1** : untidy in dress or person **2** : lazily or carelessly done : SLIPSHOD

¹slow \'slō\ *adj* **1** : SLUGGISH; *also* : dull in mind : STUPID **2** : moving, flowing, or proceeding at less than the usual speed **3** : taking more than the usual time **4** : registering behind the correct time **5** : not lively : BORING **syn** dilatory, laggard, deliberate, leisurely — **slow** *adv* — **slow·ly** *adv* — **slow·ness** *n*

²slow *vb* **1** : to make slow : hold back **2** : to go slower

slow motion *n* : motion-picture action photographed so as to appear much slower than normal — **slow–motion** *adj*

SLR *abbr* single-lens reflex

sludge \'sləj\ *n* : a slushy mass : OOZE; *esp* : solid matter produced by sewage treatment processes

slue *var of* ²SLEW

¹slug \'sləg\ *n* **1** : a small mass of metal; *esp* : BULLET **2** : a metal disk for use (as in a slot machine) in place of a coin **3** : any of numerous wormlike mollusks related to the snails **4** : a quantity of liquor drunk

²slug *vb* **slugged; slug·ging** : to strike forcibly and heavily — **slug·ger** *n*

slug·gard \'slə-gərd\ *n* : a lazy person

slug·gish \'slə-gish\ *adj* **1** : SLOTHFUL, LAZY **2** : slow in movement or flow **3** : STAGNANT, DULL — **slug·gish·ly** *adv* — **slug·gish·ness** *n*

¹sluice \'slüs\ *n* **1** : an artificial passage for water with a gate for controlling the flow; *also* : the gate so used **2** : a channel that carries off surplus water **3** : an inclined trough or flume for washing ore or floating logs

²sluice *vb* **sluiced; sluic·ing** **1** : to draw off through a sluice **2** : to wash with running water : FLUSH

¹slum \'sləm\ *n* : a thickly populated area marked by poverty and dirty or deteriorated houses

²slum *vb* **slummed; slum·ming** : to visit slums esp. out of curiosity; *also* : to go somewhere or do something that might be considered beneath one's station

¹slum·ber \'sləm-bər\ *vb* **slum·bered; slum·ber·ing** **1** : DOZE; *also* : SLEEP **2** : to be in a sluggish or torpid state

²slumber *n* : SLEEP

slum·ber·ous \'sləm-bə-rəs\ *or* **slum·brous** \-brəs\ *adj* **1** : SLUMBERING, SLEEPY **2** : PEACEFUL, INACTIVE

slum·lord \'sləm-ˌlòrd\ *n* : a landlord who receives unusually large profits from substandard properties

slump \'sləmp\ *vb* **1** : to sink down suddenly : COLLAPSE **2** : SLOUCH **3** : to decline sharply — **slump** *n*

slung *past and past part of* SLING

slunk *past and past part of* SLINK

¹slur \'slər\ *vb* **slurred; slur·ring** **1** : to slide or slip over without due mention or emphasis **2** : to perform two or more successive notes of different pitch in a smooth or connected way

²slur *n* : a curved line connecting notes to be slurred; *also* : a group of slurred notes

³slur *n* : a slighting remark : ASPERSION

slurp \'slərp\ *vb* : to eat or drink noisily — **slurp** *n*

slur·ry \'slər-ē\ *n, pl* **slur·ries** : a watery mixture of insoluble matter

slush \'sləsh\ *n* **1** : partly melted or watery snow **2** : soft mud — **slushy** *adj*

slut \'slət\ *n* **1** : a slovenly woman **2** : a lewd woman — **slut·tish** *adj*

sly \'slī\ *adj* **sli·er** *also* **sly·er** \'slī-ər\; **sli·est** *also* **sly·est** \'slī-əst\ **1** : CRAFTY, CUNNING **2** : SECRETIVE, FURTIVE **3** : ROGUISH **syn** tricky, wily, artful, foxy, guileful — **sly·ly** *adv* — **sly·ness** *n*

sm *abbr* small

Sm *symbol* samarium

SM *abbr* sergeant major

SMA *abbr* sergeant major of the army

¹smack \'smak\ *n* : characteristic flavor; *also* : a slight trace

²smack *vb* **1** : to have a taste **2** : to have a trace or suggestion

³smack *vb* **1** : to move (the lips) so as to make a sharp noise **2** : to kiss or slap with a loud noise

⁴smack *n* **1** : a sharp noise made by the lips **2** : a noisy slap

⁵smack *adv* : squarely and sharply

⁶smack *n* : a sailing ship used in fishing

⁷smack *n, slang* : HEROIN

SMaj *abbr* sergeant major

¹small \'smòl\ *adj* **1** : little in size or amount **2** : operating on a limited scale **3** : little or close to zero (as in number or value) **4** : made up of little things **5** : TRIFLING, UNIMPORTANT **6** : MEAN, PETTY **syn** diminutive, petite, wee, tiny, minute — **small·ish** *adj* — **small·ness** *n*

²small *n* : a small part or product ⟨the ∼ of the back⟩

small·pox \'smòl-ˌpäks\ *n* : a contagious virus disease of humans formerly common but now eradicated

small–time \'smòl-'tīm\ *adj* : insignificant in performance and standing : MINOR — **small–tim·er** *n*

¹smart \'smärt\ *vb* **1** : to cause or feel a stinging pain **2** : to feel or endure distress — **smart** *n*

²smart *adj* **1** : making one smart ⟨a ∼ blow⟩ **2** : mentally quick : BRIGHT **3** : WITTY, CLEVER **4** : STYLISH **5** : being a guided missile **6** : containing a microprocessor for limited computing capability ⟨∼ terminal⟩ **syn** knowing, quick-witted, intelligent, brainy, sharp — **smart·ly** *adv* — **smart·ness** *n*

smart al·eck \'smärt-ˌa-lik\ *n* : a person given to obnoxious cleverness

smart card *n* : a small plastic card that has a built-in microprocessor to store and handle data

¹smash \'smash\ *n* **1** : a smashing blow **2** : a hard, overhand stroke in tennis **3** : the act or sound of smashing **4** : collision of vehicles : CRASH **5** : COLLAPSE, RUIN; *esp* : BANKRUPTCY **6** : a striking success : HIT — **smash** *adv*

²smash *vb* **1** : to break or be broken into pieces **2** : to move forward with force and shattering effect **3** : to destroy utterly : WRECK

smat·ter·ing \'sma-tə-riŋ\ *n* **1** : superficial knowledge **2** : a small scattered number or amount

¹smear \'smir\ *n* **1** : a spot left by an oily or sticky substance **2** : material smeared on a surface (as of a microscope slide)

²smear *vb* **1** : to overspread esp. with something oily or sticky : SMUDGE, SOIL **3** : to injure by slander or insults

smell \'smel\ *vb* **smelled** \'smeld\ *or* **smelt** \'smelt\; **smell·ing** **1** : to perceive the odor of by sense organs of the nose; *also* : to detect or seek with or as if with these organs **2** : to have or give off an odor

²**smell** n 1 : ODOR, SCENT 2 : the process or power of perceiving odor; also : the special sense by which one perceives odor 3 : an act of smelling — **smelly** adj

smelling salts n pl : an aromatic preparation used as a stimulant and restorative (as to relieve faintness)

¹**smelt** \'smelt\ n, pl **smelts** or **smelt** : any of a family of small food fishes of coastal or fresh waters that are related to the trouts and salmons

²**smelt** vb : to melt or fuse (ore) in order to separate the metal; also : REFINE

smelt·er \'smel-tər\ n 1 : one that smelts 2 : an establishment for smelting

smid·gen also **smid·geon** or **smid·gin** \'smi-jən\ n : a small amount : BIT

smi·lax \'smi-ˌlaks\ n 1 : any of various mostly climbing and prickly plants related to the lilies 2 : an ornamental plant related to the asparagus

¹**smile** \'smil\ vb **smiled; smil·ing** 1 : to look with a smile 2 : to be favorable 3 : to express by a smile

²**smile** n : a change of facial expression to express amusement, pleasure, or affection

smirch \'smərch\ vb 1 : to make dirty or stained 2 : to bring disgrace on — **smirch** n

smirk \'smərk\ vb : to wear a self-conscious or conceited smile : SIMPER — **smirk** n

smite \'smīt\ vb **smote** \'smōt\; **smit·ten** \'smit-ᵊn\ or **smote; smit·ing** \'smī-tiŋ\ 1 : to strike heavily; also : to kill by striking 2 : to affect as if by a heavy blow

smith \'smith\ n : a worker in metals; esp : BLACKSMITH

smith·er·eens \ˌsmi-thə-ˈrēnz\ n pl [perh. fr. Ir smidiríní] : FRAGMENTS, BITS

smithy \'smi-thē\ n, pl **smith·ies** : a smith's workshop

¹**smock** \'smäk\ n : a loose garment worn over other clothes as a protection

²**smock** vb : to gather (cloth) in regularly spaced tucks — **smock·ing** n

smog \'smäg, 'smòg\ n [blend of smoke and fog] : a thick haze caused by the action of sunlight on air polluted by smoke and automobile exhaust fumes — **smog·gy** adj

¹**smoke** \'smōk\ n 1 : the gas from burning material (as coal, wood, or tobacco) in which are suspended particles of soot 2 : a mass or column of smoke 3 : something (as a cigarette) to smoke; also : the act of smoking — **smoke·less** adj — **smoky** adj

²**smoke** vb **smoked; smok·ing** 1 : to emit smoke 2 : to inhale and exhale the fumes of burning tobacco; also : to use in smoking ⟨~ a pipe⟩ 3 : to stupefy or drive away by smoke 4 : to discolor with smoke 5 : to cure (as meat) with smoke — **smok·er** n

smoke detector n : an alarm that sounds automatically when it detects smoke

smoke jumper n : a forest firefighter who parachutes to locations otherwise difficult to reach

smoke·stack \'smōk-ˌstak\ n : a pipe or funnel through which smoke and gases are discharged

smol·der or **smoul·der** \'smōl-dər\ vb **smol·dered** or **smoul·dered; smol·der·ing** or **smoul·der·ing** 1 : to burn and smoke without flame 2 : to burn inwardly — **smolder** n

smooch \'smüch\ vb : KISS, PET — **smooch** n

¹**smooth** \'smüth\ adj 1 : not rough or uneven 2 : not jarring or jolting 3 : BLAND, MILD 4 : fluent in speech and agreeable in manner — **smooth·ly** adv — **smooth·ness** n

²**smooth** vb 1 : to make smooth 2 : to free from trouble or difficulty

smooth muscle n : muscle with no cross striations that is typical of visceral organs (as the stomach and bladder) and is not under voluntary control

smor·gas·bord \'smòr-gəs-ˌbòrd\ n [Sw smörgåsbord, fr. smörgås open sandwich + bord table] : a luncheon or supper buffet consisting of many foods

smote past and past part of SMITE

¹**smoth·er** \'smə-thər\ n 1 : thick stifling smoke 2 : a dense cloud (as of fog or dust) 3 : a confused multitude of things

²**smother** vb **smoth·ered; smoth·er·ing** 1 : to be overcome by or die from lack of air 2 : to kill by depriving of air 3 : SUPPRESS 4 : to cover thickly

SMSgt abbr senior master sergeant

¹**smudge** \'sməj\ vb **smudged; smudg·ing** : to soil or blur by rubbing or smearing

²**smudge** n : a dirty or blurred spot — **smudgy** adj

smug \'sməg\ adj **smug·ger; smug·gest** : conscious of one's virtue and importance : SELF-SATISFIED — **smug·ly** adv — **smug·ness** n

smug·gle \'smə-gəl\ vb **smug·gled; smug·gling** 1 : to import or export secretly, illegally, or without paying the duties required by law 2 : to convey secretly — **smug·gler** \'smə-glər\ n

smut \'smət\ n 1 : something (as soot) that smudges; also : SMUDGE, SPOT 2 : any of various destructive diseases of plants caused by fungi; also : a fungus causing smut 3 : indecent language or matter — **smut·ty** adj

smutch \'sməch\ n : SMUDGE

Sn symbol [LL stannum] tin

SN abbr seaman

snack \'snak\ n : a light meal : BITE

snaf·fle \'sna-fəl\ n : a simple jointed bit for a horse's bridle

¹**snag** \'snag\ n 1 : a stump or piece of a tree esp. when under water 2 : an unexpected difficulty **syn** obstacle, obstruction, impediment, bar

²**snag** vb **snagged; snag·ging** 1 : to become caught on or as if on a snag 2 : to seize quickly : SNATCH

snail \'snāl\ n : any of numerous small gastropod mollusks with a spiral shell into which they can withdraw

snake \'snāk\ n 1 : any of numerous long-bodied limbless reptiles : SERPENT 2 : a treacherous person 3 : something that resembles a snake — **snaky** adj

snake·bite \-ˌbīt\ n : the bite of a snake and esp. a venomous snake

¹**snap** \'snap\ vb **snapped; snap·ping** 1 : to grasp or slash at something with the teeth 2 : to get or buy

quickly **3** : to utter sharp or angry words **4** : to break suddenly with a sharp sound **5** : to give a sharp cracking noise **6** : to throw with a quick motion **7** : FLASH ⟨her eyes *snapped*⟩ **8** : to put a football into play — **snap•per** *n* — **snap•pish** *adj*

²snap *n* **1** : the act or sound of snapping **2** : something very easy to do : CINCH **3** : a short period of cold weather **4** : a catch or fastening that closes with a click **5** : a thin brittle cookie **6** : ENERGY, VIM; *also* : smartness of movement **7** : the putting of the ball into play in football

snap bean *n* : a bean grown primarily for its young tender pods that are usu. broken in pieces for cooking

snap•drag•on \'snap-ˌdra-gən\ *n* : any of a genus of herbs with long spikes of showy flowers

snapping turtle *n* : either of two large American turtles with powerful jaws and a strong musky odor

snap•py \'sna-pē\ *adj* **snap•pi•er; -est 1** : quickly made or done **2** : marked by vigor **3** : STYLISH

snap•shot \'snap-ˌshät\ *n* : a photograph taken usu. with an inexpensive hand-held camera

snare \'snar\ *n* : a trap consisting of a noose for catching birds or mammals — **snare** *vb*

¹snarl \'snärl\ *vb* : to cause to become knotted and intertwined

²snarl *n* : TANGLE

³snarl *vb* : to growl angrily or threateningly

⁴snarl *n* : an angry ill-tempered growl

¹snatch \'snach\ *vb* **1** : to try to grasp something suddenly **2** : to seize or take away suddenly **syn** clutch, seize, grab, nab

²snatch *n* **1** : a short period **2** : an act of snatching **3** : something brief or fragmentary ⟨∼es of song⟩

¹sneak \'snēk\ *vb* **sneaked** \'snēkt\ *or* **snuck** \'snək\; **sneak•ing** : to move, act, or take in a furtive manner — **sneak•ing•ly** *adv*

²sneak *n* **1** : one who acts in a furtive or shifty manner **2** : a stealthy or furtive move or escape — **sneak•i•ly** \'snē-kə-lē\ *adv* — **sneaky** *adj*

sneak•er \'snē-kər\ *n* : a sports shoe with a pliable rubber sole

sneer \'snir\ *vb* : to show scorn or contempt by curling the lip or by a jeering tone — **sneer** *n*

sneeze \'snēz\ *vb* **sneezed; sneez•ing** : to force the breath out suddenly and violently as a reflex act — **sneeze** *n*

SNF *abbr* skilled nursing facility

snick•er \'sni-kər\ *n* : a partly suppressed laugh — **snicker** *vb*

snide \'snīd\ *adj* **1** : MEAN, LOW ⟨a ∼ trick⟩ **2** : slyly disparaging ⟨a ∼ remark⟩

sniff \'snif\ *vb* **1** : to draw air audibly up the nose esp. for smelling **2** : to show disdain or scorn **3** : to detect by or as if by smelling — **sniff** *n*

snif•fle \'sni-fəl\ *n* **1** *pl* : a head cold marked by nasal discharge **2** : SNUFFLE — **sniffle** *vb*

¹snip \'snip\ *n* **1** : a fragment snipped off **2** : a simple stroke of the scissors or shears

²snip *vb* **snipped; snip•ping** : to cut off by bits : CLIP; *also* : to remove by cutting off

¹snipe \'snīp\ *n, pl* **snipes** *or* **snipe** : any of several long-billed game birds esp. of marshy areas that belong to the same family as the sandpipers

²snipe *vb* **sniped; snip•ing** : to shoot at an exposed enemy from a concealed position — **snip•er** *n*

snip•py \'sni-pē\ *adj* **snip•pi•er; -est** : CURT, SNAPPISH

snips \'snips\ *n pl* : hand shears used esp. for cutting sheet metal ⟨tin ∼⟩

snitch \'snich\ *vb* **1** : INFORM, TATTLE **2** : PILFER, SNATCH

sniv•el \'sni-vəl\ *vb* **-eled** *or* **-elled; -el•ing** *or* **-el•ling 1** : to have a running nose; *also* : SNUFFLE **2** : to whine in a snuffling manner — **snivel** *n*

snob \'snäb\ *n* : one who seeks association with persons of higher social position and looks down on those considered inferior — **snob•bish** *adj* — **snob•bish•ly** *adv* — **snob•bish•ness** *n*

snob•bery \'snä-bə-rē\ *n, pl* **-ber•ies** : snobbish conduct

¹snoop \'snüp\ *vb* [D *snoepen* to buy or eat on the sly] : to pry in a furtive or meddlesome way

²snoop *n* : a prying meddlesome person

snooty \'snü-tē\ *adj* **snoot•i•er; -est** : DISDAINFUL, SNOBBISH

snooze \'snüz\ *vb* **snoozed; snooz•ing** : to take a nap : DOZE — **snooze** *n*

snore \'snōr\ *vb* **snored; snor•ing** : to breathe with a rough hoarse noise while sleeping — **snore** *n*

snor•kel \'snòr-kəl\ *n* [G *Schnorchel*] : a tube projecting above the water used by swimmers for breathing with the face under water — **snorkel** *vb*

snort \'snòrt\ *vb* **1** : to force air violently and noisily through the nose ⟨his horse ∼ed⟩ **2** : INHALE — **snort** *n*

snot \'snät\ *n* : nasal mucus

snout \'snaút\ *n* **1** : a long projecting muzzle (as of a pig) **2** : a usu. large or grotesque nose

¹snow \'snō\ *n* **1** : crystals of ice formed from water vapor in the air **2** : a descent or shower of snow crystals

²snow *vb* **1** : to fall or cause to fall in or as snow **2** : to cover or shut in with or as if with snow

¹snow•ball \'snō-ˌbòl\ *n* : a round mass of snow pressed into shape in the hand for throwing

²snowball *vb* **1** : to throw snowballs at **2** : to increase or expand at a rapidly accelerating rate

snow•bank \-ˌbaŋk\ *n* : a mound or slope of snow

snow•belt \-ˌbelt\ *n, often cap* : a region that receives an appreciable amount of annual snowfall

snow•blow•er \-ˌblō-ər\ *n* : a machine in which a rotating spiral blade picks up and propels snow aside

snow•board \-ˌbòrd\ *n* : a board like a wide ski ridden in a surfing position downhill over snow

snow•drift \-ˌdrift\ *n* : a bank of drifted snow

snow•drop \-ˌdräp\ *n* : a plant with narrow leaves and a nodding white flower that blooms early in the spring

snow•fall \-ˌfòl\ *n* : a fall of snow

snow fence *n* : a fence across the path of prevailing winds to protect something (as a road) from drifting snow

snow·field \'snō-ˌfēld\ *n* : a mass of perennial snow at the head of a glacier

snow·mo·bile \'snō-mō-ˌbēl\ *n* : any of various automotive vehicles for travel on snow — **snow·mo·bil·er** \-ˌbē-lər\ *n* — **snow·mo·bil·ing** \-liŋ\ *n*

snow pea *n* : a cultivated pea with flat edible pods

snow·plow \'snō-ˌplaù\ *n* **1** : a device for clearing away snow **2** : a skiing maneuver in which the heels of both skis are slid outward for slowing down or stopping

¹snow·shoe \-ˌshü\ *n* : a light frame of wood strung with thongs that is attached to a shoe or boot to prevent sinking down into soft snow

²snowshoe *vb* **snow·shoed; snow·shoe·ing** : to travel on snowshoes

snow·storm \-ˌstòrm\ *n* : a storm of falling snow

snow thrower *n* : SNOWBLOWER

snowy \'snō-ē\ *adj* **snow·i·er; -est 1** : marked by snow **2** : white as snow

snub \'snəb\ *vb* **snubbed; snub·bing** : to treat with disdain : SLIGHT — **snub** *n*

snub–nosed \'snəb-ˌnōzd\ *adj* : having a nose slightly turned up at the end

snuck *past and past part of* SNEAK

¹snuff \'snəf\ *vb* **1** : to pinch off the charred end of (a candle) **2** : to put out (a candle) — **snuff·er** *n*

²snuff *vb* **1** : to draw forcibly into or through the nose **2** : SMELL

³snuff *n* : SNIFF

⁴snuff *n* : pulverized tobacco

snuf·fle \'snə-fəl\ *vb* **snuf·fled; snuf·fling 1** : to snuff or sniff audibly and repeatedly **2** : to breathe with a sniffing sound — **snuf·fle** *n*

snug \'snəg\ *adj* **snug·ger; snug·gest 1** : fitting closely and comfortably **2** : CONCEALED — **snug·ly** *adv* — **snug·ness** *n*

snug·gle \'snə-gəl\ *vb* **snug·gled; snug·gling** : to curl up or draw close comfortably : NESTLE

¹so \'sō\ *adv* **1** : in the manner indicated **2** : in the same way **3** : THUS **4** : FINALLY **5** : to the extent indicated **6** : THEREFORE

²so *conj* : for that reason ⟨he wanted it, ∼ he took it⟩

³so *pron* **1** : the same ⟨became chairman and remained ∼⟩ **2** : approximately that ⟨a dozen or ∼⟩

⁴so *abbr* south; southern

SO *abbr* strikeout

¹soak \'sōk\ *vb* **1** : to remain in a liquid **2** : WET, SATURATE **3** : to draw in by or as if by absorption **syn** drench, steep, impregnate

²soak *n* **1** : the act of soaking **2** : the liquid in which something is soaked **3** : DRUNKARD

soap \'sōp\ *n* : a cleansing substance made usu. by action of alkali on fat — **soap** *vb* — **soapy** *adj*

soap opera *n* [fr. its sponsorship by soap manufacturers] : a radio or television daytime serial drama

soap·stone \'sōp-ˌstōn\ *n* : a soft talc-containing stone with a soapy feel

soar \'sōr\ *vb* : to fly upward or at a height on or as if on wings

sob \'säb\ *vb* **sobbed; sob·bing** : to weep with convulsive heavings of the chest or contractions of the throat — **sob** *n*

so·ber \'sō-bər\ *adj* **so·ber·er** \-bər-ər\; **so·ber·est** \-bə-rəst\ **1** : temperate in the use of liquor **2** : not drunk **3** : serious or grave in mood or disposition **4** : having a quiet tone or color **syn** solemn, earnest, staid, sedate — **so·ber·ly** *adv* — **so·ber·ness** *n*

so·bri·ety \sō-'brī-ə-tē\ *n* : the quality or state of being sober

so·bri·quet \'sō-bri-ˌkā, -ˌket\ *n* [F] : NICKNAME

soc *abbr* **1** social; society **2** sociology

so–called \'sō-'kòld\ *adj* : commonly but often inaccurately so termed

soc·cer \'sä-kər\ *n* [by shortening & alter. fr. *associ-*

ation football] : a game played on a field by two teams with a round inflated ball advanced chiefly by kicking

¹so·cia·ble \'sō-shə-bəl\ *adj* **1** : liking companionship : FRIENDLY **2** : characterized by pleasant social relations **syn** gracious, cordial, affable, genial — **so·cia·bil·i·ty** \ˌsō-shə-'bi-lə-tē\ *n* — **so·cia·bly** \'sō-shə-blē\ *adv*

²sociable *n* : SOCIAL

¹so·cial \'sō-shəl\ *adj* **1** : marked by pleasant companionship with one's friends **2** : naturally living and breeding in organized communities ⟨∼ insects⟩ **3** : of or relating to human society ⟨∼ institutions⟩ **4** : of, relating to, or based on rank in a particular society ⟨∼ circles⟩; *also* : of or relating to fashionable society — **so·cial·ly** *adv*

²social *n* : a social gathering

social disease *n* : VENEREAL DISEASE

so·cial·ise *Brit var of* SOCIALIZE

so·cial·ism \'sō-shə-ˌli-zəm\ *n* : any of various social systems based on shared or government ownership and administration of the means of production and distribution of goods — **so·cial·ist** \'sō-shə-list\ *n or adj* — **so·cial·is·tic** \ˌsō-shə-'lis-tik\ *adj*

so·cial·ite \'sō-shə-ˌlīt\ *n* : a person prominent in fashionable society

so·cial·ize \'sō-shə-ˌlīz\ *vb* **-ized; -iz·ing 1** : to regulate according to the theory and practice of socialism **2** : to adapt to social needs or uses **3** : to participate actively in a social gathering — **so·cial·i·za·tion** \ˌsō-shə-lə-'zā-shən\ *n*

social science *n* : a science (as economics or political science) dealing with a particular aspect of human society — **social scientist** *n*

social work *n* : services, activities, or methods providing social services esp. to the economically underprivileged and socially maladjusted — **social worker** *n*

so·ci·e·ty \sə-'sī-ə-tē\ *n, pl* **-ties** [MF *societé*, fr. L *societat-, societas*, fr. *socius* companion] **1** : COMPANIONSHIP **2** : a voluntary association of persons for common ends **3** : a part of a community bound together by common interests and standards; *esp* : the group or set of fashionable people

so·cio·eco·nom·ic \ˌsō-sē-ō-ˌe-kə-'nä-mik, ˌsō-shē-, -ˌē-kə-\ *adj* : of, relating to, or involving both social and economic factors

sociol *abbr* sociologist; sociology

so·ci·ol·o·gy \ˌsō-sē-'ä-lə-jē, ˌsō-shē-\ *n* : the science of society, social institutions, and social relationships — **so·cio·log·i·cal** \ˌsō-sē-ə-'lä-ji-kəl, ˌsō-shē-\ *adj* — **so·ci·ol·o·gist** \-'ä-lə-jist\ *n*

¹sock \'säk\ *n, pl* **socks** *or* **sox** \'säks\ : a stocking with a short leg

²sock *vb* : to hit, strike, or apply forcefully

³sock *n* : a vigorous blow : PUNCH

sock·et \'sä-kət\ *n* : an opening or hollow that forms a holder for something

socket wrench *n* : a wrench usu. in the form of a bar and removable socket made to fit a bolt or nut

¹sod \'säd\ *n* : TURF 1

²sod *vb* **sod·ded; sod·ding** : to cover with sod

so·da \'sō-də\ *n* **1** : SODIUM CARBONATE **2** : SODIUM BICARBONATE **3** : SODIUM **4** : SODA WATER **5** : SODA POP **6** : a sweet drink of soda water, flavoring, and often ice cream

soda pop *n* : a carbonated, sweetened, and flavored soft drink

soda water *n* : a beverage of water charged with carbon dioxide

sod·den \'säd-ᵊn\ *adj* **1** : lacking spirit : DULLED **2** : SOAKED, DRENCHED **3** : heavy or doughy from being improperly cooked ⟨∼ biscuits⟩

so·di·um \'sō-dē-əm\ *n* : a soft waxy silver white metallic chemical element occurring in nature in combined form (as in salt) — see ELEMENT table

sodium bicarbonate *n* : a white weakly alkaline salt

I'VE CARVED THIS LOVELY STATUE

USING ONLY MY CLAWS

AND THE SOFA

© 1990 PAWS, INC.

used esp. in baking powders, fire extinguishers, and medicine

sodium carbonate *n* : a carbonate of sodium used esp. in washing and bleaching textiles

sodium chloride *n* : SALT 1

sodium fluoride *n* : a salt used chiefly in tiny amounts to prevent tooth decay

sodium hydroxide *n* : a white brittle caustic substance used in making soap and rayon and in bleaching

sodium nitrate *n* : a crystalline salt used as a fertilizer and in curing meat

sodium thiosulfate *n* : a hygroscopic crystalline salt used as a photographic fixing agent

sod·omy \'sä-də-mē\ *n* **1** : sexual intercourse with a member of the same sex or with an animal **2** : noncoital and esp. anal or oral sexual intercourse with a member of the opposite sex — **sod·om·ize** \'sä-də-ˌmīz\ *vb*

so·ev·er \sō-'e-vər\ *adv* **1** : in any degree or manner ⟨how bad ∼⟩ **2** : at all : of any kind ⟨any help ∼⟩

so·fa \'sō-fə\ *n* [Ar ṣuffah long bench] : a couch usu. with upholstered back and arms

soft \'sȯft\ *adj* **1** : not hard or rough : NONVIOLENT **2** : RESTFUL, GENTLE, SOOTHING **3** : emotionally susceptible **4** : not prepared to endure hardship **5** : not containing certain salts that prevent lathering ⟨∼ water⟩ **6** : occurring at such a speed as to avoid destructive impact ⟨∼ landing of a spacecraft on the moon⟩ **7** : BIODEGRADABLE ⟨a ∼ detergent⟩ **8** : not alcoholic ⟨∼ drinks⟩ **9** : less detrimental than a hard narcotic ⟨∼ drugs⟩ — **soft·ly** *adv* — **soft·ness** *n*

soft·ball \'sȯft-ˌbȯl\ *n* : a game similar to baseball played with a ball larger and softer than a baseball; *also* : the ball used in this game

soft·bound \-ˌbaůnd\ *adj* : not bound in hard covers ⟨∼ books⟩

soft coal *n* : BITUMINOUS COAL

soft·en \'sȯ-fən\ *vb* : to make or become soft — **soft·en·er** *n*

soft palate *n* : the fold at the back of the hard palate that partially separates the mouth and the pharynx

soft·ware \'sȯft-ˌwar\ *n* : the entire set of programs, procedures, and related documentation associated with a system; *esp* : computer programs

soft·wood \-ˌwůd\ *n* **1** : the wood of a coniferous tree as compared to that of a broad-leaved deciduous tree **2** : a tree that yields softwood — **softwood** *adj*

sog·gy \'sä-gē\ *adj* **sog·gi·er**; **-est** : heavy with water or moisture — **sog·gi·ly** \'sä-gə-lē\ *adv* — **sog·gi·ness** \-gē-nəs\ *n*

soi·gné *or* **soi·gnée** \swän-'yā\ *adj* : elegantly maintained; *esp* : WELL-GROOMED

¹soil \'sȯil\ *vb* **1** : CORRUPT, POLLUTE **2** : to make or become dirty **3** : STAIN, DISGRACE

²soil *n* **1** : STAIN, DEFILEMENT **2** : EXCREMENT, WASTE

³soil *n* **1** : firm land : EARTH **2** : the upper layer of earth in which plants grow **3** : COUNTRY, REGION

soi·ree *or* **soi·rée** \swä-'rā\ *n* [F *soirée* evening period, evening party, fr. MF, fr. *soir* evening, fr. L *sero* at a late hour] : an evening party

so·journ \'sō-ˌjərn, sō-'jərn\ *vb* : to dwell in a place temporarily — **so·journ** *n* — **so·journ·er** *n*

¹sol \'säl, 'sōl\ *n* — see MONEY table

²sol *n* : a fluid colloidal system

³sol *abbr* **1** solicitor **2** soluble **3** solution

Sol \'säl\ *n* : SUN

¹sol·ace \'sä-ləs\ *n* : COMFORT

²solace *vb* **so·laced**; **so·lac·ing** : to give solace to : CONSOLE

so·lar \'sō-lər\ *adj* **1** : of, derived from, or relating to the sun **2** : measured by the earth's course in relation to the sun ⟨the ∼ year⟩ **3** : operated by or using the sun's light or heat ⟨∼ energy⟩

solar cell *n* : a photoelectric cell that converts light into electrical energy and is used as a power source

solar collector *n* : a device for the absorption of solar radiation for the heating of water or buildings or the production of electricity

solar flare *n* : a sudden temporary outburst of energy from a small area of the sun's surface

so·lar·i·um \sō-'lar-ē-əm\ *n*, *pl* **-ia** \-ē-ə\ *also* **-i·ums** : a room exposed to the sun; *esp* : a room (as in a hospital) for exposure of the body to sunshine

solar plexus *n* : the general area of the stomach below the sternum

solar system *n* : the sun together with the group of celestial bodies that revolve around it

solar wind *n* : plasma continuously ejected from the sun's surface

sold *past and past part of* SELL

sol·der \'sä-dər, 'sȯ-\ *n* : a metallic alloy used when melted to mend or join metallic surfaces — **solder** *vb*

soldering iron *n* : a metal device for applying heat in soldering

¹sol·dier \'sōl-jər\ *n* [ME *soudier*, fr. MF, fr. *soulde* pay, fr. LL *solidus* a Roman coin, fr. L, solid] : a person in military service; *esp* : an enlisted man or woman — **sol·dier·ly** *adj or adv*

²soldier *vb* **sol·diered**; **sol·dier·ing** **1** : to serve as a soldier **2** : to pretend to work while actually doing nothing

soldier of fortune *n* : ADVENTURER 2

sol·diery \'sōl-jə-rē\ *n* : a body of soldiers

¹sole \'sōl\ *n* : any of various flatfishes marketed for food

²sole *n* **1** : the undersurface of the foot **2** : the bottom of a shoe

³sole *vb* **soled**; **sol·ing** : to furnish (a shoe) with a sole

⁴sole *adj* : SINGLE, ONLY — **sole·ly** \'sōl-lē\ *adv*

so·le·cism \'sä-lə-ˌsi-zəm, 'sō-\ *n* **1** : a mistake in grammar **2** : a breach of etiquette

sol·emn \'sä-ləm\ *adj* **1** : marked by or observed with full religious ceremony **2** : FORMAL, CEREMONIOUS **3** : highly serious : GRAVE **4** : SOMBER, GLOOMY — **so-**

lem·ni·ty \sə-'lem-nə-tē\ *n* — **sol·emn·ly** \'sä-ləm-lē\ *adv*

sol·em·nize \'sä-ləm-ˌnīz\ *vb* **-nized; -niz·ing 1** : to observe or honor with solemnity **2** : to celebrate (a marriage) with religious rites — **sol·em·ni·za·tion** \ˌsä-ləm-nə-'zā-shən\ *n*

so·le·noid \'sō-lə-ˌnȯid, 'sä-\ *n* : a coil of wire usu. in cylindrical form that when carrying a current acts like a magnet

so·lic·it \sə-'li-sət\ *vb* **1** : ENTREAT, BEG **2** : to approach with a request or plea **3** : TEMPT, LURE — **so·lic·i·ta·tion** \-ˌli-sə-'tā-shən\ *n*

so·lic·i·tor \sə-'li-sə-tər\ *n* **1** : one that solicits **2** : LAWYER; *esp* : a legal official of a city or state

so·lic·i·tous \sə-'li-sə-təs\ *adj* **1** : WORRIED, CONCERNED **2** : EAGER, WILLING **syn** avid, impatient, keen, anxious — **so·lic·i·tous·ly** *adv*

so·lic·i·tude \sə-'li-sə-ˌtüd, -ˌtyüd\ *n* : CONCERN, ANXIETY

¹**sol·id** \'sä-ləd\ *adj* **1** : not hollow; *also* : written as one word without a hyphen ⟨a ~ compound⟩ **2** : having, involving, or dealing with three dimensions or with solids ⟨~ geometry⟩ **3** : not loose or spongy : COMPACT ⟨a ~ mass of rock⟩; *also* : neither gaseous nor liquid : HARD, RIGID ⟨~ ice⟩ **4** : of good substantial quality or kind ⟨~ comfort⟩ **5** : thoroughly dependable : RELIABLE ⟨a ~ citizen⟩; *also* : serious in purpose or character ⟨~ reading⟩ **6** : UNANIMOUS, UNITED ⟨~ for pay increases⟩ **7** : of one substance or character — **solid** *adv* — **so·lid·i·ty** \sə-'li-də-tē\ *n* — **sol·id·ly** *adv* — **sol·id·ness** *n*

²**solid** *n* **1** : a geometrical figure (as a cube or sphere) having three dimensions **2** : a solid substance

sol·i·dar·i·ty \ˌsä-lə-'dar-ə-tē\ *n* : unity based on shared interests, objectives, or standards

so·lid·i·fy \sə-'li-də-ˌfī\ *vb* **-fied; -fy·ing** : to make or become solid — **so·lid·i·fi·ca·tion** \-ˌli-də-fə-'kā-shən\ *n*

solid–state *adj* **1** : relating to the structure and properties of solid material **2** : using semiconductor devices rather than vacuum tubes

so·lil·o·quise *Brit var of* SOLILOQUIZE

so·lil·o·quize \sə-'li-lə-ˌkwīz\ *vb* **-quized; -quiz·ing** : to talk to oneself : utter a soliloquy

so·lil·o·quy \sə-'li-lə-kwē\ *n, pl* **-quies** [LL *soliloquium*, fr. L *solus* alone + *loqui* to speak] **1** : the act of talking to oneself **2** : a dramatic monologue that represents unspoken reflections by a character

sol·i·taire \'sä-lə-ˌtar\ *n* **1** : a single gem (as a diamond) set alone **2** : a card game for one person

sol·i·tary \'sä-lə-ˌter-ē\ *adj* **1** : being or living apart from others **2** : LONELY, SECLUDED **3** : SOLE, ONLY

sol·i·tude \'sä-lə-ˌtüd, -ˌtyüd\ *n* **1** : the state of being alone : SECLUSION **2** : a lonely place

soln *abbr* solution

¹**so·lo** \'sō-lō\ *n, pl* **solos** [It. fr. *solo* alone, fr. L *solus*] **1** : a piece of music for a single voice or instrument with or without accompaniment **2** : an action in which there is only one performer — **solo** *adj or vb* — **so·lo·ist** *n*

²**solo** *adv* : without a companion : ALONE

so·lon \'sō-lən\ *n* **1** : a wise and skillful lawgiver **2** : a member of a legislative body

sol·stice \'säl-stəs, 'sōl-\ *n* [ME, fr. OF, fr. L *solstitium*, fr. *sol* sun + *-stit-, -stes* standing] : the time of the year when the sun is farthest north of the equator (**summer solstice**) about June 22 or farthest south (**winter solstice**) about Dec. 22 — **sol·sti·tial** \säl-'sti-shəl, sōl-\ *adj*

sol·u·ble \'säl-yə-bəl\ *adj* **1** : capable of being dissolved in or as if in a liquid **2** : capable of being solved or explained — **sol·u·bil·i·ty** \ˌsäl-yə-'bi-lə-tē\ *n*

sol·ute \'säl-ˌyüt\ *n* : a dissolved substance

so·lu·tion \sə-'lü-shən\ *n* **1** : an action or process of solving a problem; *also* : an answer to a problem **2** : an act or the process by which one substance is homogenously mixed with another usu. liquid substance; *also* : a mixture thus formed

solve \'sälv\ *vb* **solved; solv·ing** : to find the answer to or a solution for — **solv·able** *adj*

sol·ven·cy \'säl-vən-sē\ *n* : the condition of being solvent

¹**sol·vent** \-vənt\ *adj* **1** : able or sufficient to pay all legal debts **2** : dissolving or able to dissolve

²**solvent** *n* : a usu. liquid substance capable of dissolving or dispersing one or more other substances

So·ma·lian \sō-'mäl-yən\ *n* : a native or inhabitant of Somalia — **Somalian** *adj*

so·mat·ic \sō-'ma-tik\ *adj* : of, relating to, or affecting the body in contrast to the mind or the sex cells and their precursors

som·ber *or* **som·bre** \'säm-bər\ *adj* **1** : DARK, GLOOMY **2** : GRAVE, MELANCHOLY — **som·ber·ly** *adv*

som·bre·ro \səm-'brer-ō\ *n, pl* **-ros** [Sp, fr. *sombra* shade] : a broad-brimmed felt hat worn esp. in the Southwest and in Mexico

sombrero

¹**some** \'səm\ *adj* **1** : one unspecified ⟨~ man called⟩ **2** : an unspecified or indefinite number of ⟨~ berries are ripe⟩ **3** : at least a few or a little ⟨~ years ago⟩

²**some** *pron* : a certain number or amount ⟨∼ of the berries are ripe⟩ ⟨∼ of it is missing⟩

¹**-some** \səm\ *adj suffix* : characterized by a (specified) thing, quality, state, or action ⟨awe*some*⟩ ⟨burden*some*⟩

²**-some** *n suffix* : a group of (so many) members and esp. persons ⟨four*some*⟩

¹**some•body** \ˈsəm-ˌbä-dē, -bə-\ *pron* : some person

²**somebody** *n* : a person of importance

some•day \ˈsəm-ˌdā\ *adv* : at some future time

some•how \-ˌhaů\ *adv* : by some means

some•one \-(ˌ)wən\ *pron* : some person

som•er•sault \ˈsə-mər-ˌsȯlt\ *n* [MF *sombresaut* leap, ultim. fr. L *super* over + *saltus* leap, fr. *salire* to jump] : a leap or roll in which a person turns heels over head — **somersault** *vb*

som•er•set \-ˌset\ *n or vb* : SOMERSAULT

some•thing \ˈsəm-thiŋ\ *pron* : some undetermined or unspecified thing

some•time \-ˌtīm\ *adv* **1** : at a future time **2** : at an unknown or unnamed time

some•times \-ˌtīmz\ *adv* : OCCASIONALLY

¹**some•what** \-ˌhwät, -ˌhwət\ *pron* : SOMETHING

²**somewhat** *adv* : in some degree

some•where \-ˌhwer\ *adv* : in, at, or to an unknown or unnamed place

som•nam•bu•lism \säm-ˈnam-byə-ˌli-zəm\ *n* : performance of motor acts (as walking) during sleep; *also* : an abnormal condition of sleep characterized by this — **som•nam•bu•list** \-list\ *n*

som•no•lent \ˈsäm-nə-lənt\ *adj* : SLEEPY, DROWSY — **som•no•lence** \-ləns\ *n*

son \ˈsən\ *n* **1** : a male offspring or descendant **2** *cap* : Jesus Christ **3** : a person deriving from a particular source (as a country, race, or school)

so•nar \ˈsō-ˌnär\ *n* [*sound navigation and ranging*] : a method or device for detecting and locating submerged objects (as submarines) by sound waves

so•na•ta \sə-ˈnä-tə\ *n* [It] : an instrumental composition with three or four movements differing in rhythm and mood but related in key

son•a•ti•na \ˌsä-nə-ˈtē-nə\ *n* [It, dim. of *sonata*] : a short usu. simplified sonata

song \ˈsȯŋ\ *n* **1** : vocal music; *also* : a short composition of words and music **2** : poetic composition **3** : a distinctive or characteristic sound (as of a bird) **4** : a small amount (sold for a ∼)

song•bird \ˈsȯŋ-ˌbərd\ *n* : a bird that utters a series of musical tones

Song of Sol•o•mon \-ˈsä-lə-mən\ — see BIBLE table

Song of Songs — see BIBLE table

song•ster \ˈsȯŋ-stər\ *n* : one that sings

song•stress \-strəs\ *n* : a female singer

son•ic \ˈsä-nik\ *adj* : of or relating to sound waves or the speed of sound

sonic boom *n* : an explosive sound produced by an aircraft traveling at supersonic speed

son–in–law \ˈsən-ən-ˌlȯ\ *n, pl* **sons–in–law** : the husband of one's daughter

son•net \ˈsä-nət\ *n* : a poem of 14 lines usu. in iambic pentameter with a definite rhyme scheme

so•no•rous \sə-ˈnȯr-əs, ˈsä-nə-rəs\ *adj* **1** : giving out sound when struck **2** : loud, deep, or rich in sound : RESONANT **3** : high-sounding : IMPRESSIVE — **so•nor•i•ty** \sə-ˈnȯr-ə-tē\ *n*

soon \ˈsün\ *adv* **1** : before long **2** : PROMPTLY, QUICKLY **3** *archaic* : EARLY **4** : WILLINGLY, READILY

soot \ˈsůt, ˈsət, ˈsüt\ *n* : a fine black powder consisting chiefly of carbon that is formed when something burns and that colors smoke — **sooty** *adj*

sooth \ˈsüth\ *n, archaic* : TRUTH

soothe \ˈsüth\ *vb* **soothed; sooth•ing 1** : to please by flattery or attention **2** : to calm down : COMFORT — **sooth•er** *n* — **sooth•ing•ly** *adv*

sooth•say•er \ˈsüth-ˌsā-ər\ *n* : one who foretells events — **sooth•say•ing** *n*

¹**sop** \ˈsäp\ *n* : a conciliatory bribe, gift, or concession

²**sop** *vb* **sopped; sop•ping 1** : to steep or dip in or as if in a liquid **2** : to wet thoroughly : SOAK; *also* : to mop up (a liquid)

SOP *abbr* standard operating procedure; standing operating procedure

soph *abbr* sophomore

soph•ism \ˈsä-ˌfi-zəm\ *n* **1** : an argument correct in form but embodying a subtle fallacy **2** : SOPHISTRY

soph•ist \ˈsä-fist\ *n* : PHILOSOPHER; *esp* : a captious or fallacious reasoner

so•phis•tic \sä-ˈfis-tik, sə-\ *or* **so•phis•ti•cal** \-ti-kəl\ *adj* : of or characteristic of sophists or sophistry **syn** fallacious, illogical, unreasonable, specious

so•phis•ti•cat•ed \sə-ˈfis-tə-ˌkā-təd\ *adj* **1** : COMPLEX ⟨∼ instruments⟩ **2** : made worldly-wise by wide experience **3** : intellectually appealing ⟨∼ novel⟩ — **so•phis•ti•ca•tion** \-ˌfis-tə-ˈkā-shən\ *n*

soph•ist•ry \ˈsä-fə-strē\ *n* : subtly deceptive reasoning or argument

soph•o•more \ˈsäf-ˌmȯr, ˈsä-fə-\ *n* : a student in the second year of high school or college

soph•o•mor•ic \ˌsäf-ˈmȯr-ik, ˌsä-fə-\ *adj* **1** : being overconfident of knowledge but poorly informed and immature **2** : of, relating to, or characteristic of a sophomore ⟨a ∼ prank⟩

So•pho•ni•as \ˌsä-fə-ˈnī-əs, ˌsō-\ *n* : ZEPHANIAH

sop•o•rif•ic \ˌsä-pə-ˈri-fik\ *adj* **1** : causing sleep or drowsiness **2** : LETHARGIC

so•pra•no \sə-ˈpra-nō, -ˈprä-\ *n, pl* **-nos** [It, fr. *sopra* above, fr. L *supra*] **1** : the highest singing voice; *also* : a singer with this voice **2** : the highest part in a 4-part chorus — **soprano** *adj*

sor•bet \sȯr-ˈbā\ *n* : a fruit-flavored ice served for dessert or between courses as a palate refresher

sor•cery \ˈsȯr-sə-rē\ *n* [ME *sorcerie*, fr. OF, fr. *sorcier* sorcerer, fr. (assumed) VL *sortiarius*, fr. L *sort-, sors* chance, lot] : the use of magic : WITCHCRAFT — **sor•cer•er** \-rər\ *n* — **sor•cer•ess** \-rəs\ *n*

sor•did \ˈsȯr-dəd\ *adj* **1** : marked by baseness or grossness : VILE **2** : DIRTY, SQUALID — **sor•did•ly** *adv* — **sor•did•ness** *n*

¹**sore** \ˈsȯr\ *adj* **sor•er; sor•est 1** : causing pain or distress (a ∼ bruise) **2** : painfully sensitive ⟨∼ muscles⟩ **3** : SEVERE, INTENSE **4** : IRRITATED, ANGRY — **sore•ly** *adv* — **sore•ness** *n*

²**sore** *n* **1** : a sore spot on the body; *esp* : one (as an ulcer) with the tissues broken and usu. infected **2** : a source of pain or vexation

sore•head \ˈsȯr-ˌhed, ˈsȯr-\ *n* : a person easily angered or discontented

sore throat *n* : painful throat due to inflammation

sor•ghum \ˈsȯr-gəm\ *n* : a tall variable Old World tropical grass grown widely for its edible seed, for forage, or for its sweet juice which yields a syrup

so•ror•i•ty \sə-ˈrȯr-ə-tē\ *n, pl* **-ties** [ML *sororitas* sisterhood, fr. L *soror* sister] : a club of girls or women esp. at a college

¹**sor•rel** \ˈsȯr-əl\ *n* : a brownish orange to light brown color; *also* : a sorrel-colored animal (as a horse)

²**sorrel** *n* : any of various herbs having a sour juice

sor•row \ˈsär-ō\ *n* **1** : deep distress, sadness, or regret; *also* : resultant unhappy or unpleasant state **2** : a cause of grief or sadness **3** : a display of grief or sadness — **sorrow** *vb* — **sor•row•ful** \-fəl\ *adj* — **sor•row•ful•ly** \-f(ə-)lē\ *adv*

sor•ry \ˈsär-ē\ *adj* **sor•ri•er; -est 1** : feeling sorrow, regret, or penitence **2** : MOURNFUL, SAD **3** : causing sorrow, pity, or scorn : WRETCHED

¹**sort** \ˈsȯrt\ *n* **1** : a group of persons or things that have similar characteristics : CLASS **2** : WAY, MANNER **3** : QUALITY, NATURE **4** : an instance of sorting — **out of sorts 1** : somewhat ill **2** : GROUCHY, IRRITABLE

²**sort** *vb* **1** : to put in a certain place according to kind, class, or nature **2** : to be in accord : AGREE — **sort•er** *n*

sor•tie \'sòr-tē, sòr-'tē\ *n* **1** : a sudden issuing of troops from a defensive position against the enemy **2** : one mission or attack by one airplane

sort of *adv* : to a moderate degree

SOS \ˌes-(ˌ)ō-'es\ *n* : a call or request for help or rescue

so–so \'sō-'sō\ *adv or adj* : PASSABLY

sot \'sät\ *n* : a habitual drunkard — **sot•tish** *adj* — **sot•tish•ly** *adv*

souf•flé \sü-'flā\ *n* [F, fr. *soufflé*, pp. of *souffler* to blow, puff up, fr. L *sufflare*, fr. *sub-* up + *flare* to blow] : a spongy dish made light in baking by stiffly beaten egg whites

sough \'saù, 'səf\ *vb* : to make a moaning or sighing sound — **sough** *n*

sought *past and past part of* SEEK

¹soul \'sōl\ *n* **1** : the immaterial essence of an individual life **2** : the spiritual principle embodied in human beings or the universe **3** : an active or essential part **4** : the moral and emotional nature of human beings **5** : spiritual or moral force **6** : PERSON ⟨a kindly ∼⟩ **7** : a strong, positive feeling (as of intense sensitivity and emotional fervor) conveyed esp. by black American performers; *also* : NEGRITUDE — **souled** \'sōld\ *adj* — **soul•less** \'sōl-ləs\ *adj*

²soul *adj* **1** : of, relating to, or characteristic of black Americans or their culture ⟨∼ food⟩ ⟨∼ music⟩ **2** : designed for or controlled by blacks ⟨∼ radio stations⟩

soul brother *n* : a black male

soul•ful \'sōl-fəl\ *adj* : full of or expressing deep feeling — **soul•ful•ly** *adv*

¹sound \'saùnd\ *adj* **1** : not diseased or sickly **2** : free from flaw or defect **3** : FIRM, STRONG **4** : free from error or fallacy : RIGHT **5** : LEGAL, VALID **6** : THOROUGH **7** : UNDISTURBED ⟨∼ sleep⟩ **8** : showing good judgment — **sound•ly** *adv* — **sound•ness** *n*

²sound *n* **1** : the sensation of hearing; *also* : mechanical energy transmitted by longitudinal pressure waves (**sound waves**) (as in air) that is the stimulus to hearing **2** : something heard : NOISE, TONE; *also* : hearing distance : EARSHOT **3** : a musical style — **sound•less** *adj* — **sound•less•ly** *adv* — **sound•proof** \-ˌprüf\ *adj or vb*

³sound *vb* **1** : to make or cause to make a sound **2** : to order or proclaim by a sound ⟨∼ the alarm⟩ **3** : to convey a certain impression : SEEM **4** : to examine the condition of by causing to give out sounds — **sound•able** \'saùn-də-bəl\ *adj*

⁴sound *n* : a long passage of water wider than a strait often connecting two larger bodies of water ⟨Puget ∼⟩

⁵sound *vb* **1** : to measure the depth of (water) esp. by a weighted line dropped from the surface : FATHOM **2** : PROBE **3** : to dive down suddenly ⟨the hooked fish ∼ed⟩ — **sound•ing** *n*

sound bite *n* : a brief recorded statement broadcast esp. on a news program

sound•er \'saùn-dər\ *n* : one that sounds; *esp* : a device for making soundings

sound•stage \'saùnd-ˌstāj\ *n* : the part of a motion-picture studio in which a production is filmed

soup \'süp\ *n* **1** : a liquid food with stock as its base and often containing pieces of solid food **2** : something having the consistency of soup **3** : an unfortunate predicament ⟨in the ∼⟩

soup•çon \süp-'sōⁿ\ *n* [F, lit., suspicion] : a little bit : ¹TRACE **2**

soup•spoon \'süp-ˌspün\ *n* : a spoon with a large or rounded bowl for eating soup

soup up *vb* : to increase the power of

soupy \'sü-pē\ *adj* **soup•i•er; -est 1** : having the consistency of soup **2** : densely foggy or cloudy

¹sour \'saùr\ *adj* **1** : having an acid or tart taste ⟨∼ as vinegar⟩ **2** : SPOILED, PUTRID ⟨a ∼ odor⟩ **3** : UNPLEASANT, DISAGREEABLE ⟨∼ disposition⟩ — **sour•ish** *adj* — **sour•ly** *adv* — **sour•ness** *n*

²sour *vb* : to become or make sour

source \'sòrs\ *n* **1** : ORIGIN, BEGINNING **2** : a supplier of information **3** : the beginning of a stream of water

¹souse \'saùs\ *vb* **soused; sous•ing 1** : PICKLE **2** : to plunge into a liquid **3** : DRENCH **4** : to make drunk

²souse *n* **1** : something (as pigs' feet) steeped in pickle **2** : a soaking in liquid **3** : DRUNKARD

¹south \'saùth\ *adv* : to or toward the south; *also* : into a state of decline

²south *adj* **1** : situated toward or at the south **2** : coming from the south

³south *n* **1** : the direction to the right of one facing east **2** : the compass point directly opposite to north **3** *cap* : regions or countries south of a specified or implied point; *esp* : the southeastern part of the U.S. — **south•er•ly** \'sə-thər-lē\ *adj or adv* — **south•ern** \'sə-thərn\ *adj* — **South•ern•er** *n* — **south•ern•most** \-ˌmōst\ *adj* — **south•ward** \'saùth-wərd\ *adv or adj* — **south•wards** \-wərdz\ *adv*

South African *n* : a native or inhabitant of the Republic of South Africa — **South African** *adj*

south•east \saù-'thēst, *naut* saù-'ēst\ *n* **1** : the general direction between south and east **2** : the compass point midway between south and east **3** *cap* : regions or countries southeast of a specified or implied point — **southeast** *adj or adv* — **south•east•er•ly** *adv or adj* — **south•east•ern** \-'ēs-tərn\ *adj*

south•paw \'saùth-ˌpò\ *n* : a left-handed person; *esp* : a left-handed baseball pitcher — **southpaw** *adj*

south pole *n, often cap S&P* : the southernmost point of the earth

south•west \saùth-'west, *naut* saù-'west\ *n* **1** : the general direction between south and west **2** : the compass point midway between south and west **3** *cap* : regions or countries southwest of a specified or implied point — **southwest** *adj or adv* — **south•west•er•ly** *adv or adj* — **south•west•ern** \-'wes-tərn\ *adj*

sou•ve•nir \ˌsü-və-'nir\ *n* [F] : something serving as a reminder

sou'•west•er \saù-'wes-tər\ *n* : a long waterproof coat worn in storms at sea; *also* : a waterproof hat

¹sov•er•eign \'sä-vrən, -və-rən\ *n* **1** : one possessing the supreme power and authority in a state **2** : a gold coin of the United Kingdom

²sovereign *adj* **1** : EXCELLENT, FINE **2** : supreme in power or authority **3** : CHIEF, HIGHEST **4** : having independent authority

sov•er•eign•ty \-tē\ *n, pl* **-ties 1** : supremacy in rule or power **2** : power to govern without external control **3** : the supreme political power in a state

so•vi•et \'sō-vē-ˌet, 'sä-, -ət\ *n* **1** : an elected governmental council in a Communist country **2** *pl, cap* : the people and esp. the leaders of the U.S.S.R. — **soviet** *adj, often cap* — **so•vi•et•ize** *vb, often cap*

¹sow \'saù\ *n* : an adult female swine

²sow \'sō\ *vb* **sowed; sown** \'sōn\ *or* **sowed; sow•ing 1** : to plant seed esp. by scattering **2** : to strew with seed **3** : to scatter abroad — **sow•er** \'sō-ər\ *n*

sow bug \'saù-\ *n* : WOOD LOUSE

sox *pl of* SOCK

soy \'sòi\ *n* : a sauce made from soybeans fermented in brine

soy•bean \'sòi-ˌbēn\ *n* : an Asian legume widely grown for forage and for its edible seeds that yield a valuable oil (**soybean oil**); *also* : its seed

sp *abbr* **1** special **2** species **3** specimen **4** spelling **5** spirit

Sp *abbr* Spain

SP *abbr* **1** shore patrol; shore patrolman **2** shore police **3** specialist

spa \'spä\ *n* [*Spa*, watering place in Belgium] **1** : a resort with mineral springs **2** : a health and fitness facility **3** : a hot tub with a whirlpool device

¹space \'spās\ *n* **1** : a period of time **2** : some small measurable distance, area, or volume **3** : the limitless area in which all things exist and move **4** : an empty place **5** : the region beyond the earth's atmosphere **6** : a definite place (as a seat on a train or ship)

²**space** *vb* **spaced; spac·ing** : to place at intervals — **spac·er** *n*

space–age \'spās-ₐāj\ *adj* : of or relating to the age of space exploration

space·craft \-ₐkraft\ *n* : a vehicle for travel beyond the earth's atmosphere

space·flight \-ₐflīt\ *n* : flight beyond the earth's atmosphere

space heater *n* : a usu. portable device for heating a relatively small area

space·man \'spās-ₐman, -mən\ *n* : one who travels outside the earth's atmosphere

space·ship \-ₐship\ *n* : a vehicle used for space travel

space shuttle *n* : a reusable spacecraft designed to transport people and cargo between earth and space

space station *n* : a large artificial satellite serving as a base (as for scientific observation)

space suit *n* : a suit equipped to make life in space possible for its wearer

space walk *n* : a period of activity outside a spacecraft by an astronaut in space — **space·walk** \'spās-ₐwȯk\ *vb* — **space·walk·er** *n*

spa·cious \'spā-shəs\ *adj* : very large in extent : ROOMY **syn** commodious, capacious, ample — **spa·cious·ly** *adv* — **spa·cious·ness** *n*

¹**spade** \'spād\ *n* : a shovel with a blade for digging — **spade·ful** *n*

²**spade** *vb* **spad·ed; spad·ing** : to dig with a spade — **spad·er** *n*

³**spade** *n* : any of a suit of playing cards marked with a black figure resembling an inverted heart with a short stem at the bottom

spa·dix \'spā-diks\ *n*, *pl* **spa·di·ces** \'spā-də-ₐsēz\ : a floral spike with a fleshy or succulent axis usu. enclosed in a spathe

spa·ghet·ti \spə-'ge-tē\ *n* [It, fr. pl. of *spaghetto*, dim. of *spago* cord, string] : thin solid pasta strings

¹**span** \'span\ *n* **1** : an English unit of length equal to nine inches (about 23 centimeters) **2** : a limited portion of time **3** : the spread (as of an arch) from one support to another

²**span** *vb* **spanned; span·ning 1** : MEASURE **2** : to extend across

³**span** *n* : a pair of animals (as mules) driven together

Span *abbr* Spanish

span·dex \'span-ₐdeks\ *n* : any of various elastic synthetic textile fibers

span·gle \'span-gəl\ *n* : a small disk of shining metal or plastic used esp. on a dress for ornament — **spangle** *vb*

Span·glish \'span-glish\ *n* : a combination of Spanish and English

Span·iard \'span-yərd\ *n* : a native or inhabitant of Spain

span·iel \'span-yəl\ *n* [ME *spaniell*, fr. MF *espaignol*, lit., Spaniard] : a dog of any of several breeds of mostly small and short-legged dogs usu. with long wavy hair and large drooping ears

Span·ish \'spa-nish\ *n* **1** : the chief language of Spain and of the countries colonized by the Spanish **2** **Spanish** *pl* : the people of Spain — **Spanish** *adj*

Spanish American *n* : a resident of the U.S. whose native language is Spanish; *also* : a native or inhabitant of one of the countries of America in which Spanish is the national language — **Spanish–American** *adj*

Spanish fly *n* : a preparation of dried green European beetles noted as an aphrodisiac with often highly toxic side effects but not in reputable medical use

Spanish moss *n* : a plant related to the pineapple that grows in pendent tufts of grayish green filaments on trees from the southern U.S. to Argentina

Spanish rice *n* : rice cooked with onions, green peppers, and tomatoes

spaniel

spank \'spank\ *vb* : to hit on the buttocks with the open hand — **spank** *n*

spank·ing \'span-kin\ *adj* : BRISK, LIVELY ⟨∼ breeze⟩ — **spanking** *adv*

span·ner \'span-ər\ *n*, *chiefly Brit* : WRENCH

¹**spar** \'spär\ *n* **1** : a stout pole **2** : a rounded wood or metal piece (as a mast, yard, boom, or gaff) for supporting sail rigging

²**spar** *vb* **sparred; spar·ring** : to box for practice without serious hitting; *also* : SKIRMISH, WRANGLE

¹**spare** \'spar\ *vb* **spared; spar·ing 1** : to refrain from punishing or injuring : show mercy to ⟨∼d the prisoners⟩ **2** : to exempt from something ⟨∼ me the trouble⟩ **3** : to get along without ⟨can't ∼ a dime⟩ **4** : to use frugally or rarely ⟨don't ∼ the syrup⟩

²**spare** *adj* **spar·er; spar·est 1** : held in reserve **2** : SUPERFLUOUS **3** : not liberal or profuse **4** : LEAN, THIN **5** : SCANTY **syn** meager, sparse, skimpy, exiguous, scant — **spare·ness** *n*

³**spare** *n* **1** : a duplicate kept in reserve; *esp* : a spare tire **2** : the knocking down of all the bowling pins with the first two balls

spar·ing \'spar-in\ *adj* : SAVING, FRUGAL **syn** thrifty, economical, provident — **spar·ing·ly** *adv*

¹**spark** \'spärk\ *n* **1** : a small particle of a burning substance or a hot glowing particle struck from a mass (as by steel on flint) **2** : a short bright flash of electricity between two points **3** : SPARKLE **4** : a particle capable of being kindled or developed : GERM

²**spark** *vb* **1** : to emit or produce sparks **2** : to stir to activity : INCITE

³**spark** *vb* : WOO, COURT

¹**spar·kle** \'spär-kəl\ *vb* **spar·kled; spar·kling 1** : FLASH, GLEAM **2** : to perform brilliantly **3** : EFFERVESCE — **spar·kler** *n*

²**sparkle** *n* **1** : GLEAM **2** : ANIMATION

spark plug *n* **1** : a device that produces a spark to ignite the fuel mixture in an engine cylinder **2** : one that begins something or drives something forward

spar·row \'spar-ō\ *n* : any of several small dull≈colored singing birds

sparse \'spärs\ *adj* **spars·er; spars·est** : thinly scattered : SCANTY **syn** meager, spare, skimpy, exiguous, scant — **sparse·ly** *adv* — **sparse·ness** *n*

spasm \'spa-zəm\ *n* **1** : a sudden involuntary and abnormal muscular contraction **2** : a sudden, violent, and temporary effort, feeling, or outburst

spas·mod·ic \spaz-'mä-dik\ *adj* **1** : relating to or affected or characterized by spasm ⟨∼ movements⟩; *also* : resembling a spasm **2** : INTERMITTENT — **spas·mod·i·cal·ly** \-di-k(ə-)lē\ *adv*

spas·tic \'spas-tik\ *adj* : of, relating to, marked by, or affected with muscular spasm ⟨∼ paralysis⟩ — **spastic** *n*

¹**spat** \'spat\ *past and past part of* SPIT

²**spat** *n*, *pl* **spat** *or* **spats** : a young bivalve mollusk (as an oyster)

³**spat** *n* : a gaiter covering instep and ankle

⁴**spat** *n* : a brief petty quarrel : DISPUTE

spat

⁵**spat** *vb* **spat·ted; spat·ting** : to quarrel briefly

spate \'spāt\ *n* : a sudden outburst

spathe \'spāth\ *n* : a sheathing bract or pair of bracts enclosing an inflorescence (as of the calla lily) and esp. a spadix on the same axis

spa·tial \'spā-shəl\ *adj* : of or relating to space — **spa·tial·ly** *adv*

spat·ter \'spa-tər\ *vb* **1** : to splash with drops of liquid **2** : to sprinkle around — **spatter** *n*

spat·u·la \'spa-chə-lə\ *n* : a flexible knifelike implement for scooping, spreading, or mixing soft substances

spav·in \'spa-vən\ *n* : a bony enlargement of the hock of a horse — **spav·ined** \-vənd\ *adj*

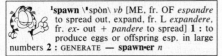

¹**spawn** \'spȯn\ *vb* [ME, fr. OF *espandre* to spread out, expand, fr. L *expandere*, fr. *ex-* out + *pandere* to spread] **1** : to produce eggs or offspring esp. in large numbers **2** : GENERATE — **spawn·er** *n*

²**spawn** *n* **1** : the eggs of water animals (as fishes or oysters) that lay many small eggs **2** : offspring esp. when produced in great quantities

spay \'spā\ *vb* **spayed; spay·ing** : to remove the ovaries of (a female animal)

SPCA *abbr* Society for the Prevention of Cruelty to Animals

SPCC *abbr* Society for the Prevention of Cruelty to Children

speak \'spēk\ *vb* **spoke** \'spōk\; **spo·ken** \'spō-kən\; **speak·ing 1** : to utter words **2** : to express orally **3** : to mention in speech or writing **4** : to address an audience **5** : to use or be able to use (a language) in talking

speak·easy \'spēk-ˌē-zē\ *n, pl* **-eas·ies** : an illicit drinking place

speak·er \'spē-kər\ *n* **1** : one that speaks **2** : the presiding officer of a deliberative assembly **3** : LOUD-SPEAKER

¹**spear** \'spir\ *n* **1** : a long-shafted weapon with a sharp point for thrusting or throwing **2** : a sharp-pointed instrument with barbs used in spearing fish — **spear·man** \-mən\ *n*

²**spear** *vb* : to strike or pierce with or as if with a spear — **spear·er** *n*

³**spear** *n* : a usu. young blade, shoot, or sprout (as of asparagus)

spear·head \-ˌhed\ *n* : a leading force, element, or influence — **spearhead** *vb*

spear·mint \-ˌmint\ *n* : a common highly aromatic garden mint

spec *abbr* **1** special **2** specifically

spe·cial \'spe-shəl\ *adj* **1** : UNCOMMON, NOTEWORTHY **2** : particularly favored **3** : INDIVIDUAL, UNIQUE **4** : EXTRA, ADDITIONAL **5** : confined to or designed for a definite field of action, purpose, or occasion — **special** *n*

special delivery *n* : delivery of mail by messenger for an extra fee

special effects *n pl* : images in a television or film production added after filming is completed to enhance believability

Special Forces *n pl* : a branch of the army composed of soldiers specially trained in guerrilla warfare

spe·cial·ise *Brit var of* SPECIALIZE

spe·cial·ist \'spe-shə-list\ *n* **1** : a person who specializes in a particular branch of learning or activity **2** : any of four enlisted ranks in the army corresponding to the grades of corporal through sergeant first class

spe·cial·ize \'spe-shə-ˌlīz\ *vb* **-ized; -iz·ing** : to concentrate one's efforts in a special activity or field; *also* : to change in an adaptive manner — **spe·cial·i·za·tion** \ˌspe-shə-lə-ˈzā-shən\ *n*

spe·cial·ly \'spe-shə-lē\ *adv* **1** : in a special manner **2** : for a special purpose : in particular

spe·cial·ty \'spe-shəl-tē\ *n, pl* **-ties 1** : a particular quality or detail **2** : a product of a special kind or of special excellence **3** : something (as a discipline) in which one specializes

spe·cie \'spē-shē, -sē\ *n* : money in coin

spe·cies \'spē-shēz, -sēz\ *n, pl* **spe·cies** [ME, fr. L, appearance, kind, species, fr. *specere* to look] **1** : SORT, KIND **2** : a category of biological classification ranking just below the genus or subgenus and comprising closely related organisms potentially able to breed with one another

specif *abbr* specific; specifically

¹**spe·cif·ic** \spi-ˈsi-fik\ *adj* **1** : having a unique effect or influence or reacting in only one way or with only one thing ⟨∼ antibodies⟩ ⟨∼ enzymes⟩ **2** : DEFINITE, EXACT **3** : of, relating to, or constituting a species — **spe·cif·i·cal·ly** \-fi-k(ə-)lē\ *adv*

²**specific** *n* : something specific : DETAIL, PARTICULAR — usu. used in pl.

spec·i·fi·ca·tion \ˌspe-sə-fə-ˈkā-shən\ *n* **1** : the act or process of specifying **2** : a description of work to be done and materials to be used (as in building) — usu. used in pl.

specific gravity *n* : the ratio of the density of a substance to the density of some substance (as water) taken as a standard when both densities are obtained by weighing in air

GARFIELD, WHAT'S THE MATTER?

JON! YOU GOTTA CLEAN OUT THE REFRIGERATOR!

WHATEVER IT IS, IT CAN'T BE THAT BAD, OLD BUDDY

THE TUNA IS SPAWNING IN THE TOMATO SOUP!

JIM DAVIS 9-25
© 1987 PAWS, INC.

spec·i·fy \'spe-sə-ˌfī\ vb **-fied; -fy·ing** : to mention or name explicitly

spec·i·men \'spe-sə-mən\ n : an item or part typical of a group or whole

spe·cious \'spē-shəs\ adj : seeming to be genuine, correct, or beautiful but not really so (∼ reasoning)

speck \'spek\ n **1** : a small spot or blemish **2** : a small particle — **speck** vb

speck·le \'spe-kəl\ n : a little speck — **speckle** vb

¹specs \'speks\ n pl : GLASSES

²specs n pl : SPECIFICATIONS

spec·ta·cle \'spek-ti-kəl\ n **1** : an unusual or impressive public display **2** pl : GLASSES — **spec·ta·cled** \-kəld\ adj

spec·tac·u·lar \spek-'ta-kyə-lər\ adj : exciting to see : SENSATIONAL

spec·ta·tor \'spek-ˌtā-tər\ n : a person who looks on (as at a sports event) syn observer, witness, bystander, onlooker, eyewitness

spec·ter or **spec·tre** \'spek-tər\ n : a visible disembodied spirit : GHOST

spec·tral \'spek-trəl\ adj **1** : of, relating to, or resembling a specter **2** : of, relating to, or made by a spectrum

spec·tro·gram \'spek-trə-ˌgram\ n : a photograph or diagram of a spectrum

spec·tro·graph \-ˌgraf\ n : an instrument for dispersing radiation into a spectrum and photographing or mapping the spectrum — **spec·tro·graph·ic** \ˌspek-trə-'gra-fik\ adj — **spec·tro·graph·i·cal·ly** \-fi-k(ə-)lē\ adv

spec·trom·e·ter \spek-'trä-mə-tər\ n : an instrument for measuring spectra — **spec·tro·met·ric** \ˌspek-trə-'me-trik\ adj — **spec·trom·e·try** \spek-'trä-mə-trē\ n

spec·tro·scope \'spek-trə-ˌskōp\ n : an instrument that produces spectra esp. of visible electromagnetic radiation — **spec·tro·scop·ic** \ˌspek-trə-'skä-pik\ adj — **spec·tro·scop·i·cal·ly** \-pi-k(ə-)lē\ adv — **spec·tros·co·pist** \spek-'träs-kə-pist\ n — **spec·tros·co·py** \-pē\ n

spec·trum \'spek-trəm\ n, pl **spec·tra** \-trə\ or **spec·trums** [NL, fr. L, appearance, fr. specere to look] **1** : a series of colors formed when a beam of white light is dispersed (as by a prism) so that its parts are arranged in the order of their wavelengths **2** : a series of radiations arranged in regular order **3** : a continuous sequence or range (a wide ∼ of political opinions)

spec·u·late \'spe-kyə-ˌlāt\ vb **-lat·ed; -lat·ing** [L speculari to spy out, examine, fr. specula watchtower, fr. specere to look, look at] **1** : to think or wonder about a subject **2** : to take a business risk in hope of gain syn reason, think, deliberate, reflect — **spec·u·la·tion** \ˌspe-kyə-'lā-shən\ n — **spec·u·la·tive** \'spe-kyə-ˌlā-tiv\ adj — **spec·u·la·tive·ly** adv — **spec·u·la·tor** \-ˌlā-tər\ n

speech \'spēch\ n **1** : the act of speaking **2** : TALK, CONVERSATION **3** : a public talk or lecture **4** : LANGUAGE, DIALECT **5** : an individual manner of speaking **6** : the power of speaking — **speech·less** adj

¹speed \'spēd\ n **1** archaic : SUCCESS **2** : SWIFTNESS, RAPIDITY **3** : rate of motion or performance **4** : a transmission gear (as of a bicycle) **5** : METHAMPHETAMINE; also : a related drug syn haste, hurry, dispatch, celerity — **speed·i·ly** \'spē-də-lē\ adv — **speedy** adj

²speed vb **sped** \'sped\ or **speed·ed; speed·ing 1** archaic : PROSPER; also : GET ALONG, FARE **2** : to go fast; esp : to go at an excessive or illegal speed **3** : to cause to go faster — **speed·er** n

speed·boat \-ˌbōt\ n : a fast motorboat

speed bump n : a low raised ridge across a roadway (as in a parking lot) to limit vehicle speed

speed·om·e·ter \spi-'dä-mə-tər\ n : an instrument for indicating speed

speed·up \'spēd-ˌəp\ n : ACCELERATION

speed·way \-ˌwā\ n : a racecourse for motor vehicles

speed·well \'spēd-ˌwel\ n : a low creeping plant that bears spikes of small usu. bluish flowers and is related to the snapdragon

¹spell \'spel\ vb **spelled** \'speld, 'spelt\; **spell·ing 1** : to name, write, or print in order the letters of a word **2** : MEAN

²spell n [ME, talk, tale, fr. OE] **1** : a magic formula : INCANTATION **2** : a controlling influence

³spell n **1** : one's turn at work or duty **2** : a stretch of a specified kind of weather **3** : a period of bodily or mental distress or disorder : ATTACK

⁴spell vb **spelled** \'speld\; **spell·ing** : to take the place of for a time in work or duty : RELIEVE

spell·bind·er \-ˌbīn-dər\ n : a speaker of compelling eloquence

spell·bound \-ˌbau̇nd\ adj : held by or as if by a spell : FASCINATED

spell·er \'spe-lər\ n **1** : one who spells words **2** : a book with exercises for teaching spelling

spelt \'spelt\ chiefly Brit past and past part of ¹SPELL

spe·lunk·er \spi-'ləŋ-kər, 'spē-ˌləŋ-kər\ n [L spelunca cave, fr. Gk spēlynx] : one who makes a hobby of exploring caves — **spe·lunk·ing** n

spend \'spend\ vb **spent** \'spent\; **spend·ing 1** : to pay out : EXPEND **2** : WEAR OUT, EXHAUST; also : to consume wastefully **3** : to cause or permit to elapse : PASS — **spend·er** n

spend·thrift \'spend-ˌthrift\ n : one who spends wastefully or recklessly

spent \'spent\ adj : drained of energy

sperm \'spərm\ n, pl **sperm** or **sperms 1** : SEMEN **2** : a male gamete

sper·ma·to·zo·on \(ˌ)spər-ˌma-tə-'zō-ˌän, -'zō-ən\ n, pl **-zoa** \-'zō-ə\ : a motile male gamete of an animal usu. with a rounded or elongated head and a long posterior flagellum

sperm cell n : SPERM 2

sper·mi·cide \'spər-mə-ˌsīd\ n : a preparation or substance used to kill sperm — **sper·mi·cid·al** \ˌspər-mə-'sī-dəl\ adj

sperm whale *n* : a whale with conical teeth, no whale-bone, and a large fluid-containing cavity in the head

spew \'spyü\ *vb* : VOMIT

SPF *abbr* sun protection factor

sp gr *abbr* specific gravity

sphag·num \'sfag-nəm\ *n* : any of a genus of atypical mosses that grow in wet acid areas where their remains become compacted with other plant debris to form peat; *also* : a mass of these mosses

sphere \'sfir\ *n* [ME *spere* globe, celestial sphere, fr. MF *espere*, fr. L *sphaera*, fr. Gk *sphaira*, lit., ball] 1 : a globe-shaped body : BALL 2 : a celestial body 3 : a solid figure so shaped that every point on its surface is an equal distance from the center 4 : range of action or influence — **spher·i·cal** \'sfir-i-kəl, 'sfer-\ *adj* — **spher·i·cal·ly** \-i-k(ə-)lē\ *adv*

spher·oid \'sfir-ˌòid, 'sfer-\ *n* : a figure similar to a sphere but not perfectly round — **sphe·roi·dal** \sfir-'òi-dəl\ *adj*

sphinc·ter \'sfiŋk-tər\ *n* : a muscular ring that closes a bodily opening

sphinx \'sfiŋks\ *n, pl* **sphinx·es** *or* **sphin·ges** \'sfin-ˌjēz\ 1 : a winged monster in Greek mythology having a woman's head and a lion's body and noted for killing anyone unable to answer its riddle 2 : an enigmatic or mysterious person 3 : an ancient Egyptian image having the body of a lion and the head of a man, ram, or hawk

spice \'spīs\ *n* 1 : any of various aromatic plant products (as pepper or nutmeg) used to season or flavor foods 2 : something that adds interest and relish — **spice** *vb* — **spicy** *adj*

spick–and–span *or* **spic–and–span** \ˌspik-ənd-'span\ *adj* : quite new; *also* : spotlessly clean

spic·ule \'spi-kyül\ *n* : a slender pointed body esp. of calcium or silica (sponge ∼s)

spi·der \'spī-dər\ *n* 1 : any of an order of arachnids that have a 2-part body, eight legs, and two or more pairs of abdominal organs for spinning threads of silk used esp. in making webs for catching prey 2 : a cast-iron frying pan — **spi·dery** *adj*

spider mite *n* : any of several small web-spinning mites that attack forage and crop plants

spider plant *n* : a houseplant of the lily family having long green leaves usu. striped with white and producing tufts of small plants on long hanging stems

spi·der·web \'spī-dər-ˌweb\ *n* : the web spun by a spider

spiel \'spēl\ *vb* : to talk in a fast, smooth, and usu. colorful manner — **spiel** *n*

spig·ot \'spi-gət, -kət\ *n* : FAUCET

¹spike \'spīk\ *n* 1 : a very large nail 2 : any of various pointed projections (as on the sole of a shoe to prevent slipping) — **spiky** *adj*

²spike *vb* **spiked; spik·ing** 1 : to fasten with spikes 2 : to put an end to : QUASH (∼ a rumor) 3 : to pierce with or impale on a spike 4 : to add alcoholic liquor to (a drink)

³spike *n* 1 : an ear of grain 2 : a long cluster of usu. stemless flowers

¹spill \'spil\ *vb* **spilled** \'spild, 'spilt\ *also* **spilt** \'spilt\; **spill·ing** 1 : to cause or allow to fall, flow, or run out esp. unintentionally 2 : to cause (blood) to be lost by wounding 3 : to run out or over with resulting loss or waste 4 : to let out : DIVULGE — **spill·able** *adj*

²spill *n* 1 : an act of spilling; *also* : a fall from a horse or vehicle or an erect position 2 : something spilled

spill·way \-ˌwā\ *n* : a passage for surplus water to run over or around an obstruction (as a dam)

¹spin \'spin\ *vb* **spun** \'spən\; **spin·ning** 1 : to draw out (fiber) and twist into thread; *also* : to form (thread) by such means 2 : to form thread by extruding a sticky quickly hardening fluid; *also* : to construct from such thread (spiders ∼ their webs) 3 : to produce slowly and by degrees (∼ a story) 4 : TWIRL 5 : WHIRL, REEL (my head is *spinning*) 6 : to move rapidly along — **spin·ner** *n*

²spin *n* 1 : a rapid rotating motion 2 : an excursion in a wheeled vehicle 3 : a particular point of view, emphasis, or interpretation

spin·ach \'spi-nich\ *n* : a dark green herb grown for its edible leaves

spi·nal \'spīn-əl\ *adj* : of or relating to the backbone or spinal cord — **spi·nal·ly** *adv*

spinal column *n* : BACKBONE

spinal cord *n* : the thick cord of nervous tissue that extends from the brain along the back in the cavity of the backbone and carries nerve impulses to and from the brain

spinal nerve *n* : any of the paired nerves which arise from the spinal cord and pass to various parts of the body and of which there are normally 31 pairs in human beings

spin·dle \'spind-əl\ *n* 1 : a round tapering stick or rod by which fibers are twisted in spinning 2 : a turned part of a piece of furniture (the ∼s of a chair) 3 : a slender pin or rod which turns or on which something else turns

spin·dling \'spind-liŋ\ *adj* : SPINDLY

spin·dly \'spind-lē\ *adj* : being long or tall and thin and usu. weak

spin·drift \'spin-ˌdrift\ *n* : spray blown from waves

spine \'spīn\ *n* 1 : BACKBONE 2 : a stiff sharp process esp. on a plant or animal 3 : the part of a book where the pages are attached — **spiny** *adj*

spi·nel \spə-'nel\ *n* : a hard crystalline mineral of variable color used as a gem

spine·less \'spīn-ləs\ *adj* 1 : having no spines, thorns, or prickles 2 : lacking a backbone 3 : lacking courage or determination

spin·et \'spi-nət\ *n* 1 : an early harpsichord having a single keyboard and only one string for each note 2 : a small upright piano

spin·na·ker \'spi-ni-kər\ *n* : a large triangular sail set on a long light pole

EAT YOUR SPINACH, GARFIELD

IT'S GOOD FOR YOU

WELL, NOW THAT'S MORE LIKE IT!

3-10

JIM DAViS

spinning jen·ny \-'je-nē\ *n* : an early multiple-spindle machine for spinning wool or cotton

spinning wheel *n* : a small machine for spinning thread or yarn in which a large wheel drives a single spindle

spin–off \'spin-ˌȯf\ *n* **1** : a usu. useful by-product **2** : something (as a TV show) derived from an earlier work — **spin off** *vb*

spin·ster \'spin-stər\ *n* : an unmarried woman past the common age for marrying — **spin·ster·hood** \-ˌhu̇d\ *n*

spiny lobster *n* : any of several edible crustaceans differing from the related lobster in lacking the large front claws and in having a very spiny carapace

¹spi·ral \'spī-rəl\ *adj* : winding or coiling around a center or axis and usu. getting closer to or farther away from it — **spi·ral·ly** *adv*

²spiral *n* **1** : something that has a spiral form; *also* : a single turn in a spiral object **2** : a continuously spreading and accelerating increase or decrease

³spiral *vb* **-raled** *or* **-ralled; -ral·ing** *or* **-ral·ling 1** : to move and esp. to rise or fall in a spiral course **2** : to form into a spiral

spi·rant \'spī-rənt\ *n* : a consonant (as \f\, \s\, \sh\) uttered with decided friction of the breath against some part of the oral passage — **spirant** *adj*

spire \'spīr\ *n* **1** : a slender tapering stalk (as of grass) **2** : a pointed tip (as of an antler) **3** : STEEPLE — **spiry** *adj*

spi·rea *or* **spi·raea** \spī-'rē-ə\ *n* : any of a genus of shrubs related to the roses with dense clusters of small white or pink flowers

¹spir·it \'spir-ət\ *n* [ME, fr. OF or L; OF, fr. L *spiritus*, lit., breath, fr. *spirare* to blow, breathe] **1** : a life-giving force; *also* : the animating principle : SOUL **2** *cap* : HOLY SPIRIT **3** : SPECTER, GHOST **4** : PERSON **5** : DISPOSITION, MOOD **6** : VIVACITY, ARDOR **7** : essential or real meaning : INTENT **8** : distilled alcoholic liquor **9** : LOYALTY (school ∼) — **spir·it·less** *adj*

²spirit *vb* : to carry off secretly or mysteriously

spir·it·ed \'spir-ə-təd\ *adj* **1** : ANIMATED, LIVELY **2** : COURAGEOUS

¹spir·i·tu·al \'spir-i-chəl, -chə-wəl\ *adj* **1** : of, relating to, consisting of, or affecting the spirit : INCORPOREAL **2** : of or relating to sacred matters **3** : ecclesiastical rather than lay or temporal — **spir·i·tu·al·i·ty** \ˌspir-i-chə-'wa-lə-tē\ *n* — **spir·i·tu·al·ize** \'spir-i-chə-ˌlīz, -chə-wə-\ *vb* — **spir·i·tu·al·ly** *adv*

²spiritual *n* : a religious song originating among blacks of the southern U.S.

spir·i·tu·al·ism \'spir-i-chə-ˌli-zəm, -chə-wə-\ *n* : a belief that spirits of the dead communicate with the living usu. through a medium — **spir·i·tu·al·ist** \-list\ *n*, *often cap* — **spir·i·tu·al·is·tic** \ˌspir-i-chə-'lis-tik, -chə-wə-\ *adj*

spir·i·tu·ous \'spir-i-chəs, -chə-wəs; 'spir-ə-təs\ *adj* : containing alcohol

spi·ro·chete *also* **spi·ro·chaete** \'spī-rə-ˌkēt\ *n* : any of an order of spirally undulating bacteria including those causing syphilis and Lyme disease

spirt *var of* SPURT

¹spit \'spit\ *n* **1** : a thin pointed rod for holding meat over a fire **2** : a point of land that runs out into the water

²spit *vb* **spit·ted; spit·ting** : to pierce with or as if with a spit

³spit *vb* **spit** *or* **spat** \'spat\; **spit·ting 1** : to eject (saliva) from the mouth **2** : to express by or as if by spitting **3** : to rain or snow lightly

⁴spit *n* **1** : SALIVA **2** : perfect likeness ⟨∼ and image of his father⟩

spit·ball \'spit-ˌbȯl\ *n* **1** : paper chewed and rolled into a ball to be thrown as a missile **2** : a baseball pitch delivered after the ball has been moistened with saliva or sweat

¹spite \'spīt\ *n* : ill will with a wish to annoy, anger, or frustrate : petty malice **syn** malignity, spleen, grudge, malevolence — **spite·ful** \-fəl\ *adj* — **spite·ful·ly** *adv* — **spite·ful·ness** *n* — **in spite of** : in defiance or contempt of : NOTWITHSTANDING

²spite *vb* **spit·ed; spit·ing** : to treat maliciously : ANNOY, OFFEND

spit·tle \'spit-əl\ *n* : SALIVA

spit·tle·bug \-ˌbəg\ *n* : any of a family of leaping insects with froth-secreting larvae that are related to aphids

spit·toon \spi-'tün\ *n* : a receptacle for spit

splash \'splash\ *vb* **1** : to dash a liquid about **2** : to scatter a liquid on : SPATTER **3** : to fall or strike with a splashing noise **syn** sprinkle, bespatter, douse, splatter — **splash** *n*

splash·down \'splash-ˌdau̇n\ *n* : the landing of a manned spacecraft in the ocean — **splash down** *vb*

splat·ter \'spla-tər\ *vb* : SPATTER — **splatter** *n*

¹splay \'splā\ *vb* : to spread outward or apart — **splay** *n*

²splay *adj* **1** : spread out : turned outward **2** : AWKWARD, CLUMSY

spleen \'splēn\ *n* **1** : a vascular organ located near the stomach in most vertebrates that is concerned esp. with the filtration and storage of blood, destruction of red blood cells, and production of lymphocytes **2** : SPITE, MALICE **syn** malignity, grudge, malevolence, ill will, spitefulness

splen·did \'splen-dəd\ *adj* [L *splendidus*, fr. *splendēre* to shine] **1** : SHINING, BRILLIANT **2** : SHOWY, GORGEOUS **3** : ILLUSTRIOUS **4** : EXCELLENT **syn** resplendent, glorious, sublime, superb — **splen·did·ly** *adv*

splen·dor \'splen-dər\ *n* **1** : BRILLIANCE **2** : POMP, MAGNIFICENCE

splen·dour *chiefly Brit var of* SPLENDOR

sple·net·ic \spli-'ne-tik\ *adj* : marked by bad temper or spite

splen·ic \'sple-nik\ *adj* : of, relating to, or located in the spleen

splice \'splīs\ *vb* **spliced; splic·ing 1** : to unite (as two ropes) by weaving the strands together **2** : to unite (as two lengths of film) by connecting the ends together — **splice** *n*

splint \'splint\ *n* **1** : a thin strip of wood interwoven with others to make something (as a basket) **2** : material or a device used to protect and keep in place an injured body part (as a broken arm)

¹splin·ter \'splin-tər\ *n* : a thin piece of something split off lengthwise : SLIVER

²splinter *vb* : to split into splinters

split \'split\ *vb* **split; split·ting 1** : to divide lengthwise or along a grain or seam **2** : to burst or break in pieces **3** : to divide into parts or sections **4** : LEAVE **syn** rend, cleave, rip, tear — **split** *n*

split–lev·el \'split-'le-vəl\ *n* : a house divided so that the floor in one part is about halfway between two floors in the other

split personality *n* : SCHIZOPHRENIA; *also* : MULTIPLE PERSONALITY

split·ting *adj* : causing a piercing sensation ⟨∼ headache⟩

splotch \'spläch\ *n* : BLOTCH

splurge \'splərj\ *vb* **splurged; splurg·ing** : to spend more than usual esp. on oneself — **splurge** *n*

splut·ter \'splə-tər\ *n* : SPUTTER — **splutter** *vb*

¹spoil \'spȯil\ *n* : PLUNDER ⟨∼s of war⟩

²spoil *vb* **spoiled** \'spȯild, 'spȯilt\ *or* **spoilt** \'spȯilt\; **spoil·ing 1** : ROB, PILLAGE **2** : to damage seriously : RUIN **3** : to impair the quality or effect of **4** : to damage the disposition of by pampering; *also* : INDULGE, CODDLE **5** : DECAY, ROT **6** : to have an eager desire

⟨~*ing* for a fight⟩ **syn** injure, harm, hurt, mar —
spoil·age \'spȯi-lij\ *n*
spoil·er \'spȯi-lər\ *n* **1** : one that spoils **2** : a device (as
on an airplane or automobile) used to disrupt airflow
and decrease lift
spoil·sport \'spȯil-ˌspȯrt\ *n* : one who spoils the fun of
others
¹**spoke** \'spōk\ *past & archaic past part of* SPEAK
²**spoke** *n* : any of the rods extending from the hub of a
wheel to the rim
spo·ken \'spō-kən\ *past part of* SPEAK
spokes·man \'spōks-mən\ *n* : a person who speaks as
the representative of another or others
spokes·per·son \-ˌpər-sən\ *n* : SPOKESMAN
spokes·wom·an \-ˌwu̇-mən\ *n* : a woman who speaks
as the representative of another or others
spo·li·a·tion \ˌspō-lē-'ā-shən\ *n* : the act of plundering
: the state of being plundered
¹**sponge** \'spənj\ *n* **1** : an elastic porous water-
absorbing mass of fibers that forms the skeleton of
various primitive sea animals; *also* : any of a phylum
of chiefly marine sea animals that are the source of
natural sponges **2** : a spongelike or porous mass or
material — **spongy** \'spən-jē\ *adj*
²**sponge** *vb* **sponged; spong·ing 1** : to bathe or wipe
with a sponge **2** : to live at another's expense **3** : to
gather sponges — **spong·er** *n*
sponge cake *n* : a light cake made without shortening
sponge rubber *n* : a cellular rubber resembling natural
sponge

spon·sor \'spän-sər\ *n* [LL, fr. L, guarantor, surety, fr. *spondēre* to promise] **1**
: one who takes the responsibility for
some other person or thing : SURETY **2**
: GODPARENT **3** : a business firm that pays the cost of
a radio or television program usu. in return for advertising time during its course — **sponsor** *vb* —
spon·sor·ship *n*

spon·ta·ne·ous \spän-'tā-nē-əs\ *adj* [LL *spontaneus*,
fr. L *sponte* of one's free will, voluntarily] **1** : done
or produced freely or naturally **2** : acting or taking
place without external force or cause **syn** impulsive,
instinctive, automatic, unpremeditated — **spon·ta-
ne·ity** \ˌspän-tə-'nē-ə-tē, -'nā-\ *n* — **spon·ta·ne·ous·-
ly** *adv*
spontaneous combustion *n* : a bursting into flame of
material through heat produced within itself by chemical action (as oxidation)
spoof \'spüf\ *vb* **1** : DECEIVE, HOAX **2** : to make good-
natured fun of — **spoof** *n*
¹**spook** \'spük\ *n* : GHOST, APPARITION — **spooky** *adj*
²**spook** *vb* : FRIGHTEN
spool \'spül\ *n* : a cylinder on which flexible material
(as thread) is wound
spoon \'spün\ *n* [ME, fr. OE *spōn* splinter, chip] **1** : an
eating or cooking implement consisting of a small
shallow bowl with a handle **2** : a metal piece used on
a fishing line as a lure — **spoon** *vb* — **spoon·ful** *n*

spoon·bill \'spün-ˌbil\ *n* : any of several wading birds
related to the ibises that have a bill with a broad flat
tip
spoon–feed \-ˌfēd\ *vb* **-fed** \-ˌfed\; **-feed·ing** : to feed
by means of a spoon
spoor \'spu̇r, 'spȯr\ *n* : a track, a trail, a scent, or
droppings esp. of a wild animal
spo·rad·ic \spə-'ra-dik\ *adj* : occurring now and then
syn occasional, rare, scarce, infrequent, uncommon
— **spo·rad·i·cal·ly** \-di-k(ə-)lē\ *adv*
spore \'spȯr\ *n* : a primitive usu. one-celled often environmentally resistant dormant or reproductive
body produced by plants and some microorganisms
¹**sport** \'spȯrt\ *vb* [ME, to divert, disport, short for *dis-
porten,* fr. MF *desporter,* fr. *des-* (fr. L *dis-* apart) +
porter to carry, fr. L *portare*] **1** : to amuse oneself
: FROLIC **2** : SHOW OFF **1** — **sport·ive** *adj*
²**sport** *n* **1** : a source of diversion : PASTIME **2** : physical
activity engaged in for pleasure **3** : JEST **4** : MOCKERY
⟨make ~ of his efforts⟩ **5** : BUTT, LAUGHINGSTOCK **6**
: one who accepts results cheerfully whether favorable or not **7** : an individual exhibiting marked deviation from its normal type esp. as a result of mutation
syn play, frolic, fun, recreation — **sporty** *adj*
³**sport** *or* **sports** *adj* : of, relating to, or suitable for sport
or casual wear ⟨~ coats⟩
sport fish *n* : a fish noted for the sport it affords an-
glers
sports·cast \'spȯrts-ˌkast\ *n* : a broadcast dealing with
sports events — **sports·cast·er** \-ˌkas-tər\ *n*
sports·man \'spȯrts-mən\ *n* **1** : a person who engages
in sports (as in hunting or fishing) **2** : one who plays
fairly and wins or loses gracefully — **sports·man-
like** \-ˌlīk\ *adj* — **sports·man·ship** *n*
sports·wom·an \-ˌwu̇-mən\ *n* : a woman who engages
in sports
sports·writ·er \-ˌrī-tər\ *n* : one who writes about sports
esp. for a newspaper — **sports·writ·ing** *n*
¹**spot** \'spät\ *n* **1** : STAIN, BLEMISH **2** : a small part different (as in color) from the main part **3** : LOCATION,
SITE — **spot·less** *adj* — **spot·less·ly** *adv* — **on the
spot 1** : at the place of action **2** : in difficulty or danger
²**spot** *vb* **spot·ted; spot·ting 1** : to mark or disfigure with
spots **2** : to pick out : RECOGNIZE, IDENTIFY
³**spot** *adj* **1** : being, done, or originating on the spot ⟨a
~ broadcast⟩ **2** : paid upon delivery **3** : made at random or at a few key points ⟨a ~ check⟩
spot–check \'spät-ˌchek\ *vb* : to make a spot check of
spot·light \-ˌlīt\ *n* **1** : a circle of brilliant light projected
upon a particular area, person, or object (as on a
stage); *also* : the device that produces this light **2**
: public notice — **spotlight** *vb*
spotted owl *n* : a rare large dark brown dark-
eyed bird of humid old growth forests and thickly
wooded canyons from British Columbia to southern
California and central Mexico
spot·ter \'spä-tər\ *n* **1** : one that keeps watch : OBSERV-
ER **2** : one that removes spots
spot·ty \'spä-tē\ *adj* **spot·ti·er; -est** : uneven in quality;

also : sparsely distributed ⟨∼ attendance⟩

spou·sal \'spaů-zəl, -səl\ *n* : MARRIAGE 2, WEDDING — usu. used in pl.

spouse \'spaůs\ *n* : one's husband or wife — **spou·sal** \'spaů-zəl, -səl\ *adj*

¹spout \'spaůt\ *vb* 1 : to eject or issue forth forcibly and freely ⟨wells ∼*ing* oil⟩ 2 : to speak pompously

²spout *n* 1 : a pipe or hole through which liquid spouts 2 : a jet of liquid; *esp* : WATERSPOUT 2

spp *abbr, pl* species

¹sprain \'sprān\ *n* : a sudden or severe twisting of a joint with stretching or tearing of ligaments; *also* : a sprained condition

²sprain *vb* : to subject to sprain

sprat \'sprat\ *n* 1 : a small European herring 2 : a young herring

sprawl \'sprôl\ *vb* 1 : to lie or sit with limbs spread out awkwardly 2 : to spread out irregularly — **sprawl** *n*

¹spray \'sprā\ *n* : a usu. flowering branch; *also* : a decorative arrangement of flowers and foliage

²spray *n* 1 : liquid flying in small drops like water blown from a wave 2 : a jet of fine vapor (as from an atomizer) 3 : an instrument (as an atomizer) for scattering fine liquid

³spray *vb* 1 : to scatter or let fall in a spray 2 : to discharge spray on or into — **spray·er** *n*

spray can *n* : a pressurized container from which aerosols are sprayed

spray gun *n* : a device for spraying liquids (as paint or insecticide)

¹spread \'spred\ *vb* **spread; spread·ing** 1 : to scatter over a surface 2 : to flatten out : open out 3 : to distribute over a period of time or among many persons 4 : to cover something with ⟨∼ rugs on the floor⟩ 5 : to prepare for a meal ⟨∼ a table⟩ 6 : to pass on from person to person 7 : to stretch, force, or push apart — **spread·er** *n*

²spread *n* 1 : the act or process of spreading 2 : EXPANSE, EXTENT 3 : a prominent display in a periodical 4 : a food to be spread on bread or crackers 5 : a cloth cover for a bed 6 : distance between two points : GAP

spread·sheet \'spred-₁shēt\ *n* : an accounting program for a computer

spree \'sprē\ *n* : an unrestrained outburst ⟨buying ∼⟩; *esp* : a drinking bout

sprig \'sprig\ *n* : a small shoot or twig

spright·ly \'sprīt-lē\ *adj* **spright·li·er; -est** : LIVELY, SPIRITED **syn** animated, vivacious, gay — **spright·li·ness** *n*

¹spring \'spriŋ\ *vb* **sprang** \'spraŋ\ *or* **sprung** \'sprəŋ\; **sprung; spring·ing** 1 : to move suddenly upward or forward 2 : to grow quickly ⟨weeds *sprang* up overnight⟩ 3 : to come from by birth or descent 4 : to move quickly by elastic force 5 : WARP 6 : to develop (a leak) through the seams 7 : to cause to close suddenly ⟨∼ a trap⟩ 8 : to make known suddenly ⟨∼ a surprise⟩ 9 : to make lame : STRAIN

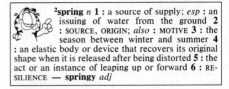

²spring *n* 1 : a source of supply; *esp* : an issuing of water from the ground 2 : SOURCE, ORIGIN; *also* : MOTIVE 3 : the season between winter and summer 4 : an elastic body or device that recovers its original shape when it is released after being distorted 5 : the act or an instance of leaping up or forward 6 : RESILIENCE — **springy** *adj*

spring·board \'spriŋ-₁bōrd\ *n* : a springy board used in jumping or vaulting or for diving

spring fever *n* : a lazy or restless feeling often associated with the onset of spring

spring tide *n* : a tide of greater-than-average range that occurs at each new moon and full moon

spring·time \'spriŋ-₁tīm\ *n* : the season of spring

¹sprin·kle \'spriŋ-kəl\ *vb* **sprin·kled; sprin·kling** : to scatter in small drops or particles — **sprin·kler** *n*

²sprinkle *n* : a light rainfall

sprin·kling *n* : SMATTERING

¹sprint \'sprint\ *vb* : to run at top speed esp. for a short distance — **sprint·er** *n*

²sprint *n* 1 : a short run at top speed 2 : a short distance race

sprite \'sprīt\ *n* 1 : GHOST, SPIRIT 2 : ELF, FAIRY

spritz *vb* : SPRAY

sprock·et \'sprä-kət\ *n* : a toothed wheel whose teeth engage the links of a chain

¹sprout \'spraůt\ *vb* : to send out new growth ⟨∼*ing* seeds⟩

²sprout *n* : a usu. young and growing plant shoot (as from a seed)

¹spruce \'sprüs\ *vb* **spruced; spruc·ing** : to make or become spruce

²spruce *adj* **spruc·er; spruc·est** : neat and smart in appearance **syn** stylish, fashionable, modish, dapper, natty

³spruce *n* : any of a genus of evergreen pyramid-shaped trees related to the pines and having soft light wood; *also* : the wood of a spruce

sprung *past and past part of* SPRING

spry \'sprī\ *adj* **spri·er** *or* **spry·er** \'sprī-ər\; **spri·est** *or* **spry·est** \'sprī-əst\ : NIMBLE, ACTIVE **syn** agile, brisk, lively, sprightly

spud \'spəd\ *n* 1 : a sharp narrow spade 2 : POTATO

spume \'spyüm\ *n* : frothy matter on liquids : FOAM — **spumy** \'spyü-mē\ *adj*

spu·mo·ni *also* **spu·mo·ne** \spů-'mō-nē\ *n* [It *spumone,* fr. *spuma* foam] : ice cream in layers of different colors, flavors, and textures often with candied fruits and nuts

spun *past and past part of* SPIN

spun glass *n* : FIBERGLASS

spunk \'spəŋk\ *n* [fr. *spunk* tinder, fr. ScGael *spong* sponge, tinder, fr. L *spongia* sponge] : PLUCK, COURAGE — **spunky** *adj*

¹spur \'spər\ *n* 1 : a pointed device fastened to a rider's boot and used to urge on a horse 2 : something that urges to action 3 : a stiff sharp spine (as on the leg of a cock); *also* : a hollow projecting appendage of a flower (as a columbine) **4** : a ridge extending sideways from a mountain **5** : a branch of railroad track extending from the main line **syn** goad, motive, impulse, incentive, inducement — **spurred** \'spərd\ *adj* — **on the spur of the moment** : on hasty impulse

²**spur** *vb* **spurred; spur·ring 1** : to urge a horse on with spurs **2** : INCITE

spurge \'spərj\ *n* : any of a genus of herbs and woody plants with bitter milky juice

spu·ri·ous \'spyŭr-ē-əs\ *adj* [LL *spurius* false, fr. L, of illegitimate birth, fr. *spurius*, n., bastard] : not genuine : FALSE

spurn \'spərn\ *vb* **1** : to kick away or trample on **2** : to reject with disdain

¹**spurt** \'spərt\ *vb* : to gush out : SPOUT

²**spurt** *n* : a sudden gushing or spouting

³**spurt** *n* **1** : a sudden brief burst of effort or speed **2** : a sharp increase of activity ⟨~ in sales⟩

⁴**spurt** *vb* : to make a spurt

sput·ter \'spə-tər\ *vb* **1** : to spit small scattered particles : SPLUTTER **2** : to utter words hastily or explosively in excitement or confusion **3** : to make small popping sounds — **sputter** *n*

spu·tum \'spyü-təm\ *n, pl* **spu·ta** \-tə\ [L] : material that is spit or coughed up and consists of saliva and mucus

¹**spy** \'spī\ *vb* **spied; spy·ing 1** : to watch or search for information secretly : act as a spy **2** : to get a momentary or quick glimpse of : SEE

²**spy** *n, pl* **spies 1** : one who secretly watches others **2** : a secret agent who tries to get information for one country in the territory of an enemy

spy·glass \'spī-ˌglas\ *n* : a small telescope

sq *abbr* **1** squadron **2** square

squab \'skwäb\ *n, pl* **squabs** *or* **squab** : a young bird and esp. a pigeon

squab·ble \'skwä-bəl\ *n* : a noisy altercation : WRANGLE **syn** quarrel, spat, row, tiff — **squabble** *vb*

squad \'skwäd\ *n* **1** : a small organized group of military personnel **2** : a small group engaged in a common effort

squad car *n* : a police car connected by two≈ way radio with headquarters

squad·ron \'skwä-drən\ *n* : any of several units of military organization

squal·id \'skwä-ləd\ *adj* **1** : filthy or degraded through neglect or poverty **2** : SORDID, DEBASED **syn** nasty, foul, dirty, grubby

squall \'skwȯl\ *n* : a sudden violent gust of wind often with rain or snow — **squally** *adj*

squa·lor \'skwä-lər\ *n* : the quality or state of being squalid

squan·der \'skwän-dər\ *vb* : to spend wastefully or foolishly

¹**square** \'skwar\ *n* **1** : an instrument used to lay out or test right angles **2** : a rectangle with all four sides equal **3** : something square **4** : the product of a number multiplied by itself **5** : an area bounded by four streets **6** : an open area in a city where streets meet **7** : a highly conventional person

²**square** *adj* **squar·er; squar·est 1** : having four equal sides and four right angles **2** : forming a right angle ⟨cut a ~ corner⟩ **3** : multiplied by itself : SQUARED ⟨x^2 is the symbol for *x* ~⟩ **4** : being a unit of square measure equal to a square each side of which measures one unit ⟨a ~ foot⟩ **5** : being of a specified length in each of two dimensions ⟨an area 10 feet ~⟩ **6** : exactly adjusted **7** : JUST, FAIR ⟨a ~ deal⟩ **8** : leaving no balance ⟨make accounts ~⟩ **9** : SUBSTANTIAL ⟨a ~ meal⟩ **10** : highly conservative or conventional — **square·ly** *adv*

³**square** *vb* **squared; squar·ing 1** : to form with four equal sides and right angles or with flat surfaces ⟨~ a timber⟩ **2** : to multiply (a number) by itself **3** : CONFORM, AGREE **4** : BALANCE, SETTLE ⟨~ an account⟩

square dance *n* : a dance for four couples arranged to form a square

square measure *n* : a unit or system of units for measuring area — see METRIC SYSTEM table, WEIGHT table

square–rigged \'skwar-ˌrigd\ *adj* : having the chief sails extended on yards that are fastened to the masts horizontally and at their center

square–rig·ger \-ˌri-gər\ *n* : a square-rigged craft

square root *n* : either of the two numbers whose squares are equal to a given number ⟨the *square root* of 9 is +3 or −3⟩

¹**squash** \'skwäsh, 'skwȯsh\ *vb* **1** : to beat or press into a pulp or flat mass **2** : QUASH, SUPPRESS

²**squash** *n* **1** : the impact of something soft and heavy; *also* : the sound of such impact **2** : a crushed mass **3** : a game played on a 4-wall court with a racket and rubber ball

³**squash** *n, pl* **squash·es** *or* **squash** : a fruit of any of various plants related to the gourds that is used esp. as a vegetable; *also* : a plant and esp. a vine bearing squashes

squash racquets *n* : SQUASH 3

¹**squat** \'skwät\ *vb* **squat·ted; squat·ting 1** : to sit down upon the hams or heels **2** : to settle on land without right or title; *also* : to settle on public land with a view to acquiring title — **squat·ter** *n*

²**squat** *n* : the act or posture of squatting

³**squat** *adj* **squat·ter; squat·test** : low to the ground; *also* : short and thick in stature **syn** thickset, stocky, heavyset, stubby

squawk \'skwȯk\ *n* : a harsh loud cry; *also* : a noisy protest — **squawk** *vb*

squeak \'skwēk\ *vb* **1** : to utter or speak in a weak shrill tone **2** : to make a thin high-pitched sound — **squeak** *n* — **squeaky** *adj*

¹**squeal** \'skwēl\ *vb* **1** : to make a shrill sound or cry **2** : to betray a secret or turn informer **3** : COMPLAIN, PROTEST

²**squeal** *n* : a shrill sharp cry or noise

squea·mish \'skwē-mish\ *adj* **1** : easily nauseated; *also* : NAUSEATED **2** : easily disgusted **syn** fussy, nice, dainty, fastidious, persnickety — **squea·mish·ness** *n*

squee·gee \'skwē-ˌjē\ *n* : a blade set crosswise on a handle and used for spreading or wiping liquid on, across, or off a surface — **squeegee** *vb*

¹**squeeze** \'skwēz\ *vb* **squeezed; squeez·ing 1** : to exert pressure on the opposite sides or parts of **2** : to obtain by pressure ⟨~ juice from a lemon⟩ **3** : to force, thrust, or cause to pass by pressure — **squeez·er** *n*

²**squeeze** *n* **1** : an act or instance of squeezing **2** : a quantity squeezed out

squeeze bottle *n* : a flexible plastic bottle that dispenses its contents when it is squeezed

squelch \'skwelch\ *vb* **1** : to suppress completely : CRUSH **2** : to move in soft mud — **squelch** *n*

squib \'skwib\ *n* : a brief witty writing or speech

squid \'skwid\ *n, pl* **squid** *or* **squids** : any of an order of long-bodied sea mollusks having eight arms and two longer tentacles and usu. a slender internal shell

squint \'skwint\ *vb* **1** : to look or aim obliquely **2** : to look or peer with the eyes partly closed **3** : to be cross≈ eyed — **squint** *n or adj*

¹**squire** \'skwīr\ *n* [ME *squier*, fr. OF *esquier*, fr. LL *scutarius*, fr. L *scutum* shield] **1** : an armor-bearer of a knight **2** : a man gallantly devoted to a lady **3** : a member of the British gentry ranking below a knight and above a gentleman; *also* : a prominent landowner **4** : a local magistrate

²**squire** *vb* **squired; squir·ing** : to attend as a squire or escort

squirm \'skwərm\ *vb* : to twist about like a worm : WRIGGLE

¹**squir·rel** \'skwər-əl\ *n, pl* **squirrels** *also* **squirrel** [ME *squirel*, fr. MF *esquireul*, fr. (assumed) VL *scuriolus*, dim. of *scurius*, alter. of L *sciurus*, fr. Gk *skiouros*,

prob. fr. *skia* shadow + *oura* tail] : any of various rodents usu. with a long bushy tail and strong hind legs; *also* : the fur of a squirrel

²squirrel *vb* **-reled** *or* **-relled; -rel·ing** *or* **-rel·ling** : to store up for future use

¹squirt \'skwərt\ *vb* : to eject liquid in a thin spurt

²squirt *n* **1** : an instrument (as a syringe) for squirting **2** : a small forcible jet of liquid

¹Sr *abbr* **1** senior **2** sister

²Sr *symbol* strontium

SR *abbr* seaman recruit

¹SRO \ˌes-(ˌ)är-'ō\ *n* [*single-room* *occupancy*] : a house or apartment building in which low-income tenants live in single rooms

²SRO *abbr* standing room only

SS *abbr* **1** saints **2** Social Security **3** steamship **4** sworn statement

SSA *abbr* Social Security Administration

SSE *abbr* south-southeast

SSG *or* **SSgt** *abbr* staff sergeant

SSI *abbr* supplemental security income

SSM *abbr* staff sergeant major

SSN *abbr* Social Security Number

ssp *abbr* subspecies

SSR *abbr* Soviet Socialist Republic

SSS *abbr* Selective Service System

SST \ˌes-(ˌ)es-'tē\ *n* [*supersonic transport*] : a supersonic passenger airplane

SSW *abbr* south-southwest

st *abbr* **1** stanza **2** state **3** stitch **4** stone **5** street

St *abbr* saint

ST *abbr* **1** short ton **2** standard time

-st — see -EST

sta *abbr* station; stationary

¹stab \'stab\ *n* **1** : a wound produced by a pointed weapon **2** : a quick thrust; *also* : a brief attempt

²stab *vb* **stabbed; stab·bing** : to pierce or wound with or as if with a pointed weapon; *also* : THRUST, DRIVE

sta·bile \'stā-ˌbēl\ *n* : an abstract sculpture or construction similar to a mobile but made to be stationary

sta·bi·lize \'stā-bə-ˌlīz\ *vb* **-lized; -liz·ing 1** : to make stable **2** : to hold steady ⟨~ prices⟩ — **sta·bi·li·za·tion** \ˌstā-bə-lə-'zā-shən\ *n* — **sta·bi·liz·er** \'stā-bə-ˌlī-zər\ *n*

¹sta·ble \'stā-bəl\ *n* : a building in which domestic animals are sheltered and fed — **sta·ble·man** \-mən, -ˌman\ *n*

²stable *vb* **sta·bled; sta·bling** : to put or keep in a stable

³stable *adj* **sta·bler; sta·blest 1** : firmly established; *also* : mentally and emotionally healthy **2** : steady in purpose : CONSTANT **3** : DURABLE, ENDURING **4** : resistant to chemical or physical change **syn** lasting, permanent, perpetual, perdurable — **sta·bil·i·ty** \stə-'bi-lə-tē\ *n*

stac·ca·to \stə-'kä-tō\ *adj or adv* [It] : cut short so as not to sound connected ⟨~ notes⟩

¹stack \'stak\ *n* **1** : a large pile (as of hay or grain) **2** : an orderly pile (as of poker chips) **3** : a large quantity **4** : a vertical pipe : SMOKESTACK **5** : a rack with shelves for storing books

²stack *vb* **1** : to pile up **2** : to arrange (cards) secretly for cheating

stack up *vb* : MEASURE UP

sta·di·um \'stā-dē-əm\ *n, pl* **-dia** \-dē-ə\ *or* **-di·ums** : a structure with tiers of seats for spectators built around a field for sports events

¹staff \'staf\ *n, pl* **staffs** \'stafs, 'stavz\ *or* **staves** \'stavz, 'stāvz\ **1** : a pole, stick, rod, or bar used for supporting, for measuring, or as a symbol of authority; *also* : CLUB, CUDGEL **2** : something that sustains ⟨bread is the ~ of life⟩ **3** : the five horizontal lines on which music is written **4** : a body of assistants to an executive **5** : a group of officers holding no command but having duties concerned with planning and managing

²staff *vb* : to supply with a staff or with workers

staff·er \'sta-fər\ *n* : a member of a staff (as of a newspaper)

staff sergeant *n* : a noncommissioned officer ranking in the army next below a sergeant first class, in the air force next below a technical sergeant, and in the marine corps next below a gunnery sergeant

¹stag \'stag\ *n, pl* **stags** *or* **stag** : an adult male of various large deer

²stag *adj* : restricted to or intended for men ⟨a ~ party⟩ ⟨~ movies⟩

³stag *adv* : unaccompanied by a date

¹stage \'stāj\ *n* **1** : a raised platform on which an orator may speak or a play may be presented **2** : the acting profession : THEATER **3** : the scene of a notable action or event **4** : a station or resting place on a traveled road **5** : STAGECOACH **6** : a degree of advance in an undertaking, process, or development **7** : a propulsion unit in a rocket — **stagy** \'stā-jē\ *adj*

²stage *vb* **staged; stag·ing** : to produce or perform on or as if on a stage — **stage·able** *adj*

stage·coach \'stāj-ˌkōch\ *n* : a horse-drawn coach that runs regularly between stations

stag·fla·tion \ˌstag-'flā-shən\ *n* : inflation with stagnant economic activity and high unemployment

¹stag·ger \'sta-gər\ *vb* **1** : to reel from side to side : TOTTER **2** : to begin to doubt : WAVER **3** : to cause to reel or waver **4** : to arrange in overlapping or alternating positions or times ⟨~ working hours⟩ **5** : ASTONISH — **stag·ger·ing·ly** *adv*

²stagger *n* **1** *sing or pl* : an abnormal condition of domestic mammals and birds associated with damage to the central nervous system and marked by lack of coordination and a reeling unsteady gait **2** : a reeling or unsteady gait or stance

stag·ing \'stā-jiŋ\ *n* **1** : SCAFFOLDING **2** : the assembling of troops and matériel in transit in a particular place

stag·nant \'stag-nənt\ *adj* **1** : not flowing : MOTIONLESS ⟨~ water in a pond⟩ **2** : DULL, INACTIVE ⟨~ business⟩

stag·nate \'stag-ˌnāt\ *vb* **stag·nat·ed; stag·nat·ing** : to be or become stagnant — **stag·na·tion** \stag-'nā-shən\ *n*

staid \'stād\ *adj* : SOBER, SEDATE **syn** grave, serious, earnest

¹stain \'stān\ *vb* **1** : DISCOLOR, SOIL **2** : TAINT, CORRUPT **3** : DISGRACE **4** : to color (as wood, paper, or cloth) by processes affecting the material itself

²stain *n* **1** : a small soiled or discolored area **2** : a taint of guilt : STIGMA **3** : a preparation (as a dye or pigment) used in staining — **stain·less** *adj*

stainless steel *n* : steel alloyed with chromium that is highly resistant to stain, rust, and corrosion

stair \'star\ *n* **1** : a series of steps or flights of steps for passing from one level to another — often used in pl. **2** : one step of a stairway

stair·case \-ˌkās\ *n* : a flight of steps with their supporting framework, casing, and balusters

stair·way \-ˌwā\ *n* : one or more flights of stairs with connecting landings

stair·well \-ˌwel\ *n* : a vertical shaft in which stairs are located

¹stake \'stāk\ *n* **1** : a pointed piece of material (as of wood) driven into the ground as a marker or a support **2** : a post to which a person is bound for death by burning; *also* : such a death **3** : something that is staked for gain or loss **4** : the prize in a contest

²stake *vb* **staked; stak·ing 1** : to mark the limits of by or as if by stakes **2** : to tie to a stake **3** : to support or secure with stakes **4** : BET, WAGER

stake·out \'stāk-ˌaút\ *n* : a surveillance by police (as of a suspected criminal)

sta·lac·tite \stə-'lak-ˌtīt\ *n* [NL *stalactites*, fr. Gk *stalaktos* dripping] : an icicle-shaped deposit hanging from the roof or sides of a cavern

sta·lag·mite \stə-'lag-ˌmīt\ *n* [NL *stalagmites*, fr. Gk *stalagma* drop *or* *stalagmos* dripping] : a deposit re-

sembling an inverted stalactite rising from the floor of a cavern

stale \'stāl\ *adj* **stal·er; stal·est 1** : having lost good taste and quality from age ⟨∼ bread⟩ **2** : used or heard so often as to be dull ⟨∼ news⟩ **3** : not as strong or effective as before ⟨∼ from lack of practice⟩ — **stale·ness** *n*

stale·mate \'stāl-ˌmāt\ *n* : a drawn contest : DEADLOCK — **stalemate** *vb*

¹stalk \'stòk\ *n* : a plant stem; *also* : any slender usu. upright supporting or connecting part — **stalked** \'stòkt\ *adj*

²stalk *vb* **1** : to pursue (game) stealthily **2** : to walk stiffly or haughtily

¹stall \'stòl\ *n* **1** : a compartment in a stable or barn for one animal **2** : a booth or counter where articles may be displayed for sale **3** : a seat in a church choir; *also* : a church pew **4** *chiefly Brit* : a front orchestra seat in a theater

²stall *vb* : to bring or come to a standstill unintentionally ⟨∼ an engine⟩

³stall *n* : the condition of an airfoil or aircraft in which lift is lost and the airfoil or aircraft tends to drop

⁴stall *n* [alter. of *stale* lure] : a ruse to deceive or delay

⁵stall *vb* : to hold off, divert, or delay by evasion or deception

stal·lion \'stal-yən\ *n* : a male horse

stal·wart \'stòl-wərt\ *adj* : STOUT, STRONG; *also* : BRAVE, VALIANT

sta·men \'stā-mən\ *n* : an organ of a flower that produces pollen

stam·i·na \'sta-mə-nə\ *n* [L, pl. of *stamen* warp, thread of life spun by the Fates] : VIGOR, ENDURANCE

sta·mi·nate \'stā-mə-nət, 'sta-mə-, -ˌnāt\ *adj* **1** : having or producing stamens **2** : having stamens but no pistils

stam·mer \'sta-mər\ *vb* : to hesitate or stumble in speaking — **stammer** *n* — **stam·mer·er** *n*

¹stamp \'stamp; *for 2 also* 'stämp *or* 'stòmp\ *vb* **1** : to pound or crush with a heavy instrument **2** : to strike or beat with the bottom of the foot **3** : IMPRESS, IMPRINT **4** : to cut out or indent with a stamp or die **5** : to attach a postage stamp to

²stamp *n* **1** : a device or instrument for stamping **2** : the mark made by stamping; *also* : a distinctive mark or quality **3** : the act of stamping **4** : a stamped or printed paper affixed to show that a charge has been paid ⟨postage ∼⟩ ⟨tax ∼⟩

¹stam·pede \stam-'pēd\ *n* : a wild headlong rush or flight esp. of frightened animals

²stampede *vb* **stam·ped·ed; stam·ped·ing 1** : to flee or cause to flee in panic **2** : to act or cause to act together suddenly and heedlessly

stance \'stans\ *n* : a way of standing

¹stanch \'stònch, 'stänch\ *vb* : to check the flowing of (as blood); *also* : to cease flowing or bleeding

²stanch *var of* ²STAUNCH

stan·chion \'stan-chən\ *n* : an upright bar, post, or support

¹stand \'stand\ *vb* **stood** \'stùd\; **standing 1** : to take or be at rest in an upright or firm position **2** : to assume a specified position **3** : to remain stationary or unchanged **4** : to be steadfast **5** : to act in resistance ⟨∼ against a foe⟩ **6** : to maintain a relative position or rank **7** : to gather slowly and remain ⟨tears *stood* in her eyes⟩ **8** : to set upright **9** : ENDURE, TOLERATE ⟨I won't ∼ for that⟩ **10** : to submit to ⟨∼ trial⟩ — **stand pat** : to oppose or resist change

²stand *n* **1** : an act of standing, staying, or resisting **2** : a stop made to give a performance **3** : POSITION, VIEWPOINT **4** : a place taken by a witness to testify in court **5** *pl* : tiered seats for spectators **6** : a raised platform (as for speakers) **7** : a structure for a small retail business **8** : a structure for supporting or holding something upright ⟨music ∼⟩ **9** : a group of plants growing in a continuous area

stand–alone \'stan-də-ˌlōn\ *adj* : SELF-CONTAINED; *esp* : capable of operation independent of a computer system

stan·dard \'stan-dərd\ *n* **1** : a figure adopted as an emblem by a people **2** : the personal flag of a ruler; *also* : FLAG **3** : something set up as a rule for measuring or as a model to be followed **4** : an upright support ⟨lamp ∼⟩ — **standard** *adj*

stan·dard–bear·er \-ˌbar-ər\ *n* : the leader of a cause

standard deviation *n* : a measure of dispersion in a set of data

stan·dard·ise *Brit var of* STANDARDIZE

stan·dard·ize \'stan-dər-ˌdīz\ *vb* **-ized; -iz·ing** : to make standard or uniform — **stan·dard·i·za·tion** \ˌstan-dər-də-'zā-shən\ *n*

standard of living : the necessities, comforts, and luxuries that a person or group is accustomed to

standard time *n* : the time established by law or by general usage over a region or country

¹stand·by \'stand-ˌbī\ *n, pl* **stand·bys** \-ˌbīz\ **1** : one that can be relied on **2** : a substitute in reserve — **on standby** : ready or available for immediate action or use

²standby *adj* **1** : ready for use **2** : relating to airline travel in which the passenger must wait for an available unreserved seat — **standby** *adv*

stand–in \'stan-ˌdin\ *n* **1** : someone employed to occupy an actor's place while lights and camera are readied **2** : SUBSTITUTE

¹stand·ing \'stan-diŋ\ *adj* **1** : ERECT **2** : not flowing : STAGNANT **3** : remaining at the same level or amount for an indefinite period ⟨∼ offer⟩ **4** : PERMANENT **5** : done from a standing position ⟨a ∼ jump⟩

²standing *n* **1** : length of service; *also* : relative position in society or in a profession : RANK **2** : DURATION

stand·off \'stan-ˌdòf\ *n* : TIE, DRAW

stand·off·ish \stan-'dò-fish\ *adj* : somewhat cold and reserved

stand·out \'stan-ˌdaùt\ *n* : something conspicuously excellent

stand·pipe \\'stand-ₐpīp\\ *n* : a high vertical pipe or reservoir for water used to produce a uniform pressure

stand·point \\-ₐpȯint\\ *n* : a position from which objects or principles are judged

stand·still \\-ₐstil\\ *n* : a state of rest

stand–up \\'stan-ₐdəp\\ *adj* : done or performing in a standing position ⟨a ~ comic⟩ ⟨~ comedy⟩

stank \\'staŋk\\ *past of* STINK

stan·za \\'stan-zə\\ *n* [It] : a group of lines forming a division of a poem

sta·pes \\'stā-ₐpēz\\ *n, pl* **stapes** *or* **sta·pe·des** \\'stā-pə-ₐdēz\\ : the small innermost bone of the ear of mammals

staph \\'staf\\ *n* : STAPHYLOCOCCUS

staph·y·lo·coc·cus \\ₐsta-fə-lō-'kä-kəs\\ *n, pl* **-coc·ci** \\-'kä-ₐkī, -'käk-ₐsī\\ : any of various spherical bacteria including some pathogens of skin and mucous membranes — **staph·y·lo·coc·cal** \\-'kä-kəl\\ *adj*

¹sta·ple \\'stā-pəl\\ *n* : a U-shaped piece of metal or wire with sharp points to be driven into a surface or through thin layers (as paper) for attaching or holding together — **staple** *vb* — **sta·pler** *n*

²staple *n* **1** : a chief commodity or product **2** : a chief part of something ⟨a ~ of their diet⟩ **3** : unmanufactured or raw material **4** : a textile fiber suitable for spinning into yarn

³staple *adj* **1** : regularly produced in large quantities **2** : PRINCIPAL, MAIN

¹star \\'stär\\ *n* **1** : a celestial body that appears as a fixed point of light; *esp* : such a body that is gaseous, self‑luminous, and of great mass **2** : a planet or configuration of planets that is held in astrology to influence one's fortune — usu. used in pl. **3** *obs* : DESTINY, FORTUNE **4** : a conventional figure representing a star; *esp* : ASTERISK **5** : an actor or actress playing the leading role **6** : a brilliant performer — **star·dom** \\'stär-dəm\\ *n* — **star·less** *adj* — **star·like** *adj* — **star·ry** *adj*

²star *vb* **starred; star·ring 1** : to adorn with stars **2** : to mark with an asterisk **3** : to play the leading role

star·board \\'stär-bərd\\ *n* [ME sterbord, fr. OE stēorbord, fr. stēor- steering oar + bord ship's side] : the right side of a ship or airplane looking forward — **starboard** *adj*

¹starch \\'stärch\\ *vb* : to stiffen with or as if with starch

²starch *n* : a complex carbohydrate that is stored in plants, is an important foodstuff, and is used in adhesives and sizes, in laundering, and in pharmacy — **starchy** *adj*

stare \\'star\\ *vb* **stared; star·ing** : to look fixedly with wide-open eyes — **stare** *n* — **star·er** *n*

star·fish \\'stär-ₐfish\\ *n* : any of a class of echinoderms usu. having five arms arranged around a central disk and feeding largely on mollusks

star fruit *n* : CARAMBOLA 1

¹stark \\'stärk\\ *adj* **1** : rigid as if in death; *also* : STRICT **2** *archaic* : STRONG, ROBUST **3** : SHEER, UTTER **4** : BARREN, DESOLATE ⟨~ landscape⟩; *also* : UNADORNED ⟨~ realism⟩ **5** : sharply delineated — **stark·ly** *adv*

²stark *adv* : WHOLLY, ABSOLUTELY ⟨~ naked⟩

star·light \\'stär-ₐlīt\\ *n* : the light given by the stars

star·ling \\'stär-liŋ\\ *n* : a dark brown or in summer glossy greenish black European bird related to the crows that is naturalized nearly worldwide and often considered a pest

¹start \\'stärt\\ *vb* **1** : to give an involuntary twitch or jerk (as from surprise) **2** : BEGIN, COMMENCE **3** : to set going **4** : to enter or cause to enter a game or contest; *also* : to be in the starting lineup — **start·er** *n*

²start *n* **1** : a sudden involuntary motion : LEAP **2** : a spasmodic and brief effort or action **3** : BEGINNING; *also* : the place of beginning

star·tle \\'stärt-ᵊl\\ *vb* **star·tled; star·tling** : to frighten or surprise suddenly : cause to start

star·tling *adj* : causing sudden fear, surprise, or anxiety

starve \\'stärv\\ *vb* **starved; starv·ing** [ME sterven to die, fr. OE steorfan] **1** : to die or cause to die from hunger **2** : to suffer extreme hunger or deprivation ⟨starving for affection⟩ **3** : to subdue by famine — **star·va·tion** \\stär-'vā-shən\\ *n*

starve·ling \\'stärv-liŋ\\ *n* : one that is thin from lack of nourishment

stash \\'stash\\ *vb* : to store in a secret place for future use — **stash** *n*

stat *abbr* **1** [L statim] immediately **2** statute

¹state \\'stāt\\ *n* [ME stat, fr. OF & L; OF estat, fr. L status, fr. stare to stand] **1** : mode or condition of being ⟨the four ~s of matter⟩ **2** : condition of mind **3** : social position **4** : a body of people occupying a territory and organized under one government; *also* : the government of such a body of people **5** : one of the constituent units of a nation having a federal government — **state·hood** \\-ₐhůd\\ *n*

²state *vb* **stat·ed; stat·ing 1** : FIX ⟨stated intervals⟩ **2** : to express in words

state·craft \\'stāt-ₐkraft\\ *n* : the art of conducting state affairs

state·house \\-ₐhaůs\\ *n* : the building in which a state legislature meets

state·ly \\'stāt-lē\\ *adj* **state·li·er; -est 1** : having lofty dignity : HAUGHTY **2** : IMPRESSIVE, MAJESTIC **syn** magnificent, imposing, august — **state·li·ness** *n*

state·ment \\'stāt-mənt\\ *n* **1** : the act or result of presenting in words **2** : a summary of a financial account

state·room \\'stāt-ₐrüm, -ₐrům\\ *n* : a private room on a ship or railroad car

state·side \\'stāt-ₐsīd\\ *adj* : of or relating to the U.S. as regarded from outside its continental limits — **stateside** *adv*

states·man \\'stāts-mən\\ *n* : a person engaged in fixing the policies and conducting the affairs of a government; *esp* : one wise and skilled in such matters — **states·man·like** *adj* — **states·man·ship** *n*

¹stat·ic \\'sta-tik\\ *adj* **1** : acting by mere weight without motion ⟨~ pressure⟩ **2** : relating to bodies at rest or forces in equilibrium **3** : not moving : not active **4** : of or relating to stationary charges of electricity **5** : of, relating to, or caused by radio static

²static *n* : noise produced in a radio or television receiver by atmospheric or other electrical disturbances

¹sta·tion \\'stā-shən\\ *n* **1** : the place where a person or thing stands or is assigned to remain **2** : a regular stopping place on a transportation route : DEPOT **3** : a place where a fleet is assigned for duty **4** : a stock farm or ranch esp. in Australia or New Zealand **5** : social standing **6** : a complete assemblage of radio or television equipment for sending or receiving

²station *vb* : to assign to a station

sta·tion·ary \\'stā-shə-ₐner-ē\\ *adj* **1** : fixed in a station, course, or mode **2** : unchanging in condition

stationary front *n* : the boundary between two air masses neither of which is advancing

station break *n* : a pause in a radio or television broadcast to announce the identity of the network or station

sta·tio·ner \\'stā-shə-nər\\ *n* : one that sells stationery

sta·tio·nery \\'stā-shə-ₐner-ē\\ *n* : materials (as paper, pens, or ink) for writing; *esp* : letter paper with envelopes

station wagon *n* : an automobile having a passenger compartment which extends to the back of the vehicle and no trunk

sta·tis·tic \\stə-'tis-tik\\ *n* **1** : a single term or datum in a collection of statistics **2** : a quantity (as the mean) that is computed from a sample

sta·tis·tics \\-tiks\\ *n sing or pl* [G Statistik study of political facts and figures, fr. NL statisticus of politics,

fr. L *status* state] : a branch of mathematics dealing with the collection, analysis, and interpretation of masses of numerical data; *also* : a collection of such numerical data — **sta·tis·ti·cal** \-ti-kəl\ *adj* — **sta·tis·ti·cal·ly** \-ti-k(ə-)lē\ *adv* — **stat·is·ti·cian** \ˌsta-tə-ˈsti-shən\ *n*

stat·u·ary \ˈsta-chə-ˌwer-ē\ *n, pl* **-ar·ies 1** : the art of making statues **2** : STATUES

stat·ue \ˈsta-chü\ *n* : a likeness (as of a person or animal) sculptured, modeled, or cast in a solid substance

stat·u·esque \ˌsta-chə-ˈwesk\ *adj* : tall and shapely

stat·u·ette \ˌsta-chə-ˈwet\ *n* : a small statue

stat·ure \ˈsta-chər\ *n* **1** : natural height (as of a person) **2** : quality or status gained (as by achievement)

sta·tus \ˈstā-təs, ˈsta-\ *n* **1** : the condition of a person in the eyes of others or of the law **2** : state of affairs

sta·tus quo \-ˈkwō\ *n* [L, state in which] : the existing state of affairs

stat·ute \ˈsta-chüt\ *n* : a law enacted by a legislative body

stat·u·to·ry \ˈsta-chə-ˌtōr-ē\ *adj* : imposed by statute : LAWFUL

statutory rape *n* : sexual intercourse with a person who is below the statutory age of consent

¹**staunch** \ˈstȯnch\ *var of* ¹STANCH

²**staunch** *adj* **1** : WATERTIGHT ⟨a ∼ ship⟩ **2** : FIRM, STRONG; *also* : STEADFAST, LOYAL **syn** resolute, constant, true, faithful — **staunch·ly** *adv*

¹**stave** \ˈstāv\ *n* **1** : CUDGEL, STAFF **2** : any of several narrow strips of wood placed edge to edge to make something (as a barrel) **3** : STANZA

²**stave** *vb* **staved** *or* **stove** \ˈstōv\; **stav·ing 1** : to break in the staves of; *also* : to break a hole in **2** : to drive or thrust away ⟨∼ off trouble⟩

staves *pl of* STAFF

¹**stay** \ˈstā\ *n* **1** : a strong rope or wire used to support a mast **2** : ¹GUY

²**stay** *vb* **stayed** \ˈstād\ *also* **staid** \ˈstād\; **stay·ing 1** : PAUSE, WAIT **2** : REMAIN **3** : to stand firm **4** : LIVE, DWELL **5** : DELAY, POSTPONE **6** : to last out (as a race)

7 : STOP, CHECK **8** : to satisfy (as hunger) for a time **syn** remain, abide, linger, tarry

³**stay** *n* **1** : STOP, HALT **2** : a residence or sojourn in a place

⁴**stay** *n* **1** : PROP, SUPPORT **2** : CORSET — usu. used in pl.

⁵**stay** *vb* : to hold up : PROP

staying power *n* : STAMINA

stbd *abbr* starboard

std *abbr* standard

STD \ˌes-(ˌ)tē-ˈdē\ *n* : SEXUALLY TRANSMITTED DISEASE

Ste *abbr* [F *sainte*] saint (female)

stead \ˈsted\ *n* **1** : ADVANTAGE ⟨stood him in good ∼⟩ **2** : the place or function ordinarily occupied or carried out by another ⟨acted in her brother's ∼⟩

stead·fast \ˈsted-ˌfast\ *adj* **1** : firmly fixed in place **2** : not subject to change **3** : firm in belief, determination, or adherence : LOYAL **syn** resolute, true, faithful, staunch — **stead·fast·ly** *adv* — **stead·fast·ness** *n*

¹**steady** \ˈste-dē\ *adj* **steadi·er; -est 1** : direct or sure in movement; *also* : CALM **2** : FIRM, FIXED **3** : STABLE **4** : CONSTANT, RESOLUTE **5** : REGULAR **6** : RELIABLE, SOBER **syn** uniform, even — **steadi·ly** \-də-lē\ *adv* — **steadi·ness** \-dē-nəs\ *n* — **steady** *adv*

²**steady** *vb* **stead·ied; steady·ing** : to make or become steady

steak \ˈstāk\ *n* : a slice of meat and esp. beef; *also* : a slice of a large fish

¹**steal** \ˈstēl\ *vb* **stole** \ˈstōl\; **sto·len** \ˈstō-lən\; **steal·ing 1** : to take and carry away without right or permission **2** : to come or go secretly or gradually **3** : to get for oneself slyly or by skill and daring ⟨∼ a kiss⟩ **4** : to gain or attempt to gain a base in baseball by running without the aid of a hit or an error **syn** pilfer, filch, purloin, swipe

²**steal** *n* **1** : an act of stealing **2** : BARGAIN

stealth \ˈstelth\ *n* **1** : secret or unobtrusive procedure **2** : an aircraft design intended to produce a weak radar return

stealthy \ˈstel-thē\ *adj* **stealth·i·er; -est** : done by stealth : FURTIVE, SLY **syn** secret, covert, clandestine, surreptitious, underhanded — **stealth·i·ly** \'stel-thə-lē\ *adv*

¹steam \'stēm\ *n* **1** : the vapor into which water is changed when heated to the boiling point **2** : water vapor when compressed so that it supplies heat and power **3** : POWER, FORCE, ENERGY — **steamy** *adj*

²steam *vb* **1** : to pass off as vapor **2** : to emit vapor **3** : to move by or as if by the agency of steam — **steam·er** *n*

steam·boat \'stēm-ˌbōt\ *n* : a boat driven by steam

steam engine *n* : a reciprocating engine having a piston driven by steam

steam·fit·ter \'stēm-ˌfi-tər\ *n* : a worker who puts in or repairs equipment (as steam pipes) for heating, ventilating, or refrigerating systems

steam·roll·er \-ˌrō-lər\ *n* : a machine for compacting roads or pavements — **steam·roll·er** *also* **steam·roll** \-ˌrōl\ *vb*

steam·ship \-ˌship\ *n* : a ship driven by steam

steed \'stēd\ *n* : HORSE

¹steel \'stēl\ *n* **1** : iron treated with intense heat and mixed with carbon to make it hard and tough **2** : an article made of steel **3** : a quality (as hardness of mind) that suggests steel — **steel** *adj* — **steely** *adj*

²steel *vb* : to fill with courage or determination

steel wool *n* : long fine steel shavings used esp. for cleaning and polishing

¹steep \'stēp\ *adj* **1** : having a very sharp slope : PRECIPITOUS **2** : too great or too high ⟨~ prices⟩ — **steep·ly** *adv* — **steep·ness** *n*

²steep *n* : a steep slope

³steep *vb* **1** : to soak in a liquid; *esp* : to extract the essence of by soaking ⟨~ tea⟩ **2** : SATURATE ⟨~ed in learning⟩

stee·ple \'stē-pəl\ *n* : a tall tapering structure built on top of a church tower; *also* : a church tower

stee·ple·chase \-ˌchās\ *n* [fr. the use of church steeples as landmarks to guide the riders] : a horse race across country; *also* : a race over a course obstructed by hurdles

¹steer \'stir\ *n* : a male bovine animal castrated before sexual maturity and usu. raised for beef

²steer *vb* **1** : to direct the course of (as by a rudder or wheel) **2** : GUIDE, CONTROL **3** : to pursue a course of action **4** : to be subject to guidance or direction — **steers·man** \'stirz-mən\ *n*

steer·age \'stir-ij\ *n* **1** : DIRECTION, GUIDANCE **2** : a section in a passenger ship for passengers paying the lowest fares

stego·sau·rus \ˌste-gə-'sòr-əs\ *n* : any of a genus of plant-eating armored dinosaurs with a series of bony plates along the backbone

stein \'stīn\ *n* : an earthenware mug

stel·lar \'ste-lər\ *adj* : of or relating to stars : resembling a star

¹stem \'stem\ *n* **1** : the main stalk of a plant; *also* : a plant part that supports another part (as a leaf or fruit) **2** : the bow of a ship **3** : a line of ancestry : STOCK **4** : that part of an inflected word which remains unchanged throughout a given inflection **5** : something resembling the stem of a plant — **stem·less** *adj* — **stemmed** \'stemd\ *adj*

²stem *vb* **stemmed; stem·ming** : to have a specified source : DERIVE

³stem *vb* **stemmed; stem·ming** : to make headway against ⟨~ the tide⟩

⁴stem *vb* **stemmed; stem·ming** : to stop or check by or as if by damming

stench \'stench\ *n* : STINK

sten·cil \'sten-səl\ *n* [ME *stanselen* to ornament with sparkling colors, fr. MF *estanceler*, fr. *estancele* spark, fr. (assumed) VL *stincilla*, alter. of L *scintilla*] : an impervious material (as metal or paper) perforated with lettering or a design through which a substance (as ink or paint) is applied to a surface to be printed — **stencil** *vb*

ste·nog·ra·phy \stə-'nä-grə-fē\ *n* : the art or process of writing in shorthand — **ste·nog·ra·pher** \-fər\ *n* — **steno·graph·ic** \ˌste-nə-'gra-fik\ *adj*

sten·to·ri·an \sten-'tȯr-ē-ən\ *adj* : extremely loud and powerful

¹step \'step\ *n* **1** : a rest for the foot in ascending or descending : STAIR **2** : an advance made by raising one foot and putting it down elsewhere **3** : manner of walking **4** : a small space or distance **5** : a degree, rank, or plane in a series **6** : a sequential measure leading to a result

²step *vb* **stepped; step·ping 1** : to advance or recede by steps **2** : to go on foot : WALK **3** : to move along briskly **4** : to press down with the foot **5** : to measure by steps **6** : to construct or arrange in or as if in steps

step·broth·er \'step-ˌbrə-thər\ *n* : the son of one's stepparent by a former marriage

step·child \-ˌchīld\ *n* : a child of one's husband or wife by a former marriage

step·daugh·ter \-ˌdȯ-tər\ *n* : a daughter of one's wife or husband by a former marriage

step down *vb* **1** : RETIRE, RESIGN **2** : to lower (a voltage) by means of a transformer

step·fa·ther \-ˌfä-thər\ *n* : the husband of one's mother by a subsequent marriage

step·lad·der \'step-ˌla-dər\ *n* : a light portable set of steps in a hinged frame

step·moth·er \-ˌmə-thər\ *n* : the wife of one's father by a subsequent marriage

step·par·ent \-ˌpar-ənt\ *n* : one's stepfather or stepmother

steppe \'step\ *n* [Russ *step'*] : dry level grass-covered treeless land in regions of wide temperature range esp. in southeastern Europe and Asia

step·sis·ter \'step-ˌsis-tər\ *n* : the daughter of one's stepparent by a former marriage

step·son \-ˌsən\ *n* : a son of one's wife or husband by a former marriage

step up *vb* **1** : to increase (a voltage) by means of a transformer **2** : INCREASE, ACCELERATE **3** : to come forward — **step–up** \'step-ˌəp\ *n*

ster *abbr* sterling

ste·reo \'ster-ē-ˌō, 'stir-\ *n, pl* **ste·re·os 1** : stereophonic reproduction **2** : a stereophonic sound system — **stereo** *adj*

ste·reo·phon·ic \ˌster-ē-ə-'fä-nik, ˌstir-\ *adj* : of or relating to sound reproduction designed to create the effect of listening to the original — **ste·reo·phon·i·cal·ly** \-'fä-ni-k(ə-)lē\ *adv*

ster·e·o·scope \'ster-ē-ə-ˌskōp, 'stir-\ *n* [Gk *stereos* solid + *-skopion* means for viewing] : an optical instrument that blends two slightly different pictures of the same subject to give the effect of depth

ste·reo·scop·ic \ˌster-ē-ə-'skä-pik, ˌstir-\ *adj* **1** : of or relating to the stereoscope **2** : characterized by the seeing of objects in three dimensions ⟨~ vision⟩ — **ste·reo·scop·i·cal·ly** \-'skä-pi-k(ə-)lē\ *adv* — **ste·re·os·co·py** \ˌster-ē-'äs-kə-pē, ˌstir-\ *n*

ste·reo·type \'ster-ē-ə-ˌtīp, 'stir-\ *n* **1** : a metal printing plate cast from a mold made from set type **2** : something agreeing with a pattern; *esp* : an idea that many people have about a thing or a group and that may often be untrue or only partly true — **stereotype** *vb* — **ste·reo·typ·i·cal** \ˌster-ē-ə-'ti-pi-kəl\ *adj* — **ste·reo·typ·i·cal·ly** \-pi-k(ə-)lē\ *adv*

ste·reo·typed \-ˌtīpt\ *adj* : lacking originality or individuality **syn** trite, clichéd, commonplace, hackneyed, stale, threadbare

ster·ile \'ster-əl\ *adj* **1** : unable to bear fruit, crops, or offspring **2** : free from living things and esp. germs — **ste·ril·i·ty** \stə-'ri-lə-tē\ *n*

ster·il·ize \'ster-ə-ˌlīz\ *vb* **-ized; -iz·ing** : to make ster-

ile; *esp* : to free from germs — **ster·il·i·za·tion** \ster-ə-lə-'zā-shən\ *n* — **ster·il·iz·er** \'ster-ə-ˌlī-zər\ *n*

¹**ster·ling** \'stər-liŋ\ *n* **1** : British money **2** : sterling silver

²**sterling** *adj* **1** : of, relating to, or calculated in terms of British sterling **2** : having a fixed standard of purity represented by an alloy of 925 parts of silver with 75 parts of copper **3** : made of sterling silver **4** : EXCELLENT

¹**stern** \'stərn\ *adj* **1** : SEVERE, AUSTERE **2** : STOUT, STURDY ⟨∼ resolve⟩ — **stern·ly** *adv* — **stern·ness** *n*

²**stern** *n* : the rear end of a boat

ster·num \'stər-nəm\ *n, pl* **sternums** *or* **ster·na** \-nə\ : a long flat bone or cartilage at the center front of the chest connecting the ribs of the two sides

ste·roid \'stir-ˌȯid\ *n* : any of numerous compounds including various hormones (as anabolic steroids) and sugar derivatives — **steroid** *or* **ste·roi·dal** \stə-'rȯid-əl\ *adj*

stetho·scope \'ste-thə-ˌskōp\ *n* : an instrument used to detect and listen to sounds produced in the body

ste·ve·dore \'stē-və-ˌdȯr\ *n* [Sp *estibador,* fr. *estibar* to pack, fr. L *stipare* to press together] : one who works at loading and unloading ships

¹**stew** \'stü, 'styü\ *n* **1** : a dish of stewed meat and vegetables served in gravy **2** : a state of agitation, worry, or resentment

²**stew** *vb* **1** : to boil slowly : SIMMER **2** : to be in a state of agitation, worry, or resentment

stew·ard \'stü-ərd, 'styü-\ *n* [ME, fr. OE *stīweard,* fr. *stī, stig* hall, sty + *weard* ward] **1** : one employed on a large estate to manage domestic concerns **2** : one who supervises the provision and distribution of food (as on a ship); *also* : an employee on a ship or airplane who serves passengers **3** : one actively concerned with the direction of the affairs of an organization — **stew·ard·ship** *n*

stew·ard·ess \'stü-ər-dəs, 'styü-\ *n* : a woman who is a steward esp. on an airplane

stg *abbr* sterling

¹**stick** \'stik\ *n* **1** : a cut or broken branch or twig; *also* : a long slender piece of wood **2** : ROD, STAFF **3** : something resembling a stick **4** : a dull uninteresting

person **5** *pl* : remote usu. rural areas

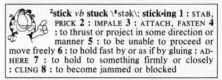

²**stick** *vb* **stuck** \'stək\; **stick·ing 1** : STAB, PRICK **2** : IMPALE **3** : ATTACH, FASTEN **4** : to thrust or project in some direction or manner **5** : to be unable to proceed or move freely **6** : to hold fast by or as if by gluing : ADHERE **7** : to hold to something firmly or closely : CLING **8** : to become jammed or blocked

stick·er \'sti-kər\ *n* : one that sticks (as a bur) or causes sticking (as glue); *esp* : an adhesive label

stick insect *n* : any of various usu. wingless insects with a long round body resembling a stick

stick·ler \'sti-klər, -kə-lər\ *n* : one who insists on exactness or completeness

stick shift *n* : a manually operated automobile gearshift usu. mounted on the floor

stick–to–it·ive·ness \stik-'tü-ə-tiv-nəs\ *n* : dogged perseverance : TENACITY

stick up *vb* : to rob at gunpoint — **stick·up** \'stik-ˌəp\ *n*

sticky \'sti-kē\ *adj* **stick·i·er; -est 1** : ADHESIVE **2** : VISCOUS, GLUEY **3** : tending to stick ⟨∼ valve⟩ **4** : DIFFICULT

¹**stiff** \'stif\ *adj* **1** : not pliant : RIGID **2** : not limber ⟨∼ joints⟩; *also* : TENSE, TAUT **3** : not flowing or working easily ⟨∼ paste⟩ **4** : not natural and easy : FORMAL **5** : STRONG, FORCEFUL ⟨∼ breeze⟩ **6** : HARSH, SEVERE **syn** inflexible, inelastic — **stiff·ly** *adv* — **stiff·ness** *n*

²**stiff** *vb* : to refuse to pay or tip

stiff·en \'sti-fən\ *vb* : to make or become stiff — **stiff·en·er** *n*

stiff–necked \'stif-'nekt\ *adj* : STUBBORN, HAUGHTY

sti·fle \'stī-fəl\ *vb* **sti·fled; sti·fling 1** : to kill by depriving of or die from lack of oxygen or air : SMOTHER **2** : to keep in check by effort : SUPPRESS ⟨∼ a sneeze⟩ — **sti·fling·ly** *adv*

stig·ma \'stig-mə\ *n, pl* **stig·ma·ta** \stig-'mä-tə, 'stig-mə-tə\ *or* **stigmas** [L] **1** : a mark of disgrace or discredit **2** *pl* : bodily marks resembling the wounds of the crucified Christ **3** : the upper part of the pistil of a flower that receives the pollen in fertilization — **stig·mat·ic** \stig-'ma-tik\ *adj*

stig·ma·tize \'stig-mə-ˌtīz\ *vb* **-tized; -tiz·ing 1** : to mark with a stigma **2** : to characterize as disgraceful

stile \'stīl\ *n* : steps used for crossing a fence or wall

sti·let·to \stə-'le-tō\ *n, pl* **-tos** *or* **-toes** [It, dim. of *stilo* stylus, dagger] : a slender dagger

¹**still** \'stil\ *adj* **1** : MOTIONLESS **2** : making no sound : SILENT — **still·ness** *n*

²**still** *vb* : to make or become still

³**still** *adv* **1** : without motion ⟨sit ~⟩ **2** : up to and during this or that time **3** : in spite of that : NEVERTHELESS **4** : EVEN ⟨ran ~ faster⟩ **5** : BESIDES, YET

⁴**still** *n* **1** : STILLNESS, SILENCE **2** : a static photograph esp. from a motion picture

⁵**still** *n* **1** : DISTILLERY **2** : apparatus used in distillation

still·birth \'stil-ˌbərth\ *n* : the birth of a dead fetus

still·born \-'bȯrn\ *adj* : born dead

still life *n, pl* **still lifes** : a picture of inanimate objects

stilt \'stilt\ *n* : one of a pair of poles for walking with each having a step or loop for the foot to elevate the wearer above the ground; *also* : a polelike support of a structure above ground or water level

stilt·ed \'stil-təd\ *adj* : not easy and natural ⟨~ language⟩

Stil·ton \'stilt-ᵊn\ *n* : a blue cheese of English origin

stim·u·lant \'sti-myə-lənt\ *n* **1** : an agent (as a drug) that temporarily increases the activity of an organism or any of its parts **2** : STIMULUS **3** : an alcoholic beverage — **stimulant** *adj*

stim·u·late \-ˌlāt\ *vb* **-lat·ed; -lat·ing** : to make active or more active : ANIMATE, AROUSE **syn** excite, provoke, motivate, quicken — **stim·u·la·tion** \ˌsti-myə-'lā-shən\ *n* — **stim·u·la·tive** \'sti-myə-ˌlā-tiv\ *adj*

stim·u·lus \'sti-myə-ləs\ *n, pl* **-li** \-ˌlī\ [L] **1** : something that moves to activity **2** : an agent that directly influences the activity of a living organism or one of its parts

¹**sting** \'stiŋ\ *vb* **stung** \'stəŋ\; **sting·ing 1** : to prick painfully esp. with a sharp or poisonous process **2** : to cause to suffer acutely — **sting·er** *n*

²**sting** *n* **1** : an act of stinging; *also* : a resultant wound, sore, or pain **2** : a pointed often venom-bearing organ (as of a bee) : STINGER **3** : an elaborate confidence game; *esp* : one worked by undercover police to trap criminals

stin·gy \'stin-jē\ *adj* **stin·gi·er; -est** : not generous : giving or spending as little as possible — **stin·gi·ness** *n*

stink \'stiŋk\ *vb* **stank** \'staŋk\ *or* **stunk** \'stəŋk\; **stunk; stink·ing** : to give forth a strong and offensive smell; *also* : to be extremely bad in quality or repute — **stink** *n* — **stink·er** *n*

stink·bug \'stiŋk-ˌbəg\ *n* : any of various true bugs that emit a disagreeable odor

¹**stint** \'stint\ *vb* **1** : to be sparing or frugal **2** : to cut short in amount

²**stint** *n* **1** : an assigned amount of work **2** : RESTRAINT, LIMITATION **3** : a period of time spent at a particular activity

sti·pend \'stī-ˌpend, -pənd\ *n* [ME, alter. of *stipendy*, fr. L *stipendium*, fr. *stips* gift + *pendere* to weigh, pay] : a fixed sum of money paid periodically for services or to defray expenses

stip·ple \'sti-pəl\ *vb* **stip·pled; stip·pling 1** : to engrave by means of dots and light strokes **2** : to apply (as paint or ink) with small short touches — **stipple** *n*

stip·u·late \'sti-pyə-ˌlāt\ *vb* **-lat·ed; -lat·ing** : to make an agreement; *esp* : to make a special demand for something as a condition in an agreement — **stip·u·la·tion** \ˌsti-pyə-'lā-shən\ *n*

¹**stir** \'stər\ *vb* **stirred; stir·ring 1** : to move slightly **2** : AROUSE, EXCITE **3** : to mix, dissolve, or make by continued circular movement ⟨~ eggs into cake batter⟩ **4** : to move to activity (as by pushing, beating, or prodding)

²**stir** *n* **1** : a state of agitation or activity **2** : an act of stirring

stir–fry \'stər-ˌfrī\ *vb* : to fry quickly over high heat while stirring continuously — **stir–fry** *n*

stir·ring \'stər-iŋ\ *adj* **1** : ACTIVE, BUSTLING **2** : ROUSING, INSPIRING

stir·rup \'stər-əp\ *n* [ME *stirop*, fr. OE *stigrāp*, lit., mounting rope] **1** : a light frame hung from a saddle to support the rider's foot **2** : STAPES

¹**stitch** \'stich\ *n* **1** : a sudden sharp pain esp. in the side **2** : one of the series of loops formed by or over a needle in sewing

²**stitch** *vb* **1** : to fasten or join with stitches **2** : to decorate with stitches **3** : SEW

stk *abbr* stock

stoat \'stōt\ *n, pl* **stoats** *also* **stoat** : the common Old and New World ermine esp. in its brown summer coat

¹**stock** \'stäk\ *n* **1** *archaic* : a block of wood **2** : a stupid person **3** : a wooden part of a thing serving as its support, frame, or handle **4** *pl* : a device for publicly punishing offenders consisting of a wooden frame with holes in which the feet and hands can be locked **5** : the original from which others derive; *also* : a group having a common origin : FAMILY **6** : LIVESTOCK **7** : a supply of goods **8** : the ownership element in a corporation divided to give the owners an interest and usu. voting power **9** : a company of actors playing at a particular theater and presenting a series of plays **10** : liquid in which meat, fish, or vegetables have been simmered that is used as a basis for soup, gravy, or sauce

stocks 4

²**stock** *vb* : to provide with stock

³**stock** *adj* : kept regularly for sale or use; *also* : commonly used : STANDARD

stock·ade \stä-'kād\ *n* [Sp *estacada*, fr. *estaca* stake, pale] : an enclosure (as of posts and stakes) for defense or confinement

stock·bro·ker \-ˌbrō-kər\ *n* : one who executes orders to buy and sell securities

stock car *n* : a racing car that is similar to a regular car

stock exchange *n* : a place where the buying and selling of securities is conducted

stock·hold·er \'stäk-ˌhōl-dər\ *n* : one who owns corporate stock

stock·i·nette *or* **stock·i·net** \ˌstä-kə-'net\ *n* : an elastic knitted fabric used esp. for infants' wear and bandages

stock·ing \'stä-kiŋ\ *n* : a close-fitting knitted covering for the foot and leg

stock market *n* **1** : STOCK EXCHANGE **2** : a market for stocks

stock·pile \'stäk-ˌpīl\ *n* : a reserve supply esp. of something essential — **stockpile** *vb*

stocky \'stä-kē\ *adj* **stock·i·er; -est** : being short and relatively thick : STURDY **syn** thickset, squat, heavyset, stubby

stock·yard \'stäk-ˌyärd\ *n* : a yard for stock; *esp* : one for livestock about to be slaughtered or shipped

stodgy \'stä-jē\ *adj* **stodg·i·er; -est 1** : HEAVY, DULL **2** : extremely old-fashioned

¹sto·ic \'stō-ik\ *n* [ME, fr. L *stoicus,* fr. Gk *stōïkos,* lit., of the portico, fr. *Stoa (Poikilē)* the Painted Portico, portico at Athens where the philosopher Zeno taught] : one who suffers without complaining

²stoic *or* **sto·i·cal** \-i-kəl\ *adj* : not affected by passion or feeling; *esp* : showing indifference to pain **syn** impassive, phlegmatic, apathetic, stolid — **sto·i·cal·ly** \-i-k(ə-)lē\ *adv* — **sto·i·cism** \'stō-ə-ˌsi-zəm\ *n*

stoke \'stōk\ *vb* **stoked; stok·ing 1** : to stir up a fire **2** : to tend and supply fuel to a furnace — **stok·er** *n*

STOL *abbr* short takeoff and landing

¹stole \'stōl\ *past of* STEAL

²stole *n* **1** : a long narrow band worn round the neck by some clergymen **2** : a long wide scarf or similar covering worn by women

stolen *past part of* STEAL

stol·id \'stä-ləd\ *adj* : not easily aroused or excited : showing little or no emotion **syn** phlegmatic, apathetic, impassive, stoic — **sto·lid·i·ty** \stä-ˈli-də-tē\ *n* — **stol·id·ly** *adv*

sto·lon \'stō-lən, -ˌlän\ *n* : RUNNER 6

¹stom·ach \'stə-mək\ *n* **1** : a saclike digestive organ of a vertebrate into which food goes from the mouth by way of the throat and which opens below into the intestine **2** : a cavity in an invertebrate animal that is analogous to a stomach **3** : ABDOMEN **4** : desire for food caused by hunger : APPETITE **5** : INCLINATION, DESIRE

²stomach *vb* : to bear without open resentment : put up with

stom·ach·ache \-ˌāk\ *n* : pain in or in the region of the stomach

stom·ach·er \'stə-mi-kər, -chər\ *n* : the front of a bodice often appearing between the laces of an outer garment (as in 16th century costume)

stomp \'stämp, 'stòmp\ *vb* : STAMP — **stomp** *n*

¹stone \'stōn\ *n* **1** : hardened earth or mineral matter : ROCK **2** : a small piece of rock **3** : a precious stone : GEM **4** : CALCULUS 3 **5** : a hard stony seed (as of a date) or one (as of a plum) with a stony covering **6** *pl usu* stone : a British unit of weight equal to 14 pounds — **stony** *also* **ston·ey** \'stō-nē\ *adj*

²stone *vb* **stoned; ston·ing 1** : to pelt or kill with stones **2** : to remove the stones of (a fruit)

Stone Age *n* : the first known period of prehistoric human culture characterized by the use of stone tools

stoned \'stōnd\ *adj* **1** : DRUNK **2** : being under the influence of a drug

stone·wall \'stōn-ˌwòl\ *vb* : to refuse to comply or cooperate with

stone·washed \'stōn-ˌwòsht, -ˌwäsht\ *adj* : having been washed with stones during manufacture to create a softer fabric (∼ jeans)

stood *past and past part of* STAND

stooge \'stüj\ *n* **1** : a person who plays a subordinate or compliant role to a principal **2** : STRAIGHT MAN

stool \'stül\ *n* **1** : a seat usu. without back or arms **2** : FOOTSTOOL **3** : a seat used while urinating or defecating **4** : a discharge of fecal matter

stool pigeon *n* : DECOY, INFORMER

¹stoop \'stüp\ *vb* **1** : to bend forward and downward **2** : CONDESCEND **3** : to lower oneself morally

²stoop *n* **1** : an act of bending forward **2** : a bent position of head and shoulders

³stoop *n* : a porch or platform at a house door

¹stop \'stäp\ *vb* **stopped; stop·ping 1** : to close (an opening) by filling or covering closely **2** : BLOCK, HALT **3** : to cease to go on **4** : to bring activity or operation to an end **5** : STAY, TARRY **syn** quit, discontinue, desist, cease

²stop *n* **1** : END, CESSATION **2** : a set of organ pipes of one tone quality; *also* : a control knob for such a set **3** : OBSTRUCTION **4** : PLUG, STOPPER **5** : an act of stopping : CHECK **6** : a delay in a journey : STAY **7** : a place

for stopping **8** *chiefly Brit* : any of several punctuation marks

stop·gap \'stäp-ˌgap\ *n* : something that serves as a temporary expedient

stop·light \-ˌlīt\ *n* : TRAFFIC LIGHT

stop·over \'stäp-ˌō-vər\ *n* **1** : a stop at an intermediate point in one's journey **2** : a stopping place on a journey

stop·page \'stä-pij\ *n* : the act of stopping : the state of being stopped

stop·per \'stä-pər\ *n* : something (as a cork) for sealing an opening

stop·watch \'stäp-ˌwäch\ *n* : a watch that can be started or stopped at will for exact timing

stor·age \'stòr-ij\ *n* **1** : space for storing; *also* : cost of storing **2** : MEMORY 6 **3** : the act of storing; *esp* : the safekeeping of goods (as in a warehouse)

storage battery *n* : a group of connected rechargeable electrochemical cells used to provide electric current

¹store \'stòr\ *vb* **stored; stor·ing 1** : to place or leave in a safe location for preservation or future use **2** : to provide esp. for a future need

²store *n* **1** : something accumulated and kept for future use **2** : a large or ample quantity **3** : STOREHOUSE **4** : a retail business establishment

store·house \-ˌhaùs\ *n* : a building for storing goods or supplies; *also* : an abundant source or supply

store·keep·er \-ˌkē-pər\ *n* : one who operates a retail store

store·room \-ˌrüm, -ˌrùm\ *n* : a room for storing goods or supplies

sto·ried \'stòr-ēd\ *adj* : celebrated in story or history

stork \'stòrk\ *n* : any of various large stout-billed Old World wading birds related to the herons and ibises

¹storm \'stòrm\ *n* **1** : a heavy fall of rain, snow, or hail with high wind **2** : a violent outbreak or disturbance **3** : a mass attack on a defended position — **storm·i·ly** \'stòr-mə-lē\ *adv* — **storm·i·ness** \-mē-nəs\ *n* — **stormy** *adj*

²storm *vb* **1** : to blow with violence; *also* : to rain, snow, or hail heavily **2** : to make a mass attack against **3** : to be violently angry : RAGE **4** : to rush along furiously

¹sto·ry \'stòr-ē\ *n, pl* **stories 1** : NARRATIVE, ACCOUNT **2** : REPORT, STATEMENT **3** : ANECDOTE **4** : SHORT STORY **5** : LIE, FALSEHOOD **6** : a news article or broadcast **syn** untruth, tale, canard

²story *also* **sto·rey** \'stòr-ē\ *n, pl* **stories** *also* **storeys** : a floor of a building or the space between two adjacent floor levels

sto·ry·tell·er \-ˌte-lər\ *n* : a teller of stories

sto·tin·ka \stō-ˈtiŋ-kə\ *n, pl* **-tin·ki** \-kē\ — see *lev* at MONEY table

¹stout \'staùt\ *adj* **1** : BRAVE **2** : FIRM **3** : STURDY **4** : STAUNCH, ENDURING **5** : SOLID **6** : FORCEFUL, VIOLENT **7** : BULKY, THICKSET **syn** fleshy, fat, portly, corpulent, obese, plump — **stout·ly** *adv* — **stout·ness** *n*

²stout *n* : a dark heavy ale

¹stove \'stōv\ *n* : an apparatus that burns fuel or uses electricity to provide heat (as for cooking or heating)

²stove *past and past part of* STAVE

stow \'stō\ *vb* **1** : HIDE, STORE **2** : to pack in a compact mass

stow·away \'stō-ə-ˌwā\ *n* : one who hides on a vehicle to ride free

STP *abbr* standard temperature and pressure

strad·dle \'strad-ᵊl\ *vb* **strad·dled; strad·dling 1** : to stand, sit, or walk with legs spread apart **2** : to favor or seem to favor two apparently opposite sides — **straddle** *n*

strafe \'strāf\ *vb* **strafed; straf·ing** [G *Gott strafe England* may God punish England, propaganda slogan during World War I] : to fire upon with machine guns from a low-flying airplane

strag·gle \'stra-gəl\ *vb* **strag·gled; strag·gling 1** : to wander from the direct course : ROVE, STRAY **2** : to become separated from others of the same kind — **strag•gler** *n* — **strag•gly** \'stra-g(ə-)lē\ *adj*

¹straight \'strāt\ *adj* **1** : free from curves, bends, angles, or irregularities **2** : not wandering from the main point or proper course ⟨∼ thinking⟩ **3** : HONEST, UPRIGHT **4** : having the elements in correct order **5** : UNMIXED, UNDILUTED ⟨∼ whiskey⟩ **6** : CONVENTIONAL, SQUARE; *also* : HETEROSEXUAL

²straight *adv* : in a straight manner

³straight *n* **1** : a straight line, course, or arrangement **2** : the part of a racetrack between the last turn and the finish **3** : a sequence of five cards in a poker hand

straight–arm \'strāt-ˌärm\ *n* : an act of warding off a football tackler with the arm fully extended — **straight–arm** *vb*

straight•away \'strā-tə-ˌwā\ *n* : a straight stretch (as at a racetrack)

straight•edge \'strāt-ˌej\ *n* : a piece of material with a straight edge for testing straight lines and surfaces or drawing straight lines

straight•en \'strāt-ᵊn\ *vb* : to make or become straight

straight flush *n* : a poker hand containing five cards of the same suit in sequence

straight•for•ward \strāt-'fȯr-wərd\ *adj* **1** : FRANK, CANDID, HONEST **2** : proceeding in a straight course or manner

straight man *n* : an entertainer who feeds lines to a comedian

straight•way \'strāt-ˌwā, -ˌwā\ *adv* : IMMEDIATELY

¹strain \'strān\ *n* [ME *streen* progeny, lineage, fr. OE *strēon* gain, acquisition] **1** : LINEAGE, ANCESTRY **2** : a group (as of people or plants) of presumed common ancestry **3** : an inherited or inherent character or quality ⟨a ∼ of madness in the family⟩ **4** : STREAK, TRACE **5** : MELODY **6** : the general style or tone

²strain *vb* [ME, fr. MF *estraindre*, fr. L *stringere* to bind or draw tight, press together] **1** : to draw taut **2** : to exert to the utmost **3** : to strive violently **4** : to injure by improper or excessive use **5** : to filter or remove by filtering **6** : to stretch beyond a proper limit — **strain•er** *n*

³strain *n* **1** : excessive tension or exertion (as of body or mind) **2** : bodily injury from excessive tension, effort, or use; *esp* : one in which muscles or ligaments are unduly stretched usu. from a wrench or twist **3** : deformation of a material body under the action of applied forces

¹strait \'strāt\ *adj* [ME, fr. OF *estreit*, fr. L *strictus* strait, strict] **1** *archaic* : STRICT **2** *archaic* : NARROW **3** *archaic* : CONSTRICTED **4** : DIFFICULT, STRAITENED

²strait *n* **1** : a narrow channel connecting two bodies of water **2** *pl* : DISTRESS

strait•en \'strāt-ᵊn\ *vb* **1** : to hem in : CONFINE **2** : to make distressing or difficult

strait•jack•et *also* **straight•jack•et** \'strāt-ˌja-kət\ *n* : a cover or garment of strong material (as canvas) used to bind the body and esp. the arms closely in restraining a violent prisoner or patient — **straitjacket** *vb*

strait•laced *or* **straight•laced** \-'lāst\ *adj* : strict in manners, morals or opinion

¹strand \'strand\ *n* : SHORE, BEACH

²strand *vb* **1** : to run, drift, or drive upon the shore ⟨a ∼ed ship⟩ **2** : to place or leave in a helpless position

³strand *n* **1** : one of the fibers twisted or plaited together into a cord, rope, or cable; *also* : a cord, rope, or cable made up of such fibers **2** : a twisted or plaited ropelike mass ⟨a ∼ of pearls⟩ — **strand•ed** \'strandəd\ *adj*

strange \'strānj\ *adj* **strang•er; strang•est** [ME, fr. OF *estrange*, fr. L *extraneus*, lit., external, fr. *extra* outside] **1** : of external origin, kind, or character **2** : NEW, UNFAMILIAR **3** : DISTANT **6 4** : UNACCUSTOMED, INEXPERIENCED **syn** singular, peculiar, eccentric, erratic, odd, queer, quaint, curious — **strange•ly** *adv* **strange•ness** *n*

strang•er \'strān-jər\ *n* **1** : FOREIGNER **2** : INTRUDER **3** : a person with whom one is unacquainted

stran•gle \'straŋ-gəl\ *vb* **stran•gled; stran•gling 1** : to choke to death : THROTTLE **2** : STIFLE, SUPPRESS — **stran•gler** *n*

stran•gu•late \'straŋ-gyə-ˌlāt\ *vb* **-lat•ed; -lat•ing 1** : STRANGLE, CONSTRICT **2** : to become so constricted as to stop circulation

stran•gu•la•tion \ˌstraŋ-gyə-'lā-shən\ *n* : the act or process of strangling or strangulating; *also* : the state of being strangled or strangulated

¹strap \'strap\ *n* : a narrow strip of flexible material used esp. for fastening, holding together, or wrapping

²strap *vb* **strapped; strap•ping 1** : to secure with a strap **2** : BIND, CONSTRICT **3** : to flog with a strap **4** : STROP

strap•less \-ləs\ *adj* : having no straps; *esp* : having no shoulder straps

¹strap•ping \'stra-piŋ\ *adj* : LARGE, STRONG, HUSKY

²strap•ping *n* : material for a strap

strat•a•gem \'stra-tə-jəm, -ˌjem\ *n* **1** : a trick to deceive or outwit the enemy; *also* : a deceptive scheme **2** : skill in deception

strat•e•gy \'stra-tə-jē\ *n, pl* **-gies** [Gk *stratēgia* generalship, fr. *stratēgos* general, fr. *stratos* camp, army + *agein* to lead] **1** : the science and art of military command aimed at meeting the enemy under conditions advantageous to one's own force **2** : a careful plan or method esp. for achieving an end — **strate•gic** \strə-'tē-jik\ *adj* — **strat•e•gist** \'stra-tə-jist\ *n*

strat•i•fy \'stra-tə-ˌfī\ *vb* **-fied; -fy•ing** : to form or arrange in layers — **strat•i•fi•ca•tion** \ˌstra-tə-fə-'kā-shən\ *n*

stra•tig•ra•phy \strə-'ti-grə-fē\ *n* : geology that deals with rock strata — **strati•graph•ic** \ˌstra-tə-'gra-fik\ *adj*

strato•sphere \'stra-tə-ˌsfir\ *n* : the part of the earth's atmosphere between about 7 miles (11 kilometers) and 31 miles (50 kilometers) above the earth — **strato•spher•ic** \ˌstra-tə-'sfir-ik, -'sfer-\ *adj*

stra•tum \'strā-təm, 'stra-\ *n, pl* **stra•ta** \'strā-tə, 'stra-\ [NL, fr. L, spread, bed, fr. neut. of *stratus*, pp. of *sternere* to spread out] **1** : a bed, layer, or sheetlike mass (as of one kind of rock lying between layers of other kinds of rock) **2** : a level of culture; *also* : a group of people representing one stage in cultural development

¹straw \'strȯ\ *n* **1** : stalks of grain after threshing; *also* : a single coarse dry stem (as of a grass) **2** : a thing of small worth : TRIFLE **3** : a tube (as of paper or plastic) for sucking up a beverage

²straw *adj* **1** : made of straw **2** : having no real force or validity ⟨a ∼ vote⟩

straw•ber•ry \'strȯ-ˌber-ē, -bə-rē\ *n* : an edible juicy usu. red pulpy fruit of any of serveral low herbs with white flowers and long slender runners; *also* : one of these herbs

straw boss *n* : a foreman of a small group of workers

straw•flow•er \'strȯ-ˌflaů-ər\ *n* : any of several plants whose flowers can be dried with little loss of form or color

¹stray \'strā\ *n* **1** : a domestic animal wandering at large or lost **2** : WAIF

²stray *vb* **1** : to wander or roam without purpose **2** : DEVIATE

³stray *adj* **1** : having strayed : separated from the group or the main body **2** : occurring at random ⟨∼ remarks⟩

¹streak \'strēk\ *n* **1** : a line or mark of a different color or texture from its background **2** : a narrow band of light; *also* : a lightning bolt **3** : a slight admixture : TRACE **4** : a brief run (as of luck); *also* : an unbroken series

²streak *vb* **1** : to form streaks in or on **2** : to move very swiftly

¹stream \'strēm\ *n* **1** : a body of water (as a river) flow-

strawberry

ing on the earth; *also* : any body of flowing fluid (as water or gas) **2** : a continuous procession ⟨a ～ of traffic⟩

²**stream** *vb* **1** : to flow in or as if in a stream **2** : to pour out streams of liquid **3** : to trail out in length **4** : to move forward in a steady stream

stream·bed \ˈstrēm-ˌbed\ *n* : the channel occupied by a stream

stream·er \ˈstrē-mər\ *n* **1** : a long narrow ribbonlike flag **2** : a long ribbon on a dress or hat **3** : a newspaper headline that runs across the entire sheet **4** *pl* : AURORA

stream·let \ˈstrēm-lət\ *n* : a small stream

stream·lined \-ˌlīnd\ *adj* **1** : made with contours to reduce resistance to motion through water or air **2** : SIMPLIFIED **3** : MODERNIZED — **streamline** *vb*

street \ˈstrēt\ *n* [ME *strete*, fr. OE *strǣt*, fr. LL *strata* paved road, fr. L, fem. of *stratus*, pp. of *sternere* to spread out] **1** : a thoroughfare esp. in a city, town, or village **2** : the occupants of the houses on a street

street·car \-ˌkär\ *n* : a passenger vehicle running on rails on city streets

street railway *n* : a company operating streetcars or buses

street·walk·er \ˈstrēt-ˌwȯ-kər\ *n* : PROSTITUTE

strength \ˈstreŋth\ *n* **1** : the quality of being strong : ability to do or endure : POWER **2** : TOUGHNESS, SOLIDITY **3** : power to resist attack **4** : INTENSITY **5** : force as measured in numbers ⟨the ～ of an army⟩

strength·en \ˈstreŋ-thən\ *vb* : to make or become stronger — **strength·en·er** *n*

stren·u·ous \ˈstren-yə-wəs\ *adj* **1** : VIGOROUS, ENERGETIC **2** : requiring energy or stamina — **stren·u·ous·ly** *adv*

strep \ˈstrep\ *n* : STREPTOCOCCUS

strep throat *n* : an inflammatory sore throat caused by streptococci and marked by fever, prostration, and toxemia

strep·to·coc·cus \ˌstrep-tə-ˈkä-kəs\ *n*, *pl* **-coc·ci** \-ˈkä-ˌkī, -ˈkäk-ˌsī, -ˈkä-ˌkē, -ˈkäk-ˌsē\ : any of various spherical bacteria that usu. grow in chains and include some causing serious diseases — **strep·to·coc·cal** \-kəl\ *adj*

strep·to·my·cin \-ˈmīs-ᵊn\ *n* : an antibiotic produced by soil bacteria and used esp. in treating tuberculosis

¹**stress** \ˈstres\ *n* **1** : PRESSURE, STRAIN; *esp* : a force that tends to distort a body **2** : a factor that induces bodily or mental tension; *also* : a state induced by such a stress **3** : EMPHASIS **4** : relative prominence of sound **5** : ACCENT; *also* : any syllable carrying the accent — **stress·ful** \ˈstres-fəl\ *adj*

²**stress** *vb* **1** : to put pressure or strain on **2** : to put emphasis on : ACCENT

¹**stretch** \ˈstrech\ *vb* **1** : to spread or reach out : EXTEND **2** : to draw out in length or breadth : EXPAND **3** : to make tense : STRAIN **4** : EXAGGERATE **5** : to become

extended without breaking ⟨rubber ～es easily⟩

²**stretch** *n* **1** : an act of extending or drawing out beyond ordinary or normal limits **2** : a continuous extent in length, area, or time **3** : the extent to which something may be stretched **4** : either of the straight sides of a racecourse

³**stretch** *adj* : easily stretched ⟨～ pants⟩

stretch·er \ˈstre-chər\ *n* **1** : one that stretches **2** : a device for carrying a sick, injured, or dead person

strew \ˈstrü\ *vb* **strewed**; **strewed** *or* **strewn** \ˈstrün\; **strew·ing 1** : to spread by scattering **2** : to cover by or as if by scattering something over or on **3** : DISSEMINATE

stria \ˈstrī-ə\ *n*, *pl* **stri·ae** \ˈstrī-ˌē\ **1** : STRIATION **3 2** : a stripe or line (as in the skin)

stri·at·ed muscle \ˈstrī-ˌā-təd-\ *n* : muscle tissue made up of long thin cells with many nuclei and alternate light and dark stripes that includes esp. the muscle of the heart and muscle that moves the vertebrate skeleton and is mostly under voluntary control

stri·a·tion \strī-ˈā-shən\ *n* **1** : the state of being marked with stripes or lines **2** : arrangement of striations or striae **3** : a minute groove, scratch, or channel esp. when one of a parallel series

strick·en \ˈstri-kən\ *adj* **1** : afflicted by or as if by disease, misfortune, or sorrow **2** : WOUNDED

strict \ˈstrikt\ *adj* **1** : allowing no evasion or escape : RIGOROUS ⟨～ discipline⟩ **2** : ACCURATE, PRECISE **syn** stringent, rigid — **strict·ly** *adv* — **strict·ness** *n*

stric·ture \ˈstrik-chər\ *n* **1** : an abnormal narrowing of a bodily passage; *also* : the narrowed part **2** : hostile criticism : a critical remark

¹**stride** \ˈstrīd\ *vb* **strode** \ˈstrōd\; **strid·den** \ˈstrid-ᵊn\; **strid·ing** : to walk or run with long regular steps — **strid·er** *n*

²**stride** *n* **1** : a long step **2** : a stage of progress **3** : manner of striding : GAIT

stri·dent \ˈstrīd-ᵊnt\ *adj* : harsh sounding : GRATING, SHRILL

strife \ˈstrīf\ *n* : CONFLICT, FIGHT, STRUGGLE **syn** discord, contention, dissension

¹**strike** \ˈstrīk\ *vb* **struck** \ˈstrək\; **struck** *also* **strick·en** \ˈstri-kən\; **strik·ing 1** : to take a course : GO ⟨*struck* off through the brush⟩ **2** : to touch or hit sharply; *also* : to deliver a blow **3** : to produce by or as if by a blow ⟨*struck* terror in the foe⟩ **4** : to lower (as a flag or sail) **5** : to collide with; *also* : to injure or destroy by collision **6** : DELETE, CANCEL **7** : to produce by impressing ⟨*struck* a medal⟩; *also* : COIN ⟨～ a new cent⟩ **8** : to cause to sound ⟨～ a bell⟩ **9** : to afflict suddenly : lay low ⟨*stricken* with a high fever⟩ **10** : to appear to; *also* : to appear to as remarkable : IMPRESS **11** : to reach by reckoning ⟨～ an average⟩ **12** : to stop work in order to obtain a change in conditions of employment **13** : to cause (a match) to ignite by rubbing **14** : to come upon ⟨～ gold⟩ **15** : TAKE ON, ASSUME ⟨～ a pose⟩ — **strik·er** *n*

²**strike** *n* **1** : an act or instance of striking **2** : a sudden discovery of rich ore or oil deposits **3** : a pitched baseball that is swung at but not hit **4** : the knocking down of all the bowling pins with the 1st ball **5** : a military attack

strike·break·er \-ˌbrā-kər\ *n* : a person hired to replace a striking worker

strike·out \-ˌaut\ *n* : an out in baseball as a result of a batter's being charged with three strikes

strike out *vb* **1** : to enter upon a course of action **2** : to start out vigorously **3** : to make an out in baseball by a strikeout

strike up *vb* **1** : to begin or cause to begin to sing or play **2** : BEGIN

strike zone *n* : the area over home plate through which a pitched baseball must pass to be called a strike

strik·ing \ˈstrī-kiŋ\ *adj* : attracting attention : very noticeable **syn** arresting, salient, conspicuous, outstanding, remarkable, prominent — **strik·ing·ly** *adv*

¹string \'striŋ\ *n* **1** : a line usu. composed of twisted threads **2** : a series of things arranged as if strung on a cord **3** : a plant fiber (as a leaf vein) **4** *pl* : the stringed instruments of an orchestra **syn** succession, progression, sequence, chain, train

²string *vb* **strung** \'strəŋ\; **string•ing 1** : to provide with strings ⟨∼ a racket⟩ **2** : to make tense **3** : to thread on or as if on a string ⟨∼ pearls⟩ **4** : to hang, tie, or fasten by a string **5** : to take the strings out of ⟨∼ beans⟩ **6** : to extend like a string

string bean *n* : a bean of one of the older varieties of kidney bean that have stringy fibers on the lines of separation of the pods; *also* : SNAP BEAN

stringed \'striŋd\ *adj* **1** : having strings ⟨∼ instruments⟩ **2** : produced by strings

strin•gen•cy \'strin-jən-sē\ *n* **1** : STRICTNESS, SEVERITY **2** : SCARCITY ⟨∼ of money⟩ — **strin•gent** \-jənt\ *adj*

string•er \'striŋ-ər\ *n* **1** : a long horizontal member in a framed structure or a bridge **2** : a news correspondent paid by the amount of copy

stringy \'striŋ-ē\ *adj* **string•i•er; -est 1** : resembling string esp. in tough, fibrous, or disordered quality ⟨∼ meat⟩ **2** : lean and sinewy in build

¹strip \'strip\ *vb* **stripped** \'stript\ *also* **stript; strip•ping 1** : to take the covering or clothing from **2** : to take off one's clothes **3** : to pull or tear off **4** : to make bare or clear (as by cutting or grazing) **5** : PLUNDER, PILLAGE **syn** divest, denude, deprive, dismantle — **strip•per** *n*

²strip *n* **1** : a long narrow flat piece **2** : AIRSTRIP

¹stripe \'strīp\ *vb* **striped** \'strīpt\; **strip•ing** : to make stripes on

²stripe *n* **1** : a line or long narrow division having a different color from the background **2** : a strip of braid (as on a sleeve) indicating military rank or length of service **3** : TYPE, CHARACTER — **striped** \'strīpt, ¹strī-pəd\ *adj*

striped bass *n* : a large marine bony fish of the Atlantic and Pacific coasts of the U.S. that is an excellent food and sport fish

strip•ling \'stri-pliŋ\ *n* : YOUTH, LAD

strip mine *n* : a mine that is worked from the earth's surface by the stripping of the topsoil — **strip–mine** *vb*

strip•tease \'strip-₁tēz\ *n* : a burlesque act in which a performer removes clothing piece by piece — **strip-teas•er** *n*

strive \'strīv\ *vb* **strove** \'strōv\ *also* **strived** \'strīvd\; **striv•en** \'stri-vən\ *or* **strived; striv•ing 1** : to make effort : labor hard **2** : to struggle in opposition : CONTEND **syn** endeavor, attempt, try, assay

strobe \'strōb\ *n* **1** : STROBOSCOPE **2** : a device for high-speed intermittent illumination (as in photography)

stro•bo•scope \'strō-bə-₁skōp\ *n* : an instrument for studying rapid motion by means of a rapidly flashing light

strode *past of* STRIDE

¹stroke \'strōk\ *vb* **stroked; strok•ing 1** : to rub gently **2** : to flatter in a manner designed to persuade

²stroke *n* **1** : the act of striking : BLOW, KNOCK **2** : a sudden action or process producing an impact ⟨∼ of lightning⟩; *also* : an unexpected result **3** : sudden weakening or loss of consciousness or the power to move or feel caused by rupture or obstruction (as by a clot) of an artery of the brain **4** : one of a series of movements against air or water to get through or over it ⟨the ∼ of a bird's wing⟩ **5** : a rower who sets the pace for a crew **6** : a vigorous effort **7** : the sound of striking (as of a clock) **8** : a single movement with or as if with a tool or implement (as a pen)

stroll \'strōl\ *vb* : to walk in a leisurely or idle manner — **stroll** *n* — **stroll•er** *n*

strong \'stròŋ\ *adj* **stron•ger** \'stròŋ-gər\; **stron•gest** \'stròŋ-gəst\ **1** : POWERFUL, VIGOROUS **2** : HEALTHY, ROBUST **3** : of a specified number ⟨an army 10 thousand ∼⟩ **4** : not mild or weak **5** : VIOLENT ⟨∼ wind⟩

6 : ZEALOUS **7** : not easily broken **8** : FIRM, SOLID **syn** stout, sturdy, stalwart, tough — **strong•ly** *adv*

strong–arm \'stròŋ-₁ärm\ *adj* : having or using undue force ⟨∼ methods⟩

strong force *n* : the physical force responsible for binding together nucleons in the atomic nucleus

strong•hold \-₁hōld\ *n* : a fortified place : FORTRESS

strong•man \-₁man\ *n* : one who leads or controls by force of will and character or by military strength

stron•tium \'strän-chē-əm, ¹strän-tē-əm\ *n* : a soft malleable metallic chemical element — see ELEMENT table

¹strop \'sträp\ *n* : STRAP; *esp* : one for sharpening a razor

²strop *vb* **stropped; strop•ping** : to sharpen a razor on a strop

stro•phe \'strō-fē\ *n* [Gk *strophē*, lit., act of turning] : a division of a poem — **stroph•ic** \'strä-fik\ *adj*

strove *past of* STRIVE

struck *past and past part of* STRIKE

struc•ture \'strək-chər\ *n* [ME, fr. L *structura*, fr. *structus*, pp. of *struere* to heap up, build] **1** : the action of building : CONSTRUCTION **2** : something built (as a house or a dam); *also* : something made up of interdependent parts in a definite pattern of organization **3** : arrangement or relationship of elements (as particles, parts, or organs) in a substance, body, or system — **struc•tur•al** *adj*

²structure *vb* **struc•tured; struc•tur•ing** : to make into a structure

stru•del \'strüd-ºl, ¹shtrüd-\ *n* [G, lit., whirlpool] : a pastry made of a thin sheet of dough rolled up with filling and baked ⟨apple ∼⟩

¹strug•gle \'strə-gəl\ *vb* **strug•gled; strug•gling 1** : to make strenuous efforts against opposition : STRIVE **2** : to proceed with difficulty or with great effort **syn** endeavor, attempt, try, assay

²struggle *n* **1** : CONTEST, STRIFE **2** : a violent effort or exertion

strum \'strəm\ *vb* **strummed; strum•ming** : to play on a stringed instrument by brushing the strings with the fingers ⟨∼ a guitar⟩

strum•pet \'strəm-pət\ *n* : PROSTITUTE

strung \'strəŋ\ *past and past part of* STRING

¹strut \'strət\ *vb* **strut•ted; strut•ting** : to walk with an affectedly proud gait

²strut *n* **1** : a bar or rod for resisting lengthwise pressure **2** : a haughty or pompous gait

strych•nine \'strik-₁nīn, -nən, -₁nēn\ *n* : a bitter poisonous plant alkaloid used as a poison (as for rats) and medicinally as a stimulant to the central nervous system

¹stub \'stəb\ *n* **1** : STUMP 2 **2** : a short blunt end **3** : a small part of each leaf (as of a checkbook) kept as a memorandum of the items on the detached part

²stub *vb* **stubbed; stub•bing** : to strike (as one's toe) against something

stub•ble \'stə-bəl\ *n* **1** : the cut stem ends of herbs and esp. grasses left in the soil after harvest **2** : a rough surface or growth resembling stubble — **stub•bly** \-b(ə-)lē\ *adj*

stub•born \'stə-bərn\ *adj* **1** : FIRM, DETERMINED **2** : done or continued in a willful, unreasonable, or persistent manner **3** : not easily controlled or remedied ⟨a ∼ cold⟩ — **stub•born•ly** *adv* — **stub•born•ness** *n*

stub•by \'stə-bē\ *adj* : short, blunt, and thick like a stub

stuc•co \'stə-kō\ *n*, *pl* **stuccos** *or* **stuccoes** [It] : plaster for coating exterior walls — **stuc•coed** \'stə-kōd\ *adj*

stuck *past and past part of* STICK

stuck–up \'stək-¹əp\ *adj* : CONCEITED

¹stud \'stəd\ *n* : a male animal and esp. a horse (**stud-horse** \-₁hòrs\) kept for breeding

²stud *n* **1** : one of the smaller uprights in a building to which the wall materials are fastened **2** : a removable

device like a button used as a fastener or ornament ⟨shirt ~s⟩ **3** : a projecting nail, pin, or rod

³stud *vb* **stud•ded; stud•ding 1** : to supply with or adorn with studs **2** : DOT

⁴stud *abbr* student

stud•book \'stəd-ˌbu̇k\ *n* : an official record of the pedigree of purebred animals (as horses or dogs)

stud•ding \'stə-diŋ\ *n* : the studs in a building or wall

stu•dent \'stüd-ᵊnt, 'styüd-\ *n* : SCHOLAR, PUPIL; *esp* : one who attends a school

stud•ied \'stə-dēd\ *adj* : INTENTIONAL ⟨a ~ insult⟩ **syn** deliberate, considered, premeditated, designed

stu•dio \'stü-dē-ˌō, 'styü-\ *n, pl* **-dios 1** : a place where an artist works; *also* : a place for the study of an art **2** : a place where motion pictures are made **3** : a place equipped for the transmission of radio or television programs

stu•di•ous \'stü-dē-əs, 'styü-\ *adj* : devoted to study — **stu•di•ous•ly** *adv*

¹study \'stə-dē\ *n, pl* **stud•ies 1** : the use of the mind to gain knowledge **2** : the act or process of learning about something **3** : careful examination **4** : INTENT, PURPOSE **5** : a branch of learning **6** : a room esp. for reading and writing

²study *vb* **stud•ied; study•ing 1** : to engage in study or the study of **2** : to consider attentively or in detail **syn** consider, contemplate, weigh

¹stuff \'stəf\ *n* **1** : personal property **2** : raw material **3** : a finished textile fabric; *esp* : a worsted fabric **4** : writing, talk, or ideas of little or transitory worth **5** : an unspecified material substance or aggregate of matter **6** : fundamental material **7** : special knowledge or capability

²stuff *vb* **1** : to fill by packing things in : CRAM **2** : to eat greedily : GORGE **3** : to prepare (as meat) by filling with a stuffing **4** : to fill (as a cushion) with a soft material **5** : to stop up : PLUG

stuffed shirt \'stəft-\ *n* : a smug, conceited, and usu. pompous and inflexibly conservative person

stuff•ing *n* : material used to fill tightly; *esp* : a mixture of bread crumbs and spices used to stuff meat and poultry

stuffy \'stə-fē\ *adj* **stuff•i•er; -est 1** : STODGY **2** : lacking fresh air : CLOSE; *also* : blocked up ⟨a ~ nose⟩

stul•ti•fy \'stəl-tə-ˌfī\ *vb* **-fied; -fy•ing 1** : to cause to appear foolish or stupid **2** : to impair, invalidate, or make ineffective **3** : to have a dulling effect on — **stul•ti•fi•ca•tion** \ˌstəl-tə-fə-'kā-shən\ *n*

stum•ble \'stəm-bəl\ *vb* **stum•bled; stum•bling 1** : to blunder morally **2** : to trip in walking or running **3** : to walk unsteadily; *also* : to speak or act in a blundering or clumsy manner **4** : to happen by chance — **stumble** *n*

stumbling block *n* : an obstacle to belief, understanding, or progress

¹stump \'stəmp\ *n* **1** : the base of a bodily part (as a leg or tooth) left after the rest is removed **2** : the part of

a plant and esp. a tree remaining with the root after the trunk is cut off **3** : a place or occasion for political public speaking — **stumpy** *adj*

²stump *vb* **1** : BAFFLE, PERPLEX **2** : to clear (land) of stumps **3** : to tour (a region) making political speeches **4** : to walk clumsily and heavily

stun \'stən\ *vb* **stunned; stun•ning 1** : to make senseless or dizzy by or as if by a blow **2** : BEWILDER, STUPEFY

stung *past and past part of* STING

stunk *past and past part of* STINK

stun•ning *adj* **1** : causing astonishment or disbelief **2** : strikingly beautiful — **stun•ning•ly** *adv*

¹stunt \'stənt\ *vb* : to hinder the normal growth or progress of

²stunt *n* : an unusual or spectacular feat

stu•pe•fy \'stü-pə-ˌfī, 'styü-\ *vb* **-fied; -fy•ing 1** : to make stupid, groggy, or insensible **2** : ASTONISH — **stu•pe•fac•tion** \ˌstü-pə-'fak-shən, ˌstyü-\ *n*

stu•pen•dous \stu̇-'pen-dəs, styü-\ *adj* : causing astonishment esp. because of great size or height **syn** tremendous, prodigious, monumental, monstrous — **stu•pen•dous•ly** *adv*

stu•pid \'stü-pəd, 'styü-\ *adj* [MF *stupide*, fr. L *stupidus*, fr. *stupēre* to be numb, be astonished] **1** : very dull in mind **2** : showing or resulting from dullness of mind — **stu•pid•i•ty** \stu̇-'pi-də-tē, styü-\ *n* — **stu•pid•ly** *adv*

stu•por \'stü-pər, 'styü-\ *n* **1** : a condition of greatly dulled or completely suspended sense or feeling **2** : a state of extreme apathy or torpor often following stress or shock — **stu•por•ous** *adj*

stur•dy \'stər-dē\ *adj* **stur•di•er; -est** [ME, brave, stubborn, fr. OF *estourdi* stunned, fr. pp. of *estourdir* to stun] **1** : RESOLUTE, UNYIELDING **2** : STRONG, ROBUST **syn** stout, stalwart, tough, tenacious — **stur•di•ly** \-də-lē\ *adv* — **stur•di•ness** \-dē-nəs\ *n*

stur•geon \'stər-jən\ *n* : any of a family of large bony fishes including some whose roe is made into caviar

sturgeon

stut•ter \'stə-tər\ *vb* : to speak with involuntary disruption or blocking of sounds — **stutter** *n*

¹sty \'stī\ *n, pl* **sties** : a pen or housing for swine

²sty *or* **stye** \'stī\ *n, pl* **sties** *or* **styes** : an inflamed swelling of a skin gland on the edge of an eyelid

¹style \'stī(ə)l\ *n* **1** : mode of address : TITLE **2** : a way of speaking or writing; *esp* : one characteristic of an individual, period, school, or nation ⟨ornate ~⟩ **3** : manner or method of acting, making, or performing; *also* : a distinctive or characteristic manner **4** : a slender pointed instrument or process; *esp* : STYLUS **5** : a fashionable manner or mode **6** : overall excellence, skill, or grace in performance, manner, or appearance **7** : the custom followed in spelling, capitalization, punctuation, and typography — **sty·lis·tic** \stī-'lis-tik\ *adj*

²**style** *vb* **styled; styl·ing 1** : NAME, DESIGNATE **2** : to make or design in accord with a prevailing mode

styl·ing \'stī-liŋ\ *n* : the way in which something is styled

styl·ise *Brit var of* STYLIZE

styl·ish \'stī-lish\ *adj* : conforming to current fashion **syn** modish, smart, chic — **styl·ish·ly** *adv* — **styl·ish·ness** *n*

styl·ist \'stī-list\ *n* **1** : one (as a writer) noted for a distinctive style **2** : a developer or designer of styles

styl·ize \'stī-ˌlīz, 'stī-ə-\ *vb* **styl·ized; styl·iz·ing** : to conform to a style; *esp* : to represent or design according to a pattern or style rather than according to nature or tradition

sty·lus \'stī-ləs\ *n, pl* **sty·li** \'stī-ˌlī\ *also* **sty·lus·es** \'stī-lə-səz\ [L *stylus, stilus* spike, stylus] **1** : a pointed implement used by the ancients for writing on wax **2** : a phonograph needle

sty·mie \'stī-mē\ *vb* **sty·mied; sty·mie·ing** : BLOCK, FRUSTRATE

styp·tic \'stip-tik\ *adj* : tending to check bleeding — **styptic** *n*

suave \'swäv\ *adj* [MF, pleasant, sweet, fr. L *suavis*] : persuasively pleasing : smoothly agreeable **syn** urbane, smooth, bland — **suave·ly** *adv* — **sua·vi·ty** \'swä-və-tē\ *n*

¹**sub** \'səb\ *n* : SUBSTITUTE — **sub** *vb*

²**sub** *n* : SUBMARINE

³**sub** *abbr* **1** subtract **2** suburb

sub- \'səb\ *prefix* **1** : under : beneath **2** : subordinate : secondary **3** : subordinate portion of : subdivision of **4** : with repetition of a process described in a simple verb so as to form, stress, or deal with subordinate parts or relations **5** : somewhat **6** : falling nearly in the category of : bordering on

subacute	subliterate
subagency	subminimal
subagent	subminimum
subaqueous	suboptimal
subarctic	suborder
subarea	subparagraph
subatmospheric	subparallel
subaverage	subphylum
subbasement	subplot
subcategory	subpopulation
subcellular	subproblem
subchapter	subprofessional
subclass	subprogram
subclassify	subregion
subcommittee	subroutine
subcontract	subsection
subcontractor	subsense
subculture	subsoil
subcutaneous	subspecies
subdiscipline	substage
subentry	substation
subfamily	subsystem
subfield	subteen
subfreezing	subthreshold
subgenre	subtopic
subgenus	subtotal
subgroup	subtreasury
subhead	subtype
subheading	subunit
subhuman	subvariety
subkingdom	subvisible
sublethal	subzero

sub·al·pine \ˌsəb-'al-ˌpīn\ *adj* **1** : of or relating to the region about the foot and lower slopes of the Alps **2** : of, relating to, or inhabiting high upland slopes esp. just below the timberline

sub·al·tern \sə-'bȯl-tərn\ *n* : SUBORDINATE; *esp* : a junior officer (as in the British army)

sub·as·sem·bly \ˌsəb-ə-'sem-blē\ *n* : an assembled unit to be incorporated with other units in a finished product

sub·atom·ic \ˌsəb-ə-'tä-mik\ *adj* : of or relating to the inside of the atom or to particles smaller than atoms

sub·clin·i·cal \ˌsəb-'kli-ni-kəl\ *adj* : not detectable by the usual clinical tests ⟨a ∼ infection⟩

sub·com·pact \'səb-'käm-ˌpakt\ *n* : an automobile smaller than a compact

¹**sub·con·scious** \ˌsəb-'kän-chəs, 'səb-\ *adj* : existing in the mind without entering conscious awareness — **sub·con·scious·ly** *adv* — **sub·con·scious·ness** *n*

²**subconscious** *n* : mental activities just below the threshold of consciousness

sub·con·ti·nent \ˌsəb-'känt-ᵊn-ənt\ *n* : a major subdivision of a continent — **sub·con·ti·nen·tal** \ˌsəb-ˌkänt-ᵊn-'ent-ᵊl\ *adj*

sub·di·vide \ˌsəb-də-'vīd, 'səb-də-ˌvīd\ *vb* : to divide the parts of into more parts; *esp* : to divide (a tract of land) into building lots — **sub·di·vi·sion** \-'vi-zhən, -ˌvi-\ *n*

sub·duc·tion \səb-'dək-shən\ *n* : the descent of the edge of one crustal plate beneath the edge of an adjacent plate

sub·due \səb-'dü, -'dyü\ *vb* **sub·dued; sub·du·ing 1** : to bring into subjection : VANQUISH **2** : to bring under control : CURB **3** : to reduce the intensity of

subj *abbr* **1** subject **2** subjunctive

¹**sub·ject** \'səb-jikt\ *n* [ME, fr. MF, fr. L *subjectus* one under authority & *subjectum* subject of a proposition, fr. *subicere* to subject, lit., to throw under, fr. *sub-* under + *jacere* to throw] **1** : a person under the authority of another **2** : a person subject to a sovereign **3** : an individual that is studied or experimented on **4** : the person or thing discussed or treated : TOPIC, THEME **5** : a word or word group denoting that of which something is predicated

²**subject** *adj* **1** : being under the power or rule of another **2** : LIABLE, EXPOSED ⟨∼ to floods⟩ **3** : dependent on some act or condition ⟨appointment ∼ to senate approval⟩ **syn** subordinate, secondary, tributary, collateral, dependent

³**sub·ject** \səb-'jekt\ *vb* **1** : to bring under control : CONQUER **2** : to make liable **3** : to cause to undergo or endure — **sub·jec·tion** \-'jek-shən\ *n*

sub·jec·tive \(ˌ)səb-'jek-tiv\ *adj* **1** : of, relating to, or constituting a subject **2** : of, relating to, or arising within one's self or mind in contrast to what is outside : PERSONAL — **sub·jec·tive·ly** *adv* — **sub·jec·tiv·i·ty** \-ˌjek-'ti-və-tē\ *n*

subject matter *n* : matter presented for consideration, discussion, or study

sub·join \(ˌ)səb-'jȯin\ *vb* : APPEND

sub ju·di·ce \(ˌ)sùb-'yü-di-ˌkā, ˌsəb-'jü-də-(ˌ)sē\ *adv* [L] : before a judge or court : not yet legally decided

sub·ju·gate \'səb-ji-ˌgāt\ *vb* **-gat·ed; -gat·ing** : CONQUER, SUBDUE; *also* : ENSLAVE **syn** reduce, overcome, overthrow, vanquish, defeat, beat — **sub·ju·ga·tion** \ˌsəb-ji-'gā-shən\ *n*

sub·junc·tive \səb-'jəŋk-tiv\ *adj* : of, relating to, or constituting a verb form that represents an act or state as contingent or possible or viewed emotionally (as with desire) ⟨the ∼ mood⟩ — **subjunctive** *n*

sub·lease \'səb-ˌlēs, -ˌlēs\ *n* : a lease by a lessee of part or all of leased premises to another person with the original lessee retaining some right under the original lease — **sublease** *vb*

¹**sub·let** \'səb-'let\ *vb* **-let; -let·ting** : to let all or a part of (a leased property) to another; *also* : to rent (a property) from a lessee

²**sublet** \-ˌlet\ *n* : property and esp. housing obtained by or available through a sublease

sub·li·mate \'sə-blə-ˌmāt\ *vb* **-mat·ed; -mat·ing 1** : SUBLIME **2** : to direct the expression of (as a desire or impulse) from a primitive to a more socially and culturally acceptable form — **sub·li·ma·tion** \ˌsə-blə-ˈmā-shən\ n

¹**sub·lime** \sə-ˈblīm\ vb **sub·limed; sub·lim·ing** : to pass or cause to pass directly from the solid to the vapor state

²**sublime** adj **1** : EXALTED, NOBLE **2** : having awe-inspiring beauty or grandeur syn glorious, splendid, superb, resplendent, gorgeous — **sub·lime·ly** adv — **sub·lim·i·ty** \-ˈbli-mə-tē\ n

sub·lim·i·nal \(ˌ)səb-ˈli-mən-ᵊl, ˈsəb-\ adj **1** : inadequate to produce a sensation or mental awareness (∼ stimuli) **2** : existing or functioning below the threshold of consciousness (the ∼ mind) (∼ advertising)

sub·ma·chine gun \ˌsəb-mə-ˈshēn-ˌgən\ n : an automatic firearm fired from the shoulder or hip

¹**sub·ma·rine** \ˈsəb-mə-ˌrēn, ˌsəb-mə-ˈrēn\ adj : UNDERWATER; esp : UNDERSEA

²**submarine** n **1** : a naval vessel designed to operate underwater **2** : a large sandwich made from a long split roll with any of a variety of fillings

sub·merge \səb-ˈmərj\ vb **sub·merged; sub·merg·ing 1** : to put or plunge under the surface of water **2** : INUNDATE — **sub·mer·gence** \-ˈmər-jəns\ n

sub·merse \səb-ˈmərs\ vb **sub·mersed; sub·mers·ing** : SUBMERGE — **sub·mer·sion** \-ˈmər-zhən\ n

¹**sub·mers·ible** \səb-ˈmər-sə-bəl\ adj : capable of being submerged

²**submersible** n : something that is submersible; esp : a small underwater craft used for deep-sea research

sub·mi·cro·scop·ic \ˌsəb-ˌmī-krə-ˈskä-pik\ adj : too small to be seen in an ordinary light microscope

sub·min·ia·ture \ˈsəb-mi-nē-ə-ˌchur, ˈsəb-, -ˈmi-ni-ˌchur, -chər\ adj : very small

sub·mit \səb-ˈmit\ vb **sub·mit·ted; sub·mit·ting 1** : to commit to the discretion or decision of another or of others **2** : YIELD, SURRENDER **3** : to put forward as an opinion — **sub·mis·sion** \-ˈmi-shən\ n — **sub·mis·sive** \-ˈmi-siv\ adj

sub·nor·mal \ˌsəb-ˈnȯr-məl\ adj : falling below what is normal; also : having less of something and esp. intelligence than is normal — **sub·nor·mal·i·ty** \ˌsəb-nȯr-ˈma-lə-tē\ n

sub·or·bit·al \ˈsəb-ˈȯr-bət-ᵊl, ˈsəb-\ adj : being or involving less than one orbit

¹**sub·or·di·nate** \sə-ˈbȯrd-ᵊn-ət\ adj **1** : of lower class or rank **2** : INFERIOR **3** : submissive to authority **4** : subordinated to other elements in a sentence : DEPENDENT (∼ clause) syn secondary, subject, tributary, collateral

²**subordinate** n : one that is subordinate

³**sub·or·di·nate** \sə-ˈbȯrd-ᵊn-ˌāt\ vb **-nat·ed; -nat·ing 1** : to place in a lower rank or class **2** : SUBDUE — **sub·or·di·na·tion** \-ˌbȯrd-ᵊn-ˈā-shən\ n

sub·orn \sə-ˈbȯrn\ vb **1** : to induce secretly to do an unlawful thing **2** : to induce to commit perjury — **sub·or·na·tion** \ˌsə-ˌbȯr-ˈnā-shən\ n

¹**sub·poe·na** \sə-ˈpē-nə\ n [ME suppena, fr. L sub poena under penalty] : a writ commanding the person named in it to attend court under penalty for failure to do so

²**subpoena** vb **-naed; -na·ing** : to summon with a subpoena

sub–Sa·ha·ran \ˌsəb-sə-ˈhar-ən\ adj : of, relating to, or being the part of Africa south of the Sahara

sub·scribe \səb-ˈskrīb\ vb **sub·scribed; sub·scrib·ing 1** : to sign one's name to a document **2** : to give consent by or as if by signing one's name **3** : to promise to contribute by signing one's name with the amount promised **4** : to place an order by signing **5** : to receive a periodical or service regularly on order **6** : FAVOR, APPROVE syn agree, acquiesce, assent, accede — **sub·scrib·er** n

sub·script \ˈsəb-ˌskript\ n : a symbol (as a letter or number) immediately below or below and to the right or left of another written character — **subscript** adj

sub·scrip·tion \səb-ˈskrip-shən\ n **1** : the act of sub-scribing : SIGNATURE **2** : a purchase by signed order

sub·se·quent \ˈsəb-si-kwənt, -sə-ˌkwent\ adj : following after : SUCCEEDING — **sub·se·quent·ly** adv

sub·ser·vi·ence \səb-ˈsər-vē-əns\ n **1** : a subordinate place or condition **2** : SERVILITY — **sub·ser·vi·en·cy** \-ən-sē\ n — **sub·ser·vi·ent** \-ənt\ adj

sub·set \ˈsəb-ˌset\ n : a set each of whose elements is an element of an inclusive set

sub·side \səb-ˈsīd\ vb **sub·sid·ed; sub·sid·ing** [L sub-sidere, fr. sub- under + sidere to sit down, sink] **1** : to settle to the bottom of a liquid **2** : to tend downward : DESCEND **3** : SINK, SUBMERGE **4** : to become quiet and tranquil syn abate, wane, moderate, slacken — **sub·sid·ence** \səb-ˈsīd-ᵊns, ˈsəb-sə-dəns\ n

¹**sub·sid·iary** \səb-ˈsi-dē-ˌer-ē\ adj **1** : furnishing aid or support **2** : of secondary importance **3** : of or relating to a subsidy syn auxiliary, contributory, subservient, accessory

²**subsidiary** n, pl **-iar·ies** : one that is subsidiary; esp : a company controlled by another

sub·si·dise Brit var of SUBSIDIZE

sub·si·dize \ˈsəb-sə-ˌdīz\ vb **-dized; -diz·ing** : to aid or furnish with a subsidy

sub·si·dy \ˈsəb-sə-dē\ n, pl **-dies** [ME, fr. L subsidium reserve troops, support, assistance, fr. sub- near + sedēre to sit] : a gift of public money to a private person or company or to another government

sub·sist \səb-ˈsist\ vb **1** : EXIST, PERSIST **2** : to have the means (as food and clothing) of maintaining life; esp : to nourish oneself

sub·sis·tence \səb-ˈsis-təns\ n **1** : EXISTENCE **2** : means of subsisting : the minimum (as of food and clothing) necessary to support life

sub·son·ic \ˌsəb-ˈsä-nik, ˈsəb-\ adj : being or relating to a speed less than that of sound; also : moving at such a speed

sub·spe·cies \ˈsəb-ˌspē-shēz, -ˌsēz\ n : a subdivision of a species; esp : a category in biological classification ranking just below a species that designates a geographic population genetically distinct from other such populations and potentially able to breed with them where its range overlaps theirs

sub·stance \ˈsəb-stəns\ n **1** : essential nature : ESSENCE (divine ∼); also : the fundamental or essential part or quality (the ∼ of the speech) **2** : physical material from which something is made or which has discrete existence; also : matter of particular or definite chemical constitution **3** : material possessions : PROPERTY, WEALTH

substance abuse n : excessive use of a drug (as alcohol or cocaine) : use of a drug without medical justification

sub·stan·dard \ˌsəb-ˈstan-dərd\ adj : falling short of a standard or norm

sub·stan·tial \səb-ˈstan-chəl\ adj **1** : existing as or in substance : MATERIAL; also : not illusory : REAL **2** : IMPORTANT, ESSENTIAL **3** : NOURISHING, SATISFYING (∼ meal) **4** : having means : WELL-TO-DO **5** : CONSIDERABLE (∼ profit) **6** : STRONG, FIRM — **sub·stan·tial·ly** adv

sub·stan·ti·ate \səb-ˈstan-chē-ˌāt\ vb **-at·ed; -at·ing 1** : to give substance or body to **2** : VERIFY, PROVE — **sub·stan·ti·a·tion** \-ˌstan-chē-ˈā-shən\ n

sub·stan·tive \ˈsəb-stən-tiv\ n : NOUN; also : a word or phrase used as a noun

¹**sub·sti·tute** \ˈsəb-stə-ˌtüt, -ˌtyüt\ n : a person or thing replacing another — **substitute** adj

²**substitute** vb **-tut·ed; -tut·ing 1** : to put or use in the place of another **2** : to serve as a substitute — **sub·sti·tu·tion** \ˌsəb-stə-ˈtü-shən, -ˈtyü-\ n

sub·strate \ˈsəb-ˌstrāt\ n **1** : the base on which a plant or animal lives **2** : a substance acted upon (as by an enzyme)

sub·stra·tum \ˈsəb-ˌstrā-təm, -ˌstra-\ n, pl **-stra·ta** \-tə\ : the layer or structure (as subsoil) lying underneath

sub·struc·ture \'səb-ˌstrək-chər\ *n* : FOUNDATION, GROUNDWORK

sub·sur·face \'səb-ˌsər-fəs\ : earth material near the surface of the ground — **subsurface** *adj*

sub·ter·fuge \'səb-tər-ˌfyüj\ *n* : a trick or device used in order to conceal, escape, or evade **syn** fraud, deception, trickery

sub·ter·ra·nean \ˌsəb-tə-'rā-nē-ən\ *adj* **1** : lying or being underground **2** : SECRET, HIDDEN

sub·tile \'sət-ᵊl\ *adj* **sub·til·er** \'sət-lər, -ᵊl-ər\; **sub·til·est** \'sət-ləst, -ᵊl-əst\ : SUBTLE

sub·ti·tle \'səb-ˌtīt-ᵊl\ *n* **1** : a secondary or explanatory title (as of a book) **2** : printed matter projected on a motion-picture screen during or between the scenes

sub·tle \'sət-ᵊl\ *adj* **sub·tler** \'sət-ᵊl-ər\; **sub·tlest** \'sət-ᵊl-əst\ **1** : hardly noticeable (∼ differences) **2** : SHREWD, PERCEPTIVE **3** : CLEVER, SLY — **sub·tle·ty** \-tē\ *n* — **sub·tly** \'sət-ᵊl-ē\ *adv*

sub·tract \səb-'trakt\ *vb* : to take away (as one part or number) from another; *also* : to perform the operation of deducting one number from another — **sub·trac·tion** \-'trak-shən\ *n*

sub·tra·hend \'səb-trə-ˌhend\ *n* : a number that is to be subtracted from another

sub·trop·i·cal \ˌsəb-'trä-pi-kəl, 'səb-\ *also* **sub·trop·ic** \-pik\ *adj* : of, relating to, or being regions bordering on the tropical zone — **sub·trop·ics** \-piks\ *n pl*

sub·urb \'sə-ˌbərb\ *n* **1** : an outlying part of a city; *also* : a small community adjacent to a city **2** *pl* : a residential area adjacent to a city — **sub·ur·ban** \sə-'bər-bən\ *adj or n* — **sub·ur·ban·ite** \sə-'bər-bə-ˌnīt\ *n*

sub·ur·bia \sə-'bər-bē-ə\ *n* **1** : SUBURBS **2** : suburban people or customs

sub·ven·tion \səb-'ven-chən\ *n* : SUBSIDY, ENDOWMENT

sub·vert \səb-'vərt\ *vb* **1** : OVERTHROW, RUIN **2** : CORRUPT — **sub·ver·sion** \-'vər-zhən\ *n* — **sub·ver·sive** \-'vər-siv\ *adj*

sub·way \'səb-ˌwā\ *n* : an underground way; *esp* : an underground electric railway

suc·ceed \sək-'sēd\ *vb* **1** : to follow next in order or next after another; *esp* : to inherit sovereignty, rank, title, or property **2** : to attain a desired object or end : be successful

suc·cess \sək-'ses\ *n* **1** : favorable or desired outcome **2** : the gaining of wealth and fame **3** : one that succeeds — **suc·cess·ful** \-fəl\ *adj* — **suc·cess·ful·ly** *adv*

suc·ces·sion \sək-'se-shən\ *n* **1** : the order, act, or right of succeeding to a property, title, or throne **2** : the act or process of following in order **3** : a series of persons or things that follow one after another **syn** progression, sequence, chain, train, string

suc·ces·sive \sək-'se-siv\ *adj* : following in order : CONSECUTIVE — **suc·ces·sive·ly** *adv*

suc·ces·sor \sək-'se-sər\ *n* : one that succeeds (as to a throne, title, estate, or office)

suc·cinct \(ˌ)sək-'siŋkt, sə-'siŋkt\ *adj* : BRIEF, CONCISE **syn** terse, laconic, summary, curt, short — **suc·cinct·ly** *adv* — **suc·cinct·ness** *n*

suc·cor \'sə-kər\ *n* [ME *succur*, fr. earlier *sucurs*, taken as pl., fr. OF *sucors*, fr. ML *succursus*, fr. L *succurrere* to run up, run to help] : AID, HELP, RELIEF — **succor** *vb*

suc·co·tash \'sə-kə-ˌtash\ *n* [Narraganset (American Indian language of Rhode Island) *msíckquatash* boiled corn kernels] : beans and corn kernels cooked together

suc·cour *chiefly Brit var of* SUCCOR

¹**suc·cu·lent** \'sə-kyə-lənt\ *adj* : full of juice : JUICY; *also* : having fleshy tissues that conserve moisture (∼ plants) — **suc·cu·lence** \-ləns\ *n*

²**succulent** *n* : a succulent plant (as a cactus)

suc·cumb \sə-'kəm\ *vb* **1** : to yield to superior strength or force or overpowering appeal or desire **2** : DIE **syn** submit, capitulate, relent, defer

¹**such** \'səch, 'sich\ *adj* **1** : of this or that kind **2** : having a quality just specified or to be specified

²**such** *pron* **1** : such a one or ones (he's a star, and acted as ∼) **2** : that or those similar or related thereto (boards and nails and ∼)

³**such** *adv* : to that degree : SO

such·like \'səch-ˌlīk\ *adj* : SIMILAR

¹**suck** \'sək\ *vb* **1** : to draw in liquid and esp. mother's milk with the mouth **2** : to draw liquid from by action of the mouth (∼ an orange) **3** : to take in or up or remove by or as if by suction

²**suck** *n* **1** : a sucking movement or force **2** : the act of sucking

suck·er \'sə-kər\ *n* **1** : one that sucks **2** : a part of an animal's body used for sucking or for clinging **3** : a fish with thick soft lips for sucking in food **4** : a shoot from the roots or lower part of a plant **5** : a person easily deceived **6** — used as a generalized term of reference (see if you can get that ∼ working again)

suck·le \'sə-kəl\ *vb* **suck·led; suck·ling** : to give or draw milk from the breast or udder; *also* : NURTURE

suck·ling \'sə-kliŋ\ *n* : a young unweaned mammal

su·cre \'sü-(ˌ)krā\ *n* — see MONEY table

su·crose \'sü-ˌkrōs, -ˌkrōz\ *n* : a sweet sugar obtained commercially esp. from sugarcane or sugar beets

suc·tion \'sək-shən\ *n* **1** : the act of sucking **2** : the act or process of drawing something (as liquid or dust) into a space (as in a vacuum cleaner or a pump) by partially exhausting the air in the space — **suc·tion·al** \-shə-nəl\ *adj*

suction cup *n* : a cup-shaped device in which a partial vacuum is produced when applied to a surface

Su·da·nese \ˌsüd-ᵊn-'ēz, -'ēs\ *n* : a native or inhabitant of Sudan — **Sudanese** *adj*

sud·den \'səd-ᵊn\ *adj* [ME *sodain*, fr. MF, fr. L *subitaneus*, fr. *subitus* sudden, fr. pp. of *subire* to come up] **1** : happening or coming unexpectedly (∼ shower); *also* : changing angle or character all at once (∼ turn) (∼ descent) **2** : HASTY, RASH (∼ decision) **3** : made or brought about in a short time : PROMPT (∼

cure) **syn** precipitate, headlong, impetuous — **sud-den·ly** adv — **sud·den·ness** n
sudden infant death syndrome n : death due to unknown causes of an apparently healthy infant usu. before one year of age and esp. during sleep
suds \'sədz\ n pl : soapy water esp. when frothy — **sudsy** \'səd-zē\ adj
sue \'sü\ vb **sued; su·ing 1** : PETITION, SOLICIT **2** : to seek justice or right by bringing legal action
suede or **suède** \'swād\ n [F gants de Suède Swedish gloves] **1** : leather with a napped surface **2** : a fabric with a suedelike nap
su·et \'sü-ət\ n : the hard fat from beef and mutton that yields tallow
suff abbr **1** sufficient **2** suffix
suf·fer \'sə-fər\ vb **suf·fered; suf·fer·ing 1** : to feel or endure pain **2** : EXPERIENCE, UNDERGO **3** : to bear loss, damage, or injury **4** : ALLOW, PERMIT **syn** endure, abide, tolerate, stand, brook, stomach — **suf·fer·able** \'sə-fə-rə-bəl\ adj — **suf·fer·er** n
suf·fer·ance \'sə-frəns, -fə-rəns\ n **1** : consent or approval implied by lack of interference or resistance **2** : ENDURANCE, PATIENCE
suf·fer·ing \'sə-friŋ, -fə-riŋ\ n : PAIN, MISERY, HARDSHIP
suf·fice \sə-'fīs\ vb **suf·ficed; suf·fic·ing 1** : to satisfy a need : be sufficient **2** : to be capable or competent
suf·fi·cien·cy \sə-'fi-shən-sē\ n **1** : a sufficient quantity to meet one's needs **2** : ADEQUACY
suf·fi·cient \sə-'fi-shənt\ adj : adequate to accomplish a purpose or meet a need — **suf·fi·cient·ly** adv
¹**suf·fix** \'sə-,fiks\ n : an affix occurring at the end of a word
²**suf·fix** \'sə-,fiks, (,)sə-'fiks\ vb : to attach as a suffix — **suf·fix·a·tion** \,sə-,fik-'sā-shən\ n
suf·fo·cate \'sə-fə-,kāt\ vb **-cat·ed; -cat·ing** : STIFLE, SMOTHER, CHOKE — **suf·fo·cat·ing·ly** adv — **suf·fo·ca·tion** \,sə-fə-'kā-shən\ n
suf·fra·gan \'sə-fri-gən\ n : an assistant bishop; esp : one not having the right of succession — **suffragan** adj
suf·frage \'sə-frij\ n [L suffragium] **1** : VOTE **2** : the right to vote : FRANCHISE
suf·frag·ette \,sə-fri-'jet\ n : a woman who advocates suffrage for women
suf·frag·ist \'sə-fri-jist\ n : one who advocates extension of the suffrage esp. to women
suf·fuse \sə-'fyüz\ vb **suf·fused; suf·fus·ing** : to spread over or through in the manner of a fluid or light **syn** infuse, imbue, ingrain, steep — **suf·fu·sion** \-'fyü-zhən\ n
¹**sug·ar** \'shù-gər\ n **1** : a sweet substance that is colorless or white when pure and is chiefly sucrose from sugarcane or sugar beets **2** : a water-soluble compound (as glucose) similar to sucrose — **sug·ary** adj
²**sugar** vb **sug·ared; sug·ar·ing 1** : to mix, cover, or sprinkle with sugar **2** : SWEETEN ⟨∼ advice with flattery⟩ **3** : to form sugar ⟨a syrup that ∼s⟩ **4** : GRANULATE

sugar beet n : a large beet with a white root from which sugar is made
sug·ar·cane \'shù-gər-,kān\ n : a tall grass widely grown in warm regions for the sugar in its stalks
sugar daddy n **1** : a well-to-do usu. older man who supports or spends lavishly on a mistress or girlfriend **2** : a generous benefactor of a cause
sugar maple n : a maple with a sweet sap; esp : one of eastern No. America with sap that is the chief source of maple syrup and maple sugar
sugar pea n : SNOW PEA

sug·ar·plum \'shù-gər-,pləm\ n : a small ball of candy

sug·gest \səg-'jest, sə-\ vb **1** : to put (as a thought, plan, or desire) into a person's mind **2** : to remind or evoke by association of ideas **syn** imply, hint, intimate, insinuate, connote
sug·gest·ible \səg-'jes-tə-bəl, sə-\ adj : easily influenced by suggestion
sug·ges·tion \-'jes-chən\ n **1** : an act or instance of suggesting; also : something suggested **2** : a slight indication
sug·ges·tive \-'jes-tiv\ adj : tending to suggest something; esp : suggesting something improper or indecent — **sug·ges·tive·ly** adv — **sug·ges·tive·ness** n
sui·cide \'sü-ə-,sīd\ n **1** : the act of killing oneself purposely **2** : one that commits or attempts suicide — **sui·cid·al** \,sü-ə-'sīd-əl\ adj
sui ge·ner·is \,sü-,ī-'je-nə-rəs, ,sü-ē-\ adj [L, of its own kind] : being in a class by itself : UNIQUE
¹**suit** \'süt\ n **1** : an action in court to recover a right or claim **2** : an act of suing or entreating; esp : COURTSHIP **3** : a number of things used together ⟨∼ of clothes⟩ **4** : one of the four sets of playing cards in a pack
²**suit** vb **1** : to be appropriate or fitting **2** : to be becoming to **3** : to meet the needs or desires of : PLEASE
suit·able \'sü-tə-bəl\ adj : FITTING, PROPER, APPROPRIATE **syn** fit, meet, apt, happy — **suit·abil·i·ty** \,sü-tə-'bi-lə-tē\ n — **suit·able·ness** \'sü-tə-bəl-nəs\ n — **suit·ably** \-tə-blē\ adv
suit·case \'süt-,kās\ n : a bag or case carried by hand and designed to hold a traveler's clothing and personal articles
suite \'swēt, for 4 also 'süt\ n **1** : RETINUE **2** : a group of rooms occupied as a unit **3** : a modern instrumental composition in several movements of different character; also : a long orchestral concert arrangement in suite form of material drawn from a longer work **4** : a set of matched furniture for a room
suit·ing \'sü-tiŋ\ n : fabric for suits of clothes
suit·or \'sü-tər\ n **1** : one who sues or petitions **2** : one who seeks to marry a woman
su·ki·ya·ki \skē-'yä-kē, ,sù-kē-'yä-\ n : thin slices of meat, bean curd, and vegetables cooked in soy sauce and sugar

sul·fa drug \\'səl-fə-\\ *n* : any of various synthetic organic bacteria-inhibiting drugs

sul·fate \\'səl-ˌfāt\\ *n* : a salt or ester of sulfuric acid

sul·fide \\'səl-ˌfīd\\ *n* : a compound of sulfur

sul·fur *also* **sul·phur** \\'səl-fər\\ *n* : a nonmetallic chemical element used esp. in the chemical and paper industries and in vulcanizing rubber — see ELEMENT table

sulfur di·ox·ide \\-dī-'äk-sīd\\ *n* : a heavy pungent toxic gas that is used esp. in bleaching, as a preservative, and as a refrigerant, and is a major air pollutant

sul·fu·ric \\ˌsəl-'fyur-ik\\ *adj* : of, relating to, or containing sulfur

sulfuric acid *or* **sul·phu·ric acid** \\ˌsəl-'fyur-ik-\\ *n* : a heavy corrosive oily strong acid

sul·fu·rous *also* **sul·phu·rous** \\'səl-fə-rəs, -fyə-, *also esp for 1* ˌsəl-'fyur-əs\\ *adj* 1 : of, relating to, or containing sulfur 2 : of or relating to brimstone or the fire of hell : INFERNAL 3 : FIERY, INFLAMED ⟨~ sermons⟩

¹**sulk** \\'səlk\\ *vb* : to be or become moodily silent or irritable

²**sulk** *n* : a sulky mood or spell

¹**sulky** \\'səl-kē\\ *adj* : inclined to sulk : MOROSE, MOODY **syn** surly, glum, sullen, gloomy — **sulk·i·ly** \\'səl-kə-lē\\ *adv* — **sulk·i·ness** \\-kē-nəs\\ *n*

²**sulky** *n, pl* **sulkies** : a light 2-wheeled horse-drawn vehicle with a seat for the driver and usu. no body

sul·len \\'sə-lən\\ *adj* 1 : gloomily silent : MOROSE 2 : DISMAL, GLOOMY ⟨a ~ sky⟩ **syn** glum, surly, dour, saturnine — **sul·len·ly** *adv* — **sul·len·ness** *n*

sul·ly \\'sə-lē\\ *vb* **sul·lied; sul·ly·ing** : SOIL, SMIRCH, DEFILE

sul·tan \\'səlt-ᵊn\\ *n* : a sovereign esp. of a Muslim state — **sul·tan·ate** \\-ˌāt\\ *n*

sul·ta·na \\ˌsəl-'ta-nə\\ *n* 1 : a female member of a sultan's family 2 : a pale seedless grape; *also* : a raisin of this grape

sul·try \\'səl-trē\\ *adj* **sul·tri·er; -est** [obs. E *sulter* to swelter, alter. of E *swelter*] : very hot and moist : SWELTERING; *also* : exciting sexual desire

¹**sum** \\'səm\\ *n* [ME *summe*, fr. OF, fr. L *summa*, fr. fem. of *summus* highest] 1 : a quantity of money 2 : the whole amount 3 : GIST 4 : the result obtained by adding numbers 5 : a problem in arithmetic

²**sum** *vb* **summed; sum·ming** : to find the sum of by adding or counting

su·mac *also* **su·mach** \\'sü-ˌmak, 'shü-\\ *n* : any of a genus of trees, shrubs, and woody vines with feathery compound leaves and spikes of red or whitish berries

sumac

sum·ma·rise *Brit var of* SUMMARIZE

sum·ma·rize \\'sə-mə-ˌrīz\\ *vb* **-rized; -riz·ing** : to tell in a summary

¹**sum·ma·ry** \\'sə-mə-rē\\ *adj* 1 : covering the main points briefly : CONCISE 2 : done without delay or formality ⟨~ punishment⟩ **syn** terse, succinct, laconic — **sum·mar·i·ly** \\(ˌ)sə-'mer-ə-lē, 'sə-mə-rə-lē\\ *adv*

²**sum·ma·ry** *n, pl* **-ries** : a concise statement of the main points

sum·ma·tion \\(ˌ)sə-'mā-shən\\ *n* : a summing up; *esp* : a speech in court summing up the arguments in a case

sum·mer \\'sə-mər\\ *n* : the season of the year in a region in which the sun shines most directly : the warmest period of the year — **sum·mery** *adj*

sum·mer·house \\'sə-mər-ˌhaus\\ *n* : a covered structure in a garden or park to provide a shady retreat

summer squash *n* : any of various garden squashes (as zucchini) used as a vegetable while immature

sum·mit \\'sə-mət\\ *n* 1 : the highest point 2 : a conference of highest-level officials

sum·mon \\'sə-mən\\ *vb* [ME *somonen*, fr. OF *somondre*, fr. (assumed) VL *summonere*, alter. of L *summonēre* to remind secretly] 1 : to call to a meeting : CONVOKE 2 : to send for; *also* : to order to appear in court 3 : to evoke esp. by an act of the will ⟨~ up courage⟩ — **sum·mon·er** *n*

sum·mons \\'sə-mənz\\ *n, pl* **sum·mons·es** 1 : an authoritative call to appear at a designated place or to attend to a duty 2 : a warning or citation to appear in court at a specified time to answer charges

sump·tu·ous \\'səmp-shə-wəs, -chə-\\ *adj* : LAVISH, LUXURIOUS

sum up *vb* : SUMMARIZE

¹**sun** \\'sən\\ *n* 1 : the shining celestial body around which the earth and other planets revolve and from which they receive light and heat 2 : a celestial body like the sun 3 : SUNSHINE — **sun·less** *adj* — **sun·ny** *adj*

²**sun** *vb* **sunned; sun·ning** 1 : to expose to or as if to the rays of the sun 2 : to sun oneself

Sun *abbr* Sunday

sun·bath \\'sən-ˌbath, -ˌbȧth\\ *n* : an exposure to sunlight or a sunlamp — **sun·bathe** \\-ˌbāth\\ *vb*

sun·beam \\-ˌbēm\\ *n* : a ray of sunlight

sun·block \\'sən-ˌbläk\\ *n* : a preparation for blocking out more of the sun's rays than a sunscreen

sun·bon·net \\-ˌbä-nət\\ *n* : a bonnet with a wide brim to shield the face and neck from the sun

¹**sun·burn** \\-ˌbərn\\ *vb* **-burned** \\-ˌbərnd\\ *or* **-burnt** \\-ˌbərnt\\; **-burn·ing** : to cause or become affected with sunburn

²**sunburn** *n* : a skin inflammation caused by overexposure to sunlight

sun·dae \\'sən-(ˌ)dā, -dē\\ *n* : ice cream served with topping

Sun·day \\'sən-dē, -ˌdā\\ *n* : the 1st day of the week : the Christian Sabbath

sun·der \\'sən-dər\\ *vb* : to force apart **syn** sever, part, disjoin, disunite

sun·di·al \\-ˌdī-(ə)l\\ *n* : a device for showing the time of day from the shadow cast on a plate by an object with a straight edge

sun·down \\-ˌdaun\\ *n* : SUNSET 2

sun·dries \\'sən-drēz\\ *n pl* : various small articles or items

sun·dry \\'sən-drē\\ *adj* : SEVERAL, DIVERS, VARIOUS

sun·fish \\'sən-ˌfish\\ *n* 1 : a huge marine fish with a deep flattened body 2 : any of numerous often brightly colored American freshwater fishes related to the perches and usu. having the body flattened from side to side

sun·flow·er \\-ˌflau-ər\\ *n* : any of a genus of tall New World plants related to the daisies and often grown for the oil-rich seeds of their yellow-petaled dark-centered flower heads

sung *past and past part of* SING

sun·glasses \\'sən-ˌgla-səz\\ *n pl* : glasses to protect the eyes from the sun

sunk *past and past part of* SINK

sunk·en \\'səŋ-kən\\ *adj* 1 : SUBMERGED 2 : fallen in : HOLLOW ⟨~ cheeks⟩ 3 : lying in a depression ⟨~ garden⟩; *also* : constructed below the general floor level ⟨~ living room⟩

sun·lamp \\'sən-ˌlamp\\ *n* : an electric lamp designed to

emit radiation of wavelengths from ultraviolet to infrared

sun·light \-ˌlīt\ n : SUNSHINE

sun·lit \-ˌlit\ adj : lighted by or as if by the sun

sun·rise \-ˌrīz\ n 1 : the apparent rising of the sun above the horizon 2 : the time at which the sun rises

sun·roof \-ˌrüf, -ˌrůf\ n : a panel in an automobile roof that can be opened

sun·screen \-ˌskrēn\ n : a substance used in suntan preparations to protect the skin

sun·set \-ˌset\ n 1 : the apparent descent of the sun below the horizon 2 : the time at which the sun sets

sun·shade \ˈsən-ˌshād\ n : something (as a parasol or awning) used as a protection from the sun's rays

sun·shine \-ˌshīn\ n : the direct light of the sun — **sunshiny** adj

sun·spot \-ˌspät\ n : any of the dark spots that appear from time to time on the sun's surface

sun·stroke \-ˌströk\ n : heatstroke caused by direct exposure to the sun

sun·tan \-ˌtan\ n : a browning of the skin from exposure to the sun's rays

sun·up \-ˌəp\ n : SUNRISE 2

¹sup \ˈsəp\ vb **supped; sup·ping** : to take or drink in swallows or gulps

²sup n : a mouthful esp. of liquor or broth; also : a small quantity of liquid

³sup vb **supped; sup·ping 1** : to eat the evening meal **2** : to make one's supper ⟨supped on roast beef⟩

⁴sup abbr **1** superior **2** supplement; supplementary **3** supply **4** supra

¹su·per \ˈsü-pər\ n : SUPERINTENDENT

²super adj **1** : very fine : EXCELLENT **2** : EXTREME, EXCESSIVE

super- \ˌsü-pər\ prefix **1** : over and above : higher in quantity, quality, or degree than : more than **2** : in addition : extra **3** : exceeding a norm **4** : in excessive degree or intensity **5** : surpassing all or most others of its kind **6** : situated above, on, or at the top of **7** : next above or higher **8** : more inclusive than **9** : superior in status or position

superabsorbent	superpatriot
superachiever	superpatriotic
superagency	superpatriotism
superblock	superpremium
superbomb	superrich
supercity	supersalesman
superclean	supersecret
superexpensive	supersize
superfine	supersized
superheat	supersmart
superheavy	supersophisticated
superhero	superspy
superhuman	superstar
superhumanly	superstate
superindividual	superstore
superliner	superstratum
superman	superstrength
supermom	superstrong
supernormal	supersubtle

supersystem	superthin
supertanker	superwoman

su·per·abun·dant \ˌsü-pər-ə-ˈbən-dənt\ adj : more than ample — **su·per·abun·dance** \-dəns\ n

su·per·an·nu·ate \ˌsü-pər-ˈan-yə-ˌwāt\ vb **-at·ed; -ating 1** : to make out-of-date **2** : to retire and pension because of age or infirmity — **su·per·an·nu·at·ed** adj

su·perb \sů-ˈpərb\ adj [L superbus excellent, proud, fr. super above] : marked to the highest degree by excellence, brilliance, or competence **syn** resplendent, glorious, gorgeous, sublime — **su·perb·ly** adv

su·per·charg·er \ˈsü-pər-ˌchär-jər\ n : a device for increasing the amount of air supplied to an internal combustion engine

su·per·cil·ious \ˌsü-pər-ˈsi-lē-əs\ adj [L superciliosus, fr. supercilium eyebrow, haughtiness] : haughtily contemptuous **syn** disdainful, overbearing, arrogant, lordly, superior

su·per·com·pu·ter \ˈsü-pər-kəm-ˌpyü-tər\ n : a large very fast mainframe

su·per·con·duc·tiv·i·ty \ˌsü-pər-ˌkän-ˌdək-ˈti-və-tē\ n : a complete disappearance of electrical resistance in a substance esp. at very low temperatures — **super·con·duc·tive** \-kən-ˈdək-tiv\ adj — **su·per·con·duc·tor** \-ˈdək-tər\ n

su·per·con·ti·nent \ˈsü-pər-ˌkänt-ᵊn-ənt\ n : a former large continent from which other continents are held to have broken off and drifted away

su·per·ego \ˌsü-pər-ˈē-gō\ n : the one of the three divisions of the psyche in psychoanalytic theory that functions to reward and punish through a system of moral attitudes, conscience, and a sense of guilt

su·per·fi·cial \ˌsü-pər-ˈfi-shəl\ adj **1** : of or relating to the surface or appearance only **2** : not thorough : SHALLOW — **su·per·fi·ci·al·i·ty** \-ˌfi-shē-ˈa-lə-tē\ n — **su·per·fi·cial·ly** adv

su·per·flu·ous \sü-ˈpər-flə-wəs\ adj : exceeding what is sufficient or necessary : SURPLUS **syn** extra, spare, supernumerary — **su·per·flu·i·ty** \ˌsü-pər-ˈflü-ə-tē\ n

su·per·high·way \ˌsü-pər-ˈhī-ˌwā\ n : a broad highway designed for high-speed traffic

su·per·im·pose \-im-ˈpōz\ vb : to lay (one thing) over or above something else

su·per·in·tend \ˌsü-pə-rin-ˈtend\ vb : to have or exercise the charge and oversight of : DIRECT — **su·perin·ten·dence** \-ˈten-dəns\ n — **su·per·in·ten·den·cy** \-dən-sē\ n — **su·per·in·ten·dent** \-dənt\ n

> **¹su·pe·ri·or** \sů-ˈpir-ē-ər\ adj **1** : situated higher up, over, or near the top; also : higher in rank or numbers **2** : of greater value or importance **3** : courageously indifferent (as to pain or misfortune) **4** : better than most others of its kind **5** : ARROGANT, HAUGHTY — **su·pe·ri·or·i·ty** \-ˌpir-ē-ˈȯr-ə-tē\ n

²superior n **1** : one who is above another in rank, office, or station; esp : the head of a religious house or order **2** : one higher in quality or merit

¹**su·per·la·tive** \su̇-'pər-lə-tiv\ *adj* **1** : of, relating to, or constituting the degree of grammatical comparison that denotes an extreme or unsurpassed level or extent **2** : surpassing others : SUPREME **syn** peerless, incomparable, superb — **su·per·la·tive·ly** *adv*

²**superlative** *n* **1** : the superlative degree or a superlative form in a language **2** : the utmost degree : ACME

su·per·mar·ket \'sü-pər-ˌmär-kət\ *n* : a self-service retail market selling foods and household merchandise

su·per·nal \su̇-'pər-nəl\ *adj* **1** : being or coming from on high **2** : of heavenly or spiritual character

su·per·nat·u·ral \ˌsü-pər-'na-chə-rəl\ *adj* : of or relating to phenomena beyond or outside of nature; *esp* : relating to or attributed to a divinity, ghost, or devil — **su·per·nat·u·ral·ly** *adv*

su·per·no·va \ˌsü-pər-'nō-və\ *n* : the explosion of a very large star

¹**su·per·nu·mer·ary** \-'nü-mə-ˌrer-ē, -'nyü-\ *adj* : exceeding the usual or required number : EXTRA **syn** surplus, superfluous, spare

²**supernumerary** *n, pl* **-ar·ies** : an extra person or thing; *esp* : an actor hired for a nonspeaking part

su·per·pose \ˌsü-pər-'pōz\ *vb* **-posed; -pos·ing** : SUPERIMPOSE — **su·per·po·si·tion** \-pə-'zi-shən\ *n*

su·per·pow·er \'sü-pər-ˌpau̇-ər\ *n* **1** : excessive or superior power **2** : one of a few politically and militarily dominant nations

su·per·sat·u·rat·ed \-'sa-chə-ˌrā-təd\ *adj* : containing an amount of a substance greater than that required for saturation

su·per·scribe \'sü-pər-ˌskrīb, ˌsü-pər-'skrīb\ *vb* **-scribed; -scrib·ing** : to write on the top or outside : ADDRESS — **su·per·scrip·tion** \ˌsü-pər-'skrip-shən\ *n*

su·per·script \'sü-pər-ˌskript\ *n* : a symbol (as a numeral or letter) written immediately above or above and to one side of another character

su·per·sede \ˌsü-pər-'sēd\ *vb* **-sed·ed; -sed·ing** [MF *superseder* to refrain from, fr. L *supersedēre* to be superior to, refrain from, fr. *super-* above + *sedēre* to sit] : to take the place of : REPLACE

su·per·son·ic \-'sä-nik\ *adj* **1** : ULTRASONIC **2** : being or relating to speeds from one to five times the speed of sound; *also* : capable of moving at such a speed ⟨a ∼ airplane⟩

su·per·sti·tion \ˌsü-pər-'sti-shən\ *n* **1** : beliefs or practices resulting from ignorance, fear of the unknown, or trust in magic or chance **2** : an unreasoning fear of nature, the unknown, or God resulting from superstition — **su·per·sti·tious** \-shəs\ *adj*

su·per·struc·ture \'sü-pər-ˌstrək-chər\ *n* : something built on a base or as a vertical extension

su·per·vene \ˌsü-pər-'vēn\ *vb* **-vened; -ven·ing** : to occur as something additional or unexpected

su·per·vise \'sü-pər-ˌvīz\ *vb* **-vised; -vis·ing** : OVERSEE, SUPERINTEND — **su·per·vi·sion** \ˌsü-pər-'vi-zhən\ *n* — **su·per·vi·sor** \'sü-pər-ˌvī-zər\ *n* — **su·per·vi·so·ry** \ˌsü-pər-'vī-zə-rē\ *adj*

su·pine \su̇-'pīn\ *adj* **1** : lying on the back or with the face upward **2** : LETHARGIC, SLUGGISH; *also* : ABJECT **syn** inactive, inert, passive, idle

supp *or* **suppl** *abbr* supplement; supplementary

sup·per \'sə-pər\ *n* : the evening meal esp. when dinner is taken at midday — **sup·per·time** \-ˌtīm\ *n*

sup·plant \sə-'plant\ *vb* **1** : to take the place of (another) esp. by force or trickery **2** : REPLACE

sup·ple \'sə-pəl\ *adj* **sup·pler; sup·plest 1** : COMPLIANT, ADAPTABLE **2** : capable of bending without breaking or creasing : LIMBER **syn** resilient, elastic, flexible

¹**sup·ple·ment** \'sə-plə-mənt\ *n* **1** : something that supplies a want or makes an addition **2** : a continuation (as of a book) containing corrections or additional material — **sup·ple·men·tal** \ˌsə-plə-'ment-ᵊl\ *adj* — **sup·ple·men·ta·ry** \-'men-tə-rē\ *adj*

²**sup·ple·ment** \'sə-plə-ˌment\ *vb* : to fill up the deficiencies of : add to

sup·pli·ant \'sə-plē-ənt\ *n* : one who supplicates : PETITIONER, PLEADER

sup·pli·cant \'sə-pli-kənt\ *n* : SUPPLIANT

sup·pli·cate \'sə-plə-ˌkāt\ *vb* **-cat·ed; -cat·ing 1** : to make a humble entreaty; *esp* : to pray to God **2** : to ask earnestly and humbly : BESEECH **syn** implore, beg, entreat, plead — **sup·pli·ca·tion** \ˌsə-plə-'kā-shən\ *n*

¹**sup·ply** \sə-'plī\ *vb* **sup·plied; sup·ply·ing** [ME *supplien*, fr. MF *soupleier*, fr. L *supplēre* to fill up, supplement, supply, fr. *sub-* under, up to + *plēre* to fill] **1** : to add as a supplement **2** : to satisfy the needs of **3** : FURNISH, PROVIDE — **sup·pli·er** *n*

²**supply** *n, pl* **supplies 1** : the quantity or amount (as of a commodity) needed or available; *also* : PROVISIONS, STORES — usu. used in pl. **2** : the act or process of filling a want or need : PROVISION **3** : the quantities of goods or services offered for sale at a particular time or at one price

sup·ply–side \sə-'plī-ˌsīd\ *adj* : of, relating to, or being an economic theory that recommends the reduction of tax rates to expand economic activity

¹**sup·port** \sə-'pōrt\ *vb* **1** : BEAR, TOLERATE **2** : to take sides with : BACK, ASSIST **3** : to provide with food, clothing, and shelter **4** : to hold up or serve as a foundation for **syn** uphold, advocate, champion — **sup·port·able** *adj* — **sup·port·er** *n*

²**support** *n* **1** : the act of supporting : the state of being supported **2** : one that supports : PROP, BASE

support group *n* : a group of people with common experiences and concerns who provide emotional and moral support for one another

sup·pose \sə-'pōz\ *vb* **sup·posed; sup·pos·ing 1** : to assume to be true (as for the sake of argument) **2** : EXPECT ⟨I am *supposed* to go⟩ **3** : to think probable — **sup·pos·al** *n*

sup·posed \sə-'pōzd, -'pō-zəd\ *adj* : BELIEVED; *also* : mistakenly believed — **sup·pos·ed·ly** \-'pō-zəd-lē, -'pōzd-lē\ *adv*

sup·pos·ing *conj* : if by way of hypothesis : on the assumption that

sup·po·si·tion \ˌsə-pə-'zi-shən\ *n* **1** : something that is supposed : HYPOTHESIS **2** : the act of supposing

sup·pos·i·to·ry \sə-'pä-zə-ˌtȯr-ē\ *n, pl* **-ries** [ML *suppositorium*, fr. LL, neut. of *suppositorius* placed beneath] : a small easily melted mass of usu. medicated material for insertion (as into the rectum)

sup·press \sə-'pres\ *vb* **1** : to put down by authority or force : SUBDUE ⟨∼ a revolt⟩ **2** : to keep from being known; *also* : to stop the publication or circulation of **3** : to hold back : REPRESS ⟨∼ anger⟩ ⟨∼ a cough⟩ — **sup·press·ible** \-'pre-sə-bəl\ *adj* — **sup·pres·sion** \-'pre-shən\ *n*

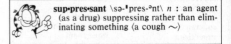

sup·pres·sant \sə-'pres-ᵊnt\ *n* : an agent (as a drug) suppressing rather than eliminating something ⟨a cough ∼⟩

sup·pu·rate \'sə-pyə-ˌrāt\ *vb* **-rat·ed; -rat·ing** : to form or give off pus — **sup·pu·ra·tion** \ˌsə-pyə-'rā-shən\ *n*

su·pra \'sü-prə, -ˌprä\ *adv* : earlier in this writing : ABOVE

su·pra·na·tion·al \ˌsü-prə-'na-shə-nəl, -ˌprä-\ *adj* : going beyond national boundaries, authority, or interests ⟨∼ organizations⟩

su·prem·a·cist \su̇-'pre-mə-sist\ *n* : an advocate of group supremacy

su·prem·a·cy \su̇-'pre-mə-sē\ *n, pl* **-cies** : supreme rank, power, or authority

I'M HUNGRY. I NEED AN APPETITE SUPPRESSANT

JON'S LEFTOVERS ALWAYS DO THE TRICK

© 1989 PAWS, INC.

9-30   JPM DAVIS

su·preme \su̇-'prēm\ adj [L supremus, superl. of supe-rus upper, fr. super over, above] 1 : highest in rank or authority 2 : highest in degree or quality ⟨~ among poets⟩ 3 : ULTIMATE ⟨the ~ sacrifice⟩ syn superlative, surpassing, peerless, incomparable — **su·preme·ly** adv — **su·preme·ness** n

Supreme Being n : GOD 1

supt abbr superintendent

sur·cease \'sər-ˌsēs\ n : CESSATION, RESPITE

¹**sur·charge** \'sər-ˌchärj\ vb 1 : to fill to excess : OVER-LOAD 2 : to apply a surcharge to (postage stamps)

²**surcharge** n 1 : an extra fee or cost 2 : an excessive load or burden 3 : something officially printed on a postage stamp esp. to change its value

sur·cin·gle \'sər-ˌsiŋ-gəl\ n : a band put around a horse's body to make something (as a saddle) fast

¹**sure** \'shu̇r\ adj **sur·er; sur·est** [ME, fr. MF sur, fr. L securus secure] 1 : firmly established 2 : TRUSTWOR-THY, RELIABLE 3 : CONFIDENT 4 : not to be disputed : UNDOUBTED 5 : bound to happen 6 : careful to re-member or attend to something ⟨be ~ to lock the door⟩ syn certain, cocksure, positive — **sure·ness** n

²**sure** adv : SURELY

sure·fire \'shu̇r-ˈfīr\ adj : certain to get results : DE-PENDABLE

sure·ly \'shu̇r-lē\ adv 1 : in a sure manner 2 : without doubt 3 : INDEED, REALLY

sure·ty \'shu̇r-ə-tē\ n, pl **-ties** 1 : SURENESS, CERTAINTY 2 : something that makes sure : GUARANTEE 3 : one who is a guarantor for another person

¹**surf** \'sərf\ n : waves that break upon the shore; also : the sound or foam of breaking waves

²**surf** vb : to ride the surf (as on a surfboard) — **surf-er** n — **surf·ing** n

¹**sur·face** \'sər-fəs\ n 1 : the outside of an object or body 2 : outward aspect or appearance — **surface** adj

²**surface** vb **sur·faced; sur·fac·ing** 1 : to give a surface to : make smooth 2 : to rise to the surface

surf·board \'sərf-ˌbȯrd\ n : a buoyant board used in surfing

¹**sur·feit** \'sər-fət\ n 1 : EXCESS, SUPERABUNDANCE 2 : excessive indulgence (as in food or drink) 3 : disgust caused by excess

²**surfeit** vb : to feed, supply, or indulge to the point of surfeit : CLOY

surg abbr surgeon; surgery; surgical

¹**surge** \'sərj\ vb **surged; surg·ing** 1 : to rise and fall ac-tively : TOSS 2 : to move in waves 3 : to rise suddenly to an excessive or abnormal value

²**surge** n 1 : a sweeping onward like a wave of the sea ⟨a ~ of emotion⟩ 2 : a large billow 3 : a transient sud-den increase of current or voltage in an electrical cir-cuit

sur·geon \'sər-jən\ n : a physician who specializes in surgery

sur·gery \'sər-jə-rē\ n, pl **-ger·ies** [ME surgerie, fr. OF cirurgie, surgerie, fr. L chirurgia, fr. Gk cheirourgia, fr. cheirourgos surgeon, fr. cheirourgos doing by hand, fr. cheir hand + ergon work] 1 : a branch of

medicine concerned with the correction of physical defects, the repair of injuries, and the treatment of disease esp. by operations 2 : a room or area where surgery is performed 3 : the work done by a surgeon

sur·gi·cal \'sər-ji-kəl\ adj : of, relating to, or associated with surgeons or surgery — **sur·gi·cal·ly** \-k(ə-)lē\ adv

sur·ly \'sər-lē\ adj **sur·li·er; -est** [alter. of ME sirly lordly, imperious, fr. sir] : having a rude unfriendly disposition syn morose, glum, sullen, sulky, gloomy — **sur·li·ness** \-lē-nəs\ n

sur·mise \sər-'mīz\ vb **sur·mised; sur·mis·ing** : GUESS syn conjecture, presume, suppose — **surmise** n

sur·mount \sər-'mau̇nt\ vb 1 : to prevail over : OVER-COME 2 : to get to or lie at the top of

sur·name \'sər-ˌnām\ n 1 : NICKNAME 2 : the name borne in common by members of a family

sur·pass \sər-'pas\ vb 1 : to be superior to in quality, degree, or performance : EXCEL 2 : to go beyond the reach or powers of syn transcend, outdo, outstrip, exceed — **sur·pass·ing·ly** adv

sur·plice \'sər-pləs\ n : a loose white outer garment worn at church services

sur·plus \'sər-(ˌ)pləs\ n 1 : quantity left over : EXCESS 2 : the excess of assets over liabilities syn superfluity, overabundance, surfeit

¹**sur·prise** \sər-'prīz\ n 1 : an attack made without warning 2 : a taking unawares 3 : something that sur-prises 4 : AMAZEMENT, ASTONISHMENT

²**surprise** also **sur·prize** vb **sur·prised; sur·pris·ing** 1 : to come upon and attack unexpectedly 2 : to take unawares 3 : AMAZE 4 : to cause astonishment or sur-prise syn astonish, astound, dumbfound — **sur·pris-ing** adj

sur·pris·ing·ly \-'prī-ziŋ-lē\ adv 1 : in a surprising man-ner or degree 2 : it is surprising that

sur·re·al \sə-'rē-əl, -'rēl\ adj 1 : having the intense ir-rational reality of a dream 2 : of or relating to surre-alism

sur·re·al·ism \sə-'rē-ə-ˌli-zəm\ n : art, literature, or theater characterized by fantastic or incongruous im-agery or effects produced by unnatural juxtapositions and combinations — **sur·re·al·ist** \-list\ n or adj — **sur·re·al·is·tic** \sə-ˌrē-ə-'lis-tik\ adj — **sur·re·al·is-ti·cal·ly** \-ti-k(ə-)lē\ adv

¹**sur·ren·der** \sə-'ren-dər\ vb **-dered; -der·ing** 1 : to yield to the power of another : give up under compul-sion 2 : RELINQUISH

²**surrender** n : the act of giving up or yielding oneself or the possession of something to another

sur·rep·ti·tious \ˌsər-əp-'ti-shəs\ adj : done, made, or acquired by stealth : CLANDESTINE syn underhand, covert, furtive — **sur·rep·ti·tious·ly** adv

sur·rey \'sər-ē\ n, pl **surreys** : a 2-seated horse-drawn carriage

☞ For illustration, see next page.

sur·ro·ga·cy \'sər-ə-gə-sē\ n : SURROGATE MOTHER-HOOD

sur·ro·gate \'sər-ə-ˌgāt, -gət\ n 1 : DEPUTY, SUBSTI-

surrey

TUTE **2** : a law officer in some states with authority in the probate of wills, the settlement of estates, and the appointment of guardians **3** : SURROGATE MOTHER
surrogate mother *n* : a woman who becomes pregnant (as by surgical implantation of a fertilized egg) in order to carry the fetus for another woman — **surrogate motherhood** *n*
sur·round \sə-'raund\ *vb* **1** : to enclose on all sides : ENCIRCLE **2** : to enclose so as to cut off retreat or escape
sur·round·ings \sə-'raun-diŋz\ *n pl* : conditions by which one is surrounded
sur·tax \'sər-₁taks\ *n* : an additional tax over and above a normal tax
sur·tout \(₁)sər-'tü\ *n* [F, fr. *sur* over (fr. L *super*) + *tout* all, fr. L *totus* whole] : a man's long close=fitting overcoat
surv *abbr* survey; surveying; surveyor
sur·veil·lance \sər-'vā-ləns\ *n* [F] : close watch; *also* : SUPERVISION
¹**sur·vey** \sər-'vā\ *vb* **sur·veyed; sur·vey·ing 1** : to look over and examine closely **2** : to find and represent the contours, measurements, and position of a part of the earth's surface (as a tract of land) **3** : to view or study something as a whole **syn** scrutinize, examine, inspect, study — **sur·vey·or** \-ər\ *n*
²**sur·vey** \'sər-₁vā\ *n, pl* **surveys** : the act or an instance of surveying; *also* : something that is surveyed
sur·vive \sər-'vīv\ *vb* **sur·vived; sur·viv·ing 1** : to remain alive or existent **2** : OUTLIVE, OUTLAST — **sur·viv·al** *n* — **sur·vi·vor** \-'vī-vər\ *n*
sus·cep·ti·ble \sə-'sep-tə-bəl\ *adj* **1** : of such a nature as to permit (words ∼ of being misunderstood) **2** : having little resistance to a stimulus or agency (∼ to colds) **3** : IMPRESSIONABLE, RESPONSIVE **syn** sensitive, subject, exposed, prone, liable, open — **sus·cep·ti·bil·i·ty** \-₁sep-tə-'bi-lə-tē\ *n*

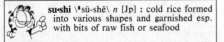

su·shi \'sü-shē\ *n* [Jp] : cold rice formed into various shapes and garnished esp. with bits of raw fish or seafood

¹**sus·pect** \'səs-₁pekt, sə-'spekt\ *adj* : regarded with suspicion; *also* : QUESTIONABLE

²**sus·pect** \'səs-₁pekt\ *n* : one who is suspected (as of a crime)
³**sus·pect** \sə-'spekt\ *vb* **1** : to have doubts of : MISTRUST **2** : to imagine to be guilty without proof **3** : SURMISE
sus·pend \sə-'spend\ *vb* **1** : to bar temporarily from a privilege, office, or function **2** : to stop temporarily : make inactive for a time **3** : to withhold (judgment) for a time **4** : HANG; *esp* : to hang so as to be free except at one point **5** : to keep from falling or sinking by some invisible support
sus·pend·er \sə-'spen-dər\ *n* : one of two supporting straps which pass over the shoulders and to which the trousers are fastened
sus·pense \sə-'spens\ *n* **1** : SUSPENSION **2** : mental uncertainty : ANXIETY **3** : excitement as to an outcome — **sus·pense·ful** *adj*
sus·pen·sion \sə-'spen-chən\ *n* **1** : the act of suspending : the state or period of being suspended **2** : the state of a substance when its particles are mixed with but undissolved in a fluid or solid; *also* : a substance in this state **3** : something suspended **4** : a device by which something is suspended
sus·pen·so·ry \sə-'spen-sə-rē\ *adj* **1** : SUSPENDED; *also* : fitted or serving to suspend something **2** : temporarily leaving undetermined
sus·pi·cion \sə-'spi-shən\ *n* **1** : the act or an instance of suspecting something wrong without proof **2** : TRACE, SOUPÇON **syn** mistrust, uncertainty, doubt, skepticism
sus·pi·cious \sə-'spi-shəs\ *adj* **1** : open to or arousing suspicion **2** : inclined to suspect **3** : showing suspicion — **sus·pi·cious·ly** *adv*
sus·tain \sə-'stān\ *vb* **1** : to provide with nourishment **2** : to keep going : PROLONG (∼*ed* effort) **3** : to hold up : PROP **4** : to hold up under : ENDURE **5** : SUFFER (∼ a broken arm) **6** : to support as true, legal, or valid **7** : PROVE, CORROBORATE — **sus·tain·able** \səs-'tā-nə-bəl\ *adj*
sus·te·nance \'səs-tə-nəns\ *n* **1** : FOOD, NOURISHMENT **2** : a supplying with the necessities of life **3** : something that sustains or supports
su·ture \'sü-chər\ *n* **1** : material or a stitch for sewing a wound together **2** : a seam or line along which two things or parts are joined by or as if by sewing
su·zer·ain \'sü-zə-rən, -₁rān\ *n* [F] **1** : a feudal lord **2** : a nation that has political control over the foreign relations of another nation — **su·zer·ain·ty** \-tē\ *n*
svc *or* **svce** *abbr* service
svelte \'sfelt\ *adj* [F, fr. It *svelto*, fr. pp. of *svellere* to pluck out, modif. of L *evellere*, fr. *e-* out + *vellere* to pluck] : SLENDER, LITHE
svgs *abbr* savings
SW *abbr* **1** shortwave **2** southwest
¹**swab** \'swäb\ *n* **1** : MOP **2** : a wad of absorbent material esp. for applying medicine or for cleaning; *also* : a sample taken with a swab **3** : SAILOR
²**swab** *vb* **swabbed; swab·bing** : to use a swab on : MOP
swad·dle \'swäd-əl\ *vb* **swad·dled; swad·dling 1** : to

bind (an infant) in bands of cloth **2** : to wrap up
: SWATHE
swaddling clothes *n pl* : bands of cloth wrapped
around an infant
swag \'swag\ *n* : stolen goods : LOOT
swag·ger \'swa-gər\ *vb* **1** : to walk with a conceited
swing or strut **2** : BOAST, BRAG — **swagger** *n*
Swa·hi·li \swä-'hē-lē\ *n* : a language that is a trade and
governmental language over much of East Africa and
the Congo region
swain \'swān\ *n* [ME *swein* boy, servant, fr. ON
sveinn] **1** : RUSTIC; *esp* : SHEPHERD **2** : ADMIRER, SUIT-
OR
SWAK *abbr* sealed with a kiss
¹**swal·low** \'swä-lō\ *n* : any of numerous small long⸗
winged migratory birds that often have a deeply
forked tail

²**swallow** *vb* **1** : to take into the stomach
through the throat **2** : to envelop or take
in as if by swallowing **3** : to accept or believe without question, protest, or anger

³**swallow** *n* **1** : an act of swallowing **2** : an amount that
can be swallowed at one time
swal·low·tail \'swä-lō-₁tāl\ *n* **1** : a deeply forked and tapering tail like that of a swallow **2** : TAILCOAT **3** : any
of various large butterflies with the border of each
hind wing usu. drawn out into a process resembling
a tail — **swal·low–tailed** \-₁tāld\ *adj*
swam *past of* SWIM
swa·mi \'swä-mē\ *n* [Hindi *svāmī*, fr. Skt *svāmin* owner, lord] : a Hindu ascetic or religious teacher
¹**swamp** \'swämp\ *n* : a spongy wetland — **swamp** *adj*
— **swampy** *adj*
²**swamp** *vb* **1** : to fill or become filled with or as if with
water **2** : OVERWHELM **3**
swamp·land \-₁land\ *n* : SWAMP
swan \'swän\ *n, pl* **swans** *also* **swan** : any of various
heavy-bodied long-necked mostly pure white swim-
ming birds related to the geese
¹**swank** \'swaŋk\ *or* **swanky** \'swaŋ-kē\ *adj* **swank-**
er *or* **swank·i·er; -est** : showily smart and dashing;
also : fashionably elegant
²**swank** *n* **1** : PRETENTIOUSNESS **2** : ELEGANCE
swans·down \'swänz-₁daùn\ *n* **1** : the very soft down
of a swan used esp. for trimming **2** : a soft thick cotton flannel
swan song *n* : a farewell appearance, act, or pro-
nouncement
swap \'swäp\ *vb* **swapped; swap·ping** : TRADE, EX-
CHANGE — **swap** *n*
sward \'swòrd\ *n* : the grassy surface of land
¹**swarm** \'swòrm\ *n* **1** : a great number of honeybees
leaving together from a hive with a queen to start a
new colony; *also* : a hive of bees **2** : a large crowd
²**swarm** *vb* **1** : to form in a swarm and depart from a
hive **2** : to throng together : gather in great numbers
swart \'swòrt\ *adj* : SWARTHY

swar·thy \'swòr-thē, -thē\ *adj* **swar·thi·er; -est** : dark
in color or complexion : dark-skinned
swash \'swäsh\ *vb* : to move about with a splashing
sound — **swash** *n*
swash·buck·ler \-₁bə-klər\ *n* : a swaggering or daring
soldier or adventurer — **swash·buck·ling** *adj*
swas·ti·ka \'swäs-ti-kə\ *n* [Skt *svastika*, fr. *svasti* well⸗
being, fr. *su-* well + *as-* to be] : a symbol or ornament
in the form of a cross with the ends of the arms bent
at right angles
swat \'swät\ *vb* **swat·ted; swat·ting** : to hit sharply ⟨~
a fly⟩ ⟨~ a ball⟩ — **swat** *n* — **swat·ter** *n*
SWAT *abbr* Special Weapons and Tactics
swatch \'swäch\ *n* : a sample piece (as of fabric) or a
collection of samples
swath \'swäth, 'swòth\ *or* **swathe** \'swäth, 'swòth,
'swäth\ *n* [ME, fr. OE *swæth* footstep, trace] **1** : a row
of cut grass or grain **2** : the sweep of a scythe or mowing machine or the path cut in mowing
swathe \'swäth, 'swòth, 'swäth\ *vb* **swathed; swath·**
ing : to bind or wrap with or as if with a bandage
¹**sway** \'swā\ *n* **1** : a gentle swinging from side to side
2 : controlling influence or power : DOMINION
²**sway** *vb* **1** : to swing gently from side to side **2** : RULE,
GOVERN **3** : to cause to swing from side to side **4**
: BEND, SWERVE; *also* : INFLUENCE **syn** oscillate, fluctuate, vibrate, waver
sway·backed \'swā-₁bakt\ *also* **sway·back** \-₁bak\ *adj*
: having an abnormally sagging back ⟨a ~ mare⟩ —
swayback *n*
swear \'swar\ *vb* **swore** \'swōr\; **sworn** \'swōrn\;
swear·ing 1 : to make a solemn statement or promise
under oath **2** : to assert or promise emphatically or
earnestly **3** : to administer an oath to **4** : to bind by
or as if by an oath **5** : to use profane or obscene language — **swear·er** *n*
swear in *vb* : to induct into office by administration of
an oath
sweat \'swet\ *vb* **sweat** *or* **sweat·ed; sweat·ing 1** : to
excrete salty moisture from glands of the skin : PER-
SPIRE **2** : to form drops of moisture on the surface **3**
: to work so that one sweats : TOIL **4** : to cause to
sweat **5** : to draw out or get rid of by or as if by sweating **6** : to make a person overwork — **sweat** *n* —
sweaty *adj*
sweat·er \'swe-tər\ *n* **1** : one that sweats **2** : a knitted
or crocheted jacket or pullover
sweat·shirt \'swet-₁shərt\ *n* : a loose collarless pullover usu. of heavy cotton jersey
sweat·shop \'swet-₁shäp\ *n* : a shop or factory in which
workers are employed for long hours at low wages
and under unhealthy conditions
Swed *abbr* Sweden
swede \'swēd\ *n* **1** *cap* : a native or inhabitant of Sweden **2** *chiefly Brit* : RUTABAGA
Swed·ish \'swē-dish\ *n* **1** : the language of Sweden **2**
Swedish *pl* : the people of Sweden — **Swedish** *adj*

¹**sweep** \'swēp\ *vb* **swept** \'swept\; **sweep-ing** **1** : to remove or clean by or as if by brushing **2** : to destroy completely; *also* : to remove or take with a single swift movement **3** : to remove from sight or consideration **4** : to move over with speed and force ⟨the tide *swept* over the shore⟩ **5** : to win an overwhelming victory in; *also* : to win all the games or contests of **6** : to move or extend in a wide curve — **sweep•er** *n*

²**sweep** *n* **1** : something (as a long oar) that operates with a sweeping motion **2** : a clearing off or away **3** : a winning of all the contests or prizes in a competition **4** : a sweeping movement **5** : CURVE, BEND **6** : RANGE, SCOPE

sweep•ing *adj* : EXTENSIVE ⟨∼ reforms⟩; *also* : indiscriminately inclusive ⟨∼ generalities⟩

sweep•ings \'swē-piŋz\ *n pl* : things collected by sweeping

sweep–sec•ond hand \'swēp-,se-kənd-\ *n* : a hand marking seconds on a timepiece

sweep•stakes \'swēp-,stāks\ *also* **sweep•stake** \-,stāk\ *n, pl* **sweepstakes** **1** : a race or contest in which the entire prize may go to the winner **2** : any of various lotteries

¹**sweet** \'swēt\ *adj* **1** : being or causing the one of the four basic taste sensations that is caused esp. by table sugar and is identified esp. by the taste buds at the front of the tongue; *also* : pleasing to the taste **2** : AGREEABLE **3** : pleasing to a sense other than taste ⟨a ∼ smell⟩ ⟨∼ music⟩ **4** : not stale or spoiled : WHOLESOME ⟨∼ milk⟩ **5** : not salted ⟨∼ butter⟩ — **sweet•ish** *adj* — **sweet•ly** *adv* — **sweet•ness** *n*

²**sweet** *n* **1** : something sweet : CANDY **2** : DARLING

sweet•bread \'swēt-,bred\ *n* : the pancreas or thymus of an animal (as a calf or lamb) used for food

sweet•bri•er *also* **sweet•bri•ar** \-,brī-ər\ *n* : a thorny Old World rose with fragrant white to deep pink flowers

sweet clover *n* : any of a genus of erect legumes widely grown for soil improvement or hay

sweet corn *n* : an Indian corn with kernels rich in sugar and cooked as a vegetable while immature

sweet•en \'swēt-ᵊn\ *vb* **sweet•ened; sweet•en•ing** : to make sweet — **sweet•en•er** *n* — **sweet•en•ing** *n*

sweet•heart \'swēt-,härt\ *n* : one who is loved

sweet•meat \-,mēt\ *n* : CANDY

sweet pea *n* : a garden plant of the legume family with climbing stems and fragrant flowers of many colors; *also* : its flower

sweet pepper *n* : a large mild thick-walled fruit of a pepper; *also* : a plant related to the potato that bears sweet peppers

sweet potato *n* : a tropical vine related to the morning glory; *also* : its sweet yellow edible root

sweet–talk \'swēt-,tȯk\ *vb* : FLATTER, COAX — **sweet talk** *n*

sweet tooth *n* : a craving or fondness for sweet food

sweet wil•liam \,swēt-'wil-yəm\ *n, often cap W* : a widely cultivated Old World pink with small white to deep red or purple flowers often showily spotted, banded, or mottled

¹**swell** \'swel\ *vb* **swelled; swelled** *or* **swol•len** \'swō-lən\; **swell•ing** **1** : to grow big or make bigger **2** : to expand or distend abnormally or excessively ⟨a *swollen* joint⟩; *also* : BULGE **3** : to fill or be filled with emotion (as pride) *syn* expand, amplify, distend, inflate, dilate — **swell•ing** *n*

²**swell** *n* **1** : a long crestless wave or series of waves in the open sea **2** : the condition of being protuberant **3** : a person dressed in the height of fashion; *also* : a person of high social position

³**swell** *adj* **1** : STYLISH; *also* : socially prominent **2** : EXCELLENT

swelled head *n* : an exaggerated opinion of oneself : SELF-CONCEIT

swell•head \'swel-,hed\ *n* : one who has a swelled head — **swell•head•ed** \-,he-dəd\ *adj*

swel•ter \'swel-tər\ *vb* [ME *sweltren,* fr. *swelten* to die, be overcome by heat, fr. OE *sweltan* to die] **1** : to be faint or oppressed with the heat **2** : to become exceedingly hot

swept *past and past part of* SWEEP

swerve \'swərv\ *vb* **swerved; swerv•ing** : to move abruptly aside from a straight line or course — **swerve** *n*

¹**swift** \'swift\ *adj* **1** : moving or capable of moving with great speed **2** : occurring suddenly **3** : READY, ALERT — **swift•ly** *adv* — **swift•ness** *n*

²**swift** *n* : any of numerous small insect-eating birds with long narrow wings

swig \'swig\ *vb* **swigged; swig•ging** : to drink in long drafts — **swig** *n*

¹**swill** \'swil\ *vb* **1** : to swallow greedily : GUZZLE **2** : to feed (as hogs) on swill

²**swill** *n* **1** : food for animals composed of edible refuse mixed with liquid **2** : GARBAGE

¹**swim** \'swim\ *vb* **swam** \'swam\; **swum** \'swəm\; **swim•ming** **1** : to propel oneself along in water by natural means (as by hands and legs, by tail, or by fins) **2** : to glide smoothly along **3** : FLOAT **4** : to be covered with or as if with a liquid **5** : to be dizzy ⟨his head *swam*⟩ **6** : to cross or go over by swimming — **swim•mer** *n*

²**swim** *n* **1** : an act of swimming **2** : the main current of activity ⟨in the ∼⟩

swim•ming *n* : the action, art, or sport of swimming and diving

swimming pool *n* : a tank (as of concrete or plastic) designed for swimming

swim•suit \'swim-,süt\ *n* : a suit for swimming or bathing

swin•dle \'swin-dᵊl\ *vb* **swin•dled; swin•dling** [fr. *swindler,* fr. G *Schwindler* giddy person, fr. *schwindeln* to be dizzy] : CHEAT, DEFRAUD — **swindle** *n* — **swin•dler** *n*

swine \'swīn\ *n, pl* **swine** **1** : any of a family of stout short-legged hoofed mammals with bristly skin and a long flexible snout; *esp* : one widely raised as a meat animal **2** : a contemptible person — **swin·ish** *adj*

¹swing \'swiŋ\ *vb* **swung** \'swəŋ\; **swing·ing 1** : to move or cause to move rapidly in an arc **2** : to sway or cause to sway back and forth **3** : to hang so as to move freely back and forth or in a curve **4** : to be executed by hanging **5** : to move or turn on a hinge or pivot **6** : to manage or handle successfully **7** : to march or walk with free swaying movements **8** : to have a steady pulsing rhythm; *also* : to play swing music **9** : to be lively and up-to-date; *also* : to engage freely in sex **syn** wield, manipulate, ply, maneuver — **swing·er** *n* — **swing·ing** *adj*

²swing *n* **1** : the act of swinging **2** : a swinging blow, movement, or rhythm **3** : the distance through which something swings : FLUCTUATION **4** : progression of an activity or process ⟨in full ∿⟩ **5** : a seat suspended by a rope or chain for swinging back and forth for pleasure **6** : jazz music played esp. by a large band and marked by a steady lively rhythm, simple harmony, and a basic melody often submerged in improvisation

³swing *adj* **1** : of or relating to swing music **2** : that may swing often decisively either way (as on an issue) ⟨∿ voters⟩

¹swipe \'swīp\ *n* : a strong sweeping blow

²swipe *vb* **swiped; swip·ing 1** : to strike or wipe with a sweeping motion **2** : PILFER, SNATCH

swirl \'swərl\ *vb* : to move or cause to move with a whirling motion — **swirl** *n* — **swirly** \'swər-lē\ *adj*

swish \'swish\ *n* **1** : a prolonged hissing sound **2** : a light sweeping or brushing sound — **swish** *vb*

Swiss \'swis\ *n* **1** *pl* **Swiss** : a native or inhabitant of Switzerland **2** : a hard cheese with large holes

Swiss chard *n* : a beet having large leaves and succulent stalks often cooked as a vegetable

¹switch \'swich\ *n* **1** : a slender flexible whip, rod, or twig **2** : a blow with a switch **3** : a shift from one thing to another; *also* : change from the usual **4** : a device for adjusting the rails of a track so that a locomotive or train may be turned from one track to another; *also* : a railroad siding **5** : a device for making, breaking, or changing the connections in an electrical circuit **6** : a heavy strand of hair often used in addition to a person's own hair for some coiffures

²switch *vb* **1** : to punish or urge on with a switch **2** : WHISK ⟨a cow ∿*ing* her tail⟩ **3** : to shift or turn by operating a switch **4** : CHANGE, EXCHANGE

switch·back \'swich-ˌbak\ *n* : a zigzag road, trail, or section of railroad tracks for climbing a steep hill

switch·blade \-ˌblād\ *n* : a pocket-knife with a spring-operated blade

switch·board \-ˌbōrd\ *n* : a panel for controlling the operation of a number of electric circuits; *esp* : one used to make and break telephone connections

switch·hit·ter \-'hi-tər\ *n* : a baseball player who bats either right-handed or left-handed — **switch·hit** \-'hit\ *vb*

switch·man \'swich-mən\ *n* : one who attends a railroad switch

Switz *abbr* Switzerland

¹swiv·el \'swi-vəl\ *n* : a device joining two parts so that one or both can turn freely

²swivel *vb* **-eled** *or* **-elled; -el·ing** *or* **-el·ling** : to swing or turn on or as if on a swivel

swiv·et \'swi-vət\ *n* : an agitated state

swiz·zle stick \'swi-zəl-\ *n* : a stick used to stir mixed drinks

swollen *past part of* SWELL

swoon \'swün\ *vb* : FAINT — **swoon** *n*

swoop \'swüp\ *vb* : to move with a sweep ⟨the eagle ∿*ed* down on its prey⟩ — **swoop** *n*

swop *chiefly Brit var of* SWAP

sword \'sōrd\ *n* **1** : a weapon with a long blade for cutting or thrusting **2** : the use of force

sword·fish \-ˌfish\ *n* : a very large ocean fish used for

food that has the upper jaw prolonged into a long swordlike beak

swordfish

sword·play \-ˌplā\ *n* : the art or skill of wielding a sword

swords·man \'sōrdz-mən\ *n* : one skilled in swordplay; *esp* : FENCER

sword·tail \'sōrd-ˌtāl\ *n* : a small brightly marked Central American fish

swore *past of* SWEAR

sworn *past part of* SWEAR

swum *past part of* SWIM

swung *past and past part of* SWING

syb·a·rite \'si-bə-ˌrīt\ *n* : a lover of luxury : VOLUPTUARY — **syb·a·rit·ic** \ˌsi-bə-'ri-tik\ *adj*

syc·a·more \'si-kə-ˌmōr\ *n* : a large spreading tree of eastern and central No. America that has light brown flaky bark and small round fruits hanging on long stalks

sy·co·phant \'si-kə-fənt\ *n* : a servile flatterer — **syc·o·phan·tic** \ˌsi-kə-'fan-tik\ *adj*

syl *or* **syll** *abbr* syllable

syl·lab·i·ca·tion \sə-ˌla-bə-'kā-shən\ *n* : the division of words into syllables

syl·lab·i·fy \sə-'la-bə-ˌfī\ *vb* **-fied; -fy·ing** : to form or divide into syllables — **syl·lab·i·fi·ca·tion** \-ˌla-bə-fə-'kā-shən\ *n*

syl·la·ble \'si-lə-bəl\ *n* [ME, fr. MF *sillabe*, fr. L *syllaba*, fr. Gk *syllabē*, fr. *syllambanein* to gather together, fr. *syn* with + *lambanein* to take] : a unit of spoken language consisting of an uninterrupted utterance and forming either a whole word (as *cat*) or a commonly recognized division of a word (as *syl* in *syl·la·ble*); *also* : one or more letters representing such a unit — **syl·lab·ic** \sə-'la-bik\ *adj*

syl·la·bus \'si-lə-bəs\ *n, pl* **-bi** \-ˌbī\ *or* **-bus·es** : a summary containing the heads or main topics of a speech, book, or course of study

syl·lo·gism \'si-lə-ˌji-zəm\ *n* : a logical scheme of a formal argument consisting of a major and a minor premise and a conclusion which must logically be true if the premises are true — **syl·lo·gis·tic** \ˌsi-lə-'jis-tik\ *adj*

sylph \'silf\ *n* **1** : an imaginary being inhabiting the air **2** : a slender graceful woman

syl·van \'sil-vən\ *adj* **1** : living or located in a wooded area; *also* : of, relating to, or characteristic of forest **2** : abounding in woods or trees

sym *abbr* **1** symbol **2** symmetrical

sym·bi·o·sis \ˌsim-ˌbī-'ō-səs, -bē-\ *n, pl* **-o·ses** \-ˌsēz\ : the living together in close association of two dissimilar organisms esp. when mutually beneficial — **sym·bi·ot·ic** \-'ä-tik\ *adj*

sym·bol \'sim-bəl\ *n* **1** : something that stands for something else; *esp* : something concrete that represents or suggests another thing that cannot in itself be pictured ⟨the lion is a ∿ of bravery⟩ **2** : a letter, character, or sign used in writing or printing to represent operations, quantities, elements, sounds, or other ideas — **sym·bol·ic** \sim-'bä-lik\ *also* **sym·bol·i·cal** \-li-kəl\ *adj* — **sym·bol·i·cal·ly** \-k(ə-)lē\ *adv*

sym·bol·ise *Brit var of* SYMBOLIZE

sym·bol·ism \'sim-bə-ˌli-zəm\ *n* : representation of abstract or intangible things by means of symbols

sym·bol·ize \'sim-bə-ˌlīz\ *vb* **-ized; -iz·ing 1** : to serve as a symbol of **2** : to represent by symbols — **sym·bol·i·za·tion** \ˌsim-bə-lə-ˈzā-shən\ *n*

sym·me·try \ˈsi-mə-trē\ *n, pl* **-tries 1** : an arrangement marked by regularity and balanced proportions **2** : correspondence in size, shape, and position of parts that are on opposite sides of a dividing line or center — **sym·met·ri·cal** \sə-ˈme-tri-kəl\ *or* **sym·met·ric** \sə-ˈme-trik\ *adj* — **sym·met·ri·cal·ly** \-k(ə-)lē\ *adv*

sympathetic nervous system *n* : the part of the autonomic nervous system that is concerned esp. with preparing the body to react to situations of stress or emergency and that tends to decrease the tone and contractility of muscle not under direct voluntary control, increase the activity of the heart and the blood pressure, and cause the contraction of blood vessels

sym·pa·thise *chiefly Brit var of* SYMPATHIZE

sym·pa·thize \ˈsim-pə-ˌthīz\ *vb* **-thized; -thiz·ing** : to feel or show sympathy — **sym·pa·thiz·er** *n*

sym·pa·thy \ˈsim-pə-thē\ *n, pl* **-thies 1** : a relationship between persons or things wherein whatever affects one similarly affects the other **2** : harmony of interests and aims **3** : FAVOR, SUPPORT **4** : the capacity for entering into and sharing the feelings or interests of another; *also* : COMPASSION, PITY **5** : an expression of sorrow for another's loss, grief, or misfortune — **sym·pa·thet·ic** \ˌsim-pə-ˈthe-tik\ *adj* — **sym·pa·thet·i·cal·ly** \-ti-k(ə-)lē\ *adv*

sym·pho·ny \ˈsim-fə-nē\ *n, pl* **-nies 1** : harmony of sounds **2** : a large and complex composition for a full orchestra **3** : a large orchestra of a kind that plays symphonies — **sym·phon·ic** \sim-ˈfä-nik\ *adj*

sym·po·sium \sim-ˈpō-zē-əm\ *n, pl* **-sia** \-zē-ə\ *or* **-siums** : a conference at which a particular topic is discussed by various speakers; *also* : a collection of opinions about a subject

symp·tom \ˈsimp-təm\ *n* [LL *symptoma,* fr. Gk *symptōma* happening, attribute, symptom, fr. *sympiptein* to happen, fr. *syn* with + *piptein* to fall] **1** : something that indicates the presence of disease or abnormality; *esp* : something (as a headache) that can be sensed only by the individual affected **2** : SIGN, INDICATION — **symp·tom·at·ic** \ˌsimp-tə-ˈma-tik\ *adj*

syn *abbr* synonym; synonymous; synonymy

syn·a·gogue *or* **syn·a·gog** \ˈsi-nə-ˌgäg\ *n* [ME *synagoge,* fr. OF, fr. LL *synagoga,* fr. Gk *synagōgē* assembly, synagogue, fr. *synagein* to bring together] **1** : a Jewish congregation **2** : the house of worship of a Jewish congregation

syn·apse \ˈsi-ˌnaps, sə-ˈnaps\ *n* : the point at which a nervous impulse passes from one neuron to another

¹sync *also* **synch** \ˈsiŋk\ *vb* **synced** *also* **synched** \ˈsiŋkt\; **sync·ing** *also* **synch·ing** \ˈsiŋ-kiŋ\ : SYNCHRONIZE

²sync *also* **synch** *n* : SYNCHRONIZATION, SYNCHRONISM — **sync** *adj*

syn·chro·nise *Brit var of* SYNCHRONIZE

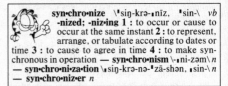
syn·chro·nize \ˈsiŋ-krə-ˌnīz, ˈsin-\ *vb* **-nized; -niz·ing 1** : to occur or cause to occur at the same instant **2** : to represent, arrange, or tabulate according to dates or time **3** : to cause to agree in time **4** : to make synchronous in operation — **syn·chro·nism** \-ˌni-zəm\ *n* — **syn·chro·ni·za·tion** \ˌsiŋ-krə-nə-ˈzā-shən, ˌsin-\ *n* — **syn·chro·niz·er** *n*

syn·chro·nous \ˈsiŋ-krə-nəs, ˈsin-\ *adj* **1** : happening at the same time : CONCURRENT **2** : working, moving, or occurring together at the same rate and at the proper time

syn·co·pa·tion \ˌsiŋ-kə-ˈpā-shən, ˌsin-\ *n* : a shifting of the regular musical accent : occurrence of accented notes on the weak beat — **syn·co·pate** \ˈsiŋ-kə-ˌpāt, ˈsin-\ *vb*

syn·co·pe \ˈsiŋ-kə-(ˌ)pē, ˈsin-\ *n* : the loss of one or more sounds or letters in the interior of a word (as in *fo'c'sle* for *forecastle*)

¹syn·di·cate \ˈsin-di-kət\ *n* **1** : a group of persons who combine to carry out a financial or industrial undertaking **2** : a loose association of racketeers **3** : a business concern that sells materials for publication in many newspapers and periodicals at the same time

²syn·di·cate \-də-ˌkāt\ *vb* **-cat·ed; -cat·ing 1** : to combine into or manage as a syndicate **2** : to publish through a syndicate — **syn·di·ca·tion** \ˌsin-də-ˈkā-shən\ *n*

syn·drome \ˈsin-ˌdrōm\ *n* : a group of signs and symptoms that occur together and characterize a particular abnormality

syn·er·gism \ˈsin-ər-ˌji-zəm\ *n* : interaction of discrete agencies (as industrial firms), agents (as drugs), or conditions such that the total effect is greater than the sum of the individual effects — **syn·er·gist** \-jist\ *n* — **syn·er·gis·tic** \ˌsi-nər-ˈjis-tik\ *adj* — **syn·er·gis·ti·cal·ly** \-ti-k(ə-)lē\ *adv*

syn·fuel \ˈsin-ˌfyül\ *n* [*synthetic*] : a fuel derived esp. from a fossil fuel

syn·od \ˈsi-nəd\ *n* : COUNCIL, ASSEMBLY; *esp* : a religious governing body — **syn·od·al** \-nəd-ᵊl, -ˌnäd-ᵊl\ *adj* — **syn·od·ic** \-dik\ *or* **syn·od·i·cal** \sə-ˈnä-di-kəl\ *adj*

syn·onym \ˈsi-nə-ˌnim\ *n* : one of two or more words in the same language which have the same or very nearly the same meaning — **syn·on·y·mous** \sə-ˈnä-nə-məs\ *adj* — **syn·on·y·my** \-mē\ *n*

syn·op·sis \sə-ˈnäp-səs\ *n, pl* **-op·ses** \-ˌsēz\ : a condensed statement or outline (as of a treatise) : ABSTRACT

syn·op·tic \sə-ˈnäp-tik\ *also* **syn·op·ti·cal** \-ti-kəl\ *adj* : characterized by or affording a comprehensive view

syn·tax \ˈsin-ˌtaks\ *n* : the way in which words are put together to form phrases, clauses, or sentences — **syn·tac·tic** \sin-ˈtak-tik\ *or* **syn·tac·ti·cal** \-ti-kəl\ *adj*

syn·the·sis \ˈsin-thə-səs\ *n, pl* **-the·ses** \-ˌsēz\ : the combination of parts or elements into a whole; *esp* : the production of a substance by union of chemical-

SYNCHRONIZED BOREDOM

ly simpler substances — **syn•the•size** \-ˌsīz\ *vb* — **syn•the•siz•er** *n*

syn•thet•ic \sin-ˈthe-tik\ *adj* : produced artificially esp. by chemical means; *also* : not genuine — **synthetic** *n* — **syn•thet•i•cal•ly** \-ti-k(ə-)lē\ *adv*

syph•i•lis \ˈsi-fə-ləs\ *n* [NL, fr. *Syphilus*, hero of the poem *Syphilis sive Morbus Gallicus* (*Syphilis or the French disease*) (1530) by Girolamo Fracastoro †1553 Ital. physician] : an infectious usu. venereal disease caused by a spirochete — **syph•i•lit•ic** \ˌsi-fə-ˈli-tik\ *adj or n*

sy•phon *var of* SIPHON

Syr•i•an \ˈsir-ē-ən\ *n* : a native or inhabitant of Syria — **Syrian** *adj*

¹**sy•ringe** \sə-ˈrinj\ *n* : a device used esp. for injecting liquids into or withdrawing them from the body

²**syringe** *vb* **sy•ringed; sy•ring•ing** : to flush or cleanse with or as if with a syringe

syr•up \ˈsir-əp, ˈsir-əp\ *n* 1 : a thick sticky solution of sugar and water often flavored or medicated 2 : the concentrated juice of a fruit or plant — **syr•upy** *adj*

syst *abbr* system

sys•tem \ˈsis-təm\ *n* 1 : a group of units so combined as to form a whole and to operate in unison 2 : the body as a functioning whole; *also* : a group of bodily organs (as the nervous system) that together carry on

some vital function 3 : a definite scheme or method of procedure or classification 4 : regular method or order — **sys•tem•at•ic** \ˌsis-tə-ˈma-tik\ *also* **sys•tem•at•i•cal** \-ti-kəl\ *adj* — **sys•tem•at•i•cal•ly** \-k(ə-)lē\ *adv*

sys•tem•a•tise *Brit var of* SYSTEMATIZE

sys•tem•a•tize \ˈsis-tə-mə-ˌtīz\ *vb* **-a•tized; -a•tiz•ing** : to make into a system : arrange methodically

¹**sys•tem•ic** \sis-ˈte-mik\ *adj* 1 : of, relating to, or affecting the whole body ⟨∼ disease⟩ 2 : of, relating to, or being a pesticide that when absorbed into the sap or bloodstream makes the entire plant or animal toxic to a pest (as an insect or fungus)

²**systemic** *n* : a systemic pesticide

systemic lupus erythematosus *n* : a systemic disease esp. of women characterized by fever, skin rash, and arthritis, often by anemia, by small hemorrhages of the skin and mucous membranes, and in serious cases by involvement of various internal organs

sys•tem•ize \ˈsis-tə-ˌmīz\ *vb* **-ized; -iz•ing** : SYSTEMATIZE

systems analyst *n* : a person who studies a procedure or business to determine its goals or purposes and to discover the best ways to accomplish them — **systems analysis** *n*

sys•to•le \ˈsis-tə-(ˌ)lē\ *n* : a rhythmically recurrent contraction of the heart — **sys•tol•ic** \sis-ˈtä-lik\ *adj*

T

¹**t** \ˈtē\ *n, pl* **t's** *or* **ts** \ˈtēz\ *often cap* : the 20th letter of the English alphabet

²**t** *abbr, often cap* 1 metric ton 2 tablespoon 3 teaspoon 4 temperature 5 ton 6 transitive 7 troy 8 true

T *abbr* 1 toddler 2 T-shirt

Ta *symbol* tantalum

TA *abbr* teaching assistant

¹**tab** \ˈtab\ *n* 1 : a short projecting flap, loop, or tag; *also* : a small insert or addition 2 : close surveillance : WATCH ⟨keep ∼s on him⟩ 3 : BILL, CHECK

²**tab** *vb* **tabbed; tab•bing** : DESIGNATE

tab•by \ˈta-bē\ *n, pl* **tabbies** : a usu. striped or mottled domestic cat; *also* : a female domestic cat

tab•er•na•cle \ˈta-bər-ˌna-kəl\ *n* [ME, fr. OF, fr. LL *tabernaculum*, fr. L, tent, fr. *taberna* hut] 1 *often cap* : a tent sanctuary used by the Israelites during the Exodus 2 : a receptacle for the consecrated elements of the Eucharist 3 : a house of worship

¹**ta•ble** \ˈtā-bəl\ *n* 1 : a flat slab or plaque : TABLET 2 : a piece of furniture consisting of a smooth flat top fixed on legs 3 : a supply of food : BOARD, FARE 4 : a group of people assembled at or as if at a table 5 : an orderly arrangement of data usu. in rows and columns 6 : a short list ⟨∼ of contents⟩ — **ta•ble•top** \-ˌtäp\ *n*

²**table** *vb* **ta•bled; ta•bling** 1 *Brit* : to place on the agen-

da 2 : to remove (a parliamentary motion) from consideration indefinitely

tab•leau \ˈta-blō\ *n, pl* **tab•leaux** \-ˌblōz\ *also* **tab•leaus** [F] : a scene or event usu. presented on a stage by costumed participants who remain silent and motionless

ta•ble•cloth \ˈtā-bəl-ˌklòth\ *n* : a covering spread over a dining table before the table is set

ta•ble d'hôte \ˌtä-bəl-ˈdōt\ *n* [F, lit., host's table] : a complete meal of several courses offered at a fixed price

ta•ble•land \ˈtā-bəl-ˌland\ *n* : PLATEAU

ta•ble•spoon \-ˌspün\ *n* 1 : a large spoon used esp. for serving 2 : a unit of measure equal to ½ fluid ounce (15 milliliters)

ta•ble•spoon•ful \-ˌfùl\ *n, pl* **-spoonfuls** \-ˌfùlz\ *also* **-spoons•ful** \-ˌspünz-ˌfùl\ : TABLESPOON 2

tab•let \ˈta-blət\ *n* 1 : a flat slab suited for or bearing an inscription 2 : a collection of sheets of paper glued together at one edge 3 : a compressed or molded block of material; *esp* : a usu. disk-shaped medicated mass

table tennis *n* : a game resembling tennis played on a tabletop with wooden paddles and a small hollow plastic ball

ta•ble•ware \ˈtā-bəl-ˌwar\ *n* : utensils (as of china or silver) for table use

¹**tab•loid** \ˈta-ˌblòid\ *adj* : condensed into small scope

²**tabloid** *n* : a newspaper marked by small pages, con-

densation of the news, and usu. many photographs; *esp* : one characterized by sensationalism

¹**ta·boo** *also* **ta·bu** \tə-'bü, ta-\ *adj* [Tongan (a Polynesian language) *tabu*] : prohibited by a taboo

²**taboo** *also* **tabu** *n, pl* **taboos** *also* **tabus** **1** : a prohibition against touching, saying, or doing something for fear of immediate harm from a supernatural force **2** : a prohibition imposed by social custom

ta·bor *also* **ta·bour** \'tā-bər\ *n* : a small drum used to accompany a pipe or fife played by the same person

tab·u·lar \'ta-byə-lər\ *adj* **1** : having a flat surface **2** : arranged in a table; *esp* : set up in rows and columns **3** : computed by means of a table

tab·u·late \-,lāt\ *vb* **-lat·ed; -lat·ing** : to put into tabular form — **tab·u·la·tion** \,ta-byə-'lā-shən\ *n* — **tab·u·la·tor** \'ta-byə-,lā-tər\ *n*

TAC \'tak\ *abbr* Tactical Air Command

tach \'tak\ *n* : TACHOMETER

ta·chom·e·ter \ta-'kä-mə-tər, tə-\ *n* [ultim. fr. Gk *tachos* speed] : a device to indicate speed of rotation

tachy·car·dia \,ta-ki-'kär-dē-ə\ *n* : relatively rapid heart action

tachy·on \'ta-kē-,än\ *n* : a hypothetical particle held to travel faster than light

tac·it \'ta-sət\ *adj* [F or L; F *tacite*, fr. L *tacitus* silent, fr. *tacēre* to be silent] **1** : expressed without words or speech **2** : implied or indicated but not actually expressed ⟨~ consent⟩ — **tac·it·ly** *adv* — **tac·it·ness** *n*

tac·i·turn \'ta-sə-,tərn\ *adj* : disinclined to talk **syn** uncommunicative, reserved, reticent, closemouthed — **tac·i·tur·ni·ty** \,ta-sə-'tər-nə-tē\ *n*

¹**tack** \'tak\ *vb* **1** : to fasten with tacks; *also* : to add on **2** : to change the direction of (a sailing ship) from one tack to another **3** : to follow a zigzag course

²**tack** *n* **1** : a small sharp nail with a broad flat head **2** : the direction toward the wind that a ship is sailing ⟨starboard ~⟩; *also* : the run of a ship on one tack **3** : a change of course from one tack to another **4** : a zigzag course **5** : a course of action

³**tack** *n* : gear for harnessing a horse

¹**tack·le** \'ta-kəl, *naut often* 'tā-\ *n* **1** : GEAR, APPARATUS, EQUIPMENT **2** : the rigging of a ship **3** : an arrangement of ropes and pulleys for hoisting or pulling heavy objects **4** : the act or an instance of tackling; *also* : a football lineman playing between guard and end

²**tackle** *vb* **tack·led; tack·ling** **1** : to attach and secure with or as if with tackle **2** : to seize, grapple with, or throw down with the intention of subduing or stopping **3** : to set about dealing with ⟨~ a problem⟩ — **tack·ler** *n*

¹**tacky** \'ta-kē\ *adj* **tack·i·er; -est** : sticky to the touch

²**tacky** *adj* **tack·i·er; -est** **1** : SHABBY, SEEDY **2** : marked by lack of style or good taste; *also* : cheaply showy

ta·co \'tä-kō\ *n, pl* **tacos** \-,kōz\ [MexSp] : a usu. fried tortilla rolled up with or folded over a filling

tact \'takt\ *n* [F, sense of touch, fr. L *tactus*, fr. *tangere* to touch] : a keen sense of what to do or say to keep good relations with others — **tact·ful** \-fəl\

adj — **tact·ful·ly** *adv* — **tact·less** *adj* — **tact·less·ly** *adv*

tac·tic \'tak-tik\ *n* : a planned action for accomplishing an end

tac·tics \'tak-tiks\ *n sing or pl* **1** : the science of maneuvering forces in combat **2** : the skill of using available means to reach an end — **tac·ti·cal** \-ti-kəl\ *adj* — **tac·ti·cian** \tak-'ti-shən\ *n*

tac·tile \'takt-əl, 'tak-,tīl\ *adj* : of, relating to, or perceptible through the sense of touch

tad·pole \'tad-,pōl\ *n* [ME *taddepol*, fr. *tode* toad + *polle* head] : an aquatic larva of a frog or toad that has a tail and gills

tae kwon do \'tī-'kwän-'dō\ *n* : a Korean martial art resembling karate

taf·fe·ta \'ta-fə-tə\ *n* : a crisp lustrous fabric (as of silk or rayon)

taff·rail \'taf-,rāl, -rəl\ *n* : the rail around a ship's stern

taf·fy \'ta-fē\ *n, pl* **taffies** : a candy usu. of molasses or brown sugar stretched until porous and light≈ colored

¹**tag** \'tag\ *n* **1** : a metal or plastic binding on an end of a shoelace **2** : a piece of hanging or attached material **3** : a hackneyed quotation or saying **4** : a descriptive or identifying epithet

²**tag** *vb* **tagged; tag·ging** **1** : to provide or mark with or as if with a tag; *esp* : IDENTIFY **2** : to attach as an addition **3** : to follow closely and persistently ⟨~s along everywhere we go⟩ **4** : to hold responsible for something

³**tag** *n* : a game in which one player chases others and tries to touch one of them

⁴**tag** *vb* **tagged; tag·ging** **1** : to touch in or as if in a game of tag **2** : SELECT

TAG *abbr* the adjutant general

tag sale *n* : GARAGE SALE

Ta·hi·tian \tə-'hē-shən\ *n* **1** : a native or inhabitant of Tahiti **2** : the Polynesian language of the Tahitians — **Tahitian** *adj*

tai·ga \'tī-gə\ *n* [Russ *taĭga*] : a swampy coniferous subarctic forest extending south from the tundra

¹**tail** \'tāl\ *n* **1** : the rear end or a process extending from the rear end of an animal **2** : something resembling an animal's tail **3** *pl* : full evening dress for men **4** : the back, last, lower, or inferior part of something; *esp* : the reverse of a coin **5** : one who follows or keeps watch on someone — **tailed** \'tāld\ *adj* — **tail·less** \'tāl-ləs\ *adj*

²**tail** *vb* : FOLLOW; *esp* : to follow for the purpose of surveillance

tail·coat \-'kōt\ *n* : a coat with tails; *esp* : a man's full≈ dress coat with two long tapering skirts at the back

¹**tail·gate** \-,gāt\ *n* : a board or gate at the back end of a vehicle that can be let down (as for loading)

²**tailgate** *vb* **tail·gat·ed; tail·gat·ing 1** : to drive dangerously close behind another vehicle **2** : to hold a tailgate picnic

³**tailgate** *adj* : relating to or being a picnic set up on the tailgate esp. of a station wagon

tail·light \-₁līt\ *n* : a usu. red warning light mounted at the rear of a vehicle

¹**tai·lor** \¹tā-lər\ *n* [ME *taillour*, fr. OF *tailleur*, fr. *taillier* to cut, fr. LL *taliare*, fr. L *talea* twig, cutting] : a person whose occupation is making or altering garments

²**tailor** *vb* **1** : to make or fashion as the work of a tailor **2** : to make or adapt to suit a special purpose

tail pipe *n* : an outlet by which the exhaust gases are removed from an engine (as of an automobile)

tail·spin \¹tāl-₁spin\ *n* : a rapid descent or downward spiral

tail wind *n* : a wind blowing in the same general direction as a course of movement (as of an aircraft)

¹**taint** \¹tānt\ *vb* **1** : CORRUPT, CONTAMINATE **2** : to affect or become affected with something bad (as putrefaction)

²**taint** *n* : a contaminating mark or influence

Tai·wan·ese \₁tī-wə-¹nēz, -¹nēs\ *n* : a native or inhabitant of Taiwan — **Taiwanese** *adj*

ta·ka \¹tä-kə\ *n* — see MONEY table

¹**take** \¹tāk\ *vb* **took** \¹tùk\; **tak·en** \¹tā-kən\; **tak·ing 1** : to get into one's hands or possession : GRASP, SEIZE **2** : CAPTURE; *also* : DEFEAT **3** : to obtain or secure for use **4** : to catch or attack through the effect of a sudden force or influence ⟨*taken* ill⟩ **5** : CAPTIVATE, DELIGHT **6** : to bring into a relation ⟨∼ a wife⟩ **7** : REMOVE, SUBTRACT **8** : to pick out : CHOOSE **9** : ASSUME, UNDERTAKE **10** : RECEIVE, ACCEPT **11** : to use for transportation ⟨∼ a bus⟩ **12** : to become impregnated with : ABSORB ⟨∼s a dye⟩ **13** : to receive into one's body (as by swallowing) ⟨∼ a pill⟩ **14** : ENDURE, UNDERGO **15** : to lead, carry, or cause to go along to another place **16** : NEED, REQUIRE **17** : to obtain as the result of a special procedure ⟨∼ a snapshot⟩ **18** : to undertake and do, make, or perform ⟨∼ a walk⟩ **19** : to take effect : ACT, OPERATE **syn** grab, clutch, snatch, seize, nab, grapple — **tak·er** *n* — **take advantage of 1** : to profit by **2** : EXPLOIT — **take after** : RESEMBLE — **take care** : to be careful — **take care of** : to care for : attend to — **take effect** : to become operative — **take exception** : OBJECT — **take for** : to suppose to be; *esp* : to mistake for — **take place** : HAPPEN — **take to 1** : to go to **2** : to apply or devote oneself to **3** : to conceive a liking for

²**take** *n* **1** : the number or quantity taken; *also* : PROCEEDS, RECEIPTS **2** : an act or the action of taking **3** : a television or movie scene filmed or taped at one time; *also* : a sound recording made at one time **4** : a distinct or personal point of view

take·off \¹tā-₁kôf\ *n* **1** : IMITATION; *esp* : PARODY **2** : an act or instance of taking off

take off *vb* **1** : REMOVE **2** : DEDUCT **3** : to set out : go away **4** : to leave the surface; *esp* : to begin flight

take on *vb* **1** : to begin to perform or deal with; *also* : to contend with as an opponent **2** : ENGAGE, HIRE **3** : to assume or acquire as or as if one's own **4** : to make an unusual show of one's feelings esp. of grief or anger

take over *vb* : to assume control or possession of or responsibility for — **take·over** \¹tā-₁kō-vər\ *n*

take up *vb* **1** : PICK UP **2** : to begin to occupy **3** : to absorb or incorporate into itself ⟨plants *taking up* nutrients⟩ **4** : to begin to engage in ⟨*took up* jogging⟩ **5** : to make tighter or shorter ⟨*take up* the slack⟩

tak·ings \¹tā-kiŋz\ *n pl* : receipts esp. of money

ta·la \¹tä-lə\ *n, pl* **tala** — see MONEY table

talc \¹talk\ *n* : a soft mineral with a soapy feel used esp. in making toilet powder (**tal·cum powder** \¹tal-kəm-\)

tale \¹tāl\ *n* **1** : a relation of a series of events **2** : a report of a confidential matter **3** : idle talk; *esp* : harm

ful gossip **4** : a usu. imaginative narrative **5** : FALSEHOOD **6** : COUNT, TALLY

tal·ent \¹ta-lənt\ *n* **1** : an ancient unit of weight and value **2** : the natural endowments of a person **3** : a special often creative or artistic aptitude **4** : mental power : ABILITY **5** : a person of talent **syn** genius, gift, faculty, aptitude, knack — **tal·ent·ed** *adj*

ta·ler \¹tä-lər\ *n* : any of numerous silver coins issued by German states from the 15th to the 19th centuries

tales·man \¹tālz-mən\ *n* : a person summoned for jury duty

tal·is·man \¹ta-ləs-mən, -ləz-\ *n, pl* **-mans** [F *talisman* or Sp *talismán* or It *talismano*, fr. Ar *ṭilsam*, fr. MGk *telesma*, fr. Gk, consecration, fr. *telein* to initiate into the mysteries, complete, fr. *telos* end] : an object thought to act as a charm

¹**talk** \¹tòk\ *vb* **1** : to express in speech : utter words : SPEAK **2** : DISCUSS ⟨∼ business⟩ **3** : to influence or cause by talking ⟨∼ed him into going⟩ **4** : to use (a language) for communicating **5** : CONVERSE **6** : to reveal confidential information; *also* : GOSSIP **7** : to give a talk : LECTURE — **talk·er** *n* — **talk back** : to answer impertinently

²**talk** *n* **1** : the act of talking **2** : a way of speaking **3** : a formal discussion **4** : REPORT, RUMOR **5** : the topic of comment or gossip ⟨the ∼ of the town⟩ **6** : an informal address or lecture

talk·ative \¹tò-kə-tiv\ *adj* : given to talking **syn** loquacious, chatty, gabby, garrulous — **talk·ative·ly** *adv* — **talk·ative·ness** *n*

talk·ing-to \¹tò-kiŋ-₁tü\ *n* : REPRIMAND, REPROOF

talk radio *n* : radio programming consisting of call= in shows

tall \¹tòl\ *adj* **1** : high in stature; *also* : of a specified height ⟨six feet ∼⟩ **2** : LARGE, FORMIDABLE ⟨a ∼ order⟩ **3** : UNBELIEVABLE, IMPROBABLE ⟨a ∼ story⟩ — **tall·ness** *n*

tal·low \¹ta-lō\ *n* : a hard white fat rendered usu. from cattle or sheep tissues and used esp. in candles

¹**tal·ly** \¹ta-lē\ *n, pl* **tallies** [ME *talye*, fr. ML *talea*, fr. L, twig, cutting] **1** : a device for visibly recording or accounting esp. business transactions **2** : a recorded account **3** : a corresponding part; *also* : CORRESPONDENCE

²**tally** *vb* **tal·lied; tal·ly·ing 1** : to mark on or as if on a tally **2** : to make a count of : RECKON; *also* : SCORE **3** : CORRESPOND, MATCH **syn** square, accord, harmonize, conform, jibe

tal·ly·ho \₁ta-lē-¹hō\ *n, pl* **-hos** : a call of a huntsman at sight of the fox

Tal·mud \¹täl-₁mùd, ¹tal-məd\ *n* [Late Heb *talmūdh*, lit., instruction] : the authoritative body of Jewish tradition — **Tal·mu·dic** \täl-¹mü-dik, -¹myü-, -¹mə-; täl-¹mù-\ *adj* — **Tal·mud·ist** \¹täl-₁mù-dist, ¹tal-mə-\ *n*

tal·on \¹ta-lən\ *n* : the claw of an animal and esp. of a bird of prey

ta·lus \¹tā-ləs, ¹ta-\ *n* : rock debris at the base of a cliff

tam \¹tam\ *n* : TAM-O'-SHANTER

ta·ma·le \tə-¹mä-lē\ *n* [MexSp *tamales*, pl. of *tamal* tamale, fr. Nahuatl (American Indian language) *tamalli* steamed cornmeal dough] : ground meat seasoned with chili, rolled in cornmeal dough, wrapped in corn husks, and steamed

tam·a·rack \¹ta-mə-₁rak\ *n* : a larch of northern No. America; *also* : its hard resinous wood

tam·a·rind \¹ta-mə-rənd, -₁rind\ *n* [Sp & Pg *tamarindo*, fr. Ar *tamr hindī*, lit., Indian date] : a tropical tree of the legume family with hard yellowish wood and feathery leaves; *also* : its acid fruit

tam·ba·la \täm-¹bä-lə\ *n, pl* **-la** *or* **-las** — see *kwacha* at MONEY table

tam·bou·rine \₁tam-bə-¹rēn\ *n* : a small shallow drum with loose disks at the sides played by shaking or striking with the hand

¹**tame** \¹tām\ *adj* **tam·er; tam·est 1** : reduced from a

state of native wildness esp. so as to be useful to humans : DOMESTICATED **2** : made docile : SUBDUED **3** : lacking spirit or interest : INSIPID **syn** submissive, domestic, domesticated — **tame·ly** *adv* — **tame·ness** *n*
[2]**tame** *vb* **tamed; tam·ing 1** : to make or become tame; *also* : to subject (land) to cultivation **2** : HUMBLE, SUBDUE — **tam·able** *or* **tame·able** \'tā-mə-bəl\ *adj* — **tame·less** *adj* — **tam·er** *n*
tam-o'-shan·ter \'ta-mə-ˌshan-tər\ *n* [fr. poem *Tam o' Shanter* (1790) by Robert Burns †1796 Scot. poet] : a Scottish woolen cap with a wide flat circular crown and usu. a pom-pom in the center
tamp \'tamp\ *vb* : to drive down or in by a series of light blows

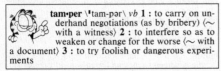

tam·per \'tam-pər\ *vb* **1** : to carry on underhand negotiations (as by bribery) ⟨∼ with a witness⟩ **2** : to interfere so as to weaken or change for the worse ⟨∼ with a document⟩ **3** : to try foolish or dangerous experiments

tam·pon \'tam-ˌpän\ *n* [F, lit., plug] : a plug (as of cotton) introduced into a body cavity usu. to absorb secretions (as from menstruation) or to arrest bleeding
[1]**tan** \'tan\ *vb* **tanned; tan·ning 1** : to change (hide) into leather esp. by soaking in a liquid containing tannin **2** : to make or become brown (as by exposure to the sun) **3** : WHIP, THRASH
[2]**tan** *n* **1** : a brown skin color induced by sun or weather **2** : a light yellowish brown color
[3]**tan** *abbr* tangent
tan·a·ger \'ta-ni-jər\ *n* : any of numerous American birds that are often brightly colored
tan·bark \'tan-ˌbärk\ *n* : bark (as of oak or sumac) that is rich in tannin and used in tanning
[1]**tan·dem** \'tan-dəm\ *n* [L, at last, at length (taken to mean "lengthwise", fr. *tam* so] **1** : a 2-seated carriage with horses hitched tandem; *also* : its team **2** : a bicycle for two persons sitting one behind the other — **in tandem** : in a tandem arrangement
[2]**tandem** *adv* : one behind another
[3]**tandem** *adj* **1** : consisting of things arranged one behind the other **2** : working in conjunction with each other
tang \'taŋ\ *n* **1** : a part in a tool that connects the blade with the handle **2** : a sharp distinctive flavor; *also* : a pungent odor — **tangy** *adj*
[1]**tan·gent** \'tan-jənt\ *adj* [L *tangent-, tangens*, prp. of *tangere* to touch] : TOUCHING; *esp* : touching a circle or sphere at only one point
[2]**tangent** *n* **1** : a tangent line, curve, or surface **2** : an abrupt change of course — **tan·gen·tial** \tan-'jen-chəl\ *adj*
tan·ger·ine \'tan-jə-ˌrēn, ˌtan-jə-'rēn\ *n* : a deep orange loose-skinned citrus fruit; *also* : a tree that bears tangerines

[1]**tan·gi·ble** \'tan-jə-bəl\ *adj* **1** : perceptible esp. by the sense of touch : PALPABLE **2** : substantially real : MATERIAL ⟨∼ rewards⟩ **3** : capable of being appraised **syn** appreciable, perceptible, sensible, discernible — **tan·gi·bil·i·ty** \ˌtan-jə-'bi-lə-tē\ *n*
[2]**tangible** *n* : something tangible; *esp* : a tangible asset
[1]**tan·gle** \'tan-gəl\ *vb* **tan·gled; tan·gling 1** : to involve so as to hamper or embarrass; *also* : ENTRAP **2** : to unite or knit together in intricate confusion : ENTANGLE
[2]**tangle** *n* **1** : a tangled twisted mass **2** : a confusedly complicated state : MUDDLE
tan·go \'tan-gō\ *n, pl* **tangos** : a dance of Latin American origin — **tango** *vb*
tank \'taŋk\ *n* **1** : a large artificial receptacle for liquids **2** : a heavily armed and armored combat vehicle that moves on tracks — **tank·ful** *n*
tan·kard \'tan-kərd\ *n* : a tall one-handled drinking vessel
tank·er \'tan-kər\ *n* : a vehicle equipped for transporting a liquid
tank top *n* : a sleeveless collarless pullover shirt with shoulder straps
tank town *n* : a small town
tan·ner \'ta-nər\ *n* : one that tans hides
tan·nery \'ta-nə-rē\ *n, pl* **-ner·ies** : a place where tanning is carried on
tan·nic acid \'ta-nik-\ *n* : TANNIN
tan·nin \'ta-nən\ *n* : any of various plant substances used esp. in tanning and dyeing, in inks, and as astringents
tan·sy \'tan-zē\ *n, pl* **tansies** [ME *tanesey*, fr. MF *tanesie*, fr. ML *athanasia*, fr. Gk, immortality, fr. *athanatos* immortal, fr. *a-* not + *thanatos* death] : a common weedy herb related to the daisies with an aromatic odor and bitter-tasting finely divided leaves
tan·ta·lise *Brit var of* TANTALIZE
tan·ta·lize \'tan-tə-ˌlīz\ *vb* **-lized; -liz·ing** [fr. *Tantalus*, king of Greek myth punished in Hades by having to stand up to his chin in water that receded as he bent to drink] : to tease or torment by presenting something desirable but keeping it out of reach — **tan·ta·liz·er** *n* — **tan·ta·liz·ing·ly** *adv*
tan·ta·lum \'tan-tə-ləm\ *n* : a hard ductile metallic chemical element — see ELEMENT table
tan·ta·mount \'tan-tə-ˌmaùnt\ *adj* : equivalent in value or meaning

tan·trum \'tan-trəm\ *n* : a fit of bad temper

Tan·za·ni·an \ˌtan-zə-'nē-ən\ *n* : a native or inhabitant of Tanzania — **Tanzanian** *adj*
Tao·ism \'taù-ˌi-zəm, 'daù-\ *n* : a Chinese mystical philosophy; *also* : a religion developed from Taoist philosophy and Buddhism — **Tao·ist** \-ist\ *adj or n*
[1]**tap** \'tap\ *n* **1** : FAUCET, COCK **2** : liquor drawn through

tapir

a tap **3** : the removing of fluid from a container or cavity by tapping **4** : a tool for forming an internal screw thread **5** : a point in an electric circuit where a connection may be made

²**tap** *vb* **tapped; tap•ping 1** : to release or cause to flow by piercing or by drawing a plug from a container or cavity **2** : to pierce so as to let out or draw off a fluid **3** : to draw from ⟨∼ resources⟩ **4** : to cut in on (a telephone wire) to get information; *also* : to cut in (an electrical circuit) on another circuit **5** : to form an internal screw thread in by means of a tap **6** : to connect (as a gas or water main) with a local supply — **tap•per** *n*

³**tap** *vb* **tapped; tap•ping 1** : to rap lightly **2** : to bring about by repeated light blows **3** : SELECT; *esp* : to elect to membership

⁴**tap** *n* **1** : a light blow or stroke; *also* : its sound **2** : a small metal plate for the sole or heel of a shoe

ta•pa \ˈtä-pə, ˈta-\ *n* [Sp, lit., cover, lid] : an hors d'oeuvre served with drinks in Spanish bars — usu. used in pl.

¹**tape** \ˈtāp\ *n* **1** : a narrow band of woven fabric **2** : a narrow flexible strip; *esp* : MAGNETIC TAPE

²**tape** *vb* **taped; tap•ing 1** : to fasten or support with tape **2** : to record on magnetic tape

tape deck *n* : a device used to play back magnetic tapes that usu. has to be connected to an audio system

tape measure *n* : a tape marked off in units (as inches) for measuring

¹**ta•per** \ˈtā-pər\ *n* **1** : a slender wax candle; *also* : a long waxed wick **2** : a gradual lessening of thickness or width in a long object

²**taper** *vb* **ta•pered; ta•per•ing 1** : to make or become gradually smaller toward one end **2** : to diminish gradually

tape–re•cord \ˌtā-pri-ˈkȯrd\ *vb* : to make a recording of on magnetic tape — **tape recorder** *n* — **tape re•cording** *n*

tap•es•try \ˈta-pə-strē\ *n, pl* **-tries** : a heavy reversible textile that has designs or pictures woven into it and is used esp. as a wall hanging

tape•worm \ˈtāp-ˌwərm\ *n* : any of a class of long flat segmented worms parasitic in vertebrate intestines

tap•i•o•ca \ˌta-pē-ˈō-kə\ *n* : a usu. granular preparation of cassava starch used esp. in puddings; *also* : a dish (as pudding) that contains tapioca

ta•pir \ˈtā-pər\ *n, pl* **tapir** *or* **tapirs** : any of a genus of large harmless hoofed mammals of tropical America and Asia from Myanmar to Sumatra

tap•pet \ˈta-pət\ *n* : a lever or projection moved by some other piece (as a cam) or intended to move something else

tap•room \ˈtap-ˌrüm, -ˌrüm\ *n* : BARROOM

tap•root \-ˌrüt, -ˌrůt\ *n* : a large main root growing straight down and giving off small side roots

taps \ˈtaps\ *n sing or pl* : the last bugle call at night blown as a signal that lights are to be put out; *also* : a similar call blown at military funerals and memorial services

tap•ster \ˈtap-stər\ *n* : BARTENDER

¹**tar** \ˈtär\ *n* **1** : a thick dark sticky liquid distilled from organic material (as wood or coal) **2** : SAILOR, SEAMAN

²**tar** *vb* **tarred; tar•ring** : to cover or smear with or as if with tar

tar•an•tel•la \ˌtar-ən-ˈte-lə\ *n* : a lively folk dance of southern Italy in 6/8 time

ta•ran•tu•la \tə-ˈran-chə-lə, -tə-lə\ *n, pl* **tarantulas** *also* **ta•ran•tu•lae** \-ˈran-chə-ˌlē, -tə-ˌlē\ : any of a family of large hairy American spiders with a sharp bite that is not very poisonous to human beings

tar•dy \ˈtär-dē\ *adj* **tar•di•er; -est 1** : moving slowly : SLUGGISH **2** : LATE **syn** behindhand, overdue, belated — **tar•di•ly** \-də-lē\ *adv* — **tar•di•ness** \-dē-nəs\ *n*

¹**tare** \ˈtar\ *n* : a weed of grainfields

²**tare** *n* : a deduction from the gross weight of a substance and its container made in allowance for the weight of the container — **tare** *vb*

¹**tar•get** \ˈtär-gət\ *n* [ME, fr. MF *targette*, dim. of *targe* light shield, of Gmc origin] **1** : a mark to shoot at **2** : an object of ridicule or criticism **3** : a goal to be achieved

²**target** *vb* : to make a target of

tar•iff \ˈtar-əf\ *n* [It *tariffa*, fr. Ar *ta'rīf* notification] **1** : a schedule of duties imposed by a government esp. on imported goods; *also* : a duty or rate of duty imposed in such a schedule **2** : a schedule of rates or charges

tar•mac \ˈtär-ˌmak\ *n* : a surface paved with crushed stone covered with tar

tarn \ˈtärn\ *n* : a small mountain lake

tar•nish \ˈtär-nish\ *vb* : to make or become dull or discolored — **tarnish** *n*

ta•ro \ˈtär-ō, ˈtar-\ *n, pl* **taros** : a tropical plant related to the arums that is grown for its edible starchy fleshy root; *also* : this root

tar•ot \ˈtar-ō\ *n* : one of a set of usu. 78 playing cards used esp. for fortune-telling

tar•pau•lin \tär-ˈpȯ-lən, ˈtär-pə-\ *n* : a piece of material (as durable plastic) used for protecting exposed objects

tar•pon \ˈtär-pən\ *n, pl* **tarpon** *or* **tarpons** : a large silvery bony fish often caught for sport in the warm coastal waters of the Atlantic esp. off Florida

tar•ra•gon \ˈtar-ə-gən\ *n* : a small widely cultivated

perennial wormwood with pungent leaves used as a flavoring; *also* : its leaves

¹tar•ry \'tar-ē\ *vb* **tar•ried; tar•ry•ing 1** : to be tardy : DELAY; *esp* : to be slow in leaving **2** : to stay in or at a place : SOJOURN **syn** remain, wait, linger, abide

²tar•ry \'tär-ē\ *adj* : of, resembling, or smeared with tar

tar sand *n* : sand or sandstone that is naturally soaked with the heavy sticky portions of petroleum

tar•sus \'tär-səs\ *n, pl* **tar•si** \-ˌsī\ [NL] : the part of a vertebrate foot between the metatarsus and the leg; *also* : the small bones that support this part — **tar•sal** \-səl\ *adj or n*

¹tart \'tärt\ *adj* **1** : agreeably sharp to the taste : PUNGENT **2** : BITING, CAUSTIC — **tart•ly** *adv* — **tart•ness** *n*

²tart *n* **1** : a small pie or pastry shell containing jelly, custard, or fruit **2** : PROSTITUTE

tar•tan \'tärt-ᵊn\ *n* : a twilled woolen fabric with a plaid design of Scottish origin consisting of stripes of varying width and color usu. patterned to designate a distinctive clan

tar•tar \'tär-tər\ *n* **1** : a substance in the juice of grapes deposited (as in wine casks) as a reddish crust or sediment **2** : a hard crust of saliva, food debris, and calcium salts on the teeth

tar•tar sauce *or* **tar•tare sauce** \'tär-tər-\ *n* : mayonnaise with chopped pickles, olives, or capers

¹task \'task\ *n* [ME *taske*, fr. OF *tasque*, fr. ML *tasca* tax or service imposed by a feudal superior, fr. *taxare* to tax] : a piece of assigned work **syn** job, duty, chore, stint, assignment

²task *vb* : to oppress with great labor

task force *n* : a temporary grouping to accomplish a particular objective

task•mas•ter \'task-ˌmas-tər\ *n* : one that imposes a task or burdens another with labor

¹tas•sel \'ta-səl, 'tä-\ *n* **1** : a hanging ornament made of a bunch of cords of even length fastened at one end **2** : something suggesting a tassel; *esp* : a male flower cluster of Indian corn

²tassel *vb* **-seled** *or* **-selled; -sel•ing** *or* **-sel•ling** : to adorn with or put forth tassels

¹taste \'tāst\ *vb* **tast•ed; tast•ing 1** : EXPERIENCE, UNDERGO **2** : to try or determine the flavor of by taking a bit into the mouth **3** : to eat or drink esp. in small quantities : SAMPLE **4** : to have a specific flavor

²taste *n* **1** : a small amount tasted **2** : BIT; *esp* : a sample of experience **3** : the special sense that identifies sweet, sour, bitter, or salty qualities and is mediated by receptors in the taste buds of the tongue **4** : a quality perceptible to the sense of taste; *also* : a complex sensation involving true taste, smell, and touch **5** : individual preference **6** : critical judgment, discernment, or appreciation; *also* : aesthetic quality **syn** tang, relish, flavor, savor — **taste•ful** \-fəl\ *adj* — **taste•ful•ly** *adv* — **taste•less** *adj* — **taste•less•ly** *adv* — **tast•er** *n*

taste bud *n* : a sense organ mediating the sensation of taste

tasty \'tā-stē\ *adj* **tast•i•er; -est** : pleasing to the taste

: SAVORY **syn** palatable, appetizing, toothsome, flavorsome — **tast•i•ness** \'tā-stē-nəs\ *n*

tat \'tat\ *vb* **tat•ted; tat•ting** : to work at or make by tatting

¹tat•ter \'ta-tər\ *vb* : to make or become ragged

²tatter *n* **1** : a part torn and left hanging **2** *pl* : tattered clothing

tat•ter•de•ma•lion \ˌta-tər-di-'māl-yən\ *n* : one that is ragged or disreputable

tat•ter•sall \'ta-tər-ˌsȯl, -səl\ *n* : a pattern of colored lines forming squares on solid background; *also* : a fabric in a tattersall pattern

tat•ting \'ta-tiŋ\ *n* : a delicate handmade lace formed usu. by looping and knotting with a single thread and a small shuttle; *also* : the act or process of making such lace

tat•tle \'tat-ᵊl\ *vb* **tat•tled; tat•tling 1** : CHATTER, PRATE **2** : to tell secrets; *also* : to inform against another — **tat•tler** *n*

tat•tle•tale \'tat-ᵊl-ˌtāl\ *n* : one that tattles : INFORMER

¹tat•too \ta-'tü\ *n, pl* **tattoos** [alter. of earlier *taptoo*, fr. D *taptoe*, fr. the phrase *tap toe!* taps shut!] **1** : a call sounded before taps as notice to go to quarters **2** : a rapid rhythmic rapping

²tattoo *vb* : to mark (the skin) with tattoos

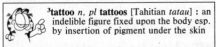

³tattoo *n, pl* **tattoos** [Tahitian *tatau*] : an indelible figure fixed upon the body esp. by insertion of pigment under the skin

tau \'taủ, 'tȯ\ *n* : the 19th letter of the Greek alphabet — T or τ

taught *past and past part of* TEACH

¹taunt \'tȯnt\ *n* : a sarcastic challenge or insult

²taunt *vb* : to reproach or challenge in a mocking manner : jeer at **syn** mock, deride, ridicule, twit — **taunt•er** *n*

taupe \'tōp\ *n* : a brownish gray

Tau•rus \'tȯr-əs\ *n* [L, lit., bull] **1** : a zodiacal constellation between Aries and Gemini usu. pictured as a bull **2** : the 2d sign of the zodiac in astrology; *also* : one born under this sign

taut \'tȯt\ *adj* **1** : tightly drawn : not slack **2** : extremely nervous : TENSE **3** : TRIM, TIDY ⟨a ∼ ship⟩ — **taut•ly** *adv* — **taut•ness** *n*

tau•tol•o•gy \tȯ-'tä-lə-jē\ *n, pl* **-gies** : needless repetition of an idea, statement, or word; *also* : an instance of such repetition — **tau•to•log•i•cal** \ˌtȯt-ᵊl-'ä-ji-kəl\ *adj* — **tau•to•log•i•cal•ly** \-ji-k(ə-)lē\ *adv* — **tau•tol•o•gous** \tȯ-'tä-lə-gəs\ *adj* — **tau•tol•o•gous•ly** *adv*

tav•ern \'ta-vərn\ *n* [ME *taverne*, fr. OF, fr. L *taberna* hut, shop] **1** : an establishment where alcoholic liquors are sold to be drunk on the premises **2** : INN

taw \'tȯ\ *n* **1** : a marble used as a shooter **2** : the line from which players shoot at marbles

taw•dry \'tȯ-drē\ *adj* **taw•dri•er; -est** [*tawdry lace* a tie of lace for the neck, fr. *St. Audrey* (St. Etheldreda) †679 queen of Northumbria] : cheap and gaudy in appearance and quality **syn** garish, flashy, chintzy, meretricious — **taw·dri·ly** adv

taw·ny \'tȯ-nē\ adj **taw·ni·er; -est** : of a brownish orange color

¹tax \'taks\ vb **1** : to levy a tax on **2** : CHARGE, ACCUSE **3** : to put under pressure — **tax·able** \'tak-sə-bəl\ adj — **tax·a·tion** \tak-'sā-shən\ n

²tax n **1** : a charge usu. of money imposed by authority on persons or property for public purposes **2** : a heavy charge : STRAIN

¹taxi \'tak-sē\ n, pl **tax·is** \-sēz\ also **tax·ies** : TAXICAB; also : a similarly operated boat or aircraft

²taxi vb **tax·ied; taxi·ing** or **taxy·ing; tax·is** or **tax·ies 1** : to move along the ground or on the water under an aircraft's own power when starting or after a landing **2** : to go by taxicab

taxi·cab \'tak-sē-ˌkab\ n : an automobile that carries passengers for a fare usu. based on the distance traveled

taxi·der·my \'tak-sə-ˌdər-mē\ n : the skill or occupation of preparing, stuffing, and mounting skins of animals — **taxi·der·mist** \-mist\ n

tax·on·o·my \tak-'sä-nə-mē\ n : classification esp. of animals or plants according to natural relationships — **tax·o·nom·ic** \ˌtak-sə-'nä-mik\ adj — **tax·on·o·mist** \tak-'sä-nə-mist\ n

tax·pay·er \'taks-ˌpā-ər\ n : one who pays or is liable for a tax — **tax·pay·ing** adj

Tay–Sachs disease \'tā-'saks-\ n : a hereditary disorder caused by the absence of an enzyme needed to break down fatty material, marked by buildup of lipids in nervous tissue, and causing death in childhood

tb abbr tablespoon; tablespoonful

Tb symbol terbium

TB \tē-'bē\ n : TUBERCULOSIS

TBA abbr, often not cap to be announced

T–bar \'tē-ˌbär\ n : a ski lift with a series of T⸗ shaped bars

tbs or **tbsp** abbr tablespoon; tablespoonful

Tc symbol technetium

TC abbr teachers college

T cell n : any of several lymphocytes (as a helper T cell) specialized esp. for activity in and control of immunity and the immune response

TD abbr **1** touchdown **2** Treasury Department

TDD abbr telecommunications device for the deaf

TDY abbr temporary duty

Te symbol tellurium

tea \'tē\ n **1** : the cured leaves and leaf buds of a shrub grown chiefly in China, Japan, India, and Sri Lanka; also : this shrub **2** : a drink made by steeping tea in boiling water **3** : refreshments usu. including tea served in late afternoon; also : a reception at which tea is served

teach \'tēch\ vb **taught** \'tȯt\; **teach·ing 1** : to cause to know something : act as a teacher **2** : to show how ⟨∼ a child to swim⟩ **3** : to make to know the disagreeable consequences of an action **4** : to guide the studies of **5** : to impart the knowledge of ⟨∼ algebra⟩ — **teach·able** adj — **teach·er** n

teach·ing n **1** : the act, practice, or profession of a teacher **2** : something taught; esp : DOCTRINE

tea·cup \'tē-ˌkəp\ n : a small cup used with a saucer for hot beverages

teak \'tēk\ n : the hard durable yellowish brown wood of a tall East Indian timber tree related to the vervains; also : this tree

tea·ket·tle \'tē-ˌket-ᵊl\ n : a covered kettle with a handle and spout for boiling water

teal \'tēl\ n, pl **teal** or **teals 1** : any of various small short-necked wild ducks **2** : a dark greenish blue color

¹team \'tēm\ n [ME teme, fr. OE tēam offspring, lineage, group of draft animals] **1** : two or more draft animals harnessed to the same vehicle or implement **2**

teal 1

: a number of persons associated in work or activity; esp : a group on one side in a match

²team vb **1** : to haul with or drive a team **2** : to form a team

³team adj : of or performed by a team; also : marked by devotion to teamwork ⟨a ∼ player⟩

team·mate \-ˌmāt\ n : a fellow member of a team

team·ster \'tēm-stər\ n : one that drives a team or truck

team·work \-ˌwərk\ n : the work or activity of a number of persons acting in close association as members of a unit

tea·pot \'tē-ˌpät\ n : a vessel with a spout for brewing and serving tea

¹tear \'tir\ n : a drop of the salty liquid that moistens the eye and inner side of the eyelids; also, pl : an act of weeping or grieving — **tear·ful** \-fəl\ adj — **tear·ful·ly** adv

²tear \'tir\ vb : to fill with or shed tears ⟨eyes ∼ing in the wind⟩

³tear \'tar\ vb **tore** \'tōr\; **torn** \'tōrn\; **tear·ing 1** : to separate parts of or pull apart by force : REND **2** : LACERATE **3** : to disrupt by the pull of contrary forces **4** : to remove by force : WRENCH **5** : to move or act with violence, haste, or force **syn** rip, split, cleave, rend

⁴tear \'tar\ n **1** : the act of tearing **2** : a hole or flaw made by tearing : RENT

tear gas \'tir-\ n : a substance that on dispersion in the atmosphere blinds the eyes with tears — **tear gas** vb

tear·jerk·er \'tir-ˌjər-kər\ n : an extravagantly pathetic story, song, play, movie, or broadcast

¹tease \'tēz\ vb **teased; teas·ing 1** : to disentangle and lay parallel by combing or carding ⟨∼ wool⟩ **2** : to scratch the surface of (cloth) so as to raise a nap **3** : to annoy persistently esp. in fun by goading, coaxing, or tantalizing **4** : to comb (hair) by taking a strand and pushing the short hairs toward the scalp with the comb **syn** harass, worry, pester, annoy

²tease n **1** : the act of teasing or state of being teased **2** : one that teases

tea·sel \'tē-zəl\ n : a prickly herb or its flower head covered with stiff bracts and used to raise the nap on cloth; also : an artificial device used for this purpose

tea·spoon \'tē-ˌspün\ n **1** : a small spoon suitable for stirring beverages **2** : a unit of measure equal to ⅙ fluid ounce (5 milliliters)

tea·spoon·ful \-ˌfül\ n, pl **-spoonfuls** also **-spoons·ful** \-ˌspünz-ˌfül\ : TEASPOON 2

teat \'tit, 'tēt\ n : the protuberance through which milk is drawn from an udder or breast

tech abbr **1** technical; technically; technician **2** technological; technology

tech·ne·tium \tek-'nē-shē-əm\ n : a metallic chemical element produced in certain nuclear reactions — see ELEMENT table

tech·nic \'tek-nik, tek-'nēk\ n : TECHNIQUE 1

tech·ni·cal \'tek-ni-kəl\ adj [Gk technikos of art, skillful, fr. technē art, craft, skill] **1** : having special knowledge esp. of a mechanical or scientific subject ⟨∼ experts⟩ **2** : of or relating to a particular and esp. a practical or scientific subject ⟨∼ training⟩ **3** : according to a strict interpretation of the rules **4** : of or relating to technique — **tech·ni·cal·ly** \-k(ə-)lē\ adv

tech·ni·cal·i·ty \ˌtek-nə-ˈka-lə-tē\ n, pl **-ties 1** : a detail meaningful only to a specialist **2** : the quality or state of being technical

technical sergeant n : a noncommissioned officer in the air force ranking next below a master sergeant

tech·ni·cian \tek-ˈni-shən\ n : a person who has acquired the technique of a specialized skill or subject

tech·nique \tek-ˈnēk\ n [F] **1** : the manner in which technical details are treated or basic physical movements are used **2** : technical methods

tech·noc·ra·cy \tek-ˈnä-krə-sē\ n : management of society by technical experts — **tech·no·crat** \ˈtek-nəˌkrat\ n — **tech·no·crat·ic** \ˌtek-nə-ˈkra-tik\ adj

tech·nol·o·gy \tek-ˈnä-lə-jē\ n, pl **-gies** : ENGINEERING; also : a manner of accomplishing a task using technical methods or knowledge — **tech·no·log·i·cal** \ˌtek-nə-ˈlä-ji-kəl\ adj

tec·ton·ics \tek-ˈtä-niks\ n sing or pl **1** : geological structural features **2** : geology dealing esp. with the faulting and folding of a planet or moon — **tec·ton·ic** \-nik\ adj

ted·dy bear \ˈte-dē-ˌbar\ n [Teddy Roosevelt; fr. a cartoon depicting the president sparing the life of a bear cub while hunting] : a stuffed toy bear

te·dious \ˈtē-dē-əs\ adj : tiresome because of length or dullness syn boring, tiring, irksome — **te·dious·ly** adv — **te·dious·ness** n

te·di·um \ˈtē-dē-əm\ n : TEDIOUSNESS; also : BOREDOM

¹tee \ˈtē\ n : a small mound or peg on which a golf ball is placed to be hit at the beginning of play on a hole; also : the area from which the ball is hit to begin play

²tee vb **teed; tee·ing** : to place (a ball) on a tee

teem \ˈtēm\ vb : to become filled to overflowing : ABOUND syn swarm, crawl, flow

teen adj : TEENAGE

teen·age \ˈtē-ˌnāj\ or **teen·aged** \-ˌnājd\ adj : of, being, or relating to people in their teens — **teen·ag·er** \-ˌnā-jər\ n

teens \ˈtēnz\ n pl : the numbers 13 to 19 inclusive; esp : the years 13 to 19 in a person's life

tee·ny \ˈtē-nē\ adj **tee·ni·er; -est** : TINY

tee·pee var of TEPEE

tee shirt var of T-SHIRT

tee·ter \ˈtē-tər\ vb **1** : to move unsteadily **2** : SEESAW — **teeter** n

teeth pl of TOOTH

teethe \ˈtēth\ vb **teethed; teeth·ing** : to grow teeth : cut one's teeth

teeth·ing n : growth of the first set of teeth through the gums with its accompanying phenomena

tee·to·tal \ˈtē-ˈtōt-əl, -ˌtōt-\ adj : of or relating to the practice of complete abstinence from alcoholic drinks — **tee·to·tal·er** or **tee·to·tal·ler** \-ˈtōt-əl-ər\ n — **tee·to·tal·ism** \-əl-ˌi-zəm\ n

TEFL abbr teaching English as a foreign language

tek·tite \ˈtek-ˌtīt\ n : a glassy body of probably meteoric origin

tel abbr **1** telegram **2** telegraph **3** telephone

tele·cast \ˈte-li-ˌkast\ vb **-cast** also **-cast·ed; -cast·**ing : to broadcast by television — **telecast** n — **tele·cast·er** n

tele·com·mu·ni·ca·tion \ˌte-li-kə-ˌmyü-nə-ˈkā-shən\ n : communication at a distance (as by telephone or radio)

tele·com·mute \ˈte-li-kə-ˌmyüt\ vb : to work at home by the use of an electronic linkup with a central office

tele·con·fer·ence \ˈte-li-ˌkän-fə-rəns\ n : a conference among people remote from one another held using telecommunications — **tele·con·fer·enc·ing** n

teleg abbr telegraphy

tele·gen·ic \ˌte-lə-ˈje-nik, -ˈjē-\ adj : markedly attractive to television viewers

tele·gram \ˈte-lə-ˌgram\ n : a message sent by telegraph

¹tele·graph \-ˌgraf\ n : an electric apparatus or system for sending messages by a code over wires — **tele·graph·ic** \ˌte-lə-ˈgra-fik\ adj

²telegraph vb : to send or communicate by or as if by telegraph — **te·leg·ra·pher** \tə-ˈle-grə-fər\ n

te·leg·ra·phy \tə-ˈle-grə-fē\ n : the use or operation of a telegraph apparatus or system

tele·mar·ket·ing \ˌte-lə-ˈmär-kə-tiŋ\ n : the marketing of goods or services by telephone — **tele·mar·ket·er** \-tər\ n

te·lem·e·try \tə-ˈle-mə-trē\ n : the transmission esp. by radio of measurements made by automatic instruments to a distant station — **tele·me·ter** \ˈte-lə-ˌmē-tər\ n

te·lep·a·thy \tə-ˈle-pə-thē\ n : apparent communication from one mind to another by extrasensory means — **tele·path·ic** \ˌte-lə-ˈpa-thik\ adj — **tele·path·i·cal·ly** \-thi-k(ə-)lē\ adv

¹tele·phone \ˈte-lə-ˌfōn\ n : an instrument for sending and receiving sounds over long distances by electricity

²telephone vb **-phoned; -phon·ing 1** : to send or communicate by telephone **2** : to speak to (a person) by telephone — **tele·phon·er** n

te·le·pho·ny \tə-ˈle-fə-nē, ˈte-lə-ˌfō-\ n : use or operation of apparatus for transmission of sounds between distant points — **tel·e·phon·ic** \ˌte-lə-ˈfä-nik\ adj

tele·pho·to \ˌte-lə-ˈfō-tō\ adj : being a camera lens giving a large image of a distant object — **tele·pho·tog·ra·phy** \-fə-ˈtä-grə-fē\ n

tele·play \ˈte-li-ˌplā\ n : a play written for television

tele·print·er \ˈte-li-ˌprin-tər\ n : TELETYPEWRITER

¹tele·scope \ˈte-lə-ˌskōp\ n **1** : a cylindrical instrument equipped with lenses or mirrors for viewing distant objects **2** : RADIO TELESCOPE

²telescope vb **-scoped; -scop·ing 1** : to slide or pass or cause to slide or pass one within another like the sections of a collapsible hand telescope **2** : COMPRESS, CONDENSE

tele·scop·ic \ˌte-lə-ˈskä-pik\ adj **1** : of or relating to a telescope **2** : seen only by a telescope **3** : able to discern objects at a distance **4** : having parts that telescope — **tele·scop·i·cal·ly** \-pi-k(ə-)lē\ *adv*

tele·text \'te-lə-ˌtekst\ *n* : a system for broadcasting text over a television signal and displaying it on a decoder-equipped television

tele·thon \'te-lə-ˌthän\ *n* : a long television program usu. to solicit funds for a charity

tele·type·writ·er \ˌte-lə-'tīp-ˌrī-tər\ *n* : a printing device resembling a typewriter used to send and receive signals over telephone lines

tele·vise \'te-lə-ˌvīz\ *vb* **-vised; -vis·ing** : to broadcast by television

tele·vi·sion \'te-lə-ˌvi-zhən\ *n* [F *télévision*, fr. Gk *tēle* far, at a distance + F *vision* vision] : a system for transmitting images and sound by converting them into electrical or radio waves which are converted back into images and sound by a receiver; *also* : a television receiving set

tell \'tel\ *vb* **told** \'tōld\; **tell·ing 1** : COUNT, ENUMERATE **2** : to relate in detail : NARRATE **3** : SAY, UTTER **4** : to make known : REVEAL **5** : to report to : INFORM **6** : ORDER, DIRECT **7** : to find out by observing **8** : to have a marked effect **9** : to serve as evidence **syn** disclose, discover, betray

tell·er \'te-lər\ *n* **1** : one that relates : NARRATOR **2** : one that counts **3** : a bank employee handling money received or paid out

tell·ing \'te-liŋ\ *adj* : producing a marked effect : EFFECTIVE **syn** cogent, convincing, sound

tell off *vb* : REPRIMAND, SCOLD

tell·tale \'tel-ˌtāl\ *n* **1** : INFORMER, TATTLETALE **2** : something that serves to disclose : INDICATION — **telltale** *adj*

tel·lu·ri·um \tə-'lùr-ē-əm\ *n* : a chemical element used esp. in alloys — see ELEMENT table

tem·blor \'tem-blər\ *n* [Sp, lit., trembling] : EARTHQUAKE

te·mer·i·ty \tə-'mer-ə-tē\ *n, pl* **-ties** : rash or presumptuous daring : BOLDNESS **syn** audacity, effrontery, gall, nerve, cheek

¹temp \'temp\ *n* **1** : TEMPERATURE **2** : a temporary worker

²temp *abbr* temporary

¹tem·per \'tem-pər\ *vb* **1** : to dilute or soften by the addition of something else ⟨∼ justice with mercy⟩ **2** : to bring (as steel) to a desired hardness by reheating and cooling **3** : to toughen (glass) by gradual heating and cooling **4** : TOUGHEN **5** : TUNE

²temper *n* **1** : characteristic tone : TENDENCY **2** : the hardness or toughness of a substance ⟨∼ of a knife blade⟩ **3** : a characteristic frame of mind : DISPOSITION **4** : calmness of mind : COMPOSURE **5** : state of feeling or frame of mind at a particular time **6** : heat of mind or emotion **syn** temperament, character, personality, makeup — **tem·pered** \'tem-pərd\ *adj*

tem·pera \'tem-pə-rə\ *n* [It] : a painting process using an albuminous or colloidal medium as a vehicle; *also* : a painting done in tempera

tem·per·a·ment \'tem-prə-mənt, -pər-mənt\ *n* **1** : characteristic or habitual inclination or mode of emotional response : DISPOSITION ⟨nervous ∼⟩ **2** : excessive sensitiveness or irritability **syn** character, personality, nature, makeup — **tem·per·a·men·tal** \ˌtem-prə-'ment-ᵊl, -pər-'ment-\ *adj*

tem·per·ance \'tem-prəns, -pə-rəns\ *n* : habitual moderation in the indulgence of the appetites or passions; *esp* : moderation in or abstinence from the use of intoxicating drink

tem·per·ate \'tem-prət, -pə-rət\ *adj* **1** : not extreme or excessive : MILD **2** : moderate in indulgence of appetite or desire **3** : moderate in the use of intoxicating liquors **4** : having a moderate climate **syn** sober, continent, abstemious

temperate zone *n, often cap T&Z* : the region between the tropic of Cancer and the arctic circle or between the tropic of Capricorn and the antarctic circle

tem·per·a·ture \'tem-pər-ˌchùr, -prə-ˌchùr, -chər\ *n* **1** : degree of hotness or coldness of something (as air, water, or the body) as shown by a thermometer **2** : FEVER

tem·pest \'tem-pəst\ *n* [ME, fr. OF *tempeste*, ultim. fr. L *tempestas* season, weather, storm, fr. *tempus* time] : a violent storm

tem·pes·tu·ous \tem-'pes-chə-wəs\ *adj* : of, involving, or resembling a tempest : STORMY — **tem·pes·tu·ous·ly** *adv* — **tem·pes·tu·ous·ness** *n*

tem·plate *also* **tem·plet** \'tem-plət\ *n* : a gauge, mold, or pattern that functions as a guide to the form or structure of something being made

¹tem·ple \'tem-pəl\ *n* **1** : an edifice for the worship of a deity **2** : a place devoted to a special or exalted purpose

²temple *n* : the flattened space on each side of the forehead esp. of humans

tem·po \'tem-pō\ *n, pl* **tem·pi** \-(ˌ)pē\ *or* **tempos** [It, lit., time] **1** : the rate of speed of a musical piece or passage **2** : rate of motion or activity : PACE

¹tem·po·ral \'tem-pə-rəl\ *adj* **1** : of, relating to, or limited by time ⟨∼ and spatial bounds⟩ **2** : of or relating to earthly life or secular concerns ⟨∼ power⟩

²temporal *adj* : of or relating to the temples or the sides of the skull

¹tem·po·rary \'tem-pə-ˌrer-ē\ *adj* : lasting for a time only : TRANSITORY **syn** transient, ephemeral, momentary, impermanent — **tem·po·rar·i·ly** \ˌtem-pə-'rer-ə-lē\ *adv*

²temporary *n, pl* **-rar·ies** : one serving for a limited time

tem·po·rise *Brit var of* TEMPORIZE

tem·po·rize \'tem-pə-ˌrīz\ *vb* **-rized; -riz·ing 1** : to adapt one's actions to the time or the dominant opinion : COMPROMISE **2** : to draw out matters so as to gain time — **tem·po·riz·er** *n*

tempt \'tempt\ *vb* **1** : to entice to do wrong by promise of pleasure or gain **2** : PROVOKE **3** : to risk the dangers of **4** : to induce to do something : INCITE **syn** inveigle, decoy, seduce, lure — **tempt·er** *n* — **tempt·ing·ly** *adv*

temp·ta·tion \temp-'tā-shən\ *n* **1** : the act of tempting : the state of being tempted **2** : something that tempts

tempt·ress \'tempt-trəs\ *n* : a woman who tempts

ten \'ten\ *n* **1** : one more than nine **2** : the 10th in a set or series **3** : something having 10 units — **ten** *adj or pron* — **tenth** \'tenth\ *adj or adv or n*

ten·a·ble \'te-nə-bəl\ *adj* : capable of being held, maintained, or defended — **ten·a·bil·i·ty** \ˌte-nə-'bi-lə-tē\ *n*

te·na·cious \tə-'nā-shəs\ *adj* **1** : not easily pulled apart : COHESIVE, TOUGH ⟨a ∼ metal⟩ **2** : holding fast ⟨∼ of his rights⟩ **3** : RETENTIVE ⟨a ∼ memory⟩ — **te·na·cious·ly** *adv* — **te·nac·i·ty** \tə-'na-sə-tē\ *n*

ten·an·cy \'te-nən-sē\ *n, pl* **-cies** : the temporary possession or occupancy of something (as a house) that belongs to another; *also* : the period of a tenant's occupancy

ten·ant \'te-nənt\ *n* **1** : one who rents or leases (as a house) from a landlord **2** : DWELLER, OCCUPANT — **tenant** *vb* — **ten·ant·less** *adj*

tenant farmer *n* : a farmer who works land owned by another and pays rent either in cash or in shares of produce

ten·ant·ry \'te-nən-trē\ *n, pl* **-ries** : the body of tenants esp. on a great estate

Ten Commandments *n pl* : the commandments of God given to Moses on Mount Sinai

¹tend \'tend\ *vb* **1** : to apply oneself ⟨∼ to your affairs⟩ **2** : to take care of ⟨∼ a plant⟩ **3** : to manage the operations of ⟨∼ a machine⟩

²tend *vb* **1** : to move or develop one's course in a particular direction **2** : to show an inclination or tendency

ten·den·cy \'ten-dən-sē\ *n, pl* **-cies 1** : DRIFT, TREND **2**

: a proneness to or readiness for a particular kind of thought or action : PROPENSITY **syn** bent, leaning, disposition, inclination

ten·den·tious \ten-ˈden-chəs\ *adj* : marked by a tendency in favor of a particular point of view : BIASED — **ten·den·tious·ly** *adv* — **ten·den·tious·ness** *n*

¹ten·der \ˈten-dər\ *adj* **1** : having a soft texture : easily broken, chewed, or cut **2** : physically weak : DELICATE; *also* : IMMATURE **3** : expressing or responsive to love or sympathy : LOVING, COMPASSIONATE **4** : SENSITIVE, TOUCHY **syn** sympathetic, warm, warmhearted — **ten·der·ly** *adv* — **ten·der·ness** *n*

²tender *n* **1** : an offer or proposal made for acceptance; *esp* : an offer of a bid for a contract **2** : something (as money) that may be offered in payment

³tender *vb* : to present for acceptance

⁴tend·er \ˈten-dər\ *n* **1** : one that tends or takes care **2** : a boat carrying passengers and freight to a larger ship **3** : a car attached to a steam locomotive for carrying fuel and water

ten·der·foot \ˈten-dər-ˌfu̇t\ *n, pl* **-feet** \-ˌfēt\ *also* **-foots** \-ˌfu̇ts\ **1** : one not hardened to frontier or rough outdoor life **2** : an inexperienced beginner

ten·der·heart·ed \ˌten-dər-ˈhär-təd\ *adj* : easily moved to love, pity, or sorrow

ten·der·ize \ˈten-də-ˌrīz\ *vb* **-ized; -iz·ing** : to make (meat) tender — **ten·der·iz·er** \ˈten-də-ˌrī-zər\ *n*

ten·der·loin \ˈten-dər-ˌlȯin\ *n* **1** : a tender strip of beef or pork from near the backbone **2** : a district of a city largely devoted to vice

ten·di·ni·tis *or* **ten·don·itis** \ˌten-də-ˈnī-təs\ *n* : inflammation of a tendon

ten·don \ˈten-dən\ *n* : a tough cord of dense white fibrous tissue uniting a muscle with another part (as a bone) — **ten·di·nous** \-də-nəs\ *adj*

ten·dril \ˈten-drəl\ *n* : a slender coiling organ by which some climbing plants attach themselves to a support

ten·e·brous \ˈte-nə-brəs\ *adj* : shut off from the light : GLOOMY, OBSCURE

ten·e·ment \ˈte-nə-mənt\ *n* **1** : a house used as a dwelling **2** : a building divided into apartments for rent to families; *esp* : one meeting only minimum standards of safety and comfort **3** : APARTMENT, FLAT

te·net \ˈte-nət\ *n* [L, he holds, fr. *tenēre* to hold] : one of the principles or doctrines held in common by members of a group (as a church or profession) **syn** doctrine, dogma, belief

ten·fold \ˈten-ˌfōld, -ˈfōld\ *adj* : being 10 times as great or as many — **ten·fold** \-ˈfōld\ *adv*

ten-gallon hat *n* : a wide-brimmed hat with a large soft crown

Tenn *abbr* Tennessee

ten·nis \ˈte-nəs\ *n* : a game played with a ball and racket on a court divided by a net

ten·on \ˈte-nən\ *n* : a projecting part in a piece of ma-

terial (as wood) for insertion into a mortise to make a joint

ten·or \ˈte-nər\ *n* **1** : the general drift of something spoken or written **2** : the highest natural adult male voice; *also* : a singer having this voice **3** : a continuing in a course, movement, or activity ⟨the ∼ of my life⟩

ten·our *chiefly Brit var of* TENOR

ten·pen·ny \ˈten-ˌpe-nē\ *adj* : amounting to, worth, or costing 10 pennies

tenpenny nail *n* : a nail three inches (about 7.6 centimeters) long

ten·pin \ˈten-ˌpin\ *n* : a bottle-shaped bowling pin set in groups of 10 and bowled at in a game (**tenpins**)

¹tense \ˈtens\ *n* [ME *tens* time, tense, fr. MF, fr. L *tempus*] : distinction of form of a verb to indicate the time of the action or state

²tense *adj* **tens·er; tens·est** [L *tensus*, fr. pp. of *tendere* to stretch] **1** : stretched tight : TAUT **2** : feeling or showing nervous tension **syn** stiff, rigid, inflexible — **tense·ly** *adv* — **tense·ness** *n* — **ten·si·ty** \ˈten-sə-tē\ *n*

³tense *vb* **tensed; tens·ing** : to make or become tense

ten·sile \ˈten-səl, -ˌsīl\ *adj* : of or relating to tension ⟨∼ strength⟩

ten·sion \ˈten-chən\ *n* **1** : the act of straining or stretching; *also* : the condition of being strained or stretched **2** : a state of mental unrest often with signs of bodily stress **3** : a state of latent hostility or opposition

ten–speed \ˈten-ˌspēd\ *n* : a bicycle with a derailleur having 10 possible combinations of gears

¹tent \ˈtent\ *n* **1** : a collapsible shelter of material stretched and supported by poles **2** : a canopy placed over the head and shoulders to retain vapors or oxygen given for medical reasons

²tent *vb* **1** : to lodge in tents **2** : to cover with or as if with a tent

ten·ta·cle \ˈten-ti-kəl\ *n* : any of various long flexible projections about the head or mouth (as of an insect, mollusk, or fish) — **ten·ta·cled** \-kəld\ *adj* — **ten·tac·u·lar** \ten-ˈta-kyə-lər\ *adj*

ten·ta·tive \ˈten-tə-tiv\ *adj* **1** : not fully worked out or developed ⟨∼ plans⟩ **2** : HESITANT, UNCERTAIN ⟨a ∼ smile⟩ — **ten·ta·tive·ly** *adv*

ten·u·ous \ˈten-yə-wəs\ *adj* **1** : not dense : RARE ⟨a ∼ fluid⟩ **2** : not thick : SLENDER ⟨a ∼ rope⟩ **3** : having little substance : FLIMSY, WEAK ⟨∼ influences⟩ **4** : lacking stability : SHAKY ⟨∼ reasoning⟩ — **te·nu·i·ty** \te-ˈnü-ə-tē, tə-, -ˈnyü-\ *n* — **ten·u·ous·ly** *adv* — **ten·u·ous·ness** *n*

ten·ure \ˈten-yər\ *n* : the act, right, manner, or period of holding something (as a landed property, an office, or a position)

ten·ured \ˈten-yərd\ *adj* : having tenure ⟨∼ faculty members⟩

te·o·sin·te \ˌtā-ō-ˈsin-tē\ *n* : a tall annual grass of Mexico and Central America closely related to maize

te·pee \ˈtē-(ˌ)pē\ *n* [Dakota *tʰípi*, fr. *tʰi-* to dwell] : an American Indian conical tent usu. of skins

tep·id \ˈte-pəd\ *adj* **1** : moderately warm : LUKEWARM **2** : HALFHEARTED

te·qui·la \tə-'kē-lə, tā-\ *n* : a Mexican liquor made from mescal

ter *abbr* **1** terrace **2** territory

ter·bi·um \'tər-bē-əm\ *n* : a metallic chemical element — see ELEMENT table

ter·cen·te·na·ry \ˌtər-ˌsen-'te-nə-rē, tər-'sent-ᵊn-ˌer-ē\ *n, pl* **-ries** : a 300th anniversary or its celebration — **tercentenary** *adj*

ter·cen·ten·ni·al \ˌtər-ˌsen-'te-nē-əl\ *adj or n* : TERCEN-TENARY

te·re·do \tə-'rē-dō, -'rā-\ *n, pl* **teredos** *or* **te·red·i·nes** \-'red-ᵊn-ˌēz\ [L] : SHIPWORM

¹term \'tərm\ *n* **1** : END, TERMINATION **2** : DURATION; *esp* : a period of time fixed esp. by law or custom **3** : a mathematical expression connected with another by a plus or minus sign; *also* : an element (as a numerator) of a fraction or proportion **4** : a word or expression that has a precise meaning in some uses or is limited to a particular subject or field **5** *pl* : PRO-VISIONS, CONDITIONS ⟨~s of a contract⟩ **6** *pl* : mutual relationship ⟨on good ~s⟩ **7** : AGREEMENT, CONCORD

²term *vb* : to apply a term to : CALL

ter·ma·gant \'tər-mə-gənt\ *n* : an overbearing or nagging woman : SHREW

¹ter·mi·nal \'tər-mən-ᵊl\ *adj* **1** : of, relating to, or forming an end, limit, or terminus **2** : being or being in the final stages of a fatal disease ⟨a ~ patient⟩ ⟨~ illness⟩ **syn** final, concluding, last, latest — **ter·mi·nal·ly** *adv*

²terminal *n* **1** : EXTREMITY, END **2** : a device at the end of a wire or on electrical equipment for making a connection **3** : either end of a transportation line (as a railroad) with its offices and freight and passenger stations; *also* : a freight or passenger station **4** : a device (as in a computer system) for data entry and display

ter·mi·nate \'tər-mə-ˌnāt\ *vb* **-nat·ed; -nat·ing** : to bring or come to an end **syn** conclude, finish, complete — **ter·mi·na·ble** \-nə-bəl\ *adj* — **ter·mi·na·tion** \ˌtər-mə-'nā-shən\ *n* — **ter·mi·na·tor** \'tər-mə-ˌnā-tər\ *n*

ter·mi·nol·o·gy \ˌtər-mə-'nä-lə-jē\ *n, pl* **-gies** : the technical or special terms used in a business, art, science, or special subject

ter·mi·nus \'tər-mə-nəs\ *n, pl* **-ni** \-ˌnī\ *or* **-nus·es** [L] **1** : final goal : END **2** : either end of a transportation line or travel route; *also* : the station or city at such a place

ter·mite \'tər-ˌmīt\ *n* : any of numerous pale soft-bodied social insects that feed on wood

tern \'tərn\ *n* : any of various chiefly marine birds with narrow wings and often a forked tail

ter·na·ry \'tər-nə-rē\ *adj* **1** : of, relating to, or proceeding by threes **2** : having three elements or parts

terr *abbr* territory

¹ter·race \'ter-əs\ *n* **1** : a flat roof or open platform **2** : a level area next to a building **3** : an embankment with level top **4** : a bank or ridge on a slope to conserve moisture and soil **5** : a row of houses on raised land; *also* : a street with such a row of houses **6** : a strip of park in the middle of a street

²terrace *vb* **ter·raced; ter·rac·ing** : to form into a terrace or supply with terraces

ter·ra–cot·ta \ˌter-ə-'kä-tə\ *n* [It *terra cotta*, lit., baked earth] : a reddish brown earthenware

terra fir·ma \-'fər-mə\ *n* [NL] : solid ground

ter·rain \tə-'rān\ *n* : the surface features of an area of land ⟨a rough ~⟩

ter·ra in·cog·ni·ta \ˌter-ə-ˌin-ˌkäg-'nē-tə\ *n, pl* **ter·rae in·cog·ni·tae** \'ter-ˌī-ˌin-ˌkäg-'nē-tī\ [L] : an unexplored area or field of knowledge

ter·ra·pin \'ter-ə-pən\ *n* : any of various turtles of fresh or brackish water

ter·rar·i·um \tə-'rar-ē-əm\ *n, pl* **-ia** \-ē-ə\ *or* **-i·ums** : a usu. transparent enclosure for keeping or raising small plants and animals indoors

ter·res·tri·al \tə-'res-trē-əl\ *adj* **1** : of or relating to the

earth or its inhabitants **2** : living or growing on land ⟨~ plants⟩ **syn** mundane, earthly, worldly

ter·ri·ble \'ter-ə-bəl\ *adj* **1** : exciting terror : FEARFUL, DREADFUL ⟨~ weapons⟩ **2** : hard to bear : DISTRESSING ⟨a ~ situation⟩ **3** : extreme in degree : INTENSE ⟨~ heat⟩ **4** : of very poor quality : AWFUL ⟨a ~ play⟩ **syn** frightful, horrible, shocking, appalling — **ter·ri·bly** \-blē\ *adv*

ter·ri·er \'ter-ē-ər\ *n* [F ⟨*chien*⟩ *terrier*, lit., earth dog, fr. *terrier* of earth, fr. ML *terrarius*, fr. L *terra* earth] : any of various usu. small dogs orig. used by hunters to drive small game animals from their holes

ter·rif·ic \tə-'ri-fik\ *adj* **1** : exciting terror **2** : EXTRAOR-DINARY, ASTOUNDING ⟨~ speed⟩ **3** : unusually good ⟨makes ~ chili⟩

ter·ri·fy \'ter-ə-ˌfī\ *vb* **-fied; -fy·ing** : to fill with terror : FRIGHTEN **syn** scare, terrorize, startle, alarm — **ter·ri·fy·ing·ly** *adv*

ter·ri·to·ry \'ter-ə-ˌtōr-ē\ *n, pl* **-ries 1** : a geographical area belonging to or under the jurisdiction of a governmental authority **2** : a part of the U.S. not included within any state but organized with a separate legislature **3** : REGION, DISTRICT; *also* : a region in which one feels at home **4** : a field of knowledge or interest **5** : an assigned area **6** : an area occupied and defended by one or a group of animals — **ter·ri·to·ri·al** \ˌter-ə-'tōr-ē-əl\ *adj*

ter·ror \'ter-ər\ *n* **1** : a state of intense fear : FRIGHT **2** : one that inspires fear **syn** panic, consternation, dread, alarm, dismay, horror, trepidation

ter·ror·ise *chiefly Brit var of* TERRORIZE

ter·ror·ism \'ter-ər-ˌi-zəm\ *n* : the systematic use of terror esp. as a means of coercion — **ter·ror·ist** \-ist\ *adj or n*

ter·ror·ize \'ter-ər-ˌīz\ *vb* **-ized; -iz·ing 1** : to fill with terror : SCARE **2** : to coerce by threat or violence **syn** terrify, frighten, alarm, startle

ter·ry \'ter-ē\ *n, pl* **terries** : an absorbent fabric with a loose pile of uncut loops

terse \'tərs\ *adj* **ters·er; ters·est** [L *tersus* clean, neat, fr. pp. of *tergēre* to wipe off] : effectively brief : CON-CISE — **terse·ly** *adv* — **terse·ness** *n*

ter·ti·ary \'tər-shē-ˌer-ē\ *adj* **1** : of third rank, importance, or value **2** *cap* : of, relating to, or being the earlier period of the Cenozoic era **3** : occurring in or being the third stage

Tertiary *n* : the Tertiary period

TESL *abbr* teaching English as a second language

TESOL *abbr* Teachers of English to Speakers of Other Languages

¹test \'test\ *n* [ME, vessel in which metals were assayed, fr. MF, fr. L *testum* earthen vessel] **1** : a critical examination or evaluation : TRIAL **2** : a means or result of testing

²test *vb* **1** : to put to test : TRY, EXAMINE **2** : to undergo or score on tests

tes·ta·ment \'tes-tə-mənt\ *n* **1** *cap* : either of two main divisions of the Bible **2** : EVIDENCE, WITNESS **3** : CRE-DO **4** : the legal instructions for the disposition of one's property after death : WILL — **tes·ta·men·ta·ry** \ˌtes-tə-'men-tə-rē\ *adj*

tes·tate \'tes-ˌtāt, -tət\ *adj* : having left a valid will

tes·ta·tor \'tes-ˌtā-tər, tes-'tā-\ *n* : a person who dies leaving a valid will

tes·ta·trix \tes-'tā-triks\ *n* : a female testator

¹tes·ter \'tēs-tər, 'tes-\ *n* : a canopy over a bed, pulpit, or altar

²test·er \'tes-tər\ *n* : one that tests

tes·ti·cle \'tes-ti-kəl\ *n* : TESTIS; *esp* : one of a higher mammal usu. with its enclosing structures

tes·ti·fy \'tes-tə-ˌfī\ *vb* **-fied; -fy·ing 1** : to make a statement based on personal knowledge or belief : bear witness **2** : to serve as evidence or proof

tes·ti·mo·ni·al \ˌtes-tə-'mō-nē-əl\ *n* **1** : a statement testifying to benefits received; *also* : a character ref-

erence **2** : an expression of appreciation : TRIBUTE —
testimonial *adj*

tes·ti·mo·ny \'tes-tə-ˌmō-nē\ *n, pl* **-nies 1** : evidence
based on observation or knowledge **2** : an outward
sign : SYMBOL **3** : a solemn declaration made by a witness under oath esp. in a court **syn** evidence, confirmation, proof, testament

tes·tis \'tes-təs\ *n, pl* **tes·tes** \'tes-ˌtēz\ [L, witness, tes-
tis] : a typically paired male reproductive gland that
produces sperm and in most mammals is contained
within the scrotum at sexual maturity

tes·tos·ter·one \te-'stäs-tə-ˌrōn\ *n* : a male sex hormone causing development of the male reproductive
system and secondary sex characteristics

test tube *n* : a glass tube closed at one end and used
esp. in chemistry and biology

tes·ty \'tes-tē\ *adj* **tes·ti·er; -est** [ME *testif*, fr. Anglo⹀
French (the French of medieval England), head-
strong, fr. OF *teste* head, fr. LL *testa* skull, fr. L,
shell] : easily annoyed; *also* : marked by ill humor

tet·a·nus \'tet-ᵊn-əs\ *n* : an infectious disease caused
by bacterial poisons and marked by muscle stiffness
and spasms esp. of the jaws — **tet·a·nal** \-əl\ *adj*

tetchy \'te-chē\ *adj* **tetchi·er; -est** : irritably or peevishly sensitive

¹tête-à-tête \'tāt-ə-ˌtāt\ *n* [F, lit., head to head] : a private conversation between two persons

²tête-à-tête \ˌtāt-ə-'tāt\ *adv* : in private

³tête-à-tête \'tāt-ə-ˌtāt\ *adj* : being face-to-face : PRI-
VATE

¹teth·er \'te-thər\ *n* **1** : something (as a rope) by which
an animal is fastened **2** : the limit of one's strength or
resources

²tether *vb* : to fasten or restrain by or as if by a tether

tet·ra·eth·yl lead \ˌte-trə-'e-thəl-\ *n* : a heavy oily poisonous liquid used as an antiknock agent in gasoline

tet·ra·he·dron \-'hē-drən\ *n, pl* **-drons** *or* **-dra** \-drə\ : a
polyhedron that has four faces — **tet·ra·he·dral**
\-drəl\ *adj*

tet·ra·hy·dro·can·nab·i·nol　\-ˌhī-drə-kə-'na-bə-ˌnôl,
-ˌnōl\ *n* : THC

te·tram·e·ter \te-'tra-mə-tər\ *n* : a line of verse consisting of four metrical feet

Teu·ton·ic \tü-'tä-nik, tyü-\ *adj* : GERMANIC

Tex *abbr* Texas

text \'tekst\ *n* **1** : the actual words of an author's work
2 : the main body of printed or written matter on a
page **3** : a scriptural passage chosen as the subject
esp. of a sermon **4** : THEME, TOPIC **5** : TEXTBOOK —
tex·tu·al \'teks-chə-wəl\ *adj*

text·book \'tekst-ˌbúk\ *n* : a book used in the study of
a subject

tex·tile \'tek-ˌstīl, 'tekst-ᵊl\ *n* : CLOTH; *esp* : a woven
or knit cloth

tex·ture \'teks-chər\ *n* **1** : the visual or tactile surface
characteristics and appearance of something (a
coarse ~) **2** : essential part **3** : basic scheme or structure : FABRIC **4** : overall structure

TGIF *abbr* thank God it's Friday

¹Th *abbr* Thursday

²Th *symbol* thorium

¹-th — see ¹-ETH

²-th *or* **-eth** *adj suffix* — used in forming ordinal numbers ⟨hundred*th*⟩

³-th *n suffix* **1** : act or process **2** : state or condition
⟨dear*th*⟩

Thai \'tī\ *n, pl* **Thai** *or* **Thais 1** : a native or inhabitant
of Thailand **2** : the official language of Thailand —
Thai *adj*

thal·a·mus \'tha-lə-məs\ *n, pl* **-mi** \-ˌmī\ [NL] : a subdivision of the brain that serves as a relay station to
and from the cerebral cortex and functions in arousal
and the integration of sensory information

thal·li·um \'tha-lē-əm\ *n* : a poisonous metallic chemical element — see ELEMENT table

¹than \'thən, ˌthan\ *conj* **1** — used after a comparative
adjective or adverb to introduce the second part of a
comparison expressing inequality ⟨older ~ I am⟩ **2**
— used after *other* or a word of similar meaning to
express a difference of kind, manner, or identity
⟨adults other ~ parents⟩

²than *prep* : in comparison with ⟨older ~ me⟩

thane \'thān\ *n* **1** : a free retainer of an Anglo⹀
Saxon lord **2** : a Scottish feudal lord

thank \'thank\ *vb* : to express gratitude to ⟨~ed them
for the present⟩

thank·ful \'thank-fəl\ *adj* **1** : conscious of
benefit received **2** : expressive of thanks
3 : GLAD — **thank·ful·ness** *n*

thank·ful·ly \-fə-lē\ *adv* **1** : in a thankful manner **2** :
makes one thankful

thank·less \'thank-kləs\ *adj* **1** : UNGRATEFUL **2** : UNAP-
PRECIATED

thanks \'thanks\ *n pl* : an expression of gratitude

thanks·giv·ing \thanks-'gi-vin\ *n* **1** : the act of giving
thanks **2** : a prayer expressing gratitude **3** *cap* : the
4th Thursday in November observed as a legal holiday for giving thanks for divine goodness

¹that \'that, thət\ *pron, pl* **those** \'thōz\ **1** : the one indicated, mentioned, or understood ⟨~ is my house⟩ **2**
: the one farther away or first mentioned ⟨this is an
elm, ~'s a maple⟩ **3** : what has been indicated or
mentioned ⟨after ~, we left⟩ **4** : the one or ones : IT,
THEY ⟨*those* who wish to leave may do so⟩

²that \thət, 'that\ *conj* **1** : the following, namely ⟨he said
~ he would⟩; *also* : which is, namely ⟨there's a
chance ~ it may fail⟩ **2** : to this end or purpose
⟨shouted ~ all might hear⟩ **3** : as to result in the following, namely ⟨so heavy ~ it can't be moved⟩ **4** : for
this reason, namely : BECAUSE ⟨we're glad ~ you
came⟩

³that *adj, pl* **those 1** : being the one mentioned, indicated, or understood ⟨~ boy⟩ ⟨*those* people⟩ **2** : being
the one farther away or less immediately under discussion ⟨this chair or ~ one⟩

⁴that \thət, 'that\ *pron* **1** : WHO, WHOM, WHICH ⟨the man
~ saw you⟩ ⟨the man ~ you saw⟩ ⟨the money ~ was

spent⟩ **2** : in, on, or at which ⟨the way ∼ he drives⟩ ⟨the day ∼ it rained⟩

⁵that \ˈthat\ *adv* : to such an extent or degree ⟨I like it, but not ∼ much⟩

¹thatch \ˈthach\ *vb* : to cover with or as if with thatch — **thatch·er** *n*

²thatch *n* **1** : plant material (as straw) for use as roofing **2** : a mat of grass clippings accumulated next to the soil on a lawn **3** : a covering of or as if of thatch ⟨a ∼ of white hair⟩

thaw \ˈthȯ\ *vb* **1** : to melt or cause to melt **2** : to become so warm as to melt ice or snow **3** : to abandon aloofness or hostility — **thaw** *n*

THC \ˌtē-(ˌ)āch-ˈsē\ *n* [*tetra*hydro*cannabinol*] : a physiologically active chemical from hemp plant resin that is the chief intoxicant in marijuana

¹the \thə, *before vowel sounds usu* thē\ *definite article* **1** : that in particular **2** — used before adjectives functioning as nouns ⟨a word to ∼ wise⟩

²the *adv* **1** : to what extent ⟨∼ sooner, the better⟩ **2** : to that extent ⟨the sooner, ∼ better⟩

theat *abbr* theater; theatrical

the·ater *or* **the·atre** \ˈthē-ə-tər\ *n* [ME *theatre*, fr. MF, fr. L *theatrum*, fr. Gk *theatron*, fr. *theasthai* to view, fr. *thea* act of seeing] **1** : a building for dramatic performances; *also* : a building or area for showing motion pictures **2** : a place of enactment of significant events ⟨∼ of war⟩ **3** : a place (as a lecture room) resembling a theater **4** : dramatic literature or performance

theater–in–the–round *n* : a theater with the stage in the center of the auditorium

the·at·ri·cal \thē-ˈa-tri-kəl\ *also* **the·at·ric** \-trik\ *adj* **1** : of or relating to the theater **2** : marked by artificiality of emotion : HISTRIONIC **3** : marked by extravagant display : SHOWY

the·at·ri·cals \-kəlz\ *n pl* : the performance of plays

the·at·rics \thē-ˈa-triks\ *n pl* **1** : THEATRICALS **2** : staged or contrived effects

the·be \ˈthā-bā\ *n, pl* **thebe** — see *pula* at MONEY table

thee \ˈt͟hē\ *pron, archaic objective case of* THOU

theft \ˈtheft\ *n* : the act of stealing

thegn \ˈthān\ *n* : THANE 1

their \t͟hər, ˈt͟her\ *adj* : of or relating to them or themselves

theirs \ˈt͟herz\ *pron* : their one : their ones

the·ism \ˈthē-ˌi-zəm\ *n* : belief in the existence of a god or gods — **the·ist** \-ist\ *n or adj* — **the·is·tic** \thē-ˈis-tik\ *adj*

them \t͟həm, ˈt͟hem\ *pron, objective case of* THEY

theme \ˈthēm\ *n* **1** : a subject or topic of discourse or of artistic representation **2** : a written exercise : COMPOSITION **3** : a melodic subject of a musical composition or movement — **the·mat·ic** \thi-ˈma-tik\ *adj*

them·selves \t͟həm-ˈselvz, them-\ *pron pl* : THEY, THEM — used reflexively, for emphasis, or in absolute constructions ⟨they govern ∼⟩ ⟨they ∼ came⟩ ⟨∼ busy, they sent me⟩

¹then \ˈt͟hen\ *adv* **1** : at that time **2** : soon after that : NEXT **3** : in addition : BESIDES **4** : in that case **5** : CONSEQUENTLY

²then *n* : that time ⟨since ∼⟩

³then *adj* : existing or acting at that time ⟨the ∼ attorney general⟩

thence \ˈt͟hens, ˈt͟hens\ *adv* **1** : from that place **2** *archaic* : THENCEFORTH **3** : from that fact : THEREFROM

thence·forth \-ˌfȯrth\ *adv* : from that time forward : THEREAFTER

thence·for·ward \t͟hens-ˈfȯr-wərd, thens-\ *also* **thence·for·wards** \-wərdz\ *adv* : onward from that place or time

the·oc·ra·cy \thē-ˈä-krə-sē\ *n, pl* **-cies 1** : government by officials regarded as divinely inspired **2** : a state governed by a theocracy — **the·o·crat·ic** \ˌthē-ə-ˈkra-tik\ *adj*

theol *abbr* theological; theology

the·ol·o·gy \thē-ˈä-lə-jē\ *n, pl* **-gies 1** : the study of religious faith, practice, and experience; *esp* : the study of God and of God's relation to the world **2** : a theory or system of theology — **the·o·lo·gian** \ˌthē-ə-ˈlō-jən\ *n* — **the·o·log·i·cal** \-ˈlä-ji-kəl\ *adj*

the·o·rem \ˈthē-ə-rəm, ˈthir-əm\ *n* **1** : a statement esp. in mathematics that has been or is to be proved **2** : an idea accepted or proposed as a demonstrable truth : PROPOSITION

the·o·ret·i·cal \ˌthē-ə-ˈre-ti-kəl\ *also* **the·o·ret·ic** \-tik\ *adj* **1** : relating to or having the character of theory **2** : existing only in theory : HYPOTHETICAL — **the·o·ret·i·cal·ly** \-ti-k(ə-)lē\ *adv*

the·o·rise *Brit var of* THEORIZE

the·o·rize \ˈthē-ə-ˌrīz\ *vb* **-rized; -riz·ing** : to form a theory : SPECULATE — **the·o·rist** \-rist\ *n*

the·o·ry \ˈthē-ə-rē, ˈthir-ē\ *n, pl* **-ries 1** : abstract thought **2** : the general principles of a subject **3** : a plausible or scientifically acceptable general principle offered to explain observed facts **4** : HYPOTHESIS, CONJECTURE

theory of games : GAME THEORY

the·os·o·phy \thē-ˈä-sə-fē\ *n* : belief about God and the world held to be based on mystical insight — **theo·soph·i·cal** \ˌthē-ə-ˈsä-fi-kəl\ *adj* — **the·os·o·phist** \thē-ˈä-sə-fist\ *n*

ther·a·peu·tic \ˌther-ə-ˈpyü-tik\ *adj* [Gk *therapeutikos*, fr. *therapeuein* to attend, treat, fr. *theraps* attendant] : of, relating to, or dealing with healing and esp. with remedies for diseases — **ther·a·peu·ti·cal·ly** \-ti-k(ə-)lē\ *adv*

ther·a·peu·tics \ˌther-ə-ˈpyü-tiks\ *n* : a branch of medical or dental science dealing with the use of remedies

ther·a·py \ˈther-ə-pē\ *n, pl* **-pies** : treatment of bodily, mental, or behavioral disorders — **ther·a·pist** \-pist\ *n*

¹there \ˈt͟her, ˈt͟her\ *adv* **1** : in or at that place — often used interjectionally **2** : to or into that place : THITHER **3** : in that matter or respect

²there \ˈt͟her, ˈt͟her, t͟hər\ *pron* — used as a function word to introduce a sentence or clause ⟨∼'s a pen here⟩

³there \ˈt͟her, ˈt͟her\ *n* **1** : that place ⟨get away from ∼⟩ **2** : that point ⟨you take it from ∼⟩

there·abouts \ˌt͟her-ə-ˈbau̇ts, ˌt͟her-; ˈt͟her-ə-ˌbau̇ts, ˈt͟her-\ *or* **there·about** \-ˈbau̇t, -ˌbau̇t\ *adv* **1** : near that place or time **2** : near that number, degree, or quantity

there·af·ter \t͟her-ˈaf-tər, t͟her-\ *adv* : after that : AFTERWARD

there·at \-ˈat\ *adv* **1** : at that place **2** : at that occurrence : on that account

there·by \t͟her-ˈbī, t͟her-, ˈt͟her-ˌbī, ˈt͟her-ˌbī\ *adv* **1** : by that : by that means **2** : connected with or with reference to that

there·for \t͟her-ˈfȯr, t͟her-\ *adv* : for or in return for that

there·fore \ˈt͟her-ˌfȯr, ˈt͟her-\ *adv* : for that reason : CONSEQUENTLY

there·from \t͟her-ˈfrəm, t͟her-\ *adv* : from that or it

there·in \t͟her-ˈin, t͟her-\ *adv* **1** : in or into that place, time, or thing **2** : in that respect

there·of \-ˈəv, -ˈäv\ *adv* **1** : of that or it **2** : from that : THEREFROM

there·on \-ˈȯn, -ˈän\ *adv* **1** : on that **2** *archaic* : THEREUPON 3

there·to \t͟her-ˈtü, t͟her-\ *adv* : to that

there·un·to \ˌt͟her-ˈən-(ˌ)tü; ˌt͟her-ən-ˈtü, ˌt͟her-\ *adv, archaic* : THERETO

there·upon \ˈt͟her-ə-ˌpȯn, ˈt͟her-, -ˌpän; ˌt͟her-ə-ˈpȯn, -ˈpän, ˌt͟her-\ *adv* **1** : on that matter **2** : THEREFORE **3** : immediately after that : at once

there·with \t͟her-ˈwith, t͟her-, -ˈwit͟h\ *adv* **1** : with that **2** *archaic* : THEREUPON, FORTHWITH

there·with·al \ˈt͟her-wi-ˌt͟hȯl, ˈt͟her-, -ˌt͟hȯl\ *adv* **1** *archaic* : BESIDES **2** : THEREWITH

therm *abbr* thermometer

ther·mal \\'thər-məl\\ adj 1 : of, relating to, or caused by heat 2 : designed to prevent the loss of body heat ⟨~ underwear⟩ — **ther·mal·ly** adv

thermal pollution n : the discharge of heated liquid (as waste water from a factory) into natural waters at a temperature harmful to the environment

therm·is·tor \\'thər-ˌmis-tər\\ n : an electrical resistor whose resistance varies sharply with temperature

ther·mo·cline \\'thər-mə-ˌklīn\\ n : the region in a thermally stratified body of water that separates warmer surface water from cold deep water

ther·mo·cou·ple \\'thər-mə-ˌkə-pəl\\ n : a device for measuring temperature by measuring the temperature-dependent potential difference created at the junction of two dissimilar metals

ther·mo·dy·nam·ics \\ˌthər-mə-dī-ˈna-miks\\ n : physics that deals with the mechanical action or relations of heat — **ther·mo·dy·nam·ic** \\-mik\\ adj — **ther·mo·dy·nam·i·cal·ly** \\-mi-k(ə-)lē\\ adv

ther·mom·e·ter \\thər-ˈmä-mə-tər\\ n [F thermomètre, fr. Gk thermē heat + metron measure] : an instrument for measuring temperature typically by the rise or fall of a liquid (as mercury) in a thin glass tube — **ther·mo·met·ric** \\ˌthər-mə-ˈme-trik\\ adj — **ther·mo·met·ri·cal·ly** \\-tri-k(ə-)lē\\ adv

ther·mo·nu·cle·ar \\ˌthər-mō-ˈnü-klē-ər, -ˈnyü-\\ adj 1 : of or relating to changes in the nucleus of atoms of low atomic weight (as hydrogen) that require a very high temperature (as in the hydrogen bomb) 2 : utilizing or relating to a thermonuclear bomb ⟨~ war⟩

ther·mo·plas·tic \\ˌthər-mə-ˈplas-tik\\ adj : capable of softening when heated and of hardening again when cooled ⟨~ resins⟩ — **thermoplastic** n

ther·mos \\'thər-məs\\ n : a cylindrical container with a vacuum between an inner and an outer wall used to keep liquids hot or cold

ther·mo·sphere \\'thər-mə-ˌsfir\\ n : the part of the earth's atmosphere that lies above the mesosphere and that is characterized by steadily increasing temperature with height

ther·mo·stat \\'thər-mə-ˌstat\\ n : a device that automatically controls temperature — **ther·mo·stat·ic** \\ˌthər-mə-ˈsta-tik\\ adj — **ther·mo·stat·i·cal·ly** \\-ti-k(ə-)lē\\ adv

the·sau·rus \\thi-ˈsȯr-əs\\ n, pl **-sau·ri** \\-ˈsȯr-ˌī\\ or **-sau·rus·es** \\-ˈsȯr-ə-səz\\ [NL, fr. L, treasure, collection, fr. Gk thēsauros] : a book of words and their synonyms — **the·sau·ral** \\-ˈsȯr-əl\\ adj

these pl of THIS

the·sis \\'thē-səs\\ n, pl **the·ses** \\'thē-ˌsēz\\ 1 : a proposition that a person advances and offers to maintain by argument 2 : an essay embodying results of original research; esp : one written for an academic degree

¹thes·pi·an \\'thes-pē-ən\\ adj, often cap [fr. Thespis, 6th cent. B.C. Greek poet and reputed originator of tragedy] : relating to the drama : DRAMATIC

²thespian n : ACTOR

Thess abbr Thessalonians

Thes·sa·lo·nians \\ˌthe-sə-ˈlō-nyənz, -nē-ənz\\ n — see BIBLE table

the·ta \\'thā-tə\\ n : the 8th letter of the Greek alphabet — Θ or θ

thew \\'thü, 'thyü\\ n : MUSCLE, SINEW — usu. used in pl.

they \\'thā\\ pron 1 : those individuals under discussion : the ones previously mentioned or referred to 2 : unspecified persons : PEOPLE

thi·a·mine \\'thī-ə-mən, -ˌmēn\\ also **thi·a·min** \\-mən\\ n : a vitamin of the vitamin B complex essential to normal metabolism and nerve function

¹thick \\'thik\\ adj 1 : having relatively great depth or extent from one surface to its opposite ⟨a ~ plank⟩; also : heavily built : THICKSET 2 : densely massed : CROWDED; also : FREQUENT, NUMEROUS 3 : dense or viscous in consistency ⟨~ syrup⟩ 4 : marked by haze,

fog, or mist ⟨~ weather⟩ 5 : measuring in thickness ⟨one meter ~⟩ 6 : imperfectly articulated : INDISTINCT ⟨~ speech⟩ 7 : STUPID, OBTUSE 8 : associated on close terms : INTIMATE 9 : EXCESSIVE syn compact, close, tight — **thick·ly** adv

²thick n 1 : the most crowded or active part 2 : the part of greatest thickness

thick·en \\'thi-kən\\ vb : to make or become thick — **thick·en·er** n

thick·et \\'thi-kət\\ n : a dense growth of bushes or small trees

thick·ness \\-nəs\\ n 1 : the smallest of three dimensions ⟨length, width, and ~⟩ 2 : the quality or state of being thick 3 : LAYER, SHEET ⟨a single ~ of canvas⟩

thick·set \\'thik-ˈset\\ adj 1 : closely placed or planted 2 : having a thick body : BURLY

thick–skinned \\-ˈskind\\ adj 1 : having a thick skin 2 : not easily bothered by criticism or insult

thief \\'thēf\\ n, pl **thieves** \\'thēvz\\ : one that steals esp. secretly

thieve \\'thēv\\ vb **thieved; thiev·ing** : STEAL, ROB syn filch, pilfer, purloin, swipe

thiev·ery \\'thē-və-rē\\ n, pl **-er·ies** : the act of stealing : THEFT

thigh \\'thī\\ n : the part of the vertebrate hind limb between the knee and the hip

thigh·bone \\'thī-ˌbōn\\ n : FEMUR

thim·ble \\'thim-bəl\\ n : a cap or guard worn on the finger to push the needle in sewing — **thim·ble·ful** n

¹thin \\'thin\\ adj **thin·ner; thin·nest** 1 : having little extent from one surface through to its opposite : not thick : SLENDER 2 : not closely set or placed : SPARSE ⟨~ hair⟩ 3 : not dense or not dense enough : more fluid or rarefied than normal ⟨~ air⟩ ⟨~ syrup⟩ 4 : lacking substance, fullness, or strength ⟨~ broth⟩ 5 : FLIMSY — **thin·ly** adv — **thin·ness** n

²thin vb **thinned; thin·ning** : to make or become thin

thine \\'thīn\\ pron, archaic : one or the ones belonging to thee

thing \\'thiŋ\\ n 1 : a matter of concern : AFFAIR ⟨~s to do⟩ 2 pl : state of affairs ⟨~s are improving⟩ 3 : EVENT, CIRCUMSTANCE ⟨the crime was a terrible ~⟩ 4 : DEED, ACT ⟨expected great ~s of him⟩ 5 : a distinct entity : OBJECT 6 : an inanimate object distinguished from a living being 7 pl : POSSESSIONS, EFFECTS 8 : an article of clothing 9 : DETAIL, POINT 10 : IDEA, NOTION 11 : something one likes to do : SPECIALTY ⟨doing her ~⟩

think \\'thiŋk\\ vb **thought** \\'thȯt\\; **think·ing** 1 : to form or have in the mind 2 : to have as an opinion : BELIEVE 3 : to reflect on : PONDER 4 : to call to mind : REMEMBER 5 : REASON 6 : to form a mental picture of : IMAGINE 7 : to devise by thinking ⟨thought up a plan to escape⟩ syn conceive, fancy, realize, envisage — **think·er** n

think tank n : an institute, corporation, or group organized for interdisciplinary research (as in technological or social problems)

thin·ner \\'thi-nər\\ n : a volatile liquid (as turpentine) used to thin paint

thin–skinned \\'thin-ˈskind\\ adj 1 : having a thin skin 2 : extremely sensitive to criticism or insult

¹third \\'thərd\\ adj : next after the second — **third** or **third·ly** adv

²third n 1 : one of three equal parts of something 2 : one that is number three in a countable series 3 : the 3d forward gear in an automotive vehicle

third degree n : the subjection of a prisoner to mental or physical torture to force a confession

third dimension n 1 : thickness, depth, or apparent thickness or depth that confers solidity on an object 2 : a quality that confers reality — **third–dimensional** adj

third world n, often cap T&W : the aggregate of the underdeveloped nations of the world

¹thirst \\'thərst\\ n 1 : a feeling of dryness in the mouth and throat associated with a desire to drink; *also* : a bodily condition producing this **2** : an ardent desire : CRAVING ⟨a ∼ for knowledge⟩ — **thirsty** *adj*

²**thirst** *vb* **1** : to need drink : suffer thirst **2** : to have a strong desire : CRAVE

thir·teen \ˌthər-ˈtēn\ *n* : one more than 12 — **thirteen** *adj or pron* — **thir·teenth** \-ˈtēnth\ *adj or n*

thir·ty \ˈthərt-ē\ *n, pl* **thirties** : three times 10 — **thir·ti·eth** \-tē-əth\ *adj or n* — **thirty** *adj or pron*

¹**this** \ˈthis\ *pron, pl* **these** \ˈthēz\ **1** : the one close or closest in time or space ⟨∼ is your book⟩ **2** : what is in the present or under immediate observation or discussion ⟨∼ is a mess⟩; *also* : what is happening or being done now ⟨after ∼ we'll leave⟩

²**this** *adj, pl* **these 1** : being the one near, present, just mentioned, or more immediately under observation ⟨∼ book⟩ **2** : constituting the immediate past or future ⟨friends all *these* years⟩

³**this** *adv* : to such an extent or degree ⟨we need a book about ∼ big⟩

this·tle \ˈthi-səl\ *n* : any of various tall prickly composite plants with often showy heads of tightly packed tubular flowers

this·tle·down \-ˌdaùn\ *n* : the down from the ripe flower head of a thistle

¹**thith·er** \ˈthi-thər\ *adv* : to that place

²**thither** *adj* : being on the farther side

thith·er·ward \-wərd\ *adv* : toward that place : THITHER

thole \ˈthōl\ *n* : a pin set in the gunwale of a boat to hold an oar in place

thong \ˈthòŋ\ *n* **1** : a strip esp. of leather or hide **2** : a sandal held on the foot by a thong between the toes

tho·rax \ˈthōr-ˌaks\ *n, pl* **tho·rax·es** *or* **tho·ra·ces** \ˈthōr-ə-ˌsēz\ **1** : the part of the body of a mammal between the neck and the abdomen; *also* : its cavity containing the heart and lungs **2** : the middle of the three main divisions of the body of an insect — **tho·rac·ic** \thə-ˈra-sik\ *adj*

tho·ri·um \ˈthōr-ē-əm\ *n* : a radioactive metallic chemical element — see ELEMENT table

thorn \ˈthòrn\ *n* **1** : a woody plant bearing sharp processes **2** : a sharp rigid plant process that is usu. a modified leafless branch **3** : something that causes distress — **thorny** *adj*

thor·ough \ˈthər-ō\ *adj* **1** : COMPLETE, EXHAUSTIVE ⟨a ∼ search⟩ **2** : very careful : PAINSTAKING ⟨a ∼ scholar⟩ **3** : having full mastery — **thor·ough·ly** *adv* — **thor·ough·ness** *n*

¹**thor·ough·bred** \ˈthər-ə-ˌbred\ *adj* **1** : bred from the best blood through a long line **2** *cap* : of or relating to the Thoroughbred breed of horses **3** : marked by high≈spirited grace

²**thoroughbred** *n* **1** *cap* : any of an English breed of light speedy horses kept chiefly for racing **2** : one (as a pedigreed animal) of excellent quality

Thoroughbred 1

thor·ough·fare \-ˌfar\ *n* : a public road or street

thor·ough·go·ing \ˌthər-ə-ˈgō-iŋ\ *adj* : marked by thoroughness or zeal

thorp \ˈthòrp\ *n, archaic* : VILLAGE

those *pl of* THAT

¹**thou** \ˈthaù\ *pron, archaic* : the person addressed

²**thou** \ˈthaù\ *n, pl* **thou** : a thousand of something (as dollars)

¹**though** \ˈthō\ *conj* **1** : despite the fact that ⟨∼ the odds are hopeless, they fight on⟩ **2** : granting that ⟨∼ it may look bad, still, all is not lost⟩

²**though** *adv* : HOWEVER, NEVERTHELESS ⟨not for long, ∼⟩

¹**thought** \ˈthòt\ *past and past part of* THINK

²**thought** *n* **1** : the process of thinking **2** : serious consideration : REGARD **3** : reasoning power **4** : the power to imagine : CONCEPTION **5** : IDEA, NOTION **6** : OPINION, BELIEF

thought·ful \ˈthòt-fəl\ *adj* **1** : absorbed in thought **2** : marked by careful thinking ⟨a ∼ essay⟩ **3** : considerate of others ⟨a ∼ host⟩ — **thought·ful·ly** *adv* — **thought·ful·ness** *n*

thought·less \-ləs\ *adj* **1** : insufficiently alert : CARELESS ⟨a ∼ worker⟩ **2** : RECKLESS ⟨a ∼ act⟩ **3** : lacking concern for others : INCONSIDERATE ⟨∼ remarks⟩ — **thought·less·ly** *adv* — **thought·less·ness** *n*

thou·sand \ˈthaùz-ᵊnd\ *n, pl* **thousands** *or* **thousand** : 10 times 100 — **thousand** *adj* — **thou·sandth** \-ᵊnth\ *adj or n*

thousands place *n* : the place four to the left of the decimal point in an Arabic number

thrall \ˈthròl\ *n* **1** : SLAVE, BONDMAN **2** : a state of servitude — **thrall·dom** *or* **thral·dom** \ˈthròl-dəm\ *n*

thrash \ˈthrash\ *vb* **1** : THRESH 1 **2** : BEAT, WHIP; *also* : DEFEAT **3** : to move about violently **4** : to go over again and again ⟨∼ over the matter⟩; *also* : to hammer out ⟨∼ out a plan⟩

¹**thrash·er** \ˈthra-shər\ *n* : one that thrashes or threshes

²**thrasher** *n* : any of various long-tailed American songbirds related to the mockingbird

¹**thread** \ˈthred\ *n* **1** : a thin continuous strand of spun and twisted textile fibers **2** : something resembling a textile thread **3** : the ridge or groove that winds around a screw **4** : a train of thought **5** : a continuing element

²**thread** *vb* **1** : to pass a thread through the eye of (a needle) **2** : to pass (as film) through something **3** : to make one's way through or between **4** : to put together on a thread ⟨∼ beads⟩ **5** : to form a screw thread on or in

thread·bare \-ˌbar\ *adj* **1** : having the nap worn off so that the thread shows : SHABBY **2** : TRITE

thready \ˈthre-dē\ *adj* **1** : consisting of or bearing fibers of filaments ⟨a ∼ bark⟩ **2** : lacking in fullness, body, or vigor

threat \ˈthret\ *n* **1** : an expression of intent to do harm **2** : one that threatens

threat·en \ˈthret-ᵊn\ *vb* **1** : to utter threats against **2** : to give signs or warning of : PORTEND **3** : to hang over as a threat : MENACE — **threat·en·ing·ly** *adv*

threat·ened *adj* : having an uncertain chance of continued survival; *esp* : likely to become an endangered species

three \ˈthrē\ *n* **1** : one more than two **2** : the 3d in a set or series **3** : something having three units — **three** *adj or pron*

3–D \ˈthrē-ˈdē\ *n* : three-dimensional form

three–dimensional *adj* **1** : relating to or having three dimensions **2** : giving the illusion of varying distances ⟨a ∼ picture⟩

three·fold \ˈthrē-ˌfōld, -ˈfōld\ *adj* **1** : having three parts : TRIPLE **2** : being three times as great or as many — **three·fold** \-ˈfōld\ *adv*

three·pence \ˈthre-pəns, ˈthri-, ˈthrə-, *US also* ˈthrē-pens\ *n* **1** *pl* **threepence** *or* **three·pence·es** : a coin worth three pennies **2** : the sum of three British pennies

three·score \'thrē-'skōr\ *adj* : being three times twenty : SIXTY

three·some \'thrē-səm\ *n* : a group of three persons or things

thren·o·dy \'thre-nə-dē\ *n, pl* **-dies** : a song of lamentation : ELEGY

thresh \'thrash, 'thresh\ *vb* **1** : to separate (as grain from straw) mechanically **2** : THRASH — **thresh·er** *n*

thresh·old \'thresh-ˌhōld\ *n* **1** : the sill of a door **2** : a point or place of beginning or entering : OUTSET **3** : a point at which a physiological or psychological effect begins to be produced

threw *past of* THROW

thrice \'thrīs\ *adv* **1** : three times **2** : in a threefold manner or degree

thrift \'thrift\ *n* [ME, fr. ON, prosperity, fr. *thrīfask* to thrive] : careful management esp. of money : FRUGALITY — **thrift·i·ly** \'thrif-tə-lē\ *adv* — **thrift·less** *adj* — **thrifty** *adj*

thrill \'thril\ *vb* [ME *thirlen, thrillen* to pierce, fr. OE *thyrlian*, fr. *thyrel* hole, fr. *thurh* through] **1** : to have or cause to have sudden sharp feeling of excitement; *also* : TINGLE, SHIVER **2** : TREMBLE, VIBRATE — **thrill** *n* — **thrill·er** *n* — **thrill·ing·ly** *adv*

thrive \'thrīv\ *vb* **throve** \'thrōv\ *or* **thrived; thriv·en** \'thri-vən\ *also* **thrived; thriv·ing 1** : to grow luxuriantly : FLOURISH **2** : to gain in wealth or possessions : PROSPER

throat \'thrōt\ *n* : the part of the neck in front of the spinal column; *also* : the passage through it to the stomach and lungs — **throat·ed** *adj*

throaty \'thrō-tē\ *adj* **throat·i·er; -est 1** : uttered or produced from low in the throat ⟨a ~ voice⟩ **2** : heavy, thick, or deep as if from the throat ⟨~ notes of a horn⟩ — **throat·i·ly** \-tə-lē\ *adv* — **throat·i·ness** \-tē-nəs\ *n*

¹throb \'thräb\ *vb* **throbbed; throb·bing** : to pulsate or pound esp. with abnormal force or rapidity : BEAT, VIBRATE

²throb *n* : BEAT, PULSE

throe \'thrō\ *n* **1** : PANG, SPASM **2** *pl* : a hard or painful struggle

throm·bo·sis \thräm-'bō-səs\ *n, pl* **-bo·ses** \-ˌsēz\ : the formation or presence of a clot in a blood vessel — **throm·bot·ic** \-'bä-tik\ *adj*

throm·bus \'thräm-bəs\ *n, pl* **throm·bi** \-ˌbī\ : a clot of blood formed within a blood vessel and remaining attached to its place of origin

throne \'thrōn\ *n* **1** : the chair of state of a sovereign or high dignitary **2** : royal power : SOVEREIGNTY

¹throng \'thròŋ\ *n* **1** : MULTITUDE **2** : a crowding together of many persons

²throng *vb* **thronged; throng·ing** : CROWD

¹throt·tle \'thrät-ᵊl\ *vb* **throt·tled; throt·tling** [ME *throtlen*, fr. *throte* throat] **1** : CHOKE, STRANGLE **2** : SUPPRESS **3** : to reduce the speed of (an engine) by closing the throttle — **throt·tler** *n*

²throttle *n* : a valve regulating the flow of steam or fuel to an engine; *also* : the lever controlling this valve

¹through \'thrü\ *prep* **1** : into at one side and out at the other side of ⟨go ~ the door⟩ **2** : by way of ⟨entered ~ a skylight⟩ **3** : in the midst of ⟨a path ~ the trees⟩ **4** : by means of ⟨succeeded ~ hard work⟩ **5** : over the whole of ⟨rumors swept ~ the office⟩ **6** : during the whole of ⟨~ the night⟩ **7** : to and including ⟨Monday ~ Friday⟩

²through *adv* **1** : from one end or side to the other **2** : from beginning to end : to completion ⟨see it ~⟩ **3** : to the core : THOROUGHLY ⟨he was wet ~⟩ **4** : into the open : OUT ⟨break ~⟩

³through *adj* **1** : permitting free passage ⟨a ~ street⟩ **2** : going from point of origin to destination without change or transfer ⟨a ~ train⟩ **3** : coming from or going to points outside a local area ⟨~ traffic⟩ **4** : FINISHED ⟨~ with the job⟩

¹through·out \thrü-'aùt\ *adv* **1** : EVERYWHERE **2** : from beginning to end

²throughout *prep* **1** : in or to every part of **2** : during the whole period of

through·put \'thrü-ˌpùt\ *n* : OUTPUT, PRODUCTION ⟨the ~ of a computer⟩

throve *past of* THRIVE

¹throw \'thrō\ *vb* **threw** \'thrü\; **thrown** \'thrōn\; **throw·ing 1** : to propel through the air esp. with a forward motion of the hand and arm ⟨~ a ball⟩ **2** : to cause to fall or fall off **3** : to put suddenly in a certain position or condition ⟨~ into panic⟩ **4** : to put on or take off hastily ⟨~ on a coat⟩ **5** : to lose intentionally ⟨~ a game⟩ **6** : to move (a lever) so as to connect or disconnect parts of something (as a clutch) **7** : to act as host for ⟨~ a party⟩ **syn** toss, fling, pitch, sling — **throw·er** *n*

²throw *n* **1** : an act of throwing, hurling, or flinging; *also* : CAST **2** : the distance a missile may be thrown **3** : a light coverlet **4** : a woman's scarf or light wrap

throw·away \'thrō-ə-ˌwā\ *n* : something that is or is designed to be thrown away esp. after one use

throw·back \-ˌbak\ *n* : reversion to an earlier type or phase; *also* : an instance or product of this

throw up *vb* **1** : to build hurriedly **2** : VOMIT

thrum \'thrəm\ *vb* **thrummed; thrum·ming** : to play or pluck a stringed instrument idly : STRUM

thrush \'thrəsh\ *n* : any of numerous small or medium-sized songbirds that are mostly of a plain color often with spotted underparts

¹thrust \'thrəst\ *vb* **thrust; thrust·ing 1** : to push or drive with force : SHOVE **2** : STAB, PIERCE **3** : INTERJECT **4** : to press the acceptance of upon someone

²thrust *n* **1** : a lunge with a pointed weapon **2** : ATTACK **3** : the pressure of one part of a construction against another (as of an arch against an abutment) **4** : the force produced by a propeller or jet or rocket engine that drives a vehicle (as an aircraft) forward **5** : a violent push : SHOVE

thrust·er *also* **thrust·or** \'thrəs-tər\ *n* : one that thrusts; *esp* : a rocket engine

thru·way \'thrü-ˌwā\ *n* : EXPRESSWAY

¹thud \'thəd\ *n* **1** : BLOW **2** : a dull sound

²thud *vb* **thud·ded; thud·ding** : to move or strike so as to make a thud

thug \'thəg\ *n* [Hindi *ṭhag*, lit., thief] : a brutal ruffian or assassin — **thug·gish** *adj*

thu·li·um \'thü-lē-əm, 'thyü-\ *n* : a rare metallic chemical element — see ELEMENT table

¹thumb \'thəm\ *n* **1** : the short thick first digit of the human hand or a corresponding digit of a lower animal **2** : the part of a glove or mitten that covers the thumb

²thumb *vb* **1** : to leaf through (pages) with the thumb **2** : to wear or soil with the thumb by frequent handling **3** : to request or obtain (a ride) in a passing automobile by signaling with the thumb

¹thumb·nail \'thəm-ˌnāl\ *n* : the nail of the thumb

²thumbnail *adj* : BRIEF, CONCISE ⟨a ~ description⟩

thumb·print \-ˌprint\ *n* : an impression made by the thumb

thumb·screw \-ˌskrü\ *n* **1** : a screw with a head that may be turned by the thumb and forefinger **2** : a device of torture for squeezing the thumb

thumb·tack \-ˌtak\ *n* : a tack with a broad flat head for pressing with one's thumb into a board or wall

¹thump \'thəmp\ *vb* **1** : to strike with or as if with something thick or heavy so as to cause a dull sound **2** : POUND

²thump *n* : a blow with or as if with something blunt or heavy; *also* : the sound made by such a blow

¹thun·der \'thən-dər\ *n* **1** : the sound following a flash of lightning; *also* : a noise like such a sound **2** : a loud utterance or threat

²thunder *vb* **1** : to produce thunder **2** : ROAR, SHOUT

thun·der·bolt \-ˌbōlt\ *n* : a flash of lightning with its accompanying thunder

thun·der·clap \-ˌklap\ *n* : a crash of thunder
thun·der·cloud \-ˌklaùd\ *n* : a dark storm cloud producing lightning and thunder
thun·der·head \-ˌhed\ *n* : a large cumulus cloud often appearing before a thunderstorm
thun·der·ous \ˈthən-də-rəs\ *adj* : producing thunder; *also* : making a noise like thunder — **thun·der·ous·ly** *adv*
thun·der·show·er \ˈthən-dər-ˌshaú-ər\ *n* : a shower accompanied by thunder and lightning
thun·der·storm \-ˌstòrm\ *n* : a storm accompanied by thunder and lightning
thun·der·struck \-ˌstrək\ *adj* : stunned as if struck by a thunderbolt
Thurs *or* **Thu** *abbr* Thursday
Thurs·day \ˈthərz-dē, -ˌdā\ *n* [ME, fr. OE *thursdæg*, fr. ON *thōrsdagr*, lit., day of Thor (Norse god)] : the 5th day of the week
thus \ˈthəs\ *adv* **1** : in this or that manner **2** : to this degree or extent : SO **3** : because of this or that : HENCE
¹**thwack** \ˈthwak\ *vb* : to strike with or as if with something flat or heavy
²**thwack** *n* : a heavy blow : WHACK
¹**thwart** \ˈthwòrt\ *vb* **1** : FOIL, BAFFLE **2** : BLOCK, DEFEAT **syn** balk, outwit, frustrate
²**thwart** \ˈthwòrt, *naut often* ˈthòrt\ *adv* : ATHWART
³**thwart** *adj* : situated or placed across something else
⁴**thwart** \ˈthwòrt\ *n* : a rower's seat extending across a boat
thy \ˈthī\ *adj, archaic* : of, relating to, or done by or to thee or thyself
thyme \ˈtīm, ˈthīm\ *n* [ME, fr. MF *thym*, fr. L *thymum*, fr. Gk *thymon*, prob. fr. *thyein* to make a burnt offering, sacrifice] : a garden mint with aromatic leaves used esp. in seasoning; *also* : its leaves so used
thy·mine \ˈthī-ˌmēn\ *n* : a pyrimidine base that is one of the four bases coding genetic information in the molecular chain of DNA
thy·mus \ˈthī-məs\ *n* : a glandular organ of the neck region that is composed largely of lymphoid tissue, functions esp. in the development of the immune system, and tends to atrophy in the adult
thy·ris·tor \thī-ˈris-tər\ *n* : a semiconductor device that acts as a switch, rectifier, or voltage regulator
thy·roid \ˈthī-ˌròid\ *also* **thy·roi·dal** \thī-ˈròid-əl\ *adj* [NL *thyroides*, fr. Gk *thyreoeidēs* shield-shaped, thyroid, fr. *thyreos* shield shaped like a door, fr. *thyra* door] : of, relating to, or being a large endocrine gland that lies at the base of the neck and produces several iodine-containing hormones that affect growth, development, and metabolism — **thyroid** *n*
thy·rox·ine *or* **thy·rox·in** \thī-ˈräk-ˌsēn, -sən\ *n* : an iodine-containing hormone that is produced by the thyroid gland, increases metabolic rate, and is used to treat thyroid disorders
thy·self \thī-ˈself\ *pron, archaic* : YOURSELF
Ti *symbol* titanium
ti·ara \tē-ˈar-ə, -ˈer-, -ˈär-\ *n* **1** : the pope's triple

crown **2** : a decorative headband or semicircle for formal wear by women
Ti·bet·an \tə-ˈbet-ən\ *n* : a native or inhabitant of Tibet — **Tibetan** *adj*
tib·ia \ˈti-bē-ə\ *n, pl* **-i·ae** \-bē-ˌē\ *also* **-i·as** [L] : the inner of the two bones of the vertebrate hind limb between the knee and the ankle
tic \ˈtik\ *n* : a local and habitual twitching of muscles esp. of the face
ti·cal \ti-ˈkäl, ˈti-kəl\ *n, pl* **ticals** *or* **tical** : BAHT

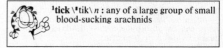
¹**tick** \ˈtik\ *n* : any of a large group of small blood-sucking arachnids

²**tick** *n* : the fabric case of a mattress or pillow; *also* : a mattress consisting of a tick and its filling
³**tick** *n* **1** : a light rhythmic audible tap or beat **2** : a small mark used to draw attention to or check something
⁴**tick** *vb* **1** : to make the sound of a tick or series of ticks **2** : to mark, count, or announce by or as if by ticking beats **3** : to mark or check with a tick **4** : to function as an operating mechanism : RUN
⁵**tick** *n, chiefly Brit* : CREDIT; *also* : a credit account
tick·er \ˈti-kər\ *n* **1** : something (as a watch) that ticks **2** : a telegraph instrument that prints information (as stock prices) on paper tape **3** *slang* : HEART
ticker tape *n* : the paper ribbon on which a telegraphic ticker prints
¹**tick·et** \ˈti-kət\ *n* [MF *etiquet, estiquette* notice attached to something, fr. *estiquier* to attach, fr. MD *steken* to stick] **1** : CERTIFICATE, LICENSE, PERMIT; *esp* : a certificate or token showing that a fare or admission fee has been paid **2** : TAG, LABEL **3** : SLATE **4** **4** : a summons issued to a traffic offender
²**ticket** *vb* **1** : to attach a ticket to **2** : to furnish or serve with a ticket
tick·ing \ˈti-kiŋ\ *n* : a strong fabric used in upholstering and as a mattress covering
tick·le \ˈti-kəl\ *vb* **tick·led; tick·ling** **1** : to excite or stir up agreeably : PLEASE, AMUSE **2** : to have a tingling sensation **3** : to touch (as a body part) lightly so as to cause uneasiness, laughter, or spasmodic movements — **tickle** *n*
tick·lish \-kə-lish\ *adj* **1** : OVERSENSITIVE, TOUCHY **2** : UNSTABLE ⟨a ~ foothold⟩ **3** : requiring delicate handling ⟨~ subject⟩ **4** : sensitive to tickling — **tick·lish·ly** *adv* — **tick·lish·ness** *n*
¹**tid·al wave** \ˈtīd-əl-\ *n* **1** : an unusually high sea wave that sometimes follows an earthquake **2** : an unusual rise of water alongshore due to strong winds
tid·bit \ˈtid-ˌbit\ *n* : a choice morsel
¹**tide** \ˈtīd\ *n* [ME, time, fr. OE *tīd*] **1** : the alternate rising and falling of the surface of the ocean **2** : something that fluctuates like the tides of the sea — **tid·al** \ˈtīd-əl\ *adj*
²**tide** *vb* **tid·ed; tid·ing** : to carry through or help along as if by the tide ⟨a loan to ~ us over⟩
tide·land \ˈtīd-ˌland, -lənd\ *n* **1** : land overflowed dur-

ing flood tide **2** : land under the ocean within a nation's territorial waters — often used in pl.

tide·wa·ter \-ˌwȯ-tər, -ˌwä-\ *n* **1** : water overflowing land at flood tide **2** : low-lying coastal land

tid·ings \'tī-diŋz\ *n pl* : NEWS, MESSAGE

¹ti·dy \'tī-dē\ *adj* **ti·di·er; -est 1** : well ordered and cared for : NEAT **2** : LARGE, SUBSTANTIAL ⟨a ∼ sum⟩ — **ti·di·ness** \'tī-dē-nəs\ *n*

²tidy *vb* **ti·died; ti·dy·ing 1** : to put in order **2** : to make things tidy

³tidy *n*, *pl* **tidies** : a decorated covering used to protect the back or arms of a chair from wear or soil

¹tie \'tī\ *n* **1** : a line, ribbon, or cord used for fastening, uniting, or closing **2** : a structural element (as a beam or rod) holding two pieces together **3** : one of the cross supports to which railroad rails are fastened **4** : a connecting link : BOND ⟨family ∼s⟩ **5** : an equality in number (as of votes or scores); *also* : an undecided or deadlocked contest **6** : NECKTIE

²tie *vb* **tied; ty·ing** *or* **tie·ing 1** : to fasten, attach, or close by means of a tie **2** : to bring together firmly : UNITE **3** : to form a knot or bow in ⟨∼ a scarf⟩ **4** : to restrain from freedom of action : CONSTRAIN **5** : to make or have an equal score with

tie·back \'tī-ˌbak\ *n* : a decorative strip for draping a curtain to the side of a window

tie–dye·ing \'tī-ˌdī-iŋ\ *n* : a method of producing patterns in textiles by tying parts of the fabric so that they will not absorb the dye — **tie–dyed** \-ˌdīd\ *adj*

tie–in \'tī-ˌin\ *n* : CONNECTION

tier \'tir\ *n* : ROW, LAYER; *esp* : one of two or more rows arranged one above another — **tiered** \'tird\ *adj*

tie–rod \'tī-ˌräd\ *n* : a rod used as a connecting member or brace

tie–up \-ˌəp\ *n* **1** : a slowing or stopping of traffic or business **2** : CONNECTION

tiff \'tif\ *n* : a petty quarrel — **tiff** *vb*

Tif·fa·ny \'tif-ə-nē\ *adj* : made of pieces of stained glass ⟨a ∼ lamp⟩

ti·ger \'tī-gər\ *n* : a very large tawny black-striped Asian cat — **ti·ger·ish** *adj*

tiger

¹tight \'tīt\ *adj* **1** : so close in structure as to prevent passage of a liquid or gas **2** : strongly fixed or held : SECURE **3** : TAUT **4** : fitting usu. too closely ⟨∼ shoes⟩ **5** : set close together : COMPACT ⟨a ∼ formation⟩ **6** : DIFFICULT, TRYING ⟨get in a ∼ spot⟩ **7** : STINGY, MISERLY **8** : evenly contested : CLOSE **9** : INTOXICATED **10** : low in supply : hard to get ⟨money is ∼⟩ — **tight·ly** *adv* — **tight·ness** *n*

²tight *adv* **1** : TIGHTLY, FIRMLY **2** : SOUNDLY ⟨sleep ∼⟩

tight·en \'tīt-ᵊn\ *vb* : to make or become tight

tight·fist·ed \'tīt-'fis-təd\ *adj* : STINGY

tight·rope \-ˌrōp\ *n* : a taut rope or wire for acrobats to perform on

tights \'tīts\ *n pl* : skintight garments covering the body esp. below the waist; *also*, *Brit* : PANTY HOSE

tight·wad \'tīt-ˌwäd\ *n* : a stingy person

ti·gress \'tī-grəs\ *n* : a female tiger

til·de \'til-də\ *n* [Sp. fr. ML *titulus* tittle] : a mark placed esp. over the letter *n* (as in Spanish *señor* sir)

to denote the sound \n^y\ or over vowels (as in Portuguese *irmã* sister) to indicate nasal quality

¹tile \'tīl\ *n* **1** : a flat or curved piece of fired clay, stone, or concrete used for roofs, floors, or walls; *also* : a pipe of earthenware or concrete used for a drain **2** : a thin piece (as of linoleum) used for covering walls or floors — **til·ing** \'tī-liŋ\ *n*

²tile *vb* **tiled; til·ing** : to cover with tiles — **til·er** *n*

¹till \'til\ *prep or conj* : UNTIL

²till *vb* : to work by plowing, sowing, and raising crops : CULTIVATE — **till·able** *adj*

³till *n* : DRAWER; *esp* : a money drawer in a store or bank

till·age \'til-ij\ *n* **1** : the work of tilling land **2** : cultivated land

¹till·er \'til-lər\ *n* [OE *telgor, telgra* twig, shoot] : a sprout or stalk esp. from the base or lower part of a plant

²till·er \'til-lər\ *n* : one that tills

³till·er \'til-lər\ *n* [ME *tiler* stock of a crossbow, fr. MF *telier*, lit., beam of a loom, fr. ML *telarium*, fr. L *tela* web] : a lever used for turning a boat's rudder from side to side

¹tilt \'tilt\ *n* **1** : a contest in which two combatants charging usu. with lances try to unhorse each other : JOUST; *also* : a tournament of tilts **2** : a verbal contest **3** : SLANT, TIP

²tilt *vb* **1** : to move or shift so as to incline : TIP **2** : to engage in or as if in combat with lances : JOUST, ATTACK

tilth \'tilth\ *n* **1** : TILLAGE **2 2** : the state of a soil esp. in relation to the suitability of its particle size and structure for growing crops

Tim *abbr* Timothy

tim·ber \'tim-bər\ *n* [ME, fr. OE, building, wood] **1** : growing trees or their wood — often used interjectionally to warn of a falling tree **2** : wood for use in making something **3** : a usu. large squared or dressed piece of wood

tim·bered \'tim-bərd\ *adj* : having walls framed by exposed timbers

tim·ber·land \'tim-bər-ˌland\ *n* : wooded land

tim·ber·line \'tim-bər-ˌlīn\ *n* : the upper limit of tree growth in mountains or high latitudes

timber rattlesnake *n* : a widely distributed rattlesnake of the eastern U.S.

timber wolf *n* : GRAY WOLF

tim·bre *also* **tim·ber** \'tam-bər, 'tim-\ *n* [F, fr. MF, bell struck by a hammer, fr. OF, drum, fr. MGk *tymbanon* kettledrum, fr. Gk *tympanon*] : the distinctive quality given to a sound by its overtones

tim·brel \'tim-brəl\ *n* : a small hand drum or tambourine

¹time \'tīm\ *n* **1** : a period during which an action, process, or condition exists or continues ⟨gone a long ∼⟩ **2** : LEISURE ⟨found ∼ to read⟩ **3** : a point or period when something occurs : OCCASION ⟨the last ∼ we met⟩ **4** : a set or customary moment or hour for something to occur ⟨arrived on ∼⟩ **5** : AGE, ERA **6** : state of affairs : CONDITIONS ⟨hard ∼s⟩ **7** : a rate of speed : TEMPO **8** : a moment, hour, day, or year as indicated by a clock or calendar ⟨what ∼ is it⟩ **9** : a system of reckoning time ⟨solar ∼⟩ **10** : one of a series of recurring instances; *also*, : added or accumulated quantities or examples ⟨five ∼s greater⟩ **11** : a person's experience during a particular period ⟨had a good ∼⟩ **12** : the hours or days of one's work; *also* : an hourly pay rate ⟨straight ∼⟩ **13** : TIME-OUT

²time *vb* **timed; tim·ing 1** : to arrange or set the time of : SCHEDULE ⟨∼s his calls conveniently⟩ **2** : to set the tempo or duration of ⟨∼ a performance⟩ **3** : to cause to keep time with **4** : to determine or record the time, duration, or rate of ⟨∼ a sprinter⟩ — **tim·er** *n*

time bomb *n* **1** : a bomb so made as to explode at a predetermined time **2** : something with a potentially dangerous delayed reaction

time clock *n* : a clock that records the time workers arrive and depart

time frame *n* : a period of time esp. with respect to some action or project

time–hon·ored \'tīm-₁ä-nərd\ *adj* : honored because of age or long usage

time·keep·er \-₁kē-pər\ *n* 1 : a clerk who keeps records of the time worked by employees 2 : one appointed to mark and announce the time in an athletic game or contest

time·less \-ləs\ *adj* 1 : ETERNAL 2 : not limited or affected by time ⟨~ works of art⟩ — time·less·ly *adv* — time·less·ness *n*

time·ly \-lē\ *adj* time·li·er; -est 1 : coming early or at the right time ⟨a ~ arrival⟩ 2 : appropriate to the time ⟨a ~ book⟩ — time·li·ness *n*

time–out \'tīm-'aùt\ *n* : a brief suspension of activity esp. in an athletic game

time·piece \-₁pēs\ *n* : a device (as a clock) to show the passage of time

times \'tīmz\ *prep* : multiplied by ⟨2 ~ 2 is 4⟩

time–shar·ing \'tīm-₁shar-iŋ\ *n* 1 : simultaneous use of a computer by many users 2 *or* time–share \-shar\ : joint ownership or rental of a vacation lodging by several persons with each taking turns using the place

times sign *n* : the symbol × used to indicate multiplication

time·ta·ble \'tīm-₁tā-bəl\ *n* 1 : a table of the departure and arrival times (as of trains) 2 : a schedule showing a planned order or sequence

time warp *n* : an anomaly, discontinuity, or suspension held to occur in the progress of time

time·worn \-₁wōrn\ *adj* 1 : worn by time 2 : HACK-NEYED, STALE

tim·id \'ti-məd\ *adj* : lacking in courage or self‑confidence : FEARFUL — ti·mid·i·ty \tə-'mi-də-tē\ *n* — tim·id·ly *adv*

tim·o·rous \'ti-mə-rəs\ *adj* : of a timid disposition : AFRAID — tim·o·rous·ly *adv* — tim·o·rous·ness *n*

tim·o·thy \'ti-mə-thē\ *n* : a grass with long cylindrical spikes widely grown for hay

Tim·o·thy \'ti-mə-thē\ *n* — see BIBLE table

tim·pa·ni \'tim-pə-nē\ *n sing or pl* [It] : a set of kettle-drums played by one performer in an orchestra — tim·pa·nist \-nist\ *n*

¹tin \'tin\ *n* 1 : a soft white crystalline metallic chemical element malleable at ordinary temperatures that is used esp. in solders and alloys — see ELEMENT table 2 : a container (as a can) made of metal (as tinplate)

²tin *vb* tinned; tin·ning 1 : to cover or plate with tin 2 : to pack in tins

TIN *abbr* taxpayer identification number

tinct \'tiŋkt\ *n* : TINCTURE, TINGE

¹tinc·ture \'tiŋk-chər\ *n* 1 *archaic* : a substance that colors 2 : a slight admixture : TRACE 3 : an alcoholic solution of a medicinal substance **syn** touch, suggestion, suspicion, tinge

²tincture *vb* tinc·tured; tinc·tur·ing 1 : COLOR, TINGE 2 : AFFECT

tin·der \'tin-dər\ *n* 1 : a very flammable substance used as kindling 2 : something serving to incite or inflame

tin·der·box \'tin-dər-₁bäks\ *n* 1 : a metal box for holding tinder and usu. flint and steel for striking a spark 2 : a highly flammable object or place

tine \'tīn\ *n* : a slender pointed part (as of a fork or an antler) : PRONG

tin·foil \'tin-₁fòil\ *n* : a thin metal sheeting usu. of aluminum or tin-lead alloy

¹tinge \'tinj\ *vb* tinged; ting·ing *or* ting·ing 1 : to color slightly : TINT 2 : to affect or modify esp. with a slight odor or taste

²tinge *n* : a slight coloring, flavor, or quality : TRACE **syn** touch, suggestion, suspicion, tincture, soupçon

tin·gle \'tiŋ-gəl\ *vb* tin·gled; tin·gling 1 : to feel a prickling or thrilling sensation 2 : TINKLE — tingle *n*

¹tin·ker \'tiŋ-kər\ *n* 1 : a usu. itinerant mender of household utensils 2 : an unskillful mender : BUNGLER

²**tinker** *vb* : to repair or adjust something in an unskillful or experimental manner — **tin·ker·er** *n*

¹**tin·kle** \'tiŋ-kəl\ *vb* **tin·kled; tin·kling** : to make or cause to make a tinkle

²**tinkle** *n* : a series of short high ringing or clinking sounds

tin·ny \'ti-nē\ *adj* **tin·ni·er; -est 1** : abounding in or yielding tin **2** : resembling tin; *also* : LIGHT, CHEAP **3** : thin in tone ⟨a ~ voice⟩ — **tin·ni·ly** \-nə-lē\ *adv* — **tin·ni·ness** \-nē-nəs\ *n*

tin·plate \'tin-'plāt\ *n* : thin sheet iron or steel coated with tin — **tin–plate** *vb*

tin·sel \'tin-səl\ *n* [MF *etincelle* spark, glitter] **1** : a thread, strip, or sheet of metal, paper, or plastic used to produce a glittering appearance **2** : something superficially attractive but of little worth

tin·smith \'tin-₁smith\ *n* : one that works with sheet metal (as tinplate)

¹**tint** \'tint\ *n* **1** : a slight or pale coloration : HUE **2** : any of various shades of a color

²**tint** *vb* : to impart a tint to : COLOR

tin·tin·nab·u·la·tion \₁tin-tə-₁na-byə-'lā-shən\ *n* **1** : the ringing of bells **2** : a tingling sound as if of bells

tin·ware \'tin-₁war\ *n* : articles and esp. utensils made of tinplate

ti·ny \'tī-nē\ *adj* **ti·ni·er; -est** : very small : MINUTE **syn** miniature, diminutive, wee, lilliputian

¹**tip** \'tip\ *vb* **tipped; tip·ping 1** : OVERTURN, UPSET **2** : LEAN, SLANT; *also* : to raise and tilt forward ⟨tipped his hat⟩

²**tip** *n* : the act or an instance of tipping

³**tip** *vb* **tipped; tip·ping 1** : to furnish with a tip **2** : to cover or adorn the tip of

⁴**tip** *n* **1** : the usu. pointed end of something **2** : a small piece or part serving as an end, cap, or point

⁵**tip** *n* : a light touch or blow

⁶**tip** *vb* **tipped; tip·ping** : to strike lightly : TAP

⁷**tip** *n* : a piece of advice or expert or confidential information : HINT

⁸**tip** *vb* **tipped; tip·ping** : to impart a piece of information about or to

⁹**tip** *vb* **tipped; tip·ping** : to give a gratuity to

¹⁰**tip** *n* : a gift or small sum given for a service performed or anticipated

tip–off \'tip-₁of\ *n* : WARNING, TIP

tip·pet \'ti-pət\ *n* : a long scarf or shoulder cape

tip·ple \'ti-pəl\ *vb* **tip·pled; tip·pling** : to drink intoxicating liquor esp. habitually or excessively — **tipple** *n* — **tip·pler** *n*

tip·ster \'tip-stər\ *n* : a person who gives or sells tips esp. for gambling

tip·sy \'tip-sē\ *adj* **tip·si·er; -est** : unsteady or foolish from the effects of alcohol — **tip·si·ly** \-sə-lē\ *adv*

¹**tip·toe** \'tip-₁tō\ *n* : the position of being balanced on the balls of the feet and toes with the heels raised; *also* : the ends of the toes

²**tiptoe** *adv or adj* : on or as if on tiptoe

³**tiptoe** *vb* **tip·toed; tip·toe·ing** : to walk or proceed on or as if on tiptoe

¹**tip–top** \'tip-'täp\ *n* : the highest point

²**tip–top** *adj* : EXCELLENT, FIRST-RATE

ti·rade \'tī-₁rād\ *n* [F, shot, tirade, fr. MF, fr. It *tirata* fr. *tirare* to draw, shoot] : a prolonged speech of abuse or condemnation

tir·a·mi·su \₁tir-ə-'mē-sü, -mē-'sü\ *n* [It *tiramisù*] : a dessert made with ladyfingers, mascarpone, chocolate, and espresso

¹**tire** \'tīr\ *vb* **tired; tir·ing 1** : to make or become weary : FATIGUE **2** : to wear out the patience of : BORE

²**tire** *n* **1** : a metal hoop that forms the tread of a wheel **2** : a rubber cushion usu. containing compressed air that encircles a wheel (as of a bike)

tired \'tīrd\ *adj* **1** : WEARY, FATIGUED **2** : HACKNEYED — **tired·ness** *n*

tire·less \'tīr-ləs\ *adj* : not tiring : UNTIRING, INDEFATIGABLE — **tire·less·ly** *adv* — **tire·less·ness** *n*

tire·some \-səm\ *adj* : tending to bore : WEARISOME, TEDIOUS — **tire·some·ly** *adv* — **tire·some·ness** *n*

ti·ro *chiefly Brit var of* TYRO

tis·sue \'ti-shü\ *n* [ME *tissu*, a rich fabric, fr. OF, fr. *tistre* to weave, fr. L *texere*] **1** : a fine lightweight often sheer fabric **2** : NETWORK, WEB **3** : a soft absorbent paper **4** : a mass or layer of cells forming a basic structural material of an animal or plant

¹**tit** \'tit\ *n* : TEAT

²**tit** *n* : TITMOUSE

Tit *abbr* Titus

ti·tan \'tīt-³n\ *n* **1** *cap* : one of a family of giants overthrown by the gods of ancient Greece **2** : one gigantic in size or power

ti·tan·ic \tī-'ta-nik\ *adj* : enormous in size, force, or power **syn** immense, gigantic, giant, colossal, mammoth

ti·ta·ni·um \tī-'tā-nē-əm\ *n* : a gray light strong metallic chemical element used esp. in alloys — see ELEMENT table

tit·bit \'tit-₁bit\ *var of* TIDBIT

tithe \'tīth\ *n* : a 10th part paid or given esp. for the support of a church — **tithe** *vb* — **tith·er** *n*

tit·il·late \'tit-³l-₁āt\ *vb* **-lat·ed; -lat·ing 1** : to excite pleasurably **2** : TICKLE — **tit·il·la·tion** \₁tit-³l-'ā-shən\ *n*

tit·i·vate *or* **tit·ti·vate** \'ti-tə-₁vāt\ *vb* **-vat·ed; -vat·ing** : to dress up : spruce up — **tit·i·va·tion** \₁ti-tə-'vā-shən\ *n*

ti·tle \'tīt-³l\ *n* **1** : CLAIM, RIGHT; *esp* : a legal right to the ownership of property **2** : the distinguishing name esp. of an artistic production (as a book) **3** : an appellation of honor, rank, or office **4** : CHAMPIONSHIP **syn** designation, denomination, appellation

ti·tled \'tīt-³ld\ *adj* : having a title esp. of nobility

title page *n* : a page of a book bearing the title and usu. the names of the author and publisher

tit·mouse \'tit-₁maus\ *n, pl* **tit·mice** \-₁mīs\ : any of numerous small long-tailed insect-eating birds

ti·tra·tion \tī-'trā-shən\ *n* : a process of finding the concentration of a solution (as of an acid) by adding small portions of a second solution of known concentration (as of a base) to a fixed amount of the first until an expected change (as in color) occurs

tit•ter \'ti-tər\ *vb* : to laugh in an affected or in a nervous or half-suppressed manner : GIGGLE — **titter** *n*

tit•tle \'tit-ᵊl\ *n* : a tiny piece : JOT

tit•tle–tat•tle \'tit-ᵊl-ˌtat-ᵊl\ *n* : idle talk : GOSSIP — **tittle–tattle** *vb*

tit•u•lar \'ti-chə-lər\ *adj* **1** : existing in title only : NOMINAL ⟨∼ ruler⟩ **2** : of, relating to, or bearing a title ⟨∼ role⟩

Ti•tus \'tī-təs\ *n* — see BIBLE table

tiz•zy \'ti-zē\ *n, pl* **tizzies** : a highly excited and distracted state of mind

tk *abbr* **1** tank **2** truck

TKO \ˌtē-ˌkā-'ō\ *n* [technical *k*nockout] : the termination of a boxing match when a boxer is declared unable to continue the fight

tkt *abbr* ticket

Tl *symbol* thallium

TLC *abbr* tender loving care

T lymphocyte *n* : T CELL

Tm *symbol* thulium

TM *abbr* trademark

T–man \'tē-ˌman\ *n* : a special agent of the U.S. Treasury Department

tn *abbr* **1** ton **2** town

TN *abbr* Tennessee

tng *abbr* training

tnpk *abbr* turnpike

TNT \ˌtē-(ˌ)en-'tē\ *n* : a flammable toxic compound used as a high explosive

¹to \tə, 'tü\ *prep* **1** : in the direction of and reaching ⟨drove ∼ town⟩ **2** : in the direction of : TOWARD **3** : ON, AGAINST ⟨apply salve ∼ a burn⟩ **4** : as far as ⟨can pay up ∼ a dollar⟩ **5** : so as to become or bring about ⟨beaten ∼ death⟩ ⟨broken ∼ pieces⟩ **6** : BEFORE ⟨it's five minutes ∼ six⟩ **7** : UNTIL ⟨from May ∼ December⟩ **8** : fitting or being a part of : FOR ⟨key ∼ the lock⟩ **9** : with the accompaniment of ⟨sing ∼ the music⟩ **10** : in relation or comparison with ⟨similar ∼ that one⟩ ⟨won 10 ∼ 6⟩ **11** : in accordance with ⟨add salt ∼ taste⟩ **12** : within the range of ⟨∼ my knowledge⟩ **13** : contained, occurring, or included in ⟨two pints ∼ a quart⟩ **14** : as regards ⟨agreeable ∼ everyone⟩ **15** : affecting as the receiver or beneficiary ⟨whispered ∼ her⟩ ⟨gave it ∼ me⟩ **16** : for no one except ⟨a room ∼ myself⟩ **17** : into the action of ⟨we got ∼ talking⟩ **18** — used for marking the following verb as an infinitive ⟨wants ∼ go⟩ and often used by itself at the end of a clause in place of an infinitive suggested by the preceding context ⟨goes to town whenever he wants ∼⟩ ⟨can leave if you'd like ∼⟩

²to \'tü\ *adv* **1** : in a direction toward ⟨run ∼ and fro⟩ **2** : into contact esp. with the frame of a door ⟨the door slammed ∼⟩ **3** : to the matter in hand ⟨fell ∼ and ate heartily⟩ **4** : to a state of consciousness or awareness ⟨came ∼ hours after the accident⟩

TO *abbr* turn over

toad \'tōd\ *n* : any of numerous tailless leaping amphibians differing typically from the related frogs in having a shorter stockier build, rough dry warty skin, and less aquatic habits

toad

toad•stool \-ˌstül\ *n* : MUSHROOM; *esp* : one that is poisonous or inedible

toady \'tō-dē\ *n, pl* **toad•ies** : a person who flatters in the hope of gaining favors : SYCOPHANT — **toady** *vb*

to–and–fro \ˌtü-ən-'frō\ *adj* : forward and backward — **to–and–fro** *n*

¹toast \'tōst\ *vb* **1** : to warm thoroughly **2** : to make (as bread) crisp, hot, and brown by heat **3** : to become toasted

²toast *n* **1** : sliced toasted bread **2** : someone or something in whose honor persons drink **3** : an act of drinking in honor of a toast

³toast *vb* : to propose or drink to as a toast

toast•er \'tō-stər\ *n* : an electrical appliance for toasting

toaster oven *n* : a portable electrical appliance that bakes, broils, and toasts

toast•mas•ter \'tōst-ˌmas-tər\ *n* : a person who presides at a banquet and introduces the after-dinner speakers

toast•mis•tress \-ˌmis-trəs\ *n* : a woman who acts as toastmaster

Tob *abbr* Tobit

to•bac•co \tə-'ba-kō\ *n, pl* **-cos** [Sp *tabaco*] **1** : a tall broad-leaved herb related to the potato; *also* : its leaves prepared for smoking or chewing or as snuff **2** : manufactured tobacco products; *also* : smoking as a practice

to•bac•co•nist \tə-'ba-kə-nist\ *n* : a dealer in tobacco

To•bi•as \tō-'bī-əs\ *n* : TOBIT

To•bit \'tō-bət\ *n* — see BIBLE table

¹to•bog•gan \tə-'bä-gən\ *n* : a long flat-bottomed light sled made of thin boards curved up at one end

²toboggan *vb* **1** : to coast on or as if on a toboggan **2** : to decline suddenly (as in value) — **to·bog·gan·er** *n*

toc·sin \'täk-sən\ *n* 1 : an alarm bell 2 : a warning signal

¹to·day \tə-'dā\ *adv* 1 : on or for this day 2 : at the present time

²today *n* : the present day, time, or age

tod·dle \'täd-ᵊl\ *vb* **tod·dled**; **tod·dling** : to walk with short tottering steps in the manner of a young child — **toddle** *n* — **tod·dler** *n*

tod·dy \'tä-dē\ *n, pl* **toddies** [Hindi *tāṛī* juice of a palm, fr. *tāṛ* a palm, fr. Skt *tāla*] : a drink made of liquor, sugar, spices, and hot water

to–do \tə-'dü\ *n, pl* **to–dos** \-'düz\ : BUSTLE, STIR, FUSS

¹toe \'tō\ *n* 1 : one of the jointed parts of the front end of a vertebrate's foot 2 : the front part of a foot or hoof

²toe *vb* **toed**; **toe·ing** : to touch, reach, or drive with the toes

toea \'toi-ə\ *n* — see *kina* at MONEY table

toe·hold \'tō-ˌhōld\ *n* 1 : a place of support for the toes 2 : a slight footing

toe·nail \'tō-ˌnāl\ *n* : a nail of a toe

tof·fee *or* **tof·fy** \'tò-fē, 'tä-\ *n, pl* **toffees** *or* **toffies** : candy of brittle but tender texture made by boiling sugar and butter together

to·fu \'tō-(ˌ)fü\ *n* [Jp *tōfu*] : a soft vegetable cheese made from soybeans

tog \'täg, 'tòg\ *vb* **togged**; **tog·ging** : to put togs on : DRESS

to·ga \'tō-gə\ *n* : the loose outer garment worn in public by citizens of ancient Rome — **to·gaed** \-gəd\ *adj*

¹to·geth·er \tə-'ge-thər\ *adv* 1 : in or into one place or group 2 : in or into contact or association ⟨mix ∼⟩ 3 : at one time : SIMULTANEOUSLY ⟨talk and work ∼⟩ 4 : in succession ⟨for days ∼⟩ 5 : in or into harmony or coherence ⟨get ∼ on a plan⟩ 6 : as a group : JOINTLY — **to·geth·er·ness** *n*

²together *adj* : composed in mind or manner

tog·gery \'tä-gə-rē, 'tò-\ *n* : CLOTHING

tog·gle switch \'tä-gəl-\ *n* : an electric switch operated by pushing a projecting lever through a small arc

To·go·lese \ˌtō-gə-'lēz, -'lēs\ *n* : a native or inhabitant of Togo — **Togolese** *adj*

togs \'tägz, 'tògz\ *n pl* : CLOTHING; *esp* : clothes for a specified use ⟨riding ∼⟩

¹toil \'tòil\ *n* 1 : laborious effort 2 : long fatiguing labor : DRUDGERY — **toil·ful** \-fəl\ *adj* — **toil·some** *adj*

²toil *vb* [ME, to argue, struggle, fr. OF *toeillier* to stir, disturb, dispute, fr. L *tudiculare* to crush, grind, fr. *tudicula* machine for crushing olives, dim. of *tudes* hammer] 1 : to work hard and long 2 : to proceed with great effort : PLOD — **toil·er** *n*

³toil *n* [ME *toile* cloth, net, fr. L *tela* cloth on a loom] : NET, TRAP — usu. used in pl.

toi·let \'tòi-lət\ *n* 1 : the act or process of dressing and grooming oneself 2 : BATHROOM 3 : a fixture for use in urinating and defecating; *esp* : one consisting essentially of a water-flushed bowl and seat — **toilet** *vb*

toi·let·ry \'tòi-lə-trē\ *n, pl* **-ries** : an article or preparation used in making one's toilet — usu. used in pl.

toi·lette \twä-'let\ *n* 1 : TOILET 1 2 : formal attire; *also* : a particular costume

toilet training *n* : the process of training a child to control bladder and bowel movements and to use the toilet — **toilet train** *vb*

toil·worn \'tòil-ˌwòrn\ *adj* : showing the effects of toil

To·kay \tō-'kā\ *n* : naturally sweet wine from Hungary

toke \'tōk\ *n, slang* : a puff on a marijuana cigarette or pipe

¹to·ken \'tō-kən\ *n* 1 : an outward sign 2 : SYMBOL, EMBLEM 3 : SOUVENIR, KEEPSAKE 4 : a small part representing the whole 5 : a piece resembling a coin issued as money or for use by a particular group on specified terms

²token *adj* 1 : done or given as a token esp. in partial fulfillment of an obligation 2 : representing only a symbolic effort : MINIMAL, PERFUNCTORY

to·ken·ism \'tō-kə-ˌni-zəm\ *n* : the policy or practice of making only a symbolic effort (as to desegregate)

told *past and past part of* TELL

tole \'tōl\ *n* : sheet metal and esp. tinplate for use in domestic and ornamental wares

tol·er·a·ble \'tä-lə-rə-bəl\ *adj* 1 : capable of being borne or endured 2 : moderately good : PASSABLE — **tol·er·a·bly** \-blē\ *adv*

tol·er·ance \'tä-lə-rəns\ *n* 1 : the act or practice of tolerating; *esp* : sympathy or indulgence for beliefs or practices differing from one's own 2 : the allowable deviation from a standard (as of size) 3 : the body's ability to become less responsive over time to something (as a drug) — **tol·er·ant** *adj* — **tol·er·ant·ly** *adv*

tol·er·ate \'tä-lə-ˌrāt\ *vb* **-at·ed**; **-at·ing** 1 : to exhibit physiological tolerance for (as a drug) 2 : to allow to be or to be done without hindrance **syn** abide, bear, suffer, stand, brook — **tol·er·a·tion** \ˌtä-lə-'rā-shən\ *n*

¹toll \'tōl\ *n* 1 : a tax paid for a privilege (as for passing over a bridge) 2 : a charge for a service (as for a long-distance telephone call) 3 : the cost in life, health, loss, or suffering

²toll *vb* 1 : to cause the slow regular sounding of (a bell) esp. by pulling a rope 2 : to give signal of : SOUND 3 : to sound with slow measured strokes 4 : to announce by tolling

³toll *n* : the sound of a tolling bell

toll·booth \'tōl-ˌbüth\ *n* : a booth where tolls are paid

toll·gate \-ˌgāt\ *n* : a point where vehicles stop to pay a toll

toll·house \-ˌhaus\ *n* : a house or booth where tolls are paid

tol·u·ene \'täl-yə-ˌwēn\ *n* : a liquid hydrocarbon used esp. as a solvent

tom \'täm\ *n* : the male of various animals (as a cat or turkey)

¹tom·a·hawk \'tä-mə-ˌhòk\ *n* : a light ax used as a missile and as a hand weapon esp. by No. American Indians

²tomahawk *vb* : to strike or kill with a tomahawk

to·ma·to \tə-'mā-tō, -'mä-\ *n, pl* **-toes** : a usu. large, rounded, and red or yellow pulpy edible berry of a widely grown tropical herb related to the potato; *also* : this herb

tomb \'tüm\ *n* 1 : a place of burial : GRAVE 2 : a house, chamber, or vault for the dead — **tomb** *vb*

tom·boy \'täm-ˌbòi\ *n* : a girl who behaves in a manner usu. considered boyish — **tom·boy·ish** *adj*

tomb·stone \'tüm-ˌstōn\ *n* : a stone marking a grave

tom·cat \'täm-ˌkat\ *n* : a male domestic cat

Tom Col·lins \ˌtäm-'kä-lənz\ *n* : a tall iced drink with a base of gin

tome \'tōm\ *n* : BOOK; *esp* : a large or weighty one

tom·fool·ery \ˌtäm-'fü-lə-rē\ *n* : playful or foolish behavior

tommy gun \'tä-mē-ˌgən\ *n* : SUBMACHINE GUN — **tommy-gun** *vb*

to·mog·ra·phy \tō-'mä-grə-fē\ *n* : a method of producing a three-dimensional image of the internal structures of a solid object (as the human body or the earth) — **to·mo·graph·ic** \ˌtō-mə-'gra-fik\ *adj*

to·mor·row \tə-'mär-ō\ *adv* : on or for the day after today — **tomorrow** *n*

tom·tit \'täm-ˌtit, täm-'tit\ *n* : any of various small active birds

tom-tom \'täm-ˌtäm\ *n* : a small-headed drum beaten with the hands

ton \'tən\ *n, pl* **tons** *also* **ton** 1 — see WEIGHT table 2 : a unit equal to the volume of a long ton weight of seawater used in reckoning the displacement of ships and equal to 35 cubic feet

to·nal·i·ty \tō-'na-lə-tē\ *n, pl* **-ties** : tonal quality

¹tone \'tōn\ *n* [ME, fr. L *tonus* tension, tone, fr. Gk *tonos*, lit., act of stretching; fr. the dependence of the pitch of a musical string on its tension] 1 : vocal or

musical sound; *esp* : sound quality **2** : a sound of definite pitch **3** : WHOLE STEP **4** : accent or inflection expressive of an emotion **5** : the pitch of a word often used to express differences of meaning **6** : style or manner of expression **7** : color quality; *also* : SHADE, TINT **8** : the effect in painting of light and shade together with color **9** : healthy and vigorous condition of a living body or bodily part; *also* : the state of partial contraction characteristic of normal muscle **10** : general character, quality, or trend **syn** atmosphere, feeling, mood, vein — **ton•al** \ˈtōn-ᵊl\ *adj*

²**tone** *vb* **toned; ton•ing 1** : to give a particular intonation or inflection to **2** : to impart tone to **3** : SOFTEN, MELLOW **4** : to harmonize in color : BLEND

tone•arm *n* : the movable part of a record player that carries the pickup and the needle

tong \ˈtäŋ, ˈtȯŋ\ *n* : a Chinese secret society in the U.S.

tongs \ˈtäŋz, ˈtȯŋz\ *n pl* : a grasping device consisting of two pieces joined at one end by a pivot or hinged like scissors — **tong** *vb*

¹**tongue** \ˈtəŋ\ *n* **1** : a fleshy movable process of the floor of the mouth used in tasting and in taking and swallowing food and in humans as a speech organ **2** : the flesh of a tongue (as of the ox) used as food **3** : the power of communication **4** : LANGUAGE **1 5** : manner or quality of utterance; *also* : intended meaning **6** : ecstatic usu. unintelligible utterance accompanying religious excitement — usu. used in pl. **7** : something resembling an animal's tongue esp. in being elongated and fastened at one end only — **tongued** \ˈtəŋd\ *adj* — **tongue•less** *adj*

²**tongue** *vb* **tongued; tongu•ing 1** : to touch or lick with the tongue **2** : to articulate notes on a wind instrument

tongue–in–cheek *adj* : characterized by insincerity, irony, or whimsical exaggeration — **tongue in cheek** *adv*

tongue–lash \ˈtəŋ-ˌlash\ *vb* : CHIDE, REPROVE — **tongue–lash•ing** \-iŋ\ *n*

tongue–tied \-ˌtīd\ *adj* : unable or disinclined to speak clearly or freely (as from shyness or a tongue impairment)

tongue twister *n* : an utterance that is difficult to articulate because of a succession of similar consonants

¹**ton•ic** \ˈtä-nik\ *adj* **1** : of, relating to, or producing a healthy physical or mental condition : INVIGORATING **2** : relating to or based on the 1st tone of a scale — **to•nic•i•ty** \tō-ˈni-sə-tē\ *n*

²**tonic** *n* **1** : something that invigorates, restores, or refreshes **2** : the 1st degree of a musical scale

tonic water *n* : a carbonated beverage flavored with a bit of quinine, lemon, and lime

¹**to•night** \tə-ˈnīt\ *adv* : on this present night or the coming night

²**tonight** *n* : the present or the coming night

ton•nage \ˈtə-nij\ *n* **1** : a duty on ships based on tons

carried **2** : ships in terms of the number of tons registered or carried **3** : total weight in tons shipped, carried, or mined

ton•sil \ˈtän-səl\ *n* : either of a pair of oval masses of lymphoid tissue that lie one on each side of the throat at the back of the mouth

ton•sil•lec•to•my \ˌtän-sə-ˈlek-tə-mē\ *n, pl* **-mies** : the surgical removal of the tonsils

ton•sil•li•tis \-ˈlī-təs\ *n* : inflammation of the tonsils

ton•so•ri•al \tän-ˈsȯr-ē-əl\ *adj* : of or relating to a barber or a barber's work

ton•sure \ˈtän-chər\ *n* [ME, fr. ML *tonsura*, fr. L, act of shearing, fr. *tonsus*, pp. of *tondēre* to shear] **1** : the rite of admission to the clerical state by the clipping or shaving of the head **2** : the shaven crown or patch worn by clerics (as monks) — **tonsure** *vb*

too \ˈtü\ *adv* **1** : in addition : ALSO **2** : EXCESSIVELY **3** : to such a degree as to be regrettable **4** : VERY

took *past of* TAKE

¹**tool** \ˈtül\ *n* **1** : a hand instrument that aids in accomplishing a task **2** : the cutting or shaping part in a machine; *also* : a machine for shaping metal in any way **3** : something used in doing a job (a scholar's books are his ~s); *also* : a means to an end **4** : a person used by another : DUPE **5** *pl* : natural ability

²**tool** *vb* **1** : to shape, form, or finish with a tool; *esp* : to letter or decorate (as a book cover) by means of hand tools **2** : to equip a plant or industry with machines and tools for production **3** : DRIVE, RIDE (~*ing* along at 60)

¹**toot** \ˈtüt\ *vb* **1** : to sound or cause to sound in short blasts **2** : to blow an instrument (as a horn) — **toot•er** *n*

²**toot** *n* : a short blast (as on a horn)

tooth \ˈtüth\ *n, pl* **teeth** \ˈtēth\ **1** : one of the hard bony structures borne esp. on the jaws of vertebrates and used for seizing and chewing food and as weapons; *also* : a hard sharp structure esp. around the mouth of an invertebrate **2** : something resembling an animal's tooth **3** : any of the projections on the edge of a wheel that fits into corresponding projections on another wheel — **toothed** \ˈtütht\ *adj* — **tooth•less** *adj*

tooth•ache \ˈtüth-ˌāk\ *n* : pain in or about a tooth

tooth•brush \-ˌbrəsh\ *n* : a brush for cleaning the teeth

tooth•paste \-ˌpāst\ *n* : a paste for cleaning the teeth

tooth•pick \-ˌpik\ *n* : a pointed instrument for removing food particles caught between the teeth

tooth powder *n* : a powder for cleaning the teeth

tooth•some \ˈtüth-səm\ *adj* **1** : AGREEABLE, ATTRACTIVE **2** : pleasing to the taste : DELICIOUS **syn** palatable, appetizing, savory, tasty

toothy \ˈtü-thē\ *adj* **tooth•i•er; -est** : having or showing prominent teeth

¹**top** \ˈtäp\ *n* **1** : the highest part, point, or level of something **2** : the stalks and leaves of a plant with edible roots (beet ~s) **3** : the upper end, edge, or surface (the ~ of a page) **4** : an upper piece, lid, or covering **5** : the highest degree, pitch, or rank

²**top** *vb* **topped; top•ping 1** : to remove or trim the top

of : PRUNE ⟨∼ a tree⟩ **2** : to cover with a top or on the top : CROWN, CAP **3** : to be superior to : EXCEL, SURPASS **4** : to go over the top of **5** : to strike (a ball) above the center **6** : to make an end or conclusion ⟨∼ off a meal with coffee⟩
³top *adj* **1** : of, relating to, or being at the top : HIGHEST **2** : CHIEF
⁴top *n* : a child's toy that has a tapering point on which it is made to spin
to·paz \ˈtō-ˌpaz\ *n* : a hard silicate of aluminum; *esp* : a yellow transparent topaz used as a gem
top·coat \ˈtäp-ˌkōt\ *n* **1** : a lightweight overcoat **2** : a protective coating (as of paint)
top dollar *n* : the highest amount being paid for a commodity or service
top–dress \-ˌdres\ *vb* : to apply material to (as land) without working it in; *esp* : to scatter fertilizer over
top·dress·ing \-ˌdre-siŋ\ *n* : a material used to topdress soil
top·flight \ˈtäp-ˈflīt\ *adj* : of, relating to, or being the highest level of excellence or rank — **top flight** *n*
top hat *n* : a tall-crowned hat usu. of beaver or silk
top–heavy \ˈtäp-ˌhe-vē\ *adj* : having the top part too heavy for the lower part
top·ic \ˈtä-pik\ *n* **1** : a heading in an outlined argument **2** : the subject of a discourse or a section of it : THEME
top·i·cal \-pi-kəl\ *adj* **1** : designed to be applied to or to work on a part (as of the body) **2** : of, relating to, or arranged by topics ⟨a ∼ outline⟩ **3** : relating to current or local events — **top·i·cal·ly** \-k(ə-)lē\ *adv*
top·knot \ˈtäp-ˌnät\ *n* **1** : an ornament (as a knot of ribbons) forming a headdress **2** : a crest of feathers or tuft of hair on the top of the head
top·less \-ləs\ *adj* **1** : wearing no clothing on the upper body **2** : featuring topless waitresses or entertainers
top·mast \ˈtäp-ˌmast, -məst\ *n* : the 2d mast above a ship's deck
top·most \ˈtäp-ˌmōst\ *adj* : highest of all : UPPERMOST
top–notch \-ˈnäch\ *adj* : of the highest quality : FIRSTRATE
to·pog·ra·phy \tə-ˈpä-grə-fē\ *n* **1** : the art of showing in detail on a map or chart the physical features of a place or region **2** : the outline of the form of a place showing its relief and the position of features (as rivers, roads, or cities) — **to·pog·ra·pher** \-fər\ *n* — **top·o·graph·ic** \ˌtä-pə-ˈgra-fik\ *or* **top·o·graph·i·cal** \-fi-kəl\ *adj*
top·ping \ˈtä-piŋ\ *n* : a food served on top of another to make it look or taste better
top·ple \ˈtä-pəl\ *vb* **top·pled; top·pling 1** : to fall from or as if from being top-heavy **2** : to push over : OVERTURN; *also* : OVERTHROW
tops \ˈtäps\ *adj* : topmost in quality or importance ⟨∼ in his field⟩
top·sail \ˈtäp-ˌsāl, -səl\ *also* **top·s'l** \-səl\ *n* : the sail next above the lowest sail on a mast in a squarerigged ship
top secret *adj* : demanding complete secrecy among those concerned
top·side \ˈtäp-ˈsīd\ *adv or adj* **1** : to or on the top or surface **2** : on deck
top·sides \-ˈsīdz\ *n pl* : the top portion of the outer surface of a ship on each side above the waterline
top·soil \ˈtäp-ˌsȯil\ *n* : surface soil usu. including the organic layer in which plants have most of their roots
top·sy–tur·vy \ˌtäp-sē-ˈtər-vē\ *adv* **1** : in utter confusion **2** : UPSIDE DOWN — **topsy-turvy** *adj*
toque \ˈtōk\ *n* : a woman's small hat without a brim
tor \ˈtȯr\ *n* : a high craggy hill
To·rah \ˈtȯr-ə\ *n* **1** : a scroll of the first five books of the Old Testament used in a synagogue; *also* : these five books **2** : the body of divine knowledge and law found in the Jewish scriptures and tradition
¹torch \ˈtȯrch\ *n* **1** : a flaming light made of something that burns brightly and usu. carried in the hand **2** : something that resembles a torch in giving light,

heat, or guidance **3** *chiefly Brit* : FLASHLIGHT **4** : a portable burner for producing a hot flame
²torch *vb* : to set fire to
torch·bear·er \ˈtȯrch-ˌbar-ər\ *n* : one who carries a torch; *also* : one in the forefront (as of a political campaign)
torch·light \-ˌlīt\ *n* : light given by torches
torch song *n* : a popular sentimental song of unrequited love
tore *past of* TEAR
to·re·ador \ˈtȯr-ē-ə-ˌdȯr\ *n* : TORERO
to·re·ro \tə-ˈrer-ō\ *n, pl* **-ros** [Sp] : BULLFIGHTER
¹tor·ment \ˈtȯr-ˌment\ *n* **1** : extreme pain or anguish of body or mind **2** : a source of vexation or pain
²tor·ment \tȯr-ˈment\ *vb* **1** : to cause severe suffering of body or mind to **2** : DISTORT, TWIST *syn* rack, afflict, try, torture — **tor·men·tor** \-ˈmen-tər\ *n*
torn *past part of* TEAR
tor·na·do \tȯr-ˈnā-dō\ *n, pl* **-does** *or* **-dos** [modif of Sp *tronada* thunderstorm, fr. *tronar* to thunder, fr. L *tonare*] : a violent destructive whirling wind accompanied by a funnel-shaped cloud that moves over a narrow path
¹tor·pe·do \tȯr-ˈpē-dō\ *n, pl* **-does** : a thin cylindrical self-propelled underwater weapon
²torpedo *vb* **tor·pe·doed; tor·pe·do·ing** : to hit or destroy with or as if with a torpedo
torpedo boat *n* : a small very fast boat for firing torpedoes
tor·pid \ˈtȯr-pəd\ *adj* **1** : having lost motion or the power of exertion : DORMANT **2** : SLUGGISH **3** : lacking vigor : DULL — **tor·pid·i·ty** \tȯr-ˈpi-də-tē\ *n*
tor·por \ˈtȯr-pər\ *n* **1** : DULLNESS, APATHY **2** : extreme sluggishness : STAGNATION *syn* stupor, lethargy, languor, lassitude
¹torque \ˈtȯrk\ *n* : a force that produces or tends to produce rotation or torsion
²torque *vb* **torqued; torqu·ing** : to impart torque to : cause to twist (as about an axis)
tor·rent \ˈtȯr-ənt\ *n* [F, fr. L *torrent-, torrens*, fr. *torrent-, torrens* burning, seething, rushing, fr. prp. of *torrēre* to parch, burn] **1** : a tumultuous outburst **2** : a rushing stream (as of water)
tor·ren·tial \tȯ-ˈren-chəl\ *adj* : relating to or resembling a torrent ⟨∼ rains⟩
tor·rid \ˈtȯr-əd\ *adj* **1** : parched with heat esp. of the sun : HOT **2** : ARDENT
torrid zone *n* : the region of the earth between the tropic of Cancer and the tropic of Capricorn
tor·sion \ˈtȯr-shən\ *n* **1** : a wrenching by which one part of a body is under pressure to turn about a longitudinal axis while the other part is held fast or is under pressure to turn in the opposite direction **2** : a twisting of a bodily organ or part on its own axis — **tor·sion·al** \ˈtȯr-shə-nəl\ *adj* — **tor·sion·al·ly** *adv*
tor·so \ˈtȯr-sō\ *n, pl* **torsos** *or* **tor·si** \ˈtȯr-ˌsē\ [It, lit., stalk] : the trunk of the human body
tort \ˈtȯrt\ *n* : a wrongful act which does not involve a breach of contract and for which the injured party can recover damages in a civil action
tor·ti·lla \tȯr-ˈtē-ə\ *n* : a round thin cake of unleavened cornmeal or wheat flour bread
tor·toise \ˈtȯr-təs\ *n* : TURTLE; *esp* : any of a family of land turtles
tor·toise·shell \-ˌshel\ *n* : the mottled horny substance of the shell of some turtles used in inlaying and in making various ornamental articles — **tortoiseshell** *adj*
tor·to·ni \tȯr-ˈtō-nē\ *n* : rich ice cream often made with minced almonds and chopped cherries and flavored with rum
tor·tu·ous \ˈtȯr-chə-wəs\ *adj* **1** : marked by twists or turns : WINDING **2** : DEVIOUS, TRICKY
¹tor·ture \ˈtȯr-chər\ *n* **1** : anguish of body or mind **2** : the infliction of severe pain esp. to punish or coerce
²torture *vb* **tor·tured; tor·tur·ing 1** : to cause intense

suffering to : TORMENT **2** : to punish or coerce by inflicting severe pain **3** : TWIST, DISTORT **syn** rack, harrow, afflict, try — **tor·tur·er** *n*

To·ry \'tōr-ē\ *n, pl* **Tories 1** : a member of a chiefly 18th century British party upholding the established church and the traditional political structure **2** : an American supporter of the British during the American Revolution **3** *often not cap* : an extreme conservative — **Tory** *adj*

¹toss \'tòs, 'täs\ *vb* **1** : to fling to and fro or up and down **2** : to throw with a quick light motion; *also* : BANDY **3** : to fling or lift with a sudden motion ⟨~*ed* her head angrily⟩ **4** : to move restlessly or turbulently ⟨~*es* on the waves⟩ **5** : to twist and turn repeatedly **6** : FLOUNCE **7** : to accomplish readily ⟨~ off an article⟩ **8** : to decide an issue by flipping a coin

²toss *n* : an act or instance of tossing; *esp* : TOSS-UP 1

toss–up \-ˌəp\ *n* **1** : a deciding by flipping a coin **2** : an even chance **3** : something that offers no clear basis for choice

¹tot \'tät\ *n* **1** : a small child **2** : a small drink of alcoholic liquor : SHOT

²tot *vb* **tot·ted; tot·ting** : to add up

³tot *abbr* total

¹to·tal \'tōt-ᵊl\ *adj* **1** : making up a whole : ENTIRE ⟨~ amount⟩ **2** : COMPLETE, UTTER ⟨a ~ failure⟩ **3** : involving a complete and unified effort esp. to achieve a desired effect — **to·tal·ly** *adv*

²total *n* **1** : SUM 4 **2** : the entire amount **syn** aggregate, whole, gross, totality

³total *vb* **to·taled** *or* **to·talled; to·tal·ing** *or* **to·tal·ling 1** : to add up : COMPUTE **2** : to amount to : NUMBER **3** : to make a total wreck of (a car)

to·tal·i·tar·i·an \tō-ˌtal-ə-'ter-ē-ən\ *adj* : of, relating to, or advocating a political regime based on subordination of the individual to the state and strict control of all aspects of life esp. by coercive measures — **to·tal·i·tar·i·an·ism** \-ē-ə-ˌni-zəm\ *n*

to·tal·i·ty \tō-'ta-lə-tē\ *n, pl* **-ties 1** : an aggregate amount : SUM, WHOLE **2** : ENTIRETY, WHOLENESS

to·tal·iza·tor *or* **to·tal·isa·tor** \'tōt-ᵊl-ə-ˌzā-tər\ *n* : a machine for registering and indicating the number of bets and the odds on a horse or dog race

¹tote \'tōt\ *vb* **tot·ed; tot·ing** : CARRY

²tote *vb* **tot·ed; tot·ing** : ADD, TOTAL — usu. used with *up*

to·tem \'tō-təm\ *n* : an object (as an animal or plant) serving as the emblem of a family or clan and often as a reminder of its ancestry; *also* : something usu. carved or painted to represent such an object

totem pole *n* : a pole that is carved with a series of totems and is erected before the houses of some northwest American Indians

tot·ter \'tä-tər\ *vb* **1** : to tremble or rock as if about to fall : SWAY **2** : to move unsteadily : STAGGER

tou·can \'tü-ˌkan\ *n* : any of a family of fruit-eating birds of tropical America with brilliant coloring and a very large beak

¹touch \'təch\ *vb* **1** : to bring a bodily part (as the hand) into contact with so as to feel **2** : to be or cause to be in contact **3** : to strike or push lightly esp. with the hand or foot **4** : DISTURB, HARM **5** : to make use of ⟨never ~*es* alcohol⟩ **6** : to induce to give or lend **7** : to get to : REACH **8** : to refer to in passing : MENTION **9** : to affect the interest of : CONCERN **10** : to leave a mark on; *also* : BLEMISH **11** : to move to sympathetic feeling **12** : to come close : VERGE **13** : to have a bearing : RELATE **14** : to make a usu. brief or incidental stop in port **syn** affect, influence, impress, strike, sway

²touch *n* **1** : a light stroke or tap **2** : the act or fact of touching or being touched **3** : the sense by which pressure or traction on the skin or mucous membrane is perceived; *also* : a particular sensation conveyed by this sense **4** : mental or moral sensitiveness : TACT **5** : a small quantity : HINT ⟨a ~ of spring in the air⟩

6 : a manner of striking or touching esp. the keys of a keyboard instrument **7** : an improving detail ⟨add a few ~*es* to the painting⟩ **8** : distinctive manner or skill ⟨the ~ of a master⟩ **9** : the state of being in contact ⟨keep in ~⟩ **syn** suggestion, suspicion, tincture, tinge

touch·down \'təch-ˌdaùn\ *n* : the act of scoring six points in American football by being lawfully in possession of the ball on, above, or behind an opponent's goal line

tou·ché \tü-'shā\ *interj* [F] — used to acknowledge a hit in fencing or the success of an argument, an accusation, or a witty point

touch football *n* : football in which touching is substituted for tackling

touch·ing *adj* : capable of stirring emotions **syn** moving, impressive, poignant, affecting

touch off *vb* **1** : to describe with precision **2** : to start by or as if by touching with fire

touch·stone \'təch-ˌstōn\ *n* : a test or criterion of genuineness or quality **syn** standard, gauge, benchmark, yardstick

touch up *vb* : to improve or perfect by small additional strokes or alterations — **touch–up** \'təch-ˌəp\ *n*

touchy \'tə-chē\ *adj* **touch·i·er; -est 1** : easily offended : PEEVISH **2** : calling for tact in treatment ⟨a ~ subject⟩ **syn** irascible, cranky, cross, tetchy, testy

¹tough \'təf\ *adj* **1** : strong or firm in texture but flexible and not brittle **2** : not easily chewed **3** : characterized by severity and determination ⟨a ~ policy⟩ **4** : capable of enduring strain or hardship : ROBUST **5** : hard to influence : STUBBORN **6** : difficult to accomplish, resolve, or cope with ⟨a ~ problem⟩ **7** : ROWDYISH **syn** tenacious, stout, sturdy, stalwart — **tough·ly** *adv* — **tough·ness** *n*

²tough *n* : a tough person : ROWDY

tough·en \'tə-fən\ *vb* **tough·ened; tough·en·ing** : to make or become tough

tou·pee \tü-'pā\ *n* [F *toupet* forelock] : a small wig for a bald spot

¹tour \'tùr, *1 is also* 'taùr\ *n* **1** : one's turn : SHIFT **2** : a journey in which one returns to the starting point

²tour *vb* : to make a tour

tour de force \ˌtùr-də-'fōrs\ *n, pl* **tours de force** *same*\ [F] : a feat of strength, skill, or ingenuity

tour·ist \'tùr-ist\ *n* : one that makes a tour for pleasure or culture

tourist class *n* : economy accommodations (as on a ship)

tour·ma·line \'tùr-mə-lən, -ˌlēn\ *n* : a mineral that when transparent is valued as a gem

tour·na·ment \'tùr-nə-mənt, 'tər-\ *n* **1** : a medieval sport in which mounted armored knights contended with blunted lances or swords **2** : a championship series of games or athletic contests

tour·ney \-nē\ *n, pl* **tourneys** : TOURNAMENT

tour·ni·quet \'tùr-ni-kət, 'tər-\ *n* : a device (as a tight bandage) for stopping bleeding or blood flow

tou·sle \'taù-zəl\ *vb* **tou·sled; tou·sling** : to disorder by rough handling : DISHEVEL, MUSS

tout \'taùt, *2 is also* 'tüt\ *vb* **1** : to give a tip or solicit bets on a racehorse **2** : to praise or publicize loudly — **tout** *n*

¹tow \'tō\ *vb* : to draw or pull along behind

²tow *n* **1** : an act of towing or condition of being towed **2** : something (as a barge) that is towed

³tow *n* : short or broken fiber (as of flax or hemp) used esp. for yarn, twine, or stuffing

to·ward \'tōrd, 'tō-ərd, tə-'wòrd\ *or* **to·wards** \'tōrdz, 'tō-ərdz, tə-'wòrdz\ *prep* **1** : in the direction of ⟨heading ~ the river⟩ **2** : along a course leading to ⟨efforts ~ reconciliation⟩ **3** : in regard to ⟨tolerance ~ minorities⟩ **4** : so as to face ⟨turn the chair ~ the window⟩ **5** : close upon ⟨it was getting along ~ sundown⟩ **6** : for part payment of ⟨here's $100 ~ your tuition⟩

tow·boat \'tō-ˌbōt\ *n* : TUGBOAT

tow•el \'taú-əl\ *n* : an absorbent cloth or paper for wiping or drying

tow•el•ing *or* **tow•el•ling** *n* : a cotton or linen fabric for making towels

¹tow•er \'taú-ər\ *n* **1** : a tall structure either isolated or built upon a larger structure ⟨an observation ∼⟩ **2** : a towering citadel — **tow•ered** *adj*

²tower *vb* : to reach or rise to a great height

tow•er•ing *adj* **1** : LOFTY ⟨∼ pines⟩ **2** : reaching high intensity ⟨a ∼ rage⟩ **3** : EXCESSIVE ⟨∼ ambition⟩

tow•head \'tō-₁hed\ *n* : a person having whitish blond hair — **tow•head•ed** \-₁he-dəd\ *adj*

to•whee \'tō-₁hē, 'tō-(₁)ē, tō-'hē\ *n* : a common finch of eastern No. America having the male black, white, and reddish; *also* : any of several closely related finches

to wit *adv* : NAMELY

town \'taún\ *n* **1** : a compactly settled area usu. larger than a village but smaller than a city **2** : CITY **3** : the inhabitants of a town **4** : a New England territorial and political unit usu. containing both rural and urban areas; *also* : a New England community in which matters of local government are decided by a general assembly (**town meeting**) of qualified voters

town house *n* **1** : the city residence of a person having a country home **2** : a single-family house of two or sometimes three stories connected to another house by a common wall

town•ie *or* **towny** \'taú-nē\ *n, pl* **townies** : a permanent resident of a town as distinguished from a member of another group

towns•folk \'taúnz-₁fōk\ *n pl* : TOWNSPEOPLE

town•ship \'taún-₁ship\ *n* **1** : TOWN 4 **2** : a unit of local government in some states **3** : an unorganized subdivision of a county; *also* : an administrative division **4** : a division of territory in surveys of U.S. public land containing 36 square miles **5** : an area in the Republic of South Africa segregated for occupation by persons of non-European descent

towns•man \'taúnz-mən\ *n* **1** : a native or resident of a town or city **2** : a fellow citizen of a town

towns•peo•ple \-₁pē-pəl\ *n pl* **1** : the inhabitants of a town or city **2** : town-bred persons

towns•wom•an \-₁wú-mən\ *n* **1** : a woman who is a native or resident of a town or city **2** : a woman who is a fellow citizen of a town

tow•path \'tō-₁path, -₁pȧth\ *n* : a path (as along a canal) traveled esp. by draft animals towing boats

tow truck *n* : a truck equipped for towing disabled vehicles

tox•emia \täk-'sē-mē-ə\ *n* : a bodily disorder associated with the presence of toxic substances in the blood

tox•ic \'täk-sik\ *adj* [LL *toxicus*, fr. L *toxicum* poison, fr. Gk *toxikon* arrow poison, fr. neut. of *toxikos* of a bow, fr. *toxon* bow, arrow] : of, relating to, or caused by poison or a toxin : POISONOUS — **tox•ic•i•ty** \täk-'si-sə-tē\ *n*

tox•i•col•o•gy \₁täk-si-'kä-lə-jē\ *n* : a science that deals with poisons and esp. with problems of their use and control — **tox•i•co•log•i•cal** \-kə-'lä-ji-kəl\ *or* **tox•i•co•log•ic** \-kə-'lä-jik\ *adj* — **tox•i•col•o•gist** \-'kä-lə-jist\ *n*

toxic shock syndrome *n* : an acute disease associated with the presence of a bacterium that is characterized by fever, diarrhea, nausea, diffuse erythema, and shock and occurs esp. in menstruating females using tampons

tox•in \'täk-sən\ *n* : a poisonous substance produced by metabolic activities of a living organism that is usu. unstable, very toxic when introduced into the tissues, and usu. capable of inducing antibodies

¹toy \'tói\ *n* **1** : something trifling **2** : a small ornament : BAUBLE **3** : something for a child to play with

²toy *vb* **1** : to deal with something lightly : TRIFLE **2** : FLIRT **3** : to amuse oneself as if with a plaything

³toy *adj* **1** : DIMINUTIVE **2** : designed for use as a toy

tp *abbr* **1** title page **2** township

tpk *or* **tpke** *abbr* turnpike

tr *abbr* **1** translated; translation; translator **2** transpose **3** troop

¹trace \'trās\ *n* **1** : a mark (as a footprint or track) left by something that has passed **2** : a minute or barely detectable amount

²trace *vb* **traced; trac•ing 1** : to mark out : SKETCH **2** : to form (as letters) carefully **3** : to copy (a drawing) by marking lines on transparent paper laid over the drawing to be copied **4** : to follow the trail of : track down **5** : to study out and follow the development of — **trace•able** *adj*

³trace *n* : either of two lines of a harness for fastening a draft animal to a vehicle

trac•er \'trā-sər\ *n* **1** : one that traces **2** : ammunition containing a chemical to mark the flight of projectiles by a trail of smoke or fire

trac•ery \'trā-sə-rē\ *n, pl* **-er•ies** : ornamental work having a design with branching or interlacing lines

tra•chea \'trā-kē-ə\ *n, pl* **-che•ae** \-kē-₁ē\ *also* **-che•as** : the main tube by which air enters the lungs of vertebrates : WINDPIPE — **tra•che•al** \-kē-əl\ *adj*

tra•che•ot•o•my \₁trā-kē-'ä-tə-mē\ *n, pl* **-mies** : the surgical operation of cutting into the trachea esp. through the skin

trac•ing *n* **1** : the act of one that traces **2** : something that is traced **3** : a graphic record made by an instrument for measuring vibrations or pulsations

¹track \'trak\ *n* **1** : a mark left in passing **2** : PATH, ROUTE, TRAIL **3** : a course laid out for racing; *also* : track-and-field sports **4** : one of a series of paths along which material (as music) is recorded (as on magnetic tape) **5** : the course along which something moves; *esp* : a way made by two parallel lines of metal rails **6** : awareness of a fact or progression ⟨lost ∼ of time⟩ **7** : either of two endless metal belts on which a vehicle (as a bulldozer) travels

²track *vb* **1** : to follow the tracks or traces of : TRAIL **2** : to observe the moving path of (as a missile) **3** : to make tracks on **4** : to carry (as mud) on the feet and deposit — **track•er** *n*

track•age \'tra-kij\ *n* : lines of railway track

track–and–field *adj* : of or relating to athletic contests held on a running track or on the adjacent field

¹tract \'trakt\ *n* **1** : an area without precise boundaries ⟨huge ∼s of land⟩ **2** : a defined area of land **3** : a system of body parts or organs that act together to perform some function ⟨the digestive ∼⟩

²tract *n* : a pamphlet of political or religious propaganda

trac•ta•ble \'trak-tə-bəl\ *adj* : easily controlled : DOCILE **syn** amenable, obedient, biddable

tract house *n* : any of many similar houses built on a tract of land

trac•tion \'trak-shən\ *n* **1** : the act of drawing : the state of being drawn **2** : the drawing of a vehicle by motive power; *also* : the particular form of motive power used **3** : the adhesive friction of a body on a surface on which it moves **4** : a pulling force applied to a skeletal structure (as a broken bone) by using a special device; *also* : a state of tension created by such a pulling force ⟨a leg in ∼⟩ — **trac•tion•al** \-shə-nəl\ *adj* — **trac•tive** \'trak-tiv\ *adj*

trac•tor \'trak-tər\ *n* **1** : an automotive vehicle used esp. for drawing farm equipment **2** : a truck for hauling a trailer

¹trade \'trād\ *n* **1** : one's regular business or work : OCCUPATION **2** : an occupation requiring manual or mechanical skill **3** : the persons engaged in a business or industry **4** : the business of buying and selling or bartering commodities **5** : an act of trading : TRANSACTION

²**trade** *vb* **trad•ed; trad•ing 1** : to give in exchange for another commodity : BARTER **2** : to engage in the exchange, purchase, or sale of goods **3** : to deal regularly as a customer — **trade on** : EXPLOIT ⟨*trades on* his family name⟩

trade–in \'trād-ₗin\ *n* : an item of merchandise traded in

trade in *vb* : to turn in as part payment for a purchase

¹**trade•mark** \'trād-ₗmärk\ *n* : a device (as a word or mark) that points distinctly to the origin or ownership of merchandise to which it is applied and that is legally reserved for the exclusive use of the owner; *also* : something that identifies a person or thing

²**trademark** *vb* : to secure the trademark rights for

trade name *n* : a name that is given by a manufacturer or merchant to a product to distinguish it as made of or sold by him and that may be used and protected as a trademark

trad•er \'trā-dər\ *n* **1** : a person whose business is buying or selling **2** : a ship engaged in trade

trades•man \'trādz-mən\ *n* **1** : one who runs a retail store : SHOPKEEPER **2** : CRAFTSMAN

trades•peo•ple \-ₗpē-pəl\ *n pl* : people engaged in trade

trade union *n* : LABOR UNION

trade wind *n* : a wind blowing almost constantly in one direction

trading stamp *n* : a printed stamp given as a premium to a retail customer that when accumulated may be redeemed for merchandise

tra•di•tion \trə-'di-shən\ *n* **1** : an inherited, established, or customary pattern of thought or action **2** : the handing down of beliefs and customs by word of mouth or by example without written instruction; *also* : a belief or custom thus handed down — **tra•di•tion•al** \-ₗdi-shə-nəl\ *adj* — **tra•di•tion•al•ly** *adv*

tra•duce \trə-'düs, -'dyüs\ *vb* **tra•duced; tra•duc•ing** : to lower the reputation of : DEFAME, SLANDER **syn** malign, libel, calumniate — **tra•duc•er** *n*

¹**traf•fic** \'tra-fik\ *n* **1** : the business of bartering or buying and selling **2** : communication or dealings between individuals or groups **3** : the movement (as of vehicles) along a route; *also* : the vehicles, people, ships, or planes moving along a route **4** : the passengers or cargo carried by a transportation system

²**traffic** *vb* **traf•ficked; traf•fick•ing** : to carry on traffic — **traf•fick•er** *n*

traffic circle *n* : ROTARY 2

traffic light *n* : an electrically operated visual signal for controlling traffic

tra•ge•di•an \trə-'jē-dē-ən\ *n* **1** : a writer of tragedies **2** : an actor who plays tragic roles

tra•ge•di•enne \trə-ₗjē-dē-'en\ *n* [F] : an actress who plays tragic roles

trag•e•dy \'tra-jə-dē\ *n, pl* **-dies** [ME *tragedie*, fr. MF, fr. L *tragoedia*, fr. Gk *tragōidia*, fr. *tragos* goat + *aeidein* to sing] **1** : a serious drama with a sorrowful or disastrous conclusion **2** : a disastrous event : CALAMITY; *also* : MISFORTUNE **3** : tragic quality or element ⟨the ∼ of life⟩

trag•ic \'tra-jik\ *also* **trag•i•cal** \-ji-kəl\ *adj* **1** : of, relating to, or expressive of tragedy **2** : appropriate to tragedy **3** : LAMENTABLE, UNFORTUNATE — **trag•i•cal•ly** \-ji-k(ə-)lē\ *adv*

¹**trail** \'trāl\ *vb* **1** : to hang down so as to drag along or sweep the ground **2** : to draw or drag along behind **3** : to extend over a surface in a straggling manner **4** : to lag behind **5** : to follow the track of : PURSUE **6** : DWINDLE ⟨her voice ∼*ed* off⟩

²**trail** *n* **1** : something that trails or is trailed ⟨a ∼ of smoke⟩ **2** : a trace or mark left by something that has passed or been drawn along : SCENT, TRACK ⟨a ∼ of blood⟩ **3** : a beaten path; *also* : a marked path through woods

trail bike *n* : a small motorcycle for off-road use

trail•blaz•er \-ₗblā-zər\ *n* : PATHFINDER, PIONEER — **trail•blaz•ing** *adj or n*

trail•er \'trā-lər\ *n* **1** : one that trails; *esp* : a creeping plant (as an ivy) **2** : a vehicle that is hauled by another (as a tractor) **3** : a vehicle equipped to serve wherever parked as a dwelling or place of business

trailing arbutus *n* : a trailing spring-flowering plant of the heath family with fragrant pink or white flowers; *also* : its flower

¹**train** \'trān\ *n* **1** : a part of a gown that trails behind the wearer **2** : RETINUE **3** : a moving file of persons, vehicles, or animals **4** : a connected series ⟨a ∼ of thought⟩ **5** : AFTERMATH **6** : a connected line of railroad cars usu. hauled by a locomotive **syn** succession, sequence, procession, chain

²**train** *vb* **1** : to cause to grow as desired ⟨∼ a vine on a trellis⟩ **2** : to form by instruction, discipline, or drill **3** : to make or become prepared (as by exercise) for a test of skill **4** : to aim or point at an object ⟨∼ guns on a fort⟩ **syn** discipline, school, educate, instruct — **train•er** *n*

train•ee \trā-'nē\ *n* : one who is being trained esp. for a job

train•ing *n* **1** : the act, process, or method of one who trains **2** : the skill, knowledge, or experience gained by one who trains

train•man \-mən\ *n* : a member of a train crew

traipse \'trāps\ *vb* **traipsed; traips•ing** : TRAMP, WALK

trait \'trāt\ *n* **1** : a distinguishing quality (as of personality) : PECULIARITY **2** : an inherited characteristic

trai•tor \'trā-tər\ *n* [ME *traitre*, fr. OF, fr. L *traditor*, fr. *tradere* to hand over, deliver, betray, fr. *trans-* across + *dare* to give] **1** : one who betrays another's trust or is false to an obligation **2** : one who commits treason — **trai•tor•ous** *adj*

tra•jec•to•ry \trə-'jek-tə-rē\ *n, pl* **-ries** : the curve that a body (as a planet in its orbit) describes in space

tram \'tram\ *n* **1** : a boxlike car running on a railway **(tram•way** \-ₗwā\) in a mine **2** *chiefly Brit* : STREETCAR **3** : an overhead cable car

¹**tram•mel** \'tra-məl\ *n* [ME *tramayle*, a kind of net, fr. MF *tremail*, fr. LL *tremaculum*, fr. L *tres* three + *macula* mesh, spot] : something impeding activity, progress, or freedom

²**trammel** *vb* **-meled** *or* **-melled; -mel•ing** *or* **-mel•ling**

1 : to catch and hold in or as if in a net **2** : HAMPER **syn** clog, fetter, shackle, hobble

¹**tramp** \'tramp, *1 & 3 are also* 'trämp, 'tromp\ *vb* **1** : to walk, tread, or step heavily **2** : to walk about or through; *also* : HIKE **3** : to tread on forcibly and repeatedly

²**tramp** \'tramp, *5 is also* 'trämp, 'tromp\ *n* **1** : a foot traveler **2** : a begging or thieving vagrant **3** : an immoral woman; *esp* : PROSTITUTE **4** : a walking trip : HIKE **5** : the succession of sounds made by the beating of feet on a road **6** : a ship that does not follow a regular course but takes cargo to any port

tram·ple \'tram-pəl\ *vb* **tram·pled; tram·pling 1** : to tread heavily so as to bruise, crush, or injure **2** : to inflict injury or destruction **3** : to press down or crush by or as if by treading — **trample** *n* — **tram·pler** *n*

tram·po·line \₁tram-pə-'lēn, 'tram-pə-₁lēn\ *n* [It *trampolino* springboard] : a resilient sheet or web (as of nylon) supported by springs in a metal frame and used as a springboard in tumbling — **tram·po·lin·ist** \-'lē-nist, -₁lē-\ *n*

trance \'trans\ *n* [ME, fr. MF *transe,* fr. *transir* to pass away, swoon, fr. L *transire* to pass, pass away, fr. *trans-* across + *ire* to go] **1** : a living state in which the vital bodily and mental activities slow down greatly **2** : a sleeplike state (as of deep hypnosis) **3** : a state of very deep absorption

tran·quil \'traŋ-kwəl, 'tran-\ *adj* : free from agitation or disturbance : QUIET **syn** serene, placid, peaceful — **tran·quil·li·ty** *or* **tran·quil·i·ty** \tran-'kwi-lə-tē, traŋ-\ *n* — **tran·quil·ly** *adv*

tran·quil·ize *also* **tran·quil·lize** \'traŋ-kwə-₁līz, 'tran-\ *vb* **-ized** *also* **-lized; -iz·ing** *also* **-liz·ing** : to make or become tranquil; *esp* : to relieve of mental tension and anxiety by means of drugs

tran·quil·iz·er *also* **tran·quil·liz·er** \-₁lī-zər\ *n* : a drug used to relieve mental disturbance (as tension and anxiety)

trans *abbr* **1** transaction **2** transitive **3** translated; translation; translator **4** transmission **5** transportation **6** transverse

trans·act \tran-'zakt, -'sakt\ *vb* : CARRY OUT, PERFORM; *also* : CONDUCT

trans·ac·tion \-'zak-shən, -'sak-\ *n* **1** : something transacted; *esp* : a business deal **2** : an act or process of transacting **3** *pl* : the records of the proceedings of a society or organization

trans·at·lan·tic \₁trans-ət-'lan-tik, ₁tranz-\ *adj* : crossing or extending across or situated beyond the Atlantic Ocean

trans·ax·le \trans-'ak-səl\ *n* : a unit combining the transmission and the front axle of a front-wheel-drive automobile

trans·ceiv·er \tran-'sē-vər\ *n* : a radio transmitter-receiver that uses many of the same components for both transmission and reception

trans·cend \tran-'send\ *vb* **1** : to rise above the limits of **2** : SURPASS **syn** exceed, outdo, outshine, outstrip

tran·scen·dent \-'sen-dənt\ *adj* **1** : exceeding usual limits : SURPASSING **2** : transcending material existence **syn** superlative, supreme, peerless, incomparable

tran·scen·den·tal \₁tran-₁sen-'dent-ᵊl, -sən-\ *adj* **1** : TRANSCENDENT **2** : of, relating to, or characteristic of transcendentalism; *also* : ABSTRUSE

tran·scen·den·tal·ism \-ᵊl-₁i-zəm\ *n* : a philosophy holding that ultimate reality is unknowable or asserting the primacy of the spiritual over the material and empirical — **tran·scen·den·tal·ist** \-ᵊl-ist\ *adj or n*

trans·con·ti·nen·tal \₁trans-₁känt-ᵊn-'ent-ᵊl\ *adj* : extending or going across a continent

tran·scribe \trans-'krīb\ *vb* **tran·scribed; tran·scrib·ing 1** : to write a copy of **2** : to make a copy of (dictated or recorded matter) in longhand or on a typewriter **3** : to represent (speech sounds) by means of

phonetic symbols; *also* : to make a musical transcription of

tran·script \'tran-₁skript\ *n* **1** : a written, printed, or typed copy **2** : an official copy esp. of a student's educational record

tran·scrip·tion \tran-'skrip-shən\ *n* **1** : an act or process of transcribing **2** : COPY, TRANSCRIPT **3** : an arrangement of a musical composition for some instrument or voice other than the original

tran·scrip·tion·ist \-shə-nist\ *n* : one that transcribes; *esp* : a typist who transcribes medical reports

trans·der·mal \trans-'dər-məl, 'tranz-\ *adj* : relating to, being, or supplying a medication in a form for absorption through the skin ⟨~ nicotine patch⟩

trans·duc·er \trans-'dü-sər, tranz-, -'dyü-\ *n* : a device that is actuated by power from one system and supplies power usu. in another form to a second system

tran·sept \'tran-₁sept\ *n* : the part of a cruciform church that crosses at right angles to the greatest length; *also* : either of the projecting ends

¹**trans·fer** \trans-'fər, 'trans-₁fər\ *vb* **trans·ferred; trans·fer·ring 1** : to pass or cause to pass from one person, place, or situation to another : TRANSPORT, TRANSMIT **2** : to make over the possession of : CONVEY **3** : to print or copy from one surface to another by contact **4** : to change from one vehicle or transportation line to another — **trans·fer·able** \trans-'fər-ə-bəl\ *adj* — **trans·fer·al** \-əl\ *n*

²**trans·fer** \'trans-₁fər\ *n* **1** : conveyance of right, title, or interest in property from one person to another **2** : an act or process of transferring **3** : one that transfers or is transferred **4** : a ticket entitling a passenger to continue a trip on another route

trans·fer·ence \trans-'fər-əns\ *n* : an act, process, or instance of transferring

trans·fig·ure \trans-'fi-gyər\ *vb* **-ured; -ur·ing 1** : to change the form or appearance of **2** : EXALT, GLORIFY — **trans·fig·u·ra·tion** \₁trans-₁fi-gyə-'rä-shən, -gə-\ *n*

trans·fix \trans-'fiks\ *vb* **1** : to pierce through with or as if with a pointed weapon **2** : to hold motionless by or as if by piercing

trans·form \trans-'förm\ *vb* : to change in structure, appearance, or character **syn** transmute, transfigure, transmogrify — **trans·for·ma·tion** \₁trans-fər-'mä-shən\ *n*

trans·form·er \trans-'för-mər\ *n* : one that transforms; *esp* : a device for converting variations of current in one circuit into variations of voltage and current in another circuit

trans·fuse \trans-'fyüz\ *vb* **trans·fused; trans·fus·ing 1** : to cause to pass from one to another **2** : to diffuse into or through **3** : to transfer (as blood) into a vein of a person or animal — **trans·fu·sion** \-'fyü-zhən\ *n*

trans·gress \trans-'gres, tranz-\ *vb* [F *transgresser,* L *transgressus,* pp. of *transgredi* to step beyond or across, fr. *trans-* across + *gradi* to step] **1** : to go beyond the limits set by ⟨~ the divine law⟩ **2** : to go beyond : EXCEED **3** : SIN — **trans·gres·sion** \-'gre-shən\ *n* — **trans·gres·sor** \-'gre-sər\ *n*

¹**tran·sient** \'tran-shənt, -sē-ənt, -shē-, -zē-\ *adj* **1** : not lasting long : SHORT-LIVED **2** : passing through a place with only a brief stay **syn** transitory, passing, momentary, fleeting — **tran·sient·ly** *adv*

²**transient** *n* : one that is transient; *esp* : a transient guest

tran·sis·tor \tran-'zis-tər, -'sis-\ *n* [*transfer* + *resistor;* fr. its transferring an electrical signal across a resistor] **1** : a small electronic semiconductor device used in electronic equipment **2** : a radio having transistors

tran·sis·tor·ized \-tə-₁rīzd\ *adj* : having or using transistors

tran·sit \'tran-sət, -zət\ *n* **1** : a passing through, across, or over : PASSAGE **2** : conveyance of persons or things from one place to another **3** : usu. local transportation esp. of people by public conveyance **4** : a surveyor's instrument for measuring angles

tran·si·tion \tran-'si-shən, -'zi-\ *n* : passage from one state, place, stage, or subject to another : CHANGE — **tran·si·tion·al** \-'si-shə-nəl, 'zi-\ *adj*

tran·si·tive \'tran-sə-tiv, -zə-\ *adj* **1** : having or containing an object required to complete the meaning **2** : TRANSITIONAL — **tran·si·tive·ly** *adv* — **tran·si·tiveness** *n* — **tran·si·tiv·i·ty** \ˌtran-sə-'ti-və-tē, -zə-\ *n*

tran·si·to·ry \'tran-sə-ˌtȯr-ē, -zə-\ *adj* : of brief duration : SHORT-LIVED, TEMPORARY **syn** transient, passing, momentary, fleeting

transl *abbr* translated; translation

trans·late \trans-'lāt, tranz-\ *vb* **trans·lat·ed; translat·ing 1** : to change from one place, state, or form to another **2** : to convey to heaven without death **3** : to turn into one's own or another language — **translat·able** *adj* — **trans·la·tion** \-'lā-shən\ *n* — **transla·tor** \-'lā-tər\ *n*

trans·lit·er·ate \trans-'li-tə-ˌrāt, tranz-\ *vb* **-at·ed; -at·ing** : to represent or spell in the characters of another alphabet — **trans·lit·er·a·tion** \ˌtrans-ˌli-tə-'rā-shən, ˌtranz-\ *n*

trans·lu·cent \trans-'lüs-ᵊnt, tranz-\ *adj* : not transparent but clear enough to allow light to pass through — **trans·lu·cence** \-ᵊns\ *n* — **trans·lu·cen·cy** \-ᵊn-sē\ *n* — **trans·lu·cent·ly** *adv*

trans·mi·grate \-'mī-ˌgrāt\ *vb* : to pass at death from one body or being to another — **trans·mi·gra·tion** \ˌtrans-mī-'grā-shən, ˌtranz-\ *n* — **trans·mi·gra·to·ry** \-'mī-grə-ˌtȯr-ē\ *adj*

trans·mis·sion \-'mi-shən\ *n* **1** : an act or process of transmitting **2** : the passage of radio waves between transmitting stations and receiving stations **3** : the gears by which power is transmitted from the engine of an automobile to the axle that propels the vehicle **4** : something transmitted

trans·mit \-'mit\ *vb* **trans·mit·ted; trans·mit·ting 1** : to transfer from one person or place to another : FORWARD **2** : to pass on by or as if by inheritance **3** : to cause or allow to spread abroad or to another ⟨∼ a disease⟩ **4** : to cause (as light, electricity, or force) to pass through space or a material **5** : to send out (radio or television signals) **syn** convey, communicate, impart — **trans·mis·si·ble** \-'mi-sə-bəl\ *adj* — **transmit·ta·ble** \-'mi-tə-bəl\ *adj* — **trans·mit·tal** \-'mit-ᵊl\ *n*

trans·mit·ter \-'mi-tər\ *n* : one that transmits; *esp* : an apparatus for transmitting telegraph, radio, or television signals

trans·mog·ri·fy \trans-'mä-grə-ˌfī, tranz-\ *vb* **-fied; -fy·ing** : to change or alter often with grotesque or humorous effect — **trans·mog·ri·fi·ca·tion** \-ˌmä-grə-fə-'kā-shən\ *n*

trans·mute \-'myüt\ *vb* **trans·muted; trans·mut·ing** : to change or alter in form, appearance, or nature **syn** transform, convert, transfigure, metamorphose — **trans·mu·ta·tion** \ˌtrans-myü-'tā-shən, ˌtranz-\ *n*

trans·na·tion·al \-'na-shə-nəl\ *adj* : extending beyond national boundaries

trans·oce·an·ic \ˌtrans-ˌō-shē-'a-nik, ˌtranz-\ *adj* **1** : lying or dwelling beyond the ocean **2** : crossing or extending across the ocean

tran·som \'tran-səm\ *n* **1** : a piece (as a crossbar in the frame of a window or door) that lies crosswise in a structure **2** : a window above an opening (as a door) built on and often hinged to a horizontal crossbar

tran·son·ic *also* **trans–son·ic** \trans-'sä-nik\ *adj* : being or relating to speeds near that of sound in air or about 741 miles (1185 kilometers) per hour

trans·pa·cif·ic \ˌtrans-pə-'si-fik\ *adj* : crossing, extending across, or situated beyond the Pacific Ocean

trans·par·ent \trans-'par-ənt\ *adj* **1** : clear enough to be seen through **2** : SHEER, DIAPHANOUS ⟨a ∼ fabric⟩ **3** : readily understood : CLEAR; *also* : easily detected

⟨a ∼ lie⟩ **syn** lucid, translucent, lucent — **trans·paren·cy** \-ən-sē\ *n* — **trans·par·ent·ly** *adv*

tran·spire \trans-'pīr\ *vb* **trans·pired; trans·pir·ing** [MF *transpirer*, fr. L *trans*- across + *spirare* to breathe] **1** : to pass or give off (as water vapor) through pores or a membrane **2** : to become known **3** : to take place : HAPPEN — **tran·spi·ra·tion** \ˌtrans-pə-'rā-shən\ *n*

¹trans·plant \trans-'plant\ *vb* **1** : to dig up and plant elsewhere **2** : to remove from one place and settle or introduce elsewhere : TRANSPORT **3** : to transfer (an organ or tissue) from one part or individual to another — **trans·plan·ta·tion** \ˌtrans-ˌplan-'tā-shən\ *n*

²trans·plant \'trans-ˌplant\ *n* **1** : a person or thing transplanted **2** : the act or process of transplanting

trans·po·lar \trans-'pō-lər\ *adj* : going or extending across either of the polar regions

trans·pon·der \tran-'spän-dər\ *n* [*trans*mitter + re*sponder*] : a radio or radar set that upon receiving a certain signal emits a signal of its own and that is used esp. for the identification and location of objects

¹trans·port \trans-'pȯrt\ *vb* **1** : to convey from one place to another : CARRY **2** : to carry away by strong emotion : ENRAPTURE **3** : to send to a penal colony overseas **syn** bear, ferry — **trans·por·ta·tion** \ˌtrans-pər-'tā-shən\ *n* — **trans·port·er** *n*

²trans·port \'trans-ˌpȯrt\ *n* **1** : an act of transporting **2** : strong or intensely pleasurable emotion ⟨∼s of joy⟩ **3** : a ship used in transporting troops or supplies; *also* : a vehicle (as a truck or plane) used to transport persons or goods

trans·pose \trans-'pōz\ *vb* **trans·posed; trans·posing 1** : to change the position or sequence of ⟨∼ the letters in a word⟩ **2** : to write or perform (a musical composition) in a different key — **trans·po·si·tion** \ˌtrans-pə-'zi-shən\ *n*

trans·sex·u·al \(ˌ)trans-'sek-shə-wəl\ *n* : a person with a psychological urge to belong to the opposite sex that may be carried to the point of undergoing surgery to modify the sex organs to mimic the opposite sex

trans·ship \tran-'ship, trans-\ *vb* : to transfer for further transportation from one ship or conveyance to another — **trans·ship·ment** *n*

tran·sub·stan·ti·a·tion \ˌtran-səb-ˌstan-chē-'ā-shən\ *n* : the change in the eucharistic elements from the substance of bread and wine to the substance of the body of Christ with only the appearances of bread and wine remaining

trans·verse \trans-'vərs, tranz-\ *adj* : lying across : set crosswise — **transverse** \'trans-ˌvərs, 'tranz-\ *n* — **trans·verse·ly** *adv*

trans·ves·tite \trans-'ves-ˌtīt, tranz-\ *n* : a person and esp. a male who adopts the dress and often the behavior of the opposite sex — **transvestite** *adj* — **trans·ves·tism** \-ˌti-zəm\ *n*

¹trap \'trap\ *n* **1** : a device for catching animals **2** : something by which one is caught unawares; *also* : a situation from which escape is difficult or impossible **3** : a machine for throwing clay pigeons into the air; *also* : SAND TRAP **4** : a light one-horse carriage on springs **5** : a device to allow some one thing to pass through while keeping other things out ⟨a ∼ in a drainpipe⟩ **6** *pl* : a group of percussion instruments (as in a dance orchestra)

²trap *vb* **trapped; trap·ping 1** : to catch in or as if in a trap; *also* : CONFINE **2** : to provide or set (a place) with traps **3** : to set traps for animals esp. as a business **syn** snare, entrap, ensnare, bag, lure, decoy — **trap·per** *n*

trap·door \'trap-'dȯr\ *n* : a lifting or sliding door covering an opening in a floor or roof

tra·peze \tra-'pēz\ *n* : a gymnastic apparatus consisting of a horizontal bar suspended by two parallel ropes

trap·e·zoid \'tra-pə-ˌzȯid\ *n* [NL *trapezoïdes*, fr. Gk *trapezoeidēs* trapezoidal, fr. *trapeza* table, fr. *tra-four* + *peza* foot] : a plane 4-sided figure with two and only two sides parallel — **trap·e·zoi·dal** \ˌtra-pə-ˈzȯid-ᵊl\ *adj*

trap·pings \ˈtra-piŋz\ *n pl* **1** : CAPARISON 1 **2** : outward decoration or dress; *also* : outward sign ⟨∼ of success⟩

traps \ˈtraps\ *n pl* : personal belongings : LUGGAGE

trap·shoot·ing \ˈtrap-ˌshü-tiŋ\ *n* : shooting at clay pigeons sprung from a trap into the air away from the shooter

¹**trash** \ˈtrash\ *n* **1** : something of little worth : RUBBISH **2** : a worthless person; *also* : such persons as a group : RIFFRAFF — **trashy** *adj*

²**trash** *vb* **1** : VANDALIZE, DESTROY **2** : ATTACK **3** : SPOIL, RUIN **4** : to criticize or disparage harshly

trau·ma \ˈtraù-mə, ˈtrò-\ *n, pl* **traumas** *also* **trau·ma·ta** \-mə-tə\ [Gk] : a bodily or mental injury usu. caused by an external agent; *also* : a cause of trauma — **trau·mat·ic** \trə-ˈma-tik, trò-, traù-\ *adj*

trau·ma·tize \ˈtraù-mə-ˌtīz, ˈtrò-\ *vb* **-tized; -tiz·ing** : to inflict a trauma on

¹**tra·vail** \trə-ˈvāl, ˈtra-ˌvāl\ *n* **1** : painful work or exertion : TOIL **2** : AGONY, TORMENT **3** : CHILDBIRTH, LABOR

²**travail** *vb* : to labor hard : TOIL

¹**trav·el** \ˈtra-vəl\ *vb* **-eled** *or* **-elled; -el·ing** *or* **-el·ling** [ME *travailen* to labor, journey, fr. OF *travaillier* to torture, labor, fr. (assumed) VL *trepaliare* to torture, fr. LL *trepalium* instrument of torture] **1** : to go on or as if on a trip or tour : JOURNEY **2** : to move as if by traveling ⟨news ∼s fast⟩ **3** : ASSOCIATE **4** : to go from place to place as a sales representative **5** : to move from point to point ⟨light waves ∼ very fast⟩ **6** : to journey over or through ⟨∼ing the highways⟩ — **trav·el·er** *or* **trav·el·ler** *n*

²**travel** *n* **1** : the act of traveling : PASSAGE **2** : JOURNEY, TRIP — often used in pl. **3** : the number traveling : TRAFFIC **4** : the motion of a piece of machinery and esp. when to and fro

traveler's check *n* : a check paid for in advance that is signed when bought and signed again when cashed

traveling bag *n* : SUITCASE

trav·el·ogue *or* **trav·el·og** \ˈtra-və-ˌlòg, -ˌläg\ *n* : a usu. illustrated lecture on travel

¹**tra·verse** \ˈtra-vərs\ *n* : something that crosses or lies across

²**tra·verse** \trə-ˈvərs, tra-ˈvərs *or* ˈtra-vərs\ *vb* **tra·versed; tra·vers·ing** **1** : to go or travel across or over **2** : to move or pass along or through **3** : to extend over **4** : SWIVEL

³**tra·verse** \ˈtra-ˌvərs\ *adj* : TRANSVERSE

trav·er·tine \ˈtra-vər-ˌtēn, -tən\ *n* : a crystalline mineral formed by deposition from spring waters

¹**trav·es·ty** \ˈtra-və-stē\ *vb* **-tied; -ty·ing** : to make a travesty of

²**travesty** *n, pl* **-ties** [obs. E *travesty* disguised, parodied, fr. F *travesti*, pp. of *travestir* to disguise, fr. It *travestire*, fr. *tra-* across (fr. L *trans-*) + *vestire* to dress] : an imitation that makes crude fun of something; *also* : an inferior imitation

¹**trawl** \ˈtròl\ *vb* : to fish or catch with a trawl — **trawl·er** *n*

²**trawl** *n* **1** : a large conical net dragged along the sea bottom in fishing **2** : a long heavy fishing line equipped with many hooks in series

tray \ˈtrā\ *n* : an open receptacle with flat bottom and low rim for holding, carrying, or exhibiting articles

treach·er·ous \ˈtre-chə-rəs\ *adj* **1** : characterized by treachery **2** : UNTRUSTWORTHY, UNRELIABLE **3** : providing insecure footing or support **syn** traitorous, faithless, false, disloyal — **treach·er·ous·ly** *adv*

treach·ery \ˈtre-chə-rē\ *n, pl* **-er·ies** : violation of allegiance or trust

trea·cle \ˈtrē-kəl\ *n* [ME *triacle* a medicinal compound, fr. MF, fr. L *theriaca*, fr. Gk *thēriakē* anti-dote against a poisonous bite, fr. *thērion* wild animal] *chiefly Brit* : MOLASSES — **trea·cly** \-k(ə-)lē\ *adj*

¹**tread** \ˈtred\ *vb* **trod** \ˈträd\; **trod·den** \ˈträd-ᵊn\ *or* **trod; tread·ing** **1** : to step or walk on or over **2** : to move on foot : WALK; *also* : DANCE **3** : to beat or press with the feet

²**tread** *n* **1** : a mark made by or as if by treading **2** : the manner or sound of stepping **3** : the part of a wheel that makes contact with a road **4** : the horizontal part of a step

trea·dle \ˈtred-ᵊl\ *n* : a lever device pressed by the foot to drive a machine — **treadle** *vb*

tread·mill \ˈtred-ˌmil\ *n* **1** : a mill worked by persons who tread on steps around the edge of a wheel or by animals that walk on an endless belt **2** : a device with an endless belt on which a person walks or runs in place **3** : a wearisome routine

treas *abbr* treasurer; treasury

trea·son \ˈtrēz-ᵊn\ *n* : the offense of attempting to overthrow the government of one's country or of assisting its enemies in war — **trea·son·able** \-ᵊn-ə-bəl\ *adj* — **trea·son·ous** \-ᵊn-əs\ *adj*

¹**trea·sure** \ˈtre-zhər, ˈtrā-\ *n* **1** : wealth stored up or held in reserve **2** : something of great value

²**treasure** *vb* **trea·sured; trea·sur·ing** **1** : HOARD **2** : to keep as precious : CHERISH **syn** prize, value, appreciate, esteem

trea·sur·er *n* : an officer of a club, business, or government who has charge of money taken in and paid out

treasure trove \-ˌtrōv\ *n* **1** : treasure of unknown ownership found buried or hidden **2** : a valuable discovery

trea·sury \ˈtre-zhə-rē, ˈtrā-\ *n, pl* **-sur·ies** **1** : a place in which stores of wealth are kept **2** : the place where collected funds are stored and paid out **3** *cap* : a governmental department in charge of finances

¹**treat** \ˈtrēt\ *vb* **1** : NEGOTIATE **2** : to deal with esp. in writing; *also* : HANDLE **3** : to pay for the food or entertainment of **4** : to behave or act toward ⟨∼ them well⟩ **5** : to regard in a specified manner ⟨∼ as inferiors⟩ **6** : to give medical or surgical care to **7** : to subject to some action ⟨∼ soil with lime⟩

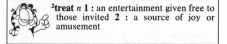

²**treat** *n* **1** : an entertainment given free to those invited **2** : a source of joy or amusement

trea·tise \ˈtrē-təs\ *n* : a systematic written exposition or argument

treat·ment \ˈtrēt-mənt\ *n* : the act or manner or an instance of treating someone or something; *also* : a substance or method used in treating

trea·ty \ˈtrē-tē\ *n, pl* **treaties** : an agreement made by negotiation or diplomacy esp. between two or more states or governments

¹**tre·ble** \ˈtre-bəl\ *n* **1** : the highest of the four voice parts in vocal music : SOPRANO **2** : a high-pitched or shrill voice or sound **3** : the upper half of the musical pitch range

²**treble** *adj* **1** : triple in number or amount **2** : relating to or having the range of a musical treble **3** : high-pitched : SHRILL — **tre·bly** *adv*

³**treble** *vb* **tre·bled; tre·bling** : to make or become three times the size, amount, or number

¹**tree** \ˈtrē\ *n* **1** : a woody perennial plant usu. with a single main stem and a head of branches and leaves at the top **2** : a piece of wood adapted to a particular use ⟨a shoe ∼⟩ **3** : something resembling a tree ⟨a genealogical ∼⟩ — **tree·less** *adj*

²**tree** *vb* **treed; tree·ing** : to drive to or up a tree ⟨∼ a raccoon⟩

tree farm *n* : an area of forest land managed to ensure continuous commercial production

tree line *n* : TIMBERLINE

tree of heaven : a Chinese ailanthus that is widely grown as a shade and ornamental tree

tree surgery *n* : operative treatment of diseased trees esp. for control of decay — **tree surgeon** *n*

tre·foil \'trē-ˌfȯil, 'tre-\ *n* **1** : an herb (as clover) with leaves with three leaflets **2** : a decorative design with three leaflike parts

¹trek \'trek\ *vb* **trekked; trek·king 1** *chiefly southern Africa* : to travel or migrate by ox wagon **2** : to make one's way arduously

²trek *n* **1** *chiefly southern Africa* : a migration esp. of settlers by ox wagon **2** : a slow or difficult journey

¹trel·lis \'tre-ləs\ *n* [ME *trelis*, fr. MF *treliz* fabric of coarse weave, trellis, fr. (assumed) VL *trilicius* woven with triple thread, fr. L *tres* three + *licium* thread] : a frame of latticework used esp. for climbing plants

²trellis *vb* : to provide with a trellis; *esp* : to train (as a vine) on a trellis

trem·a·tode \'tre-mə-ˌtōd\ *n* : any of a class of parasitic worms

¹trem·ble \'trem-bəl\ *vb* **trem·bled; trem·bling 1** : to shake involuntarily (as with fear or cold) : SHIVER **2** : to move, sound, pass, or come to pass as if shaken or tremulous **3** : to be affected with fear or doubt

²tremble *n* : a spell of shaking or quivering

tre·men·dous \tri-'men-dəs\ *adj* **1** : causing dread, awe, or terror : TERRIFYING **2** : unusually large, powerful, great, or excellent **syn** stupendous, monumental, monstrous — **tre·men·dous·ly** *adv*

trem·o·lo \'tre-mə-ˌlō\ *n, pl* **-los** [It] : a rapid fluttering of a tone or alternating tones

trem·or \'tre-mər\ *n* **1** : a trembling or shaking esp. from weakness, emotional stress, or disease **2** : a quivering motion of the earth (as during an earthquake)

trem·u·lous \'trem-yə-ləs\ *adj* **1** : marked by trembling or tremors : QUIVERING **2** : TIMOROUS, TIMID — **trem·u·lous·ly** *adv*

¹trench \'trench\ *n* [ME *trenche* track cut through a wood, fr. MF, act of cutting, fr. *trenchier* to cut, prob. fr. (assumed) VL *trinicare* to cut in three, fr. L *trini* three each] **1** : a long narrow cut in the ground : DITCH; *esp* : a ditch protected by banks of earth and used to shelter soldiers **2** *pl* : a place or situation likened to trench warfare **3** : a long narrow steep-sided depression in the ocean floor

²trench *vb* **1** : to cut or dig trenches in **2** : to protect (troops) with trenches **3** : to come close : VERGE

tren·chant \'tren-chənt\ *adj* **1** : vigorously effective; *also* : CAUSTIC **2** : sharply perceptive : KEEN **3** : CLEAR-CUT, DISTINCT

tren·cher \'tren-chər\ *n* : a wooden platter for serving food

tren·cher·man \'tren-chər-mən\ *n* : a hearty eater

trench foot *n* : a painful foot disorder resembling frostbite and resulting from exposure to cold and wet

trench mouth *n* : a progressive painful disease of the mouth and adjacent parts that is marked by ulcera-

tion and associated with a great increase in certain bacteria normally present in the mouth

¹trend \'trend\ *vb* **1** : to have or take a general direction : TEND **2** : to show a tendency : INCLINE

²trend *n* **1** : a general direction taken (as by a stream or mountain range) **2** : a prevailing tendency : DRIFT **3** : a current style or preference : VOGUE

trendy \'tren-dē\ *adj* **trend·i·er; -est** : very fashionable; *also* : marked by superficial or faddish appeal or taste

trep·i·da·tion \ˌtre-pə-'dā-shən\ *n* : nervous agitation : APPREHENSION **syn** horror, terror, panic, consternation, dread, fright, dismay

¹tres·pass \'tres-pəs, -ˌpas\ *n* **1** : SIN, OFFENSE **2** : unlawful entry on someone else's land **syn** transgression, violation, infraction, infringement

²trespass *vb* **1** : to commit an offense : ERR, SIN **2** : INTRUDE, ENCROACH; *esp* : to enter unlawfully upon the land of another — **tres·pass·er** *n*

tress \'tres\ *n* : a long lock of hair — usu. used in pl.

tres·tle *also* **tres·sel** \'tre-səl\ *n* **1** : a supporting framework consisting usu. of a horizontal piece with spreading legs at each end **2** : a braced framework of timbers, piles, or steel for carrying a road or railroad over a depression

trey \'trā\ *n, pl* **treys** : a card or the side of a die with three spots

tri·ad \'trī-ˌad, -əd\ *n* : a union or group of three usu. closely related persons or things

tri·age \trē-'äzh, 'trē-ˌäzh\ *n* [F, sorting] : the sorting of and allocation of treatment to patients and esp. battle or disaster victims according to a system of priorities designed to maximize the number of survivors

tri·al \'trī-əl\ *n* **1** : the action or process of trying or putting to the proof : TEST **2** : the hearing and judgment of a matter in issue before a competent tribunal **3** : a source of vexation or annoyance **4** : an experiment to test quality, value, or usefulness **5** : EFFORT, ATTEMPT **syn** cross, ordeal, tribulation, affliction — **trial** *adj*

tri·an·gle \'trī-ˌaŋ-gəl\ *n* **1** : a plane figure that has three sides and three angles : a polygon having three sides **2** : something shaped like a triangle — **tri·an·gu·lar** \trī-'aŋ-gyə-lər\ *adj* — **tri·an·gu·lar·ly** *adv*

triangle 1: *1* equilateral, *2* isosceles, *3* right triangle

tri·an·gu·la·tion \(ˌ)trī-ˌaŋ-gyə-'lā-shən\ *n* : a method using trigonometry to find the location of a point using bearings from two fixed points a known distance apart — **tri·an·gu·late** \trī-'aŋ-gyə-ˌlāt\ *vb*

Tri·as·sic \trī-'a-sik\ *adj* : of, relating to, or being the earliest period of the Mesozoic era marked by the first appearance of the dinosaurs — **Triassic** *n*

trib *abbr* tributary

tribe \'trīb\ *n* **1** : a social group comprising numerous families, clans, or generations **2** : a group of persons having a common character, occupation, or interest **3** : a group of related plants or animals ⟨the cat ∼⟩ — **trib·al** \'trī-bəl\ *adj*

tribes·man \'trībz-mən\ *n* : a member of a tribe

trib·u·la·tion \ˌtri-byə-'lā-shən\ *n* [ME *tribulacion*, fr. OF, fr. L *tribulatio*, fr. *tribulare* to press, oppress, fr. *tribulum* drag used in threshing] : distress or suffering resulting from oppression or persecution; *also* : a trying experience **syn** trial, affliction, cross, ordeal

tri·bu·nal \trī-'byün-ᵊl, tri-\ *n* **1** : the seat of a judge **2** : a court of justice **3** : something that decides or determines ⟨the ∼ of public opinion⟩

tri·bune \'tri-ˌbyün, tri-'byün\ *n* **1** : an official in ancient Rome with the function of protecting the interests of plebeian citizens from the patricians **2** : a defender of the people

¹**trib·u·tary** \'tri-byə-ˌter-ē\ *adj* **1** : paying tribute : SUBJECT **2** : flowing into a larger stream or a lake **syn** subordinate, secondary, dependent

²**tributary** *n*, *pl* **-tar·ies 1** : a ruler or state that pays tribute **2** : a tributary stream

trib·ute \'tri-(ˌ)byüt, -byət\ *n* **1** : a payment by one ruler or nation to another as an act of submission or price of protection **2** : a usu. excessive tax, rental, or levy exacted by a sovereign or superior **3** : a gift or service showing respect, gratitude, or affection; *also* : PRAISE **syn** eulogy, citation, encomium, panegyric

trice \'trīs\ *n* : INSTANT, MOMENT

tri·ceps \'trī-ˌseps\ *n*, *pl* **triceps** : a large muscle along the back of the upper arm that is attached at its upper end by three main parts and acts to extend the forearm at the elbow joint

tri·cer·a·tops \(ˌ)trī-'ser-ə-ˌtäps\ *n*, *pl* **-tops** *also* **-topses** [NL, fr. Gk *tri-* three + *kerat-*, *keras* horn + *ōps* face] : any of a genus of large plant-eating Cretaceous dinosaurs with three horns, a bony crest on the neck, and hoofed toes

tri·chi·na \tri-'kī-nə\ *n*, *pl* **-nae** \-(ˌ)nē\ *also* **-nas** : a small slender nematode worm that in the larval state is parasitic in the voluntary muscles of flesh= eating mammals (as the hog and humans)

trich·i·no·sis \ˌtri-kə-'nō-səs\ *n* : infestation with or disease caused by trichinae and marked esp. by pain, fever, and swelling

¹**trick** \'trik\ *n* **1** : a crafty procedure meant to deceive **2** : a mischievous action : PRANK **3** : a childish action **4** : a deceptive or ingenious feat designed to puzzle or amuse **5** : PECULIARITY, MANNERISM **6** : a quick or artful way of getting a result : KNACK **7** : the cards played in one round of a card game **8** : a tour of duty : SHIFT **syn** ruse, maneuver, artifice, wile, feint

²**trick** *vb* **1** : to deceive by cunning or artifice : CHEAT **2** : to dress ornately

trick·ery \'tri-kə-rē\ *n* : deception by tricks and stratagems

trick·le \'tri-kəl\ *vb* **trick·led; trick·ling 1** : to run or fall in drops **2** : to flow in a thin gentle stream — **trickle** *n*

trick·ster \'trik-stər\ *n* : one who tricks or cheats

tricky \'tri-kē\ *adj* **trick·i·er; -est 1** : inclined to trickery **2** : requiring skill or caution ⟨a ∼ situation to handle⟩ **3** : UNRELIABLE ⟨a ∼ lock⟩

tri·col·or \'trī-ˌkə-lər\ *n* : a flag of three colors ⟨the French ∼⟩

tri·cy·cle \'trī-(ˌ)si-kəl\ *n* : a 3-wheeled vehicle usu. propelled by pedals

tri·dent \'trīd-ᵊnt\ *n* [L *trident-*, *tridens*, fr. *tri-* three + *dent-*, *dens* tooth] : a 3-pronged spear

tried \'trīd\ *adj* **1** : found trustworthy through testing **2** : subjected to trials

tri·en·ni·al \trī-'e-nē-əl\ *adj* **1** : occurring or being done every three years **2** : lasting for three years — **tri·en·ni·al** *n*

¹**tri·fle** \'trī-fəl\ *n* : something of little value or importance

²**trifle** *vb* **tri·fled; tri·fling 1** : to talk in a jesting or mocking manner **2** : to treat someone or something as unimportant **3** : DALLY, FLIRT **4** : to handle idly : TOY — **tri·fler** *n*

tri·fling \'trī-fliŋ\ *adj* **1** : FRIVOLOUS **2** : TRIVIAL, INSIGNIFICANT **syn** petty, paltry, measly, inconsequential

tri·fo·cals \trī-'fō-kəlz\ *n pl* : eyeglasses with lenses having one part for close focus, one for intermediate focus, and one for distant focus

tri·fo·li·ate \trī-'fō-lē-ət\ *adj* : having three leaves or leaflets

¹**trig** \'trig\ *adj* : stylishly trim : SMART

²**trig** *n* : TRIGONOMETRY

¹**trig·ger** \'tri-gər\ *n* [alter. of earlier *tricker*, fr. D *trekker*, fr. MD *trecker* one that pulls, fr. *trecken* to pull] : a movable lever that activates a device when it is squeezed; *esp* : the part of a firearm lock moved by the finger to fire a gun — **trigger** *adj* — **trig·gered** *adj*

²**trigger** *vb* **1** : to fire by pulling a trigger **2** : to initiate, actuate, or set off as if by a trigger

tri·glyc·er·ide *n* : any of a group of fats and oils that are derived from glycerol and fatty acids and are widespread in animal tissue

trig·o·nom·e·try \ˌtri-gə-'nä-mə-trē\ *n* : the branch of mathematics dealing with the properties of triangles and esp. with finding unknown angles or sides given the size or length of some angles or sides — **trig·o·no·met·ric** \-nə-'me-trik\ *also* **trig·o·no·met·ri·cal** \-tri-kəl\ *adj*

trike \'trīk\ *n* : TRICYCLE

¹**trill** \'tril\ *n* **1** : the alternation of two musical tones a scale degree apart **2** : WARBLE **3** : the rapid vibration of one speech organ against another (as of the tip of the tongue against the teeth)

²**trill** *vb* : to utter as or with a trill

tril·lion \'tril-yən\ *n* **1** : a thousand billions **2** *Brit* : a million billions — **trillion** *adj* — **tril·lionth** \-yənth\ *adj or n*

tril·li·um \'tri-lē-əm\ *n* : any of a genus of herbs of the lily family with an erect stem bearing a whorl of three leaves and a large solitary usu. spring-blooming flower with three petals

tril·o·gy \'tri-lə-jē\ *n*, *pl* **-gies** : a series of three dramas or literary or musical compositions that are closely related and develop one theme

¹**trim** \'trim\ *vb* **trimmed; trim·ming** [OE *trymian*, *trymman* to strengthen, arrange, fr. *trum* strong, firm] **1** : to put ornaments on : ADORN **2** : to defeat esp. resoundingly **3** : to make trim, neat, regular, or less bulky by or as if by cutting ⟨∼ a beard⟩ ⟨∼ a budget⟩ **4** : to cause (a boat) to assume a desired position in the water by arrangement of the load; *also* : to adjust (as a submarine or airplane) esp. for horizontal motion **5** : to adjust (a sail) to a desired position **6** : to change one's views for safety or expediency — **trim·ly** *adv* — **trim·mer** *n* — **trim·ness** *n*

²**trim** *adj* **trim·mer; trim·mest** : showing neatness, good order, or compactness ⟨a ∼ figure⟩ **syn** tidy, trig, smart, spruce, shipshape

³**trim** *n* **1** : good condition : FITNESS **2** : material used for ornament or trimming; *esp* : the woodwork in the finish of a house esp. around doors and windows **3** : the position of a ship or boat esp. with reference to the horizontal; *also* : the relation between the plane of a sail and the direction of a ship **4** : the position of an airplane at which it will continue in level flight with no adjustments to the controls **5** : something that is trimmed off

tri·ma·ran \'trī-mə-ˌran, ˌtrī-mə-'ran\ *n* : a sailboat with three hulls

tri·mes·ter \trī-ˈmes-tər, ˈtrī-ˌmes-tər\ *n* **1** : a period of three or about three months (as in pregnancy) **2** : one of three terms into which an academic year is sometimes divided

trim·e·ter \ˈtri-mə-tər\ *n* : a line of verse consisting of three metrical feet

trim·ming \ˈtri-miŋ\ *n* **1** : DEFEAT **2** : the action of one that trims **3** : something that trims, ornaments, or completes

tri·month·ly \trī-ˈmənth-lē\ *adj* : occurring every three months

trine \ˈtrīn\ *adj* : THREEFOLD, TRIPLE

Trin·i·da·di·an \ˌtri-nə-ˈdä-dē-ən, -ˈda-\ *n* : a native or inhabitant of the island of Trinidad — **Trinidadian** *adj*

Trin·i·tar·i·an \ˌtri-nə-ˈter-ē-ən\ *n* : a believer in the doctrine of the Trinity — **Trin·i·tar·i·an·ism** \-ē-ə-ˌni-zəm\ *n*

Trin·i·ty \ˈtri-nə-tē\ *n* **1** : the unity of Father, Son, and Holy Spirit as three persons in one Godhead **2** *not cap* : TRIAD

trin·ket \ˈtriŋ-kət\ *n* **1** : a small ornament (as a jewel or ring) **2** : TRIFLE

trio \ˈtrē-ō\ *n, pl* **tri·os** **1** : a musical composition for three voices or three instruments **2** : the performers of a trio **3** : a group or set of three

¹trip \ˈtrip\ *vb* **tripped; trip·ping** **1** : to move with light quick steps **2** : to catch the foot against something so as to stumble or cause to stumble **3** : to make a mistake : SLIP; *also* : to detect in a misstep : EXPOSE **4** : to release (as a spring or switch) by moving a catch; *also* : ACTIVATE **5** : to get high on a drug and esp. a hallucinatory drug

²trip *n* **1** : JOURNEY, VOYAGE **2** : a quick light step **3** : a false step : STUMBLE; *also* : ERROR **4** : the action of tripping mechanically; *also* : a device for tripping **5** : an intense drug-induced hallucinatory experience **6** : absorption in an attitude or state of mind (an ego ∼)

tri·par·tite \trī-ˈpär-ˌtīt\ *adj* **1** : divided into three parts **2** : having three corresponding parts or copies **3** : made between three parties (a ∼ treaty)

tripe \ˈtrīp\ *n* **1** : stomach tissue of a ruminant and esp. an ox used as food **2** : something poor, worthless, or offensive : TRASH

¹tri·ple \ˈtri-pəl\ *vb* **tri·pled; tri·pling** **1** : to make or become three times as great or as many **2** : to hit a triple

²triple *n* **1** : a triple quantity **2** : a group of three **3** : a hit in baseball that lets the batter reach third base

³triple *adj* **1** : being three times as great or as many **2** : having three units or members **3** : repeated three times

triple bond *n* : a chemical bond in which three pairs of electrons are shared by two atoms in a molecule

triple point *n* : the condition of temperature and pressure under which the gaseous, liquid, and solid forms of a substance can exist in equilibrium

trip·let \ˈtri-plət\ *n* **1** : a unit of three lines of verse **2** : a group of three of a kind **3** : one of three offspring born at one birth

tri·plex \ˈtri-ˌpleks, ˈtrī-\ *adj* : THREEFOLD, TRIPLE

¹trip·li·cate \ˈtri-pli-kət\ *adj* : made in three identical copies

²trip·li·cate \-plə-ˌkāt\ *vb* **-cat·ed; -cat·ing** **1** : TRIPLE **2** : to provide three copies of (∼ a document)

³trip·li·cate \-pli-kət\ *n* : three copies all alike — used with *in* (typed in ∼)

tri·ply \ˈtri-plē, ˈtri-pə-lē\ *adv* : in a triple degree, amount, or manner

tri·pod \ˈtrī-ˌpäd\ *n* : something (as a caldron, stool, or camera stand) that rests on three legs — **tripod** *or* **tri·po·dal** \ˈtri-pəd-ᵊl, ˈtrī-ˌpäd-\ *adj*

trip·tych \ˈtrip-tik\ *n* : a picture or carving in three panels side by side

tri·reme \ˈtrī-ˌrēm\ *n* : an ancient galley having three banks of oars

tri·sect \ˈtrī-ˌsekt, trī-ˈsekt\ *vb* : to divide into three

usu. equal parts — **tri·sec·tion** \ˈtrī-ˌsek-shən\ *n*

trite \ˈtrīt\ *adj* **trit·er; trit·est** [L *tritus,* fr. pp. of *terere* to rub, wear away] : used so commonly that the novelty is worn off : STALE **syn** hackneyed, stereotyped, commonplace, clichéd

tri·ti·um \ˈtri-tē-əm, ˈtri-shē-\ *n* : a radioactive form of hydrogen with atoms of three times the mass of ordinary hydrogen atoms

tri·ton \ˈtrīt-ᵊn\ *n* : any of various large marine gastropod mollusks with a heavy elongated conical shell; *also* : the shell of a triton

trit·u·rate \ˈtri-chə-ˌrāt\ *vb* **-rat·ed; -rat·ing** : to rub or grind to a fine powder

¹tri·umph \ˈtrī-əmf\ *n, pl* **tri·umphs** **1** : the joy or exultation of victory or success **2** : VICTORY, CONQUEST — **tri·um·phal** \trī-ˈəm-fəl\ *adj*

²triumph *vb* **1** : to obtain victory : PREVAIL **2** : to celebrate victory or success exultantly — **tri·um·phant** \trī-ˈəm-fənt\ *adj* — **tri·um·phant·ly** *adv*

tri·um·vir \trī-ˈəm-vər\ *n, pl* **-virs** *also* **-vi·ri** \-və-ˌrī\ : a member of a triumvirate

tri·um·vi·rate \-və-rət\ *n* : a ruling body of three persons

tri·une \ˈtrī-ˌün, -ˌyün\ *adj, often cap* : being three in one (the ∼ God)

triv·et \ˈtri-vət\ *n* **1** : a 3-legged stand : TRIPOD **2** : a usu. metal stand with short feet for use under a hot dish

triv·ia \ˈtri-vē-ə\ *n sing or pl* : unimportant matters : TRIFLES

triv·i·al \ˈtri-vē-əl\ *adj* [L *trivialis* found everywhere, commonplace, fr. *trivium* crossroads, fr. *tri-* three + *via* way] : of little importance — **triv·i·al·i·ty** \ˌtri-vē-ˈa-lə-tē\ *n*

triv·i·um \ˈtri-vē-əm\ *n, pl* **triv·ia** \-vē-ə\ : the three liberal arts of grammar, rhetoric, and logic in a medieval university

tri·week·ly \trī-ˈwē-klē\ *adj* **1** : occurring or appearing three times a week **2** : occurring or appearing every three weeks — **triweekly** *adv*

tro·che \ˈtrō-kē\ *n* : a medicinal lozenge

tro·chee \ˈtrō-(ˌ)kē\ *n* : a metrical foot of one accented syllable followed by one unaccented syllable — **tro·cha·ic** \trō-ˈkā-ik\ *adj*

trod *past and past part of* TREAD

trodden *past part of* TREAD

troi·ka \ˈtròi-kə\ *n* [Russ *troĭka,* fr. *troe* three] : a group of three; *esp* : an administrative or ruling body of three

¹troll \ˈtrōl\ *vb* **1** : to sing the parts of (a song) in succession **2** : to fish by trailing a lure or baited hook from a moving boat **3** : to sing or play jovially

²troll *n* : a lure used in trolling; *also* : the line with its lure

³troll *n* : a dwarf or giant in Scandinavian folklore inhabiting caves or hills

trol·ley *also* **trol·ly** \ˈträ-lē\ *n, pl* **trolleys** *also* **trollies** **1** : a device (as a grooved wheel on the end of a pole) to carry current from a wire to an electrically driven vehicle **2** : a streetcar powered electrically through a trolley **3** : a wheeled carriage running on an overhead rail or track

trol·ley·bus \ˈträ-lē-ˌbəs\ *n* : a bus powered electrically through a trolley

trolley car *n* : TROLLEY 2

trol·lop \ˈträ-ləp\ *n* : a disreputable woman; *esp* : one who engages in sex promiscuously

trom·bone \träm-ˈbōn, ˈträm-ˌbōn\ *n* [It, lit., big trumpet, fr. *tromba* trumpet] : a brass wind instrument that consists of a long metal tube with two turns and a flaring end and that usu. has a movable slide to vary the pitch — **trom·bon·ist** \-ˈbō-nist, -ˌbō-\ *n*

☞ For illustration, see next page.

tromp \ˈträmp, ˈtrömp\ *vb* **1** : TRAMP, MARCH **2** : to stamp with the foot **3** : DEFEAT

¹troop \ˈtrüp\ *n* **1** : a cavalry unit corresponding to an

trombone

infantry company **2** *pl* : armed forces : SOLDIERS **3** : a collection of people or things **4** : a unit of Girl Scouts or Boy Scouts under an adult leader

²**troop** *vb* : to move or gather in crowds

troop•er \'trü-pər\ *n* **1** : an enlisted cavalryman; *also* : a cavalry horse **2** : a mounted or a state police officer

troop•ship \'trüp-ˌship\ *n* : a ship for carrying troops

trope \'trōp\ *n* : a word or expression used in a figurative sense

tro•phy \'trō-fē\ *n*, *pl* **trophies** : something gained or given in conquest or victory esp. when preserved or mounted as a memorial

trop•ic \'trä-pik\ *n* [ME *tropik*, fr. L *tropicus* of the solstice, fr. Gk *tropikos*, fr. *tropē* turn] **1** : either of the two parallels of latitude approximately 23½ degrees north (**tropic of Can•cer** \-'kan-sər\) or south (**tropic of Cap•ri•corn** \-'ka-prə-ˌkȯrn\) of the equator where the sun is directly overhead when it reaches its most northerly or southerly point in the sky **2** *pl, often cap* : the region lying between the tropics — **trop•i•cal** \-pi-kəl\ *or* **tropic** *adj*

tro•pism \'trō-ˌpi-zəm\ *n* : an automatic movement by an organism in response to a source of stimulation; *also* : a reflex reaction involving this

tro•po•sphere \'trō-pə-ˌsfir, 'trä-\ *n* : the part of the atmosphere between the earth's surface and the stratosphere in which most weather changes occur — **tro•po•spher•ic** \ˌtrō-pə-'sfir-ik, ˌträ-, -'sfer-\ *adj*

¹**trot** \'trät\ *n* **1** : a moderately fast gait of a 4-footed animal (as a horse) in which the legs move in diagonal pairs **2** : a human jogging gait between a walk and a run

²**trot** *vb* **trot•ted; trot•ting 1** : to ride, drive, or go at a trot **2** : to proceed briskly : HURRY — **trot•ter** *n*

troth \'träth, 'trȯth, 'trōth\ *n* **1** : pledged faithfulness **2** : one's pledged word; *also* : BETROTHAL

trou•ba•dour \'trü-bə-ˌdȯr\ *n* [F, fr. OProv *trobador*, fr. *trobar* to compose] : any of a class of poet‑ musicians flourishing esp. in southern France and northern Italy during the 11th, 12th, and 13th centuries

¹**trou•ble** \'trə-bəl\ *vb* **trou•bled; trou•bling 1** : to agitate mentally or spiritually : DISTURB, WORRY **2** : to produce physical disorder in : AFFLICT **3** : to put to inconvenience **4** : RUFFLE ⟨~ the waters⟩ **5** : to make an effort **syn** distress, ail, upset — **trou•ble•some** *adj* — **trou•ble•some•ly** *adv* — **trou•blous** \-bə-ləs\ *adj*

²**trouble** *n* **1** : the quality or state of being troubled esp. mentally **2** : an instance of distress or annoyance **3** : DISEASE, AILMENT ⟨heart ~⟩ **4** : EXERTION, PAINS ⟨took the ~ to phone⟩ **5** : a cause of disturbance or distress

trou•ble•mak•er \-ˌmā-kər\ *n* : a person who causes trouble

trou•ble•shoot•er \-ˌshü-tər\ *n* **1** : a worker employed to locate trouble and make repairs in equipment **2** : an expert in resolving disputes or problems — **trouble•shoot** *vb*

trough \'trȯf, 'trȯth, *by bakers often* 'trō\ *n*, *pl* **troughs** \'trȯfs, 'trȯvz; 'trȯths, 'trȯthz; 'trōz\ **1** : a long shallow open boxlike container esp. for water or feed for livestock **2** : a gutter along the eaves of a house **3** : a long channel or depression (as between waves or hills) **4** : an elongated area of low barometric pressure

trounce \'traủns\ *vb* **trounced; trounc•ing 1** : to thrash or punish severely **2** : to defeat decisively

troupe \'trüp\ *n* : COMPANY; *esp* : a group of performers on the stage — **troup•er** *n*

trou•sers \'traủ-zərz\ *n pl* [alter. of earlier *trouse*, fr. ScGael *triubhas*] : an outer garment covering each leg separately and usu. extending from the waist to the ankle — **trouser** *adj*

trous•seau \'trü-sō, trü-'sō\ *n*, *pl* **trousseaux** \-sōz, -ˈsōz\ *or* **trousseaus** [F] : the personal outfit of a bride

trout \'traủt\ *n*, *pl* **trout** *also* **trouts** [ME, fr. OE *trūht*, fr. LL *tructa*, a fish with sharp teeth, fr. Gk *trōktēs*, lit., gnawer] : any of various mostly freshwater food and game fishes usu. smaller than the related salmons

trow \'trō\ *vb*, *archaic* : THINK, SUPPOSE

trow•el \'traủ-əl\ *n* **1** : a hand tool used for spreading, shaping, or smoothing loose or plastic material (as mortar or plaster) **2** : a small flat or scooplike implement used in gardening — **trowel** *vb*

troy \'trȯi\ *adj* : expressed in troy weight ⟨~ ounce⟩

troy weight *n* : a system of weights based on a pound of 12 ounces and an ounce of 480 grains (31 grams) — see WEIGHT table

tru•ant \'trü-ənt\ *n* [ME, vagabond, idler, fr. OF, vagrant] : a student who stays out of school without permission — **tru•an•cy** \-ən-sē\ *n* — **truant** *adj*

truce \'trüs\ *n* **1** : ARMISTICE **2** : a respite esp. from something unpleasant

¹**truck** \'trək\ *vb* **1** : EXCHANGE, BARTER **2** : to have dealings : TRAFFIC

²**truck** *n* **1** : BARTER **2** : small goods or merchandise; *esp* : vegetables grown for market **3** : DEALINGS

³**truck** *n* **1** : a wheeled vehicle (as a strong heavy automobile) designed for carrying heavy articles or hauling a trailer **2** : a swiveling frame with springs and one or more pairs of wheels used to carry and guide one end of a locomotive or railroad car

⁴**truck** *vb* **1** : to transport on a truck **2** : to be employed in driving a truck — **truck•er** *n*

truck farm *n* : a farm growing vegetables for market — **truck farmer** *n*

truck•le \'trə-kəl\ *vb* **truck•led; truck•ling** : to yield slavishly to the will of another : SUBMIT **syn** fawn, toady, cringe, cower

truc•u•lent \'trə-kyə-lənt\ *adj* **1** : feeling or showing ferocity : SAVAGE **2** : aggressively self-assertive : PUGNACIOUS — **truc•u•lence** \-ləns\ *n* — **truc•u•len•cy** \-lən-sē\ *n* — **truc•u•lent•ly** *adv*

trudge \'trəj\ *vb* **trudged; trudg•ing** : to walk or march steadily and usu. laboriously

¹**true** \'trü\ *adj* **tru•er; tru•est 1** : STEADFAST, LOYAL **2** : agreeing with facts or reality ⟨a ~ description⟩ **3** : CONSISTENT ⟨~ to expectations⟩ **4** : properly so called ⟨~ love⟩ **5** : RIGHTFUL ⟨~ and lawful king⟩ **6** : conformable to a standard or pattern; *also* : placed or formed accurately **syn** constant, staunch, resolute, steadfast

²**true** *adv* **1** : TRUTHFULLY **2** : ACCURATELY ⟨the bullet flew straight and ~⟩; *also* : without variation from type ⟨breed ~⟩

³**true** *n* **1** : TRUTH, REALITY — usu. used with *the* **2** : the state of being accurate (as in alignment) ⟨out of ~⟩

⁴**true** *vb* **trued; tru•ing** *also* **tru•ing** : to bring or restore to a desired precision

true–blue *adj* : marked by unswerving loyalty

true bug *n* : BUG 2

true•heart•ed \'trü-ˌhär-təd\ *adj* : FAITHFUL, LOYAL

truf•fle \'trə-fəl, 'trü-\ *n* **1** : the usu. dark and wrinkled edible fruit of any of several European underground fungi; *also* : one of these fungi **2** : a candy made of chocolate, butter, and sugar shaped into balls and coated with cocoa

tru•ism \'trü-ˌi-zəm\ *n* : an undoubted or self‑evident truth **syn** commonplace, platitude, bromide, cliché

tru·ly \'trü-lē\ *adv* **1** : in all sincerity **2** : in agreement with fact **3** : ACCURATELY **4** : in a proper or suitable manner

¹trump \'trəmp\ *n* : TRUMPET

²trump *n* : a card of a designated suit any of whose cards will win over a card that is not of this suit; *also* : the suit itself — often used in pl.

³trump *vb* : to take with a trump

trumped–up \'trəmpt-'əp\ *adj* : fraudulently concocted : SPURIOUS

trum·pery \'trəm-pə-rē\ *n* **1** : NONSENSE **2** : trivial articles : JUNK

¹trum·pet \'trəm-pət\ *n* **1** : a wind instrument consisting of a long curved metal tube flaring at one end and with a cup-shaped mouthpiece at the other **2** : something that resembles a trumpet or its tonal quality **3** : a funnel-shaped instrument for collecting, directing, or intensifying sound

²trumpet *vb* **1** : to blow a trumpet **2** : to proclaim on or as if on a trumpet — **trum·pet·er** *n*

¹trun·cate \'trəŋ-ˌkāt, 'trən-\ *adj* : having the end square or blunt

²truncate *vb* **trun·cat·ed; trun·cat·ing** : to shorten by or as if by cutting : LOP — **trun·ca·tion** \ˌtrəŋ-'kā-shən\ *n*

trun·cheon \'trən-chən\ *n* : a police officer's club

trun·dle \'trənd-ᵊl\ *vb* **trun·dled; trun·dling** : to roll along : WHEEL

trundle bed *n* : a low bed that can be stored under a higher bed

trunk \'trəŋk\ *n* **1** : the main stem of a tree **2** : the body of a person or animal apart from the head and limbs **3** : the main or central part of something **4** : a box or chest used to hold usu. clothes or personal effects (as of a traveler); *also* : the enclosed luggage space in the rear of an automobile **5** : the long muscular nose of an elephant **6** *pl* : men's shorts worn chiefly for sports **7** : a usu. major channel or passage

trunk line *n* : a system handling long-distance through traffic

¹truss \'trəs\ *vb* **1** : to secure tightly : BIND **2** : to arrange for cooking by binding close the wings or legs of (a fowl) **3** : to support, strengthen, or stiffen by or as if by a truss

²truss *n* **1** : a collection of structural parts (as beams) forming a rigid framework (as in bridge or building construction) **2** : a device worn to reduce a hernia by pressure

¹trust \'trəst\ *n* **1** : assured reliance on the character, strength, or truth of someone or something **2** : a basis of reliance, faith, or hope **3** : confident hope **4** : financial credit **5** : a property interest held by one person for the benefit of another **6** : a combination of firms formed by a legal agreement; *esp* : one that reduces competition **7** : something entrusted to one to be cared for in the interest of another **8** : CARE, CUSTODY **syn** confidence, dependence, faith, reliance

²trust *vb* **1** : to place confidence : DEPEND **2** : to be confident : HOPE **3** : ENTRUST **4** : to permit to stay or go or to do something without fear or misgiving **5** : to rely on or on the truth of : BELIEVE **6** : to extend credit to

trust·ee \ˌtrəs-'tē\ *n* **1** : a person to whom property is legally committed in trust **2** : a country charged with the supervision of a trust territory

trust·ee·ship \ˌtrəs-'tē-ˌship\ *n* **1** : the office or function of a trustee **2** : supervisory control by one or more nations over a trust territory

trust·ful \'trəst-fəl\ *adj* : full of trust : CONFIDING — **trust·ful·ly** *adv* — **trust·ful·ness** *n*

trust territory *n* : a non-self-governing territory placed under a supervisory authority by the Trusteeship Council of the United Nations

trust·wor·thy \-ˌwər-thē\ *adj* : worthy of confidence : DEPENDABLE **syn** trusty, tried, reliable — **trust·wor·thi·ness** *n*

¹trusty \'trəs-tē\ *adj* **trust·i·er; -est** : TRUSTWORTHY, DEPENDABLE

²trusty \'trəs-tē, ˌtrəs-'tē\ *n, pl* **trust·ies** : a trusted person; *esp* : a convict considered trustworthy and allowed special privileges

truth \'trüth\ *n, pl* **truths** \'trüthz, 'trüths\ **1** : TRUTHFULNESS, HONESTY **2** : the real state of things : FACT **3** : the body of real events or facts : ACTUALITY **4** : a true or accepted statement or proposition ⟨the ~s of

science) **5** : agreement with fact or reality : CORRECT-
NESS **syn** veracity, verity
truth·ful \'trüth-fəl\ *adj* : telling or disposed to tell the
truth — **truth·ful·ly** *adv* — **truth·ful·ness** *n*
truth serum *n* : a drug held to induce a subject under
questioning to talk freely
¹**try** \'trī\ *vb* **tried; try·ing 1** : to examine or investigate
judicially **2** : to conduct the trial of **3** : to put to test
or trial **4** : to subject to strain, affliction, or annoyance **5** : to extract or clarify (as lard) by melting **6** : to
make an effort to do something : ATTEMPT, ENDEAV-
OR **syn** essay, assay, strive, struggle
²**try** *n*, *pl* **tries** : an experimental trial
try·ing *adj* : severely straining the powers of endurance
try on *vb* : to put on (a garment) to test the fit and looks
try out *vb* : to participate in competition esp. for a position on an athletic team or a part in a play — **try·
out** \'trī-ˌaut\ *n*
tryst \'trist\ *n* **1** : an agreement (as between lovers) to
meet **2** : an appointed meeting or meeting place —
tryst *vb* — **tryst·er** *n*
tsar \'zär, 'tsär, 'sär\ *var of* CZAR
tset·se fly \'tset-sē-, 'tsēt-, 'tet-, 'tēt-, 'set-, 'sēt-\ *n*
: any of several sub-Saharan African dipteran flies including the vector of sleeping sickness
TSgt *abbr* technical sergeant
T–shirt \'tē-ˌshərt\ *n* : a collarless short-sleeved or
sleeveless cotton undershirt; *also* : an outer shirt of
similar design — **T–shirt·ed** \-ˌshər-təd\ *adj*
tsp *abbr* teaspoon; teaspoonful
T square *n* : a ruler with a crosspiece at one end for
making parallel lines
tsu·na·mi \sù-'nä-mē, tsú-\ *n* [Jp] : a tidal wave caused
by an underwater earthquake or volcanic eruption
TT *abbr* Trust Territories
TTY *abbr* teletypewriter
Tu *abbr* Tuesday
tub \'təb\ *n* **1** : a wide low bucketlike vessel **2** : BATH-
TUB; *also* : BATH **3** : the amount that a tub will hold
tu·ba \'tü-bə, 'tyü-\ *n* : a large low-pitched brass wind
instrument
tub·al \'tü-bəl, 'tyü-\ *adj* : of, relating to, or involving
a tube and esp. a fallopian tube
tube \'tüb, 'tyüb\ *n* **1** : any of various usu. cylindrical
structures or devices; *esp* : one to convey fluids **2** : a
slender hollow anatomical part (as a fallopian tube)
functioning as a channel in a plant or animal body
: DUCT **3** : a soft round container from which a paste
is squeezed **4** : a tunnel for vehicular or rail travel **5**
: INNER TUBE **6** : ELECTRON TUBE **7** : TELEVISION —
tubed *adj* — **tube·less** *adj*
tu·ber \'tü-bər, 'tyü-\ *n* : a short fleshy usu. underground stem (as of a potato plant) bearing minute
scalelike leaves each with a bud at its base
tu·ber·cle \'tü-bər-kəl, 'tyü-\ *n* **1** : a small knobby
prominence or outgrowth esp. on an animal or plant
2 : a small abnormal lump in an organ or on the skin;
esp : one caused by tuberculosis
tubercle bacillus *n* : a bacterium that is the cause of
tuberculosis
tu·ber·cu·lar \tù-'bər-kyə-lər, tyü-\ *adj* **1** : TUBERCU-
LOUS **2** : of, resembling, or being a tubercle
tu·ber·cu·lin \tù-'bər-kyə-lən, tyü-\ *n* : a sterile liquid
extracted from the tubercle bacillus and used in the
diagnosis of tuberculosis esp. in children and cattle
tu·ber·cu·lo·sis \tù-ˌbər-kyə-'lō-səs, tyü-\ *n*, *pl* **-lo-
ses** \-ˌsēz\ : a communicable bacterial disease typically marked by wasting, fever, and formation of cheesy
tubercles often in the lungs — **tu·ber·cu·lous** \-'bər-
kyə-ləs\ *adj*
tube·rose \'tüb-ˌrōz, 'tyüb-\ *n* : a bulbous herb related
to the agaves and often grown for its spike of fragrant
waxy-white flowers
tu·ber·ous \'tü-bə-rəs, 'tyü-\ *adj* : of, resembling, or
being a tuber

tub·ing \'tü-biŋ, 'tyü-\ *n* **1** : material in the form of a
tube; *also* : a length of tube **2** : a series or system of
tubes
tu·bu·lar \'tü-byə-lər, 'tyü-\ *adj* : having the form of or
consisting of a tube; *also* : made with tubes
tu·bule \'tü-byül, 'tyü-\ *n* : a small tube
¹**tuck** \'tək\ *n* **1** : a fold stitched into cloth to shorten,
decorate, or control fullness **2** : a cosmetic surgical
operation for the removal of excess skin or fat ⟨a tum-
my ∼⟩
²**tuck** *vb* **1** : to pull up into a fold ⟨∼ed up her skirt⟩ **2**
: to make tucks in **3** : to put into a snug often concealing place ⟨∼ a book under the arm⟩ **4** : to secure
in place by pushing the edges under ⟨∼ in a blanket⟩
5 : to cover by tucking in bedclothes
tuck·er \'tə-kər\ *vb* **tuck·ered; tuck·er·ing** : EXHAUST,
FATIGUE
Tues *or* **Tue** *abbr* Tuesday
Tues·day \'tüz-dē, 'tyüz-, -dā\ *n* : the 3d day of the
week
tu·fa \'tü-fə, 'tyü-\ *n* : a porous rock formed as a deposit from springs or streams
tuff \'təf\ *n* : a rock composed of volcanic detritus
¹**tuft** \'təft\ *n* **1** : a small cluster of long flexible outgrowths (as hairs); *also* : a bunch of soft fluffy
threads cut off short and used as ornament **2** : CLUMP,
CLUSTER — **tuft·ed** *adj*
²**tuft** *vb* **1** : to provide or adorn with a tuft **2** : to make
(as a mattress) firm by stitching at intervals and sewing on tufts — **tuft·er** *n*
¹**tug** \'təg\ *vb* **tugged; tug·ging 1** : to pull hard **2** : to
struggle in opposition : CONTEND **3** : to move by pulling hard : HAUL **4** : to tow with a tugboat
²**tug** *n* **1** : a harness trace **2** : an act of tugging : PULL **3**
: a straining effort **4** : a struggle between opposing
people or forces **5** : TUGBOAT
tug·boat \-ˌbōt\ *n* : a strongly built boat used for towing or pushing
tug–of–war \ˌtəg-əv-'wòr\ *n*, *pl* **tugs–of–war 1** : a
struggle for supremacy **2** : an athletic contest in
which two teams pull against each other at opposite
ends of a rope
tu·grik *or* **tu·ghrik** \'tü-grik\ *n* — see MONEY table
tu·ition \tù-'i-shən, tyü-\ *n* : money paid for instruction
⟨college ∼⟩
tu·la·re·mia \ˌtü-lə-'rē-mē-ə, ˌtyü-\ *n* : an infectious
bacterial disease esp. of wild rabbits, rodents, humans, and some domestic animals that in humans is
marked by symptoms (as fever) of toxemia
tu·lip \'tü-ləp, 'tyü-\ *n* [NL *tulipa*, fr. Turk *tülbent* tur-
ban] : any of a genus of Eurasian bulbous herbs re-
lated to the lilies and grown for their large showy
erect cup-shaped flowers; *also* : a flower or bulb of a
tulip
tulip tree *n* : a tall American timber tree with greenish
tulip-shaped flowers and soft white wood that is related to the magnolias
tulle \'tül\ *n* : a sheer often stiffened silk, rayon, or nylon net ⟨a veil of ∼⟩
¹**tum·ble** \'təm-bəl\ *vb* **tum·bled; tum·bling** [ME, fr.
tumben to dance, fr. OE *tumbian*] **1** : to fall or cause
to fall suddenly and helplessly **2** : to fall into ruin **3**
: to perform gymnastic feats of rolling and turning **4**
: to roll over and over : TOSS **5** : to issue forth hurriedly and confusedly **6** : to come to understand **7** : to
throw together in a confused mass
²**tumble** *n* **1** : a disorderly state **2** : an act or instance of
tumbling
tum·ble·down \'təm-bəl-ˌdaùn\ *adj* : DILAPIDATED,
RAMSHACKLE
tum·bler \'təm-blər\ *n* **1** : one that tumbles; *esp* : AC-
ROBAT **2** : a drinking glass without foot or stem **3** : a
movable obstruction in a lock that must be adjusted
to a particular position (as by a key) before the bolt
can be thrown
tum·ble·weed \'təm-bəl-ˌwēd\ *n* : a plant that breaks

away from its roots in autumn and is driven about by the wind

tum·brel *or* **tum·bril** \'təm-brəl\ *n* **1** : CART **2** : a vehicle carrying condemned persons (as during the French Revolution) to a place of execution

tu·mid \'tü-məd, 'tyü-\ *adj* **1** : SWOLLEN, DISTENDED **2** : BOMBASTIC, TURGID

tum·my \'tə-mē\ *n, pl* **tummies** : BELLY, ABDOMEN, STOMACH

tu·mor \'tü-mər, 'tyü-\ *n* : an abnormal and functionless mass of tissue that is not inflammatory and arises from preexistent tissue — **tu·mor·ous** *adj*

tu·mour *chiefly Brit var of* TUMOR

tu·mult \'tü-ˌməlt, 'tyü-\ *n* **1** : UPROAR **2** : violent agitation of mind or feelings

tu·mul·tu·ous \tu̇-'məl-chə-wəs, tyu̇-, -chəs\ *adj* **1** : marked by tumult **2** : tending to incite a tumult **3** : marked by violent upheaval

tun \'tən\ *n* : a large cask

tu·na \'tü-nə, 'tyü-\ *n, pl* **tuna** *or* **tunas** [Sp] : any of several mostly large marine fishes related to the mackerels and caught for food and sport; *also* : the flesh of a tuna

tuna

tun·able \'tü-nə-bəl, 'tyü-\ *adj* : capable of being tuned — **tun·abil·i·ty** \ˌtü-nə-'bi-lə-tē, ˌtyü-\ *n*

tun·dra \'tən-drə\ *n* [Russ] : a treeless plain of arctic and subarctic regions

¹tune \'tün, 'tyün\ *n* **1** : a succession of pleasing musical tones : MELODY **2** : correct musical pitch **3** : harmonious relationship : AGREEMENT ⟨in ∼ with the times⟩ **4** : general attitude ⟨changed his ∼⟩ **5** : AMOUNT, EXTENT ⟨in debt to the ∼ of millions⟩

²tune *vb* **tuned; tun·ing 1** : to adjust in musical pitch **2** : to bring or come into harmony : ATTUNE **3** : to put in good working order **4** : to adjust a radio or television receiver so as to receive a broadcast **5** : to adjust the frequency of the output of (a device) to a chosen frequency — **tun·er** *n*

tune·ful \-fəl\ *adj* : MELODIOUS, MUSICAL — **tune·ful·ly** *adv* — **tune·ful·ness** *n*

tune·less \-ləs\ *adj* **1** : UNMELODIOUS **2** : not producing music — **tune·less·ly** *adv*

tune–up \'tün-ˌəp, 'tyün-\ *n* : an adjustment to ensure efficient functioning (an engine ∼)

tung·sten \'təŋ-stən\ *n* [Sw, fr. *tung* heavy + *sten* stone] : a white hard heavy ductile metallic chemical element used esp. for electrical purposes and in alloys — see ELEMENT table

tu·nic \'tü-nik, 'tyü-\ *n* **1** : a usu. knee-length belted under or outer garment worn by ancient Greeks and Romans **2** : a hip-length or longer blouse or jacket

tuning fork *n* : a 2-pronged metal implement that gives a fixed tone when struck and is useful for tuning musical instruments

Tu·ni·sian \tü-'nē-zhən, tyü-, -'ni-\ *n* : a native or inhabitant of Tunisia — **Tunisian** *adj*

¹tun·nel \'tən-əl\ *n* : an enclosed passage (as a tube or conduit); *esp* : one underground (as in a mine)

²tunnel *vb* **-neled** *or* **-nelled; -nel·ing** *or* **-nel·ling** : to make a tunnel through or under

tun·ny \'tə-nē\ *n, pl* **tunnies** *also* **tunny** : TUNA

tuque \'tük, 'tyük\ *n* [CanF] : a warm knitted cone-shaped cap

tur·ban \'tər-bən\ *n* **1** : a headdress worn esp. by Muslims and made of a cap around which is wound a long

cloth **2** : a headdress resembling a turban; *esp* : a woman's close-fitting hat without a brim

tur·bid \'tər-bəd\ *adj* [L *turbidus* confused, turbid, fr. *turba* confusion, crowd] **1** : cloudy or discolored by suspended particles (a ∼ stream) **2** : CONFUSED, MUDDLED — **tur·bid·i·ty** \ˌtər-'bi-də-tē\ *n*

tur·bine \'tər-bən, -ˌbīn\ *n* [F, fr. L *turbin-, turbo* top, whirlwind, whirl] : an engine whose central driveshaft is fitted with curved vanes spun by the pressure of water, steam, or gas

tur·bo·fan \'tər-bō-ˌfan\ *n* : a jet engine having a fan driven by a turbine for supplying air for combustion

tur·bo·jet \-ˌjet\ *n* : an airplane powered by a jet engine (**turbojet engine**) having a turbine-driven air compressor supplying compressed air to the combustion chamber

tur·bo·prop \-ˌpräp\ *n* : an airplane powered by a jet engine (**turboprop engine**) having a turbine-driven propeller

tur·bot \'tər-bət\ *n, pl* **turbot** *also* **turbots** : a European flatfish that is a popular food fish; *also* : any of several similar flatfishes

tur·bu·lence \'tər-byə-ləns\ *n* : the quality or state of being turbulent

tur·bu·lent \-lənt\ *adj* **1** : causing violence or disturbance **2** : marked by agitation or tumult : TEMPESTUOUS — **tur·bu·lent·ly** *adv*

tu·reen \tə-'rēn, tyu̇-\ *n* [F *terrine*, fr. MF, fr. fem. of *terrin* of earth] : a deep bowl from which foods (as soup) are served at table

¹turf \'tərf\ *n, pl* **turfs** \'tərfs\ *also* **turves** \'tərvz\ **1** : the upper layer of soil bound by grass and roots into a close mat; *also* : a piece of this **2** : an artificial substitute for turf (as on a playing field) **3** : a piece of peat dried for fuel **4** : a track or course for horse racing; *also* : horse racing as a sport or business

²turf *vb* : to cover with turf

tur·gid \'tər-jəd\ *adj* **1** : being in a swollen state **2** : excessively embellished in style or language : BOMBASTIC — **tur·gid·i·ty** \ˌtər-'ji-də-tē\ *n*

Turk \'tərk\ *n* : a native or inhabitant of Turkey

tur·key \'tər-kē\ *n, pl* **turkeys** [*Turkey,* country in western Asia and southeastern Europe; fr. confusion with the guinea fowl, supposed to be imported from Turkish territory] : a large American bird related to the domestic chicken and widely raised for food; *also* : its flesh

turkey buzzard *n* : TURKEY VULTURE

turkey vulture *n* : an American vulture with a red head and whitish bill

Turk·ish \'tər-kish\ *n* : the language of Turkey — **Turkish** *adj*

tur·mer·ic \'tər-mə-rik\ *n* : a spice or dyestuff obtained from the large aromatic deep-yellow rhizome of an East Indian perennial herb related to the ginger; *also* : this herb

tur·moil \'tər-ˌmȯil\ *n* : an extremely confused or agitated condition

¹turn \'tərn\ *vb* **1** : to move or cause to move around an axis or center : ROTATE, REVOLVE ⟨∼ a wheel⟩ **2** : to effect a desired end by turning something ⟨∼ the oven on⟩ **3** : WRENCH ⟨∼ an ankle⟩ **4** : to change or cause to change position by moving through an arc of a circle ⟨∼ed her chair to the fire⟩ **5** : to cause to move around a center so as to show another side of ⟨∼ a page⟩ **6** : to revolve mentally : PONDER **7** : to become dizzy : REEL **8** : to reverse the sides or surfaces of ⟨∼ a pancake⟩ **9** : UPSET, DISORDER ⟨things were ∼ed topsy-turvy⟩ **10** : to set in another esp. contrary direction **11** : to change one's course or direction **12** : to go around ⟨∼ a corner⟩ **13** : BECOME ⟨my hair ∼ed gray⟩ ⟨∼ed twenty-one⟩ **14** : to direct toward or away from something; *also* : DEVOTE, APPLY **15** : to have recourse **16** : to become or make hostile **17** : to cause to become of a specified nature or appearance ⟨∼s the leaves yellow⟩ **18** : to make or become spoiled

: SOUR **19** : to pass from one state to another 〈water ∼s to ice〉 **20** : CONVERT, TRANSFORM **21** : TRANSLATE, PARAPHRASE **22** : to give a rounded form to; *esp* : to shape by means of a lathe **23** : to gain by passing in trade 〈∼ a quick profit〉 — **turn color 1** : BLUSH **2** : to become pale — **turn loose** : to set free

²**turn** *n* **1** : a turning about a center or axis : REVOLUTION, ROTATION **2** : the action or an act of giving or taking a different direction 〈make a left ∼〉 **3** : a change of course or tendency 〈a ∼ for the better〉 **4** : a place at which something turns : BEND, CURVE **5** : a short walk or trip round about 〈take a ∼ around the block〉 **6** : an act affecting another 〈did him a good ∼〉 **7** : a place, time, or opportunity accorded in a scheduled order 〈waited his ∼ in line〉 **8** : a period of duty : SHIFT **9** : a short act esp. in a variety show **10** : a special purpose or requirement 〈the job serves his ∼〉 **11** : a skillful fashioning 〈neat ∼ of phrase〉 **12** : a single round (as of rope passed around an object) **13** : natural or special aptitude **14** : a usu. sudden and brief disorder of body or spirits; *esp* : a spell of nervous shock or faintness

turn·about \'tər-nə-ₜbau̇t\ *n* **1** : a reversal of direction, trend, or policy **2** : RETALIATION

turn·buck·le \'tərn-ₜbə-kəl\ *n* : a link with a screw thread at one or both ends for tightening a rod or stay

turn·coat \-ₜkōt\ *n* : one who switches to an opposing side or party : TRAITOR

turn down *vb* : to decline to accept : REJECT — **turn·down** \'tərn-ₜdau̇n\ *n*

turn·er \'tər-nər\ *n* **1** : one that turns or is used for turning **2** : one that forms articles with a lathe

turn·ery \'tər-nə-rē\ *n, pl* **-er·ies** : the work, products, or shop of a turner

turn in *vb* **1** : to deliver up **2** : to inform on **3** : to acquit oneself of 〈*turn in* a good job〉 **4** : to go to bed

turn·ing *n* **1** : the act or course of one that turns **2** : a place of a change of direction

tur·nip \'tər-nəp\ *n* **1** : a garden herb related to the cabbage with a thick edible usu. white root **2** : RUTABAGA **3** : the root of a turnip

turn·key \'tərn-ₖkē\ *n, pl* **turnkeys** : one who has charge of a prison's keys

turn·off \'tərn-ₒȯf\ *n* : a place for turning off esp. from an expressway

turn off *vb* **1** : to deviate from a straight course or a main road **2** : to stop the functioning or flow of **3** : to cause to lose interest; *also* : to evoke a negative feeling in

turn on *vb* **1** : to cause to flow, function, or operate **2** : to get high or cause to get high as a result of using a drug (as marijuana) **3** : EXCITE, STIMULATE

turn·out \'tərn-ₐau̇t\ *n* **1** : an act of turning out **2** : the number of people who participate or attend an event **3** : a widened place in a highway for vehicles to pass or park **4** : manner of dress **5** : net yield : OUTPUT

turn out *vb* **1** : EXPEL, EVICT **2** : PRODUCE **3** : to come forth and assemble **4** : to get out of bed **5** : to prove to be in the end

¹**turn·over** \'tər-ₙnō-vər\ *n* **1** : UPSET **2** : SHIFT, REVERSAL **3** : a filled pastry made by turning half of the crust over the other half **4** : the volume of business done **5** : movement (as of goods or people) into, through, and out of a place **6** : the number of persons hired within a period to replace those leaving or dropped **7** : an instance of a team's losing possession of the ball esp. through error

²**turnover** *adj* : capable of being turned over

turn over *vb* : TRANSFER 〈*turn* the job *over* to her〉

turn·pike \'tərn-ₚpīk\ *n* [ME *turnepike* revolving frame bearing spikes and serving as a barrier, fr. *turnen* to turn + *pike*] **1** : TOLLGATE; *also* : an expressway on which tolls are charged **2** : a main road

turn·stile \-ₛstīl\ *n* : a post with arms pivoted on the top set in a passageway so that persons can pass through only on foot one by one

turn·ta·ble \-ₜtā-bəl\ *n* : a circular platform that revolves (as for turning a locomotive or a phonograph record)

turn to *vb* : to apply oneself to work

turn up *vb* **1** : to come to light or bring to light : DISCOVER, APPEAR **2** : to arrive at an appointed time or place **3** : to happen unexpectedly

---

tur·pen·tine \'tər-pən-ₜtīn\ *n* **1** : a mixture of oil and resin obtained from various cone-bearing trees (as pines) **2** : an oil distilled from turpentine or pine wood and used as a solvent and paint thinner

---

tur·pi·tude \'tər-pə-ₜtüd, -ₜtyüd\ *n* : inherent baseness : DEPRAVITY

tur·quoise *also* **tur·quois** \'tər-ₖȯiz, -ₖkwȯiz\ *n* [ME *turkeis, turcas*, fr. MF *turquoyse*, fr. fem. of *turquoys* Turkish, fr. OF, fr. *Turc* Turk] **1** : a blue, bluish green, or greenish gray mineral that is valued as a gem **2** : a light greenish blue color

tur·ret \'tər-ət\ *n* **1** : a little tower often at an angle of a larger structure and merely ornamental **2** : a low usu. revolving structure (as on a tank or warship) in which one or more guns are mounted

¹**tur·tle** \'tərt-ᵊl\ *n, archaic* : TURTLEDOVE

²**turtle** *n, pl* **turtles** *also* **turtle** : any of an order of horny-beaked land, freshwater, or sea reptiles with the trunk enclosed in a bony shell

tur·tle·dove \'tərt-ᵊl-ₜdəv\ *n* : any of several small pigeons noted for plaintive cooing

tur·tle·neck \-ₙnek\ *n* : a high close-fitting turnover collar (as on a sweater); *also* : a sweater or shirt with a turtleneck — **tur·tle·necked** \-ₙnekt\ *adj*

turves *pl of* TURF

Tus·ca·ro·ra \ₜtəs-kə-ˈrȯr-ə\ *n, pl* **Tuscarora** *or* **Tuscaroras** : a member of an American Indian people of No. Carolina and later of New York and Ontario

tusk \'təsk\ *n* : a long enlarged protruding tooth (as of an elephant, walrus, or boar) used esp. to dig up food or as a weapon — **tusked** \'təskt\ *adj*

tusk·er \'təs-kər\ *n* : an animal with tusks; *esp* : a male elephant with two normally developed tusks

¹**tus·sle** \'tə-səl\ *n* **1** : a physical struggle : SCUFFLE **2** : an intense argument, controversy, or struggle

²**tussle** *vb* **tus·sled; tus·sling** : to struggle roughly

tus·sock \'tə-sək\ *n* : a dense tuft esp. of grass or sedge; *also* : a hummock in a marsh or bog bound together by roots — **tus·socky** *adj*

tu·te·lage \'tüt-ᵊl-ij, 'tyüt-\ *n* **1** : an act of guarding or protecting **2** : the state of being under a guardian or tutor **3** : instruction esp. of an individual

tu·te·lary \'tüt-ᵊl-ᵢer-ē, 'tyüt-\ *adj* : acting as a guardian ⟨~ deity⟩

¹**tu·tor** \'tü-tər, 'tyü-\ *n* **1** : a person charged with the instruction and guidance of another **2** : a private teacher

²**tutor** *vb* **1** : to have the guardianship of **2** : to teach or guide individually : COACH ⟨~ed her in Latin⟩ **3** : to receive instruction esp. privately

tu·to·ri·al \tü-'tōr-ē-əl, tyü-\ *n* : a class conducted by a tutor for one student or a small number of students

tut·ti \'tü-tē, 'tü-, -ᵢtē\ *adj or adv* [It., pl. of *tutto* all] : with all voices and instruments playing together — used as a direction in music

tut·ti-frut·ti \ᵢtü-ti-'frü-tē, ᵢtü-\ *n* [It, lit., all fruits] : a confection or ice cream containing chopped usu. candied fruits

tux·e·do \ᵢtək-'sē-dō\ *n, pl* **-dos** *or* **-does** [*Tuxedo* Park, N.Y.] **1** : a usu. black or blackish blue jacket **2** : semiformal evening clothes for men

TV \'tē-'vē\ *n* : TELEVISION

TVA *abbr* Tennessee Valley Authority

TV dinner *n* : a frozen packaged dinner that needs only heating before serving

twad·dle \'twäd-ᵊl\ *n* : silly idle talk : DRIVEL — **twad·dle** *vb*

twain \'twān\ *n* **1** : TWO **2** : PAIR

¹**twang** \'twaŋ\ *n* **1** : a harsh quick ringing sound like that of a plucked bowstring **2** : nasal speech or resonance **3** : the characteristic speech of a region

²**twang** *vb* **twanged; twang·ing 1** : to sound or cause to sound with a twang **2** : to speak with a nasal twang

tweak \'twēk\ *vb* : to pinch and pull with a sudden jerk and twitch — **tweak** *n*

tweed \'twēd\ *n* **1** : a rough woolen fabric made usu. in twill weaves **2** *pl* : tweed clothing; *esp* : a tweed suit

tweedy \'twē-dē\ *adj* **tweed·i·er; -est 1** : of or resembling tweed **2** : given to wearing tweeds **3** : suggestive of the outdoors in taste or habits

tween \'twēn\ *prep* : BETWEEN

tweet \'twēt\ *n* : a chirping note — **tweet** *vb*

tweet·er \'twē-tər\ *n* : a small loudspeaker that reproduces sounds of high pitch

twee·zers \'twē-zərz\ *n pl* [obs. E *tweeze*, n., case for small implements, short for obs. E *etweese*, fr. pl. of obs. E *etwee*, fr. F *étui*] : a small pincerlike implement held between the thumb and forefinger for grasping something

twelve \'twelv\ *n* **1** : one more than 11 **2** : the 12th in a set or series **3** : something having 12 units — **twelfth** \'twelfth\ *adj or n* — **twelve** *adj or pron*

twelve·month \-ᵢmənth\ *n* : YEAR

twen·ty \'twen-tē\ *n, pl* **twenties** : two times 10 — **twen·ti·eth** \-tē-əth\ *adj or n* — **twenty** *adj or pron*

twenty-twenty *or* **20/20** \ᵢtwen-tē-'twen-tē\ *adj* : characterized by a visual capacity for seeing detail that is normal for the human eye ⟨~ vision⟩

twice \'twīs\ *adv* **1** : on two occasions **2** : two times ⟨~ two is four⟩

¹**twid·dle** \'twid-ᵊl\ *vb* **twid·dled; twid·dling 1** : to be busy with trifles; *also* : to play idly with something **2** : to rotate lightly or idly

²**twiddle** *n* : TURN, TWIST

twig \'twig\ *n* : a small branch — **twig·gy** *adj*

twi·light \'twī-ᵢlīt\ *n* **1** : the light from the sky between full night and sunrise or between sunset and full night **2** : a state of imperfect clarity; *also* : a period of decline

twilight zone *n* **1** : TWILIGHT 2; *also* : an area just beyond ordinary legal or ethical limits **2** : a world of fantasy or unreality

twill \'twil\ *n* [ME *twyll*, fr. OE *twilic* having a double thread, part trans. of L *bilic-, bilix*, fr. *bi-* two + *licium* thread] **1** : a fabric with a twill weave **2** : a textile weave that gives an appearance of diagonal lines

twilled \'twild\ *adj* : made with a twill weave

¹**twin** \'twin\ *n* **1** : either of two offspring produced at a birth **2** : one of two persons or things closely related to or resembling each other

²**twin** *vb* **twinned; twin·ning 1** : to be coupled with another **2** : to bring forth twins

³**twin** *adj* **1** : born with one another or as a pair at one birth ⟨~ brother⟩ ⟨~ girls⟩ **2** : made up of two similar or related members or parts **3** : being one of a pair ⟨~ city⟩

¹**twine** \'twīn\ *n* **1** : a strong thread of two or three strands twisted together **2** : an act of entwining or interlacing — **twiny** *adj*

²**twine** *vb* **twined; twin·ing 1** : to twist together; *also* : to form by twisting **2** : INTERLACE, WEAVE **3** : to coil about a support **4** : to stretch or move in a sinuous manner — **twin·er** *n*

¹**twinge** \'twinj\ *vb* **twinged; twing·ing** *or* **twinge·ing** : to affect with or feel a sharp sudden pain

²**twinge** *n* : a sudden sharp stab (as of pain or distress)

¹**twin·kle** \'twiŋ-kəl\ *vb* **twin·kled; twin·kling 1** : to shine or cause to shine with a flickering or sparkling light **2** : to appear bright with merriment **3** : to flutter or flit rapidly — **twin·kler** *n*

²**twinkle** *n* **1** : a wink of the eyelids; *also* : the duration of a wink **2** : an intermittent radiance **3** : a rapid flashing motion — **twin·kly** \'twiŋ-klē\ *adj*

twin·kling \'twiŋ-kliŋ\ *n* : the time required for a wink : INSTANT

¹**twirl** \'twərl\ *vb* : to turn or cause to turn rapidly ⟨~ a baton⟩ *syn* revolve, rotate, circle, spin, swirl, pirouette — **twirl·er** *n*

²**twirl** *n* **1** : an act of twirling **2** : COIL, WHORL — **twirly** \'twər-lē\ *adj*

¹**twist** \'twist\ *vb* **1** : to unite by winding one thread or strand round another **2** : WREATHE, TWINE **3** : to turn so as to hurt ⟨~ed her ankle⟩ **4** : to twirl into spiral shape **5** : to subject (as a shaft) to torsion **6** : to turn from the true form or meaning **7** : to pull off or break by torsion **8** : to follow a winding course **9** : to turn around

²**twist** *n* **1** : something formed by twisting or winding **2** : an act of twisting : the state of being twisted **3** : a spiral turn or curve; *also* : SPIN **4** : a turning aside **5** : ECCENTRICITY **6** : a distortion of meaning **7** : an unexpected turn or development **8** : DEVICE, TRICK **9** : a variant approach or method

twist·er \'twis-tər\ *n* **1** : one that twists; *esp* : a ball with a forward and spinning motion **2** : TORNADO; *also* : WATERSPOUT 2

¹**twit** \'twit\ *n* : FOOL

²**twit** *vb* **twit·ted; twit·ting** : to ridicule as a fault; *also* : TAUNT *syn* deride, mock, razz

¹**twitch** \'twich\ *vb* **1** : to move or pull with a sudden motion : JERK **2** : to move jerkily : QUIVER

²**twitch** *n* **1** : an act or movement of twitching **2** : a short sharp contraction of muscle fibers

twit·ter \'twi-tər\ *vb* **1** : to make a succession of chirping noises **2** : to talk in a chattering fashion **3** : to tremble with agitation : FLUTTER

²**twitter** *n* **1** : a slight agitation of the nerves **2** : a small tremulous intermittent noise (as made by a swallow) **3** : a light chattering

twixt \'twikst\ *prep* : BETWEEN

two \'tü\ *n, pl* **twos 1** : one more than one **2** : the second in a set or series **3** : something having two units — **two** *adj or pron*

two cents *n* **1** : a sum or object of very small value **2**

or **two cents worth** : an opinion offered on a topic under discussion

two–faced \'tü-ˌfāst\ *adj* **1** : DOUBLE-DEALING, FALSE **2** : having two faces

two·fold \'tü-ˌfōld, -'fōld\ *adj* **1** : having two units or members **2** : being twice as much or as many — **two·fold** \-'fōld\ *adv*

2,4–D \ˌtü-ˌfōr-'dē\ *n* : an irritant compound used esp. as a weed killer

2,4,5–T \-ˌfīv-'tē\ *n* : an irritant compound used esp. as an herbicide and defoliant

two·pence \'tə-pəns, *US also* 'tü-ˌpens\ *n* : the sum of two pence

two·pen·ny \'tə-pə-nē, *US also* 'tü-ˌpe-nē\ *adj* : of the value of or costing twopence

two–ply \'tü-'plī\ *adj* **1** : woven as a double cloth **2** : consisting of two strands or thicknesses

two·some \'tü-səm\ *n* **1** : a group of two persons or things : COUPLE **2** : a golf match between two players

two–step \'tü-ˌstep\ *n* : a ballroom dance performed with a sliding step in march or polka time; *also* : a piece of music for this dance — **two–step** *vb*

two–time \'tü-ˌtīm\ *vb* : to betray (a spouse or lover) by secret lovemaking with another — **two–tim·er** *n*

two–way *adj* : involving two elements or allowing movement or use in two directions or manners

2WD *abbr* two-wheel drive

twp *abbr* township

TWX *abbr* teletypewriter exchange

TX *abbr* Texas

-ty *n suffix* : quality : condition : degree ⟨real*ty*⟩

ty·coon \tī-'kün\ *n* [Jp *taikun*] **1** : a masterful leader (as in politics) **2** : a powerful businessman or industrialist

tying *pres part of* TIE

tyke \'tīk\ *n* : a small child

tym·pan·ic membrane \tim-'pa-nik-\ *n* : EARDRUM

tym·pa·num \'tim-pə-nəm\ *n, pl* **-na** \-nə\ *also* **-nums** : EARDRUM; *also* : MIDDLE EAR — **tym·pan·ic** \tim-'pa-nik\ *adj*

¹type \'tīp\ *n* [ME, fr. LL *typus*, fr. L & Gk; L *typus* image, fr. Gk *typos* blow, impression, model, fr. *typtein* to strike, beat] **1** : a person, thing, or event that foreshadows another to come : TOKEN, SYMBOL **2** : MODEL, EXAMPLE **3** : a distinctive stamp, mark, or sign : EMBLEM **4** : rectangular blocks usu. of metal each having a face so shaped as to produce a character when printed **5** : the letters or characters printed from or as if from type **6** : general character or form common to a number of individuals and setting them off as a distinguishable class ⟨horses of draft ∼⟩ **7** : a class, kind, or group set apart by common characteristics ⟨a seedless ∼ of orange⟩; *also* : something distinguishable as a variety ⟨reactions of this ∼⟩ **syn** sort, nature, character, description

²type *vb* **typed; typ·ing 1** : to represent beforehand as a type **2** : to produce a copy of; *also* : REPRESENT, TYPIFY **3** : to write with a typewriter **4** : to identify as belonging to a type **5** : TYPECAST

type·cast \-ˌkast\ *vb* **-cast; -cast·ing 1** : to cast (an actor) in a part calling for characteristics possessed by the actor **2** : to cast repeatedly in the same type of role

type·face \-ˌfās\ *n* : all type of a single design

type·script \'tīp-ˌskript\ *n* : typewritten matter

type·set \-ˌset\ *vb* **-set; -set·ting** : to set in type : COMPOSE — **type·set·ter** *n*

type·write \-ˌrīt\ *vb* **-wrote** \-ˌrōt\; **-writ·ten** \-ˌrit-ᵊn\ : TYPE **3**

type·writ·er \-ˌrī-tər\ *n* **1** : a machine for writing in characters similar to those produced by printers' type by means of types striking a ribbon to transfer ink or carbon impressions onto paper **2** : TYPIST

type·writ·ing \-ˌrī-tiŋ\ *n* : the use of a typewriter ⟨teach ∼⟩; *also* : writing produced with a typewriter

¹ty·phoid \'tī-ˌfȯid, tī-'fȯid\ *adj* : of, relating to, or being a communicable bacterial disease (**typhoid fever**) marked by fever, diarrhea, prostration, and intestinal inflammation

²typhoid *n* : TYPHOID FEVER

ty·phoon \tī-'fün\ *n* : a tropical cyclone in the region of the Philippines or the China sea

ty·phus \'tī-fəs\ *n* : a severe infectious disease transmitted esp. by body lice, caused by a rickettsia, and marked by high fever, stupor and delirium, intense headache, and a dark red rash

typ·i·cal \'ti-pi-kəl\ *adj* **1** : being or having the nature of a type **2** : exhibiting the essential characteristics of a group **3** : conforming to a type — **typ·i·cal·i·ty** \ˌti-pə-'ka-lə-tē\ *n* — **typ·i·cal·ness** *n*

typ·i·cal·ly \-pi-k(ə-)lē\ *adv* **1** : in a typical manner **2** : in typical circumstances

typ·i·fy \'ti-pə-ˌfī\ *vb* **-fied; -fy·ing 1** : to represent by an image, form, model, or resemblance **2** : to embody the essential or common characteristics of

typ·ist \'tī-pist\ *n* : one who operates a typewriter

ty·po \'tī-pō\ *n, pl* **typos** : an error in typing or in setting type

ty·pog·ra·pher \tī-'pä-grə-fər\ *n* : one who designs or arranges printing

ty·pog·ra·phy \tī-'pä-grə-fē\ *n* : the art of printing with type; *also* : the style, arrangement, or appearance of printed matter — **ty·po·graph·ic** \ˌtī-pə-'gra-fik\ *or* **ty·po·graph·i·cal** \-fi-kəl\ *adj* — **ty·po·graph·i·cal·ly** *adv*

ty·ran·ni·cal \tə-'ra-ni-kəl, tī-\ *also* **ty·ran·nic** \-nik\ *adj* : of or relating to a tyrant : DESPOTIC **syn** arbitrary, absolute, autocratic — **ty·ran·ni·cal·ly** \-ni-k(ə-)lē\ *adv*

tyr·an·nise *Brit var of* TYRANNIZE

tyr·an·nize \'tir-ə-ˌnīz\ *vb* **-nized; -niz·ing** : to act as a tyrant : rule with unjust severity — **tyr·an·niz·er** *n*

ty·ran·no·saur \tə-'ra-nə-ˌsȯr\ *n* : a very large American flesh-eating dinosaur of the Cretaceous that had small forelegs and walked on its hind legs

ty·ran·no·sau·rus \tə-ˌra-nə-'sȯr-əs\ *n* : TYRANNOSAUR

tyr·an·nous \'tir-ə-nəs\ *adj* : TYRANNICAL — **tyr·an·nous·ly** *adv*

tyr·an·ny \'tir-ə-nē\ *n, pl* **-nies 1** : oppressive power **2** : the rule or authority of a tyrant : government in which absolute power is vested in a single ruler **3** : a tyrannical act

ty·rant \'tī-rənt\ *n* **1** : an absolute ruler : DESPOT **2** : a ruler who governs oppressively or brutally **3** : one who uses authority or power harshly

tyre *chiefly Brit var of* ²TIRE

ty·ro \'tī-rō\ *n, pl* **tyros** [ML, fr. L *tiro* young soldier, tyro] : a beginner in learning : NOVICE

tzar \'zär, 'tsär, 'sär\ *var of* CZAR

U

¹u \'yü\ *n, pl* **u's** *or* **us** \'yüz\ *often cap* : the 21st letter of the English alphabet

²u *abbr, often cap* unit

¹U \'yü\ *adj* : characteristic of the upper classes

²U *abbr* **1** [abbr. of *Union of Orthodox Hebrew Congregations*] kosher certification — often enclosed in a circle **2** university **3** unsatisfactory

³U *symbol* uranium

UAE *abbr* United Arab Emirates

UAR *abbr* United Arab Republic

UAW *abbr* United Automobile Workers

ubiq·ui·tous \yü-'bi-kwə-təs\ *adj* : existing or being everywhere at the same time : OMNIPRESENT — **ubiq·ui·tous·ly** *adv* — **ubiq·ui·ty** \-kwə-tē\ *n*

U–boat \'yü-ˌbōt\ *n* [trans. of G *U-boot,* short for *Unterseeboot,* lit., undersea boat] : a German submarine

UC *abbr* uppercase

ud·der \'ə-dər\ *n* : an organ (as of a cow) consisting of two or more milk glands enclosed in a large hanging sac and each provided with a nipple

UFO \ˌyü-(ˌ)ef-'ō\ *n, pl* **UFO's** *or* **UFOs** \-'ōz\ : an unidentified flying object; *esp* : FLYING SAUCER

Ugan·dan \ü-'gan-dən, yü-, -'gän-\ *n* : a native or inhabitant of Uganda — **Ugandan** *adj*

ug·ly \'ə-glē\ *adj* **ug·li·er; -est** [ME, fr. ON *uggligr,* fr. *uggr* fear] **1** : FRIGHTFUL, DIRE **2** : offensive to the sight : HIDEOUS **3** : offensive or unpleasant to any sense **4** : morally objectionable : REPULSIVE **5** : likely to cause inconvenience or discomfort **6** : SURLY, QUARRELSOME ⟨an ∼ disposition⟩ — **ug·li·ness** \-glē-nəs\ *n*

UHF *abbr* ultrahigh frequency

UK *abbr* United Kingdom

ukase \yü-'kās, -'kāz\ *n* [F & Russ; F, fr. Russ *ukaz,* fr. *ukazat'* to show, order] : an edict esp. of a Russian emperor or government

Ukrai·ni·an \yü-'krā-nē-ən\ *n* : a native or inhabitant of Ukraine — **Ukrainian** *adj*

uku·le·le *also* **uke·le·le** \ˌyü-kə-'lā-lē\ *n* [Hawaiian *'ukulele,* fr. *'uku* flea + *lele* jumping] : a small usu. 4-stringed guitar popularized in Hawaii

ul·cer \'əl-sər\ *n* **1** : an open eroded sore of skin or mucous membrane often discharging pus **2** : something that festers and corrupts like an open sore — **ul·cer·ous** *adj*

ul·cer·ate \'əl-sə-ˌrāt\ *vb* **-at·ed; -at·ing** : to become affected with an ulcer — **ul·cer·a·tive** \'əl-sə-ˌrā-tiv\ *adj*

ul·cer·a·tion \ˌəl-sə-'rā-shən\ *n* **1** : the process of forming or state of having an ulcer **2** : ULCER 1

ul·na \'əl-nə\ *n* : the bone on the little-finger side of the human forearm; *also* : a corresponding bone of the forelimb of vertebrates above fishes

ul·ster \'əl-stər\ *n* : a long loose overcoat

ult *abbr* **1** ultimate **2** ultimo

ul·te·ri·or \ˌəl-'tir-ē-ər\ *adj* **1** : lying farther away : more remote **2** : situated beyond or on the farther side **3** : going beyond what is openly said or shown : HIDDEN ⟨∼ motives⟩

¹ul·ti·mate \'əl-tə-mət\ *adj* **1** : most remote in space or time : FARTHEST **2** : last in a progression : FINAL **3** : the best or most extreme of its kind **4** : arrived at as the last resort **5** : FUNDAMENTAL, ABSOLUTE, SUPREME ⟨∼ reality⟩ **6** : incapable of further analysis or division : ELEMENTAL **7** : MAXIMUM **syn** concluding, eventual, latest, terminal — **ul·ti·mate·ly** *adv*

²ultimate *n* : something ultimate

ul·ti·ma·tum \ˌəl-tə-'mā-təm, -'mä-\ *n, pl* **-tums** *or* **-ta** \-tə\ : a final condition or demand whose rejection will bring about a resort to forceful action

ul·ti·mo \'əl-tə-ˌmō\ *adj* [L *ultimo mense* in the last month] : of or occurring in the month preceding the present

¹ul·tra \'əl-trə\ *adj* : going beyond others or beyond due limits : EXTREME

²ultra *n* : EXTREMIST

ul·tra·con·ser·va·tive \-kən-'sər-və-tiv\ *adj* : extremely conservative

ul·tra·high frequency \-'hī-\ *n* : a radio frequency between 300 and 3000 megahertz

¹ul·tra·light \'əl-trə-ˌlīt\ *adj* : extremely light esp. in weight

²ultralight *n* : a very light recreational aircraft typically carrying only one person

ul·tra·ma·rine \ˌəl-trə-mə-'rēn\ *n* **1** : a deep blue pigment **2** : a very bright deep blue color

ul·tra·mi·cro·scop·ic \-ˌmī-krə-'skä-pik\ *adj* : too small to be seen with an ordinary microscope

ul·tra·mod·ern \-'mä-dərn\ *adj* : extremely or excessively modern in idea, style, or tendency

ul·tra·mon·tane \-'män-ˌtān, -ˌmän-'tān\ *adj* **1** : of or relating to countries or peoples beyond the mountains (as the Alps) **2** : favoring greater or absolute supremacy of papal over national or diocesan authority in the Roman Catholic Church — **ultramontane** *n, often cap* — **ul·tra·mon·tan·ism** \-'mänt-ᵊn-ˌi-zəm\ *n*

ul·tra·pure \-'pyu̇r\ *adj* : of the utmost purity

ul·tra·short \-'shȯrt\ *adj* **1** : having a wavelength below 10 meters **2** : very short in duration

ul·tra·son·ic \ˌəl-trə-'sä-nik\ *adj* : having a frequency too high to be heard by the human ear — **ul·tra·son·i·cal·ly** \-ni-k(ə-)lē\ *adv*

ul·tra·son·ics \-'sä-niks\ *n sing or pl* **1** : ultrasonic vibrations **2** : the science of ultrasonic phenomena

ul·tra·sound \-ˌsau̇nd\ *n* **1** : ultrasonic vibrations **2** : the diagnostic or therapeutic use of ultrasound to form a two-dimensional image of internal body structures **3** : a diagnostic examination using ultrasound

HERE YOU GO, GARFIELD

THAT'S MILK

IT'LL MAKE YOUR COAT NICE AND SHINY

I THINK I'LL OPT TO MOLT

ALL CATS LOVE MILK!

WHEN I WAS YOUNG I WAS FRIGHTENED BY AN UDDER

JIM DAVIS 5·30

ul·tra·vi·o·let \-ˈvī-ə-lət\ *adj* : having a wavelength shorter than those of visible light and longer than those of X rays ⟨∼ radiation⟩; *also* : producing or employing ultraviolet radiation — **ultraviolet** *n*

ul·tra vi·res \ˈəl-trə-ˈvī-rēz\ *adv or adj* [NL, lit., beyond power] : beyond the scope of legal power or authority

ul·u·late \ˈəl-yə-ˌlāt\ *vb* **-lat·ed; -lat·ing** : HOWL, WAIL

um·bel \ˈəm-bəl\ *n* : a flat-topped or rounded flower cluster in which the individual flower stalks all arise near one point on the main stem

um·ber \ˈəm-bər\ *n* : a brown earthy substance valued as a pigment either in its raw state or burnt — **umber** *adj*

umbilical cord *n* : a cord containing blood vessels that connects the navel of a fetus with the placenta of its mother

um·bi·li·cus \ˌəm-ˈbi-li-kəs, ˌəm-bə-ˈlī-\ *n, pl* **um·bi·li·ci** \ˌəm-ˈbi-lə-ˌkī; ˌəm-bə-ˈlī-ˌkī, -ˌsī\ *or* **um·bi·li·cus·es** : NAVEL — **um·bil·i·cal** \ˌəm-ˈbi-li-kəl\ *adj*

um·bra \ˈəm-brə\ *n, pl* **umbras** *or* **um·brae** \-(ˌ)brē, -ˌbrī\ **1** : SHADE, SHADOW **2** : the conical part of the shadow of a celestial body from which the sun's light is completely blocked

um·brage \ˈəm-brij\ *n* **1** : SHADE; *also* : FOLIAGE **2** : RESENTMENT, OFFENSE ⟨take ∼ at a remark⟩

um·brel·la \ˌəm-ˈbre-lə\ *n* **1** : a collapsible shade for protection against weather consisting of fabric stretched over hinged ribs radiating from a center pole **2** : something that resembles an umbrella in shape or purpose

umi·ak \ˈü-mē-ˌak\ *n* : an open Eskimo boat made of a wooden frame covered with skins

umiak

um·pire \ˈəm-ˌpīr\ *n* [ME *oumpere*, alter. of *noumpere* (the phrase *a noumpere* being understood as *an oumpere*), fr. MF *nomper* not equal, not paired, fr. *non* not + *per* equal, fr. L *par*] **1** : one having authority to decide finally a controversy or question between parties **2** : an official in a sport who rules on plays — **umpire** *vb*

ump·teen \ˈəmp-ˌtēn\ *adj* : very many : indefinitely numerous — **ump·teenth** \-ˌtēnth\ *adj*

UN *abbr* United Nations

un- \ˌən, ˈən\ *prefix* **1** : not : IN-, NON- **2** : opposite of : contrary to

unabashed	unalike
unabated	unaltered
unabsorbed	unambiguous
unabsorbent	unambiguously
unacademic	unambitious
unaccented	unanchored
unacceptable	unannounced
unacclimatized	unanswerable
unaccommodating	unanswered
unaccredited	unanticipated
unacknowledged	unapologetic
unacquainted	unapparent
unadapted	unappealing
unadjusted	unappeased
unadorned	unappetizing
unadventurous	unappreciated
unadvertised	unappreciative
unaesthetic	unapproachable
unaffiliated	unappropriated
unafraid	unapproved
unaggressive	unarguable
unaided	unarguably

unarmored	uncomprehending
unartistic	unconcealed
unashamed	unconfined
unasked	unconfirmed
unassertive	unconformable
unassisted	uncongenial
unathletic	unconnected
unattainable	unconquered
unattended	unconsecrated
unattested	unconsidered
unattractive	unconsolidated
unauthentic	unconstrained
unauthorized	unconsumed
unavailable	unconsummated
unavowed	uncontaminated
unawakened	uncontested
unbaked	uncontrolled
unbaptized	uncontroversial
unbeloved	unconverted
unbleached	unconvincing
unblemished	uncooked
unblinking	uncooperative
unbound	uncoordinated
unbranched	uncorrected
unbranded	uncorroborated
unbreakable	uncountable
unbridgeable	uncreative
unbruised	uncredited
unbrushed	uncropped
unbudging	uncrowded
unburied	uncrowned
unburned	uncrystallized
uncanceled	uncultivated
uncanonical	uncultured
uncap	uncured
uncapitalized	uncurious
uncared–for	uncurtained
uncataloged	uncustomary
uncaught	undamaged
uncensored	undamped
uncensured	undated
unchallenged	undecided
unchangeable	undecipherable
unchanged	undeclared
unchanging	undecorated
unchaperoned	undefeated
uncharacteristic	undefended
unchaste	undefiled
unchastely	undefinable
unchasteness	undefined
unchastity	undemanding
unchecked	undemocratic
unchivalrous	undenominational
unchristened	undependable
unclad	undeserved
unclaimed	undeserving
unclassified	undesired
uncleaned	undetected
unclear	undetermined
uncleared	undeterred
unclouded	undeveloped
uncluttered	undifferentiated
uncoated	undigested
uncollected	undignified
uncolored	undiluted
uncombed	undiminished
uncombined	undimmed
uncomely	undiplomatic
uncomic	undirected
uncommercial	undisciplined
uncompensated	undisclosed
uncomplaining	undiscovered
uncompleted	undiscriminating
uncomplicated	undisguised
uncomplimentary	undismayed
uncompounded	undisputed

undissolved
undistinguished
undistributed
undisturbed
undivided
undocumented
undogmatic
undomesticated
undone
undoubled
undramatic
undraped
undreamed
undressed
undrinkable
undulled
undutiful
undyed
uneager
uneatable
uneaten
uneconomic
uneconomical
unedifying
unedited
uneducated
unembarrassed
unemotional
unemphatic
unenclosed
unencumbered
unendurable
unenforceable
unenforced
unenlightened
unenterprising
unenthusiastic
unenviable
unequipped
unessential
unethical
unexamined
unexcelled
unexceptional
unexcited
unexciting
unexpired
unexplained
unexploded
unexplored
unexposed
unexpressed
unexpurgated
unfading
unfaltering
unfashionable
unfashionably
unfathomable
unfavorable
unfavorably
unfeasible
unfeminine
unfenced
unfermented
unfertilized
unfilled
unfiltered
unfitted
unflagging
unflattering
unflavored
unfocused
unfolded
unforced
unforeseeable
unforeseen

unforgivable
unforgiving
unformulated
unfortified
unframed
unfree
unfulfilled
unfunded
unfunny
unfurnished
unfussy
ungentle
ungentlemanly
ungerminated
unglamorous
unglazed
ungoverned
ungraceful
ungracefully
ungraded
ungrammatical
unground
ungrudging
unguided
unhackneyed
unhampered
unhardened
unharmed
unharvested
unhatched
unhealed
unhealthful
unheated
unheeded
unhelpful
unheralded
unheroic
unhesitating
unhindered
unhistorical
unhonored
unhoused
unhurried
unhurt
unhygienic
unidentifiable
unidentified
unidiomatic
unimaginable
unimaginative
unimpaired
unimpassioned
unimpeded
unimportant
unimposing
unimpressed
unimpressive
unimproved
unincorporated
uninfected
uninfluenced
uninformative
uninformed
uninhabitable
uninhabited
uninitiated
uninjured
uninspired
uninstructed
uninstructive
uninsured
unintended
unintentional
unintentionally
uninteresting
uninvited

uninviting
unjointed
unjustifiable
unjustified
unkept
unknowable
unknowledgeable
unlabeled
unladylike
unlamented
unleavened
unlicensed
unlighted
unlikable
unlimited
unlined
unlit
unliterary
unlivable
unlovable
unloved
unloving
unmade
unmalicious
unmanageable
unmanned
unmapped
unmarked
unmarketable
unmarred
unmarried
unmasculine
unmatched
unmeant
unmeasurable
unmeasured
unmelodious
unmentioned
unmerited
unmilitary
unmilled
unmixed
unmodified
unmolested
unmotivated
unmounted
unmovable
unmoved
unmusical
unnameable
unnamed
unnecessary
unneeded
unnewsworthy
unnoticeable
unnoticed
unobjectionable
unobservant
unobserved
unobstructed
unobtainable
unofficial
unofficially
unopened
unopposed
unoriginal
unorthodox
unorthodoxy
unostentatious
unowned
unpaged
unpaid
unpainted
unpaired
unpalatable
unpardonable

unpasteurized
unpatriotic
unpaved
unpeeled
unperceived
unperceptive
unperformed
unpersuaded
unpersuasive
unperturbed
unplanned
unplanted
unpleasing
unplowed
unpoetic
unpolished
unpolitical
unpolluted
unposed
unpractical
unpredictable
unpredictability
unprejudiced
unpremeditated
unprepared
unpreparedness
unprepossessing
unpressed
unpretending
unpretty
unprivileged
unprocessed
unproductive
unprofessed
unprofessional
unprogrammed
unprogressive
unpromising
unprompted
unpronounceable
unpropitious
unprotected
unproven
unprovided
unprovoked
unpublished
unpunished
unquenchable
unquestioned
unraised
unrated
unratified
unreachable
unreadable
unready
unrealistic
unrealized
unrecognizable
unrecognized
unrecorded
unrecoverable
unredeemable
unrefined
unreflecting
unreflective
unregistered
unregulated
unrehearsed
unrelated
unreliable
unrelieved
unremarkable
unremembered
unremovable
unrepentant
unreported

unrepresentative
unrepresented
unrepressed
unresistant
unresisting
unresolved
unresponsive
unresponsiveness
unrestful
unrestricted
unreturnable
unrewarding
unrhymed
unrhythmic
unripened
unromantic
unromantically
unsafe
unsaid
unsalable
unsalted
unsanctioned
unsanitary
unsatisfactory
unsatisfied
unscented
unscheduled
unscholarly
unsealed
unseasoned
unseaworthy
unsegmented
unself–conscious
unself–consciously
unsensational
unsentimental
unserious
unserviceable
unsexual
unshaded
unshakable
unshaken
unshapely
unshaven
unshorn
unsifted
unsigned
unsinkable
unsmiling
unsociable
unsoiled
unsold
unsoldierly
unsolicited
unsolvable
unsolved
unsorted
unspecified
unspectacular
unspent
unspiritual
unspoiled
unspoken
unsportsmanlike
unstained
unstated
unsterile
unstructured
unstylish
unsubdued
unsubstantiated
unsubtle
unsuccessful
unsuccessfully
unsuitable
unsuited

unsullied
unsupervised
unsupportable
unsupported
unsure
unsurpassed
unsurprising
unsurprisingly
unsuspected
unsuspecting
unsuspicious
unsweetened
unsymmetrical
unsympathetic
unsystematic
untactful
untainted
untalented
untamed
untanned
untapped
untarnished
untaxed
unteachable
untenable
untenanted
untended
untested
unthrifty
untidy
untilled
untitled
untraceable
untraditional
untrained
untrammeled
untranslatable
untranslated
untraveled
untraversed
untreated
untrimmed
untrod
untroubled
untrustworthy
untruthful
untypical
unusable
unvaried
unvarying
unventilated
unverifiable
unverified
unversed
unvisited
unwanted
unwarranted
unwary
unwashed
unwavering
unweaned
unwearable
unwearied
unweathered
unwed
unwelcome
unwilling
unwillingly
unwillingness
unwomanly
unworkable
unworn
unworried
unwounded
unwoven

un·able \,ən-'ā-bəl\ adj 1 : not able 2 : UNQUALIFIED, INCOMPETENT
un·abridged \,ən-ə-'brijd\ adj 1 : not abridged ⟨an ∼ edition of Shakespeare⟩ 2 : complete of its class : not based on one larger ⟨an ∼ dictionary⟩
un·ac·com·pa·nied \,ən-ə-'kəm-pə-nēd\ adj : not accompanied; esp : being without instrumental accompaniment
un·ac·count·able \,ən-ə-'kaủn-tə-bəl\ adj 1 : not to be accounted for : INEXPLICABLE 2 : not responsible — **un·ac·count·ably** \-blē\ adv
un·ac·count·ed \-'kaủn-təd\ adj : not accounted ⟨the loss was ∼ for⟩
un·ac·cus·tomed \,ən-ə-'kəs-təmd\ adj 1 : not customary : not usual or common 2 : not accustomed or habituated ⟨∼ to noise⟩
un·adul·ter·at·ed \,ən-ə-'dəl-tə-,rā-təd\ adj : PURE, UNMIXED syn absolute, sheer, simple, unalloyed, undiluted, unmitigated
un·af·fect·ed \,ən-ə-'fek-təd\ adj 1 : not influenced or changed mentally, physically, or chemically 2 : free from affectation : NATURAL, GENUINE — **un·af·fect·ed·ly** adv
un·alien·able \-'āl-yə-nə-bəl, -'ā-lē-ə-\ adj : INALIENABLE
un·aligned \,ən-ə-'līnd\ adj : not associated with any one of competing international blocs ⟨∼ nations⟩
un·al·loyed \,ən-ə-'lȯid\ adj : UNMIXED, UNQUALIFIED, PURE ⟨∼ happiness⟩
un·al·ter·able \,ən-'ȯl-tə-rə-bəl\ adj : not capable of being altered or changed — **un·al·ter·ably** \-blē\ adv
un–Amer·i·can \,ən-ə-'mer-ə-kən\ adj : not characteristic of or consistent with American customs or principles
unan·i·mous \yủ-'na-nə-məs\ adj [L unanimus, fr. unus one + animus mind] 1 : being of one mind : AGREEING 2 : formed with or indicating the agreement of all — **una·nim·i·ty** \yü-nə-'ni-mə-tē\ n — **unan·i·mous·ly** adv
un·arm \,ən-'ärm\ vb : DISARM
un·armed \-'ärmd\ adj : not armed or armored
un·as·sail·able \,ən-ə-'sā-lə-bəl\ adj : not liable to doubt, attack, or question
un·as·sum·ing \,ən-ə-'sü-miŋ\ adj : MODEST, RETIRING syn humble, lowly, meek
un·at·tached \,ən-ə-'tacht\ adj 1 : not married or engaged 2 : not joined or united
un·avail·ing \,ən-ə-'vā-liŋ\ adj : being of no avail — **un·avail·ing·ly** adv
un·avoid·able \,ən-ə-'vȯi-də-bəl\ adj : not avoidable : INEVITABLE syn certain, ineluctable, inescapable, necessary — **un·avoid·ably** \-blē\ adv
¹**un·aware** \,ən-ə-'war\ adv : UNAWARES
²**unaware** adj : not aware : IGNORANT — **un·aware·ness** n
un·awares \-'warz\ adv 1 : without knowing : UNINTENTIONALLY 2 : without warning : by surprise ⟨taken ∼⟩
un·bal·anced \,ən-'ba-lənst\ adj 1 : not in a state of balance 2 : mentally disordered 3 : not adjusted so as to make credits equal to debits
un·bar \-'bär\ vb : UNBOLT, OPEN
un·bear·able \,ən-'bar-ə-bəl\ adj : greater than can be borne ⟨∼ pain⟩ syn insufferable, insupportable, intolerable, unendurable, unsupportable — **un·bear·ably** \-blē\ adv
un·beat·able \-'bē-tə-bəl\ adj : not capable of being defeated syn indomitable, invincible, invulnerable, unconquerable
un·beat·en \-'bēt-°n\ adj 1 : not pounded, beaten, or whipped 2 : UNTROD 3 : UNDEFEATED
un·be·com·ing \,ən-bi-'kə-miŋ\ adj : not becoming : UNSUITABLE, IMPROPER syn indecorous, indecent, indelicate, unseemly — **un·be·com·ing·ly** adv
un·be·knownst \,ən-bi-'nȯnst\ also **un·be·known** \-'nȯn\ adj : happening without one's knowledge

un·be·lief \ˌən-bə-ˈlēf\ *n* : the withholding or absence of belief : DOUBT — **un·be·liev·ing** \-ˈlē-viŋ\ *adj*

un·be·liev·able \-ˈlē-və-bəl\ *adj* : too improbable for belief; *also* : of such a superlative degree as to be hard to believe ⟨an ∼ catch for a touchdown⟩ **syn** inconceivable, unimaginable, unthinkable — **un·be·liev·ably** \-blē\ *adv*

un·be·liev·er \-ˈlē-vər\ *n* 1 : DOUBTER 2 : INFIDEL

un·bend \-ˈbend\ *vb* -**bent** \-ˈbent\; -**bend·ing** 1 : to free from being bent : make or become straight 2 : UNTIE 3 : to make or become less stiff or more affable : RELAX

un·bend·ing *adj* : formal and distant in manner : INFLEXIBLE

un·bi·ased \ˌən-ˈbī-əst\ *adj* : free from bias; *esp* : UNPREJUDICED **syn** disinterested, dispassionate, impartial, nondiscriminatory, nonpartisan, objective, uncolored

un·bid·den \-ˈbid-ᵊn\ *also* **un·bid** \-ˈbid\ *adj* : not bidden : UNASKED

un·bind \-ˈbīnd\ *vb* -**bound** \-ˈbau̇nd\; -**bind·ing** 1 : to remove bindings from : UNTIE 2 : RELEASE

un·blessed *also* **un·blest** \ˌən-ˈblest\ *adj* 1 : not blessed 2 : EVIL

un·block \-ˈbläk\ *vb* : to free from being blocked

un·blush·ing \-ˈblə-shiŋ\ *adj* 1 : not blushing 2 : SHAMELESS — **un·blush·ing·ly** *adv*

un·bod·ied \-ˈbä-dēd\ *adj* 1 : having no body; *also* : DISEMBODIED 2 : FORMLESS

un·bolt \ˌən-ˈbōlt\ *vb* : to open or unfasten by withdrawing a bolt

un·bolt·ed \-ˈbōl-təd\ *adj* : not fastened by bolts

un·born \-ˈbȯrn\ *adj* : not yet born

un·bos·om \-ˈbu̇-zəm, -ˈbü-\ *vb* 1 : DISCLOSE, REVEAL 2 : to disclose the thoughts or feelings of oneself

un·bound·ed \-ˈbau̇n-dəd\ *adj* : having no bounds or limits ⟨∼ enthusiasm⟩ **syn** boundless, endless, immeasurable, limitless, measureless, unlimited

un·bowed \ˌən-ˈbau̇d\ *adj* 1 : not bowed down 2 : UNSUBDUED

un·bri·dled \-ˈbrīd-ᵊld\ *adj* 1 : UNRESTRAINED 2 : not confined by a bridle

un·bro·ken \-ˈbrō-kən\ *adj* 1 : not damaged 2 : not subdued or tamed 3 : not interrupted : CONTINUOUS

un·buck·le \-ˈbə-kəl\ *vb* : to loose the buckle of : UNFASTEN ⟨∼ a belt⟩

un·bur·den \-ˈbərd-ᵊn\ *vb* 1 : to free or relieve from a burden 2 : to relieve oneself of (as cares or worries)

un·but·ton \-ˈbət-ᵊn\ *vb* : to unfasten the buttons of ⟨∼ your coat⟩

un·called–for \ˌən-ˈkȯld-ˌfȯr\ *adj* : not called for, needed, or wanted

un·can·ny \-ˈka-nē\ *adj* 1 : GHOSTLY, MYSTERIOUS, EERIE 2 : suggesting superhuman or supernatural powers **syn** spooky, unearthly, weird — **un·can·ni·ly** \-ˈkan-ᵊl-ē\ *adv*

un·ceas·ing \-ˈsē-siŋ\ *adj* : never ceasing **syn** ceaseless, continuous, endless, interminable, unending, unremitting — **un·ceas·ing·ly** *adv*

un·cer·e·mo·ni·ous \ˌən-ˌser-ə-ˈmō-nē-əs\ *adj* : acting without or lacking ordinary courtesy : ABRUPT — **un·cer·e·mo·ni·ous·ly** *adv*

un·cer·tain \ˌən-ˈsərt-ᵊn\ *adj* 1 : not determined or fixed ⟨an ∼ quantity⟩ 2 : subject to chance or change : not dependable ⟨∼ weather⟩ 3 : not definitely known 4 : not sure ⟨∼ of the truth⟩ — **un·cer·tain·ly** *adv*

un·cer·tain·ty \-ᵊn-tē\ *n* 1 : lack of certainty : DOUBT 2 : something that is uncertain **syn** concern, doubt, dubiety, incertitude, skepticism, suspicion

un·chain \ˌən-ˈchān\ *vb* : to free by or as if by removing a chain

un·charged \ˌən-ˈchärjd\ *adj* : having no electrical charge

un·char·i·ta·ble \-ˈchar-ə-tə-bəl\ *adj* : not charitable;

esp : severe in judging others — **un·char·i·ta·ble·ness** *n* — **un·char·i·ta·bly** \-blē\ *adv*

un·chart·ed \-ˈchär-təd\ *adj* 1 : not recorded on a map, chart, or plan 2 : UNKNOWN

un·chris·tian \-ˈkris-chən\ *adj* 1 : not of the Christian faith 2 : contrary to the Christian spirit

un·churched \-ˈchərcht\ *adj* : not belonging to or connected with a church

un·cial \ˈən-shəl, -chəl; ˈən-sē-əl\ *adj* : relating to or written in a form of script with rounded letters used esp. in early Greek and Latin manuscripts — **uncial** *n*

un·cir·cu·lat·ed \ˌən-ˈsər-kyə-ˌlā-təd\ *adj* : issued for use as money but kept out of circulation

un·cir·cum·cised \ˌən-ˈsər-kəm-ˌsīzd\ *adj* : not circumcised; *also* : HEATHEN

un·civ·il \ˌən-ˈsi-vəl\ *adj* 1 : not civilized : BARBAROUS 2 : DISCOURTEOUS, ILL-MANNERED, IMPOLITE

un·civ·i·lized \-ˈsi-və-ˌlīzd\ *adj* 1 : not civilized : BARBAROUS 2 : remote from civilization : WILD

un·clasp \-ˈklasp\ *vb* : to open by or as if by loosing the clasp

un·cle \ˈəŋ-kəl\ *n* [ME, fr. OF, fr. L *avunculus* mother's brother] : the brother of one's father or mother; *also* : the husband of one's aunt

un·clean \ˌən-ˈklēn\ *adj* 1 : morally or spiritually impure 2 : prohibited by ritual law for use or contact 3 : DIRTY, SOILED — **un·clean·li·ness** \-lē-nəs\ *n* — **un·clean·ly** *adj* — **un·clean·ness** *n*

un·clench \-ˈklench\ *vb* : to open from a clenched position : RELAX

Uncle Tom \-ˈtäm\ *n* [fr. *Uncle Tom*, faithful slave in Harriet Beecher Stowe's novel *Uncle Tom's Cabin* (1851-52)] : a black eager to win the approval of whites

un·cloak \ˌən-ˈklōk\ *vb* 1 : to remove a cloak or cover from 2 : UNMASK, REVEAL

un·clog \-ˈkläg\ *vb* : to remove an obstruction from

un·close \-ˈklōz\ *vb* : OPEN — **un·closed** \-ˈklōzd\ *adj*

un·clothe \-ˈklōth\ *vb* : to strip of clothes or a covering — **un·clothed** \-ˈklōthd\ *adj*

un·coil \ˌən-ˈkȯil\ *vb* : to release or become released from a coiled state

un·com·fort·able \ˌən-ˈkəmf-tə-bəl, -ˈkəm-fər-tə-\ *adj* 1 : causing discomfort 2 : feeling discomfort — **un·com·fort·ably** \-blē\ *adv*

un·com·mit·ted \ˌən-kə-ˈmi-təd\ *adj* : not committed; *esp* : not pledged to a particular belief, allegiance, or program

un·com·mon \ˌən-ˈkä-mən\ *adj* 1 : not ordinarily encountered : UNUSUAL, RARE 2 : REMARKABLE, EXCEPTIONAL **syn** extraordinary, phenomenal, singular, unique — **un·com·mon·ly** *adv*

un·com·mu·ni·ca·tive \ˌən-kə-ˈmyü-nə-ˌkā-tiv, -ni-kə-\ *adj* : not inclined to talk or impart information : RESERVED **syn** closemouthed, reticent, silent, taciturn

un·com·pro·mis·ing \ˌən-ˈkäm-prə-ˌmī-ziŋ\ *adj* : not making or accepting a compromise : UNYIELDING **syn** adamant, inflexible, obdurate, rigid, unbending

un·con·cern \ˌən-kən-ˈsərn\ *n* 1 : lack of care or interest : INDIFFERENCE 2 : freedom from excessive concern

un·con·cerned \-ˈsərnd\ *adj* 1 : not having any part or interest 2 : not anxious or upset : free of worry **syn** aloof, detached, incurious, remote, uncurious, uninterested — **un·con·cern·ed·ly** \-ˈsər-nəd-lē\ *adv*

un·con·di·tion·al \ˌən-kən-ˈdi-shə-nəl\ *adj* : not limited in any way — **un·con·di·tion·al·ly** *adv*

un·con·di·tioned \-ˈdi-shənd\ *adj* 1 : not subject to conditions 2 : not acquired or learned : NATURAL ⟨∼ responses⟩ 3 : producing an unconditioned response ⟨∼ stimuli⟩

un·con·quer·able \ˌən-ˈkäŋ-kə-rə-bəl\ *adj* : incapable of being conquered or overcome : INDOMITABLE

un·con·scio·na·ble \-ˈkän-shə-nə-bəl\ *adj* 1 : not guided or controlled by conscience 2 : not in accordance with what is right or just **syn** unreasonable, undue, unjustifiable, unwarrantable, unwarranted — **un·con·scio·na·bly** \-blē\ *adv*

¹**un·con·scious** \ˌən-ˈkän-chəs, -shəs\ *adj* **1** : not knowing or perceiving : not aware **2** : not done consciously or on purpose **3** : having lost consciousness **4** : of or relating to the unconscious — **un·con·scious·ly** *adv* — **un·con·scious·ness** *n*

²**unconscious** *n* : the part of one's mental life of which one is not ordinarily aware but which is often a powerful force in controlling behavior

un·con·sti·tu·tion·al \ˌən-ˌkän-stə-ˈtü-shə-nəl, -ˈtyü-\ *adj* : not according to or consistent with the constitution of a state or society — **un·con·sti·tu·tion·al·i·ty** \-tü-shə-ˈna-lə-tē, -ˈtyü-\ *n* — **un·con·sti·tu·tion·al·ly** \-ˈtü-shə-nə-lē, -ˈtyü-\ *adv*

un·con·trol·la·ble \ˌən-kən-ˈtrō-lə-bəl\ *adj* : incapable of being controlled : UNGOVERNABLE — **un·con·trol·la·bly** \-blē\ *adv*

un·con·ven·tion·al \-ˈven-chə-nəl\ *adj* : not conventional : being out of the ordinary — **un·con·ven·tion·al·i·ty** \-ˌven-chə-ˈna-lə-tē\ *n* — **un·con·ven·tion·al·ly** \-ˈven-chə-nə-lē\ *adv*

un·cork \ˌən-ˈkȯrk\ *vb* **1** : to draw a cork from **2** : to release from a sealed or pent-up state; *also* : to let go

un·count·ed \ˌən-ˈkau̇n-təd\ *adj* **1** : not counted **2** : INNUMERABLE

un·cou·ple \-ˈkə-pəl\ *vb* : DISCONNECT

un·couth \-ˈküth\ *adj* [ME, unfamiliar, fr. OE *uncūth*, fr. *un-* + *cūth* known] **1** : strange, awkward, and clumsy in shape or appearance **2** : vulgar in conduct or speech : RUDE **syn** discourteous, ill-mannered, impolite, ungracious, unmannered, unmannerly

un·cov·er \-ˈkə-vər\ *vb* **1** : to make known : DISCLOSE, REVEAL **2** : to expose to view by removing some covering **3** : to take the cover from **4** : to remove the hat from; *also* : to take off the hat as a token of respect — **un·covered** *adj*

un·crit·i·cal \ˌən-ˈkri-ti-kəl\ *adj* **1** : not critical : lacking in discrimination **2** : showing lack or improper use of critical standards or procedures — **un·crit·i·cal·ly** \-k(ə-)lē\ *adv*

un·cross \-ˈkrȯs\ *vb* : to change from a crossed position ⟨∼ed his legs⟩

unc·tion \ˈəŋk-shən\ *n* **1** : the act of anointing as a rite of consecration or healing **2** : exaggerated or insincere earnestness of language or manner

unc·tu·ous \ˈəŋk-chə-wəs\ *adj* [ME, fr. MF or ML; MF *unctueux*, fr. ML *unctuosus*, fr. L *unctus* act of anointing, fr. *unguere* to anoint] **1** : FATTY, OILY **2** : insincerely smooth in speech and manner — **unc·tu·ous·ly** *adv*

un·curl \ˌən-ˈkərl\ *vb* : to make or become straightened out from a curled or coiled position

un·cut \ˌən-ˈkət\ *adj* **1** : not cut down or into **2** : not shaped by cutting ⟨an ∼ diamond⟩ **3** : not having the folds of the leaves slit ⟨an ∼ book⟩ **4** : not abridged or curtailed ⟨the ∼ version of the film⟩ **5** : not diluted ⟨∼ heroin⟩

un·daunt·ed \-ˈdȯn-təd\ *adj* : not daunted : not discouraged or dismayed **syn** bold, brave, dauntless, fearless, intrepid, valiant — **un·daunt·ed·ly** *adv*

un·de·ceive \ˌən-di-ˈsēv\ *vb* : to free from deception, illusion, or error

un·de·mon·stra·tive \ˌən-di-ˈmän-strə-tiv\ *adj* : restrained in expression of feeling : RESERVED

un·de·ni·able \ˌən-di-ˈnī-ə-bəl\ *adj* **1** : plainly true : INCONTESTABLE **2** : unquestionably excellent or genuine **syn** incontrovertible, indisputable, indubitable, unquestionable — **un·de·ni·ably** \-blē\ *adv*

¹**un·der** \ˈən-dər\ *adv* **1** : in or into a position below or beneath something **2** : below some quantity, level, or limit ⟨$10 or ∼⟩ **3** : in or into a condition of subjection, subordination, or unconsciousness ⟨the ether put him ∼⟩

²**un·der** \ˌən-dər, ˈən-\ *prep* **1** : lower than and over-

hung, surmounted, or sheltered by ⟨∼ a tree⟩ **2** : subject to the authority or guidance of ⟨served ∼ him⟩ ⟨was ∼ contract⟩ **3** : subject to the action or effect of ⟨∼ the influence of alcohol⟩ **4** : within the division or grouping of ⟨items ∼ this heading⟩ **5** : less or lower than ⟨as in size, amount, or rank⟩ ⟨earns ∼ $5000⟩

³**under** \ˈən-dər\ *adj* **1** : lying below, beneath, or on the ventral side **2** : facing or protruding downward **3** : SUBORDINATE **4** : lower than usual, proper, or desired in amount, quality, or degree

un·der·achiev·er \ˌən-dər-ə-ˈchē-vər\ *n* : one who performs below an expected level of proficiency

un·der·act \-ˈakt\ *vb* : to perform feebly or with restraint

un·der·ac·tive \-ˈak-tiv\ *adj* : characterized by abnormally low activity ⟨∼ glands⟩ — **un·der·ac·tiv·i·ty** \-ˌak-ˈti-və-tē\ *n*

un·der·age \-ˈāj\ *adj* : of less than mature or legal age

un·der·arm \-ˈärm\ *adj* **1** : UNDERHAND **2** ⟨an ∼ throw⟩ **2** : placed under or on the underside of the arms ⟨∼ seams⟩ — **underarm** *adv or n*

un·der·bel·ly \ˈən-dər-ˌbe-lē\ *n* **1** : the underside of a body or mass **2** : a vulnerable area

un·der·bid \ˌən-dər-ˈbid\ *vb* -**bid**; -**bid·ding 1** : to bid less than another **2** : to bid too low

un·der·body \ˈən-dər-ˌbä-dē\ *n* : the lower parts of the body of a vehicle

un·der·bred \ˌən-dər-ˈbred\ *adj* : marked by lack of good breeding

un·der·brush \ˈən-dər-ˌbrəsh\ *n* : shrubs, bushes, or small trees growing beneath large trees

un·der·car·riage \ˈən-dər-ˌkar-ij\ *n* **1** : a supporting framework (as of an automobile) **2** *chiefly Brit* : the landing gear of an airplane

un·der·charge \ˌən-dər-ˈchärj\ *vb* : to charge (as a person) too little — **undercharge** \ˈən-dər-ˌchärj\ *n*

un·der·class·man \ˌən-dər-ˈklas-mən\ *n* : a member of the freshman or sophomore class

un·der·clothes \ˈən-dər-ˌklō(th)z\ *n pl* : UNDERWEAR

un·der·cloth·ing \-ˌklō-thiŋ\ *n* : UNDERWEAR

un·der·coat \-ˌkōt\ *n* **1** : a coat worn under another **2** : a growth of short hair or fur partly concealed by the longer and usu. coarser hairs of a mammal **3** : a coat of paint under another

un·der·coat·ing \-ˌkō-tiŋ\ *n* : a special waterproof coating applied to the underside of a vehicle

un·der·cov·er \ˌən-dər-ˈkə-vər\ *adj* : acting or executed in secret; *esp* : employed or engaged in secret investigation ⟨an ∼ agent⟩

un·der·croft \ˈən-dər-ˌkrȯft\ *n* [ME, fr. *under* + *crofte* crypt, fr. MD, fr. ML *crupta*, fr. L *crypta*] : a vaulted chamber under a church

un·der·cur·rent \-ˌkər-ənt\ *n* **1** : a current below the surface **2** : a hidden tendency of feeling or opinion

un·der·cut \ˌən-dər-ˈkət\ *vb* -**cut**; -**cut·ting 1** : to cut away the underpart of **2** : to offer to sell or to work at a lower rate than **3** : to strike (the ball) obliquely downward so as to give a backward spin or elevation to the shot — **un·der·cut** \ˈən-dər-ˌkət\ *n*

un·der·de·vel·oped \ˌən-dər-di-ˈve-ləpt\ *adj* **1** : not normally or adequately developed ⟨∼ muscles⟩ **2** : having a relatively low level of economic development ⟨the ∼ nations⟩

un·der·dog \ˈən-dər-ˌdȯg\ *n* : the loser or predicted loser in a struggle

un·der·done \ˌən-dər-ˈdən\ *adj* : not thoroughly done or cooked : RARE

un·der·draw·ers \ˈən-dər-ˌdrȯrz, -ˌdrȯ-ərz\ *n pl* : UNDERPANTS

un·der·em·pha·size \ˌən-dər-ˈem-fə-ˌsīz\ *vb* : to emphasize inadequately — **un·der·em·pha·sis** \-səs\ *n*

un·der·em·ployed \-im-ˈplȯid\ *adj* : having less than full-time or adequate employment

un·der·es·ti·mate \-ˈes-tə-ˌmāt\ *vb* : to set too low a value on

un·der·ex·pose \-ik-ˈspōz\ *vb* : to expose (a photographic plate or film) for less time than is needed — **un·der·ex·po·sure** \-'spō-zhər\ n

un·der·feed \ˌən-dər-'fēd\ vb -**fed** \-'fed\; -**feed·ing** : to feed with too little food

un·der·foot \-'fut\ adv **1** : under the feet ⟨flowers trampled ∼⟩ **2** : close about one's feet : in the way

un·der·fur \'ən-dər-ˌfər\ n : an undercoat of fur esp. when thick and soft

un·der·gar·ment \-ˌgär-mənt\ n : a garment to be worn under another

un·der·gird \ˌən-dər-'gərd\ vb : to brace up : STRENGTHEN

un·der·go \ˌən-dər-'gō\ vb -**went** \-'went\; -**gone** \-'gon, -'gän\; -**go·ing 1** : to submit to : ENDURE **2** : to go through : EXPERIENCE

un·der·grad \'ən-dər-ˌgrad\ n : UNDERGRADUATE

un·der·grad·u·ate \ˌən-dər-'gra-jə-wət, -jə-ˌwāt\ n : a student at a university or college who has not taken a first degree

¹un·der·ground \ˌən-dər-'graund\ adv **1** : beneath the surface of the earth **2** : in or into hiding or secret operation

²un·der·ground \'ən-dər-ˌgraund\ n **1** : a space under the surface of the ground; esp : SUBWAY **2** : a secret political movement or group; esp : an organized body working in secret to overthrow a government or an occupying power **3** : an avant-garde group or movement that operates outside the establishment

³underground \'ən-dər-ˌgraund\ adj **1** : being, growing, operating, or located below the surface of the ground ⟨∼ stems⟩ **2** : conducted by secret means **3** : produced or published by the underground ⟨∼ publications⟩; also : of or relating to the avant-garde underground

un·der·growth \'ən-dər-ˌgrōth\ n : low growth (as of herbs and shrubs) on the floor of a forest

¹un·der·hand \'ən-dər-ˌhand\ adv **1** : in an underhanded or secret manner **2** : with an underhand motion

²underhand adj **1** : UNDERHANDED **2** : made with the hand kept below the level of the shoulder

¹un·der·hand·ed \ˌən-dər-'han-dəd\ adv : UNDERHAND

²underhanded adj : marked by secrecy and deception — **un·der·hand·ed·ly** adv — **un·der·hand·ed·ness** n

un·der·lie \-'lī\ vb -**lay** \-'lā\; -**lain** \-'lān\; -**ly·ing** \-'lī-iŋ\ **1** : to lie or be situated under **2** : to be at the basis of : form the foundation of : SUPPORT

un·der·line \'ən-dər-ˌlīn\ vb **1** : to draw a line under **2** : EMPHASIZE, STRESS — **underline** n

un·der·ling \'ən-dər-liŋ\ n : SUBORDINATE, INFERIOR

un·der·lip \ˌən-dər-'lip\ n : the lower lip

un·der·ly·ing \ˌən-dər-ˌlī-iŋ\ adj **1** : lying under or below **2** : FUNDAMENTAL, BASIC ⟨∼ principles⟩

un·der·mine \-'mīn\ vb **1** : to excavate beneath **2** : to weaken or wear away secretly or gradually

un·der·most \'ən-dər-ˌmōst\ adj : lowest in relative position — **undermost** adv

¹un·der·neath \ˌən-dər-'nēth\ prep **1** : directly under **2** : under subjection to

²underneath adv **1** : below a surface or object : BENEATH **2** : on the lower side

un·der·nour·ished \ˌən-dər-'nər-isht\ adj : supplied with insufficient nourishment — **un·der·nour·ish·ment** \-'nər-ish-mənt\ n

un·der·pants \'ən-dər-ˌpants\ n pl : a usu. short undergarment for the lower trunk : DRAWERS

un·der·part \-ˌpärt\ n : a part lying on the lower side esp. of a bird or mammal

un·der·pass \-ˌpas\ n : a crossing of a highway and another way (as a road) at different levels; also : the lower level

un·der·pay \ˌən-dər-'pā\ vb : to pay too little

un·der·pin·ning \'ən-dər-ˌpi-niŋ\ n : the material and construction (as a foundation) used for support of a structure — **un·der·pin** \ˌən-dər-'pin\ vb

un·der·play \ˌən-dər-'plā\ vb : to treat or handle with restraint; esp : to play a role with subdued force

un·der·pop·u·lat·ed \ˌən-dər-'pä-pyə-ˌlā-təd\ adj : having a lower than normal or desirable density of population

un·der·priv·i·leged \-'priv-lijd, -'pri-və-lijd\ adj : having fewer esp. economic and social privileges than others

un·der·pro·duc·tion \ˌən-dər-prə-'dək-shən\ n : the production of less than enough to satisfy the demand or of less than the usual supply

un·der·rate \-'rāt\ vb : to rate or value too low

un·der·rep·re·sent·ed \-ˌre-pri-'zen-təd\ adj : inadequately represented

un·der·score \ˌən-dər-'skōr\ vb **1** : to draw a line under : UNDERLINE **2** : EMPHASIZE — **underscore** n

¹un·der·sea \ˌən-dər-'sē\ adj : being, carried on, or used beneath the surface of the sea

²undersea or **un·der·seas** \-'sēz\ adv : beneath the surface of the sea

un·der·sec·re·tary \ˌən-dər-'se-krə-ˌter-ē\ n : a secretary immediately subordinate to a principal secretary ⟨∼ of state⟩

un·der·sell \-'sel\ vb -**sold** \-'sōld\; -**sell·ing** : to sell articles cheaper than

un·der·sexed \-'sekst\ adj : deficient in sexual desire

un·der·shirt \-'shərt\ n : a collarless undergarment with or without sleeves

un·der·shoot \ˌən-dər-'shüt\ vb -**shot** \-'shät\; -**shoot·ing 1** : to shoot short of or below (a target) **2** : to fall short of (a runway) in landing an airplane

un·der·shorts \'ən-dər-ˌshorts\ n pl : SHORT 2

un·der·shot \'ən-dər-ˌshät\ adj **1** : moved by water passing beneath ⟨an ∼ waterwheel⟩ **2** : having the lower front teeth projecting beyond the upper when the mouth is closed

un·der·side \'ən-dər-ˌsīd, ˌən-dər-'sīd\ n : the side or surface lying underneath

un·der·signed \'ən-dər-ˌsīnd\ n, pl **undersigned** : one whose name is signed at the end of a document

un·der·sized \ˌən-dər-'sīzd\ also **un·der·size** \-'sīz\ adj : of a size less than is common, proper, or normal

un·der·skirt \\'ən-dər-ˌskərt\ *n* : a skirt worn under an outer skirt; *esp* : PETTICOAT

un·der·staffed \ˌən-dər-'staft\ *adj* : inadequately staffed

un·der·stand \ˌən-dər-'stand\ *vb* **-stood** \-'stůd\; **-stand·ing 1** : to grasp the meaning of : COMPREHEND **2** : to have thorough or technical acquaintance with or expertness in ⟨~ finance⟩ **3** : to have reason to believe ⟨I ~ you are leaving tomorrow⟩ **4** : INTERPRET ⟨we ~ this to be a refusal⟩ **5** : to have a sympathetic attitude **6** : to accept as settled ⟨it is *understood* that he will pay the expenses⟩ — **un·der·stand·able** \-'stan-də-bəl\ *adj*

un·der·stand·ably \-blē\ *adv* : as can be easily understood

¹**un·der·stand·ing** \ˌən-dər-'stan-diŋ\ *n* **1** : knowledge and ability to judge : INTELLIGENCE ⟨a person of ~⟩ **2** : agreement of opinion or feeling **3** : a mutual agreement informally or tacitly entered into

²**understanding** *adj* : endowed with understanding : TOLERANT, SYMPATHETIC

un·der·state \ˌən-dər-'stāt\ *vb* **1** : to represent as less than is the case **2** : to state with restraint esp. for effect — **un·der·state·ment** *n*

un·der·stood \ˌən-dər-'stůd\ *adj* **1** : agreed upon **2** : IMPLICIT

un·der·sto·ry \'ən-dər-ˌstōr-ē, -ˌstòr-\ *n* : the vegetative layer between the top layer of a forest and the ground cover

un·der·study \'ən-dər-ˌstə-dē, ˌən-dər-'stə-dē\ *vb* : to study another actor's part in order to substitute in an emergency — **understudy** \'ən-dər-ˌstə-dē\ *n*

un·der·sur·face \'ən-dər-ˌsər-fəs\ *n* : UNDERSIDE

un·der·take \ˌən-dər-'tāk\ *vb* **-took** \-'tůk\; **-tak·en** \-'tā-kən\; **-tak·ing 1** : to take upon oneself : set about ⟨~ a task⟩ **2** : to put oneself under obligation **3** : GUARANTEE, PROMISE

un·der·tak·er \'ən-dər-ˌtā-kər\ *n* : one whose business is to prepare the dead for burial and to arrange and manage funerals

un·der·tak·ing \'ən-dər-ˌtā-kiŋ, ˌən-dər-'tā-kiŋ; *2 is* 'ən-dər-ˌtā-kiŋ *only*\ *n* **1** : the act of one who undertakes or engages in any project **2** : the business of an undertaker **3** : something undertaken **4** : PROMISE, GUARANTEE

under–the–counter *adj* : UNLAWFUL, ILLICIT ⟨~ sale of drugs⟩

un·der·tone \'ən-dər-ˌtōn\ *n* **1** : a low or subdued tone or utterance **2** : a subdued color (as seen through and modifying another color)

un·der·tow \-ˌtō\ *n* : the current beneath the surface that flows seaward when waves are breaking upon the shore

un·der·trick \-ˌtrik\ *n* : a trick by which a declarer in bridge falls short of making the contract

un·der·val·ue \ˌən-dər-'val-yü\ *vb* **1** : to value or estimate below the real worth **2** : to esteem lightly

un·der·wa·ter \ˌən-dər-'wò-tər, -'wä-\ *adj* : lying, growing, worn, or operating below the surface of the water — **un·der·wa·ter** *adv*

under way \-'wā\ *adv* **1** : into motion from a standstill **2** : in progress

un·der·wear \'ən-dər-ˌwar\ *n* : clothing or a garment worn next to the skin and under other clothing

un·der·weight \ˌən-dər-'wāt\ *n* : weight below what is normal, average, or necessary — **underweight** *adj*

un·der·world \'ən-dər-ˌwərld\ *n* **1** : the place of departed souls : HADES **2** : the side of the world opposite to one **3** : the world of organized crime

un·der·write \'ən-dər-ˌrīt, ˌən-dər-'rīt\ *vb* **-wrote** \-ˌrōt, -'rōt\; **-writ·ten** \-ˌrit-ᵊn, -'rit-ᵊn\; **-writ·ing 1** : to write under or at the end of something else **2** : to set one's name to an insurance policy and thereby become answerable for a designated loss or damage

3 : to subscribe to : agree to **4** : to guarantee financial support of — **un·der·writ·er** *n*

un·de·sign·ing \ˌən-di-'zī-niŋ\ *adj* : having no artful, ulterior, or fraudulent purpose : SINCERE

un·de·sir·able \-'zī-rə-bəl\ *adj* : not desirable — **undesirable** *n*

un·de·vi·at·ing \ˌən-'dē-vē-ˌā-tiŋ\ *adj* : keeping a true course

un·dies \'ən-dēz\ *n pl* : UNDERWEAR; *esp* : women's underwear

un·do \ˌən-'dü\ *vb* **-did** \-'did\; **-done** \-'dən\; **-do·ing 1** : to make or become unfastened or loosened : OPEN **2** : to make null or as if not done : REVERSE **3** : to bring to ruin; *also* : UPSET

un·do·ing *n* : a cause of ruin

un·doubt·ed \-'daů-təd\ *adj* : not doubted or called into question : CERTAIN — **un·doubt·ed·ly** *adv*

¹**un·dress** \ˌən-'dres\ *vb* : to remove the clothes or covering of : STRIP, DISROBE

²**undress** *n* **1** : informal dress; *esp* : a loose robe or dressing gown **2** : ordinary dress **3** : NUDITY

un·due \-'dü, -'dyü\ *adj* **1** : not due **2** : exceeding or violating propriety or fitness : EXCESSIVE

un·du·lant \'ən-jə-lənt, 'ən-də-, -dyə-\ *adj* : UNDULATING

undulant fever *n* : a human disease caused by bacteria from infected domestic animals or their products and marked by intermittent fever, pain and swelling in the joints, and great weakness

un·du·late \-ˌlāt\ *vb* **-lat·ed; -lat·ing** [LL *undula* small wave, fr. L *unda* wave] **1** : to have a wavelike motion or appearance **2** : to rise and fall in pitch or volume

un·du·la·tion \ˌən-jə-'lā-shən, ˌən-də-, -dyə-\ *n* **1** : wavy or wavelike motion **2** : pulsation of sound **3** : a wavy appearance or outline — **un·du·la·to·ry** \'ən-jə-lə-ˌtōr-ē, 'ən-də-, -dyə-\ *adj*

un·du·ly \ˌən-'dü-lē, 'ən-, -'dyü-\ *adv* : in an undue manner; *esp* : EXCESSIVELY

un·dy·ing \-'dī-iŋ\ *adj* : not dying : IMMORTAL, PERPETUAL

un·earned \-'ərnd\ *adj* : not earned by labor, service, or skill ⟨~ income⟩

un·earth \-'ərth\ *vb* **1** : to dig up out of or as if out of the earth ⟨~ buried treasure⟩ **2** : to bring to light : DISCOVER ⟨~ a secret⟩

un·earth·ly \-lē\ *adj* **1** : not of or belonging to the earth **2** : SUPERNATURAL, WEIRD; *also* : ABSURD

un·easy \ˌən-'ē-zē\ *adj* **1** : AWKWARD, EMBARRASSED ⟨~ among strangers⟩ **2** : disturbed by pain or worry; *also* : RESTLESS **3** : UNSTABLE ⟨an ~ truce⟩ — **un·eas·i·ly** \-'ē-zə-lē\ *adv* — **un·eas·i·ness** \-'ē-zē-nəs\ *n*

un·em·ployed \ˌən-im-'plòid\ *adj* : not being used; *also* : having no job

un·em·ploy·ment \-'plòi-mənt\ *n* **1** : lack of employment **2** : money paid at regular intervals (as by a government agency) to an unemployed person

un·end·ing \ˌən-'en-diŋ\ *adj* : having no ending : ENDLESS

un·equal \ˌən-'ē-kwəl\ *adj* **1** : not alike (as in size, amount, number, or value) **2** : not uniform : VARIABLE **3** : badly balanced or matched **4** : INADEQUATE, INSUFFICIENT ⟨~ to the task⟩ — **un·equal·ly** *adv*

un·equaled *or* **un·equalled** \-kwəld\ *adj* : not equaled : UNPARALLELED

un·equiv·o·cal \ˌən-i-'kwi-və-kəl\ *adj* : leaving no doubt : CLEAR — **un·equiv·o·cal·ly** *adv*

un·err·ing \ˌən-'er-iŋ, ˌən-'ər-\ *adj* : making no errors : CERTAIN, UNFAILING — **un·err·ing·ly** *adv*

UNES·CO \yü-'nes-kō\ *abbr* United Nations Educational, Scientific, and Cultural Organization

un·even \ˌən-'ē-vən\ *adj* **1** : ODD **3 2** : not even : not level or smooth : RUGGED, RAGGED **3** : IRREGULAR; *also* : varying in quality — **un·even·ly** *adv* — **un·even·ness** *n*

un·event·ful \ˌən-i-ˈvent-fəl\ adj : lacking interesting or noteworthy incidents — **un·event·ful·ly** adv

un·ex·am·pled \ˌən-ig-ˈzam-pəld\ adj : UNPRECEDENTED, UNPARALLELED

un·ex·cep·tion·able \ˌən-ik-ˈsep-shə-nə-bəl\ adj : not open to exception or objection : beyond reproach

un·ex·pect·ed \ˌən-ik-ˈspek-təd\ adj : not expected : UNFORESEEN — **un·ex·pect·ed·ly** adv

un·fail·ing \ˌən-ˈfā-liŋ\ adj 1 : not failing, flagging, or waning : CONSTANT 2 : INEXHAUSTIBLE 3 : INFALLIBLE, SURE — **un·fail·ing·ly** adv

un·fair \-ˈfar\ adj 1 : marked by injustice, partiality, or deception : UNJUST 2 : not equitable in business dealings — **un·fair·ly** adv — **un·fair·ness** n

un·faith·ful \ˌən-ˈfāth-fəl\ adj 1 : not observant of vows, allegiance, or duty : DISLOYAL 2 : INACCURATE, UNTRUSTWORTHY — **un·faith·ful·ly** adv — **un·faith·ful·ness** n

un·fa·mil·iar \ˌən-fə-ˈmil-yər\ adj 1 : not well-known : STRANGE ⟨an ∼ place⟩ 2 : not acquainted ⟨∼ with the subject⟩ — **un·fa·mil·iar·i·ty** \-ˌmil-lē-ˈar-, -ˈyar-\ n

un·fas·ten \ˌən-ˈfas-ᵊn\ vb : to make or become loose : UNDO, DETACH

un·feel·ing \-ˈfē-liŋ\ adj 1 : lacking feeling : INSENSATE 2 : HARDHEARTED, CRUEL — **un·feel·ing·ly** adv

un·feigned \-ˈfānd\ adj : not feigned : not hypocritical : GENUINE

un·fet·ter \-ˈfe-tər\ vb 1 : to free from fetters 2 : LIBERATE

un·fil·ial \ˌən-ˈfi-lē-əl, -ˈfil-yəl\ adj : not observing the obligations of a child to a parent : UNDUTIFUL

un·fin·ished \ˌən-ˈfi-nisht\ adj 1 : not brought to an end 2 : being in a rough or unpolished state

¹**un·fit** \-ˈfit\ adj : not fit or suitable; esp : physically or mentally unsound — **un·fit·ness** n

²**unfit** vb : DISABLE, DISQUALIFY

un·fix \-ˈfiks\ vb 1 : to loosen from a fastening : DETACH 2 : UNSETTLE

un·flap·pa·ble \-ˈfla-pə-bəl\ adj : not easily upset or panicked — **un·flap·pa·bly** adv

un·fledged \ˌən-ˈflejd\ adj : not feathered or ready for flight; also : IMMATURE, CALLOW

un·flinch·ing \-ˈflin-chiŋ\ adj : not flinching or shrinking : STEADFAST — **un·flinch·ing·ly** adv

un·fold \-ˈfōld\ vb 1 : to open the folds of : open up 2 : to lay open to view : DISCLOSE 3 : BLOSSOM, DEVELOP

un·for·get·ta·ble \ˌən-fər-ˈge-tə-bəl\ adj : incapable of being forgotten — **un·for·get·ta·bly** \-blē\ adv

un·formed \-ˈfòrmd\ adj : not regularly formed or ordered : UNDEVELOPED

un·for·tu·nate \-ˈfòr-chə-nət\ adj 1 : not fortunate : UNLUCKY 2 : attended with misfortune 3 : UNSUITABLE — **unfortunate** n

un·for·tu·nate·ly \-nət-lē\ adv 1 : in an unfortunate manner 2 : it is unfortunate

un·found·ed \ˌən-ˈfaùn-dəd\ adj : lacking a sound basis : GROUNDLESS

un·freeze \-ˈfrēz\ vb **-froze** \-ˈfrōz\; **-fro·zen** \-ˈfrōz-ᵊn\; **-freez·ing** 1 : to cause to thaw 2 : to remove from a freeze ⟨∼ prices⟩

un·fre·quent·ed \ˌən-frē-ˈkwen-təd; ˌən-ˈfrē-kwən-\ adj : seldom visited or traveled over

un·friend·ly \ˌən-ˈfrend-lē\ adj 1 : not friendly or kind : HOSTILE 2 : UNFAVORABLE — **un·friend·li·ness** \-lē-nəs\ n

un·frock \-ˈfräk\ vb : DEFROCK

un·fruit·ful \-ˈfrüt-fəl\ adj 1 : not producing fruit or offspring : BARREN 2 : yielding no valuable result : UNPROFITABLE — **un·fruit·ful·ness** n

un·furl \-ˈfərl\ vb : to loose from a furled state : UNFOLD

un·gain·ly \-ˈgān-lē\ adj [un- + obs. gainly proper, becoming, fr. gain direct, handy, fr. ME geyn, fr. OE gēn, fr. ON gegn] : CLUMSY, AWKWARD — **un·gain·li·ness** \-lē-nəs\ n

un·gen·er·ous \ˌən-ˈje-nə-rəs\ adj : not generous or liberal : STINGY

un·glued \ˌən-ˈglüd\ adj : UPSET, DISORDERED

un·god·ly \ˌən-ˈgäd-lē, -ˈgòd-\ adj 1 : IMPIOUS, IRRELIGIOUS 2 : SINFUL, WICKED 3 : OUTRAGEOUS ⟨an ∼ hour⟩ — **un·god·li·ness** \-lē-nəs\ n

un·gov·ern·able \-ˈgə-vər-nə-bəl\ adj : not capable of being governed, guided, or restrained : UNRULY

un·gra·cious \-ˈgrā-shəs\ adj 1 : not courteous : RUDE 2 : not pleasing : DISAGREEABLE

un·grate·ful \ˌən-ˈgrāt-fəl\ adj 1 : not thankful for favors 2 : DISAGREEABLE; also : THANKLESS — **un·grate·ful·ly** adv — **un·grate·ful·ness** n

un·guard·ed \-ˈgär-dəd\ adj 1 : UNPROTECTED 2 : DIRECT, INCAUTIOUS ⟨∼ remarks⟩

un·guent \ˈəŋ-gwənt, ˈən-\ n : a soothing or healing salve : OINTMENT

¹**un·gu·late** \ˈəŋ-gyə-lət, ˈən-, -ˌlāt\ adj [LL ungulatus, fr. L ungula hoof, fr. unguis nail, hoof] : having hoofs

²**ungulate** n : a hoofed mammal (as a cow, horse, or rhinoceros)

Unh symbol unnilhexium

un·hal·lowed \ˌən-ˈha-lōd\ adj 1 : not consecrated : UNHOLY 2 : IMPIOUS, PROFANE 3 : contrary to accepted standards : IMMORAL

un·hand \ˌən-ˈhand\ vb : to remove the hand from : let go

un·hand·some \-ˈhan-səm\ adj 1 : not beautiful or handsome : HOMELY 2 : UNBECOMING 3 : DISCOURTEOUS, RUDE

un·handy \-ˈhan-dē\ adj : INCONVENIENT; also : AWKWARD

un·hap·py \-ˈha-pē\ adj 1 : UNLUCKY, UNFORTUNATE 2 : SAD, MISERABLE 3 : INAPPROPRIATE — **un·hap·pi·ly** \-ˈha-pə-lē\ adv — **un·hap·pi·ness** \-pē-nəs\ n

un·har·ness \-ˈhär-nəs\ vb : to remove the harness from (as a horse)

un·healthy \-ˈhel-thē\ adj 1 : not conducive to health : UNWHOLESOME 2 : SICKLY, DISEASED

un·heard \-ʹhərd\ *adj* **1** : not heard **2** : not granted a hearing

unheard–of *adj* : previously unknown; *esp* : UNPRECEDENTED

un·hinge \ˌən-ʹhinj\ *vb* **1** : to take from the hinges **2** : to make unstable esp. mentally

un·hitch \-ʹhich\ *vb* : UNFASTEN, LOOSE

un·ho·ly \-ʹhō-lē\ *adj* : not holy : PROFANE, WICKED — **un·ho·li·ness** \-lē-nəs\ *n*

un·hook \-ʹhůk\ *vb* : to loose from a hook

un·horse \-ʹhòrs\ *vb* : to dislodge from or as if from a horse

uni·cam·er·al \ˌyü-ni-ʹka-mə-rəl\ *adj* : having a single legislative house or chamber

UNI·CEF \ʹyü-nə-ˌsef\ *abbr* [United Nations International Children's Emergency Fund, its former name] United Nations Children's Fund

uni·cel·lu·lar \ˌyü-ni-ʹsel-yə-lər\ *adj* : having or consisting of a single cell

uni·corn \ʹyü-nə-ˌkòrn\ *n* [ME *unicorne*, fr. OF, fr. LL *unicornis*, fr. L, having one horn, fr. *unus* one + *cornu* horn] : a mythical animal with one horn in the middle of the forehead

uni·cy·cle \ʹyü-ni-ˌsī-kəl\ *n* : a vehicle having a single wheel and is usu. propelled by pedals

uni·di·rec·tion·al \ˌyü-ni-də-ʹrek-shə-nəl, -dī-\ *adj* : having, moving in, or responsive in a single direction

uni·fi·ca·tion \ˌyü-nə-fə-ʹkā-shən\ *n* : the act, process, or result of unifying : the state of being unified

¹uni·form \ʹyü-nə-ˌfòrm\ *adj* **1** : not varying **2** : of the same form with others ⟨∼ procedures⟩ — **uni·form·ly** *adv*

²uniform *vb* : to clothe with a uniform

³uniform *n* : distinctive dress worn by members of a particular group (as an army or a police force)

uni·for·mi·ty \ˌyü-nə-ʹfòr-mə-tē\ *n, pl* **-ties** : the state of being uniform

uni·fy \ʹyü-nə-ˌfī\ *vb* **-fied; -fy·ing** : to make into a coherent whole : UNITE

uni·lat·er·al \ˌyü-nə-ʹla-tə-rəl\ *adj* : of, having, affecting, or done by one side only — **uni·lat·er·al·ly** *adv*

un·im·peach·able \ˌən-im-ʹpē-chə-bəl\ *adj* : not liable to accusation : BLAMELESS, IRREPROACHABLE

un·in·hib·it·ed \ˌən-in-ʹhi-bə-təd\ *adj* : free from inhibition; *also* : boisterously informal — **un·in·hib·it·ed·ly** *adv*

un·in·tel·li·gent \-ʹte-lə-jənt\ *adj* : lacking intelligence

un·in·tel·li·gi·ble \-jə-bəl\ *adj* : not intelligible : OBSCURE — **un·in·tel·li·gi·bly** \-blē\ *adv*

un·in·ter·est·ed \ˌən-ʹin-trəs-təd, -tə-rəs-, -tə-ˌres-\ *adj* : not interested : not having the mind or feelings engaged or aroused

un·in·ter·rupt·ed \ˌən-ˌin-tə-ʹrəp-təd\ *adj* : not interrupted : CONTINUOUS

union \ʹyü-nyən\ *n* **1** : an act or instance of uniting two or more things into one : the state of being so united : COMBINATION, JUNCTION **2** : a uniting in marriage **3** : something formed by a combining of parts or members; *esp* : a confederation of independent individuals (as nations or persons) for some common purpose **4** : an organization of workers (as a labor union or a trade union) formed to advance its members' interests esp. in respect to wages and working conditions **5** : a device emblematic of union used on or as a national flag; *also* : the upper inner corner of a flag **6** : a device for connecting parts (as of a machine); *esp* : a coupling for pipes

union·ise *Brit var of* UNIONIZE

union·ism \ʹyü-nyə-ˌni-zəm\ *n* **1** : the principle or policy of forming or adhering to a union; *esp, cap* : adherence to the policy of a firm federal union before or during the U.S. Civil War **2** : the principles or system of trade unions — **union·ist** *n*

union·ize \ʹyü-nyə-ˌnīz\ *vb* **-ized; -iz·ing** : to form into

or cause to join a labor union — **union·i·za·tion** \ˌyü-nyə-nə-ʹzā-shən\ *n*

union jack *n* **1** : a flag consisting of the part of a national flag that signifies union **2** *cap U&J* : the national flag of the United Kingdom

unique \yů-ʹnēk\ *adj* **1** : being the only one of its kind : SINGLE, SOLE **2** : very unusual : NOTABLE — **unique·ly** *adv* — **unique·ness** *n*

uni·sex \ʹyü-nə-ˌseks\ *adj* : not distinguishable as male or female; *also* : suitable or designed for both males and females — **unisex** *n*

uni·sex·u·al \ˌyü-nə-ʹsek-shə-wəl\ *adj* **1** : having only male or only female sex organs **2** : UNISEX

uni·son \ʹyü-nə-sən, -zən\ *n* [MF, fr. ML *unisonus* having the same sound, fr. L *unus* one + *sonus* sound] **1** : sameness or identity in musical pitch **2** : the condition of being tuned or sounded at the same pitch or in octaves ⟨sing in ∼⟩ **3** : harmonious agreement or union : ACCORD

unit \ʹyü-nət\ *n* **1** : the smallest whole number greater than zero : ONE **2** : a definite amount or quantity used as a standard of measurement **3** : a single thing, person, or group that is a constituent of a whole; *also* : a part of a military establishment that has a prescribed organization — **unit** *adj*

Uni·tar·i·an \ˌyü-nə-ʹter-ē-ən\ *n* : a member of a religious denomination stressing individual freedom of belief — **Uni·tar·i·an·ism** *n*

uni·tary \ʹyü-nə-ˌter-ē\ *adj* **1** : of or relating to a unit **2** : not divided — **uni·tar·i·ly** \ˌyü-nə-ʹter-ə-lē\ *adv*

unite \yů-ʹnīt\ *vb* **unit·ed; unit·ing** **1** : to put or join together so as to make one : COMBINE, COALESCE **2** : to join by a legal or moral bond; *also* : to join in interest or fellowship **3** : AMALGAMATE, CONSOLIDATE **4** : to act in concert

unit·ed \yů-ʹnī-təd\ *adj* **1** : made one : COMBINED **2** : relating to or produced by joint action **3** : being in agreement : HARMONIOUS

unit·ize \ʹyü-nə-ˌtīz\ *vb* **-ized; -iz·ing** **1** : to form or convert into a unit **2** : to divide into units

uni·ty \ʹyü-nə-tē\ *n, pl* **-ties** **1** : the quality or state of being or being made one : ONENESS **2** : a definite quantity or combination of quantities taken as one or for which 1 is made to stand in calculation **3** : CONCORD, ACCORD, HARMONY **4** : continuity without change ⟨∼ of purpose⟩ **5** : reference of all the parts of a literary or artistic composition to a single main idea **6** : totality of related parts **syn** solidarity, union, integrity

univ *abbr* **1** universal **2** university

uni·valve \ʹyü-ni-ˌvalv\ *n* : a mollusk having a shell with only one piece; *esp* : GASTROPOD — **univalve** *adj*

uni·ver·sal \ˌyü-nə-ʹvər-səl\ *adj* **1** : including, covering, or affecting the whole without limit or exception : UNLIMITED, GENERAL ⟨a ∼ rule⟩ **2** : present or occurring everywhere **3** : used or for use among all ⟨a ∼ language⟩ — **uni·ver·sal·ly** *adv*

uni·ver·sal·i·ty \-vər-ʹsa-lə-tē\ *n* : the quality or state of being universal

uni·ver·sal·ize \-ʹvər-sə-ˌlīz\ *vb* **-ized; -iz·ing** : to make universal : GENERALIZE — **uni·ver·sal·i·za·tion** \-ˌvər-sə-lə-ʹzā-shən\ *n*

universal joint *n* : a shaft coupling for transmitting rotation from one shaft to another not in a straight line with it

universal joint

Universal Product Code *n* : a combination of a bar code and numbers by which a scanner can identify a product and usu. assign a price

uni·verse \\'yü-nə-ˌvərs\ *n* [L *universum*, fr. neut. of *universus* entire, whole, fr. *unus* one + *versus* turned toward, fr. pp. of *vertere* to turn] : the whole body of things observed or assumed : COSMOS

uni·ver·si·ty \ˌyü-nə-'vər-sə-tē\ *n, pl* **-ties** : an institution of higher learning authorized to confer degrees in various special fields (as theology, law, and medicine) as well as in the arts and sciences generally

un·just \ˌən-'jəst\ *adj* : characterized by injustice — **un·just·ly** *adv*

un·kempt \-'kempt\ *adj* **1** : lacking order or neatness; *also* : ROUGH, UNPOLISHED **2** : not combed : DISHEVELED

un·kind \-'kīnd\ *adj* : not kind or sympathetic ⟨an ∼ remark⟩ — **un·kind·ly** *adv* — **un·kind·ness** *n*

un·kind·ly \-'kīnd-lē\ *adj* : UNKIND — **un·kind·li·ness** *n*

un·know·ing \ˌən-'nō-iŋ\ *adj* : not knowing — **un·know·ing·ly** *adv*

un·known \-'nōn\ *adj* : not known or not well-known — **unknown** *n*

un·lace \ˌən-'lās\ *vb* : to loose by undoing a lace

un·lade \-'lād\ *vb* **-lad·ed; -laded** *or* **-lad·en** \-'lād-ᵊn\; **-lad·ing** : to take the load or cargo from : UNLOAD

un·latch \-'lach\ *vb* **1** : to open or loose by lifting the latch **2** : to become loosed or opened

un·law·ful \ˌən-'lȯ-fəl\ *adj* **1** : not lawful : ILLEGAL **2** : ILLEGITIMATE — **un·law·ful·ly** *adv*

un·lead·ed \-'le-dəd\ *adj* : not treated or mixed with lead or lead compounds

un·learn \-'lərn\ *vb* : to put out of one's knowledge or memory; *also* : to discard the habit of

un·learned \-'lər-nəd *for 1;* -'lərnd *for 2*\ *adj* **1** : UNEDUCATED, ILLITERATE **2** : not gained by study or training

un·leash \-'lēsh\ *vb* : to free from or as if from a leash : let loose

un·less \ən-'les, 'ən-ˌles\ *conj* : except on condition that ⟨won't go ∼ you do⟩

un·let·tered \ˌən-'le-tərd\ *adj* : not educated : ILLITERATE

¹**un·like** \-'līk\ *adj* **1** : not like : DISSIMILAR, DIFFERENT **2** : UNEQUAL — **un·like·ness** *n*

²**unlike** *prep* **1** : different from ⟨she's quite ∼ her sister⟩ **2** : unusual for ⟨it's ∼ you to be late⟩ **3** : differently from ⟨behaves ∼ his brother⟩

un·like·li·hood \ˌən-'lī-klē-ˌhůd\ *n* : IMPROBABILITY

un·like·ly \-'lī-klē\ *adj* **1** : not likely : IMPROBABLE **2** : likely to fail

un·lim·ber \ˌən-'lim-bər\ *vb* : to get ready for action

un·list·ed \ˌən-'lis-təd\ *adj* **1** : not appearing on a list; *esp* : not appearing in a telephone book **2** : not listed on a stock exchange

un·load \-'lōd\ *vb* **1** : to take away or off : REMOVE ⟨∼

cargo from a hold⟩; *also* : to get rid of **2** : to take a load from ⟨∼ the ship⟩; *also* : to relieve or set free : UNBURDEN ⟨∼ one's mind of worries⟩ **3** : to draw the charge from ⟨∼*ed* the gun⟩ **4** : to sell in volume

un·lock \-'läk\ *vb* **1** : to open or unfasten through release of a lock **2** : RELEASE ⟨∼ a flood of emotions⟩ **3** : DISCLOSE, REVEAL ⟨∼ nature's secrets⟩

un·looked–for \-'lůkt-fȯr\ *adj* : UNEXPECTED

un·loose \ˌən-'lüs\ *vb* : to relax the strain of : set free; *also* : UNTIE

un·loos·en \-'lüs-ᵊn\ *vb* : UNLOOSE

un·love·ly \-'ləv-lē\ *adj* : having no charm or appeal : not amiable

un·luck·i·ly \-'lə-kə-lē\ *adv* : UNFORTUNATELY

un·lucky \-'lə-kē\ *adj* **1** : UNFORTUNATE, ILL-FATED **2** : likely to bring misfortune : INAUSPICIOUS **3** : REGRETTABLE

un·man \ˌən-'man\ *vb* **1** : to deprive of manly courage **2** : CASTRATE

un·man·ly \-'man-lē\ *adj* : not manly : COWARDLY; *also* : EFFEMINATE

un·man·ner·ly \-'ma-nər-lē\ *adj* : RUDE, IMPOLITE — **unmannerly** *adv*

un·mask \ˌən-'mask\ *vb* **1** : to strip of a mask or a disguise : EXPOSE **2** : to remove one's mask

un·mean·ing \-'mē-niŋ\ *adj* : having no meaning : SENSELESS

un·me·di·at·ed \ˌən-'mē-dē-ˌā-təd\ *adj* : not mediated : not communicated or transformed by an intervening agency

un·meet \-'mēt\ *adj* : not meet or fit : UNSUITABLE, IMPROPER

un·men·tion·able \-'men-chə-nə-bəl\ *adj* : not fit or proper to be talked about

un·mer·ci·ful \-'mər-si-fəl\ *adj* : not merciful : CRUEL, MERCILESS — **un·mer·ci·ful·ly** *adv*

un·mind·ful \-'mīnd-fəl\ *adj* : not mindful : CARELESS, UNAWARE

un·mis·tak·able \ˌən-mə-'stā-kə-bəl\ *adj* : not capable of being mistaken or misunderstood : CLEAR, OBVIOUS — **un·mis·tak·ably** \-blē\ *adv*

un·mit·i·gat·ed \ˌən-'mi-tə-ˌgā-təd\ *adj* **1** : not softened or lessened **2** : ABSOLUTE, DOWNRIGHT ⟨an ∼ liar⟩

un·moor \-'můr\ *vb* : to loose from or as if from moorings

un·mor·al \-'mȯr-əl\ *adj* : having no moral perception or quality : AMORAL — **un·mo·ral·i·ty** \ˌən-mə-'ra-lə-tē\ *n*

un·muz·zle \-'mə-zəl\ *vb* : to remove a muzzle from

un·nat·u·ral \ˌən-'na-chə-rəl\ *adj* : contrary to or acting contrary to nature or natural instincts; *also* : ABNORMAL — **un·nat·u·ral·ly** *adv* — **un·nat·u·ral·ness** *n*

un·nec·es·sar·i·ly \ˌən-ˌne-sə-'ser-ə-lē\ *adv* **1** : not by necessity **2** : to an unnecessary degree ⟨∼ harsh⟩

un·nerve \ˌən-'nərv\ *vb* : to deprive of courage, strength, or steadiness; *also* : UPSET

un·nil·hex·i·um \ˌyün-ᵊl-'hek-sē-əm\ *n* [NL, fr. *unnil*- (fr. L *unus* one + *nil* zero) + Gk *hex* six + NL *-ium*]

: the chemical element of atomic number 106 — see ELEMENT table

un·nil·pen·ti·um \-'pen-tē-əm\ *n* : the chemical element of atomic number 105 — see ELEMENT table

un·nil·qua·di·um \-'kwä-dē-əm\ *n* : the chemical element of atomic number 104 — see ELEMENT table

un·num·bered \ən-'nəm-bərd\ *adj* : not numbered or counted : INNUMERABLE

un·ob·tru·sive \ən-əb-'trü-siv\ *adj* : not obtrusive or forward : not bold : INCONSPICUOUS — **un·ob·tru·sive·ly** *adv*

un·oc·cu·pied \ən-'ä-kyə-ıpīd\ *adj* 1 : not busy : UNEMPLOYED 2 : not occupied : EMPTY, VACANT

un·or·ga·nized \-'ȯr-gə-ınīzd\ *adj* 1 : not formed or brought into an integrated or ordered whole 2 : not organized into unions (∼ labor)

Unp *symbol* unnilpentium

un·pack \ən-'pak\ *vb* 1 : to separate and remove things packed 2 : to open and remove the contents of

un·par·al·leled \ən-'par-ə-ıleld\ *adj* : having no parallel; *esp* : having no equal or match

un·par·lia·men·ta·ry \ən-ıpär-lə-'men-tə-rē\ *adj* : contrary to parliamentary practice

un·peg \ən-'peg\ *vb* 1 : to remove a peg from 2 : to unfasten by or as if by removing a peg

un·per·son \'ən-ıpərs-ᵊn, -ıpərs-\ *n* : a person who usu. for political or ideological reasons is removed from recognition or consideration

un·pile \ən-'pīl\ *vb* : to take or disentangle from a pile

un·pin \-'pin\ *vb* : to remove a pin from : UNFASTEN

un·pleas·ant \-'plez-ᵊnt\ *adj* : not pleasant : DISAGREEABLE — **un·pleas·ant·ly** *adv* — **un·pleas·ant·ness** *n*

un·plug \ən-'pləg\ *vb* 1 : UNCLOG 2 : to remove (a plug) from a receptacle; *also* : to disconnect from an electric circuit by removing a plug

un·plumbed \-'pləmd\ *adj* 1 : not tested or measured with a plumb line 2 : not thoroughly explored

un·pop·u·lar \ən-'pä-pyə-lər\ *adj* : not popular : looked upon or received unfavorably — **un·pop·u·lar·i·ty** \-ın-ıpä-pyə-'lar-ə-tē\ *n*

un·prec·e·dent·ed \ən-'pre-sə-ıden-təd\ *adj* : having no precedent : NOVEL

un·pre·ten·tious \ən-pri-'ten-chəs\ *adj* : not pretentious : MODEST

un·prin·ci·pled \ən-'prin-sə-pəld\ *adj* : lacking sound or honorable principles : UNSCRUPULOUS

un·print·able \-'prin-tə-bəl\ *adj* : unfit to be printed

un·prof·it·able \ən-'prä-fə-tə-bəl\ *adj* : not profitable : USELESS, VAIN

Unq *symbol* unnilquadium

un·qual·i·fied \ən-'kwä-lə-ıfīd\ *adj* 1 : not having requisite qualifications 2 : not modified or restricted by reservations : COMPLETE — **un·qual·i·fied·ly** \-ıfī-əd-lē\ *adv*

un·ques·tion·able \-'kwes-chə-nə-bəl\ *adj* : not questionable : INDISPUTABLE — **un·ques·tion·ably** \-blē\ *adv*

un·ques·tion·ing \-chə-niŋ\ *adj* : not questioning : accepting without examination or hesitation — **un·ques·tion·ing·ly** *adv*

un·qui·et \-'kwī-ət\ *adj* 1 : not quiet : AGITATED, DISTURBED 2 : physically, emotionally, or mentally restless : UNEASY

un·quote \'ən-ıkwōt\ *n* — used orally to indicate the end of a direct quotation

un·rav·el \ən-'ra-vəl\ *vb* 1 : to separate the threads of 2 : SOLVE (∼ a mystery) 3 : to become unraveled

un·read \-'red\ *adj* 1 : not read; *also* : left unexamined 2 : lacking the benefits or the experience of reading

un·re·al \-'rēl\ *adj* : lacking in reality, substance, or genuineness — **un·re·al·i·ty** \ən-rē-'a-lə-tē\ *n*

un·rea·son·able \-'rēz-ᵊn-ə-bəl\ *adj* 1 : not governed by or acting according to reason; *also* : not conformable to reason : ABSURD 2 : exceeding the bounds of reason or moderation — **un·rea·son·able·ness** *n* — **un·rea·son·ably** *adv*

un·rea·soned \-'rēz-ᵊnd\ *adj* : not based on reason or reasoning

un·rea·son·ing \-'rēz-ᵊn-iŋ\ *adj* : not using or showing the use of reason as a guide or control

un·re·con·struct·ed \ən-ırē-kən-'strək-təd\ *adj* : not reconciled to some political, economic, or social change; *esp* : holding stubbornly to a particular belief, view, place, or style

un·reel \ən-'rēl\ *vb* 1 : to unwind from or as if from a reel 2 : to perform successfully

un·re·gen·er·ate \ən-ri-'je-nə-rət\ *adj* : not regenerated or reformed

un·re·lent·ing \-'len-tiŋ\ *adj* 1 : not yielding in determination : STERN (∼ leader) 2 : not letting up or weakening in vigor or pace : CONSTANT — **un·re·lent·ing·ly** *adv*

un·re·mit·ting \-'mi-tiŋ\ *adj* : CONTINUOUS, INCESSANT, PERSEVERING — **un·re·mit·ting·ly** *adv*

un·re·quit·ed \ən-ri-'kwī-təd\ *adj* : not requited : not reciprocated or returned in kind (∼ love)

un·re·served \-'zərvd\ *adj* 1 : not limited or partial (∼ enthusiasm) 2 : not cautious or reticent : FRANK, OPEN 3 : not set aside for special use — **un·re·serv·ed·ly** \-'zər-vəd-lē\ *adv*

un·rest \ən-'rest\ *n* : a disturbed or uneasy state : TURMOIL

un·re·strained \ən-ri-'strānd\ *adj* 1 : IMMODERATE, UNCONTROLLED 2 : SPONTANEOUS

un·re·straint \-ri-'strānt\ *n* : lack of restraint

un·rid·dle \ən-'rid-ᵊl\ *vb* : to find the explanation of : SOLVE

un·righ·teous \-'rī-chəs\ *adj* 1 : SINFUL, WICKED 2 : UNJUST — **un·righ·teous·ness** *n*

un·ripe \-'rīp\ *adj* : not ripe : IMMATURE

un·ri·valed *or* **un·ri·valled** \ən-'rī-vəld\ *adj* : having no rival : SUPREME

un·robe \-'rōb\ *vb* : DISROBE, UNDRESS

un·roll \-'rōl\ *vb* 1 : to unwind a roll of : open out 2 : DISPLAY, DISCLOSE 3 : to become unrolled or spread out

un·roof \-'rüf, -'rüf\ *vb* : to strip off the roof or covering of

un·ruf·fled \ən-'rə-fəld\ *adj* 1 : not agitated or upset 2 : not ruffled : SMOOTH (∼ water)

un·ru·ly \-'rü-lē\ *adj* [ME *unreuly*, fr. *un-* + *reuly* disciplined, fr. *reule* rule, fr. OF, fr. L *regula* straightedge, rule, fr. *regere* to direct] : not submissive to rule or restraint : TURBULENT (∼ passions) — **un·rul·i·ness** \-'rü-lē-nəs\ *n*

un·sad·dle \ən-'sad-ᵊl\ *vb* 1 : to remove the saddle from a horse 2 : UNHORSE

un·sat·u·rat·ed \-'sa-chə-ıra-təd\ *adj* 1 : capable of absorbing or dissolving more of something 2 : containing double or triple bonds between carbon atoms (∼ fats or oils) — **un·sat·u·rate** \-rət\ *n*

un·saved \ən-'sāvd\ *adj* : not saved; *esp* : not rescued from eternal punishment

un·sa·vory \-'sā-və-rē\ *adj* 1 : TASTELESS 2 : unpleasant to taste or smell 3 : morally offensive

un·say \-'sā\ *vb* **-said** \-'sed\; **-say·ing** : to take back (something said) : RETRACT, WITHDRAW

un·scathed \-'skāthd\ *adj* : wholly unharmed : not injured

un·schooled \-'sküld\ *adj* : not schooled : UNTAUGHT, UNTRAINED

un·sci·en·tif·ic \ən-ısī-ən-'ti-fik\ *adj* : not scientific : not in accord with the principles and methods of science

un·scram·ble \ən-'skram-bəl\ *vb* 1 : RESOLVE, CLARIFY 2 : to restore (as a radio message) to intelligible form

un·screw \-'skrü\ *vb* 1 : to draw the screws from 2 : to loosen by turning

un·scru·pu·lous \-'skrü-pyə-ləs\ *adj* : not scrupulous : UNPRINCIPLED — **un·scru·pu·lous·ly** *adv* — **un·scru·pu·lous·ness** *n*

un·seal \-'sēl\ *vb* : to break or remove the seal of
: OPEN

un·search·able \-'sər-chə-bəl\ *adj* : not capable of being searched or explored

un·sea·son·able \-'sēz-ᵊn-ə-bəl\ *adj* : not seasonable
: happening or coming at the wrong time : UNTIMELY
— **un·sea·son·ably** \-blē\ *adv*

un·seat \-'sēt\ *vb* 1 : to throw from one's seat esp. on
horseback 2 : to remove from political office

un·seem·ly \-'sēm-lē\ *adj* : not according with established standards of good form or taste; *also* : not suitable — **un·seem·li·ness** *n*

un·seen \ᵊən-'sēn\ *adj* : not seen : INVISIBLE

un·seg·re·gat·ed \-'se-gri-ᵢgā-təd\ *adj* : not segregated;
esp : free from racial segregation

un·self·ish \-'sel-fish\ *adj* : not selfish : GENEROUS —
un·self·ish·ly *adv* — **un·self·ish·ness** *n*

un·set·tle \ᵊən-'set-ᵊl\ *vb* : to move or loosen from a
settled position : DISPLACE, DISTURB

un·set·tled \-'set-ᵊld\ *adj* 1 : not settled : not fixed (as
in position or character) 2 : not calm : DISTURBED 3
: not decided in mind : UNDETERMINED 4 : not paid ⟨∼
accounts⟩ 5 : not occupied by settlers

un·shack·le \-'sha-kəl\ *vb* : to free from shackles

un·shaped \-'shāpt\ *adj* : not shaped; *esp* : not being in
finished, final, or perfect form ⟨∼ ideas⟩ ⟨∼ timber⟩

un·sheathe \ᵊən-'shēth\ *vb* : to draw from or as if from
a sheath

un·ship \-'ship\ *vb* 1 : to remove from a ship 2 : to remove or become removed from position ⟨∼ an oar⟩

un·shod \ᵊən-'shäd\ *adj* : not wearing or provided with
shoes

un·sight·ly \ᵊən-'sīt-lē\ *adj* : unpleasant to the sight
: UGLY

un·skilled \-'skild\ *adj* 1 : not skilled; *esp* : not skilled
in a specified branch of work 2 : not requiring skill

un·skill·ful \-'skil-fəl\ *adj* : lacking in skill or proficiency — **un·skill·ful·ly** *adv*

un·sling \-'sliŋ\ *vb* **-slung** \-'sləŋ\; **-sling·ing** : to remove from being slung

un·snap \-'snap\ *vb* : to loosen or free by or as if by
undoing a snap

un·snarl \-'snärl\ *vb* : to remove snarls from : UNTAN-
GLE

un·so·phis·ti·cat·ed \ᵢən-sə-'fis-tə-ᵢkā-təd\ *adj* 1 : not
worldly-wise : lacking sophistication 2 : SIMPLE

un·sought \ᵢən-'sòt\ *adj* : not sought : not searched for
or asked for : not obtained by effort ⟨∼ honors⟩

un·sound \-'saùnd\ *adj* 1 : not healthy or whole; *also*
: not mentally normal 2 : not valid 3 : not firmly made
or fixed — **un·sound·ly** *adv* — **un·sound·ness** *n*

un·spar·ing \-'spar-iŋ\ *adj* 1 : HARD, RUTHLESS 2 : not
frugal : LIBERAL, PROFUSE

un·speak·able \-'spē-kə-bəl\ *adj* 1 : impossible to express in words 2 : extremely bad — **un·speak·ably**
\-blē\ *adv*

un·spot·ted \-'spä-təd\ *adj* : not spotted or stained; *esp*
: free from moral stain

un·sprung \-'sprəŋ\ *adj* : not sprung; *esp* : not
equipped with springs

un·sta·ble \-'stā-bəl\ *adj* 1 : not stable 2 : FICKLE, VAC-
ILLATING; *also* : lacking effective emotional control 3
: readily changing (as by decomposing) in chemical or
physical composition or in biological activity ⟨an ∼
atomic nucleus⟩

un·steady \ᵢən-'ste-dē\ *adj* : not steady : UNSTABLE —
un·stead·i·ly \-'sted-ᵊl-ē\ *adv* — **un·stead·i·ness**
\-'ste-dē-nəs\ *n*

un·stint·ing \-'stin-tiŋ\ *adj* 1 : not restricting or holding
back 2 : giving or being given freely or generously ⟨∼
praise⟩

un·stop \-'stäp\ *vb* 1 : UNCLOG 2 : to remove a stopper
from

un·stop·pa·ble \ᵢən-'stä-pə-bəl\ *adj* : incapable of being stopped

un·strap \-'strap\ *vb* : to remove or loose a strap from

un·stressed \ᵢən-'strest\ *adj* : not stressed; *esp* : not
bearing a stress or accent

un·strung \-'strəŋ\ *adj* 1 : having the strings loose or
detached 2 : nervously tired or anxious

un·stud·ied \-'stə-dēd\ *adj* 1 : not acquired by study 2
: NATURAL, UNFORCED ⟨moved with ∼ grace⟩

un·sub·stan·tial \ᵢən-səb-'stan-chəl\ *adj* : INSUBSTAN-
TIAL

un·sung \ᵢən-'səŋ\ *adj* 1 : not sung 2 : not celebrated
in song or verse ⟨∼ heroes⟩

un·swerv·ing \ᵢən-'swer-viŋ\ *adj* 1 : not swerving or
turning aside 2 : STEADY

un·tan·gle \-'taŋ-gəl\ *vb* 1 : DISENTANGLE 2 : to
straighten out : RESOLVE ⟨∼ a problem⟩

un·taught \-'tòt\ *adj* 1 : not instructed or taught : IG-
NORANT 2 : NATURAL, SPONTANEOUS ⟨∼ kindness⟩

un·think·able \-'thiŋ-kə-bəl\ *adj* : not to be thought of
or considered as possible ⟨∼ cruelty⟩

un·think·ing \ᵢən-'thiŋ-kiŋ\ *adj* : not thinking; *esp*
: THOUGHTLESS, HEEDLESS — **un·think·ing·ly** *adv*

un·thought \ᵢən-'thòt\ *adj* : not anticipated : UNEX-
PECTED — often used with *of* ⟨unthought-of develop-
ment⟩

un·tie \-'tī\ *vb* **-tied**; **-ty·ing** *or* **-tie·ing** 1 : to free from
something that ties, fastens, or restrains : UNBIND 2
: DISENTANGLE, RESOLVE 3 : to become loosened or
unbound

¹**un·til** \ᵢən-'til\ *prep* : up to the time of ⟨worked ∼ 5
o'clock⟩

²**until** *conj* 1 : up to the time that ⟨wait ∼ he calls⟩ 2 : to
the point or degree that ⟨ran ∼ she was breathless⟩

¹**un·time·ly** \ᵢən-'tīm-lē\ *adv* : at an inopportune time
: UNSEASONABLY; *also* : PREMATURELY

²**untimely** *adj* : PREMATURE ⟨∼ death⟩; *also* : INOPPOR-
TUNE, UNSEASONABLE

un·tir·ing \ᵢən-'tī-riŋ\ *adj* : not becoming tired : INDE-
FATIGABLE — **un·tir·ing·ly** *adv*

un·to \'ᵊən-ᵢtü\ *prep* : TO

un·told \ᵢən-'tōld\ *adj* 1 : not counted : VAST, NUMBER-
LESS 2 : not told : not revealed

¹**un·touch·able** \ᵢən-'tə-chə-bəl\ *adj* : forbidden to the
touch

²**untouchable** *n* : a member of the lowest social class in
India having in traditional Hindu belief the quality of
defiling by contact a member of a higher caste

un·touched \ᵢən-'təcht\ *adj* 1 : not subjected to touching 2 : not described or dealt with 3 : not tasted 4 : being in a primeval state or condition 5 : UNAFFECTED

un·to·ward \ᵢən-'tōrd, -'tō-ərd; ᵢən-tə-'wòrd\ *adj* 1
: difficult to manage : STUBBORN, WILLFUL ⟨an ∼
child⟩ 2 : INCONVENIENT, TROUBLESOME ⟨an ∼ en-
counter⟩

un·tried \ᵢən-'trīd\ *adj* : not tested or proved by experience or trial; *also* : not tried in court

un·true \-'trü\ *adj* 1 : not faithful : DISLOYAL 2 : not
according with a standard of correctness 3 : FALSE

un·truth \ᵢən-'trüth, 'ᵊən-ᵢtrüth\ *n* 1 : lack of truthfulness 2 : FALSEHOOD

un·tune \-'tün, -'tyün\ *vb* 1 : to put out of tune 2 : DIS-
ARRANGE, DISCOMPOSE

un·tu·tored \-'tü-tərd, -'tyü-\ *adj* : UNTAUGHT, UN-
LEARNED, IGNORANT

un·twine \-'twīn\ *vb* : UNWIND, DISENTANGLE

un·twist \ᵢən-'twist\ *vb* 1 : to separate the twisted
parts of : UNTWINE 2 : to become untwined

un·used \-'yüst, -'yüzd *for 1;* -'yüzd *for 2*\ *adj* 1 : UN-
ACCUSTOMED 2 : not used

un·usu·al \-'yü-zhə-wəl\ *adj* : not usual : UNCOMMON,
RARE — **un·usu·al·ly** *adv*

un·ut·ter·able \ᵢən-'ə-tə-rə-bəl\ *adj* : being beyond the
powers of description : INEXPRESSIBLE — **un·ut·ter·**
ably \-blē\ *adv*

un·var·nished \-'vär-nisht\ *adj* 1 : not varnished 2 : not
embellished : PLAIN ⟨the ∼ truth⟩

un·veil \ᵢən-'vāl\ *vb* 1 : to remove a veil or covering
from : DISCLOSE 2 : to remove a veil : reveal oneself

un·voiced \-'vȯist\ *adj* **1** : not verbally expressed : UN-SPOKEN **2** : VOICELESS 2

un·war·rant·able \-'wȯr-ən-tə-bəl\ *adj* : not justifiable : INEXCUSABLE — **un·war·rant·ably** \-blē\ *adv*

un·weave \-'wēv\ *vb* -**wove** \-'wōv\; -**wo·ven** \-'wō-vən\; -**weav·ing** : DISENTANGLE, RAVEL

un·well \ˌən-'wəl\ *adj* : SICK, AILING

un·whole·some \-'hōl-səm\ *adj* **1** : harmful to physical, mental, or moral well-being **2** : CORRUPT, UNSOUND; *also* : offensive to the senses : LOATHSOME

un·wieldy \-'wēl-dē\ *adj* : not easily managed, handled, or used (as because of bulk, weight, or complexity) : AWKWARD ⟨an ~ tool⟩

un·wind \-'wīnd\ *vb* -**wound** \-'waȯnd\; -**wind·ing 1** : to undo something that is wound : loose from coils **2** : to become unwound : be capable of being unwound **3** : RELAX

un·wise \ˌən-'wīz\ *adj* : not wise : FOOLISH — **un·wise·ly** *adv*

un·wit·ting \-'wi-tiŋ\ *adj* **1** : not knowing : UNAWARE **2** : not intended : INADVERTENT ⟨~ mistake⟩ — **un·wit·ting·ly** *adv*

un·wont·ed \-'wȯn-təd, -'wōn-\ *adj* **1** : RARE, UNUSUAL **2** : not accustomed by experience — **un·wont·ed·ly** *adv*

un·world·ly \-'wərld-lē\ *adj* **1** : not of this world; *esp* : SPIRITUAL **2** : NAIVE **3** : not swayed by worldly considerations — **un·world·li·ness** \-lē-nəs\ *n*

un·wor·thy \ˌən-'wər-thē\ *adj* **1** : BASE, DISHONORABLE **2** : not meritorious : not worthy : UNDESERVING **3** : not deserved : UNMERITED ⟨~ treatment⟩ — **un·wor·thi·ly** \-thə-lē\ *adv* — **un·wor·thi·ness** \-thē-nəs\ *n*

un·wrap \-'rap\ *vb* : to remove the wrapping from : DISCLOSE

un·writ·ten \-'rit-ᵊn\ *adj* **1** : not in writing : ORAL, TRADITIONAL ⟨an ~ law⟩ **2** : containing no writing : BLANK

un·yield·ing \ˌən-'yēl-diŋ\ *adj* **1** : characterized by lack of softness or flexibility **2** : characterized by firmness or obduracy

un·yoke \-'yōk\ *vb* : to remove a yoke from; *also* : SEPARATE, DISCONNECT

un·zip \-'zip\ *vb* : to zip open : open by means of a zipper

¹up \'əp\ *adv* **1** : in or to a higher position or level; *esp* : away from the center of the earth **2** : from beneath a surface (as ground or water) **3** : from below the horizon **4** : in or into an upright position; *esp* : out of bed **5** : with greater intensity ⟨speak ~⟩ **6** : in or into a better or more advanced state or a state of greater intensity or activity ⟨stir ~ a fire⟩ **7** : into existence, evidence, or knowledge ⟨the missing book turned ~⟩ **8** : into consideration ⟨brought the matter ~⟩ **9** : to or at bat **10** : into possession or custody ⟨gave himself ~⟩ **11** : ENTIRELY, COMPLETELY ⟨eat it ~⟩ **12** — used for emphasis ⟨clean ~ a room⟩ **13** : ASIDE, BY ⟨lay ~ supplies⟩ **14** : so as to arrive or approach ⟨ran ~ the path⟩ **15** : in a direction opposite to down **16** : in or into parts ⟨tear ~ paper⟩ **17** : to a stop ⟨pull ~ at the curb⟩ **18** : for each side ⟨the score was 15 ~⟩

²up *adj* **1** : risen above the horizon ⟨the sun is ~⟩ **2** : being out of bed ⟨~ by 6 o'clock⟩ **3** : relatively high ⟨prices are ~⟩ **4** : RAISED, LIFTED ⟨windows are ~⟩ **5** : BUILT, CONSTRUCTED ⟨the house is ~⟩ **6** : grown above a surface ⟨the corn is ~⟩ **7** : moving, inclining, or directed upward **8** : marked by agitation, excitement, or activity **9** : READY; *esp* : highly prepared **10** : going on : taking place ⟨find out what is ~⟩ **11** : EXPIRED, ENDED ⟨the time is ~⟩ **12** : well informed ⟨~ on the news⟩ **13** : being ahead or in advance of an opponent ⟨one hole ~ in a match⟩ **14** : presented for or being under consideration **15** : charged before a court ⟨~ for robbery⟩

³up *prep* **1** : to, toward, or at a higher point of ⟨~ a ladder⟩ **2** : to or toward the source of ⟨~ the river⟩ **3** : to

or toward the northern part of ⟨~ the coast⟩ **4** : to or toward the interior of ⟨traveling ~ the country⟩ **5** : ALONG ⟨walk ~ the street⟩

⁴up *n* **1** : an upward course or slope **2** : a period or state of prosperity or success ⟨he had his ~s and downs⟩

⁵up *vb* **upped** \'əpt\ *or in 2* **up; upped; up·ping; ups** *or in 2* **up 1** : to rise from a lying or sitting position **2** : to act abruptly or surprisingly ⟨she *upped* and left home⟩ **3** : to move or cause to move upward ⟨*upped* the prices⟩

Upa·ni·shad \ü-'pän-i-ˌshäd\ *n* : one of a set of Vedic philosophical treatises

¹up·beat \'əp-ˌbēt\ *n* : an unaccented beat in a musical measure; *esp* : the last beat of the measure

²upbeat *adj* : OPTIMISTIC, CHEERFUL

up·braid \ˌəp-'brād\ *vb* : to criticize, reproach, or scold severely

up·bring·ing \'əp-ˌbriŋ-iŋ\ *n* : the process of bringing up and training

UPC *abbr* Universal Product Code

up·chuck \'əp-ˌchək\ *vb* : VOMIT

up·com·ing \'əp-ˌkə-miŋ\ *adj* : FORTHCOMING, APPROACHING

up—coun·try \'əp-ˌkən-trē\ *adj* : of or relating to the interior of a country or a region — **up–country** \'əp-'kən-\ *adv*

up·date \ˌəp-'dāt\ *vb* : to bring up to date — **update** \'əp-ˌdāt\ *n*

up·draft \'əp-ˌdraft, -ˌdraft\ *n* : an upward movement of gas (as air)

up·end \ˌəp-'end\ *vb* : to set, stand, or rise on end; *also* : OVERTURN

up–front \'əp-ˌfrənt, ˌəp-'frənt\ *adj* **1** : HONEST, CANDID **2** : ADVANCE ⟨~ payment⟩

up front *adv* : in advance ⟨paid *up front*⟩

¹up·grade \'əp-ˌgrād\ *n* **1** : an upward grade or slope **2** : INCREASE, RISE

²up·grade \'əp-ˌgrād, ˌəp-'grād\ *vb* : to raise to a higher grade or position; *esp* : to advance to a job requiring a higher level of skill

up·growth \'əp-ˌgrōth\ *n* : the process of growing upward : DEVELOPMENT; *also* : a product or result of this

up·heav·al \ˌəp-'hē-vəl\ *n* **1** : the action or an instance of uplifting esp. of part of the earth's crust **2** : a violent agitation or change

¹up·hill \'əp-'hil\ *adv* : upward on a hill or incline; *also* : against difficulties

²up·hill \-ˌhil\ *adj* **1** : situated on elevated ground **2** : ASCENDING **3** : DIFFICULT, LABORIOUS

up·hold \ˌəp-'hōld\ *vb* -**held** \-'held\; -**hold·ing 1** : to give support to **2** : to support against an opponent **3** : to keep elevated — **up·hold·er** *n*

up·hol·ster \ˌəp-'hōl-stər\ *vb* : to furnish with or as if with upholstery — **up·hol·ster·er** *n*

up·hol·stery \-stə-rē\ *n, pl* -**ster·ies** [ME *upholdester* upholsterer, fr. *upholden* to uphold, fr. *up* + *holden* to hold] : materials (as fabrics, padding, and springs) used to make a soft covering esp. for a seat

UPI *abbr* United Press International

up·keep \'əp-ˌkēp\ *n* : the act or cost of keeping up or maintaining; *also* : the state of being maintained

up·land \'əp-lənd, -ˌland\ *n* : high land esp. at some distance from the sea — **upland** *adj*

¹up·lift \ˌəp-'lift\ *vb* **1** : to lift or raise up : ELEVATE **2** : to improve the condition of esp. morally, socially, or intellectually

²up·lift \'əp-ˌlift\ *n* **1** : a lifting up; *esp* : an upheaval of the earth's surface **2** : moral or social improvement; *also* : a movement to make such improvement

up·mar·ket \ˌəp-'mär-kət\ *adj* : appealing to wealthy consumers

up·most \'əp-ˌmōst\ *adj* : UPPERMOST

up·on \ə-'pȯn, -'pän\ *prep* : ON

¹up·per \'ə-pər\ *adj* **1** : higher in physical position, rank, or order **2** : constituting the smaller and more restricted branch of a bicameral legislature **3** *cap* : being a later part or formation of a specific geological period **4** : being toward the interior ⟨the ∼ Amazon⟩ **5** : NORTHERN ⟨∼ New York State⟩

²**upper** *n* : one that is upper; *esp* : the parts of a shoe or boot above the sole

up·per·case \ˌə-pər-ˈkās\ *adj* : CAPITAL 1 — **upper-case** *n*

upper class *n* : a social class occupying a position above the middle class and having the highest status in a society — **upper–class** *adj*

up·per·class·man \ˌə-pər-ˈklas-mən\ *n* : a junior or senior in a college or high school

upper crust *n* : the highest social class or group; *esp* : the highest circle of the upper class

up·per·cut \ˈə-pər-ˌkət\ *n* : a short swinging punch delivered (as in boxing) in an upward direction usu. with a bent arm

upper hand *n* : MASTERY, ADVANTAGE

up·per·most \ˈə-pər-ˌmōst\ *adv* : in or into the highest or most prominent position — **uppermost** *adj*

up·pish \ˈə-pish\ *adj* : UPPITY

up·pi·ty \ˈə-pə-tē\ *adj* : ARROGANT, PRESUMPTUOUS

up·raise \ˌəp-ˈrāz\ *vb* : to lift up : ELEVATE

¹**up·right** \ˈəp-ˌrīt\ *adj* **1** : PERPENDICULAR, VERTICAL **2** : erect in carriage or posture **3** : morally correct : JUST — **upright** *adv* — **up·right·ly** *adv* — **up·right·ness** *n*

²**upright** *n* **1** : the state of being upright : a vertical position **2** : something that stands upright

upright piano *n* : a piano whose strings run vertically

up·ris·ing \ˈəp-ˌrī-ziŋ\ *n* : INSURRECTION, REVOLT, REBELLION

up·riv·er \ˈəp-ˈri-vər\ *adv or adj* : toward or at a point nearer the source of a river

up·roar \ˈəp-ˌrōr\ *n* [D *oproer*, fr. MD, fr. *op* up + *roer* motion] : a state of commotion, excitement, or violent disturbance

up·roar·i·ous \ˌəp-ˈrōr-ē-əs\ *adj* **1** : marked by uproar **2** : extremely funny — **up·roar·i·ous·ly** *adv*

up·root \ˌəp-ˈrüt, -ˈrút\ *vb* : to remove by or as if by pulling up by the roots

¹**up·set** \ˌəp-ˈset\ *vb* **-set; -set·ting** **1** : to force or be forced out of the usual upright, level, or proper position **2** : to disturb emotionally : WORRY; *also* : to make somewhat ill **3** : UNSETTLE, DISARRANGE **4** : to defeat unexpectedly

²**up·set** \ˈəp-ˌset\ *n* **1** : an upsetting or being upset; *esp* : a minor illness **2** : a derangement of plans or ideas **3** : an unexpected defeat

³**up·set** \(ˌ)əp-ˈset\ *adj* : emotionally disturbed or agitated

up·shot \ˈəp-ˌshät\ *n* : the final result

¹**up·side** \ˈəp-ˌsīd\ *n* : the upper side

²**up·side** \ˌəp-ˈsīd\ *prep* : up on or against the side of ⟨knocked him ∼ the head⟩

up·side down \ˌəp-ˌsīd-ˈdaún\ *adv* **1** : with the upper and the lower parts reversed in position **2** : in or into confusion or disorder — **upside–down** *adj*

up·si·lon \ˈüp-sə-ˌlän, ˈyúp-, ˈəp-\ *n* : the 20th letter of the Greek alphabet — Y or υ

¹**up·stage** \ˈəp-ˈstāj\ *adv or adj* : toward or at the rear of a theatrical stage

²**up·stage** \ˌəp-ˈstāj\ *vb* : to draw attention away from (as an actor)

¹**up·stairs** \ˌəp-ˈstarz\ *adv* **1** : up the stairs : to or on a higher floor **2** : to or at a higher position

²**up·stairs** \ˈəp-ˈstarz\ *adj* : situated above the stairs esp. on an upper floor ⟨∼ bedroom⟩

³**up·stairs** \ˈəp-ˌstarz, ˈəp-ˌstarz\ *n sing or pl* : the part of a building above the ground floor

up·stand·ing \ˌəp-ˈstan-diŋ, ˈəp-\ *adj* **1** : ERECT **2** : STRAIGHTFORWARD, HONEST

¹**up·start** \ˈəp-ˈstärt\ *vb* : to jump up suddenly

²**up·start** \ˈəp-ˌstärt\ *n* : one that has risen suddenly; *esp* : one that claims more personal importance than is warranted — **up·start** \-ˈstärt\ *adj*

up·state \ˈəp-ˈstāt\ *adj* : of, relating to, or characteristic of a part of a state away from a large city and esp. to the north — **upstate** *adv* — **upstate** *n*

up·stream \ˈəp-ˈstrēm\ *adv* : at or toward the source of a stream — **upstream** *adj*

up·stroke \ˈəp-ˌstrōk\ *n* : an upward stroke (as of a pen)

up·surge \-ˌsərj\ *n* : a rapid or sudden rise

up·swept \ˈəp-ˌswept\ *adj* : swept upward ⟨∼ hairdo⟩

up·swing \ˈəp-ˌswiŋ\ *n* : an upward swing; *esp* : a marked increase or rise (as in activity)

up·take \ˈəp-ˌtāk\ *n* **1** : UNDERSTANDING, COMPREHENSION ⟨quick on the ∼⟩ **2** : the process or an instance of absorbing and incorporating esp. into a living organism

up·thrust \ˈəp-ˌthrəst\ *n* : an upward thrust (as of the earth's crust) — **upthrust** *vb*

up·tight \ˈəp-ˈtīt\ *adj* **1** : TENSE, NERVOUS, UNEASY; *also* : ANGRY, INDIGNANT **2** : rigidly conventional

up–to–date *adj* **1** : extending up to the present time **2** : abreast of the times : MODERN — **up–to–date·ness** *n*

up·town \ˈəp-ˌtaún\ *n* : the upper part of a town or city; *esp* : the residential district — **up·town** \ˈəp-ˈtaún\ *adj or adv*

¹**up·turn** \ˈəp-ˌtərn, ˌəp-ˈtərn\ *vb* **1** : to turn (as earth) up or over **2** : to turn or direct upward

²**up·turn** \ˈəp-ˌtərn\ *n* : an upward turn esp. toward better conditions or higher prices

¹**up·ward** \ˈəp-wərd\ *or* **up·wards** \-wərdz\ *adv* **1** : in a direction from lower to higher **2** : toward a higher or better condition **3** : toward a greater amount or higher number, degree, or rate

²**upward** *adj* : directed or moving toward or situated in a higher place or level : ASCENDING — **up·ward·ly** *adv*

upwards of *also* **upward of** *adv* : more than : in excess of ⟨they cost *upwards of* $25 each⟩

up·well \ˌəp-ˈwel\ *vb* : to move or flow upward

up·well·ing \-ˈwe-liŋ\ *n* : a rising or an appearance of rising to the surface and flowing outward; *esp* : the movement of deep cold usu. nutrient-rich ocean water to the surface

up·wind \ˈəp-ˈwind\ *adv or adj* : in the direction from which the wind is blowing

ura·cil \ˈyúr-ə-ˌsil\ *n* : a pyrimidine base that is one of the four bases coding genetic information in the molecular chain of RNA

ura·ni·um \yú-ˈrā-nē-əm\ *n* : a silvery heavy radioactive metallic chemical element used as a source of atomic energy — see ELEMENT table

Ura·nus \ˈyúr-ə-nəs, yú-ˈrā-\ *n* [LL, the sky personified as a god, fr. Gk *Ouranos*, fr. *ouranos* sky, heaven] : the planet 7th in order from the sun — see PLANET table

ur·ban \ˈər-bən\ *adj* : of, relating to, characteristic of, or constituting a city

ur·bane \ˌər-ˈbān\ *adj* [L *urbanus* urban, urbane, fr. *urbs* city] : very polite and polished in manner : SUAVE

ur·ban·ise *Brit var of* URBANIZE

ur·ban·ite \ˈər-bə-ˌnīt\ *n* : a person who lives in a city

ur·ban·i·ty \ˌər-ˈba-nə-tē\ *n, pl* **-ties** : the quality or state of being urbane

ur·ban·ize \ˈər-bə-ˌnīz\ *vb* **-ized; -iz·ing** : to cause to take on urban characteristics — **ur·ban·i·za·tion** \ˌər-bə-nə-ˈzā-shən\ *n*

ur·chin \ˈər-chən\ *n* [ME, hedgehog, fr. MF *herichon*, ultim. fr. L *ericius*] : a pert or mischievous youngster

Ur·du \ˈúr-dü, ˈər-\ *n* [Hindi *urdū*, fr. Per *zabān-e-urdū-e-muallā* language of the Exalted Comp (the imperial bazaar in Delhi)] : an official language of Pakistan that is widely used by Muslims in urban areas of India

urea \yú-ˈrē-ə\ *n* : a soluble nitrogenous compound that is the chief solid constituent of mammalian urine

ure•mia \yu̇-'rē-mē-ə\ *n* : accumulation in the blood of materials normally passed off in the urine resulting in a poisoned condition — **ure•mic** \-mik\ *adj*

ure•ter \'yu̇r-ə-tər\ *n* : a duct that carries the urine from a kidney to the bladder

ure•thra \yu̇-'rē-thrə\ *n, pl* **-thras** *or* **-thrae** \-(͵)thrē\ : the canal that in most mammals carries off the urine from the bladder and in the male also serves to carry semen from the body — **ure•thral** \-thrəl\ *adj*

ure•thri•tis \͵yu̇r-i-'thrī-təs\ *n* : inflammation of the urethra

¹**urge** \'ərj\ *vb* **urged; urg•ing 1 :** to present, advocate, or demand earnestly **2 :** to try to persuade or sway ⟨∼ a guest to stay⟩ **3 :** to serve as a motive or reason for **4 :** to impress or impel to some course or activity ⟨the dog *urged* the sheep onward⟩

²**urge** *n* **1 :** the act or process of urging **2 :** a force or impulse that urges or drives

ur•gent \'ər-jənt\ *adj* **1 :** calling for immediate attention : PRESSING **2 :** urging insistently — **ur•gen•cy** \-jən-sē\ *n* — **ur•gent•ly** *adv*

uric \'yu̇r-ik\ *adj* : of, relating to, or found in urine

uric acid *n* : a nearly insoluble acid that is the chief nitrogenous excretory product of birds but is present in only small amounts in mammalian urine

uri•nal \'yu̇r-ən-ᵊl\ *n* **1 :** a receptacle for urine **2 :** a place for urinating

uri•nal•y•sis \͵yu̇r-ə-'na-lə-səs\ *n* : chemical analysis of urine

uri•nary \'yu̇r-ə-͵ner-ē\ *adj* **1 :** relating to, occurring in, or being organs for the formation and discharge of urine **2 :** of, relating to, or for urine

urinary bladder *n* : a membranous sac in many vertebrates that serves for the temporary retention of urine and discharges by the urethra

uri•nate \'yu̇r-ə-͵nāt\ *vb* **-nat•ed; -nat•ing :** to release or give off urine — **uri•na•tion** \͵yu̇r-ə-'nā-shən\ *n*

urine \'yu̇r-ən\ *n* : a waste material from the kidneys that is usu. a yellowish watery liquid in mammals but is semisolid in birds and reptiles

urn \'ərn\ *n* **1 :** a vessel that typically has the form of a vase on a pedestal and often is used to hold the ashes of the dead **2 :** a closed vessel usu. with a spout for serving a hot beverage

uro•gen•i•tal \͵yu̇r-ō-'je-nət-ᵊl\ *adj* : of, relating to, or being the excretory and reproductive organs or functions

urol•o•gy \yu̇-'rä-lə-jē\ *n* : a branch of medical science dealing with the urinary or urogenital tract and its disorders — **uro•log•ic** \͵yu̇r-ə-'lä-jik\ *or* **uro•log•i•cal** \-ji-kəl\ *adj* — **urol•o•gist** \yu̇-'rä-lə-jist\ *n*

Ur•sa Ma•jor \͵ər-sə-'mā-jər\ *n* [L, lit., greater bear] : the northern constellation that contains the stars which form the Big Dipper

Ursa Mi•nor \-'mī-nər\ *n* [L, lit., lesser bear] : the constellation including the north pole of the heavens and the stars that form the Little Dipper with the North Star at the tip of the handle

ur•sine \'ər-͵sīn\ *adj* : of, relating to, or resembling a bear

ur•ti•car•ia \͵ər-tə-'kar-ē-ə\ *n* [NL, fr. L *urtica* nettle] : HIVES

Uru•guay•an \͵u̇r-ə-'gwī-ən, ͵yu̇r-ə-'gwä-\ *n* : a native or inhabitant of Uruguay — **Uruguayan** *adj*

us \'əs\ *pron, objective case of* WE

US *abbr* United States

USA *abbr* **1** United States Army **2** United States of America

us•able *also* **use•able** \'yü-zə-bəl\ *adj* : suitable or fit for use — **us•abil•i•ty** \͵yü-zə-'bi-lə-tē\ *n*

USAF *abbr* United States Air Force

us•age \'yü-sij, -zij\ *n* **1 :** habitual or customary practice or procedure **2 :** the way in which words and phrases are actually used **3 :** the action or mode of using **4 :** manner of treating

USCG *abbr* United States Coast Guard

USDA *abbr* United States Department of Agriculture

¹**use** \'yüs\ *n* **1 :** the act or practice of using or employing something : EMPLOYMENT, APPLICATION **2 :** the fact or state of being used **3 :** the way of using **4 :** USAGE, CUSTOM **5 :** the privilege or benefit of using something **6 :** the ability or power to use something (as a limb) **7 :** the legal enjoyment of property that consists in its employment, occupation, or exercise; *also* : the benefit or profit esp. from property held in trust **8 :** USEFULNESS, UTILITY; *also* : the end served : OBJECT, FUNCTION **9 :** the occasion or need to employ ⟨he had no more ∼ for it⟩ **10 :** ESTEEM, LIKING ⟨had no ∼ for modern art⟩

²**use** \'yüz\ *vb* **used** \'yüzd; "*used to*" *usu* 'yüs-tə\; **us•ing 1 :** to put into action or service : EMPLOY **2 :** to consume or take (as drugs) : UTILIZE ⟨∼ tact⟩; *also* : MANIPULATE ⟨*used* his friends to get ahead⟩ **4 :** to expend or consume by putting to use **5 :** to behave toward : TREAT ⟨*used* the horse cruelly⟩ **6 :** to benefit from ⟨house could ∼ a coat of paint⟩ **7 :** — used in the past with *to* to indicate a former practice, fact, or state ⟨we *used* to work harder⟩ — **us•er** *n*

used \'yüzd\ *adj* **1 :** having been used by another : SECONDHAND ⟨∼ cars⟩ **2 :** ACCUSTOMED, HABITUATED ⟨∼ to the heat⟩

use•ful \'yüs-fəl\ *adj* : capable of being put to use : ADVANTAGEOUS; *esp* : serviceable for a beneficial end — **use•ful•ly** *adv* — **use•ful•ness** *n*

use•less \-ləs\ *adj* : having or being of no use : WORTHLESS — **use•less•ly** *adv* — **use•less•ness** *n*

USES *abbr* United States Employment Service

use up *vb* : to consume completely

¹**ush•er** \'ə-shər\ *n* [ME *ussher*, fr. MF *ussier*, fr. (assumed) VL *ustiarius* doorkeeper, fr. L *ostium, ustium* door, mouth of a river] **1 :** an officer who walks before a person of rank **2 :** one who escorts people to their seats (as in a church or theater)

²**usher** *vb* **1 :** to conduct to a place **2 :** to precede as an usher, forerunner, or harbinger **3 :** INAUGURATE, INTRODUCE ⟨∼ in a new era⟩

ush•er•ette \͵ə-shə-'ret\ *n* : a girl or woman who is an usher (as in a theater)

USIA *abbr* United States Information Agency

USMC *abbr* United States Marine Corps

USN *abbr* United States Navy

USO *abbr* United Service Organizations

USP *abbr* United States Pharmacopeia

USPS *abbr* United States Postal Service

USS *abbr* United States ship

USSR *abbr* Union of Soviet Socialist Republics

usu *abbr* usual; usually

usu•al \'yü-zhə-wəl\ *adj* **1 :** accordant with usage, custom, or habit : NORMAL **2 :** commonly or ordinarily used **3 :** ORDINARY **syn** customary, habitual, accustomed, routine — **usu•al•ly** \'yü-zhə-wə-lē, 'yü-zhə-lē\ *adv*

usu•fruct \'yü-zə-͵frəkt\ *n* [L *ususfructus*, fr. *usus et fructus* use and enjoyment] : the legal right to use and enjoy the benefits and profits of something belonging to another

usu•rer \'yü-zhər-ər\ *n* : one that lends money esp. at an exorbitant rate

usu•ri•ous \yü-'zhu̇r-ē-əs\ *adj* : practicing, involving, or constituting usury ⟨a ∼ rate of interest⟩

usurp \yü-'sərp, -'zərp\ *vb* [ME, fr. MF *usurper*, fr. L *usurpare*, lit., to take possession of without legal claim, fr. *usu* (abl. of *usus* use) + *rapere* to seize] : to seize and hold by force or without right ⟨∼ a throne⟩ — **usur•pa•tion** \͵yü-sər-'pā-shən, -zər-\ *n* — **usurp•er** \yü-'sər-pər, -'zər-\ *n*

usu•ry \'yü-zhə-rē\ *n, pl* **-ries 1 :** the lending of money with an interest charge for its use **2 :** an excessive rate or amount of interest charged; *esp* : interest above an established legal rate

UT *abbr* Utah

Ute \'yüt\ *n, pl* **Ute** *or* **Utes** : a member of an American Indian people orig. ranging through Utah, Colorado, Arizona, and New Mexico

uten·sil \yu̇-'ten-səl\ *n* [ME, vessels for domestic use, fr. MF *utensile*, fr. L *utensilia*, fr. neut. pl. of *utensilis* useful, fr. *uti* to use] **1** : an instrument or vessel used in a household and esp. a kitchen **2** : a useful tool

uter·ine tube \'yü-tə-₁rīn-, -rən-\ *n* : FALLOPIAN TUBE

uter·us \'yü-tə-rəs\ *n, pl* **uteri** \'yü-tə-₁rī\ *also* **uter·us·es** : the muscular organ of a female mammal in which the young develop before birth — **uter·ine** \-₁rīn, -rən\ *adj*

utile \'yüt-əl, 'yü-₁tīl\ *adj* : USEFUL

uti·lise *Brit var of* UTILIZE

¹util·i·tar·i·an \yü-₁ti-lə-'ter-ē-ən\ *n* : a person who believes in utilitarianism

²utilitarian *adj* **1** : of or relating to utilitarianism **2** : of or relating to utility : aiming at usefulness rather than beauty; *also* : serving a useful purpose

util·i·tar·i·an·ism \-ē-ə-ə-₁ni-zəm\ *n* : a theory that the greatest good for the greatest number should be the main consideration in making a choice of actions

¹util·i·ty \yü-'ti-lə-tē\ *n, pl* **-ties** **1** : USEFULNESS **2** : something useful or designed for use **3** : a business organization performing a public service and subject to special governmental regulation **4** : a public service or a commodity (as electricity or water) provided by a public utility; *also* : equipment to provide such or a similar service

²utility *adj* **1** : capable of serving esp. as a substitute in various uses or positions (a ∼ outfielder) (a ∼ knife) **2** : being of a usable but poor quality (∼ beef)

uti·lize \'yüt-əl-₁īz\ *vb* **-lized; -liz·ing** : to make use of : turn to profitable account or use — **uti·li·za·tion** \₁yüt-əl-ə-'zā-shən\ *n*

ut·most \'ət-₁mōst\ *adj* **1** : situated at the farthest or most distant point : EXTREME **2** : of the greatest or highest degree, quantity, number, or amount — **utmost** *n*

uto·pia \yu̇-'tō-pē-ə\ *n* [*Utopia*, imaginary island described in Sir Thomas More's *Utopia*, fr. Gk *ou* not, no + *topos* place] **1** *often cap* : a place of ideal perfection esp. in laws, government, and social conditions **2** : an impractical scheme for social improvement

¹uto·pi·an \-pē-ən\ *adj, often cap* **1** : of, relating to, or resembling a utopia **2** : proposing ideal social and political schemes that are impractical **3** : VISIONARY

²utopian *n* **1** : a believer in the perfectibility of human society **2** : one that proposes or advocates utopian schemes

¹ut·ter \'ə-tər\ *adj* [ME, remote, fr. OE *ūtera* outer, compar. adj. fr. *ūt* out, adv.] : ABSOLUTE, TOTAL (∼ ruin) — **ut·ter·ly** *adv*

²utter *vb* [ME *uttren*, fr. *utter* outside, adv., fr. OE *ūtor*, compar. of *ūt* out] **1** : to send forth as a sound : express in usu. spoken words : PRONOUNCE, SPEAK **2** : to put (as currency) into circulation — **ut·ter·er** *n*

ut·ter·ance \'ə-tə-rəns\ *n* **1** : something uttered; *esp* : an oral or written statement **2** : the action of uttering with the voice : SPEECH **3** : power, style, or manner of speaking

ut·ter·most \'ə-tər-₁mōst\ *adj* : EXTREME, UTMOST (the ∼ parts of the earth) — **uttermost** *n*

U–turn \'yü-₁tərn\ *n* : a turn resembling the letter U; *esp* : a 180-degree turn made by a vehicle in a road

UV *abbr* ultraviolet

uvu·la \'yü-vyə-lə\ *n, pl* **-las** *or* **-lae** \-₁lē, -₁lī\ : the fleshy lobe hanging at the back of the roof of the mouth — **uvu·lar** \-lər\ *adj*

UW *abbr* underwriter

ux·o·ri·ous \₁ək-'sōr-ē-əs, ₁əg-'zōr-\ *adj* : excessively devoted or submissive to a wife

V

¹v \'vē\ *n, pl* **v's** *or* **vs** \'vēz\ *often cap* : the 22d letter of the English alphabet

²v *abbr, often cap* **1** vector **2** velocity **3** verb **4** verse **5** versus **6** very **7** victory **8** vide **9** voice **10** voltage **11** volume **12** vowel

V *symbol* **1** vanadium **2** volt

Va *abbr* Virginia

VA *abbr* **1** Veterans Administration **2** vice admiral **3** Virginia

va·can·cy \'vā-kən-sē\ *n, pl* **-cies** **1** : a vacating esp. of an office, position, or piece of property **2** : a vacant office, position, or tenancy; *also* : the period during which it stands vacant **3** : empty space : VOID **4** : the state of being vacant

va·cant \'vā-kənt\ *adj* **1** : not occupied (∼ seat) (∼ room) **2** : EMPTY (∼ space) **3** : free from business or care (a few ∼ hours) **4** : devoid of thought, reflection, or expression (a ∼ smile) — **va·cant·ly** *adv*

va·cate \'vā-₁kāt\ *vb* **va·cat·ed; va·cat·ing** **1** : to make void : ANNUL **2** : to make vacant (as an office or house); *also* : to give up the occupancy of

¹va·ca·tion \vā-'kā-shən, və-\ *n* : a period of rest from work : HOLIDAY

²vacation *vb* : to take or spend a vacation — **va·ca·tion·er** *n*

va·ca·tion·ist \-shə-nist\ *n* : a person taking a vacation

va·ca·tion·land \-shən-₁land\ *n* : an area with recreational attractions and facilities for vacationists

vac·ci·nate \'vak-sə-₁nāt\ *vb* **-nat·ed; -nat·ing** : to administer a vaccine to usu. by injection; *also* : to produce immunity to smallpox by inoculating (a person) with the related cowpox virus

vac·ci·na·tion \₁vak-sə-'nā-shən\ *n* **1** : the act of vaccinating **2** : the scar left by vaccinating

vac·cine \vak-'sēn, 'vak-₁sēn\ *n* [L *vaccinus* of or from cows, fr. *vacca* cow; so called from the derivation of smallpox vaccine from cows] : material (as a preparation of killed or weakened virus or bacteria) used in vaccinating to induce immunity to a disease

vac·cin·ia \vak-'si-nē-ə\ *n* : COWPOX

vac·il·late \'va-sə-₁lāt\ *vb* **-lat·ed; -lat·ing** **1** : SWAY, TOTTER; *also* : FLUCTUATE **2** : to incline first to one course or opinion and then to another : WAVER — **vac·il·la·tion** \₁va-sə-'lā-shən\ *n*

va·cu·ity \va-'kyü-ə-tē\ *n, pl* **-ities** **1** : an empty space **2** : the state, fact, or quality of being vacuous **3** : something that is vacuous

vac·u·ole \'va-kyə-₁wōl\ *n* : a usu. fluid-filled cavity esp. in the cytoplasm of an individual cell — **vac·u·o·lar** \₁va-kyə-'wō-lər, -₁lär\ *adj*

vac·u·ous \'va-kyə-wəs\ *adj* **1** : EMPTY, VACANT, BLANK **2** : DULL, STUPID, INANE — **vac·u·ous·ly** *adv* — **vac·u·ous·ness** *n*

¹vac·u·um \'va-(₁)kyüm, -kyəm\ *n, pl* **vacuums** *or* **vac·ua** \-kyə-wə\ [L, fr. neut. of *vacuus* empty] **1** : a space entirely empty of matter **2** : a space from which most of the air has been removed (as by a pump) **3** : VOID, GAP **4** : VACUUM CLEANER — **vacuum** *adj*

²vacuum *vb* : to use a vacuum device (as a vacuum cleaner) on

vacuum bottle *n* : THERMOS

vacuum cleaner *n* : a household appliance for cleaning (as floors or rugs) by suction

vacuum–packed *adj* : having much of the air removed before being hermetically sealed

vacuum tube *n* : an electron tube from which most of the air has been removed

va·de me·cum \₁vä-dē-ˈmē-kəm, ₁vä-dē-ˈmä-\ *n, pl* **vade mecums** [L, go with me] : something (as a handbook or manual) carried as a constant companion

VADM *abbr* vice admiral

¹**vag·a·bond** \ˈva-gə-₁bänd\ *adj* **1** : WANDERING, HOMELESS **2** : of, characteristic of, or leading the life of a vagrant or tramp **3** : leading an unsettled or irresponsible life

²**vagabond** *n* : one leading a vagabond life; *esp* : TRAMP

va·gar·i·ous \vä-ˈger-ē-əs\ *adj* : marked by vagaries : CAPRICIOUS — **va·gar·i·ous·ly** *adv*

va·ga·ry \ˈvä-gə-rē, və-ˈger-ē\ *n, pl* **-ries** : an odd or eccentric idea or action : WHIM, CAPRICE

va·gi·na \və-ˈjī-nə\ *n, pl* **-nae** \-(₁)nē\ *or* **-nas** [L, lit., sheath] : a canal that leads from the uterus to the external opening of the female sex organs — **vag·i·nal** \ˈva-jən-ᵊl\ *adj*

vag·i·ni·tis \₁va-jə-ˈnī-təs\ *n* : inflammation of the vagina

va·gran·cy \ˈvā-grən-sē\ *n, pl* **-cies** **1** : the quality or state of being vagrant; *also* : a vagrant act or notion **2** : the offense of being a vagrant

¹**va·grant** \ˈvā-grənt\ *n* : a person who has no job and wanders from place to place

²**vagrant** *adj* **1** : of, relating to, or characteristic of a vagrant **2** : following no fixed course : RANDOM, CAPRICIOUS ⟨~ thoughts⟩ — **va·grant·ly** *adv*

vague \ˈvāg\ *adj* **vagu·er; vagu·est** [MF, fr. L *vagus*, lit., wandering] **1** : not clear, definite, or distinct **2** : not clearly felt or analyzed ⟨a ~ unrest⟩ **syn** obscure, dark, enigmatic, ambiguous, equivocal — **vague·ly** *adv* — **vague·ness** *n*

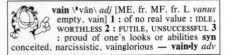

vain \ˈvān\ *adj* [ME, fr. MF, fr. L *vanus* empty, vain] **1** : of no real value : IDLE, WORTHLESS **2** : FUTILE, UNSUCCESSFUL **3** : proud of one's looks or abilities **syn** conceited, narcissistic, vainglorious — **vain·ly** *adv*

vain·glo·ri·ous \₁vān-ˈglōr-ē-əs\ *adj* : marked by vainglory : BOASTFUL

vain·glo·ry \ˈvān-₁glōr-ē\ *n* **1** : excessive or ostentatious pride esp. in one's own achievements **2** : vain display : VANITY

val *abbr* value; valued

va·lance \ˈva-ləns, ˈvā-\ *n* **1** : drapery hanging from an edge (as of an altar, table, or bed) **2** : a drapery or a decorative frame across the top of a window

vale \ˈvāl\ *n* : VALLEY, DALE

vale·dic·tion \₁va-lə-ˈdik-shən\ *n* [L *valedicere* to say farewell, fr. *vale* farewell + *dicere* to say] : an act or utterance of leave-taking : FAREWELL

vale·dic·to·ri·an \-₁dik-ˈtōr-ē-ən\ *n* : the student usu. of the highest rank in a graduating class who delivers the valedictory address at commencement

vale·dic·to·ry \-ˈdik-tə-rē\ *adj* : bidding farewell : delivered as a valediction ⟨a ~ address⟩ — **valedictory** *n*

va·lence \ˈvā-ləns\ *n* [LL *valentia* power, capacity, fr. L *valēre* to be strong] : the combining power of an atom as shown by the number of its electrons that are lost, gained, or shared in the formation of chemical bonds

Va·len·ci·ennes \və-₁len-sē-ˈen, ₁va-lən-sē-, -ˈenz\ *n* : a fine handmade lace

val·en·tine \ˈva-lən-₁tīn\ *n* : a sweetheart chosen or complimented on St. Valentine's Day; *also* : a greeting card sent on this day

Valentine's Day *also* **Valentine Day** *n* : SAINT VALENTINE'S DAY

¹**va·let** \ˈva-lət, -(₁)lā; va-ˈlā\ *n* **1** : a male servant who takes care of a man's clothes and performs personal services **2** : an attendant in a hotel who performs personal services for customers

²**valet** *vb* : to serve as a valet

val·e·tu·di·nar·i·an \₁va-lə-₁tüd-ᵊn-ˈer-ē-ən, -₁tyüd-\ *n* : a person of a weak or sickly constitution; *esp* : one whose chief concern is being or becoming an invalid — **val·e·tu·di·nar·i·an·ism** \-ē-ə-₁ni-zəm\ *n*

val·iant \ˈval-yənt\ *adj* : having or showing valor : BRAVE, HEROIC **syn** valorous, doughty, courageous, bold, audacious, dauntless, undaunted, intrepid — **val·iant·ly** *adv*

val·id \ˈva-ləd\ *adj* **1** : having legal force ⟨a ~ contract⟩ **2** : founded on truth or fact : capable of being justified or defended : SOUND ⟨a ~ argument⟩ ⟨~ reasons⟩ — **va·lid·i·ty** \və-ˈli-də-tē\ *n* — **val·id·ly** *adv*

val·i·date \ˈva-lə-₁dāt\ *vb* **-dat·ed; -dat·ing** **1** : to make legally valid **2** : to confirm the validity of **3** : VERIFY — **val·i·da·tion** \₁va-lə-ˈdā-shən\ *n*

va·lise \və-ˈlēs\ *n* [F] : SUITCASE

val·ley \ˈva-lē\ *n, pl* **valleys** : a long depression between ranges of hills or mountains

val·or \ˈva-lər\ *n* [ME, fr. MF *valour*, fr. ML *valor* value, valor, fr. L *valēre* to be strong] : personal bravery **syn** heroism, prowess, gallantry — **val·or·ous** \ˈva-lə-rəs\ *adj*

val·o·ri·za·tion \₁va-lə-rə-ˈzā-shən\ *n* : the support of commodity prices by any of various forms of government subsidy — **val·o·rize** \ˈva-lə-₁rīz\ *vb*

val·our *chiefly Brit var of* VALOR

valse \ˈväls\ *n* [F] : WALTZ; *esp* : a concert waltz

¹**valu·able** \ˈval-yə-bəl, -yə-wə-bəl\ *adj* **1** : having money value **2** : having great money value **3** : of great use or service **syn** invaluable, priceless, costly, expensive, dear, precious

²**valuable** *n* : a usu. personal possession of considerable value ⟨their ~s were stolen⟩

val·u·ate \ˈval-yə-₁wāt\ *vb* **-at·ed; -at·ing** : to place a value on : APPRAISE — **val·u·a·tor** \-₁wā-tər\ *n*

val·u·a·tion \₁val-yə-ˈwā-shən\ *n* **1** : the act or process of valuing; *esp* : appraisal of property **2** : the estimated or determined market value of a thing

¹**val·ue** \ˈval-yü\ *n* **1** : a fair return or equivalent in money, goods, or services for something exchanged **2** : the monetary worth of a thing; *also* : relative worth, utility, or importance ⟨nothing of ~ to say⟩ **3** : an assigned or computed numerical quantity ⟨the ~ of x in

an equation⟩ **4** : relative lightness or darkness of a color : LUMINOSITY **5** : the relative length of a tone or note **6** : something (as a principle or ideal) intrinsically valuable or desirable ⟨human rather than material ∼s⟩ — **val·ue·less** *adj*

²**value** *vb* **val·ued; valu·ing 1** : to estimate the monetary worth of : APPRAISE **2** : to rate in usefulness, importance, or general worth **3** : to consider or rate highly : PRIZE, ESTEEM — **val·u·er** *n*

val·ue–add·ed tax *n* : an incremental excise tax that is levied on the value added at each stage of the processing of a raw material or the production and distribution of a commodity

valve \'valv\ *n* **1** : a structure (as in a vein) that temporarily closes a passage or that permits movement in one direction only **2** : a device by which the flow of a fluid material may be regulated by a movable part; *also* : the movable part of such a device **3** : a device in a brass wind instrument for quickly varying the tube length in order to change the fundamental tone by some definite interval **4** : one of the separate usu. hinged pieces of which the shell of some animals and esp. bivalve mollusks consists **5** : one of the pieces into which a ripe seed capsule or pod separates — **valved** \'valvd\ *adj* — **valve·less** *adj*

val·vu·lar \'val-vyə-lər\ *adj* : of, relating to, or affecting a valve esp. of the heart ⟨∼ heart disease⟩

va·moose \və-'müs, va-\ *vb* **va·moosed; va·moos·ing** [Sp *vamos* let us go] : to leave or go away quickly

¹**vamp** \'vamp\ *vb* **1** : to provide with a new vamp **2** : to patch up with a new part **3** : INVENT, IMPROVISE ⟨∼ up an excuse⟩

²**vamp** *n* **1** : the part of a boot or shoe upper covering esp. the front part of the foot **2** : a short introductory musical passage often repeated

³**vamp** *n* : a woman who uses her charm or wiles to seduce and exploit men

⁴**vamp** *vb* : to practice seductive wiles on

vam·pire \'vam-ˌpīr\ *n* **1** : a night≠ wandering bloodsucking ghost **2** : a person who preys on other people; *esp* : a woman who exploits and ruins her lover **3** : VAMPIRE BAT

vampire bat *n* : any of various bats of Central and South America that feed on the blood of animals; *also* : any of several other bats that do not feed on blood but are sometimes reputed to do so

¹**van** \'van\ *n* : VANGUARD

²**van** *n* : a usu. enclosed wagon or motortruck for moving goods or animals; *also* : a versatile enclosed box≠ like motor vehicle

va·na·di·um \və-'nā-dē-əm\ *n* : a soft grayish ductile metallic chemical element used esp. to form alloys — see ELEMENT table

Van Al·len belt \van-'a-lən-\ *n* : a belt of intense radiation in the magnetosphere composed of charged particles trapped by earth's magnetic field

van·dal \'vand-ᵊl\ *n* **1** *cap* : a member of a Germanic

people who sacked Rome in A.D. 455 **2** : a person who willfully mars or destroys property

van·dal·ise *Brit var of* VANDALIZE

van·dal·ism \-ˌi-zəm\ *n* : willful or malicious destruction or defacement of public or private property

van·dal·ize \-ˌīz\ *vb* **-ized; -iz·ing** : to subject to vandalism : DAMAGE

Van·dyke \van-'dīk\ *n* : a trim pointed beard

vane \'vān\ *n* [ME, fr. OE *fana* banner] **1** : a movable device attached to a high object for showing wind direction **2** : a thin flat or curved object that is rotated about an axis by a flow of fluid or that rotates to cause a fluid to flow or that redirects a flow of fluid ⟨the ∼s of a windmill⟩

van·guard \'van-ˌgärd\ *n* **1** : the troops moving at the front of an army **2** : the forefront of an action or movement

va·nil·la \və-'ni-lə\ *n* [NL, genus name, fr. Sp *vainilla* vanilla (plant and fruit), dim. of *vaina* sheath, fr. L *vagina*] : a flavoring extract obtained from the long beanlike pods (**vanilla beans**) of a tropical American climbing orchid or made synthetically; *also* : this orchid

van·ish \'va-nish\ *vb* : to pass from sight or existence : disappear completely — **van·ish·er** *n*

van·i·ty \'va-nə-tē\ *n, pl* **-ties 1** : something that is vain, empty, or useless **2** : the quality or fact of being useless or futile : FUTILITY **3** : undue pride in oneself or one's appearance : CONCEIT **4** : a small case for cosmetics : COMPACT

vanity plate *n* : an automobile license plate bearing distinctive letters or numbers designated by the owner

van·quish \'vaŋ-kwish, 'van-\ *vb* **1** : to overcome in battle or in a contest **2** : to gain mastery over (as an emotion)

van·tage \'van-tij\ *n* **1** : superiority in a contest **2** : a position giving a strategic advantage or a commanding perspective

va·pid \'va-pəd, 'vā-\ *adj* : lacking spirit, liveliness, or zest : FLAT, INSIPID — **va·pid·i·ty** \va-'pi-də-tē\ *n* — **vap·id·ly** *adv* — **vap·id·ness** *n*

va·por \'vā-pər\ *n* **1** : fine separated particles (as fog or smoke) floating in the air and clouding it **2** : a substance in the gaseous state; *esp* : one that is liquid under ordinary conditions **3** : something insubstantial or fleeting **4** *pl* : a depressed or hysterical nervous condition

va·por·ing \'vā-pə-riŋ\ *n* : an idle, boastful, or high-flown expression or speech — usu. used in pl.

va·por·ise *Brit var of* VAPORIZE

va·por·ize \'vā-pə-ˌrīz\ *vb* **-ized; -iz·ing** : to convert into vapor — **va·por·iza·tion** \ˌvā-pə-rə-'zā-shən\ *n*

va·por·iz·er \-ˌrī-zər\ *n* : a device that vaporizes something (as a medicated liquid)

vapor lock *n* : an interruption of flow of a fluid (as fuel in an engine) caused by the formation of vapor in the feeding system

va·por·ous \'vā-pə-rəs\ *adj* **1** : full of vapors : FOGGY,

MISTY **2** : UNSUBSTANTIAL, VAGUE — **va·por·ous·ly** *adv* — **va·por·ous·ness** *n*

va·pory \'vā-pǝ-rē\ *adj* : MISTY

va·pour *chiefly Brit var of* VAPOR

va·que·ro \vä-'ker-ō\ *n, pl* **-ros** [Sp, fr. *vaca* cow, fr. L *vacca*] : a ranch hand : COWBOY

var *abbr* **1** variable **2** variant; variation **3** variety **4** various

¹var·i·able \'ver-ē-ǝ-bǝl\ *adj* **1** : able or apt to vary : CHANGEABLE **2** : FICKLE **3** : not true to type : ABERRANT ⟨a ∼ wheat⟩ — **var·i·abil·i·ty** \ˌver-ē-ǝ-'bi-lǝ-tē, ˌvar-\ *n* — **var·i·ably** \-blē\ *adv*

²variable *n* **1** : a quantity that may take on any of a set of values; *also* : a mathematical symbol representing a variable **2** : something that is variable

var·i·ance \'ver-ē-ǝns\ *n* **1** : variation or a degree of variation : DEVIATION **2** : DISAGREEMENT, DISPUTE **3** : a license to do something contrary to the usual rule ⟨a zoning ∼⟩ **4** : the square of the standard deviation **syn** discord, contention, dissension, strife, conflict

¹var·i·ant \'ver-ē-ǝnt\ *adj* **1** : differing from others of its kind or class **2** : varying usu. slightly from the standard or type

²variant *n* **1** : one that exhibits variation from a type or norm **2** : one of two or more different spellings or pronunciations of a word

var·i·a·tion \ˌver-ē-'ā-shǝn\ *n* **1** : the act, process, or an instance of varying : a change in form, position, or condition : MODIFICATION, ALTERATION **2** : extent of change or difference **3** : divergence in the characteristics of an organism from those typical or usual for its group; *also* : one exhibiting such variation **4** : repetition of a musical theme with modifications in rhythm, tune, harmony, or key

vari·col·ored \'ver-i-ˌkǝ-lǝrd\ *adj* : having various colors : VARIEGATED

var·i·cose \'var-ǝ-ˌkōs\ *adj* : abnormally swollen and dilated ⟨∼ veins⟩ — **var·i·cos·i·ty** \ˌvar-ǝ-'kä-sǝ-tē\ *n*

var·ied \'ver-ēd\ *adj* **1** : having many forms or types : DIVERSE **2** : VARIEGATED — **var·ied·ly** *adv*

var·ie·gat·ed \'ver-ē-ǝ-ˌgā-tǝd\ *adj* **1** : having patches, stripes, or marks of different colors ⟨∼ flowers⟩ **2** : VARIED **1** — **var·ie·gate** \-ˌgāt\ *vb* — **var·ie·ga·tion** \ˌver-ē-ǝ-'gā-shǝn\ *n*

¹va·ri·etal \vǝ-'rī-ǝt-ǝl\ *adj* : of or relating to a variety; *esp* : of, relating to, or producing a varietal

²varietal *n* : a wine bearing the name of the principal grape from which it is made

va·ri·ety \vǝ-'rī-ǝ-tē\ *n, pl* **-et·ies 1** : the state of being varied or various : DIVERSITY **2** : a collection of different things : ASSORTMENT **3** : something varying from others of the same general kind **4** : any of various groups of plants or animals within a species distinguished by characteristics insufficient to separate species : SUBSPECIES **5** : entertainment such as is given in a stage presentation comprising a series of performances (as songs, dances, or acrobatic acts)

var·i·o·rum \ˌver-ē-'ōr-ǝm\ *n* : an edition or text of a work containing notes by various persons or variant readings of the text

var·i·ous \'ver-ē-ǝs\ *adj* **1** : VARICOLORED **2** : of differing kinds : MULTIFARIOUS **3** : UNLIKE ⟨animals as ∼ as the jaguar and the sloth⟩ **4** : having a number of different aspects **5** : NUMEROUS, MANY **6** : INDIVIDUAL, SEPARATE **syn** divergent, disparate, different, dissimilar, diverse, unalike — **var·i·ous·ly** *adv*

var·let \'vär-lǝt\ *n* **1** : ATTENDANT **2** : SCOUNDREL, KNAVE

var·mint \'vär-mǝnt\ *n* [alter. of *vermin*] **1** : an animal considered a pest; *esp* : one classed as vermin and unprotected by game law **2** : a contemptible person : RASCAL

¹var·nish \'vär-nish\ *n* **1** : a liquid preparation that is spread on a surface and dries into a hard glossy coating; *also* : the glaze of this coating **2** : something suggesting varnish by its gloss **3** : outside show : deceptive or superficial appearance

²varnish *vb* **1** : to cover with varnish **2** : to cover or conceal with something that gives a fair appearance : GLOSS

var·si·ty \'vär-sǝ-tē\ *n, pl* **-ties** [by shortening & alter. fr. *university*] **1** *Brit* : UNIVERSITY **2** : the principal team representing a college, school, or club

vary \'ver-ē\ *vb* **var·ied; vary·ing 1** : ALTER, CHANGE **2** : to make or be of different kinds : introduce or have variety : DIVERSIFY, DIFFER **3** : DEVIATE, SWERVE **4** : to change in bodily structure or function away from what is usual for members of a group

vas·cu·lar \'vas-kyǝ-lǝr\ *adj* [NL *vascularis*, fr. L *vasculum* small vessel, dim. of *vas* vase, vessel] : of or relating to a channel or system of channels for the conveyance of a body fluid (as blood or sap); *also* : supplied with or containing such vessels and esp. blood vessels

vascular plant *n* : a plant having a specialized system for carrying fluids that includes xylem and phloem

vase \'vās, 'vāz\ *n* : a usu. round vessel of greater depth than width used chiefly for ornament or for flowers

va·sec·to·my \vǝ-'sek-tǝ-mē, vā-'zek-\ *n, pl* **-mies** : surgical excision of all or part of the sperm-carrying ducts of the testis usu. to induce sterility

va·so·con·stric·tion \ˌvas-ō-kǝn-'strik-shǝn, ˌvāz-\ *n* : narrowing of the interior diameter of blood vessels

va·so·con·stric·tor \-tǝr\ *n* : an agent (as a nerve fiber or a drug) that initiates or induces vasoconstriction

vas·sal \'va-sǝl\ *n* **1** : a person under the protection of a feudal lord to whom he owes homage and loyalty : a feudal tenant **2** : one occupying a dependent or subordinate position — **vassal** *adj*

vas·sal·age \-sǝ-lij\ *n* **1** : the state of being a vassal **2** : the homage and loyalty due from a vassal **3** : SERVITUDE, SUBJECTION

vast \'vast\ *adj* : very great in size, amount, degree, intensity, or esp. extent **syn** enormous, huge, gigantic, colossal, mammoth — **vast·ly** *adv* — **vast·ness** *n*

²vast *n* : a great expanse : IMMENSITY

vasty \'vas-tē\ *adj* : VAST, IMMENSE

vat \'vat\ *n* : a large vessel (as a tub or barrel) esp. for holding liquids in manufacturing processes

VAT *abbr* value-added tax

vat·ic \'va-tik\ *adj* : PROPHETIC, ORACULAR

Vat·i·can \'va-ti-kǝn\ *n* **1** : the papal headquarters in Rome **2** : the papal government

vaude·ville \'vȯd-vǝl, 'väd-, 'vȯd-, -ˌvil\ *n* [F, fr. MF, satirical song, alter. of *vaudevire*, fr. *vau-de-Vire* valley of Vire, town in northwest France where such songs were composed] : a stage entertainment consisting of unrelated acts (as of acrobats, comedians, dancers, or singers)

¹vault \'vȯlt\ *n* **1** : an arched masonry structure usu. forming a ceiling or roof; *also* : something (as the sky) resembling a vault **2** : a room or space covered by a vault esp. when underground **3** : a room or compartment for the safekeeping of valuables **4** : a burial chamber; *also* : a usu. metal or concrete case in which a casket is enclosed at burial — **vaulty** *adj*

²vault *vb* **1** : to form or cover with a vault

³vault *vb* : to leap vigorously esp. by aid of the hands or a pole — **vault·er** *n*

⁴vault *n* : an act of vaulting : LEAP

vault·ed *adj* **1** : built in the form of a vault : ARCHED **2** : covered with a vault

vault·ing *adj* : reaching for the heights ⟨∼ ambition⟩

vaunt \'vȯnt\ *vb* [ME, fr. MF *vanter*, fr. LL *vanitare*, ultim. fr. L *vanus* vain] : BRAG, BOAST — **vaunt** *n*

vaunt·ed *adj* : much praised or boasted of

vb *abbr* verb; verbal

VCR \ˌvē-(ˌ)sē-'är\ *n* [*videocassette recorder*] : a videotape recorder that uses videocassettes

VD *abbr* venereal disease

VDT *abbr* video display terminal

veal \'vēl\ *n* : the flesh of a young calf

vec•tor \'vek-tər\ *n* **1** : a quantity that has magnitude and direction **2** : an organism (as a fly or tick) that transmits disease germs

Ve•da \'vā-də\ *n* [Skt, lit., knowledge] : any of a class of Hindu sacred writings — **Ve•dic** \'vā-dik\ *adj*

Ve•dan•ta \vā-'dän-tə, və-, -'dan-\ *n* : an orthodox Hindu philosophy based on the Upanishads

vee•jay \'vē-ˌjā\ *n* : an announcer of a program featuring music videos

veep \'vēp\ *n* : VICE PRESIDENT

veer \'vir\ *vb* : to shift from one direction or course to another syn turn, avert, deflect, divert — **veer** *n*

veg•an \'vē-gən, 'vā-; 've-jən, -ˌjan\ *n* : a strict vegetarian who consumes no animal food or dairy products — **veg•an•ism** \'vē-gə-ˌni-zəm, 'vā-, 've-\ *n*

¹veg•e•ta•ble \'vej-tə-bəl, 've-jə-\ *adj* [ME, fr. ML *vegetabilis* vegetative, fr. *vegetare* to grow, fr. L, to animate, fr. *vegetus* lively, fr. *vegēre* to enliven] **1** : of, relating to, or growing like plants ⟨the ∼ kingdom⟩ **2** : made or obtained from plants ⟨∼ oils⟩ **3** : suggesting that of a plant (as in inertness) ⟨a ∼ existence⟩

²vegetable *n* **1** : PLANT 1 **2** : a usu. herbaceous plant grown for an edible part that is usu. eaten as part of a meal; *also* : such an edible part

veg•e•tal \'ve-jət-ᵊl\ *adj* **1** : VEGETABLE **2** : VEGETATIVE

veg•e•tar•i•an \ˌve-jə-'ter-ē-ən\ *n* : one that believes in or practices living on a diet of vegetables, fruits, grains, nuts, and sometimes animal products (as milk and cheese) — **vegetarian** *adj* — **veg•e•tar•i•an•ism** \-ē-ə-ˌni-zəm\ *n*

veg•e•tate \'ve-jə-ˌtāt\ *vb* **-tat•ed; -tat•ing** : to live or grow in the manner of a plant; *esp* : to lead a dull inert life

veg•e•ta•tion \ˌve-jə-'tā-shən\ *n* **1** : the act or process of vegetating; *also* : inert existence **2** : plant life or cover (as of an area) — **veg•e•ta•tion•al** \-shə-nəl\ *adj*

veg•e•ta•tive \'ve-jə-ˌtā-tiv\ *adj* **1** : of or relating to nutrition and growth esp. as contrasted with reproduction **2** : of, relating to, or composed of vegetation **3** : VEGETABLE 3

veg out \'vej-\ *vb* **vegged out; vegging out** [short for *vegetate*] : to spend time idly or passively

ve•he•ment \'vē-ə-mənt\ *adj* **1** : marked by great force or energy **2** : marked by strong feeling or expression : PASSIONATE, FERVID — **ve•he•mence** \-məns\ *n* — **ve•he•ment•ly** *adv*

ve•hi•cle \'vē-ə-kəl, 'vē-ˌhi-\ *n* **1** : a medium by which a thing is applied or administered ⟨linseed oil is a ∼ for pigments⟩ **2** : a medium through or by means of which something is conveyed or expressed **3** : a means of transporting persons or goods syn instrument, agent, agency, organ, channel — **ve•hic•u•lar** \vē-'hi-kyə-lər\ *adj*

¹veil \'vāl\ *n* **1** : a piece of often sheer or diaphanous material used to screen or curtain something or to cover the head or face **2** : the state of becoming a nun ⟨take the ∼⟩ **3** : something that hides or obscures like a veil

²veil *vb* : to cover with or as if with a veil : wear a veil

¹vein \'vān\ *n* **1** : a fissure in rock filled with mineral matter; *also* : a bed of useful mineral matter **2** : any of the tubular branching vessels that carry blood from the capillaries toward the heart **3** : any of the bundles of vascular vessels forming the framework of a leaf **4** : any of the thickened ribs that stiffen the wings of an insect **5** : something (as a wavy variegation in marble) suggesting veins **6** : a distinctive style of expression **7** : a distinctive element or quality : STRAIN **8** : MOOD, HUMOR — **veined** \'vānd\ *adj*

²vein *vb* : to pattern with or as if with veins — **vein•ing** *n*

vel *abbr* velocity

ve•lar \'vē-lər\ *adj* : of or relating to a velum and esp. that of the soft palate

veld *or* **veldt** \'velt, 'felt\ *n* [Afrikaans *veld*, fr. D, field] : an open grassland esp. in southern Africa usu. with few shrubs or trees

vel•lum \'ve-ləm\ *n* [ME *velim*, fr. MF *veelin*, fr. *veelin*, adj., of a calf, fr. *veel* calf] **1** : a fine-grained lambskin, kidskin, or calfskin prepared for writing on or for binding books **2** : a strong cream-colored paper — **vellum** *adj*

ve•loc•i•pede \və-'lä-sə-ˌpēd\ *n* : an early bicycle

ve•loc•i•ty \və-'lä-sə-tē\ *n, pl* **-ties** : quickness of motion : SPEED ⟨the ∼ of light⟩

ve•lour *or* **ve•lours** \və-'lu̇r\ *n, pl* **velours** \-'lu̇rz\ : any of various textile fabrics with pile like that of velvet

ve•lum \'vē-ləm\ *n, pl* **ve•la** \-lə\ : a membranous body part (as the soft palate) resembling a veil

vel•vet \'vel-vət\ *n* [ME *veluet, velvet*, fr. MF *velu* shaggy, ultim. fr. L *villus* shaggy hair] **1** : a fabric having a short soft dense warp pile **2** : something resembling or suggesting velvet (as in softness or luster) **3** : the soft skin covering the growing antlers of deer — **velvet** *adj* — **velvety** *adj*

vel•ve•teen \ˌvel-və-'tēn\ *n* **1** : a fabric woven usu. of cotton in imitation of velvet **2** *pl* : clothes made of velveteen

Ven *abbr* venerable

ve•nal \'vēn-ᵊl\ *adj* : capable of being bought or bribed : MERCENARY, CORRUPT — **ve•nal•i•ty** \vi-'nal-ə-tē\ *n* — **ve•nal•ly** \'vēn-ᵊl-ē\ *adv*

ve•na•tion \ve-'nā-shən, vē-\ *n* : an arrangement or system of veins ⟨the ∼ of the hand⟩ ⟨leaf ∼⟩

venation

vend \'vend\ *vb* : SELL; *esp* : to sell as a hawker or peddler — **vend•ible** *adj*

vend•ee \ven-'dē\ *n* : one to whom a thing is sold : BUYER

ven•det•ta \ven-'de-tə\ *n* : a feud marked by acts of revenge

vending machine *n* : a coin-operated machine for selling merchandise

ven•dor \'ven-dər, *for 1 also* ven-'dȯr\ *n* **1** : one that vends : SELLER **2** : VENDING MACHINE

¹ve•neer \və-'nir\ *n* [G *Furnier*, fr. *furnieren* to veneer, fr. F *fournir* to furnish] **1** : a thin usu. superficial layer of material ⟨brick ∼⟩; *esp* : a thin layer of fine wood glued over a cheaper wood **2** : superficial display : GLOSS

²veneer *vb* : to overlay with a veneer

ven•er•a•ble \'ve-nə-rə-bəl\ *adj* **1** : deserving to be venerated — often used as a religious title **2** : made sacred by association

ven•er•ate \'ve-nə-ˌrāt\ *vb* **-at•ed; -at•ing** : to regard with reverential respect syn adore, revere, reverence, worship — **ven•er•a•tion** \ˌve-nə-'rā-shən\ *n*

ve•ne•re•al \və-'nir-ē-əl\ *adj* : of or relating to sexual intercourse or to diseases transmitted by it ⟨a ∼ infection⟩

NOW TO THE ENTERTAINMENT PORTION OF OUR SHOW

AN AMAZING FEAT OF VENTRILOQUISM

FEATURING MY OVERQUALIFIED ASSISTANT

JIM DAVIS   3-2

venereal disease *n* : a contagious disease (as gonorrhea or syphilis) usu. acquired by having sexual intercourse with someone who already has it

ve·ne·tian blind \və-ˈnē-shən-\ *n* : a blind having thin horizontal parallel slats that can be adjusted to admit a desired amount of light

Ven·e·zue·lan \ˌve-nə-ˈzwā-lən\ *n* : a native or inhabitant of Venezuela — **Venezuelan** *adj*

ven·geance \ˈven-jəns\ *n* : punishment inflicted in retaliation for an injury or offense : REVENGE

venge·ful \ˈvenj-fəl\ *adj* : filled with a desire for revenge : VINDICTIVE — **venge·ful·ly** *adv*

ve·nial \ˈvē-nē-əl\ *adj* : capable of being forgiven : EXCUSABLE ⟨∼ sin⟩

ve·ni·re \və-ˈnī-rē\ *n* : a panel from which a jury is drawn

ve·ni·re fa·ci·as \-ˈfā-shē-əs\ *n* [ME, fr. ML, you should cause to come] : a writ summoning persons to appear in court to serve as jurors

ve·ni·re·man \və-ˈnī-rē-mən, -ˈnir-ē-\ *n* : a member of a venire

ven·i·son \ˈven-ə-sən, -zən\ *n, pl* **venisons** *also* **venison** [ME, fr. OF *veneison* hunting, game, fr. L *venatio,* fr. *venari* to hunt, pursue] : the edible flesh of a deer

ven·om \ˈve-nəm\ *n* [ME *venim, venom,* fr. OF *venim,* ultim. fr. L *venenum* magic charm, drug, poison] **1** : poisonous material secreted by some animals (as snakes, spiders, or bees) and transmitted usu. by biting or stinging **2** : ILL WILL, MALEVOLENCE

ven·om·ous \ˈve-nə-məs\ *adj* **1** : full of venom : POISONOUS **2** : SPITEFUL, MALEVOLENT **3** : secreting and using venom ⟨∼ snakes⟩ — **ven·om·ous·ly** *adv*

ve·nous \ˈvē-nəs\ *adj* **1** : of, relating to, or full of veins **2** : being purplish red oxygen-deficient blood rich in carbon dioxide that is present in most veins

¹vent \ˈvent\ *vb* **1** : to provide with a vent **2** : to serve as a vent for **3** : EXPEL, DISCHARGE **4** : to give vigorous or emotional expression to

²vent *n* **1** : an opportunity or way of escape or passage : OUTLET **2** : an opening for the escape of a gas or liquid or for the relief of pressure

³vent *n* : a slit in a garment esp. in the lower part of a seam (as of a jacket or skirt)

ven·ti·late \ˈvent-əl-ˌāt\ *vb* **-lat·ed; -lat·ing 1** : to discuss freely and openly ⟨∼ a question⟩ **2** : to give vent to ⟨∼ one's grievances⟩ **3** : to cause fresh air to circulate through (as a room or mine) so as to replace foul air **4** : to provide with a vent or outlet **syn** express, vent, air, utter, voice, broach — **ven·ti·la·tor** \-ᵊl-ˌā-tər\ *n*

ven·ti·la·tion \ˌvent-ᵊl-ˈā-shən\ *n* **1** : the act or process of ventilating **2** : circulation of air (as in a room) **3** : a system or means of providing fresh air

ven·tral \ˈven-trəl\ *adj* **1** : of or relating to the belly : ABDOMINAL **2** : of, relating to, or located on or near the surface of the body that in humans is the front but in most other animals is the lower surface — **ven·tral·ly** *adv*

ven·tri·cle \ˈven-tri-kəl\ *n* **1** : a chamber of the heart that receives blood from the atrium of the same side

and pumps it into the arteries **2** : any of the communicating cavities of the brain that are continuous with the central canal of the spinal cord

ven·tril·o·quism \ven-ˈtri-lə-ˌkwi-zəm\ *n* [LL *ventriloquus* ventriloquist, fr. L *venter* belly + *loqui* to speak; fr. the belief that the voice is produced from the ventriloquist's stomach] : the production of the voice in such a manner that the sound appears to come from a source other than the speaker — **ven·tril·o·quist** \-kwist\ *n*

ven·tril·o·quy \-kwē\ *n* : VENTRILOQUISM

¹ven·ture \ˈven-chər\ *vb* **ven·tured; ven·tur·ing 1** : to expose to hazard : RISK **2** : to undertake the risks of : BRAVE **3** : to offer at the risk of rebuff, rejection, or censure ⟨∼ an opinion⟩ **4** : to proceed despite danger : DARE

²venture *n* **1** : an undertaking involving chance or risk; *esp* : a speculative business enterprise **2** : something risked in a speculative venture : STAKE

ven·ture·some \ˈven-chər-səm\ *adj* **1** : involving risk : DANGEROUS, HAZARDOUS **2** : inclined to venture : BOLD, DARING **syn** adventurous, venturous, rash, reckless, foolhardy — **ven·ture·some·ly** *adv* — **ven·ture·some·ness** *n*

ven·tur·ous \ˈven-chə-rəs\ *adj* : VENTURESOME — **ven·tur·ous·ly** *adv* — **ven·tur·ous·ness** *n*

ven·ue \ˈven-yü\ *n* : the place in which the alleged events from which a legal action arises took place; *also* : the place from which the jury is taken and where the trial is held

Ve·nus \ˈvē-nəs\ *n* : the planet 2d in order from the sun — see PLANET table

Ve·nu·sian \vi-ˈnü-zhən, -ˈnyü-\ *adj* : of or relating to the planet Venus

Ve·nus's-fly·trap \ˈvē-nə-səz-ˈflī-ˌtrap\ *or* **Venus fly·trap** *n* : an insect-eating plant of the Carolina coast that has the leaf tip modified into an insect trap

ve·ra·cious \və-ˈrā-shəs\ *adj* **1** : TRUTHFUL, HONEST **2** : TRUE, ACCURATE — **ve·ra·cious·ly** *adv*

ve·rac·i·ty \və-ˈra-sə-tē\ *n, pl* **-ties 1** : devotion to truth : TRUTHFULNESS **2** : conformity with fact : ACCURACY **3** : something true

ve·ran·da *or* **ve·ran·dah** \və-ˈran-də\ *n* : a long open usu. roofed porch

verb \ˈvərb\ *n* : a word that is the grammatical center of a predicate and expresses an act, occurrence, or mode of being

¹ver·bal \ˈvər-bəl\ *adj* **1** : of, relating to, or consisting of words; *esp* : having to do with words rather than with the ideas to be conveyed **2** : expressed in usu. spoken words : not written : ORAL ⟨a ∼ contract⟩ **3** : of, relating to, or formed from a verb **4** : LITERAL, VERBATIM — **ver·bal·ly** *adv*

²verbal *n* : a word that combines characteristics of a verb with those of a noun or adjective

verbal auxiliary *n* : an auxiliary verb

ver·bal·ize \ˈvər-bə-ˌlīz\ *vb* **-ized; -iz·ing 1** : to speak or write in wordy or empty fashion **2** : to express something in words : describe verbally **3** : to convert into a verb — **ver·bal·i·za·tion** \ˌvər-bə-lə-ˈzā-shən\ n

verbal noun n : a noun derived directly from a verb or verb stem and in some uses having the sense and constructions of a verb

ver·ba·tim \(ˌ)vər-ˈbā-təm\ adv or adj : in the same words : word for word

ver·be·na \(ˌ)vər-ˈbē-nə\ n : VERVAIN; esp : any of several garden plants of hybrid origin with showy spikes of bright often fragrant flowers

ver·biage \ˈvər-bē-ij, -bij\ n **1** : superfluity of words usu. of little or obscure content **2** : DICTION, WORDING

ver·bose \(ˌ)vər-ˈbōs\ adj : using more words than are needed : WORDY syn prolix, diffuse, redundant, windy — **ver·bos·i·ty** \-ˈbä-sə-tē\ n

ver·bo·ten \vər-ˈbōt-ᵊn, fər-\ adj [G] : forbidden usu. by dictate

ver·dant \ˈvər-dᵊnt\ adj : green with growing plants — **ver·dant·ly** adv

ver·dict \ˈvər-(ˌ)dikt\ n [alter. of ME verdit, fr. Anglo-French (the French of medieval England), fr. OF ver true (fr. L verus) + dit saying, dictum, fr. L dictum, fr. dicere to say] **1** : the finding or decision of a jury **2** : DECISION, JUDGMENT

ver·di·gris \ˈvər-də-ˌgrēs, -ˌgris\ n : a green or bluish deposit that forms on copper, brass, or bronze surfaces

ver·dure \ˈvər-jər\ n : the greenness of growing vegetation; also : such vegetation

¹**verge** \ˈvərj\ n **1** : a staff carried as an emblem of authority or office **2** : something that borders or bounds : EDGE, MARGIN **3** : BRINK, THRESHOLD

²**verge** vb **verged; verg·ing 1** : to be contiguous **2** : to be on the verge

³**verge** vb **verged; verg·ing 1** : to move or extend in some direction or toward some condition : INCLINE **2** : to be in transition or change

verg·er \ˈvər-jər\ n **1** chiefly Brit : an attendant who carries a verge (as before a bishop) **2** : SEXTON

ve·rid·i·cal \və-ˈri-di-kəl\ adj **1** : TRUTHFUL **2** : not illusory : GENUINE

ver·i·fy \ˈver-ə-ˌfī\ vb **-fied; -fy·ing 1** : to confirm in law by oath **2** : to establish the truth, accuracy, or reality of syn authenticate, corroborate, substantiate, validate — **ver·i·fi·able** adj — **ver·i·fi·ca·tion** \ˌver-ə-fə-ˈkā-shən\ n

ver·i·ly \ˈver-ə-lē\ adv **1** : in very truth : CERTAINLY **2** : TRULY, CONFIDENTLY

ver·i·si·mil·i·tude \ˌver-ə-sə-ˈmi-lə-ˌtüd, -ˌtyüd\ n : the quality or state of appearing to be true

ver·i·ta·ble \ˈver-ə-tə-bəl\ adj : ACTUAL, GENUINE, TRUE — **ver·i·ta·bly** adv

ver·i·ty \ˈver-ə-tē\ n, pl **-ties 1** : the quality or state of being true or real : TRUTH, REALITY **2** : something (as a statement) that is true **3** : HONESTY, VERACITY

ver·meil n [MF] **1** \ˈvər-məl, -ˌmāl\ : VERMILION **2** \ver-ˈmā\ : gilded silver

ver·mi·cel·li \ˌvər-mə-ˈche-lē, -ˈse-\ n [It, fr. pl. of ver-

micello, dim. of verme worm] : a pasta made in thinner strings than spaghetti

ver·mic·u·lite \vər-ˈmi-kyə-ˌlīt\ n : any of various lightweight water-absorbent minerals derived from mica

ver·mi·form appendix \ˈvər-mə-ˌform-\ n : APPENDIX 2

ver·mil·ion also **ver·mil·lion** \vər-ˈmil-yən\ n : a bright reddish orange color; also : any of various red pigments

ver·min \ˈvər-mən\ n, pl **vermin 1** : small common harmful or objectionable animals (as lice or mice) that are difficult to get rid of **2** : birds and mammals that prey on game — **ver·min·ous** adj

ver·mouth \vər-ˈmüth\ n [F vermout, fr. G Wermut wormwood] : a dry or sweet wine flavored with herbs and often used in mixed drinks

¹**ver·nac·u·lar** \vər-ˈna-kyə-lər\ adj [L vernaculus native, fr. verna slave born in the master's house, native] **1** : of, relating to, or being a language or dialect native to a region or country rather than a literary, cultured, or foreign language **2** : of, relating to, or being the normal spoken form of a language **3** : applied to a plant or animal in common speech as distinguished from biological nomenclature ⟨∼ names⟩

²**vernacular** n **1** : a vernacular language **2** : the mode of expression of a group or class **3** : a vernacular name of a plant or animal

ver·nal \ˈvərn-ᵊl\ adj : of, relating to, or occurring in the spring

ver·ni·er \ˈvər-nē-ər\ n : a short scale made to slide along the divisions of a graduated instrument to indicate parts of divisions

ve·ron·i·ca \və-ˈrä-ni-kə\ n : SPEEDWELL

ver·sa·tile \ˈvər-sət-ᵊl\ adj : turning with ease from one thing or position to another; esp : having many aptitudes — **ver·sa·til·i·ty** \ˌvər-sə-ˈti-lə-tē\ n

¹**verse** \ˈvərs\ n **1** : a line of poetry; also : STANZA **2** : metrical writing distinguished from poetry esp. by its lower level of intensity **3** : POETRY **4** : POEM **5** : one of the short divisions of a chapter in the Bible

²**verse** vb **versed; vers·ing** : to familiarize by experience, study, or practice ⟨well versed in the theater⟩

ver·si·cle \ˈvər-si-kəl\ n : a verse or sentence said or sung by a leader in public worship and followed by a response from the people

ver·si·fi·ca·tion \ˌvər-sə-fə-ˈkā-shən\ n **1** : the making of verses **2** : metrical structure

ver·si·fy \ˈvər-sə-ˌfī\ vb **-fied; -fy·ing 1** : to write verse **2** : to turn into verse — **ver·si·fi·er** \-ˌfī-ər\ n

ver·sion \ˈvər-zhən\ n **1** : TRANSLATION; esp : a translation of the Bible **2** : an account or description from a particular point of view esp. as contrasted with another **3** : a form or variant of a type or original

vers li·bre \ver-ˈlēbrᵉ\ n, pl **vers li·bres** \same\ [F] : FREE VERSE

ver·so \ˈvər-sō\ n, pl **versos** : a left-hand page

ver·sus \ˈvər-səs\ prep **1** : AGAINST 1 ⟨the champion ∼

the challenger⟩ **2** : in contrast or as an alternative to ⟨free trade ∼ protection⟩

vert *abbr* vertical

ver·te·bra \'vər-tə-brə\ *n, pl* **-brae** \-ˌbrā, -ˌ(ˌ)brē\ *or* **-bras** [L] : one of the segments of bone or cartilage making up the backbone

ver·te·bral \(ˌ)vər-tē-brəl, 'vər-tə-\ *adj* : of, relating to, or made up of vertebrae : SPINAL

vertebral column *n* : BACKBONE

¹ver·te·brate \'vər-tə-brət, -ˌbrāt\ *adj* **1** : having a backbone **2** : of or relating to the vertebrates

²vertebrate *n* : any of a large group of animals (as mammals, birds, reptiles, amphibians, or fishes) that have a backbone or in some primitive forms (as a lamprey) a flexible rod of cells and that have a tubular nervous system arranged along the back and divided into a brain and spinal cord

ver·tex \'vər-ˌteks\ *n, pl* **ver·ti·ces** \'vər-tə-ˌsēz\ *also* **ver·tex·es** [L *vertex, vortex* whirl, whirlpool, top of the head, summit, fr. *vertere* to turn] **1** : the point opposite to and farthest from the base of a geometrical figure **2** : the point where the sides of an angle or three or more edges of a polyhedron (as a cube) meet **3** : the highest point : TOP, SUMMIT

ver·ti·cal \'vər-ti-kəl\ *adj* **1** : of, relating to, or located at the vertex : directly overhead **2** : rising perpendicularly from a level surface : UPRIGHT — **vertical** *n* — **ver·ti·cal·i·ty** \ˌvər-tə-'ka-lə-tē\ *n* — **ver·ti·cal·ly** \-k(ə-)lē\ *adv*

ver·tig·i·nous \(ˌ)vər-'ti-jə-nəs\ *adj* : marked by, affected with, or tending to cause dizziness

ver·ti·go \'vər-ti-ˌgō\ *n, pl* **-goes** *or* **-gos** : DIZZINESS, GIDDINESS

ver·vain \'vər-ˌvān\ *n* : any of a genus of chiefly American herbs or low woody plants with often showy heads or spikes of tubular flowers

verve \'vərv\ *n* : liveliness of imagination; *also* : VIVACITY

¹very \'ver-ē\ *adj* **veri·er; -est** [ME *verray, verry,* fr. OF *verai,* ultim. fr. L *verax* truthful, fr. *verus* true] **1** : EXACT, PRECISE ⟨the ∼ heart of the city⟩ **2** : exactly suitable ⟨the ∼ tool for the job⟩ **3** : ABSOLUTE, UTTER ⟨the *veriest* nonsense⟩ **4** — used as an intensive esp. to emphasize identity (before my ∼ eyes) **5** : MERE, BARE ⟨the ∼ idea scared him⟩ **6** : SELFSAME, IDENTICAL ⟨the ∼ man I saw⟩

²very *adv* **1** : in actual fact : TRULY **2** : to a high degree : EXTREMELY

very high frequency *n* : a radio frequency of between 30 and 300 megahertz

ves·i·cant \'ve-si-kənt\ *n* : an agent that causes blistering — **vesicant** *adj*

ves·i·cle \'ve-si-kəl\ *n* : a membranous and usu. fluid‑filled cavity in a plant or animal; *also* : BLISTER — **ve·sic·u·lar** \və-'si-kyə-lər\ *adj*

¹ves·per \'ves-pər\ *n* **1** *cap, archaic* : EVENING STAR **2** : a vesper bell **3** *archaic* : EVENING, EVENTIDE

²vesper *adj* : of or relating to vespers or the evening

ves·pers \-pərz\ *n pl, often cap* : a late afternoon or evening worship service

ves·sel \'ve-səl\ *n* **1** : a container (as a barrel, bottle, bowl, or cup) for holding something **2** : a person held to be the recipient of a quality (as grace) **3** : a craft bigger than a rowboat **4** : a tube in which a body fluid (as blood or sap) is contained and circulated

¹vest \'vest\ *vb* **1** : to place or give into the possession or distinction of some person or authority **2** : to grant or endow with a particular authority, right, or property **3** : to become legally vested **4** : to clothe with or as if with a garment; *esp* : to garb in ecclesiastical vestments

²vest *n* **1** : a man's sleeveless garment for the upper body usu. worn under a suit coat; *also* : a similar garment for women **2** *chiefly Brit* : a man's sleeveless undershirt **3** : a front piece of a dress resembling the front of a vest

¹ves·tal \'vest-ᵊl\ *adj* : CHASTE

²vestal *n* : VESTAL VIRGIN

vestal virgin *n* **1** : a virgin consecrated to the Roman goddess Vesta and to the service of watching the sacred fire perpetually kept burning on her altar **2** : a chaste woman

vest·ed *adj* : fully and unconditionally guaranteed as a legal right, benefit, or privilege

vested interest *n* : an interest (as in an existing political, economic, or social arrangement) to which the holder has a strong commitment; *also* : one (as a corporation) having a vested interest

ves·ti·bule \'ves-tə-ˌbyül\ *n* **1** : any of various bodily cavities forming or suggesting an entrance to some other cavity or space **2** : a passage or room between the outer door and the interior of a building — **ves·tib·u·lar** \ve-'sti-byə-lər\ *adj*

ves·tige \'ves-tij\ *n* [F, fr. L *vestigium* footprint, track, vestige] : a trace or visible sign left by something lost or vanished; *also* : a minute remaining amount — **ves·ti·gial** \ve-'sti-jē-əl, -jəl\ *adj* — **ves·ti·gial·ly** *adv*

vest·ing \'ves-tiŋ\ *n* : the conveying to an employee of inalienable rights to share in a pension fund; *also* : the right so conveyed

vest·ment \'vest-mənt\ *n* **1** : an outer garment; *esp* : a ceremonial or official robe **2** *pl* : CLOTHING, GARB **3** : a garment or insignia worn by a clergyman when officiating or assisting at a religious service

vest–pocket *adj* : very small ⟨a ∼ park⟩

ves·try \'ves-trē\ *n, pl* **vestries 1** : a room in a church for vestments, altar linens, and sacred vessels **2** : a room used for church meetings and classes **3** : a body administering the temporal affairs of an Episcopal parish

ves·try·man \-mən\ *n* : a member of a vestry

ves·ture \'ves-chər\ *n* **1** : a covering garment **2** : CLOTHING, APPAREL

¹vet \'vet\ *n* : VETERINARIAN

²vet *adj or n* : VETERAN

vetch \'vech\ *n* : any of a genus of twining herbs related to the garden pea including some grown for fodder and green manure

vet·er·an \'ve-tron, -tə-rən\ *n* [L *veteranus,* fr. *veteranus* old, of long experience, fr. *veter-, vetus* old] **1** : an old soldier of long service **2** : a former member of the armed forces **3** : a person of long experience in an occupation or skill — **veteran** *adj*

Veterans Day *n* : November 11 observed as a legal holiday in commemoration of the end of hostilities in 1918 and 1945

vet·er·i·nar·i·an \ˌve-trə-'ner-ē-ən, ˌve-tə-rə-\ *n* : one qualified and authorized to practice veterinary medicine

¹vet·er·i·nary \'ve-trə-ˌner-ē, 've-tə-rə-\ *adj* : of, relating to, or being the medical care of animals and esp. domestic animals

²veterinary *n, pl* **-nar·ies** : VETERINARIAN

¹ve·to \'vē-tō\ *n, pl* **vetoes** [L, I forbid] **1** : an authoritative prohibition **2** : a power of one part of a government to forbid the carrying out of projects attempted by another part; *esp* : a power vested in a chief executive to prevent the carrying out of measures adopted by a legislature **3** : the exercise of the power of veto

²veto *vb* **1** : FORBID, PROHIBIT **2** : to refuse assent to (a legislative bill) so as to prevent enactment or cause reconsideration — **ve·to·er** *n*

vex \'veks\ *vb* **vexed** *also* **vext; vex·ing 1** : to bring trouble, distress, or agitation to **2** : to annoy continually with little irritations

vex·a·tion \vek-'sā-shən\ *n* **1** : the act of vexing **2** : the quality or state of being vexed : IRRITATION **3** : a cause of trouble or annoyance

vex·a·tious \-shəs\ *adj* **1** : causing vexation : ANNOYING **2** : full of distress or annoyance : TROUBLED — **vex·a·tious·ly** *adv* — **vex·a·tious·ness** *n*

vexed \'vekst\ *adj* : fully debated or discussed ⟨a ∼ question⟩

VF *abbr* **1** video frequency **2** visual field

VFD *abbr* volunteer fire department

VFW *abbr* Veterans of Foreign Wars

VG *abbr* **1** very good **2** vicar-general

VHF *abbr* very high frequency

VI *abbr* Virgin Islands

via \'vī-ə, 'vē-ə\ *prep* **1** : by way of **2** : by means of

vi·a·ble \'vī-ə-bəl\ *adj* **1** : capable of living; *esp* : capable of surviving outside the mother's womb without artificial support ⟨a ∼ fetus⟩ **2** : capable of growing and developing ⟨∼ seeds⟩ **3** : capable of being put into practice : WORKABLE **4** : having a reasonable chance of succeeding ⟨a ∼ candidate⟩ — **vi·a·bil·i·ty** \ˌvī-ə-'bi-lə-tē\ *n* — **vi·a·bly** \'vī-ə-blē\ *adv*

via·duct \'vī-ə-ˌdəkt\ *n* : a long elevated roadway usu. consisting of a series of short spans supported on arches, piers, or columns

viaduct

vi·al \'vī-əl\ *n* : a small vessel for liquids

vi·and \'vī-ənd\ *n* : an article of food

vi·at·i·cum \vī-'a-ti-kəm, vē-\ *n, pl* **-cums** *or* **-ca** \-kə\ **1** : the Christian Eucharist given to a person in danger of death **2** : an allowance esp. in money for traveling needs and expenses

vibes \'vībz\ *n pl* **1** : VIBRAPHONE **2** : VIBRATIONS

vi·brant \'vī-brənt\ *adj* **1** : VIBRATING, PULSATING **2** : pulsating with vigor or activity **3** : readily set in vibration : RESPONSIVE **4** : sounding from vibration — **vi·bran·cy** \-brən-sē\ *n*

vi·bra·phone \'vī-brə-ˌfōn\ *n* : a percussion instrument like the xylophone but with metal bars and motor-driven resonators

vi·brate \'vī-ˌbrāt\ *vb* **vi·brat·ed; vi·brat·ing 1** : OSCILLATE **2** : to set in vibration **3** : to be in vibration **4** : WAVER, FLUCTUATE **5** : to respond sympathetically : THRILL

vi·bra·tion \vī-'brā-shən\ *n* **1** : a rapid to-and-fro motion of the particles of an elastic body or medium (as a stretched cord) that produces sound **2** : an act of vibrating : a state of being vibrated : OSCILLA-

TION **3** : a trembling motion **4** : VACILLATION **5** : a feeling or impression that someone or something gives off — usu. used in pl. ⟨good ∼s⟩ — **vi·bra·tion·al** \-shə-nəl\ *adj*

vi·bra·to \vi-'brä-tō\ *n, pl* **-tos** [It] : a slightly tremulous effect imparted to vocal or instrumental music

vi·bra·tor \'vī-ˌbrā-tər\ *n* : one that vibrates or causes vibration; *esp* : a vibrating electrical device used in massage or for sexual stimulation

vi·bra·to·ry \'vī-brə-ˌtōr-ē\ *adj* : consisting of, capable of, or causing vibration

vi·bur·num \vī-'bər-nəm\ *n* : any of a genus of widely distributed shrubs or trees related to the honeysuckle and bearing small usu. white flowers in broad clusters

vic *abbr* vicinity

Vic *abbr* Victoria

vic·ar \'vi-kər\ *n* **1** : an administrative deputy **2** : a minister in charge of a church who serves under the authority of another minister — **vic·ar·i·ate** \vī-'ker-ē-ət\ *n*

vic·ar·age \'vi-kə-rij\ *n* : a vicar's home

vicar–general *n, pl* **vicars–general** : an administrative deputy (as of a Roman Catholic or Anglican bishop)

vi·car·i·ous \vī-'ker-ē-əs, -'kar-\ *adj* **1** : acting for another **2** : done or suffered by one person on behalf of another or others ⟨a ∼ sacrifice⟩ **3** : sharing in someone else's experience through the use of the imagination or sympathetic feelings — **vi·car·i·ous·ly** *adv* — **vi·car·i·ous·ness** *n*

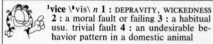

¹vice \'vīs\ *n* **1** : DEPRAVITY, WICKEDNESS **2** : a moral fault or failing **3** : a habitual usu. trivial fault **4** : an undesirable behavior pattern in a domestic animal

²vice *chiefly Brit var of* VISE

³vi·ce \'vī-sē\ *prep* : in the place of; *also* : rather than

vice admiral *n* : a commissioned officer in the navy or coast guard ranking above a rear admiral

vice·ge·rent \'vīs-'jir-ənt\ *n* : an administrative deputy of a king or magistrate — **vice·ge·ren·cy** \-ən-sē\ *n*

vi·cen·ni·al \vī-'se-nē-əl\ *adj* : occurring once every 20 years

vice presidency *n* : the office of vice president

vice president *n* **1** : an officer ranking next to a president and usu. empowered to act for the president during an absence or disability **2** : any of several of a president's deputies

vice·re·gal \'vīs-'rē-gəl\ *adj* : of or relating to a viceroy

vice·roy \'vīs-ˌrȯi\ *n* : the governor of a country or province who rules as representative of the sovereign — **vice·roy·al·ty** \-əl-tē\ *n*

vice ver·sa \vī-si-'vər-sə, 'vīs-'vər-\ *adv* : with the order reversed

vi·chys·soise \ˌvi-shē-'swäz, ˌvē-\ *n* [F] : a soup made esp. from leeks or onions and potatoes, cream, and chicken stock and usu. served cold

vic·in·age \'vis-ᵊn-ij\ *n* : a neighboring or surrounding district : VICINITY

vi·cin·i·ty \və-'si-nə-tē\ *n, pl* **-ties** [MF *vicinité*, fr. L

vicinitas, fr. vicinus neighboring, fr. vicus row of houses, village] **1** : NEARNESS, PROXIMITY **2** : a surrounding area : NEIGHBORHOOD

vi·cious \ˈvi-shəs\ adj **1** : having the quality of vice : WICKED, DEPRAVED **2** : DEFECTIVE, FAULTY; also : INVALID **3** : IMPURE, FOUL **4** : having a savage disposition; also : marked by violence or ferocity **5** : MALICIOUS, SPITEFUL **6** : worsened by internal causes that augment each other ⟨~ wage-price spiral⟩ — **vi·cious·ly** adv — **vi·cious·ness** n

vi·cis·si·tude \və-ˈsi-sə-ˌtüd, vī-, -ˌtyüd\ n : an irregular, unexpected, or surprising change
vic·tim \ˈvik-təm\ n **1** : a living being offered as a sacrifice in a religious rite **2** : an individual injured or killed (as by disease or accident) **3** : a person cheated, fooled, or injured ⟨a ~ of circumstances⟩
vic·tim·ise Brit var of VICTIMIZE
vic·tim·ize \ˈvik-tə-ˌmīz\ vb **-ized; -iz·ing** : to make a victim of — **vic·tim·i·za·tion** \ˌvik-tə-mə-ˈzā-shən\ n — **vic·tim·iz·er** \ˈvik-tə-ˌmī-zər\ n
vic·tim·less adj : having no victim ⟨considered gambling to be a ~ crime⟩
vic·tor \ˈvik-tər\ n : WINNER, CONQUEROR
vic·to·ria \vik-ˈtōr-ē-ə\ n : a low 4-wheeled carriage with a folding top and a raised driver's seat in front
¹**Vic·to·ri·an** \vik-ˈtōr-ē-ən\ adj **1** : of or relating to the reign of Queen Victoria of England or the art, letters, or tastes of her time **2** : typical of the standards, attitudes, or conduct of the age of Victoria esp. when considered prudish or narrow
²**Victorian** n **1** : a person and esp. an author of the Victorian period **2** : a typically large ornate house built during Queen Victoria's reign
vic·to·ri·ous \vik-ˈtōr-ē-əs\ adj **1** : having won a victory **2** : of, relating to, or characteristic of victory — **vic·to·ri·ous·ly** adv
vic·to·ry \ˈvik-tə-rē\ n, pl **-ries 1** : the overcoming of an enemy or an antagonist **2** : achievement of mastery or success in a struggle or endeavor
¹**vict·ual** \ˈvit-ᵊl\ n **1** : food fit for humans **2** pl : food supplies
²**victual** vb **-ualed** or **-ualled; -ual·ing** or **-ual·ling 1** : to supply with food **2** : to store up provisions
vict·ual·ler or **vict·ual·er** \ˈvit-ᵊl-ər\ n : one that supplies provisions (as to an army or a ship)
vi·cu·ña or **vi·cu·na** \vi-ˈkün-yə, vī-; vī-ˈkü-nə, -ˈkyü-\ n **1** : a So. American wild mammal related to the llama and alpaca; also : its wool **2** : a soft fabric woven from the wool of the vicuña; also : a sheep's wool imitation of this
vi·de \ˈvī-dē, ˈvē-ˌdā\ vb imper [L] : SEE — used to direct a reader to another item
vi·de·li·cet \və-ˈde-lə-ˌset, vī-; vi-ˈdā-li-ˌket\ adv [ME, fr. L, fr. vidēre to see + licet it is permitted] : that is to say : NAMELY

¹**vid·eo** \ˈvi-dē-ˌō\ n **1** : TELEVISION **2** : VIDEOTAPE **3** : a videotaped performance ⟨music ~s⟩
²**video** adj **1** : relating to or used in transmission or reception of the television image **2** : relating to or being images on a television screen or computer display ⟨a ~ terminal⟩
vid·eo·cas·sette \ˌvi-dē-ō-kə-ˈset\ n **1** : a case containing videotape for use with a VCR **2** : a recording (as of a movie) on a videocassette
videocassette recorder n : VCR
vid·eo·disc or **vid·eo·disk** \ˈvi-dē-ō-ˌdisk\ n **1** : a disc similar in appearance and use to a phonograph record on which programs have been recorded for playback on a television set; also : OPTICAL DISK **2** : a recording (as of a movie) on a videodisc
video game n : an electronic game played on a video screen
vid·eo·phone \ˈvid-ē-ə-ˌfōn\ n : a telephone for transmitting both audio and video signals
¹**vid·eo·tape** \ˈvid-ē-ō-ˌtāp\ n : a recording of visual images and sound made on magnetic tape; also : the magnetic tape used for such a recording
²**videotape** vb : to make a videotape of
videotape recorder n : a device for recording and playing back videotapes
vie \ˈvī\ vb **vied; vy·ing** \ˈvī-iŋ\ : to compete for superiority : CONTEND — **vi·er** \ˈvī-ər\ n
Viet·cong \vē-ˈet-ˈkäŋ, ˌvē-ət-, -ˈkòŋ\ n, pl **Vietcong** : a guerrilla soldier of the Vietnamese communist movement
Viet·nam·ese \vē-ˌet-nə-ˈmēz, ˌvē-ət-, -ˈmēs\ n, pl **Vietnamese** : a native or inhabitant of Vietnam — **Vietnamese** adj
¹**view** \ˈvyü\ n **1** : the act of seeing or examining : INSPECTION; also : SURVEY **2** : a way of looking at or regarding something **3** : ESTIMATE, JUDGMENT ⟨stated his ~s⟩ **4** : a sight (as of a landscape) regarded for its pictorial quality **5** : extent or range of vision ⟨within ~⟩ **6** : OBJECT, PURPOSE ⟨done with a ~ to promotion⟩ **7** : a picture of a scene
²**view** vb **1** : to look at attentively : EXAMINE **2** : SEE, WATCH **3** : to examine mentally : CONSIDER — **view·er** n
view·er·ship \ˈvyü-ər-ˌship\ n : a television audience esp. with respect to size or makeup
view·find·er \ˈvyü-ˌfīn-dər\ n : a device on a camera for showing the view to be included in the picture
view·point \-ˌpòint\ n : POINT OF VIEW, STANDPOINT
vi·ges·i·mal \vī-ˈje-sə-məl\ adj : based on the number 20
vig·il \ˈvi-jəl\ n **1** : a religious observance formerly held on the night before a religious feast **2** : the day before a religious feast observed as a day of spiritual preparation **3** : evening or nocturnal devotions or prayers — usu. used in pl. **4** : an act or a time of keeping awake when sleep is customary; esp : WATCH 1
vig·i·lance \ˈvi-jə-ləns\ n : the quality or state of being vigilant
vigilance committee n : a committee of vigilantes

vig·i·lant \\'vi-jə-lənt\\ *adj* : alertly watchful esp. to avoid danger — **vig·i·lant·ly** *adv*

vig·i·lan·te \\ₔvi-jə-'lan-tē\\ *n* : a member of a volunteer committee organized to suppress and punish crime summarily (as when the processes of law appear inadequate); *also* : a self-appointed doer of justice — **vig·i·lan·tism** \\-'lan-ₔti-zəm\\ *n*

¹vi·gnette \\vin-'yet\\ *n* [F, fr. MF *vignete*, fr. dim. of *vigne* vine] **1** : a small decorative design **2** : a picture (as an engraving or a photograph) that shades off gradually into the surrounding ground **3** : a short descriptive literary sketch

²vignette *vb* **vi·gnett·ed; vi·gnett·ing 1** : to finish (as a photograph) in the manner of a vignette **2** : to describe briefly

vig·or \\'vi-gər\\ *n* **1** : active strength or energy of body or mind **2** : INTENSITY, FORCE

vig·or·ous \\'vi-g-rəs\\ *adj* **1** : having vigor : ROBUST **2** : done with force and energy — **vig·or·ous·ly** *adv* — **vig·or·ous·ness** *n*

vig·our *chiefly Brit var of* VIGOR

Vi·king \\'vī-kiŋ\\ *n* [ON *vīkingr*] : any of the pirate Norsemen who raided or invaded the coasts of Europe in the 8th to 10th centuries

vil *abbr* village

vile \\'vīl\\ *adj* **vil·er; vil·est 1** : morally despicable **2** : physically repulsive : FOUL **3** : of little worth **4** : DEGRADING, IGNOMINIOUS **5** : utterly bad or contemptible ⟨~ weather⟩ — **vile·ly** \\'vīl-lē\\ *adv* — **vile·ness** *n*

vil·i·fy \\'vi-lə-ₔfī\\ *vb* **-fied; -fy·ing** : to blacken the character of with abusive language : DEFAME **syn** malign, calumniate, slander, libel, traduce — **vil·i·fi·ca·tion** \\ₔvi-lə-fə-'kā-shən\\ *n* — **vil·i·fi·er** \\'vi-lə-ₔfī-ər\\ *n*

vil·la \\'vi-lə\\ *n* **1** : a country estate **2** : the rural or suburban residence of a wealthy person

---

vil·lage \\'vi-lij\\ *n* **1** : a settlement usu. larger than a hamlet and smaller than a town **2** : an incorporated minor municipality **3** : the people of a village

vil·lag·er \\'vi-li-jər\\ *n* : an inhabitant of a village

vil·lain \\'vi-lən\\ *n* **1** : VILLEIN **2** : an evil person : SCOUNDREL

vil·lain·ess \\-lə-nəs\\ *n* : a woman who is a villain

vil·lain·ous \\-lə-nəs\\ *adj* **1** : befitting a villain : WICKED, EVIL **2** : highly objectionable : DETESTABLE **syn** vicious, iniquitous, nefarious, infamous, corrupt, degenerate — **vil·lain·ous·ly** *adv* — **vil·lain·ous·ness** *n*

vil·lainy \\-lə-nē\\ *n, pl* **-lain·ies 1** : villainous conduct; *also* : a villainous act **2** : villainous character or nature

vil·lein \\'vi-lən, -ₔlān\\ *n* **1** : a free villager of Anglo-Saxon times **2** : an unfree peasant having the status of a slave to a feudal lord

vil·len·age \\'vil-ə-nij\\ *n* **1** : the holding of land at the will of a feudal lord **2** : the status of a villein

vil·lous \\'vi-ləs\\ *adj* : covered with fine hairs or villi

vil·lus \\'vi-ləs\\ *n, pl* **vil·li** \\-ₔlī, -(ₔ)lē\\ : a slender usu. vascular process; *esp* : one of the tiny projections of the mucous membrane of the small intestine that function in the absorption of food

vim \\'vim\\ *n* : robust energy and enthusiasm : VITALITY

VIN *abbr* vehicle identification number

vin·ai·grette \\ₔvi-ni-'gret\\ *n* [F] : a sauce made typically of oil and vinegar, onions, parsley, and herbs

vin·ci·ble \\'vin-sə-bəl\\ *adj* : capable of being overcome or subdued

vin·di·cate \\'vin-də-ₔkāt\\ *vb* **-cat·ed; -cat·ing 1** : AVENGE **2** : EXONERATE, ABSOLVE **3** : CONFIRM, SUBSTANTIATE **4** : to provide defense for : JUSTIFY **5** : to maintain a right to : ASSERT — **vin·di·ca·tor** \\-ₔkā-tər\\ *n*

vin·di·ca·tion \\ₔvin-də-'kā-shən\\ *n* : a vindicating or being vindicated; *esp* : justification against denial or censure : DEFENSE

vin·dic·tive \\vin-'dik-tiv\\ *adj* **1** : disposed to revenge **2** : intended for or involving revenge **3** : VICIOUS, SPITEFUL — **vin·dic·tive·ly** *adv* — **vin·dic·tive·ness** *n*

vine \\'vīn\\ *n* [ME, fr. OF *vigne*, fr. L *vinea* vine, vineyard, fr. fem. of *vineus* of wine, fr. *vinum* wine] **1** : GRAPE **2 2** : a plant whose stem requires support and which climbs (as by tendrils) or trails along the ground; *also* : the stem of such a plant

vin·e·gar \\'vi-ni-gər\\ *n* [ME *vinegre*, fr. OF *vinaigre*, fr. *vin* wine + *aigre* keen, sour] : a sour liquid obtained by fermentation (as of cider, wine, or malt) and used in cookery and pickling

vin·e·gary \\-gə-rē\\ *adj* **1** : resembling vinegar : SOUR **2** : disagreeable in manner or disposition : CRABBED

vine·yard \\'vin-yərd\\ *n* **1** : a field of grapevines esp. to produce grapes for wine production **2** : a sphere of activity : field of endeavor

vi·nous \\'vī-nəs\\ *adj* **1** : of, relating to, or made with wine ⟨~ medications⟩ **2** : showing the effects of the use of wine ⟨~ bloodshot eyes⟩

¹vin·tage \\'vin-tij\\ *n* **1** : a season's yield of grapes or wine **2** : WINE; *esp* : a usu. superior wine which comes from a single year **3** : the act or period of gathering grapes or making wine **4** : a period of origin ⟨clothes of 1890 ~⟩

²vintage *adj* **1** : of, relating to, or produced in a particular vintage **2** : of old, recognized, and enduring interest, importance, or quality : CLASSIC ⟨~ cars⟩ **3** : of the best and most characteristic — used with a proper noun

vint·ner \\'vint-nər\\ *n* : a dealer in wines

vi·nyl \\'vīn-ᵊl\\ *n* **1** : a chemical derived from ethylene by the removal of one hydrogen atom **2** : a polymer of a vinyl compound or a product (as a textile fiber) made from one

vinyl chloride *n* : a flammable gaseous carcinogenic compound used esp. to make vinyl resins

vi·ol \\'vī-əl\\ *n* : a bowed stringed instrument chiefly of the 16th and 17th centuries having a fretted neck and usu. six strings

¹**vi·o·la** \vī-ˈō-lə, ˈvī-ə-lə\ *n* : VIOLET 1; *esp* : any of various hybrid garden plants with white, yellow, purple, or variously colored flowers that resemble but are smaller than the related pansies

²**vi·o·la** \vē-ˈō-lə\ *n* : an instrument of the violin family slightly larger and tuned lower than a violin — **vi·o·list** \-list\ *n*

vi·o·la·ble \ˈvī-ə-lə-bəl\ *adj* : capable of being violated

vi·o·late \ˈvī-ə-ˌlāt\ *vb* **-lat·ed; -lat·ing 1** : BREAK, DISREGARD ⟨∼ a law⟩ ⟨∼ a frontier⟩ **2** : RAPE **3** : PROFANE, DESECRATE **4** : INTERRUPT, DISTURB ⟨*violated* his privacy⟩ — **vi·o·la·tor** \-ˌlā-tər\ *n*

vi·o·la·tion \ˌvī-ə-ˈlā-shən\ *n* : an act or instance of violating : the state of being violated **syn** breach, infraction, trespass, infringement, transgression

vi·o·lence \ˈvī-ləns, ˈvī-ə-\ *n* **1** : exertion of physical force so as to injure or abuse **2** : injury by or as if by infringement or profanation **3** : intense or furious often destructive action or force **4** : vehement feeling or expression : INTENSITY **5** : jarring quality : DISCORDANCE **syn** compulsion, coercion, duress, constraint

vi·o·lent \-lənt\ *adj* **1** : marked by extreme force or sudden intense activity **2** : caused by or showing strong feeling ⟨∼ words⟩ **3** : EXTREME, INTENSE **4** : emotionally agitated to the point of loss of self-control **5** : caused by force : not natural ⟨∼ death⟩ — **vi·o·lent·ly** *adv*

vi·o·let \ˈvī-ə-lət\ *n* **1** : any of a genus of chiefly herbs usu. with heart-shaped leaves and both aerial and underground flowers; *esp* : one with small usu. solid-colored flowers **2** : a reddish blue color

vi·o·lin \ˌvī-ə-ˈlin\ *n* : a bowed stringed instrument with four strings that has a shallow body, a fingerboard without frets, and a curved bridge — **vi·o·lin·ist** \-ˈli-nist\ *n*

violin

vi·o·lon·cel·lo \ˌvī-ə-lən-ˈche-lō\ *n* [It] : CELLO — **vi·o·lon·cel·list** \-list\ *n*

VIP \ˌvē-ˌī-ˈpē\ *n, pl* **VIPs** \-ˈpēz\ [*very important person*] : a person of great influence or prestige; *esp* : a high official with special privileges

vi·per \ˈvī-pər\ *n* **1** : a common stout-bodied Eurasian venomous snake having a bite only rarely fatal to humans; *also* : any snake (as a pit viper) of the same family as the viper **2** : any venomous or reputedly venomous snake **3** : a vicious or treacherous person — **vi·per·ine** \-pə-ˌrīn\ *adj*

vi·ra·go \və-ˈrä-gō, -ˈrā-\ *n, pl* **-goes** *or* **-gos** [ME, fr. L, strong or heroic woman, fr. *vir* man] **1** : a loud overbearing woman **2** : a woman of great strength and courage

vi·ral \ˈvī-rəl\ *adj* : of, relating to, or caused by a virus

vir·eo \ˈvir-ē-ˌō\ *n, pl* **-e·os** [L, a small bird, fr. *virēre* to be green] : any of various small insect-eating American songbirds mostly olive green and grayish in color

¹**vir·gin** \ˈvər-jən\ *n* **1** : an unmarried woman devoted to religion **2** : an unmarried girl or woman **3** *cap* : the mother of Jesus **4** : a person who has not had sexual intercourse

²**virgin** *adj* **1** : free from stain : PURE, SPOTLESS **2** : CHASTE **3** : befitting a virgin : MODEST **4** : FRESH, UNSPOILED; *esp* : not altered by human activity ⟨∼ forest⟩ **5** : INITIAL, FIRST

¹**vir·gin·al** \ˈvər-jən-əl\ *adj* : of, relating to, or characteristic of a virgin or virginity — **vir·gin·al·ly** *adv*

²**virginal** *n* : a small rectangular spinet without legs popular in the 16th and 17th centuries

Vir·gin·ia creeper \vər-ˈjin-yə-\ *n* : a No. American vine related to the grapes that has leaves with five leaflets and bluish black berries

Virginia reel *n* : an American country-dance

vir·gin·i·ty \vər-ˈji-nə-tē\ *n, pl* **-ties 1** : the quality or state of being virgin; *esp* : MAIDENHOOD **2** : the unmarried life : CELIBACY

Vir·go \ˈvər-ˌgō\ *n* [L, lit., virgin] **1** : a zodiacal constellation between Leo and Libra usu. pictured as a young woman **2** : the 6th sign of the zodiac in astrology; *also* : one born under this sign

vir·gule \ˈvər-gyül\ *n* : a mark / used typically to denote "or" (as in *and/or*) or "per" (as in *feet/second*)

vir·i·des·cent \ˌvir-ə-ˈdes-ᵊnt\ *adj* : slightly green : GREENISH

vir·ile \ˈvir-əl\ *adj* **1** : having the nature, powers, or qualities of a man **2** : MASCULINE, MALE **3** : MASTERFUL, FORCEFUL — **vi·ril·i·ty** \və-ˈri-lə-tē\ *n*

vi·ri·on \ˈvī-rē-ˌän, ˈvir-ē-\ *n* : a complete virus particle consisting of an RNA or DNA core with a protein coat

vi·rol·o·gy \vī-ˈrä-lə-jē\ *n* : a branch of science that deals with viruses — **vi·rol·o·gist** \-jist\ *n*

vir·tu \vər-ˈtü, vir-\ *n* [It *virtù*, lit., virtue] **1** : a love of or taste for objects of art **2** : objects of art (as curios and antiques)

vir·tu·al \ˈvər-chə-wəl\ *adj* : being in essence or in effect though not formally recognized or admitted ⟨a ∼ dictator⟩

vir·tu·al·ly \ˈvər-chə-wə-lē\ *adv* **1** : almost entirely : NEARLY **2** : for all practical purposes

virtual reality *n* : an artificial environment that is experienced through sensory stimuli (as sights and sounds) provided by an interactive computer program

vir·tue \ˈvər-chü\ *n* [ME *virtu*, fr. OF, fr. L *virtus* strength, manliness, virtue, fr. *vir* man] **1** : conformity to a standard of right : MORALITY **2** : a particular moral excellence **3** : manly strength or courage : VALOR **4** : a commendable quality : MERIT **5** : active power to accomplish a given effect : POTENCY, EFFICACY **6** : chastity esp. in a woman

vir·tu·os·i·ty \ˌvər-chə-ˈwä-sə-tē\ *n, pl* **-ties** : great technical skill in the practice of a fine art

vir·tu·o·so \ˌvər-chə-ˈwō-sō, -zō\ *n, pl* **-sos** *or* **-si** \-sē, -zē\ [It] **1** : one skilled in or having a taste for the fine arts **2** : one who excels in the technique of an art; *esp* : a highly skilled musical performer **syn** expert, adept, artist, doyen, master — **virtuoso** *adj*

vir·tu·ous \ˈvər-chə-wəs\ *adj* **1** : having or showing virtue and esp. moral virtue **2** : CHASTE — **vir·tu·ous·ly** *adv*

vir·u·lent \ˈvir-ə-lənt, ˈvir-yə-\ *adj* **1** : highly infectious ⟨a ∼ germ⟩; *also* : marked by a rapid, severe, and often deadly course ⟨a ∼ disease⟩ **2** : extremely poisonous or venomous : NOXIOUS **3** : full of malice : MALIGNANT — **vir·u·lence** \-ləns\ *n* — **vir·u·lent·ly** *adv*

vi·rus \ˈvī-rəs\ *n* [L, venom, poisonous emanation] **1** : any of a large group of submicroscopic infectious agents that have an outside coat of protein around a core of RNA or DNA, that can grow and multiply only in living cells, and that cause important diseases in human beings, lower animals, and plants; *also* : a disease caused by a virus **2** : something (as a corrupting influence) that poisons the mind or spirit **3** : a computer program usu. hidden within another program that reproduces itself and inserts the copies into other programs and that usu. performs a malicious action (as destroying data)

vis *abbr* **1** visibility **2** visual

¹**vi·sa** \ˈvē-zə, -sə\ *n* [F] **1** : an endorsement by the proper authorities on a passport to show that it has been examined and the bearer may proceed **2** : a signature

by a superior official signifying approval of a document

²vi·sa \vb **vi·saed** \-zəd, -səd\; **vi·sa·ing** \-zə-iŋ, -sə-\ : to give a visa to (a passport)

vis·age \'vi-zij\ n : the face or countenance of a person or sometimes an animal; also : LOOK, APPEARANCE

¹vis-à-vis \ˌvēz-ə-'vē, ˌvēs-\ prep [F, lit., face-to-face] **1** : face-to-face with : OPPOSITE **2** : in relation to **3** : as compared with

²vis-à-vis n, pl **vis-à-vis** \same or -'vēz\ **1** : one that is face-to-face with another **2** : ESCORT **3** : COUNTERPART **4** : TÊTE-À-TÊTE

³vis-à-vis adv : in company : TOGETHER

viscera pl of VISCUS

vis·cer·al \'vi-sə-rəl\ adj **1** : felt in or as if in the viscera **2** : not intellectual : INSTINCTIVE **3** : of or relating to the viscera — **vis·cer·al·ly** adv

vis·cid \'vi-səd\ adj : VISCOUS — **vis·cid·i·ty** \vi-'si-də-tē\ n

vis·cos·i·ty \vis-'kä-sə-tē\ n, pl **-ties** : the quality of being viscous; esp : the property of resistance to flow in a fluid

vis·count \'vī-ˌkaunt\ n : a member of the British peerage ranking below an earl and above a baron

vis·count·ess \-ˌkaùn-təs\ n **1** : the wife or widow of a viscount **2** : a woman who holds the rank of viscount in her own right

vis·cous \'vis-kəs\ adj [ME viscouse, fr. LL viscosus full of birdlime, viscous, fr. L viscum mistletoe, birdlime] **1** : having the sticky consistency of glue **2** : having or characterized by viscosity

vis·cus \'vis-kəs\ n, pl **vis·cera** \'vi-sə-rə\ : an internal organ of the body; esp : one (as the heart or liver) located in the cavity of the trunk

vise \'vīs\ n [MF vis something winding, fr. L vitis vine] : a tool with two jaws for holding work that typically close by a screw or lever

vis·i·bil·i·ty \ˌvi-zə-'bi-lə-tē\ n, pl **-ties 1** : the quality, condition, or degree of being visible **2** : the degree of clearness of the atmosphere

vis·i·ble \'vi-zə-bəl\ adj : capable of being seen ⟨∼ stars⟩; also : MANIFEST, APPARENT ⟨has no ∼ means of support⟩ — **vis·i·bly** \-blē\ adv

¹vi·sion \'vi-zhən\ n **1** : something seen otherwise than by ordinary sight (as in a dream or trance) **2** : a vivid picture created by the imagination **3** : the act or power of imagination **4** : unusual wisdom in foreseeing what is going to happen **5** : the act or power of seeing : SIGHT **6** : something seen; esp : a lovely sight

²vision vb : IMAGINE, ENVISION

¹vi·sion·ary \'vi-zhə-ˌner-ē\ adj **1** : of the nature of a vision : ILLUSORY, UNREAL **2** : not practical : UTOPIAN **3** : seeing or likely to see visions : given to dreaming or imagining **syn** imaginary, fantastic, chimerical, quixotic

²visionary n, pl **-ar·ies 1** : one whose ideas or projects are impractical : DREAMER **2** : one who sees visions

¹vis·it \'vi-zət\ vb **1** : to go to see in order to comfort or help **2** : to call on either as an act of courtesy or friendship **3** : to dwell with for a time as a guest **4** : to come to or upon as a reward, affliction, or punishment **5** : INFLICT **6** : to make a visit or regular or frequent visits **7** : CHAT, CONVERSE — **vis·it·able** adj

²visit n **1** : a short stay : CALL **2** : a brief residence as a guest **3** : a journey to and stay at a place **4** : a formal or professional call (as by a doctor)

vis·i·tant \'vi-zənt\ n : VISITOR

vis·i·ta·tion \ˌvi-zə-'tā-shən\ n **1** : VISIT; esp : an official visit **2** : a special dispensation of divine favor or wrath; also : a severe trial

visiting nurse n : a nurse employed to visit sick persons or perform public health services in a community

vis·i·tor \'vi-zə-tər\ n : one that visits

vi·sor \'vī-zər\ n **1** : the front piece of a helmet; esp : a movable upper piece **2** : VIZARD **3** : a projecting part

(as on a cap) to shade the eyes — **vi·sored** \-zərd\ adj

vis·ta \'vis-tə\ n **1** : a distant view through or along an avenue or opening **2** : an extensive mental view over a series of years or events

VISTA abbr Volunteers in Service to America

¹vi·su·al \'vi-zhə-wəl\ adj **1** : of, relating to, or used in vision ⟨∼ organs⟩ **2** : perceived by vision ⟨a ∼ impression⟩ **3** : VISIBLE **4** : done by sight only ⟨∼ navigation⟩ **5** : of or relating to instruction by means of sight ⟨∼ aids⟩ — **vi·su·al·ly** adv

²visual n : something (as a picture, chart, or film) that appeals to the sight and is used for illustration, demonstration, or promotion — usu. used in pl.

vi·su·al·ise Brit var of VISUALIZE

vi·su·al·ize \'vi-zhə-wə-ˌlīz\ vb **-ized; -iz·ing** : to make visible; esp : to form a mental image of — **vi·su·al·i·za·tion** \ˌvi-zhə-wə-lə-'zā-shən\ n — **vi·su·al·iz·er** n

vi·ta \'vē-tə, 'vī-\ n, pl **vi·tae** \'vē-ˌtī, 'vī-tē\ [L, lit., life] : a brief autobiographical sketch

vi·tal \'vīt-ᵊl\ adj **1** : concerned with or necessary to the maintenance of life **2** : full of life and vigor : ANIMATED **3** : of, relating to, or characteristic of life or living beings **4** : FATAL, MORTAL ⟨∼ wound⟩ **5** : FUNDAMENTAL, INDISPENSABLE — **vi·tal·ly** adv

vi·tal·i·ty \vī-'ta-lə-tē\ n, pl **-ties 1** : the property distinguishing the living from the nonliving **2** : mental and physical vigor **3** : enduring quality **4** : ANIMATION, LIVELINESS

vi·tal·ize \'vīt-ᵊl-ˌīz\ vb **-ized; -iz·ing** : to impart life or vigor to : ANIMATE — **vi·tal·i·za·tion** \ˌvīt-ᵊl-ə-'zā-shən\ n

vi·tals \'vīt-ᵊlz\ n pl **1** : vital organs (as the heart and brain) **2** : essential parts

vital signs n pl : the pulse rate, respiratory rate, body temperature, and often blood pressure of a person

vital statistics n pl : statistics dealing with births, deaths, marriages, health, and disease

vi·ta·min \'vī-tə-mən\ n : any of various organic substances that are essential in tiny amounts to the nutrition of most animals and some plants and are mostly obtained from foods

vitamin A n : any of several vitamins (as from egg yolk or fish-liver oils) required esp. for good vision

vitamin B n **1** : VITAMIN B COMPLEX **2** or **vitamin B₁** : THIAMINE

vitamin B complex n : a group of vitamins that are found widely in foods and are essential for normal function of certain enzymes and for growth

vitamin B₆ \-'bē-'siks\ n : any of several compounds that are considered essential to vertebrate nutrition

vitamin B₁₂ \-'bē-'twelv\ n : a complex cobalt=containing compound that occurs esp. in liver and is essential to normal blood formation, neural function, and growth; also : any of several compounds of similar action

vitamin C n : a vitamin found esp. in fruits and vegetables that is needed by the body to prevent scurvy

vitamin D n : any or all of several vitamins that are needed for normal bone and tooth structure and are found esp. in fish-liver oils, egg yolk, and milk or are produced by the body in response to ultraviolet light

vitamin E n : any of various oily fat-soluble liquid vitamins whose absence in the body is associated with such ailments as infertility, the breakdown of muscles, and vascular problems and which are found esp. in leaves and in seed germ oils

vitamin K n [Dan koagulation coagulation] : any of several vitamins needed for blood to clot properly

vi·ti·ate \'vi-shē-ˌāt\ vb **-at·ed; -at·ing 1** : CONTAMINATE, POLLUTE; also : DEBASE, PERVERT **2** : to make legally ineffective : INVALIDATE — **vi·ti·a·tion** \ˌvi-shē-'ā-shən\ n — **vi·ti·a·tor** \'vi-shē-ˌā-tər\ n

vi·ti·cul·ture \'vi-tə-ˌkəl-chər\ n : the growing of grapes — **vi·ti·cul·tur·al** \ˌvi-tə-'kəl-chə-rəl\ adj — **vi·ti·cul·tur·ist** \-rist\ n

vit·re·ous \'vi-trē-əs\ adj **1** : of, relating to, or resembling glass : GLASSY ⟨∼ rocks⟩ **2** : of, relating to, or being the clear colorless transparent jelly (**vitreous humor**) behind the lens in the eyeball

vit·ri·ol \'vi-trē-əl\ *n* : something resembling acid in being caustic, corrosive, or biting — **vit·ri·ol·ic** \ˌvi-trē-'ä-lik\ *adj*

vit·tles \'vit-ᵊlz\ *n pl* : VICTUALS

vi·tu·per·ate \vī-'tü-pə-ˌrāt, və-, -'tyü-\ *vb* -**at·ed**; -**at·ing** : to abuse in words : SCOLD **syn** revile, berate, rate, upbraid, rail, lash — **vi·tu·per·a·tive** \-'tü-pə-rə-tiv, -ˌrā-\ *adj* — **vi·tu·per·a·tive·ly** *adv*

vi·tu·per·a·tion \(ˌ)vī-tü-pə-'rā-shən, və-, -tyü-\ *n* : lengthy harsh criticism or abuse

vi·va \'vē-və\ *interj* [It & Sp, long live] — used to express goodwill or approval

vi·va·ce \vē-'vä-chä\ *adv or adj* [It] : in a brisk spirited manner — used as a direction in music

vi·va·cious \və-'vā-shəs, vī-\ *adj* : lively in temper, conduct, or spirit : SPRIGHTLY — **vi·va·cious·ly** *adv* — **vi·va·cious·ness** *n*

vi·vac·i·ty \-'va-sə-tē\ *n* : the quality or state of being vivacious

vi·va vo·ce \ˌvī-və-'vō-sē, ˌvē-və-'vō-ˌchā\ *adj* [ML, with the living voice] : expressed or conducted by word of mouth : ORAL — **viva voce** *adv*

viv·id \'vi-vəd\ *adj* **1** : having the appearance of vigorous life **2** : BRILLIANT, INTENSE ⟨a ∼ red⟩ **3** : producing a strong impression on the senses; *esp* : producing distinct mental pictures ⟨a ∼ description⟩ — **viv·id·ly** *adv* — **viv·id·ness** *n*

viv·i·fy \'vi-və-ˌfī\ *vb* -**fied**; -**fy·ing 1** : to put life into : ANIMATE **2** : to make vivid — **viv·i·fi·ca·tion** \ˌvi-və-fə-'kā-shən\ *n* — **viv·i·fi·er** *n*

vi·vip·a·rous \vī-'vi-pə-rəs, və-\ *adj* : producing living young from within the body rather than from eggs — **vi·vi·par·i·ty** \ˌvī-və-'par-ə-tē, ˌvi-\ *n*

viv·i·sec·tion \ˌvi-və-'sek-shən, 'vi-və-ˌsek-\ *n* : the cutting of or operation on a living animal; *also* : animal experimentation esp. if causing distress to the subject

vix·en \'vik-sən\ *n* **1** : an ill-tempered scolding woman **2** : a female fox

viz *abbr* videlicet

viz·ard \'vi-zərd\ *n* : a mask for disguise or protection

vi·zier \və-'zir\ *n* : a high executive officer of many Muslim countries

VJ *abbr* veejay

VOA *abbr* Voice of America

voc *abbr* **1** vocational **2** vocative

vocab *abbr* vocabulary

vo·ca·ble \'vō-kə-bəl\ *n* : TERM, NAME; *esp* : a word as such without regard to its meaning

vo·cab·u·lary \vō-'ka-byə-ˌler-ē\ *n, pl* -**lar·ies 1** : a list or collection of words usu. alphabetically arranged and defined or explained : LEXICON **2** : a stock of words in a language used by a class or individual or in relation to a subject

vocabulary entry *n* : a word (as the noun *book*), hyphened or open compound (as the verb *cross-refer* or the noun *boric acid*), word element (as the affix *-an*), abbreviation (as *agt*), verbalized symbol (as *Na*), or term (as *master of ceremonies*) entered alphabetically in a dictionary for the purpose of definition or identification or expressly included as an inflected form (as the noun *mice* or the verb *saw*) or as a derived form (as the noun *godlessness* or the adverb *globally*) or related phrase (as in *spite of*) run on at its base word and usu. set in a type (as boldface) readily distinguishable from that of the lightface running text which defines, explains, or identifies the entry

¹vo·cal \'vō-kəl\ *adj* **1** : uttered by the voice : ORAL **2** : relating to, composed or arranged for, or sung by the human voice ⟨∼ music⟩ **3** : given to expressing oneself freely or insistently : OUTSPOKEN **4** : of or relating to the voice

²vocal *n* **1** : a vocal sound **2** : a vocal composition or its performance

vocal cords *n pl* : either of two pairs of elastic folds of mucous membrane that project into the cavity of the larynx and function in the production of vocal sounds

vo·cal·ic \vō-'ka-lik\ *adj* : of, relating to, or functioning as a vowel

vo·cal·ise *Brit var of* VOCALIZE

vo·cal·ist \'vō-kə-list\ *n* : SINGER

vo·cal·ize \-ˌlīz\ *vb* -**ized**; -**iz·ing 1** : to give vocal expression to : UTTER; *esp* : SING **2** : to make voiced rather than voiceless — **vo·cal·iz·er** *n*

vo·ca·tion \vō-'kā-shən\ *n* **1** : a summons or strong inclination to a particular state or course of action ⟨religious ∼⟩ **2** : regular employment : OCCUPATION, PROFESSION — **vo·ca·tion·al** \-shə-nəl\ *adj*

vo·ca·tion·al·ism \-shə-nə-ˌli-zəm\ *n* : emphasis on vocational training in education

voc·a·tive \'vä-kə-tiv\ *adj* : of, relating to, or constituting a grammatical case marking the one addressed — **vocative** *n*

vo·cif·er·ate \vō-'si-fə-ˌrāt\ *vb* -**at·ed**; -**at·ing** [L *vociferari*, fr. *voc-, vox* voice + *ferre* to bear] : to cry out loudly : CLAMOR, SHOUT — **vo·cif·er·a·tion** \-ˌsi-fə-'rā-shən\ *n*

vo·cif·er·ous \vō-'si-fə-rəs\ *adj* : making or given to loud outcry — **vo·cif·er·ous·ly** *adv* — **vo·cif·er·ous·ness** *n*

vod·ka \'väd-kə\ *n* [Russ, fr. *voda* water] : a colorless liquor distilled from a mash

vogue \'vōg\ *n* [MF, action of rowing, course, fashion, fr. It *voga*, fr. *vogare* to row] **1** : popular acceptance or favor : POPULARITY **2** : a period of popularity **3** : one that is in fashion at a particular time **syn** mode, fad, rage, craze, trend, fashion

vogu·ish \'vō-gish\ *adj* **1** : FASHIONABLE, SMART **2** : suddenly or temporarily popular

¹voice \'vȯis\ *n* **1** : sound produced through the mouth by vertebrates and esp. by human beings in speaking or shouting **2** : musical sound produced by the vocal cords : the power to produce such sound; *also* : one of the melodic parts in a vocal or instrumental composition **3** : the vocal organs as a means of tone production ⟨train the ∼⟩ **4** : sound produced by vibration of the vocal cords as heard in vowels and some consonants **5** : the power of speaking **6** : a sound suggesting a voice ⟨the ∼ of the sea⟩ **7** : an instrument or medium of expression **8** : a choice, opinion, or wish openly expressed; *also* : right of expression **9** : distinction of form of a verb to indicate the relation of the subject to the action expressed by the verb

²voice *vb* **voiced; voic·ing** : to give voice or expression to : UTTER ⟨∼ a complaint⟩ **syn** express, vent, air, ventilate

voice box *n* : LARYNX

voiced \'vȯist\ *adj* **1** : having a voice ⟨soft-*voiced*⟩ **2** : uttered with voice ⟨a ∼ consonant⟩ — **voiced·ness** \'vȯist-nəs, 'vȯi-səd-nəs\ *n*

voice·less \'vȯis-ləs\ *adj* **1** : having no voice **2** : not pronounced with voice — **voice·less·ly** *adv* — **voice·less·ness** *n*

voice mail *n* : an electronic communication system in which spoken messages are recorded for later playback to the intended recipient

voice-over *n* : the voice in a film or television program of a person who is heard but not seen or not seen talking

voice·print \'vȯis-ˌprint\ *n* : an individually distinctive pattern of voice characteristics that is spectrographically produced

¹void \'vȯid\ *adj* **1** : UNOCCUPIED, VACANT **2** : containing nothing : EMPTY **3** : LACKING, DEVOID ⟨proposals ∼ of sense⟩ **4** : VAIN, USELESS **5** : of no legal force or effect : NULL

²void *n* **1** : empty space : EMPTINESS, VACUUM **2** : a feeling of want or hollowness

³**void** *vb* **1** : to make or leave empty; *also* : VACATE, LEAVE **2** : DISCHARGE, EMIT ⟨∼ urine⟩ **3** : to render void : ANNUL, NULLIFY ⟨∼ a contract⟩ — **void•able** *adj* — **void•er** *n*

voi•là \vwä-ˈlä\ *interj* [F] — used to call attention or to express satisfaction or approval

voile \ˈvȯil\ *n* : a sheer fabric used for women's clothing and curtains

vol *abbr* **1** volume **2** volunteer

vol•a•tile \ˈvä-lət-ᵊl\ *adj* **1** : readily becoming a vapor at a relatively low temperature ⟨a ∼ liquid⟩ **2** : likely to change suddenly ⟨a ∼ temper⟩ — **vol•a•til•i•ty** \ˌvä-lə-ˈti-lə-tē\ *n* — **vol•a•til•ize** \ˈvä-lət-ᵊl-ˌīz\ *vb*

vol•ca•nic \väl-ˈka-nik\ *adj* **1** : of, relating to, or produced by a volcano **2** : explosively violent

vol•ca•nism \ˈväl-kə-ˌni-zəm\ *n* : volcanic action or activity

vol•ca•no \ˈväl-ˈkā-nō\ *n, pl* **-noes** *or* **-nos** [It *vulcano*, fr. L *Volcanus, Vulcanus* Roman god of fire and metalworking] : an opening in the earth's crust from which molten rock and steam issue; *also* : a hill or mountain composed of the ejected material

vol•ca•nol•o•gy \ˌväl-kə-ˈnä-lə-jē\ *n* : a branch of geology that deals with volcanic phenomena — **vol•ca•nol•o•gist** \-kə-ˈnä-lə-jist\ *n*

vole \ˈvōl\ *n* : any of various small rodents that are closely related to the lemmings and muskrats

vo•li•tion \vō-ˈli-shən\ *n* **1** : the act or the power of making a choice or decision : WILL **2** : a choice or decision made — **vo•li•tion•al** \-ˈli-shə-nəl\ *adj*

¹**vol•ley** \ˈvä-lē\ *n, pl* **volleys 1** : a flight of missiles (as arrows) **2** : simultaneous discharge of a number of missile weapons **3** : an act of volleying **4** : a burst of many things at once ⟨a ∼ of angry letters⟩

²**volley** *vb* **vol•leyed; vol•ley•ing 1** : to discharge or become discharged in or as if in a volley **2** : to hit an object of play in the air before it touches the ground

vol•ley•ball \-ˌbȯl\ *n* : a game played by volleying an inflated ball over a net; *also* : the ball used in this game

volt \ˈvōlt\ *n* : the meter-kilogram-second unit of electrical potential difference and electromotive force equal to the difference in potential between two points in a wire carrying a constant current of one ampere when the power dissipated between the points is equal to one watt

volt•age \ˈvōl-tij\ *n* : potential difference measured in volts

volt•a•ic \väl-ˈtā-ik, vōl-\ *adj* : of, relating to, or producing direct electric current by chemical action

volte–face \ˌvȯlt-ˈfäs, ˌvȯl-tə-\ *n* : a reversal in policy : ABOUT-FACE

volt•me•ter \ˈvōlt-ˌmē-tər\ *n* : an instrument for measuring in volts the difference in potential between different points of an electrical circuit

vol•u•ble \ˈväl-yə-bəl\ *adj* : fluent and smooth in speech : GLIB **syn** garrulous, loquacious, talkative — **vol•u•bil•i•ty** \ˌväl-yə-ˈbi-lə-tē\ *n* — **vol•u•bly** \ˈväl-yə-blē\ *adv*

vol•ume \ˈväl-yəm\ *n* [ME, fr. MF, fr. L *volumen* roll, scroll, fr. *volvere* to roll] **1** : a series of printed sheets bound typically in book form; *also* : an arbitrary number of issues of a periodical **2** : space occupied as measured by cubic units ⟨the ∼ of a cylinder⟩ **3** : sufficient matter to fill a book ⟨her glance spoke ∼s⟩ **4** : AMOUNT ⟨increasing ∼ of business⟩ **5** : the degree of loudness of a sound **syn** body, bulk, mass

vo•lu•mi•nous \və-ˈlü-mə-nəs\ *adj* : having or marked by great volume or bulk : LARGE — **vo•lu•mi•nous•ly** *adv* — **vo•lu•mi•nous•ness** *n*

¹**vol•un•tary** \ˈvä-lən-ˌter-ē\ *adj* **1** : done, made, or given freely and without compulsion ⟨a ∼ sacrifice⟩ **2** : done on purpose : INTENTIONAL ⟨∼ manslaughter⟩ **3** : of, relating to, or regulated by the will ⟨∼ behavior⟩ **4** : having power of free choice **5** : provided or supported by voluntary action ⟨a ∼ organization⟩ **syn** deliberate, willful, willing, witting — **vol•un•tar•i•ly** \ˌvä-lən-ˈter-ə-lē\ *adv*

²**voluntary** *n, pl* **-tar•ies** : an organ solo played in a religious service

voluntary muscle *n* : muscle (as most striated muscle) under voluntary control

¹**vol•un•teer** \ˌvä-lən-ˈtir\ *n* **1** : a person who voluntarily undertakes a service or duty **2** : a plant growing spontaneously esp. from seeds lost from a previous crop

²**volunteer** *vb* **1** : to offer or give voluntarily **2** : to offer oneself as a volunteer

vo•lup•tu•ary \və-ˈləp-chə-ˌwer-ē\ *n, pl* **-ar•ies** : a person whose chief interest in life is the indulgence of sensual appetites

vo•lup•tu•ous \-chə-wəs\ *adj* **1** : giving sensual gratification **2** : given to or spent in enjoyment of luxury or pleasure **syn** luxurious, epicurean, sensuous — **vo•lup•tu•ous•ly** *adv* — **vo•lup•tu•ous•ness** *n*

vo•lute \və-ˈlüt\ *n* : a spiral or scroll-shaped decoration

¹**vom•it** \ˈvä-mət\ *n* : an act or instance of throwing up the contents of the stomach through the mouth; *also* : the matter thrown up

²**vomit** *vb* **1** : to throw up the contents of the stomach through the mouth **2** : to belch forth : GUSH

voo•doo \ˈvü-dü\ *n, pl* **voodoos 1** : a religion that is derived from African polytheism and is practiced chiefly in Haiti **2** : a person who deals in spells and necromancy; *also* : ¹SPELL 1 **3** : a charm used in voodoo — **voodoo** *adj*

voo•doo•ism \-ˌi-zəm\ *n* **1** : VOODOO 1 **2** : the practice of witchcraft

vo•ra•cious \vȯ-ˈrā-shəs, və-\ *adj* **1** : having a huge appetite : RAVENOUS **2** : very eager ⟨a ∼ reader⟩ **syn** gluttonous, ravening, rapacious — **vo•ra•cious•ly** *adv* — **vo•ra•cious•ness** *n* — **vo•rac•i•ty** \-ˈra-sə-tē\ *n*

vor•tex \ˈvȯr-ˌteks\ *n, pl* **vor•ti•ces** \ˈvȯr-tə-ˌsēz\ *also* **vor•tex•es** \ˈvȯr-ˌtek-səz\ : WHIRLPOOL; *also* : something resembling a whirlpool

vo•ta•ry \ˈvō-tə-rē\ *n, pl* **-ries 1** : ENTHUSIAST, DEVO-

TEE; *also* : a devoted adherent or admirer **2** : a devout or zealous worshiper

¹**vote** \'vōt\ *n* [ME, fr. L *votum* vow, wish, fr. *vovēre* to vow] **1** : a choice or opinion of a person or body of persons expressed usu. by a ballot, spoken word, or raised hand; *also* : the ballot, word, or gesture used to express a choice or opinion **2** : the decision reached by voting **3** : the right of suffrage **4** : a group of voters with some common characteristics ⟨the big city ∼⟩ — **vote·less** *adj*

²**vote** *vb* **vot·ed; vot·ing 1** : to cast a vote **2** : to elect, decide, pass, defeat, grant, or make legal by a vote **3** : to declare by general agreement **4** : to offer as a suggestion : PROPOSE **5** : to cause to vote esp. in a given way — **vot·er** *n*

vo·tive \'vō-tiv\ *adj* : consisting of or expressing a vow, wish, or desire

vou *abbr* voucher

vouch \'vaùch\ *vb* **1** : PROVE, SUBSTANTIATE **2** : to verify by examining documentary evidence **3** : to give a guarantee **4** : to supply supporting evidence or testimony; *also* : to give personal assurance

vouch·er \'vaù-chər\ *n* **1** : an act of vouching **2** : one that vouches for another **3** : a documentary record of a business transaction **4** : a written affidavit or authorization **5** : a form indicating a credit against future purchases or expenditures

vouch·safe \vaùch-'sāf\ *vb* **vouch·safed; vouch·saf·ing** : to grant or give as or as if a privilege or a special favor — **vouch·safe·ment** *n*

¹**vow** \'vaù\ *n* : a solemn promise or statement; *esp* : one by which a person is bound to an act, service, or condition ⟨marriage ∼s⟩

²**vow** *vb* **1** : to make a vow or as a vow **2** : to bind or commit by a vow — **vow·er** *n*

vow·el \'vaù-əl\ *n* **1** : a speech sound produced without obstruction or friction in the mouth **2** : a letter representing such a sound

vox po·pu·li \'väks-'pä-pyə-ˌlī\ *n* [L, voice of the people] : popular sentiment

¹**voy·age** \'vòi-ij\ *n* [ME, fr. OF *voiage,* fr. LL *viaticum,* fr. L, traveling money, fr. neut. of *viaticus* of a journey, fr. *via* way] : a journey esp. by water from one place or country to another

²**voyage** *vb* **voy·aged; voy·ag·ing** : to take or make a voyage — **voy·ag·er** *n*

voya·geur \ˌvòi-ə-'zhər, ˌvwä-yä-\ *n* [CanF] : a person employed by a fur company to transport goods to and from remote stations esp. in the Canadian Northwest

voy·eur \vwä-'yər, vòi-'ər\ *n* : one who habitually seeks sexual stimulation by visual means — **voy·eur·ism** \-ˌi-zəm\ *n*

VP *abbr* **1** verb phrase **2** vice president

vs *abbr* **1** verse **2** versus

vss *abbr* **1** verses **2** versions

V/STOL *abbr* vertical or short takeoff and landing

Vt *or* **VT** *abbr* Vermont

VTOL *abbr* vertical takeoff and landing

VTR *abbr* videotape recorder

vul·ca·nise *Brit var of* VULCANIZE

vul·ca·nize \'vəl-kə-ˌnīz\ *vb* **-nized; -niz·ing** : to treat rubber or rubberlike material chemically to give useful properties (as elasticity and strength)

Vulg *abbr* Vulgate

vul·gar \'vəl-gər\ *adj* [ME, fr. L *vulgaris* of the mob, vulgar, fr. *vulgus* mob, common people] **1** : VERNACULAR ⟨the ∼ tongue⟩ **2** : of or relating to the common people : GENERAL, COMMON **3** : lacking cultivation or refinement : BOORISH; *also* : offensive to good taste or refined feelings **syn** gross, obscene, ribald, dirty, indecent, profane — **vul·gar·ly** *adv*

vul·gar·ian \ˌvəl-'gar-ē-ən\ *n* : a vulgar person

vul·gar·ism \'vəl-gə-ˌri-zəm\ *n* **1** : VULGARITY **2** : a word or expression originated or used chiefly by illiterate persons **3** : a coarse expression : OBSCENITY

vul·gar·i·ty \ˌvəl-'gar-ə-tē\ *n, pl* **-ties 1** : something vulgar **2** : the quality or state of being vulgar

vul·gar·ize \'vəl-gə-ˌrīz\ *vb* **-ized; -iz·ing** : to make vulgar — **vul·gar·i·za·tion** \ˌvəl-gə-rə-'zā-shən\ *n* — **vul·gar·iz·er** \'vəl-gə-ˌrī-zər\ *n*

Vul·gate \'vəl-ˌgāt\ *n* [ML *vulgata,* fr. LL *vulgata editio* edition in general circulation] : a Latin version of the Bible used by the Roman Catholic Church

vul·ner·a·ble \'vəl-nə-rə-bəl\ *adj* **1** : capable of being wounded : susceptible to wounds **2** : open to attack **3** : liable to increased penalties in contract bridge — **vul·ner·a·bil·i·ty** \ˌvəl-nə-rə-'bi-lə-tē\ *n* — **vul·ner·a·bly** \'vəl-nə-rə-blē\ *adv*

vul·pine \'vəl-ˌpīn\ *adj* : of, relating to, or resembling a fox esp. in cunning

vul·ture \'vəl-chər\ *n* **1** : any of various large birds (as a turkey vulture) related to the hawks, eagles, and falcons but having weaker claws and the head usu. naked and living chiefly on carrion **2** : a rapacious person

vul·va \'vəl-və\ *n, pl* **vul·vae** \-ˌvē\ [NL, fr. L, womb, female genitals] : the external parts of the female genital organs

vv *abbr* **1** verses **2** vice versa

vying *pres part of* VIE

W

¹**w** \'də-bəl-(ˌ)yü\ *n, pl* **w's** *or* **ws** *often cap* : the 23d letter of the English alphabet

²**w** *abbr, often cap* **1** water **2** watt **3** week **4** weight **5** west; western **6** wide; width **7** wife **8** with

W *symbol* [G *Wolfram*] tungsten

WA *abbr* **1** Washington **2** Western Australia

wacky \'wa-kē\ *adj* **wack·i·er; -est** : ECCENTRIC, CRAZY

¹**wad** \'wäd\ *n* **1** : a little mass, bundle, or tuft ⟨∼s of clay⟩ **2** : a soft mass of usu. light fibrous material **3** : a pliable plug (as of felt) used to retain a powder charge (as in a cartridge) **4** : a considerable amount (as of money) **5** : a roll of paper money

²**wad** *vb* **wad·ded; wad·ding 1** : to push a wad into ⟨∼ a gun⟩ **2** : to form into a wad **3** : to hold in by a wad ⟨∼ a bullet in a gun⟩ **4** : to stuff or line with a wad : PAD

wad·ding \'wä-diŋ\ *n* **1** : WADS; *also* : material for making wads **2** : a soft mass or sheet of short loose fibers used for stuffing or padding

wad·dle \'wäd-ᵊl\ *vb* **wad·dled; wad·dling** : to walk with short steps swaying from side to side like a duck — **waddle** *n*

wade \'wäd\ *vb* **wad·ed; wad·ing 1** : to step in or through a medium (as water) more resistant than air **2** : to move or go with difficulty or labor and often with determination ⟨∼ through a dull book⟩ — **wad·able** *or* **wade·able** \'wä-də-bəl\ *adj* — **wade** *n*

wad·er \'wä-dər\ *n* **1** : one that wades **2** : SHOREBIRD; *also* : WADING BIRD **3** *pl* : a waterproof garment consisting of pants with attached boots for wading

wa·di \'wä-dē\ *n* [Ar *wādiy*] : a streambed of southwest Asia and northern Africa that is dry except in the rainy season

wading bird *n* : any of an order of long-legged birds (as sandpipers, cranes, or herons) that wade in water in search of food

wa·fer \'wä-fər\ *n* **1** : a thin crisp cake or cracker **2** : a thin round piece of unleavened bread used in the Eucharist **3** : something (as a piece of candy) that resembles a wafer

waf·fle \'wä-fəl\ *n* : a soft but crisped cake of batter cooked in a special hinged metal utensil (**waffle iron**)

¹**waft** \'wäft, 'waft\ *vb* : to cause to move or go lightly by or as if by the impulse of wind or waves

²waft *n* **1** : a slight breeze : PUFF **2** : the act of waving

¹wag \\'wag\\ *vb* **wagged; wag·ging 1** : to sway or swing shortly from side to side or to-and-fro ⟨the dog *wagged* his tail⟩ **2** : to move in chatter or gossip ⟨scandal caused tongues to ~⟩

²wag *n* : an act of wagging : a wagging movement

³wag *n* : WIT, JOKER

¹wage \\'wāj\\ *n* **1** : payment for labor or services usu. according to contract **2** *pl* : RECOMPENSE, REWARD

²wage *vb* **waged; wag·ing 1** : to engage in : CARRY ON ⟨~ a war⟩ **2** : to be in process of being waged

¹wa·ger \\'wā-jər\\ *n* **1** : BET, STAKE **2** : something on which bets are laid : GAMBLE

²wager *vb* : BET — **wa·ger·er** *n*

wag·gery \\'wa-gə-rē\\ *n, pl* **-ger·ies 1** : mischievous merriment : PLEASANTRY **2** : JEST, TRICK

wag·gish \\'wa-gish\\ *adj* **1** : resembling or characteristic of a wag : MISCHIEVOUS **2** : SPORTIVE, HUMOROUS

wag·gle \\'wa-gəl\\ *vb* **wag·gled; wag·gling** : to move backward and forward or from side to side : WAG — **waggle** *n*

wag·on chiefly Brit var of WAGON

wag·on \\'wa-gən\\ *n* **1** : a 4-wheeled vehicle; *esp* : one drawn by animals and used for freight or merchandise **2** : PADDY WAGON **3** : a child's 4-wheeled cart **4** : STATION WAGON

wag·on·er \\'wa-gə-nər\\ *n* : the driver of a wagon

wag·on·ette \\,wa-gə-'net\\ *n* : a light wagon with two facing seats along the sides behind a cross seat in front

wa·gon-lit \\,và-gōⁿ-'lē\\ *n, pl* **wagons–lits** *or* **wagon–lits** \\same *or* -'lēz\\ [F, fr. *wagon* railroad car + *lit* bed] : a railroad sleeping car

wagon train *n* : a column of wagons traveling overland

wag·tail \\'wag-,tāl\\ *n* : any of various slender-bodied mostly Old World birds with a long tail that jerks up and down

wa·hi·ne \\wä-'hē-nē, -,nä\\ *n* **1** : a Polynesian woman **2** : a female surfer

wa·hoo \\'wä-,hü\\ *n, pl* **wahoos** : a large vigorous food and sport fish related to the mackerel and found in warm seas

waif \\'wāf\\ *n* **1** : something found without an owner and esp. by chance **2** : a stray person or animal; *esp* : a homeless child

wail \\'wāl\\ *vb* **1** : LAMENT, WEEP **2** : to make a sound suggestive of a mournful cry **3** : COMPLAIN — **wail** *n*

wail·ful \\-fəl\\ *adj* : SORROWFUL, MOURNFUL **syn** melancholy, doleful, lugubrious, lamentable, plaintive, woeful — **wail·ful·ly** *adv*

wain \\'wān\\ *n* : a usu. large heavy farm wagon

wain·scot \\'wān-skət, -,skōt, -,skät\\ *n* **1** : a usu. paneled wooden lining of an interior wall of a room **2** : the lower part of an interior wall when finished differently from the rest — **wainscot** *vb*

wain·scot·ing *or* **wain·scot·ting** \\-,skō-tiŋ, -,skä-, -skə-\\ *n* : material for a wainscot; *also* : WAINSCOT

waist \\'wāst\\ *n* **1** : the narrowed part of the body between the chest and hips **2** : a part resembling the human waist esp. in narrowness or central position ⟨the

~ of a ship⟩ **3** : a garment or part of a garment (as a blouse or bodice) for the upper part of the body

waist·band \\-,band\\ *n* : a band (as on trousers or a skirt) that fits around the waist

waist·coat \\'wes-kət, 'wāst-,kōt\\ *n, chiefly Brit* : VEST 1

waist·line \\'wāst-,līn\\ *n* **1** : a line around the waist at its narrowest part; *also* : the length of this **2** : the line at which the bodice and skirt of a dress meet

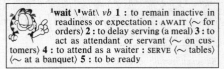

¹wait \\'wāt\\ *vb* **1** : to remain inactive in readiness or expectation ⟨~ for orders⟩ **2** : to delay serving (a meal) **3** : to act as attendant or servant ⟨~ on customers⟩ **4** : to attend as a waiter : SERVE ⟨~ tables⟩ ⟨~ at a banquet⟩ **5** : to be ready

²wait *n* **1** : a position of concealment usu. with intent to attack or surprise ⟨lie in ~⟩ **2** : an act or period of waiting

wait·er \\'wā-tər\\ *n* **1** : one that waits on another; *esp* : a person who waits tables **2** : TRAY

waiting game *n* : a strategy in which one or more participants withhold action in the hope of an opportunity for more effective action later

waiting room *n* : a room (as at a doctor's office) for the use of persons who are waiting

wait·per·son \\'wāt-,pər-sən\\ *n* : a waiter or waitress

wait·ress \\'wā-trəs\\ *n* : a woman who waits tables

waive \\'wāv\\ *vb* **waived; waiv·ing** [ME *weiven*, fr. OF *weyver*, fr. *waif* lost, unclaimed] **1** : to give up claim to ⟨*waived* his right to a trial⟩ **2** : POSTPONE

waiv·er \\'wā-vər\\ *n* : the act of waiving right, claim, or privilege; *also* : a document containing a declaration of such an act

¹wake \\'wāk\\ *vb* **woke** \\'wōk\\ *also* **waked** \\'wākt\\; **woken** \\'wō-kən\\ *also* **waked** *or* **woke; wak·ing 1** : to be or remain awake; *esp* : to keep watch (as over a corpse) **2** : AWAKE, AWAKEN ⟨the baby *woke* up early⟩

²wake *n* **1** : the state of being awake **2** : a watch held over the body of a dead person prior to burial

³wake *n* : the track left by a ship in the water; *also* : a track left behind

wake·ful \\'wāk-fəl\\ *adj* : not sleeping or able to sleep : SLEEPLESS, ALERT — **wake·ful·ness** *n*

wak·en \\'wā-kən\\ *vb* : WAKE

wake-rob·in \\'wāk-,rä-bən\\ *n* : TRILLIUM

wak·ing \\'wā-kiŋ\\ *adj* : passed in a conscious or alert state ⟨every ~ hour⟩

wale \\'wāl\\ *n* : a ridge esp. on cloth; *also* : the texture esp. of a fabric

¹walk \\'wok\\ *vb* [partly fr. ME *walken*, fr. OE *wealcan* to roll, toss and partly fr. ME *walkien*, fr. OE *wealcian* to roll up, muffle up] **1** : to move or cause to move on foot usu. at a natural unhurried gait ⟨~ to town⟩ ⟨~ a horse⟩ **2** : to pass over, through, or along by walking ⟨~ the streets⟩ **3** : to perform or accomplish by walking ⟨~ guard⟩ **4** : to follow a course of action or way of life ⟨~ humbly in the sight of God⟩

I CAN WAIT, BIRD

SOONER OR LATER, YOU'VE GOTTA COME OUT OF THERE AGAIN

JRM DAVIS 3-14

5 : WALK OUT **6** : to receive a base on balls; *also* : to give a base on balls to — **walk·er** *n*

²**walk** *n* **1** : a going on foot ⟨go for a ∼⟩ **2** : a place, path, or course for walking **3** : distance to be walked ⟨a quarter-mile ∼ from here⟩ **4** : manner of living : CONDUCT, BEHAVIOR **5** : social or economic status ⟨various ∼s of life⟩ **6** : manner of walking : GAIT; *esp* : a slow 4-beat gait of a horse **7** : BASE ON BALLS

walk·away \'wȯ-kə-₁wā\ *n* : an easily won contest

walk·ie-talk·ie \₁wȯ-kē-'tȯ-kē\ *n* : a small portable radio transmitting and receiving set

¹**walk–in** \'wȯk-₁in\ *adj* : large enough to be walked into ⟨a ∼ refrigerator⟩

²**walk–in** *n* **1** : an easy election victory **2** : one that walks in

walking papers *n pl* : DISMISSAL, DISCHARGE

walking stick *n* **1** : a stick used in walking **2** *usu* **walking·stick** : STICK INSECT; *esp* : one common in parts of the U.S.

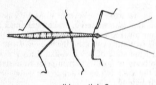

walking stick 2

walk–on \'wȯk-₁ȯn, -₁än\ *n* : a small part in a dramatic production

walk·out \-₁aȯt\ *n* **1** : a labor strike **2** : the action of leaving a meeting or organization as an expression of disapproval

walk out *vb* **1** : to leave suddenly often as an expression of disapproval **2** : to go on strike

walk·over \-₁ō-vər\ *n* : a one-sided contest : an easy victory

walk–up \'wȯk-₁əp\ *n* : a building or apartment house without an elevator — **walk–up** *adj*

walk·way \-₁wā\ *n* : a passage for walking

¹**wall** \'wȯl\ *n* [ME, fr. OE *weall*, fr. L *vallum* rampart, fr. *vallus* stake, palisade] **1** : a structure (as of stone or brick) intended for defense or security or for enclosing something **2** : one of the upright enclosing parts of a building or room **3** : the inside surface of a cavity or container ⟨the ∼ of a boiler⟩ **4** : something like a wall in appearance, function, or effect ⟨a tariff ∼⟩ — **walled** \'wȯld\ *adj*

²**wall** *vb* **1** : to provide, separate, or surround with or as if with a wall ⟨∼ in a garden⟩ **2** : to close (an opening) with or as if with a wall ⟨∼ up a door⟩

wal·la·by \'wä-lə-bē\ *n, pl* **wallabies** *also* **wallaby** : any of various small or medium-sized kangaroos

wall·board \'wȯl-₁bȯrd\ *n* : a structural material (as of wood pulp or plaster) made in large sheets and used for sheathing interior walls and ceilings

wal·let \'wä-lət\ *n* **1** : a bag or sack for carrying things on a journey **2** : a pocketbook with compartments (as

for personal papers and usu. unfolded money) : BILLFOLD

wall·eye \'wȯ-₁lī\ *n* **1** : an eye with a whitish iris or an opaque white cornea **2** : a large vigorous No. American food and sport fish related to the perches — **wall·eyed** \-₁līd\ *adj*

wall·flow·er \'wȯl-₁flaȯ-ər\ *n* **1** : any of several Old World plants related to the mustards; *esp* : one with showy fragrant flowers **2** : a person who usu. from shyness or unpopularity remains alone (as at a dance)

Wal·loon \wä-'lün\ *n* : a member of a people of southern and southeastern Belgium and adjacent parts of France — **Walloon** *adj*

¹**wal·lop** \'wä-ləp\ *vb* [ME *walopen* to gallop, fr. OF *waloper*] **1** : to beat soundly : TROUNCE **2** : to hit hard : SOCK **syn** batter, beat, lambaste, pound, pummel, thrash

²**wallop** *n* **1** : a powerful blow or impact **2** : the ability to hit hard **3** : emotional, sensory, or psychological force : IMPACT

wal·lop·ing \'wä-lə-piŋ\ *adj* **1** : LARGE, WHOPPING **2** : exceptionally fine or impressive

¹**wal·low** \'wä-lō\ *vb* **1** : to roll oneself about sluggishly in or as if in deep mud ⟨hogs ∼*ing* in the mire⟩ **2** : to indulge oneself excessively ⟨∼ in luxury⟩ **3** : to become or remain helpless ⟨∼ in ignorance⟩ **syn** bask, indulge, luxuriate, revel, welter

²**wallow** *n* : a muddy or dust-filled area where animals wallow

wall·pa·per \'wȯl-₁pā-pər\ *n* : decorative paper for the walls of a room — **wallpaper** *vb*

wall–to–wall *adj* **1** : covering the entire floor ⟨wall-to-wall carpeting⟩ **2** : covering or filling one entire space or time ⟨crowds of *wall-to-wall* people⟩

wal·nut \'wȯl-(₁)nət\ *n* [ME *walnot*, fr. OE *wealhhnutu*, lit., foreign nut, fr. *Wealh* Welshman, foreigner + *hnutu* nut] **1** : a nut with a furrowed usu. rough shell and an adherent husk from any of a genus of trees related to the hickories; *esp* : the large edible nut of a Eurasian tree **2** : a tree that bears walnuts **3** : the usu. reddish to dark brown wood of a walnut used esp. in cabinetwork and veneers

wal·rus \'wȯl-rəs, 'wäl-\ *n, pl* **walrus** *or* **wal·rus·es** : a large mammal of northern seas related to the seals and having ivory tusks

¹**waltz** \'wȯlts\ *n* [G *Walzer*, fr. *walzen* to roll, dance] **1** : a gliding dance done to music having three beats to the measure **2** : music for or suitable for waltzing

²**waltz** *vb* **1** : to dance a waltz **2** : to move or advance easily, successfully, or conspicuously ⟨he ∼*ed* off with the championship⟩

wam·ble \'wäm-bəl\ *vb* **wam·bled; wam·bling** : to progress unsteadily or with a lurching shambling gait

wam·pum \'wäm-pəm\ *n* [short for *wampumpeag*, fr. Massachuset (a North American Indian language) *wampompeag*, fr. *wampan* white + *api* string + *-ag*, pl. suffix] **1** : beads made of shells strung in strands, belts, or sashes and used by No. American Indians as money and ornaments **2** *slang* : MONEY

wan \\'wän\\ *adj* **wan·ner; wan·nest 1** : SICKLY, PALLID; *also* : FEEBLE **2** : DIM, FAINT **3** : LANGUID ⟨a ~ smile⟩ **syn** ashen, blanched, doughy, livid, pale, waxen — **wan·ly** *adv* — **wan·ness** *n*

wand \\'wänd\\ *n* **1** : a slender staff carried in a procession **2** : the staff of a fairy, diviner, or magician

wan·der \\'wän-dər\\ *vb* **1** : to move about aimlessly or without a fixed course or goal : RAMBLE **2** : to go astray in conduct or thought; *esp* : to become delirious **syn** gad, gallivant, meander, range, roam, rove — **wan·der·er** *n*

wandering Jew *n* : either of two trailing or creeping plants cultivated for their showy and often white-striped foliage

wan·der·lust \\'wän-dər-₁ləst\\ *n* : strong longing for or impulse toward wandering

¹**wane** \\'wän\\ *vb* **waned; wan·ing 1** : to grow gradually smaller or less ⟨the moon ~s⟩ ⟨his strength *waned*⟩ **2** : to lose power, prosperity, or influence **3** : to draw near an end ⟨summer is *waning*⟩ **syn** abate, ebb, moderate, relent, slacken, subside

²**wane** *n* : a waning (as in size or power); *also* : a period in which something is waning

wan·gle \\'waŋ-gəl\\ *vb* **wan·gled; wan·gling 1** : to obtain by sly or devious means; *also* : to use trickery or questionable means to achieve an end **2** : MANIPULATE; *also* : FINAGLE

wan·na·be \\'wä-nə-₁bē\\ *n* : a person who wants or aspires to be someone or something else or who tries to look or act like someone else

¹**want** \\'wȯnt, 'wänt\\ *vb* **1** : to fail to possess : LACK ⟨they ~ the necessities of life⟩ **2** : to feel or suffer the need of **3** : NEED, REQUIRE ⟨the house ~s painting⟩ **4** : to desire earnestly : WISH

²**want** *n* **1** : a lack of a required or usual amount : SHORTAGE **2** : dire need : DESTITUTION **3** : something wanted : DESIRE **4** : personal defect : FAULT

¹**want·ing** \\'wȯn-tiŋ, 'wän-\\ *adj* **1** : not present or in evidence : ABSENT **2** : falling below standards or expectations **3** : lacking in ability or capacity : DEFICIENT ⟨~ in common sense⟩

²**wanting** *prep* **1** : LESS, MINUS ⟨a month ~ two days⟩ **2** : WITHOUT ⟨a book ~ a cover⟩

¹**wan·ton** \\'wȯnt-ᵊn, 'wänt-\\ *adj* [ME, undisciplined, fr. *wan-* deficient, wrong + *towen*, pp. of *teen* to draw, train, discipline] **1** : UNCHASTE, LEWD, LUSTFUL; *also* : SENSUAL **2** : having no regard for justice or for other persons' feelings, rights, or safety : MERCILESS, INHUMANE ⟨~ cruelty⟩ **3** : having no just cause ⟨a ~ attack⟩ — **wan·ton·ly** *adv* — **wan·ton·ness** *n*

²**wanton** *n* : a wanton individual; *esp* : a lewd or immoral person

³**wanton** *vb* **1** : to be wanton : act wantonly **2** : to pass or waste wantonly

wa·pi·ti \\'wä-pə-tē\\ *n, pl* **wapiti** *or* **wapitis** : ELK 2

¹**war** \\'wȯr\\ *n* **1** : a state or period of usu. open and declared armed fighting between states or nations **2** : the art or science of warfare **3** : a state of hostility, conflict, or antagonism **4** : a struggle between opposing forces or for a particular end ⟨~ against disease⟩ — **war·less** \\-ləs\\ *adj*

²**war** *vb* **warred; war·ring** : to engage in warfare : be in conflict

³**war** *abbr* warrant

¹**war·ble** \\'wȯr-bəl\\ *n* **1** : a melodious succession of low pleasing sounds **2** : a musical trill

²**warble** *vb* **war·bled; war·bling 1** : to sing or utter in a trilling manner or with variations **2** : to express by or as if by warbling

³**warble** *n* : a swelling under the hide esp. of the back of cattle, horses, and wild mammals caused by the maggot of a fly (**warble fly**); *also* : its maggot

war·bler \\'wȯr-blər\\ *n* **1** : SONGSTER **2** : any of various small slender-billed Old World singing birds related

to the thrushes and noted for their song **3** : any of numerous small bright-colored American insect-eating birds with a usu. weak and unmusical song

war·bon·net \\'wȯr-₁bä-nət\\ *n* : a feathered American Indian ceremonial headdress

war cry *n* **1** : a cry used by fighters in war **2** : a slogan used esp. to rally people to a cause

¹**ward** \\'wȯrd\\ *n* **1** : a guarding or being under guard or guardianship; *esp* : CUSTODY **2** : a body of guards **3** : a division of a prison **4** : a division in a hospital **5** : a division of a city for electoral or administrative purposes **6** : a person (as a child) under the protection of a guardian or a law court **7** : a person or body of persons under the protection or tutelage of a government **8** : a means of defense : PROTECTION

²**ward** *vb* : to turn aside : DEFLECT — usu. used with *off* ⟨~ off a blow⟩

¹**-ward** \\wərd\\ *also* **-wards** \\wərdz\\ *adj suffix* **1** : that moves, tends, faces, or is directed toward ⟨wind*ward*⟩ **2** : that occurs or is situated in the direction of ⟨sea*ward*⟩

²**-ward** *or* **-wards** *adv suffix* **1** : in a (specified) direction ⟨up*wards*⟩ ⟨after*ward*⟩ **2** : toward a (specified) point, position, or area ⟨sky*ward*⟩

war dance *n* : a dance performed (as by American Indians) before going to war or in celebration of victory

war·den \\'wȯrd-ᵊn\\ *n* **1** : GUARDIAN, KEEPER **2** : the governor of a town, district, or fortress **3** : an official charged with special supervisory or enforcement duties ⟨game ~⟩ ⟨air raid ~⟩ **4** : an official in charge of the operation of a prison **5** : one of two ranking lay officers of an Episcopal parish **6** : any of various British college officials

ward·er \\'wȯr-dər\\ *n* : WATCHMAN, WARDEN

ward heel·er \\-₁hē-lər\\ *n* : a local worker for a political boss

ward·robe \\'wȯr-₁drōb\\ *n* [ME *warderobe,* fr. OF, fr. *warder* to guard + *robe* robe] **1** : a room or closet where clothes are kept; *also* : CLOTHESPRESS **2** : a collection of wearing apparel ⟨his summer ~⟩

ward·room \\-₁drüm, -₁drum\\ *n* : the dining area for officers aboard a warship

ward·ship \\'wȯrd-₁ship\\ *n* **1** : GUARDIANSHIP **2** : the state of being under care of a guardian

ware \\'war\\ *n* **1** : manufactured articles or products of art or craft : GOODS ⟨glass*ware*⟩ **2** : an article of merchandise ⟨a peddler hawking his ~s⟩ **3** : items (as dishes) of fired clay : POTTERY

ware·house \\-₁haus\\ *n* : a place for the storage of merchandise or commodities : STOREHOUSE — **warehouse** *vb* — **ware·house·man** \\-mən\\ *n* — **ware·hous·er** \\-₁haù-zər, -zər\\ *n*

ware·room \\'war-₁rüm, -₁rum\\ *n* : a room in which goods are exhibited for sale

war·fare \\'wȯr-₁far\\ *n* **1** : military operations between enemies : WAR; *also* : an activity undertaken by one country to weaken or destroy another ⟨economic ~⟩ **2** : STRUGGLE, CONFLICT

war·fa·rin \\'wȯr-fə-rən\\ *n* : an anticoagulant compound used as a rodent poison and in medicine

war·head \\'wȯr-₁hed\\ *n* : the section of a missile containing the charge

war·horse \\-₁hȯrs\\ *n* **1** : a horse for use in war **2** : a veteran soldier or public person (as a politician)

war·like \\-₁līk\\ *adj* **1** : fond of war ⟨~ peoples⟩ **2** : of, relating to, or useful in war : MILITARY, MARTIAL ⟨~ supplies⟩ **3** : befitting or characteristic of war or of soldiers ⟨~ attitudes⟩

war·lock \\-₁läk\\ *n* [ME *warloghe,* fr. OE *wǣrloga* one that breaks faith, the Devil, fr. *wǣr* faith, troth + *-loga* (fr. *lēogan* to lie)] : SORCERER, WIZARD

war·lord \\-₁lȯrd\\ *n* **1** : a high military leader **2** : a military commander exercising local civil power by force ⟨former Chinese ~s⟩

¹**warm** \\'wȯrm\\ *adj* **1** : having or giving out heat to a

moderate or adequate degree ⟨∼ milk⟩ ⟨a ∼ stove⟩ **2** : serving to retain heat ⟨∼ clothes⟩ **3** : feeling or inducing sensations of heat ⟨∼ from exercise⟩ ⟨a ∼ climb⟩ **4** : showing or marked by strong feeling : ARDENT ⟨∼ support⟩ **5** : marked by tense excitement or hot anger ⟨a ∼ campaign⟩ **6** : giving a pleasant impression of warmth, cheerfulness, or friendliness ⟨∼ colors⟩ ⟨a ∼ tone of voice⟩ **7** : marked by or tending toward injury, distress, or pain ⟨made things ∼ for the enemy⟩ **8** : newly made : FRESH ⟨a ∼ scent⟩ **9** : near to a goal ⟨getting ∼ in a search⟩ — **warm·ly** *adv*

²**warm** *vb* **1** : to make or become warm **2** : to give a feeling of warmth or vitality to **3** : to experience feelings of affection or pleasure ⟨she ∼ed to her guest⟩ **4** : to reheat for eating ⟨∼ed over the roast⟩ **5** : to make ready for operation or performance by preliminary exercise or operation ⟨∼ up the motor⟩ **6** : to become increasingly ardent, interested, or competent ⟨the speaker ∼ed to his topic⟩ — **warm·er** *n*

warm–blood·ed \-ˈblə-dəd\ *adj* : able to maintain a relatively high and constant body temperature relatively independent of that of the surroundings

warmed–over \ˈwȯrmd-ˈō-vər\ *adj* **1** : REHEATED ⟨∼ cabbage⟩ **2** : not fresh or new ⟨∼ ideas⟩

warm front *n* : an advancing edge of a warm air mass

warm·heart·ed \ˈwȯrm-ˈhär-təd\ *adj* : marked by warmth of feeling : CORDIAL — **warm·heart·ed·ness** *n*

warming pan *n* : a long-handled covered pan filled with live coals and formerly used to warm a bed

war·mon·ger \ˈwȯr-ˌmən-gər, -ˌmäŋ-\ *n* : one who urges or attempts to stir up war

warmth \ˈwȯrmth\ *n* **1** : the quality or state of being warm **2** : ZEAL, ARDOR, FERVOR

warm up *vb* : to engage in exercise or practice esp. before entering a game or contest — **warm–up** \ˈwȯrm-ˌəp\ *n*

warn \ˈwȯrn\ *vb* **1** : to put on guard : CAUTION; *also* : ADMONISH, COUNSEL **2** : to notify esp. in advance : INFORM **3** : to order to go or keep away

¹**warn·ing** \ˈwȯr-niŋ\ *n* **1** : the act of warning : the state of being warned **2** : something that warns or serves to warn

²**warning** *adj* : serving as an alarm, signal, summons, or admonition ⟨∼ bell⟩ — **warn·ing·ly** *adv*

¹**warp** \ˈwȯrp\ *n* **1** : the lengthwise threads on a loom or in a woven fabric **2** : a twist out of a true plane or straight line ⟨a ∼ in a board⟩

²**warp** *vb* [ME, fr. OE *weorpan* to throw] **1** : to turn or twist out of shape; *also* : to become so twisted **2** : to lead astray; *also* : PERVERT; *also* : FALSIFY, DISTORT

war paint *n* : paint put on the face and body by American Indians as a sign of going to war

war·path \ˈwȯr-ˌpath, -ˌpȧth\ *n* : the course taken by a party of American Indians going on a hostile expedition — **on the warpath** : ready to fight or argue

war·plane \-ˌplān\ *n* : a military airplane; *esp* : one armed for combat

¹**war·rant** \ˈwȯr-ənt, ˈwär-\ *n* **1** : AUTHORIZATION; *also* : JUSTIFICATION, GROUND **2** : evidence (as a document) of authorization; *esp* : a legal writ authorizing an officer to take action (as in making an arrest, seizure, or search) **3** : a certificate of appointment issued to an officer of lower rank than a commissioned officer

²**warrant** *vb* **1** : to guarantee security or immunity to : SECURE **2** : to declare or maintain positively ⟨I ∼ this is so⟩ **3** : to assure (a person) of the truth of what is said **4** : to guarantee to be as it appears or as it is represented ⟨∼ goods as of the first quality⟩ **5** : SANCTION, AUTHORIZE **6** : to give proof of : ATTEST; *also* : GUARANTEE **7** : JUSTIFY ⟨his need ∼s the expenditure⟩

warrant officer *n* **1** : an officer in the armed forces ranking next below a commissioned officer **2** : a commissioned officer ranking below an ensign in the navy or coast guard and below a second lieutenant in the marine corps

war·ran·ty \ˈwȯr-ən-tē, ˈwär-\ *n, pl* **-ties** : an expressed or implied statement that some situation or thing is as it appears to be or is represented to be; *esp* : a usu. written guarantee of the integrity of a product and of the maker's responsibility for the repair or replacement of defective parts

war·ren \ˈwȯr-ən, ˈwär-\ *n* **1** : an area where rabbits breed; *also* : a structure where rabbits are bred or kept **2** : a crowded tenement or district

war·rior \ˈwȯr-yər; ˈwȯr-ē-ər, ˈwär-\ *n* : a man engaged or experienced in warfare

war·ship \ˈwȯr-ˌship\ *n* : a naval vessel

wart \ˈwȯrt\ *n* **1** : a small usu. horny projecting growth on the skin; *esp* : one caused by a virus **2** : a protuberance resembling a wart (as on a plant) — **warty** *adj*

wart·hog \ˈwȯrt-ˌhȯg, -ˌhäg\ *n* : a wild African hog which has large tusks and the males of which have two pairs of rough warty protuberances below the eyes

war·time \ˈwȯr-ˌtīm\ *n* : a period during which a war is in progress

wary \ˈwar-ē\ *adj* **war·i·er; -est** : very cautious; *esp* : careful in guarding against danger or deception

was *past 1st & 3d sing of* BE

¹**wash** \ˈwȯsh, ˈwäsh\ *vb* **1** : to clean with water and usu. soap or detergent ⟨∼ clothes⟩ ⟨∼ your hands⟩ **2** : to wet thoroughly : DRENCH **3** : to flow along the border of ⟨waves ∼ the shore⟩ **4** : to pour or flow in a stream or current **5** : to move or remove by or as if by the action of water **6** : to cover or daub lightly with a liquid (as whitewash) **7** : to run water over (as gravel or ore) in order to separate valuable matter from refuse ⟨∼ sand for gold⟩ **8** : to undergo laundering ⟨a dress that doesn't ∼ well⟩ **9** : to stand a test ⟨that story will not ∼⟩ **10** : to be worn away by water

²**wash** *n* **1** : the act or process or an instance of washing or being washed **2** : articles to be washed or being washed **3** : the flow or action of a mass of water (as a wave) **4** : erosion by waves (as of the sea) **5** *West* : the dry bed of a stream **6** : worthless esp. liquid waste : REFUSE, SWILL **7** : a thin coat of paint (as watercolor) **8** : a disturbance in the air caused by the passage of a wing or propeller

³**wash** *adj* : WASHABLE

Wash *abbr* Washington

wash·able \ˈwȯ-shə-bəl, ˈwä-\ *adj* : capable of being washed without damage

wash–and–wear *adj* : of, relating to, or being a fabric or garment that needs little or no ironing after washing

wash·ba·sin \ˈwȯsh-ˌbās-ᵊn, ˈwäsh-\ *n* : WASHBOWL

wash·board \-ˌbȯrd\ *n* : a grooved board to scrub clothes on

wash·bowl \-ˌbōl\ *n* : a large bowl for water for washing hands and face

wash·cloth \-ˌklȯth\ *n* : a cloth used for washing one's face and body

washed–out \ˈwȯsht-ˈaut, ˈwäsht-\ *adj* **1** : faded in color **2** : EXHAUSTED ⟨felt ∼ after working all night⟩

washed–up \-ˈəp\ *adj* : no longer successful, popular, skillful, or needed

wash·er \ˈwȯ-shər, ˈwä-\ *n* **1** : a ring or perforated plate used around a bolt or screw to ensure tightness or relieve friction **2** : one that washes; *esp* : a machine for washing

wash·er·wom·an \-ˌwu̇-mən\ *n* : a woman whose occupation is washing clothes

wash·house \\'wȯsh-ˌhaùs, 'wäsh-\ n : a house or building for washing clothes

wash·ing \\'wȯ-shiṇ, 'wä-\ n 1 : material obtained by washing 2 : articles washed or to be washed

washing soda n : SODIUM CARBONATE

Wash·ing·ton's Birthday \\'wȯ-shiṇ-tǝnz-, 'wä-\ n : the 3d Monday in February observed as a legal holiday

wash·out \\'wȯsh-ˌaùt, 'wäsh-\ n 1 : the washing away of earth (as from a road); also : a place where earth is washed away 2 : a complete failure

wash·room \-ˌrüm, -ˌrùm\ n : BATHROOM

wash·stand \-ˌstand\ n 1 : a stand holding articles needed for washing face and hands 2 : LAVATORY 1

wash·tub \-ˌtǝb\ n : a tub for washing or soaking clothes

wash·wom·an \\'wȯsh-ˌwù-mǝn, 'wäsh-\ n : WASHERWOMAN

washy \\'wȯ-shē, 'wä-\ adj **wash·i·er; -est** 1 : WEAK, WATERY 2 : PALLID 3 : lacking in vigor, individuality, or definiteness

wasp \\'wäsp, 'wȯsp\ n : any of numerous social or solitary winged insects related to the bees and ants with biting mouthparts and in females and workers an often formidable sting

WASP or **Wasp** n [white Anglo-Saxon Protestant] : an American of northern European and esp. British ancestry and of Protestant background

wasp·ish \\'wäs-pish, 'wȯs-\ adj 1 : SNAPPISH, IRRITABLE 2 : resembling a wasp in form; esp : slightly built **syn** fractious, fretful, huffy, peevish, petulant, querulous

wasp waist n : a very slender waist

¹**was·sail** \\'wä-sǝl, wä-'sāl\ n [ME wæs hæil, fr. ON ves heill be well] 1 : an early English toast to someone's health 2 : a hot drink made with wine, beer, or cider, spices, sugar, and usu. baked apples and traditionally served at Christmas 3 : riotous drinking : REVELRY

²**wassail** vb 1 : CAROUSE 2 : to drink to the health of — **was·sail·er** n

Was·ser·mann test \\'wä-sǝr-mǝn-, 'vä-\ n : a blood test for infection with syphilis

wast·age \\'wā-stij\ n : WASTE 3

¹**waste** \\'wāst\ n 1 : a sparsely settled or barren region

: DESERT; also : uncultivated land 2 : the act or an instance of wasting : the state of being wasted 3 : gradual loss or decrease by use, wear, or decay 4 : material left over, rejected, or thrown away; also : an unwanted by-product of a manufacturing or chemical process 5 : refuse (as garbage) that accumulates about habitations 6 : material (as feces) produced but not used by a living organism — **waste·ful** \-fǝl\ adj — **waste·ful·ly** adv — **waste·ful·ness** n

²**waste** vb **wast·ed; wast·ing** 1 : DEVASTATE 2 : to wear away or diminish gradually : CONSUME 3 : to spend or use carelessly or uselessly : SQUANDER 4 : to lose or cause to lose weight, strength, or energy ⟨wasting away from fever⟩ 5 : to become diminished in bulk or substance : DWINDLE **syn** depredate, desolate, despoil, ravage, spoil, strip — **wast·er** n

³**waste** adj 1 : being wild and uninhabited : BARREN, DESOLATE; also : UNCULTIVATED 2 : being in a ruined condition 3 : discarded as worthless after being used ⟨~ water⟩ 4 : excreted from or stored in inert form in a living organism as a by-product of vital activity ⟨~ matter from birds⟩

waste·bas·ket \\'wāst-ˌbas-kǝt\ n : a receptacle for refuse

waste·land \-ˌland, -lǝnd\ n : land that is barren or unfit for cultivation

waste·pa·per \-'pā-pǝr\ n : paper thrown away as used, not needed, or not fit for use

wast·rel \\'wā-strǝl\ n : one that wastes : SPENDTHRIFT

¹**watch** \\'wäch, 'wȯch\ vb 1 : to be or stay awake intentionally : keep vigil ⟨~ed by the patient's bedside⟩ ⟨~ and pray⟩ 2 : to be on the lookout for danger : be on one's guard 3 : to keep guard ⟨~ outside the door⟩ 4 : OBSERVE ⟨~ a game⟩ 5 : to keep in view so as to prevent harm or warn of danger ⟨~ a brush fire carefully⟩ 6 : to keep oneself informed about ⟨~ his progress⟩ 7 : to lie in wait for esp. so as to take advantage of ⟨~ed her opportunity⟩ — **watch·er** n

²**watch** n 1 : the act of keeping awake to guard, protect, or attend; also : a state of alert and continuous attention 2 : a public weather alert ⟨tornado ~⟩ 3 : close

observation **4** : LOOKOUT, WATCHMAN, GUARD **5** : a period during which a part of a ship's crew is on duty; *also* : the part of a crew on duty during a watch **6** : a portable timepiece carried on the person

watch•band \'wäch-ˌband, 'wȯch-\ *n* : the bracelet or strap of a wristwatch

watch•dog \-ˌdȯg\ *n* **1** : a dog kept to guard property **2** : one that guards or protects

watch•ful \-fəl\ *adj* : steadily attentive and alert esp. to danger : VIGILANT — **watch•ful•ly** *adv* — **watch-ful•ness** *n*

watch•mak•er \-ˌmā-kər\ *n* : one that makes or repairs watches — **watch•mak•ing** \-ˌmā-kiŋ\ *n*

watch•man \-mən\ *n* : a person assigned to watch : GUARD

watch night *n* : a devotional service lasting until after midnight esp. on New Year's Eve

watch•tow•er \'wäch-ˌtaů-ər, 'wȯch-\ *n* : a tower for a lookout

watch•word \-ˌwərd\ *n* **1** : a secret word used as a signal or sign of recognition **2** : a word or motto used as a slogan or rallying cry

¹wa•ter \'wȯ-tər, 'wä-\ *n* **1** : the liquid that descends as rain and forms rivers, lakes, and seas **2** : a natural mineral water — usu. used in pl. **3** *pl* : the water occupying or flowing in a particular bed; *also* : a band of seawater bordering on and under the control of a country ⟨sailing Canadian ∼s⟩ **4** : any of various liquids containing or resembling water; *esp* : a watery fluid (as tears, urine, or sap) formed or circulating in a living organism **5** : a specified degree of thoroughness or completeness ⟨a scoundrel of the first ∼⟩

²water *vb* **1** : to supply with or get or take water ⟨∼ horses⟩ ⟨the ship ∼ed at each port⟩ **2** : to treat (as cloth) so as to give a lustrous appearance in wavy lines **3** : to dilute by or as if by adding water to **4** : to form or secrete water or watery matter ⟨her eyes ∼ed⟩ ⟨my mouth ∼ed⟩

water bed *n* : a bed whose mattress is a watertight bag filled with water

wa•ter•borne \-ˌbȯrn\ *adj* : supported or carried by water

water buffalo *n* : a common oxlike often domesticated Asian bovine

water buffalo

water chestnut *n* : a whitish crunchy vegetable used esp. in Chinese cooking that is the peeled tuber of a widely cultivated Asian sedge; *also* : the tuber or the sedge itself

water closet *n* : a compartment or room with a toilet bowl : BATHROOM; *also* : a toilet bowl along with its accessories

wa•ter•col•or \'wȯ-tər-ˌkə-lər, 'wä-\ *n* **1** : a paint whose liquid part is water **2** : the art of painting with watercolors **3** : a picture made with watercolors

wa•ter•course \-ˌkȯrs\ *n* : a stream of water; *also* : the bed of a stream

wa•ter•craft \-ˌkraft\ *n* : a craft for water transport : SHIP, BOAT

wa•ter•cress \-ˌkres\ *n* : a perennial European cress with white flowers that is naturalized in the U.S. and is used esp. in salads

wa•ter•fall \-ˌfȯl\ *n* : a very steep descent of the water of a stream

wa•ter•fowl \'wȯ-tər-ˌfaůl, 'wä-\ *n* **1** : a bird that frequents water **2** **waterfowl** *pl* : wild ducks and geese hunted as game

wa•ter•front \-ˌfrənt\ *n* : land or a section of a town fronting or abutting on a body of water

water gap *n* : a pass in a mountain ridge through which a stream runs

water glass *n* : a drinking glass

water hyacinth *n* : a showy floating aquatic plant of tropical America that often clogs waterways (as in the southern U.S.)

watering place *n* : a resort that features mineral springs or bathing

water lily *n* : any of various aquatic plants with floating roundish leaves and showy solitary flowers

wa•ter•line \'wȯ-tər-ˌlīn, 'wä-\ *n* : a line that marks the level of the surface of water on something (as a ship or the shore)

wa•ter•logged \-ˌlȯgd, -ˌlägd\ *adj* : so filled or soaked with water as to be heavy or unmanageable ⟨a ∼ boat⟩

wa•ter•loo \ˌwȯ-tər-'lü, ˌwä-\ *n*, *pl* **-loos** [*Waterloo*, Belgium, scene of Napoleon's defeat in 1815] : a decisive or final defeat or setback

¹wa•ter•mark \'wȯ-tər-ˌmärk, 'wä-\ *n* **1** : a mark indicating height to which water has risen **2** : a marking in paper visible when the paper is held up to the light

²watermark *vb* : to mark (paper) with a watermark

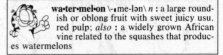

wa•ter•mel•on \-ˌme-lən\ *n* : a large roundish or oblong fruit with sweet juicy usu. red pulp; *also* : a widely grown African vine related to the squashes that produces watermelons

water moccasin *n* : a venomous pit viper chiefly of the southeastern U.S. that is related to the copperhead

water ou•zel \-'ü-zəl\ *n* : DIPPER 1

water pipe *n* : a pipe for smoking that has a long flexible tube whereby the smoke is cooled by passing through water

water polo *n* : a team game played in a swimming pool with a ball resembling a soccer ball

wa·ter·pow·er \\'wȯ-tər-ˌpau̇-ər, 'wä-\ *n* : the power of moving water used to run machinery

¹**wa·ter·proof** \\'wȯ-tər-ˌpru̇f, 'wä-\ *adj* : not letting water through; *esp* : covered or treated with a material to prevent permeation by water — **wa·ter·proof·ing** *n*

²**waterproof** *n* **1** : a waterproof fabric **2** *chiefly Brit* : RAINCOAT

³**waterproof** *vb* : to make waterproof

wa·ter–re·pel·lent \ˌwȯ-tər-ri-'pe-lənt, ˌwä-\ *adj* : treated with a finish that is resistant to water penetration

wa·ter–re·sis·tant \-ri-'zis-tənt\ *adj* : WATER= REPELLENT

wa·ter·shed \\'wȯ-tər-ˌshed, 'wä-\ *n* **1** : a dividing ridge between two drainage areas **2** : the region or area drained by a particular body of water

wa·ter·side \-ˌsīd\ *n* : the land bordering a body of water

water ski *n* : a ski used on water when the wearer is towed — **wa·ter–ski** *vb* — **wa·ter–ski·er** \-ˌskē-ər\ *n*

wa·ter·spout \\'wȯ-tər-ˌspau̇t, 'wä-\ *n* **1** : a pipe for carrying water from a roof **2** : a funnel-shaped cloud extending from a cloud down to a spray torn up by whirling winds from an ocean or lake

water strider *n* : any of various long-legged bugs that move about swiftly on the surface of water

water table *n* : the upper limit of the portion of the ground wholly saturated with water

wa·ter·tight \ˌwȯ-tər-'tīt, ˌwä-\ *adj* **1** : constructed so as to keep water out **2** : allowing no possibility for doubt or uncertainty ⟨a ∼ case against the accused⟩

wa·ter·way \\'wȯ-tər-ˌwā, 'wä-\ *n* : a navigable body of water

wa·ter·wheel \-ˌhwēl\ *n* : a wheel made to turn by water flowing against it

water wings *n pl* : an air-filled device to give support to a person's body esp. when learning to swim

wa·ter·works \\'wȯ-tər-ˌwərks, 'wä-\ *n pl* : a system for supplying water (as to a city)

wa·tery \\'wȯ-tə-rē, 'wä-\ *adj* **1** : containing, full of, or giving out water ⟨∼ clouds⟩ **2** : being like water : THIN, WEAK ⟨∼ lemonade⟩; *also* : being soft and soggy ⟨∼ turnips⟩

WATS \\'wäts\ *abbr* Wide-Area Telecommunications Service

watt \\'wät\ *n* [James *Watt* †1819 Scottish engineer and inventor] : the metric unit of power equal to the work done at the rate of one joule per second or to the power produced by a current of one ampere across a potential difference of one volt

watt·age \\'wä-tij\ *n* : amount of power expressed in watts

wat·tle \\'wät-ᵊl\ *n* **1** : a framework of rods with flexible branches or reeds interlaced used esp. formerly in building; *also* : material for this framework **2** : a naked fleshy process hanging usu. from the head or neck (as of a bird) — **wat·tled** \-ᵊld\ *adj*

W Aust *abbr* Western Australia

¹**wave** \\'wāv\ *vb* **waved; wav·ing 1** : FLUTTER ⟨flags *waving* in the breeze⟩ **2** : to motion with the hands or with something held in them in signal or salute **3** : to become moved or brandished to-and-fro; *also* : BRANDISH, FLOURISH ⟨∼ a sword⟩ **4** : to move before the wind with a wavelike motion ⟨fields of *waving* grain⟩ **5** : to curve up and down like a wave : UNDULATE

²**wave** *n* **1** : a moving ridge or swell on the surface of water **2** : a wavelike formation or shape ⟨a ∼ in the hair⟩ **3** : the action or process of making wavy or curly **4** : a waving motion; *esp* : a signal made by wav-

ing something **5** : FLOW, GUSH ⟨a ∼ of anger swept over her⟩ **6** : a peak of activity ⟨a ∼ of selling⟩ **7** : a disturbance that transfers energy progressively from point to point in a medium ⟨light travels in ∼s⟩ ⟨a sound ∼⟩ **8** : a period of hot or cold weather — **wave·like** *adj*

wave·length \\'wāv-ˌleŋth\ *n* **1** : the distance in the line of advance of a wave from any one point (as a crest) to the next corresponding point **2** : a line of thought that reveals a common understanding

wave·let \-lət\ *n* : a little wave : RIPPLE

wa·ver \\'wā-vər\ *vb* **1** : to fluctuate in opinion, allegiance, or direction **2** : REEL, TOTTER; *also* : QUIVER, FLICKER ⟨∼*ing* flames⟩ **3** : FALTER **4** : to give an unsteady sound : QUAVER **syn** falter, hesitate, shilly= shally, vacillate — **waver** *n* — **wa·ver·er** *n* — **wa·ver·ing·ly** *adv*

wavy \\'wā-vē\ *adj* **wav·i·er; -est** : having waves : moving in waves

¹**wax** \\'waks\ *n* **1** : a yellowish plastic substance secreted by bees for constructing the honeycomb **2** : any of various substances like beeswax

²**wax** *vb* : to treat or rub with wax

³**wax** *vb* **1** : to increase in size, numbers, strength, volume, or duration **2** : to increase in apparent size ⟨the moon ∼*es* toward the full⟩ **3** : to take on a quality or state : BECOME ⟨∼*ed* indignant⟩ ⟨the party ∼*ed* merry⟩

wax bean *n* : a kidney bean with pods that turn creamy yellow to bright yellow when mature enough to use as snap beans

wax·en \\'wak-sən\ *adj* **1** : made of or covered with wax **2** : resembling wax (as in color or consistency)

wax myrtle *n* : any of a genus of shrubs or trees with aromatic leaves; *esp* : an evergreen shrub of the eastern U.S. that produces small hard berries with a thick coating of white wax used for candles

wax·wing \\'waks-ˌwiŋ\ *n* : any of a genus of chiefly brown to gray singing birds with a showy crest and red waxy material on the tips of some wing feathers

wax·work \-ˌwərk\ *n* **1** : an effigy usu. of a person in wax **2** *pl* : an exhibition of wax figures

waxy \\'wak-sē\ *adj* **wax·i·er; -est 1** : made of or full of wax **2** : WAXEN 2

way \\'wā\ *n* **1** : a thoroughfare for travel or passage : ROAD, PATH, STREET **2** : ROUTE **3** : a course of action ⟨chose the easy ∼⟩; *also* : opportunity, capability, or fact of doing as one pleases ⟨always had your own ∼⟩ **4** : a possible course : POSSIBILITY ⟨no two ∼s about it⟩ **5** : METHOD, MODE ⟨this ∼ of thinking⟩ ⟨a new ∼ of painting⟩ **6** : FEATURE, RESPECT ⟨a good worker in many ∼s⟩ **7** : the usual or characteristic state of affairs ⟨as is the ∼ with old people⟩; *also* : individual characteristic or peculiarity ⟨used to her ∼s⟩ **8** : DISTANCE ⟨a short ∼ from here⟩ ⟨a long ∼ from success⟩ **9** : progress along a course ⟨working my ∼ through college⟩ **10** : something having direction : LOCALITY ⟨out our ∼⟩ **11** : STATE, CONDITION ⟨the ∼ things are⟩ **12** *pl* : an inclined structure upon which a ship is built or is supported in launching **13** : CATEGORY, KIND ⟨get what you need in the ∼ of supplies⟩ **14** : motion or speed of a boat through the water — **by the way** : by way of interjection or digression — **by way of 1** : for the purpose of ⟨*by way of* illustration⟩ **2** : by the route through : VIA — **out of the way 1** : WRONG, IMPROPER **2** : SECLUDED, REMOTE

way·bill \\'wā-ˌbil\ *n* : a paper that accompanies a freight shipment and gives details of goods, route, and charges

way·far·er \\'wā-ˌfar-ər\ *n* : a traveler esp. on foot — **way·far·ing** \-ˌfar-iŋ\ *adj*

way·lay \\'wā-ˌlā\ *vb* **-laid** \-ˌlād\; **-lay·ing** : to lie in wait for or attack from ambush

way–out \'wā-ˌaut\ *adj* : FAR-OUT

-ways \ˌwāz\ *adv suffix* : in (such) a way, course, direction, or manner ⟨side*ways*⟩

ways and means *n pl* : methods and resources esp. for raising revenues needed by a state; *also* : a legislative committee concerned with this function

way·side \'wā-ˌsīd\ *n* : the side of or land adjacent to a road or path

way station *n* : an intermediate station on a line of travel (as a railroad)

way·ward \'wā-wərd\ *adj* [ME, short for *awayward* turned away, fr. *away*, adv. + *-ward* directed toward] **1** : following one's own capricious or wanton inclinations ⟨∼ children⟩ **2** : UNPREDICTABLE, IRREGULAR ⟨a ∼ act⟩

WBC *abbr* white blood cells

WC *abbr* **1** water closet **2** without charge

WCTU *abbr* Women's Christian Temperance Union

we \'wē\ *pron* **1** — used of a group that includes the speaker or writer **2** — used for the singular *I* by a monarch, editor, or writer

weak \'wēk\ *adj* **1** : lacking strength or vigor : FEEBLE **2** : not able to sustain or resist much weight, pressure, or strain **3** : deficient in vigor of mind or character; *also* : resulting from or indicative of such deficiency ⟨a ∼ policy⟩ ⟨a ∼ will⟩ ⟨*weak*-minded⟩ **4** : not supported by truth or logic ⟨a ∼ argument⟩ **5** : lacking skill or proficiency; *also* : indicative of a lack of skill or aptitude **6** : lacking vigor of expression or effect **7** : of less than usual strength ⟨∼ tea⟩ **8** : not having or exerting authority ⟨∼ government⟩; *also* : INEFFECTIVE, IMPOTENT **9** : of, relating to, or constituting a verb or verb conjugation that forms the past tense and past participle by adding *-ed* or *-d* or *-t* — **weak·ly** *adv*

weak·en \'wē-kən\ *vb* : to make or become weak **syn** enfeeble, debilitate, undermine, sap, cripple, disable

weak·fish \'wēk-ˌfish\ *n* [obs. D *weekvis*, fr. D *week* soft + *vis* fish; fr. its tender flesh] : a common marine fish of the Atlantic coast of the U.S. caught for food and sport; *also* : any of several related food fishes

weak force *n* : the physical force responsible for particle decay processes in radioactivity

weak–kneed \'wēk-ˌnēd\ *adj* : lacking willpower or resolution

weak·ling \'wē-kliŋ\ *n* : a person who is physically, mentally, or morally weak

weak·ly \'wē-klē\ *adj* : FEEBLE, WEAK

weak·ness \'wēk-nəs\ *n* **1** : the quality or state of being weak; *also* : an instance or period of being weak ⟨in a moment of ∼ he agreed to go⟩ **2** : FAULT, DEFECT **3** : an object of special desire or fondness ⟨chocolate is her ∼⟩

¹weal \'wēl\ *n* : WELL-BEING, PROSPERITY

²weal *n* : WELT

weald \'wēld\ *n* [The *Weald*, wooded district in England, fr. ME *Weeld* the Weald, fr. OE *weald* forest] **1** : FOREST **2** : WOLD

wealth \'welth\ *n* [ME *welthe* welfare, prosperity, fr. *wele* weal] **1** : abundance of possessions or resources : AFFLUENCE, RICHES **2** : abundant supply : PROFUSION ⟨a ∼ of detail⟩ **3** : all property that has a money or an exchange value; *also* : all objects or resources that have economic value **syn** fortune, property, substance, worth

wealthy \'wel-thē\ *adj* **wealth·i·er; -est** : having wealth : RICH

wean \'wēn\ *vb* **1** : to accustom (a young mammal) to take food by means other than nursing **2** : to free from a source of dependence; *also* : to free from a usu. unwholesome habit or interest

weap·on \'we-pən\ *n* **1** : something (as a gun, knife, or club) used to injure, defeat, or destroy **2** : a means of contending against another — **weap·on·less** \-ləs\ *adj*

weap·on·ry \-rē\ *n* : WEAPONS

¹wear \'war\ *vb* **wore** \'wōr\; **worn** \'wōrn\; **wear·ing** **1** : to use as an article of clothing or adornment ⟨∼ a coat⟩ ⟨∼s earrings⟩; *also* : to carry on the person ⟨∼ a gun⟩ **2** : EXHIBIT, PRESENT ⟨∼ a smile⟩ **3** : to impair, diminish, or decay by use or by scraping or rubbing ⟨clothes *worn* to shreds⟩; *also* : to produce gradually by friction, rubbing, or wasting away ⟨∼ a hole in the rug⟩ **4** : to exhaust or lessen the strength of : WEARY, FATIGUE ⟨*worn* by care and toil⟩ **5** : to endure use : last under use or the passage of time ⟨this cloth ∼s well⟩ **6** : to diminish or fail with the passage of time ⟨the day ∼s on⟩ ⟨the effect of the drug *wore* off⟩ **7** : to grow or become by attrition, use, or age ⟨the coin was *worn* thin⟩ — **wear·able** \'war-ə-bəl\ *adj* — **wear·er** *n*

²wear *n* **1** : the act of wearing : the state of being worn ⟨clothes for everyday ∼⟩ **2** : clothing usu. of a particular kind or for a special occasion or use ⟨children's ∼⟩ **3** : wearing or lasting quality ⟨the coat still has lots of ∼ in it⟩ **4** : the result of wearing or use : impairment due to use ⟨the suit shows ∼⟩

wear and tear *n* : the loss, injury, or stress to which something is subjected in the course of use; *esp* : normal depreciation

wear down *vb* : to weary and overcome by persistent resistance or pressure

wea·ri·some \'wir-ē-səm\ *adj* : causing weariness : TIRESOME — **wea·ri·some·ly** *adv* — **wea·ri·some·ness** *n*

wear out *vb* **1** : TIRE **2** : to make or become useless by wear

¹wea·ry \'wir-ē\ *adj* **wea·ri·er; -est 1** : worn out in strength, energy, or freshness **2** : expressing or characteristic of weariness ⟨a ∼ sigh⟩ **3** : having one's patience, tolerance, or pleasure exhausted ⟨∼ of war⟩ — **wea·ri·ly** \'wir-ə-lē\ *adv* — **wea·ri·ness** \-ē-nəs\ *n*

²weary *vb* **wea·ried; wea·ry·ing** : to become or make weary : TIRE

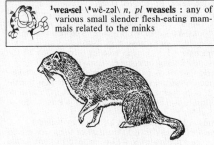

weasel

¹wea·sel \'wē-zəl\ *n, pl* **weasels** : any of various small slender flesh-eating mammals related to the minks

²weasel *vb* **wea·seled; wea·sel·ing 1** : to use weasel words : EQUIVOCATE **2** : to escape from or evade a situation or obligation — often used with *out*

weasel word *n* [fr. the weasel's reputed habit of sucking the contents out of an egg while leaving the shell superficially intact] : a word used to avoid a direct or forthright statement or position

¹weath·er \'we-t͟hər\ *n* **1** : the state of the atmosphere with respect to heat or cold, wetness or dryness, calm or storm, clearness or cloudiness **2** : a particular and esp. a disagreeable atmospheric state : RAIN, STORM

²weather *vb* **1** : to expose to or endure the action of weather; *also* : to alter (as in color or texture) by such exposure **2** : to bear up against successfully ⟨~ a storm⟩ ⟨~ troubles⟩

³weather *adj* : WINDWARD

weath·er–beat·en \'we-t͟hər-ˌbēt-ᵊn\ *adj* : worn or damaged by exposure to the weather; *also* : toughened or tanned by the weather ⟨~ face⟩

weath·er·cock \-ˌkäk\ *n* : a weather vane shaped like a rooster

weath·er·ing \'we-t͟hə-riŋ\ *n* : the action of the weather in altering the color, texture, composition, or form of exposed objects; *also* : alteration thus effected

weath·er·ize \'we-t͟hə-ˌrīz\ *vb* **-ized; -iz·ing** : to make (as a house) better protected against winter weather (as by adding insulation)

weath·er·man \-ˌman\ *n* : one who reports and forecasts the weather : METEOROLOGIST

weath·er·per·son \-ˌpər-sən\ *n* : a person who reports and forecasts the weather : METEOROLOGIST

weath·er·proof \'we-t͟hər-ˌprüf\ *adj* : able to withstand exposure to weather — **weatherproof** *vb*

weather stripping *n* : material used to seal a door or window at the edges

weather vane *n* : VANE 1

weath·er·worn \'we-t͟hər-ˌwōrn\ *adj* : worn by exposure to the weather

¹weave \'wēv\ *vb* **wove** \'wōv\ *or* **weaved; wo·ven** \'wō-vən\ *or* **weaved; weav·ing 1** : to form by interlacing strands of material; *esp* : to make on a loom by interlacing warp and filling threads ⟨~ cloth⟩ **2** : to interlace (as threads) into a fabric and esp. cloth **3** : SPIN 2 **4** : to make as if by weaving together parts **5** : to insert as a part : work in **6** : to move in a winding or zigzag course esp. to avoid obstacles ⟨we *wove* our way through the crowd⟩ — **weav·er** *n*

²weave *n* : something woven; *also* : a pattern or method of weaving ⟨a loose ~⟩

¹web \'web\ *n* **1** : a fabric on a loom or coming from a loom **2** : COBWEB; *also* : SNARE, ENTANGLEMENT ⟨caught in a ~ of deceit⟩ **3** : an animal or plant membrane; *esp* : one uniting the toes (as in many birds) **4** : NETWORK ⟨a ~ of highways⟩ **5** : the series of barbs on each side of the shaft of a feather — **webbed** \'webd\ *adj*

²web *vb* **webbed; web·bing 1** : to make a web **2** : to cover or provide with webs or a network **3** : ENTANGLE, ENSNARE

web·bing \'we-biŋ\ *n* : a strong closely woven tape designed for bearing weight and used esp. for straps, harness, or upholstery

web–foot·ed \'web-ˈfu̇-təd\ *adj* : having webbed feet

wed \'wed\ *vb* **wed·ded** *also* **wed; wed·ding 1** : to take, give, enter into, or join in marriage : MARRY **2** : to unite firmly

Wed *abbr* Wednesday

wed·ding \'we-diŋ\ *n* **1** : a marriage ceremony usu. with accompanying festivities : NUPTIALS **2** : a joining in close association **3** : a wedding anniversary or its celebration

¹wedge \'wej\ *n* **1** : a piece of wood or metal that tapers to a thin edge and is used to split logs or rocks or to raise heavy weights **2** : something (as an action or policy) that serves to open up a way for a breach, change, or intrusion **3** : a wedge-shaped object or part ⟨a ~ of pie⟩

²wedge *vb* **wedged; wedg·ing 1** : to hold firm by or as if by driving in a wedge **2** : to force (something) into a narrow space

wed·lock \'wed-ˌläk\ *n* [ME *wedlok*, fr. OE *wedlāc* marriage bond, fr. *wedd* pledge + *-lāc*, suffix denoting activity] : the state of being married : MARRIAGE, MATRIMONY

Wednes·day \'wenz-dē, -(ˌ)dā\ *n* [ME, fr. OE *wōdnesdæg*, lit., day of Woden (supreme god of the pagan Anglo-Saxons)] : the 4th day of the week

wee \'wē\ *adj* [ME *we*, fr. *we*, n., little bit, fr. OE *wæge* weight] **1** : very small : TINY **2** : very early ⟨~ hours of the morning⟩

¹weed \'wēd\ *n* : a plant that tends to grow thickly where it is not wanted and to choke out more desirable plants

²weed *vb* **1** : to clear of or remove weeds or something harmful, inferior, or superfluous ⟨~ a garden⟩ **2** : to get rid of ⟨~ out the troublemakers⟩ — **weed·er** *n*

³weed *n* : mourning clothes — usu. used in pl. ⟨widow's ~s⟩

weedy \'wē-dē\ *adj* **1** : full of weeds **2** : resembling a weed esp. in vigor of growth or spread **3** : noticeably lean and scrawny : LANKY

week \'wēk\ *n* **1** : seven successive days; *esp* : a calendar period of seven days beginning with Sunday and ending with Saturday **2** : the working or school days of the calendar week

week·day \'wēk-ˌdā\ *n* : a day of the week except Sunday or sometimes except Saturday and Sunday

¹week·end \-ˌend\ *n* : the period between the close of one working or business or school week and the beginning of the next

²weekend *vb* : to spend the weekend

¹week·ly \'wē-klē\ *adj* **1** : occurring, appearing, or done every week **2** : computed in terms of one week — **weekly** *adv*

²weekly *n, pl* **weeklies** : a weekly publication

ween \'wēn\ *vb, archaic* : SUPPOSE 3

wee·ny \'wē-nē\ *also* **ween·sy** \'wēn-sē\ *adj* : exceptionally small

weep \'wēp\ *vb* **wept** \'wept\; **weep·ing** **1** : to express emotion and esp. sorrow by shedding tears : BEWAIL, CRY **2** : to give off fluid slowly : OOZE — **weep·er** *n*

weep·ing *adj* **1** : TEARFUL **2** : having slender drooping branches

weeping willow *n* : a willow with slender drooping branches

weepy \'wē-pē\ *adj* : inclined to weep

wee·vil \'wē-vəl\ *n* : any of a large group of mostly small beetles with a long head usu. curved into a snout and larvae that feed esp. in fruits or seeds — **wee·vily** *or* **wee·vil·ly** \'wē-və-lē\ *adj*

weft \'weft\ *n* **1** : a filling thread or yarn in weaving **2** : WEB, FABRIC; *also* : something woven

¹weigh \'wā\ *vb* [ME *weyen*, fr. OE *wegan* to move, carry, weigh] **1** : to find the heaviness of **2** : to have weight or a specified weight **3** : to consider carefully : PONDER **4** : to merit consideration as important : COUNT ⟨evidence ∼*ing* against him⟩ **5** : to raise before sailing ⟨∼ anchor⟩ **6** : to press down with or as if with a heavy weight

²weigh *n* [alter. of *way*] : WAY — used in the phrase *under weigh*

¹weight \'wāt\ *n* **1** : the amount that something weighs; *also* : the standard amount that something should weigh **2** : a quantity or object weighing a usu. specified amount **3** : a unit (as a pound or kilogram) of weight or mass; *also* : a system of such units **4** : a heavy object for holding or pressing something down; *also* : a heavy object for throwing or lifting in an athletic contest **5** : a mental or emotional burden **6** : IMPORTANCE; *also* : INFLUENCE ⟨threw his ∼ around⟩ **7** : overpowering force **8** : relative thickness (as of a textile) ⟨summer-*weight* clothes⟩ **syn** significance, moment, consequence, import, authority, prestige, credit

☞ For table, see next page.

²weight *vb* **1** : to load with or as if with a weight **2** : to oppress with a burden ⟨∼*ed* down with cares⟩

weight·less \'wāt-ləs\ *adj* : having little weight : lacking apparent gravitational pull — **weight·less·ly** *adv* — **weight·less·ness** *n*

weighty \'wā-tē\ *adj* **weight·i·er; -est** **1** : of much importance or consequence : MOMENTOUS, SERIOUS ⟨∼ problems⟩ **2** : SOLEMN ⟨a ∼ manner⟩ **3** : HEAVY **4** : POWERFUL, TELLING ⟨∼ arguments⟩

weir \'war, 'wir\ *n* **1** : a fence set in a waterway for catching fish **2** : a dam in a stream to raise the water level or divert its flow

weird \'wird\ *adj* [ME *wird, werd* fate, destiny, fr. OE *wyrd*] **1** : MAGICAL **2** : UNEARTHLY, MYSTERIOUS **3** : ODD, UNUSUAL **syn** eerie, uncanny, spooky — **weird·ly** *adv* — **weird·ness** *n*

weirdo \'wir-(ˌ)dō\ *n, pl* **weird·os** : a person who is extraordinarily strange or eccentric

Welch \'welch\ *var of* WELSH

¹wel·come \'wel-kəm\ *vb* **wel·comed; wel·com·ing** **1** : to greet cordially or courteously **2** : to accept, meet, or face with pleasure ⟨he ∼*s* criticism⟩

²welcome *adj* **1** : received gladly into one's presence ⟨a ∼ visitor⟩ **2** : giving pleasure : PLEASING ⟨∼ news⟩ **3** : willingly permitted or admitted ⟨all are ∼ to use the books⟩ **4** — used in the phrase "You're welcome" as a reply to an expression of thanks

³welcome *n* **1** : a cordial greeting or reception **2** : the state of being welcome ⟨overstayed their ∼⟩

¹weld \'weld\ *vb* **1** : to unite (metal or plastic parts) either by heating and allowing the parts to flow together or by hammering or pressing together **2** : to unite closely or intimately ⟨∼*ed* together in friendship⟩ — **weld·er** *n*

²weld *n* **1** : a welded joint **2** : union by welding

wel·fare \'wel-ˌfar\ *n* **1** : the state of doing well esp. in respect to happiness, well-being, or prosperity **2** : aid in the form of money or necessities for those in need; *also* : the agency through which the aid is given

welfare state *n* : a nation or state that assumes primary responsibility for the individual and social welfare of its citizens

wel·kin \'wel-kən\ *n* : SKY; *also* : AIR

¹well \'wel\ *n* **1** : a spring with its pool : FOUNTAIN; *also* : a source of supply ⟨a ∼ of information⟩ **2** : a hole sunk in the earth to obtain a natural deposit (as of water, oil, or gas) **3** : an open space (as for a staircase) extending vertically through floors of a structure **4** : something suggesting a well

²well *vb* : to rise up and flow out

³well *adv* **bet·ter** \'be-tər\; **best** \'best\ **1** : in a good or proper manner : RIGHTLY; *also* : EXCELLENTLY, SKILLFULLY **2** : SATISFACTORILY, FORTUNATELY ⟨the party turned out ∼⟩ **3** : ABUNDANTLY ⟨eat ∼⟩ **4** : with reason or courtesy : PROPERLY ⟨I cannot ∼ refuse⟩ **5** : COMPLETELY, FULLY, QUITE ⟨∼ worth the price⟩ ⟨*well*-hidden⟩ **6** : INTIMATELY, CLOSELY ⟨I know him ∼⟩ **7** : CONSIDERABLY, FAR ⟨∼ over a million⟩ ⟨∼ ahead⟩ **8** : without trouble or difficulty ⟨we could ∼ have gone⟩ **9** : EXACTLY, DEFINITELY ⟨remember it ∼⟩

⁴well *adj* **1** : PROSPEROUS; *also* : being in satisfactory condition or circumstances **2** : SATISFACTORY, PLEASING ⟨all is ∼⟩ **3** : ADVISABLE, DESIRABLE ⟨it is not ∼ to anger him⟩ **4** : free or recovered from ill health : HEALTHY **5** : FORTUNATE ⟨it is ∼ that this has happened⟩

well–ad·just·ed \ˌwel-ə-'jəs-təd\ *adj* : WELL-BALANCED 2

well–ad·vised \-əd-'vīzd\ *adj* **1** : PRUDENT **2** : resulting from, based on, or showing careful deliberation or wise counsel ⟨∼ plans⟩

well–ap·point·ed \-ə-'pȯin-təd\ *adj* : properly fitted out

well–ba·lanced \'wel-'ba-lənst\ *adj* **1** : nicely or evenly balanced or arranged **2** : emotionally or psychologically untroubled

well–be·ing \-'bē-iŋ\ *n* : the state of being happy, healthy, or prosperous

well·born \-'bȯrn\ *adj* : born of noble or wealthy lineage

well·bred \-'bred\ *adj* : having or indicating good breeding : REFINED

well–de·fined \-di-'fīnd\ *adj* : having clearly distinguishable limits or boundaries

well–dis·posed \-di-'spōzd\ *adj* : disposed to be friendly, favorable, or sympathetic

well–done \'wel-'dən\ *adj* **1** : rightly or properly performed **2** : cooked thoroughly

well–fa·vored \-'fā-vərd\ *adj* : GOOD-LOOKING, HANDSOME

well–fixed \-'fikst\ *adj* : WELL-HEELED

well–found·ed \-'faùn-dəd\ *adj* : based on good reasons

well–groomed \-'grümd, -'grùmd\ *adj* : neatly dressed or cared for

WEIGHTS AND MEASURES[1]

UNIT	ABBREVIATION OR SYMBOL	EQUIVALENT IN OTHER U.S. UNITS	METRIC EQUIVALENT
		WEIGHT avoirdupois (ordinary commodities)	
ton			
short ton		20 short hundredweight, 2000 pounds	0.907 metric ton
long ton		20 long hundredweight, 2240 pounds	1.016 metric tons
hundredweight	cwt		
short hundredweight		100 pounds, 0.05 short ton	45.359 kilograms
long hundredweight		112 pounds, 0.05 long ton	50.802 kilograms
pound	lb *or* lb avdp *also* #	16 ounces, 7000 grains (1.215 apothecaries' or troy pound)	0.454 kilogram
ounce	oz *or* oz avdp	16 drams, 437.5 grains (0.911 apothecaries' or troy ounce)	28.350 grams
dram	dr *or* dr avdp	27.344 grains, 0.0625 ounce	1.772 grams
grain	gr	0.037 dram, 0.002286 ounce	0.0648 gram
		troy (precious metals, jewels)	
pound	lb t	12 ounces, 240 pennyweight, 5760 grains (0.823 avoirdupois pound, 1.0 apothecaries' pound)	0.373 kilogram
ounce	oz t	20 pennyweight, 480 grains (1.097 avoirdupois ounce, 1.0 apothecaries' ounce)	31.103 grams
pennyweight	dwt *also* pwt	24 grains, 0.05 ounce	1.555 grams
grain	gr	0.042 pennyweight, 0.002083 ounce	0.0648 gram
		apothecaries' (drugs)	
pound	lb ap	12 ounces, 5760 grains (0.822 avoirdupois pound, 1.0 troy pound)	0.373 kilogram
ounce	oz ap *or* ℥	8 drams, 480 grains (1.097 avoirdupois ounce, 1.0 troy ounce)	31.103 grams
dram	dr ap *or* ℨ	0.125 ounce, 60 grains	3.888 grams
grain	gr	0.0166 dram, 0.002083 ounce	0.0648 gram
		CAPACITY U.S. liquid measure	
gallon	gal	4 quarts (231 cubic inches)	3.785 liters
quart	qt	2 pints (57.75 cubic inches)	0.946 liter
pint	pt	4 gills (28.875 cubic inches)	0.473 liter
gill	gi	4 fluid ounces (7.219 cubic inches)	118.294 milliliters
fluid ounce	fl oz *or* f ℥	8 fluid drams (1.805 cubic inches)	29.573 milliliters
fluid dram	fl dr *or* f ℨ	60 minims (0.226 cubic inch)	3.697 milliliters
minim	min *or* ♏	¹⁄₆₀ fluid dram (0.003760 cubic inch)	0.061610 milliliter
		U.S. dry measure	
bushel	bu	4 pecks (2150.42 cubic inches)	35.239 liters
peck	pk	8 quarts (537.605 cubic inches)	8.810 liters
quart	qt	2 pints (67.201 cubic inches)	1.101 liters
pint	pt	½ quart (33.600 cubic inches)	0.551 liter
		LENGTH	
mile	mi	5280 feet, 320 rods, 1760 yards	1.609 kilometers
rod	rd	5.50 yards, 16.5 feet	5.029 meters
yard	yd	3 feet, 36 inches	0.9144 meter
foot	ft *or* '	12 inches, 0.333 yard	30.48 centimeters
inch	in *or* "	0.083 foot, 0.028 yard	2.54 centimeters
		AREA	
square mile	sq mi *or* mi²	640 acres, 102,400 square rods	2.590 square kilometers
acre		4840 square yards, 43,560 square feet	4047 square meters
square rod	sq rd *or* rd²	30.25 square yards, 0.00625 acre	25.293 square meters
square yard	sq yd *or* yd²	1296 square inches, 9 square feet	0.836 square meter
square foot	sq ft *or* ft²	144 square inches, 0.111 square yard	0.093 square meter
square inch	sq in *or* in²	0.0069 square foot, 0.00077 square yard	6.452 square centimeters
		VOLUME	
cubic yard	cu yd *or* yd³	27 cubic feet, 46.656 cubic inches	0.765 cubic meter
cubic foot	cu ft *or* ft³	1728 cubic inches, 0.0370 cubic yard	0.028 cubic meter
cubic inch	cu in *or* in³	0.00058 cubic foot, 0.000021 cubic yard	16.387 cubic centimeters

[1]For U.S. equivalents of metric units see Metric System table

well–ground·ed \-'graùn-dəd\ *adj* **1** : having a firm foundation **2** : WELL-FOUNDED

well·head \-₁hed\ *n* **1** : the source of a spring or a stream **2** : principal source **3** : the top of or a structure built over a well

well–heeled \-'hēld\ *adj* : financially well-off

well–known \-'nōn\ *adj* : fully or widely known

well–mean·ing \-'mē-niŋ\ *adj* : having or based on good intentions

well·ness \-nəs\ *n* : good health esp. as an actively sought goal ⟨∼ clinics⟩ ⟨lifestyles that promote ∼⟩

well–nigh \-'nī\ *adv* : ALMOST, NEARLY

well–off \-'ȯf\ *adj* : being in good condition or circumstances; *esp* : WELL-TO-DO

well–or·dered \-'ȯr-dərd\ *adj* : having an orderly procedure or arrangement

well–read \-'red\ *adj* : well informed through reading

well–round·ed \-'raùn-dəd\ *adj* **1** : broadly trained, educated, and experienced **2** : COMPREHENSIVE ⟨a ∼ program of activities⟩

well–spo·ken \'wel-'spō-kən\ *adj* **1** : speaking well and esp. courteously **2** : spoken with propriety ⟨∼ words⟩

well·spring \-₁spriŋ\ *n* : a source of continuous supply

well–timed \-'tīmd\ *adj* : TIMELY

well–to–do \₁wel-tə-'dü\ *adj* : having more than adequate financial resources : PROSPEROUS

well–turned \'wel-'tərnd\ *adj* **1** : pleasingly shaped ⟨a ∼ ankle⟩ **2** : pleasingly expressed ⟨a ∼ phrase⟩

well–wish·er \'wel-₁wi-shər\ *n* : one that wishes well to another — **well–wish·ing** *adj or n*

welsh \'welsh, 'welch\ *vb* **1** : to avoid payment **2** : to break one's word ⟨∼ed on his promises⟩

Welsh \'welsh\ *n* **1** **Welsh** *pl* : the people of Wales **2** : the Celtic language of Wales — **Welsh** *adj* — **Welsh·man** \-mən\ *n*

Welsh cor·gi \-'kȯr-gē\ *n* [W *corgi*, fr. *cor* dwarf + *ci* dog] : a short-legged long-backed dog with foxy head of either of two breeds of Welsh origin

Welsh rabbit *n* : melted often seasoned cheese served over toast or crackers

Welsh rare·bit \-'rar-bət\ *n* : WELSH RABBIT

¹welt \'welt\ *n* **1** : the narrow strip of leather between a shoe upper and sole to which other parts are stitched **2** : a doubled edge, strip, insert, or seam for ornament or reinforcement **3** : a ridge or lump raised on the skin usu. by a blow; *also* : a heavy blow

²welt *vb* **1** : to furnish with a welt **2** : to hit hard

¹wel·ter \'wel-tər\ *vb* **1** : WRITHE, TOSS; *also* : WALLOW **2** : to rise and fall or toss about in or with waves **3** : to become deeply sunk, soaked, or involved **4** : to be in turmoil

²welter *n* **1** : TURMOIL **2** : a chaotic mass or jumble

wel·ter·weight \'wel-tər-₁wāt\ *n* : a boxer weighing more than 135 but not over 147 pounds

wen \'wen\ *n* : an abnormal growth or a cyst protruding from a surface esp. of the skin

wench \'wench\ *n* [ME *wenche*, short for *wenchel* child, fr. OE *wencel*] **1** : a young woman **2** : a female servant

wend \'wend\ *vb* : to direct one's course : proceed on (one's way)

went *past of* GO

wept *past and past part of* WEEP

were *past 2d sing, past pl, or past subjunctive of* BE

were·wolf \'wer-₁wùlf, 'wir-, 'wər-\ *n, pl* **were·wolves** \-₁wùlvz\ [ME, fr. OE *werwulf*, fr. *wer* man + *wulf* wolf] : a person transformed into a wolf or capable of assuming a wolf's form

wes·kit \'wes-kət\ *n* : VEST 1

¹west \'west\ *adv* : to or toward the west

²west *adj* **1** : situated toward or at the west **2** : coming from the west

³west *n* **1** : the general direction of sunset **2** : the compass point directly opposite to east **3** *cap* : regions or countries west of a specified or implied point **4** *cap* : Europe and the Americas — **west·er·ly** \'wes-tər-lē\ *adv or adj* — **west·ward** *adv or adj* — **west·wards** *adv*

¹west·ern \'wes-tərn\ *adj* **1** : lying toward or coming from the west **2** *cap* : of, relating to, or characteristic of a region conventionally designated West **3** *cap* : of or relating to the Roman Catholic or Protestant segment of Christianity — **West·ern·er** *n*

²western *n, often cap* : a novel, story, film, or radio or television show about life in the western U.S. during the latter half of the 19th century

west·ern·ise *Brit var of* WESTERNIZE

west·ern·ize \'wes-tər-₁nīz\ *vb* **-ized; -iz·ing** : to give western characteristics to

¹wet \'wet\ *adj* **wet·ter; wet·test** **1** : consisting of or covered or soaked with liquid (as water) **2** : RAINY **3** : not dry ⟨∼ paint⟩ **4** : permitting or advocating the manufacture and sale of alcoholic beverages ⟨a ∼ town⟩ ⟨a ∼ candidate⟩ **syn** damp, dank, moist, humid — **wet·ly** *adv* — **wet·ness** *n*

²wet *n* **1** : WATER; *also* : WETNESS, MOISTURE **2** : rainy weather : RAIN **3** : an advocate of a wet liquor policy

³wet *vb* **wet** *or* **wet·ted; wet·ting** : to make or become wet

wet blanket *n* : one that quenches or dampens enthusiasm or pleasure

weth·er \'we-thər\ *n* : a castrated male sheep or goat

wet·land \'wet-₁land, -lənd\ *n* : land or areas (as swamps) containing much soil moisture — usu. used in pl.

wet nurse *n* : a woman who cares for and suckles children not her own

wet suit *n* : a rubber suit for swimmers that acts to retain body heat by keeping a layer of water against the body as insulation

wh *abbr* **1** which **2** white

¹whack \'hwak\ *vb* **1** : to strike with a smart or resounding blow **2** : to cut with or as if with a whack

²whack *n* **1** : a smart or resounding blow; *also* : the sound of such a blow **2** : PORTION, SHARE **3** : CONDITION, STATE ⟨the machine is out of ∼⟩ **4** : an opportunity or attempt to do something : CHANCE **5** : a single action or occasion ⟨made three pies at a ∼⟩

¹whale \'hwāl\ *n, pl* **whales** *or* **whale** **1** : CETACEAN; *esp* : one (as a sperm whale or killer whale) of large size **2** : a person or thing impressive in size or quality ⟨a ∼ of a story⟩

²whale *vb* **whaled; whal·ing** : to fish or hunt for whales

³whale *vb* **whaled; whal·ing** **1** : THRASH **2** : to strike or hit vigorously

whale·boat \-₁bōt\ *n* : a long narrow rowboat originally used by whalers

whale·bone \-₁bōn\ *n* : BALEEN

whal·er \'hwā-lər\ *n* **1** : a person or ship that hunts whales **2** : WHALEBOAT

wham·my \'hwa-mē\ *n, pl* **wham·mies** : JINX, HEX

wharf \'hwȯrf\ *n, pl* **wharves** \'hwȯrvz\ *also* **wharfs** : a structure alongside which ships lie to load and unload

¹what \'hwät, 'hwət\ *pron* **1** — used to inquire about the identity or nature of a being, an object, or some matter or situation ⟨∼ is he, a salesman⟩ ⟨∼'s that⟩ ⟨∼ happened⟩ **2** : that which ⟨I know ∼ you want⟩ **3** : WHATEVER 1 ⟨take ∼ you want⟩

²what *adv* **1** : in what respect : HOW ⟨∼ does he care⟩ **2** — used with *with* to introduce a prepositional phrase that expresses cause ⟨kept busy ∼ with school and work⟩

³what *adj* **1** — used to inquire about the identity or nature of a person, object, or matter ⟨∼ books do you read⟩ **2** : how remarkable or surprising ⟨∼ an idea⟩ : WHATEVER

¹what·ev·er \hwät-'e-vər\ *pron* **1** : anything or everything that ⟨does ∼ he wants to⟩ **2** : no matter what ⟨∼ you do, don't cheat⟩ **3** : WHAT 1 — used as an intensive ⟨∼ do you mean⟩

²whatever *adj* : of any kind at all ⟨no food ∼⟩

¹**what·not** \'hwät-ˌnät\ *pron* : any of various other things that might also be mentioned ⟨needles, pins, and ∼⟩

²**whatnot** *n* : a light open set of shelves for small ornaments

what·so·ev·er \ˌhwät-sō-'e-vər\ *pron or adj* : WHATEVER

wheal \'hwēl\ *n* : a rapidly formed flat slightly raised itching or burning patch on the skin; *also* : WELT

wheat \'hwēt\ *n* : a cereal grain that yields a fine white flour and is the chief breadstuff of temperate regions; *also* : any of several grasses yielding wheat — **wheat·en** *adj*

wheat germ *n* : the vitamin-rich wheat embryo separated in milling

whee·dle \'hwēd-ᵊl\ *vb* **whee·dled; whee·dling** 1 : to entice by flattery 2 : to gain or get by wheedling

¹**wheel** \'hwēl\ *n* 1 : a disk or circular frame that turns on a central axis 2 : a device whose main part is a wheel 3 : something resembling a wheel in shape or motion 4 : a curving or circular movement 5 : machinery that imparts motion : moving power ⟨the ∼s of government⟩ 6 : a person of importance 7 *pl, slang* : AUTOMOBILE — **wheeled** \'hwēld\ *adj* — **wheel·less** *adj*

²**wheel** *vb* 1 : ROTATE, REVOLVE 2 : to change direction as if turning on a pivot 3 : to convey or move on wheels or in a vehicle

wheel·bar·row \-ˌbar-ō\ *n* : a vehicle with handles and usu. one wheel for carrying small loads

wheel·base \-ˌbās\ *n* : the distance in inches between the front and rear axles of an automotive vehicle

wheel·chair \-ˌcher\ *n* : a chair mounted on wheels esp. for the use of disabled persons

wheel·er \'hwē-lər\ *n* 1 : one that wheels 2 : WHEEL-HORSE 3 : something that has wheels — used in combination ⟨a side-*wheeler*⟩

wheel·er–deal·er \ˌhwē-lər-'dē-lər\ *n* : a shrewd operator esp. in business or politics

wheel·horse \'hwēl-ˌhȯrs\ *n* 1 : a horse in a position nearest the front wheels of a wagon 2 : a steady and effective worker esp. in a political body

wheel·house \-ˌhaüs\ *n* : PILOTHOUSE

wheel–thrown \'hwēl-ˌthrōn\ *adj* : made on a potter's wheel

wheel·wright \-ˌrīt\ *n* : a maker and repairer of wheels and wheeled vehicles

¹**wheeze** \'hwēz\ *vb* **wheezed; wheez·ing** : to breathe with difficulty usu. with a whistling sound

²**wheeze** *n* 1 : a sound of wheezing 2 : an often repeated and well-known joke 3 : a trite saying

wheezy \'hwē-zē\ *adj* **wheez·i·er; -est** 1 : inclined to wheeze 2 : having a wheezing sound — **wheez·i·ly** \-zə-lē\ *adv* — **wheez·i·ness** \-zē-nəs\ *n*

whelk \'hwelk\ *n* : a large sea snail; *esp* : one much used as food in Europe

whelm \'hwelm\ *vb* : to overcome or engulf completely : OVERWHELM

¹**whelp** \'hwelp\ *n* : any of the young of various carnivorous mammals (as a dog)

²**whelp** *vb* : to give birth to (whelps); *also* : bring forth young

¹**when** \'hwen\ *adv* 1 : at what time ⟨∼ will you return⟩ 2 : at or during which time ⟨a time ∼ things were better⟩

²**when** *conj* 1 : at or during the time that ⟨leave ∼ I do⟩ 2 : every time that ⟨they all clapped ∼ he sang⟩ 3 : in the event that : IF ⟨disqualified ∼ you cheat⟩ 4 : ALTHOUGH ⟨quit politics ∼ he might have had a great career in it⟩

³**when** *pron* : what or which time ⟨since ∼ have you been the boss⟩

⁴**when** *n* : the time of a happening

whence \'hwens\ *adv or conj* : from what place, source, or cause

when·ev·er \hwe-'ne-vər, hwə-\ *conj or adv* : at whatever time

when·so·ev·er \'hwen-sō-ˌe-vər\ *conj* : at whatever time

¹**where** \'hwer\ *adv* 1 : at, in, or to what place ⟨∼ is it⟩ ⟨∼ will we go⟩ 2 : at, in, or to what situation, position, direction, circumstances, or respect ⟨∼ does this road lead⟩

²**where** *conj* 1 : at, in, or to what place ⟨knows ∼ the house is⟩ 2 : at, in, or to what situation, position, direction, circumstances, or respect ⟨shows ∼ the road leads⟩ 3 : WHEREVER ⟨goes ∼ she likes⟩ 4 : at, in, or to which place ⟨the town ∼ we live⟩ 5 : at, in, or to the place at, in, or to which ⟨stay ∼ you are⟩ 6 : in a case, situation, or respect in which ⟨outstanding ∼ endurance is called for⟩

³**where** *n* : PLACE, LOCATION ⟨the ∼ and how of the accident⟩

¹**where·abouts** \-ə-ˌbaùts\ *also* **where·about** \-ˌbaùt\ *adv* : about where : near what place ⟨∼ does he live⟩

²**whereabouts** *n sing or pl* : the place where a person or thing is ⟨his present ∼ are unknown⟩

where·as \hwer-'az\ *conj* 1 : while on the contrary; *also* : ALTHOUGH 2 : in view of the fact that : SINCE

where·at \-'at\ *conj* 1 : at or toward which 2 : in consequence of which : WHEREUPON

where·by \-'bī\ *conj* : by, through, or in accordance with which ⟨the means ∼ we achieved our goals⟩

¹**where·fore** \'hwer-ˌfȯr\ *adv* 1 : for what reason or purpose : WHY 2 : THEREFORE

²**wherefore** *n* : an answer or statement giving an explanation : REASON

¹**where·in** \hwer-'in\ *adv* : in what : in what respect ⟨∼ was I wrong⟩

²**wherein** *conj* 1 : in which : WHERE ⟨the city ∼ we live⟩ 2 : during which 3 : in what way : HOW ⟨showed me ∼ I was wrong⟩

where·of \-'əv, -'äv\ *conj* 1 : of what ⟨knows ∼ he speaks⟩ 2 : of which or whom ⟨books ∼ the best are lost⟩

where·on \-ˈȯn, -ˈän\ *conj* : on which ⟨the base ~ it rests⟩

where·so·ev·er \ˈhwer-sō-ˌe-vər\ *conj* : WHEREVER

where·to \ˈhwer-ˌtü\ *conj* : to which

where·up·on \ˈhwer-ə-ˌpȯn, -ˌpän\ *conj* 1 : on which 2 : closely following and in consequence of which

¹**wher·ev·er** \hwer-ˈe-vər\ *adv* : where in the world ⟨~ did he get that tie⟩

²**wherever** *conj* 1 : at, in, or to whatever place 2 : in any circumstance in which

where·with \ˈhwer-ˌwith, -ˌwith\ *conj* : with or by means of which

where·with·al \ˈhwer-wi-ˌthȯl, -ˌthȯl\ *n* : MEANS, RESOURCES; *esp* : MONEY

wher·ry \ˈhwer-ē\ *n, pl* **wherries** : a long light rowboat sharp at both ends

whet \ˈhwet\ *vb* **whet·ted; whet·ting** 1 : to sharpen by rubbing on or with something abrasive (as a whetstone) 2 : to make keen : STIMULATE ⟨~ the appetite⟩

wheth·er \ˈhwe-thər\ *conj* 1 : if it is or was true that ⟨ask ~ he is going⟩ 2 : if it is or was better ⟨uncertain ~ to go or stay⟩ 3 : whichever is or was the case, namely that ⟨~ we succeed or fail, we must try⟩ 4 : EITHER ⟨turned out well ~ by accident or design⟩

whet·stone \ˈhwet-ˌstōn\ *n* : a stone for sharpening blades

whey \ˈhwā\ *n* : the watery part of milk that separates after the milk sours and thickens

¹**which** \ˈhwich\ *adj* 1 : being what one or ones out of a group ⟨~ shirt should I wear⟩ 2 : WHICHEVER

²**which** *pron* 1 : which one or ones ⟨~ is yours⟩ ⟨~ are his⟩ ⟨it's in May or June, I'm not sure ~⟩ 2 : WHICHEVER ⟨we have all kinds; take ~ you like⟩ 3 — used to introduce a relative clause and to serve as a substitute therein for the noun modified by the clause ⟨the money ~ is coming to me⟩

¹**which·ev·er** \hwich-ˈe-vər\ *adj* : no matter which ⟨~ way you go⟩

²**whichever** *pron* : whatever one or ones

which·so·ev·er \ˌhwich-sō-ˈe-vər\ *pron or adj* : WHICHEVER

whick·er \ˈhwi-kər\ *vb* : NEIGH, WHINNY — **whicker** *n*

¹**whiff** \ˈhwif\ *n* 1 : a quick puff or slight gust (as of air) 2 : an inhalation of odor, gas, or smoke 3 : a slight trace 4 : STRIKEOUT

²**whiff** *vb* 1 : to expel, puff out, or blow away in or as if in whiffs 2 : to inhale an odor 3 : STRIKE OUT 3

whif·fle·tree \ˈhwi-fəl-(ˌ)trē\ *n* : the pivoted swinging bar to which the traces of a harness are fastened

Whig \ˈhwig\ *n* [short for *Whiggamore*, member of a Scottish group that marched to Edinburgh in 1648 to oppose the court party] 1 : a member or supporter of a British political group of the late 17th through early 19th centuries seeking to limit royal authority and increase parliamentary power 2 : an American favoring independence from Great Britain during the American Revolution 3 : a member or supporter of an American political party formed about 1834 to oppose the Democrats

¹**while** \ˈhwīl\ *n* 1 : a period of time ⟨stay a ~⟩ 2 : the time and effort used : TROUBLE ⟨worth your ~⟩

²**while** *conj* 1 : during the time that ⟨she called ~ you were out⟩ 2 : AS LONG AS ⟨~ there's life there's hope⟩ 3 : ALTHOUGH ⟨~ he's respected, he's not liked⟩

³**while** *vb* **whiled; whil·ing** : to cause to pass esp. pleasantly ⟨~ away an hour⟩

¹**whi·lom** \ˈhwī-ləm\ *adv* [ME, lit., at times, fr. OE *hwīlum*, dat. pl. of *hwīl* time, while] *archaic* : FORMERLY

²**whilom** *adj* : FORMER ⟨his ~ friends⟩

whilst \ˈhwīlst\ *conj, chiefly Brit* : WHILE

whim \ˈhwim\ *n* : a sudden wish, desire, or change of mind

whim·per \ˈhwim-pər\ *vb* : to make a low whining plaintive or broken sound — **whimper** *n*

whim·si·cal \ˈhwim-zi-kəl\ *adj* 1 : full of whims : CAPRICIOUS 2 : resulting from or characterized by whim or caprice : ERRATIC — **whim·si·cal·i·ty** \ˌhwim-zə-ˈka-lə-tē\ *n* — **whim·si·cal·ly** \ˈhwim-zi-k(ə-)lē\ *adv*

whim·sy *or* **whim·sey** \ˈhwim-zē\ *n, pl* **whimsies** *or* **whimseys** 1 : WHIM, CAPRICE 2 : a fanciful or fantastic device, object, or creation esp. in writing or art

whine \ˈhwīn\ *vb* **whined; whin·ing** [ME, fr. OE *hwīnan* to whiz] 1 : to utter a usu. high-pitched plaintive or distressed cry; *also* : to make a sound similar to such a cry 2 : to complain with or as if with a whine — **whine** *n* — **whin·er** *n* — **whiny** *also* **whin·ey** \ˈhwī-nē\ *adj*

¹**whin·ny** \ˈhwi-nē\ *vb* **whin·nied; whin·ny·ing** : to neigh usu. in a low or gentle manner

²**whinny** *n, pl* **whinnies** : NEIGH

¹**whip** \ˈhwip\ *vb* **whipped; whip·ping** 1 : to move, snatch, or jerk quickly or forcefully ⟨~ out a gun⟩ 2 : to strike with a slender lithe implement (as a lash) esp. as a punishment; *also* : SPANK 3 : to drive or urge on by or as if by using a whip 4 : to bind or wrap (as a rope or rod) with cord in order to protect and strengthen; *also* : to wind or wrap around something 5 : DEFEAT 6 : to stir up : INCITE ⟨~ up enthusiasm⟩ 7 : to produce in a hurry ⟨~ up a meal⟩ 8 : to beat (as eggs or cream) into a froth 9 : to proceed nimbly or briskly; *also* : to flap about forcefully ⟨flags *whipping* in the wind⟩ — **whip·per** *n* — **whip into shape** : to bring forcefully to a desired state or condition

²**whip** *n* 1 : a flexible instrument used for whipping 2 : a stroke or cut with or as if with a whip 3 : a dessert made by whipping a portion of the ingredients ⟨prune ~⟩ 4 : a person who handles a whip 5 : a member of a legislative body appointed by a party to enforce party discipline 6 : a whipping or thrashing motion

whip·cord \-ˌkȯrd\ *n* 1 : a thin tough braided cord 2 : a strong cloth with fine diagonal cords or ribs

whip hand *n* : positive control : ADVANTAGE

whip·lash \ˈhwip-ˌlash\ *n* 1 : the lash of a whip 2 : injury resulting from a sudden sharp movement of the neck and head (as of a person in a vehicle that is struck from the rear)

whip·per·snap·per \ˈhwi-pər-ˌsna-pər\ *n* : a small, insignificant, or presumptuous person

whip·pet \ˈhwi-pət\ *n* : any of a breed of small swift slender dogs that are used for racing

whipping boy *n* : SCAPEGOAT

whip·ple·tree \ˈhwi-pəl-(ˌ)trē\ *n* : WHIFFLETREE

whip·poor·will \ˈhwi-pər-ˌwil\ *n* : an American insect-eating bird with dull variegated plumage whose call at nightfall and just before dawn is suggestive of its name

whippoorwill

whip·saw \ˈhwip-ˌsȯ\ *vb* : to beset with two or more adverse conditions or situations at once

¹**whir** *also* **whirr** \ˈhwər\ *vb* **whirred; whir·ring** : to move, fly, or revolve with a whir

²**whir** *also* **whirr** *n* : a continuous fluttering or vibratory sound made by something in rapid motion

¹**whirl** \ˈhwərl\ *vb* 1 : to move or drive in a circle or curve esp. with force or speed 2 : to turn or cause to

turn rapidly in circles **3** : to turn abruptly : WHEEL **4** : to move or go quickly **5** : to become dizzy or giddy : REEL

²whirl *n* **1** : a rapid rotating or circling movement; *also* : something whirling **2** : COMMOTION, BUSTLE ⟨the social ~⟩ **3** : a state of mental confusion **4** : TRY ⟨gave it a ~⟩

whirl·i·gig \'hwər-li-ˌgig\ *n* [ME *whirlegigg*, fr. *whirlen* to whirl + *gigg* top] **1** : a child's toy having a whirling motion **2** : something that continuously whirls or changes

whirl·pool \-ˌpül\ *n* : water moving rapidly in a circle so as to produce a depression in the center into which floating objects may be drawn

whirl·wind \-ˌwind\ *n* **1** : a small whirling windstorm **2** : a confused rush **3** : a violent or destructive force

whirly·bird \'hwər-lē-ˌbərd\ *n* : HELICOPTER

¹whish \'hwish\ *vb* : to move with a whish or swishing sound

²whish *n* : a rushing sound : SWISH

¹whisk \'hwisk\ *n* **1** : a quick light sweeping or brushing motion **2** : a usu. wire kitchen implement for beating food by hand **3** : WHISK BROOM

²whisk *vb* **1** : to move nimbly and quickly **2** : to move or convey briskly ⟨~ed the children off to bed⟩ **3** : to beat or whip lightly ⟨~ eggs⟩ **4** : to brush or wipe off lightly ⟨~ a coat⟩

whisk broom *n* : a small broom with a short handle used esp. as a clothes brush

whis·ker \'hwis-kər\ *n* **1** : one hair of the beard **2** *pl* : the part of the beard that grows on the sides of the face or on the chin **3** : one of the long bristles or hairs growing near the mouth of an animal (as a cat or mouse) — **whis·kered** \-kərd\ *adj*

whis·key *or* **whis·ky** \'hwis-kē\ *n, pl* **whiskeys** *or* **whiskies** [Ir *uisce beathadh* & ScGael *uisge beatha*, lit., water of life] : a liquor distilled from the fermented mash of grain (as rye, corn, or barley)

¹whis·per \'hwis-pər\ *vb* **1** : to speak very low or under the breath; *also* : to tell or utter by whispering ⟨~ a secret⟩ **2** : to make a low rustling sound ⟨~ing leaves⟩

²whisper *n* **1** : something communicated by or as if by whispering : HINT, RUMOR **2** : an act or instance of whispering

whist \'hwist\ *n* : a card game played by four players in two partnerships with a deck of 52 cards

¹whis·tle \'hwi-səl\ *n* **1** : a device by which a shrill sound is produced ⟨steam ~⟩ ⟨tin ~⟩ **2** : a shrill clear sound made by forcing breath out or air in through the puckered lips **3** : the sound or signal produced by a whistle or as if by whistling **4** : the shrill clear note of an animal (as a bird)

²whistle *vb* **whis·tled; whis·tling 1** : to utter a shrill clear sound by blowing or drawing air through the puckered lips **2** : to utter a shrill note or call resembling a whistle **3** : to make a shrill clear sound esp. by rapid movements ⟨the wind *whistled*⟩ **4** : to blow or sound a whistle **5** : to signal or call by a whistle **6** : to produce, utter, or express by whistling ⟨~ a tune⟩ — **whis·tler** *n*

whis·tle–blow·er \'hwi-səl-ˌblō-ər\ *n* : INFORMER

whis·tle–stop \-ˌstäp\ *n* : a brief personal appearance by a political candidate orig. on the rear platform of a touring train

whit \'hwit\ *n* [prob. alter. of ME *wiht, wight* creature, thing, fr. OE *wiht*] : the smallest part or particle : BIT

¹white \'hwīt\ *adj* **whit·er; whit·est 1** : free from color **2** : of the color of new snow or milk; *esp* : of the color white **3** : light or pallid in color ⟨lips ~ with fear⟩ **4** : SILVERY; *also* : made of silver **5** : of, relating to, or being a member of a group or race characterized by light-colored skin **6** : free from spot or blemish : PURE, INNOCENT **7** : BLANK 2 ⟨~ space in printed matter⟩ **8** : not intended to cause harm ⟨a ~ lie⟩ **9** : wearing white ⟨~ friars⟩ **10** : marked by snow ⟨~ Christmas⟩ **11** : consisting of a wide range of frequencies ⟨~ light⟩ — **white·ness** \-nəs\ *n* — **whit·ish** \'hwī-tish\ *adj*

²white *n* **1** : the color of maximal lightness that characterizes objects which both reflect and transmit light : the opposite of black **2** : a white or light-colored part or thing ⟨the ~ of an egg⟩; *also, pl* : white garments **3** : the light-colored pieces in a 2-player board game; *also* : the person by whom these are played **4** : one that is or approaches the color white **5** : a person of a light-skinned race

white ant *n* : TERMITE

white blood cell *n* : a colorless blood cell (as a lymphocyte) that does not contain hemoglobin but does have a nucleus

white–bread \'hwīt-'bred\ *adj* : being, typical of, or having qualities (as blandness) associated with the white middle class

white·cap \'hwīt-ˌkap\ *n* : a wave crest breaking into white foam

white chocolate *n* : a whitish chocolate candy

white–col·lar \'hwīt-'kä-lər\ *adj* : of, relating to, or constituting the class of salaried workers whose duties do not require the wearing of work clothes or protective clothing

white dwarf *n* : a small very dense whitish star of low luminosity

white elephant *n* **1** : an Indian elephant of a pale color that is sometimes venerated in India, Sri Lanka, Thailand, and Myanmar **2** : something requiring much care and expense and giving little profit or enjoyment

white feather *n* [fr. the superstition that a white feather in the plumage of a gamecock is a mark of a poor fighter] : a mark or symbol of cowardice

white·fish \'hwīt-ˌfish\ *n* : any of various freshwater food fishes related to the salmons and trouts

white flag *n* : a flag of pure white used to signify truce or surrender

white gold *n* : a pale alloy of gold resembling platinum in appearance

white goods *n pl* : white fabrics or articles (as sheets or towels) typically made of cotton or linen

White·hall \'hwīt-ˌhȯl\ *n* : the British government

white·head \-ˌhed\ *n* : a small whitish lump in the skin due to retention of secretion in an oil gland duct

white heat *n* : a temperature higher than red heat at which a body becomes brightly incandescent

white–hot *adj* **1** : being at or radiating white heat **2** : FERVID

White House \-ˌhaus\ *n* **1** : the executive department of the U.S. government **2** : a residence of the president of the U.S.

white lead *n* : a heavy white poisonous carbonate of lead used esp. as a pigment in exterior paints

white matter *n* : whitish nerve tissue that consists largely of nerve-cell processes enclosed in a fatty material and that lies under the gray matter of the brain and spinal cord or is collected into nerves

whit·en \'hwīt-ᵊn\ *vb* : to make or become white **syn** blanch, bleach — **whit·en·er** *n*

white pine *n* : a tall-growing pine of eastern No. America with needles in clusters of five; *also* : its wood

white sale *n* : a sale on white goods

white shark *n* : GREAT WHITE SHARK

white slave *n* : a woman or girl held unwillingly for purposes of prostitution — **white slavery** *n*

white·tail \'hwīt-ˌtāl\ *n* : WHITE-TAILED DEER

white–tailed deer *n* : a No. American deer with a rather long tail white on the underside the males of which have forward-arching antlers

white·wall \'hwīt-ˌwȯl\ *n* : an automobile tire having a white band on the sidewall

¹white·wash \-ˌwȯsh, -ˌwäsh\ *vb* **1** : to whiten with whitewash **2** : to clear of a charge of wrongdoing by offering excuses, hiding facts, or conducting a perfunctory investigation **3** : SHUT OUT 2

²whitewash *n* **1** : a liquid mixture (as of lime and water) for whitening a surface **2** : a clearing of wrongdoing by whitewashing

white·wood \-ˌwud\ *n* : any of various trees and esp. a tulip tree having light-colored wood; *also* : such wood

¹whith·er \'hwi-thər\ *adv* **1** : to what place **2** : to what situation, position, degree, or end ⟨∼ will this drive him⟩

²whither *conj* **1** : to the place at, in, or to which; *also* : to which place **2** : to whatever place

whith·er·so·ev·er \ˌhwi-thər-sō-ˈe-vər\ *conj* : to whatever place

¹whit·ing \'hwī-tiŋ\ *n* : any of several usu. light or silvery food fishes (as a hake) found mostly near seacoasts

²whiting *n* : calcium carbonate in powdered form used esp. as a pigment and in putty

whit·low \'hwit-ˌlō\ *n* : a deep inflammation of a finger or toe with pus formation

Whit·sun·day \'hwit-ˈsən-dē, -ˌsən-ˌdā\ *n* [ME *Whitsonday*, fr. OE *hwīta sunnandæg*, lit., white Sunday; prob. fr. the custom of wearing white robes by those newly baptized at this season] : PENTECOST

whit·tle \'hwit-ᵊl\ *vb* **whit·tled; whit·tling 1** : to pare or cut off chips from the surface of (wood) with a knife; *also* : to cut or shape by such paring **2** : to reduce as if by paring down ⟨∼ down expenses⟩

¹whiz *or* **whizz** \'hwiz\ *vb* **whizzed; whiz·zing** : to hum, whir, or hiss like a speeding object (as an arrow or ball) passing through air

²whiz *or* **whizz** *n, pl* **whiz·zes** : a hissing, buzzing, or whizzing sound

³whiz *n, pl* **whiz·zes** : WIZARD 2

who \'hü\ *pron* **1** : what or which person or persons ⟨∼ did it⟩ ⟨∼ is he⟩ ⟨∼ are they⟩ **2** : the person or persons that ⟨knows ∼ did it⟩ **3** — used to introduce a relative clause and to serve as a substitute therein for the substantive modified by the clause ⟨the man ∼ lives there is rich⟩

WHO *abbr* World Health Organization

whoa \'wō, 'hwō, 'hō\ *vb imper* — a command to an animal to stand still

who·dun·it *also* **who·dun·nit** \hü-ˈdə-nət\ *n* : a detective or mystery story

who·ev·er \hü-ˈe-vər\ *pron* : whatever person : no matter who

¹whole \'hōl\ *adj* [ME *hool* healthy, unhurt, entire, fr. OE *hāl*] **1** : being in healthy or sound condition : free from defect or damage **2** : having all its proper parts or elements ⟨∼ milk⟩ **3** : constituting the total sum of : ENTIRE ⟨owns the ∼ island⟩ **4** : each or all of the ⟨the ∼ family⟩ **5** : not scattered or divided : CONCENTRATED ⟨gave me his ∼ attention⟩ **6** : seemingly complete or total ⟨the ∼ idea is to hide, not hinder⟩ **syn** perfect, intact, sound — **whole·ness** *n*

²whole *n* **1** : a complete amount or sum **2** : something whole or entire — **on the whole 1** : in view of all the circumstances or conditions **2** : in general

whole·heart·ed \'hōl-ˈhär-təd\ *adj* : undivided in purpose, enthusiasm, or will : HEARTY, ZESTFUL, SINCERE

whole note *n* : a musical note equal to one measure of four beats

whole number *n* : any of the set of nonnegative integers; *also* : INTEGER

¹whole·sale \'hōl-ˌsāl\ *n* : the sale of goods in quantity usu. for resale by a retail merchant

²wholesale *adj* **1** : performed on a large scale without discrimination ⟨∼ slaughter⟩ **2** : of, relating to, or engaged in wholesaling — **wholesale** *adv*

³wholesale *vb* **whole·saled; whole·sal·ing** : to sell at wholesale — **whole·sal·er** *n*

whole·some \'hōl-səm\ *adj* **1** : promoting mental, spiritual, or bodily health or well-being ⟨a ∼ environment⟩ **2** : sound in body, mind, or morals : HEALTHY **3** : PRUDENT ⟨∼ respect for the law⟩ — **whole·some·ness** *n*

whole step *n* : a musical interval comprising two half steps (as C–D or F♯–G♯)

whole wheat *adj* : made of ground entire wheat kernels
whol·ly \ˈhōl-lē\ *adv* **1** : COMPLETELY, TOTALLY **2** : SOLELY, EXCLUSIVELY
whom \ˈhüm\ *pron, objective case of* WHO
whom·ev·er \hü-ˈme-vər\ *pron, objective case of* WHOEVER
whom·so·ev·er \ˌhüm-sō-ˈe-vər\ *pron, objective case of* WHOSOEVER
¹**whoop** \ˈhwüp, ˈhwůp, ˈhüp, ˈhůp\ *vb* **1** : to shout or call loudly and vigorously **2** : to make the characteristic whoop of whooping cough **3** : to go or pass with a loud noise **4** : to utter or express with a whoop; *also* : to urge, drive, or cheer with a whoop
²**whoop** *n* **1** : a whooping sound or utterance : SHOUT, HOOT **2** : a crowing intake of breath after a fit of coughing in whooping cough
whooping cough *n* : an infectious bacterial disease esp. of children marked by convulsive coughing fits often followed by a shrill gasping intake of breath
whooping crane *n* : a large white nearly extinct No. American crane noted for its loud whooping call

whooping crane

whoop·la \ˈhwüp-ˌlä, ˈhwůp-\ *n* **1** : HOOPLA **2** : boisterous merrymaking
whop·per \ˈhwä-pər\ *n* : something unusually large or extreme of its kind; *esp* : a monstrous lie
whop·ping \ˈhwä-piŋ\ *adj* : extremely large
whore \ˈhōr\ *n* : PROSTITUTE
whorl \ˈhwȯrl, ˈhwərl\ *n* **1** : a group of parts (as leaves or petals) encircling an axis and esp. a plant stem **2** : something that whirls or coils around a center : COIL, SPIRAL **3** : one of the turns of a snail shell
whorled \ˈhwȯrld, ˈhwərld\ *adj* : having or arranged in whorls
¹**whose** \ˈhüz\ *adj* : of or relating to whom or which esp. as possessor or possessors, agent or agents, or object or objects of an action ⟨asked ∼ bag it was⟩
²**whose** *pron* : whose one or ones ⟨∼ is this car⟩ ⟨∼ are those books⟩
who·so \ˈhü-ˌsō\ *pron* : WHOEVER
who·so·ev·er \ˌhü-sō-ˈe-vər\ *pron* : WHOEVER
whs *or* **whse** *abbr* warehouse
whsle *abbr* wholesale
¹**why** \ˈhwī\ *adv* : for what reason, cause, or purpose ⟨∼ did you do it⟩
²**why** *conj* **1** : the cause, reason, or purpose for which ⟨that is ∼ you did it⟩ **2** : for which : on account of which ⟨knows the reason ∼ you did it⟩
³**why** *n, pl* **whys** : REASON, CAUSE ⟨the ∼s of racial prejudice⟩
⁴**why** \ˈwī, ˈhwī\ *interj* — used to express surprise, hesitation, approval, disapproval, or impatience ⟨∼, here's what I was looking for⟩
WI *abbr* **1** West Indies **2** Wisconsin
WIA *abbr* wounded in action
wick \ˈwik\ *n* : a loosely bound bundle of soft fibers that draws up oil, tallow, or wax to be burned in a candle, oil lamp, or stove
wick·ed \ˈwi-kəd\ *adj* **1** : morally bad : EVIL, SINFUL **2** : FIERCE, VICIOUS **3** : ROGUISH ⟨a ∼ glance⟩ **4** : REPUGNANT, VILE ⟨a ∼ odor⟩ **5** : HARMFUL, DANGEROUS ⟨a ∼ attack⟩ **6** : impressively excellent ⟨throws a ∼ fastball⟩ — **wick·ed·ly** *adv* — **wick·ed·ness** *n*
wick·er \ˈwi-kər\ *n* **1** : a small pliant branch (as an osier or a withe) **2** : WICKERWORK — **wicker** *adj*
wick·er·work \-ˌwərk\ *n* : work made of osiers, twigs, or rods : BASKETRY
wick·et \ˈwi-kət\ *n* **1** : a small gate or door; *esp* : one forming a part of or placed near a larger one **2** : a window-like opening usu. with a grille or grate (as at a ticket office) **3** : a set of three upright rods topped by two crosspieces bowled at in cricket **4** : an arch or hoop in croquet
wick·i·up \ˈwi-kē-ˌəp\ *n* : a hut used by nomadic Indians of the western and southwestern U.S. with a usu. oval base and a rough frame covered with reed mats, grass, or brushwood
wid *abbr* widow, widower

¹**wide** \ˈwīd\ *adj* **wider; wid·est** **1** : covering a vast area **2** : measured across or at right angles to the length **3** : not narrow : BROAD; *also* : ROOMY **4** : opened to full width ⟨eyes ∼ with wonder⟩ **5** : not limited : EXTENSIVE ⟨∼ experience⟩ **6** : far from the goal, mark, or truth ⟨a ∼ guess⟩ — **wide·ly** *adv*

²**wide** *adv* **wid·er; wid·est** **1** : over a great distance or extent : WIDELY ⟨searched far and ∼⟩ **2** : over a specified distance, area, or extent **3** : so as to leave a wide space between ⟨∼ apart⟩ **4** : so as to clear by a considerable distance ⟨ran ∼ around left end⟩ **5** : COMPLETELY, FULLY ⟨opened her eyes ∼⟩
wide–awake \ˌwīd-ə-ˈwāk\ *adj* : fully awake; *also* : KNOWING, ALERT
wide–body \ˈwīd-ˌbä-dē\ *n* : a large jet aircraft
wide–eyed \ˈwīd-ˈīd\ *adj* **1** : having the eyes wide open esp. with wonder or astonishment **2** : NAIVE
wide·mouthed \-ˈmau̇thd, -ˈmau̇tht\ *adj* **1** : having one's mouth opened wide (as in awe) **2** : having a wide mouth ⟨∼ jars⟩
wid·en \ˈwīd-ᵊn\ *vb* : to increase in width, scope, or extent
wide·spread \ˈwīd-ˈspred\ *adj* **1** : widely scattered or prevalent **2** : widely extended or spread out ⟨∼ wings⟩

© 1987 PAWS, INC.

JiM DAViS   10-10

¹**wid·ow** \'wi-dō\ *n* : a woman who has lost her husband by death and has not married again — **wid·ow·hood** *n*

²**widow** *vb* : to cause to become a widow or widower

wid·ow·er \'wi-də-wər\ *n* : a man who has lost his wife by death and has not married again

width \'width\ *n* **1** : a distance from side to side : the measurement taken at right angles to the length : BREADTH **2** : largeness of extent or scope; *also* : FULLNESS **3** : a measured and cut piece of material ⟨a ~ of calico⟩

wield \'wēld\ *vb* **1** : to use or handle esp. effectively ⟨~ a broom⟩ **2** : to exert authority by means of : EMPLOY ⟨~ influence⟩ — **wield·er** *n*

wie·ner \'wē-nər\ *n* [short for *wienerwurst*, fr. G, lit., Vienna sausage] : FRANKFURTER

wife \'wīf\ *n, pl* **wives** \'wīvz\ **1** *dial* : WOMAN **2** : a woman acting in a specified capacity — used in combination **3** : a female partner in a marriage — **wife·hood** *n* — **wife·less** *adj* — **wife·ly** *adj*

wig \'wig\ *n* [short for *periwig*, fr. MF *perruque*, fr. It *parrucca, perrucca* hair, wig] : a manufactured covering of natural or synthetic hair for the head; *also* : TOUPEE

wi·geon *or* **wid·geon** \'wi-jən\ *n, pl* **wigeon** *or* **wigeons** *or* **widgeon** *or* **widgeons** : any of several mediums sized freshwater ducks

wig·gle \'wi-gəl\ *vb* **wig·gled; wig·gling 1** : to move to and fro with quick jerky or shaking movements : JIGGLE **2** : WRIGGLE — **wiggle** *n*

wig·gler \'wi-glər, -gə-lər\ *n* **1** : a larva or pupa of a mosquito **2** : one that wiggles

wig·gly \'wi-glē, -gə-lē\ *adj* **1** : tending to wiggle ⟨a ~ worm⟩ **2** : WAVY ⟨~ lines⟩

wight \'wīt\ *n* : a living being : CREATURE

wig·let \'wi-glət\ *n* : a small wig used esp. to enhance a hairstyle

¹**wig·wag** \'wig-ˌwag\ *vb* **1** : to signal by or as if by a flag or light waved according to a code **2** : to make or cause to make a signal (as with the hand or arm)

²**wigwag** *n* : the art or practice of wigwagging

wig·wam \'wig-ˌwäm\ *n* : a hut of the Indians of the eastern U.S. having typically an arched framework of poles overlaid with bark, rush mats, or hides

¹**wild** \'wīld\ *adj* **1** : living in a state of nature and not ordinarily tamed ⟨~ ducks⟩ **2** : growing or produced without human aid or care ⟨~ honey⟩ ⟨~ plants⟩ **3** : WASTE, DESOLATE ⟨~ country⟩ **4** : UNCONTROLLED, UNRESTRAINED, UNRULY ⟨~ passions⟩ ⟨a ~ young stallion⟩ **5** : TURBULENT, STORMY ⟨a ~ night⟩ **6** : EXTRAVAGANT, FANTASTIC, CRAZY ⟨~ ideas⟩ **7** : indicative of strong passion, desire, or emotion ⟨a ~ stare⟩ **8** : UNCIVILIZED, SAVAGE **9** : deviating from the natural or expected course : ERRATIC ⟨a ~ throw⟩ **10** : having a denomination determined by the holder ⟨deuces ~⟩ — **wild·ly** *adv* — **wild·ness** *n*

²**wild** *adv* **1** : WILDLY **2** : without regulation or control ⟨running ~⟩

³**wild** *n* **1** : WILDERNESS **2** : a natural or undomesticated state or existence

wild boar *n* : an Old World wild hog from which most domestic swine have been derived

wild carrot *n* : QUEEN ANNE'S LACE

¹**wild·cat** \'wīld-ˌkat\ *n, pl* **wildcats 1** : any of various small or medium-sized cats (as a lynx or ocelot) **2** : a quick-tempered hard-fighting person

²**wildcat** *adj* **1** : not sound or safe ⟨~ schemes⟩ **2** : initiated by a group of workers without formal union approval ⟨~ strike⟩

³**wildcat** *vb* **wild·cat·ted; wild·cat·ting** : to drill an oil or gas well in a region not known to be productive

wil·de·beest \'wil-də-ˌbēst\ *n, pl* **wildebeests** *also* **wildebeest** [Afrikaans *wildebees*, fr. *wilde* wild + *bees* ox] : GNU

wil·der·ness \'wil-dər-nəs\ *n* [ME, fr. *wildern* wild, fr.

OE *wilddēoren* of wild beasts] : an uncultivated and uninhabited region

wild·fire \'wīld-ˌfīr\ *n* : an uncontrollable fire — **like wildfire** : very rapidly

wild·fowl \-ˌfaůl\ *n* : a bird and esp. a waterfowl (as a wild duck or goose) hunted as game

wild–goose chase *n* : the pursuit of something unattainable

wild·life \'wīld-ˌlīf\ *n* : nonhuman living things and esp. wild animals living in their natural environment

wild oat *n* **1** : any of several wild grasses **2** *pl* : offenses and indiscretions attributed to youthful exuberance — usu. used in the phrase *sow one's wild oats*

wild rice *n* : a No. American aquatic grass; *also* : its edible seed

wild·wood \'wīld-ˌwůd\ *n* : a wood unaltered or unfrequented by humans

¹**wile** \'wīl\ *n* **1** : a trick or stratagem intended to ensnare or deceive; *also* : a playful trick **2** : TRICKERY, GUILE

²**wile** *vb* **wiled; wil·ing** : LURE, ENTICE

¹**will** \'wil\ *vb, past* **would** \'wůd\; *pres sing & pl* **will 1** : WISH, DESIRE ⟨call it what you ~⟩ **2** — used as an auxiliary verb to express (1) desire, willingness, or in negative constructions refusal ⟨~ you have another⟩ ⟨he *won't* do it⟩, (2) customary or habitual action ⟨~ get angry over nothing⟩, (3) simple futurity ⟨tomorrow we ~ go shopping⟩, (4) capability or sufficiency ⟨the back seat ~ hold three⟩, (5) determination or willfulness ⟨I ~ go despite them⟩, (6) probability ⟨that ~ be the mailman⟩, (7) inevitability ⟨accidents ~ happen⟩, or (8) a command ⟨you ~ do as I say⟩

²**will** *n* **1** : wish or desire often combined with determination ⟨the ~ to win⟩ **2** : something desired; *esp* : a choice or determination of one having authority or power **3** : the act, process, or experience of willing : VOLITION **4** : the mental powers manifested as wishing, choosing, desiring, or intending **5** : a disposition to act according to principles or ends **6** : power of controlling one's own actions or emotions ⟨a leader of iron ~⟩ **7** : a legal document in which a person declares to whom his or her possessions are to go after death

³**will** *vb* **1** : to dispose of by or as if by a will : BEQUEATH **2** : to determine by an act of choice; *also* : DECREE, ORDAIN **3** : INTEND, PURPOSE; *also* : CHOOSE

will·ful *or* **wil·ful** \'wil-fəl\ *adj* **1** : governed by will without regard to reason : OBSTINATE **2** : INTENTIONAL ⟨~ murder⟩ — **will·ful·ly** *adv*

wil·lies \'wi-lēz\ *n pl* : a fit of nervousness : JITTERS — used with *the*

will·ing \'wi-liŋ\ *adj* **1** : inclined or favorably disposed in mind : READY ⟨~ to go⟩ **2** : prompt to act or respond ⟨~ workers⟩ **3** : done, borne, or accepted voluntarily or without reluctance **4** : of or relating to the will : VOLITIONAL — **will·ing·ly** *adv* — **will·ing·ness** *n*

wil·li·waw \'wi-lē-ˌwô\ *n* : a sudden violent gust of cold land air common along mountainous coasts of high latitudes

will-o'-the-wisp \ˌwil-ə-thə-'wisp\ *n* **1** : a light that appears at night over marshy grounds **2** : a misleading or elusive goal or hope

wil·low \'wi-lō\ *n* **1** : any of a genus of quicks growing shrubs and trees with tough pliable shoots **2** : an object made of willow wood

wil·low·ware \-ˌwar\ *n* : dinnerware that is usu. blue and white and that is decorated with a story- telling design featuring a large willow tree by a little bridge

wil·lowy \'wi-lə-wē\ *adj* : PLIANT; *also* : gracefully tall and slender

will·pow·er \'wil-ˌpaů-ər\ *n* : energetic determination : RESOLUTENESS

wil·ly-nil·ly \ˌwi-lē-'ni-lē\ *adv or adj* [alter. of *will I nill I or will ye nill ye or will he nill he*; *nill* fr. archaic

nill to be unwilling, fr. ME *nilen,* fr. OE *nyllan,* fr. *ne* not + *wyllan* to wish] : without regard for one's choice : by compulsion ⟨they rushed us along ∼⟩

¹**wilt** \'wilt\ *vb* **1** : to lose or cause to lose freshness and become limp esp. from lack of water : DROOP **2** : to grow weak or faint : LANGUISH

²**wilt** *n* : any of various plant disorders marked by wilting and often shriveling

wily \'wī-lē\ *adj* **wil·i·er; -est** : full of guile : TRICKY — **wil·i·ness** \-lē-nəs\ *n*

> **wimp** \'wimp\ *n* : a weak, cowardly, or ineffectual person — **wimpy** \'wim-pē\ *adj*

¹**wim·ple** \'wim-pəl\ *n* : a cloth covering worn over the head and around the neck and chin by women esp. in the late medieval period and by some nuns

²**wimple** *vb* **wim·pled; wim·pling 1** : to cover with or as if with a wimple **2** : to ripple or cause to ripple

¹**win** \'win\ *vb* **won** \'wən\; **win·ning** [ME *winnen,* fr. OE *winnan* to struggle] **1** : to get possession of esp. by effort : GAIN; *also* : to obtain by work : EARN **2** : to gain in or as if in battle or contest; *also* : to be the victor in ⟨*won* the war⟩ **3** : to solicit and gain the favor of; *esp* : to induce to accept oneself in marriage

²**win** *n* : VICTORY; *esp* : 1st place at the finish (as of a horse race)

wince \'wins\ *vb* **winced; winc·ing** : to shrink back involuntarily (as from pain) : FLINCH — **wince** *n*

winch \'winch\ *n* : a machine that has a drum on which is wound a rope or cable for hauling or hoisting — **winch** *vb*

¹**wind** \'wind\ *n* **1** : a movement of the air **2** : a prevailing force or influence : TENDENCY, TREND **3** : BREATH ⟨he had the ∼ knocked out of him⟩ **4** : gas produced in the stomach or intestines **5** : something insubstantial; *esp* : idle words **6** : air carrying a scent (as of game) **7** : INTIMATION ⟨they got ∼ of our plans⟩ **8** : WIND INSTRUMENTS; *also, pl* : players of wind instruments

²**wind** *vb* **1** : to get a scent of ⟨the dogs ∼*ed* the game⟩ **2** : to cause to be out of breath ⟨he was ∼*ed* from the climb⟩ **3** : to allow (as a horse) to rest so as to recover breath

³**wind** \'wīnd, 'wind\ *vb* **wind·ed** \'wīn-dəd, 'win-\ *or* **wound** \'waùnd\; **wind·ing** : to sound by blowing ⟨∼ a horn⟩

⁴**wind** \'wīnd\ *vb* **wound** \'waùnd\ *also* **wind·ed; wind·ing 1** : ENTANGLE, INVOLVE **2** : to introduce stealthily : INSINUATE **3** : to encircle or cover with something pliable : WRAP, COIL, TWINE ⟨∼ a bobbin⟩ **4** : to hoist or haul by a rope or chain and a winch **5** : to tighten the spring of; *also* : CRANK **6** : to raise to a high level (as of excitement) **7** : to cause to move in a curving line or path **8** : to have a curving course or shape ⟨a river ∼*ing* through the valley⟩ **9** : to move or lie so as to encircle

⁵**wind** \'wīnd\ *n* : COIL, TURN

wind·age \'win-dij\ *n* : the influence of the wind in deflecting the course of a projectile through the air; *also* : the amount of such deflection

wind·bag \'wind-ˌbag\ *n* : an overly talkative person

wind·blown \-ˌblōn\ *adj* : blown by the wind; *also* : having the appearance of being blown by the wind

wind·break \-ˌbrāk\ *n* : a growth of trees or shrubs serving to break the force of the wind; *also* : a shelter from the wind

wind·break·er \-ˌbrā-kər\ *n* : a light jacket made of material that can resist the wind

wind–bro·ken \-ˌbrō-kən\ *adj* : having the power of breathing impaired by disease — used of a horse

wind·burned \-ˌbərnd\ *adj* : irritated and inflamed by exposure to the wind — **wind·burn** \-ˌbərn\ *n*

wind·chill \-ˌchil\ *n* : a still-air temperature that would have the same cooling effect on exposed human skin as a given combination of temperature and wind speed

windchill factor *n* : WINDCHILL

wind·er \'wīn-dər\ *n* : one that winds

wind·fall \'wind-ˌfȯl\ *n* **1** : something (as a tree or fruit) blown down by the wind **2** : an unexpected or sudden gift, gain, or advantage

wind·flow·er \-ˌflaù-ər\ *n* : ANEMONE

¹**wind·ing** \'wīn-diŋ\ *n* : material (as wire) wound or coiled about an object

²**winding** *adj* **1** : having a pronounced curve or spiral ⟨∼ stairs⟩ **2** : having a course that winds ⟨a ∼ road⟩

wind·ing–sheet \-ˌshēt\ *n* : SHROUD

wind instrument *n* : a musical instrument (as a flute or horn) sounded by wind and esp. by the breath

wind·jam·mer \'wind-ˌja-mər\ *n* : a sailing ship; *also* : one of its crew

wind·lass \'wind-ləs\ *n* [ME *wyndlas,* alter. of *wyndas,* fr. ON *vindáss,* fr. *vinda* to wind + *áss* pole] : a winch used esp. on ships for hoisting or hauling

wind·mill \'wind-ˌmil\ *n* : a mill or machine worked by the wind turning sails or vanes that radiate from a central shaft

win·dow \'win-dō\ *n* [ME *windowe,* fr. ON *vindauga,* fr. *vindr* wind + *auga* eye] **1** : an opening in the wall of a building to let in light and air; *also* : the framework with fittings that closes such an opening **2** : WINDOWPANE **3** : an opening resembling or suggesting that of a window in a building **4** : an interval of time during which certain conditions or an opportunity exists **5** : an area of a computer display on which different information may be displayed independently — **win·dow·less** *adj*

window box *n* : a box for growing plants in or by a window

window dressing *n* **1** : display of merchandise in a store window **2** : a showing made to create a deceptively favorable impression

win·dow·pane \'win-dō-ˌpān\ *n* : a pane in a window

win·dow–shop \-ˌshäp\ *vb* : to look at the displays in store windows without going inside the stores to make purchases — **win·dow–shop·per** *n*

win·dow·sill \-ˌsil\ *n* : the horizontal member at the bottom of a window

wind·pipe \'wind-ˌpīp\ *n* : the passage for the breath from the larynx to the lungs

wind·proof \-'prüf\ *adj* : impervious to wind ⟨a ∼ jacket⟩

wind·row \'wind-ˌrō\ *n* 1 : hay raked up into a row to dry 2 : a row of something (as dry leaves) swept up by or as if by the wind

wind shear *n* : a radical shift in wind speed and direction that occurs over a very short distance

wind·shield \'wind-ˌshēld\ *n* : a transparent screen (as of glass) in front of the occupants of a vehicle

wind sock *n* : an open-ended truncated cloth cone mounted in an elevated position to indicate wind direction

wind·storm \-ˌstȯrm\ *n* : a storm with high wind and little or no rain

wind·surf·ing \-ˌsər-fiŋ\ *n* : the sport or activity of riding a sailboard — **wind·surf** \-ˌsərf\ *vb* — **wind·surf·er** *n*

wind·swept \'wind-ˌswept\ *adj* : swept by or as if by wind ⟨∼ plains⟩

wind tunnel *n* : an enclosed passage through which air is blown to investigate air flow around an object

wind·up \'wīn-ˌdəp\ *n* 1 : CONCLUSION, FINISH 2 : a series of regular and distinctive motions made by a pitcher preliminary to delivering a pitch

wind up *vb* 1 : to bring or come to a conclusion : END 2 : to put in order for the purpose of bringing to an end 3 : to arrive in a place, situation, or condition at the end or as a result of a course of action ⟨wound up as paupers⟩ 4 : to make a pitching windup

¹wind·ward \'win-dwərd\ *n* : the side or direction from which the wind is blowing

²windward *adj* : being in or facing the direction from which the wind is blowing

windy \'win-dē\ *adj* **wind·i·er; -est** 1 : having wind : exposed to winds ⟨a ∼ day⟩ ⟨a ∼ prairie⟩ 2 : STORMY 3 : FLATULENT 4 : indulging in or characterized by useless talk : VERBOSE

¹wine \'wīn\ *n* 1 : fermented grape juice used as a beverage 2 : the usu. fermented juice of a plant product (as fruit) used as a beverage ⟨rice ∼⟩

²wine *vb* **wined; win·ing** : to treat to or drink wine

wine cellar *n* : a room for storing wines; *also* : a stock of wines

wine·grow·er \-ˌgrō-ər\ *n* : one that cultivates a vineyard and makes wine

wine·press \-ˌpres\ *n* : a vat in which juice is pressed from grapes

¹wing \'wiŋ\ *n* 1 : one of the movable feathered or membranous paired appendages by means of which a bird, bat, or insect flies 2 : something suggesting a wing; *esp* : an airfoil that develops the lift which supports an aircraft in flight 3 : a plant or animal appendage or part likened to a wing 4 : a turned-back or extended edge on an article of clothing 5 : a means of flight or rapid progress 6 : the act or manner of flying : FLIGHT 7 *pl* : the area at the side of the stage out of sight 8 : one of the positions or players on either side of a center position or line 9 : either of two opposing groups within an organization : FACTION 10 : a unit in military aviation consisting of two or more squadrons — **wing·less** *adj* — **on the wing** : in flight : FLYING — **under one's wing** : in one's charge or care

²wing *vb* 1 : to fit with wings; *also* : to enable to fly easily 2 : to pass through in flight : FLY ⟨∼ the air⟩ ⟨swallows ∼ing southward⟩ 3 : to let fly : DISPATCH 4 : to wound in the wing ⟨∼ a bird⟩; *also* : to wound without killing 5 : to perform without preparation : IMPROVISE ⟨∼ing it⟩

wing·ding \'wiŋ-ˌdiŋ\ *n* : a wild, lively, or lavish party

winged \'wiŋd, 'wiŋ-əd, *in compounds* 'wiŋd\ *adj* 1 : having wings esp. of a specified character 2 : soaring with or as if with wings : ELEVATED 3 : SWIFT, RAPID

wing·span \'wiŋ-ˌspan\ *n* : the distance between the tips of a pair of wings

wing·spread \-ˌspred\ *n* : the spread of the wings; *esp* : the distance between the tips of the fully extended wings of a winged animal

¹wink \'wiŋk\ *vb* 1 : to close and open one eye quickly as a signal or hint 2 : to close and open the eyes quickly : BLINK 3 : to avoid seeing or noticing something ⟨∼ at a traffic violation⟩ 4 : TWINKLE, FLICKER — **wink·er** \'wiŋ-kər\ *n*

²wink *n* 1 : a brief period of sleep : NAP 2 : an act of winking; *esp* : a hint or sign given by winking 3 : INSTANT ⟨dries in a ∼⟩

win·ner \'wi-nər\ *n* : one that wins

¹win·ning \'wi-niŋ\ *n* 1 : VICTORY 2 : something won; *esp* : money won at gambling ⟨large ∼s⟩

²winning *adj* 1 : successful esp. in competition 2 : ATTRACTIVE, CHARMING

win·now \'wi-nō\ *vb* 1 : to remove (as chaff) by a current of air; *also* : to free (as grain) from waste in this manner 2 : to sort or separate as if by winnowing

wino \'wī-nō\ *n, pl* **win·os** : one who is addicted to drinking wine

win·some \'win-səm\ *adj* [ME *winsum*, fr. OE *wynsum*, fr. *wynn* joy] 1 : generally pleasing and engaging 2 : CHEERFUL, GAY — **win·some·ly** *adv* — **win·some·ness** *n*

¹win·ter \'win-tər\ *n* : the season of the year in any region in which the noonday sun shines most obliquely : the coldest period of the year

²winter *adj* : sown in autumn for harvesting in the following spring or summer ⟨∼ wheat⟩

win·ter·green \'win-tər-ˌgrēn\ *n* 1 : a low evergreen plant of the heath family with white bell-shaped flowers and spicy red berries 2 : an aromatic oil from the common wintergreen or its flavor or something flavored with it

win·ter·ize \'win-tə-ˌrīz\ *vb* **-ized; -iz·ing** : to make ready for winter

win·ter·kill \'win-tər-ˌkil\ *vb* : to kill or die by exposure to winter weather

winter squash *n* : any of various hard-shelled squashes that keep well in storage

win·ter·tide \-ˌtīd\ *n* : WINTER

win·ter·time \-ˌtīm\ *n* : WINTER

win·try \'win-trē\ *also* **win·tery** \'win-tə-rē\ *adj* **win·tri·er; -est** 1 : of, relating to, or characteristic of winter ⟨∼ weather⟩ 2 : CHILLING, CHEERLESS ⟨a ∼ welcome⟩

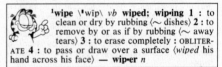

¹wipe \'wīp\ *vb* **wiped; wip·ing** 1 : to clean or dry by rubbing ⟨∼ dishes⟩ 2 : to remove by or as if by rubbing ⟨∼ away tears⟩ 3 : to erase completely : OBLITERATE 4 : to pass or draw over a surface ⟨wiped his hand across his face⟩ — **wip·er** *n*

²wipe *n* 1 : an act or instance of wiping; *also* : BLOW, STRIKE, SWIPE 2 : something used for wiping

wipe out *vb* : to destroy completely

¹wire \'wīr\ *n* 1 : metal in the form of a thread or slender rod; *also* : a thread or rod of metal 2 : hidden or secret influences controlling the action of a person or organization — usu. used in pl. ⟨pull ∼s⟩ 3 : a line of wire for conducting electric current 4 : a telegraph or telephone wire or system 5 : TELEGRAM, CABLEGRAM 6 : the finish line of a race

²wire *vb* **wired; wir·ing** 1 : to provide or equip with wire ⟨∼ a house⟩ 2 : to bind, string, or mount with wire 3 : to send or send word to by telegraph

wire·hair \'wīr-ˌhar\ *n* : a wirehaired dog or cat

wire·haired \-'hard\ *adj* : having a stiff wiry outer coat of hair

¹**wire·less** \-ləs\ *adj* **1** : having no wire or wires **2** *chiefly Brit* : RADIO

²**wireless** *n* **1** : wireless telegraphy **2** *chiefly Brit* : RADIO

wire–pull·er \-ˌpu̇-lər\ *n* : one who uses secret or underhanded means to influence the acts of a person or organization — **wire–pull·ing** *n*

wire service *n* : a news agency that sends out syndicated news copy to subscribers by wire or satellite

wire·tap \-ˌtap\ *n* : the act or an instance of tapping a telephone or telegraph wire to get information; *also* : an electrical connection used for such tapping — **wiretap** *vb* — **wire·tap·per** \-ˌta-pər\ *n*

wire·worm \-ˌwərm\ *n* : any of various slender hard‑coated beetle larvae esp. destructive to plant roots

wir·ing \'wīr-iŋ\ *n* : a system of wires

wiry \'wīr-ē\ *adj* **wir·i·er** \'wī-rē-ər\; **-est 1** : made of or resembling wire **2** : slender yet strong and sinewy — **wir·i·ness** \'wī-rē-nəs\ *n*

Wis *or* **Wisc** *abbr* Wisconsin

Wisd *abbr* Wisdom

wis·dom \'wiz-dəm\ *n* [ME, fr. OE *wīsdom*, fr. *wīs* wise] **1** : accumulated philosophic or scientific learning : KNOWLEDGE; *also* : INSIGHT **2** : good sense : JUDGMENT **3** : a wise attitude or course of action

Wisdom *n* — see BIBLE table

wisdom of Sol·o·mon \-ˈsä-lə-mən\ — see BIBLE table

wisdom tooth *n* : the last tooth of the full set on each half of each human jaw

¹**wise** \'wīz\ *n* : WAY, MANNER, FASHION ⟨in no ∼⟩ ⟨in this ∼⟩

²**wise** *adj* **wis·er; wis·est 1** : having wisdom : SAGE **2** : having or showing good sense or good judgment **3** : aware of what is going on : KNOWING; *also* : CRAFTY, SHREWD **4** : possessing inside information — **wise·ly** *adv*

-wise \-ˌwīz\ *adv comb form* : in the manner or direction of ⟨slant*wise*⟩

wise·acre \'wī-ˌzā-kər\ *n* [MD *wijssegger* soothsayer] : SMART ALECK

¹**wise·crack** \'wīz-ˌkrak\ *n* : a clever, smart, or flippant remark

²**wisecrack** *vb* : to make a wisecrack

wise guy *n* : SMART ALECK

¹**wish** \'wish\ *vb* **1** : to have a desire : long for ⟨∼ you

were here⟩ ⟨∼ for a puppy⟩ **2** : to form or express a wish concerning ⟨∼ed him a happy birthday⟩ **3** : BID ⟨he ∼ed me good morning⟩ **4** : to request by expressing a desire ⟨I ∼ you to go now⟩

²**wish** *n* **1** : an act or instance of wishing or desire : WANT; *also* : GOAL **2** : an expressed will or desire

wish·bone \-ˌbōn\ *n* : a forked bone in front of the breastbone in most birds

wish·ful \'wish-fəl\ *adj* **1** : expressive of a wish; *also* : having a wish **2** : according with wishes rather than fact ⟨∼ thinking⟩

wishy–washy \'wi-shē-ˌwȯ-shē, -ˌwä-\ *adj* : WEAK, INSIPID; *also* : morally feeble

wisp \'wisp\ *n* **1** : a small handful (as of hay or straw) **2** : a thin strand, strip, or fragment ⟨a ∼ of hair⟩; *also* : a thready streak ⟨a ∼ of smoke⟩ **3** : something frail, slight, or fleeting ⟨a ∼ of a smile⟩ — **wispy** *adj*

wis·te·ria \wis-ˈtir-ē-ə\ *or* **wis·tar·ia** \-ˈtir-ē-ə *also* -ˈter-\ *n* : any of a genus of chiefly Asian mostly woody vines related to the peas and widely grown for their long showy clusters of blue, white, purple, or rose flowers

wist·ful \'wist-fəl\ *adj* : feeling or showing a timid desire — **wist·ful·ly** *adv* — **wist·ful·ness** *n*

wit \'wit\ *n* **1** : reasoning power : INTELLIGENCE **2** : mental soundness : SANITY — usu. used in pl. **3** : RESOURCEFULNESS, INGENUITY; *esp* : quickness and cleverness in handling words and ideas **4** : a talent for making clever remarks; *also* : a person noted for making witty remarks — **wit·ted** \'wi-təd\ *adj* — **at one's wit's end** : at a loss for a means of solving a problem

¹**witch** \'wich\ *n* **1** : a person believed to have magic power; *esp* : SORCERESS **2** : an ugly old woman : HAG **3** : a charming or alluring girl or woman

²**witch** *vb* : BEWITCH

witch·craft \'wich-ˌkraft\ *n* : the power or practices of a witch : SORCERY

witch doctor *n* : a person in a primitive society who uses magic to treat sickness and to fight off evil spirits

witch·ery \'wi-chə-rē\ *n, pl* **-er·ies 1** : SORCERY **2** : FASCINATION, CHARM

witch·grass \'wich-ˌgras\ *n* : any of several grasses that are weeds in cultivated areas

witch ha·zel \'wich-ˌhā-zəl\ *n* **1** : a shrub of eastern No. America bearing small yellow flowers in the fall **2** : a soothing alcoholic lotion made from witch hazel bark

witch–hunt \'wich-ˌhənt\ *n* **1** : a searching out and persecution of persons accused of witchcraft **2** : the searching out and deliberate harassment esp. of political opponents

witch·ing \'wi-chiŋ\ *adj* : of, relating to, or suitable for sorcery or supernatural occurrences

with \'with, 'with\ *prep* **1** : AGAINST ⟨a fight ∼ his brother⟩ **2** : FROM ⟨parting ∼ friends⟩ **3** : in mutual relation to ⟨talk ∼ a friend⟩ **4** : in the company of ⟨went there ∼ her⟩ **5** : AS REGARDS, TOWARD ⟨is patient ∼ children⟩ **6** : compared to ⟨on equal terms ∼ another⟩ **7** : in support of ⟨I'm ∼ you all the way⟩ **8** : in the presence of ⟨CONTAINING ⟨tea ∼ sugar⟩ **9** : in the opinion of : as judged by ⟨their arguments had weight ∼ her⟩ **10** : BECAUSE OF, THROUGH ⟨pale ∼ anger⟩; *also* : by means of ⟨hit him ∼ a club⟩ **11** : in a manner indicating ⟨work ∼ a will⟩ **12** : GIVEN, GRANTED ⟨∼ your permission I'll leave⟩ **13** : HAVING ⟨came ∼ good news⟩ ⟨stood there ∼ his mouth open⟩ **14** : at the time of : right after ⟨∼ that we left⟩ **15** : DESPITE ⟨∼ all her cleverness, she failed⟩ **16** : in the direction of ⟨swim ∼ the tide⟩

with·al \wi-'thȯl, -'thäl\ *adv* **1** : together with this : BESIDES **2** : on the other hand : NEVERTHELESS

with·draw \with-'drȯ, with-\ *vb* **-drew** \-'drü\; **-drawn** \-'drȯn\; **-draw·ing** \-'drȯ-iŋ\ **1** : to take back or away : REMOVE **2** : to call back (as from consideration); *also* : RETRACT **3** : to go away : RETREAT, LEAVE **4** : to terminate one's participation in or use of something

with·draw·al \-'drȯ-əl\ *n* **1** : an act or instance of withdrawing **2** : the discontinuance of the use or administration of a drug and esp. an addicting drug; *also* : the period following such discontinuance marked by often painful physiological and psychological symptoms **3** : a pathological retreat from the real world (as in some schizophrenic states)

with·drawn \with-'drȯn\ *adj* **1** : ISOLATED, SECLUDED **2** : socially detached and unresponsive

withe \'with\ *n* : a slender flexible twig or branch

with·er \'wi-thər\ *vb* **1** : to shrivel from or as if from loss of bodily moisture and esp. sap **2** : to lose or cause to lose vitality, force, or freshness **3** : to cause to feel shriveled ⟨∼ed him with a glance⟩

with·ers \'wi-thərz\ *n pl* : the ridge between the shoulder bones of a horse; *also* : the corresponding part in other 4-footed animals

with·hold \with-'hōld, with-\ *vb* **-held** \-'held\; **-holding 1** : to hold back : RESTRAIN; *also* : RETAIN **2** : to refrain from granting, giving, or allowing ⟨∼ permission⟩ ⟨∼ names⟩

withholding tax *n* : a tax on income withheld at the source

¹**with·in** \wi-'thin, -'thin-\ *adv* **1** : in or into the interior : INSIDE **2** : inside oneself : INWARDLY

²**within** *prep* **1** : inside the limits or influence of ⟨∼ call⟩ **2** : in the limits or compass of ⟨∼ a mile⟩ **3** : in or to the inner part of ⟨∼ the room⟩

with–it \'wi-thət, -thət\ *adj* : socially or culturally up-to-date

¹**with·out** \wi-'thaut, -'thaut\ *prep* **1** : OUTSIDE **2** : LACKING ⟨∼ hope⟩; *also* : not accompanied by or showing ⟨spoke ∼ thinking⟩

²**without** *adv* **1** : on the outside : EXTERNALLY **2** : with something lacking or absent ⟨has learned to do ∼⟩

with·stand \with-'stand, with-\ *vb* **-stood** \-'stud\; **-stand·ing** : to stand against : RESIST; *esp* : to oppose (as an attack) successfully

wit·less \'wit-ləs\ *adj* : lacking wit or understanding : FOOLISH — **wit·less·ly** *adv* — **wit·less·ness** *n*

¹**wit·ness** \'wit-nəs\ *n* [ME *witnesse,* fr. OE *witnes* knowledge, testimony, witness, fr. *wit* mind, intelligence] **1** : TESTIMONY ⟨bear ∼ to the fact⟩ **2** : one that gives evidence; *esp* : one who testifies in a cause or before a court **3** : one present at a transaction so as to be able to testify that it has taken place **4** : one who has personal knowledge or experience of something **5** : something serving as evidence or proof : SIGN

²**witness** *vb* **1** : to bear witness : TESTIFY **2** : to act as legal witness of **3** : to furnish proof of : BETOKEN **4** : to be a witness of **5** : to be the scene of ⟨this region has ∼ed many wars⟩

wit·ti·cism \'wi-tə-ˌsi-zəm\ *n* : a witty saying or phrase

wit·ting \'wi-tiŋ\ *adj* : done knowingly : INTENTIONAL — **wit·ting·ly** *adv*

wit·ty \'wi-tē\ *adj* **wit·ti·er; -est** : marked by or full of wit : AMUSING ⟨a ∼ writer⟩ ⟨a ∼ remark⟩ **syn** humorous, facetious, jocular, jocose — **wit·ti·ly** \-tə-lē\ *adv* — **wit·ti·ness** \-tē-nəs\ *n*

wive \'wīv\ *vb* **wived; wiv·ing** : to take a wife

wives *pl of* WIFE

wiz·ard \'wi-zərd\ *n* [ME *wysard* wise man, fr. *wys* wise] **1** : MAGICIAN, SORCERER **2** : a very clever or skillful person ⟨a ∼ at chess⟩

wiz·ard·ry \'wi-zər-drē\ *n, pl* **-ries 1** : magic skill : SORCERY **2** : great skill or cleverness in an activity

wiz·en \'wiz-ᵊn, 'wēz-\ *vb* : to become or cause to become dry, shrunken, or wrinkled

wk *abbr* **1** week **2** work

WL *abbr* wavelength

wmk *abbr* watermark

WNW *abbr* west-northwest

WO *abbr* warrant officer

w/o *abbr* without

woad \'wōd\ *n* : a European herb related to the mustards; *also* : a blue dyestuff made from its leaves

wob·ble \'wä-bəl\ *vb* **wob·bled; wob·bling 1** : to move or cause to move with an irregular rocking or side-to-side motion **2** : TREMBLE, QUAVER **3** : WAVER, VACILLATE — **wobble** *n* — **wob·bly** \-bə-lē\ *adj*

woe \'wō\ *n* **1** : deep suffering from misfortune, affliction, or grief **2** : TROUBLE, MISFORTUNE ⟨economic ∼s⟩

woe·be·gone \'wō-bi-ˌgȯn\ *adj* : exhibiting woe, sorrow, or misery; *also* : being in a sorry condition

woe·ful *also* **wo·ful** \'wō-fəl\ *adj* **1** : full of woe : AFFLICTED **2** : involving, bringing, or relating to woe **3** : DEPLORABLE — **woe·ful·ly** *adv*

wok \'wäk\ *n* : a bowl-shaped cooking utensil used esp. in stir-frying

woke *past of* WAKE

woken *past part of* WAKE

wold \'wōld\ *n* : an upland plain or stretch of rolling land without woods

¹**wolf** \'wulf\ *n, pl* **wolves** \'wulvz\ **1** : any of several large erect-eared bushy-tailed doglike predatory mammals that live and hunt in packs; *esp* : GRAY WOLF **2** : a fierce or destructive person — **wolf·ish** *adj*

²**wolf** *vb* : to eat greedily : DEVOUR

wolf·hound \-ˌhaund\ *n* : any of several large dogs orig. used in hunting wolves

wol·fram \'wul-frəm\ *n* : TUNGSTEN

wol·ver·ine \ˌwul-və-'rēn\ *n, pl* **wolverines** *also* **wolverine** : a dark shaggy-coated flesh-eating mammal of northern forests and associated tundra that is related to the weasels

wom·an \'wu-mən\ *n, pl* **wom·en** \'wi-mən\ [ME, fr. OE *wīfman,* fr. *wīf* woman, wife + *man* human being, man] **1** : an adult female person **2** : WOMANKIND **3** : feminine nature : WOMANLINESS **4** : a female servant or attendant

wom·an·hood \'wu-mən-ˌhud\ *n* **1** : the state of being

a woman : the distinguishing qualities of a woman or of womankind **2** : WOMEN, WOMANKIND

wom·an·ish \'wů-mə-nish\ *adj* **1** : of, relating to, or characteristic of a woman **2** : suitable to a woman rather than to a man : EFFEMINATE

wom·an·kind \'wů-mən-ˌkīnd\ *n* : the females of the human race : WOMEN

wom·an·like \-ˌlīk\ *adj* : WOMANLY

wom·an·ly \-lē\ *adj* : having qualities characteristic of a woman — **wom·an·li·ness** \-lē-nəs\ *n*

woman suffrage *n* : possession and exercise of suffrage by women

womb \'wüm\ *n* **1** : UTERUS **2** : a place where something is generated

wom·bat \'wäm-ˌbat\ *n* : any of several stocky burrowing Australian marsupials that resemble small bears

wom·en·folk \'wi-mən-ˌfōk\ *also* **wom·en·folks** \-ˌfōks\ *n pl* : WOMEN

¹won \'wən\ *past and past part of* WIN

²won \'wòn\ *n, pl* **won** — see MONEY table

¹won·der \'wən-dər\ *n* **1** : a cause of astonishment or surprise : MARVEL; *also* : MIRACLE **2** : the quality of exciting wonder ⟨the charm and ∼ of the scene⟩ **3** : a feeling (as of awed astonishment or uncertainty) aroused by something extraordinary or affecting

> **²wonder** *vb* **1** : to feel surprise or amazement **2** : to feel curiosity or doubt

wonder drug *n* : MIRACLE DRUG

won·der·ful \'wən-dər-fəl\ *adj* **1** : exciting wonder : MARVELOUS, ASTONISHING **2** : unusually good : ADMIRABLE — **won·der·ful·ly** \-f(ə-)lē\ *adv* — **won·der·ful·ness** *n*

won·der·land \-ˌland, -lənd\ *n* **1** : an imaginary place of delicate beauty or magical charm **2** : a place that excites admiration or wonder

won·der·ment \-mənt\ *n* **1** : ASTONISHMENT, SURPRISE **2** : a cause of or occasion for wonder **3** : curiosity about something

won·drous \'wən-drəs\ *adj* : WONDERFUL, MARVELOUS — **won·drous·ly** *adv* — **won·drous·ness** *n*

¹wont \'wònt, 'wōnt\ *adj* [ME *woned, wont*, fr. pp. of *wonen* to dwell, be used to, fr. OE *wunian*] **1** : ACCUSTOMED, USED ⟨as we are ∼ to do⟩ **2** : INCLINED, APT

²wont *n* : CUSTOM, USAGE, HABIT ⟨according to her ∼⟩

won't \'wōnt\ : will not

wont·ed \'wòn-təd, 'wōn-\ *adj* : ACCUSTOMED, CUSTOMARY ⟨his ∼ courtesy⟩

woo \'wü\ *vb* **1** : to try to gain the love of : COURT **2** : SOLICIT, ENTREAT **3** : to try to gain or bring about ⟨∼ public favor⟩ — **woo·er** *n*

¹wood \'wůd\ *n* **1** : a dense growth of trees usu. larger than a grove and smaller than a forest — often used in pl. **2** : a hard fibrous substance that is basically xy-

lem and forms the bulk of trees and shrubs beneath the bark; *also* : this material fit or prepared for some use (as burning or building) **3** : something made of wood

²wood *adj* **1** : WOODEN **2** : suitable for holding, cutting, or working with wood **3** *or* **woods** \'wůdz\ : living or growing in woods

³wood *vb* **1** : to supply or load with wood esp. for fuel **2** : to cover with a growth of trees

wood alcohol *n* : METHANOL

wood·bine \'wůd-ˌbīn\ *n* : any of several honeysuckles; *also* : VIRGINIA CREEPER

wood·block \-ˌbläk\ *n* : WOODCUT

wood·chop·per \-ˌchä-pər\ *n* : one engaged esp. in chopping down trees

wood·chuck \-ˌchək\ *n* : a thickset grizzled marmot of Alaska, Canada, and the northeastern U.S.

wood·cock \'wůd-ˌkäk\ *n, pl* **woodcocks** : a brown eastern No. American game bird with a short neck and long bill that is related to the snipe; *also* : a related and similar Old World bird

wood·craft \-ˌkraft\ *n* **1** : skill and practice in matters relating to the woods and esp. in how to take care of oneself in them **2** : skill in shaping or constructing articles from wood

wood·cut \-ˌkət\ *n* **1** : a relief printing surface engraved on a block of wood **2** : a print from a woodcut

wood·cut·ter \-ˌkə-tər\ *n* : a person who cuts wood

wood·ed \'wů-dəd\ *adj* : covered with woods or trees ⟨∼ slopes⟩

wood·en \'wů-ᵊn\ *adj* **1** : made of wood **2** : lacking flexibility : awkwardly stiff — **wood·en·ly** *adv* — **wood·en·ness** *n*

wood·en·ware \'wůd-ᵊn-ˌwar\ *n* : articles made of wood for domestic use

wood·land \'wůd-lənd, -ˌland\ *n* : land covered with trees : FOREST — **woodland** *adj*

wood·lot \'wůd-ˌlät\ *n* : a restricted area of woodland usu. privately kept to meet fuel and timber needs ⟨a farm ∼⟩

wood louse *n* : any of various small flat crustaceans that live esp. in ground litter and under stones and bark

wood·man \'wůd-mən\ *n* : WOODSMAN

wood·note \-ˌnōt\ *n* : verbal expression that is natural and artless

wood nymph *n* : a nymph living in the woods

wood·peck·er \'wůd-ˌpe-kər\ *n* : any of numerous usu. brightly marked climbing birds with stiff spiny tail feathers and a chisellike bill used to drill into trees for insects

wood·pile \-ˌpīl\ *n* : a pile of wood and esp. firewood

wood·shed \-ˌshed\ *n* : a shed for storing wood and esp. firewood

woods·man \'wůdz-mən\ *n* : a person who frequents or works in the woods; *esp* : one skilled in woodcraft

woodsy \'wůd-zē\ *adj* : relating to or suggestive of woods

wood·wind \'wůd-ˌwind\ *n* : one of a group of wind instruments including flutes, clarinets, oboes, bassoons, and sometimes saxophones

wood•work \-ˌwərk\ *n* : work made of wood; *esp* : interior fittings (as moldings or stairways) of wood

woody \ˈwu̇d-ē\ *adj* **wood•i•er; -est 1** : abounding or overgrown with woods **2** : of or containing wood or wood fibers **3** : characteristic or suggestive of wood — **wood•i•ness** \ˈwu̇d-ē-nəs\ *n*

woof \ˈwu̇f\ *n* [alter. of ME *oof*, fr. OE *ōwef*, fr. *ō-* (fr. *on* on) + *wefan* to weave] **1** : WEFT 1 **2** : a woven fabric; *also* : its texture

woof•er \ˈwu̇f-ər\ *n* : a loudspeaker that reproduces sounds of low pitch

wool \ˈwu̇l\ *n* **1** : the soft wavy or curly hair of some mammals and esp. the domestic sheep; *also* : something (as a textile or garment) made of wool **2** : material that resembles a mass of wool — **wooled** \ˈwu̇ld\ *adj*

¹wool•en *or* **wool•len** \ˈwu̇l-ən\ *adj* **1** : made of wool **2** : of or relating to the manufacture or sale of woolen products 〈~ mills〉

²woolen *or* **woollen** *n* **1** : a fabric made of wool **2** : garments of woolen fabric — usu. used in pl.

wool•gath•er•ing \-ˌga-thə-riŋ\ *n* : idle daydreaming

¹wool•ly *also* **wooly** \ˈwu̇l-ē\ *adj* **wool•li•er; -est 1** : of, relating to, or bearing wool **2** : consisting of or resembling wool **3** : mentally confused 〈~ thinking〉 **4** : marked by a lack of order or restraint 〈the wild and ~ West〉

²wool•ly *also* **wool•ie** *or* **wooly** \ˈwu̇l-ē\ *n, pl* **wool•lies** : a garment made from wool; *esp* : underclothing of knitted wool — usu. used in pl.

woolly bear *n* : any of numerous very hairy moth caterpillars

woo•zy \ˈwü-zē\ *adj* **woo•zi•er; -est 1** : BEFUDDLED **2** : somewhat dizzy, nauseated, or weak — **woo•zi•ness** \ˈwü-zē-nəs\ *n*

¹word \ˈwərd\ *n* **1** : something that is said; *esp* : a brief remark **2** : a speech sound or series of speech sounds that communicates a meaning; *also* : a graphic representation of such a sound or series of sounds **3** : ORDER, COMMAND **4** *often cap* : the 2d person of the Trinity; *also* : GOSPEL **5** : NEWS, INFORMATION **6** : PROMISE **7** *pl* : QUARREL, DISPUTE **8** : a verbal signal : PASSWORD — **word•less** *adj*

²word *vb* : to express in words : PHRASE

word•age \ˈwər-dij\ *n* **1** : WORDS **2** : number of words **3** : WORDING

word•book \ˈwərd-ˌbu̇k\ *n* : VOCABULARY, DICTIONARY

word•ing \ˈwər-diŋ\ *n* : verbal expression : PHRASEOLOGY

word of mouth : oral communication

word•play \ˈwərd-ˌplā\ *n* : verbal wit

word processing *n* : the production of typewritten documents with automated and usu. computerized text-editing equipment — **word process** *vb*

word processor *n* : a keyboard-operated terminal for use in word processing; *also* : software to perform word processing

wordy \ˈwər-dē\ *adj* **word•i•er; -est** : using many words : VERBOSE **syn** prolix, diffuse, redundant — **word•i•ness** \-dē-nəs\ *n*

wore *past of* WEAR

¹work \ˈwərk\ *n* **1** : TOIL, LABOR; *also* : EMPLOYMENT 〈out of ~〉 **2** : TASK, JOB 〈have ~ to do〉 **3** : the energy used when a force is applied over a given distance **4** : DEED, ACHIEVEMENT **5** : a fortified structure **6** *pl* : engineering structures **7** *pl* : a place where industrial labor is done : PLANT, FACTORY **8** *pl* : the moving parts of a mechanism **9** : something produced by mental effort or physical labor; *esp* : an artistic production (as a book or needlework) **10** : WORKMANSHIP 〈careless ~〉 **11** : material in the process of manufac-

ture **12** *pl* : everything possessed, available, or belonging 〈the whole ~s went overboard〉; *also* : drastic treatment 〈gave him the ~s〉 **syn** occupation, employment, business, pursuit, calling — **in the works** : in process of preparation

²work *adj* **1** : used for work 〈~ elephants〉 **2** : suitable or styled for wear while working 〈~ clothes〉

³work *vb* **worked** \ˈwərkt\ *or* **wrought** \ˈrȯt\; **work•ing 1** : to bring to pass : EFFECT **2** : to fashion or create a useful or desired product through labor or exertion **3** : to prepare for use (as by kneading) **4** : to bring into a desired form by a manufacturing process 〈~ cold steel〉 **5** : to set or keep in operation : OPERATE 〈a pump ~ed by hand〉 **6** : to solve by reasoning or calculation 〈~ out a problem〉 **7** : to cause to toil or labor 〈~ed the men hard〉; *also* : to make use of 〈~ a mine〉 **8** : to pay for with labor or service 〈~ off a debt〉 **9** : to bring or get into some position or condition by stages 〈the stream ~ed itself clear〉 〈the knot ~ed loose〉 **10** : CONTRIVE, ARRANGE 〈~ it so you can leave early〉 **11** : to practice trickery or cajolery on 〈~ed the management for a free ticket〉 **12** : EXCITE, PROVOKE 〈~ed himself into a rage〉 **13** : to exert oneself physically or mentally; *esp* : to perform work regularly for wages **14** : to function according to plan or design **15** : to produce a desired effect : SUCCEED 〈the plan ~ed〉 **16** : to make way slowly and with difficulty 〈he ~ed forward through the crowd〉 **17** : to permit of being worked 〈this wood ~s easily〉 **18** : to be in restless motion; *also* : FERMENT 1 — **work on 1** : AFFECT **2** : to try to influence or persuade — **work upon** : to have effect upon : operate on : INFLUENCE

work•able \ˈwər-kə-bəl\ *adj* **1** : capable of being worked **2** : PRACTICABLE, FEASIBLE — **work•able•ness** *n*

work•a•day \ˈwər-kə-ˌdā\ *adj* **1** : relating to or suited for working days **2** : PROSAIC, ORDINARY

work•a•hol•ic \ˌwər-kə-ˈhȯ-lik, -ˈhä-\ *n* : a compulsive worker

work•bench \-ˌbench\ *n* : a bench on which work esp. of mechanics, machinists, and carpenters is performed

work•book \-ˌbu̇k\ *n* **1** : a worker's manual **2** : a student's book of problems to be answered directly on the pages

work•day \ˈwərk-ˌdā\ *n* **1** : a day on which work is done as distinguished from a day off **2** : the period of time in a day when work is performed

work•er \ˈwər-kər\ *n* **1** : one that works; *esp* : a person who works for wages **2** : any of the sexually undeveloped individuals of a colony of social insects (as bees, ants, or termites) that perform the work of the community

workers' compensation *n* : a system of insurance that reimburses an employer for damages paid to an employee who was injured while working

work ethic *n* : belief in work as a moral good

work farm *n* : a farm on which persons guilty of minor law violations are confined

work•horse \ˈwərk-ˌhȯrs\ *n* **1** : a horse used for hard work **2** : a person who does most of the work of a group task **3** : a strong useful machine or vehicle

work•house \-ˌhau̇s\ *n* **1** *Brit* : POORHOUSE **2** : a house of correction for persons guilty of minor law violations

¹work•ing \ˈwər-kiŋ\ *n* **1** : manner of functioning — usu. used in pl. **2** *pl* : an excavation made in mining or tunneling

²working *adj* **1** : engaged in work 〈a ~ journalist〉 **2** : adequate to allow work to be done 〈a ~ majority〉 〈a ~ knowledge of French〉 **3** : adopted or assumed to help further work or activity 〈a ~ model of the car〉 **4** : spent at work 〈~ life〉

work•ing•man \ˈwər-kiŋ-ˌman\ *n* : WORKER 1

work·man \\'wərk-mən\ *n* **1** : WORKER 1 **2** : ARTISAN, CRAFTSMAN

work·man·like \-ˌlīk\ *adj* : worthy of a good workman : SKILLFUL

work·man·ship \-ˌship\ *n* : the art or skill of a workman : CRAFTSMANSHIP; *also* : the quality of a piece of work ⟨a vase of exquisite ∼⟩

work·out \\'wərk-ˌaut\ *n* **1** : a practice or exercise to test or improve one's fitness, ability, or performance **2** : a test or trial to determine ability or capacity or suitability

work out *vb* **1** : to bring about esp. by resolving difficulties **2** : DEVELOP, ELABORATE **3** : to prove effective, practicable, or suitable **4** : to amount to a total or calculated figure — used with *at* **5** : to engage in a workout

work·room \\'wərk-ˌrüm, -ˌrum\ *n* : a room used for work

work·shop \-ˌshäp\ *n* **1** : a shop where manufacturing or handicrafts are carried on **2** : a seminar emphasizing exchange of ideas and practical methods

work·sta·tion \-ˌstā-shən\ *n* : an area with equipment for the performance of a specialized task; *also* : an intelligent terminal or personal computer usu. connected to a computer network

world \\'wərld\ *n* [ME, fr. OE *woruld* human existence, this world, age, fr. a prehistoric compound whose first constituent is represented by OE *wer* man and whose second constituent is akin to OE *eald* old] **1** : the earth with its inhabitants and all things upon it **2** : people in general : MANKIND **3** : human affairs ⟨withdraw from the ∼⟩ **4** : UNIVERSE, CREATION **5** : a state of existence : scene of life and action ⟨the ∼ of the future⟩ **6** : a distinctive class of persons or their sphere of interest ⟨the musical ∼⟩ **7** : a part or section of the earth or its inhabitants by itself **8** : a great number or quantity ⟨a ∼ of troubles⟩ **9** : a celestial body

world–beat·er \-ˌbē-tər\ *n* : one that excels all others of its kind : CHAMPION

world·ling \-liŋ\ *n* : a person absorbed in the concerns of the present world

world·ly \-lē\ *adj* **1** : of, relating to, or devoted to this world and its pursuits rather than to religion or spiritual affairs **2** : WORLDLY-WISE, SOPHISTICATED — **world·li·ness** \-lē-nəs\ *n*

world·ly–wise \-ˌwīz\ *adj* : possessing a practical and often shrewd understanding of human affairs

world·wide \\'wərld-ˌwīd\ *adj* : extended throughout the entire world — **worldwide** *adv*

¹worm \\'wərm\ *n* **1** : any of various small long usu. naked and soft-bodied round or flat invertebrate animals (as an earthworm, nematode, tapeworm, or maggot) **2** : a human being who is an object of contempt, loathing, or pity : WRETCH **3** : something that inwardly torments or devours **4** *pl* : infestation with or disease caused by parasitic worms **5** : a spiral or wormlike thing (as the thread of a screw) — **wormy** *adj*

²worm *vb* **1** : to move or cause to move or proceed slowly and deviously **2** : to insinuate or introduce (oneself) by devious or subtle means **3** : to obtain or extract by artful or insidious pleading, asking, or persuading ⟨∼ed the truth out of him⟩ **4** : to treat (an animal) with a drug to destroy or expel parasitic worms

worm–eat·en \\'wərm-ˌēt-ᵊn\ *adj* : eaten or burrowed by worms

worm gear *n* : a mechanical linkage consisting of a short rotating screw whose threads mesh with the teeth of a gear wheel

worm·hole \\'wərm-ˌhōl\ *n* : a hole or passage burrowed by a worm

worm·wood \-ˌwud\ *n* **1** : any of a genus of aromatic woody plants (as a sagebrush) : *esp* : one of Europe used in absinthe **2** : something bitter or grievous : BITTERNESS

worn *past part of* WEAR

worn–out \\'wōrn-ˈaut\ *adj* : exhausted or used up by or as if by wear

wor·ri·some \\'wər-ē-səm\ *adj* **1** : causing distress or worry **2** : inclined to worry or fret

¹wor·ry \\'wər-ē\ *vb* **wor·ried; wor·ry·ing 1** : to shake and mangle with the teeth ⟨a terrier ∼*ing* a rat⟩ **2** : to make anxious or upset ⟨her poor health *worries* me⟩ **3** : to feel or express great care or anxiety : FRET — **wor·ri·er** *n*

²worry *n, pl* **worries 1** : ANXIETY **2** : a cause of anxiety : TROUBLE

wor·ry·wart \\'wər-ē-ˌwort\ *n* : one who is inclined to worry unduly

¹worse \\'wərs\ *adj, comparative of* BAD *or of* ILL **1** : bad or evil in a greater degree : less good **2** : more unfavorable, unpleasant, or painful; *also* : SICKER

²worse *n* **1** : one that is worse **2** : a greater degree of ill or badness ⟨a turn for the ∼⟩

³worse *adv, comparative of* BAD *or of* ILL : in a worse manner : to a worse extent or degree

wors·en \\'wərs-ᵊn\ *vb* : to make or become worse

¹wor·ship \\'wər-shəp\ *n* [ME *worshipe* worthiness, respect, reverence paid to a divine being, fr. OE *weorthscipe* worthiness, respect, fr. *weorth* worthy, worth + -*scipe* -ship, suffix denoting quality or condition] **1** *chiefly Brit* : a person of importance — used as a title for officials **2** : reverence toward a divine being or supernatural power; *also* : the expression of such reverence **3** : extravagant respect or admiration or devotion ⟨∼ of the dollar⟩

²worship *vb* **-shiped** *or* **-shipped; -ship·ing** *or* **-ship·ping 1** : to honor or reverence as a divine being or supernatural power **2** : IDOLIZE **3** : to perform or take part in worship — **wor·ship·er** *or* **wor·ship·per** *n*

wor·ship·ful \\'wər-shəp-fəl\ *adj* **1** *archaic* : NOTABLE, DISTINGUISHED **2** *chiefly Brit* — used as a title for various persons or groups of rank or distinction **3** : VENERATING, WORSHIPING

¹worst \\'wərst\ *adj, superlative of* BAD *or of* ILL **1** : most

bad, evil, ill, or corrupt **2 :** most unfavorable, unpleasant, or painful; *also* : most unsuitable, faulty, or unattractive **3 :** least skillful or efficient

²worst *adv, superlative of* ILL *or of* BAD *or* BADLY **1 :** to the extreme degree of badness or inferiority : in the worst manner **2 :** MOST ⟨those who need help ∼⟩

³worst *n* : one that is worst

⁴worst *vb* : DEFEAT

wor•sted \ˈwus-təd, ˈwər-stəd\ *n* [ME, fr. *Worsted* (now *Worstead*), England] : a smooth compact yarn from long wool fibers; *also* : a fabric made from such yarn

wort \ˈwərt, ˈwȯrt\ *n* : a solution obtained by infusion from malt and fermented to form beer

¹worth \ˈwərth\ *n* **1 :** monetary value; *also* : the equivalent of a specified amount or figure ⟨$5 ∼ of gas⟩ **2 :** the value of something measured by its qualities **3 :** MERIT, EXCELLENCE

²worth *prep* **1 :** equal in value to; *also* : having possessions or income equal to **2 :** deserving of ⟨well ∼ the effort⟩

worth•less \ˈwərth-ləs\ *adj* **1 :** lacking worth : VALUELESS; *also* : USELESS **2 :** LOW, DESPICABLE — **worth•less•ness** *n*

worth•while \ˈwərth-ˈhwīl\ *adj* : being worth the time or effort spent

¹wor•thy \ˈwər-ᵵẖē\ *adj* **wor•thi•er; -est 1 :** having worth or value : ESTIMABLE **2 :** HONORABLE, MERITORIOUS **3 :** having sufficient worth ⟨∼ of the honor⟩ — **wor•thi•ly** \ˈwər-ᵵẖə-lē\ *adv* — **wor•thi•ness** \-ᵵẖē-nəs\ *n*

²worthy *n, pl* **worthies :** a worthy person

would \ˈwud\ *past of* WILL **1** *archaic* : wish for : WANT **2 :** strongly desire : WISH ⟨I ∼ I were young again⟩ **3** — used as an auxiliary to express (1) preference ⟨∼ rather run than fight⟩, (2) wish, desire, or intent ⟨those who ∼ forbid gambling⟩, (3) habitual action ⟨we ∼ meet often for lunch⟩, (4) a contingency or possibility ⟨if he were coming, he ∼ be here by now⟩, (5) probability ⟨∼ have won if he hadn't tripped⟩, or (6) a request ⟨∼ you help us⟩ **4 :** COULD **5 :** SHOULD

would–be \ˈwud-ˈbē\ *adj* : desiring or pretending to be ⟨a ∼ artist⟩

¹wound \ˈwünd\ *n* **1 :** an injury involving cutting or breaking of bodily tissue (as by violence, accident, or surgery) **2 :** an injury or hurt to feelings or reputation

²wound *vb* : to inflict a wound to or in

³wound \ˈwaund\ *past and past part of* WIND

wove *past of* WEAVE

woven *past part of* WEAVE

¹wow \ˈwau\ *n* : a striking success : HIT

²wow *vb* : to arouse enthusiastic approval

WP *abbr* word processing; word processor

WPM *abbr* words per minute

wpn *abbr* weapon

wrack \ˈrak\ *n* [ME, fr. OE *wræc* misery, punishment, something driven by the sea] : violent or total destruction

wraith \ˈrāth\ *n, pl* **wraiths** \ˈrāths, ˈrāᵵẖz\ **1 :** GHOST, SPECTER **2 :** an insubstantial appearance : SHADOW

¹wran•gle \ˈraŋ-gəl\ *vb* **wran•gled; wran•gling 1 :** to quarrel angrily or peevishly : BICKER **2 :** ARGUE **3 :** to obtain by persistent arguing **4 :** to herd and care for (livestock) on the range — **wran•gler** *n*

²wrangle *n* : an angry, noisy, or prolonged dispute; *also* : CONTROVERSY

¹wrap \ˈrap\ *vb* **wrapped; wrap•ping 1 :** to cover esp. by winding or folding **2 :** to envelop and secure for transportation or storage **3 :** to enclose wholly : ENFOLD **4 :** to coil, fold, draw, or twine about something **5 :** SURROUND, ENVELOP ⟨*wrapped* in mystery⟩ **6 :** INVOLVE, ENGROSS ⟨*wrapped* up in a hobby⟩ **7 :** to complete filming or videotaping

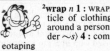 **²wrap** *n* **1 :** WRAPPER, WRAPPING **2 :** an article of clothing that may be wrapped around a person **3** *pl* : SECRECY ⟨kept under ∼s⟩ **4 :** completion of filming or videotaping

wrap•around \ˈra-pə-ˌraund\ *n* : a garment (as a dress) adjusted to the figure by wrapping around

wrap•per \ˈra-pər\ *n* **1 :** that in which something is wrapped **2 :** one that wraps **3 :** an article of clothing worn wrapped around the body

wrap•ping \ˈra-piŋ\ *n* : something used to wrap an object : WRAPPER

wrap–up \ˈrap-ˌəp\ *n* : SUMMARY

wrap up *vb* **1 :** SUMMARIZE, SUM UP **2 :** to bring to a usu. successful conclusion

wrasse \ˈras\ *n* : any of a large family of usu. brightly colored marine fishes including many food fishes

wrath \ˈrath\ *n* **1 :** violent anger : RAGE **2 :** divine punishment **syn** indignation, ire, fury, anger

wrath•ful \-fəl\ *adj* **1 :** filled with wrath : very angry **2 :** showing, marked by, or arising from anger — **wrath•ful•ly** *adv* — **wrath•ful•ness** *n*

wreak \ˈrēk\ *vb* **1 :** to exact as a punishment : INFLICT ⟨∼ vengeance on an enemy⟩ **2 :** to give free scope or rein to ⟨∼ed his wrath⟩ **3 :** BRING ABOUT, CAUSE ⟨∼ havoc⟩

wreath \ˈrēth\ *n, pl* **wreaths** \ˈrēᵵẖz, ˈrēths\ : something (as boughs or flowers) intertwined into a circular shape

wreathe \ˈrēᵵẖ\ *vb* **wreathed; wreath•ing 1 :** to shape or take on the shape of a wreath **2 :** to crown, decorate, or cover with or as if with a wreath ⟨a face *wreathed* in smiles⟩

¹wreck \ˈrek\ *n* **1 :** something (as goods) cast up on the land by the sea after a shipwreck **2 :** SHIPWRECK **3 :** the action of breaking up or destroying something **4 :** broken remains (as of a vehicle after a crash) **5 :** something disabled or in a state of ruin; *also* : an individual broken in health or strength

²wreck *vb* **1 :** SHIPWRECK **2 :** to ruin or damage by breaking up : involve in disaster or ruin

wreck•age \ˈre-kij\ *n* **1 :** the act of wrecking : the state of being wrecked : RUIN **2 :** the remains of a wreck

wreck•er \ˈre-kər\ *n* **1 :** one that searches for or works upon the wrecks of ships **2 :** TOW TRUCK **3 :** one that wrecks; *esp* : one whose work is the demolition of buildings

wren \'ren\ *n* : any of a family of small mostly brown singing birds with short wings and often a tail that points upward

¹**wrench** \'rench\ *vb* **1** : to move with a violent twist **2** : to pull, strain, or tighten with violent twisting or force **3** : to injure or disable by a violent twisting or straining **4** : to snatch forcibly : WREST

²**wrench** *n* **1** : a forcible twisting; *also* : an injury (as to one's ankle) by twisting **2** : a tool for holding, twisting, or turning (as nuts or bolts)

¹**wrest** \'rest\ *vb* **1** : to pull or move by a forcible twisting movement **2** : to gain with difficulty by or as if by force or violence ⟨∼ control of the government from the dictator⟩

²**wrest** *n* : a forcible twist : WRENCH

¹**wres·tle** \'re-səl, 'ra-\ *vb* **wres·tled; wres·tling 1** : to scuffle with and try to throw down an opponent **2** : to compete against in wrestling **3** : to struggle for control (as of something difficult) ⟨∼ with a problem⟩ — **wres·tler** \'res-lər, 'ras-\ *n*

²**wrestle** *n* : the action or an instance of wrestling : STRUGGLE

wres·tling \'res-liŋ\ *n* : the sport in which two opponents wrestle each other

wretch \'rech\ *n* [ME *wrecche*, fr. OE *wrecca* outcast, exile] **1** : a miserable unhappy person **2** : a base, despicable, or vile person

wretch·ed \'re-chəd\ *adj* **1** : deeply afflicted, dejected, or distressed : MISERABLE **2** : WOEFUL, GRIEVOUS ⟨a ∼ accident⟩ **3** : DESPICABLE ⟨a ∼ trick⟩ **4** : poor in quality or ability : INFERIOR ⟨∼ workmanship⟩ — **wretch·ed·ly** *adv* — **wretch·ed·ness** *n*

wrig·gle \'ri-gəl\ *vb* **wrig·gled; wrig·gling 1** : to twist or move to and fro like a worm : SQUIRM ⟨wriggled in his chair⟩ ⟨∼ your toes⟩; *also* : to move along by twisting and turning ⟨a snake *wriggled* along the path⟩ **2** : to extricate oneself as if by wriggling ⟨∼ out of difficulty⟩ — **wriggle** *n*

wrig·gler *n* **1** : one that wriggles **2** : WIGGLER 1

wring \'riŋ\ *vb* **wrung** \'rəŋ\; **wring·ing** \'riŋ-iŋ\ **1** : to squeeze or twist esp. so as to make dry or to extract moisture or liquid ⟨∼ wet clothes⟩ **2** : to get by or as if by twisting or pressing ⟨∼ the truth out of him⟩ **3** : to twist so as to strain or sprain : CONTORT ⟨∼ his neck⟩ **4** : to twist together as a sign of anguish ⟨*wrung* her hands⟩ **5** : to affect painfully as if by wringing : TORMENT ⟨her plight *wrung* my heart⟩

wring·er \'riŋ-ər\ *n* : one that wrings; *esp* : a device for squeezing out liquid or moisture ⟨clothes ∼⟩

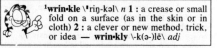

¹**wrin·kle** \'riŋ-kəl\ *n* **1** : a crease or small fold on a surface (as in the skin or in cloth) **2** : a clever or new method, trick, or idea — **wrin·kly** \-k(ə-)lē\ *adj*

²**wrinkle** *vb* **wrin·kled; wrin·kling** : to develop or cause to develop wrinkles

wrist \'rist\ *n* : the joint or region between the hand and the arm; *also* : a corresponding part in a lower animal

wrist·band \-ıband\ *n* : a band or the part of a sleeve encircling the wrist

wrist·let \-lət\ *n* : WRISTBAND; *esp* : a close-fitting knitted band attached to the top of a glove or the end of a sleeve

wrist·watch \-ıwäch\ *n* : a small watch attached to a bracelet or strap to fasten about the wrist

writ \'rit\ *n* **1** : something written **2** : a written legal order signed by a court officer

write \'rit\ *vb* **wrote** \'rōt\; **writ·ten** \'rit-ᵊn\ *also* **writ** \'rit\; **writ·ing** \'rī-tiŋ\ [ME, fr. OE *wrītan* to scratch, draw, inscribe] **1** : to form characters, letters, or words on a surface ⟨learn to read and ∼⟩ **2** : to form the letters or the words of ⟨∼ your name⟩ ⟨∼ a check⟩ **3** : to put down on paper : express in writing **4** : to make up and set down for others to read ⟨∼ a book⟩ ⟨∼ music⟩ **5** : to write a letter to **6** : to communicate by letter : CORRESPOND

write–in \'rīt-ıin\ *n* : a vote cast by writing in the name of a candidate; *also* : a candidate whose name is written in

write in *vb* : to insert (a name not listed on a ballot) in an appropriate space; *also* : to cast (a vote) in this manner

write off *vb* **1** : to reduce the estimated value of : DE-PRECIATE **2** : CANCEL ⟨*write off* a bad debt⟩

writ·er \'rī-tər\ *n* : one that writes esp. as a business or occupation : AUTHOR

writer's cramp *n* : a painful spasmodic cramp of muscles of the hand or fingers brought on by excessive writing

write–up \'rīt-ıəp\ *n* : a written account (as in a newspaper); *esp* : a flattering article

writhe \'rīth\ *vb* **writhed; writh·ing 1** : to twist and turn this way and that ⟨∼ in pain⟩ **2** : to suffer with shame or confusion

writ·ing *n* **1** : the act of one that writes; *also* : HAND-WRITING **2** : something that is written or printed **3** : a style or form of composition **4** : the occupation of a writer

wrnt *abbr* warrant

¹**wrong** \'röŋ\ *n* **1** : an injurious, unfair, or unjust act **2** : a violation of the legal rights of another person **3** : something that is wrong : wrong principles, practices, or conduct ⟨know right from ∼⟩ **4** : the state, position, or fact of being wrong

²**wrong** *adj* **wrong·er** \'röŋ-ər\; **wrong·est** \'röŋ-əst\ **1** : SINFUL, IMMORAL **2** : not right according to a standard or code : IMPROPER **3** : INCORRECT ⟨a ∼ solution⟩ **4** : UNSATISFACTORY **5** : UNSUITABLE, INAPPROPRIATE **6** : constituting a surface that is considered the back, bottom, inside, or reverse of something ⟨iron only on the ∼ side of the fabric⟩ **syn** false, erroneous, incorrect, inaccurate, untrue — **wrong·ly** *adv*

³**wrong** *adv* **1** : INCORRECTLY **2** : in a wrong direction, manner, or relation

⁴**wrong** *vb* **wronged; wrong·ing 1** : to do

wrong to : INJURE, HARM **2** : to treat unjustly : DIS-HONOR, MALIGN **syn** oppress, persecute, aggrieve
wrong·do·er \'róṅ-ɪdü-ər\ *n* : a person who does wrong and esp. moral wrong — **wrong·do·ing** \-ɪdü-iṅ\ *n*
wrong·ful \'róṅ-fəl\ *adj* **1** : WRONG, UNJUST **2** : UNLAWFUL — **wrong·ful·ly** *adv* — **wrong·ful·ness** *n*
wrong·head·ed \-'he-dəd\ *adj* : stubborn in clinging to wrong opinion or principles — **wrong·head·ed·ly** *adv* — **wrong·head·ed·ness** *n*
wrote *past of* WRITE
wroth \'róth, 'róth\ *adj* : filled with wrath : ANGRY
wrought \'rót\ *adj* [ME, fr. pp. of *worken* to work] **1** : FASHIONED, FORMED ⟨carefully ∼ essays⟩ **2** : ORNAMENTED **3** : beaten into shape by tools : HAMMERED ⟨∼ metals⟩ **4** : deeply stirred : EXCITED ⟨gets easily ∼ up⟩
wrought iron *n* : a commercial form of iron that is tough, malleable, and relatively soft — **wrought-iron** *adj*
wrung *past and past part of* WRING
wry \'rī\ *adj* **wry·er** \'rī-ər\; **wry·est** \'rī-əst\ **1** : having a bent or twisted shape ⟨a ∼ smile⟩; *esp* : turned abnormally to one side : CONTORTED ⟨a ∼ neck⟩ **2** : cleverly and often ironically humorous — **wry·ly** *adv* — **wry·ness** *n*
wry·neck \'rī-ɪnek\ *n* **1** : either of two Old World woodpeckers that differ from typical woodpeckers in having a peculiar manner of twisting the head and neck **2** : an abnormal twisting of the neck and head to one side caused by muscle spasms
WSW *abbr* west-southwest
wt *abbr* weight
wurst \'wərst, 'wùrst\ *n* : SAUSAGE
wuss \'wùs\ *n* : WIMP — **wussy** \'wù-sē\ *adj*
WV *or* **W Va** *abbr* West Virginia
WW *abbr* World War
w/w *abbr* wall-to-wall
WY *or* **Wyo** *abbr* Wyoming
WYS·I·WYG \'wi-zē-ɪwig\ *adj* [*w*hat *y*ou *s*ee *i*s *w*hat *y*ou *g*et] : of, relating to, or being a computer display that shows a document exactly as it will appear when printed out

X

¹x \'eks\ *n, pl* **x's** *or* **xs** \'ek-səz\ *often cap* **1** : the 24th letter of the English alphabet **2** : an unknown quantity
²x *vb* **x-ed** *also* **x'd** *or* **xed** \'ekst\; **x-ing** *or* **x'ing** \'ek-siṅ\ : to cancel or obliterate with a series of *x*'s — usu. used with *out*
³x *abbr* **1** ex **2** experimental
⁴x *symbol* **1** times ⟨3 x 2 is 6⟩ **2** by ⟨a 3 x 5 index card⟩ **3** *often cap* power of magnification
Xan·a·du \'za-nə-ɪdü, -ɪdyü\ *n* [fr. *Xanadu*, locality in Kubla Khan (1798), poem by Eng. poet Samuel Taylor Coleridge †1834] : an idyllic, exotic, or luxurious place
Xan·thip·pe \zan-'thi-pē, -'ti-\ *or* **Xan·tip·pe** \-'ti-pē\ *n* [Gk *Xanthippē*, shrewish wife of Socrates] : an ill-tempered woman
x–ax·is \'eks-ɪak-səs\ *n* : the axis of a graph or of a system of coordinates in a plane parallel to which abscissas are measured
X–C *abbr* cross-country
X chromosome *n* : a sex chromosome that usually occurs paired in each female cell and single in each male cell in organisms (as human beings) in which the male normally has two unlike sex chromosomes
Xe *symbol* xenon
xe·non \'zē-ɪnän, 'ze-\ *n* [Gk, neut. of *xenos* strange] : a heavy gaseous chemical element occurring in minute quantities in air — see ELEMENT table
xe·no·pho·bia \ɪze-nə-'fō-bē-ə, ɪzē-\ *n* : fear and hatred of strangers or foreigners or of what is strange or foreign — **xe·no·phobe** \'ze-nə-ɪfōb, 'zē-\ *n* — **xe·no·pho·bic** \ɪze-nə-'fō-bik, ɪzē-\ *adj*
xe·ric \'zir-ik, 'zer-\ *adj* : characterized by or requiring only a small amount of moisture ⟨a ∼ habitat⟩
xe·rog·ra·phy \zə-'rä-grə-fē\ *n* : a process for copying printed matter by the action of light on an electrically charged surface in which the latent image usu. is developed with a powder — **xe·ro·graph·ic** \ɪzir-ə-'gra-fik\ *adj*
xe·ro·phyte \'zir-ə-ɪfīt\ *n* : a plant adapted for growth with a limited water supply — **xe·ro·phyt·ic** \ɪzir-ə-'fi-tik\ *adj*
xi \'zī, 'ksī\ *n* : the 14th letter of the Greek alphabet — Ξ *or* ξ
XL *abbr* **1** extra large **2** extra long
Xmas \'kris-məs *also* 'eks-məs\ *n* [*X* (symbol for *Christ*, fr. the Gk letter chi (X), initial of *Christos* Christ) + *-mas* (in *Christmas*)] : CHRISTMAS
XO *abbr* executive officer
x–ra·di·a·tion \ɪeks-ɪrā-dē-'ā-shən\ *n, often cap* **1** : exposure to X rays **2** : radiation consisting of X rays
x–ray \'eks-ɪrā\ *vb, often cap* : to examine, treat, or photograph with X rays
X ray \'eks-ɪrā\ *n* **1** : a radiation of the same nature as light rays but of extremely short wavelength that is able to penetrate through various thicknesses of solids and to act on photographic film **2** : a photograph taken with X rays — **X–ray** *adj*
XS *abbr* extra small
xu \'sü\ *n, pl* **xu** — see *dong* at MONEY table
xy·lem \'zī-ləm, -ɪlem\ *n* : a woody tissue of vascular plants that transports water and dissolved materials upward, functions in support and storage, and lies central to the phloem
xy·lo·phone \'zī-lə-ɪfōn\ *n* [Gk *xylon* wood + *phōnē* voice, sound] : a musical instrument consisting of a series of wooden bars graduated in length to produce the musical scale, supported on belts of straw or felt, and sounded by striking with two small wooden hammers — **xy·lo·phon·ist** \-ɪfō-nist\ *n*

Y

¹**y** \'wī\ *n, pl* **y's** *or* **ys** \'wīz\ *often cap* : the 25th letter of the English alphabet

²**y** *abbr* **1** yard **2** year

¹**Y** \'wī\ *n* : YMCA, YWCA

²**Y** *symbol* yttrium

¹**-y** *also* **-ey** \ē\ *adj suffix* **1** : characterized by : full of ⟨dirty⟩ ⟨clay*ey*⟩ **2** : having the character of : composed of ⟨icy⟩ **3** : like : like that of ⟨home*y*⟩ ⟨wintry⟩ ⟨stagy⟩ **4** : tending or inclined to ⟨sleepy⟩ ⟨chatty⟩ **5** : giving occasion for (specified) action ⟨teary⟩ **6** : performing (specified) action ⟨curly⟩

²**-y** \ē\ *n suffix, pl* **-ies** **1** : state : condition : quality ⟨beggary⟩ **2** : activity, place of business, or goods dealt with ⟨laundry⟩ **3** : whole body or group ⟨soldiery⟩

³**-y** *n suffix, pl* **-ies** : instance of a (specified) action ⟨entreaty⟩ ⟨inquiry⟩

YA *abbr* young adult

¹**yacht** \'yät\ *n* [obs. D *jaght*, fr. Middle Low German *jacht*, short for *jachtschip*, lit., hunting ship] : a usu. large recreational watercraft

²**yacht** *vb* : to race or cruise in a yacht

yacht·ing *n* : the sport of racing or cruising in a yacht

yachts·man \'yäts-mən\ *n* : a person who owns or sails a yacht

ya·hoo \'yā-hü, 'yä-\ *n, pl* **yahoos** [fr. *Yahoo*, one of a race of brutes having the form of men in Jonathan Swift's *Gulliver's Travels*] : a boorish, crass, or stupid person

Yah·weh \'yä-ɪwā\ *also* **Yah·veh** \-ɪvä\ *n* : GOD 1 — used esp. by the Hebrews

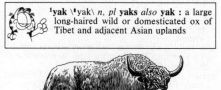

¹**yak** \'yak\ *n, pl* **yaks** *also* **yak** : a large long-haired wild or domesticated ox of Tibet and adjacent Asian uplands

yak

²**yak** *also* **yack** \'yak\ *n* : persistent or voluble talk — **yak** *also* **yack** *vb*

yam \'yam\ *n* **1** : the edible starchy root of a twining vine that largely replaces the potato as food in the tropics; *also* : a plant that produces yams **2** : a usu. deep orange sweet potato

yam·mer \'ya-mər\ *vb* [ME *yameren*, alter. of *yomeren* to murmur, be sad, fr. OE *gēomrian*] **1** : WHIMPER **2** : CHATTER — **yammer** *n*

¹**yank** \'yaŋk\ *n* : a strong sudden pull : JERK

²**yank** *vb* : to pull with a quick vigorous movement

Yank \'yaŋk\ *n* : YANKEE

Yan·kee \'yaŋ-kē\ *n* **1** : a native or inhabitant of New England; *also* : a native or inhabitant of the northern U.S. **2** : AMERICAN 2

yan·qui \'yäŋ-kē\ *n, often cap* [Sp] : a citizen of the U.S. as distinguished from a Latin American

¹**yap** \'yap\ *vb* **yapped; yap·ping 1** : BARK, YELP **2** : GAB

²**yap** *n* **1** : a quick sharp bark **2** : CHATTER

¹**yard** \'yärd\ *n* [ME, fr. OE *geard* enclosure, yard] **1** : a small enclosed area open to the sky and adjacent to a building **2** : the grounds of a building **3** : the grounds surrounding a house usu. covered with grass **4** : an enclosure for livestock **5** : an area set aside for a particular business or activity **6** : a system of railroad tracks for storing cars and making up trains

²**yard** *n* [ME *yarde*, fr. OE *gierd* twig, measure, yard] **1** — see WEIGHT table **2** : a long spar tapered toward the ends that supports and spreads the head of a sail — **the whole nine yards** : all of a set of circumstances, conditions, or details

yard·age \'yär-dij\ *n* : an aggregate number of yards; *also* : the length, extent, or volume of something as measured in yards

yard·arm \'yärd-ɪärm\ *n* : either end of the yard of a square-rigged ship

yard·man \-mən, -ɪman\ *n* : a person employed in or about a yard

yard·mas·ter \-ɪmas-tər\ *n* : the person in charge of a railroad yard

yard·stick \-ɪstik\ *n* **1** : a graduated measuring stick three feet long **2** : a standard for making a critical judgment : CRITERION **syn** gauge, touchstone, benchmark, measure

yar·mul·ke *also* **yar·mel·ke** \'yä-mə-kə, 'yär-, -məl-\ *n* : a skullcap worn esp. by Jewish males in the synagogue and the home

yarn \'yärn\ *n* **1** : a continuous often plied strand composed of fibers or filaments and used in weaving and knitting to form cloth **2** : STORY; *esp* : a tall tale

yar·row \'yar-ō\ *n* : a strong-scented herb related to the daisies that has white or pink flowers in flat clusters

yaw \'yò\ *vb* : to deviate erratically from a course ⟨the ship ~ed in the heavy seas⟩ — **yaw** *n*

yawl \'yòl\ *n* : a 2-masted sailboat with the shorter mast aft of the rudder

¹**yawn** \'yòn\ *vb* : to open wide; *esp* : to open the mouth wide usu. as an involuntary reaction to fatigue or boredom — **yawn·er** *n*

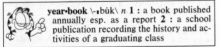

²yawn *n* : a deep usu. involuntary intake of breath through the wide-open mouth

yawp *or* **yaup** \'yȯp\ *vb* 1 : to make a raucous noise : SQUAWK 2 : CLAMOR, COMPLAIN — **yawp·er** *n*

yaws \'yȯz\ *n pl* : an infectious tropical disease caused by a spirochete closely resembling the causative agent of syphilis

y–ax·is \'wī-ˌak-səs\ *n* : the axis of a graph or of a system of coordinates in a plane parallel to which the ordinates are measured

Yb *symbol* ytterbium

YB *abbr* yearbook

Y chromosome *n* : a sex chromosome that is characteristic of male cells in organisms (as humans) in which the male typically has two unlike sex chromosomes

yd *abbr* yard

¹ye \'yē\ *pron* : YOU 1

²ye \yē, yə, *originally same as* THE\ *definite article, archaic* : THE — used by early printers to represent the manuscript word *þe (the)*

¹yea \'yā\ *adv* 1 : YES — used in oral voting 2 : INDEED, TRULY

²yea *n* : an affirmative vote; *also* : a person casting such a vote

year \'yir\ *n* 1 : the period of about 365¼ solar days required for one revolution of the earth around the sun 2 : a cycle of 365 or 366 days beginning with January 1; *also* : a calendar year specified usu. by a number 3 *pl* : a time of special significance ⟨their glory ∼s⟩ 4 *pl* : AGE ⟨advanced in ∼s⟩ 5 : a period of time other than a calendar year ⟨the school ∼⟩

year·book \-ˌbu̇k\ *n* 1 : a book published annually esp. as a report 2 : a school publication recording the history and activities of a graduating class

year·ling \'yir-liŋ, 'yər-lən\ *n* 1 : one that is a year old 2 : a racehorse between January 1st of the year after the year in which it was born and the next January 1st

year·long \'yir-ˌlȯŋ\ *adj* : lasting through a year

¹year·ly \'yir-lē\ *adj* : ANNUAL

²yearly *adv* : every year

yearn \'yərn\ *vb* 1 : to feel a longing or craving 2 : to feel tenderness or compassion **syn** long, pine, hanker, hunger, thirst

yearn·ing *n* : a tender or urgent longing

year–round \'yir-'rau̇nd\ *adj* : effective, employed, or operating for the full year : not seasonal ⟨a ∼ resort⟩

yeast \'yēst\ *n* 1 : a surface froth or a sediment in sugary liquids (as fruit juices) that consists largely of cells of a tiny fungus and is used in making alcoholic liquors and as a leaven in baking 2 : a commercial product containing yeast plants in a moist or dry medium 3 : a minute one-celled fungus present and functionally active in yeast that reproduces by budding; *also* : any of several similar fungi 4 *archaic* : the foam of waves : SPUME 5 : something that causes ferment or activity

yeasty \'yē-stē\ *adj* **yeast·i·er; -est** 1 : of, relating to, or resembling yeast 2 : UNSETTLED 3 : full of vitality; *also* : FRIVOLOUS

yegg \'yeg\ *n* : one that breaks open safes to steal; *also* : ROBBER

¹yell \'yel\ *vb* : to utter a loud cry or scream : SHOUT

²yell *n* 1 : SHOUT 2 : a cheer used esp. to encourage an athletic team (as at a college)

¹yel·low \'ye-lō\ *adj* 1 : of the color yellow 2 : having a yellow complexion or skin 3 : SENSATIONAL ⟨∼ journalism⟩ 4 : COWARDLY — **yel·low·ish** \'ye-lə-wish\ *adj*

²yellow *n* 1 : a color between green and orange in the spectrum : the color of ripe lemons or sunflowers 2 : something yellow; *esp* : the yolk of an egg 3 *pl* : any of several plant diseases marked by stunted growth and yellowing of foliage

³yellow *vb* : to make or turn yellow

yellow birch *n* : a No. American birch with thin lustrous gray or yellow bark; *also* : its strong hard wood

yellow fever *n* : an acute destructive virus disease marked by prostration, jaundice, fever, and often hemorrhage and transmitted by a mosquito

yellow jack *n* : YELLOW FEVER

yellow jacket *n* : any of various small social wasps having the body barred with bright yellow

yelp \\'yelp\ *vb* [ME, to boast, cry out, fr. OE *gielpan* to boast, exult] : to utter a sharp quick shrill cry — **yelp** *n*

Ye·me·ni \\'ye-mə-nē\ *n* : YEMENITE — **Yemeni** *adj*

Ye·men·ite \\'ye-mə-ᵢnīt\ *n* : a native or inhabitant of Yemen — **Yemenite** *adj*

¹**yen** \\'yen\ *n, pl* **yen** — see MONEY table

²**yen** *n* [obs. E argot *yen-yen* craving for opium, fr. Chin (Guangdong dial.) *yīn-yáhn*, fr. *yīn* opium + *yáhn* craving] : a strong desire : LONGING

yeo·man \\'yō-mən\ *n* **1** : an attendant or officer in a royal or noble household **2** : a naval petty officer who performs clerical duties **3** : a person who owns and cultivates a small farm; *esp* : one of a class of English freeholders below the gentry

yeo·man·ry \-rē\ *n* : the body of yeomen and esp. of small landed proprietors

-yer — see -ER

¹**yes** \\'yes\ *adv* — used as a function word esp. to express assent or agreement or to introduce a more emphatic or explicit phrase

²**yes** *n* : an affirmative reply

ye·shi·va *or* **ye·shi·vah** \yə-'shē-və\ *n, pl* **yeshivas** *or* **ye·shi·voth** \-ᵢshē-'vōt, -'vōth\ : a Jewish school esp. for religious instruction

yes–man \\'yes-ᵢman\ *n* : a person who endorses uncritically every opinion or proposal of a superior

¹**yes·ter·day** \\'yes-tər-dē, -ᵢdā\ *adv* **1** : on the day preceding today **2** : only a short time ago

²**yesterday** *n* **1** : the day last past **2** : time not long past

yes·ter·year \\'yes-tər-ᵢyir\ *n* **1** : last year **2** : the recent past

¹**yet** \\'yet\ *adv* **1** : in addition : BESIDES; *also* : EVEN **6 2** : up to now; *also* : STILL **3** : so soon as now (not time to go ~) **4** : EVENTUALLY **5** : NEVERTHELESS, HOWEVER

²**yet** *conj* : but nevertheless : BUT

ye·ti \\'ye-tē, 'yä-\ *n* [Tibetan] : ABOMINABLE SNOWMAN

yew \\'yü\ *n* **1** : any of a genus of evergreen trees and shrubs with dark stiff poisonous needles and fleshy fruits **2** : the wood of a yew; *esp* : that of an Old World yew

Yid·dish \\'yi-dish\ *n* [Yiddish *yidish*, short for *yidish daytsh*, lit., Jewish German] : a language derived from medieval German and spoken by Jews esp. of eastern European origin — **Yiddish** *adj*

¹**yield** \\'yēld\ *vb* **1** : to give as fitting, owed, or required **2** : GIVE UP; *esp* : to give up possession of on claim or demand **3** : to bear as a natural product **4** : PRODUCE, SUPPLY **5** : to bring in : RETURN **6** : to give way (as to force or influence) **7** : to give place **syn** relinquish, cede, waive, surrender

²**yield** *n* : something yielded; *esp* : the amount or quantity produced or returned

yield·ing \\'yēl-diŋ\ *adj* **1** : not rigid or stiff : FLEXIBLE **2** : SUBMISSIVE, COMPLIANT

yikes \\'yīks\ *interj* — used to express fear or astonishment

yip \\'yip\ *vb* **yipped; yip·ping** : YAP

YMCA \ᵢwī-ᵢem-(ᵢ)sē-'ā\ *n* : Young Men's Christian Association

YMHA \ᵢwī-ᵢem-ᵢäch-'ā\ *n* : Young Men's Hebrew Association

yo \\'yō\ *interj* — used to call attention, indicate attentiveness, or express affirmation

YOB *abbr* year of birth

yo·del \\'yōd-ᵊl\ *vb* **yo·deled** *or* **yo·delled; yo·del·ing** *or* **yo·del·ling** : to sing by suddenly changing from chest voice to falsetto and back; *also* : to shout or call in this manner — **yodel** *n* — **yo·del·er** *n*

yo·ga \\'yō-gə\ *n* [Skt, lit., yoking, fr. *yunakti* he yokes] **1** *cap* : a Hindu theistic philosophy teaching the suppression of all activity of body, mind, and will in order that the self may realize its distinction from them

and attain liberation **2** : a system of exercises for attaining bodily or mental control and well-being

yo·gi \\'yō-gē\ *also* **yo·gin** \-gən, -ᵢgin\ *n* **1** : a person who practices yoga **2** *cap* : an adherent of Yoga philosophy

yo·gurt *also* **yo·ghurt** \\'yō-gərt\ *n* [Turk *yoğurt*] : a soured slightly acid often flavored semisolid milk food made of skimmed cow's milk and milk solids to which cultures of bacteria have been added

¹**yoke** \\'yōk\ *n, pl* **yokes** **1** : a wooden bar or frame by which two draft animals (as oxen) are coupled at the heads or necks for working together; *also* : a frame fitted to a person's shoulders to carry a load in two equal portions **2** : a clamp that embraces two parts to hold or unite them in position **3** *pl usu* **yoke** : two animals yoked together **4** : SERVITUDE, BONDAGE **5** : TIE, LINK (the ~ of matrimony) **6** : a fitted or shaped piece esp. at the shoulder of a garment **syn** couple, pair, brace

yoke 1

²**yoke** *vb* **yoked; yok·ing** **1** : to put a yoke on : couple with a yoke **2** : to attach a draft animal to ⟨~ a plow⟩ **3** : JOIN; *esp* : MARRY

yo·kel \\'yō-kəl\ *n* : a naive or gullible country person

yolk \\'yōk\ *n* **1** : the yellow rounded inner mass of the egg of a bird or reptile **2** : the stored food material of an egg consisting chiefly of proteins, lecithin, and cholesterol — **yolked** \\'yōkt\ *adj*

Yom Kip·pur \ᵢyōm-ki-'pur, ᵢyäm-, -'ki-pər\ *n* [Heb *yōm kippūr*, lit., day of atonement] : a Jewish holiday observed in September or October with fasting and prayer as a day of atonement

¹**yon** \\'yän\ *adj* : YONDER

²**yon** *adv* **1** : YONDER **2** : THITHER ⟨ran hither and ~⟩

yon·der \\'yän-dər\ *adv* : at or to that place

²**yonder** *adj* **1** : more distant ⟨the ~ side of the river⟩ **2** : being at a distance within view ⟨~ hills⟩

yore \\'yōr\ *n* [ME, fr. *yore*, adv., long ago, fr. OE *geāra*, fr. *gēar* year] : time long past ⟨in days of ~⟩

York·ie \\'yȯr-kē\ *n* : YORKSHIRE TERRIER

York·shire terrier \\'yȯrk-ᵢshir-, -shər-\ *n* : any of a breed of compact toy terriers with long straight silky hair

you \\'yü\ *pron* **1** : the person or persons addressed ⟨~ are a nice person⟩ ⟨~ are nice people⟩ **2** : ONE **2** ⟨~ turn this knob to open it⟩

¹**young** \\'yəŋ\ *adj* **youn·ger** \\'yəŋ-gər\; **youn·gest** \\'yəŋ-gəst\ **1** : being in the first or an early stage of life, growth, or development **2** : having little experience **3** : recently come into being **4** : YOUTHFUL **5** *cap* : belonging to or representing a new or revived usu. political group or movement — **young·ish** \\'yəŋ-ish\ *adj*

²**young** *n, pl* **young** : young persons; *also* : young animals

young·ling \\'yəŋ-liŋ\ *n* : one that is young — **youngling** *adj*

young·ster \-stər\ *n* **1** : a young person **2** : CHILD

your \\'yu̇r, 'yȯr, yər\ *adj* : of or relating to you or yourself

yours \\'yu̇rz, 'yȯrz\ *pron* : one or the ones belonging to you

your·self \yər-'self\ *pron, pl* **yourselves** \-'selvz\ : YOU — used reflexively, for emphasis, or in absolute constructions ⟨you'll hurt ~⟩ ⟨do it ~⟩

youth \\'yüth\ *n, pl* **youths** \\'yü<u>th</u>z, 'yüths\ **1** : the pe-

riod of life between childhood and maturity **2** : a young man; *also* : young persons **3** : YOUTHFULNESS
youth·ful \'yüth-fəl\ *adj* **1** : of, relating to, or appropriate to youth **2** : being young and not yet mature **3** : FRESH, VIGOROUS — **youth·ful·ly** *adv* — **youthful·ness** *n*
youth hostel *n* : HOSTEL 2
yowl \'yaúl\ *vb* : to utter a loud long mournful cry : WAIL — **yowl** *n*
yo-yo \'yō-(₁)yō\ *n, pl* **yo-yos** : a thick grooved double disk with a string attached to its center which is made to fall and rise to the hand by unwinding and rewinding on the string
yr *abbr* **1** year **2** your
yrbk *abbr* yearbook
YT *abbr* Yukon Territory
yt·ter·bi·um \i-'tər-bē-əm\ *n* : a rare metallic chemical element — see ELEMENT table
yt·tri·um \'i-trē-əm\ *n* : a rare metallic chemical element — see ELEMENT table
yu·an \'yü-ən, yü-'än\ *n, pl* **yuan 1** — see MONEY table **2** : the dollar of the Republic of China (Taiwan)
yuc·ca \'yə-kə\ *n* : any of a genus of plants related to the agaves that grow esp. in warm dry regions and

bear large clusters of white cup-shaped flowers atop a long stiff stalk
yuck \'yək\ *interj* — used to express rejection or disgust
Yu·go·slav \₁yü-gō-'släv, -'slav\ *n* : a native or inhabitant of Yugoslavia — **Yugoslav** *adj* — **Yu·go·sla·vi·an** \-'slä-vē-ən\ *adj or n*
yule \'yül\ *n, often cap* : CHRISTMAS
Yule log *n* : a large log formerly put onthe hearth on Christmas Eve as the foundation of the fire
yule·tide \'yül-₁tīd\ *n, often cap* : CHRISTMASTIDE
yum·my \'yə-mē\ *adj* **yum·mi·er; -est** : highly attractive or pleasing
yup·pie \'yə-pē\ *n* [prob. fr. *young urban professional* + *-ie* (as in *hippie*)] : a young college-educated adult employed in a well-paying profession and living and working in or near a large city
yurt \'yürt\ *n* : a light round tent of skins or felt stretched over a lattice framework used by pastoral peoples of inner Asia
YWCA \₁wī-₁də-bəl-yü-(₁)sē-'ā\ *n* : Young Women's Christian Association
YWHA \-₁āch-'ā\ *n* : Young Women's Hebrew Association

Z

¹z \'zē\ *n, pl* **z's** *or* **zs** *often cap* : the 26th letter of the English alphabet
²z *abbr* **1** zero **2** zone
Z *symbol* atomic number
Zach *abbr* Zacharias
Zach·a·ri·as \₁za-kə-'rī-əs\ *n* : ZECHARIAH
zaire \'zīr, zä-'ir\ *n, pl* **zaires** *or* **zaire** — see MONEY table
Zair·ian \zä-'ir-ē-ən\ *n* : a native or inhabitant of Zaire — **Zairian** *adj*
Zam·bi·an \'zam-bē-ən\ *n* : a native or inhabitant of Zambia — **Zambian** *adj*
¹za·ny \'zā-nē\ *n, pl* **zanies** [It *zanni*, a traditional masked clown, fr. It dial. *Zanni*, nickname for It *Giovanni* John] **1** : CLOWN, BUFFOON **2** : a silly or foolish person
²zany *adj* **za·ni·er; -est 1** : characteristic of a zany **2** : CRAZY, FOOLISH — **za·ni·ly** \'zā-nə-lē, 'zān-ᵊl-ē\ *adv* — **za·ni·ness** \'zā-nē-nəs\ *n*
zap \'zap\ *vb* **zapped; zap·ping 1** : DESTROY, KILL **2** : to irradiate esp. with microwaves
zeal \'zēl\ *n* : eager and ardent interest in the pursuit of something : FERVOR **syn** enthusiasm, passion, ardor
zeal·ot \'ze-lət\ *n* : a zealous person; *esp* : a fanatical partisan **syn** enthusiast, bigot
zeal·ous \'ze-ləs\ *adj* : filled with, characterized by, or due to zeal — **zeal·ous·ly** *adv* — **zeal·ous·ness** *n*
ze·bra \'zē-brə\ *n, pl* **zebras** *also* **zebra** : any of several African mammals related to the horse but conspicuously striped with black or brown and white or buff
ze·bu \'zē-bü, -byü\ *n* : an ox of any of various breeds developed in India that have a large fleshy hump over the shoulders, a dewlap, drooping ears, and marked resistance to heat and to insect attack
Zech *abbr* Zechariah
Zech·a·ri·ah \₁ze-kə-'rī-ə\ *n* — see BIBLE table
zed \'zed\ *n, chiefly Brit* : the letter *z*
zeit·geist \'tsīt-₁gīst, 'zīt-\ *n* [G, fr. *Zeit* time + *Geist* spirit] : the general intellectual, moral, and cultural state of an era
Zen \'zen\ *n* : a Japanese Buddhist sect that teaches self-discipline, meditation, and attainment of enlightenment through direct intuitive insight
ze·na·na \zə-'nä-nə\ *n* : HAREM
ze·nith \'zē-nəth\ *n* **1** : the point in the heavens directly

zebu

overhead **2** : the highest point : ACME **syn** culmination, pinnacle, apex
ze·o·lite \'zē-ə-₁līt\ *n* : any of various feldsparlike silicates used esp. as water softeners
Zeph *abbr* Zephaniah
Zeph·a·ni·ah \₁ze-fə-'nī-ə\ *n* — see BIBLE table
zeph·yr \'ze-fər\ *n* : a breeze from the west; *also* : a gentle breeze
zep·pe·lin \'ze-plən, -pə-lən\ *n* [Count Ferdinand von *Zeppelin* †1917 Ger. airship manufacturer] : a cylindrical rigid blimplike airship
¹ze·ro \'zē-rō, 'zir-ō\ *n, pl* **zeros** *also* **zeroes** [ultim. fr. Ar *şifr*] **1** : the numerical symbol 0 **2** : the number represented by the symbol 0 **3** : the point at which the graduated degrees or measurements on a scale (as of a thermometer) begin **4** : the lowest point
²zero *adj* **1** : of, relating to, or being a zero **2** : having no magnitude or quantity **3** : ABSENT, LACKING; *esp* : having no modified inflectional form
³zero *vb* : to adjust the sights of a firearm to hit the point aimed at ⟨∼ in⟩
zero hour *n* : the time at which an event (as a military operation) is scheduled to begin
zest \'zest\ *n* **1** : a quality of enhancing enjoyment : PIQUANCY **2** : keen enjoyment : GUSTO — **zest·ful** \-fəl\ *adj* — **zest·ful·ly** *adv* — **zest·ful·ness** *n*
ze·ta \'zā-tə, 'zē-\ *n* : the 6th letter of the Greek alphabet — Z or ζ
zi·do·vu·dine \zi-'dō-vyü-₁dēn\ *n* : AZT
¹zig·zag \'zig-₁zag\ *n* : one of a series of short sharp

turns, angles, or alterations in a course; *also* : something marked by such a series
²zigzag *adv* : in or by a zigzag path
³zigzag *adj* : having short sharp turns or angles
⁴zigzag *vb* **zig·zagged; zig·zag·ging** : to form into or proceed along a zigzag

zil·lion \'zil-yən\ *n* : a large indeterminate number

Zim·ba·bwe·an \zim-'bä-bwē-ən\ *n* : a native or inhabitant of Zimbabwe — **Zimbabwean** *adj*
zinc \'ziŋk\ *n* : a bluish white crystalline metallic chemical element that is commonly found in minerals and is used esp. as a protective coating for iron and steel — see ELEMENT table
zinc ointment *n* : ZINC OXIDE OINTMENT
zinc oxide *n* : a white solid used esp. as a pigment, in compounding rubber, and in ointments
zinc oxide ointment *n* : an ointment containing zinc oxide and used for skin disorders
zing \'ziŋ\ *n* **1** : a shrill humming noise **2** : VITALITY 4 — **zing** *vb*
zing·er \'ziŋ-ər\ *n* : a pointed witty remark or retort
zin·nia \'zi-nē-ə, 'zēn-yə\ *n* : any of a small genus of tropical American herbs related to the daisies and widely grown for their showy long-lasting flower heads
Zi·on \'zī-ən\ *n* **1** : the Jewish people **2** : the Jewish homeland as a symbol of Judaism or of Jewish national aspiration **3** : HEAVEN **4** : UTOPIA
Zi·on·ism \'zī-ə-ˌni-zəm\ *n* : an international movement orig. for the establishment of a Jewish national or religious community in Palestine and later for the support of modern Israel — **Zi·on·ist** \-nist\ *adj or n*
¹zip \'zip\ *vb* **zipped; zip·ping** : to move, act, or function with speed or vigor
²zip *n* **1** : a sudden sharp hissing sound **2** : ENERGY, VIM
³zip *n* : NOTHING, ZERO
⁴zip *vb* **zipped; zip·ping** : to close or open with a zipper
zip code *n, often cap Z&I&P* [*zone improvement plan*]

: a number that identifies each postal delivery area in the U.S.
zip·per \'zi-pər\ *n* : a fastener consisting of two rows of metal or plastic teeth on strips of tape and a sliding piece that closes an opening by drawing the teeth together
zip·py \'zi-pē\ *adj* **zip·pi·er; -est** : BRISK, SNAPPY
zir·con \'zər-ˌkän\ *n* : a zirconium-containing mineral transparent varieties of which are used as gems
zir·co·ni·um \ˌzər-'kō-nē-əm\ *n* : a gray corrosion-resistant metallic chemical element used esp. in alloys and ceramics — see ELEMENT table
zit \'zit\ *n* : PIMPLE
zith·er \'zi-thər, -thər\ *n* : a musical instrument having 30 to 40 strings played with plectrum and fingers
zi·ti \'zē-tē\ *n, pl* **ziti** [It] : medium-size tubular pasta
zlo·ty \'zlȯ-tē\ *n, pl* **zlo·tys** \-tēz\ *or* **zloty** — see MONEY table
Zn *symbol* zinc
zo·di·ac \'zō-dē-ˌak\ *n* [ME, fr. MF *zodiaque*, fr. L *zodiacus*, fr. Gk *zōidiakos*, fr. *zōidion* carved figure, sign of the zodiac, fr. dim. of *zōion* living being, figure] **1** : an imaginary belt in the heavens that encompasses the paths of most of the planets and that is divided into 12 constellations or signs **2** : a figure representing the signs of the zodiac and their symbols — **zo·di·a·cal** \zō-'dī-ə-kəl\ *adj*

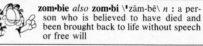

zom·bie *also* **zom·bi** \'zäm-bē\ *n* : a person who is believed to have died and been brought back to life without speech or free will

zon·al \'zōn-ᵊl\ *adj* : of, relating to, or having the form of a zone — **zon·al·ly** *adv*
¹zone \'zōn\ *n* [ME, fr. L *zona* belt, zone, fr. Gk *zōnē*] **1** : any of five great divisions of the earth's surface made according to latitude and temperature and including the torrid zone about the equator, the two temperate zones lying between the torrid zone and the polar circles, and the two frigid zones lying between the polar circles and the poles **2** : an encircling band or girdle ⟨a ~ of trees⟩ **3** : a section of an area

or territory created for a particular purpose ⟨business ~⟩ ⟨postal ~⟩

²**zone** *vb* **zoned; zon•ing 1 :** ENCIRCLE **2 :** to arrange in or mark off into zones; *esp* : to divide (as a city) into sections reserved for different purposes

zonked \'zäŋkt\ *adj* : being or acting as if under the influence of alcohol or a drug : HIGH

zoo \'zü\ *n, pl* **zoos :** a zoological garden or collection of living animals usu. for public display

zoo•ge•og•ra•phy \ˌzō-ə-jē-'ä-grə-fē\ *n* : a branch of biogeography concerned with the geographical distribution of animals — **zoo•ge•og•ra•pher** \-fər\ *n* — **zoo•geo•graph•ic** \-ˌjē-ə-'gra-fik\ *also* **zoo•geo•graph•i•cal** \-fi-kəl\ *adj*

zoo•keep•er \'zü-ˌkē-pər\ *n* : a person who cares for animals in a zoo

zool *abbr* zoological; zoology

zoological garden *n* : a garden or park where wild animals are kept for exhibition

zo•ol•o•gy \zō-'ä-lə-jē\ *n* : a branch of biology that deals with the classification and the properties and vital phenomena of animals — **zo•o•log•i•cal** \ˌzō-ə-'lä-ji-kəl\ *adj* — **zo•ol•o•gist** \zō-'ä-lə-jist\ *n*

zoom \'züm\ *vb* **1 :** to move with a loud hum or buzz **2 :** to gain altitude quickly **3 :** to focus a camera or microscope using a special lens that permits the apparent distance of the object to be varied — **zoom** *n*

zoom lens *n* : a camera lens in which the image size can be varied continuously while the image remains in focus

zoo•mor•phic \ˌzō-ə-'mòr-fik\ *adj* **1 :** having the form of an animal **2 :** of, relating to, or being the representation of a deity in the form or with the attributes of an animal

zoo•plank•ton \ˌzō-ə-'plaŋk-tən, -ˌtän\ *n* : animal life of the plankton

zoo•spore \'zō-ə-ˌspòr\ *n* : a motile spore

zoot suit \'züt-\ *n* : a flashy suit of extreme cut typically consisting of a thigh-length jacket with wide padded shoulders and trousers that are wide at the top and narrow at the bottom — **zoot•suit•er** \-ˌsü-tər\ *n*

Zo•ro•as•tri•an•ism \ˌzòr-ə-'was-trē-ə-ˌni-zəm\ *n* : a religion founded by the Persian prophet Zoroaster — **Zo•ro•as•tri•an** \-trē-ən\ *adj or n*

Zou•ave \zù-'äv\ *n* : a member of a French infantry unit orig. composed of Algerians wearing a brilliant uniform and conducting a quick spirited drill; *also* : a member of a military unit modeled on the Zouaves

zounds \'zaùndz\ *interj* [euphemism for *God's wounds*] — used as a mild oath

zoy•sia \'zòi-shə, -zhə, -sē-ə, -zē-ə\ *n* : any of a genus of creeping perennial grasses having fine wiry leaves and including some used as lawn grasses

ZPG *abbr* zero population growth

Zr *symbol* zirconium

zuc•chet•to \zü-'ke-tō, tsü-\ *n, pl* **-tos** [It] : a small round skullcap worn by Roman Catholic ecclesiastics

zuc•chi•ni \zù-'kē-nē\ *n, pl* **-ni** *or* **-nis** [It] : a summer squash of bushy growth with smooth cylindrical dark green fruits; *also* : its fruit

Zu•lu \'zü-ˌlü\ *n, pl* **Zulu** *or* **Zulus :** a member of a Bantu-speaking people of South Africa; *also* : the Bantu language of the Zulus

Zu•ni \'zü-nē\ *or* **Zu•ñi** \-nyē\ *n, pl* **Zuni** *or* **Zunis** *or* **Zuñi** *or* **Zuñis :** a member of an American Indian people of western New Mexico; *also* : the language of the Zuni people

zwie•back \'swē-ˌbak, 'swī-, 'zwē-, 'zwī-, -ˌbäk\ *n* [G, lit., twice baked, fr. *zwie-* twice + *backen* to bake] : a usu. sweetened bread that is baked and then sliced and toasted until dry and crisp

Zwing•li•an \'zwiŋ-glē-ən, 'swiŋ-, -lē-; 'tsfiŋ-lē-\ *adj* : of or relating to the Swiss religious reformer Ulrich Zwingli or his teachings — **Zwinglian** *n*

zy•de•co \'zī-də-ˌkō\ *n* : popular music of southern Louisiana that combines tunes of French origin with elements of Caribbean music and the blues

zy•gote \'zī-ˌgōt\ *n* : a cell formed by the union of two sexual cells; *also* : the developing individual produced from such a cell — **zy•got•ic** \zī-'gä-tik\ *adj*

Common English Given Names

The following vocabulary presents given names that are most frequent in English use. The list is not exhaustive either of the names themselves or the variant spellings of those names which are entered. Compound or double names and surnames used as given names are not entered except in cases where long-continued or common use gives them an independent character.

Besides the pronunciations of the names, the list usually provides at least one of the following kinds of information at each entry: (1) etymology, indicating the language source but not the original form of the name, and (2) meaning where known or ascertainable with reasonable certainty.

Names of Men

Aar·on \'ar-ən, 'er-\ [Heb]
Abra·ham \'ā-brə-ˌham\ [Heb]
Ad·am \'ad-əm\ [Heb] man
Ad·di·son \'ad-ə-sən\ [fr. a surname]
Adolph \'ad-ˌälf, 'ā-ˌdälf\ [Gmc] noble wolf, *i.e.*, noble hero
Adri·an \'ā-drē-ən\ [L] of Hadria, ancient town in central Italy
Al \al\ *dim of* ALAN, ALBERT, *etc.*
Al·an \'al-ən\ [Celt]
Al·bert \'al-bərt\ [Gmc] illustrious through nobility
Al·den \'ȯl-dən\ [OE] old friend
Al·ex \'al-iks\ *or* **Al·ec** \'al-ik\ *dim of* ALEXANDER
Al·ex·an·der \ˌal-ig-'zan-dər\ [Gk] a defender of men
Al·fred \'al-frəd, -fərd\ [OE] elf counsel, *i.e.*, good counsel
Al·len *or* **Al·lan** *or* **Al·lyn** \'al-ən\ *var of* ALAN
Al·ton \'ȯlt-ᵊn, 'alt-\ [prob. fr. a surname]
Al·va *or* **Al·vah** \'al-və\ [Heb]
Al·vin \'al-vən\ [Gmc]
Amos \'ā-məs\ [Heb]
An·dre \'än-(ˌ)drā\ [F] *var of* ANDREW
An·drew \'an-(ˌ)drü\ [Gk] manly
An·dy \'an-dē\ *dim of* ANDREW
An·ge·lo \'an-jə-ˌlō\ [It, fr. Gk] angel, messenger
An·gus \'aŋ-gəs\ [Celt]
An·tho·ny \'an(t)-thə-nē, *chiefly Brit* 'an-tə-\ [L]
An·ton \'ant-ᵊn, 'an-ˌtän\ [G & Slav] *var of* ANTHONY
An·to·nio \an-'tō-nē-ˌō\ [It] *var of* ANTHONY
Ar·chi·bald \'är-chə-ˌbȯld, -bəld\ [Gmc]
Ar·chie \'är-chē\ *dim of* ARCHIBALD
Ar·den \'ärd-ᵊn\ [prob. fr. a surname]
Ar·len *or* **Ar·lin** \'är-lən\ [prob. fr. a surname]
Ar·lo \'är-(ˌ)lō\
Ar·mand \'är-ˌmänd, -mənd\ [F] *var of* HERMAN
Arne \'ärn\ [Scand] eagle
Ar·nold \'ärn-ᵊld\ [Gmc] power of an eagle
Art \'ärt\ *dim of* ARTHUR
Ar·thur \'är-thər\ [prob. L]
Au·brey \'ȯ-brē\ [Gmc] elf ruler
Au·gust \'ȯ-gəst\ [L] August, majestic
Aus·tin \'ȯs-tən, 'äs-\ *alter of* Augustine

Bai·ley \'bā-lē\ [fr. a surname]
Bar·clay \'bär-klē\ [fr. a surname]
Bar·net *or* **Bar·nett** \bär-'net\ [fr. a surname]
Bar·ney \'bär-nē\ *dim of* BERNARD
Bar·rett \'bar-ət\ [fr. a surname]
Bar·ry *or* **Bar·rie** \'bar-ē\ [Ir]
Bart \'bärt\ *dim of* Bartholomew
Bar·ton \'bärt-ᵊn\ [fr. a surname]
Ba·sil \'baz-əl, 'bäs-, 'bās-, 'bāz-\ [Gk] kingly, royal
Ben \'ben\ *or* **Ben·nie** *or* **Ben·ny** \'ben-ē\ *dim of* BENJAMIN
Ben·e·dict \'ben-ə-ˌdikt\ [L] blessed
Ben·ja·min \'benj-(ə-)mən\ [Heb] son of the right hand
Ben·nett \'ben-ət\ [OF] *var of* BENEDICT

Ben·ton \'bent-ᵊn\ [fr. a surname]
Ber·nard \'bər-nərd, (ˌ)bər-'närd\ *or* **Bern·hard** \'bərn-ˌhärd\ [Gmc] bold as a bear
Ber·nie \'bər-nē\ *dim of* BERNARD
Bert *or* **Burt** \'bərt\ *dim of* BERTRAM, ALBERT, etc.
Ber·tram \'bər-trəm\ [Gmc] bright raven
Bill \'bil\ *or* **Bil·ly** *or* **Bil·lie** \'bil-ē\ *dim of* WILLIAM
Blaine \'blān\ [fr. a surname]
Blair \'bla(ə)r, 'ble(ə)r\ [fr. a surname]
Bob·by \'bäb-ē\ *or* **Bob** \'bäb\ *dim of* ROBERT
Bo·ris \'bȯr-əs, 'bȯr-, 'bär-\ [Russ]
Boyd \'bȯid\ [fr. a surname]
Brad·ford \'brad-fərd\ [fr. a surname]
Brad·ley \'brad-lē\ [fr. a surname]
Bran·don \'bran-dən\ [fr. a surname]
Bren·dan \'bren-dən\ [Celt]
Brent \'brent\ [fr. a surname]
Brett *or* **Bret** \'bret\ [IrGael]
Bri·an *or* **Bry·an** \'brī-ən\ [Celt]
Brooks \'brùks\ [fr. a surname]
Bruce \'brüs\ [fr. a surname]
Bru·no \'brü-(ˌ)nō\ [It, fr. Gmc] brown
Bryce *or* **Brice** \'brīs\ [fr. a surname]
Bud·dy \'bəd-ē\ [prob. alter. of *brother*]
Bu·ford \'byü-fərd\ [fr. a surname]
Burke \'bərk\ [fr. a surname]
Bur·ton \'bərt-ᵊn\ [fr. a surname]
By·ron \'bī-rən\ [fr. a surname]

Cal·vin \'kal-vən\ [fr. a surname]
Cam·er·on \'kam-(ə-)rən\ [fr. a surname]
Carl \'kärl\ *var of* KARL
Car·los \'kär-ləs, -ˌlōs\ [Sp] *var of* CHARLES
Carl·ton *or* **Carle·ton** \'kär(-ə)l-tən, 'kärlt-ᵊn\ [fr. a surname]
Car·lyle \kär-'lī(ə)l, 'kär-ˌ\ [fr. a surname]
Car·men \'kär-mən\ [Sp, fr. L] song
Car·roll \'kar-əl\ [fr. a surname]
Car·son \'kärs-ᵊn\ [fr. a surname]
Car·ter \'kärt-ər\ [fr. a surname]
Cary *or* **Car·ey** \'ka(ə)r-ē, 'ke(ə)r-ē\ [fr. a surname]
Ce·cil \'sē-səl, 'ses-əl\ [L]
Chad \'chad\ [Gmc]
Charles \'chär(-ə)lz\ [Gmc] man of the common people
Ches·ter \'ches-tər\ [fr. a surname]
Chris \'kris\ *dim of* CHRISTOPHER
Chris·tian \'kris(h)-chən\ [Gk] Christian (the believer)
Chris·to·pher \'kris-tə-fər\ [Gk] Christ bearer
Clar·ence \'klar-ən(t)s\ [fr. the English dukedom]
Clark *or* **Clarke** \'klärk\ [fr. a surname]
Claude *or* **Claud** \'klȯd\ [L]
Clay \'klā\ *dim of* CLAYTON
Clay·ton \'klāt-ᵊn\ [fr. a surname]
Clem \'klem\ *dim of* CLEMENT
Clem·ent \'klem-ənt\ [L] mild, merciful
Clif·ford \'klif-ərd\ [fr. a surname]
Clif·ton \'klif-tən\ [fr. a surname]
Clint \'klint\ *dim of* CLINTON
Clin·ton \'klint-ᵊn\ [fr. a surname]
Clyde \'klīd\ [fr. a surname]

Cole \'kōl\ [fr. a surname]
Co·lin \'käl-ən, 'kō-lən\ *or* **Col·lin** \'käl-ən\ *dim of* NICHOLAS
Con·rad \'kän-ˌrad, -rəd\ [Gmc] bold counsel
Con·stan·tine \'kän(t)-stən-ˌtēn, -ˌtīn\ [L]
Cor·ey \'kòr-ē\ [fr. a surname]
Cor·ne·lius \kòr-'nēl-yəs\ [L]
Craig \'krāg\ [fr. a surname]
Cur·tis \'kərt-əs\ [OF] courteous
Cyr·il \'sir-əl\ [Gk] lordly
Cy·rus \'sī-rəs\ [OPer]

Dale \'dā(ə)l\ [fr. a surname]
Dal·las \'dal-əs\ [fr. a surname]
Dal·ton \'dòlt-ᵊn\ [fr. a surname]
Dan \'dan\ [Heb] judge
Da·na \'dā-nə\ [fr. a surname]
Dan·iel \'dan-yəl *also* 'dan-ᵊl\ [Heb] God has judged
Dan·ny \'dan-ē\ *dim of* DANIEL
Dar·old \'dar-əld\ *perh alter of* DARRELL
Dar·rell *or* **Dar·rel** *or* **Dar·ryl** *or* **Dar·yl** \'dar-əl\ [fr. a surname]
Dar·win \'där-wən\ [fr. a surname]
Dave \'dāv\ *dim of* DAVID
Da·vid \'dā-vəd\ [Heb] beloved
Da·vis \'dā-vəs\ [fr. a surname]
Dean *or* **Deane** \'dēn\ [fr. a surname]
Del·a·no \'del-ə-ˌnō\ [fr. a surname]
Del·bert \'del-bərt\ *dim of* Adalbert
Del·mar \'del-mər, -ˌmär\ *or* **Del·mer** \-mər\ [fr. a surname]
Den·nis *or* **Den·is** \'den-əs\ [OF, fr. Gk] belonging to Dionysus, god of wine
Den·ny \'den-ē\ *dim of* DENNIS
Den·ton \'dent-ᵊn\ [fr. a surname]
Der·ek \'der-ik\ [Middle Dutch, fr. Gmc] ruler of the people
Dew·ey \'d(y)ü-ē\ [fr. a surname]
De·witt \di-'wit\ [fr. a surname]
Dex·ter \'dek-stər\ [L] on the right hand, fortunate
Dick \'dik\ *dim of* RICHARD
Dirk \'dərk\ [Dutch] *var of* DEREK
Dom·i·nic *or* **Dom·i·nick** \'däm-ə-(ˌ)nik\ [L] belonging to the Lord
Don *or* **Donn** \'dän\ *dim of* DONALD
Don·al \'dän-ᵊl\ *var of* DONALD
Don·ald \'dän-ᵊld\ [ScGael] world ruler
Don·nie \'dän-ē\ *dim of* DON
Don·o·van \'dän-ə-vən, 'dən-\ [fr. a surname]
Doug \'dəg\ *dim of* DOUGLAS
Doug·las *or* **Doug·lass** \'dəg-ləs\ [fr. a surname]
Duane \dü-'ān, 'dwān\ [fr. a surname]
Dud·ley \'dəd-lē\ [fr. a surname]
Dun·can \'dəŋ-kən\ [ScGael] brown head
Dur·ward \'dər-wərd\ [fr. a surname]
Dwayne *or* **Dwaine** \'dwān\ [fr. a surname]
Dwight \'dwīt\ [fr. a surname]
Dy·lan \'dil-ən\ [W]

Earl *or* **Earle** \'ər(-ə)l\ [OE] warrior, noble
Ed \'ed\ *dim of* EDWARD, EDGAR, etc.
Ed·die *or* **Ed·dy** \'ed-ē\ *dim of* ED
Ed·gar \'ed-gər\ [OE] spear of wealth
Ed·mund *or* **Ed·mond** \'ed-mənd\ [OE] protector of wealth
Ed·son \'ed-sən\ [fr. a surname]
Ed·ward \'ed-wərd\ [OE] guardian of wealth
Ed·win \'ed-wən\ [OE] friend of wealth
El·bert \'el-bərt\ *var of* ALBERT
Eli \'ē-ˌlī\ [Heb] high
E·li·as \i-'lī-əs\ [Gk] *var of* Elijah
El·liott *or* **El·liot** *or* **El·iot** \'el-ē-ət, 'el-yət\ [fr. a surname]
El·lis \'el-əs\ *var of* ELIAS
Ells·worth \'elz-(ˌ)wərth\ [fr. a surname]
El·mer \'el-mər\ [fr. a surname]

El·mo \'el-(ˌ)mō\ [It, fr. Gk] lovable
El·ton \'elt-ᵊn\ [fr. a surname]
El·vin \'el-vən\ [fr. a surname]
El·wood *or* **Ell·wood** \'el-ˌwüd\ [fr. a surname]
Em·man·u·el *or* **Eman·u·el** \i-'man-yə(-wə)l\ [Heb] God with us
Em·er·son \'em-ər-sən\ [fr. a surname]
Emil \'ā-məl\ *or* **Emile** \ā-'mē(ə)l\ [L]
Em·mett \'em-ət\ [fr. a surname]
Em·o·ry *or* **Em·ery** \'em-(ə-)rē\ [Gmc]
Er·ic *or* **Er·ich** *or* **Er·ik** \'er-ik\ [Scand]
Er·nest *or* **Ear·nest** \'ər-nəst\ [G] earnestness
Er·nie \'ər-nē\ *dim of* ERNEST
Ernst \'ərn(t)st, 'e(ə)rn(t)st\ [G] *var of* ERNEST
Er·rol \'er-əl\ [prob. fr. a surname]
Ethan \'ē-thən\ [Heb] strength
Eu·gene \yü-'jēn, 'yü-ˌ\ [Gk] wellborn
Ev·an \'ev-ən\ [W] *var of* JOHN
Ev·er·ett \'ev-(ə-)rət\ [fr. a surname]

Fe·lix \'fē-liks\ [L] happy, prosperous
Fer·di·nand \'fərd-ᵊn-ˌand\ [Gmc]
Fer·nan·do \fər-'nan-(ˌ)dō\ [Sp] *var of* FERDINAND
Fletch·er \'flech-ər\ [fr. a surname]
Floyd \'flòid\ [fr. a surname]
For·rest *or* **For·est** \'fòr-əst, 'fär-\ [fr. a surname]
Fos·ter \'fòs-tər, 'fäs-\ [fr. a surname]
Fran·cis \'fran(t)-səs\ [OIt & OF] Frenchman
Fran·cis·co \fran-'sis-(ˌ)kō\ [Sp] *var of* FRANCIS
Frank \'fraŋk\ [Gmc] freeman, Frank
Frank·lin *or* **Frank·lyn** \'fraŋ-klən\ [fr. a surname]
Fred \'fred\ *dim of* FREDERICK, ALFRED
Fred·die \'fred-ē\ *dim of* FREDERICK
Fred·er·ick *or* **Fred·er·ic** *or* **Fred·rick** *or* **Fred·ric** \'fred-(ə-)rik\ [Gmc] peaceful ruler
Free·man \'frē-mən\ [fr. a surname]
Fritz \'frits\ [G] *dim of* Friedrich

Ga·bri·el \'gā-brē-əl\ [Heb] man of God
Gar·land \'gär-lənd\ [fr. a surname]
Gar·rett \'gar-ət\ [fr. a surname]
Garth \'gärth\ [fr. a surname]
Gary \'gar-ē, 'ger-ē\ *or* **Gar·ry** \'gar-\ [prob. fr. a surname]
Gay·lord \'gā-ˌlò(ə)rd\ [fr. a surname]
Gene \'jēn\ *dim of* EUGENE
Geof·frey \'jef-rē\ [OF, fr. Gmc]
George \'jò(ə)rj\ [Gk] of or relating to a farmer
Ger·ald \'jer-əld\ [Gmc] spear dominion
Ge·rard \jə-'rärd, *chiefly Brit* 'jer-ˌärd, -ərd\ *or* **Ger·hard** \'ge(ə)r-ˌhärd\ [Gmc] strong with the spear
Ger·ry \'jer-ē\ *var of* JERRY
Gil·bert \'gil-bərt\ [Gmc] *prob* illustrious through hostages
Giles \'jī(ə)lz\ [OF, fr. LL]
Glenn *or* **Glen** \'glen\ [fr. a surname]
Gor·don \'gòrd-ᵊn\ [fr. a surname]
Gra·ham \'grā-əm, 'gra(-ə)m\ [fr. a surname]
Grant \'grant\ [fr. a surname]
Gran·ville \'gran-ˌvil\ [fr. a surname]
Gray \'grā\ [fr. a surname]
Gregg *or* **Greg** \'greg\ *dim of* GREGORY
Greg·o·ry \'greg-(ə-)rē\ [LGk] vigilant
Gro·ver \'grō-vər\ [fr. a surname]
Gus \'gəs\ *dim of* Gustav *or* Augustus
Guy \'gī\ [OF, fr. Gmc]

Hal \'hal\ *dim of* HENRY
Hall \'hòl\ [fr. a surname]
Ham·il·ton \'ham-əl-tən, -əlt-ᵊn\ [fr. a surname]
Hans \'hanz, 'hän(t)s\ [G] *dim of* Johannes
Har·lan \'här-lən\ *or* **Har·land** \-lənd\ [fr. a surname]
Har·ley \'här-lē\ [fr. a surname]
Har·low \'här-(ˌ)lō\ [fr. a surname]
Har·mon \'här-mən\ [fr. a surname]
Har·old \'har-əld\ [OE] army dominion

Har·ris \'har-əs\ [fr. a surname]
Har·ri·son \'har-ə-sən\ [fr. a surname]
Har·ry \'har-ē\ dim of HENRY
Har·vey \'här-vē\ [fr. a surname]
Hec·tor \'hek-tər\ [Gk] holding fast
Hel·mut \'hel-mət, -ˌmüt\ [G] helmet courage
Hen·ry \'hen-rē\ [Gmc] ruler of the home
Her·bert \'hər-bərt\ [Gmc] illustrious by reason of an army
Her·man or **Her·mann** \'hər-mən\ [Gmc] warrior
Her·schel or **Her·shel** \'hər-shəl\ [fr. a surname]
Hi·ram \'hī-rəm\ [Phoenician]
Ho·bart \'hō-bərt, -ˌbärt\ [fr. a surname]
Hol·lis \'häl-əs\ [fr. a surname]
Ho·mer \'hō-mər\ [Gk]
Hor·ace \'hòr-əs, 'här-\ [L]
How·ard \'haů-(ə)rd\ [fr. a surname]
How·ell \'haů(-ə)l\ [W]
Hu·bert \'hyü-bərt\ [Gmc] bright in spirit
Hud·son \'həd-sən\ [fr. a surname]
Hugh \'hyü\ or **Hu·go** \'hyü-(ˌ)gō\ [Gmc] prob mind, spirit

Ian \'ē-ən\ [ScGael] var of JOHN
Ira \'ī-rə\ [Heb]
Ir·ving \'ər-viŋ\ or **Ir·vin** \-vən\ [fr. a surname]
Ir·win \'ər-wən\ [fr. a surname]
Isaac \'ī-zik, -zək\ [Heb] he laughs
Ivan \'ī-vən\ [Russ] var of JOHN

Jack \'jak\ dim of JOHN
Jack·son \'jak-sən\ [fr. a surname]
Ja·cob \'jā-kəb, -kəp\ [Heb] one who supplants
Jacques or **Jacque** \'zhäk\ [F] var of JAMES
Jake \'jāk\ dim of JACOB
James \'jāmz\ [OF, fr. LL Jacobus] var of JACOB
Ja·mie \'jā-mē\ dim of JAMES
Jan \'jan\ [Dutch & LG] var of JOHN
Jar·ed \'jar-əd, 'jer-\ [Heb] descent
Ja·son \'jās-ᵊn\ [Gk]
Jay \'jā\ [prob. fr. a surname]
Jed \'jed\ dim of Jedidiah
Jef·frey or **Jeff·ery** or **Jef·fry** \'jef-(ə-)rē\ var of GEOFFREY
Jer·ald or **Jer·old** or **Jer·rold** \'jer-əld\ var of GERALD
Jer·e·my \'jer-ə-mē\ or **Jer·e·mi·ah** \ˌjer-ə-'mī-ə\ [Heb] prob Yahweh exalts
Je·rome \jə-'rōm, Brit also 'jer-əm\ [Gk] bearing a holy name
Jer·ry or **Jere** \'jer-ē\ dim of GERALD
Jes·se \'jes-ē\ [Heb]
Jim \'jim\ or **Jim·my** or **Jim·mie** \'jim-ē\ dim of JAMES
Jo·dy \'jō-dē\ perh alter of JOSEPH
Joe \'jō\ dim of JOSEPH
Jo·el \'jō-əl\ [Heb] Yahweh is God
John \'jän\ [Heb] Yahweh is gracious
Jon \'jän\ var of JOHN
Jo·nah \'jō-nə\ [Heb]
Jon·a·than \'jän-ə-thən\ [Heb] Yahweh has given
Jor·dan \'jòrd-ᵊn\ [fr. a surname]
Jo·seph or **Jo·sef** \'jō-zəf also -səf\ [Heb] he shall add
Josh·ua \'jäsh-(ə-)wə\ [Heb] Yahweh saves
Judd \'jəd\ [fr. a surname]
Jud·son \'jəd-sən\ [fr. a surname]
Jules \'jülz\ [F] var of JULIUS
Ju·lian or **Ju·lien** \'jül-yən\ [L] sprung from or belonging to Julius
Ju·lius \'jül-yəs\ or **Ju·lio** \-(ˌ)yō\ [L]
Jus·tin \'jəs-tən\ or **Jus·tus** \-təs\ [L] just

Karl \'kär(-ə)l\ [G & Scand] var of CHARLES
Keith \'kēth\ [fr. a surname]
Kel·ly \'kel-ē\ [fr. a surname]
Ken \'ken\ dim of KENNETH
Ken·dall \'ken-dᵊl\ [fr. a surname]
Ken·neth \'ken-əth\ [ScGael]

Kent \'kent\ [prob. fr. a surname]
Ken·ton \'kent-ᵊn\ [fr. a surname]
Ker·mit \'kər-mət\ [prob. fr. a surname]
Ker·ry \'ker-ē\ [prob. fr. the county of Ireland]
Kev·in \'kev-ən\ [OIr]
Kir·by \'kər-bē\ [fr. a surname]
Kirk \'kərk\ [fr. a surname]
Klaus \'klaůs, 'klòs\ [G] dim of Nikolaus
Kurt \'kərt, 'ků(ə)rt\ [G] dim of CONRAD
Kyle \'kī(ə)l\ [Celt]

La·mar \lə-'mär\ [fr. a surname]
Lance \'lan(t)s\ dim of Lancelot
Lane \'lān\ [fr. a surname]
Lan·ny \'lan-ē\ prob dim of LAWRENCE
Lar·ry \'lar-ē\ dim of LAWRENCE
Lars \'lärz\ [Sw] var of LAWRENCE
Law·rence or **Lau·rence** \'lòr-ən(t)s, 'lär-\ [L] of Laurentum, ancient city in central Italy
Lee or **Leigh** \'lē\ [fr. a surname]
Leigh·ton or **Lay·ton** \'lāt-ᵊn\ [fr. a surname]
Le·land \'lē-lənd\ [fr. a surname]
Len \'len\ dim of LEONARD
Leo \'lē-(ˌ)ō\ [L] lion
Le·on \'lē-ˌän, -ən\ [Sp] var of LEO
Leon·ard \'len-ərd\ [G] strong or brave as a lion
Le·roy \li-'ròi, 'lē-ˌ\ [OF] royal
Les·lie \'les-lē, 'lez-\ [fr. a surname]
Les·ter \'les-tər\ [fr. a surname]
Lew·is \'lü-əs\ var of LOUIS
Li·am \'lē-əm\ [Ir]
Lin·coln \'liŋ-kən\ [fr. a surname]
Li·o·nel \'lī-ən-ᵊl, -ə-ˌnel\ [OF] young lion
Lloyd or **Loyd** \'lòid\ [W] gray
Lo·gan \'lō-gən\ [fr. a surname]
Lon \'län\ dim of Alonzo
Lon·nie or **Lon·ny** \'län-ē\ dim of LON
Lo·ren \'lòr-ən, 'lòr-\ dim of Lorenzo
Lou·ie \'lü-ē\ var of LOUIS
Lou·is or **Lu·is** \'lü-əs, 'lü-ē\ [Gmc] famous warrior
Low·ell \'lō-əl\ [fr. a surname]
Lu·cian \'lü-shən\ [Gk]
Lud·wig \'ləd-(ˌ)wig, 'lüd-\ [G] var of LOUIS
Luke \'lük\ [Gk] prob dim of LUCIUS
Lu·ther \'lü-thər\ [fr. a surname]
Lyle \'lī(ə)l\ [fr. a surname]
Ly·man \'lī-mən\ [fr. a surname]
Lynn \'lin\ [fr. a surname]

Mack or **Mac** \'mak\ [fr. surnames beginning with Mc or Mac, fr. Gael mac son]
Mal·colm \'mal-kəm\ [ScGael] servant of (St.) Columba
Man·fred \'man-frəd\ [Gmc] peace among men
Man·u·el \'man-yə(-wə)l\ [Sp & Pg] var of EMMANUEL
Mar·cus \'mär-kəs\ [L]
Ma·rio \'mär-ē-ˌō\ [It] var of MARIUS
Mar·i·on \'mer-ē-ən, 'mar-\ [fr. a surname]
Mark or **Marc** \'märk\ var of MARCUS
Mar·lin \'mär-lən\ [prob. fr. a surname]
Mar·shall or **Mar·shal** \'mär-shəl\ [fr. a surname]
Mar·tin \'märt-ᵊn\ [LL] of Mars
Mar·vin \'mär-vən\ [prob. fr. a surname]
Ma·son \'mās-ᵊn\ [fr. a surname]
Matt \'mat\ dim of MATTHEW
Mat·thew \'math-(ˌ)yü also 'math-(ˌ)ü\ [Heb] gift of Yahweh
Mau·rice \'mòr-əs, 'mär-; mò-'rēs\ [LL] prob Moorish
Max \'maks\ dim of MAXIMILIAN
Max·well \'mak-ˌswel, -swəl\ [fr. a surname]
May·nard \'mā-nərd\ [Gmc] bold in strength
Mel·ville \'mel-ˌvil\ [fr. a surname]
Mel·vin or **Mel·vyn** \'mel-vən\ [prob. fr. a surname]
Mer·e·dith \'mer-əd-əth\ [W]
Merle \'mər(-ə)l\ [F] blackbird

Mer·lin *or* Mer·lyn \'mər-lən\ [Celt]
Mer·rill \'mer-əl\ [fr. a surname]
Mi·chael \'mī-kəl\ [Heb] who is like God?
Mick·ey \'mik-ē\ *dim of* MICHAEL
Mike \'mīk\ *dim of* MICHAEL
Mi·lan \'mī-lən\ [prob. fr. the city in Italy]
Miles *or* Myles \'mī(ə)lz\ [Gmc]
Mil·ford \'mil-fərd\ [fr. a surname]
Mil·lard \'mil-ərd, mil-'ärd\ [fr. a surname]
Mi·lo \'mī-(ˌ)lō\ [prob. L]
Mil·ton \'milt-ᵊn\ [fr. a surname]
Mitch·ell \'mich-əl\ [fr. a surname]
Mon·roe \mən-'rō, 'mən-ˌ\ [fr. a surname]
Mon·te *or* Mon·ty \'mänt-ē\ *dim of* MONTAGUE
Mor·gan \'mòr-gən\ [W] *prob* dweller on the sea
Mor·ris \'mòr-əs, 'mär-\ *var of* MAURICE
Mor·ton \'mòrt-ᵊn\ [fr. a surname]
Mur·ray \'mər-ē, 'mə-rē\ [fr. a surname]
My·ron \'mī-rən\ [Gk]

Na·than \nā-thən\ [Heb] given, gift
Na·than·iel \nə-'than-yəl\ [Heb] gift of God
Ned \'ned\ *dim of* EDWARD, EDWIN
Neil *or* Neal \'nē(ə)l\ [Celt]
Nel·son \'nel-sən\ [fr. a surname]
Nev·ille \'nev-əl\ [fr. a surname]
Nev·in \'nev-ən\ [fr. a surname]
New·ell \'n(y)ü-əl\ [fr. a surname]
New·ton \'n(y)üt-ᵊn\ [fr. a surname]
Nich·o·las \'nik-(ə-)ləs\ [Gk] victorious among the people
Nick \'nik\ *dim of* NICHOLAS
Niles \'nī(ə)lz\ [fr. a surname]
Nils \'nils, 'nē(ə)ls\ [Scand]
No·ah \'nō-ə\ [Heb] rest
No·el \'nō-əl\ [F, fr. L] Christmas
No·lan \'nō-lən\ [fr. a surname]
Nor·man \'nòr-mən\ [Gmc] Norseman, Norman
Nor·ris \'nòr-əs, 'när-\ [fr. a surname]
Nor·ton \'nòrt-ᵊn\ [fr. a surname]

Ol·i·ver \'äl-ə-vər\ [OF]
Ol·lie \'äl-ē\ *dim of* OLIVER
Or·lan·do \òr-'lan-(ˌ)dō\ [It] *var of* ROLAND
Or·rin \'òr-ən, 'är-\ *or* Orin *or* Oren \'òr-, 'är-, 'ōr-\ [prob. fr. a surname]
Or·ville *or* Or·val \'òr-vəl\ [prob. fr. a surname]
Os·car \'äs-kər\ [OE] spear of a deity
Otis \'ōt-əs\ [fr. a surname]
Ot·to \'ät-(ˌ)ō\ [Gmc]
Ow·en \'ō-ən\ [OW]

Palm·er \'päm-ər, 'päl-mər\ [fr. a surname]
Par·ker \'pär-kər\ [fr. a surname]
Pat \'pat\ *dim of* PATRICK
Pat·rick \'pa-trik\ [L] patrician
Paul \'pòl\ [L] little
Pe·dro \'pē-(ˌ)drō, 'pä-\ [Sp] *var of* PETER
Per·cy \'pər-sē\ [fr. a surname]
Per·ry \'per-ē\ [fr. a surname]
Pete \'pēt\ *dim of* PETER
Pe·ter \'pēt-ər\ [Gk] rock
Phil \'fil\ *dim of* PHILIP
Phil·ip *or* Phil·lip \'fil-əp\ [Gk] lover of horses
Pierre \pē-'e(ə)r\ [F] *var of* PETER
Por·ter \'pōrt-ər, 'pòrt-\ [fr. a surname]
Pres·ton \'pres-tən\ [fr. a surname]

Quen·tin \'kwent-ᵊn\ [LL] of or relating to the fifth

Ra·fa·el *or* Ra·pha·el \'raf-ē-əl, 'rä-fē-\ [Heb] God has healed
Ra·leigh \'ròl-ē, 'räl-\ [fr. a surname]
Ralph \'ralf, *Brit also* 'räf\ [Gmc] wolf in counsel
Ra·mon \rə-'mōn, 'rä-mən\ [Sp] *var of* RAYMOND
Ran·dall *or* Ran·dal \'ran-dᵊl\ *var of* RANDOLPH

Ran·dolph \'ran-ˌdälf\ [Gmc] shield wolf
Ran·dy \'ran-dē\ *dim of* RANDOLPH
Ray \'rā\ *dim of* RAYMOND
Ray·mond \'rā-mənd\ [Gmc] wise protection
Reed *or* Reid \'rēd\ [fr. a surname]
Reg·gie \'rej-ē\ *dim of* REGINALD
Reg·i·nald \'rej-ən-ᵊld\ [Gmc] wise dominion
Re·gis \'rē-jəs\ [fr. a proper name]
Re·ne \'ren-(ˌ)ā, rə-'nā, 'rä-nē, 'rē-nē\ [F, fr. L] reborn
Reu·ben *or* Ru·ben \'rü-bən\ [Heb]
Rex \'reks\ [L] king
Reyn·old \'ren-ᵊld\ *var of* REGINALD
Rich·ard \'rich-ərd\ [Gmc] strong in rule
Rob·ert \'räb-ərt\ [Gmc] bright in fame
Ro·ber·to \rə-'bərt-(ˌ)ō, rō-, -'bert-\ [Sp & It] *var of* ROBERT
Rob·in \'räb-ən\ *dim of* ROBERT
Rod·er·ick \'räd-(ə-)rik\ [Gmc] famous ruler
Rod·ney \'räd-nē\ [fr. a surname]
Rog·er *or* Rod·ger \'räj-ər\ [Gmc] famous spear
Rog·ers \'räj-ərz\ [fr. a surname]
Ro·land \'rō-lənd\ *or* Rol·land \'räl-ənd\ *or* Row·land \'rō-lənd\ [Gmc] famous land
Rolf \'rälf\ *var of* RUDOLPH
Rol·lin \'räl-ən\ *var of* ROLAND
Ron \'rän\ *dim of* RONALD
Ron·al \'rän-ᵊl\ *var of* RONALD
Ron·ald \'rän-ᵊld\ [ON] *var of* REGINALD
Ron·nie *or* Ron·ny \'rän-ē\ *dim of* RONALD
Ros·coe \'räs-(ˌ)kō, 'ròs-\ [fr. a surname]
Ross \'ròs\ [fr. a surname]
Roy \'ròi\ [ScGael]
Roy·al \'ròi(-ə)l\ [prob. fr. a surname]
Royce \'ròis\ [fr. a surname]
Ru·dolph *or* Ru·dolf \'rü-ˌdälf\ [Gmc] famous wolf
Ru·dy \'rüd-ē\ *dim of* RUDOLPH
Ru·fus \'rü-fəs\ [L] red, red-haired
Ru·pert \'rü-pərt\ *var of* ROBERT
Rus·sell *or* Rus·sel \'rəs-əl\ [fr. a surname]
Ry·an \'rī-ən\ [IrGael]

Sal·va·tore \'sal-və-ˌtō(ə)r, -ˌtò(ə)r; ˌsal-və-'tōr-ē, -'tòr-\ [It] savior
Sam \'sam\ *dim of* SAMUEL
Sam·my *or* Sam·mie \'sam-ē\ *dim of* SAM
Sam·u·el \'sam-yə(-wə)l\ [Heb] name of God
San·ford \'san-fərd\ [fr. a surname]
Saul \'sòl\ [Heb] asked for
Scott \'skät\ [fr. a surname]
Sean \'shòn\ [Ir] *var of* JOHN
Seth \'seth\ [Heb]
Sey·mour \'sē-ˌmō(ə)r, -ˌmò(ə)r\ [fr. a surname]
Shel·by \'shel-bē\ [fr. a surname]
Shel·don \'shel-dən\ [fr. a surname]
Sher·i·dan \'sher-əd-ᵊn\ [fr. a surname]
Sher·man \'shər-mən\ [fr. a surname]
Sher·win \'shər-wən\ [fr. a surname]
Sher·wood \'shər-ˌwu̇d, 'she(ə)r-\ [fr. a surname]
Sid·ney *or* Syd·ney \'sid-nē\ [fr. a surname]
Sieg·fried \'sig-ˌfrēd, 'sēg-\ [Gmc] victorious peace
Sig·mund \'sig-mənd\ [Gmc] victorious protection
Si·mon \'sī-mən\ [Heb]
Sol·o·mon \'säl-ə-mən\ [Heb] peaceable
Spen·cer \'spen(t)-sər\ [fr. a surname]
Sta·cy *or* Sta·cey \'stā-sē\ [ML]
Stan \'stan\ *dim of* STANLEY
Stan·ford \'stan-fərd\ [fr. a surname]
Stan·ley \'stan-lē\ [fr. a surname]
Stan·ton \'stant-ᵊn\ [fr. a surname]
Ste·fan \'stef-ən, -ˌän\ [Pol] *var of* STEPHEN
Ste·phen *or* Ste·ven *or* Ste·phan \'stē-vən\ [Gk] crown
Steve \'stēv\ *dim of* STEVEN
Ster·ling \'stər-liŋ\ [fr. a surname]
Stu·art *or* Stew·art \'st(y)ü-ərt, 'st(y)ü(-ə)rt\ [fr. a surname]

Syl·ves·ter \sil-'ves-tər\ [L] woodsy, of the woods

Tay·lor \'tā-lər\ [fr. a surname]
Ted \'ted\ *or* **Ted·dy** \'ted-ē\ *dim of* EDWARD, THE-ODORE
Ter·ence *or* **Ter·rance** *or* **Ter·rence** \'ter-ən(t)s\ [L]
Ter·rell *or* **Ter·rill** \'ter-əl\ [fr. a surname]
Ter·ry \'ter-ē\ *dim of* TERENCE
Thad \'thad\ *dim of* THADDEUS
Thad·de·us \'thad-ē-əs\ [Gk]
The·o·dore \'thē-ə-ˌdō(ə)r, -ˌdȯ(ə)r, -əd-ər\ [Gk] gift of God
Thom·as \'täm-əs\ [Aram] twin
Thur·man \'thər-mən\ [fr. a surname]
Tim \'tim\ *dim of* TIMOTHY
Tim·o·thy \'tim-ə-thē\ [Gk] revering God
To·by \'tō-bē\ *dim of* TOBIAS
Todd \'täd\ [prob. fr. a surname]
Tom \'täm\ *or* **Tom·my** *or* **Tom·mie** \'täm-ē\ *dim of* THOMAS
To·ny \'tō-nē\ *dim of* ANTHONY
Tra·cy \'trā-sē\ [fr. a surname]
Trav·is \'trav-əs\ [fr. a surname]
Trent \'trent\ [fr. a surname]
Tre·vor \'trev-ər\ [Celt]
Troy \'trȯi\ [prob. fr. a surname]
Tru·man \'trü-mən\ [fr. a surname]
Ty·ler \'tī-lər\ [fr. a surname]
Ty·rone \'tī-ˌrōn, tī-'; tir-'ōn\ [prob. fr. the county in Ireland]

Val \'val\ *dim of* VALENTINE
Van \'van\ [fr. surnames beginning with *Van,* fr. Dutch *van* of]
Vance \'van(t)s\ [fr. a surname]
Vaughn \'vȯn, 'vän\ [fr. a surname]
Verne *or* **Vern** \'vərn\ *prob alter of* VERNON
Ver·non \'vər-nən\ [prob. fr. a surname]
Vic·tor \'vik-tər\ [L] conqueror
Vin·cent \'vin(t)-sənt\ [LL] of or relating to the conquering one
Vir·gil \'vər-jəl\ [L]

Wade \'wād\ [fr. a surname]
Wal·lace *or* **Wal·lis** \'wäl-əs\ [fr. a surname]
Walt \'wȯlt\ *dim of* WALTER
Wal·ter \'wȯl-tər\ [Gmc] army of dominion
Wal·ton \'wȯlt-ᵊn\ [fr. a surname]
Ward \'wȯ(ə)rd\ [fr. a surname]
War·ner \'wȯr-nər\ [fr. a surname]
War·ren \'wȯr-ən, 'wär-\ [fr. a surname]
Wayne \'wān\ [fr. a surname]
Wel·don \'wel-dən\ [fr. a surname]
Wen·dell \'wen-dᵊl\ [fr. a surname]
Wer·ner \'wər-nər, 'we(ə)r-\ [Gmc] army of the Varini, a Germanic people
Wes·ley \'wes-lē *also* 'wez-\ [fr. a surname]
Wil·bur *or* **Wil·ber** \'wil-bər\ [fr. a surname]
Wi·ley *or* **Wy·lie** \'wī-lē\ [fr. a surname]
Wil·ford \'wil-fərd\ [fr. a surname]
Wil·fred \'wil-frəd\ [OE] desired peace
Will \'wil\ *or* **Wil·lie** \-ē\ *dim of* WILLIAM
Wil·lard \'wil-ərd\ [fr. a surname]
Wil·liam \'wil-yəm\ [Gmc] desired helmet
Wil·lis \'wil-əs\ [fr. a surname]
Wil·mer \'wil-mər\ [fr. a surname]
Wil·son \'wil-sən\ [fr. a surname]
Wil·ton \'wilt-ᵊn\ [fr. a surname]
Win·field \'win-ˌfēld\ [fr. a surname]
Win·fred \'win-frəd\ [OE] *prob* joyous peace
Win·ston \'win(t)-stən\ [fr. a surname]
Win·ton \'wint-ᵊn\ [fr. a surname]
Wood·row \'wu̇d-(ˌ)rō\ [fr. a surname]
Wy·att \'wī-ət\ [fr. a surname]

Yale \'yā(ə)l\ [fr. a surname]

Zach·a·ry \'zak-ə-rē\ *dim of* ZACHARIAH
Zane \'zān\ [fr. a surname]

Names of Women

Ab·by \'ab-ē\ *dim of* ABIGAIL
Ab·i·gail \'ab-ə-ˌgāl\ [Heb] *prob* source of joy
Ada \'ād-ə\ [Heb] *prob* ornament
Ad·di·son \'ad-ə-sən\ [fr. a surname]
Ad·e·laide \'ad-ᵊl-ˌād\ [Gmc] of noble rank
Adele \ə-'del\ [Gmc] noble
Adri·enne \'ā-drē-ˌen, -ən\ [F] *fem of* ADRIEN
Ag·nes \'ag-nəs\ [LL]
Ai·leen \ī-'lēn\ [IrGael] *var of* HELEN
Al·ber·ta \al-'bərt-ə\ *fem of* ALBERT
Al·ex·an·dra \ˌal-ig-'zan-drə\ [Gk] *fem of* ALEXANDER
Alex·is \ə-'lek-səs\ [Gk]
Al·ice *or* **Al·yce** \'al-əs\ [OF] *var of* ADELAIDE
Ali·cia \ə-'lish-ə\ [ML] *var of* ADELAIDE
Al·i·son *or* **Al·li·son** \'al-ə-sən\ [OF] *dim of* ALICE
Al·ma \'al-mə\ [L] nourishing, cherishing
Al·va \'al-və\ [Sp, fr. L] white
Aman·da \ə-'man-də\ [L] worthy to be loved
Am·ber \'am-bər\ [E]
Ame·lia \ə-'mēl-yə\ [Gmc]
Amy \'ā-mē\ [L] beloved
An·as·ta·sia \ˌan-ə-'stā-zh(ē-)ə\ [LGk] of the resurrection
An·drea \'an-drē-ə, an-'drā-ə\ *fem of* ANDREW
An·ge·la \'an-jə-lə\ [It, fr. Gk] angel
An·gel·i·ca \an-'jel-i-kə\ *var of* ANGELA
An·ge·line \'an-jə-ˌlīn, -ˌlēn\ *dim of* ANGELA
Ani·ta \ə-'nēt-ə\ [Sp] *dim of* ANN
Ann *or* **Anne** \'an\ *or* **An·na** \'an-ə\ [Heb] grace
An·na·belle \'an-ə-ˌbel\ *prob var of* MABEL
An·nette \a-'net, ə-\ *or* **An·net·ta** \-'net-ə\ [F] *dim of* ANN
An·nie \'an-ē\ *dim of* ANN
An·toi·nette \ˌan-t(w)ə-'net\ [F] *dim of* ANTONIA
April \'ā-prəl\ [E] April (the month)
Ar·dell *or* **Ar·delle** \är-'del\ *var of* ADELE
Ar·lene *or* **Ar·leen** *or* **Ar·line** \är-'lēn\
Ash·ley \'ash-lē\ [OE] ash-tree meadow
As·trid \'as-trəd\ [Scand] beautiful as a deity
Au·dra \'ȯ-drə\ *var of* AUDREY
Au·drey \'ȯ-drē\ [OE] noble strength

Ba·bette \ba-'bet\ [F] *dim of* ELIZABETH
Bar·ba·ra \'bär-b(ə-)rə\ [Gk] foreign
Be·atrice \'bē-ə-trəs\ [It, fr. ML] she that makes happy
Becky \'bek-ē\ *dim of* REBECCA
Ber·na·dette \ˌbər-nə-'det\ [F] *fem of* BERNARD
Ber·na·dine \'bər-nə-ˌdēn\ *fem of* BERNARD
Ber·nice \(ˌ)bər-'nēs, 'bər-nəs\ [Gk] bringing victory
Ber·tha \'bər-thə\ [Gmc] bright
Ber·yl \'ber-əl\ [Gk] beryl (the mineral)
Bes·sie \'bes-ē\ *dim of* ELIZABETH
Beth \'beth\ *dim of* ELIZABETH
Bet·sy *or* **Bet·sey** \'bet-sē\ *dim of* ELIZABETH
Bet·ty *or* **Bet·te** *or* **Bet·tye** *or* **Bet·tie** \'bet-ē\ *dim of* ELIZABETH
Beu·lah \'byü-lə\ [Heb] married
Bev·er·ly *or* **Bev·er·ley** \'bev-ər-lē\ [prob. fr. a surname]
Bil·lie \'bil-ē\ *fem of* BILLY
Blair \'ble(ə)r\ [fr. a surname]
Blake \'blāk\ [fr. a surname]
Blanche \'blanch\ [OF, fr. Gmc] white
Bob·bie \'bäb-ē\ *dim of* ROBERTA
Bo·ni·ta \bə-'nēt-ə\ [Sp] pretty
Bon·nie \'bän-ē\ [ME] pretty
Bran·dy \'bran-dē\ [E]

Bren·da \\'bren-də\ [Scand]
Bri·gitte \\'brij-ət, brə-'jit\ [G] *var of* BRIDGET
Brit·tany \\'brit-ᵊn-ē\ [E]
Brooke \\'brůk\ [OE] brook

Cait·lin \\'kāt-lin\ [Ir] *var of* CATHERINE
Ca·mil·la \kə-'mil-ə\ [L] freeborn girl attendant at a sacrifice
Ca·mille \kə-'mē(ə)l\ [F] *var of* CAMILLA
Can·da·ce \\'kan-dəs, kan-'dā-sē\ [Gk]
Car·la \\'kär-lə\ [It] *fem of* Carlo
Car·lene \kär-'lēn\ *var of* CARLA
Car·lot·ta \kär-'lät-ə\ [It] *var of* CHARLOTTE
Car·men \\'kär-mən\ *or* **Car·mine** \kär-'mēn, 'kär-mən\ [Sp, fr. L] song
Car·ol *or* **Car·ole** *or* **Car·yl** \\'kar-əl\ *dim of* CAROLYN
Car·o·lyn \\'kar-ə-lən\ *or* **Car·o·line** \-lən, -ₗlīn\ [It] *fem of* CHARLES
Car·rie \\'kar-ē\ *dim of* CAROLINE
Cath·er·ine *or* **Cath·a·rine** \\'kath-(ə-)rən\ [LGk]
Cath·leen \kath-'lēn\ [IrGael] *var of* CATHERINE
Cath·ryn \\'kath-rən\ *var of* CATHERINE
Cathy *or* **Cath·ie** \\'kath-ē\ *dim of* CATHERINE
Ce·cile \sə-'sē(ə)l\ *var of* CECILIA
Ce·ci·lia \sə-'sēl-yə, -'sil-\ *or* **Ce·ce·lia** \-'sēl-\ [L] *fem of* CECIL
Ce·leste \sə-'lest\ [L] heavenly
Ce·lia \\'sēl-yə\ *dim of* CECILIA
Char·lene \shär-'lēn\ *fem of* CHARLES
Char·lotte \\'shär-lət\ [F] *fem dim of* CHARLES
Cher·ie \\'sher-ē\ [F] dear
Cher·ry \\'cher-ē\ [E] cherry
Cher·yl \\'cher-əl, 'sher-\ *prob var of* CHERRY
Chloe \\'klō-ē\ [Gk] young verdure
Chris·tie \\'kris-tē\ *dim of* CHRISTINE
Chris·tine \kris-'tēn\ *or* **Chris·ti·na** \-'tē-nə\ [Gk] Christian
Cin·dy \\'sin-dē\ *dim of* LUCINDA
Claire *or* **Clare** \\'kla(ə)r, 'kle(ə)r\ *var of* CLARA
Clara \\'klar-ə\ [L] bright
Cla·rice \\'klar-əs, klə-'rēs\ *dim of* CLARA
Clau·dette \klȯ-'det\ [F] *fem of* CLAUDE
Clau·dia \\'klȯd-ē-ə\ [L] *fem of* CLAUDE
Clau·dine \klȯ-'dēn\ [F] *fem of* CLAUDE
Cleo \\'klē-(ₗ)ō\ *dim of* Cleopatra
Co·lette \kä-'let\ [OF] *fem dim of* NICHOLAS
Col·leen \kä-'lēn\ [IrGael] girl
Con·nie \\'kän-ē\ *dim of* CONSTANCE
Con·stance \\'kän(t)-stən(t)s\ [L] constancy
Co·ra \\'kōr-ə, 'kȯr-\ [Gk] maiden
Cor·ey \\'kȯr-ē\ [Ir]
Co·rinne *or* **Cor·rine** \kə-'rin, -'rēn\ [Gk] *dim of* CORA
Cor·ne·lia \kȯr-'nēl-yə\ [L] *fem of* CORNELIUS
Court·ney \\'kȯ(ə)rt-nē, 'kȯ(ə)rt-\ [OE] of the court
Crys·tal \\'kris-tᵊl\ [E]
Cyn·thia \\'sin(t)-thē-ə\ [Gk] she of Mount Cynthus on the island of Delos

Dai·sy \\'dā-zē\ [E] daisy
Dale \\'dā(ə)l\ [E] valley
Da·na \\'dā-nə\ [fr. a surname]
Dan·ielle \dän-'yel\ [F] *fem of* DANIEL
Daph·ne \\'daf-nē\ [Gk] laurel
Dar·la \\'där-lə\ [deriv. of *darling*]
Dar·lene \där-'lēn\ [deriv. of *darling*]
Dawn \\'dȯn, 'dän\ [E] dawn
De·an·na \dē-'an-ə\ *or* **De·anne** \-'an\ *var of* DIANA
Deb·bie *or* **Deb·by** \\'deb-ē\ *dim of* DEBORAH
Deb·o·rah *or* **Deb·o·ra** \\'deb-(ə-)rə\ [Heb] bee
Deb·ra \\'deb-rə\ *var of* DEBORAH
Dee \\'dē\ *prob dim of* EDITH
Deir·dre \\'di(ə)r-drē, 'de(ə)r-\ [IrGael]
De·lia \\'dēl-yə\ [Gk] she of Delos (i.e. the goddess Artemis)
Del·la \\'del-ə\ *dim of* ADELAIDE, DELIA
De·lo·res \də-'lōr-əs, -'lȯr-\ *var of* DOLORES

De·na *or* **Dee·na** \\'dē-nə\ *dim of* GERALDINE
De·nise \də-'nēz, -'nēs\ [F] *fem of* DENIS
Di·ana *or* **Di·an·na** \dī-'an-ə\ [L]
Di·ane *or* **Di·anne** *or* **Di·an** *or* **Di·ann** \dī-'an\ [F] *var of* DIANA
Di·na *or* **Di·nah** \\'dī-nə\ [Heb] judged
Dix·ie \\'dik-sē\ [E] *prob* Dixie (nickname for the southern states of the U.S.)
Do·lo·res \də-'lōr-əs, -'lȯr-\ [Sp, fr. L] sorrows (i.e. those of the Virgin Mary)
Don·na \\'dän-ə\ *or* **Do·na** \\'dän-ə, 'dō-nə\ [It, fr. L] lady
Do·ra \\'dōr-ə, 'dȯr-\ *dim of* THEODORA, Eudora
Do·reen \dȯ-'rēn, də-\ [IrGael]
Dor·is \\'dȯr-əs, 'där-\ [Gk] *prob* Dorian (a member of an ancient Hellenic race)
Dor·o·thy \\'dȯr-ə-thē, 'där-\ *or* **Dor·o·thea** \ₗdȯr-ə-'thē-ə, ₗdär-\ [LGk] goddess of gifts
Dot·tie *or* **Dot·ty** \\'dät-ē\ *dim of* DOROTHY

Edith *or* **Edythe** \\'ēd-əth\ [OE]
Ed·na \\'ed-nə\ [Aram]
Ed·wi·na \e-'dwē-nə, -'dwin-ə\ *fem of* EDWIN
Ef·fie \\'ef-ē\ *dim of* Euphemia
Ei·leen \ī-'lēn\ [IrGael] *var of* HELEN
Elaine \i-'lān\ [OF] *var of* HELEN
El·ea·nor *or* **El·i·nor** *or* **El·ea·nore** \\'el-ə-nər, -ₗnȯ(ə)r, -ₗnō(ə)r\ [OProv] *var of* HELEN
Ele·na \\'el-ə-nə, ə-'lē-nə\ [It] *var of* HELEN
Elise \ə-'lēz, -'lēs\ [F] *var of* ELIZABETH
Eliz·a·beth *or* **Elis·a·beth** \i-'liz-ə-bəth\ [Heb] God has sworn
El·la \\'el-ə\ [OF]
El·len *or* **El·lyn** \\'el-ən\ *var of* HELEN
El·o·ise \\'el-ə-ₗwēz, ₗel-ə-'\ [OF, fr. Gmc]
El·sa \\'el-sə\ [G] *dim of* ELIZABETH
El·sie \\'el-sē\ *dim of* ELIZABETH
El·va \\'el-və\ [Gmc] elf
Em·i·ly *or* **Em·i·lie** \\'em-(ə-)lē\ [L] *fem of* EMIL
Em·ma \\'em-ə\ [Gmc] *var of* ERMA
Enid \\'ē-nəd\ [W]
Er·i·ka \\'er-i-kə\ *fem of* ERIC
Er·in \\'er-ən\ [IrGael]
Er·ma \\'ər-mə\ [Gmc]
Er·nes·tine \\'ər-nə-ₗstēn\ *fem of* ERNEST
Es·telle \e-'stel\ *or* **Es·tel·la** \e-'stel-ə\ [OProv, fr. L] star
Es·ther \\'es-tər\ [prob. fr. Per] *prob* star
Eth·el \\'eth-əl\ [OE] noble
Et·ta \\'et-ə\ *dim of* HENRIETTA
Eu·ge·nia \yů-'jēn-yə\ *or* **Eu·ge·nie** \-'jē-nē\ *fem of* EUGENE
Eu·nice \\'yü-nəs\ [Gk] having (i.e. bringing) happy victory
Eva \\'ē-və\ *var of* EVE
Evan·ge·line \i-'van-jə-lən, -ₗlēn, -ₗlīn\ [Gk] bringing good news
Eve \\'ēv\ [Heb] life, living
Eve·lyn \\'ev-(ə-)lən, *chiefly Brit* 'ēv-\ [OF, fr. Gmc]

Faith \\'fāth\ [E] faith
Faye *or* **Fay** \\'fā\ *dim of* FAITH
Fe·lice \fə-'lēs\ [L] happiness
Fern *or* **Ferne** \\'fərn\ [E] fern
Flo·ra \\'flōr-ə, 'flȯr-\ [L] goddess of flowers
Flor·ence \\'flȯr-ən(t)s, 'flär-\ [L] bloom, prosperity
Fran·ces \\'fran(t)-səs, -ₗsəz\ *fem of* FRANCIS
Fran·cine \fran-'sēn\ [F] *prob dim of* FRANCES
Fre·da *or* **Frie·da** \\'frēd-ə\ *dim of* WINIFRED
Fred·er·ic·ka *or* **Fred·er·i·ca** \ₗfred-(ə-)'rē-kə, -'rik-ə\ *fem of* FREDERICK

Gail *or* **Gayle** *or* **Gale** \\'gā(ə)l\ *dim of* ABIGAIL
Gay \\'gā\ [E] gay
Ge·ne·va \jə-'nē-və\ *var of* GENEVIEVE
Gen·e·vieve \\'jen-ə-ₗvēv\ [prob. fr. Celt]

George·ann \jòr-'jan\ [*George* + *Ann*]
Geor·gette \jòr-'jet\ *fem of* GEORGE
Geor·gia \'jòr-jə\ *fem of* GEORGE
Geor·gi·na \jòr-'jē-nə\ *fem of* GEORGE
Ger·al·dine \'jer-əl-ˌdēn\ *fem of* GERALD
Ger·trude \'gər-ˌtrüd\ [Gmc] spear strength
Gil·li·an \'jil-ē-ən\ *var of* JULIANA
Gin·ger \'jin-jər\ [E] ginger
Gi·sela \jə-'sel-ə, -'zel-\ [Gmc] pledge
Gi·selle \jə-'zel\ *var of* GISELA
Glad·ys \'glad-əs\ [W]
Glen·da \'glen-də\ *prob var of* GLENNA
Glen·na \'glen-ə\ *fem of* GLENN
Glo·ria \'glōr-ē-ə, 'glòr-\ [L] glory
Grace \'grās\ [L] favor, grace
Gre·ta \'grēt-ə, 'gret-\ *dim of* MARGARET
Gretch·en \'grech-ən\ [G] *dim of* MARGARET
Gwen \'gwen\ *dim of* GWENDOLYN
Gwen·do·lyn \'gwen-də-lən\ [W]

Han·nah \'han-ə\ [Heb] *var of* ANN
Har·ri·et *or* **Har·ri·ett** *or* **Har·ri·ette** \'har-ē-ət\ *var of* HENRIETTA
Hat·tie \'hat-ē\ *dim of* HARRIET
Ha·zel \'hā-zəl\ [E] hazel
Heath·er \'heth-ər\ [ME] heather (the shrub)
Hei·di \'hīd-ē\ [G] *dim of* ADELAIDE
He·laine \hə-'lān\ *var of* HELEN
Hel·en \'hel-ən\ *or* **He·le·na** \'hel-ə-nə, hə-'lē-nə\ [Gk]
He·lene \hə-'lēn\ [F] *var of* HELEN
Hel·ga \'hel-gə\ [Scand] holy
Hen·ri·et·ta \ˌhen-rē-'et-ə\ [MF] *fem of* HENRY
Her·mine \'hər-ˌmēn\ [G] *prob fem of* HERMAN
Hes·ter \'hes-tər\ *var of* ESTHER
Hil·ary *or* **Hil·la·ry** \'hil-ə-rē\ [L] cheerful
Hil·da \'hil-də\ [OE] battle
Hil·de·gard *or* **Hil·de·garde** \'hil-də-ˌgärd\ [Gmc] *prob* battle enclosure
Hol·ly \'häl-ē\ [E] holly
Hope \'hōp\ [E] hope

Ida \'īd-ə\ [Gmc]
Ilene \ī-'lēn\ *var of* EILEEN
Imo·gene \'im-ə-ˌjēn, 'ī-mə-\
Ina \'ī-nə\
Inez \ī-'nez, 'ī-nəz\ [Sp] *var of* AGNES
In·grid \'iŋ-grəd\ [Scand] beautiful as Ing (an ancient Germanic god)
Irene \ī-'rēn\ [Gk] peace
Iris \'ī-rəs\ [Gk] rainbow
Ir·ma \'ər-mə\ *var of* ERMA
Is·a·bel *or* **Is·a·belle** \'iz-ə-ˌbel\ [OProv] *var of* ELIZABETH

Jack·ie *or* **Jacky** \'jak-ē\ *dim of* JACQUELINE
Jac·que·line *or* **Jac·que·lyn** *or* **Jac·que·lin** \'jak-(w)ə-lən, -ˌlēn\ [OF] *fem of* JACOB
Ja·mie \'jā-mē\ *fem of* JAMES
Jan \'jan\ *dim of* JANET
Jane *or* **Jayne** \'jān\ [OF] *var of* JOAN
Ja·net *or* **Ja·nette** \'jan-ət, jə-'net\ *dim of* JANE
Ja·nice \'jan-əs, jə-'nēs\ *or* **Jan·is** \'jan-əs\ *prob dim of* JANE
Ja·nie \'jā-nē\ *dim of* JANE
Jean *or* **Jeanne** \'jēn\ [OF] *var of* JOAN
Jea·nette *or* **Jean·nette** \jə-'net\ [F] *dim of* JEANNE
Jean·nie *or* **Jean·ie** \jē-nē\ *dim of* JEAN
Jean·nine *or* **Jea·nine** \jə-'nēn\ [F] *dim of* JEANNE
Jen·nie *or* **Jen·ny** \'jen-ē\ *dim of* JANE
Jen·ni·fer \'jen-ə-fər\ [Celt]
Jer·al·dine \'jer-əl-ˌdēn\ *var of* GERALDINE
Jer·i·lyn \'jer-ə-lən\ *var of* GERALDINE
Jer·ry *or* **Jeri** *or* **Jer·rie** \'jer-ē\ *dim of* GERALDINE
Jes·si·ca \'jes-i-kə\ [prob. Heb]
Jes·sie \'jes-ē\ [Sc] *dim of* JANET
Jew·el *or* **Jew·ell** \'jü(-ə)l\ [E] jewel

Jill \'jil\ *dim of* JULIANA
Jo \'jō\ *dim of* JOSEPHINE
Joan *or* **Joann** *or* **Joanne** \'jō(-ə)n, jō-'an\ [Gk] *fem of* JOHN
Jo·an·na \jō-'an-ə\ *or* **Jo·han·na** \-'(h)an-ə\ *var of* JOAN
Joc·e·lyn \'jäs-(ə-)lən\ [OF, fr. Gmc]
Jo·dy *or* **Jo·die** \'jō-dē\ *alter of* JUDITH
Jo·lene \jō-'lēn\ *prob dim of* JO
Jo·se·phine \'jō-zə-ˌfēn *also* 'jō-sə-\ *fem of* JOSEPH
Joy \'jòi\ [E] joy
Joyce \'jòis\ [OF]
Jua·ni·ta \wä-'nēt-ə\ [Sp] *fem dim of* JOHN
Ju·dith \'jüd-əth\ [Heb] Jewess
Ju·dy *or* **Ju·di** *or* **Ju·die** \'jüd-ē\ *dim of* JUDITH
Ju·lia \'jül-yə\ [L] *fem of* JULIUS
Ju·li·ana \ˌjü-lē-'an-ə\ [LL] *fem of* JULIAN
Ju·li·anne *or* **Ju·li·ann** \ˌjü-lē-'an, jül-'yan\ *var of* JULIANA
Ju·lie \'jü-lē\ [MF] *var of* JULIA
Ju·liet \'jül-yət, -ē-ˌet, -ē-ət; ˌjül-ē-'et, jül-'yet, 'jül-ˌyet\ [It] *dim of* JULIA
June \'jün\ [E] June (the month)
Jus·tine \ˌjəs-'tēn\ [F] *fem of* JUSTIN

Ka·ra \'kär-ə, 'kar-ə\ *var of* CATHERINE
Kar·en *or* **Kar·in** *or* **Kaa·ren** \'kar-ən, 'kär-\ [Scand]
Kar·la \'kär-lə\ *var of* CARLA
Kar·ol \'kar-əl\ *var of* CAROL
Kar·o·lyn \'kar-ə-lən\ *var of* CAROLYN
Kate \'kāt\ *dim of* CATHERINE
Kath·er·ine *or* **Kath·a·rine** *or* **Kath·ryn** \'kath-(ə-)rən\ *var of* CATHERINE
Kath·leen \kath-'lēn\ [IrGael] *var of* CATHERINE
Kathy \'kath-ē\ *dim of* CATHERINE
Ka·tie \kāt-ē\ *dim of* KATE
Kay *or* **Kaye** \'kā\ *dim of* CATHERINE
Kel·ly \'kel-ē\ [fr. a surname]
Ker·ry \'ker-ē\ [prob. fr. the county of Ireland]
Kim \'kim\ *prob dim of* KIMBERLY
Kim·ber·ly \'kim-bər-lē\ [OE]
Kit·ty \'kit-ē\ *dim of* CATHERINE
Kris·tin \'kris-tən\ [Scand] *var of* CHRISTINE
Kris·tine \kris-'tēn\ *var of* CHRISTINE

La·na \'lan-ə, 'län-ə, 'lä-nə\
Lau·ra \'lòr-ə, 'lär-\ [ML] *prob fem dim of* LAWRENCE
Lau·rel \'lòr-əl, 'lär-\ [E] laurel
Lau·ren \'lòr-ən, 'lär-\ *var of* LAURA
Lau·rie \'lòr-ē, 'lär-\ *dim of* LAURA
La·verne *or* **La·vern** \lə-'vərn\
Le·ah \'lē-ə\ [Heb] *prob* wild cow
Le·anne \lē-'an\ [prob. fr. *Lee* + *Ann*]
Lee \'lē\ [fr. a surname]
Leigh \'lē\ *var of* LEE
Lei·la *or* **Le·la** \'lē-lə\ [Per] dark as night
Le·lia \'lēl-yə\ [L]
Le·na \'lē-nə\ [G] *dim of* HELENA, Magdalena
Le·nore \lə-'nō(ə)r, -'nò(ə)r\ *or* **Le·no·ra** \lə-'nōr-ə, -'nòr-\ *var of* LEONORA
Le·o·na \lē-'ō-nə\ *fem of* LEON
Le·o·no·ra \ˌlē-ə-'nōr-ə, -'nòr-\ *var of* ELEANOR
Les·lie *or* **Les·ley** \'les-lē *also* 'lez-\ [fr. a surname]
Le·ti·tia \li-'tish-ə, -'tē-shə\ [L] gladness
Lib·by \'lib-ē\ *dim of* ELIZABETH
Li·la \'lī-lə\ *var of* LEILA
Lil·lian \'lil-yən, 'lil-ē-ən\ *prob dim of* ELIZABETH
Lil·lie \'lil-ē\ *dim of* LILLIAN
Lily \'lil-ē\ [E] lily
Lin·da *or* **Lyn·da** \'lin-də\ *dim of* MELINDA, Belinda
Lind·sey *or* **Lind·say** \'lin-zē\ [OE] linden isle
Li·sa \'lē-sə, 'lī-zə\ *dim of* ELIZABETH
Lo·is \'lō-əs\ [Gk]
Lo·la \'lō-lə\ [Sp] *dim of* DOLORES
Lon·na \'län-ə\ *fem of* LON

Lo·ra \'lōr-ə, 'lòr-\ *var of* LAURA
Lo·re·lei \'lōr-ə-ˌlī, 'lòr-\ [G]
Lo·rene \lò-'rēn\ *dim of* LORA
Lo·ret·ta \lə-'ret-ə, lò-\ [ML] *var of* Lauretta
Lo·ri \'lōr-ē, 'lòr-\ *var of* LAURA
Lor·na \'lòr-nə\
Lor·raine *or* **Lo·raine** \lə-'rān, lò-\ [prob. fr. *Lorraine*, region in northeast France]
Lou \'lü\ *dim of* LOUISE
Lou·ise \lů-'ēz\ *or* **Lou·i·sa** \-'ē-zə\ *fem of* LOUIS
Lu·anne \lü-'an\ [*Lu-* + *Anne*]
Lu·cille *or* **Lu·cile** \lü-'sē(ə)l\ [L] *prob dim of* LUCIA
Lu·cin·da \lü-'sin-də\ [L] *var of* LUCY
Lu·cre·tia \lü-'krē-shə\ [L]
Lu·cy \'lü-sē\ *or* **Lu·cia** \'lü-shə\ [L] *fem of* Lucius
Lu·el·la \lů-'el-ə\ [prob. fr. *Lou* (dim. of *Louise*) + *Ella*]
Lyd·ia \'lid-ē-ə\ [Gk] woman of Lydia, ancient country in Asia Minor
Ly·nette \lə-'net\ [W]
Lynne *or* **Lynn** \'lin\ *dim of* CAROLYN, JACQUELYN, etc.

Ma·bel \'mā-bəl\ [L] lovable
Mac·ken·zie \mə-'ken-zē\ [fr. a surname]
Mad·e·line *or* **Mad·e·leine** *or* **Mad·e·lyn** \'mad-ᵊl-ən\ [Gk] woman of Magdala, ancient town in northern Palestine
Madge \'maj\ *dim of* MARGARET
Mal·lory \'mal-(ə-)rē\ [fr. a surname]
Ma·mie \'mā-mē\ *dim of* MARGARET
Ma·ra \'mär-ə\ *var of* MARY
Mar·cel·la \mär-'sel-ə\ [L] *fem of* Marcellus
Mar·cia \'mär-shə\ [L] *fem of* MARCUS
Mar·ga·ret \'mär-g(ə-)rət\ [Gk] pearl
Mar·gery \'märj-(ə-)rē\ [OF] *var of* MARGARET
Mar·gie \'mär-jē\ *dim of* MARGARET
Mar·go \'mär-(ˌ)gō\ *var of* MARGOT
Mar·got \'mär-(ˌ)gō, -gət\ *dim of* MARGARET
Mar·gue·rite \ˌmär-g(y)ə-'rēt\ [OF] *var of* MARGARET
Ma·ria \mə-'rē-ə *also* -'rī-\ *var of* MARY
Mar·i·an \'mer-ē-ən, 'mar-\ *var of* MARIANNE
Mar·i·anne \ˌmer-ē-'an, ˌmar-\ *or* **Mar·i·an·na** \-'an-ə\ [F] *dim of* MARY
Ma·rie \mə-'rē\ [OF] *var of* MARY
Mar·i·et·ta \ˌmer-ē-'et-ə, ˌmar-\ *dim of* MARY
Mar·i·lee \'mer-ə-(ˌ)lē, 'mar-\ [prob. fr. *Mary* + *Lee*]
Mar·i·lyn *or* **Mar·i·lynn** *or* **Mar·y·lyn** \'mer-ə-lən, 'mar-\ [prob. fr. *Mary* + *-lyn*]
Ma·ri·na \mə-'rē-nə\ [LGk]
Mar·i·on \'mer-ē-ən, 'mar-\ *dim of* MARY
Mar·jo·rie *or* **Mar·jo·ry** \'märj-(ə-)rē\ *var of* MARGERY
Mar·la \'mär-lə\ *prob dim of* MARLENE
Mar·lene \mär-'lēn(-ə), -'lā-nə\ [G] *dim of* Magdalene
Mar·lyn \'mär-lən\ *prob var of* MARLENE
Mar·sha \'mär-shə\ *var of* MARCIA
Mar·ta \'märt-ə\ [It] *var of* MARTHA
Mar·tha \'mär-thə\ [Aram] lady
Mar·va \'mär-və\ *prob fem of* MARVIN
Mary \'me(ə)r-ē, 'mā-rē\ [Gk, fr. Heb]
Mary·ann *or* **Mary·anne** \ˌmer-ē-'an, ˌmā-rē-\ [*Mary* + *Ann*]
Mary·el·len \ˌmer-ē-'el-ən, ˌmā-rē-\ [*Mary* + *Ellen*]
Mary·lon \'mer-ə-lən, 'mar-\ *var of* MARILYN
Maude \'mòd\ [OF] *var of* Matilda
Mau·reen *or* **Mau·rine** \mò-'rēn\ [Ir] *dim of* MARY
Max·ine \mak-'sēn\ [F] *fem dim of* Maximilian
May *or* **Mae** \'mā\ *dim of* MARY
Me·gan \'meg-ən, 'mē-gən\ [Ir]
Mel·a·nie \'mel-ə-nē\ [Gk] blackness
Mel·ba \'mel-bə\ [E] woman of Melbourne, Australia
Me·lin·da \mə-'lin-də\ *prob alter of* Belinda
Me·lis·sa \mə-'lis-ə\ [Gk] bee
Mel·va \'mel-və\ *prob fem of* MELVIN
Mer·e·dith \'mer-əd-əth\ [W]
Merle \'mər(-ə)l\ [F] blackbird

Mer·ri·ly \'mer-ə-lē\ *alter of* MARILEE
Mer·ry \'mer-ē\ [E] merry
Mia \'mē-ə\ [It]
Mi·chele *or* **Mi·chelle** \mi-'shel\ [F] *fem of* MICHAEL
Mil·dred \'mil-drəd\ [OE] gentle strength
Mil·li·cent \'mil-ə-sənt\ [Gmc]
Mil·lie \'mil-ē\ *dim of* MILDRED
Min·nie \'min-ē\ [Sc] *dim of* MARY
Mir·an·da \mə-'ran-də\ [L] admirable
Mir·i·am \'mir-ē-əm\ [Heb] *var of* MARY
Mit·zi \'mit-sē\ *prob dim of* MARGARET
Mol·ly *or* **Mol·lie** \'mäl-ē\ *dim of* MARY
Mo·na \'mō-nə\ [IrGael]
Mon·i·ca \'män-i-kə\ [LL]
Mu·ri·el \'myůr-ē-əl\ [prob. Celt]
My·ra \'mī-rə\
Myr·na \'mər-nə\
Myr·tle \'mərt-ᵊl\ [Gk] myrtle

Na·dine \nä-'dēn, nə-\ [F, fr. Russ] hope
Nan \'nan\ *dim of* ANN
Nan·cy \'nan(t)-sē\ *dim of* ANN
Nan·nette *or* **Na·nette** \na-'net, nə-\ [F] *dim of* ANN
Na·o·mi \nä-'ō-mē\ [Heb] pleasant
Nat·a·lie \'nat-ᵊl-ē\ [LL] of or relating to Christmas
Nel·lie \'nel-ē\ *or* **Nell** \'nel\ *dim of* ELLEN, HELEN, ELEANOR
Net·tie \'net-ē\ [Sc] *dim of* JANET
Ni·cole \nē-'kòl\ [F] *fem of* NICHOLAS
Ni·na \'nē-nə\ [Russ] *dim of* ANN
Ni·ta \'nēt-ə\ [Sp] *dim of* JUANITA
No·na \'nō-nə\ [L] ninth
No·ra \'nōr-ə, 'nòr-\ *dim of* LEONORA, ELEANOR, Honora
No·reen \nò-'rēn\ [IrGael] *dim of* NORA
Nor·ma \'nòr-mə\ [It]

Ol·ga \'äl-gə, 'ōl-\ [Russ] *var of* HELGA
Ol·ive \'äl-iv, -əv\ *or* **O·liv·ia** \ə-'liv-ē-ə, ō-\ [L] olive
Opal \'ō-pəl\ [E] opal

Pam \'pam\ *dim of* PAMELA
Pa·me·la \'pam-ə-lə; pə-'mē-lə, pa-\
Pa·tri·cia \pə-'trish-ə, -'trē-shə\ [L] *fem of* PATRICK
Pat·sy \'pat-sē\ *dim of* PATRICIA
Pat·ty *or* **Pat·ti** *or* **Pat·tie** \'pat-ē\ *dim of* PATRICIA
Pau·la \'pò-lə\ [L] *fem of* PAUL
Pau·lette \pò-'let\ *fem dim of* PAUL
Pau·line \pò-'lēn\ *fem dim of* PAUL
Pearl \'pər(-ə)l\ [E] pearl
Peg·gy \'peg-ē\ *dim of* MARGARET
Pe·nel·o·pe \pə-'nel-ə-pē\ [Gk]
Pen·ny \'pen-ē\ *dim of* PENELOPE
Phoe·be \'fē-bē\ [Gk] shining
Phyl·lis \'fil-əs\ [Gk] green leaf
Pol·ly \'päl-ē\ *dim of* MARY
Por·tia \'pōr-shə, 'pòr-\ [L]
Pris·cil·la \prə-'sil-ə\ [L]
Pru·dence \'prüd-ᵊn(t)s\ [E] prudence

Ra·chel \'rā-chəl\ [Heb] ewe
Rae \'rā\ *dim of* RACHEL
Ra·mo·na \rə-'mō-nə\ [Sp] *fem of* RAMON
Re·ba \'rē-bə\ *dim of* REBECCA
Re·bec·ca \ri-'bek-ə\ [Heb]
Re·gi·na \ri-'jē-nə, -'jī-\ [L] queen
Re·nee \rə-'nā, 'ren-(ˌ)ā, 'rā-nē, 'rē-nē\ [F] reborn
Rhea \'rē-ə\ [Gk]
Rho·da \'rōd-ə\ [Gk] rose
Ri·ta \'rēt-ə\ [It] *dim of* MARGARET
Ro·ber·ta \rə-'bərt-ə, rō-\ *fem of* ROBERT
Rob·in *or* **Rob·yn** \'räb-ən\ [E] robin
Ro·chelle \rō-'shel\ [prob. fr. a surname]
Ro·na *or* **Rho·na** \'rō-nə\
Ron·da \'rän-də\ *var of* Rhonda
Ron·nie \'rän-ē\ *dim of* VERONICA

Ro•sa•lie \'rō-zə-(ˌ)lē, 'räz-ə-\ [L] festival of roses
Ro•sa•lind \'räz-(ə-)lənd, 'rō-zə-lənd\ [Sp]
Rose \'rōz\ or Ro•sa \'rō-zə\ [L] rose
Rose•anne \rō-'zan\ [*Rose* + *Anne*]
Rose•mary \'rōz-ˌmer-ē\ or Rose•ma•rie \ˌrōz-mə-'rē\ [E] rosemary
Ro•set•ta \rō-'zet-ə\ *dim of* ROSE
Ros•lyn \'räz-lən\ or Ro•sa•lyn or Ro•se•lyn \'räz-(ə-)lən, 'rō-zə-lən\ *var of* ROSALIND
Ro•we•na \rə-'wē-nə\ [perh. fr. OE]
Rox•anne \räk-'san\ [OPer]
Ru•by \'rü-bē\ [E] ruby
Ruth \'rüth\ [Heb]
Ruth•ann \rü-'than\ [*Ruth* + *Ann*]

Sa•bra \'sä-brə\ *dim of* Sabrina
Sa•die \'sād-ē\ *dim of* SARA
Sal•ly or Sal•lie \'sal-ē\ *dim of* SARA
Sa•man•tha \sə-'man-thə\ [Aram]
San•dra \'san-drə, 'sän-\ *dim of* ALEXANDRA
San•dy \'san-dē\ *dim of* ALEXANDRA
Sar•ah or Sara \'ser-ə, 'sar-ə, 'sä-rə\ [Heb] princess
Sara•lee \'ser-ə-(ˌ)lē, 'sar-\ [prob. fr. *Sara* + *Lee*]
Saun•dra \'sòn-drə, 'sän-\ *var of* SANDRA
Sel•ma \'sel-mə\ [Sw] *fem dim of* Anselm
Shari \'sha(ə)r-ē, 'she(ə)r-\ *dim of* SHARON
Shar•lene \shär-'lēn\ *var of* CHARLENE
Shar•on or Shar•ron \'shar-ən, 'sher-\ [Heb]
Shei•la \'shē-lə\ [IrGael] *dim of* CECILIA
She•lia \'shēl-yə\ *var of* SHEILA
Shel•ley \'shel-ē\ [fr. a surname]
Sher•rill or Sher•yl \'sher-əl\ [prob. fr. a surname]
Sher•ry or Sher•rie or Sheri \'sher-ē\
Shir•ley \'shər-lē\ [fr. a surname]
Sig•rid \'sig-rəd\ [Scand] beautiful as victory
Son•dra \'sän-drə\ *var of* SANDRA
So•nia or So•nya or So•nja \'sō-nyə, 'sò-\ [Russ] *dim of* SOPHIA
So•phia \sə-'fē-ə, -'fī-\ or So•phie \'sō-fē\ [Gk] wisdom
Sta•cy or Sta•cey \'stā-sē\ *dim of* ANASTASIA
Stel•la \'stel-ə\ [L] star
Steph•a•nie \'stef-ə-nē\ *fem of* STEPHEN
Sue \'sü\ or Su•sie \'sü-zē\ *dim of* SUSAN
Su•el•len \sü-'el-ən\ [*Sue* + *Ellen*]
Su•san or Su•zan \'süz-ᵊn\ *dim of* SUSANNA
Su•san•na or Su•san•nah \sü-'zan-ə\ [Heb] lily
Su•zanne or Su•sanne or Su•zann \sü-'zan\ [F] *var of* SUSAN
Syb•il \'sib-əl\ [Gk] sibyl

Syl•via \'sil-vē-ə\ [L] she of the forest

Ta•mara \tə-'mar-ə\ [prob. fr. Georgian (language of the Republic of Georgia)]
Tan•ya \'tan-yə\ [Russ] *dim of* TATIANA
Ta•ra \'tär-ə\ [IrGael]
Tat•i•ana \ˌtät-ē-'än-ə\ [Russ]
Te•re•sa \tə-'rē-sə\ *var of* THERESA
Ter•ry or Ter•ri \'ter-ē\ *dim of* THERESA
Thel•ma \'thel-mə\
The•o•do•ra \ˌthē-ə-'dōr-ə, -'dòr-\ [LGk] *fem of* THEODORE
The•re•sa or Te•re•sa \tə-'rē-sə\ [LL]
The•rese \tə-'rēs\ *var of* THERESA
Tif•fa•ny \'tif-ə-nē\ [Gk]
Ti•na \'tē-nə\ *dim of* CHRISTINA
To•by \'tō-bē\
To•ni \'tō-nē\ *dim of* Antonia
Tra•cy \'trā-sē\ [fr. a surname]
Tru•dy \'trüd-ē\ *dim of* GERTRUDE

Ur•su•la \'ər-sə-lə\ [LL] little she-bear

Val•er•ie \'val-ə-rē\ [L] *prob* strong
Van•es•sa \və-'nes-ə\
Vel•ma \'vel-mə\
Ve•ra \'vir-ə\ [Russ] faith
Ver•na \'vər-nə\ *prob fem of* VERNON
Ve•ron•i•ca \və-'rän-i-kə\ [LL]
Vicki or Vicky or Vick•ie \'vik-ē\ *dim of* VICTORIA
Vic•to•ria \vik-'tōr-ē-ə, -'tòr-\ [L] victory
Vi•da \'vēd-ə, 'vīd-\ *fem dim of* DAVID
Vi•o•la \vī-'ō-lə, vē-'ō-, 'vī-ə-, 'vē-ə-\ [L] violet
Vi•o•let \'vī-ə-lət\ [OF, fr. L] violet
Vir•gin•ia \vər-'jin-yə, -'jin-ē-ə\ [L]
Viv•i•an \'viv-ē-ən\ [LL]

Wan•da \'wän-də\ [Pol]
Wen•dy \'wen-dē\
Whit•ney \'hwit-nē, 'wit-\ [OE]
Wil•da \'wil-də\ *var of* WILLA
Wil•la \'wil-ə\ or Wil•lie \'wil-ē\ *prob fem dim of* WILLIAM
Wil•ma \'wil-mə\ *prob fem dim of* WILLIAM
Win•i•fred \'win-ə-frəd\ [W]

Yvette \i-'vet\ [F]
Yvonne \i-'vän\ [F]

Zel•da \'zel-də\ *dim of* Griselda

Foreign Words and Phrases

ab·eunt stu·dia in mo·res \'ä-be-ˌ u̇ nt-'stü-dē-ˌ ä-ˌ in-'mō-ˌ räs\ [L] : practices zealously pursued pass into habits

à bien·tôt \ä-byanⁿ-tō\ [F] : so long

ab in·cu·na·bu·lis \ˌ äb-ˌ iŋ-ku̇-'nä-bu̇-ˌ lēs\ [L] : from the cradle : from infancy

à bon chat, bon rat \ä-bōⁿ-'shà-bōⁿ-'rà\ [F] : to a good cat, a good rat : retaliation in kind

à bouche ou·verte \ä-bü-shü-vert\ [F] : with open mouth : eagerly : uncritically

ab ovo us·que ad ma·la \ˌ äb-'ō-vō-ˌ u̇ s-kwe-ˌ äd-'mä-lä\ [L] : from egg to apples : from soup to nuts : from beginning to end

à bras ou·verts \à-brà-zü-ver\ [F] : with open arms : cordially

ab·sit in·vi·dia \'äb-ˌ sit-in-'wi-dē-ˌ ä\ [L] : let there be no envy or ill will

ab uno dis·ce om·nes \äb-'ü-nō-ˌ dis-ke-'òm-ˌ nās\ [L] : from one learn to know all

ab ur·be con·di·ta \äb-'u̇ r-be-'kòn-di-ˌ tä\ [L] : from the founding of the city (Rome, founded 753 B.C.) — used by the Romans in reckoning dates

ab·usus non tol·lit usum \'ä-ˌ bü-sùs-ˌ nōn-ˌ tò-lit-'ü-sùm\ [L] : abuse does not take away use, i.e., is not an argument against proper use

à compte \à-kōⁿt\ [F] : on account

à coup sûr \à-kü-su̇ ē r\ [F] : with sure stroke : surely

acte gra·tuit \àk-tə-grà-twᵉē\ [F] : gratuitous impulsive act

ad ar·bi·tri·um \ˌ ad-är-'bi-trē-ùm\ [L] : at will : arbitrarily

ad as·tra per as·pe·ra \ad-'as-trə-ˌ pər-'as-pə-rə\ [L] : to the stars by hard ways — motto of Kansas

ad ex·tre·mum \ˌ ad-ik-'strē-məm\ [L] : to the extreme : at last

ad ka·len·das Grae·cas \ˌ äd-kä-'len-däs-'grī-ˌ käs\ [L] : at the Greek calends : never (since the Greeks had no calends)

ad ma·jo·rem Dei glo·ri·am \ˌ äd-mä-'yòr-ˌ em-'de-ˌ ē-'glòr-ē-ˌ äm\ [L] : to the greater glory of God — motto of the Society of Jesus

ad pa·tres \ad-'pä-ˌ träs\ [L] : (gathered) to his fathers : deceased

ad re·fe·ren·dum \ˌ äd-ˌ re-fe-'ren-dùm\ [L] : for reference : for further consideration by one having the authority to make a final decision

à droite \à-drwät\ [F] : to or on the right hand

ad un·guem \äd-'u̇ ŋ-ˌ gwem\ [L] : to the fingernail : to a nicety : exactly (from the use of the fingernail to test the smoothness of marble)

ad utrum·que pa·ra·tus \ˌ äd-u̇-'trüm-kwe-pä-'rä-tùs\ [L] : prepared for either (event)

ad vi·vum \äd-'wē-ˌ wùm\ [L] : to the life

ae·gri som·nia \'ī-grē-'sòm-nē-ˌ ä\ [L] : a sick man's dreams

ae·quam ser·va·re men·tem \'ī-ˌ kwäm-ser-'wä-rä-'men-ˌ tem\ [L] : to preserve a calm mind

ae·quo ani·mo \'ī-ˌ kwō-'ä-ni-ˌ mō\ [L] : with even mind : calmly

ae·re per·en·ni·us \'ī-rä-pe-'re-nē-ˌ ùs\ [L] : more lasting than bronze

à gauche \à-gōsh\ [F] : to or on the left hand

age quod agis \'ä-ge-ˌ kwòd-'ä-gis\ [L] : do what you are doing : to the business at hand

à grands frais \à-gränⁿ-fre\ [F] : at great expense

à huis clos \à-wᵉē-klō\ [F] : with closed doors

aide–toi, le ciel t'ai·dera \ed-twà-lə-'syel-te-drà\ [F] : help yourself (and) heaven will help you

aî·né \e-nā\ [F] : elder : senior (masc.)

aî·née \e-nā\ [F] : elder : senior (fem.)

à l'aban·don \à-là-bäⁿ-dōⁿ\ [F] : carelessly : in disorder

à la belle étoile \à-là-bel-ā-twàl\ [F] : under the beautiful star : in the open air at night

à la bonne heure \à-là-bò-nœr\ [F] : at a good time : well and good : all right

à la fran·çaise \à-là-fränⁿ-sez\ [F] : in the French manner

à l'amé·ri·caine \à-là-mä-rē-ken\ [F] : in the American manner : of the American kind

à l'an·glaise \à-länⁿ-glez\ [F] : in the English manner

à la page \à-là-päzh\ [F] : at the page : up-to⸗the-minute

à la russe \à-là-rūēs\ [F] : in the Russian manner

alea jac·ta est \'ä-lē-ä-ˌ yäk-tä-'est\ [L] : the die is cast

à l'im·pro·viste \à-laⁿ-prò-vēst\ [F] : unexpectedly

ali·quan·do bo·nus dor·mi·tat Ho·me·rus \ä-li-'kwän-dō-'bò-nùs-dòr-'mē-tät-hō-'mer-ùs\ [L] : sometimes (even) good Homer nods

alis vo·lat pro·pri·is \'ä-ˌ lēs-'wò-ˌ lät-'prò-prē-ˌ ēs\ [L] : she flies with her own wings — motto of Oregon

al–ki \'al-ˌ kī\ [Chinook Jargon] : by and by — motto of Washington

alo·ha oe \ä-'lō-hä-'òi, -'ō-ē\ [Hawaiian] : love to you : greetings : farewell

al·ter idem \ˌ òl-tər-'ī-ˌ dem, ˌ äl-ter-'ē-\ [L] : second self

a max·i·mis ad mi·ni·ma \ä-'mäk-si-ˌ mēs-ˌ äd-'mi-ni-ˌ mä\ [L] : from the greatest to the least

ami·cus hu·ma·ni ge·ne·ris \ä-'mē-kùs-hü-'mä-nē-'ge-ne-ris\ [L] : friend of the human race

ami·cus us·que ad aras \-ˌ ùs-kwe-ˌ äd-'är-ˌ äs\ [L] : a friend as far as to the altars, i.e., except in what is contrary to one's religion; *also* : a friend to the last extremity

ami de cour \à-mē-də-kùr\ [F] : court friend : insincere friend

amor pa·tri·ae \'ä-ˌ mòr-'pä-trē-ˌ ī\ [L] : love of one's country

amor vin·cit om·nia \'ä-ˌ mòr-'wiŋ-kit-'òm-nē-ä\ [L] : love conquers all things

an·cienne no·blesse \äⁿ-syen-nò-bles\ [F] : old-time nobility : the French nobility before the Revolution of 1789

an·guis in her·ba \'äŋ-gwis-in-'her-ˌ bä\ [L] : snake in the grass

ani·mal bi·pes im·plu·me \'ä-ni-ˌ mäl-'bi-ˌ pās-im-'plü-me\ [L] : two-legged animal without feathers (i.e., the human race)

ani·mis opi·bus·que pa·ra·ti \'ä-ni-ˌ mēs-ˌ ò-pi-'bùs-kwe-pä-'rä-tē\ [L] : prepared in mind and resources — one of the mottoes of South Carolina

an·no ae·ta·tis su·ae \'ä-nō-ī-'tä-tis-'sü-ˌ ī\ [L] : in the (specified) year of his or her age

an·no mun·di \'ä-nō-'mùn-dē\ [L] : in the year of the world — used in reckoning dates from the supposed period of the creation of the world, esp. as fixed by James Ussher at 4004 B.C. or by the Jews at 3761 B.C.

an·no ur·bis con·di·tae \'ä-nō-'ùr-bis-'kòn-di-ˌ tī\ [L] : in the year of the founded city (Rome, founded 753 B.C.)

an·nu·it coep·tis \'ä-nù-ˌ wit-'kòip-ˌ tēs\ [L] : He (God) has approved our beginnings — motto on the reverse of the Great Seal of the United States

à peu près \à-pœ-pre\ [F] : nearly : approximately

à pied \à-pyä\ [F] : on foot

après moi le déluge \à-pre-mwà-lə-dā-lūēzh\ *or* **après nous le déluge** \à-pre-nü-\ [F] : after me the deluge — attributed to Louis XV

à pro·pos de bottes \à-prə-pô-də-bȯt\ [F] : apropos of boots — used to change the subject

à pro·pos de rien \-ryaⁿ\ [F] : apropos of nothing

aqua et ig·ni in·ter·dic·tus \ˈäk-wä-et-ˈig-nē-ˌin-terˈdik-tùs\ [L] : forbidden to be furnished with water and fire : outlawed

Ar·ca·des am·bo \ˈär-kä-ˌdes-ˈäm-bō\ [L] : both Arcadians : two persons of like occupations or tastes; *also* : two rascals

ar·rec·tis au·ri·bus \ä-ˈrek-ˌtēs-ˈaú-ri-ˌbús\ [L] : with ears pricked up : attentively

ar·ri·ve·der·ci \ä-ˌrē-ve-ˈder-chē\ [It] : till we meet again : farewell

ars est ce·la·re ar·tem \ˈärs-ˌest-kä-ˈlär-ä-ˈär-ˌtem\ [L] : it is (true) art to conceal art

ars lon·ga, vi·ta bre·vis \ˈärs-ˈlȯṇ-ˌgä-ˈwē-ˌtä-ˈbre-wis\ [L] : art is long, life is short

a ter·go \ä-ˈter-(ˌ)gō\ [L] : from behind

à tort et à tra·vers \à-tȯr-ä-à-trà-ver\ [F] : wrong and crosswise : at random : without rhyme or reason

au bout de son la·tin \ō-bü-də-sōⁿ-là-taⁿ\ [F] : at the end of one's Latin : at the end of one's mental resources

au con·traire \ō-kōⁿ-trer\ [F] : on the contrary

au·de·mus ju·ra nos·tra de·fen·de·re \aú-ˈdā-mùs-ˈyúr-ä-ˈnȯ-strä-dä-ˈfen-de-rä\ [L] : we dare defend our rights — motto of Alabama

au·den·tes for·tu·na ju·vat \aú-ˈden-ˌtās-fȯr-ˈtü-nä-ˌyù-ˌwät\ [L] : fortune favors the bold

au·di al·ter·am par·tem \ˈaú-ˌdē-ˈäl-te-ˌräm-ˈpär-ˌtem\ [L] : hear the other side

au fait \ō-fet, -fe\ [F] : to the point : fully competent : fully informed : socially correct

au fond \ō-fōⁿ\ [F] : at bottom : fundamentally

au grand sé·rieux \ō-gräⁿ-sä-ryœ̄\ [F] : in all seriousness

au pays des aveugles les borgnes sont rois \ō-pā-ē-dä-zà-vœglᵊ-lā-bȯrnʸ-ə-sōⁿ-rwä\ [F] : in the country of the blind the one-eyed men are kings

au·rea me·di·o·cri·tas \ˈaú-rē-ä-ˌme-dē-ˈȯ-kri-ˌtäs\ [L] : the golden mean

au reste \ō-rest\ [F] : for the rest : besides

aus·si·tôt dit, aus·si·tôt fait \ō-sē-tō-dē-ō-sē-tō-fe\ [F] : no sooner said than done

aut Cae·sar aut ni·hil \aút-ˈkī-sär-aút-ˈni-ˌhil\ [L] : either a Caesar or nothing

aut Caesar aut nul·lus \-ˈnú-lùs\ [L] : either a Caesar or a nobody

au·tres temps, au·tres mœurs \ō-trə-täⁿ-ō-trə-mœrs\ [F] : other times, other customs

aut vin·ce·re aut mo·ri \aút-ˈwiṇ-ke-rä-ˌaút-ˈmȯ-ˌrē\ [L] : either to conquer or to die

aux armes \ō-zàrm\ [F] : to arms

avant la lettre \à-väⁿ-lä-letrᵊ\ [F] : before the letter : before a (specified) name existed

ave at·que va·le \ˈä-ˌwä-ˌät-kwe-ˈwä-ˌlā\ [L] : hail and farewell

à vo·tre san·té \à-vȯt-säⁿ-tā, -vȯ-trə-\ [F] : to your health — used as a toast

beaux yeux \bō-zyœ̄\ [F] : beautiful eyes : beauty of face

bel·la fi·gu·ra \ˈbel-lä-fē-ˈgü-rä\ [It] : fine appearance or impression

belle laide \bel-led\ [F] : beautiful ugly woman : a woman who is attractive though not conventionally beautiful

bien en·ten·du \byaⁿ-näⁿ-täⁿ-dǖ\ [F] : well understood : of course

bien-pen·sant \byaⁿ-päⁿ-säⁿ\ [F] : right-minded : one who holds orthodox views

bien·sé·ance \byaⁿ-sä-äⁿs\ [F] : propriety

bis dat qui ci·to dat \ˈbis-ˌdät-kwē-ˈki-tō-ˌdät\ [L] : he or she gives twice who gives promptly

bon ap·pé·tit \bȯ-nà-pā-tē\ [F] : good appetite : enjoy your meal

bon gré, mal gré \ˈbōⁿ-ˌgrä-ˈmál-ˌgrä\ [F] : whether with good grace or bad : willy-nilly

bo·nis avi·bus \ˈbȯ-ˌnēs-ˈä-wi-ˌbús\ [L] : under good auspices

bon·jour \bōⁿ-zhür\ [F] : good day : good morning

bonne foi \bȯn-fwä\ [F] : good faith

bon·soir \bōⁿ-swàr\ [F] : good evening

bru·tum ful·men \ˈbrü-tùm-ˈfùl-men\ [L] : insensible thunderbolt : a futile threat or display of force

buon gior·no \bwȯn-ˈjȯr-nō\ [It] : good day

ca·dit quae·stio \ˈkä-dit-ˈkwī-stē-ˌō\ [L] : the question drops : the argument collapses

cau·sa si·ne qua non \ˈkaú-ˌsä-ˌsi-nä-kwä-ˈnōn\ [L] : an indispensable cause or condition

ça va sans dire \sà-và-säⁿ-dēr\ [F] : it goes without saying

ca·ve ca·nem \ˈkä-wā-ˈkä-ˌnem\ [L] : beware the dog

ce·dant ar·ma to·gae \ˈkä-ˌdänt-ˈär-mə-ˈtō-ˌgī\ [L] : let arms yield to the toga : let military power give way to civil power — motto of Wyoming

ce n'est que le pre·mier pas qui coûte \snek-lə-prə-myä-pä-kē-küt\ [F] : it is only the first step that costs

c'est-à-dire \se-tà-dēr\ [F] : that is to say : namely

c'est au·tre chose \se-tōt-shōz, -tō-trə-\ [F] : that's a different thing

c'est la guerre \se-là-ger\ [F] : that's war : it cannot be helped

c'est la vie \se-là-vē\ [F] : that's life : that's how things happen

c'est plus qu'un crime, c'est une faute \se-plǖ-kœⁿkrēm-se-tūēn-fōt\ [F] : it is worse than a crime, it is a blunder

ce·te·ra de·sunt \ˈkä-te-ˌrä-ˈdā-ˌsùnt\ [L] : the rest is missing

cha·cun à son goût \shà-kœⁿ-nà-sōⁿ-gü\ [F] : everyone to his or her taste

châ·teau en Es·pagne \shä-tō-äⁿ-nes-pànʸ\ [F] : castle in Spain : a visionary project

cher·chez la femme \sher-shä-là-fàm\ [F] : look for the woman

che sa·rà, sa·rà \ˌkä-sä-ˌrä-sä-ˈrä\ [It] : what will be, will be

che·val de ba·taille \shə-vál-də-bà-täʸ\ [F] : war-horse : argument constantly relied on : favorite subject

co·gi·to, er·go sum \ˈkō-gi-ˌtō-ˌer-gō-ˈsùm\ [L] : I think, therefore I exist

co·mé·die hu·maine \kò-mä-dē-ūē-men\ [F] : human comedy : the whole variety of human life

comme ci, comme ça \kòm-sē-kòm-sà\ [F] : so-so

com·pa·gnon de voy·age \kōⁿ-pà-nʸōⁿ-də-vwà-yàzh\ [F] : traveling companion

compte ren·du \kōⁿt-räⁿ-dūē\ [F] : report (as of proceedings in an investigation)

con·cor·dia dis·cors \kòn-ˈkòr-dē-ä-ˈdis-ˌkòrs\ [L] : discordant harmony

cor·rup·tio op·ti·mi pes·si·ma \kò-ˈrùp-tē-ˌō-ˈäp-ti-ˌmē-ˈpe-si-ˌmä\ [L] : the corruption of the best is the worst of all

coup de maî·tre \küd-metrᵉ, kü-də-\ [F] : masterstroke

coup d'es·sai \kü-dä-se\ [F] : experiment : trial

coûte que coûte \küt-kə-küt\ [F] : cost what it may

cre·do quia ab·sur·dum est \ˈkrä-dō-ˈkwē-ä-äp-ˈsùr-dùm-ˈest\ [L] : I believe it because it is absurd

cres·cit eun·do \ˈkres-kit-ˈeùn-dō\ [L] : it grows as it goes — motto of New Mexico

crise de nerfs or crise des nerfs \krēz-də-ner\ [F] : crisis of nerves : nervous collapse : hysterical fit

crux cri·ti·co·rum \ˈkrùks-ˌkri-ti-ˈkòr-ùm\ [L] : crux of critics

cu·jus re·gio, ej·us re·li·gio \ˈkü-yùs-ˈre-gē-ˌō-ˈe-yùs-re-ˈli-gē-ˌō\ [L] : whose region, his or her religion : subjects are to accept the religion of their ruler

cum gra·no sa·lis \kùm-ˈgrä-nō-ˈsä-lis\ [L] : with a grain of salt

cur·sus ho·no·rum \ˈkùr-sùs-hò-ˈnō-rùm\ [L] : course of honors : succession of offices of increasing importance

cus·tos mo·rum \ˈkùs-tōs-ˈmōr-ùm\ [L] : guardian of manners or morals : censor

d'ac·cord \dà-kòr\ [F] : in accord : agreed

dame d'hon·neur \dàm-dò-nœr\ [F] : lady-in-waiting

dam·nant quod non in·tel·li·gunt \ˈdäm-ˌnänt-ˌkwòd-ˈnòn-in-ˈte-li-ˌgùnt\ [L] : they condemn what they do not understand

de bonne grâce \də-bòn-gräs\ [F] : with good grace : willingly

de gus·ti·bus non est dis·pu·tan·dum \dä-ˈgùs-ti-ˌbùs-ˈnòn-ˌest-ˌdis-pù-ˈtän-ˌdùm\ [L] : there is no disputing about tastes

Dei gra·tia \ˈde-ē-ˈgrä-tē-ˌä\ [L] : by the grace of God

de in·te·gro \dä-ˈin-te-ˌgrō\ [L] : anew : afresh

de l'au·dace, en·core de l'au·dace, et tou·jours de l'au·dace \də-lō-däs-äⁿ-kōr-də-lō-däs-ä-tü-zhür-də-lō-däs\ [F] : audacity, more audacity, and ever more audacity

de·len·da est Car·tha·go \dä-ˈlen-dä-ˌest-kär-ˈtä-gō\ [L] : Carthage must be destroyed

de·li·ne·a·vit \dä-ˌlē-nä-ˈä-wit\ [L] : he or she drew it

de mal en pis \də-mà-läⁿ-pē\ [F] : from bad to worse

de mi·ni·mis non cu·rat lex \dä-ˈmi-ni-ˌmēs-ˌnòn-ˈkü-ˌrät-ˈleks\ [L] : the law takes no account of trifles

de mor·tu·is nil ni·si bo·num \dä-ˈmòr-tù-ˌwēs-ˌnēl-ˌni-sē-ˈbò-ˌnùm\ [L] : of the dead (say) nothing but good

de nos jours \də-nō-zhür\ [F] : of our time : contem-

porary — used postpositively esp. after a proper name

Deo fa·ven·te \ˌdā-ō-fä-ˈven-tä\ [L] : with God's favor

Deo gra·ti·as \ˌdä-ō-ˈgrä-tē-ˌäs\ [L] : thanks (be) to God

de pro·fun·dis \ˌdä-prō-ˈfùn-dēs\ [L] : out of the depths

der Geist der stets ver·neint \dər-ˈgīst-dər-ˌshtäts-fer-ˈnīnt\ [G] : the spirit that ever denies — applied originally to Mephistopheles

de·si·pe·re in lo·co \dä-ˈsi-pe-rä-in-ˈlò-kō\ [L] : to indulge in trifling at the proper time

Deus vult \ˈdā-ùs-ˈwùlt\ [L] : God wills it — rallying cry of the First Crusade

di·es fau·stus \ˈdē-ˌäs-ˈfaù-stùs\ [L] : lucky day

dies in·fau·stus \-ˈin-ˌfaù-stùs\ [L] : unlucky day

dies irae \-ˈē-ˌrī\ [L] : day of wrath — used of the Judgment Day

Dieu et mon droit \dyē-ā-mòⁿ-drwä\ [F] : God and my right — motto on the British royal arms

Dieu vous garde \dyœ-vü-gàrd\ [F] : God keep you

di·ri·go \ˈdē-ri-ˌgō\ [L] : I direct — motto of Maine

dis ali·ter vi·sum \ˈdēs-ˈä-li-ˌter-ˈwē-ˌsùm\ [L] : the Gods decreed otherwise

di·tat De·us \ˈdē-ˌtät-ˈdä-ˌùs\ [L] : God enriches — motto of Arizona

di·vi·de et im·pe·ra \ˈdē-wi-ˌde-ˌet-ˈim-pe-ˌrä\ [L] : divide and rule

do·cen·do dis·ci·mus \dò-ˌken-dō-ˈdis-ki-ˌmùs\ [L] : we learn by teaching

Do·mi·ne di·ri·ge nos \ˈdò-mi-ˌne-ˈdē-ri-ge-ˈnōs\ [L] : Lord, direct us — motto of the City of London

Do·mi·nus vo·bis·cum \ˈdò-mi-ˌnùs-wō-ˈbēs-ˌkùm\ [L] : the Lord be with you

dul·ce et de·co·rum est pro pa·tria mo·ri \ˈdùl-ˌkä-et-de-ˈkōr-ùm-ˌest-prō-ˈpä-trē-ˌä-ˈmò-ˌrē\ [L] : it is sweet and seemly to die for one's country

dum spi·ro, spe·ro \dùm-ˈspē-rō-ˈspä-rō\ [L] : while I breathe I hope — one of the mottoes of South Carolina

dum vi·vi·mus vi·va·mus \dùm-ˈwē-wē-ˌmùs-wē-ˈwä-mùs\ [L] : while we live, let us live

d'un certain âge \dœⁿ-ser-te-nàzh\ [F] : of a certain age : no longer young

dux fe·mi·na fac·ti \ˈdùks-ˈfä-mi-nä-ˈfäk-ˌtē\ [L] : a woman was leader of the exploit

ec·ce sig·num \ˈe-ke-ˈsig-ˌnùm\ [L] : behold the sign : look at the proof

e con·tra·rio \ˌä-kòn-ˈträr-ē-ˌō\ [L] : on the contrary

écra·sez l'in·fâme \ä-krä-zā-laⁿ-fäm\ [F] : crush the infamous thing

eheu fu·ga·ces la·bun·tur an·ni \ˈä-ˌheù-fù-ˈgä-ˌkäs-lä-ˌbùn-ˌtùr-ˈän-ˌrē\ [L] : alas! the fleeting years glide on

ein' fes·te Burg ist un·ser Gott \īn-ˌfes-tə-ˈbùrk-ist-ˌùn-zər-ˈgòt\ [G] : a mighty fortress is our God

em·bar·ras de ri·chesses or embarras de ri·chesse \äⁿ-bä-rä-də-rē-shes\ [F] : embarrassing surplus of riches : confusing abundance

em·bar·ras de choix \äⁿ-bä-rä-də-shwà\ or embarras du choix \-dūē-shwà\ [F] : embarrassing variety of choice

en ami \äⁿ-nä-mē\ [F] : as a friend

en ef·fet \äⁿ-nä-fe\ [F] : in fact : indeed

en fa·mille \äⁿ-fä-mēy\ [F] : in or with one's family : at home : informally

en·fant ché·ri \äⁿ-fäⁿ-shä-rē\ [F] : loved or pampered child : one that is highly favored

en·fant gâ·té \äⁿ-fäⁿ-gä-tä\ [F] : spoiled child

en·fants per·dus \äⁿ-fäⁿ-per-dē\ [F] : lost children : soldiers sent to a dangerous post

en·fin \äⁿ-faⁿ\ [F] : in conclusion : in a word

en gar·çon \äⁿ-gàr-sōⁿ\ [F] : as or like a bachelor

en garde \äⁿ-gàrd\ [F] : on guard

en pan·tou·fles \äⁿ-päⁿ-tüflᵃ\ [F] : in slippers : at ease : informally

en plein air \äⁿ-ple-ner\ [F] : in the open air

en plein jour \äⁿ-plaⁿ-zhür\ [F] : in broad day

en règle \äⁿ-regl⁰\ [F] : in order : in due form

en re·tard \äⁿ-rə-tàr\ [F] : behind time : late

en re·traite \äⁿ-rə-tret\ [F] : in retreat : in retirement

en re·vanche \äⁿ-rə-väⁿsh\ [F] : in return : in compensation

en se·condes noces \äⁿ-sə-gōⁿd-nòs\ [F] : in a second marriage

en·se pe·tit pla·ci·dam sub li·ber·ta·te qui·e·tem \ᵛen-se-ᵖpe-tit-ᵖplä-ki-ˌdäm-sùb-ᵖlē-ber-ˌtä-te-kwē-ᵖä-ˌtem\ [L] : with the sword he seeks calm repose under liberty : by the sword we seek peace, but peace only under liberty — motto of Massachusetts

eo ip·so \ˌā-ō-ᵖip-(ˌ)sō\ [L] : by that itself : by that fact alone

épa·ter le bour·geois \ā-pà-tä-lə-bür-zhwà\ [F] : to shock the middle classes

e plu·ri·bus unum \ˌē-ᵖplùr-ə-bəs-ᵖyü-nəm, ˌā-ᵖplùr-i-bùs-ᵖü-nùm\ [L] : one out of many — used on the Great Seal of the U.S. and on several U.S. coins

ep·pur si muo·ve \äp-ᵖpür-sē-ᵖmwò-vä\ [It] : and yet it does move — attributed to Galileo after recanting his assertion of the earth's motion

Erin go bragh \ᵛer-ən-gə-ᵖbrò, -gō-ᵖbrä\ [Ir *go brách* or *go bráth*, lit., till doomsday] : Ireland forever

er·ra·re hu·ma·num est \e-ᵖrär-e-hü-ᵖmä-nùm-ᵖest\ [L] : to err is human

es·prit de l'es·ca·lier \es-prēd-les-kà-lyä\ or **es·prit d'es·ca·lier** \-prē-des-\ [F] : staircase wit : repartee thought of only too late

es·se quam vi·de·ri \ᵛe-sä-ˌkwäm-wi-ᵖdä-rē\ [L] : to be rather than to seem — motto of North Carolina

est mo·dus in re·bus \est-ᵖmò-ˌdùs-in-ᵖrä-ˌbùs\ [L] : there is a proper measure in things, i.e., the golden mean should always be observed

es·to per·pe·tua \ᵛes-ˌtō-per-ᵖpe-tù-ˌwä\ [L] : may she endure forever — motto of Idaho

et hoc ge·nus om·ne \et-ᵖhōk-ᵖge-nùs-ᵖòm-ne\ or **et id genus omne** \et-ˌid-\ [L] : and everything of this kind

et in Ar·ca·dia ego \et-in-är-ᵖkä-dē-ä-ᵖe-gō\ [L] : I too (lived) in Arcadia

et sic de si·mi·li·bus \et-ᵖsēk-dä-si-ᵖmi-li-ˌbùs\ [L] : and so of like things

et tu Bru·te \et-ᵖtü-ᵖbrü-te\ [L] : thou too, Brutus — exclamation attributed to Julius Caesar on seeing his friend Brutus among his assassins

eu·re·ka \yù-ᵖrē-kə\ [Gk] : I have found it — motto of California

Ewig–Weib·li·che \ˌā-vik̲-ᵖvīp-li-k̲ə\ [G] : eternal feminine

ex·al·té \eg-zàl-tä\ [F] : emotionally excited or elated : fanatic

ex ani·mo \eks-ᵖä-ni-ˌmō\ [L] : from the heart : sincerely

ex·cel·si·or \ik-ᵖsel-sē-ər, eks-ᵖkel-sē-ˌòr\ [L] : still higher — motto of New York

ex·cep·tio pro·bat re·gu·lam de re·bus non ex·cep·tis \eks-ᵖkep-tē-ˌō-ᵖprō-bät-ᵖrä-gù-ˌläm-dä-ᵖrä-ˌbùs-ᵖnōn-eks-ᵖkep-ˌtēs\ [L] : an exception establishes the rule as to things not excepted

ex·cep·tis ex·ci·pi·en·dis \eks-ᵖkep-ˌtēs-eks-ˌki-pē-ᵖen-ˌdēs\ [L] : with the proper or necessary exceptions

ex·i·tus ac·ta pro·bat \ᵛek-si-ˌtùs-ᵖäk-tä-ᵖprò-ˌbät\ [L] : the outcome justifies the deed

ex li·bris \eks-ᵖlē-bris\ [L] : from the books of — used on bookplates

ex me·ro mo·tu \ˌeks-ᵖmer-ō-ᵖmō-tü\ [L] : out of mere impulse : of one's own accord

ex ne·ces·si·ta·te rei \ˌeks-ne-ˌke-si-ᵖtä-te-ᵖrä-ˌē\ [L] : from the necessity of the case

ex ni·hi·lo ni·hil fit \eks-ᵖni-hi-ˌlō-ᵖni-ˌhil-ᵖfit\ [L] : from nothing nothing is produced

ex pe·de Her·cu·lem \eks-ᵖpe-de-ᵖher-kù-ˌlem\ [L] : from the foot (we may judge of the size of) Hercules : from a part we may judge of the whole

ex·per·to cre·de \eks-ᵖper-tō-ᵖkrä-de\ or **experto cre·di·te** \-ᵖkrä-di-ˌte\ [L] : believe one who has had experience

ex un·gue le·o·nem \eks-ᵖùŋ-gwe-le-ᵖō-ˌnem\ [L] : from the claw (we may judge of) the lion : from a part we may judge of the whole

ex vi ter·mi·ni \eks-ᵖwē-ᵖter-mi-ˌnē\ [L] : from the force of the term

fa·ci·le prin·ceps \ᵛfä-ki-le-ᵖpriŋ-ˌkeps\ [L] : easily first

fa·ci·lis de·scen·sus Aver·no \ᵛfä-ki-ˌlis-dä-ᵖskän-ˌsùs-ä-ᵖwer-nò\ or **facilis descensus Aver·ni** \-(ˌ)nē\ [L] : the descent to Avernus is easy : the road to evil is easy

fa·çon de par·ler \fà-sōⁿ-də-pàr-lä\ [F] : manner of speaking : figurative or conventional expression

faire suivre \fer-swᵞēvrᵃ\ [F] : have forwarded : please forward

fas est et ab ho·ste do·ce·ri \ˌfäs-ᵖest-et-äb-ᵖhò-ste-dò-ᵖkä-(ˌ)rē\ [L] : it is right to learn even from an enemy

Fa·ta vi·am in·ve·ni·ent \ᵛfä-tä-ᵛwē-ˌäm-in-ᵖwe-nē-ˌent\ [L] : the Fates will find a way

fat·ti mas·chii, pa·ro·le fe·mi·ne \ᵛfät-tē-ᵖmäs-ˌkē-pä-ᵖrò-lä-ᵖfä-mē-ˌnä\ [It] : deeds are males, words are females : deeds are more effective than words — motto of Maryland, where it is generally interpreted as meaning "manly deeds, womanly words"

faux bon·homme \fō-bò-nòm\ [F] : pretended good fellow

faux–naïf \fōē-nà-ēf\ [F] : spuriously or affectedly childlike : artfully simple

fe·lix cul·pa \ᵛfä-liks-ᵖkùl-pä\ [L] : fortunate fault — used esp. of original sin in relation to the consequent coming of Christ

femme de cham·bre \fäm-də-shäⁿbrᵃ\ [F] : chambermaid : lady's maid

fes·ti·na len·te \fe-ᵖstē-nä-ᵖlen-ˌtä\ [L] : make haste slowly

feux d'ar·ti·fice \fōē-dàr-tē-fēs\ [F] : fireworks : display of wit

fi·at ex·pe·ri·men·tum in cor·po·re vi·li \ᵛfē-ät-ek-ˌsper-ē-ᵖmen-ˌtùm-in-ᵖkòr-pò-re-ᵖwē-lē\ [L] : let experiment be made on a worthless body

fi·at ju·sti·tia, ru·at cae·lum \ᵛfē-ät-yùs-ᵖti-tē-ä-ᵖrù-ˌät-ᵖkī-ˌlùm\ [L] : let justice be done though the heavens fall

fi·at lux \ᵛfē-ˌät-ᵖlùks\ [L] : let there be light

Fi·dei De·fen·sor \ᵛfi-de-ˌē-dä-ᵖfän-ˌsòr\ [L] : Defender of the Faith — a title of the sovereigns of England

fi·dus Acha·tes \ˌfē-dùs-ä-ᵖkä-ˌtäs\ [L] : faithful Achates : trusty friend

fille de cham·bre \fēy-də-shäⁿbrᵃ\ [F] : lady's maid

fille d'hon·neur \fēy-dò-nœr\ [F] : maid of honor

fils \fēs\ [F] : son — used orig. after French and now also after other family names to distinguish a son from his father

fi·nem re·spi·ce \ᵛfē-ˌnem-ᵖrä-spi-ˌke\ [L] : consider the end

fi·nis co·ro·nat opus \ˌfē-nis-kò-ᵖrō-ˌnät-ᵖō-ˌpùs\ [L] : the end crowns the work

flo·re·at \ᵛflō-rē-ˌät\ [L] : may (he, she, or it) flourish — usu. followed by a name

fluc·tu·at nec mer·gi·tur \ᵛflùk-tù-ˌwät-nek-ᵖmer-gi-ˌtùr\ [L] : it is tossed by the waves but does not sink — motto of Paris

fo·lie de gran·deur or **fo·lie des gran·deurs** \fò-lē-də-gräⁿ-dœr\ [F] : delusion of greatness : megalomania

force de frappe \fòrs-də-fràp\ [F] : military striking force esp. with nuclear weapons

fors·an et haec olim me·mi·nis·se ju·va·bit \ᵛfòr-ˌsän-ˌet-ᵖhīk-ᵖō-lim-ˌme-mi-ᵖni-se-yù-ᵖwä-bit\ [L] : perhaps this too will be a pleasure to look back on one day

for·tes for·tu·na ju·vat \ᵛfòr-ˌtäs-fòr-ᵖtü-nä-ᵖyù-ˌwät\ [L] : fortune favors the brave

fron·ti nul·la fi·des \\'frȯn-ˌtē-ˌnu̇-lä-'fi-ˌdās\ [L] : no reliance can be placed on appearance

fu·it Il·i·um \\'fu̇-it-'i-lē-ˌu̇m\ [L] : Troy has been (i.e., is no more)

fu·ror lo·quen·di \\'fu̇r-ˌȯr-lȯ-'kwen-(ˌ)dē\ [L] : rage for speaking

furor po·e·ti·cus \-pȯ-'ā-ti-ku̇s\ [L] : poetic frenzy

furor scri·ben·di \-skrē-'ben-(ˌ)dē\ [L] : rage for writing

Gal·li·ce \\'gä-li-ˌke\ [L] : in French : after the French manner

gar·çon d'hon·neur \gàr-sōⁿ-dȯ-nœr\ [F] : bridegroom's attendant

garde du corps \gàrd-dǖ-kȯr\ [F] : bodyguard

gar·dez la foi \gàr-dā-là-fwà\ [F] : keep faith

gau·de·a·mus igi·tur \ˌgau̇d-ē-'ä-mu̇s-'i-gi-ˌtu̇r\ [L] : let us then be merry

gens d'é·glise \zhäⁿ-dā-glēz\ [F] : church people : clergy

gens de guerre \zhäⁿ-də-ger\ [F] : military people : soldiery

gens du monde \zhäⁿ-dǖ-mōⁿd\ [F] : people of the world : fashionable people

gno·thi se·au·ton \\'gnō-thē-ˌse-au̇-'tȯn\ [Gk] : know thyself

grand monde \grän-mōⁿd\ [F] : great world : high society

gros·so mo·do \\'grȯs-(ˌ)sō-'mō-(ˌ)dō\ [It] : roughly

guerre à ou·trance \ger-à-ü-träⁿs\ [F] : war to the uttermost

gu·ten Tag \\'gut-ᵊn-'täk\ [G] : good day

has·ta la vis·ta \\'äs-tä-lä-'vēs-tä\ [Sp] : good-bye

haut goût \ȯ-gü\ [F] : high flavor : slight taint of decay

hic et nunc \\'hēk-et-'nu̇ŋk\ [L] : here and now

hic et ubi·que \\'hēk-et-ù-'bē-kwe\ [L] : here and everywhere

hic ja·cet \hik-'jä-sət, hēk-'yä-ket\ [L] : here lies — used preceding a name on a tombstone

hinc il·lae la·cri·mae \\'hiŋk-'i-ˌlī-'lä-kri-ˌmī\ [L] : hence those tears

hoc age \hȯk-'äg-e\ [L] : do this : apply yourself to what you are about

hoc opus, hic la·bor est \ˌhȯk-'ȯ-ˌpu̇s-ˌhēk-'lä-ˌbȯr-'est\ [L] : this is the hard work, this is the toil

homme d'af·faires \ȯm-dà-fer\ [F] : man of business : business agent

homme d'es·prit \-des-prē\ [F] : man of wit

homme moyen sen·suel \ȯm-mwà-yaⁿ-säⁿ-swʸel\ [F] : the average nonintellectual man

ho·mo sum: hu·ma·ni nil a me ali·e·num pu·to \\'hȯ-mō-ˌsu̇m-hü-'mä-nē-'nēl-ä-ˌmä-ˌä-lē-'ä-nu̇m-'pü-tō\ [L] : I am a human being : I regard nothing of human concern as foreign to my interests

ho·ni soit qui mal y pense \ȯ-nē-swà-kē-màl-ē-päⁿs\ [F] : shamed be he who thinks evil of it — motto of the Order of the Garter

hu·ma·num est er·ra·re \hü-'mä-nu̇m-ˌest-e-'rär-e\ [L] : to err is human

ich dien \ik-'dēn\ [G] : I serve — motto of the Prince of Wales

ici on parle fran·cais \ē-sē-ōⁿ-pàrl-fräⁿ-se\ [F] : French is spoken here

idées re·çues \ē-dā-rə-sw̄e\ [F] : received ideas : conventional opinions

id est \id-'est\ [L] : that is

ig·no·ran·tia ju·ris ne·mi·nem ex·cu·sat \ˌig-nə-'rän-tē-ä-'yu̇r-is-'nä-mi-ˌnem-eks-'kü-ˌsät\ [L] : ignorance of the law excuses no one

ig·no·tum per ig·no·ti·us \ig-'nō-tu̇m-ˌper-ig-'nō-tē-ˌu̇s\ [L] : (explaining) the unknown by means of the more unknown

il faut cul·ti·ver no·tre jar·din \ēl-fō-kw̄el-tē-vä-nȯt-zhàr-daⁿ, -nȯ-trə-zhàr-\ [F] : we must cultivate our garden : we must tend to our own affairs

in ae·ter·num \ˌin-ī-'ter-ˌnu̇m\ [L] : forever

in du·bio \in-'dúb-ē-ˌō\ [L] : in doubt : undetermined

in fu·tu·ro \ˌin-fü-'tu̇r-ō\ [L] : in the future

in hoc sig·no vin·ces \ˌin-ˌhōk-'sig-nō-'wiŋ-ˌkās\ [L] : by this sign (the Cross) you will conquer

in li·mi·ne \in-'lē-mi-ˌne\ [L] : on the threshold : at the beginning

in om·nia pa·ra·tus \in-'ȯm-nē-ä-pä-'rä-ˌtu̇s\ [L] : ready for all things

in par·ti·bus in·fi·de·li·um \in-'pär-ti-ˌbu̇s-ˌin-fə-'dä-lē-ˌu̇m\ [L] : in the regions of the infidels — used of a titular bishop having no diocesan jurisdiction, usu. in non-Christian countries

in prae·sen·ti \ˌin-prī-'sen-ˌtē\ [L] : at the present time

in sae·cu·la sae·cu·lo·rum \in-'sī-kù-ˌlä-ˌsī-kù-'lȯr-ùm, -'sä-kù-ˌlä-ˌsä-\ [L] : for ages of ages : forever and ever

insh·al·lah \ˌin-shä-'lä\ [Ar] : if Allah wills : God willing

in sta·tu quo an·te bel·lum \in-ˌstä-ˌtü-kwō-'än-te-'be-lùm\ [L] : in the same state as before the war

in·te·ger vi·tae sce·le·ris·que pu·rus \\'in-te-ˌger-'wē-ˌtī-ˌiske-le-'ris-kwe-'pü-rùs\ [L] : upright of life and free from wickedness

in·ter nos \ˌin-tər-'nōs\ [L] : between ourselves

in·tra mu·ros \ˌin-trä-'mü-ˌrōs\ [L] : within the walls

in usum Del·phi·ni \in-'ü-sùm-del-'fē-nē\ [L] : for the use of the Dauphin : expurgated

in utrum·que pa·ra·tus \ˌin-ü-'trüm-kwe-pä-'rä-ˌtu̇s\ [L] : prepared for either (event)

in·ve·nit \in-'wä-nit\ [L] : he or she devised it

in vi·no ve·ri·tas \in-'wē-nō-'wä-ri-ˌtäs\ [L] : there is truth in wine

in·vi·ta Mi·ner·va \in-'wē-ˌtä-mi-'ner-ˌwä\ [L] : Minerva being unwilling : without natural talent or inspiration

ip·sis·si·ma ver·ba \ip-'si-si-ˌmä-'wer-ˌbä\ [L] : the very words

ira fu·ror bre·vis est \\'ē-rä-'fùr-ˌȯr-'bre-wis-'est\ [L] : anger is a brief madness

j'ac·cuse \zhà-kw̄ez\ [F] : I accuse : bitter denunciation

jac·ta alea est \\'yäk-ˌtä-'ä-lē-ä-'est\ [L] : the die is cast

j'adoube \zhà-düb\ [F] : I adjust — used in chess when touching a piece without intending to move it

ja·nu·is clau·sis \ˌyä-nù-ˌwēs-'klau̇-ˌsēs\ [L] : behind closed doors

je main·tien·drai \zhə-maⁿ-tyaⁿ-drä\ [F] : I will maintain — motto of the Netherlands

jeu de mots \zhœ̄-də-mō\ [F] : play on words : pun

Jo·an·nes est no·men eius \yō-'ä-näs-est-'nō-men-ā-yùs\ [L] : John is his name — motto of Puerto Rico

jo·lie laide \zhȯ-lē-led\ [F] : good-looking ugly woman : woman who is attractive though not conventionally pretty

jour·nal in·time \zhür-nàl-aⁿ-tēm\ [F] : intimate journal : private diary

jus di·vi·num \\'yüs-di-'wē-ˌnùm\ [L] : divine law

jus·ti·tia om·ni·bus \yùs-'ti-tē-ˌä-'ȯm-ni-ˌbùs\ [L] : justice for all — motto of the District of Columbia

j'y suis, j'y reste \zhē-sw̄e-zhē-rest\ [F] : here I am, here I remain

la belle dame sans mer·ci \là-bel-dàm-säⁿ-mer-sē\ [F] : the beautiful lady without mercy

la·bo·ra·re est ora·re \ˌlä-bō-'rär-ä-ˌest-'ō-ˌrär-ä\ [L] : to work is to pray

la·bor om·nia vin·cit \\'lä-ˌbȯr-ˌȯm-nē-ä-'wiŋ-kit\ [L] : labor conquers all things — motto of Oklahoma

la·cri·mae re·rum \\'lä-kri-ˌmī-'rä-rùm\ [L] : tears for things : pity for misfortune; also : tears in things : tragedy in life

lais·sez–al·ler or **lais·ser–al·ler** \le-sä-à-lä\ [F] : letting go : lack of restraint

lap·sus ca·la·mi \\'läp-sùs-'kä-lä-ˌmē\ [L] : slip of the pen

lap·sus lin·guae \-'liŋ-ˌgwī\ [L] : slip of the tongue

la reine le veut \là-ren-lə-vȫ\ [F] : the queen wills it

la scia·te ogni spe·ran·za, voi ch'en·tra·te \läsh-'shä-tä-ₗō-nʸē-spä-ˈrän-tsä-ₗvō-ē-kân-ˈträ-tä\ [It] : abandon all hope, ye who enter

lau·da·tor tem·po·ris ac·ti \laù-ˈdä-ₗtòr-ₗtem-pò-ris-ˈäk-ₗtē\ [L] : one who praises past times

laus Deo \laùs-ˈdā-ō\ [L] : praise (be) to God

Le·bens·welt \ˈlā-bəns-ₗvelt\ [G] : life world : world of lived experience

le cœur a ses rai·sons que la rai·son ne con·naît point \lə-kœr-à-sä-re-zōⁿk-là-re-zōⁿ-nə-kò-ne-pwaⁿ\ [F] : the heart has its reasons that reason knows nothing of

le roi est mort, vive le roi \lə-rwä-e-mòr-vēv-lə-rwä\ [F] : the king is dead, long live the king

le roi le veut \-lə-vœ̄\ [F] : the king wills it

le roi s'avi·se·ra \-sà-vēz-rà\ [F] : the king will consider

le style, c'est l'homme \lə-stēl-se-lòm\ [F] : the style is the man

l'état, c'est moi \lā-tà-se-mwà\ [F] : the state, it is I

l'étoile du nord \lā-twàl-dœ̄-nò̇r\ [F] : the star of the north — motto of Minnesota

Lie·der·kranz \ˈlē-dər-ₗkränts\ [G] : wreath of songs : German singing society

lit·tera scrip·ta ma·net \ˈli-te-ₗrä-ˈskrip-tä-ˈmä-net\ [L] : the written letter abides

lo·cus in quo \ˈlò-kùs-in-ˈkwō\ [L] : place in which

l'union fait la force \lœ̄-nyōⁿ-fe-là-fòrs\ [F] : union makes strength — motto of Belgium

lu·sus na·tu·rae \ˈlü-sùs-nä-ˈtùr-ē, -ˈtùr-ₗī\ [L] : freak of nature

ma foi \mà-fwà\ [F] : my faith! : indeed

mag·na est ve·ri·tas et prae·va·le·bit \ˈmäg-nä-ₗest-ˈwä-ri-ₗtäs-et-ₗprī-wä-ˈlä-bit\ [L] : truth is mighty and will prevail

mag·ni no·mi·nis um·bra \ˈmäg-nē-ˈnō-mi-nis-ˈùm-brä\ [L] : the shadow of a great name

ma·ha·lo \ˈmä-hä-lō\ [Hawaiian] : thank you

mai·son de san·té \mä-zōⁿ-də-sä̃n-tä\ [F] : private hospital : asylum

ma·lade ima·gi·naire \mà-làd-ē-mà-zhē-ner\ [F] : imaginary invalid : hypochondriac

ma·lis avi·bus \ˈmä-ₗlēs-ä-wi-ₗbùs\ [L] : under evil auspices

ma·no a ma·no \ˈmä-nō-ä-ˈmä-nō\ [Sp] : hand to hand : in direct competition or confrontation

man spricht Deutsch \ₗmän-ₗshprik̲t-ˈdòich\ [G] : German spoken

ma·riage de con·ve·nance \mà-ryàzh-də-kōⁿv-näⁿs\ [F] : marriage of convenience

mau·vaise honte \mò-vez-ōⁿt\ [F] : bad shame : bashfulness

mau·vais quart d'heure \mò-ve-kàr-dœr\ [F] : bad quarter hour : an uncomfortable though brief experience

me·dio tu·tis·si·mus ibis \ˈme-dē-ₗō-tü-ˈti-si-mùs-ˈē-bis\ [L] : you will go most safely by the middle course

me ju·di·ce \mä-ˈyü-di-ke\ [L] : I being judge : in my judgment

mens sa·na in cor·po·re sa·no \ˈmäns-ˈsä-nä-in-ˈkòr-pò-re-ˈsä-nō\ [L] : a sound mind in a sound body

me·um et tu·um \ˈmē-ùm-ₗet-ˈtü-ùm, ˈmä-ùm-\ [L] : mine and thine : distinction of private property

mi·ra·bi·le vi·su \mi-ˈrä-bi-lä-ˈwē-sü\ [L] : wonderful to behold

mi·ra·bi·lia \ₗmir-ä-ˈbi-lē-ä\ [L] : wonders : miracles

mœurs \mœr, mœrs\ [F] : mores : attitudes, customs, and manners of a society

mo·le ru·it sua \ˈmō-le-ˈrù-it-ˈsù-ä\ [L] : it collapses from its own bigness

monde \mōⁿd\ [F] : world : fashionable world : society

mon·ta·ni sem·per li·be·ri \mòn-ˈtä-nē-ˈsem-per-ˈlē-be-ₗrē\ [L] : mountaineers are always free — motto of West Virginia

mo·nu·men·tum ae·re per·en·ni·us \ₗmò-nù-ˈmentùm-ₗī-re-pe-ˈre-nē-ùs\ [L] : a monument more lasting than bronze — used of an immortal work of art or literature

mo·ri·tu·ri te sa·lu·ta·mus \ₗmòr-i-ˈtùr-ē-ₗtä-ₗsä-lù-ˈtä-mùs\ or morituri te sa·lu·tant \-ˈsä-lù-ₗtänt\ [L] : we (or those) who are about to die salute thee

mul·tum in par·vo \ˈmùl-tùm-in-ˈpär-vō\ [L] : much in little

mu·ta·to no·mi·ne de te fa·bu·la nar·ra·tur \mü-ˈtä-tō-ˈnō-mi-ne-ₗdä-ˈtä-ˈfä-bù-lä-nä-ˈrä-ₗtùr\ [L] : with the name changed the story applies to you

my·ste·ri·um tre·men·dum \mi-ˈster-ē-ₗùm-tre-ˈmen-dùm\ [L] : overwhelming mystery

na·tu·ram ex·pel·las fur·ca, ta·men us·que re·cur·ret \nä-ˈtü-ₗräm-ek-ₗspe-läs-ˈfùr-ₗkä-ₗtä-men-ˈùs-kwe-re-ˈkùr-et\ [L] : you may drive nature out with a pitchfork, but she will keep coming back

na·tu·ra non fa·cit sal·tum \nä-ˈtü-rä-ₗnòn-ˈfä-kit-ˈsäl-ₗtùm\ [L] : nature makes no leap

ne ce·de ma·lis \nä-ˈkä-de-ˈmä-ₗlēs\ [L] : yield not to misfortunes

ne·mo me im·pu·ne la·ces·sit \ˈnä-mō-ˈmä-im-ˈpü-nä-lä-ˈke-sit\ [L] : no one attacks me with impunity — motto of Scotland and of the Order of the Thistle

ne quid ni·mis \ₗnä-ₗkwid-ˈni-mis\ [L] : not anything in excess

n'est-ce pas? \nes-pä\ [F] : isn't it so?

nicht wahr? \nikt-ˈvär\ [G] : not true? : isn't it so?

nil ad·mi·ra·ri \ˈnēl-ₗäd-mi-ˈrär-ē\ [L] : to be excited by nothing : equanimity

nil de·spe·ran·dum \ˈnēl-ₗdä-spä-ˈrän-dùm\ [L] : never despair

nil si·ne nu·mi·ne \ˈnēl-ₗsi-nä-ˈnü-mi-ne\ [L] : nothing without the divine will — motto of Colorado

n'im·porte \naⁿ-pòrt\ [F] : it's no matter

no·lens vo·lens \ˈnō-ₗlenz-ˈvō-ₗlenz\ [L] : unwilling (or) willing : willy-nilly

non om·nia pos·su·mus om·nes \nōn-ˈòm-nē-ä-ₗpò-sù-mùs-ˈòm-ₗnäs\ [L] : we can't all (do) all things

non om·nis mo·ri·ar \nōn-ˈòm-nis-ˈmòr-ē-ₗär\ [L] : I shall not wholly die

non sans droict \nōⁿ-sän-drwä\ [OF] : not without right — motto on Shakespeare's coat of arms

non sum qua·lis eram \nōⁿ-ₗsùm-ˈkwä-lis-ˈer-ₗäm\ [L] : I am not what I used to be

nos·ce te ip·sum \ˈnòs-ke-ₗtä-ˈip-ₗsùm\ [L] : know thyself

nos·tal·gie de la boue \nòs-tàl-zhē-də-là-bü\ [F] : yearning for the mud : attraction to what is unworthy, crude, or degrading

nous avons chan·gé tout ce·la \nü-zà-vōⁿ-shäⁿ-zhä-tü-sə-là\ [F] : we have changed all that

nous ver·rons ce que nous ver·rons \nü-ve-rōⁿ-sə-kə-nü-ve-rōⁿ\ [F] : we shall see what we shall see

no·vus ho·mo \ˈnò-wùs-ˈhò-mō\ [L] : new man : man newly ennobled : upstart

no·vus or·do se·clo·rum \-ˈòr-ₗdō-sä-ˈklōr-ùm\ [L] : a new cycle of the ages — motto on the reverse of the Great Seal of the United States

nu·gae \ˈnü-ₗgī\ [L] : trifles

nuit blanche \nwʸē-blä̃nsh\ [F] : white night : a sleepless night

nyet \ˈnyet\ [Russ] : no

ob·iit \ˈò-bē-ₗit\ [L] : he or she died

ob·scu·rum per ob·scu·ri·us \òb-ˈskyùr-ùm-ₗper-òb-ˈskyùr-ē-ùs\ [L] : (explaining) the obscure by means of the more obscure

ode·rint dum me·tu·ant \ˈò-de-ₗrint-ₗdùm-ˈme-tù-ₗwänt\ [L] : let them hate, so long as they fear

odi et amo \ˈò-dē-et-ˈä-(ₗ)mō\ [L] : I hate and I love

omer·tà \ò-ˈmer-tä\ [It] : submission : code chiefly among members of the criminal underworld that enjoins private vengeance and the refusal to give information to outsiders (as the police)

om·ne ig·no·tum pro mag·ni·fi·co \ˈòm-ne-ig-ˈnō-ₗtùm-prō-mäg-ˈni-fi-ₗkō\ [L] : everything unknown (is taken) as grand : the unknown tends to be exaggerated in importance or difficulty

om·nia mu·tan·tur, nos et mu·ta·mur in il·lis \ˈòm-nē-ä-mü-**'**tän-**'**tur-**'**nôs-**'**et-mü-**'**tä-mûr-in-**'**i-**'**lēs\ [L] : all things are changing, and we are changing with them

om·nia vin·cit amor **'**òm-nē-ä-**'**win-kit-**'**ä-**'**mòr\ [L] : love conquers all

onus pro·ban·di **'**ō-nùs-prō-**'**ban-**'**dī, -dē\ [L] : burden of proof

ora pro no·bis **'**ō-rä-prō-**'**nō-**'**bēs\ [L] : pray for us

ore ro·tun·do **'**ōr-ä-rō-**'**tùn-dō\ [L] : with round mouth : eloquently

oro y pla·ta **'**ōr-ō-ē-**'**plä-tä\ [Sp] : gold and silver — motto of Montana

o tem·pora! o mo·res! \ō-**'**tem-pò-rä-ō-**'**mō-**'**rās\ [L] : oh the times! oh the manners!

oti·um cum dig·ni·ta·te **'**ō-tē-**'**ùm-kùm-**'**dig-ni-**'**tä-te\ [L] : leisure with dignity

où sont les neiges d'an·tan? \ü-sōⁿ-lä-nezh-däⁿ-tä^m\ [F] : where are the snows of yesteryear?

outre–mer \ütr^ə-mer\ [F] : overseas : distant lands

pal·li·da Mors **'**pa-li-də-**'**mòrz\ [L] : pale Death

pa·nem et cir·cen·ses **'**pän-**'**em-et-kir-**'**kän-**'**säs\ [L] : bread and circuses : provision of the means of life and recreation by government to appease discontent

pan·ta rhei **'**pän-**'**tä-**'**rä\ [Gk] : all things are in flux

par avance \pär-à-väⁿs\ [F] : in advance : by anticipation

par avion \pär-à-vyō^m\ [F] : by airplane — used on airmail

par ex·em·ple \pär-äg-zäⁿpl^ə\ [F] : for example

pars pro to·to **'**pärs-**'**prō-**'**tō-(**'**)tō\ [L] : part (taken) for the whole

par·tu·ri·unt mon·tes, nas·ce·tur ri·di·cu·lus mus \pär-**'**tùr-ē-**'**ùnt-**'**mòn-**'**täs-näs-**'**kä-**'**tùr-ri-**'**di-kù-lùs-**'**müs\ [L] : the mountains are in labor, and a ridiculous mouse will be brought forth

pa·ter pa·tri·ae **'**pä-**'**ter-**'**pä-trē-**'**ī\ [L] : father of his country

pau·cis ver·bis **'**paù-kēs-**'**wer-**'**bēs\ [L] : in a few words

pax vo·bis·cum **'**päks-vō-**'**bēs-**'**kùm\ [L] : peace (be) with you

peine forte et dure \pen-fòr-tä-dēr\ [F] : strong and hard punishment : torture

per an·gus·ta ad au·gus·ta \per-**'**än-**'**gùs-tä-äd-**'**aù-**'**gùs-tä\ [L] : through difficulties to honors

père \per\ [F] : father — used orig. after French and now also after other family names to distinguish a father from his son

per·eant qui an·te nos nos·tra dix·e·runt **'**per-e-**'**änt-kwē-**'**än-te-**'**nōs-**'**nòs-trä-dēk-**'**sä-**'**rùnt\ [L] : may they perish who have expressed our bright ideas before us

per·fide Al·bion \per-fēd-àl-byō^m\ [F] : perfidious Albion (England)

peu à peu \pœ̄-à-pœ̄\ [F] : little by little

peu de chose \pœ̄-də-shōz\ [F] : a trifle

pièce d'oc·ca·sion \pyes-dò-kä-zyō^m\ [F] : piece for a special occasion

pinx·it **'**piŋk-sit\ [L] : he or she painted it

place aux dames \plàs-ō-dàm\ [F] : (make) room for the ladies

ple·no ju·re **'**plä-nō-**'**yùr-e\ [L] : with full right

plus ça change, plus c'est la même chose \plœ̄-sà-shäⁿzh-plœ̄-se-lä-mem-shōz\ [F] : the more that changes, the more it's the same thing — often shortened to *plus ça change*

plus roy·a·liste que le roi \plœ̄-rwà-yà-lēst-kəl-rwà\ [F] : more royalist than the king

po·cas pa·la·bras **'**pō-käs-pä-**'**lä-vräs\ [Sp] : few words

po·eta nas·ci·tur, non fit \pò-**'**ä-tä-**'**näs-ki-**'**tùr-nōn-**'**fit\ [L] : a poet is born, not made

pol·li·ce ver·so **'**pò-li-ke-**'**ver-sō\ [L] : with thumb turned : with a gesture or expression of condemnation

post hoc, er·go prop·ter hoc **'**pòst-**'**hōk-**'**er-gō-**'**pròp-ter-**'**hōk\ [L] : after this, therefore on account of it (a fallacy of argument)

post ob·itum \pòst-**'**ō-bi-**'**tùm\ [L] : after death

pour ac·quit \pür-à-kē\ [F] : received payment

pour le mé·rite \pür-lə-mä-rēt\ [F] : for merit

pri·mum non no·ce·re **'**prē-mùm-**'**nōn-nō-**'**kä-re\ [L] : the first thing (is) to do no harm

pro aris et fo·cis \prō-**'**ä-**'**rēs-et-**'**fō-**'**kēs\ [L] : for altars and firesides

pro bo·no pu·bli·co \prō-**'**bò-nō-**'**pü-bli-**'**kō\ [L] : for the public good

pro hac vi·ce \prō-**'**häk-**'**wi-ke\ [L] : for this occasion

pro pa·tria \prō-**'**pä-trē-**'**ä\ [L] : for one's country

pro re·ge, le·ge, et gre·ge \prō-**'**rä-ge-**'**lä-ge-et-**'**gre-ge\ [L] : for the king, the law, and the people

pro re na·ta \prō-**'**rä-**'**nä-tä\ [L] : for an occasion that has arisen : as needed — used in medical prescriptions

quand même \käⁿ-mem\ [F] : even so : all the same

quan·tum mu·ta·tus ab il·lo **'**kwän-tùm-mü-**'**tä-tis-äb-**'**i-lō\ [L] : how changed from what he once was

quan·tum suf·fi·cit **'**kwän-tùm-**'**sə-fi-kit\ [L] : as much as suffices : a sufficient quantity — used chiefly in medical prescriptions

¿quién sa·be? \kyän-**'**sä-vä\ [Sp] : who knows?

qui fa·cit per ali·um fa·cit per se \kwē-**'**fä-kit-**'**per-**'**ä-lē-**'**ùm-**'**fä-kit-**'**per-**'**sä\ [L] : he who does (something) through another does it through himself

quis cus·to·di·et ip·sos cus·to·des? **'**kwis-kùs-**'**tō-dē-**'**et-ip-**'**sōs-kùs-**'**tō-**'**däs\ [L] : who will keep the keepers themselves?

qui s'ex·cuse s'ac·cuse \kē-sek-skū̄ez-sà-kū̄ez\ [F] : he who excuses himself accuses himself

quis se·pa·ra·bit? \kwis-**'**sä-pä-**'**rä-bit\ [L] : who shall separate (us)? — motto of the Order of St. Patrick

qui trans·tu·lit sus·ti·net \kwē-**'**träns-tù-**'**lit-**'**sùs-ti-**'**net\ [L] : He who transplanted sustains (us) — motto of Connecticut

qui va là? \kē-và-lä\ [F] : who goes there?

quo·ad hoc **'**kwò-**'**äd-**'**hōk\ [L] : as far as this : to this extent

quod erat de·mon·stran·dum **'**kwòd-**'**er-**'**ät-**'**de-mòn-**'**strän-dùm\ [L] : which was to be proved

quod erat fa·ci·en·dum **'**fä-kē-**'**en-**'**dùm\ [L] : which was to be done

quod sem·per, quod ubi·que, quod ab om·ni·bus \kwòd-**'**sem-**'**per-kwòd-**'**ù-bi-**'**kwä-kwòd-äb-**'**òm-ni-**'**bùs\ [L] : what (has been held) always, everywhere, by everybody

quod vi·de \kwòd-**'**wi-**'**de\ [L] : which see

quo·rum pars mag·na fui **'**kwòr-ùm-**'**pärs-**'**mäg-nə-**'**fü-ē\ [L] : in which I played a great part

quos de·us vult per·de·re pri·us de·men·tat \kwòs-**'**de-ùs-**'**wùlt-**'**per-de-**'**re-**'**prē-ùs-dä-**'**men-**'**tät\ [L] : those whom a god wishes to destroy he first drives mad

quot ho·mi·nes, tot sen·ten·ti·ae \kwòt-**'**hò-mi-**'**näs-**'**tòt-sen-**'**ten-tē-**'**ī\ [L] : there are as many opinions as there are men

quo va·dis? \kwò-**'**vä-dis, -**'**wä-\ [L] : whither are you going?

rai·son d'état \re-zōⁿ-dä-tà\ [F] : reason of state

re·cu·ler pour mieux sau·ter \rə-kū̄e-lä-pür-myœ̄-sō-tä\ [F] : to draw back in order to make a better jump

reg·nat po·pu·lus **'**reg-nät-**'**pò-pù-lùs\ [L] : the people rule — motto of Arkansas

re in·fec·ta \rä-in-**'**fek-tä\ [L] : the business being unfinished : without accomplishing one's purpose

re·li·gio lo·ci \re-**'**li-gē-ō-**'**lò-kē\ [L] : religious sanctity of a place

rem acu te·ti·gis·ti \rem-**'**ä-kü-te-ti-**'**gis-tē\ [L] : you have touched the point with a needle : you have hit the nail on the head

ré·pon·dez s'il vous plaît \rä-pōⁿ-dä-sēl-vü-ple\ [F] : reply, if you please

re·qui·es·cat in pa·ce \re-kwē-**'**es-**'**kät-in-**'**pä-ke,

ˌrā-kwē-ˈes-ˌkät-in-ˈpä-ˌchä\ [L] : may he or she rest in peace — used on tombstones

re·spi·ce fi·nem \ˈrä-spi-ˌke-ˈfē-ˌnem\ [L] : look to the end : consider the outcome

re·sur·gam \re-ˈsu̇r-ˌgäm\ [L] : I shall rise again

re·te·nue \rət-nǖ\ [F] : self-restraint : reserve

re·ve·nons à nos mou·tons \rəv-nōⁿ-à-nō-mü-tōⁿ\ [F] : let us return to our sheep : let us get back to the subject

ruse de guerre \rǖz-də-ger\ [F] : war stratagem

rus in ur·be \ˈrüs-in-ˈu̇r-ˌbe\ [L] : country in the city

sae·va in·dig·na·tio \ˈsī-wä-ˌin-dig-ˈnä-tē-ō\ [L] : fierce indignation

sal At·ti·cum \ˈsal-ˈa-ti-kəm\ [L] : Attic salt : wit

salle à man·ger \sàl-à-mäⁿ-zhā\ [F] : dining room

sa·lon des re·fu·sés \sà-lòⁿ-dā-rə-fǖ-zā\ [F] : salon of the refused : exhibition of art that has been rejected by an official body

sa·lus po·pu·li su·pre·ma lex es·to \ˈsäl-ˌüs-ˈpò-pu̇-ˌlē-sù-ˈprä-mä-ˌleks-ˈes-tō\ [L] : let the welfare of the people be the supreme law — motto of Missouri

sanc·ta sim·pli·ci·tas \ˌsäŋk-tä-sim-ˈpli-ki-ˌtäs\ [L] : holy simplicity — often used ironically in reference to another's naïveté

sans doute \säⁿ-düt\ [F] : without doubt

sans gêne \säⁿ-zhen\ [F] : without embarrassment or constraint

sans peur et sans re·proche \säⁿ-pœr-ä-säⁿ-rə-pròsh\ [F] : without fear and without reproach

sans sou·ci \säⁿ-sü-sē\ [F] : without worry

sa·yo·na·ra \ˌsä-yō-ˈnär-ä\ [Jp] : good-bye

sculp·sit \ˈsku̇lp-sit\ [L] : he or she carved it

scu·to bo·nae vo·lun·ta·tis tu·ae co·ro·nas·ti nos \ˈskü-ˌtō-ˈbò-ˌnī-vò-lùn-ˈtä-tis-ˈtù-ˌī-ˌkòr-ò-ˈnäs-tē-ˈnōs\ [L] : Thou hast crowned us with the shield of Thy good will — a motto on the Great Seal of Maryland

se·cun·dum ar·tem \se-ˈku̇n-du̇m-ˈär-ˌtem\ [L] : according to the art : according to the accepted practice of a profession or trade

secundum na·tu·ram \-nä-ˈtü-ˌräm\ [L] : according to nature : naturally

se de·fen·den·do \ˈsä-ˌdā-ˌfen-ˈden-dō\ [L] : in self-defense

se ha·bla es·pa·ñol \sā-ˌäb-lä-ˌäs-pä-ˈnʸòl\ [Sp] : Spanish spoken

sem·per ea·dem \ˈsem-ˌper-ˈe-ä-ˌdem\ [L] : always the same (fem.) — motto of Queen Elizabeth I

sem·per fi·de·lis \ˈsem-pər-fi-ˈdä-lis\ [L] : always faithful — motto of the U.S. Marine Corps

sem·per idem \ˈsem-ˌper-ˈē-ˌdem\ [L] : always the same (masc.)

sem·per pa·ra·tus \ˌsem-pər-pä-ˈrä-təs\ [L] : always prepared — motto of the U.S. Coast Guard

se non è ve·ro, è ben tro·va·to \sä-nōn-e-ˈvä-rō-e-ˌben-trō-ˈvä-tō\ [It] : even if it is not true, it is well conceived

sic itur ad as·tra \ˌsēk-ˈi-ˌtu̇r-ˌäd-ˈäs-trä\ [L] : thus one goes to the stars : such is the way to immortality

sic sem·per ty·ran·nis \ˌsik-ˈsem-pər-ti-ˈra-nis\ [L] : thus ever to tyrants — motto of Virginia

sic trans·it glo·ria mun·di \ˌsēk-ˈträn-sit-ˈglōr-ē-ä-ˈmùn-dē\ [L] : so passes away the glory of the world

si jeu·nesse sa·vait, si vieil·lesse pou·vait! \sē-zhœ-nes-sà-ve-sē-vye-yes-pü-ve\ [F] : if youth only knew, if age only could!

si·lent le·ges in·ter ar·ma \ˈsi-ˌlent-ˈlä-ˌgäs-ˌin-ter-ˈär-mä\ [L] : the laws are silent in the midst of arms

s'il vous plaît \sēl-vü-ple\ [F] : if you please

si·mi·lia si·mi·li·bus cu·ran·tur \sē-ˈmi-lē-ä-si-ˈmi-li-bùs-kü-ˈrän-ˌtu̇r\ [L] : like is cured by like

si·mi·lis si·mi·li gau·det \ˈsi-mi-lis-ˈsi-mi-lē-ˈgaù-ˌdet\ [L] : like takes pleasure in like

si mo·nu·men·tum re·qui·ris, cir·cum·spi·ce \ˌsē-ˌmò-nü-ˈmen-tu̇m-re-ˈkwē-ris-kir-ˈku̇m-spi-ke\ [L] : if you seek his monument, look around — epitaph of

Sir Christopher Wren in St. Paul's, London, of which he was architect

sim·pliste \saⁿ-plēst\ [F] : simplistic : overly simple or naive

si quae·ris pen·in·su·lam amoe·nam, cir·cum·spi·ce \sē-ˈkwī-ris-pä-ˈnin-sü-ˌläm-ä-ˈmòi-ˌnäm-kir-ˈku̇m-spi-ke\ [L] : if you seek a beautiful peninsula, look around — motto of Michigan

sis·te vi·a·tor \ˈsis-te-wē-ˈä-ˌtòr\ [L] : stop, traveler — used on Roman roadside tombs

si vis pa·cem, pa·ra bel·lum \ˌsē-ˈwēs-ˈpä-ˌkem-ˌpä-rä-ˈbe-ˌlùm\ [L] : if you wish peace, prepare for war

sol·vi·tur am·bu·lan·do \ˈsòl-wi-ˌtu̇r-ˌäm-bù-ˈlän-dō\ [L] : it is solved by walking : the problem is solved by a practical experiment

splen·di·de men·dax \ˈsplen-di-ˌdä-ˈmen-ˌdäks\ [L] : nobly untruthful

spo·lia opi·ma \ˈspò-lē-ä-ō-ˈpē-mä\ [L] : rich spoils : the arms taken by the victorious from the vanquished general

sta·tus in quo \ˈstä-tùs-ˌin-ˈkwō\ [L] : state in which : the existing state

status quo an·te bel·lum \-kwō-ˌän-te-ˈbe-lùm\ [L] : the state existing before the war

sua·vi·ter in mo·do, for·ti·ter in re \ˈswä-wi-ˌter-in-ˈmò-dō-ˈfòr-ti-ˌter-in-ˈrä\ [L] : gently in manner, strongly in deed

sub ver·bo \ˌsu̇b-ˈwer-bō\ *or* **sub vo·ce** \ˌsu̇b-ˈwō-ke\ [L] : under the word — introducing a cross-reference in a dictionary or index

sunt la·cri·mae re·rum \ˌsu̇nt-ˌlä-kri-ˌmī-ˈrä-rùm\ [L] : there are tears for things : tears attend trials

suo ju·re \ˌsü-ō-ˈyu̇r-e\ [L] : in his or her own right

suo lo·co \-ˈlò-kò\ [L] : in its proper place

suo Mar·te \-ˈmär-te\ [L] : by one's own exertions

su·um cui·que \ˌsü-u̇m-ˈkwi-kwe\ [L] : to each his own

tant mieux \täⁿ-myœ̄\ [F] : so much the better

tant pis \-pē\ [F] : so much the worse : too bad

tem·po·ra mu·tan·tur, nos et mu·ta·mur in il·lis \ˈtem-pò-rä-mü-ˈtän-ˌtu̇r-ˈnōs-ˌet-mü-ˈtä-mu̇r-in-ˈi-ˌlēs\ [L] : the times are changing, and we are changing with them

tem·pus edax re·rum \ˈtem-pu̇s-ˌe-ˌdäks-ˈrä-rùm\ [L] : time, that devours all things

tem·pus fu·git \ˈtem-pəs-ˈfyü-jət, ˈtem-pu̇s-ˈfü-git\ [L] : time flies

ti·meo Da·na·os et do·na fe·ren·tes \ˈti-mē-ˌō-ˈdä-nä-ˌōs-ˌet-ˈdō-nä-fe-ˈren-ˌtäs\ [L] : I fear the Greeks even when they bring gifts

to·ti·dem ver·bis \ˈtō-ti-ˌdem-ˈwer-ˌbēs\ [L] : in so many words

to·tis vi·ri·bus \ˈtō-ˌtēs-ˈwē-ri-ˌbùs\ [L] : with all one's might

to·to cae·lo \ˈtō-tō-ˈkī-lō\ *or* **toto coe·lo** \-ˈkòi-lō\ [L] : by the whole extent of the heavens : diametrically

tou·jours per·drix \tü-zhür-per-drē\ [F] : always partridge : too much of a good thing

tour d'ho·ri·zon \tür-dò-rē-zōⁿ\ [F] : circuit of the horizon : general survey

tous frais faits \tü-fre-fe\ [F] : all expenses defrayed

tout à fait \tü-tà-fe\ [F] : altogether : quite

tout au con·traire \tü-tō-kōⁿ-trer\ [F] : quite the contrary

tout à vous \tü-tà-vü\ [F] : wholly yours : at your service

tout bien ou rien \tü-byaⁿ-nü-ryaⁿ\ [F] : everything well (done) or nothing (attempted)

tout com·pren·dre c'est tout par·don·ner \tü-kōⁿ-präⁿ-drə-se-tü-pàr-dò-nä\ [F] : to understand all is to forgive all

tout court \tü-kür\ [F] : quite short and nothing more : simply : just; *also* : brusquely

tout de même \tüt-mem\ [F] : all the same : nevertheless

tout de suite \tüt-swʸēt\ [F] : immediately; *also* : all at once : consecutively

tout en·sem·ble \tü-tän-sänbl⁀\ [F] : all together : general effect

tout est per·du fors l'hon·neur \tü-te-per-dǖ-fȯr-lȯ-nœr\ *or* **tout est perdu hors l'honneur** \-dǖ-ȯr-\ [F] : all is lost save honor

tout le monde \tül-mōⁿd\ [F] : all the world : everybody

tra·hi·son des clercs \trȧ-ē-zȯⁿ-dä-klerk\ [F] : treason of the intellectuals

tranche de vie \träⁿsh-də-vē\ [F] : slice of life

trist·esse \trē-stes\ [F] : melancholy

tru·di·tur di·es die \'trü-di-ı̣tu̇r-'di-ı̣äs-'di-ı̣ä\ [L] : day is pushed forth by day : one day hurries on another

tu·e·bor \tu̇-'ā-ı̣bȯr\ [L] : I will defend — a motto on the Great Seal of Michigan

ua mau ke ea o ka ai·na i ka po·no \u̇-ä-'mä-u̇-ke-'e-ä-ō-kä-'ä-ē-nä-ı̣ē-kä-'pō-nō\ [Hawaiian] : the life of the land is established in righteousness — motto of Hawaii

über alles [G] : above everything else

ue·ber·mensch \'ē-bər-ı̣mensh\ [G] : superman

ul·ti·ma ra·tio re·gum \'u̇l-ti-mä-ı̣rä-tē-ō-'rä-gu̇m\ [L] : the final argument of kings, i.e., war

und so wei·ter \u̇nt-zō-'vī-tər\ [G] : and so on

uno ani·mo \'ü-nō-'ä-ni-ı̣mō\ [L] : with one mind : unanimously

ur·bi et or·bi \'u̇r-bē-ı̣et-'ȯr-bē\ [L] : to the city (Rome) and the world : to everyone

uti·le dul·ci \'ü-ti-le-'du̇l-ı̣kē\ [L] : the useful with the agreeable

ut in·fra \u̇t-'in-frä\ [L] : as below

ut su·pra \u̇t-'sü-prä\ [L] : as above

va·de re·tro me, Sa·ta·na \'wä-de-'rä-trō-ı̣mä-'sä-tä-ı̣nä\ [L] : get thee behind me, Satan

vae vic·tis \wī-'wik-ı̣tēs\ [L] : woe to the vanquished

va·ria lec·tio \'wär-ē-ä-'lek-tē-ı̣ō\ *pl* **va·ri·ae lec·ti·o·nes** \'wär-ē-ı̣ī-ı̣lek-tē-'ō-ı̣nās\ [L] : variant reading

va·ri·um et mu·ta·bi·le sem·per fe·mi·na \'wär-ē-u̇m-ı̣et-ı̣mü-'tä-bi-le-'sem-ı̣per-'fä-mi-nä\ [L] : woman is ever a fickle and changeable thing

ve·di Na·po·li e poi mo·ri \'vā-dē-'nä-pō-lē-ā-ı̣pȯ-ē-'mȯ-rē\ [It] : see Naples and then die

ve·ni, vi·di, vi·ci \'wä-nē-'wē-dē-'wē-kē\ [L] : I came, I saw, I conquered

ven·tre à terre \väⁿ-trä-ter\ [F] : belly to the ground : at very great speed

ver·ba·tim ac lit·te·ra·tim \wer-'bä-tim-ı̣äk-ı̣li-te-'rä-tim\ [L] : word for word and letter for letter

ver·bum sat sa·pi·en·ti est \'wer-bu̇m-'sät-ı̣sä-pē-'en-tē-'est\ [L] : a word to the wise is sufficient

vieux jeu \vyœ̄-zhœ̄\ [F] : old game : old hat

vin·cit om·nia ve·ri·tas \'wiŋ-ket-'ȯm-nē-ä-'wä-ri-ı̣täs\ [L] : truth conquers all things

vin·cu·lum ma·tri·mo·nii \'wiŋ-ku̇-lu̇m-ı̣mä-tri-'mō-nē-ı̣ē\ [L] : bond of marriage

vin du pays \vaⁿ-dǖ-pä-ē\ *or* **vin de pays** \vaⁿ-də-\ [F] : wine of the locality

vir·gi·ni·bus pu·e·ris·que \wir-'gi-ni-bu̇s-ı̣pu̇-e-'rēs-kwe\ [L] : for girls and boys

vir·go in·tac·ta \'vīr-ı̣gō-in-'täk-tä\ [L] : untouched virgin

vir·tu·te et ar·mis \wir-'tü-te-ı̣et-'är-mēs\ [L] : by valor and arms — motto of Mississippi

vis me·di·ca·trix na·tu·rae \'wēs-ı̣me-di-'kä-triks-nä-'tü-ı̣rī\ [L] : the healing power of nature

vive la dif·fé·rence \vēv-lä-dē-fä-räⁿs\ [F] : long live the difference (between the sexes)

vive la reine \vēv-lä-ren\ [F] : long live the queen

vive le roi \vēv-lə-rwä\ [F] : long live the king

vix·e·re for·tes an·te Aga·mem·no·na \wik-'sä-re-'fȯr-ı̣täs-ı̣än-te-ı̣ä-gä-'mem-nȯ-ı̣nä\ [L] : brave men lived before Agamemnon

vogue la ga·lère \vȯg-lä-gȧ-ler\ [F] : let the galley be kept rowing : keep on, whatever may happen

voi·là tout \vwȧ-lȧ-tü\ [F] : that's all

vox et prae·te·rea ni·hil \'wȯks-et-prī-'ter-e-ä-'ni-ı̣hil\ [L] : voice and nothing more

vox po·pu·li vox Dei \'wȯks-'pȯ-pü-ı̣lē-'wȯks-'de-ē\ [L] : the voice of the people is the voice of God

Wan·der·jahr \'vän-dər-ı̣yär\ [G] : year of wandering

wie geht's? \vē-'gäts\ [G] : how goes it?

wun·der·bar \'vu̇n-dər-ı̣bär\ [G] : wonderful

Biographical, Biblical, and Mythological Names

This section is a listing of the names of important figures from recorded history, biblical tradition, classical mythology, popular legend, and current events. Figures from the Bible, myth, or legend are clearly identified as such. In cases where figures have alternate names, they are entered under the name by which they are best known. The part of the name shown in boldface type is either the family name or the common shorter name for that figure. The dates following the name or pronunciation are the birth and death dates. Other dates in the entry refer to the dates of a particular office, honor, or achievement. Italicized names within an entry refer to a person's nickname, original name, title, or other name.

Aar·on \'ar-ən, 'er-\ brother of Moses and first high priest of the Hebrews in the Bible

Abel \'ā-bəl\ son of Adam and Eve and brother of Cain in the Bible

Abra·ham \'ā-brə-ˌham\ patriarch and founder of the Hebrew people in the Bible

Achil·les \ə-'kil-ēz\ Greek hero in the Trojan War in mythology

Ad·am \'ad-əm\ the first man in the Bible

Ad·ams \'ad-əmz\ Abigail 1744–1818 American writer; wife of John Adams

Adams John 1735–1826 2d president of the U.S. (1797–1801)

Adams John Quin·cy \'kwin-zē, 'kwin(t)-sē\ 1767–1848 6th president of the U.S. (1825–29); son of John and Abigail Adams

Adams Samuel 1722–1803 patriot in the American Revolutionary War

Ad·dams \'ad-əmz\ Jane 1860–1935 American social worker; Nobel Prize winner (1931)

Ado·nis \ə-'dän-əs, -'dō-nəs\ beautiful youth in Greek mythology who is loved by Aphrodite

Ae·ne·as \i-'nē-əs\ Trojan hero in Greek and Roman mythology

Ae·o·lus \'ē-ə-ləs\ god of the winds in Greek mythology

Aes·chy·lus \'es-kə-ləs, 'ēs-\ 525–456 B.C. Greek dramatist

Aes·cu·la·pi·us \ˌes-kyə-'lā-pē-əs\ god of medicine in Roman mythology — compare ASCLEPIUS

Ae·sop \'ē-ˌsäp, -səp\ legendary Greek writer of fables

Ag·a·mem·non \ˌag-ə-'mem-ˌnän, -nən\ leader of the Greeks during the Trojan War in Greek mythology

Ag·nes \'ag-nəs\ Saint died 304 A.D. Christian martyr

Ahab \'ā-ˌhab\ king of Israel in the 9th century B.C. and husband of Jezebel

Ajax \'ā-ˌjaks\ hero in Greek mythology who kills himself because the armor of Achilles is awarded to Odysseus during the Trojan War

Alad·din \ə-'lad-ᵊn\ youth in the *Arabian Nights' Entertainments* who comes into possession of a magic lamp and ring

Al·cott \'ȯl-kət, 'al-, -ˌkät\ Louisa May 1832–1888 American author

Al·ex·an·der \ˌal-ig-'zan-dər, ˌel-\ name of eight popes: especially VI (Rodrigo Borgia) 1431–1503 (pope 1492–1503)

Alexander III of Macedon 356–323 B.C. *the Great* king (336–323)

Al·fred \'al-frəd, -fərd\ 849–899 *the Great* king of the West Saxons (871–899)

Ali Ba·ba \ˌal-ē-'bäb-ə\ a woodcutter in the *Arabian Nights' Entertainments* who enters the cave of the Forty Thieves by using the password *Sesame*

Al·len \'al-ən\ Ethan 1738–1789 American Revolutionary soldier

Amerigo Vespucci — see VESPUCCI

Am·herst \'am-(ˌ)ərst\ Jeffrey 1717–1797 *Baron Amherst* British general in America

Amund·sen \'äm-ən-sən\ Roald 1872–1928 Norwegian explorer and discoverer of the South Pole (1911)

An·a·ni·as \ˌan-ə-'nī-əs\ early Christian struck dead for lying

An·der·sen \'an-dər-sən\ Hans Christian 1805–1875 Danish writer of fairy tales

An·der·son \'an-dər-sən\ Marian 1897–1993 American contralto

Anne \'an\ 1665–1714 queen of Great Britain (1702–14)

An·tho·ny \'an(t)-thə-nē\ Susan Brownell 1820–1906 American suffragist

An·tig·o·ne \an-'tig-ə-nē\ daughter of Oedipus and Jocasta in Greek mythology

An·to·ni·us \an-'tō-nē-əs\ Marcus *about* 82–30 B.C. *Mark* or *Marc An·to·ny* or *An·tho·ny* \'an(t)-thə-nē, -tə-nē\ Roman general

Aph·ro·di·te \ˌaf-rə-'dīt-ē\ goddess of love and beauty in Greek mythology — compare VENUS

Apol·lo \ə-'päl-ō\ god of sunlight, prophecy, music, and poetry in Greek and Roman mythology

Aqui·nas \ə-'kwī-nəs\ Saint Thomas 1224 (or 1225)–1274 Italian theologian

Ar·chi·me·des \ˌär-kə-'mēd-ēz\ *about* 287–212 B.C. Greek mathematician

Ares \'a(ə)r-ēz, 'e(ə)r-\ god of war in Greek mythology — compare MARS

Ar·is·toph·a·nes \ˌar-ə-'stäf-ə-ˌnēz\ *about* 450–*about* 388 B.C. Greek dramatist

Ar·is·tot·le \'ar-ə-ˌstät-ᵊl\ 384–322 B.C. Greek philosopher

Arm·strong \'ärm-ˌstrȯŋ\ Louis 1901–1971 *Satchmo* \'sach-ˌmō\ American jazz musician

Armstrong Neil Alden 1930– American astronaut and first man on the moon (1969)

Ar·nold \'ärn-ᵊld\ Benedict 1741–1801 American Revolutionary general and traitor

Ar·te·mis \'ärt-ə-məs\ goddess of the moon, wild animals, and hunting in Greek mythology — compare DIANA

Ar·thur \'är-thər\ legendary king of the Britons whose story is based on traditions of a 6th century military leader — **Ar·thu·ri·an** \är-'th(y)ùr-ē-ən\ *adj*

Arthur Chester Alan 1829–1886 21st president of the U.S. (1881–85)

As·cle·pi·us \ə-'sklē-pē-əs\ god of medicine in Greek mythology — compare AESCULAPIUS

As·tor \'as-tər\ John Jacob 1763–1848 American (German-born) fur trader and capitalist

Athe·na \ə-'thē-nə\ *or* **Athe·ne** \-nē\ goddess of wisdom in Greek mythology — compare MINERVA

At·las \'at-ləs\ Titan in Greek mythology forced to bear the heavens on his shoulders

At·ti·la \ə-'til-ə, 'at-ᵊl-ə\ 406?–453 A.D. *the Scourge of God* king of the Huns

Biographical, Biblical, and Mythological Names   734

At•tucks \'at-əks\ Crispus 1723?–1770 American patriot; one of five men killed in Boston Massacre

Au•du•bon \'ȯd-ə-₁bän, -bən\ John James 1785–1851 American (Haitian-born) artist and naturalist

Au•gus•tine \'ȯ-gə-₁stēn; ȯ-'gəs-tən, ə-\ Saint 354–430 A.D. church father; bishop of Hippo (396–430)

Au•gus•tus \ȯ-'gəs-təs, ə-\ or Augustus Caesar or Oc•ta•vi•an \äk-'tā-vē-ən\ 63 B.C.–14 A.D. 1st Roman emperor (27 B.C.–14 A.D.)

Aus•ten \'ȯs-tən, 'äs-\ Jane 1775–1817 English author

Bac•chus \'bak-əs\ — see DIONYSUS

Bach \'bäk, 'bäk\ Johann Sebastian 1685–1750 German composer and organist

Ba•con \'bā-kən\ Francis 1561–1626 English philosopher and author

Ba•den–Pow•ell \₁bād-ᵊn-'pō-əl\ Robert Stephenson Smyth 1857–1941 English founder of Boy Scout movement

Baf•fin \'baf-ən\ William about 1584–1622 English navigator

Bal•boa, de \bal-'bō-ə\ Vasco Núñez 1475–1519 Spanish explorer and first European to sight Pacific Ocean (1513)

Bal•ti•more \'bȯl-tə-₁mō(ə)r, -₁mȯ(ə)r\ Lord — see George CALVERT

Bal•zac, de \'bȯl-₁zak, 'bal-\ Honoré 1799–1850 French author

Ba•rab•bas \bə-'rab-əs\ prisoner released in preference to Jesus at the demand of the multitude

Bar•num \'bär-nəm\ Phineas Taylor 1810–1891 American show-business manager

Bar•rie \'bar-ē\ Sir James Matthew 1860–1937 Scottish author

Bar•thol•di \bär-'täl-dē, -'tȯl-, -'thäl-, -'thȯl-\ Frédéric-Auguste 1834–1904 French sculptor who designed the Statue of Liberty

Bar•ton \'bärt-ᵊn\ Clara 1821–1912 founder of American Red Cross Society

Beau•re•gard \'bōr-ə-₁gärd, 'bȯr-\ Pierre Gustave Toutant 1818–1893 American Confederate general

Beck•et, à \ə-'bek-ət, ä-\ Saint Thomas about 1118–1170 archbishop of Canterbury (1162–1170)

Bee•tho•ven \'bā-₁tō-vən\ Ludwig van 1770–1827 German composer

Bell \'bel\ Alexander Graham 1847–1922 American (Scottish-born) inventor of the telephone

Ben•e•dict \'ben-ə-₁dikt\ name of 15 popes: especially XIV (Prospero Lambertini) 1675–1758 (pope 1740–58); XV (Giacomo della Chiesa) 1854–1922 (pope 1914–22)

Be•nét \bə-'nā\ Stephen Vincent 1898–1943 American author

Ben•ja•min \'benj-(ə-)mən\ youngest son of Jacob and ancestor of one of the 12 tribes of Israel in the Bible

Ben•ton \'bent-ᵊn\ Thomas Hart 1889–1975 American painter

Be•o•wulf \'bā-ə-₁wùlf\ legendary warrior and hero of the Old English poem Beowulf

Be•ring \'bi(ə)r-iŋ, 'be(ə)r-\ Vitus 1681–1741 Danish navigator; explored Bering sea and strait for Russia

Ber•lin \(₁)bər-'lin\ Irving 1888–1989 American (Russian-born) composer

Ber•ni•ni \bər-'nē-nē\ Gian Lorenzo 1598–1680 Italian sculptor, architect, and painter

Bes•se•mer \'bes-ə-mər\ Sir Henry 1813–1898 English engineer and inventor

Be•thune \bə-'th(y)ün\ Mary 1875–1955 née McLeod American educator

Bi•zet \bē-'zā\ Alexandre-César-Léopold 1838–1875 called Georges French composer

Black Hawk \'blak-₁hȯk\ 1767–1838 American Indian chief

Black•well \'blak-₁wel, -wəl\ Elizabeth 1821–1910 American (English-born) physician

Blake \'blāk\ William 1757–1827 English poet and artist

Bloom•er \'blü-mər\ Amelia Jenks 1818–1894 American social reformer

Boc•cac•cio \bō-'käch-(ē-₁)ō\ Giovanni 1313–1375 Italian author

Bohr \'bō(ə)r, 'bȯ(ə)r\ Niels 1885–1962 Danish physicist; Nobel prize winner (1922)

Bo•leyn \bù-'lin, 'bùl-ən\ Anne 1507?–1536 2d wife of Henry VIII and mother of Elizabeth I of England

Bo•lí•var \si-'mȯn \sē-₁mōn-bə-'lē-₁vär, ₁sī-mən-'bäl-ə-vər\ 1783–1830 South American liberator

Bon•i•face \'bän-ə-fəs, -₁fās\ name of nine popes: especially VIII (Benedetto Caetani) about 1235 (or 1240)–1303 (pope 1294–1303)

Boone \'bün\ Daniel 1734–1820 American pioneer

Booth \'büth\ John Wilkes 1838–1865 assassin of Abraham Lincoln

Bo•re•as \'bōr-ē-əs, 'bȯr-\ god of the north wind in Greek mythology

Bot•ti•cel•li \₁bät-ə-'chel-ē\ Sandro 1445–1510 Italian painter

Bow•ie \'bü-ē, 'bō-\ James 1796–1836 hero of Texas revolution

Boyle \'bȯi(ə)l\ Robert 1627–1691 English physicist and chemist

Brad•bury \'brad-₁ber-ē, -b(ə-)rē\ Ray Douglas 1920– American author

Brad•dock \'brad-ək\ Edward 1695–1755 British general in America

Brad•ford \'brad-fərd\ William 1590–1657 Pilgrim leader

Brad•street \'brad-₁strēt\ Anne about 1612–1672 American poet

Bra•dy \'brād-ē\ Mathew B. 1823?–1896 American photographer

Brah•ma \'bräm-ə\ creator god of the Hindu sacred triad — compare SIVA, VISHNU

Brahms \'brämz\ Johannes 1833–1897 German composer

Braille \'brā(ə)l, 'brī\ Louis 1809–1852 French blind teacher of the blind

Braun \'braùn\ Wernher von 1912–1977 American (German-born) engineer

Brezh•nev \'brezh-₁nef\ Leonid Ilyich 1906–1982 Russian politician; 1st secretary of Communist party (1964–82); president of the U.S.S.R. (1960–64; 1977–82)

Brid•ger \'brij-ər\ James 1804–1881 American pioneer and scout

Bron•të \'bränt-ē, 'brän-₁tā\ family of English writers: Charlotte 1816–1855 and her sisters Emily 1818–1848 and Anne 1820–1849

Brooks \'brùks\ Gwendolyn Elizabeth 1917– American poet

Brown \'braùn\ John Old Brown of Osa•wat•o•mie \₁ō-sə-'wät-ə-mē\ 1800–1859 American abolitionist

Brow•ning \'braù-niŋ\ Elizabeth Barrett 1806–1861 English poet; wife of Robert

Browning Robert 1812–1889 English poet; husband of Elizabeth

Bru•tus \'brüt-əs\ Marcus Junius 85–42 B.C. Roman politician; one of Julius Caesar's assassins

Bry•an \'brī-ən\ William Jennings 1860–1925 American lawyer and politician

Bu•chan•an \byü-'kan-ən, bə-\ James 1791–1868 15th president of the U.S. (1857–61)

Buck \'bək\ Pearl 1892–1973 American author; Nobel Prize winner (1938)

Buddha — see GAUTAMA BUDDHA

Buffalo Bill — see William Frederick CODY

Bun•yan \'bən-yən\ John 1628–1688 English preacher and author

Bur•bank \'bər-₁baŋk\ Luther 1849–1926 American horticulturist

Bur•goyne \(₁)bər-'gȯin, 'bər-₁gȯin\ John 1722–1792 British general in America

Burns \'bərnz\ Robert 1759–1796 Scottish poet

Burn·side \\'bərn-₁sīd\\ Ambrose Everett 1824–1881 American general

Burr \\'bər\\ Aaron 1756–1836 vice president of the U.S. (1801–05)

Bush \\'bush\\ George Herbert Walker 1924–   41st president of the U.S. (1989–93)

By·ron \\'bī-rən\\ Lord 1788–1824 *George Gordon Byron* English poet

Cab·ot \\'kab-ət\\ John *about* 1450–*about* 1499 Italian navigator; explored coast of North America for England

Cabot Sebastian 1476?–1557 English navigator; son of John Cabot

Ca·bri·ni \\kə-'brē-nē\\ Saint Frances Xavier 1850–1917 *Mother Cabrini* first American (Italian-born) saint (1946)

Cae·sar \\'sē-zər\\ Gaius Julius 100–44 B.C. Roman general, political leader, and writer

Cain \\'kān\\ brother of Abel in the Bible

Cal·houn \\kal-'hün\\ John Caldwell 1782–1850 vice president of the U.S. (1825–32)

Ca·lig·u·la \\kə-'lig-yə-lə\\ 12–41 A.D. *Gaius Caesar* Roman emperor (37–41)

Cal·li·ope \\kə-'lī-ə-₁pē\\ muse of heroic poetry in Greek mythology

Cal·vert \\'kal-vərt\\ George 1580?–1632 1st Baron *Baltimore* English colonist in America

Cal·vin \\'kal-vən\\ John 1509–1564 French theologian and reformer

Ca·nute \\kə-'n(y)üt\\ *died* 1035 *the Great* king of England (1016–35); of Denmark (1018–35); of Norway (1028–35)

Car·ne·gie \\'kär-nə-gē, kär-'neg-ē\\ Andrew 1835–1919 American (Scottish-born) industrialist and philanthropist

Carroll Lewis — see Charles Lutwidge DODGSON

Car·son \\'kärs-ᵊn\\ Christopher 1809–1868 *Kit* American soldier and guide

Carson Rachel Louise 1907–1964 American scientist

Car·ter \\'kärt-ər\\ James Earl, Jr. 1924–   *Jimmy* 39th president of the U.S. (1977–81)

Car·tier \\kär-'tyā, 'kärt-ē-₁ā\\ Jacques 1491–1557 French navigator; explored Saint Lawrence river

Ca·ru·so \\kə-'rü-sō, -zō\\ En·ri·co \\en-'rē-kō\\ 1873–1921 Italian tenor

Car·ver \\'kär-vər\\ George Washington *about* 1864–1943 American botanist

Ca·sa·no·va \\₁kaz-ə-'nō-və, ₁kas-\\ Giovanni Giacomo 1725–1798 Italian adventurer

Cas·san·dra \\kə-'san-drə\\ daughter of Priam in Greek mythology who is endowed with the gift of prophecy but fated never to be believed

Cas·satt \\kə-'sat\\ Mary 1845–1926 American painter

Cas·tro \\'kas-trō, 'käs-\\ **(Ruz)** \\'rüs\\ Fi·del \\fē-'del\\ 1926–   Cuban premier (1959–)

Cath·er \\'kath-ər\\ Willa Sibert 1873–1947 American author

Cath·er·ine \\'kath-(ə-)rən\\ name of 1st, 5th, and 6th wives of Henry VIII of England: Catherine of Aragon 1485–1536; Catherine Howard 1520?–1542; Catherine Parr 1512–1548

Catherine I 1684–1727 wife of Peter the Great; empress of Russia (1725–27)

Catherine II 1729–1796 *the Great* empress of Russia (1762–96)

Cav·en·dish \\'kav-ən-(₁)dish\\ Henry 1731–1810 English scientist

Ce·ci·lia \\sə-'sēl-yə, -'sil-\\ Saint 2d or 3d century A.D. Roman martyr; patron saint of music

Ce·res \\'si(ə)r-₁ēz\\ the goddess of agriculture in Roman mythology — compare DEMETER

Cer·van·tes \\sər-'van-₁tēz\\ Miguel de 1547–1616 Spanish author

Cé·zanne \\sā-'zan\\ Paul 1839–1906 French painter

Cha·gall \\shə-'gäl, -'gal\\ Marc 1887–1985 Russian painter

Cham·plain \\(')sham-'plān\\ Samuel de *about* 1567–1635 French explorer in America; founder of Quebec

Chap·lin \\'chap-lən\\ Sir Charles Spencer 1889–1977 British actor and producer

Chap·man \\'chap-mən\\ John 1774–1845 *Johnny Appleseed* \\'ap-əl-₁sēd\\ American pioneer

Char·le·magne \\'shär-lə-₁mān\\ 742–814 A.D. *Charles the Great* or *Charles I* Frankish king (768–814); emperor of the West (800–814)

Charles \\'chär(-ə)lz\\ name of 10 kings of France: especially **I** 823–877 A.D. (reigned 840–77) *the Bald*; Holy Roman emperor as *Charles II* (875–77); **IV** 1294–1328 (reigned 1322–28) *the Fair*; **V** 1337–1380 (reigned 1364–80) *the Wise*; **VI** 1368–1422 (reigned 1380–1422) *the Mad* or *the Beloved*; **VII** 1403–1461 (reigned 1422–61) *the Victorious*; **IX** 1550–1574 (reigned 1560–74); **X** 1757–1836 (reigned 1824–30)

Charles name of two kings of Great Britain: **I** 1600–1649 (reigned 1625–49) *Charles Stuart*; **II** 1630–1685 (reigned 1660–85) son of Charles I

Charles V 1500–1558 Holy Roman emperor (1519–56); king of Spain as *Charles I* (1516–56)

Charles Edward Stuart 1720–1788 *the Young Pretender*; *(Bonnie) Prince Charlie* English prince

Charles Mar·tel \\mär-'tel\\ *about* 688–741 A.D. Frankish ruler (719–41); grandfather of Charlemagne

Cha·ryb·dis \\kə-'rib-dəs, shə-, chə-\\ a whirlpool off the coast of Sicily personified in Greek mythology as a female monster

Chau·cer \\'chȯ-sər\\ Geoffrey *about* 1342–1400 English poet

Che·khov \\'chek-₁ȯf, -₁ȯv\\ Anton Pavlovich 1860–1904 Russian author

Cheops — see KHUFU

Ches·ter·ton \\'ches-tərt-ᵊn\\ Gilbert Keith 1874–1936 English author

Cho·pin \\'shō-₁pan\\ Frédéric François 1810–1849 Polish pianist and composer

Chou En·lai \\'jō-'en-'lī\\ 1898–1976 Chinese Communist politician; premier (1949–76)

Christ Jesus — see JESUS

Chris·tie \\'kris-tē\\ Agatha 1890–1976 English author

Chur·chill \\'chər-₁chil, 'chərch-₁hil\\ Sir Winston Leonard Spencer 1874–1965 British prime minister (1940–45; 1951–55)

Clark \\'klärk\\ George Rogers 1752–1818 American soldier and pioneer

Clark William 1770–1838 American explorer

Clay \\'klā\\ Henry 1777–1852 American politician and orator

Clem·ens \\'klem-ənz\\ Samuel Langhorne 1835–1910 pseudonym *Mark Twain* \\'twān\\ American author

Cle·o·pa·tra \\₁klē-ə-'pa-trə, -'pä-, -'pä-\\ 69–30 B.C. queen of Egypt (51–30)

Cleve·land \\'klēv-lənd\\ (Stephen) Grover 1837–1908 22d and 24th president of the U.S. (1885–89; 1893–97)

Clin·ton \\'klin-tᵊn\\ William Jefferson 1946–   42d president of the U.S. (1993–)

Cly·tem·nes·tra \\₁klīt-əm-'nes-trə\\ wife of Agamemnon in Greek mythology

Cobb \\'käb\\ Tyrus Raymond 1886–1961 *Ty* American baseball player

Co·chise \\kō-'chēs\\ 1812?–1874 Apache chief

Co·dy \\'kōd-ē\\ William Frederick 1846–1917 *Buffalo Bill* American hunter, guide, and entertainer

Co·han \\'kō-₁han\\ George Michael 1878–1942 American actor and composer

Cole·ridge \\'kōl-rij, 'kō-lə-rij\\ Samuel Taylor 1772–1834 English poet

Co·lette \\kȯ-'let\\ Sidonie-Gabrielle 1873–1954 French author

Co·lum·bus \\kə-'ləm-bəs\\ Christopher 1451–1506 Genoese navigator; discovered America for Spain (1492)

Con·fu·cius \\kən-'fyü-shəs\\ 551–479 B.C. Chinese philosopher

Con·rad \\'kän-₁rad\\ Joseph 1857–1924 British (Ukrainian-born of Polish parents) author

Con·sta·ble \\'kən(t)-stə-bəl, 'kän(t)-\\ John 1776–1837 English painter

Con·stan·tine \\'kän(t)-stən-₁tēn, -₁tīn\\ *died* 337 A.D. *the Great* Roman emperor (306–37)

Cook \\'kúk\\ Captain James 1728–1779 English navigator

Coo·lidge \\'kü-lij\\ (John) Calvin 1872–1933 30th president of the U.S. (1923–29)

Coo·per \\'kü-pər, 'kúp-ər\\ James Fen·i·more \\'fen-ə-₁mō(ə)r, -₁mò(ə)r\\ 1789–1851 American author

Co·per·ni·cus \\kō-'pər-ni-kəs\\ Nicolaus 1473–1543 Polish astronomer

Cop·land \\'kō-plənd\\ Aaron 1900–1990 American composer

Cop·ley \\'käp-lē\\ John Sin·gle·ton \\'siŋ-gəl-tən\\ 1738–1815 American portrait painter

Corn·wal·lis \\kòrn-'wäl-əs\\ 1st Marquis 1738–1805 *Charles Cornwallis* British general in America

Co·ro·na·do \\₁kòr-ə-'näd-ō, ₁kär-\\ Francisco Vásquez de *about* 1510–1554 Spanish explorer of southwestern U.S.

Cor·tés \\kòr-'tez, 'kòr-₁tez\\ Hernán *or* Hernando 1485–1547 Spanish conqueror of Mexico

Cous·teau \\kü-'stō\\ Jacques-Yves 1910–1997 French marine explorer

Crane \\'krān\\ Stephen 1871–1900 American author

Crazy Horse \\'krā-zē-₁hòrs\\ 1842–1877 Sioux chief

Crock·ett \\'kräk-ət\\ David 1786–1836 *Davy* American pioneer

Crom·well \\'kräm-₁wel, 'krəm-, -wəl\\ Oliver 1599–1658 English general and political leader; lord protector of England (1653–58)

Cro·nus \\'krō-nəs, 'krän-əs\\ a Titan in Greek mythology overthrown by his son Zeus

Cum·mings \\'kəm-iŋz\\ Edward Estlin 1894–1962 known as *e. e. cummings* American poet

Cu·pid \\'kyü-pəd\\ god of love in Roman mythology — compare EROS

Cu·rie \\kyù-'rē, 'kyü(ə)r-ē\\ Marie 1867–1934 French (Polish-born) chemist; Nobel Prize winner (1903, 1911)

Curie Pierre 1859–1906 French chemist; Nobel Prize winner (1903)

Cus·ter \\'kəs-tər\\ George Armstrong 1839–1876 American general

Cy·ra·no de Ber·ge·rac \\₁sir-ə-₁nō-də-'ber-zhə-₁rak\\ Savinien de 1619–1655 French poet and soldier

Dae·da·lus \\'ded-əl-əs, 'dēd-\\ builder in Greek mythology of the Cretan labyrinth and inventor of wings by which he and his son Icarus escape from it

Dal·ton \\'dòlt-ᵊn\\ John 1766–1844 English chemist and physicist

Da·na \\'dā-nə\\ Richard Henry 1815–1882 American author

Dan·iel \\'dan-yəl\\ a prophet in the Bible who is held captive in Babylon and delivered by God from a den of lions

Dan·te \\'dän-tā, 'dan-, -tē\\ 1265–1321 Italian poet

Dare \\'da(ə)r, 'de(ə)r\\ Virginia 1587–? first child born in America of English parents

Da·ri·us I \\də-'rī-əs\\ 550–486 B.C. *the Great* king of Persia (522–486)

Dar·row \\'dar-ō\\ Clarence Seward 1857–1938 American lawyer

Dar·win \\'där-wən\\ Charles Robert 1809–1882 English naturalist

Da·vid \\'dā-vəd\\ a youth in the Bible who slays Goliath and succeeds Saul as king of Israel

Da·vis \\'dā-vəs\\ Jefferson 1808–1889 president of the Confederate States of America (1861–65)

Dawes \\'dòz\\ William 1745–1799 American patriot

Debs \\'debz\\ Eugene Victor 1855–1926 American socialist

De·bus·sy \\₁deb-yü-'sē, ₁dāb-; də-'byü-sē\\ (Achille-) Claude 1862–1918 French composer

De·ca·tur \\di-'kāt-ər\\ Stephen 1779–1820 American naval officer

De·foe \\di-'fō\\ Daniel 1660–1731 English author

De·gas \\də-'gä\\ (Hilaire-Germain-) Edgar 1834–1917 French painter

de Gaulle \\di-'gōl, -'gòl\\ Charles-André-Joseph-Marie 1890–1970 French general; president of Fifth Republic (1958–69)

De·li·lah \\di-'lī-lə\\ mistress and betrayer of Samson in the Bible

De·me·ter \\di-'mēt-ər\\ goddess of agriculture in Greek mythology — compare CERES

de Mille \\də-'mil\\ Agnes George 1905–1993 American dancer and choreographer

Des·cartes \\dā-'kärt\\ René 1596–1650 French mathematician and philosopher

de So·to \\di-'sōt-ō\\ Hernando 1496 (or 1499 or 1500)–1542 Spanish explorer in America

Dew·ey \\'d(y)ü-ē\\ George 1837–1917 American admiral

Dewey John 1859–1952 American philosopher and educator

Dewey Melvil 1851–1931 American librarian

Di·ana \\dī-'an-ə\\ goddess of the forest and of childbirth in ancient Italian mythology who was identified with Artemis by the Romans

Dick·ens \\'dik-ənz\\ Charles John Huffam 1812–1870 pseudonym *Boz* \\'bäz, 'bōz\\ English author

Dick·in·son \\'dik-ən-sən\\ Emily Elizabeth 1830–1886 American poet

Di·do \\'dīd-ō\\ legendary queen of Carthage who falls in love with Aeneas and kills herself when he leaves her

Di·o·ny·sus \\₁dī-ə-'nī-səs, -'nē-\\ god of wine and ecstasy in Greek mythology — called also *Bacchus* — **Di·o·ny·sian** \\dī-ə-'nizh-ē-ən\\ *adj*

Dis·ney \\'diz-nē\\ Walter Elias 1901–1966 American film producer

Dis·rae·li \\diz-'rā-lē\\ Benjamin 1804–1881 1st Earl of *Bea·cons·field* \\'bē-kənz-₁fēld\\ British prime minister (1868; 1874–80)

Dix \\'diks\\ Dorothea Lynde 1802–1887 American social reformer

Dodg·son \\'däj-sən, 'däd-\\ Charles Lut·widge \\'lət-wij\\ 1832–1898 pseudonym *Lewis Car·roll* \\'kar-əl\\ English author and mathematician

Donne \\'dən\\ John 1572–1631 English poet and minister

Don Qui·xote \\₁dän-kē-'(h)ōt-ē, ₁däŋ-; dän-'kwik-sət\\ the idealistic and impractical hero of Cervantes' *Don Quixote*

Dos·to·yev·ski \\₁däs-tə-'yef-skē, -'yev-\\ Fyodor Mikhaylovich 1821–1881 Russian novelist

Doug·las \\'dəg-ləs\\ Stephen Arnold 1813–1861 American politician

Doug·lass \\'dəg-ləs\\ Frederick 1817–1895 American abolitionist

Doyle \\'dòi(ə)l\\ Sir Arthur Co·nan \\'kō-nən\\ 1859–1930 British physician, novelist, and detective-story writer

Drake \\'drāk\\ Sir Francis 1540 (or 1543)–1596 English navigator and admiral

Drei·ser \\'drī-sər, -zər\\ Theodore 1871–1945 American author

Du Bois \\d(y)ü-'bòis\\ William Edward Burghardt 1868–1963 American educator and writer

Du·mas \\d(y)ü-'mä, 'd(y)ü-₁mä\\ Alexandre 1802–1870 *Dumas père* \\'pe(ə)r\\ French author

Dumas Alexandre 1824–1895 *Dumas fils* \\'fēs\\ French author

Dun·can \\'dəŋ-kən\\ Isadora 1877–1927 American dancer

Dü·rer \\'d(y)ùr-ər\\ Albrecht 1471–1528 German painter and engraver

Ea·kins \\'ā-kənz\\ Thomas 1844–1916 American artist

Ear·hart \\'e(ə)r-ˌhärt, -'i(ə)r-\\ Amelia 1897–1937 American aviator

Ed·dy \\'ed-ē\\ Mary Baker 1821–1910 American founder of the Christian Science Church

Ed·i·son \\'ed-ə-sən\\ Thomas Alva 1847–1931 American inventor

Ed·ward \\'ed-wərd\\ name of eight post-Norman kings of England: **I** 1239–1307 (reigned 1272–1307) *Longshanks*; **II** 1284–1327 (reigned 1307–27); **III** 1312–1377 (reigned 1327–77); **IV** 1442–1483 (reigned 1461–70; 1471–83); **V** 1470–1483 (reigned 1483); **VI** 1537–1553 (reigned 1547–53) son of Henry VIII and Jane Seymour; **VII** 1841–1910 (reigned 1901–10) *Albert Edward* son of Queen Victoria; **VIII** 1894–1972 (reigned 1936; abdicated) *Duke of Windsor* son of George V

Ein·stein \\'īn-ˌstīn\\ Albert 1879–1955 American (German-born) physicist; Nobel Prize winner (1921)

Ei·sen·how·er \\'īz-ᵊn-ˌhaů(-ə)r\\ Dwight David 1890–1969 American general; 34th president of the U.S. (1953–61)

Elec·tra \\i-'lek-trə\\ sister of Orestes in Greek mythology who with her brother avenges their father's murder

Eli·jah \\i-'lī-jə\\ Hebrew prophet of the 9th century B.C.

El·iot \\'el-ē-ət, 'el-yət\\ George 1819–1880 pseudonym of *Mary Ann Evans* English author

Eliot Thomas Stearns 1888–1965 British (American-born) poet and critic

Eliz·a·beth I \\i-'liz-ə-bəth\\ 1533–1603 daughter of Henry VIII and Anne Boleyn; queen of England (1558–1603)

Elizabeth II 1926–   queen of the United Kingdom (1952–)

Em·er·son \\'em-ər-sən\\ Ralph Waldo 1803–1882 American essayist and poet

En·dym·i·on \\en-'dim-ē-ən\\ beautiful youth in Greek mythology loved by the goddess of the moon

Ep·i·cu·rus \\ep-i-'kyúr-əs\\ 341–270 B.C. Greek philosopher

Er·ik \\'er-ik\\ *the Red* 10th century Norwegian navigator; explored Greenland coast

Eriksson Leif — see LEIF ERIKSSON

Eros \\'e(ə)r-ˌäs, 'i(ə)r-\\ god of love in Greek mythology — compare CUPID

Esau \\'ē-(ˌ)sȯ\\ son of Isaac and Rebekah and elder twin brother of Jacob in the Bible

Es·ther \\'es-tər\\ Hebrew woman in the Bible who as the queen of Persia delivers her people from destruction

Eu·clid \\'yü-kləd\\ *flourished about* 300 B.C. Greek mathematician

Eu·rip·i·des \\yu-'rip-ə-ˌdēz\\ *about* 484–406 B.C. Greek dramatist

Eu·ro·pa \\yu-'rō-pə\\ a princess in Greek mythology who was carried off by Zeus disguised as a white bull

Eu·ryd·i·ce \\yü-'rid-ə-sē\\ the wife of Orpheus whom he attempts to bring back from Hades

Eve \\'ēv\\ the first woman in the Bible

Eze·kiel \\i-'zē-kyəl, -kē-əl\\ Hebrew prophet of the 6th century B.C.

Fahr·en·heit \\'far-ən-ˌhīt, 'fär-\\ Daniel Gabriel 1686–1736 German physicist

Far·a·day \\'far-ə-ˌdā, -əd-ē\\ Michael 1791–1867 English chemist and physicist

Far·ra·gut \\'far-ə-gət\\ David Glasgow 1801–1870 American admiral

Faulk·ner \\'fȯk-nər\\ William 1897–1962 American author; Nobel Prize winner (1949)

Faust \\'faůst\\ *or* **Fau·stus** \\'faů-stəs, 'fȯ-\\ a legendary German magician who sells his soul to the devil

Fawkes \\'fȯks\\ Guy 1570–1606 English conspirator

Fer·di·nand \\'fərd-ᵊn-ˌand\\ **II** of Aragon *or* **V** of Castile 1452–1516 *the Catholic* king of Castile (1474–1504); of Aragon (1479–1516); of Naples (1504–16); founder of the Spanish monarchy

Fer·mi \\'fe(ə)r-mē\\ Enrico 1901–1954 American (Italian-born) physicist; Nobel Prize winner (1938)

Field·ing \\'fē(ə)l-diŋ\\ Henry 1707–1754 English author

Fill·more \\'fil-ˌmō(ə)r, -ˌmȯ(ə)r\\ Millard 1800–1874 13th president of the U.S. (1850–53)

Fitz·ger·ald \\fits-'jer-əld\\ Francis Scott Key 1896–1940 American author

Flem·ing \\'flem-iŋ\\ Sir Alexander 1881–1955 British bacteriologist; Nobel Prize winner (1945)

Flo·ra \\'flōr-ə, 'flȯr-\\ goddess of flowers in Roman mythology

Flying Dutchman legendary Dutch mariner condemned to sail the seas until Judgment Day

Ford \\'fō(ə)rd, 'fȯ(ə)rd\\ Gerald Rudolph 1913– 38th president of the U.S. (1974–77)

Ford Henry 1863–1947 American automobile manufacturer

Fos·ter \\'fȯs-tər, 'fäs-\\ Stephen Collins 1826–1864 American songwriter

Francis \\'fran(t)-səs\\ **of As·si·si** \\ə-'sis-ē, -'sis-ē, -'sē-zē, -'sē-sē, -'siz-ē\\ Saint 1181 (*or* 1182)–1226 Italian friar; founder of Franciscan order

Frank·lin \\'fraŋ-klən\\ Benjamin 1706–1790 American patriot, author, and inventor

Fred·er·ick I \\'fred-(ə-)rik\\ *about* 1123–1190 *Frederick Bar·ba·ros·sa* \\ˌbär-bə-'räs-ə, -'rȯs-\\ Holy Roman emperor (1152–90)

Frederick II 1712–1786 *the Great* king of Prussia (1740–86)

Fré·mont \\'frē-ˌmänt\\ John Charles 1813–1890 American general and explorer

French \\'french\\ Daniel Chester 1850–1931 American sculptor

Freud \\'frȯid\\ Sigmund 1856–1939 Austrian neurologist; founder of psychoanalysis

Frig·ga \\'frig-ə\\ wife of Odin and goddess of married love and the hearth in Norse mythology

Frost \\'frȯst\\ Robert Lee 1874–1963 American poet

Ful·ler \\'fůl-ər\\ (Richard) Buckminster 1895–1983 American engineer

Fuller (Sarah) Margaret 1810–1850 American author and reformer

Ful·ton \\'fúlt-ᵊn\\ Robert 1765–1815 American inventor

Ga·bri·el \\'gā-brē-əl\\ one of the four archangels named in Hebrew tradition — compare MICHAEL, RAPHAEL, URIEL

Ga·ga·rin \\gə-'gär-ən\\ Yu·ry \\'yü(ə)r-ē\\ Alekseyevich 1934–1968 Russian astronaut; first man in space

Gage \\'gāj\\ Thomas 1721–1787 British general in America

Gal·a·had \\'gal-ə-ˌhad\\ knight of the Round Table who finds the Holy Grail

Gal·a·tea \\ˌgal-ə-'tē-ə\\ a female figure sculpted by Pygmalion in Greek mythology and given life by Aphrodite in answer to the sculptor's prayer

Ga·len \\'gā-lən\\ 129–about 199 A.D. Greek physician and writer

Ga·li·le·i \\ˌgal-ə-'lā-ē\\ Ga·li·leo \\ˌgal-ə-'lē-ō, -'lā-\\ 1564–1642 usually called Galileo Italian astronomer and physicist — **Gal·i·le·an** \\ˌgal-ə-'lē-ən\\ adj

Gall \\'gȯl\\ 1840?–1894 Sioux leader

Ga·ma, da \\'gam-ə, 'gäm-\\ Vasco about 1460–1524 Portuguese navigator

Gan·dhi \\'gän-dē, 'gan-\\ Mohandas Karamchand 1869–1948 Ma·hat·ma \\mə-'hät-mə, -'hat-\\ Indian leader

Gar·field \\'gär-ˌfēld\\ James Abram 1831–1881 20th president of the U.S. (1881)

Gar·i·bal·di \\ˌgar-ə-'bȯl-dē\\ Giuseppe 1807–1882 Italian patriot

Gar·ri·son \\'gar-ə-sən\\ William Lloyd 1805–1879 American abolitionist

Gau·guin \\gō-gan\\ (Eugène-Henri-) Paul 1848–1903 French painter

Gau·ta·ma Bud·dha \\ˌgaùt-ə-mə-'büd-ə, -'bùd-\\ about 563–about 483 B.C. The Buddha Indian philosopher; founder of Buddhism

Gen·ghis Khan \\ˌjeŋ-gə-'skän, ˌgeŋ-\\ about 1162–1227 Mongol conqueror

George \\'jȯ(ə)rj\\ name of six kings of Great Britain: **I** 1660–1727 (reigned 1714–27); **II** 1683–1760 (reigned 1727–60); **III** 1738–1820 (reigned 1760–1820); **IV** 1762–1830 (reigned 1820–30); **V** 1865–1936 (reigned 1910–36); **VI** 1895–1952 (reigned 1936–52)

Ge·ron·i·mo \\jə-'rän-ə-ˌmō\\ 1829–1909 Apache leader

Gersh·win \\'gərsh-wən\\ George 1898–1937 American composer

Gid·e·on \\'gid-ē-ən\\ Hebrew hero in the Bible

Gil·bert \\'gil-bərt\\ Sir William Schwenck 1836–1911 English librettist and poet; collaborator with Sir Arthur Sullivan

Glad·stone \\'glad-ˌstōn, chiefly British -stən\\ William Ewart 1809–1898 British prime minister (1868–74; 1880–85; 1886; 1892–94)

Glenn \\'glen\\ John Herschel 1921– American astronaut and politician; first American to orbit the earth (1962)

Go·di·va \\gə-'dī-və\\ an English gentlewoman who in legend rode naked through Coventry to save its citizens from a tax

Goe·thals \\'gō-thəlz\\ George Washington 1858–1928 American general and engineer

Goe·the \\'gə(r)-tə\\ Johann Wolfgang von 1749–1832 German author

Gogh, van \\van-'gō, -'gäk, -'kȯk\\ Vincent Willem 1853–1890 Dutch painter

Go·li·ath \\gə-'lī-əth\\ Philistine giant who is killed by David in the Bible

Gom·pers \\'gäm-pərz\\ Samuel 1850–1924 American (British-born) labor leader

Good·year \\'gùd-ˌyi(ə)r, 'gùj-ˌi(ə)r\\ Charles 1800–1860 American inventor

Gor·gas \\'gȯr-gəs\\ William Crawford 1854–1920 American army surgeon

Gra·ham \\'grā-əm, 'gra(-ə)m\\ Martha 1893–1991 American dancer and choreographer

Grant \\'grant\\ Ulysses 1822–1885 originally Hiram Ulysses Grant American general; 18th president of the U.S. (1869–77)

Gre·co, El \\el-'grek-ō\\ 1541–1614 Doménikos Theotokópoulos Spanish (Cretan-born) painter

Gree·ley \\'grē-lē\\ Horace 1811–1872 American journalist and politician

Greene \\'grēn\\ Graham 1904–1991 British novelist

Greene Nathanael 1742–1786 American Revolutionary general

Greg·o·ry \\'greg-(ə-)rē\\ name of 16 popes: especially **I** Saint about 540–604 the Great (pope 590–604); **VII** Saint about 1020–1085 (pope 1073–85); **XIII** 1502–1585 (pope 1572–85)

Grey \\'grā\\ Lady Jane 1537–1554 English noblewoman beheaded as a possible rival for the throne of Mary I

Grey Zane 1875–1939 American novelist

Grimm \\'grim\\ Jacob 1785–1863 and his brother Wilhelm 1786–1859 German philologists and folklorists

Guin·e·vere \\'gwin-ə-ˌvi(ə)r\\ wife of King Arthur and lover of Lancelot

Gu·ten·berg \\'güt-ᵊn-ˌbərg\\ Johannes about 1390–1468 German inventor of printing from movable type

Ha·des \\'hād-ˌēz\\ — see PLUTO

Ha·dri·an \\'hā-drē-ən\\ 76–138 A.D. Roman emperor (117–138)

Ha·gar \\'hā-ˌgär, -gər\\ mistress of Abraham and mother of Ishmael in the Bible

Hai·le Se·las·sie \\hī-lē-sə-'las-ē, -'läs-\\ 1892–1975 emperor of Ethiopia (1930–36; 1941–74)

Hale \\'hā(ə)l\\ Edward Everett 1822–1909 American minister and author

Hale Nathan 1755–1776 American Revolutionary hero

Hal·ley \\'hal-ē, 'hā-lē\\ Edmond or Edmund 1656–1742 English astronomer

Hal·sey \\'hȯl-sē, -zē\\ William Frederick 1882–1959 American admiral

Ham·il·ton \\'ham-əl-tən\\ Alexander 1755–1804 American political leader

Ham·mu·ra·bi \\ham-ə-'räb-ē\\ or **Ham·mu·ra·pi** \\-'räp-ē\\ died 1750 B.C. king of Babylon (1792–50)

Han·cock \\'han-ˌkäk\\ John 1737–1793 American Revolutionary patriot

Han·del \\'han-dᵊl\\ George Frideric 1685–1759 British (German-born) composer

Han·dy \\'han-dē\\ William Christopher 1873–1958 American blues musician

Han·ni·bal \\'han-ə-bəl\\ 247–183 B.C. Carthaginian general

Har·ding \\'härd-iŋ\\ Warren Gamaliel 1865–1923 29th president of the U.S. (1921–23)

Har·dy \\'härd-ē\\ Thomas 1840–1928 English author

Har·ri·son \\'har-ə-sən\\ Benjamin 1833–1901 23d president of the U.S. (1889–93)

Harrison William Henry 1773–1841 9th president of the U.S. (1841)

Harte \\'härt\\ Francis Brett 1836–1902 known as Bret American author

Har·vey \\'här-vē\\ William 1578–1657 English physician and anatomist

Haw·thorne \\'hȯ-ˌthȯ(ə)rn\\ Nathaniel 1804–1864 American author

Hayes \\'hāz\\ Rutherford Birchard 1822–1893 19th president of the U.S. (1877–81)

Hearst \\'hərst\\ William Randolph 1863–1951 American newspaper publisher

Hec·tor \\'hek-tər\\ son of Priam and Trojan hero slain by Achilles in Greek mythology

Hec·u·ba \\'hek-yə-bə\\ wife of Priam in Greek mythology

Hel·en of Troy \\ˌhel-ə-nəv-'trȯi\\ wife of Menelaus whose abduction by Paris in Greek mythology caused the Trojan War

He·li·os \\'hē-lē-əs, -ōs\\ god of the sun in Greek mythology

Hem·ing·way \\'hem-iŋ-ıwä\\ Ernest Miller 1899–1961 American author; Nobel Prize winner (1954)

Hen·ry \\'hen-rē\\ name of eight kings of England: **I** 1068–1135 (reigned 1100–35); **II** 1133–1189 (reigned 1154–89); **III** 1207–1272 (reigned 1216–72); **IV** 1367–1413 (reigned 1399–1413); **V** 1387–1422 (reigned 1413–22); **VI** 1421–1471 (reigned 1422–61; 1470–71); **VII** 1457–1509 (reigned 1485–1509); **VIII** 1491–1547 (reigned 1509–47)

Henry name of 4 kings of France: **I** 1008–1060 (reigned 1031–60); **II** 1519–1559 (reigned 1547–59); **III** 1551–1589 (reigned 1574–89); **IV** 1553–1610 *Henry of Navarre* (reigned 1589–1610)

Henry O. — see William Sydney PORTER

Henry Patrick 1736–1799 American patriot and orator

He·phaes·tus \\hi-'fes-təs, -'fēs-\\ god of fire and of metalworking in Greek mythology — compare VULCAN

He·ra \\'hir-ə, 'hē-rə\\ sister and wife of Zeus and goddess of women and marriage in Greek mythology — compare JUNO

Her·cu·les \\'hər-kyə-ılēz\\ *or* **Her·a·cles** \\'her-ə-ıklēz\\ hero in Greek mythology noted for his strength and for performing 12 labors imposed on him by Hera

Her·maph·ro·di·tus \\(ı)hər-ımaf-rə-'dīt-əs\\ son of Hermes and Aphrodite who in Greek mythology is joined with a nymph into one body

Her·mes \\'hər-mēz\\ god of commerce, eloquence, invention, travel, and theft who serves as herald and messenger of the other gods in Greek mythology

Her·od \\'her-əd\\ 73–4 B.C. *the Great* Roman king of Judea (37–4)

Herod An·ti·pas \\'ant-ə-ıpas, -pəs\\ 21 B.C.–39 A.D. Roman governor of Galilee (4 B.C.–39 A.D.); son of Herod the Great

Hey·er·dahl \\'hā-ər-ıdäl, 'hī-\\ Thor 1914– Norwegian explorer and author

Hi·a·wa·tha \\ıhī-ə-'wȯ-thə, ıhē-ə-, -'wäth-ə\\ legendary Iroquois chief

Hick·ok \\'hik-ıäk\\ James Butler 1837–1876 *Wild Bill* American scout and United States marshal

Hil·ton \\'hilt-ᵊn\\ James 1900–1954 English novelist

Hip·poc·ra·tes \\hip-'äk-rə-ıtēz\\ *about* 460–*about* 377 B.C. *founder of medicine* Greek physician

Hi·ro·hi·to \\ıhir-ō-'hē-tō\\ 1901–1989 emperor of Japan (1926–89)

Hit·ler \\'hit-lər\\ Adolf 1889–1945 German (Austrian≈born) chancellor (1933–45)

Holmes \\'hōmz, 'hōlmz\\ Oliver Wendell 1809–1894 American physician and author

Holmes Oliver Wendell 1841–1935 American jurist; son of the preceding

Ho·mer \\'hō-mər\\ 9th–8th? century B.C. Greek epic poet — **Ho·mer·ic** \\hō-'mer-ik\\ *adj*

Homer Winslow 1836–1910 American painter

Hooke \\'hùk\\ Robert 1635–1703 English scientist

Hook·er \\'hùk-ər\\ Thomas 1586?–1647 English colonist; a founder of Connecticut

Hoc·ver \\'hü-vər\\ Herbert Clark 1874–1964 31st president of the U.S. (1929–33)

Hoover John Edgar 1895–1972 American criminologist; director of the Federal Bureau of Investigation (1924–72)

Hou·di·ni \\hü-'dē-nē\\ Harry 1874–1926 originally *Ehrich Weiss* American magician

Hous·ton \\'(h)yü-stən\\ Samuel 1793–1863 *Sam* American general; president of the Republic of Texas (1836–38; 1841–44)

Howe \\'haù\\ Elias 1819–1867 American inventor

Howe Julia 1819–1910 née *Ward* American suffragist and reformer

Hud·son \\'həd-sən\\ Henry *died* 1611 English navigator and explorer

Hughes \\'hyüz *also* 'yüz\\ (James) Langston 1902–1967 American author

Hus·sein I \\hü-'sān\\ 1935–1999 king of Jordan (1952–1999)

Hutch·in·son \\'həch-ə(n)-sən\\ Anne 1591–1643 religious leader in America

Hutchinson Thomas 1711–1780 American colonial administrator

Hux·ley \\'hək-slē\\ Aldous Leonard 1894–1963 English author

Hy·men \\'hī-mən\\ god of marriage in Greek mythology

Ib·sen \\'ib-sən, 'ip-\\ Henrik 1828–1906 Norwegian dramatist and poet

Ic·a·rus \\'ik-ə-rəs\\ son of Daedalus who in Greek mythology falls into the sea when the wax of his artificial wings melts as he flies too near the sun

Ig·na·tius \\ig-'nä-sh(ē-)əs\\ *Saint Ignatius of Loy·o·la* \\lȯi-'ō-lə\\ 1491–1556 Spanish soldier and priest; founded the Society of Jesus

In·no·cent \\'in-ə-sənt\\ name of 13 popes: especially **II** died 1143 (pope 1130–43); **III** 1160 (or 1161)–1216 (pope 1198–1216); **IV** died 1254 (pope 1243–54); **XI** 1611–1689 (pope 1676–89)

Ir·ving \\'ər-viŋ\\ Washington 1783–1859 American author

Isaac \\'ī-zik, -zək\\ son of Abraham and father of Jacob in the Bible

Is·a·bel·la I \\ıiz-ə-'bel-ə\\ 1451–1504 queen of Castile (1474–1504) and of Aragon (1479–1504); wife of Ferdinand V of Castile

Isa·iah \\ī-'zā-ə\\ Hebrew prophet of the 8th century B.C.

Ish·ma·el \\'ish-(ı)mä-əl, -mē-\\ outcast son of Abraham and Hagar in the Bible

Ives \\'īvz\\ Charles Edward 1874–1954 American composer

Jack·son \\'jak-sən\\ Andrew 1767–1845 American general; 7th president of the U.S. (1829–37)

Jackson Thomas Jonathan 1824–1863 *Stonewall* American Confederate general

Ja·cob \\'jā-kəb\\ son of Isaac and Rebekah and younger twin brother of Esau in the Bible

James \\'jāmz\\ one of the 12 apostles in the Bible

James *the Less* one of the 12 apostles in the Bible

James name of two kings of Great Britain: **I** 1566–1625 (reigned 1603–25); king of Scotland as *James VI* (reigned 1567–1603); **II** 1633–1701 (reigned 1685–88)

James Henry 1843–1916 British (American-born) author

Ja·nus \\'jā-nəs\\ god of gates and doors and of beginnings and endings in Roman mythology who is usually pictured as having two opposite faces

Ja·son \\'jās-ᵊn\\ hero in Greek mythology noted for his successful quest of the Golden Fleece

Jay \\'jā\\ John 1745–1829 American jurist and political leader; 1st chief justice of the U.S. Supreme Court (1789–95)

Jef·fer·son \\'jef-ər-sən\\ Thomas 1743–1826 3d president of the U.S. (1801–09) — **Jef·fer·so·nian** \\ıjef-ər-'sō-nē-ən, -nyən\\ *adj*

Jer·e·mi·ah \\ıjer-ə-'mī-ə\\ Hebrew prophet of the 6th and 7th centuries B.C.

Je·sus \\'jē-zəs, -zəz\\ *or* **Jesus Christ** \\'krīst\\ *or* **Christ** *Jesus about* 6 B.C.–*about* 30 A.D. source of the Christian religion and Savior in the Christian faith

Jez·e·bel \\'jez-ə-ıbel\\ queen of Israel and wife of Ahab who was noted for her wickedness

Joan of Arc \\ıjō-nə-'värk\\ *Saint about* 1412–1431 *the Maid of Orleans* French national heroine

Job \\'jōb\\ man in the Bible who has many sufferings but keeps his faith

Jo·cas·ta \\jō-'kas-tə\\ queen of Thebes in Greek mythology who unknowingly marries her son Oedipus

John \\'jän\\ *the Baptist* prophet and baptizer of Jesus in the Bible

John one of the 12 apostles believed to be the author of the fourth Gospel, three Epistles, and the Book of Revelation

John name of 21 popes: especially **XXIII** 1881–1963 (pope 1958–63)

John 1167–1216 *John Lack•land* \'lak-₁land\ king of England (1199–1216)

John•son \'jän(t)-sən\ Andrew 1808–1875 17th president of the U.S. (1865–69)

Johnson Lyndon Baines 1908–1973 36th president of the U.S. (1963–69)

Johnson Samuel 1709–1784 *Dr. Johnson* English lexicographer and author

Jol•liet *or* **Jo•liet** \zhól-'yä, ₁jō-lē-'et\ Louis 1645–1700 French explorer in America

Jo•nah \'jō-nə\ Hebrew prophet who in the Bible spends three days in the belly of a great fish

Jones \'jōnz\ John Paul 1747–1792 American (Scottish-born) naval officer

Jop•lin \'jäp-lən\ Scott 1868–1917 American pianist and composer

Jo•seph \'jō-zəf *also* -səf \ a son of Jacob in the Bible who rose to high office in Egypt after being sold into slavery by his brothers

Joseph *about* 1840–1904 Nez Percé Indian chief

Joseph Saint husband of Mary, the mother of Jesus, in the Bible

Josh•ua \'jäsh-(ə-)wə\ Hebrew leader in the Bible who succeeds Moses during the settlement of the Israelites in Canaan

Ju•dah \'jüd-ə\ son of Jacob and ancestor of one of the 12 tribes of Israel in the Bible

Ju•das \'jüd-əs\ *or* **Judas Is•car•i•ot** \-is-'kar-ē-ət\ one of the 12 apostles and the betrayer of Jesus in the Bible

Ju•no \'jü-nō\ the queen of heaven in Roman mythology, wife of Jupiter, and goddess of light, birth, women, and marriage — compare HERA

Ju•pi•ter \'jü-pət-ər\ the chief god in Roman mythology, husband of Juno, and the god of light, of the sky and weather, and of the state

Kalb \'kälp, 'kalb\ Johann 1721–1780 Baron *de Kalb* \di-'kalb\ German general in American Revolutionary army

Keats \'kēts\ John 1795–1821 English poet

Kel•ler \'kel-ər\ Helen Adams 1880–1968 American deaf and blind lecturer

Kel•vin \'kel-vən\ 1st Baron 1824–1907 *William Thomson* British mathematician and physicist

Ken•ne•dy \'ken-əd-ē\ John Fitzgerald 1917–1963 35th president of the U.S. (1961–63)

Kennedy Robert Francis 1925–1968 American politician; attorney general of the U.S. (1961–64); brother of John F. Kennedy

Ke•o•kuk \'kē-ə-₁kək\ 1788?–?1848 American Indian chief

Key \'kē\ Francis Scott 1779–1843 American lawyer; author of "The Star-Spangled Banner"

Khayyám Omar — see OMAR KHAYYÁM

Khru•shchev \krüsh-'(ch)óf, -'(ch)óv, -'(ch)ef\ Ni•ki•ta \nə-'kēt-ə\ Sergeyevich 1894–1971 premier of U.S.S.R. (1958–64)

Khu•fu \'kü-fü\ *or Greek* **Che•ops** \'kē-₁äps\ 26th century B.C. king of Egypt and pyramid builder

Kidd \'kid\ William *about* 1645–1701 *Captain Kidd* Scottish pirate

King \'kiŋ\ Martin Luther, Jr. 1929–1968 American minister and civil rights leader; Nobel Prize winner (1964)

Kip•ling \'kip-liŋ\ Rud•yard \'rəd-yərd, 'rəj-ərd\ 1865–1936 English author

Kis•sin•ger \'kis-ᵊn-jər\ Henry Alfred 1923– American (German-born) scholar and government official; U.S. secretary of state (1973–77); Nobel Prize winner (1973)

Knox \'näks\ John *about* 1514–1572 Scottish religious reformer

Koch \'kók, 'kȯk\ Robert 1843–1910 German bacteriologist; Nobel Prize winner (1905)

Koś•ciusz•ko \₁käs-ē-'əs-₁kō, kȯsh-'chüsh-kō\ Ta-

deusz 1746–1817 Polish patriot and general in American Revolutionary army

Krish•na \'krish-nə\ god worshipped in later Hinduism

Kriss Kringle — see SANTA CLAUS

Ku•blai Khan \₁kü-blə-'kän, -₁blī-\ 1215–1294 founder of Mongol dynasty in China

La•fa•yette \₁läf-ē-'et, ₁laf-\ Marquis de 1757–1834 French general in American Revolutionary army

La•ius \'lä-(y)əs, 'lī-əs\ king of Thebes who in Greek mythology is killed by his son Oedipus

Lan•ce•lot \'lan(t)-sə-₁lät\ legendary knight of the Round Table and lover of Queen Guinevere

La Salle \lə-'sal\ Sieur de 1643–1687 French explorer in America

La•voi•sier \lǝv-'wäz-ē-₁ā\ Antoine-Laurent 1743–1794 French chemist

Law•rence \'lȯr-ən(t)s, 'lär-\ Thomas Edward 1888–1935 *Lawrence of Arabia* later surnamed *Shaw* British archaeologist, soldier, and author

Laz•a•rus \'laz-(ə-)rəs\ brother of Mary and Martha who in the Bible is raised by Jesus from the dead

Lazarus beggar in the biblical parable of the rich man and the beggar

Le•da \'lēd-ə\ a queen of Sparta in Greek mythology who is courted by Zeus in the form of a swan

Lee \'lē\ Ann 1736–1784 English mystic; founder of Shaker society in the U.S.

Lee Henry 1756–1818 *Light-Horse Harry* American general

Lee Robert Edward 1807–1870 American Confederate general

Leeu•wen•hoek \'lā-vən-₁hùk\ Antonie van 1632–1723 Dutch naturalist

Leif Er•iks•son \₁lā-'ver-ik-sən, ₁lē-'fer-\ *or* **Er•ics•son** *flourished* 1000 Norwegian explorer; son of Erik the Red

Le•nin \'len-ən\ 1870–1924 originally *Vladimir Ilyich Ul•ya•nov* \ül-'yän-əf, -₁ȯf, -₁ȯv\ Russian Communist leader

Leo \'lē-ō\ name of 13 popes: especially **I** Saint *died* 461 (pope 440–61); **III** Saint *died* 816 (pope 795–816); **XIII** 1810–1903 (pope 1878–1903)

Le•o•nar•do da Vin•ci \₁lē-ə-'närd-₁ōd-ə- 'vin-chē, ₁lä-, -'vēn-\ 1452–1519 Italian painter, sculptor, architect, and engineer

Lew•is \'lü-əs\ John Llewellyn 1880–1969 American labor leader

Lewis Meriwether 1774–1809 American explorer (with William Clark)

Lewis (Harry) Sinclair 1885–1951 American author; Nobel Prize winner (1930)

Lin•coln \'liŋ-kən\ Abraham 1809–1865 16th president of the U.S. (1861–65)

Lind•bergh \'lin(d)-₁bərg\ Charles Augustus 1902–1974 American aviator

Lin•nae•us \lə-'nē-əs, -'nā-\ Carolus 1707–1778 Swedish *Carl von Lin•né* \lə-'nā\ Swedish botanist

Lis•ter \'lis-tər\ Joseph 1827–1912 English surgeon

Liszt \'list\ Franz 1811–1886 Hungarian pianist and composer

Liv•ing•stone \'liv-iŋ-stən\ David 1813–1873 Scottish explorer in Africa

Long•fel•low \'lȯŋ-₁fel-ō\ Henry Wads•worth \'wädz-(₁)wərth\ 1807–1882 American poet

Lou•is \'lü-ē, 'lü-əs\ name of 18 kings of France: especially **IX** Saint 1214–1270 (reigned 1226–70); **XI** 1423–1483 (reigned 1461–83); **XII** 1462–1515 (reigned 1498–1515); **XIII** 1601–1643 (reigned 1610–43); **XIV** 1638–1715 (reigned 1643–1715); **XV** 1710–1774 (reigned 1715–74); **XVI** 1754–1793 (reigned 1774–92; guillotined); **XVII** 1785–1795 (reigned in name 1793–95); **XVIII** 1755–1824 (reigned 1814–15; 1815–24)

Low **'**lō\ Juliette Gordon 1860–1927 American founder of the Girl Scouts

Low·ell **'**lō-əl\ Amy 1874–1925 American poet

Lowell James Russell 1819–1891 American author

Luke **'**lük\ physician and companion of the apostle Paul believed to be the author of the third Gospel and the Book of Acts

Lu·ther **'**lü-thər\ Martin 1483–1546 German Reformation leader

Ly·on **'**lī-ən\ Mary 1797–1849 American educator

Mac·Ar·thur \mə-**'**kär-thər\ Douglas 1880–1964 American general

Mc·Car·thy \mə-**'**kär-thē\ Joseph Raymond 1908–1957 American politician

Mc·Clel·lan \mə-**'**klel-ən\ George Brinton 1826–1885 American general

Mc·Cor·mick \mə-**'**kȯr-mik\ Cyrus Hall 1809–1884 American inventor

Mc·Kin·ley \mə-**'**kin-lē\ William 1843–1901 25th president of the U.S. (1897–1901)

Ma·cy **'**mā-sē\ Anne Sullivan 1866–1936 American educator; teacher of Helen Keller

Mad·i·son **'**mad-ə-sən\ James 1751–1836 4th president of the U.S. (1809–17)

Ma·gel·lan \mə-**'**jel-ən\ Ferdinand *about* 1480–1521 Portuguese navigator

Mal·colm X \mal-kə-**'**meks\ 1925–1965 American civil rights leader

Ma·net \ma-**'**nā, mä-\ Édouard 1832–1883 French painter

Mann **'**man\ Horace 1796–1859 American educator

Mao Tse–tung \maú(d)-zə-**'**dúŋ, ˌmaút-sə-\ 1893–1976 Chinese Communist; leader of People's Republic of China (1949–76)

Mar·co·ni \mär-**'**kō-nē\ Guglielmo 1874–1937 Italian physicist and inventor; Nobel Prize winner (1909)

Ma·rie An·toi·nette \mə-**'**rē-ˌan-t(w)ə-**'**net\ 1755–1793 wife of Louis XVI

Mar·i·on **'**mer-ē-ən, **'**mar-ē-\ Francis 1732?–1795 *the Swamp Fox* American commander in Revolution

Mark **'**märk\ evangelist believed to be the author of the second Gospel

Mar·quette \mär-**'**ket\ Jacques 1637–1675 French-born Jesuit missionary and explorer in America

Mars **'**märz\ the god of war in Roman mythology

Mar·shall **'**mär-shəl\ George Catlett 1880–1959 American general and diplomat

Marshall John 1755–1835 American jurist; chief justice of the U.S. Supreme Court (1801–35)

Mar·tha **'**mär-thə\ sister of Lazarus and Mary and friend of Jesus in the Bible

Mar·tin **'**märt-ᵊn\ Saint *about* 316–397 *Martin of Tours* \-**'**tú(ə)r\ patron saint of France

Marx **'**märks\ Karl 1818–1883 German political philosopher and socialist

Mary **'**me(ə)r-ē, **'**ma(ə)r-ē\ mother of Jesus

Mary sister of Lazarus and Martha in the Bible

Mary I 1516–1558 *Mary Tudor; Bloody Mary* queen of England (1553–58)

Mary II 1662–1694 joint British sovereign with William III (1689–94)

Mary Mag·da·lene \-**'**mag-də-ˌlən, -ˌlēn\ woman in the Bible who was healed of evil spirits by Jesus and who later saw the risen Christ

Mary Stuart 1542–1587 *Mary, Queen of Scots* queen of Scotland (1542–87)

Mas·sa·soit \ˌmas-ə-**'**sȯit\ *died* 1661 Indian chief in eastern Massachusetts

Math·er **'**math-ər, **'**math-\ Cotton 1663–1728 American religious leader and author

Mather Increase 1639–1723 American minister and author; father of Cotton Mather

Mat·thew **'**math-yü\ apostle believed to be the author of the first Gospel

Mau·pas·sant \ˌmō-pə-**'**sänt\ (Henri-René-Albert-) Guy de 1850–1893 French short-story writer

Mead **'**mēd\ Margaret 1901–1978 American anthropologist

Meade **'**mēd\ George Gordon 1815–1872 American general

Mea·ny **'**mē-nē\ George 1894–1980 American labor leader

Me·dea \mə-**'**dē-ə\ woman with magic powers in Greek mythology who helps Jason to win the Golden Fleece and who kills her children when he leaves her

Me·di·ci, de' **'**med-ə-chē\ Catherine 1519–1589 French *Catherine de Médicis* \ˌmäd-ə-**'**sē(s)\ queen of Henry II of France

Me·ir \me-**'**i(ə)r\ Golda 1898–1978 prime minister of Israel (1969–74)

Mel·ville **'**mel-ˌvil\ Herman 1819–1891 American author

Men·del **'**men-dᵊl\ Gregor Johann 1822–1884 Austrian botanist

Men·e·la·us \ˌmen-ᵊl-**'**ā-əs\ king of Sparta, brother of Agamemnon, and husband of Helen of Troy in Greek mythology

Meph·is·toph·e·les \ˌmef-ə-**'**stäf-ə-ˌlēz\ chief devil in the Faust legend

Mer·ca·tor \(ˌ)mər-**'**kāt-ər\ Gerardus 1512–1594 Flemish mapmaker

Mer·cu·ry **'**mər-kyə-rē, -k(ə-)rē\ god of commerce, eloquence, travel, and theft who serves as herald and messenger of the other gods in Roman mythology

Mer·lin **'**mər-lən\ prophet and magician in the legend of King Arthur

Mi·chael **'**mī-kəl\ one of the four archangels named in Hebrew tradition — compare GABRIEL, RAPHAEL, URIEL

Mi·chel·an·ge·lo \ˌmī-kə-**'**lan-jə-ˌlō, ˌmik-ə-**'**lan-, ˌmē-kə-**'**län-\ 1475–1564 Italian sculptor, painter, architect, and poet

Mi·das **'**mīd-əs\ legendary king who was given the power to turn everything he touched into gold

Mil·lay \mil-**'**ā\ Edna St. Vincent 1892–1950 American poet

Mil·ler **'**mil-ər\ Arthur 1915– American author

Mil·ton **'**milt-ᵊn\ John 1608–1674 English poet

Mi·ner·va \mə-'nər-və\ goddess of wisdom in Roman mythology — compare ATHENA

Mi·no·taur \'min-ə-ıtȯ(ə)r, 'mī-nə-\ monster in Greek mythology shaped half like a man and half like a bull

Min·u·it \'min-yə-wət\ Peter 1580–1638 Dutch colonial administrator in America

Mitch·ell \'mich-əl\ Maria 1818–1889 American astronomer

Mo·lière \mōl-'ye(ə)r, 'mōl-ıye(ə)r\ 1622–1673 originally *Jean-Baptiste Poquelin* French actor and dramatist

Mo·net \mō-'nā\ Claude 1840–1926 French painter

Mon·roe \mən-'rō\ James 1758–1831 5th president of the U.S. (1817–25)

Mont·calm de Saint-Vé·ran \mänt-'käm-də-ısan-vā-'rän, -'kälm-\ Marquis de 1712–1759 French field marshal in Canada

Mon·tes·so·ri \ımänt-ə-'sōr-ē, -'sȯr-\ Maria 1870–1952 Italian physician and educator

Mon·te·zu·ma II \ımänt-ə-'zü-mə\ 1466–1520 last Aztec emperor of Mexico (1502–20)

Moore \'mō(ə)r, 'mȯ(ə)r, 'mü(ə)r\ Marianne Craig 1887–1972 American poet

More \'mō(ə)r, 'mȯ(ə)r\ Sir Thomas 1478–1535 *Saint* English public official and author

Mor·gan \'mȯr-gən\ John Pierpont 1837–1913 American financier

Mor·ri·son \'mȯr-ə-sən, ımär-\ Toni 1931–   American author

Morse \'mō(ə)rs\ Samuel Finley Breese 1791–1872 American artist and inventor

Mo·ses \'mō-zəz *also* -zəs\ Hebrew prophet and lawgiver who in the Bible freed the Israelites from slavery in Egypt

Mott \'mät\ Lucretia 1793–1880 American reformer

> **Mo·zart** \'mōt-ısärt\ Wolfgang Amadeus 1756–1791 Austrian composer

Mu·ham·mad \mō-'ham-əd, -'häm- *also* mü-\ *about* 570–632 Arab prophet and founder of Islam

Mus·so·li·ni \ımü-sə-'lē-nē, ımüs-ə-\ Be·ni·to \bə-'nēt-ō\ 1883–1945 *Il Du·ce* \ĕl-'dü-chā\ Italian fascist premier (1922–43)

Na·po·léon I \nə-'pōl-yən, -'pō-lē-ən\ *or* Napoléon Bo·na·parte \'bō-nə-ıpärt\ 1769–1821 emperor of the French (1804–15) — **Na·po·le·on·ic** \nə-ıpō-lē-'än-ik\ *adj*

Nar·cis·sus \när-'sis-əs\ a beautiful youth in Greek mythology who pines away for love of his own reflection and is then turned into the narcissus flower

Nash \'nash\ Ogden 1902–1971 American poet

Na·tion \'nā-shən\ Car·ry \'kar-ē\ Amelia 1846–1911 American social reformer

Neb·u·cha·drez·zar II \ıneb-(y)ə-kə-'drez-ər\ *also* **Neb·u·chad·nez·zar** \-kəd-'nez-\ *about* 630–562 B.C. Chaldean king of Babylon (605–562)

Neh·ru \'ne(ə)r-ıü, 'nā-rü\ Ja·wa·har·lal \jə-'wä-hər-ıläl\ 1889–1964 Indian nationalist; 1st prime minister (1947–64)

Nel·son \'nel-sən\ Horatio 1758–1805 Viscount *Nelson* British admiral

Nem·e·sis \'nem-ə-səs\ the goddess of reward and punishment in Greek mythology

Nep·tune \'nep-ıt(y)ün\ the god of the sea in Roman mythology

Ne·ro \'nē-ırō, 'ni(ə)r-ō\ 37–68 A.D. Roman emperor (54–68)

New·ton \'n(y)üt-ᵊn\ Sir Isaac 1642–1727 English mathematician and physicist

Nich·o·las \'nik-(ə-)ləs\ Saint 4th century Christian bishop

Nicholas I 1796–1855 czar of Russia (1825–55)

Nicholas II 1868–1918 czar of Russia (1894–1917)

Night·in·gale \'nīt-ᵊn-ıgāl, -iŋ-\ Florence 1820–1910 English nurse and philanthropist

Ni·ke \'nī-kē\ the goddess of victory in Greek mythology

Ni·o·be \'nī-ə-bē\ a daughter of Tantalus in Greek mythology who while weeping for her slain children is turned into a stone from which her tears continue to flow

Nix·on \'nik-sən\ Richard Mil·hous \'mil-ıhaüs\ 1913–1994 37th president of the U.S. (1969–74)

No·ah \'nō-ə\ Old Testament builder of the ark in which he, his family, and living creatures of every kind survived the Flood

No·bel \nō-'bel\ Alfred Bernhard 1833–1896 Swedish manufacturer, inventor, and philanthropist

Oce·a·nus \ō-'sē-ə-nəs\ a Titan who rules over a great river encircling the earth in Greek mythology

Odin \'ōd-ᵊn\ *or* **Wo·den** \'wōd-ᵊn\ god of war and patron of heroes in Norse mythology

Odys·seus \ō-'dis-ē-əs, -'dis-yəs, -'dish-əs, -'dish-ıüs\ *or* **Ulys·ses** \yü-'lis-ēz\ king of Ithaca and hero in Greek mythology who after the Trojan War wanders for 10 years before reaching home

Oe·di·pus \'ed-ə-pəs, 'ēd-\ son of Laius and Jocasta who in Greek mythology kills his father and marries his mother not knowing their identity

Ogle·thorpe \'ō-gəl-ıthȯrp\ James Edward 1696–1785 English general and philanthropist; founder of Georgia

O'·Keeffe \ō-'kēf\ Georgia 1887–1986 American painter

Omar Khay·yám \ıō-ımär-ıkī-'(y)äm, ıō-mər-, -'(y)am\ 1048?–1122 Persian poet and astronomer

O'·Neill \ō-'nē(ə)l\ Eugene Gladstone 1888–1953 American dramatist; Nobel Prize winner (1936)

Or·pheus \'ȯr-ıfyüs, -fē-əs\ poet and musician in Greek mythology who almost rescues his wife Eurydice from Hades by charming Pluto and Persephone with his lyre

Or·well \'ȯr-ıwel, -wəl\ George 1903–1950 pseudonym of *Eric Blair* English author — **Or·well·ian** \ȯr-'wel-ē-ən\ *adj*

Osce·o·la \ıäs-ē-'ō-lə, ıō-sē-\ *about* 1800–1838 Seminole chief

Otis \'ōt-əs\ James 1725–1783 American Revolutionary patriot

Ov·id \'äv-əd\ 43 B.C.–17 A.D.? Roman poet

Ow·en \'ō-ən\ Robert 1771–1858 Welsh social reformer

Ow·ens \'ō-ənz\ Jesse 1913–1980 originally *James Cleveland* American athlete

Paine \'pān\ Thomas 1737–1809 American (English-born) political philosopher and author

Pan \'pan\ god of forests, pastures, flocks, and shepherds in Greek mythology who is represented as having the legs, ears, and horns of a goat

Pan·do·ra \pan-'dōr-ə, -'dȯr-\ woman in Greek mythology who out of curiosity opens a box and lets loose all of the evils that trouble humans

Par·is \'par-əs\ son of Priam whose abduction of Helen of Troy in Greek mythology led to the Trojan War

Park·man \'pärk-mən\ Francis 1823–1893 American historian

Pas·cal \pas-'kal\ Blaise 1623–1662 French mathematician and philosopher

Pas·ter·nak \'pas-tər-ˌnak\ Boris Leonidovich 1890–1960 Russian author; Nobel Prize winner (1958)

Pas·teur \pas-'tər\ Louis 1822–1895 French chemist and microbiologist

Pat·rick \'pa-trik\ Saint 5th century apostle and patron saint of Ireland

Pat·ton \'pat-ᵊn\ George Smith 1885–1945 American general

Paul \'pȯl\ Saint *died between* 62 *and* 68 A.D. author of several New Testament epistles — Pau·line \'pȯ-ˌlīn\ *adj*

Paul name of six popes: especially III 1468–1549 (pope 1534–49); V 1552–1621 (pope 1605–21); VI 1897–1978 (pope 1963–78)

Paul Bun·yan \'pȯl-'bən-yən\ giant lumberjack in American folklore

Pau·ling \'pȯ-liŋ\ Linus Carl 1901–1994 American chemist; Nobel Prize winner (1954, 1962)

Pav·lov \'päv-ˌlȯf, 'pav-, -ˌlȯv\ Ivan Petrovich 1849–1936 Russian physiologist; Nobel Prize winner (1904)

Pav·lo·va \'pav-lə-və, pav-'lō-və\ Anna 1882–1931 Russian ballerina

Pea·ry \'pi(ə)r-ē\ Robert Edwin 1856–1920 American arctic explorer

Pe·cos Bill \ˌpā-kəs-'bil\ a cowboy in American folklore known for his extraordinary feats

Peg·a·sus \'peg-ə-səs\ winged horse in Greek mythology

Penn \'pen\ William 1644–1718 English Quaker; founder of Pennsylvania

Per·i·cles \'per-ə-ˌklēz\ *about* 495–429 B.C. Athenian political leader

Per·ry \'per-ē\ Matthew Calbraith 1794–1858 American commodore

Perry Oliver Hazard 1785–1819 American naval officer

Per·seph·o·ne \pər-'sef-ə-nē\ daughter of Zeus and Demeter who in Greek mythology is abducted by Pluto to rule with him over the underworld

Per·shing \'pər-shiŋ, -zhiŋ\ John Joseph 1860–1948 American general

Pe·ter \'pēt-ər\ Saint *died about* 64 A.D. *Si·mon Peter* \'sī-mən-\ one of the 12 apostles in the Bible

Peter I 1672–1725 *the Great* czar of Russia (1682–1725)

Phil·ip \'fil-əp\ one of the 12 apostles in the Bible

Philip 1639?–1676 American Indian chief

Philip name of six kings of France: especially II *or* Philip Augustus 1165–1223 (reigned 1179–1223); IV 1268–1314 (reigned 1285–1314) *the Fair*; VI 1293–1350 (reigned 1328–50)

Philip name of five kings of Spain: especially II 1527–1598 (reigned 1556–98); V 1683–1746 (reigned 1700–46)

Philip II 382–336 B.C. king of Macedon (359–336); father of Alexander the Great

Pi·cas·so \pi-'käs-ō, -'kas-\ Pablo 1881–1973 Spanish painter and sculptor in France

Pick·ett \'pik-ət\ George Edward 1825–1875 American Confederate general

Pierce \'pi(ə)rs\ Franklin 1804–1869 14th president of the U.S. (1853–57)

Pi·late \'pī-lət\ Pon·tius \'pän-chəs, 'pən-chəs\ *died after* 36 A.D. Roman governor of Judea

Pitt \'pit\ William 1759–1806 English prime minister (1783–1801; 1804–6)

Pi·us \'pī-əs\ name of 12 popes: especially VII 1742–1823 (pope 1800–23); IX 1792–1878 (pope 1846–78); X 1835–1914 (pope 1903–14); XI 1857–1939 (pope 1922–39); XII 1876–1958 (pope 1939–58)

Pi·zar·ro \pə-'zär-ō\ Francisco *about* 1475–1541 Spanish conqueror of Peru

Pla·to \'plāt-ō\ *about* 428–348 (*or* 347) B.C. Greek philosopher

Plu·to \'plüt-ō\ god of the dead and the underworld in Greek mythology

Po·ca·hon·tas \ˌpō-kə-'hänt-əs\ *about* 1595–1617 American Indian princess

Poe \'pō\ Edgar Allan 1809–1849 American author

Polk \'pōk\ James Knox 1795–1849 11th president of the U.S. (1845–49)

Po·lo \'pō-lō\ Mar·co \'mär-kō\ 1254–1324 Venetian traveler

Poly·phe·mus \ˌpäl-ə-'fē-məs\ a Cyclops in Greek mythology who is blinded by Odysseus

Ponce de Le·ón \ˌpän(t)-sə-ˌdā-lē-'ōn, ˌpän(t)s-də-'lē-ən\ Juan 1460–1521 Spanish explorer and discoverer of Florida (1513)

Pon·ti·ac \'pänt-ē-ˌak\ *about* 1720–1769 Ottawa chief

Por·ter \'pōrt-ər, 'pȯrt-\ Cole Albert 1891–1964 American composer and songwriter

Porter David Dixon 1813–1891 American admiral

Porter Katherine Anne 1890–1980 American author

Porter William Sydney 1862–1910 pseudonym *O. Henry* \(ˈ)ō-'hen-rē\ American author

Po·sei·don \pə-'sīd-ᵊn\ god of the sea in Greek mythology — compare NEPTUNE

Pot·ter \'pät-ər\ Beatrix 1866–1943 British author and illustrator

Pow·ha·tan \ˌpau̇-ə-'tan, pau̇-'hat-ᵊn\ 1550?–1618 American Indian chief

Pri·am \'prī-əm, -ˌam\ king of Troy during the Trojan War in Greek mythology

Pro·me·theus \prə-'mē-th(y)üs, -thē-əs\ a Titan in Greek mythology who is punished by Zeus for stealing fire from heaven and giving it to human beings

Pro·teus \'prō-ˌt(y)üs, 'prōt-ē-əs\ sea god in Greek mythology who is capable of assuming different forms

Puc·ci·ni \pü-'chē-nē\ Giacomo 1858–1924 Italian composer

Pu·las·ki \pə-'las-kē, pyü-\ Kazimierz 1747–1779 Polish soldier in American Revolutionary army

Pu·lit·zer \'pu̇l-ət-sər, 'pyü-lət-sər\ Joseph 1847–1911 American (Hungarian-born) journalist

Pyg·ma·lion \pig-'māl-yən, -'mā-lē-ən\ a sculptor in Greek mythology who falls in love with a statue which is then brought to life

Py·thag·o·ras \pə-'thag-ə-rəs, pī-\ *about* 580–*about* 500 B.C. Greek philosopher and mathematician

Ra \'rä, 'rȯ\ god of the sun and chief deity of ancient Egypt

Ra·leigh *or* Ra·legh \'rȯl-ē, 'räl- *also* 'ral-\ Sir Walter 1554–1618 English navigator and historian

Ram·ses \'ram-ˌsēz\ *or* Ram·e·ses \'ram-ə-ˌsēz\ name of 12 kings of Egypt: especially II (reigned 1304–1237 B.C.); III (reigned 1198–66 B.C.)

Ran·dolph \'ran-ˌdälf\ Asa Philip 1889–1979 American labor leader

Ra·pha·el \'raf-ē-əl, 'rä-fē-\ one of the four archangels named in Hebrew tradition — compare GABRIEL, MICHAEL, URIEL

Ra·pha·el \'raf-ē-əl, 'rä-fē-, 'räf-ē-\ 1483–1520 Italian painter

Ras·pu·tin \ra-'sp(y)üt-ᵊn, -'spüt-\ Grigory Yefimovich 1872–1916 Russian mystic

Rea·gan \'rā-gən *also* 'rē-\ Ronald Wilson 1911– 40th president of the U.S. (1981–89)

Re·bek·ah *or* **Re·bec·ca** \ri-'bek-ə\ wife of Isaac in the Bible

Red Cloud \'red-ıklaúd\ 1822–1909 American Indian chief

Reed \'rēd\ Walter 1851–1902 American army surgeon

Rem·brandt \'rem-ıbrant *also* -ıbränt\ 1606–1669 Dutch painter

Re·mus \'rē-məs\ son of Mars who in Roman mythology is killed by his twin brother Romulus

Re·noir \'ren-ıwär, rən-'wär\ Pierre-Auguste 1841–1919 French painter

Re·vere \ri-'vi(ə)r\ Paul 1735–1818 American patriot and silversmith

Rich·ard \'rich-ərd\ name of three kings of England: **I** 1157–1199 (reigned 1189–99) *the Lion-Hearted;* **II** 1367–1400 (reigned 1377–99); **III** 1452–1485 (reigned 1483–85)

Rob·in Good·fel·low \ıräb-ən-'gúd-ıfel-ō\ mischievous elf in English folklore

Rob·in·son \'räb-ən-sən\ Edwin Arlington 1869–1935 American poet

Rob·in·son Cru·soe \ıräb-ə(n)-sən-'krü-sō\ a shipwrecked sailor in Daniel Defoe's *Robinson Crusoe* who lives for many years on a desert island

Ro·cham·beau \ırō-ısham-'bō\ Comte de 1725–1807 French general in American Revolution

Rocke·fel·ler \'räk-i-ıfel-ər, 'räk-ıfel-\ John Davison father 1839–1937 and son 1874–1960 American oil magnates and philanthropists

Ro·ma·nov *or* **Ro·ma·noff** \rō-'män-əf, 'rō-mə-ınäf\ Michael 1596–1645 1st czar (1613–45) of Russian Romanov dynasty (1613–1917)

Rom·u·lus \'räm-yə-ləs\ son of Mars in Roman mythology who was the twin brother of Remus and the founder of Rome

Rönt·gen *or* **Roent·gen** \'rent-gən, 'rənt-, -jən\ Wilhelm Conrad 1845–1923 German physicist; Nobel Prize winner (1901)

Roo·se·velt \'rō-zə-vəlt (*Roosevelts' usual pronunciation*), -ıvelt *also* 'rü-\ (Anna) Eleanor 1884–1962 American lecturer and writer; wife of Franklin Delano Roosevelt

Roosevelt Franklin Del·a·no \'del-ə-ınō\ 1882–1945 32d president of the U.S. (1933–45)

Roosevelt Theodore 1858–1919 26th president of the U.S. (1901–09); Nobel Prize winner (1906)

Ross \'rös\ Betsy 1752–1836 reputed maker of first American flag

Ros·si·ni \rö-'sē-nē, rə-\ Gioacchino Antonio 1792–1868 Italian composer

Ru·bens \'rü-bənz\ Peter Paul 1577–1640 Flemish painter

Rus·sell \'rəs-əl\ Bertrand Arthur William 1872–1970 English mathematician and philosopher; Nobel Prize winner (1950)

Ruth \'rüth\ woman in the Bible who was one of the ancestors of King David

Ruth George Herman 1895–1948 *Babe* American baseball player

Ruth·er·ford \'rəth-ə(r)-fərd, 'rəth-\ Ernest 1871–1937 1st Baron *Rutherford of Nelson* British physicist

Sa·bin \'sā-bin\ Albert Bruce 1906–1993 American physician

Sac·a·ga·wea \ısak-ə-jə-'wē-ə, -'wä-ə\ 1786?–1812 Shoshone interpreter and guide to Lewis and Clark

Sä·dät \sə-'dat, -'dät\ Anwar el- 1918–1981 president of Egypt (1970–81)

Saint Nicholas — see NICHOLAS, SANTA CLAUS

Sal·in·ger \'sal-ən-jər\ Jerome David 1919– American author

Salk \'sök, 'sölk\ Jonas Edward 1914–1995 American physician

Sa·lo·me \sə-'lō-mē\ niece of Herod Antipas who in the Bible is given the head of John the Baptist as a reward for her dancing

Sa·mo·set \'sam-ə-ıset, sə-'mäs-ət\ *died about* 1653 Abenaki leader

Sam·son \'sam(p)-sən\ powerful Hebrew hero in the Bible who fought against the Philistines

Sam·u·el \'sam-yə(-wə)l\ Hebrew judge in the Bible who appointed Saul and then David king

Sand·burg \'san(d)-ıbərg\ Carl 1878–1967 American author

San·ta Claus \'sant-ē-ıklöz, 'sant-ə-\ *or* **Saint Nich·o·las** \sänt-'nik-(ə-)ləs, sənt-\ *or* **Kriss Krin·gle** \'kris-'krin-gəl\ a fat jolly old man in modern folklore who delivers presents to good children at Christmastime

Sap·pho \'saf-ō\ *flourished about* 610–*about* 580 B.C. Greek poet

Sa·rah \'ser-ə, 'sar-ə, 'sä-rə\ wife of Abraham and mother of Isaac in the Bible

Sar·gent \'sär-jənt\ John Singer 1856–1925 American painter

Sat·urn \'sat-ərn\ a god of agriculture in Roman mythology

Saul \'söl\ first king of Israel in the Bible

Saul *or* **Saul of Tar·sus** \-'tär-səs\ the apostle Paul

Sche·her·a·zade \shə-ıher-ə-'zäd(-ə), -'zäd(-ē)\ fictional oriental queen and narrator of the tales in the *Arabian Nights' Entertainments*

Schu·bert \'shü-bərt, -ıbərt\ Franz Peter 1797–1828 Austrian composer

Schweit·zer \'shwīt-sər, 'swīt-, 'shvīt-\ Albert 1875–1965 French Protestant minister, philosopher, physician, and music scholar; Nobel Prize winner (1952)

Scott \'skät\ Dred \'dred\ 1795?–1858 American slave

Scott Sir Walter 1771–1832 Scottish author

Scott Winfield 1786–1866 American general

Scyl·la \'sil-ə\ a nymph in Greek mythology who is changed into a monster and inhabits a cave opposite the whirlpool Charybdis off the coast of Sicily

Se·quoya \si-'kwói-ə\ *about* 1760–1843 Cherokee linguist

Ser·ra \'ser-ə\ Junípero 1713–1784 Spanish missionary in Mexico and California

Se·ton \'sēt-ᵊn\ Saint Elizabeth Ann Bayley 1774–1821 *Mother Seton* American religious leader

Sew·ard \'sü-ərd, 'sú(-ə)rd\ William Henry 1801–1872 American politician; secretary of state (1861–69)

Shake·speare \'shāk-ıspi(ə)r\ William 1564–1616 English dramatist and poet

Shaw \'shó\ George Bernard 1856–1950 British author

Shel·ley \'shel-ē\ Mary Woll·stone·craft \'wúl-stən-ıkraft\ 1797–1851 English novelist; wife of Percy Bysshe Shelley

Shelley Percy Bysshe \'bish\ 1792–1822 English poet

Shep·ard \'shep-ərd\ Alan Bartlett 1923–1998 American astronaut; first American in space (1961)

Sher·i·dan \'sher-əd-ᵊn\ Philip Henry 1831–1888 American general

Sher·lock Holmes \'shər-ıläk-'hōmz, -'hōlmz\ detective in stories by Sir Arthur Conan Doyle

Sher·man \'shər-mən\ John 1823–1900 American politician

Sherman William Tecumseh 1820–1891 American general

Sieg·fried \'sig-ıfrēd, 'sēg-\ hero in Germanic legend who kills a dragon guarding a gold hoard

Si·mon \'sī-mən\ *or* **Simon the Zealot** one of the 12 apostles

Sind·bad the Sailor \'sin-ıbad-\ citizen of Baghdad whose adventures are narrated in the *Arabian Nights' Entertainments*

Sis·y·phus \'sis-ə-fəs\ king of Corinth who in Greek mythology is condemned to roll a heavy stone up a hill in Hades only to have it roll down again as it nears the top

Sit·ting Bull \ˌsit-iŋ-ˈbůl\ *about* 1831–90 Sioux Indian leader

Si·va \ˈshiv-ə, ˈsiv-; ˈshē-və, ˈsē-\ god of destruction in the Hindu sacred triad — compare BRAHMA, VISHNU

Smith \ˈsmith\ Bessie 1894 (or 1898)–1937 American blues singer

Smith John *about* 1580–1631 English colonist in America

Smith Joseph 1805–1844 American founder of the Mormon Church

Soc·ra·tes \ˈsäk-rə-ˌtēz\ *about* 470–399 B.C. Greek philosopher

Sol·o·mon \ˈsäl-ə-mən\ son of David and 10th-century B.C. king of Israel noted for his wisdom

Soph·o·cles \ˈsäf-ə-ˌklēz\ *about* 496–406 B.C. Greek dramatist

Sou·sa \ˈsü-zə, ˈsü-sə\ John Philip 1854–1932 American bandmaster and composer

Spar·ta·cus \ˈspärt-ə-kəs\ *died* 71 B.C. Roman slave and gladiator; leader of a slave rebellion

Sphinx \ˈsfiŋ(k)s\ monster in Greek mythology having a lion's body, wings, and the head and bust of a woman

Squan·to \ˈskwän-tō\ *died* 1622 Indian friend of the Pilgrims

Sta·lin \ˈstäl-ən, ˈstal-, -ˌēn\ Joseph 1879–1953 Soviet leader

Stan·dish \ˈstan-dish\ Myles *or* Miles 1584?–1656 American colonist

Stan·ley \ˈstan-lē\ Sir Henry Morton 1841–1904 British explorer in Africa

Stan·ton \ˈstant-ⁿn\ Elizabeth Cady 1815–1902 American suffragist

Stein \ˈstīn\ Gertrude 1874–1946 American author

Stein·beck \ˈstīn-ˌbek\ John Ernst 1902–1968 American author; Nobel Prize winner (1962)

Steu·ben, von \ˈst(y)ü-bən, ˈshtoi-\ Baron Friedrich Wilhelm Ludolf Gerhard Augustin 1730–1794 Prussian-born general in American Revolution

Ste·ven·son \ˈstē-vən-sən\ Adlai Ewing 1900–1965 American politician

Stevenson Robert Louis Balfour 1850–1894 Scottish author

Stowe \ˈstō\ Harriet Elizabeth Beecher 1811–1896 American author

Stra·di·va·ri \ˌstrad-ə-ˈvär-ē, -ˈvar-, -ˈver-\ Antonio 1644–1737 Latin *Antonius Strad·i·var·i·us* \ˌstrad-ə-ˈvar-ē-əs, -ˈver-\ Italian violin maker

Strauss \ˈstraůs, ˈshtraůs\ Johann father 1804–1849 and his sons Johann 1825–1899 and Josef 1827–1870 Austrian composers

Stu·art \ˈst(y)ü-ərt, ˈst(y)ů(-ə)rt\ — see CHARLES I, MARY STUART

Stuart Charles—CHARLES EDWARD STUART

Stuart Gilbert Charles 1755–1828 American painter

Stuart James Ewell Brown 1833–1864 *Jeb* American Confederate general

Stuy·ve·sant \ˈstī-və-sənt\ Peter *about* 1610–1672 Dutch colonial administrator in America

Sul·li·van \ˈsəl-ə-vən\ Sir Arthur Seymour 1842–1900 English composer; collaborator with Sir William Gilbert

Sullivan Louis Henri 1856–1924 American architect

Sum·ner \ˈsəm-nər\ Charles 1811–1874 American politician

Swift \ˈswift\ Jonathan 1667–1745 English author

Taft \ˈtaft\ William Howard 1857–1930 27th president of the U.S. (1909–13); chief justice of the U.S. Supreme Court (1921–30)

Ta·ney \ˈtȯ-nē\ Roger Brooke 1777–1864 American jurist; chief justice of the U.S. Supreme Court (1836–64)

Tan·ta·lus \ˈtant-ᵊl-əs\ king in Greek mythology who is

condemned to stand up to his chin in a pool of water in Hades and beneath fruit-laden boughs only to have the water or fruit go out of reach at each attempt to drink or eat

Tay·lor \ˈtā-lər\ Zachary 1784–1850 12th president of the U.S. (1849–50)

Tchai·kov·sky \chī-ˈkòf-skē, chə-, -ˈkòv-\ Pyotr Ilich 1840–1893 Russian composer

Te·cum·seh \tə-ˈkəm(p)-sə, -sē\ 1768–1813 Shawnee chief

Ten·ny·son \ˈten-ə-sən\ Alfred 1809–1892 known as *Alfred, Lord Tennyson* English poet

Te·re·sa \tə-ˈrā-zə, -ˈrē-sə\ of Á·vi·la \ˈäv-i-lə\ Saint 1515–1582 Spanish nun and mystic

The·seus \ˈthē-ˌsüs, -sē-əs\ hero in Greek mythology who kills the Minotaur and conquers the Amazons

Thom·as \ˈtäm-əs\ apostle in the Bible who demanded proof of Christ's resurrection

Thomas à Becket — see BECKET, À

Thor \ˈthò(ə)r\ god of thunder, weather, and crops in Norse mythology

Tho·reau \thə-ˈrō, thò-; ˈthòr-ō\ Henry David 1817–1862 American author

Thur·ber \ˈthər-bər\ James Grover 1894–1961 American author

Ti·be·ri·us \tī-ˈbir-ē-əs\ 42 B.C.–37 A.D. Roman emperor (14–37)

Tocque·ville \ˈtōk-ˌvil, ˈtòk-, ˈtäk-, -ˌvēl, -vəl\ Alexis⸗ Charles-Henri Clérel de 1805–1859 French politician and author

Tol·kien \ˈtòl-ˌkēn, ˈtòl-, ˈtäl-\ John Ronald Reuel 1892–1973 English author

Tol·stoy \tòl-ˈstòi, tōl-ˈstòi, täl-ˈstòi, ˈtòl-ˌstòi, ˈtōl-ˌstòi, ˈtäl-ˌstòi\ Count Lev Nikolayevich 1828–1910 Russian author

Tri·ton \ˈtrīt-ᵊn\ sea god in Greek mythology who is half man and half fish

Trots·ky \ˈträt-skē, ˈtròt-\ Leon 1879–1940 originally *Lev Davidovich Bronstein* Russian Communist

Tru·man \ˈtrü-mən\ Harry S. 1884–1972 33d president of the U.S. (1945–53)

Truth \ˈtrüth\ Sojourner 1797?–1883 American abolitionist

Tub·man \ˈtəb-mən\ Harriet *about* 1820–1913 American abolitionist

Tut·ankh·a·men \ˌtüt-ˌäŋ-ˈkäm-ən, -ˌtäŋ-\ *or* **Tut·ankh·a·ten** \-ˈkät-ᵊn\ *about* 1370–1352 B.C. king of Egypt (1361–1352 B.C.)

Twain Mark — see CLEMENS

Tweed \ˈtwēd\ William Marcy 1823–1878 *Boss Tweed* American politician

Ty·ler \ˈtī-lər\ John 1790–1862 10th president of the U.S. (1841–45)

Ulysses — see ODYSSEUS

Ura·nus \ˈyůr-ə-nəs, yù-ˈrā-\ the sky personified as a god and father of the Titans in Greek mythology

Ur·ban \ˈər-bən\ name of eight popes: especially **II** *about* 1035–1099 (pope 1088–99)

Uri·el \ˈyůr-ē-əl\ one of the four archangels named in Hebrew tradition — compare GABRIEL, MICHAEL, RAPHAEL

Val·en·tine \ˈval-ən-ˌtīn\ Saint 3d century Christian martyr

Van Bu·ren \van-ˈbyůr-ən, vən-\ Martin 1782–1862 8th president of the U.S. (1837–41)

Van Dyck *or* **Van·dyke** \van-ˈdīk, vən-\ Sir Anthony 1599–1641 Flemish painter

Ve·láz·quez \və-ˈlas-kəs\ Diego Rodríguez de Silva 1599–1660 Spanish painter

Ve·nus \ˈvē-nəs\ the goddess of love and beauty in Roman mythology — compare APHRODITE

Ver·di \ˈve(ə)rd-ē\ Giuseppe Fortunio Francesco 1813–1901 Italian composer

Ver·meer \vər-ˈme(ə)r, -ˈmi(ə)r\ Jan 1632–1675 also called *Jan van der Meer van Delft* Dutch painter

Verne Jules \ˈjülz-ˈvərn\ 1828–1905 French author

Ves·puc·ci \ve-'spü-chē\ Ame·ri·go \ˌäm-ə-'rē-gō\ 1454–1512 Latin *Amer·i·cus Ves·pu·cius* \ə-'mer-ə-kəs-ˌves-'pyü-sh(ē-)əs\ Italian navigator for whom America was named

Vic·to·ria \vik-'tōr-ē-ə, -'tȯr-\ 1819–1901 *Alexandrina Victoria* queen of Great Britain (1837–1901)

Vinci, da Leonardo — see LEONARDO DA VINCI

Vir·gil *also* **Ver·gil** \'vər-jəl\ 70–19 B.C. Roman poet

Vish·nu \'vish-nü\ god of preservation in the Hindu sacred triad — compare BRAHMA, SIVA

Vol·ta \'vōl-tə, 'väl-, 'vȯl-\ Count Alessandro Giuseppe Antonio Anastasio 1745–1827 Italian physicist

Vol·taire \vōl-'ta(ə)r, vȯl-, väl-, -'te(ə)r\ 1694–1778 originally *François-Marie Arouet* French author

Vul·can \'vəl-kən\ the god of fire and metalworking in Roman mythology — compare HEPHAESTUS

Wag·ner \'väg-nər\ (Wilhelm) Ri·chard \'rik-ärt, 'rik-\ 1813–1883 German composer

Walk·er \'wȯ-kər\ Alice Malsenior 1944–   American author

War·ren \'wȯr-ən, 'wär-\ Earl 1891–1974 American jurist; chief justice of the U.S. Supreme Court (1953–69)

Wash·ing·ton \'wȯsh-iŋ-tən, 'wäsh-\ Book·er \'bu̇k-ər\ Tal·ia·ferro \'täl-ə-vər\ 1856–1915 American educator

Washington George 1732–1799 American general; 1st president of the U.S. (1789–97)

Watt \'wät\ James 1736–1819 Scottish inventor

Wayne \'wān\ Anthony 1745–1796 *Mad Anthony* American general

Web·ster \'web-stər\ Daniel 1782–1852 American politician

Webster Noah 1758–1843 American lexicographer

Wel·ling·ton \'wel-iŋ-tən\ 1st Duke of 1769–1852 *Arthur Wellesley*; *the Iron Duke* British general and politician

Wells \'welz\ Herbert George 1866–1946 English author and historian

Wes·ley \'wes-lē, 'wez-\ John 1703–1791 English founder of Methodism

Wes·ting·house \'wes-tiŋ-ˌhau̇s\ George 1846–1914 American inventor

Whar·ton \'hwȯrt-ᵊn, 'wȯrt-\ Edith Newbold 1862–1937 American author

Whis·tler \'hwis-lər, 'wis-\ James Abbott McNeill 1834–1903 American artist

Whit·man \'hwit-mən, 'wit-\ Walt 1819–1892 American poet

Whit·ney \'hwit-nē, 'wit-\ Eli 1765–1825 American inventor

Whit·ti·er \'hwit-ē-ər, 'wit-\ John Greenleaf 1807–1892 American poet

Wilde \'wi(ə)ld\ Oscar Fingal O'Flahertie Wills 1854–1900 Irish author

Wil·der \'wil-dər\ Thornton Niven 1897–1975 American author

Wil·liam \'wil-yəm\ name of four kings of England: **I** *(the Conqueror) about* 1028–1087 (reigned 1066–87); **II** *(Rufus* \'rü-fəs\) *about* 1056–1100 (reigned 1087–1100); **III** 1650–1702 (reigned 1689–1702); **IV** 1765–1837 (reigned 1830–37)

Wil·liam Tell \ˌwil-yəm-'tel\ legendary Swiss patriot commanded to shoot an apple from his son's head

Wil·liams \'wil-yəmz\ Roger 1603?–1683 English colonist; founder of Rhode Island

Williams Tennessee 1911–1983 originally *Thomas Lanier Williams* American dramatist

Wil·son \'wil-sən\ (Thomas) Wood·row \'wu̇d-ˌrō\ 1856–1924 28th president of the U.S. (1913–21); Nobel Prize winner (1919)

Win·throp \'win(t)-thrəp\ John 1588–1649 1st governor of Massachusetts Bay Colony

Woden — see ODIN

Woolf \'wu̇lf\ Virginia 1882–1941 English author

Words·worth \'wərdz-(ˌ)wərth\ William 1770–1850 English poet

Wren \'ren\ Sir Christopher 1632–1723 English architect

Wright \'rīt\ Frank Lloyd 1867–1959 American architect

Wright Or·ville \'ȯr-vəl\ 1871–1948 and his brother Wilbur 1867–1912 American pioneers in aviation

Wright Richard 1908–1960 American author

Wy·eth \'wī-əth\ Andrew Newell 1917–   American painter

Yeats \'yāts\ William Butler 1865–1939 Irish author

Young \'yəŋ\ Brig·ham \'brig-əm\ 1801–1877 American Mormon leader

Zech·a·ri·ah \ˌzek-ə-'rī-ə\ Hebrew prophet of the 6th century B.C.

Zeng·er \'zeŋ-(g)ər\ John Peter 1697–1746 American (German-born) journalist and printer

Zeph·y·rus \'zef-ə-rəs\ god of the west wind in Greek mythology

Zeus \'züs\ chief god, ruler of the sky and weather (as lightning and rain), and husband of Hera in Greek mythology

Geographical Names

This section contains definitions of current and historical place-names likely to be of interest to the student. It adds to the general vocabulary by entering many adjectives and nouns formed from geographical names, such as **Florentine** at Florence and **Libyan** at Libya. In the entries the letters N, E, S, and W singly or in combination indicate direction and are not part of a place name. They may represent either the name of the direction (as *north*) or the adjective derived from it (as *northern*); thus, west-northwest of Santiago appears as WNW of Santiago and southern California appears as S California. The only other special abbreviations used in this section are U.S. for United States, and U.S.S.R. for Union of Soviet Socialist Republics. All heights and distances are given in metric units.

Ab·er·deen \ˌab-ər-ˈdēn\ city NE Scotland in Grampian region — **Ab·er·do·ni·an** \-ˈdō-nē-ən\ *adj or n*
Ab·i·djan \ˌab-i-ˈjän\ city, seat of government of Ivory Coast
Abu Dha·bi \ˌäb-ü-ˈdäb-ē\ city, capital of United Arab Emirates
Abu·ja \ä-ˈbü-jä\ city, official capital of Nigeria
Ab·ys·sin·ia \ˌab-ə-ˈsin-ē-ə, -ˈsin-yə\ — see ETHIOPIA — **Ab·ys·sin·i·an** \-ē-ən, -yən\ *adj or n*
Aca·dia \ə-ˈkäd-ē-ə\ *or French* **Aca·die** \à-kà-dē\ NOVA SCOTIA — an early name — **Aca·di·an** \-ē-ən\ *adj or n*
Aca·pul·co \ˌäk-ə-ˈpül-kō, ˌak-\ city S Mexico on the Pacific
Ac·cra \ə-ˈkrä\ city, capital of Ghana
Acon·ca·gua \ˌak-ən-ˈkäg-wə, ˌäk-, -əŋ-\ mountain 6960 meters W Argentina; highest in the Andes & in North America & South America
Ad·dis Aba·ba \ˌad-ə-ˈsab-ə-bə\ city, capital of Ethiopia
Ad·e·laide \ˈad-əl-ˌād\ city, capital of South Australia
Aden \ˈäd-ən, ˈäd-, ˈad-\ city S Yemen; formerly capital of People's Democratic Republic of Yemen
Aden, Gulf of arm of Indian ocean between Yemen (Arabia) & Somalia (Africa)
Ad·i·ron·dack \ˌad-ə-ˈrän-ˌdak\ mountains NE New York; highest Mount Marcy 1629 meters
Ad·mi·ral·ty \ˈad-m(ə-)rəl-tē\ **1** island SE Alaska in N Alexander island group **2** islands W Pacific N of New Guinea; belong to Papua New Guinea
Adri·at·ic \ˌā-drē-ˈat-ik, ˌad-rē-\ sea arm of Mediterranean between Italy & Balkan peninsula
Ae·ge·an \i-ˈjē-ən\ sea arm of Mediterranean between Asia Minor & Greece
Af·ghan·i·stan \af-ˈgan-ə-ˌstan\ country W Asia E of Iran; capital, Kabul
Af·ri·ca \ˈaf-ri-kə\ continent S of Mediterranean
Aga·na \ə-ˈgän-yə\ town, capital of Guam
Agra \ˈäg-rə\ city N India
Aguas·ca·lien·tes \ˌäg-wə-skäl-ˈyen-ˌtās\ city central Mexico, NE of Guadalajara
Agul·has, Cape \ə-ˈgəl-əs\ cape Republic of South Africa in S Western Cape Province; most southerly point of Africa, at 34°50′ S latitude
Ahag·gar \ə-ˈhäg-ər, ˌä-hə-ˈgär\ mountains S Algeria in W central Sahara
Ah·mad·abad *or* **Ah·med·abad** \ˈäm-əd-ə-ˌbäd\ city W India
Ak·ron \ˈak-rən\ city NE Ohio
Al·a·bama \ˌal-ə-ˈbam-ə\ state SE U.S.; capital, Montgomery — **Al·a·bam·i·an** \-ˈbam-ē-ən\ *or* **Al·a·bam·an** \-ˈbam-ən\ *adj or n*
Alas·ka \ə-ˈlas-kə\ **1** peninsula SW Alaska SW of Cook inlet **2** state of U.S. in NW North America; capital, Juneau **3** mountain range S Alaska extending from Alaska peninsula to Yukon boundary — **Alas·kan** \-kən\ *adj or n*
Alaska, Gulf of inlet of Pacific off S Alaska between Alaska peninsula on W & Alexander island group on E

Al·ba·nia \al-ˈbā-nē-ə, -nyə\ country S Europe in Balkan peninsula on Adriatic; capital, Tirane
Al·ba·ny \ˈȯl-bə-nē\ city, capital of New York
Al·be·marle \ˈal-bə-ˌmärl\ inlet of Atlantic in NE North Carolina
Al·bert, Lake \-ˈal-bərt\ lake E Africa between Uganda & Democratic Republic of the Congo in course of Nile
Al·ber·ta \al-ˈbərt-ə\ province W Canada; capital, Edmonton — **Al·ber·tan** \-ˈbərt-ᵊn\ *adj or n*
Al·bu·quer·que \ˈal-bə-ˌkər-kē\ city central New Mexico
Al·ca·traz \ˈal-kə-ˌtraz\ island California in San Francisco Bay
Al·da·bra \ˈal-də-brə\ island NW Indian ocean N of Madagascar; belongs to Seychelles
Al·der·ney \ˈȯl-dər-nē\ island in English channel — see CHANNEL
Alep·po \ə-ˈlep-ō\ city N Syria
Aleu·tian \ə-ˈlü-shən\ islands SW Alaska extending W from Alaska peninsula
Al·ex·an·der \ˌal-ig-ˈzan-dər, ˌel-\ island group SE Alaska
Al·ex·an·dria \ˌal-ig-ˈzan-drē-ə, ˌel-\ **1** city N Virginia **2** city N Egypt on Mediterranean — **Al·ex·an·dri·an** \-drē-ən\ *adj or n*
Al·ge·ria \al-ˈjir-ē-ə\ country NW Africa on Mediterranean; capital, Algiers — **Al·ge·ri·an** \-ē-ən\ *adj or n*
Al·giers \al-ˈji(ə)rz\ city, capital of Algeria — **Al·ge·rine** \ˌal-jə-ˈrēn\ *adj or n*
Al·lah·abad \ˈal-ə-hə-ˌbad, -ˌbäd\ city N India
Al·le·ghe·ny \ˌal-ə-ˈgā-nē\ **1** river 523 kilometers long W Pennsylvania & SW New York **2** mountains of Appalachian system E U.S. in Pennsylvania, Maryland, Virginia, & West Virginia
Al·len·town \ˈal-ən-ˌtaün\ city E Pennsylvania
Al·ma-Ata \ˌal-ˈmä-ə-ˈtä, ˌal-mə-ə-ˈtä\ *or* **Al·maty** \ˈal-ˈmä-tē\ city, former capital of Kazakhstan
Alps \ˈalps\ mountain system central Europe — see MONT BLANC
Al·tai \ˈal-ˌtī\ mountain system central Asia between Mongolia & W China & between Kazakhstan & Russia; highest peak Tabun Bogdo 4653 meters
Ama·ga·sa·ki \ˌam-ə-gə-ˈsäk-ē\ city Japan in W central Honshu
Am·a·ril·lo \ˌam-ə-ˈril-ō, -ˈril-ə\ city NW Texas
Am·a·zon \ˈam-ə-ˌzän, -zən\ river about 6275 kilometers long N South America flowing from Peruvian Andes into Atlantic in N Brazil
Amer·i·ca \ə-ˈmer-ə-kə\ **1** either continent (North America or South America) of western hemisphere **2** *or the* **Amer·i·cas** \-kəz\ lands of western hemisphere including North, Central, & South America & West Indies **3** UNITED STATES OF AMERICA
American Falls — see NIAGARA FALLS
American Samoa islands SW central Pacific; capital, Pago Pago (on Tutuila island)
Am·man \ä-ˈmän, -ˈman\ city, capital of Jordan
Am·ster·dam \ˈam(p)-stər-ˌdam\ city, official capital of the Netherlands

Amur \ä-'mu̇(ə)r\ river 2865 kilometers long E Asia flowing into the Pacific & forming part of boundary between China & Russia

An·a·heim \'an-ə-ˌhīm\ city SW California E of Long Beach

An·a·to·lia \ˌan-ə-'tō-lē-ə, -'tōl-yə\ — see ASIA MINOR — **An·a·to·li·an** \-'tō-lē-ən, -'tōl-yən\ adj or n

An·chor·age \'aŋ-k(ə-)rij\ city S central Alaska

An·da·man \'an-də-mən, -ˌman\ 1 islands India in Bay of Bengal S of Myanmar & N of Nicobar islands 2 sea arm of Bay of Bengal S of Myanmar — **An·da·man·ese** \ˌan-də-mə-'nēz, -'nēs\ adj or n

An·des \'an-dēz\ mountain system W South America extending from Panama to Tierra del Fuego — see ACONCAGUA — **An·de·an** \'an-(ˌ)dē-ən, an-'dē-\ adj — **An·dine** \'an-ˌdēn, -ˌdīn\ adj

An·dor·ra \an-'dȯr-ə, -där-ə\ country SW Europe in E Pyrenees between France & Spain; capital, Andorra la Vella — **An·dor·ran** \-ən\ adj or n

An·dros \'an-drəs\ island, largest of Bahamas

An·gel Falls \ˌān-jəl-\ waterfall 979 meters SE Venezuela; world's highest waterfall

Ang·kor \'aŋ-ˌkȯ(ə)r\ ruins of ancient city NW Cambodia

An·gle·sey \'aŋ-gəl-sē\ island NW Wales

An·go·la \aŋ-'gō-lə, an-\ country SW Africa S of mouth of Congo river; until 1975 a dependency of Portugal; capital, Luanda — **An·go·lan** \-lən\ adj or n

An·i·ak·chak Crater \ˌan-ē-'ak-ˌchak-\ volcano 1347 meters SW Alaska on Alaska peninsula; crater 10 kilometers in diameter

An·ka·ra \'aŋ-kə-rə, äŋ-\ city, capital of Turkey in N central Anatolia

An·nap·o·lis \ə-'nap-(ə-)ləs\ city, capital of Maryland

Ann Ar·bor \a-'när-bər\ city SE Michigan

An·shan \'än-'shän\ city NE China

An·ta·nan·a·ri·vo \ˌan-tə-ˌnan-ə-'rē-vō\ city, capital of Madagascar

Ant·arc·ti·ca \(')ant-'ärk-ti-kə, -'ärt-i-\ or **Ant·arc·tic continent** \-'ärk-tik-, -'ärt-ik-\ body of land around the South Pole; plateau covered by great ice cap

An·ti·gua \an-'tē-gə\ island West Indies in the Leewards E of Nevis; capital, Saint Johns; part of independent Antigua and Barbuda

Antigua and Barbuda country West Indies in the Leewards; capital, St. Johns

An·til·les \an-'til-ēz\ the West Indies except for the Bahamas — see GREATER ANTILLES, LESSER ANTILLES — **An·til·le·an** \-'til-ē-ən\ adj

An·trim \'an-trəm\ 1 district E Northern Ireland 2 town in Antrim district

Aorangi — see COOK, MOUNT

Ap·en·nines \'ap-ə-ˌnīnz\ mountain chain Italy extending length of the peninsula; highest point Monte Corno (NE of Rome) 2914 meters — **Ap·en·nine** \-ˌnīn\ adj

Apia \ə-'pē-ə\ town, capital of independent Samoa

Apo, Mount \-'ä-pō\ volcano Philippines in SE Mindanao 2954 meters; highest peak in the Philippines

Ap·pa·la·chia \ˌap-ə-'lā-chə, -'lach-ə, -'lā-shə\ region E U.S. including Appalachian mountains from S central New York to central Alabama

Ap·pa·la·chian \ˌap-ə-'lā-ch(ē-)ən, -'lach(-ē)-ən, -'lāsh(ē-)ən\ mountain system E North America extending from S Quebec to central Alabama — see MITCHELL, MOUNT

'Aqa·ba, Gulf of \-'äk-ə-bə, -'ak-\ arm of Red sea E of Sinai peninsula

Aquid·neck Island \ə-'kwid-ˌnek-\ or **Rhode Island** island SE Rhode Island in Narragansett Bay

Ara·bia \ə-'rā-bē-ə\ peninsula of SW Asia including Saudi Arabia, Yemen, Oman, & Persian Gulf States

Ara·bi·an \ə-'rā-bē-ən\ sea NW section of Indian ocean between Arabia & India

Ar·a·fu·ra \ˌar-ə-'fu̇r-ə\ sea between N Australia & W New Guinea

Ar·al sea \'ar-əl-\ or formerly **Lake Aral** lake W Asia between Kazakhstan & Uzbekistan

Ar·a·rat \'ar-ə-ˌrat\ mountain 5165 meters E Turkey near border of Iran

Arc·tic \'ärk-tik, 'ärt-ik\ 1 ocean N of Arctic circle 2 Arctic regions 3 island group N Canada in N & E Northwest Territories

Ar·da·bil or **Ar·de·bil** \ˌär-də-'bē(ə)l\ city NW Iran

Ards \'ärdz\ district E Northern Ireland

Ar·gen·ti·na \ˌär-jən-'tē-nə\ country S South America between the Andes & the Atlantic; capital, Buenos Aires — **Argentine** \'är-jən-ˌtēn, -ˌtīn\ adj or n — **Ar·gen·tin·ean** or **Ar·gen·tin·i·an** \ˌär-jən-'tin-ē-ən\ adj or n

Ar·gos \'är-ˌgäs, -gəs\ ancient Greek city & state S Greece

Ar·i·zo·na \ˌar-ə-'zō-nə\ state SW U.S.; capital, Phoenix — **Ar·i·zo·nan** \-nən\ or **Ar·i·zo·nian** \-nē-ən, -nyən\ adj or n

Ar·kan·sas \'är-kən-ˌsȯ; 1 is also är-'kan-zəs\ 1 river 2335 kilometers long SW central U.S. flowing SE into the Mississippi 2 state S central U.S.; capital, Little Rock — **Ar·kan·san** \är-'kan-zən\ adj or n

Ar·ling·ton \'är-liŋ-tən\ city N Texas

Ar·magh \är-'mä, 'är-ˌmä\ 1 district S Northern Ireland 2 town in Armagh district

Ar·me·nia \är-'mē-nē-ə, -nyə\ 1 region W Asia in mountainous area SE of Black sea & SW of Caspian sea divided between Iran, Turkey, & Armenia (country) 2 country E Europe; capital, Yerevan; a republic of U.S.S.R. 1936–91 — **Ar·me·ni·an** \-nē-ən, -nyən\ adj or n

Arn·hem Land \'är-nəm-\ region N Australia on N coast of Northern Territory

Ar·no \'är-nō\ river 241 kilometers long central Italy flowing through Florence

Aru·ba \ə-'rü-bə\ island Netherlands Antilles off coast of NW Venezuela

Ashkh·a·bad \'ash-kə-ˌbad, -ˌbäd\ or **Ash·ga·bat** \'äsh-gä-ˌbät\ city, capital of Turkmenistan

Asia \'ā-zhə, -shə\ continent of eastern hemisphere N of equator — see EURASIA

Asia Mi·nor \-'mī-nər\ or **Anatolia** peninsula in modern Turkey between Black sea on N & the Mediterranean on S

As·ma·ra \az-'mär-ə, -'mar-ə\ city, capital of Eritrea

As·syr·ia \ə-'sir-ē-ə\ ancient empire W Asia extending along the middle Tigris & over foothills to the E — **As·syr·i·an** \-ē-ən\ adj or n

As·ta·na \ə-'stä-nə\ city, capital of Kazakhstan

Asun·ción \ə-ˌsün(t)-sē-'ōn, (ˌ)ä-\ city, capital of Paraguay

As·wân \a-'swän, ä-\ city S Egypt on the Nile near site of **Aswân High Dam**

Ata·ca·ma \ˌat-ə-'käm-ə\ desert N Chile

Atchaf·a·laya \(ə-)ˌchaf-ə-'lī-ə\ river 362 kilometers long S Louisiana flowing S into Gulf of Mexico

Ath·a·bas·ca or **Ath·a·bas·ka** \ˌath-ə-'bas-kə\ river 1231 kilometers long NE Alberta flowing into Lake Athabasca

Athabasca, Lake lake W central Canada on Alberta-Saskatchewan border

Ath·ens \'ath-ənz\ city, capital of Greece — **Athe·nian** \ə-'thē-nē-ən, -nyən\ adj or n

At·lan·ta \ət-'lant-ə, at-\ city, capital of Georgia

At·lan·tic \ət-'lant-ik, at-\ ocean separating North America & South America from Europe & Africa — **Atlantic** adj

At·las \'at-ləs\ mountains NW Africa extending from SW Morocco to N Tunisia

At·ti·ca \'at-i-kə\ ancient division & state E Greece; chief city Athens — **At·tic** \'at-ik\ adj

Auck·land \'ȯ-klənd\ city N New Zealand on NW North island

Au·gus·ta \ȯ-'gəst-ə, ə-\ city, capital of Maine

Au·ro·ra \ə-'rȯr-ə, ȯ-, -'rȯr-\ city NE central Colorado

ONE OF THE SMALLER CONTINENTS

Aus·tin \ˈȯs-tən, ˈäs-\ city, capital of Texas

Aus·tral·asia \ˌȯs-trə-ˈlā-zhə, ˌäs-, -ˈlā-shə\ Australia, Tasmania, New Zealand, & Melanesia — **Aus·tral·asian** \-zhən, -shən\ adj or n

 **Aus·tra·lia** \ò-ˈstrāl-yə, ä-, ə-\ **1** continent of eastern hemisphere SE of Asia **2** independent country in the Commonwealth including continent of Australia & island of Tasmania; capital, Canberra — **Aus·tra·lian** \-yən\ adj or n

Australian Alps mountain range SE Australia in E Victoria & SE New South Wales; part of Great Dividing range

Australian Capital Territory district SE Australia including two areas, one containing Canberra (capital of Australia) & the other on Jervis Bay; surrounded by New South Wales

Aus·tria \ˈȯs-trē-ə, ˈäs-\ country central Europe; capital, Vienna — **Aus·tri·an** \-ən\ adj or n

Aus·tria–Hun·ga·ry \-ˈhəŋ-gə-rē\ country 1867–1918 central Europe including Bohemia, Moravia, Bukovina, Transylvania, Galicia, and what are now Austria, Hungary, Slovenia, Croatia, & part of NE Italy — **Aus·tro–Hun·gar·i·an** \ˈȯs-(ˌ)trō-ˌhəŋ-ˈgar-ē-ən, ˈäs-, -ˈger-\ adj or n

Aus·tro·ne·sia \ˌȯs-trə-ˈnē-zhə, ˌäs-, -ˈnē-shə\ **1** islands of the S Pacific **2** area extending from Madagascar through Malay peninsula & island group to Hawaii & Easter island — **Aus·tro·ne·sian** \-zhən, -shən\ adj or n

Avon \ˈā-vən, ˈav-ən, in the U.S. also ˈā-ˌvän\ **1** river 155 kilometers long central England flowing WSW into the Severn **2** county SW England

Ayles·bury \ˈā(ə)lz-b(ə-)rē, in the U.S. also -ˌber-ē\ borough SE central England in Buckinghamshire

Ayr \ˈa(ə)r, ˈe(ə)r\ or **Ayr·shire** \-ˌshi(ə)r, -shər\ former county SW Scotland

Az·ca·po·tzal·co \ˌäs-kə-pət-ˈsäl-(ˌ)kō, ˌäz-gə-\ city central Mexico, NW of Mexico City

Azer·bai·jan \ˌaz-ər-ˌbī-ˈjän, ˌäz-\ country SE Europe bordering on Caspian sea; capital, Baku; a republic of U.S.S.R. 1936–91

Azores \ˈā-ˌzō(ə)rz, -ˌzȯ(ə)rz; ə-ˈzō(ə)rz, -ˈzȯ(ə)rz\ islands N Atlantic belonging to Portugal & lying 1290 kilometers W of Portuguese coast — **Azor·e·an** or **Azor·i·an** \ā-ˈzōr-ē-ən, ə-, -ˈzȯr-\ adj or n

Bab·y·lon \ˈbab-ə-lən, -ˌlän\ ancient city, capital of Babylonia; site about 89 kilometers S of Baghdad near the Euphrates — **Bab·y·lo·nian** \ˌbab-ə-ˈlō-nyən, -nē-ən\ adj or n

Bab·y·lo·nia \ˌbab-ə-ˈlō-nyə, -nē-ə\ ancient country W Asia in valley of lower Euphrates and Tigris rivers; capital, Babylon — **Bab·y·lo·nian** \-nyən, -nē-ən\ adj or n

Bac·tria \ˈbak-trē-ə\ ancient country W Asia in present NE Afghanistan — **Bac·tri·an** \-ən\ adj or n

Bad Lands barren region SW South Dakota & NW Nebraska

Baf·fin \ˈbaf-ən\ island NE Canada in Arctic island group N of Hudson strait

Baffin Bay inlet of the Atlantic between W Greenland & E Baffin island

Bagh·dad \ˈbag-ˌdad\ city, capital of Iraq on the Tigris

Ba·guio \ˌbäg-ē-ˈō\ city, formerly summer capital of the Philippines in NW central Luzon

Ba·ha·mas \bə-ˈhäm-əz, by outsiders also -ˈhä-məz\ islands in N Atlantic SE of Florida; an independent member of the Commonwealth; capital, Nassau — **Ba·ha·mi·an** \bə-ˈhä-mē-ən, -ˈhäm-ē-ən\ or **Ba·ha·man** \-ˈhä-mən, -ˈhäm-ən\ adj or n

Bahia — see SALVADOR

Bah·rain \bä-ˈrān\ islands in Persian gulf off coast of Arabia; an independent country; capital, Manama

Bai·kal, Lake \-bī-ˈkȯl, -ˈkäl\ lake Russia, in mountains N of Mongolia

Ba·ja California \ˌbä-(ˌ)hä-\ peninsula NW Mexico W of Gulf of California

Ba·kers·field \ˈbā-kərz-ˌfēld\ city S California

Ba·ku \bä-ˈkü\ city, capital of Azerbaijan on W coast of Caspian sea

Bal·a·ton \ˈbal-ə-ˌtän, ˈbȯl-ə-ˌtōn\ lake W Hungary

Bal·boa Heights \(ˌ)bal-ˌbō-ə-\ town Panama; formerly the center of administration for Canal Zone

Ba·li \ˈbäl-ē\ island Indonesia off E end of Java — **Ba·li·nese** \ˌbäl-i-ˈnēz, ˌbal-, -ˈnēs\ adj or n

Bal·kan \ˈbȯl-kən\ **1** mountains N Bulgaria extending from Yugoslavia border to Black sea; highest about 2380 meters **2** peninsula SE Europe between Adriatic & Ionian seas on the W & Aegean & Black seas on the E

Bal·kans \ˈbȯl-kənz\ or **Balkan States** countries occupying the Balkan peninsula: Slovenia, Croatia, Bosnia and Herzegovina, Macedonia, Yugoslavia, Romania, Bulgaria, Albania, Greece, Turkey (in Europe)

Bal·ly·cas·tle \ˌbal-ē-ˈkas-əl\ town N Northern Ireland in Moyle district

Bal·ly·me·na \ˌbal-ē-ˈmē-nə\ district NE central Northern Ireland

Bal·ly·mon·ey \ˌbal-ē-ˈmən-ē\ district N central Northern Ireland

Bal·tic \ˈbȯl-tik\ sea arm of the Atlantic N Europe E of Scandinavian peninsula

Bal·ti·more \ˈbȯl-tə-ˌmō(ə)r, -ˌmȯ(ə)r; ˈbȯl-(tə-)mər\ city N central Maryland

Ba·ma·ko \ˌbäm-ə-ˈkō\ city, capital of Mali on the Niger

Ban·bridge \ban-ˈbrij\ district SE central Northern Ireland

Ban·dar Se·ri Be·ga·wan \ˌbən-dər-ˌser-ē-bə-ˈgä-wən\ town, capital of Brunei

Ban·dung \ˈbän-ˌdùŋ\ city Indonesia in W Java SE of Jakarta

Ban·ga·lore \ˈbaŋ-gə-ˌlō(ə)r, -ˌlȯ(ə)r\ city S India W of Madras

Bang·kok \\'baŋ-ˌkäk, baŋ-'käk\ city, capital of Thailand

Ban·gla·desh \ˌbäŋ-gle-'desh, ˌbaŋ-, -'däsh\ country S Asia E of India; formerly part of Pakistan; an independent state since 1971; capital, Dhaka — see EAST PAKISTAN

Ban·gor \\'baŋ-ˌgȯ(ə)r, 'ban-ˌgȯ(ə)r, 'baŋ-gər\ city area E Northern Ireland in North Down district

Ban·gui \bäŋ-'gē\ city, capital of Central African Republic

Ban·jul \'bän-ˌjül\ or formerly **Bath·urst** \'bath-(ˌ)ərst\ city, capital of Gambia

Bao·tou or **Pao–t'ou** \'baù-'tō\ city N China

Bar·ba·dos \bär-'bād-əs, -ōz, -äs, -ōs\ island West Indies in Lesser Antilles E of Windward Islands; an independent country in the Commonwealth since 1966; capital, Bridgetown — **Bar·ba·di·an** \-'bäd-ē-ən\ adj or n

Bar·bu·da \bär-'büd-ə\ island West Indies; part of independent Antigua and Barbuda

Bar·ce·lo·na \ˌbär-sə-'lō-nə\ city NE Spain on the Mediterranean; chief city of Catalonia

Bar·king \'bär-kiŋ\ city area of E Greater London county, England

Bar·na·ul \ˌbär-nə-'ül\ city S Russia

Bar·net \'bär-nət\ city area of N Greater London county, England

Bar·ran·qui·lla \ˌbar-ən-'kē-(y)ə\ city N Colombia

Barren Grounds treeless plains N Canada W of Hudson bay

Bar·row, Point \-'bar-ō\ most northerly point of Alaska & of United States at about 71°25′N latitude

Ba·si·lan \ˌbä-sē-ˌlän\ island S Philippines

Bas·il·don \'baz-əl-dən\ town SE England in Essex county

Bass \'bas\ strait separating Tasmania & continent of Australia

Basse·terre \bas-'te(ə)r, bäs-\ seaport St. Kitts, capital of Saint Kitts-Nevis

Basutoland — see LESOTHO

Batavia — see JAKARTA

Bathurst — see BANJUL

Bat·on Rouge \ˌbat-ᵊn-'rüzh\ city, capital of Louisiana

Ba·var·ia \bə-'ver-ē-ə, -'var-\ or German **Bay·ern** \'bī-ərn\ state SE Germany bordering on Czech Republic & Austria — **Ba·var·i·an** \bə-'ver-ē-ən, -'var-\ adj or n

Ba·ya·mon \ˌbī-ə-'mōn\ city NE central Puerto Rico

Beau·fort \'bō-fərt\ sea consisting of part of Arctic ocean NE of Alaska & NW of Canada

Beau·mont \'bō-ˌmänt, bō-'mänt\ city SE Texas

Bech·u·a·na·land \ˌbech-(ə-)'wän-ə-ˌland\ 1 region S Africa N of Orange river 2 — see BOTSWANA — **Bech·u·a·na** \ˌbech-(ə-)'wän-ə\ adj or n

Bed·ford·shire \'bed-fərd-ˌshi(ə)r, -shər\ or **Bedford** county SE England

Bedloe's or **Bedloe** — see LIBERTY

Bei·jing \'bā-'jiŋ\ or **Pe·king** \'pē-'kiŋ, 'pā-\ city, capital of China

Bei·rut \bā-'rüt\ city, capital of Lebanon

Be·la·rus \ˌbē-lə-'rüs, ˌbyel-ə-\ or **Bye·la·rus** \bē-ˌel-ə-, ˌbyel-ə-\ country central Europe; capital, Minsk

Belau — see PALAU

Be·lém \bə-'lem\ city N Brazil

Bel·fast \'bel-ˌfast, bel-'fast\ 1 district E Northern Ireland 2 city, capital of Northern Ireland in Antrim district

Belgian Congo — see CONGO 2

Bel·gium \'bel-jəm\ or French **Bel·gique** \bel-zhēk\ or Flemish **Bel·gië** \'bel-gē-ə\ county W Europe; capital, Brussels — **Bel·gian** \'bel-jən\ adj or n

Bel·grade \'bel-ˌgrād, -ˌgräd, -'grad\ or **Beo·grad** \'beù-ˌgräd\ city, capital of Yugoslavia on the Danube

Be·lize \bə-'lēz\ or formerly **British Honduras** country

Central America on the Caribbean; capital, Belmopan

Bel·mo·pan \ˌbel-mō-'pan\ city, capital of Belize

Be·lo Ho·ri·zon·te \'bä-lō-ˌhȯr-ə-'zänt-ē, 'bel-ō-, -ˌhär-\ city E Brazil N of Rio de Janeiro

Be·lo·rus·sia \ˌbel-ō-'rəsh-ə, ˌbyel-\ or **Bye·lo·rus·sia** \bē-ˌel-ō-, ˌbyel-ō-\ former republic of U.S.S.R.; became independent Belarus in 1991 — **Belorussian** adj or n

Ben·gal \ben-'gȯl, beŋ-\ region S Asia including delta of Ganges & Brahmaputra rivers; divided between Bangladesh & India — **Ben·gal·ese** \ˌbeŋ-gə-'lēz, ˌben-, -'lēs\ adj or n

Bengal, Bay of arm of Indian ocean between India & Myanmar

Be·nin \bə-'nin, -'nēn\ or formerly **Da·ho·mey** \də-'hō-mē\ country W Africa on Gulf of Guinea; capital, Porto-Novo — **Ben·i·nese** \bə-ˌnin-'ēz, -ˌnēn-; ˌben-i-'nēz, -'nēs\ adj or n

Ben Nev·is \ben-'nev-əs\ mountain 1343 meters W Scotland in the Grampians; highest in Great Britain

Ber·gen \'bər-gən, 'be(ə)r-\ city SW Norway

Be·ring \'bi(ə)r-iŋ, 'be(ə)r-\ 1 sea arm of the N Pacific between Alaska & NE Siberia 2 strait about 90 kilometers wide between North America (Alaska) and Asia (Russia)

Berke·ley \'bər-klē\ city W California on San Francisco Bay N of Oakland

Berk·shire \'bərk-ˌshi(ə)r, -shər, for 2 British usually 'bärk-\ 1 hills W Massachusetts; highest point Mount Greylock 1064 meters 2 county S England W of London

Ber·lin \(ˌ)bər-'lin\ city, official capital of Germany; divided 1945–90 into **East Berlin** (capital of East Germany) & **West Berlin** (city of West Germany lying within East Germany) — **Ber·lin·er** \-'lin-ər\ n

Ber·mu·da \(ˌ)bər-'myüd-ə\ islands W Atlantic ESE of Cape Hatteras; a British colony; capital, Hamilton — **Ber·mu·dan** \-'myüd-ᵊn\ or **Ber·mu·di·an** \-'myüd-ē-ən\ adj or n

Bern or **Berne** \'bərn, 'be(ə)rn\ city, capital of Switzerland — **Ber·nese** \(ˌ)bər-'nēz, -'nēs\ adj or n

Bes·sa·ra·bia \ˌbes-ə-'rä-bē-ə\ region SE Europe now chiefly in Moldova — **Bes·sa·ra·bi·an** \-bē-ən\ adj or n

Beth·le·hem \'beth-li-ˌhem, -lē-həm, -lē-əm\ town of ancient Palestine in Judea SW of Jerusalem in area occupied by Israel since 1967

Bev·er·ly Hills \ˌbev-ər-lē-'hilz\ city SW California within city of Los Angeles

Bex·ley \'bek-slē\ city area of E Greater London county, England

Bho·pal \bō-'päl\ city N central India

Bhu·tan \bü-'tan, -'tän\ country S Asia in the Himalayas on NE border of India; capital, Thimphu — **Bhu·ta·nese** \ˌbüt-ᵊn-'ēz, -'ēs\ adj or n

Bi·ki·ni \bə-'kē-nē\ island W Pacific in Marshall islands

Bil·lings \'bil-iŋz\ city S central Montana; largest in state

Bi·lox·i \bə-'lək-sē, -'läk-\ city SE Mississippi on Gulf of Mexico

Bi·o·ko \bē-'ō-kō\ or formerly **Fer·nan·do Po** \fər-ˌnan-(ˌ)dō-'pō\ or 1973–79 **Ma·cí·as Ngue·ma Bi·yo·go** \'mä-thē-ə-sən-'(g)wä-mə-bi-'yō-(ˌ)gō\ island portion of Equatorial Guinea in Gulf of Guinea

Bir·ken·head \'bər-kən-ˌhed, ˌbər-kən-'hed\ city area NW England in Merseyside county

Bir·ming·ham \'bər-miŋ-ˌham, British usually -miŋ-əm\ 1 city N central Alabama 2 city W central England in West Midlands county

Bisayas — see VISAYAN

Bis·cay, Bay of \'bis-ˌkā, -kē\ inlet of the Atlantic between W coast of France & N coast of Spain

Bish·kek \bish-'kek\ or 1926–91 **Frunze** \'frün-zə\ city, capital of Kyrgyzstan

Bis·marck \'biz-₁märk\ **1** city, capital of North Dakota **2** island group W Pacific N of E end of New Guinea

Bis·sau \bis-'aü\ city, capital of Guinea-Bissau

Bi·thyn·ia \bə-'thin-ē-ə\ ancient country NW Asia Minor bordering on Sea of Marmara and Black sea — **Bi·thyn·i·an** \-ē-ən\ adj or n

Bit·ter·root Range \'bit-ə(r)-₁rüt-, -₁rüt-\ range of the Rockies along Idaho-Montana boundary

Black·burn \'blak-(₁)bərn\ city area NW England in Lancashire

Black Forest forested mountain region SW Germany along E bank of the upper Rhine

Black hills mountains W South Dakota & NE Wyoming; highest Harney Peak 2207 meters

Black·pool \'blak-₁pül\ city area NW England in Lancashire

Black sea or ancient **Pon·tus Eux·i·nus** \'pänt-əs-₁yük-'sī-nəs\ or **Pon·tus** sea between Europe & Asia connected with Aegean sea through the Bosporus, Sea of Marmara, & Dardanelles

Blanc, Mont — see MONT BLANC

Bloem·fon·tein \'blüm-fən-₁tān, -₁fän-\ city Republic of South Africa, capital of Free State & judicial capital of the country

Blue Ridge E range of the Applachians E U.S. extending from S Pennsylvania to N Georgia

Boe·o·tia \bē-'ō-sh(ē-)ə\ ancient state E central Greece NW of Attica; chief ancient city, Thebes — **Boe·o·tian** \bē-'ō-shən\ adj or n

Bo·go·tá \₁bō-gə-'tò, -'tä\ city, capital of Colombia

Bo Hai or **Po Hai** \'bō-'hī\ or **Gulf of Chih·li** \'chē-lē, 'jir-\ arm of Yellow Sea NE China

Bo·he·mia \bō-'hē-mē-ə\ region W Czech Republic; once a kingdom; chief city, Prague

Bo·hol \bō-'hòl\ island S central Philippines

Boi·se \'bòi-sē, -zē\ city, capital of Idaho

Bo·liv·ia \bə-'liv-ē-ə\ country W central South America; administrative capital, La Paz; constitutional capital, Sucre — **Bo·liv·i·an** \-ē-ən\ adj or n

Bol·ton \'bōlt-ⁿn\ or in full **Bolton–le–Moors** \-lə-₁mü(ə)rz\ city area NW England in Greater Manchester county

Bom·bay \bäm-'bā\ or **Mum·bai** \'məm-₁bī\ city W India

Bonn \'bän, 'bòn\ city Germany on the Rhine SSE of Cologne; seat of German parliament and formerly capital of West Germany

Boo·thia \'bü-thē-ə\ peninsula N Canada W of Baffin island; its N tip is most northerly point in North America except for islands

Bor·ders \'bòrd-ərz\ region SE Scotland; established 1975

Bor·neo \'bòr-nē-₁ō\ island Malay group SW of the Philippines; divided between Brunei, Indonesia, and Malaysia

Bos·nia \'bäz-nē-ə\ region S Europe; with Herzegovina forms independent **Bosnia and Her·ze·go·vi·na** \₁hert-sə-gō-'vē-nə, ₁hərt-, -'gō-və-nə\; capital, Sarajevo — **Bos·ni·an** \-nē-ən\ adj or n

Bos·po·rus \'bäs-p(ə-)rəs\ or ancient **Bosporus Thra-**

ci·us \-'thrā-sh(ē-)əs\ strait about 29 kilometers long between Turkey in Europe & Turkey in Asia connecting Sea of Marmara & Black sea

Bos·ton \'bò-stən\ city, capital of Massachusetts — **Bos·to·nian** \bò-'stō-nē-ən, -nyən\ adj or n

Bot·a·ny Bay \'bät-ⁿn-ē-, 'bät-nē-\ inlet of S Pacific SE Australia in New South Wales S of Sydney

Both·nia, Gulf of \-'bäth-nē-ə\ arm of Baltic sea between Sweden & Finland

Bo·tswa·na \bät-'swän-ə\ country S Africa; formerly (as Bechuanaland) dependent on Britain; now an independent state; capital, Gaborone

Boul·der \'bōl-dər\ city N central Colorado

Boulder Dam — see HOOVER DAM

Bourne·mouth \'bō(ə)rn-məth, 'bò(ə)rn-, 'bù(ə)rn-\ town S England in Dorset county on English channel

Brad·ford \'brad-fərd\ city N England in West Yorkshire

Brah·ma·pu·tra \₁bräm-ə-'p(y)ü-trə\ river 2900 kilometers long S Asia flowing from the Himalayas in Tibet to Ganges delta

Bra·sí·lia \brə-'zil-yə\ city, capital of Brazil

Bra·ti·sla·va \₁brat-ə-'släv-ə, ₁brät-\ city on the Danube; capital of Slovakia

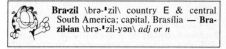

Bra·zil \brə-'zil\ country E & central South America; capital, Brasília — **Bra·zil·ian** \brə-'zil-yən\ adj or n

Braz·za·ville \'braz-ə-₁vil, 'bräz-ə-₁vēl\ city, capital of Republic of the Congo on W bank of lower Congo river

Bre·men \'brem-ən, 'brā-mən\ city NW Germany

Bren·ner \'bren-ər\ pass 1371 meters in the Alps between Austria & Italy

Brent \'brent\ city area of W Greater London county, England

Bret·on, Cape \kăp-'bret-ⁿn, kə-'bret-, -'brit-\ cape Canada; most easterly point of Cape Breton Island & of Nova Scotia

Bridge·port \'brij-₁pō(ə)rt, -₁pò(ə)rt\ city SW Connecticut

Bridge·town \'brij-₁taùn\ city, capital of Barbados

Brigh·ton \'brīt-ⁿn\ city area S England in East Sussex county on English channel

Bris·bane \'briz-bən, -₁bān\ city E Australia, capital of Queensland

Bris·tol \'bris-tⁿl\ **1** city SW England in Avon **2** channel between S Wales & SW England

Brit·ain \'brit-ⁿn\ **1** the island of Great Britain **2** UNITED KINGDOM

British Columbia province W Canada on Pacific coast; capital, Victoria

British Commonwealth of Nations — see COMMONWEALTH, THE

British Guiana — see GUYANA

British Honduras — see BELIZE

British India the part of India formerly under direct British administration

British Indian Ocean Territory British colony in Indian ocean consisting of Chagos island group

British Isles island group W Europe consisting of Great Britain, Ireland, & nearby islands

British Virgin Islands E islands of Virgin islands group; a British possession

British West Indies islands of the West Indies belonging to the Commonwealth & including Jamaica, Trinidad and Tobago, Bahamas, & Cayman Islands, Windward Islands, Leeward Islands, & British Virgin Islands

Brit·ta·ny \'brit-ᵊn-ē\ region NW France SW of Normandy

Brom·ley \'bräm-lē\ city area of SE Greater London county, England

Bronx \'bräŋ(k)s\ or **The Bronx** section of New York City NE of Manhattan island

Brook·lyn \'brük-lən\ section of New York City at SW end of Long Island

Brooks Range \'brüks-\ mountains N Alaska

Browns·ville \'braunz-₁vil, -vəl\ city S Texas on the Rio Grande

Bru·nei \brü-'nī, 'brü-₁nī\ country NE Borneo; formerly under British authority; capital, Bandar Seri Begawan

Brus·sels \'brəs-əlz\ city, capital of Belgium

Bu·cha·rest \'b(y)ü-kə-₁rest\ city, capital of Romania

Buck·ing·ham·shire \'bək-iŋ-əm-₁shi(ə)r, -shər, in the U.S. also -iŋ-₁ham-\ or **Buckingham** county SE central England

Bu·da·pest \'büd-ə-₁pest also 'byüd-, 'bud-, -₁pesht\ city, capital of Hungary

Bue·nos Ai·res \₁bwā-nə-'sa(ə)r-ēz, ₁bō-nə-, -'se(ə)r-, -'sī(ə)r-\ city, capital of Argentina

Buf·fa·lo \'bəf-ə-₁lō\ city W New York on Lake Erie

Bu·jum·bu·ra \₁bü-jəm-'bur-ə\ city, capital of Burundi

Bu·ko·vi·na \₁bü-kə-'vē-nə\ region E central Europe in foothills of E Carpathians

Bul·gar·ia \₁bəl-'gar-ē-ə, bul-, -'ger-\ country SE Europe on Black sea; capital, Sofia

Bull Run \'bul-'rən\ stream NE Virginia

Bun·ker Hill \₁bəŋ-kər-\ height in Boston, Massachusetts

Bur·gun·dy \'bər-gən-dē\ region E France — **Bur·gun·di·an** \(₁)bər-'gən-dē-ən\ adj or n

Bur·ki·na Fa·so \bür-'kē-nə-'fä-sō\ or formerly **Upper Volta** \-'vōl-tə, -'völ-\ country W Africa N of Ivory Coast, Ghana, & Togo; capital, Ouagadougou

Bur·ling·ton \'bər-liŋ-tən\ city NW Vermont; largest in state

Bur·ma \'bər-mə\ — see MYANMAR

Bu·run·di \bu-'rün-dē\ country E central Africa; capital, Bujumbura — see RUANDA-URUNDI

Bute \'byüt\ island SW Scotland in Firth of Clyde

Butte \'byüt\ city SW Montana

Byelarus — see BELARUS

Byelorussia — see BELORUSSIA

Byz·an·tine Empire \'biz-ᵊn-₁tēn, 'bīz-, -₁tīn; bə-'zan-₁tēn, -tīn, bi-\ empire of SE and S Europe and W Asia from 4th to 15th century

Byz·an·ti·um \bə-'zan-sh(ē-)əm, -'zant-ē-əm\ ancient city on site of modern Istanbul

Caer·nar·von \kär-'när-vən, kə(r)-\ city area NW Wales in Gwynedd county

Cai·ro \'kī-rō\ city, capital of Egypt — **Cai·rene** \kī-'rēn\ adj or n

Ca·la·bria \kə-'lä-brē-ə, -'läb-rē-\ district of ancient Italy consisting of area forming heel of Italian peninsula — **Ca·la·bri·an** \kə-'lä-brē-ən, -'läb-rē-\ adj or n

Cal·cut·ta \kal-'kət-ə\ city E India on Hooghly river — **Cal·cut·tan** \-'kət-ᵊn\ adj or n

Cal·e·do·nia \₁kal-ə-'dō-nyə, -nē-ə\ — see SCOTLAND — **Cal·e·do·nian** \-nyən, -nē-ən\ adj or n

Cal·ga·ry \'kal-gə-rē\ city SW Alberta, Canada

Ca·li \'käl-ē\ city W Colombia

Cal·i·for·nia \₁kal-ə-'för-nyə\ state SW U.S.; capital, Sacramento — **Cal·i·for·nian** \-nyən\ adj or n

California, Gulf of arm of the Pacific NW Mexico

Cal·va·ry \'kalv-(ə-)rē\ place outside ancient Jerusalem where Christ was crucified

Cam·bay, Gulf of \-kam-'bā\ inlet of Arabian sea India N of Bombay

Cam·bo·dia \kam-'bōd-ē-ə\ or **Kam·pu·chea** \₁kam-pə-'chē-ə\ or 1970–75 **Khmer Republic** \kə-'me(ə)r-\ country SE Asia in S Indochina; capital, Phnom Penh

Cam·bria \'kam-brē-ə\ WALES — an old name

Cam·bridge \'kām-brij\ city E England in Cambridgeshire

Cam·bridge·shire \'kām-brij-₁shi(ə)r, -shər\ or **Cambridge** county E England

Cam·den \'kam-dən\ city area of N Greater London county, England

Cam·er·oon or French **Cam·er·oun** \₁kam-ə-'rün\ country W Africa; capital, Yaoundé — **Cam·er·oo·nian** \-'rü-nē-ən, -rü-nyən\ adj or n

Ca·mi·guin \₁kam-ə-'gēn\ island Philippines, off N coast of Mindanao

Ca·naan \'kā-nən\ ancient region SW Asia; approximately the area later called Palestine — **Ca·naan·ite** \'kā-nə-₁nīt\ adj or n

Can·a·da \'kan-ə-də\ country N North America; independent state in the Commonwealth; capital, Ottawa — **Ca·na·di·an** \kə-'nād-ē-ən\ adj or n

Canadian Falls — see NIAGARA FALLS

Canadian Shield or **Lau·ren·tian Plateau** \lò-'ren-chən-\ region E Canada & NE U.S. extending from Mackenzie basin E to Davis strait & S to S Quebec, S central Ontario, NE Minnesota, N Wisconsin, NW Michigan, and NE New York including the Adirondacks

Canal Zone or **Panama Canal Zone** strip of territory Panama formerly leased to U.S. for Panama canal

Ca·nary \kə-'ne(ə)r-ē\ islands in the Atlantic off NW coast of Africa belonging to Spain

Ca·nav·er·al, Cape \-kə-'nav-(ə-)rəl\ or 1963–1973 **Cape Ken·ne·dy** \-'ken-ə-dē\ cape E Florida in the Atlantic on Canaveral peninsula E of Indian river

Can·ber·ra \'kan-b(ə-)rə, -₁ber-ə\ city, capital of Australia in Australian Capital Territory

Can·on City \₁kan-yən\ city S central Colorado on Arkansas river

Can·ter·bury \'kant-ə(r)-₁ber-ē, -b(ə-)rē\ **1** city SE Australia in E New South Wales **2** city SE England in Kent county

Canton — see GUANGZHOU

Cape Bret·on Island \kāp-'bret-ᵊn-, kə-'bret-, -'brit-\ island NE Nova Scotia

Cape Horn — see HORN, CAPE

Cape of Good Hope 1 — see GOOD HOPE, CAPE OF **2** — see CAPE PROVINCE

Cape Province or **Cape of Good Hope** or formerly **Cape Colony** former province S Republic of South Africa; capital, Cape Town

Cape Town \'kāp-₁taun\ city, legislative capital of Republic of South Africa and capital of former Cape Province

Cape Verde \-'vərd\ islands in the N Atlantic off W Africa; an independent country; capital, Praia; until 1975 belonged to Portugal

Cape York peninsula \-'yò(ə)rk-\ peninsula NE Australia in N Queensland

Ca·pri \ka-'prē, kə-; 'käp-rē, 'kap-\ island Italy S of Bay of Naples

Ca·ra·cas \kə-'rak-əs, -'räk-\ city, capital of Venezuela

Car·diff \'kärd-əf\ city, capital of Wales in South Glamorgan county

Ca·rib·be·an \₁kar-ə-'bē-ən, kə-'rib-ē-\ sea arm of the Atlantic; on N & E are the West Indies, on S is South

America, & on W is Central America — **Caribbean** *adj*

Car·lisle \kär-'lī(ə)l, kər-, 'kär-ılī(ə)l\ city NW England in Cumbria county

Carls·bad Caverns \'kär(-ə)lz-ıbad-\ series of caves SE New Mexico

Car·mar·then \kär-'mär-thən, kə(r)-\ port S Wales in Dyfed county

Car·o·li·na \ıkar-ə-'lī-nə\ English colony on E coast of North America founded 1663 & divided 1729 into North Carolina & South Carolina (the **Carolinas**) — **Car·o·lin·i·an** \-'lin-e-ən\ *adj or n*

Ca·ro·li·na \ıkär-ə-'lē-nə\ city NE Puerto Rico

Car·o·line \'kar-ə-ılīn, -lən\ islands W Pacific E of S Philippines; formerly part of Trust Territory of the Pacific Islands

Car·pa·thi·an \kär-'pā-thē-ən\ mountains E central Europe along boundary between Slovakia & Poland & in N & central Romania; highest Gerlachovka 2655 meters

Car·pen·tar·ia, Gulf of \-ıkär-pən-'ter-ē-ə, -tar-\ inlet of Arafura sea N of Australia

Car·rick·fer·gus \ıkar-ik-'fər-gəs\ district E Northern Ireland

Car·son City \'kärs-ən-\ city, capital of Nevada

Car·thage \'kär-thij\ ancient city N Africa NE of modern Tunis; capital of an empire that once included much of NW Africa, E Spain, & Sicily — **Car·tha·gin·i·an** \ıkär-thə-'jin-yən, -'jin-ē-ən\ *adj or n*

Ca·sa·blan·ca \ıkas-ə-'blaŋ-kə, ıkaz-\ city W Morocco on the Atlantic

Cas·cade Range \(')kas-'kād-\ mountains NW U.S. in Washington, Oregon, & N California — see RAINIER, MOUNT

Cas·per \'kas-pər\ city central Wyoming

Cas·pi·an sea \'kas-pē-ən-\ salt lake between Europe and Asia about 27 meters below sea level

Cas·tile \kas-'tē(ə)l\ *or in full* **Cas·til·la** \kä-'stē-yä\ region & ancient kingdom central & N Spain

Cast·le·reagh \'kas-əl-rā\ district E Northern Ireland

Cas·tries \'kas-ıtrēz, -ıtrēs\ seaport, capital of Saint Lucia

Cat·a·lo·nia \ıkat-əl-'ō-nyə, -nē-ə\ region NE Spain bordering on France & the Mediterranean; chief city, Barcelona — **Cat·a·lo·nian** \-'ō-nyən, -nē-ən\ *adj or n*

Ca·tan·dua·nes \ıkät-ən-'dwän-əs\ island E Philippines

Ca·thay \kath-'ā\ an old name for China

Cats·kill \'kat-ıskil\ mountains in Appalachian system SE New York W of the Hudson

Cau·ca·sus \'kò-kə-səs\ mountain system SE Europe between Black and Caspian seas in Russia, Georgia, Azerbaijan, & Armenia

Cay·enne \kī-'en, kā-\ city, capital of French Guiana

Cay·man Islands \(')kā-'man, 'kā-mən\ islands West Indies NW of Jamaica; a British colony

Ce·bu \sā-'bü\ island E central Philippines

Ce·dar Rapids \'sēd-ər-\ city E Iowa

Celebes — see SULAWESI

Cel·tic \'kel-tik, 'sel-\ sea inlet of the Atlantic in British Isles SE of Ireland, SW of Wales, & W of Cornwall and Isles of Scilly county, England

Central region central Scotland; established 1975

Central African Republic country N central Africa; capital, Bangui

Central America narrow portion of North America from S border of Mexico to South America — **Central American** *adj or n*

Central Valley valley of Sacramento & San Joaquin rivers in California between Sierra Nevada & Coast ranges

Cey·lon \si-'län, sā-\ 1 island in Indian ocean off S India 2 — see SRI LANKA — **Cey·lon·ese** \ısä-lə-'nēz, ısē-lə-, 'sel-ə-, -'nēs\ *adj or n*

Chad \'chad\ country N central Africa; capital, N'Djamena — **Chad·ian** \'chad-ē-ən\ *adj or n*

Chad, Lake shallow lake N central Africa at junction of boundaries of Chad, Niger, & Nigeria

Cha·gos \'chä-gəs\ island group central Indian ocean; forms British Indian Ocean Territory — see DIEGO GARCIA

Chal·dea \kal-'dē-ə\ ancient region SW Asia on Euphrates river & Persian gulf — **Chal·de·an** \-'dē-ən\ *adj or n* — **Chal·dee** \'kal-ıdē\ *n*

Cham·pagne \sham-'pän\ region NE France

Champlain, Lake \sham-'plän\ lake between New York & Vermont extending N into Quebec

Chan·di·garh \'chən-dē-gər\ city N India N of Delhi

Chang \'chäŋ\ *or* **Yang·tze** \'yaŋ-'sē, 'yaŋ(k)t-'sē\ river 5525 kilometers long central China flowing into East China sea

Chang·chun \'chäŋ-'chùn\ city NE China

Chang·sha \'chäŋ-'shä\ city SE central China

Channel 1 — see SANTA BARBARA 2 islands in English channel including Jersey, Guernsey, & Alderney & belonging to United Kingdom

Charles \'chär(ə)lz\ river 76 kilometers long E Massachusetts flowing into Boston harbor

Charles, Cape cape E Virginia N of entrance to Chesapeake Bay

Charles·ton \'chärl-stən\ 1 seaport SE South Carolina 2 city, capital of West Virginia

Char·lotte \'shär-lət\ city S North Carolina

Charlotte Ama·lie \-'am-ə-lē\ city, capital of Virgin Islands of the U.S.; on Saint Thomas island

Char·lottes·ville \'shär-ləts-ıvil, -vəl\ city central Virginia

Char·lotte·town \'shär-lət-ıtaùn\ city, capital of Prince Edward Island, Canada

Chat·ta·noo·ga \ıchat-ə-'nü-gə, ıchat-ən-'ü-\ city SE Tennessee

Chelms·ford \'chelm-sfərd, 'chem-\ city area SE England in Essex county

Che·lya·binsk \chel-'yä-bən(t)sk\ city W Russia, S of Sverdlovsk

Cheng–chou — see ZHENGZHOU

Cheng·du *or* **Ch'eng–tu** \'chəŋ-'dü\ city SW central China

Ches·a·peake \'ches-(ə-)ıpēk\ city SE Virginia

Chesapeake Bay inlet of the Atlantic in Virginia & Maryland

Chesh·ire \'chesh-ər, 'chesh-ıi(ə)r\ *or* **Ches·ter** \'chestər\ county W England bordering on Wales

Ches·ter \'ches-tər\ city NW England in Cheshire

Chev·i·ot \'chev-ē-ət, 'chē-vē-ət\ hills along English–Scottish border

Chey·enne \shī-'an, -'en\ city, capital of Wyoming

Chi·ba \'chē-bə\ city E Japan in Honshu on Tokyo Bay E of Tokyo

Chi·ca·go \shə-'käg-ō, -'kòg-\ city NE Illinois — **Chica·go·an** \-'käg-ə-wən, -'kòg-\ *n*

Chi·chén It·zá \chə-ıchen-ət-'sä\ ruined Mayan city SE Mexico in Yucatán

Chich·es·ter \'chich-ə-stər\ city S England in West Sussex county

Ch'i–ch'i–ha–erh — see QIQIHAR

Chihli, Gulf of — see BO HAI

Chi·le \'chil-ē\ country SW South America; capital, Santiago — **Chil·ean** \'chil-ē-ən, chə-'lā-ən\ *adj or n*

Chim·bo·ra·zo \ıchim-bə-'räz-ō, ıshim-\ mountain 6267 meters W central Ecuador

Chi·na \'chī-nə\ 1 country E Asia; capital, Beijing — see TAIWAN 2 sea section of the W Pacific; divided at Taiwan strait into East China & South China seas

Chin–chou *or* **Chinchow** — see JINZHOU

Chi·si·nau \ıkē-shē-'naù\ *or* **Kishi·nev** \'ki-shi-ınef\ city central Moldova; its capital

Chit·ta·gong \'chit-ə-ıgäŋ, -ıgòŋ\ city SE Bangladesh on Bay of Bengal

Chong·qing *or* **Ch'ung–ch'ing** \'chùŋ-'chiŋ\ *or* **Chung·king** \'chùŋ-'kiŋ\ city SW central China

Christ·church \'krīs(t)-ˌchərch\ city New Zealand on E coast of South island

Christ·mas \'kris-məs\ island E Indian ocean SW of Java; governed by Australia

Cin·cin·na·ti \ˌsin(t)-sə-'nat-ē, -'nat-ə\ city SW Ohio

Ciudad Trujillo — see SANTO DOMINGO

Cleve·land \'klēv-lənd\ **1** city NE Ohio **2** county N England N of North Yorkshire

Clwyd \'klüid\ county NE Wales; established 1974

Clyde \'klīd\ river 171 kilometers long SW Scotland flowing into **Firth of Clyde** (estuary)

Coast mountains mountain range W British Columbia, Canada; the N continuation of Cascade Range

Coast ranges chain of mountain ranges W North America extending along Pacific coast W of Sierra Nevada & Cascade Range & through Vancouver island into S Alaska to Kenai peninsula & Kodiak island

Cod, Cape \-'käd\ peninsula SE Massachusetts

Coim·ba·tore \ˌkoim-bə-'tō(ə)r, -'tò(ə)r\ city S India

Cole·raine \kōl-'rān, 'kōl-ˌran\ **1** county N Northern Ireland **2** port in Coleraine county

Co·logne \kə-'lōn\ city W Germany on the Rhine

Co·lom·bia \kə-'ləm-bē-ə\ country NW South America; capital, Bogotá — **Co·lom·bi·an** \-bē-ən\ adj or n

Co·lom·bo \kə-'ləm-bō\ city, capital of Sri Lanka

Col·o·ra·do \ˌkäl-ə-'rad-ō, -'räd-\ **1** river 2335 kilometers long SW U.S. & NW Mexico flowing from N Colorado into Gulf of California **2** desert SE California **3** plateau region SW U.S. W of Rocky mountains **4** state W U.S.; capital, Denver — **Col·o·rad·an** \-'rad-ən, -'räd-\ or **Co·lo·ra·do·an** \-'rad-ə-wən, -'räd-\ adj or n

Colorado Springs city central Colorado

Co·lum·bia \kə-'ləm-bē-ə\ **1** river 1953 kilometers long SW Canada & NW U.S. flowing S & W from SE British Columbia into the Pacific **2** plateau in Columbia river basin in E Washington, E Oregon, & SW Idaho **3** city, capital of South Carolina **4** — see UNITED STATES OF AMERICA

Co·lum·bus \kə-'ləm-bəs\ **1** city W Georgia **2** city, capital of Ohio

Com·mon·wealth, the \'käm-ən-ˌwel(t)th\ or **Commonwealth of Nations** or formerly **British Commonwealth of Nations** the United Kingdom & most of the countries formerly dependent on it

Com·o·ros \'käm-ə-ˌrōz\ islands off SE Africa NW of Madagascar; formerly a French possession; an independent country (except for Mayotte Island remaining French) since 1975; capital, Moroni

Con·a·kry \'kän-ə-krē\ city, capital of Guinea

Con·cord \'käŋ-kərd\ **1** city W California **2** city, capital of New Hampshire **3** town E Massachusetts NW of Boston

Con·go \'käŋ-gō\ **1** or **Zaire** \'zī(ə)r, zä-'i(ə)r\ river 4344 kilometers long W Africa flowing into the Atlantic **2** or **Democratic Republic of the Congo** or formerly **Zaire** or earlier **Belgian Congo** country central Africa consisting of most of Congo River basin E of lower Congo River; capital, Kinshasa **3** or **Republic of the Congo** country W central Africa W of lower Congo River; capital, Brazzaville — **Con·go·lese** \ˌkäŋ-gə-'lēz, -'lēs\ adj or n

Con·nacht \'kän-ˌòt\ province W Ireland

Con·nect·i·cut \kə-'net-i-kət\ **1** river 655 kilometers long NE U.S. flowing S from N New Hampshire into Long Island Sound **2** state NE U.S.; capital, Hartford

Constantinople — see ISTANBUL

Con·ti·nen·tal Di·vide \ˌkänt-ən-ˌent-əl-di-'vīd\ line of highest points of land separating the waters flowing W from those flowing N or E and extending SSE from NW Canada across N U.S. through Mexico & Central America to South America where it joins the Andes mountains

Cook \'kùk\ **1** inlet of the Pacific S Alaska W of Kenai peninsula **2** islands S Pacific SW of Society islands

belonging to New Zealand **3** strait New Zealand between North island & South island

Cook, Mount or formerly **Ao·rangi** \aù-'räŋ-ē\ mountain 3764 meters New Zealand in W central South island in Southern Alps; highest in New Zealand

Cooks·town \'kùk-ˌstaùn\ district central Northern Ireland

Co·pen·ha·gen \ˌkō-pən-'hā-gən, -'häg-ən\ city, capital of Denmark

Cor·al \'kòr-əl, 'kär-\ sea arm of the W Pacific NE of Australia

Cór·do·ba \'kòrd-ə-bə, -ə-və\ city N central Argentina

Cor·inth \'kòr-ən(t)th, 'kär-\ **1** region of ancient Greece **2** ancient city, its capital; site SW of present city of Corinth — **Co·rin·thi·an** \kə-'rin(t)-thē-ən\ adj or n

Corinth, Gulf of inlet of Ionian sea central Greece N of the Peloponnisos

Cork \'kò(ə)rk\ city S Ireland in Munster

Corn·wall \'kòrn-ˌwòl, -wəl\ area and once a county SW England

Cornwall and Isles of Scilly county SW England

Cor·pus Chris·ti \ˌkòr-pə-'skris-tē\ city S Texas

Cor·reg·i·dor \kə-'reg-ə-ˌdò(ə)r\ island Philippines at entrance to Manila Bay

Cor·si·ca \'kòr-si-kə\ island France in the Mediterranean N of Sardinia — **Cor·si·can** \'kòr-si-kən\ adj or n

Cos·ta Ri·ca \ˌkäs-tə-'rē-kə, ˌkòs-, ˌkōs-\ country Central America between Nicaragua & Panama; capital, San José — **Cos·ta Ri·can** \-'rē-kən\ adj or n

Côte d'Ivoire — see IVORY COAST

Cots·wold \'kät-ˌswōld\ hills SW central England

Cov·en·try \'kəv-ən-trē, 'kəv-\ city central England in West Midlands county

Cow·pens \'kaù-ˌpenz\ town NW South Carolina

Craig·av·on \krā-'gav-ən\ district central Northern Ireland

Cra·ter \'krāt-ər\ lake 589 meters deep SW Oregon in Cascade range — see MAZAMA, MOUNT

Crete \'krēt\ island Greece in E Mediterranean — **Cre·tan** \'krēt-ən\ adj or n

Cri·mea \krī-'mē-ə, krə-\ peninsula SE Europe, extending into Black sea — **Cri·me·an** \krī-'mē-ən, krə-\ adj

Cro·atia \krō-'ā-sh(ē-)ə\ country SE Europe; capital, Zagreb; a republic of Yugoslavia 1946-91

Croy·don \'kròid-ən\ city area of S Greater London county, England

Cu·ba \'kyü-bə\ island in the West Indies; an independent country; capital, Havana — **Cu·ban** \-bən\ adj or n

Cum·ber·land \'kəm-bər-lənd\ river 1106 kilometers long S Kentucky & N Tennessee

Cumberland Gap pass through Cumberland plateau NE Tennessee

Cumberland plateau or **Cumberland mountains** mountain region E U.S.; part of S Appalachian mountains extending from S West Virginia to NE Alabama

Cum·bria \'kəm-brē-ə\ county NW England — **Cum·bri·an** \-ən\ adj or n

Cumbrian mountains NW England chiefly in Cumbria county

Cu·par \'kü-pər\ town E Scotland in Fife region

Cu·ri·ti·ba \ˌkùr-ə-'tē-bə\ city S Brazil SW of São Paulo

Cush \'kəsh, 'kùsh\ ancient country NE Africa in upper Nile valley S of Egypt — **Cush·ite** \-ˌīt\ n — **Cush·it·ic** \ˌkəsh-'it-ik, kùsh-\ adj

Cuz·co \'kü-skō\ city S central Peru

Cymru — see WALES

Cy·prus \'sī-prəs\ island E Mediterranean S of Turkey; an independent country in the Commonwealth; capital, Nicosia — **Cyp·ri·ot** \'sip-rē-ət, -rē-ˌät\ or **Cyp·ri·ote** \-ˌōt, -ət\ adj or n

Cy·re·na·i·ca \ˌsir-ə-ˈnā-ə-kə, ˌsī-rə-\ ancient region N Africa on coast W of Egypt; capital, Cyrene — **Cy·re·na·i·can** \-kən\ *adj or n*

Czecho·slo·va·kia \ˌchek-ə-slō-ˈväk-ē-ə, -ˈvak-\ former country central Europe; capital, Prague; since January 1, 1993 divided into the independent states of the Czech Republic and Slovakia — **Czecho·slo·vak** \-ˈslō-ˌväk, -ˌvak\ *adj or n* — **Czecho·slo·va·ki·an** \ˌslō-ˈväk-ē-ən, -ˈvak-\ *adj or n*

Czech Republic \ˈchek-\ country central Europe; capital, Prague; formerly part of Czechoslovakia

Dacca — see DHAKA

Dahomey — see BENIN

Da·kar \ˈdak-ˌär,də-ˈkär\ city, capital of Senegal

Da·ko·ta \də-ˈkōt-ə\ *or* **James** \ˈjāmz\ river 1145 kilometers long North Dakota and South Dakota flowing S into the Missouri

Dakota Territory territory 1861–89 NW U.S. divided 1889 into states of North Dakota & South Dakota (the **Da·ko·tas** \də-ˈkōt-əz\)

Da·lian *or* **Ta–lien** \ˈdä-ˈlyen\ *or* **Dai·ren** \ˈdī-ˈren\ *or* **Lü·da** *or* **Lü–ta** \ˈlē-ˈdä\ city NE China

Dal·las \ˈdal-əs, -is\ city NE Texas

Dal·ma·tia \dal-ˈmā-sh(ē-)ə\ region W Balkan peninsula on the Adriatic — **Dal·ma·tian** \-shən\ *adj or n*

Da·mas·cus \də-ˈmas-kəs\ city, capital of Syria

Dan·ube \ˈdan-yüb\ river 2850 kilometers long S Europe flowing from SW Germany into Black sea — **Da·nu·bi·an** \da-ˈnyü-bē-ən\ *adj*

Dar·da·nelles \ˌdärd-ᵊn-ˈelz\ *or* **Hel·les·pont** \ˈhel-ə-ˌspänt\ strait NW Turkey connecting Sea of Marmara & the Aegean

Dar es Sa·laam \ˌdär-ˌes-sə-ˈläm\ city, capital of Tanzania

Dar·ling \ˈdär-liŋ\ river 2739 kilometers long SE Australia in Queensland & New South Wales flowing SW into the Murray

Dar·win \ˈdär-wən\ city Australia, capital of Northern Territory

Da·vao \ˈdäv-ˌaů, dä-ˈvaů\ city S Philippines in E Mindanao on Davao Gulf

Dav·en·port \ˈdav-ən-ˌpō(ə)rt, -ˌpȯ(ə)rt\ city E Iowa

Da·vis \ˈdā-vəs\ strait between SW Greenland & E Baffin island connecting Baffin Bay & the Atlantic

Day·ton \ˈdāt-ᵊn\ city SW Ohio

Dead sea \ˈded-\ salt lake between Israel & Jordan; 397 meters below sea level

Death Valley \ˈdeth-\ dry valley E California & S Nevada containing lowest point in U.S. (86 meters below sea level)

Dec·can \ˈdek-ən, -ˌan\ plateau region S India

Del·a·ware \ˈdel-ə-ˌwa(ə)r, -ˌwe(ə)r, -wər\ 1 river 451 kilometers long E U.S. flowing S from S New York into Delaware Bay 2 state E U.S.; capital, Dover — **Del·a·war·ean** *or* **Del·a·war·ian** \ˌdel-ə-ˈwar-ē-ən, -ˈwer-\ *adj or n*

Delaware Bay inlet of the Atlantic between SW New Jersey & E Delaware

Del·hi \ˈdel-ē\ city N India — see NEW DELHI

De·los \ˈdē-ˌläs\ island Greece — **De·lian** \ˈdē-lē-ən, ˈdēl-yən\ *adj or n*

Del·phi \ˈdel-ˌfī\ ancient town central Greece on S slope of Parnassus

Democratic Republic of the Congo — see CONGO 2

Denali — see MCKINLEY, MOUNT

Den·mark \ˈden-ˌmärk\ country N Europe occupying most of Jutland & neighboring islands; capital, Copenhagen

Den·ver \ˈden-vər\ city, capital of Colorado

Der·by \ˈdär-bē, *chiefly in the U.S.* ˈdər-bē\ city area N central England in Derbyshire

Der·by·shire \ˈdär-bē-ˌshi(ə)r, -shər, *U.S. also* ˈdər-\ *or* **Derby** county N central England

Der·ry \ˈder-ē\ *or* **Lon·don·der·ry** \ˌlən-dən-ˈder-ē; ˈlən-dən-ˌder-ē, -d(ə-)rē\ 1 district NW Northern Ireland 2 seaport in Londonderry district

Des Moines \di-ˈmȯin\ city, capital of Iowa

De·troit \di-ˈtrȯit\ 1 river 50 kilometers long between SE Michigan & Ontario connecting Lake Saint Clair & Lake Erie 2 city SE Michigan

Dev·on \ˈdev-ən\ *or* **De·von·shire** \-ˌshi(ə)r, -shər\ county SW England

Dha·ka *or* **Dac·ca** \ˈdak-ə, ˈdäk-\ city, capital of Bangladesh

Die·go Gar·cia \dē-ˌä-gō-ˌgär-ˈsē-ə\ island in Indian ocean; chief island of Chagos island group

Di·nar·ic Alps \də-ˌnar-ik-\ range of the E Alps in W Slovenia, W Croatia, Bosnia and Herzegovina, & Montenegro

District of Co·lum·bia \-kə-ˈləm-bē-ə\ federal district E U.S. coextensive with city of Washington

Djakarta — see JAKARTA

Dji·bou·ti \jə-ˈbüt-ē\ 1 country E Africa on Gulf of Aden 2 city, its capital

Dne·pro·pe·trovsk *or* **Dni·pro·pe·trovs'k** \də-ˌnyep-rə-pē-ˈtrȯfsk\ city E central Ukraine

Dodge City \ˈdäj-\ city S Kansas on Arkansas river

Do·do·ma \dō-ˈdō-ˌmä\ town, capital of Tanzania

Do·ha \ˈdō-hä\ city & port, capital of Qatar on Persian gulf

Dom·i·ni·ca \ˌdäm-ə-ˈnē-kə, də-ˈmin-ə-kə\ island West Indies in the Leeward Islands; an independent country; capital, Roseau

Do·min·i·can Republic \də-ˌmin-i-kən\ country West Indies in E Hispaniola; capital, Santo Domingo — **Do·min·i·can** \də-ˈmin-i-kən\ *adj or n*

Don \ˈdän\ river 1930 kilometers long SW Russia

Do·netsk \də-ˈnetsk\ city E Ukraine

Dor·ches·ter \ˈdȯr-chə-stər, -ˌches-tər\ city area S England in Dorset county

Dor·set \ˈdȯr-sət\ *or* **Dor·set·shire** \-ˌshi(ə)r, -shər\ county S England on English channel

Dort·mund \ˈdȯ(ə)rt-ˌmùnt, -mənd\ city W Germany in the Ruhr

Dou·ro \ˈdȯr-ü, ˈdȯr-\ *or Spanish* **Due·ro** \ˈdwe(ə)r-ō\ *or ancient* **Du·ri·us** \ˈd(y)ùr-ē-əs\ river 895 kilometers long N Spain & N Portugal flowing into the Atlantic

Do·ver \ˈdō-vər\ city, capital of Delaware

Dover, Strait of channel between SE England & N France; the most easterly section of English channel

Down \ˈdaůn\ district SE Northern Ireland

Down·pat·rick \daůn-ˈpa-trik\ city district E Northern Ireland in Down district

Dra·kens·berg \ˈdräk-ənz-ˌbərg\ mountain range E Republic of South Africa & Lesotho; highest peak Thabana Ntlenyana 3482 meters

Dres·den \ˈdrez-dən\ city E Germany

Dub·lin \ˈdəb-lən\ *or ancient* **Eb·la·na** \ˈeb-lə-nə\ city, capital of Ireland in Leinster

Dud·ley \ˈdəd-lē\ city area W central England in West Midlands county

Duis·burg \ˈdü-əs-ˌbərg; ˈd(y)üz-ˌbərg\ city W Germany at junction of Rhine & Ruhr rivers

Du·luth \də-ˈlüth\ city NE Minnesota

Dum·fries \ˌdəm-ˈfrēs\ town S Scotland in Dumfries and Galloway region

Dumfries and Gal·lo·way \-ˈgal-ə-ˌwä\ region S Scotland; established 1975

Dun·dee \ˌdən-ˈdē\ city E Scotland in Tayside region

Dun·gan·non \dən-ˈgan-ən\ district W Northern Ireland

Dur·ban \ˈdər-bən\ city E Republic of South Africa in E KwaZulu-Natal

Dur·ham \ˈdər-əm, ˈdə-rəm, ˈdùr-əm\ 1 city N central North Carolina 2 county N England on North sea 3 city area in Durham county

Du·shan·be \d(y)ü-ˈsham-bə, -ˈshäm-\ city, capital of Tajikistan

Düs·sel·dorf \ˈd(y)üs-əl-ˌdȯrf\ city W Germany on the Rhine

Dutch East Indies — see NETHERLANDS EAST INDIES

CLIMBER'S LOG: 12,000 FEET UP MT. EVEREST AND THE GOING IS SLOW

AT THIS ALTITUDE OXYGEN IS SCARCE. THE EXPERIENCED CLIMBER KNOWS HE MUST REST OFTEN

NOW I'VE SEEN EVERYTHING

JIM DAVIS 2-26

© 1988 PAWS, INC.

Dy·fed \'dəv-ed, -əd\ county SW Wales; established 1974

Ea·ling \'ē-liŋ\ city area of W Greater London county, England

East An·glia \-aŋ-glē-ə\ region E England including Norfolk & Suffolk counties

East China sea — see CHINA

Eas·ter \'ē-stər\ island SE Pacific 3220 kilometers W of Chilean coast; belongs to Chile

Eastern Cape province S Republic of South Africa

Eastern Ghats \-'gòts\ chain of low mountains SE India along coast

Eastern Roman Empire the Byzantine Empire from 395 to 474

East Germany the German Democratic Republic — see GERMANY

East Indies the Malay island group — **East Indian** adj or n

East London city S Republic of South Africa in SE Eastern Cape

East Pakistan the former E division of Pakistan consisting of E portion of Bengal; now the independent country of Bangladesh

East river strait SE New York connecting upper New York Bay & Long Island Sound & separating Manhattan island and Long Island

East Sus·sex \-'səs-iks, U.S. also -ˌeks\ county SE England

Eblana — see DUBLIN

Ebro \'ā-brō\ river 909 kilometers long NE Spain flowing into the Mediterranean

Ec·ua·dor \'ek-wə-ˌdò(ə)r\ country W South America; capital, Quito — **Ec·ua·dor·an** \ˌek-wə-'dòr-ən, -'dòr-\ or **Ec·ua·dor·ean** or **Ec·ua·dor·ian** \-ē-ən\ adj or n

Ed·in·burgh \'ed-ᵊn-ˌbər-ə,-ˌbə-rə, -b(ə-)rə\ city, capital of Scotland, in Lothian region

Ed·mon·ton \'ed-mən-tən\ city, capital of Alberta, Canada

Edom \'ēd-əm\ ancient country SW Asia S of Judea & Dead sea — **Edom·ite** \'ēd-ə-ˌmīt\ n

Egypt \'ē-jəpt\ country NE Africa & Sinai peninsula of SW Asia bordering on Mediterranean & Red seas; capital, Cairo

Eire — see IRELAND

Elam \'ē-ləm\ ancient country SW Asia at head of Persian gulf E of Babylonia — **Elam·ite** \'ē-lə-ˌmīt\ n

Elbe \'el-bə, 'elb\ river 1160 kilometers long N Czech Republic & NE Germany flowing NW into North sea

El·bert, Mount \-'el-bərt\ mountain 4399 meters W central Colorado; highest in Colorado & the Rocky mountains

El·burz \el-'bù(ə)rz\ mountains N Iran

Eliz·a·beth \i-'liz-ə-bəth\ city NE New Jersey

Elles·mere \'elz-ˌmi(ə)r\ island N Canada in Northwest Territories

Ellice — see TUVALU

El Paso \el-'pas-ō\ city W Texas on Rio Grande

El Sal·va·dor \el-'sal-və-ˌdò(ə)r, -ˌsal-və-'dò(ə)r\ country Central America bordering on the Pacific; capital, San Salvador

Ely, Isle of \-'ē-lē\ district E England in Cambridgeshire

En·field \'en-ˌfēld\ city area of N Greater London county, England

En·gland \'iŋ-glənd also 'iŋ-lənd\ country S Great Britain; a division of United Kingdom; capital, London

English channel arm of the Atlantic between S England & N France

En·nis·kil·len \ˌen-ə-'skil-ən\ city district SW Northern Ireland in Fermanagh district

Ephra·im \'ē-frē-əm\ 1 hilly region N Jordan E of Jordan river 2 — see ISRAEL — **Ephra·im·ite** \'ē-frē-ə-ˌmīt\ n

Equatorial Guinea or formerly **Spanish Guinea** country W Africa including Río Muni & Bioko; capital, Malabo

Erie \'i(ə)r-ē\ 1 city NW Pennsylvania 2 canal New York between Hudson river at Albany & Lake Erie at Buffalo; built 1817–25; now superseded by New York State Barge Canal

Erie, Lake lake E North America in U.S. & Canada; one of the Great Lakes

Er·in \'er-ən\ poetic name of Ireland

Er·i·trea \ˌer-ə-'trē-ə, -'trā-\ country NE Africa; capital, Asmara

Española — see HISPANIOLA

Es·sen \'es-ᵊn\ city W Germany in the Ruhr

Es·sex \'es-iks\ county SE England on North sea

Es·to·nia \e-'stō-nē-ə, -nyə\ country E Europe on Baltic sea; capital, Tallinn; a republic of U.S.S.R. 1940–91

Ethi·o·pia \ˌē-thē-'ō-pē-ə\ or **Ab·ys·sin·ia** \ˌab-ə-'sin-yə, -'sin-ē-ə\ country E Africa; capital, Addis Ababa — **Ethi·o·pi·an** \-pē-ən\ adj or n

Et·na \'et-nə\ volcano 3323 meters Italy in NE Sicily

Eto·bi·coke \et-'ō-bi-ˌkō\ city Canada in SE Ontario

Etru·ria \i-'trùr-ē-ə\ ancient country central Italy

Eu·gene \yü-'jēn\ city W Oregon

Eu·phra·tes \yù-'frāt-ēz\ river 3596 kilometers long SW Asia flowing from E Turkey & uniting with the Tigris to form the Shatt-al-Arab

Eur·asia \yù-'rā-zhə, -shə\ landmass consisting of Europe & Asia — **Eur·asian** \-zhən, -shən\ adj or n

Eu·rope \'yùr-əp\ continent of the eastern hemisphere between Asia & the Atlantic

Ev·ans·ville \'ev-ənz-ˌvil\ city SW Indiana

Ev·er·est, Mount \-'ev-(ə-)rəst\ mountain 8848 meters S Asia in the Himalayas on border between Nepal & Tibet; highest in the world

Ev·er·glades \'ev-ər-ˌglādz\ swamp region S Florida now partly drained

Ex·e·ter \'ek-sət-ər\ 1 town SE New Hampshire 2 city SW England in Devon county

Faer·oe or **Far·oe** \'fa(ə)r-ō, 'fe(ə)r-\ islands NE Atlan-

tic NW of the Shetlands belonging to Denmark —
Faer·oese \ˌfar-ə-ˈwēz, ˌfer-, -ˈwēs\ *adj or n*
Fair·field \ˈfa(ə)r-ˌfēld, ˈfe(ə)r-\ city SE Australia in E
New South Wales
Fai·sa·la·bad \ˌfī-ˌsäl-ə-ˈbäd, -ˌsal-ə-ˈbad\ *or formerly* **Ly·all·pur** \lē-ˌäl-ˈpu̇(ə)r\ city NE Pakistan W of
Lahore
Falk·land \ˈfȯ(l)-klənd\ *or Spanish* **Is·las Mal·vi·nas**
\ˌēz-läz-mäl-ˈvē-näs\ islands SW Atlantic E of S end
of Argentina; a British colony; capital, Stanley
Far East the countries of E Asia & the Malay island
group — usually thought to consist of the Asian
countries bordering on the Pacific but sometimes including also India, Sri Lanka, Bangladesh, Tibet, &
Myanmar — **Far Eastern** *adj*
Far·go \ˈfär-gō\ city E North Dakota; largest in state
Fear, Cape \-ˈfi(ə)r\ cape SE North Carolina at mouth
of Cape Fear river
Fer·man·agh \fər-ˈman-ə\ district SW Northern Ireland
Fernando Po — see BIOKO
Fez \ˈfez\ city N central Morocco
Fife \ˈfīf\ region E Scotland
Fi·ji \ˈfē-jē\ islands SW Pacific; an independent country in the Commonwealth; capital, Suva — **Fi·ji·an**
\-jē-ən\ *adj or n*
Fin·land \ˈfin-lənd\ country NE Europe; capital, Helsinki — **Fin·land·er** *n*
Flan·ders \ˈflan-dərz\ region W Belgium & N France
on North sea
Flat·tery, Cape \-ˈflat-ə-rē\ cape NW Washington at
entrance to Strait of Juan de Fuca
Flint \ˈflint\ city SE Michigan
Flor·ence \ˈflȯr-ən(t)s, ˈflär-\ *or Italian* **Fi·ren·ze** \fē-ˈrent-sä\ *or ancient* **Flo·ren·tia** \flə-ˈren-chə, -chē-ə\
city central Italy — **Flor·en·tine** \ˈflȯr-ən-ˌtēn, ˈflär-,
-ˌtīn\ *adj or n*
Flor·i·da \ˈflȯr-əd-ə, ˈflär-\ state SE U.S.; capital, Tallahassee — **Flo·rid·i·an** \flə-ˈrid-ē-ən\ *or* **Flor·i·dan**
\ˈflȯr-əd-ᵊn, ˈflär-\ *adj or n*
Florida, Straits of channel between Florida Keys on
NW & Cuba & Bahamas on S & E connecting Gulf of
Mexico & the Atlantic
Florida Keys chain of islands off S tip of Florida
Foochow — see FUZHOU
For·a·ker, Mount \-ˈfȯr-i-kər, -ˈfär-\ mountain 5304
meters S central Alaska in Alaska range
For·mo·sa \fȯr-ˈmō-sə, fər-, -zə\ — see TAIWAN —
For·mo·san \-ˈmōs-ᵊn, -ˈmōz-\ *adj or n*
For·ta·le·za \ˌfȯrt-ᵊl-ˈā-zə\ city NE Brazil
Fort–de–France \ˌfȯrd-ə-ˈfräns\ city West Indies,
capital of Martinique on W coast
Forth \ˈfō(ə)rth, ˈfȯ(ə)rth\ river S central Scotland
flowing E into North sea through **Firth of Forth**
Fort Knox \-ˈnäks\ military reservation N central Kentucky SSW of Louisville; location of U.S. Gold Bullion Depository
Fort Lau·der·dale \-ˈlȯd-ər-ˌdāl\ city SE Florida
Fort Wayne \-ˈwān\ city NE Indiana
Fort Worth \-ˈwərth\ city NE Texas
Fox \ˈfäks\ islands SW Alaska in the E Aleutians
Foxe Basin \ˈfäks-\ inlet of the Atlantic N Canada in E
Northwest Territories W of Baffin island
France \ˈfran(t)s\ country W Europe between the English channel & the Mediterranean; capital, Paris
Frank·fort \ˈfraŋk-fərt\ city, capital of Kentucky
Frank·furt \ˈfraŋk-fərt, ˈfrän-ˌfu̇(ə)rt\ *or in full* **Frankfurt am Main** \-(ˌ)äm-ˈmīn\ *or* **Frankfort on the Main**
city W Germany on Main river
Frank·lin \ˈfraŋ-klən\ former district N Canada in
Northwest Territories including Arctic islands &
Boothia & Melville peninsulas
Fra·ser \ˈfrā-zər, -zhər\ river 1370 kilometers long
Canada in S central British Columbia flowing into the
Pacific

Fred·er·ic·ton \ˈfred-(ə-)rik-tən\ city, capital of New
Brunswick, Canada
Free State province E central Republic of South Africa
Free·town \ˈfrē-ˌtau̇n\ city, capital of Sierra Leone
Fre·mont \ˈfrē-mänt\ city W California
French Guiana country N South America on the Atlantic; an overseas division of France; capital, Cayenne
French Indochina — see INDOCHINA
Fres·no \ˈfrez-nō\ city S central California
Frunze — see BISHKEK
Fu·ji \ˈf(y)ü-jē\ *or* **Fu·ji·ya·ma** \ˌf(y)ü-jē-ˈ(y)äm-ə\
mountain 3776 meters Japan in S central Honshu;
highest in Japan
Fu·ku·o·ka \ˌfü-kə-ˈwō-kə\ city Japan in N Kyushu
Ful·ler·ton \ˈfu̇l-ərt-ᵊn\ city SW California
Fu·na·fu·ti \ˌf(y)ü-nə-ˈf(y)üt-ē\ city, capital of Tuvalu
Fun·dy, Bay of \-ˈfən-dē\ inlet of the Atlantic SE Canada between New Brunswick & Nova Scotia
Fu·shun \ˈfü-ˈshu̇n\ city NE China E of Shenyang
Fu·zhou \ˈfü-ˈjō\ *or* **Foo·chow** \ˈfü-ˈjō, -ˈchau̇\ city SE
China
Ga·bon \ga-ˈbōn\ country W Africa on the equator;
capital, Libreville — **Gab·o·nese** \ˌgab-ə-ˈnēz, -ˈnēs\
adj or n
Ga·bo·rone \ˌgäb-ə-ˈrōn\ city, capital of Botswana
Gads·den Purchase \ˈgadz-dən-\ area of land S of Gila
river in present Arizona & New Mexico purchased
1853 by the U.S. from Mexico
Ga·la·pa·gos islands \gə-ˈläp-ə-gəs-, -ˈlap-\ island
group Ecuador in the Pacific 965 kilometers W of
South America
Ga·la·tia \gə-ˈlā-sh(ē-)ə\ ancient country central Asia
Minor in region around modern Ankara, Turkey —
Ga·la·tian \-shən\ *adj or n*
Ga·li·cia \gə-ˈlish-(ē-)ə\ **1** region E central Europe now
divided between Poland & Ukraine **2** region NW
Spain on the Atlantic — **Ga·li·cian** \-ˈlish-ən\ *adj or
n*
Gal·i·lee \ˈgal-ə-ˌlē\ hilly region N Israel — **Gal·i·le·an** \ˌgal-ə-ˈlē-ən\ *adj or n*
Galilee, Sea of *or* **Lake of** **Gen·nes·a·ret** \-gə-ˈnəs-ə-ˌret, -rət\ lake N Israel on Syrian border; crossed by
Jordan river
Gal·lo·way \ˈgal-ə-ˌwā\ district SW Scotland — see
DUMFRIES AND GALLOWAY
Gam·bia \ˈgam-bē-ə\ country W Africa; capital, Banjul
— **Gam·bi·an** \-bē-ən\ *adj or n*
Gan·ges \ˈgan-ˌjēz\ river 2495 kilometers long N India
flowing from the Himalayas SE & E to unite with the
Brahmaputra & empty into Bay of Bengal through a
vast delta — **Gan·get·ic** \gan-ˈjet-ik\ *adj*
Garden Grove city SW California
Gar·land \ˈgär-lənd\ city NE Texas
Ga·ronne \gə-ˈrän, -ˈrōn\ river 571 kilometers long SE
France flowing NW
Gary \ˈga(ə)r-ē, ˈge(ə)r-ē\ city NW Indiana on Lake
Michigan
Gas·co·ny \ˈgas-kə-nē\ region SW France — **Gas·con** \ˈgas-kən\ *adj or n*
Gas·pé \gas-ˈpā, ˈgas-ˌpā\ peninsula SE Quebec E of
mouth of the Saint Lawrence — **Gas·pe·sian** \ga-ˈspē-zhən\ *adj or n*
Gaul \ˈgȯl\ *or Latin* **Gal·lia** \ˈgal-ē-ə\ ancient country
W Europe chiefly consisting of region occupied by
modern France & Belgium but at one time including
also Po valley in N Italy
Gau·teng \ˈgau̇-ˌteŋ\ province central NE Republic of
South Africa
Ga·za Strip \ˈgäz-ə-\ district NE Sinai Peninsula on the
Mediterranean
Gee·long \jə-ˈlȯŋ\ city SE Australia in S Victoria
Ge·ne·va \jə-ˈnē-və\ city SW Switzerland on Lake of
Geneva — **Ge·ne·van** \-vən\ *adj or n* — **Gen·e·vese**
\ˌjen-ə-ˈvēz, -ˈvēs\ *adj or n*

Geneva, Lake of lake on border between SW Switzerland & E France; crossed by the Rhone

Gen·oa \'jen-ə-wə\ *or Italian* **Ge·no·va** \'je-nō-vä\ city NW Italy — **Gen·o·ese** \ˌjen-ə-'wēz, -'wēs\ *or* **Gen·o·vese** \-ə-'vēz, -'vēs\ *adj or n*

George·town \'jȯ(ə)rj-ˌtaùn\ 1 a W section of Washington, District of Columbia 2 city, capital of Guyana

Geor·gia \'jȯr-jə\ state SE U.S.; capital, Atlanta — **Geor·gian** \-jən\ *adj or n*

Georgia, Republic of country SE Europe on Black sea S of Caucasus mountains; capital, Tbilisi; a republic of U.S.S.R. 1936–91 — **Georgian** *adj or n*

Georgia, Strait of channel Canada & U.S. between Vancouver Island & main part of British Columbia NW of Puget Sound

Georgian Bay inlet of Lake Huron in S Ontario

Ger·man·town \'jər-mən-ˌtaùn\ a NW section of Philadelphia, Pennsylvania

Ger·ma·ny \'jərm-(ə-)nē\ country central Europe bordering on North & Baltic seas; official capital, Berlin; divided 1946–90 into two independent states: the Federal Republic of Germany (capital, Bonn) & the German Democratic Republic (capital, East Berlin)

Get·tys·burg \'get-ēz-ˌbərg\ town S Pennsylvania

Gha·na \'gän-ə, 'gan-ə\ *or formerly* **Gold Coast** country W Africa on Gulf of Guinea; an independent state in the Commonwealth; capital, Accra — **Gha·na·ian** \gä-'nā-ən, ga-, -yən; 'nī-ən\ *or* **Gha·ni·an** \'gän-ē-ən, 'gän-yən, 'gan-\ *adj or n*

Ghats \'gȯts\ two mountain chains S India — see EASTERN GHATS, WESTERN GHATS

Ghent \'gent\ *or* **Gent** \'kent\ city NW central Belgium

Gi·bral·tar \jə-'brȯl-tər\ British colony on S coast of Spain including Rock of Gibraltar

Gibraltar, Rock of cape on S coast of Spain in Gibraltar colony at E end of Strait of Gibraltar; highest point 426 meters

Gibraltar, Strait of passage between Spain & Africa connecting the Atlantic & the Mediterranean

Gi·la \'hē-lə\ river 1015 kilometers long SW New Mexico and S Arizona flowing W into the Colorado

Gil·bert and El·lice Islands \'gil-bərt-ən(d)-'el-əs-\ island group W Pacific; until 1976 a British colony; now divided into the independent states of Kiribati and Tuvalu

Gil·e·ad \'gil-ē-əd\ mountain region NE Palestine E of Jordan river; now in NW Jordan — **Gil·e·ad·ite** \-ē-ə-ˌdīt\ *n*

Gi·za \'gē-zə\ city N Egypt on the Nile SW of Cairo

Gla·cier Bay \ˌglā-shər\ inlet SE Alaska at S end of Saint Elias range

Glas·gow \'glas-kō, 'glas-gō, 'glaz-gō\ city S central Scotland in Strathclyde region on the Clyde — **Glas·we·gian** \glas-'wē-jən\ *adj or n*

Glen·dale \'glen-ˌdāl\ city S California just N of Los Angeles

Glou·ces·ter \'gläs-tər, 'glòs-\ city area SW central England in Gloucestershire

Glou·ces·ter·shire \'gläs-tər-ˌshi(ə)r, 'glòs-, -shər\ *or* **Gloucester** county SW central England

Goa \'gō-ə\ district W India on Malabar coast belonging to Portugal before 1962

Goat Island island W New York in Niagara river — see NIAGARA FALLS

Go·bi \'gō-bē\ desert E central Asia in Mongolia & N China

Godt·haab \'gȯt-ˌhȯb, 'gät-\ town, capital of Greenland on SW coast

Godwin Austen — see K2

Go·lan Heights \ˌgō-ˌlän-, -lən-\ hilly region NE of Sea of Galilee

Gol·con·da \gäl-'kän-də\ ruined city central India W of Hyderabad

Gold Coast 1 — see GHANA 2 coast region W Africa on N shore of Gulf of Guinea E of Ivory Coast

Golden Gate strait W California

Good Hope, Cape of \-ˌgùd-'hȯp\ cape S Republic of South Africa in SW Western Cape

Gor·ki *or* **Gor'kii** *or* **Gor'kiy** *or* **Gorky** — see NIZHNI NOVGOROD

Gram·pi·an \'gram-pē-ən\ 1 hills N central Scotland 2 region NE central Scotland; established 1975

Grand Banks shallow area in the W Atlantic SE of Newfoundland

Grand Canyon gorge of Colorado river NW Arizona

Grand Canyon of the Snake — see HELLS CANYON

Grande, Rio — see RIO GRANDE

Grand Rapids city SW Michigan

Great Australian Bight wide bay on S coast of Australia

Great Barrier Reef coral reef Australia off NE coast of Queensland

Great Basin region W U.S. between Sierra Nevada & Wasatch mountains including most of Nevada & parts of California, Idaho, Utah, Wyoming, and Oregon; has no drainage to ocean

Great Bear lake Canada in W Northwest Territories draining through Great Bear river into Mackenzie river

Great Brit·ain \-'brit-ᵊn\ 1 island W Europe NW of France consisting of England, Scotland, & Wales 2 UNITED KINGDOM

Great Dividing range mountain system E Australia & Tasmania extending S from Cape York peninsula — see KOSCIUSKO, MOUNT

Greater An·til·les \-an-'til-ēz\ group of islands of the West Indies including Cuba, Hispaniola, Jamaica, & Puerto Rico — see LESSER ANTILLES

Greater London county SE England consisting of City of London & 32 surrounding city areas

Greater Manchester county NW England including city of Manchester

Great Lakes chain of five lakes (Superior, Michigan, Huron, Erie, & Ontario) central North America in U.S. & Canada

Great Plains elevated plains region W central U.S. & W Canada E of the Rockies; extending from W Texas to NE British Columbia & NW Alberta

Great Rift valley \-'rift-\ basin SW Asia & E Africa extending with several breaks from valley of the Jordan S to central Mozambique

Great Salt lake N Utah having salty waters & no outlet

Great Slave lake NW Canada in S Northwest Territories drained by Mackenzie river

Great Smoky mountains between W North Carolina & E Tennessee; highest Clingmans Dome 2024 meters

Greece \'grēs\ country S Europe at S end of Balkan peninsula; capital, Athens

Green \'grēn\ **1** mountains E North America in the Appalachians extending from S Quebec S through Vermont into W Massachusetts **2** river 1175 kilometers long W U.S. flowing from W Wyoming S into the Colorado in SE Utah

Green Bay inlet of NW Lake Michigan 193 kilometers long in NW Michigan & NE Wisconsin

Green·land \'grēn-lənd, -ˌland\ island in the N Atlantic off NE North America belonging to Denmark; capital, Godthaab

Greens·boro \'grēnz-ˌbər-ə, -ˌbə-rə\ city N central North Carolina

Green·wich \'grin-ij, 'gren-, -ich\ city area of SE Greater London county, England

Green·wich Village \ˌgren-ich-, ˌgrin-, -ij-\ section of New York City in Manhattan on lower W side

Gre·na·da \grə-'nād-ə\ island West Indies in S Windward Islands; an independent country; capital, Saint George's

Gua·da·la·ja·ra \ˌgwäd-ə-lə-'här-ə\ city W central Mexico

Gua·dal·ca·nal \ˌgwäd-ᵊl-kə-'nal, ˌgwäd-ə-kə-\ island W Pacific in the SE Solomons

Gua·dal·qui·vir \ˌgwäd-ᵊl-'kwiv-ər, -ki-'vi(ə)r\ river 656 kilometers long S Spain flowing into the Atlantic

Gua·de·loupe \'gwäd-ᵊl-ˌüp\ two islands separated by a narrow channel in West Indies in central Leeward Islands; an overseas division of France

Gua·lla·ti·ri \ˌgwä-yə-'tir-ē, ˌgwī-ə-\ volcano 6060 meters N Chile; highest volcano in world

Guam \'gwäm\ island W Pacific in S Marianas belonging to U.S.; capital, Agana — **Gua·ma·ni·an** \gwä-'mä-nē-ən\ adj or n

Gua·na·ba·ra Bay \ˌgwän-ə-'bar-ə, -'bär-\ inlet of the Atlantic SE Brazil on which city of Rio de Janeiro is located

Guang·zhou \'gwäŋ-'jō\ or **Can·ton** \'kan-ˌtän, kan-'\ city SE China

Guan·tá·na·mo Bay \gwän-'tän-ə-ˌmō\ inlet of the Caribbean in SE Cuba; site of U.S. naval station

Gua·te·ma·la \ˌgwät-ə-'mäl-ə\ **1** country Central America **2** or **Guatemala City** city, its capital — **Gua·te·ma·lan** \-'mäl-ən\ adj or n

Gua·ya·quil \ˌgwī-ə-'kē(ə)l, -'kil\ city W Ecuador

Guern·sey \'gərn-zē\ island in English channel — see CHANNEL

Gui·a·na \gē-'an-ə, -'än-ə; gī-'an-ə\ region N South America on the Atlantic; includes Guyana, French Guiana, Suriname, & nearby parts of Brazil & Venezuela — **Gui·a·nan** \-ən\ adj or n

Guin·ea \'gin-ē\ **1** region W Africa on the Atlantic extending along coast from Gambia to Angola **2** country W Africa N of Sierra Leone & Liberia; capital, Conakry — **Guin·ean** \'gin-ē-ən\ adj or n

Guinea, Gulf of arm of the Atlantic W central Africa

Guin·ea–Bis·sau \ˌgin-ē-bis-'aú\ country W Africa; an independent state since 1974; capital, Bissau

Gui·yang \'gwē-'yäŋ\ or **Kuei–yang** \'gwä-'yäŋ\ city S China

Gulf States states of U.S. bordering on Gulf of Mexico: Florida, Alabama, Mississippi, Louisiana, and Texas

Gulf Stream warm current of the Atlantic ocean flowing from Gulf of Mexico NE along coast of U.S. to Nantucket island and from there eastward

Guy·ana \gī-'an-ə\ or formerly **British Guiana** country N South America on the Atlantic; an independent state in the Commonwealth since 1970; capital, Georgetown

Gwent \'gwent\ county SE Wales; established 1974

Gwyn·edd \'gwin-eth\ county NW Wales; established 1974

Hack·ney \'hak-nē\ city area of N Greater London county, England

Hague, The \thə-'häg\ city SW Netherlands; a capital of the Netherlands

Haidarabad — see HYDERABAD

Hai·kou \'hī-'kō\ city SE China

Hai·ti \'hät-ē\ **1** — see HISPANIOLA **2** country West Indies in W Hispaniola; capital, Port-au-Prince — **Haitian** \'hā-shən\ adj or n

Ha·le·a·ka·la Crater \ˌhäl-ē-ˌäk-ə-'lä\ crater more than 762 meters deep Hawaii in E Maui Island

Hal·i·fax \'hal-ə-ˌfaks\ city, capital of Nova Scotia, Canada

Ham·burg \'ham-ˌbərg, 'häm-ˌbù(ə)rg\ city N Germany on the Elbe — **Ham·burg·er** \-ˌbər-gər, -ˌbúr-\ n

Ham·il·ton \'ham-əl-tən, -əlt-ᵊn\ **1** city S Ontario, Canada **2** town, capital of Bermuda

Ham·mer·smith \'ham-ər-ˌsmith\ city area of SW Greater London county, England

Hamp·shire \'ham(p)-ˌshi(ə)r, -shər\ county S England on English channel

Hamp·ton \'ham(p)-tən\ city SE Virginia

Hampton Roads channel SE Virginia through which James river flows into Chesapeake Bay

Hang·zhou \'häŋ-'jō\ or **Hang·chow** \'häŋ-'jō\ or **Hang–chou** \'häŋ-'jō\ city E China

Han·ni·bal \'han-ə-bəl\ city NE Missouri on the Mississippi river

Han·no·ver or **Han·o·ver** \'han-ō-vər, 'han-ə-vər; German hä-'nō-vər\ city N central Germany

Ha·noi \ha-'nòi, hə-, hä-\ city, capital of Vietnam

Ha·ra·re \hə-'rä-rā\ or formerly **Salis·bury** \'sölz-ˌber-ē, -b(ə-)rē\ city, capital of Zimbabwe

Har·bin \'här-bən, här-'bin\ or **Ha–erh–pin** \'hä-'er-'bin\ city NE China

Har·in·gey \'har-iŋ-ˌgā\ city area of N Greater London county, England

Har·lem \'här-ləm\ section of New York City in N Manhattan

Har·ris·burg \'har-əs-ˌbərg\ city, capital of Pennsylvania

Har·row \'har-ō\ city area of NW Greater London county, England

Hart·ford \'härt-fərd\ city, capital of Connecticut

Hat·ter·as, Cape \-'hat-ə-rəs, -'ha-trəs\ cape, North Carolina on Cape Hatteras Island

Ha·vana \hə-'van-ə\ city, capital of Cuba

Hav·ant and Wa·ter·loo \'hav-ənt-ᵊn-ˌwòt-ər-'lü, -ˌwät-\ town S England in Hampshire

Ha·ver·ing \'hāv-(ə-)riŋ\ city area of NE Greater London county, England

Ha·waii \hə-'wä-(y)ē, -'wī-, -'wò-\ **1** or formerly **Sand·wich islands** \san-(d)wich-\ group of islands central Pacific belonging to U.S. **2** island, largest of the group **3** state of U.S. consisting of Hawaiian Islands except Midway; capital, Honolulu

Heb·ri·des \'heb-rə-ˌdēz\ islands W Scotland in the Atlantic consisting of **Outer Hebrides** (to W) and **Inner Hebrides** (to E) — see WESTERN ISLES — **Heb·ri·de·an** \ˌheb-rə-'dē-ən\ adj or n

Hel·e·na \'hel-ə-nə\ city, capital of Montana

Hellespont — see DARDANELLES

Hells Canyon \'helz-\ or **Grand Canyon of the Snake** canyon of Snake river on Idaho–Oregon boundary

Hel·sin·ki \'hel-ˌsiŋ-kē, hel-'siŋ-\ city, capital of Finland

Henry, Cape \-'hen-rē\ cape E Virginia S of entrance to Chesapeake Bay

Her·e·ford and Wor·ces·ter \'her-ə-fərd-ᵊn-¦wu̇s-tər, *in the U.S. also* 'hər-fərd-\ county W England bordering on Wales

Hert·ford·shire \'här-fərd-₁shi(ə)r, -shər, *also* 'härt-, *in the U.S. also* 'hərt-\ *or* **Hertford** county SE England

Hi·a·le·ah \₁hī-ə-'lē-ə\ city SE Florida

Hi·ber·nia \hī-'bər-nē-ə\ — see IRELAND — **Hi·ber·ni·an** \-ən\ *adj or n*

Hi·ga·shi·ōsa·ka \hē-₁gä-shē-ō-'säk-ə\ city Japan in S Honshu E of Osaka

High·land \'hī-lənd\ region NW Scotland

High·lands \'hī-lən(d)z\ the mountainous N part of Scotland lying N & W of the Lowlands

High Plains the Great Plains especially from Nebraska southward

Hil·ling·don \'hil-iŋ-dən\ city area of W Greater London county, England

Hi·ma·la·ya \₁him-ə-'lā-ə, hə-'mäl-(ə-)yə\ mountain system S Asia on border between India & Tibet & in Kashmir, Nepal, & Bhutan — see EVEREST, MOUNT — **Hi·ma·la·yan** \₁him-ə-'lā-ən, hə-'mäl-(ə-)yən\ *adj*

Hin·du Kush \₁hin-(₁)dü-'ku̇sh, -'kəsh\ mountain range central Asia SW of the Pamirs on border of Kashmir & in Afghanistan

Hin·du·stan \₁hin-(₁)dü-'stan, -də-, -'stän\ **1** region N India **2** the subcontinent of India **3** the country of India

Hi·ro·shi·ma \₁hir-ə-'shē-mə, hə-'rō-shə-mə\ city Japan in SW Honshu on Inland sea

His·pan·io·la \₁his-pən-'yō-lə\ *or Spanish* **Es·pa·ño·la** \₁es-₁pän-'yō-lə\ *or formerly* **Hai·ti** \'hāt-ē\ island West Indies in Greater Antilles divided between Haiti on W & Dominican Republic on E

Ho·bart \'hō-₁bärt\ city Australia, capital of Tasmania

Ho Chi Minh City \hō-₁chē-₁min-, -₁shē-\ *or formerly* **Sai·gon** \sī-'gän, 'sī-₁gän\ city S Vietnam

Hoh·hot \'hō-'hōt\ *or* **Hu·he·hot** \'hü-₁hä-'hōt\ city N China, capital of Inner Mongolia

Hok·kai·do \hä-'kīd-ō\ island N Japan N of Honshu

Hol·land \'häl-ənd\ **1** county of Holy Roman Empire bordering on North sea & consisting of area now forming part of W Netherlands **2** — see NETHERLANDS — **Hol·land·er** \-ən-dər\ *n*

Hol·ly·wood \'häl-ē-₁wu̇d\ **1** section of Los Angeles, California, NW of downtown district **2** city SE Florida

Holy Land PALESTINE

Holy Roman Empire empire consisting mainly of German and Italian territories and existing from the 9th or 10th century to 1806

Hon·du·ras \hän-'d(y)u̇r-əs\ country Central America; capital, Tegucigalpa — **Hon·du·ran** \-ən\ *or* **Hon·du·ra·ne·an** *or* **Hon·du·ra·ni·an** \₁hän-d(y)u̇-'rä-nē-ən\ *adj or n*

Hong Kong \'häŋ-₁käŋ, -'käŋ; 'hȯŋ-₁kȯŋ, -'kȯŋ\ special administrative region China on SE coast; formerly a British colony

Ho·ni·a·ra \₁hō-nē-'är-ə\ town, capital of Solomon Islands

Ho·no·lu·lu \₁hän-ᵊl-'ü-lü, ₁hōn-ᵊl-\ city, capital of Hawaii on Oahu Island

Hon·shu \'hän-shü\ *or* **Hon·do** \'hän-dō\ island Japan; largest of the four chief islands

Hood, Mount \'hu̇d\ mountain 3424 meters NW Oregon in Cascade Range

Hoo·ver Dam \₁hü-vər-\ *or formerly* **Boul·der Dam** \'bōl-dər-\ dam 221 meters high in Colorado river between Arizona & Nevada — see MEAD, LAKE

Horn, Cape \-'hȯ(ə)rn\ cape S Chile on an island in Tierra del Fuego; the most southerly point of South America at 55°59′ S latitude

Horseshoe Falls — see NIAGARA FALLS

Houns·low \'hau̇nz-₁lō\ city area of SW Greater London county, England

Hous·ton \'(h)yü-stən\ city SE Texas

How·rah \'hau̇-rə\ city E India on Hugli river opposite Calcutta

Huang *or* **Hwang** \'hwäŋ\ *or* **Yellow** river 4830 kilometers long N China flowing into Bo Hai

Hud·ders·field \'həd-ərz-₁fēld\ city area N England in West Yorkshire NE of Manchester

Hud·son \'həd-sən\ **1** river 492 kilometers long E New York flowing S **2** bay inlet of the Atlantic in N Canada **3** strait NE Canada connecting Hudson bay & the Atlantic

Hu·gli *or* **Hoo·ghly** \'hü-glē\ river 195 kilometers long E India flowing S into Bay of Bengal; most westerly channel of the Ganges in its delta

Huhehot — see HOHHOT

Hull \'həl\ *or* **Kings·ton upon Hull** \'kiŋ(k)-stən-\ city N England in Humberside county

Hum·ber·side \'həm-bər-₁sīd\ county E England

Hun·ga·ry \'həŋ-g(ə-)rē\ country central Europe; capital, Budapest

Hunt·ing·ton Beach \'hənt-iŋ-tən-\ city SW California

Hunts·ville \'hən(t)s-₁vil, -vəl\ city N Alabama

Hu·ron, Lake \-'(h)yu̇r-ən, -'(h)yu̇(ə)r-₁än\ lake E central North America in U.S. & Canada; one of the Great Lakes

Hy·der·abad \'hīd-(ə-)rə-₁bad, -₁bäd\ **1** *or* **Hai·dar·abad** city S central India **2** city SE Pakistan on the Indus

Iba·dan \i-'bäd-ᵊn, -'bad-\ city SW Nigeria

Ibe·ri·an \ī-'bir-ē-ən\ peninsula SW Europe occupied by Spain & Portugal

Ice·land \'ī-slənd, -₁sland\ island SE of Greenland between Arctic & Atlantic oceans; capital, Reykjavik — **Ice·land·er** \-₁slan-dər, -slən-dər\ *n*

Ida·ho \'īd-ə-₁hō\ state NW U.S.; capital, Boise — **Ida·ho·an** \₁īd-ə-'hō-ən\ *adj or n*

Igua·çu *or Spanish* **Igua·zú** \₁ē-gwə-'sü\ river S Brazil flowing W

IJs·sel *or* **Ijs·sel** \'ī-səl\ river 113 kilometers long E Netherlands flowing out of Rhine N into IJsselmeer

IJs·sel·meer \₁ī-səl-'me(ə)r\ *or* **Lake Ijs·sel** freshwater lake N Netherlands separated from North sea by a dike; part of former Zuider Zee (inlet of North sea)

Ilium *or* **Ilion** — see TROY

Il·li·nois \₁il-ə-'nȯi *also* -'nȯiz\ state N central U.S.; capital, Springfield — **Il·li·nois·an** \-'nȯi-ən, -'nȯiz-ᵊn\ *adj or n*

Il·lyr·ia \il-'ir-ē-ə\ ancient country S Europe and Balkan peninsula on the Adriatic — **Il·lyr·i·an** \-ē-ən\ *adj or n*

Im·pe·ri·al Valley \im-'pir-ē-əl-\ valley SE corner of California & partly in Baja California, Mexico

In·chon \'in-₁chän\ city South Korea on Yellow sea

In·de·pen·dence \₁in-də-'pen-dən(t)s\ city W Missouri E of Kansas City

In·dia \'in-dē-ə\ **1** subcontinent S Asia S of the Himalayas between Bay of Bengal & Arabian sea **2** *or* **Bha·rat** \'bər-ət, 'bə-rət\ country consisting of major portion of the subcontinent; an independent state in the Commonwealth; capital, New Delhi **3** *or* **Indian Empire** before 1947 those parts of the Indian subcontinent under British rule or protection

In·di·an \'in-dē-ən\ ocean E of Africa, S of Asia, W of Australia, & N of Antarctica

In·di·ana \₁in-dē-'an-ə\ state E central U.S.; capital, Indianapolis — **In·di·an·an** \-'an-ən\ *or* **In·di·an·i·an** \-'an-ē-ən\ *adj or n*

In·di·a·nap·o·lis \₁in-dē-ə-'nap-(ə-)ləs\ city, capital of Indiana

Indian river lagoon 266 kilometers long E Florida between main part of the state & coastal islands

Indian Territory former territory S U.S. in present state of Oklahoma

In·dies \'in-dēz\ **1** EAST INDIES **2** WEST INDIES

In·do·chi·na \'in-(₁)dō-'chī-nə\ **1** peninsula SE Asia including Myanmar, Malay peninsula, Thailand, Cambodia, Laos, & Vietnam **2** *or* **French Indochina** former country SE Asia consisting of area now forming Cambodia, Laos, & Vietnam — **In·do–Chi·nese** \-chī-'nēz, -'nēs\ *adj or n*

In·do·ne·sia \₁in-də-'nē-zhə, -shə\ country SE Asia in Malay island group consisting of Sumatra, Java, S & E Borneo, Sulawesi, W New Guinea, & many smaller islands; capital, Jakarta — see NETHERLANDS EAST INDIES — **In·do·ne·sian** \-zhən, -shən\ *adj or n*

In·dore \in-'dō(ə)r, -'dò(ə)r\ city W central India

In·dus \'in-dəs\ river 2900 kilometers long S Asia flowing from Tibet NW & SSW through Pakistan into Arabian sea

In·gle·wood \'iŋ-gəl-₁wùd\ city SW California

In·land \'in-₁land, -lənd\ sea inlet of the Pacific in SW Japan between Honshu on N and Shikoku and Kyushu on S

Inner Hebrides — see HEBRIDES

Inner Mon·go·lia \-män-'gōl-yə, mäŋ-, -'gō-lē-ə\ region N China

Inside Passage *or* **Inland Passage** protected shipping route between Puget Sound, Washington, & Skagway, Alaska

In·ver·ness \₁in-vər-'nes\ town NW Scotland in Highland region

Io·ni·an \ī-'ō-nē-ən\ **1** sea arm of the Mediterranean between SE Italy & W Greece **2** islands W Greece in Ionian sea

Io·wa \'ī-ə-wə\ state N central U.S.; capital, Des Moines — **Io·wan** \-wən\ *adj or n*

Ips·wich \'ip-(₁)swich\ city area SE England in Suffolk county

Iran \i-'rän, -'ran; ī-'ran\ *or formerly* **Per·sia** \'pərzhə\ country SW Asia; capital, Tehran — **Irani** \i-'rän-ē, -'ran-\ *adj or n* — **Ira·nian** \ir-'ā-nē-ən, -'anē-, -'än-ē-\ *adj or n*

Iraq \i-'räk, -'rak\ country SW Asia in Mesopotamia; capital, Baghdad — **Iraqi** \-'räk-ē, -'rak-\ *adj or n*

Ire·land \'ī(ə)r-lənd\ **1** *or Latin* **Hi·ber·nia** \hī-'bərnē-ə\ island W Europe in the Atlantic; one of the British Isles **2** *or* **Irish Republic** *or* **Ei·re** \'ar-ə, 'ar-ē, 'er-, 'är-, 'ir-\ country occupying major portion of the island; capital, Dublin

Iri·an Ja·ya \'ir-ē-₁än-'jä-yä\ *or* **West Irian** territory of Indonesia consisting of W half of New Guinea

Irish sea \'ir-ish-\ arm of the Atlantic between Great Britain & Ireland

Ir·kutsk \ir(ə)r-'kütsk, ₁ər-\ city S Russia near Lake Baikal

Ir·ra·wad·dy \₁ir-ə-'wäd-ē\ river 2092 kilometers long Myanmar flowing S into Bay of Bengal

Ir·tysh \i(ə)r-'tish, ₁ər-\ river over 4200 kilometers long central Asia flowing NW & N from Altai mountains in China, through Kazakhstan, and into W central Russia

Ir·ving \'ər-viŋ\ city NE Texas NW of Dallas

Is·fa·han \₁is-fə-'hän, -'han\ *or formerly* **Is·pa·han** \₁ispə-\ city W central Iran

Is·lam·abad \is-'läm-ə-₁bäd, iz-'lam-ə-₁bad\ city, capital of Pakistan

Isle of Man — see MAN, ISLE OF

Isle of Wight \-'wīt\ island and county S England in English channel

Isle Roy·ale \('')ī(ə)l-'ròi(-ə)l\ island Michigan in Lake Superior

Isles of Scilly — see CORNWALL AND ISLES OF SCILLY; SCILLY

Is·ling·ton \'iz-liŋ-tən\ city area of N Greater London county, England

Is·ra·el \'iz-rē-əl, -rā-əl, -rəl\ **1** ancient kingdom Palestine consisting of lands occupied by the Hebrew people **2** *or* **Ephra·im** \'ē-frē-əm\ the N part of the Hebrew kingdom after about 933 B.C. **3** country SW

Asia in Palestine; established 1948; capital, Jerusalem — **Is·rae·li** \iz-'rā-lē\ *adj or n*

Is·tan·bul \₁is-təm-'bùl, -₁täm-, -₁tam-, -₁tän-\ *or formerly* **Con·stan·ti·no·ple** \₁kän-₁stant-ᵊn-'ō-pəl\ city NW Turkey on the Bosporus & Sea of Marmara; former capital of Turkey

Is·tria \'is-trē-ə\ peninsula in Croatia & Slovenia extending into the N Adriatic — **Is·tri·an** \-trē-ən\ *adj or n*

It·a·ly \'it-ᵊl-ē\ country comprising a peninsula 1220 kilometers long and the islands of Sicily and Sardinia S Europe; capital Rome

Itas·ca, Lake \-ī-'tas-kə\ lake NW central Minnesota; source of the Mississippi

Ivory Coast *or* **French Côte d'Ivoire** \₁kōt-dē-'vwär\ country W Africa on Gulf of Guinea; capital, Yamoussoukro; seat of government, Abidjan

Iwo Ji·ma \₁ē-(₁)wō-'jē-mə\ island Japan in W Pacific

Ix·ta·pa·la·pa \₁ē-stə-pə-'läp-ə\ city S central Mexico SE of Mexico City

Izhevsk \'ē-₁zhefsk\ *or 1985-87* **Usti·nov** \'üs-ti-₁nòf, -₁nòv\ city W Russia

Iz·mir \iz-'mi(ə)r\ *or formerly* **Smyr·na** \'smər-nə\ city W Turkey

Jack·son \'jak-sən\ city, capital of Mississippi

Jack·son·ville \'jak-sən-₁vil\ city NE Florida

Jai·pur \'jī-₁pù(ə)r\ city NW India

Ja·kar·ta *or* **Dja·kar·ta** \jə-'kär-tə\ *or formerly* **Ba·ta·via** \bə-'tā-vē-ə\ city, capital of Indonesia in NW Java

Ja·mai·ca \jə-'mā-kə\ island West Indies in Greater Antilles; an independent country in the Commonwealth; capital, Kingston — **Ja·mai·can** \-kən\ *adj or n*

James \'jāmz\ **1** — see DAKOTA **2** river 550 kilometers long Virginia flowing E into Chesapeake Bay

James Bay the S extension of Hudson bay between NE Ontario & W Quebec

James·town \'jām-₁staùn\ ruined village E Virginia on James river; first permanent English settlement in America (1607)

Jam·shed·pur \'jäm-₁shed-₁pù(ə)r\ city E India

Ja·pan \jə-'pan, ji-, ja-\ *or Japanese* **Nip·pon** \nip-'än\ country E Asia consisting of Honshu, Hokkaido, Kyushu, Shikoku, & other islands in W Pacific; capital, Tokyo

Japan, Sea of arm of the Pacific between Japan & main part of Asia

Ja·va \'jäv-ə, 'jav-ə\ island Indonesia SW of Borneo; chief city, Jakarta — **Ja·van** \-ən\ *adj or n*

Jef·fer·son \'jef-ər-sən\ city, capital of Missouri

Jer·sey \'jər-zē\ island in English channel — see CHANNEL — **Jer·sey·ite** \-zē-₁īt\ *n*

Jersey City city NE New Jersey on Hudson river

Je·ru·sa·lem \jə-'rü-s(ə-)ləm, -'rüz-(ə-)ləm\ city NW of Dead sea divided 1948–67 between Israel & Jordan; capital of Israel since 1950 & formerly of ancient kingdom of Israel

Jid·da \'jid-ə\ city W Saudi Arabia on Red sea

Ji·lin \jē-'lin\ *or* **Ki·rin** \'kē-'rin\ city NE China

Ji·nan *or* **Tsi·nan** \jē-'nän\ city E China

Jin·zhou *or* **Chin–chou** *or* **Chin·chow** \'jin-'jō\ city NE China

Jo·han·nes·burg \jō-'han-əs-₁bərg, -'hän-\ city NE Republic of South Africa in S Gauteng province

Jor·dan \'jòrd-ᵊn\ **1** river 320 kilometers long Israel & Jordan flowing S from Syria into Dead sea **2** country SW Asia in NW Arabia; capital, Amman — **Jor·da·ni·an** \jòr-'dā-nē-ən\ *adj or n*

Juan de Fu·ca, Strait of \-₁(h)wän-də-'fyü-kə\ strait 160 kilometers long between Vancouver Island, British Columbia, & Olympic peninsula, Washington

Ju·dea *or* **Ju·daea** \jù-'dē-ə, -'dā-\ ancient region Palestine forming the S division (Judah) of the country under Persian, Greek, & Roman rule — **Ju·dean** \-ᵊn\ *adj or n*

Ju·neau \'jü-nō, jü-'nō\ city, capital of Alaska

Ju·ra \'jur-ə\ mountain range extending along boundary between France & Switzerland N of Lake of Geneva

Jut·land \'jət-lənd\ 1 peninsula N Europe extending into North sea & consisting of main part of Denmark & N portion of Germany 2 the main part of Denmark

Ka·bul \'käb-əl, kä-'bül\ city, capital of Afghanistan

Ka Lae \kä-'lä-ā\ or **South Cape** or **South Point** most southerly point of Hawaii & of U.S.

Kal·a·ha·ri \ˌkal-ə-'här-ē\ desert region S Africa N of Orange river in S Botswana & NW Republic of South Africa

Kalgan — see ZHANGJIAKOU

Ka·li·man·tan \ˌkal-ə-'man-ˌtan, ˌkäl-ə-'män-ˌtän\ 1 BORNEO — its Indonesian name 2 the S & E portion of Borneo belonging to Indonesia; formerly part of Netherlands East Indies

Kam·chat·ka \kam-'chat-kə\ peninsula 1205 kilometers long E Russia

Kam·pa·la \käm-'päl-ə\ city, capital of Uganda

Kampuchea — see CAMBODIA

Ka·no \'kän-ō\ city N central Nigeria

Kan·pur \'kän-ˌpu̇(ə)r\ city N India on the Ganges

Kan·sas \'kan-zəs\ state W central U.S.; capital, Topeka — **Kan·san** \-zən\ adj or n

Kansas City 1 city NE Kansas bordering on Kansas City, Missouri 2 city W Missouri

Kao·hsiung \'kau̇-shē-'u̇ŋ, 'gau̇-\ city China in SW Taiwan

Ka·ra·chi \kə-'räch-ē\ city S Pakistan on Arabian sea

Ka·ra·gan·da \ˌkar-ə-gən-'dä\ city central Kazakhstan

Ka·re·lia \kə-'rē-lē-ə, -'rēl-yə\ region NE Europe in Finland & Russia — **Ka·re·lian** \-'rē-lē-ən, -'rēl-yən\ adj or n

Kar·roo \kə-'rü\ plateau region W Republic of South Africa W of Drakensberg mountains

Kash·mir \'kash-ˌmi(ə)r, 'kazh-, kash-'mi(ə)r, kazh-'mi(ə)r\ region and former state N Indian subcontinent — **Kash·miri** \kash-'mi(ə)r-ē, kazh-\ adj or n

Ka·thi·a·war \ˌkät-ē-ə-'wär\ peninsula W India N of Gulf of Cambay

Kath·man·du or **Kat·man·du** \ˌkat-ˌman-'dü\ city, capital of Nepal

Kat·mai, Mount \-'kat-ˌmī\ volcano 2047 meters S Alaska on Alaska peninsula

Kat·te·gat \'kat-i-ˌgat\ arm of North sea between Sweden & E coast of Jutland peninsula of Denmark

Kau·ai \'kau̇-ˌī\ island Hawaii NW of Oahu

Ka·wa·sa·ki \ˌkä-wə-'säk-ē\ city Japan in E Honshu S of Tokyo

Ka·zakh·stan \kə-ˌzak-'stan; kə-ˌzak-'stän, ˌkä-\ country NW central Asia; capital, Astana; a republic (**Ka·zakh Soviet Socialist Republic** \kə-ˌzak-, -ˌzäk-\) of U.S.S.R. 1936–91

Ka·zan \kə-'zan, -'zän\ city W Russia

Kee·wa·tin \kē-'wāt-ᵊn\ former district N Canada in E Northwest Territories NW of Hudson bay

Ke·me·ro·vo \'kem-ə-rə-və, -ˌrō-və, -rə-ˌvō\ city S central Russia

Ke·nai \'kē-ˌnī\ peninsula S Alaska E of Cook inlet

Kennedy, Cape — see CANAVERAL, CAPE

Ken·sing·ton and Chel·sea \'ken-ziŋ-tən-ən-'chel-sē, 'ken(t)-siŋ-\ city area of W Greater London county, England

Kent \'kent\ county SE England — **Kent·ish** \'kent-ish\ adj

Ken·tucky \kən-'tək-ē\ state E central U.S.; capital, Frankfort — **Ken·tuck·i·an** \-ē-ən\ adj or n

Ken·ya \'ken-yə, 'kēn-\ 1 mountain 5194 meters central Kenya 2 country E Africa S of Ethiopia; capital, Nairobi — **Ken·yan** \-yən\ adj or n

Key West \'kē-'west\ city SW Florida on Key West island

Kha·ba·rovsk \kə-'bär-əfsk\ city SE Russia

Khar·kov \'kär-ˌkȯf, -ˌkȯv, -kəf\ city NE Ukraine

Khar·toum \kär-'tüm\ city, capital of Sudan

Khmer Republic — see CAMBODIA

Khy·ber \'kī-bər\ pass 53 kilometers long on border between Afghanistan & Pakistan

Ki·bo \'kē-bō\ mountain peak 5895 meters NE Tanzania; highest peak of Kilimanjaro & highest point in Africa

Kiel \'kē(ə)l\ or **Nord–Ost·see** \ˌnȯrt-ˌȯst-'zä\ canal 98 kilometers long N Germany across base of Jutland peninsula connecting Baltic sea & North sea

Ki·ev or Russian **Ki·yev** \'kē-ˌ(y)ef, -(y)ev, -(y)əf\ city, capital of Ukraine

Ki·ga·li \ki-'gäl-ē\ city, capital of Rwanda

Ki·lau·ea \ˌkē-ˌlau̇-'ā-ə\ volcanic crater Hawaii on Hawaii island on E slope of Mauna Loa

Kil·i·man·ja·ro \ˌkil-ə-mən-'jär-ō, -'jar-\ mountain NE Tanzania; highest in Africa — see KIBO

Kil·lar·ney, Lakes of \-kil-'är-nē\ three lakes SW Ireland

Kings·ton \'kiŋ-stən\ city, capital of Jamaica

Kingston upon Hull — see HULL

Kingston upon Thames \-'temz\ city area of SW Greater London county, England

Kings·town \'kiŋ-ˌstau̇n\ seaport, capital of Saint Vincent and the Grenadines

Kin·sha·sa \kin-'shäs-ə\ city, capital of Democratic Republic of the Congo

Kirgiz Republic or **Kirghiz Republic** or **Kirghizia** — see KYRGYZSTAN

Ki·ri·bati \'kir-ə-ˌbas\ island group W Pacific; an independent country; capital, Tarawa

Kirin — see JILIN

Kirk·wall \'kər-ˌkwȯl\ town and port N Scotland in Orkney region

Kishinev — see CHISINAU

Ki·ta·kyu·shu \kē-'tä-kē-'ü-shü\ city Japan in N Kyushu

Kitch·en·er \'kich-(ə-)nər\ city SE Ontario, Canada

Kit·ty Hawk \'kit-ē-ˌhȯk\ village E North Carolina

Klon·dike \'klän-ˌdīk\ region NW Canada in central Yukon Territory in valley of Klondike river

Knox·ville \'näks-ˌvil, -vəl\ city E Tennessee

Ko·be \'kō-bē, -ˌbā\ city Japan in S Honshu

Ko·di·ak \'kōd-ē-ˌak\ island S Alaska E of Alaska peninsula

Ko·la \'kō-lə\ peninsula NW Russia

Ko·rea \kə-'rē-ə, especially South kō-\ former kingdom E Asia between Yellow sea & Sea of Japan; capital, Seoul; divided after World War II at 38th parallel of latitude into independent countries of North Korea & South Korea

Korea, North country E Asia; capital Pyongyang

Korea, South country E Asia; capital Seoul

Kos·ci·us·ko, Mount \-ˌkäz-ē-'əs-kō\ mountain 2230 meters SE Australia in SE New South Wales; highest in Greater Dividing range & in Australia

Kow·loon \'kau̇-'lün\ 1 peninsula SE China in Hong Kong colony opposite Hong Kong island 2 city on Kowloon peninsula

Kra·ka·toa \ˌkrak-ə-'tō-ə\ or **Krak·a·tau** \-'tau̇\ island & volcano Indonesia between Sumatra & Java

Kra·kow \'kräk-ˌau̇, 'krak-, 'kräk-, -ō, Polish 'kräk-ˌüf\ city S Poland

Kras·no·dar \'kras-nə-ˌdär\ city SW Russia

Kras·no·yarsk \ˌkras-nə-'yärsk\ city S central Russia

Kri·voy Rog \ˌkriv-ˌȯi-'rȯg, -'rȯk\ or **Kry·vyy Rih** \ˌkri-vi-'rik\ city SE central Ukraine

K2 \ˌkä-'tü\ or **God·win Aus·ten** \ˌgäd-wə-'nȯs-tən, -'näs-tən\ mountain 8611 meters N Kashmir in Karakoram range; second highest in the world

Kua·la Lum·pur \ˌkwäl-ə-'lu̇m-ˌpu̇(ə)r, -'ləm-\ city, capital of Malaysia

Kuei·yang — see GUIYANG

Kun·lun \'kün-'lün\ mountain system W China extending E from the Pamirs; highest peak Ulugh Muztagh 7724 meters

888

88888888888866

Kun·ming \'kun-'miŋ\ city S China

Kur·di·stan \ˌkur-də-'stan, ˌkər-, -'stän; 'kər-də-ˌ\ region SW Asia chiefly in E Turkey, NW Iran, & N Iraq

Ku·ril or **Ku·rile** \'kyur-ˌēl, 'kur-; kyu-'rē(ə)l, ku-\ islands Russia in W Pacific between Kamchatka peninsula & Hokkaido island

Ku·wait \kə-'wāt\ 1 country SW Asia in Arabia at head of Persian gulf 2 city, its capital — **Ku·waiti** \-'wāt-ē\ adj or n

Kuybyshev — see SAMARA

Kuz·netsk basin \kuz-'netsk-\ or **Kuz·bass** or **Kuzbas** \'kuz-ˌbas\ basin S central Russia

Kwa·ja·lein \'kwäj-ə-lən, -ˌlān\ island W Pacific in Marshall islands

Kwang·ju \'gwäŋ-jü, 'kwäŋ-\ city SW South Korea

Kwa·Zu·lu–Na·tal \kwä-'zü-lü-nä-'täl\ province E Republic of South Africa

Kyo·to \kē-'ōt-ō\ city Japan in W central Honshu; formerly capital of Japan

Kyr·gyz·stan \ˌkir-gi-'stan, -'stän; 'kir-gi-ˌ\ country W central Asia; capital, Bishkek; a republic (**Kir·giz Republic** or **Kir·ghiz Republic** \(ˌ)kir-'gēz-\ or **Kir·ghi·zia** \kir-'gē-zh(ē-)ə, -zē-ə\) of U.S.S.R. 1936–91

Kyu·shu \kē-'ü-shü\ island Japan S of W end of Honshu

Lab·ra·dor \'lab-rə-ˌdó(ə)r\ 1 peninsula E Canada between Hudson bay & the Atlantic divided between Quebec & Newfoundland 2 the part of the peninsula belonging to Newfoundland — **Lab·ra·dor·ean** or **Lab·ra·dor·ian** \ˌlab-rə-'dór-ē-ən, -'dór-\ adj or n

Lac·ca·dive \'lak-ə-ˌdēv, -ˌdīv\ islands India in Arabian sea N of Maldive islands

Lac·e·dae·mon \ˌlas-ə-'dē-mən\ — see SPARTA — **Lac·e·dae·mo·nian** \ˌlas-əd-i-'mō-nē-ən, -nyən\ adj or n

La·co·nia \lə-'kō-nē-ə, -nyə\ ancient country S Greece in SE Peloponnisos; capital, Sparta — **La·co·nian** \-nē-ən, -nyən\ adj or n

La·gos \'lā-ˌgäs\ city, former capital of Nigeria

La·hore \lə-'hō(ə)r, -'hó(ə)r\ city E Pakistan

Lake District region NW England in Cumbria county & NW Lancashire containing many lakes & mountains

Lake·hurst \'lāk-(ˌ)hərst\ town E New Jersey

Lake·wood \'lā-ˌkwud\ city central Colorado

Lam·beth \'lam-bəth, -ˌbeth\ city area of S Greater London county, England

La·nai \lə-'nī\ island Hawaii W of Maui

Lan·ca·shire \'laŋ-kə-shi(ə)r, -ˌshər\ or **Lan·cas·ter** \'laŋ-kə-stər\ county NW England — **Lan·cas·tri·an** \laŋ-'kas-trē-ən, lan-\ adj or n

Lan·cas·ter \'laŋ-kə-stər; 'lan-ˌkas-tər, 'laŋ-\ city area, capital of Lancashire, England

Land's End \'lan(d)-'zend\ cape SW England; most westerly point of England, at 5°41′ W longitude

Lan·sing \'lan(t)-siŋ\ city, capital of Michigan

Lan·zhou or **Lan–chou** \'län-'jō\ city W China

Laos \'laus, 'lā-ˌäs, 'lā-ōs\ country SE Asia in Indochina NE of Thailand; capital, Vientiane

La Paz \lə-'paz, -'päz, -'päs\ city, administrative capital of Bolivia

Lap·land \'lap-ˌland, -lənd\ region N Europe above the arctic circle in N Norway, N Sweden, N Finland, & Kola peninsula of Russia — **Lap·land·er** \-ˌlan-dər, -lən-\ n

La·re·do \lə-'rā-(ˌ)dō\ city S Texas on the Rio Grande

Larne \'lärn\ district NE Northern Ireland

Las·sen Peak \'las-ᵊn-\ volcano 3187 meters N California at S end of Cascade Range

Las Vegas \läs-'vā-gəs\ city SE Nevada

Latin America 1 Spanish America and Brazil 2 all of the Americas S of the U.S. — **Latin–American** adj — **Latin American** n

Latin Quarter section of Paris, France S of the Seine

Lat·via \'lat-vē-ə\ country E Europe on Baltic sea; capital, Riga; a republic of U.S.S.R. 1940–91

Lau·ren·tian \ló-'ren-chən\ mountains E Canada in S Quebec N of the Saint Lawrence on S edge of Canadian Shield

Laurentian Plateau — see CANADIAN SHIELD

La·val \lə-'val\ city S Quebec NW of Montreal

Law·rence \'lór-ən(t)s, 'lär-\ city NE corner of Massachusetts

Leb·a·non \'leb-ə-nən, -ˌnän\ 1 mountains Lebanon running parallel to coast; highest Dahr el Qadib 3088 meters 2 country SW Asia on the Mediterranean; capital, Beirut — **Leb·a·nese** \ˌleb-ə-'nēz, -'nēs\ adj or n

Leeds \'lēdz\ city N England in West Yorkshire

Lee·ward Islands \'lē-wərd-\ 1 islands Hawaii extending WNW from main islands of the group 2 islands S Pacific in W Society islands 3 islands West Indies in N Lesser Antilles extending from Virgin islands (on N) to Dominica (on S)

Le Ha·vre \lə-'hävrᵊ\ city N France on English channel

Leh·man Caves \'lē-mən-\ limestone caverns E Nevada

Leices·ter \'les-tər\ city central England in Leicestershire ENE of Birmingham

Leices·ter·shire \'les-tər-ˌshi(ə)r, -shər\ or **Leicester** county central England

Lein·ster \'len(t)-stər\ province E Ireland

Leip·zig \'līp-sig, -sik\ city E Germany

Le·na \'lē-nə, 'lā-\ river over 4300 kilometers long E Russia, flowing NE & N from mountains W of Lake Baikal into Arctic ocean

Leningrad — see SAINT PETERSBURG

Le·ón \lā-'ōn\ city central Mexico

Ler·wick \'lər-(ˌ)wik, 'le(ə)r-\ town and port N Scotland in Shetland region

Le·so·tho \lə-'sō-tō, -'sü-(ˌ)tü\ country S Africa surrounded by Republic of South Africa; formerly British territory of **Ba·su·to·land** \bə-'süt-ə-ˌland\, now an independent country in the Commonwealth; capital, Maseru

Lesser An·til·les \-an-'til-ēz\ islands in the West Indies including Virgin Islands, Leeward Islands, & Windward Islands, Barbados, Trinidad, Tobago, & islands in the S Caribbean N of Venezuela — see GREATER ANTILLES

Le·vant \lə-'vant\ the countries bordering on the E Mediterranean — **Lev·an·tine** \'lev-ən-ˌtīn, -ˌtēn, lə-'van-\ adj or n

Lew·es \'lü-əs\ city area S England in East Sussex county

Lew·i·sham \'lü-ə-shəm\ city area of SE Greater London county, England

Lewis with Har·ris \ˌlü-ə-swath-'har-əs, -swoth-\ island NW Scotland in Outer Hebrides

Lex·ing·ton \'lek-siŋ-tən\ 1 city N central Kentucky 2 town NE Massachusetts

Ley·te \'lāt-ē\ island Philippines S of Samar

Lha·sa \'läs-ə, 'las-\ city SW China, capital of Tibet

Li·be·ria \lī-'bir-ē-ə\ country W Africa on the Atlantic; capital, Monrovia — **Li·be·ri·an** \-ē-ən\ adj or n

Lib·er·ty \'lib-ərt-ē\ or formerly **Bed·loe's** \'bed-ˌlōz\ or **Bed·loe** \-ˌlō\ island SE New York; the Statue of Liberty is on it

Li·bre·ville \'lē-brə-ˌvil, -ˌvē(ə)l\ city, capital of Gabon

Lib·ya \'lib-ē-ə\ 1 the part of Africa N of the Sahara and just W of Egypt — an ancient name 2 northern Africa W of Egypt — an ancient name 3 country N Africa on the Mediterranean W of Egypt; capital, Tripoli — **Lib·y·an** \'lib-ē-ən\ adj or n

Libyan desert N Africa W of the Nile in Libya, Egypt, & Sudan

Liech·ten·stein \'lik-tən-ˌstīn, -ˌshtīn\ country W Europe between Austria & Switzerland; capital, Vaduz — **Liech·ten·stein·er** \-ˌstī-nər, -ˌshtī-\ n

Lif·fey \'lif-ē\ river 80 kilometers long E Ireland

Li·gu·ria \lə-ˈgyu̇r-ē-ə\ ancient region SW Europe — **Li·gu·ri·an** \-ē-ən\ adj or n

Ligurian sea arm of the Mediterranean N of Corsica

Li·lon·gwe \li-ˈlȯŋ-wä\ city, capital of Malawi

Li·ma \ˈlē-mə\ city, capital of Peru

Lim·a·vady \ˌlim-ə-ˈvad-ē\ district NW Northern Ireland

Lim·po·po \lim-ˈpō-pō\ river Africa flowing from Gauteng into Indian ocean in Mozambique

Lin·coln \ˈliŋ-kən\ 1 city, capital of Nebraska 2 city E England in Lincolnshire

Lin·coln·shire \ˈliŋ-kən-ˌshi(ə)r, -shər\ or **Lincoln** county E England

Line \ˈlīn\ islands Kiribati S of Hawaii; formerly divided between U.S. & United Kingdom

Lis·bon \ˈliz-bən\ or Portuguese **Lis·boa** \lēzh-ˈvō-ə\ city, capital of Portugal

Lis·burn \ˈliz-(ˌ)bərn\ district E Northern Ireland

Lith·u·a·nia \ˌlith-(y)ə-ˈwā-nē-ə, -nyə\ country E Europe; capital, Vilnius; a republic of U.S.S.R. 1940–91

Lit·tle Rock \ˈlit-ᵊl-ˌräk\ city, capital of Arkansas

Liv·er·pool \ˈliv-ər-ˌpu̇l\ city NW England in Merseyside county

Li·vo·nia \lə-ˈvō-nē-ə, -nyə\ city SE Michigan

Lju·blja·na \lē-ˌu̇-blē-ˈän-ə\ city, capital of Slovenia

Llan·drin·dod Wells \hlan-ˈdrin-ˌdȯd-, lan-\ town E Wales in Powys county

Lla·no Es·ta·ca·do \ˈlan-(ˌ)ō-ˌes-ta-ˈkäd-ō, ˈlän-\ or **Staked Plain** \ˈstäk(t)-\ plateau region SE New Mexico & NW Texas

Lodz \ˈlüj, ˈlädz\ city central Poland WSW of Warsaw

Lo·fo·ten \ˈlō-ˌfōt-ᵊn\ islands NW Norway

Lo·gan, Mount \-ˈlō-gən\ mountain 5951 meters NW Canada in Saint Elias range; highest in Canada & second highest in North America

Loire \lə-ˈwär\ river 1020 kilometers long central France flowing NW & W into Bay of Biscay

Lo·mé \lō-ˈmā\ city, capital of Togo

Lo·mond, Loch \-ˈlō-mənd\ lake S central Scotland

Lon·don \ˈlən-dən\ 1 city S Ontario, Canada 2 city, capital of England & of United Kingdom on the Thames; consists of **City of London** & Greater London county — **Lon·don·er** \-də-nər\ n

Londonderry — see DERRY

Long Beach city SW California S of Los Angeles

Long Island island 190 kilometers long SE New York S of Connecticut

Long Island Sound inlet of the Atlantic between Connecticut & Long Island, New York

Lon·gueuil \lȯŋ-ˈgā(ə)l\ city Canada in S Quebec E of Montreal

Lor·raine \lə-ˈrān, lȯ-\ region NE France

Los An·ge·les \lȯ-ˈsan-jə-ləs also -ˈsaŋ-g(ə-)ləs\ city SW California

Lo·thi·an \ˈlō-thē-ən\ region SE Scotland S of Firth of Forth; established 1975; includes Edinburgh

Lou·ise, Lake \-lü-ˈēz\ lake SW Alberta, Canada

Lou·i·si·ana \lü-ˌē-zē-ˈan-ə, ˌlü-ə-zē-, ˌlü-zē-\ state S U.S.; capital, Baton Rouge — **Lou·i·si·an·ian** \-ˈan-ē-ən, -ˈan-yən\ or **Lou·i·si·an·an** \-ˈan-ən\ adj or n

Louisiana Purchase area W central U.S. between Rocky mountains & the Mississippi purchased 1803 from France

Lou·is·ville \ˈlü-ē-ˌvil, -vəl\ city N Kentucky on the Ohio river

Low Countries region W Europe consisting of modern Belgium, Luxembourg, & the Netherlands

Lower 48 the continental states of the U.S. excluding Alaska

Low·lands \ˈlō-lən(d)z, -ˌlan(d)z\ the central & E part of Scotland

Lu·an·da \lü-ˈan-də\ city, capital of Angola

Lub·bock \ˈləb-ək\ city NW Texas

Luck·now \ˈlək-ˌnau̇\ city N India

Lü·da or **Lü·ta** — see DALIAN

Lu·ray Caverns \ˈlü-ˌrā-, lü-ˈrā-\ series of caves N Virginia

Lu·sa·ka \lü-ˈsäk-ə\ city, capital of Zambia

Lü·shun \ˈlü-ˈshu̇n\ or **Port Ar·thur** \-ˈär-thər\ city NE China

Lu·ton \ˈlüt-ᵊn\ city area SE central England in Bedfordshire

Lux·em·bourg or **Lux·em·burg** \ˈlək-səm-ˌbərg, ˈlu̇k-səm-ˌbu̇(ə)rg\ 1 country W Europe bordered by Belgium, France, & Germany 2 city, its capital — **Lux·em·bourg·er** \-ˌbər-gər, -ˌbu̇r-\ n — **Lux·em·bourg·ian** \ˌlək-səm-ˈbər-gē-ən, ˌlu̇k-səm-ˈbu̇r-\ adj

Lu·zon \lü-ˈzän\ island N Philippines

Lviv \lə-ˈvē-u̇, -ˈvēf\ or **Lvov** \lə-ˈvȯf, -ˈvȯv\ or Polish **Lwów** \lə-ˈvu̇f, -ˈvu̇v\ city W Ukraine

Lyallpur — see FAISALABAD

Lyd·ia \ˈlid-ē-ə\ ancient country W Asia Minor on the Aegean — **Lyd·i·an** \-ē-ən\ adj or n

Lynn \ˈlin\ city NE corner of Massachusetts

Ma·cao or Portuguese **Ma·cau** \mə-ˈkau̇\ 1 Portuguese territory on coast of SE China W of Hong Kong 2 city, its capital — **Mac·a·nese** \ˌmak-ə-ˈnēz, -ˈnēs\ n

Mac·e·do·nia \ˌmas-ə-ˈdō-nyə, -nē-ə\ region S Europe in Balkan peninsula in NE Greece, the country of Macedonia, and SW Bulgaria including territory of ancient kingdom of Macedonia (**Mac·e·don** \ˈmas-əd-ən, -ə-ˌdän\) — **Mac·e·do·nian** \ˌmas-ə-ˈdō-nyən, -nē-ən\ adj or n

Macedonia, Republic of country S central Balkan peninsula; capital, Skopje; a former republic of Yugoslavia

Mac·gil·li·cud·dy's Reeks \mə-ˌgil-ə-ˌkəd-ēz-ˈrēks\ mountains SW Ireland; highest Carrantuo hill 1041 meters

Ma·chu Pic·chu \ˌmäch-ü-ˈpēk-chü\ site SE Peru of ancient Inca city

Macías Nguema Biyogo — see BIOKO

Mac·ken·zie \mə-ˈken-zē\ 1 river 1800 kilometers long NW Canada flowing from Great Slave lake NW into Beaufort sea 2 former district NW Canada in W Northwest Territories in basin of Mackenzie river

Mack·i·nac, Straits of \-ˈmak-ə-ˌnak, -ˌnȯ\ channel N Michigan connecting Lake Huron & Lake Michigan

Mc·Kin·ley, Mount \mə-ˈkin-lē\ or **De·na·li** \də-ˈnäl-ē\ mountain 6194 meters S central Alaska in Alaska range; highest in U.S. & North America

Ma·con \ˈmā-kən\ city central Georgia

Mad·a·gas·car \ˌmad-ə-ˈgas-kər\ or formerly **Mal·a·gasy Republic** \ˌmal-ə-ˌgas-ē-\ island W Indian ocean off SE Africa; an independent country; capital, Antananarivo — **Mad·a·gas·can** \ˌmad-ə-ˈgas-kən\ adj or n

Ma·dei·ra \mə-ˈdir-ə, -ˈder-\ 1 river over 3200 kilometers long W Brazil flowing NE into the Amazon 2 islands in the N Atlantic N of the Canary islands belonging to Portugal 3 island; chief of the Madeira group — **Ma·dei·ran** \-ən\ adj or n

Ma·di·nat ash Sha'b \mə-ˈdē-ˌnat-ash-ˈshab\ town S Yemen

Mad·i·son \ˈmad-ə-sən\ city, capital of Wisconsin

Ma·dras \mə-ˈdras, -ˈdräs\ city SE India

Ma·drid \mə-ˈdrid\ city, capital of Spain

Ma·du·rai \ˌmäd-ə-ˈrī\ city S India

Magh·er·a·felt \ˈmär-ə-ˌfelt, ˈmak-ə-rə-ˌfelt\ district central Northern Ireland

Maid·stone \ˈmād-stən, -ˌstōn\ city district SE England in Kent county

Main \ˈmīn, ˈmän\ river 523 kilometers long S central Germany flowing W into the Rhine

Maine \ˈmān\ state NE U.S.; capital, Augusta

Ma·jor·ca \mə-ˈjȯr-kə, -ˈyȯr-\ or Spanish **Ma·llor·ca** \mə-ˈyȯr-kə\ island Spain in W Mediterranean — **Ma·jor·can** \-ˈjȯr-kən, -ˈyȯr-\ adj or n

Mal·a·bar \ˈmal-ə-ˌbär\ coast region SW India on Arabian sea

Ma·la·bo \mä-ˈlä-bō\ city, capital of Equatorial Guinea

Ma·lac·ca, Strait of \-mə-ˈlak-ə, -ˈläk-\ channel between S Malay peninsula & island of Sumatra

Ma·la·wi \mə-ˈlä-wē, -ˈlaů-ē\ *or formerly* **Ny·asa·land** \nī-ˈas-ə-ˌland, nē-\ country SE Africa on Lake Nyasa; an independent state since 1964; capital, Lilongwe

Ma·lay \mə-ˈlā, ˈmä-lā\ **1** island group SE Asia including Sumatra, Java, Borneo, Sulawesi, Moluccas, & Timor; usually thought to include the Philippines & sometimes New Guinea **2** peninsula about 1100 kilometers long SE Asia divided between Thailand and Malaysia (country)

Ma·laya \mə-ˈlā-ə, mä-\ **1** the Malay peninsula **2** former country SE Asia on Malay peninsula; since 1963 part of Malaysia — *see* MALAYSIA

Ma·lay·sia \mə-ˈlā-zh(ē-)ə, -sh(ē-)ə\ **1** the Malay island group **2** the Malay peninsula & Malay island group **3** country SE Asia, a union of Malaya, Sabah, Sarawak, & (until 1965) Singapore; capital, Kuala Lumpur — **Ma·lay·sian** \mə-ˈlā-zhən, -shən\ *adj or n*

Mal·dive \ˈmȯl-ˌdēv, -ˌdīv\ islands in Indian ocean S of the Laccadives; formerly under British protection; since 1965 an independent country; capital, Male — **Mal·div·i·an** \mȯl-ˈdiv-ē-ən\ *adj or n*

Ma·li \ˈmäl-ē, ˈmal-ē\ country W Africa; capital, Bamako — **Ma·li·an** \-ē-ən\ *adj or n*

Mal·ta \ˈmȯl-tə\ islands in the Mediterranean S of Sicily; a former British colony; an independent country since 1964; capital, Valletta

Malvinas, Islas — *see* FALKLAND

Mam·moth Cave \ˌmam-əth-\ limestone caverns SW central Kentucky

Man, Isle of \-ˈman\ island British Isles in Irish sea; has own legislature & laws

Ma·na·gua \mə-ˈnäg-wə\ city, capital of Nicaragua

Ma·na·ma \mə-ˈnam-ə\ city, capital of Bahrain

Man·ches·ter \ˈman-ˌches-tər, -chə-stər\ **1** city S central New Hampshire; largest in state **2** city NW England in Greater Manchester county

Man·chu·ria \man-ˈchůr-ē-ə\ region NE China S of the Amur — **Man·chu·ri·an** \man-ˈchůr-ē-ən\ *adj or n*

Man·hat·tan \man-ˈhat-ᵊn, mən-\ **1** island SE New York in New York City **2** section of New York City consisting chiefly of Manhattan island

Ma·nila \mə-ˈnil-ə\ city, capital of Philippines in W Luzon

Man·i·to·ba \ˌman-ə-ˈtō-bə\ province central Canada; capital, Winnipeg — **Man·i·to·ban** \-ˈtō-bən\ *adj or n*

Man·i·tou·lin \ˌman-ə-ˈtü-lən\ island 130 kilometers long S Ontario in Lake Huron

Ma·pu·to \mä-ˈpü-tō\ city, capital of Mozambique

Mar·a·cai·bo \ˌmar-ə-ˈkī-bō\ city NW Venezuela

Maracaibo, Lake extension of a gulf NW Venezuela

Mar·a·thon \ˈmar-ə-ˌthän, -thən\ plain E Greece NE of Athens

Mar·i·ana \ˌmar-ē-ˈan-ə, ˌmer-\ islands W Pacific N of Caroline islands; comprise Commonwealth of Northern Mariana Islands & Guam

Mariana Trench ocean trench W Pacific extending from SE of Guam to NW of Mariana islands; deepest in world

Ma·rin·du·que \ˌmar-ən-ˈdü-kā, ˌmär-\ island central Philippines

Maritime Provinces the Canadian provinces of New Brunswick, Nova Scotia, & Prince Edward Island & sometimes thought to include Newfoundland

Ma·ri·u·pol \ˌmar-ē-ˈü-ˌpȯl\ *or 1949–89* **Zhda·nov** \zhə-ˈdän-əf\ city E Ukraine

Mar·ma·ra, Sea of \ˈmär-mə-rə\ sea NW Turkey connected with Black sea by the Bosporus & with Aegean sea by the Dardanelles

Marne \ˈmärn\ river 523 kilometers long NE France flowing W into the Seine

Mar·que·sas \mär-ˈkā-zəz, -zəs, -səz, -səs\ islands S Pacific — **Mar·que·san** \-zən, -sən\ *adj or n*

Mar·seilles \mär-ˈsā, -ˈsā(ə)lz\ *or* **Mar·seille** \mär-ˈsā\ *or ancient* **Mas·sil·ia** \mə-ˈsil-ē-ə\ city SE France

Mar·shall \ˈmär-shəl\ islands W Pacific E of the Carolines; formerly part of Trust Territory of the Pacific Islands

Mar·tha's Vineyard \ˌmär-thəz-\ island SE Massachusetts off SW coast of Cape Cod WNW of Nantucket

Mar·ti·nique \ˌmärt-ᵊn-ˈēk\ island West Indies in the Windward Islands; an overseas division of France; capital, Fort-de-France

Mary·land \ˈmer-ə-lənd\ state E U.S.; capital, Annapolis — **Mary·land·er** \-lən-dər, -ˌlan-\ *n*

Mas·ba·te \mäz-ˈbät-ē\ island central Philippines

Mas·e·ru \ˈmaz-ə-ˌrü\ city, capital of Lesotho

Mash·had \mə-ˈshad\ city NE Iran

Ma·son–Dix·on line \ˌmäs-ᵊn-ˈdik-sən-\ boundary between Maryland & Pennsylvania; was in part boundary between free & slave states

Mas·qat \ˈməs-ˌkät\ *or* **Mus·cat** \ˈməs-ˌkät, -kət\ town E Arabia, capital of Oman

Mas·sa·chu·setts \ˌmas-(ə)-ˈchü-səts, -zəts\ state NE U.S.; capital, Boston

Mat·a·be·le·land \ˌmat-ə-ˈbē-lē-ˌland\ region SW Zimbabwe

Mat·lock \ˈmat-ˌläk\ town N England in Derbyshire

Mat·ter·horn \ˈmat-ər-ˌhȯ(ə)rn, ˈmät-\ mountain 4478 meters on border between Switzerland & Italy

Maui \ˈmaů-ē\ island Hawaii NW of Hawaii island

Mau·na Kea \ˌmaů-nə-ˈkä-ə\ extinct volcano 4205 meters Hawaii in N central Hawaii island

Mau·na Loa \ˌmaů-nə-ˈlō-ə\ volcano 4170 meters Hawaii in S central Hawaii island

Mau·re·ta·nia *or* **Mau·ri·ta·nia** \ˌmȯr-ə-ˈtā-nē-ə, ˌmär-, -nyə\ ancient country NW Africa in modern Morocco & W Algeria — **Mau·re·ta·ni·an** \-nē-ən, -nyən\ *adj or n*

Mauritania country NW Africa on the Atlantic N of Senegal river; capital, Nouakchott — **Mauritanian** *adj or n*

Mau·ri·tius \mȯ-ˈrish-(ē-)əs\ island in Indian ocean E of Madagascar; an independent country in the Commonwealth; capital, Port Louis — **Mau·ri·tian** \-ˈrish-ən\ *adj or n*

May, Cape \-ˈmā\ cape S New Jersey at entrance to Delaware Bay

Ma·yon \mä-ˈyȯn\ volcano 2462 meters Philippines in SE Luzon

Ma·yotte Island \mä-ˈyät-\ island Comoro group — *see* COMOROS

Ma·za·ma, Mount \-mə-ˈzäm-ə\ prehistoric mountain SW Oregon the collapse of whose top formed Crater lake

Mba·bane \ˌem-bə-ˈbän\ city, capital of Swaziland

Mbi·ni \em-ˈbē-nē\ *or formerly* **Río Mu·ni** \ˌrē-ō-ˈmü-nē\ mainland portion of Equatorial Guinea

Mead, Lake \-ˈmēd\ reservoir NW Arizona & SE Nevada formed by Hoover Dam in Colorado river

Mec·ca \ˈmek-ə\ city W Saudi Arabia containing the Great Mosque of Islam

Me·dan \mā-ˈdän\ city Indonesia in N Sumatra

Me·del·lín \ˌmed-ᵊl-ˈēn, ˌmä-thə-ˈyēn\ city NW Colombia

Med·i·ter·ra·nean \ˌmed-ə-tə-ˈrā-nē-ən, -nyən\ sea 3750 kilometers long between Europe & Africa connecting with the Atlantic through Strait of Gibraltar

Me·kong \ˈmā-ˌkȯŋ, -ˈkäŋ\ river 4185 kilometers long SE Asia flowing from E Tibet S & SE into South China sea in S Vietnam

Mel·a·ne·sia \ˌmel-ə-ˈnē-zhə, -shə\ islands of the Pacific NE of Australia & S of Micronesia including Bismarck, the Solomons, Vanuatu, New Caledonia, & Fiji

Mel·bourne \ˈmel-bərn\ city SE Australia, capital of Victoria

Me·los \'mē-₁läs\ island Greece — **Me·li·an** \'mē-lē-ən\ *adj or n*

Mel·ville \'mel-₁vil\ **1** island N Canada in N Northwest Territories **2** peninsula E Northwest Territories, Canada

Mem·phis \'mem(p)-fəs\ **1** city SW Tennessee **2** ancient city N Egypt S of modern Cairo

Men·do·ci·no, Cape \-₁men-də-'sē-nō\ cape NW California

Mer·cia \'mər-sh(ē-)ə\ ancient Anglo-Saxon kingdom central England — **Mer·cian** \'mər-shən\ *adj or n*

Mer·sey \'mər-zē\ river 110 kilometers long NW England flowing NW & W into Irish sea

Mer·sey·side \'mər-zē-₁sīd\ county NW England; includes Liverpool

Mer·ton \'mərt-ᵊn\ city area of SW Greater London county, England

Me·sa \'mā-sə\ city S central Arizona

Me·sa·bi range \mə-'säb-ē\ region NE Minnesota that contains iron ore

Mes·o·po·ta·mia \₁mes-(ə-)pə-'tā-mē-ə, -myə\ **1** region SW Asia between Euphrates & Tigris rivers **2** the entire Tigris-Euphrates valley — **Mes·o·po·ta·mian** \-mē-ən, -myən\ *adj or n*

Meuse \'myüz, 'mə(r)z\ river 933 kilometers long W Europe flowing from NE France into North sea in the Netherlands

Mex·i·co \'mek-si-₁kō\ **1** country S North America **2** *or* **Mexico City** city, its capital

Mexico, Gulf of inlet of the Atlantic SE North America

Mi·ami \mī-'am-ē, -'am-ə\ city SE Florida

Miami Beach city SE Florida

Mich·i·gan \'mish-i-gən\ state N central U.S.; capital, Lansing — **Mich·i·gan·der** \₁mish-i-'gan-dər\ *n* — **Mich·i·gan·ite** \'mish-i-gə-₁nīt\ *n*

Michigan, Lake lake N central U.S.; one of the Great Lakes

Mi·cro·ne·sia \₁mī-krə-'nē-zhə, -shə\ islands of the W Pacific E of the Philippines & N of Melanesia including Caroline, Kiribati, Mariana, & Marshall groups — **Mi·cro·ne·sian** \-zhən, -shən\ *adj or n*

Middle East the countries of SW Asia & N Africa — usually thought to include the countries extending from Libya on the W to Afghanistan on the E — **Middle Eastern** *or* **Mid·east·ern** \'mid-'ē-stərn\ *adj*

Mid·dles·brough \'mid-ᵊlz-brə\ town N England in Cleveland county

Mid Gla·mor·gan \'mid-glə-'mòr-gən\ county SE Wales; established 1974

Mid·i·an \'mid-ē-ən\ ancient region NW Arabia E of Gulf of 'Aqaba — **Mid·i·an·ite** \-ē-ə-₁nīt\ *n*

Mid·lands \'mid-lən(d)z\ the central counties of England usually thought to consist of Bedfordshire, Buckinghamshire, Cambridgeshire, Derbyshire, Leicestershire, Lincolnshire, Northamptonshire, Nottinghamshire, Oxfordshire, Staffordshire, Warwickshire, West Midlands, & part of Hereford and Worcester

Mid·way \'mid-₁wā\ islands central Pacific in Hawaiian group 2090 kilometers WNW of Honolulu belonging to U.S.; not included in state of Hawaii

Mid·west \₁mid-'west\ *or* **Middle West** region N central U.S. including area around Great Lakes & in upper Mississippi valley from Ohio on the E to North Dakota, South Dakota, Nebraska, & Kansas on the W — **Mid·west·ern** \₁mid-'wes-tərn\ *or* **Middle Western** *adj* — **Mid·west·ern·er** \₁mid-'wes-tə(r)-nər\ *or* **Middle Westerner** *n*

Mi·lan \mə-'lan, -'län\ *or Italian* **Mi·la·no** \mi-'län-ō\ city NW Italy — **Mil·a·nese** \₁mil-ə-'nēz, -'nēs\ *adj or n*

Mil·wau·kee \mil-'wò-kē\ city SE Wisconsin

Mi·nas Basin \₁mī-nəs-\ bay central Nova Scotia; NE extension of Bay of Fundy

Min·da·nao \₁min-də-'nä-ō, -'naù\ island S Philippines

Min·do·ro \min-'dōr-ō, -'dòr-\ island central Philippines

Min·ne·ap·o·lis \₁min-ē-'ap-(ə-)ləs\ city SE Minnesota

Min·ne·so·ta \₁min-ə-'sōt-ə\ state N central U.S.; capital, Saint Paul — **Min·ne·so·tan** \-'sōt-ᵊn\ *adj or n*

Mi·nor·ca \mə-'nòr-kə\ island Spain in W Mediterranean — **Mi·nor·can** \mə-'nòr-kən\ *adj or n*

Minsk \'min(t)sk\ city, capital of Belarus

Mis·sis·sip·pi \₁mis-(ə-)'sip-ē\ **1** river 3765 kilometers long central U.S. flowing into Gulf of Mexico — see ITASCA, LAKE **2** state S U.S.; capital, Jackson

Mis·sou·ri \mə-'zù(ə)r-ē, -'zùr-ə\ **1** river 3968 kilometers long W U.S. flowing from SW Montana to the Mississippi in E Missouri **2** state central U.S.; capital, Jefferson City — **Mis·sou·ri·an** \-'zùr-ē-ən\ *adj or n*

Mitch·ell, Mount \-'mich-əl\ mountain 2037 meters W North Carolina in the Appalachians; highest in U.S. E of the Mississippi

Mo·bile \mō-'bē(ə)l, 'mō-₁bēl\ city SW Alabama on Mobile Bay

Mo·des·to \mə-'dəs-tō\ city central California

Mog·a·di·shu \₁mäg-ə-'dish-ü, -'dēsh-\ *or* **Mog·a·di·scio** \-ō\ city, capital of Somalia

Mo·hawk \'mō-₁hòk\ river E central New York flowing into the Hudson

Mo·ja·ve *or* **Mo·ha·ve** \mə-'häv-ē\ desert S California SE of S end of Sierra Nevada

Mold \'mōld\ town NE Wales in Clwyd county

Mol·da·via \mäl-'dā-vē-ə, -vyə\ **1** region E Europe in NE Romania & Moldova **2** former republic of U.S.S.R. bordered by Ukraine, Black sea, & Romania; became independent (as Moldova) 1991 — **Mol·da·vian** \-vē-ən, -vyən\ *adj or n*

Mol·do·va \mäl-'dō-və, mòl-\ country E Europe in E Moldavia region; capital, Chisinau

Mol·o·kai \₁mäl-ə-'kī, ₁mō-lə-\ island Hawaii ESE of Oahu

Mo·luc·cas \mə-'lək-əz\ islands Indonesia E of Sulawesi — **Mo·luc·ca** \mə-'lək-ə\ *adj* — **Mo·luc·can** \-ən\ *adj or n*

Mo·na·co \'män-ə-₁kō *also* mə-'näk-ō\ country W Europe on Mediterranean coast of France; capital, Monaco — **Mo·na·can** \'män-ə-kən, mə-'näk-ən\ *adj or n* — **Mon·e·gasque** \₁män-i-'gask\ *n*

Mon·go·lia \män-'gōl-yə, mäŋ-, -'gō-lē-ə\ **1** region E Asia E of Altai mountains; includes Gobi desert **2** country E Asia consisting of major portion of Mongolia region; capital Ulan Bator

Mo·non·ga·he·la \mə-₁nän-gə-'hē-lə, -₁näŋ-gə-, -'hā-lə\ river N West Virginia & SW Pennsylvania

Mon·ro·via \(₁)mən-'rō-vē-ə\ city, capital of Liberia

Mon·tana \män-'tan-ə\ state NW U.S.; capital, Helena — **Mon·tan·an** \-ən\ *adj or n*

Mont Blanc \mōn-'blän(k)\ mountain 4807 meters SE France on Italian border; highest in the Alps

Mon·te·ne·gro \₁män-tə-'nē-(₁)grō, -'nā-\ region SW Yugoslavia on the Adriatic sea

Mon·ter·rey \₁mänt-ə-'rā\ city NE Mexico

Mon·te·vi·deo \₁mänt-ə-və-'dā-ō, -'vid-ē-₁ō\ city, capital of Uruguay

Mont·gom·ery \(₁)mən(t)-'gəm-(ə-)rē, män(t)-, -'gäm-\ city, capital of Alabama

Mont·pe·lier \mänt-'pēl-yər, -'pil-\ city, capital of Vermont

Mont·re·al \₁män-trē-'òl, ₁mən-\ city S Quebec, Canada on Montreal Island in the Saint Lawrence

Mont·ser·rat \₁män(t)-sə-'rat\ island West Indies in the Leeward Islands

Mo·ra·via \mə-'rā-vē-ə\ region E Czech Republic — **Mo·ra·vi·an** \mə-'rā-vē-ən\ *adj or n*

Mo·rea \mə-'rē-ə\ PELOPONNISOS — an old name — **Mo·re·an** \-'rē-ən\ *adj or n*

Mo·roc·co \mə-'räk-ō\ country NW Africa; a kingdom; capital, Rabat — **Mo·roc·can** \-'räk-ən\ *adj or n*

Mo·ro·ni \mō-'rō-nē\ city, capital of Comoros

Mos·cow \\'mäs-ı kaù, -kō\ *or Russian* **Mos·kva** \mäsk-ı vä\ city, capital of Russia and formerly of U.S.S.R. and of Russian Soviet Federated Socialist Republic

Mourne \\'mō(ə)rn, 'mò(ə)rn\ district S Northern Ireland

Moyle \\'mòi(ə)l\ district N Northern Ireland

Mo·zam·bique \ı mō-zəm-'bēk\ **1** channel SE Africa between Mozambique & Madagascar **2** country SE Africa; capital, Maputo

Mpu·ma·lan·ga \əm-ı pü-mä-'läŋ-gä\ province NE Republic of South Africa

Mukden — see SHENYANG

Mul·tan \mùl-'tän\ city NE Pakistan SW of Lahore

Mumbai — see BOMBAY

Mu·nich \\'myü-nik\ *or German* **Mün·chen** \\'m(y)ün-kən\ city S Germany in Bavaria

Mun·ster \\'mən(t)-stər\ province S Ireland

Mur·cia \\'mər-sh(ē-)ə\ region & ancient kingdom SE Spain — **Mur·cian** \-shən\ *adj or n*

Mur·ray \\'mər-ē, 'mə-rē\ river 2589 kilometers long SE Australia flowing W from E Victoria into Indian ocean in South Australia — see DARLING

Mur·rum·bidg·ee \ı mər-əm-'bij-ē, ı mə-rəm-\ river SE Australia in New South Wales flowing W into the Murray

Muscat — see MASQAT

Myan·mar \\'myän-ı mär\ *or formerly* **Bur·ma** \\'bər-mə\ country SE Asia; capital, Yangon

My·ce·nae \mī-'sē-nē\ ancient city S Greece in NE Peloponnisos

My·sore \mī-'sō(ə)r, -'sò(ə)r\ city S India

Nab·a·taea *or* **Nab·a·tea** \ı nab-ə-'tē-ə\ ancient Arab kingdom SE of Palestine — **Nab·a·tae·an** *or* **Nab·a·te·an** \-'tē-ən\ *adj or n*

Na·goya \nə-'gòi-ə, 'näg-ə-ı yä\ city Japan in S central Honshu

Nag·pur \\'näg-ı pù(ə)r\ city E central India

Nai·ro·bi \nī-'rō-bē\ city, capital of Kenya

Na·mib·ia \nə-'mib-ē-ə\ *or formerly* **South–West Africa** country SW Africa on the Atlantic; capital, Windhoek

Nan·chang \\'nän-'jäŋ\ city SE China

Nan·jing \\'nän-'jiŋ\ *or* **Nan·king** \\'nan-'kiŋ, 'nän-\ city E China

Nan·tuck·et \nan-'tək-ət\ island SE Massachusetts S of Cape Cod

Na·ples \\'nā-pəlz\ *or Italian* **Na·po·li** \\'näp-ə-lē\ *or ancient* **Ne·ap·o·lis** \nē-'ap-ə-ləs\ city S Italy on Bay of Naples — **Ne·a·pol·i·tan** \ı nē-ə-'päl-ət-ªn\ *adj or n*

Nar·ra·gan·sett Bay \ı nar-ə-'gan(t)-sət\ inlet of the Atlantic SE Rhode Island

Nash·ville \\'nash-ı vil, -vəl\ city, capital of Tennessee

Nas·sau \\'nas-ı ò\ city, capital of Bahamas on New Providence island

Na·tal \nə-'tal, -'täl\ former province E Republic of South Africa, now part of KwaZulu-Natal

Na·u·ru \nä-'ü-rü\ island W Pacific 42 kilometers S of the equator; formerly a shared British, New Zealand, & Australian trust territory; an independent country in the Commonwealth since 1968

Naz·a·reth \\'naz-(ə-)rəth\ town of ancient Palestine in central Galilee; now a city of N Israel

N'Dja·me·na \en-'jäm-ə-nə\ city, capital of Chad

Neagh, Lough \läk-'nä\ lake Northern Ireland; largest in British Isles

Near East the countries of NE Africa & SW Asia — **Near Eastern** *adj*

Ne·bras·ka \nə-'bras-kə\ state central U.S.; capital, Lincoln — **Ne·bras·kan** \-kən\ *adj or n*

Neg·ev \\'neg-ı ev\ desert region S Israel

Ne·gros \\'nā-(ı)grōs\ island central Philippines

Ne·pal \nə-'pòl, -'päl, -'pal\ country Asia on NE border of India in the Himalayas; a kingdom; capital, Kathmandu — **Nep·a·lese** \nep-ə-'lēz, -'lēs\ *adj or n* — **Ne·pali** \nə-'pòl-ē, -'päl-, -'pal-\ *adj or n*

Ness, Loch \-'nes\ lake NW Scotland

Neth·er·lands \\'neth-ər-lən(d)z\ **1** *or Dutch* **Ne·der·land** \\'nād-ər-ı länt\ *also* **Holland** country NW Europe on North sea; a kingdom; capitals, Amsterdam and The Hague **2** LOW COUNTRIES — an historical usage — **Neth·er·land** \\'neth-ər-lənd\ *adj* — **Neth·er·land·er** \-ı lan-dər, -lən-\ *n* — **Neth·er·land·ish** \-dish\ *adj*

Netherlands An·til·les \-an-'til-ēz\ islands of the West Indies belonging to the Netherlands

Netherlands East Indies *or* **Netherlands India** *or* **Dutch East Indies** former Dutch possessions in the East Indies including Indonesia

Ne·va \\'nē-və, 'nä-\ river 65 kilometers long W Russia; flows through Saint Petersburg

Ne·vada \nə-'vad-ə, -'väd-ə\ state W U.S.; capital, Carson City — **Ne·vad·an** \-'vad-ªn, -'väd-ªn\ *or* **Ne·vad·i·an** \-'vad-ē-ən, -'väd-\ *adj or n*

Ne·vis \\'nē-vəs\ island West Indies in the Leeward Islands — see SAINT KITTS

New Am·ster·dam \-'am(p)-stər-ı dam\ town founded 1625 on Manhattan island by the Dutch; renamed New York 1664 by the British

New·ark \\'n(y)ü-ərk, 'n(y)ù(-ə)rk\ city NE New Jersey

New Brit·ain \-'brit-ªn\ island W Pacific

New Bruns·wick \-'brənz-(ı)wik\ province SE Canada; capital, Fredericton

New Cal·e·do·nia \-ı kal-ə-'dō-nyə, -nē-ə\ island SW Pacific SW of Vanuatu; an overseas department of France; capital, Nouméa

New·cas·tle \\'n(y)ü-ı kas-əl\ city SE Australia in E New South Wales

Newcastle *or* **New·cas·tle up·on Tyne** \n(y)ü-'kas-əl-ə-ı pòn-'tīn\ city N England in Tyne and Wear county

New Del·hi \-'del-ē\ city, capital of India S of Delhi

New England section of U.S. consisting of states of Maine, New Hampshire, Vermont, Massachusetts, Rhode Island, & Connecticut — **New En·gland·er** \-'iŋ-glən-dər *also* -'iŋ-lən-\ *n*

New·found·land \\'n(y)ü-fən-(d)lənd, -ı d(ı)land; n(y)ü-fən-'(d)land\ **1** island Canada in the Atlantic **2** province E Canada consisting of Newfoundland island & Labrador; capital, Saint John's — **New·found·land·er** \-(d)lən-dər, -'(d)lan-dər\ *n*

New France the possessions of France in North America before 1763

New Guin·ea \-'gin-ē\ **1** island W Pacific N of E Australia divided between Irian Jaya & Papua New Guinea **2** the NE portion of the island of New Guinea together with some nearby islands; now part of Papua New Guinea — **New Guin·e·an** \-'gin-ē-ən\ *adj or n*

New·ham \\'n(y)ü-əm\ city area of E Greater London county, England

New Hamp·shire \-'ham(p)-shər, -ı shi(ə)r\ state NE U.S.; capital, Concord — **New Hamp·shire·man** \-mən\ *n* — **New Hamp·shir·ite** \-ı rīt\ *n*

New Ha·ven \-'hā-vən\ city S Connecticut

New Hebrides — see VANUATU

New Jer·sey \-'jər-zē\ state E U.S.; capital, Trenton — **New Jer·sey·ite** \-ı rīt\ *n*

New Mex·i·co \-'mek-si-ı kō\ state SW U.S.; capital, Santa Fe — **New Mex·i·can** \-si-kən\ *adj or n*

New Neth·er·land \-'neth-ər-lənd\ former Dutch colony (1613–64) North America along Hudson & lower Delaware rivers; capital, New Amsterdam

New Or·leans \-'òr-lē-ənz, -'òrl-(y)ənz, -(ı)òr-'lēnz\ city SE Louisiana

New·port \\'n(y)ü-ı pō(ə)rt, -ı pò(ə)rt\ **1** city area S England in Isle of Wight **2** city SE Wales in Gwent county

Newport News \ı n(y)ü-ı pòrt-'n(y)üz, -ı pòrt-, -pərt-\ city SE Virginia

New Prov·i·dence \-'präv-əd-ən(t)s, -ə-ı den(t)s\ island NW central Bahamas; chief town, Nassau

New·ry \\'n(y)ù(ə)r-ē\ city district S Northern Ireland in Mourne district

New South Wales state SE Australia; capital, Sydney

New Spain former Spanish possessions in North America, Central America, West Indies, & the Philippines; capital, Mexico City

New Sweden former Swedish colony (1638–55) North America on W bank of Delaware river

New·town·ab·bey \ n(y)üt-ªn-ªab-ē\ district E Northern Ireland

New·town·ards \ n(y)üt-ªn-ªärdz\ town E Northern Ireland in Ards district

Newtown Saint Bos·wells \-sənt-ªbäz-wəlz, -sänt-\ village S Scotland in Borders region

New World the western hemisphere including North America and South America

New York \-ªyò(ə)rk\ **1** state NE U.S.; capital, Albany **2** or **New York City** city SE New York — **New York·er** \-ªyòr-kər\ n

New York State Barge Canal — see ERIE

New Zea·land \-ªzē-lənd\ country SW Pacific ESE of Australia; an independent country in the Commonwealth; capital, Wellington — **New Zea·land·er** \-lən-dər\ n

Ni·ag·a·ra Falls \(ˌ)nī-ªag-(ə-)rə-\ falls New York & Ontario in **Niagara river** (58 kilometers long flowing N from Lake Erie into Lake Ontario); divided by Goat Island into Horseshoe Falls or Canadian Falls (48 meters high, 800 meters wide) & American Falls (51 meters high, 300 meters wide)

Nia·mey \nē-ªäm-ā, nyä-ªmä\ city, capital of Niger

Ni·caea \nī-ªsē-ə\ or **Nice** \ªnīs\ ancient city W Bithynia; site at modern village in NW Turkey — **Ni·cae·an** \nī-ªsē-ən\ adj or n — **Ni·cene** \ªnī-ˌsēn, nī-ªsēn\ adj

Ni·ca·ra·gua \ˌnik-ə-ªräg-wə\ **1** lake 160 kilometers long S Nicaragua **2** country Central America; capital, Managua — **Ni·ca·ra·guan** \-wən\ adj or n

Nic·o·bar \ªnik-ə-ˌbär\ islands India in Bay of Bengal S of the Andamans — see ANDAMAN

Nic·o·sia \ˌnik-ə-ªsē-ə\ city, capital of Cyprus

Ni·ger \ªnī-jər\ **1** river 4185 kilometers long W Africa flowing into Gulf of Guinea **2** country W Africa N of Nigeria; capital, Niamey

Ni·ge·ria \nī-ªjir-ē-ə\ country W Africa on Gulf of Guinea; an independent state in the Commonwealth; official capital, Abuja — **Ni·ge·ri·an** \-ē-ən\ adj or n

Nii·hau \ªnē-ˌhaù\ island Hawaii WSW of Kauai

Nile \ªnī(ə)l\ river 6693 kilometers long E Africa flowing from Lake Victoria in Uganda N into the Mediterranean in Egypt

Nil·gi·ri \ªnil-gə-rē\ hills S India

Nin·e·veh \ªnin-ə-və\ ancient city, capital of Assyria; ruins in Iraq on the Tigris

Nip·i·gon, Lake \-ªnip-ə-ˌgän\ lake Canada in W Ontario N of Lake Superior

Nip·pon \nip-ªän\ — see JAPAN — **Nip·pon·ese** \ˌnip-ə-ªnēz, -ªnēs\ adj or n

Nizh·ni Nov·go·rod or **Nizh·niy Nov·go·rod** or **Nizh·ny Nov·go·rod** \ˌnizh-nē-ªnäv-gə-ˌräd, -ªnòv-gə-rət\ or **1932-90 Gor·ki** or **Gor'·kii** or **Gor'·kiy** or **Gor·ky** \ªgòr-kē\ city W Russia

Nord–Ostsee — see KIEL

Nor·folk \ªnòr-fək, in the U.S. also -ˌfòk\ **1** city SE Virginia **2** county E England on North sea

Nor·man·dy \ªnòr-mən-dē\ region NW France NE of Brittany

North 1 river estuary of the Hudson between NE New Jersey & SE New York **2** sea arm of the Atlantic E of Great Britain **3** island N New Zealand

North·al·ler·ton \nòr-ªthal-ərt-ªn\ town N England in North Yorkshire

North America continent of western hemisphere NW of South America & N of the equator — **North American** adj or n

North·amp·ton \nòrth-ª(h)am(p)-tən\ city area central England in Northamptonshire

North·amp·ton·shire \nòrth-ª(h)am(p)-tən-ˌshi(ə)r, -shər\ or **Northampton** county central England

North Cape cape New Zealand at N end of North island

North Car·o·li·na \-ˌkar-ə-ªlī-nə\ state E U.S.; capital, Raleigh — **North Car·o·lin·ian** \-ªlin-ē-ən, -ªlin-yən\ adj or n

North Da·ko·ta \-də-ªkòt-ə\ state N U.S.; capital, Bismarck — **North Da·ko·tan** \-ªkòt-ªn\ adj or n

North Down district E Northern Ireland

Northern province NE Republic of South Africa

Northern Cape province W Republic of South Africa

Northern Cook \-ªkùk\ islands S central Pacific N of Cook islands

Northern Ireland region N Ireland comprising 26 districts of Ulster; a division of United Kingdom; capital, Belfast

Northern Mar·i·ana Islands \-ˌmar-ē-ªan-ə-, -ˌmer-\ islands W Pacific; a U.S. commonwealth since 1986

Northern Rhodesia — see ZAMBIA

Northern Territory territory N & central Australia; capital, Darwin

North Korea — see KOREA

North Slope region N Alaska between Brooks Range & Arctic ocean

North·um·ber·land \nòr-ªthəm-bər-lənd\ county N England — **North·um·bri·an** \-ªthəm-brē-ən\ adj or n

North·um·bria \nòr-ªthəm-brē-ə\ ancient country Great Britain in what is now N England and S Scotland — **North·um·bri·an** \-brē-ən\ adj or n

North Vietnam — see VIETNAM

North West province N Republic of South Africa

Northwest Territories territory N Canada consisting of the arctic islands, the mainland N of 60° between Yukon Territory & Hudson bay, & the islands in Hudson bay

North Yorkshire county N England

Nor·way \ªnò(ə)r-ˌwä\ country N Europe in Scandinavia; a kingdom; capital, Oslo

Nor·wich \ªnò(ə)r-(ˌ)wich; ªnòr-ich, ªnär-\ city E England in Norfolk county

Not·ting·ham \ªnät-iŋ-əm, in the U.S. also -ˌham\ city N central England in Nottinghamshire

Not·ting·ham·shire \ªnät-iŋ-əm-shi(ə)r, -shər, in the U.S. also -ˌham-\ or **Nottingham** county N central England

Nouak·chott \nù-ªäk-ˌshät\ city, capital of Mauritania

Nou·méa \nü-ªmā-ə\ city, capital of New Caledonia

No·va Sco·tia \ˌnō-və-ªskō-shə\ province SE Canada; capital, Halifax — **No·va Sco·tian** \-ªskō-shən\ adj or n

No·vo·kuz·netsk \ˌnō-(ˌ)vō-kùz-ªnetsk\ city S Russia

No·vo·si·birsk \ˌnō-(ˌ)vō-sə-ªbi(ə)rsk\ city S Russia

Nu·bia \ªn(y)ü-bē-ə\ region NE Africa in Nile valley in S Egypt & N Sudan — **Nu·bi·an** \-bē-ən\ adj or n

Nu·ku·a·lo·fa \ˌnü-kə-wə-ªlò-fə\ seaport, capital of Tonga

Nu·mid·ia \n(y)ù-ªmid-ē-ə\ ancient country N Africa E of Mauretania in modern Algeria — **Nu·mid·i·an** \-ē-ən\ adj or n

Ny·asa, Lake \-nī-ªas-ə, -nē-\ lake SE Africa in Malawi, Mozambique, & Tanzania

Nyasaland — see MALAWI

Oa·hu \ə-ªwä-hü\ island Hawaii; site of Honolulu

Oak·land \ªō-klənd\ city W California on San Francisco Bay E of San Francisco

Oce·a·nia \ˌō-shē-ªan-ē-ə, -ªä-nē-ə\ lands of the central & S Pacific: Micronesia, Melanesia, Polynesia including New Zealand, & sometimes Australia & Malay island group — **Oce·a·ni·an** \-ªan-ē-ən, -ªä-nē-\ adj or n

Oder \ªōd-ər\ or **Odra** \ªò-drə\ river 906 kilometers long central Europe flowing from Silesia NW into Baltic sea; forms part of boundary between Poland & Germany

Odes·sa \ō-ªdes-ə\ city & port S Ukraine on Black sea

Ohio \ō-ªhī-ō\ **1** river 1579 kilometers long E U.S. flowing from W Pennsylvania into the Mississippi **2**

state E central U.S.; capital, Columbus — **Ohio·an** \ō-'hī-ə-wən\ *adj or n*

Oka·ya·ma \ō-kə-'yäm-ə\ city Japan in W Honshu on Inland sea

Okee·cho·bee, Lake \ō-kə-'chō-bē\ lake S central Florida

Oke·fe·no·kee \ō-kə-fə-'nō-kē\ swamp SE Georgia & NE Florida

Oki·na·wa \ō-kə-'nä-wə, -'naù-ə\ **1** islands Japan in central Ryukyus **2** island, chief of group — **Oki·na·wan** \-'nä-wən, -'naù-ən\ *adj or n*

Okla·ho·ma \ō-klə-'hō-mə\ state S U.S.; capital, Oklahoma City — **Okla·ho·man** \-mən\ *adj or n*

Oklahoma City city, capital of Oklahoma

Old·ham \'ōl-dəm\ city NW England in Greater Manchester county

Old Point Comfort cape SE Virginia N of entrance to Hampton Roads

Ol·du·vai Gorge \'ōl-də-ˌvī-\ canyon N Tanzania SE of Serengeti Plain; site of fossil beds

Old World the half of the earth to the east of the Atlantic ocean including Europe, Asia, and Africa; *esp* : the continent of Europe

Olym·pia \ə-'lim-pē-ə, ō-\ **1** city, capital of Washington **2** plain S Greece in NW Peloponnisos

Olym·pic \ə-'lim-pik, ō-\ mountains NW Washington on Olympic peninsula; highest Mt. Olympus 2428 meters

Olym·pus \ə-'lim-pəs, ō-\ mountains NE Greece

Omagh \'ō-mə\ **1** district W Northern Ireland **2** town in Omagh district

Oma·ha \'ō-mə-ˌhò, -ˌhä\ city E Nebraska

Oman \ō-'män, -'man\ country SW Asia in SE Arabia; a sultanate; capital, Masqat — see UNITED ARAB EMIRATES

Oman, Gulf of arm of Arabian sea between Oman & SE Iran

Omsk \'òm(p)sk, 'äm(p)sk\ city S Russia

On·tar·io \än-'ter-ē-ˌō, -'tar-\ province E Canada; capital, Toronto — **On·tar·i·an** \-ē-ən\ *adj or n*

Ontario, Lake lake E central North America in U.S. & Canada; one of the Great Lakes

Or·ange \'òr-inj, 'är-, -ənj\ river 2090 kilometers long S Africa flowing W from Drakensberg mountains into the Atlantic

Or·e·gon \'òr-i-gən, 'är-, -ˌgän\ state NW U.S.; capital, Salem — **Or·e·go·nian** \ˌòr-i-'gō-nē-ən, ˌär-, -nyən\ *adj or n*

Oregon Trail pioneer route to the Pacific Northwest about 3220 kilometers long from Missouri to Washington

Ori·no·co \ˌōr-ə-'nō-kō, ˌòr-\ river 2061 kilometers long Venezuela flowing into the Atlantic

Ork·ney \'òrk-nē\ islands N Scotland forming a region

Or·lan·do \òr-'lan-dō\ city central Florida

Osa·ka \ō-'säk-ə\ city Japan in S Honshu

Osh·a·wa \'äsh-ə-ˌwä\ city SE Ontario, Canada on Lake Ontario ENE of Toronto

Os·lo \'äz-lō, 'äs-\ city, capital of Norway

Ot·ta·wa \'ät-ə-ˌwä, -wə, -ˌwò\ city, capital of Canada in SE Ontario on Ottawa river

Ottoman Empire \ät-ə-mən-\ former Turkish sultanate in SE Europe, W Asia, & N Africa

Oua·ga·dou·gou \ˌwäg-ə-'dü-ˌgü\ city, capital of Burkina Faso

Outer Hebrides — see HEBRIDES

Ox·ford \'äks-fərd\ city central England in Oxfordshire

Ox·ford·shire \'äks-fərd-ˌshi(ə)r, -shər\ *or* **Oxford** county central England

Ox·nard \'äk-ˌsnärd\ city SW California

Ozark plateau \'ō-ˌzärk-\ *or* **Ozark mountains** eroded plateau N Arkansas, S Missouri, & NE Oklahoma with E extension into S Illinois

Pa·cif·ic \pə-'sif-ik\ ocean extending from arctic circle to the equator (North Pacific) and from the equator to the antarctic regions (South Pacific) & from W North America & W South America to E Asia & Australia — **Pacific** *adj*

Pacific Islands, Trust Territory of the grouping of islands in W Pacific formerly under U.S. administration: the Carolines & the Marshalls

Pa·dang \'pä-ˌdäŋ\ city Indonesia in W Sumatra

Pa·dre \'päd-rē, 'pad-\ island about 182 kilometers long S Texas in Gulf of Mexico

Pa·go Pa·go \ˌpäŋ-(g)ō-'päŋ-(g)ō, ˌpäg-ō-'päg-ō\ town, capital of American Samoa on Tutuila island

Painted Desert region N central Arizona

Pak·i·stan \'pak-i-ˌstan, ˌpäk-i-'stän\ country S Asia NW of India; until 1971 included also an eastern division E of India; capital, Islamabad — see EAST PAKISTAN — **Pak·i·stani** \-'stan-ē, -'stän-ē\ *adj or n*

Pa·lau \pə-'laù\ *or* **Be·lau** \bə-'laù\ island group W Pacific in the W Carolines

Pa·la·wan \pə-'lä-wən, -ˌwän\ island W Philippines between South China & Sulu seas

Pa·lem·bang \ˌpäl-əm-'bäŋ\ city Indonesia in SE Sumatra

Pa·ler·mo \pə-'lər-mō, -'le(ə)r-\ city Italy, capital of Sicily

Pal·es·tine \'pal-ə-ˌstīn, -ˌstēn\ region SW Asia between Syrian Desert & the Mediterranean now divided between Israel & Jordan — **Pal·es·tin·ian** \ˌpal-ə-'stin-ē-ən, -'stin-yən\ *adj or n*

Pal·i·sades \ˌpal-ə-'sädz\ line of high cliffs 24 kilometers long on W bank of the Hudson in SE New York & NE New Jersey

Pa·mirs \pə-'mi(ə)rz\ *or* **Pa·mir** \pə-'mi(ə)r\ elevated mountainous region central Asia in E Tajikistan & on borders of China, India, Pakistan, & Afghanistan; many peaks over 6000 meters

Pam·li·co \'pam-li-ˌkō\ inlet of the Atlantic E North Carolina between main part of the state & offshore islands

Pam·pa \'pam-pə\ city NW Texas

Pan·a·ma \'pan-ə-ˌmä, -ˌmò, ˌpan-ə-'mä, -'mò\ **1** country S Central America **2** *or* **Panama City** city, its capital on the Pacific **3** canal 82 kilometers long Panama connecting Atlantic & Pacific oceans — **Pan·a·ma·ni·an** \ˌpan-ə-'mä-nē-ən\ *adj or n*

Panama, Isthmus of *or formerly* **Isthmus of Dar·i·en** \-ˌdar-ē-'en\ strip of land central Panama connecting North America & South America

Panama Canal Zone — see CANAL ZONE

Pa·nay \pə-'nī\ island central Philippines

Pao–t'ou — see BAOTOU

Pap·ua, Territory of \-'pap-yə-wə, -'päp-ə-wə\ former British territory consisting of SE New Guinea & offshore islands; now part of Papua New Guinea

Papua New Guinea country combining former territories of Papua & New Guinea; formerly a United Nations trust territory governed by Australia; independent since 1975; capital, Port Moresby

Par·a·guay \'par-ə-ˌgwī, -ˌgwā\ **1** river 2549 kilometers long central South America flowing from Brazil S into the Paraná in Paraguay **2** country central South America; capital, Asunción — **Par·a·guay·an** \ˌpar-ə-'gwī-ən, -'gwä-\ *adj or n*

Par·a·mar·i·bo \ˌpar-ə-'mar-ə-ˌbō\ city, capital of Suriname

Pa·ra·ná \ˌpar-ə-'nä\ river about 4875 kilometers long central South America flowing S from Brazil into Argentina

Pa·ri·cu·tín \pə-ˌrē-kə-ˌtēn\ **1** former village Mexico **2** volcano on site of former village of Paricutín

Par·is \'par-əs\ city, capital of France — **Pa·ri·sian** \pə-'rizh-ən, -'rēzh-\ *adj or n*

Par·nas·sus \pär-'nas-əs\ mountain central Greece

Par·os \'par-ˌäs, 'per-\ island Greece — **Par·i·an** \'par-ē-ən, 'per-\ *adj*

Par·ra·mat·ta \ˌpar-ə-'mat-ə\ city SE Australia in New South Wales NW of Sydney

Par·thia \\'pär-thē-ə\ ancient country SW Asia in NE modern Iran — **Par·thi·an** \-thē-ən\ adj or n

Pas·a·de·na \ˌpas-ə-'dē-nə\ 1 city SW California just NE of Los Angeles 2 city SE Texas

Pat·a·go·nia \ˌpat-ə-'gō-nyə, -nē-ə\ region South America S of about 40° S latitude in S Argentina & S tip of Chile; sometimes thought to include Tierra del Fuego — **Pat·a·go·nian** \-nyən, -nē-ən\ adj or n

Pat·er·son \'pat-ər-sən\ city NE New Jersey

Pat·mos \'pat-məs\ island Greece SSW of Samos

Pat·na \'pat-nə\ city NE India on the Ganges

Pearl Harbor inlet Hawaii on S coast of Oahu W of Honolulu

Peking — see BEIJING

Pe·li·on, Mount \-'pē-lē-ən\ mountain 1551 meters NE Greece

Pel·o·pon·ni·sos \ˌpel-ə-pə-'nē-səs\ peninsula forming S part of mainland of Greece

Pen·nine Chain \'pen-ˌīn-\ mountains N England; highest Cross Fell 893 meters

Penn·syl·va·nia \ˌpen(t)-səl-'vā-nyə, -nē-ə\ state E U.S.; capital, Harrisburg

People's Democratic Republic of Yemen — see YEMEN

Pe·o·ria \pē-'ȯr-ē-ə, -'ōr-\ city N central Illinois

Per·ga·mum \'pər-gə-məm\ or **Per·ga·mus** \-məs\ ancient Greek kingdom including most of Asia Minor; at its height 263–133 B.C.; capital, Pergamum (in what is now W Turkey)

Perm \'pərm, 'pe(ə)rm\ city W Russia

Pernambuco — see RECIFE

Persia — see IRAN

Per·sian \'pər-zhən\ gulf arm of Arabian sea between Iran & Arabia

Perth \'pərth\ city, capital of Western Australia

Pe·ru \pə-'rü\ country W South America; capital, Lima — **Pe·ru·vi·an** \pə-'rü-vē-ən\ adj or n

Pe·ter·bor·ough \'pēt-ər-ˌbər-ə, -ˌbə-rə, -b(ə-)rə\ town central England in Cambridgeshire

Pe·tra \'pē-trə, 'pe-trə\ ancient city NW Arabia; site in SW Jordan

Petrograd — see SAINT PETERSBURG

Phil·a·del·phia \ˌfil-ə-'del-fyə, -fē-ə\ city SE Pennsylvania — **Phil·a·del·phian** \-fyən, -fē-ən\ adj or n

Phil·ip·pines \ˌfil-ə-'pēnz, 'fil-ə-ˌpēnz\ island group approximately 800 kilometers off SE coast of Asia; an independent country; capital, Manila — **Phil·ippine** \-'pēn, -ˌpēn\ adj

Phnom Penh \(pə-)'nȯm-'pen, (pə-)'näm-\ city, capital of Cambodia

Phoe·ni·cia \fi-'nish-(ē-)ə, -'nēsh-\ ancient country SW Asia on the Mediterranean in modern Syria & Lebanon

Phoe·nix \'fē-niks\ city, capital of Arizona

Phry·gia \'frij-(ē-)ə\ ancient country W central Asia Minor

Pied·mont \'pēd-ˌmänt\ plateau region E U.S. E of the Appalachians between SE New York & NE Alabama — **Pied·mon·tese** \ˌpēd-mən-'tēz, -(ˌ)män-, -'tēs\ adj or n

Pierre \'pi(ə)r\ city, capital of South Dakota

Pie·ter·mar·itz·burg \ˌpēt-ər-'mar-əts-ˌbərg\ city E Republic of South Africa, in KwaZulu-Natal

Pikes Peak \'pīks-\ mountain 4301 meters E central Colorado in a range of the Rockies

Pin·dus \'pin-dəs\ mountains W Greece; highest point 2480 meters

Pi·sa \'pē-zə\ city W central Italy W of Florence

Pit·cairn \'pit-ˌka(ə)rn, -ˌke(ə)rn\ island S Pacific; a British colony

Pitts·burgh \'pits-ˌbərg\ city SW Pennsylvania

Plac·id, Lake \-'plas-əd\ lake NE New York

Plym·outh \'plim-əth\ 1 town SE Massachusetts 2 city SW England in Devon county

Po \'pō\ river 652 kilometers N Italy flowing into the Adriatic

Po Hai — see BO HAI

Po·land \'pō-lənd\ country central Europe on Baltic sea; capital, Warsaw

Pol·y·ne·sia \ˌpäl-ə-'nē-zhə, -shə\ islands of the central & S Pacific including Hawaii, the Line, Tonga, Cook, & Samoa islands, & often New Zealand among others

Pom·er·a·nia \ˌpäm-ə-'rā-nē-ə, -nyə\ region N Europe on Baltic sea; formerly in Germany, now mostly in Poland

Pom·peii \päm-'pā, -'pā-ˌē\ ancient city S Italy SE of Naples destroyed 79 A.D. by eruption of Vesuvius — **Pom·pe·ian** \-'pā-ən\ adj or n

Po·na·pe \'pō-nə-ˌpä\ island W Pacific in the E Carolines

Pon·ce \'pȯn(t)-sä\ city S Puerto Rico

Pon·do·land \'pän-(ˌ)dō-ˌland\ territory Republic of South Africa in Eastern Cape province

Pon·ta Del·ga·da \ˌpän-tə-del-'gäd-ə, -'gad-\ city & port Portugal, largest in the Azores

Pont·char·train, Lake \-'pän-chər-ˌtrān, -ˌpän-chər-'trān\ lake SE Louisiana E of the Mississippi & N of New Orleans

Pon·tus \'pänt-əs\ 1 ancient country NE Asia Minor 2 or **Pontus Euxinus** — see BLACK SEA — **Pon·tic** \'pänt-ik\ adj or n

Poole \'pül\ city area S England in Dorset county on English Channel

Poo·na \'pü-nə\ city W India, ESE of Bombay

Po·po·ca·te·petl \ˌpō-pə-ˌkat-ə-'pet-əl\ volcano 5452 meters SE central Mexico

Port Arthur — see LÜSHUN

Port–au–Prince \ˌpȯrt-ō-'prin(t)s, ˌpȯrt-\ city, capital of Haiti

Port Jack·son \-'jak-sən\ inlet of S Pacific SE Australia in New South Wales; harbor of Sydney

Port·land \'pȯrt-lənd, 'pȯrt-\ 1 city SW Maine; largest in state 2 city NW Oregon

Port Lou·is \-'lü-əs, -'lü-ē, -lü-'ē\ city, capital of Mauritius

Port Mores·by \-'mō(ə)rz-bē, -'mȯ(ə)rz-\ city, capital of Papua New Guinea

Pôr·to Ale·gre \ˌpȯrt-ō-ə-'leg-rə, ˌpȯrt-\ city S Brazil

Port of Spain city NW Trinidad, capital of Trinidad and Tobago

Por·to–No·vo \ˌpȯrt-ə-'nō-vō, ˌpȯrt-\ city, capital of Benin

Port Phil·lip Bay \-'fil-əp-\ inlet of S Pacific SE Australia in Victoria; harbor of Melbourne

Ports·mouth \'pȯrt-sməth, 'pȯrt-\ 1 city SE Virginia 2 city S England in Hampshire

Por·tu·gal \'pȯr-chi-gəl, 'pȯr-\ country SW Europe; capital, Lisbon

Portuguese India former Portuguese possession on W coast of India; became part of India 1962

Po·to·mac \pə-'tō-mək, -mik\ river 462 kilometers long flowing from West Virginia into Chesapeake Bay & forming boundary between Maryland & Virginia

Pough·keep·sie \pə-'kip-sē, pō-\ city and river port SE New York on the Hudson

Po·wys \'pō-əs\ county E central Wales; established 1974

Prague \'präg\ or Czech **Pra·ha** \'prä-hä\ city, capital of Czech Republic & formerly of Czechoslovakia

Praia \'prī-ə\ town, capital of Cape Verde

Prairie Provinces the Canadian provinces of Alberta, Manitoba, & Saskatchewan

Pres·ton \'pres-tən\ city area NW England in Lancashire

Pre·to·ria \pri-'tōr-ē-ə, -'tȯr-\ city Republic of South Africa, in Gauteng; administrative capital of the country

Prib·i·lof \'prib-ə-ˌlȯf\ islands Alaska in Bering sea

Prince Ed·ward Island \-ˌed-wərd-\ island SE Canada in Gulf of Saint Lawrence; a province; capital, Charlottetown

Prince Ru·pert's Land \-ˈrü-pərts-\ historical region N & W Canada consisting of drainage basin of Hudson bay granted 1670 by King Charles II to Hudson's Bay Company

Prince·ton \ˈprin(t)-stən\ town W central New Jersey

Prín·ci·pe \ˈprin(t)-sə-pə\ island W Africa in Gulf of Guinea — see SÃO TOMÉ AND PRÍNCIPE

Prom·on·to·ry \ˈpräm-ən-ˌtōr-ē, -ˌtòr-\ locality NW Utah

Pro·vence \prə-ˈvän(t)s\ region SE France on the Mediterranean

Prov·i·dence \ˈpräv-əd-ən(t)s, -ə-ˌden(t)s\ city, capital of Rhode Island

Prus·sia \ˈprəsh-ə\ former kingdom &, later, state Germany; capital, Berlin — **Prus·sian** \-ən\ adj or n

Pueb·lo \ˈpü-ˈeb-lō, ˈpweb-, pyü-ˈeb-\ city SE central Colorado SSE of Colorado Springs

Puer·to Ri·co \ˌpòrt-ə-ˈrē-kō, ˌpòrt-, ˌpwert-\ island West Indies E of Hispaniola; a self-governing commonwealth associated with U.S.; capital, San Juan — **Puer·to Ri·can** \-ˈrē-kən\ adj or n

Pu·get Sound \ˌpyü-jət-\ arm of the Pacific W Washington

Pun·jab \ˌpən-ˈjäb, -ˈjab, ˈpen-ˌjäb, -ˌjab\ region in Pakistan & NW India in valley of the Indus

Pu·san \ˈpü-ˌsän\ city SE South Korea

Pyong·yang \pē-ˈòŋ-ˌyäŋ, pē-ˈəŋ-, -ˌyaŋ\ city, capital of North Korea

Pyr·e·nees \ˈpir-ə-ˌnēz\ mountains on French-Spanish border extending from Bay of Biscay to the Mediterranean; highest Pico de Aneto 3404 meters

Qa·tar \ˈkät-ər, ˈgät-, ˈgət-\ independent country E Arabia on peninsula extending into Persian gulf; capital, Doha

Qing·dao \ˈchiŋ-ˈdaù\ or **Tsing·tao** \ˈchiŋ-ˈdaù, ˈ(t)siŋ-\ city & port E China

Qi·qi·har \ˈchē-ˈchē-ˈhär\ or **Ch'i-ch'i-ha-erh** \ˈchē-ˈchē-ˈhä-ˈər\ city NE China

Que·bec \kwi-ˈbek, ki-\ or French **Qué·bec** \kā-bek\ **1** province E Canada **2** city, its capital, on the Saint Lawrence

Queens \ˈkwēnz\ section of New York City on Long Island E of Brooklyn

Queens·land \ˈkwēnz-ˌland, -lənd\ state NE Australia; capital, Brisbane — **Queens·land·er** \-ər\ n

Que·zon City \ˈkā-ˌsòn-\ city Philippines in Luzon; formerly capital of the country

Qui·to \ˈkē-tō\ city, capital of Ecuador

Ra·bat \rə-ˈbät\ city, capital of Morocco

Rai·nier, Mount \rə-ˈni(ə)r, -rā-\ mountain 4392 meters W central Washington; highest in Cascade Range

Rajasthan — see RAJPUTANA

Raj·pu·ta·na \ˌräj-pə-ˈtän-ə\ or **Ra·ja·sthan** \ˈräj-ə-ˌstän\ region NW India S of Punjab

Ra·leigh \ˈrò-lē, ˈräl-ē\ city, capital of North Carolina

Rand — see WITWATERSRAND

Rand·wick \ˈran-(ˌ)dwik\ city SE Australia in E New South Wales

Rangoon — see YANGON

Ra·wal·pin·di \ˌrä-wəl-ˈpin-dē, raùl-ˈpin-, ròl-ˈpin-\ city NE Pakistan NNW of Lahore

Read·ing \ˈred-iŋ\ city area S England in Berkshire

Re·ci·fe \rə-ˈsē-fə\ or formerly **Per·nam·bu·co** \ˌpər-nəm-ˈb(y)ü-kō, ˌper-nəm-ˈbü-\ city NE Brazil

Red \ˈred\ **1** river 1638 kilometers long flowing E on Oklahoma-Texas boundary & into the Atchafalaya & the Mississippi in Louisiana **2** sea between Arabia & NE Africa

Red·bridge \ˈred-(ˌ)brij\ city area of NE Greater London county, England

Re·gi·na \ri-ˈjī-nə\ city, capital of Saskatchewan, Canada

Re·no \ˈrē-nō\ city NW Nevada

Republic of the Congo — see CONGO 3

Ré·union \rē-ˈyün-yən\ island W Indian ocean; an overseas division of France; capital Saint-Denis

Reyk·ja·vik \ˈrāk-(y)ə-ˌvik, -ˌvēk\ city, capital of Iceland

Rhine \ˈrīn\ river 1320 kilometers long W Europe flowing from SE Switzerland to North sea in the Netherlands — **Rhen·ish** \ˈren-ish, ˈrē-nish\ adj or n

Rhine·land \ˈrīn-ˌland, -lənd\ or German **Rhein·land** \ˈrīn-ˌlänt\ the part of Germany W of the Rhine — **Rhine·land·er** \ˈrīn-ˌlan-dər, -lən-\ n

Rhode Is·land \rō-ˈdī-lənd\ **1** or officially **Rhode Island and Providence Plantations** state NE U.S.; capital, Providence **2** — see AQUIDNECK ISLAND — **Rhode Is·land·er** \-lən-dər\ n

Rho·de·sia \rō-ˈdē-zh(ē-)ə\ — see ZIMBABWE — **Rho·de·sian** \-zh(ē-)ən\ adj or n

Rhone or French **Rhône** \ˈrōn\ or ancient **Rhod·a·nus** \ˈräd-ən-əs\ river 813 kilometers long Switzerland & SE France

Rich·mond \ˈrich-mənd\ **1** — see STATEN ISLAND **2** city, capital of Virginia

Richmond upon Thames \-ˈtemz\ city area of SW Greater London county, England

Ri·ga \ˈrē-gə\ city, capital of Latvia

Rio \ˈrē-ō\ RIO DE JANEIRO

Rio de Ja·nei·ro \ˈrē-ō-ˌdā-zhə-ˈne(ə)r-ō, -ˌdē-, -də-, -jə-ˈne(ə)r-\ city SE Brazil on Guanabara Bay

Rio Grande \ˌrē-(ˌ)ō-ˈgrand(-ē)\ or Mexican **Rio Bra·vo** \-ˈbräv-ō\ river 3035 kilometers long SW U.S. forming part of U.S.-Mexico boundary & flowing into Gulf of Mexico

Río Muni — see MBINI

Riv·er·side \ˈriv-ər-ˌsīd\ city S California

Riv·i·era \ˌriv-ē-ˈer-ə\ coast region SE France & NW Italy

Ri·yadh \rē-ˈ(y)äd\ city, capital of Saudi Arabia

Ro·a·noke \ˈrō-(ə-)ˌnōk\ city W Virginia

Roanoke Island island North Carolina S of entrance to Albemarle sound

Rob·son, Mount \ˈräb-sən\ mountain 3954 meters W Canada in E British Columbia; highest in the Canadian Rockies

Roch·es·ter \ˈräch-ə-stər, ˈräch-ˌes-tər\ city W New York

Rock·ford \ˈräk-fərd\ city N Illinois

Rocky \ˈräk-ē\ mountains W North America extending SE from N Alaska to central New Mexico — see ELBERT, MOUNT; ROBSON, MOUNT

Roman Empire the empire of ancient Rome

Ro·ma·nia \rō-ˈmä-nē-ə, -nyə\ or **Ru·ma·nia** \rù-\ country SE Europe on Black sea; capital, Bucharest

Rom·blon \räm-ˈblōn\ island group central Philippines

Rome \ˈrōm\ **1** or Italian **Ro·ma** \ˈrō-mä\ city, capital of Italy **2** the Roman Empire

Ro·sa·rio \rō-ˈzär-ē-ˌō, -ˈsär-\ city E central Argentina

Ro·seau \rō-ˈzō\ seaport, capital of Dominica

Ros·tov \rə-ˈstòf, -ˈstòv\ city SW Russia, on the Don

Ros·well \ˈräz-ˌwel, -wəl\ city SE New Mexico

Ro·ta \ˈrōt-ə\ island W Pacific in Marianas

Rot·ter·dam \ˈrät-ər-ˌdam\ city SW Netherlands

Ru·an·da-Urun·di \rù-ˈän-də-ù-ˈrün-dē\ former territory E central Africa bordering on Lake Tanganyika & administered by Belgium; divided into Burundi & Rwanda 1962

Ru·dolf, Lake \-ˈrü-ˌdälf\ lake N Kenya in Great Rift valley

Ruhr \ˈrù(ə)r\ industrial district W Germany E of the Rhine in valley of Ruhr river

Rupert's Land — see PRINCE RUPERT'S LAND

Rush·more, Mount \-ˈrəsh-ˌmō(ə)r, -ˌmò(ə)r\ mountain 1707 meters W South Dakota in Black hills

Rus·sia \ˈrəsh-ə\ **1** former empire largely having the same boundaries as U.S.S.R.; capital, Petrograd (Saint Petersburg) **2** : UNION OF SOVIET SOCIALIST REPUBLICS **3** country E Europe & N Asia; capital, Moscow; a republic (**Russian Soviet Federated Socialist Republic** or **Soviet Russia**) of U.S.S.R. 1922-91

Ru·the·nia \rü-ˈthē-nyə, -nē-ə\ region W Ukraine W of

the N Carpathians — **Ru·the·nian** \rü-'thē-nyən, -'nē-ən\ *adj or n*

Ru·wen·zo·ri \ˌrü-(w)ən-'zōr-ē, -'zor-\ mountain group E central Africa between Uganda & Democratic Republic of the Congo; highest Mount Margherita 5109 meters

Rwan·da *or formerly* **Ru·an·da** \rü-'än-də\ country E central Africa, until 1962 part of Ruanda-Urundi trust territory; capital, Kigali — **Rwan·dan** \-dən\ *adj or n*

Ryu·kyu \rē-'(y)ü-k(y)ü\ islands W Pacific extending in an arc from Kyushu, Japan, to Taiwan, China; belong to Japan — **Ryu·kyu·an** \-ˌ(y)ü-'k(y)ü-ən\ *adj or n*

Saar \'sär, 'zär\ **1** river Europe flowing from E France to W Germany **2** *or* **Saar·land** \'sär-ˌland, 'zär-\ district W Europe in valley of Saar river between France and Germany

Sa·bah \'säb-ə\ part of Malaysia in NE Borneo

Sac·ra·men·to \ˌsak-rə-'ment-ō\ **1** river 615 kilometers long N California flowing S into Suisun Bay **2** city, capital of California

Sag·ue·nay \'sag-ə-ˌnā, ˌsag-ə-'nā\ river Canada in S Quebec flowing E into the Saint Lawrence

Sa·ha·ra \sə-'har-ə, -'her-, -'här-\ desert region N Africa N of Sudan region extending from Atlantic coast to Red sea or, as sometimes thought, to the Nile — **Sa·ha·ran** \-ən\ *adj*

Sa·hel \'sa-hil, sə-'hil\ the S fringe of the Sahara

Saigon — see HO CHI MINH CITY

Saint Al·bans \-'òl-bənz\ city area SE England in Hertfordshire

Saint Cath·a·rines \-'kath-(ə-)rənz\ city Canada in SE Ontario

Saint Chris·to·pher — see SAINT KITTS

Saint Clair, Lake \-'kla(ə)r, -'kle(ə)r\ lake SE Michigan & SE Ontario connected by **Saint Clair river** (64 kilometers long) with Lake Huron & draining by Detroit river into Lake Erie

Saint Croix \sänt-'kroi, sənt-\ **1** river 120 kilometers long Canada & U.S. on border between New Brunswick & Maine **2** island West Indies; largest of Virgin Islands of the U.S.

Saint Eli·as, Mount \-ˌsänt-əl-'ī-əs\ mountain 6050 meters on Alaska-Canada boundary in **Saint Elias range**

Saint George's \-'jòr-jəz\ town, capital of Grenada

Saint George's Channel channel British Isles between SW Wales & Ireland

Saint Gott·hard \sänt-'gät-ərd, -'gäth-, sənt-\ **1** pass S central Switzerland in Saint Gotthard range of the Alps **2** tunnel 15 kilometers long near the pass

Saint He·le·na \ˌsänt-əl-'ē-nə, ˌsänt-hə-'lē-\ island S Atlantic; a British colony

Saint Hel·ens \sänt-'hel-ənz, sənt-\ city area NW England in Merseyside county ENE of Liverpool

Saint Helens, Mount volcano S Washington

Saint John \sänt-'jän, sənt-\ city Canada in New Brunswick

Saint Johns \sänt-'jänz, sənt-\ city, capital of Antigua and Barbuda

Saint John's \sänt-'jänz, sənt-\ city, capital of Newfoundland, Canada

Saint Kitts \-'kits\ *or* **Saint Chris·to·pher** \-'kris-tə-fər\ island West Indies in the Leeward islands; with Nevis forms independent **Saint Kitts-Nevis** (Saint Christopher-Nevis); capital, Basseterre (on Saint Kitts)

Saint Law·rence \sänt-'lòr-ən(t)s, sənt-, -'lär-\ **1** river 1225 kilometers long E Canada in Ontario & Quebec bordering on U.S. in New York & flowing from Lake Ontario NE into the **Gulf of Saint Lawrence** (inlet of the Atlantic) **2** seaway Canada & U.S. in & along the Saint Lawrence between Lake Ontario & Montreal

Saint Lou·is \sänt-'lü-əs, sənt-\ city E Missouri on the Mississippi

Saint Lu·cia \sänt-'lü-shə, sənt-\ island West Indies in the Windwards S of Martinique; an independent country; capital, Castries

Saint Paul \-'pòl\ city, capital of Minnesota

Saint Pe·ters·burg \-'pēt-ərz-ˌbərg\ **1** city W Florida **2** *or* *1914–24* **Pet·ro·grad** \'pe-trə-ˌgrad, -ˌgräd\ *or* *1924–91* **Le·nin·grad** \'len-ən-ˌgrad, -ˌgräd\ city W Russia

Saint Thom·as \-'täm-əs\ island West Indies, one of Virgin Islands of the U.S.; chief town, Charlotte Amalie

Saint Vin·cent \sänt-'vin(t)-sənt, sənt-\ island West Indies in the central Windward Islands; with N Grenadines forms independent **Saint Vincent and the Grenadines**; capital, Kingstown (on Saint Vincent)

Sai·pan \sī-'pan, -'pän; 'sī-ˌpan, -ˌpän\ island W Pacific in S central Marianas

Sa·kai \('\sä-'kī\ city Japan in S Honshu

Sa·kha·lin \'sak-ə-ˌlēn, -lən; ˌsak-ə-'lēn\ island SE Russia W Pacific N of Hokkaido, Japan; until 1945 divided between Japan & U.S.S.R.

Sal·a·mis \'sal-ə-məs\ **1** ancient city Cyprus on E coast **2** island Greece off Attica

Sa·lem \'sā-ləm\ city, capital of Oregon

Sal·ford \'sòl-fərd\ city area NW England in Greater Manchester county

Salisbury — see HARARE

Sa·lo·ni·ka \sə-'län-i-kə, ˌsal-ə-'nē-kə\ *or* **Thes·sa·lo·ni·ca** \ˌthes-ə-lə-'nī-kə, -'län-i-kə\ city N Greece in Macedonia

Salop — see SHROPSHIRE

Salt Lake City city, capital of Utah

Sal·va·dor \'sal-və-ˌdò(ə)r, ˌsal-və-'dò(ə)r\ *or* **Ba·hia** \bä-'ē-ə\ city NE Brazil on the Atlantic — **Sal·va·dor·an** \ˌsal-və-'dòr-ən, -'dòr-\ *or* **Sal·va·dor·ean** *or* **Sal·va·dor·ian** \-ē-ən\ *adj or n*

Sal·ween \'sal-ˌwēn\ river 2415 kilometers long SE Asia flowing S

Sa·mar \'säm-ˌär\ island central Philippines

Sa·ma·ra \sə-'mär-ə\ *or* *1935–91* **Kuy·by·shev** \'kwē-bə-ˌshef, -ˌshev\ city W Russia, on the Volga

Sam·ni·um \'sam-nē-əm\ ancient country S central Italy — **Sam·nite** \'sam-ˌnīt\ *adj or n*

Sa·moa \sə-'mō-ə\ **1** islands SW central Pacific N of Tonga islands; divided at longitude 171° W into American Samoa & independent Samoa **2** *or formerly* **Western Samoa** independent country SW central Pacific W of American Samoa; capital, Apia — **Sa·mo·an** \-ən\ *adj or n*

Sa·mos \'sā-ˌmäs\ island Greece in the Aegean off coast of Turkey — **Sa·mi·an** \-mē-ən\ *adj or n*

San·'a *or* **San·a·'a** \'san-ˌä, san-'ä\ city SW Arabia, capital of Yemen & formerly of Yemen Arab Republic

San An·to·nio \ˌsan-ən-'tō-nē-ˌō\ city S Texas

San Ber·nar·di·no \ˌsan-ˌbər-nə(r)-'dē-nō\ city S California

San Di·ego \ˌsan-dē-'ā-gō\ city SW California

Sand·wich \'san-(ˌ)d\wich\ town SE England

Sandwich islands — see HAWAII

San Fran·cis·co \ˌsan-frən-'sis-kō\ city W California on San Francisco Bay & Pacific ocean

San Joa·quin \ˌsan-wä-'kēn, -wò\ river 563 kilometers long central California flowing NW into the Sacramento

San Jo·se \ˌsan-ə-'zā\ city W California SE of San Francisco

San Jo·sé \ˌsan-ə-'zā, -ō-'zā, -hō-'zā\ city, capital of Costa Rica

San Juan \san-'hwän, -'wän\ city, capital of Puerto Rico

San Ma·ri·no \ˌsan-mə-'rē-nō\ **1** country S Europe on Italian peninsula ENE of Florence near Adriatic sea **2** town, its capital

San Sal·va·dor \san-'sal-və-ˌdò(ə)r\ **1** island central Bahamas **2** city, capital of El Salvador

San·ta Ana \ˌsant-ə-ˈan-ə\ city SW California ESE of Long Beach

San·ta Bar·ba·ra \-ˈbär-b(ə-)rə\ *or* Channel islands California in the Pacific off SW coast

San·ta Fe \ˌsant-ə-ˈfā\ city, capital of New Mexico

Santa Fe Trail pioneer route to the Southwest 1930 kilometers long used especially 1821–80 from vicinity of Kansas City, Missouri, to Santa Fe, New Mexico

San·ti·a·go \ˌsant-ē-ˈäg-ō, ˌsänt-\ city, capital of Chile

San·to Do·min·go \ˌsant-əd-ə-ˈmiŋ-gō\ *or formerly* Ci·u·dad Tru·ji·llo \ˌsē-ü-ˌthä-trü-ˈhē-(y)ō, ˌsē-ü-ˌdad-\ city, capital of Dominican Republic

São Pau·lo \ˌsä-ō-ˈpaü-lō\ city SE Brazil

São To·mé \ˌsä-ō-tō-ˈmā\ town, capital of São Tomé and Príncipe

São Tomé and Príncipe country W Africa; formerly a Portuguese colony; became independent 1975; capital São Tomé

Sap·po·ro \ˈsäp-ə-ˌrō; sə-ˈpōr-ō, -ˈpòr-\ city Japan on W Hokkaido

Sa·ra·tov \sə-ˈrät-əf\ city W Russia, on the Volga

Sa·ra·wak \sə-ˈrä-(ˌ)wä(k), -ˌwak\ part of Malaysia in N Borneo

Sar·din·ia \sär-ˈdin-ē-ə, -ˈdin-yə\ island Italy in the Mediterranean S of Corsica — Sar·din·ian \-ˈdin-ē-ən, -ˈdin-yən\ *adj or n*

Sar·gas·so sea \sär-ˌgas-ō-\ area of nearly still water in the N Atlantic lying chiefly between 25° & 35° N latitude & 40°& 70° W longitude

Sas·katch·e·wan \sə-ˈskach-ə-wən, sa-, -ˌwän\ province W Canada; capital, Regina

Sas·ka·toon \ˌsas-kə-ˈtün\ city central Saskatchewan, Canada

Sau·di Ara·bia \ˌsaüd-ē-ə-ˈrä-bē-ə, ˌsòd-ē-, sä-ˌüd-ē-\ country SW Asia occupying largest part of Arabian peninsula; a kingdom; capital, Riyadh — Saudi *adj or n* — Saudi Arabian *adj or n*

Sault Sainte Ma·rie canals \ˌsü-(ˌ)sänt-mə-ˈrē-\ *or* Soo canals \ˌsü-\ three ship canals, two in U.S. (Michigan) & one in Canada (Ontario), at rapids in river connecting Lake Superior & Lake Huron

Sa·vaii \sə-ˈvī-ˌē\ island, largest in Western Samoa

Sa·van·nah \sə-ˈvan-ə\ city E Georgia

Sa·voy \sə-ˈvòi\ *or French* Sa·voie \sà-ˈvwà\ region SE France SW of Switzerland bordering on Italy — Sa·voy·ard \sə-ˈvòi-ˌärd, ˌsav-ˌòi-ˈärd; ˌsav-ˌwä-ˈyär(d)\ *adj or n*

Sca·fell Pike \ˈskò-ˈfel-\ mountain 978 meters NW England in Cumbria county; highest in Cumbrian mountains & in England

Scan·di·na·via \ˌskan-də-ˈnā-vē-ə, -vyə\ 1 peninsula N Europe occupied by Norway & Sweden 2 Denmark, Norway, Sweden, & sometimes also Iceland & Finland — Scan·di·na·vian \-vē-ən,-vyən\ *adj or n*

Scar·bor·ough \ˈskär-ˌbər-ə, -b(ə-)rə\ city Canada in SE Ontario near Toronto

Schel·de \ˈskel-də\ *or* Scheldt \ˈskelt\ *or ancient* Scal·dis \ˈskal-dəs\ river 435 kilometers long W Europe flowing from N France through Belgium into North sea in Netherlands

Scil·ly \ˈsil-ē\ islands SW England off Land's End in Cornwall and Isles of Scilly county

Sco·tia \ˈskō-shə\ SCOTLAND — the Medieval Latin name

Scot·land \ˈskät-lənd\ *or Latin* Cal·e·do·nia \ˌkal-ə-ˈdō-nyə, -nē-ə\ country N Great Britain; a division of United Kingdom of Great Britain and Northern Ireland; capital, Edinburgh

Scyth·ia \ˈsith-ē-ə, ˈsith-\ ancient area of Europe & Asia N & NE of Black sea & E of Aral sea — Scyth·i·an \-ē-ən\ *adj or n*

Se·at·tle \sē-ˈat-əl\ city W Washington

Seine \ˈsān, ˈsen\ river 773 kilometers long N France flowing NW into English channel

Sel·kirk \ˈsel-ˌkərk\ range of the Rocky mountains SE

British Columbia, Canada; highest peak over 3500 meters

Se·ma·rang \sə-ˈmär-ˌäŋ\ city Indonesia in central Java

Sen·dai \(ˈ)sen-ˈdī\ city Japan in NE Honshu

Sen·e·ca Falls \ˈsen-i-kə-\ village W central New York

Sen·e·gal \ˌsen-i-ˈgòl\ 1 river 1633 kilometers long W Africa flowing W into the Atlantic 2 country W Africa; capital, Dakar — Sen·e·ga·lese \ˌsen-i-gə-ˈlēz, -ˈlēs\ *adj or n*

Seoul \ˈsōl\ city, capital of South Korea

Ser·bia \ˈsər-bē-ə\ region in the Balkans comprising the largest part of Yugoslavia

Ser·en·ge·ti Plain \ˌser-ən-ˈget-ē\ area N Tanzania

Seven Hills the seven hills upon and about which was built the city of Rome

Sev·ern \ˈsev-ərn\ river 338 kilometers long Wales & England flowing from E central Wales into Bristol channel

Se·ville \sə-ˈvil\ *or Spanish* Se·vi·lla \sā-ˈvē-(y)ä\ city SW Spain

Sey·chelles \sā-ˈshel(z)\ islands W Indian ocean NE of Madagascar; formerly a British colony; became independent 1976; capital, Victoria

Shang·hai \shaŋ-ˈhī\ city E China

Shan·non \ˈshan-ən\ river 370 kilometers long W Ireland flowing S & W into the Atlantic

Shas·ta, Mount \-ˈshas-tə\ mountain 4317 meters N California in Cascade Range

Shatt–al–Ar·ab \ˌshat-ˌal-ˈar-əb\ river 193 kilometers long SE Iraq formed by flowing together of Euphrates & Tigris rivers & flowing SE into Persian gulf

Shef·field \ˈshef-ˌēld\ city N England in South Yorkshire

Shen·an·do·ah Valley \ˌshen-ən-ˈdō-ə-, ˌshan-ə-ˈdō-ə-\ valley Virginia between the Allegheney & Blue Ridge mountains

Shen·yang \ˈshən-ˈyäŋ\ *or* Muk·den \ˈmùk-dən, ˈmək-; mùk-ˈden\ city NE China; chief city of Manchuria

Sher·brooke \ˈshər-ˌbrùk\ city Quebec, Canada E of Montreal

Sher·wood Forest \ˌshər-ˌwùd-\ ancient royal forest central England chiefly in Nottinghamshire

Shet·land \ˈshet-lənd\ 1 islands N Scotland NE of the Orkneys 2 *or* Zet·land \ˈzet-\ region consisting of the Shetland islands

Shi·jia·zhuang *or* Shih·kia·chwang \ˈshi(ə)r-jē-ˈäj-ˈwäŋ, ˈshē-jē-\ city NE China

Shi·ko·ku \shi-ˈkō-kü\ island S Japan E of Kyushu

Shreve·port \ˈshrēv-ˌpō(ə)rt, -ˌpò(ə)rt\ city NW Louisiana

Shrews·bury \ˈsh(r)üz-ˌber-ē, ˈshròz-\ city area W England in Shropshire county

Shrop·shire \ˈshräp-shər, -ˌshir\ *or 1974–80* Sal·op \ˈsa-ləp, -ˌläp\ county W England bordering on Wales

Siam — see THAILAND

Siam, Gulf of — see THAILAND, GULF OF

Sian — see XI'AN

Si·be·ria \sī-ˈbir-ē-ə\ region N Asia in Russia between the Urals & the Pacific — Si·be·ri·an \-ē-ən\ *adj or n*

Sic·i·ly \ˈsis-(ə-)lē\ *or Italian* Si·ci·lia \sē-ˈchēl-yä\ island S Italy SW of toe of Italian peninsula; capital, Palermo — Si·cil·ian \sə-ˈsil-yən\ *adj or n*

Si·er·ra Le·one \sē-ˌer-ə-lē-ˈōn, ˌsir-ə-\ country W Africa on the Atlantic; capital, Freetown — Si·er·ra Le·on·ean \-ˈō-nē-ən\ *adj or n*

Si·er·ra Ma·dre \sē-ˌer-ə-ˈmäd-rē\ mountain system Mexico including Sierra Madre Oc·ci·den·tal \-ˌäk-sə-ˌden-ˈtäl\ range W of the central plateau, Sierra Madre Ori·en·tal \-ˌòr-ē-ˌen-ˈtäl, -ˌòr-\ range E of the plateau, & Sierra del Sur \sē-ˌer-ə-ˌdel-ˈsü(ə)r\ range to the S

Sierra Ne·va·da \-nə-ˈvad-ə, -ˈväd-\ 1 mountain range E California & W Nevada — see WHITNEY, MOUNT 2 mountain range S Spain; highest peak Mulhacén 3477 meters, highest in Spain

Sik·kim \'sik-əm, -,im\ former country SE Asia on S slope of the Himalayas between Nepal & Bhutan; part of India (country) since 1975; capital, Gangtok

Si·le·sia \sī-'lē-zh(ē-)ə, -sh(ē-)ə, sə-\ region E central Europe in valley of the upper Oder; formerly chiefly in Germany now chiefly in E Czech Republic & SW Poland — **Si·le·sian** \-zh(ē-)ən, -sh(ē-)ən\ *adj or n*

Sim·coe, Lake \-'sim-kō\ lake Canada in SE Ontario

Si·nai \'sī-,nī\ 1 mountain on Sinai peninsula where according to the Bible the Law was given to Moses 2 peninsula extension of continent of Asia NE Egypt between Red sea & the Mediterranean

Sin·ga·pore \'siŋ-(g)ə-,pō(ə)r, -,pô(ə)r\ 1 island off S end of Malay peninsula; an independent country in the Commonwealth 2 city, its capital — **Sin·ga·por·ean** \,siŋ-(g)ə-'pōr-ē-ən, -'pôr-\ *adj or n*

Sinkiang Uighur — see XINJIANG UYGUR

Sioux Falls \'sü-\ city SE South Dakota; largest in state

Skag·er·rak \'skag-ə-,rak\ arm of North sea between S Norway & N Denmark

Skag·way \'skag-wā\ city SE Alaska

Sla·vo·nia \slə-'vō-nē-ə, -nyə\ region E Croatia — **Sla·vo·ni·an** \-nē-ən, -nyən\ *adj or n*

Slo·va·kia \slō-'väk-ē-ə, -'vak-\ country central Europe; capital, Bratislava; formerly part of Czechoslovakia

Slo·ve·nia \slō-'vē-nē-ə, -nyə\ country S Europe; capital, Ljubljana; a republic of Yugoslavia 1946–91

Smyrna — see IZMIR

Snake \'snāk\ river NW U.S. flowing from NW Wyoming into the Columbia in SE Washington

Snow·don \'snōd-ən\ massif 1085 meters NW Wales; highest point in Wales

Snow·do·nia \snō-'dō-nē-ə, -nyə\ mountainous district NW Wales in area around Snowdon

So·ci·e·ty \sə-'sī-ət-ē\ islands S Pacific; belong to France; chief island, Tahiti

So·fia \'sō-fē-ə, 'sò-, sō-'fē-\ city, capital of Bulgaria

So·ho \'sō-,hō\ district of central London, England, in Westminster

So·li·hull \,sō-li-'həl\ city area central England in West Midlands county

Sol·o·mon \'säl-ə-mən\ 1 islands W Pacific E of New Guinea divided between Papua New Guinea & independent Solomon Islands (capital, Honiara) 2 sea arm of Coral sea W of the Solomons

So·ma·lia \sō-'mäl-ē-ə, sə-, 'mäl-yə\ country E Africa on Gulf of Aden & Indian ocean; capital, Mogadishu — **So·ma·li·an** \-'mäl-ē-ən, -'mäl-yən\ *adj or n*

So·ma·li·land \sō-'mäl-ē-,land, sə-\ region E Africa consisting of Somalia, Djibouti, & part of E Ethiopia — **So·ma·li** \sō-'mäl-ē\ *n*

Som·er·set \'səm-ər-,set, -sət\ *or* **Som·er·set·shire** \-,shi(ə)r, -,shər\ county SW England

So·nor·an \sə-'nōr-ən, -'nòr-\ *or* **Sonora** desert SW U.S. & NW Mexico

Soo canals — see SAULT SAINTE MARIE CANALS

South island S New Zealand

South Africa, Republic of country S Africa; formerly (as **Union of South Africa**) a British dominion; became independent 1961; administrative capital, Pretoria; legislative capital, Cape Town; judicial capital, Bloemfontein — **South African** *adj or n*

South America continent of western hemisphere SE of North America & chiefly S of the equator — **South American** *adj or n*

South·amp·ton \saùth-'(h)am(p)-tən\ city S England in Hampshire

South Australia state S Australia; capital, Adelaide — **South Australian** *adj or n*

South Bend \-'bend\ city N Indiana

South Cape *or* **South Point** — see KA LAE

South Car·o·li·na \-,kar-ə-'lī-nə\ state SE U.S.; capital, Columbia — **South Car·o·lin·i·an** \-'lin-ē-ən, -'lin-yən\ *adj or n*

South China sea — see CHINA

South Da·ko·ta \-də-'kōt-ə\ state NW central U.S.; capital, Pierre — **South Da·ko·tan** \-'kōt-ən\ *adj or n*

South·end on Sea \,saù-'thend-\ city area SE England in Essex county E of London

Southern Alps mountain range New Zealand in W South island extending almost the length of the island

Southern Rhodesia — see ZIMBABWE

South Gla·mor·gan \-glə-'mòr-gən\ county SE Wales; established 1974; includes Cardiff

South Korea — see KOREA

South seas the areas of the Atlantic, Indian, & Pacific oceans in the southern hemisphere

South Shields \-'shē(ə)l(d)z\ city N England in Tyne and Wear county

South Vietnam — see VIETNAM

South·wark \'səth-ərk, 'saùth-wərk\ city area of S Greater London county, England

South–West Africa territory SW Africa; under administration of Union (later Republic) of South Africa 1919–90 — see NAMIBIA

South Yorkshire county N England; includes Barnsley

Soviet Central Asia portion of central & SW Asia formerly belonging to U.S.S.R. & including Kirghiz Soviet Socialist Republic, Tadzhik Soviet Socialist Republic, Turkmen Soviet Socialist Republic, Uzbek Soviet Socialist Republic & sometimes Kazakhstan

Soviet Russia — see RUSSIA 2 — see UNION OF SOVIET SOCIALIST REPUBLICS

Soviet Union — see UNION OF SOVIET SOCIALIST REPUBLICS

Spain \'spān\ country SW Europe in Iberian peninsula; a kingdom; capital, Madrid

Spanish America 1 the Spanish-speaking countries of America 2 the parts of America settled & formerly governed by the Spanish

Spanish Guinea — see EQUATORIAL GUINEA

Spanish Sahara — see WESTERN SAHARA

Spar·ta \'spärt-ə\ *or* **Lac·e·dae·mon** \,las-ə-'dē-mən\ ancient city S Greece in Peloponnisos; capital of Laconia

Spo·kane \spō-'kan\ city E Washington

Spring·field \'spriŋ-,fēld\ 1 city, capital of Illinois 2 city SW Massachusetts 3 city SW Missouri

Sri Lan·ka \(')srē-'läŋ-kə, (')shrē-\ *or formerly* **Cey·lon** \si-'län, sā-\ country having the same boundaries as island of Ceylon; an independent state in the Commonwealth; capital, Colombo

Sri·na·gar \sri-'nəg-ər\ city N India

Staked Plain — see LLANO ESTACADO

Staf·ford \'staf-ərd\ city area W central England in Staffordshire

Staf·ford·shire \'staf-ərd-,shi(ə)r, -shər\ *or* **Stafford** county W central England

Stam·ford \'stam(p)-fərd\ city SW Connecticut

Stan·ley \'stan-lē\ town, capital of Falkland islands

Stat·en Island \'stat-ən-\ 1 island SE New York SW of mouth of the Hudson 2 *or formerly* **Rich·mond** \'rich-mənd\ section of New York City including Staten Island

Sterling Heights city SE Michigan

Stir·ling \'stər-liŋ\ town central Scotland in Central region

Stock·holm \'stäk-,hō(l)m\ city, capital of Sweden

Stock·port \'stäk-,pō(ə)rt, -,pò(ə)rt\ city area NW England in Greater Manchester county

Stock·ton \'stäk-tən\ city central California

Stoke on Trent \,stō-,kòn-'trent, -,kän-\ city central England in Staffordshire

Stone Mountain mountain 514 meters NW Georgia E of Atlanta

Stor·no·way \'stòr-nə-,wä\ town NW Scotland in Western Isles region

Stra·bane \strə-ˈban\ district W Northern Ireland

Strath·clyde \strath-ˈklīd\ region SW Scotland; established 1975; includes Glasgow

Strom·bo·li \ˈsträm-bə-lē\ volcano 927 meters Italy on Stromboli Island

Stutt·gart \ˈshtút-ˌgärt, ˈstút-, ˈstət-\ city SW Germany

Styx \ˈstiks\ chief river of the underworld in Greek mythology

Süchow — see XUZHOU

Su·cre \ˈsü-krä\ city, constitutional capital of Bolivia

Su·dan \sü-ˈdan, -ˈdän\ **1** region N Africa S of the Sahara between the Atlantic & the upper Nile **2** country NE Africa S of Egypt; capital, Khartoum — **Su·da·nese** \ˌsüd-ᵊn-ˈēz, -ˈēs\ adj or n

Sud·bury \ˈsəd-ˌber-ē, -b(ə-)rē\ city SE Ontario, Canada

Su·ez \sü-ˈez, ˈsü-ˌez\ canal 163 kilometers long NE Egypt across Isthmus of Suez

Suez, Gulf of arm of Red sea

Suez, Isthmus of isthmus NE Egypt between Mediterranean & Red seas connecting Africa & Asia

Suf·folk \ˈsəf-ək\ county E England on North sea

Sui·sun Bay \sə-ˈsün-\ inlet of San Francisco Bay, W central California

Su·la·we·si \ˌsü-lə-ˈwä-sē\ or **Ce·le·bes** \ˈsel-ə-ˌbēz, sə-ˈlē-bēz\ island Indonesia E of Borneo

Su·lu \ˈsü-lü\ **1** island group SW Philippines SW of Mindanao **2** sea W Philippines

Su·ma·tra \sü-ˈmä-trə\ island W Indonesia S of Malay peninsula — **Su·ma·tran** \-trən\ adj or n

Su·mer \ˈsü-mər\ the S division of ancient Babylonia — **Su·me·ri·an** \sü-ˈmer-ē-ən, -ˈmir-\ adj or n

Sun·da \ˈsən-də\ strait between Java & Sumatra

Sun·der·land \ˈsən-dər-lənd\ city area N England in Tyne and Wear county

Sun·ny·vale \ˈsən-ē-ˌvāl\ city W California

Sun Valley resort center central Idaho

Su·pe·ri·or, Lake \-sú-ˈpir-ē-ər\ lake E central North America in U.S. & Canada; largest of the Great Lakes

Su·ra·ba·ja \ˌsúr-ə-ˈbī-ə\ city Indonesia in NE Java

Su·ri·na·me \ˌsúr-ə-ˈnäm-ə\ or **Su·ri·nam** \ˈsúr-ə-ˌnam, ˌsúr-ə-ˈnäm\ country N South America between Guyana & French Guiana; formerly a territory of the Netherlands; became independent 1975; capital, Paramaribo

Sur·rey \ˈsər-ē, ˈsə-rē\ **1** county SE England SW of London **2** city Canada in SW British Columbia

Sut·ton \ˈsət-ᵊn\ city area of S Greater London county, England

Su·va \ˈsü-və\ city, capital of Fiji on Viti Levu island

Sverdlovsk — se YEKATERINBURG

Swan·sea \ˈswän-zē\ city SE Wales in West Glamorgan county

Swa·zi·land \ˈswäz-ē-ˌland\ country SE Africa between Mpumalanga & Mozambique; an independent kingdom; capital, Mbabane — **Swa·zi** \ˈswäz-ē\ adj or n

Swe·den \ˈswēd-ᵊn\ country N Europe on Scandinavian peninsula bordering on Baltic sea; a kingdom; capital, Stockholm

Swit·zer·land \ˈswit-sər-lənd\ country W Europe in the Alps; capital, Bern

Syd·ney \ˈsid-nē\ city SE Australia, capital of New South Wales

Syr·a·cuse \ˈsir-ə-ˌkyüs, -kyüz\ city central New York

Syr·ia \ˈsir-ē-ə\ **1** ancient region SW Asia bordering on the Mediterranean **2** former area under administration of France (1920–44) including present Syria & Lebanon **3** country S of Turkey; capital, Damascus — **Syr·i·an** \ˈsir-ē-ən\ adj or n

Syrian Desert desert region between Mediterranean coast & the Euphrates in N Saudi Arabia, SE Syria, W Iraq, & NE Jordan

Ta·ble Bay harbor of Cape Town, Republic of South Africa

Ta·briz \tə-ˈbrēz\ city NW Iran

Ta·co·ma \tə-ˈkō-mə\ city W Washington

Tae·gu \ta-ˈgü, tī-\ city South Korea NNW of Pusan

Tae·jon \ta-ˈjön, tī-\ city South Korea NW of Taegu

Ta·gus \ˈtā-gəs\ or Spanish **Ta·jo** \ˈtä-hō\ or Portuguese **Te·jo** \ˈtä-zhü\ river 1007 kilometers long Spain & Portugal flowing W into the Atlantic

Ta·hi·ti \tə-ˈhēt-ē\ island S Pacific in Society islands — **Ta·hi·tian** \-ˈhē-shən\ adj or n

Tai·chung \ˈtī-ˈchúŋ\ city China in W Taiwan

Tai·nan \ˈtī-ˈnän\ city China in SW Taiwan

Tai·pei \ˈtī-ˈpā, -ˈbā\ or formerly **Tai·ho·ku** \ˈtī-ˈhō-ˌkü\ city, capital of (Nationalist) China in N Taiwan

Tai·wan \ˈtī-ˈwän\ or **For·mo·sa** \fȯr-ˈmō-sə, fər-, -zə\ **1** island China off SE coast; since 1949 seat of government of (Nationalist) Republic of China; capital, Taipei **2** strait between Taiwan & main part of China connecting East China & South China seas — **Tai·wan·ese** \ˌtī-wə-ˈnēz, -ˈnēs\ adj or n

Tai·yuan \ˈtī-yü-ˈän\ city N China

Ta·jik·i·stan \tä-ˌjik-i-ˈstan, -ˈstän, -ˈjik-i-ˌ, -ˈjēk-\ country W central Asia bordering on China & Afghanistan; capital, Dushanbe; a republic (**Ta·dzhik Soviet Socialist Republic** \tä-ˈjik-, -ˈjēk-\ or **Ta·dzhik·i·stan** \same as TAJIKISTAN\) of U.S.S.R. 1929–91

Ta·kli·ma·kan or **Ta·kla Ma·kan** \ˌtäk-lə-mə-ˈkän\ desert W China

Ta–lien — see DALIAN

Tal·la·has·see \ˌtal-ə-ˈhas-ē\ city, capital of Florida

Tal·linn \ˈtal-ən, ˈtäl-\ city, capital of Estonia

Tam·pa \ˈtam-pə\ city W Florida on Tampa Bay

Tan·gan·yi·ka \ˌtan-gən-ˈyē-kə, ˌtaŋ-gən-, -gə-ˈnē-\ former country E Africa S of Kenya; became part of Tanzania 1964

Tanganyika, Lake lake E Africa between Tanzania & Democratic Republic of the Congo

Tang·shan \ˈdäŋ-ˈshän, ˈtaŋ-\ city NE China

Tan·za·nia \ˌtan-zə-ˈnē-ə, ˌtän-\ country E Africa on Indian ocean; formed 1964 by union of Tanganyika & Zanzibar; capital, Dodoma; seat of government, Dar es Salaam — **Tan·za·ni·an** \-ˈnē-ən\ adj or n

Ta·ra·wa \tə-ˈrä-wə, ˈtar-ə-wə\ island central Pacific, capital of Kiribati

Tar·lac \ˈtär-ˌläk\ city Philippines in central Luzon

Tar·ry·town \ˈtar-ē-ˌtaún\ village SE New York

Tar·sus \ˈtär-səs\ ancient city of S Asia Minor; now a city in S Turkey

Tash·kent \tash-ˈkent\ city, capital of Uzbekistan

Tas·man \ˈtaz-mən\ sea consisting of the part of the S Pacific between SE Australia & New Zealand

Tas·ma·nia \taz-ˈmä-nē-ə, -nyə\ or earlier **Van Diemen's Land** \van-ˈdē-mənz-\ island SE Australia S of Victoria; a state; capital, Hobart — **Tas·ma·nian** \-nē-ən, -nyən\ adj or n

Ta·try \ˈtä-trē\ or **Ta·tra** \ˈtä-trə\ mountains N Slovakia & S Poland in central Carpathian mountains

Taun·ton \ˈtȯnt-ᵊn, ˈtänt-, ˈtant-\ city area SW England in Somerset county

Tay·side \ˈtä-ˌsīd\ region E central Scotland; established 1975

Tbi·li·si \tə-ˈbil-ə-sē\ or **Tif·lis** \ˈtif-ləs, tə-ˈflēs\ city, capital of Republic of Georgia

Te·gu·ci·gal·pa \tə-ˌgü-sə-ˈgal-pə\ city, capital of Honduras

Teh·ran \ˌtā-ˈran, -ˈrän\ city, capital of Iran; at foot of S slope of Elburz mountains

Tel Aviv \ˌtel-ə-ˈvēv\ city W Israel

Tem·pe \ˈtem-ˌpē\ city S central Arizona

Ten·nes·see \ˌten-ə-ˈsē, ˈten-ə-ˌsē\ **1** river 1049 kilometers long in Tennessee, N Alabama, & W Kentucky **2** state E central U.S.; capital, Nashville

Te·noch·ti·tlan \tä-ˌnȯch-tē-ˈtlän\ ancient name of Mexico City

Tex·as \'tek-səs, -siz\ state S U.S.; capital, Austin — **Tex·an** \-sən\ *adj or n*

Thai·land \'tī-₁land, -lənd\ *or formerly* **Si·am** \sī-'am\ country SE Asia on Gulf of Thailand; capital, Bangkok — **Thai·land·er** \'tī-₁lan-dər, -lən-dər\ *n*

Thailand, Gulf of *or formerly* **Gulf of Siam** arm of South China sea between Indochina and Malay peninsula

Thames \'temz\ river 338 kilometers long S England flowing E from the Cotswolds in Gloucestershire into the North sea

Thar \'tär\ desert E Pakistan & NW India (country) E of Indus river

Thebes \'thēbz\ **1** *or ancient* **The·bae** \'thē-bē\ ancient city S Egypt on the Nile **2** ancient city E Greece NNW of Athens on site of modern village of Thivai — **The·ban** \'thē-bən\ *adj or n*

Thes·sa·lo·ni·ca \₁thes-ə-lə-'nī-kə, -'län-i-kə\ — see SALONIKA — **Thes·sa·lo·nian** \-'lō-nē-ən, -'lō-nyən\ *adj or n*

Thim·phu \thim-'bü\ city, capital of Bhutan

Thousand islands Canada & U.S. in the Saint Lawrence in Ontario & New York

Thrace \'thrās\ *or ancient* **Thra·cia** \'thrā-sh(ē-)ə\ region SE Europe in Balkan peninsula N of the Aegean now divided between Greece & Turkey; in ancient times extended N to the Danube — **Thra·cian** \'thrā-shən\ *adj or n*

Three Rivers *or* **Trois–Ri·vières** \₁t(r)wä-riv-'ye(ə)r\ city S Quebec, Canada

Thunder Bay city SW Ontario, Canada

Thur·rock \'thər-ək, 'thə-rək\ district SE England in Essex county

Tian·jin \tē-'än-'jin\ *or* **Tien·tsin** \tē-'en(t)-'sin\ city NE China SE of Beijing

Tian Shan *or* **Tien Shan** \tē-'en-'shän, tē-'än-\ mountain system central Asia extending NE from Pamirs

Ti·ber \'tī-bər\ *or Italian* **Te·ve·re** \'tä-vä-rä\ *or ancient* **Ti·ber·is** \'tī-bə-rəs\ river 405 kilometers long central Italy flowing through Rome into Tyrrhenian sea

Ti·bes·ti \tə-'bes-tē\ mountains N central Africa in central Sahara in NW Chad; highest 3415 meters

Ti·bet \tə-'bet\ region SW China on high plateau (average altitude 4875 meters) N of the Himalayas; capital, Lhasa

Tier·ra del Fue·go \tē-'er-ə-₁del-f(y)ù-'ā-gō\ **1** island group off S South America **2** chief island of the group; divided between Argentina & Chile

Tiflis — see TBILISI

Ti·gris \'tī-grəs\ river 1899 kilometers long Turkey & Iraq flowing SSE & uniting with the Euphrates to form the Shatt-al-Arab

Ti·mor \'tē-₁mò(ə)r, tē-'mò(ə)r\ island Indonesia SE of Sulawesi; W half formerly belonged to Netherlands, E half to Portugal

Ti·ra·ne *or* **Ti·ra·na** \ti-'rän-ə\ city, capital of Albania

Ti·rol *or* **Ty·rol** \tə-'rōl; 'tī-₁rōl, tī-'rōl\ *or Italian* **Ti·ro·lo** \tē-'rò-lō\ region in E Alps in W Austria & NE Italy — **Ti·ro·le·an** \tə-'rō-lē-ən, tī-; ₁tir-ə-'lē-,

₁tī-rə-'lē-\ *or* **Tir·o·lese** \₁tir-ə-'lēz, ₁tī-rə-, -'lēs\ *adj or n*

Ti·ti·ca·ca, Lake \-₁tit-i-'käk-ə\ lake on Bolivia-Peru boundary at altitude of 3810 meters

To·ba·go \tə-'bä-gō\ island West Indies NE of Trinidad; part of independent Trinidad and Tobago

To·go \'tō-gō\ country W Africa on Gulf of Guinea; capital, Lomé — **To·go·lese** \₁tō-gə-'lēz, -'lēs\ *adj or n*

To·kyo \'tō-kē-₁ō\ city, capital of Japan in SE Honshu on Tokyo Bay — **To·kyo·ite** \'tō-kē-(₁)ō-₁īt\ *n*

To·le·do \tə-'lēd-ō, -'lēd-ə\ city NW Ohio

Tol'·yat·ti \tòl-'yät-ē\ city W Russia; NW of Samara

Ton·ga \'täŋ-(g)ə\ islands SW Pacific E of Fiji islands; a kingdom in the Commonwealth; capital, Nukualofa — **Ton·gan** \-(g)ən\ *adj or n*

To·pe·ka \tə-'pē-kə\ city, capital of Kansas

Tor·bay \(')tòr-'bā\ town SW England in Devon county

To·ron·to \tə-'ränt-ō, -'ränt-ə\ city, capital of Ontario, Canada

Tor·rance \'tòr-ən(t)s, 'tär-\ city SW California

Tor·res \'tòr-əs\ strait between New Guinea & Cape York peninsula, Australia

Tower Hamlets city area of E Greater London county, England

To·yo·na·ka \₁tòi-ə-'näk-ə\ city Japan on Honshu; a suburb of Osaka

Trans·vaal \tran(t)s-'väl, tranz-\ former province NE Republic of South Africa; capital, Pretoria

Tran·syl·va·nia \₁tran(t)s-əl-'vā-nyə, -nē-ə\ region N Romania — **Tran·syl·va·nian** \-nyən, -nē-ən\ *adj or n*

Transylvanian Alps a S extension of Carpathian mountains in central Romania

Tren·ton \'trent-ᵊn\ city, capital of New Jersey

Trin·i·dad \'trin-ə-₁dad\ island West Indies off NE coast of Venezuela; with Tobago forms (since 1962) the independent country of **Trinidad and Tobago**; capital, Port of Spain — **Trin·i·da·di·an** \₁trin-ə-'däd-ē-ən, -'dad-\ *adj or n*

Trip·o·li \'trip-ə-lē\ city, capital of Libya

Tris·tan da Cu·nha \₁tris-tən-də-'kü-nə, -nyə\ island S Atlantic, chief of the Tristan da Cunha islands belonging to British colony of Saint Helena

Tri·van·drum \triv-'an-drəm\ city S India

Tro·bri·and \'trō-brē-₁änd\ islands SW Pacific in Solomon sea belonging to Papua New Guinea

Trois–Rivières — see THREE RIVERS

Trow·bridge \'trō-(₁)brij\ town S England in Wiltshire

Troy \'tròi\ *or* **Il·i·um** \'il-ē-əm\ *or* **Il·i·on** \'il-ē-₁än, -ən\ *or ancient* **Troia** \'tròi-ə, 'trō-yə\ *or* **Tro·ja** \'trō-jə, -yə\ ancient city NW Asia Minor SW of the Dardanelles

Truk \'trək, 'trùk\ islands W Pacific in central Carolines

Tru·ro \'trü(ə)r-ō\ city SW England in Cornwall and Isles of Scilly county

Trust Territory of the Pacific Islands — see PACIFIC ISLANDS, TRUST TERRITORY OF THE

Tsinan — see JINAN

Tsingtao — see QINGDAO

Tuc·son \tü-'sän, 'tü-ˌsän\ city SE Arizona

Tu·la \'tü-lə\ city W Russia S of Moscow

Tul·sa \'təl-sə\ city NE Oklahoma

Tu·nis \'t(y)ü-nəs\ city, capital of Tunisia

Tu·ni·sia \t(y)ü-'nē-zh(ē-)ə, -'nizh-(ē-)ə\ country N Africa on the Mediterranean E of Algeria; capital, Tunis — **Tu·ni·sian** \-'nē-zh(ē-)ən, -'nizh-(ē-)ən\ adj or n

Tu·rin \'t(y)ür-ən, t(y)ù-'rin\ city NW Italy on the Po

Tur·key \'tər-kē\ country W Asia & SE Europe between Mediterranean & Black seas; capital, Ankara

Turk·men·i·stan \(ˌ)tərk-ˌmen-ə-'stan, -'stän; -'men-ə-ˌ\ country central Asia; capital, Ashkhabad; a republic (**Turk·men Soviet Socialist Republic** \'tərk-mən-\) of U.S.S.R. 1925–91 — **Turk·me·ni·an** \ˌtərk-'mē-nē-ən\ adj

Turks and Cai·cos \ˌtərk-sən-'kā-kəs\ two groups of islands West Indies at SE end of the Bahamas; a British colony

Tu·tu·ila \ˌtüt-ə-'wē-lə\ island S Pacific, chief of American Samoa group

Tu·va·lu \tü-'väl-ü, -'vär-\ or formerly **El·lice** \'el-əs\ islands W Pacific N of Fiji; an independent country in the Commonwealth; capital, Funafuti — see GILBERT AND ELLICE ISLANDS

Tyne and Wear \'tī-nən-'(d)wi(ə)r\ county N England; includes Newcastle

Tyre \'tī(ə)r\ ancient city, capital of Phoenicia; now a town of S Lebanon — **Tyr·i·an** \'tir-ē-ən\ adj or n

Tyrol — see TIROL — **Tyrolean** adj or n — **Tyrolese** adj or n

Tyr·rhe·ni·an \tə-'rē-nē-ən\ sea, part of the Mediterranean SW of Italy, N of Sicily, & E of Sardinia & Corsica

Ufa \ü-'fä\ city W Russia NE of Samara

Ugan·da \yü-'gan-də, -'gän-, -'gän-\ country E Africa N of Lake Victoria; an independent state in the Commonwealth; capital, Kampala — **Ugan·dan** \-dən\ adj or n

Ukraine \yü-'krān, 'yü-ˌkrān\ or the **Ukraine** country E Europe on N coast of Black sea; capital, Kiev; a republic of U.S.S.R. 1923–91

Ulan Ba·tor \ˌü-ˌlän-'bä-ˌtò(ə)r\ city, capital of Mongolia

Ul·ster \'əl-stər\ 1 region N Ireland (island) consisting of Northern Ireland & N Ireland (country) 2 province N Ireland (country) 3 NORTHERN IRELAND

Um·bria \'əm-brē-ə\ region central Italy in the Apennines

Un·ga·va \ˌən-'gav-ə\ 1 bay inlet of Hudson strait NE Canada 2 peninsula region NE Canada in N Quebec

Union of South Africa — see SOUTH AFRICA, REPUBLIC OF

Union of Soviet Socialist Republics or **Soviet Union** or **Soviet Russia** country 1922–91 E Europe & N Asia; a union of 15 now independent republics; capital, Moscow

United Arab Emir·ates \-i-'mi(ə)r-əts, -ˌāts\ country E Arabia on Persian Gulf; composed of seven emirates; capital, Abu Dhabi

United Kingdom or in full **United Kingdom of Great Britain and Northern Ireland** country W Europe in British Isles consisting of England, Scotland, Wales, Northern Ireland, Channel islands, & Isle of Man; capital, London

United Nations international political association; headquarters, New York City

United States of America or **United States** country North America bordering on Atlantic, Pacific, & Arctic oceans & including Hawaii; capital, Washington

Upper Volta — see BURKINA FASO — **Upper Vol·tan** \-'vält-ᵊn, -'vōlt-, -'vòlt-\ adj or n

Ural \'yùr-əl\ 1 mountains Russia & Kazakhstan; usually thought of as dividing line between Europe & Asia; highest about 1894 meters 2 river over 2400 kilometers long Russia & Kazakhstan flowing from S end of Ural mountains into Caspian sea

Uru·guay \'(y)ùr-ə-ˌgwī, 'yùr-ə-ˌgwä\ 1 river about 1600 kilometers long SE South America 2 country SE South America; capital, Montevideo — **Uru·guay·an** \ˌ(y)ùr-ə-'gwī-ən, ˌyùr-ə-'gwä-\ adj or n

Ürüm·qi \'ǖ-'rǖm-'chē\ or **Urum·chi** \ù-'rùm-chē, ˌùr-əm-'chē\ city NW China

Us·pa·lla·ta \ˌü-spə-'yät-ə, -'zhät-\ mountain pass 3840 meters S South America in the Andes between Argentina & Chile

Ustinov — see IZHEVSK

Utah \'yü-ˌtò, -ˌtä\ state W U.S.; capital, Salt Lake City — **Utah·an** \-ˌtò(-ə)n, -ˌtä(-ə)n\ adj or n — **Utahn** \-ˌtò(-ə)n, -ˌtä(-ə)n\ n

Uz·bek·i·stan \(ˌ)ùz-ˌbek-i-'stan, -'stän; -'bek-i-ˌ\ country W central Asia between Aral sea & Afghanistan; capital, Tashkent; a republic (**Uz·bek Soviet Socialist Republic** \'ùz-ˌbek, 'əz-; ùz-'\) of U.S.S.R. 1924–91

Va·duz \vä-'düts\ town, capital of Liechtenstein

Val·dez \val-'dēz\ town and port S Alaska

Va·len·cia \və-'len-ch(ē-)ə, -'len(t)-sē-ə\ 1 region & ancient kingdom E Spain 2 city, its capital, on the Mediterranean

Valley Forge locality SE Pennsylvania

Val·let·ta \və-'let-ə\ city, capital of Malta

Van·cou·ver \van-'kü-vər\ 1 island W Canada in SW British Columbia 2 city SW British Columbia, Canada

Van Diemen's Land — see TASMANIA

Van·u·atu \ˌvan-ˌwä-'tü, ˌvän-, -'wä-ˌtü\ or formerly **New Heb·ri·des** \-'heb-rə-ˌdēz\ islands SW Pacific W of Fiji; formerly under shared British and French administration; became independent 1980; capital, Vila

Va·ra·na·si \və-'rä-nə-ˌsē\ city N India

Vat·i·can \'vat-i-kən\ independent state within Rome, Italy; created 1929 as headquarters for the Pope

Ven·e·zu·e·la \ˌven-əz(-ə)-'wä-lə, -'wē-\ country N South America; capital, Caracas — **Ven·e·zu·e·lan** \-lən\ adj or n

Ven·ice \'ven-əs\ or Italian **Ve·ne·zia** \vā-'net-sē-ə\ city N Italy on islands in Lagoon of Venice

Ve·ra·cruz \ˌver-ə-'krüz, -'krüs\ city E Mexico

Ver·mont \vər-'mänt\ state NE U.S.; capital, Montpelier — **Ver·mont·er** \-ər\ n

Ve·ro·na \və-'rō-nə\ city N Italy W of Venice

Ve·su·vi·us \və-'sü-vē-əs\ volcano about 1277 meters S Italy near Bay of Naples

Vicks·burg \'viks-ˌbərg\ city W Mississippi

Vic·to·ria \vik-'tōr-ē-ə, -'tòr-\ 1 city, capital of British Columbia, Canada on Vancouver island 2 island N Canada in Arctic island group 3 state SE Australia; capital, Melbourne 4 city, former capital of Hong Kong 5 seaport, capital of Seychelles — **Vic·to·ri·an** \-ē-ən\ adj or n

Victoria, Lake lake E Africa in Tanzania, Kenya, & Uganda

Vi·en·na \vē-'en-ə\ or ancient **Vin·dob·o·na** \vin-'däb-ə-nə\ or **Vin·dob·na** \-'däb-nə\ city, capital of Austria on the Danube — **Vi·en·nese** \ˌvē-ə-'nēz, -'nēs\ adj or n

Vien·tiane \(ˈ)vyen-'tyän\ city, capital of Laos

Viet·nam \vē-'et-'näm, vyet-, ˌvē-ət-, -'nam\ country SE Asia in Indochina; capital, Hanoi; established 1945–46 & divided 1954–75 at 17th parallel into the independent states of **North Vietnam** (capital, Hanoi) & **South Vietnam** (capital, Saigon)

Vi·la \'vē-lə\ city, capital of Vanuatu

Vil·ni·us \\'vil-nē-əs\ *or Russian* **Vil·na** \\'vil-nə\ *or* **Vil·no** \-nō\ city, capital of Lithuania

Vin·land \\'vin-lənd\ a portion of the coast of North America visited and so called by Norse voyagers about 1000 A.D.; perhaps Newfoundland

Vir·gin·ia \vər-'jin-yə, -'jin-ē-ə\ state E U.S.; capital, Richmond — **Vir·gin·ian** \-yən, -ē-ən\ *adj or n*

Virginia Beach city SE Virginia

Virginia City village W Nevada

Vir·gin Islands \ˌvər-jən-\ island group West Indies E of Puerto Rico — see BRITISH VIRGIN ISLANDS; VIRGIN ISLANDS OF THE UNITED STATES

Virgin Islands of the United States the W islands of the Virgin Islands group; capital, Charlotte Amalie (on Saint Thomas)

Vi·sa·yan \və-'sī-ən\ *or* **Bi·sa·yas** \bə-'sī-əz\ islands central Philippines

Vish·a·kha·pat·nam \vi-ˌshäk-ə-'pət-nəm\ *or* **Vis·a·kha·pat·nam** \-ˌsä-\ city E India

Vis·tu·la \\'vis(h)-chə-lə, 'vis-tə-lə\ river about 1100 kilometers long Poland flowing N from the Carpathians

Vi·ti Le·vu \ˌvēt-ē-'lev-ü\ island SW Pacific; largest of the Fiji group

Vlad·i·vos·tok \ˌvlad-ə-və-'stäk, -'väs-ˌtäk\ city & port SE Russia on Sea of Japan

Vol·ga \\'väl-gə, 'vól-, 'vōl-\ river 3689 kilometers long W Russia; longest river in Europe

Vol·go·grad \\'väl-gə-ˌgrad, 'vól-, 'vōl-\ city SW Russia, on the Volga

Vol·ta \\'väl-tə, 'vól-\ river 1600 kilometers long Ghana including Lake Volta (reservoir) and emptying into Gulf of Guinea

Vo·ro·nezh \və-'rò-nish\ city SW Russia

Vosges \\'vōzh\ mountains NE France on W side of Rhine valley; highest 1423 meters

Wa·co \\'wā-kō\ city central Texas

Wake \\'wāk\ island N Pacific N of Marshall islands; belongs to U.S.

Wake·field \\'wāk-ˌfēld\ city N England in West Yorkshire

Wa·la·chia *or* **Wal·la·chia** \wä-'lā-kē-ə\ region S Romania between Transylvanian Alps & the Danube

Wales \\'wā(ə)lz\ *or Welsh* **Cym·ru** \\'kəm-ˌrē\ principality SW Great Britain; a division of United Kingdom; capital, Cardiff

Wal·sall \\'wól-ˌsòl, -səl\ city area W central England in West Midlands county

Wal·tham Forest \ˌwòl-thəm-\ city area of NE Greater London county, England

Wands·worth \\'wän(d)z-(ˌ)wərth\ city area of SW Greater London county, England

War·ley \\'wòr-lē\ city area W central England in West Midlands county

War·ren \\'wòr-ən, 'wär-\ city SE Michigan

War·saw \\'wòr-ˌsò\ *or Polish* **War·sza·wa** \vär-'shäv-ə\ city, capital of Poland

War·wick \\'wär-ik\ city area central England in Warwickshire

War·wick·shire \\'wär-ik-ˌshi(ə)r, -shər\ *or* **Warwick**-county central England

Wa·satch \\'wò-ˌsach\ range of the Rockies SE Idaho & N central Utah; highest Mount Timpanogos 3660 meters (in Utah)

Wash·ing·ton \\'wòsh-iŋ-tən, 'wäsh-\ **1** state NW U.S.; capital, Olympia **2** city, capital of U.S.; having the same boundaries as District of Columbia — **Washing·to·nian** \ˌwòsh-iŋ-'tō-nē-ən, ˌwäsh-, -nyən\ *adj or n*

Washington, Mount mountain 1917 meters N New Hampshire; highest in White mountains

Wa·ter·bury \\'wòt-ə(r)-ˌber-ē, 'wät-\ city W central Connecticut

Wa·ver·ley \\'wā-vər-lē\ city SE Australia in E New South Wales

Wei·mar Republic \\'vī-ˌmär-\ the German republic 1919–33

Wel·land \\'wel-ənd\ canal 44 kilometers long SE Ontario connecting Lake Erie & Lake Ontario

Wel·ling·ton \\'wel-iŋ-tən\ city, capital of New Zealand

Wes·sex \\'wes-iks\ ancient kingdom S England; capital, Winchester

West Bank area Palestine W of Jordan river

West Brom·wich \-'bräm-ij, -'bräm-, -ich\ city area W central England in West Midlands county

Western Australia state W Australia; capital, Perth — **Western Australian** *adj or n*

Western Cape province SW Republic of South Africa

Western Ghats \-'gòts\ chain of low mountains SW India

Western Isles region W Scotland consisting of the Outer Hebrides; established 1975

Western Sahara *or formerly* **Spanish Sahara** region NW Africa; occupied by Morocco

Western Samoa — see SAMOA 2

West Germany the Federal Republic of Germany — see GERMANY

West Gla·mor·gan \-glə-'mòr-gən\ county S Wales; established 1974

West Indies islands lying between SE North America & N South America & consisting of the Greater Antilles, Lesser Antilles, & Bahamas — **West Indian** *adj or n*

West Irian — see IRIAN JAYA

West Midlands county W central England; includes Birmingham

West·min·ster \\'wes(t)-ˌmin(t)-stər\ *or* **City of Westminster** city area of W central Greater London county, England

West Pakistan the former W division of Pakistan now having the same boundaries as Pakistan

West·pha·lia \wes(t)-'fāl-yə, -'fā-lē-ə\ region W Germany E of the Rhine — **West·pha·lian** \-'fāl-yən, -'fā-lē-ən\ *adj or n*

West Point U.S. military post SE New York

West Quod·dy Head \-ˌkwäd-ē-\ cape; most easterly point of Maine & of the Lower 48 states

West Sus·sex \-'səs-iks\ county SE England — **West Virginian** *adj or n*

West Virginia state E U.S.; capital, Charleston — **West Virginian** *adj or n*

West York·shire \-'yòrk-ˌshi(ə)r, -shər\ county NW England; includes Wakefield

White mountains N New Hampshire in the Appalachians — see WASHINGTON, MOUNT

White·horse \\'hwit-ˌhò(ə)rs, 'wīt-\ city, capital of Yukon Territory, Canada

White sea sea inlet NW Russia

Whit·ney, Mount \-'hwit-nē, -'wit-\ mountain 4418 meters SE central California in Sierra Nevada; highest in U.S. outside of Alaska

Wich·i·ta \\'wich-ə-ˌtò\ city S Kansas

Wight, Isle of \-'wīt\ — see ISLE OF WIGHT

Wil·lem·stad \\'vil-əm-ˌstät\ city, capital of Netherlands Antilles

Wil·liams·burg \\'wil-yəmz-ˌbərg\ city SE Virginia

Wil·ming·ton \\'wil-miŋ-tən\ city N Delaware; largest in state

Wilt·shire \\'wilt-ˌshi(ə)r, 'wil-chər, 'wilt-shər\ county S England

Win·ches·ter \\'win-ˌches-tər, -chə-stər\ city area S England in Hampshire

Win·der·mere \\'win-də(r)-ˌmi(ə)r\ lake NW England in Lake District

Wind·hoek \\'vint-ˌhùk\ city, capital of Namibia

Wind·sor \\'win-zər\ city S Ontario, Canada on Detroit river

Wind·ward Islands \-win-dwərd-\ islands West Indies in the S Lesser Antilles extending S from Martinique but not including Barbados, Tobago, or Trinidad

Win·ni·peg \\'win-ə-ˌpeg\ city, capital of Manitoba, Canada

Winnipeg, Lake lake S central Manitoba, Canada

Win·ni·pe·sau·kee, Lake \-ˌwin-ə-pə-ˈsȯ-kē\ lake central New Hampshire

Win·ston–Sa·lem \ˌwin(t)-stən-ˈsā-ləm\ city N central North Carolina

Wis·con·sin \wis-ˈkän(t)-sən\ state N central U.S.; capital, Madison — **Wis·con·sin·ite** \-sə-ˌnīt\ *n*

Wit·wa·ters·rand \ˈwit-ˌwȯt-ərz-ˌrand, -ˌwät-, -ˌränd, -ˌränt\ *or* **Rand** \ˈrand, ˈränd, ˈränt\ ridge of gold-bearing rock NE Republic of South Africa in North West and Gauteng provinces

Wol·lon·gong \ˈwul-ən-ˌgäŋ, -ˌgȯŋ\ city SE Australia in E New South Wales S of Sydney

Wol·ver·hamp·ton \ˈwul-vər-ˌham(p)-tən\ city area W central England in West Midlands county NW of Birmingham

Worces·ter \ˈwus-tər\ **1** city E central Massachusetts **2** city W central England in Hereford and Worcester county

Wran·gell, Mount \ˈraŋ-gəl\ volcano 4317 meters S Alaska in Wrangell range

Wro·claw \ˈvrȯt-ˌsläf, -ˌsläv\ city SW Poland in Silesia

Wu·han \ˈwü-ˈhän\ city S China

Wu·sih *or* **Wu–hsi** \ˈwü-ˈshē\ city E China

Wy·o·ming \wī-ˈō-miŋ\ state NW U.S.; capital, Cheyenne — **Wy·o·ming·ite** \-miŋ-ˌīt\ *n*

Xi'·an *or* **Si·an** \ˈshē-ˈän\ city E central China

Xin·jiang Uy·gur *or* **Sin·kiang Ui·ghur** \ˈshin-jē-ˈäŋ-ˈwē-gər\ region W China

Xu·zhou \ˈshü-ˈjō\ *or* **Sü·chow** \ˈshü-ˈjō, ˈsü-; ˈsü-ˈchaü\ city E China

Yak·i·ma \ˈyak-ə-ˌmò\ city S central Washington

Ya·lu \ˈyäl-ü\ river about 800 kilometers long SE Manchuria & North Korea

Ya·mous·sou·kro \ˌyä-mü-ˈsü-krō\ town, capital of Ivory Coast

Yan·gon \ˌyän-ˈgōn\ *or formerly* **Ran·goon** \ran-ˈgün, raŋ-\ city, capital of Myanmar

Yangtze — see CHANG

Yaoun·dé \yaún-ˈdā\ city, capital of Cameroon

Yap \ˈyap, ˈyäp\ island W Pacific in the W Carolines

Ya·ro·slavl \ˌyär-ə-ˈsläv-əl\ city W Russia, NE of Moscow

Yaz·oo \ya-ˈzü, ˈyaz-ü\ river W central Mississippi

Ye·ka·te·rin·burg \yi-ˈkat-ə-rən-ˌbərg, -ˈkät-, -ˌbərk\ *or 1924–91* **Sverd·lovsk** \sverd-ˈlȯfsk\ city W Russia, in central Ural mountains

Yellow 1 — see HUANG **2** sea section of East China sea between N China, North Korea, & South Korea

Yel·low·knife \ˈyel-ə-ˌnīf\ town, capital of Northwest Territories, Canada

Ye·men \ˈyem-ən\ country S Arabia bordering on Red sea & Gulf of Aden; capital, San'a; before 1990 divided into the independent states of **Yemen Arab Republic** (capital, San'a) & **People's Democratic Republic of Yemen** (capital, Aden) — **Ye·me·ni** \ˈyem-ə-nē\ *adj or n* — **Ye·men·ite** \-ə-ˌnīt\ *n*

Yen·i·sey \ˌyen-ə-ˈsā\ river over 4100 kilometers long central Russia, flowing N into Arctic ocean

Ye·re·van \ˌyer-ə-ˈvän\ city, capital of Armenia

Yo·ko·ha·ma \ˌyō-kə-ˈhäm-ə\ city Japan in SE Honshu on Tokyo Bay S of Tokyo

Yon·kers \ˈyäŋ-kərz\ city SE New York N of New York City

York \ˈyȯ(ə)rk\ city N England in North Yorkshire

York, Cape cape NE Australia in Queensland at N tip of Cape York peninsula

York·shire \ˈyȯrk-ˌshi(ə)r, -shər\ former county N England

Yo·sem·i·te Falls \yō-ˌsem-ət-ē-\ waterfall E California in Yosemite valley; includes two falls, the upper 436 meters & the lower 98 meters

Youngs·town \ˈyəŋ-ˌstaún\ city NE Ohio

Yu·ca·tán \ˌyü-kə-ˈtan, -ˈtän\ peninsula SE Mexico & N Central America including Belize & N Guatemala

Yu·go·sla·via \ˌyü-gō-ˈsläv-ē-ə\ country S Europe including Serbia & Montenegro and formerly also the now independent Slovenia, Croatia, Bosnia and Herzegovina, & Republic of Macedonia; capital, Belgrade — **Yu·go·slav** \ˌyü-gō-ˈsläv, -ˈslav\ *or* **Yu·go·sla·vi·an** \-ˈsläv-ē-ən\ *adj or n*

Yu·kon \ˈyü-ˌkän\ **1** river 3185 kilometers long NW Canada & Alaska flowing into Bering sea **2** *or* **Yukon Territory** territory NW Canada; capital, Whitehorse

Yu·ma \ˈyü-mə\ city SW corner of Arizona on the Colorado

Za·greb \ˈzäg-ˌreb\ city, capital of Croatia

Zaire \zä-ˈi(ə)r *also* ˈzī(ə)r\ **1** river in Africa — see CONGO **1 2** country in Africa — see CONGO **2**

Zam·be·zi *or* **Zam·be·si** \zam-ˈbē-zē\ river SE Africa flowing from NW Zambia into Mozambique channel

Zam·bia \ˈzam-bē-ə\ country S Africa N of the Zambezi; formerly (as **Northern Rhodesia**) dependent on Britain; became independent 1964; capital, Lusaka

Zan·zi·bar \ˈzan-zə-ˌbär\ island Tanzania off NE Tanganyika coast; formerly a sultanate; became independent 1963; united 1964 with Tanganyika forming Tanzania

Za·po·rizh·zhya *or* **Za·po·ro·zh'ye** \ˌzäp-ə-ˈrȯ-zhə\ city SE Ukraine

Zetland — see SHETLAND

Zhang·jia·kou \ˈjäŋ-jē-ˈä-ˈkō\ *or* **Kal·gan** \ˈkal-ˈgan\ city NE China NW of Beijing

Zhdanov — see MARIUPOL

Zheng·zhou *or* **Cheng–chou** \ˈjəŋ-ˈjō\ city NE central China

Zim·ba·bwe \zim-ˈbäb-wē, -wā\ *or formerly* **Rhodesia** country S Africa S of Zambezi river; an independent state in the Commonwealth; capital, Harare

Zui·der Zee \ˌzīd-ər-ˈzä, -ˈzē\ former inlet of North sea N Netherlands — see IJSSELMEER

Zu·lu·land \ˈzü-(ˌ)lü-ˌland\ territory E Republic of South Africa in NE KwaZulu-Natal on Indian ocean

Zu·rich \ˈzú(ə)r-ik\ city N Switzerland

Signs and Symbols

Astronomy

☉ the sun; Sunday
◑, ☾, *or* ☽ the moon; Monday
● new moon
☽, ◑, ◐, ☽ first quarter
○ *or* ☺ full moon
☾, ◑, ◑, ☾ last quarter
☿ Mercury; Wednesday
♀ Venus; Friday

⊕, ⊖, *or* ♁ the earth
♂ Mars; Tuesday
♃ Jupiter; Thursday
♄ *or* ♄ Saturn; Saturday
♅, ⯑, *or* ♅ Uranus
♆, ⯓, *or* ♆ Neptune
♇ Pluto
☄ comet
✳ *or* ✶ fixed star

Business

a/c account ⟨in a/c with⟩
@ at; each ⟨4 apples @ 5¢ = 20¢⟩
/ *or* ℔ per
c/o care of
number if it precedes a numeral ⟨track #3⟩; pounds if it follows ⟨a 5# sack of sugar⟩
℔ pound; pounds

% percent
‰ per thousand
$ dollars
¢ cents
£ pounds
/ shillings
© copyrighted
® registered trademark

Mathematics

+ plus; positive ⟨a + b=c⟩—used also to indicate omitted figures or an approximation

− minus; negative

± plus or minus ⟨the square root of $4a^2$ is ± 2a⟩

× multiplied by; times ⟨6×4=24⟩—also indicated by placing a dot between the factors ⟨6·4=24⟩ or by writing the factors one after the other, often enclosed in parentheses, without explicitly indicating multiplication ⟨(4)(5)(3)=60⟩ ⟨−4abc⟩

÷ *or* : divided by ⟨24÷6=4⟩—also indicated by writing the divisor under the dividend with a line between ⟨$\frac{24}{6}$=4⟩ or by writing the divisor after the dividend with an oblique line between ⟨3/8⟩

= equals ⟨6+2=8⟩

≠ *or* ≠ is not equal to

> is greater than ⟨6>5⟩

< is less than ⟨3<4⟩

≧ *or* ≥ is greater than or equal to

≦ *or* ≤ is less than or equal to

∝ varies directly as; is proportional to

: is to; the ratio of

∴ therefore

∞ infinity

∠ angle; the angle ⟨∠ABC⟩

∟ right angle ⟨∟ABC⟩

⊥ the perpendicular; is perpendicular to ⟨AB⊥CD⟩

‖	parallel; is parallel to ⟨AB ‖ CD⟩
⊙ *or* ○	circle
⌒	arc of a circle
△	triangle
□	square
▭	rectangle
√ ̄ *or* √	root—used without a figure to indicate a square root (as in $\sqrt{4}=2$) or with an index above the sign to indicate a higher degree (as in $\sqrt[3]{3},\sqrt[3]{7}$); also denoted by a fractional index at the right of a number whose denominator expresses the degree of the root ⟨$3^{1/3}=\sqrt[3]{3}$⟩
( )	parentheses ⎫ indicate that the quantities
[ ]	brackets ⎬ enclosed by them are to be
{ }	braces ⎭ taken together
s	standard deviation of a sample taken from a population
σ	standard deviation of a population
x̄	arithmetic mean of a sample of a variable *x*
μ	arithmetic mean of a population
$μ_2$ *or* $σ^2$	variance
π	pi; the number 3.14159265 +; the ratio of the circumference of a circle to its diameter
°	degree ⟨60°⟩
′	minute; foot ⟨30′⟩—used also to distinguish between different values of the same variable or between different variables (as *a′, a″, a‴,* usually read *a* prime, *a* double prime, *a* triple prime)
″	second; inch ⟨30″⟩
$0, 1, 2, 3$, etc.	—used as exponents placed above and at the right of an expression to indicate that it is raised to a power whose degree is indicated by the figure ⟨a^0 equals 1⟩ ⟨a^1 equals *a*⟩ ⟨a^2 is the square of *a*⟩
$-1, -2, -3$, etc.	—used as exponents placed above and at the right of an expression to indicate that the reciprocal of the expression is raised to the power whose degree is indicated by the figure ⟨a^{-1} equals $1/a$⟩ ⟨a^{-2} equals $1/a^2$⟩
!	factorial ⟨$n! = n\ (n-1)(n-2) \ldots 1$⟩
n	an unspecified number esp. when an integer
⊂	is included in, is a subset of
⊃	contains as a subset
∈ *or* ϵ	is an element of
∉	is not an element of

Medicine

A̅A̅, Ā, *or* āā	of each
℞	take—used on prescriptions; prescription; treatment
☠	poison

Miscellaneous

&	and
&c	et cetera; and so forth
" *or* "	ditto marks
/	virgule; used to mean "or" (as in *and/or*), "and/or" (as in *dead/wounded*), "per" (as in *feet/second*), indicates end of a line of verse; separates the figures of a date (4/8/74)
☞	index *or* fist

<	derived from
>	whence derived
+	and

} used in linguistics

*	hypothetical, ungrammatical
†	died—used esp. in genealogies
✚	cross
☧	monogram from Greek XP signifying Christ
✡	Judaism
☥	ankh
℣	versicle
℟	response
✶	—used in Roman Catholic and Anglican service books to divide each verse of a psalm, indicating where the response begins
✠ or +	—used in some service books to indicate where the sign of the cross is to be made; also used by certain Roman Catholic and Anglican prelates as a sign of the cross preceding their signatures
LXX	Septuagint
fl or f:	relative aperture of a photographic lens
⊕	civil defense
☮	peace
卐	swastika

Reference marks

*	asterisk or star	§	section or numbered clause
†	dagger	‖	parallels
‡	double dagger	¶ or ℙ	paragraph

Stamps and stamp collecting

★ or *	unused
★★ or **	unused with original gum intact and never mounted with a stamp hinge
⊙ or ○ or 0	used
⊞	block of four or more
⊠	entire cover or card

Weather

H or Ⓗ	high pressure region	∞	haze
L or Ⓛ	low pressure region	◗	hurricane
◎	calm	⌇	tropical storm
○	clear	•	rain
◐	cloudy (partly)	⚡	rain and snow
●	cloudy (completely overcast)	⚞	frost
⤋	drifting or blowing snow	⇝	sandstorm or dust storm
𝟫	drizzle	▽	shower(s)
≡	fog	▿	shower of rain
∾	freezing rain	△	shower of hail
▲▲▲▲	cold front	△	sleet
━━	warm front	✳	snow
∿∿	stationary front	☇	thunderstorm
)(	funnel clouds	⌐	visibility reduced by smoke

A Handbook of Style

Punctuation

The English writing system uses punctuation marks to separate groups of words for meaning and emphasis; to convey an idea of the variations of pitch, volume, pauses, and intonations of speech; and to help avoid contextual ambiguity. The use of the standard English punctuation marks is discussed in the following pages; examples are provided to illustrate the general rules.

Apostrophe '

1. Indicates the possessive case of nouns and indefinite pronouns. The possessive case of almost all singular nouns may be formed by adding 's. Traditionally, however, only the apostrophe is added when the s would not be pronounced in normal speech. The possessive case of plural nouns ending in s or in an \s\ or \z\ sound is generally formed by adding an apostrophe only; the possessive of irregular plurals is formed by adding 's.

> her mother-in-law's car
>
> anyone's guess
>
> the boy's mother
>
> the boys' mothers
>
> Degas's drawings
>
> Knox's products
>
> Aristophanes' play
>
> for righteousness' sake
>
> the Stephenses' house
>
> children's laughter

2. Marks omission of letters in contracted words.

> didn't
>
> o'clock
>
> hang 'em up

3. Marks omission of digits in numbers.

> class of '83

4. Is often used to form plurals of letters, figures, punctuated abbreviations, symbols, and words referred to as words.

> Dot your *i*'s and cross your *t*'s.
>
> Two of the junior faculty have Ph.D's.
>
> She has trouble pronouncing her *the*'s.

Brackets [ ]

1. Set off interpolated editorial matter within quoted material.

He wrote, "I ain't [sic] going."

> Vaulting ambition, which o'erleaps itself
> And falls on the other [side].
> —Shakespeare

2. Function as parentheses within parentheses.

> Bowman Act (22 Stat., ch. 4, § [or sec.] 4, p. 50)

3. Set off phonetic symbols and transcriptions.

> [t] in British *duty*
>
> the word is pronounced [ˈek-sə-jənt]

Colon :

1. Introduces a clause or phrase that explains, illustrates, amplifies, or restates what has gone before.

> The sentence was poorly constructed: it lacked both unity and coherence.

2. Directs attention to an appositive.

> He had only one pleasure: eating.

3. Introduces a series.

> Three abstained: England, France, and Belgium.

4. Introduces lengthy quoted material set off from the rest of a text by indentation but not by quotation marks.

> I quote from the text of Chapter One:

5. Separates elements in page references, in bibliographical and biblical citations, and in set formulas used to express ratios and time.

> *Journal of the American Medical Association* 48:356
>
> Stendhal, *Love* (New York: Penguin, 1975)
>
> John 4:10
>
> a ratio of 3:5
>
> 8:30 a.m.

6. Separates titles and subtitles (as of books).

Battle Cry of Freedom: The Era of the Civil War

7. Follows the salutation in formal correspondence.

> Dear Sir or Madam:
>
> Ladies and Gentlemen:

8. Punctuates headings in memorandums and formal correspondence.

> TO: VIA:
>
> SUBJECT: REFERENCE:

, Comma

1. Separates main clauses joined by a coordinating conjunction (such as *and, but, or, nor*, or *for*) and sometimes short parallel clauses not joined by conjunctions.

> She knew very little about him, and he volunteered nothing.
>
> I came, I saw, I conquered.

2. Sets off an adverbial clause or a long adverbial phrase that precedes or interrupts the main clause.

> When she discovered the answer, she reported it to us.
>
> The report, after being read aloud, was put up for consideration.

3. Sets off transitional words and expressions (such as *on the contrary, on the other hand*), conjunctive adverbs (such as *consequently, furthermore, however*), and expressions that introduce an illustration or example (such as *namely, for example*).

> My partner, on the other hand, remains unconvinced.
>
> The regent's whim, however, threw the negotiations into chaos.
>
> She responded as completely as she could; that is, she answered each individual question specifically.

4. Sets off contrasting and opposing expressions within sentences.

> The cost is not $65.00, but $56.65.
>
> He changed his style, not his ethics.

5. Separates words, phrases, or clauses in series. (Many omit the comma before the conjunction introducing the last item in a series when no ambiguity results.)

> He was young, eager, and restless.
>
> It requires one to travel constantly, to have no private life, and to live on almost nothing.
>
> Be sure to pack a flashlight, a sweater and an extra pair of socks.

6. Separates coordinate adjectives modifying a noun. However, a comma is not used between two adjectives when the first modifies the combination of the second adjective and the word or phrase it modifies.

> The harsh, damp, piercing wind cut through his jacket.
>
> a low common denominator

7. Sets off parenthetical elements such as nonrestrictive clauses and phrases.

> Our guide, who wore a blue beret, was an experienced traveler.
>
> We visited Gettysburg, site of the famous battle.
>
> The book's author, Marie Jones, was an accomplished athlete.

8. Introduces a direct quotation, terminates a direct quotation that is neither a question nor an exclamation, and sets off split quotations. The comma is not used with quotations that are tightly integrated into the sentences in which they appear (e.g., as subject or predicate nominatives) or those that do not represent actual dialogue.

> Mary said, "I am leaving."
>
> "I am leaving," Mary said.
>
> "I am leaving," Mary said with determination, "even if you want me to stay."
>
> "The computer is down" was the reply she feared.
>
> The fact that he said he was about to "faint from hunger" doesn't mean he actually fainted.

9. Sets off words in direct address, absolute phrases, and mild interjections.

> You may go, John, if you wish.
>
> I fear their encounter, his temper being what it is.
>
> Ah, that's my idea of an excellent dinner.

10. Separates a tag question from the rest of the sentence.

> It's a fine day, isn't it?

11. Indicates the omission of a word or words used in a parallel construction earlier in the sentence. When the meaning of the sentence is quite clear without the comma, the comma is omitted.

> Common stocks are preferred by some investors; bonds, by others.
>
> He was in love with her and she with him.

12. Is used to avoid ambiguity that might arise from adjacent words.

> To Mary, Jane was someone special.

13. Is used to to divide digits in numbers into groups of three; however, it is generally not used in pagination, in dates, or in street numbers, and sometimes not used in numbers with four digits.

> Smithville, pop. 100,000
>
> 4,550 cars
>
> *but*
>
> page 1411 4507 Main St.
>
> 3600 rpm the year 1983

14. Punctuates an inverted name.

Morton, William A.

15. Separates a surname from a following title or degree and often from the words "Junior" and "Senior" and their abbreviations.

Sandra H. Cobb, Vice President

Jesse Ginsburg, D.D.M.

16. Sets off geographical names (such as state or country from city), elements of dates, and addresses. When just the month and the year are given in a date, the comma is usually omitted.

Shreveport, Louisiana, is the site of a large air base.

On Sunday, June 23, 1940, he was wounded.

Number 10 Downing Street, London, is a famous address.

She began her career in April 1993 at a modest salary.

17. Follows the salutation in informal correspondence, and follows the complimentary close of a letter.

Dear Mark,

Affectionately,

Very truly yours,

Dash   —

1. Usually marks an abrupt change or break in the continuity of a sentence.

When in 1960 the stockpile was sold off—indeed, dumped as surplus—natural rubber sales were hard hit.—Barry Commoner.

2. Is sometimes used in place of commas or parentheses when special emphasis is required.

The presentations—and especially the one by Ms. Dow—impressed the audience.

3. Introduces a statement that explains, summarizes, or expands on what precedes it.

Oil, steel, and wheat—these are the sinews of industrialization.

The motion was then tabled—that is, removed indefinitely from consideration.

4. Often precedes the attribution of a quotation.

My foot is on my native heath. . .

—Sir Walter Scott

5. Sets off an interrupting clause or phrase. The dash takes the place of a comma that would ordinarily set off the clause, but an exclamation point or question mark is retained.

If we don't succeed—and the critics say we won't—then the whole project is in jeopardy.

They are demanding that everything—even the marshland!—be transferred to the new trust.

Your question—it was *your* question, wasn't it, Mr. Jones?—just can't be answered.

Ellipsis (or Suspension Points)   . . .   .

1. Indicates the omission of one or more words within a quoted passage. When four dots are used, the ellipsis indicates the omission of one or more sentences within the passage or the omission of words at the end of a sentence. The first or the last of the four dots is a period.

In the little world in which children have their existence, . . . there is nothing so finely perceived and so finely felt as injustice.—Charles Dickens

Security is mostly a superstition. . . . Avoiding danger is no safer in the long run than outright exposure. . . . Life is either a daring adventure or nothing.—Helen Keller

2. Usually indicates omission of one or more lines of poetry when ellipsis is extended the length of the line.

I think that I shall never see

A poem lovely as a tree

. . . .

Poems are made by fools like me,

But only God can make a tree.

—Joyce Kilmer

3. Indicates halting speech or an unfinished sentence in dialogue.

"I'd like to. . . that is. . . if you don't mind. . . ."

Exclamation Point   !

1. Ends an emphatic phrase or sentence.

Get out of here!

Her notorious ostentation—she flew her friends to Bangkok for her birthday parties!—was feasted on by the popular press.

2. Ends an emphatic interjection.

Encore!

All of this proves—at long last!—that we were right from the start.

Hyphen   -

The hyphen is often used between parts of a compound. The styling of such words varies; when in doubt, see the entry in the dictionary at its own place or in a list of undefined words at an individual prefix. For unentered compounds, advice will be found in *Webster's Standard American Style Manual* or a comparable guide.

1. Is often used between a prefix and root, especially whenever the root is capitalized, when two identical vowels come together, or when the resulting word could be confused with another identically spelled word.

pre-Renaissance co-opted

anti-inflationary

re-cover a sofa

but

recover from an illness

2. Is used in some compounds, especially those containing prepositions.

president-elect   sister-in-law

good-for-nothing over-the-counter

falling-out   write-off

3. Is often used in compound modifiers in attributive position.

traveling in a fast-moving van

She has gray-green eyes.

a come-as-you-are party

4. Suspends the first element of a hyphenated compound or a prefix (hyphenated or not) when the second element or base word is part of a following hyphenated compound or derived form.

a six- or eight-cylinder engine

pre- and postadolescent trauma

5. Marks division of a word at the end of a line.

The ruling pas-
sion of his life

6. Is used in writing out compound numbers between 21 and 99.

thirty-four

one hundred and thirty-eight

7. Is often used between the numerator and the denominator in writing out fractions, especially when they are used as modifiers. However, fractions used as nouns are often written as open compounds, especially when either the numerator or the denominator already contains a hyphen.

a two-thirds majority of the vote

three fifths of her paycheck

one seventy-second of an inch

8. Serves as an equivalent of *through* or (*up*) *to and including* when used between indicators of range such as numbers and dates. (In typeset material the longer en dash is used.)

pages 40–98

the years 1980–89

9. Serves as the equivalent of *to, and,* or *versus* in indicating linkage or opposition. (In typeset material the longer en dash is used.)

the New York–Paris flight

the Hardy–Weinberg law

the Lincoln–Douglas Debates

The final score was 7–2.

⸗   Hyphen, Double

Is used at the end-of-line division of a hyphenated compound to indicate that the compound is hyphenated and not closed.

self⸗ [end of line] seeker

but

self- [end of line] same

( )   Parentheses

1. Enclose words, numbers, phrases, or clauses that provide examples, explanations, or supplementary material that does not essentially alter the meaning of the sentence.

Three old destroyers (all now out of commission) will be scrapped.

He has followed the fortunes of the modern renaissance (*al-Nahdad*) in the Arabic-speaking world.

2. Enclose numerals that confirm a written number in a text.

Delivery will be made in thirty (30) days.

3. Enclose numbers or letters in a series.

We must set forth (1) our long-term goals, (2) our immediate objectives, and (3) the means at our disposal.

4. Enclose abbreviations that follow their spelled-out forms or spelled-out forms that follow their abbreviations.

a ruling by the Federal Communications Commission (FCC)

the manufacture and disposal of PVC (polyvinyl chloride)

5. Indicate alternative terms.

Please indicate the lecture(s) you would like to attend.

6. Enclose publication data in footnotes and endnotes.

Marguerite Yourcenar, *The Dark Brain of Piranesi and Other Essays* (New York: Farrar, Straus and Giroux, 1985), p. 9.

7. Are used with other punctuation marks in the following ways:

If the parenthetic expression is an independent sentence standing alone, its first word is capitalized and a period is included *inside* the last parenthesis. However, if the parenthetic expression, even if it could stand alone as a sentence, occurs within a sentence, it is uncapitalized and has no sentence period but may have an exclamation point, a question mark, a period for an abbreviation, or quotation marks within the closing parenthesis.

The discussion was held in the boardroom. (The results are still confidential.)

Although we liked the restaurant (their Italian food was the best), we seldom went there.

After waiting in line for an hour (why do we do these things?), we finally left.

Years ago, someone (I wish I could remember who!) told me about it.

What was once informally known as A.B.D. status is now often recognized by the degree of Master of Philosophy (M. Phil.).

He was depressed ("I must resign") and refused to do anything.

No punctuation mark should be placed directly before parenthetical material in a sentence; if a break is required, punctuation should be placed *after* the final parenthesis.

I'll get back to you tomorrow (Friday), when I have more details.

Period   .

1. Ends sentences or sentence fragments that are neither interrogatory nor exclamatory.

Not bad.

Give it your best.

I gave it my best.

He asked if she had given it her best.

2. Follows some abbreviations and contractions.

Dr.   A.D.   ibid.   i.e.

Jr.   etc.   cont.

3. Is normally used with an individual's initials.

F. Scott Fitzgerald

T. S. Eliot

4. Is used after numerals and letters in vertical enumerations and outlines.

Required skills are:
1. Shorthand
2. Typing
3. Transcription
I. Objectives
   A. Economy
      1. low initial cost
      2. low maintenance cost
   B. Ease of operation

Question Mark   ?

1. Ends a direct question.

How did she do it?

"How did she do it?" he asked.

2. Ends a question that is part of a larger sentence, but not an indirect question.

How did she do it? was the question on each person's mind.

He wondered, Will it work?

He wondered whether it would work.

3. Indicates the writer's ignorance or uncertainty.

Geoffrey Chaucer, English poet (1342?–1400)

Quotation Marks, Double   "   "

1. Enclose direct quotations but not indirect quotations.

She said, "I am leaving."

She said that she was leaving.

2. Enclose words or phrases borrowed from others, words used in a special way, and words of marked informality when introduced into formal writing.

Much of the population in the hellish future he envisions is addicted to "derms," patches that deliver potent drug doses instantaneously through the skin.

He called himself "emperor," but he was really just a dictator.

He was arrested for smuggling "smack."

3. Enclose titles of poems, short stories, articles, lectures, chapters of books, short musical compositions, and radio and TV programs.

Robert Frost's "After Apple-Picking"

Cynthia Ozick's "Rosa"

The third chapter of *Treasure Island* is entitled "The Black Spot."

"All the Things You Are"

Debussy's "Clair de lune"

NBC's "Today Show"

4. Are used with other punctuation marks in the following ways:

The period and the comma fall *within* the quotation marks.

"I am leaving," she said.

It was unclear how she maintained such an estate on "a small annuity."

The colon and semicolon fall *outside* the quotation marks.

There was only one thing to do when he said, "I may not run": promise him a large campaign contribution.

He spoke of his "little cottage in the country"; he might better have called it a mansion.

The dash, the question mark, and the exclamation point fall *within* the quotation marks when they refer to the quoted matter only; they fall *outside* when they refer to the whole sentence.

"I can't see how—" he started to say.

He asked, "When did she leave?"

What is the meaning of "the open door"?

The sergeant shouted "Halt!"

Save us from his "mercy"!

5. Are not used with *yes* or *no* except in direct discourse.

She said yes to all our requests.

6. Are not used with lengthy quotations set off from the text.

He took the title for his biography of Thoreau from a passage in *Walden*:

I long ago lost a hound, a bay horse, and a turtledove, and am still on their trail. . . . I have met one or two who had heard the hound, and the tramp of the horse, and even seen the dove disappear behind a cloud, and they seemed as anxious to recover them as if they had lost them themselves.

However, the title *A Hound, a Bay Horse, and a Turtle-Dove* probably puzzled some readers.

' ' Quotation Marks, Single

1. Enclose a quotation within a quotation in American usage. When both single and double quotation marks occur at the end of a sentence, the period typically falls within *both* sets of marks.

The witness said, "I distinctly heard him say, 'Don't be late,' and then heard the door close."

The witness said, "I distinctly heard him say, 'Don't be late.'"

2. Are sometimes used in place of double quotation marks especially in British usage. In this case a quotation within a quotation is set off by double quotation marks.

The witness said, 'I distinctly heard him say, "Don't be late," and then heard the door close.'

Semicolon ;

1. Links independent clauses not joined by a coordinating conjunction.

Some people have the ability to write well; others do not.

2. Links clauses joined by a conjunctive adverb

(such as *consequently, furthermore, however*).

Speeding is illegal; furthermore, it is very dangerous.

3. Often occurs before expressions that introduce expansions or series (such as *for example, for instance, that is, e.g.,* or *i.e.*).

As a manager she tried to do the best job she could; that is, to keep her project on schedule and under budget.

4. Separates phrases that contain commas.

The country's resources consist of large ore deposits; lumber, waterpower, and fertile soils; and a strong, rugged people.

Send copies to our offices in Portland, Maine; Springfield, Illinois; and Savannah, Georgia.

5. Is placed outside quotation marks and parentheses.

They again demanded "complete autonomy"; the demand was again rejected.

/ Virgule (or Slash)

1. Separates alternatives.

high-heat and/or high-speed applications

. . . sit hour after hour. . . and finally year after year in a catatonic/frenzied trance rewriting the Bible —William Saroyan

2. Replaces the word *to* or *and* between related terms that are compounded.

the fiscal year 1983/1984

in the May/June issue

3. Divides run-in lines of poetry.

Say, sages, what's the charm on earth/Can turn death's dart aside?—Robert Burns

4. Divides elements in dates and divides numerators and denominators in fractions.

offer expires 5/19/94

Fifteen and 44/100 dollars

5. Often represents *per* or *to* when used with units of measure or to indicate the terms of a ratio.

9 ft/sec

risk/reward trade-off

6. Sets off phonemes of phonemic transcription.

/b/ as in *but*

Capitalization

Capitals are used for two broad purposes in English: they mark a beginning (as of a sentence) and they signal a proper noun, pronoun, or adjective. The following principles, each with examples, describe the most common uses of capital letters.

Beginnings

1. The first word of a sentence or sentence fragment is capitalized.

> The play lasted nearly three hours.
>
> How are you feeling?
>
> Bravo!

2. The first word of a sentence contained within parentheses is capitalized if it does not occur within another sentence. The first word of a parenthetical sentence within another sentence is not capitalized.

> The discussion was held in the boardroom. (The results are still confidential.)
>
> Although we liked the restaurant (their Italian food was the best), we seldom ate there.
>
> After waiting in line for an hour (why do we do these things?), we finally left.

3. The first word of a direct quotation is capitalized. However, if the quotation is interrupted in the middle of a sentence, the second part does not begin with a capital. When a quotation, whether a sentence fragment or a complete sentence, is syntactically dependent on the sentence in which it occurs, the quotation does not begin with a capital.

> The President said, "We have rejected this report entirely."
>
> "We have rejected this report entirely," the President said, "and we will not comment on it further."
>
> The President made it clear that "there is no room for compromise."

4. The first word of a sentence within a sentence is usually capitalized when it represents a direct question, a motto or aphorism, or spoken or unspoken dialogue. The first word following a colon may be either lowercased or capitalized if it introduces a complete sentence. While the former is more usual, the latter is common when the sentence is fairly lengthy and distinctly separate from the preceding clause.

> That question, as Disraeli said, is this: Is man an ape or an angel?
>
> My first thought was, How can I avoid this assignment?
>
> The advantage of this particular system is clear: it's inexpensive.
>
> The situation is critical: This company

cannot hope to recoup the fourth-quarter losses that were sustained in five operating divisions.

5. The first word of a line of poetry is traditionally capitalized; however, in much twentieth-century poetry the line beginnings are lowercased.

> The best lack all conviction, while the worst
> Are full of passionate intensity.
> —W. B. Yeats

6. The first words of run-in enumerations that form complete sentences are capitalized, as are usually the first words of vertical lists and enumerations. However, enumerations of words or phrases run in with the introductory text are generally lowercased.

> Do the following tasks at the end of the day: 1. Clear your desktop of papers. 2. Cover office machines. 3. Straighten the contents of your desk drawers, cabinets, and bookcases.
>
> This is the agenda:
> Call to order
> Roll call
> Minutes of the previous meeting
> Treasurer's report
>
> On the agenda will be (1) call to order, (2) roll call, (3) minutes of the previous meeting, (4) treasurer's report. . . .

7. The first word in an outline heading is capitalized.

> I. Editorial tasks
> II. Production responsibilities
>   A. Cost estimates
>   B. Bids

8. The first word of the salutation of a letter and the first word of a complimentary close are capitalized.

> Dear Mary,
>
> Ladies and Gentlemen:
>
> Sincerely yours,

Proper Nouns, Pronouns, and Adjectives

Capitals are used with almost all proper nouns—that is, nouns that name particular persons, places, or things (including abstract entities), distinguishing them from others of the same class—and proper adjectives—that is, adjectives that take their meaning from what is named by the proper noun. The essential distinction in the use of capitals and lowercase letters at the beginnings of words lies in this individualizing significance of capitals as against the generalizing significance of lowercase. The following subject headings are in alphabetical order.

ARMED FORCES

1. Branches and units of the armed forces are capitalized, as are easily recognized short forms of full branch and unit designations. However, the words *army, navy,* etc., are lowercased when used in their plural forms or when they are not part of an official title.

> United States Army
>
> a contract with the Army
>
> Corps of Engineers
>
> a bridge built by the Engineers
>
> allied armies

AWARDS

2. Names of awards and prizes are capitalized.

> the Nobel Prize in Chemistry
>
> Distinguished Service Cross
>
> Academy Award

DERIVATIVES OF PROPER NAMES

3. Derivatives of proper names are capitalized when used in their primary sense. However, if the derived term has taken on a specialized meaning, it is usually not capitalized.

> Roman customs
>
> Shakespearean comedies
>
> Edwardian era
>
> *but*
>
> quixotic
>
> herculean
>
> bohemian tastes

GEOGRAPHICAL REFERENCES

4. Divisions of the earth's surface and names of distinct areas, regions, places, or districts are capitalized, as are most derivative adjectives and some derivative nouns and verbs.

> The Eastern Hemisphere
>
> Midwest
>
> Tropic of Cancer
>
> Springfield, Massachusetts
>
> the Middle Eastern situation
>
> an Americanism
>
> *but*
>
> french fries
>
> a japan finish
>
> manila envelope

5. Popular names of localities are capitalized.

> the Corn Belt   the Loop

> The Big Apple   the Gold Coast
>
> the Pacific Rim

6. Words designating global, national, regional, or local political divisions are capitalized when they are essential elements of specific names. However, they are usually lowercased when they precede a proper name or stand alone. (In legal documents, these words are often capitalized regardless of position.)

> the British Empire   Washington State
>
> New York City   Ward 1
>
> *but*
>
> the fall of the empire   the state of
>   Washington
>
> the city of New York   fires in three wards

7. Generic geographical terms (such as *lake, mountain, river, valley*) are capitalized if they are part of a specific proper name.

> Hudson Bay   Long Island
>
> Niagara Falls   Crater Lake
>
> the Shenandoah Valley

8. Generic terms preceding names are usually capitalized.

> Lakes Michigan and Superior
>
> Mounts Whitney and Rainier

9. Generic terms following names are usually lowercased, as are singular or plural generic terms that are used descriptively or alone.

> the Himalaya and Andes mountains
>
> the Atlantic coast of Labrador
>
> the Hudson valley
>
> the river valley
>
> the valley

10. Compass points are capitalized when they refer to a geographical region or when they are part of a street name, but they are lowercased when they refer to simple direction.

> up North
>
> back East
>
> the Northwest
>
> West Columbus Avenue
>
> Park Avenue South
>
> *but*
>
> west of the Rockies
>
> the east coast of Florida

11. Adjectives derived from compass points and nouns designating the inhabitants of some geographical regions are capitalized. When in doubt, see the entry in the dictionary.

> a Southern accent
>
> Northerners

12. Terms designating public places are capitalized if they are part of a proper name.

> Brooklyn Bridge
>
> Lincoln Park

the St. Regis Hotel
Independence Hall
but
Wisconsin and Connecticut avenues
the Plaza and St. Regis hotels

GOVERNMENTAL AND JUDICIAL BODIES

13. Full names of legislative, deliberative, executive, and administrative bodies are capitalized, as are short forms of these names. However, nonspecific noun and adjective references to them are usually lowercased.

the U.S. House of Representatives
the House
the Federal Bureau of Investigation
but
both houses of Congress
a federal agency

14. Names of international courts, the U.S. Supreme Court, and other higher courts are capitalized. However, names of city and county courts are usually lowercased.

The International Court of Arbitration
the Supreme Court of the United States
the Supreme Court
the United States Court of Appeals for the Second Circuit
the Michigan Court of Appeals
Lawton municipal court
Newark night court

HISTORICAL PERIODS AND EVENTS

15. Names of congresses, councils, and expositions are capitalized.

the Yalta Conference
the Republican National Convention

16. Names of historical events, some historical periods, and some cultural periods and movements are capitalized. When in doubt, consult the entry in the dictionary, especially for periods.

the Boston Tea Party
Renaissance
Prohibition
the Augustan Age
the Enlightenment
but
the space age
neoclassicism

17. Numerical designations of historical time periods are capitalized when they are part of a proper name; otherwise they are lowercased.

the Third Reich
the Roaring Twenties
but
the eighteenth century
the eighties

18. Names of treaties, laws, and acts are capitalized.

Treaty of Versailles
The Clear Air Act of 1990

ORGANIZATIONS

19. Names of firms, corporations, schools, and organizations and their members are capitalized. However, common nouns occurring after the names of two or more organizations are lowercased. The word *the* at the beginning of such names is only capitalized when the full legal name is used.

Thunder's Mouth Press
University of Wisconsin
European Community
Rotary International
Kiwanians
American and United airlines

20. Words such as *group, division, department, office,* or *agency* that designate a corporate and organizational unit are capitalized only when used with its specific name.

in the Editorial Department of Merriam-Webster
but
a notice to all department heads

PEOPLE

21. Names of persons are capitalized. However, the capitalization of particles such as *de, della, der, du, l', la, ten,* and *van* varies widely, especially in names of people in English-speaking countries.

Noah Webster
W.E.B. Du Bois
Daphne du Maurier
Werner Von Braun
Anthony Van Dyck

22. Titles preceding the name of a person and epithets instead of a name are capitalized. However, titles following a name or used alone are usually lowercased.

President Roosevelt
Professor Kaiser
Queen Elizabeth
Old Hickory
the Iron Chancellor
but
Henry VIII, king of England

23. Corporate titles are capitalized when used with an individual's name; otherwise, they are lowercased.

Lisa Dominguez, Vice President
The sales manager called me.

24. Words of family relationship preceding or used in place of a person's name are capitalized; how-

ever, these words are lowercased if they are part of a noun phrase used in place of a name.

> Cousin Julia
> I know when Mother's birthday is.
> > *but*
> I know when my mother's birthday is.

25. Words designating peoples, nationalities, religious groups, tribes, races, and languages are capitalized. Other terms used to refer to groups of people are often lowercased. Designations based on color are usually lowercased.

Canadians	Iroquois
Ibo	African-American
Latin	Indo-European

> highlander (an inhabitant of a highland)
> Highlander (an inhabitant of the Highlands of Scotland)

black	white

PERSONIFICATIONS

26. Personifications are capitalized.

> She dwells with Beauty—Beauty, that must die;
> And Joy, whose hand is ever at his lips
> Bidding adieu.
> > —John Keats

> obey the commands of Nature

PRONOUNS

27. The pronoun *I* is capitalized. For pronouns referring to the Deity, see rule 29 below.

> . . . no one but I myself had yet printed any of my work.—Paul Bowles

RELIGIOUS TERMS

28. Words designating the Deity are capitalized.

> An anthropomorphic, vengeful Jehovah became a spiritual, benevolent Supreme Being.—A. R. Katz

29. Personal pronouns referring to the Deity are usually capitalized, even when they closely follow their antecedent. However, many writers never capitalize such pronouns.

> All Thy works, O Lord, shall bless Thee.
> > —*Oxford American Hymnal*

> God's in his heaven—
> All's right with the world!
> > —Robert Browning

30. Traditional designations of revered persons, such as prophets, apostles, and saints, are often capitalized.

> our Lady
> the Prophet
> the Lawgiver

31. Names of religions, creeds and confessions, denominations, and religious orders are capitalized, as is the word *Church* when used as part of a proper name.

Judaism
Apostles' Creed
the Thirty-nine Articles of the Church of England
Society of Jesus
Hunt Memorial Church
> *but*
the local Baptist church

32. Names for the Bible or parts, versions, or editions of it and names of other sacred books are capitalized but not italicized. Adjectives derived from the names of sacred books are irregularly capitalized or lowercased; when in doubt, see the entry in the dictionary.

Authorized Version	New English Bible
Old Testament	Pentateuch
Apocrypha	Gospel of Saint Mark
Talmud	Koran
biblical	Koranic

SCIENTIFIC TERMS

33. Names of planets and their satellites, asteroids, stars, constellations and groups of stars, and other unique celestial objects are capitalized. However, the words *sun, earth,* and *moon* are usually lowercased unless they occur with other astronomical names.

Venus	Ganymede
Sirius	Pleiades

> the Milky Way
> enjoying the beauty of the moon
> probes heading for the Moon and Mars

34. New Latin genus names in zoology and botany are capitalized; the second term in binomial scientific names, identifying the species, is not.

> a cabbage butterfly (*Pieris rapae*)
> a common buttercup (*Ranunculus acris*)

35. New Latin names of all groups above genus in zoology and botany (such as class or family) are capitalized; however, their derivative adjectives and nouns are not.

> Gastropoda *but* gastropod
> Mantidae *but* mantid

36. Names of geological eras, periods, epochs, and strata and names of prehistoric divisions are capitalized.

Silurian period	Pleistocene epoch
Age of Reptiles	Neolithic age

SEASONS, MONTHS, DAYS

37. Names of months, days of the week, and holidays and holy days are capitalized.

January	Ramadan
Tuesday	Thanksgiving
Yom Kippur	Easter

38. Names of seasons are not capitalized except when personified.

last spring

the sweet breath of Spring

TITLES OF PRINTED MATTER AND WORKS OF ART

39. Words in titles are capitalized, with the exception of internal conjunctions, prepositions, and articles. In some publications, prepositions of five or more letters are capitalized also.

Of Mice and Men

"The Man Who Would Be King"

"To His Coy Mistress"

Slouching Toward Bethlehem

40. Capitalization of the titles of movies, plays, paintings, sculpture, and musical compositions follow similar conventions. For more details, see the Italicization section below.

41. Major sections of books, long articles, or reports are capitalized when they are referred to within the same material.

See the Appendix for further information.

The Introduction explains the scope of this book.

discussed later in Chapter 4

42. Nouns used with numbers or letters to designate major reference headings are capitalized. Nouns designating minor elements are typically lowercased.

Volume V	Table 3
page 101	note 10

TRADEMARKS

43. Registered trademarks and service marks are capitalized.

Express Mail	Orlon
Kleenex	Walkman

VEHICLES

44. Names of ships, aircraft, and spacecraft are capitalized.

Titanic

Lindbergh's *Spirit of St. Louis*

Apollo 13

Italicization

The following are usually italicized in print and underlined in manuscript and typescript.

1. Words and passages that are to be emphasized.

This was their fatal error: there *was* no cache of supplies in the now-abandoned depot.

2. Titles of books, magazines, newspapers, plays, long poems, movies, paintings, sculpture, and long musical compositions (but not musical compositions identified by the name of their genre).

Dickens's *Bleak House*
National Geographic
Christian Science Monitor
Shakespeare's *Othello*
Eliot's *The Waste Land*
the movie *Back to the Future*
Gainsborough's *Blue Boy*
Mozart's *Don Giovanni*
but
Schubert's Sonata in B-flat Major, D. 960

NOTE: In the plurals of such italicized titles, the *s* or *es* endings are usually in roman type.

hidden under a stack of *New Yorker*s

3. Names of ships, aircraft, and spacecraft.

Titanic
Lindbergh's *Spirit of St. Louis*
Apollo 13

4. Words, letters, and figures when referred to as such.

The *g* in *align* is silent.
The first *2* and the last *0* are barely legible.

5. Unfamiliar words when first introduced and defined in a text.

Heart failure is often accompanied by *edema*, an accumulation of fluid which tends to produce swelling of the lower extremities.

6. Foreign words and phrases that have not been naturalized in English. In general, any word entered in the main A–Z vocabulary of this dictionary need not be italicized.

c'est la vie
aere perennius
che sarà, sarà
sans peur et sans reproche
but
pasta   ad hoc   ex officio

7. New Latin scientific names of genera, species, subspecies, races, and varieties (but not groups of higher rank, such as phyla, classes, or orders) in botanical or zoological names.

a thick-shelled American clam (*Mercenaria mercenaria*)
a mallard (*Anas platyrhynchos*)
but
the family Hominidae

8. Case titles in legal citations, both in full and shortened form; "v" for "versus" is set in either roman or italic.

Jones v. *Ohio*
Smith et al v. Jones
the *Jones* case
Jones

Documentation of Sources

Writers and editors use various methods to indicate the source of a quotation or piece of information borrowed from another work. In works published for the general public and traditionally in scholarly works in the humanities, footnotes or endnotes have been preferred. In this system, sequential numbers within the text refer the reader to notes at the bottom of the page or at the end of the article, chapter, or book; these notes contain full bibliographical information of the works cited. In scholarly works in the social and natural sciences, and increasingly in the humanities as well, parenthetical references within the text refer the reader to an alphabetically arranged list of sources at the end of the work. The system of footnotes or endnotes is the more flexible, in that it allows for commentary on the work or subject and can also be used for brief peripheral discussions not tied to any specific work. However, style manuals tend to encourage the use of parenthetical references in addition to or instead of footnotes or endnotes, since for most kinds of material they are efficient and convenient for both writer and reader. In a carefully documented work, a bibliography or list of sources normally follows the entire text (including any endnotes) regardless of which system is used.

Though different publishers and journals have adopted slightly varying styles, the following examples illustrate standard styles for references, notes, and bibliographic entries. For more extensive treatment than can be provided here, *Webster's Standard American Style Manual*, *The Chicago Manual of Style*, *The MLA Style Manual*, or the *Publication Manual of the American Psychological Association* may be consulted.

Footnotes and Endnotes

Footnotes and endnotes are indicated by superscript Arabic numerals placed immediately after the material to be documented. The numbering is consecutive throughout an article or monograph; in a book, it usually starts over with each new chapter or section. Footnotes appear at the bottom of the page; endnotes, which take the same form as footnotes, are gathered at the end of the article, chapter, or book. Endnotes are generally preferred over footnotes by writers and publishers because they are easier to handle when preparing both manuscript and printed pages, though they can be less convenient for the reader. All of the examples shown reflect humanities citation style. All of the cited works appear again in the Lists of Sources section below.

Books

One author

[1]Elizabeth Bishop, *The Complete Poems: 1927–1979* (New York: Farrar, Straus & Giroux, 1983), 46.

Two or more authors

[2]Bert Holldobler and Edward O. Wilson, *The Ants* (Cambridge, Mass.: Belknap–Harvard Univ. Press, 1990), 119.

[3]Randolph Quirk et al., *A Comprehensive Grammar of the English Language* (London: Longman, 1985), 135.

Edition and/or translation

[4]Arthur S. Banks, ed. *Political Handbook of the World: 1992* (Binghamton, N.Y.: CSA Publications, 1992), 293–95.

[5]Simone de Beauvoir, *The Second Sex*, trans. and ed. H.M. Parshley (New York: Knopf, 1953; Random House, 1974), 446.

Second or later edition

[6]Albert C. Baugh and Thomas Cable, *A History of the English Language*, 3d ed. (Englewood Cliffs, N.J.: Prentice Hall, 1978), 14.

Article in a collection or festschrift

[7]Ernst Mayr, "Processes of Speciation in Animals," in *Mechanisms of Speciation*, ed. C. Barigozzi (New York: Alan R. Liss, 1982), 1–3.

Work in two or more volumes

[8]Ronald M. Nowak, *Walker's Mammals of the World*, 5th ed. (Baltimore: Johns Hopkins Univ. Press, 1991), 2:661.

Corporate author

[9]Commission of the Humanities. *The Humanities in American Life* (Berkeley: Univ. of California Press, 1980), 46.

Book lacking publication data

[10]*Photographic View Album of Cambridge* [England], n.p., n.d., n.pag.

Subsequent reference

[11]Baugh and Cable, 18–19.

Articles

Journal paginated consecutively throughout annual volume

[12]Stephen Jay Gould and Niles Eldredge, "Punctuated Equilibria: The Tempo and Mode of Evolution Reconsidered," *Paleobiology* 3 (1977): 121.

Journal paginated consecutively only within each issue

[13]Roseann Duenas Gonzalez, "Teaching Mexican American Students to Write: Capitalizing on the Culture," *English Journal* 71.7 (Nov. 1982): 22–24.

Monthly magazine

[14]John Lukacs, "The End of the Twentieth Century," *Harper's*, Jan. 1993: 40.

Weekly magazine

[15]Richard Preston, "A Reporter at Large: Crisis in the Hot Zone," *New Yorker*, 26 Oct. 1992: 58.

Newspaper

[16]William J. Broad, "Big Science Squeezes Small-Scale Researchers," *New York Times*, 29 Dec. 1992: C1.

Signed review

[17]George Steiner, review of *Oeuvres en Prose Complètes, Tome 3*, by Charles Péguy, *Times Literary Supplement*, 25 Dec. 1992: 3.

Parenthetical References

Parenthetical references are highly abbreviated bibliographical citations that appear within the text itself, enclosed in parentheses. Such references direct the reader to a detailed bibliography or list of sources at the end of the work, often removing the need for footnotes or endnotes. The parenthetical references usually include only the author's last name and a page reference. (In the social and natural sciences, the year of publication is included after the author's name, and the page number is often omitted.) Any element of the reference that is clear from the context may be omitted. To distinguish among cited works published by the same author, the author's name may be followed by the specific work's title, which is usually shortened. (If the author-date system is being used, a lowercase letter can be added after the year—e.g., 1992a, 1992b—to distinguish between works published in the same year.) Each of the following references is keyed to an entry in the Lists of Sources section below.

Humanities style

(Quirk et al., 135)
(Baugh and Cable, *History*, 14)
(Commission on the Humanities, 46)

Sciences style   (Mayr 1982, 1–3)
                                  (Nowak 1991, 2:661)
                                  (Gould and Eldredge 1977)

Lists of Sources

A bibliography or list of sources in alphabetical order usually appears at the
end of the work. The following lists of cited works illustrate standard styles
employed in, respectively, the humanities and the social and natural sciences. The principal differences between the two styles are these. In the sciences, (1) an initial is generally used instead of the author's first name, (2)
the date is placed directly after the author's name, (3) all words in titles are
lowercased except the first word and the first word of any subtitle as well
as proper nouns and adjectives, and (4) article titles are not set off by quotation marks. (In some scientific publications, book and journal titles are not
italicized.)

Humanities style   Baugh, Albert C., and Thomas Cable. *A History of the English
                                  Language.* 3d ed. Englewood Cliffs, N.J.: Prentice Hall, 1978.

                                  Beauvoir, Simone de. *The Second Sex.* Trans. and ed. H. M.
                                  Parshley. New York: Alfred A. Knopf, 1953. Reprint. New York:
                                  Random House, 1974.

                                  Bishop, Elizabeth. *The Complete Poems: 1927–1979.* New York:
                                  Farrar, Straus & Giroux, 1983.

                                  Commission on the Humanities. *The Humanities in American Life.*
                                  Berkeley: University of California Press, 1980.

                                  Gonzalez, Roseann Duenas. "Teaching Mexican American Students
                                  to Write: Capitalizing on the Culture." *English Journal* 71.7
                                  (November 1982): 22–24.

                                  Lukacs, John. "The End of the Twentieth Century." *Harper's,*
                                  January 1993: 39–58.

                                  Photographic View Album of Cambridge [England]. N.d., n.p., n.
                                  pag.

                                  Quirk, Randolph, Sidney Greenbaum, Geoffrey Leech, and Jan
                                  Svartvik. *A Comprehensive Grammar of the English Language.*
                                  London: Longman, 1985.

                                  Steiner, George. Review of *Oeuvres en Prose Complètes, Tome 3,*
                                  by Charles Péguy. *Times Literary Supplement,* 25 December 1992:
                                  3–4.

Sciences style   Banks, A. S., ed. 1992. *Political handbook of the world: 1992.*
                                  Binghamton, N.Y.: CSA Publications.

                                  Broad, W. J. 1992. Big science squeezes small-scale researchers.
                                  New York Times, 29 Dec.: C1 + .

                                  Gould, S. J., and N. Eldredge. 1977. Punctuated equilibria: The tempo
                                  and mode of evolution reconsidered. *Paleobiology* 3: 115–151.

                                  Holldobler, B., and E. O. Wilson. 1990. *The ants.* Cambridge,
                                  Mass.: Belknap–Harvard Univ. Press.

                                  Mayr, E. 1982. Processes of speciation in animals. In C. Barigozzi,
                                  ed., *Mechanisms of speciation.* New York: Alan R. Liss: 1–19.

                                  Nowak, R.M. 1991. *Walker's mammals of the world.* 5th ed. 2 vols.
                                  Baltimore: Johns Hopkins Univ. Press.

                                  Preston, R. 1992. A reporter at large: Crisis in the hot zone. *New
                                  Yorker,* 26 Oct.: 58–81.

Garfield's Daffy Definitions

© PAWS

alarm clock: A device for waking people who don't have kids or pets.

Arbuckle: From the Latin *arbuculus,* "wiener-chested"; a geek; a nerd; a geeky nerd; you get the picture.

bed: Furniture piece designed for that most exciting of all activities—sleep.

bird: A feathered, flying cat snack.

brother: A common household pest; synonymous with "bother."

calories: The best-tasting bits of any food. Take thousands, they're small.

car: An automotive machine that almost any doofus is allowed to operate; but can a cat get a license? Noooooooo!

cat: A highly intelligent and attractive animal of the feline persuasion; nature's most perfect pet.

chocolate: A sweet, highly fattening substance; one of the four basic food groups.

Christmas: December holiday that promotes the spirit of getting; also has some religious significance.

claw: A cat's best friend; a drape's worst nightmare.

diet: Like "die" with a "t"; an eating program that removes excess pounds and your will to live.

dog: A brainless, four-legged flea magnet whose breath could stun a moose.

dream: A fantasy, like no-cal lasagna, or a woman who thinks Jon is cool.

eat: What one does between naps.

exercise: Any completely unnecessary physical activity, such as jogging or rolling over.

fat: Overweight; obese; Santa-waisted; in other words, just right.

french fries: Slivers of potato cooked in hot oil; best when eaten or stuck in your nose.

Halloween: Ancient Celtic celebration of the dead that has evolved quite nicely into an excuse to eat candy until you explode.

homework: Cruel and unusual punishment best suffered in front of the TV.

kitten: A small, cuddly animal used to trick people into buying cats.

lasagna: Nature's most perfect food.

lazy: Indolent, slothful; in extreme cases, comatose.

mailman: One who delivers the mail; see also scratching post.

mouse: Furry, germ-infested, cheese-licking rodent. This is suitable cat cuisine? I don't think so.

morning: The bad end to a good night; would be much better if it started later.

Nermal: The world's cutest kitten; soon to become extinct.

Odie: A type of dog or fungus; it's hard to tell.

parent: An adult keeper of children; not easily understood, but at least they provide snacks and TV.

party: A type of fun assembly guaranteed by the Constitution; see also soiree, wingding, riot.

pet: A domestic animal who provides love and companionship in exchange for blind obedience and twelve square meals a day.

pizza: Delicious tomato and cheese plant that scientists have trained to grow in flat, cardboard boxes. It's true!

Pooky: A huggable "beddy" bear who never says a harsh word . . . or anything else.

school: An educational institution designed to train your brain, assuming they can find it.

sister: An annoying female sibling usually found in the bathroom.

sleep: A state of unconsciousness best experienced in large quantities; also the perfect exercise.

snoring: The loud, irritating breathing of a sleeper; easily remedied with a pair of cymbals.

spider: Web-spinning, eight-legged insect; generally harmless, especially if bludgeoned with a sledgehammer.

teacher: One who instructs; comes in "good," "bad," and "ogre" models.

telephone: A communication device permanently attached to an adolescent's ear.

television: Device that receives mind-numbing video signals; don't grow up without it.

tomorrow: The best time for starting anything unpleasant, like homework or a diet.

veterinarian: A doctor who treats animals, whether they like it or not; synonymous with "needles as long as your arm."